Third Edition

O*NET

Dictionary of Occupational Titles

Based on information obtained from the U.S. Department of Labor, the U.S. Census Bureau, and other reliable sources

Developed under the direction of Michael Farr
with database work by Laurence Shatkin, Ph.D.

jist
Works
America's Career Publisher

O*NET Dictionary of Occupational Titles, Third Edition

© 2004 by JIST Publishing, Inc.

Published by JIST Works, an imprint of JIST Publishing, Inc.
8902 Otis Avenue
Indianapolis, IN 46216-1033

Phone: 1-800-648-JIST   Fax: 1-800-JIST-FAX
E-mail: info@jist.com   Web site: www.jist.com

Acquisitions Editor: Susan Pines
Development Editor: Stephanie Koutek
Cover Designer: Honeymoon Image & Design, Inc.
Interior Designer: Aleata Howard
Interior Layout: Carolyn J. Newland
Proofreaders: David Faust, Jeanne Clark

Printed in the United States of America

08 07 06 05 04 03   9 8 7 6 5 4 3 2 1

Library of Congress Cataloging-in-Publication Data

O*NET dictionary of occupational titles.-- 3rd ed.
        p. cm.
"Based on information obtained from the U.S. Department of Labor, the
U.S. Census Bureau, and other reliable sources."
"Developed under the direction of Michael Farr, with database work by
Laurence Shatkin, Ph.D."
    ISBN 1-56370-963-5 — ISBN 1-56370-962-7 (pbk.)
    1. Occupations—United States—Dictionaries. 2. Occupations—United
States—Classification. I. Farr, J. Michael. II. Shatkin, Laurence.
III. United States. Dept. of Labor. IV. JIST Works, Inc.
    HB2595.O16 2004
    331.7'003—dc22

                                2003025153

ISBN 1-56370-962-7 Softcover
ISBN 1-56370-963-5 Hardcover

This Book Is Easier to Use Than It Looks

Please don't be intimidated by the formal look and large size of this book, as it is very helpful and easy to use. This reference puts the more than 1,100 job descriptions from the nation's main occupational information database into practical print form, which makes it useful to job seekers, students, educators, career counselors, businesses, and others. In addition to the job descriptions, this book features facts that do not appear in the database (called the Occupational Information Network, or O*NET for short), including information on earnings, education and training required, and growth.

Part I provides five easy methods to find job descriptions that interest you. You can (1) browse the jobs by O*NET number; (2) review lists of jobs organized by interest; (3) find jobs according to the education or training required; (4) use the lists of jobs with highest earnings, fastest growth, and most openings; or (5) look for jobs alphabetically by their job title. When you find a job title that interests you, look it up in Part II. Simple.

The Best and Most Up-to-Date Source of Career Information

The information database used to create this book was developed by the U.S. Department of Labor (DOL) and replaces an older information system used in the *Dictionary of Occupational Titles*. This database represents a major change from the past. Many governmental, business, educational, and other organizations now rely on the O*NET system as the standard occupational classification and information system.

The O*NET is clearly an important information source. But the government is maintaining the O*NET in electronic form only. As a result, the DOL releases the O*NET database to developers so they can adapt the data into print and software formats that reach a wide audience.

This book uses the most recent O*NET 5.1 database and includes the following new features:

- New and revised job descriptions present a better picture of tasks that are core to the occupations.

- Easier than ever to use with several ways to quickly find the job information you need.

- Most current information on wages, growth, and openings.

- Latest Classification of Instructional Programs information, including new programs.

Important Notice on the Limitations of Use of This Book

Occupational information in this book reflects jobs as they have been found to occur, but they may not coincide in every respect with jobs as performed in particular establishments or at certain localities. Readers demanding specific job information should supplement it with local data.

Note that the U.S. Department of Labor and JIST Publishing have no responsibility for establishing wage levels or settling jurisdictional matters for occupations. In preparing vocational definitions, no data were collected concerning these and related matters. Therefore, the occupational information in this book cannot be regarded as determining standards for any aspect of the employer-employee relationship. Data contained in this publication should not be considered a judicial or legislative standard for wages, hours, or other contractual or bargaining elements.

Credits

Although two people have their names on the cover, this book represents many years of work by hundreds of dedicated individuals. The O*NET database that serves as this book's basis was created by researchers and developers under the direction of the U.S. Department of Labor. They, in turn, were assisted by thousands of employers who provided details on the nature of work in many thousands of job samplings used in the database's development.

While the O*NET database was first released several years ago, it is based on the substantial work done on an earlier database used to develop the *Dictionary of Occupational Titles* (DOT). That DOT database was first used in the 1939 DOT edition and had its final update in 1991. The DOT formed the basis for much of the occupational information used by employers, job seekers, career counselors, educational and training institutions, researchers, policy makers, and others.

Because of their large numbers, most who worked on the occupational material used in this book are not credited. Even so, we appreciate their efforts and present this book in their honor and in the honor of the good people at the U.S. Department of Labor who made the O*NET database and earlier sources of career information possible. Thanks.

Other Career Information Sources to Consider

Here are other career information resources that may interest you. Many are available at your library or bookstore, or go to www.jist.com for details.

Occupational Outlook Handbook　　　　　　*300 Best Jobs Without a Four-Year Degree*
Enhanced Occupational Outlook Handbook　*200 Best Jobs for College Graduates*
Guide for Occupational Exploration　　　　*Career Guide to America's Top Industries*
Best Jobs for the 21st Century　　　　　　www.careeroink.com (for free information on 14,000 job titles)

Table of Contents

Quick Summary of Major Sections

Introduction. Provides a brief overview of the O*NET system and this book. Includes a sample O*NET job description and reviews its many elements, such as job duties, education required, earnings, skills, abilities, personality type, working conditions, and more. Offers tips to help students, job seekers, career changers, employers, career counselors, and others use this reference. *The introduction starts on page 1.*

Part I: Five Easy Ways to Find O*NET Jobs of Interest. Presents a variety of ways to find jobs to explore:

Part II: O*NET Job Descriptions. This large section provides information-packed descriptions for the more than 1,100 jobs in the O*NET database. Descriptions are arranged by their O*NET number and within logical groupings of related jobs. The major job groups, subgroups, and jobs are listed starting in the column to the right, with the major groups listed below. *The job descriptions start on page 55.*

Management Occupations 11-0000
Business and Financial Operations Occupations 13-0000
Computer and Mathematical Occupations 15-0000
Architecture and Engineering Occupations 17-0000
Life, Physical, and Social Science Occupations 19-0000
Community and Social Services Occupations 21-0000
Legal Occupations 23-0000
Education, Training, and Library Occupations 25-0000
Arts, Design, Entertainment, Sports, and Media Occupations 27-0000
Healthcare Practitioners and Technical Occupations 29-0000
Healthcare Support Occupations 31-0000
Protective Service Occupations 33-0000
Food Preparation and Serving Related Occupations 35-0000
Building and Grounds Cleaning and Maintenance Occupations 37-0000
Personal Care and Service Occupations 39-0000
Sales and Related Occupations 41-0000
Office and Administrative Support Occupations 43-0000
Farming, Fishing, and Forestry Occupations 45-0000
Construction and Extraction Occupations 47-0000
Installation, Maintenance, and Repair Occupations 49-0000
Production Occupations 51-0000
Transportation and Material Moving Occupations 53-0000
Military Specific Occupations 55-0000

Index of O*NET Job Titles. All job titles in the O*NET database (and, therefore, in this book) appear here in alphabetical order. *The index starts on page 685.*

The list that follows presents all the job titles in Part II and the page numbers where they can be found, organized within the job groupings used in the O*NET. Major O*NET job groups are in large bold type and related subgroups are in regular-size bold type. The O*NET job titles themselves are presented in regular type within the various groupings, along with the number assigned to each job in the O*NET system. Descriptions for all of these jobs can be found in Part II, presented in the same order as in the list that follows.

List of Occupations in Related O*NET Job Groupings

Introduction

We know that many people skip the introduction and dive directly into the book. Our objective was to make this introduction easy to read and nontechnical. We admit that some information here is, well, dull. But we tried to format it so you can quickly browse the headings and disregard or read material as desired. For example, this introduction presents a sample job description with its elements pointed out and explained, which is very helpful in understanding the book's second part.

Also, please note that although there may be technical differences between the terms *occupation* and *job,* we use them interchangeably in this book.

What Is the O*NET?

The O*NET is not a book—it is a computerized database of information on occupations. Developed by the U.S. Department of Labor, O*NET is short for "The Occupational Information Network," the database's formal name.

In its current form (Version 5.1, the one we used in this book), the O*NET database provides information on about 1,100 occupations. In the years to come, occupations will be added and deleted, and the information on all occupations will be updated regularly. For example, this book's third edition includes many changes made to the O*NET database since the first edition was released in 1998.

The Department of Labor has stated that its role is to create and maintain the O*NET database, and it has no plans to release it in print. The *O*NET Dictionary of Occupational Titles* was the first book to provide the O*NET in a useful printed form. This new edition presents the newest O*NET updates, including new and revised descriptions that present a better picture of core occupational tasks.

*The O*NET Replaces an Older Occupational Information System*

The O*NET was designed to replace an earlier occupational information system, also developed by the Department of Labor. This older system was used as the basis for a book titled the *Dictionary of Occupational Titles*, published for the final time in 1991.

The old DOT gave details on 12,741 occupational titles. Although this is far more than the approximately 1,100 jobs in the O*NET database, many old DOT jobs were highly specialized or employed few people, and their descriptions were not included in the O*NET. The result is a list of O*NET occupations that is smaller and far more useful for many purposes.

The new O*NET and the old DOT system have similarities because the new O*NET is built on the solid foundation provided by the older DOT system. If you are familiar with the *Dictionary of Occupational Titles*, you will probably feel quite comfortable with the O*NET descriptions in this book. Because this book bridges the new O*NET and the DOT, we refer to both systems in the title—*O*NET Dictionary of Occupational Titles*.

The O*NET Has Too Much Information to Be Useful for Many Purposes

Remember that the O*NET is not a book—it is a database with many details about each occupation. The O*NET database includes a narrative description of each job, plus details on almost 450 data element descriptors. If you were to print the complete O*NET information for one occupation, you would have a very long, boring, and confusing description.

Consider this: If you were asked to describe your best friend, you would most likely omit many details. For example, you probably would not mention your friend's blood type, cholesterol level, mom's name, if he or she were good at reading maps, and what he or she had for breakfast, lunch, and dinner. Instead, you would select details that you felt best described this person. More specific details could be very important to someone at some time, but not in many situations.

In a similar way, if you looked at all the information available for each occupation in the O*NET database, you would quickly understand why printing it in book form would not make sense. For example, on the next page is the summary information on just one of the almost 450 O*NET data elements available for one occupation.

Rate control is very important for a job such as Aircraft Pilot, but it means little to most office workers, for example. So including rate control information on each occupation would not be helpful—and giving details on the almost 450 data elements for every job would create many pages of little interest to most people.

In addition, a book with all this information would be thousands of pages long and require many volumes. Who would buy or read it? For this reason, we used a variety of techniques to reduce the information provided for each occupation and increase the usefulness of each description for most readers.

Sample of One O*NET Data Element

Element:	Rate Control
Description:	The ability to time the adjustments of a movement or equipment control in anticipation of changes in the speed and/or direction of a continuously moving object or scene.
Content Model Key:	I.A.2.b.4

           I. Worker Characteristics
              A. Abilities
                  2. Psychomotor Abilities
                      b. Control Movement Abilities
                        4. Rate Control

Variable	Variable Description	File Name	Field Values	Scale, Ques Codes
A28LV00M	Rate Control-Level	Means_AB	1-7,0(NR)	LV,A

Left Label	Value	Right Value
Requires precisely timed control adjustments to random changes of a high-speed object moving in several directions.	7.00	
	6.50	Operating aircraft controls used to land a jet on an aircraft carrier in rough weather.
	4.80	Shooting a duck in flight.
	3.60	Keeping up with a car you are following when the speed of that car changes.
	2.40	Riding a bicycle alongside a jogger.
Requires timed control adjustments to a slow-moving, almost predictable object moving in a single direction.	1.00	

A28IM00M	Rate Control-Importance	Means_AB	1-5	IM,A

If You Want More Details About the O*NET Occupations

You may want more detailed information about occupations than we can provide in this book. For example, you may want to know the rate control measures for an occupation. If so, we suggest that you access the O*NET database. It is available on the Internet at http://www.onetcenter.org.

The O*NET database on the Internet can be difficult to understand, since it includes an enormous amount of detailed information on each job. Software and Web sites from other sources, including JIST Publishing, include the O*NET information in electronic form. In some cases, this makes it much easier to find and use the details in the O*NET you really want. Please contact or JIST or visit careerOINK.com if you are interested in software or a Web site that includes the O*NET data. CareerOINK.com offers job information at free and paid levels.

How This Book Is Organized

This book is organized in two parts. Part I shows you five ways to find job descriptions that interest you. You can browse the jobs by O*NET number; by interest area; by amount of education and training required; by ranking on earnings, growth, and openings lists; and by title. You can read more about these criteria later in the following section and in Part I. Part II presents the job descriptions in order by O*NET number.

A Sample O*NET Description—and What It Includes

It would take more than 10 pages to print all the data on one job in the O*NET database, and much of that data would be in coded form that is not easy to understand without study. That's simply too much information for most people, and it would result in a book of more than 10,000 pages. So our challenge was to create a description of each O*NET occupation that would be useful to most people and would also be practical in book form.

We stayed up late many nights considering how to do this. The result is the carefully thought-out job descriptions you find in this book. Because a picture is worth a thousand words, we provide a sample O*NET job description next. To help you understand all that it includes, we point out its many elements and then explain each one.

O*NET Occupational Title

O*NET Number

13-1071.01 Employment Interviewers, Private or Public Employment Service

Education — ● Education/Training Required: Bachelor's degree

Employed — ● Employed: No data available.

Openings — ● Annual Earnings: $38,010

Projected Growth — ● Growth: 17.6%

Earnings — ● Annual Job Openings: 19,000

Lead Description

Interview job applicants in employment office and refer them to prospective employers for consideration. Search application files, notify selected applicants of job openings, and refer qualified applicants to prospective employers. Contact employers to verify referral results. Record and evaluate various pertinent data.

O*NET Occupational Description

Occupational Task List

Conduct or arrange for skill, intelligence, or psychological testing of applicants and current employees. Contact employers to solicit orders for job vacancies, determining their requirements and recording relevant data such as job descriptions. Hire workers and place them with employers needing temporary help. Inform applicants of job openings and details such as duties and responsibilities, compensation, benefits, schedules, working conditions, and promotion opportunities. Interview job applicants to match their qualifications with employers' needs, recording and evaluating applicant experience, education, training, and skills. Maintain records of applicants not selected for employment. Perform reference and background checks on applicants. Provide background information on organizations with which interviews are scheduled. Review employment applications and job orders to match applicants with job requirements, using manual or computerized file searches. Search for and recruit applicants for open positions through campus job fairs and advertisements. Select qualified applicants or refer them to employers according to organization policy. Administer assessment tests to identify skill-building needs. Conduct workshops and demonstrate the use of job listings to assist applicants with skill building. Evaluate selection and testing techniques by conducting research or follow-up activities and conferring with management and supervisory

Related DOT Jobs

personnel. Refer applicants to services such as vocational counseling, literacy or language instruction, transportation assistance, vocational training, and child care. Instruct job applicants in presenting a positive image by providing help with resume writing, personal appearance, and interview techniques.

GOE INFORMATION—Interest Area: 13. General Management and Support. **Work Group:** 13.02. Management Support. **Personality Type**—Social. Social occupations frequently involve working with, communicating with, and teaching people. These occupations often involve helping or providing service to others. **Work Values**—Social Service; Good Working Conditions; Pleasant Co-workers; Supervision, Technical; Supervision, Human Relations. **Skills**—Speaking; Active Listening; Complex Problem Solving; Reading Comprehension; Judgment and Decision Making; Writing; Management of Personnel Resources. **Abilities**—*Cognitive:* Oral Comprehension; Oral Expression; Fluency of Ideas; Written Expression; Written Comprehension. *Psychomotor:* None met the criteria. *Physical:* None met the criteria. *Sensory:* Speech Recognition; Speech Clarity. **General Work Activities**—*Information Input:* Getting Information; Identifying Objects, Actions, and Events; Estimating Needed Characteristics. *Mental Process:* Judging Qualities of Things, Services, or Other People's Work; Processing Information; Analyzing Data or Information. *Work Output:* Documenting or Recording Information; Handling and Moving Objects; Interacting with Computers. *Interacting with Others:* Performing for or Working with the Public; Establishing and Maintaining Relationships; Communicating with Persons Outside Organization. **Physical Work Conditions**—Sitting; Indoors. **Other Job Characteristics**—Consequence of Error; Importance of Being Exact or Accurate; Importance of Repeating Same Tasks.

Experience—Job Zone 3. Previous work-related skill, knowledge, or experience is required. **Job Preparation:** SVP 6.0 to less than 7.0—more than one year and less than four years. **Knowledge**—Personnel and Human Resources; Therapy and Counseling; Psychology; Clerical; Administration and Management. **Instructional Programs**—Human Resources Management/Personnel Administration, General; Labor and Industrial Relations.

Related DOT Jobs—166.267-010 Employment Interviewer.

Labels on right side: GOE Interest Area and Work Group; Personality Type; Work Values; Skills; Abilities; General Work Activities; Physical Work Conditions; Other Job Characteristics; Experience; Job Preparation; Knowledge; Instructional Programs

Details on Each Information Element in the Job Descriptions

While short, each description is packed with useful information that will be quite helpful for most readers. Most content is easy enough to understand, although some details will interest only those who require them. Other elements require some explanation. Following are details on each information element included in the job descriptions. Some of this information may be more detail than you need, so skim the content to find what you want to know.

We tried to keep our explanation nontechnical. However, some of the O*NET is technical, and some readers have inquiring minds that want to know such details. For this

reason, we felt compelled to add more information than some of you might want. Too much, too little—it's a balancing act we hope gives most of you what you need.

O*NET Number

Each O*NET occupation is assigned a unique number. These are not random numbers because they are based on the Standard Occupational Classification (SOC) system established by the federal government. The SOC is a structure for organizing jobs based on the work performed, and it is being adopted by all federal agencies that collect and distribute data. Since the O*NET numbering system puts job titles into groupings of related jobs, it's pretty logical to use. You can see how this system works by looking at the list of O*NET occupations in the Table of Contents.

Occupations in this book are presented in numerical order, using their assigned O*NET number. Although some numbers appear to be missing, these absent numbers allow for future expansion of the numbering system.

Quick tip on how to use this information: The O*NET number allows you to quickly cross-reference other O*NET information sources, including the government's Web site that provides more details on the O*NET jobs.

O*NET Occupational Title

This title, which appears in bold, is assigned to the job by the Department of Labor. We include the newest O*NET titles, which are based on those used in the SOC system.

Education/Training Required

This line lists the education or training typically required for entry into a job. Please note, however, that some (or many) who work in the job may have higher or lower levels of education than indicated. Certification or licensing may be required for some jobs, but accurate information on such requirements is not available yet from the O*NET database. You need to determine such requirements from other sources, such as the *Occupational Outlook Handbook*.

The Department of Labor uses 11 levels of education or training to classify the education, training, and experience needs of a job. One of these levels is assigned to each job in this book.

The 11 Education and Training Levels

Short-term on-the-job training. It is possible to work in these occupations and achieve an average level of performance within a few days or weeks through on-the-job training.

Moderate-term on-the-job training. Occupations that require this type of training can be performed adequately after a 1- to 12-month period of combined on-the-job and informal training. Typically, untrained workers observe experienced workers perform tasks and are gradually moved into progressively more difficult assignments.

Long-term on-the-job training. This training requires more than 12 months of on-the-job training or combined work experience and formal classroom instruction. This includes occupations that use formal apprenticeships for training workers that may take up to 4 years. It also includes intensive occupation-specific, employer-sponsored training like police academies. Furthermore, it includes occupations that require natural talent that must be developed over many years.

Work experience in a related occupation. This type of job requires experience in a related occupation. For example, police detectives are selected based on their experience as police patrol officers.

Postsecondary vocational training. This requirement can vary from training that involves a few months to usually less than 1 year. In a few instances, there may be as many as 4 years of training.

Associate's degree. This degree usually requires 2 years of full-time academic work beyond high school.

Bachelor's degree. This degree requires approximately 4 to 5 years of full-time academic work beyond high school.

Work experience plus degree. Jobs in this category are often management-related and require some experience in a related nonmanagerial position.

Master's degree. Completion of a master's degree usually requires 1 to 2 years of full-time study beyond the bachelor's degree.

Doctoral degree. This degree normally requires 2 or more years of full-time academic work beyond the bachelor's degree.

First professional degree. This type of degree normally requires a minimum of 2 years of education beyond the bachelor's degree and frequently requires 3 years.

Quick tip on how to use this information: We put this information at the top of the description to give you a quick idea of the job's education or training requirements.

Employed

The number of people employed in the occupation can be used to estimate job availability. This information, released in 1998, comes from the Department of Labor's Bureau of Labor Statistics (BLS) and is the most current available.

Quick tip on how to use this information: Occupations employing a large number of people often have more openings than those employing smaller numbers. This is one useful measure of job opportunity.

Annual Earnings

This figure represents the median earnings for all people in the job. The median means that half the people earn more and half earn less. This annual amount, released in 2001, comes from the BLS and is the most current available.

Quick tips on how to use this information: Earnings figures can be misleading for several reasons. For example, new or recent entrants to the occupation often earn substantially less because they usually have much less experience than the average person working in the job. Pay rates also often vary considerably in different regions of the country. In addition, smaller employers often pay less. So consider the earnings information as a guideline that may not apply to your situation. You can often obtain local earnings information from your state employment service or other sources; ask your librarian for help. You also can ask people employed in an occupation what workers in your geographic area earn at differing experience levels.

Growth

This part of the description lists the percent of projected new jobs for the 10-year period ending in 2010. The figure comes from BLS and is the most up-to-date available.

Quick tip on how to use this information: Jobs with high projected growth frequently provide many opportunities. Low and negative growth numbers may reflect stagnant or declining areas.

Annual Job Openings

The number of openings available each year for the job appears next. It is based on the new jobs created plus openings due to resignations, terminations, retirement, and death. This data, released in 2001, comes from BLS and is the most current available.

Quick tip on how to use this information: Occupations with many annual openings often offer opportunity and may be easier to obtain.

O*NET Occupational Description

This section gives you a brief but useable description for each job. The first part is the lead description, which is printed in italics. This text is sometimes followed by statements (also in italics) such as "Include wholesale or retail trade merchandising managers" or "Exclude procurement managers" that provide related titles that may be described in other O*NET occupations. This section is then followed, in regular type, by an occupational task list that describes occupational tasks specific to the job.

Quick tips on how to use this information: The brief lead information gives you a quick way to understand the job. If it interests you, the more detailed task statement gives you a good review of the work that someone in the job does.

GOE Interest Area and Work Group

The Guide for Occupational Exploration is a system for organizing jobs based on interests. Developed by the U.S. Department of Labor, the GOE was designed as an intuitive way to help counselors, students, job seekers, career changers, and others identify occupations for further exploration. Since the GOE system is widely used for exploring career and learning options, we provide GOE information in the descriptions so you can cross-reference other systems that use it.

The GOE organizes all jobs into 14 major interest groupings and then into more specific subgroups (called *work groups*) of related jobs. Note that we use the latest GOE interest group and work group names and numbers throughout this book. This new GOE information comes from a major revision of the GOE system released in a book titled *Guide for Occupational Exploration,* Third Edition (JIST Works). The many changes and improvements make the old GOE system obsolete.

We include the four-digit GOE work group number for each job. The first two numbers represent the major interest area where the job is assigned. The last two digits indicate the GOE work group where the job is found.

Here is a list of the GOE's 14 major interest areas.

The 14 GOE Interest Areas

01	Arts, Entertainment, and Media
02	Science, Math, and Engineering
03	Plants and Animals
04	Law, Law Enforcement, and Public Safety
05	Mechanics, Installers, and Repairers
06	Construction, Mining, and Drilling
07	Transportation
08	Industrial Production
09	Business Detail
10	Sales and Marketing
11	Recreation, Travel, and Other Personal Services
12	Education and Social Service
13	General Management and Support
14	Medical and Health Services

Quick tips on how to use this information: The GOE information is a very helpful way to find jobs that you might otherwise overlook. GOE codes in the job descriptions allow you to cross-reference any career information system using the new GOE structure. Also, Part I lists all the O*NET jobs that fall into each interest area. If you take an interest assessment that gives you a GOE code or group, Part I allows you to cross-reference it to related O*NET jobs.

Personality Type

This information is useful for those who use a career interest inventory titled the *Self-Directed Search* or related career information systems based on these personality types. The SDS author developed a popular theory that suggests a person's interests can be classified into 1 of 6 personality types. Each personality type relates to jobs that fit the descriptions listed next.

The 6 Personality Types

Artistic. These occupations frequently involve working with forms, designs, and patterns. They often require self-expression, and the work can be done without following a clear set of rules.

Conventional. These occupations frequently involve following set procedures and routines. These occupations can include working with data and details more than with ideas. Usually there is a clear line of authority to follow.

Enterprising. These occupations frequently involve starting up and carrying out projects. These occupations can involve leading people and making many decisions. They sometimes require risk taking and often deal with business.

Investigative. These occupations frequently involve working with ideas and require an extensive amount of thinking. These occupations can involve searching for facts and figuring out problems mentally.

Realistic. These occupations frequently involve work activities that include practical, hands-on problems and solutions. They often deal with plants, animals, and real-world materials like wood, tools, and machinery. Many of the occupations require working outside and do not involve a lot of paperwork or working closely with others.

Social. These occupations frequently involve working with, communicating with, and teaching people. These occupations often involve helping or providing service to others.

Quick tips on how to use this information: The SDS and other career interest inventories, like the *Strong Campbell Interest Inventory* and the *Armed Services Vocational Battery,* use the SDS personality types. If you have used one of these popular tests, you might recall your personality type and use it to identify jobs that match it. You can also use the personality type information even if you haven't taken one of the assessments. Simply read the personality type definitions and determine the one that most closely describes jobs that interest you. Then compare jobs you have held or are considering to see if they are close matches.

The Personality Types Easily Cross-Reference to GOE Interest Areas

Most career information systems use groupings of related jobs that can be easily cross-referenced. For example, here we include a table that cross-references the 14 GOE interest areas to the 6 SDS personality types. This "crosswalk" allows you to identify potential jobs based on interests and personality types. We hope you find this information interesting and useful, whatever your situation.

GOE Interest Area	Personality Type
01 Arts, Entertainment, and Media	Artistic
02 Science, Math, and Engineering	Investigative
03 Plants and Animals	Realistic
04 Law, Law Enforcement, and Public Safety	Realistic, Social
05 Mechanics, Installers, and Repairers	Realistic
06 Construction, Mining, and Drilling	Realistic
07 Transportation	Realistic
08 Industrial Production	Realistic
09 Business Detail	Conventional
10 Sales and Marketing	Enterprising
11 Recreation, Travel, and Other Personal Services	Social, Conventional
12 Education and Social Service	Social
13 General Management and Support	Enterprising, Social
14 Medical and Health Services	Investigative, Social

Work Values

The O*NET database includes information on 21 work values for each job. The work values information helps you identify jobs that match your personal values, such as wanting security or independence in the work you do. For most jobs, relatively few work values receive high ratings, so giving numeric data for all 21 values is not useful. Instead, we selected the work values for each job that exceeded an "average" rating by the greatest amount. In most cases, we include the top 5 work values.

The 21 work values are arranged into 6 major groupings.

The 21 Work Values

Achievement. **Occupations that satisfy these work values are results-oriented and allow employees to use their strongest abilities, giving them a feeling of accomplishment.**

Ability Utilization. Workers on this job make use of their individual abilities.

Achievement. Workers on this job get a feeling of accomplishment.

(continues)

(continued)

Altruism. Occupations that satisfy these work values allow employees to provide service to others and work with co-workers in a friendly, noncompetitive environment.

Moral Values. Workers on this job are never pressured to do things that go against their sense of right and wrong.

Pleasant Co-workers. Workers on this job have co-workers who are easy to get along with.

Social Service. Workers on this job have work where they do things for other people.

Autonomy. Occupations that satisfy this work value allow employees to work on their own and make decisions.

Autonomy. Workers on this job plan their work with little supervision.

Creativity. Workers on this job try out their own ideas.

Responsibility. Workers on this job make decisions on their own.

Comfort. Occupations that satisfy these work values offer job security and good working conditions.

Activity. Workers on this job are busy all the time.

Compensation. Workers on this job are paid well in comparison with other workers.

Good Working Conditions. Workers on this job have good working conditions.

Independence. Workers on this job do their work alone.

Security. Workers on this job have steady employment.

Variety. Workers on this job have something different to do every day.

Safety. Occupations that satisfy these work values offer supportive management that stands behind employees and provides a predictable and stable work environment.

Company Policies and Practices. Workers on this job are treated fairly by the company.

Supervision, Human Relations. Workers on this job have supervisors who back up their workers with management.

Supervision, Technical. Workers on this job have supervisors who train their workers well.

Status. Occupations that satisfy these work values offer advancement and potential for leadership and are often considered prestigious.

Advancement. Workers on this job have opportunities for advancement.

Authority. Workers on this job give directions and instructions to others.

Recognition. Workers on this job receive recognition for the work they do.

Social Status. Workers on this job are looked up to by others in their company and their community.

Quick tips on how to use this information: While often overlooked by job seekers, work values are a very important part of what makes a job enjoyable or miserable. So think about which work values are particularly important to include in your career and write down those that are most important to you. Later, as you review the job descriptions, look for ones that meet your criteria.

Skills

This section lists skills needed to perform in each job. Depending on the occupation, some of these skills are quite complex, while others are relatively basic. All of us possess thousands of skills, although we take most of them for granted. For example, have you ever considered the complexity of physical skills needed to drive a car? This task is so complex that the most sophisticated machines cannot do it nearly as well as most 16-year-olds. While all of the many skills we possess are not listed in the O*NET database, it does include many skills that are important across a range of jobs. To avoid overwhelming you with details, only those skills with higher numerical ratings in the database are listed for each job.

The O*NET database provides measures for 35 skills for each job. Each skill is rated on two scales. One rates the skill on its importance to the job, and the other rates the skill on the level of performance required for the job. To create useful skills information for the job descriptions, we used the level-of-performance measure, since that is, we believe, the more useful measure.

For each job, we included skills whose scores exceeded the average for all jobs by the greatest amount. We included as many as 8 such skills for each job, and we ranked them by the extent to which their rating exceeds the average.

Some jobs have fewer than 8 and sometimes no skills with numeric measures higher than the average measure for all jobs for each skill. For example, no skill is rated higher than average for Maids. Skills with the highest ratings include active listening, learning strategies, coordination, and reading comprehension. However, the respective ratings for these 4 skills are 1.83, 1.83, 1.33, and 1.33. On a scale of 0 to 7, all are considerably below the average. You can understand why listing these skills would not be an accurate representation of skills needed to perform this job. So, in these situations, we include the phrase "None met the criteria."

Following are the 35 skills used in the job descriptions, along with brief explanations for each one. These skills are classified as either Basic Skills or Cross-Functional Skills.

The 35 Skills

Basic Skills. **These capacities facilitate the acquisition of new knowledge and skills.**

Active Learning. Working with new material or information to grasp its implications.

Active Listening. Listening to what other people are saying and asking questions as appropriate.

Critical Thinking. Using logic and analysis to identify the strengths and weaknesses of different approaches.

Learning Strategies. Using multiple approaches when learning or teaching new things.

Mathematics. Using mathematics to solve problems.

Monitoring. Assessing how well one is doing when learning or doing something.

Reading Comprehension. Understanding written sentences and paragraphs in work-related documents.

Science. Using scientific methods to solve problems.

Speaking. Talking to others to effectively convey information.

Writing. Communicating effectively with others in writing as indicated by the needs of the audience.

Cross-Functional Skills. **These skills facilitate performance in a variety of job settings.**

Complex Problem Solving. Identifying complex problems, reviewing the options, and implementing solutions.

Coordination. Adjusting actions in relation to others' actions.

Equipment Maintenance. Performing routine maintenance and determining when and what kind of maintenance is needed.

Equipment Selection. Determining the kind of tools and equipment needed to do a job.

Installation. Installing equipment, machines, wiring, or programs to meet specifications.

Instructing. Teaching others how to do something.

Judgment and Decision Making. Weighing the relative costs and benefits of a potential action.

Management of Financial Resources. Determining how money will be spent to get the work done and accounting for these expenditures.

Management of Material Resources. Obtaining and seeing to the appropriate use of equipment, facilities, and materials needed to do certain work.

Management of Personnel Resources. Motivating, developing, and directing people as they work, identifying the best people for the job.

Negotiation. Bringing others together and trying to reconcile differences.

Operation and Control. Controlling operations of equipment or systems.

Operation Monitoring. Watching gauges, dials, or other indicators to make sure a machine is working properly.

Operations Analysis. Analyzing needs and product requirements to create a design.

Persuasion. Persuading others to approach things differently.

Programming. Writing computer programs for various purposes.

Quality Control Analysis. Evaluating the quality or performance of products, services, or processes.

Repairing. Repairing machines or systems using the needed tools.

Service Orientation. Actively looking for ways to help people.

Social Perceptiveness. Being aware of others' reactions and understanding why they react the way they do.

Synthesis and Reorganization. Reorganizing information to get a better approach to problems or tasks.

Systems Evaluation. Looking at many indicators of system performance, taking into account their accuracy.

Technology Design. Generating or adapting equipment and technology to serve user needs.

Time Management. Managing one's time and the time of others.

Troubleshooting. Determining what is causing an operating error and deciding what to do about it.

Quick tips on how to use this information: A big part of successful career decision-making depends on your knowing what skills you enjoy and are good at. So look over the list of skills and write down those that you would most like to use in your next job. These are the ones to include in your career planning as much as possible. If you are looking for a job, the skills in the job descriptions are those you should emphasize in the interview, since they are the ones likely to be valued by employers.

Abilities

This section contains "enduring attributes" that influence the job performance of workers. These attributes don't change over long periods of time. Abilities affect how quickly a person can learn new skills and the level of skill that can be achieved. Sometimes people refer to this as aptitude or even talent. Usually an ability increases your interest in learning and practicing a skill. For example, you may find that math is easy for you. So when you are taught a concept like calculating the mean and standard deviation (to help control product quality, for example), you are able to quickly learn how to use this in your job.

The O*NET database provides measures on 52 abilities for each job. (I trust that you are now beginning to understand our wisdom in including only the more important measures in each job description.) The abilities are organized into four subgroups: Cognitive (with 21 abilities), Psychomotor (10 abilities), Physical (9 abilities), and Sensory (12 abilities).

We used the O*NET's level-of-ability rating to select the top abilities (as many as 5) in each subgroup. We set a requirement that an ability must have a measure higher than the average of that ability for all jobs, and we ranked the abilities by the extent to which their rating exceeds the average. For example, the highest-ranked physical abilities for Employment Interviewers include trunk strength, gross body coordination, and extent flexibility—but the numeric ratings for these abilities are only 1.2, 0.4, and 0.4 on a scale of 0 to 7. Obviously, these are not important abilities for an Employment Interviewer, and that is why we set the average as a minimum. When no ability has a rating higher than the average for all jobs, we write "None met the criteria."

Here are the 52 abilities that are included in the job descriptions, along with brief explanations for each.

The 52 Abilities

Cognitive Abilities. These are mental processes that influence the acquisition and application of knowledge in problem solving.

Category Flexibility. The ability to produce many rules so that each rule tells how to group or combine a set of things in a different way.

Deductive Reasoning. The ability to apply general rules to specific problems to come up with logical answers. It involves deciding if an answer makes sense or provides a logical explanation for why a series of seemingly unrelated events occur together.

Flexibility of Closure. The ability to identify or detect a known pattern (a figure, object, word, or sound) that is hidden in other distracting material.

Fluency of Ideas. The ability to come up with a number of ideas about a given topic. It concerns the number of ideas produced and not the quality, correctness, or creativity of the ideas.

Inductive Reasoning. The ability to combine separate pieces of information, or specific answers to problems, to form general rules or conclusions. It includes coming up with a logical explanation for why a series of seemingly unrelated events occur together.

Information Ordering. The ability to correctly follow a given rule or set of rules in order to arrange things or actions in a certain order. The things or actions can include numbers, letters, words, pictures, procedures, sentences, and mathematical or logical operations.

Mathematical Reasoning. The ability to understand and organize a problem and then to select a mathematical method or formula to solve the problem.

Memorization. The ability to remember information such as words, numbers, pictures, and procedures.

Number Facility. The ability to add, subtract, multiply, or divide quickly and correctly.

Oral Comprehension. The ability to listen to and understand information and ideas presented through spoken words and sentences.

Oral Expression. The ability to communicate information and ideas in speaking so others will understand.

Originality. The ability to come up with unusual or clever ideas about a given topic or situation or to develop creative ways to solve a problem.

Perceptual Speed. The ability to quickly and accurately compare letters, numbers, objects, pictures, or patterns. The things to be compared may be presented at the same time or one after the other. This ability also includes comparing a presented object with a remembered object.

Problem Sensitivity. The ability to tell when something is wrong or is likely to go wrong. It does not involve solving the problem, only recognizing that there is a problem.

Selective Attention. The ability to concentrate and not be distracted while performing a task over a period of time.

Spatial Orientation. The ability to know one's location in relation to the environment or to know where other objects are in relation to one's self.

Speed of Closure. The ability to quickly make sense of information that seems to be without meaning or organization. It involves quickly combining and organizing different pieces of information into a meaningful pattern.

Time Sharing. The ability to efficiently shift back and forth between two or more activities or sources of information (such as speech, sounds, touch, or other sources).

Visualization. The ability to imagine how something will look after it is moved around or when its parts are moved or rearranged.

Written Comprehension. The ability to read and understand information and ideas presented in writing.

Written Expression. The ability to communicate information and ideas in writing so others will understand.

Psychomotor Abilities. These abilities influence the capacity to manipulate and control objects primarily using fine motor skills.

Arm-Hand Steadiness. The ability to keep the hand and arm steady while making an arm movement or while holding the arm and hand in one position.

Control Precision. The ability to quickly and repeatedly make precise adjustments in moving the controls of a machine or vehicle to exact positions.

Finger Dexterity. The ability to make precisely coordinated movements of the fingers of one or both hands to grasp, manipulate, or assemble very small objects.

Manual Dexterity. The ability to quickly make coordinated movements of one hand, a hand together with its arm, or two hands to grasp, manipulate, or assemble objects.

Multilimb Coordination. The ability to coordinate movements of two or more limbs together (for example, two arms, two legs, or one leg and one arm) while sitting, standing, or lying down. It does not involve performing the activities while the body is in motion.

Rate Control. The ability to time the adjustments of a movement or equipment control in anticipation of changes in the speed and/or direction of a continuously moving object or scene.

Reaction Time. The ability to quickly respond (with the hand, finger, or foot) to one signal (sound, light, picture, and so on) when it appears.

Response Orientation. The ability to choose quickly and correctly between two or more movements in response to two or more signals (lights, sounds, pictures, and so on). It includes the speed with which the correct response is started with the hand, foot, or other body parts.

Speed of Limb Movement. The ability to quickly move the arms or legs.

Wrist-Finger Speed. The ability to make fast, simple, repeated movements of the fingers, hands, and wrists.

Physical Strength Abilities. These abilities influence strength, endurance, flexibility, balance, and coordination.

Dynamic Flexibility. The ability to quickly and repeatedly bend, stretch, twist, or reach out with the body, arms, and/or legs.

Dynamic Strength. The ability to exert muscle force repeatedly or continuously over time. This involves muscular endurance and resistance to muscle fatigue.

Explosive Strength. The ability to use short bursts of muscle force to propel oneself (as in jumping or sprinting) or to throw an object.

Extent Flexibility. The ability to bend, stretch, twist, or reach out with the body, arms, and/or legs.

Gross Body Coordination. The ability to coordinate the movement of the arms, legs, and torso together in activities where the whole body is in motion.

Gross Body Equilibrium. The ability to keep or regain one's body balance or stay upright when in an unstable position.

Stamina. The ability to exert one's self physically over long periods of time without getting winded or out of breath.

Static Strength. The ability to exert maximum muscle force to lift, push, pull, or carry objects.

Trunk Strength. The ability to use one's abdominal and lower back muscles to support part of the body repeatedly or continuously over time without giving out or fatiguing.

***Sensory Abilities.* These abilities influence visual, auditory, and speech perception.**

Auditory Attention. The ability to focus on a single source of auditory (hearing) information in the presence of other distracting sounds.

Depth Perception. The ability to judge which of several objects is closer or farther away from the observer or to judge the distance between an object and the observer.

Far Vision. The ability to see details at a distance.

Glare Sensitivity. The ability to see objects in the presence of glare or bright lighting.

Hearing Sensitivity. The ability to detect or tell the difference between sounds that vary over broad ranges of pitch and loudness.

Near Vision. The ability to see details of objects at a close range (within a few feet of the observer).

Night Vision. The ability to see under low light conditions.

Peripheral Vision. The ability to see objects or movement of objects to one's side when the eyes are focused forward.

Sound Localization. The ability to tell the direction from which a sound originated.

Speech Clarity. The ability to speak clearly so that it is understandable to a listener.

Speech Recognition. The ability to identify and understand the speech of another person.

Visual Color Discrimination. The ability to match or detect differences between colors, including shades of color and brightness.

Quick tips on how to use this information: Many of the abilities are similar to the skills. This overlap should not concern you, because skills and abilities are alike in some important ways. As with skills, you can select abilities that are important to you and look for career options that include them.

Abilities and Disabilities

We encourage you to use the data on abilities with care. The O*NET information does not take into account how a person with a disability might perform a job. Many jobs can be redesigned to accommodate disabilities. For this reason, the O*NET data should not be used to exclude people from jobs.

This is but one example of how even carefully collected data can lead to inaccurate conclusions. Data has its limitations, and you need to use common sense in interpreting the contents of this book and other references.

General Work Activities

This section lists the general types of activities involved in performing the job described. As with the skills section, some jobs list very complex activities as well as more basic ones. There are four subgroups within general work activities: Information Input (5 activities), Mental Process (10 activities), Work Output (9 activities), and Interacting with Others (17 activities). For each job, we included work activities whose rating exceeded the average for all jobs by the greatest amount, and we ranked them by the extent to which their rating exceeds the average. For each subgroup of activities, we listed as many as 3.

Here are brief descriptions for the 41 general work activities in the O*NET database.

The 41 General Work Activities

Information Input

Estimating Needed Characteristics. Estimating the characteristics of materials, products, events, or information: Estimating sizes, distances, and quantities or determining time, costs, resources, or materials needed to perform a work activity.

Getting Information. Observing, receiving, and otherwise obtaining information from all relevant sources.

Identifying Objects, Actions, and Events. Identifying information received by making estimates or categorizations, recognizing differences or similarities, or sensing.

Inspecting Equipment, Structures, or Materials. Inspecting or diagnosing equipment, structures, or materials to identify the causes of errors or other problems or defects.

Monitoring Processes, Materials, or Surroundings. Monitoring and reviewing information from materials, events, or the environment, often to detect problems or to find out when things are finished.

Mental Process

Analyzing Data or Information. Identifying underlying principles, reasons, or facts by breaking down information or data into separate parts.

Developing Objectives and Strategies. Establishing long-range objectives and specifying the strategies and actions to achieve these objectives.

Evaluating Information Against Standards. Evaluating information against a set of standards and verifying that it is correct.

Judging Qualities of Things, Services, or Other People's Work. Making judgments about or assessing the value, importance, or quality of things or people's work.

Making Decisions and Solving Problems. Combining, evaluating, and reasoning with information and data to make decisions and solve problems. These processes involve making decisions about the relative importance of information and choosing the best solution.

Organizing, Planning, and Prioritizing. Developing plans to accomplish work and prioritizing and organizing one's work.

Processing Information. Compiling, coding, categorizing, calculating, tabulating, auditing, verifying, or processing information or data.

Scheduling Work and Activities. Scheduling events, programs, and activities, as well as the work of others.

Thinking Creatively. Originating, inventing, designing, or creating new applications, ideas, relationships, systems, or products, including artistic contributions.

Updating and Using Relevant Knowledge. Keeping up-to-date technically and knowing the functions of one's job and related jobs.

Work Output

Controlling Machines and Processes. Using either control mechanisms or direct physical activity to operate machines or processes (not including computers or vehicles).

Documenting or Recording Information. Entering, transcribing, recording, storing, or maintaining information either in written form or by electronic/magnetic recording.

Drafting and Specifying Technical Devices. Providing documentation, detailed instructions, drawings, or specifications to inform others about how devices, parts, equipment, or structures are to be fabricated, constructed, assembled, modified, maintained, or used.

Handling and Moving Objects. Using one's hands and arms in handling, installing, forming, positioning, and moving materials or in manipulating things. Includes the use of keyboards.

Interacting with Computers. Controlling computer functions by using programs, setting up functions, writing software, or otherwise communicating with computer systems.

Operating Vehicles or Equipment. Running, maneuvering, navigating, or driving vehicles or mechanized equipment, such as forklifts, passenger vehicles, aircraft, or watercraft.

Performing General Physical Activities. Performing physical activities that require moving one's whole body, such as in climbing, lifting, balancing, walking, and stooping, where the activities often also require considerable use of the arms and legs, such as in the physical handling of materials.

Repairing and Maintaining Electronic Equipment. Fixing, servicing, adjusting, regulating, calibrating, fine-tuning, or testing machines, devices, and equipment that operate primarily on the basis of electrical or electronic (not mechanical) principles.

Repairing and Maintaining Mechanical Equipment. Fixing, servicing, aligning, setting up, adjusting, and testing machines, devices, moving parts, and equipment that operate primarily on the basis of mechanical (not electronic) principles.

Interacting with Others

Assisting and Caring for Others. Providing assistance or personal care to others.

Coaching and Developing Others. Identifying developmental needs of others and coaching or otherwise helping others to improve their knowledge or skills.

Communicating with Other Workers. Providing information to supervisors, fellow workers, and subordinates. This information can be exchanged face-to-face, in writing, or via telephone/electronic transfer.

Communicating with Persons Outside Organization. Communicating with persons outside the organization and representing the organization to customers, the public, government, and other external sources. Information can be exchanged face-to-face, in writing, or via telephone/electronic transfer.

Coordinating Work and Activities of Others. Coordinating members of a work group to accomplish tasks.

Developing and Building Teams. Encouraging and building mutual trust, respect, and cooperation among team members.

Establishing and Maintaining Relationships. Developing constructive and cooperative working relationships with others.

Guiding, Directing, and Motivating Subordinates. Providing guidance and direction to subordinates, including setting performance standards and monitoring subordinates.

Influencing Others or Selling. Convincing others to buy merchandise/goods or otherwise changing their minds or actions.

Interpreting Meaning of Information to Others. Translating or explaining what information means and how it can be understood or used to support responses or feedback to others.

Monitoring and Controlling Resources. Monitoring and controlling resources and overseeing the spending of money.

Performing Administrative Activities. Approving requests, handling paperwork, and performing day-to-day administrative tasks.

Performing for or Working with the Public. Performing for people or dealing directly with the public, including serving persons in restaurants and stores and receiving clients or guests.

Providing Consultation and Advice to Others. Providing consultation and expert advice to management or other groups on technical, systems-related, or process-related topics.

Resolving Conflict and Negotiating with Others. Handling complaints, arbitrating disputes, resolving grievances, or otherwise negotiating with others.

Staffing Organizational Units. Recruiting, interviewing, selecting, hiring, and promoting persons for the organization.

Teaching Others. Identifying educational needs, developing formal training programs or classes, and teaching or instructing others.

Quick tip on how to use this information: This information gives you a good idea of the types of activities that require higher-than-average skills for the job. So, for example, if a job requires higher-than-average skills in "staffing organizational units, " you need to decide if you have or want to develop these skills to perform well on this job.

Physical Work Conditions

The O*NET provides 25 measures on a variety of work environments and working conditions, including work setting, environmental conditions, job hazards, body positioning, and work attire. (The present edition of the O*NET has only incomplete ratings for these measures, so we used the ratings from O*NET release 4.0.) We included physical work conditions for jobs only when their rating exceeded the average for all jobs, and we ranked them by the extent to which their rating exceeds the average. We included as many as 5 for each job. Brief descriptions for each measure follow. Here are all the physical work conditions in the O*NET database, as well as brief descriptions of each.

The 25 Physical Work Conditions

Bending or Twisting the Body. Amount of bending or twisting.

Climbing Ladders, Scaffolds, Poles, etc. Covers all climbing to elevated locations.

Common Protective or Safety Attire. Examples are safety shoes, glasses, gloves, hearing protection, hard hat, and personal flotation device.

Contaminants. Contaminants present like pollutants, gases, dust, odors, and so on.

(continues)

(continued)

Cramped Work Space or Awkward Positions. Cramped work space that requires getting into awkward positions.

Diseases or Infections. Potential diseases/infections (for example, patient care, some laboratory work, and sanitation control).

Distracting Sounds and Noise Levels. Sounds and noise levels that are distracting and uncomfortable.

Extremely Bright or Inadequate Lighting. Extremely bright or inadequate lighting conditions.

Hazardous Conditions. For example, high-voltage electricity, combustibles, explosives, chemicals; does not include hazardous equipment or situations.

Hazardous Equipment. For example, saws and machinery/mechanical parts. Includes exposure to vehicular traffic but not driving a vehicle.

Minor Burns, Cuts, Bites or Stings. Amount job involves likelihood of cuts, bites, stings, or minor burns.

High Places. For example, heights above 8 feet on ladders, poles, scaffolding, and catwalks.

Indoors. Amount job requires working indoors.

Keeping or Regaining Balance. Amount of keeping or regaining balance.

Kneeling, Crouching, or Crawling. Amount of kneeling, stooping, crouching, or crawling.

Making Repetitive Motions. Need to make repetitive motions.

Outdoors. Amount job requires working outdoors.

Radiation. Potential exposure to radiation.

Sitting. Amount of sitting required.

Specialized Protective or Safety Attire. Examples are breathing apparatus, safety harness, full protection suit, and radiation protection.

Standing. Amount of standing required.

Using Hands on Objects, Tools, or Controls. Using hands to handle, control, or feel objects, tools, or controls.

Very Hot or Cold. Very hot (above 90°F) or very cold (under 32°F) temperatures.

Walking or Running. Amount of walking or running.

Whole Body Vibration. For example, operating a jackhammer or earthmoving equipment.

Quick tips on how to use this information: For people with physical limitations or reactions to chemicals, for example, the importance of these measures is obvious. You can use this information to avoid jobs that are likely to

cause you problems or provide tasks you cannot handle. All of us have limitations of some kind, and all of us have preferences for our working conditions. All jobs require some compromise, and the information here helps you clearly understand what a job may require of you.

Other Job Characteristics

This section of the job description provides other information you may find helpful. There are 5 job characteristics presented below. For each job, we included those whose score exceeded the average for all jobs by the greatest amount. We included as many as 5 such characteristics for each job, and we ranked them by the extent to which their rating exceeds the average. Here are brief definitions for these characteristics.

The 5 Other Job Characteristics

Consequence of Error. The degree to which a mistake would cause a serious problem that was not readily correctable.

Degree of Automation. The level of automation of this job.

Importance of Being Exact or Accurate. The importance of being very exact or highly accurate in performing this job.

Importance of Repeating Same Tasks. The importance of repeating the same physical activities (for example, key entry) or mental activities (for example, checking entries in a ledger) over and over—without stopping.

Pace Determined by Speed of Equipment. The degree to which the pace is determined by the speed of equipment or machinery. (This does not refer to keeping busy at all times on this job.)

Quick tip on how to use this information: As you see, several of these items overlap with other data collected in the O*NET database. Still, we think you will find this information useful in helping you consider one job over another.

Experience

This section of the job description presents information the O*NET refers to as "job zones." The information presented in the O*NET job zones is a bit technical and hard to interpret, so we extracted one easily understood element from the job zones that gives the level of experience needed for each job. The O*NET assigns 1 of 5 levels of experience for each job, and we included this information in our job descriptions. Please note that sometimes discrepancies occur between the education data listed at a job description's beginning and the job zone data because the information comes from different agencies within the Department of Labor.

Here are the 5 levels the O*NET provides to help define the experience needed for entry into various jobs.

The 5 Levels of Experience

Job Zone 1. Little or no preparation needed. No previous work-related skill, knowledge, or experience is needed for these occupations. For example, a person can become a general office clerk even if the person has never worked in an office before.

Job Zone 2. Some preparation needed. Some previous work-related skill, knowledge, or experience may be helpful in these occupations but usually is not needed. For example, a drywall installer might benefit from experience installing drywall, but an inexperienced person could still learn to be an installer with little difficulty.

Job Zone 3. Medium preparation needed. Previous work-related skill, knowledge, or experience is required for these occupations. For example, an electrician must have completed 3 or 4 years of apprenticeship or several years of vocational training and often must have passed a licensing exam to perform the job.

Job Zone 4. Considerable preparation needed. A minimum of 2 to 4 years of work-related skill, knowledge, or experience is needed for these occupations. For example, an accountant must complete 4 years of college and work for several years in accounting to be considered qualified.

Job Zone 5. Extensive preparation needed. Extensive skill, knowledge, and experience are needed for these occupations. Many require more than 5 years of experience. For example, surgeons must complete 4 years of college and an additional 5 to 7 years of specialized medical training to be able to do the job.

Quick tip on how to use this information: This helps you understand the amount of training or education needed to qualify for entry into a job.

Job Preparation

The Department of Labor uses a system called the Standard Vocational Preparation (SVP) to assign 1 of 5 levels of training or education to a job. This SVP system has been used by the department for many years in standard reference systems such as the *Dictionary of Occupational Titles,* and SVP information has been included in the O*NET database. Please note that sometimes discrepancies occur between the education data listed at a job description's beginning and the job preparation data because the information comes from different agencies within the Department of Labor.

The 5 Standard Vocational Preparation (SVP) Codes

SVP below 4.0—Less than six months.

SVP 4.0 to less than 6.0—Six months to less than two years.

SVP 6.0 to less than 7.0—More than one year and less than four years.

SVP 7.0 to less than 8.0—Two years to less than 10 years.

SVP 8.0 and above—Four years to more than 10 years.

Quick tip on how to use this information: This measure is very similar to the one used for experience and can be used in a similar way to consider jobs that interest you.

Knowledge

Our job descriptions include information from the O*NET on the knowledge required to successfully perform in the occupation described. The knowledge may have been obtained from formal or informal sources, including high school or college courses or majors, training programs, self-employment, military, paid or volunteer work experience, and other life experiences. There are 33 O*NET knowledge descriptors. We selected the 5 whose ratings exceeded the average rating on that knowledge for all jobs, and we ranked them by the extent to which their rating exceeds the average.

Here are brief descriptions of the 33 knowledge items used in the O*NET and included in our job descriptions. They are arranged within the useful clusters shown here.

The 33 Knowledge Descriptors

Arts and Humanities

English Language. Knowledge of the structure and content of the English language, including the meaning and spelling of words, rules of composition, and grammar.

Fine Arts. Knowledge of theory and techniques required to produce, compose, and perform works of music, dance, visual arts, drama, and sculpture.

Foreign Language. Knowledge of the structure and content of a foreign (non-English) language, including the meaning and spelling of words, rules of composition and grammar, and pronunciation.

History and Archeology. Knowledge of past historical events and their causes, indicators, and impact on particular civilizations and cultures.

Philosophy and Theology. Knowledge of different philosophical systems and religions, including their basic principles, values, ethics, ways of thinking, customs, and practices and their impact on human culture.

(continues)

(continued)

Business and Management

Administration and Management. Knowledge of principles and processes involved in business and organizational planning, coordination, and execution. This includes strategic planning, resource allocation, manpower modeling, leadership techniques, and production methods.

Clerical. Knowledge of administrative and clerical procedures and systems such as word-processing systems, filing and records management systems, stenography and transcription, forms design principles, and other office procedures and terminology.

Customer and Personal Service. Knowledge of principles and processes for providing customer and personal services, including needs assessment techniques, quality service standards, alternative delivery systems, and customer satisfaction evaluation techniques.

Economics and Accounting. Knowledge of economic and accounting principles and practices, the financial markets, banking, and the analysis and reporting of financial data.

Personnel and Human Resources. Knowledge of policies and practices involved in personnel/human resource functions. This includes recruitment, selection, training, and promotion regulations and procedures; compensation and benefits packages; labor relations and negotiation strategies; and personnel information systems.

Sales and Marketing. Knowledge of principles and methods involved in showing, promoting, and selling products or services. This includes marketing strategies and tactics, product demonstration and sales techniques, and sales control systems.

Communications

Communications and Media. Knowledge of media production, communication, and dissemination techniques and methods, including alternative ways to inform and entertain via written, oral, and visual media.

Telecommunications. Knowledge of transmission, broadcasting, switching, control, and operation of telecommunications systems.

Education and Training

Education and Training. Knowledge of instructional methods and training techniques, including curriculum design principles, learning theory, group and individual teaching techniques, design of individual development plans, and test design principles.

Health Services

Medicine and Dentistry. Knowledge of the information and techniques needed to diagnose and treat injuries, diseases, and deformities. This includes symptoms, treatment alternatives, drug properties and interactions, and preventive health-care measures.

Therapy and Counseling. Knowledge of information and techniques needed to rehabilitate physical and mental ailments and to provide career guidance, including alternative treatments, rehabilitation equipment and its proper use, and methods to evaluate treatment effects.

Law and Public Safety

Law and Government. Knowledge of laws, legal codes, court procedures, precedents, government regulations, executive orders, agency rules, and the democratic political process.

Public Safety and Security. Knowledge of weaponry; public safety; security operations, rules, regulations, precautions, and prevention; and the protection of people, data, and property.

Manufacturing and Production

Building and Construction. Knowledge of materials, methods, and the appropriate tools to construct objects, structures, and buildings.

Computers and Electronics. Knowledge of electric circuit boards, processors, chips, and computer hardware and software, including applications and programming.

Design. Knowledge of design techniques, principles, tools, and instruments involved in the production and use of precision technical plans, blueprints, drawings, and models.

Engineering and Technology. Knowledge of equipment, tools, mechanical devices, and their uses to produce motion, light, power, technology, and other applications.

Food Production. Knowledge of techniques and equipment for planting, growing, and harvesting of food for consumption, including crop rotation methods, animal husbandry, and food storage/handling techniques.

Mechanical. Knowledge of machines and tools, including their designs, uses, benefits, repair, and maintenance.

Production and Processing. Knowledge of inputs, outputs, raw materials, waste, quality control, costs, and techniques for maximizing the manufacture and distribution of goods.

Mathematics and Science

Biology. Knowledge of plant and animal living tissue, cells, organisms, and entities, including their functions, interdependencies, and interactions with each other and the environment.

Chemistry. Knowledge of the composition, structure, and properties of substances and of the chemical processes and transformations that they undergo. This includes uses of chemicals and their interactions, danger signs, production techniques, and disposal methods.

Geography. Knowledge of various methods for describing the location and distribution of land, sea, and air masses, including their physical locations, relationships, and characteristics.

Mathematics. Knowledge of numbers and their operations and interrelationships, including arithmetic, algebra, geometry, calculus, statistics, and their applications.

Physics. Knowledge and prediction of physical principles, laws, and applications, including air, water, material dynamics, light, atomic principles, heat, electric theory, earth formations, and meteorological and related natural phenomena.

Psychology. Knowledge of human behavior and performance, mental processes, psychological research methods, and the assessment and treatment of behavioral and affective disorders.

Sociology and Anthropology. Knowledge of group behavior and dynamics, societal trends and influences, cultures, their history, migrations, ethnicity, and origins.

Transportation

Transportation. Knowledge of principles and methods for moving people or goods by air, rail, sea, or road, including their relative costs, advantages, and limitations.

Quick tips on how to use this information: If you are considering additional education or training, this section gives you some idea of the courses or programs that would be helpful for each job. It also helps you to identify if you have some or all of the knowledge needed for a new job and what you need to improve on through additional training.

Instructional Programs

The Classification of Instructional Programs (CIP) is a system of naming and categorizing training and educational programs and courses. Developed by the U.S. Department of Education, the CIP is widely used in occupational, education, and training reference systems. We listed the latest CIP program or course names related to each occupation.

Quick tip on how to use this information: The CIP information helps you identify the names of training or educational programs that prepare you for a job. The U.S. Department of Education has a reference guide describing all of the CIP programs. Titled the *Classification of Instructional Programs*, it should be available through state libraries and directly from the Department of Education at www.ed.gov.

Related DOT Jobs

At the end of each description is one or more job titles related to the O*NET job title. We obtained these by cross-referencing the O*NET title to another occupational classification system titled the *Dictionary of Occupational Titles*.

The DOT is an older occupational reference system developed by the Department of Labor that has been replaced by the O*NET. We also included the DOT number assigned to each job title to allow you to cross-reference career information systems using the DOT system.

Quick tips on how to use this information: Even if you never use the DOT, the alternative titles help you identify the wide range of specialized jobs that are available. The DOT has over 12,000 job titles, and most of them are now merged into the more general job titles used in the O*NET. This makes the O*NET much easier to use when identifying jobs that interest you, and the DOT job titles can give you ideas on more specialized jobs that may interest you even more. If you wish, you can then learn more about the more specialized DOT jobs by reading their descriptions in the *Dictionary of Occupational Titles*. One of these specialized jobs may be just what you want to do with your career.

An Explanation of Some Curious Things in the Job Descriptions

As you read the job descriptions in this book, you may notice some odd things. For example, some job descriptions do not include information found in most other descriptions. And other details here and there may not seem right to you. We explain some of these points here, although you may notice others.

The basic reason for apparent errors is that the job descriptions are based on data we assemble from and cross-reference to several enormous databases of information. These databases are not perfect. They may have missing data, may not provide precise cross-references to other systems, and may have other limitations. We did our best to create a useful resource but had to base it on the limitations of our information sources. So here are explanations of a few things you may notice as you read the job descriptions.

Information in the Descriptions May Overlap

As you read the job descriptions, you may note that information in one section of a description is similar to information in another. This is not an error, as the O*NET data sometimes overlaps. For example, the general work activities statements are often similar to the occupational task list section. The skills statements may be similar to content provided elsewhere in the description.

The reason lies in how the information was developed. The occupational task lists were written specifically for each job, based on information collected from employer surveys and other sources. Work values, knowledge, abilities, skills, general work activities, and physical work conditions were created quite differently. For these, a list of characteristics was developed that applies to many or all jobs. Each occupation was given a numerical rating for each characteristic, with higher numbers referring to higher levels of competence. Since there are so many measures, listing them all for each job would be impractical and, we think, confusing. Instead, we developed a method for listing the more important characteristics for each job—the ones that are most important to have or develop.

"None Met the Criteria"

The criteria we used to select data for inclusion in the job descriptions differs from one part to another. These criteria were explained earlier in this introduction.

When you see the statement "None met the criteria" in the abilities or other parts of a job description, this doesn't mean abilities are not important in these jobs. Rather, the job had no measure high enough to meet our criteria for inclusion. We adjusted our criteria to keep this situation from occurring too often, but you see this statement in some descriptions.

Information That Seems Incorrect

You may notice that some information in a job descriptions seems contradictory, inaccurate, or incorrect. This is simply a reflection of the data that was available from the database. So, as you review the descriptions, keep in mind that data has its limitations.

For example, you may notice that several jobs in a row share the same education, openings, growth, and salary data. The O*NET system is used for most information in this book, but we used the Occupational Employment Survey (OES) system as the information source for the education requirements, employment data, projected growth, and earnings for each occupation. The OES is used by the U.S. Bureau of Labor Statistics (BLS) to collect wage and employment data. Therefore, you see the same education level, employment data and projections, and earnings data for jobs that share OES titles, even though their O*NET titles differ.

"No Data Available"

When you see this statement in a job description, it means just what it says. This tends to happen for recent O*NET job entries, where the data has not yet been collected or processed for one or more of that job's measures.

"Others"

You see this statement at the end of some job descriptions in the Instructional Programs or Related DOT Jobs sections. We did this only when there is a very long list of similar or related instructional programs or DOT jobs. When this is so, we listed the first 20 DOT job titles, and we cut off the program names at 2000 characters. Since this section's purpose is to introduce you to the many specialized programs and jobs related to each O*NET title, we think that listing these amounts of information gives you a good idea of the many related occupations and programs. For some O*NET job titles, there are hundreds of related DOT titles. Many of these jobs are similar to each other, like "Manager, Bakery" and "Manager, Cemetery," and going on and on with similar job titles isn't helpful.

Some Job Descriptions Are Shorter Than Others

Some job descriptions are substantially shorter than others. When this occurs, you see the statement "The Department of Labor has not collected some data for this job, so it has fewer details than the other descriptions."

One reason for the shorter descriptions is that some jobs have been recently added to the O*NET database, and these do not yet have data available for them.

Another reason is that sometimes one job title encapsulates other detailed jobs as part of the numbering structure, and the one job title has a briefer description. To get full information, you need to review the detailed jobs' descriptions. For example, Accountants and Auditors is listed as one job (with a shorter description), but it is then followed by longer, separate descriptions for Accountants and then Auditors.

Tips for Using This Book

The O*NET is now the major and most authoritative source of occupational information for employers, job seekers, students, career changers, and many others. Most occupational information sources will rely on or cross-reference the O*NET as the standard for detailed, reliable data on jobs.

As a major revision, the *O*NET Dictionary of Occupational Titles,* Third Edition, is intended for use by a variety of audiences. Following are brief tips for the major users of this book. Note that these tips are in addition to the quick tips we provide throughout our explanation of the various data elements included in the job descriptions.

Tips for Employers and Human Resource Development Professionals

The O*NET descriptions in this book provide a variety of valuable information for use in business. Some of these uses include the following.

- **Write job descriptions.** Each O*NET description has been carefully constructed to accurately reflect the tasks, skills, abilities, and other attributes required. These details provide an excellent source of objective information to use in writing job descriptions. As an example, look back at the sample description for Employment Interviewers presented earlier in the introduction. You find the key skills needed in the position, the responsibility level required, the education and training required, and the knowledge needed to succeed in the job—most of the content for a solid job description. Of course, you will need to customize the information for your organization, but the O*NET descriptions provide an excellent starting point.

- **Structure employment interviews and hiring decisions.** You can use the O*NET descriptions to identify key skills and experiences to look for when screening applicants during interviews. This can be done informally, or a formal list of required competencies could be developed and then used by interviewers to more objectively rate each applicant. Of course, employer-specific requirements should be added as needed to the basic requirements for job performance provided by the O*NET descriptions.

- **Set pay levels.** We have noted the limitations for using pay information, and those same cautions apply when used by employers setting pay levels. The salary information does, however, provide some guidance on the pay rate for an experienced worker. Entry-level workers are often paid less (sometimes much less), and local conditions often determine the going rate to attract the employee skills needed. There are no hard guidelines, so use your judgment.

- **Identify training requirements.** You can use the descriptions to identify training needed for current or prospective employees to gain proficiency in various jobs. You may also identify skills or other weaknesses in a potential employee that can be corrected through brief training and therefore increase the applicant pool for certain positions.

The O*NET information is also helpful for existing employees seeking upward mobility to a more challenging or different job with the same employer. It can help them identify skills, training, knowledge, and other factors that they need to develop for success.

Tips for People Exploring Career Alternatives

Virtually all workers in North America work in one of the occupations described in this book. While the descriptions are quite brief, they provide substantial information that can be used as a preliminary source for identifying one or more career options to explore more thoroughly.

If you are using this book to explore career options, the best way to begin is by identifying jobs or clusters of jobs that interest you most. Part I presents five ways to find jobs in the O*NET: by SOC number, by interest area, by education and training requirements, by placement in three best jobs lists, and alphabetically by job title. Read the O*NET descriptions for those jobs that most interest you and, for those you want to know even more about, use one of the resources that follow:

- **Read the *Occupational Outlook Handbook*.** Each O*NET description relates to one or more job titles found in a separate book titled the *Occupational Outlook Handbook*. We like the OOH and recommend it highly. Its descriptions are longer and provide details that are useful to anyone considering the occupation. The OOH is available in most libraries and through many bookstores. The OOH descriptions are also provided in a book titled *America's Top 300 Jobs* (JIST Works). One of these books should be available in most libraries and bookstores.

- **Read the *Dictionary of Occupational Titles* and the *Guide for Occupational Exploration*.** The DOT and GOE are widely used reference books with organizational systems cross-referenced by many other books, interest inventories, and other materials. The O*NET descriptions in this book include related DOT and GOE numbers and job titles or interest groups, allowing you to cross-reference these important systems. The DOT was published by the U.S. Department of Labor and provides brief descriptions for over 12,000 job titles. The last edition of the DOT was released in 1991. Since the O*NET database replaces the older DOT database of occupational information, there are no plans to update the DOT in the future. Even so, it will remain a rich source of information on many specific job titles that are simply not described elsewhere. The *Guide for Occupational Exploration* (JIST Works) organizes jobs into groupings based on interests and provides useful information on these groupings and the jobs within the groups.

- **Get additional information from the library or the Internet.** Ask a librarian to direct you to books, periodicals, and other sources of information on an occupation that interests you. Professional journals are often available for a wide variety of occupations and industries. You can also often obtain substantial information from professional associations and sources on the Internet. JIST's Web site provides links to other career-related sites. Visit the company at www.jist.com.

- **Talk to people who work in the jobs that interest you.** The best source of information is often overlooked—the people who work in jobs that interest you. They are often willing to answer your questions and to give you sources of additional information.

Tips for Those Considering Education or Training Options

People with more training or education tend to earn more than those with less. While most training and education benefits you in some way, many people do not spend enough time investigating such an important decision. Before you spend substantial time and money on courses or training programs, spend some time investigating what you hope to gain.

Each O*NET description provides several sources of education and training information. The education section of each job description is the most obvious one, but additional information is found in the knowledge and instructional programs sections. Following are some details on how each of these sections can be used to better understand the training or education needed for a given job.

- **The education section.** This includes information on the training or education level typically required for entry into the listed occupation.

- **The knowledge section.** This section gives you some idea of the courses or programs that would be helpful for each job.

- **The instructional program section.** Each occupational description includes one or more CIP titles. This refers to the Classification of Instructional Pro-

grams, a widely used system for organizing training and education programs. The CIP title tells you the type of training or educational programs typically available for preparing for that occupation. Program names used in various schools and training programs may differ from those listed in the CIP, but the CIP information gives you some idea of the programs available.

While the O*NET descriptions provide some information on the level of training, education, and experience required for various occupations, you obviously need more detail. As with occupational data, a wide variety of training and education information is available. Bookstores and libraries have many books on the topic, much is available on the Internet, and local schools and training programs provide orientation and admission information. All these resources should be used before making an important decision on education or training.

Tips for Job Seekers

The O*NET job descriptions in this book can help you in two important ways:

- **Identify new job targets.** Many job seekers miss employment opportunities by overlooking jobs they can do but with which they are not familiar. For this reason, you should carefully review all the O*NET job titles, with particular emphasis on those in clusters you are already considering. A listing of O*NET jobs within clusters appears in the table of contents. Review it if you are looking for a job. As you identify possible new job targets, look up their O*NET descriptions to determine if you might qualify. If you do, consider pursuing these jobs. In the interview, point out the qualities that you have and state that you can quickly learn any needed skills.

- **Prepare for interviews.** The O*NET descriptions offer very useful information in preparing for interviews. For example, once you have set up an interview for a position, carefully review the O*NET description for that job. Doing so helps you identify skills and experience you should emphasize. We also encourage you to carefully review the O*NET descriptions of jobs you have held in the past. Doing so identifies skills and other characteristics that you can present in your interview for a new position.

Even past jobs that seem unrelated to your current interests often provide skills and experience that you can use to convince an employer that you can handle the position you seek. Careful interview preparation can make the difference between getting a job offer or not. We have often found that better-prepared job seekers get jobs over those with superior credentials. The difference is in how well they present themselves in interviews. Those who read and understand the skills they have to do the job they seek—and communicate this to an employer—have a distinct advantage.

Tips for Teachers and Educators

O*NET descriptions provide excellent information on the skill and knowledge needed to succeed in a given job. If you are responsible for developing or teaching a course or curriculum for a school or training program, the descriptions provide exact points that need to be learned. An outcome-oriented program could be developed to teach specific, measurable knowledge or competencies. Remember that the O*NET database provides specific measures for many elements included in this book, and these measures can be obtained by accessing the database itself.

Tips for Those Researching Technical and Legal Issues— "Caveat Datum"

You have probably heard of "caveat emptor," which is Latin for "let the buyer beware." We think "caveat datum," which (loosely translated) means "beware of the data," is particularly appropriate as our advice regarding the O*NET data as the basis for settling legal and other important issues.

The O*NET database—and the O*NET descriptions in this book—provide substantial technical information on jobs and their many characteristics and requirements. The U.S. government provides this information, and great care has been taken to make it both accurate and reliable. Even so, the information does have limitations. For example, the O*NET job title Sales Managers has enormous differences in requirements from one employer to another in such points as responsibility, stress, travel requirements, computer literacy requirements, product knowledge, and physical lifting of samples. These differences can simply not be included in one description database, and many job-to-job

differences exist. That is why the U.S. Department of Labor has never approved or encouraged the use of its occupational information to support formal litigation or as the final, authoritative basis for legal and other formal matters.

In a similar way, we urge you to understand that the validity of the underlying information has limitations. For example, an occupation that lists a bachelor's degree as a typical training requirement for entry often has some or even many people successfully working in the job with less education—or much more.

One information source can simply not cover all variations of a given job. Too many differences exist in the requirements for the same job title among different employers. That is why we recommend that you use your own judgment in understanding the information. While it has been carefully collected and reviewed, it has limitations and should not be used as the final authoritative source for legal or technical issues.

Your Suggestions Are Welcome

While it was impractical to include details on all data elements for each occupation found in the O*NET database, the O*NET descriptions in this book include substantial details in a useful format. In addition to the narrative description, we include higher-than-average requirements for many data elements for each occupation—plus the cross-walk information for the GOE, CIP, and DOT (all explained earlier). While some compromises were involved in constructing helpful descriptions, we think the information is valuable for many uses. We hope you agree.

Because we intend to revise this book as updated O*NET data becomes available, please let us know what you would like us to include in future editions. Please send your comments and suggestions to Editor, *O*NET Dictionary of Occupational Titles*, JIST Works, 8902 Otis Ave., Indianapolis, IN 46216-1033. You can also send an e-mail to info@jist.com. Thanks!

Five Easy Ways to Find O*NET Jobs of Interest

This book provides over 1,100 job descriptions, so how do you pinpoint those that are most relevant to you? This part provides five easy ways for you to find job descriptions. The lists included in this part can help you narrow the selection and consider jobs that you qualify for or are interested in. Several kinds of lists sort the jobs in helpful ways:

- Interest area lists sort jobs according to fourteen career interest areas
- Education and training level lists sort jobs according to their education and training requirements
- Best-paying, fastest-growing, and most openings lists present the top 50+ jobs in each of those three categories

You can also browse the job titles alphabetically or by O*NET number.

Method 1: Browse the Jobs by O*NET Number

The jobs are listed in the Table of Contents by their O*NET numbers, which are based on the Standard Occupational Classification (SOC) system. The SOC is a structure established by the federal government that organizes the jobs according to the work performed.

If you know the O*NET number for a job, look it up in the Table of Contents and then turn to the corresponding page for the complete job description. The Table of Contents starts on page v.

When to Use This Method: You may have obtained the O*NET number for a job in several ways, including in the *Occupational Outlook Handbook,* another resource by the U.S. Department of Labor. The *OOH* lists the O*NET numbers for over 250 jobs held by about 90 percent of the labor force. Use the O*NET number to locate the job description in Part II of this book. You can also browse other descriptions in the same section, as they are likely to have similar tasks and responsibilities.

Method 2: Browse the Jobs Based on Your Interests

You can use the following lists to find jobs that fall into each of the 14 Guide for Occupational Exploration (GOE) career interest areas. This system is explained in more detail in the Introduction. The jobs within each interest area are listed alphabetically, and each job is listed with its O*NET number to help you locate it in Part II.

When to Use This Method: If certain types of careers interest you, the following lists help you narrow your search. Simply find the career areas that interest you most, review the list of related jobs, and then look up their descriptions in Part II using the O*NET number.

01: Arts, Entertainment, and Media

O*NET Number	Job Title
27-2011.00	Actors
13-1011.00	Agents and Business Managers of Artists, Performers, and Athletes
27-1011.00	Art Directors
27-1019.99	Artists and Related Workers, All Other
27-2021.00	Athletes and Sports Competitors
27-4011.00	Audio and Video Equipment Technicians
27-3021.00	Broadcast News Analysts
27-4012.00	Broadcast Technicians
51-5022.04	Camera Operators
27-4031.00	Camera Operators, Television, Video, and Motion Picture
27-3043.03	Caption Writers
27-1013.03	Cartoonists
27-2032.00	Choreographers
27-2022.00	Coaches and Scouts
27-1021.00	Commercial and Industrial Designers
27-2041.03	Composers
27-3043.04	Copy Writers
39-3092.00	Costume Attendants
27-1012.00	Craft Artists
27-3043.02	Creative Writers
27-2031.00	Dancers
27-1029.99	Designers, All Other
43-9031.00	Desktop Publishers
27-2012.02	Directors—Stage, Motion Pictures, Television, and Radio
51-5022.08	Dot Etchers
27-3041.00	Editors
51-5022.09	Electronic Masking System Operators
51-9194.06	Engravers, Hand
51-9194.02	Engravers/Carvers
27-2099.99	Entertainers and Performers, Sports and Related Workers, All Other
51-9194.03	Etchers
51-9194.00	Etchers and Engravers
51-9194.05	Etchers, Hand
27-1027.02	Exhibit Designers
27-1022.00	Fashion Designers
27-4032.00	Film and Video Editors
27-1013.00	Fine Artists, Including Painters, Sculptors, and Illustrators
39-9031.00	Fitness Trainers and Aerobics Instructors
27-1023.00	Floral Designers
51-9195.04	Glass Blowers, Molders, Benders, and Finishers
27-1024.00	Graphic Designers
27-1025.00	Interior Designers
27-3091.00	Interpreters and Translators
39-5091.00	Makeup Artists, Theatrical and Performance
27-4099.99	Media and Communication Equipment Workers, All Other
27-3099.99	Media and Communication Workers, All Other
27-1026.00	Merchandise Displayers and Window Trimmers
41-9012.00	Models
27-1014.00	Multi-Media Artists and Animators
27-2041.02	Music Arrangers and Orchestrators
27-2041.01	Music Directors
27-2041.00	Music Directors and Composers
27-2042.00	Musicians and Singers
27-2042.02	Musicians, Instrumental
27-1013.01	Painters and Illustrators
51-9194.04	Pantograph Engravers
51-5022.02	Paste-Up Workers
51-5022.03	Photoengravers
27-4021.00	Photographers
27-3043.01	Poets and Lyricists
51-9195.05	Potters
51-9194.01	Precision Etchers and Engravers, Hand or Machine
27-2012.01	Producers
27-2012.00	Producers and Directors
27-4021.01	Professional Photographers
27-2012.03	Program Directors

27-3012.00	Public Address System and Other Announcers
27-3031.00	Public Relations Specialists
27-3011.00	Radio and Television Announcers
27-4013.00	Radio Operators
27-3022.00	Reporters and Correspondents
27-1013.04	Sculptors
27-1027.00	Set and Exhibit Designers
27-1027.01	Set Designers
27-2042.01	Singers
27-1013.02	Sketch Artists
27-4014.00	Sound Engineering Technicians
27-2012.04	Talent Directors
27-2012.05	Technical Directors/Managers
27-3042.00	Technical Writers
27-2023.00	Umpires, Referees, and Other Sports Officials
27-3043.00	Writers and Authors

02: Science, Math, and Engineering

O*NET Number	Job Title
15-2011.00	Actuaries
17-3021.00	Aerospace Engineering and Operations Technicians
17-2011.00	Aerospace Engineers
19-4011.00	Agricultural and Food Science Technicians
17-2021.00	Agricultural Engineers
19-4011.01	Agricultural Technicians
19-1011.00	Animal Scientists
19-3091.01	Anthropologists
19-3091.00	Anthropologists and Archeologists
19-3091.02	Archeologists
17-1011.00	Architects, Except Landscape and Naval
17-3011.00	Architectural and Civil Drafters
17-3011.01	Architectural Drafters
19-2011.00	Astronomers
19-2021.00	Atmospheric and Space Scientists
19-1021.01	Biochemists
19-1021.00	Biochemists and Biophysicists
19-1029.99	Biological Scientists, All Other
19-4021.00	Biological Technicians
19-1020.01	Biologists
17-2031.00	Biomedical Engineers
19-1021.02	Biophysicists
17-3023.02	Calibration and Instrumentation Technicians
17-1021.00	Cartographers and Photogrammetrists
17-2041.00	Chemical Engineers
19-4031.00	Chemical Technicians
19-2031.00	Chemists
19-4061.01	City Planning Aides
17-3011.02	Civil Drafters
17-3022.00	Civil Engineering Technicians
17-2051.00	Civil Engineers
15-1011.00	Computer and Information Scientists, Research

11-3021.00	Computer and Information Systems Managers
17-2061.00	Computer Hardware Engineers
15-1021.00	Computer Programmers
15-1071.01	Computer Security Specialists
15-1031.00	Computer Software Engineers, Applications
15-1032.00	Computer Software Engineers, Systems Software
15-1099.99	Computer Specialists, All Other
15-1041.00	Computer Support Specialists
15-1051.00	Computer Systems Analysts
19-1031.00	Conservation Scientists
47-4011.00	Construction and Building Inspectors
15-1061.00	Database Administrators
17-3019.99	Drafters, All Other
19-3011.00	Economists
17-3023.00	Electrical and Electronic Engineering Technicians
17-3012.00	Electrical and Electronics Drafters
17-3012.02	Electrical Drafters
17-3023.03	Electrical Engineering Technicians
17-2071.00	Electrical Engineers
17-3024.00	Electro-Mechanical Technicians
17-3012.01	Electronic Drafters
17-3023.01	Electronics Engineering Technicians
17-2072.00	Electronics Engineers, Except Computer
11-9041.00	Engineering Managers
17-3029.99	Engineering Technicians, Except Drafters, All Other
17-2199.99	Engineers, All Other
17-3025.00	Environmental Engineering Technicians
17-2081.00	Environmental Engineers
19-4091.00	Environmental Science and Protection Technicians, Including Health
19-2041.00	Environmental Scientists and Specialists, Including Health
19-1041.00	Epidemiologists
17-2111.02	Fire-Prevention and Protection Engineers
19-4011.02	Food Science Technicians
19-1012.00	Food Scientists and Technologists
19-1032.00	Foresters
19-3092.00	Geographers
19-4041.00	Geological and Petroleum Technicians
19-4041.01	Geological Data Technicians
19-4041.02	Geological Sample Test Technicians
19-2042.01	Geologists
19-2042.00	Geoscientists, Except Hydrologists and Geographers
17-2111.00	Health and Safety Engineers, Except Mining Safety Engineers and Inspectors
19-3093.00	Historians
19-2043.00	Hydrologists
17-3026.00	Industrial Engineering Technicians
17-2112.00	Industrial Engineers
17-2111.01	Industrial Safety and Health Engineers

(continues)

(continued)

02: Science, Math, and Engineering

O*NET Number	Job Title
19-3032.00	Industrial-Organizational Psychologists
17-1012.00	Landscape Architects
19-1099.99	Life Scientists, All Other
19-4099.99	Life, Physical, and Social Science Technicians, All Other
17-3031.02	Mapping Technicians
17-2121.02	Marine Architects
17-2121.01	Marine Engineers
17-2121.00	Marine Engineers and Naval Architects
17-2131.00	Materials Engineers
19-2032.00	Materials Scientists
15-2099.99	Mathematical Science Occupations, All Other
15-2091.00	Mathematical Technicians
15-2021.00	Mathematicians
17-3013.00	Mechanical Drafters
17-3027.00	Mechanical Engineering Technicians
17-2141.00	Mechanical Engineers
19-1042.00	Medical Scientists, Except Epidemiologists
19-1022.00	Microbiologists
17-2151.00	Mining and Geological Engineers, Including Mining Safety Engineers
11-9121.00	Natural Sciences Managers
15-1071.00	Network and Computer Systems Administrators
15-1081.00	Network Systems and Data Communications Analysts
17-2161.00	Nuclear Engineers
19-4051.01	Nuclear Equipment Operation Technicians
19-4051.00	Nuclear Technicians
51-4012.00	Numerical Tool and Process Control Programmers
15-2031.00	Operations Research Analysts
17-2171.00	Petroleum Engineers
27-4021.02	Photographers, Scientific
19-2099.99	Physical Scientists, All Other
19-2012.00	Physicists
19-1013.01	Plant Scientists
19-3094.00	Political Scientists
13-1041.05	Pressure Vessel Inspectors
17-2111.03	Product Safety Engineers
19-3039.99	Psychologists, All Other
19-1031.02	Range Managers
41-9031.00	Sales Engineers
19-4061.00	Social Science Research Assistants
19-3099.99	Social Scientists and Related Workers, All Other
19-3041.00	Sociologists
19-1013.00	Soil and Plant Scientists
19-1031.01	Soil Conservationists
19-1013.02	Soil Scientists
43-9111.00	Statistical Assistants
15-2041.00	Statisticians
19-3022.00	Survey Researchers
17-3031.00	Surveying and Mapping Technicians
17-3031.01	Surveying Technicians
17-1022.00	Surveyors
19-3051.00	Urban and Regional Planners
19-1023.00	Zoologists and Wildlife Biologists

03: Plants and Animals

O*NET Number	Job Title
11-9011.02	Agricultural Crop Farm Managers
45-2091.00	Agricultural Equipment Operators
45-2099.99	Agricultural Workers, All Other
45-2021.00	Animal Breeders
39-2011.00	Animal Trainers
45-4021.00	Fallers
45-1012.00	Farm Labor Contractors
11-9012.00	Farmers and Ranchers
45-2092.00	Farmworkers and Laborers, Crop, Nursery, and Greenhouse
45-2093.00	Farmworkers, Farm and Ranch Animals
45-1011.01	First-Line Supervisors and Manager/Supervisors—Agricultural Crop Workers
45-1011.03	First-Line Supervisors and Manager/Supervisors—Animal Care Workers, Except Livestock
45-1011.02	First-Line Supervisors and Manager/Supervisors—Animal Husbandry Workers
45-1011.06	First-Line Supervisors and Manager/Supervisors—Fishery Workers
45-1011.04	First-Line Supervisors and Manager/Supervisors—Horticultural Workers
37-1012.02	First-Line Supervisors and Manager/Supervisors—Landscaping Workers
45-1011.05	First-Line Supervisors and Manager/Supervisors—Logging Workers
45-1011.00	First-Line Supervisors/Managers of Farming, Fishing, and Forestry Workers
37-1012.00	First-Line Supervisors/Managers of Landscaping, Lawn Service, and Groundskeeping Workers
11-9011.03	Fish Hatchery Managers
45-3011.00	Fishers and Related Fishing Workers
19-4093.00	Forest and Conservation Technicians
45-4011.00	Forest and Conservation Workers
45-2092.02	General Farmworkers
37-3019.99	Grounds Maintenance Workers, All Other
45-3021.00	Hunters and Trappers
37-3011.00	Landscaping and Groundskeeping Workers
37-1012.01	Lawn Service Managers
45-4022.00	Logging Equipment Operators
45-4022.01	Logging Tractor Operators
45-4029.99	Logging Workers, All Other
39-2021.00	Nonfarm Animal Caretakers
11-9011.01	Nursery and Greenhouse Managers

45-2092.01	Nursery Workers
37-2021.00	Pest Control Workers
37-3012.00	Pesticide Handlers, Sprayers, and Applicators, Vegetation
37-3013.00	Tree Trimmers and Pruners
29-1131.00	Veterinarians
31-9096.00	Veterinary Assistants and Laboratory Animal Caretakers
29-2056.00	Veterinary Technologists and Technicians

04: Law, Law Enforcement, and Public Safety

O*NET Number	Job Title
23-1021.00	Administrative Law Judges, Adjudicators, and Hearing Officers
45-2011.00	Agricultural Inspectors
55-3011.00	Air Crew Members
55-1011.00	Air Crew Officers
55-1012.00	Aircraft Launch and Recovery Officers
55-3012.00	Aircraft Launch and Recovery Specialists
33-9011.00	Animal Control Workers
23-1022.00	Arbitrators, Mediators, and Conciliators
55-3013.00	Armored Assault Vehicle Crew Members
55-1013.00	Armored Assault Vehicle Officers
55-3014.00	Artillery and Missile Crew Members
55-1014.00	Artillery and Missile Officers
53-6051.01	Aviation Inspectors
33-3011.00	Bailiffs
33-3021.04	Child Support, Missing Persons, and Unemployment Insurance Fraud Investigators
55-1015.00	Command and Control Center Officers
55-3015.00	Command and Control Center Specialists
13-1041.00	Compliance Officers, Except Agriculture, Construction, Health and Safety, and Transportation
33-3012.00	Correctional Officers and Jailers
33-3021.03	Criminal Investigators and Special Agents
33-9091.00	Crossing Guards
33-3021.00	Detectives and Criminal Investigators
13-1061.00	Emergency Management Specialists
29-2041.00	Emergency Medical Technicians and Paramedics
13-1041.01	Environmental Compliance Inspectors
13-1041.03	Equal Opportunity Representatives and Officers
13-2061.00	Financial Examiners
33-2011.00	Fire Fighters
33-2021.01	Fire Inspectors
33-2021.00	Fire Inspectors and Investigators
33-2021.02	Fire Investigators
55-2011.00	First-Line Supervisors/Managers of Air Crew Members
55-2013.00	First-Line Supervisors/Managers of All Other Tactical Operations Specialists
33-1011.00	First-Line Supervisors/Managers of Correctional Officers
33-1021.00	First-Line Supervisors/Managers of Fire Fighting and Prevention Workers
33-1012.00	First-Line Supervisors/Managers of Police and Detectives
55-2012.00	First-Line Supervisors/Managers of Weapons Specialists/Crew Members
33-1099.99	First-Line Supervisors/Managers, Protective Service Workers, All Other
33-3031.00	Fish and Game Wardens
19-4092.00	Forensic Science Technicians
33-2011.02	Forest Fire Fighters
33-1021.02	Forest Fire Fighting and Prevention Supervisors
33-2022.00	Forest Fire Inspectors and Prevention Specialists
33-9031.00	Gaming Surveillance Officers and Gaming Investigators
13-1041.04	Government Property Inspectors and Investigators
33-3051.02	Highway Patrol Pilots
33-3021.05	Immigration and Customs Inspectors
55-3016.00	Infantry
55-1016.00	Infantry Officers
23-1023.00	Judges, Magistrate Judges, and Magistrates
23-2092.00	Law Clerks
23-1011.00	Lawyers
23-2099.99	Legal Support Workers, All Other
13-1041.02	Licensing Examiners and Inspectors
33-9092.00	Lifeguards, Ski Patrol, and Other Recreational Protective Service Workers
53-6051.03	Marine Cargo Inspectors
55-3019.99	Military Enlisted Tactical Operations and Air/Weapons Specialists and Crew Members, All Other
55-1019.99	Military Officer Special and Tactical Operations Leaders/Managers, All Other
33-2011.01	Municipal Fire Fighters
33-1021.01	Municipal Fire Fighting and Prevention Supervisors
19-4051.02	Nuclear Monitoring Technicians
29-9011.00	Occupational Health and Safety Specialists
29-9012.00	Occupational Health and Safety Technicians
23-2011.00	Paralegals and Legal Assistants
33-3041.00	Parking Enforcement Workers
33-3051.00	Police and Sheriff's Patrol Officers
33-3021.01	Police Detectives
33-3021.02	Police Identification and Records Officers
33-3051.01	Police Patrol Officers
33-9021.00	Private Detectives and Investigators
33-9099.99	Protective Service Workers, All Other
53-6051.02	Public Transportation Inspectors
55-3017.00	Radar and Sonar Technicians
33-9032.00	Security Guards
33-3051.03	Sheriffs and Deputy Sheriffs
55-3018.00	Special Forces
55-1017.00	Special Forces Officers

(continues)

(continued)

04: Law, Law Enforcement, and Public Safety

O*NET Number	Job Title
23-2093.02	Title Examiners and Abstractors
23-2093.00	Title Examiners, Abstractors, and Searchers
23-2093.01	Title Searchers
33-3052.00	Transit and Railroad Police

05: Mechanics, Installers, and Repairers

O*NET Number	Job Title
49-3011.03	Aircraft Body and Bonded Structure Repairers
49-3011.02	Aircraft Engine Specialists
49-3011.00	Aircraft Mechanics and Service Technicians
49-3011.01	Airframe-and-Power-Plant Mechanics
49-3021.00	Automotive Body and Related Repairers
49-3022.00	Automotive Glass Installers and Repairers
49-3023.01	Automotive Master Mechanics
49-3023.00	Automotive Service Technicians and Mechanics
49-3023.02	Automotive Specialty Technicians
49-2091.00	Avionics Technicians
49-2092.03	Battery Repairers
49-3091.00	Bicycle Repairers
53-6011.00	Bridge and Lock Tenders
49-3031.00	Bus and Truck Mechanics and Diesel Engine Specialists
49-9061.00	Camera and Photographic Equipment Repairers
49-2022.01	Central Office and PBX Installers and Repairers
49-9091.00	Coin, Vending, and Amusement Machine Servicers and Repairers
49-2022.03	Communication Equipment Mechanics, Installers, and Repairers
49-2011.00	Computer, Automated Teller, and Office Machine Repairers
49-9012.00	Control and Valve Installers and Repairers, Except Mechanical Door
49-2011.02	Data Processing Equipment Repairers
49-2092.01	Electric Home Appliance and Power Tool Repairers
49-9012.01	Electric Meter Installers and Repairers
49-2092.02	Electric Motor and Switch Assemblers and Repairers
49-2092.00	Electric Motor, Power Tool, and Related Repairers
49-2093.00	Electrical and Electronics Installers and Repairers, Transportation Equipment
49-2094.00	Electrical and Electronics Repairers, Commercial and Industrial Equipment
49-2095.00	Electrical and Electronics Repairers, Powerhouse, Substation, and Relay
49-2092.05	Electrical Parts Reconditioners
49-9051.00	Electrical Power-Line Installers and Repairers
49-2096.00	Electronic Equipment Installers and Repairers, Motor Vehicles
49-2097.00	Electronic Home Entertainment Equipment Installers and Repairers
47-4021.00	Elevator Installers and Repairers
49-3041.00	Farm Equipment Mechanics
49-1011.00	First-Line Supervisors/Managers of Mechanics, Installers, and Repairers
49-2022.02	Frame Wirers, Central Office
49-9031.02	Gas Appliance Repairers
49-2092.06	Hand and Portable Power Tool Repairers
49-9021.01	Heating and Air Conditioning Mechanics
49-9021.00	Heating, Air Conditioning, and Refrigeration Mechanics and Installers
47-3013.00	Helpers—Electricians
49-9098.00	Helpers—Installation, Maintenance, and Repair Workers
49-9031.01	Home Appliance Installers
49-9031.00	Home Appliance Repairers
49-9041.00	Industrial Machinery Mechanics
49-9099.99	Installation, Maintenance, and Repair Workers, All Other
49-9063.01	Keyboard Instrument Repairers and Tuners
49-9094.00	Locksmiths and Safe Repairers
49-9042.00	Maintenance and Repair Workers, General
49-9043.00	Maintenance Workers, Machinery
49-9011.00	Mechanical Door Repairers
51-9082.00	Medical Appliance Technicians
49-9062.00	Medical Equipment Repairers
49-9012.03	Meter Mechanics
49-9044.00	Millwrights
49-3042.00	Mobile Heavy Equipment Mechanics, Except Engines
49-3051.00	Motorboat Mechanics
49-3052.00	Motorcycle Mechanics
49-9063.00	Musical Instrument Repairers and Tuners
49-2011.03	Office Machine and Cash Register Servicers
51-9083.00	Ophthalmic Laboratory Technicians
51-9083.02	Optical Instrument Assemblers
49-3053.00	Outdoor Power Equipment and Other Small Engine Mechanics
51-9122.00	Painters, Transportation Equipment
49-9063.04	Percussion Instrument Repairers and Tuners
49-9069.99	Precision Instrument and Equipment Repairers, All Other
49-2021.00	Radio Mechanics
49-3043.00	Rail Car Repairers
53-6051.04	Railroad Inspectors
49-3092.00	Recreational Vehicle Service Technicians
49-9063.03	Reed or Wind Instrument Repairers and Tuners
49-9021.02	Refrigeration Mechanics
49-9097.00	Signal and Track Switch Repairers
49-2022.05	Station Installers and Repairers, Telephone
49-9063.02	Stringed Instrument Repairers and Tuners
49-2022.00	Telecommunications Equipment Installers and Repairers, Except Line Installers

49-2022.04	Telecommunications Facility Examiners
49-9052.00	Telecommunications Line Installers and Repairers
49-3093.00	Tire Repairers and Changers
49-2092.04	Transformer Repairers
49-9012.02	Valve and Regulator Repairers
49-9064.00	Watch Repairers

06: Construction, Mining, and Drilling

O*NET Number	Job Title
47-2031.05	Boat Builders and Shipwrights
47-2011.00	Boilermakers
47-2031.06	Brattice Builders
47-2021.00	Brickmasons and Blockmasons
47-2031.03	Carpenter Assemblers and Repairers
47-2031.00	Carpenters
47-2041.00	Carpet Installers
47-2081.01	Ceiling Tile Installers
47-2051.00	Cement Masons and Concrete Finishers
49-9092.00	Commercial Divers
47-4099.99	Construction and Related Workers, All Other
47-2031.01	Construction Carpenters
47-5021.01	Construction Drillers
47-2061.00	Construction Laborers
11-9021.00	Construction Managers
47-5041.00	Continuous Mining Machine Operators
47-5011.00	Derrick Operators, Oil and Gas
47-2081.00	Drywall and Ceiling Tile Installers
47-2081.02	Drywall Installers
47-5021.00	Earth Drillers, Except Oil and Gas
47-2111.00	Electricians
53-7032.01	Excavating and Loading Machine Operators
47-5031.00	Explosives Workers, Ordnance Handling Experts, and Blasters
47-5099.99	Extraction Workers, All Other
47-4031.00	Fence Erectors
47-1011.01	First-Line Supervisors and Manager/Supervisors —Construction Trades Workers
47-1011.02	First-Line Supervisors and Manager/Supervisors —Extractive Workers
47-1011.00	First-Line Supervisors/Managers of Construction Trades and Extraction Workers
47-2042.00	Floor Layers, Except Carpet, Wood, and Hard Tiles
47-2043.00	Floor Sanders and Finishers
47-2121.00	Glaziers
47-2073.01	Grader, Bulldozer, and Scraper Operators
53-7062.02	Grips and Set-Up Workers, Motion Picture Sets, Studios, and Stages
47-4041.00	Hazardous Materials Removal Workers
47-3019.99	Helpers, Construction Trades, All Other
47-3011.00	Helpers—Brickmasons, Blockmasons, Stonemasons, and Tile and Marble Setters
47-3012.00	Helpers—Carpenters
47-5081.00	Helpers—Extraction Workers
47-3014.00	Helpers—Painters, Paperhangers, Plasterers, and Stucco Masons
47-3015.00	Helpers—Pipelayers, Plumbers, Pipefitters, and Steamfitters
47-3016.00	Helpers—Roofers
47-4051.00	Highway Maintenance Workers
47-2131.00	Insulation Workers, Floor, Ceiling, and Wall
47-2132.00	Insulation Workers, Mechanical
53-7033.00	Loading Machine Operators, Underground Mining
49-9095.00	Manufactured Building and Mobile Home Installers
47-5042.00	Mine Cutting and Channeling Machine Operators
47-5049.99	Mining Machine Operators, All Other
47-2073.02	Operating Engineers
47-2073.00	Operating Engineers and Other Construction Equipment Operators
47-2141.00	Painters, Construction and Maintenance
47-2142.00	Paperhangers
47-2071.00	Paving, Surfacing, and Tamping Equipment Operators
47-2072.00	Pile-Driver Operators
47-2152.01	Pipe Fitters
47-2151.00	Pipelayers
47-2152.03	Pipelaying Fitters
47-2161.00	Plasterers and Stucco Masons
47-2152.02	Plumbers
47-2152.00	Plumbers, Pipefitters, and Steamfitters
47-4061.00	Rail-Track Laying and Maintenance Equipment Operators
49-9045.00	Refractory Materials Repairers, Except Brickmasons
47-2171.00	Reinforcing Iron and Rebar Workers
49-9096.00	Riggers
47-5051.00	Rock Splitters, Quarry
47-5061.00	Roof Bolters, Mining
47-2181.00	Roofers
47-5012.00	Rotary Drill Operators, Oil and Gas
47-2031.02	Rough Carpenters
47-5071.00	Roustabouts, Oil and Gas
49-2098.00	Security and Fire Alarm Systems Installers
47-4091.00	Segmental Pavers
47-4071.00	Septic Tank Servicers and Sewer Pipe Cleaners
47-5013.00	Service Unit Operators, Oil, Gas, and Mining
47-2211.00	Sheet Metal Workers
47-2031.04	Ship Carpenters and Joiners
53-7111.00	Shuttle Car Operators
51-9195.03	Stone Cutters and Carvers
47-2022.00	Stonemasons
47-2221.00	Structural Iron and Steel Workers
47-2082.00	Tapers

(continues)

(continued)

06: Construction, Mining, and Drilling

O*NET Number	Job Title
47-2053.00	Terrazzo Workers and Finishers
47-2044.00	Tile and Marble Setters
47-5021.02	Well and Core Drill Operators

07: Transportation

O*NET Number	Job Title
53-5011.01	Able Seamen
53-2021.00	Air Traffic Controllers
53-2022.00	Airfield Operations Specialists
53-2011.00	Airline Pilots, Copilots, and Flight Engineers
53-3011.00	Ambulance Drivers and Attendants, Except Emergency Medical Technicians
53-3022.00	Bus Drivers, School
53-3021.00	Bus Drivers, Transit and Intercity
53-5021.00	Captains, Mates, and Pilots of Water Vessels
53-2012.00	Commercial Pilots
53-7031.00	Dredge Operators
53-3031.00	Driver/Sales Workers
53-1031.00	First-Line Supervisors/Managers of Transportation and Material-Moving Machine and Vehicle Operators
53-6051.06	Freight Inspectors
53-4011.00	Locomotive Engineers
53-4012.00	Locomotive Firers
53-5021.02	Mates—Ship, Boat, and Barge
53-3099.99	Motor Vehicle Operators, All Other
53-5022.00	Motorboat Operators
53-5011.02	Ordinary Seamen and Marine Oilers
53-6021.00	Parking Lot Attendants
53-5021.03	Pilots, Ship
53-4099.99	Rail Transportation Workers, All Other
53-4013.00	Rail Yard Engineers, Dinkey Operators, and Hostlers
53-4021.00	Railroad Brake, Signal, and Switch Operators
53-4031.00	Railroad Conductors and Yardmasters
53-4021.02	Railroad Yard Workers
53-5011.00	Sailors and Marine Oilers
53-5021.01	Ship and Boat Captains
53-7062.01	Stevedores, Except Equipment Operators
53-4041.00	Subway and Streetcar Operators
53-3041.00	Taxi Drivers and Chauffeurs
53-3032.02	Tractor-Trailer Truck Drivers
53-6041.00	Traffic Technicians
53-4021.01	Train Crew Members
53-6051.00	Transportation Inspectors
11-3071.01	Transportation Managers
53-6099.99	Transportation Workers, All Other
53-3032.01	Truck Drivers, Heavy
53-3032.00	Truck Drivers, Heavy and Tractor-Trailer
53-3033.00	Truck Drivers, Light or Delivery Services

08: Industrial Production

O*NET Number	Job Title
51-2011.03	Aircraft Rigging Assemblers
51-2011.01	Aircraft Structure Assemblers, Precision
51-2011.00	Aircraft Structure, Surfaces, Rigging, and Systems Assemblers
51-2011.02	Aircraft Systems Assemblers, Precision
51-2099.99	Assemblers and Fabricators, All Other
51-8013.02	Auxiliary Equipment Operators, Power
51-3011.02	Bakers, Manufacturing
51-9071.04	Bench Workers, Jewelry
51-5011.02	Bindery Machine Operators and Tenders
51-5011.01	Bindery Machine Setters and Set-Up Operators
51-5011.00	Bindery Workers
51-8021.01	Boiler Operators and Tenders, Low Pressure
51-5012.00	Bookbinders
51-4121.05	Brazers
51-4033.02	Buffing and Polishing Set-Up Operators
51-7011.00	Cabinetmakers and Bench Carpenters
51-4072.05	Casting Machine Set-Up Operators
51-9191.00	Cementing and Gluing Machine Operators and Tenders
51-9011.01	Chemical Equipment Controllers and Operators
51-9011.00	Chemical Equipment Operators and Tenders
51-9011.02	Chemical Equipment Tenders
51-8091.00	Chemical Plant and System Operators
51-9192.00	Cleaning, Washing, and Metal Pickling Equipment Operators and Tenders
51-9121.02	Coating, Painting, and Spraying Machine Operators and Tenders
51-9121.01	Coating, Painting, and Spraying Machine Setters and Set-Up Operators
51-9121.00	Coating, Painting, and Spraying Machine Setters, Operators, and Tenders
51-2021.00	Coil Winders, Tapers, and Finishers
51-4081.02	Combination Machine Tool Operators and Tenders, Metal and Plastic
51-4081.01	Combination Machine Tool Setters and Set-Up Operators, Metal and Plastic
51-4011.00	Computer-Controlled Machine Tool Operators, Metal and Plastic
53-7011.00	Conveyor Operators and Tenders
51-9193.00	Cooling and Freezing Equipment Operators and Tenders
53-7021.00	Crane and Tower Operators
51-9021.00	Crushing, Grinding, and Polishing Machine Setters, Operators, and Tenders
51-9031.00	Cutters and Trimmers, Hand
51-9032.04	Cutting and Slicing Machine Operators and Tenders
51-9032.00	Cutting and Slicing Machine Setters, Operators, and Tenders

51-4031.00	Cutting, Punching, and Press Machine Setters, Operators, and Tenders, Metal and Plastic
51-9081.00	Dental Laboratory Technicians
51-5023.04	Design Printing Machine Setters and Set-Up Operators
53-7032.02	Dragline Operators
51-4032.00	Drilling and Boring Machine Tool Setters, Operators, and Tenders, Metal and Plastic
51-2022.00	Electrical and Electronic Equipment Assemblers
51-9061.04	Electrical and Electronic Inspectors and Testers
51-4193.02	Electrolytic Plating and Coating Machine Operators and Tenders, Metal and Plastic
51-4193.01	Electrolytic Plating and Coating Machine Setters and Set-Up Operators, Metal and Plastic
51-2023.00	Electromechanical Equipment Assemblers
51-5022.10	Electrotypers and Stereotypers
51-5023.07	Embossing Machine Set-Up Operators
51-2031.00	Engine and Other Machine Assemblers
51-5023.08	Engraver Set-Up Operators
53-7032.00	Excavating and Loading Machine and Dragline Operators
51-4021.00	Extruding and Drawing Machine Setters, Operators, and Tenders, Metal and Plastic
51-6091.01	Extruding and Forming Machine Operators and Tenders, Synthetic or Glass Fibers
51-6091.00	Extruding and Forming Machine Setters, Operators, and Tenders, Synthetic and Glass Fibers
51-9041.02	Extruding, Forming, Pressing, and Compacting Machine Operators and Tenders
51-9041.01	Extruding, Forming, Pressing, and Compacting Machine Setters and Set-Up Operators
51-9041.00	Extruding, Forming, Pressing, and Compacting Machine Setters, Operators, and Tenders
51-6092.00	Fabric and Apparel Patternmakers
51-9032.01	Fiber Product Cutting Machine Setters and Set-Up Operators
51-2091.00	Fiberglass Laminators and Fabricators
51-9131.04	Film Laboratory Technicians
53-1021.00	First-Line Supervisors/Managers of Helpers, Laborers, and Material Movers, Hand
51-1011.00	First-Line Supervisors/Managers of Production and Operating Workers
51-2041.02	Fitters, Structural Metal—Precision
51-3091.00	Food and Tobacco Roasting, Baking, and Drying Machine Operators and Tenders
51-3092.00	Food Batchmakers
51-3093.00	Food Cooking Machine Operators and Tenders
51-4022.00	Forging Machine Setters, Operators, and Tenders, Metal and Plastic
51-4071.00	Foundry Mold and Coremakers
53-7062.03	Freight, Stock, and Material Movers, Hand
51-9051.00	Furnace, Kiln, Oven, Drier, and Kettle Operators and Tenders
51-7021.00	Furniture Finishers
53-7071.00	Gas Compressor and Gas Pumping Station Operators
53-7071.02	Gas Compressor Operators
51-8092.02	Gas Distribution Plant Operators
51-8092.00	Gas Plant Operators
51-8092.01	Gas Processing Plant Operators
53-7071.01	Gas Pumping Station Operators
51-8093.03	Gaugers
51-9071.06	Gem and Diamond Workers
51-9032.03	Glass Cutting Machine Setters and Set-Up Operators
45-2041.00	Graders and Sorters, Agricultural Products
51-9022.00	Grinding and Polishing Workers, Hand
51-4033.01	Grinding, Honing, Lapping, and Deburring Machine Set-Up Operators
51-4033.00	Grinding, Lapping, Polishing, and Buffing Machine Tool Setters, Operators, and Tenders, Metal and Plastic
51-5022.01	Hand Compositors and Typesetters
51-4191.00	Heat Treating Equipment Setters, Operators, and Tenders, Metal and Plastic
51-4191.02	Heat Treating, Annealing, and Tempering Machine Operators and Tenders, Metal and Plastic
51-4191.03	Heaters, Metal and Plastic
51-4191.01	Heating Equipment Setters and Set-Up Operators, Metal and Plastic
51-9198.00	Helpers—Production Workers
53-7041.00	Hoist and Winch Operators
11-3051.00	Industrial Production Managers
53-7051.00	Industrial Truck and Tractor Operators
51-9061.00	Inspectors, Testers, Sorters, Samplers, and Weighers
47-4041.01	Irradiated-Fuel Handlers
51-9071.01	Jewelers
51-9071.00	Jewelers and Precious Stone and Metal Workers
51-5021.00	Job Printers
53-7062.00	Laborers and Freight, Stock, and Material Movers, Hand
51-4034.00	Lathe and Turning Machine Tool Setters, Operators, and Tenders, Metal and Plastic
51-4192.00	Lay-Out Workers, Metal and Plastic
51-5023.03	Letterpress Setters and Set-Up Operators
45-4023.00	Log Graders and Scalers
53-7063.00	Machine Feeders and Offbearers
51-4041.00	Machinists
51-5023.05	Marking and Identification Printing Machine Setters and Set-Up Operators
53-7199.99	Material Moving Workers, All Other
51-9061.01	Materials Inspectors
51-3022.00	Meat, Poultry, and Fish Cutters and Trimmers
51-9061.02	Mechanical Inspectors
51-2041.01	Metal Fabricators, Structural Metal Products

(continues)

(continued)

08: Industrial Production

O*NET Number	Job Title
51-4072.04	Metal Molding, Coremaking, and Casting Machine Operators and Tenders
51-4072.03	Metal Molding, Coremaking, and Casting Machine Setters and Set-Up Operators
51-4199.99	Metal Workers and Plastic Workers, All Other
51-4051.00	Metal-Refining Furnace Operators and Tenders
51-4035.00	Milling and Planing Machine Setters, Operators, and Tenders, Metal and Plastic
51-9023.00	Mixing and Blending Machine Setters, Operators, and Tenders
51-9071.03	Model and Mold Makers, Jewelry
51-4061.00	Model Makers, Metal and Plastic
51-7031.00	Model Makers, Wood
51-9195.06	Mold Makers, Hand
51-9195.00	Molders, Shapers, and Casters, Except Metal and Plastic
51-9195.07	Molding and Casting Workers
51-4072.00	Molding, Coremaking, and Casting Machine Setters, Operators, and Tenders, Metal and Plastic
53-6051.05	Motor Vehicle Inspectors
51-4081.00	Multiple Machine Tool Setters, Operators, and Tenders, Metal and Plastic
51-4193.04	Nonelectrolytic Plating and Coating Machine Operators and Tenders, Metal and Plastic
51-4193.03	Nonelectrolytic Plating and Coating Machine Setters and Set-Up Operators, Metal and Plastic
51-8011.00	Nuclear Power Reactor Operators
51-4011.01	Numerical Control Machine Tool Operators and Tenders, Metal and Plastic
51-5023.02	Offset Lithographic Press Setters and Set-Up Operators
51-9111.00	Packaging and Filling Machine Operators and Tenders
53-7064.00	Packers and Packagers, Hand
51-9123.00	Painting, Coating, and Decorating Workers
51-9196.00	Paper Goods Machine Setters, Operators, and Tenders
51-4062.00	Patternmakers, Metal and Plastic
51-7032.00	Patternmakers, Wood
51-8093.01	Petroleum Pump System Operators
51-8093.00	Petroleum Pump System Operators, Refinery Operators, and Gaugers
51-8093.02	Petroleum Refinery and Control Panel Operators
51-9071.05	Pewter Casters and Finishers
51-5022.13	Photoengraving and Lithographing Machine Operators and Tenders
51-9131.03	Photographic Hand Developers
51-9131.00	Photographic Process Workers
51-9132.00	Photographic Processing Machine Operators
51-9131.02	Photographic Reproduction Technicians
51-9131.01	Photographic Retouchers and Restorers
51-8099.99	Plant and System Operators, All Other
51-4072.02	Plastic Molding and Casting Machine Operators and Tenders
51-4072.01	Plastic Molding and Casting Machine Setters and Set-Up Operators
51-5022.11	Plate Finishers
51-5022.07	Platemakers
51-4193.00	Plating and Coating Machine Setters, Operators, and Tenders, Metal and Plastic
51-4052.00	Pourers and Casters, Metal
51-8012.00	Power Distributors and Dispatchers
51-8013.01	Power Generating Plant Operators, Except Auxiliary Equipment Operators
51-8013.00	Power Plant Operators
51-9061.03	Precision Devices Inspectors and Testers
51-9083.01	Precision Lens Grinders and Polishers
51-9195.01	Precision Mold and Pattern Casters, except Nonferrous Metals
51-9195.02	Precision Pattern and Die Casters, Nonferrous Metals
51-5023.01	Precision Printing Workers
51-5022.00	Prepress Technicians and Workers
51-4031.03	Press and Press Brake Machine Setters and Set-Up Operators, Metal and Plastic
51-6021.02	Pressing Machine Operators and Tenders—Textile, Garment, and Related Materials
51-5023.00	Printing Machine Operators
51-5023.09	Printing Press Machine Operators and Tenders
51-9198.02	Production Helpers
51-9061.05	Production Inspectors, Testers, Graders, Sorters, Samplers, Weighers
51-9198.01	Production Laborers
51-9199.99	Production Workers, All Other
53-7072.00	Pump Operators, Except Wellhead Pumpers
51-4031.02	Punching Machine Setters and Set-Up Operators, Metal and Plastic
53-7081.00	Refuse and Recyclable Material Collectors
51-4023.00	Rolling Machine Setters, Operators, and Tenders, Metal and Plastic
51-7041.02	Sawing Machine Operators and Tenders
51-7041.01	Sawing Machine Setters and Set-Up Operators
51-7041.00	Sawing Machine Setters, Operators, and Tenders, Wood
51-4031.01	Sawing Machine Tool Setters and Set-Up Operators, Metal and Plastic
51-5022.05	Scanner Operators
51-5023.06	Screen Printing Machine Setters and Set-Up Operators
51-9141.00	Semiconductor Processors
51-9012.00	Separating, Filtering, Clarifying, Precipitating, and Still Machine Setters, Operators, and Tenders

51-6051.00 Sewers, Hand
51-6031.00 Sewing Machine Operators
51-6031.01 Sewing Machine Operators, Garment
51-6031.02 Sewing Machine Operators, Non-Garment
51-4031.04 Shear and Slitter Machine Setters and Set-Up Operators, Metal and Plastic
53-5031.00 Ship Engineers
51-6042.00 Shoe Machine Operators and Tenders
51-9071.02 Silversmiths
51-3023.00 Slaughterers and Meat Packers
51-4121.04 Solderers
51-4122.04 Soldering and Brazing Machine Operators and Tenders
51-4122.03 Soldering and Brazing Machine Setters and Set-Up Operators
51-8021.02 Stationary Engineers
51-8021.00 Stationary Engineers and Boiler Operators
51-9032.02 Stone Sawyers
51-5022.06 Strippers
51-2041.00 Structural Metal Fabricators and Fitters
53-7121.00 Tank Car, Truck, and Ship Loaders
51-2092.00 Team Assemblers
51-6061.00 Textile Bleaching and Dyeing Machine Operators and Tenders
51-6062.00 Textile Cutting Machine Setters, Operators, and Tenders
51-6063.00 Textile Knitting and Weaving Machine Setters, Operators, and Tenders
51-6064.00 Textile Winding, Twisting, and Drawing Out Machine Setters, Operators, and Tenders
51-2093.00 Timing Device Assemblers, Adjusters, and Calibrators
51-9197.00 Tire Builders
51-4111.00 Tool and Die Makers
51-4194.00 Tool Grinders, Filers, and Sharpeners
51-8031.00 Water and Liquid Waste Treatment Plant and System Operators
51-4121.03 Welder-Fitters
51-4121.02 Welders and Cutters
51-4121.00 Welders, Cutters, Solderers, and Brazers
51-4121.01 Welders, Production
51-4122.02 Welding Machine Operators and Tenders
51-4122.01 Welding Machine Setters and Set-Up Operators
51-4122.00 Welding, Soldering, and Brazing Machine Setters, Operators, and Tenders
53-7073.00 Wellhead Pumpers
51-7099.99 Woodworkers, All Other
51-7042.02 Woodworking Machine Operators and Tenders, Except Sawing
51-7042.01 Woodworking Machine Setters and Set-Up Operators, Except Sawing
51-7042.00 Woodworking Machine Setters, Operators, and Tenders, Except Sawing

09: Business Detail

O*NET Number	Job Title
43-4051.01	Adjustment Clerks
11-3011.00	Administrative Services Managers
49-2011.01	Automatic Teller Machine Servicers
43-3011.00	Bill and Account Collectors
43-3021.00	Billing and Posting Clerks and Machine Operators
43-3021.02	Billing, Cost, and Rate Clerks
43-3021.03	Billing, Posting, and Calculating Machine Operators
43-3031.00	Bookkeeping, Accounting, and Auditing Clerks
43-4011.00	Brokerage Clerks
43-5011.00	Cargo and Freight Agents
41-2011.00	Cashiers
43-2021.02	Central Office Operators
43-4061.01	Claims Takers, Unemployment Benefits
43-2099.99	Communications Equipment Operators, All Other
43-9011.00	Computer Operators
43-4021.00	Correspondence Clerks
41-2021.00	Counter and Rental Clerks
43-5021.00	Couriers and Messengers
43-4031.01	Court Clerks
23-2091.00	Court Reporters
43-4031.00	Court, Municipal, and License Clerks
43-4041.01	Credit Authorizers
43-4041.00	Credit Authorizers, Checkers, and Clerks
43-4041.02	Credit Checkers
43-4051.00	Customer Service Representatives
43-4051.02	Customer Service Representatives, Utilities
43-9021.00	Data Entry Keyers
43-2021.01	Directory Assistance Operators
43-5032.00	Dispatchers, Except Police, Fire, and Ambulance
43-9071.01	Duplicating Machine Operators
43-4061.00	Eligibility Interviewers, Government Programs
43-6011.00	Executive Secretaries and Administrative Assistants
43-4071.00	File Clerks
43-1011.02	First-Line Supervisors, Administrative Support
43-1011.01	First-Line Supervisors, Customer Service
43-1011.00	First-Line Supervisors/Managers of Office and Administrative Support Workers
43-3041.00	Gaming Cage Workers
41-2012.00	Gaming Change Persons and Booth Cashiers
43-4161.00	Human Resources Assistants, Except Payroll and Timekeeping
43-4199.99	Information and Record Clerks, All Other
43-9041.00	Insurance Claims and Policy Processing Clerks
43-9041.01	Insurance Claims Clerks
43-9041.02	Insurance Policy Processing Clerks

(continues)

(continued)

09: Business Detail

O*NET Number	Job Title
43-4111.00	Interviewers, Except Eligibility and Loan
43-6012.00	Legal Secretaries
43-4031.03	License Clerks
43-4131.00	Loan Interviewers and Clerks
43-9051.00	Mail Clerks and Mail Machine Operators, Except Postal Service
43-9051.02	Mail Clerks, Except Mail Machine Operators and Postal Service
43-9051.01	Mail Machine Operators, Preparation and Handling
43-5081.02	Marking Clerks
29-2071.00	Medical Records and Health Information Technicians
43-6013.00	Medical Secretaries
31-9094.00	Medical Transcriptionists
43-5041.00	Meter Readers, Utilities
43-4031.02	Municipal Clerks
43-4141.00	New Accounts Clerks
43-9199.99	Office and Administrative Support Workers, All Other
43-9061.00	Office Clerks, General
43-9071.00	Office Machine Operators, Except Computer
43-4151.00	Order Clerks
43-5081.04	Order Fillers, Wholesale and Retail Sales
43-3051.00	Payroll and Timekeeping Clerks
43-5031.00	Police, Fire, and Ambulance Dispatchers
43-5051.00	Postal Service Clerks
43-5052.00	Postal Service Mail Carriers
43-5053.00	Postal Service Mail Sorters, Processors, and Processing Machine Operators
43-3061.00	Procurement Clerks
43-5061.00	Production, Planning, and Expediting Clerks
43-9081.00	Proofreaders and Copy Markers
43-4171.00	Receptionists and Information Clerks
43-6014.00	Secretaries, Except Legal, Medical, and Executive
43-5071.00	Shipping, Receiving, and Traffic Clerks
43-3021.01	Statement Clerks
43-5081.00	Stock Clerks and Order Fillers
43-5081.03	Stock Clerks—Stockroom, Warehouse, or Storage Yard
43-2011.00	Switchboard Operators, Including Answering Service
13-2082.00	Tax Preparers
43-2021.00	Telephone Operators
43-3071.00	Tellers
43-4181.01	Travel Clerks
51-5022.12	Typesetting and Composing Machine Operators and Tenders
43-5111.00	Weighers, Measurers, Checkers, and Samplers, Recordkeeping
43-4061.02	Welfare Eligibility Workers and Interviewers
43-9022.00	Word Processors and Typists

10: Sales and Marketing

O*NET Number	Job Title
11-2011.00	Advertising and Promotions Managers
41-3011.00	Advertising Sales Agents
41-9011.00	Demonstrators and Product Promoters
41-9091.00	Door-To-Door Sales Workers, News and Street Vendors, and Related Workers
41-1012.00	First-Line Supervisors/Managers of Non-Retail Sales Workers
41-1011.00	First-Line Supervisors/Managers of Retail Sales Workers
41-3021.00	Insurance Sales Agents
11-2021.00	Marketing Managers
41-2022.00	Parts Salespersons
41-9021.00	Real Estate Brokers
41-9022.00	Real Estate Sales Agents
41-2031.00	Retail Salespersons
41-3031.02	Sales Agents, Financial Services
41-3031.01	Sales Agents, Securities and Commodities
41-9099.99	Sales and Related Workers, All Other
11-2022.00	Sales Managers
41-4011.01	Sales Representatives, Agricultural
41-4011.02	Sales Representatives, Chemical and Pharmaceutical
41-4011.03	Sales Representatives, Electrical/Electronic
41-4011.06	Sales Representatives, Instruments
41-4011.04	Sales Representatives, Mechanical Equipment and Supplies
41-4011.05	Sales Representatives, Medical
41-3099.99	Sales Representatives, Services, All Other
41-4012.00	Sales Representatives, Wholesale and Manufacturing, Except Technical and Scientific Products
41-4011.00	Sales Representatives, Wholesale and Manufacturing, Technical and Scientific Products
41-3031.00	Securities, Commodities, and Financial Services Sales Agents
53-6031.00	Service Station Attendants
43-5081.01	Stock Clerks, Sales Floor
41-9041.00	Telemarketers
41-3041.00	Travel Agents

11: Recreation, Travel, and Other Personal Services

O*NET Number	Job Title
53-1011.00	Aircraft Cargo Handling Supervisors
39-3091.00	Amusement and Recreation Attendants
39-6011.00	Baggage Porters and Bellhops
51-3011.00	Bakers

51-3011.01	Bakers, Bread and Pastry
39-5011.00	Barbers
35-3011.00	Bartenders
37-2019.99	Building Cleaning Workers, All Other
51-3021.00	Butchers and Meat Cutters
35-1011.00	Chefs and Head Cooks
53-7061.00	Cleaners of Vehicles and Equipment
35-3021.00	Combined Food Preparation and Serving Workers, Including Fast Food
39-6012.00	Concierges
35-2019.99	Cooks, All Other
35-2011.00	Cooks, Fast Food
35-2012.00	Cooks, Institution and Cafeteria
35-2013.00	Cooks, Private Household
35-2014.00	Cooks, Restaurant
35-2015.00	Cooks, Short Order
35-3022.00	Counter Attendants, Cafeteria, Food Concession, and Coffee Shop
51-6052.02	Custom Tailors
35-9011.00	Dining Room and Cafeteria Attendants and Bartender Helpers
35-9021.00	Dishwashers
39-4011.00	Embalmers
39-3099.99	Entertainment Attendants and Related Workers, All Other
49-9093.00	Fabric Menders, Except Garment
35-1012.00	First-Line Supervisors/Managers of Food Preparation and Serving Workers
37-1011.00	First-Line Supervisors/Managers of Housekeeping and Janitorial Workers
39-1021.00	First-Line Supervisors/Managers of Personal Service Workers
39-6031.00	Flight Attendants
35-9099.99	Food Preparation and Serving Related Workers, All Other
35-2021.00	Food Preparation Workers
35-3041.00	Food Servers, Nonrestaurant
11-9051.00	Food Service Managers
39-4021.00	Funeral Attendants
39-3012.00	Gaming and Sports Book Writers and Runners
39-3011.00	Gaming Dealers
11-9071.00	Gaming Managers
39-3019.99	Gaming Service Workers, All Other
39-1011.00	Gaming Supervisors
39-5012.00	Hairdressers, Hairstylists, and Cosmetologists
35-9031.00	Hosts and Hostesses, Restaurant, Lounge, and Coffee Shop
43-4081.00	Hotel, Motel, and Resort Desk Clerks
37-1011.01	Housekeeping Supervisors
37-1011.02	Janitorial Supervisors
37-2011.00	Janitors and Cleaners, Except Maids and Housekeeping Cleaners
51-6011.03	Laundry and Drycleaning Machine Operators and Tenders, Except Pressing

51-6011.00	Laundry and Dry-Cleaning Workers
39-3093.00	Locker Room, Coatroom, and Dressing Room Attendants
11-9081.00	Lodging Managers
37-2012.00	Maids and Housekeeping Cleaners
39-5092.00	Manicurists and Pedicurists
13-1121.00	Meeting and Convention Planners
39-3021.00	Motion Picture Projectionists
39-9021.00	Personal and Home Care Aides
39-9099.99	Personal Care and Service Workers, All Other
51-6011.02	Precision Dyers
51-6021.01	Pressers, Delicate Fabrics
51-6021.03	Pressers, Hand
51-6021.00	Pressers, Textile, Garment, and Related Materials
39-9032.00	Recreation Workers
43-4181.02	Reservation and Transportation Ticket Agents
43-4181.00	Reservation and Transportation Ticket Agents and Travel Clerks
39-5093.00	Shampooers
51-6041.00	Shoe and Leather Workers and Repairers
51-6052.01	Shop and Alteration Tailors
39-5094.00	Skin Care Specialists
39-1012.00	Slot Key Persons
51-6011.01	Spotters, Dry Cleaning
51-6052.00	Tailors, Dressmakers, and Custom Sewers
51-6099.99	Textile, Apparel, and Furnishings Workers, All Other
39-6021.00	Tour Guides and Escorts
39-6032.00	Transportation Attendants, Except Flight Attendants and Baggage Porters
39-6022.00	Travel Guides
51-6093.00	Upholsterers
39-3031.00	Ushers, Lobby Attendants, and Ticket Takers
35-3031.00	Waiters and Waitresses

12: Education and Social Service

O*NET Number	Job Title
25-3011.00	Adult Literacy, Remedial Education, and GED Teachers and Instructors
25-1041.00	Agricultural Sciences Teachers, Postsecondary
25-1061.00	Anthropology and Archeology Teachers, Postsecondary
25-1031.00	Architecture Teachers, Postsecondary
25-4011.00	Archivists
25-1062.00	Area, Ethnic, and Cultural Studies Teachers, Postsecondary
25-1121.00	Art, Drama, and Music Teachers, Postsecondary
25-1051.00	Atmospheric, Earth, Marine, and Space Sciences Teachers, Postsecondary
25-9011.00	Audio-Visual Collections Specialists
25-1042.00	Biological Science Teachers, Postsecondary
25-1011.00	Business Teachers, Postsecondary
25-1052.00	Chemistry Teachers, Postsecondary

(continues)

(continued)

12: Education and Social Service

O*NET Number	Job Title
39-9011.00	Child Care Workers
21-1021.00	Child, Family, and School Social Workers
21-2011.00	Clergy
19-3031.02	Clinical Psychologists
19-3031.00	Clinical, Counseling, and School Psychologists
25-1122.00	Communications Teachers, Postsecondary
21-1099.99	Community and Social Service Specialists, All Other
25-1021.00	Computer Science Teachers, Postsecondary
19-3031.03	Counseling Psychologists
21-1019.99	Counselors, All Other
25-1111.00	Criminal Justice and Law Enforcement Teachers, Postsecondary
25-4012.00	Curators
21-2021.00	Directors, Religious Activities and Education
25-1063.00	Economics Teachers, Postsecondary
11-9039.99	Education Administrators, All Other
11-9032.00	Education Administrators, Elementary and Secondary School
11-9033.00	Education Administrators, Postsecondary
11-9031.00	Education Administrators, Preschool and Child Care Center/Program
25-1081.00	Education Teachers, Postsecondary
25-9099.99	Education, Training, and Library Workers, All Other
19-3031.01	Educational Psychologists
21-1012.00	Educational, Vocational, and School Counselors
25-2021.00	Elementary School Teachers, Except Special Education
25-1032.00	Engineering Teachers, Postsecondary
25-1123.00	English Language and Literature Teachers, Postsecondary
25-1053.00	Environmental Science Teachers, Postsecondary
25-9021.00	Farm and Home Management Advisors
25-1124.00	Foreign Language and Literature Teachers, Postsecondary
25-1043.00	Forestry and Conservation Science Teachers, Postsecondary
25-1064.00	Geography Teachers, Postsecondary
25-1191.00	Graduate Teaching Assistants
25-1071.00	Health Specialties Teachers, Postsecondary
25-1125.00	History Teachers, Postsecondary
25-1192.00	Home Economics Teachers, Postsecondary
25-9031.00	Instructional Coordinators
25-2012.00	Kindergarten Teachers, Except Special Education
25-1112.00	Law Teachers, Postsecondary
25-4021.00	Librarians
43-4121.00	Library Assistants, Clerical
25-1082.00	Library Science Teachers, Postsecondary
25-4031.00	Library Technicians
21-1013.00	Marriage and Family Therapists
25-1022.00	Mathematical Science Teachers, Postsecondary
21-1022.00	Medical and Public Health Social Workers
21-1023.00	Mental Health and Substance Abuse Social Workers
21-1014.00	Mental Health Counselors
25-2022.00	Middle School Teachers, Except Special and Vocational Education
25-4013.00	Museum Technicians and Conservators
25-1072.00	Nursing Instructors and Teachers, Postsecondary
19-1031.03	Park Naturalists
13-2052.00	Personal Financial Advisors
25-1126.00	Philosophy and Religion Teachers, Postsecondary
25-1054.00	Physics Teachers, Postsecondary
25-1065.00	Political Science Teachers, Postsecondary
25-1199.99	Postsecondary Teachers, All Other
25-2011.00	Preschool Teachers, Except Special Education
21-1092.00	Probation Officers and Correctional Treatment Specialists
25-1066.00	Psychology Teachers, Postsecondary
25-1193.00	Recreation and Fitness Studies Teachers, Postsecondary
21-1015.00	Rehabilitation Counselors
21-2099.99	Religious Workers, All Other
39-9041.00	Residential Advisors
25-2031.00	Secondary School Teachers, Except Special and Vocational Education
25-3021.00	Self-Enrichment Education Teachers
11-9151.00	Social and Community Service Managers
21-1093.00	Social and Human Service Assistants
25-1069.99	Social Sciences Teachers, Postsecondary, All Other
25-1113.00	Social Work Teachers, Postsecondary
21-1029.99	Social Workers, All Other
25-1067.00	Sociology Teachers, Postsecondary
25-2042.00	Special Education Teachers, Middle School
25-2041.00	Special Education Teachers, Preschool, Kindergarten, and Elementary School
25-2043.00	Special Education Teachers, Secondary School
21-1011.00	Substance Abuse and Behavioral Disorder Counselors
25-9041.00	Teacher Assistants
25-3099.99	Teachers and Instructors, All Other
25-2023.00	Vocational Education Teachers, Middle School
25-1194.00	Vocational Education Teachers, Postsecondary
25-2032.00	Vocational Education Teachers, Secondary School

13: General Management and Support

O*NET Number	Job Title
13-2011.01	Accountants
13-2011.00	Accountants and Auditors

13-2021.00	Appraisers and Assessors of Real Estate
13-2021.02	Appraisers, Real Estate
13-2021.01	Assessors
13-2011.02	Auditors
13-2031.00	Budget Analysts
13-1199.99	Business Operations Specialists, All Other
11-1011.00	Chief Executives
13-1031.00	Claims Adjusters, Examiners, and Investigators
13-1031.01	Claims Examiners, Property and Casualty Insurance
11-3041.00	Compensation and Benefits Managers
13-1072.00	Compensation, Benefits, and Job Analysis Specialists
13-1051.00	Cost Estimators
13-2041.00	Credit Analysts
13-1071.01	Employment Interviewers, Private or Public Employment Service
13-1071.00	Employment, Recruitment, and Placement Specialists
11-9011.00	Farm, Ranch, and Other Agricultural Managers
13-2051.00	Financial Analysts
11-3031.00	Financial Managers
11-3031.02	Financial Managers, Branch or Department
13-2099.99	Financial Specialists, All Other
11-9061.00	Funeral Directors
11-1021.00	General and Operations Managers
11-1011.01	Government Service Executives
11-3040.00	Human Resources Managers
11-3049.99	Human Resources Managers, All Other
13-1079.99	Human Resources, Training, and Labor Relations Specialists, All Other
13-1031.02	Insurance Adjusters, Examiners, and Investigators
13-1032.00	Insurance Appraisers, Auto Damage
13-2053.00	Insurance Underwriters
11-1031.00	Legislators
13-2071.00	Loan Counselors
13-2072.00	Loan Officers
13-1081.00	Logisticians
13-1111.00	Management Analysts
11-9199.99	Managers, All Other
19-3021.00	Market Research Analysts
13-1071.02	Personnel Recruiters
11-9131.00	Postmasters and Mail Superintendents
11-1011.02	Private Sector Executives
11-9141.00	Property, Real Estate, and Community Association Managers
11-2031.00	Public Relations Managers
13-1021.00	Purchasing Agents and Buyers, Farm Products
13-1023.00	Purchasing Agents, Except Wholesale, Retail, and Farm Products
11-3061.00	Purchasing Managers
11-3071.02	Storage and Distribution Managers
13-2081.00	Tax Examiners, Collectors, and Revenue Agents
11-3042.00	Training and Development Managers
13-1073.00	Training and Development Specialists
11-3071.00	Transportation, Storage, and Distribution Managers
13-3031.01	Treasurers, Controllers, and Chief Financial Officers
13-1022.00	Wholesale and Retail Buyers, Except Farm Products

14: Medical and Health Services

O*NET Number	Job Title
29-1061.00	Anesthesiologists
29-9091.00	Athletic Trainers
29-1121.00	Audiologists
29-2031.00	Cardiovascular Technologists and Technicians
29-1011.00	Chiropractors
13-1041.06	Coroners
31-9091.00	Dental Assistants
29-2021.00	Dental Hygienists
29-1029.99	Dentists, All Other Specialists
29-1021.00	Dentists, General
29-2032.00	Diagnostic Medical Sonographers
29-2051.00	Dietetic Technicians
29-1031.00	Dietitians and Nutritionists
29-1062.00	Family and General Practitioners
29-1199.99	Health Diagnosing and Treating Practitioners, All Other
21-1091.00	Health Educators
29-2099.99	Health Technologists and Technicians, All Other
29-9099.99	Healthcare Practitioners and Technical Workers, All Other
31-9099.99	Healthcare Support Workers, All Other
31-1011.00	Home Health Aides
29-1063.00	Internists, General
29-2061.00	Licensed Practical and Licensed Vocational Nurses
31-9011.00	Massage Therapists
29-2012.00	Medical and Clinical Laboratory Technicians
29-2011.00	Medical and Clinical Laboratory Technologists
11-9111.00	Medical and Health Services Managers
31-9092.00	Medical Assistants
31-9093.00	Medical Equipment Preparers
29-2033.00	Nuclear Medicine Technologists
31-1012.00	Nursing Aides, Orderlies, and Attendants
29-1064.00	Obstetricians and Gynecologists
31-2012.00	Occupational Therapist Aides
31-2011.00	Occupational Therapist Assistants
29-1122.00	Occupational Therapists
29-2081.00	Opticians, Dispensing
29-1041.00	Optometrists
29-1022.00	Oral and Maxillofacial Surgeons
29-1023.00	Orthodontists
29-2091.00	Orthotists and Prosthetists

(continues)

(continued)

14: Medical and Health Services

O*NET Number	Job Title
29-1065.00	Pediatricians, General
29-1051.00	Pharmacists
31-9095.00	Pharmacy Aides
29-2052.00	Pharmacy Technicians
31-2022.00	Physical Therapist Aides
31-2021.00	Physical Therapist Assistants
29-1123.00	Physical Therapists
29-1071.00	Physician Assistants
29-1069.99	Physicians and Surgeons, All Other
29-1081.00	Podiatrists
29-1024.00	Prosthodontists
31-1013.00	Psychiatric Aides
29-2053.00	Psychiatric Technicians
29-1066.00	Psychiatrists
29-1124.00	Radiation Therapists
29-2034.02	Radiologic Technicians
29-2034.01	Radiologic Technologists
29-2034.00	Radiologic Technologists and Technicians
29-1125.00	Recreational Therapists
29-1111.00	Registered Nurses
29-1126.00	Respiratory Therapists
29-2054.00	Respiratory Therapy Technicians
29-1127.00	Speech-Language Pathologists
29-1067.00	Surgeons
29-2055.00	Surgical Technologists
29-1129.99	Therapists, All Other

Method 3: Browse the Jobs by Education and Training Requirements

The following lists sort the jobs according to the amount of education and training that they require. You can find descriptions of the various education and training levels in the Introduction, and O*NET numbers are included for the jobs so that you can find the descriptions in Part II easily. The jobs are listed alphabetically in each level, and jobs without education or training information have not been included in the lists.

When to Use This Method: If you have achieved, are working toward, or are considering a certain level of education and training, these lists help you find the jobs that meet your qualifications. Simply find your education or training level here, review the list of related jobs, and then look up their descriptions in Part II using the O*NET number.

Jobs Requiring Short-Term On-the-Job Training

O*NET Number	Job Title
53-5011.01	Able Seamen
53-2022.00	Airfield Operations Specialists
39-3091.00	Amusement and Recreation Attendants

O*NET Number	Job Title
39-6011.00	Baggage Porters and Bellhops
35-3011.00	Bartenders
43-3011.00	Bill and Account Collectors
43-3021.02	Billing, Cost, and Rate Clerks
43-3021.03	Billing, Posting, and Calculating Machine Operators
51-5011.02	Bindery Machine Operators and Tenders
51-4121.05	Brazers
53-6011.00	Bridge and Lock Tenders
53-3022.00	Bus Drivers, School
41-2011.00	Cashiers
43-2021.02	Central Office Operators
39-9011.00	Child Care Workers
53-7061.00	Cleaners of Vehicles and Equipment
51-9121.00	Coating, Painting, and Spraying Machine Setters, Operators, and Tenders
51-2021.00	Coil Winders, Tapers, and Finishers
35-3021.00	Combined Food Preparation and Serving Workers, Including Fast Food
39-6012.00	Concierges
53-7011.00	Conveyor Operators and Tenders
35-2011.00	Cooks, Fast Food
35-2012.00	Cooks, Institution and Cafeteria
35-2013.00	Cooks, Private Household
35-2015.00	Cooks, Short Order
43-4021.00	Correspondence Clerks
41-2021.00	Counter and Rental Clerks
35-3022.00	Counter Attendants, Cafeteria, Food Concession, and Coffee Shop
43-5021.00	Couriers and Messengers
43-4031.01	Court Clerks
43-4031.00	Court, Municipal, and License Clerks
43-4041.01	Credit Authorizers
43-4041.00	Credit Authorizers, Checkers, and Clerks
43-4041.02	Credit Checkers
33-9091.00	Crossing Guards
51-9031.00	Cutters and Trimmers, Hand
51-9032.04	Cutting and Slicing Machine Operators and Tenders
35-9011.00	Dining Room and Cafeteria Attendants and Bartender Helpers
43-2021.01	Directory Assistance Operators
35-9021.00	Dishwashers
41-9091.00	Door-To-Door Sales Workers, News and Street Vendors, and Related Workers
53-3031.00	Driver/Sales Workers
43-9071.01	Duplicating Machine Operators
51-2022.00	Electrical and Electronic Equipment Assemblers
51-2023.00	Electromechanical Equipment Assemblers
51-2031.00	Engine and Other Machine Assemblers
51-9041.02	Extruding, Forming, Pressing, and Compacting Machine Operators and Tenders
51-9041.00	Extruding, Forming, Pressing, and Compacting Machine Setters, Operators, and Tenders

49-9093.00	Fabric Menders, Except Garment
45-2092.00	Farmworkers and Laborers, Crop, Nursery, and Greenhouse
45-2093.00	Farmworkers, Farm and Ranch Animals
43-4071.00	File Clerks
45-3011.00	Fishers and Related Fishing Workers
51-3091.00	Food and Tobacco Roasting, Baking, and Drying Machine Operators and Tenders
51-3092.00	Food Batchmakers
51-3093.00	Food Cooking Machine Operators and Tenders
35-2021.00	Food Preparation Workers
35-3041.00	Food Servers, Nonrestaurant
53-7062.03	Freight, Stock, and Material Movers, Hand
39-4021.00	Funeral Attendants
41-2012.00	Gaming Change Persons and Booth Cashiers
45-2092.02	General Farmworkers
51-9032.03	Glass Cutting Machine Setters and Set-Up Operators
53-7062.02	Grips and Set-Up Workers, Motion Picture Sets, Studios, and Stages
47-3019.99	Helpers, Construction Trades, All Other
47-3011.00	Helpers—Brickmasons, Blockmasons, Stonemasons, and Tile and Marble Setters
47-3012.00	Helpers—Carpenters
47-3013.00	Helpers—Electricians
47-5081.00	Helpers—Extraction Workers
49-9098.00	Helpers—Installation, Maintenance, and Repair Workers
47-3014.00	Helpers—Painters, Paperhangers, Plasterers, and Stucco Masons
47-3015.00	Helpers—Pipelayers, Plumbers, Pipefitters, and Steamfitters
51-9198.00	Helpers—Production Workers
47-3016.00	Helpers—Roofers
31-1011.00	Home Health Aides
35-9031.00	Hosts and Hostesses, Restaurant, Lounge, and Coffee Shop
43-4081.00	Hotel, Motel, and Resort Desk Clerks
43-4161.00	Human Resources Assistants, Except Payroll and Timekeeping
53-7051.00	Industrial Truck and Tractor Operators
43-4199.99	Information and Record Clerks, All Other
43-9041.00	Insurance Claims and Policy Processing Clerks
43-4111.00	Interviewers, Except Eligibility and Loan
37-2011.00	Janitors and Cleaners, Except Maids and Housekeeping Cleaners
53-7062.00	Laborers and Freight, Stock, and Material Movers, Hand
37-3011.00	Landscaping and Groundskeeping Workers
51-6011.00	Laundry and Dry-Cleaning Workers
43-4121.00	Library Assistants, Clerical
25-4031.00	Library Technicians
43-4031.03	License Clerks

33-9092.00	Lifeguards, Ski Patrol, and Other Recreational Protective Service Workers
43-4131.00	Loan Interviewers and Clerks
39-3093.00	Locker Room, Coatroom, and Dressing Room Attendants
53-7063.00	Machine Feeders and Offbearers
37-2012.00	Maids and Housekeeping Cleaners
43-9051.00	Mail Clerks and Mail Machine Operators, Except Postal Service
43-9051.02	Mail Clerks, Except Mail Machine Operators and Postal Service
43-9051.01	Mail Machine Operators, Preparation and Handling
51-5023.05	Marking and Identification Printing Machine Setters and Set-Up Operators
43-5081.02	Marking Clerks
51-3022.00	Meat, Poultry, and Fish Cutters and Trimmers
31-9093.00	Medical Equipment Preparers
51-4072.04	Metal Molding, Coremaking, and Casting Machine Operators and Tenders
43-5041.00	Meter Readers, Utilities
39-3021.00	Motion Picture Projectionists
43-4031.02	Municipal Clerks
51-4193.04	Nonelectrolytic Plating and Coating Machine Operators and Tenders, Metal and Plastic
39-2021.00	Nonfarm Animal Caretakers
45-2092.01	Nursery Workers
31-1012.00	Nursing Aides, Orderlies, and Attendants
31-2012.00	Occupational Therapist Aides
43-9061.00	Office Clerks, General
43-9071.00	Office Machine Operators, Except Computer
43-4151.00	Order Clerks
53-5011.02	Ordinary Seamen and Marine Oilers
51-9111.00	Packaging and Filling Machine Operators and Tenders
53-7064.00	Packers and Packagers, Hand
51-9123.00	Painting, Coating, and Decorating Workers
33-3041.00	Parking Enforcement Workers
53-6021.00	Parking Lot Attendants
43-3051.00	Payroll and Timekeeping Clerks
39-9021.00	Personal and Home Care Aides
51-9132.00	Photographic Processing Machine Operators
51-4072.02	Plastic Molding and Casting Machine Operators and Tenders
43-5051.00	Postal Service Clerks
43-5052.00	Postal Service Mail Carriers
43-5053.00	Postal Service Mail Sorters, Processors, and Processing Machine Operators
51-6021.03	Pressers, Hand
51-6021.02	Pressing Machine Operators and Tenders—Textile, Garment, and Related Materials
51-5023.09	Printing Press Machine Operators and Tenders
43-3061.00	Procurement Clerks
51-9198.02	Production Helpers

(continues)

(continued)

Jobs Requiring Short-Term On-the-Job Training

O*NET Number	Job Title
51-9061.05	Production Inspectors, Testers, Graders, Sorters, Samplers, Weighers
51-9198.01	Production Laborers
43-5061.00	Production, Planning, and Expediting Clerks
43-9081.00	Proofreaders and Copy Markers
31-1013.00	Psychiatric Aides
43-4171.00	Receptionists and Information Clerks
49-9045.00	Refractory Materials Repairers, Except Brickmasons
53-7081.00	Refuse and Recyclable Material Collectors
43-4181.02	Reservation and Transportation Ticket Agents
43-4181.00	Reservation and Transportation Ticket Agents and Travel Clerks
41-2031.00	Retail Salespersons
49-9096.00	Riggers
47-5071.00	Roustabouts, Oil and Gas
53-5011.00	Sailors and Marine Oilers
33-9032.00	Security Guards
53-6031.00	Service Station Attendants
51-6051.00	Sewers, Hand
39-5093.00	Shampooers
43-5071.00	Shipping, Receiving, and Traffic Clerks
39-5094.00	Skin Care Specialists
39-1012.00	Slot Key Persons
51-4121.04	Solderers
51-4122.04	Soldering and Brazing Machine Operators and Tenders
51-6011.01	Spotters, Dry Cleaning
43-3021.01	Statement Clerks
53-7062.01	Stevedores, Except Equipment Operators
43-5081.00	Stock Clerks and Order Fillers
43-5081.01	Stock Clerks, Sales Floor
43-2011.00	Switchboard Operators, Including Answering Service
53-3041.00	Taxi Drivers and Chauffeurs
25-9041.00	Teacher Assistants
41-9041.00	Telemarketers
43-2021.00	Telephone Operators
43-3071.00	Tellers
49-3093.00	Tire Repairers and Changers
39-6021.00	Tour Guides and Escorts
53-6041.00	Traffic Technicians
39-6032.00	Transportation Attendants, Except Flight Attendants and Baggage Porters
43-4181.01	Travel Clerks
37-3013.00	Tree Trimmers and Pruners
53-3032.01	Truck Drivers, Heavy
53-3033.00	Truck Drivers, Light or Delivery Services
39-3031.00	Ushers, Lobby Attendants, and Ticket Takers
31-9096.00	Veterinary Assistants and Laboratory Animal Caretakers
35-3031.00	Waiters and Waitresses
43-5111.00	Weighers, Measurers, Checkers, and Samplers, Recordkeeping
51-4121.01	Welders, Production

Jobs Requiring Moderate-Term On-the-Job Training

O*NET Number	Job Title
43-4051.01	Adjustment Clerks
41-3011.00	Advertising Sales Agents
19-4011.00	Agricultural and Food Science Technicians
45-2091.00	Agricultural Equipment Operators
55-3011.00	Air Crew Members
55-3012.00	Aircraft Launch and Recovery Specialists
53-3011.00	Ambulance Drivers and Attendants, Except Emergency Medical Technicians
33-9011.00	Animal Control Workers
39-2011.00	Animal Trainers
55-3013.00	Armored Assault Vehicle Crew Members
55-3014.00	Artillery and Missile Crew Members
25-9011.00	Audio-Visual Collections Specialists
33-3011.00	Bailiffs
49-2092.03	Battery Repairers
49-3091.00	Bicycle Repairers
43-3021.00	Billing and Posting Clerks and Machine Operators
51-5011.01	Bindery Machine Setters and Set-Up Operators
51-5011.00	Bindery Workers
51-8021.01	Boiler Operators and Tenders, Low Pressure
51-5012.00	Bookbinders
43-3031.00	Bookkeeping, Accounting, and Auditing Clerks
47-2031.06	Brattice Builders
43-4011.00	Brokerage Clerks
51-4033.02	Buffing and Polishing Set-Up Operators
53-3021.00	Bus Drivers, Transit and Intercity
49-9061.00	Camera and Photographic Equipment Repairers
27-4031.00	Camera Operators, Television, Video, and Motion Picture
27-3043.03	Caption Writers
43-5011.00	Cargo and Freight Agents
47-2031.03	Carpenter Assemblers and Repairers
47-2041.00	Carpet Installers
47-2081.01	Ceiling Tile Installers
51-9191.00	Cementing and Gluing Machine Operators and Tenders
51-9011.01	Chemical Equipment Controllers and Operators
51-9011.00	Chemical Equipment Operators and Tenders
51-9011.02	Chemical Equipment Tenders
43-4061.01	Claims Takers, Unemployment Benefits
51-9192.00	Cleaning, Washing, and Metal Pickling Equipment Operators and Tenders

51-9121.02	Coating, Painting, and Spraying Machine Operators and Tenders
51-9121.01	Coating, Painting, and Spraying Machine Setters and Set-Up Operators
49-9091.00	Coin, Vending, and Amusement Machine Servicers and Repairers
51-4081.02	Combination Machine Tool Operators and Tenders, Metal and Plastic
51-4081.01	Combination Machine Tool Setters and Set-Up Operators, Metal and Plastic
55-3015.00	Command and Control Center Specialists
49-9092.00	Commercial Divers
43-9011.00	Computer Operators
51-4011.00	Computer-Controlled Machine Tool Operators, Metal and Plastic
47-4099.99	Construction and Related Workers, All Other
47-5021.01	Construction Drillers
47-2061.00	Construction Laborers
47-5041.00	Continuous Mining Machine Operators
49-9012.00	Control and Valve Installers and Repairers, Except Mechanical Door
51-9193.00	Cooling and Freezing Equipment Operators and Tenders
33-3012.00	Correctional Officers and Jailers
39-3092.00	Costume Attendants
53-7021.00	Crane and Tower Operators
51-9021.00	Crushing, Grinding, and Polishing Machine Setters, Operators, and Tenders
43-4051.00	Customer Service Representatives
43-4051.02	Customer Service Representatives, Utilities
51-9032.00	Cutting and Slicing Machine Setters, Operators, and Tenders
51-4031.00	Cutting, Punching, and Press Machine Setters, Operators, and Tenders, Metal and Plastic
43-9021.00	Data Entry Keyers
41-9011.00	Demonstrators and Product Promoters
31-9091.00	Dental Assistants
47-5011.00	Derrick Operators, Oil and Gas
29-2051.00	Dietetic Technicians
43-5032.00	Dispatchers, Except Police, Fire, and Ambulance
53-7032.02	Dragline Operators
53-7031.00	Dredge Operators
51-4032.00	Drilling and Boring Machine Tool Setters, Operators, and Tenders, Metal and Plastic
47-2081.00	Drywall and Ceiling Tile Installers
47-2081.02	Drywall Installers
47-5021.00	Earth Drillers, Except Oil and Gas
49-9012.01	Electric Meter Installers and Repairers
51-9061.04	Electrical and Electronic Inspectors and Testers
49-2092.05	Electrical Parts Reconditioners
51-4193.02	Electrolytic Plating and Coating Machine Operators and Tenders, Metal and Plastic
43-4061.00	Eligibility Interviewers, Government Programs
51-9194.05	Etchers, Hand
53-7032.00	Excavating and Loading Machine and Dragline Operators
53-7032.01	Excavating and Loading Machine Operators
43-6011.00	Executive Secretaries and Administrative Assistants
47-5031.00	Explosives Workers, Ordnance Handling Experts, and Blasters
51-4021.00	Extruding and Drawing Machine Setters, Operators, and Tenders, Metal and Plastic
51-6091.01	Extruding and Forming Machine Operators and Tenders, Synthetic or Glass Fibers
51-6091.00	Extruding and Forming Machine Setters, Operators, and Tenders, Synthetic and Glass Fibers
51-9041.01	Extruding, Forming, Pressing, and Compacting Machine Setters and Set-Up Operators
45-4021.00	Fallers
47-4031.00	Fence Erectors
51-9032.01	Fiber Product Cutting Machine Setters and Set-Up Operators
51-2091.00	Fiberglass Laminators and Fabricators
51-9131.04	Film Laboratory Technicians
33-2021.01	Fire Inspectors
33-2021.00	Fire Inspectors and Investigators
51-2041.02	Fitters, Structural Metal—Precision
47-2042.00	Floor Layers, Except Carpet, Wood, and Hard Tiles
47-2043.00	Floor Sanders and Finishers
27-1023.00	Floral Designers
45-4011.00	Forest and Conservation Workers
33-2022.00	Forest Fire Inspectors and Prevention Specialists
51-4022.00	Forging Machine Setters, Operators, and Tenders, Metal and Plastic
51-4071.00	Foundry Mold and Coremakers
51-9051.00	Furnace, Kiln, Oven, Drier, and Kettle Operators and Tenders
43-3041.00	Gaming Cage Workers
53-7071.00	Gas Compressor and Gas Pumping Station Operators
53-7071.02	Gas Compressor Operators
53-7071.01	Gas Pumping Station Operators
51-9071.06	Gem and Diamond Workers
47-2073.01	Grader, Bulldozer, and Scraper Operators
51-9022.00	Grinding and Polishing Workers, Hand
51-4033.01	Grinding, Honing, Lapping, and Deburring Machine Set-Up Operators
51-4033.00	Grinding, Lapping, Polishing, and Buffing Machine Tool Setters, Operators, and Tenders, Metal and Plastic
49-2092.06	Hand and Portable Power Tool Repairers
47-4041.00	Hazardous Materials Removal Workers
51-4191.00	Heat Treating Equipment Setters, Operators, and Tenders, Metal and Plastic

(continues)

(continued)

Jobs Requiring Moderate-Term On-the-Job Training

O*NET Number	Job Title
51-4191.02	Heat Treating, Annealing, and Tempering Machine Operators and Tenders, Metal and Plastic
51-4191.03	Heaters, Metal and Plastic
47-4051.00	Highway Maintenance Workers
53-7041.00	Hoist and Winch Operators
45-3021.00	Hunters and Trappers
55-3016.00	Infantry
47-2131.00	Insulation Workers, Floor, Ceiling, and Wall
47-2132.00	Insulation Workers, Mechanical
43-9041.01	Insurance Claims Clerks
43-9041.02	Insurance Policy Processing Clerks
47-4041.01	Irradiated-Fuel Handlers
51-4034.00	Lathe and Turning Machine Tool Setters, Operators, and Tenders, Metal and Plastic
51-6011.03	Laundry and Drycleaning Machine Operators and Tenders, Except Pressing
51-5023.03	Letterpress Setters and Set-Up Operators
53-7033.00	Loading Machine Operators, Underground Mining
49-9094.00	Locksmiths and Safe Repairers
45-4023.00	Log Graders and Scalers
45-4022.00	Logging Equipment Operators
45-4022.01	Logging Tractor Operators
45-4029.99	Logging Workers, All Other
49-9095.00	Manufactured Building and Mobile Home Installers
17-3031.02	Mapping Technicians
51-9061.01	Materials Inspectors
49-9011.00	Mechanical Door Repairers
27-4099.99	Media and Communication Equipment Workers, All Other
31-9092.00	Medical Assistants
49-9062.00	Medical Equipment Repairers
27-1026.00	Merchandise Displayers and Window Trimmers
51-2041.01	Metal Fabricators, Structural Metal Products
51-4072.03	Metal Molding, Coremaking, and Casting Machine Setters and Set-Up Operators
51-4051.00	Metal-Refining Furnace Operators and Tenders
49-9012.03	Meter Mechanics
51-4035.00	Milling and Planing Machine Setters, Operators, and Tenders, Metal and Plastic
47-5042.00	Mine Cutting and Channeling Machine Operators
47-5049.99	Mining Machine Operators, All Other
51-9023.00	Mixing and Blending Machine Setters, Operators, and Tenders
51-4061.00	Model Makers, Metal and Plastic
41-9012.00	Models
51-9195.06	Mold Makers, Hand
51-9195.07	Molding and Casting Workers
51-4072.00	Molding, Coremaking, and Casting Machine Setters, Operators, and Tenders, Metal and Plastic
53-5022.00	Motorboat Operators
47-2073.02	Operating Engineers
47-2073.00	Operating Engineers and Other Construction Equipment Operators
51-9083.00	Ophthalmic Laboratory Technicians
51-9083.02	Optical Instrument Assemblers
43-5081.04	Order Fillers, Wholesale and Retail Sales
49-3053.00	Outdoor Power Equipment and Other Small Engine Mechanics
47-2141.00	Painters, Construction and Maintenance
51-9122.00	Painters, Transportation Equipment
51-9194.04	Pantograph Engravers
51-9196.00	Paper Goods Machine Setters, Operators, and Tenders
47-2142.00	Paperhangers
41-2022.00	Parts Salespersons
51-4062.00	Patternmakers, Metal and Plastic
47-2071.00	Paving, Surfacing, and Tamping Equipment Operators
37-2021.00	Pest Control Workers
37-3012.00	Pesticide Handlers, Sprayers, and Applicators, Vegetation
31-9095.00	Pharmacy Aides
29-2052.00	Pharmacy Technicians
51-5022.13	Photoengraving and Lithographing Machine Operators and Tenders
51-9131.03	Photographic Hand Developers
51-9131.00	Photographic Process Workers
51-9131.02	Photographic Reproduction Technicians
51-9131.01	Photographic Retouchers and Restorers
47-2072.00	Pile-Driver Operators
47-2151.00	Pipelayers
47-2152.03	Pipelaying Fitters
51-4072.01	Plastic Molding and Casting Machine Setters and Set-Up Operators
51-4193.00	Plating and Coating Machine Setters, Operators, and Tenders, Metal and Plastic
43-5031.00	Police, Fire, and Ambulance Dispatchers
51-4052.00	Pourers and Casters, Metal
51-9061.03	Precision Devices Inspectors and Testers
51-9083.01	Precision Lens Grinders and Polishers
51-9195.01	Precision Mold and Pattern Casters, except Nonferrous Metals
51-5023.01	Precision Printing Workers
51-4031.03	Press and Press Brake Machine Setters and Set-Up Operators, Metal and Plastic
51-6021.01	Pressers, Delicate Fabrics
51-6021.00	Pressers, Textile, Garment, and Related Materials
51-5023.00	Printing Machine Operators
53-7072.00	Pump Operators, Except Wellhead Pumpers

51-4031.02 Punching Machine Setters and Set-Up Operators, Metal and Plastic
55-3017.00 Radar and Sonar Technicians
27-3011.00 Radio and Television Announcers
53-4021.00 Railroad Brake, Signal, and Switch Operators
47-4061.00 Rail-Track Laying and Maintenance Equipment Operators
39-9041.00 Residential Advisors
47-5051.00 Rock Splitters, Quarry
51-4023.00 Rolling Machine Setters, Operators, and Tenders, Metal and Plastic
47-5061.00 Roof Bolters, Mining
47-2181.00 Roofers
47-5012.00 Rotary Drill Operators, Oil and Gas
47-2031.02 Rough Carpenters
41-4011.01 Sales Representatives, Agricultural
41-4011.02 Sales Representatives, Chemical and Pharmaceutical
41-4011.03 Sales Representatives, Electrical/Electronic
41-4011.06 Sales Representatives, Instruments
41-4011.04 Sales Representatives, Mechanical Equipment and Supplies
41-4011.05 Sales Representatives, Medical
41-4012.00 Sales Representatives, Wholesale and Manufacturing, Except Technical and Scientific Products
41-4011.00 Sales Representatives, Wholesale and Manufacturing, Technical and Scientific Products
51-7041.02 Sawing Machine Operators and Tenders
51-7041.01 Sawing Machine Setters and Set-Up Operators
51-7041.00 Sawing Machine Setters, Operators, and Tenders, Wood
51-4031.01 Sawing Machine Tool Setters and Set-Up Operators, Metal and Plastic
51-5023.06 Screen Printing Machine Setters and Set-Up Operators
43-6014.00 Secretaries, Except Legal, Medical, and Executive
47-4091.00 Segmental Pavers
51-9012.00 Separating, Filtering, Clarifying, Precipitating, and Still Machine Setters, Operators, and Tenders
47-4071.00 Septic Tank Servicers and Sewer Pipe Cleaners
47-5013.00 Service Unit Operators, Oil, Gas, and Mining
51-6031.00 Sewing Machine Operators
51-6031.01 Sewing Machine Operators, Garment
51-6031.02 Sewing Machine Operators, Non-Garment
51-4031.04 Shear and Slitter Machine Setters and Set-Up Operators, Metal and Plastic
47-2211.00 Sheet Metal Workers
47-2031.04 Ship Carpenters and Joiners
51-6042.00 Shoe Machine Operators and Tenders
53-7111.00 Shuttle Car Operators

51-3023.00 Slaughterers and Meat Packers
21-1093.00 Social and Human Service Assistants
51-4122.03 Soldering and Brazing Machine Setters and Set-Up Operators
51-8021.00 Stationary Engineers and Boiler Operators
43-9111.00 Statistical Assistants
43-5081.03 Stock Clerks—Stockroom, Warehouse, or Storage Yard
51-9195.03 Stone Cutters and Carvers
51-9032.02 Stone Sawyers
51-2041.00 Structural Metal Fabricators and Fitters
53-4041.00 Subway and Streetcar Operators
17-3031.00 Surveying and Mapping Technicians
53-7121.00 Tank Car, Truck, and Ship Loaders
47-2082.00 Tapers
13-2082.00 Tax Preparers
51-2092.00 Team Assemblers
51-6061.00 Textile Bleaching and Dyeing Machine Operators and Tenders
51-6062.00 Textile Cutting Machine Setters, Operators, and Tenders
51-6064.00 Textile Winding, Twisting, and Drawing Out Machine Setters, Operators, and Tenders
51-2093.00 Timing Device Assemblers, Adjusters, and Calibrators
51-9197.00 Tire Builders
23-2093.00 Title Examiners, Abstractors, and Searchers
23-2093.01 Title Searchers
51-4194.00 Tool Grinders, Filers, and Sharpeners
53-3032.02 Tractor-Trailer Truck Drivers
39-6022.00 Travel Guides
53-3032.00 Truck Drivers, Heavy and Tractor-Trailer
51-5022.12 Typesetting and Composing Machine Operators and Tenders
49-9012.02 Valve and Regulator Repairers
51-4122.02 Welding Machine Operators and Tenders
51-4122.00 Welding, Soldering, and Brazing Machine Setters, Operators, and Tenders
43-4061.02 Welfare Eligibility Workers and Interviewers
53-7073.00 Wellhead Pumpers
51-7042.02 Woodworking Machine Operators and Tenders, Except Sawing
51-7042.01 Woodworking Machine Setters and Set-Up Operators, Except Sawing
51-7042.00 Woodworking Machine Setters, Operators, and Tenders, Except Sawing
43-9022.00 Word Processors and Typists

Jobs Requiring Long-Term On-the-Job Training

O*NET Number	Job Title
27-2011.00	Actors
55-1011.00	Air Crew Officers
53-2021.00	Air Traffic Controllers

(continues)

(continued)

Jobs Requiring Long-Term On-the-Job Training

O*NET Number	Job Title
55-1012.00	Aircraft Launch and Recovery Officers
51-2011.03	Aircraft Rigging Assemblers
51-2011.01	Aircraft Structure Assemblers, Precision
51-2011.00	Aircraft Structure, Surfaces, Rigging, and Systems Assemblers
51-2011.02	Aircraft Systems Assemblers, Precision
55-1013.00	Armored Assault Vehicle Officers
55-1014.00	Artillery and Missile Officers
27-1019.99	Artists and Related Workers, All Other
27-2021.00	Athletes and Sports Competitors
27-4011.00	Audio and Video Equipment Technicians
49-2011.01	Automatic Teller Machine Servicers
49-3021.00	Automotive Body and Related Repairers
49-3022.00	Automotive Glass Installers and Repairers
51-8013.02	Auxiliary Equipment Operators, Power
51-3011.00	Bakers
51-3011.01	Bakers, Bread and Pastry
51-3011.02	Bakers, Manufacturing
51-9071.04	Bench Workers, Jewelry
47-2031.05	Boat Builders and Shipwrights
47-2011.00	Boilermakers
47-2021.00	Brickmasons and Blockmasons
51-3021.00	Butchers and Meat Cutters
51-7011.00	Cabinetmakers and Bench Carpenters
51-5022.04	Camera Operators
53-5021.00	Captains, Mates, and Pilots of Water Vessels
47-2031.00	Carpenters
27-1013.03	Cartoonists
47-2051.00	Cement Masons and Concrete Finishers
51-8091.00	Chemical Plant and System Operators
13-1031.00	Claims Adjusters, Examiners, and Investigators
13-1031.01	Claims Examiners, Property and Casualty Insurance
27-2022.00	Coaches and Scouts
55-1015.00	Command and Control Center Officers
13-1041.00	Compliance Officers, Except Agriculture, Construction, Health and Safety, and Transportation
47-2031.01	Construction Carpenters
35-2014.00	Cooks, Restaurant
27-2031.00	Dancers
51-9081.00	Dental Laboratory Technicians
51-5022.08	Dot Etchers
49-2092.01	Electric Home Appliance and Power Tool Repairers
49-2092.02	Electric Motor and Switch Assemblers and Repairers
49-2092.00	Electric Motor, Power Tool, and Related Repairers
49-9051.00	Electrical Power-Line Installers and Repairers
47-2111.00	Electricians
51-5022.09	Electronic Masking System Operators
51-5022.10	Electrotypers and Stereotypers
47-4021.00	Elevator Installers and Repairers
51-5023.08	Engraver Set-Up Operators
51-9194.06	Engravers, Hand
51-9194.02	Engravers/Carvers
13-1041.01	Environmental Compliance Inspectors
13-1041.03	Equal Opportunity Representatives and Officers
51-9194.03	Etchers
51-6092.00	Fabric and Apparel Patternmakers
11-9012.00	Farmers and Ranchers
27-1013.00	Fine Artists, Including Painters, Sculptors, and Illustrators
33-2011.00	Fire Fighters
33-3031.00	Fish and Game Wardens
39-6031.00	Flight Attendants
33-2011.02	Forest Fire Fighters
51-7021.00	Furniture Finishers
33-9031.00	Gaming Surveillance Officers and Gaming Investigators
49-9031.02	Gas Appliance Repairers
51-8092.02	Gas Distribution Plant Operators
51-8092.00	Gas Plant Operators
51-8092.01	Gas Processing Plant Operators
51-8093.03	Gaugers
51-9195.04	Glass Blowers, Molders, Benders, and Finishers
47-2121.00	Glaziers
13-1041.04	Government Property Inspectors and Investigators
51-5022.01	Hand Compositors and Typesetters
49-9021.01	Heating and Air Conditioning Mechanics
49-9021.00	Heating, Air Conditioning, and Refrigeration Mechanics and Installers
33-3051.02	Highway Patrol Pilots
49-9031.01	Home Appliance Installers
49-9041.00	Industrial Machinery Mechanics
55-1016.00	Infantry Officers
13-1031.02	Insurance Adjusters, Examiners, and Investigators
13-1032.00	Insurance Appraisers, Auto Damage
27-3091.00	Interpreters and Translators
51-9071.00	Jewelers and Precious Stone and Metal Workers
51-5021.00	Job Printers
49-9063.01	Keyboard Instrument Repairers and Tuners
13-1041.02	Licensing Examiners and Inspectors
51-4041.00	Machinists
49-9042.00	Maintenance and Repair Workers, General
49-9043.00	Maintenance Workers, Machinery
51-9061.02	Mechanical Inspectors
27-3099.99	Media and Communication Workers, All Other
51-9082.00	Medical Appliance Technicians
55-1019.99	Military Officer Special and Tactical Operations Leaders/Managers, All Other

49-9044.00	Millwrights
51-9071.03	Model and Mold Makers, Jewelry
51-7031.00	Model Makers, Wood
49-3051.00	Motorboat Mechanics
49-3052.00	Motorcycle Mechanics
33-2011.01	Municipal Fire Fighters
49-9063.00	Musical Instrument Repairers and Tuners
27-2042.00	Musicians and Singers
27-2042.02	Musicians, Instrumental
51-8011.00	Nuclear Power Reactor Operators
51-4011.01	Numerical Control Machine Tool Operators and Tenders, Metal and Plastic
51-4012.00	Numerical Tool and Process Control Programmers
49-2011.03	Office Machine and Cash Register Servicers
51-5023.02	Offset Lithographic Press Setters and Set-Up Operators
29-2081.00	Opticians, Dispensing
27-1013.01	Painters and Illustrators
51-5022.02	Paste-Up Workers
51-7032.00	Patternmakers, Wood
49-9063.04	Percussion Instrument Repairers and Tuners
51-8093.01	Petroleum Pump System Operators
51-8093.00	Petroleum Pump System Operators, Refinery Operators, and Gaugers
51-8093.02	Petroleum Refinery and Control Panel Operators
51-5022.03	Photoengravers
27-4021.00	Photographers
27-4021.02	Photographers, Scientific
47-2152.01	Pipe Fitters
47-2161.00	Plasterers and Stucco Masons
51-5022.11	Plate Finishers
51-5022.07	Platemakers
47-2152.02	Plumbers
47-2152.00	Plumbers, Pipefitters, and Steamfitters
33-3051.00	Police and Sheriff's Patrol Officers
33-3051.01	Police Patrol Officers
51-9195.05	Potters
51-8012.00	Power Distributors and Dispatchers
51-8013.01	Power Generating Plant Operators, Except Auxiliary Equipment Operators
51-8013.00	Power Plant Operators
51-9194.01	Precision Etchers and Engravers, Hand or Machine
49-9069.99	Precision Instrument and Equipment Repairers, All Other
51-9195.02	Precision Pattern and Die Casters, Nonferrous Metals
51-5022.00	Prepress Technicians and Workers
13-1041.05	Pressure Vessel Inspectors
27-4021.01	Professional Photographers
27-4013.00	Radio Operators
49-3043.00	Rail Car Repairers
49-3092.00	Recreational Vehicle Service Technicians

49-9063.03	Reed or Wind Instrument Repairers and Tuners
49-9021.02	Refrigeration Mechanics
47-2171.00	Reinforcing Iron and Rebar Workers
51-5022.05	Scanner Operators
27-1013.04	Sculptors
33-3051.03	Sheriffs and Deputy Sheriffs
53-5021.01	Ship and Boat Captains
51-6041.00	Shoe and Leather Workers and Repairers
51-9071.02	Silversmiths
27-2042.01	Singers
27-1013.02	Sketch Artists
55-3018.00	Special Forces
55-1017.00	Special Forces Officers
51-8021.02	Stationary Engineers
47-2022.00	Stonemasons
49-9063.02	Stringed Instrument Repairers and Tuners
51-5022.06	Strippers
47-2221.00	Structural Iron and Steel Workers
17-3031.01	Surveying Technicians
27-2012.04	Talent Directors
27-2012.05	Technical Directors/Managers
49-2022.04	Telecommunications Facility Examiners
49-9052.00	Telecommunications Line Installers and Repairers
47-2053.00	Terrazzo Workers and Finishers
51-6063.00	Textile Knitting and Weaving Machine Setters, Operators, and Tenders
47-2044.00	Tile and Marble Setters
23-2093.02	Title Examiners and Abstractors
51-4111.00	Tool and Die Makers
49-2092.04	Transformer Repairers
33-3052.00	Transit and Railroad Police
27-2023.00	Umpires, Referees, and Other Sports Officials
51-6093.00	Upholsterers
49-9064.00	Watch Repairers
51-8031.00	Water and Liquid Waste Treatment Plant and System Operators
51-4121.03	Welder-Fitters
51-4121.02	Welders and Cutters
51-4121.00	Welders, Cutters, Solderers, and Brazers
47-5021.02	Well and Core Drill Operators

Jobs Requiring Work Experience in a Related Occupation

O*NET Number	Job Title
11-9011.02	Agricultural Crop Farm Managers
45-2011.00	Agricultural Inspectors
53-1011.00	Aircraft Cargo Handling Supervisors
53-6051.01	Aviation Inspectors
33-3021.04	Child Support, Missing Persons, and Unemployment Insurance Fraud Investigators
27-2032.00	Choreographers
47-4011.00	Construction and Building Inspectors

(continues)

(continued)

Jobs Requiring Work Experience in a Related Occupation

O*NET Number	Job Title
13-1041.06	Coroners
33-3021.03	Criminal Investigators and Special Agents
51-6052.02	Custom Tailors
33-3021.00	Detectives and Criminal Investigators
13-1061.00	Emergency Management Specialists
45-1012.00	Farm Labor Contractors
11-9011.00	Farm, Ranch, and Other Agricultural Managers
37-1012.02	First-Line Supervisors and Manager/Supervisors—Landscaping Workers
47-1011.01	First-Line Supervisors and Manager/Supervisors—Construction Trades Workers
47-1011.02	First-Line Supervisors and Manager/Supervisors—Extractive Workers
43-1011.02	First-Line Supervisors, Administrative Support
43-1011.01	First-Line Supervisors, Customer Service
55-2011.00	First-Line Supervisors/Managers of Air Crew Members
55-2013.00	First-Line Supervisors/Managers of All Other Tactical Operations Specialists
47-1011.00	First-Line Supervisors/Managers of Construction Trades and Extraction Workers
33-1011.00	First-Line Supervisors/Managers of Correctional Officers
45-1011.00	First-Line Supervisors/Managers of Farming, Fishing, and Forestry Workers
33-1021.00	First-Line Supervisors/Managers of Fire Fighting and Prevention Workers
35-1012.00	First-Line Supervisors/Managers of Food Preparation and Serving Workers
53-1021.00	First-Line Supervisors/Managers of Helpers, Laborers, and Material Movers, Hand
37-1011.00	First-Line Supervisors/Managers of Housekeeping and Janitorial Workers
37-1012.00	First-Line Supervisors/Managers of Landscaping, Lawn Service, and Groundskeeping Workers
49-1011.00	First-Line Supervisors/Managers of Mechanics, Installers, and Repairers
41-1012.00	First-Line Supervisors/Managers of Non-Retail Sales Workers
43-1011.00	First-Line Supervisors/Managers of Office and Administrative Support Workers
39-1021.00	First-Line Supervisors/Managers of Personal Service Workers
33-1012.00	First-Line Supervisors/Managers of Police and Detectives
51-1011.00	First-Line Supervisors/Managers of Production and Operating Workers
41-1011.00	First-Line Supervisors/Managers of Retail Sales Workers
53-1031.00	First-Line Supervisors/Managers of Transportation and Material-Moving Machine and Vehicle Operators
55-2012.00	First-Line Supervisors/Managers of Weapons Specialists/Crew Members
33-1099.99	First-Line Supervisors/Managers, Protective Service Workers, All Other
11-9011.03	Fish Hatchery Managers
11-9051.00	Food Service Managers
33-1021.02	Forest Fire Fighting and Prevention Supervisors
53-6051.06	Freight Inspectors
45-2041.00	Graders and Sorters, Agricultural Products
37-1011.01	Housekeeping Supervisors
33-3021.05	Immigration and Customs Inspectors
37-1011.02	Janitorial Supervisors
37-1012.01	Lawn Service Managers
11-1031.00	Legislators
53-4011.00	Locomotive Engineers
11-9081.00	Lodging Managers
53-6051.03	Marine Cargo Inspectors
53-5021.02	Mates—Ship, Boat, and Barge
53-6051.05	Motor Vehicle Inspectors
33-1021.01	Municipal Fire Fighting and Prevention Supervisors
43-4141.00	New Accounts Clerks
11-9011.01	Nursery and Greenhouse Managers
33-3021.01	Police Detectives
33-3021.02	Police Identification and Records Officers
11-9131.00	Postmasters and Mail Superintendents
33-9021.00	Private Detectives and Investigators
53-6051.02	Public Transportation Inspectors
13-1021.00	Purchasing Agents and Buyers, Farm Products
53-4013.00	Rail Yard Engineers, Dinkey Operators, and Hostlers
53-4031.00	Railroad Conductors and Yardmasters
53-6051.04	Railroad Inspectors
53-4021.02	Railroad Yard Workers
41-9021.00	Real Estate Brokers
25-3021.00	Self-Enrichment Education Teachers
51-6052.01	Shop and Alteration Tailors
11-3071.02	Storage and Distribution Managers
51-6052.00	Tailors, Dressmakers, and Custom Sewers
53-4021.01	Train Crew Members
53-6051.00	Transportation Inspectors
11-3071.01	Transportation Managers
11-3071.00	Transportation, Storage, and Distribution Managers
25-1194.00	Vocational Education Teachers, Postsecondary

Jobs Requiring Postsecondary Vocational Training

O*NET Number	Job Title
49-3011.03	Aircraft Body and Bonded Structure Repairers
49-3011.02	Aircraft Engine Specialists
49-3011.00	Aircraft Mechanics and Service Technicians
49-3011.01	Airframe-and-Power-Plant Mechanics
13-2021.00	Appraisers and Assessors of Real Estate

13-2021.02	Appraisers, Real Estate
17-3011.00	Architectural and Civil Drafters
13-2021.01	Assessors
49-3023.01	Automotive Master Mechanics
49-3023.00	Automotive Service Technicians and Mechanics
49-3023.02	Automotive Specialty Technicians
49-2091.00	Avionics Technicians
39-5011.00	Barbers
27-4012.00	Broadcast Technicians
49-3031.00	Bus and Truck Mechanics and Diesel Engine Specialists
51-4072.05	Casting Machine Set-Up Operators
49-2022.01	Central Office and PBX Installers and Repairers
35-1011.00	Chefs and Head Cooks
17-3011.02	Civil Drafters
53-2012.00	Commercial Pilots
49-2022.03	Communication Equipment Mechanics, Installers, and Repairers
15-1099.99	Computer Specialists, All Other
49-2011.00	Computer, Automated Teller, and Office Machine Repairers
23-2091.00	Court Reporters
49-2011.02	Data Processing Equipment Repairers
51-5023.04	Design Printing Machine Setters and Set-Up Operators
43-9031.00	Desktop Publishers
49-2093.00	Electrical and Electronics Installers and Repairers, Transportation Equipment
49-2094.00	Electrical and Electronics Repairers, Commercial and Industrial Equipment
49-2095.00	Electrical and Electronics Repairers, Powerhouse, Substation, and Relay
51-4193.01	Electrolytic Plating and Coating Machine Setters and Set-Up Operators, Metal and Plastic
17-3012.01	Electronic Drafters
49-2096.00	Electronic Equipment Installers and Repairers, Motor Vehicles
49-2097.00	Electronic Home Entertainment Equipment Installers and Repairers
39-4011.00	Embalmers
51-5023.07	Embossing Machine Set-Up Operators
29-2041.00	Emergency Medical Technicians and Paramedics
51-9194.00	Etchers and Engravers
49-3041.00	Farm Equipment Mechanics
39-9031.00	Fitness Trainers and Aerobics Instructors
49-2022.02	Frame Wirers, Central Office
39-3012.00	Gaming and Sports Book Writers and Runners
39-3011.00	Gaming Dealers
39-1011.00	Gaming Supervisors
39-5012.00	Hairdressers, Hairstylists, and Cosmetologists
51-4191.01	Heating Equipment Setters and Set-Up Operators, Metal and Plastic
49-9031.00	Home Appliance Repairers
51-9061.00	Inspectors, Testers, Sorters, Samplers, and Weighers

51-9071.01	Jewelers
51-4192.00	Lay-Out Workers, Metal and Plastic
43-6012.00	Legal Secretaries
29-2061.00	Licensed Practical and Licensed Vocational Nurses
53-4012.00	Locomotive Firers
39-5091.00	Makeup Artists, Theatrical and Performance
39-5092.00	Manicurists and Pedicurists
31-9011.00	Massage Therapists
17-3013.00	Mechanical Drafters
43-6013.00	Medical Secretaries
49-3042.00	Mobile Heavy Equipment Mechanics, Except Engines
51-9195.00	Molders, Shapers, and Casters, Except Metal and Plastic
51-4081.00	Multiple Machine Tool Setters, Operators, and Tenders, Metal and Plastic
51-4193.03	Nonelectrolytic Plating and Coating Machine Setters and Set-Up Operators, Metal and Plastic
51-9071.05	Pewter Casters and Finishers
51-6011.02	Precision Dyers
29-2053.00	Psychiatric Technicians
49-2021.00	Radio Mechanics
41-9022.00	Real Estate Sales Agents
29-2054.00	Respiratory Therapy Technicians
49-2098.00	Security and Fire Alarm Systems Installers
53-5031.00	Ship Engineers
49-9097.00	Signal and Track Switch Repairers
27-4014.00	Sound Engineering Technicians
49-2022.05	Station Installers and Repairers, Telephone
29-2055.00	Surgical Technologists
49-2022.00	Telecommunications Equipment Installers and Repairers, Except Line Installers
41-3041.00	Travel Agents
51-4122.01	Welding Machine Setters and Set-Up Operators

Jobs Requiring an Associate's Degree

O*NET Number	Job Title
17-3021.00	Aerospace Engineering and Operations Technicians
19-4011.01	Agricultural Technicians
45-2021.00	Animal Breeders
17-3011.01	Architectural Drafters
19-4021.00	Biological Technicians
17-3023.02	Calibration and Instrumentation Technicians
29-2031.00	Cardiovascular Technologists and Technicians
19-4031.00	Chemical Technicians
19-4061.01	City Planning Aides
17-3022.00	Civil Engineering Technicians
15-1041.00	Computer Support Specialists
27-1012.00	Craft Artists
29-2021.00	Dental Hygienists
29-2032.00	Diagnostic Medical Sonographers

(continues)

(continued)

Jobs Requiring an Associate's Degree

O*NET Number	Job Title
17-3023.00	Electrical and Electronic Engineering Technicians
17-3012.00	Electrical and Electronics Drafters
17-3012.02	Electrical Drafters
17-3023.03	Electrical Engineering Technicians
17-3024.00	Electro-Mechanical Technicians
17-3023.01	Electronics Engineering Technicians
17-3029.99	Engineering Technicians, Except Drafters, All Other
17-3025.00	Environmental Engineering Technicians
19-4091.00	Environmental Science and Protection Technicians, Including Health
45-1011.01	First-Line Supervisors and Manager/Supervisors —Agricultural Crop Workers
45-1011.03	First-Line Supervisors and Manager/Supervisors —Animal Care Workers, Except Livestock
45-1011.02	First-Line Supervisors and Manager/Supervisors —Animal Husbandry Workers
45-1011.06	First-Line Supervisors and Manager/Supervisors —Fishery Workers
45-1011.04	First-Line Supervisors and Manager/Supervisors —Horticultural Workers
19-4011.02	Food Science Technicians
19-4092.00	Forensic Science Technicians
19-4093.00	Forest and Conservation Technicians
11-9061.00	Funeral Directors
19-4041.00	Geological and Petroleum Technicians
19-4041.01	Geological Data Technicians
19-4041.02	Geological Sample Test Technicians
17-3026.00	Industrial Engineering Technicians
19-4099.99	Life, Physical, and Social Science Technicians, All Other
17-3027.00	Mechanical Engineering Technicians
29-2012.00	Medical and Clinical Laboratory Technicians
29-2071.00	Medical Records and Health Information Technicians
31-9094.00	Medical Transcriptionists
19-4051.01	Nuclear Equipment Operation Technicians
29-2033.00	Nuclear Medicine Technologists
19-4051.02	Nuclear Monitoring Technicians
19-4051.00	Nuclear Technicians
29-9012.00	Occupational Health and Safety Technicians
31-2011.00	Occupational Therapist Assistants
23-2011.00	Paralegals and Legal Assistants
31-2022.00	Physical Therapist Aides
31-2021.00	Physical Therapist Assistants
27-3012.00	Public Address System and Other Announcers
29-1124.00	Radiation Therapists
29-2034.02	Radiologic Technicians
29-2034.01	Radiologic Technologists
29-2034.00	Radiologic Technologists and Technicians
29-1111.00	Registered Nurses
29-1126.00	Respiratory Therapists
51-9141.00	Semiconductor Processors
19-4061.00	Social Science Research Assistants
29-2056.00	Veterinary Technologists and Technicians

Jobs Requiring a Bachelor's Degree

O*NET Number	Job Title
13-2011.01	Accountants
13-2011.00	Accountants and Auditors
25-3011.00	Adult Literacy, Remedial Education, and GED Teachers and Instructors
17-2011.00	Aerospace Engineers
17-2021.00	Agricultural Engineers
53-2011.00	Airline Pilots, Copilots, and Flight Engineers
19-1011.00	Animal Scientists
19-3091.01	Anthropologists
19-3091.00	Anthropologists and Archeologists
19-3091.02	Archeologists
17-1011.00	Architects, Except Landscape and Naval
29-9091.00	Athletic Trainers
19-2021.00	Atmospheric and Space Scientists
13-2011.02	Auditors
17-2031.00	Biomedical Engineers
27-3021.00	Broadcast News Analysts
13-2031.00	Budget Analysts
17-1021.00	Cartographers and Photogrammetrists
17-2041.00	Chemical Engineers
19-2031.00	Chemists
21-1021.00	Child, Family, and School Social Workers
17-2051.00	Civil Engineers
27-1021.00	Commercial and Industrial Designers
13-1072.00	Compensation, Benefits, and Job Analysis Specialists
17-2061.00	Computer Hardware Engineers
15-1021.00	Computer Programmers
15-1071.01	Computer Security Specialists
15-1031.00	Computer Software Engineers, Applications
15-1032.00	Computer Software Engineers, Systems Software
15-1051.00	Computer Systems Analysts
19-1031.00	Conservation Scientists
11-9021.00	Construction Managers
27-3043.04	Copy Writers
13-1051.00	Cost Estimators
21-1019.99	Counselors, All Other
27-3043.02	Creative Writers
13-2041.00	Credit Analysts
15-1061.00	Database Administrators
29-1031.00	Dietitians and Nutritionists
21-2021.00	Directors, Religious Activities and Education
19-3011.00	Economists
27-3041.00	Editors

17-2071.00	Electrical Engineers
17-2072.00	Electronics Engineers, Except Computer
25-2021.00	Elementary School Teachers, Except Special Education
13-1071.01	Employment Interviewers, Private or Public Employment Service
13-1071.00	Employment, Recruitment, and Placement Specialists
17-2199.99	Engineers, All Other
17-2081.00	Environmental Engineers
19-2041.00	Environmental Scientists and Specialists, Including Health
27-1027.02	Exhibit Designers
25-9021.00	Farm and Home Management Advisors
27-1022.00	Fashion Designers
27-4032.00	Film and Video Editors
13-2051.00	Financial Analysts
13-2061.00	Financial Examiners
13-2099.99	Financial Specialists, All Other
33-2021.02	Fire Investigators
17-2111.02	Fire-Prevention and Protection Engineers
45-1011.05	First-Line Supervisors and Manager/Supervisors —Logging Workers
19-1012.00	Food Scientists and Technologists
19-1032.00	Foresters
19-3092.00	Geographers
19-2042.01	Geologists
19-2042.00	Geoscientists, Except Hydrologists and Geographers
27-1024.00	Graphic Designers
17-2111.00	Health and Safety Engineers, Except Mining Safety Engineers and Inspectors
19-3093.00	Historians
13-1079.99	Human Resources, Training, and Labor Relations Specialists, All Other
19-2043.00	Hydrologists
17-2112.00	Industrial Engineers
11-3051.00	Industrial Production Managers
17-2111.01	Industrial Safety and Health Engineers
41-3021.00	Insurance Sales Agents
13-2053.00	Insurance Underwriters
27-1025.00	Interior Designers
25-2012.00	Kindergarten Teachers, Except Special Education
17-1012.00	Landscape Architects
23-2092.00	Law Clerks
13-2071.00	Loan Counselors
13-2072.00	Loan Officers
13-1081.00	Logisticians
17-2121.02	Marine Architects
17-2121.01	Marine Engineers
17-2121.00	Marine Engineers and Naval Architects
19-3021.00	Market Research Analysts
17-2131.00	Materials Engineers
19-2032.00	Materials Scientists

15-2091.00	Mathematical Technicians
17-2141.00	Mechanical Engineers
29-2011.00	Medical and Clinical Laboratory Technologists
21-1022.00	Medical and Public Health Social Workers
13-1121.00	Meeting and Convention Planners
25-2022.00	Middle School Teachers, Except Special and Vocational Education
17-2151.00	Mining and Geological Engineers, Including Mining Safety Engineers
27-1014.00	Multi-Media Artists and Animators
27-2041.02	Music Arrangers and Orchestrators
15-1071.00	Network and Computer Systems Administrators
15-1081.00	Network Systems and Data Communications Analysts
17-2161.00	Nuclear Engineers
29-1122.00	Occupational Therapists
29-2091.00	Orthotists and Prosthetists
19-1031.03	Park Naturalists
13-2052.00	Personal Financial Advisors
13-1071.02	Personnel Recruiters
17-2171.00	Petroleum Engineers
19-2099.99	Physical Scientists, All Other
29-1071.00	Physician Assistants
19-1013.01	Plant Scientists
27-3043.01	Poets and Lyricists
25-2011.00	Preschool Teachers, Except Special Education
21-1092.00	Probation Officers and Correctional Treatment Specialists
17-2111.03	Product Safety Engineers
11-9141.00	Property, Real Estate, and Community Association Managers
27-3031.00	Public Relations Specialists
13-1023.00	Purchasing Agents, Except Wholesale, Retail, and Farm Products
19-1031.02	Range Managers
39-9032.00	Recreation Workers
29-1125.00	Recreational Therapists
21-1015.00	Rehabilitation Counselors
27-3022.00	Reporters and Correspondents
41-3031.02	Sales Agents, Financial Services
41-3031.01	Sales Agents, Securities and Commodities
41-9031.00	Sales Engineers
25-2031.00	Secondary School Teachers, Except Special and Vocational Education
41-3031.00	Securities, Commodities, and Financial Services Sales Agents
27-1027.00	Set and Exhibit Designers
27-1027.01	Set Designers
11-9151.00	Social and Community Service Managers
21-1029.99	Social Workers, All Other
19-1013.00	Soil and Plant Scientists
19-1031.01	Soil Conservationists
19-1013.02	Soil Scientists
25-2042.00	Special Education Teachers, Middle School

(continues)

(continued)

Jobs Requiring a Bachelor's Degree

O*NET Number	Job Title
25-2041.00	Special Education Teachers, Preschool, Kindergarten, and Elementary School
25-2043.00	Special Education Teachers, Secondary School
19-3022.00	Survey Researchers
17-1022.00	Surveyors
13-2081.00	Tax Examiners, Collectors, and Revenue Agents
25-3099.99	Teachers and Instructors, All Other
27-3042.00	Technical Writers
13-1073.00	Training and Development Specialists
25-2023.00	Vocational Education Teachers, Middle School
25-2032.00	Vocational Education Teachers, Secondary School
13-1022.00	Wholesale and Retail Buyers, Except Farm Products
27-3043.00	Writers and Authors

Jobs Requiring Work Experience Plus Degree

O*NET Number	Job Title
15-2011.00	Actuaries
23-1021.00	Administrative Law Judges, Adjudicators, and Hearing Officers
11-3011.00	Administrative Services Managers
11-2011.00	Advertising and Promotions Managers
13-1011.00	Agents and Business Managers of Artists, Performers, and Athletes
23-1022.00	Arbitrators, Mediators, and Conciliators
27-1011.00	Art Directors
11-1011.00	Chief Executives
11-3041.00	Compensation and Benefits Managers
11-3021.00	Computer and Information Systems Managers
27-2012.02	Directors—Stage, Motion Pictures, Television, and Radio
11-9039.99	Education Administrators, All Other
11-9032.00	Education Administrators, Elementary and Secondary School
11-9033.00	Education Administrators, Postsecondary
11-9031.00	Education Administrators, Preschool and Child Care Center/Program
11-9041.00	Engineering Managers
11-3031.00	Financial Managers
11-3031.02	Financial Managers, Branch or Department
11-9071.00	Gaming Managers
11-1021.00	General and Operations Managers
11-1011.01	Government Service Executives
11-3040.00	Human Resources Managers
11-3049.99	Human Resources Managers, All Other
23-1023.00	Judges, Magistrate Judges, and Magistrates
13-1111.00	Management Analysts
11-2021.00	Marketing Managers

O*NET Number	Job Title
11-9111.00	Medical and Health Services Managers
11-9121.00	Natural Sciences Managers
53-5021.03	Pilots, Ship
11-1011.02	Private Sector Executives
27-2012.01	Producers
27-2012.00	Producers and Directors
27-2012.03	Program Directors
11-2031.00	Public Relations Managers
11-3061.00	Purchasing Managers
11-2022.00	Sales Managers
11-3042.00	Training and Development Managers
11-3031.01	Treasurers, Controllers, and Chief Financial Officers

Jobs Requiring a Master's Degree

O*NET Number	Job Title
25-1041.00	Agricultural Sciences Teachers, Postsecondary
25-1061.00	Anthropology and Archeology Teachers, Postsecondary
25-1031.00	Architecture Teachers, Postsecondary
25-4011.00	Archivists
25-1062.00	Area, Ethnic, and Cultural Studies Teachers, Postsecondary
25-1121.00	Art, Drama, and Music Teachers, Postsecondary
25-1051.00	Atmospheric, Earth, Marine, and Space Sciences Teachers, Postsecondary
29-1121.00	Audiologists
25-1042.00	Biological Science Teachers, Postsecondary
25-1011.00	Business Teachers, Postsecondary
25-1052.00	Chemistry Teachers, Postsecondary
19-3031.02	Clinical Psychologists
19-3031.00	Clinical, Counseling, and School Psychologists
25-1122.00	Communications Teachers, Postsecondary
27-2041.03	Composers
25-1021.00	Computer Science Teachers, Postsecondary
19-3031.03	Counseling Psychologists
25-1111.00	Criminal Justice and Law Enforcement Teachers, Postsecondary
25-4012.00	Curators
25-1063.00	Economics Teachers, Postsecondary
25-1081.00	Education Teachers, Postsecondary
19-3031.01	Educational Psychologists
21-1012.00	Educational, Vocational, and School Counselors
25-1032.00	Engineering Teachers, Postsecondary
25-1123.00	English Language and Literature Teachers, Postsecondary
25-1053.00	Environmental Science Teachers, Postsecondary
25-1124.00	Foreign Language and Literature Teachers, Postsecondary
25-1043.00	Forestry and Conservation Science Teachers, Postsecondary
25-1064.00	Geography Teachers, Postsecondary
25-1191.00	Graduate Teaching Assistants

21-1091.00	Health Educators
25-1071.00	Health Specialties Teachers, Postsecondary
25-1125.00	History Teachers, Postsecondary
25-1192.00	Home Economics Teachers, Postsecondary
19-3032.00	Industrial-Organizational Psychologists
25-9031.00	Instructional Coordinators
25-4021.00	Librarians
25-1082.00	Library Science Teachers, Postsecondary
21-1013.00	Marriage and Family Therapists
25-1022.00	Mathematical Science Teachers, Postsecondary
15-2021.00	Mathematicians
21-1023.00	Mental Health and Substance Abuse Social Workers
21-1014.00	Mental Health Counselors
25-4013.00	Museum Technicians and Conservators
27-2041.01	Music Directors
27-2041.00	Music Directors and Composers
25-1072.00	Nursing Instructors and Teachers, Postsecondary
29-9011.00	Occupational Health and Safety Specialists
15-2031.00	Operations Research Analysts
25-1126.00	Philosophy and Religion Teachers, Postsecondary
29-1123.00	Physical Therapists
25-1054.00	Physics Teachers, Postsecondary
25-1065.00	Political Science Teachers, Postsecondary
19-3094.00	Political Scientists
25-1199.99	Postsecondary Teachers, All Other
19-3039.99	Psychologists, All Other
25-1066.00	Psychology Teachers, Postsecondary
25-1193.00	Recreation and Fitness Studies Teachers, Postsecondary
25-1069.99	Social Sciences Teachers, Postsecondary, All Other
19-3099.99	Social Scientists and Related Workers, All Other
25-1113.00	Social Work Teachers, Postsecondary
19-3041.00	Sociologists
25-1067.00	Sociology Teachers, Postsecondary
29-1127.00	Speech-Language Pathologists
15-2041.00	Statisticians
21-1011.00	Substance Abuse and Behavioral Disorder Counselors
19-3051.00	Urban and Regional Planners

Jobs Requiring a Doctoral Degree

O*NET Number	Job Title
19-2011.00	Astronomers
19-1021.01	Biochemists
19-1021.00	Biochemists and Biophysicists
19-1029.99	Biological Scientists, All Other
19-1020.01	Biologists
19-1021.02	Biophysicists
15-1011.00	Computer and Information Scientists, Research

19-1041.00	Epidemiologists
19-1042.00	Medical Scientists, Except Epidemiologists
19-1022.00	Microbiologists
19-2012.00	Physicists
19-1023.00	Zoologists and Wildlife Biologists

Jobs Requiring a First Professional Degree

O*NET Number	Job Title
29-1061.00	Anesthesiologists
29-1011.00	Chiropractors
21-2011.00	Clergy
29-1029.99	Dentists, All Other Specialists
29-1021.00	Dentists, General
29-1062.00	Family and General Practitioners
29-1063.00	Internists, General
25-1112.00	Law Teachers, Postsecondary
23-1011.00	Lawyers
29-1064.00	Obstetricians and Gynecologists
29-1041.00	Optometrists
29-1022.00	Oral and Maxillofacial Surgeons
29-1023.00	Orthodontists
29-1065.00	Pediatricians, General
29-1051.00	Pharmacists
29-1069.99	Physicians and Surgeons, All Other
29-1081.00	Podiatrists
29-1024.00	Prosthodontists
29-1066.00	Psychiatrists
29-1067.00	Surgeons
29-1131.00	Veterinarians

Method 4: Browse the Best Jobs in Three Categories

If you are interested in jobs with high pay, a high percentage of growth, or a high number of annual openings, you can find more than 50 of the highest-rated jobs in each of these three categories in the lists in this section. Occupations with a high rate of growth can be desirable because growth provides opportunities for advancement, and occupations with many openings can provide more opportunities for new workers to enter the field and can make it easier for workers to move from one position to another. The lists actually contain more than 50 jobs because the last several jobs on each list have tied scores for earnings, growth, or openings.

When to Use This Method: If you are looking for jobs that provide good growth potential, many opportunities, or good wages, the following lists help you narrow your search. Simply find the category that is important to you, review the list of related jobs, and then look up their descriptions in Part II using the O*NET number.

For more lists of "best jobs," consult *Best Jobs for the 21st Century*, also from JIST Publishing. Also available are *300 Best Jobs Without a Four-Year Degree* and *200 Best Jobs for College Graduates*.

The 50+ Best-Paying Jobs

This list contains more than 50 jobs because the last several jobs have tied scores for earnings.

Rank	O*NET Number	Job Title	Annual Earnings
1.	29-1061.00	Anesthesiologists	GREATER THAN $145,600
2.	29-1063.00	Internists, General	GREATER THAN $145,600
3.	29-1064.00	Obstetricians and Gynecologists	GREATER THAN $145,600
4.	29-1067.00	Surgeons	GREATER THAN $145,600
5.	29-1021.00	Dentists, General	$128,910
6.	29-1022.00	Oral and Maxillofacial Surgeons	$128,910
7.	29-1023.00	Orthodontists	$128,910
8.	29-1024.00	Prosthodontists	$128,910
9.	29-1066.00	Psychiatrists	$126,460
10.	29-1065.00	Pediatricians, General	$126,430
11.	11-1011.00	Chief Executives	$120,450
12.	11-1011.01	Government Service Executives	$120,450
13.	11-1011.02	Private Sector Executives	$120,450
14.	29-1062.00	Family and General Practitioners	$118,390
15.	53-2011.00	Airline Pilots, Copilots, and Flight Engineers	$109,800
16.	29-1081.00	Podiatrists	$95,390
17.	23-1011.00	Lawyers	$88,760
18.	53-2021.00	Air Traffic Controllers	$87,930
19.	11-9041.00	Engineering Managers	$87,490
20.	23-1023.00	Judges, Magistrate Judges, and Magistrates	$87,260
21.	29-1041.00	Optometrists	$85,650
22.	19-2012.00	Physicists	$83,670
23.	11-3021.00	Computer and Information Systems Managers	$82,480
24.	17-2171.00	Petroleum Engineers	$81,420
25.	19-3094.00	Political Scientists	$81,350
26.	11-9121.00	Natural Sciences Managers	$80,420
27.	17-2161.00	Nuclear Engineers	$80,080
28.	25-1112.00	Law Teachers, Postsecondary	$77,920
29.	19-2011.00	Astronomers	$77,570
30.	15-1011.00	Computer and Information Scientists, Research	$75,130
31.	29-1051.00	Pharmacists	$74,890
32.	15-2021.00	Mathematicians	$74,790
33.	11-2021.00	Marketing Managers	$74,370
34.	15-1032.00	Computer Software Engineers, Systems Software	$73,280
35.	11-2022.00	Sales Managers	$71,620
36.	17-2061.00	Computer Hardware Engineers	$71,560
37.	17-2011.00	Aerospace Engineers	$70,370
38.	15-1031.00	Computer Software Engineers, Applications	$70,210
39.	11-3031.00	Financial Managers	$70,210
40.	11-3031.02	Financial Managers, Branch or Department	$70,210
41.	11-3031.01	Treasurers, Controllers, and Chief Financial Officers	$70,210
42.	17-2041.00	Chemical Engineers	$70,180
43.	11-9032.00	Education Administrators, Elementary and Secondary School	$69,240
44.	29-1011.00	Chiropractors	$68,420
45.	17-2072.00	Electronics Engineers, Except Computer	$68,350
46.	15-2011.00	Actuaries	$68,120
47.	25-1032.00	Engineering Teachers, Postsecondary	$67,310
48.	19-3011.00	Economists	$67,050
49.	17-2071.00	Electrical Engineers	$66,890
50.	17-2121.02	Marine Architects	$66,830
51.	17-2121.01	Marine Engineers	$66,830
52.	17-2121.00	Marine Engineers and Naval Architects	$66,830

The 50+ Fastest-Growing Jobs

This list contains more than 50 jobs because the last several jobs have tied scores for growth.

Rank	O*NET Number	Job Title	Percent Growth Through 2010
1.	15-1031.00	Computer Software Engineers, Applications	100.0%
2.	15-1041.00	Computer Support Specialists	97.0%
3.	15-1032.00	Computer Software Engineers, Systems Software	89.7%
4.	15-1071.01	Computer Security Specialists	81.9%
5.	15-1071.00	Network and Computer Systems Administrators	81.9%
6.	15-1081.00	Network Systems and Data Communications Analysts	77.5%
7.	43-9031.00	Desktop Publishers	66.7%
8.	15-1061.00	Database Administrators	65.9%
9.	39-9021.00	Personal and Home Care Aides	62.5%
10.	15-1099.99	Computer Specialists, All Other	60.7%
11.	15-1051.00	Computer Systems Analysts	59.7%
12.	31-9092.00	Medical Assistants	57.0%
13.	21-1093.00	Social and Human Service Assistants	54.2%
14.	29-1071.00	Physician Assistants	53.5%
15.	29-2071.00	Medical Records and Health Information Technicians	49.0%
16.	11-3021.00	Computer and Information Systems Managers	47.9%
17.	31-1011.00	Home Health Aides	47.3%
18.	31-2022.00	Physical Therapist Aides	46.3%
19.	31-2012.00	Occupational Therapist Aides	45.2%
20.	31-2021.00	Physical Therapist Assistants	44.8%
21.	29-1121.00	Audiologists	44.7%
22.	21-1099.99	Community and Social Service Specialists, All Other	44.5%

23.	15-1011.00	Computer and Information Scientists, Research	40.3%
24.	39-9031.00	Fitness Trainers and Aerobics Instructors	40.3%
25.	31-9096.00	Veterinary Assistants and Laboratory Animal Caretakers	39.8%
26.	31-2011.00	Occupational Therapist Assistants	39.7%
27.	29-2056.00	Veterinary Technologists and Technicians	39.3%
28.	29-1127.00	Speech-Language Pathologists	39.2%
29.	21-1023.00	Mental Health and Substance Abuse Social Workers	39.1%
30.	31-9091.00	Dental Assistants	37.2%
31.	29-2021.00	Dental Hygienists	37.1%
32.	25-2041.00	Special Education Teachers, Preschool, Kindergarten, and Elementary School	36.8%
33.	29-2052.00	Pharmacy Technicians	36.4%
34.	11-2031.00	Public Relations Managers	36.3%
35.	41-2012.00	Gaming Change Persons and Booth Cashiers	36.1%
36.	27-3031.00	Public Relations Specialists	36.1%
37.	33-9032.00	Security Guards	35.4%
38.	21-1011.00	Substance Abuse and Behavioral Disorder Counselors	35.0%
39.	29-2031.00	Cardiovascular Technologists and Technicians	34.9%
40.	29-1126.00	Respiratory Therapists	34.8%
41.	29-2055.00	Surgical Technologists	34.7%
42.	29-2054.00	Respiratory Therapy Technicians	34.6%
43.	19-3022.00	Survey Researchers	34.5%
44.	11-2011.00	Advertising and Promotions Managers	34.3%
45.	13-2052.00	Personal Financial Advisors	34.0%
46.	29-1122.00	Occupational Therapists	33.9%
47.	53-3011.00	Ambulance Drivers and Attendants, Except Emergency Medical Technicians	33.7%
48.	43-4081.00	Hotel, Motel, and Resort Desk Clerks	33.4%
49.	43-4111.00	Interviewers, Except Eligibility and Loan	33.4%
50.	29-1123.00	Physical Therapists	33.3%
51.	23-2011.00	Paralegals and Legal Assistants	33.2%
52.	29-1129.99	Therapists, All Other	33.2%

The 50+ Jobs with the Most Openings

This list contains more than 50 jobs because the last several jobs have tied scores for openings.

Rank	O*NET Number	Job Title	Annual Openings
1.	41-2011.00	Cashiers	1,125,000
2.	41-2031.00	Retail Salespersons	1,124,000
3.	35-3021.00	Combined Food Preparation and Serving Workers, Including Fast Food	737,000
4.	43-9061.00	Office Clerks, General	676,000
5.	35-3031.00	Waiters and Waitresses	596,000
6.	53-7062.03	Freight, Stock, and Material Movers, Hand	519,000
7.	53-7062.02	Grips and Set-Up Workers, Motion Picture Sets, Studios, and Stages	519,000
8.	53-7062.00	Laborers and Freight, Stock, and Material Movers, Hand	519,000
9.	53-7062.01	Stevedores, Except Equipment Operators	519,000
10.	37-2011.00	Janitors and Cleaners, Except Maids and Housekeeping Cleaners	507,000
11.	43-5081.02	Marking Clerks	467,000
12.	43-5081.04	Order Fillers, Wholesale and Retail Sales	467,000
13.	43-5081.00	Stock Clerks and Order Fillers	467,000
14.	43-5081.01	Stock Clerks, Sales Floor	467,000
15.	43-5081.03	Stock Clerks—Stockroom, Warehouse, or Storage Yard	467,000
16.	39-9011.00	Child Care Workers	370,000
17.	43-4051.01	Adjustment Clerks	359,000
18.	43-4051.00	Customer Service Representatives	359,000
19.	43-4051.02	Customer Service Representatives, Utilities	359,000
20.	37-2012.00	Maids and Housekeeping Cleaners	346,000
21.	43-3031.00	Bookkeeping, Accounting, and Auditing Clerks	298,000
22.	51-2092.00	Team Assemblers	283,000
23.	43-4171.00	Receptionists and Information Clerks	269,000
24.	31-1012.00	Nursing Aides, Orderlies, and Attendants	268,000
25.	25-9041.00	Teacher Assistants	256,000
26.	53-7064.00	Packers and Packagers, Hand	242,000
27.	33-9032.00	Security Guards	242,000
28.	53-3032.02	Tractor-Trailer Truck Drivers	240,000
29.	53-3032.01	Truck Drivers, Heavy	240,000
30.	53-3032.00	Truck Drivers, Heavy and Tractor-Trailer	240,000
31.	43-6014.00	Secretaries, Except Legal, Medical, and Executive	239,000
32.	47-2061.00	Construction Laborers	236,000
33.	11-1021.00	General and Operations Managers	235,000
34.	35-2021.00	Food Preparation Workers	231,000
35.	35-3022.00	Counter Attendants, Cafeteria, Food Concession, and Coffee Shop	216,000
36.	41-1011.00	First-Line Supervisors/Managers of Retail Sales Workers	206,000
37.	37-3011.00	Landscaping and Grounds-keeping Workers	193,000

(continues)

(continued)

The 50+ Jobs with the Most Openings

Rank	O*NET Number	Job Title	Annual Openings
38.	45-2092.00	Farmworkers and Laborers, Crop, Nursery, and Greenhouse	192,000
39.	45-2093.00	Farmworkers, Farm and Ranch Animals	192,000
40.	45-2092.02	General Farmworkers	192,000
41.	45-2092.01	Nursery Workers	192,000
42.	43-6011.00	Executive Secretaries and Administrative Assistants	185,000
43.	25-1041.00	Agricultural Sciences Teachers, Postsecondary	184,000
44.	25-1061.00	Anthropology and Archeology Teachers, Postsecondary	184,000
45.	25-1031.00	Architecture Teachers, Postsecondary	184,000
46.	25-1062.00	Area, Ethnic, and Cultural Studies Teachers, Postsecondary	184,000
47.	25-1121.00	Art, Drama, and Music Teachers, Postsecondary	184,000
48.	25-1051.00	Atmospheric, Earth, Marine, and Space Sciences Teachers, Postsecondary	184,000
49.	25-1042.00	Biological Science Teachers, Postsecondary	184,000
50.	25-1011.00	Business Teachers, Postsecondary	184,000
51.	25-1052.00	Chemistry Teachers, Postsecondary	184,000
52.	25-1122.00	Communications Teachers, Postsecondary	184,000
53.	25-1021.00	Computer Science Teachers, Postsecondary	184,000
54.	25-1111.00	Criminal Justice and Law Enforcement Teachers, Postsecondary	184,000
55.	25-1063.00	Economics Teachers, Postsecondary	184,000
56.	25-1081.00	Education Teachers, Postsecondary	184,000
57.	25-1032.00	Engineering Teachers, Postsecondary	184,000
58.	25-1123.00	English Language and Literature Teachers, Postsecondary	184,000
59.	25-1053.00	Environmental Science Teachers, Postsecondary	184,000
60.	25-1124.00	Foreign Language and Literature Teachers, Postsecondary	184,000
61.	25-1043.00	Forestry and Conservation Science Teachers, Postsecondary	184,000
62.	25-1064.00	Geography Teachers, Postsecondary	184,000
63.	25-1191.00	Graduate Teaching Assistants	184,000
64.	25-1071.00	Health Specialties Teachers, Postsecondary	184,000
65.	25-1125.00	History Teachers, Postsecondary	184,000
66.	25-1192.00	Home Economics Teachers, Postsecondary	184,000
67.	25-1112.00	Law Teachers, Postsecondary	184,000
68.	25-1082.00	Library Science Teachers, Postsecondary	184,000
69.	25-1022.00	Mathematical Science Teachers, Postsecondary	184,000
70.	25-1072.00	Nursing Instructors and Teachers, Postsecondary	184,000
71.	25-1126.00	Philosophy and Religion Teachers, Postsecondary	184,000
72.	25-1054.00	Physics Teachers, Postsecondary	184,000
73.	25-1065.00	Political Science Teachers, Postsecondary	184,000
74.	25-1199.99	Postsecondary Teachers, All Other	184,000
75.	25-1066.00	Psychology Teachers, Postsecondary	184,000
76.	25-1193.00	Recreation and Fitness Studies Teachers, Postsecondary	184,000
77.	25-1069.99	Social Sciences Teachers, Postsecondary, All Other	184,000
78.	25-1113.00	Social Work Teachers, Postsecondary	184,000
79.	25-1067.00	Sociology Teachers, Postsecondary	184,000
80.	25-1194.00	Vocational Education Teachers, Postsecondary	184,000

Method 5: Browse an Alphabetical Listing of Job Titles

Another way you can use the book is to find jobs by their titles. The index, which starts on page 685, contains an alphabetical listing of all job titles.

When to Use This Method: If you are interested in more information about certain jobs, use the index to find the job title. Then turn to the page listed to find the complete job description.

PART II

O*NET Job Descriptions

This is the book's main section, and it provides information-packed descriptions for the 1,100-plus jobs in the O*NET database. Descriptions are arranged by their O*NET number and in logical groupings of related jobs.

See the introduction for more details on how this section is organized. In addition, a sample job description points out the important features of each entry. The introduction also offers helpful information on how to use and interpret the descriptions.

If you are looking for a list of the job descriptions included here, see the table of contents. Also, all job titles appear alphabetically in the index.

11-0000

Management Occupations

11-1000 Top Executives

11-1011.00 Chief Executives

- **Education/Training Required: Work experience plus degree**
- **Employed: 547,042**
- **Annual Earnings: $120,450**
- **Growth: 17.2%**
- **Annual Job Openings: 48,000**

Determine and formulate policies and provide the overall direction of companies or private and public sector organizations within the guidelines set up by a board of directors or similar governing body. Plan, direct, or coordinate operational activities at the highest level of management with the help of subordinate executives and staff managers.

No task data available.

GOE INFORMATION—Interest Area: 13. General Management and Support. **Work Group:** 13.01. General Management Work and Management of Support Functions. **Note:** The Department of Labor has not collected some data for this job, so it has fewer details than the other descriptions.

Instructional Programs—Business Administration and Management, General; Business/Commerce, General; Entrepreneurship/Entrepreneurial Studies; International Business/Trade/Commerce; Public Administration; Public Administration and Social Service Professions, Other; Public Policy Analysis.

Related DOT Jobs—189.117-026 President; 189.117-034 Vice President.

11-1011.01 Government Service Executives

- **Education/Training Required: Work experience plus degree**
- **Employed: No data available.**
- **Annual Earnings: $120,450**
- **Growth: 17.2%**
- **Annual Job Openings: 48,000**

Determine and formulate policies and provide overall direction of federal, state, local, or international government activities. Plan, direct, and coordinate operational activities at the highest level of management with the help of subordinate managers.

Directs organization charged with administering and monitoring regulated activities to interpret and clarify laws and ensure compliance with laws. Administers, interprets, and explains policies, rules, regulations, and laws to organizations and individuals under authority of commission or applicable legislation. Develops, plans, organizes, and administers policies and procedures for organization to ensure administrative and operational objectives are met. Directs and coordinates activities of workers in public organization to ensure continuing operations, maximize returns on investments, and increase productivity. Prepares budget and directs and monitors expenditures of department funds. Directs and conducts studies and research; prepares reports and other publications relating to operational trends and program objectives and accomplishments. Consults with staff and others in government, business, and private organizations to discuss issues, coordinate activities, and resolve problems. Negotiates contracts and agreements with federal and state agencies and other organizations and prepares budget for funding and implementation of programs. Evaluates findings of investigations, surveys, and studies to formulate policies and techniques and recommend improvements for personnel

actions, programs, or business services. Implements corrective action plan to solve problems. Directs, coordinates, and conducts activities between United States Government and foreign entities to provide information to promote international interest and harmony. Reviews and analyzes legislation, laws, and public policy and recommends changes to promote and support interests of general population as well as special groups. Prepares, reviews, and submits reports concerning activities, expenses, budget, government statutes and rulings, and other items affecting business or program services. Develops, directs, and coordinates testing, hiring, training, and evaluation of staff personnel. Conducts or directs investigations or hearings to resolve complaints and violations of laws. Establishes and maintains comprehensive and current record-keeping system of activities and operational procedures in business office. Plans, promotes, organizes, and coordinates public community service program and maintains cooperative working relationships among public and agency participants. Delivers speeches, writes articles, and presents information for organization at meetings or conventions to promote services, exchange ideas, and accomplish objectives. Participates in activities to promote business and expand services; provides technical assistance in conducting of conferences, seminars, and workshops. Testifies in court, before control or review board, or at legislature.

GOE INFORMATION—Interest Area: 13. General Management and Support. **Work Group:** 13.01. General Management Work and Management of Support Functions. **Personality Type**—Enterprising. Enterprising occupations frequently involve starting up and carrying out projects. These occupations can involve leading people and making many decisions. They sometimes require risk taking and often deal with business. **Work Values**—Authority; Variety; Social Status; Good Working Conditions; Creativity. **Skills**—Management of Financial Resources; Systems Analysis; Systems Evaluation; Coordination; Management of Personnel Resources; Complex Problem Solving; Judgment and Decision Making; Monitoring. **Abilities**—*Cognitive:* Written Expression; Mathematical Reasoning; Deductive Reasoning; Oral Comprehension; Oral Expression. *Psychomotor:* None met the criteria. *Physical:* Trunk Strength. *Sensory:* Speech Clarity; Speech Recognition; Near Vision; Auditory Attention; Night Vision. **General Work Activities**—*Information Input:* Getting Information; Monitoring Processes, Materials, or Surroundings; Estimating Needed Characteristics. *Mental Process:* Making Decisions and Solving Problems; Analyzing Data or Information; Developing Objectives and Strategies. *Work Output:* Documenting or Recording Information; Interacting with Computers; Handling and Moving Objects. *Interacting with Others:* Performing Administrative Activities; Communicating with Persons Outside Organization; Communicating with Other Workers. **Physical Work Conditions**—Sitting; Walking or Running; Indoors. **Other Job Characteristics**—Consequence of Error; Importance of Being Exact or Accurate; Degree of Automation.

Experience—Job Zone 4. A minimum of two to four years of work-related skill, knowledge, or experience is needed. **Job Preparation:** SVP 7.0 to less than 8.0—two years to less than 10 years. **Knowledge**—Administration and Management; Personnel and Human Resources; Law and Government; Education and Training; Economics and Accounting. **Instructional Programs**—Business Administration and Management, General; Business/Commerce, General; Entrepreneurship/Entrepreneurial Studies; International Business/Trade/Commerce; Public Administration; Public Administration and Social Service Professions, Other; Public Policy Analysis.

Related DOT Jobs—050.117-010 Director, Employment Research and Planning; 079.167-010 Community-Services-and-Health-Education Officer; 137.137-010 Director, Translation; 168.167-090 Manager, Regulated Program; 169.117-010 Executive Secretary, State Board of Nursing; 185.167-062 Supervisor, Liquor Stores and Agencies; 186.117-022 Deputy Insurance Commissioner; 187.117-018 Director, Institution; 187.117-054

Superintendent, Recreation; 188.117-014 Business-Enterprise Officer; 188.117-018 Chief, Fishery Division; 188.117-022 Civil Preparedness Officer; 188.117-026 Commissioner, Conservation of Resources; 188.117-030 Commissioner, Public Works; 188.117-034 Director, Aeronautics Commission; 188.117-038 Director, Agricultural Services; 188.117-042 Director, Arts-and-Humanities Council; 188.117-046 Director, Compliance; 188.117-050 Director, Consumer Affairs; 188.117-054 Director, Correctional Agency; others.

11-1011.02 Private Sector Executives

- **Education/Training Required: Work experience plus degree**
- **Employed: No data available.**
- **Annual Earnings: $120,450**
- **Growth: 17.2%**
- **Annual Job Openings: 48,000**

Determine and formulate policies and business strategies and provide overall direction of private sector organizations. Plan, direct, and coordinate operational activities at the highest level of management with the help of subordinate managers.

Directs, plans, and implements policies and objectives of organization or business in accordance with charter and board of directors. Directs activities of organization to plan procedures, establish responsibilities, and coordinate functions among departments and sites. Confers with board members, organization officials, and staff members to establish policies and formulate plans. Analyzes operations to evaluate performance of company and staff and to determine areas of cost reduction and program improvement. Reviews financial statements and sales and activity reports to ensure that organization's objectives are achieved. Directs and coordinates organization's financial and budget activities to fund operations, maximize investments, and increase efficiency. Assigns or delegates responsibilities to subordinates. Directs and coordinates activities of business or department concerned with production, pricing, sales, and/or distribution of products. Directs and coordinates activities of business involved with buying and selling investment products and financial services. Directs non-merchandising departments of business, such as advertising, purchasing, credit, and accounting. Establishes internal control procedures. Prepares reports and budgets. Presides over or serves on board of directors, management committees, or other governing boards. Negotiates or approves contracts with suppliers and distributors and with maintenance, janitorial, and security providers. Promotes objectives of institution or business before associations, public, government agencies, or community groups. Screens, selects, hires, transfers, and discharges employees. Administers program for selection of sites, construction of buildings, and provision of equipment and supplies. Directs inservice training of staff.

GOE INFORMATION—Interest Area: 13. General Management and Support. **Work Group:** 13.01. General Management Work and Management of Support Functions. **Personality Type—**Enterprising. Enterprising occupations frequently involve starting up and carrying out projects. These occupations can involve leading people and making many decisions. They sometimes require risk taking and often deal with business. **Work Values—**Authority; Social Status; Autonomy; Good Working Conditions; Creativity. **Skills—**Management of Financial Resources; Systems Analysis; Systems Evaluation; Management of Personnel Resources; Judgment and Decision Making; Coordination; Management of Material Resources; Complex Problem Solving. **Abilities—**Cognitive: Written Expression; Originality; Fluency of Ideas; Oral Expression; Written Comprehension. *Psychomotor:* None met the criteria. *Physical:* Trunk Strength. *Sensory:* Speech Clarity; Speech Recognition; Near Vision; Auditory Attention; Far Vision. **General Work Activities—***Information*

Input: Getting Information; Identifying Objects, Actions, and Events; Monitoring Processes, Materials, or Surroundings. *Mental Process:* Developing Objectives and Strategies; Making Decisions and Solving Problems; Organizing, Planning, and Prioritizing. *Work Output:* Documenting or Recording Information; Interacting with Computers; Handling and Moving Objects. *Interacting with Others:* Communicating with Other Workers; Monitoring and Controlling Resources; Providing Consultation and Advice to Others. **Physical Work Conditions—**Sitting; Indoors; Walking or Running. **Other Job Characteristics—**Consequence of Error; Degree of Automation; Importance of Being Exact or Accurate.

Experience—Job Zone 5. Extensive skill, knowledge, and experience are needed for these occupations. **Job Preparation:** SVP 8.0 and above—four years to more than 10 years. **Knowledge—**Economics and Accounting; Production and Processing; Administration and Management; Sales and Marketing; Personnel and Human Resources. **Instructional Programs—**Business Administration and Management, General; Business/Commerce, General; Entrepreneurship/Entrepreneurial Studies; International Business/Trade/Commerce; Public Administration; Public Administration and Social Service Professions, Other; Public Policy Analysis.

Related DOT Jobs—090.117-034 President, Educational Institution; 099.117-022 Superintendent, Schools; 137.137-010 Director, Translation; 185.117-010 Manager, Department Store; 186.117-034 Manager, Brokerage Office; 186.117-054 President, Financial Institution; 187.167-074 Manager, Cemetery; 189.117-022 Manager, Industrial Organization; 189.117-038 User Representative, International Accounting; 189.117-046 Manager, Bakery; 189.167-022 Manager, Department; 189.167-030 Program Manager.

11-1021.00 General and Operations Managers

- **Education/Training Required: Work experience plus degree**
- **Employed: 2,397,567**
- **Annual Earnings: $65,010**
- **Growth: 15.2%**
- **Annual Job Openings: 235,000**

Plan, direct, or coordinate the operations of companies or public and private sector organizations. Duties and responsibilities include formulating policies, managing daily operations, and planning the use of materials and human resources, but are too diverse and general in nature to be classified in any one functional area of management or administration, such as personnel, purchasing, or administrative services. Includes owners and managers who head small business establishments whose duties are primarily managerial.

Determine staffing requirements and interview, hire and train new employees or oversee those personnel processes. Direct and coordinate organization's financial and budget activities to fund operations, maximize investments, and increase efficiency. Establish and implement departmental policies, goals, objectives, and procedures, conferring with board members, organization officials, and staff members as necessary. Manage staff, preparing work schedules and assigning specific duties. Monitor businesses and agencies to ensure that they efficiently and effectively provide needed services while staying within budgetary limits. Plan and direct activities such as sales promotions, coordinating with other department heads as required. Review financial statements, sales and activity reports, and other performance data to measure productivity and goal achievement and to determine areas needing cost reduction and program improvement. Determine goods and services to be sold and set prices and credit terms based on forecasts of customer demand. Develop and implement product marketing strategies, including advertising campaigns and sales promotions. Direct and coordinate activities of businesses or departments concerned with the production, pricing, sales, and/or distribution of products. Direct non-merchandising departments of businesses, such as advertising and purchasing. Locate, select, and procure merchandise for resale, representing management in purchase negotiations. Manage the movement of goods into and out of production facilities. Oversee activities directly related to making products or providing services. Plan store layouts and design displays. Recommend locations for new facilities or oversee the remodeling of current facilities. Perform sales floor work, such as greeting and assisting customers, stocking shelves, and taking inventory.

GOE INFORMATION—Interest Area: 13. General Management and Support. **Work Group:** 13.01. General Management Work and Management of Support Functions. **Note:** The Department of Labor has not collected some data for this job, so it has fewer details than the other descriptions.

Instructional Programs—Business Administration and Management, General; Business/Commerce, General; Entrepreneurship/Entrepreneurial Studies; International Business/Trade/Commerce; Public Administration.

Related DOT Jobs—185.117-010 Manager, Department Store; 189.117-022 Manager, Industrial Organization.

11-1031.00 Legislators

- **Education/Training Required: Work experience in a related occupation**
- **Employed: 54,336**
- **Annual Earnings: $14,650**
- **Growth: 12.7%**
- **Annual Job Openings: 5,000**

Develop laws and statutes at the federal, state, or local level.

No task data available.

GOE INFORMATION—Interest Area: 13. General Management and Support. **Work Group:** 13.01. General Management Work and Management of Support Functions. **Note:** The Department of Labor has not collected some data for this job, so it has fewer details than the other descriptions.

Instructional Programs—Public Administration; Public Administration and Social Service Professions, Other; Public Policy Analysis.

Related DOT Jobs—No related DOT jobs.

11-2000 Advertising, Marketing, Promotions, Public Relations, and Sales Managers

11-2011.00 Advertising and Promotions Managers

- **Education/Training Required: Work experience plus degree**
- **Employed: 100,475**
- **Annual Earnings: $55,940**
- **Growth: 34.3%**
- **Annual Job Openings: 7,000**

Plan and direct advertising policies and programs or produce collateral materials, such as posters, contests, coupons, or giveaways, to create extra interest in the purchase of a product or service for a department or an entire organization or on an account basis.

Confer with clients to provide marketing or technical advice. Confer with department heads and/or staff to discuss topics such as contracts, selection of advertising media, or product to be advertised. Coordinate activities of departments, such as sales, graphic arts, media, finance, and research. Coordinate with the media to disseminate advertising. Formulate plans to extend business with established accounts and to transact business as agent for advertising accounts. Gather and organize information to plan advertising campaigns. Identify and develop contacts for promotional campaigns and industry programs that meet identified buyer targets such as dealers, distributors, or consumers. Inspect layouts and advertising copy and edit scripts, audio- and videotapes, and other promotional material for adherence to specifications. Monitor and analyze sales promotion results to determine cost-effectiveness of promotion campaigns. Plan and execute advertising policies and strategies for organizations. Plan and prepare advertising and promotional material to increase sales of products or services, working with customers, company officials, sales departments and advertising agencies. Prepare and negotiate advertising and sales contracts. Provide presentation and product demonstration support during the introduction of new products and services to field staff and customers. Track program budgets and expenses and campaign response rates to evaluate each campaign based on program objectives and industry norms. Assist with annual budget development. Consult publications to learn about conventions and social functions and to organize prospect files for promotional purposes. Read trade journals and professional literature to stay informed on trends, innovations, and changes that affect media planning. Represent company at trade association meetings to promote products. Train and direct workers engaged in developing and producing advertisements. Assemble and communicate with a strong, diverse coalition of organizations and/or public figures, securing their cooperation, support, and action to further campaign goals. Contact organizations to explain services and facilities offered. Direct and coordinate product research and development. Direct, motivate, and monitor the mobilization of a campaign team to advance campaign goals. Prepare budgets and submit estimates for program costs as part of campaign plan development.

GOE INFORMATION—Interest Area: 10. Sales and Marketing. **Work Group:** 10.01. Managerial Work in Sales and Marketing. **Personality Type**—Artistic. Artistic occupations frequently involve working with forms, designs, and patterns. They often require self-expression, and the work can be done without following a clear set of rules. **Work Values**—Creativity; Authority; Good Working Conditions; Ability Utilization; Compensation. **Skills**—Systems Evaluation; Complex Problem Solving; Systems Analysis; Coordination; Management of Material Resources; Management of Personnel Resources; Management of Financial Resources; Judgment and Decision Making. **Abilities**—*Cognitive:* Originality; Fluency of Ideas; Written Expression; Oral Expression; Memorization. *Psychomotor:* Response Orientation. *Physical:* Trunk Strength. *Sensory:* Speech Clarity; Speech Recognition; Visual Color Discrimination; Far Vision; Near Vision. **General Work Activities**—*Information Input:* Getting Information; Identifying Objects, Actions, and Events; Estimating Needed Characteristics. *Mental Process:* Organizing, Planning, and Prioritizing; Scheduling Work and Activities; Thinking Creatively. *Work Output:* Documenting or Recording Information; Interacting with Computers; Handling and Moving Objects. *Interacting with Others:* Influencing Others or Selling; Communicating with Persons Outside Organization; Communicating with Other Workers. **Physical Work Conditions**—Sitting; Indoors; Walking or Running; Outdoors. **Other**

Job Characteristics—Consequence of Error; Importance of Being Exact or Accurate; Degree of Automation.

Experience—Job Zone 4. A minimum of two to four years of work-related skill, knowledge, or experience is needed. **Job Preparation:** SVP 7.0 to less than 8.0—two years to less than 10 years. **Knowledge**—Sales and Marketing; Communications and Media; Administration and Management; Customer and Personal Service; Fine Arts. **Instructional Programs**—Advertising; Marketing/Marketing Management, General; Public Relations/Image Management.

Related DOT Jobs—159.167-022 Executive Producer, Promos; 163.117-018 Manager, Promotion; 164.117-010 Manager, Advertising; 164.117-014 Manager, Advertising Agency; 164.117-018 Media Director; 164.167-010 Account Executive.

11-2021.00 Marketing Managers

- Education/Training Required: **Work experience plus degree**
- Employed: **190,324**
- Annual Earnings: **$74,370**
- Growth: **29.1%**
- Annual Job Openings: **12,000**

Determine the demand for products and services offered by a firm and its competitors and identify potential customers. Develop pricing strategies with the goal of maximizing the firm's profits or share of the market while ensuring that the firm's customers are satisfied. Oversee product development or monitor trends that indicate the need for new products and services.

Compile lists describing product or service offerings. Confer with legal staff to resolve problems, such as copyright infringement and royalty sharing, with outside producers and distributors. Consult with product development personnel on product specifications such as design, color, and packaging. Develop pricing strategies, balancing firm objectives and customer satisfaction. Evaluate the financial aspects of product development, such as budgets, expenditures, research and development appropriations, and return-on-investment and profit-loss projections. Formulate, direct, and coordinate marketing activities and policies to promote products and services, working with advertising and promotion managers. Identify, develop, and evaluate marketing strategy, based on knowledge of establishment objectives, market characteristics, and cost and markup factors. Initiate market research studies and analyze their findings. Negotiate contracts with vendors and distributors to manage product distribution, establishing distribution networks and developing distribution strategies. Use sales forecasting and strategic planning to ensure the sale and profitability of products, lines, or services, analyzing business developments and monitoring market trends. Consult with buying personnel to gain advice regarding the types of products or services expected to be in demand. Coordinate and participate in promotional activities and trade shows, working with developers, advertisers, and production managers to market products and services. Direct the hiring, training, and performance evaluations of marketing and sales staff and oversee their daily activities. Select products and accessories to be displayed at trade or special production shows. Advise business and other groups on local, national, and international factors affecting the buying and selling of products and services. Conduct economic and commercial surveys to identify potential markets for products and services.

GOE INFORMATION—Interest Area: 10. Sales and Marketing. **Work Group:** 10.01. Managerial Work in Sales and Marketing. **Personality Type**—Enterprising. Enterprising occupations frequently involve starting up and carrying out projects. These occupations can involve leading people and making many decisions. They sometimes require risk taking and often deal with business. **Work Values**—Creativity; Good Working Conditions; Authority; Recognition; Ability Utilization. **Skills**—Systems Analysis; Management of Financial Resources; Complex Problem Solving; Negotiation; Judgment and Decision Making; Systems Evaluation; Coordination; Speaking. **Abilities**—*Cognitive:* Originality; Fluency of Ideas; Category Flexibility; Oral Expression; Oral Comprehension. *Psychomotor:* Response Orientation. *Physical:* Trunk Strength. *Sensory:* Speech Clarity; Speech Recognition; Visual Color Discrimination; Near Vision; Auditory Attention. **General Work Activities**—*Information Input:* Identifying Objects, Actions, and Events; Getting Information; Estimating Needed Characteristics. *Mental Process:* Developing Objectives and Strategies; Making Decisions and Solving Problems; Organizing, Planning, and Prioritizing. *Work Output:* Documenting or Recording Information; Interacting with Computers; Handling and Moving Objects. *Interacting with Others:* Influencing Others or Selling; Communicating with Other Workers; Providing Consultation and Advice to Others. **Physical Work Conditions**—Sitting; Indoors; Walking or Running. **Other Job Characteristics**—Consequence of Error; Degree of Automation; Importance of Being Exact or Accurate.

Experience—Job Zone 4. A minimum of two to four years of work-related skill, knowledge, or experience is needed. **Job Preparation:** SVP 7.0 to less than 8.0—two years to less than 10 years. **Knowledge**—Sales and Marketing; Communications and Media; Geography; Economics and Accounting; Administration and Management. **Instructional Programs**—Apparel and Textile Marketing Management; Consumer Merchandising/Retailing Management; International Marketing; Marketing Research; Marketing, Other; Marketing/Marketing Management, General.

Related DOT Jobs—162.117-034 Media Buyer; 163.117-022 Director, Media Marketing; 164.117-022 Media Planner; 185.157-010 Fashion Coordinator; 185.157-014 Supervisor of Sales; 187.167-170 Manager, World Trade and Maritime Division.

11-2022.00 Sales Managers

- Education/Training Required: **Work experience plus degree**
- Employed: **342,726**
- Annual Earnings: **$71,620**
- Growth: **32.8%**
- Annual Job Openings: **21,000**

Direct the actual distribution or movement of a product or service to the customer. Coordinate sales distribution by establishing sales territories, quotas, and goals and establish training programs for sales representatives. Analyze sales statistics gathered by staff to determine sales potential and inventory requirements and monitor the preferences of customers.

Resolve customer complaints regarding sales and service. Monitor customer preferences to determine focus of sales efforts. Direct and coordinate activities involving sales of manufactured products, services, commodities, real estate, or other subjects of sale. Determine price schedules and discount rates. Review operational records and reports to project sales and determine profitability. Direct, coordinate, and review activities in sales and service accounting and record-keeping and in receiving and shipping operations. Confer or consult with department heads to plan advertising services and to secure information on equipment and customer specifications. Advise dealers and distributors on policies and operating procedures to ensure functional effectiveness of business. Prepare budgets and approve budget expenditures. Represent company at trade association meetings to promote products. Plan and direct staffing, training, and performance evaluations to develop and control sales and service programs. Visit franchised dealers to stimulate interest in establishment or expansion of leasing programs. Confer with potential customers regarding equipment needs and advise customers on types of equipment to purchase. Oversee regional and local sales managers and their staffs. Direct clerical staff to keep records of export correspondence, bid requests, and credit collections and to maintain current information on tariffs, licenses, and restrictions. Direct foreign sales and service outlets of an organization. Assess marketing potential of new and existing store locations, considering statistics and expenditures.

GOE INFORMATION—Interest Area: 10. Sales and Marketing. **Work Group:** 10.01. Managerial Work in Sales and Marketing. **Personality Type**—Enterprising. Enterprising occupations frequently involve starting up and carrying out projects. These occupations can involve leading people and making many decisions. They sometimes require risk taking and often deal with business. **Work Values**—Authority; Creativity; Compensation; Advancement; Autonomy. **Skills**—Negotiation; Service Orientation; Management of Personnel Resources; Persuasion; Time Management; Monitoring; Instructing; Complex Problem Solving. **Abilities**—*Cognitive:* Mathematical Reasoning; Originality; Fluency of Ideas; Category Flexibility; Deductive Reasoning. *Psychomotor:* Multilimb Coordination; Finger Dexterity. *Physical:* Stamina; Gross Body Coordination. *Sensory:* Speech Recognition; Speech Clarity; Depth Perception; Near Vision; Auditory Attention. **General Work Activities**—*Information Input:* Getting Information; Identifying Objects, Actions, and Events; Monitoring Processes, Materials, or Surroundings. *Mental Process:* Organizing, Planning, and Prioritizing; Making Decisions and Solving Problems; Thinking Creatively. *Work Output:* Interacting with Computers; Handling and Moving Objects; Documenting or Recording Information. *Interacting with Others:* Communicating with Persons Outside Organization; Establishing and Maintaining Relationships; Communicating with Other Workers. **Physical Work Conditions**—Sitting; Walking or Running; Indoors. **Other Job Characteristics**—Consequence of Error; Degree of Automation; Importance of Being Exact or Accurate.

Experience—Job Zone 4. A minimum of two to four years of work-related skill, knowledge, or experience is needed. **Job Preparation:** SVP 7.0 to less than 8.0—two years to less than 10 years. **Knowledge**—Sales and Marketing; Computers and Electronics; Customer and Personal Service; Mathematics; Administration and Management. **Instructional Programs**—Business Administration and Management, General; Business/Commerce, General; Consumer Merchandising/Retailing Management; Marketing, Other; Marketing/Marketing Management, General.

Related DOT Jobs—163.117-014 Manager, Export; 163.167-010 Manager, Advertising; 163.167-018 Manager, Sales; 163.167-022 Manager, Utility Sales and Service; 163.267-010 Field Representative; 185.117-014 Area Supervisor, Retail Chain Store; 185.167-042 Manager, Professional Equipment Sales-and-Service; 187.167-162 Manager, Vehicle Leasing and Rental; 189.117-018 Manager, Customer Technical Services.

11-2031.00 *Public Relations Managers*

- Education/Training Required: Work experience plus degree
- Employed: 73,893
- Annual Earnings: $57,200
- Growth: 36.3%
- Annual Job Openings: 7,000

Plan and direct public relations programs designed to create and maintain a favorable public image for employer or client, or if engaged in fundraising, plan and direct activities to solicit and maintain funds for special projects and nonprofit organizations.

Assign, supervise, and review the activities of public relations staff. Confer with labor relations managers to develop internal communications that keep employees informed of company activities. Direct activities of external agencies, establishments, and departments that develop and implement communication strategies and information programs. Establish and maintain effective working relationships with local and municipal government officials and media representatives. Evaluate advertising and promotion programs for compatibility with public relations efforts. Facilitate consumer relations or the relationship between parts of the company such as the managers and employees or different branch offices. Formulate policies and procedures related to public information programs, working with public relations executives. Identify main client groups and audiences and determine the best way to communicate publicity information to them. Manage special events such as sponsorship of races, parties introducing new products, or other activities the firm supports in order to gain public attention through the media without advertising directly. Observe and report on social, economic, and political trends that might affect employers. Respond to requests for information about employers' activities or status. Write interesting and effective press releases, prepare information for media kits, and develop and maintain company Internet or intranet Web pages. Develop and maintain the company's corporate image and identity, which includes the use of logos and signage. Draft speeches for company executives and arrange interviews and other forms of contact for them. Establish goals for soliciting funds, develop policies for collection and safeguarding of contributions, and coordinate disbursement of funds. Manage in-house communication courses. Manage communications budgets. Maintain company archives. Produce films and other video products, regulate their distribution, and operate film library.

GOE INFORMATION—Interest Area: 13. General Management and Support. **Work Group:** 13.01. General Management Work and Management of Support Functions. **Note:** The Department of Labor has not collected some data for this job, so it has fewer details than the other descriptions.

Instructional Programs—Public Relations/Image Management.

Related DOT Jobs—163.117-026 Director, Underwriter Solicitation; 165.117-010 Director, Fundraising; 165.117-014 Director, Funds Development; 165.167-014 Public-Relations Representative; 293.157-010 Fund Raiser I.

11-3000 Operations Specialties Managers

11-3011.00 *Administrative Services Managers*

- Education/Training Required: Work experience plus degree
- Employed: 362,038
- Annual Earnings: $49,810
- Growth: 20.4%
- Annual Job Openings: 31,000

Plan, direct, or coordinate supportive services of an organization, such as record-keeping, mail distribution, telephone operator/receptionist, and other office support services. May oversee facilities planning and maintenance and custodial operations.

Monitor the facility to ensure that it remains safe, secure, and well maintained. Direct or coordinate the supportive services department of a business, agency, or organization. Set goals and deadlines for the department. Prepare and review operational reports and schedules to ensure accuracy and efficiency. Analyze internal processes and recommend and implement procedural or policy changes to improve operations such as supply changes or the disposal of records. Acquire, distribute, and store supplies. Plan, administer, and control budgets for contracts, equipment, and supplies. Oversee construction and renovation projects to improve efficiency and to ensure that facilities meet environmental, health, and security standards and comply with government regulations. Hire and terminate clerical and administrative personnel. Oversee the maintenance and repair of machinery, equipment, and electrical and mechanical systems. Manage leasing of facility space. Participate in architectural and engineering planning and design, including space and installation management. Conduct classes to teach procedures to staff. Dispose of, or oversee the disposal of, surplus or unclaimed property.

GOE INFORMATION—Interest Area: 09. Business Detail. **Work Group:** 09.01. Managerial Work in Business Detail. **Personality Type—**Enterprising. Enterprising occupations frequently involve starting up and carrying out projects. These occupations can involve leading people and making many decisions. They sometimes require risk taking and often deal with business. **Work Values—**Authority; Good Working Conditions; Responsibility; Autonomy; Advancement. **Skills—**Management of Personnel Resources; Service Orientation; Coordination; Management of Financial Resources; Monitoring; Speaking; Writing; Programming. **Abilities—***Cognitive:* Written Expression; Originality; Oral Expression; Category Flexibility; Fluency of Ideas. *Psychomotor:* Control Precision; Finger Dexterity. *Physical:* Trunk Strength. *Sensory:* Speech Recognition; Near Vision; Far Vision; Speech Clarity; Auditory Attention. **General Work Activities—***Information Input:* Identifying Objects, Actions, and Events; Getting Information; Monitoring Processes, Materials, or Surroundings. *Mental Process:* Organizing, Planning, and Prioritizing; Making Decisions and Solving Problems; Updating and Using Relevant Knowledge. *Work Output:* Documenting or Recording Information; Interacting with Computers; Handling and Moving Objects. *Interacting with Others:* Establishing and Maintaining Relationships; Communicating with Other Workers; Resolving Conflict and Negotiating with Others. **Physical Work Conditions—**Sitting; Walking or Running; Indoors. **Other Job Characteristics—**Degree of Automation; Consequence of Error; Importance of Being Exact or Accurate.

Experience—Job Zone 4. A minimum of two to four years of work-related skill, knowledge, or experience is needed. **Job Preparation:** SVP 7.0 to less than 8.0—two years to less than 10 years. **Knowledge—**Personnel and Human Resources; Customer and Personal Service; Clerical; Economics and Accounting; Administration and Management. **Instructional Programs—**Business Administration and Management, General; Business/Commerce, General; Medical/Health Management and Clinical Assistant/Specialist; Public Administration; Purchasing, Procurement/Acquisitions, and Contracts Management.

Related DOT Jobs—169.167-034 Manager, Office; 187.117-062 Radiology Administrator; 188.117-130 Court Administrator; 189.167-014 Director, Service.

11-3021.00 Computer and Information Systems Managers

- **Education/Training Required: Work experience plus degree**
- **Employed: 312,953**
- **Annual Earnings: $82,480**
- **Growth: 47.9%**
- **Annual Job Openings: 28,000**

Plan, direct, or coordinate activities in such fields as electronic data processing, information systems, systems analysis, and computer programming.

Assign and review the work of systems analysts, programmers, and other computer-related workers. Consult with users, management, vendors, and technicians to assess computing needs and system requirements. Develop computer information resources, providing for data security and control, strategic computing, and disaster recovery. Evaluate data processing proposals to assess project feasibility and requirements. Direct daily operations of department, analyzing workflow, establishing priorities, developing standards, and setting deadlines. Evaluate the organization's technology use and needs and recommend improvements, such as hardware and software upgrades. Control operational budget and expenditures. Develop and interpret organizational goals, policies, and procedures. Manage backup, security, and user help systems. Meet with department heads, managers, supervisors, vendors, and others to solicit cooperation and resolve problems. Prepare and review operational reports or project progress reports. Purchase necessary equipment. Recruit, hire, train, and supervise staff and/or participate in staffing decisions. Review project plans in order to plan and coordinate project activity. Review and approve all systems charts and programs prior to their implementation. Stay abreast of advances in technology.

GOE INFORMATION—Interest Area: 02. Science, Math, and Engineering. **Work Group:** 02.01. Managerial Work in Science, Math, and Engineering. **Personality Type—**Enterprising. Enterprising occupations frequently involve starting up and carrying out projects. These occupations can involve leading people and making many decisions. They sometimes require risk taking and often deal with business. **Work Values—**Authority; Good Working Conditions; Creativity; Responsibility; Ability Utilization. **Skills—**Management of Material Resources; Management of Personnel Resources; Management of Financial Resources; Systems Evaluation; Systems Analysis; Complex Problem Solving; Operations Analysis; Coordination. **Abilities—***Cognitive:* Category Flexibility; Written Expression; Mathematical Reasoning; Deductive Reasoning; Oral Expression. *Psychomotor:* Finger Dexterity; Response Orientation; Wrist-Finger Speed. *Physical:* Trunk Strength. *Sensory:* Speech Clarity; Speech Recognition; Near Vision; Visual Color Discrimination; Auditory Attention. **General Work Activities—***Information Input:* Getting Information; Identifying Objects, Actions, and Events; Monitoring Processes, Materials, or Surroundings. *Mental Process:* Updating and Using Relevant Knowledge; Making Decisions and Solving Problems; Analyzing Data or Information. *Work Output:* Interacting with Computers; Documenting or Recording Information; Handling and Moving Objects. *Interacting with Others:* Guiding, Directing, and Motivating Subordinates; Communicating with Other Workers; Coordinating the Work and Activities of Others. **Physical Work Conditions—**Sitting; Indoors; Walking or Running. **Other Job Characteristics—**Degree of Automation; Importance of Being Exact or Accurate; Consequence of Error.

Experience—Job Zone 5. Extensive skill, knowledge, and experience are needed for these occupations. **Job Preparation:** SVP 8.0 and above—four years to more than 10 years. **Knowledge—**Computers and Electronics; Personnel and Human Resources; Economics and Accounting; Administration and Management; Customer and Personal Service. **Instructional Programs—**Computer and Information Sciences, General; Computer Science; Information Resources Management/CIO Training; Information Science/Studies; Knowledge Management; Management Information Systems, General; Operations Management and Supervision; System Administration/Administrator.

Related DOT Jobs—169.167-030 Manager, Data Processing; 169.167-082 Manager, Computer Operations.

11-3031.00 Financial Managers

- **Education/Training Required:** Work experience plus degree
- **Employed:** 657,944
- **Annual Earnings:** $70,210
- **Growth:** 18.5%
- **Annual Job Openings:** 53,000

Plan, direct, and coordinate accounting, investing, banking, insurance, securities, and other financial activities of a branch, office, or department of an establishment.

No task data available.

GOE INFORMATION—Interest Area: 13. General Management and Support. **Work Group:** 13.01. General Management Work and Management of Support Functions. **Note:** The Department of Labor has not collected some data for this job, so it has fewer details than the other descriptions.

Instructional Programs—Accounting and Business/Management; Accounting and Finance; Credit Management; Finance and Financial Management Services, Other; Finance, General; International Finance; Public Finance.

Related DOT Jobs—160.167-058 Controller; 161.117-018 Treasurer; 169.167-086 Manager, Credit and Collection; 186.117-066 Risk and Insurance Manager; 186.117-070 Treasurer, Financial Institution; 186.117-074 Trust Officer; 186.117-078 Vice President, Financial Institution; 186.117-082 Foreign-Exchange Dealer; 186.117-086 Manager, Exchange Floor; 186.137-014 Operations Officer; 186.167-054 Reserve Officer; 186.167-070 Assistant Branch Manager, Financial Institution; 186.167-082 Factor; 186.167-086 Manager, Financial Institution.

11-3031.01 Treasurers, Controllers, and Chief Financial Officers

- **Education/Training Required:** Work experience plus degree
- **Employed:** No data available.
- **Annual Earnings:** $70,210
- **Growth:** 18.5%
- **Annual Job Openings:** 53,000

Plan, direct, and coordinate the financial activities of an organization at the highest level of management. Includes financial reserve officers.

Analyze the financial details of past, present, and expected operations in order to identify development opportunities and areas where improvement is needed. Delegate authority for the receipt, disbursement, banking, protection, and custody of funds, securities, and financial instruments. Evaluate needs for procurement of funds and investment of surpluses and make appropriate recommendations. Lead staff training and development in budgeting and financial management areas. Maintain current knowledge of organizational policies and procedures, federal and state policies and directives, and current accounting standards. Supervise employees performing financial reporting, accounting, billing, collections, payroll, and budgeting duties. Conduct or coordinate audits of company accounts and financial transactions to ensure compliance with state and federal requirements and statutes. Develop and maintain relationships with banking, insurance, and non-organizational accounting personnel in order to facilitate financial activities. Monitor and evaluate the performance of accounting and other financial staff; recommend and implement personnel actions such as promotions and dismissals. Monitor

financial activities and details such as reserve levels to ensure that all legal and regulatory requirements are met. Perform tax planning work. Provide direction and assistance to other organizational units regarding accounting and budgeting policies and procedures and efficient control and utilization of financial resources. Receive and record requests for disbursements; authorize disbursements in accordance with policies and procedures. Compute, withhold, and account for all payroll deductions. Determine depreciation rates to apply to capitalized items and advise management on actions regarding the purchase, lease, or disposal of such items. Prepare and file annual tax returns or prepare financial information so that outside accountants can complete tax returns. Receive cash and checks and deposit funds. Coordinate and direct the financial planning, budgeting, procurement, or investment activities of all or part of an organization. Develop internal control policies, guidelines, and procedures for activities such as budget administration, cash and credit management, and accounting. Prepare or direct preparation of financial statements, business activity reports, financial position forecasts, annual budgets, and/or reports required by regulatory agencies. Advise management on short-term and long-term financial objectives, policies, and actions.

GOE INFORMATION—Interest Area: 13. General Management and Support. **Work Group:** 13.01. General Management Work and Management of Support Functions. **Personality Type**—Enterprising. Enterprising occupations frequently involve starting up and carrying out projects. These occupations can involve leading people and making many decisions. They sometimes require risk taking and often deal with business. **Work Values**—Authority; Good Working Conditions; Advancement; Ability Utilization; Activity. **Skills**—Management of Financial Resources; Systems Analysis; Systems Evaluation; Judgment and Decision Making; Complex Problem Solving; Mathematics; Critical Thinking; Management of Personnel Resources. **Abilities**—*Cognitive:* Mathematical Reasoning; Deductive Reasoning; Fluency of Ideas; Originality; Number Facility. *Psychomotor:* None met the criteria. *Physical:* Trunk Strength. *Sensory:* Speech Clarity; Near Vision; Speech Recognition; Auditory Attention; Night Vision. **General Work Activities**—*Information Input:* Getting Information; Identifying Objects, Actions, and Events; Estimating Needed Characteristics. *Mental Process:* Analyzing Data or Information; Processing Information; Developing Objectives and Strategies. *Work Output:* Documenting or Recording Information; Interacting with Computers; Handling and Moving Objects. *Interacting with Others:* Providing Consultation and Advice to Others; Monitoring and Controlling Resources; Communicating with Other Workers. **Physical Work Conditions**—Indoors; Sitting; Walking or Running. **Other Job Characteristics**—Consequence of Error; Importance of Being Exact or Accurate; Degree of Automation.

Experience—Job Zone 5. Extensive skill, knowledge, and experience are needed for these occupations. **Job Preparation:** SVP 8.0 and above—four years to more than 10 years. **Knowledge**—Economics and Accounting; Administration and Management; Law and Government; Mathematics; English Language. **Instructional Programs**—Accounting and Business/Management; Accounting and Finance; Credit Management; Finance and Financial Management Services, Other; Finance, General; International Finance; Public Finance.

Related DOT Jobs—160.167-058 Controller; 161.117-018 Treasurer; 186.117-070 Treasurer, Financial Institution; 186.117-078 Vice President, Financial Institution; 186.167-054 Reserve Officer.

11-3031.02 Financial Managers, Branch or Department

- Education/Training Required: Work experience plus degree
- Employed: No data available.
- Annual Earnings: $70,210
- Growth: 18.5%
- Annual Job Openings: 53,000

Direct and coordinate financial activities of workers in a branch, office, or department of an establishment, such as branch bank, brokerage firm, risk and insurance department, or credit department.

Directs and coordinates activities of workers engaged in conducting credit investigations and collecting delinquent accounts of customers. Plans, directs, and coordinates risk and insurance programs of establishment to control risks and losses. Manages branch or office of financial institution. Directs and coordinates activities to implement institution policies, procedures, and practices concerning granting or extending lines of credit and loans. Prepares financial and regulatory reports required by law, regulations, and board of directors. Analyzes and classifies risks as to frequency and financial impact of risk on company. Selects appropriate technique to minimize loss, such as avoidance and loss prevention and reduction. Prepares operational and risk reports for management analysis. Directs floor operations of brokerage firm engaged in buying and selling securities at exchange. Establishes procedures for custody and control of assets, records, loan collateral, and securities to ensure safekeeping. Evaluates effectiveness of current collection policies and procedures. Directs insurance negotiations, selects insurance brokers and carriers, and places insurance. Evaluates data pertaining to costs to plan budget. Reviews collection reports to ascertain status of collections and balances outstanding. Monitors order flow and transactions that brokerage firm executes on floor of exchange. Reviews reports of securities transactions and price lists to analyze market conditions. Establishes credit limitations on customer account. Examines, evaluates, and processes loan applications. Submits delinquent accounts to attorney or outside agency for collection.

GOE INFORMATION—Interest Area: 13. General Management and Support. Work Group: 13.01. General Management Work and Management of Support Functions. Personality Type—Enterprising. Enterprising occupations frequently involve starting up and carrying out projects. These occupations can involve leading people and making many decisions. They sometimes require risk taking and often deal with business. Work Values—Authority; Good Working Conditions; Recognition; Ability Utilization; Responsibility. Skills—Management of Financial Resources; Systems Analysis; Management of Personnel Resources; Systems Evaluation; Complex Problem Solving; Monitoring; Writing; Mathematics. Abilities—*Cognitive:* Written Expression; Mathematical Reasoning; Number Facility; Speed of Closure; Deductive Reasoning. *Psychomotor:* Wrist-Finger Speed; Response Orientation. *Physical:* Trunk Strength. *Sensory:* Speech Recognition; Speech Clarity; Far Vision; Near Vision; Auditory Attention. General Work Activities—*Information Input:* Getting Information; Identifying Objects, Actions, and Events; Estimating Needed Characteristics. *Mental Process:* Processing Information; Analyzing Data or Information; Making Decisions and Solving Problems. *Work Output:* Documenting or Recording Information; Interacting with Computers; Handling and Moving Objects. *Interacting with Others:* Communicating with Other Workers; Monitoring and Controlling Resources; Performing Administrative Activities. Physical Work Conditions—Sitting; Indoors; Walking or Running. Other Job Characteristics—Consequence of Error; Degree of Automation; Importance of Being Exact or Accurate.

Experience—Job Zone 4. A minimum of two to four years of work-related skill, knowledge, or experience is needed. Job Preparation: SVP 7.0 to less than 8.0—two years to less than 10 years. Knowledge—Economics and Accounting; Administration and Management; Law and Government; Mathematics; Personnel and Human Resources. Instructional Programs—Accounting and Business/Management; Accounting and Finance; Credit Management; Finance and Financial Management Services, Other; Finance, General; International Finance; Public Finance.

Related DOT Jobs—169.167-086 Manager, Credit and Collection; 186.117-066 Risk and Insurance Manager; 186.117-074 Trust Officer; 186.117-082 Foreign-Exchange Dealer; 186.117-086 Manager, Exchange Floor; 186.137-014 Operations Officer; 186.167-070 Assistant Branch Manager, Financial Institution; 186.167-082 Factor; 186.167-086 Manager, Financial Institution.

11-3040.00 Human Resources Managers

- Education/Training Required: Work experience plus degree
- Employed: 218,582
- Annual Earnings: $61,880
- Growth: 12.7%
- Annual Job Openings: 14,000

Plan, direct, and coordinate human resource management activities of an organization to maximize the strategic use of human resources and maintain functions such as employee compensation, recruitment, personnel policies, and regulatory compliance.

Administer compensation, benefits, and performance management systems and safety and recreation programs. Advise managers on organizational policy matters, such as equal employment opportunity and sexual harassment, and recommend needed changes. Allocate human resources, ensuring appropriate matches between personnel. Analyze statistical data and reports to identify and determine causes of personnel problems and develop recommendations for improvement of organization's personnel policies and practices. Analyze training needs to design employee development, language training, and health and safety programs. Conduct exit interviews to identify reasons for employee termination. Develop, administer, and evaluate applicant tests. Identify staff vacancies and recruit, interview, and select applicants. Maintain records and compile statistical reports concerning personnel-related data such as hires, transfers, performance appraisals, and absenteeism rates. Negotiate bargaining agreements and help interpret labor contracts. Oversee the evaluation, classification, and rating of occupations and job positions. Perform difficult staffing duties, including dealing with understaffing, refereeing disputes, firing employees, and administering disciplinary procedures. Plan and conduct new employee orientation to foster positive attitude toward organizational objectives. Plan, direct, supervise, and coordinate work activities of subordinates and staff relating to employment, compensation, labor relations, and employee relations. Plan, organize, direct, control, or coordinate the personnel, training, or labor relations activities of an organization. Prepare and follow budgets for personnel operations. Prepare personnel forecast to project employment needs. Provide current and prospective employees with information about policies, job duties, working conditions, wages, opportunities for promotion, and employee benefits. Provide terminated employees with outplacement or relocation assistance. Serve as a link between management and employees by handling questions, interpreting and administering contracts, and helping resolve work-related problems. Analyze and modify compensation and benefits policies to establish competitive programs and ensure compliance with legal requirements. Develop and/or administer special projects in areas such as pay equity, savings bond programs, day care, and employee awards. Represent organization at personnel-related hearings and investigations. Study legislation, arbitration decisions, and collective bargaining contracts to assess industry trends. Contract with vendors to provide employee services, such as food service, transportation, or relocation service. Investigate and report on industrial accidents for insurance carriers.

GOE INFORMATION—Interest Area: 13. General Management and Support. **Work Group:** 13.01. General Management Work and Management of Support Functions. **Personality Type—**Enterprising. Enterprising occupations frequently involve starting up and carrying out projects. These occupations can involve leading people and making many decisions. They sometimes require risk taking and often deal with business. **Work Values—**Authority; Social Service; Good Working Conditions; Ability Utilization; Autonomy. **Skills—**Management of Personnel Resources; Systems Analysis; Systems Evaluation; Management of Financial Resources; Negotiation; Programming; Complex Problem Solving; Speaking. **Abilities—***Cognitive:* Originality; Written Expression; Deductive Reasoning; Inductive Reasoning; Mathematical Reasoning. *Psychomotor:* Response Orientation; Reaction Time. *Physical:* Gross Body Equilibrium; Gross Body Coordination. *Sensory:* Far Vision; Speech Clarity; Speech Recognition; Near Vision; Auditory Attention. **General Work Activities—***Information Input:* Getting Information; Identifying Objects, Actions, and Events; Monitoring Processes, Materials, or Surroundings. *Mental Process:* Organizing, Planning, and Prioritizing; Analyzing Data or Information; Scheduling Work and Activities. *Work Output:* Documenting or Recording Information; Interacting with Computers; Handling and Moving Objects. *Interacting with Others:* Communicating with Other Workers; Staffing Organizational Units; Performing Administrative Activities. **Physical Work Conditions—**Sitting; Indoors. **Other Job Characteristics—**Consequence of Error; Importance of Being Exact or Accurate; Degree of Automation.

Experience—Job Zone 4. A minimum of two to four years of work-related skill, knowledge, or experience is needed. **Job Preparation:** SVP 7.0 to less than 8.0–two years to less than 10 years. **Knowledge—**Personnel and Human Resources; Administration and Management; Education and Training; Psychology; Law and Government. **Instructional Programs—**Human Resources Development; Human Resources Management/Personnel Administration, General; Labor and Industrial Relations; Labor Studies.

Related DOT Jobs—166.117-010 Director, Industrial Relations; 166.117-018 Manager, Personnel; 166.167-018 Manager, Benefits; 166.167-022 Manager, Compensation; 166.167-030 Manager, Employment; 188.117-086 Director, Merit System.

11-3041.00 Compensation and Benefits Managers

- ● **Education/Training Required: Work experience plus degree**
- ● **Employed: No data available.**
- ● **Annual Earnings: $61,880**
- ● **Growth: 12.7%**
- ● **Annual Job Openings: 14,000**

Plan, direct, or coordinate compensation and benefits activities and staff of an organization.

Administer, direct, and review employee benefit programs, including the integration of benefit programs following mergers and acquisitions. Analyze compensation policies, government regulations, and prevailing wage rates to develop competitive compensation plan. Analyze statistical data and reports to identify and determine causes of personnel problems and develop recommendations for improvement of organization's personnel policies and practices. Design, evaluate, and modify benefits policies to ensure that programs are current, competitive, and in compliance with legal requirements. Develop methods to improve employment policies, processes, and practices; recommend changes to management. Direct preparation and distribution of written and verbal information to inform employees of benefits, compensation, and personnel policies. Formulate policies, procedures, and programs for recruitment, testing, placement, classification, orientation, benefits and compensation, and labor and industrial relations. Fulfill all reporting requirements of all relevant government rules and regulations, including the Employee Retirement Income Security Act (ERISA). Identify and implement benefits to increase the quality of life for employees by working with brokers and researching benefits issues. Manage the design and development of tools to assist employees in benefits selection and to guide managers through compensation decisions. Mediate between benefits providers and employees, such as by assisting in handling employees' benefits-related questions or taking suggestions. Plan and conduct new employee orientations to foster positive attitude toward organizational objectives. Plan, direct, supervise, and coordinate work activities of subordinates and staff relating to employment, compensation, labor relations, and employee relations. Prepare detailed job descriptions and classification systems and define job levels and families in partnership with other managers. Advise management on such matters as equal employment opportunity, sexual harassment, and discrimination. Conduct exit interviews to identify reasons for employee termination. Maintain records and compile statistical reports concerning personnel-related data such as hires, transfers, performance appraisals, and absenteeism rates. Negotiate bargaining agreements. Prepare budgets for personnel operations. Prepare personnel forecasts to project employment needs. Resolve labor disputes and grievances. Study legislation, arbitration decisions, and collective bargaining contracts to assess industry trends. Contract with vendors to provide employee services, such as food services, transportation, or relocation service. Investigate and report on industrial accidents for insurance carriers. Represent organization at personnel-related hearings and investigations.

GOE INFORMATION—Interest Area: 13. General Management and Support. **Work Group:** 13.01. General Management Work and Management of Support Functions. **Personality Type—**Enterprising. Enterprising occupations frequently involve starting up and carrying out projects. These occupations can involve leading people and making many decisions. They sometimes require risk taking and often deal with business. **Work Values—**Authority; Social Service; Good Working Conditions; Ability Utilization; Autonomy. **Skills—**Management of Personnel Resources; Systems Analysis; Systems Evaluation; Management of Financial Resources; Negotiation; Programming; Complex Problem Solving; Speaking. **Abilities—***Cognitive:* Originality; Written Expression; Deductive Reasoning; Inductive Reasoning; Mathematical Reasoning. *Psychomotor:* Response Orientation; Reaction Time. *Physical:* Gross Body Equilibrium; Gross Body Coordination. *Sensory:* Far Vision; Speech Clarity; Speech Recognition; Near Vision; Auditory Attention. **General Work Activities—***Information Input:* Getting Information; Identifying Objects, Actions, and Events; Monitoring Processes, Materials, or Surroundings. *Mental Process:* Organizing, Planning, and Prioritizing; Analyzing Data or Information; Scheduling Work and Activities. *Work Output:* Documenting or Recording Information; Interacting with Computers; Handling and Moving Objects. *Interacting with Others:* Communicating with Other Workers; Staffing Organizational Units; Performing Administrative Activities. **Physical Work Conditions—**Sitting; Indoors. **Other Job Characteristics—**Consequence of Error; Importance of Being Exact or Accurate; Degree of Automation.

Experience—Job Zone 4. A minimum of two to four years of work-related skill, knowledge, or experience is needed. **Job Preparation:** SVP 7.0 to less than 8.0–two years to less than 10 years. **Knowledge—**

Personnel and Human Resources; Administration and Management; Education and Training; Psychology; Law and Government. **Instructional Programs**—Human Resources Management/Personnel Administration, General; Labor and Industrial Relations.

Related DOT Jobs—166.117-018 Manager, Personnel; 166.167-022 Manager, Personnel.

11-3042.00 Training and Development Managers

- **Education/Training Required: Work experience plus degree**
- **Employed: No data available.**
- **Annual Earnings: $61,880**
- **Growth: 12.7%**
- **Annual Job Openings: 14,000**

Plan, direct, or coordinate the training and development activities and staff of an organization.

Analyze training needs to develop new training programs or modify and improve existing programs. Conduct or arrange for ongoing technical training and personal development classes for staff members. Conduct orientation sessions and arrange on-the-job training for new hires. Confer with management and conduct surveys to identify training needs based on projected production processes, changes, and other factors. Develop and organize training manuals, multimedia visual aids, and other educational materials. Develop testing and evaluation procedures. Evaluate instructor performance and the effectiveness of training programs, providing recommendations for improvement. Plan, develop, and provide training and staff development programs, using knowledge of the effectiveness of methods such as classroom training, demonstrations, on-the-job training, meetings, conferences, and workshops. Train instructors and supervisors in techniques and skills for training and dealing with employees. Coordinate established courses with technical and professional courses provided by community schools and designate training procedures. Prepare training budget for department or organization. Review and evaluate training and apprenticeship programs for compliance with government standards.

GOE INFORMATION—**Interest Area:** 13. General Management and Support. **Work Group:** 13.01. General Management Work and Management of Support Functions. **Personality Type**—Enterprising. Enterprising occupations frequently involve starting up and carrying out projects. These occupations can involve leading people and making many decisions. They sometimes require risk taking and often deal with business. **Work Values**—Authority; Social Service; Pleasant Co-workers; Good Working Conditions; Creativity. **Skills**—Management of Personnel Resources; Instructing; Complex Problem Solving; Systems Analysis; Critical Thinking; Learning Strategies; Speaking; Operations Analysis. **Abilities**—*Cognitive:* Written Expression; Oral Expression; Speed of Closure; Originality; Deductive Reasoning. *Psychomotor:* Response Orientation; Rate Control. *Physical:* None met the criteria. *Sensory:* Far Vision; Near Vision; Speech Clarity; Sound Localization; Auditory Attention. **General Work Activities**—*Information Input:* Getting Information; Identifying Objects, Actions, and Events; Monitoring Processes, Materials, or Surroundings. *Mental Process:* Organizing, Planning, and Prioritizing; Scheduling Work and Activities; Making Decisions and Solving Problems. *Work Output:* Documenting or Recording Information; Interacting with Computers; Handling and Moving Objects. *Interacting with Others:* Communicating with Other Workers; Providing Consultation and Advice to Others; Coaching and Developing Others. **Physical Work Conditions**—Indoors; Sitting. **Other Job Characteristics**—Consequence of Error; Importance of Being Exact or Accurate; Importance of Repeating Same Tasks.

Experience—Job Zone 4. A minimum of two to four years of work-related skill, knowledge, or experience is needed. **Job Preparation:** SVP 7.0 to less than 8.0—two years to less than 10 years. **Knowledge**—Education and Training; Administration and Management; Personnel and Human Resources; Psychology; Law and Government. **Instructional Programs**—Human Resources Development; Human Resources Management/Personnel Administration, General.

Related DOT Jobs—166.167-026 Manager, Education and Training; 188.117-010 Apprenticeship Consultant; 375.167-054 Police Academy Program Coordinator.

11-3049.99 Human Resources Managers, All Other

- **Education/Training Required: Work experience plus degree**
- **Employed: No data available.**
- **Annual Earnings: No data available.**
- **Growth: 12.7%**
- **Annual Job Openings: 14,000**

All Human Resources Managers not listed separately.

No task data available.

GOE INFORMATION—**Interest Area:** 13. General Management and Support. **Work Group:** 13.01. General Management Work and Management of Support Functions. **Note:** The Department of Labor has not collected some data for this job, so it has fewer details than the other descriptions.

Instructional Programs—Human Resources Management/Personnel Administration, General; Labor and Industrial Relations; Labor Studies.

Related DOT Jobs—166.117-014 Manager, Employee Welfare; 166.167-014 Director Of Placement.

11-3051.00 Industrial Production Managers

- **Education/Training Required: Bachelor's degree**
- **Employed: 255,418**
- **Annual Earnings: $64,510**
- **Growth: 6.2%**
- **Annual Job Openings: 22,000**

Plan, direct, or coordinate the work activities and resources necessary for manufacturing products in accordance with cost, quality, and quantity specifications.

Maintain current knowledge of the quality control field, relying on current literature pertaining to materials use, technological advances, and statistical studies. Negotiate materials prices with suppliers. Direct and coordinate production, processing, distribution, and marketing activities of industrial organization. Develop budgets and approve expenditures for supplies, materials, and human resources, ensuring that materials, labor, and equipment are used efficiently to meet production targets. Review processing schedules and production orders to make decisions concerning inventory requirements, staffing requirements, work procedures, and duty assignments, considering budgetary limitations and time constraints. Review operations and confer with technical or administrative staff to resolve production or processing problems. Hire, train, evaluate, and discharge staff and resolve personnel grievances. Initiate and coordinate inventory and cost control programs. Prepare and maintain production reports and personnel records. Set and monitor product standards, examining samples of raw products or directing testing during processing, to ensure finished products are of prescribed quality. Develop and implement production tracking and quality control systems, analyzing production, quality control, maintenance, and other operational reports, to detect production problems. Review plans and confer with research and support staff to develop new products and processes. Institute employee suggestion or involvement programs. Coordinate and recommend procedures for facility and equipment maintenance or modification, including the replacement of machines.

GOE INFORMATION—Interest Area: 08. Industrial Production. **Work Group:** 08.01. Managerial Work in Industrial Production. **Personality Type—**Enterprising. Enterprising occupations frequently involve starting up and carrying out projects. These occupations can involve leading people and making many decisions. They sometimes require risk taking and often deal with business. **Work Values—**Authority; Autonomy; Creativity; Responsibility; Variety. **Skills—**Equipment Selection; Management of Material Resources; Monitoring; Coordination; Systems Evaluation; Complex Problem Solving; Management of Personnel Resources; Quality Control Analysis. **Abilities—***Cognitive:* Originality; Deductive Reasoning; Inductive Reasoning; Category Flexibility; Mathematical Reasoning. *Psychomotor:* Reaction Time; Rate Control; Finger Dexterity; Response Orientation. *Physical:* Trunk Strength. *Sensory:* Speech Recognition; Depth Perception; Far Vision; Auditory Attention; Speech Clarity. **General Work Activities—***Information Input:* Monitoring Processes, Materials, or Surroundings; Identifying Objects, Actions, and Events; Getting Information. *Mental Process:* Organizing, Planning, and Prioritizing; Making Decisions and Solving Problems; Scheduling Work and Activities. *Work Output:* Documenting or Recording Information; Controlling Machines and Processes; Performing General Physical Activities. *Interacting with Others:* Guiding, Directing, and Motivating Subordinates; Coordinating the Work and Activities of Others; Developing and Building Teams. **Physical Work Conditions—**Sitting; Walking or Running; Distracting Sounds and Noise Levels; Hazardous Conditions; High Places. **Other Job Characteristics—**Consequence of Error; Degree of Automation; Importance of Being Exact or Accurate.

Experience—Job Zone 4. A minimum of two to four years of work-related skill, knowledge, or experience is needed. **Job Preparation:** SVP 7.0 to less than 8.0—two years to less than 10 years. **Knowledge—**Production and Processing; Education and Training; Personnel and Human Resources; Administration and Management; Customer and Personal Service. **Instructional Programs—**Business Administration and Management, General; Business/Commerce, General; Operations Management and Supervision.

Related DOT Jobs—180.167-054 Superintendent; 182.167-022 Superintendent, Concrete-Mixing Plant; 183.117-010 Manager, Branch; 183.117-014 Production Superintendent; 183.161-014 Wine Maker; 183.167-010 Brewing Director; 183.167-014 General Superintendent, Milling; 183.167-018 General Supervisor; 183.167-022 General Supervisor; 183.167-026 Manager, Food Processing Plant; 183.167-034 Superintendent, Car Construction; 187.167-090 Manager, Dental Laboratory; 188.167-094 Superintendent, Industries, Correctional Facility.

11-3061.00 Purchasing Managers

- ● **Education/Training Required: Work experience plus degree**
- ● **Employed: 131,805**
- ● **Annual Earnings: $56,680**
- ● **Growth: –5.5%**
- ● **Annual Job Openings: 17,000**

Plan, direct, or coordinate the activities of buyers, purchasing officers, and related workers involved in purchasing materials, products, and services.

Analyze market and delivery systems in order to assess present and future material availability. Control purchasing department budgets. Develop and implement purchasing and contract management instructions, policies, and procedures. Direct and coordinate activities of personnel engaged in buying, selling, and distributing materials, equipment, machinery, and supplies. Interview and hire staff; oversee staff training. Participate in the development of specifications for equipment, products, or substitute materials. Prepare reports regarding market conditions and merchandise costs. Resolve vendor or contractor grievances and claims against suppliers. Review purchase order claims and contracts for conformance to company policy. Review, evaluate, and approve specifications for issuing and awarding bids. Administer online purchasing systems. Arrange for disposal of surplus materials. Locate vendors of materials, equipment, or supplies and interview them in order to determine product availability and terms of sales. Maintain records of goods ordered and received. Prepare and process requisitions and purchase orders for supplies and equipment. Prepare bid awards requiring board approval. Represent companies in negotiating contracts and formulating policies with suppliers.

GOE INFORMATION—Interest Area: 13. General Management and Support. **Work Group:** 13.01. General Management Work and Management of Support Functions. **Personality Type—**Enterprising. Enterprising occupations frequently involve starting up and carrying out projects. These occupations can involve leading people and making many decisions. They sometimes require risk taking and often deal with business. **Work Values—**Authority; Good Working Conditions; Activity; Advancement; Pleasant Co-workers. **Skills—**Management of Material Resources; Management of Financial Resources; Management of Personnel Resources; Negotiation; Judgment and Decision Making; Systems Analysis; Complex Problem Solving; Systems Evaluation. **Abilities—***Cognitive:* Mathematical Reasoning; Category Flexibility; Number Facility; Fluency of Ideas; Written Expression. *Psychomotor:* None met the criteria. *Physical:* None met the criteria. *Sensory:* Speech Clarity; Speech Recognition. **General Work Activities—***Information Input:* Getting Information; Identifying Objects, Actions, and Events; Monitoring Processes, Materials, or Surroundings. *Mental Process:* Organizing, Planning, and Prioritizing; Analyzing Data or Information; Making Decisions and Solving Problems. *Work Output:* Documenting or Recording Information; Handling and Moving Objects; Performing General Physical Activities. *Interacting with Others:* Communicating with Other Workers; Communicating with Persons Outside Organization; Monitoring and Controlling Resources. **Physical Work Conditions—**Sitting; Indoors. **Other Job Characteristics—**Consequence of Error; Importance of Being Exact or Accurate; Pace Determined by Speed of Equipment.

Experience—Job Zone 4. A minimum of two to four years of work-related skill, knowledge, or experience is needed. **Job Preparation:** SVP 7.0 to less than 8.0—two years to less than 10 years. **Knowledge—**Administration and Management; Economics and Accounting; Sales and Marketing; Production and Processing; Personnel and Human Resources. **Instructional Programs—**Purchasing, Procurement/Acquisitions, and Contracts Management.

Related DOT Jobs—162.167-014 Buyer, Tobacco, Head; 162.167-022 Manager, Procurement Services; 184.117-078 Superintendent, Commissary; 185.167-034 Manager, Merchandise.

11-3071.00 Transportation, Storage, and Distribution Managers

- **Education/Training Required: Work experience in a related occupation**
- **Employed: 149,266**
- **Annual Earnings: $57,240**
- **Growth: 20.2%**
- **Annual Job Openings: 13,000**

Plan, direct, or coordinate transportation, storage, or distribution activities in accordance with governmental policies and regulations.

No task data available.

GOE INFORMATION—Interest Area: 13. General Management and Support. **Work Group:** 13.01. General Management Work and Management of Support Functions. **Note:** The Department of Labor has not collected some data for this job, so it has fewer details than the other descriptions.

Instructional Programs—Aeronautics/Aviation/Aerospace Science and Technology, General; Aviation/Airway Management and Operations; Business Administration and Management, General; Business/Commerce, General; Logistics and Materials Management; Public Administration.

Related DOT Jobs—180.167-062 Manager, Aerial Planting and Cultivation; 181.117-010 Manager, Bulk Plant; 184.117-014 Director, Transportation; 184.117-018 District Supervisor; 184.117-022 Import-Export Agent; 184.117-026 Manager, Airport; 184.117-034 Manager, Automotive Services; 184.117-038 Manager, Flight Operations; 184.117-042 Manager, Harbor Department; 184.117-050 Manager, Operations; 184.117-054 Manager, Regional; 184.117-058 Manager, Schedule Planning; 184.117-066 Manager, Traffic; 184.117-086 Manager, Car Inspection and Repair; 184.117-090 Regional Superintendent, Railroad Car Inspection and Repair; 184.161-014 Superintendent, Water-And-Sewer Systems; 184.167-010 Boat Dispatcher; 184.167-038 Dispatcher, Chief I; 184.167-042 General Agent, Operations; 184.167-054 Manager, Bus Transportation; others.

11-3071.01 Transportation Managers

- **Education/Training Required: Work experience in a related occupation**
- **Employed: No data available.**
- **Annual Earnings: $57,240**
- **Growth: 20.2%**
- **Annual Job Openings: 13,000**

Plan, direct, and coordinate the transportation operations within an organization or the activities of organizations that provide transportation services.

Analyze expenditures and other financial information in order to develop plans, policies, and budgets for increasing profits and improving services. Collaborate with other managers and staff members in order to formulate and implement policies, procedures, goals, and objectives. Direct activities related to dispatching, routing, and tracking transportation vehicles, such as aircraft and railroad cars. Direct and coordinate, through subordinates, activities of operations department in order to obtain use of equipment, facilities, and human resources. Direct procurement processes, including equipment research and testing, vendor contracts, and requisitions approval. Implement schedule and policy changes. Monitor operations to ensure that staff members comply with administrative policies and procedures, safety rules, union contracts, and government regulations. Monitor spending to ensure that expenses are consistent with approved budgets. Negotiate and authorize contracts with equipment and materials suppliers; monitor contract fulfillment. Plan, organize, and manage the work of subordinate staff to ensure that the work is accomplished in a manner consistent with organizational requirements. Prepare management recommendations, such as proposed fee and tariff increases or schedule changes. Promote safe work activities by conducting safety audits, attending company safety meetings, and meeting with individual staff members. Recommend or authorize capital expenditures for acquisition of new equipment or property in order to increase efficiency and services of operations department. Set operations policies and standards, including determination of safety procedures for the handling of dangerous goods. Conduct employee training sessions on subjects such as hazardous material handling, employee orientation, quality improvement, and computer use. Conduct investigations in cooperation with government agencies to determine causes of transportation accidents and to improve safety procedures. Develop criteria, application instructions, procedural manuals, and contracts for federal and state public transportation programs. Direct activities of staff performing repairs and maintenance to equipment, vehicles, and facilities. Direct investigations to verify and resolve customer or shipper complaints. Participate in union contract negotiations and settlements of grievances. Promote public transportation issues at state and local levels by representing the organization before commissions or regulatory bodies during rate increase hearings. Provide administrative and technical assistance to those receiving transportation-related grants. Serve as contact persons for all workers within assigned territories. Supervise workers assigning tariff classifications and preparing billing.

GOE INFORMATION—Interest Area: 07. Transportation. **Work Group:** 07.01. Managerial Work in Transportation. **Personality Type**—Enterprising. Enterprising occupations frequently involve starting up and carrying out projects. These occupations can involve leading people and making many decisions. They sometimes require risk taking and often deal with business. **Work Values**—Authority; Autonomy; Ability Utilization; Variety; Creativity. **Skills**—Management of Material Resources; Management of Personnel Resources; Management of Financial Resources; Systems Analysis; Systems Evaluation; Negotiation; Coordination; Equipment Selection. **Abilities**—*Cognitive:* Originality; Mathematical Reasoning; Oral Comprehension; Oral Expression; Written Comprehension. *Psychomotor:* None met the criteria. *Physical:* None met the criteria. *Sensory:* Speech Clarity; Speech Recognition; Glare Sensitivity. **General Work Activities**—*Information Input:* Getting Information; Identifying Objects, Actions, and Events; Monitoring Processes, Materials, or Surroundings. *Mental Process:* Scheduling Work and Activities; Evaluating Information Against Standards; Organizing, Planning, and Prioritizing. *Work Output:* Documenting or Recording Information; Repairing and Maintaining Mechanical Equipment; Interacting with Computers. *Interacting with Others:* Communicating with Other Workers; Resolving Conflict and Negotiating with Others; Monitoring and Controlling Resources. **Physical Work Conditions**—Sitting; Outdoors. **Other Job Characteristics**—Consequence of Error; Importance of Being Exact or Accurate; Pace Determined by Speed of Equipment.

Experience—Job Zone 4. A minimum of two to four years of work-related skill, knowledge, or experience is needed. **Job Preparation:** SVP 7.0 to less than 8.0–two years to less than 10 years. **Knowledge**—Personnel and Human Resources; Economics and Accounting; Administration and Management; Law and Government; Mathematics. **Instructional Programs**—Aeronautics/Aviation/Aerospace Science and Technology, General; Aviation/Airway Management and Operations; Business Administration and Management, General; Business/Commerce, General; Logistics and Materials Management; Public Administration.

Related DOT Jobs—180.167-062 Manager, Aerial Planting and Cultivation; 184.117-014 Director, Transportation; 184.117-018 District Supervisor; 184.117-026 Manager, Airport; 184.117-034 Manager, Automotive

Services; 184.117-038 Manager, Flight Operations; 184.117-042 Manager, Harbor Department; 184.117-050 Manager, Operations; 184.117-054 Manager, Regional; 184.117-058 Manager, Schedule Planning; 184.117-066 Manager, Traffic; 184.117-086 Manager, Car Inspection and Repair; 184.117-090 Regional Superintendent, Railroad Car Inspection and Repair; 184.167-010 Boat Dispatcher; 184.167-042 General Agent, Operations; 184.167-054 Manager, Bus Transportation; 184.167-058 Manager, Cargo-and-Ramp-Services; 184.167-066 Manager, Flight Control; 184.167-070 Manager, Flight-Reservations; 184.167-082 Manager, Station; others.

11-3071.02 Storage and Distribution Managers

- Education/Training Required: Work experience in a related occupation
- Employed: No data available.
- Annual Earnings: $57,240
- Growth: 20.2%
- Annual Job Openings: 13,000

Plan, direct, and coordinate the storage and distribution operations within an organization or the activities of organizations that are engaged in storing and distributing materials and products.

Advise sales and billing departments of transportation charges for customers' accounts. Arrange for necessary shipping documentation and contact customs officials in order to effect release of shipments. Arrange for storage facilities when required. Confer with department heads to coordinate warehouse activities, such as production, sales, records control, and purchasing. Develop and document standard and emergency operating procedures for receiving, handling, storing, shipping, or salvaging products or materials. Evaluate freight costs and the inventory costs associated with transit times in order to ensure that costs are appropriate. Examine invoices and shipping manifests for conformity to tariff and customs regulations. Inspect physical conditions of warehouses, vehicle fleets, and equipment; order testing, maintenance, repair, or replacement as necessary. Issue shipping instructions and provide routing information to ensure that delivery times and locations are coordinated. Negotiate with carriers, warehouse operators, and insurance company representatives for services and preferential rates. Participate in setting transportation and service rates. Plan, develop, and implement warehouse safety and security programs and activities. Prepare and manage departmental budgets. Respond to customers' or shippers' questions and complaints regarding storage and distribution services. Review invoices, work orders, consumption reports, and demand forecasts in order to estimate peak delivery periods and issue work assignments. Schedule and monitor air or surface pickup, delivery, or distribution of products or materials. Supervise the activities of workers engaged in receiving, storing, testing, and shipping products or materials. Track and trace goods while they are en route to their destinations, expediting orders when necessary. Develop and implement plans for facility modification or expansion, such as equipment purchase or changes in space allocation or structural design. Evaluate locations for new warehouses and distribution networks in order to determine their potential usefulness. Examine products or materials in order to estimate quantities or weight and type of container required for storage or transport. Interview, select, and train warehouse and supervisory personnel. Prepare or direct preparation of correspondence; reports; and operations, maintenance, and safety manuals.

GOE INFORMATION—Interest Area: 13. General Management and Support. Work Group: 13.01. General Management Work and Management of Support Functions. Personality Type—Enterprising. Enterprising occupations frequently involve starting up and carrying out projects. These occupations can involve leading people and making many deci-

sions. They sometimes require risk taking and often deal with business. Work Values—Authority; Creativity; Autonomy; Responsibility; Company Policies and Practices. Skills—Management of Personnel Resources; Negotiation; Management of Material Resources; Systems Analysis; Operations Analysis; Systems Evaluation; Complex Problem Solving; Equipment Selection. Abilities—*Cognitive:* Mathematical Reasoning; Visualization; Written Comprehension; Written Expression; Deductive Reasoning. *Psychomotor:* None met the criteria. *Physical:* Dynamic Flexibility. *Sensory:* Speech Clarity; Speech Recognition. General Work Activities—*Information Input:* Identifying Objects, Actions, and Events; Getting Information; Monitoring Processes, Materials, or Surroundings. *Mental Process:* Scheduling Work and Activities; Organizing, Planning, and Prioritizing; Updating and Using Relevant Knowledge. *Work Output:* Performing General Physical Activities; Handling and Moving Objects; Documenting or Recording Information. *Interacting with Others:* Resolving Conflict and Negotiating with Others; Communicating with Other Workers; Monitoring and Controlling Resources. Physical Work Conditions—Climbing Ladders, Scaffolds, Poles, etc.; High Places; Indoors; Distracting Sounds and Noise Levels; Outdoors. Other Job Characteristics—Consequence of Error; Importance of Being Exact or Accurate; Degree of Automation.

Experience—Job Zone 4. A minimum of two to four years of work-related skill, knowledge, or experience is needed. Job Preparation: SVP 7.0 to less than 8.0—two years to less than 10 years. Knowledge—Personnel and Human Resources; Administration and Management; Production and Processing; Education and Training; Design. Instructional Programs—Aeronautics/Aviation/Aerospace Science and Technology, General; Aviation/Airway Management and Operations; Business Administration and Management, General; Business/Commerce, General; Logistics and Materials Management; Public Administration.

Related DOT Jobs—181.117-010 Manager, Bulk Plant; 184.117-022 Import-Export Agent; 184.167-038 Dispatcher, Chief I; 184.167-114 Manager, Warehouse; 184.167-118 Operations Manager; 184.167-146 Superintendent, Compressor Stations; 184.167-190 Superintendent, Measurement; 189.167-038 Superintendent, Ammunition Storage.

11-9000 Other Management Occupations

11-9011.00 Farm, Ranch, and Other Agricultural Managers

- Education/Training Required: Work experience in a related occupation
- Employed: 168,716
- Annual Earnings: $42,170
- Growth: 6.0%
- Annual Job Openings: 14,000

On a paid basis, manage farms, ranches, aquacultural operations, greenhouses, nurseries, timber tracts, cotton gins, packing houses, or other agricultural establishments for employers. Carry out production, financial, and marketing decisions relating to the managed operations, following guidelines from the owner. May contract tenant farmers or producers to carry out the day-to-day activities of the managed operation. May supervise planting, cultivating, harvesting, and marketing activities. May prepare cost, production, and other records. May perform physical work and operate machinery.

No task data available.

GOE INFORMATION—Interest Area: 13. General Management and Support. **Work Group:** 13.01. General Management Work and Management of Support Functions. **Note:** The Department of Labor has not collected some data for this job, so it has fewer details than the other descriptions.

Instructional Programs—Agribusiness/Agricultural Business Operations; Agricultural Animal Breeding; Agricultural Business and Management, General; Agricultural Business and Management, Other; Agricultural Production Operations, General; Agricultural Production Operations, Other; Agronomy and Crop Science; Animal Nutrition; Animal Sciences, General; Animal/Livestock Husbandry and Production; Crop Production; Dairy Husbandry and Production; Dairy Science; Farm/Farm and Ranch Management; Greenhouse Operations and Management; Horse Husbandry/Equine Science and Management; Horticultural Science; Livestock Management; Ornamental Horticulture; Plant Nursery Operations and Management; Plant Protection and Integrated Pest Management; Plant Sciences, General; Poultry Science; Range Science and Management.

Related DOT Jobs—180.117-010 Manager, Christmas-Tree Farm; 180.161-010 Manager, Production, Seed Corn; 180.161-014 Superintendent, Horticulture; 180.167-018 General Manager, Farm; 180.167-030 Manager, Fish Hatchery; 180.167-042 Manager, Nursery; 180.167-058 Superintendent, Production; 180.167-066 Manager, Orchard.

11-9011.01 Nursery and Greenhouse Managers

- **Education/Training Required: Work experience in a related occupation**
- **Employed: No data available.**
- **Annual Earnings: $42,170**
- **Growth: 6.0%**
- **Annual Job Openings: 14,000**

Plan, organize, direct, control, and coordinate activities of workers engaged in propagating, cultivating, and harvesting horticultural specialties, such as trees, shrubs, flowers, mushrooms, and other plants.

Manages nursery to grow horticultural plants for sale to trade or retail customers, for display or exhibition, or for research. Hires workers and directs supervisors and workers planting seeds, controlling plant growth and disease, potting, or cutting plants for marketing. Determines type and quantity of horticultural plants to be grown, such as trees, shrubs, flowers, ornamental plants, or vegetables, based on budget, projected sales volume, or executive directive. Grows horticultural plants under controlled conditions hydroponically. Considers such factors as whether plants need hothouse/greenhouse or natural weather growing conditions. Selects and purchases seed, plant nutrients, and disease control chemicals. Tours work areas to observe work being done, to inspect crops, and to evaluate plant and soil conditions. Confers with horticultural personnel in planning facility renovations or additions. Coordinates clerical, record-keeping, inventory, requisition, and marketing activities. Negotiates contracts for lease of lands or trucks or for purchase of trees.

GOE INFORMATION—Interest Area: 03. Plants and Animals. **Work Group:** 03.01. Managerial Work in Plants and Animals. **Personality Type**—Enterprising. Enterprising occupations frequently involve starting up and carrying out projects. These occupations can involve leading people and making many decisions. They sometimes require risk taking and often deal with business. **Work Values**—Authority; Creativity; Autonomy; Ability Utilization; Responsibility. **Skills**—Management of Personnel Resources; Management of Material Resources; Management of Financial Resources; Negotiation; Complex Problem Solving; Speaking; Coordination; Systems Analysis. **Abilities**—*Cognitive:* Written Expression; Originality; Mathematical Reasoning; Number Facility; Oral Comprehension. *Psychomotor:* None met the criteria. *Physical:* Gross Body Coordination; Gross Body Equilibrium; Trunk Strength. *Sensory:* Speech Recognition; Speech Clarity; Visual Color Discrimination; Glare Sensitivity. **General Work Activities**—*Information Input:* Getting Information; Identifying Objects, Actions, and Events; Monitoring Processes, Materials, or Surroundings. *Mental Process:* Making Decisions and Solving Problems; Scheduling Work and Activities; Thinking Creatively. *Work Output:* Handling and Moving Objects; Performing General Physical Activities; Documenting or Recording Information. *Interacting with Others:* Monitoring and Controlling Resources; Communicating with Persons Outside Organization; Resolving Conflict and Negotiating with Others. **Physical Work Conditions**—Kneeling, Crouching, or Crawling; Outdoors; Very Hot or Cold; Climbing Ladders, Scaffolds, Poles, etc.; Minor Burns, Cuts, Bites, or Stings. **Other Job Characteristics**—Importance of Repeating Same Tasks; Pace Determined by Speed of Equipment; Consequence of Error.

Experience—Job Zone 4. A minimum of two to four years of work-related skill, knowledge, or experience is needed. **Job Preparation:** SVP 7.0 to less than 8.0—two years to less than 10 years. **Knowledge**—Biology; Administration and Management; Personnel and Human Resources; Food Production; Chemistry. **Instructional Programs**—Agribusiness/Agricultural Business Operations; Agricultural Business and Management, General; Agricultural Business and Management, Other; Agricultural Production Operations, General; Agricultural Production Operations, Other; Agronomy and Crop Science; Crop Production; Farm/Farm and Ranch Management; Greenhouse Operations and Management; Horticultural Science; Ornamental Horticulture; Plant Nursery Operations and Management; Plant Protection and Integrated Pest Management; Plant Sciences, General; Range Science and Management.

Related DOT Jobs—180.117-010 Manager, Christmas-Tree Farm; 180.161-014 Superintendent, Horticulture; 180.167-042 Manager, Nursery.

11-9011.02 Agricultural Crop Farm Managers

- **Education/Training Required: Work experience in a related occupation**
- **Employed: No data available.**
- **Annual Earnings: $42,170**
- **Growth: 6.0%**
- **Annual Job Openings: 14,000**

Direct and coordinate, through subordinate supervisory personnel, activities of workers engaged in agricultural crop production for corporations, cooperatives, or other owners.

Directs and coordinates worker activities, such as planting, irrigation, chemical application, harvesting, grading, payroll, and record-keeping. Contracts with farmers or independent owners for raising of crops or for management of crop production. Coordinates growing activities with those of engineering, equipment maintenance, packing houses, and other related departments. Analyzes market conditions to determine acreage allocations. Evaluates financial statements and makes budget proposals. Negotiates with bank officials to obtain credit from bank. Hires, discharges, transfers, and promotes workers; enforces safety regulations; and interprets policies. Confers with purchasers and arranges for sale of crops. Purchases machinery, equipment, and supplies, such as tractors, seed, fertilizer, and chemicals. Records information, such as production, farm management practices, and parent stock, and prepares financial and operational reports. Plans and directs development and production of hybrid plant varieties with high yield or disease- and insect-resistant characteristics. Determines procedural changes in drying, grading, storage, and shipment for greater efficiency and accuracy. Inspects orchards and fields to determine maturity dates of crops or to estimate potential crop damage from weather. Analyzes soil to determine type and quantity of fertilizer required for maximum production. Inspects equipment to ensure proper functioning.

GOE INFORMATION—Interest Area: 03. Plants and Animals. **Work Group:** 03.01. Managerial Work in Plants and Animals. **Personality Type—**Enterprising. Enterprising occupations frequently involve starting up and carrying out projects. These occupations can involve leading people and making many decisions. They sometimes require risk taking and often deal with business. **Work Values—**Authority; Creativity; Autonomy; Responsibility; Variety. **Skills—**Management of Financial Resources; Management of Material Resources; Management of Personnel Resources; Negotiation; Coordination; Equipment Selection; Systems Analysis; Speaking. **Abilities—***Cognitive:* Mathematical Reasoning; Written Expression; Inductive Reasoning; Originality; Deductive Reasoning. *Psychomotor:* None met the criteria. *Physical:* Trunk Strength. *Sensory:* Near Vision; Speech Clarity; Far Vision. **General Work Activities—***Information Input:* Getting Information; Identifying Objects, Actions, and Events; Estimating Needed Characteristics. *Mental Process:* Organizing, Planning, and Prioritizing; Making Decisions and Solving Problems; Analyzing Data or Information. *Work Output:* Documenting or Recording Information; Performing General Physical Activities; Interacting with Computers. *Interacting with Others:* Communicating with Other Workers; Communicating with Persons Outside Organization; Monitoring and Controlling Resources. **Physical Work Conditions—**Outdoors; Minor Burns, Cuts, Bites, or Stings; Contaminants; Hazardous Equipment; Standing. **Other Job Characteristics—**Consequence of Error; Importance of Being Exact or Accurate; Importance of Repeating Same Tasks.

Experience—Job Zone 4. A minimum of two to four years of work-related skill, knowledge, or experience is needed. **Job Preparation:** SVP 7.0 to less than 8.0—two years to less than 10 years. **Knowledge—**Food Production; Economics and Accounting; Administration and Management; Production and Processing; Personnel and Human Resources. **Instructional Programs—**Agribusiness/Agricultural Business Operations; Agricultural Business and Management, General; Agricultural Business and Management, Other; Agricultural Production Operations, General; Agricultural Production Operations, Other; Agronomy and Crop Science; Crop Production; Dairy Husbandry and Production; Farm/Farm and Ranch Management; Greenhouse Operations and Management; Horticultural Science; Ornamental Horticulture; Plant Nursery Operations and Management; Plant Protection and Integrated Pest Management; Plant Sciences, General; Range Science and Management.

Related DOT Jobs—180.161-010 Manager, Production, Seed Corn; 180.167-018 General Manager, Farm; 180.167-058 Superintendent, Production; 180.167-066 Manager, Orchard.

11-9011.03 Fish Hatchery Managers

- **Education/Training Required: Work experience in a related occupation**
- **Employed: No data available.**
- **Annual Earnings: $42,170**
- **Growth: 6.0%**
- **Annual Job Openings: 14,000**

Direct and coordinate, through subordinate supervisory personnel, activities of workers engaged in fish hatchery production for corporations, cooperatives, or other owners.

Determines, administers, and executes policies relating to administration, standards of hatchery operations, and facility maintenance. Oversees trapping and spawning of fish, egg incubation, and fry rearing, applying knowledge of management and fish culturing techniques. Oversees movement of mature fish to lakes, ponds, streams, or commercial tanks. Confers with biologists and other fishery personnel to obtain data concerning fish habits, food, and environmental requirements. Collects information regarding techniques for collecting, fertilizing, and incubating spawn and treatment of spawn and fry. Prepares budget reports. Prepares reports required by state and federal laws. Accounts for and dispenses funds. Approves employment and discharge of employees, signs payrolls, and performs personnel duties.

GOE INFORMATION—Interest Area: 03. Plants and Animals. **Work Group:** 03.01. Managerial Work in Plants and Animals. **Personality Type—**Enterprising. Enterprising occupations frequently involve starting up and carrying out projects. These occupations can involve leading people and making many decisions. They sometimes require risk taking and often deal with business. **Work Values—**Authority; Creativity; Autonomy; Responsibility; Variety. **Skills—**Management of Financial Resources; Management of Personnel Resources; Management of Material Resources; Reading Comprehension; Writing; Systems Analysis; Science; Complex Problem Solving. **Abilities—***Cognitive:* Flexibility of Closure; Number Facility; Selective Attention; Written Expression; Spatial Orientation. *Psychomotor:* Response Orientation; Reaction Time; Speed of Limb Movement; Rate Control. *Physical:* Gross Body Equilibrium; Gross Body Coordination. *Sensory:* Far Vision; Sound Localization; Peripheral Vision; Auditory Attention; Glare Sensitivity. **General Work Activities—***Information Input:* Getting Information; Identifying Objects, Actions, and Events; Monitoring Processes, Materials, or Surroundings. *Mental Process:* Making Decisions and Solving Problems; Processing Information; Organizing, Planning, and Prioritizing. *Work Output:* Documenting or Recording Information; Controlling Machines and Processes; Performing General Physical Activities. *Interacting with Others:* Monitoring and Controlling Resources; Communicating with Other Workers; Staffing Organizational Units. **Physical Work Conditions—**Outdoors; Contaminants; Extremely Bright or Inadequate Lighting; Disease or Infections; Minor Burns, Cuts, Bites, or Stings. **Other Job Characteristics—**Consequence of Error; Importance of Being Exact or Accurate; Importance of Repeating Same Tasks.

Experience—Job Zone 4. A minimum of two to four years of work-related skill, knowledge, or experience is needed. **Job Preparation:** SVP 7.0 to less than 8.0—two years to less than 10 years. **Knowledge—**Food Production; Administration and Management; Personnel and Human Resources; Economics and Accounting; Biology. **Instructional Programs—**Agribusiness/Agricultural Business Operations; Agricultural Animal Breeding; Agricultural Business and Management, General; Agricultural Business and Management, Other; Agricultural Production Operations, General; Agricultural Production Operations, Other; Animal Nutrition; Animal Sciences, General; Animal/Livestock Husbandry and Production; Farm/Farm and Ranch Management; Livestock Management.

Related DOT Jobs—180.167-030 Manager, Fish Hatchery.

11-9012.00 Farmers and Ranchers

- **Education/Training Required: Long-term on-the-job training**
- **Employed: 1,293,664**
- **Annual Earnings: $42,170**
- **Growth: −25.4%**
- **Annual Job Openings: 146,000**

On an ownership or rental basis, operate farms, ranches, greenhouses, nurseries, timber tracts, or other agricultural production establishments that produce crops, horticultural specialties, livestock, poultry, finfish, shellfish, or animal specialties. May plant, cultivate, harvest, perform post-harvest activities on, and market crops and livestock; may hire, train, and supervise farm workers or supervise a farm labor contractor; may prepare cost, production, and other records. May maintain and operate machinery and perform physical work.

Harvests crops and collects specialty products, such as royal jelly from queen bee cells and honey from honeycombs. Sets up and operates farm machinery to till soil for, plant, prune, fertilize, apply herbicides and pesticides to, and haul harvested crops. Inspects growing environment to maintain optimum growing or breeding conditions. Plans harvesting, considering ripeness and maturity of crop and weather conditions. Determines kind and quantity of crops or livestock to be raised, according to market conditions, weather, and farm size. Destroys diseased or superfluous crops, such as queen bee cells, bee colonies, parasites, and vermin. Selects and purchases supplies and equipment, such as seed, tree stock, fertilizers, farm machinery, implements, livestock, and feed. Breeds and raises stock, such as animals, poultry, honeybees, or earthworms. Grows out-of-season crops in greenhouse or early crops in cold-frame bed or buds and grafts plant stock. Arranges with buyers for sale and shipment of crops. Installs irrigation systems and irrigates fields. Hires and directs workers engaged in planting, cultivating, irrigating, harvesting, and marketing crops and raising livestock. Demonstrates and explains farm work techniques and safety regulations to workers. Assembles, positions, and secures structures, such as trellises or beehives, using hand tools. Grades and packages crop for marketing. Lubricates, adjusts, and makes minor repairs on farm equipment, using oilcan, grease gun, and hand tools. Maintains employee and financial records.

GOE INFORMATION—Interest Area: 03. Plants and Animals. **Work Group:** 03.01. Managerial Work in Plants and Animals. **Personality Type**—Realistic. Realistic occupations frequently involve work activities that include practical, hands-on problems and solutions. They often deal with plants, animals, and real-world materials like wood, tools, and machinery. Many of the occupations require working outside and do not involve a lot of paperwork or working closely with others. **Work Values**—Autonomy; Creativity; Responsibility; Authority; Variety. **Skills**—Equipment Selection; Management of Financial Resources; Operation and Control; Installation; Management of Material Resources; Repairing; Management of Personnel Resources; Operation Monitoring. **Abilities**—*Cognitive:* Deductive Reasoning; Number Facility; Information Ordering; Visualization; Inductive Reasoning. *Psychomotor:* Control Precision; Multilimb Coordination; Manual Dexterity; Speed of Limb Movement; Wrist-Finger Speed. *Physical:* Stamina; Dynamic Strength; Static Strength; Trunk Strength; Explosive Strength. *Sensory:* Far Vision; Glare Sensitivity; Sound Localization; Near Vision; Peripheral Vision. **General Work Activities**—*Information Input:* Getting Information; Identifying Objects, Actions, and Events; Monitoring Processes, Materials, or Surroundings. *Mental Process:* Organizing, Planning, and Prioritizing; Analyzing Data or Information; Scheduling Work and Activities. *Work Output:* Performing General Physical Activities; Handling and Moving Objects; Controlling Machines and Processes. *Interacting with Others:* Monitoring and Controlling Resources; Communicating with Persons Outside Organization; Coordinating the Work and Activities of Others. **Physical Work Conditions**—Outdoors; Hazardous Equipment; Minor Burns, Cuts, Bites, or Stings; Using Hands on Objects, Tools, or Controls; Contaminants. **Other Job Characteristics**—Consequence of Error; Pace Determined by Speed of Equipment; Importance of Repeating Same Tasks.

Experience—Job Zone 3. Previous work-related skill, knowledge, or experience is required. **Job Preparation:** SVP 6.0 to less than 7.0—more than one year and less than four years. **Knowledge**—Food Production; Personnel and Human Resources; Economics and Accounting; Sales and Marketing; Production and Processing. **Instructional Programs**—Agribusiness/Agricultural Business Operations; Agricultural Animal Breeding; Agricultural Business and Management, General; Agricultural Production Operations, General; Agricultural Production Operations, Other; Agronomy and Crop Science; Animal Nutrition; Animal Sciences, General; Animal/Livestock Husbandry and Production; Aquaculture; Crop Production; Dairy Husbandry and Production; Dairy Science; Farm/Farm and Ranch Management; Greenhouse Operations and Management; Horticultural Science; Livestock Management; Ornamental Horticulture; Plant Nursery Operations and Management; Plant Protection and Integrated Pest Management; Plant Sciences, General; Poultry Science; Range Science and Management.

Related DOT Jobs—401.161-010 Farmer, Cash Grain; 402.161-010 Farmer, Vegetable; 403.161-010 Farmer, Tree-Fruit-and-Nut Crops; 403.161-014 Farmer, Fruit Crops, Bush and Vine; 404.161-010 Farmer, Field Crop; 407.161-010 Farmer, Diversified Crops; 413.161-010 Beekeeper; 413.161-018 Worm Grower; 421.161-010 Farmer, General.

11-9021.00 Construction Managers

- **Education/Training Required: Bachelor's degree**
- **Employed: 307,826**
- **Annual Earnings: $61,050**
- **Growth: 16.3%**
- **Annual Job Openings: 26,000**

Plan, direct, coordinate, or budget, usually through subordinate supervisory personnel, activities concerned with the construction and maintenance of structures, facilities, and systems. Participate in the conceptual development of a construction project and oversee its organization, scheduling, and implementation.

Confer with supervisory personnel, owners, contractors, and design professionals to discuss and resolve matters such as work procedures, complaints, and construction problems. Determine labor requirements and dispatch workers to construction sites. Direct and supervise workers. Interpret and explain plans and contract terms to administrative staff, workers, and clients, representing the owner or developer. Plan, organize, and direct activities concerned with the construction and maintenance of structures, facilities, and systems. Prepare and submit budget estimates and progress and cost tracking reports. Schedule the project in logical steps and budget time required to meet deadlines. Select, contract, and oversee workers who complete specific pieces of the project, such as painting or plumbing. Study job specifications to determine appropriate construction methods. Develop and implement quality control programs. Direct acquisition of land for construction projects. Evaluate construction methods and determine cost-effectiveness of plans, using computers. Inspect and review projects to monitor compliance with building and safety codes and other regulations. Investigate damage, accidents, or delays at construction sites to ensure that proper procedures are being carried out. Obtain all necessary permits and licenses. Prepare contracts and negotiate revisions, changes, and additions to contractual agreements with architects, consultants, clients, suppliers, and subcontractors. Requisition supplies and materials to complete construction projects. Take actions to deal with the results of delays, bad weather, or emergencies at construction site.

GOE INFORMATION—Interest Area: 06. Construction, Mining, and Drilling. **Work Group:** 06.01. Managerial Work in Construction, Mining, and Drilling. **Personality Type**—Enterprising. Enterprising occupations frequently involve starting up and carrying out projects. These occupations can involve leading people and making many decisions. They sometimes require risk taking and often deal with business. **Work Values**—Authority; Autonomy; Variety; Responsibility; Creativity. **Skills**—Management of Personnel Resources; Management of Financial Resources; Management of Material Resources; Coordination; Equipment Selection; Operations Analysis; Time Management; Mathematics. **Abilities**—*Cognitive:* Written Expression; Oral Expression; Written Comprehension; Oral Comprehension; Fluency of Ideas. *Psychomotor:* None met the criteria. *Physical:* None met the criteria. *Sensory:* Speech Recognition; Speech Clarity; Far Vision; Near Vision. **General Work Activities**—*Information Input:* Getting Information; Monitoring Processes, Materials, or Surroundings; Identifying Objects, Actions, and Events. *Mental Process:* Organizing, Planning, and Prioritizing; Updating and Using Relevant Knowledge; Making Decisions and Solving Problems. *Work Output:* Documenting or Recording Information; Handling and Moving Objects; Performing General Physical Activities. *Interacting with Others:* Coordinating the Work and Activities of Others; Guiding, Directing, and Motivating Subordinates; Communicating with Other Workers. **Physical Work Conditions**—High Places; Outdoors; Distracting Sounds and Noise Levels; Climbing Ladders, Scaffolds, Poles, etc.; Very Hot or Cold. **Other Job Characteristics**—Consequence of Error; Importance of Being Exact or Accurate; Pace Determined by Speed of Equipment.

Experience—Job Zone 4. A minimum of two to four years of work-related skill, knowledge, or experience is needed. **Job Preparation:** SVP 7.0 to less than 8.0—two years to less than 10 years. **Knowledge**—Building and Construction; Administration and Management; Personnel and Human Resources; Public Safety and Security; Design. **Instructional Programs**—Business Administration and Management, General; Business/Commerce, General; Construction Engineering Technology/Technician; Operations Management and Supervision.

Related DOT Jobs—182.167-010 Contractor; 182.167-018 Railroad-Construction Director; 182.167-026 Superintendent, Construction; 182.167-030 Superintendent, Maintenance of Way; 182.167-034 Supervisor, Bridges and Buildings.

11-9031.00 Education Administrators, Preschool and Child Care Center/Program

- **Education/Training Required: Work experience plus degree**
- **Employed: No data available.**
- **Annual Earnings: $31,860**
- **Growth: 13.4%**
- **Annual Job Openings: 35,000**

Plan, direct, or coordinate the academic and nonacademic activities of preschool and child care centers or programs.

Direct and coordinate activities of teachers or administrators at day care centers, schools, public agencies, and/or institutions. Plan, direct, and monitor instructional methods and content of educational, vocational, or student activity programs. Recruit, hire, train, and evaluate primary and supplemental staff and recommend personnel actions for programs and services. Determine allocations of funds for staff, supplies, materials, and equipment; authorize purchases. Determine the scope of educational program offerings and prepare drafts of program schedules and descriptions in order to estimate staffing and facility requirements. Organize and direct committees of specialists, volunteers, and staff to provide technical and advisory assistance for programs. Prepare and submit budget requests or grant proposals to solicit program funding. Prepare and maintain attendance, activity, planning, accounting, or personnel reports and records for officials and agencies or direct preparation and maintenance activities. Review and evaluate new and current programs to determine their efficiency, effectiveness, and compliance with state, local, and federal regulations; recommend any necessary modifications. Review and interpret government codes and develop procedures to meet codes and to ensure facility safety, security, and maintenance. Set educational standards and goals and help establish policies, procedures, and programs to carry them out. Collect and analyze survey data, regulatory information, and demographic and employment trends in order to forecast enrollment patterns and the need for curriculum changes. Confer with parents and staff to discuss educational activities and policies and students' behavioral or learning problems. Inform businesses, community groups, and governmental agencies about educational needs, available programs, and program policies. Monitor students' progress and provide students and teachers with assistance in resolving any problems. Teach classes or courses and/or provide direct care to children. Write articles, manuals, and other publications and assist in the distribution of promotional literature about programs and facilities.

GOE INFORMATION—Interest Area: 12. Education and Social Service. **Work Group:** 12.01. Managerial Work in Education and Social Service. **Personality Type**—Social. Social occupations frequently involve working with, communicating with, and teaching people. These occupations often involve helping or providing service to others. **Work Values**—Authority; Ability Utilization; Creativity; Social Status; Recognition. **Skills**—Management of Personnel Resources; Management of Financial Resources; Management of Material Resources; Systems Analysis; Systems Evaluation; Learning Strategies; Coordination; Writing. **Abilities**—*Cognitive:* Written Expression; Originality; Fluency of Ideas; Oral Expression; Oral Comprehension. *Psychomotor:* None met the criteria. *Physical:* None met the criteria. *Sensory:* Speech Clarity; Speech Recognition; Far Vision; Near Vision; Auditory Attention. **General Work Activities**—*Information Input:* Getting Information; Identifying Objects, Actions, and Events; Monitoring Processes, Materials, or Surroundings. *Mental Process:* Organizing, Planning, and Prioritizing; Processing Information; Analyzing Data or Information. *Work Output:* Documenting or Recording Information; Interacting with Computers; Handling and Moving Objects. *Interacting with Others:* Communicating with Other Workers; Communicating with Persons Outside Organization; Monitoring and Controlling Resources. **Physical Work Conditions**—Indoors; Sitting; Walking or Running. **Other Job Characteristics**—Consequence of Error; Degree of Automation; Importance of Being Exact or Accurate.

Experience—Job Zone 4. A minimum of two to four years of work-related skill, knowledge, or experience is needed. **Job Preparation:** SVP 7.0 to less than 8.0—two years to less than 10 years. **Knowledge**—Education and Training; Sales and Marketing; Personnel and Human Resources; Administration and Management; Economics and Accounting. **Instructional Programs**—Educational Administration and Supervision, Other; Educational Leadership and Administration, General; Educational, Instructional, and Curriculum Supervision.

Related DOT Jobs—092.167-010 Director, Day Care Center; 094.167-014 Director, Special Education; 097.167-010 Director, Vocational Training; 099.117-010 Director, Educational Program; 099.117-018 Principal.

11-9032.00 Education Administrators, Elementary and Secondary School

- **Education/Training Required: Work experience plus degree**
- **Employed: No data available.**
- **Annual Earnings: $69,240**
- **Growth: 13.4%**
- **Annual Job Openings: 35,000**

Plan, direct, or coordinate the academic, clerical, or auxiliary activities of public or private elementary or secondary-level schools.

Direct and coordinate activities of teachers, administrators, and support staff at schools, public agencies, and institutions. Evaluate curricula, teaching methods, and programs to determine their effectiveness, efficiency, and utilization and to ensure that school activities comply with federal, state, and local regulations. Collaborate with teachers to develop and maintain curriculum standards, develop mission statements, and set performance goals and objectives. Determine allocations of funds for staff, supplies, materials, and equipment; authorize purchases. Determine the scope of educational program offerings and prepare drafts of course schedules and descriptions in order to estimate staffing and facility requirements. Observe teaching methods and examine learning materials in order to evaluate and standardize curricula and teaching techniques and to determine areas where improvement is needed. Plan and develop instructional methods and content for educational, vocational, or student activity programs. Prepare and submit budget requests and recommendations or grant proposals to solicit program funding. Prepare, maintain, or oversee the preparation/maintenance of attendance, activity, planning, or personnel reports and records. Recommend personnel actions related to programs and services. Recruit, hire, train, and evaluate primary and supplemental staff. Review and approve new programs or recommend modifications to existing programs, submitting program proposals for school board approval as necessary. Set educational standards and goals and help establish policies and procedures to carry them out. Collect and analyze survey data, regulatory information, and data on demographic and employment trends to forecast enrollment patterns and curriculum change needs. Confer with parents and staff to discuss educational activities, policies, and student behavioral or learning problems. Counsel and provide guidance to students regarding personal, academic, vocational, or behavioral issues. Develop partnerships with businesses, communities, and other organizations to help meet identified educational needs and to provide school-to-work programs. Direct and coordinate school maintenance services and the use of school facilities. Enforce discipline and attendance rules. Organize and direct committees of specialists, volunteers, and staff to provide technical and advisory assistance for programs. Review and interpret government codes and develop programs to ensure adherence to codes and facility safety, security, and maintenance. Teach classes or courses to students. Write articles, manuals, and other publications and assist in the distribution of promotional literature about facilities and programs. Advocate for new schools to be built or for existing facilities to be repaired or remodeled. Establish, coordinate, and oversee particular programs across school districts, such as programs to evaluate student academic achievement.

GOE INFORMATION—Interest Area: 12. Education and Social Service. **Work Group:** 12.01. Managerial Work in Education and Social Service. **Personality Type—**Social. Social occupations frequently involve working with, communicating with, and teaching people. These occupations often involve helping or providing service to others. **Work Values—**Authority; Ability Utilization; Creativity; Social Status; Recognition. **Skills—**Management of Personnel Resources; Management of Financial Resources; Management of Material Resources; Systems Analysis; Systems Evaluation; Learning Strategies; Coordination; Writing. **Abilities—**

Cognitive: Written Expression; Originality; Fluency of Ideas; Oral Expression; Oral Comprehension. *Psychomotor:* None met the criteria. *Physical:* None met the criteria. *Sensory:* Speech Clarity; Speech Recognition; Far Vision; Near Vision; Auditory Attention. **General Work Activities—***Information Input:* Getting Information; Identifying Objects, Actions, and Events; Estimating Needed Characteristics. *Mental Process:* Organizing, Planning, and Prioritizing; Processing Information; Analyzing Data or Information. *Work Output:* Documenting or Recording Information; Interacting with Computers; Handling and Moving Objects. *Interacting with Others:* Communicating with Other Workers; Communicating with Persons Outside Organization; Establishing and Maintaining Relationships. **Physical Work Conditions—**Indoors; Sitting; Walking or Running. **Other Job Characteristics—**Consequence of Error; Degree of Automation; Importance of Being Exact or Accurate.

Experience—Job Zone 4. A minimum of two to four years of work-related skill, knowledge, or experience is needed. **Job Preparation:** SVP 7.0 to less than 8.0–two years to less than 10 years. **Knowledge—**Education and Training; Sales and Marketing; Personnel and Human Resources; Administration and Management; Economics and Accounting. **Instructional Programs—**Educational Administration and Supervision, Other; Educational Leadership and Administration, General; Educational, Instructional, and Curriculum Supervision; Elementary and Middle School Administration/Principalship; Secondary School Administration/Principalship.

Related DOT Jobs—091.107-010 Assistant Principal; 094.117-010 Director, Commission for the Blind; 094.167-014 Director, Special Education; 097.167-010 Director, Vocational Training; 099.117-010 Director, Educational Program; 099.117-018 Principal.

11-9033.00 Education Administrators, Postsecondary

- **Education/Training Required: Work experience plus degree**
- **Employed: No data available.**
- **Annual Earnings: $61,700**
- **Growth: 13.4%**
- **Annual Job Openings: 35,000**

Plan, direct, or coordinate research, instructional, student administration and services, and other educational activities at postsecondary institutions, including universities, colleges, and junior and community colleges.

Direct activities of administrative departments, such as admissions, registration, and career services. Direct, coordinate, and evaluate the activities of personnel engaged in administering academic institutions, departments, and/or alumni organizations. Establish operational policies and procedures and make any necessary modifications based on analysis of operations, demographics, and other research information. Appoint individuals to faculty positions and evaluate their performance. Confer with other academic staff to explain and formulate admission requirements and course credit policies. Develop curricula and recommend curricula revisions and additions. Participate in faculty and college committee activities. Participate in student recruitment, selection, and admission, making admissions recommendations when required to do so. Plan, administer, and control budgets, maintain financial records, and produce financial reports. Provide assistance to faculty and staff in duties such as teaching classes, conducting orientation programs, issuing transcripts, and scheduling events. Recruit, hire, train, and terminate departmental personnel. Represent institutions at community and campus events, in meetings with other institution personnel, and during accreditation processes. Review registration statistics and consult with faculty officials to develop registration policies. Audit the financial status of student organizations and facility accounts. Coordinate the production and dissemination of university publications such as course catalogs and class schedules. Determine course schedules and coordinate teaching assignments and room assignments in order to ensure optimum use of buildings and equipment. Direct and participate in institutional fundraising activities and encourage alumni participation in such activities. Direct scholarship, fellowship, and loan programs, performing activities such as selecting recipients and distributing aid. Plan and promote sporting events and social, cultural, and recreational activities. Review student misconduct reports requiring disciplinary action and counsel students regarding such reports. Supervise coaches. Teach courses within their department. Assess and collect tuition and fees. Consult with government regulatory and licensing agencies in order to ensure the institution's conformance with applicable standards. Negotiate with foundation and industry representatives on issues such as securing loans and determining construction costs and materials.

GOE INFORMATION—Interest Area: 12. Education and Social Service. **Work Group:** 12.01. Managerial Work in Education and Social Service. **Personality Type—**Enterprising. Enterprising occupations frequently involve starting up and carrying out projects. These occupations can involve leading people and making many decisions. They sometimes require risk taking and often deal with business. **Work Values—**Authority; Social Status; Good Working Conditions; Recognition; Creativity. **Skills—**Management of Financial Resources; Systems Evaluation; Management of Personnel Resources; Management of Material Resources; Systems Analysis; Coordination; Complex Problem Solving; Monitoring. **Abilities—***Cognitive:* Written Expression; Oral Expression; Oral Comprehension; Mathematical Reasoning; Memorization. *Psychomotor:* None met the criteria. *Physical:* Trunk Strength. *Sensory:* Speech Clarity; Speech Recognition; Far Vision; Near Vision; Auditory Attention. **General Work Activities—***Information Input:* Getting Information; Identifying Objects, Actions, and Events; Estimating Needed Characteristics. *Mental Process:* Making Decisions and Solving Problems; Developing Objectives and Strategies; Analyzing Data or Information. *Work Output:* Documenting or Recording Information; Interacting with Computers; Handling and Moving Objects. *Interacting with Others:* Performing Administrative Activities; Communicating with Persons Outside Organization; Resolving Conflict and Negotiating with Others. **Physical Work Conditions—**Sitting; Walking or Running; Outdoors. **Other Job Characteristics—**Consequence of Error; Importance of Being Exact or Accurate; Degree of Automation.

Experience—Job Zone 5. Extensive skill, knowledge, and experience are needed for these occupations. **Job Preparation:** SVP 8.0 and above—four years to more than 10 years. **Knowledge—**Education and Training; Administration and Management; Economics and Accounting; Personnel and Human Resources; Law and Government. **Instructional Programs—**Community College Education; Educational Administration and Supervision, Other; Educational Leadership and Administration, General; Educational, Instructional, and Curriculum Supervision; Higher Education/Higher Education Administration.

Related DOT Jobs—090.117-010 Academic Dean; 090.117-014 Alumni Secretary; 090.117-018 Dean of Students; 090.117-022 Director, Athletic; 090.117-026 Director, Extension Work; 090.117-030 Financial-Aid Officer; 090.167-010 Department Head, College or University; 090.167-014 Director of Admissions; 090.167-018 Director of Institutional Research; 090.167-022 Director of Student Affairs; 090.167-026 Director, Summer Sessions; 090.167-030 Registrar, College or University; 186.117-010 Business Manager, College or University.

11-9039.99 Education Administrators, All Other

- Education/Training Required: Work experience plus degree
- Employed: No data available.
- Annual Earnings: No data available.
- Growth: 13.4%
- Annual Job Openings: 35,000

All education administrators not listed separately.

No task data available.

GOE INFORMATION—Interest Area: 12. Education and Social Service. **Work Group:** 12.01. Managerial Work in Education and Social Service. **Note:** The Department of Labor has not collected some data for this job, so it has fewer details than the other descriptions.

Instructional Programs—Administration of Special Education; Adult and Continuing Education Administration; Educational Leadership and Administration, General; Educational, Instructional, and Curriculum Supervision; Elementary and Middle School Administration/Principalship; Higher Education/Higher Education Administration; Superintendency and Educational System Administration; Urban Education and Leadership.

Related DOT Jobs—075.117-018 Director, Educational, Community-Health Nursing; 099.117-014 Education Supervisor, Correctional Institution; 099.117-030 Director, Education.

11-9041.00 Engineering Managers

- Education/Training Required: Work experience plus degree
- Employed: 282,051
- Annual Earnings: $87,490
- Growth: 8.0%
- Annual Job Openings: 24,000

Plan, direct, or coordinate activities in such fields as architecture and engineering or research and development in these fields.

Analyze technology, resource needs, and market demand to plan and assess the feasibility of projects. Confer with management, production, and marketing staff to discuss project specifications and procedures. Coordinate and direct projects, making detailed plans to accomplish goals and directing the integration of technical activities. Direct, review, and approve product design and changes. Prepare budgets, bids, and contracts and direct the negotiation of research contracts. Set scientific and technical goals within broad outlines provided by top management. Confer with and report to officials and the public to provide information and solicit support for projects. Consult or negotiate with clients to prepare project specifications. Develop and implement policies, standards, and procedures for the engineering and technical work performed in the department, service, laboratory, or firm. Perform administrative functions, such as reviewing and writing reports, approving expenditures, enforcing rules, and making decisions about the purchase of materials or services. Plan and direct the installation, testing, operation, maintenance, and repair of facilities and equipment. Present and explain proposals, reports, and findings to clients. Recruit employees; assign, direct, and evaluate their work; and oversee the development and maintenance of staff competence. Review and recommend or approve contracts and cost estimates. Administer highway planning, construction, and maintenance. Direct the engineering of water control, treatment, and distribution projects. Plan and direct oil field development, gas and oil production, and geothermal drilling. Plan, direct, and coordinate survey work with other staff activities, such as certifying survey work and writing land legal descriptions.

GOE INFORMATION—Interest Area: 02. Science, Math, and Engineering. **Work Group:** 02.01. Managerial Work in Science, Math, and Engineering. **Personality Type—**Enterprising. Enterprising occupations frequently involve starting up and carrying out projects. These occupations can involve leading people and making many decisions. They sometimes require risk taking and often deal with business. **Work Values—**Authority; Compensation; Autonomy; Creativity; Good Working Conditions. **Skills—**Operations Analysis; Troubleshooting; Systems Analysis; Management of Material Resources; Quality Control Analysis; Science; Technology Design; Equipment Selection. **Abilities—***Cognitive:* Mathematical Reasoning; Written Expression; Originality; Deductive Reasoning; Fluency of Ideas. *Psychomotor:* Response Orientation. *Physical:* Gross Body Equilibrium; Trunk Strength. *Sensory:* Speech Clarity; Speech Recognition; Far Vision; Visual Color Discrimination; Near Vision. **General Work Activities—***Information Input:* Getting Information; Identifying Objects, Actions, and Events; Monitoring Processes, Materials, or Surroundings. *Mental Process:* Organizing, Planning, and Prioritizing; Updating and Using Relevant Knowledge; Analyzing Data or Information. *Work Output:* Documenting or Recording Information; Drafting and Specifying Technical Devices; Interacting with Computers. *Interacting with Others:* Coordinating the Work and Activities of Others; Communicating with Other Workers; Developing and Building Teams. **Physical Work Conditions—**Outdoors; High Places; Very Hot or Cold; Walking or Running; Hazardous Conditions. **Other Job Characteristics—**Consequence of Error; Importance of Being Exact or Accurate; Degree of Automation.

Experience—Job Zone 5. Extensive skill, knowledge, and experience are needed for these occupations. **Job Preparation:** SVP 8.0 and above—four years to more than 10 years. **Knowledge—**Engineering and Technology; Design; Physics; Administration and Management; Economics and Accounting. **Instructional Programs—**Aerospace, Aeronautical, and Astronautical Engineering; Agricultural/Biological Engineering and Bioengineering; Architectural Engineering; Architecture (BArch, BA/BS, MArch, MA/MS, PhD); Biomedical/Medical Engineering; Ceramic Sciences and Engineering; Chemical Engineering; City/Urban, Community, and Regional Planning; Civil Engineering, General; Civil Engineering, Other; Computer Engineering, General; Computer Engineering, Other; Computer Hardware Engineering; Computer Software Engineering; Construction Engineering; Electrical, Electronics, and Communications Engineering; Engineering Mechanics; Engineering Physics; Engineering Science; Engineering, General; Engineering, Other; Environmental Design/Architecture; Environmental/Environmental Health Engineering; Forest Engineering; Geological/Geophysical Engineering; Geotechnical Engineering; Industrial Engineering; Interior Architecture; Landscape Architecture (BS, BSLA, BLA, MSLA, MLA, PhD); Manufacturing Engineering; Materials Engineering; Materials Science; Mechanical Engineering; Metallurgical Engineering; Mining and Mineral Engineering; Naval Architecture and Marine Engineering; Nuclear Engineering; Ocean Engineering; Petroleum Engineering; Polymer/Plastics Engineering; Structural Engineering; Surveying Engineering; Systems Engineering; Textile Sciences and Engineering; Transportation and Highway Engineering; Water Resources Engineering.

Related DOT Jobs—010.161-014 Chief Petroleum Engineer; 010.167-018 Superintendent, Oil-Well Services; 018.167-022 Manager, Land Surveying; 019.167-014 Project Engineer; 162.117-030 Research-Contracts Supervisor; 316.703-034 Engineer-in-Charge, Transmitter; 316.707-070 Engineering Manager, Electronics; 516.701-010 Chief Engineer, Waterworks; 516.702-022 Highway-Administrative Engineer; 716.701-014 Plant Engineer.

11-9051.00 Food Service Managers

- **Education/Training Required: Work experience in a related occupation**
- **Employed: 465,172**
- **Annual Earnings: $33,630**
- **Growth: 15.0%**
- **Annual Job Openings: 55,000**

Plan, direct, or coordinate activities of an organization or department that serves food and beverages.

Monitor compliance with health and fire regulations regarding food preparation and serving and with building maintenance in lodging and dining facilities. Plan menus and food utilization based on anticipated number of guests, nutritional value, palatability, popularity, and costs. Organize and direct worker training programs, resolve personnel problems, hire new staff, and evaluate employee performance in dining and lodging facilities. Coordinate assignments of cooking personnel in order to ensure economical use of food and timely preparation. Estimate food, liquor, wine, and other beverage consumption in order to anticipate amounts to be purchased or requisitioned. Monitor food preparation methods, portion sizes, and garnishing and presentation of food in order to ensure that food is prepared and presented in an acceptable manner. Monitor budgets and payroll records and review financial transactions in order to ensure that expenditures are authorized and budgeted. Investigate and resolve complaints regarding food quality, service, or accommodations. Review menus and analyze recipes in order to determine labor and overhead costs and assign prices to menu items. Establish and enforce nutritional standards for dining establishments based on accepted industry standards. Keep records required by government agencies regarding sanitation and food subsidies when appropriate. Test cooked food by tasting and smelling it in order to ensure palatability and flavor conformity. Create specialty dishes and develop recipes to be used in dining facilities. Arrange for equipment maintenance and repairs; coordinate a variety of services, such as waste removal and pest control. Assess staffing needs and recruit staff by using methods such as newspaper advertisements or attendance at job fairs. Establish standards for personnel performance and customer service. Greet guests, escort them to their seats, and present them with menus and wine lists. Maintain food and equipment inventories and keep inventory records. Monitor employee and patron activities in order to ensure liquor regulations are obeyed. Order and purchase equipment and supplies. Perform some food preparation or service tasks, such as cooking, clearing tables, and serving food and drinks when necessary. Record the number, type, and cost of items sold in order to determine which items may be unpopular or less profitable. Review work procedures and operational problems in order to determine ways to improve service, performance, and/or safety. Schedule and receive food and beverage deliveries, checking delivery contents in order to verify product quality and quantity. Schedule staff hours and assign duties. Schedule use of facilities or catering services for events such as banquets or receptions and negotiate details of arrangements with clients.

GOE INFORMATION—Interest Area: 11. Recreation, Travel, and Other Personal Services. **Work Group:** 11.01. Managerial Work in Recreation, Travel, and Other Personal Services. **Personality Type—**Enterprising. Enterprising occupations frequently involve starting up and carrying out projects. These occupations can involve leading people and making many decisions. They sometimes require risk taking and often deal with business. **Work Values—**Authority; Creativity; Autonomy; Responsibility; Security. **Skills—**Management of Personnel Resources; Management of Financial Resources; Coordination; Management of Material Resources; Time Management; Speaking; Monitoring; Complex Problem Solving. **Abilities—***Cognitive:* Originality; Mathematical Reasoning; Memorization; Number Facility; Oral Expression. *Psychomotor:* Reaction Time; Wrist-Finger Speed; Rate Control; Speed of Limb Movement; Arm-Hand Steadiness. *Physical:* Gross Body Equilibrium; Trunk Strength; Stamina. *Sensory:* Visual Color Discrimination; Speech Clarity; Speech Recognition; Peripheral Vision; Auditory Attention. **General Work Activities—** *Information Input:* Identifying Objects, Actions, and Events; Getting Information; Monitoring Processes, Materials, or Surroundings. *Mental Process:* Making Decisions and Solving Problems; Scheduling Work and Activities; Organizing, Planning, and Prioritizing. *Work Output:* Handling and Moving Objects; Performing General Physical Activities; Documenting or Recording Information. *Interacting with Others:* Communicating with Other Workers; Monitoring and Controlling Resources; Staffing Organizational Units. **Physical Work Conditions—** Walking or Running; Standing; Indoors; Very Hot or Cold; Minor Burns, Cuts, Bites, or Stings. **Other Job Characteristics—**Consequence of Error; Degree of Automation; Importance of Being Exact or Accurate.

Experience—Job Zone 4. A minimum of two to four years of work-related skill, knowledge, or experience is needed. **Job Preparation:** SVP 7.0 to less than 8.0—two years to less than 10 years. **Knowledge—**Administration and Management; Personnel and Human Resources; Customer and Personal Service; Economics and Accounting; Education and Training. **Instructional Programs—**Hospitality Administration/Management, General; Hotel/Motel Administration/Management; Restaurant, Culinary, and Catering Management/Manager; Restaurant/Food Services Management.

Related DOT Jobs—185.137-010 Manager, Fast Food Services; 187.161-010 Executive Chef; 187.167-026 Director, Food Services; 187.167-050 Manager, Agricultural-Labor Camp; 187.167-066 Manager, Camp; 187.167-106 Manager, Food Service; 187.167-126 Manager, Liquor Establishment; 187.167-206 Dietary Manager; 187.167-210 Director, Food and Beverage; 319.137-014 Manager, Flight Kitchen; 319.137-018 Manager, Industrial Cafeteria; 320.137-010 Manager, Boarding House.

11-9061.00 Funeral Directors

- ● **Education/Training Required: Associate's degree**
- ● **Employed: 31,504**
- ● **Annual Earnings: $42,020**
- ● **Growth: 3.0%**
- ● **Annual Job Openings: 3,000**

Perform various tasks to arrange and direct funeral services, such as coordinating transportation of body to mortuary for embalming, interviewing family or other authorized person to arrange details, selecting pallbearers, procuring official for religious rites, and providing transportation for mourners.

Arrange for clergy members to perform needed services. Arrange for pallbearers and inform pallbearers and honorary groups of their duties. Close caskets and lead funeral corteges to churches or burial sites. Consult with families and/or friends of the deceased to arrange funeral details such as obituary notice wording, casket selection, and plans for services. Contact cemeteries to schedule the opening and closing of graves. Discuss and negotiate pre-arranged funerals with clients. Obtain information needed to complete legal documents such as death certificates and burial permits. Offer counsel and comfort to bereaved families and friends. Oversee the preparation and care of the remains of people who have died. Plan placement of caskets at funeral sites and place and adjust lights, fixtures, and floral displays. Plan, schedule, and coordinate funerals, burials, and cremations, arranging such details as the time and place of services. Provide information on funeral service options, products, and merchandise; maintain a casket display area. Provide or arrange

transportation between sites for the remains, mourners, pallbearers, clergy, and flowers. Receive and usher people to their seats for services. Direct preparations and shipment of bodies for out-of-state burial. Inform survivors of benefits for which they may be eligible. Maintain financial records, order merchandise, and prepare accounts. Manage funeral home operations, including hiring and supervising embalmers, funeral attendants, and other staff. Perform embalming duties as necessary.

GOE INFORMATION—Interest Area: 13. General Management and Support. **Work Group:** 13.01. General Management Work and Management of Support Functions. **Personality Type—**Enterprising. Enterprising occupations frequently involve starting up and carrying out projects. These occupations can involve leading people and making many decisions. They sometimes require risk taking and often deal with business. **Work Values—**Social Service; Autonomy; Authority; Security; Compensation. **Skills—**Social Perceptiveness; Management of Material Resources; Service Orientation; Speaking; Coordination; Management of Personnel Resources. **Abilities—***Cognitive:* Oral Comprehension; Oral Expression; Memorization; Written Comprehension; Written Expression. *Psychomotor:* None met the criteria. *Physical:* None met the criteria. *Sensory:* None met the criteria. **General Work Activities—***Information Input:* Getting Information; Identifying Objects, Actions, and Events; Monitoring Processes, Materials, or Surroundings. *Mental Process:* Making Decisions and Solving Problems; Organizing, Planning, and Prioritizing; Scheduling Work and Activities. *Work Output:* Handling and Moving Objects; Documenting or Recording Information; Performing General Physical Activities. *Interacting with Others:* Communicating with Persons Outside Organization; Coordinating the Work and Activities of Others; Establishing and Maintaining Relationships. **Physical Work Conditions—**Sitting; Outdoors; Disease or Infections; Specialized Protective or Safety Attire; Indoors. **Other Job Characteristics—**Consequence of Error; Pace Determined by Speed of Equipment; Importance of Repeating Same Tasks.

Experience—Job Zone 4. A minimum of two to four years of work-related skill, knowledge, or experience is needed. **Job Preparation:** SVP 7.0 to less than 8.0—two years to less than 10 years. **Knowledge—** Customer and Personal Service; Administration and Management; Sales and Marketing; Psychology; Therapy and Counseling. **Instructional Programs—**Funeral Direction/Service; Funeral Service and Mortuary Science, General.

Related DOT Jobs—187.167-030 Director, Funeral.

11-9071.00 Gaming Managers

- ● **Education/Training Required: Work experience plus degree**
- ● **Employed: 4,160**
- ● **Annual Earnings: $53,450**
- ● **Growth: 30.0%**
- ● **Annual Job Openings: Fewer than 500**

Plan, organize, direct, control, or coordinate gaming operations in a casino. Formulate gaming policies for their area of responsibility.

Circulate among gaming tables to ensure that operations are conducted properly, that dealers follow house rules, and that players are not cheating. Direct the distribution of complimentary hotel rooms, meals, and other discounts or free items given to players based on their length of play and betting totals. Direct workers compiling summary sheets that show wager amounts and payoffs for races and events. Establish policies on issues such as the type of gambling offered and the odds, the extension of credit, and the serving of food and beverages. Maintain familiarity with all games used at a facility, as well as strategies and tricks employed in those games. Monitor credit extended to players. Monitor staffing levels to ensure that games and tables are adequately staffed for each shift, arranging for staff rotations and breaks and locating substitute employees as necessary. Prepare work schedules and station assignments; keep attendance records. Resolve customer complaints regarding problems such as payout errors. Review operational expenses, budget estimates, betting accounts, and collection reports for accuracy. Set and maintain a bank and table limit for each game. Track supplies of money to tables and perform any required paperwork. Explain and interpret house rules, such as game rules and betting limits. Interview and hire workers. Notify board attendants of table vacancies so that waiting patrons can play. Record, collect, and pay off bets, issuing receipts as necessary. Remove suspected cheaters, such as card counters and other players who may have systems that shift the odds of winning to their favor. Train new workers and evaluate their performance.

GOE INFORMATION—Interest Area: 11. Recreation, Travel, and Other Personal Services. **Work Group:** 11.01. Managerial Work in Recreation, Travel, and Other Personal Services. **Personality Type—**Enterprising. Enterprising occupations frequently involve starting up and carrying out projects. These occupations can involve leading people and making many decisions. They sometimes require risk taking and often deal with business. **Work Values—**Authority; Social Service; Responsibility; Creativity; Autonomy. **Skills—**Management of Financial Resources; Management of Personnel Resources; Management of Material Resources; Speaking; Negotiation; Critical Thinking; Systems Evaluation; Time Management. **Abilities—***Cognitive:* Mathematical Reasoning; Number Facility; Time Sharing; Problem Sensitivity; Oral Comprehension. *Psychomotor:* None met the criteria. *Physical:* None met the criteria. *Sensory:* Far Vision; Near Vision; Night Vision; Sound Localization; Peripheral Vision. **General Work Activities—***Information Input:* Getting Information; Identifying Objects, Actions, and Events; Monitoring Processes, Materials, or Surroundings. *Mental Process:* Analyzing Data or Information; Scheduling Work and Activities; Organizing, Planning, and Prioritizing. *Work Output:* Documenting or Recording Information; Performing General Physical Activities; Handling and Moving Objects. *Interacting with Others:* Monitoring and Controlling Resources; Communicating with Other Workers; Establishing and Maintaining Relationships. **Physical Work Conditions—**Indoors; Sitting; Walking or Running; Standing. **Other Job Characteristics—**Consequence of Error; Importance of Being Exact or Accurate; Degree of Automation.

Experience—Job Zone 3. Previous work-related skill, knowledge, or experience is required. **Job Preparation:** SVP 6.0 to less than 7.0—more than one year and less than four years. **Knowledge—**Economics and Accounting; Administration and Management; Personnel and Human Resources; Customer and Personal Service; Mathematics. **Instructional Programs—**Personal and Culinary Services, Other.

Related DOT Jobs—187.167-014 Bookmaker; 187.167-070 Manager, Casino; 187.167-134 Manager, Mutuel Department; 343.137-010 Manager, Cardroom.

11-9081.00 Lodging Managers

- **Education/Training Required: Work experience in a related occupation**
- **Employed: 68,387**
- **Annual Earnings: $32,860**
- **Growth: 9.3%**
- **Annual Job Openings: 8,000**

Plan, direct, or coordinate activities of an organization or department that provides lodging and other accommodations.

Coordinate front-office activities of hotels or motels and resolve problems. Manage and maintain temporary or permanent lodging facilities. Answer inquiries pertaining to hotel policies and services and resolve occupants' complaints. Confer and cooperate with other managers in order to ensure coordination of hotel activities. Interview and hire applicants. Assign duties to workers and schedule shifts. Purchase supplies and arrange for outside services, such as deliveries, laundry, maintenance and repair, and trash collection. Receive and process advance registration payments, send out letters of confirmation, and return checks when registrations cannot be accepted. Show, rent, or assign accommodations. Collect payments and record data pertaining to funds and expenditures. Greet and register guests. Arrange telephone answering services, deliver mail and packages, and answer questions regarding locations for eating and entertainment. Observe and monitor staff performance in order to ensure efficient operations and adherence to facility's policies and procedures. Inspect guest rooms, public areas, and grounds for cleanliness and appearance. Book tickets for guests for local tours and attractions. Develop and implement policies and procedures for the operation of a department or establishment. Meet with clients in order to schedule and plan details of conventions, banquets, receptions, and other functions. Organize and coordinate the work of staff and convention personnel for meetings to be held at a particular facility. Participate in financial activities such as the setting of room rates, the establishment of budgets, and the allocation of funds to departments. Perform marketing and public relations activities. Prepare required paperwork pertaining to departmental functions. Provide assistance to staff members by performing activities such as inspecting rooms, setting tables, and doing laundry. Train staff members in their duties.

GOE INFORMATION—Interest Area: 11. Recreation, Travel, and Other Personal Services. **Work Group:** 11.01. Managerial Work in Recreation, Travel, and Other Personal Services. **Personality Type—**Enterprising. Enterprising occupations frequently involve starting up and carrying out projects. These occupations can involve leading people and making many decisions. They sometimes require risk taking and often deal with business. **Work Values—**Authority; Autonomy; Social Service; Responsibility; Good Working Conditions. **Skills—**Management of Material Resources; Management of Personnel Resources; Service Orientation; Management of Financial Resources; Coordination; Repairing; Time Management; Operation and Control. **Abilities—***Cognitive:* Mathematical Reasoning; Perceptual Speed; Spatial Orientation; Flexibility of Closure; Time Sharing. *Psychomotor:* Response Orientation; Speed of Limb Movement; Wrist-Finger Speed; Multilimb Coordination; Rate Control. *Physical:* Dynamic Strength; Stamina; Gross Body Equilibrium; Static Strength; Trunk Strength. *Sensory:* Speech Recognition; Night Vision; Far Vision; Speech Clarity; Peripheral Vision. **General Work Activities—***Information Input:* Getting Information; Identifying Objects, Actions, and Events; Monitoring Processes, Materials, or Surroundings. *Mental Process:* Scheduling Work and Activities; Organizing, Planning, and Prioritizing; Making Decisions and Solving Problems. *Work Output:* Performing General Physical Activities; Handling and Moving Objects; Documenting or Recording Information. *Interacting with Others:* Monitoring and Controlling Resources; Communicating with Other Workers; Performing for or Working with the Public. **Physical Work Conditions—**Outdoors; Very Hot or Cold; Walking or Running; High Places; Minor Burns, Cuts, Bites, or Stings. **Other Job Characteristics—**Consequence of Error; Degree of Automation; Pace Determined by Speed of Equipment.

Experience—Job Zone 3. Previous work-related skill, knowledge, or experience is required. **Job Preparation:** SVP 6.0 to less than 7.0—more than one year and less than four years. **Knowledge—**Customer and Personal Service; Administration and Management; Personnel and Human Resources; Public Safety and Security; Sales and Marketing. **Instructional**

Programs—Hospitality Administration/Management, General; Hospitality and Recreation Marketing Operations; Hotel/Motel Administration/Management; Resort Management; Selling Skills and Sales Operations.

Related DOT Jobs—187.117-038 Manager, Hotel or Motel; 187.137-018 Manager, Front Office; 320.137-014 Manager, Lodging Facilities.

11-9111.00 Medical and Health Services Managers

- ● **Education/Training Required: Work experience plus degree**
- ● **Employed: 249,515**
- ● **Annual Earnings: $59,220**
- ● **Growth: 32.3%**
- ● **Annual Job Openings: 27,000**

Plan, direct, or coordinate medicine and health services in hospitals, clinics, managed care organizations, public health agencies, or similar organizations.

Direct, supervise, and evaluate work activities of medical, nursing, technical, clerical, service, maintenance, and other personnel. Establish objectives and evaluative or operational criteria for units they manage. Direct or conduct recruitment, hiring, and training of personnel. Develop and maintain computerized record management systems to store and process data, such as personnel activities and information, and to produce reports. Develop and implement organizational policies and procedures for the facility or medical unit. Conduct and administer fiscal operations, including accounting, planning budgets, authorizing expenditures, establishing rates for services, and coordinating financial reporting. Establish work schedules and assignments for staff according to workload, space and equipment availability. Maintain communication between governing boards, medical staff, and department heads by attending board meetings and coordinating interdepartmental functioning. Monitor the use of diagnostic services, inpatient beds, facilities, and staff to ensure effective use of resources and assess the need for additional staff, equipment, and services. Maintain awareness of advances in medicine, computerized diagnostic and treatment equipment, data processing technology, government regulations, health insurance changes, and financing options. Manage change in integrated health care delivery systems, such as work restructuring, technological innovations, and shifts in the focus of care. Prepare activity reports to inform management of the status and implementation plans of programs, services, and quality initiatives. Plan, implement, and administer programs and services in a health care or medical facility, including personnel administration, training, and coordination of medical, nursing, and physical plant staff. Consult with medical, business, and community groups to discuss service problems, respond to community needs, enhance public relations, coordinate activities and plans, and promote health programs. Inspect facilities and recommend building or equipment modifications to ensure emergency readiness and compliance to access, safety, and sanitation regulations. Review and analyze facility activities and data to aid planning and cash and risk management and to improve service utilization. Develop or expand and implement medical programs or health services that promote research, rehabilitation, and community health. Develop instructional materials and conduct in-service and community-based educational programs.

GOE INFORMATION—**Interest Area:** 14. Medical and Health Services. **Work Group:** 14.01. Managerial Work in Medical and Health Services. **Personality Type**—Enterprising. Enterprising occupations frequently involve starting up and carrying out projects. These occupations can involve leading people and making many decisions. They sometimes require risk taking and often deal with business. **Work Values**—Authority; Social Service; Creativity; Good Working Conditions; Social Status. **Skills**—Management of Personnel Resources; Critical Thinking; Monitoring; Service Orientation; Management of Material Resources; Persuasion; Learning Strategies; Social Perceptiveness. **Abilities**—*Cognitive:* Originality; Mathematical Reasoning; Deductive Reasoning; Oral Comprehension; Category Flexibility. *Psychomotor:* Finger Dexterity. *Physical:* Trunk Strength; Gross Body Coordination. *Sensory:* Speech Recognition; Speech Clarity; Far Vision; Near Vision; Auditory Attention. **General Work Activities**—*Information Input:* Monitoring Processes, Materials, or Surroundings; Getting Information; Identifying Objects, Actions, and Events. *Mental Process:* Organizing, Planning, and Prioritizing; Updating and Using Relevant Knowledge; Making Decisions and Solving Problems. *Work Output:* Interacting with Computers; Documenting or Recording Information; Handling and Moving Objects. *Interacting with Others:* Establishing and Maintaining Relationships; Resolving Conflict and Negotiating with Others; Guiding, Directing, and Motivating Subordinates. **Physical Work Conditions**—Indoors; Sitting; Disease or Infections; Radiation. **Other Job Characteristics**—Consequence of Error; Importance of Being Exact or Accurate; Degree of Automation.

Experience—Job Zone 5. Extensive skill, knowledge, and experience are needed for these occupations. **Job Preparation:** SVP 7.0 to less than 8.0—two years to less than 10 years. **Knowledge**—Therapy and Counseling; Customer and Personal Service; Education and Training; Personnel and Human Resources; Medicine and Dentistry. **Instructional Programs**—Community Health and Preventive Medicine; Health and Medical Administrative Services, Other; Health Information/Medical Records Administration/Administrator; Health Services Administration; Health Unit Manager/Ward Supervisor; Health/Health Care Administration/Management; Hospital and Health Care Facilities Administration/Management; Medical Staff Services Technology/Technician; Nursing Administration (MSN, MS, PhD); Public Health, General (MPH, DPH).

Related DOT Jobs—076.117-010 Coordinator of Rehabilitation Services; 079.117-010 Emergency Medical Services Coordinator; 079.167-014 Medical-Record Administrator; 169.167-090 Quality Assurance Coordinator; 187.117-010 Administrator, Health Care Facility; 187.117-058 Director, Outpatient Services.

11-9121.00 Natural Sciences Managers

- ● **Education/Training Required: Work experience plus degree**
- ● **Employed: 41,741**
- ● **Annual Earnings: $80,420**
- ● **Growth: 7.6%**
- ● **Annual Job Openings: 4,000**

Plan, direct, or coordinate activities in such fields as life sciences, physical sciences, mathematics, and statistics, as well as research and development in these fields.

Confer with scientists, engineers, regulators, and others to plan and review projects and to provide technical assistance. Design and coordinate successive phases of problem analysis, solution proposals, and testing. Determine scientific and technical goals within broad outlines provided by top management and make detailed plans to accomplish these goals. Develop and implement policies, standards, and procedures for the architectural, scientific, and technical work performed to ensure regulatory compliance and operations enhancement. Plan and direct research, development, and production activities. Prepare project proposals. Advise and assist in obtaining patents or meeting other legal requirements. Conduct own research in field of expertise. Develop client relationships and communicate with clients to explain proposals, present research findings, establish specifications, or discuss project status. Develop innovative technology and train staff for its implementation. Hire, supervise, and evaluate engineers, technicians, researchers, and other staff. Prepare and administer budget, approve and review expenditures, and prepare financial reports. Recruit personnel and oversee the development and maintenance of staff competence. Review project activities and prepare and review research, testing, and operational reports. Make presentations at professional meetings to further knowledge in the field. Provide for stewardship of plant and animal resources and habitats, studying land use, monitoring animal populations, and/or providing shelter, resources, and medical treatment for animals.

GOE INFORMATION—Interest Area: 02. Science, Math, and Engineering. **Work Group:** 02.01. Managerial Work in Science, Math, and Engineering. **Personality Type**—Investigative. Investigative occupations frequently involve working with ideas and require an extensive amount of thinking. These occupations can involve searching for facts and figuring out problems mentally. **Work Values**—Authority; Creativity; Good Working Conditions; Responsibility; Autonomy. **Skills**—Management of Material Resources; Management of Financial Resources; Science; Management of Personnel Resources; Systems Analysis; Systems Evaluation; Coordination; Complex Problem Solving. **Abilities**—*Cognitive:* Mathematical Reasoning; Fluency of Ideas; Written Expression; Written Comprehension; Originality. *Psychomotor:* None met the criteria. *Physical:* None met the criteria. *Sensory:* Speech Clarity; Speech Recognition; Near Vision; Far Vision; Visual Color Discrimination. **General Work Activities**—*Information Input:* Getting Information; Identifying Objects, Actions, and Events; Estimating Needed Characteristics. *Mental Process:* Updating and Using Relevant Knowledge; Analyzing Data or Information; Making Decisions and Solving Problems. *Work Output:* Documenting or Recording Information; Interacting with Computers; Drafting and Specifying Technical Devices. *Interacting with Others:* Communicating with Other Workers; Providing Consultation and Advice to Others; Developing and Building Teams. **Physical Work Conditions**—Sitting; Indoors; Specialized Protective or Safety Attire; Hazardous Conditions; Extremely Bright or Inadequate Lighting. **Other Job Characteristics**—Consequence of Error; Degree of Automation; Importance of Being Exact or Accurate.

Experience—Job Zone 5. Extensive skill, knowledge, and experience are needed for these occupations. **Job Preparation:** SVP 8.0 and above—four years to more than 10 years. **Knowledge**—Chemistry; Administration and Management; Economics and Accounting; Law and Government; Biology. **Instructional Programs**—Acoustics; Algebra and Number Theory; Analysis and Functional Analysis; Analytical Chemistry; Anatomy; Animal Genetics; Animal Physiology; Applied Mathematics; Applied Mathematics, Other; Astronomy; Astrophysics; Atmospheric Chemistry and Climatology; Atmospheric Physics and Dynamics; Atmospheric Sciences and Meteorology, General; Atmospheric Sciences and Meteorology, Other; Atomic/Molecular Physics; Biochemistry; Biological and Biomedical Sciences, Other; Biological and Physical Sciences; Biology/Biological Sciences, General; Biometry/Biometrics; Biophysics; Biopsychology; Biostatistics; Biotechnology; Botany/Plant Biology; Botany/Plant Biology, Other; Cell/Cellular Biology and Anatomical Sciences, Other; Cell/Cellular Biology and Histology; Chemical Physics; Chemistry, General; Chemistry, Other; Computational Mathematics; Ecology; Ecology, Evolution, Systematics, and Population Biology, Other; Elementary Particle Physics; Entomology; Evolutionary Biology; Geochemistry; Geochemistry and Petrology; Geological and Earth Sciences/Geosciences, Other; Geology/Earth Science, General; Geometry/Geometric Analysis; Geophysics and Seismology; Hydrology and Water Resources Science; Immunology; Inorganic Chemistry; Logic; Marine Biology and Biological Oceanography; Mathematics and Computer Science; Mathematics and Statistics, Other; Mathematics, General; Medical Microbiology and Bacteriology; Meteorology; Microbiology, General;

Molecular Biology; Natural Sciences; Neuroscience; Nuclear Physics; Nutrition Sciences; Oceanography, Chemical and Physical; Operations Research; Optics/Optical Sciences; Organic Chemistry; Paleontology; Parasitology; Pathology/Experimental Pathology; Pharmacology; Physical and Theoretical Chemistry; Physical Sciences; Physical Sciences, Other; Physics, General; Physics, Other; Planetary Astronomy and Science; Plant Genetics; Plant Pathology/Phytopathology; Plant Physiology; Plasma and High-Temperature Physics; Polymer Chemistry; others.

Related DOT Jobs—022.161-010 Chemical Laboratory Chief; 029.167-014 Project Manager, Environmental Research; 816.701-010 Technical Director, Chemical Plant.

11-9131.00 Postmasters and Mail Superintendents

- **Education/Training Required: Work experience in a related occupation**
- **Employed: 24,887**
- **Annual Earnings: $44,500**
- **Growth: 2.5%**
- **Annual Job Openings: 2,000**

Direct and coordinate operational, administrative, management, and supportive services of a U.S. post office or coordinate activities of workers engaged in postal and related work in assigned post office.

Confer with suppliers to obtain bids for proposed purchases and to requisition supplies; disburse funds according to federal regulations. Direct and coordinate operational, management, and supportive services of one or a number of postal facilities. Hire and train employees and evaluate their performance. Organize and supervise activities such as the processing of incoming and outgoing mail. Prepare and submit detailed and summary reports of post office activities to designated supervisors. Prepare employee work schedules. Resolve customer complaints. Collect rents for post office boxes. Inform the public of available services and of postal laws and regulations. Issue and cash money orders. Negotiate labor disputes. Select and train postmasters and managers of associate postal units.

GOE INFORMATION—Interest Area: 13. General Management and Support. **Work Group:** 13.01. General Management Work and Management of Support Functions. **Personality Type**—Enterprising. Enterprising occupations frequently involve starting up and carrying out projects. These occupations can involve leading people and making many decisions. They sometimes require risk taking and often deal with business. **Work Values**—Authority; Security; Company Policies and Practices; Good Working Conditions; Compensation. **Skills**—Management of Financial Resources; Negotiation; Management of Personnel Resources; Systems Evaluation; Systems Analysis; Management of Material Resources; Complex Problem Solving; Coordination. **Abilities**—*Cognitive:* Written Expression; Oral Comprehension; Oral Expression; Written Comprehension; Time Sharing. *Psychomotor:* None met the criteria. *Physical:* None met the criteria. *Sensory:* Speech Recognition; Speech Clarity. **General Work Activities**—*Information Input:* Getting Information; Monitoring Processes, Materials, or Surroundings; Identifying Objects, Actions, and Events. *Mental Process:* Making Decisions and Solving Problems; Scheduling Work and Activities; Organizing, Planning, and Prioritizing. *Work Output:* Documenting or Recording Information; Performing General Physical Activities; Handling and Moving Objects. *Interacting with Others:* Resolving Conflict and Negotiating with Others; Communicating with Other Workers; Guiding, Directing, and Motivating Subordinates. **Physical Work Conditions**—Indoors. **Other Job Characteristics**—Importance of Being Exact or Accurate; Consequence of Error; Importance of Repeating Same Tasks.

Experience—Job Zone 4. A minimum of two to four years of work-related skill, knowledge, or experience is needed. **Job Preparation:** SVP 7.0 to less than 8.0—two years to less than 10 years. **Knowledge**—Personnel and Human Resources; Administration and Management; Education and Training; Economics and Accounting; Customer and Personal Service. **Instructional Programs**—Public Administration.

Related DOT Jobs—188.167-066 Postmaster; 188.167-086 Sectional Center Manager, Postal Service.

11-9141.00 Property, Real Estate, and Community Association Managers

- **Education/Training Required: Bachelor's degree**
- **Employed: 270,116**
- **Annual Earnings: $36,290**
- **Growth: 22.7%**
- **Annual Job Openings: 24,000**

Plan, direct, or coordinate selling, buying, leasing, or governance activities of commercial, industrial, or residential real estate properties.

Act as liaisons between on-site managers or tenants and owners. Confer regularly with community association members to ensure that their needs are being met. Determine and certify the eligibility of prospective tenants, following government regulations. Direct and coordinate the activities of staff and contract personnel and evaluate their performance. Direct collection of monthly assessments, rental fees, and deposits and payment of insurance premiums, mortgage, taxes, and incurred operating expenses. Inspect grounds, facilities, and equipment routinely to determine necessity of repairs or maintenance. Investigate complaints, disturbances, and violations; and resolve problems, following management rules and regulations. Maintain records of sales, rental, or usage activity; special permits issued; maintenance and operating costs; or property availability. Manage and oversee operations, maintenance, administration, and improvement of commercial, industrial, or residential properties. Market vacant space to prospective tenants through leasing agents, advertising, or other methods. Meet with prospective tenants to show properties, explain terms of occupancy, and provide information about local areas. Negotiate the sale, lease, or development of property; complete or review appropriate documents and forms. Plan, schedule, and coordinate general maintenance, major repairs, and remodeling or construction projects for commercial or residential properties. Prepare and administer contracts for provision of property services such as cleaning, maintenance, and security services. Prepare detailed budgets and financial reports for properties. Purchase building and maintenance supplies, equipment, or furniture. Analyze information on property values, taxes, zoning, population growth, and traffic volume and patterns in order to determine if properties should be acquired. Clean common areas, change light bulbs, and make minor property repairs. Confer with legal authorities to ensure that renting and advertising practices are not discriminatory and that properties comply with state and federal regulations. Maintain contact with insurance carriers, fire and police departments, and other agencies to ensure protection and compliance with codes and regulations. Meet with boards of directors and committees to discuss and resolve legal and environmental issues or disputes between neighbors. Meet with clients to negotiate management and service contracts, determine priorities, and discuss the financial and operational status of properties. Review rents to ensure that they are in line with rental markets. Solicit and analyze bids from contractors for repairs, renovations, and maintenance. Contract with architectural firms to draw up detailed plans for new structures. Negotiate short- and long-term loans to finance construction and ownership of structures.

GOE INFORMATION—**Interest Area:** 13. General Management and Support. **Work Group:** 13.01. General Management Work and Management of Support Functions. **Personality Type**—Enterprising. Enterprising occupations frequently involve starting up and carrying out projects. These occupations can involve leading people and making many decisions. They sometimes require risk taking and often deal with business. **Work Values**—Authority; Autonomy; Responsibility; Variety; Activity. **Skills**—Management of Financial Resources; Management of Personnel Resources; Management of Material Resources; Negotiation; Systems Evaluation; Coordination; Systems Analysis; Judgment and Decision Making. **Abilities**—*Cognitive:* Mathematical Reasoning; Number Facility; Written Expression; Oral Expression; Oral Comprehension. *Psychomotor:* None met the criteria. *Physical:* None met the criteria. *Sensory:* Speech Recognition; Speech Clarity; Sound Localization; Auditory Attention; Night Vision. **General Work Activities**—*Information Input:* Getting Information; Identifying Objects, Actions, and Events; Estimating Needed Characteristics. *Mental Process:* Organizing, Planning, and Prioritizing; Scheduling Work and Activities; Evaluating Information Against Standards. *Work Output:* Documenting or Recording Information; Performing General Physical Activities; Handling and Moving Objects. *Interacting with Others:* Communicating with Other Workers; Monitoring and Controlling Resources; Resolving Conflict and Negotiating with Others. **Physical Work Conditions**—Outdoors; Walking or Running; Sitting; Indoors; Kneeling, Crouching, or Crawling. **Other Job Characteristics**—Consequence of Error; Importance of Being Exact or Accurate; Degree of Automation.

Experience—Job Zone 4. A minimum of two to four years of work-related skill, knowledge, or experience is needed. **Job Preparation:** SVP 7.0 to less than 8.0—two years to less than 10 years. **Knowledge**—Administration and Management; Sales and Marketing; Law and Government; Personnel and Human Resources; Economics and Accounting. **Instructional Programs**—Real Estate.

Related DOT Jobs—186.117-062 Rental Manager, Public Events Facilities; 186.167-018 Manager, Apartment House; 186.167-030 Manager, Housing Project; 186.167-042 Manager, Market; 186.167-046 Manager, Property; 186.167-062 Condominium Manager; 186.167-066 Manager, Real-Estate Firm; 187.167-190 Superintendent, Building.

11-9151.00 Social and Community Service Managers

- **Education/Training Required: Bachelor's degree**
- **Employed: 128,030**
- **Annual Earnings: $41,260**
- **Growth: 24.8%**
- **Annual Job Openings: 13,000**

Plan, organize, or coordinate the activities of a social service program or community outreach organization. Oversee the program or organization's budget and policies regarding participant involvement, program requirements, and benefits. Work may involve directing social workers, counselors, or probation officers.

Act as consultants to agency staff and other community programs regarding the interpretation of program-related federal, state, and county regulations and policies. Direct activities of professional and technical staff members and volunteers. Direct fundraising activities and the preparation of public relations materials. Establish and maintain relationships with other agencies and organizations in community in order to meet community needs and to ensure that services are not duplicated. Establish and oversee administrative procedures to meet objectives set by boards of directors or senior management. Evaluate the work of staff and volunteers in order to ensure that programs are of appropriate quality and that resources are used effectively. Implement and evaluate staff training programs. Participate in the determination of organizational policies regarding such issues as participant eligibility, program requirements, and program benefits. Plan and administer budgets for programs, equipment, and support services. Prepare and maintain records and reports, such as budgets, personnel records, or training manuals. Recruit, interview, and hire or sign up volunteers and staff. Research and analyze member or community needs in order to determine program directions and goals. Speak to community groups to explain and interpret agency purposes, programs, and policies. Analyze proposed legislation, regulations, or rule changes in order to determine how agency services could be impacted. Represent organizations in relations with governmental and media institutions.

GOE INFORMATION—Interest Area: 12. Education and Social Service. **Work Group:** 12.01. Managerial Work in Education and Social Service. **Personality Type—**Social. Social occupations frequently involve working with, communicating with, and teaching people. These occupations often involve helping or providing service to others. **Work Values—**Social Service; Authority; Autonomy; Security; Creativity. **Skills—**Management of Financial Resources; Service Orientation; Speaking; Systems Analysis; Instructing; Social Perceptiveness; Complex Problem Solving; Coordination. **Abilities—***Cognitive:* Fluency of Ideas; Mathematical Reasoning; Written Expression; Originality; Perceptual Speed. *Psychomotor:* Response Orientation. *Physical:* Gross Body Equilibrium. *Sensory:* Speech Clarity; Far Vision; Speech Recognition; Sound Localization; Near Vision. **General Work Activities—***Information Input:* Getting Information; Identifying Objects, Actions, and Events; Monitoring Processes, Materials, or Surroundings. *Mental Process:* Organizing, Planning, and Prioritizing; Judging Qualities of Things, Services, or Other People's Work; Making Decisions and Solving Problems. *Work Output:* Documenting or Recording Information; Handling and Moving Objects; Performing General Physical Activities. *Interacting with Others:* Communicating with Other Workers; Providing Consultation and Advice to Others; Communicating with Persons Outside Organization. **Physical Work Conditions—**Sitting; Indoors; Disease or Infections. **Other Job Characteristics—**Consequence of Error; Importance of Being Exact or Accurate; Degree of Automation.

Experience—Job Zone 4. A minimum of two to four years of work-related skill, knowledge, or experience is needed. **Job Preparation:** SVP 7.0 to less than 8.0—two years to less than 10 years. **Knowledge—**Education and Training; Customer and Personal Service; Personnel and Human Resources; Administration and Management; Sociology and Anthropology. **Instructional Programs—**Business Administration and Management, General; Business, Management, Marketing, and Related Support Services, Other; Business/Commerce, General; Community Organization and Advocacy; Entrepreneurship/Entrepreneurial Studies; Human Services, General; Non-Profit/Public/Organizational Management; Public Administration.

Related DOT Jobs—187.117-022 District Adviser; 187.117-026 Executive Director, Sheltered Workshop; 187.117-046 Program Director, Group Work; 187.117-066 Executive Director, Red Cross; 187.167-022 Coordinator, Volunteer Services; 187.167-038 Director, Volunteer Services; 187.167-214 Director, Service; 187.167-234 Director, Community Organization; 195.117-010 Administrator, Social Welfare; 195.167-022 Director, Field; 195.167-038 Rehabilitation Center Manager.

11-9199.99 Managers, All Other

- **Education/Training Required: No data available.**
- **Employed: No data available.**
- **Annual Earnings: No data available.**
- **Growth: 9.5%**
- **Annual Job Openings: 96,000**

All managers not listed separately.

No task data available.

GOE INFORMATION—Interest Area: 13. General Management and Support. **Work Group:** 13.01. General Management Work and Management of Support Functions. **Note:** The Department of Labor has not collected some data for this job, so it has fewer details than the other descriptions.

Instructional Programs—Arts Management; Business Administration and Management, General; Business Administration, Management, and Operations, Other; Business, Management, Marketing, and Related Support Services, Other; Business/Commerce, General; Entrepreneurial and Small Business Operations, Other; Entrepreneurship/Entrepreneurial Studies; Franchising and Franchise Operations; Hospitality Administration/Management, Other; Non-Profit/Public/Organizational Management; Public Administration; Public Administration and Social Service Professions, Other; Small Business Administration/Management; Theatre/Theatre Arts Management; Tourism and Travel Services Management.

Related DOT Jobs—072.117-010 Director, Dental Services; 075.117-010 Consultant, Educational, State Board Of Nursing; 075.117-034 Executive Director, Nurses' Association; 090.164-010 Laboratory Manager; 090.167-034 Director, Field Services; 096.161-010 Home-Service Director; 096.167-010 District Extension Service Agent; 096.167-014 Specialist-In-Charge, Extension Service; 153.137-010 Manager, Pool; 168.167-066 Quality-Control Coordinator; 169.267-022 Secretary, Board-Of-Education; 181.167-010 Manager, Field Party, Geophysical Prospecting; 183.167-030 Service Supervisor, Leased Machinery And Equipment; 184.117-030 Manager, Area Development; 184.117-046 Manager, Irrigation District; 184.117-062 Manager, Station; 184.117-070 Operations Manager; 184.117-074 Revenue-Settlements Administrator; 184.117-082 Superintendent, Communications; 184.161-010 Cable Supervisor; others.

13-0000

Business and Financial Operations Occupations

13-1000 Business Operations Specialists

13-1011.00 Agents and Business Managers of Artists, Performers, and Athletes

- Education/Training Required: Work experience plus degree
- Employed: 17,461
- Annual Earnings: $55,550
- Growth: 27.9%
- Annual Job Openings: 2,000

Represent and promote artists, performers, and athletes to prospective employers. May handle contract negotiation and other business matters for clients.

Negotiates with management, promoters, union officials, and other persons to obtain contracts for clients, such as entertainers, artists, and athletes. Manages business affairs for clients, such as obtaining travel and lodging accommodations, selling tickets, marketing and advertising, and paying expenses. Schedules promotional or performance engagements for clients. Advises clients on financial and legal matters, such as investments and taxes. Collects fees, commission, or other payment, according to contract terms. Obtains information and inspects facilities, equipment, and accommodations of potential performance venue. Hires trainer or coach to advise client on performance matters, such as training techniques or presentation of act. Prepares periodic accounting statements for clients concerning financial affairs. Conducts auditions or interviews new clients.

GOE INFORMATION—Interest Area: 01. Arts, Entertainment, and Media. **Work Group:** 01.01. Managerial Work in Arts, Entertainment, and Media. **Personality Type**—Enterprising. Enterprising occupations frequently involve starting up and carrying out projects. These occupations can involve leading people and making many decisions. They sometimes require risk taking and often deal with business. **Work Values**—Social Service; Autonomy; Authority; Good Working Conditions; Variety. **Skills**—Negotiation; Management of Financial Resources; Speaking; Time Management; Management of Personnel Resources; Service Orientation; Complex Problem Solving; Critical Thinking. **Abilities**—*Cognitive:* Oral Expression; Fluency of Ideas; Originality; Mathematical Reasoning; Oral Comprehension. *Psychomotor:* None met the criteria. *Physical:* None met the criteria. *Sensory:* Speech Clarity; Speech Recognition; Auditory Attention. **General Work Activities**—*Information Input:* Getting Information; Identifying Objects, Actions, and Events; Monitoring Processes, Materials, or Surroundings. *Mental Process:* Organizing, Planning, and Prioritizing; Scheduling Work and Activities; Making Decisions and Solving Problems. *Work Output:* Documenting or Recording Information; Performing General Physical Activities; Handling and Moving Objects. *Interacting with Others:* Resolving Conflict and Negotiating with Others; Monitoring and Controlling Resources; Communicating with Persons Outside Organization. **Physical Work Conditions**—Outdoors; Sitting. **Other Job Characteristics**—Consequence of Error; Degree of Automation; Importance of Repeating Same Tasks.

Experience—Job Zone 3. Previous work-related skill, knowledge, or experience is required. **Job Preparation:** SVP 6.0 to less than 7.0—more than one year and less than four years. **Knowledge**—Sales and Marketing; Personnel and Human Resources; Economics and Accounting; Administration and Management; Fine Arts. **Instructional Programs**—Arts Management; Purchasing, Procurement/Acquisitions, and Contracts Management.

Related DOT Jobs—153.117-014 Manager, Athlete; 191.117-010 Artist's Manager; 191.117-014 Booking Manager; 191.117-018 Business Manager; 191.117-022 Circus Agent; 191.117-026 Jockey Agent; 191.117-034 Literary Agent; 191.117-038 Manager, Touring Production; 191.167-010 Advance Agent.

13-1021.00 Purchasing Agents and Buyers, Farm Products

- Education/Training Required: Work experience in a related occupation
- Employed: 19,600
- Annual Earnings: $38,680
- Growth: 16.8%
- Annual Job Openings: 2,000

Purchase farm products for further processing or resale.

Negotiates contracts with farmers for production or purchase of agricultural products such as milk, grains, and Christmas trees. Arranges sales, loans, or financing for supplies such as equipment, seed, feed, fertilizer, and chemicals. Reviews orders and determines product types and quantities required to meet demand. Plans and arranges for transportation for crops, milk, or other products to dairy or processing facility. Inspects and tests crops or other farm products to determine quality and to detect evidence of disease or insect damage. Estimates production possibilities by surveying property and studying factors such as history of crop rotation, soil fertility, and irrigation facilities. Maintains records of business transactions. Advises farm groups and growers on land preparation and livestock care to maximize quantity and quality of production. Coordinates and directs activities or workers engaged in cutting, transporting, storing, or milling products and in maintaining records. Writes articles for publication.

GOE INFORMATION—Interest Area: 13. General Management and Support. **Work Group:** 13.02. Management Support. **Personality Type**—Enterprising. Enterprising occupations frequently involve starting up and carrying out projects. These occupations can involve leading people and making many decisions. They sometimes require risk taking and often deal with business. **Work Values**—Pleasant Co-workers; Responsibility; Authority; Autonomy; Advancement. **Skills**—Negotiation; Writing; Mathematics; Speaking; Management of Financial Resources; Management of Material Resources; Coordination; Persuasion. **Abilities**—*Cognitive:* Written Expression; Mathematical Reasoning; Number Facility; Oral Expression; Category Flexibility. *Psychomotor:* None met the criteria. *Physical:* Gross Body Equilibrium; Stamina; Dynamic Flexibility. *Sensory:* Speech Clarity; Speech Recognition; Glare Sensitivity; Near Vision; Far Vision. **General Work Activities**—*Information Input:* Identifying Objects, Actions, and Events; Getting Information; Inspecting Equipment, Structures, or Materials. *Mental Process:* Making Decisions and Solving Problems; Judging Qualities of Things, Services, or Other People's Work; Organizing, Planning, and Prioritizing. *Work Output:* Documenting or Recording Information; Interacting with Computers; Drafting and Specifying Technical Devices. *Interacting with Others:* Communicating with Persons Outside Organization; Resolving Conflict and Negotiating with Others; Providing Consultation and Advice to Others. **Physical Work Conditions**—Walking or Running; Outdoors; Extremely Bright or Inadequate Lighting; Sitting; Hazardous Equipment. **Other Job Characteristics**—Importance of Being Exact or Accurate; Consequence of Error; Pace Determined by Speed of Equipment.

Experience—Job Zone 4. A minimum of two to four years of work-related skill, knowledge, or experience is needed. **Job Preparation:** SVP 7.0 to less than 8.0—two years to less than 10 years. **Knowledge**—Food Production; Production and Processing; Biology; Communications and Media; Economics and Accounting. **Instructional Programs**—Agricultural/Farm Supplies Retailing and Wholesaling.

Related DOT Jobs—162.117-010 Christmas-Tree Contractor; 162.117-022 Field Contractor; 162.117-026 Field-Contact Technician; 162.167-010 Buyer, Grain; 162.167-018 Clean-Rice Broker.

13-1022.00 Wholesale and Retail Buyers, Except Farm Products

- **Education/Training Required: Bachelor's degree**
- **Employed: 147,726**
- **Annual Earnings: $38,590**
- **Growth: −8.7%**
- **Annual Job Openings: 18,000**

Buy merchandise or commodities, other than farm products, for resale to consumers at the wholesale or retail level, including both durable and nondurable goods. Analyze past buying trends, sales records, price, and quality of merchandise to determine value and yield. Select, order, and authorize payment for merchandise according to contractual agreements. May conduct meetings with sales personnel and introduce new products.

Examine, select, order, and purchase at the most favorable price merchandise consistent with quality, quantity, and specification requirements and other factors. Negotiate prices, discount terms, and transportation arrangements for merchandise. Analyze and monitor sales records, trends, and economic conditions to anticipate consumer buying patterns and determine what the company will sell and how much inventory is needed. Interview and work closely with vendors to obtain and develop desired products. Authorize payment of invoices or return of merchandise. Inspect merchandise or products to determine value or yield. Set or recommend mark-up rates, mark-down rates, and selling prices for merchandise. Confer with sales and purchasing personnel to obtain information about customer needs and preferences. Consult with store or merchandise managers about budget and goods to be purchased. Conduct staff meetings with sales personnel to introduce new merchandise. Manage the department for which they buy. Use computers to organize and locate inventory; operate spreadsheet and word-processing software. Train and supervise sales and clerical staff. Provide clerks with information to print on price tags, such as price, mark-ups or mark-downs, manufacturer number, season code, and style number. Determine which products should be featured in advertising, the advertising medium to be used, and when the ads should be run. Monitor competitors' sales activities by following their advertisements in newspapers and other media.

GOE INFORMATION—**Interest Area:** 13. General Management and Support. **Work Group:** 13.02. Management Support. **Personality Type**—Enterprising. Enterprising occupations frequently involve starting up and carrying out projects. These occupations can involve leading people and making many decisions. They sometimes require risk taking and often deal with business. **Work Values**—Advancement; Good Working Conditions; Creativity; Variety; Responsibility. **Skills**—Management of Material Resources; Management of Financial Resources; Equipment Selection; Service Orientation; Negotiation; Quality Control Analysis; Critical Thinking; Instructing. **Abilities**—*Cognitive:* Mathematical Reasoning; Deductive Reasoning; Inductive Reasoning; Category Flexibility; Flexibility of Closure. *Psychomotor:* None met the criteria. *Physical:*

None met the criteria. *Sensory:* Speech Recognition; Speech Clarity; Near Vision; Visual Color Discrimination; Far Vision. **General Work Activities**—*Information Input:* Estimating Needed Characteristics; Monitoring Processes, Materials, or Surroundings; Inspecting Equipment, Structures, or Materials. *Mental Process:* Organizing, Planning, and Prioritizing; Updating and Using Relevant Knowledge; Thinking Creatively. *Work Output:* Performing General Physical Activities; Interacting with Computers; Handling and Moving Objects. *Interacting with Others:* Establishing and Maintaining Relationships; Performing for or Working with the Public; Influencing Others or Selling. **Physical Work Conditions**—Walking or Running; Indoors; Sitting; Climbing Ladders, Scaffolds, Poles, etc. **Other Job Characteristics**—Consequence of Error; Importance of Being Exact or Accurate; Degree of Automation.

Experience—Job Zone 3. Previous work-related skill, knowledge, or experience is required. **Job Preparation:** SVP 6.0 to less than 7.0—more than one year and less than four years. **Knowledge**—Sales and Marketing; Customer and Personal Service; Clerical; Economics and Accounting; Administration and Management. **Instructional Programs**—Apparel and Accessories Marketing Operations; Apparel and Textile Marketing Management; Fashion Merchandising; Merchandising and Buying Operations; Sales, Distribution, and Marketing Operations, General.

Related DOT Jobs—162.157-018 Buyer; 162.157-022 Buyer, Assistant.

13-1023.00 Purchasing Agents, Except Wholesale, Retail, and Farm Products

- **Education/Training Required: Bachelor's degree**
- **Employed: 236,919**
- **Annual Earnings: $43,230**
- **Growth: 12.3%**
- **Annual Job Openings: 23,000**

Purchase machinery, equipment, tools, parts, supplies, or services necessary for the operation of an establishment. Purchase raw or semi-finished materials for manufacturing.

Analyze price proposals, financial reports, and other data and information to determine reasonable prices. Confer with staff, users, and vendors to discuss defective or unacceptable goods or services and determine corrective action. Evaluate and monitor contract performance to ensure compliance with contractual obligations and to determine need for changes. Interview vendors and visit suppliers' plants and distribution centers to examine and learn about products, services, and prices. Maintain and review computerized or manual records of items purchased, costs, delivery, product performance, and inventories. Monitor shipments to ensure that goods come in on time; and in the event of problems, trace shipments and follow up on undelivered goods. Negotiate or renegotiate and administer contracts with suppliers, vendors, and other representatives. Prepare purchase orders, solicit bid proposals, and review requisitions for goods and services. Purchase the highest quality merchandise at the lowest possible price and in correct amounts. Research and evaluate suppliers based on price, quality, selection, service, support, availability, reliability, production and distribution capabilities, and the supplier's reputation and history. Review catalogs, industry periodicals, directories, trade journals, and Internet sites and consult with other department personnel to locate necessary goods and services. Study sales records and inventory levels of current stock to develop strategic purchasing programs that facilitate employee access to supplies. Write and review product specifications, maintaining a working technical knowledge of the goods or services to be purchased. Arrange the payment of duty and freight charges. Attend meetings, trade shows, conferences, conventions, and seminars to network with people in other purchasing departments.

Formulate policies and procedures for bid proposals and procurement of goods and services. Hire, train, and/or supervise purchasing clerks, buyers, and expediters. Monitor and follow applicable laws and regulations. Monitor changes affecting supply and demand, tracking market conditions, price trends, or futures markets. Negotiate leases of land and rights-of-way.

GOE INFORMATION—Interest Area: 13. General Management and Support. **Work Group:** 13.02. Management Support. **Personality Type—**Enterprising. Enterprising occupations frequently involve starting up and carrying out projects. These occupations can involve leading people and making many decisions. They sometimes require risk taking and often deal with business. **Work Values—**Authority; Variety; Advancement; Compensation; Autonomy. **Skills—**Management of Financial Resources; Negotiation; Persuasion; Judgment and Decision Making; Mathematics; Systems Evaluation; Management of Material Resources; Systems Analysis. **Abilities—***Cognitive:* Oral Expression; Mathematical Reasoning; Written Expression; Written Comprehension; Number Facility. *Psychomotor:* None met the criteria. *Physical:* None met the criteria. *Sensory:* Speech Recognition. **General Work Activities—***Information Input:* Getting Information; Monitoring Processes, Materials, or Surroundings; Identifying Objects, Actions, and Events. *Mental Process:* Making Decisions and Solving Problems; Analyzing Data or Information; Judging Qualities of Things, Services, or Other People's Work. *Work Output:* Documenting or Recording Information; Handling and Moving Objects; Interacting with Computers. *Interacting with Others:* Resolving Conflict and Negotiating with Others; Communicating with Other Workers; Communicating with Persons Outside Organization. **Physical Work Conditions—**Sitting; Indoors. **Other Job Characteristics—**Consequence of Error; Importance of Being Exact or Accurate; Pace Determined by Speed of Equipment.

Experience—Job Zone 4. A minimum of two to four years of work-related skill, knowledge, or experience is needed. **Job Preparation:** SVP 7.0 to less than 8.0—two years to less than 10 years. **Knowledge—**Administration and Management; Economics and Accounting; Sales and Marketing; Computers and Electronics; Law and Government. **Instructional Programs—**Sales, Distribution, and Marketing Operations, General.

Related DOT Jobs—162.117-018 Contract Specialist; 162.157-030 Outside Property Agent; 162.157-038 Purchasing Agent; 163.117-010 Manager, Contracts.

13-1031.00 Claims Adjusters, Examiners, and Investigators

- Education/Training Required: Long-term on-the-job training
- Employed: 193,989
- Annual Earnings: $42,440
- Growth: 15.1%
- Annual Job Openings: 25,000

Review settled claims to determine that payments and settlements have been made in accordance with company practices and procedures, ensuring that proper methods have been followed. Report overpayments, underpayments, and other irregularities. Confer with legal counsel on claims requiring litigation.

No task data available.

GOE INFORMATION—Interest Area: 13. General Management and Support. **Work Group:** 13.02. Management Support. **Note:** The Department of Labor has not collected some data for this job, so it has fewer details than the other descriptions.

Instructional Programs—Health/Medical Claims Examiner; Insurance.

Related DOT Jobs—168.267-014 Claim Examiner; 191.167-014 Claim Agent; 241.217-010 Claim Adjuster; 241.267-018 Claim Examiner.

13-1031.01 Claims Examiners, Property and Casualty Insurance

- Education/Training Required: Long-term on-the-job training
- Employed: No data available.
- Annual Earnings: $42,440
- Growth: 15.1%
- Annual Job Openings: 25,000

Review settled insurance claims to determine that payments and settlements have been made in accordance with company practices and procedures. Report overpayments, underpayments, and other irregularities. Confer with legal counsel on claims requiring litigation.

Adjust reserves and provide reserve recommendations to ensure that reserving activities are consistent with corporate policies. Communicate with reinsurance brokers to obtain information necessary for processing claims. Confer with legal counsel on claims requiring litigation. Contact and/or interview claimants, doctors, medical specialists, or employers to get additional information. Examine claims investigated by insurance adjusters, further investigating questionable claims to determine whether to authorize payments. Investigate, evaluate, and settle claims, applying technical knowledge and human relations skills to effect fair and prompt disposal of cases and to contribute to a reduced loss ratio. Pay and process claims within designated authority level. Present cases and participate in their discussion at claim committee meetings. Report overpayments, underpayments, and other irregularities. Resolve complex severe exposure claims by using high-service-oriented file handling. Supervise claims adjusters to ensure that adjusters have followed proper methods. Verify and analyze data used in settling claims to ensure that claims are valid and that settlements are made according to company practices and procedures. Conduct detailed bill reviews to implement sound litigation management and expense control. Enter claim payments, reserves, and new claims on computer system, inputting concise yet sufficient file documentation. Maintain claim files, such as records of settled claims and an inventory of claims requiring detailed analysis. Prepare reports to be submitted to company's data processing department.

GOE INFORMATION—Interest Area: 13. General Management and Support. **Work Group:** 13.02. Management Support. **Personality Type—**Conventional. Conventional occupations frequently involve following set procedures and routines. These occupations can include working with data and details more than with ideas. Usually there is a clear line of authority to follow. **Work Values—**Advancement; Supervision, Human Relations; Company Policies and Practices; Good Working Conditions; Responsibility. **Skills—**Mathematics; Reading Comprehension; Writing; Monitoring; Judgment and Decision Making; Critical Thinking; Speaking; Complex Problem Solving. **Abilities—***Cognitive:* Number Facility; Mathematical Reasoning; Oral Comprehension; Written Comprehension; Oral Expression. *Psychomotor:* None met the criteria. *Physical:* None met the criteria. *Sensory:* Speech Clarity. **General Work Activities—***Information Input:* Getting Information; Identifying Objects, Actions, and Events; Monitoring Processes, Materials, or Surroundings. *Mental Process:* Analyzing Data or Information; Making Decisions and Solving Problems; Evaluating Information Against Standards. *Work Output:* Documenting or Recording Information; Interacting with Computers; Handling and Moving Objects. *Interacting with Others:* Communicating with Other Workers; Communicating with Persons Outside Organization; Interpreting Meaning of Information for Others. **Physical Work

Conditions—Sitting; Indoors. **Other Job Characteristics**—Importance of Being Exact or Accurate; Consequence of Error; Importance of Repeating Same Tasks.

Experience—Job Zone 4. A minimum of two to four years of work-related skill, knowledge, or experience is needed. **Job Preparation:** SVP 7.0 to less than 8.0—two years to less than 10 years. **Knowledge**—Law and Government; Economics and Accounting; Mathematics; Communications and Media; Computers and Electronics. **Instructional Programs**—Health/Medical Claims Examiner; Insurance.

Related DOT Jobs—168.267-014 Claim Examiner.

13-1031.02 Insurance Adjusters, Examiners, and Investigators

- Education/Training Required: **Long-term on-the-job training**
- Employed: **No data available.**
- Annual Earnings: **$42,440**
- Growth: **15.1%**
- Annual Job Openings: **25,000**

Investigate, analyze, and determine the extent of insurance company's liability concerning personal, casualty, or property loss or damages and attempt to effect settlement with claimants. Correspond with or interview medical specialists, agents, witnesses, or claimants to compile information. Calculate benefit payments and approve payment of claims within a certain monetary limit.

Investigate and assess damage to property. Interview or correspond with claimant and witnesses, consult police and hospital records, and inspect property damage to determine extent of liability. Interview or correspond with agents and claimants to correct errors or omissions and to investigate questionable claims. Analyze information gathered by investigation and report findings and recommendations. Negotiate claim settlements and recommend litigation when settlement cannot be negotiated. Examine titles to property to determine validity and act as company agent in transactions with property owners. Examine claims form and other records to determine insurance coverage. Collect evidence to support contested claims in court. Prepare report of findings of investigation. Communicate with former associates to verify employment record and to obtain background information regarding persons or businesses applying for credit. Refer questionable claims to investigator or claims adjuster for investigation or settlement. Obtain credit information from banks and other credit services.

GOE INFORMATION—Interest Area: 13. General Management and Support. **Work Group:** 13.02. Management Support. **Personality Type**—Enterprising. Enterprising occupations frequently involve starting up and carrying out projects. These occupations can involve leading people and making many decisions. They sometimes require risk taking and often deal with business. **Work Values**—Advancement; Company Policies and Practices; Ability Utilization; Responsibility; Supervision, Human Relations. **Skills**—Systems Evaluation; Active Listening; Writing; Critical Thinking; Speaking; Complex Problem Solving; Reading Comprehension; Judgment and Decision Making. **Abilities**—*Cognitive:* Written Expression; Oral Expression; Mathematical Reasoning; Written Comprehension; Number Facility. *Psychomotor:* None met the criteria. *Physical:* None met the criteria. *Sensory:* Near Vision; Speech Clarity; Far Vision; Speech Recognition; Auditory Attention. **General Work Activities**—*Information Input:* Getting Information; Identifying Objects, Actions, and Events; Monitoring Processes, Materials, or Surroundings. *Mental Process:* Evaluating Information Against Standards; Judging Quali-

ties of Things, Services, or Other People's Work; Processing Information. *Work Output:* Documenting or Recording Information; Handling and Moving Objects; Performing General Physical Activities. *Interacting with Others:* Communicating with Other Workers; Communicating with Persons Outside Organization; Establishing and Maintaining Relationships. **Physical Work Conditions**—Sitting; Cramped Work Space or Awkward Positions; Climbing Ladders, Scaffolds, Poles, etc.; Radiation; Keeping or Regaining Balance. **Other Job Characteristics**—Importance of Repeating Same Tasks; Pace Determined by Speed of Equipment; Degree of Automation.

Experience—Job Zone 3. Previous work-related skill, knowledge, or experience is required. **Job Preparation:** SVP 6.0 to less than 7.0—more than one year and less than four years. **Knowledge**—Personnel and Human Resources; Economics and Accounting; Law and Government; Public Safety and Security; Mathematics. **Instructional Programs**—Health/Medical Claims Examiner; Insurance.

Related DOT Jobs—191.167-014 Claim Agent; 241.217-010 Claim Adjuster; 241.267-018 Claim Examiner.

13-1032.00 Insurance Appraisers, Auto Damage

- Education/Training Required: **Long-term on-the-job training**
- Employed: **12,739**
- Annual Earnings: **$41,810**
- Growth: **14.3%**
- Annual Job Openings: **2,000**

Appraise automobile or other vehicle damage to determine cost of repair for insurance claim settlement and seek agreement with automotive repair shop on cost of repair. Prepare insurance forms to indicate repair cost or cost estimates and recommendations.

Examine damaged vehicle to determine extent of structural, body, mechanical, electrical, or interior damage. Arrange to have damage appraised by another appraiser to resolve disagreement with shop on repair cost. Determine salvage value on total-loss vehicle. Evaluate practicality of repair as opposed to payment of market value of vehicle before accident. Estimate parts and labor to repair damage, using standard automotive labor- and parts-cost manuals and knowledge of automotive repair. Review repair-cost estimates with automobile repair shop to secure agreement on cost of repairs. Prepare insurance forms to indicate repair-cost estimates and recommendations.

GOE INFORMATION—Interest Area: 13. General Management and Support. **Work Group:** 13.02. Management Support. **Personality Type**—Conventional. Conventional occupations frequently involve following set procedures and routines. These occupations can include working with data and details more than with ideas. Usually there is a clear line of authority to follow. **Work Values**—Advancement; Company Policies and Practices; Responsibility; Supervision, Human Relations; Social Service. **Skills**—Mathematics; Negotiation. **Abilities**—*Cognitive:* Mathematical Reasoning; Number Facility; Written Expression; Written Comprehension; Deductive Reasoning. *Psychomotor:* None met the criteria. *Physical:* Gross Body Coordination. *Sensory:* Speech Recognition. **General Work Activities**—*Information Input:* Getting Information; Identifying Objects, Actions, and Events; Estimating Needed Characteristics. *Mental Process:* Processing Information; Making Decisions and Solving Problems; Judging Qualities of Things, Services, or Other People's Work. *Work Output:* Documenting or Recording Information; Handling and Moving Objects; Performing General Physical Activities. *Interacting with Others:* Communicating with Other Workers; Establishing and Maintaining Relationships; Performing Administrative Activities. **Physical Work Conditions**—Outdoors; Bending or Twisting the Body; Kneeling, Crouching, or Crawling; Sitting; Very Hot or Cold. **Other Job Characteristics**—Importance of Being Exact or Accurate; Importance of Repeating Same Tasks; Pace Determined by Speed of Equipment.

Experience—Job Zone 4. A minimum of two to four years of work-related skill, knowledge, or experience is needed. **Job Preparation:** SVP 7.0 to less than 8.0—two years to less than 10 years. **Knowledge**—Economics and Accounting; Mechanical; Clerical; Administration and Management; Mathematics. **Instructional Programs**—Insurance.

Related DOT Jobs—241.267-014 Appraiser, Automobile Damage.

13-1041.00 Compliance Officers, Except Agriculture, Construction, Health and Safety, and Transportation

- **Education/Training Required: Long-term on-the-job training**
- **Employed: 139,736**
- **Annual Earnings: $42,640**
- **Growth: 8.9%**
- **Annual Job Openings: 9,000**

Examine, evaluate, and investigate eligibility for or conformity with laws and regulations governing contract compliance of licenses and permits; other compliance and enforcement inspection activities not classified elsewhere.

No task data available.

GOE INFORMATION—Interest Area: 04. Law, Law Enforcement, and Public Safety. **Work Group:** 04.04. Public Safety. **Note:** The Department of Labor has not collected some data for this job, so it has fewer details than the other descriptions.

Instructional Programs—No data available.

Related DOT Jobs—168.161-010 Coroner; 168.167-014 Equal-Opportunity Representative; 168.167-026 Inspector, Boiler; 168.167-074 Reviewing Officer, Driver's License; 168.264-018 Gas Inspector; 168.267-034 Driver's License Examiner; 168.267-050 Inspector, Government Property; 168.267-054 Inspector, Industrial Waste; 168.267-062 Investigator; 168.267-066 License Inspector; 168.267-082 Agricultural-Chemicals Inspector; 168.267-086 Hazardous-Waste Management Specialist; 168.267-090 Inspector, Water-Pollution Control; 168.267-098 Pesticide-Control Inspector; 168.267-106 Registration Specialist, Agricultural Chemicals; 168.267-110 Sanitation Inspector; 168.267-114 Equal Opportunity Officer; 168.287-014 Inspector, Quality Assurance; 169.267-014 Examiner; 169.267-030 Passport-Application Examiner; others.

13-1041.01 Environmental Compliance Inspectors

- **Education/Training Required: Long-term on-the-job training**
- **Employed: No data available.**
- **Annual Earnings: $42,640**
- **Growth: 8.9%**
- **Annual Job Openings: 9,000**

Inspect and investigate sources of pollution to protect the public and environment and ensure conformance with federal, state, and local regulations and ordinances.

Inspects solid waste disposal and treatment facilities, wastewater treatment facilities, or other water courses or sites for conformance with regulations. Inspects establishments to ensure that handling, storage, and disposal of fertilizers, pesticides, and other hazardous chemicals conform with regulations. Investigates complaints and suspected violations concerning illegal dumping, pollution, pesticides, product quality, or labeling laws. Conducts field tests and collects samples for laboratory analysis. Interviews individuals to determine nature of suspected violations and to obtain evidence of violation. Examines permits, licenses, applications, and records to ensure compliance with licensing requirements. Conducts research on hazardous waste management projects to determine magnitude of disposal problem, treatment, and disposal alternatives and costs. Reviews and evaluates applications for registration of products containing dangerous materials or pollution control discharge permits. Advises individuals and groups concerning pollution control regulations and inspection and investigation findings; encourages voluntary action to correct problems or issues citations for violations. Studies laws and statutes to determine nature of code violation and type of action to be taken. Evaluates label information for accuracy and conformance to regulatory requirements. Prepares, organizes, and maintains records to document activities, recommend action, provide reference materials, and prepare technical and evidentiary reports. Assists in development of spill prevention programs and hazardous waste rules and regulations; recommends corrective action in event of hazardous spill.

GOE INFORMATION—Interest Area: 04. Law, Law Enforcement, and Public Safety. **Work Group:** 04.04. Public Safety. **Personality Type**—Investigative. Investigative occupations frequently involve working with ideas and require an extensive amount of thinking. These occupations can involve searching for facts and figuring out problems mentally. **Work Values**—Supervision, Human Relations; Advancement; Achievement; Authority; Autonomy. **Skills**—Science; Reading Comprehension; Systems Evaluation; Speaking; Systems Analysis; Critical Thinking; Complex Problem Solving; Writing. **Abilities**—*Cognitive:* Problem Sensitivity; Written Expression; Written Comprehension; Inductive Reasoning; Category Flexibility. *Psychomotor:* Multilimb Coordination. *Physical:* Gross Body Coordination; Gross Body Equilibrium; Explosive Strength. *Sensory:* Speech Clarity; Near Vision; Visual Color Discrimination; Speech Recognition; Night Vision. **General Work Activities**—*Information Input:* Identifying Objects, Actions, and Events; Getting Information; Inspecting Equipment, Structures, or Materials. *Mental Process:* Processing Information; Evaluating Information Against Standards; Analyzing Data or Information. *Work Output:* Documenting or Recording Information; Drafting and Specifying Technical Devices; Handling and Moving Objects. *Interacting with Others:* Communicating with Persons Outside Organization; Communicating with Other Workers; Providing Consultation and Advice to Others. **Physical Work Conditions**—Contaminants; Climbing Ladders, Scaffolds, Poles, etc.; Disease or Infections; Hazardous Conditions; Walking or Running. **Other Job Characteristics**—Importance of Being Exact or Accurate; Consequence of Error; Degree of Automation.

Experience—Job Zone 3. Previous work-related skill, knowledge, or experience is required. **Job Preparation:** SVP 6.0 to less than 7.0—more than one year and less than four years. **Knowledge**—Chemistry; Public Safety and Security; Law and Government; Biology; Physics. **Instructional Programs**—No data available.

Related DOT Jobs—168.267-054 Inspector, Industrial Waste; 168.267-082 Agricultural-Chemicals Inspector; 168.267-086 Hazardous-Waste Management Specialist; 168.267-090 Inspector, Water-Pollution Control; 168.267-098 Pesticide-Control Inspector; 168.267-106 Registration Specialist, Agricultural Chemicals; 168.267-110 Sanitation Inspector.

13-1041.02 Licensing Examiners and Inspectors

- **Education/Training Required: Long-term on-the-job training**
- **Employed: No data available.**
- **Annual Earnings: $42,640**
- **Growth: 8.9%**
- **Annual Job Openings: 9,000**

Examine, evaluate, and investigate eligibility for, conformity with, or liability under licenses or permits.

Evaluates applications, records, and documents to determine relevant eligibility information or liability incurred. Determines eligibility or liability and approves or disallows application or license. Administers oral, written, road, or flight test to determine applicant's eligibility for licensing. Scores tests and rates ability of applicant through observation of equipment operation and control. Visits establishments to determine that valid licenses and permits are displayed and that licensing standards are being upheld. Issues licenses to individuals meeting standards. Confers with officials or technical or professional specialists and interviews individuals to obtain information or clarify facts. Prepares reports of activities, evaluations, recommendations, and decisions. Prepares correspondence to inform concerned parties of decisions made and appeal rights. Warns violators of infractions or penalties. Provides information and answers questions of individuals or groups concerning licensing, permit, or passport regulations.

GOE INFORMATION—Interest Area: 04. Law, Law Enforcement, and Public Safety. **Work Group:** 04.04. Public Safety. **Personality Type—** Conventional. Conventional occupations frequently involve following set procedures and routines. These occupations can include working with data and details more than with ideas. Usually there is a clear line of authority to follow. **Work Values—**Social Service; Authority; Supervision, Human Relations; Company Policies and Practices; Security. **Skills—** Speaking; Monitoring; Active Listening; Reading Comprehension; Writing. **Abilities—***Cognitive:* Written Expression; Oral Expression; Written Comprehension; Problem Sensitivity; Perceptual Speed. *Psychomotor:* None met the criteria. *Physical:* Gross Body Coordination. *Sensory:* Speech Clarity; Speech Recognition; Near Vision. **General Work Activities—***Information Input:* Getting Information; Identifying Objects, Actions, and Events; Monitoring Processes, Materials, or Surroundings. *Mental Process:* Evaluating Information Against Standards; Judging Qualities of Things, Services, or Other People's Work; Making Decisions and Solving Problems. *Work Output:* Documenting or Recording Information; Handling and Moving Objects; Interacting with Computers. *Interacting with Others:* Communicating with Persons Outside Organization; Interpreting Meaning of Information for Others; Communicating with Other Workers. **Physical Work Conditions—**Sitting; Outdoors; Walking or Running; Climbing Ladders, Scaffolds, Poles, etc.; High Places. **Other Job Characteristics—**Importance of Being Exact or Accurate; Consequence of Error; Importance of Repeating Same Tasks.

Experience—Job Zone 3. Previous work-related skill, knowledge, or experience is required. **Job Preparation:** SVP 6.0 to less than 7.0—more than one year and less than four years. **Knowledge—**Law and Government; Clerical; English Language; Communications and Media; Sales and Marketing. **Instructional Programs—**No data available.

Related DOT Jobs—168.167-074 Reviewing Officer, Driver's License; 168.267-034 Driver's License Examiner; 168.267-066 License Inspector; 169.267-014 Examiner; 169.267-030 Passport-Application Examiner; 196.163-010 Flight-Operations Inspector.

13-1041.03 Equal Opportunity Representatives and Officers

- **Education/Training Required: Long-term on-the-job training**
- **Employed: No data available.**
- **Annual Earnings: $42,640**
- **Growth: 8.9%**
- **Annual Job Openings: 9,000**

Monitor and evaluate compliance with equal opportunity laws, guidelines, and policies to ensure that employment practices and contracting arrangements give equal opportunity without regard to race, religion, color, national origin, sex, age, or disability.

Interprets civil rights laws and equal opportunity governmental regulations for individuals and employers. Investigates employment practices and alleged violations of law to document and correct discriminatory factors. Studies equal opportunity complaints to clarify issues. Prepares report of findings and recommendations for corrective action. Consults with community representatives to develop technical assistance agreements in accordance with governmental regulations. Conducts surveys and evaluates findings to determine existence of systematic discrimination. Reviews contracts to determine company actions required to meet governmental equal opportunity provisions. Confers with management or other personnel to resolve or settle equal opportunity issues and disputes. Acts as representative between minority placement agencies and employers. Develops guidelines for nondiscriminatory employment practices for use by employers.

GOE INFORMATION—Interest Area: 04. Law, Law Enforcement, and Public Safety. **Work Group:** 04.04. Public Safety. **Personality Type—** Social. Social occupations frequently involve working with, communicating with, and teaching people. These occupations often involve helping or providing service to others. **Work Values—**Good Working Conditions; Social Service; Responsibility; Social Status; Supervision, Human Relations. **Skills—**Speaking; Negotiation; Writing; Complex Problem Solving; Active Listening; Reading Comprehension; Systems Analysis; Persuasion. **Abilities—***Cognitive:* Written Comprehension; Written Expression; Oral Expression; Deductive Reasoning; Inductive Reasoning. *Psychomotor:* None met the criteria. *Physical:* Gross Body Equilibrium. *Sensory:* Speech Clarity; Auditory Attention; Speech Recognition; Near Vision. **General Work Activities—***Information Input:* Getting Information; Monitoring Processes, Materials, or Surroundings; Identifying Objects, Actions, and Events. *Mental Process:* Evaluating Information Against Standards; Updating and Using Relevant Knowledge; Judging Qualities of Things, Services, or Other People's Work. *Work Output:* Documenting or Recording Information; Interacting with Computers; Performing General Physical Activities. *Interacting with Others:* Communicating with Other Workers; Communicating with Persons Outside Organization; Resolving Conflict and Negotiating with Others. **Physical Work Conditions—**Sitting; Indoors; Walking or Running; Radiation. **Other Job Characteristics—**Importance of Being Exact or Accurate; Consequence of Error; Importance of Repeating Same Tasks.

Experience—Job Zone 4. A minimum of two to four years of work-related skill, knowledge, or experience is needed. **Job Preparation:** SVP 7.0 to less than 8.0—two years to less than 10 years. **Knowledge—**Personnel and Human Resources; Law and Government; Sociology and Anthropology; English Language; Therapy and Counseling. **Instructional Programs—**No data available.

Related DOT Jobs—168.167-014 Equal-Opportunity Representative; 168.267-114 Equal Opportunity Officer.

13-1041.04 Government Property Inspectors and Investigators

- Education/Training Required: Long-term on-the-job training
- Employed: No data available.
- Annual Earnings: $42,640
- Growth: 8.9%
- Annual Job Openings: 9,000

Investigate or inspect government property to ensure compliance with contract agreements and government regulations.

Investigates regulated activities to detect violation of law relating to such activities as revenue collection, employment practices, or fraudulent benefit claims. Inspects manufactured or processed products to ensure compliance with contract specifications and legal requirements. Locates and interviews plaintiffs, witnesses, or representatives of business or government to gather facts relevant to inspection or alleged violation. Inspects government-owned equipment and materials in hands of private contractors to prevent waste, damage, theft, and other irregularities. Examines records, reports, and documents to establish facts and detect discrepancies. Investigates character of applicant for special license or permit and misuses of license or permit. Submits samples of product to government laboratory for testing as indicated by departmental procedures. Prepares correspondence, reports of inspections or investigations, and recommendations for administrative or legal authorities. Testifies in court or at administrative proceedings concerning findings of investigation.

GOE INFORMATION—Interest Area: 04. Law, Law Enforcement, and Public Safety. Work Group: 04.04. Public Safety. Personality Type—Enterprising. Enterprising occupations frequently involve starting up and carrying out projects. These occupations can involve leading people and making many decisions. They sometimes require risk taking and often deal with business. Work Values—Advancement; Variety; Supervision, Human Relations; Company Policies and Practices; Social Status. Skills—Speaking; Systems Analysis; Negotiation; Reading Comprehension; Judgment and Decision Making; Critical Thinking; Writing; Systems Evaluation. Abilities—*Cognitive:* Oral Expression; Written Expression; Problem Sensitivity; Written Comprehension; Inductive Reasoning. *Psychomotor:* Wrist-Finger Speed; Multilimb Coordination. *Physical:* Gross Body Coordination; Dynamic Strength; Gross Body Equilibrium; Trunk Strength; Dynamic Flexibility. *Sensory:* Speech Clarity; Near Vision; Auditory Attention; Speech Recognition; Hearing Sensitivity. General Work Activities—*Information Input:* Getting Information; Identifying Objects, Actions, and Events; Inspecting Equipment, Structures, or Materials. *Mental Process:* Evaluating Information Against Standards; Judging Qualities of Things, Services, or Other People's Work; Analyzing Data or Information. *Work Output:* Documenting or Recording Information; Handling and Moving Objects; Interacting with Computers. *Interacting with Others:* Communicating with Other Workers; Communicating with Persons Outside Organization; Interpreting Meaning of Information for Others. Physical Work Conditions—Walking or Running; Distracting Sounds and Noise Levels; Extremely Bright or Inadequate Lighting; Climbing Ladders, Scaffolds, Poles, etc.; Specialized Protective or Safety Attire. Other Job Characteristics—Importance of Being Exact or Accurate; Consequence of Error; Importance of Repeating Same Tasks.

Experience—Job Zone 3. Previous work-related skill, knowledge, or experience is required. Job Preparation: SVP 6.0 to less than 7.0—more than one year and less than four years. Knowledge—Law and Government; Personnel and Human Resources; Public Safety and Security; English Language; Production and Processing. Instructional Programs—No data available.

Related DOT Jobs—168.267-050 Inspector, Government Property; 168.267-062 Investigator; 168.287-014 Inspector, Quality Assurance.

13-1041.05 Pressure Vessel Inspectors

- Education/Training Required: Long-term on-the-job training
- Employed: No data available.
- Annual Earnings: $42,640
- Growth: 8.9%
- Annual Job Openings: 9,000

Inspect pressure vessel equipment for conformance with safety laws and standards regulating their design, fabrication, installation, repair, and operation.

Inspects drawings, designs, and specifications for piping, boilers, and other vessels. Evaluates factors such as materials used, safety devices, regulators, construction quality, riveting, welding, pitting, corrosion, cracking, and safety valve operation. Performs standard tests to verify condition of equipment and calibration of meters and gauges, using test equipment and hand tools. Inspects gas mains to determine that rate of flow, pressure, location, construction, or installation conform to standards. Calculates allowable limits of pressure, strength, and stresses. Recommends or orders actions to correct violations of legal requirements or to eliminate unsafe conditions. Examines permits and inspection records to determine that inspection schedule and remedial actions conform to procedures and regulations. Witnesses acceptance and installation tests. Keeps records and prepares reports of inspections and investigations for administrative or legal authorities. Confers with engineers, manufacturers, contractors, owners, and operators concerning problems in construction, operation, and repair. Investigates accidents to determine causes and to develop methods of preventing recurrences.

GOE INFORMATION—Interest Area: 02. Science, Math, and Engineering. Work Group: 02.08. Engineering Technology. Personality Type—Realistic. Realistic occupations frequently involve work activities that include practical, hands-on problems and solutions. They often deal with plants, animals, and real-world materials like wood, tools, and machinery. Many of the occupations require working outside and do not involve a lot of paperwork or working closely with others. Work Values—Autonomy; Independence; Responsibility; Supervision, Human Relations; Authority. Skills—Quality Control Analysis; Operation Monitoring; Mathematics; Operations Analysis; Systems Evaluation. Abilities—*Cognitive:* Mathematical Reasoning; Oral Expression; Deductive Reasoning; Written Expression; Problem Sensitivity. *Psychomotor:* None met the criteria. *Physical:* None met the criteria. *Sensory:* None met the criteria. General Work Activities—*Information Input:* Inspecting Equipment, Structures, or Materials; Monitoring Processes, Materials, or Surroundings; Identifying Objects, Actions, and Events. *Mental Process:* Evaluating Information Against Standards; Updating and Using Relevant Knowledge; Processing Information. *Work Output:* Controlling Machines and Processes; Documenting or Recording Information; Handling and Moving Objects. *Interacting with Others:* Communicating with Other Workers; Communicating with Persons Outside Organization; Establishing and Maintaining Relationships. Physical Work Conditions—Cramped Work Space or Awkward Positions; Very Hot or Cold; Standing; Distracting Sounds and Noise Levels; Common Protective or Safety Attire. Other Job Characteristics—Consequence of Error; Importance of Being Exact or Accurate; Importance of Repeating Same Tasks.

Experience—Job Zone 4. A minimum of two to four years of work-related skill, knowledge, or experience is needed. Job Preparation: SVP 7.0 to less than 8.0—two years to less than 10 years. Knowledge—Physics; Public Safety and Security; Mechanical; Engineering and Technology; Law and Government. Instructional Programs—No data available.

Related DOT Jobs—168.167-026 Inspector, Boiler; 168.264-018 Gas Inspector.

13-1041.06 Coroners

- Education/Training Required: **Work experience in a related occupation**
- Employed: **No data available.**
- Annual Earnings: **$42,640**
- Growth: **8.9%**
- Annual Job Openings: **9,000**

Direct activities such as autopsies, pathological and toxicological analyses, and inquests relating to the investigation of deaths occurring within a legal jurisdiction to determine cause of death or to fix responsibility for accidental, violent, or unexplained deaths.

Directs activities of physicians and technologists conducting autopsies and pathological and toxicological analyses to determine cause of death. Directs investigations into circumstances of deaths to fix responsibility for accidental, violent, or unexplained death. Confers with officials of public health and law enforcement agencies to coordinate interdepartmental activities. Directs activities of workers involved in preparing documents for permanent records. Testifies at inquests, hearings, and court trials. Coordinates activities for disposition of unclaimed corpse and personal effects of deceased. Provides information concerning death circumstance to relatives of deceased.

GOE INFORMATION—Interest Area: 14. Medical and Health Services. **Work Group:** 14.01. Managerial Work in Medical and Health Services. **Personality Type**—Investigative. Investigative occupations frequently involve working with ideas and require an extensive amount of thinking. These occupations can involve searching for facts and figuring out problems mentally. **Work Values**—Authority; Autonomy; Responsibility; Security; Ability Utilization. **Skills**—Science; Speaking; Reading Comprehension; Complex Problem Solving; Critical Thinking; Writing; Mathematics; Equipment Selection. **Abilities**—*Cognitive:* Inductive Reasoning; Speed of Closure; Written Expression; Flexibility of Closure; Deductive Reasoning. *Psychomotor:* Arm-Hand Steadiness; Manual Dexterity; Finger Dexterity; Wrist-Finger Speed; Speed of Limb Movement. *Physical:* Gross Body Coordination; Explosive Strength. *Sensory:* Speech Clarity; Visual Color Discrimination; Near Vision; Depth Perception; Night Vision. **General Work Activities**—*Information Input:* Identifying Objects, Actions, and Events; Getting Information; Inspecting Equipment, Structures, or Materials. *Mental Process:* Analyzing Data or Information; Making Decisions and Solving Problems; Judging Qualities of Things, Services, or Other People's Work. *Work Output:* Documenting or Recording Information; Handling and Moving Objects; Drafting and Specifying Technical Devices. *Interacting with Others:* Communicating with Other Workers; Coordinating the Work and Activities of Others; Providing Consultation and Advice to Others. **Physical Work Conditions**—Disease or Infections; Common Protective or Safety Attire; Contaminants; Outdoors; Hazardous Equipment. **Other Job Characteristics**—Consequence of Error; Importance of Being Exact or Accurate; Importance of Repeating Same Tasks.

Experience—Job Zone 4. A minimum of two to four years of work-related skill, knowledge, or experience is needed. **Job Preparation:** SVP 7.0 to less than 8.0—two years to less than 10 years. **Knowledge**—Medicine and Dentistry; Biology; Chemistry; Administration and Management; Law and Government. **Instructional Programs**—No data available.

Related DOT Jobs—168.161-010 Coroner.

13-1051.00 Cost Estimators

- Education/Training Required: **Bachelor's degree**
- Employed: **210,920**
- Annual Earnings: **$46,960**
- Growth: **16.5%**
- Annual Job Openings: **28,000**

Prepare cost estimates for product manufacturing, construction projects, or services to aid management in bidding on or determining price of product or service. May specialize according to particular service performed or type of product manufactured.

Analyze blueprints and other documentation to prepare time, cost, materials, and labor estimates. Assess cost effectiveness of products, projects, or services, tracking actual costs relative to bids as the project develops. Consult with clients, vendors, personnel in other departments, or construction foremen to discuss and formulate estimates and resolve issues. Confer with engineers, architects, owners, contractors, and subcontractors on changes and adjustments to cost estimates. Prepare estimates used by management for purposes such as planning, organizing, and scheduling work. Prepare estimates for use in selecting vendors or subcontractors. Review material and labor requirements to decide whether it is more cost-effective to produce or purchase components. Prepare cost and expenditure statements and other necessary documentation at regular intervals for the duration of the project. Prepare and maintain a directory of suppliers, contractors, and subcontractors. Set up cost monitoring and reporting systems and procedures. Establish and maintain tendering process and conduct negotiations. Conduct special studies to develop and establish standard hour and related cost data or to effect cost reduction. Visit site and record information about access, drainage and topography, and availability of services such as water and electricity.

GOE INFORMATION—Interest Area: 13. General Management and Support. **Work Group:** 13.02. Management Support. **Personality Type**—Conventional. Conventional occupations frequently involve following set procedures and routines. These occupations can include working with data and details more than with ideas. Usually there is a clear line of authority to follow. **Work Values**—Good Working Conditions; Independence; Responsibility; Advancement; Autonomy. **Skills**—Equipment Selection; Mathematics; Complex Problem Solving; Coordination; Active Listening; Management of Financial Resources; Negotiation; Monitoring. **Abilities**—*Cognitive:* Mathematical Reasoning; Number Facility; Inductive Reasoning; Category Flexibility; Oral Comprehension. *Psychomotor:* Reaction Time. *Physical:* None met the criteria. *Sensory:* Near Vision; Speech Recognition; Speech Clarity; Depth Perception; Far Vision. **General Work Activities**—*Information Input:* Monitoring Processes, Materials, or Surroundings; Identifying Objects, Actions, and Events; Estimating Needed Characteristics. *Mental Process:* Scheduling Work and Activities; Organizing, Planning, and Prioritizing; Making Decisions and Solving Problems. *Work Output:* Drafting and Specifying Technical Devices; Interacting with Computers; Documenting or Recording Information. *Interacting with Others:* Resolving Conflict and Negotiating with Others; Coordinating the Work and Activities of Others; Communicating with Other Workers. **Physical Work Conditions**—Sitting; Indoors. **Other Job Characteristics**—Importance of Being Exact or Accurate; Consequence of Error; Importance of Repeating Same Tasks.

Experience—Job Zone 4. A minimum of two to four years of work-related skill, knowledge, or experience is needed. **Job Preparation:** SVP 7.0 to less than 8.0—two years to less than 10 years. **Knowledge**—Administration and Management; Sales and Marketing; Production and Processing; Clerical; Economics and Accounting. **Instructional Programs**—Business Administration and Management, General; Business/Commerce, General; Construction Engineering; Construction Engineering Technology/Technician; Manufacturing Engineering; Materials Engineering; Mechanical Engineering.

Related DOT Jobs—169.267-038 Estimator.

13-1061.00 *Emergency Management Specialists*

- **Education/Training Required: Work experience in a related occupation**
- **Employed: 10,219**
- **Annual Earnings: $41,770**
- **Growth: 18.1%**
- **Annual Job Openings: 1,000**

Coordinate disaster response or crisis management activities, provide disaster preparedness training, and prepare emergency plans and procedures for natural (e.g., hurricanes, floods, earthquakes), wartime, or technological (e.g., nuclear power plant emergencies, hazardous materials spills) disasters or hostage situations.

Collaborate with other officials in order to prepare and analyze damage assessments following disasters or emergencies. Conduct surveys to determine the types of emergency-related needs that will need to be addressed in disaster planning or provide technical support to others conducting such surveys. Consult with officials of local and area governments, schools, hospitals, and other institutions in order to determine their needs and capabilities in the event of a natural disaster or other emergency. Coordinate disaster response or crisis management activities such as ordering evacuations, opening public shelters, and implementing special needs plans and programs. Design and administer emergency/disaster preparedness training courses that teach people how to effectively respond to major emergencies and disasters. Develop and maintain liaisons with municipalities, county departments, and similar entities in order to facilitate plan development, response effort coordination, and exchanges of personnel and equipment. Develop and perform tests and evaluations of emergency management plans in accordance with state and federal regulations. Inspect facilities and equipment such as emergency management centers and communications equipment in order to determine their operational and functional capabilities in emergency situations. Keep informed of activities or changes that could affect the likelihood of an emergency as well as those that could affect response efforts and details of plan implementation. Keep informed of federal, state, and local regulations affecting emergency plans and ensure that plans adhere to these regulations. Maintain and update all resource materials associated with emergency preparedness plans. Prepare emergency situation status reports that describe response and recovery efforts, needs, and preliminary damage assessments. Prepare plans that outline operating procedures to be used in response to disasters/emergencies such as hurricanes, nuclear accidents, and terrorist attacks and in recovery from these events. Propose alteration of emergency response procedures based on regulatory changes, technological changes, or knowledge gained from outcomes of previous emergency situations. Review emergency plans of individual organizations such as medical facilities in order to ensure their adequacy. Study emergency plans used elsewhere in order to gather information for plan development. Apply for federal funding for emergency management-related needs; administer such grants and report on their progress. Attend meetings, conferences, and workshops related to emergency management in order to learn new information and to develop working relationships with other emergency management specialists. Develop and implement training procedures and strategies for radiological protection, detection, and decontamination.

Develop instructional materials for the public and make presentations to citizens' groups in order to provide information on emergency plans and their implementation process. Inventory and distribute nuclear, biological, and chemical detection and contamination equipment, providing instruction in its maintenance and use. Provide communities with assistance in applying for federal funding for emergency management facilities, radiological instrumentation, and other related items. Train local groups in the preparation of long-term plans that are compatible with federal and state plans.

GOE INFORMATION—Interest Area: 04. Law, Law Enforcement, and Public Safety. **Work Group:** 04.01. Managerial Work in Law, Law Enforcement, and Public Safety. **Note:** The Department of Labor has not collected some data for this job, so it has fewer details than the other descriptions.

Instructional Programs—Community Organization and Advocacy; Public Administration.

Related DOT Jobs—188.117-022 Civil Preparedness Officer.

13-1071.00 *Employment, Recruitment, and Placement Specialists*

- **Education/Training Required: Bachelor's degree**
- **Employed: 198,907**
- **Annual Earnings: $38,010**
- **Growth: 17.6%**
- **Annual Job Openings: 19,000**

Recruit and place workers.

No task data available.

GOE INFORMATION—Interest Area: 13. General Management and Support. **Work Group:** 13.02. Management Support. **Note:** The Department of Labor has not collected some data for this job, so it has fewer details than the other descriptions.

Instructional Programs—Human Resources Management/Personnel Administration, General; Labor and Industrial Relations.

Related DOT Jobs—099.167-010 Certification and Selection Specialist; 166.267-010 Employment Interviewer; 166.267-026 Recruiter; 166.267-034 Job Development Specialist; 166.267-038 Personnel Recruiter; 205.367-050 Supervisor, Contingents.

13-1071.01 *Employment Interviewers, Private or Public Employment Service*

- **Education/Training Required: Bachelor's degree**
- **Employed: No data available.**
- **Annual Earnings: $38,010**
- **Growth: 17.6%**
- **Annual Job Openings: 19,000**

Interview job applicants in employment office and refer them to prospective employers for consideration. Search application files, notify selected applicants of job openings, and refer qualified applicants to prospective employers. Contact employers to verify referral results. Record and evaluate various pertinent data.

Conduct or arrange for skill, intelligence, or psychological testing of applicants and current employees. Contact employers to solicit orders for job vacancies, determining their requirements and recording relevant data such as job descriptions. Hire workers and place them with employers needing temporary help. Inform applicants of job openings and details such as duties and responsibilities, compensation, benefits, schedules, working conditions, and promotion opportunities. Interview job applicants to match their qualifications with employers' needs, recording and evaluating applicant experience, education, training, and skills. Maintain records of applicants not selected for employment. Perform reference and background checks on applicants. Provide background information on organizations with which interviews are scheduled. Review employment applications and job orders to match applicants with job requirements, using manual or computerized file searches. Search for and recruit applicants for open positions through campus job fairs and advertisements. Select qualified applicants or refer them to employers according to organization policy. Administer assessment tests to identify skill-building needs. Conduct workshops and demonstrate the use of job listings to assist applicants with skill building. Evaluate selection and testing techniques by conducting research or follow-up activities and conferring with management and supervisory personnel. Refer applicants to services such as vocational counseling, literacy or language instruction, transportation assistance, vocational training, and child care. Instruct job applicants in presenting a positive image by providing help with resume writing, personal appearance, and interview techniques.

GOE INFORMATION—Interest Area: 13. General Management and Support. **Work Group:** 13.02. Management Support. **Personality Type—** Social. Social occupations frequently involve working with, communicating with, and teaching people. These occupations often involve helping or providing service to others. **Work Values—**Social Service; Good Working Conditions; Pleasant Co-workers; Supervision, Technical; Supervision, Human Relations. **Skills—**Speaking; Active Listening; Complex Problem Solving; Reading Comprehension; Judgment and Decision Making; Writing; Management of Personnel Resources. **Abilities—***Cognitive:* Oral Comprehension; Oral Expression; Fluency of Ideas; Written Expression; Written Comprehension. *Psychomotor:* None met the criteria. *Physical:* None met the criteria. *Sensory:* Speech Recognition; Speech Clarity. **General Work Activities—***Information Input:* Getting Information; Identifying Objects, Actions, and Events; Estimating Needed Characteristics. *Mental Process:* Judging Qualities of Things, Services, or Other People's Work; Processing Information; Analyzing Data or Information. *Work Output:* Documenting or Recording Information; Handling and Moving Objects; Interacting with Computers. *Interacting with Others:* Performing for or Working with the Public; Establishing and Maintaining Relationships; Communicating with Persons Outside Organization. **Physical Work Conditions—**Sitting; Indoors. **Other Job Characteristics—**Consequence of Error; Importance of Being Exact or Accurate; Importance of Repeating Same Tasks.

Experience—Job Zone 3. Previous work-related skill, knowledge, or experience is required. **Job Preparation:** SVP 6.0 to less than 7.0—more than one year and less than four years. **Knowledge—**Personnel and Human Resources; Therapy and Counseling; Psychology; Clerical; Administration and Management. **Instructional Programs—**Human Resources Management/Personnel Administration, General; Labor and Industrial Relations.

Related DOT Jobs—166.267-010 Employment Interviewer.

13-1071.02 Personnel Recruiters

- **Education/Training Required: Bachelor's degree**
- **Employed: No data available.**
- **Annual Earnings: $38,010**
- **Growth: 17.6%**
- **Annual Job Openings: 19,000**

Seek out, interview, and screen applicants to fill existing and future job openings and promote career opportunities within an organization.

Arrange for interviews and provide travel arrangements as necessary. Advise management on organizing, preparing, and implementing recruiting and retention programs. Conduct reference and background checks on applicants. Contact applicants to inform them of employment possibilities, consideration, and selection. Establish and maintain relationships with hiring managers to stay abreast of current and future hiring and business needs. Evaluate recruitment and selection criteria to ensure conformance to professional, statistical, and testing standards, recommending revision as needed. Inform potential applicants about facilities, operations, benefits, and job or career opportunities in organizations. Interview applicants to obtain information on work history, training, education, and job skills. Maintain current knowledge of Equal Employment Opportunity (EEO) and affirmative action guidelines and laws, such as the Americans with Disabilities Act. Perform searches for qualified candidates according to relevant job criteria, using computer databases, networking, Internet recruiting resources, cold calls, media, recruiting firms, and employee referrals. Recruit applicants for open positions, arranging job fairs with college campus representatives. Review and evaluate applicant qualifications or eligibility for specified licensing according to established guidelines and designated licensing codes. Screen and refer applicants to hiring personnel in the organization, making hiring recommendations when appropriate. Address civic and social groups and attend conferences to disseminate information concerning possible job openings and career opportunities. Advise managers and employees on staffing policies and procedures. Hire applicants and authorize paperwork assigning them to positions. Prepare and maintain employment records. Project yearly recruitment expenditures for budgetary consideration and control. Serve on selection and examination boards to evaluate applicants according to test scores, contacting promising candidates for interviews. Supervise personnel clerks performing filing, typing, and record-keeping duties.

GOE INFORMATION—Interest Area: 13. General Management and Support. **Work Group:** 13.02. Management Support. **Personality Type—** Enterprising. Enterprising occupations frequently involve starting up and carrying out projects. These occupations can involve leading people and making many decisions. They sometimes require risk taking and often deal with business. **Work Values—**Good Working Conditions; Social Service; Supervision, Human Relations; Responsibility; Company Policies and Practices. **Skills—**Management of Personnel Resources; Management of Financial Resources; Systems Analysis; Active Listening; Complex Problem Solving; Speaking; Systems Evaluation; Writing. **Abilities—***Cognitive:* Mathematical Reasoning; Written Expression; Originality; Number Facility; Oral Expression. *Psychomotor:* None met the criteria. *Physical:* None met the criteria. *Sensory:* Speech Clarity; Speech Recognition; Auditory Attention; Near Vision; Night Vision. **General Work Activities—***Information Input:* Identifying Objects, Actions, and Events; Getting Information; Estimating Needed Characteristics. *Mental Process:* Judging Qualities of Things, Services, or Other People's Work; Organizing, Planning, and Prioritizing; Making Decisions and Solving Problems. *Work Output:* Documenting or Recording Information; Interacting with Computers; Performing General Physical Activities. *Interacting with Others:* Staffing Organizational Units; Communicating with Persons Outside Organization; Communicating with Other Workers. **Physical Work Conditions—**Sitting; Indoors; Disease or Infections; Walking or Running. **Other Job Characteristics—**Consequence of Error; Importance of Repeating Same Tasks; Importance of Being Exact or Accurate.

Experience—Job Zone 3. Previous work-related skill, knowledge, or experience is required. **Job Preparation:** SVP 6.0 to less than 7.0—more than one year and less than four years. **Knowledge**—Personnel and Human Resources; Psychology; Sales and Marketing; Administration and Management; Computers and Electronics. **Instructional Programs**—Human Resources Management/Personnel Administration, General; Labor and Industrial Relations.

Related DOT Jobs—099.167-010 Certification and Selection Specialist; 166.267-026 Recruiter; 166.267-038 Personnel Recruiter; 205.367-050 Supervisor, Contingents.

13-1072.00 Compensation, Benefits, and Job Analysis Specialists

- **Education/Training Required: Bachelor's degree**
- **Employed: 86,611**
- **Annual Earnings: $43,330**
- **Growth: 15.7%**
- **Annual Job Openings: 8,000**

Conduct programs of compensation and benefits and job analysis for employer. May specialize in specific areas, such as position classification and pension programs.

Analyze organizational, occupational, and industrial data to facilitate organizational functions and provide technical information to business, industry, and government. Assess need for and develop job analysis instruments and materials. Consult with or serve as a technical liaison between business, industry, government, and union officials. Develop, implement, administer, and evaluate personnel and labor relations programs, including performance appraisal, affirmative action, and employment equity programs. Ensure company compliance with federal and state laws, including reporting requirements. Evaluate job positions, determining classification, exempt or non-exempt status, and salary. Observe, interview, and survey employees and conduct focus group meetings to collect job, organizational, and occupational information. Perform multifactor data and cost analyses that may be used in areas such as support of collective bargaining agreements. Plan and develop curricula and materials for training programs and conduct training. Plan, develop, evaluate, improve, and communicate methods and techniques for selecting, promoting, compensating, evaluating, and training workers. Prepare occupational classifications, job descriptions, and salary scales. Provide advice on the resolution of classification and salary complaints. Research employee benefit and health and safety practices and recommend changes or modifications to existing policies. Research job and worker requirements, structural and functional relationships among jobs and occupations, and occupational trends. Advise managers and employees on state and federal employment regulations, collective agreements, benefit and compensation policies, personnel procedures, and classification programs. Advise staff of individuals' qualifications. Assist in preparing and maintaining personnel records and handbooks. Negotiate collective agreements on behalf of employers or workers and mediate labor disputes and grievances. Prepare reports, such as organization and flow charts and career path reports, to summarize job analysis and evaluation and compensation analysis information. Prepare research results for publication in form of journals, books, manuals, and film. Review occupational data on Alien Employment Certification Applications to determine the appropriate occupational title and code; provide local offices with information about immigration and occupations. Work with the Department of Labor and promote its use with employers. Administer employee insurance, pension, and savings plans, working with insurance brokers and plan carriers. Speak at conferences and events to promote apprenticeships and related training programs.

GOE INFORMATION—**Interest Area:** 13. General Management and Support. **Work Group:** 13.02. Management Support. **Personality Type**—Investigative. Investigative occupations frequently involve working with ideas and require an extensive amount of thinking. These occupations can involve searching for facts and figuring out problems mentally. **Work Values**—Good Working Conditions; Responsibility; Pleasant Co-workers; Authority; Ability Utilization. **Skills**—Systems Evaluation; Systems Analysis; Writing; Complex Problem Solving; Speaking; Reading Comprehension; Learning Strategies; Operations Analysis. **Abilities**—*Cognitive:* Written Expression; Deductive Reasoning; Oral Expression; Originality; Oral Comprehension. *Psychomotor:* None met the criteria. *Physical:* None met the criteria. *Sensory:* Speech Clarity; Near Vision; Night Vision; Auditory Attention; Far Vision. **General Work Activities**—*Information Input:* Getting Information; Identifying Objects, Actions, and Events; Monitoring Processes, Materials, or Surroundings. *Mental Process:* Analyzing Data or Information; Organizing, Planning, and Prioritizing; Judging Qualities of Things, Services, or Other People's Work. *Work Output:* Documenting or Recording Information; Performing General Physical Activities; Interacting with Computers. *Interacting with Others:* Communicating with Other Workers; Communicating with Persons Outside Organization; Providing Consultation and Advice to Others. **Physical Work Conditions**—Sitting; Walking or Running; Disease or Infections; High Places; Indoors. **Other Job Characteristics**—Importance of Repeating Same Tasks; Importance of Being Exact or Accurate; Degree of Automation.

Experience—Job Zone 3. Previous work-related skill, knowledge, or experience is required. **Job Preparation:** SVP 6.0 to less than 7.0—more than one year and less than four years. **Knowledge**—Psychology; Personnel and Human Resources; Education and Training; Administration and Management; Computers and Electronics. **Instructional Programs**—Human Resources Management/Personnel Administration, General; Labor and Industrial Relations.

Related DOT Jobs—166.067-010 Occupational Analyst; 166.267-018 Job Analyst.

13-1073.00 Training and Development Specialists

- **Education/Training Required: Bachelor's degree**
- **Employed: 204,442**
- **Annual Earnings: $41,780**
- **Growth: 19.4%**
- **Annual Job Openings: 20,000**

Conduct training and development programs for employees.

Keep up with developments in area of expertise by reading current journals, books, and magazine articles. Present information, using a variety of instructional techniques and formats such as role playing, simulations, team exercises, group discussions, videos, and lectures. Schedule classes based on availability of classrooms, equipment, and instructors. Organize and develop, or obtain, training procedure manuals and guides and course materials such as handouts and visual materials. Offer specific training programs to help workers maintain or improve job skills. Monitor, evaluate, and record training activities and program effectiveness. Attend meetings and seminars to obtain information for use in training programs or to inform management of training program status. Coordinate recruitment and placement of training program participants. Evaluate training materials prepared by instructors, such as outlines, text, and handouts. Develop alternative training methods if expected improvements are not seen. Assess training needs through surveys, interviews with employees, focus groups, and/or consultation with managers, instructors, or customer representatives. Screen, hire, and assign workers to positions based on qualifications. Select and assign instructors to conduct training. Devise programs to develop executive potential among employees in lower-level positions. Design, plan, organize, and direct orientation and training for employees or customers of industrial or commercial establishment. Negotiate contracts with clients, including desired training outcomes, fees, and expenses. Supervise instructors, evaluate instructor performance, and refer instructors to classes for skill development. Monitor training costs to ensure budget is not exceeded and prepare budget reports to justify expenditures. Refer trainees to employer relations representatives, to locations offering job placement assistance, or to appropriate social services agencies if warranted.

GOE INFORMATION—Interest Area: 13. General Management and Support. **Work Group:** 13.02. Management Support. **Personality Type—** Social. Social occupations frequently involve working with, communicating with, and teaching people. These occupations often involve helping or providing service to others. **Work Values—**Authority; Social Service; Creativity; Pleasant Co-workers; Good Working Conditions. **Skills—**Speaking; Writing; Instructing; Service Orientation; Social Perceptiveness; Learning Strategies; Critical Thinking; Time Management. **Abilities—***Cognitive:* Oral Expression; Originality; Fluency of Ideas; Written Expression; Written Comprehension. *Psychomotor:* Finger Dexterity. *Physical:* Trunk Strength; Extent Flexibility; Gross Body Coordination. *Sensory:* Speech Clarity; Speech Recognition; Far Vision; Auditory Attention; Near Vision. **General Work Activities—***Information Input:* Getting Information; Identifying Objects, Actions, and Events; Monitoring Processes, Materials, or Surroundings. *Mental Process:* Organizing, Planning, and Prioritizing; Updating and Using Relevant Knowledge; Thinking Creatively. *Work Output:* Interacting with Computers; Documenting or Recording Information; Handling and Moving Objects. *Interacting with Others:* Communicating with Other Workers; Teaching Others; Establishing and Maintaining Relationships. **Physical Work Conditions—**Indoors; Sitting; Walking or Running; Disease or Infections; Standing. **Other Job Characteristics—**Consequence of Error; Importance of Repeating Same Tasks; Importance of Being Exact or Accurate.

Experience—Job Zone 4. A minimum of two to four years of work-related skill, knowledge, or experience is needed. **Job Preparation:** SVP 7.0 to less than 8.0—two years to less than 10 years. **Knowledge—**Customer and Personal Service; Psychology; Education and Training; Personnel and Human Resources; Sociology and Anthropology. **Instructional Programs—**Human Resources Management/Personnel Administration, General; Organizational Behavior Studies.

Related DOT Jobs—079.127-010 Inservice Coordinator, Auxiliary Personnel; 166.167-038 Port Purser; 166.167-054 Technical Training Coordinator; 169.167-062 Coordinator, Skill-Training Program; 239.137-010 Commercial-Instructor Supervisor.

13-1079.99 Human Resources, Training, and Labor Relations Specialists, All Other

- Education/Training Required: Bachelor's degree
- Employed: No data available.
- Annual Earnings: No data available.
- Growth: 18.0%
- Annual Job Openings: 96,000

All human resources, training, and labor relations specialists not listed separately.

No task data available.

GOE INFORMATION—Interest Area: 13. General Management and Support. **Work Group:** 13.02. Management Support. **Note:** The Department of Labor has not collected some data for this job, so it has fewer details than the other descriptions.

Instructional Programs—Human Resources Management and Services, Other; Human Resources Management/Personnel Administration, General; Labor and Industrial Relations; Organizational Behavior Studies.

Related DOT Jobs—166.167-042 Senior Enlisted Advisor; 166.167-050 Program Specialist, Employee-Health Maintenance; 166.257-010 Employer Relations Representative; 166.267-030 Retirement Officer; 166.267-042 Employee Relations Specialist; 166.267-046 Human Resource Advisor; 169.107-010 Arbitrator; 169.207-010 Conciliator.

13-1081.00 Logisticians

- Education/Training Required: Bachelor's degree
- Employed: No data available.
- Annual Earnings: No data available.
- Growth: 16.1%
- Annual Job Openings: 86,000

Analyze and coordinate the logistical functions of a firm or organization. Responsible for the entire life cycle of a product, including acquisition, distribution, internal allocation, delivery, and final disposal of resources.

Develop and implement technical project management tools such as plans, schedules, and responsibility and compliance matrices. Develop proposals that include documentation for estimates. Direct and support the compilation and analysis of technical source data necessary for product development. Direct availability and allocation of materials, supplies, and finished products. Direct team activities, establishing task priorities, scheduling and tracking work assignments, providing guidance, and ensuring the availability of resources. Manage the logistical aspects of product life cycles, including coordination or provisioning of samples and the minimization of obsolescence. Participate in the assessment and review of design alternatives and design change proposal impacts. Perform system life-cycle cost analysis and develop component studies. Plan, organize, and execute logistics support activities such as maintenance planning, repair analysis, and test equipment recommendations. Provide project management services, including the provision and analysis of technical data. Redesign the movement of goods in order to maximize value and minimize costs. Report project plans, progress, and results. Stay informed of logistics technology advances and apply appropriate technology in order to improve logistics processes. Collaborate with other departments as necessary to meet customer requirements, to take advantage of sales opportunities, or, in the case of shortages, to minimize negative impacts on a business. Develop an understanding of customers' needs and take actions to ensure that such needs are met. Explain proposed solutions to customers, management, or other interested parties through written proposals and oral presentations. Maintain and develop positive business relationships with a customer's key personnel involved in or directly relevant to a logistics activity. Manage subcontractor activities, reviewing proposals, developing performance specifications, and serving as liaisons between subcontractors and organizations. Protect and control proprietary materials. Review logistics performance with customers against targets, benchmarks, and service agreements. Support the development of training materials and technical manuals.

GOE INFORMATION—Interest Area: 13. General Management and Support. **Work Group:** 13.02. Management Support. **Note:** The Department of Labor has not collected some data for this job, so it has fewer details than the other descriptions.

Instructional Programs—Logistics and Materials Management; Operations Management and Supervision.

Related DOT Jobs—019.167-010 Logistics Engineer.

13-1111.00 Management Analysts

- **Education/Training Required: Work experience plus degree**
- **Employed: 500,910**
- **Annual Earnings: $57,970**
- **Growth: 28.9%**
- **Annual Job Openings: 50,000**

Conduct organizational studies and evaluations, design systems and procedures, conduct work simplifications and measurement studies, and prepare operations and procedures manuals to assist management in operating more efficiently and effectively. Includes program analysts and management consultants.

Review forms and reports; confer with management and users about format, distribution, and purpose and to identify problems and improvements. Develop and implement records management program for filing, protection, and retrieval of records and assure compliance with program. Interview personnel and conduct on-site observation to ascertain unit functions, work performed, and methods, equipment, and personnel used. Prepare manuals and train workers in use of new forms, reports, procedures, or equipment according to organizational policy. Design, evaluate, recommend, and approve changes of forms and reports. Recommend purchase of storage equipment; design area layout to locate equipment in space available. Plan study of work problems and procedures, such as organizational change, communications, information flow, integrated production methods, inventory control, or cost analysis. Gather and organize information on problems or procedures. Analyze data gathered and develop solutions or alternative methods of proceeding. Document findings of study and prepare recommendations for implementation of new systems, procedures, or organizational changes. Confer with personnel concerned to ensure successful functioning of newly implemented systems or procedures.

GOE INFORMATION—Interest Area: 13. General Management and Support. **Work Group:** 13.02. Management Support. **Personality Type**—Enterprising. Enterprising occupations frequently involve starting up and carrying out projects. These occupations can involve leading people and making many decisions. They sometimes require risk taking and often deal with business. **Work Values**—Creativity; Authority; Good Working Conditions; Achievement; Social Status. **Skills**—Systems Evaluation; Systems Analysis; Complex Problem Solving; Management of Personnel Resources; Management of Material Resources; Operations Analysis; Equipment Selection; Monitoring. **Abilities**—*Cognitive:* Originality; Fluency of Ideas; Problem Sensitivity; Written Expression; Visualization. *Psychomotor:* Wrist-Finger Speed. *Physical:* None met the criteria. *Sensory:* Speech Clarity; Near Vision; Speech Recognition. **General Work Activities**—*Information Input:* Getting Information; Identifying Objects, Actions, and Events; Monitoring Processes, Materials, or Surroundings. *Mental Process:* Organizing, Planning, and Prioritizing; Analyzing Data or Information; Making Decisions and Solving Problems. *Work Output:* Documenting or Recording Information; Interacting with Computers; Drafting and Specifying Technical Devices. *Interacting with Others:* Communicating with Other Workers; Providing Consultation and Advice to Others; Establishing and Maintaining Relationships. **Physical Work Conditions**—Indoors; Sitting. **Other Job Characteristics**—Consequence of Error; Importance of Being Exact or Accurate; Degree of Automation.

Experience—Job Zone 4. A minimum of two to four years of work-related skill, knowledge, or experience is needed. **Job Preparation:** SVP

7.0 to less than 8.0—two years to less than 10 years. **Knowledge**—Administration and Management; Education and Training; Personnel and Human Resources; Economics and Accounting; Clerical. **Instructional Programs**—Business Administration and Management, General; Business/Commerce, General.

Related DOT Jobs—161.117-014 Director, Records Management; 161.167-010 Management Analyst; 161.167-014 Manager, Forms Analysis; 161.167-018 Manager, Records Analysis; 161.167-022 Manager, Reports Analysis; 161.267-010 Clerical-Methods Analyst; 161.267-018 Forms Analyst; 161.267-022 Records-Management Analyst; 161.267-026 Reports Analyst.

13-1121.00 Meeting and Convention Planners

- **Education/Training Required: Bachelor's degree**
- **Employed: 33,882**
- **Annual Earnings: $36,550**
- **Growth: 23.3%**
- **Annual Job Openings: 3,000**

Coordinate activities of staff and convention personnel to make arrangements for group meetings and conventions.

Arrange the availability of audiovisual equipment, transportation, displays, and other event needs. Confer with staff at a chosen event site in order to coordinate details. Consult with customers in order to determine objectives and requirements for events such as meetings, conferences, and conventions. Coordinate services for events, such as accommodation and transportation for participants, facilities, catering, signage, displays, special needs requirements, printing, and event security. Direct administrative details such as financial operations, dissemination of promotional materials, and responses to inquiries. Evaluate and select providers of services according to customer requirements. Hire, train, and supervise volunteers and support staff required for events. Inspect event facilities in order to ensure that they conform to customer requirements. Meet with sponsors and organizing committees in order to plan scope and format of events, to establish and monitor budgets, and to review administrative procedures and event progress. Monitor event activities in order to ensure compliance with applicable regulations and laws, satisfaction of participants, and resolution of any problems that arise. Negotiate contracts with such service providers and suppliers as hotels, convention centers, and speakers. Organize registration of event participants. Plan and develop programs, agendas, budgets, and services according to customer requirements. Conduct post-event evaluations in order to determine how future events could be improved. Design and implement efforts to publicize events and promote sponsorships. Develop event topics and choose featured speakers. Maintain records of event aspects, including financial details. Obtain permits from fire and health departments to erect displays and exhibits and serve food at events. Promote conference, convention, and trades show services by performing tasks such as meeting with professional and trade associations and producing brochures and other publications. Read trade publications, attend seminars, and consult with other meeting professionals in order to keep abreast of meeting management standards and trends. Review event bills for accuracy and approve payment.

GOE INFORMATION—Interest Area: 11. Recreation, Travel, and Other Personal Services. **Work Group:** 11.01. Managerial Work in Recreation, Travel, and Other Personal Services. **Personality Type**—Enterprising. Enterprising occupations frequently involve starting up and carrying out projects. These occupations can involve leading people and making many decisions. They sometimes require risk taking and often deal with business. **Work Values**—Authority; Good Working Conditions;

Creativity; Social Service; Recognition. **Skills**—Management of Personnel Resources; Coordination; Service Orientation; Negotiation; Management of Material Resources; Speaking; Complex Problem Solving; Social Perceptiveness. **Abilities**—*Cognitive:* Oral Comprehension; Oral Expression; Written Expression; Fluency of Ideas; Category Flexibility. *Psychomotor:* None met the criteria. *Physical:* None met the criteria. *Sensory:* Speech Recognition; Speech Clarity; Auditory Attention. **General Work Activities**—*Information Input:* Getting Information; Identifying Objects, Actions, and Events; Monitoring Processes, Materials, or Surroundings. *Mental Process:* Scheduling Work and Activities; Organizing, Planning, and Prioritizing; Thinking Creatively. *Work Output:* Performing General Physical Activities; Handling and Moving Objects; Documenting or Recording Information. *Interacting with Others:* Communicating with Other Workers; Communicating with Persons Outside Organization; Coordinating the Work and Activities of Others. **Physical Work Conditions**—Sitting; Outdoors; High Places; Radiation. **Other Job Characteristics**—Consequence of Error; Importance of Being Exact or Accurate; Importance of Repeating Same Tasks.

Experience—Job Zone 4. A minimum of two to four years of work-related skill, knowledge, or experience is needed. **Job Preparation:** SVP 7.0 to less than 8.0—two years to less than 10 years. **Knowledge**—Customer and Personal Service; Administration and Management; Sales and Marketing; Economics and Accounting; Communications and Media. **Instructional Programs**—Selling Skills and Sales Operations.

Related DOT Jobs—169.117-022 Meeting Planner; 187.167-078 Manager, Convention.

13-1199.99 Business Operations Specialists, All Other

- Education/Training Required: No data available.
- Employed: No data available.
- Annual Earnings: No data available.
- Growth: 16.1%
- Annual Job Openings: 86,000

All business operations specialists not listed separately.

No task data available.

GOE INFORMATION—Interest Area: 13. General Management and Support. **Work Group:** 13.01. General Management Work and Management of Support Functions; 13.02. Management Support. **Note:** The Department of Labor has not collected some data for this job, so it has fewer details than the other descriptions.

Instructional Programs—Business, Management, Marketing, and Related Support Services, Other.

Related DOT Jobs—100.117-014 Library Consultant; 110.167-010 Bar Examiner; 152.067-018 Cue Selector; 162.167-030 Purchase-Price Analyst; 166.267-014 Hospital-Insurance Representative; 168.267-026 Dealer-Compliance Representative; 168.367-010 Attendance Officer; 168.367-014 Rater, Travel Accommodations; 169.117-014 Grant Coordinator; 169.117-018 Provider Relations Representative; 169.167-022 Fire Assistant; 169.167-026 Laboratory Assistant, Liaison Inspection; 169.167-066 Legislative Assistant; 169.167-078 Utilization Coordinator; 169.262-010 Caseworker; 184.167-250 Tariff Publishing Agent; 186.117-018 Customs Broker; 187.167-034 Director, Nurses' Registry; 187.167-062 Manager, Branch Operation Evaluation; 189.117-050 Consultant; others.

13-2000 Financial Specialists

13-2011.00 Accountants and Auditors

- Education/Training Required: Bachelor's degree
- Employed: 975,783
- Annual Earnings: $45,380
- Growth: 18.5%
- Annual Job Openings: 100,000

Examine, analyze, and interpret accounting records for the purpose of giving advice or preparing statements. Install or advise on systems of recording costs or other financial and budgetary data.

No task data available.

GOE INFORMATION—Interest Area: 13. General Management and Support. **Work Group:** 13.02. Management Support. **Note:** The Department of Labor has not collected some data for this job, so it has fewer details than the other descriptions.

Instructional Programs—Accounting; Accounting and Business/Management; Accounting and Computer Science; Accounting and Finance; Auditing; Taxation.

Related DOT Jobs—160.162-010 Accountant, Tax; 160.162-018 Accountant; 160.162-022 Accountant, Budget; 160.162-026 Accountant, Cost; 160.162-030 Auditor, Data Processing; 160.167-022 Accountant, Property; 160.167-026 Accountant, Systems; 160.167-030 Auditor, County or City; 160.167-034 Auditor, Internal; 160.167-038 Auditor, Tax; 160.167-042 Bursar; 160.167-054 Auditor; 160.267-014 Director, Utility Accounts.

13-2011.01 Accountants

- Education/Training Required: Bachelor's degree
- Employed: No data available.
- Annual Earnings: $45,380
- Growth: 18.5%
- Annual Job Openings: 100,000

Analyze financial information and prepare financial reports to determine or maintain record of assets, liabilities, profit and loss, tax liability, or other financial activities within an organization.

Prepare, examine, and analyze accounting records, financial statements, and other financial reports to assess accuracy, completeness, and conformance to reporting and procedural standards. Compute taxes owed and prepare tax returns, ensuring compliance with payment, reporting, and other tax requirements. Analyze business operations, trends, costs, revenues, financial commitments, and obligations to project future revenues and expenses or to provide advice. Report to management regarding the finances of establishment. Establish tables of accounts and assign entries to proper accounts. Develop, maintain, and analyze budgets, preparing periodic reports that compare budgeted costs to actual costs. Develop, implement, modify, and document record-keeping and accounting systems, making use of current computer technology. Prepare forms and manuals for accounting and bookkeeping personnel and direct their work activities. Survey operations to ascertain accounting needs and to recommend, develop, and maintain solutions to business and financial problems. Work as Internal Revenue Service agents. Advise management about issues such as resource utilization, tax strategies, and the assumptions underlying budget forecasts. Provide internal and external auditing services for businesses and individuals. Advise clients in areas such as compensation, employee health care benefits, the design of accounting and data processing systems, and long-range tax and estate plans. Investigate bankruptcies and other complex financial transactions and prepare reports summarizing the findings. Represent clients before taxing authorities and provide support during litigation involving financial issues. Appraise, evaluate, and inventory real property and equipment, recording information such as the property's description, value, and location. Maintain and examine the records of government agencies. Serve as bankruptcy trustees and business valuators.

GOE INFORMATION—Interest Area: 13. General Management and Support. **Work Group:** 13.02. Management Support. **Personality Type—** Conventional. Conventional occupations frequently involve following set procedures and routines. These occupations can include working with data and details more than with ideas. Usually there is a clear line of authority to follow. **Work Values—**Good Working Conditions; Compensation; Social Status; Security; Ability Utilization. **Skills—**Systems Analysis; Management of Financial Resources; Systems Evaluation; Operations Analysis; Judgment and Decision Making; Time Management; Monitoring; Mathematics. **Abilities—***Cognitive:* Mathematical Reasoning; Number Facility; Deductive Reasoning; Flexibility of Closure; Category Flexibility. *Psychomotor:* Finger Dexterity. *Physical:* None met the criteria. *Sensory:* Near Vision; Speech Recognition; Speech Clarity. **General Work Activities—***Information Input:* Getting Information; Identifying Objects, Actions, and Events; Estimating Needed Characteristics. *Mental Process:* Processing Information; Organizing, Planning, and Prioritizing; Analyzing Data or Information. *Work Output:* Interacting with Computers; Documenting or Recording Information; Handling and Moving Objects. *Interacting with Others:* Communicating with Other Workers; Establishing and Maintaining Relationships; Providing Consultation and Advice to Others. **Physical Work Conditions—**Sitting; Indoors; Making Repetitive Motions; Using Hands on Objects, Tools, or Controls; Disease or Infections. **Other Job Characteristics—**Importance of Being Exact or Accurate; Consequence of Error; Degree of Automation.

Experience—Job Zone 4. A minimum of two to four years of work-related skill, knowledge, or experience is needed. **Job Preparation:** SVP 7.0 to less than 8.0—two years to less than 10 years. **Knowledge—**Economics and Accounting; Clerical; Customer and Personal Service; Law and Government; Mathematics. **Instructional Programs—**Accounting; Accounting and Business/Management; Accounting and Computer Science; Accounting and Finance; Auditing; Taxation.

Related DOT Jobs—160.162-010 Accountant, Tax; 160.162-018 Accountant; 160.162-022 Accountant, Budget; 160.162-026 Accountant, Cost; 160.167-022 Accountant, Property; 160.167-026 Accountant, Systems; 160.167-042 Bursar.

13-2011.02 Auditors

- **Education/Training Required: Bachelor's degree**
- **Employed: No data available.**
- **Annual Earnings: $45,380**
- **Growth: 18.5%**
- **Annual Job Openings: 100,000**

Examine and analyze accounting records to determine financial status of establishment and prepare financial reports concerning operating procedures.

Audit payroll and personnel records to determine unemployment insurance premiums, workers' compensation coverage, liabilities, and compliance with tax laws. Collect and analyze data to detect deficient controls, duplicated effort, extravagance, fraud, or non-compliance with laws, regulations, and management policies. Examine and evaluate financial and information systems, recommending controls to ensure system reliability and data integrity. Examine inventory to verify journal and ledger entries. Examine records and interview workers to ensure recording of transactions and compliance with laws and regulations. Inspect account books and accounting systems for efficiency, effectiveness, and use of accepted accounting procedures to record transactions. Inspect cash on hand, notes receivable and payable, negotiable securities, and canceled checks to confirm records are accurate. Prepare detailed reports on audit findings. Prepare, analyze, and verify annual reports, financial statements, and other records, using accepted accounting and statistical procedures to assess financial condition and facilitate financial planning. Report to management about asset utilization and audit results and recommend changes in operations and financial activities. Review data about material assets, net worth, liabilities, capital stock, surplus, income, and expenditures. Supervise auditing of establishments and determine scope of investigation required. Conduct pre-implementation audits to determine if systems and programs under development will work as planned. Confer with company officials about financial and regulatory matters. Direct activities of personnel engaged in filing, recording, compiling, and transmitting financial records. Evaluate taxpayer finances to determine tax liability, using knowledge of interest and discount rates, annuities, valuation of stocks and bonds, and amortization valuation of depletable assets. Examine records, tax returns, and related documents pertaining to settlement of decedent's estate. Produce up-to-the-minute information, using internal computer systems, to allow management to base decisions on actual, not historical, data. Review taxpayer accounts and conduct audits on-site, by correspondence, or by summoning taxpayer to office. Examine whether the organization's objectives are reflected in its management activities and whether employees understand the objectives.

GOE INFORMATION—Interest Area: 13. General Management and Support. **Work Group:** 13.02. Management Support. **Personality Type—** Conventional. Conventional occupations frequently involve following set procedures and routines. These occupations can include working with data and details more than with ideas. Usually there is a clear line of authority to follow. **Work Values—**Authority; Advancement; Good Working Conditions; Compensation; Pleasant Co-workers. **Skills—**Systems Evaluation; Systems Analysis; Complex Problem Solving; Mathematics; Critical Thinking; Monitoring; Judgment and Decision Making; Speaking. **Abilities—***Cognitive:* Number Facility; Written Expression; Speed of Closure; Mathematical Reasoning; Inductive Reasoning. *Psychomotor:* Finger Dexterity; Control Precision; Multilimb Coordination. *Physical:* None met the criteria. *Sensory:* Near Vision; Speech Clarity; Speech Recognition; Glare Sensitivity. **General Work Activities—***Information Input:* Getting Information; Identifying Objects, Actions, and Events; Estimating Needed Characteristics. *Mental Process:* Processing Information; Analyzing Data or Information; Evaluating Information Against Standards. *Work Output:* Documenting or Recording Information; Interacting with Computers; Handling and Moving Objects. *Interacting with Others:* Communicating with Other Workers; Providing Consultation and Advice to Others; Communicating with Persons Outside Organization. **Physical Work Conditions—**Sitting; Indoors; Disease or Infections. **Other Job Characteristics—**Importance of Being Exact or Accurate; Consequence of Error; Importance of Repeating Same Tasks.

Experience—Job Zone 4. A minimum of two to four years of work-related skill, knowledge, or experience is needed. **Job Preparation:** SVP 7.0 to less than 8.0—two years to less than 10 years. **Knowledge—**Economics and Accounting; Mathematics; Administration and Management; Law and Government; Clerical. **Instructional Programs—**Accounting; Accounting and Business/Management; Accounting and Computer Science; Accounting and Finance; Auditing; Taxation.

Related DOT Jobs—160.167-030 Auditor, County or City; 160.167-034 Auditor, Internal; 160.167-038 Auditor, Tax; 160.167-054 Auditor; 160.267-014 Director, Utility Accounts.

13-2021.00 Appraisers and Assessors of Real Estate

- **Education/Training Required: Postsecondary vocational training**
- **Employed: 56,811**
- **Annual Earnings: $38,950**
- **Growth: 18.0%**
- **Annual Job Openings: 6,000**

Appraise real property to determine its fair value. May assess taxes in accordance with prescribed schedules.

No task data available.

GOE INFORMATION—Interest Area: 13. General Management and Support. **Work Group:** 13.02. Management Support. **Note:** The Department of Labor has not collected some data for this job, so it has fewer details than the other descriptions.

Instructional Programs—Real Estate.

Related DOT Jobs—188.167-010 Appraiser; 191.267-010 Appraiser, Real Estate.

13-2021.01 Assessors

- **Education/Training Required: Postsecondary vocational training**
- **Employed: No data available.**
- **Annual Earnings: $38,950**
- **Growth: 18.0%**
- **Annual Job Openings: 6,000**

Appraise real and personal property to determine its fair value. May assess taxes in accordance with prescribed schedules.

Analyze trends in sales prices, construction costs, and rents in order to assess property values and/or determine the accuracy of assessments. Approve applications for property tax exemptions or deductions. Calculate tax bills for properties by multiplying assessed values by jurisdiction tax rates. Complete and maintain assessment rolls that show the assessed values and status of all property in a municipality. Conduct regular reviews of property within jurisdictions in order to determine changes in property due to construction or demolition. Determine taxability and value of properties, using methods such as field inspection, structural measurement, calculation, sales analysis, market trend studies, and income and expense analysis. Establish uniform and equitable systems for assessing all classes and kinds of property. Explain assessed values to property owners and defend appealed assessments at public hearings. Identify the ownership of each piece of taxable property. Inspect new construction and major improvements to existing structures in order to determine values. Inspect properties, considering factors such as market value, location, and building or replacement costs to determine appraisal value. Issue notices of assessments and taxes. Maintain familiarity with aspects of local real estate markets. Prepare and maintain current data on each parcel assessed, including maps of boundaries, inventories of land and structures, property characteristics, and any applicable exemptions. Write and submit appraisal and tax reports for public record. Hire staff members. Provide sales analyses to be used for equalization of school aid. Review information about transfers of property to ensure its accuracy, checking basic information on buyers, sellers, and sales prices and making corrections as necessary. Serve on assessment review boards.

GOE INFORMATION—Interest Area: 13. General Management and Support. **Work Group:** 13.02. Management Support. **Personality Type—**Conventional. Conventional occupations frequently involve following set procedures and routines. These occupations can include working with data and details more than with ideas. Usually there is a clear line of authority to follow. **Work Values**—Responsibility; Independence; Autonomy; Compensation; Security. **Skills**—Judgment and Decision Making; Systems Analysis; Reading Comprehension; Mathematics; Writing. **Abilities**—*Cognitive:* Mathematical Reasoning; Written Expression; Inductive Reasoning; Number Facility; Category Flexibility. *Psychomotor:* None met the criteria. *Physical:* Gross Body Equilibrium. *Sensory:* Speech Clarity; Far Vision. **General Work Activities**—*Information Input:* Getting Information; Identifying Objects, Actions, and Events; Estimating Needed Characteristics. *Mental Process:* Processing Information; Analyzing Data or Information; Judging Qualities of Things, Services, or Other People's Work. *Work Output:* Documenting or Recording Information; Performing General Physical Activities; Operating Vehicles or Equipment. *Interacting with Others:* Communicating with Other Workers; Providing Consultation and Advice to Others; Interpreting Meaning of Information for Others. **Physical Work Conditions**—Outdoors; Walking or Running; Climbing Ladders, Scaffolds, Poles, etc.; High Places; Standing. **Other Job Characteristics**—Importance of Being Exact or Accurate; Importance of Repeating Same Tasks; Consequence of Error.

Experience—Job Zone 4. A minimum of two to four years of work-related skill, knowledge, or experience is needed. **Job Preparation:** SVP 7.0 to less than 8.0—two years to less than 10 years. **Knowledge**—Economics and Accounting; Law and Government; Mathematics; Geography; Building and Construction. **Instructional Programs**—Real Estate.

Related DOT Jobs—188.167-010 Appraiser.

13-2021.02 Appraisers, Real Estate

- **Education/Training Required: Postsecondary vocational training**
- **Employed: No data available.**
- **Annual Earnings: $38,950**
- **Growth: 18.0%**
- **Annual Job Openings: 6,000**

Appraise real property to determine its value for purchase, sales, investment, mortgage, or loan purposes.

Compute final estimation of property values, taking into account such factors as depreciation, replacement costs, value comparisons of similar properties, and income potential. Draw land diagrams that will be used in appraisal reports to support findings. Estimate building replacement costs using building valuation manuals and professional cost estimators. Evaluate land and neighborhoods where properties are situated, considering locations and trends or impending changes that could influence future values. Examine the type and location of nearby services such as shopping centers, schools, parks, and other neighborhood features in order to evaluate their impact on property values. Inspect properties to evaluate construction, condition, special features, and functional design and to take property measurements. Obtain county land values and sales information about nearby properties in order to aid in establishment of property values. Photograph interiors and exteriors of properties in order to assist in estimating property value, substantiate findings, and complete appraisal reports. Prepare written reports that estimate property values, outline methods by which the estimations were made, and meet appraisal standards. Search public records for transactions such as sales, leases, and assessments. Verify legal descriptions of properties by comparing them to county records. Check building codes and zoning bylaws in order to determine any effects on the properties being appraised. Examine income records and operating costs of income properties. Interview persons familiar with properties and immediate surroundings, such as contractors, homeowners, and realtors, in order to obtain pertinent information. Testify in court as to the value of a piece of real estate property.

GOE INFORMATION—Interest Area: 13. General Management and Support. **Work Group:** 13.02. Management Support. **Personality Type—**Enterprising. Enterprising occupations frequently involve starting up and carrying out projects. These occupations can involve leading people and making many decisions. They sometimes require risk taking and often deal with business. **Work Values—**Responsibility; Autonomy; Independence; Social Status; Good Working Conditions. **Skills—**Writing; Mathematics; Speaking; Reading Comprehension; Complex Problem Solving; Systems Analysis; Active Listening; Management of Personnel Resources. **Abilities—***Cognitive:* Deductive Reasoning; Number Facility; Written Expression; Mathematical Reasoning; Written Comprehension. *Psychomotor:* Wrist-Finger Speed. *Physical:* None met the criteria. *Sensory:* Far Vision; Speech Clarity; Speech Recognition. **General Work Activities—***Information Input:* Getting Information; Identifying Objects, Actions, and Events; Inspecting Equipment, Structures, or Materials. *Mental Process:* Judging Qualities of Things, Services, or Other People's Work; Updating and Using Relevant Knowledge; Analyzing Data or Information. *Work Output:* Documenting or Recording Information; Performing General Physical Activities; Handling and Moving Objects. *Interacting with Others:* Communicating with Other Workers; Guiding, Directing, and Motivating Subordinates; Communicating with Persons Outside Organization. **Physical Work Conditions—**Outdoors; Sitting; Walking or Running; Standing; Distracting Sounds and Noise Levels. **Other Job Characteristics—**Importance of Being Exact or Accurate; Consequence of Error; Importance of Repeating Same Tasks.

Experience—Job Zone 4. A minimum of two to four years of work-related skill, knowledge, or experience is needed. **Job Preparation:** SVP 7.0 to less than 8.0—two years to less than 10 years. **Knowledge—**Personnel and Human Resources; Building and Construction; Economics and Accounting; Law and Government; Geography. **Instructional Programs—**Real Estate.

Related DOT Jobs—191.267-010 Appraiser, Real Estate.

13-2031.00 Budget Analysts

- **Education/Training Required: Bachelor's degree**
- **Employed: 70,019**
- **Annual Earnings: $50,510**
- **Growth: 14.6%**
- **Annual Job Openings: 8,000**

Examine budget estimates for completeness, accuracy, and conformance with procedures and regulations. Analyze budgeting and accounting reports for the purpose of maintaining expenditure controls.

Analyze monthly department budgeting and accounting reports to maintain expenditure controls. Compile and analyze accounting records and other data to determine the financial resources required to implement a program. Direct the preparation of regular and special budget reports. Examine budget estimates for completeness, accuracy, and conformance with procedures and regulations. Interpret budget directives and establish policies for carrying out directives. Perform cost-benefits analyses to compare operating programs, review financial requests, and explore alternative financing methods. Review operating budgets to analyze trends affecting budget needs. Summarize budgets and submit recommendations for the approval or disapproval of funds requests.

Consult with managers to ensure that budget adjustments are made in accordance with program changes. Match appropriations for specific programs with appropriations for broader programs, including items for emergency funds. Provide advice and technical assistance with cost analysis, fiscal allocation, and budget preparation. Seek new ways to improve efficiency and increase profits. Testify before examining and fund-granting authorities, clarifying and promoting the proposed budgets.

GOE INFORMATION—Interest Area: 13. General Management and Support. **Work Group:** 13.02. Management Support. **Personality Type—**Conventional. Conventional occupations frequently involve following set procedures and routines. These occupations can include working with data and details more than with ideas. Usually there is a clear line of authority to follow. **Work Values—**Advancement; Good Working Conditions; Authority; Supervision, Human Relations; Compensation. **Skills—**Management of Financial Resources; Systems Analysis; Systems Evaluation; Judgment and Decision Making; Complex Problem Solving; Mathematics; Critical Thinking; Management of Personnel Resources. **Abilities—***Cognitive:* Mathematical Reasoning; Number Facility; Written Comprehension; Written Expression; Oral Expression. *Psychomotor:* None met the criteria. *Physical:* None met the criteria. *Sensory:* Near Vision; Speech Recognition. **General Work Activities—***Information Input:* Identifying Objects, Actions, and Events; Getting Information; Estimating Needed Characteristics. *Mental Process:* Processing Information; Analyzing Data or Information; Making Decisions and Solving Problems. *Work Output:* Documenting or Recording Information; Interacting with Computers; Handling and Moving Objects. *Interacting with Others:* Monitoring and Controlling Resources; Communicating with Other Workers; Providing Consultation and Advice to Others. **Physical Work Conditions—**Indoors; Sitting. **Other Job Characteristics—**Importance of Being Exact or Accurate; Consequence of Error; Degree of Automation.

Experience—Job Zone 4. A minimum of two to four years of work-related skill, knowledge, or experience is needed. **Job Preparation:** SVP 7.0 to less than 8.0—two years to less than 10 years. **Knowledge—**Economics and Accounting; Administration and Management; Mathematics; Personnel and Human Resources; Computers and Electronics. **Instructional Programs—**Accounting; Finance, General.

Related DOT Jobs—161.117-010 Budget Officer; 161.267-030 Budget Analyst.

13-2041.00 Credit Analysts

- **Education/Training Required: Bachelor's degree**
- **Employed: 60,035**
- **Annual Earnings: $41,650**
- **Growth: 16.0%**
- **Annual Job Openings: 7,000**

Analyze current credit data and financial statements of individuals or firms to determine the degree of risk involved in extending credit or lending money. Prepare reports with this credit information for use in decision-making.

Analyze credit data and financial statements to determine the degree of risk involved in extending credit or lending money. Analyze financial data such as income growth, quality of management, and market share to determine expected profitability of loans. Confer with credit association and other business representatives to exchange credit information. Evaluate customer records and recommend payment plans based on earnings, savings data, payment history, and purchase activity. Generate financial ratios, using computer programs, to evaluate customers' financial status. Prepare reports that include the degree of risk involved in extending credit or lending money. Compare liquidity, profitability, and credit histories of establishments being evaluated with those of similar establishments in the same industries and geographic locations. Complete loan applications, including credit analyses and summaries of loan requests, and submit to loan committees for approval. Consult with customers to resolve complaints and verify financial and credit transactions. Review individual or commercial customer files to identify and select delinquent accounts for collection.

GOE INFORMATION—Interest Area: 13. General Management and Support. **Work Group:** 13.02. Management Support. **Personality Type—**Conventional. Conventional occupations frequently involve following set procedures and routines. These occupations can include working with data and details more than with ideas. Usually there is a clear line of authority to follow. **Work Values—**Advancement; Good Working Conditions; Supervision, Human Relations; Company Policies and Practices; Activity. **Skills—**Systems Evaluation; Systems Analysis; Complex Problem Solving; Mathematics; Critical Thinking; Speaking; Judgment and Decision Making; Active Listening. **Abilities—***Cognitive:* Mathematical Reasoning; Number Facility; Written Expression; Deductive Reasoning; Oral Expression. *Psychomotor:* None met the criteria. *Physical:* None met the criteria. *Sensory:* Speech Recognition; Near Vision; Speech Clarity; Auditory Attention; Night Vision. **General Work Activities—***Information Input:* Getting Information; Identifying Objects, Actions, and Events; Monitoring Processes, Materials, or Surroundings. *Mental Process:* Processing Information; Analyzing Data or Information; Judging Qualities of Things, Services, or Other People's Work. *Work Output:* Interacting with Computers; Documenting or Recording Information; Handling and Moving Objects. *Interacting with Others:* Communicating with Other Workers; Communicating with Persons Outside Organization; Establishing and Maintaining Relationships. **Physical Work Conditions—**Sitting; Indoors; Disease or Infections. **Other Job Characteristics—**Consequence of Error; Degree of Automation; Importance of Repeating Same Tasks.

Experience—Job Zone 4. A minimum of two to four years of work-related skill, knowledge, or experience is needed. **Job Preparation:** SVP 7.0 to less than 8.0—two years to less than 10 years. **Knowledge—**Economics and Accounting; Computers and Electronics; Law and Government; Mathematics; Geography. **Instructional Programs—**Accounting; Credit Management; Finance, General.

Related DOT Jobs—160.267-022 Credit Analyst; 186.267-022 Loan Review Analyst; 241.267-022 Credit Analyst.

13-2051.00 Financial Analysts

- **Education/Training Required:** Bachelor's degree
- **Employed:** 144,730
- **Annual Earnings:** $55,120
- **Growth:** 25.5%
- **Annual Job Openings:** 20,000

Conduct quantitative analyses of information affecting investment programs of public or private institutions.

Analyze financial information to produce forecasts of business, industry, and economic conditions for use in making investment decisions. Assemble spreadsheets and draw charts and graphs used to illustrate technical reports, using computer. Evaluate and compare the relative quality of various securities in a given industry. Interpret data affecting investment programs, such as price, yield, stability, future trends in investment risks, and economic influences. Maintain knowledge and stay abreast of developments in the fields of industrial technology, business, finance, and economic theory. Monitor fundamental economic,

industrial, and corporate developments through the analysis of information obtained from financial publications and services, investment banking firms, government agencies, trade publications, company sources, and personal interviews. Prepare plans of action for investment based on financial analyses. Present oral and written reports on general economic trends, individual corporations, and entire industries. Recommend investments and investment timing to companies, investment firm staff, or the investing public. Collaborate with investment bankers to attract new corporate clients to securities firms. Contact brokers and purchase investments for companies according to company policy. Determine the prices at which securities should be syndicated and offered to the public.

GOE INFORMATION—Interest Area: 13. General Management and Support. **Work Group:** 13.02. Management Support. **Personality Type—**Investigative. Investigative occupations frequently involve working with ideas and require an extensive amount of thinking. These occupations can involve searching for facts and figuring out problems mentally. **Work Values—**Autonomy; Compensation; Creativity; Recognition; Social Status. **Skills—**Judgment and Decision Making; Systems Analysis; Critical Thinking; Systems Evaluation; Mathematics; Reading Comprehension; Complex Problem Solving; Management of Financial Resources. **Abilities—***Cognitive:* Number Facility; Mathematical Reasoning; Deductive Reasoning; Written Expression; Speed of Closure. *Psychomotor:* None met the criteria. *Physical:* Trunk Strength. *Sensory:* Near Vision; Speech Recognition; Speech Clarity; Auditory Attention. **General Work Activities—***Information Input:* Identifying Objects, Actions, and Events; Getting Information; Monitoring Processes, Materials, or Surroundings. *Mental Process:* Analyzing Data or Information; Updating and Using Relevant Knowledge; Judging Qualities of Things, Services, or Other People's Work. *Work Output:* Documenting or Recording Information; Interacting with Computers; Handling and Moving Objects. *Interacting with Others:* Communicating with Other Workers; Providing Consultation and Advice to Others; Communicating with Persons Outside Organization. **Physical Work Conditions—**Sitting; Indoors. **Other Job Characteristics—**Degree of Automation; Consequence of Error; Importance of Being Exact or Accurate.

Experience—Job Zone 5. Extensive skill, knowledge, and experience are needed for these occupations. **Job Preparation:** SVP 8.0 and above—four years to more than 10 years. **Knowledge—**Economics and Accounting; Mathematics; Law and Government; Computers and Electronics; Sales and Marketing. **Instructional Programs—**Accounting and Business/Management; Accounting and Finance; Finance, General.

Related DOT Jobs—160.267-026 Investment Analyst.

13-2052.00 Personal Financial Advisors

- **Education/Training Required:** Bachelor's degree
- **Employed:** 93,964
- **Annual Earnings:** $57,710
- **Growth:** 34.0%
- **Annual Job Openings:** 13,000

Advise clients on financial plans utilizing knowledge of tax and investment strategies, securities, insurance, pension plans, and real estate. Duties include assessing clients' assets, liabilities, cash flow, insurance coverage, tax status, and financial objectives to establish investment strategies.

Interviews client with debt problems to determine available monthly income after living expenses to meet credit obligations. Counsels client on financial problems, such as excessive spending and borrowing of funds. Establishes payment priorities to plan payoff method and estimate time for debt liquidation. Explains to individuals and groups financial assistance available to college and university students, such as loans, grants, and scholarships. Calculates amount of debt and funds available. Interviews students to obtain information and compares data on students' applications with eligibility requirements to determine eligibility for assistance program. Determines amount of aid to be granted, considering such factors as funds available, extent of demand, and needs of students. Contacts creditors to arrange for payment adjustments so that payments are feasible for client and agreeable to creditors. Opens account for client and disburses funds from account to creditors as agent for client. Prepares required records and reports. Authorizes release of funds to students. Assists in selection of candidates for specific financial awards or aid.

GOE INFORMATION—Interest Area: 12. Education and Social Service. **Work Group:** 12.03. Educational Services. **Personality Type—**Social. Social occupations frequently involve working with, communicating with, and teaching people. These occupations often involve helping or providing service to others. **Work Values—**Social Service; Good Working Conditions; Social Status; Authority; Pleasant Co-workers. **Skills—**Speaking; Service Orientation; Active Listening; Mathematics; Management of Financial Resources; Judgment and Decision Making; Critical Thinking; Complex Problem Solving. **Abilities—***Cognitive:* Mathematical Reasoning; Number Facility; Problem Sensitivity; Written Expression; Oral Comprehension. *Psychomotor:* None met the criteria. *Physical:* None met the criteria. *Sensory:* Speech Clarity; Speech Recognition. **General Work Activities—***Information Input:* Getting Information; Identifying Objects, Actions, and Events; Estimating Needed Characteristics. *Mental Process:* Analyzing Data or Information; Processing Information; Developing Objectives and Strategies. *Work Output:* Documenting or Recording Information; Interacting with Computers; Handling and Moving Objects. *Interacting with Others:* Communicating with Persons Outside Organization; Communicating with Other Workers; Establishing and Maintaining Relationships. **Physical Work Conditions—**Sitting; Indoors. **Other Job Characteristics—**Importance of Being Exact or Accurate; Consequence of Error; Importance of Repeating Same Tasks.

Experience—Job Zone 3. Previous work-related skill, knowledge, or experience is required. **Job Preparation:** SVP 6.0 to less than 7.0—more than one year and less than four years. **Knowledge—**Economics and Accounting; Mathematics; Customer and Personal Service; Administration and Management; Therapy and Counseling. **Instructional Programs—**Finance, General; Financial Planning and Services.

Related DOT Jobs—160.207-010 Credit Counselor; 169.267-018 Financial-Aid Counselor.

13-2053.00 Insurance Underwriters

- **Education/Training Required: Bachelor's degree**
- **Employed: 106,547**
- **Annual Earnings: $44,060**
- **Growth: 2.0%**
- **Annual Job Openings: 11,000**

Review individual applications for insurance to evaluate degree of risk involved and determine acceptance of applications.

Examine documents to determine degree of risk from such factors as applicant financial standing and value and condition of property. Decline excessive risks. Evaluate possibility of losses due to catastrophe or excessive insurance. Review company records to determine amount of insurance in force on single risk or group of closely related risks. Write to field representatives, medical personnel, and others to obtain further information, quote rates, or explain company underwriting policies. Decrease value of policy when risk is substandard and specify applicable endorsements or apply rating to ensure safe profitable distribution of

risks, using reference materials. Authorize reinsurance of policy when risk is high.

GOE INFORMATION—Interest Area: 13. General Management and Support. **Work Group:** 13.02. Management Support. **Personality Type—**Conventional. Conventional occupations frequently involve following set procedures and routines. These occupations can include working with data and details more than with ideas. Usually there is a clear line of authority to follow. **Work Values—**Advancement; Responsibility; Supervision, Human Relations; Good Working Conditions; Company Policies and Practices. **Skills—**Mathematics; Judgment and Decision Making; Critical Thinking; Writing; Reading Comprehension; Complex Problem Solving. **Abilities—***Cognitive:* Mathematical Reasoning; Written Comprehension; Written Expression; Problem Sensitivity; Number Facility. *Psychomotor:* None met the criteria. *Physical:* None met the criteria. *Sensory:* Near Vision. **General Work Activities—***Information Input:* Getting Information; Identifying Objects, Actions, and Events; Monitoring Processes, Materials, or Surroundings. *Mental Process:* Processing Information; Analyzing Data or Information; Making Decisions and Solving Problems. *Work Output:* Documenting or Recording Information; Handling and Moving Objects; Interacting with Computers. *Interacting with Others:* Communicating with Persons Outside Organization; Communicating with Other Workers; Interpreting Meaning of Information for Others. **Physical Work Conditions—**Sitting; Indoors. **Other Job Characteristics—**Consequence of Error; Importance of Being Exact or Accurate; Importance of Repeating Same Tasks.

Experience—Job Zone 4. A minimum of two to four years of work-related skill, knowledge, or experience is needed. **Job Preparation:** SVP 7.0 to less than 8.0—two years to less than 10 years. **Knowledge—**Economics and Accounting; Mathematics; Clerical; Administration and Management; Law and Government. **Instructional Programs—**Insurance.

Related DOT Jobs—169.267-046 Underwriter.

13-2061.00 Financial Examiners

- **Education/Training Required: Bachelor's degree**
- **Employed: 24,830**
- **Annual Earnings: $55,030**
- **Growth: 10.2%**
- **Annual Job Openings: 2,000**

Enforce or ensure compliance with laws and regulations governing financial and securities institutions and financial and real estate transactions. May examine, verify correctness of, or establish authenticity of records.

Direct and participate in formal and informal meetings with bank directors, trustees, senior management, counsels, outside accountants, and consultants in order to gather information and discuss findings. Investigate activities of institutions in order to enforce laws and regulations and to ensure legality of transactions and operations or financial solvency. Prepare reports, exhibits, and other supporting schedules that detail an institution's safety and soundness, compliance with laws and regulations, and recommended solutions to questionable financial conditions. Recommend actions to ensure compliance with laws and regulations or to protect solvency of institutions. Resolve problems concerning the overall financial integrity of banking institutions, including loan investment portfolios, capital, earnings, and specific or large troubled accounts. Review audit reports of internal and external auditors in order to monitor adequacy of scope of reports or to discover specific weaknesses in internal routines. Review balance sheets, operating income and expense accounts, and loan documentation in order to confirm institution assets and liabilities. Verify and inspect cash reserves, assigned collateral, and bank-owned securities in order to check internal control procedures. Confer with officials of real estate, securities, or financial institution industries in order to exchange views and discuss issues or pending cases. Establish guidelines for procedures and policies that comply with new and revised regulations and direct their implementation. Evaluate data processing applications for institutions under examination in order to develop recommendations for coordinating existing systems with examination procedures. Examine the minutes of meetings of directors, stockholders, and committees in order to investigate the specific authority extended at various levels of management. Plan, supervise, and review work of assigned subordinates. Review and analyze new, proposed, or revised laws, regulations, policies, and procedures in order to interpret their meaning and determine their impact. Review applications for mergers, acquisitions, establishment of new institutions, acceptance in Federal Reserve System, or registration of securities sales in order to determine their public interest value and conformance to regulations and recommend acceptance or rejection. Train other examiners in the financial examination process.

GOE INFORMATION—Interest Area: 04. Law, Law Enforcement, and Public Safety. **Work Group:** 04.04. Public Safety. **Personality Type—** Enterprising. Enterprising occupations frequently involve starting up and carrying out projects. These occupations can involve leading people and making many decisions. They sometimes require risk taking and often deal with business. **Work Values—**Good Working Conditions; Authority; Advancement; Social Status; Compensation. **Skills—**Reading Comprehension; Writing; Judgment and Decision Making; Mathematics; Speaking; Negotiation; Systems Analysis; Active Listening. **Abilities—***Cognitive:* Mathematical Reasoning; Number Facility; Written Expression; Problem Sensitivity; Written Comprehension. *Psychomotor:* None met the criteria. *Physical:* Trunk Strength. *Sensory:* Near Vision; Speech Recognition; Speech Clarity. **General Work Activities—***Information Input:* Identifying Objects, Actions, and Events; Getting Information; Monitoring Processes, Materials, or Surroundings. *Mental Process:* Evaluating Information Against Standards; Updating and Using Relevant Knowledge; Processing Information. *Work Output:* Documenting or Recording Information; Interacting with Computers; Drafting and Specifying Technical Devices. *Interacting with Others:* Communicating with Persons Outside Organization; Providing Consultation and Advice to Others; Communicating with Other Workers. **Physical Work Conditions—**Sitting; Indoors; Walking or Running; Radiation. **Other Job Characteristics—**Consequence of Error; Importance of Being Exact or Accurate; Importance of Repeating Same Tasks.

Experience—Job Zone 4. A minimum of two to four years of work-related skill, knowledge, or experience is needed. **Job Preparation:** SVP 7.0 to less than 8.0—two years to less than 10 years. **Knowledge—**Economics and Accounting; Education and Training; Law and Government; Administration and Management; Mathematics. **Instructional Programs—**Accounting; Taxation.

Related DOT Jobs—160.167-046 Chief Bank Examiner; 186.117-090 Compliance Officer; 188.167-038 Director, Securities and Real Estate.

13-2071.00 Loan Counselors

- **Education/Training Required: Bachelor's degree**
- **Employed: 28,738**
- **Annual Earnings: $31,470**
- **Growth: 16.0%**
- **Annual Job Openings: 3,000**

Provide guidance to prospective loan applicants who have problems qualifying for traditional loans. Guidance may include determining the best type of loan and explaining loan requirements or restrictions.

Analyze applicants' financial status, credit, and property evaluations to determine feasibility of granting loans. Approve loans within specified limits. Calculate amount of debt and funds available in order to plan methods of payoff and to estimate time for debt liquidation. Check loan agreements to ensure that they are complete and accurate according to policies. Contact applicants or creditors to resolve questions about applications or to assist with completion of paperwork. Interview applicants and request specified information for loan applications. Maintain and review account records, updating and recategorizing them according to status changes. Maintain current knowledge of credit regulations. Refer loans to loan committees for approval. Review accounts to determine write-offs for collection agencies. Submit applications to credit analysts for verification and recommendation. Analyze potential loan markets to find opportunities to promote loans and financial services. Arrange for maintenance and liquidation of delinquent properties. Assist in selection of financial award candidates, using electronic databases to certify loan eligibility. Authorize and sign mail collection letters. Compare data on student aid applications with eligibility requirements of assistance programs. Confer with underwriters to resolve mortgage application problems. Contact borrowers with delinquent accounts to obtain payment in full or to negotiate repayment plans. Contact creditors to explain clients' financial situations and to arrange for payment adjustments so that payments are feasible for clients and agreeable to creditors. Counsel clients on personal and family financial problems, such as excessive spending and borrowing of funds. Establish payment priorities according to credit terms and interest rates in order to reduce clients' overall costs. Inform individuals and groups about the financial assistance available to college or university students. Locate debtors using post office directories, utility services account listings, and mailing lists. Match students' needs and eligibility with available financial aid programs in order to provide informed recommendations. Open accounts for clients and disburse funds from clients' accounts to creditors. Petition courts to transfer titles and deeds of collateral to banks.

GOE INFORMATION—Interest Area: 13. General Management and Support. **Work Group:** 13.02. Management Support. **Personality Type—** Enterprising. Enterprising occupations frequently involve starting up and carrying out projects. These occupations can involve leading people and making many decisions. They sometimes require risk taking and often deal with business. **Work Values—**Advancement; Good Working Conditions; Pleasant Co-workers; Social Service; Responsibility. **Skills—** Speaking; Management of Personnel Resources; Mathematics; Reading Comprehension; Judgment and Decision Making; Active Listening; Writing; Complex Problem Solving. **Abilities—***Cognitive:* Number Facility; Written Expression; Oral Expression; Mathematical Reasoning; Written Comprehension. *Psychomotor:* Wrist-Finger Speed; Response Orientation. *Physical:* None met the criteria. *Sensory:* Speech Recognition; Speech Clarity; Near Vision. **General Work Activities—***Information Input:* Getting Information; Identifying Objects, Actions, and Events; Monitoring Processes, Materials, or Surroundings. *Mental Process:* Analyzing Data or Information; Processing Information; Evaluating Information Against Standards. *Work Output:* Documenting or Recording Information; Interacting with Computers; Handling and Moving Objects. *Interacting with Others:* Communicating with Persons Outside Organization; Establishing and Maintaining Relationships; Communicating with Other Workers. **Physical Work Conditions—**Sitting; Indoors. **Other Job Characteristics—**Importance of Being Exact or Accurate; Degree of Automation; Consequence of Error.

Experience—Job Zone 4. A minimum of two to four years of work-related skill, knowledge, or experience is needed. **Job Preparation:** SVP 7.0 to less than 8.0—two years to less than 10 years. **Knowledge**—Economics and Accounting; Law and Government; Sales and Marketing; Customer and Personal Service; Mathematics. **Instructional Programs**—Banking and Financial Support Services; Finance and Financial Management Services, Other.

Related DOT Jobs—160.207-010 Credit Counselor; 169.267-018 Financial-Aid Counselor.

13-2072.00 Loan Officers

- **Education/Training Required: Bachelor's degree**
- **Employed: 235,952**
- **Annual Earnings: $43,210**
- **Growth: 4.9%**
- **Annual Job Openings: 28,000**

Evaluate, authorize, or recommend approval of commercial, real estate, or credit loans. Advise borrowers on financial status and methods of payments. Includes mortgage loan officers and agents, collection analysts, loan servicing officers, and loan underwriters.

Analyze applicants' financial status, credit, and property evaluations to determine feasibility of granting loans. Analyze potential loan markets and develop referral networks in order to locate prospects for loans. Approve loans within specified limits and refer loan applications outside those limits to management for approval. Compute payment schedules. Explain to customers the different types of loans and credit options that are available, as well as the terms of those services. Meet with applicants to obtain information for loan applications and to answer questions about the process. Negotiate payment arrangements with customers who have delinquent loans. Obtain and compile copies of loan applicants' credit histories, corporate financial statements, and other financial information. Prepare reports to send to customers whose accounts are delinquent; forward irreconcilable accounts for collector action. Review and update credit and loan files. Review loan agreements to ensure that they are complete and accurate according to policy. Submit applications to credit analysts for verification and recommendation. Work with clients to identify their financial goals and to find ways of reaching those goals. Arrange for maintenance and liquidation of delinquent properties. Confer with underwriters to aid in resolving mortgage application problems. Handle customer complaints and take appropriate action to resolve them. Interview, hire, and train new employees. Market bank products to individuals and firms, promoting bank services that may meet customers' needs. Petition courts to transfer titles and deeds of collateral to banks. Provide special services such as investment banking for clients with more specialized needs. Set credit policies, credit lines, procedures, and standards in conjunction with senior managers. Stay abreast of new types of loans and other financial services and products in order to better meet customers' needs. Supervise loan personnel.

GOE INFORMATION—Interest Area: 13. General Management and Support. **Work Group:** 13.02. Management Support. **Personality Type**—Enterprising. Enterprising occupations frequently involve starting up and carrying out projects. These occupations can involve leading people and making many decisions. They sometimes require risk taking and often deal with business. **Work Values**—Advancement; Good Working Conditions; Pleasant Co-workers; Social Service; Responsibility. **Skills**—Speaking; Management of Personnel Resources; Mathematics; Reading Comprehension; Judgment and Decision Making; Active Listening; Writing; Complex Problem Solving. **Abilities**—*Cognitive:* Number Facility; Written Expression; Oral Expression; Mathematical Reasoning; Written Comprehension. *Psychomotor:* Wrist-Finger Speed; Response Orienta-

tion. *Physical:* None met the criteria. *Sensory:* Speech Recognition; Speech Clarity; Near Vision. **General Work Activities**—*Information Input:* Getting Information; Identifying Objects, Actions, and Events; Monitoring Processes, Materials, or Surroundings. *Mental Process:* Analyzing Data or Information; Processing Information; Evaluating Information Against Standards. *Work Output:* Documenting or Recording Information; Interacting with Computers; Handling and Moving Objects. *Interacting with Others:* Communicating with Persons Outside Organization; Establishing and Maintaining Relationships; Communicating with Other Workers. **Physical Work Conditions**—Sitting; Indoors. **Other Job Characteristics**—Importance of Being Exact or Accurate; Degree of Automation; Consequence of Error.

Experience—Job Zone 4. A minimum of two to four years of work-related skill, knowledge, or experience is needed. **Job Preparation:** SVP 7.0 to less than 8.0—two years to less than 10 years. **Knowledge**—Economics and Accounting; Law and Government; Sales and Marketing; Customer and Personal Service; Mathematics. **Instructional Programs**—Credit Management; Finance, General.

Related DOT Jobs—186.167-078 Commercial Loan Collection Officer; 186.267-018 Loan Officer.

13-2081.00 Tax Examiners, Collectors, and Revenue Agents

- **Education/Training Required: Bachelor's degree**
- **Employed: 79,428**
- **Annual Earnings: $42,860**
- **Growth: 8.3%**
- **Annual Job Openings: 6,000**

Determine tax liability or collect taxes from individuals or business firms according to prescribed laws and regulations.

Check tax forms in order to verify that names and taxpayer identification numbers are correct, that computations have been performed correctly, and that amounts match those on supporting documentation. Collect taxes from individuals or businesses according to prescribed laws and regulations. Conduct independent field audits and investigations of income tax returns in order to verify information and/or to amend tax liabilities. Confer with taxpayers or their representatives in order to discuss the issues, laws, and regulations involved in returns and to resolve problems with returns. Contact taxpayers by mail or telephone in order to address discrepancies and to request supporting documentation. Determine appropriate methods of debt settlement, such as offers of compromise, wage garnishment, or seizure and sale of property. Examine accounting systems and records in order to determine whether accounting methods used were appropriate and in compliance with statutory provisions. Examine and analyze tax assets and liabilities in order to determine resolution of delinquent tax problems. Impose payment deadlines on delinquent taxpayers and monitor payments in order to ensure that deadlines are met. Investigate claims of inability to pay taxes by researching court information for the status of liens, mortgages, or financial statements or by locating assets through third parties. Maintain knowledge of tax code changes and of accounting procedures and theory in order to properly evaluate financial information. Maintain records for each case, including contacts, telephone numbers, and actions taken. Process individual and corporate income tax returns and sales and excise tax returns. Review filed tax returns in order to determine whether claimed tax credits and deductions are allowed by law. Review selected tax returns in order to determine the nature and extent of audits to be performed on them. Secure a taxpayer's agreement to discharge a tax assessment or submit contested determinations to other administrative or judicial conferees for appeals hearings. Direct service of legal documents, such as subpoenas, warrants, notices of assessment, and garnishments. Enter tax return information into computers for processing. Install systems of recording costs or other financial and budgetary data or provide advice on such systems based on examination of current financial records. Notify taxpayers of any overpayment or underpayment and either issue a refund or request further payment. Participate in informal appeals hearings on contested cases from other agents. Prepare briefs and assist in searching and seizing records in order to prepare charges and documentation for court cases. Recommend criminal prosecutions and/or civil penalties. Request that the state or federal revenue service prepare a return on a taxpayer's behalf in cases where taxes have not been filed. Send notices to taxpayers when accounts are delinquent. Serve as members of regional appeals board in order to re-examine unresolved issues in terms of relevant laws and regulations.

GOE INFORMATION—Interest Area: 13. General Management and Support. **Work Group:** 13.02. Management Support. **Personality Type—**Conventional. Conventional occupations frequently involve following set procedures and routines. These occupations can include working with data and details more than with ideas. Usually there is a clear line of authority to follow. **Work Values—**Good Working Conditions; Supervision, Human Relations; Security; Authority; Company Policies and Practices. **Skills—**Mathematics; Complex Problem Solving; Reading Comprehension; Judgment and Decision Making; Critical Thinking; Speaking; Active Listening; Writing. **Abilities—***Cognitive:* Mathematical Reasoning; Number Facility; Written Comprehension; Deductive Reasoning; Oral Expression. *Psychomotor:* None met the criteria. *Physical:* None met the criteria. *Sensory:* Speech Recognition; Near Vision; Speech Clarity. **General Work Activities—***Information Input:* Getting Information; Identifying Objects, Actions, and Events; Estimating Needed Characteristics. *Mental Process:* Analyzing Data or Information; Evaluating Information Against Standards; Updating and Using Relevant Knowledge. *Work Output:* Documenting or Recording Information; Interacting with Computers; Handling and Moving Objects. *Interacting with Others:* Providing Consultation and Advice to Others; Communicating with Persons Outside Organization; Interpreting Meaning of Information for Others. **Physical Work Conditions—**Sitting; Indoors. **Other Job Characteristics—**Importance of Being Exact or Accurate; Consequence of Error; Importance of Repeating Same Tasks.

Experience—Job Zone 4. A minimum of two to four years of work-related skill, knowledge, or experience is needed. **Job Preparation:** SVP 7.0 to less than 8.0—two years to less than 10 years. **Knowledge—**Economics and Accounting; Law and Government; Mathematics; Administration and Management; English Language. **Instructional Programs—**Accounting; Taxation.

Related DOT Jobs—160.167-050 Revenue Agent; 188.167-074 Revenue Officer.

13-2082.00 Tax Preparers

- **Education/Training Required: Moderate-term on-the-job training**
- **Employed: 68,557**
- **Annual Earnings: $27,680**
- **Growth: 17.4%**
- **Annual Job Openings: 8,000**

Prepare tax returns for individuals or small businesses but do not have the background or responsibilities of an accredited or certified public accountant.

Check data input or verify totals on forms prepared by others to detect errors in arithmetic, data entry, or procedures. Compute taxes owed or overpaid, using adding machines or personal computers, and complete entries on forms, following tax form instructions and tax tables. Interview clients to obtain additional information on taxable income and deductible expenses and allowances. Prepare or assist in preparing simple to complex tax returns for individuals or small businesses. Review financial records such as income statements and documentation of expenditures in order to determine forms needed to prepare tax returns. Use all appropriate adjustments, deductions, and credits to keep clients' taxes to a minimum. Calculate form preparation fees according to return complexity and processing time required. Consult tax law handbooks or bulletins in order to determine procedures for preparation of atypical returns. Furnish taxpayers with sufficient information and advice in order to ensure correct tax form completion.

GOE INFORMATION—Interest Area: 09. Business Detail. **Work Group:** 09.03. Bookkeeping, Auditing, and Accounting. **Personality Type—**Conventional. Conventional occupations frequently involve following set procedures and routines. These occupations can include working with data and details more than with ideas. Usually there is a clear line of authority to follow. **Work Values—**Good Working Conditions; Social Service; Independence; Pleasant Co-workers; Compensation. **Skills—**Mathematics; Speaking; Reading Comprehension; Active Listening. **Abilities—***Cognitive:* Number Facility; Mathematical Reasoning; Deductive Reasoning; Oral Expression; Written Comprehension. *Psychomotor:* None met the criteria. *Physical:* None met the criteria. *Sensory:* Speech Recognition; Near Vision; Speech Clarity. **General Work Activities—***Information Input:* Getting Information; Identifying Objects, Actions, and Events; Estimating Needed Characteristics. *Mental Process:* Processing Information; Evaluating Information Against Standards; Analyzing Data or Information. *Work Output:* Documenting or Recording Information; Handling and Moving Objects; Interacting with Computers. *Interacting with Others:* Communicating with Persons Outside Organization; Performing Administrative Activities; Performing for or Working with the Public. **Physical Work Conditions—**Sitting; Making Repetitive Motions; Indoors. **Other Job Characteristics—**Importance of Being Exact or Accurate; Consequence of Error; Importance of Repeating Same Tasks.

Experience—Job Zone 2. Some previous work-related skill, knowledge, or experience may be helpful, but usually is not needed. **Job Preparation:** SVP 4.0 to less than 6.0—six months to less than two years. **Knowledge—**Economics and Accounting; Law and Government; Clerical; Mathematics; Customer and Personal Service. **Instructional Programs—**Accounting Technology/Technician and Bookkeeping; Taxation.

Related DOT Jobs—219.362-070 Tax Preparer.

13-2099.99 Financial Specialists, All Other

- **Education/Training Required: Bachelor's degree**
- **Employed: No data available.**
- **Annual Earnings: No data available.**
- **Growth: 28.0%**
- **Annual Job Openings: 20,000**

All financial specialists not listed separately.

No task data available.

GOE INFORMATION—Interest Area: 13. General Management and Support. **Work Group:** 13.01. General Management Work and Management of Support Functions. **Note:** The Department of Labor has not collected some data for this job, so it has fewer details than the other descriptions.

Instructional Programs—Finance, General.

Related DOT Jobs—169.267-042 Letter-Of-Credit Document Examiner.

15-0000

Computer and Mathematical Occupations

15-1000 Computer Specialists

15-1011.00 Computer and Information Scientists, Research

- Education/Training Required: Doctoral degree
- Employed: 28,046
- Annual Earnings: $75,130
- Growth: 40.3%
- Annual Job Openings: 2,000

Conduct research into fundamental computer and information science as theorists, designers, or inventors. Solve or develop solutions to problems in the field of computer hardware and software.

No task data available.

GOE INFORMATION—Interest Area: 02. Science, Math, and Engineering. Work Group: 02.06. Mathematics and Computers. Note: The Department of Labor has not collected some data for this job, so it has fewer details than the other descriptions.

Instructional Programs—Artificial Intelligence and Robotics; Computer and Information Sciences and Support Services, Other; Computer and Information Sciences, General; Computer Science; Computer Systems Analysis/Analyst; Information Science/Studies; Medical Informatics.

Related DOT Jobs—030.062-010 Software Engineer.

15-1021.00 Computer Programmers

- Education/Training Required: Bachelor's degree
- Employed: 585,386
- Annual Earnings: $60,120
- Growth: 16.2%
- Annual Job Openings: 36,000

Convert project specifications and statements of problems and procedures to detailed logical flow charts for coding into computer language. Develop and write computer programs to store, locate, and retrieve specific documents, data, and information. May program Web sites.

Compile and write documentation of program development and subsequent revisions, inserting comments in the coded instructions so others can understand the program. Conduct trial runs of programs and software applications to be sure that they will produce the desired information and that the instructions are correct. Consult with managerial, engineering, and technical personnel to clarify program intent, identify problems, and suggest changes. Correct errors by making appropriate changes and then rechecking the program to ensure that the desired results are produced. Investigate whether networks, workstations, the central processing unit of the system, and/or peripheral equipment are responding to a program's instructions. Perform or direct revision, repair, or expansion of existing programs to increase operating efficiency or adapt to new requirements. Perform systems analysis and programming tasks to maintain and control the use of computer systems software as a systems programmer. Prepare detailed workflow charts and diagrams that describe input, output, and logical operation and convert them into a series of instructions coded in a computer language. Write, analyze, review, and rewrite programs, using workflow chart and diagram and applying knowledge of computer capabilities, subject matter, and symbolic logic. Write, update, and maintain computer programs or software packages to handle specific jobs, such as tracking inventory, storing or retrieving data, or controlling other equipment. Assign, coordinate, and review work and activities of programming personnel. Collaborate with computer manufacturers and other users to develop new programming methods. Consult with and assist computer operators or system analysts to define and resolve problems in running computer programs. Train subordinates in programming and program coding. Write or contribute to instructions or manuals to guide end users.

GOE INFORMATION—Interest Area: 02. Science, Math, and Engineering. Work Group: 02.06. Mathematics and Computers. Personality Type—Investigative. Investigative occupations frequently involve working with ideas and require an extensive amount of thinking. These occupations can involve searching for facts and figuring out problems mentally. Work Values—Creativity; Ability Utilization; Advancement; Autonomy; Compensation. Skills—Programming; Troubleshooting; Technology Design; Quality Control Analysis; Operations Analysis; Complex Problem Solving; Writing; Instructing. Abilities—*Cognitive:* Written Expression; Mathematical Reasoning; Inductive Reasoning; Speed of Closure; Originality. *Psychomotor:* Wrist-Finger Speed; Finger Dexterity. *Physical:* Trunk Strength. *Sensory:* Near Vision; Speech Clarity; Visual Color Discrimination; Speech Recognition; Hearing Sensitivity. General Work Activities—*Information Input:* Getting Information; Identifying Objects, Actions, and Events; Monitoring Processes, Materials, or Surroundings. *Mental Process:* Updating and Using Relevant Knowledge; Thinking Creatively; Processing Information. *Work Output:* Interacting with Computers; Documenting or Recording Information; Drafting and Specifying Technical Devices. *Interacting with Others:* Communicating with Other Workers; Providing Consultation and Advice to Others; Interpreting Meaning of Information for Others. Physical Work Conditions—Sitting; Indoors; Making Repetitive Motions; Walking or Running. Other Job Characteristics—Degree of Automation; Importance of Being Exact or Accurate; Consequence of Error.

Experience—Job Zone 4. A minimum of two to four years of work-related skill, knowledge, or experience is needed. Job Preparation: SVP 7.0 to less than 8.0—two years to less than 10 years. Knowledge—Computers and Electronics; Education and Training; Mathematics; Clerical; Communications and Media. Instructional Programs—Artificial Intelligence and Robotics; Bioinformatics; Computer Graphics; Computer Programming, Specific Applications; Computer Programming, Vendor/Product Certification; Computer Programming/Programmer, General; E-Commerce/Electronic Commerce; Management Information Systems, General; Medical Informatics; Medical Office Computer Specialist/Assistant; Web Page, Digital/Multimedia, and Information Resources Design; Web/Multimedia Management and Webmaster.

Related DOT Jobs—030.162-010 Computer Programmer; 030.162-018 Programmer, Engineering and Scientific; 030.167-010 Chief, Computer Programmer.

15-1031.00 Computer Software Engineers, Applications

- Education/Training Required: Bachelor's degree
- Employed: 379,969
- Annual Earnings: $70,210
- Growth: 100.0%
- Annual Job Openings: 28,000

Develop, create, and modify general computer applications software or specialized utility programs. Analyze user needs and develop software solutions. Design software or customize software for client use with the aim of optimizing operational efficiency. May analyze and design databases within an application area, working individually or coordinating database development as part of a team.

Analyze information to determine, recommend, and plan computer specifications and layouts and peripheral equipment modifications. Analyze user needs and software requirements to determine feasibility of design within time and cost constraints. Confer with systems analysts, engineers, programmers, and others to design system and to obtain information on project limitations and capabilities, performance requirements, and interfaces. Coordinate software system installation and monitor equipment functioning to ensure specifications are met. Design, develop, and modify software systems, using scientific analysis and mathematical models to predict and measure outcome and consequences of design. Determine system performance standards. Develop and direct software system testing and validation procedures, programming, and documentation. Modify existing software to correct errors, to allow it to adapt to new hardware, or to improve its performance. Obtain and evaluate information on factors such as reporting formats required, costs, and security needs to determine hardware configuration. Store, retrieve, and manipulate data for analysis of system capabilities and requirements. Consult with customers about software system design and maintenance. Recommend purchase of equipment to control dust, temperature, and humidity in area of system installation. Specify power supply requirements and configuration. Supervise the work of programmers, technologists and technicians, and other engineering and scientific personnel. Train users to use new or modified equipment.

GOE INFORMATION—Interest Area: 02. Science, Math, and Engineering. **Work Group:** 02.07. Engineering. **Personality Type—**Investigative. Investigative occupations frequently involve working with ideas and require an extensive amount of thinking. These occupations can involve searching for facts and figuring out problems mentally. **Work Values—**Creativity; Ability Utilization; Good Working Conditions; Responsibility; Social Status. **Skills—**Programming; Troubleshooting; Installation; Operations Analysis; Technology Design; Management of Material Resources; Science; Equipment Selection. **Abilities—***Cognitive:* Mathematical Reasoning; Inductive Reasoning; Deductive Reasoning; Oral Expression; Written Expression. *Psychomotor:* Response Orientation; Wrist-Finger Speed. *Physical:* Gross Body Coordination. *Sensory:* Speech Clarity; Speech Recognition; Near Vision; Auditory Attention; Visual Color Discrimination. **General Work Activities—***Information Input:* Identifying Objects, Actions, and Events; Getting Information; Monitoring Processes, Materials, or Surroundings. *Mental Process:* Updating and Using Relevant Knowledge; Analyzing Data or Information; Thinking Creatively. *Work Output:* Interacting with Computers; Drafting and Specifying Technical Devices; Documenting or Recording Information. *Interacting with Others:* Providing Consultation and Advice to Others; Communicating with Other Workers; Communicating with Persons Outside Organization. **Physical Work Conditions—**Sitting; Indoors; Making Repetitive Motions; Walking or Running. **Other Job Characteristics—**Degree of Automation; Importance of Being Exact or Accurate; Pace Determined by Speed of Equipment.

Experience—Job Zone 4. A minimum of two to four years of work-related skill, knowledge, or experience is needed. **Job Preparation:** SVP 7.0 to less than 8.0—two years to less than 10 years. **Knowledge—**Computers and Electronics; Mathematics; Engineering and Technology; Design; Education and Training. **Instructional Programs—**Artificial Intelligence and Robotics; Bioinformatics; Computer Engineering Technologies/Technicians, Other; Computer Engineering, General; Computer Science; Computer Software Engineering; Information Technology; Medical Illustration and Informatics, Other; Medical Informatics.

Related DOT Jobs—030.062-010 Software Engineer.

15-1032.00 Computer Software Engineers, Systems Software

- **Education/Training Required: Bachelor's degree**
- **Employed: 316,858**
- **Annual Earnings: $73,280**
- **Growth: 89.7%**
- **Annual Job Openings: 23,000**

Research, design, develop, and test operating systems-level software, compilers, and network distribution software for medical, industrial, military, communications, aerospace, business, scientific, and general computing applications. Set operational specifications and formulate and analyze software requirements. Apply principles and techniques of computer science, engineering, and mathematical analysis.

Analyze information to determine, recommend, and plan installation of a new system or modification of an existing system. Confer with data processing and project managers to obtain information on limitations and capabilities for data processing projects. Consult with engineering staff to evaluate interface between hardware and software, develop specifications and performance requirements, and resolve customer problems. Coordinate installation of software system. Design and develop software systems, using scientific analysis and mathematical models to predict and measure outcome and consequences of design. Develop and direct software system testing and validation procedures. Direct software programming and development of documentation. Evaluate factors such as reporting formats required, cost constraints, and need for security restrictions to determine hardware configuration. Modify existing software to correct errors, to adapt it to new hardware, or to upgrade interfaces and improve performance. Monitor functioning of equipment to ensure system operates in conformance with specifications. Store, retrieve, and manipulate data for analysis of system capabilities and requirements. Advise customer about, or perform, maintenance of software system. Consult with customers and/or other departments on project status, proposals, and technical issues such as software system design and maintenance. Prepare reports and correspondence concerning project specifications, activities, and status. Recommend purchase of equipment to control dust, temperature, and humidity in area of system installation. Specify power supply requirements and configuration. Supervise and assign work to programmers, designers, technologists and technicians, and other engineering and scientific personnel. Train users to use new or modified equipment. Utilize microcontrollers to develop control signals, implement control algorithms, and measure process variables such as temperatures, pressures, and positions.

GOE INFORMATION—Interest Area: 02. Science, Math, and Engineering. **Work Group:** 02.07. Engineering. **Personality Type—**Investigative. Investigative occupations frequently involve working with ideas and require an extensive amount of thinking. These occupations can involve searching for facts and figuring out problems mentally. **Work Values—**Creativity; Ability Utilization; Good Working Conditions; Responsibility; Social Status. **Skills—**Programming; Troubleshooting; Installation; Operations Analysis; Technology Design; Management of Material Resources; Science; Equipment Selection. **Abilities—***Cognitive:* Mathematical Reasoning; Inductive Reasoning; Deductive Reasoning; Oral Expression; Written Expression. *Psychomotor:* Response Orientation; Wrist-Finger Speed. *Physical:* Gross Body Coordination. *Sensory:* Speech Clarity; Speech Recognition; Near Vision; Auditory Attention; Visual Color Discrimination. **General Work Activities—***Information Input:* Identifying Objects, Actions, and Events; Getting Information; Estimating Needed Characteristics. *Mental Process:* Updating and Using Relevant Knowledge; Analyzing Data or Information; Thinking Creatively.

Work Output: Interacting with Computers; Drafting and Specifying Technical Devices; Documenting or Recording Information. *Interacting with Others:* Providing Consultation and Advice to Others; Communicating with Other Workers; Communicating with Persons Outside Organization. **Physical Work Conditions**—Sitting; Indoors; Making Repetitive Motions; Walking or Running. **Other Job Characteristics**—Degree of Automation; Importance of Being Exact or Accurate; Pace Determined by Speed of Equipment.

Experience—Job Zone 4. A minimum of two to four years of work-related skill, knowledge, or experience is needed. **Job Preparation:** SVP 7.0 to less than 8.0—two years to less than 10 years. **Knowledge**—Computers and Electronics; Mathematics; Engineering and Technology; Design; Education and Training. **Instructional Programs**—Artificial Intelligence and Robotics; Computer Engineering Technologies/Technicians, Other; Computer Engineering, General; Computer Science; Information Science/Studies; Information Technology.

Related DOT Jobs—030.062-010 Software Engineer.

15-1041.00 Computer Support Specialists

- **Education/Training Required: Associate's degree**
- **Employed: 505,616**
- **Annual Earnings: $38,560**
- **Growth: 97.0%**
- **Annual Job Openings: 40,000**

Provide technical assistance to computer system users. Answer questions or resolve computer problems for clients in person, via telephone, or from remote location. May provide assistance concerning the use of computer hardware and software, including printing, installation, word processing, electronic mail, and operating systems.

Develop training materials and procedures and/or train users in the proper use of hardware and software. Inspect equipment and read order sheets to prepare for delivery to users. Install and perform minor repairs to hardware, software, and peripheral equipment, following design or installation specifications. Modify and customize commercial programs for internal needs. Oversee the daily performance of computer systems. Prepare evaluations of software or hardware and recommend improvements or upgrades. Set up equipment for employee use, performing or ensuring proper installation of cable, operating systems, and appropriate software. Supervise and coordinate workers engaged in problem-solving, monitoring, and installing data communication equipment and software. Answer users' inquiries regarding computer software and hardware operation to resolve problems. Enter commands and observe system functioning to verify correct operations and detect errors. Maintain record of daily data communication transactions, problems and remedial action taken, and installation activities. Read technical manuals, confer with users, and conduct computer diagnostics to investigate and resolve problems and to provide technical assistance and support. Read trade magazines and technical manuals and attend conferences and seminars to maintain knowledge of hardware and software. Refer major hardware or software problems or defective products to vendors or technicians for service. Conduct office automation feasibility studies, including workflow analysis, space design, and cost comparison analysis. Confer with staff, users, and management to establish requirements for new systems or modifications.

GOE INFORMATION—Interest Area: 02. Science, Math, and Engineering. **Work Group:** 02.06. Mathematics and Computers. **Personality Type**—Investigative. Investigative occupations frequently involve working with ideas and require an extensive amount of thinking. These

occupations can involve searching for facts and figuring out problems mentally. **Work Values**—Creativity; Advancement; Variety; Social Service; Autonomy. **Skills**—Programming; Troubleshooting; Quality Control Analysis; Installation; Equipment Selection; Technology Design; Systems Analysis; Complex Problem Solving. **Abilities**—*Cognitive:* Written Comprehension; Originality; Written Expression; Deductive Reasoning; Oral Expression. *Psychomotor:* Finger Dexterity; Arm-Hand Steadiness; Wrist-Finger Speed; Manual Dexterity; Control Precision. *Physical:* Extent Flexibility; Gross Body Coordination; Dynamic Flexibility. *Sensory:* Speech Clarity; Near Vision; Visual Color Discrimination; Speech Recognition; Auditory Attention. **General Work Activities**—*Information Input:* Getting Information; Monitoring Processes, Materials, or Surroundings; Identifying Objects, Actions, and Events. *Mental Process:* Updating and Using Relevant Knowledge; Judging Qualities of Things, Services, or Other People's Work; Analyzing Data or Information. *Work Output:* Interacting with Computers; Repairing and Maintaining Electronic Equipment; Handling and Moving Objects. *Interacting with Others:* Communicating with Other Workers; Teaching Others; Providing Consultation and Advice to Others. **Physical Work Conditions**—Sitting; Indoors; Using Hands on Objects, Tools, or Controls; Cramped Work Space or Awkward Positions; Making Repetitive Motions. **Other Job Characteristics**—Degree of Automation; Pace Determined by Speed of Equipment; Importance of Being Exact or Accurate.

Experience—Job Zone 4. A minimum of two to four years of work-related skill, knowledge, or experience is needed. **Job Preparation:** SVP 7.0 to less than 8.0—two years to less than 10 years. **Knowledge**—Computers and Electronics; Education and Training; Design; Telecommunications; Customer and Personal Service. **Instructional Programs**—Accounting and Computer Science; Agricultural Business Technology; Computer Hardware Technology/Technician; Computer Software Technology/Technician; Data Processing and Data Processing Technology/Technician; Medical Office Computer Specialist/Assistant.

Related DOT Jobs—031.132-010 Supervisor, Network Control Operators; 031.262-014 Network Control Operator; 032.132-010 User Support Analyst Supervisor; 032.262-010 User Support Analyst; 033.162-018 Technical Support Specialist; 039.264-010 Microcomputer Support Specialist.

15-1051.00 Computer Systems Analysts

- **Education/Training Required: Bachelor's degree**
- **Employed: 431,428**
- **Annual Earnings: $61,990**
- **Growth: 59.7%**
- **Annual Job Openings: 34,000**

Analyze science, engineering, business, and all other data processing problems for application to electronic data processing systems. Analyze user requirements, procedures, and problems to automate or improve existing systems and review computer system capabilities, workflow, and scheduling limitations. May analyze or recommend commercially available software. May supervise computer programmers.

Analyze information processing or computation needs and plan and design computer systems, using techniques such as structured analysis, data modeling, and information engineering. Assess the usefulness of pre-developed application packages and adapt them to a user environment. Confer with clients regarding the nature of the information processing or computation needs a computer program is to address. Define the goals of the system and devise flow charts and diagrams describing logical operational steps of programs. Determine computer software or hardware needed to set up or alter system. Develop, document, and revise system design procedures, test procedures, and quality standards. Expand or modify system to serve new purposes or improve work flow. Interview or survey workers, observe job performance, and/or perform the job in order to determine what information is processed and how it is processed. Provide staff and users with assistance solving computer-related problems, such as malfunctions and program problems. Recommend new equipment or software packages. Review and analyze computer printouts and performance indicators to locate code problems; correct errors by correcting codes. Specify inputs accessed by the system and plan the distribution and use of the results. Test, maintain, and monitor computer programs and systems, including coordinating the installation of computer programs and systems. Train staff and users to work with computer systems and programs. Use object-oriented programming languages, as well as client/server applications development processes and multimedia and Internet technology. Consult with management to ensure agreement on system principles. Coordinate and link the computer systems within an organization to increase compatibility and so that information can be shared. Prepare cost-benefit and return-on-investment analyses to aid in decisions on system implementation. Read manuals, periodicals, and technical reports to learn how to develop programs that meet staff and user requirements. Supervise computer programmers or other systems analysts or serve as project leaders for particular systems projects. Utilize the computer in the analysis and solution of business problems, such as the development of integrated production and inventory control and cost analysis systems.

GOE INFORMATION—Interest Area: 02. Science, Math, and Engineering. **Work Group:** 02.06. Mathematics and Computers. **Personality Type**—Investigative. Investigative occupations frequently involve working with ideas and require an extensive amount of thinking. These occupations can involve searching for facts and figuring out problems mentally. **Work Values**—Creativity; Ability Utilization; Compensation; Responsibility; Company Policies and Practices. **Skills**—Programming; Troubleshooting; Installation; Quality Control Analysis; Technology Design; Operations Analysis; Complex Problem Solving; Writing. **Abilities**—*Cognitive:* Written Expression; Deductive Reasoning; Mathematical Reasoning; Speed of Closure; Originality. *Psychomotor:* Wrist-Finger Speed; Response Orientation; Reaction Time; Arm-Hand Steadiness. *Physical:* Trunk Strength. *Sensory:* Speech Clarity; Near Vision; Visual Color Discrimination; Speech Recognition; Sound Localization. **General Work Activities**—*Information Input:* Getting Information; Identifying Objects, Actions, and Events; Inspecting Equipment, Structures, or Materials. *Mental Process:* Thinking Creatively; Updating and Using Relevant Knowledge; Analyzing Data or Information. *Work Output:* Interacting with Computers; Documenting or Recording Information; Drafting and Specifying Technical Devices. *Interacting with Others:* Providing Consultation and Advice to Others; Communicating with Other Workers; Communicating with Persons Outside Organization. **Physical Work Conditions**—Sitting; Indoors; Making Repetitive Motions; Walking or Running. **Other Job Characteristics**—Degree of Automation; Importance of Being Exact or Accurate; Consequence of Error.

Experience—Job Zone 3. Previous work-related skill, knowledge, or experience is required. **Job Preparation:** SVP 6.0 to less than 7.0—more than one year and less than four years. **Knowledge**—Computers and Electronics; Education and Training; English Language; Mathematics; Telecommunications. **Instructional Programs**—Computer and Information Sciences, General; Computer Systems Analysis/Analyst; Information Technology; Web/Multimedia Management and Webmaster.

Related DOT Jobs—030.162-014 Programmer-Analyst; 030.162-022 Systems Programmer; 030.167-014 Systems Analyst; 033.262-010 Quality Assurance Analyst.

15-1061.00 Database Administrators

- **Education/Training Required: Bachelor's degree**
- **Employed: 106,007**
- **Annual Earnings: $54,850**
- **Growth: 65.9%**
- **Annual Job Openings: 8,000**

Coordinate changes to computer databases; test and implement the database, applying knowledge of database management systems. May plan, coordinate, and implement security measures to safeguard computer databases.

Develop data model describing data elements and how they are used, following procedures and using pen, template, or computer software. Develop standards and guidelines to guide the use and acquisition of software and to protect vulnerable information. Establish and calculate optimum values for database parameters, using manuals and calculator. Modify existing databases and database management systems or direct programmers and analysts to make changes. Plan, coordinate, and implement security measures to safeguard information in computer files against accidental or unauthorized damage, modification or disclosure. Review procedures in database management system manuals for making changes to database. Review project requests describing database user needs to estimate time and cost required to accomplish project. Review workflow charts developed by programmer analyst to understand tasks computer will perform, such as updating records. Select and enter codes to monitor database performance and to create production database. Specify users and user access levels for each segment of database. Test programs or databases, correct errors, and make necessary modifications. Write and code logical and physical database descriptions and specify identifiers of database to management system or direct others in coding descriptions. Approve, schedule, plan, and supervise the installation and testing of new products and improvements to computer systems, such as the installation of new databases. Develop methods for integrating different products so they work properly together, such as customizing commercial databases to fit specific needs. Identify and evaluate industry trends in database systems to serve as a source of information and advice for upper management. Revise company definition of data as defined in data dictionary. Train users and answer questions. Work as part of a project team to coordinate database development and determine project scope and limitations.

GOE INFORMATION—Interest Area: 02. Science, Math, and Engineering. **Work Group:** 02.06. Mathematics and Computers. **Personality Type**—Investigative. Investigative occupations frequently involve working with ideas and require an extensive amount of thinking. These occupations can involve searching for facts and figuring out problems mentally. **Work Values**—Creativity; Compensation; Security; Responsibility; Company Policies and Practices. **Skills**—Programming; Technology Design; Operations Analysis; Mathematics; Systems Analysis; Installation; Quality Control Analysis; Troubleshooting. **Abilities**—*Cognitive:* Category Flexibility; Mathematical Reasoning; Speed of Closure; Originality; Number Facility. *Psychomotor:* Wrist-Finger Speed; Response Orientation; Finger Dexterity; Manual Dexterity; Reaction Time. *Physical:* Trunk Strength. *Sensory:* Near Vision; Glare Sensitivity; Sound Localization; Auditory Attention. **General Work Activities**—*Information Input:* Getting Information; Monitoring Processes, Materials, or Surroundings; Estimating Needed Characteristics. *Mental Process:* Updating and Using Relevant Knowledge; Processing Information; Analyzing Data or Information. *Work Output:* Interacting with Computers; Documenting or Recording Information; Handling and Moving Objects. *Interacting with Others:* Communicating with Other Workers; Teaching Others;

Establishing and Maintaining Relationships. **Physical Work Conditions**—Sitting; Indoors; Using Hands on Objects, Tools, or Controls; Making Repetitive Motions; Walking or Running. **Other Job Characteristics**—Degree of Automation; Importance of Being Exact or Accurate; Consequence of Error.

Experience—Job Zone 4. A minimum of two to four years of work-related skill, knowledge, or experience is needed. **Job Preparation:** SVP 7.0 to less than 8.0—two years to less than 10 years. **Knowledge**—Computers and Electronics; Administration and Management; Education and Training; Mathematics; Clerical. **Instructional Programs**—Computer and Information Sciences, General; Computer and Information Systems Security; Computer Systems Analysis/Analyst; Data Modeling/Warehousing and Database Administration; Management Information Systems, General.

Related DOT Jobs—039.162-010 Data Base Administrator; 039.162-014 Data Base Design Analyst; 109.067-010 Information Scientist.

15-1071.00 Network and Computer Systems Administrators

- Education/Training Required: Bachelor's degree
- Employed: 228,537
- Annual Earnings: $53,770
- Growth: 81.9%
- Annual Job Openings: 18,000

Install, configure, and support an organization's local area network (LAN), wide area network (WAN), and Internet system or a segment of a network system. Maintain network hardware and software. Monitor network to ensure network availability to all system users and perform necessary maintenance to support network availability. May supervise other network support and client server specialists and plan, coordinate, and implement network security measures.

Confer with network users about how to solve existing system problems. Design, configure, and test computer hardware, networking software, and operating system software. Diagnose hardware and software problems and replace defective components. Maintain and administer computer networks and related computing environments, including computer hardware, systems software, applications software, and all configurations. Monitor network performance in order to determine whether adjustments need to be made and where changes will need to be made in the future. Operate master consoles in order to monitor the performance of computer systems and networks and to coordinate computer network access and use. Perform data backups and disaster recovery operations. Perform routine network startup and shutdown procedures and maintain control records. Plan, coordinate, and implement network security measures in order to protect data, software, and hardware. Recommend changes to improve systems and network configurations and determine hardware or software requirements related to such changes. Train people in computer system use. Analyze equipment performance records in order to determine the need for repair or replacement. Coordinate with vendors and with company personnel in order to facilitate purchases. Gather data pertaining to customer needs; use the information to identify, predict, interpret, and evaluate system and network requirements. Load computer tapes and disks; install software and printer paper or forms. Maintain an inventory of parts for emergency repairs. Maintain logs related to network functions, as well as maintenance and repair records. Research new technology and implement it or recommend its implementation.

GOE INFORMATION—Interest Area: 02. Science, Math, and Engineering. **Work Group:** 02.06. Mathematics and Computers. **Note:** The Department of Labor has not collected some data for this job, so it has fewer details than the other descriptions.

Instructional Programs—Computer and Information Sciences and Support Services, Other; Computer and Information Sciences, General; Computer and Information Systems Security; Computer Systems Analysis/Analyst; Computer Systems Networking and Telecommunications; Information Science/Studies; System Administration/Administrator; System, Networking, and LAN/WAN Management/Manager.

Related DOT Jobs—033.162-010 Computer Security Coordinator; 033.162-014 Data Recovery Planner; 033.362-010 Computer Security Specialist.

15-1071.01 Computer Security Specialists

- Education/Training Required: Bachelor's degree
- Employed: 228,537
- Annual Earnings: $53,770
- Growth: 81.9%
- Annual Job Openings: 18,000

Plan, coordinate, and implement security measures for information systems to regulate access to computer data files and prevent unauthorized modification, destruction, or disclosure of information.

Confer with users to discuss issues such as computer data access needs, security violations, and programming changes. Develop plans to safeguard computer files against accidental or unauthorized modification, destruction, or disclosure and to meet emergency data processing needs. Document computer security and emergency measures policies, procedures, and tests. Encrypt data transmissions and erect firewalls to conceal confidential information as it is being transmitted and to keep out tainted digital transfers. Modify computer security files to incorporate new software, correct errors, or change individual access status. Monitor current reports of computer viruses to determine when to update virus protection systems. Monitor use of data files and regulate access to safeguard information in computer files. Perform risk assessments and execute tests of data processing system to ensure functioning of data processing activities and security measures. Review violations of computer security procedures and discuss procedures with violators to ensure violations are not repeated. Coordinate implementation of computer system plan with establishment personnel and outside vendors. Train users and promote security awareness to ensure system security and to improve server and network efficiency. Maintain permanent fleet cryptologic and carry-on direct support systems required in special land, sea surface, and subsurface operations.

GOE INFORMATION—Interest Area: 02. Science, Math, and Engineering. **Work Group:** 02.06. Mathematics and Computers. **Personality Type**—Investigative. Investigative occupations frequently involve working with ideas and require an extensive amount of thinking. These occupations can involve searching for facts and figuring out problems mentally. **Work Values**—Good Working Conditions; Compensation; Creativity; Responsibility; Autonomy. **Skills**—Programming; Installation; Technology Design; Operations Analysis; Equipment Selection; Complex Problem Solving; Quality Control Analysis; Management of Material Resources. **Abilities**—*Cognitive:* Deductive Reasoning; Fluency of Ideas; Information Ordering; Written Comprehension; Written Expression. *Psychomotor:* None met the criteria. *Physical:* None met the criteria. *Sensory:* Near Vision; Sound Localization; Speech Clarity; Hearing Sensitivity; Far Vision. **General Work Activities**—*Information In-*

put: Getting Information; Monitoring Processes, Materials, or Surroundings; Identifying Objects, Actions, and Events. *Mental Process:* Updating and Using Relevant Knowledge; Analyzing Data or Information; Organizing, Planning, and Prioritizing. *Work Output:* Interacting with Computers; Documenting or Recording Information; Repairing and Maintaining Electronic Equipment. *Interacting with Others:* Communicating with Other Workers; Providing Consultation and Advice to Others; Coordinating the Work and Activities of Others. **Physical Work Conditions**—Indoors; Sitting. **Other Job Characteristics**—Consequence of Error; Importance of Being Exact or Accurate; Degree of Automation.

Experience—Job Zone 4. A minimum of two to four years of work-related skill, knowledge, or experience is needed. **Job Preparation:** SVP 7.0 to less than 8.0—two years to less than 10 years. **Knowledge**—Computers and Electronics; Public Safety and Security; Administration and Management; Philosophy and Theology; Telecommunications. **Instructional Programs**—Computer and Information Sciences and Support Services, Other; Computer and Information Sciences, General; Computer and Information Systems Security; Computer Systems Analysis/Analyst; Computer Systems Networking and Telecommunications; Information Science/Studies; System Administration/Administrator; System, Networking, and LAN/WAN Management/Manager.

Related DOT Jobs—033.162-010 Computer Security Coordinator; 033.162-014 Data Recovery Planner; 033.362-010 Computer Security Specialist.

15-1081.00 Network Systems and Data Communications Analysts

- Education/Training Required: Bachelor's degree
- Employed: 118,684
- Annual Earnings: $57,470
- Growth: 77.5%
- Annual Job Openings: 9,000

Analyze, design, test, and evaluate network systems, such as local area networks (LAN), wide area networks (WAN), and Internet, intranet, and other data communications systems. Perform network modeling, analysis, and planning. Research and recommend network and data communications hardware and software. Includes telecommunications specialists who deal with the interfacing of computer and communications equipment. May supervise computer programmers.

Consult customers, visit workplaces, or conduct surveys to determine present and future user needs. Design and implement network configurations, network architecture (including hardware and software technology, site locations, and integration of technologies), and systems. Identify areas of operation that need upgraded equipment such as modems, fiber-optic cables, and telephone wires. Monitor system performance and provide security measures, troubleshooting, and maintenance as needed. Read technical manuals and brochures to determine which equipment meets establishment requirements. Set up user accounts, regulating and monitoring file access to ensure confidentiality and proper use. Test and evaluate hardware and software to determine efficiency, reliability, and compatibility with existing system; make purchase recommendations. Visit vendors, attend conferences or training, and study technical journals to keep up with changes in technology. Work with other engineers, systems analysts, programmers, technicians, scientists, and top-level managers in the design, testing and evaluation of systems. Adapt and modify existing software to meet specific needs. Assist users to diagnose and solve data communication problems. Develop and write procedures for installation, use, and troubleshooting of communications hardware

and software. Maintain needed files by adding and deleting files on the network server and backing up files to guarantee their safety in the event of problems with the network. Maintain the peripherals, such as printers, that are connected to the network. Train users in use of equipment.

GOE INFORMATION—Interest Area: 02. Science, Math, and Engineering. **Work Group:** 02.06. Mathematics and Computers. **Personality Type**—Investigative. Investigative occupations frequently involve working with ideas and require an extensive amount of thinking. These occupations can involve searching for facts and figuring out problems mentally. **Work Values**—Compensation; Creativity; Ability Utilization; Advancement; Autonomy. **Skills**—Programming; Management of Material Resources; Troubleshooting; Equipment Selection; Operations Analysis; Quality Control Analysis; Technology Design; Systems Analysis. **Abilities**—*Cognitive:* Written Expression; Originality; Oral Comprehension; Oral Expression; Written Comprehension. *Psychomotor:* Wrist-Finger Speed; Finger Dexterity; Reaction Time; Response Orientation; Control Precision. *Physical:* None met the criteria. *Sensory:* Speech Clarity; Near Vision; Hearing Sensitivity; Speech Recognition; Sound Localization. **General Work Activities**—*Information Input:* Getting Information; Monitoring Processes, Materials, or Surroundings; Identifying Objects, Actions, and Events. *Mental Process:* Updating and Using Relevant Knowledge; Analyzing Data or Information; Processing Information. *Work Output:* Interacting with Computers; Drafting and Specifying Technical Devices; Repairing and Maintaining Electronic Equipment. *Interacting with Others:* Providing Consultation and Advice to Others; Communicating with Other Workers; Teaching Others. **Physical Work Conditions**—Sitting; Indoors; Radiation; Keeping or Regaining Balance; Cramped Work Space or Awkward Positions. **Other Job Characteristics**—Degree of Automation; Consequence of Error; Pace Determined by Speed of Equipment.

Experience—Job Zone 4. A minimum of two to four years of work-related skill, knowledge, or experience is needed. **Job Preparation:** SVP 7.0 to less than 8.0—two years to less than 10 years. **Knowledge**—Computers and Electronics; Telecommunications; Sales and Marketing; Education and Training; Customer and Personal Service. **Instructional Programs**—Computer and Information Sciences, General; Computer and Information Systems Security; Computer Systems Analysis/Analyst; Computer Systems Networking and Telecommunications; Information Technology.

Related DOT Jobs—031.262-010 Data Communications Analyst.

15-1099.99 Computer Specialists, All Other

- Education/Training Required: Postsecondary vocational training
- Employed: No data available.
- Annual Earnings: No data available.
- Growth: 60.7%
- Annual Job Openings: 16,000

All computer specialists not listed separately.

No task data available.

GOE INFORMATION—Interest Area: 02. Science, Math, and Engineering. **Work Group:** 02.06. Mathematics and Computers. **Note:** The Department of Labor has not collected some data for this job, so it has fewer details than the other descriptions.

Instructional Programs—Bioinformatics; Biomathematics and Bioinformatics, Other; Computer and Information Sciences and Support Services, Other; Computer and Information Sciences, General; Computer Science; Data Processing and Data Processing Technology/Technician; Information Science/Studies; Management Information Systems and Services, Other.

Related DOT Jobs—019.062-010 Geographic Information System Specialist; 033.167-010 Computer Systems Hardware Analyst.

15-2000 Mathematical Science Occupations

15-2011.00 *Actuaries*

- Education/Training Required: Work experience plus degree
- Employed: 14,271
- Annual Earnings: $68,120
- Growth: 5.4%
- Annual Job Openings: 1,000

Analyze statistical data, such as mortality, accident, sickness, disability, and retirement rates and construct probability tables to forecast risk and liability for payment of future benefits. May ascertain premium rates required and cash reserves necessary to ensure payment of future benefits.

Analyze statistical information to estimate mortality, accident, sickness, disability, and retirement rates. Construct probability tables for events such as fires, natural disasters, and unemployment, based on analysis of statistical data and other pertinent information. Ascertain premium rates required and cash reserves and liabilities necessary to ensure payment of future benefits. Collaborate with programmers, underwriters, accounts, claims experts, and senior management to help companies develop plans for new lines of business or improving existing business. Design, review, and help administer insurance, annuity, and pension plans, determining financial soundness and calculating premiums. Determine equitable basis for distributing surplus earnings under participating insurance and annuity contracts in mutual companies. Determine or help determine company policy and explain complex technical matters to company executives, government officials, shareholders, policyholders, and/or the public. Determine policy contract provisions for each type of insurance. Explain changes in contract provisions to customers. Manage credit and help price corporate security offerings. Provide advice to clients on a contract basis, working as a consultant. Provide expertise to help financial institutions manage risks and maximize returns associated with investment products or credit offerings. Testify before public agencies on proposed legislation affecting businesses. Testify in court as expert witness or to provide legal evidence on matters such as the value of potential lifetime earnings of a person who is disabled or killed in an accident.

GOE INFORMATION—Interest Area: 02. Science, Math, and Engineering. **Work Group:** 02.06. Mathematics and Computers. **Personality Type**—Conventional. Conventional occupations frequently involve following set procedures and routines. These occupations can include working with data and details more than with ideas. Usually there is a clear line of authority to follow. **Work Values**—Autonomy; Good Working Conditions; Advancement; Recognition; Independence. **Skills**—Mathematics; Systems Evaluation; Complex Problem Solving; Systems Analysis; Critical Thinking; Monitoring; Judgment and Decision Making; Reading Comprehension. **Abilities**—*Cognitive:* Number Facility; Mathematical Reasoning; Deductive Reasoning; Flexibility of Closure; Speed

of Closure. *Psychomotor:* Finger Dexterity; Wrist-Finger Speed; Manual Dexterity. *Physical:* None met the criteria. *Sensory:* Near Vision; Glare Sensitivity. **General Work Activities**—*Information Input:* Getting Information; Identifying Objects, Actions, and Events; Estimating Needed Characteristics. *Mental Process:* Analyzing Data or Information; Processing Information; Evaluating Information Against Standards. *Work Output:* Documenting or Recording Information; Interacting with Computers; Handling and Moving Objects. *Interacting with Others:* Monitoring and Controlling Resources; Interpreting Meaning of Information for Others; Communicating with Other Workers. **Physical Work Conditions**—Sitting. **Other Job Characteristics**—Importance of Being Exact or Accurate; Degree of Automation; Importance of Repeating Same Tasks.

Experience—Job Zone 5. Extensive skill, knowledge, and experience are needed for these occupations. **Job Preparation:** SVP 8.0 and above—four years to more than 10 years. **Knowledge**—Economics and Accounting; Mathematics; Sociology and Anthropology; Law and Government; Philosophy and Theology. **Instructional Programs**—Actuarial Science.

Related DOT Jobs—020.167-010 Actuary.

15-2021.00 *Mathematicians*

- Education/Training Required: Master's degree
- Employed: 3,618
- Annual Earnings: $74,790
- Growth: −1.9%
- Annual Job Openings: Fewer than 500

Conduct research in fundamental mathematics or in application of mathematical techniques to science, management, and other fields. Solve or direct solutions to problems in various fields by mathematical methods.

Address the relationships of quantities, magnitudes, and forms through the use of numbers and symbols. Apply mathematical theories and techniques to the solution of practical problems in business, engineering, or the sciences. Assemble sets of assumptions and explore the consequences of each set. Conduct research to extend mathematical knowledge in traditional areas, such as algebra, geometry, probability, and logic. Develop new principles and new relationships between existing mathematical principles to advance mathematical science. Perform computations and apply methods of numerical analysis to data. Maintain knowledge in the field by reading professional journals, talking with other mathematicians, and attending professional conferences. Design, analyze, and decipher encryption systems designed to transmit military, political, financial, or law enforcement–related information in code.

GOE INFORMATION—Interest Area: 02. Science, Math, and Engineering. **Work Group:** 02.06. Mathematics and Computers. **Personality Type**—Investigative. Investigative occupations frequently involve working with ideas and require an extensive amount of thinking. These occupations can involve searching for facts and figuring out problems mentally. **Work Values**—Autonomy; Ability Utilization; Creativity; Good Working Conditions; Independence. **Skills**—Mathematics; Learning Strategies; Complex Problem Solving; Critical Thinking; Reading Comprehension; Writing. **Abilities**—*Cognitive:* Mathematical Reasoning; Number Facility; Originality; Fluency of Ideas; Inductive Reasoning. *Psychomotor:* None met the criteria. *Physical:* None met the criteria. *Sensory:* None met the criteria. **General Work Activities**—*Information Input:* Identifying Objects, Actions, and Events; Getting Information; Estimating Needed Characteristics. *Mental Process:* Processing Information; Analyzing Data or Information; Updating and Using Relevant Knowledge. *Work Output:* Interacting with Computers; Documenting or Recording Information;

Handling and Moving Objects. *Interacting with Others:* Interpreting Meaning of Information for Others; Communicating with Other Workers; Providing Consultation and Advice to Others. **Physical Work Conditions**—Sitting; Indoors. **Other Job Characteristics**—Importance of Being Exact or Accurate; Consequence of Error; Degree of Automation.

Experience—Job Zone 5. Extensive skill, knowledge, and experience are needed for these occupations. **Job Preparation:** SVP 8.0 and above—four years to more than 10 years. **Knowledge**—Mathematics; Economics and Accounting; Engineering and Technology; Computers and Electronics; Physics. **Instructional Programs**—Algebra and Number Theory; Analysis and Functional Analysis; Applied Mathematics; Applied Mathematics, Other; Computational Mathematics; Geometry/Geometric Analysis; Logic; Mathematical Statistics and Probability; Mathematics and Statistics, Other; Mathematics, General; Mathematics, Other; Topology and Foundations.

Related DOT Jobs—020.067-014 Mathematician.

15-2031.00 Operations Research Analysts
- **Education/Training Required: Master's degree**
- **Employed: 47,215**
- **Annual Earnings: $55,470**
- **Growth: 8.0%**
- **Annual Job Openings: 4,000**

Formulate and apply mathematical modeling and other optimizing methods, using a computer to develop and interpret information that assists management with decision making, policy formulation, or other managerial functions. May develop related software, service, or products. Frequently concentrates on collecting and analyzing data and developing decision support software. May develop and supply optimal time, cost, or logistics networks for program evaluation, review, or implementation.

Analyzes problem in terms of management information and conceptualizes and defines problem. Prepares model of problem in form of one or several equations that relates constants and variables, restrictions, alternatives, conflicting objectives, and their numerical parameters. Specifies manipulative or computational methods to be applied to model. Performs validation and testing of model to ensure adequacy or determines need for reformulation. Evaluates implementation and effectiveness of research. Designs, conducts, and evaluates experimental operational models where insufficient data exists to formulate model. Develops and applies time and cost networks to plan and control large projects. Defines data requirements and gathers and validates information, applying judgment and statistical tests. Studies information and selects plan from competitive proposals that afford maximum probability of profit or effectiveness relating to cost or risk. Prepares for management reports defining problem, evaluation, and possible solution.

GOE INFORMATION—**Interest Area:** 02. Science, Math, and Engineering. **Work Group:** 02.06. Mathematics and Computers. **Personality Type**—Investigative. Investigative occupations frequently involve working with ideas and require an extensive amount of thinking. These occupations can involve searching for facts and figuring out problems mentally. **Work Values**—Creativity; Autonomy; Ability Utilization; Responsibility; Recognition. **Skills**—Systems Evaluation; Systems Analysis; Mathematics; Complex Problem Solving; Monitoring; Judgment and Decision Making; Critical Thinking; Operations Analysis. **Abilities**—*Cognitive:* Mathematical Reasoning; Fluency of Ideas; Number Facility; Written Expression; Deductive Reasoning. *Psychomotor:* None met the criteria. *Physical:* None met the criteria. *Sensory:* None met the criteria. **General**

Work Activities—*Information Input:* Getting Information; Identifying Objects, Actions, and Events; Monitoring Processes, Materials, or Surroundings. *Mental Process:* Analyzing Data or Information; Making Decisions and Solving Problems; Processing Information. *Work Output:* Interacting with Computers; Documenting or Recording Information; Handling and Moving Objects. *Interacting with Others:* Providing Consultation and Advice to Others; Communicating with Other Workers; Communicating with Persons Outside Organization. **Physical Work Conditions**—Sitting; Indoors. **Other Job Characteristics**—Consequence of Error; Importance of Being Exact or Accurate; Importance of Repeating Same Tasks.

Experience—Job Zone 4. A minimum of two to four years of work-related skill, knowledge, or experience is needed. **Job Preparation:** SVP 7.0 to less than 8.0—two years to less than 10 years. **Knowledge**—Mathematics; Economics and Accounting; Administration and Management; Production and Processing; Computers and Electronics. **Instructional Programs**—Management Science, General; Management Sciences and Quantitative Methods, Other; Operations Research.

Related DOT Jobs—020.067-018 Operations-Research Analyst.

15-2041.00 Statisticians
- **Education/Training Required: Master's degree**
- **Employed: 19,482**
- **Annual Earnings: $54,030**
- **Growth: 2.3%**
- **Annual Job Openings: 2,000**

Engage in the development of mathematical theory or apply statistical theory and methods to collect, organize, interpret, and summarize numerical data to provide usable information. May specialize in fields such as bio-statistics, agricultural statistics, business statistics, economic statistics, or other fields.

Adapt statistical methods in order to solve specific problems in many fields, such as economics, biology, and engineering. Analyze and interpret statistical data in order to identify significant differences in relationships among sources of information. Apply sampling techniques or utilize complete enumeration bases in order to determine and define groups to be surveyed. Design research projects that apply valid scientific techniques and utilize information obtained from baselines or historical data in order to structure uncompromised and efficient analyses. Develop and test experimental designs, sampling techniques, and analytical methods. Evaluate sources of information in order to determine any limitations in terms of reliability or usability. Evaluate the statistical methods and procedures used to obtain data in order to ensure validity, applicability, efficiency, and accuracy. Examine theories such as those of probability and inference in order to discover mathematical bases for new or improved methods of obtaining and evaluating numerical data. Identify relationships and trends in data, as well as any factors that could affect the results of research. Plan data collection methods for specific projects and determine the types and sizes of sample groups to be used. Process large amounts of data for statistical modeling and graphic analysis, using computers. Report results of statistical analyses, including information in the form of graphs, charts, and tables. Develop an understanding of fields to which statistical methods are to be applied in order to determine whether methods and results are appropriate. Prepare data for processing by organizing information, checking for any inaccuracies, and adjusting and weighting the raw data. Supervise and provide instructions for workers collecting and tabulating data.

GOE INFORMATION—**Interest Area:** 02. Science, Math, and Engineering. **Work Group:** 02.06. Mathematics and Computers. **Personality**

Type—Investigative. Investigative occupations frequently involve working with ideas and require an extensive amount of thinking. These occupations can involve searching for facts and figuring out problems mentally. **Work Values**—Autonomy; Ability Utilization; Creativity; Independence; Good Working Conditions. **Skills**—Mathematics; Complex Problem Solving; Systems Evaluation; Critical Thinking; Science; Systems Analysis; Judgment and Decision Making; Reading Comprehension. **Abilities**—*Cognitive:* Speed of Closure; Mathematical Reasoning; Number Facility; Inductive Reasoning; Written Expression. *Psychomotor:* Finger Dexterity; Control Precision; Wrist-Finger Speed. *Physical:* None met the criteria. *Sensory:* Near Vision; Speech Clarity; Glare Sensitivity. **General Work Activities**—*Information Input:* Getting Information; Identifying Objects, Actions, and Events; Estimating Needed Characteristics. *Mental Process:* Analyzing Data or Information; Processing Information; Organizing, Planning, and Prioritizing. *Work Output:* Documenting or Recording Information; Interacting with Computers; Handling and Moving Objects. *Interacting with Others:* Interpreting Meaning of Information for Others; Communicating with Other Workers; Communicating with Persons Outside Organization. **Physical Work Conditions**—Sitting; Indoors. **Other Job Characteristics**—Importance of Being Exact or Accurate; Degree of Automation; Pace Determined by Speed of Equipment.

Experience—Job Zone 4. A minimum of two to four years of work-related skill, knowledge, or experience is needed. **Job Preparation:** SVP 7.0 to less than 8.0—two years to less than 10 years. **Knowledge**—Mathematics; Computers and Electronics; Economics and Accounting; English Language; Administration and Management. **Instructional Programs**—Applied Mathematics; Biostatistics; Business Statistics; Mathematical Statistics and Probability; Mathematics, General; Statistics, General; Statistics, Other.

Related DOT Jobs—020.067-022 Statistician, Mathematical; 020.167-026 Statistician, Applied.

15-2091.00 Mathematical Technicians

- Education/Training Required: Bachelor's degree
- Employed: No data available.
- Annual Earnings: $36,570
- Growth: 5.9%
- Annual Job Openings: Fewer than 500

Apply standardized mathematical formulas, principles, and methodology to technological problems in engineering and physical sciences in relation to specific industrial and research objectives, processes, equipment, and products.

Process data for analysis, using computers. Reduce raw data to meaningful terms, using the most practical and accurate combination and sequence of computational methods. Translate data into numbers, equations, flow charts, graphs, or other forms. Confer with scientific or engineering personnel to plan projects. Modify standard formulas so that they conform to project needs and data processing methods. Apply standardized mathematical formulas, principles, and methodology to the solution of technological problems involving engineering or physical science.

GOE INFORMATION—Interest Area: 02. Science, Math, and Engineering. **Work Group:** 02.06. Mathematics and Computers. **Personality Type**—Investigative. Investigative occupations frequently involve working with ideas and require an extensive amount of thinking. These occupations can involve searching for facts and figuring out problems mentally. **Work Values**—Advancement; Good Working Conditions; Ability Utilization; Supervision, Human Relations; Creativity. **Skills**—Mathematics; Programming; Critical Thinking; Complex Problem Solving; Equipment Selection; Science; Active Listening; Operations Analysis. **Abilities**—*Cognitive:* Mathematical Reasoning; Number Facility; Deductive Reasoning; Oral Comprehension; Oral Expression. *Psychomotor:* Wrist-Finger Speed. *Physical:* None met the criteria. *Sensory:* Glare Sensitivity; Near Vision. **General Work Activities**—*Information Input:* Getting Information; Identifying Objects, Actions, and Events; Estimating Needed Characteristics. *Mental Process:* Processing Information; Analyzing Data or Information; Updating and Using Relevant Knowledge. *Work Output:* Interacting with Computers; Documenting or Recording Information; Handling and Moving Objects. *Interacting with Others:* Communicating with Other Workers; Interpreting Meaning of Information for Others; Establishing and Maintaining Relationships. **Physical Work Conditions**—Sitting; Indoors. **Other Job Characteristics**—Importance of Being Exact or Accurate; Degree of Automation; Importance of Repeating Same Tasks.

Experience—Job Zone 4. A minimum of two to four years of work-related skill, knowledge, or experience is needed. **Job Preparation:** SVP 7.0 to less than 8.0—two years to less than 10 years. **Knowledge**—Mathematics; Computers and Electronics; Engineering and Technology; English Language; Clerical. **Instructional Programs**—Applied Mathematics.

Related DOT Jobs—020.162-010 Mathematical Technician.

15-2099.99 Mathematical Science Occupations, All Other

- Education/Training Required: No data available.
- Employed: No data available.
- Annual Earnings: No data available.
- Growth: 2.7%
- Annual Job Openings: Fewer than 500

All mathematical scientists not listed separately.

No task data available.

GOE INFORMATION—Interest Area: 02. Science, Math, and Engineering. **Work Group:** 02.06. Mathematics and Computers. **Note:** The Department of Labor has not collected some data for this job, so it has fewer details than the other descriptions.

Instructional Programs—Applied Mathematics; Applied Mathematics, Other; Computational Mathematics; Mathematics and Statistics, Other; Mathematics, General.

Related DOT Jobs—199.267-014 Cryptanalyst.

17-0000
Architecture and Engineering Occupations

17-1000 Architects, Surveyors, and Cartographers

17-1011.00 Architects, Except Landscape and Naval

- Education/Training Required: Bachelor's degree
- Employed: 102,403
- Annual Earnings: $55,470
- Growth: 18.5%
- Annual Job Openings: 4,000

Plan and design structures, such as private residences, office buildings, theaters, factories, and other structural property.

Prepare information regarding design, structure specifications, materials, color, equipment, estimated costs, and construction time. Consult with client to determine functional and spatial requirements of structure. Direct activities of workers engaged in preparing drawings and specification documents. Plan layout of project. Prepare contract documents for building contractors. Prepare scale drawings. Integrate engineering element into unified design. Conduct periodic on-site observation of work during construction to monitor compliance with plans. Administer construction contracts. Represent client in obtaining bids and awarding construction contracts. Prepare operating and maintenance manuals, studies, and reports.

GOE INFORMATION—Interest Area: 02. Science, Math, and Engineering. Work Group: 02.07. Engineering. Personality Type—Artistic. Artistic occupations frequently involve working with forms, designs, and patterns. They often require self-expression, and the work can be done without following a clear set of rules. Work Values—Creativity; Recognition; Ability Utilization; Social Status; Achievement. Skills—Complex Problem Solving; Operations Analysis; Coordination; Management of Financial Resources; Management of Personnel Resources; Negotiation; Active Listening; Persuasion. Abilities—*Cognitive:* Originality; Deductive Reasoning; Visualization; Category Flexibility; Fluency of Ideas. *Psychomotor:* Finger Dexterity; Arm-Hand Steadiness; Control Precision. *Physical:* None met the criteria. *Sensory:* Speech Recognition; Far Vision; Near Vision; Visual Color Discrimination; Speech Clarity. General Work Activities—*Information Input:* Getting Information; Inspecting Equipment, Structures, or Materials; Identifying Objects, Actions, and Events. *Mental Process:* Thinking Creatively; Organizing, Planning, and Prioritizing; Making Decisions and Solving Problems. *Work Output:* Drafting and Specifying Technical Devices; Interacting with Computers; Documenting or Recording Information. *Interacting with Others:* Coordinating the Work and Activities of Others; Establishing and Maintaining Relationships; Communicating with Persons Outside Organization. Physical Work Conditions—High Places; Climbing Ladders, Scaffolds, Poles, etc.; Sitting; Outdoors; Common Protective or Safety Attire. Other Job Characteristics—Consequence of Error; Importance of Being Exact or Accurate; Degree of Automation.

Experience—Job Zone 5. Extensive skill, knowledge, and experience are needed for these occupations. Job Preparation: SVP 7.0 to less than 8.0—two years to less than 10 years. Knowledge—Building and Construction; Design; Engineering and Technology; Law and Government; Public Safety and Security. Instructional Programs—Architectural History and Criticism, General; Architecture (BArch, BA/BS, MArch, MA/MS, PhD); Architecture and Related Services, Other; Environmental Design/Architecture.

Related DOT Jobs—106.101-010 Architect; 116.701-010 School-Plant Consultant.

17-1012.00 Landscape Architects

- Education/Training Required: Bachelor's degree
- Employed: 21,747
- Annual Earnings: $46,710
- Growth: 31.1%
- Annual Job Openings: 1,000

Plan and design land areas for such projects as parks and other recreational facilities, airports, highways, hospitals, schools, land subdivisions, and commercial, industrial, and residential sites.

Prepare site plans, specifications, and cost estimates for land development, coordinating arrangement of existing and proposed land features and structures. Confer with clients, engineering personnel, and architects on overall program. Compile and analyze data on conditions, such as location, drainage, and location of structures for environmental reports and landscaping plans. Inspect landscape work to ensure compliance with specifications, approve quality of materials and work, and advise client and construction personnel.

GOE INFORMATION—Interest Area: 02. Science, Math, and Engineering. Work Group: 02.07. Engineering. Personality Type—Artistic. Artistic occupations frequently involve working with forms, designs, and patterns. They often require self-expression, and the work can be done without following a clear set of rules. Work Values—Creativity; Ability Utilization; Social Status; Recognition; Achievement. Skills—Coordination; Operations Analysis; Complex Problem Solving; Management of Financial Resources; Social Perceptiveness; Equipment Selection; Mathematics; Critical Thinking. Abilities—*Cognitive:* Originality; Fluency of Ideas; Visualization; Category Flexibility; Written Expression. *Psychomotor:* Multilimb Coordination; Reaction Time; Finger Dexterity; Arm-Hand Steadiness; Control Precision. *Physical:* Gross Body Equilibrium. *Sensory:* Far Vision; Speech Recognition; Near Vision; Depth Perception; Visual Color Discrimination. General Work Activities—*Information Input:* Getting Information; Monitoring Processes, Materials, or Surroundings; Identifying Objects, Actions, and Events. *Mental Process:* Thinking Creatively; Making Decisions and Solving Problems; Organizing, Planning, and Prioritizing. *Work Output:* Drafting and Specifying Technical Devices; Documenting or Recording Information; Interacting with Computers. *Interacting with Others:* Coordinating the Work and Activities of Others; Communicating with Persons Outside Organization; Communicating with Other Workers. Physical Work Conditions—Outdoors; Sitting; High Places; Distracting Sounds and Noise Levels; Contaminants. Other Job Characteristics—Consequence of Error; Importance of Being Exact or Accurate; Degree of Automation.

Experience—Job Zone 4. A minimum of two to four years of work-related skill, knowledge, or experience is needed. Job Preparation: SVP 8.0 and above—four years to more than 10 years. Knowledge—Design; Building and Construction; Geography; Engineering and Technology; Biology. Instructional Programs—Environmental Design/Architecture; Landscape Architecture (BS, BSLA, BLA, MSLA, MLA, PhD).

Related DOT Jobs—106.101-018 Landscape Architect.

17-1021.00 Cartographers and Photogrammetrists

- **Education/Training Required: Bachelor's degree**
- **Employed: 6,995**
- **Annual Earnings: $41,500**
- **Growth: 18.5%**
- **Annual Job Openings: 1,000**

Collect, analyze, and interpret geographic information provided by geodetic surveys, aerial photographs, and satellite data. Research, study, and prepare maps and other spatial data in digital or graphic form for legal, social, political, educational, and design purposes. May work with Geographic Information Systems (GIS). May design and evaluate algorithms, data structures, and user interfaces for GIS and mapping systems.

Compile data required for map preparation, including aerial photographs, survey notes, records, reports, and original maps. Delineate aerial photographic detail, such as control points, hydrography, topography, and cultural features, using precision stereoplotting apparatus or drafting instruments. Determine guidelines that specify which source material is acceptable for use. Determine map content and layout, as well as production specifications such as scale, size, projection, and colors; direct production in order to ensure that specifications are followed. Examine and analyze data from ground surveys, reports, aerial photographs, and satellite images in order to prepare topographic maps, aerial-photograph mosaics, and related charts. Identify, scale, and orient geodetic points, elevations, and other planimetric or topographic features, applying standard mathematical formulas. Inspect final compositions in order to ensure completeness and accuracy. Prepare and alter trace maps, charts, tables, detailed drawings, and three-dimensional optical models of terrain, using stereoscopic plotting and computer graphics equipment. Revise existing maps and charts, making all necessary corrections and adjustments. Build and update digital databases. Collect information about specific features of the Earth, using aerial photography and other digital remote sensing techniques. Select aerial photographic and remote sensing techniques and plotting equipment needed to meet required standards of accuracy. Study legal records in order to establish boundaries of local, national, and international properties. Travel over photographed areas in order to observe, identify, record, and verify all relevant features.

GOE INFORMATION—Interest Area: 02. Science, Math, and Engineering. **Work Group:** 02.08. Engineering Technology. **Personality Type—**Conventional. Conventional occupations frequently involve following set procedures and routines. These occupations can include working with data and details more than with ideas. Usually there is a clear line of authority to follow. **Work Values—**Autonomy; Responsibility; Ability Utilization; Good Working Conditions; Creativity. **Skills—**Mathematics; Equipment Selection; Programming; Reading Comprehension; Operations Analysis; Management of Material Resources; Complex Problem Solving; Writing. **Abilities—***Cognitive:* Spatial Orientation; Flexibility of Closure; Mathematical Reasoning; Speed of Closure; Number Facility. *Psychomotor:* Arm-Hand Steadiness; Wrist-Finger Speed; Finger Dexterity. *Physical:* Stamina; Gross Body Coordination; Gross Body Equilibrium. *Sensory:* Far Vision; Visual Color Discrimination; Near Vision; Night Vision; Depth Perception. **General Work Activities—***Information Input:* Getting Information; Identifying Objects, Actions, and Events; Monitoring Processes, Materials, or Surroundings. *Mental Process:* Analyzing Data or Information; Processing Information; Updating and Using Relevant Knowledge. *Work Output:* Drafting and Specifying Technical Devices; Documenting or Recording Information; Handling and Moving Objects. *Interacting with Others:* Interpreting Meaning of Information for Others; Communicating with Other Workers; Communicating with Persons Outside Organization. **Physical Work Conditions—**Outdoors; Walking or Running; Disease or Infections; Sitting; High Places. **Other Job Characteristics—**Importance of Being Exact or Accurate; Importance of Repeating Same Tasks; Degree of Automation.

Experience—Job Zone 4. A minimum of two to four years of work-related skill, knowledge, or experience is needed. **Job Preparation:** SVP 7.0 to less than 8.0—two years to less than 10 years. **Knowledge—**Geography; Design; Computers and Electronics; Fine Arts; Education and Training. **Instructional Programs—**Cartography; Surveying Technology/Surveying.

Related DOT Jobs—018.131-010 Supervisor, Cartography; 018.261-010 Drafter, Cartographic; 018.261-026 Photogrammetrist; 018.262-010 Field-Map Editor.

17-1022.00 Surveyors

- **Education/Training Required: Bachelor's degree**
- **Employed: 58,260**
- **Annual Earnings: $39,240**
- **Growth: 8.1%**
- **Annual Job Openings: 7,000**

Make exact measurements and determine property boundaries. Provide data relevant to the shape, contour, gravitation, location, elevation, or dimension of land or land features on or near the earth's surface for engineering, mapmaking, mining, land evaluation, construction, and other purposes.

Calculate heights, depths, relative positions, property lines, and other characteristics of terrain. Compute geodetic measurements and interpret survey data in order to determine positions, shapes, and elevations of geomorphic and topographic features. Determine longitudes and latitudes of important features and boundaries in survey areas, using theodolites, transits, levels, and satellite-based global positioning systems (GPS). Direct or conduct surveys in order to establish legal boundaries for properties, based on legal deeds and titles. Establish fixed points for use in making maps, using geodetic and engineering instruments. Plan and conduct ground surveys designed to establish baselines, elevations, and other geodetic measurements. Prepare and maintain sketches, maps, reports, and legal descriptions of surveys in order to describe, certify, and assume liability for work performed. Prepare or supervise preparation of all data, charts, plots, maps, records, and documents related to surveys. Record the results of surveys, including the shape, contour, location, elevation, and dimensions of land or land features. Verify the accuracy of survey data, including measurements and calculations conducted at survey sites. Write descriptions of property boundary surveys for use in deeds, leases, or other legal documents. Adjust surveying instruments in order to maintain their accuracy. Conduct research in surveying and mapping methods, using knowledge of techniques of photogrammetric map compilation and electronic data processing. Coordinate findings with the work of engineering and architectural personnel, clients, and others concerned with projects. Determine specifications for photographic equipment to be used for aerial photography, as well as altitudes from which to photograph terrain. Develop criteria for survey methods and procedures. Direct aerial surveys of specified geographical areas. Locate and mark sites selected for geophysical prospecting activities, such as efforts to locate petroleum or other mineral products. Search legal records, survey records, and land titles in order to obtain information about property boundaries in areas to be surveyed. Survey bodies of water in order to determine navigable channels and to secure data for construction of breakwaters, piers, and other marine structures. Train assistants and helpers; direct their work in such activities as performing surveys or drafting maps. Develop criteria for the design and modification of survey instruments. Analyze survey objectives and specifications in order to prepare survey proposals or to direct others in survey proposal preparation.

GOE INFORMATION—Interest Area: 02. Science, Math, and Engineering. **Work Group:** 02.08. Engineering Technology. **Personality Type—** Investigative. Investigative occupations frequently involve working with ideas and require an extensive amount of thinking. These occupations can involve searching for facts and figuring out problems mentally. **Work Values—**Achievement; Autonomy; Social Status; Authority; Variety. **Skills—**Mathematics; Science; Management of Material Resources; Management of Financial Resources; Management of Personnel Resources; Equipment Selection; Programming; Writing. **Abilities—***Cognitive:* Spatial Orientation; Mathematical Reasoning; Number Facility; Written Expression; Deductive Reasoning. *Psychomotor:* Arm-Hand Steadiness; Control Precision; Speed of Limb Movement; Multilimb Coordination. *Physical:* Stamina; Gross Body Equilibrium; Gross Body Coordination; Dynamic Strength; Explosive Strength. *Sensory:* Far Vision; Near Vision; Speech Recognition; Glare Sensitivity; Night Vision. **General Work Activities—***Information Input:* Getting Information; Estimating Needed Characteristics; Identifying Objects, Actions, and Events. *Mental Process:* Analyzing Data or Information; Processing Information; Organizing, Planning, and Prioritizing. *Work Output:* Documenting or Recording Information; Drafting and Specifying Technical Devices; Handling and Moving Objects. *Interacting with Others:* Communicating with Other Workers; Communicating with Persons Outside Organization; Providing Consultation and Advice to Others. **Physical Work Conditions—**Outdoors; Walking or Running; Extremely Bright or Inadequate Lighting; High Places; Very Hot or Cold. **Other Job Characteristics—**Importance of Being Exact or Accurate; Pace Determined by Speed of Equipment; Degree of Automation.

Experience—Job Zone 4. A minimum of two to four years of work-related skill, knowledge, or experience is needed. **Job Preparation:** SVP 7.0 to less than 8.0—two years to less than 10 years. **Knowledge—**Geography; Design; Education and Training; Mathematics; Administration and Management. **Instructional Programs—**Surveying Technology/Surveying.

Related DOT Jobs—018.161-010 Surveyor, Mine; 018.167-018 Land Surveyor; 018.167-026 Photogrammetric Engineer; 018.167-038 Surveyor, Geodetic; 018.167-042 Surveyor, Geophysical Prospecting; 018.167-046 Surveyor, Marine; 024.061-014 Geodesist; 184.167-026 Director, Photogrammetry Flight Operations.

17-2000 Engineers

17-2011.00 Aerospace Engineers

- **Education/Training Required: Bachelor's degree**
- **Employed: 50,434**
- **Annual Earnings: $70,370**
- **Growth: 13.9%**
- **Annual Job Openings: 2,000**

Perform a variety of engineering work in designing, constructing, and testing aircraft, missiles, and spacecraft. May conduct basic and applied research to evaluate adaptability of materials and equipment to aircraft design and manufacture. May recommend improvements in testing equipment and techniques.

Develop design criteria for aeronautical or aerospace products or systems, including testing methods, production costs, quality standards, and completion dates. Analyze project requests and proposals and engineering data to determine feasibility, productibility, cost, and production time of aerospace or aeronautical product. Formulate conceptual design of aeronautical or aerospace products or systems to meet customer requirements. Formulate mathematical models or other methods of computer analysis to develop, evaluate, or modify design according to customer engineering requirements. Plan and conduct experimental, environmental, operational, and stress tests on models and prototypes of aircraft and aerospace systems and equipment. Evaluate product data and design from inspections and reports for conformance to engineering principles, customer requirements, and quality standards. Direct and coordinate activities of engineering or technical personnel designing, fabricating, modifying, or testing of aircraft or aerospace products. Direct research and development programs. Review performance reports and documentation from customers and field engineers; inspect malfunctioning or damaged products to determine problem. Plan and coordinate activities concerned with investigating and resolving customers' reports of technical problems with aircraft or aerospace vehicles. Write technical reports and other documentation, such as handbooks and bulletins, for use by engineering staff, management, and customers. Maintain records of performance reports for future reference. Evaluate and approve selection of vendors by study of past performance and new advertisements.

GOE INFORMATION—Interest Area: 02. Science, Math, and Engineering. **Work Group:** 02.07. Engineering. **Personality Type—**Investigative. Investigative occupations frequently involve working with ideas and require an extensive amount of thinking. These occupations can involve searching for facts and figuring out problems mentally. **Work Values—**Creativity; Ability Utilization; Social Status; Authority; Responsibility. **Skills—**Technology Design; Science; Mathematics; Troubleshooting; Quality Control Analysis; Programming; Equipment Selection; Operations Analysis. **Abilities—***Cognitive:* Mathematical Reasoning; Number Facility; Written Expression; Written Comprehension; Deductive Reasoning. *Psychomotor:* Control Precision. *Physical:* None met the criteria. *Sensory:* Depth Perception; Speech Clarity; Visual Color Discrimination; Speech Recognition. **General Work Activities—***Information Input:* Getting Information; Identifying Objects, Actions, and Events; Inspecting Equipment, Structures, or Materials. *Mental Process:* Updating and Using Relevant Knowledge; Processing Information; Analyzing Data or Information. *Work Output:* Drafting and Specifying Technical Devices; Documenting or Recording Information; Interacting with Computers. *Interacting with Others:* Interpreting Meaning of Information for Others; Communicating with Other Workers; Communicating with Persons Outside Organization. **Physical Work Conditions—**Sitting; Outdoors; Specialized Protective or Safety Attire; High Places. **Other Job Characteristics—**Importance of Being Exact or Accurate; Consequence of Error; Degree of Automation.

Experience—Job Zone 5. Extensive skill, knowledge, and experience are needed for these occupations. **Job Preparation:** SVP 8.0 and above—four years to more than 10 years. **Knowledge—**Engineering and Technology; Design; Physics; Mathematics; Production and Processing. **Instructional Programs—**Aerospace, Aeronautical, and Astronautical Engineering.

Related DOT Jobs—206.101-010 Aerodynamicist; 206.101-014 Aeronautical Engineer; 206.101-018 Aeronautical Test Engineer; 206.102-022 Aeronautical-Design Engineer; 206.102-026 Aeronautical-Research Engineer; 206.103-030 Stress Analyst; 216.701-010 Value Engineer; 216.701-014 Field-Service Engineer; 216.701-018 Aeronautical Project Engineer.

17-2021.00 Agricultural Engineers

- **Education/Training Required: Bachelor's degree**
- **Employed: 2,400**
- **Annual Earnings: $49,070**
- **Growth: 14.8%**
- **Annual Job Openings: Fewer than 500**

Apply knowledge of engineering technology and biological science to agricultural problems concerned with power and machinery, electrification, structures, soil and water conservation, and processing of agricultural products.

Design agricultural machinery components and equipment, using computer-aided design technology. Design sensing, measuring, and recording devices and other instrumentation used to study plant or animal life. Design structures for crop storage, animal shelter and loading, and animal and crop processing; supervise their construction. Discuss plans with clients, contractors, consultants, and other engineers so that they can be evaluated and necessary changes made. Meet with clients, such as district or regional councils, farmers, and developers, to discuss their needs. Plan and direct construction of rural electric-power distribution systems and irrigation, drainage, and flood control systems for soil and water conservation. Prepare reports, sketches, working drawings, specifications, proposals, and budgets for proposed sites or systems. Test agricultural machinery and equipment to ensure adequate performance. Design and supervise environmental and land reclamation projects in agriculture and related industries. Design food processing plants and related mechanical systems. Provide advice on water quality and issues related to pollution management, river control, and ground and surface water resources. Visit sites to observe environmental problems, to consult with contractors, and/or to monitor construction activities. Conduct educational programs that provide farmers or farm cooperative members with information that can help them improve agricultural productivity. Supervise food processing or manufacturing plant operations.

GOE INFORMATION—**Interest Area:** 02. Science, Math, and Engineering. **Work Group:** 02.07. Engineering. **Personality Type**—Investigative. Investigative occupations frequently involve working with ideas and require an extensive amount of thinking. These occupations can involve searching for facts and figuring out problems mentally. **Work Values**—Creativity; Ability Utilization; Responsibility; Autonomy; Social Status. **Skills**—Technology Design; Operations Analysis; Science; Mathematics; Complex Problem Solving; Equipment Selection; Systems Analysis; Quality Control Analysis. **Abilities**—*Cognitive:* Originality; Visualization; Written Expression; Deductive Reasoning; Mathematical Reasoning. *Psychomotor:* Finger Dexterity; Multilimb Coordination; Control Precision; Rate Control. *Physical:* Dynamic Flexibility; Gross Body Coordination. *Sensory:* Speech Clarity; Far Vision; Visual Color Discrimination; Near Vision; Night Vision. **General Work Activities**—*Information Input:* Getting Information; Identifying Objects, Actions, and Events; Monitoring Processes, Materials, or Surroundings. *Mental Process:* Thinking Creatively; Analyzing Data or Information; Updating and Using Relevant Knowledge. *Work Output:* Drafting and Specifying Technical Devices; Documenting or Recording Information; Handling and Moving Objects. *Interacting with Others:* Communicating with Other Workers; Coordinating the Work and Activities of Others; Communicating with Persons Outside Organization. **Physical Work Conditions**—Outdoors; Hazardous Conditions; Hazardous Equipment; Extremely Bright or Inadequate Lighting; Very Hot or Cold. **Other Job Characteristics**—Consequence of Error; Importance of Being Exact or Accurate; Degree of Automation.

Experience—Job Zone 5. Extensive skill, knowledge, and experience are needed for these occupations. **Job Preparation:** SVP 8.0 and above—four years to more than 10 years. **Knowledge**—Biology; Food Production; Engineering and Technology; Design; Building and Construction. **Instructional Programs**—Agricultural/Biological Engineering and Bioengineering.

Related DOT Jobs—013.061-010 Agricultural Engineer; 013.061-014 Agricultural-Research Engineer; 013.061-018 Design-Engineer, Agricultural Equipment; 013.061-022 Test Engineer, Agricultural Equipment.

17-2031.00 Biomedical Engineers

- **Education/Training Required: Bachelor's degree**
- **Employed: 7,221**
- **Annual Earnings: $59,790**
- **Growth: 31.4%**
- **Annual Job Openings: Fewer than 500**

Apply knowledge of engineering, biology, and biomechanical principles to the design, development, and evaluation of biological and health systems and products, such as artificial organs, prostheses, instrumentation, medical information systems, and health management and care delivery systems.

Advise and assist in the application of instrumentation in clinical environments. Conduct research, along with life scientists, chemists, and medical scientists, on the engineering aspects of the biological systems of humans and animals. Design and develop medical diagnostic and clinical instrumentation, equipment, and procedures, utilizing the principles of engineering and bio-behavioral sciences. Develop models or computer simulations of human bio-behavioral systems in order to obtain data for measuring or controlling life processes. Evaluate the safety, efficiency, and effectiveness of biomedical equipment. Install, adjust, maintain, and/or repair biomedical equipment. Research new materials to be used for products such as implanted artificial organs. Adapt or design computer hardware or software for medical science uses. Advise hospital administrators on the planning, acquisition, and use of medical equipment. Analyze new medical procedures in order to forecast likely outcomes. Design and deliver technology to assist people with disabilities. Develop new applications for energy sources, such as using nuclear power for biomedical implants. Diagnose and interpret bioelectric data, using signal processing techniques. Teach biomedical engineering or disseminate knowledge about field through writing or consulting.

GOE INFORMATION—**Interest Area:** 02. Science, Math, and Engineering. **Work Group:** 02.07. Engineering. **Note:** The Department of Labor has not collected some data for this job, so it has fewer details than the other descriptions.

Instructional Programs—Biomedical/Medical Engineering.

Related DOT Jobs—019.061-010 Biomedical Engineer.

17-2041.00 Chemical Engineers

- **Education/Training Required: Bachelor's degree**
- **Employed: 32,883**
- **Annual Earnings: $70,180**
- **Growth: 4.1%**
- **Annual Job Openings: 2,000**

Design chemical plant equipment and devise processes for manufacturing chemicals and products, such as gasoline, synthetic rubber, plastics, detergents, cement, paper, and pulp, by applying principles and technology of chemistry, physics, and engineering.

Develop processes to separate components of liquids or gases or generate electrical currents, using controlled chemical processes. Conduct research to develop new and improved chemical manufacturing processes. Design and plan layout of equipment. Design measurement and control systems for chemical plants based on data collected in laboratory experiments and in pilot plant operations. Determine most effective arrangement of operations, such as mixing, crushing, heat transfer, distillation, and drying. Perform laboratory studies of steps in manufacture of new product and test proposed process in small-scale operation (pilot plant). Perform tests throughout stages of production to determine degree of control over variables, including temperature, density, specific gravity, and pressure. Develop safety procedures to be employed by workers operating equipment or working in close proximity to on-going chemical reactions. Prepare estimate of production costs and production progress reports for management. Direct activities of workers who operate or who are engaged in constructing and improving absorption, evaporation, or electromagnetic equipment.

GOE INFORMATION—Interest Area: 02. Science, Math, and Engineering. **Work Group:** 02.07. Engineering. **Personality Type**—Investigative. Investigative occupations frequently involve working with ideas and require an extensive amount of thinking. These occupations can involve searching for facts and figuring out problems mentally. **Work Values**—Creativity; Ability Utilization; Social Status; Authority; Responsibility. **Skills**—Operation Monitoring; Science; Quality Control Analysis; Operations Analysis; Troubleshooting; Equipment Selection; Technology Design; Complex Problem Solving. **Abilities**—*Cognitive:* Mathematical Reasoning; Originality; Category Flexibility; Deductive Reasoning; Written Comprehension. *Psychomotor:* Response Orientation; Control Precision; Reaction Time; Finger Dexterity; Arm-Hand Steadiness. *Physical:* Gross Body Equilibrium; Extent Flexibility. *Sensory:* Visual Color Discrimination; Speech Clarity; Depth Perception; Near Vision; Hearing Sensitivity. **General Work Activities**—*Information Input:* Getting Information; Identifying Objects, Actions, and Events; Estimating Needed Characteristics. *Mental Process:* Updating and Using Relevant Knowledge; Analyzing Data or Information; Making Decisions and Solving Problems. *Work Output:* Drafting and Specifying Technical Devices; Documenting or Recording Information; Controlling Machines and Processes. *Interacting with Others:* Communicating with Other Workers; Providing Consultation and Advice to Others; Interpreting Meaning of Information for Others. **Physical Work Conditions**—Common Protective or Safety Attire; Hazardous Conditions; Contaminants; Specialized Protective or Safety Attire; Sitting. **Other Job Characteristics**—Consequence of Error; Degree of Automation; Importance of Being Exact or Accurate.

Experience—Job Zone 5. Extensive skill, knowledge, and experience are needed for these occupations. **Job Preparation:** SVP 8.0 and above—four years to more than 10 years. **Knowledge**—Chemistry; Design; Physics; Engineering and Technology; Mathematics. **Instructional Programs**—Chemical Engineering.

Related DOT Jobs—806.101-010 Absorption-and-Adsorption Engineer; 806.101-014 Chemical Design Engineer, Processes; 806.101-018 Chemical Engineer; 806.102-022 Chemical Research Engineer; 806.102-026 Chemical-Test Engineer.

17-2051.00 Civil Engineers

- **Education/Training Required: Bachelor's degree**
- **Employed: 232,046**
- **Annual Earnings: $58,420**
- **Growth: 10.2%**
- **Annual Job Openings: 4,000**

Perform engineering duties in planning, designing, and overseeing construction and maintenance of building structures and facilities, such as roads, railroads, airports, bridges, harbors, channels, dams, irrigation projects, pipelines, power plants, water and sewage systems, and waste disposal units. Includes architectural, structural, traffic, ocean, and geo-technical engineers.

Analyze survey reports, maps, drawings, blueprints, aerial photography, and other topographical or geologic data to plan projects. Plan and design transportation or hydraulic systems and structures, following construction and government standards, using design software and drawing tools. Compute load and grade requirements, water flow rates, and material stress factors to determine design specifications. Inspect project sites to monitor progress and ensure conformance to design specifications and safety or sanitation standards. Direct construction, operations, and maintenance activities at project site. Direct or participate in surveying to lay out installations and establish reference points, grades, and elevations to guide construction. Estimate quantities and cost of materials, equipment, or labor to determine project feasibility. Prepare or present public reports, such as bid proposals, deeds, environmental impact statements, and property and right-of-way descriptions. Test soils and materials to determine the adequacy and strength of foundations, concrete, asphalt, or steel. Provide technical advice regarding design, construction, or program modifications and structural repairs to industrial and managerial personnel. Conduct studies of traffic patterns or environmental conditions to identify engineering problems and assess the potential impact of projects.

GOE INFORMATION—Interest Area: 02. Science, Math, and Engineering. **Work Group:** 02.07. Engineering. **Personality Type**—Realistic. Realistic occupations frequently involve work activities that include practical, hands-on problems and solutions. They often deal with plants, animals, and real-world materials like wood, tools, and machinery. Many of the occupations require working outside and do not involve a lot of paperwork or working closely with others. **Work Values**—Creativity; Ability Utilization; Autonomy; Social Status; Authority. **Skills**—Mathematics; Complex Problem Solving; Coordination; Negotiation; Science; Equipment Selection; Persuasion; Operations Analysis. **Abilities**—*Cognitive:* Deductive Reasoning; Originality; Visualization; Inductive Reasoning; Speed of Closure. *Psychomotor:* Control Precision; Finger Dexterity; Reaction Time; Multilimb Coordination; Arm-Hand Steadiness. *Physical:* None met the criteria. *Sensory:* Auditory Attention; Far Vision; Speech Recognition; Near Vision; Speech Clarity. **General Work Activities**—*Information Input:* Getting Information; Monitoring Processes, Materials, or Surroundings; Estimating Needed Characteristics. *Mental Process:* Making Decisions and Solving Problems; Organizing, Planning, and Prioritizing; Updating and Using Relevant Knowledge. *Work Output:* Interacting with Computers; Drafting and Specifying Technical Devices; Documenting or Recording Information. *Interacting with Others:* Resolving Conflict and Negotiating with Others; Communicating with Other Workers; Coordinating the Work and Activities of Others. **Physical Work Conditions**—Outdoors; High Places; Hazardous Conditions; Climbing Ladders, Scaffolds, Poles, etc.; Contaminants. **Other Job Characteristics**—Consequence of Error; Importance of Being Exact or Accurate; Importance of Repeating Same Tasks.

Experience—Job Zone 4. A minimum of two to four years of work-related skill, knowledge, or experience is needed. **Job Preparation:** SVP 7.0 to less than 8.0—two years to less than 10 years. **Knowledge**—Design; Engineering and Technology; Building and Construction; Customer and Personal Service; Mathematics. **Instructional Programs**—Civil Engineering, General; Civil Engineering, Other; Transportation and Highway Engineering; Water Resources Engineering.

Related DOT Jobs—019.167-018 Resource-Recovery Engineer; 506.101-010 Airport Engineer; 506.101-014 Civil Engineer; 506.101-018 Hydraulic Engineer; 506.102-022 Irrigation Engineer; 506.102-026 Railroad Engineer; 506.103-030 Sanitary Engineer; 506.103-034 Structural Engineer; 506.103-038 Transportation Engineer; 516.701-014 Drainage-Design Coordinator; 516.701-018 Forest Engineer; 516.702-026 Production Engineer, Track.

17-2061.00 Computer Hardware Engineers

- Education/Training Required: Bachelor's degree
- Employed: 59,964
- Annual Earnings: $71,560
- Growth: 24.9%
- Annual Job Openings: 3,000

Research, design, develop, and test computer or computer-related equipment for commercial, industrial, military, or scientific use. May supervise the manufacturing and installation of computer or computer-related equipment and components.

Analyze information to determine, recommend, and plan layout, including type of computers and peripheral equipment modifications. Analyze user needs and recommend appropriate hardware. Build, test and modify product prototypes, using working models or theoretical models constructed using computer simulation. Confer with engineering staff and consult specifications to evaluate interface between hardware and software and operational and performance requirements of overall system. Design and develop computer hardware and support peripherals, including central processing units (CPUs), support logic, microprocessors, custom integrated circuits, and printers and disk drives. Evaluate factors such as reporting formats required, cost constraints, and need for security restrictions to determine hardware configuration. Monitor functioning of equipment and make necessary modifications to ensure system operates in conformance with specifications. Specify power supply requirements and configuration, drawing on system performance expectations and design specifications. Store, retrieve, and manipulate data for analysis of system capabilities and requirements. Test and verify hardware and support peripherals to ensure that they meet specifications and requirements, analyzing and recording test data. Write detailed functional specifications that document the hardware development process and support hardware introduction. Assemble and modify existing pieces of equipment to meet special needs. Direct technicians, engineering designers, or other technical support personnel as needed. Provide technical support to designers, marketing and sales departments, suppliers, engineers, and other team members throughout the product development and implementation process. Provide training and support to system designers and users. Recommend purchase of equipment to control dust, temperature, and humidity in area of system installation. Select hardware and material, assuring compliance with specifications and product requirements. Update knowledge and skills to keep up with rapid advancements in computer technology.

GOE INFORMATION—Interest Area: 02. Science, Math, and Engineering. Work Group: 02.07. Engineering. Personality Type—Investigative. Investigative occupations frequently involve working with ideas and require an extensive amount of thinking. These occupations can involve searching for facts and figuring out problems mentally. Work Values—Creativity; Ability Utilization; Good Working Conditions; Responsibility; Social Status. Skills—Programming; Troubleshooting; Installation; Operations Analysis; Technology Design; Management of Material Resources; Science; Equipment Selection. Abilities—*Cognitive:* Mathematical Reasoning; Inductive Reasoning; Deductive Reasoning; Oral Expression; Written Expression. *Psychomotor:* Response Orientation; Wrist-Finger Speed. *Physical:* Gross Body Coordination. *Sensory:* Speech Clarity; Speech Recognition; Near Vision; Auditory Attention; Visual Color Discrimination. General Work Activities—*Information Input:* Identifying Objects, Actions, and Events; Getting Information; Estimating Needed Characteristics. *Mental Process:* Updating and Using Relevant Knowledge; Analyzing Data or Information; Thinking Creatively. *Work Output:* Interacting with Computers; Drafting and Specifying Technical Devices; Documenting or Recording Information. *Interacting with Others:* Providing Consultation and Advice to Others; Communicating with Other Workers; Communicating with Persons Outside Organization. Physical Work Conditions—Sitting; Indoors; Making Repetitive Motions; Walking or Running. Other Job Characteristics—Degree of Automation; Importance of Being Exact or Accurate; Pace Determined by Speed of Equipment.

Experience—Job Zone 4. A minimum of two to four years of work-related skill, knowledge, or experience is needed. Job Preparation: SVP 7.0 to less than 8.0—two years to less than 10 years. Knowledge—Computers and Electronics; Mathematics; Engineering and Technology; Design; Education and Training. Instructional Programs—Computer Engineering, General; Computer Hardware Engineering.

Related DOT Jobs—003.061-030 Electronics Engineer.

17-2071.00 Electrical Engineers

- Education/Training Required: Bachelor's degree
- Employed: 157,188
- Annual Earnings: $66,890
- Growth: 11.3%
- Annual Job Openings: 8,000

Design, develop, test, or supervise the manufacturing and installation of electrical equipment, components, or systems for commercial, industrial, military, or scientific use.

Confer with engineers, customers, and others to discuss existing or potential engineering projects and products. Design, implement, maintain, and improve electrical instruments, equipment, facilities, components, products, and systems for commercial, industrial, and domestic purposes. Direct and coordinate manufacturing, construction, installation, maintenance, support, documentation, and testing activities to ensure compliance with specifications, codes, and customer requirements. Inspect completed installations and observe operations to ensure conformance to design and equipment specifications and compliance with operational and safety standards. Perform detailed calculations to compute and establish manufacturing, construction, and installation standards and specifications. Plan and implement research methodology and procedures to apply principles of electrical theory to engineering projects. Plan layout of electric power generating plants and distribution lines and stations. Prepare and study technical drawings, specifications of electrical systems, and topographical maps to ensure that installation and operations conform to standards and customer requirements. Assist in developing capital project programs for new equipment and major repairs. Collect data relating to commercial and residential development, population, and power system interconnection to determine operating efficiency of electrical systems. Compile data and write reports regarding existing and potential engineering studies and projects. Conduct field surveys and study maps, graphs, diagrams, and other data to identify and correct power system problems. Develop budgets, estimating labor, material, and construction costs. Investigate customer or public complaints, determine nature and extent of problem, and recommend remedial measures.

Oversee project production efforts to assure projects are completed satisfactorily, on time, and within budget. Prepare specifications for purchase of materials and equipment. Supervise and train project team members as necessary. Investigate and test vendors' and competitors' products. Operate computer-assisted engineering and design software and equipment to perform engineering tasks.

GOE INFORMATION—Interest Area: 02. Science, Math, and Engineering. **Work Group:** 02.07. Engineering. **Personality Type—**Investigative. Investigative occupations frequently involve working with ideas and require an extensive amount of thinking. These occupations can involve searching for facts and figuring out problems mentally. **Work Values—**Creativity; Ability Utilization; Social Status; Responsibility; Autonomy. **Skills—**Programming; Technology Design; Mathematics; Equipment Selection; Science; Critical Thinking; Operation Monitoring; Operations Analysis. **Abilities—***Cognitive:* Mathematical Reasoning; Originality; Number Facility; Written Expression; Written Comprehension. *Psychomotor:* Finger Dexterity; Wrist-Finger Speed; Manual Dexterity; Arm-Hand Steadiness; Control Precision. *Physical:* Gross Body Coordination; Gross Body Equilibrium; Stamina; Trunk Strength. *Sensory:* Visual Color Discrimination; Near Vision; Depth Perception; Hearing Sensitivity; Far Vision. **General Work Activities—***Information Input:* Getting Information; Identifying Objects, Actions, and Events; Inspecting Equipment, Structures, or Materials. *Mental Process:* Analyzing Data or Information; Updating and Using Relevant Knowledge; Processing Information. *Work Output:* Drafting and Specifying Technical Devices; Interacting with Computers; Documenting or Recording Information. *Interacting with Others:* Communicating with Other Workers; Communicating with Persons Outside Organization; Providing Consultation and Advice to Others. **Physical Work Conditions—**Sitting; Hazardous Conditions; Walking or Running; Extremely Bright or Inadequate Lighting; Climbing Ladders, Scaffolds, Poles, etc. **Other Job Characteristics—**Importance of Being Exact or Accurate; Degree of Automation; Consequence of Error.

Experience—Job Zone 5. Extensive skill, knowledge, and experience are needed for these occupations. **Job Preparation:** SVP 8.0 and above—four years to more than 10 years. **Knowledge—**Engineering and Technology; Design; Building and Construction; Computers and Electronics; Production and Processing. **Instructional Programs—**Electrical, Electronics, and Communications Engineering.

Related DOT Jobs—306.101-010 Electrical Engineer; 306.101-014 Electrical Test Engineer; 306.101-018 Electrical-Design Engineer; 306.102-022 Electrical-Prospecting Engineer; 306.102-026 Electrical-Research Engineer; 306.104-046 Illuminating Engineer; 316.701-014 Distribution-Field Engineer; 316.701-018 Electrical Engineer, Power System; 316.702-022 Electrolysis-and-Corrosion-Control Engineer; 316.702-026 Engineer of System Development; 316.703-038 Induction-Coordination Power Engineer; 316.704-046 Power-Distribution Engineer; 316.705-050 Power-Transmission Engineer; 316.705-054 Protection Engineer.

17-2072.00 Electronics Engineers, Except Computer

- **Education/Training Required: Bachelor's degree**
- **Employed: 130,366**
- **Annual Earnings: $68,350**
- **Growth: 10.4%**
- **Annual Job Openings: 6,000**

Research, design, develop, and test electronic components and systems for commercial, industrial, military, or scientific use, utilizing knowledge of electronic theory and materials properties. Design

electronic circuits and components for use in fields such as telecommunications, aerospace guidance and propulsion control, acoustics, or instruments and controls.

Analyze system requirements, capacity, cost, and customer needs to determine feasibility of project and develop system plan. Confer with engineers, customers, vendors, and others to discuss existing and potential engineering projects or products. Design electronic components and software, products, and systems for commercial, industrial, medical, military, and scientific applications. Develop and perform operational, maintenance, and testing procedures for electronic products, components, equipment, and systems. Direct and coordinate activities concerned with manufacture, construction, installation, maintenance, operation, and modification of electronic equipment, products, and systems. Evaluate operational systems, prototypes, and proposals and recommend repair or design modifications based on factors such as environment, service, cost, and system capabilities. Inspect electronic equipment, instruments, products, and systems to ensure conformance to specifications, safety standards, and applicable codes and regulations. Plan and develop applications and modifications for electronic properties used in components, products, and systems to improve technical performance. Plan and implement research, methodology, and procedures to apply principles of electronic theory to engineering projects. Prepare engineering sketches and specifications for construction, relocation, and installation of equipment, facilities, products, and systems. Determine material and equipment needs and order supplies. Prepare, review, and maintain maintenance schedules, design documentation, and operational reports and charts. Provide technical support and instruction to staff and customers regarding equipment standards and help solve specific, difficult in-service engineering problems. Review and evaluate work of others, inside and outside the organization, to ensure effectiveness, technical adequacy, and compatibility in the resolution of complex engineering problems. Review or prepare budget and cost estimates for equipment, construction, and installation projects; control expenditures. Operate computer-assisted engineering and design software and equipment to perform engineering tasks. Prepare documentation containing information such as confidential descriptions and specifications of proprietary hardware and software, product development and introduction schedules, product costs, and information about product performance weaknesses. Prepare necessary criteria, procedures, reports, and plans for successful conduct of the program/project with consideration given to site preparation, facility validation, installation, quality assurance, and testing. Represent employer at conferences, meetings, boards, panels, committees, and working groups to present, explain, and defend findings and recommendations, negotiate compromises and agreements, and exchange information.

GOE INFORMATION—Interest Area: 02. Science, Math, and Engineering. **Work Group:** 02.07. Engineering. **Personality Type—**Investigative. Investigative occupations frequently involve working with ideas and require an extensive amount of thinking. These occupations can involve searching for facts and figuring out problems mentally. **Work Values—**Creativity; Ability Utilization; Responsibility; Social Status; Autonomy. **Skills—**Mathematics; Science; Writing; Equipment Selection; Systems Analysis; Reading Comprehension; Judgment and Decision Making; Technology Design. **Abilities—***Cognitive:* Mathematical Reasoning; Originality; Number Facility; Written Expression; Visualization. *Psychomotor:* Wrist-Finger Speed; Finger Dexterity; Manual Dexterity; Multilimb Coordination; Response Orientation. *Physical:* Dynamic Flexibility; Gross Body Coordination. *Sensory:* Near Vision; Speech Clarity; Visual Color Discrimination; Depth Perception; Hearing Sensitivity. **General Work Activities—***Information Input:* Getting Information; Inspecting Equipment, Structures, or Materials; Identifying Objects, Actions, and Events. *Mental Process:* Analyzing Data or Information; Updating and Using Relevant Knowledge; Processing Information. *Work Output:* Drafting and Specifying Technical Devices; Documenting or Recording Information; Repairing and Maintaining Electronic Equipment. *Interacting with Others:* Communicating with Other Workers; Communicating with Persons Outside Organization; Coordinating the Work and Activities of Others. **Physical Work Conditions**—Hazardous Conditions; Sitting; Using Hands on Objects, Tools, or Controls; Walking or Running; Climbing Ladders, Scaffolds, Poles, etc. **Other Job Characteristics**—Importance of Being Exact or Accurate; Consequence of Error; Degree of Automation.

Experience—Job Zone 5. Extensive skill, knowledge, and experience are needed for these occupations. **Job Preparation:** SVP 8.0 and above—four years to more than 10 years. **Knowledge**—Design; Engineering and Technology; Computers and Electronics; Telecommunications; Production and Processing. **Instructional Programs**—Electrical, Electronics, and Communications Engineering.

Related DOT Jobs—031.167-018 Telecommunications Specialist; 306.103-030 Electronics Engineer; 306.103-034 Electronics-Design Engineer; 306.103-038 Electronics-Research Engineer; 306.104-042 Electronics-Test Engineer; 306.105-050 Planning Engineer, Central Office Facilities; 316.701-010 Cable Engineer, Outside Plant; 316.703-030 Engineer-in-Charge, Studio Operations; 316.704-042 Outside-Plant Engineer; 316.705-058 Supervisor, Microwave; 316.706-066 Transmission-and-Protection Engineer; 318.701-010 Central-Office Equipment Engineer; 318.701-014 Commercial Engineer; 318.701-018 Customer-Equipment Engineer.

17-2081.00 Environmental Engineers

- Education/Training Required: Bachelor's degree
- Employed: 52,421
- Annual Earnings: $61,250
- Growth: 26.0%
- Annual Job Openings: 3,000

Design, plan, or perform engineering duties in the prevention, control, and remediation of environmental health hazards utilizing various engineering disciplines. Work may include waste treatment, site remediation, or pollution control technology.

Advise corporations and government agencies of procedures to follow in cleaning up contaminated sites in order to protect people and the environment. Advise industries and government agencies about environmental policies and standards. Assess the existing or potential environmental impact of land use projects on air, water, and land. Coordinate and manage environmental protection programs and projects, assigning and evaluating work. Design systems, processes, and equipment for control, management, and remediation of water, air, and soil quality. Develop proposed project objectives and targets; report to management on progress in attaining them. Develop site-specific health and safety protocols, such as spill contingency plans and methods for loading and transporting waste. Inform company employees and other interested parties of environmental issues. Inspect industrial and municipal facilities and programs in order to evaluate operational effectiveness and ensure compliance with environmental regulations. Monitor progress of environmental improvement programs. Prepare, review, and update environmental investigation and recommendation reports. Provide environmental engineering assistance in network analysis, regulatory analysis, and planning or reviewing database development. Provide technical-level support for environmental remediation and litigation projects, including remediation system design and determination of regulatory applicability. Serve as liaison with federal, state, and local agencies and officials on issues pertaining to solid and hazardous waste program requirements. Serve on teams conducting multimedia inspections at complex facilities, providing assistance with planning, quality assurance, safety inspection protocols, and sampling. Assess, sort, characterize, and pack known and unknown materials. Assist in budget implementation, forecasts, and administration. Collaborate with environmental scientists, planners, hazardous waste technicians, engineers, and other specialists and experts in law and business to address environmental problems. Develop and present environmental compliance training or orientation sessions. Develop, implement, and manage plans and programs related to conservation and management of natural resources. Maintain, write, and revise quality-assurance documentation and procedures. Obtain, update, and maintain plans, permits, and standard operating procedures. Prepare hazardous waste manifests and land disposal restriction notifications. Provide administrative support for projects by collecting data, providing project documentation, training staff, and performing other general administrative duties. Request bids from suppliers or consultants.

GOE INFORMATION—Interest Area: 02. Science, Math, and Engineering. **Work Group:** 02.07. Engineering. **Note:** The Department of Labor has not collected some data for this job, so it has fewer details than the other descriptions.

Instructional Programs—Environmental/Environmental Health Engineering.

Related DOT Jobs—019.081-018 Pollution-Control Engineer; 029.081-010 Environmental Analyst.

17-2111.00 Health and Safety Engineers, Except Mining Safety Engineers and Inspectors

- Education/Training Required: Bachelor's degree
- Employed: 44,368
- Annual Earnings: $57,560
- Growth: 10.9%
- Annual Job Openings: 3,000

Promote worksite or product safety by applying knowledge of industrial processes, mechanics, chemistry, psychology, and industrial health and safety laws.

No task data available.

GOE INFORMATION—Interest Area: 02. Science, Math, and Engineering. **Work Group:** 02.07. Engineering. **Note:** The Department of Labor has not collected some data for this job, so it has fewer details than the other descriptions.

Instructional Programs—Environmental/Environmental Health Engineering.

Related DOT Jobs—012.061-010 Product-Safety Engineer; 012.061-014 Safety Engineer; 012.167-022 Fire-Prevention Research Engineer; 012.167-026 Fire-Protection Engineer; 012.167-034 Industrial-Health Engineer; 012.167-058 Safety Manager.

17-2111.01 Industrial Safety and Health Engineers

- Education/Training Required: Bachelor's degree
- Employed: 44,368
- Annual Earnings: $57,560
- Growth: 10.9%
- Annual Job Openings: 3,000

Plan, implement, and coordinate safety programs requiring application of engineering principles and technology to prevent or correct unsafe environmental working conditions.

Devises and implements safety or industrial health program to prevent, correct, or control unsafe environmental conditions. Examines plans and specifications for new machinery or equipment to determine if all safety requirements have been included. Conducts or coordinates training of workers concerning safety laws and regulations; use of safety equipment, devices, and clothing; and first aid. Inspects facilities, machinery, and safety equipment to identify and correct potential hazards and ensure compliance with safety regulations. Conducts or directs testing of air quality, noise, temperature, or radiation to verify compliance with health and safety regulations. Provides technical guidance to organizations regarding how to handle health-related problems, such as water and air pollution. Compiles, analyzes, and interprets statistical data related to exposure factors concerning occupational illnesses and accidents. Installs or directs installation of safety devices on machinery. Investigates causes of industrial accidents or injuries to develop solutions to minimize or prevent recurrence. Conducts plant or area surveys to determine safety levels for exposure to materials and conditions. Checks floors of plant to ensure that they are strong enough to support heavy machinery. Designs and builds safety devices for machinery or safety clothing. Prepares reports of findings from investigation of accidents, inspection of facilities, or testing of environment. Maintains liaison with outside organizations, such as fire departments, mutual aid societies, and rescue teams.

GOE INFORMATION—**Interest Area:** 02. Science, Math, and Engineering. **Work Group:** 02.07. Engineering. **Personality Type**—Investigative. Investigative occupations frequently involve working with ideas and require an extensive amount of thinking. These occupations can involve searching for facts and figuring out problems mentally. **Work Values**—Creativity; Authority; Social Status; Responsibility; Autonomy. **Skills**—Operations Analysis; Technology Design; Mathematics; Equipment Selection; Quality Control Analysis; Instructing; Science; Complex Problem Solving. **Abilities**—*Cognitive:* Mathematical Reasoning; Inductive Reasoning; Written Expression; Number Facility; Deductive Reasoning. *Psychomotor:* Multilimb Coordination; Control Precision. *Physical:* Extent Flexibility; Gross Body Coordination; Trunk Strength; Explosive Strength. *Sensory:* Peripheral Vision; Depth Perception; Sound Localization; Near Vision; Speech Clarity. **General Work Activities**—*Information Input:* Getting Information; Inspecting Equipment, Structures, or Materials; Monitoring Processes, Materials, or Surroundings. *Mental Process:* Analyzing Data or Information; Updating and Using Relevant Knowledge; Processing Information. *Work Output:* Drafting and Specifying Technical Devices; Documenting or Recording Information; Interacting with Computers. *Interacting with Others:* Providing Consultation and Advice to Others; Interpreting Meaning of Information for Others; Communicating with Other Workers. **Physical Work Conditions**—Specialized Protective or Safety Attire; Indoors; Radiation; Sitting; Common Protective or Safety Attire. **Other Job Characteristics**—Consequence of Error; Importance of Being Exact or Accurate; Importance of Repeating Same Tasks.

Experience—Job Zone 4. A minimum of two to four years of work-related skill, knowledge, or experience is needed. **Job Preparation:** SVP 7.0 to less than 8.0—two years to less than 10 years. **Knowledge**—Engineering and Technology; Design; Public Safety and Security; Physics; Administration and Management. **Instructional Programs**—Environmental/Environmental Health Engineering.

Related DOT Jobs—012.061-014 Safety Engineer; 012.167-034 Industrial-Health Engineer; 012.167-058 Safety Manager.

17-2111.02 Fire-Prevention and Protection Engineers

- **Education/Training Required: Bachelor's degree**
- **Employed: No data available.**
- **Annual Earnings: $57,560**
- **Growth: 10.9%**
- **Annual Job Openings: 3,000**

Research causes of fires, determine fire protection methods, and design or recommend materials or equipment such as structural components or fire-detection equipment to assist organizations in safeguarding life and property against fire, explosion, and related hazards.

Determines fire causes and methods of fire prevention. Studies buildings to evaluate fire prevention factors, resistance of construction, contents, water supply and delivery, and exits. Recommends and advises on use of fire detection equipment, extinguishing devices, or methods to alleviate conditions conducive to fire. Conducts research on fire retardants and fire safety of materials and devices to determine cause and methods of fire prevention. Advises and plans for prevention of destruction by fire, wind, water, or other causes of damage. Evaluates fire departments and laws and regulations affecting fire prevention or fire safety. Organizes and trains personnel to carry out fire protection programs. Designs fire detection equipment, alarm systems, fire extinguishing devices and systems, or structural components protection.

GOE INFORMATION—**Interest Area:** 02. Science, Math, and Engineering. **Work Group:** 02.07. Engineering. **Personality Type**—Investigative. Investigative occupations frequently involve working with ideas and require an extensive amount of thinking. These occupations can involve searching for facts and figuring out problems mentally. **Work Values**—Creativity; Social Status; Authority; Responsibility; Autonomy. **Skills**—Technology Design; Operations Analysis; Instructing; Equipment Selection; Complex Problem Solving; Systems Evaluation; Speaking; Quality Control Analysis. **Abilities**—*Cognitive:* Inductive Reasoning; Deductive Reasoning; Category Flexibility; Written Expression; Oral Expression. *Psychomotor:* None met the criteria. *Physical:* None met the criteria. *Sensory:* Speech Clarity; Night Vision. **General Work Activities**—*Information Input:* Getting Information; Inspecting Equipment, Structures, or Materials; Monitoring Processes, Materials, or Surroundings. *Mental Process:* Analyzing Data or Information; Updating and Using Relevant Knowledge; Making Decisions and Solving Problems. *Work Output:* Drafting and Specifying Technical Devices; Documenting or Recording Information; Performing General Physical Activities. *Interacting with Others:* Providing Consultation and Advice to Others; Communicating with Persons Outside Organization; Teaching Others. **Physical Work Conditions**—Specialized Protective or Safety Attire; Climbing Ladders, Scaffolds, Poles, etc.; Cramped Work Space or Awkward Positions; Kneeling, Crouching, or Crawling; Sitting. **Other Job Characteristics**—Consequence of Error; Importance of Being Exact or Accurate; Pace Determined by Speed of Equipment.

Experience—Job Zone 4. A minimum of two to four years of work-related skill, knowledge, or experience is needed. **Job Preparation:** SVP 7.0 to less than 8.0—two years to less than 10 years. **Knowledge**—Public Safety and Security; Education and Training; Engineering and Technology; Design; Chemistry. **Instructional Programs**—Environmental/Environmental Health Engineering.

Related DOT Jobs—012.167-022 Fire-Prevention Research Engineer; 012.167-026 Fire-Protection Engineer.

17-2111.03 Product Safety Engineers

- **Education/Training Required: Bachelor's degree**
- **Employed: No data available.**
- **Annual Earnings: $57,560**
- **Growth: 10.9%**
- **Annual Job Openings: 3,000**

Develop and conduct tests to evaluate product safety levels and recommend measures to reduce or eliminate hazards.

Conducts research to evaluate safety levels for products. Evaluates potential health hazards or damage which could occur from misuse of product and engineers solutions to improve safety. Investigates causes of accidents, injuries, or illnesses from product usage to develop solutions to minimize or prevent recurrence. Advises and recommends procedures for detection, prevention, and elimination of physical, chemical, or other product hazards. Participates in preparation of product usage and precautionary label instructions. Prepares reports of findings from investigation of accidents.

GOE INFORMATION—Interest Area: 02. Science, Math, and Engineering. **Work Group:** 02.07. Engineering. **Personality Type**—Investigative. Investigative occupations frequently involve working with ideas and require an extensive amount of thinking. These occupations can involve searching for facts and figuring out problems mentally. **Work Values**—Creativity; Ability Utilization; Achievement; Autonomy; Responsibility. **Skills**—Quality Control Analysis; Operations Analysis; Mathematics; Complex Problem Solving; Technology Design; Science; Troubleshooting; Writing. **Abilities**—*Cognitive:* Deductive Reasoning; Written Expression; Fluency of Ideas; Problem Sensitivity; Inductive Reasoning. *Psychomotor:* None met the criteria. *Physical:* None met the criteria. *Sensory:* Sound Localization; Speech Clarity; Speech Recognition. **General Work Activities**—*Information Input:* Getting Information; Identifying Objects, Actions, and Events; Monitoring Processes, Materials, or Surroundings. *Mental Process:* Processing Information; Analyzing Data or Information; Making Decisions and Solving Problems. *Work Output:* Documenting or Recording Information; Interacting with Computers; Handling and Moving Objects. *Interacting with Others:* Interpreting Meaning of Information for Others; Providing Consultation and Advice to Others; Communicating with Other Workers. **Physical Work Conditions**—Specialized Protective or Safety Attire; Indoors; Radiation; Whole Body Vibration; Disease or Infections. **Other Job Characteristics**—Importance of Being Exact or Accurate; Consequence of Error; Pace Determined by Speed of Equipment.

Experience—Job Zone 5. Extensive skill, knowledge, and experience are needed for these occupations. **Job Preparation:** SVP 8.0 and above—four years to more than 10 years. **Knowledge**—Chemistry; Engineering and Technology; Physics; Public Safety and Security; Biology. **Instructional Programs**—Environmental/Environmental Health Engineering.

Related DOT Jobs—012.061-010 Product-Safety Engineer.

17-2112.00 Industrial Engineers

- **Education/Training Required: Bachelor's degree**
- **Employed: 153,636**
- **Annual Earnings: $60,770**
- **Growth: 4.5%**
- **Annual Job Openings: 10,000**

Design, develop, test, and evaluate integrated systems for managing industrial production processes, including human work factors, quality control, inventory control, logistics and material flow, cost analysis, and production coordination.

Analyze statistical data and product specifications to determine standards and establish quality and reliability objectives of finished product. Develop manufacturing methods, labor utilization standards, and cost analysis systems to promote efficient staff and facility utilization. Draft and design layout of equipment, materials, and workspace to illustrate maximum efficiency, using drafting tools and computer. Plan and establish sequence of operations to fabricate and assemble parts or products and to promote efficient utilization. Review production schedules, engineering specifications, orders, and related information to obtain knowledge of manufacturing methods, procedures, and activities. Study operations sequence, material flow, functional statements, organization charts, and project information to determine worker functions and responsibilities. Formulate sampling procedures and designs and develop forms and instructions for recording, evaluating, and reporting quality and reliability data. Apply statistical methods and perform mathematical calculations to determine manufacturing processes, staff requirements, and production standards. Coordinate quality control objectives and activities to resolve production problems, maximize product reliability, and minimize cost. Communicate with management and user personnel to develop production and design standards. Recommend methods for improving utilization of personnel, material, and utilities. Estimate production cost and effect of product design changes for management review, action, and control. Complete production reports, purchase orders, and material, tool, and equipment lists. Direct workers engaged in product measurement, inspection, and testing activities to ensure quality control and reliability. Record or oversee recording of information to ensure currency of engineering drawings and documentation of production problems. Regulate and alter workflow schedules according to established manufacturing sequences and lead times to expedite production operations. Implement methods and procedures for disposition of discrepant material and defective or damaged parts and assess cost and responsibility. Evaluate precision and accuracy of production and testing equipment and engineering drawings to formulate corrective action plan. Confer with vendors, staff, and management personnel regarding purchases, procedures, product specifications, manufacturing capabilities, and project status. Schedule deliveries based on production forecasts, material substitutions, storage and handling facilities, and maintenance requirements.

GOE INFORMATION—Interest Area: 02. Science, Math, and Engineering. **Work Group:** 02.07. Engineering. **Personality Type**—Enterprising. Enterprising occupations frequently involve starting up and carrying out projects. These occupations can involve leading people and making many decisions. They sometimes require risk taking and often deal with business. **Work Values**—Creativity; Authority; Ability Utilization; Autonomy; Social Status. **Skills**—Management of Material Resources; Mathematics; Operations Analysis; Systems Evaluation; Science; Complex Problem Solving; Reading Comprehension; Technology Design. **Abilities**—*Cognitive:* Mathematical Reasoning; Written Expression; Fluency of Ideas; Originality; Number Facility. *Psychomotor:* None met the criteria. *Physical:* None met the criteria. *Sensory:* Speech Recognition; Speech Clarity. **General Work Activities**—*Information Input:* Getting Information; Identifying Objects, Actions, and Events; Monitoring Processes, Materials, or Surroundings. *Mental Process:* Processing Information; Analyzing Data or Information; Updating and Using Relevant Knowledge. *Work Output:* Documenting or Recording Information; Interacting with Computers; Drafting and Specifying Technical Devices. *Interacting with Others:* Communicating with Other Workers; Coordinating the Work and Activities of Others; Providing Consultation and Advice to Others. **Physical Work Conditions**—Sitting; Specialized Protective or Safety Attire; Indoors; Walking or Running; Whole Body Vibration.

Other Job Characteristics—Consequence of Error; Pace Determined by Speed of Equipment; Degree of Automation.

Experience—Job Zone 4. A minimum of two to four years of work-related skill, knowledge, or experience is needed. **Job Preparation:** SVP 7.0 to less than 8.0—two years to less than 10 years. **Knowledge**—Engineering and Technology; Design; Production and Processing; Administration and Management; Mathematics. **Instructional Programs**—Industrial Engineering.

Related DOT Jobs—011.161-010 Supervisor, Metallurgical-and-Quality-Control-Testing; 012.061-018 Standards Engineer; 012.067-010 Metrologist; 012.167-010 Configuration Management Analyst; 012.167-014 Manager, Quality Control; 012.167-018 Factory Lay-Out Engineer; 012.167-030 Industrial Engineer; 012.167-038 Liaison Engineer; 012.167-042 Manufacturing Engineer; 012.167-046 Production Engineer; 012.167-050 Production Planner; 012.167-054 Quality Control Engineer; 012.167-062 Supervisor, Vendor Quality; 012.167-070 Time-Study Engineer; 012.167-074 Tool Planner; 012.167-078 Documentation Engineer; 012.167-082 Material Scheduler; 012.187-014 Shoe-Lay-Out Planner; 019.167-010 Logistics Engineer; 822.261-014 Equipment Inspector.

17-2121.00 Marine Engineers and Naval Architects

- Education/Training Required: Bachelor's degree
- Employed: 5,117
- Annual Earnings: $66,830
- Growth: 2.1%
- Annual Job Openings: Fewer than 500

Design, develop, and evaluate the operation of marine vessels, ship machinery, and related equipment, such as power supply and propulsion systems.

No task data available.

GOE INFORMATION—Interest Area: 02. Science, Math, and Engineering. **Work Group:** 02.07. Engineering. **Note:** The Department of Labor has not collected some data for this job, so it has fewer details than the other descriptions.

Instructional Programs—Naval Architecture and Marine Engineering.

Related DOT Jobs—001.061-014 Architect, Marine; 014.061-010 Design Engineer, Marine Equipment; 014.061-014 Marine Engineer; 014.061-018 Research Engineer, Marine Equipment; 014.061-022 Test Engineer, Marine Equipment; 014.167-010 Marine Surveyor; 014.167-014 Port Engineer.

17-2121.01 Marine Engineers

- Education/Training Required: Bachelor's degree
- Employed: 5,117
- Annual Earnings: $66,830
- Growth: 2.1%
- Annual Job Openings: Fewer than 500

Design, develop, and take responsibility for the installation of ship machinery and related equipment, including propulsion machines and power supply systems.

Design and oversee testing, installation, and repair of marine apparatus and equipment. Conduct analytical, environmental, operational, or performance studies in order to develop designs for products such as marine engines, equipment, and structures. Prepare or direct the preparation of product or system layouts and detailed drawings and schematics. Evaluate operation of marine equipment during acceptance testing and shakedown cruises. Analyze data in order to determine feasibility of product proposals. Confer with research personnel in order to clarify or resolve problems and to develop or modify designs. Investigate and observe tests on machinery and equipment for compliance with standards. Conduct environmental, operational, or performance tests on marine machinery and equipment. Determine conditions under which tests are to be conducted, as well as sequences and phases of test operations. Maintain and coordinate repair of marine machinery and equipment for installation on vessels. Inspect marine equipment and machinery in order to draw up work requests and job specifications. Review work requests and compare them with previous work completed on ships in order to ensure that costs are economically sound. Prepare technical reports for use by engineering, management, or sales personnel. Maintain contact with, and formulate reports for, contractors and clients in order to ensure completion of work at minimum cost. Coordinate activities with regulatory bodies in order to ensure repairs and alterations are at minimum cost consistent with safety. Procure materials needed to repair marine equipment and machinery. Act as liaisons between ships' captains and shore personnel in order to ensure that schedules and budgets are maintained and that ships are operated safely and efficiently. Check, test, and maintain automatic controls and alarm systems. Maintain records of engineering department activities, including expense records and details of equipment maintenance and repairs. Perform monitoring activities in order to ensure that ships comply with international regulations and standards for lifesaving equipment and pollution preventatives. Prepare plans, estimates, design and construction schedules, and contract specifications, including any special provisions. Schedule machine overhauls and the servicing of electrical, heating, ventilation, refrigeration, water, and sewage systems. Supervise other engineers and crew members and train them for routine and emergency duties.

GOE INFORMATION—Interest Area: 02. Science, Math, and Engineering. **Work Group:** 02.07. Engineering. **Personality Type**—Realistic. Realistic occupations frequently involve work activities that include practical, hands-on problems and solutions. They often deal with plants, animals, and real-world materials like wood, tools, and machinery. Many of the occupations require working outside and do not involve a lot of paperwork or working closely with others. **Work Values**—Creativity; Ability Utilization; Authority; Autonomy; Social Status. **Skills**—Equipment Selection; Quality Control Analysis; Science; Troubleshooting; Mathematics; Installation; Systems Analysis; Complex Problem Solving. **Abilities**—*Cognitive:* Written Expression; Originality; Inductive Reasoning; Speed of Closure; Deductive Reasoning. *Psychomotor:* Control Precision; Finger Dexterity; Manual Dexterity; Multilimb Coordination; Response Orientation. *Physical:* Gross Body Equilibrium; Gross Body Coordination; Dynamic Flexibility. *Sensory:* Speech Clarity; Hearing Sensitivity; Night Vision; Far Vision; Glare Sensitivity. **General Work Activities**—*Information Input:* Getting Information; Inspecting Equipment, Structures, or Materials; Monitoring Processes, Materials, or Surroundings. *Mental Process:* Updating and Using Relevant Knowledge; Analyzing Data or Information; Evaluating Information Against Standards. *Work Output:* Drafting and Specifying Technical Devices; Repairing and Maintaining Mechanical Equipment; Documenting or Recording Information. *Interacting with Others:* Communicating with Other Workers; Coordinating the Work and Activities of Others; Communicating with Persons Outside Organization. **Physical Work Conditions**—Hazardous Equipment; Hazardous Conditions; Minor Burns, Cuts, Bites, or Stings; Distracting Sounds and Noise Levels; Sitting. **Other Job Characteristics**—Consequence of Error; Importance of Being Exact or Accurate; Degree of Automation.

Experience—Job Zone 5. Extensive skill, knowledge, and experience are needed for these occupations. **Job Preparation:** SVP 8.0 and above—four years to more than 10 years. **Knowledge**—Engineering and Technology; Mechanical; Design; Physics; Building and Construction. **Instructional Programs**—Naval Architecture and Marine Engineering.

Related DOT Jobs—014.061-010 Design Engineer, Marine Equipment; 014.061-014 Marine Engineer; 014.061-018 Research Engineer, Marine Equipment; 014.061-022 Test Engineer, Marine Equipment; 014.167-010 Marine Surveyor; 014.167-014 Port Engineer.

17-2121.02 Marine Architects
- **Education/Training Required: Bachelor's degree**
- **Employed: No data available.**
- **Annual Earnings: $66,830**
- **Growth: 2.1%**
- **Annual Job Openings: Fewer than 500**

Design and oversee construction and repair of marine craft and floating structures such as ships, barges, tugs, dredges, submarines, torpedoes, floats, and buoys. May confer with marine engineers.

Oversee construction and testing of prototype in model basin and develop sectional and waterline curves of hull to establish center of gravity, ideal hull form, and buoyancy and stability data. Confer with marine engineering personnel to establish arrangement of boiler room equipment and propulsion machinery, heating and ventilating systems, refrigeration equipment, piping, and other functional equipment. Design complete hull and superstructure according to specifications and test data in conformity with standards of safety, efficiency, and economy. Design layout of craft interior, including cargo space, passenger compartments, ladder wells, and elevators. Study design proposals and specifications to establish basic characteristics of craft, such as size, weight, speed, propulsion, displacement, and draft. Evaluate performance of craft during dock and sea trials to determine design changes and conformance with national and international standards.

GOE INFORMATION—**Interest Area:** 02. Science, Math, and Engineering. **Work Group:** 02.07. Engineering. **Personality Type**—Realistic. Realistic occupations frequently involve work activities that include practical, hands-on problems and solutions. They often deal with plants, animals, and real-world materials like wood, tools, and machinery. Many of the occupations require working outside and do not involve a lot of paperwork or working closely with others. **Work Values**—Creativity; Ability Utilization; Social Status; Achievement; Recognition. **Skills**—Quality Control Analysis; Mathematics; Technology Design; Complex Problem Solving; Systems Analysis; Monitoring; Science; Equipment Selection. **Abilities**—*Cognitive:* Originality; Visualization; Fluency of Ideas; Deductive Reasoning; Written Comprehension. *Psychomotor:* Finger Dexterity; Rate Control; Multilimb Coordination; Manual Dexterity. *Physical:* Gross Body Equilibrium; Dynamic Flexibility; Gross Body Coordination. *Sensory:* Far Vision; Glare Sensitivity; Speech Clarity; Near Vision; Night Vision. **General Work Activities**—*Information Input:* Inspecting Equipment, Structures, or Materials; Getting Information; Identifying Objects, Actions, and Events. *Mental Process:* Thinking Creatively; Organizing, Planning, and Prioritizing; Updating and Using Relevant Knowledge. *Work Output:* Drafting and Specifying Technical Devices; Documenting or Recording Information; Handling and Moving Objects. *Interacting with Others:* Communicating with Other Workers; Coordinating the Work and Activities of Others; Communicating with Persons Outside Organization. **Physical Work Conditions**—Keeping or Regaining Balance; Hazardous Equipment; Extremely Bright or Inadequate Lighting; Distracting Sounds and Noise Levels; Sitting. **Other Job**

Characteristics—Importance of Being Exact or Accurate; Consequence of Error; Degree of Automation.

Experience—Job Zone 5. Extensive skill, knowledge, and experience are needed for these occupations. **Job Preparation:** SVP 8.0 and above—four years to more than 10 years. **Knowledge**—Design; Engineering and Technology; Physics; Building and Construction; Mathematics. **Instructional Programs**—Naval Architecture and Marine Engineering.

Related DOT Jobs—106.101-014 Architect, Marine.

17-2131.00 Materials Engineers
- **Education/Training Required: Bachelor's degree**
- **Employed: 33,491**
- **Annual Earnings: $61,260**
- **Growth: 5.3%**
- **Annual Job Openings: 2,000**

Evaluate materials and develop machinery and processes to manufacture materials for use in products that must meet specialized design and performance specifications. Develop new uses for known materials. Includes those working with composite materials or specializing in one type of material, such as graphite, metal and metal alloys, ceramics and glass, plastics and polymers, and naturally occurring materials.

Analyze product failure data and laboratory test results in order to determine causes of problems and develop solutions. Conduct or supervise tests on raw materials or finished products in order to ensure their quality. Design and direct the testing and/or control of processing procedures. Determine appropriate methods for fabricating and joining materials. Evaluate technical specifications and economic factors relating to process or product design objectives. Monitor material performance and evaluate material deterioration. Plan and implement laboratory operations for the purpose of developing material and fabrication procedures that meet cost, product specification, and performance standards. Review new product plans and make recommendations for material selection based on design objectives, such as strength, weight, heat resistance, electrical conductivity, and cost. Solve problems in a number of engineering fields, such as mechanical, chemical, electrical, civil, nuclear, and aerospace. Supervise production and testing processes in industrial settings such as metal refining facilities, smelting or foundry operations, or non-metallic materials production operations. Conduct training sessions on new material products, applications, or manufacturing methods for customers and their employees. Design processing plants and equipment. Guide technical staff engaged in developing materials for specific uses in projected products or devices. Modify properties of metal alloys, using thermal and mechanical treatments. Perform managerial functions such as preparing proposals and budgets, analyzing labor costs, and writing reports. Plan and evaluate new projects, consulting with other engineers and corporate executives as necessary. Remove metals from ores, and refine and alloy them to obtain useful metal. Replicate the characteristics of materials and their components with computers. Supervise the work of technologists, technicians, and other engineers and scientists. Sell and service metal products. Teach in colleges and universities. Write for technical magazines, journals, and trade association publications.

GOE INFORMATION—**Interest Area:** 02. Science, Math, and Engineering. **Work Group:** 02.07. Engineering. **Personality Type**—Investigative. Investigative occupations frequently involve working with ideas and require an extensive amount of thinking. These occupations can involve searching for facts and figuring out problems mentally. **Work Values**—Creativity; Ability Utilization; Responsibility; Autonomy;

Social Status. **Skills**—Operations Analysis; Science; Technology Design; Mathematics; Complex Problem Solving; Judgment and Decision Making; Systems Evaluation; Equipment Selection. **Abilities**—*Cognitive:* Mathematical Reasoning; Written Expression; Visualization; Written Comprehension; Inductive Reasoning. *Psychomotor:* Rate Control; Control Precision. *Physical:* None met the criteria. *Sensory:* Speech Clarity. **General Work Activities**—*Information Input:* Getting Information; Identifying Objects, Actions, and Events; Monitoring Processes, Materials, or Surroundings. *Mental Process:* Analyzing Data or Information; Updating and Using Relevant Knowledge; Making Decisions and Solving Problems. *Work Output:* Drafting and Specifying Technical Devices; Documenting or Recording Information; Interacting with Computers. *Interacting with Others:* Communicating with Other Workers; Providing Consultation and Advice to Others; Communicating with Persons Outside Organization. **Physical Work Conditions**—Sitting; Indoors. **Other Job Characteristics**—Consequence of Error; Pace Determined by Speed of Equipment; Importance of Being Exact or Accurate.

Experience—Job Zone 5. Extensive skill, knowledge, and experience are needed for these occupations. **Job Preparation:** SVP 8.0 and above—four years to more than 10 years. **Knowledge**—Engineering and Technology; Design; Mathematics; Production and Processing; Physics. **Instructional Programs**—Ceramic Sciences and Engineering; Materials Engineering; Metallurgical Engineering.

Related DOT Jobs—019.061-014 Materials Engineer.

17-2141.00 Mechanical Engineers

- Education/Training Required: Bachelor's degree
- Employed: 221,443
- Annual Earnings: $61,440
- Growth: 13.1%
- Annual Job Openings: 7,000

Perform engineering duties in planning and designing tools, engines, machines, and other mechanically functioning equipment. Oversee installation, operation, maintenance, and repair of such equipment as centralized heat, gas, water, and steam systems.

Conduct research that tests and analyzes the feasibility, design, operation, and performance of equipment, components, and systems. Confer with engineers and other personnel to implement operating procedures, resolve system malfunctions, and provide technical information. Design test control apparatus and equipment and develop procedures for testing products. Develop and test models of alternate designs and processing methods to assess feasibility, operating condition effects, possible new applications, and necessity of modification. Establish and coordinate the maintenance and safety procedures, service schedule, and supply of materials required to maintain machines and equipment in the prescribed condition. Investigate equipment failures and difficulties in order to diagnose faulty operation and make recommendations to maintenance crew. Oversee installation, operation, maintenance, and repair to ensure that machines and equipment are installed and functioning according to specifications. Recommend design modifications to eliminate machine or system malfunctions. Research and analyze customer design proposals, specifications, manuals, and other data to evaluate the feasibility, cost, and maintenance requirements of designs or applications. Research, design, evaluate, install, operate, and maintain mechanical products, equipment, systems, and processes to meet requirements, applying knowledge of engineering principles. Specify system components or direct modification of products to ensure conformance with engineering design and performance specifications. Assist drafters in developing the structural design of products, using drafting tools or computer-assisted design/drafting equipment and software. Develop, coordinate, and monitor all aspects of production, including selection of manufacturing methods, fabrication, and operation of product designs. Perform personnel functions, such as supervision of production workers, technicians, technologists, and other engineers, and design of evaluation programs. Provide feedback to design engineers on customer problems and needs. Study industrial processes to determine where and how application of equipment can be made. Write performance requirements for product development or engineering projects. Apply engineering principles and practices to emerging fields, such as robotics, waste management, and biomedical engineering. Estimate costs and submit bids for engineering, construction, or extraction projects and prepare contract documents. Read and interpret blueprints, technical drawings, schematics, and computer-generated reports. Solicit new business and provide technical customer service.

GOE INFORMATION—**Interest Area:** 02. Science, Math, and Engineering. **Work Group:** 02.07. Engineering. **Personality Type**—Realistic. Realistic occupations frequently involve work activities that include practical, hands-on problems and solutions. They often deal with plants, animals, and real-world materials like wood, tools, and machinery. Many of the occupations require working outside and do not involve a lot of paperwork or working closely with others. **Work Values**—Creativity; Autonomy; Social Status; Authority; Ability Utilization. **Skills**—Technology Design; Mathematics; Operations Analysis; Science; Equipment Selection; Quality Control Analysis; Complex Problem Solving; Troubleshooting. **Abilities**—*Cognitive:* Mathematical Reasoning; Number Facility; Deductive Reasoning; Fluency of Ideas; Visualization. *Psychomotor:* Arm-Hand Steadiness; Finger Dexterity; Response Orientation; Manual Dexterity; Rate Control. *Physical:* Extent Flexibility; Trunk Strength; Gross Body Equilibrium. *Sensory:* Visual Color Discrimination; Near Vision; Hearing Sensitivity; Sound Localization; Speech Clarity. **General Work Activities**—*Information Input:* Getting Information; Identifying Objects, Actions, and Events; Inspecting Equipment, Structures, or Materials. *Mental Process:* Updating and Using Relevant Knowledge; Thinking Creatively; Analyzing Data or Information. *Work Output:* Drafting and Specifying Technical Devices; Interacting with Computers; Documenting or Recording Information. *Interacting with Others:* Communicating with Other Workers; Providing Consultation and Advice to Others; Interpreting Meaning of Information for Others. **Physical Work Conditions**—Hazardous Equipment; Sitting; Walking or Running; Hazardous Conditions; High Places. **Other Job Characteristics**—Degree of Automation; Consequence of Error; Importance of Being Exact or Accurate.

Experience—Job Zone 4. A minimum of two to four years of work-related skill, knowledge, or experience is needed. **Job Preparation:** SVP 7.0 to less than 8.0—two years to less than 10 years. **Knowledge**—Design; Engineering and Technology; Physics; Computers and Electronics; Mathematics. **Instructional Programs**—Mechanical Engineering.

Related DOT Jobs—706.101-010 Automotive Engineer; 706.101-014 Mechanical Engineer; 706.101-018 Mechanical-Design Engineer, Facilities; 706.102-022 Mechanical-Design Engineer, Products; 706.102-026 Tool Designer; 706.103-030 Tool-Designer Apprentice; 706.103-034 Utilization Engineer; 706.103-038 Applications Engineer, Manufacturing; 706.104-042 Stress Analyst; 716.102-022 Mechanical Research Engineer; 716.103-034 Test Engineer, Mechanical Equipment; 716.103-038 Solar-Energy-Systems Designer.

17-2151.00 Mining and Geological Engineers, Including Mining Safety Engineers

- Education/Training Required: Bachelor's degree
- Employed: 6,483
- Annual Earnings: $62,180
- Growth: −1.3%
- Annual Job Openings: Fewer than 500

Determine the location and plan the extraction of coal, metallic ores, nonmetallic minerals, and building materials, such as stone and gravel. Work involves conducting preliminary surveys of deposits or undeveloped mines and planning their development; examining deposits or mines to determine whether they can be worked at a profit; making geological and topographical surveys; evolving methods of mining best suited to character, type, and size of deposits; and supervising mining operations.

Design, implement, and monitor the development of mines, facilities, systems, and equipment. Examine maps, deposits, drilling locations, and/or mines in order to determine the location, size, accessibility, contents, value, and potential profitability of mineral, oil, and gas deposits. Lay out, direct, and supervise mine construction operations, such as the construction of shafts and tunnels. Monitor mine production rates in order to assess operational effectiveness. Prepare schedules, reports, and estimates of the costs involved in developing and operating mines. Select locations and plan underground or surface mining operations, specifying processes, labor usage, and equipment that will result in safe, economical, and environmentally sound extraction of minerals and ores. Select or develop mineral location, extraction, and production methods, based on factors such as safety, cost, and deposit characteristics. Select or devise materials-handling methods and equipment to transport ore, waste materials, and mineral products efficiently and economically. Test air to detect toxic gases and recommend measures to remove them, such as installation of ventilation shafts. Conduct or direct mining experiments in order to test or prove research findings. Design mining and mineral treatment equipment and machinery in collaboration with other engineering specialists. Design, develop, and implement computer applications for use in mining operations such as mine design, modeling, or mapping or for monitoring mine conditions. Devise solutions to problems of land reclamation and water and air pollution, such as methods of storing excavated soil and returning exhausted mine sites to natural states. Evaluate data in order to develop new mining products, equipment, or processes. Implement and coordinate mine safety programs, including the design and maintenance of protective and rescue equipment and safety devices. Inspect mining areas for unsafe structures, equipment, and working conditions. Prepare technical reports for use by mining, engineering, and management personnel. Supervise and coordinate the work of technicians, technologists, survey personnel, engineers, scientists, and other mine personnel.

GOE INFORMATION—Interest Area: 02. Science, Math, and Engineering. Work Group: 02.07. Engineering. Personality Type—Investigative. Investigative occupations frequently involve working with ideas and require an extensive amount of thinking. These occupations can involve searching for facts and figuring out problems mentally. Work Values—Authority; Responsibility; Creativity; Autonomy; Social Status. Skills—Equipment Selection; Operations Analysis; Science; Technology Design; Systems Analysis; Complex Problem Solving; Mathematics; Systems Evaluation. Abilities—*Cognitive:* Originality; Fluency of Ideas; Deductive Reasoning; Speed of Closure; Written Expression. *Psychomo-*tor: Finger Dexterity; Manual Dexterity; Control Precision; Rate Control; Multilimb Coordination. *Physical:* Gross Body Equilibrium; Explosive Strength. *Sensory:* Far Vision; Night Vision; Speech Clarity; Sound Localization; Glare Sensitivity. General Work Activities—*Information Input:* Getting Information; Identifying Objects, Actions, and Events; Inspecting Equipment, Structures, or Materials. *Mental Process:* Organizing, Planning, and Prioritizing; Updating and Using Relevant Knowledge; Processing Information. *Work Output:* Drafting and Specifying Technical Devices; Documenting or Recording Information; Performing General Physical Activities. *Interacting with Others:* Communicating with Other Workers; Coordinating the Work and Activities of Others; Interpreting Meaning of Information for Others. Physical Work Conditions—Hazardous Conditions; Hazardous Equipment; Common Protective or Safety Attire; Contaminants; Outdoors. Other Job Characteristics—Consequence of Error; Importance of Being Exact or Accurate; Degree of Automation.

Experience—Job Zone 4. A minimum of two to four years of work-related skill, knowledge, or experience is needed. Job Preparation: SVP 7.0 to less than 8.0—two years to less than 10 years. Knowledge—Engineering and Technology; Physics; Design; Administration and Management; Mathematics. Instructional Programs—Mining and Mineral Engineering.

Related DOT Jobs—010.061-010 Design Engineer, Mining-and-Oil-Field Equipment; 010.061-014 Mining Engineer; 010.061-022 Research Engineer, Mining-and-Oil-Well Equipment; 010.061-026 Safety Engineer, Mines; 010.061-030 Test Engineer, Mining-and-Oil-Field Equipment.

17-2161.00 Nuclear Engineers

- Education/Training Required: Bachelor's degree
- Employed: 13,900
- Annual Earnings: $80,080
- Growth: 1.8%
- Annual Job Openings: 1,000

Conduct research on nuclear engineering problems or apply principles and theory of nuclear science to problems concerned with release, control, and utilization of nuclear energy and nuclear waste disposal.

Analyze available data and consult with other scientists in order to determine parameters of experimentation and suitability of analytical models. Conduct tests of nuclear fuel behavior and cycles and performance of nuclear machinery and equipment in order to optimize performance of existing plants. Design and develop nuclear equipment such as reactor cores, radiation shielding, and associated instrumentation and control mechanisms. Design and direct nuclear research projects in order to discover facts, to test or modify theoretical models, or to develop new theoretical models or new uses for current models. Examine accidents in order to obtain data that can be used to design preventive measures. Formulate equations that describe phenomena occurring during fission of nuclear fuels and develop research models based on the equations. Keep abreast of developments and changes in the nuclear field by reading technical journals and by independent study and research. Monitor nuclear facility operations in order to identify any design, construction, or operation practices that violate safety regulations and laws or that could jeopardize the safety of operations. Perform experiments that will provide information about acceptable methods of nuclear material usage, nuclear fuel reclamation, and waste disposal. Recommend preventive measures to be taken in the handling of nuclear technology, based on data obtained from operations monitoring or from evaluation of test results. Synthesize analyses of test results and use the results to prepare technical reports of findings and recommendations. Design and oversee construction and operation of nuclear reactors and power plants and nuclear fuels reprocessing and reclamation systems. Develop new medical scanning technologies. Direct operating and maintenance activities of operational nuclear power plants in order to ensure efficiency and conformity to safety standards. Initiate corrective actions and/or order plant shutdowns in emergency situations. Prepare construction project proposals that include cost estimates and discuss proposals with interested parties such as vendors, contractors, and nuclear facility review boards. Write operational instructions to be used in nuclear plant operation and nuclear fuel and waste handling and disposal. Design and develop nuclear weapons.

GOE INFORMATION—Interest Area: 02. Science, Math, and Engineering. **Work Group:** 02.07. Engineering. **Personality Type—**Investigative. Investigative occupations frequently involve working with ideas and require an extensive amount of thinking. These occupations can involve searching for facts and figuring out problems mentally. **Work Values—**Creativity; Ability Utilization; Social Status; Responsibility; Authority. **Skills—**Science; Technology Design; Quality Control Analysis; Operation Monitoring; Operations Analysis; Systems Analysis; Systems Evaluation; Mathematics. **Abilities—***Cognitive:* Mathematical Reasoning; Deductive Reasoning; Written Expression; Inductive Reasoning; Originality. *Psychomotor:* Response Orientation; Control Precision; Reaction Time; Rate Control; Multilimb Coordination. *Physical:* None met the criteria. *Sensory:* Speech Clarity; Hearing Sensitivity; Auditory Attention; Speech Recognition; Far Vision. **General Work Activities—***Information Input:* Getting Information; Inspecting Equipment, Structures, or Materials; Monitoring Processes, Materials, or Surroundings. *Mental Process:* Analyzing Data or Information; Processing Information; Updating and Using Relevant Knowledge. *Work Output:* Drafting and Specifying Technical Devices; Documenting or Recording Information; Interacting with Computers. *Interacting with Others:* Communicating with Other Workers; Interpreting Meaning of Information for Others; Providing Consultation and Advice to Others. **Physical Work Conditions—**Radiation; Hazardous Conditions; Specialized Protective or Safety Attire; High Places; Common Protective or Safety Attire. **Other Job Characteristics—**Consequence of Error; Importance of Being Exact or Accurate; Degree of Automation.

Experience—Job Zone 5. Extensive skill, knowledge, and experience are needed for these occupations. **Job Preparation:** SVP 8.0 and above—four years to more than 10 years. **Knowledge—**Engineering and Technology; Physics; Design; Mathematics; Administration and Management. **Instructional Programs—**Nuclear Engineering.

Related DOT Jobs—015.061-010 Design Engineer, Nuclear Equipment; 015.061-014 Nuclear Engineer; 015.061-018 Research Engineer, Nuclear Equipment; 015.061-022 Test Engineer, Nuclear Equipment; 015.061-026 Nuclear-Fuels Reclamation Engineer; 015.061-030 Nuclear-Fuels Research Engineer; 015.067-010 Nuclear-Criticality Safety Engineer; 015.137-010 Radiation-Protection Engineer; 015.167-010 Nuclear-Plant Technical Advisor; 015.167-014 Nuclear-Test-Reactor Program Coordinator; 506.104-042 Waste-Management Engineer, Radioactive Materials.

17-2171.00 Petroleum Engineers

- **Education/Training Required: Bachelor's degree**
- **Employed: 8,972**
- **Annual Earnings: $81,420**
- **Growth: −7.2%**
- **Annual Job Openings: Fewer than 500**

Devise methods to improve oil and gas well production and determine the need for new or modified tool designs. Oversee drilling and offer technical advice to achieve economical and satisfactory progress.

Design or modify mining and oil field machinery and tools, applying engineering principles. Conduct engineering research experiments in order to improve or modify mining and oil machinery and operations. Develop plans for oil and gas field drilling and for product recovery and treatment. Confer with scientific, engineering, and technical personnel in order to resolve design, research, and testing problems. Evaluate findings in order to develop, design, or test equipment or processes. Monitor production rates and plan rework processes in order to improve production. Analyze data in order to recommend placement of wells and supplementary processes to enhance production. Assist engineering and other personnel to solve operating problems. Coordinate activities of workers engaged in research, planning, and development. Inspect oil and gas wells in order to determine that installations are completed. Assign work to staff in order to obtain maximum utilization of personnel. Interpret drilling and testing information for personnel. Test machinery and equipment in order to ensure that it is safe and conforms to performance specifications. Write technical reports for engineering and management personnel. Assess costs and estimate the production capabilities and economic value of oil and gas wells in order to evaluate the economic viability of potential drilling sites. Coordinate the installation, maintenance, and operation of mining and oil field equipment. Design and implement environmental controls on oil and gas operations. Direct and monitor the completion and evaluation of wells, well testing, and well surveys. Maintain records of drilling and production operations. Simulate reservoir performance for different recovery techniques, using computer models. Specify and supervise well modification and stimulation programs in order to maximize oil and gas recovery. Supervise the removal of drilling equipment, the removal of any waste, and the safe return of land to structural stability when wells or pockets are exhausted. Take samples in order to assess the amount and quality of oil, the depth at which resources lie, and the equipment needed to properly extract them.

GOE INFORMATION—Interest Area: 02. Science, Math, and Engineering. **Work Group:** 02.07. Engineering. **Personality Type—**Realistic. Realistic occupations frequently involve work activities that include practical, hands-on problems and solutions. They often deal with plants, animals, and real-world materials like wood, tools, and machinery. Many of the occupations require working outside and do not involve a lot of paperwork or working closely with others. **Work Values—**Creativity; Social Status; Authority; Ability Utilization; Autonomy. **Skills—**Mathematics; Technology Design; Quality Control Analysis; Operations Analysis; Science; Systems Evaluation; Installation; Complex Problem Solving. **Abilities—***Cognitive:* Originality; Mathematical Reasoning; Deductive Reasoning; Number Facility; Written Expression. *Psychomotor:* Rate Control; Response Orientation; Manual Dexterity; Reaction Time; Finger Dexterity. *Physical:* Gross Body Equilibrium; Dynamic Strength; Stamina; Explosive Strength; Dynamic Flexibility. *Sensory:* Hearing Sensitivity; Peripheral Vision; Depth Perception; Auditory Attention; Sound Localization. **General Work Activities—***Information Input:* Getting Information; Inspecting Equipment, Structures, or Materials; Identifying Objects, Actions, and Events. *Mental Process:* Processing Information; Updating and Using Relevant Knowledge; Analyzing Data or Information. *Work Output:* Drafting and Specifying Technical Devices; Documenting or Recording Information; Handling and Moving Objects. *Interacting with Others:* Communicating with Other Workers; Coordinating the Work and Activities of Others; Providing Consultation and Advice to Others. **Physical Work Conditions—**Hazardous Conditions; Outdoors; Hazardous Equipment; Walking or Running; Distracting Sounds and Noise Levels. **Other Job Characteristics—**Consequence of Error; Importance of Being Exact or Accurate; Degree of Automation.

Experience—Job Zone 5. Extensive skill, knowledge, and experience are needed for these occupations. **Job Preparation:** SVP 8.0 and above—four years to more than 10 years. **Knowledge—**Engineering and Technology; Physics; Design; Mathematics; Production and Processing. **Instructional Programs**—Petroleum Engineering.

Related DOT Jobs—010.061-010 Design Engineer, Mining-and-Oil-Field Equipment; 010.061-018 Petroleum Engineer; 010.061-022 Research Engineer, Mining-and-Oil-Well Equipment; 010.061-030 Test Engineer, Mining-and-Oil-Field Equipment; 010.161-010 Chief Engineer, Research; 010.167-010 Chief Engineer; 010.167-014 District Supervisor, Mud-Analysis Well Logging.

17-2199.99 Engineers, All Other

- **Education/Training Required: Bachelor's degree**
- **Employed: No data available.**
- **Annual Earnings: No data available.**
- **Growth: 0.4%**
- **Annual Job Openings: 15,000**

All engineers not listed separately.

No task data available.

GOE INFORMATION—Interest Area: 02. Science, Math, and Engineering. **Work Group:** 02.07. Engineering. **Note:** The Department of Labor has not collected some data for this job, so it has fewer details than the other descriptions.

Instructional Programs—Architectural Engineering; Assistive/Augmentative Technology and Rehabilitation Engineering; Construction Engineering; Engineering Mechanics; Engineering Physics; Engineering Science; Engineering, General; Engineering, Other; Forest Engineering; Geological/Geophysical Engineering; Manufacturing Engineering; Ocean Engineering; Polymer/Plastics Engineering; Surveying Engineering; Systems Engineering; Textile Sciences and Engineering.

Related DOT Jobs—019.061-010 Biomedical Engineer; 019.061-018 Optical Engineer; 019.061-022 Ordnance Engineer; 019.061-026 Reliability Engineer; 019.081-010 Maintainability Engineer; 019.081-014 Photographic Engineer; 019.187-010 Packaging Engineer.

17-3000 Drafters, Engineering, and Mapping Technicians

17-3011.00 Architectural and Civil Drafters

- **Education/Training Required: Postsecondary vocational training**
- **Employed: 101,853**
- **Annual Earnings: $37,010**
- **Growth: 20.8%**
- **Annual Job Openings: 12,000**

Prepare detailed drawings of architectural and structural features of buildings or drawings and topographical relief maps used in civil engineering projects, such as highways, bridges, and public works. Utilize knowledge of building materials, engineering practices, and mathematics to complete drawings.

No task data available.

GOE INFORMATION—Interest Area: 02. Science, Math, and Engineering. **Work Group:** 02.08. Engineering Technology. **Note:** The Depart-

ment of Labor has not collected some data for this job, so it has fewer details than the other descriptions.

Instructional Programs—Architectural Drafting and Architectural CAD/CADD; Architectural Technology/Technician; CAD/CADD Drafting and/or Design Technology/Technician; Civil Drafting and Civil Engineering CAD/CADD; Drafting and Design Technology/Technician, General.

Related DOT Jobs—001.261-010 Drafter, Architectural; 001.261-014 Drafter, Landscape; 005.281-010 Drafter, Civil; 005.281-014 Drafter, Structural; 010.281-010 Drafter, Directional Survey; 010.281-014 Drafter, Geological; 010.281-018 Drafter, Geophysical; 014.281-010 Drafter, Marine; 017.261-026 Drafter, Commercial; 017.261-034 Drafter, Heating and Ventilating; 017.261-038 Drafter, Plumbing; 017.281-018 Drafter, Assistant; 017.281-030 Drafter, Oil and Gas.

17-3011.01 Architectural Drafters

- **Education/Training Required: Associate's degree**
- **Employed: 101,853**
- **Annual Earnings: $37,010**
- **Growth: 20.8%**
- **Annual Job Openings: 12,000**

Prepare detailed drawings of architectural designs and plans for buildings and structures according to specifications provided by architect.

Analyze building codes, by-laws, space and site requirements, and other technical documents and reports to determine their effect on architectural designs. Operate computer-aided drafting equipment or conventional drafting station to produce designs, working drawings, charts, forms, and records. Coordinate structural, electrical, and mechanical designs and determine a method of presentation in order to graphically represent building plans. Obtain and assemble data to complete architectural designs, visiting job sites to compile measurements as necessary. Draw rough and detailed scale plans for foundations, buildings, and structures, based on preliminary concepts, sketches, engineering calculations, specification sheets, and other data. Lay out and plan interior room arrangements for commercial buildings, using computer-assisted drafting (CAD) equipment and software. Supervise, coordinate, and inspect the work of draftspersons, technicians, and technologists on construction projects. Represent architect on construction site, ensuring builder compliance with design specifications and advising on design corrections under architect's supervision. Check dimensions of materials to be used and assign numbers to lists of materials. Determine procedures and instructions to be followed according to design specifications and quantity of required materials. Analyze technical implications of architect's design concept, calculating weights, volumes, and stress factors. Create freehand drawings and lettering to accompany drawings. Prepare colored drawings of landscape and interior designs for presentation to client. Reproduce drawings on copy machines or trace copies of plans and drawings, using transparent paper or cloth, ink, pencil, and standard drafting instruments. Prepare cost estimates, contracts, bidding documents, and technical reports for specific projects under an architect's supervision. Calculate heat loss and gain of buildings and structures to determine required equipment specifications, following standard procedures. Build landscape, architectural, and display models.

GOE INFORMATION—Interest Area: 02. Science, Math, and Engineering. **Work Group:** 02.08. Engineering Technology. **Personality Type**—Realistic. Realistic occupations frequently involve work activities that include practical, hands-on problems and solutions. They often deal with plants, animals, and real-world materials like wood, tools, and machinery. Many of the occupations require working outside and do not involve a lot of paperwork or working closely with others. **Work Values**—Good Working Conditions; Independence; Ability Utilization; Social Status; Compensation. **Skills**—Coordination; Operations Analysis; Complex Problem Solving; Mathematics; Critical Thinking; Technology Design; Monitoring; Speaking. **Abilities**—*Cognitive:* Visualization; Deductive Reasoning; Originality; Mathematical Reasoning; Flexibility of Closure. *Psychomotor:* Finger Dexterity; Arm-Hand Steadiness; Manual Dexterity; Control Precision. *Physical:* None met the criteria. *Sensory:* Far Vision; Visual Color Discrimination; Near Vision; Depth Perception; Speech Recognition. **General Work Activities**—*Information Input:* Monitoring Processes, Materials, or Surroundings; Getting Information; Identifying Objects, Actions, and Events. *Mental Process:* Thinking Creatively; Organizing, Planning, and Prioritizing; Evaluating Information Against Standards. *Work Output:* Drafting and Specifying Technical Devices; Interacting with Computers; Documenting or Recording Information. *Interacting with Others:* Communicating with Persons Outside Organization; Establishing and Maintaining Relationships; Communicating with Other Workers. **Physical Work Conditions**—Using Hands on Objects, Tools, or Controls; Sitting; Indoors; Radiation. **Other Job Characteristics**—Importance of Being Exact or Accurate; Consequence of Error; Importance of Repeating Same Tasks.

Experience—Job Zone 3. Previous work-related skill, knowledge, or experience is required. **Job Preparation:** SVP 7.0 to less than 8.0–two years to less than 10 years. **Knowledge**—Design; Building and Construction; Computers and Electronics; Customer and Personal Service; Engineering and Technology. **Instructional Programs**—Architectural Drafting and Architectural CAD/CADD; Architectural Technology/Technician; CAD/CADD Drafting and/or Design Technology/Technician; Civil Drafting and Civil Engineering CAD/CADD; Drafting and Design Technology/Technician, General.

Related DOT Jobs—014.281-010 Drafter, Marine; 017.261-026 Drafter, Commercial; 017.261-034 Drafter, Heating and Ventilating; 017.261-038 Drafter, Plumbing; 017.281-018 Drafter, Assistant; 017.281-030 Drafter, Oil and Gas; 126.101-010 Drafter, Architectural; 126.101-014 Drafter, Landscape; 528.101-014 Drafter, Structural.

17-3011.02 Civil Drafters

- **Education/Training Required: Postsecondary vocational training**
- **Employed: No data available.**
- **Annual Earnings: $37,010**
- **Growth: 20.8%**
- **Annual Job Openings: 12,000**

Prepare drawings and topographical and relief maps used in civil engineering projects such as highways, bridges, pipelines, flood control projects, and water and sewerage control systems.

Correlate, interpret, and modify data obtained from topographical surveys, well logs, and geophysical prospecting reports. Draft plans and detailed drawings for structures, installations, and construction projects such as highways, sewage disposal systems, and dikes, working from sketches or notes. Draw maps, diagrams, and profiles, using cross-sections and surveys, to represent elevations, topographical contours, subsurface formations, and structures. Finish and duplicate drawings and documentation packages according to required mediums and specifications for reproduction, using blueprinting, photography, or other duplicating methods. Review rough sketches, drawings, specifications, and other engineering data received from civil engineers to ensure that they conform to design concepts. Supervise or conduct field surveys, inspections, or technical investigations to obtain data required to revise

construction drawings. Calculate excavation tonnage and prepare graphs and fill-hauling diagrams for use in earth-moving operations. Calculate weights, volumes, and stress factors and their implications for technical aspects of designs. Determine the order of work and method of presentation, such as orthographic or isometric drawing. Explain drawings to production or construction teams and provide adjustments as necessary. Locate and identify symbols located on topographical surveys to denote geological and geophysical formations or oil field installations. Plot characteristics of boreholes for oil and gas wells from photographic subsurface survey recordings and other data, representing depth, degree, and direction of inclination. Supervise and train other technologists, technicians, and drafters. Determine quality, cost, strength, and quantity of required materials and enter figures on materials lists. Produce drawings using computer assisted drafting systems (CAD) or drafting machines or by hand using compasses, dividers, protractors, triangles, and other drafting devices.

GOE INFORMATION—**Interest Area:** 02. Science, Math, and Engineering. **Work Group:** 02.08. Engineering Technology. **Personality Type**—Realistic. Realistic occupations frequently involve work activities that include practical, hands-on problems and solutions. They often deal with plants, animals, and real-world materials like wood, tools, and machinery. Many of the occupations require working outside and do not involve a lot of paperwork or working closely with others. **Work Values**—Good Working Conditions; Ability Utilization; Autonomy; Moral Values; Advancement. **Skills**—Mathematics; Programming; Operations Analysis; Complex Problem Solving. **Abilities**—*Cognitive:* Number Facility; Mathematical Reasoning; Written Comprehension; Oral Comprehension; Inductive Reasoning. *Psychomotor:* Wrist-Finger Speed; Arm-Hand Steadiness; Finger Dexterity. *Physical:* Trunk Strength. *Sensory:* Near Vision; Visual Color Discrimination; Far Vision; Speech Recognition. **General Work Activities**—*Information Input:* Getting Information; Identifying Objects, Actions, and Events; Estimating Needed Characteristics. *Mental Process:* Processing Information; Updating and Using Relevant Knowledge; Analyzing Data or Information. *Work Output:* Drafting and Specifying Technical Devices; Interacting with Computers; Handling and Moving Objects. *Interacting with Others:* Communicating with Other Workers; Interpreting Meaning of Information for Others; Establishing and Maintaining Relationships. **Physical Work Conditions**—Sitting; Outdoors; Indoors. **Other Job Characteristics**—Importance of Being Exact or Accurate; Consequence of Error; Importance of Repeating Same Tasks.

Experience—Job Zone 3. Previous work-related skill, knowledge, or experience is required. **Job Preparation:** SVP 6.0 to less than 7.0—more than one year and less than four years. **Knowledge**—Design; Physics; Geography; Engineering and Technology; Mathematics. **Instructional Programs**—Architectural Drafting and Architectural CAD/CADD; Architectural Technology/Technician; CAD/CADD Drafting and/or Design Technology/Technician; Civil Drafting and Civil Engineering CAD/CADD; Drafting and Design Technology/Technician, General.

Related DOT Jobs—010.281-010 Drafter, Directional Survey; 010.281-014 Drafter, Geological; 010.281-018 Drafter, Geophysical; 528.101-010 Drafter, Civil.

17-3012.00 Electrical and Electronics Drafters

- **Education/Training Required: Associate's degree**
- **Employed: 41,069**
- **Annual Earnings: $40,070**
- **Growth: 23.3%**
- **Annual Job Openings: 5,000**

Prepare wiring diagrams, circuit board assembly diagrams, and layout drawings used for manufacture, installation, and repair of electrical equipment in factories, power plants, and buildings.

No task data available.

GOE INFORMATION—Interest Area: 02. Science, Math, and Engineering. **Work Group:** 02.08. Engineering Technology. **Note:** The Department of Labor has not collected some data for this job, so it has fewer details than the other descriptions.

Instructional Programs—Electrical/Electronics Drafting and Electrical/Electronics CAD/CADD.

Related DOT Jobs—003.131-010 Supervisor, Drafting and Printed Circuit Design; 003.261-018 Integrated Circuit Layout Designer; 003.261-022 Printed Circuit Designer; 003.281-010 Drafter, Electrical; 003.281-014 Drafter, Electronic; 003.362-010 Design Technician, Computer-Aided; 017.261-014 Design Drafter, Electromechanisms; 019.161-010 Supervisor, Estimator and Drafter; 019.261-014 Estimator and Drafter; 726.364-014 Test Fixture Designer.

17-3012.01 Electronic Drafters

- **Education/Training Required: Postsecondary vocational training**
- **Employed: 41,069**
- **Annual Earnings: $40,070**
- **Growth: 23.3%**
- **Annual Job Openings: 5,000**

Draw wiring diagrams, circuit board assembly diagrams, schematics, and layout drawings used for manufacture, installation, and repair of electronic equipment.

Compare logic element configuration on display screen with engineering schematics and calculate figures to convert, redesign, and modify element. Consult with engineers to discuss and interpret design concepts and determine requirements of detailed working drawings. Draft detail and assembly drawings of design components, circuitry, and printed circuit boards, using computer-assisted equipment or standard drafting techniques and devices. Examine electronic schematics and supporting documents to develop, compute, and verify specifications for drafting data, such as configuration of parts, dimensions, and tolerances. Key and program specified commands and engineering specifications into computer system to change functions and test final layout. Plot electrical test points on layout sheets and draw schematics for wiring test fixture heads to frames. Review work orders and procedural manuals and confer with vendors and design staff to resolve problems and modify design. Copy drawings of printed circuit board fabrication, using print machine or blueprinting procedure. Generate computer tapes of final layout design to produce layered photo masks and photo plotting design onto film. Locate files relating to specified design project in database library, load program into computer, and record completed job data. Review blueprints to determine customer requirements and consult with assembler regarding schematics, wiring procedures, and conductor paths. Select drill size to drill test head, according to test design and specifications, and submit guide layout to designated department. Supervise and coordinate work activities of workers engaged in drafting, designing layouts, assembling, and testing printed circuit boards. Train students to use drafting machines and to prepare schematic diagrams, block diagrams, control drawings, logic diagrams, integrated circuit drawings, and interconnection diagrams.

GOE INFORMATION—Interest Area: 02. Science, Math, and Engineering. **Work Group:** 02.08. Engineering Technology. **Personality Type—**

Realistic. Realistic occupations frequently involve work activities that include practical, hands-on problems and solutions. They often deal with plants, animals, and real-world materials like wood, tools, and machinery. Many of the occupations require working outside and do not involve a lot of paperwork or working closely with others. **Work Values**—Good Working Conditions; Ability Utilization; Social Status; Compensation; Authority. **Skills**—Programming; Technology Design; Mathematics; Operations Analysis; Equipment Selection; Quality Control Analysis; Troubleshooting; Management of Material Resources. **Abilities**—*Cognitive:* Visualization; Number Facility; Category Flexibility; Information Ordering; Deductive Reasoning. *Psychomotor:* Arm-Hand Steadiness; Wrist-Finger Speed; Manual Dexterity; Finger Dexterity; Control Precision. *Physical:* Trunk Strength; Dynamic Flexibility. *Sensory:* Visual Color Discrimination; Near Vision; Speech Clarity; Speech Recognition. **General Work Activities**—*Information Input:* Getting Information; Identifying Objects, Actions, and Events; Inspecting Equipment, Structures, or Materials. *Mental Process:* Analyzing Data or Information; Processing Information; Making Decisions and Solving Problems. *Work Output:* Drafting and Specifying Technical Devices; Interacting with Computers; Handling and Moving Objects. *Interacting with Others:* Communicating with Other Workers; Coordinating the Work and Activities of Others; Providing Consultation and Advice to Others. **Physical Work Conditions**—Using Hands on Objects, Tools, or Controls; Sitting; Indoors; Walking or Running; Making Repetitive Motions. **Other Job Characteristics**—Importance of Being Exact or Accurate; Degree of Automation; Consequence of Error.

Experience—Job Zone 3. Previous work-related skill, knowledge, or experience is required. **Job Preparation:** SVP 6.0 to less than 7.0—more than one year and less than four years. **Knowledge**—Design; Computers and Electronics; Engineering and Technology; Mathematics; Administration and Management. **Instructional Programs**—Electrical/Electronics Drafting and Electrical/Electronics CAD/CADD.

Related DOT Jobs—017.261-014 Design Drafter, Electromechanisms; 313.101-010 Supervisor, Drafting and Printed Circuit Design; 326.101-018 Integrated Circuit Layout Designer; 326.102-022 Printed Circuit Designer; 328.101-014 Drafter, Electronic; 336.201-010 Design Technician, Computer-Aided; 726.364-014 Test Fixture Designer.

17-3012.02 Electrical Drafters

- **Education/Training Required: Associate's degree**
- **Employed: No data available.**
- **Annual Earnings: $40,070**
- **Growth: 23.3%**
- **Annual Job Openings: 5,000**

Develop specifications and instructions for installation of voltage transformers, overhead or underground cables, and related electrical equipment used to conduct electrical energy from transmission lines or high-voltage distribution lines to consumers.

Assemble documentation packages and produce drawing sets which are then checked by an engineer or an architect. Confer with engineering staff and other personnel to resolve problems. Draft working drawings, wiring diagrams, wiring connection specifications, or cross-sections of underground cables as required for instructions to installation crew. Draw master sketches to scale showing relation of proposed installations to existing facilities and exact specifications and dimensions. Measure factors that affect installation and arrangement of equipment, such as distances to be spanned by wire and cable. Study work order requests to determine type of service, such as lighting or power, demanded by installation. Visit proposed installation sites and draw rough sketches of location. Determine the order of work and the method of presentation, such as orthographic or isometric drawing. Explain drawings to production or construction teams and provide adjustments as necessary. Prepare and interpret specifications, calculating weights, volumes, and stress factors. Reproduce working drawings on copy machines or trace drawings in ink. Review completed construction drawings and cost estimates for accuracy and conformity to standards and regulations. Supervise and train other technologists, technicians, and drafters. Write technical reports and draw charts that display statistics and data. Use computer-aided drafting equipment and/or conventional drafting stations, technical handbooks, tables, calculators, and traditional drafting tools such as boards, pencils, protractors, and T-squares.

GOE INFORMATION—Interest Area: 02. Science, Math, and Engineering. **Work Group:** 02.08. Engineering Technology. **Personality Type—** Conventional. Conventional occupations frequently involve following set procedures and routines. These occupations can include working with data and details more than with ideas. Usually there is a clear line of authority to follow. **Work Values—**Authority; Ability Utilization; Autonomy; Creativity; Advancement. **Skills—**Operations Analysis; Management of Personnel Resources; Equipment Selection; Complex Problem Solving; Mathematics; Systems Analysis; Judgment and Decision Making; Management of Material Resources. **Abilities—***Cognitive:* Speed of Closure; Originality; Spatial Orientation; Number Facility; Visualization. *Psychomotor:* Finger Dexterity. *Physical:* Dynamic Flexibility; Stamina; Trunk Strength. *Sensory:* Far Vision; Night Vision; Glare Sensitivity; Depth Perception; Near Vision. **General Work Activities—***Information Input:* Getting Information; Inspecting Equipment, Structures, or Materials; Estimating Needed Characteristics. *Mental Process:* Analyzing Data or Information; Updating and Using Relevant Knowledge; Making Decisions and Solving Problems. *Work Output:* Drafting and Specifying Technical Devices; Documenting or Recording Information; Handling and Moving Objects. *Interacting with Others:* Communicating with Other Workers; Guiding, Directing, and Motivating Subordinates; Coordinating the Work and Activities of Others. **Physical Work Conditions—**Hazardous Conditions; Radiation; Outdoors; High Places; Hazardous Equipment. **Other Job Characteristics—**Importance of Being Exact or Accurate; Consequence of Error; Degree of Automation.

Experience—Job Zone 4. A minimum of two to four years of work-related skill, knowledge, or experience is needed. **Job Preparation:** SVP 7.0 to less than 8.0—two years to less than 10 years. **Knowledge—**Design; Engineering and Technology; Building and Construction; Administration and Management; Economics and Accounting. **Instructional Programs—**Electrical/Electronics Drafting and Electrical/Electronics CAD/CADD.

Related DOT Jobs—019.161-010 Supervisor, Estimator and Drafter; 019.261-014 Estimator and Drafter; 328.101-010 Drafter, Electrical.

17-3013.00 Mechanical Drafters

- **Education/Training Required: Postsecondary vocational training**
- **Employed: 70,194**
- **Annual Earnings: $39,620**
- **Growth: 15.4%**
- **Annual Job Openings: 8,000**

Prepare detailed working diagrams of machinery and mechanical devices, including dimensions, fastening methods, and other engineering information.

Check dimensions of materials to be used and assign numbers to the materials. Design scale or full-size blueprints of specialty items, such as furniture and automobile body or chassis components. Develop detailed design drawings and specifications for mechanical equipment, dies/tools, and controls, using computer-assisted drafting (CAD) equipment. Lay out and draw schematic, orthographic, or angle views to depict functional relationships of components, assemblies, systems, and machines. Lay out, draw, and reproduce illustrations for reference manuals and technical publications to describe operation and maintenance of mechanical systems. Position instructions and comments onto drawings. Review and analyze specifications, sketches, drawings, ideas, and related data to assess factors affecting component designs and the procedures and instructions to be followed. Compute mathematical formulas to develop and design detailed specifications for components or machinery, using computer-assisted equipment. Confer with customer representatives to review schematics and answer questions pertaining to installation of systems. Coordinate with and consult other workers in order to design, lay out, or detail components and systems and to resolve design or other problems. Draw freehand sketches of designs, trace finished drawings onto designated paper for the reproduction of blueprints, and reproduce working drawings on copy machines. Modify and revise designs to correct operating deficiencies or to reduce production problems. Shade or color drawings to clarify and emphasize details and dimensions and eliminate background, using ink, crayon, airbrush, and overlays. Supervise and train other drafters, technologists, and technicians.

GOE INFORMATION—Interest Area: 02. Science, Math, and Engineering. **Work Group:** 02.08. Engineering Technology. **Personality Type—** Realistic. Realistic occupations frequently involve work activities that include practical, hands-on problems and solutions. They often deal with plants, animals, and real-world materials like wood, tools, and machinery. Many of the occupations require working outside and do not involve a lot of paperwork or working closely with others. **Work Values—**Authority; Good Working Conditions; Ability Utilization; Creativity; Moral Values. **Skills—**Mathematics; Technology Design; Programming; Operations Analysis; Operation Monitoring; Quality Control Analysis; Systems Evaluation; Systems Analysis. **Abilities—***Cognitive:* Visualization; Mathematical Reasoning; Number Facility; Deductive Reasoning; Fluency of Ideas. *Psychomotor:* Arm-Hand Steadiness; Manual Dexterity; Finger Dexterity; Control Precision; Wrist-Finger Speed. *Physical:* Gross Body Coordination; Trunk Strength; Explosive Strength. *Sensory:* Visual Color Discrimination; Near Vision; Depth Perception; Speech Recognition; Glare Sensitivity. **General Work Activities—***Information Input:* Getting Information; Inspecting Equipment, Structures, or Materials; Identifying Objects, Actions, and Events. *Mental Process:* Updating and Using Relevant Knowledge; Analyzing Data or Information; Organizing, Planning, and Prioritizing. *Work Output:* Drafting and Specifying Technical Devices; Interacting with Computers; Handling and Moving Objects. *Interacting with Others:* Communicating with Persons Outside Organization; Communicating with Other Workers; Establishing and Maintaining Relationships. **Physical Work Conditions—**Sitting; Using Hands on Objects, Tools, or Controls; Making Repetitive Motions; Hazardous Equipment; Radiation. **Other Job Characteristics—**Importance of Being Exact or Accurate; Consequence of Error; Degree of Automation.

Experience—Job Zone 4. A minimum of two to four years of work-related skill, knowledge, or experience is needed. **Job Preparation:** SVP 7.0 to less than 8.0—two years to less than 10 years. **Knowledge—**Design; Engineering and Technology; Mathematics; Computers and Electronics; Physics. **Instructional Programs—**Mechanical Drafting and Mechanical Drafting CAD/CADD.

Related DOT Jobs—017.261-018 Detailer; 017.261-022 Detailer, Furniture; 017.261-030 Drafter, Detail; 017.261-042 Drafter, Automotive Design; 017.281-010 Auto-Design Detailer; 017.281-014 Drafter Apprentice; 017.281-

026 Drafter, Automotive Design Layout; 017.281-034 Technical Illustrator; 226.101-010 Drafter, Aeronautical; 326.101-014 Controls Designer; 716.101-010 Die Designer; 716.101-014 Die-Designer Apprentice; 716.101-018 Engineering Assistant, Mechanical Equipment; 726.101-014 Drafter, Castings; 726.101-018 Drafter, Patent; 726.102-022 Drafter, Tool Design; 728.101-010 Drafter, Mechanical.

17-3019.99 Drafters, All Other

- Education/Training Required: No data available.
- Employed: No data available.
- Annual Earnings: No data available.
- Growth: 23.2%
- Annual Job Openings: 16,000

All drafters not listed separately.

No task data available.

GOE INFORMATION—Interest Area: 02. Science, Math, and Engineering. **Work Group:** 02.08. Engineering Technology. **Note:** The Department of Labor has not collected some data for this job, so it has fewer details than the other descriptions.

Instructional Programs—Drafting and Design Technology/Technician, General; Drafting/Design Engineering Technologies/Technicians, Other.

Related DOT Jobs—007.261-010 Chief Drafter; 017.161-010 Drafter, Chief, Design.

17-3021.00 Aerospace Engineering and Operations Technicians

- Education/Training Required: Associate's degree
- Employed: 21,062
- Annual Earnings: $50,480
- Growth: 5.6%
- Annual Job Openings: 2,000

Operate, install, calibrate, and maintain integrated computer/communications systems consoles, simulators, and other data acquisition, test, and measurement instruments and equipment to launch, track, position, and evaluate air and space vehicles. May record and interpret test data.

Adjust, repair, or replace faulty components of test setups and equipment. Construct and maintain test facilities for aircraft parts and systems according to specifications. Fabricate and install parts and systems to be tested in test equipment, using hand tools, power tools, and test instruments. Identify required data, data acquisition plans, and test parameters, setting up equipment to conform to these specifications. Inspect, diagnose, maintain, and operate test setups and equipment to detect malfunctions. Operate and calibrate computer systems and devices to comply with test requirements and to perform data acquisition and analysis. Test aircraft systems under simulated operational conditions, performing systems readiness tests and pre- and post-operational checkouts, to establish design or fabrication parameters. Confer with engineering personnel regarding details and implications of test procedures and results. Exchange cooling system components in various vehicles. Finish vehicle instrumentation and deinstrumentation. Record and interpret test data on parts, assemblies, and mechanisms.

GOE INFORMATION—Interest Area: 02. Science, Math, and Engineering. **Work Group:** 02.08. Engineering Technology. **Personality Type—**

Investigative. Investigative occupations frequently involve working with ideas and require an extensive amount of thinking. These occupations can involve searching for facts and figuring out problems mentally. **Work Values**—Activity; Good Working Conditions; Compensation; Advancement; Achievement. **Skills**—Science; Programming; Installation; Operation Monitoring; Mathematics; Repairing; Quality Control Analysis; Operation and Control. **Abilities**—*Cognitive:* Number Facility; Mathematical Reasoning; Written Expression; Deductive Reasoning; Written Comprehension. *Psychomotor:* Wrist-Finger Speed; Response Orientation; Reaction Time; Finger Dexterity; Arm-Hand Steadiness. *Physical:* Trunk Strength; Stamina; Extent Flexibility; Dynamic Flexibility. *Sensory:* Near Vision; Far Vision; Sound Localization; Peripheral Vision; Night Vision. **General Work Activities**—*Information Input:* Monitoring Processes, Materials, or Surroundings; Inspecting Equipment, Structures, or Materials; Getting Information. *Mental Process:* Processing Information; Analyzing Data or Information; Updating and Using Relevant Knowledge. *Work Output:* Interacting with Computers; Documenting or Recording Information; Repairing and Maintaining Electronic Equipment. *Interacting with Others:* Communicating with Other Workers; Interpreting Meaning of Information for Others; Providing Consultation and Advice to Others. **Physical Work Conditions**—Hazardous Equipment; Using Hands on Objects, Tools, or Controls; Indoors; Sitting; Common Protective or Safety Attire. **Other Job Characteristics**—Importance of Being Exact or Accurate; Consequence of Error; Degree of Automation.

Experience—Job Zone 4. A minimum of two to four years of work-related skill, knowledge, or experience is needed. **Job Preparation:** SVP 7.0 to less than 8.0–two years to less than 10 years. **Knowledge**—Computers and Electronics; Engineering and Technology; Physics; Mechanical; Mathematics. **Instructional Programs**—Aeronautical/Aerospace Engineering Technology/Technician.

Related DOT Jobs—226.101-014 Research Mechanic; 226.201-010 Flight-Test Data Acquisition Technician; 710.361-014 Test Equipment Mechanic; 869.261-026 Wind Tunnel Mechanic.

17-3022.00 Civil Engineering Technicians

- Education/Training Required: Associate's degree
- Employed: 93,503
- Annual Earnings: $37,410
- Growth: 11.9%
- Annual Job Openings: 9,000

Apply theory and principles of civil engineering in planning, designing, and overseeing construction and maintenance of structures and facilities under the direction of engineering staff or physical scientists.

Inspect project site and evaluate contractor work to detect design malfunctions and ensure conformance to design specifications and applicable codes. Analyze proposed site factors and design maps, graphs, tracings, and diagrams to illustrate findings. Plan and conduct field surveys to locate new sites and analyze details of project sites. Draft detailed dimensional drawings and design layouts for projects and to ensure conformance to specifications. Develop plans and estimate costs for installation of systems, utilization of facilities, or construction of structures. Read and review project blueprints and structural specifications to determine dimensions of structure or system and material requirements. Calculate dimensions, square footage, profile and component specifications, and material quantities, using calculator or computer. Report maintenance problems occurring at project site to supervisor and negotiate changes to resolve system conflicts. Conduct materials test and analysis, using tools and equipment and applying engineering knowledge. Confer with supervisor to determine project details, such as plan preparation, acceptance testing, and evaluation of field conditions. Prepare reports and document project activities and data. Evaluate facility to determine suitability for occupancy and square footage availability. Respond to public suggestions and complaints.

GOE INFORMATION—Interest Area: 02. Science, Math, and Engineering. **Work Group:** 02.08. Engineering Technology. **Personality Type—**Realistic. Realistic occupations frequently involve work activities that include practical, hands-on problems and solutions. They often deal with plants, animals, and real-world materials like wood, tools, and machinery. Many of the occupations require working outside and do not involve a lot of paperwork or working closely with others. **Work Values—**Advancement; Good Working Conditions; Ability Utilization; Supervision, Human Relations; Activity. **Skills—**Operations Analysis; Equipment Selection; Complex Problem Solving; Mathematics; Quality Control Analysis; Science; Systems Evaluation; Judgment and Decision Making. **Abilities—***Cognitive:* Mathematical Reasoning; Number Facility; Written Expression; Category Flexibility; Problem Sensitivity. *Psychomotor:* Rate Control; Control Precision; Multilimb Coordination. *Physical:* Gross Body Equilibrium. *Sensory:* Depth Perception; Glare Sensitivity; Night Vision; Speech Clarity; Far Vision. **General Work Activities—***Information Input:* Getting Information; Identifying Objects, Actions, and Events; Monitoring Processes, Materials, or Surroundings. *Mental Process:* Evaluating Information Against Standards; Organizing, Planning, and Prioritizing; Updating and Using Relevant Knowledge. *Work Output:* Drafting and Specifying Technical Devices; Documenting or Recording Information; Performing General Physical Activities. *Interacting with Others:* Communicating with Other Workers; Providing Consultation and Advice to Others; Establishing and Maintaining Relationships. **Physical Work Conditions—**High Places; Outdoors; Climbing Ladders, Scaffolds, Poles, etc.; Hazardous Conditions; Walking or Running. **Other Job Characteristics—**Importance of Being Exact or Accurate; Consequence of Error; Pace Determined by Speed of Equipment.

Experience—Job Zone 4. A minimum of two to four years of work-related skill, knowledge, or experience is needed. **Job Preparation:** SVP 7.0 to less than 8.0—two years to less than 10 years. **Knowledge—**Design; Engineering and Technology; Building and Construction; Mathematics; Computers and Electronics. **Instructional Programs—**Civil Engineering Technology/Technician; Construction Engineering Technology/Technician.

Related DOT Jobs—019.261-018 Facility Planner; 019.261-026 Fire-Protection Engineering Technician; 199.261-014 Parking Analyst; 526.101-014 Civil Engineering Technician.

17-3023.00 *Electrical and Electronic Engineering Technicians*

- **Education/Training Required: Associate's degree**
- **Employed: 232,736**
- **Annual Earnings: $42,130**
- **Growth: 10.8%**
- **Annual Job Openings: 22,000**

Apply electrical and electronic theory and related knowledge, usually under the direction of engineering staff, to design, build, repair, calibrate, and modify electrical components, circuitry, controls, and machinery for subsequent evaluation and use by engineering staff in making engineering design decisions.

No task data available.

GOE INFORMATION—Interest Area: 02. Science, Math, and Engineering. **Work Group:** 02.08. Engineering Technology. **Note:** The Department of Labor has not collected some data for this job, so it has fewer details than the other descriptions.

Instructional Programs—Computer Engineering Technology/Technician; Computer Technology/Computer Systems Technology; Electrical and Electronic Engineering Technologies/Technicians, Other; Electrical, Electronic, and Communications Engineering Technology/Technician; Telecommunications Technology/Technician.

Related DOT Jobs—003.161-010 Electrical Technician; 003.161-014 Electronics Technician; 003.161-018 Technician, Semiconductor Development; 003.261-010 Instrumentation Technician; 019.281-010 Calibration Laboratory Technician; 710.261-010 Instrument Repairer; 710.281-026 Instrument Mechanic; 710.281-030 Instrument Technician; 710.281-042 Instrument-Technician Apprentice; 711.281-014 Instrument Mechanic, Weapons System; 725.381-010 Tube Rebuilder; 726.261-010 Electronics Assembler, Developmental; 726.261-014 Electrician, Research; 729.281-026 Electrical-Instrument Repairer; 828.261-018 Senior Technician, Controls.

17-3023.01 *Electronics Engineering Technicians*

- **Education/Training Required: Associate's degree**
- **Employed: 232,736**
- **Annual Earnings: $42,130**
- **Growth: 10.8%**
- **Annual Job Openings: 22,000**

Lay out, build, test, troubleshoot, repair, and modify developmental and production electronic components, parts, equipment, and systems, such as computer equipment, missile control instrumentation, electron tubes, test equipment, and machine tool numerical controls, applying principles and theories of electronics, electrical circuitry, engineering mathematics, electronic and electrical testing, and physics. Usually work under direction of engineering staff.

Adjust and replace defective or improperly functioning circuitry and electronics components, using hand tools and soldering iron. Assemble, test, and maintain circuitry or electronic components according to engineering instructions, technical manuals, and knowledge of electronics, using hand and power tools. Build prototypes from rough sketches or plans. Fabricate parts, such as coils, terminal boards, and chassis, using bench lathes, drills, or other machine tools. Read blueprints, wiring diagrams, schematic drawings, and engineering instructions for assembling electronics units, applying knowledge of electronic theory and components. Test electronics units, using standard test equipment, and analyze results to evaluate performance and determine need for adjustment. Design basic circuitry and draft sketches for clarification of details and design documentation under engineers' direction, using drafting instruments and computer-aided design equipment. Develop and upgrade preventative maintenance procedures for components, equipment, parts, and systems. Identify and resolve equipment malfunctions, working with manufacturers and field representatives as necessary to procure replacement parts. Maintain system logs and manuals to document testing and operation of equipment. Maintain working knowledge of state-of-the-art tools, software, etc., through reading and/or attending conferences, workshops, or other training. Perform preventative maintenance and calibration of equipment and systems. Procure parts and maintain inventory and related documentation. Provide user applications and engineering support and recommendations for new and existing equipment with regard to installation, upgrades, and enhancement. Research equipment and component needs, sources, competitive prices, delivery times, and ongoing operational costs. Write computer or microprocessor software programs. Write reports and record data on testing techniques, laboratory equipment, and specifications to assist engineers. Provide customer support and education, working with users to identify needs, determine sources of problems, and provide information on product use. Survey satellite receival sites for proper signal level and provide technical assistance in dish location and installation, transporting dishes as necessary.

GOE INFORMATION—Interest Area: 02. Science, Math, and Engineering. **Work Group:** 02.08. Engineering Technology. **Personality Type—**Realistic. Realistic occupations frequently involve work activities that include practical, hands-on problems and solutions. They often deal with plants, animals, and real-world materials like wood, tools, and machinery. Many of the occupations require working outside and do not involve a lot of paperwork or working closely with others. **Work Values—**Advancement; Good Working Conditions; Ability Utilization; Achievement; Activity. **Skills—**Installation; Technology Design; Troubleshooting; Operations Analysis; Quality Control Analysis; Repairing; Mathematics; Operation Monitoring. **Abilities—***Cognitive:* Mathematical Reasoning; Visualization; Written Comprehension; Written Expression; Deductive Reasoning. *Psychomotor:* Arm-Hand Steadiness; Control Precision; Finger Dexterity. *Physical:* None met the criteria. *Sensory:* Speech Clarity; Sound Localization. **General Work Activities—***Information Input:* Inspecting Equipment, Structures, or Materials; Getting Information; Identifying Objects, Actions, and Events. *Mental Process:* Updating and Using Relevant Knowledge; Evaluating Information Against Standards; Thinking Creatively. *Work Output:* Repairing and Maintaining Electronic Equipment; Interacting with Computers; Drafting and Specifying Technical Devices. *Interacting with Others:* Communicating with Other Workers; Performing Administrative Activities; Communicating with Persons Outside Organization. **Physical Work Conditions—**Hazardous Equipment; Hazardous Conditions; Indoors; Common Protective or Safety Attire; Extremely Bright or Inadequate Lighting. **Other Job Characteristics—**Degree of Automation; Importance of Being Exact or Accurate; Pace Determined by Speed of Equipment.

Experience—Job Zone 4. A minimum of two to four years of work-related skill, knowledge, or experience is needed. **Job Preparation:** SVP 7.0 to less than 8.0—two years to less than 10 years. **Knowledge—**Design; Computers and Electronics; Engineering and Technology; Mathematics; Production and Processing. **Instructional Programs—**Computer Engineering Technology/Technician; Computer Technology/Computer Systems Technology; Electrical and Electronic Engineering Technologies/Technicians, Other; Electrical, Electronic, and Communications Engineering Technology/Technician; Telecommunications Technology/Technician.

Related DOT Jobs—316.101-014 Electronics Technician; 316.101-018 Technician, Semiconductor Development; 725.381-010 Tube Rebuilder; 726.261-010 Electronics Assembler, Developmental.

17-3023.02 Calibration and Instrumentation Technicians

- ● **Education/Training Required: Associate's degree**
- ● **Employed: No data available.**
- ● **Annual Earnings: $42,130**
- ● **Growth: 10.8%**
- ● **Annual Job Openings: 22,000**

Develop, test, calibrate, operate, and repair electrical, mechanical, electromechanical, electrohydraulic, or electronic measuring and recording instruments, apparatus, and equipment.

Plans sequence of testing and calibration program for instruments and equipment according to blueprints, schematics, technical manuals, and other specifications. Sets up test equipment and conducts tests on performance and reliability of mechanical, structural, or electromechanical equipment. Modifies performance and operation of component parts and circuitry to specifications, using test equipment and precision instruments. Selects sensing, telemetering, and recording instrumentation and circuitry. Disassembles and reassembles instruments and equipment, using hand tools, and inspects instruments and equipment for defects. Sketches plans for developing jigs, fixtures, instruments, and related nonstandard apparatus. Analyzes and converts test data, using mathematical formulas, and reports results and proposed modifications. Performs preventative and corrective maintenance of test apparatus and peripheral equipment. Confers with engineers, supervisor, and other technical workers to assist with equipment installation, maintenance, and repair techniques.

GOE INFORMATION—Interest Area: 02. Science, Math, and Engineering. **Work Group:** 02.08. Engineering Technology. **Personality Type—**Realistic. Realistic occupations frequently involve work activities that include practical, hands-on problems and solutions. They often deal with plants, animals, and real-world materials like wood, tools, and machinery. Many of the occupations require working outside and do not involve a lot of paperwork or working closely with others. **Work Values—**Supervision, Human Relations; Good Working Conditions; Social Status; Supervision, Technical; Company Policies and Practices. **Skills—**Technology Design; Equipment Selection; Quality Control Analysis; Troubleshooting; Operation Monitoring; Installation; Repairing; Mathematics. **Abilities—***Cognitive:* Mathematical Reasoning; Information Ordering; Deductive Reasoning; Written Comprehension; Fluency of Ideas. *Psychomotor:* Control Precision; Finger Dexterity; Wrist-Finger Speed; Arm-Hand Steadiness. *Physical:* None met the criteria. *Sensory:* None met the criteria. **General Work Activities—***Information Input:* Identifying Objects, Actions, and Events; Inspecting Equipment, Structures, or Materials; Monitoring Processes, Materials, or Surroundings. *Mental Process:* Processing Information; Analyzing Data or Information; Making Decisions and Solving Problems. *Work Output:* Repairing and Maintaining Mechanical Equipment; Handling and Moving Objects; Controlling Machines and Processes. *Interacting with Others:* Communicating with Other Workers; Establishing and Maintaining Relationships; Interpreting Meaning of Information for Others. **Physical Work Conditions—**Indoors; Sitting; Standing. **Other Job Characteristics—**Importance of Being Exact or Accurate; Consequence of Error; Pace Determined by Speed of Equipment.

Experience—Job Zone 4. A minimum of two to four years of work-related skill, knowledge, or experience is needed. **Job Preparation:** SVP 7.0 to less than 8.0—two years to less than 10 years. **Knowledge—**Design; Mathematics; Computers and Electronics; Engineering and Technology; Mechanical. **Instructional Programs—**Computer Engineering Technology/Technician; Computer Technology/Computer Systems Technology; Electrical and Electronic Engineering Technologies/Technicians, Other; Electrical, Electronic, and Communications Engineering Technology/Technician; Telecommunications Technology/Technician.

Related DOT Jobs—019.281-010 Calibration Laboratory Technician; 326.101-010 Instrumentation Technician; 828.261-018 Senior Technician, Controls.

17-3023.03 Electrical Engineering Technicians

- **Education/Training Required: Associate's degree**
- **Employed: No data available.**
- **Annual Earnings: $42,130**
- **Growth: 10.8%**
- **Annual Job Openings: 22,000**

Apply electrical theory and related knowledge to test and modify developmental or operational electrical machinery and electrical control equipment and circuitry in industrial or commercial plants and laboratories. Usually work under direction of engineering staff.

Analyze and interpret test information to resolve design-related problems. Assemble electrical and electronic systems and prototypes according to engineering data and knowledge of electrical principles, using hand tools and measuring instruments. Build, calibrate, maintain, troubleshoot, and repair electrical instruments or testing equipment. Collaborate with electrical engineers and other personnel to identify, define, and solve developmental problems. Modify electrical prototypes, parts, assemblies, and systems to correct functional deviations. Plan method and sequence of operations for developing and testing experimental electronic and electrical equipment. Set up and operate test equipment to evaluate performance of developmental parts, assemblies, or systems under simulated operating conditions and record results. Conduct inspections for quality control and assurance programs, reporting findings and recommendations. Draw or modify diagrams and write engineering specifications to clarify design details and functional criteria of experimental electronics units. Evaluate engineering proposals, shop drawings, and design comments for sound electrical engineering practice and conformance with established safety and design criteria and recommend approval or disapproval. Install and maintain electrical control systems and solid-state equipment. Perform supervisory duties such as recommending work assignments, approving leaves, and completing performance evaluations. Plan, schedule, and monitor work of support personnel to assist supervisor. Prepare project cost and work-time estimates. Provide technical assistance and resolution when electrical or engineering problems are encountered before, during, and after construction. Review existing electrical engineering criteria to identify necessary revisions, deletions, or amendments to outdated material. Prepare contracts and initiate, review, and coordinate modifications to contract specifications and plans throughout the construction process. Visit construction sites to observe conditions impacting design and to identify solutions to technical design problems involving electrical systems equipment that arise during construction. Write commissioning procedures for electrical installations.

GOE INFORMATION—Interest Area: 02. Science, Math, and Engineering. **Work Group:** 02.08. Engineering Technology. **Personality Type—**Realistic. Realistic occupations frequently involve work activities that include practical, hands-on problems and solutions. They often deal with plants, animals, and real-world materials like wood, tools, and machinery. Many of the occupations require working outside and do not involve a lot of paperwork or working closely with others. **Work Values—**Advancement; Good Working Conditions; Ability Utilization; Achievement; Activity. **Skills—**Technology Design; Troubleshooting; Operations Analysis; Equipment Selection; Quality Control Analysis; Operation Monitoring; Installation; Complex Problem Solving. **Abilities—***Cognitive:* Visualization; Mathematical Reasoning; Deductive Reasoning; Information Ordering; Fluency of Ideas. *Psychomotor:* Control Precision; Wrist-Finger Speed; Manual Dexterity. *Physical:* None met the criteria. *Sensory:* Visual Color Discrimination; Speech Recognition. **General Work Activities—**

Information Input: Monitoring Processes, Materials, or Surroundings; Inspecting Equipment, Structures, or Materials; Identifying Objects, Actions, and Events. *Mental Process:* Analyzing Data or Information; Updating and Using Relevant Knowledge; Processing Information. *Work Output:* Repairing and Maintaining Electronic Equipment; Drafting and Specifying Technical Devices; Handling and Moving Objects. *Interacting with Others:* Communicating with Other Workers; Interpreting Meaning of Information for Others; Providing Consultation and Advice to Others. **Physical Work Conditions—**Hazardous Conditions; Indoors; Sitting; Minor Burns, Cuts, Bites, or Stings; Specialized Protective or Safety Attire. **Other Job Characteristics—**Consequence of Error; Importance of Being Exact or Accurate; Degree of Automation.

Experience—Job Zone 4. A minimum of two to four years of work-related skill, knowledge, or experience is needed. **Job Preparation:** SVP 7.0 to less than 8.0—two years to less than 10 years. **Knowledge—**Design; Engineering and Technology; Computers and Electronics; Physics; Mathematics. **Instructional Programs—**Computer Engineering Technology/Technician; Computer Technology/Computer Systems Technology; Electrical and Electronic Engineering Technologies/Technicians, Other; Electrical, Electronic, and Communications Engineering Technology/Technician; Telecommunications Technology/Technician.

Related DOT Jobs—316.101-010 Electrical Technician; 726.261-014 Electrician, Research.

17-3024.00 Electro-Mechanical Technicians

- **Education/Training Required: Associate's degree**
- **Employed: 43,451**
- **Annual Earnings: $38,150**
- **Growth: 14.5%**
- **Annual Job Openings: 4,000**

Operate, test, and maintain unmanned, automated, servo-mechanical, or electromechanical equipment. May operate unmanned submarines, aircraft, or other equipment at worksites, such as oil rigs, deep ocean exploration, or hazardous waste removal. May assist engineers in testing and designing robotics equipment.

Operates metalworking machines to fabricate housings, jigs, fittings, and fixtures. Aligns, fits, and assembles component parts, using hand tools, power tools, fixtures, templates, and microscope. Installs electrical and electronic parts and hardware in housing or assembly, using soldering equipment and hand tools. Tests performance of electromechanical assembly, using test instruments such as oscilloscope, electronic voltmeter, and bridge. Repairs, reworks, and calibrates assemblies to meet operational specifications and tolerances. Verifies dimensions and clearances of parts to ensure conformance to specifications, using precision measuring instruments. Inspects parts for surface defects. Analyzes and records test results and prepares written documentation. Reads blueprints, schematics, diagrams, and technical orders to determine method and sequence of assembly.

GOE INFORMATION—Interest Area: 02. Science, Math, and Engineering. **Work Group:** 02.08. Engineering Technology. **Personality Type—**Realistic. Realistic occupations frequently involve work activities that include practical, hands-on problems and solutions. They often deal with plants, animals, and real-world materials like wood, tools, and machinery. Many of the occupations require working outside and do not involve a lot of paperwork or working closely with others. **Work Values—**Independence; Moral Values; Supervision, Technical; Supervision, Human Relations; Company Policies and Practices. **Skills—**Repairing; Troubleshooting;

Quality Control Analysis; Installation; Operation Monitoring; Operation and Control; Equipment Selection; Science. **Abilities**—*Cognitive:* Visualization; Information Ordering; Perceptual Speed; Written Comprehension; Memorization. *Psychomotor:* Finger Dexterity; Arm-Hand Steadiness; Manual Dexterity; Control Precision; Speed of Limb Movement. *Physical:* Dynamic Flexibility; Gross Body Coordination; Explosive Strength; Dynamic Strength; Extent Flexibility. *Sensory:* Visual Color Discrimination; Depth Perception; Near Vision; Peripheral Vision; Far Vision. **General Work Activities**—*Information Input:* Inspecting Equipment, Structures, or Materials; Monitoring Processes, Materials, or Surroundings; Getting Information. *Mental Process:* Updating and Using Relevant Knowledge; Analyzing Data or Information; Judging Qualities of Things, Services, or Other People's Work. *Work Output:* Repairing and Maintaining Electronic Equipment; Handling and Moving Objects; Controlling Machines and Processes. *Interacting with Others:* Communicating with Other Workers; Interpreting Meaning of Information for Others; Performing Administrative Activities. **Physical Work Conditions**—Hazardous Equipment; Using Hands on Objects, Tools, or Controls; Minor Burns, Cuts, Bites, or Stings; Radiation; Distracting Sounds and Noise Levels. **Other Job Characteristics**—Degree of Automation; Importance of Repeating Same Tasks; Importance of Being Exact or Accurate.

Experience—Job Zone 4. A minimum of two to four years of work-related skill, knowledge, or experience is needed. **Job Preparation:** SVP 7.0 to less than 8.0—two years to less than 10 years. **Knowledge**—Mechanical; Production and Processing; Engineering and Technology; Computers and Electronics; Design. **Instructional Programs**—Engineering Technologies/Technicians, Other.

Related DOT Jobs—710.281-018 Electromechanical Technician; 828.381-018 Assembler, Electromechanical.

17-3025.00 *Environmental Engineering Technicians*

- **Education/Training Required: Associate's degree**
- **Employed: 18,325**
- **Annual Earnings: $36,590**
- **Growth: 29.1%**
- **Annual Job Openings: 2,000**

Apply theory and principles of environmental engineering to modify, test, and operate equipment and devices used in the prevention, control, and remediation of environmental pollution, including waste treatment and site remediation. May assist in the development of environmental pollution remediation devices under direction of engineer.

Maintain process parameters and evaluate process anomalies. Perform environmental quality work in field and office settings. Receive, set up, test, and decontaminate equipment. Arrange for the disposal of lead, asbestos, and other hazardous materials. Assist in the cleanup of hazardous material spills. Conduct pollution surveys, collecting and analyzing samples such as air and ground water. Develop work plans, including writing specifications and establishing material, manpower, and facilities needs. Improve chemical processes to reduce toxic emissions. Inspect facilities to monitor compliance with regulations governing substances such as asbestos, lead, and wastewater. Maintain project logbook records and computer program files. Obtain product information, identify vendors and suppliers, and order materials and equipment to maintain inventory. Oversee support staff. Perform laboratory work such as logging numerical and visual observations, preparing and packaging samples, recording test results, and performing photo documentation. Perform statistical analysis and correction of air and/or water pollution data

submitted by industry and other agencies. Produce environmental assessment reports, tabulating data and preparing charts, graphs, and sketches. Provide technical engineering support in the planning of projects, such as wastewater treatment plants, to ensure compliance with environmental regulations and policies. Review technical documents to ensure completeness and conformance to requirements. Review work plans to schedule activities. Work with customers to assess the environmental impact of proposed construction and to develop pollution prevention programs. Manage Government Impact Card purchases with environmental laboratories to support customers' projects.

GOE INFORMATION—**Interest Area:** 02. Science, Math, and Engineering. **Work Group:** 02.08. Engineering Technology. **Note:** The Department of Labor has not collected some data for this job, so it has fewer details than the other descriptions.

Instructional Programs—Environmental Engineering Technology/Environmental Technology; Hazardous Materials Information Systems Technology/Technician.

Related DOT Jobs—012.261-010 Air Analyst; 029.261-014 Pollution-Control Technician.

17-3026.00 *Industrial Engineering Technicians*

- **Education/Training Required: Associate's degree**
- **Employed: 52,118**
- **Annual Earnings: $40,970**
- **Growth: 10.1%**
- **Annual Job Openings: 5,000**

Apply engineering theory and principles to problems of industrial layout or manufacturing production, usually under the direction of engineering staff. May study and record time, motion, method, and speed involved in performance of production, maintenance, clerical, and other worker operations for such purposes as establishing standard production rates or improving efficiency.

Study time, motion, methods, and speed involved in maintenance, production, and other operations to establish standard production rate and improve efficiency. Observe workers operating equipment or performing tasks to determine time involved and fatigue rate, using timing devices. Prepare charts, graphs, and diagrams to illustrate workflow, routing, floor layouts, material handling, and machine utilization. Recommend revision to methods of operation, material handling, equipment layout, or other changes to increase production or improve standards. Record test data, applying statistical quality control procedures. Observe worker using equipment to verify that equipment is being operated and maintained according to quality assurance standards. Recommend modifications to existing quality or production standards to achieve optimum quality within limits of equipment capability. Evaluate data and write reports to validate or indicate deviations from existing standards. Aid in planning work assignments in accordance with worker performance, machine capacity, production schedules, and anticipated delays. Prepare graphs or charts of data or enter data into computer for analysis. Interpret engineering drawings, schematic diagrams, or formulas and confer with management or engineering staff to determine quality and reliability standards. Read worker logs, product processing sheets, and specification sheets to verify that records adhere to quality assurance specifications. Compile and evaluate statistical data to determine and maintain quality and reliability of products. Select products for tests at specified stages in production process and test products for performance characteristics and adherence to specifications.

GOE INFORMATION—Interest Area: 02. Science, Math, and Engineering. **Work Group:** 02.08. Engineering Technology. **Personality Type—** Investigative. Investigative occupations frequently involve working with ideas and require an extensive amount of thinking. These occupations can involve searching for facts and figuring out problems mentally. **Work Values—**Advancement; Supervision, Human Relations; Ability Utilization; Achievement; Supervision, Technical. **Skills—**Quality Control Analysis; Systems Evaluation; Systems Analysis; Equipment Selection; Operations Analysis; Complex Problem Solving; Mathematics; Science. **Abilities—***Cognitive:* Speed of Closure; Originality; Mathematical Reasoning; Number Facility; Written Expression. *Psychomotor:* Finger Dexterity; Manual Dexterity. *Physical:* Dynamic Flexibility; Gross Body Coordination; Gross Body Equilibrium. *Sensory:* Far Vision; Auditory Attention; Sound Localization; Peripheral Vision; Speech Clarity. **General Work Activities—***Information Input:* Getting Information; Monitoring Processes, Materials, or Surroundings; Identifying Objects, Actions, and Events. *Mental Process:* Processing Information; Analyzing Data or Information; Evaluating Information Against Standards. *Work Output:* Documenting or Recording Information; Interacting with Computers; Drafting and Specifying Technical Devices. *Interacting with Others:* Communicating with Other Workers; Interpreting Meaning of Information for Others; Establishing and Maintaining Relationships. **Physical Work Conditions—**Extremely Bright or Inadequate Lighting; Distracting Sounds and Noise Levels; Sitting; Contaminants; Very Hot or Cold. **Other Job Characteristics—**Importance of Being Exact or Accurate; Degree of Automation; Pace Determined by Speed of Equipment.

Experience—Job Zone 3. Previous work-related skill, knowledge, or experience is required. **Job Preparation:** SVP 6.0 to less than 7.0—more than one year and less than four years. **Knowledge—**Production and Processing; Engineering and Technology; Design; Physics; Mathematics. **Instructional Programs—**Engineering/Industrial Management; Industrial Production Technologies/Technicians, Other; Industrial Technology/Technician; Manufacturing Technology/Technician.

Related DOT Jobs—012.261-014 Quality Control Technician; 012.267-010 Industrial Engineering Technician; 168.367-022 Personnel Quality Assurance Auditor.

17-3027.00 Mechanical Engineering Technicians

- **Education/Training Required:** Associate's degree
- **Employed:** 58,108
- **Annual Earnings:** $40,910
- **Growth:** 13.9%
- **Annual Job Openings:** 5,000

Apply theory and principles of mechanical engineering to modify, develop, and test machinery and equipment under direction of engineering staff or physical scientists.

Review project instructions and blueprints to ascertain test specifications, procedures, and objectives and test nature of technical problems, such as redesign. Set up and conduct tests of complete units and components under operational conditions to investigate proposals for improving equipment performance. Devise, fabricate, and assemble new or modified mechanical components for products, such as industrial machinery or equipment, and measuring instruments. Test equipment, using test devices attached to generator, voltage regulator, or other electrical parts, such as generators or spark plugs. Review project instructions and specifications to identify, modify, and plan requirements fabrication, assembly, and testing. Set up prototype and test apparatus and operate test controlling equipment to observe and record prototype test results. Estimate cost factors, including labor and material for purchased and fabricated parts and costs for assembly, testing, and installing. Inspect lines and figures for clarity and return erroneous drawings to designer for correction. Prepare parts sketches and write work orders and purchase requests to be furnished by outside contractors. Read dials and meters to determine amperage, voltage, and electrical output and input at specific operating temperature to analyze parts performance. Operate drill press, grinders, engine lathe, or other machines to modify parts tested or to fabricate experimental parts for testing. Evaluate tool drawing designs by measuring drawing dimensions and comparing with original specifications for form and function, using engineering skills. Confer with technicians, submit reports of test results to engineering department, and recommend design or material changes. Record test procedures and results, numerical and graphical data, and recommendations for changes in product or test methods. Draft detail drawing or sketch for drafting room completion or to request parts fabrication by machine, sheet, or wood shops. Calculate required capacities for equipment of proposed system to obtain specified performance and submit data to engineering personnel for approval. Discuss changes in design, method of manufacture and assembly, and drafting techniques and procedures with staff and coordinate corrections. Analyze test results in relation to design or rated specifications and test objectives; modify or adjust equipment to meet specifications.

GOE INFORMATION—Interest Area: 02. Science, Math, and Engineering. **Work Group:** 02.08. Engineering Technology. **Personality Type—** Realistic. Realistic occupations frequently involve work activities that include practical, hands-on problems and solutions. They often deal with plants, animals, and real-world materials like wood, tools, and machinery. Many of the occupations require working outside and do not involve a lot of paperwork or working closely with others. **Work Values—**Advancement; Achievement; Variety; Supervision, Human Relations; Social Status. **Skills—**Technology Design; Operation and Control; Operation Monitoring; Mathematics; Quality Control Analysis; Equipment Selection; Complex Problem Solving; Systems Analysis. **Abilities—***Cognitive:* Mathematical Reasoning; Oral Comprehension; Visualization; Written Expression; Problem Sensitivity. *Psychomotor:* Rate Control; Wrist-Finger Speed; Control Precision; Reaction Time; Manual Dexterity. *Physical:* Explosive Strength; Dynamic Flexibility; Dynamic Strength; Gross Body Coordination. *Sensory:* Sound Localization; Speech Clarity; Speech Recognition; Auditory Attention; Visual Color Discrimination. **General Work Activities—***Information Input:* Getting Information; Identifying Objects, Actions, and Events; Monitoring Processes, Materials, or Surroundings. *Mental Process:* Updating and Using Relevant Knowledge; Processing Information; Analyzing Data or Information. *Work Output:* Controlling Machines and Processes; Drafting and Specifying Technical Devices; Handling and Moving Objects. *Interacting with Others:* Communicating with Other Workers; Establishing and Maintaining Relationships; Interpreting Meaning of Information for Others. **Physical Work Conditions—**Hazardous Equipment; Hazardous Conditions; Common Protective or Safety Attire; Climbing Ladders, Scaffolds, Poles, etc.; Using Hands on Objects, Tools, or Controls. **Other Job Characteristics—**Importance of Being Exact or Accurate; Degree of Automation; Pace Determined by Speed of Equipment.

Experience—Job Zone 4. A minimum of two to four years of work-related skill, knowledge, or experience is needed. **Job Preparation:** SVP 7.0 to less than 8.0—two years to less than 10 years. **Knowledge—**Design; Engineering and Technology; Mechanical; Mathematics; Physics. **Instructional Programs—**Mechanical Engineering Related Technologies/Technicians, Other; Mechanical Engineering/Mechanical Technology/Technician.

Related DOT Jobs—017.261-010 Auto-Design Checker; 716.102-026 Mechanical-Engineering Technician; 716.103-030 Optomechanical Technician; 716.701-010 Die-Drawing Checker; 718.101-010 Heat-Transfer Technician; 726.701-010 Drawings Checker, Engineering; 726.701-014 Tool Design Checker.

17-3029.99 Engineering Technicians, Except Drafters, All Other

- Education/Training Required: Associate's degree
- Employed: No data available.
- Annual Earnings: No data available.
- Growth: 23.2%
- Annual Job Openings: 16,000

All engineering technicians, except drafters, not listed separately.

No task data available.

GOE INFORMATION—Interest Area: 02. Science, Math, and Engineering. **Work Group:** 02.08. Engineering Technology. **Note:** The Department of Labor has not collected some data for this job, so it has fewer details than the other descriptions.

Instructional Programs—Architectural Engineering Technology/Technician; Energy Management and Systems Technology/Technician; Engineering Technologies/Technicians, Other; Environmental Control Technologies/Technicians, Other; Hydraulics and Fluid Power Technology/Technician; Laser and Optical Technology/Technician; Metallurgical Technology/Technician; Mining and Petroleum Technologies/Technicians, Other; Mining Technology/Technician; Plastics Engineering Technology/Technician; Solar Energy Technology/Technician.

Related DOT Jobs—011.261-010 Metallurgical Technician; 011.261-014 Welding Technician; 011.261-018 Nondestructive Tester; 011.261-022 Laboratory Assistant, Metallurgical; 011.281-014 Spectroscopist; 011.361-010 Tester; 013.161-010 Agricultural-Engineering Technician; 019.261-022 Test Technician; 196.263-026 Controller, Remotely-Piloted Vehicle; 196.263-042 Test Pilot.

17-3031.00 Surveying and Mapping Technicians

- Education/Training Required: Moderate-term on-the-job training
- Employed: 55,489
- Annual Earnings: $28,210
- Growth: 25.3%
- Annual Job Openings: 7,000

Perform surveying and mapping duties, usually under the direction of a surveyor, cartographer, or photogrammetrist, to obtain data used for construction, mapmaking, boundary location, mining, or other purposes. May calculate mapmaking information and create maps from source data, such as surveying notes, aerial photography, satellite data, or other maps, to show topographical features, political boundaries, and other features. May verify accuracy and completeness of topographical maps.

No task data available.

GOE INFORMATION—Interest Area: 02. Science, Math, and Engineering. **Work Group:** 02.08. Engineering Technology. **Note:** The Department of Labor has not collected some data for this job, so it has fewer details than the other descriptions.

Instructional Programs—Cartography; Surveying Technology/Surveying.

Related DOT Jobs—018.167-010 Chief of Party; 018.167-014 Geodetic Computator; 018.167-030 Supervisor, Mapping; 018.167-034 Surveyor Assistant, Instruments; 018.260-580 Photogrammetric Technician; 018.261-018 Editor, Map; 018.261-022 Mosaicist; 018.281-010 Stereo-Plotter Operator; 029.167-010 Aerial-Photograph Interpreter.

17-3031.01 Surveying Technicians

- Education/Training Required: Long-term on-the-job training
- Employed: 55,489
- Annual Earnings: $28,210
- Growth: 25.3%
- Annual Job Openings: 7,000

Adjust and operate surveying instruments, such as the theodolite and electronic distance-measuring equipment, and compile notes, make sketches, and enter data into computers.

Adjust and operate surveying instruments such as prisms, theodolites, and electronic distance-measuring equipment. Compile information necessary to stake projects for construction, using engineering plans. Conduct surveys to ascertain the locations of natural features and human-made structures on the Earth's surface, underground, and underwater, using electronic distance-measuring equipment and other surveying instruments. Lay out grids and determine horizontal and vertical controls. Operate and manage land-information computer systems, performing tasks such as storing data, making inquiries, and producing plots and reports. Perform calculations to determine earth curvature corrections, atmospheric impacts on measurements, traverse closures and adjustments, azimuths, level runs, and placement of markers. Place and hold measuring tapes when electronic distance-measuring equipment is not used. Position and hold the vertical rods, or targets, that theodolite operators use for sighting in order to measure angles, distances, and elevations. Record survey measurements and descriptive data, using notes, drawings, sketches, and inked tracings. Run rods for benches and cross-section elevations. Search for section corners, property irons, and survey points. Set out and recover stakes, marks, and other monumentation. Collect information needed to carry out new surveys, using source maps, previous survey data, photographs, computer records, and other relevant information. Compare survey computations with applicable standards in order to determine adequacy of data. Direct and supervise work of subordinate members of surveying parties. Maintain equipment and vehicles used by surveying crews. Perform manual labor, such as cutting brush for lines; carrying stakes, rebar, and other heavy items; and stacking rods. Provide assistance in the development of methods and procedures for conducting field surveys. Prepare topographic and contour maps of land surveyed, including site features and other relevant information such as charts, drawings, and survey notes.

GOE INFORMATION—Interest Area: 02. Science, Math, and Engineering. **Work Group:** 02.08. Engineering Technology. **Personality Type—**Realistic. Realistic occupations frequently involve work activities that include practical, hands-on problems and solutions. They often deal with plants, animals, and real-world materials like wood, tools, and machinery. Many of the occupations require working outside and do not involve a lot of paperwork or working closely with others. **Work Values**—Authority; Moral Values; Advancement; Supervision, Technical; Company Policies and Practices. **Skills**—None met the criteria. **Abilities**—*Cognitive:* Spatial Orientation; Written Expression; Mathematical Reasoning. *Psychomotor:* None met the criteria. *Physical:* None met the criteria. *Sensory:* Far Vision. **General Work Activities**—*Information Input:* Getting Information; Identifying Objects, Actions, and Events; Monitoring Processes,

Materials, or Surroundings. *Mental Process:* Processing Information; Updating and Using Relevant Knowledge; Analyzing Data or Information. *Work Output:* Controlling Machines and Processes; Documenting or Recording Information; Performing General Physical Activities. *Interacting with Others:* Communicating with Other Workers; Guiding, Directing, and Motivating Subordinates; Coordinating the Work and Activities of Others. **Physical Work Conditions**—Outdoors; Very Hot or Cold; Extremely Bright or Inadequate Lighting; Standing; Kneeling, Crouching, or Crawling. **Other Job Characteristics**—Importance of Being Exact or Accurate; Consequence of Error; Pace Determined by Speed of Equipment.

Experience—Job Zone 4. A minimum of two to four years of work-related skill, knowledge, or experience is needed. **Job Preparation:** SVP 7.0 to less than 8.0—two years to less than 10 years. **Knowledge**—Design; Geography; Engineering and Technology; Mathematics; Computers and Electronics. **Instructional Programs**—Cartography; Surveying Technology/Surveying.

Related DOT Jobs—018.167-010 Chief of Party; 018.167-034 Surveyor Assistant, Instruments.

17-3031.02 Mapping Technicians

- **Education/Training Required: Moderate-term on-the-job training**
- **Employed: No data available.**
- **Annual Earnings: $28,210**
- **Growth: 25.3%**
- **Annual Job Openings: 7,000**

Calculate mapmaking information from field notes; draw and verify accuracy of topographical maps.

Analyze aerial photographs in order to detect and interpret significant military, industrial, resource, or topographical data. Calculate latitudes, longitudes, angles, areas, and other information for mapmaking, using survey field notes and reference tables. Check all layers of maps in order to ensure accuracy, identifying and marking errors and making corrections. Compare topographical features and contour lines with images from aerial photographs, old maps, and other reference materials in order to verify the accuracy of their identification. Compute and measure scaled distances between reference points in order to establish relative positions of adjoining prints and enable the creation of photographic mosaics. Form three-dimensional images of aerial photographs taken from different locations, using mathematical techniques and plotting instruments. Lay out and match aerial photographs in sequences in which they were taken and identify any areas missing from photographs. Monitor mapping work and the updating of maps in order to ensure accuracy, the inclusion of new and/or changed information, and compliance with rules and regulations. Produce and update overlay maps in order to show information boundaries, water locations, and topographic features on various base maps and at different scales. Redraw and correct maps, such as revising parcel maps to reflect tax code area changes, using information from official records and surveys. Trace contours and topographic details in order to generate maps that denote specific land and property locations and geographic attributes. Trim, align, and join prints in order to form photographic mosaics, maintaining scaled distances between reference points. Complete detailed source and method notes detailing the location of routine and complex

land parcels. Create survey description pages and historical records related to the mapping activities and specifications of section plats. Determine scales, line sizes, and colors to be used for hard copies of computerized maps, using plotters. Enter GPS data, legal deeds, field notes, and land survey reports into GIS workstations so that information can be transformed into graphic land descriptions, such as maps and drawings. Identify and compile database information in order to create maps in response to requests. Identify, research, and resolve anomalies in legal land descriptions, referring issues to title and survey experts as appropriate. Research and combine existing property information in order to describe property boundaries in relation to adjacent properties, taking into account parcel splits, combinations, and land boundary adjustments. Research resources such as survey maps and legal descriptions in order to verify property lines and to obtain information needed for mapping. Supervise and coordinate activities of workers engaged in plotting data and drafting maps or in producing blueprints, photostats, and photographs. Answer questions and provide information to the public and to staff members regarding assessment maps, surveys, boundaries, easements, property ownership, roads, zoning, and similar matters. Produce representations of surface and mineral ownership layers by interpreting legal survey plans. Train staff members in duties such as tax mapping, the use of computerized mapping equipment, and the interpretation of source documents.

GOE INFORMATION—**Interest Area:** 02. Science, Math, and Engineering. **Work Group:** 02.08. Engineering Technology. **Personality Type**—Conventional. Conventional occupations frequently involve following set procedures and routines. These occupations can include working with data and details more than with ideas. Usually there is a clear line of authority to follow. **Work Values**—Authority; Moral Values; Autonomy; Achievement; Activity. **Skills**—Mathematics; Technology Design; Management of Personnel Resources. **Abilities**—*Cognitive:* Spatial Orientation; Mathematical Reasoning; Flexibility of Closure; Number Facility; Speed of Closure. *Psychomotor:* Wrist-Finger Speed; Arm-Hand Steadiness; Finger Dexterity; Speed of Limb Movement. *Physical:* None met the criteria. *Sensory:* Near Vision; Visual Color Discrimination; Far Vision; Depth Perception; Glare Sensitivity. **General Work Activities**—*Information Input:* Getting Information; Identifying Objects, Actions, and Events; Inspecting Equipment, Structures, or Materials. *Mental Process:* Processing Information; Updating and Using Relevant Knowledge; Analyzing Data or Information. *Work Output:* Drafting and Specifying Technical Devices; Interacting with Computers; Documenting or Recording Information. *Interacting with Others:* Communicating with Other Workers; Coordinating the Work and Activities of Others; Guiding, Directing, and Motivating Subordinates. **Physical Work Conditions**—Sitting; Using Hands on Objects, Tools, or Controls; Indoors; Making Repetitive Motions; Radiation. **Other Job Characteristics**—Importance of Being Exact or Accurate; Importance of Repeating Same Tasks; Consequence of Error.

Experience—Job Zone 3. Previous work-related skill, knowledge, or experience is required. **Job Preparation:** SVP 6.0 to less than 7.0—more than one year and less than four years. **Knowledge**—Geography; Design; Computers and Electronics; Mathematics; Administration and Management. **Instructional Programs**—Cartography; Surveying Technology/Surveying.

Related DOT Jobs—018.167-014 Geodetic Computator; 018.167-030 Supervisor, Mapping; 018.261-018 Editor, Map; 018.261-022 Mosaicist; 018.281-010 Stereo-Plotter Operator; 029.167-010 Aerial-Photograph Interpreter.

19-0000
Life, Physical, and Social Science Occupations

19-1000 Life Scientists

19-1011.00 Animal Scientists

- Education/Training Required: Bachelor's degree
- Employed: No data available.
- Annual Earnings: $48,400
- Growth: 8.8%
- Annual Job Openings: 1,000

Conduct research in the genetics, nutrition, reproduction, growth, and development of domestic farm animals.

Studies nutritional requirements of animals and nutritive value of feed materials for animals and poultry. Studies effects of management practices, processing methods, feed, and environmental conditions on quality and quantity of animal products, such as eggs and milk. Researches and controls selection and breeding practices to increase efficiency of production and improve quality of animals. Develops improved practices in incubation, brooding, and artificial insemination. Develops improved practices in feeding, housing, sanitation, and parasite and disease control of animals and poultry. Determines generic composition of animal population and heritability of traits, utilizing principles of genetics. Crossbreeds animals with existing strains or crosses strains to obtain new combinations of desirable characteristics.

GOE INFORMATION—Interest Area: 02. Science, Math, and Engineering. **Work Group:** 02.03. Life Sciences. **Personality Type—**Investigative. Investigative occupations frequently involve working with ideas and require an extensive amount of thinking. These occupations can involve searching for facts and figuring out problems mentally. **Work Values—**Autonomy; Creativity; Independence; Responsibility; Ability Utilization. **Skills—**Science; Operations Analysis; Complex Problem Solving; Quality Control Analysis; Critical Thinking; Equipment Selection; Reading Comprehension; Mathematics. **Abilities—***Cognitive:* Written Expression; Inductive Reasoning; Deductive Reasoning; Oral Comprehension; Written Comprehension. *Psychomotor:* None met the criteria. *Physical:* None met the criteria. *Sensory:* Speech Clarity; Near Vision; Speech Recognition. **General Work Activities—***Information Input:* Getting Information; Identifying Objects, Actions, and Events; Monitoring Processes, Materials, or Surroundings. *Mental Process:* Analyzing Data or Information; Processing Information; Making Decisions and Solving Problems. *Work Output:* Documenting or Recording Information; Controlling Machines and Processes; Interacting with Computers. *Interacting with Others:* Interpreting Meaning of Information for Others; Providing Consultation and Advice to Others; Communicating with Other Workers. **Physical Work Conditions—**Disease or Infections; Minor Burns, Cuts, Bites, or Stings; Specialized Protective or Safety Attire; Sitting; Kneeling, Crouching, or Crawling. **Other Job Characteristics—**Importance of Being Exact or Accurate; Consequence of Error; Pace Determined by Speed of Equipment.

Experience—Job Zone 5. Extensive skill, knowledge, and experience are needed for these occupations. **Job Preparation:** SVP 8.0 and above—four years to more than 10 years. **Knowledge—**Biology; Food Production; Medicine and Dentistry; Chemistry; History and Archeology. **Instructional Programs—**Agricultural Animal Breeding; Agriculture, General; Animal Health; Animal Nutrition; Animal Sciences, General; Animal Sciences, Other; Dairy Science; Poultry Science; Range Science and Management.

Related DOT Jobs—040.061-014 Animal Scientist; 040.061-018 Dairy Scientist; 040.061-042 Poultry Scientist; 041.061-014 Animal Breeder.

19-1012.00 Food Scientists and Technologists

- Education/Training Required: Bachelor's degree
- Employed: No data available.
- Annual Earnings: $48,400
- Growth: 8.8%
- Annual Job Openings: 1,000

Use chemistry, microbiology, engineering, and other sciences to study the principles underlying the processing and deterioration of foods; analyze food content to determine levels of vitamins, fat, sugar, and protein; discover new food sources; research ways to make processed foods safe, palatable, and healthful; and apply food science knowledge to determine best ways to process, package, preserve, store, and distribute food.

Check raw ingredients for maturity or stability for processing and finished products for safety, quality, and nutritional value. Develop food standards and production specifications, safety and sanitary regulations, and waste management and water supply specifications. Develop new or improved ways of preserving, processing, packaging, storing, and delivering foods, using knowledge of chemistry, microbiology, and other sciences. Search for substitutes for harmful or undesirable additives, such as nitrites. Study methods to improve aspects of foods such as chemical composition, flavor, color, texture, nutritional value, and convenience. Study the structure and composition of food or the changes foods undergo in storage and processing. Test new products for flavor, texture, color, nutritional content, and adherence to government and industry standards. Confer with process engineers, plant operators, flavor experts, and packaging and marketing specialists in order to resolve problems in product development. Evaluate food processing and storage operations and assist in the development of quality assurance programs for such operations. Inspect food processing areas in order to ensure compliance with government regulations and standards for sanitation, safety, quality, and waste management standards. Demonstrate products to clients.

GOE INFORMATION—Interest Area: 02. Science, Math, and Engineering. **Work Group:** 02.03. Life Sciences. **Personality Type—**Investigative. Investigative occupations frequently involve working with ideas and require an extensive amount of thinking. These occupations can involve searching for facts and figuring out problems mentally. **Work Values—**Creativity; Autonomy; Responsibility; Security; Ability Utilization. **Skills—**Science; Equipment Selection; Complex Problem Solving; Quality Control Analysis; Mathematics; Critical Thinking; Reading Comprehension; Systems Analysis. **Abilities—***Cognitive:* Written Comprehension; Fluency of Ideas; Inductive Reasoning; Deductive Reasoning; Originality. *Psychomotor:* None met the criteria. *Physical:* None met the criteria. *Sensory:* Speech Clarity. **General Work Activities—***Information Input:* Getting Information; Identifying Objects, Actions, and Events; Inspecting Equipment, Structures, or Materials. *Mental Process:* Analyzing Data or Information; Making Decisions and Solving Problems; Processing Information. *Work Output:* Documenting or Recording Information; Handling and Moving Objects; Controlling Machines and Processes. *Interacting with Others:* Interpreting Meaning of Information for Others; Communicating with Other Workers; Providing Consultation and Advice to Others. **Physical Work Conditions—**Indoors; Sitting; Minor Burns, Cuts, Bites, or Stings. **Other Job Characteristics—**Pace Determined by Speed of Equipment; Consequence of Error; Importance of Being Exact or Accurate.

Experience—Job Zone 4. A minimum of two to four years of work-related skill, knowledge, or experience is needed. **Job Preparation:** SVP

7.0 to less than 8.0—two years to less than 10 years. **Knowledge**—Food Production; Production and Processing; Biology; Chemistry; Law and Government. **Instructional Programs**—Agriculture, General; Food Science; Food Technology and Processing; International Agriculture.

Related DOT Jobs—041.081-010 Food Technologist.

19-1013.00 Soil and Plant Scientists

- Education/Training Required: Bachelor's degree
- Employed: No data available.
- Annual Earnings: $48,400
- Growth: 8.8%
- Annual Job Openings: 1,000

Conduct research in breeding, physiology, production, yield, and management of crops and agricultural plants, their growth in soils, and control of pests or study the chemical, physical, biological, and mineralogical composition of soils as they relate to plant or crop growth. May classify and map soils and investigate effects of alternative practices on soil and crop productivity.

No task data available.

GOE INFORMATION—Interest Area: 02. Science, Math, and Engineering. **Work Group:** 02.03. Life Sciences. **Note:** The Department of Labor has not collected some data for this job, so it has fewer details than the other descriptions.

Instructional Programs—Agricultural and Horticultural Plant Breeding; Agriculture, General; Agronomy and Crop Science; Horticultural Science; Plant Protection and Integrated Pest Management; Plant Sciences, General; Plant Sciences, Other; Range Science and Management; Soil Chemistry and Physics; Soil Microbiology; Soil Science and Agronomy, General.

Related DOT Jobs—040.061-010 Agronomist; 040.061-038 Horticulturist; 040.061-058 Soil Scientist; 041.061-018 Apiculturist; 041.061-038 Botanist; 041.061-046 Entomologist; 041.061-082 Plant Breeder; 041.061-086 Plant Pathologist.

19-1013.01 Plant Scientists

- Education/Training Required: Bachelor's degree
- Employed: No data available.
- Annual Earnings: $48,400
- Growth: 8.8%
- Annual Job Openings: 1,000

Conduct research in breeding, production, and yield of plants or crops and control of pests.

Conducts research to determine best methods of planting, spraying, cultivating, and harvesting horticultural products. Experiments to develop new or improved varieties of products having specific features, such as higher yield, resistance to disease, size, or maturity. Studies crop production to discover effects of various climatic and soil conditions on crops. Develops methods for control of noxious weeds, crop diseases, and insect pests. Conducts experiments and investigations to determine methods of storing, processing, and transporting horticultural products. Studies insect distribution and habitat and recommends methods to prevent importation and spread of injurious species. Aids in control and elimination of agricultural, structural, and forest pests by developing new and improved pesticides. Conducts experiments regarding causes of bee diseases and factors affecting yields of nectar pollen on various plants visited by bees. Identifies and classifies species of insects and allied forms, such as mites and spiders. Improves bee strains, utilizing selective breeding by artificial insemination.

GOE INFORMATION—Interest Area: 02. Science, Math, and Engineering. **Work Group:** 02.03. Life Sciences. **Personality Type**—Investigative. Investigative occupations frequently involve working with ideas and require an extensive amount of thinking. These occupations can involve searching for facts and figuring out problems mentally. **Work Values**—Autonomy; Creativity; Independence; Responsibility; Ability Utilization. **Skills**—Science; Writing; Critical Thinking; Complex Problem Solving; Quality Control Analysis; Reading Comprehension; Operations Analysis; Mathematics. **Abilities**—*Cognitive:* Inductive Reasoning; Category Flexibility; Deductive Reasoning; Written Comprehension; Oral Comprehension. *Psychomotor:* None met the criteria. *Physical:* None met the criteria. *Sensory:* Visual Color Discrimination; Speech Clarity; Far Vision; Speech Recognition. **General Work Activities**—*Information Input:* Getting Information; Identifying Objects, Actions, and Events; Monitoring Processes, Materials, or Surroundings. *Mental Process:* Analyzing Data or Information; Processing Information; Updating and Using Relevant Knowledge. *Work Output:* Documenting or Recording Information; Interacting with Computers; Handling and Moving Objects. *Interacting with Others:* Providing Consultation and Advice to Others; Interpreting Meaning of Information for Others; Communicating with Persons Outside Organization. **Physical Work Conditions**—Outdoors; Minor Burns, Cuts, Bites, or Stings; Specialized Protective or Safety Attire; Very Hot or Cold; Kneeling, Crouching, or Crawling. **Other Job Characteristics**—Importance of Being Exact or Accurate; Consequence of Error; Importance of Repeating Same Tasks.

Experience—Job Zone 5. Extensive skill, knowledge, and experience are needed for these occupations. **Job Preparation:** SVP 8.0 and above—four years to more than 10 years. **Knowledge**—Food Production; Biology; Chemistry; English Language; Education and Training. **Instructional Programs**—Agricultural and Horticultural Plant Breeding; Agriculture, General; Agronomy and Crop Science; Horticultural Science; Plant Protection and Integrated Pest Management; Plant Sciences, General; Plant Sciences, Other; Range Science and Management; Soil Chemistry and Physics; Soil Microbiology; Soil Science and Agronomy, General.

Related DOT Jobs—040.061-010 Agronomist; 040.061-038 Horticulturist; 041.061-018 Apiculturist; 041.061-046 Entomologist; 041.061-082 Plant Breeder.

19-1013.02 Soil Scientists

- Education/Training Required: Bachelor's degree
- Employed: No data available.
- Annual Earnings: $48,400
- Growth: 8.8%
- Annual Job Openings: 1,000

Research or study soil characteristics, map soil types, and investigate responses of soils to known management practices to determine use capabilities of soils and effects of alternative practices on soil productivity.

Studies soil characteristics and classifies soils according to standard types. Investigates responses of specific soil types to soil management practices, such as fertilization, crop rotation, and industrial waste control. Conducts experiments on farms or experimental stations to determine best soil types for different plants. Performs chemical analysis on microorganism content of soil to determine microbial reactions and chemical mineralogical relationship to plant growth. Provides advice on rural or urban land use.

GOE INFORMATION—Interest Area: 02. Science, Math, and Engineering. **Work Group:** 02.03. Life Sciences. **Personality Type—**Investigative. Investigative occupations frequently involve working with ideas and require an extensive amount of thinking. These occupations can involve searching for facts and figuring out problems mentally. **Work Values—**Creativity; Autonomy; Independence; Ability Utilization; Responsibility. **Skills—**Science; Reading Comprehension; Writing; Operations Analysis; Critical Thinking; Complex Problem Solving; Mathematics; Quality Control Analysis. **Abilities—***Cognitive:* Inductive Reasoning; Category Flexibility; Mathematical Reasoning; Deductive Reasoning; Originality. *Psychomotor:* None met the criteria. *Physical:* None met the criteria. *Sensory:* Speech Clarity; Speech Recognition. **General Work Activities—***Information Input:* Identifying Objects, Actions, and Events; Getting Information; Monitoring Processes, Materials, or Surroundings. *Mental Process:* Analyzing Data or Information; Making Decisions and Solving Problems; Processing Information. *Work Output:* Documenting or Recording Information; Interacting with Computers; Handling and Moving Objects. *Interacting with Others:* Providing Consultation and Advice to Others; Interpreting Meaning of Information for Others; Communicating with Persons Outside Organization. **Physical Work Conditions—**Outdoors; Minor Burns, Cuts, Bites, or Stings; Very Hot or Cold; Kneeling, Crouching, or Crawling; Hazardous Conditions. **Other Job Characteristics—**Importance of Being Exact or Accurate; Pace Determined by Speed of Equipment; Importance of Repeating Same Tasks.

Experience—Job Zone 5. Extensive skill, knowledge, and experience are needed for these occupations. **Job Preparation:** SVP 8.0 and above—four years to more than 10 years. **Knowledge—**Food Production; Chemistry; Biology; Geography; Mathematics. **Instructional Programs—**Agricultural and Horticultural Plant Breeding; Agriculture, General; Agronomy and Crop Science; Horticultural Science; Plant Protection and Integrated Pest Management; Plant Sciences, General; Plant Sciences, Other; Range Science and Management; Soil Chemistry and Physics; Soil Microbiology; Soil Science and Agronomy, General.

Related DOT Jobs—040.061-058 Soil Scientist.

19-1020.01 Biologists

- **Education/Training Required: Doctoral degree**
- **Employed: 73,101**
- **Annual Earnings: $44,770**
- **Growth: 21.0%**
- **Annual Job Openings: 5,000**

Research or study basic principles of plant and animal life, such as origin, relationship, development, anatomy, and functions.

Develop and maintain liaisons and effective working relations with groups and individuals, agencies, and the public to encourage cooperative management strategies or to develop information and interpret findings. Program and use computers to store, process, and analyze data. Collect and analyze biological data about relationships among and between organisms and their environment. Study aquatic plants and animals and environmental conditions affecting them, such as radioactivity or pollution. Communicate test results to state and federal representatives and general public. Identify, classify, and study structure, behavior, ecology, physiology, nutrition, culture, and distribution of plant and animal species. Prepare environmental impact reports for industry, government, or publication. Represent employer in a technical capacity at conferences. Plan and administer biological research programs for government, research firms, medical industries, or manufacturing firms. Research environmental effects of present and potential uses of land and water areas, determining methods of improving environmental conditions

or such outputs as crop yields. Review reports such as those relating to land use classifications and recreational development for accuracy and adequacy. Measure salinity, acidity, light, oxygen content, and other physical conditions of water to determine their relationship to aquatic life. Teach, supervise students, and perform research at universities and colleges. Supervise biological technicians and technologists and other scientists. Study basic principles of plant and animal life, such as origin, relationship, development, anatomy, and functions. Study and manage wild animal populations. Prepare requests for proposals or statements of work. Cultivate, breed, and grow aquatic life, such as lobsters, clams, or fish. Prepare plans for management of renewable resources. Develop methods and apparatus for securing representative plant, animal, aquatic, or soil samples. Study reactions of plants, animals, and marine species to parasites. Develop pest management and control measures and conduct risk assessments related to pest exclusion, using scientific methods.

GOE INFORMATION—Interest Area: 02. Science, Math, and Engineering. **Work Group:** 02.03. Life Sciences. **Personality Type—**Investigative. Investigative occupations frequently involve working with ideas and require an extensive amount of thinking. These occupations can involve searching for facts and figuring out problems mentally. **Work Values—**Creativity; Autonomy; Ability Utilization; Recognition; Independence. **Skills—**Judgment and Decision Making; Negotiation; Management of Financial Resources; Persuasion; Science; Critical Thinking; Equipment Selection; Management of Material Resources. **Abilities—***Cognitive:* Inductive Reasoning; Category Flexibility; Oral Expression; Written Expression; Flexibility of Closure. *Psychomotor:* Finger Dexterity. *Physical:* None met the criteria. *Sensory:* Speech Clarity; Speech Recognition; Near Vision; Visual Color Discrimination; Auditory Attention. **General Work Activities—***Information Input:* Identifying Objects, Actions, and Events; Monitoring Processes, Materials, or Surroundings; Getting Information. *Mental Process:* Processing Information; Updating and Using Relevant Knowledge; Organizing, Planning, and Prioritizing. *Work Output:* Documenting or Recording Information; Interacting with Computers; Handling and Moving Objects. *Interacting with Others:* Establishing and Maintaining Relationships; Communicating with Other Workers; Communicating with Persons Outside Organization. **Physical Work Conditions—**Common Protective or Safety Attire; Disease or Infections; Contaminants; Outdoors; Specialized Protective or Safety Attire. **Other Job Characteristics—**Importance of Being Exact or Accurate; Consequence of Error; Importance of Repeating Same Tasks.

Experience—Job Zone 5. Extensive skill, knowledge, and experience are needed for these occupations. **Job Preparation:** SVP 8.0 and above—four years to more than 10 years. **Knowledge—**Biology; Law and Government; Chemistry; Geography; Computers and Electronics. **Instructional Programs—**Biochemistry; Biochemistry/Biophysics and Molecular Biology; Biology/Biological Sciences, General; Biophysics; Cell/Cellular Biology and Anatomical Sciences, Other; Molecular Biochemistry; Soil Microbiology.

Related DOT Jobs—041.061-022 Aquatic Biologist; 041.061-030 Biologist; 041.061-066 Nematologist.

19-1021.00 Biochemists and Biophysicists

- **Education/Training Required: Doctoral degree**
- **Employed: No data available.**
- **Annual Earnings: $57,100**
- **Growth: 21.0%**
- **Annual Job Openings: 5,000**

Study the chemical composition and physical principles of living cells and organisms, their electrical and mechanical energy, and related phenomena. May conduct research to further understanding of the complex chemical combinations and reactions involved in metabolism, reproduction, growth, and heredity. May determine the effects of foods, drugs, serums, hormones, and other substances on tissues and vital processes of living organisms.

No task data available.

GOE INFORMATION—Interest Area: 02. Science, Math, and Engineering. **Work Group:** 02.03. Life Sciences. **Note:** The Department of Labor has not collected some data for this job, so it has fewer details than the other descriptions.

Instructional Programs—Biochemistry; Biochemistry/Biophysics and Molecular Biology; Biophysics; Cell/Cellular Biology and Anatomical Sciences, Other; Molecular Biochemistry; Molecular Biophysics; Soil Chemistry and Physics; Soil Microbiology.

Related DOT Jobs—022.081-010 Toxicologist; 041.061-026 Biochemist; 041.061-034 Biophysicist; 041.061-094 Staff Toxicologist.

19-1021.01 Biochemists

- **Education/Training Required: Doctoral degree**
- **Employed: No data available.**
- **Annual Earnings: $57,100**
- **Growth: 21.0%**
- **Annual Job Openings: 5,000**

Research or study chemical composition and processes of living organisms that affect vital processes such as growth and aging to determine chemical actions and effects on organisms such as the action of foods, drugs, or other substances on body functions and tissues.

Studies chemistry of living processes, such as cell development, breathing, and digestion, and living energy changes, such as growth, aging, and death. Researches methods of transferring characteristics, such as resistance to disease, from one organism to another. Researches and determines chemical action of substances such as drugs, serums, hormones, and food on tissues and vital processes. Examines chemical aspects of formation of antibodies and researches chemistry of cells and blood corpuscles. Isolates, analyzes, and identifies hormones, vitamins, allergens, minerals, and enzymes and determines their effects on body functions. Develops and executes tests to detect disease, genetic disorders, or other abnormalities. Develops methods to process, store, and use food, drugs, and chemical compounds. Develops and tests new drugs and medications used for commercial distribution. Prepares reports and recommendations based upon research outcomes. Design and build laboratory equipment needed for special research projects. Cleans, purifies, refines, and otherwise prepares pharmaceutical compounds for commercial distribution. Analyzes foods to determine nutritional value and effects of cooking, canning, and processing on this value.

GOE INFORMATION—Interest Area: 02. Science, Math, and Engineering. **Work Group:** 02.03. Life Sciences. **Personality Type**—Investigative. Investigative occupations frequently involve working with ideas and require an extensive amount of thinking. These occupations can involve searching for facts and figuring out problems mentally. **Work Values**—Creativity; Ability Utilization; Autonomy; Responsibility; Independence. **Skills**—Science; Equipment Selection; Reading Comprehension; Writing; Complex Problem Solving; Programming; Mathematics; Critical Thinking. **Abilities**—*Cognitive:* Inductive Reasoning; Written

Expression; Written Comprehension; Deductive Reasoning; Category Flexibility. *Psychomotor:* Finger Dexterity; Arm-Hand Steadiness. *Physical:* Trunk Strength. *Sensory:* Near Vision; Glare Sensitivity. **General Work Activities**—*Information Input:* Identifying Objects, Actions, and Events; Getting Information; Monitoring Processes, Materials, or Surroundings. *Mental Process:* Analyzing Data or Information; Processing Information; Updating and Using Relevant Knowledge. *Work Output:* Documenting or Recording Information; Controlling Machines and Processes; Interacting with Computers. *Interacting with Others:* Interpreting Meaning of Information for Others; Providing Consultation and Advice to Others; Communicating with Other Workers. **Physical Work Conditions**—Disease or Infections; Contaminants; Common Protective or Safety Attire; Indoors; Using Hands on Objects, Tools, or Controls. **Other Job Characteristics**—Importance of Being Exact or Accurate; Consequence of Error; Importance of Repeating Same Tasks.

Experience—Job Zone 5. Extensive skill, knowledge, and experience are needed for these occupations. **Job Preparation:** SVP 8.0 and above—four years to more than 10 years. **Knowledge**—Biology; Chemistry; Building and Construction; Mathematics; English Language. **Instructional Programs**—Biochemistry; Biochemistry/Biophysics and Molecular Biology; Biophysics; Cell/Cellular Biology and Anatomical Sciences, Other; Molecular Biochemistry; Molecular Biophysics; Soil Chemistry and Physics; Soil Microbiology.

Related DOT Jobs—041.061-026 Biochemist.

19-1021.02 Biophysicists

- **Education/Training Required: Doctoral degree**
- **Employed: No data available.**
- **Annual Earnings: $57,100**
- **Growth: 21.0%**
- **Annual Job Openings: 5,000**

Research or study physical principles of living cells and organisms, their electrical and mechanical energy, and related phenomena.

Studies physical principles of living cells and organisms and their electrical and mechanical energy. Researches manner in which characteristics of plants and animals are carried through successive generations. Researches transformation of substances in cells, using atomic isotopes. Investigates damage to cells and tissues caused by X rays and nuclear particles. Studies spatial configuration of submicroscopic molecules, such as proteins, using X-ray and electron microscope. Investigates transmission of electrical impulses along nerves and muscles. Investigates dynamics of seeing and hearing. Analyzes functions of electronic and human brains, such as learning, thinking, and memory. Researches cancer treatment, using radiation and nuclear particles. Studies absorption of light by chlorophyll in photosynthesis or by pigments of eye involved in vision.

GOE INFORMATION—Interest Area: 02. Science, Math, and Engineering. **Work Group:** 02.03. Life Sciences. **Personality Type**—Investigative. Investigative occupations frequently involve working with ideas and require an extensive amount of thinking. These occupations can involve searching for facts and figuring out problems mentally. **Work Values**—Autonomy; Ability Utilization; Responsibility; Creativity; Independence. **Skills**—Science; Reading Comprehension; Mathematics; Writing; Complex Problem Solving; Critical Thinking; Equipment Selection; Programming. **Abilities**—*Cognitive:* Inductive Reasoning; Category Flexibility; Written Expression; Written Comprehension; Oral Comprehension. *Psychomotor:* Arm-Hand Steadiness; Response Orientation; Finger Dexterity; Control Precision. *Physical:* Trunk Strength. *Sensory:* Near Vision; Night Vision; Visual Color Discrimination; Sound Localization; Glare Sensitivity. **General Work Activities**—*Information*

Input: Identifying Objects, Actions, and Events; Getting Information; Monitoring Processes, Materials, or Surroundings. *Mental Process:* Analyzing Data or Information; Updating and Using Relevant Knowledge; Processing Information. *Work Output:* Documenting or Recording Information; Interacting with Computers; Controlling Machines and Processes. *Interacting with Others:* Interpreting Meaning of Information for Others; Providing Consultation and Advice to Others; Communicating with Other Workers. **Physical Work Conditions**—Radiation; Common Protective or Safety Attire; Indoors; Disease or Infections; Contaminants. **Other Job Characteristics**—Importance of Being Exact or Accurate; Consequence of Error; Importance of Repeating Same Tasks.

Experience—Job Zone 5. Extensive skill, knowledge, and experience are needed for these occupations. **Job Preparation:** SVP 8.0 and above—four years to more than 10 years. **Knowledge**—Biology; Physics; Chemistry; Mathematics; Medicine and Dentistry. **Instructional Programs**—Biochemistry; Biochemistry/Biophysics and Molecular Biology; Biophysics; Cell/Cellular Biology and Anatomical Sciences, Other; Molecular Biochemistry; Molecular Biophysics; Soil Chemistry and Physics; Soil Microbiology.

Related DOT Jobs—041.061-034 Biophysicist.

19-1022.00 Microbiologists

- Education/Training Required: Doctoral degree
- Employed: No data available.
- Annual Earnings: $49,880
- Growth: 21.0%
- Annual Job Openings: 5,000

Investigate the growth, structure, development, and other characteristics of microscopic organisms, such as bacteria, algae, or fungi. Includes medical microbiologists who study the relationship between organisms and disease or the effects of antibiotics on microorganisms.

Conduct chemical analyses of substances, such as acids, alcohols, and enzymes. Examine physiological, morphological, and cultural characteristics, using microscope, to identify and classify microorganisms in human, water, and food specimens. Investigate the relationship between organisms and disease, including the control of epidemics and the effects of antibiotics on microorganisms. Isolate and make cultures of bacteria or other microorganisms in prescribed media, controlling moisture, aeration, temperature, and nutrition. Observe action of microorganisms upon living tissues of plants, higher animals, and other microorganisms, and on dead organic matter. Perform tests on water, food, and the environment to detect harmful microorganisms and to obtain information about sources of pollution and contamination. Prepare technical reports and recommendations based upon research outcomes. Research use of bacteria and microorganisms to develop vitamins, antibiotics, amino acids, grain alcohol, sugars, and polymers. Study growth, structure, development, and general characteristics of bacteria and other microorganisms to understand their relationship to human, plant, and animal health. Study the structure and function of human, animal, and plant tissues, cells, pathogens, and toxins. Conduct research to address agricultural issues such as increasing crop yield, combating crop damage, and determining the effects of microorganisms on soil and agricultural products and insect control. Isolate and tend microorganisms that break down pollutants or produce alternate sources of energy. Provide laboratory services for health departments, for community environmental health programs, and for physicians needing information for diagnosis and treatment. Supervise biological technologists and technicians and other scientists. Use biotechnology in such applications as the production

of specialty biologicals, for gene transfer, or to advance knowledge of cell reproduction and human disease. Develop new products and new methods of food and pharmaceutical supply preservation. Use a variety of specialized equipment such as electron microscopes, gas chromatographs and high-pressure liquid chromatographs, electrophoresis units, thermocyclers, fluorescence-activated cell sorters, and phosphoimagers.

GOE INFORMATION—Interest Area: 02. Science, Math, and Engineering. **Work Group:** 02.03. Life Sciences. **Personality Type**—Investigative. Investigative occupations frequently involve working with ideas and require an extensive amount of thinking. These occupations can involve searching for facts and figuring out problems mentally. **Work Values**—Creativity; Autonomy; Ability Utilization; Social Status; Independence. **Skills**—Science; Writing; Reading Comprehension; Equipment Selection; Complex Problem Solving; Mathematics; Operation and Control; Critical Thinking. **Abilities**—*Cognitive:* Inductive Reasoning; Category Flexibility; Speed of Closure; Written Expression; Oral Comprehension. *Psychomotor:* Reaction Time; Arm-Hand Steadiness; Finger Dexterity; Speed of Limb Movement; Control Precision. *Physical:* Extent Flexibility; Gross Body Coordination; Dynamic Flexibility. *Sensory:* Near Vision; Visual Color Discrimination; Speech Clarity; Glare Sensitivity; Night Vision. **General Work Activities**—*Information Input:* Identifying Objects, Actions, and Events; Getting Information; Monitoring Processes, Materials, or Surroundings. *Mental Process:* Analyzing Data or Information; Updating and Using Relevant Knowledge; Processing Information. *Work Output:* Documenting or Recording Information; Controlling Machines and Processes; Interacting with Computers. *Interacting with Others:* Communicating with Other Workers; Interpreting Meaning of Information for Others; Providing Consultation and Advice to Others. **Physical Work Conditions**—Disease or Infections; Common Protective or Safety Attire; Indoors; Hazardous Conditions; Specialized Protective or Safety Attire. **Other Job Characteristics**—Importance of Being Exact or Accurate; Consequence of Error; Pace Determined by Speed of Equipment.

Experience—Job Zone 5. Extensive skill, knowledge, and experience are needed for these occupations. **Job Preparation:** SVP 8.0 and above—four years to more than 10 years. **Knowledge**—Biology; Chemistry; Mathematics; English Language; Administration and Management. **Instructional Programs**—Biochemistry/Biophysics and Molecular Biology; Cell/Cellular Biology and Anatomical Sciences, Other; Microbiology, General; Neuroanatomy; Soil Microbiology; Structural Biology.

Related DOT Jobs—041.061-058 Microbiologist.

19-1023.00 Zoologists and Wildlife Biologists

- Education/Training Required: Doctoral degree
- Employed: No data available.
- Annual Earnings: $46,220
- Growth: 21.0%
- Annual Job Openings: 5,000

Study the origins, behavior, diseases, genetics, and life processes of animals and wildlife. May specialize in wildlife research and management, including the collection and analysis of biological data to determine the environmental effects of present and potential use of land and water areas.

Analyze characteristics of animals to identify and classify them. Collect and dissect animal specimens and examine specimens under microscope. Inventory or estimate plant and wildlife populations. Organize and conduct experimental studies with live animals in controlled or natural surroundings. Prepare collections of preserved specimens or microscopic slides for species identification and study of development or disease. Study animals in their natural habitats, assessing effects of environment and industry on animals, interpreting findings, and recommending alternative operating conditions for industry. Study characteristics of animals, such as origin, interrelationships, classification, life histories and diseases, development, genetics, and distribution. Disseminate information by writing reports and scientific papers or journal articles and by making presentations and giving talks for schools, clubs, interest groups, and park interpretive programs. Make recommendations on management systems and planning for wildlife populations and habitat, consulting with stakeholders and the public at large to explore options. Raise specimens for study and observation or for use in experiments. Coordinate preventive programs to control the outbreak of wildlife diseases. Design zoo education programs. Oversee the care and distribution of zoo animals, working with curators and zoo directors to determine the best way to contain animals, maintain their habitats, and manage facilities. Perform administrative duties such as fundraising, public relations, budgeting, and supervision of zoo staff. Procure animals for zoo exhibition and locate mates for them.

GOE INFORMATION—Interest Area: 02. Science, Math, and Engineering. **Work Group:** 02.03. Life Sciences. **Personality Type—**Investigative. Investigative occupations frequently involve working with ideas and require an extensive amount of thinking. These occupations can involve searching for facts and figuring out problems mentally. **Work Values—**Creativity; Autonomy; Achievement; Ability Utilization; Responsibility. **Skills—**Science; Reading Comprehension; Equipment Selection; Complex Problem Solving; Writing; Mathematics; Critical Thinking; Operation Monitoring. **Abilities—***Cognitive:* Category Flexibility; Inductive Reasoning; Flexibility of Closure; Speed of Closure; Information Ordering. *Psychomotor:* Reaction Time; Response Orientation; Arm-Hand Steadiness; Rate Control; Finger Dexterity. *Physical:* Gross Body Equilibrium; Stamina; Dynamic Flexibility; Dynamic Strength; Static Strength. *Sensory:* Auditory Attention; Far Vision; Sound Localization; Night Vision; Glare Sensitivity. **General Work Activities—***Information Input:* Getting Information; Identifying Objects, Actions, and Events; Monitoring Processes, Materials, or Surroundings. *Mental Process:* Analyzing Data or Information; Processing Information; Updating and Using Relevant Knowledge. *Work Output:* Documenting or Recording Information; Handling and Moving Objects; Controlling Machines and Processes. *Interacting with Others:* Interpreting Meaning of Information for Others; Monitoring and Controlling Resources; Communicating with Other Workers. **Physical Work Conditions—**Minor Burns, Cuts, Bites, or Stings; Outdoors; Disease or Infections; Common Protective or Safety Attire; Specialized Protective or Safety Attire. **Other Job Characteristics—**Importance of Being Exact or Accurate; Consequence of Error; Importance of Repeating Same Tasks.

Experience—Job Zone 5. Extensive skill, knowledge, and experience are needed for these occupations. **Job Preparation:** SVP 8.0 and above—four years to more than 10 years. **Knowledge—**Biology; Chemistry; Mathematics; Clerical. **Instructional Programs—**Animal Behavior and Ethology; Animal Physiology; Cell/Cellular Biology and Anatomical Sciences, Other; Ecology; Entomology; Wildlife and Wildlands Science and Management; Wildlife Biology; Zoology/Animal Biology; Zoology/Animal Biology, Other.

Related DOT Jobs—041.061-090 Zoologist.

19-1029.99 Biological Scientists, All Other

- **Education/Training Required: Doctoral degree**
- **Employed: No data available.**
- **Annual Earnings: No data available.**
- **Growth: 21.0%**
- **Annual Job Openings: 5,000**

All biological scientists not listed separately.

No task data available.

GOE INFORMATION—Interest Area: 02. Science, Math, and Engineering. **Work Group:** 02.03. Life Sciences. **Note:** The Department of Labor has not collected some data for this job, so it has fewer details than the other descriptions.

Instructional Programs—Anatomy; Animal Genetics; Animal Physiology; Aquatic Biology/Limnology; Behavioral Sciences; Biology/Biological Sciences, General; Biometry/Biometrics; Biostatistics; Biotechnology; Botany/Plant Biology; Botany/Plant Biology, Other; Cell Biology and Anatomy; Cell/Cellular and Molecular Biology; Cell/Cellular Biology and Anatomical Sciences, Other; Cell/Cellular Biology and Histology; Conservation Biology; Developmental Biology and Embryology; Ecology; Ecology, Evolution, Systematics, and Population Biology, Other; Entomology; Environmental Biology; Evolutionary Biology; Genetics, General; Genetics, Other; Immunology; Marine Biology and Biological Oceanography; Medical Microbiology and Bacteriology; Microbial and Eukaryotic Genetics; Molecular Biology; Molecular Genetics; Mycology; Neuroanatomy; Neuroscience; Nutrition Sciences; Parasitology; Pathology/Experimental Pathology; Pharmacology; Photobiology; Plant Genetics; Plant Molecular Biology; Plant Pathology/Phytopathology; Plant Physiology; Population Biology; Radiation Biology/Radiobiology; Systematic Biology/Biological Systematics; Toxicology; Virology.

Related DOT Jobs—No related DOT jobs.

19-1031.00 Conservation Scientists

- **Education/Training Required: Bachelor's degree**
- **Employed: 16,192**
- **Annual Earnings: $48,970**
- **Growth: 8.3%**
- **Annual Job Openings: 1,000**

Manage, improve, and protect natural resources to maximize their use without damaging the environment. May conduct soil surveys and develop plans to eliminate soil erosion or to protect rangelands from fire and rodent damage. May instruct farmers, agricultural production managers, or ranchers in best ways to use crop rotation, contour plowing, or terracing to conserve soil and water; in the number and kind of livestock and forage plants best suited to particular ranges; and in range and farm improvements, such as fencing and reservoirs for stock watering.

No task data available.

GOE INFORMATION—Interest Area: 02. Science, Math, and Engineering. **Work Group:** 02.03. Life Sciences. **Note:** The Department of Labor has not collected some data for this job, so it has fewer details than the other descriptions.

Instructional Programs—Forest Management/Forest Resources Management; Forest Sciences and Biology; Forestry, General; Forestry, Other; Land Use Planning and Management/Development; Natural Resources and Conservation, Other; Natural Resources Management and Policy; Natural Resources Management and Policy, Other; Natural Resources/Conservation, General; Water, Wetlands, and Marine Resources Management; Wildlife and Wildlands Science and Management.

Related DOT Jobs—040.061-046 Range Manager; 040.061-054 Soil Conservationist; 049.127-010 Park Naturalist.

19-1031.01 Soil Conservationists

- **Education/Training Required: Bachelor's degree**
- **Employed: 16,192**
- **Annual Earnings: $48,970**
- **Growth: 8.3%**
- **Annual Job Openings: 1,000**

Plan and develop coordinated practices for soil erosion control, soil and water conservation, and sound land use.

Advise land users such as farmers and ranchers on conservation plans, problems, and alternative solutions and provide technical and planning assistance. Analyze results of investigations to determine measures needed to maintain or restore proper soil management. Compute design specifications for implementation of conservation practices, using survey and field information technical guides, engineering manuals, and calculator. Develop, conduct, and/or participate in surveys, studies, and investigations of various land uses, gathering information for use in developing corrective action plans. Monitor projects during and after construction to ensure projects conform to design specifications. Plan soil management and conservation practices, such as crop rotation, reforestation, permanent vegetation, contour plowing, or terracing, to maintain soil and conserve water. Provide information, knowledge, expertise, and training to government agencies at all levels to solve water and soil management problems and to assure coordination of resource protection activities. Compile and interpret wetland biodata to determine extent and type of wetland and to aid in program formulation. Compute cost estimates of different conservation practices based on needs of land users, maintenance requirements, and life expectancy of practices. Conduct fact-finding and mediation sessions among government units, landowners, and other agencies in order to resolve disputes. Coordinate and implement technical, financial, and administrative assistance programs for local government units to ensure efficient program implementation and timely responses to requests for assistance. Initiate, schedule, and conduct annual audits and compliance checks of program implementation by local government. Manage field offices and involve staff in cooperative ventures. Participate on work teams to plan, develop, and implement water and land management programs and policies. Provide access to programs and training to assist in completion of government groundwater protection plans. Respond to complaints and questions on wetland jurisdiction, providing information and clarification. Review and approve amendments to comprehensive local water plans and conservation district plans. Review annual reports of counties, conservation districts, and watershed management organizations, certifying compliance with mandated reporting requirements. Review grant applications and make funding recommendations. Review proposed wetland restoration easements and provide technical recommendations. Revisit land users to view implemented land use practices and plans. Survey property to mark locations and measurements, using surveying instruments. Visit areas affected by erosion problems to seek sources and solutions. Apply principles of specialized fields of science, such as agronomy, soil science, forestry, or agriculture, to achieve conservation objectives. Develop and maintain working relationships with local government staff and board members.

GOE INFORMATION—**Interest Area:** 02. Science, Math, and Engineering. **Work Group:** 02.03. Life Sciences. **Personality Type**—Investigative. Investigative occupations frequently involve working with ideas and require an extensive amount of thinking. These occupations can involve searching for facts and figuring out problems mentally. **Work Values**—Autonomy; Creativity; Responsibility; Ability Utilization; Independence. **Skills**—Systems Analysis; Complex Problem Solving; Mathematics; Systems Evaluation; Monitoring; Science; Judgment and Decision Making; Reading Comprehension. **Abilities**—*Cognitive:* Originality; Written Expression; Fluency of Ideas; Inductive Reasoning; Speed of Closure. *Psychomotor:* Multilimb Coordination; Finger Dexterity. *Physical:* Gross Body Equilibrium. *Sensory:* Far Vision; Depth Perception; Glare Sensitivity; Speech Clarity; Auditory Attention. **General Work Activities**—*Information Input:* Getting Information; Identifying Objects, Actions, and Events; Monitoring Processes, Materials, or Surroundings. *Mental Process:* Analyzing Data or Information; Organizing, Planning, and Prioritizing; Making Decisions and Solving Problems. *Work Output:* Documenting or Recording Information; Performing General Physical Activities; Drafting and Specifying Technical Devices. *Interacting with Others:* Communicating with Persons Outside Organization; Providing Consultation and Advice to Others; Interpreting Meaning of Information for Others. **Physical Work Conditions**—Outdoors; Extremely Bright or Inadequate Lighting; Very Hot or Cold; Contaminants; Walking or Running. **Other Job Characteristics**—Consequence of Error; Importance of Being Exact or Accurate; Degree of Automation.

Experience—Job Zone 4. A minimum of two to four years of work-related skill, knowledge, or experience is needed. **Job Preparation:** SVP 7.0 to less than 8.0—two years to less than 10 years. **Knowledge**—Biology; Food Production; Chemistry; Engineering and Technology; Mathematics. **Instructional Programs**—Forest Management/Forest Resources Management; Forest Sciences and Biology; Forestry, General; Forestry, Other; Land Use Planning and Management/Development; Natural Resources and Conservation, Other; Natural Resources Management and Policy; Natural Resources Management and Policy, Other; Natural Resources/Conservation, General; Water, Wetlands, and Marine Resources Management; Wildlife and Wildlands Science and Management.

Related DOT Jobs—040.061-054 Soil Conservationist; 040.261-010 Soil-Conservation Technician.

19-1031.02 Range Managers

- **Education/Training Required: Bachelor's degree**
- **Employed: No data available.**
- **Annual Earnings: $48,970**
- **Growth: 8.3%**
- **Annual Job Openings: 1,000**

Research or study range land management practices to provide sustained production of forage, livestock, and wildlife.

Develop technical standards and specifications used to manage, protect, and improve the natural resources of range lands and related grazing lands. Develop methods for protecting range from fire and rodent damage and for controlling poisonous plants. Maintain soil stability and vegetation for non-grazing uses, such as wildlife habitats and outdoor recreation. Manage forage resources through fire, herbicide use, or revegetation to maintain a sustainable yield from the land. Regulate grazing and help ranchers plan and organize grazing systems in order to manage, improve, and protect rangelands and maximize their use. Plan and direct construction and maintenance of range improvements such as fencing, corrals, stock-watering reservoirs, and soil-erosion control structures. Study forage plants and their growth requirements to determine varieties best suited to particular range. Study rangeland management practices and research range problems to provide sustained production of forage, livestock, and wildlife. Study grazing patterns to determine number and kind of livestock that can be most profitably grazed and to determine the best grazing seasons. Develop new and improved instruments and techniques for activities such as range reseeding. Measure and assess vegetation resources for biological assessment companies, environmental impact statements, and rangeland monitoring programs. Mediate agreements among rangeland users and preservationists as to appropriate land use and management. Offer advice to rangeland users on water management, forage production methods, and control of brush. Plan and implement revegetation of disturbed sites. Tailor conservation plans to landowners' goals, such as livestock support, wildlife, or recreation. Manage private livestock operations.

GOE INFORMATION—Interest Area: 02. Science, Math, and Engineering. **Work Group:** 02.03. Life Sciences. **Personality Type—**Investigative. Investigative occupations frequently involve working with ideas and require an extensive amount of thinking. These occupations can involve searching for facts and figuring out problems mentally. **Work Values—**Autonomy; Creativity; Independence; Responsibility; Ability Utilization. **Skills—**Operations Analysis; Systems Evaluation; Systems Analysis; Judgment and Decision Making; Complex Problem Solving; Equipment Selection; Science; Critical Thinking. **Abilities—***Cognitive:* Spatial Orientation; Flexibility of Closure; Oral Expression; Fluency of Ideas; Problem Sensitivity. *Psychomotor:* None met the criteria. *Physical:* Stamina; Explosive Strength. *Sensory:* Far Vision; Peripheral Vision; Glare Sensitivity; Night Vision. **General Work Activities—***Information Input:* Getting Information; Estimating Needed Characteristics; Identifying Objects, Actions, and Events. *Mental Process:* Making Decisions and Solving Problems; Processing Information; Organizing, Planning, and Prioritizing. *Work Output:* Documenting or Recording Information; Performing General Physical Activities; Drafting and Specifying Technical Devices. *Interacting with Others:* Providing Consultation and Advice to Others; Communicating with Other Workers; Interpreting Meaning of Information for Others. **Physical Work Conditions—**Outdoors; Walking or Running; Minor Burns, Cuts, Bites, or Stings; Very Hot or Cold; Kneeling, Crouching, or Crawling. **Other Job Characteristics—**Consequence of Error; Importance of Repeating Same Tasks; Importance of Being Exact or Accurate.

Experience—Job Zone 5. Extensive skill, knowledge, and experience are needed for these occupations. **Job Preparation:** SVP 8.0 and above—four years to more than 10 years. **Knowledge—**Food Production; Building and Construction; Biology; Administration and Management; Law and Government. **Instructional Programs—**Forest Management/Forest Resources Management; Forest Sciences and Biology; Forestry, General; Forestry, Other; Land Use Planning and Management/Development; Natural Resources and Conservation, Other; Natural Resources Management and Policy; Natural Resources Management and Policy, Other; Natural Resources/Conservation, General; Water, Wetlands, and Marine Resources Management; Wildlife and Wildlands Science and Management.

Related DOT Jobs—040.061-046 Range Manager.

19-1031.03 *Park Naturalists*

- **Education/Training Required: Bachelor's degree**
- **Employed: No data available.**
- **Annual Earnings: $48,970**
- **Growth: 8.3%**
- **Annual Job Openings: 1,000**

Plan, develop, and conduct programs to inform public of historical, natural, and scientific features of national, state, or local park.

Conduct field trips to point out scientific, historic, and natural features of parks, forests, historic sites, or other attractions. Confer with park staff to determine subjects and schedules for park programs. Construct historical, scientific, and nature visitor-center displays. Interview specialists in desired fields to obtain and develop data for park information programs. Plan and develop audiovisual devices for public programs. Prepare and present illustrated lectures and interpretive talks about park features. Provide visitor services by explaining regulations; answering visitor requests, needs, and complaints; and providing information about the park and surrounding areas. Assist with operations of general facilities, such as visitor centers. Compile and maintain official park photographic and information files. Plan, organize, and direct activities of seasonal staff members. Prepare brochures and write newspaper articles. Research stories regarding the area's natural history or environment. Survey park to determine forest conditions and distribution and abundance of fauna and flora. Take photographs and motion pictures for use in lectures and publications and to develop displays. Perform emergency duties to protect human life, government property, and natural features of park. Perform routine maintenance on park structures.

GOE INFORMATION—Interest Area: 12. Education and Social Service. **Work Group:** 12.01. Managerial Work in Education and Social Service. **Personality Type—**Social. Social occupations frequently involve working with, communicating with, and teaching people. These occupations often involve helping or providing service to others. **Work Values—**Autonomy; Creativity; Responsibility; Recognition; Variety. **Skills—**Service Orientation; Management of Personnel Resources; Systems Analysis; Management of Material Resources; Speaking; Equipment Selection; Writing; Complex Problem Solving. **Abilities—***Cognitive:* Spatial Orientation; Visualization; Time Sharing; Oral Expression; Written Expression. *Psychomotor:* Rate Control. *Physical:* Stamina; Dynamic Strength; Gross Body Equilibrium; Static Strength; Explosive Strength. *Sensory:* Far Vision; Night Vision; Speech Clarity; Sound Localization; Glare Sensitivity. **General Work Activities—***Information Input:* Getting Information; Identifying Objects, Actions, and Events; Estimating Needed Characteristics. *Mental Process:* Thinking Creatively; Organizing, Planning, and Prioritizing; Processing Information. *Work Output:* Performing General Physical Activities; Handling and Moving Objects; Documenting or Recording Information. *Interacting with Others:* Communicating with Persons Outside Organization; Performing for or Working with the Public; Establishing and Maintaining Relationships. **Physical Work Conditions—**Outdoors; Walking or Running; Minor Burns, Cuts, Bites, or Stings; Extremely Bright or Inadequate Lighting; Very Hot or Cold. **Other Job Characteristics—**Importance of Repeating Same Tasks; Pace Determined by Speed of Equipment; Degree of Automation.

Experience—Job Zone 4. A minimum of two to four years of work-related skill, knowledge, or experience is needed. **Job Preparation:** SVP 7.0 to less than 8.0—two years to less than 10 years. **Knowledge—**Biology; History and Archeology; Education and Training; Fine Arts; Administration and Management. **Instructional Programs—**Forest Management/Forest Resources Management; Forest Sciences and Biology; Forestry, General; Forestry, Other; Land Use Planning and Management/Development; Natural Resources and Conservation, Other; Natural Resources Management and Policy; Natural Resources Management and Policy, Other; Natural Resources/Conservation, General; Water, Wetlands, and Marine Resources Management; Wildlife and Wildlands Science and Management.

Related DOT Jobs—049.127-010 Park Naturalist.

19-1032.00 Foresters

- **Education/Training Required: Bachelor's degree**
- **Employed: 12,440**
- **Annual Earnings: $46,080**
- **Growth: 7.0%**
- **Annual Job Openings: 1,000**

Manage forested lands for economic, recreational, and conservation purposes. May inventory the type, amount, and location of standing timber, appraise the timber's worth, negotiate the purchase, and draw up contracts for procurement. May determine how to conserve wildlife habitats, creek beds, water quality, and soil stability and how best to comply with environmental regulations. May devise plans for planting and growing new trees, monitor trees for healthy growth, and determine the best time for harvesting. Develop forest management plans for public and privately-owned forested lands.

Monitor contract compliance and results of forestry activities to assure adherence to government regulations. Establish short- and long-term plans for management of forest lands and forest resources. Supervise activities of other forestry workers. Choose and prepare sites for new trees, using controlled burning, bulldozers, or herbicides to clear weeds, brush, and logging debris. Plan and supervise forestry projects, such as determining the type, number, and placement of trees to be planted; managing tree nurseries; thinning forest; and monitoring growth of new seedlings. Negotiate terms and conditions of agreements and contracts for forest harvesting, forest management, and leasing of forest lands. Direct and participate in forest-fire suppression. Determine methods of cutting and removing timber with minimum waste and environmental damage. Analyze effect of forest conditions on tree growth rates, tree species prevalence, and the yield, duration, seed production, growth viability, and germination of different species. Monitor forest-cleared lands to ensure that they are reclaimed to their most suitable end use. Plan and implement projects for conservation of wildlife habitats and soil and water quality. Plan and direct forest surveys and related studies and prepare reports and recommendations. Perform inspections of forests or forest nurseries. Map forest area soils and vegetation to estimate the amount of standing timber and future value and growth. Conduct public educational programs on forest care and conservation. Procure timber from private landowners. Subcontract with loggers or pulpwood cutters for tree removal and to aid in road layout. Plan cutting programs and manage timber sales from harvested areas, assisting companies to achieve production goals. Monitor wildlife populations and assess the impacts of forest operations on population and habitats. Plan and direct construction and maintenance of recreation facilities, fire towers, trails, roads, and bridges, ensuring that they comply with guidelines and regulations set for forested public lands. Contact local forest owners and gain permission to take inventory of the type, amount, and location of all standing timber on the property. As a consultant on forestry issues, provide advice and recommendations to private woodlot owners, firefighters, government agencies, or companies. Study different tree species' classification, life history, light and soil requirements, adaptation to new environmental conditions, and resistance to disease and insects. Develop new techniques for wood or residue use. Develop techniques for measuring and identifying trees.

GOE INFORMATION—Interest Area: 02. Science, Math, and Engineering. **Work Group:** 02.03. Life Sciences. **Personality Type—**Realistic. Realistic occupations frequently involve work activities that include practical, hands-on problems and solutions. They often deal with plants, animals, and real-world materials like wood, tools, and machinery. Many of the occupations require working outside and do not involve a lot of paperwork or working closely with others. **Work Values—**Autonomy; Responsibility; Creativity; Authority; Ability Utilization. **Skills—**Management of Financial Resources; Coordination; Quality Control Analysis; Mathematics; Time Management; Equipment Selection; Complex Problem Solving; Operations Analysis. **Abilities—***Cognitive:* Originality; Category Flexibility; Flexibility of Closure; Fluency of Ideas; Problem Sensitivity. *Psychomotor:* Multilimb Coordination; Control Precision; Reaction Time; Speed of Limb Movement; Rate Control. *Physical:* Static Strength; Dynamic Strength; Trunk Strength; Stamina; Gross Body Equilibrium. *Sensory:* Auditory Attention; Night Vision; Far Vision; Depth Perception; Speech Recognition. **General Work Activities—***Information Input:* Monitoring Processes, Materials, or Surroundings; Identifying Objects, Actions, and Events; Getting Information. *Mental Process:* Organizing, Planning, and Prioritizing; Making Decisions and Solving Problems; Processing Information. *Work Output:* Performing General Physical Activities; Documenting or Recording Information; Handling and Moving Objects. *Interacting with Others:* Communicating with Other Workers; Performing for or Working with the Public; Resolving Conflict and Negotiating with Others. **Physical Work Conditions—**Outdoors; Minor Burns, Cuts, Bites, or Stings; Extremely Bright or Inadequate Lighting; Very Hot or Cold; Climbing Ladders, Scaffolds, Poles, etc. **Other Job Characteristics—**Consequence of Error; Importance of Repeating Same Tasks; Degree of Automation.

Experience—Job Zone 4. A minimum of two to four years of work-related skill, knowledge, or experience is needed. **Job Preparation:** SVP 7.0 to less than 8.0—two years to less than 10 years. **Knowledge—**Biology; Geography; Administration and Management; Computers and Electronics; Building and Construction. **Instructional Programs—**Forest Management/Forest Resources Management; Forest Resources Production and Management; Forest Sciences and Biology; Forestry, General; Forestry, Other; Natural Resources and Conservation, Other; Natural Resources Management and Policy; Natural Resources Management and Policy, Other; Natural Resources/Conservation, General; Urban Forestry; Wood Science and Wood Products/Pulp and Paper Technology.

Related DOT Jobs—040.061-030 Forest Ecologist; 040.061-050 Silviculturist; 040.167-010 Forester.

19-1041.00 Epidemiologists

- **Education/Training Required: Doctoral degree**
- **Employed: No data available.**
- **Annual Earnings: $52,710**
- **Growth: 26.5%**
- **Annual Job Openings: 2,000**

Investigate and describe the determinants and distribution of disease, disability, and other health outcomes and develop the means for prevention and control.

Identify and analyze public health issues related to foodborne parasitic diseases and their impact on public policies or scientific studies or surveys. Investigate diseases or parasites to determine cause and risk factors, progress, life cycle, or mode of transmission. Plan and direct studies to investigate human or animal disease, preventive methods, and treatments for disease. Prepare and analyze samples to study effects of drugs, gases, pesticides, or microorganisms on cell structure and tissue. Standardize drug dosages, methods of immunization, and procedures for manufacture of drugs and medicinal compounds. Conduct research to develop methodologies, instrumentation, and procedures for medical application, analyzing data and presenting findings. Consult with and advise physicians, educators, researchers, government health officials, and others regarding medical applications of sciences, such as physics, biology, and chemistry. Oversee public health programs, including statistical analysis, health care planning, surveillance systems, and public health improvement. Plan, administer, and evaluate health safety standards and programs to improve public health, conferring with health department, industry personnel, physicians, and others. Provide expertise in the design, management, and evaluation of study protocols and health status questionnaires, sample selection, and analysis. Supervise professional, technical, and clerical personnel. Teach principles of medicine and medical and laboratory procedures to physicians, residents, students, and technicians.

GOE INFORMATION—Interest Area: 02. Science, Math, and Engineering. **Work Group:** 02.03. Life Sciences. **Personality Type**—Investigative. Investigative occupations frequently involve working with ideas and require an extensive amount of thinking. These occupations can involve searching for facts and figuring out problems mentally. **Work Values**—Social Status; Creativity; Achievement; Recognition; Ability Utilization. **Skills**—Instructing; Science; Systems Analysis; Systems Evaluation; Writing; Reading Comprehension; Complex Problem Solving; Critical Thinking. **Abilities**—*Cognitive:* Inductive Reasoning; Written Expression; Fluency of Ideas; Originality; Problem Sensitivity. *Psychomotor:* Arm-Hand Steadiness; Finger Dexterity; Control Precision; Manual Dexterity; Reaction Time. *Physical:* None met the criteria. *Sensory:* Speech Clarity; Near Vision; Night Vision; Auditory Attention; Visual Color Discrimination. **General Work Activities**—*Information Input:* Getting Information; Identifying Objects, Actions, and Events; Monitoring Processes, Materials, or Surroundings. *Mental Process:* Analyzing Data or Information; Updating and Using Relevant Knowledge; Processing Information. *Work Output:* Documenting or Recording Information; Controlling Machines and Processes; Interacting with Computers. *Interacting with Others:* Teaching Others; Interpreting Meaning of Information for Others; Communicating with Other Workers. **Physical Work Conditions**—Disease or Infections; Common Protective or Safety Attire; Specialized Protective or Safety Attire; Radiation; Indoors. **Other Job Characteristics**—Consequence of Error; Importance of Being Exact or Accurate; Degree of Automation.

Experience—Job Zone 4. A minimum of two to four years of work-related skill, knowledge, or experience is needed. **Job Preparation:** SVP 7.0 to less than 8.0—two years to less than 10 years. **Knowledge**—Biology; Medicine and Dentistry; Chemistry; Education and Training; Mathematics. **Instructional Programs**—Cell/Cellular Biology and Histology; Epidemiology; Medical Scientist (MS, PhD).

Related DOT Jobs—041.061-054 Histopathologist; 041.167-010 Environmental Epidemiologist.

19-1042.00 Medical Scientists, Except Epidemiologists

- **Education/Training Required:** Doctoral degree
- **Employed:** No data available.
- **Annual Earnings:** $55,960
- **Growth:** 26.5%
- **Annual Job Openings:** 2,000

Conduct research dealing with the understanding of human diseases and the improvement of human health. Engage in clinical investigation or other research, production, technical writing, or related activities.

Conduct research to develop methodologies, instrumentation, and procedures for medical application, analyzing data and presenting findings. Evaluate effects of drugs, gases, pesticides, parasites, and microorganisms

at various levels. Follow strict safety procedures when handling toxic materials to avoid contamination. Investigate cause, progress, life cycle, or mode of transmission of diseases or parasites. Plan and direct studies to investigate human or animal disease, preventive methods, and treatments for disease. Prepare and analyze organ, tissue, and cell samples to identify toxicity, bacteria, or microorganisms or to study cell structure. Standardize drug dosages, methods of immunization, and procedures for manufacture of drugs and medicinal compounds. Confer with health department, industry personnel, physicians, and others to develop health safety standards and public health improvement programs. Study animal and human health and physiological processes. Consult with and advise physicians, educators, researchers, and others regarding medical applications of physics, biology, and chemistry. Teach principles of medicine and medical and laboratory procedures to physicians, residents, students, and technicians. Use equipment such as atomic absorption spectrometers, electron microscopes, flow cytometers, and chromatography systems.

GOE INFORMATION—Interest Area: 02. Science, Math, and Engineering. **Work Group:** 02.03. Life Sciences. **Personality Type**—Investigative. Investigative occupations frequently involve working with ideas and require an extensive amount of thinking. These occupations can involve searching for facts and figuring out problems mentally. **Work Values**—Social Status; Creativity; Achievement; Recognition; Ability Utilization. **Skills**—Instructing; Science; Systems Analysis; Systems Evaluation; Writing; Reading Comprehension; Complex Problem Solving; Critical Thinking. **Abilities**—*Cognitive:* Inductive Reasoning; Written Expression; Fluency of Ideas; Originality; Problem Sensitivity. *Psychomotor:* Arm-Hand Steadiness; Finger Dexterity; Control Precision; Manual Dexterity; Reaction Time. *Physical:* None met the criteria. *Sensory:* Speech Clarity; Near Vision; Night Vision; Auditory Attention; Visual Color Discrimination. **General Work Activities**—*Information Input:* Identifying Objects, Actions, and Events; Getting Information; Monitoring Processes, Materials, or Surroundings. *Mental Process:* Analyzing Data or Information; Updating and Using Relevant Knowledge; Processing Information. *Work Output:* Documenting or Recording Information; Controlling Machines and Processes; Interacting with Computers. *Interacting with Others:* Teaching Others; Interpreting Meaning of Information for Others; Communicating with Other Workers. **Physical Work Conditions**—Disease or Infections; Common Protective or Safety Attire; Specialized Protective or Safety Attire; Radiation; Indoors. **Other Job Characteristics**—Consequence of Error; Importance of Being Exact or Accurate; Degree of Automation.

Experience—Job Zone 4. A minimum of two to four years of work-related skill, knowledge, or experience is needed. **Job Preparation:** SVP 7.0 to less than 8.0—two years to less than 10 years. **Knowledge**—Biology; Medicine and Dentistry; Chemistry; Education and Training; Mathematics. **Instructional Programs**—Anatomy; Biochemistry; Biomedical Sciences, General; Biophysics; Biostatistics; Cardiovascular Science; Cell Physiology; Cell/Cellular Biology and Histology; Endocrinology; Environmental Toxicology; Epidemiology; Exercise Physiology; Human/Medical Genetics; Immunology; Medical Microbiology and Bacteriology; Medical Scientist (MS, PhD); Molecular Biology; Molecular Pharmacology; Molecular Physiology; Molecular Toxicology; Neurobiology and Neurophysiology; Neuropharmacology; Oncology and Cancer Biology; Pathology/Experimental Pathology; Pharmacology; Pharmacology and Toxicology; Pharmacology and Toxicology, Other; Physiology, General; Physiology, Pathology, and Related Sciences, Other; Reproductive Biology; Toxicology; Vision Science/Physiological Optics.

Related DOT Jobs—041.061-010 Anatomist; 041.061-070 Parasitologist; 041.061-074 Pharmacologist; 041.067-010 Medical Coordinator, Pesticide Use; 079.021-014 Medical Physicist.

19-1099.99 Life Scientists, All Other

- Education/Training Required: **No data available.**
- Employed: **No data available.**
- Annual Earnings: **No data available.**
- Growth: **15.9%**
- Annual Job Openings: **1,000**

All life scientists not listed separately.

No task data available.

GOE INFORMATION—Interest Area: 02. Science, Math, and Engineering. **Work Group:** 02.03. Life Sciences. **Note:** The Department of Labor has not collected some data for this job, so it has fewer details than the other descriptions.

Instructional Programs—Behavioral Sciences; Biological and Biomedical Sciences, Other; Biology/Biological Sciences, General; Ecology; Ecology, Evolution, Systematics, and Population Biology, Other; Natural Sciences; Nutrition Sciences.

Related DOT Jobs—041.261-010 Public-Health Microbiologist.

19-2000 Physical Scientists

19-2011.00 Astronomers

- Education/Training Required: **Doctoral degree**
- Employed: **No data available.**
- Annual Earnings: **$77,570**
- Growth: **10.5%**
- Annual Job Openings: **1,000**

Observe, research, and interpret celestial and astronomical phenomena to increase basic knowledge and apply such information to practical problems.

Studies celestial phenomena from ground or above atmosphere, using various optical devices such as telescopes situated on ground or attached to satellites. Studies history, structure, extent, and evolution of stars, stellar systems, and universe. Calculates orbits and determines sizes, shapes, brightness, and motions of different celestial bodies. Computes positions of sun, moon, planets, stars, nebulae, and galaxies. Determines exact time by celestial observations and conducts research into relationships between time and space. Analyzes wave lengths of radiation from celestial bodies, as observed in all ranges of spectrum. Develops mathematical tables giving positions of sun, moon, planets, and stars at given times for use by air and sea navigators. Designs optical, mechanical, and electronic instruments for astronomical research.

GOE INFORMATION—Interest Area: 02. Science, Math, and Engineering. **Work Group:** 02.02. Physical Sciences. **Personality Type—**Investigative. Investigative occupations frequently involve working with ideas and require an extensive amount of thinking. These occupations can involve searching for facts and figuring out problems mentally. **Work Values—**Autonomy; Creativity; Independence; Ability Utilization; Responsibility. **Skills—**Science; Mathematics; Technology Design; Critical Thinking; Programming; Equipment Selection; Operations Analysis; Complex Problem Solving. **Abilities—***Cognitive:* Mathematical Reasoning; Inductive Reasoning; Number Facility; Written Expression; Deductive Reasoning. *Psychomotor:* Control Precision. *Physical:* None met the criteria. *Sensory:* Night Vision; Depth Perception; Far Vision; Glare Sensitivity; Peripheral Vision. **General Work Activities—***Information Input:* Monitoring Processes, Materials, or Surroundings; Getting Information; Identifying Objects, Actions, and Events. *Mental Process:* Processing Information; Analyzing Data or Information; Updating and Using Relevant Knowledge. *Work Output:* Drafting and Specifying Technical Devices; Documenting or Recording Information; Interacting with Computers. *Interacting with Others:* Interpreting Meaning of Information for Others; Providing Consultation and Advice to Others; Communicating with Other Workers. **Physical Work Conditions—**Outdoors; High Places; Extremely Bright or Inadequate Lighting; Sitting; Very Hot or Cold. **Other Job Characteristics—**Importance of Being Exact or Accurate; Importance of Repeating Same Tasks; Pace Determined by Speed of Equipment.

Experience—Job Zone 5. Extensive skill, knowledge, and experience are needed for these occupations. **Job Preparation:** SVP 8.0 and above—four years to more than 10 years. **Knowledge—**Physics; Mathematics; History and Archeology; Design; Engineering and Technology. **Instructional Programs—**Astronomy; Astronomy and Astrophysics, Other; Astrophysics; Planetary Astronomy and Science.

Related DOT Jobs—021.067-010 Astronomer.

19-2012.00 Physicists

- Education/Training Required: **Doctoral degree**
- Employed: **No data available.**
- Annual Earnings: **$83,670**
- Growth: **10.5%**
- Annual Job Openings: **1,000**

Conduct research into the phases of physical phenomena, develop theories and laws on the basis of observation and experiments, and devise methods to apply laws and theories to industry and other fields.

Analyze data from research conducted to detect and measure physical phenomena. Describe and express observations and conclusions in mathematical terms. Design computer simulations to model physical data so that it can be better understood. Develop theories and laws on the basis of observation and experiments and apply these theories and laws to problems in areas such as nuclear energy, optics, and aerospace technology. Observe the structure and properties of matter and the transformation and propagation of energy, using equipment such as masers, lasers, and telescopes in order to explore and identify the basic principles governing these phenomena. Perform complex calculations as part of the analysis and evaluation of data, using computers. Report experimental results by writing papers for scientific journals or by presenting information at scientific conferences. Collaborate with other scientists in the design, development, and testing of experimental, industrial, or medical equipment, instrumentation, and procedures. Conduct application evaluations and analyze results in order to determine commercial, industrial, scientific, medical, military, or other uses for electro-optical devices. Develop manufacturing, assembly, and fabrication processes of lasers, masers, infrared, and other light-emitting and light-sensitive devices. Provide support services for activities such as radiation therapy, diagnostic imaging, or seismology. Teach physics to students. Advise authorities of procedures to be followed in radiation incidents or hazards and assist in civil defense planning. Conduct research pertaining to potential environmental impacts of atomic energy-related industrial development in order to determine licensing qualifications. Develop standards of permissible concentrations of radioisotopes in liquids and gases. Direct testing and monitoring of contamination of radioactive equipment and recording of personnel and plant area radiation exposure data.

GOE INFORMATION—**Interest Area:** 02. Science, Math, and Engineering. **Work Group:** 02.02. Physical Sciences. **Personality Type**—Investigative. Investigative occupations frequently involve working with ideas and require an extensive amount of thinking. These occupations can involve searching for facts and figuring out problems mentally. **Work Values**—Creativity; Autonomy; Recognition; Ability Utilization; Social Status. **Skills**—Science; Mathematics; Writing; Technology Design; Reading Comprehension; Complex Problem Solving; Critical Thinking; Equipment Selection. **Abilities**—*Cognitive:* Mathematical Reasoning; Deductive Reasoning; Written Comprehension; Inductive Reasoning; Written Expression. *Psychomotor:* None met the criteria. *Physical:* None met the criteria. *Sensory:* Speech Recognition; Speech Clarity; Hearing Sensitivity. **General Work Activities**—*Information Input:* Getting Information; Identifying Objects, Actions, and Events; Monitoring Processes, Materials, or Surroundings. *Mental Process:* Processing Information; Analyzing Data or Information; Updating and Using Relevant Knowledge. *Work Output:* Drafting and Specifying Technical Devices; Interacting with Computers; Documenting or Recording Information. *Interacting with Others:* Interpreting Meaning of Information for Others; Communicating with Persons Outside Organization; Providing Consultation and Advice to Others. **Physical Work Conditions**—Specialized Protective or Safety Attire; Sitting; Indoors; Radiation; Hazardous Conditions. **Other Job Characteristics**—Importance of Being Exact or Accurate; Consequence of Error; Importance of Repeating Same Tasks.

Experience—Job Zone 5. Extensive skill, knowledge, and experience are needed for these occupations. **Job Preparation:** SVP 8.0 and above—four years to more than 10 years. **Knowledge**—Physics; Education and Training; Mathematics; Engineering and Technology; Design. **Instructional Programs**—Acoustics; Astrophysics; Atomic/Molecular Physics; Elementary Particle Physics; Health/Medical Physics; Nuclear Physics; Optics/Optical Sciences; Physics, General; Physics, Other; Plasma and High-Temperature Physics; Solid State and Low-Temperature Physics; Theoretical and Mathematical Physics.

Related DOT Jobs—015.021-010 Health Physicist; 023.061-010 Electro-Optical Engineer; 023.061-014 Physicist; 023.067-010 Physicist, Theoretical.

19-2021.00 Atmospheric and Space Scientists

- ● **Education/Training Required: Bachelor's degree**
- ● **Employed: 6,894**
- ● **Annual Earnings: $61,530**
- ● **Growth: 17.1%**
- ● **Annual Job Openings: Fewer than 500**

Investigate atmospheric phenomena and interpret meteorological data gathered by surface and air stations, satellites, and radar to prepare reports and forecasts for public and other uses.

Analyzes and interprets meteorological data gathered by surface and upper air stations, satellites, and radar to prepare reports and forecasts. Studies and interprets synoptic reports, maps, photographs, and prognostic charts to predict long- and short-range weather conditions. Prepares special forecasts and briefings for air and sea transportation, agriculture, fire prevention, air-pollution control, and school groups. Operates computer graphic equipment to produce weather reports and maps for analysis, distribution, or use in televised weather broadcast. Conducts basic or applied research in meteorology. Issues hurricane and other severe weather warnings. Broadcasts weather forecast over television or radio. Directs forecasting services at weather station or at radio or television broadcasting facility.

GOE INFORMATION—**Interest Area:** 02. Science, Math, and Engineering. **Work Group:** 02.02. Physical Sciences. **Personality Type**—Investigative. Investigative occupations frequently involve working with ideas and require an extensive amount of thinking. These occupations can involve searching for facts and figuring out problems mentally. **Work Values**—Social Status; Recognition; Responsibility; Autonomy; Ability Utilization. **Skills**—Science; Equipment Selection; Critical Thinking; Complex Problem Solving; Speaking; Management of Personnel Resources; Systems Analysis; Reading Comprehension. **Abilities**—*Cognitive:* Speed of Closure; Inductive Reasoning; Written Expression; Flexibility of Closure; Originality. *Psychomotor:* Finger Dexterity. *Physical:* None met the criteria. *Sensory:* Speech Clarity; Glare Sensitivity; Peripheral Vision; Far Vision; Night Vision. **General Work Activities**—*Information Input:* Monitoring Processes, Materials, or Surroundings; Getting Information; Identifying Objects, Actions, and Events. *Mental Process:* Updating and Using Relevant Knowledge; Analyzing Data or Information; Processing Information. *Work Output:* Interacting with Computers; Documenting or Recording Information; Handling and Moving Objects. *Interacting with Others:* Communicating with Other Workers; Performing for or Working with the Public; Interpreting Meaning of Information for Others. **Physical Work Conditions**—Extremely Bright or Inadequate Lighting; Sitting; Very Hot or Cold; Outdoors; Disease or Infections. **Other Job Characteristics**—Degree of Automation; Importance of Repeating Same Tasks; Importance of Being Exact or Accurate.

Experience—Job Zone 4. A minimum of two to four years of work-related skill, knowledge, or experience is needed. **Job Preparation:** SVP 7.0 to less than 8.0—two years to less than 10 years. **Knowledge**—Geography; Physics; Communications and Media; Telecommunications; Administration and Management. **Instructional Programs**—Atmospheric Chemistry and Climatology; Atmospheric Physics and Dynamics; Atmospheric Sciences and Meteorology, General; Atmospheric Sciences and Meteorology, Other; Meteorology.

Related DOT Jobs—025.062-010 Meteorologist.

19-2031.00 Chemists

- ● **Education/Training Required: Bachelor's degree**
- ● **Employed: 84,323**
- ● **Annual Earnings: $51,860**
- ● **Growth: 19.1%**
- ● **Annual Job Openings: 6,000**

Conduct qualitative and quantitative chemical analyses or chemical experiments in laboratories for quality or process control or to develop new products or knowledge.

Analyze organic and inorganic compounds to determine chemical and physical properties, composition, structure, relationships, and reactions, utilizing chromatography, spectroscopy, and spectrophotometry techniques. Induce changes in composition of substances by introducing heat, light, energy, and chemical catalysts for quantitative and qualitative analysis. Develop, improve, and customize products, equipment, formulas, processes, and analytical methods. Compile and analyze test information to determine process or equipment operating efficiency and to diagnose malfunctions. Study effects of various methods of processing, preserving, and packaging on composition and properties of foods. Prepare test solutions, compounds, and reagents for laboratory personnel to conduct test. Confer with scientists and engineers to conduct analyses of research projects, interpret test results, or develop nonstandard tests. Write technical papers and reports and prepare standards and specifications for processes, facilities, products, and tests. Direct, coordinate, and advise personnel in test procedures for analyzing components and physical properties of materials.

GOE INFORMATION—**Interest Area:** 02. Science, Math, and Engineering. **Work Group:** 02.02. Physical Sciences. **Personality Type—**Investigative. Investigative occupations frequently involve working with ideas and require an extensive amount of thinking. These occupations can involve searching for facts and figuring out problems mentally. **Work Values—**Creativity; Ability Utilization; Responsibility; Autonomy; Achievement. **Skills—**Science; Writing; Complex Problem Solving; Quality Control Analysis; Operations Analysis; Reading Comprehension; Equipment Selection; Technology Design. **Abilities—***Cognitive:* Mathematical Reasoning; Written Expression; Oral Comprehension; Oral Expression; Problem Sensitivity. *Psychomotor:* Response Orientation; Arm-Hand Steadiness; Finger Dexterity. *Physical:* None met the criteria. *Sensory:* Visual Color Discrimination; Speech Clarity; Speech Recognition; Near Vision; Glare Sensitivity. **General Work Activities—***Information Input:* Getting Information; Identifying Objects, Actions, and Events; Monitoring Processes, Materials, or Surroundings. *Mental Process:* Processing Information; Analyzing Data or Information; Updating and Using Relevant Knowledge. *Work Output:* Documenting or Recording Information; Controlling Machines and Processes; Drafting and Specifying Technical Devices. *Interacting with Others:* Communicating with Other Workers; Providing Consultation and Advice to Others; Coordinating the Work and Activities of Others. **Physical Work Conditions—**Hazardous Conditions; Contaminants; Common Protective or Safety Attire; Disease or Infections; Minor Burns, Cuts, Bites, or Stings. **Other Job Characteristics—**Importance of Being Exact or Accurate; Consequence of Error; Importance of Repeating Same Tasks.

Experience—Job Zone 4. A minimum of two to four years of work-related skill, knowledge, or experience is needed. **Job Preparation:** SVP 7.0 to less than 8.0—two years to less than 10 years. **Knowledge—**Chemistry; Mathematics; Biology; English Language; Engineering and Technology. **Instructional Programs—**Analytical Chemistry; Chemical Physics; Chemistry, General; Chemistry, Other; Inorganic Chemistry; Organic Chemistry; Physical and Theoretical Chemistry; Polymer Chemistry.

Related DOT Jobs—022.061-010 Chemist; 022.061-014 Chemist, Food; 022.137-010 Laboratory Supervisor.

19-2032.00 *Materials Scientists*

- **Education/Training Required: Bachelor's degree**
- **Employed: 7,710**
- **Annual Earnings: $62,750**
- **Growth: 19.8%**
- **Annual Job Openings: 1,000**

Research and study the structures and chemical properties of various natural and manmade materials, including metals, alloys, rubber, ceramics, semiconductors, polymers, and glass. Determine ways to strengthen or combine materials or develop new materials with new or specific properties for use in a variety of products and applications.

Conduct research into the structures and properties of materials such as metals, alloys, polymers, and ceramics in order to obtain information that could be used to develop new products or enhance existing ones. Determine ways to strengthen or combine materials or develop new materials with new or specific properties for use in a variety of products and applications. Devise testing methods to evaluate the effects of various conditions on particular materials. Plan laboratory experiments to confirm feasibility of processes and techniques used in the production of materials having special characteristics. Prepare reports of materials study findings for the use of other scientists and requestors. Recommend materials for reliable performance in various environments. Research methods of

processing, forming, and firing materials in order to develop such products as ceramic fillings for teeth, unbreakable dinner plates, and telescope lenses. Study the nature, structure, and physical properties of metals and their alloys and their responses to applied forces. Test material samples for tolerance under tension, compression, and shear to determine the cause of metal failures. Confer with customers in order to determine how materials can be tailored to suit their needs. Monitor production processes in order to ensure that equipment is used efficiently and that projects are completed within appropriate time frames and budgets. Receive molten metal from smelters and further alloy and refine it in oxygen, open-hearth, or other kinds of furnaces. Teach in colleges and universities. Test individual parts and products in order to ensure that manufacturer and governmental quality and safety standards are met. Test metals in order to determine whether they meet specifications of mechanical strength, strength-weight ratio, ductility, magnetic and electrical properties, and resistance to abrasion, corrosion, heat, and cold. Visit suppliers of materials or users of products in order to gather specific information.

GOE INFORMATION—**Interest Area:** 02. Science, Math, and Engineering. **Work Group:** 02.02. Physical Sciences. **Personality Type—**Investigative. Investigative occupations frequently involve working with ideas and require an extensive amount of thinking. These occupations can involve searching for facts and figuring out problems mentally. **Work Values—**Creativity; Autonomy; Ability Utilization; Responsibility; Social Status. **Skills—**Science; Writing; Mathematics; Quality Control Analysis; Reading Comprehension; Operations Analysis; Speaking; Complex Problem Solving. **Abilities—***Cognitive:* Originality; Mathematical Reasoning; Written Expression; Fluency of Ideas; Number Facility. *Psychomotor:* None met the criteria. *Physical:* None met the criteria. *Sensory:* Near Vision. **General Work Activities—***Information Input:* Getting Information; Identifying Objects, Actions, and Events; Monitoring Processes, Materials, or Surroundings. *Mental Process:* Analyzing Data or Information; Updating and Using Relevant Knowledge; Processing Information. *Work Output:* Documenting or Recording Information; Controlling Machines and Processes; Handling and Moving Objects. *Interacting with Others:* Communicating with Other Workers; Interpreting Meaning of Information for Others; Guiding, Directing, and Motivating Subordinates. **Physical Work Conditions—**Sitting; Indoors; Common Protective or Safety Attire; Using Hands on Objects, Tools, or Controls. **Other Job Characteristics—**Importance of Being Exact or Accurate; Consequence of Error; Degree of Automation.

Experience—Job Zone 4. A minimum of two to four years of work-related skill, knowledge, or experience is needed. **Job Preparation:** SVP 7.0 to less than 8.0—two years to less than 10 years. **Knowledge—**Chemistry; Engineering and Technology; Physics; Mathematics; Administration and Management. **Instructional Programs—**Materials Science.

Related DOT Jobs—029.081-014 Materials Scientist.

19-2041.00 *Environmental Scientists and Specialists, Including Health*

- **Education/Training Required: Bachelor's degree**
- **Employed: 63,723**
- **Annual Earnings: $47,330**
- **Growth: 22.3%**
- **Annual Job Openings: 4,000**

Conduct research or perform investigation for the purpose of identifying, abating, or eliminating sources of pollutants or hazards that affect either the environment or the health of the population.

Utilizing knowledge of various scientific disciplines, may collect, synthesize, study, report, and take action based on data derived from measurements or observations of air, food, soil, water, and other sources.

Analyze data to determine validity, quality, and scientific significance and to interpret correlations between human activities and environmental effects. Collect, synthesize, and analyze data derived from pollution emission measurements, atmospheric monitoring, meteorological and mineralogical information, and soil or water samples. Conduct environmental audits and inspections and investigations of violations. Design and direct studies to obtain technical environmental information about planned projects. Determine data collection methods to be employed in research projects and surveys. Develop methods to minimize the impact of production processes on the environment, based on the study and assessment of industrial production, environmental legislation, and physical, biological, and social environments. Evaluate violations or problems discovered during inspections in order to determine appropriate regulatory actions or to provide advice on the development and prosecution of regulatory cases. Investigate and report on accidents affecting the environment. Monitor effects of pollution and land degradation and recommend means of prevention or control. Monitor environmental impacts of development activities. Plan and develop research models using knowledge of mathematical and statistical concepts. Prepare charts or graphs from data samples and provide summary information on the environmental relevance of the data. Provide technical guidance, support, and oversight to environmental programs, industry, and the public. Research sources of pollution to determine their effects on the environment and to develop theories or methods of pollution abatement or control. Communicate scientific and technical information through oral briefings, written documents, workshops, conferences, and public hearings. Conduct applied research on topics such as waste control and treatment and pollution control methods. Develop programs designed to obtain the most productive, non-damaging use of land. Develop the technical portions of legal documents, administrative orders, or consent decrees. Provide advice on proper standards and regulations and the development of policies, strategies, and codes of practice for environmental management. Review and implement environmental technical standards, guidelines, policies, and formal regulations that meet all appropriate requirements. Supervise environmental technologists and technicians.

GOE INFORMATION—Interest Area: 02. Science, Math, and Engineering. **Work Group:** 02.03. Life Sciences. **Personality Type**—Investigative. Investigative occupations frequently involve working with ideas and require an extensive amount of thinking. These occupations can involve searching for facts and figuring out problems mentally. **Work Values**—Autonomy; Creativity; Ability Utilization; Achievement; Recognition. **Skills**—Science; Mathematics; Complex Problem Solving; Reading Comprehension; Systems Analysis; Operations Analysis; Systems Evaluation; Writing. **Abilities**—*Cognitive:* Mathematical Reasoning; Number Facility; Written Expression; Deductive Reasoning; Written Comprehension. *Psychomotor:* None met the criteria. *Physical:* None met the criteria. *Sensory:* None met the criteria. **General Work Activities**—*Information Input:* Getting Information; Identifying Objects, Actions, and Events; Estimating Needed Characteristics. *Mental Process:* Analyzing Data or Information; Processing Information; Making Decisions and Solving Problems. *Work Output:* Documenting or Recording Information; Interacting with Computers; Drafting and Specifying Technical Devices. *Interacting with Others:* Communicating with Other Workers; Interpreting Meaning of Information for Others; Communicating with Persons Outside Organization. **Physical Work Conditions**—Outdoors; Contaminants; Disease or Infections; Common Protective or Safety Attire; Specialized Protective or Safety Attire. **Other Job Characteristics**—

Importance of Being Exact or Accurate; Consequence of Error; Degree of Automation.

Experience—Job Zone 5. Extensive skill, knowledge, and experience are needed for these occupations. **Job Preparation:** SVP 8.0 and above—four years to more than 10 years. **Knowledge**—Biology; Chemistry; Mathematics; Physics; Engineering and Technology. **Instructional Programs**—Environmental Science; Environmental Studies.

Related DOT Jobs—019.081-018 Pollution-Control Engineer; 029.081-010 Environmental Analyst.

19-2042.00 Geoscientists, Except Hydrologists and Geographers
- **Education/Training Required: Bachelor's degree**
- **Employed: 25,497**
- **Annual Earnings: $58,280**
- **Growth: 18.1%**
- **Annual Job Openings: 2,000**

Study the composition, structure, and other physical aspects of the earth. May use geological, physics, and mathematics knowledge in exploration for oil, gas, minerals, or underground water or in waste disposal, land reclamation, or other environmental problems. May study the earth's internal composition, atmospheres, and oceans and its magnetic, electrical, and gravitational forces. Includes mineralogists, crystallographers, paleontologists, stratigraphers, geodesists, and seismologists.

No task data available.

GOE INFORMATION—Interest Area: 02. Science, Math, and Engineering. **Work Group:** 02.02. Physical Sciences. **Note:** The Department of Labor has not collected some data for this job, so it has fewer details than the other descriptions.

Instructional Programs—Geochemistry; Geochemistry and Petrology; Geological and Earth Sciences/Geosciences, Other; Geology/Earth Science, General; Geophysics and Seismology; Oceanography, Chemical and Physical; Paleontology.

Related DOT Jobs—024.061-010 Crystallographer; 024.061-018 Geologist; 024.061-022 Geologist, Petroleum; 024.061-026 Geophysical Prospector; 024.061-038 Mineralogist; 024.061-042 Paleontologist; 024.061-046 Petrologist; 024.061-054 Stratigrapher; 024.161-010 Engineer, Soils; 024.284-010 Prospector.

19-2042.01 Geologists
- **Education/Training Required: Bachelor's degree**
- **Employed: No data available.**
- **Annual Earnings: $58,280**
- **Growth: 18.1%**
- **Annual Job Openings: 3,000**

Study composition, structure, and history of the earth's crust; examine rocks, minerals, and fossil remains to identify and determine the sequence of processes affecting the development of the earth; apply knowledge of chemistry, physics, biology, and mathematics to explain these phenomena and to help locate mineral and petroleum deposits and underground water resources; prepare geologic reports and maps; and interpret research data to recommend further action for study.

Analyze and interpret geological, geochemical, and geophysical information from sources such as survey data, well logs, boreholes, and aerial photos. Identify risks for natural disasters such as mudslides, earthquakes, and volcanic eruptions and provide advice on ways in which potential damage can be mitigated. Investigate the composition, structure, and history of the Earth's crust through the collection, examination, measurement, and classification of soils, minerals, rocks, and fossil remains. Measure characteristics of the Earth, such as gravity and magnetic fields, using equipment such as seismographs, gravimeters, torsion balances, and magnetometers. Plan and conduct geological, geochemical, and geophysical field studies and surveys; sample collection; and drilling and testing programs used to collect data for research and/or application. Test industrial diamonds and abrasives, soil, or rocks in order to determine their geological characteristics, using optical, X-ray, heat, acid, and precision instruments. Advise construction firms and government agencies on dam and road construction, foundation design, and land use and resource management. Assess ground and surface water movement in order to provide advice regarding issues such as waste management, route and site selection, and the restoration of contaminated sites. Communicate geological findings by writing research papers, participating in conferences, and/or teaching geological science at universities. Conduct geological and geophysical studies to provide information for use in regional development, site selection, and the development of public works projects. Develop applied software for the analysis and interpretation of geological data. Develop instruments for geological work, such as diamond tools and dies, jeweled bearings, and grinding laps and wheels. Identify deposits of construction materials and assess the materials' characteristics and suitability for use as concrete aggregates or road fill or in other applications. Inspect construction projects in order to analyze engineering problems, applying geological knowledge and using test equipment and drilling machinery. Locate and estimate probable natural gas, oil, and mineral ore deposits and underground water resources, using aerial photographs, charts, and research and survey results. Prepare geological maps, cross-sectional diagrams, charts, and reports concerning mineral extraction, land use, and resource management, using results of field work and laboratory research.

GOE INFORMATION—Interest Area: 02. Science, Math, and Engineering. **Work Group:** 02.02. Physical Sciences. **Personality Type—**Investigative. Investigative occupations frequently involve working with ideas and require an extensive amount of thinking. These occupations can involve searching for facts and figuring out problems mentally. **Work Values—**Responsibility; Ability Utilization; Autonomy; Creativity; Achievement. **Skills—**Technology Design; Mathematics; Equipment Selection; Science; Operations Analysis; Complex Problem Solving; Writing; Programming. **Abilities—***Cognitive:* Written Expression; Category Flexibility; Mathematical Reasoning; Written Comprehension; Flexibility of Closure. *Psychomotor:* Control Precision; Arm-Hand Steadiness; Finger Dexterity. *Physical:* None met the criteria. *Sensory:* Visual Color Discrimination; Glare Sensitivity; Near Vision. **General Work Activities—***Information Input:* Getting Information; Identifying Objects, Actions, and Events; Monitoring Processes, Materials, or Surroundings. *Mental Process:* Processing Information; Analyzing Data or Information; Making Decisions and Solving Problems. *Work Output:* Controlling Machines and Processes; Documenting or Recording Information; Interacting with Computers. *Interacting with Others:* Interpreting Meaning of Information for Others; Communicating with Other Workers; Providing Consultation and Advice to Others. **Physical Work Conditions—**Outdoors; Very Hot or Cold; Specialized Protective or Safety Attire; Contaminants; Extremely Bright or Inadequate Lighting. **Other Job Characteristics—**Importance of Being Exact or Accurate; Consequence of Error; Pace Determined by Speed of Equipment.

Experience—Job Zone 5. Extensive skill, knowledge, and experience are needed for these occupations. **Job Preparation:** SVP 8.0 and above—

four years to more than 10 years. **Knowledge—**Physics; Geography; Engineering and Technology; History and Archeology; Chemistry. **Instructional Programs—**Geochemistry; Geochemistry and Petrology; Geological and Earth Sciences/Geosciences, Other; Geology/Earth Science, General; Geophysics and Seismology; Oceanography, Chemical and Physical; Paleontology.

Related DOT Jobs—024.061-010 Crystallographer; 024.061-018 Geologist; 024.061-022 Geologist, Petroleum; 024.061-026 Geophysical Prospector; 024.061-038 Mineralogist; 024.061-042 Paleontologist; 024.061-046 Petrologist; 024.061-054 Stratigrapher; 024.161-010 Engineer, Soils; 024.284-010 Prospector.

19-2043.00 *Hydrologists*

- **Education/Training Required: Bachelor's degree**
- **Employed: 7,837**
- **Annual Earnings: $56,400**
- **Growth: 25.7%**
- **Annual Job Openings: 1,000**

Research the distribution, circulation, and physical properties of underground and surface waters; study the form and intensity of precipitation, its rate of infiltration into the soil, its movement through the earth, and its return to the ocean and atmosphere.

Studies and analyzes physical aspects of earth, including atmosphere and hydrosphere, and interior structure. Studies, measures, and interprets seismic, gravitational, electrical, thermal, and magnetic forces and data affecting the earth. Studies, maps, and charts distribution, disposition, and development of waters of land areas, including form and intensity of precipitation. Studies waters of land areas to determine modes of return to ocean and atmosphere. Investigates origin and activity of glaciers, volcanoes, and earthquakes. Compiles and evaluates data to prepare navigational charts and maps, predict atmospheric conditions, and prepare environmental reports. Evaluates data in reference to project planning, such as flood and drought control, water power and supply, drainage, irrigation, and inland navigation. Prepares and issues maps and reports indicating areas of seismic risk to existing or proposed construction or development.

GOE INFORMATION—Interest Area: 02. Science, Math, and Engineering. **Work Group:** 02.02. Physical Sciences. **Personality Type—**Investigative. Investigative occupations frequently involve working with ideas and require an extensive amount of thinking. These occupations can involve searching for facts and figuring out problems mentally. **Work Values—**Autonomy; Creativity; Ability Utilization; Responsibility; Independence. **Skills—**Science; Mathematics; Systems Analysis; Critical Thinking; Writing; Complex Problem Solving; Judgment and Decision Making; Reading Comprehension. **Abilities—***Cognitive:* Written Comprehension; Mathematical Reasoning; Deductive Reasoning; Oral Comprehension; Flexibility of Closure. *Psychomotor:* None met the criteria. *Physical:* None met the criteria. *Sensory:* None met the criteria. **General Work Activities—***Information Input:* Getting Information; Identifying Objects, Actions, and Events; Monitoring Processes, Materials, or Surroundings. *Mental Process:* Processing Information; Analyzing Data or Information; Updating and Using Relevant Knowledge. *Work Output:* Documenting or Recording Information; Interacting with Computers; Handling and Moving Objects. *Interacting with Others:* Interpreting Meaning of Information for Others; Providing Consultation and Advice to Others; Communicating with Other Workers. **Physical Work Conditions—**Outdoors; Very Hot or Cold; Extremely Bright or Inadequate Lighting; High Places; Specialized Protective or Safety Attire. **Other Job Characteristics—**Importance of Being Exact or Accurate; Consequence of Error; Importance of Repeating Same Tasks.

Experience—Job Zone 5. Extensive skill, knowledge, and experience are needed for these occupations. **Job Preparation:** SVP 8.0 and above—four years to more than 10 years. **Knowledge**—Physics; Geography; Mathematics; Chemistry; History and Archeology. **Instructional Programs**—Geology/Earth Science, General; Hydrology and Water Resources Science; Oceanography, Chemical and Physical.

Related DOT Jobs—024.061-030 Geophysicist; 024.061-034 Hydrologist; 024.061-050 Seismologist; 024.167-010 Geophysical-Laboratory Chief.

19-2099.99 Physical Scientists, All Other

- **Education/Training Required: Bachelor's degree**
- **Employed: No data available.**
- **Annual Earnings: No data available.**
- **Growth: 9.4%**
- **Annual Job Openings: 3,000**

All physical scientists not listed separately.

No task data available.

GOE INFORMATION—**Interest Area:** 02. Science, Math, and Engineering. **Work Group:** 02.02. Physical Sciences. **Note:** The Department of Labor has not collected some data for this job, so it has fewer details than the other descriptions.

Instructional Programs—Natural Sciences; Physical Sciences, Other.

Related DOT Jobs—040.061-062 Wood Technologist.

19-3000 Social Scientists and Related Workers

19-3011.00 Economists

- **Education/Training Required: Bachelor's degree**
- **Employed: 21,702**
- **Annual Earnings: $67,050**
- **Growth: 18.5%**
- **Annual Job Openings: 3,000**

Conduct research, prepare reports, or formulate plans to aid in solution of economic problems arising from production and distribution of goods and services. May collect and process economic and statistical data using econometric and sampling techniques.

Compile, analyze, and report data to explain economic phenomena and forecast market trends, applying mathematical models and statistical techniques. Develop economic guidelines and standards and prepare points of view used in forecasting trends and formulating economic policy. Forecast production and consumption of renewable resources and supply, consumption, and depletion of non-renewable resources. Study economic and statistical data in area of specialization, such as finance, labor, or agriculture. Formulate recommendations, policies, or plans to solve economic problems or to interpret markets. Provide advice and consultation on economic relationships to businesses, public and private agencies, and other employers. Supervise research projects and students' study projects. Teach theories, principles, and methods of economics. Testify at regulatory or legislative hearings concerning the estimated effects of changes in legislation or public policy and present recommendations based on cost-benefit analyses.

GOE INFORMATION—**Interest Area:** 02. Science, Math, and Engineering. **Work Group:** 02.04. Social Sciences. **Personality Type**—Investigative. Investigative occupations frequently involve working with ideas and require an extensive amount of thinking. These occupations can involve searching for facts and figuring out problems mentally. **Work Values**—Autonomy; Authority; Creativity; Ability Utilization; Good Working Conditions. **Skills**—Systems Evaluation; Systems Analysis; Complex Problem Solving; Judgment and Decision Making; Persuasion; Mathematics; Writing; Monitoring. **Abilities**—*Cognitive:* Written Expression; Mathematical Reasoning; Oral Expression; Number Facility; Deductive Reasoning. *Psychomotor:* None met the criteria. *Physical:* None met the criteria. *Sensory:* Speech Clarity; Near Vision; Speech Recognition; Auditory Attention; Far Vision. **General Work Activities**—*Information Input:* Getting Information; Identifying Objects, Actions, and Events; Monitoring Processes, Materials, or Surroundings. *Mental Process:* Updating and Using Relevant Knowledge; Analyzing Data or Information; Processing Information. *Work Output:* Documenting or Recording Information; Interacting with Computers; Performing General Physical Activities. *Interacting with Others:* Providing Consultation and Advice to Others; Teaching Others; Communicating with Other Workers. **Physical Work Conditions**—Sitting; Indoors. **Other Job Characteristics**—Importance of Being Exact or Accurate; Consequence of Error; Degree of Automation.

Experience—Job Zone 5. Extensive skill, knowledge, and experience are needed for these occupations. **Job Preparation:** SVP 8.0 and above—four years to more than 10 years. **Knowledge**—Economics and Accounting; Education and Training; Mathematics; Personnel and Human Resources; Production and Processing. **Instructional Programs**—Agricultural Economics; Applied Economics; Business/Managerial Economics; Development Economics and International Development; Econometrics and Quantitative Economics; Economics, General; Economics, Other; International Economics.

Related DOT Jobs—050.067-010 Economist.

19-3021.00 Market Research Analysts

- **Education/Training Required: Bachelor's degree**
- **Employed: 90,021**
- **Annual Earnings: $53,450**
- **Growth: 24.4%**
- **Annual Job Openings: 13,000**

Research market conditions in local, regional, or national areas to determine potential sales of a product or service. May gather information on competitors, prices, sales, and methods of marketing and distribution. May use survey results to create a marketing campaign based on regional preferences and buying habits.

Collect and analyze data on customer demographics, preferences, needs, and buying habits to identify potential markets and factors affecting product demand. Conduct research on consumer opinions and marketing strategies, collaborating with marketing professionals, statisticians, pollsters, and other professionals. Develop and implement procedures for identifying advertising needs. Devise and evaluate methods and procedures for collecting data (such as surveys, opinion polls, or questionnaires) or arrange to obtain existing data. Forecast and track marketing and sales trends, analyzing collected data. Gather data on competitors and analyze their prices, sales, and method of marketing and distribution. Measure and assess customer and employee satisfaction. Measure the effectiveness of marketing, advertising, and communications programs and strategies. Monitor industry statistics and follow trends in trade literature. Prepare reports of findings, illustrating data graphically and translating complex findings into written text. Attend staff conferences to provide management with information and proposals concerning the promotion, distribution, design, and pricing of company products or services. Direct trained survey interviewers. Seek and provide information to help companies determine their position in the marketplace.

GOE INFORMATION—Interest Area: 13. General Management and Support. **Work Group:** 13.02. Management Support. **Personality Type—** Investigative. Investigative occupations frequently involve working with ideas and require an extensive amount of thinking. These occupations can involve searching for facts and figuring out problems mentally. **Work Values—**Autonomy; Good Working Conditions; Recognition; Advancement; Creativity. **Skills—**Writing; Systems Analysis; Programming; Mathematics; Complex Problem Solving; Systems Evaluation; Monitoring; Operations Analysis. **Abilities—**_Cognitive:_ Mathematical Reasoning; Number Facility; Inductive Reasoning; Speed of Closure; Deductive Reasoning. _Psychomotor:_ None met the criteria. _Physical:_ None met the criteria. _Sensory:_ Auditory Attention; Near Vision; Speech Clarity; Speech Recognition; Night Vision. **General Work Activities—**_Information Input:_ Getting Information; Identifying Objects, Actions, and Events; Monitoring Processes, Materials, or Surroundings. _Mental Process:_ Analyzing Data or Information; Processing Information; Organizing, Planning, and Prioritizing. _Work Output:_ Documenting or Recording Information; Interacting with Computers; Performing General Physical Activities. _Interacting with Others:_ Communicating with Other Workers; Interpreting Meaning of Information for Others; Communicating with Persons Outside Organization. **Physical Work Conditions—**Sitting; Disease or Infections; Indoors; Walking or Running; Radiation. **Other Job Characteristics—**Importance of Being Exact or Accurate; Consequence of Error; Importance of Repeating Same Tasks.

Experience—Job Zone 4. A minimum of two to four years of work-related skill, knowledge, or experience is needed. **Job Preparation:** SVP 7.0 to less than 8.0—two years to less than 10 years. **Knowledge—**Sales and Marketing; Psychology; Computers and Electronics; Economics and Accounting; Mathematics. **Instructional Programs—**Applied Economics; Business/Managerial Economics; Econometrics and Quantitative Economics; Economics, General; International Economics; Marketing Research.

Related DOT Jobs—050.067-014 Market-Research Analyst I; 169.267-034 Research Analyst.

19-3022.00 Survey Researchers

- **Education/Training Required: Bachelor's degree**
- **Employed: 22,581**
- **Annual Earnings: $23,230**
- **Growth: 34.5%**
- **Annual Job Openings: 3,000**

Design or conduct surveys. May supervise interviewers who conduct the survey in person or over the telephone. May present survey results to client.

Collaborate with other researchers in the planning, implementation, and evaluation of surveys. Conduct surveys and collect data, using methods such as interviews, questionnaires, focus groups, market analysis surveys, public opinion polls, literature reviews, and file reviews. Consult with clients in order to identify survey needs and any specific requirements, such as special samples. Determine and specify details of survey projects, including sources of information, procedures to be used, and the design of survey instruments and materials. Direct and review the work of staff members, including survey support staff and interviewers who gather survey data. Direct updates and changes in survey implementation and

methods. Monitor and evaluate survey progress and performance, using sample disposition reports and response rate calculations. Prepare and present summaries and analyses of survey data, including tables, graphs, and fact sheets that describe survey techniques and results. Produce documentation of the questionnaire development process, data collection methods, sampling designs, and decisions related to sample statistical weighting. Support, plan, and coordinate operations for single or multiple surveys. Analyze data from surveys, old records, and/or case studies, using statistical software programs. Conduct research in order to gather information about survey topics. Hire and train recruiters and data collectors. Review, classify, and record survey data in preparation for computer analysis. Write training manuals to be used by survey interviewers.

GOE INFORMATION—Interest Area: 02. Science, Math, and Engineering. **Work Group:** 02.04. Social Sciences. **Note:** The Department of Labor has not collected some data for this job, so it has fewer details than the other descriptions.

Instructional Programs—Applied Economics; Business/Managerial Economics; Economics, General; Marketing Research.

Related DOT Jobs—No related DOT jobs.

19-3031.00 Clinical, Counseling, and School Psychologists

- **Education/Training Required: Master's degree**
- **Employed: No data available.**
- **Annual Earnings: $50,420**
- **Growth: 18.1%**
- **Annual Job Openings: 18,000**

Diagnose and treat mental disorders; learning disabilities; and cognitive, behavioral, and emotional problems by using individual, child, family, and group therapies. May design and implement behavior modification programs.

No task data available.

GOE INFORMATION—Interest Area: 12. Education and Social Service. **Work Group:** 12.02. Social Services. **Note:** The Department of Labor has not collected some data for this job, so it has fewer details than the other descriptions.

Instructional Programs—Clinical Child Psychology; Clinical Psychology; Counseling Psychology; Developmental and Child Psychology; Psychoanalysis and Psychotherapy; Psychology, General; School Psychology.

Related DOT Jobs—045.061-010 Psychologist, Developmental; 045.061-018 Psychologist, Experimental; 045.067-010 Psychologist, Educational; 045.067-018 Psychometrist; 045.107-022 Clinical Psychologist; 045.107-026 Psychologist, Counseling; 045.107-034 Psychologist, School; 045.107-046 Psychologist, Chief; 045.107-050 Clinical Therapist.

19-3031.01 Educational Psychologists

- **Education/Training Required: Master's degree**
- **Employed: No data available.**
- **Annual Earnings: $50,420**
- **Growth: 18.1%**
- **Annual Job Openings: 18,000**

Investigate processes of learning and teaching and develop psychological principles and techniques applicable to educational problems.

Assess an individual child's needs, limitations, and potential, using observation, review of school records, and consultation with parents and school personnel. Counsel children and families to help solve conflicts and problems in learning and adjustment. Collect and analyze data to evaluate the effectiveness of academic programs and other services, such as behavioral management systems. Collaborate with other educational professionals to develop teaching strategies and school programs. Compile and interpret students' test results, along with information from teachers and parents, in order to diagnose conditions and to help assess eligibility for special services. Design classes and programs to meet the needs of special students. Develop individualized educational plans in collaboration with teachers and other staff members. Promote an understanding of child development and its relationship to learning and behavior. Provide consultation to parents, teachers, administrators, and others on topics such as learning styles and behavior modification techniques. Provide educational programs on topics such as classroom management, teaching strategies, or parenting skills. Refer students and their families to appropriate community agencies for medical, vocational, or social services. Select, administer, and score psychological tests. Serve as a resource to help families and schools deal with crises, such as separation and loss. Attend workshops, seminars, and/or professional meetings in order to remain informed of new developments in school psychology. Conduct research to generate new knowledge that can be used to address learning and behavior issues. Initiate and direct efforts to foster tolerance, understanding, and appreciation of diversity in school communities. Maintain student records, including special education reports, confidential records, records of services provided, and behavioral data. Report any pertinent information to the proper authorities in cases of child endangerment, neglect, or abuse.

GOE INFORMATION—Interest Area: 12. Education and Social Service. **Work Group:** 12.03. Educational Services. **Personality Type—**Investigative. Investigative occupations frequently involve working with ideas and require an extensive amount of thinking. These occupations can involve searching for facts and figuring out problems mentally. **Work Values—**Social Service; Creativity; Autonomy; Ability Utilization; Achievement. **Skills—**Systems Evaluation; Social Perceptiveness; Complex Problem Solving; Systems Analysis; Learning Strategies; Science; Mathematics; Writing. **Abilities—***Cognitive:* Category Flexibility; Written Expression; Inductive Reasoning; Speed of Closure; Oral Expression. *Psychomotor:* Reaction Time; Response Orientation. *Physical:* None met the criteria. *Sensory:* Auditory Attention; Sound Localization; Speech Clarity; Speech Recognition; Near Vision. **General Work Activities—***Information Input:* Getting Information; Identifying Objects, Actions, and Events; Monitoring Processes, Materials, or Surroundings. *Mental Process:* Judging Qualities of Things, Services, or Other People's Work; Analyzing Data or Information; Processing Information. *Work Output:* Documenting or Recording Information; Handling and Moving Objects; Interacting with Computers. *Interacting with Others:* Communicating with Other Workers; Interpreting Meaning of Information for Others; Communicating with Persons Outside Organization. **Physical Work Conditions—**Sitting; Walking or Running; Indoors; Disease or Infections; Radiation. **Other Job Characteristics—**Importance of Being Exact or Accurate; Consequence of Error; Importance of Repeating Same Tasks.

Experience—Job Zone 4. A minimum of two to four years of work-related skill, knowledge, or experience is needed. **Job Preparation:** SVP 7.0 to less than 8.0—two years to less than 10 years. **Knowledge—**Education and Training; Psychology; Therapy and Counseling; Sociology and Anthropology; Administration and Management. **Instructional Programs—**Clinical Child Psychology; Clinical Psychology; Counseling Psychology; Developmental and Child Psychology; Psychoanalysis and Psychotherapy; Psychology, General; School Psychology.

Related DOT Jobs—045.067-010 Psychologist, Educational; 045.067-018 Psychometrist; 045.107-034 Psychologist, School.

19-3031.02 Clinical Psychologists

- **Education/Training Required: Master's degree**
- **Employed: No data available.**
- **Annual Earnings: $50,420**
- **Growth: 18.1%**
- **Annual Job Openings: 18,000**

Diagnose or evaluate mental and emotional disorders of individuals through observation, interview, and psychological tests;, formulate and administer programs of treatment.

Observes individual at play, in group interactions, or in other situations to detect indications of mental deficiency, abnormal behavior, or maladjustment. Develops treatment plan, including type, frequency, intensity, and duration of therapy, in collaboration with psychiatrist and other specialists. Analyzes information to assess client problems, determine advisability of counseling, and refer client to other specialists, institutions, or support services. Conducts individual and group counseling sessions regarding psychological or emotional problems, such as stress, substance abuse, and family situations. Responds to client reactions, evaluates effectiveness of counseling or treatment, and modifies plan as needed. Interviews individuals, couples, or families and reviews records to obtain information on medical, psychological, emotional, relationship, or other problems. Selects, administers, scores, and interprets psychological tests to obtain information on individual's intelligence, achievement, interests, and personality. Utilizes treatment methods such as psychotherapy, hypnosis, behavior modification, stress reduction therapy, psychodrama, and play therapy. Plans and develops accredited psychological service programs in psychiatric center or hospital in collaboration with psychiatrists and other professional staff. Consults reference material, such as textbooks, manuals, and journals, to identify symptoms, make diagnoses, and develop approach to treatment. Assists clients to gain insight, define goals, and plan action to achieve effective personal, social, educational, and vocational development and adjustment. Provides occupational, educational, and other information to enable individual to formulate realistic educational and vocational plans. Plans, supervises, and conducts psychological research in fields such as personality development and diagnosis, treatment, and prevention of mental disorders. Directs, coordinates, and evaluates activities of psychological staff and student interns engaged in patient evaluation and treatment in psychiatric facility. Provides psychological services and advice to private firms and community agencies on individual cases or mental health programs. Develops, directs, and participates in staff training programs.

GOE INFORMATION—Interest Area: 12. Education and Social Service. **Work Group:** 12.02. Social Services. **Personality Type—**Investigative. Investigative occupations frequently involve working with ideas and require an extensive amount of thinking. These occupations can involve searching for facts and figuring out problems mentally. **Work Values—**Social Service; Creativity; Autonomy; Responsibility; Ability Utilization. **Skills—**Social Perceptiveness; Active Listening; Systems Evaluation; Complex Problem Solving; Speaking; Systems Analysis; Reading Comprehension; Persuasion. **Abilities—***Cognitive:* Written Expression; Inductive Reasoning; Problem Sensitivity; Oral Comprehension; Written Comprehension. *Psychomotor:* None met the criteria. *Physical:* None met the criteria. *Sensory:* Speech Clarity; Speech Recognition; Near Vision; Auditory Attention; Far Vision. **General Work Activities—***Information Input:* Getting Information; Identifying Objects, Actions, and Events; Monitoring Processes, Materials, or Surroundings. *Mental Process:* Analyzing Data or Information; Updating and Using Relevant

Knowledge; Making Decisions and Solving Problems. *Work Output:* Documenting or Recording Information; Interacting with Computers; Handling and Moving Objects. *Interacting with Others:* Communicating with Persons Outside Organization; Communicating with Other Workers; Assisting and Caring for Others. **Physical Work Conditions**—Sitting; Indoors; Disease or Infections. **Other Job Characteristics**—Consequence of Error; Importance of Being Exact or Accurate; Importance of Repeating Same Tasks.

Experience—Job Zone 4. A minimum of two to four years of work-related skill, knowledge, or experience is needed. **Job Preparation:** SVP 7.0 to less than 8.0—two years to less than 10 years. **Knowledge**—Therapy and Counseling; Psychology; Customer and Personal Service; Administration and Management; Sociology and Anthropology. **Instructional Programs**—Clinical Child Psychology; Clinical Psychology; Counseling Psychology; Developmental and Child Psychology; Psychoanalysis and Psychotherapy; Psychology, General; School Psychology.

Related DOT Jobs—045.107-022 Clinical Psychologist; 045.107-046 Psychologist, Chief; 045.107-050 Clinical Therapist.

19-3031.03 Counseling Psychologists
- **Education/Training Required: Master's degree**
- **Employed: No data available.**
- **Annual Earnings: $50,420**
- **Growth: 18.1%**
- **Annual Job Openings: 18,000**

Assess and evaluate individuals' problems through the use of case history, interview, and observation and provide individual or group counseling services to assist individuals in achieving more effective personal, social, educational, and vocational development and adjustment.

Counsels clients to assist them in understanding personal or interactive problems, defining goals, and developing realistic action plans. Collects information about individuals or clients, using interviews, case histories, observational techniques, and other assessment methods. Develops therapeutic and treatment plans based on individual interests, abilities, or needs of clients. Selects, administers, or interprets psychological tests to assess intelligence, aptitude, ability, or interests. Advises clients on the potential benefits of counseling or makes referrals to specialists or other institutions for non-counseling problems. Analyzes data such as interview notes, test results, and reference manuals and texts to identify symptoms and diagnose the nature of client's problems. Evaluates results of counseling methods to determine the reliability and validity of treatments. Consults with other professionals to discuss therapy or treatment, counseling resources, or techniques and to share occupational information. Conducts research to develop or improve diagnostic or therapeutic counseling techniques.

GOE INFORMATION—**Interest Area:** 12. Education and Social Service. **Work Group:** 12.02. Social Services. **Personality Type**—Social. Social occupations frequently involve working with, communicating with, and teaching people. These occupations often involve helping or providing service to others. **Work Values**—Social Service; Creativity; Autonomy; Achievement; Good Working Conditions. **Skills**—Social Perceptiveness; Active Listening; Critical Thinking; Learning Strategies; Reading Comprehension; Complex Problem Solving; Speaking; Monitoring. **Abilities**—*Cognitive:* Problem Sensitivity; Inductive Reasoning; Oral Expression; Oral Comprehension; Written Comprehension. *Psychomotor:* None met the criteria. *Physical:* None met the criteria. *Sensory:* Speech Recognition; Speech Clarity; Night Vision. **General Work Activities**—*Information Input:* Identifying Objects, Actions, and Events; Getting Information;

Monitoring Processes, Materials, or Surroundings. *Mental Process:* Analyzing Data or Information; Making Decisions and Solving Problems; Thinking Creatively. *Work Output:* Documenting or Recording Information; Interacting with Computers; Handling and Moving Objects. *Interacting with Others:* Communicating with Persons Outside Organization; Establishing and Maintaining Relationships; Assisting and Caring for Others. **Physical Work Conditions**—Sitting; Indoors; Disease or Infections. **Other Job Characteristics**—Consequence of Error; Importance of Being Exact or Accurate; Pace Determined by Speed of Equipment.

Experience—Job Zone 5. Extensive skill, knowledge, and experience are needed for these occupations. **Job Preparation:** SVP 8.0 and above—four years to more than 10 years. **Knowledge**—Therapy and Counseling; Psychology; Philosophy and Theology; Sociology and Anthropology; Education and Training. **Instructional Programs**—Clinical Child Psychology; Clinical Psychology; Counseling Psychology; Developmental and Child Psychology; Psychoanalysis and Psychotherapy; Psychology, General; School Psychology.

Related DOT Jobs—045.107-026 Psychologist, Counseling; 045.107-054 Counselor, Marriage and Family.

19-3032.00 Industrial-Organizational Psychologists
- **Education/Training Required: Master's degree**
- **Employed: No data available.**
- **Annual Earnings: $66,010**
- **Growth: 18.1%**
- **Annual Job Openings: 18,000**

Apply principles of psychology to personnel, administration, management, sales, and marketing problems. Activities may include policy planning; employee screening, training, and development; and organizational development and analysis. May work with management to reorganize the work setting to improve worker productivity.

Analyze data, using statistical methods and applications, in order to evaluate the outcomes and effectiveness of workplace programs. Analyze job requirements and content in order to establish criteria for classification, selection, training, and other related personnel functions. Conduct research studies of physical work environments, organizational structures, communication systems, group interactions, morale, and motivation in order to assess organizational functioning. Develop and implement employee selection and placement programs. Develop interview techniques, rating scales, and psychological tests used to assess skills, abilities, and interests for the purpose of employee selection, placement, and promotion. Facilitate organizational development and change. Formulate and implement training programs, applying principles of learning and individual differences. Identify training and development needs. Observe and interview workers in order to obtain information about the physical, mental, and educational requirements of jobs as well as information about aspects such as job satisfaction. Study organizational effectiveness, productivity, and efficiency, including the nature of workplace supervision and leadership. Advise management concerning personnel, managerial, and marketing policies and practices and their potential effects on organizational effectiveness and efficiency. Assess employee performance. Counsel workers about job and career-related issues. Participate in mediation and dispute resolution. Study consumers' reactions to new products and package designs and to advertising efforts, using surveys and tests. Write reports on research findings and implications in order to contribute to general knowledge and to suggest potential changes in organizational functioning.

GOE INFORMATION—Interest Area: 02. Science, Math, and Engineering. Work Group: 02.04. Social Sciences. Personality Type—Investigative. Investigative occupations frequently involve working with ideas and require an extensive amount of thinking. These occupations can involve searching for facts and figuring out problems mentally. Work Values—Creativity; Autonomy; Good Working Conditions; Compensation; Authority. Skills—Systems Evaluation; Complex Problem Solving; Systems Analysis; Mathematics; Management of Personnel Resources; Writing; Reading Comprehension; Science. Abilities—Cognitive: Originality; Written Expression; Mathematical Reasoning; Oral Expression; Oral Comprehension. Psychomotor: None met the criteria. Physical: None met the criteria. Sensory: Speech Clarity; Speech Recognition; Night Vision. General Work Activities—Information Input: Getting Information; Identifying Objects, Actions, and Events; Monitoring Processes, Materials, or Surroundings. Mental Process: Analyzing Data or Information; Processing Information; Updating and Using Relevant Knowledge. Work Output: Documenting or Recording Information; Interacting with Computers; Handling and Moving Objects. Interacting with Others: Providing Consultation and Advice to Others; Communicating with Other Workers; Teaching Others. Physical Work Conditions—Indoors; Sitting. Other Job Characteristics—Consequence of Error; Importance of Being Exact or Accurate; Degree of Automation.

Experience—Job Zone 5. Extensive skill, knowledge, and experience are needed for these occupations. Job Preparation: SVP 8.0 and above—four years to more than 10 years. Knowledge—Personnel and Human Resources; Psychology; Education and Training; Administration and Management; Therapy and Counseling. Instructional Programs—Industrial and Organizational Psychology; Psychology, General.

Related DOT Jobs—045.061-014 Psychologist, Engineering; 045.107-030 Psychologist, Industrial-Organizational.

19-3039.99 Psychologists, All Other

- Education/Training Required: Master's degree
- Employed: No data available.
- Annual Earnings: No data available.
- Growth: 18.1%
- Annual Job Openings: 18,000

All psychologists not listed separately.

No task data available.

GOE INFORMATION—Interest Area: 02. Science, Math, and Engineering. Work Group: 02.04. Social Sciences. Note: The Department of Labor has not collected some data for this job, so it has fewer details than the other descriptions.

Instructional Programs—Behavioral Sciences; Cognitive Psychology and Psycholinguistics; Community Psychology; Comparative Psychology; Developmental and Child Psychology; Educational Psychology; Environmental Psychology; Experimental Psychology; Family Psychology; Forensic Psychology; Geropsychology; Health/Medical Psychology; Personality Psychology; Physiological Psychology/Psychobiology; Psychology, General; Psychology, Other; Psychometrics and Quantitative Psychology; Psychopharmacology; Social Psychology.

Related DOT Jobs—045.067-014 Psychologist, Social.

19-3041.00 Sociologists

- Education/Training Required: Master's degree
- Employed: No data available.
- Annual Earnings: $54,880
- Growth: 17.2%
- Annual Job Openings: 2,000

Study human society and social behavior by examining the groups and social institutions that people form, as well as various social, religious, political, and business organizations. May study the behavior and interaction of groups, trace their origin and growth, and analyze the influence of group activities on individual members.

Collects and analyzes scientific data concerning social phenomena, such as community, associations, social institutions, ethnic minorities, and social change. Plans and directs research on crime and prevention, group relations in industrial organization, urban communities, and physical environment and technology. Observes group interaction and interviews group members to identify problems and collect data related to factors such as group organization and authority relationships. Develops research designs on basis of existing knowledge and evolving theory. Develops approaches to solution of group's problems, based on findings and incorporating sociological research and study in related disciplines. Constructs and tests methods of data collection. Collects information and makes judgments through observation, interview, and review of documents. Analyzes and evaluates data. Develops intervention procedures, utilizing techniques such as interviews, consultations, role-playing, and participant observation of group interaction, to facilitate solution. Monitors group interaction and role affiliations to evaluate progress and to determine need for additional change. Consults with lawmakers, administrators, and other officials who deal with problems of social change. Interprets methods employed and findings to individuals within agency and community. Prepares publications and reports on subjects such as social factors which affect health, demographic characteristics, and social and racial discrimination in society. Collaborates with research workers in other disciplines. Directs work of statistical clerks, statisticians, and others.

GOE INFORMATION—Interest Area: 02. Science, Math, and Engineering. Work Group: 02.04. Social Sciences. Personality Type—Investigative. Investigative occupations frequently involve working with ideas and require an extensive amount of thinking. These occupations can involve searching for facts and figuring out problems mentally. Work Values—Creativity; Autonomy; Responsibility; Good Working Conditions; Ability Utilization. Skills—Writing; Mathematics; Complex Problem Solving; Systems Analysis; Social Perceptiveness; Critical Thinking; Systems Evaluation; Reading Comprehension. Abilities—Cognitive: Written Expression; Mathematical Reasoning; Oral Comprehension; Written Comprehension; Originality. Psychomotor: None met the criteria. Physical: None met the criteria. Sensory: Speech Recognition; Speech Clarity; Auditory Attention. General Work Activities—Information Input: Getting Information; Identifying Objects, Actions, and Events; Monitoring Processes, Materials, or Surroundings. Mental Process: Analyzing Data or Information; Processing Information; Making Decisions and Solving Problems. Work Output: Documenting or Recording Information; Interacting with Computers; Handling and Moving Objects. Interacting with Others: Providing Consultation and Advice to Others; Communicating with Other Workers; Interpreting Meaning of Information for Others. Physical Work Conditions—Sitting; Indoors; Disease or Infections. Other Job Characteristics—Consequence of Error; Importance of Being Exact or Accurate; Pace Determined by Speed of Equipment.

Experience—Job Zone 3. Previous work-related skill, knowledge, or experience is required. Job Preparation: SVP 6.0 to less than 7.0—more than one year and less than four years. Knowledge—Sociology and Anthropology; Education and Training; Philosophy and Theology; Psychology; English Language. Instructional Programs—Criminology; Demography and Population Studies; Sociology; Urban Studies/Affairs.

Related DOT Jobs—054.067-010 Research Worker, Social Welfare; 054.067-014 Sociologist; 054.107-010 Clinical Sociologist.

19-3051.00 Urban and Regional Planners

- Education/Training Required: Master's degree
- Employed: 29,822
- Annual Earnings: $48,530
- Growth: 16.4%
- Annual Job Openings: 3,000

Develop comprehensive plans and programs for use of land and physical facilities of local jurisdictions, such as towns, cities, counties, and metropolitan areas.

Design, promote, and administer government plans and policies affecting land use, zoning, public utilities, community facilities, housing, and transportation. Hold public meetings and confer with government, social scientists, lawyers, developers, the public, and special interest groups to formulate and develop land use or community plans. Recommend approval, denial, or conditional approval of proposals. Determine the effects of regulatory limitations on projects. Assess the feasibility of proposals and identify necessary changes. Create, prepare, or requisition graphic and narrative reports on land use data, including land area maps overlaid with geographic variables such as population density. Advise planning officials on project feasibility, cost-effectiveness, regulatory conformance, and possible alternatives. Conduct field investigations, surveys, impact studies, or other research in order to compile and analyze data on economic, social, regulatory, and physical factors affecting land use. Discuss with planning officials the purpose of land use projects such as transportation, conservation, residential, commercial, industrial, and community use. Keep informed about economic and legal issues involved in zoning codes, building codes, and environmental regulations. Mediate community disputes and assist in developing alternative plans and recommendations for programs or projects. Coordinate work with economic consultants and architects during the formulation of plans and the design of large pieces of infrastructure. Review and evaluate environmental impact reports pertaining to private and public planning projects and programs. Supervise and coordinate the work of urban planning technicians and technologists. Investigate property availability.

GOE INFORMATION—Interest Area: 02. Science, Math, and Engineering. **Work Group:** 02.04. Social Sciences. **Personality Type—**Investigative. Investigative occupations frequently involve working with ideas and require an extensive amount of thinking. These occupations can involve searching for facts and figuring out problems mentally. **Work Values—**Creativity; Autonomy; Ability Utilization; Achievement; Social Status. **Skills—**Complex Problem Solving; Persuasion; Coordination; Speaking; Service Orientation; Writing; Time Management; Social Perceptiveness. **Abilities—***Cognitive:* Originality; Category Flexibility; Written Expression; Deductive Reasoning; Visualization. *Psychomotor:* Finger Dexterity; Multilimb Coordination. *Physical:* Gross Body Coordination. *Sensory:* Far Vision; Speech Recognition; Near Vision; Speech Clarity; Depth Perception. **General Work Activities—***Information Input:* Identifying Objects, Actions, and Events; Getting Information; Monitoring Processes, Materials, or Surroundings. *Mental Process:* Making Decisions and Solving Problems; Organizing, Planning, and Prioritizing; Updating and Using Relevant Knowledge. *Work Output:* Documenting or Recording Information; Interacting with Computers; Handling and Moving Objects. *Interacting with Others:* Establishing and Maintaining Relationships; Communicating with Persons Outside Organization; Performing for or Working with the Public. **Physical Work Conditions—**Sitting; Outdoors; Extremely Bright or Inadequate Lighting; Very Hot or Cold; Disease or Infections. **Other Job Characteristics—**Importance of Being Exact or Accurate; Degree of Automation; Importance of Repeating Same Tasks.

Experience—Job Zone 4. A minimum of two to four years of work-related skill, knowledge, or experience is needed. **Job Preparation:** SVP 7.0 to less than 8.0—two years to less than 10 years. **Knowledge—**Customer and Personal Service; Design; Geography; Building and Construction; Law and Government. **Instructional Programs—**City/Urban, Community, and Regional Planning.

Related DOT Jobs—188.167-110 Planner, Program Services; 199.167-014 Urban Planner.

19-3091.00 Anthropologists and Archeologists

- Education/Training Required: Bachelor's degree
- Employed: No data available.
- Annual Earnings: $38,890
- Growth: 17.2%
- Annual Job Openings: 2,000

Study the origin, development, and behavior of humans. May study the way of life, language, or physical characteristics of existing people in various parts of the world. May engage in systematic recovery and examination of material evidence, such as tools or pottery remaining from past human cultures, in order to determine the history, customs, and living habits of earlier civilizations.

No task data available.

GOE INFORMATION—Interest Area: 02. Science, Math, and Engineering. **Work Group:** 02.04. Social Sciences. **Note:** The Department of Labor has not collected some data for this job, so it has fewer details than the other descriptions.

Instructional Programs—Anthropology; Archeology; Physical Anthropology.

Related DOT Jobs—055.067-010 Anthropologist; 055.067-014 Anthropologist, Physical; 055.067-018 Archeologist; 055.067-022 Ethnologist.

19-3091.01 Anthropologists

- Education/Training Required: Bachelor's degree
- Employed: No data available.
- Annual Earnings: $38,890
- Growth: 17.2%
- Annual Job Openings: 2,000

Research or study the origins and physical, social, and cultural development and behavior of humans and the cultures and organizations they have created.

Compare the customs, values, and social patterns of different cultures. Formulate general rules that describe how cultures and societies develop and behave. Study the origin and physical, social, or cultural development of humans, including physical attributes, cultural traditions, possessions, beliefs, languages, and settlement patterns. Study linguistics, chemistry, nutrition, or behavioral science in order to apply those disciplines' methodologies to the study of culture. Study specific groups in the field, observing and interviewing members to obtain information about topics such as group and family relationships and activities. Write about and present research findings. Advise government agencies and private organizations on matters such as the concerns of different groups and cultures. Examine museum collections of human fossils to determine how they fit into evolutionary theory. Gather and analyze artifacts and skeletal remains in order to increase knowledge of ancient cultures.

Observe and measure bodily variations and physical attributes in different human groups. Collaborate with police departments and pathologists in forensic activities such as tooth and bone structure identification. Teach anthropology.

GOE INFORMATION—Interest Area: 02. Science, Math, and Engineering. **Work Group:** 02.04. Social Sciences. **Personality Type**—Investigative. Investigative occupations frequently involve working with ideas and require an extensive amount of thinking. These occupations can involve searching for facts and figuring out problems mentally. **Work Values**—Creativity; Autonomy; Ability Utilization; Responsibility; Variety. **Skills**—Writing; Complex Problem Solving; Science; Critical Thinking; Social Perceptiveness; Reading Comprehension; Mathematics; Speaking. **Abilities**—*Cognitive:* Written Expression; Oral Comprehension; Written Comprehension; Inductive Reasoning; Fluency of Ideas. *Psychomotor:* None met the criteria. *Physical:* None met the criteria. *Sensory:* Speech Clarity; Speech Recognition; Night Vision; Auditory Attention; Far Vision. **General Work Activities**—*Information Input:* Getting Information; Identifying Objects, Actions, and Events; Estimating Needed Characteristics. *Mental Process:* Processing Information; Analyzing Data or Information; Judging Qualities of Things, Services, or Other People's Work. *Work Output:* Documenting or Recording Information; Interacting with Computers; Handling and Moving Objects. *Interacting with Others:* Interpreting Meaning of Information for Others; Providing Consultation and Advice to Others; Communicating with Other Workers. **Physical Work Conditions**—Sitting; Outdoors; Kneeling, Crouching, or Crawling. **Other Job Characteristics**—Importance of Being Exact or Accurate; Importance of Repeating Same Tasks; Pace Determined by Speed of Equipment.

Experience—Job Zone 4. A minimum of two to four years of work-related skill, knowledge, or experience is needed. **Job Preparation:** SVP 7.0 to less than 8.0—two years to less than 10 years. **Knowledge**—Sociology and Anthropology; History and Archeology; Biology; Geography; Philosophy and Theology. **Instructional Programs**—Anthropology; Archeology; Physical Anthropology.

Related DOT Jobs—055.067-010 Anthropologist; 055.067-014 Anthropologist, Physical; 055.067-022 Ethnologist.

19-3091.02 Archeologists

- Education/Training Required: Bachelor's degree
- Employed: No data available.
- Annual Earnings: $38,890
- Growth: 17.2%
- Annual Job Openings: 2,000

Conduct research to reconstruct record of past human life and culture from human remains, artifacts, architectural features, and structures recovered through excavation, underwater recovery, or other means of discovery.

Clean, restore, and preserve artifacts. Collect artifacts made of stone, bone, metal, and other materials, placing them in bags and marking them to show where they were found. Compare findings from one site with archeological data from other sites to find similarities or differences. Consult site reports, existing artifacts, and topographic maps to identify archaeological sites. Create a grid of each site and draw and update maps of unit profiles, stratum surfaces, features, and findings. Create artifact typologies to organize and make sense of past material cultures. Describe artifacts' physical properties or attributes, such as the materials from which artifacts are made and their size, shape, function, and decoration. Develop and test theories concerning the origin and development of past cultures. Record the exact locations and conditions of artifacts uncovered in diggings or surveys, using drawings and photographs as necessary. Research, survey, and assess sites of past societies and cultures in search of answers to specific research questions. Study objects and structures recovered by excavation to identify, date, and/or authenticate them and to interpret their significance. Write, present, and publish reports that record site history, methodology, and artifact analysis results, along with recommendations for conserving and interpreting findings. Assess archaeological sites for resource management, development, or conservation purposes and recommend methods for site protection. Lead field training sites and train field staff, students, and volunteers in excavation methods. Teach archaeology at colleges and universities.

GOE INFORMATION—Interest Area: 02. Science, Math, and Engineering. **Work Group:** 02.04. Social Sciences. **Personality Type**—Investigative. Investigative occupations frequently involve working with ideas and require an extensive amount of thinking. These occupations can involve searching for facts and figuring out problems mentally. **Work Values**—Autonomy; Creativity; Responsibility; Achievement; Recognition. **Skills**—Science; Complex Problem Solving; Writing; Critical Thinking; Reading Comprehension; Equipment Selection; Judgment and Decision Making. **Abilities**—*Cognitive:* Inductive Reasoning; Deductive Reasoning; Category Flexibility; Written Comprehension; Written Expression. *Psychomotor:* None met the criteria. *Physical:* Extent Flexibility; Gross Body Coordination; Gross Body Equilibrium. *Sensory:* Visual Color Discrimination; Peripheral Vision. **General Work Activities**—*Information Input:* Getting Information; Identifying Objects, Actions, and Events; Estimating Needed Characteristics. *Mental Process:* Judging Qualities of Things, Services, or Other People's Work; Processing Information; Analyzing Data or Information. *Work Output:* Documenting or Recording Information; Handling and Moving Objects; Performing General Physical Activities. *Interacting with Others:* Interpreting Meaning of Information for Others; Communicating with Other Workers; Communicating with Persons Outside Organization. **Physical Work Conditions**—Outdoors; Kneeling, Crouching, or Crawling; Very Hot or Cold; Cramped Work Space or Awkward Positions; Bending or Twisting the Body. **Other Job Characteristics**—Importance of Being Exact or Accurate; Consequence of Error; Pace Determined by Speed of Equipment.

Experience—Job Zone 4. A minimum of two to four years of work-related skill, knowledge, or experience is needed. **Job Preparation:** SVP 7.0 to less than 8.0—two years to less than 10 years. **Knowledge**—History and Archeology; Sociology and Anthropology; Geography; Foreign Language; Philosophy and Theology. **Instructional Programs**—Anthropology; Archeology; Physical Anthropology.

Related DOT Jobs—055.067-018 Archeologist.

19-3092.00 Geographers

- Education/Training Required: Bachelor's degree
- Employed: No data available.
- Annual Earnings: $48,410
- Growth: 17.2%
- Annual Job Openings: 2,000

Study nature and use of areas of earth's surface, relating and interpreting interactions of physical and cultural phenomena. Conduct research on physical aspects of a region, including land forms, climates, soils, plants, and animals, and conduct research on the spatial implications of human activities within a given area, including social characteristics, economic activities, and political organization, as well as researching interdependence between regions at scales ranging from local to global.

Analyze geographic distributions of physical and cultural phenomena on local, regional, continental, and global scales. Collect data on physical characteristics of specified areas, such as geological formations, climates, and vegetation, using surveying or meteorological equipment. Create and modify maps, graphs, and diagrams, using geographical information software and related equipment and principles of cartography such as coordinate systems, longitude, latitude, elevation, topography, and map scales. Gather and compile geographic data from sources including censuses, field observations, satellite imagery, aerial photographs, and existing maps. Locate and obtain existing geographic information databases. Write and present reports of research findings. Conduct fieldwork at outdoor sites. Develop, operate, and maintain geographical information (GIS) computer systems, including hardware, software, plotters, digitizers, printers, and video cameras. Provide consulting services in fields including resource development and management, business location and market area analysis, environmental hazards, regional cultural history, and urban social planning. Provide geographical information systems support to the private and public sectors. Study the economic, political, and cultural characteristics of a specific region's population. Teach geography.

GOE INFORMATION—Interest Area: 02. Science, Math, and Engineering. **Work Group:** 02.02. Physical Sciences. **Personality Type—**Investigative. Investigative occupations frequently involve working with ideas and require an extensive amount of thinking. These occupations can involve searching for facts and figuring out problems mentally. **Work Values—**Autonomy; Creativity; Ability Utilization; Responsibility; Social Status. **Skills—**Writing; Mathematics; Reading Comprehension; Critical Thinking; Complex Problem Solving; Science; Speaking. **Abilities—***Cognitive:* Written Expression; Spatial Orientation; Flexibility of Closure; Oral Expression; Written Comprehension. *Psychomotor:* Arm-Hand Steadiness; Rate Control. *Physical:* None met the criteria. *Sensory:* Night Vision; Far Vision; Visual Color Discrimination; Depth Perception; Glare Sensitivity. **General Work Activities—***Information Input:* Getting Information; Identifying Objects, Actions, and Events; Estimating Needed Characteristics. *Mental Process:* Processing Information; Analyzing Data or Information; Updating and Using Relevant Knowledge. *Work Output:* Documenting or Recording Information; Controlling Machines and Processes; Handling and Moving Objects. *Interacting with Others:* Communicating with Other Workers; Communicating with Persons Outside Organization; Interpreting Meaning of Information for Others. **Physical Work Conditions—**Outdoors; Kneeling, Crouching, or Crawling; Bending or Twisting the Body; Very Hot or Cold; Keeping or Regaining Balance. **Other Job Characteristics—**Importance of Being Exact or Accurate; Importance of Repeating Same Tasks; Pace Determined by Speed of Equipment.

Experience—Job Zone 4. A minimum of two to four years of work-related skill, knowledge, or experience is needed. **Job Preparation:** SVP 7.0 to less than 8.0—two years to less than 10 years. **Knowledge—**Geography; Sociology and Anthropology; Biology; Physics; History and Archeology. **Instructional Programs—**Geography.

Related DOT Jobs—029.067-010 Geographer; 029.067-014 Geographer, Physical.

19-3093.00 Historians

- **Education/Training Required: Bachelor's degree**
- **Employed: No data available.**
- **Annual Earnings: $42,940**
- **Growth: 17.2%**
- **Annual Job Openings: 2,000**

Research, analyze, record, and interpret the past as recorded in sources such as government and institutional records, newspapers and other periodicals, photographs, interviews, films, and unpublished manuscripts, such as personal diaries and letters.

Conduct historical research as a basis for the identification, conservation, and reconstruction of historic places and materials. Conduct historical research and publish or present findings and theories. Determine which topics to research or pursue research topics specified by clients or employers. Gather historical data from sources such as archives, court records, diaries, news files, and photographs, as well as collect data sources such as books, pamphlets, and periodicals. Organize data and analyze and interpret its authenticity and relative significance. Organize information for publication and for other means of dissemination, such as use in CD-ROMs or Internet sites. Research the history of a particular country or region or of a specific time period. Trace historical development in a particular field, such as social, cultural, political, or diplomatic history. Advise or consult with individuals and institutions regarding issues such as the historical authenticity of materials or the customs of a specific historical period. Collect detailed information on individuals for use in biographies. Coordinate activities of workers engaged in cataloging and filing materials. Interview people in order to gather information about historical events and to record oral histories. Prepare publications and exhibits or review those prepared by others in order to ensure their historical accuracy. Present historical accounts in terms of individuals or social, ethnic, political, economic, or geographic groupings. Research and prepare manuscripts in support of public programming and the development of exhibits at historic sites, museums, libraries, and archives. Teach and conduct research in colleges, universities, museums, and other research agencies and schools. Translate or request translation of reference materials. Edit historical society publications. Recommend actions related to historical art, such as which items to add to a collection or which items to display in an exhibit. Speak to various groups, organizations, and clubs in order to promote the aims and activities of historical societies.

GOE INFORMATION—Interest Area: 02. Science, Math, and Engineering. **Work Group:** 02.04. Social Sciences. **Personality Type—**Investigative. Investigative occupations frequently involve working with ideas and require an extensive amount of thinking. These occupations can involve searching for facts and figuring out problems mentally. **Work Values—**Autonomy; Good Working Conditions; Creativity; Responsibility; Achievement. **Skills—**Writing; Speaking; Reading Comprehension; Management of Personnel Resources; Complex Problem Solving; Critical Thinking; Management of Financial Resources; Management of Material Resources. **Abilities—***Cognitive:* Written Expression; Written Comprehension; Memorization; Oral Comprehension; Oral Expression. *Psychomotor:* None met the criteria. *Physical:* None met the criteria. *Sensory:* Speech Clarity; Speech Recognition; Near Vision. **General Work Activities—***Information Input:* Getting Information; Identifying Objects, Actions, and Events; Estimating Needed Characteristics. *Mental Process:* Judging Qualities of Things, Services, or Other People's Work; Analyzing Data or Information; Processing Information. *Work Output:* Documenting or Recording Information; Interacting with Computers; Handling and Moving Objects. *Interacting with Others:* Communicating with Persons Outside Organization; Interpreting Meaning of Information for Others; Communicating with Other Workers. **Physical Work Conditions—**Sitting; Indoors; Disease or Infections. **Other Job Characteristics—**Importance of Being Exact or Accurate; Consequence of Error; Pace Determined by Speed of Equipment.

Experience—Job Zone 4. A minimum of two to four years of work-related skill, knowledge, or experience is needed. **Job Preparation:** SVP 7.0 to less than 8.0—two years to less than 10 years. **Knowledge—**History and Archeology; Sociology and Anthropology; Communications and

Media; Philosophy and Theology; English Language. **Instructional Programs**—American History (United States); Ancient Studies/Civilization; Architectural History and Criticism, General; Asian History; Canadian History; Classical, Ancient Mediterranean, and Near Eastern Studies and Archaeology; Cultural Resource Management and Policy Analysis; European History; Historic Preservation and Conservation; Historic Preservation and Conservation, Other; History and Philosophy of Science and Technology; History, General; History, Other; Holocaust and Related Studies; Medieval and Renaissance Studies.

Related DOT Jobs—052.067-014 Director, State-Historical Society; 052.067-022 Historian; 052.067-026 Historian, Dramatic Arts; 052.167-010 Director, Research.

19-3094.00 Political Scientists
- **Education/Training Required: Master's degree**
- **Employed: No data available.**
- **Annual Earnings: $81,350**
- **Growth: 17.2%**
- **Annual Job Openings: 2,000**

Study the origin, development, and operation of political systems. Research a wide range of subjects, such as relations between the United States and foreign countries, the beliefs and institutions of foreign nations, or the politics of small towns or a major metropolis. May study topics such as public opinion, political decision making, and ideology. May analyze the structure and operation of governments as well as various political entities. May conduct public opinion surveys, analyze election results, or analyze public documents.

Conducts research into political philosophy and theories of political systems, such as governmental institutions, public laws, and international law. Analyzes and interprets results of studies and prepares reports detailing findings, recommendations, or conclusions. Consults with government officials, civic bodies, research agencies, and political parties. Organizes and conducts public opinion surveys and interprets results. Recommends programs and policies to institutions and organizations. Prepares reports detailing findings and conclusions.

GOE INFORMATION—**Interest Area:** 02. Science, Math, and Engineering. **Work Group:** 02.04. Social Sciences. **Personality Type**—Investigative. Investigative occupations frequently involve working with ideas and require an extensive amount of thinking. These occupations can involve searching for facts and figuring out problems mentally. **Work Values**—Autonomy; Creativity; Good Working Conditions; Responsibility; Ability Utilization. **Skills**—Systems Analysis; Writing; Mathematics; Complex Problem Solving; Systems Evaluation; Speaking; Reading Comprehension; Social Perceptiveness. **Abilities**—*Cognitive:* Written Expression; Written Comprehension; Inductive Reasoning; Oral Comprehension; Oral Expression. *Psychomotor:* None met the criteria. *Physical:* None met the criteria. *Sensory:* Speech Recognition; Speech Clarity; Auditory Attention. **General Work Activities**—*Information Input:* Getting Information; Identifying Objects, Actions, and Events; Estimating Needed Characteristics. *Mental Process:* Processing Information; Analyzing Data or Information; Making Decisions and Solving Problems. *Work Output:* Documenting or Recording Information; Interacting with Computers; Handling and Moving Objects. *Interacting with Others:* Providing Consultation and Advice to Others; Communicating with Persons Outside Organization; Communicating with Other Workers. **Physical Work Conditions**—Sitting; Indoors. **Other Job Characteristics**—Importance of Being Exact or Accurate; Pace Determined by Speed of Equipment; Importance of Repeating Same Tasks.

Experience—Job Zone 5. Extensive skill, knowledge, and experience are needed for these occupations. **Job Preparation:** SVP 8.0 and above—four years to more than 10 years. **Knowledge**—Law and Government; Philosophy and Theology; History and Archeology; Sociology and Anthropology; Communications and Media. **Instructional Programs**—American Government and Politics (United States); Canadian Government and Politics; International/Global Studies; Political Science and Government, General; Political Science and Government, Other.

Related DOT Jobs—051.067-010 Political Scientist.

19-3099.99 Social Scientists and Related Workers, All Other
- **Education/Training Required: Master's degree**
- **Employed: No data available.**
- **Annual Earnings: No data available.**
- **Growth: 17.1%**
- **Annual Job Openings: 5,000**

All social scientists and related workers not listed separately.

No task data available.

GOE INFORMATION—**Interest Area:** 02. Science, Math, and Engineering. **Work Group:** 02.04. Social Sciences. **Note:** The Department of Labor has not collected some data for this job, so it has fewer details than the other descriptions.

Instructional Programs—Behavioral Sciences; Gerontology; Social Sciences, General; Social Sciences, Other.

Related DOT Jobs—059.067-010 Philologist; 059.067-014 Scientific Linguist; 059.167-010 Intelligence Research Specialist; 059.267-010 Intelligence Specialist; 059.267-014 Intelligence Specialist.

19-4000 Life, Physical, and Social Science Technicians

19-4011.00 Agricultural and Food Science Technicians
- **Education/Training Required: Moderate-term on-the-job training**
- **Employed: 17,604**
- **Annual Earnings: $27,530**
- **Growth: 15.2%**
- **Annual Job Openings: 3,000**

Work with agricultural scientists in food, fiber, and animal research, production, and processing; assist with animal breeding and nutrition work; under supervision, conduct tests and experiments to improve yield and quality of crops or to increase the resistance of plants and animals to disease or insects. Includes technicians who assist food scientists or food technologists in the research, development, production technology, quality control, packaging, processing, and use of foods.

No task data available.

GOE INFORMATION—**Interest Area:** 02. Science, Math, and Engineering. **Work Group:** 02.03. Life Sciences. **Note:** The Department of Labor has not collected some data for this job, so it has fewer details than the other descriptions.

Instructional Programs—Agricultural Animal Breeding; Agronomy and Crop Science; Animal Nutrition; Animal Sciences, General; Animal/Livestock Husbandry and Production; Crop Production; Dairy Science; Food Science.

Related DOT Jobs—022.261-014 Malt-Specifications-Control Assistant; 022.381-010 Yeast-Culture Developer; 029.361-010 Bottle-House Quality-Control Technician; 029.361-014 Food Tester; 040.361-014 Seed Analyst; 049.364-010 Feed-Research Aide; 049.364-018 Biological Aide; 199.251-010 Tester, Food Products; 411.364-010 Blood Tester, Fowl; 526.381-018 Baker, Test; 559.384-010 Laboratory Assistant, Culture Media.

19-4011.01 *Agricultural Technicians*

- **Education/Training Required: Associate's degree**
- **Employed: No data available.**
- **Annual Earnings: $27,530**
- **Growth: 15.2%**
- **Annual Job Openings: 15,000**

Set up and maintain laboratory and collect and record data to assist scientist in biology or related agricultural science experiments.

Adjust testing equipment and prepare culture media, following standard procedures. Collect samples from crops or animals so testing can be performed. Examine animals and specimens in order to determine the presence of diseases or other problems. Measure or weigh ingredients used in testing or for purposes such as animal feed. Operate laboratory equipment such as spectrometers, nitrogen determination apparatus, air samplers, centrifuges, and PH meters in order to perform tests. Prepare data summaries, reports, and analyses that include results, charts, and graphs in order to document research findings and results. Receive and prepare laboratory samples for analysis, following proper protocols in order to ensure that they will be stored, prepared, and disposed of efficiently and effectively. Record data pertaining to experimentation, research, and animal care. Set up laboratory or field equipment and prepare sites for testing. Conduct insect and plant disease surveys. Devise cultural methods and environmental controls for plants for which guidelines are sketchy or nonexistent. Maintain and repair agricultural facilities, equipment, and tools in order to ensure operational readiness, safety, and cleanliness. Measure and mark plot areas and plow, disc, level, and otherwise prepare land for cultivated crops, orchards, and vineyards. Operate farm machinery, including tractors, plows, mowers, combines, balers, sprayers, earthmoving equipment, and trucks. Perform crop production duties such as tilling, hoeing, pruning, weeding, and harvesting crops. Perform general nursery duties such as propagating standard varieties of plant materials, collecting and germinating seeds, maintaining cuttings of plants, and controlling environmental conditions. Plant seeds in specified areas and count the resulting plants in order to determine the percentage of seeds that germinated. Provide food and water to livestock and laboratory animals and record details of their food consumption. Provide routine animal care such as taking and recording body measurements, applying identification, and assisting in the birthing process. Respond to inquiries and requests from the public that do not require specialized scientific knowledge or expertise. Supervise pest or weed control operations, including locating and identifying pests or weeds, selecting chemicals and application methods, scheduling application, and training operators. Transplant trees, vegetables, and/or horticultural plants. Conduct inspections of apiaries in order to locate diseases and destroy contaminated bees and hives. Prepare and present agricultural demonstrations. Supervise and train agricultural technicians and farm laborers.

GOE INFORMATION—**Interest Area:** 02. Science, Math, and Engineering. **Work Group:** 02.03. Life Sciences. **Personality Type**—Realistic. Realistic occupations frequently involve work activities that include practical, hands-on problems and solutions. They often deal with plants, animals, and real-world materials like wood, tools, and machinery. Many of the occupations require working outside and do not involve a lot of paperwork or working closely with others. **Work Values**—Supervision, Technical; Variety; Advancement. **Skills**—None met the criteria. **Abilities**—*Cognitive:* Category Flexibility; Mathematical Reasoning; Perceptual Speed; Flexibility of Closure; Written Expression. *Psychomotor:* Reaction Time; Manual Dexterity; Response Orientation; Finger Dexterity; Arm-Hand Steadiness. *Physical:* Dynamic Strength; Static Strength; Dynamic Flexibility; Explosive Strength; Stamina. *Sensory:* Sound Localization. **General Work Activities**—*Information Input:* Identifying Objects, Actions, and Events; Monitoring Processes, Materials, or Surroundings; Inspecting Equipment, Structures, or Materials. *Mental Process:* Updating and Using Relevant Knowledge; Evaluating Information Against Standards; Analyzing Data or Information. *Work Output:* Handling and Moving Objects; Performing General Physical Activities; Controlling Machines and Processes. *Interacting with Others:* Communicating with Other Workers; Performing Administrative Activities; Establishing and Maintaining Relationships. **Physical Work Conditions**—Disease or Infections; Kneeling, Crouching, or Crawling; Keeping or Regaining Balance; Outdoors; Contaminants. **Other Job Characteristics**—Importance of Being Exact or Accurate; Importance of Repeating Same Tasks; Pace Determined by Speed of Equipment.

Experience—Job Zone 2. Some previous work-related skill, knowledge, or experience may be helpful, but usually is not needed. **Job Preparation:** SVP 4.0 to less than 6.0—six months to less than two years. **Knowledge**—Biology; Food Production; Medicine and Dentistry; Chemistry. **Instructional Programs**—Agricultural Animal Breeding; Agronomy and Crop Science; Animal Nutrition; Animal Sciences, General; Animal/Livestock Husbandry and Production; Crop Production; Dairy Science; Food Science.

Related DOT Jobs—040.361-014 Seed Analyst; 049.364-010 Feed-Research Aide; 049.364-018 Biological Aide; 411.364-010 Blood Tester, Fowl; 559.384-010 Laboratory Assistant, Culture Media.

19-4011.02 *Food Science Technicians*

- **Education/Training Required: Associate's degree**
- **Employed: 17,604**
- **Annual Earnings: $27,530**
- **Growth: 15.2%**
- **Annual Job Openings: 15,000**

Perform standardized qualitative and quantitative tests to determine physical or chemical properties of food or beverage products.

Analyze test results to classify products or compare results with standard tables. Compute moisture or salt content, percentages of ingredients, formulas, or other product factors, using mathematical and chemical procedures. Conduct standardized tests on food, beverages, additives, and preservatives in order to ensure compliance with standards and regulations regarding factors such as color, texture, and nutrients. Examine chemical and biological samples in order to identify cell structures and to locate bacteria or extraneous material, using microscope. Prepare slides and incubate slides with cell cultures. Provide assistance to food scientists and technologists in research and development, production technology, and quality control. Record and compile test results and prepare graphs, charts, and reports. Clean and sterilize laboratory equipment. Measure, test, and weigh bottles, cans, and other containers in order to ensure hardness, strength, and dimensions that meet specifications. Mix, blend, or cultivate ingredients in order to make reagents or to manufacture food or beverage products. Order supplies needed to maintain inventories in laboratories or in storage facilities of food or beverage processing plants. Taste or smell foods or beverages in order to ensure that flavors meet specifications or to select samples with specific characteristics.

GOE INFORMATION—Interest Area: 02. Science, Math, and Engineering. **Work Group:** 02.03. Life Sciences. **Personality Type—**Realistic. Realistic occupations frequently involve work activities that include practical, hands-on problems and solutions. They often deal with plants, animals, and real-world materials like wood, tools, and machinery. Many of the occupations require working outside and do not involve a lot of paperwork or working closely with others. **Work Values—**Security; Good Working Conditions; Variety; Supervision, Human Relations; Advancement. **Skills—**Mathematics; Science; Quality Control Analysis; Operation Monitoring; Equipment Selection; Reading Comprehension; Writing; Critical Thinking. **Abilities—***Cognitive:* Category Flexibility; Number Facility; Mathematical Reasoning; Written Expression; Information Ordering. *Psychomotor:* Control Precision; Manual Dexterity; Arm-Hand Steadiness; Finger Dexterity; Multilimb Coordination. *Physical:* Extent Flexibility; Gross Body Coordination. *Sensory:* Visual Color Discrimination; Near Vision. **General Work Activities—***Information Input:* Identifying Objects, Actions, and Events; Getting Information; Monitoring Processes, Materials, or Surroundings. *Mental Process:* Analyzing Data or Information; Updating and Using Relevant Knowledge; Judging Qualities of Things, Services, or Other People's Work. *Work Output:* Documenting or Recording Information; Handling and Moving Objects; Controlling Machines and Processes. *Interacting with Others:* Interpreting Meaning of Information for Others; Communicating with Other Workers; Monitoring and Controlling Resources. **Physical Work Conditions—**Indoors; Common Protective or Safety Attire; Using Hands on Objects, Tools, or Controls; Hazardous Conditions; Contaminants. **Other Job Characteristics—**Importance of Being Exact or Accurate; Degree of Automation; Consequence of Error.

Experience—Job Zone 2. Some previous work-related skill, knowledge, or experience may be helpful, but usually is not needed. **Job Preparation:** SVP 4.0 to less than 6.0—six months to less than two years. **Knowledge—**Chemistry; Biology; Food Production; Mathematics; Production and Processing. **Instructional Programs—**Food Science.

Related DOT Jobs—022.261-014 Malt-Specifications-Control Assistant; 022.381-010 Yeast-Culture Developer; 029.361-010 Bottle-House Quality-Control Technician; 029.361-014 Food Tester; 199.251-010 Tester, Food Products; 526.381-018 Baker, Test.

19-4021.00 Biological Technicians

- **Education/Training Required: Associate's degree**
- **Employed: 41,465**
- **Annual Earnings: $32,280**
- **Growth: 26.4%**
- **Annual Job Openings: 7,000**

Assist biological and medical scientists in laboratories. Set up, operate, and maintain laboratory instruments and equipment; monitor experiments; make observations; and calculate and record results. May analyze organic substances, such as blood, food, and drugs.

Analyze experimental data and interpret results to write reports and summaries of findings. Clean, maintain, and prepare supplies and work areas. Conduct or assist in conducting research, including the collection of information and samples, such as blood, water, soil, plants, and animals. Conduct standardized biological, microbiological, and biochemical tests and laboratory analyses to evaluate the quantity or quality of physical or

chemical substances in food and other products. Examine animals and specimens to detect the presence of disease or other problems. Feed livestock and laboratory animals. Measure or weigh compounds and solutions for use in testing or animal feed. Monitor and observe experiments, recording production and test data for evaluation by research personnel. Provide technical support and services for scientists and engineers working in fields such as agriculture, environmental science, resource management, biology, and health sciences. Set up, adjust, calibrate, clean, maintain, and troubleshoot laboratory and field equipment. Isolate, identify, and prepare specimens for examination. Keep detailed logs of all work-related activities. Monitor laboratory work to ensure compliance with set standards. Participate in the research, development, and manufacturing of medicinal and pharmaceutical preparations. Conduct or supervise operational programs such as fish hatcheries, greenhouses, and livestock production programs. Use computers, computer-interfaced equipment, robotics, and high-technology industrial applications to perform work duties.

GOE INFORMATION—Interest Area: 02. Science, Math, and Engineering. **Work Group:** 02.05. Laboratory Technology. **Personality Type—**Realistic. Realistic occupations frequently involve work activities that include practical, hands-on problems and solutions. They often deal with plants, animals, and real-world materials like wood, tools, and machinery. Many of the occupations require working outside and do not involve a lot of paperwork or working closely with others. **Work Values—**Supervision, Technical; Variety; Advancement. **Skills—**None met the criteria. **Abilities—***Cognitive:* Category Flexibility; Mathematical Reasoning; Perceptual Speed; Flexibility of Closure; Written Expression. *Psychomotor:* Reaction Time; Manual Dexterity; Response Orientation; Finger Dexterity; Arm-Hand Steadiness. *Physical:* Dynamic Strength; Static Strength; Dynamic Flexibility; Explosive Strength; Stamina. *Sensory:* Sound Localization. **General Work Activities—***Information Input:* Identifying Objects, Actions, and Events; Monitoring Processes, Materials, or Surroundings; Inspecting Equipment, Structures, or Materials. *Mental Process:* Updating and Using Relevant Knowledge; Evaluating Information Against Standards; Analyzing Data or Information. *Work Output:* Handling and Moving Objects; Performing General Physical Activities; Controlling Machines and Processes. *Interacting with Others:* Communicating with Other Workers; Performing Administrative Activities; Establishing and Maintaining Relationships. **Physical Work Conditions—**Disease or Infections; Kneeling, Crouching, or Crawling; Keeping or Regaining Balance; Outdoors; Contaminants. **Other Job Characteristics—**Importance of Being Exact or Accurate; Importance of Repeating Same Tasks; Pace Determined by Speed of Equipment.

Experience—Job Zone 2. Some previous work-related skill, knowledge, or experience may be helpful, but usually is not needed. **Job Preparation:** SVP 4.0 to less than 6.0—six months to less than two years. **Knowledge—**Biology; Food Production; Medicine and Dentistry; Chemistry. **Instructional Programs—**Biology Technician/Biotechnology Laboratory Technician.

Related DOT Jobs—040.361-014 Seed Analyst; 049.364-010 Feed-Research Aide; 049.364-018 Biological Aide; 411.364-010 Blood Tester, Fowl; 559.384-010 Laboratory Assistant, Culture Media.

19-4031.00 Chemical Technicians

- **Education/Training Required: Associate's degree**
- **Employed: 73,454**
- **Annual Earnings: $36,190**
- **Growth: 15.0%**
- **Annual Job Openings: 13,000**

Conduct chemical and physical laboratory tests to assist scientists in making qualitative and quantitative analyses of solids, liquids, and gaseous materials for purposes such as research and development of new products or processes, quality control, maintenance of environmental standards, and other work involving experimental, theoretical, or practical application of chemistry and related sciences.

Compile and interpret results of tests and analyses. Conduct chemical and physical laboratory tests to assist scientists in making qualitative and quantitative analyses of solids, liquids, and gaseous materials. Maintain, clean, and sterilize laboratory instruments and equipment. Monitor product quality to ensure compliance to standards and specifications. Prepare chemical solutions for products and processes following standardized formulas or create experimental formulas. Provide technical support and assistance to chemists and engineers. Set up and conduct chemical experiments, tests, and analyses using techniques such as chromatography, spectroscopy, physical and chemical separation techniques, and microscopy. Design and fabricate experimental apparatus to develop new products and processes. Develop and conduct programs of sampling and analysis to maintain quality standards of raw materials, chemical intermediates, and products. Develop new chemical engineering processes or production techniques. Direct or monitor other workers producing chemical products. Operate experimental pilot plants, assisting with experimental design. Order and inventory materials in order to maintain supplies. Write technical reports or prepare graphs and charts to document experimental results.

GOE INFORMATION—Interest Area: 02. Science, Math, and Engineering. **Work Group:** 02.05. Laboratory Technology. **Personality Type—** Realistic. Realistic occupations frequently involve work activities that include practical, hands-on problems and solutions. They often deal with plants, animals, and real-world materials like wood, tools, and machinery. Many of the occupations require working outside and do not involve a lot of paperwork or working closely with others. **Work Values—**Advancement; Supervision, Technical; Variety; Supervision, Human Relations; Pleasant Co-workers. **Skills—**Science; Mathematics; Operation and Control; Equipment Selection; Critical Thinking; Quality Control Analysis; Reading Comprehension; Writing. **Abilities—***Cognitive:* Written Expression; Mathematical Reasoning; Category Flexibility; Number Facility; Information Ordering. *Psychomotor:* Control Precision; Arm-Hand Steadiness; Manual Dexterity; Finger Dexterity; Multilimb Coordination. *Physical:* Gross Body Coordination; Explosive Strength; Gross Body Equilibrium; Trunk Strength; Dynamic Flexibility. *Sensory:* Visual Color Discrimination; Near Vision; Depth Perception. **General Work Activities—***Information Input:* Identifying Objects, Actions, and Events; Monitoring Processes, Materials, or Surroundings; Getting Information. *Mental Process:* Updating and Using Relevant Knowledge; Processing Information; Analyzing Data or Information. *Work Output:* Documenting or Recording Information; Controlling Machines and Processes; Handling and Moving Objects. *Interacting with Others:* Communicating with Other Workers; Interpreting Meaning of Information for Others; Assisting and Caring for Others. **Physical Work Conditions—**Hazardous Conditions; Contaminants; Common Protective or Safety Attire; Indoors; Hazardous Equipment. **Other Job Characteristics—**Importance of Being Exact or Accurate; Degree of Automation; Importance of Repeating Same Tasks.

Experience—Job Zone 3. Previous work-related skill, knowledge, or experience is required. **Job Preparation:** SVP 6.0 to less than 7.0—more than one year and less than four years. **Knowledge—**Chemistry; Biology; Mathematics; English Language; Physics. **Instructional Programs—**Chemical Technology/Technician; Food Science.

Related DOT Jobs—019.261-030 Laboratory Technician; 022.161-018 Perfumer; 022.261-010 Chemical Laboratory Technician; 029.261-010 Laboratory Tester.

19-4041.00 Geological and Petroleum Technicians

- **Education/Training Required: Associate's degree**
- **Employed: 10,105**
- **Annual Earnings: $38,540**
- **Growth: 6.5%**
- **Annual Job Openings: 2,000**

Assist scientists in the use of electrical, sonic, or nuclear measuring instruments in both laboratory and production activities to obtain data indicating potential sources of metallic ore, gas, or petroleum. Analyze mud and drill cuttings. Chart pressure, temperature, and other characteristics of wells or bore holes. Investigate and collect information leading to the possible discovery of new oil fields.

No task data available.

GOE INFORMATION—Interest Area: 02. Science, Math, and Engineering. **Work Group:** 02.05. Laboratory Technology. **Note:** The Department of Labor has not collected some data for this job, so it has fewer details than the other descriptions.

Instructional Programs—Petroleum Technology/Technician.

Related DOT Jobs—010.131-010 Well-Logging Captain, Mud Analysis; 010.161-018 Observer, Seismic Prospecting; 010.261-010 Field Engineer, Specialist; 010.261-014 Observer, Electrical Prospecting; 010.261-018 Observer, Gravity Prospecting; 010.261-022 Surveyor, Oil-Well Directional; 010.261-026 Test-Engine Evaluator; 010.267-010 Scout; 010.281-022 Well-Logging Operator, Mud Analysis; 024.267-010 Geological Aide; 024.381-010 Laboratory Assistant; 029.261-018 Test-Engine Operator; 029.261-022 Tester; 194.382-010 Section-Plotter Operator; 930.167-010 Technical Operator.

19-4041.01 Geological Data Technicians

- **Education/Training Required: Associate's degree**
- **Employed: No data available.**
- **Annual Earnings: $38,540**
- **Growth: 6.5%**
- **Annual Job Openings: 15,000**

Measure, record, and evaluate geological data, using sonic, electronic, electrical, seismic, or gravity-measuring instruments to prospect for oil or gas. May collect and evaluate core samples and cuttings.

Measure geological characteristics used in prospecting for oil or gas, using measuring instruments. Record readings in order to compile data used in prospecting for oil or gas. Evaluate and interpret core samples and cuttings and other geological data used in prospecting for oil or gas. Operate and adjust equipment and apparatus used to obtain geological data. Read and study reports in order to compile information and data for geological and geophysical prospecting. Set up or direct setup of instruments used to collect geological data. Collect samples and cuttings, using equipment and hand tools. Interview individuals and research public databases in order to obtain information. Assemble, maintain, and distribute information for library or record systems. Plan and direct activities of workers who operate equipment to collect data. Develop and print photographic recordings of information, using equipment. Diagnose and repair malfunctioning instruments and equipment, using manufacturers' manuals and hand tools. Develop and design packing materials and handling procedures for shipping of objects. Prepare and attach packing instructions to shipping containers. Prepare notes, sketches, geological maps, and cross-sections. Supervise oil, water, and gas well drilling activities.

GOE INFORMATION—Interest Area: 02. Science, Math, and Engineering. **Work Group:** 02.05. Laboratory Technology. **Personality Type—** Realistic. Realistic occupations frequently involve work activities that include practical, hands-on problems and solutions. They often deal with plants, animals, and real-world materials like wood, tools, and machinery. Many of the occupations require working outside and do not involve a lot of paperwork or working closely with others. **Work Values—**Variety; Authority; Creativity; Compensation; Supervision, Technical. **Skills—** Reading Comprehension; Science; Mathematics; Speaking; Complex Problem Solving; Repairing; Equipment Selection; Installation. **Abilities—***Cognitive:* Speed of Closure; Mathematical Reasoning; Fluency of Ideas; Written Comprehension; Flexibility of Closure. *Psychomotor:* Control Precision; Reaction Time; Rate Control; Wrist-Finger Speed; Finger Dexterity. *Physical:* Gross Body Coordination; Gross Body Equilibrium; Dynamic Flexibility; Extent Flexibility; Explosive Strength. *Sensory:* Visual Color Discrimination; Far Vision; Speech Clarity; Night Vision; Auditory Attention. **General Work Activities—***Information Input:* Getting Information; Identifying Objects, Actions, and Events; Estimating Needed Characteristics. *Mental Process:* Updating and Using Relevant Knowledge; Analyzing Data or Information; Processing Information. *Work Output:* Handling and Moving Objects; Performing General Physical Activities; Repairing and Maintaining Mechanical Equipment. *Interacting with Others:* Communicating with Other Workers; Coordinating the Work and Activities of Others; Communicating with Persons Outside Organization. **Physical Work Conditions—**Outdoors; Hazardous Equipment; Extremely Bright or Inadequate Lighting; Very Hot or Cold; Contaminants. **Other Job Characteristics—**Pace Determined by Speed of Equipment; Importance of Being Exact or Accurate; Degree of Automation.

Experience—Job Zone 3. Previous work-related skill, knowledge, or experience is required. **Job Preparation:** SVP 6.0 to less than 7.0—more than one year and less than four years. **Knowledge—**Physics; Clerical; Administration and Management; Production and Processing; Engineering and Technology. **Instructional Programs—**Petroleum Technology/Technician.

Related DOT Jobs—010.161-018 Observer, Seismic Prospecting; 010.261-014 Observer, Electrical Prospecting; 010.261-018 Observer, Gravity Prospecting; 010.261-022 Surveyor, Oil-Well Directional; 010.267-010 Scout; 024.267-010 Geological Aide; 194.382-010 Section-Plotter Operator; 930.167-010 Technical Operator.

19-4041.02 Geological Sample Test Technicians

- **Education/Training Required: Associate's degree**
- **Employed: 10,105**
- **Annual Earnings: $38,540**
- **Growth: 6.5%**
- **Annual Job Openings: 15,000**

Test and analyze geological samples, crude oil, or petroleum products to detect presence of petroleum, gas, or mineral deposits indicating potential for exploration and production or to determine physical and chemical properties to ensure that products meet quality standards.

Assemble, operate, and maintain field and laboratory testing, measuring, and mechanical equipment, working as part of a crew when required. Collect and prepare solid and fluid samples for analysis. Compile and record testing and operational data for review and further analysis. Plot

information from aerial photographs, well logs, section descriptions, and other databases. Prepare notes, sketches, geological maps, and cross sections. Prepare, transcribe, and/or analyze seismic, gravimetric, well log, or other geophysical and survey data. Test and analyze samples in order to determine their content and characteristics, using laboratory apparatus and testing equipment. Adjust and repair testing, electrical, and mechanical equipment and devices. Assess the environmental impacts of development projects on subsurface materials. Collaborate with hydro-geologists in order to evaluate groundwater and well circulation. Participate in geological, geophysical, geochemical, hydrographic, or oceanographic surveys; prospecting field trips; exploratory drilling; well logging; or underground mine survey programs. Participate in the evaluation of possible mining locations. Inspect engines for wear and defective parts, using equipment and measuring devices. Supervise well exploration and drilling activities and well completions.

GOE INFORMATION—Interest Area: 02. Science, Math, and Engineering. **Work Group:** 02.05. Laboratory Technology. **Personality Type—** Realistic. Realistic occupations frequently involve work activities that include practical, hands-on problems and solutions. They often deal with plants, animals, and real-world materials like wood, tools, and machinery. Many of the occupations require working outside and do not involve a lot of paperwork or working closely with others. **Work Values—**Advancement; Supervision, Technical; Authority; Compensation; Company Policies and Practices. **Skills—**Science; Quality Control Analysis; Repairing; Management of Personnel Resources; Operation and Control; Equipment Selection; Operation Monitoring; Troubleshooting. **Abilities—***Cognitive:* Flexibility of Closure; Mathematical Reasoning; Inductive Reasoning; Number Facility; Information Ordering. *Psychomotor:* Wrist-Finger Speed; Finger Dexterity; Arm-Hand Steadiness; Manual Dexterity; Speed of Limb Movement. *Physical:* Stamina; Dynamic Strength; Extent Flexibility; Gross Body Coordination; Gross Body Equilibrium. *Sensory:* Visual Color Discrimination; Near Vision; Sound Localization; Speech Clarity; Hearing Sensitivity. **General Work Activities—***Information Input:* Identifying Objects, Actions, and Events; Getting Information; Inspecting Equipment, Structures, or Materials. *Mental Process:* Analyzing Data or Information; Updating and Using Relevant Knowledge; Processing Information. *Work Output:* Documenting or Recording Information; Performing General Physical Activities; Handling and Moving Objects. *Interacting with Others:* Communicating with Other Workers; Establishing and Maintaining Relationships; Interpreting Meaning of Information for Others. **Physical Work Conditions—**Outdoors; Hazardous Conditions; Minor Burns, Cuts, Bites, or Stings; Contaminants; Common Protective or Safety Attire. **Other Job Characteristics—** Pace Determined by Speed of Equipment; Degree of Automation; Importance of Being Exact or Accurate.

Experience—Job Zone 3. Previous work-related skill, knowledge, or experience is required. **Job Preparation:** SVP 6.0 to less than 7.0—more than one year and less than four years. **Knowledge—**Personnel and Human Resources; Mechanical; Physics; Chemistry; Engineering and Technology. **Instructional Programs—**Petroleum Technology/Technician.

Related DOT Jobs—010.131-010 Well-Logging Captain, Mud Analysis; 010.261-010 Field Engineer, Specialist; 010.261-026 Test-Engine Evaluator; 010.281-022 Well-Logging Operator, Mud Analysis; 024.381-010 Laboratory Assistant; 029.261-018 Test-Engine Operator; 029.261-022 Tester.

19-4051.00 Nuclear Technicians

- **Education/Training Required: Associate's degree**
- **Employed: 3,330**
- **Annual Earnings: $59,690**
- **Growth: 20.7%**
- **Annual Job Openings: Fewer than 500**

Assist scientists in both laboratory and production activities by performing technical tasks involving nuclear physics, primarily in operation, maintenance, production, and quality control support activities.

No task data available.

GOE INFORMATION—Interest Area: 02. Science, Math, and Engineering. **Work Group:** 02.05. Laboratory Technology. **Note:** The Department of Labor has not collected some data for this job, so it has fewer details than the other descriptions.

Instructional Programs—Industrial Radiologic Technology/Technician; Nuclear and Industrial Radiologic Technologies/Technicians, Other; Nuclear Engineering Technology/Technician; Nuclear/Nuclear Power Technology/Technician; Radiation Protection/Health Physics Technician.

Related DOT Jobs—015.261-010 Chemical-Radiation Technician; 015.362-010 Accelerator Operator; 015.362-014 Gamma-Facilities Operator; 015.362-018 Hot-Cell Technician; 015.362-022 Radioisotope-Production Operator; 015.362-026 Reactor Operator, Test-and-Research; 015.384-010 Scanner; 199.167-010 Radiation Monitor; 199.384-010 Decontaminator.

19-4051.01 Nuclear Equipment Operation Technicians

- **Education/Training Required: Associate's degree**
- **Employed: No data available.**
- **Annual Earnings: $59,690**
- **Growth: 20.7%**
- **Annual Job Openings: 15,000**

Operate equipment used for the release, control, and utilization of nuclear energy to assist scientists in laboratory and production activities.

Adjust controls of equipment in order to control particle beam movement, pulse rates, energy and intensity, or radiation, according to specifications. Clear personnel from particle beam areas before operations begin. Control laboratory compounding equipment enclosed in protective hot cells in order to prepare radioisotopes and other radioactive materials. Follow policies and procedures for radiation workers in order to ensure personnel safety. Install instrumentation leads in reactor cores in order to measure operating temperatures and pressures according to mockups, blueprints, and diagrams. Monitor instruments, gauges, and recording devices in control rooms during operation of equipment under direction of nuclear experimenters. Notify experimenters in target control rooms when particle beam parameters meet specifications. Position fuel elements in geometric configurations around tubes in reactors or gamma facilities according to radiation intensity specifications, using slave manipulators or extension tools. Review experiment schedules in order to determine specifications, such as subatomic particle energy, intensity, and repetition rate parameters. Set control panel switches according to standard procedures in order to route electric power from sources and direct particle beams through injector units. Transfer capsules of experimental materials to and from tubes, chambers, or tunnels leading to reactor cores, using slave manipulators or extension tools. Calculate equipment operating factors, such as radiation times, dosages, temperatures, gamma intensities, and pressures, using standard formulas and conversion tables. Collaborate with accelerator and beamline physicists in order to make experimental measurements. Communicate with accelerator maintenance personnel in order to ensure readiness of support systems, such as vacuum, water cooling, and radiofrequency power sources. Diagnose routine problems affecting accelerator performance. Direct the work of accelerator support

service personnel. Disassemble, clean, and decontaminate hot cells and reactor parts during maintenance shutdowns, using slave manipulators, cranes, and hand tools. Modify, devise, and maintain equipment used in operations. Perform testing, maintenance, repair, and upgrading of accelerator systems. Set up and operate machines to cut fuel elements to size to fit into shielding boxes or to polish test pieces, following blueprints and other specifications and using extension tools. Submit computations to supervisors for review. Test physical, chemical, or metallurgical properties of experimental materials according to standardized procedures, using test equipment and measuring instruments. Warn maintenance workers of radiation hazards and direct workers to vacate hazardous areas. Write summaries of activities and record experimental data, such as accelerator performance, systems status, particle beam specification, and beam conditions obtained.

GOE INFORMATION—Interest Area: 02. Science, Math, and Engineering. **Work Group:** 02.05. Laboratory Technology. **Personality Type—**Realistic. Realistic occupations frequently involve work activities that include practical, hands-on problems and solutions. They often deal with plants, animals, and real-world materials like wood, tools, and machinery. Many of the occupations require working outside and do not involve a lot of paperwork or working closely with others. **Work Values—**Compensation; Supervision, Technical; Ability Utilization; Supervision, Human Relations; Company Policies and Practices. **Skills—**Installation; Science; Operation Monitoring; Operation and Control; Mathematics; Equipment Selection; Quality Control Analysis; Troubleshooting. **Abilities—***Cognitive:* Perceptual Speed; Information Ordering; Number Facility; Memorization; Mathematical Reasoning. *Psychomotor:* Reaction Time; Control Precision; Arm-Hand Steadiness; Manual Dexterity; Response Orientation. *Physical:* Explosive Strength; Static Strength; Gross Body Coordination; Stamina; Dynamic Flexibility. *Sensory:* Peripheral Vision; Visual Color Discrimination; Depth Perception; Far Vision; Near Vision. **General Work Activities—***Information Input:* Monitoring Processes, Materials, or Surroundings; Inspecting Equipment, Structures, or Materials; Identifying Objects, Actions, and Events. *Mental Process:* Updating and Using Relevant Knowledge; Processing Information; Analyzing Data or Information. *Work Output:* Controlling Machines and Processes; Documenting or Recording Information; Handling and Moving Objects. *Interacting with Others:* Communicating with Other Workers; Coordinating the Work and Activities of Others; Interpreting Meaning of Information for Others. **Physical Work Conditions—**Radiation; Specialized Protective or Safety Attire; Hazardous Conditions; Contaminants; Common Protective or Safety Attire. **Other Job Characteristics—**Importance of Being Exact or Accurate; Consequence of Error; Degree of Automation.

Experience—Job Zone 3. Previous work-related skill, knowledge, or experience is required. **Job Preparation:** SVP 6.0 to less than 7.0—more than one year and less than four years. **Knowledge—**Physics; Engineering and Technology; Chemistry; Public Safety and Security; Production and Processing. **Instructional Programs—**Industrial Radiologic Technology/Technician; Nuclear and Industrial Radiologic Technologies/Technicians, Other; Nuclear Engineering Technology/Technician; Nuclear/Nuclear Power Technology/Technician; Radiation Protection/Health Physics Technician.

Related DOT Jobs—015.362-010 Accelerator Operator; 015.362-014 Gamma-Facilities Operator; 015.362-018 Hot-Cell Technician; 015.362-022 Radioisotope-Production Operator; 015.362-026 Reactor Operator, Test-and-Research.

19-4051.02 Nuclear Monitoring Technicians

- Education/Training Required: Associate's degree
- Employed: 3,330
- Annual Earnings: $59,690
- Growth: 20.7%
- Annual Job Openings: 15,000

Collect and test samples to monitor results of nuclear experiments and contamination of humans, facilities, and environment.

Calibrate and maintain chemical instrumentation sensing elements and sampling system equipment, using calibration instruments and hand tools. Collect samples of air, water, gases, and solids in order to determine radioactivity levels of contamination. Determine intensities and types of radiation in work areas, equipment, and materials, using radiation detectors and other instruments. Determine or recommend radioactive decontamination procedures according to the size and nature of equipment and the degree of contamination. Immerse samples in chemical compounds in order to prepare them for testing. Inform supervisors when individual exposures or area radiation levels approach maximum permissible limits. Monitor personnel in order to determine the amounts and intensities of radiation exposure. Operate manipulators from outside cells to move specimens into and out of shielded containers, to remove specimens from cells, or to place specimens on benches or equipment work stations. Place irradiated nuclear fuel materials in environmental chambers for testing and observe reactions through cell windows. Provide initial response to abnormal events and to alarms from radiation monitoring equipment. Set up equipment that automatically detects area radiation deviations and test detection equipment in order to ensure its accuracy. Test materials' physical, chemical, or metallurgical properties, using equipment such as tensile testers, hardness testers, metallographic units, micrometers, and gauges. Weigh and mix decontamination chemical solutions in tanks and immerse objects in solutions for specified times, using hoists. Calculate safe radiation exposure times for personnel, using plant contamination readings and prescribed safe levels of radiation. Confer with scientists directing projects in order to determine significant events to monitor during tests. Decontaminate objects by cleaning with soap or solvents or by abrading with wire brushes, buffing wheels, or sandblasting machines. Enter data into computers in order to record characteristics of nuclear events and locating coordinates of particles. Instruct personnel in radiation safety procedures and demonstrate use of protective clothing and equipment. Observe projected photographs to locate particle tracks and events; compile lists of events from particle detectors. Place radioactive waste, such as sweepings and broken sample bottles, into containers for disposal. Prepare reports describing contamination tests, material and equipment decontaminated, and methods used in decontamination processes. Scan photographic emulsions exposed to direct radiation in order to compute track properties from standard formulas, using microscopes with scales and protractors. Set up and operate machines that cut, lap, and polish test pieces, following blueprints, X-ray negatives, and sketches.

GOE INFORMATION—Interest Area: 04. Law, Law Enforcement, and Public Safety. **Work Group:** 04.04. Public Safety. **Personality Type—** Realistic. Realistic occupations frequently involve work activities that include practical, hands-on problems and solutions. They often deal with plants, animals, and real-world materials like wood, tools, and machinery. Many of the occupations require working outside and do not involve a lot of paperwork or working closely with others. **Work Values—**Compensation; Supervision, Technical; Company Policies and Practices; Social Status; Recognition. **Skills—**Science; Operation Monitoring; Operation and Control; Mathematics; Installation; Speaking; Equipment Selection; Critical Thinking. **Abilities—***Cognitive:* Problem Sensitivity; Inductive Reasoning; Category Flexibility; Number Facility; Deductive Reasoning. *Psychomotor:* Control Precision; Manual Dexterity; Finger Dexterity; Reaction Time; Response Orientation. *Physical:* Dynamic Flexibility; Stamina; Dynamic Strength; Gross Body Equilibrium; Extent Flexibility. *Sensory:* Near Vision; Speech Clarity; Far Vision; Visual Color Discrimination; Night Vision. **General Work Activities—***Information Input:* Monitoring Processes, Materials, or Surroundings; Identifying Objects, Actions, and Events; Getting Information. *Mental Process:* Updating and Using Relevant Knowledge; Processing Information; Analyzing Data or Information. *Work Output:* Documenting or Recording Information; Controlling Machines and Processes; Handling and Moving Objects. *Interacting with Others:* Communicating with Other Workers; Interpreting Meaning of Information for Others; Providing Consultation and Advice to Others. **Physical Work Conditions—**Specialized Protective or Safety Attire; Radiation; Hazardous Conditions; Contaminants; Hazardous Equipment. **Other Job Characteristics—**Consequence of Error; Importance of Being Exact or Accurate; Degree of Automation.

Experience—Job Zone 3. Previous work-related skill, knowledge, or experience is required. **Job Preparation:** SVP 6.0 to less than 7.0—more than one year and less than four years. **Knowledge—**Physics; Chemistry; Public Safety and Security; Education and Training; Biology. **Instructional Programs—**Industrial Radiologic Technology/Technician; Nuclear and Industrial Radiologic Technologies/Technicians, Other; Nuclear Engineering Technology/Technician; Nuclear/Nuclear Power Technology/Technician; Radiation Protection/Health Physics Technician.

Related DOT Jobs—015.261-010 Chemical-Radiation Technician; 015.384-010 Scanner; 199.167-010 Radiation Monitor; 199.384-010 Decontaminator.

19-4061.00 Social Science Research Assistants

- Education/Training Required: Associate's degree
- Employed: No data available.
- Annual Earnings: No data available.
- Growth: 20.0%
- Annual Job Openings: 15,000

Assist social scientists in laboratory, survey, and other social research. May perform publication activities, laboratory analysis, quality control, or data management. Normally these individuals work under the direct supervision of a social scientist and assist in those activities which are more routine.

Perform descriptive and multivariate statistical analyses of data, using computer software. Recruit and schedule research participants. Administer standardized tests to research subjects and/or interview them in order to collect research data. Code data in preparation for computer entry. Conduct Internet-based and library research. Develop and implement research quality control procedures. Edit and submit protocols and other required research documentation. Obtain informed consent of research subjects and/or their guardians. Prepare tables, graphs, fact sheets, and written reports summarizing research results. Prepare, manipulate, and manage extensive databases. Provide assistance in the design of survey instruments such as questionnaires. Screen potential subjects in order to determine their suitability as study participants. Track research participants and perform any necessary followup tasks. Verify the accuracy and validity of data entered in databases; correct any errors. Allocate and manage laboratory space and resources. Design and create special programs for tasks such as statistical analysis and data entry and cleaning. Perform data entry and other clerical work as required for project completion. Perform needs assessments and/or consult with clients in order to determine the types of research and information that are required. Present research findings to groups of people. Provide assistance with the preparation of project-related reports, manuscripts, and presentations. Supervise the work of survey interviewers. Track laboratory supplies and expenses such as participant reimbursement. Collect specimens such as blood samples as required by research projects.

GOE INFORMATION—Interest Area: 02. Science, Math, and Engineering. **Work Group:** 02.04. Social Sciences. **Note:** The Department of Labor has not collected some data for this job, so it has fewer details than the other descriptions.

Instructional Programs—Social Sciences, General.

Related DOT Jobs—199.364-010 City Planning Aide.

19-4061.01 City Planning Aides
- **Education/Training Required: Associate's degree**
- **Employed: No data available.**
- **Annual Earnings: No data available.**
- **Growth: 20.0%**
- **Annual Job Openings: 15,000**

Compile data from various sources, such as maps, reports, and field and file investigations, for use by city planner in making planning studies.

Participate in and support team planning efforts. Prepare, develop, and maintain maps and databases. Prepare, maintain, and update files and records, including land use data and statistics. Research, compile, analyze, and organize information from maps, reports, investigations, and books for use in reports and special projects. Respond to public inquiries and complaints. Serve as a liaison between planning department and other departments and agencies. Conduct interviews, surveys, and site inspections concerning factors that affect land usage, such as zoning, traffic flow, and housing. Inspect sites and review plans for minor development permit applications. Perform clerical duties such as composing, typing, and proofreading documents; scheduling appointments and meetings; handling mail; and posting public notices. Perform code enforcement tasks. Prepare reports, using statistics, charts, and graphs, to illustrate planning studies in areas such as population, land use, or zoning. Provide and process zoning and project permits and applications.

GOE INFORMATION—Interest Area: 02. Science, Math, and Engineering. **Work Group:** 02.04. Social Sciences. **Personality Type—**Conventional. Conventional occupations frequently involve following set procedures and routines. These occupations can include working with data and details more than with ideas. Usually there is a clear line of authority to follow. **Work Values—**Good Working Conditions; Advancement; Supervision, Human Relations; Company Policies and Practices; Variety. **Skills—**Writing; Mathematics; Speaking; Active Listening. **Abilities—***Cognitive:* Written Expression; Oral Comprehension; Oral Expression; Written Comprehension; Mathematical Reasoning. *Psychomotor:* None met the criteria. *Physical:* None met the criteria. *Sensory:* Speech Clarity; Speech Recognition; Near Vision. **General Work Activities—***Information Input:* Getting Information; Identifying Objects, Actions, and Events; Estimating Needed Characteristics. *Mental Process:* Analyzing Data or Information; Processing Information; Thinking Creatively. *Work Output:* Handling and Moving Objects; Documenting or Recording Information; Interacting with Computers. *Interacting with Others:* Communicating with Persons Outside Organization; Communicating

with Other Workers; Establishing and Maintaining Relationships. **Physical Work Conditions—**Sitting; Outdoors; Indoors; Radiation. **Other Job Characteristics—**Importance of Being Exact or Accurate; Importance of Repeating Same Tasks; Consequence of Error.

Experience—Job Zone 3. Previous work-related skill, knowledge, or experience is required. **Job Preparation:** SVP 6.0 to less than 7.0—more than one year and less than four years. **Knowledge—**Geography; Clerical; Mathematics; Law and Government; Sociology and Anthropology. **Instructional Programs—**Social Sciences, General.

Related DOT Jobs—199.364-010 City Planning Aide.

19-4091.00 Environmental Science and Protection Technicians, Including Health
- **Education/Training Required: Associate's degree**
- **Employed: 27,133**
- **Annual Earnings: $34,690**
- **Growth: 24.5%**
- **Annual Job Openings: 3,000**

Performs laboratory and field tests to monitor the environment and investigate sources of pollution, including those that affect health. Under direction of an environmental scientist or specialist, may collect samples of gases, soil, water, and other materials for testing and take corrective actions as assigned.

Calculate amount of pollutant in samples or compute air pollution or gas flow in industrial processes, using chemical and mathematical formulas. Collect samples of gases, soils, water, industrial wastewater, and asbestos products to conduct tests on pollutant levels and identify sources of pollution. Examine and analyze material for presence and concentration of contaminants such as asbestos, using variety of microscopes. Initiate procedures to close down or fine establishments violating environmental and/or health regulations. Inspect sanitary conditions at public facilities. Inspect workplaces to ensure the absence of health and safety hazards such as high noise levels, radiation, or potential lighting hazards. Make recommendations to control or eliminate unsafe conditions at workplaces or public facilities. Prepare samples or photomicrographs for testing and analysis. Record test data and prepare reports, summaries, and charts that interpret test results. Respond to and investigate hazardous conditions or spills or outbreaks of disease or food poisoning, collecting samples for analysis. Set up equipment or stations to monitor and collect pollutants from sites such as smoke stacks, manufacturing plants, or mechanical equipment. Weigh, analyze, and measure collected sample particles, such as lead, coal dust, or rock, to determine concentration of pollutants. Calibrate microscopes and test instruments. Conduct standardized tests to ensure materials and supplies used throughout power supply systems meet processing and safety specifications. Determine amounts and kinds of chemicals to use in destroying harmful organisms and removing impurities from purification systems. Develop and implement programs for monitoring of environmental pollution and radiation. Develop testing procedures and direct activities of workers in laboratory. Discuss test results and analyses with customers. Distribute permits, closure plans, and cleanup plans. Maintain files such as hazardous waste databases, chemical usage data, personnel exposure information, and diagrams showing equipment locations. Perform statistical analysis of environmental data. Provide information and technical and program assistance to government representatives, employers, and the general public on the issues of public health, environmental protection, or workplace safety.

GOE INFORMATION—Interest Area: 02. Science, Math, and Engineering. Work Group: 02.05. Laboratory Technology. Personality Type—Investigative. Investigative occupations frequently involve working with ideas and require an extensive amount of thinking. These occupations can involve searching for facts and figuring out problems mentally. Work Values—Recognition; Creativity; Security; Independence; Variety. Skills—Science; Mathematics; Operation and Control; Operation Monitoring; Equipment Selection; Writing; Installation; Reading Comprehension. Abilities—*Cognitive:* Written Expression; Category Flexibility; Flexibility of Closure; Mathematical Reasoning; Number Facility. *Psychomotor:* Control Precision; Finger Dexterity; Arm-Hand Steadiness; Manual Dexterity; Wrist-Finger Speed. *Physical:* Explosive Strength; Dynamic Flexibility; Dynamic Strength; Gross Body Coordination; Gross Body Equilibrium. *Sensory:* Far Vision; Near Vision; Visual Color Discrimination; Speech Clarity; Glare Sensitivity. General Work Activities—*Information Input:* Getting Information; Monitoring Processes, Materials, or Surroundings; Identifying Objects, Actions, and Events. *Mental Process:* Updating and Using Relevant Knowledge; Analyzing Data or Information; Processing Information. *Work Output:* Documenting or Recording Information; Controlling Machines and Processes; Handling and Moving Objects. *Interacting with Others:* Communicating with Other Workers; Communicating with Persons Outside Organization; Interpreting Meaning of Information for Others. Physical Work Conditions—Contaminants; Hazardous Conditions; Outdoors; Common Protective or Safety Attire; Climbing Ladders, Scaffolds, Poles, etc. Other Job Characteristics—Importance of Being Exact or Accurate; Consequence of Error; Degree of Automation.

Experience—Job Zone 3. Previous work-related skill, knowledge, or experience is required. Job Preparation: SVP 6.0 to less than 7.0—more than one year and less than four years. Knowledge—Chemistry; Public Safety and Security; Mathematics; Biology; Physics. Instructional Programs—Environmental Science; Environmental Studies; Physical Science Technologies/Technicians, Other; Science Technologies/Technicians, Other.

Related DOT Jobs—012.261-010 Air Analyst; 012.281-010 Smoke Tester; 022.261-018 Chemist, Instrumentation; 022.261-022 Chemist, Wastewater-Treatment Plant; 022.281-014 Chemist, Water Purification; 029.261-014 Pollution-Control Technician; 029.261-030 Microscopist, Asbestos; 029.361-018 Laboratory Assistant.

19-4092.00 Forensic Science Technicians

- Education/Training Required: Associate's degree
- Employed: 6,399
- Annual Earnings: $38,370
- Growth: 13.0%
- Annual Job Openings: 1,000

Collect, identify, classify, and analyze physical evidence related to criminal investigations. Perform tests on weapons or substances such as fiber, hair, and tissue to determine significance to investigation. May testify as expert witnesses on evidence or crime laboratory techniques. May serve as specialists in area of expertise, such as ballistics, fingerprinting, handwriting, or biochemistry.

Analyze and classify biological fluids using DNA typing or serological techniques. Analyze gunshot residue and bullet paths in order to determine how shootings occurred. Analyze handwritten and machine-produced textual evidence to decipher altered or obliterated text or to determine authorship, age, and/or source. Collect evidence from crime scenes, storing it in conditions that preserve its integrity. Collect impressions of dust from surfaces in order to obtain and identify fingerprints. Compare objects such as tools with impression marks in order to determine whether a specific object is responsible for a specific mark. Confer with ballistics, fingerprinting, handwriting, documents, electronics, medical, chemical, or metallurgical experts concerning evidence and its interpretation. Determine types of bullets used in shooting and whether they were fired from a specific weapon. Examine DNA samples to determine if they match other samples. Examine physical evidence such as hair, fiber, wood, or soil residues in order to obtain information about its source and composition. Identify and quantify drugs and poisons found in biological fluids and tissues, in foods, and at crime scenes. Interpret laboratory findings and test results in order to identify and classify substances, materials, and other evidence collected at crime scenes. Keep records and prepare reports detailing findings, investigative methods, and laboratory techniques. Reconstruct crime scenes in order to determine relationships among pieces of evidence. Examine firearms in order to determine mechanical condition and legal status, performing restoration work on damaged firearms in order to obtain information such as serial numbers. Interpret the pharmacological effects of a drug or a combination of drugs on an individual. Operate and maintain laboratory equipment and apparatus. Prepare solutions, reagents, and sample formulations needed for laboratory work. Testify in court about investigative and analytical methods and findings. Visit morgues, examine scenes of crimes, or contact other sources in order to obtain evidence or information to be used in investigations. Perform polygraph examination by explaining tests to subjects, attaching equipment to measure physiological responses, questioning subjects, and recording and interpreting subsequent machine readouts. Test racehorses and racing dogs for substances that may affect their performances.

GOE INFORMATION—Interest Area: 04. Law, Law Enforcement, and Public Safety. Work Group: 04.03. Law Enforcement. Personality Type—Investigative. Investigative occupations frequently involve working with ideas and require an extensive amount of thinking. These occupations can involve searching for facts and figuring out problems mentally. Work Values—Autonomy; Recognition; Creativity; Variety; Achievement. Skills—Science; Equipment Selection; Operation and Control; Mathematics; Operation Monitoring; Speaking; Complex Problem Solving; Systems Analysis. Abilities—*Cognitive:* Inductive Reasoning; Speed of Closure; Category Flexibility; Flexibility of Closure; Written Expression. *Psychomotor:* Arm-Hand Steadiness; Wrist-Finger Speed; Manual Dexterity; Finger Dexterity; Speed of Limb Movement. *Physical:* Gross Body Coordination; Trunk Strength; Dynamic Flexibility; Dynamic Strength; Gross Body Equilibrium. *Sensory:* Near Vision; Night Vision; Visual Color Discrimination; Depth Perception; Speech Clarity. General Work Activities—*Information Input:* Getting Information; Identifying Objects, Actions, and Events; Monitoring Processes, Materials, or Surroundings. *Mental Process:* Analyzing Data or Information; Judging Qualities of Things, Services, or Other People's Work; Making Decisions and Solving Problems. *Work Output:* Documenting or Recording Information; Handling and Moving Objects; Controlling Machines and Processes. *Interacting with Others:* Communicating with Persons Outside Organization; Communicating with Other Workers; Interpreting Meaning of Information for Others. Physical Work Conditions—Outdoors; Disease or Infections; Common Protective or Safety Attire; Kneeling, Crouching, or Crawling; Contaminants. Other Job Characteristics—Importance of Being Exact or Accurate; Consequence of Error; Degree of Automation.

Experience—Job Zone 4. A minimum of two to four years of work-related skill, knowledge, or experience is needed. Job Preparation: SVP 7.0 to less than 8.0—two years to less than 10 years. Knowledge—Chemistry; Public Safety and Security; Law and Government; Medicine and Dentistry; Biology. Instructional Programs—Forensic Science and Technology.

Related DOT Jobs—029.261-026 Criminalist; 199.267-010 Ballistics Expert, Forensic.

19-4093.00 Forest and Conservation Technicians

- Education/Training Required: Associate's degree
- Employed: 18,013
- Annual Earnings: $30,440
- Growth: 3.2%
- Annual Job Openings: 2,000

Compile data pertaining to size, content, condition, and other characteristics of forest tracts under direction of foresters; train and lead forest workers in forest propagation, fire prevention, and suppression. May assist conservation scientists in managing, improving, and protecting rangelands and wildlife habitats and help provide technical assistance regarding the conservation of soil, water, and related natural resources.

Inspect trees and collect samples of plants, seeds, foliage, bark, and roots to locate insect and disease damage. Manage forest protection activities, including fire control, fire crew training, and coordination of fire detection and public education programs. Patrol park or forest areas to protect resources and prevent damage. Perform reforestation (forest renewal), including nursery and silviculture operations, site preparation, seeding and tree planting programs, cone collection, and tree improvement. Select and mark trees for thinning or logging, drawing detailed plans that include access roads. Supervise forest nursery operations, timber harvesting, land use activities such as livestock grazing, and disease or insect control programs. Thin and space trees and control weeds and undergrowth, using manual tools and chemicals, or supervise workers performing these tasks. Train and lead forest and conservation workers in seasonal activities, such as planting tree seedlings, putting out forest fires, and maintaining recreational facilities. Conduct laboratory or field experiments with plants, animals, insects, diseases, and soils. Install gauges, stream flow recorders, and soil moisture measuring instruments; collect and record data from them to assist with watershed analysis. Issue fire permits, timber permits, and other forest use licenses. Measure distances, clean site-lines, and record data to help survey crews. Monitor activities of logging companies and contractors. Plan and supervise construction of access routes and forest roads. Provide forestry education and general information, advice, and recommendations to woodlot owners, community organizations, and the general public. Provide information about, and enforce, regulations such as those concerning environmental protection, resource utilization, fire safety, and accident prevention. Provide technical support to forestry research programs in areas such as

tree improvement, seed orchard operations, insect and disease surveys, or experimental forestry and forest engineering research. Survey, measure, and map access roads and forest areas such as burns, cut-over areas, experimental plots, and timber sales sections. Develop and maintain computer databases. Keep records of the amount and condition of logs taken to mills.

GOE INFORMATION—Interest Area: 03. Plants and Animals. **Work Group:** 03.03. Hands-on Work in Plants and Animals. **Note:** The Department of Labor has not collected some data for this job, so it has fewer details than the other descriptions.

Instructional Programs—Forest Management/Forest Resources Management; Forest Resources Production and Management; Forest Sciences and Biology; Forest Technology/Technician; Forestry, General; Forestry, Other; Land Use Planning and Management/Development; Natural Resources and Conservation, Other; Natural Resources Management and Policy, Other; Natural Resources/Conservation, General; Urban Forestry; Water, Wetlands, and Marine Resources Management.

Related DOT Jobs—040.261-010 Soil-Conservation Technician; 452.364-010 Forester Aide.

19-4099.99 Life, Physical, and Social Science Technicians, All Other

- Education/Training Required: Associate's degree
- Employed: No data available.
- Annual Earnings: No data available.
- Growth: 20.0%
- Annual Job Openings: 15,000

All life, physical, and social science technicians not listed separately.

No task data available.

GOE INFORMATION—Interest Area: 02. Science, Math, and Engineering. **Work Group:** 02.04. Social Sciences; 02.05. Laboratory Technology. **Note:** The Department of Labor has not collected some data for this job, so it has fewer details than the other descriptions.

Instructional Programs—Physical Science Technologies/Technicians, Other; Science Technologies/Technicians, Other.

Related DOT Jobs—019.261-034 Laser Technician; 022.161-014 Colorist; 024.364-010 Paleontological Helper; 025.264-010 Hydrographer; 025.267-010 Oceanographer, Assistant; 025.267-014 Weather Observer; 029.383-010 Pilot, Submersible; 049.364-014 Vector Control Assistant; 199.364-014 Scientific Helper; 850.684-010 Excavator.

21-0000
Community and Social Services Occupations

21-1000 Counselors, Social Workers, and Other Community and Social Service Specialists

21-1011.00 Substance Abuse and Behavioral Disorder Counselors

- **Education/Training Required: Master's degree**
- **Employed: 60,947**
- **Annual Earnings: $29,870**
- **Growth: 35.0%**
- **Annual Job Openings: 7,000**

Counsel and advise individuals with alcohol, tobacco, drug, or other problems, such as gambling and eating disorders. May counsel individuals, families, or groups or engage in prevention programs.

Complete and maintain accurate records and reports regarding the patients' histories and progress, services provided, and other required information. Coordinate counseling efforts with mental health professionals and other health professionals such as doctors, nurses, and social workers. Counsel clients and patients, individually and in group sessions, to assist in overcoming dependencies, adjusting to life, and making changes. Develop client treatment plans based on research, clinical experience, and client histories. Interview clients, review records, and confer with other professionals in order to evaluate individuals' mental and physical condition and to determine their suitability for participation in a specific program. Modify treatment plans to comply with changes in client status. Participate in case conferences and staff meetings. Plan and implement follow-up and aftercare programs for clients to be discharged from treatment programs. Provide clients or family members with information about addiction issues and about available services and programs, making appropriate referrals when necessary. Review and evaluate clients' progress in relation to measurable goals described in treatment and care plans. Act as liaisons between clients and medical staff. Attend training sessions in order to increase knowledge and skills. Conduct chemical dependency program orientation sessions. Confer with family members or others close to clients in order to keep them informed of treatment planning and progress. Coordinate activities with courts, probation officers, community services, and other post-treatment agencies. Counsel family members to assist them in understanding, dealing with, and supporting clients or patients. Develop, implement, and evaluate public education, prevention, and health promotion programs, working in collaboration with organizations, institutions, and communities. Follow progress of discharged patients in order to determine effectiveness of treatments. Instruct others in program methods, procedures, and functions. Intervene as advocate for clients or patients in order to resolve emergency problems in crisis situations. Supervise and direct other workers providing services to clients or patients.

GOE INFORMATION—Interest Area: 12. Education and Social Service. **Work Group:** 12.02. Social Services. **Personality Type**—Social. Social occupations frequently involve working with, communicating with, and teaching people. These occupations often involve helping or providing service to others. **Work Values**—Social Service; Creativity; Autonomy; Responsibility; Achievement. **Skills**—Social Perceptiveness; Management of Financial Resources; Service Orientation; Systems Analysis; Management of Personnel Resources; Instructing; Systems Evaluation; Complex Problem Solving. **Abilities**—*Cognitive:* Oral Expression; Problem Sensitivity; Fluency of Ideas; Written Expression; Originality. *Psychomotor:* None met the criteria. *Physical:* None met the criteria. *Sensory:* Speech Recognition; Speech Clarity; Auditory Attention; Near Vision; Night Vision. **General Work Activities**—*Information Input:* Getting Information; Identifying Objects, Actions, and Events; Monitoring Processes, Materials, or Surroundings. *Mental Process:* Making Decisions and Solving Problems; Analyzing Data or Information; Organizing, Planning, and Prioritizing. *Work Output:* Documenting or Recording Information; Handling and Moving Objects; Interacting with Computers. *Interacting with Others:* Establishing and Maintaining Relationships; Assisting and Caring for Others; Communicating with Persons Outside Organization. **Physical Work Conditions**—Sitting; Disease or Infections; High Places; Walking or Running; Radiation. **Other Job Characteristics**—Consequence of Error; Importance of Repeating Same Tasks; Pace Determined by Speed of Equipment.

Experience—Job Zone 4. A minimum of two to four years of work-related skill, knowledge, or experience is needed. **Job Preparation:** SVP 7.0 to less than 8.0—two years to less than 10 years. **Knowledge**—Therapy and Counseling; Psychology; Customer and Personal Service; Medicine and Dentistry; Education and Training. **Instructional Programs**—Clinical/Medical Social Work; Mental and Social Health Services and Allied Professions, Other; Substance Abuse/Addiction Counseling.

Related DOT Jobs—045.107-058 Substance Abuse Counselor.

21-1012.00 Educational, Vocational, and School Counselors

- **Education/Training Required: Master's degree**
- **Employed: 205,482**
- **Annual Earnings: $43,470**
- **Growth: 25.3%**
- **Annual Job Openings: 22,000**

Counsel individuals and provide group educational and vocational guidance services.

Counsel individuals to help them understand and overcome personal, social, or behavioral problems affecting their educational or vocational situations. Counsel students regarding educational issues such as course and program selection, class scheduling, school adjustment, truancy, study habits, and career planning. Evaluate individuals' abilities, interests, and personality characteristics, using tests, records, interviews, and professional sources. Address community groups, faculty, and staff members to explain available counseling services. Assess needs for assistance such as rehabilitation, financial aid, or additional vocational training and refer clients to the appropriate services. Compile and study occupational, educational, and economic information to assist counselees in determining and carrying out vocational and educational objectives. Conduct follow-up interviews with counselees to determine if their needs have been met. Confer with parents or guardians, teachers, other counselors, and administrators to resolve students' behavioral, academic, and other problems. Enforce all administration policies and rules governing students. Establish and enforce behavioral rules and procedures to maintain order among students. Establish and supervise peer counseling and peer tutoring programs. Instruct individuals in career development techniques such as job search and application strategies, resume writing, and interview skills. Interview clients to obtain information about employment history, educational background, and career goals and to identify barriers to employment. Maintain accurate and complete student records as required by laws, district policies, and administrative regulations. Meet with other professionals to discuss individual students' needs and progress. Meet with parents and guardians to discuss their children's progress and to determine their priorities for their children and their resource needs. Observe and evaluate students' performance, behavior, social development, and physical health. Plan and conduct orientation programs and group conferences to promote the adjustment of individuals to new life experiences such as starting college. Plan and promote career and employment-related programs such as work-experience programs. Prepare reports on students and activities as required by administration. Prepare students for later educational experiences by encouraging them to explore learning opportunities and to persevere with challenging tasks. Provide crisis intervention to students when difficult situations occur at schools. Provide students with information on such topics as college degree programs and admission requirements, financial aid opportunities, trade and technical schools, and apprenticeship programs. Refer qualified counselees to employers or employment services for job placement. Refer students to degree programs based on interests, aptitudes, or educational assessments. Review transcripts to ensure that students meet graduation or college entrance requirements and write letters of recommendation. Teach classes and present self-help or information sessions on subjects related to education and career planning. Attend staff meetings and serve on committees as required. Attend professional meetings, educational conferences, and teacher training workshops in order to maintain and improve professional competence. Collaborate with teachers and administrators in the development, evaluation, and revision of school programs. Encourage students and/or parents to seek additional assistance from mental health professionals when necessary. Identify cases involving domestic abuse or other family problems affecting students' development. Observe children during classroom and play activities to gain additional information about them. Perform administrative duties such as hall and cafeteria monitoring and bus loading and unloading. Provide disabled students with assistive devices, supportive technology, and assistance accessing facilities such as restrooms. Provide information for teachers and staff members involved in helping students or graduates identify and pursue employment opportunities. Provide information to businesses regarding human resource and employment issues. Provide special services such as alcohol and drug prevention programs and classes that teach students to handle conflicts without resorting to violence. Sponsor extracurricular activities such as clubs, student organizations, and academic contests.

GOE INFORMATION—Interest Area: 12. Education and Social Service. Work Group: 12.03. Educational Services. Personality Type—Social. Social occupations frequently involve working with, communicating with, and teaching people. These occupations often involve helping or providing service to others. Work Values—Social Service; Authority; Achievement; Creativity; Good Working Conditions. Skills—Service Orientation; Social Perceptiveness; Active Listening; Speaking; Complex Problem Solving; Systems Evaluation; Reading Comprehension; Instructing. Abilities—*Cognitive:* Oral Expression; Oral Comprehension; Written Expression; Fluency of Ideas; Written Comprehension. *Psychomotor:* None met the criteria. *Physical:* None met the criteria. *Sensory:* Speech Clarity; Speech Recognition. General Work Activities—*Information Input:* Getting Information; Identifying Objects, Actions, and Events; Monitoring Processes, Materials, or Surroundings. *Mental Process:* Judging Qualities of Things, Services, or Other People's Work; Analyzing Data or Information; Making Decisions and Solving Problems. *Work Output:* Documenting or Recording Information; Interacting with Computers; Handling and Moving Objects. *Interacting with Others:* Establishing and Maintaining Relationships; Communicating with Persons Outside Organization; Assisting and Caring for Others. Physical Work Conditions—Sitting; Indoors. Other Job Characteristics—Importance of Being Exact or Accurate; Consequence of Error; Importance of Repeating Same Tasks.

Experience—Job Zone 4. A minimum of two to four years of work-related skill, knowledge, or experience is needed. Job Preparation: SVP 7.0 to less than 8.0—two years to less than 10 years. Knowledge—Therapy

and Counseling; Psychology; Education and Training; Sociology and Anthropology; Personnel and Human Resources. Instructional Programs—College Student Counseling and Personnel Services; Counselor Education/School Counseling and Guidance Services.

Related DOT Jobs—045.107-010 Counselor; 045.107-014 Counselor, Nurses' Association; 045.107-018 Director of Counseling; 045.107-038 Residence Counselor; 045.107-042 Vocational Rehabilitation Counselor; 045.117-010 Director of Guidance in Public Schools; 090.107-010 Foreign-Student Adviser; 094.224-022 Employment Training Specialist; 169.267-026 Supervisor, Special Services; 187.167-198 Veterans Contact Representative.

21-1013.00 Marriage and Family Therapists

- Education/Training Required: Master's degree
- Employed: 21,107
- Annual Earnings: $32,720
- Growth: 29.9%
- Annual Job Openings: 2,000

Diagnose and treat mental and emotional disorders, whether cognitive, affective, or behavioral, within the context of marriage and family systems. Apply psychotherapeutic and family systems theories and techniques in the delivery of professional services to individuals, couples, and families for the purpose of treating such diagnosed nervous and mental disorders.

Ask questions that will help clients identify their feelings and behaviors. Collect information about clients, using techniques such as testing, interviewing, discussion, and observation. Confer with clients in order to develop plans for post-treatment activities. Counsel clients on concerns such as unsatisfactory relationships, divorce and separation, child rearing, home management, and financial difficulties. Determine whether clients should be counseled or referred to other specialists in such fields as medicine, psychiatry, and legal aid. Develop and implement individualized treatment plans addressing family relationship problems. Encourage individuals and family members to develop and use skills and strategies for confronting their problems in a constructive manner. Maintain case files that include activities, progress notes, evaluations, and recommendations. Confer with other counselors in order to analyze individual cases and to coordinate counseling services. Contact doctors, schools, social workers, juvenile counselors, law enforcement personnel, and others to gather information in order to make recommendations to courts for the resolution of child custody or visitation disputes. Follow up on results of counseling programs and clients' adjustments in order to determine effectiveness of programs. Provide family counseling and treatment services to inmates participating in substance abuse programs. Provide instructions to clients on how to obtain help with legal, financial, and other personal issues. Supervise other counselors, social service staff, and assistants. Write evaluations of parents and children for use by courts deciding divorce and custody cases, testifying in court if necessary. Provide public education and consultation to other professionals or groups regarding counseling services, issues, and methods.

GOE INFORMATION—Interest Area: 12. Education and Social Service. Work Group: 12.02. Social Services. Note: The Department of Labor has not collected some data for this job, so it has fewer details than the other descriptions.

Instructional Programs—Clinical Pastoral Counseling/Patient Counseling; Marriage and Family Therapy/Counseling; Social Work.

Related DOT Jobs—045.107-054 Counselor, Marriage and Family.

21-1014.00 Mental Health Counselors

- Education/Training Required: **Master's degree**
- Employed: 67,195
- Annual Earnings: $29,050
- Growth: 21.7%
- Annual Job Openings: 7,000

Counsel with emphasis on prevention. Work with individuals and groups to promote optimum mental health. May help individuals deal with addictions and substance abuse; family, parenting, and marital problems; suicide; stress management; problems with self-esteem; and issues associated with aging and mental and emotional health.

Act as client advocates in order to coordinate required services or to resolve emergency problems in crisis situations. Collaborate with other staff members to perform clinical assessments and develop treatment plans. Collect information about clients through interviews, observation, and tests. Counsel clients and patients, individually and in group sessions, to assist in overcoming dependencies, adjusting to life, and making changes. Develop and implement treatment plans based on clinical experience and knowledge. Discuss with individual patients their plans for life after leaving therapy. Encourage clients to express their feelings and discuss what is happening in their lives and help them to develop insight into themselves and their relationships. Evaluate clients' physical or mental condition based on review of client information. Evaluate the effectiveness of counseling programs and clients' progress in resolving identified problems and moving towards defined objectives. Guide clients in the development of skills and strategies for dealing with their problems. Maintain confidentiality of records relating to clients' treatment. Modify treatment activities and approaches as needed in order to comply with changes in clients' status. Plan, organize, and lead structured programs of counseling, work, study, recreation, and social activities for clients. Prepare and maintain all required treatment records and reports. Refer patients, clients, or family members to community resources or to specialists as necessary. Counsel family members to assist them in understanding, dealing with, and supporting clients or patients. Gather information about community mental health needs and resources that could be used in conjunction with therapy. Learn about new developments in their field by reading professional literature, attending courses and seminars, and establishing and maintaining contact with other social service agencies. Meet with families, probation officers, police, and other interested parties in order to exchange necessary information during the treatment process. Monitor clients' use of medications. Supervise other counselors, social service staff, and assistants. Plan and conduct programs to prevent substance abuse or improve community health and counseling services. Run workshops and courses about mental health issues.

GOE INFORMATION—Interest Area: 12. Education and Social Service. **Work Group:** 12.02. Social Services. **Personality Type**—Social. Social occupations frequently involve working with, communicating with, and teaching people. These occupations often involve helping or providing service to others. **Work Values**—Social Service; Creativity; Autonomy; Responsibility; Achievement. **Skills**—Social Perceptiveness; Management of Financial Resources; Service Orientation; Systems Analysis; Management of Personnel Resources; Instructing; Systems Evaluation; Complex Problem Solving. **Abilities**—*Cognitive:* Oral Expression; Problem Sensitivity; Fluency of Ideas; Written Expression; Originality. *Psychomotor:* None met the criteria. *Physical:* None met the criteria. *Sensory:* Speech Recognition; Speech Clarity; Auditory Attention; Near Vision; Night Vision. **General Work Activities**—*Information Input:* Getting Information; Identifying Objects, Actions, and Events; Monitoring Processes, Materials, or Surroundings. *Mental Process:* Making Decisions and Solv-ing Problems; Organizing, Planning, and Prioritizing; Analyzing Data or Information. *Work Output:* Documenting or Recording Information; Handling and Moving Objects; Performing General Physical Activities. *Interacting with Others:* Establishing and Maintaining Relationships; Communicating with Persons Outside Organization; Assisting and Caring for Others. **Physical Work Conditions**—Sitting; Disease or Infections; High Places; Walking or Running; Radiation. **Other Job Characteristics**—Consequence of Error; Importance of Repeating Same Tasks; Pace Determined by Speed of Equipment.

Experience—Job Zone 4. A minimum of two to four years of work-related skill, knowledge, or experience is needed. **Job Preparation:** SVP 7.0 to less than 8.0—two years to less than 10 years. **Knowledge**—Therapy and Counseling; Psychology; Customer and Personal Service; Medicine and Dentistry; Education and Training. **Instructional Programs**—Clinical/Medical Social Work; Mental and Social Health Services and Allied Professions, Other; Mental Health Counseling/Counselor; Substance Abuse/Addiction Counseling.

Related DOT Jobs—195.107-050 Bereavement Counselor.

21-1015.00 Rehabilitation Counselors

- Education/Training Required: **Bachelor's degree**
- Employed: 110,345
- Annual Earnings: $25,610
- Growth: 23.6%
- Annual Job Openings: 12,000

Counsel individuals to maximize the independence and employability of persons coping with personal, social, and vocational difficulties that result from birth defects, illness, disease, accidents, or the stress of daily life. Coordinate activities for residents of care and treatment facilities. Assess client needs and design and implement rehabilitation programs that may include personal and vocational counseling, training, and job placement.

No task data available.

GOE INFORMATION—Interest Area: 12. Education and Social Service. **Work Group:** 12.02. Social Services. **Note:** The Department of Labor has not collected some data for this job, so it has fewer details than the other descriptions.

Instructional Programs—Assistive/Augmentative Technology and Rehabilitation Engineering; Vocational Rehabilitation Counseling/Counselor.

Related DOT Jobs—045.107-042 Vocational Rehabilitation Counselor; 076.117-010 Coordinator of Rehabilitation Services; 094.117-018 Vocational Rehabilitation Consultant.

21-1019.99 Counselors, All Other

- Education/Training Required: **Bachelor's degree**
- Employed: No data available.
- Annual Earnings: No data available.
- Growth: 18.8%
- Annual Job Openings: 33,000

All counselors not listed separately.

No task data available.

GOE INFORMATION—Interest Area: 12. Education and Social Service. **Work Group:** 12.02. Social Services. **Note:** The Department of Labor has not collected some data for this job, so it has fewer details than the other descriptions.

Instructional Programs—Genetic Counseling/Counselor; Mental and Social Health Services and Allied Professions, Other; Social Work.

Related DOT Jobs—No related DOT jobs.

21-1021.00 Child, Family, and School Social Workers

- Education/Training Required: Bachelor's degree
- Employed: 281,306
- Annual Earnings: $32,950
- Growth: 26.9%
- Annual Job Openings: 35,000

Provide social services and assistance to improve the social and psychological functioning of children and their families and to maximize the family well-being and the academic functioning of children. May assist single parents, arrange adoptions, and find foster homes for abandoned or abused children. In schools, they address such problems as teenage pregnancy, misbehavior, and truancy. May also advise teachers on how to deal with problem children.

Interview clients individually, in families, or in groups, assessing their situations, capabilities, and problems, to determine what services are required to meet their needs. Counsel individuals, groups, families, or communities regarding issues including mental health, poverty, unemployment, substance abuse, physical abuse, rehabilitation, social adjustment, child care, and/or medical care. Maintain case history records and prepare reports. Counsel students whose behavior, school progress, or mental or physical impairment indicate a need for assistance, diagnosing students' problems and arranging for needed services. Consult with parents, teachers, and other school personnel to determine causes of problems such as truancy and misbehavior and to implement solutions. Counsel parents with child-rearing problems, interviewing the child and family to determine whether further action is required. Develop and review service plans in consultation with clients and perform follow-ups assessing the quantity and quality of services provided. Collect supplementary information needed to assist client, such as employment records, medical records, or school reports. Address legal issues, such as child abuse and discipline, assisting with hearings and providing testimony to inform custody arrangements. Provide, find, or arrange for support services, such as child care, homemaker service, prenatal care, substance abuse treatment, job training, counseling, or parenting classes, to prevent more serious problems from developing. Refer clients to community resources for services such as job placement, debt counseling, legal aid, housing, medical treatment, or financial assistance and provide concrete information, such as where to go and how to apply. Arrange for medical, psychiatric, and other tests that may disclose causes of difficulties and indicate remedial measures. Work in child and adolescent residential institutions. Administer welfare programs. Evaluate personal characteristics and home conditions of foster home or adoption applicants. Serve as liaisons between students, homes, schools, family services, child guidance clinics, courts, protective services, doctors, and other contacts to help children who face problems such as disabilities, abuse, or poverty. Place children in foster or adoptive homes, institutions, or medical treatment centers. Supervise other social workers. Recommend temporary foster care and advise foster or adoptive parents. Determine clients' eligibility for financial assistance. Conduct social research. Lead group counseling sessions that provide support in such areas as grief, stress, or chemical dependency. Serve on policymaking committees, assist in community development, and assist client groups by lobbying for solutions to problems. Collaborate with other professionals to evaluate patients' medical or physical condition and to assess client needs. Investigate child abuse or neglect cases and take authorized protective action when necessary. Refer patient, client, or family to community resources to assist in recovery from mental or physical illness and to provide access to services such as financial assistance, legal aid, housing, job placement, or education. Counsel clients and patients in individual and group sessions to help them overcome dependencies, recover from illness, and adjust to life. Organize support groups or counsel family members to assist them in understanding, dealing with, and supporting the client or patient. Advocate for clients or patients to resolve crises. Identify environmental impediments to client or patient progress through interviews and review of patient records. Utilize consultation data and social work experience to plan and coordinate client or patient care and rehabilitation, following through to ensure service efficacy. Modify treatment plans to comply with changes in clients' status. Monitor, evaluate, and record client progress according to measurable goals described in treatment and care plan. Supervise and direct other workers providing services to clients or patients. Develop and advise on social policy and assist in community development. Oversee Medicaid- and Medicare-related paperwork and record-keeping in hospitals. Conduct social research to advance knowledge in the social work field. Plan and conduct programs to combat social problems, prevent substance abuse, or improve community health and counseling services. Counsel clients in individual and group sessions to assist them in dealing with substance abuse, mental and physical illness, poverty, unemployment, or physical abuse. Interview clients, review records, and confer with other professionals to evaluate mental or physical condition of client or patient. Collaborate with counselors, physicians, and nurses to plan and coordinate treatment, drawing on social work experience and patient needs. Monitor, evaluate, and record client progress with respect to treatment goals. Refer patient, client, or family to community resources for housing or treatment to assist in recovery from mental or physical illness, following through to ensure service efficacy. Counsel and aid family members to assist them in understanding, dealing with, and supporting the client or patient. Modify treatment plans according to changes in client status. Plan and conduct programs to prevent substance abuse, to combat social problems, or to improve health and counseling services in community. Supervise and direct other workers who provide services to clients or patients. Develop or advise on social policy and assist in community development.

GOE INFORMATION—Interest Area: 12. Education and Social Service. **Work Group:** 12.02. Social Services. **Personality Type**—Social. Social occupations frequently involve working with, communicating with, and teaching people. These occupations often involve helping or providing service to others. **Work Values**—Social Service; Autonomy; Authority; Activity; Variety. **Skills**—Social Perceptiveness; Service Orientation; Speaking; Monitoring; Learning Strategies; Active Listening; Writing; Negotiation. **Abilities**—*Cognitive:* Problem Sensitivity; Inductive Reasoning; Originality; Written Expression; Oral Expression. *Psychomotor:* None met the criteria. *Physical:* Trunk Strength. *Sensory:* Speech Recognition; Speech Clarity; Near Vision; Auditory Attention; Depth Perception. **General Work Activities**—*Information Input:* Identifying Objects, Actions, and Events; Getting Information; Monitoring Processes, Materials, or Surroundings. *Mental Process:* Organizing, Planning, and Prioritizing; Making Decisions and Solving Problems; Evaluating Information Against Standards. *Work Output:* Documenting or Recording Information; Interacting with Computers; Performing General Physical Activities. *Interacting with Others:* Establishing and Maintaining Relationships; Communicating with Other Workers; Resolving Conflict and Negotiating with Others. **Physical Work Conditions**—Sitting; Outdoors; Disease or Infections; Indoors. **Other Job Characteristics**—Importance of Being Exact or Accurate; Consequence of Error; Degree of Automation.

Experience—Job Zone 5. Extensive skill, knowledge, and experience are needed for these occupations. **Job Preparation:** SVP 7.0 to less than

8.0—two years to less than 10 years. **Knowledge**—Therapy and Counseling; Psychology; Customer and Personal Service; Sociology and Anthropology; Philosophy and Theology. **Instructional Programs**—Juvenile Corrections; Social Work; Youth Services/Administration.

Related DOT Jobs—195.107-010 Caseworker; 195.107-014 Caseworker, Child Welfare; 195.107-018 Caseworker, Family; 195.107-022 Social Group Worker; 195.107-026 Social Worker, Delinquency Prevention; 195.107-038 Social Worker, School; 195.137-010 Casework Supervisor.

21-1022.00 Medical and Public Health Social Workers

- **Education/Training Required: Bachelor's degree**
- **Employed: 103,695**
- **Annual Earnings: $36,410**
- **Growth: 31.6%**
- **Annual Job Openings: 13,000**

Provide persons, families, or vulnerable populations with the psychosocial support needed to cope with chronic, acute, or terminal illnesses, such as Alzheimer's, cancer, or AIDS. Services include advising family caregivers, providing patient education and counseling, and making necessary referrals for other social services.

Collaborate with other professionals to evaluate patients' medical or physical condition and to assess client needs. Investigate child abuse or neglect cases and take authorized protective action when necessary. Refer patient, client, or family to community resources to assist in recovery from mental or physical illness and to provide access to services such as financial assistance, legal aid, housing, job placement, or education. Counsel clients and patients in individual and group sessions to help them overcome dependencies, recover from illness, and adjust to life. Organize support groups or counsel family members to assist them in understanding, dealing with, and supporting the client or patient. Advocate for clients or patients to resolve crises. Identify environmental impediments to client or patient progress through interviews and review of patient records. Utilize consultation data and social work experience to plan and coordinate client or patient care and rehabilitation, following through to ensure service efficacy. Modify treatment plans to comply with changes in clients' status. Monitor, evaluate, and record client progress according to measurable goals described in treatment and care plan. Supervise and direct other workers providing services to clients or patients. Develop or advise on social policy and assist in community development. Oversee Medicaid- and Medicare-related paperwork and record-keeping in hospitals. Conduct social research to advance knowledge in the social work field. Plan and conduct programs to combat social problems, prevent substance abuse, or improve community health and counseling services.

GOE INFORMATION—Interest Area: 12. Education and Social Service. **Work Group:** 12.02. Social Services. **Personality Type**—Social. Social occupations frequently involve working with, communicating with, and teaching people. These occupations often involve helping or providing service to others. **Work Values**—Social Service; Creativity; Autonomy; Responsibility; Achievement. **Skills**—Social Perceptiveness; Service Orientation; Negotiation; Coordination; Active Listening; Critical Thinking; Speaking; Learning Strategies. **Abilities**—*Cognitive:* Problem Sensitivity; Speed of Closure; Inductive Reasoning; Category Flexibility; Originality. *Psychomotor:* Response Orientation; Reaction Time. *Physical:* Explosive Strength. *Sensory:* Speech Recognition; Speech Clarity; Far Vision; Near Vision; Auditory Attention. **General Work Activities**—*Information Input:* Identifying Objects, Actions, and Events; Getting Information; Monitoring Processes, Materials, or Surroundings. *Mental Process:* Making Decisions and Solving Problems; Updating and Using

Relevant Knowledge; Judging Qualities of Things, Services, or Other People's Work. *Work Output:* Documenting or Recording Information; Interacting with Computers; Performing General Physical Activities. *Interacting with Others:* Establishing and Maintaining Relationships; Resolving Conflict and Negotiating with Others; Communicating with Persons Outside Organization. **Physical Work Conditions**—Sitting; Disease or Infections; High Places; Walking or Running; Radiation. **Other Job Characteristics**—Consequence of Error; Importance of Repeating Same Tasks; Pace Determined by Speed of Equipment.

Experience—Job Zone 5. Extensive skill, knowledge, and experience are needed for these occupations. **Job Preparation:** SVP 7.0 to less than 8.0—two years to less than 10 years. **Knowledge**—Psychology; Therapy and Counseling; Customer and Personal Service; Philosophy and Theology; Sociology and Anthropology. **Instructional Programs**—Clinical/Medical Social Work.

Related DOT Jobs—195.107-030 Social Worker, Medical.

21-1023.00 Mental Health and Substance Abuse Social Workers

- **Education/Training Required: Master's degree**
- **Employed: 83,125**
- **Annual Earnings: $32,080**
- **Growth: 39.1%**
- **Annual Job Openings: 10,000**

Assess and treat individuals with mental, emotional, or substance abuse problems, including abuse of alcohol, tobacco, and/or other drugs. Activities may include individual and group therapy, crisis intervention, case management, client advocacy, prevention, and education.

Counsel clients in individual and group sessions to assist them in dealing with substance abuse, mental and physical illness, poverty, unemployment, or physical abuse. Interview clients, review records, and confer with other professionals to evaluate mental or physical condition of client or patient. Collaborate with counselors, physicians, and nurses to plan and coordinate treatment, drawing on social work experience and patient needs. Monitor, evaluate, and record client progress with respect to treatment goals. Refer patient, client, or family to community resources for housing or treatment to assist in recovery from mental or physical illness, following through to ensure service efficacy. Counsel and aid family members to assist them in understanding, dealing with, and supporting the client or patient. Modify treatment plans according to changes in client status. Plan and conduct programs to prevent substance abuse, to combat social problems, or to improve health and counseling services in community. Supervise and direct other workers who provide services to clients or patients. Develop or advise on social policy and assist in community development. Conduct social research to advance knowledge in the social work field.

GOE INFORMATION—Interest Area: 12. Education and Social Service. **Work Group:** 12.02. Social Services. **Personality Type**—Social. Social occupations frequently involve working with, communicating with, and teaching people. These occupations often involve helping or providing service to others. **Work Values**—Social Service; Creativity; Autonomy; Responsibility; Achievement. **Skills**—Social Perceptiveness; Service Orientation; Active Listening; Complex Problem Solving; Negotiation; Critical Thinking; Persuasion; Speaking. **Abilities**—*Cognitive:* Problem Sensitivity; Originality; Inductive Reasoning; Oral Expression; Written Expression. *Psychomotor:* Response Orientation; Reaction Time. *Physical:* Explosive Strength; Gross Body Coordination; Gross Body Equilibrium.

Sensory: Speech Recognition; Speech Clarity; Auditory Attention. **General Work Activities**—*Information Input:* Getting Information; Identifying Objects, Actions, and Events; Monitoring Processes, Materials, or Surroundings. *Mental Process:* Making Decisions and Solving Problems; Organizing, Planning, and Prioritizing; Updating and Using Relevant Knowledge. *Work Output:* Documenting or Recording Information; Interacting with Computers; Operating Vehicles or Equipment. *Interacting with Others:* Establishing and Maintaining Relationships; Assisting and Caring for Others; Resolving Conflict and Negotiating with Others. **Physical Work Conditions**—Sitting; Disease or Infections; High Places; Walking or Running; Radiation. **Other Job Characteristics**—Consequence of Error; Importance of Repeating Same Tasks; Pace Determined by Speed of Equipment.

Experience—Job Zone 5. Extensive skill, knowledge, and experience are needed for these occupations. **Job Preparation:** SVP 7.0 to less than 8.0—two years to less than 10 years. **Knowledge**—Psychology; Therapy and Counseling; Customer and Personal Service; Sociology and Anthropology; Medicine and Dentistry. **Instructional Programs**—Clinical/Medical Social Work.

Related DOT Jobs—195.107-034 Social Worker, Psychiatric; 195.167-050 Case Manager.

21-1029.99 Social Workers, All Other

- Education/Training Required: Bachelor's degree
- Employed: No data available.
- Annual Earnings: No data available.
- Growth: 18.8%
- Annual Job Openings: 33,000

All social workers not listed separately.

No task data available.

GOE INFORMATION—Interest Area: 12. Education and Social Service. **Work Group:** 12.02. Social Services. **Note:** The Department of Labor has not collected some data for this job, so it has fewer details than the other descriptions.

Instructional Programs—Social Work.

Related DOT Jobs—No related DOT jobs.

21-1091.00 Health Educators

- Education/Training Required: Master's degree
- Employed: 43,053
- Annual Earnings: $35,230
- Growth: 23.5%
- Annual Job Openings: 7,000

Promote, maintain, and improve individual and community health by assisting individuals and communities to adopt healthy behaviors. Collect and analyze data to identify community needs prior to planning, implementing, monitoring, and evaluating programs designed to encourage healthy lifestyles, policies, and environments. May also serve as a resource to assist individuals, other professionals, or the community and may administer fiscal resources for health education programs.

Plans and provides educational opportunities for health personnel. Collaborates with health specialists and civic groups to ascertain community health needs, determine availability of services, and develop goals. Promotes health discussions in schools, industry, and community

agencies. Conducts community surveys to ascertain health needs, develop desirable health goals, and determine availability of professional health services. Prepares and disseminates educational and informational materials. Develops and maintains cooperation between public, civic, professional, and voluntary agencies.

GOE INFORMATION—Interest Area: 14. Medical and Health Services. **Work Group:** 14.08. Health Protection and Promotion. **Personality Type**—Social. Social occupations frequently involve working with, communicating with, and teaching people. These occupations often involve helping or providing service to others. **Work Values**—Social Service; Authority; Creativity; Social Status; Achievement. **Skills**—Speaking; Complex Problem Solving; Systems Analysis; Coordination; Writing; Systems Evaluation; Active Listening; Persuasion. **Abilities**—*Cognitive:* Oral Expression; Written Expression; Inductive Reasoning; Originality; Oral Comprehension. *Psychomotor:* None met the criteria. *Physical:* None met the criteria. *Sensory:* Speech Clarity; Speech Recognition; Night Vision. **General Work Activities**—*Information Input:* Getting Information; Identifying Objects, Actions, and Events; Estimating Needed Characteristics. *Mental Process:* Updating and Using Relevant Knowledge; Making Decisions and Solving Problems; Processing Information. *Work Output:* Documenting or Recording Information; Interacting with Computers; Performing General Physical Activities. *Interacting with Others:* Communicating with Persons Outside Organization; Communicating with Other Workers; Teaching Others. **Physical Work Conditions**—Sitting; Indoors; Disease or Infections; Specialized Protective or Safety Attire. **Other Job Characteristics**—Consequence of Error; Importance of Being Exact or Accurate; Importance of Repeating Same Tasks.

Experience—Job Zone 5. Extensive skill, knowledge, and experience are needed for these occupations. **Job Preparation:** SVP 8.0 and above—four years to more than 10 years. **Knowledge**—Education and Training; Sales and Marketing; Therapy and Counseling; Medicine and Dentistry; Communications and Media. **Instructional Programs**—Community Health Services/Liaison/Counseling; Health Communication; International Public Health/International Health; Maternal and Child Health; Public Health Education and Promotion.

Related DOT Jobs—079.117-014 Public Health Educator.

21-1092.00 Probation Officers and Correctional Treatment Specialists

- Education/Training Required: Bachelor's degree
- Employed: 84,409
- Annual Earnings: $38,780
- Growth: 23.8%
- Annual Job Openings: 14,000

Provide social services to assist in rehabilitation of law offenders in custody or on probation or parole. Make recommendations for actions involving formulation of rehabilitation plan and treatment of offender, including conditional release and education and employment stipulations.

Arrange for medical, mental health, or substance abuse treatment services according to individual needs and/or court orders. Arrange for post-release services such as employment, housing, counseling, education, and social activities. Assess the suitability of penitentiary inmates for release under parole and statutory release programs and submit recommendations to parole boards. Conduct prehearing and presentencing investigations and testify in court regarding offenders' backgrounds and recommended sentences and sentencing conditions. Develop liaisons and networks with other parole officers, community agencies, staff in correctional institutions, psychiatric facilities, and after-care agencies in order to make plans for helping offenders with life adjustments. Develop rehabilitation programs for assigned offenders or inmates, establishing rules of conduct, goals, and objectives. Gather information about offenders' backgrounds by talking to offenders, their families and friends, and other people who have relevant information. Identify and approve work placements for offenders with community service sentences. Inform offenders or inmates of requirements of conditional release, such as office visits, restitution payments, or educational and employment stipulations. Interview probationers and parolees regularly to evaluate their progress in accomplishing goals and maintaining the terms specified in their probation contracts and rehabilitation plans. Investigate alleged parole violations, using interviews, surveillance, and search and seizure. Prepare and maintain case folder for each assigned inmate or offender. Recommend remedial action or initiate court action when terms of probation or parole are not complied with. Develop and prepare packets containing information about social service agencies and assistance organizations and programs that might be useful for inmates or offenders. Discuss with offenders how such issues as drug and alcohol abuse and anger management problems might have played roles in their criminal behavior. Participate in decisions about whether cases should go before courts and which court should hear them. Provide offenders or inmates with assistance in matters concerning detainers, sentences in other jurisdictions, writs, and applications for social assistance. Recommend appropriate penitentiary for initial placement of an offender. Supervise people on community-based sentences, including people on electronically monitored home detention. Write reports describing offenders' progress.

GOE INFORMATION—Interest Area: 12. Education and Social Service. **Work Group:** 12.02. Social Services. **Personality Type**—Social. Social occupations frequently involve working with, communicating with, and teaching people. These occupations often involve helping or providing service to others. **Work Values**—Social Service; Authority; Supervision, Human Relations; Autonomy; Security. **Skills**—Service Orientation; Active Listening; Speaking; Systems Evaluation; Complex Problem Solving; Judgment and Decision Making; Social Perceptiveness; Systems Analysis. **Abilities**—*Cognitive:* Oral Expression; Written Expression; Oral Comprehension; Problem Sensitivity; Written Comprehension. *Psychomotor:* None met the criteria. *Physical:* None met the criteria. *Sensory:* Speech Clarity; Speech Recognition; Glare Sensitivity. **General Work Activities**—*Information Input:* Getting Information; Identifying Objects, Actions, and Events; Monitoring Processes, Materials, or Surroundings. *Mental Process:* Judging Qualities of Things, Services, or Other People's Work; Making Decisions and Solving Problems; Organizing, Planning, and Prioritizing. *Work Output:* Documenting or Recording Information; Performing General Physical Activities; Handling and Moving Objects. *Interacting with Others:* Communicating with Persons Outside Organization; Communicating with Other Workers; Establishing and Maintaining Relationships. **Physical Work Conditions**—Walking or Running; Indoors; Sitting; Specialized Protective or Safety Attire. **Other Job Characteristics**—Consequence of Error; Importance of Being Exact or Accurate; Degree of Automation.

Experience—Job Zone 3. Previous work-related skill, knowledge, or experience is required. **Job Preparation:** SVP 6.0 to less than 7.0—more than one year and less than four years. **Knowledge**—Therapy and Counseling; Psychology; Sociology and Anthropology; Law and Government; Public Safety and Security. **Instructional Programs**—Social Work.

Related DOT Jobs—166.267-022 Prisoner-Classification Interviewer; 195.107-042 Correctional-Treatment Specialist; 195.107-046 Probation-and-Parole Officer; 195.367-026 Preparole-Counseling Aide.

21-1093.00 Social and Human Service Assistants

- **Education/Training Required: Moderate-term on-the-job training**
- **Employed: 270,849**
- **Annual Earnings: $23,070**
- **Growth: 54.2%**
- **Annual Job Openings: 45,000**

Assist professionals from a wide variety of fields, such as psychology, rehabilitation, or social work, to provide client services as well as support for families. May assist clients in identifying available benefits and social and community services and help clients obtain them. May assist social workers with developing, organizing, and conducting programs to prevent and resolve problems relevant to substance abuse, human relationships, rehabilitation, or adult daycare.

Visit individuals in homes or attend group meetings to provide information on agency services, requirements, and procedures. Advise clients regarding food stamps, child care, food, money management, sanitation, and housekeeping. Interview individuals and family members to compile information on social, educational, criminal, institutional, or drug history. Provide information on and refer individuals to public or private agencies and community services for assistance. Assist clients with preparation of forms, such as tax or rent forms. Assist in locating housing for displaced individuals. Assist in planning of food budget, utilizing charts and sample budgets. Monitor free supplementary meal program to ensure cleanliness of facility and ensure that eligibility guidelines are met for persons receiving meals. Meet with youth groups to acquaint them with consequences of delinquent acts. Observe clients' food selections and recommend alternate economical and nutritional food choices. Observe and discuss meal preparation and suggest alternate methods of food preparation. Consult with supervisor concerning programs for individual families. Oversee day-to-day group activities of residents in institution. Transport and accompany clients to shopping area and to appointments, using automobile. Explain rules established by owner or management, such as sanitation and maintenance requirements and parking regulations. Demonstrate use and care of equipment for tenant use. Inform tenants of facilities such as laundries and playgrounds. Submit to and review reports and problems with superior. Keep records and prepare reports for owner or management concerning visits with clients. Care for children in client's home during client's appointments.

GOE INFORMATION—Interest Area: 12. Education and Social Service. **Work Group:** 12.02. Social Services. **Personality Type**—Social. Social occupations frequently involve working with, communicating with, and teaching people. These occupations often involve helping or providing service to others. **Work Values**—Social Service; Authority; Variety; Supervision, Technical; Supervision, Human Relations. **Skills**—Service Orientation; Social Perceptiveness; Speaking; Active Listening; Critical Thinking; Learning Strategies; Systems Evaluation; Complex Problem Solving. **Abilities**—*Cognitive:* Oral Expression; Oral Comprehension; Time Sharing; Written Comprehension; Written Expression. *Psychomotor:* None met the criteria. *Physical:* None met the criteria. *Sensory:* Speech Recognition. **General Work Activities**—*Information Input:* Getting Information; Identifying Objects, Actions, and Events; Monitoring Processes, Materials, or Surroundings. *Mental Process:* Organizing, Planning, and Prioritizing; Processing Information; Updating and Using Relevant Knowledge. *Work Output:* Documenting or Recording Information; Performing General Physical Activities; Handling and Moving Objects. *Interacting with Others:* Assisting and Caring for Others; Establishing and Maintaining Relationships; Communicating with Other Workers. **Physical Work**

Conditions—Disease or Infections; Outdoors; Walking or Running; Very Hot or Cold; Sitting. **Other Job Characteristics**—Consequence of Error; Importance of Repeating Same Tasks; Importance of Being Exact or Accurate.

Experience—Job Zone 2. Some previous work-related skill, knowledge, or experience may be helpful, but usually is not needed. **Job Preparation:** SVP 4.0 to less than 6.0—six months to less than two years. **Knowledge**—Therapy and Counseling; Customer and Personal Service; Psychology; Sociology and Anthropology; Food Production. **Instructional Programs**—Mental and Social Health Services and Allied Professions, Other.

Related DOT Jobs—195.367-010 Case Aide; 195.367-014 Management Aide; 195.367-022 Food-Management Aide; 195.367-034 Social-Services Aide.

21-1099.99 Community and Social Service Specialists, All Other

- **Education/Training Required:** No data available.
- **Employed:** No data available.
- **Annual Earnings:** No data available.
- **Growth:** 44.5%
- **Annual Job Openings:** 33,000

All community and social service specialists not listed separately.

No task data available.

GOE INFORMATION—Interest Area: 12. Education and Social Service. **Work Group:** 12.02. Social Services. **Note:** The Department of Labor has not collected some data for this job, so it has fewer details than the other descriptions.

Instructional Programs—Behavioral Sciences; Mental and Social Health Services and Allied Professions, Other.

Related DOT Jobs—No related DOT jobs.

21-2000 Religious Workers

21-2011.00 Clergy

- **Education/Training Required:** First professional degree
- **Employed:** 171,337
- **Annual Earnings:** $33,840
- **Growth:** 15.0%
- **Annual Job Openings:** 12,000

Conduct religious worship and perform other spiritual functions associated with beliefs and practices of religious faith or denomination. Provide spiritual and moral guidance and assistance to members.

Administer religious rites or ordinances. Study and interpret religious laws, doctrines, and/or traditions. Counsel individuals and groups concerning their spiritual, emotional, and personal needs. Organize and lead regular religious services. Conduct special ceremonies such as weddings, funerals, and confirmations. Instruct people who seek conversion to a particular faith. Pray and promote spirituality. Prepare and deliver sermons and other talks. Prepare people for participation in religious ceremonies. Read from sacred texts such as the Bible, Torah, or Koran. Collaborate with committees and individuals to address financial and administrative issues pertaining to congregations. Devise ways in which congregation membership can be expanded. Organize and engage in interfaith, community, civic, educational, and recreational activities sponsored by or related to their religion. Participate in fundraising activities to support congregation activities and facilities. Perform administrative duties such as overseeing building management, ordering supplies, contracting for services and repairs, and supervising the work of staff members and volunteers. Plan and lead religious education programs for their congregations. Refer people to community support services, psychologists, and/or doctors as necessary. Respond to requests for assistance during emergencies or crises. Share information about religious issues by writing articles, giving speeches, or teaching. Train leaders of church, community, and youth groups. Visit people in homes, hospitals, and prisons to provide them with comfort and support.

GOE INFORMATION—Interest Area: 12. Education and Social Service. **Work Group:** 12.02. Social Services. **Personality Type**—Social. Social occupations frequently involve working with, communicating with, and teaching people. These occupations often involve helping or providing service to others. **Work Values**—Social Service; Social Status; Autonomy; Achievement; Recognition. **Skills**—Service Orientation; Social Perceptiveness; Speaking; Writing; Active Listening; Reading Comprehension; Learning Strategies; Complex Problem Solving. **Abilities**—*Cognitive:* Oral Expression; Written Expression; Fluency of Ideas; Written Comprehension; Problem Sensitivity. *Psychomotor:* None met the criteria. *Physical:* None met the criteria. *Sensory:* Speech Clarity; Speech Recognition. **General Work Activities**—*Information Input:* Getting Information; Identifying Objects, Actions, and Events; Monitoring Processes, Materials, or Surroundings. *Mental Process:* Organizing, Planning, and Prioritizing; Making Decisions and Solving Problems; Judging Qualities of Things, Services, or Other People's Work. *Work Output:* Performing General Physical Activities; Documenting or Recording Information; Handling and Moving Objects. *Interacting with Others:* Assisting and Caring for Others; Establishing and Maintaining Relationships; Performing for or Working with the Public. **Physical Work Conditions**—Indoors; Standing; Sitting; Disease or Infections. **Other Job Characteristics**—Consequence of Error; Pace Determined by Speed of Equipment; Degree of Automation.

Experience—Job Zone 5. Extensive skill, knowledge, and experience are needed for these occupations. **Job Preparation:** SVP 8.0 and above—four years to more than 10 years. **Knowledge**—Philosophy and Theology; Education and Training; Therapy and Counseling; Psychology; English Language. **Instructional Programs**—Clinical Pastoral Counseling/Patient Counseling; Divinity/Ministry (BD, MDiv.); Pastoral Counseling and Specialized Ministries, Other; Pastoral Studies/Counseling; Pre-Theology/Pre-Ministerial Studies; Rabbinical Studies; Theological and Ministerial Studies, Other; Theology and Religious Vocations, Other; Theology/Theological Studies; Youth Ministry.

Related DOT Jobs—120.107-010 Clergy Member.

21-2021.00 Directors, Religious Activities and Education

- **Education/Training Required:** Bachelor's degree
- **Employed:** 121,300
- **Annual Earnings:** $27,420
- **Growth:** 15.9%
- **Annual Job Openings:** 23,000

Direct and coordinate activities of a denominational group to meet religious needs of students. Plan, direct, or coordinate church school programs designed to promote religious education among church membership. May provide counseling and guidance relative to marital, health, financial, and religious problems.

Coordinates activities with religious advisers, councils, and university officials to meet religious needs of students. Counsels individuals regarding marital, health, financial, and religious problems. Plans congregational activities and projects to encourage participation in religious education programs. Develops, organizes, and directs study courses and religious education programs within congregation. Supervises instructional staff in religious education program. Promotes student participation in extracurricular congregational activities. Assists and advises groups in promoting interfaith understanding. Plans and conducts conferences dealing with interpretation of religious ideas and convictions. Solicits support, participation, and interest in religious education programs from congregation members, organizations, officials, and clergy. Analyzes member participation and changes in congregation emphasis to determine needs for religious education. Interprets policies of university to community religious workers. Interprets religious education to public through speaking, leading discussions, and writing articles for local and national publications. Analyzes revenue and program cost data to determine budget priorities. Orders and distributes school supplies.

GOE INFORMATION—Interest Area: 12. Education and Social Service. Work Group: 12.02. Social Services. Personality Type—Social. Social occupations frequently involve working with, communicating with, and teaching people. These occupations often involve helping or providing service to others. Work Values—Social Service; Social Status; Creativity; Autonomy; Achievement. Skills—Management of Financial Resources; Social Perceptiveness; Service Orientation; Management of Personnel Resources; Management of Material Resources; Systems Analysis; Speaking; Instructing. Abilities—Cognitive: Oral Expression; Fluency of Ideas; Oral Comprehension; Mathematical Reasoning; Problem Sensitivity. Psychomotor: None met the criteria. Physical: None met the criteria. Sensory: Speech Clarity; Speech Recognition. General Work Activities—Information Input: Getting Information; Monitoring Processes, Materials, or Surroundings; Identifying Objects, Actions, and Events. Mental Process: Organizing, Planning, and Prioritizing; Making Decisions and Solving Problems; Scheduling Work and Activities. Work Output: Documenting or Recording Information; Performing General Physical Activities; Handling and Moving Objects. Interacting with Others: Communicating with Other Workers; Communicating with Persons Outside Organization; Establishing and Maintaining Relationships. Physical Work Conditions—Indoors; Sitting; Walking or Running; Disease or Infections. Other Job Characteristics—Consequence of Error; Importance of Being Exact or Accurate; Pace Determined by Speed of Equipment.

Experience—Job Zone 5. Extensive skill, knowledge, and experience are needed for these occupations. Job Preparation: SVP 8.0 and above—four years to more than 10 years. Knowledge—Therapy and Counseling; Philosophy and Theology; Administration and Management; Education and Training; Sociology and Anthropology. Instructional Programs—Bible/Biblical Studies; Missions/Missionary Studies and Missiology; Religious Education; Youth Ministry.

Related DOT Jobs—129.107-018 Director of Religious Activities; 129.107-022 Director, Religious Education.

21-2099.99 Religious Workers, All Other

- Education/Training Required: No data available.
- Employed: No data available.
- Annual Earnings: No data available.
- Growth: 15.4%
- Annual Job Openings: 33,000

All religious workers not listed separately.

No task data available.

GOE INFORMATION—Interest Area: 12. Education and Social Service. Work Group: 12.02. Social Services. Note: The Department of Labor has not collected some data for this job, so it has fewer details than the other descriptions.

Instructional Programs—Pastoral Studies/Counseling; Theological and Ministerial Studies, Other.

Related DOT Jobs—129.027-010 Cantor; 129.107-010 Christian Science Nurse; 129.107-014 Christian Science Practitioner; 129.107-026 Pastoral Assistant; 129.271-010 Mohel; 199.207-010 Dianetic Counselor.

23-0000
Legal
Occupations

23-1000 Lawyers, Judges, and Related Workers

23-1011.00 Lawyers

- Education/Training Required: First professional degree
- Employed: 680,794
- Annual Earnings: $88,760
- Growth: 18.0%
- Annual Job Openings: 35,000

Represent clients in criminal and civil litigation and other legal proceedings, draw up legal documents, and manage or advise clients on legal transactions. May specialize in a single area or may practice broadly in many areas of law.

Act as agent, trustee, guardian, or executor for businesses or individuals. Advise clients concerning business transactions, claim liability, advisability of prosecuting or defending lawsuits, or legal rights and obligations. Analyze the probable outcomes of cases, using knowledge of legal precedents. Present and summarize cases to judges and juries. Evaluate findings and develop strategies and arguments in preparation for presentation of cases. Examine legal data to determine advisability of defending or prosecuting lawsuit. Gather evidence to formulate defense or to initiate legal actions by such means as interviewing clients and witnesses to ascertain the facts of a case. Interpret laws, rulings, and regulations for individuals and businesses. Negotiate settlements of civil disputes. Prepare and draft legal documents, such as wills, deeds, patent applications, mortgages, leases, and contracts. Prepare legal briefs and opinions; file appeals in state and federal courts of appeal. Present evidence to defend clients or prosecute defendants in criminal or civil litigation. Probate wills and represent and advise executors and administrators of estates. Represent clients in court or before government agencies. Search for and examine public and other legal records to write opinions or establish ownership. Select jurors, argue motions, meet with judges, and question witnesses during the course of a trial. Study Constitution, statutes, decisions, regulations, and ordinances of quasi-judicial bodies to determine ramifications for cases. Confer with colleagues with specialties in appropriate areas of legal issue to establish and verify bases for legal proceedings. Perform administrative and management functions related to the practice of law. Supervise legal assistants. Help develop federal and state programs, draft and interpret laws and legislation, and establish enforcement procedures. Work as law school faculty member or administrator. Work in environmental law, representing public interest groups, waste disposal companies, or construction firms in their dealings with state and federal agencies.

GOE INFORMATION—Interest Area: 04. Law, Law Enforcement, and Public Safety. Work Group: 04.02. Law. Personality Type—Enterprising. Enterprising occupations frequently involve starting up and carrying out projects. These occupations can involve leading people and making many decisions. They sometimes require risk taking and often deal with business. Work Values—Autonomy; Compensation; Ability Utilization; Social Service; Creativity. Skills—Persuasion; Speaking; Critical Thinking; Reading Comprehension; Complex Problem Solving; Systems Analysis; Writing; Negotiation. Abilities—*Cognitive:* Oral Expression; Written Expression; Written Comprehension; Oral Comprehension; Deductive Reasoning. *Psychomotor:* None met the criteria. *Physical:* None met the criteria. *Sensory:* Speech Clarity; Speech Recognition; Auditory Attention. General Work Activities—*Information Input:* Getting Information; Identifying Objects, Actions, and Events; Monitoring Processes, Materials, or Surroundings. *Mental Process:* Updating and Using Relevant Knowledge; Evaluating Information Against Standards; Analyzing Data or Information. *Work Output:* Documenting or Recording Information; Handling and Moving Objects; Interacting with Computers. *Interacting with Others:* Influencing Others or Selling; Providing Consultation and Advice to Others; Communicating with Persons Outside Organization. Physical Work Conditions—Indoors; Sitting. Other Job Characteristics—Consequence of Error; Importance of Being Exact or Accurate; Pace Determined by Speed of Equipment.

Experience—Job Zone 5. Extensive skill, knowledge, and experience are needed for these occupations. Job Preparation: SVP 8.0 and above—four years to more than 10 years. Knowledge—Law and Government; Education and Training; English Language; Therapy and Counseling; Administration and Management. Instructional Programs—Advanced Legal Research/Studies, General (LL.M., M.C.L., M.L.I., M.S.L., J.S.D./ S.J.D.); American/U.S. Law/Legal Studies/Jurisprudence (LL.M., M.C.J., J.S.D./S.J.D.); Banking, Corporate, Finance, and Securities Law (LL.M., J.S.D./S.J.D.); Canadian Law/Legal Studies/Jurisprudence (LL.M., M.C.J., J.S.D./S.J.D.); Comparative Law (LL.M., M.C.L., J.S.D./S.J.D.); Energy, Environment, and Natural Resources Law (LL.M., M.S., J.S.D./S.J.D.); Health Law (LL.M., M.J., J.S.D./S.J.D.); International Business, Trade, and Tax Law (LL.M., J.S.D./S.J.D.); International Law and Legal Studies (LL.M., J.S.D./S.J.D.); Law (LL.B., J.D.); Legal Professions and Studies, Other; Legal Research and Advanced Professional Studies, Other; Programs for Foreign Lawyers (LL.M., M.C.L.); Tax Law/Taxation (LL.M, J.S.D./S.J.D.).

Related DOT Jobs—110.107-010 Lawyer; 110.107-014 Lawyer, Criminal; 110.117-010 District Attorney; 110.117-014 Insurance Attorney; 110.117-018 Lawyer, Admiralty; 110.117-022 Lawyer, Corporation; 110.117-026 Lawyer, Patent; 110.117-030 Lawyer, Probate; 110.117-034 Lawyer, Real Estate; 110.117-038 Tax Attorney; 110.117-042 Title Attorney.

23-1021.00 Administrative Law Judges, Adjudicators, and Hearing Officers

- Education/Training Required: Work experience plus degree
- Employed: 14,261
- Annual Earnings: $50,210
- Growth: 1.1%
- Annual Job Openings: 1,000

Conduct hearings to decide or recommend decisions on claims concerning government programs or other government-related matters and prepare decisions. Determine penalties or the existence and the amount of liability, recommend the acceptance or rejection of claims, or compromise settlements.

Authorize payment of valid claims and determine method of payment. Conduct hearings to review and decide claims regarding issues such as social program eligibility, environmental protection, and enforcement of health and safety regulations. Confer with individuals or organizations involved in cases in order to obtain relevant information. Determine existence and amount of liability according to current laws, administrative and judicial precedents, and available evidence. Explain to claimants how they can appeal rulings that go against them. Issue subpoenas and administer oaths in preparation for formal hearings. Monitor and direct the activities of trials and hearings to ensure that they are conducted fairly and that courts administer justice while safeguarding the legal rights of all involved parties. Prepare written opinions and decisions. Recommend the acceptance or rejection of claims or compromise settlements according to laws, regulations, policies, and precedent decisions. Research and analyze laws, regulations, policies, and precedent decisions to prepare for hearings and to determine conclusions.

Review and evaluate data on documents such as claim applications, birth or death certificates, and physician or employer records. Rule on exceptions, motions, and admissibility of evidence. Conduct studies of appeals procedures in field agencies to ensure adherence to legal requirements and to facilitate determination of cases.

GOE INFORMATION—Interest Area: 04. Law, Law Enforcement, and Public Safety. **Work Group:** 04.02. Law. **Personality Type**—Enterprising. Enterprising occupations frequently involve starting up and carrying out projects. These occupations can involve leading people and making many decisions. They sometimes require risk taking and often deal with business. **Work Values**—Autonomy; Good Working Conditions; Responsibility; Security; Authority. **Skills**—Judgment and Decision Making; Critical Thinking; Active Listening; Speaking; Writing; Reading Comprehension; Complex Problem Solving; Negotiation. **Abilities**—*Cognitive:* Written Comprehension; Oral Comprehension; Memorization; Deductive Reasoning; Inductive Reasoning. *Psychomotor:* None met the criteria. *Physical:* None met the criteria. *Sensory:* Speech Clarity; Speech Recognition; Auditory Attention. **General Work Activities**—*Information Input:* Getting Information; Identifying Objects, Actions, and Events; Estimating Needed Characteristics. *Mental Process:* Making Decisions and Solving Problems; Evaluating Information Against Standards; Processing Information. *Work Output:* Documenting or Recording Information; Handling and Moving Objects; Interacting with Computers. *Interacting with Others:* Communicating with Other Workers; Communicating with Persons Outside Organization; Providing Consultation and Advice to Others. **Physical Work Conditions**—Sitting; Indoors; Disease or Infections. **Other Job Characteristics**—Importance of Being Exact or Accurate; Consequence of Error; Importance of Repeating Same Tasks.

Experience—Job Zone 5. Extensive skill, knowledge, and experience are needed for these occupations. **Job Preparation:** SVP 8.0 and above—four years to more than 10 years. **Knowledge**—Law and Government; Therapy and Counseling; Psychology; Administration and Management; English Language. **Instructional Programs**—Law (LL.B., J.D.); Legal Professions and Studies, Other.

Related DOT Jobs—119.107-010 Hearing Officer; 119.117-010 Appeals Reviewer, Veteran; 119.167-010 Adjudicator; 119.267-014 Appeals Referee; 169.267-010 Claims Adjudicator.

23-1022.00 Arbitrators, Mediators, and Conciliators

- **Education/Training Required: Work experience plus degree**
- **Employed: 4,422**
- **Annual Earnings: $46,660**
- **Growth: 27.2%**
- **Annual Job Openings: Fewer than 500**

Facilitate negotiation and conflict resolution through dialogue. Resolve conflicts outside of the court system by mutual consent of parties involved.

Arranges and conducts hearings to obtain information and evidence relative to disposition of claim. Determines existence and amount of liability according to law, administrative and judicial precedents, and evidence. Counsels parties and recommends acceptance or rejection of compromise settlement offers. Prepares written opinions and decisions. Analyzes evidence and applicable law, regulations, policy, and precedent decisions to determine conclusions. Interviews or corresponds with claimants or agents to elicit information. Questions witnesses to obtain information. Reviews and evaluates data on documents such as claim applications, birth or death certificates, and physician or employer records.

Rules on exceptions, motions, and admissibility of evidence. Researches laws, regulations, policies, and precedent decisions to prepare for hearings. Participates in court proceedings. Issues subpoenas and administers oaths to prepare for formal hearing. Obtains additional information to clarify evidence. Authorizes payment of valid claims. Notifies claimant of denied claim and appeal rights. Conducts studies of appeals procedures in field agencies to ensure adherence to legal requirements and to facilitate determination of cases.

GOE INFORMATION—Interest Area: 04. Law, Law Enforcement, and Public Safety. **Work Group:** 04.02. Law. **Personality Type**—Enterprising. Enterprising occupations frequently involve starting up and carrying out projects. These occupations can involve leading people and making many decisions. They sometimes require risk taking and often deal with business. **Work Values**—Autonomy; Good Working Conditions; Responsibility; Security; Authority. **Skills**—Judgment and Decision Making; Critical Thinking; Active Listening; Speaking; Writing; Reading Comprehension; Complex Problem Solving; Negotiation. **Abilities**—*Cognitive:* Written Comprehension; Oral Comprehension; Memorization; Deductive Reasoning; Inductive Reasoning. *Psychomotor:* None met the criteria. *Physical:* None met the criteria. *Sensory:* Speech Clarity; Speech Recognition; Auditory Attention. **General Work Activities**—*Information Input:* Getting Information; Identifying Objects, Actions, and Events; Estimating Needed Characteristics. *Mental Process:* Making Decisions and Solving Problems; Processing Information; Evaluating Information Against Standards. *Work Output:* Documenting or Recording Information; Handling and Moving Objects; Interacting with Computers. *Interacting with Others:* Communicating with Other Workers; Communicating with Persons Outside Organization; Resolving Conflict and Negotiating with Others. **Physical Work Conditions**—Sitting; Indoors; Disease or Infections. **Other Job Characteristics**—Importance of Being Exact or Accurate; Consequence of Error; Importance of Repeating Same Tasks.

Experience—Job Zone 5. Extensive skill, knowledge, and experience are needed for these occupations. **Job Preparation:** SVP 8.0 and above—four years to more than 10 years. **Knowledge**—Law and Government; Therapy and Counseling; Psychology; Administration and Management; English Language. **Instructional Programs**—Law (LL.B., J.D.); Legal Professions and Studies, Other.

Related DOT Jobs—169.107-010 Arbitrator; 169.207-010 Conciliator.

23-1023.00 Judges, Magistrate Judges, and Magistrates

- **Education/Training Required: Work experience plus degree**
- **Employed: 24,008**
- **Annual Earnings: $87,260**
- **Growth: 1.1%**
- **Annual Job Openings: 2,000**

Arbitrate, advise, adjudicate, or administer justice in a court of law. May sentence defendant in criminal cases according to government statutes. May determine liability of defendant in civil cases. May issue marriage licenses and perform wedding ceremonies.

Advise attorneys, juries, litigants, and court personnel regarding conduct, issues, and proceedings. Award compensation for damages to litigants in civil cases in relation to findings by juries or by the court. Conduct preliminary hearings to decide issues such as whether there is reasonable and probable cause to hold defendants in felony cases. Grant divorces and divide assets between spouses. Impose restrictions upon parties in civil cases until trials can be held. Instruct juries on applicable laws, direct juries to deduce the facts from the evidence presented, and hear their verdicts. Interpret and enforce rules of procedure or establish new rules in situations where there are no procedures already established by law. Monitor proceedings to ensure that all applicable rules and procedures are followed. Preside over hearings and listen to allegations made by plaintiffs to determine whether the evidence supports the charges. Read documents on pleadings and motions to ascertain facts and issues. Research legal issues and write opinions on the issues. Rule on admissibility of evidence and methods of conducting testimony. Rule on custody and access disputes and enforce court orders regarding custody and support of children. Sentence defendants in criminal cases, on conviction by jury, according to applicable government statutes. Settle disputes between opposing attorneys. Write decisions on cases. Participate in judicial tribunals to help resolve disputes. Perform wedding ceremonies. Supervise other judges, court officers, and the court's administrative staff.

GOE INFORMATION—Interest Area: 04. Law, Law Enforcement, and Public Safety. **Work Group:** 04.02. Law. **Personality Type**—Enterprising. Enterprising occupations frequently involve starting up and carrying out projects. These occupations can involve leading people and making many decisions. They sometimes require risk taking and often deal with business. **Work Values**—Responsibility; Autonomy; Social Status; Recognition; Authority. **Skills**—Judgment and Decision Making; Critical Thinking; Active Listening; Reading Comprehension; Systems Analysis; Speaking; Writing; Complex Problem Solving. **Abilities**—*Cognitive:* Speed of Closure; Memorization; Deductive Reasoning; Problem Sensitivity; Written Comprehension. *Psychomotor:* None met the criteria. *Physical:* None met the criteria. *Sensory:* Speech Clarity; Night Vision; Auditory Attention; Speech Recognition; Near Vision. **General Work Activities**—*Information Input:* Getting Information; Identifying Objects, Actions, and Events; Monitoring Processes, Materials, or Surroundings. *Mental Process:* Evaluating Information Against Standards; Judging Qualities of Things, Services, or Other People's Work; Updating and Using Relevant Knowledge. *Work Output:* Documenting or Recording Information; Performing General Physical Activities; Handling and Moving Objects. *Interacting with Others:* Resolving Conflict and Negotiating with Others; Interpreting Meaning of Information for Others; Communicating with Other Workers. **Physical Work Conditions**—Sitting; Indoors; Disease or Infections. **Other Job Characteristics**—Consequence of Error; Importance of Being Exact or Accurate; Pace Determined by Speed of Equipment.

Experience—Job Zone 5. Extensive skill, knowledge, and experience are needed for these occupations. **Job Preparation:** SVP 8.0 and above—four years to more than 10 years. **Knowledge**—Law and Government; Philosophy and Theology; Sociology and Anthropology; Public Safety and Security; History and Archeology. **Instructional Programs**—Law (LL.B., J.D.); Legal Professions and Studies, Other.

Related DOT Jobs—111.107-010 Judge; 111.107-014 Magistrate.

23-2000 Legal Support Workers

23-2011.00 Paralegals and Legal Assistants

- Education/Training Required: Associate's degree
- Employed: 188,214
- Annual Earnings: $36,670
- Growth: 33.2%
- Annual Job Openings: 23,000

Assist lawyers by researching legal precedent, investigating facts, or preparing legal documents. Conduct research to support a legal proceeding, to formulate a defense, or to initiate legal action.

Gather and analyze research data, such as statutes, decisions, and legal articles, codes, and documents. Prepare legal documents, including briefs, pleadings, appeals, wills, contracts, and real estate closing statements. Investigate facts and law of cases to determine causes of action and to prepare cases. Prepare affidavits or other documents, maintain document file, and file pleadings with court clerk. Appraise and inventory real and personal property for estate planning. Arbitrate disputes between parties and assist in real estate closing process. Call upon witnesses to testify at hearing. Answer questions regarding legal issues pertaining to civil service hearings. Direct and coordinate law office activity, including delivery of subpoenas. Keep and monitor legal volumes to ensure that law library is up-to-date. Present arguments and evidence to support appeal at appeal hearing.

GOE INFORMATION—Interest Area: 04. Law, Law Enforcement, and Public Safety. **Work Group:** 04.02. Law. **Personality Type**—Enterprising. Enterprising occupations frequently involve starting up and carrying out projects. These occupations can involve leading people and making many decisions. They sometimes require risk taking and often deal with business. **Work Values**—Good Working Conditions; Social Service; Variety; Advancement; Autonomy. **Skills**—Negotiation; Critical Thinking; Speaking; Reading Comprehension; Persuasion; Complex Problem Solving; Writing; Mathematics. **Abilities**—*Cognitive:* Written Expression; Written Comprehension; Deductive Reasoning; Oral Comprehension; Oral Expression. *Psychomotor:* Wrist-Finger Speed. *Physical:* None met the criteria. *Sensory:* Speech Clarity; Near Vision. **General Work Activities**—*Information Input:* Getting Information; Identifying Objects, Actions, and Events; Monitoring Processes, Materials, or Surroundings. *Mental Process:* Processing Information; Evaluating Information Against Standards; Analyzing Data or Information. *Work Output:* Documenting or Recording Information; Handling and Moving Objects; Interacting with Computers. *Interacting with Others:* Communicating with Other Workers; Resolving Conflict and Negotiating with Others; Interpreting Meaning of Information for Others. **Physical Work Conditions**—Sitting; Indoors. **Other Job Characteristics**—Importance of Being Exact or Accurate; Consequence of Error; Importance of Repeating Same Tasks.

Experience—Job Zone 4. A minimum of two to four years of work-related skill, knowledge, or experience is needed. **Job Preparation:** SVP 7.0 to less than 8.0—two years to less than 10 years. **Knowledge**—Clerical; Law and Government; Economics and Accounting; English Language; Administration and Management. **Instructional Programs**—Legal Assistant/Paralegal.

Related DOT Jobs—119.167-014 Patent Agent; 119.267-022 Legal Investigator; 119.267-026 Paralegal.

23-2091.00 Court Reporters

- Education/Training Required: Postsecondary vocational training
- Employed: 18,385
- Annual Earnings: $40,410
- Growth: 16.2%
- Annual Job Openings: 2,000

Use verbatim methods and equipment to capture, store, retrieve, and transcribe pretrial and trial proceedings or other information. Includes stenocaptioners who operate computerized stenographic captioning equipment to provide captions of live or prerecorded broadcasts for hearing-impaired viewers.

Ask speakers to clarify inaudible statements. File a legible transcript of records of a court case with the court clerk's office. Provide transcripts of proceedings upon request of judges, lawyers, or the public. Record verbatim proceedings of courts, legislative assemblies, committee meetings, and other proceedings, using computerized recording equipment, electronic stenograph machines, or stenomasks. Respond to requests during court sessions to read portions of the proceedings already recorded. Transcribe recorded proceedings in accordance with established formats. Verify accuracy of transcripts by checking copies against original records of proceedings and accuracy of rulings by checking with judges. Caption news, emergency broadcasts, sporting events, and other programming for television networks or cable stations. File and store shorthand notes of court session. Record depositions and other proceedings for attorneys. Record symbols on computer disks or CD-ROM and then translate and display them as text in computer-aided transcription process. Take notes in shorthand or use a stenotype or shorthand machine that prints letters on a paper tape.

GOE INFORMATION—Interest Area: 09. Business Detail. **Work Group:** 09.07. Records Processing. **Note:** The Department of Labor has not collected some data for this job, so it has fewer details than the other descriptions.

Instructional Programs—Court Reporting/Court Reporter.

Related DOT Jobs—202.362-010 Shorthand Reporter; 202.362-014 Stenographer; 202.362-018 Stenographer, Print Shop; 202.362-022 Stenotype Operator; 202.382-010 Stenocaptioner; 203.362-026 Caption Writer.

23-2092.00 Law Clerks

- **Education/Training Required: Bachelor's degree**
- **Employed: 31,290**
- **Annual Earnings: $30,180**
- **Growth: 13.2%**
- **Annual Job Openings: 3,000**

Assist lawyers or judges by researching or preparing legal documents. May meet with clients or assist lawyers and judges in court.

Prepare affidavits of documents and maintain document files and case correspondence. Research and analyze law sources to prepare drafts of briefs or arguments for review, approval, and use by attorney. Review and file pleadings, petitions, and other documents relevant to court actions. Search for and study legal documents to investigate facts and law of cases, to determine causes of action, and to prepare cases. Search patent files to ascertain originality of patent applications. Store, catalog, and maintain currency of legal volumes. Communicate and arbitrate disputes between parties. Appraise and inventory real and personal property for estate planning. Arrange transportation and accommodation for witnesses and jurors if required. Deliver or direct delivery of subpoenas to witnesses and parties to action. Prepare real estate closing statements and assist in closing process. Serve copies of pleas to opposing counsel.

GOE INFORMATION—Interest Area: 04. Law, Law Enforcement, and Public Safety. **Work Group:** 04.02. Law. **Personality Type**—Enterprising. Enterprising occupations frequently involve starting up and carrying out projects. These occupations can involve leading people and making many decisions. They sometimes require risk taking and often deal with business. **Work Values**—Good Working Conditions; Social Service; Advancement; Variety; Social Status. **Skills**—Critical Thinking; Writing; Reading Comprehension; Negotiation; Persuasion; Complex Problem Solving; Active Listening; Speaking. **Abilities**—*Cognitive:* Written Comprehension; Number Facility; Written Expression; Oral Comprehension; Oral Expression. *Psychomotor:* None met the criteria. *Physical:* None met

the criteria. *Sensory:* Speech Recognition; Speech Clarity; Near Vision. **General Work Activities**—*Information Input:* Getting Information; Identifying Objects, Actions, and Events; Estimating Needed Characteristics. *Mental Process:* Analyzing Data or Information; Updating and Using Relevant Knowledge; Evaluating Information Against Standards. *Work Output:* Documenting or Recording Information; Handling and Moving Objects; Interacting with Computers. *Interacting with Others:* Resolving Conflict and Negotiating with Others; Communicating with Other Workers; Communicating with Persons Outside Organization. **Physical Work Conditions**—Sitting; Indoors. **Other Job Characteristics**—Consequence of Error; Importance of Being Exact or Accurate; Degree of Automation.

Experience—Job Zone 4. A minimum of two to four years of work-related skill, knowledge, or experience is needed. **Job Preparation:** SVP 7.0 to less than 8.0—two years to less than 10 years. **Knowledge**—Clerical; Law and Government; English Language; Personnel and Human Resources; Economics and Accounting. **Instructional Programs**—Law (LL.B., J.D.).

Related DOT Jobs—119.267-026 Paralegal.

23-2093.00 Title Examiners, Abstractors, and Searchers

- **Education/Training Required: Moderate-term on-the-job training**
- **Employed: 48,291**
- **Annual Earnings: $31,770**
- **Growth: 1.0%**
- **Annual Job Openings: 5,000**

Search real estate records, examine titles, or summarize pertinent legal or insurance details for a variety of purposes. May compile lists of mortgages, contracts, and other instruments pertaining to titles by searching public and private records for law firms, real estate agencies, or title insurance companies.

Confer with realtors, lending institution personnel, buyers, sellers, contractors, surveyors, and courthouse personnel in order to exchange title-related information or to resolve problems. Copy or summarize recorded documents, such as mortgages, trust deeds, and contracts, that affect property titles. Enter into record-keeping systems appropriate data needed to create new title records or update existing ones. Examine documentation such as mortgages, liens, judgments, easements, plat books, maps, contracts, and agreements in order to verify factors such as properties' legal descriptions, ownership, or restrictions. Examine individual titles in order to determine if restrictions, such as delinquent taxes, will affect titles and limit property use. Obtain maps or drawings delineating properties from company title plants, county surveyors, and/or assessors' offices. Prepare lists of all legal instruments applying to a specific piece of land and the buildings on it. Prepare reports describing any title encumbrances encountered during searching activities and outlining actions needed to clear titles. Read search requests in order to ascertain types of title evidence required and to obtain descriptions of properties and names of involved parties. Direct activities of workers who search records and examine titles, assigning, scheduling, and evaluating work and providing technical guidance as necessary. Prepare and issue title commitments and title insurance policies based on information compiled from title searches. Retrieve and examine real estate closing files for accuracy and to ensure that information included is recorded and executed according to regulations. Summarize pertinent legal or insurance details or sections of statutes or case law from reference books so that they can be used in examinations or as proofs or ready reference. Assess fees related to registration of property-related documents. Determine whether land-related documents can be registered under the relevant legislation such as the Land Titles Act. Prepare real estate closing statements, utilizing knowledge and expertise in real estate procedures. Verify accuracy and completeness of land-related documents accepted for registration; prepare rejection notices when documents are not acceptable.

GOE INFORMATION—Interest Area: 04. Law, Law Enforcement, and Public Safety. **Work Group:** 04.02. Law. **Note:** The Department of Labor has not collected some data for this job, so it has fewer details than the other descriptions.

Instructional Programs—Legal Assistant/Paralegal.

Related DOT Jobs—119.167-018 Title Supervisor; 119.267-010 Abstractor; 119.287-010 Title Examiner; 162.267-010 Title Clerk; 209.367-046 Title Searcher.

23-2093.01 Title Searchers

- **Education/Training Required: Moderate-term on-the-job training**
- **Employed: No data available.**
- **Annual Earnings: $31,770**
- **Growth: 1.0%**
- **Annual Job Openings: 11,000**

Compile list of mortgages, deeds, contracts, judgments, and other instruments (chain) pertaining to title by searching public and private records of real estate or title insurance company.

Searches lot books, geographic and general indices, and assessor's rolls to compile lists of transactions pertaining to property. Reads search request to ascertain type of title evidence required and to obtain description of property and names of involved parties. Compares legal description of property with legal description contained in records and indices to verify such factors as deed ownership. Compiles information and documents required for title binder. Requisitions maps or drawings delineating property from company title plant, county surveyor, or assessor's office. Examines title to determine if there are restrictions limiting use of property, lists restrictions, and indicates action needed for clear title. Uses computerized system to retrieve additional documentation needed to complete real estate transaction. Confers with realtors, lending institution personnel, buyers, sellers, contractors, surveyors, and courthouse personnel to obtain additional information. Retrieves and examines closing files for accuracy and to ensure that information included is recorded and executed according to regulations. Prepares title commitment and final policy of title insurance based on information compiled from title search. Prepares closing statement, utilizing knowledge and expertise in real estate procedures.

GOE INFORMATION—Interest Area: 04. Law, Law Enforcement, and Public Safety. **Work Group:** 04.02. Law. **Personality Type**—Conventional. Conventional occupations frequently involve following set procedures and routines. These occupations can include working with data and details more than with ideas. Usually there is a clear line of authority to follow. **Work Values**—Independence; Good Working Conditions; Supervision, Technical; Company Policies and Practices; Advancement. **Skills**—Writing; Speaking; Reading Comprehension; Critical Thinking; Active Listening. **Abilities**—*Cognitive:* Written Expression; Written Comprehension; Speed of Closure; Deductive Reasoning; Oral Expression. *Psychomotor:* Wrist-Finger Speed. *Physical:* None met the criteria.

Sensory: Near Vision. **General Work Activities**—*Information Input:* Getting Information; Identifying Objects, Actions, and Events; Estimating Needed Characteristics. *Mental Process:* Processing Information; Evaluating Information Against Standards; Updating and Using Relevant Knowledge. *Work Output:* Documenting or Recording Information; Interacting with Computers; Handling and Moving Objects. *Interacting with Others:* Communicating with Persons Outside Organization; Communicating with Other Workers; Establishing and Maintaining Relationships. **Physical Work Conditions**—Sitting; Indoors; Disease or Infections. **Other Job Characteristics**—Importance of Being Exact or Accurate; Degree of Automation; Importance of Repeating Same Tasks.

Experience—Job Zone 2. Some previous work-related skill, knowledge, or experience may be helpful, but usually is not needed. **Job Preparation:** SVP 4.0 to less than 6.0—six months to less than two years. **Knowledge**—Law and Government; Clerical; Geography; English Language; Economics and Accounting. **Instructional Programs**—Legal Assistant/Paralegal.

Related DOT Jobs—209.367-046 Title Searcher.

23-2093.02 Title Examiners and Abstractors

- **Education/Training Required: Long-term on-the-job training**
- **Employed: 48,291**
- **Annual Earnings: $31,770**
- **Growth: 1.0%**
- **Annual Job Openings: 11,000**

Title Examiners: Search public records and examine titles to determine legal condition of property title. Copy or summarize (abstracts) recorded documents which affect condition of title to property (e.g., mortgages, trust deeds, and contracts). May prepare and issue policy that guarantees legality of title. Abstractors: Summarize pertinent legal or insurance details or sections of statutes or case law from reference books for purpose of examination, proof, or ready reference. Search out titles to determine if title deed is correct.

Copies or summarizes recorded documents, such as mortgages, trust deeds, and contracts, affecting title to property. Examines mortgages, liens, judgments, easements, plat books, maps, contracts, and agreements to verify legal description, ownership, restrictions, or conformity to requirements. Analyzes encumbrances to title, statutes, and case law and prepares report outlining encumbrances and actions required to clear title. Prepares and issues title insurance policy. Searches records to determine if delinquent taxes are due. Prepares correspondence and other records. Confers with interested parties to resolve problems and impart information. Directs activities of workers searching records and examining titles to real property.

GOE INFORMATION—Interest Area: 04. Law, Law Enforcement, and Public Safety. **Work Group:** 04.02. Law. **Personality Type**—Conventional. Conventional occupations frequently involve following set procedures and routines. These occupations can include working with data and details more than with ideas. Usually there is a clear line of authority to follow. **Work Values**—Company Policies and Practices; Independence; Social Service; Autonomy; Good Working Conditions. **Skills**—Reading Comprehension; Management of Personnel Resources; Critical Thinking; Speaking; Writing; Complex Problem Solving; Mathematics; Active Listening. **Abilities**—*Cognitive:* Written Comprehension; Written Expression; Speed of Closure; Number Facility; Deductive Reasoning. *Psychomotor:* None met the criteria. *Physical:* None met the criteria. *Sensory:* Near Vision; Glare Sensitivity; Speech Clarity; Speech Recognition.

General Work Activities—*Information Input:* Getting Information; Identifying Objects, Actions, and Events; Estimating Needed Characteristics. *Mental Process:* Analyzing Data or Information; Evaluating Information Against Standards; Processing Information. *Work Output:* Documenting or Recording Information; Handling and Moving Objects; Performing General Physical Activities. *Interacting with Others:* Communicating with Persons Outside Organization; Communicating with Other Workers; Resolving Conflict and Negotiating with Others. **Physical Work Conditions—**Indoors; Sitting; Disease or Infections; Making Repetitive Motions. **Other Job Characteristics—**Importance of Being Exact or Accurate; Degree of Automation; Importance of Repeating Same Tasks.

Experience—Job Zone 3. Previous work-related skill, knowledge, or experience is required. **Job Preparation:** SVP 6.0 to less than 7.0—more than one year and less than four years. **Knowledge—**Law and Government; Clerical; Administration and Management; Economics and Accounting; English Language. **Instructional Programs—**Legal Assistant/Paralegal.

Related DOT Jobs—119.167-018 Title Supervisor; 119.267-010 Abstractor; 119.287-010 Title Examiner; 162.267-010 Title Clerk.

23-2099.99 Legal Support Workers, All Other

- **Education/Training Required: No data available.**
- **Employed: No data available.**
- **Annual Earnings: No data available.**
- **Growth: 20.2%**
- **Annual Job Openings: 11,000**

All legal support workers not listed separately.

No task data available.

GOE INFORMATION—Interest Area: 04. Law, Law Enforcement, and Public Safety. **Work Group:** 04.02. Law. **Note:** The Department of Labor has not collected some data for this job, so it has fewer details than the other descriptions.

Instructional Programs—Legal Assistant/Paralegal.

Related DOT Jobs—119.267-018 Contract Clerk; 119.367-010 Escrow Officer; 186.167-074 Closer.

25-0000
Education, Training, and Library Occupations

25-1000 Postsecondary Teachers

25-1011.00 Business Teachers, Postsecondary

- **Education/Training Required:** Master's degree
- **Employed:** No data available.
- **Annual Earnings:** $54,280
- **Growth:** 23.5%
- **Annual Job Openings:** 184,000

Teach courses in business administration and management, such as accounting, finance, human resources, labor relations, marketing, and operations research.

Evaluate and grade students' class work, assignments, and papers. Prepare and deliver lectures to undergraduate and/or graduate students on topics such as financial accounting, principles of marketing, and operations management. Advise students on academic and vocational curricula and on career issues. Compile, administer, and grade examinations or assign this work to others. Compile bibliographies of specialized materials for outside reading assignments. Initiate, facilitate, and moderate classroom discussions. Keep abreast of developments in their field by reading current literature, talking with colleagues, and participating in professional organizations and conferences. Maintain regularly scheduled office hours in order to advise and assist students. Maintain student attendance records, grades, and other required records. Plan, evaluate, and revise curricula, course content, and course materials and methods of instruction. Prepare course materials such as syllabi, homework assignments, and handouts. Select and obtain materials and supplies, such as textbooks. Supervise undergraduate and/or graduate teaching, internship, and research work. Act as advisers to student organizations. Collaborate with colleagues to address teaching and research issues. Collaborate with members of the business community to improve programs, to develop new programs, and to provide student access to learning opportunities such as internships. Conduct research in a particular field of knowledge and publish findings in professional journals, books, and/or electronic media. Participate in campus and community events. Participate in student recruitment, registration, and placement activities. Perform administrative duties such as serving as department head. Provide professional consulting services to government and/or industry. Serve on academic or administrative committees that deal with institutional policies, departmental matters, and academic issues. Write grant proposals to procure external research funding.

GOE INFORMATION—Interest Area: 12. Education and Social Service. **Work Group:** 12.03. Educational Services. **Note:** The Department of Labor has not collected some data for this job, so it has fewer details than the other descriptions.

Instructional Programs—Accounting; Actuarial Science; Business Administration and Management, General; Business Statistics; Business Teacher Education; Business/Commerce, General; Business/Corporate Communications; Entrepreneurship/Entrepreneurial Studies; Finance, General; Financial Planning and Services; Franchising and Franchise Operations; Human Resources Management/Personnel Administration, General; Insurance; International Business/Trade/Commerce; International Finance; International Marketing; Investments and Securities; Labor and Industrial Relations; Logistics and Materials Management; Management Science, General; Marketing Research; Marketing/Marketing Management, General; Operations Management and Supervision; Organizational Behavior Studies; Public Finance; Purchasing, Procurement/Acquisitions, and Contracts Management.

Related DOT Jobs—090.222-010 Instructor, Business Education; 090.227-010 Faculty Member, College or University.

25-1021.00 Computer Science Teachers, Postsecondary

- **Education/Training Required:** Master's degree
- **Employed:** No data available.
- **Annual Earnings:** $49,050
- **Growth:** 23.5%
- **Annual Job Openings:** 184,000

Teach courses in computer science. May specialize in a field of computer science, such as the design and function of computers or operations and research analysis.

Evaluate and grade students' class work, laboratory work, assignments, and papers. Prepare and deliver lectures to undergraduate and/or graduate students on topics such as programming, data structures, and software design. Advise students on academic and vocational curricula and on career issues. Compile, administer, and grade examinations or assign this work to others. Compile bibliographies of specialized materials for outside reading assignments. Initiate, facilitate, and moderate classroom discussions. Keep abreast of developments in their field by reading current literature, talking with colleagues, and participating in professional conferences. Maintain regularly scheduled office hours in order to advise and assist students. Maintain student attendance records, grades, and other required records. Plan, evaluate, and revise curricula, course content, and course materials and methods of instruction. Prepare course materials such as syllabi, homework assignments, and handouts. Select and obtain materials and supplies, such as textbooks and laboratory equipment. Supervise students' laboratory work. Supervise undergraduate and/or graduate teaching, internship, and research work. Act as advisers to student organizations. Collaborate with colleagues to address teaching and research issues. Conduct research in a particular field of knowledge and publish findings in professional journals, books, and/or electronic media. Direct research of other teachers or of graduate students working for advanced academic degrees. Participate in campus and community events. Participate in student recruitment, registration, and placement activities. Perform administrative duties such as serving as department head. Provide professional consulting services to government and/or industry. Serve on academic or administrative committees that deal with institutional policies, departmental matters, and academic issues. Write grant proposals to procure external research funding.

GOE INFORMATION—Interest Area: 12. Education and Social Service. **Work Group:** 12.03. Educational Services. **Personality Type—**Investigative. Investigative occupations frequently involve working with ideas and require an extensive amount of thinking. These occupations can involve searching for facts and figuring out problems mentally. **Work Values—**Authority; Social Service; Creativity; Ability Utilization; Achievement. **Skills—**Programming; Instructing; Writing; Learning Strategies; Mathematics; Complex Problem Solving; Speaking; Reading Comprehension. **Abilities—***Cognitive:* Written Expression; Oral Expression; Originality; Deductive Reasoning; Written Comprehension. *Psychomotor:* Finger Dexterity; Wrist-Finger Speed; Response Orientation; Multilimb Coordination. *Physical:* Gross Body Coordination; Gross Body Equilibrium. *Sensory:* Speech Clarity; Far Vision; Night Vision; Sound Localization; Near Vision. **General Work Activities—***Information Input:* Getting Information; Monitoring Processes, Materials, or Surroundings; Identifying Objects, Actions, and Events. *Mental Process:* Updating and Using Relevant Knowledge; Analyzing Data or Information; Thinking Creatively. *Work Output:* Interacting with Computers; Handling and Moving Objects; Documenting or Recording Information. *Interacting with*

Others: Teaching Others; Communicating with Persons Outside Organization; Providing Consultation and Advice to Others. **Physical Work Conditions**—Indoors; Sitting; Using Hands on Objects, Tools, or Controls; Disease or Infections; Extremely Bright or Inadequate Lighting. **Other Job Characteristics**—Degree of Automation; Pace Determined by Speed of Equipment; Importance of Repeating Same Tasks.

Experience—Job Zone 5. Extensive skill, knowledge, and experience are needed for these occupations. **Job Preparation:** SVP 8.0 and above—four years to more than 10 years. **Knowledge**—Education and Training; Computers and Electronics; Mathematics; English Language; Physics. **Instructional Programs**—Computer and Information Sciences, General; Computer Programming/Programmer, General; Computer Science; Computer Systems Analysis/Analyst; Information Science/Studies.

Related DOT Jobs—090.227-010090.227-010 Faculty Member, College or University.

25-1022.00 Mathematical Science Teachers, Postsecondary

- ● **Education/Training Required: Master's degree**
- ● **Employed: No data available.**
- ● **Annual Earnings: $49,420**
- ● **Growth: 23.5%**
- ● **Annual Job Openings: 184,000**

Teach courses pertaining to mathematical concepts, statistics, and actuarial science and to the application of original and standardized mathematical techniques in solving specific problems and situations.

Evaluate and grade students' class work, assignments, and papers. Prepare and deliver lectures to undergraduate and/or graduate students on topics such as linear algebra, differential equations, and discrete mathematics. Advise students on academic and vocational curricula and on career issues. Compile, administer, and grade examinations or assign this work to others. Compile bibliographies of specialized materials for outside reading assignments. Initiate, facilitate, and moderate classroom discussions. Keep abreast of developments in their field by reading current literature, talking with colleagues, and participating in professional conferences. Maintain regularly scheduled office hours in order to advise and assist students. Maintain student attendance records, grades, and other required records. Plan, evaluate, and revise curricula, course content, and course materials and methods of instruction. Prepare course materials such as syllabi, homework assignments, and handouts. Select and obtain materials and supplies, such as textbooks. Supervise undergraduate and/or graduate teaching, internship, and research work. Act as advisers to student organizations. Collaborate with colleagues to address teaching and research issues. Conduct research in a particular field of knowledge and publish findings in books, professional journals, and/or electronic media. Participate in campus and community events. Participate in student recruitment, registration, and placement activities. Perform administrative duties such as serving as department head. Provide professional consulting services to government and/or industry. Serve on academic or administrative committees that deal with institutional policies, departmental matters, and academic issues. Write grant proposals to procure external research funding.

GOE INFORMATION—**Interest Area:** 12. Education and Social Service. **Work Group:** 12.03. Educational Services. **Personality Type**—Investigative. Investigative occupations frequently involve working with ideas and require an extensive amount of thinking. These occupations can involve searching for facts and figuring out problems mentally. **Work Values**—Authority; Social Service; Creativity; Ability Utilization; Achievement. **Skills**—Mathematics; Instructing; Learning Strategies; Reading

Comprehension; Writing; Complex Problem Solving; Critical Thinking; Speaking. **Abilities**—*Cognitive:* Mathematical Reasoning; Number Facility; Written Expression; Oral Expression; Written Comprehension. *Psychomotor:* None met the criteria. *Physical:* None met the criteria. *Sensory:* Speech Clarity. **General Work Activities**—*Information Input:* Getting Information; Monitoring Processes, Materials, or Surroundings; Identifying Objects, Actions, and Events. *Mental Process:* Analyzing Data or Information; Updating and Using Relevant Knowledge; Processing Information. *Work Output:* Documenting or Recording Information; Handling and Moving Objects; Interacting with Computers. *Interacting with Others:* Teaching Others; Coaching and Developing Others; Communicating with Other Workers. **Physical Work Conditions**—Sitting; Standing. **Other Job Characteristics**—Importance of Being Exact or Accurate; Pace Determined by Speed of Equipment; Degree of Automation.

Experience—Job Zone 5. Extensive skill, knowledge, and experience are needed for these occupations. **Job Preparation:** SVP 8.0 and above—four years to more than 10 years. **Knowledge**—Education and Training; Mathematics; English Language; Clerical; Administration and Management. **Instructional Programs**—Algebra and Number Theory; Analysis and Functional Analysis; Applied Mathematics; Business Statistics; Geometry/Geometric Analysis; Logic; Mathematical Statistics and Probability; Mathematics and Statistics, Other; Mathematics, General; Mathematics, Other; Statistics, General; Topology and Foundations.

Related DOT Jobs—090.227-010 Faculty Member, College or University.

25-1031.00 Architecture Teachers, Postsecondary

- ● **Education/Training Required: Master's degree**
- ● **Employed: No data available.**
- ● **Annual Earnings: $54,480**
- ● **Growth: 23.5%**
- ● **Annual Job Openings: 184,000**

Teach courses in architecture and architectural design, such as architectural environmental design, interior architecture/design, and landscape architecture.

Evaluate and grade students' work, including work performed in design studios. Prepare and deliver lectures to undergraduate and/or graduate students on topics such as architectural design methods, aesthetics and design, and structures and materials. Advise students on academic and vocational curricula and on career issues. Compile, administer, and grade examinations or assign this work to others. Compile bibliographies of specialized materials for outside reading assignments. Initiate, facilitate, and moderate classroom discussions. Keep abreast of developments in their field by reading current literature, talking with colleagues, and participating in professional conferences. Maintain regularly scheduled office hours in order to advise and assist students. Maintain student attendance records, grades, and other required records. Plan, evaluate, and revise curricula, course content, and course materials and methods of instruction. Prepare course materials such as syllabi, homework assignments, and handouts. Select and obtain materials and supplies, such as textbooks and laboratory equipment. Supervise undergraduate and/or graduate teaching, internship, and research work. Act as advisers to student organizations. Collaborate with colleagues to address teaching and research issues. Conduct research in a particular field of knowledge and publish findings in professional journals, books, and/or electronic media. Participate in campus and community events. Participate in student recruitment, registration, and placement activities. Perform administrative duties such as serving as department head. Provide professional consulting services to government and/or industry. Serve on academic or administrative committees that deal with institutional policies, departmental matters, and academic issues. Write grant proposals to procure external research funding.

GOE INFORMATION—Interest Area: 12. Education and Social Service. **Work Group:** 12.03. Educational Services. **Note:** The Department of Labor has not collected some data for this job, so it has fewer details than the other descriptions.

Instructional Programs—Architectural Engineering; Architecture (BArch, BA/BS, MArch, MA/MS, PhD); City/Urban, Community, and Regional Planning; Environmental Design/Architecture; Interior Architecture; Landscape Architecture (BS, BSLA, BLA, MSLA, MLA, PhD); Teacher Education and Professional Development, Specific Subject Areas, Other.

Related DOT Jobs—090.227-010 Faculty Member, College or University.

25-1032.00 Engineering Teachers, Postsecondary

- Education/Training Required: Master's degree
- Employed: No data available.
- Annual Earnings: $67,310
- Growth: 23.5%
- Annual Job Openings: 184,000

Teach courses pertaining to the application of physical laws and principles of engineering for the development of machines, materials, instruments, processes, and services. Includes teachers of subjects such as chemical, civil, electrical, industrial, mechanical, mineral, and petroleum engineering. Includes both teachers primarily engaged in teaching and those who do a combination of both teaching and research.

Evaluate and grade students' class work, laboratory work, assignments, and papers. Prepare and deliver lectures to undergraduate and/or graduate students on topics such as mechanics, hydraulics, and robotics. Advise students on academic and vocational curricula and on career issues. Compile, administer, and grade examinations or assign this work to others. Compile bibliographies of specialized materials for outside reading assignments. Initiate, facilitate, and moderate class discussions. Keep abreast of developments in their field by reading current literature, talking with colleagues, and participating in professional conferences. Maintain regularly scheduled office hours in order to advise and assist students. Maintain student attendance records, grades, and other required records. Plan, evaluate, and revise curricula, course content, and course materials and methods of instruction. Prepare course materials such as syllabi, homework assignments, and handouts. Select and obtain materials and supplies, such as textbooks and laboratory equipment. Supervise students' laboratory work. Supervise undergraduate and/or graduate teaching, internship, and research work. Act as advisers to student organizations. Collaborate with colleagues to address teaching and research issues. Conduct research in a particular field of knowledge and publish findings in professional journals, books, and/or electronic media. Participate in campus and community events. Participate in student recruitment, registration, and placement activities. Perform administrative duties such as serving as department head. Provide professional consulting services to government and/or industry. Serve on academic or administrative committees that deal with institutional policies, departmental matters, and academic issues. Write grant proposals to procure external research funding.

GOE INFORMATION—Interest Area: 12. Education and Social Service. **Work Group:** 12.03. Educational Services. **Personality Type—**Investi-

gative. Investigative occupations frequently involve working with ideas and require an extensive amount of thinking. These occupations can involve searching for facts and figuring out problems mentally. **Work Values—**Authority; Social Service; Creativity; Ability Utilization; Achievement. **Skills—**Science; Mathematics; Technology Design; Instructing; Critical Thinking; Learning Strategies; Reading Comprehension; Complex Problem Solving. **Abilities—***Cognitive:* Written Expression; Oral Expression; Mathematical Reasoning; Written Comprehension; Oral Comprehension. *Psychomotor:* None met the criteria. *Physical:* None met the criteria. *Sensory:* Speech Clarity; Sound Localization; Far Vision; Night Vision; Auditory Attention. **General Work Activities—***Information Input:* Getting Information; Monitoring Processes, Materials, or Surroundings; Identifying Objects, Actions, and Events. *Mental Process:* Analyzing Data or Information; Processing Information; Updating and Using Relevant Knowledge. *Work Output:* Documenting or Recording Information; Handling and Moving Objects; Interacting with Computers. *Interacting with Others:* Teaching Others; Coaching and Developing Others; Communicating with Other Workers. **Physical Work Conditions—**Indoors; Sitting. **Other Job Characteristics—**Importance of Being Exact or Accurate; Consequence of Error; Pace Determined by Speed of Equipment.

Experience—Job Zone 5. Extensive skill, knowledge, and experience are needed for these occupations. **Job Preparation:** SVP 8.0 and above—four years to more than 10 years. **Knowledge—**Education and Training; Engineering and Technology; Physics; Chemistry; Design. **Instructional Programs—**Aerospace, Aeronautical, and Astronautical Engineering; Agricultural/Biological Engineering and Bioengineering; Architectural Engineering; Biomedical/Medical Engineering; Ceramic Sciences and Engineering; Chemical Engineering; Civil Engineering, General; Civil Engineering, Other; Computer Engineering, General; Computer Engineering, Other; Computer Hardware Engineering; Computer Software Engineering; Construction Engineering; Electrical, Electronics, and Communications Engineering; Engineering Mechanics; Engineering Physics; Engineering Science; Engineering, General; Engineering, Other; Environmental/Environmental Health Engineering; Forest Engineering; Geological/Geophysical Engineering; Geotechnical Engineering; Industrial Engineering; Manufacturing Engineering; Materials Engineering; Materials Science; Mechanical Engineering; Metallurgical Engineering; Mining and Mineral Engineering; Naval Architecture and Marine Engineering; Nuclear Engineering; Ocean Engineering; Petroleum Engineering; Polymer/Plastics Engineering; Structural Engineering; Surveying Engineering; Systems Engineering; Teacher Education and Professional Development, Specific Subject Areas, Other; Textile Sciences and Engineering; Transportation and Highway Engineering; Water Resources Engineering.

Related DOT Jobs—090.227-010 Faculty Member, College or University.

25-1041.00 Agricultural Sciences Teachers, Postsecondary

- Education/Training Required: Master's degree
- Employed: No data available.
- Annual Earnings: $64,500
- Growth: 23.5%
- Annual Job Openings: 184,000

Teach courses in the agricultural sciences. Includes teachers of agronomy, dairy sciences, fisheries management, horticultural sciences, poultry sciences, range management, and agricultural soil conservation.

Evaluate and grade students' class work, laboratory work, assignments, and papers. Prepare and deliver lectures to undergraduate and/or graduate students on topics such as crop production, plant genetics, and soil chemistry. Advise students on academic and vocational curricula and on career issues. Compile, administer, and grade examinations or assign this work to others. Compile bibliographies of specialized materials for outside reading assignments. Initiate, facilitate, and moderate classroom discussions. Keep abreast of developments in their field by reading current literature, talking with colleagues, and participating in professional conferences. Maintain regularly scheduled office hours in order to advise and assist students. Maintain student attendance records, grades, and other required records. Plan, evaluate, and revise curricula, course content, and course materials and methods of instruction. Prepare course materials such as syllabi, homework assignments, and handouts. Select and obtain materials and supplies, such as textbooks and laboratory equipment. Supervise laboratory sessions and fieldwork; coordinate laboratory operations. Supervise undergraduate and/or graduate teaching, internship, and research work. Act as advisers to student organizations. Collaborate with colleagues to address teaching and research issues. Conduct research in a particular field of knowledge and publish findings in professional journals, books, and/or electronic media. Participate in campus and community events. Participate in student recruitment, registration, and placement activities. Perform administrative duties such as serving as department head. Provide professional consulting services to government and/or industry. Serve on academic or administrative committees that deal with institutional policies, departmental matters, and academic issues. Write grant proposals to procure external research funding.

GOE INFORMATION—Interest Area: 12. Education and Social Service. **Work Group:** 12.03. Educational Services. **Personality Type**—Investigative. Investigative occupations frequently involve working with ideas and require an extensive amount of thinking. These occupations can involve searching for facts and figuring out problems mentally. **Work Values**—Authority; Social Service; Creativity; Achievement; Social Status. **Skills**—Instructing; Science; Learning Strategies; Reading Comprehension; Critical Thinking; Writing; Mathematics; Complex Problem Solving. **Abilities**—*Cognitive:* Written Expression; Oral Expression; Oral Comprehension; Written Comprehension; Mathematical Reasoning. *Psychomotor:* None met the criteria. *Physical:* None met the criteria. *Sensory:* Speech Clarity; Speech Recognition; Night Vision. **General Work Activities**—*Information Input:* Getting Information; Monitoring Processes, Materials, or Surroundings; Identifying Objects, Actions, and Events. *Mental Process:* Processing Information; Analyzing Data or Information; Updating and Using Relevant Knowledge. *Work Output:* Documenting or Recording Information; Handling and Moving Objects; Interacting with Computers. *Interacting with Others:* Teaching Others; Coaching and Developing Others; Interpreting Meaning of Information for Others. **Physical Work Conditions**—Indoors; Sitting. **Other Job Characteristics**—Consequence of Error; Importance of Being Exact or Accurate; Pace Determined by Speed of Equipment.

Experience—Job Zone 5. Extensive skill, knowledge, and experience are needed for these occupations. **Job Preparation:** SVP 8.0 and above—four years to more than 10 years. **Knowledge**—Biology; Education and Training; Medicine and Dentistry; Therapy and Counseling; Chemistry. **Instructional Programs**—Agribusiness/Agricultural Business Operations; Agricultural and Domestic Animal Services, Other; Agricultural and Food Products Processing; Agricultural and Horticultural Plant Breeding; Agricultural Animal Breeding; Agricultural Business and Management, General; Agricultural Business and Management, Other; Agricultural Economics; Agricultural Mechanization, General; Agricultural Mechanization, Other; Agricultural Power Machinery Operation; Agricultural Production Operations, General; Agricultural Production Operations, Other; Agricultural Teacher Education; Agricultural/Farm Supplies Retailing and Wholesaling; Agriculture, Agriculture Operations,

and Related Sciences, Other; Agriculture, General; Agronomy and Crop Science; Animal Health; Animal Nutrition; Animal Sciences, General; Animal Sciences, Other; Animal Training; Animal/Livestock Husbandry and Production; Applied Horticulture/Horticultural Business Services, Other; Applied Horticulture/Horticultural Operations, General; Aquaculture; Crop Production; Dairy Science; Equestrian/Equine Studies; Farm/Farm and Ranch Management; Food Science; Greenhouse Operations and Management; Horticultural Science; International Agriculture; Landscaping and Groundskeeping; Livestock Management; Ornamental Horticulture; Plant Nursery Operations and Management; Plant Protection and Integrated Pest Management; Plant Sciences, General; Plant Sciences, Other; Poultry Science; Range Science and Management; Soil Science and Agronomy, General; Turf and Turfgrass Management.

Related DOT Jobs—090.227-010 Faculty Member, College or University.

25-1042.00 Biological Science Teachers, Postsecondary

- **Education/Training Required: Master's degree**
- **Employed: No data available.**
- **Annual Earnings: $57,240**
- **Growth: 23.5%**
- **Annual Job Openings: 184,000**

Teach courses in biological sciences.

Evaluate and grade students' class work, laboratory work, assignments, and papers. Prepare and deliver lectures to undergraduate and/or graduate students on topics such as molecular biology, marine biology, and botany. Advise students on academic and vocational curricula and on career issues. Compile, administer, and grade examinations or assign this work to others. Compile bibliographies of specialized materials for outside reading assignments. Initiate, facilitate, and moderate classroom discussions. Keep abreast of developments in their field by reading current literature, talking with colleagues, and participating in professional conferences. Maintain regularly scheduled office hours in order to advise and assist students. Maintain student attendance records, grades, and other required records. Plan, evaluate, and revise curricula, course content, and course materials and methods of instruction. Prepare course materials such as syllabi, homework assignments, and handouts. Select and obtain materials and supplies, such as textbooks and laboratory equipment. Supervise students' laboratory work. Supervise undergraduate and/or graduate teaching, internship, and research work. Act as advisers to student organizations. Collaborate with colleagues to address teaching and research issues. Conduct research in a particular field of knowledge and publish findings in professional journals, books, and/or electronic media. Participate in campus and community events. Participate in student recruitment, registration, and placement activities. Perform administrative duties such as serving as department head. Provide professional consulting services to government and/or industry. Serve on academic or administrative committees that deal with institutional policies, departmental matters, and academic issues. Write grant proposals to procure external research funding.

GOE INFORMATION—Interest Area: 12. Education and Social Service. **Work Group:** 12.03. Educational Services. **Personality Type**—Investigative. Investigative occupations frequently involve working with ideas and require an extensive amount of thinking. These occupations can involve searching for facts and figuring out problems mentally. **Work Values**—Authority; Social Service; Creativity; Achievement; Social Status. **Skills**—Instructing; Science; Learning Strategies; Reading Comprehension; Critical Thinking; Writing; Mathematics; Complex Problem Solving. **Abilities**—*Cognitive:* Written Expression; Oral Expression; Oral

Comprehension; Written Comprehension; Mathematical Reasoning. *Psychomotor:* None met the criteria. *Physical:* None met the criteria. *Sensory:* Speech Clarity; Speech Recognition; Night Vision. **General Work Activities—***Information Input:* Getting Information; Monitoring Processes, Materials, or Surroundings; Identifying Objects, Actions, and Events. *Mental Process:* Processing Information; Analyzing Data or Information; Updating and Using Relevant Knowledge. *Work Output:* Documenting or Recording Information; Handling and Moving Objects; Interacting with Computers. *Interacting with Others:* Teaching Others; Coaching and Developing Others; Interpreting Meaning of Information for Others. **Physical Work Conditions—**Indoors; Sitting. **Other Job Characteristics—**Consequence of Error; Importance of Being Exact or Accurate; Pace Determined by Speed of Equipment.

Experience—Job Zone 5. Extensive skill, knowledge, and experience are needed for these occupations. **Job Preparation:** SVP 8.0 and above—four years to more than 10 years. **Knowledge—**Biology; Education and Training; Medicine and Dentistry; Therapy and Counseling; Chemistry. **Instructional Programs—**Anatomy; Animal Physiology; Biochemistry; Biological and Biomedical Sciences, Other; Biology/Biological Sciences, General; Biometry/Biometrics; Biophysics; Biotechnology; Botany/Plant Biology; Cell/Cellular Biology and Histology; Ecology; Ecology, Evolution, Systematics, and Population Biology, Other; Entomology; Evolutionary Biology; Immunology; Marine Biology and Biological Oceanography; Microbiology, General; Molecular Biology; Neuroscience; Nutrition Sciences; Parasitology; Pathology/Experimental Pathology; Pharmacology; Plant Genetics; Plant Pathology/Phytopathology; Plant Physiology; Radiation Biology/Radiobiology; Toxicology; Virology; Zoology/Animal Biology.

Related DOT Jobs—090.227-010 Faculty Member, College or University.

25-1043.00 Forestry and Conservation Science Teachers, Postsecondary

- Education/Training Required: Master's degree
- Employed: No data available.
- Annual Earnings: $63,460
- Growth: 23.5%
- Annual Job Openings: 184,000

Teach courses in environmental and conservation science.

Evaluate and grade students' class work, assignments, and papers. Prepare and deliver lectures to undergraduate and/or graduate students on topics such as forest resource policy, forest pathology, and mapping. Advise students on academic and vocational curricula and on career issues. Compile, administer, and grade examinations or assign this work to others. Compile bibliographies of specialized materials for outside reading assignments. Initiate, facilitate, and moderate classroom discussions. Keep abreast of developments in their field by reading current literature, talking with colleagues, and participating in professional conferences. Maintain regularly scheduled office hours in order to advise and assist students. Maintain student attendance records, grades, and other required records. Plan, evaluate, and revise curricula, course content, and course materials and methods of instruction. Prepare course materials such as syllabi, homework assignments, and handouts. Select and obtain materials and supplies, such as textbooks and laboratory equipment. Supervise students' laboratory and/or fieldwork. Supervise undergraduate and/or graduate teaching, internship, and research work. Act as advisers to student organizations. Collaborate with colleagues to address teaching and research issues. Conduct research in a particular field of knowledge and publish findings in books, professional journals, and/or electronic media. Participate in campus and community events. Participate in student

recruitment, registration, and placement activities. Perform administrative duties such as serving as department head. Provide professional consulting services to government and/or industry. Serve on academic or administrative committees that deal with institutional policies, departmental matters, and academic issues. Write grant proposals to procure external research funding.

GOE INFORMATION—Interest Area: 12. Education and Social Service. **Work Group:** 12.03. Educational Services. **Personality Type—**Investigative. Investigative occupations frequently involve working with ideas and require an extensive amount of thinking. These occupations can involve searching for facts and figuring out problems mentally. **Work Values—**Authority; Social Service; Creativity; Achievement; Social Status. **Skills—**Instructing; Science; Learning Strategies; Reading Comprehension; Critical Thinking; Writing; Mathematics; Complex Problem Solving. **Abilities—***Cognitive:* Written Expression; Oral Expression; Oral Comprehension; Written Comprehension; Mathematical Reasoning. *Psychomotor:* None met the criteria. *Physical:* None met the criteria. *Sensory:* Speech Clarity; Speech Recognition; Night Vision. **General Work Activities—***Information Input:* Getting Information; Monitoring Processes, Materials, or Surroundings; Identifying Objects, Actions, and Events. *Mental Process:* Processing Information; Analyzing Data or Information; Updating and Using Relevant Knowledge. *Work Output:* Documenting or Recording Information; Handling and Moving Objects; Interacting with Computers. *Interacting with Others:* Teaching Others; Coaching and Developing Others; Providing Consultation and Advice to Others. **Physical Work Conditions—**Indoors; Sitting. **Other Job Characteristics—**Consequence of Error; Importance of Being Exact or Accurate; Pace Determined by Speed of Equipment.

Experience—Job Zone 5. Extensive skill, knowledge, and experience are needed for these occupations. **Job Preparation:** SVP 8.0 and above—four years to more than 10 years. **Knowledge—**Biology; Education and Training; Medicine and Dentistry; Therapy and Counseling; Chemistry. **Instructional Programs—**Science Teacher Education/General Science Teacher Education.

Related DOT Jobs—090.227-010 Faculty Member, College or University.

25-1051.00 Atmospheric, Earth, Marine, and Space Sciences Teachers, Postsecondary

- Education/Training Required: Master's degree
- Employed: No data available.
- Annual Earnings: $60,230
- Growth: 23.5%
- Annual Job Openings: 184,000

Teach courses in the physical sciences, except chemistry and physics.

Evaluate and grade students' class work, assignments, and papers. Prepare and deliver lectures to undergraduate and/or graduate students on topics such as structural geology, micrometeorology, and atmospheric thermodynamics. Advise students on academic and vocational curricula and on career issues. Compile, administer, and grade examinations or assign this work to others. Compile bibliographies of specialized materials for outside reading assignments. Initiate, facilitate, and moderate classroom discussions. Keep abreast of developments in their field by reading current literature, talking with colleagues, and participating in professional conferences. Maintain regularly scheduled office hours in order to advise and assist students. Maintain student attendance records, grades, and other required records. Plan, evaluate, and revise curricula, course content, and course materials and methods of instruction. Prepare course materials such as syllabi, homework assignments, and handouts. Select and obtain materials and supplies, such as textbooks and laboratory equipment. Supervise laboratory work and fieldwork. Supervise undergraduate and/or graduate teaching, internship, and research work. Act as advisers to student organizations. Collaborate with colleagues to address teaching and research issues. Conduct research in a particular field of knowledge and publish findings in professional journals, books, and/or electronic media. Participate in campus and community events. Participate in student recruitment, registration, and placement activities. Perform administrative duties such as serving as department head. Provide professional consulting services to government and/or industry. Serve on academic or administrative committees that deal with institutional policies, departmental matters, and academic issues. Write grant proposals to procure external research funding.

GOE INFORMATION—Interest Area: 12. Education and Social Service. **Work Group:** 12.03. Educational Services. **Note:** The Department of Labor has not collected some data for this job, so it has fewer details than the other descriptions.

Instructional Programs—Acoustics; Astronomy; Astrophysics; Atmospheric Chemistry and Climatology; Atmospheric Physics and Dynamics; Atmospheric Sciences and Meteorology, General; Atmospheric Sciences and Meteorology, Other; Atomic/Molecular Physics; Elementary Particle Physics; Geochemistry; Geochemistry and Petrology; Geological and Earth Sciences/Geosciences, Other; Geology/Earth Science, General; Geophysics and Seismology; Hydrology and Water Resources Science; Meteorology; Nuclear Physics; Oceanography, Chemical and Physical; Optics/Optical Sciences; Paleontology; Physics Teacher Education; Physics, Other; Planetary Astronomy and Science; Plasma and High-Temperature Physics; Science Teacher Education/General Science Teacher Education; Solid State and Low-Temperature Physics; Theoretical and Mathematical Physics.

Related DOT Jobs—090.227-010 Faculty Member, College or University.

25-1052.00 Chemistry Teachers, Postsecondary

- **Education/Training Required: Master's degree**
- **Employed: No data available.**
- **Annual Earnings: $53,750**
- **Growth: 23.5%**
- **Annual Job Openings: 184,000**

Teach courses pertaining to the chemical and physical properties and compositional changes of substances. Work may include instruction in the methods of qualitative and quantitative chemical analysis. Includes both teachers primarily engaged in teaching and those who do a combination of both teaching and research.

Evaluate and grade students' class work, laboratory performance, assignments, and papers. Prepare and deliver lectures to undergraduate and/or graduate students on topics such as organic chemistry, analytical chemistry, and chemical separation. Advise students on academic and vocational curricula and on career issues. Compile, administer, and grade examinations or assign this work to others. Compile bibliographies of specialized materials for outside reading assignments. Initiate, facilitate, and moderate classroom discussions. Keep abreast of developments in their field by reading current literature, talking with colleagues, and participating in professional conferences. Maintain regularly scheduled office hours in order to advise and assist students. Maintain student attendance records, grades, and other required records. Plan, evaluate, and revise curricula, course content, and course materials and methods

of instruction. Prepare course materials such as syllabi, homework assignments, and handouts. Select and obtain materials and supplies, such as textbooks and laboratory equipment. Supervise students' laboratory work. Supervise undergraduate and/or graduate teaching, internship, and research work. Act as advisers to student organizations. Collaborate with colleagues to address teaching and research issues. Conduct research in a particular field of knowledge and publish findings in professional journals, books, and/or electronic media. Participate in campus and community events. Participate in student recruitment, registration, and placement activities. Perform administrative duties such as serving as department head. Provide professional consulting services to government and/or industry. Serve on academic or administrative committees that deal with institutional policies, departmental matters, and academic issues. Write grant proposals to procure external research funding. Perform administrative duties such as serving as a department head. Prepare and submit required reports related to instruction. Provide professional consulting services to government and/or industry.

GOE INFORMATION—Interest Area: 12. Education and Social Service. **Work Group:** 12.03. Educational Services. **Personality Type**—Investigative. Investigative occupations frequently involve working with ideas and require an extensive amount of thinking. These occupations can involve searching for facts and figuring out problems mentally. **Work Values**—Authority; Social Service; Creativity; Achievement; Social Status. **Skills**—Instructing; Writing; Science; Learning Strategies; Reading Comprehension; Complex Problem Solving; Speaking; Mathematics. **Abilities**—*Cognitive:* Written Expression; Originality; Oral Expression; Fluency of Ideas; Inductive Reasoning. *Psychomotor:* Finger Dexterity; Reaction Time; Arm-Hand Steadiness; Manual Dexterity; Control Precision. *Physical:* None met the criteria. *Sensory:* Speech Clarity; Far Vision; Night Vision; Glare Sensitivity; Near Vision. **General Work Activities**—*Information Input:* Getting Information; Identifying Objects, Actions, and Events; Monitoring Processes, Materials, or Surroundings. *Mental Process:* Analyzing Data or Information; Updating and Using Relevant Knowledge; Organizing, Planning, and Prioritizing. *Work Output:* Documenting or Recording Information; Interacting with Computers; Handling and Moving Objects. *Interacting with Others:* Teaching Others; Communicating with Persons Outside Organization; Interpreting Meaning of Information for Others. **Physical Work Conditions**—Hazardous Conditions; Contaminants; Disease or Infections; Common Protective or Safety Attire; Indoors. **Other Job Characteristics**—Degree of Automation; Importance of Being Exact or Accurate; Consequence of Error.

Experience—Job Zone 5. Extensive skill, knowledge, and experience are needed for these occupations. **Job Preparation:** SVP 8.0 and above—four years to more than 10 years. **Knowledge**—Chemistry; Education and Training; Mathematics; English Language; Administration and Management. **Instructional Programs**—Analytical Chemistry; Chemical Physics; Chemistry, General; Chemistry, Other; Geochemistry; Inorganic Chemistry; Organic Chemistry; Physical and Theoretical Chemistry; Polymer Chemistry.

Related DOT Jobs—090.227-010 Faculty Member, College or University.

25-1053.00 Environmental Science Teachers, Postsecondary

- **Education/Training Required: Master's degree**
- **Employed: No data available.**
- **Annual Earnings: $57,160**
- **Growth: 23.5%**
- **Annual Job Openings: 184,000**

Teach courses in environmental science.

Evaluate and grade students' class work, laboratory work, assignments, and papers. Prepare and deliver lectures to undergraduate and/or graduate students on topics such as hazardous waste management, industrial safety, and environmental toxicology. Advise students on academic and vocational curricula and on career issues. Compile, administer, and grade examinations or assign this work to others. Compile bibliographies of specialized materials for outside reading assignments. Initiate, facilitate, and moderate classroom discussions. Keep abreast of developments in their field by reading current literature, talking with colleagues, and participating in professional conferences. Maintain regularly scheduled office hours in order to advise and assist students. Maintain student attendance records, grades, and other required records. Plan, evaluate, and revise curricula, course content, and course materials and methods of instruction. Prepare course materials such as syllabi, homework assignments, and handouts. Select and obtain materials and supplies, such as textbooks and laboratory equipment. Supervise students' laboratory work and fieldwork. Supervise undergraduate and/or graduate teaching, internship, and research work. Act as advisers to student organizations. Collaborate with colleagues to address teaching and research issues. Conduct research in a particular field of knowledge and publish findings in professional journals, books, and/or electronic media. Participate in campus and community events. Participate in student recruitment, registration, and placement activities. Perform administrative duties such as serving as department head. Provide professional consulting services to government and/or industry. Serve on academic or administrative committees that deal with institutional policies, departmental matters, and academic issues. Write grant proposals to procure external research funding.

GOE INFORMATION—Interest Area: 12. Education and Social Service. **Work Group:** 12.03. Educational Services. **Note:** The Department of Labor has not collected some data for this job, so it has fewer details than the other descriptions.

Instructional Programs—Environmental Science; Environmental Studies; Science Teacher Education/General Science Teacher Education.

Related DOT Jobs—090.227-010 Faculty Member, College or University.

25-1054.00 Physics Teachers, Postsecondary

- **Education/Training Required: Master's degree**
- **Employed: No data available.**
- **Annual Earnings: $61,300**
- **Growth: 23.5%**
- **Annual Job Openings: 184,000**

Teach courses pertaining to the laws of matter and energy. Includes both teachers primarily engaged in teaching and those who do a combination of both teaching and research.

Evaluate and grade students' class work, laboratory work, assignments, and papers. Prepare and deliver lectures to undergraduate and/or graduate students on topics such as quantum mechanics, particle physics, and optics. Advise students on academic and vocational curricula and on career issues. Compile, administer, and grade examinations or assign this work to others. Compile bibliographies of specialized materials for outside reading assignments. Initiate, facilitate, and moderate classroom discussions. Keep abreast of developments in their field by reading current literature, talking with colleagues, and participating in professional conferences. Maintain regularly scheduled office hours in order to advise and assist students. Maintain student attendance records, grades, and

other required records. Plan, evaluate, and revise curricula, course content, and course materials and methods of instruction. Prepare course materials such as syllabi, homework assignments, and handouts. Select and obtain materials and supplies, such as textbooks and laboratory equipment. Supervise students' laboratory work. Supervise undergraduate and/or graduate teaching, internship, and research work. Act as advisers to student organizations. Collaborate with colleagues to address teaching and research issues. Conduct research in a particular field of knowledge and publish findings in professional journals, books, and/or electronic media. Participate in campus and community events. Participate in student recruitment, registration, and placement activities. Perform administrative duties such as serving as department head. Provide professional consulting services to government and/or industry. Serve on academic or administrative committees that deal with institutional policies, departmental matters, and academic issues. Write grant proposals to procure external research funding.

GOE INFORMATION—Interest Area: 12. Education and Social Service. **Work Group:** 12.03. Educational Services. **Personality Type—**Investigative. Investigative occupations frequently involve working with ideas and require an extensive amount of thinking. These occupations can involve searching for facts and figuring out problems mentally. **Work Values—**Authority; Social Service; Creativity; Achievement; Social Status. **Skills—**Science; Instructing; Writing; Learning Strategies; Complex Problem Solving; Reading Comprehension; Critical Thinking; Speaking. **Abilities—***Cognitive:* Mathematical Reasoning; Number Facility; Written Expression; Deductive Reasoning; Oral Expression. *Psychomotor:* Rate Control; Reaction Time; Response Orientation. *Physical:* None met the criteria. *Sensory:* Speech Clarity; Night Vision; Far Vision; Sound Localization; Speech Recognition. **General Work Activities—***Information Input:* Getting Information; Identifying Objects, Actions, and Events; Estimating Needed Characteristics. *Mental Process:* Updating and Using Relevant Knowledge; Analyzing Data or Information; Thinking Creatively. *Work Output:* Documenting or Recording Information; Interacting with Computers; Handling and Moving Objects. *Interacting with Others:* Teaching Others; Communicating with Persons Outside Organization; Interpreting Meaning of Information for Others. **Physical Work Conditions—**Indoors; Sitting; Radiation; Disease or Infections; Common Protective or Safety Attire. **Other Job Characteristics—**Degree of Automation; Importance of Repeating Same Tasks; Pace Determined by Speed of Equipment.

Experience—Job Zone 5. Extensive skill, knowledge, and experience are needed for these occupations. **Job Preparation:** SVP 8.0 and above—four years to more than 10 years. **Knowledge—**Physics; Education and Training; Mathematics; English Language; Administration and Management. **Instructional Programs—**Acoustics; Atomic/Molecular Physics; Elementary Particle Physics; Nuclear Physics; Optics/Optical Sciences; Physics, General; Physics, Other; Plasma and High-Temperature Physics; Solid State and Low-Temperature Physics; Theoretical and Mathematical Physics.

Related DOT Jobs—090.227-010 Faculty Member, College or University.

25-1061.00 Anthropology and Archeology Teachers, Postsecondary

- **Education/Training Required: Master's degree**
- **Employed: No data available.**
- **Annual Earnings: $59,000**
- **Growth: 23.5%**
- **Annual Job Openings: 184,000**

Teach courses in anthropology or archeology.

Evaluate and grade students' class work, assignments, and papers. Prepare and deliver lectures to undergraduate and/or graduate students on topics such as research methods, urban anthropology, and language and culture. Advise students on academic and vocational curricula, career issues, and laboratory and field research. Compile, administer, and grade examinations or assign this work to others. Compile bibliographies of specialized materials for outside reading assignments. Initiate, facilitate, and moderate classroom discussions. Keep abreast of developments in their field by reading current literature, talking with colleagues, and participating in professional conferences. Maintain regularly scheduled office hours in order to advise and assist students. Maintain student attendance records, grades, and other required records. Plan, evaluate, and revise curricula, course content, and course materials and methods of instruction. Prepare course materials such as syllabi, homework assignments, and handouts. Select and obtain materials and supplies, such as textbooks and laboratory equipment. Supervise students' laboratory work or fieldwork. Supervise undergraduate and/or graduate teaching, internship, and research work. Act as advisers to student organizations. Collaborate with colleagues to address teaching and research issues. Conduct research in a particular field of knowledge and publish findings in professional journals, books, and/or electronic media. Participate in campus and community events. Participate in student recruitment, registration, and placement activities. Perform administrative duties such as serving as department head. Provide professional consulting services to government and/or industry. Serve on academic or administrative committees that deal with institutional policies, departmental matters, and academic issues. Write grant proposals to procure external research funding.

GOE INFORMATION—Interest Area: 12. Education and Social Service. **Work Group:** 12.03. Educational Services. **Personality Type—**Social. Social occupations frequently involve working with, communicating with, and teaching people. These occupations often involve helping or providing service to others. **Work Values—**Authority; Social Service; Creativity; Achievement; Social Status. **Skills—**Instructing; Speaking; Reading Comprehension; Learning Strategies; Complex Problem Solving; Writing; Critical Thinking; Active Listening. **Abilities—***Cognitive:* Written Expression; Oral Expression; Oral Comprehension; Written Comprehension; Mathematical Reasoning. *Psychomotor:* None met the criteria. *Physical:* None met the criteria. *Sensory:* Speech Clarity; Speech Recognition; Far Vision. **General Work Activities—***Information Input:* Getting Information; Identifying Objects, Actions, and Events; Monitoring Processes, Materials, or Surroundings. *Mental Process:* Analyzing Data or Information; Processing Information; Organizing, Planning, and Prioritizing. *Work Output:* Documenting or Recording Information; Handling and Moving Objects; Interacting with Computers. *Interacting with Others:* Teaching Others; Coaching and Developing Others; Communicating with Other Workers. **Physical Work Conditions—**Indoors; Sitting; Standing. **Other Job Characteristics—**Consequence of Error; Importance of Being Exact or Accurate; Pace Determined by Speed of Equipment.

Experience—Job Zone 5. Extensive skill, knowledge, and experience are needed for these occupations. **Job Preparation:** SVP 8.0 and above—four years to more than 10 years. **Knowledge—**History and Archeology; Sociology and Anthropology; Education and Training; Psychology; Economics and Accounting. **Instructional Programs—**Anthropology; Archeology; Physical Anthropology; Social Science Teacher Education.

Related DOT Jobs—090.227-010 Faculty Member, College or University.

25-1062.00 Area, Ethnic, and Cultural Studies Teachers, Postsecondary

- **Education/Training Required: Master's degree**
- **Employed: No data available.**
- **Annual Earnings: $54,700**
- **Growth: 23.5%**
- **Annual Job Openings: 184,000**

Teach courses pertaining to the culture and development of an area (e.g., Latin America), an ethnic group, or any other group (e.g., women's studies, urban affairs).

Evaluate and grade students' class work, assignments, and papers. Prepare and deliver lectures to undergraduate and/or graduate students on topics such as race and ethnic relations, gender studies, and cross-cultural perspectives. Advise students on academic and vocational curricula and on career issues. Compile, administer, and grade examinations or assign this work to others. Compile bibliographies of specialized materials for outside reading assignments. Incorporate experiential/site visit components into courses. Initiate, facilitate, and moderate classroom discussions. Keep abreast of developments in their field by reading current literature, talking with colleagues, and participating in professional conferences. Maintain regularly scheduled office hours in order to advise and assist students. Maintain student attendance records, grades, and other required records. Plan, evaluate, and revise curricula, course content, and course materials and methods of instruction. Prepare course materials such as syllabi, homework assignments, and handouts. Select and obtain materials and supplies, such as textbooks. Supervise undergraduate and/or graduate teaching, internship, and research work. Act as advisers to student organizations. Collaborate with colleagues to address teaching and research issues. Conduct research in a particular field of knowledge and publish findings in professional journals, books, and/or electronic media. Participate in campus and community events. Participate in student recruitment, registration, and placement activities. Perform administrative duties such as serving as department head. Provide professional consulting services to government and/or industry. Serve on academic or administrative committees that deal with institutional policies, departmental matters, and academic issues. Write grant proposals to procure external research funding.

GOE INFORMATION—Interest Area: 12. Education and Social Service. **Work Group:** 12.03. Educational Services. **Personality Type—**Social. Social occupations frequently involve working with, communicating with, and teaching people. These occupations often involve helping or providing service to others. **Work Values—**Authority; Social Service; Creativity; Achievement; Social Status. **Skills—**Instructing; Speaking; Reading Comprehension; Learning Strategies; Complex Problem Solving; Writing; Critical Thinking; Active Listening. **Abilities—***Cognitive:* Written Expression; Oral Expression; Oral Comprehension; Written Comprehension; Mathematical Reasoning. *Psychomotor:* None met the criteria. *Physical:* None met the criteria. *Sensory:* Speech Clarity; Speech Recognition; Far Vision. **General Work Activities—***Information Input:* Getting Information; Identifying Objects, Actions, and Events; Monitoring Processes, Materials, or Surroundings. *Mental Process:* Analyzing Data or Information; Processing Information; Organizing, Planning, and Prioritizing. *Work Output:* Documenting or Recording Information; Interacting with Computers; Handling and Moving Objects. *Interacting with Others:* Teaching Others; Coaching and Developing Others; Communicating with Other Workers. **Physical Work Conditions—**Indoors; Sitting; Standing. **Other Job Characteristics—**Consequence of Error; Importance of Being Exact or Accurate; Pace Determined by Speed of Equipment.

Experience—Job Zone 5. Extensive skill, knowledge, and experience are needed for these occupations. **Job Preparation:** SVP 8.0 and above—four years to more than 10 years. **Knowledge**—History and Archeology; Sociology and Anthropology; Education and Training; Psychology; Economics and Accounting. **Instructional Programs**—African Studies; African-American/Black Studies; American Indian/Native American Studies; American/United States Studies/Civilization; Area Studies, Other; Area, Ethnic, Cultural, and Gender Studies, Other; Asian Studies/Civilization; Asian-American Studies; Balkans Studies; Baltic Studies; Canadian Studies; Caribbean Studies; Central/Middle and Eastern European Studies; Chinese Studies; Commonwealth Studies; East Asian Studies; Ethnic, Cultural Minority, and Gender Studies, Other; European Studies/Civilization; French Studies; Gay/Lesbian Studies; German Studies; Hispanic-American, Puerto Rican, and Mexican-American/Chicano Studies; Intercultural/Multicultural and Diversity Studies; Islamic Studies; Italian Studies; Japanese Studies; Jewish/Judaic Studies; Korean Studies; Latin American Studies; Near and Middle Eastern Studies; Pacific Area/Pacific Rim Studies; Polish Studies; Regional Studies (U.S., Canadian, Foreign); Religion/Religious Studies, Other; Russian Studies; Scandinavian Studies; Slavic Studies; Social Studies Teacher Education; South Asian Studies; Southeast Asian Studies; Spanish and Iberian Studies; Tibetan Studies; Ukraine Studies; Ural-Altaic and Central Asian Studies; Western European Studies; Women's Studies.

Related DOT Jobs—090.227-010 Faculty Member, College or University.

25-1063.00 Economics Teachers, Postsecondary

- **Education/Training Required: Master's degree**
- **Employed: No data available.**
- **Annual Earnings: $62,820**
- **Growth: 23.5%**
- **Annual Job Openings: 184,000**

Teach courses in economics.

Evaluate and grade students' class work, assignments, and papers. Prepare and deliver lectures to undergraduate and/or graduate students on topics such as econometrics, price theory, and macroeconomics. Advise students on academic and vocational curricula and on career issues. Compile, administer, and grade examinations or assign this work to others. Compile bibliographies of specialized materials for outside reading assignments. Initiate, facilitate, and moderate classroom discussions. Keep abreast of developments in their field by reading current literature, talking with colleagues, and participating in professional conferences. Maintain regularly scheduled office hours in order to advise and assist students. Maintain student attendance records, grades, and other required records. Plan, evaluate, and revise curricula, course content, and course materials and methods of instruction. Prepare course materials such as syllabi, homework assignments, and handouts. Select and obtain materials and supplies, such as textbooks. Supervise undergraduate and/or graduate teaching, internship, and research work. Act as advisers to student organizations. Collaborate with colleagues to address teaching and research issues. Conduct research in a particular field of knowledge and publish findings in professional journals, books, and/or electronic media. Participate in campus and community events. Participate in student recruitment, registration, and placement activities. Perform administrative duties such as serving as department head. Provide professional consulting services to government and/or industry. Serve on academic or administrative committees that deal with institutional policies, departmental matters, and academic issues. Write grant proposals to procure external research funding.

GOE INFORMATION—**Interest Area:** 12. Education and Social Service. **Work Group:** 12.03. Educational Services. **Personality Type**—Social. Social occupations frequently involve working with, communicating with, and teaching people. These occupations often involve helping or providing service to others. **Work Values**—Authority; Social Service; Creativity; Achievement; Social Status. **Skills**—Instructing; Speaking; Reading Comprehension; Learning Strategies; Complex Problem Solving; Writing; Critical Thinking; Active Listening. **Abilities**—*Cognitive:* Written Expression; Oral Expression; Oral Comprehension; Written Comprehension; Mathematical Reasoning. *Psychomotor:* None met the criteria. *Physical:* None met the criteria. *Sensory:* Speech Clarity; Speech Recognition; Far Vision. **General Work Activities**—*Information Input:* Getting Information; Identifying Objects, Actions, and Events; Monitoring Processes, Materials, or Surroundings. *Mental Process:* Analyzing Data or Information; Processing Information; Organizing, Planning, and Prioritizing. *Work Output:* Documenting or Recording Information; Interacting with Computers; Handling and Moving Objects. *Interacting with Others:* Teaching Others; Coaching and Developing Others; Communicating with Other Workers. **Physical Work Conditions**—Indoors; Sitting; Standing. **Other Job Characteristics**—Consequence of Error; Importance of Being Exact or Accurate; Pace Determined by Speed of Equipment.

Experience—Job Zone 5. Extensive skill, knowledge, and experience are needed for these occupations. **Job Preparation:** SVP 8.0 and above—four years to more than 10 years. **Knowledge**—History and Archeology; Sociology and Anthropology; Education and Training; Psychology; Economics and Accounting. **Instructional Programs**—Applied Economics; Business/Managerial Economics; Development Economics and International Development; Econometrics and Quantitative Economics; Economics, General; Economics, Other; International Economics; Social Science Teacher Education.

Related DOT Jobs—090.227-010 Faculty Member, College or University.

25-1064.00 Geography Teachers, Postsecondary

- **Education/Training Required: Master's degree**
- **Employed: No data available.**
- **Annual Earnings: $55,250**
- **Growth: 23.5%**
- **Annual Job Openings: 184,000**

Teach courses in geography.

Evaluate and grade students' class work, assignments, and papers. Prepare and deliver lectures to undergraduate and/or graduate students on topics such as urbanization, environmental systems, and cultural geography. Advise students on academic and vocational curricula and on career issues. Compile, administer, and grade examinations or assign this work to others. Compile bibliographies of specialized materials for outside reading assignments. Initiate, facilitate, and moderate classroom discussions. Keep abreast of developments in their field by reading current literature, talking with colleagues, and participating in professional conferences. Maintain regularly scheduled office hours in order to advise and assist students. Maintain student attendance records, grades, and other required records. Plan, evaluate, and revise curricula, course content, and course materials and methods of instruction. Prepare course materials such as syllabi, homework assignments, and handouts. Select and obtain materials and supplies, such as textbooks. Supervise students' laboratory work and fieldwork. Supervise undergraduate and/or graduate teaching, internship, and research work. Act as advisers to student organizations. Collaborate with colleagues to address teaching and research issues.

Conduct research in a particular field of knowledge and publish findings in professional journals, books, and/or electronic media. Maintain geographic information systems laboratories, performing duties such as updating software. Participate in campus and community events. Participate in student recruitment, registration, and placement activities. Perform administrative duties such as serving as department head. Perform spatial analysis and modeling, using geographic information system techniques. Provide professional consulting services to government and/or industry. Serve on academic or administrative committees that deal with institutional policies, departmental matters, and academic issues. Write grant proposals to procure external research funding.

GOE INFORMATION—Interest Area: 12. Education and Social Service. **Work Group:** 12.03. Educational Services. **Note:** The Department of Labor has not collected some data for this job, so it has fewer details than the other descriptions.

Instructional Programs—Geography; Geography Teacher Education.

Related DOT Jobs—090.227-010 Faculty Member, College or University.

25-1065.00 Political Science Teachers, Postsecondary

- Education/Training Required: Master's degree
- Employed: No data available.
- Annual Earnings: $54,930
- Growth: 23.5%
- Annual Job Openings: 184,000

Teach courses in political science, international affairs, and international relations.

Evaluate and grade students' class work, assignments, and papers. Prepare and deliver lectures to undergraduate and/or graduate students on topics such as classical political thought, international relations, and democracy and citizenship. Advise students on academic and vocational curricula and on career issues. Compile, administer, and grade examinations or assign this work to others. Compile bibliographies of specialized materials for outside reading assignments. Initiate, facilitate, and moderate classroom discussions. Keep abreast of developments in their field by reading current literature, talking with colleagues, and participating in professional conferences. Maintain regularly scheduled office hours in order to advise and assist students. Maintain student attendance records, grades, and other required records. Plan, evaluate, and revise curricula, course content, and course materials and methods of instruction. Prepare course materials such as syllabi, homework assignments, and handouts. Select and obtain materials and supplies, such as textbooks. Supervise undergraduate and/or graduate teaching, internship, and research work. Act as advisers to student organizations. Collaborate with colleagues to address teaching and research issues. Conduct research in a particular field of knowledge and publish findings in professional journals, books, and/or electronic media. Participate in campus and community events. Participate in student recruitment, registration, and placement activities. Perform administrative duties such as serving as department head. Provide professional consulting services to government and/or industry. Serve on academic or administrative committees that deal with institutional policies, departmental matters, and academic issues. Write grant proposals to procure external research funding.

GOE INFORMATION—Interest Area: 12. Education and Social Service. **Work Group:** 12.03. Educational Services. **Personality Type**—Social. Social occupations frequently involve working with, communicating with, and teaching people. These occupations often involve helping or providing service to others. **Work Values**—Authority; Social Service; Creativity; Achievement; Social Status. **Skills**—Instructing; Speaking; Reading Comprehension; Learning Strategies; Complex Problem Solving; Writing; Critical Thinking; Active Listening. **Abilities**—*Cognitive:* Written Expression; Oral Expression; Oral Comprehension; Written Comprehension; Mathematical Reasoning. *Psychomotor:* None met the criteria. *Physical:* None met the criteria. *Sensory:* Speech Clarity; Speech Recognition; Far Vision. **General Work Activities**—*Information Input:* Getting Information; Identifying Objects, Actions, and Events; Monitoring Processes, Materials, or Surroundings. *Mental Process:* Analyzing Data or Information; Processing Information; Organizing, Planning, and Prioritizing. *Work Output:* Documenting or Recording Information; Interacting with Computers; Handling and Moving Objects. *Interacting with Others:* Teaching Others; Coaching and Developing Others; Providing Consultation and Advice to Others. **Physical Work Conditions**—Indoors; Sitting; Standing. **Other Job Characteristics**—Consequence of Error; Importance of Being Exact or Accurate; Pace Determined by Speed of Equipment.

Experience—Job Zone 5. Extensive skill, knowledge, and experience are needed for these occupations. **Job Preparation:** SVP 8.0 and above—four years to more than 10 years. **Knowledge**—History and Archeology; Sociology and Anthropology; Education and Training; Psychology; Economics and Accounting. **Instructional Programs**—American Government and Politics (United States); Political Science and Government, General; Political Science and Government, Other; Social Science Teacher Education.

Related DOT Jobs—090.227-010 Faculty Member, College or University.

25-1066.00 Psychology Teachers, Postsecondary

- Education/Training Required: Master's degree
- Employed: No data available.
- Annual Earnings: $53,120
- Growth: 23.5%
- Annual Job Openings: 184,000

Teach courses in psychology, such as child, clinical, and developmental psychology and psychological counseling.

Evaluate and grade students' class work, laboratory work, assignments, and papers. Prepare and deliver lectures to undergraduate and/or graduate students on topics such as abnormal psychology, cognitive processes, and work motivation. Advise students on academic and vocational curricula and on career issues. Compile, administer, and grade examinations or assign this work to others. Compile bibliographies of specialized materials for outside reading assignments. Initiate, facilitate, and moderate classroom discussions. Keep abreast of developments in their field by reading current literature, talking with colleagues, and participating in professional conferences. Maintain regularly scheduled office hours in order to advise and assist students. Maintain student attendance records, grades, and other required records. Plan, evaluate, and revise curricula, course content, and course materials and methods of instruction. Prepare course materials such as syllabi, homework assignments, and handouts. Select and obtain materials and supplies, such as textbooks. Supervise students' laboratory work. Supervise undergraduate and/or graduate teaching, internship, and research work. Act as advisers to student organizations. Collaborate with colleagues to address teaching and research issues. Conduct research in a particular field of knowledge and publish findings in professional journals, books, and/or electronic media. Participate in campus and community events. Participate in student recruitment, registration, and placement activities. Perform administrative duties such as serving as department head. Provide professional consulting services to government and/or industry. Serve on academic or administrative committees that deal with institutional policies, departmental matters, and academic issues. Write grant proposals to procure external research funding.

GOE INFORMATION—Interest Area: 12. Education and Social Service. **Work Group:** 12.03. Educational Services. **Personality Type**—Social. Social occupations frequently involve working with, communicating with, and teaching people. These occupations often involve helping or providing service to others. **Work Values**—Authority; Social Service; Creativity; Achievement; Social Status. **Skills**—Instructing; Speaking; Reading Comprehension; Learning Strategies; Complex Problem Solving; Writing; Critical Thinking; Active Listening. **Abilities**—*Cognitive:* Written Expression; Oral Expression; Oral Comprehension; Written Comprehension; Mathematical Reasoning. *Psychomotor:* None met the criteria. *Physical:* None met the criteria. *Sensory:* Speech Clarity; Speech Recognition; Far Vision. **General Work Activities**—*Information Input:* Getting Information; Identifying Objects, Actions, and Events; Monitoring Processes, Materials, or Surroundings. *Mental Process:* Analyzing Data or Information; Processing Information; Organizing, Planning, and Prioritizing. *Work Output:* Documenting or Recording Information; Handling and Moving Objects; Interacting with Computers. *Interacting with Others:* Teaching Others; Coaching and Developing Others; Communicating with Other Workers. **Physical Work Conditions**—Indoors; Sitting; Standing. **Other Job Characteristics**—Consequence of Error; Importance of Being Exact or Accurate; Pace Determined by Speed of Equipment.

Experience—Job Zone 5. Extensive skill, knowledge, and experience are needed for these occupations. **Job Preparation:** SVP 8.0 and above—four years to more than 10 years. **Knowledge**—History and Archeology; Sociology and Anthropology; Education and Training; Psychology; Economics and Accounting. **Instructional Programs**—Clinical Psychology; Cognitive Psychology and Psycholinguistics; Community Psychology; Comparative Psychology; Counseling Psychology; Developmental and Child Psychology; Educational Psychology; Experimental Psychology; Industrial and Organizational Psychology; Marriage and Family Therapy/Counseling; Personality Psychology; Physiological Psychology/Psychobiology; Psychology Teacher Education; Psychology, General; Psychology, Other; Psychometrics and Quantitative Psychology; School Psychology; Social Psychology; Social Science Teacher Education.

Related DOT Jobs—090.227-010 Faculty Member, College or University.

25-1067.00 Sociology Teachers, Postsecondary

- Education/Training Required: Master's degree
- Employed: No data available.
- Annual Earnings: $51,110
- Growth: 23.5%
- Annual Job Openings: 184,000

Teach courses in sociology.

Evaluate and grade students' class work, assignments, and papers. Prepare and deliver lectures to undergraduate and/or graduate students on topics such as race and ethnic relations, measurement and data collection, and workplace social relations. Advise students on academic and vocational curricula and on career issues. Compile, administer, and grade examinations or assign this work to others. Compile bibliographies of specialized materials for outside reading assignments. Initiate, facilitate, and moderate classroom discussions. Keep abreast of developments in their field by reading current literature, talking with colleagues, and

participating in professional conferences. Maintain regularly scheduled office hours in order to advise and assist students. Maintain student attendance records, grades, and other required records. Plan, evaluate, and revise curricula, course content, and course materials and methods of instruction. Prepare course materials such as syllabi, homework assignments, and handouts. Select and obtain materials and supplies, such as textbooks and laboratory equipment. Supervise students' laboratory work and fieldwork. Supervise undergraduate and/or graduate teaching, internship, and research work. Act as advisers to student organizations. Collaborate with colleagues to address teaching and research issues. Conduct research in a particular field of knowledge and publish findings in professional journals, books, and/or electronic media. Participate in campus and community events. Participate in student recruitment, registration, and placement activities. Perform administrative duties such as serving as department head. Provide professional consulting services to government and/or industry. Serve on academic or administrative committees that deal with institutional policies, departmental matters, and academic issues. Write grant proposals to procure external research funding.

GOE INFORMATION—Interest Area: 12. Education and Social Service. **Work Group:** 12.03. Educational Services. **Personality Type**—Social. Social occupations frequently involve working with, communicating with, and teaching people. These occupations often involve helping or providing service to others. **Work Values**—Authority; Social Service; Creativity; Achievement; Social Status. **Skills**—Instructing; Speaking; Reading Comprehension; Learning Strategies; Complex Problem Solving; Writing; Critical Thinking; Active Listening. **Abilities**—*Cognitive:* Written Expression; Oral Expression; Oral Comprehension; Written Comprehension; Mathematical Reasoning. *Psychomotor:* None met the criteria. *Physical:* None met the criteria. *Sensory:* Speech Clarity; Speech Recognition; Far Vision. **General Work Activities**—*Information Input:* Getting Information; Identifying Objects, Actions, and Events; Monitoring Processes, Materials, or Surroundings. *Mental Process:* Analyzing Data or Information; Processing Information; Organizing, Planning, and Prioritizing. *Work Output:* Documenting or Recording Information; Interacting with Computers; Handling and Moving Objects. *Interacting with Others:* Teaching Others; Coaching and Developing Others; Communicating with Other Workers. **Physical Work Conditions**—Indoors; Sitting; Standing. **Other Job Characteristics**—Consequence of Error; Importance of Being Exact or Accurate; Pace Determined by Speed of Equipment.

Experience—Job Zone 5. Extensive skill, knowledge, and experience are needed for these occupations. **Job Preparation:** SVP 8.0 and above—four years to more than 10 years. **Knowledge**—History and Archeology; Sociology and Anthropology; Education and Training; Psychology; Economics and Accounting. **Instructional Programs**—Social Science Teacher Education; Sociology.

Related DOT Jobs—090.227-010 Faculty Member, College or University.

25-1069.99 Social Sciences Teachers, Postsecondary, All Other

- Education/Training Required: Master's degree
- Employed: No data available.
- Annual Earnings: No data available.
- Growth: 23.5%
- Annual Job Openings: 184,000

All postsecondary social sciences teachers not listed separately.

No task data available.

GOE INFORMATION—**Interest Area:** 12. Education and Social Service. **Work Group:** 12.03. Educational Services. **Note:** The Department of Labor has not collected some data for this job, so it has fewer details than the other descriptions.

Instructional Programs—Social Science Teacher Education; Social Sciences, General.

Related DOT Jobs—090.227-010 Faculty Member, College or University.

25-1071.00 Health Specialties Teachers, Postsecondary

- Education/Training Required: Master's degree
- Employed: No data available.
- Annual Earnings: $59,100
- Growth: 23.5%
- Annual Job Openings: 184,000

Teach courses in health specialties, such as veterinary medicine, dentistry, pharmacy, therapy, laboratory technology, and public health.

Evaluate and grade students' class work, assignments, and papers. Prepare and deliver lectures to undergraduate and/or graduate students on topics such as public health, stress management, and worksite health promotion. Advise students on academic and vocational curricula and on career issues. Compile, administer, and grade examinations or assign this work to others. Compile bibliographies of specialized materials for outside reading assignments. Initiate, facilitate, and moderate classroom discussions. Keep abreast of developments in their field by reading current literature, talking with colleagues, and participating in professional conferences. Maintain regularly scheduled office hours in order to advise and assist students. Maintain student attendance records, grades, and other required records. Plan, evaluate, and revise curricula, course content, and course materials and methods of instruction. Prepare course materials such as syllabi, homework assignments, and handouts. Select and obtain materials and supplies, such as textbooks and laboratory equipment. Supervise laboratory sessions. Supervise undergraduate and/or graduate teaching, internship, and research work. Act as advisers to student organizations. Collaborate with colleagues to address teaching and research issues. Conduct research in a particular field of knowledge and publish findings in professional journals, books, and/or electronic media. Participate in campus and community events. Participate in student recruitment, registration, and placement activities. Perform administrative duties such as serving as department head. Provide professional consulting services to government and/or industry. Serve on academic or administrative committees that deal with institutional policies, departmental matters, and academic issues. Write grant proposals to procure external research funding.

GOE INFORMATION—**Interest Area:** 12. Education and Social Service. **Work Group:** 12.03. Educational Services. **Personality Type**—Investigative. Investigative occupations frequently involve working with ideas and require an extensive amount of thinking. These occupations can involve searching for facts and figuring out problems mentally. **Work Values**—Authority; Social Service; Creativity; Achievement; Social Status. **Skills**—Science; Writing; Reading Comprehension; Instructing; Complex Problem Solving; Critical Thinking; Speaking; Learning Strategies. **Abilities**—*Cognitive:* Written Expression; Oral Expression; Written Comprehension; Oral Comprehension; Mathematical Reasoning. *Psychomotor:* None met the criteria. *Physical:* None met the criteria. *Sensory:* Speech Clarity; Speech Recognition; Sound Localization; Auditory Attention. **General Work Activities**—*Information Input:* Getting Informa-

tion; Monitoring Processes, Materials, or Surroundings; Identifying Objects, Actions, and Events. *Mental Process:* Updating and Using Relevant Knowledge; Analyzing Data or Information; Organizing, Planning, and Prioritizing. *Work Output:* Documenting or Recording Information; Handling and Moving Objects; Interacting with Computers. *Interacting with Others:* Teaching Others; Coaching and Developing Others; Communicating with Other Workers. **Physical Work Conditions**—Disease or Infections; Indoors; Radiation; Standing; Specialized Protective or Safety Attire. **Other Job Characteristics**—Importance of Being Exact or Accurate; Importance of Repeating Same Tasks; Pace Determined by Speed of Equipment.

Experience—Job Zone 5. Extensive skill, knowledge, and experience are needed for these occupations. **Job Preparation:** SVP 8.0 and above—four years to more than 10 years. **Knowledge**—Biology; Education and Training; Medicine and Dentistry; Therapy and Counseling; English Language. **Instructional Programs**—Allied Health and Medical Assisting Services, Other; Allied Health Diagnostic, Intervention, and Treatment Professions, Other; Art Therapy/Therapist; Asian Bodywork Therapy; Audiology/Audiologist and Hearing Sciences; Audiology/Audiologist and Speech-Language Pathology/Pathologist; Biostatistics; Blood Bank Technology Specialist; Cardiovascular Technology/Technologist; Chiropractic (DC); Clinical Laboratory Science/Medical Technology/Technologist; Clinical/Medical Laboratory Assistant; Clinical/Medical Laboratory Technician; Communication Disorders, General; Cytotechnology/Cytotechnologist; Dance Therapy/Therapist; Dental Assisting/Assistant; Dental Clinical Sciences, General (MS, PhD); Dental Hygiene/Hygienist; Dental Laboratory Technology/Technician; Dental Services and Allied Professions, Other; Dentistry (DDS, DMD); Diagnostic Medical Sonography/Sonographer and Ultrasound Technician; Electrocardiograph Technology/Technician; Electroneurodiagnostic/Electroencephalographic Technology/Technologist; Emergency Medical Technology/Technician (EMT Paramedic); Environmental Health; Epidemiology; Health Occupations Teacher Education; Health/Medical Physics; Health/Medical Preparatory Programs, Other; Hematology Technology/Technician; Hypnotherapy/Hypnotherapist; Massage Therapy/Therapeutic Massage; Medical Radiologic Technology/Science—Radiation Therapist; Music Therapy/Therapist; Nuclear Medical Technology/Technologist; Occupational Health and Industrial Hygiene; Occupational Therapist Assistant; Occupational Therapy/Therapist; Orthotist/Prosthetist; Perfusion Technology/Perfusionist; Pharmacy (PharmD [USA] PharmD, BS/BPharm [Canada]); Pharmacy Administration and Pharmacy Policy and Regulatory Affairs (MS, PhD); Pharmacy Technician/Assistant; Pharmacy, Pharmaceutical Sciences, and Administration, Other; Physical Therapist Assistant; Physical Therapy/Therapist; Physician Assistant; Pre-Dentistry Studies; Pre-Medicine/Pre-Medical Studies; Pre-Nursing Studies; others.

Related DOT Jobs—090.227-010 Faculty Member, College or University.

25-1072.00 Nursing Instructors and Teachers, Postsecondary

- Education/Training Required: Master's degree
- Employed: No data available.
- Annual Earnings: $49,470
- Growth: 23.5%
- Annual Job Openings: 184,000

Demonstrate and teach patient care in classroom and clinical units to nursing students. Includes both teachers primarily engaged in teaching and those who do a combination of both teaching and research.

Evaluate and grade students' class work, laboratory and clinic work, assignments, and papers. Prepare and deliver lectures to undergraduate and/or graduate students on topics such as pharmacology, mental health nursing, and community health care practices. Advise students on academic and vocational curricula and on career issues. Compile, administer, and grade examinations or assign this work to others. Compile bibliographies of specialized materials for outside reading assignments. Demonstrate patient care in clinical units of hospitals. Initiate, facilitate, and moderate classroom discussions. Keep abreast of developments in their field by reading current literature, talking with colleagues, and participating in professional conferences. Maintain regularly scheduled office hours in order to advise and assist students. Maintain student attendance records, grades, and other required records. Plan, evaluate, and revise curricula, course content, and course materials and methods of instruction. Prepare course materials such as syllabi, homework assignments, and handouts. Select and obtain materials and supplies, such as textbooks and laboratory equipment. Supervise students' laboratory and clinical work. Supervise undergraduate and/or graduate teaching, internship, and research work. Act as advisers to student organizations. Assess clinical education needs and patient and client teaching needs, utilizing a variety of methods. Collaborate with colleagues to address teaching and research issues. Conduct research in a particular field of knowledge and publish findings in professional journals, books, and/or electronic media. Coordinate training programs with area universities, clinics, hospitals, health agencies, and/or vocational schools. Participate in campus and community events. Participate in student recruitment, registration, and placement activities. Perform administrative duties such as serving as department head. Provide professional consulting services to government and/or industry. Serve on academic or administrative committees that deal with institutional policies, departmental matters, and academic issues. Write grant proposals to procure external research funding.

GOE INFORMATION—Interest Area: 12. Education and Social Service. **Work Group:** 12.03. Educational Services. **Personality Type—**Social. Social occupations frequently involve working with, communicating with, and teaching people. These occupations often involve helping or providing service to others. **Work Values—**Authority; Social Service; Achievement; Social Status; Ability Utilization. **Skills—**Learning Strategies; Instructing; Management of Personnel Resources; Science; Reading Comprehension; Speaking; Service Orientation; Systems Analysis. **Abilities—***Cognitive:* Oral Expression; Written Expression; Deductive Reasoning; Written Comprehension; Fluency of Ideas. *Psychomotor:* Arm-Hand Steadiness; Reaction Time; Manual Dexterity; Response Orientation; Control Precision. *Physical:* Static Strength; Stamina; Extent Flexibility; Gross Body Equilibrium; Trunk Strength. *Sensory:* Speech Clarity; Visual Color Discrimination; Speech Recognition; Sound Localization; Near Vision. **General Work Activities—***Information Input:* Getting Information; Monitoring Processes, Materials, or Surroundings; Identifying Objects, Actions, and Events. *Mental Process:* Updating and Using Relevant Knowledge; Organizing, Planning, and Prioritizing; Judging Qualities of Things, Services, or Other People's Work. *Work Output:* Documenting or Recording Information; Performing General Physical Activities; Handling and Moving Objects. *Interacting with Others:* Teaching Others; Communicating with Other Workers; Coaching and Developing Others. **Physical Work Conditions—**Disease or Infections; Common Protective or Safety Attire; Indoors; Walking or Running; Specialized Protective or Safety Attire. **Other Job Characteristics—**Importance of Being Exact or Accurate; Consequence of Error; Degree of Automation.

Experience—Job Zone 5. Extensive skill, knowledge, and experience are needed for these occupations. **Job Preparation:** SVP 8.0 and above—four years to more than 10 years. **Knowledge—**Education and Training; Medicine and Dentistry; Biology; Psychology; Therapy and Counseling.

Instructional Programs—Adult Health Nurse/Nursing; Clinical Nurse Specialist; Family Practice Nurse/Nurse Practitioner; Maternal/Child Health and Neonatal Nurse/Nursing; Nurse Anesthetist; Nurse Midwife/Nursing Midwifery; Nursing—Registered Nurse Training (RN, ASN, BSN, MSN); Nursing Science (MS, PhD); Nursing, Other; Pediatric Nurse/Nursing; Perioperative/Operating Room and Surgical Nurse/Nursing; Pre-Nursing Studies; Psychiatric/Mental Health Nurse/Nursing; Public Health/Community Nurse/Nursing.

Related DOT Jobs—075.124-018 Nurse, Instructor.

25-1081.00 Education Teachers, Postsecondary

- **Education/Training Required: Master's degree**
- **Employed: No data available.**
- **Annual Earnings: $47,060**
- **Growth: 23.5%**
- **Annual Job Openings: 184,000**

Teach courses pertaining to education, such as counseling, curriculum, guidance, instruction, teacher education, and teaching English as a second language.

Evaluate and grade students' class work, assignments, and papers. Prepare and deliver lectures to undergraduate and/or graduate students on topics such as children's literature, learning and development, and reading instruction. Advise students on academic and vocational curricula and on career issues. Compile, administer, and grade examinations or assign this work to others. Compile bibliographies of specialized materials for outside reading assignments. Initiate, facilitate, and moderate classroom discussions. Keep abreast of developments in their field by reading current literature, talking with colleagues, and participating in professional conferences. Maintain regularly scheduled office hours in order to advise and assist students. Maintain student attendance records, grades, and other required records. Plan, evaluate, and revise curricula, course content, and course materials and methods of instruction. Prepare course materials such as syllabi, homework assignments, and handouts. Select and obtain materials and supplies, such as textbooks. Supervise students' fieldwork, internship, and research work. Act as advisers to student organizations. Collaborate with colleagues to address teaching and research issues. Conduct research in a particular field of knowledge and publish findings in professional journals, books, and/or electronic media. Participate in campus and community events. Participate in student recruitment, registration, and placement activities. Perform administrative duties such as serving as department head. Provide professional consulting services to government and/or industry. Serve on academic or administrative committees that deal with institutional policies, departmental matters, and academic issues. Write grant proposals to procure external research funding. Advise and instruct teachers employed in school systems by providing activities such as in-service seminars.

GOE INFORMATION—Interest Area: 12. Education and Social Service. **Work Group:** 12.03. Educational Services. **Note:** The Department of Labor has not collected some data for this job, so it has fewer details than the other descriptions.

Instructional Programs—Agricultural Teacher Education; Art Teacher Education; Biology Teacher Education; Business Teacher Education; Chemistry Teacher Education; Computer Teacher Education; Drama and Dance Teacher Education; Driver and Safety Teacher Education; Education, General; English/Language Arts Teacher Education; Family and Consumer Sciences/Home Economics Teacher Education; Foreign Language Teacher Education; French Language Teacher Education; Geography Teacher Education; German Language Teacher Education; Health Occupations Teacher Education; Health Teacher Education; History Teacher Education; Mathematics Teacher Education; Music Teacher Education; Physical Education Teaching and Coaching; Physics Teacher Education; Reading Teacher Education; Sales and Marketing Operations/Marketing and Distribution Teacher Education; Science Teacher Education/General Science Teacher Education; Social Science Teacher Education; Social Studies Teacher Education; Spanish Language Teacher Education; Speech Teacher Education; Teacher Education and Professional Development, Specific Subject Areas, Other; Technical Teacher Education; Technology Teacher Education/Industrial Arts Teacher Education; Trade and Industrial Teacher Education.

Related DOT Jobs—090.227-010 Faculty Member, College or University.

25-1082.00 Library Science Teachers, Postsecondary

- Education/Training Required: Master's degree
- Employed: No data available.
- Annual Earnings: $51,050
- Growth: 23.5%
- Annual Job Openings: 184,000

Teach courses in library science.

Evaluate and grade students' class work, assignments, and papers. Prepare and deliver lectures to undergraduate and/or graduate students on topics such as collection development, archival methods, and indexing and abstracting. Advise students on academic and vocational curricula and on career issues. Compile, administer, and grade examinations or assign this work to others. Compile bibliographies of specialized materials for outside reading assignments. Initiate, facilitate, and moderate classroom discussions. Keep abreast of developments in their field by reading current literature, talking with colleagues, and participating in professional conferences. Maintain regularly scheduled office hours in order to advise and assist students. Maintain student attendance records, grades, and other required records. Plan, evaluate, and revise curricula, course content, and course materials and methods of instruction. Prepare course materials such as syllabi, homework assignments, and handouts. Select and obtain materials and supplies, such as textbooks. Supervise undergraduate and/or graduate teaching, internship, and research work. Act as advisers to student organizations. Collaborate with colleagues to address teaching and research issues. Conduct research in a particular field of knowledge and publish findings in professional journals, books, and/or electronic media. Participate in campus and community events. Participate in student recruitment, registration, and placement activities. Perform administrative duties such as serving as department head. Provide professional consulting services to government and/or industry. Serve on academic or administrative committees that deal with institutional policies, departmental matters, and academic issues. Write grant proposals to procure external research funding.

GOE INFORMATION—Interest Area: 12. Education and Social Service. Work Group: 12.03. Educational Services. Note: The Department of Labor has not collected some data for this job, so it has fewer details than the other descriptions.

Instructional Programs—Library Science/Librarianship; Teacher Education and Professional Development, Specific Subject Areas, Other.

Related DOT Jobs—090.227-010 Faculty Member, College or University.

25-1111.00 Criminal Justice and Law Enforcement Teachers, Postsecondary

- Education/Training Required: Master's degree
- Employed: No data available.
- Annual Earnings: $43,770
- Growth: 23.5%
- Annual Job Openings: 184,000

Teach courses in criminal justice, corrections, and law enforcement administration.

Evaluate and grade students' class work, assignments, and papers. Prepare and deliver lectures to undergraduate and/or graduate students on topics such as criminal law, defensive policing, and investigation techniques. Advise students on academic and vocational curricula and on career issues. Compile, administer, and grade examinations or assign this work to others. Compile bibliographies of specialized materials for outside reading assignments. Initiate, facilitate, and moderate classroom discussions. Keep abreast of developments in their field by reading current literature, talking with colleagues, and participating in professional conferences. Maintain regularly scheduled office hours in order to advise and assist students. Maintain student attendance records, grades, and other required records. Plan, evaluate, and revise curricula, course content, and course materials and methods of instruction. Prepare course materials such as syllabi, homework assignments, and handouts. Select and obtain materials and supplies, such as textbooks. Supervise undergraduate and/or graduate teaching, internship, and research work. Act as advisers to student organizations. Collaborate with colleagues to address teaching and research issues. Conduct research in a particular field of knowledge and publish findings in professional journals, books, and/or electronic media. Participate in campus and community events. Participate in student recruitment, registration, and placement activities. Perform administrative duties such as serving as department head. Provide professional consulting services to government and/or industry. Serve on academic or administrative committees that deal with institutional policies, departmental matters, and academic issues. Write grant proposals to procure external research funding.

GOE INFORMATION—Interest Area: 12. Education and Social Service. Work Group: 12.03. Educational Services. Note: The Department of Labor has not collected some data for this job, so it has fewer details than the other descriptions.

Instructional Programs—Corrections; Corrections Administration; Corrections and Criminal Justice, Other; Criminal Justice/Law Enforcement Administration; Criminal Justice/Police Science; Criminal Justice/Safety Studies; Criminalistics and Criminal Science; Forensic Science and Technology; Juvenile Corrections; Security and Loss Prevention Services; Teacher Education and Professional Development, Specific Subject Areas, Other.

Related DOT Jobs—090.227-010 Faculty Member, College or University.

25-1112.00 Law Teachers, Postsecondary

- Education/Training Required: First professional degree
- Employed: No data available.
- Annual Earnings: $77,920
- Growth: 23.5%
- Annual Job Openings: 184,000

Teach courses in law.

Evaluate and grade students' class work, assignments, papers, and oral presentations. Prepare and deliver lectures to undergraduate and/or graduate students on topics such as civil procedure, contracts, and torts. Advise students on academic and vocational curricula and on career issues. Assign cases for students to hear and try. Compile, administer, and grade examinations or assign this work to others. Compile bibliographies of specialized materials for outside reading assignments. Initiate, facilitate, and moderate classroom discussions. Keep abreast of developments in their field by reading current literature, talking with colleagues, and participating in professional conferences. Maintain regularly scheduled office hours in order to advise and assist students. Maintain student attendance records, grades, and other required records. Plan, evaluate, and revise curricula, course content, and course materials and methods of instruction. Prepare course materials such as syllabi, homework assignments, and handouts. Select and obtain materials and supplies, such as textbooks. Supervise undergraduate and/or graduate teaching, internship, and research work. Act as advisers to student organizations. Collaborate with colleagues to address teaching and research issues. Conduct research in a particular field of knowledge and publish findings in professional journals, books, and/or electronic media. Participate in campus and community events. Participate in student recruitment, registration, and placement activities. Perform administrative duties such as serving as department head. Provide professional consulting services to government and/or industry. Serve on academic or administrative committees that deal with institutional policies, departmental matters, and academic issues. Write grant proposals to procure external research funding.

GOE INFORMATION—Interest Area: 12. Education and Social Service. **Work Group:** 12.03. Educational Services. **Note:** The Department of Labor has not collected some data for this job, so it has fewer details than the other descriptions.

Instructional Programs—Law (LL.B., J.D.); Legal Studies, General.

Related DOT Jobs—090.227-010 Faculty Member, College or University.

25-1113.00 Social Work Teachers, Postsecondary

- **Education/Training Required: Master's degree**
- **Employed: No data available.**
- **Annual Earnings: $50,250**
- **Growth: 23.5%**
- **Annual Job Openings: 184,000**

Teach courses in social work.

Evaluate and grade students' class work, assignments, and papers. Prepare and deliver lectures to undergraduate and/or graduate students on topics such as family behavior, child and adolescent mental health, and social intervention evaluation. Advise students on academic and vocational curricula and on career issues. Compile, administer, and grade examinations or assign this work to others. Compile bibliographies of specialized materials for outside reading assignments. Initiate, facilitate, and moderate classroom discussions. Keep abreast of developments in their field by reading current literature, talking with colleagues, and participating in professional conferences. Maintain regularly scheduled office hours in order to advise and assist students. Maintain student attendance records, grades, and other required records. Plan, evaluate, and revise curricula, course content, and course materials and methods of instruction. Prepare course materials such as syllabi, homework assignments, and handouts. Select and obtain materials and supplies, such as textbooks and laboratory equipment. Supervise students' laboratory work and fieldwork. Supervise undergraduate and/or graduate

teaching, internship, and research work. Act as advisers to student organizations. Collaborate with colleagues and with community agencies in order to address teaching and research issues. Conduct research in a particular field of knowledge and publish findings in professional journals, books, and/or electronic media. Participate in campus and community events. Participate in student recruitment, registration, and placement activities. Perform administrative duties such as serving as department head. Provide professional consulting services to government and/or industry. Serve on academic or administrative committees that deal with institutional policies, departmental matters, and academic issues. Write grant proposals to procure external research funding.

GOE INFORMATION—Interest Area: 12. Education and Social Service. **Work Group:** 12.03. Educational Services. **Note:** The Department of Labor has not collected some data for this job, so it has fewer details than the other descriptions.

Instructional Programs—Clinical/Medical Social Work; Social Work; Teacher Education and Professional Development, Specific Subject Areas, Other.

Related DOT Jobs—090.227-010 Faculty Member, College or University.

25-1121.00 Art, Drama, and Music Teachers, Postsecondary

- **Education/Training Required: Master's degree**
- **Employed: No data available.**
- **Annual Earnings: $47,080**
- **Growth: 23.5%**
- **Annual Job Openings: 184,000**

Teach courses in drama, music, and the arts, including fine and applied art, such as painting and sculpture, or design and crafts.

Evaluate and grade students' class work, performances, projects, assignments, and papers. Prepare and deliver lectures to undergraduate and/or graduate students on topics such as acting techniques, fundamentals of music, and art history. Advise students on academic and vocational curricula and on career issues. Compile, administer, and grade examinations or assign this work to others. Compile bibliographies of specialized materials for outside reading assignments. Explain and demonstrate artistic techniques. Initiate, facilitate, and moderate classroom discussions. Keep abreast of developments in their field by reading current literature, talking with colleagues, and participating in professional conferences. Maintain regularly scheduled office hours in order to advise and assist students. Maintain student attendance records, grades, and other required records. Plan, evaluate, and revise curricula, course content, and course materials and methods of instruction. Prepare course materials such as syllabi, homework assignments, and handouts. Prepare students for performances, exams, or assessments. Select and obtain materials and supplies, such as textbooks and performance pieces. Supervise undergraduate and/or graduate teaching, internship, and research work. Act as advisers to student organizations. Collaborate with colleagues to address teaching and research issues. Conduct research in a particular field of knowledge and publish findings in professional journals, books, and/or electronic media. Display students' work in schools, galleries, and exhibitions. Keep students informed of community events such as plays and concerts. Organize performance groups and direct their rehearsals. Participate in campus and community events. Participate in student recruitment, registration, and placement activities. Perform administrative duties such as serving as department head. Provide professional consulting services to government and/or industry. Serve on academic or administrative committees that deal with institutional policies, departmental matters, and academic issues. Write grant proposals to procure external research funding.

GOE INFORMATION—**Interest Area:** 12. Education and Social Service. **Work Group:** 12.03. Educational Services. **Personality Type**—Artistic. Artistic occupations frequently involve working with forms, designs, and patterns. They often require self-expression, and the work can be done without following a clear set of rules. **Work Values**—Authority; Social Service; Creativity; Ability Utilization; Achievement. **Skills**—Instructing; Learning Strategies; Speaking; Writing; Complex Problem Solving; Reading Comprehension; Critical Thinking; Time Management. **Abilities**—*Cognitive:* Written Expression; Oral Expression; Written Comprehension; Originality; Fluency of Ideas. *Psychomotor:* Wrist-Finger Speed. *Physical:* Stamina. *Sensory:* Visual Color Discrimination; Speech Clarity; Hearing Sensitivity; Far Vision; Near Vision. **General Work Activities**—*Information Input:* Getting Information; Monitoring Processes, Materials, or Surroundings; Identifying Objects, Actions, and Events. *Mental Process:* Analyzing Data or Information; Thinking Creatively; Judging Qualities of Things, Services, or Other People's Work. *Work Output:* Handling and Moving Objects; Documenting or Recording Information; Performing General Physical Activities. *Interacting with Others:* Teaching Others; Coaching and Developing Others; Communicating with Other Workers. **Physical Work Conditions**—Indoors; Sitting; Using Hands on Objects, Tools, or Controls; Standing. **Other Job Characteristics**—Importance of Being Exact or Accurate; Consequence of Error; Pace Determined by Speed of Equipment.

Experience—Job Zone 5. Extensive skill, knowledge, and experience are needed for these occupations. **Job Preparation:** SVP 8.0 and above—four years to more than 10 years. **Knowledge**—Fine Arts; Education and Training; English Language; Administration and Management; Therapy and Counseling. **Instructional Programs**—Art History, Criticism, and Conservation; Art/Art Studies, General; Arts Management; Ceramic Arts and Ceramics; Cinematography and Film/Video Production; Commercial Photography; Conducting; Crafts/Craft Design, Folk Art, and Artisanry; Dance, General; Design and Applied Arts, Other; Design and Visual Communications, General; Directing and Theatrical Production; Drama and Dramatics/Theatre Arts, General; Dramatic/Theatre Arts and Stagecraft, Other; Fashion/Apparel Design; Fiber, Textile, and Weaving Arts; Film/Cinema Studies; Film/Video and Photographic Arts, Other; Fine Arts and Art Studies, Other; Fine/Studio Arts, General; Graphic Design; Industrial Design; Interior Design; Intermedia/Multimedia; Jazz/Jazz Studies; Metal and Jewelry Arts; Music History, Literature, and Theory; Music Management and Merchandising; Music Pedagogy; Music Performance, General; Music Theory and Composition; Music, Other; Musicology and Ethnomusicology; Painting; Photography; Piano and Organ; Playwriting and Screenwriting; Printmaking; Sculpture; Technical Theatre/Theatre Design and Technology; Theatre Literature, History, and Criticism; Theatre/Theatre Arts Management; Violin, Viola, Guitar, and Other Stringed Instruments; Visual and Performing Arts, General; Visual and Performing Arts, Other; Voice and Opera.

Related DOT Jobs—090.227-010 Faculty Member, College or University.

25-1122.00 Communications Teachers, Postsecondary

- Education/Training Required: Master's degree
- Employed: No data available.
- Annual Earnings: $47,110
- Growth: 23.5%
- Annual Job Openings: 184,000

Teach courses in communications, such as organizational communications, public relations, radio/television broadcasting, and journalism.

Evaluate and grade students' class work, assignments, and papers. Prepare and deliver lectures to undergraduate and/or graduate students on topics such as public speaking, media criticism, and oral traditions. Advise students on academic and vocational curricula and on career issues. Compile, administer, and grade examinations or assign this work to others. Compile bibliographies of specialized materials for outside reading assignments. Initiate, facilitate, and moderate classroom discussions. Keep abreast of developments in their field by reading current literature, talking with colleagues, and participating in professional conferences. Maintain regularly scheduled office hours in order to advise and assist students. Maintain student attendance records, grades, and other required records. Plan, evaluate, and revise curricula, course content, and course materials and methods of instruction. Prepare course materials such as syllabi, homework assignments, and handouts. Select and obtain materials and supplies, such as textbooks. Supervise undergraduate and/or graduate teaching, internship, and research work. Act as advisers to student organizations. Collaborate with colleagues to address teaching and research issues. Conduct research in a particular field of knowledge and publish findings in professional journals, books, and/or electronic media. Participate in campus and community events. Participate in student recruitment, registration, and placement activities. Perform administrative duties such as serving as department head. Provide professional consulting services to government and/or industry. Serve on academic or administrative committees that deal with institutional policies, departmental matters, and academic issues. Write grant proposals to procure external research funding.

GOE INFORMATION—**Interest Area:** 12. Education and Social Service. **Work Group:** 12.03. Educational Services. **Note:** The Department of Labor has not collected some data for this job, so it has fewer details than the other descriptions.

Instructional Programs—Advertising; Broadcast Journalism; Communication Studies/Speech Communication and Rhetoric; Communication, Journalism, and Related Programs, Other; Digital Communication and Media/Multimedia; Health Communication; Journalism; Journalism, Other; Mass Communication/Media Studies; Political Communication; Public Relations/Image Management; Radio and Television.

Related DOT Jobs—090.227-010 Faculty Member, College or University.

25-1123.00 English Language and Literature Teachers, Postsecondary

- Education/Training Required: Master's degree
- Employed: No data available.
- Annual Earnings: $45,590
- Growth: 23.5%
- Annual Job Openings: 184,000

Teach courses in English language and literature, including linguistics and comparative literature.

Evaluate and grade students' class work, assignments, and papers. Prepare and deliver lectures to undergraduate and/or graduate students on topics such as poetry, novel structure, and translation and adaptation. Advise students on academic and vocational curricula and on career issues. Compile, administer, and grade examinations or assign this work to others. Compile bibliographies of specialized materials for outside reading assignments. Initiate, facilitate, and moderate classroom discussions. Keep abreast of developments in their field by reading current literature, talking with colleagues, and participating in professional conferences. Maintain regularly scheduled office hours in order to advise and assist students. Maintain student attendance records, grades, and other required records.

Plan, evaluate, and revise curricula, course content, and course materials and methods of instruction. Prepare course materials such as syllabi, homework assignments, and handouts. Select and obtain materials and supplies, such as textbooks. Supervise undergraduate and/or graduate teaching, internship, and research work. Provide assistance to students in college writing centers. Act as advisers to student organizations. Collaborate with colleagues to address teaching and research issues. Conduct research in a particular field of knowledge and publish findings in professional journals, books, and/or electronic media. Participate in campus and community events. Participate in student recruitment, registration, and placement activities. Perform administrative duties such as serving as department head. Provide professional consulting services to government and/or industry. Recruit, train, and supervise student writing instructors. Serve on academic or administrative committees that deal with institutional policies, departmental matters, and academic issues. Write grant proposals to procure external research funding.

GOE INFORMATION—Interest Area: 12. Education and Social Service. **Work Group:** 12.03. Educational Services. **Personality Type—**Artistic. Artistic occupations frequently involve working with forms, designs, and patterns. They often require self-expression, and the work can be done without following a clear set of rules. **Work Values—**Authority; Social Service; Creativity; Achievement; Ability Utilization. **Skills—**Instructing; Speaking; Learning Strategies; Reading Comprehension; Writing; Critical Thinking; Complex Problem Solving; Active Listening. **Abilities—***Cognitive:* Written Expression; Oral Expression; Written Comprehension; Oral Comprehension; Fluency of Ideas. *Psychomotor:* None met the criteria. *Physical:* None met the criteria. *Sensory:* Speech Clarity; Speech Recognition; Sound Localization. **General Work Activities—***Information Input:* Getting Information; Monitoring Processes, Materials, or Surroundings; Identifying Objects, Actions, and Events. *Mental Process:* Analyzing Data or Information; Processing Information; Updating and Using Relevant Knowledge. *Work Output:* Documenting or Recording Information; Interacting with Computers; Handling and Moving Objects. *Interacting with Others:* Teaching Others; Communicating with Other Workers; Communicating with Persons Outside Organization. **Physical Work Conditions—**Indoors; Sitting. **Other Job Characteristics—**Importance of Being Exact or Accurate; Consequence of Error; Pace Determined by Speed of Equipment.

Experience—Job Zone 5. Extensive skill, knowledge, and experience are needed for these occupations. **Job Preparation:** SVP 8.0 and above—four years to more than 10 years. **Knowledge—**Foreign Language; Education and Training; English Language; Communications and Media; Therapy and Counseling. **Instructional Programs—**American Literature (Canadian); American Literature (United States); Comparative Literature; Creative Writing; English Composition; English Language and Literature, General; English Language and Literature/Letters, Other; English Literature (British and Commonwealth); Technical and Business Writing.

Related DOT Jobs—090.227-010 Faculty Member, College or University.

25-1124.00 Foreign Language and Literature Teachers, Postsecondary

- **Education/Training Required: Master's degree**
- **Employed: No data available.**
- **Annual Earnings: $45,030**
- **Growth: 23.5%**
- **Annual Job Openings: 184,000**

Teach courses in foreign (i.e., other than English) languages and literature.

Evaluate and grade students' class work, assignments, and papers. Prepare and deliver lectures to undergraduate and/or graduate students on topics such as how to speak and write a foreign language and the cultural aspects of areas where a particular language is used. Advise students on academic and vocational curricula and on career issues. Compile, administer, and grade examinations or assign this work to others. Compile bibliographies of specialized materials for outside reading assignments. Initiate, facilitate, and moderate classroom discussions. Keep abreast of developments in their field by reading current literature, talking with colleagues, and participating in professional organizations and activities. Maintain regularly scheduled office hours in order to advise and assist students. Maintain student attendance records, grades, and other required records. Plan, evaluate, and revise curricula, course content, and course materials and methods of instruction. Prepare course materials such as syllabi, homework assignments, and handouts. Select and obtain materials and supplies, such as textbooks. Supervise undergraduate and/or graduate teaching, internship, and research work. Act as advisers to student organizations. Collaborate with colleagues to address teaching and research issues. Conduct research in a particular field of knowledge and publish findings in scholarly journals, books, and/or electronic media. Participate in campus and community events. Participate in student recruitment, registration, and placement activities. Perform administrative duties such as serving as department head. Provide professional consulting services to government and/or industry. Serve on academic or administrative committees that deal with institutional policies, departmental matters, and academic issues. Write grant proposals to procure external research funding.

GOE INFORMATION—Interest Area: 12. Education and Social Service. **Work Group:** 12.03. Educational Services. **Personality Type—**Artistic. Artistic occupations frequently involve working with forms, designs, and patterns. They often require self-expression, and the work can be done without following a clear set of rules. **Work Values—**Authority; Social Service; Creativity; Achievement; Ability Utilization. **Skills—**Instructing; Speaking; Learning Strategies; Reading Comprehension; Writing; Critical Thinking; Complex Problem Solving; Active Listening. **Abilities—***Cognitive:* Written Expression; Oral Expression; Written Comprehension; Oral Comprehension; Fluency of Ideas. *Psychomotor:* None met the criteria. *Physical:* None met the criteria. *Sensory:* Speech Clarity; Speech Recognition; Sound Localization. **General Work Activities—***Information Input:* Getting Information; Monitoring Processes, Materials, or Surroundings; Identifying Objects, Actions, and Events. *Mental Process:* Analyzing Data or Information; Processing Information; Updating and Using Relevant Knowledge. *Work Output:* Documenting or Recording Information; Interacting with Computers; Handling and Moving Objects. *Interacting with Others:* Teaching Others; Communicating with Other Workers; Communicating with Persons Outside Organization. **Physical Work Conditions—**Indoors; Sitting. **Other Job Characteristics—**Importance of Being Exact or Accurate; Consequence of Error; Pace Determined by Speed of Equipment.

Experience—Job Zone 5. Extensive skill, knowledge, and experience are needed for these occupations. **Job Preparation:** SVP 8.0 and above—four years to more than 10 years. **Knowledge—**Foreign Language; Education and Training; English Language; Communications and Media; Therapy and Counseling. **Instructional Programs—**African Languages, Literatures, and Linguistics; Albanian Language and Literature; American Indian/Native American Languages, Literatures, and Linguistics; Ancient Near Eastern and Biblical Languages, Literatures, and Linguistics; Ancient/Classical Greek Language and Literature; Arabic Language and Literature; Australian/Oceanic/Pacific Languages, Literatures, and Linguistics; Bahasa Indonesian/Bahasa Malay Languages and Literatures; Baltic Languages, Literatures, and Linguistics; Bengali Language and Literature; Bulgarian Language and Literature; Burmese Language and

Literature; Catalan Language and Literature; Celtic Languages, Literatures, and Linguistics; Chinese Language and Literature; Classics and Classical Languages, Literatures, and Linguistics, General; Classics and Classical Languages, Literatures, and Linguistics, Other; Czech Language and Literature; Danish Language and Literature; Dutch/Flemish Language and Literature; East Asian Languages, Literatures, and Linguistics, General; East Asian Languages, Literatures, and Linguistics, Other; Filipino/Tagalog Language and Literature; Finnish and Related Languages, Literatures, and Linguistics; Foreign Languages and Literatures, General; Foreign Languages, Literatures, and Linguistics, Other; French Language and Literature; German Language and Literature; Germanic Languages, Literatures, and Linguistics, General; Germanic Languages, Literatures, and Linguistics, Other; Hebrew Language and Literature; Hindi Language and Literature; Hungarian/Magyar Language and Literature; Iranian/Persian Languages, Literatures, and Linguistics; Italian Language and Literature; Japanese Language and Literature; Khmer/Cambodian Language and Literature; Korean Language and Literature; Language Interpretation and Translation; Lao/Laotian Language and Literature; Latin Language and Literature; Latin Teacher Education; Linguistics; Middle/Near Eastern and Semitic Languages, Literatures, and Linguistics, Other; others.

Related DOT Jobs—090.227-010 Faculty Member, College or University.

25-1125.00 *History Teachers, Postsecondary*

- **Education/Training Required: Master's degree**
- **Employed: No data available.**
- **Annual Earnings: $50,400**
- **Growth: 23.5%**
- **Annual Job Openings: 184,000**

Teach courses in human history and historiography.

Evaluate and grade students' class work, assignments, and papers. Prepare and deliver lectures to undergraduate and/or graduate students on topics such as ancient history, postwar civilizations, and the history of third-world countries. Advise students on academic and vocational curricula and on career issues. Compile, administer, and grade examinations or assign this work to others. Compile bibliographies of specialized materials for outside reading assignments. Initiate, facilitate, and moderate classroom discussions. Keep abreast of developments in their field by reading current literature, talking with colleagues, and participating in professional conferences. Maintain regularly scheduled office hours in order to advise and assist students. Maintain student attendance records, grades, and other required records. Plan, evaluate, and revise curricula, course content, and course materials and methods of instruction. Prepare course materials such as syllabi, homework assignments, and handouts. Select and obtain materials and supplies, such as textbooks. Supervise undergraduate and/or graduate teaching, internship, and research work. Act as advisers to student organizations. Collaborate with colleagues to address teaching and research issues. Conduct research in a particular field of knowledge and publish findings in professional journals, books, and/or electronic media. Participate in campus and community events. Participate in student recruitment, registration, and placement activities. Perform administrative duties such as serving as department head. Provide professional consulting services to government, educational institutions, and/or industry. Serve on academic or administrative committees that deal with institutional policies, departmental matters, and academic issues. Write grant proposals to procure external research funding.

GOE INFORMATION—Interest Area: 12. Education and Social Service. **Work Group:** 12.03. Educational Services. **Personality Type**—Social. Social occupations frequently involve working with, communicating with, and teaching people. These occupations often involve helping or providing service to others. **Work Values**—Authority; Social Service; Creativity; Achievement; Social Status. **Skills**—Instructing; Speaking; Reading Comprehension; Learning Strategies; Complex Problem Solving; Writing; Critical Thinking; Active Listening. **Abilities**—*Cognitive:* Written Expression; Oral Expression; Oral Comprehension; Written Comprehension; Mathematical Reasoning. *Psychomotor:* None met the criteria. *Physical:* None met the criteria. *Sensory:* Speech Clarity; Speech Recognition; Far Vision. **General Work Activities**—*Information Input:* Getting Information; Identifying Objects, Actions, and Events; Monitoring Processes, Materials, or Surroundings. *Mental Process:* Analyzing Data or Information; Processing Information; Organizing, Planning, and Prioritizing. *Work Output:* Documenting or Recording Information; Interacting with Computers; Handling and Moving Objects. *Interacting with Others:* Teaching Others; Coaching and Developing Others; Communicating with Other Workers. **Physical Work Conditions**—Indoors; Sitting; Standing. **Other Job Characteristics**—Consequence of Error; Importance of Being Exact or Accurate; Pace Determined by Speed of Equipment.

Experience—Job Zone 5. Extensive skill, knowledge, and experience are needed for these occupations. **Job Preparation:** SVP 8.0 and above—four years to more than 10 years. **Knowledge**—History and Archeology; Sociology and Anthropology; Education and Training; Psychology; Economics and Accounting. **Instructional Programs**—American History (United States); Asian History; Canadian History; European History; History and Philosophy of Science and Technology; History, General; History, Other; Public/Applied History and Archival Administration.

Related DOT Jobs—090.227-010 Faculty Member, College or University.

25-1126.00 *Philosophy and Religion Teachers, Postsecondary*

- **Education/Training Required: Master's degree**
- **Employed: No data available.**
- **Annual Earnings: $47,740**
- **Growth: 23.5%**
- **Annual Job Openings: 184,000**

Teach courses in philosophy, religion, and theology.

Evaluate and grade students' class work, assignments, and papers. Prepare and deliver lectures to undergraduate and/or graduate students on topics such as ethics, logic, and contemporary religious thought. Advise students on academic and vocational curricula and on career issues. Compile, administer, and grade examinations or assign this work to others. Compile bibliographies of specialized materials for outside reading assignments. Initiate, facilitate, and moderate classroom discussions. Keep abreast of developments in their field by reading current literature, talking with colleagues, and participating in professional conferences. Maintain regularly scheduled office hours in order to advise and assist students. Maintain student attendance records, grades, and other required records. Plan, evaluate, and revise curricula, course content, and course materials and methods of instruction. Prepare course materials such as syllabi, homework assignments, and handouts. Select and obtain materials and supplies, such as textbooks. Supervise undergraduate and/or graduate teaching, internship, and research work. Act as advisers to student organizations. Collaborate with colleagues to address teaching and research issues. Conduct research in a particular field of knowledge and publish findings in professional journals, books, and/or electronic media. Participate in campus and community events. Participate in student recruitment, registration, and placement activities. Perform administrative duties such as serving as department head. Provide professional consulting services to government and/or industry. Serve on academic or administrative committees that deal with institutional policies, departmental matters, and academic issues. Write grant proposals to procure external research funding.

GOE INFORMATION—Interest Area: 12. Education and Social Service. Work Group: 12.03. Educational Services. Note: The Department of Labor has not collected some data for this job, so it has fewer details than the other descriptions.

Instructional Programs—Bible/Biblical Studies; Buddhist Studies; Christian Studies; Divinity/Ministry (BD, MDiv.); Ethics; Hindu Studies; Missions/Missionary Studies and Missiology; Pastoral Counseling and Specialized Ministries, Other; Pastoral Studies/Counseling; Philosophy; Philosophy and Religious Studies, Other; Philosophy, Other; Pre-Theology/Pre-Ministerial Studies; Rabbinical Studies; Religion/Religious Studies; Religious Education; Religious/Sacred Music; Talmudic Studies; Theological and Ministerial Studies, Other; Theology and Religious Vocations, Other; Theology/Theological Studies.

Related DOT Jobs—090.227-010 Faculty Member, College or University.

25-1191.00 Graduate Teaching Assistants

- Education/Training Required: Master's degree
- Employed: No data available.
- Annual Earnings: $22,150
- Growth: 23.5%
- Annual Job Openings: 184,000

Assist department chairperson, faculty members, or other professional staff members in college or university by performing teaching or teaching-related duties, such as teaching lower-level courses, developing teaching materials, preparing and giving examinations, and grading examinations or papers. Graduate assistants must be enrolled in a graduate school program. Graduate assistants who primarily perform non-teaching duties, such as laboratory research, should be reported in the occupational category related to the work performed.

Evaluate and grade examinations, assignments, and papers; record grades. Lead discussion sections, tutorials, and laboratory sections. Teach undergraduate level courses. Develop teaching materials such as syllabi, visual aids, answer keys, supplementary notes, and course Web sites. Attend lectures given by the instructor whom they are assisting. Complete laboratory projects prior to assigning them to students so that any needed modifications can be made. Copy and distribute classroom materials. Demonstrate use of laboratory equipment and enforce laboratory rules. Inform students of the procedures for completing and submitting class work such as lab reports. Meet with supervisors to discuss students' grades and to complete required grade-related paperwork. Notify instructors of errors or problems with assignments. Order or obtain materials needed for classes. Prepare and proctor examinations. Return assignments to students in accordance with established deadlines. Schedule and maintain regular office hours to meet with students. Arrange for supervisors to conduct teaching observations; meet with supervisors to receive feedback about teaching performance. Assist faculty members or staff with student conferences. Provide assistance to faculty members or staff with laboratory or field research. Provide instructors with assistance in the use of audiovisual equipment. Provide assistance to library staff in maintaining library collections.

GOE INFORMATION—Interest Area: 12. Education and Social Service. Work Group: 12.03. Educational Services. Personality Type—Social. Social occupations frequently involve working with, communicating

with, and teaching people. These occupations often involve helping or providing service to others. Work Values—Social Service; Authority; Pleasant Co-workers; Good Working Conditions; Creativity. Skills—Instructing; Speaking; Learning Strategies; Reading Comprehension; Writing; Mathematics; Critical Thinking; Complex Problem Solving. Abilities—Cognitive: Oral Expression; Oral Comprehension; Written Comprehension; Written Expression; Fluency of Ideas. Psychomotor: None met the criteria. Physical: None met the criteria. Sensory: Speech Clarity; Speech Recognition. General Work Activities—Information Input: Getting Information; Identifying Objects, Actions, and Events; Monitoring Processes, Materials, or Surroundings. Mental Process: Updating and Using Relevant Knowledge; Analyzing Data or Information; Organizing, Planning, and Prioritizing. Work Output: Documenting or Recording Information; Handling and Moving Objects; Interacting with Computers. Interacting with Others: Teaching Others; Communicating with Other Workers; Communicating with Persons Outside Organization. Physical Work Conditions—Indoors; Standing; Sitting. Other Job Characteristics—Importance of Repeating Same Tasks; Pace Determined by Speed of Equipment; Importance of Being Exact or Accurate.

Experience—Job Zone 5. Extensive skill, knowledge, and experience are needed for these occupations. Job Preparation: SVP 8.0 and above—four years to more than 10 years. Knowledge—Education and Training; English Language; Clerical; Administration and Management; Computers and Electronics. Instructional Programs—No data available.

Related DOT Jobs—090.227-014 Graduate Assistant.

25-1192.00 Home Economics Teachers, Postsecondary

- Education/Training Required: Master's degree
- Employed: No data available.
- Annual Earnings: $48,040
- Growth: 23.5%
- Annual Job Openings: 184,000

Teach courses in child care, family relations, finance, nutrition, and related subjects as pertaining to home management.

Evaluate and grade students' class work, laboratory work, projects, assignments, and papers. Prepare and deliver lectures to undergraduate and/or graduate students on topics such as food science, nutrition, and child care. Advise students on academic and vocational curricula and on career issues. Compile, administer, and grade examinations or assign this work to others. Compile bibliographies of specialized materials for outside reading assignments. Initiate, facilitate, and moderate classroom discussions. Keep abreast of developments in their field by reading current literature, talking with colleagues, and participating in professional conferences. Maintain regularly scheduled office hours in order to advise and assist students. Maintain student attendance records, grades, and other required records. Plan, evaluate, and revise curricula, course content, and course materials and methods of instruction. Prepare course materials such as syllabi, homework assignments, and handouts. Select and obtain materials and supplies, such as textbooks. Supervise undergraduate and/or graduate teaching, internship, and research work. Act as advisers to student organizations. Collaborate with colleagues to address teaching and research issues. Conduct research in a particular field of knowledge and publish findings in professional journals, books, and/or electronic media. Participate in campus and community events. Participate in student recruitment, registration, and placement activities. Perform administrative duties such as serving as department head. Provide professional consulting services to government and/or industry. Serve on academic or administrative committees that deal with institutional policies, departmental matters, and academic issues. Write grant proposals to procure external research funding.

GOE INFORMATION—Interest Area: 12. Education and Social Service. **Work Group:** 12.03. Educational Services. **Note:** The Department of Labor has not collected some data for this job, so it has fewer details than the other descriptions.

Instructional Programs—Business Family and Consumer Sciences/ Human Sciences; Child Care and Support Services Management; Family and Consumer Sciences/Human Sciences, General; Foodservice Systems Administration/Management; Human Development and Family Studies, General.

Related DOT Jobs—090.227-010 Faculty Member, College or University; 096.121-014 Home Economist.

25-1193.00 Recreation and Fitness Studies Teachers, Postsecondary

- **Education/Training Required: Master's degree**
- **Employed: No data available.**
- **Annual Earnings: $42,140**
- **Growth: 23.5%**
- **Annual Job Openings: 184,000**

Teach courses pertaining to recreation, leisure, and fitness studies, including exercise physiology and facilities management.

Evaluate and grade students' class work, assignments, and papers. Prepare and deliver lectures to undergraduate and/or graduate students on topics such as anatomy, therapeutic recreation, and conditioning theory. Advise students on academic and vocational curricula and on career issues. Compile, administer, and grade examinations or assign this work to others. Compile bibliographies of specialized materials for outside reading assignments. Initiate, facilitate, and moderate classroom discussions. Keep abreast of developments in their field by reading current literature, talking with colleagues, and participating in professional conferences. Maintain regularly scheduled office hours in order to advise and assist students. Maintain student attendance records, grades, and other required records. Plan, evaluate, and revise curricula, course content, and course materials and methods of instruction. Prepare course materials such as syllabi, homework assignments, and handouts. Select and obtain materials and supplies, such as textbooks. Supervise undergraduate and/or graduate teaching, internship, and research work. Act as advisers to student organizations. Collaborate with colleagues to address teaching and research issues. Conduct research in a particular field of knowledge and publish findings in professional journals, books, and/or electronic media. Participate in campus and community events. Participate in student recruitment, registration, and placement activities. Perform administrative duties such as serving as department heads. Prepare students to act as sports coaches. Provide professional consulting services to government and/or industry. Serve on academic or administrative committees that deal with institutional policies, departmental matters, and academic issues. Write grant proposals to procure external research funding.

GOE INFORMATION—Interest Area: 12. Education and Social Service. **Work Group:** 12.03. Educational Services. **Note:** The Department of Labor has not collected some data for this job, so it has fewer details than the other descriptions.

Instructional Programs—Health and Physical Education, General; Parks, Recreation, and Leisure Studies; Sport and Fitness Administration/Management.

Related DOT Jobs—090.227-010 Faculty Member, College or University; 099.224-010 Instructor, Physical Education.

25-1194.00 Vocational Education Teachers, Postsecondary

- **Education/Training Required: Work experience in a related occupation**
- **Employed: No data available.**
- **Annual Earnings: $38,540**
- **Growth: 23.5%**
- **Annual Job Openings: 184,000**

Teach or instruct vocational or occupational subjects at the postsecondary level (but at less than the baccalaureate) to students who have graduated or left high school. Includes correspondence school instructors; industrial, commercial, and government training instructors; and adult education teachers and instructors who prepare persons to operate industrial machinery and equipment and transportation and communications equipment. Teaching may take place in public or private schools whose primary business is education or in a school associated with an organization whose primary business is other than education.

Conduct on-the-job training, classes, or training sessions to teach and demonstrate principles, techniques, procedures, and/or methods of designated subjects. Present lectures and conduct discussions to increase students' knowledge and competence, using visual aids such as graphs, charts, videotapes, and slides. Administer oral, written, or performance tests in order to measure progress and to evaluate training effectiveness. Advise students on course selection, career decisions, and other academic and vocational concerns. Determine training needs of students or workers. Develop curricula and plan course content and methods of instruction. Integrate academic and vocational curricula so that students can obtain a variety of skills. Observe and evaluate students' work to determine progress, provide feedback, and make suggestions for improvement. Participate in conferences, seminars, and training sessions to keep abreast of developments in the field and integrate relevant information into training programs. Prepare outlines of instructional programs and training schedules and establish course goals. Provide individualized instruction and tutorial and/or remedial instruction. Select and assemble books, materials, supplies, and equipment for training, courses, or projects. Supervise and monitor students' use of tools and equipment. Supervise independent or group projects, field placements, laboratory work, or other training. Arrange for lectures by experts in designated fields. Develop teaching aids such as instructional software, multimedia visual aids, or study materials. Prepare reports and maintain records such as student grades, attendance rolls, and training activity details. Review enrollment applications and correspond with applicants to obtain additional information. Serve on faculty and school committees concerned with budgeting, curriculum revision, and course and diploma requirements.

GOE INFORMATION—Interest Area: 12. Education and Social Service. **Work Group:** 12.03. Educational Services. **Personality Type**—Social. Social occupations frequently involve working with, communicating with, and teaching people. These occupations often involve helping or providing service to others. **Work Values**—Authority; Social Service; Creativity; Achievement; Responsibility. **Skills**—Instructing; Speaking; Writing; Complex Problem Solving; Service Orientation; Learning Strategies; Active Listening; Equipment Selection. **Abilities**—*Cognitive:* Oral Expression; Originality; Fluency of Ideas; Written Expression; Oral Comprehension. *Psychomotor:* None met the criteria. *Physical:* None met the criteria. *Sensory:* Speech Clarity; Auditory Attention; Sound Localization; Speech Recognition; Near Vision. **General Work Activities**—*Information Input:* Getting Information; Monitoring Processes, Materials, or Surroundings; Identifying Objects, Actions, and Events. *Mental Process:* Thinking Creatively; Updating and Using Relevant Knowledge; Organizing, Planning, and Prioritizing. *Work Output:* Handling and Moving Objects; Interacting with Computers; Documenting or Recording Information. *Interacting with Others:* Teaching Others; Communicating with Persons Outside Organization; Assisting and Caring for Others. **Physical Work Conditions**—Walking or Running; Indoors; Standing; Making Repetitive Motions. **Other Job Characteristics**—Importance of Being Exact or Accurate; Consequence of Error; Pace Determined by Speed of Equipment.

Experience—Job Zone 4. A minimum of two to four years of work-related skill, knowledge, or experience is needed. **Job Preparation:** SVP 7.0 to less than 8.0—two years to less than 10 years. **Knowledge**—Education and Training; English Language; Philosophy and Theology; Administration and Management; Sociology and Anthropology. **Instructional Programs**—Agricultural Teacher Education; Business Teacher Education; Health Occupations Teacher Education; Sales and Marketing Operations/ Marketing and Distribution Teacher Education; Teacher Education and Professional Development, Specific Subject Areas, Other; Technical Teacher Education; Technology Teacher Education/Industrial Arts Teacher Education; Trade and Industrial Teacher Education.

Related DOT Jobs—075.127-010 Instructor, Psychiatric Aide; 090.222-010 Instructor, Business Education; 097.221-010 Instructor, Vocational Training; 099.227-014 Instructor, Correspondence School; 099.227-018 Instructor, Ground Services; 166.221-010 Instructor, Technical Training; 166.227-010 Training Representative; 235.222-010 Private-Branch-Exchange Service Adviser; 239.227-010 Customer-Service-Representative Instructor; 375.227-010 Police-Academy Instructor; 378.227-010 Marksmanship Instructor; 522.264-010 Training Technician; 621.221-010 Field-Service Representative; 683.222-010 Instructor, Weaving; 689.324-010 Instructor; 715.221-010 Instructor, Watch Assembly; 740.221-010 Instructor, Decorating; 788.222-010 Instructor; 789.222-010 Instructor, Apparel Manufacture; 919.223-010 Instructor, Bus, Trolley, and Taxi; others.

25-1199.99 *Postsecondary Teachers, All Other*

- ● **Education/Training Required: Master's degree**
- ● **Employed: No data available.**
- ● **Annual Earnings: No data available.**
- ● **Growth: 23.5%**
- ● **Annual Job Openings: 184,000**

All postsecondary teachers not listed separately.

No task data available.

GOE INFORMATION—Interest Area: 12. Education and Social Service. **Work Group:** 12.03. Educational Services. **Note:** The Department of Labor has not collected some data for this job, so it has fewer details than the other descriptions.

Instructional Programs—Creative Writing; General Studies; Humanities/Humanistic Studies; Liberal Arts and Sciences, General Studies, and Humanities, Other; Liberal Arts and Sciences/Liberal Studies; Speech and Rhetorical Studies.

Related DOT Jobs—090.227-010 Faculty Member, College or University.

25-2000 Primary, Secondary, and Special Education School Teachers

25-2011.00 *Preschool Teachers, Except Special Education*

- ● **Education/Training Required: Bachelor's degree**
- ● **Employed: 422,588**
- ● **Annual Earnings: $18,640**
- ● **Growth: 20.0%**
- ● **Annual Job Openings: 55,000**

Instruct children (normally up to 5 years of age) in activities designed to promote social, physical, and intellectual growth needed for primary school in preschool, day care center, or other child development facility. May be required to hold state certification.

Establish clear objectives for all lessons, units, and projects and communicate those objectives to children. Organize and lead activities designed to promote physical, mental, and social development, such as games, arts and crafts, music, storytelling, and field trips. Plan and conduct activities for a balanced program of instruction, demonstration, and work time that provides students with opportunities to observe, question, and investigate. Prepare materials and classrooms for class activities. Teach basic skills such as color, shape, number, and letter recognition; personal hygiene; and social skills. Plan and supervise class projects, field trips, visits by guests, or other experiential activities and guide students in learning from those activities. Adapt teaching methods and instructional materials to meet students' varying needs and interests. Arrange indoor and outdoor space to facilitate creative play, motor-skill activities, and safety. Assimilate arriving children to the school environment by greeting them, helping them remove outerwear, and selecting activities of interest to them. Attend to children's basic needs by feeding them, dressing them, and changing their diapers. Confer with other staff members to plan and schedule lessons promoting learning, following approved curricula. Demonstrate activities to children. Enforce all administration policies and rules governing students. Establish and enforce rules for behavior and procedures for maintaining order. Identify children showing signs of emotional, developmental, or health-related problems and discuss them with supervisors, parents or guardians, and child development specialists. Maintain accurate and complete student records as required by laws, district policies, and administrative regulations. Meet with other professionals to discuss individual students' needs and progress. Meet with parents and guardians to discuss their children's progress and needs, determine their priorities for their children, and suggest ways that they can promote learning and development. Observe and evaluate children's performance, behavior, social development, and physical health. Organize and label materials and display students' work in a manner appropriate for their ages and perceptual skills. Prepare and implement remedial programs for students requiring extra help. Prepare reports on students and activities as required by administration. Provide a variety of materials and resources for children to explore, manipulate, and use, both in learning activities and in imaginative play. Read books to entire classes or to small groups. Serve meals and snacks in accordance with nutritional guidelines. Supervise, evaluate, and plan assignments for teacher assistants and volunteers. Teach proper eating habits and personal hygiene. Administer tests to help determine children's developmental levels, needs, and potential. Attend professional meetings, educational conferences, and teacher training workshops in order to maintain and improve professional competence. Attend staff meetings and serve on committees as required. Collaborate with other teachers and administrators in the development, evaluation, and revision of preschool programs. Perform administrative duties such as hall and cafeteria monitoring and bus loading and unloading. Provide disabled students with assistive devices, supportive technology, and assistance accessing facilities such as restrooms. Select, store, order, issue, and inventory classroom equipment, materials, and supplies.

GOE INFORMATION—Interest Area: 12. Education and Social Service. **Work Group:** 12.03. Educational Services. **Personality Type—**Social. Social occupations frequently involve working with, communicating with, and teaching people. These occupations often involve helping or providing service to others. **Work Values—**Social Service; Authority; Creativity; Responsibility; Achievement. **Skills—**Learning Strategies; Social Perceptiveness; Monitoring; Speaking. **Abilities—***Cognitive:* Time Sharing; Originality; Fluency of Ideas; Memorization; Written Expression. *Psychomotor:* Response Orientation; Reaction Time. *Physical:* Stamina; Dynamic Flexibility; Static Strength; Trunk Strength; Extent Flexibility. *Sensory:* Far Vision; Speech Recognition; Peripheral Vision; Speech Clarity; Hearing Sensitivity. **General Work Activities—***Information Input:* Getting Information; Monitoring Processes, Materials, or Surroundings; Identifying Objects, Actions, and Events. *Mental Process:* Organizing, Planning, and Prioritizing; Thinking Creatively; Updating and Using Relevant Knowledge. *Work Output:* Performing General Physical Activities; Handling and Moving Objects; Documenting or Recording Information. *Interacting with Others:* Assisting and Caring for Others; Establishing and Maintaining Relationships; Resolving Conflict and Negotiating with Others. **Physical Work Conditions—**Kneeling, Crouching, or Crawling; Outdoors; Walking or Running; Disease or Infections; Very Hot or Cold. **Other Job Characteristics—**Importance of Repeating Same Tasks; Importance of Being Exact or Accurate; Degree of Automation.

Experience—Job Zone 4. A minimum of two to four years of work-related skill, knowledge, or experience is needed. **Job Preparation:** SVP 7.0 to less than 8.0—two years to less than 10 years. **Knowledge—**Customer and Personal Service; Education and Training; Psychology; Therapy and Counseling; Fine Arts. **Instructional Programs—**Child Care and Support Services Management; Early Childhood Education and Teaching; Kindergarten/Preschool Education and Teaching.

Related DOT Jobs—092.227-018 Teacher, Preschool.

25-2012.00 Kindergarten Teachers, Except Special Education

- **Education/Training Required: Bachelor's degree**
- **Employed: 174,658**
- **Annual Earnings: $38,740**
- **Growth: 14.5%**
- **Annual Job Openings: 23,000**

Teach elemental natural and social science, personal hygiene, music, art, and literature to children from 4 to 6 years old. Promote physical, mental, and social development. May be required to hold state certification.

Instruct students individually and in groups, adapting teaching methods to meet students' varying needs and interests. Observe and evaluate children's performance, behavior, social development, and physical health. Teach basic skills such as color, shape, number, and letter recognition; personal hygiene; and social skills. Demonstrate activities to children. Assimilate arriving children to the school environment by greeting them, helping them remove outerwear, and selecting activities of interest to

them. Confer with other staff members to plan and schedule lessons promoting learning, following approved curricula. Confer with parents or guardians, other teachers, counselors, and administrators to resolve students' behavioral and academic problems. Establish and enforce rules for behavior and policies and procedures to maintain order among students. Establish clear objectives for all lessons, units, and projects and communicate those objectives to children. Guide and counsel students with adjustment and/or academic problems or special academic interests. Identify children showing signs of emotional, developmental, or health-related problems and discuss them with supervisors, parents or guardians, and child development specialists. Instruct and monitor students in the use and care of equipment and materials in order to prevent injuries and damage. Maintain accurate and complete student records and prepare reports on children and activities as required by laws, district policies, and administrative regulations. Meet with other professionals to discuss individual students' needs and progress. Meet with parents and guardians to discuss their children's progress and to determine their priorities for their children and their resource needs. Organize and label materials and display children's work in a manner appropriate for their sizes and perceptual skills. Organize and lead activities designed to promote physical, mental, and social development such as games, arts and crafts, music, and storytelling. Plan and conduct activities for a balanced program of instruction, demonstration, and work time that provides students with opportunities to observe, question, and investigate. Plan and supervise class projects, field trips, visits by guests, or other experiential activities and guide students in learning from those activities. Prepare and implement remedial programs for students requiring extra help. Prepare children for later grades by encouraging them to explore learning opportunities and to persevere with challenging tasks. Prepare for assigned classes and show written evidence of preparation upon request of immediate supervisors. Prepare materials, classrooms, and other indoor and outdoor spaces to facilitate creative play, learning and motor-skill activities, and safety. Prepare objectives and outlines for courses of study, following curriculum guidelines or requirements of states and schools. Prepare, administer, and grade tests and assignments to evaluate children's progress. Provide a variety of materials and resources for children to explore, manipulate, and use, both in learning activities and in imaginative play. Read books to entire classes or to small groups. Supervise, evaluate, and plan assignments for teacher assistants and volunteers. Administer standardized ability and achievement tests and interpret results to determine children's developmental levels and needs. Attend professional meetings, educational conferences, and teacher training workshops in order to maintain and improve professional competence. Attend staff meetings and serve on committees as required. Collaborate with other teachers and administrators in the development, evaluation, and revision of kindergarten programs. Involve parent volunteers and older students in children's activities in order to facilitate involvement in focused, complex play. Perform administrative duties such as assisting in school libraries, hall and cafeteria monitoring, and bus loading and unloading. Provide disabled students with assistive devices, supportive technology, and assistance accessing facilities such as restrooms. Select, store, order, issue, and inventory classroom equipment, materials, and supplies. Use computers, audiovisual aids, and other equipment and materials to supplement presentations.

GOE INFORMATION—Interest Area: 12. Education and Social Service. **Work Group:** 12.03. Educational Services. **Personality Type—**Social. Social occupations frequently involve working with, communicating with, and teaching people. These occupations often involve helping or providing service to others. **Work Values—**Social Service; Authority; Creativity; Responsibility; Achievement. **Skills—**Learning Strategies; Service Orientation; Monitoring; Speaking; Social Perceptiveness. **Abilities—***Cognitive:* Time Sharing; Originality; Flexibility of Closure; Fluency of Ideas; Memorization. *Psychomotor:* Speed of Limb Movement;

Response Orientation; Reaction Time; Rate Control; Multilimb Coordination. *Physical:* Trunk Strength; Extent Flexibility; Gross Body Coordination; Static Strength; Stamina. *Sensory:* Far Vision; Peripheral Vision; Sound Localization; Speech Recognition; Hearing Sensitivity. **General Work Activities**—*Information Input:* Getting Information; Identifying Objects, Actions, and Events; Monitoring Processes, Materials, or Surroundings. *Mental Process:* Organizing, Planning, and Prioritizing; Thinking Creatively; Updating and Using Relevant Knowledge. *Work Output:* Performing General Physical Activities; Documenting or Recording Information; Handling and Moving Objects. *Interacting with Others:* Establishing and Maintaining Relationships; Communicating with Persons Outside Organization; Assisting and Caring for Others. **Physical Work Conditions**—Outdoors; Disease or Infections; Walking or Running; Kneeling, Crouching, or Crawling; Standing. **Other Job Characteristics**—Importance of Repeating Same Tasks; Degree of Automation; Consequence of Error.

Experience—Job Zone 4. A minimum of two to four years of work-related skill, knowledge, or experience is needed. **Job Preparation:** SVP 7.0 to less than 8.0—two years to less than 10 years. **Knowledge**—Education and Training; Customer and Personal Service; Psychology; Sociology and Anthropology; Therapy and Counseling. **Instructional Programs**—Early Childhood Education and Teaching; Kindergarten/Preschool Education and Teaching.

Related DOT Jobs—092.227-014 Teacher, Kindergarten.

25-2021.00 Elementary School Teachers, Except Special Education

- Education/Training Required: Bachelor's degree
- Employed: 1,532,103
- Annual Earnings: $41,080
- Growth: 13.2%
- Annual Job Openings: 144,000

Teach pupils in public or private schools at the elementary level basic academic, social, and other formative skills.

Establish clear objectives for all lessons, units, and projects and communicate those objectives to students. Instruct students individually and in groups, using various teaching methods such as lectures, discussions, and demonstrations. Prepare, administer, and grade tests and assignments in order to evaluate students' progress. Assign and grade class work and homework. Adapt teaching methods and instructional materials to meet students' varying needs and interests. Confer with other staff members to plan and schedule lessons promoting learning, following approved curricula. Confer with parents or guardians, teachers, counselors, and administrators in order to resolve students' behavioral and academic problems. Enforce administration policies and rules governing students. Establish and enforce rules for behavior and procedures for maintaining order among the students for whom they are responsible. Guide and counsel students with adjustment and/or academic problems or special academic interests. Instruct and monitor students in the use and care of equipment and materials in order to prevent injuries and damage. Maintain accurate and complete student records as required by laws, district policies, and administrative regulations. Meet with other professionals to discuss individual students' needs and progress. Meet with parents and guardians to discuss their children's progress and to determine their priorities for their children and their resource needs. Observe and evaluate students' performance, behavior, social development, and physical health. Organize and label materials and display students' work. Organize and lead activities designed to promote physical, mental, and social development, such as games, arts

and crafts, music, and storytelling. Plan and conduct activities for a balanced program of instruction, demonstration, and work time that provides students with opportunities to observe, question, and investigate. Plan and supervise class projects, field trips, visits by guest speakers, or other experiential activities and guide students in learning from those activities. Prepare and implement remedial programs for students requiring extra help. Prepare for assigned classes and show written evidence of preparation upon request of immediate supervisors. Prepare materials and classrooms for class activities. Prepare objectives and outlines for courses of study, following curriculum guidelines or requirements of states and schools. Prepare reports on students and activities as required by administration. Prepare students for later grades by encouraging them to explore learning opportunities and to persevere with challenging tasks. Provide a variety of materials and resources for children to explore, manipulate, and use, both in learning activities and in imaginative play. Read books to entire classes or small groups. Supervise, evaluate, and plan assignments for teacher assistants and volunteers. Administer standardized ability and achievement tests and interpret results to determine student strengths and areas of need. Attend professional meetings, educational conferences, and teacher training workshops in order to maintain and improve professional competence. Attend staff meetings and serve on committees as required. Collaborate with other teachers and administrators in the development, evaluation, and revision of elementary school programs. Involve parent volunteers and older students in children's activities in order to facilitate involvement in focused, complex play. Perform administrative duties such as assisting in school libraries, hall and cafeteria monitoring, and bus loading and unloading. Provide disabled students with assistive devices, supportive technology, and assistance accessing facilities such as restrooms. Select, store, order, issue, and inventory classroom equipment, materials, and supplies. Sponsor extracurricular activities such as clubs, student organizations, and academic contests. Use computers, audiovisual aids, and other equipment and materials to supplement presentations.

GOE INFORMATION—Interest Area: 12. Education and Social Service. **Work Group:** 12.03. Educational Services. **Personality Type**—Social. Social occupations frequently involve working with, communicating with, and teaching people. These occupations often involve helping or providing service to others. **Work Values**—Authority; Social Service; Creativity; Responsibility; Achievement. **Skills**—Learning Strategies; Instructing; Social Perceptiveness; Speaking; Complex Problem Solving; Reading Comprehension; Service Orientation; Mathematics. **Abilities**—*Cognitive:* Time Sharing; Originality; Category Flexibility; Memorization; Number Facility. *Psychomotor:* Response Orientation; Speed of Limb Movement; Reaction Time; Arm-Hand Steadiness. *Physical:* Gross Body Equilibrium; Gross Body Coordination; Static Strength; Stamina; Explosive Strength. *Sensory:* Speech Clarity; Far Vision; Speech Recognition; Peripheral Vision; Night Vision. **General Work Activities**—*Information Input:* Getting Information; Monitoring Processes, Materials, or Surroundings; Identifying Objects, Actions, and Events. *Mental Process:* Updating and Using Relevant Knowledge; Organizing, Planning, and Prioritizing; Thinking Creatively. *Work Output:* Handling and Moving Objects; Documenting or Recording Information; Performing General Physical Activities. *Interacting with Others:* Establishing and Maintaining Relationships; Coaching and Developing Others; Communicating with Persons Outside Organization. **Physical Work Conditions**—Outdoors; Very Hot or Cold; Walking or Running; Disease or Infections; Kneeling, Crouching, or Crawling. **Other Job Characteristics**—Importance of Being Exact or Accurate; Importance of Repeating Same Tasks; Degree of Automation.

Experience—Job Zone 4. A minimum of two to four years of work-related skill, knowledge, or experience is needed. **Job Preparation:** SVP 7.0 to less than 8.0—two years to less than 10 years. **Knowledge**—Geography; Education and Training; History and Archeology; Sociology and

Anthropology; Therapy and Counseling. **Instructional Programs**—Elementary Education and Teaching; Teacher Education, Multiple Levels.

Related DOT Jobs—092.227-010 Teacher, Elementary School.

25-2022.00 Middle School Teachers, Except Special and Vocational Education

- Education/Training Required: Bachelor's degree
- Employed: 570,009
- Annual Earnings: $41,220
- Growth: 9.6%
- Annual Job Openings: 54,000

Teach students in public or private schools in one or more subjects at the middle, intermediate, or junior high level, which falls between elementary and senior high school as defined by applicable state laws and regulations.

Establish clear objectives for all lessons, units, and projects and communicate these objectives to students. Instruct through lectures, discussions, and demonstrations in one or more subjects, such as English, mathematics, or social studies. Prepare, administer, and grade tests and assignments in order to evaluate students' progress. Assign lessons and correct homework. Adapt teaching methods and instructional materials to meet students' varying needs and interests. Confer with other staff members to plan and schedule lessons promoting learning, following approved curricula. Confer with parents or guardians, other teachers, counselors, and administrators in order to resolve students' behavioral and academic problems. Enforce all administration policies and rules governing students. Establish and enforce rules for behavior and procedures for maintaining order among the students for whom they are responsible. Guide and counsel students with adjustment and/or academic problems or special academic interests. Instruct and monitor students in the use and care of equipment and materials in order to prevent injury and damage. Maintain accurate, complete, and correct student records as required by laws, district policies, and administrative regulations. Meet with other professionals to discuss individual students' needs and progress. Meet with parents and guardians to discuss their children's progress and to determine their priorities for their children and their resource needs. Observe and evaluate students' performance, behavior, social development, and physical health. Organize and label materials and display students' work. Organize and supervise games and other recreational activities to promote physical, mental, and social development. Plan and conduct activities for a balanced program of instruction, demonstration, and work time that provides students with opportunities to observe, question, and investigate. Plan and supervise class projects, field trips, visits by guest speakers, or other experiential activities and guide students in learning from such activities. Prepare and implement remedial programs for students requiring extra help. Prepare for assigned classes and show written evidence of preparation upon request of immediate supervisors. Prepare materials and classrooms for class activities. Prepare objectives and outlines for courses of study, following curriculum guidelines or requirements of states and schools. Prepare reports on students and activities as required by administration. Prepare students for later grades by encouraging them to explore learning opportunities and to persevere with challenging tasks. Supervise, evaluate, and plan assignments for teacher assistants and volunteers. Administer standardized ability and achievement tests and interpret results to determine student strengths and areas of need. Attend professional meetings, educational conferences, and teacher training workshops in order to maintain and improve professional competence. Attend staff meetings and serve on staff committees as required. Collaborate with other teachers and administrators in the development, evaluation, and

revision of middle school programs. Perform administrative duties such as assisting in school libraries, hall and cafeteria monitoring, and bus loading and unloading. Provide disabled students with assistive devices, supportive technology, and assistance accessing facilities such as restrooms. Select, store, order, issue, and inventory classroom equipment, materials, and supplies. Sponsor extracurricular activities such as clubs, student organizations, and academic contests. Use computers, audiovisual aids, and other equipment and materials to supplement presentations.

GOE INFORMATION—**Interest Area:** 12. Education and Social Service. **Work Group:** 12.03. Educational Services. **Personality Type**—Social. Social occupations frequently involve working with, communicating with, and teaching people. These occupations often involve helping or providing service to others. **Work Values**—Social Service; Authority; Creativity; Responsibility; Achievement. **Skills**—Learning Strategies; Speaking; Instructing; Mathematics; Social Perceptiveness; Reading Comprehension; Monitoring; Complex Problem Solving. **Abilities**—*Cognitive:* Oral Comprehension; Oral Expression; Written Comprehension; Written Expression; Originality. *Psychomotor:* None met the criteria. *Physical:* None met the criteria. *Sensory:* Speech Clarity; Speech Recognition; Auditory Attention; Sound Localization. **General Work Activities**—*Information Input:* Getting Information; Identifying Objects, Actions, and Events; Monitoring Processes, Materials, or Surroundings. *Mental Process:* Updating and Using Relevant Knowledge; Judging Qualities of Things, Services, or Other People's Work; Analyzing Data or Information. *Work Output:* Documenting or Recording Information; Handling and Moving Objects; Performing General Physical Activities. *Interacting with Others:* Establishing and Maintaining Relationships; Teaching Others; Communicating with Persons Outside Organization. **Physical Work Conditions**—Disease or Infections; Outdoors; Standing; Distracting Sounds and Noise Levels. **Other Job Characteristics**—Importance of Being Exact or Accurate; Importance of Repeating Same Tasks; Degree of Automation.

Experience—Job Zone 4. A minimum of two to four years of work-related skill, knowledge, or experience is needed. **Job Preparation:** SVP 7.0 to less than 8.0–two years to less than 10 years. **Knowledge**—Education and Training; Therapy and Counseling; History and Archeology; English Language; Sociology and Anthropology. **Instructional Programs**—Art Teacher Education; Computer Teacher Education; English/Language Arts Teacher Education; Family and Consumer Sciences/Home Economics Teacher Education; Foreign Language Teacher Education; Health Occupations Teacher Education; Health Teacher Education; History Teacher Education; Junior High/Intermediate/Middle School Education and Teaching; Mathematics Teacher Education; Music Teacher Education; Physical Education Teaching and Coaching; Reading Teacher Education; Science Teacher Education/General Science Teacher Education; Social Science Teacher Education; Social Studies Teacher Education; Teacher Education and Professional Development, Specific Subject Areas, Other; Technology Teacher Education/Industrial Arts Teacher Education.

Related DOT Jobs—091.227-010 Teacher, Secondary School; 099.224-010 Instructor, Physical Education.

25-2023.00 Vocational Education Teachers, Middle School

- Education/Training Required: Bachelor's degree
- Employed: 19,556
- Annual Earnings: $41,460
- Growth: 13.1%
- Annual Job Openings: 2,000

Teach or instruct vocational or occupational subjects at the middle school level.

Establish clear objectives for all lessons, units, and projects and communicate those objectives to students. Instruct students individually and in groups, using various teaching methods such as lectures, discussions, and demonstrations. Prepare, administer, and grade tests and assignments to evaluate students' progress. Adapt teaching methods and instructional materials to meet students' varying needs and interests. Assign and grade class work and homework. Confer with other staff members to plan and schedule lessons promoting learning, following approved curricula. Confer with parents or guardians, other teachers, counselors, and administrators in order to resolve students' behavioral and academic problems. Enforce all administration policies and rules governing students. Establish and enforce rules for behavior and procedures for maintaining order among the students for whom they are responsible. Guide and counsel students with adjustment and/or academic problems or special academic interests. Instruct and monitor students in the use and care of equipment and materials in order to prevent injuries and damage. Maintain accurate and complete student records as required by laws, district policies, and administrative regulations. Meet with other professionals to discuss individual students' needs and progress. Meet with parents and guardians to discuss their children's progress and to determine their priorities for their children and their resource needs. Observe and evaluate students' performance, behavior, social development, and physical health. Plan and conduct activities for a balanced program of instruction, demonstration, and work time that provides students with opportunities to observe, question, and investigate. Plan and supervise class projects, field trips, visits by guest speakers, or other experiential activities and guide students in learning from those activities. Prepare and implement remedial programs for students requiring extra help. Prepare for assigned classes and show written evidence of preparation upon request of immediate supervisors. Prepare materials and classrooms for class activities. Prepare objectives and outlines for courses of study, following curriculum guidelines or requirements of states and schools. Prepare reports on students and activities as required by administration. Prepare students for later educational experiences by encouraging them to explore learning opportunities and to persevere with challenging tasks. Attend professional meetings, educational conferences, and teacher training workshops in order to maintain and improve professional competence. Attend staff meetings and serve on committees as required. Collaborate with other teachers and administrators in the development, evaluation, and revision of middle school programs. Perform administrative duties such as assisting in school libraries, hall and cafeteria monitoring, and bus loading and unloading. Provide disabled students with assistive devices, supportive technology, and assistance accessing facilities such as restrooms. Select, store, order, issue, and inventory classroom equipment, materials, and supplies. Sponsor extracurricular activities such as clubs, student organizations, and academic contests. Use computers, audiovisual aids, and other equipment and materials to supplement presentations.

GOE INFORMATION—Interest Area: 12. Education and Social Service. **Work Group:** 12.03. Educational Services. **Personality Type—**Social. Social occupations frequently involve working with, communicating with, and teaching people. These occupations often involve helping or providing service to others. **Work Values—**Social Service; Authority; Creativity; Responsibility; Achievement. **Skills—**Learning Strategies; Speaking; Instructing; Mathematics; Social Perceptiveness; Reading Comprehension; Monitoring; Complex Problem Solving. **Abilities—***Cognitive:* Oral Comprehension; Oral Expression; Written Comprehension; Written Expression; Originality. *Psychomotor:* None met the criteria. *Physical:* None met the criteria. *Sensory:* Speech Clarity; Speech Recognition; Auditory Attention; Sound Localization. **General Work Activities—***In-formation Input:* Getting Information; Identifying Objects, Actions, and Events; Monitoring Processes, Materials, or Surroundings. *Mental Process:* Updating and Using Relevant Knowledge; Judging Qualities of Things, Services, or Other People's Work; Analyzing Data or Information. *Work Output:* Documenting or Recording Information; Handling and Moving Objects; Performing General Physical Activities. *Interacting with Others:* Establishing and Maintaining Relationships; Teaching Others; Communicating with Persons Outside Organization. **Physical Work Conditions—**Disease or Infections; Outdoors; Standing; Distracting Sounds and Noise Levels. **Other Job Characteristics—**Importance of Being Exact or Accurate; Importance of Repeating Same Tasks; Degree of Automation.

Experience—Job Zone 4. A minimum of two to four years of work-related skill, knowledge, or experience is needed. **Job Preparation:** SVP 7.0 to less than 8.0—two years to less than 10 years. **Knowledge—**Education and Training; Therapy and Counseling; History and Archeology; English Language; Sociology and Anthropology. **Instructional Programs—**Technology Teacher Education/Industrial Arts Teacher Education.

Related DOT Jobs—091.221-010 Teacher, Industrial Arts.

25-2031.00 Secondary School Teachers, Except Special and Vocational Education

- **Education/Training Required: Bachelor's degree**
- **Employed: 1,003,679**
- **Annual Earnings: $43,280**
- **Growth: 18.6%**
- **Annual Job Openings: 60,000**

Instruct students in secondary public or private schools in one or more subjects at the secondary level, such as English, mathematics, or social studies. May be designated according to subject matter specialty, such as typing instructors, commercial teachers, or English teachers.

Establish clear objectives for all lessons, units, and projects and communicate those objectives to students. Instruct through lectures, discussions, and demonstrations in one or more subjects, such as English, mathematics, or social studies. Prepare, administer, and grade tests and assignments to evaluate students' progress. Assign and grade class work and homework. Adapt teaching methods and instructional materials to meet students' varying needs and interests. Confer with other staff members to plan and schedule lessons promoting learning, following approved curricula. Confer with parents or guardians, other teachers, counselors, and administrators in order to resolve students' behavioral and academic problems. Enforce all administration policies and rules governing students. Establish and enforce rules for behavior and procedures for maintaining order among the students for whom they are responsible. Guide and counsel students with adjustment and/or academic problems or special academic interests. Instruct and monitor students in the use and care of equipment and materials in order to prevent injuries and damage. Maintain accurate and complete student records as required by laws, district policies, and administrative regulations. Meet with other professionals to discuss individual students' needs and progress. Meet with parents and guardians to discuss their children's progress and to determine their priorities for their children and their resource needs. Observe and evaluate students' performance, behavior, social development, and physical health. Plan and conduct activities for a balanced program of instruction, demonstration, and work time that provides students with opportunities to observe, question, and investigate. Plan and supervise class projects, field trips, visits by guest speakers, or other experiential activities and guide students in learning from those activities. Prepare and implement remedial programs for students requiring extra help. Prepare for assigned classes and show written evidence of preparation upon request of immediate supervisors. Prepare materials and classrooms for class activities. Prepare objectives and outlines for courses of study, following curriculum guidelines or requirements of states and schools. Prepare reports on students and activities as required by administration. Prepare students for later grades by encouraging them to explore learning opportunities and to persevere with challenging tasks. Administer standardized ability and achievement tests and interpret results to determine students' strengths and areas of need. Attend professional meetings, educational conferences, and teacher training workshops in order to maintain and improve professional competence. Attend staff meetings and serve on committees as required. Collaborate with other teachers and administrators in the development, evaluation, and revision of secondary school programs. Perform administrative duties such as assisting in school libraries, hall and cafeteria monitoring, and bus loading and unloading. Provide disabled students with assistive devices, supportive technology, and assistance accessing facilities such as restrooms. Select, store, order, issue, and inventory classroom equipment, materials, and supplies. Sponsor extracurricular activities such as clubs, student organizations, and academic contests. Use computers, audiovisual aids, and other equipment and materials to supplement presentations.

GOE INFORMATION—Interest Area: 12. Education and Social Service. Work Group: 12.03. Educational Services. Personality Type—Social. Social occupations frequently involve working with, communicating with, and teaching people. These occupations often involve helping or providing service to others. Work Values—Social Service; Authority; Creativity; Responsibility; Achievement. Skills—Learning Strategies; Speaking; Instructing; Mathematics; Social Perceptiveness; Reading Comprehension; Monitoring; Complex Problem Solving. Abilities—*Cognitive:* Oral Comprehension; Oral Expression; Written Comprehension; Written Expression; Originality. *Psychomotor:* None met the criteria. *Physical:* None met the criteria. *Sensory:* Speech Clarity; Speech Recognition; Auditory Attention; Sound Localization. General Work Activities—*Information Input:* Getting Information; Identifying Objects, Actions, and Events; Monitoring Processes, Materials, or Surroundings. *Mental Process:* Updating and Using Relevant Knowledge; Analyzing Data or Information; Judging Qualities of Things, Services, or Other People's Work. *Work Output:* Documenting or Recording Information; Handling and Moving Objects; Performing General Physical Activities. *Interacting with Others:* Establishing and Maintaining Relationships; Teaching Others; Communicating with Persons Outside Organization. Physical Work Conditions—Disease or Infections; Outdoors; Standing; Distracting Sounds and Noise Levels. Other Job Characteristics—Importance of Being Exact or Accurate; Importance of Repeating Same Tasks; Degree of Automation.

Experience—Job Zone 4. A minimum of two to four years of work-related skill, knowledge, or experience is needed. Job Preparation: SVP 7.0 to less than 8.0—two years to less than 10 years. Knowledge—Education and Training; Therapy and Counseling; History and Archeology; English Language; Sociology and Anthropology. Instructional Programs—Agricultural Teacher Education; Art Teacher Education; Biology Teacher Education; Business Teacher Education; Chemistry Teacher Education; Computer Teacher Education; Drama and Dance Teacher Education; Driver and Safety Teacher Education; English/Language Arts Teacher Education; Family and Consumer Sciences/Home Economics Teacher Education; Foreign Language Teacher Education; French Language Teacher Education; Geography Teacher Education; German Language Teacher Education; Health Occupations Teacher Education; Health Teacher Education; History Teacher Education; Junior High/Intermediate/Middle School Education and Teaching; Latin Teacher Education; Mathematics

Teacher Education; Music Teacher Education; Physical Education Teaching and Coaching; Physics Teacher Education; Reading Teacher Education; Sales and Marketing Operations/Marketing and Distribution Teacher Education; Science Teacher Education/General Science Teacher Education; Secondary Education and Teaching; Social Science Teacher Education; Social Studies Teacher Education; Spanish Language Teacher Education; Speech Teacher Education; Teacher Education and Professional Development, Specific Subject Areas, Other; Teacher Education, Multiple Levels; Technology Teacher Education/Industrial Arts Teacher Education.

Related DOT Jobs—091.227-010 Teacher, Secondary School; 099.224-010 Instructor, Physical Education; 099.227-022 Instructor, Military Science.

25-2032.00 Vocational Education Teachers, Secondary School

- **Education/Training Required: Bachelor's degree**
- **Employed: 108,876**
- **Annual Earnings: $43,590**
- **Growth: 13.4%**
- **Annual Job Openings: 7,000**

Teach or instruct vocational or occupational subjects at the secondary school level.

Instruct students in the knowledge and skills required in a specific occupation or occupational field, using a systematic plan of lectures; discussions; audiovisual presentations; and laboratory, shop, and field studies. Instruct students individually and in groups, using various teaching methods such as lectures, discussions, and demonstrations. Prepare, administer, and grade tests and assignments in order to evaluate students' progress. Assign and grade class work and homework. Confer with other staff members to plan and schedule lessons promoting learning, following approved curricula. Confer with parents or guardians, other teachers, counselors, and administrators in order to resolve students' behavioral and academic problems. Enforce all administration policies and rules governing students. Establish and enforce rules for behavior and procedures for maintaining order among the students for whom they are responsible. Establish clear objectives for all lessons, units, and projects and communicate those objectives to students. Guide and counsel students with adjustment and/or academic problems or special academic interests. Instruct and monitor students in the use and care of equipment and materials in order to prevent injury and damage. Maintain accurate and complete student records as required by law, district policy, and administrative regulations. Meet with other professionals to discuss individual students' needs and progress. Meet with parents and guardians to discuss their children's progress and to determine their priorities for their children and their resource needs. Observe and evaluate students' performance, behavior, social development, and physical health. Place students in jobs or make referrals to job placement services. Plan and conduct activities for a balanced program of instruction, demonstration, and work time that provides students with opportunities to observe, question, and investigate. Plan and supervise class projects, field trips, visits by guest speakers, or other experiential activities and guide students in learning from those activities. Plan and supervise work-experience programs in businesses, industrial shops, and school laboratories. Prepare and implement remedial programs for students requiring extra help. Prepare materials and classroom for class activities. Prepare objectives and outlines for courses of study, following curriculum guidelines or requirements of states and schools. Prepare reports on students and activities as required by administration. Prepare students for later grades by encouraging them to explore learning opportunities and to persevere with challenging tasks. Attend professional meetings, educational conferences, and teacher training workshops in order to maintain and improve professional competence. Attend staff meetings and serve on committees as required. Collaborate with other teachers and administrators in the development, evaluation, and revision of secondary school programs. Keep informed about trends in education and subject matter specialties. Perform administrative duties such as assisting in school libraries, hall and cafeteria monitoring, and bus loading and unloading. Provide disabled students with assistive devices, supportive technology, and assistance accessing facilities such as restrooms. Select, order, store, issue, and inventory classroom equipment, materials, and supplies. Sponsor extracurricular activities such as clubs, student organizations, and academic contests. Use computers, audiovisual aids, and other equipment and materials to supplement presentations.

GOE INFORMATION—Interest Area: 12. Education and Social Service. **Work Group:** 12.03. Educational Services. **Personality Type**—Social. Social occupations frequently involve working with, communicating with, and teaching people. These occupations often involve helping or providing service to others. **Work Values**—Social Service; Authority; Creativity; Responsibility; Achievement. **Skills**—Learning Strategies; Speaking; Instructing; Mathematics; Social Perceptiveness; Reading Comprehension; Monitoring; Complex Problem Solving. **Abilities**—*Cognitive:* Oral Comprehension; Oral Expression; Written Comprehension; Written Expression; Originality. *Psychomotor:* None met the criteria. *Physical:* None met the criteria. *Sensory:* Speech Clarity; Speech Recognition; Auditory Attention; Sound Localization. **General Work Activities**—*Information Input:* Getting Information; Identifying Objects, Actions, and Events; Monitoring Processes, Materials, or Surroundings. *Mental Process:* Updating and Using Relevant Knowledge; Analyzing Data or Information; Judging Qualities of Things, Services, or Other People's Work. *Work Output:* Documenting or Recording Information; Handling and Moving Objects; Performing General Physical Activities. *Interacting with Others:* Establishing and Maintaining Relationships; Teaching Others; Communicating with Persons Outside Organization. **Physical Work Conditions**—Disease or Infections; Outdoors; Standing; Distracting Sounds and Noise Levels. **Other Job Characteristics**—Importance of Being Exact or Accurate; Importance of Repeating Same Tasks; Degree of Automation.

Experience—Job Zone 4. A minimum of two to four years of work-related skill, knowledge, or experience is needed. **Job Preparation:** SVP 7.0 to less than 8.0—two years to less than 10 years. **Knowledge**—Education and Training; Therapy and Counseling; History and Archeology; English Language; Sociology and Anthropology. **Instructional Programs**—Technology Teacher Education/Industrial Arts Teacher Education.

Related DOT Jobs—091.221-010 Teacher, Industrial Arts.

25-2041.00 Special Education Teachers, Preschool, Kindergarten, and Elementary School

- **Education/Training Required: Bachelor's degree**
- **Employed: 233,986**
- **Annual Earnings: $42,110**
- **Growth: 36.8%**
- **Annual Job Openings: 15,000**

Teach elementary and preschool school subjects to educationally and physically handicapped students. Includes teachers who specialize and work with audibly and visually handicapped students and those who teach basic academic and life processes skills to the mentally impaired.

Develop and implement strategies to meet the needs of students with a variety of handicapping conditions. Instruct students in academic subjects, using a variety of techniques such as phonetics, multisensory learning, and repetition, in order to reinforce learning and to meet students' varying needs and interests. Instruct students in daily living skills required for independent maintenance and self-sufficiency, such as hygiene, safety, and food preparation. Confer with parents, administrators, testing specialists, social workers, and professionals to develop individual educational plans designed to promote students' educational, physical, and social development. Modify the general education curriculum for special-needs students based upon a variety of instructional techniques and technologies. Confer with other staff members to plan and schedule lessons promoting learning, following approved curricula. Confer with parents or guardians, teachers, counselors, and administrators in order to resolve students' behavioral and academic problems. Coordinate placement of students with special needs into mainstream classes. Employ special educational strategies and techniques during instruction to improve the development of sensory- and perceptual-motor skills, language, cognition, and memory. Establish and enforce rules for behavior and policies and procedures to maintain order among the students for whom they are responsible. Establish clear objectives for all lessons, units, and projects and communicate those objectives to students. Guide and counsel students with adjustment and/or academic problems or special academic interests. Instruct and monitor students in the use and care of equipment and materials in order to prevent injuries and damage. Maintain accurate and complete student records and prepare reports on children and activities as required by laws, district policies, and administrative regulations. Meet with parents and guardians to discuss their children's progress and to determine their priorities for their children and their resource needs. Meet with parents to provide guidance in using community resources and to teach skills for dealing with students' impairments. Monitor teachers and teacher assistants to ensure that they adhere to inclusive special education program requirements. Observe and evaluate students' performance, behavior, social development, and physical health. Organize and label materials and display students' work in a manner appropriate for their eye levels and perceptual skills. Organize and supervise games and other recreational activities to promote physical, mental, and social development. Plan and conduct activities for a balanced program of instruction, demonstration, and work time that provides students with opportunities to observe, question, and investigate. Plan and supervise class projects, field trips, visits by guest speakers, or other experiential activities and guide students in learning from those activities. Prepare classrooms for class activities and provide a variety of materials and resources for children to explore, manipulate, and use, both in learning activities and in imaginative play. Prepare for assigned classes and show written evidence of preparation upon request of immediate supervisors. Prepare objectives and outlines for courses of study, following curriculum guidelines or requirements of states and schools. Prepare students for later grades by encouraging them to explore learning opportunities and to persevere with challenging tasks. Prepare, administer, and grade tests and assignments to evaluate students' progress. Provide interpretation and transcription of regular classroom materials through Braille and sign language. Supervise, evaluate, and plan assignments for teacher assistants and volunteers. Teach socially acceptable behavior, employing techniques such as behavior modification and positive reinforcement. Teach students personal development skills such as goal setting, independence, and self-advocacy. Administer standardized ability and achievement tests and interpret results to determine students' strengths and areas of need. Attend professional meetings, educational conferences, and teacher training workshops in order to maintain and improve professional competence. Attend staff meetings and serve on committees as required. Collaborate with other teachers and administrators in the development, evaluation, and revision of preschool, kindergarten, or elementary school programs. Perform administrative duties such as assisting in school libraries, hall and cafeteria monitoring, and bus loading and unloading. Provide assistive devices, supportive technology, and assistance accessing facilities such as restrooms. Select, store, order, issue, and inventory classroom equipment, materials, and supplies. Visit schools to tutor students with sensory impairments and to consult with teachers regarding students' special needs. Use computers, audiovisual aids, and other equipment and materials to supplement presentations.

GOE INFORMATION—Interest Area: 12. Education and Social Service. **Work Group:** 12.03. Educational Services. **Personality Type—**Social. Social occupations frequently involve working with, communicating with, and teaching people. These occupations often involve helping or providing service to others. **Work Values—**Social Service; Authority; Creativity; Achievement; Responsibility. **Skills—**Learning Strategies; Social Perceptiveness; Instructing; Speaking; Monitoring; Complex Problem Solving; Active Listening; Writing. **Abilities—***Cognitive:* Written Expression; Oral Expression; Written Comprehension; Oral Comprehension; Problem Sensitivity. *Psychomotor:* None met the criteria. *Physical:* None met the criteria. *Sensory:* Speech Clarity; Speech Recognition; Auditory Attention. **General Work Activities—***Information Input:* Getting Information; Identifying Objects, Actions, and Events; Monitoring Processes, Materials, or Surroundings. *Mental Process:* Making Decisions and Solving Problems; Updating and Using Relevant Knowledge; Analyzing Data or Information. *Work Output:* Documenting or Recording Information; Handling and Moving Objects; Performing General Physical Activities. *Interacting with Others:* Assisting and Caring for Others; Establishing and Maintaining Relationships; Performing for or Working with the Public. **Physical Work Conditions—**Sitting; Disease or Infections; Indoors. **Other Job Characteristics—**Importance of Repeating Same Tasks; Importance of Being Exact or Accurate; Pace Determined by Speed of Equipment.

Experience—Job Zone 4. A minimum of two to four years of work-related skill, knowledge, or experience is needed. **Job Preparation:** SVP 7.0 to less than 8.0—two years to less than 10 years. **Knowledge—**Therapy and Counseling; Education and Training; Psychology; Medicine and Dentistry; Customer and Personal Service. **Instructional Programs—**Education/Teaching of Individuals with Autism; Education/Teaching of Individuals with Emotional Disturbances; Education/Teaching of Individuals with Hearing Impairments, Including Deafness; Education/Teaching of Individuals with Mental Retardation; Education/Teaching of Individuals with Multiple Disabilities; Education/Teaching of Individuals with Orthopedic and Other Physical Health Impairments; Education/Teaching of Individuals with Specific Learning Disabilities; Education/Teaching of Individuals with Speech or Language Impairments; Education/Teaching of Individuals with Traumatic Brain Injuries; Education/Teaching of Individuals with Vision Impairments, Including Blindness; Special Education and Teaching, General; Special Education and Teaching, Other.

Related DOT Jobs—094.224-010 Teacher, Hearing Impaired; 094.224-014 Teacher, Physically Impaired; 094.224-018 Teacher, Visually Impaired; 094.227-010 Teacher, Emotionally Impaired; 094.227-022 Teacher, Mentally Impaired; 094.227-030 Teacher, Learning Disabled; 099.227-042 Teacher, Resource.

25-2042.00 Special Education Teachers, Middle School

- **Education/Training Required: Bachelor's degree**
- **Employed: 95,740**
- **Annual Earnings: $40,010**
- **Growth: 24.4%**
- **Annual Job Openings: 6,000**

Teach middle school subjects to educationally and physically handicapped students. Includes teachers who specialize and work with audibly and visually handicapped students and those who teach basic academic and life processes skills to the mentally impaired.

Develop and implement strategies to meet the needs of students with a variety of handicapping conditions. Instruct students in daily living skills required for independent maintenance and self-sufficiency, such as hygiene, safety, and food preparation. Instruct through lectures, discussions, and demonstrations in one or more subjects, such as English, mathematics, or social studies. Confer with parents, administrators, testing specialists, social workers, and professionals to develop individual educational plans designed to promote students' educational, physical, and social development. Employ special educational strategies and techniques during instruction to improve the development of sensory- and perceptual-motor skills, language, cognition, and memory. Modify the general education curriculum for special-needs students based upon a variety of instructional techniques and instructional technology. Confer with other staff members to plan and schedule lessons promoting learning, following approved curricula. Confer with parents or guardians, other teachers, counselors, and administrators in order to resolve students' behavioral and academic problems. Coordinate placement of students with special needs into mainstream classes. Establish and enforce rules for behavior and policies and procedures to maintain order among students. Establish clear objectives for all lessons, units, and projects and communicate those objectives to students. Guide and counsel students with adjustment and/or academic problems or special academic interests. Instruct and monitor students in the use and care of equipment and materials in order to prevent injuries and damage. Maintain accurate and complete student records and prepare reports on children and activities as required by laws, district policies, and administrative regulations. Meet with parents and guardians to discuss their children's progress and to determine their priorities for their children and their resource needs. Meet with parents and guardians to provide guidance in using community resources and to teach skills for dealing with students' impairments. Monitor teachers and teacher assistants to ensure that they adhere to inclusive special education program requirements. Observe and evaluate students' performance, behavior, social development, and physical health. Organize and label materials and display students' work. Organize and supervise games and other recreational activities to promote physical, mental, and social development. Plan and conduct activities for a balanced program of instruction, demonstration, and work time that provides students with opportunities to observe, question, and investigate. Plan and supervise class projects, field trips, visits by guest speakers, or other experiential activities and guide students in learning from those activities. Prepare for assigned classes and show written evidence of preparation upon request of immediate supervisors. Prepare materials and classrooms for class activities. Prepare objectives and outlines for courses of study, following curriculum guidelines or requirements of states and schools. Prepare, administer, and grade tests and assignments to evaluate students' progress. Provide additional instruction in vocational areas. Provide interpretation and transcription of regular classroom materials through Braille and sign language. Supervise, evaluate, and plan assignments for teacher assistants and volunteers. Teach socially acceptable behavior, employing techniques such as behavior modification and positive reinforcement. Teach students personal development skills such as goal setting, independence, and self-advocacy. Administer standardized ability and achievement tests and interpret results to determine students' strengths and areas of need. Attend professional meetings, educational conferences, and teacher training workshops in order to maintain and improve professional competence. Attend staff meetings and serve on committees as required. Perform administrative duties such as assisting in school libraries, hall and cafeteria monitoring, and bus loading and unloading. Provide assistive devices, supportive technology, and assistance accessing facilities such as restrooms. Select, store, order, issue, and inventory classroom equipment, materials, and supplies. Sponsor extracurricular activities such as clubs, student organizations, and academic contests. Use computers, audiovisual aids, and other equipment and materials to supplement presentations. Visit schools to tutor students with sensory impairments and to consult with teachers regarding students' special needs.

GOE INFORMATION—Interest Area: 12. Education and Social Service. **Work Group:** 12.03. Educational Services. **Personality Type**—Social. Social occupations frequently involve working with, communicating with, and teaching people. These occupations often involve helping or providing service to others. **Work Values**—Social Service; Authority; Creativity; Achievement; Responsibility. **Skills**—Learning Strategies; Social Perceptiveness; Instructing; Speaking; Monitoring; Complex Problem Solving; Active Listening; Writing. **Abilities**—*Cognitive:* Written Expression; Oral Expression; Written Comprehension; Oral Comprehension; Problem Sensitivity. *Psychomotor:* None met the criteria. *Physical:* None met the criteria. *Sensory:* Speech Clarity; Speech Recognition; Auditory Attention. **General Work Activities**—*Information Input:* Getting Information; Identifying Objects, Actions, and Events; Monitoring Processes, Materials, or Surroundings. *Mental Process:* Updating and Using Relevant Knowledge; Making Decisions and Solving Problems; Analyzing Data or Information. *Work Output:* Documenting or Recording Information; Handling and Moving Objects; Performing General Physical Activities. *Interacting with Others:* Assisting and Caring for Others; Establishing and Maintaining Relationships; Teaching Others. **Physical Work Conditions**—Sitting; Disease or Infections; Indoors. **Other Job Characteristics**—Importance of Repeating Same Tasks; Importance of Being Exact or Accurate; Pace Determined by Speed of Equipment.

Experience—Job Zone 4. A minimum of two to four years of work-related skill, knowledge, or experience is needed. **Job Preparation:** SVP 7.0 to less than 8.0—two years to less than 10 years. **Knowledge**—Therapy and Counseling; Education and Training; Psychology; Medicine and Dentistry; Customer and Personal Service. **Instructional Programs**—Special Education and Teaching, General.

Related DOT Jobs—094.224-010 Teacher, Hearing Impaired; 094.224-014 Teacher, Physically Impaired; 094.224-018 Teacher, Visually Impaired; 094.224-018 Teacher, Vocational Training; 094.227-010 Teacher, Emotionally Impaired; 094.227-022 Teacher, Mentally Impaired; 094.227-030 Teacher, Learning Disabled; 099.227-042 Teacher, Resource.

25-2043.00 Special Education Teachers, Secondary School

- **Education/Training Required: Bachelor's degree**
- **Employed: 122,778**
- **Annual Earnings: $42,780**
- **Growth: 24.6%**
- **Annual Job Openings: 8,000**

Teach secondary school subjects to educationally and physically handicapped students. Includes teachers who specialize and work with audibly and visually handicapped students and those who teach basic academic and life processes skills to the mentally impaired.

Develop and implement strategies to meet the needs of students with a variety of handicapping conditions. Instruct students in daily living skills required for independent maintenance and self-sufficiency, such as hygiene, safety, and food preparation. Instruct through lectures, discussions, and demonstrations in one or more subjects, such as English, mathematics, or social studies. Confer with parents, administrators, testing specialists, social workers, and professionals to develop individual educational plans designed to promote students' educational, physical, and social development. Modify the general education curriculum for special-needs students, based upon a variety of instructional techniques and technologies. Confer with other staff members to plan and schedule lessons promoting learning, following approved curricula. Confer with parents or guardians, other teachers, counselors, and administrators in order to resolve students' behavioral and academic problems. Coordinate placement of students with special needs into mainstream classes. Employ special educational strategies and techniques during instruction to improve the development of sensory- and perceptual-motor skills, language, cognition, and memory. Establish and enforce rules for behavior and policies and procedures to maintain order among students. Establish clear objectives for all lessons, units, and projects and communicate those objectives to students. Guide and counsel students with adjustment and/or academic problems or special academic interests. Instruct and monitor students in the use and care of equipment and materials in order to prevent injuries and damage. Maintain accurate and complete student records and prepare reports on children and activities as required by laws, district policies, and administrative regulations. Meet with other professionals to discuss individual students' needs and progress. Meet with parents and guardians to discuss their children's progress and to determine their priorities for their children and their resource needs. Meet with parents and guardians to provide guidance in using community resources and to teach skills for dealing with students' impairments. Observe and evaluate students' performance, behavior, social development, and physical health. Plan and conduct activities for a balanced program of instruction, demonstration, and work time that provides students with opportunities to observe, question, and investigate. Plan and supervise class projects, field trips, visits by guest speakers, or other experiential activities and guide students in learning from those activities. Prepare for assigned classes and show written evidence of preparation upon request of immediate supervisors. Prepare materials and classrooms for class activities. Prepare objectives and outlines for courses of study, following curriculum guidelines or requirements of states and schools. Prepare students for later grades by encouraging them to explore learning opportunities and to persevere with challenging tasks. Prepare, administer, and grade tests and assignments to evaluate students' progress. Provide interpretation and transcription of regular classroom materials through Braille and sign language. Teach personal development skills such as goal setting, independence, and self-advocacy. Teach socially acceptable behavior, employing techniques such as behavior modification and positive reinforcement. Administer standardized ability and achievement tests, and interpret results to determine students' strengths and areas of need. Attend professional meetings, educational conferences, and teacher training workshops to maintain and improve professional competence. Attend staff meetings and serve on committees as required. Collaborate with other teachers and administrators in the development, evaluation, and revision of secondary school programs. Monitor teachers and teacher assistants to ensure that they adhere to inclusive special education program requirements. Perform administrative duties such as assisting in school libraries, hall and cafeteria monitoring, and bus loading and unloading. Provide additional instruction in vocational areas. Provide assistive devices, supportive technology, and assistance accessing facilities such as restrooms. Select, store, order, issue, and inventory classroom equipment, materials, and supplies. Sponsor extracurricular activities such as clubs, student organizations, and academic contests. Visit schools to tutor students with sensory impairments and to consult with teachers regarding students' special needs. Use computers, audiovisual aids, and other equipment and materials to supplement presentations.

GOE INFORMATION—Interest Area: 12. Education and Social Service. **Work Group:** 12.03. Educational Services. **Personality Type**—Social. Social occupations frequently involve working with, communicating with, and teaching people. These occupations often involve helping or providing service to others. **Work Values**—Social Service; Authority; Creativity; Achievement; Responsibility. **Skills**—Learning Strategies; Social Perceptiveness; Instructing; Speaking; Monitoring; Complex Problem Solving; Active Listening; Writing. **Abilities**—*Cognitive:* Written Expression; Oral Expression; Written Comprehension; Oral Comprehension; Problem Sensitivity. *Psychomotor:* None met the criteria. *Physical:* None met the criteria. *Sensory:* Speech Clarity; Speech Recognition; Auditory Attention. **General Work Activities**—*Information Input:* Getting Information; Identifying Objects, Actions, and Events; Monitoring Processes, Materials, or Surroundings. *Mental Process:* Making Decisions and Solving Problems; Updating and Using Relevant Knowledge; Analyzing Data or Information. *Work Output:* Documenting or Recording Information; Handling and Moving Objects; Performing General Physical Activities. *Interacting with Others:* Assisting and Caring for Others; Establishing and Maintaining Relationships; Performing for or Working with the Public. **Physical Work Conditions**—Sitting; Disease or Infections; Indoors. **Other Job Characteristics**—Importance of Repeating Same Tasks; Importance of Being Exact or Accurate; Pace Determined by Speed of Equipment.

Experience—Job Zone 4. A minimum of two to four years of work-related skill, knowledge, or experience is needed. **Job Preparation:** SVP 7.0 to less than 8.0—two years to less than 10 years. **Knowledge**—Therapy and Counseling; Education and Training; Psychology; Medicine and Dentistry; Customer and Personal Service. **Instructional Programs**—Special Education and Teaching, General.

Related DOT Jobs—094.107-010 Work-Study Coordinator, Special Education; 094.224-010 Teacher, Hearing Impaired; 094.224-014 Teacher, Physically Impaired; 094.224-018 Teacher, Visually Impaired; 094.227-010 Teacher, Emotionally Impaired; 094.227-022 Teacher, Mentally Impaired; 094.227-026 Teacher, Vocational Training; 094.227-030 Teacher, Learning Disabled; 099.227-042 Teacher, Resource.

25-3000 Other Teachers and Instructors

25-3011.00 Adult Literacy, Remedial Education, and GED Teachers and Instructors

- Education/Training Required: Bachelor's degree
- Employed: 66,569
- Annual Earnings: $35,220
- Growth: 19.4%
- Annual Job Openings: 12,000

Teach or instruct out-of-school youths and adults in remedial education classes, preparatory classes for the General Educational Development test, literacy, or English as a Second Language. Teaching may or may not take place in a traditional educational institution.

Conduct classes, workshops, and demonstrations to teach principles, techniques, or methods in subjects such as basic English language skills, life skills, and workforce entry skills. Instruct students individually and in groups, using various teaching methods such as lectures, discussions, and demonstrations. Assign and grade class work and homework. Adapt teaching methods and instructional materials to meet students' varying needs, abilities, and interests. Confer with other staff members to plan and schedule lessons that promote learning, following approved curricula.

Enforce administration policies and rules governing students. Establish and enforce rules for behavior and procedures for maintaining order among the students for whom they are responsible. Establish clear objectives for all lessons, units, and projects and communicate those objectives to students. Guide and counsel students with adjustment and/or academic problems or special academic interests. Maintain accurate and complete student records as required by laws or administrative policies. Meet with other professionals to discuss individual students' needs and progress. Observe and evaluate students' work to determine progress and make suggestions for improvement. Observe students to determine qualifications, limitations, abilities, interests, and other individual characteristics. Plan and conduct activities for a balanced program of instruction, demonstration, and work time that provides students with opportunities to observe, question, and investigate. Plan and supervise class projects, field trips, visits by guest speakers, contests, or other experiential activities and guide students in learning from those activities. Prepare and administer written, oral, and performance tests and issue grades in accordance with performance. Prepare and implement remedial programs for students requiring extra help. Prepare for assigned classes and show written evidence of preparation upon request of immediate supervisors. Prepare materials and classrooms for class activities. Prepare objectives and outlines for courses of study, following curriculum guidelines or requirements of states and schools. Prepare reports on students and activities as required by administration. Prepare students for further education by encouraging them to explore learning opportunities and to persevere with challenging tasks. Provide information, guidance, and preparation for the General Equivalency Diploma (GED) examination. Review instructional content, methods, and student evaluations to assess strengths and weaknesses and to develop recommendations for course revision, development, or elimination. Advise students on internships, prospective employers, and job placement services. Attend professional meetings, conferences, and workshops in order to maintain and improve professional competence. Attend staff meetings and serve on committees as required. Collaborate with other teachers and professionals in the development of instructional programs. Confer with leaders of government and community groups to coordinate student training or to find opportunities for students to fulfill curriculum requirements. Observe and evaluate the performance of other instructors. Participate in publicity planning, community awareness efforts, and student recruitment. Provide disabled students with assistive devices, supportive technology, and assistance accessing facilities such as restrooms. Register, orient, and assess new students according to standards and procedures. Select and schedule class times to ensure maximum attendance. Select, order, and issue books, materials, and supplies for courses or projects. Train and assist tutors and community literacy volunteers. Write grants to obtain program funding. Write instructional articles on designated subjects. Use computers, audiovisual aids, and other equipment and materials to supplement presentations.

GOE INFORMATION—**Interest Area:** 12. Education and Social Service. **Work Group:** 12.03. Educational Services. **Personality Type**—Social. Social occupations frequently involve working with, communicating with, and teaching people. These occupations often involve helping or providing service to others. **Work Values**—Authority; Social Service; Creativity; Achievement; Responsibility. **Skills**—Instructing; Speaking; Writing; Complex Problem Solving; Learning Strategies; Active Listening; Reading Comprehension; Systems Evaluation. **Abilities**—*Cognitive:* Written Expression; Oral Expression; Oral Comprehension; Fluency of Ideas; Originality. *Psychomotor:* None met the criteria. *Physical:* Gross Body Equilibrium. *Sensory:* Speech Clarity; Auditory Attention; Speech Recognition; Sound Localization. **General Work Activities**—*Information Input:* Getting Information; Monitoring Processes, Materials, or Surroundings; Identifying Objects, Actions, and Events. *Mental Process:* Organizing, Planning, and Prioritizing; Updating and Using Relevant

Knowledge; Scheduling Work and Activities. *Work Output:* Documenting or Recording Information; Performing General Physical Activities; Handling and Moving Objects. *Interacting with Others:* Teaching Others; Communicating with Persons Outside Organization; Coaching and Developing Others. **Physical Work Conditions**—Indoors; Sitting; Walking or Running; Standing. **Other Job Characteristics**—Importance of Being Exact or Accurate; Importance of Repeating Same Tasks; Pace Determined by Speed of Equipment.

Experience—Job Zone 4. A minimum of two to four years of work-related skill, knowledge, or experience is needed. **Job Preparation:** SVP 7.0 to less than 8.0—two years to less than 10 years. **Knowledge**—Education and Training; English Language; Philosophy and Theology; History and Archeology; Fine Arts. **Instructional Programs**—Adult and Continuing Education and Teaching; Adult Literacy Tutor/Instructor; Bilingual and Multilingual Education; Multicultural Education; Teaching English as a Second or Foreign Language/ESL Language Instructor.

Related DOT Jobs—099.227-030 Teacher, Adult Education.

25-3021.00 Self-Enrichment Education Teachers

- **Education/Training Required: Work experience in a related occupation**
- **Employed: 185,676**
- **Annual Earnings: $28,880**
- **Growth: 18.5%**
- **Annual Job Openings: 34,000**

Teach or instruct courses other than those that normally lead to an occupational objective or degree. Courses may include self-improvement, nonvocational, and nonacademic subjects. Teaching may or may not take place in a traditional educational institution.

Conduct classes, workshops, and demonstrations and provide individual instruction to teach topics and skills such as cooking, dancing, writing, physical fitness, photography, personal finance, and flying. Instruct students individually and in groups, using various teaching methods such as lectures, discussions, and demonstrations. Adapt teaching methods and instructional materials to meet students' varying needs and interests. Assign and grade class work and homework. Confer with other teachers and professionals to plan and schedule lessons promoting learning and development. Enforce policies and rules governing students. Establish clear objectives for all lessons, units, and projects and communicate those objectives to students. Instruct and monitor students in use and care of equipment and materials in order to prevent injury and damage. Maintain accurate and complete student records as required by administrative policy. Meet with other instructors to discuss individual students and their progress. Monitor students' performance in order to make suggestions for improvement and to ensure that they satisfy course standards, training requirements, and objectives. Observe students to determine qualifications, limitations, abilities, interests, and other individual characteristics. Plan and conduct activities for a balanced program of instruction, demonstration, and work time that provides students with opportunities to observe, question, and investigate. Plan and supervise class projects, field trips, visits by guest speakers, contests, or other experiential activities and guide students in learning from those activities. Prepare and administer written, oral, and performance tests and issue grades in accordance with performance. Prepare and implement remedial programs for students requiring extra help. Prepare instructional program objectives, outlines, and lesson plans. Prepare materials and classrooms for class activities. Prepare students for further development by encouraging them to explore learning opportunities and to persevere with challenging tasks. Review instructional content, methods, and student evaluations in order to assess strengths and weaknesses and to develop recommendations for course revision, development, or elimination. Attend professional meetings, conferences, and workshops in order to maintain and improve professional competence. Attend staff meetings and serve on committees as required. Meet with parents and guardians to discuss their children's progress and to determine their priorities for their children. Observe and evaluate the performance of other instructors. Organize and supervise games and other recreational activities to promote physical, mental, and social development. Participate in publicity planning and student recruitment. Schedule class times to ensure maximum attendance. Select, order, and issue books, materials, and supplies for courses or projects. Write instructional articles on designated subjects. Use computers, audiovisual aids, and other equipment and materials to supplement presentations.

GOE INFORMATION—**Interest Area:** 12. Education and Social Service. **Work Group:** 12.03. Educational Services. **Personality Type**—Social. Social occupations frequently involve working with, communicating with, and teaching people. These occupations often involve helping or providing service to others. **Work Values**—Authority; Social Service; Creativity; Achievement; Responsibility. **Skills**—Instructing; Speaking; Writing; Complex Problem Solving; Learning Strategies; Active Listening; Reading Comprehension; Systems Evaluation. **Abilities**—*Cognitive:* Written Expression; Oral Expression; Oral Comprehension; Fluency of Ideas; Originality. *Psychomotor:* None met the criteria. *Physical:* Gross Body Equilibrium. *Sensory:* Speech Clarity; Auditory Attention; Speech Recognition; Sound Localization. **General Work Activities**—*Information Input:* Getting Information; Monitoring Processes, Materials, or Surroundings; Identifying Objects, Actions, and Events. *Mental Process:* Organizing, Planning, and Prioritizing; Updating and Using Relevant Knowledge; Scheduling Work and Activities. *Work Output:* Documenting or Recording Information; Performing General Physical Activities; Handling and Moving Objects. *Interacting with Others:* Teaching Others; Communicating with Persons Outside Organization; Coaching and Developing Others. **Physical Work Conditions**—Indoors; Sitting; Walking or Running; Standing. **Other Job Characteristics**—Importance of Being Exact or Accurate; Importance of Repeating Same Tasks; Pace Determined by Speed of Equipment.

Experience—Job Zone 4. A minimum of two to four years of work-related skill, knowledge, or experience is needed. **Job Preparation:** SVP 7.0 to less than 8.0—two years to less than 10 years. **Knowledge**—Education and Training; English Language; Philosophy and Theology; History and Archeology; Fine Arts. **Instructional Programs**—Adult and Continuing Education and Teaching.

Related DOT Jobs—090.227-018 Instructor, Extension Work; 097.227-010 Instructor, Flying II; 099.223-010 Instructor, Driving; 099.224-014 099.Teacher, Adventure Education; 099.227-026 Instructor, Modeling; 099.227-030 Teacher, Adult Education; 099.227-038 Teacher; 149.021-010 Teacher, Art; 150.027-014 Teacher, Drama; 151.027-014 Instructor, Dancing; 152.021-010 Teacher, Music; 159.227-010 Instructor, Bridge; 169.127-010 Civil Preparedness Training Officer.

25-3099.99 Teachers and Instructors, All Other

- **Education/Training Required: Bachelor's degree**
- **Employed: No data available.**
- **Annual Earnings: No data available.**
- **Growth: 19.4%**
- **Annual Job Openings: 119,000**

All teachers and instructors not listed separately.

No task data available.

GOE INFORMATION—Interest Area: 12. Education and Social Service. **Work Group:** 12.03. Educational Services. **Note:** The Department of Labor has not collected some data for this job, so it has fewer details than the other descriptions.

Instructional Programs—Education, Other; Multicultural Education; Teacher Education and Professional Development, Specific Levels and Methods, Other.

Related DOT Jobs—076.224-014 Orientation And Mobility Therapist For The Blind; 090.227-018 Instructor, Extension Work; 099.227-034 Tutor.

25-4000 Librarians, Curators, and Archivists

25-4011.00 Archivists

- **Education/Training Required: Master's degree**
- **Employed: No data available.**
- **Annual Earnings: $34,190**
- **Growth: 11.9%**
- **Annual Job Openings: 1,000**

Appraise, edit, and direct safekeeping of permanent records and historically valuable documents. Participate in research activities based on archival materials.

Authenticate and appraise historical documents and archival materials. Create and maintain accessible, retrievable computer archives and databases, incorporating current advances in electric information storage technology. Direct activities of workers who assist in arranging, cataloguing, exhibiting, and maintaining collections of valuable materials. Locate new materials and direct their acquisition and display. Organize archival records and develop classification systems to facilitate access to archival materials. Prepare archival records, such as document descriptions, to allow easy access to information. Preserve records, documents, and objects, copying records to film, videotape, audiotape, disk, or computer formats as necessary. Research and record the origins and historical significance of archival materials. Select and edit documents for publication and display, applying knowledge of subject, literary expression, and presentation techniques. Coordinate educational and public outreach programs, such as tours, workshops, lectures, and classes. Establish and administer policy guidelines concerning public access and use of materials. Provide reference services and assistance for users needing archival materials. Specialize in an area of history or technology, researching topics or items relevant to collections to determine what should be retained or acquired.

GOE INFORMATION—Interest Area: 12. Education and Social Service. **Work Group:** 12.03. Educational Services. **Personality Type**—Investigative. Investigative occupations frequently involve working with ideas and require an extensive amount of thinking. These occupations can involve searching for facts and figuring out problems mentally. **Work Values**—Good Working Conditions; Authority; Creativity; Autonomy; Ability Utilization. **Skills**—Management of Personnel Resources; Writing; Management of Material Resources; Complex Problem Solving; Reading Comprehension; Speaking; Systems Evaluation; Judgment and Decision Making. **Abilities**—*Cognitive:* Written Comprehension; Category Flexibility; Memorization; Written Expression; Oral Expression.

Psychomotor: None met the criteria. *Physical:* None met the criteria. *Sensory:* Speech Clarity; Near Vision. **General Work Activities**—*Information Input:* Identifying Objects, Actions, and Events; Getting Information; Estimating Needed Characteristics. *Mental Process:* Judging Qualities of Things, Services, or Other People's Work; Processing Information; Analyzing Data or Information. *Work Output:* Documenting or Recording Information; Handling and Moving Objects; Performing General Physical Activities. *Interacting with Others:* Communicating with Other Workers; Monitoring and Controlling Resources; Communicating with Persons Outside Organization. **Physical Work Conditions**—Indoors; Sitting; Walking or Running. **Other Job Characteristics**—Importance of Being Exact or Accurate; Consequence of Error; Importance of Repeating Same Tasks.

Experience—Job Zone 5. Extensive skill, knowledge, and experience are needed for these occupations. **Job Preparation:** SVP 8.0 and above—four years to more than 10 years. **Knowledge**—History and Archeology; Administration and Management; Sociology and Anthropology; Communications and Media; Philosophy and Theology. **Instructional Programs**—Art History, Criticism, and Conservation; Cultural Resource Management and Policy Analysis; Historic Preservation and Conservation; Historic Preservation and Conservation, Other; Museology/Museum Studies; Public/Applied History and Archival Administration.

Related DOT Jobs—101.167-010 Archivist.

25-4012.00 Curators

- **Education/Training Required: Master's degree**
- **Employed: No data available.**
- **Annual Earnings: $34,190**
- **Growth: 11.9%**
- **Annual Job Openings: 1,000**

Administer affairs of museum and conduct research programs. Direct instructional, research, and public service activities of institution.

Attend meetings, conventions, and civic events to promote use of institution's services, to seek financing, and to maintain community alliances. Conduct or organize tours, workshops, and instructional sessions to acquaint individuals with an institution's facilities and materials. Confer with the board of directors to formulate and interpret policies, to determine budget requirements, and to plan overall operations. Negotiate and authorize purchase, sale, exchange, or loan of collections. Plan and organize the acquisition, storage, and exhibition of collections and related materials, including the selection of exhibition themes and designs. Provide information from the institution's holdings to other curators and to the public. Schedule events and organize details, including refreshment, entertainment, decorations, and the collection of any fees. Train and supervise curatorial, fiscal, technical, research, and clerical staff, as well as volunteers or interns. Arrange insurance coverage for objects on loan or for special exhibits and recommend changes in coverage for the entire collection. Develop and maintain an institution's registration, cataloging, and basic record-keeping systems, using computer databases. Establish specifications for reproductions and oversee their manufacture or select items from commercially available replica sources. Inspect premises to assess the need for repairs and to ensure that climate and pest-control issues are addressed. Plan and conduct special research projects in area of interest or expertise. Study, examine, and test acquisitions to authenticate their origin, composition, and history and to assess their current value. Write and review grant proposals, journal articles, institutional reports, and publicity materials.

GOE INFORMATION—Interest Area: 12. Education and Social Service. **Work Group:** 12.03. Educational Services. **Personality Type**—Artistic.

Artistic occupations frequently involve working with forms, designs, and patterns. They often require self-expression, and the work can be done without following a clear set of rules. **Work Values**—Authority; Creativity; Good Working Conditions; Responsibility; Pleasant Co-workers. **Skills**—Management of Financial Resources; Management of Personnel Resources; Management of Material Resources; Writing; Systems Evaluation; Systems Analysis; Complex Problem Solving; Judgment and Decision Making. **Abilities**—*Cognitive:* Category Flexibility; Written Expression; Memorization; Fluency of Ideas; Oral Comprehension. *Psychomotor:* None met the criteria. *Physical:* None met the criteria. *Sensory:* Speech Clarity; Auditory Attention; Far Vision; Sound Localization; Glare Sensitivity. **General Work Activities**—*Information Input:* Getting Information; Identifying Objects, Actions, and Events; Estimating Needed Characteristics. *Mental Process:* Judging Qualities of Things, Services, or Other People's Work; Organizing, Planning, and Prioritizing; Analyzing Data or Information. *Work Output:* Documenting or Recording Information; Handling and Moving Objects; Drafting and Specifying Technical Devices. *Interacting with Others:* Monitoring and Controlling Resources; Communicating with Persons Outside Organization; Communicating with Other Workers. **Physical Work Conditions**—Indoors; Walking or Running. **Other Job Characteristics**—Importance of Being Exact or Accurate; Consequence of Error; Degree of Automation.

Experience—Job Zone 4. A minimum of two to four years of work-related skill, knowledge, or experience is needed. **Job Preparation:** SVP 7.0 to less than 8.0—two years to less than 10 years. **Knowledge**—History and Archeology; Administration and Management; Fine Arts; Philosophy and Theology; Sociology and Anthropology. **Instructional Programs**—Art History, Criticism, and Conservation; Museology/Museum Studies; Public/Applied History and Archival Administration.

Related DOT Jobs—099.167-030 Educational Resource Coordinator; 102.017-010 Curator; 102.117-010 Supervisor, Historic Sites; 102.117-014 Director, Museum-or-Zoo; 102.167-014 Historic-Site Administrator; 102.167-018 Registrar, Museum.

25-4013.00 Museum Technicians and Conservators

- ● **Education/Training Required: Master's degree**
- ● **Employed: No data available.**
- ● **Annual Earnings: $34,190**
- ● **Growth: 11.9%**
- ● **Annual Job Openings: 1,000**

Prepare specimens, such as fossils, skeletal parts, lace, and textiles, for museum collection and exhibits. May restore documents or install, arrange, and exhibit materials.

Classify and assign registration numbers to artifacts and supervise inventory control. Clean objects, such as paper, textiles, wood, metal, glass, rock, pottery, and furniture, using cleansers, solvents, soap solutions, and polishes. Coordinate exhibit installations, assisting with design, constructing displays, dioramas, display cases, and models and ensuring the availability of necessary materials. Determine whether objects need repair and choose the safest and most effective method of repair. Install, arrange, assemble, and prepare artifacts for exhibition, ensuring the artifacts' safety, reporting their status and condition, and identifying and correcting any problems with the setup. Prepare artifacts for storage and shipping. Preserve or direct preservation of objects, using plaster, resin, sealants, hardeners, and shellac. Repair, restore, and reassemble artifacts, designing and fabricating missing or broken parts, to restore them to their original appearance and prevent deterioration. Construct skeletal mounts of fossils, replicas of archaeological artifacts, or duplicate specimens, using a variety of materials and hand tools. Direct and supervise curatorial and technical staff in the handling, mounting, care, and storage of art objects. Estimate cost of restoration work. Notify superior when restoration of artifacts requires outside experts. Perform tests and examinations to establish storage and conservation requirements, policies, and procedures. Plan and conduct research to develop and improve methods of restoring and preserving specimens. Prepare reports on the operation of conservation laboratories, documenting the condition of artifacts, treatment options, and the methods of preservation and repair used. Recommend preservation procedures, such as control of temperature and humidity, to curatorial and building staff. Study object documentation or conduct standard chemical and physical tests to ascertain the object's age, composition, original appearance, need for treatment or restoration, and appropriate preservation method. Supervise and work with volunteers. Build, repair, and install wooden steps, scaffolds, and walkways to gain access to or permit improved view of exhibited equipment. Cut and weld metal sections in reconstruction or renovation of exterior structural sections and accessories of exhibits. Perform on-site field work, which may involve interviewing people, inspecting and identifying artifacts, note-taking, viewing sites and collections, and repainting exhibition spaces. Present public programs and tours. Specialize in particular materials or types of object, such as documents and books, paintings, decorative arts, textiles, metals, or architectural materials.

GOE INFORMATION—**Interest Area:** 12. Education and Social Service. **Work Group:** 12.03. Educational Services. **Personality Type**—Artistic. Artistic occupations frequently involve working with forms, designs, and patterns. They often require self-expression, and the work can be done without following a clear set of rules. **Work Values**—Good Working Conditions; Pleasant Co-workers; Ability Utilization; Achievement; Authority. **Skills**—Repairing; Installation; Equipment Selection; Writing; Management of Material Resources; Operations Analysis; Complex Problem Solving; Reading Comprehension. **Abilities**—*Cognitive:* Visualization; Written Expression; Flexibility of Closure; Oral Comprehension; Written Comprehension. *Psychomotor:* Wrist-Finger Speed; Manual Dexterity; Arm-Hand Steadiness; Speed of Limb Movement; Finger Dexterity. *Physical:* Explosive Strength; Dynamic Flexibility; Dynamic Strength. *Sensory:* Visual Color Discrimination; Near Vision; Speech Clarity; Depth Perception; Night Vision. **General Work Activities**—*Information Input:* Getting Information; Identifying Objects, Actions, and Events; Inspecting Equipment, Structures, or Materials. *Mental Process:* Judging Qualities of Things, Services, or Other People's Work; Processing Information; Organizing, Planning, and Prioritizing. *Work Output:* Handling and Moving Objects; Performing General Physical Activities; Drafting and Specifying Technical Devices. *Interacting with Others:* Communicating with Other Workers; Interpreting Meaning of Information for Others; Providing Consultation and Advice to Others. **Physical Work Conditions**—Kneeling, Crouching, or Crawling; Climbing Ladders, Scaffolds, Poles, etc.; Keeping or Regaining Balance; Walking or Running; Indoors. **Other Job Characteristics**—Pace Determined by Speed of Equipment; Importance of Repeating Same Tasks; Consequence of Error.

Experience—Job Zone 3. Previous work-related skill, knowledge, or experience is required. **Job Preparation:** SVP 6.0 to less than 7.0—more than one year and less than four years. **Knowledge**—History and Archeology; Fine Arts; Building and Construction; Chemistry; Design. **Instructional Programs**—Art History, Criticism, and Conservation; Museology/Museum Studies; Public/Applied History and Archival Administration.

Related DOT Jobs—055.381-010 Conservator, Artifacts; 102.167-010 Art Conservator; 102.261-010 Conservation Technician; 102.361-010 Restorer, Lace and Textiles; 102.361-014 Restorer, Ceramic; 102.367-010 Fine Arts Packer; 102.381-010 Museum Technician; 109.281-010 Armorer Technician; 109.361-010 Restorer, Paper-and-Prints; 779.381-018 Repairer, Art

Objects; 899.384-010 Transportation-Equipment-Maintenance Worker; 979.361-010 Document Restorer.

25-4021.00 Librarians

- **Education/Training Required: Master's degree**
- **Employed: 149,325**
- **Annual Earnings: $42,670**
- **Growth: 7.0%**
- **Annual Job Openings: 6,000**

Administer libraries and perform related library services. Work in a variety of settings, including public libraries, schools, colleges and universities, museums, corporations, government agencies, law firms, non-profit organizations, and health care providers. Tasks may include selecting, acquiring, cataloguing, classifying, circulating, and maintaining library materials and furnishing reference, bibliographical, and readers' advisory services. May perform in-depth strategic research and synthesize, analyze, edit, and filter information. May set up or work with databases and information systems to catalogue and access information.

Analyze patrons' requests to determine needed information and assist in furnishing or locating that information. Arrange for interlibrary loans of materials not available in a particular library. Assemble and arrange display materials. Code, classify, and catalog books, publications, films, audiovisual aids, and other library materials based on subject matter or standard library classification systems. Collect and organize books, pamphlets, manuscripts, and other materials in specific fields, such as rare books, genealogy, or music. Compile lists of books, periodicals, articles, and audiovisual materials on particular subjects. Develop library policies and procedures. Direct and train library staff in duties such as receiving, shelving, researching, cataloging, and equipment use. Evaluate materials to determine outdated or unused items to be discarded. Explain use of library facilities, resources, equipment, and services and provide information about library policies. Keep records of circulation and materials. Locate unusual or unique information in response to specific requests. Organize collections of books, publications, documents, audiovisual aids, and other reference materials for convenient access. Plan and deliver client-centered programs and services such as special services for corporate clients, storytelling for children, newsletters, or programs for special groups. Review and evaluate resource material, such as book reviews and catalogs, in order to select and order print, audiovisual, and electronic resources. Search standard reference materials, including online sources and the Internet, in order to answer patrons' reference questions. Supervise budgeting, planning, and personnel activities. Teach library patrons to search for information using databases. Check books in and out of the library. Compile lists of overdue materials and notify borrowers that their materials are overdue. Confer with teachers, parents, and community organizations to develop, plan, and conduct programs in reading, viewing, and communication skills. Design information storage and retrieval systems and develop procedures for collecting, organizing, interpreting, and classifying information. Develop and index databases that provide information for library users. Develop information access aids such as indexes and annotated bibliographies, Web pages, electronic pathfinders, and online tutorials. Perform public relations work for the library, such as giving televised book reviews and community talks. Plan and participate in fundraising drives.

GOE INFORMATION—Interest Area: 12. Education and Social Service. **Work Group:** 12.03. Educational Services. **Personality Type—**Artistic. Artistic occupations frequently involve working with forms, designs, and patterns. They often require self-expression, and the work can be done without following a clear set of rules. **Work Values—**Authority; Good Working Conditions; Social Service; Pleasant Co-workers; Responsibility. **Skills—**Reading Comprehension; Speaking; Complex Problem Solving; Service Orientation; Management of Material Resources; Learning Strategies; Active Listening; Writing. **Abilities—***Cognitive:* Category Flexibility; Written Comprehension; Written Expression; Speed of Closure; Fluency of Ideas. *Psychomotor:* Wrist-Finger Speed; Response Orientation; Manual Dexterity. *Physical:* Gross Body Equilibrium; Dynamic Flexibility; Extent Flexibility; Static Strength; Trunk Strength. *Sensory:* Speech Recognition; Near Vision; Speech Clarity; Far Vision; Sound Localization. **General Work Activities—***Information Input:* Getting Information; Estimating Needed Characteristics; Identifying Objects, Actions, and Events. *Mental Process:* Processing Information; Judging Qualities of Things, Services, or Other People's Work; Scheduling Work and Activities. *Work Output:* Handling and Moving Objects; Documenting or Recording Information; Performing General Physical Activities. *Interacting with Others:* Communicating with Persons Outside Organization; Communicating with Other Workers; Monitoring and Controlling Resources. **Physical Work Conditions—**Indoors; Sitting; Walking or Running; High Places; Kneeling, Crouching, or Crawling. **Other Job Characteristics—**Degree of Automation; Importance of Being Exact or Accurate; Importance of Repeating Same Tasks.

Experience—Job Zone 4. A minimum of two to four years of work-related skill, knowledge, or experience is needed. **Job Preparation:** SVP 7.0 to less than 8.0—two years to less than 10 years. **Knowledge—**Clerical; Education and Training; Customer and Personal Service; English Language; Communications and Media. **Instructional Programs—**Library Science, Other; Library Science/Librarianship; School Librarian/School Library Media Specialist.

Related DOT Jobs—100.117-010 Library Director; 100.127-010 Chief Librarian, Branch or Department; 100.127-014 Librarian; 100.167-010 Audiovisual Librarian; 100.167-014 Bookmobile Librarian; 100.167-018 Children's Librarian; 100.167-022 Institution Librarian; 100.167-026 Librarian, Special Library; 100.167-030 Media Specialist, School Library; 100.167-034 Young-Adult Librarian; 100.167-038 News Librarian; 100.267-010 Acquisitions Librarian; 100.267-014 Librarian, Special Collections; 100.367-022 Music Librarian; 100.367-026 Music Librarian, International Broadcast.

25-4031.00 Library Technicians

- **Education/Training Required: Short-term on-the-job training**
- **Employed: 108,904**
- **Annual Earnings: $23,790**
- **Growth: 19.5%**
- **Annual Job Openings: 29,000**

Assist librarians by helping readers in the use of library catalogs, databases, and indexes to locate books and other materials and by answering questions that require only brief consultation of standard reference. Compile records, sort and shelve books, remove or repair damaged books, register patrons, and check materials in and out of the circulation process. Replace materials in shelving area (stacks) or files. Includes bookmobile drivers who operate bookmobiles or light trucks that pull trailers to specific locations on a predetermined schedule and assist with providing services in mobile libraries.

Answer routine reference inquiries and refer patrons needing further assistance to librarians. Collect fines and respond to complaints about fines. Compile and maintain records relating to circulation, materials, and equipment. Conduct children's programs and other specialized programs such as library tours. Conduct reference searches, using printed materials and in-house and online databases. Deliver and retrieve items throughout the library by hand or using pushcart. Enter and update patrons' records on computers. File catalog cards according to system used. Guide patrons in finding and using library resources, including reference materials, audiovisual equipment, computers, and electronic resources. Issue identification cards to borrowers. Operate and maintain audiovisual equipment such as projectors, tape recorders, and videocassette recorders. Organize and maintain periodicals and reference materials. Prepare order slips for materials to be acquired, checking prices and figuring costs. Prepare volumes for binding. Process interlibrary loans for patrons. Process print and non-print library materials to prepare them for inclusion in library collections. Provide assistance to teachers and students by locating materials and helping to complete special projects. Repair damaged books. Reserve, circulate, renew, and discharge books and other materials. Review subject matter of materials to be classified and select classification numbers and headings according to classification systems. Send out notices about lost or overdue books. Sort books, publications, and other items according to procedure and return them to shelves, files, or other designated storage areas. Verify bibliographical data for materials, including author, title, publisher, publication date, and edition. Collaborate with archivists to arrange for the safe storage of historical records and documents. Compile bibliographies and prepare abstracts on subjects of interest to particular organizations or groups. Compose explanatory summaries of contents of books and other reference materials.

GOE INFORMATION—Interest Area: 12. Education and Social Service. **Work Group:** 12.03. Educational Services. **Personality Type—**Conventional. Conventional occupations frequently involve following set procedures and routines. These occupations can include working with data and details more than with ideas. Usually there is a clear line of authority to follow. **Work Values—**Good Working Conditions; Social Service; Pleasant Co-workers; Authority; Advancement. **Skills—**Service Orientation. **Abilities—***Cognitive:* Category Flexibility; Perceptual Speed; Time Sharing; Speed of Closure; Memorization. *Psychomotor:* Finger Dexterity. *Physical:* Dynamic Flexibility; Extent Flexibility. *Sensory:* Speech Clarity; Near Vision; Far Vision; Peripheral Vision. **General Work Activities—***Information Input:* Getting Information; Identifying Objects, Actions, and Events; Monitoring Processes, Materials, or Surroundings. *Mental Process:* Updating and Using Relevant Knowledge; Organizing, Planning, and Prioritizing; Scheduling Work and Activities. *Work Output:* Handling and Moving Objects; Documenting or Recording Information; Interacting with Computers. *Interacting with Others:* Communicating with Persons Outside Organization; Communicating with Other Workers; Establishing and Maintaining Relationships. **Physical Work Conditions—**Indoors; Walking or Running; Bending or Twisting the Body; Climbing Ladders, Scaffolds, Poles, etc.; Kneeling, Crouching, or Crawling. **Other Job Characteristics—**Importance of Being Exact or Accurate; Pace Determined by Speed of Equipment; Importance of Repeating Same Tasks.

Experience—Job Zone 2. Some previous work-related skill, knowledge, or experience may be helpful, but usually is not needed. **Job Preparation:** SVP 4.0 to less than 6.0—six months to less than two years. **Knowledge—**Clerical; Customer and Personal Service; English Language; Communications and Media; Computers and Electronics. **Instructional Programs—**Library Assistant/Technician.

Related DOT Jobs—100.367-010 Bibliographer; 100.367-014 Classifier; 100.367-018 Library Technical Assistant; 100.387-010 Catalog Librarian.

25-9000 Other Education, Training, and Library Occupations

25-9011.00 Audio-Visual Collections Specialists

- **Education/Training Required: Moderate-term on-the-job training**
- **Employed: 11,473**
- **Annual Earnings: $29,840**
- **Growth: 13.6%**
- **Annual Job Openings: 2,000**

Prepare, plan, and operate audiovisual teaching aids for use in education. May record, catalogue, and file audiovisual materials.

Confer with teachers in order to select course materials and to determine which training aids are best suited to particular grade levels. Construct and position properties, sets, lighting equipment, and other equipment. Determine formats, approaches, content, levels, and mediums necessary to meet production objectives effectively and within budgetary constraints. Develop manuals, texts, workbooks, or related materials for use in conjunction with production materials. Develop preproduction ideas and incorporate them into outlines, scripts, story boards, and graphics. Instruct users in the selection, use, and design of audiovisual materials and assist them in the preparation of instructional materials and the rehearsal of presentations. Locate and secure settings, properties, effects, and other production necessities. Maintain hardware and software, including computers, scanners, color copiers, and color laser printers. Perform simple maintenance tasks such as cleaning monitors and lenses and changing batteries and light bulbs. Plan and prepare audiovisual teaching aids and methods for use in school systems. Set up, adjust, and operate audiovisual equipment such as cameras, film and slide projectors, and recording equipment for meetings, events, classes, seminars, and video conferences. Acquire, catalog, and maintain collections of audiovisual material such as films, video- and audiotapes, photographs, and software programs. Attend conventions and conferences, read trade journals, and communicate with industry insiders in order to keep abreast of industry developments. Direct and coordinate activities of assistants and other personnel during production. Narrate presentations and productions. Offer presentations and workshops on the role of multimedia in effective presentations. Produce rough and finished graphics and graphic designs.

GOE INFORMATION—Interest Area: 12. Education and Social Service. **Work Group:** 12.03. Educational Services. **Personality Type—**Conventional. Conventional occupations frequently involve following set procedures and routines. These occupations can include working with data and details more than with ideas. Usually there is a clear line of authority to follow. **Work Values—**Good Working Conditions; Authority; Pleasant Co-workers; Ability Utilization; Social Service. **Skills—**Complex Problem Solving; Learning Strategies; Writing; Instructing; Speaking; Operations Analysis; Management of Material Resources; Technology Design. **Abilities—***Cognitive:* Originality; Fluency of Ideas; Visualization; Time Sharing; Written Expression. *Psychomotor:* Rate Control; Control Precision; Reaction Time; Speed of Limb Movement; Wrist-Finger Speed. *Physical:* Explosive Strength; Dynamic Flexibility; Extent Flexibility; Gross Body Equilibrium; Static Strength. *Sensory:* Speech Clarity; Glare Sensitivity; Hearing Sensitivity; Sound Localization; Peripheral Vision. **General Work Activities—***Information Input:* Getting Information; Identifying

Objects, Actions, and Events; Monitoring Processes, Materials, or Surroundings. *Mental Process:* Thinking Creatively; Organizing, Planning, and Prioritizing; Updating and Using Relevant Knowledge. *Work Output:* Handling and Moving Objects; Drafting and Specifying Technical Devices; Performing General Physical Activities. *Interacting with Others:* Communicating with Other Workers; Establishing and Maintaining Relationships; Coordinating the Work and Activities of Others. **Physical Work Conditions**—Cramped Work Space or Awkward Positions; Kneeling, Crouching, or Crawling; Bending or Twisting the Body; Using Hands on Objects, Tools, or Controls; Disease or Infections. **Other Job Characteristics**—Degree of Automation; Pace Determined by Speed of Equipment; Consequence of Error.

Experience—Job Zone 4. A minimum of two to four years of work-related skill, knowledge, or experience is needed. **Job Preparation:** SVP 7.0 to less than 8.0—two years to less than 10 years. **Knowledge**—Communications and Media; Education and Training; Fine Arts; Telecommunications; Administration and Management. **Instructional Programs**—No data available.

Related DOT Jobs—149.061-010 Audiovisual Production Specialist.

25-9021.00 *Farm and Home Management Advisors*

- **Education/Training Required: Bachelor's degree**
- **Employed: 10,682**
- **Annual Earnings: $39,620**
- **Growth: 6.1%**
- **Annual Job Openings: 2,000**

Advise, instruct, and assist individuals and families engaged in agriculture, agricultural-related processes, or home economics activities. Demonstrate procedures and apply research findings to solve problems; instruct and train in product development, sales, and the utilization of machinery and equipment to promote general welfare. Includes county agricultural agents, feed and farm management advisers, home economists, and extension service advisors.

Advises farmers in matters such as feeding and health maintenance of livestock, cultivation, growing and harvesting practices, and budgeting. Advises individuals and families on home management practices, such as budget planning, meal preparation, energy conservation, clothing, and home furnishings. Conducts classes to educate others in subjects such as nutrition, home management, home furnishing, child care, and farming techniques. Plans, develops, organizes, and evaluates training programs in subjects such as home management, horticulture, and consumer information. Collects and evaluates data to ascertain needs and develop programs beneficial to community. Delivers lectures to organizations or talks over radio and television to disseminate information and promote objectives of program. Organizes, advises, and participates in community activities and organizations such as county and state fair events and 4-H Clubs. Prepares leaflets, pamphlets, and visual aids for educational and informational purposes.

GOE INFORMATION—**Interest Area:** 12. Education and Social Service. **Work Group:** 12.03. Educational Services. **Personality Type**—Social. Social occupations frequently involve working with, communicating with, and teaching people. These occupations often involve helping or providing service to others. **Work Values**—Social Service; Authority; Creativity; Autonomy; Responsibility. **Skills**—Systems Analysis; Persuasion; Service Orientation; Instructing; Complex Problem Solving; Learning Strategies; Speaking; Writing. **Abilities**—*Cognitive:* Oral Expression; Originality; Mathematical Reasoning; Written Expression; Number Facility. *Psychomotor:* Multilimb Coordination. *Physical:* Gross Body Equi-librium; Stamina. *Sensory:* Speech Clarity; Far Vision; Speech Recognition; Near Vision; Auditory Attention. **General Work Activities**—*Information Input:* Getting Information; Identifying Objects, Actions, and Events; Estimating Needed Characteristics. *Mental Process:* Analyzing Data or Information; Organizing, Planning, and Prioritizing; Making Decisions and Solving Problems. *Work Output:* Documenting or Recording Information; Performing General Physical Activities; Handling and Moving Objects. *Interacting with Others:* Communicating with Persons Outside Organization; Providing Consultation and Advice to Others; Establishing and Maintaining Relationships. **Physical Work Conditions**—Very Hot or Cold; Contaminants; Outdoors; Extremely Bright or Inadequate Lighting; Disease or Infections. **Other Job Characteristics**—Importance of Repeating Same Tasks; Degree of Automation; Pace Determined by Speed of Equipment.

Experience—Job Zone 4. A minimum of two to four years of work-related skill, knowledge, or experience is needed. **Job Preparation:** SVP 7.0 to less than 8.0—two years to less than 10 years. **Knowledge**—Food Production; Education and Training; Economics and Accounting; Administration and Management; Biology. **Instructional Programs**—Adult Development and Aging; Agricultural and Extension Education Services; Animal Nutrition; Animal/Livestock Husbandry and Production; Apparel and Textiles, General; Business Family and Consumer Sciences/Human Sciences; Child Development; Consumer Economics; Consumer Merchandising/Retailing Management; Consumer Services and Advocacy; Crop Production; Family and Community Services; Family and Consumer Economics and Related Services, Other; Family and Consumer Sciences/Human Sciences, General; Family and Consumer Sciences/Human Sciences, Other; Family Resource Management Studies, General; Family Systems; Farm/Farm and Ranch Management; Home Furnishings and Equipment Installers; Housing and Human Environments, General; Housing and Human Environments, Other; Human Development, Family Studies, and Related Services, Other.

Related DOT Jobs—096.121-010 County Home-Demonstration Agent; 096.121-014 Home Economist; 096.127-010 County-Agricultural Agent; 096.127-014 Extension Service Specialist; 096.127-018 Feed and Farm Management Adviser; 096.127-022 Four-H Club Agent.

25-9031.00 *Instructional Coordinators*

- **Education/Training Required: Master's degree**
- **Employed: 80,847**
- **Annual Earnings: $46,600**
- **Growth: 25.0%**
- **Annual Job Openings: 15,000**

Develop instructional material, coordinate educational content, and incorporate current technology in specialized fields that provide guidelines to educators and instructors for developing curricula and conducting courses.

Advise teaching and administrative staff in curriculum development, use of materials and equipment, and implementation of state and federal programs and procedures. Research, evaluate, and prepare recommendations on curricula, instructional methods, and materials for school systems. Update the content of educational programs to ensure that students are being trained with equipment and processes that are technologically current. Confer with members of educational committees and advisory groups to obtain knowledge of subject areas and to relate curriculum materials to specific subjects, individual student needs, and occupational areas. Coordinate activities of workers engaged in cataloging, distributing, and maintaining educational materials and equipment in curriculum libraries and laboratories. Develop classroom-based and distance learning training courses, using needs assessments and skill level analyses.

Develop instructional materials to be used by educators and instructors. Develop tests, questionnaires, and procedures that measure the effectiveness of curricula and use these tools to determine whether program objectives are being met. Organize production and design of curriculum materials. Prepare or approve manuals, guidelines, and reports on state educational policies and practices for distribution to school districts. Recommend, order, or authorize purchase of instructional materials, supplies, equipment, and visual aids designed to meet student educational needs and district standards. Advise and teach students. Conduct or participate in workshops, committees, and conferences designed to promote the intellectual, social, and physical welfare of students. Inspect instructional equipment to determine if repairs are needed; authorize necessary repairs. Observe work of teaching staff in order to evaluate performance and to recommend changes that could strengthen teaching skills. Plan and conduct teacher training programs and conferences dealing with new classroom procedures, instructional materials and equipment, and teaching aids. Prepare grant proposals, budgets, and program policies and goals or assist in their preparation. Address public audiences to explain program objectives and to elicit support. Interpret and enforce provisions of state education codes and rules and regulations of state education boards.

GOE INFORMATION—Interest Area: 12. Education and Social Service. **Work Group:** 12.01. Managerial Work in Education and Social Service. **Personality Type—**Social. Social occupations frequently involve working with, communicating with, and teaching people. These occupations often involve helping or providing service to others. **Work Values—**Authority; Creativity; Autonomy; Social Service; Responsibility. **Skills—**Learning Strategies; Instructing; Speaking; Systems Analysis; Writing; Management of Personnel Resources; Complex Problem Solving; Equipment Selection. **Abilities—***Cognitive:* Written Comprehension; Originality; Written Expression; Oral Expression; Fluency of Ideas. *Psychomotor:* None met the criteria. *Physical:* None met the criteria. *Sensory:* Speech Clarity; Speech Recognition. **General Work Activities—***Information Input:* Getting Information; Identifying Objects, Actions, and Events; Monitoring Processes, Materials, or Surroundings. *Mental Process:* Judging Qualities of Things, Services, or Other People's Work; Processing Information; Analyzing Data or Information. *Work Output:* Interacting with Computers; Documenting or Recording Information; Handling and Moving Objects. *Interacting with Others:* Communicating with Other Workers; Communicating with Persons Outside Organization; Providing Consultation and Advice to Others. **Physical Work Conditions—**Sitting; Indoors; Disease or Infections. **Other Job Characteristics—**Importance of Being Exact or Accurate; Consequence of Error; Pace Determined by Speed of Equipment.

Experience—Job Zone 5. Extensive skill, knowledge, and experience are needed for these occupations. **Job Preparation:** SVP 8.0 and above—four years to more than 10 years. **Knowledge—**Education and Training; Personnel and Human Resources; Psychology; Administration and Management; English Language. **Instructional Programs—**Curriculum and Instruction; Educational/Instructional Media Design.

Related DOT Jobs—094.167-010 Supervisor, Special Education; 099.117-026 Supervisor, Education; 099.167-014 Consultant, Education; 099.167-018 Director, Instructional Material; 099.167-022 Educational Specialist; 099.167-026 Music Supervisor.

25-9041.00 Teacher Assistants

- **Education/Training Required: Short-term on-the-job training**
- **Employed: 1,261,531**
- **Annual Earnings: $18,070**
- **Growth: 23.9%**
- **Annual Job Openings: 256,000**

Perform duties that are instructional in nature or deliver direct services to students or parents. Serve in a position for which a teacher or another professional has ultimate responsibility for the design and implementation of educational programs and services.

Discuss assigned duties with classroom teachers in order to coordinate instructional efforts. Prepare lesson materials, bulletin board displays, exhibits, equipment, and demonstrations. Present subject matter to students under the direction and guidance of teachers, using lectures, discussions, or supervised role-playing methods. Tutor and assist children individually or in small groups in order to help them master assignments and to reinforce learning concepts presented by teachers. Supervise students in classrooms, halls, cafeterias, school yards, and gymnasiums or on field trips. Conduct demonstrations to teach such skills as sports, dancing, and handicrafts. Distribute teaching materials such as textbooks, workbooks, papers, and pencils to students. Distribute tests and homework assignments and collect them when they are completed. Enforce administration policies and rules governing students. Grade homework and tests and compute and record results, using answer sheets or electronic marking devices. Instruct and monitor students in the use and care of equipment and materials in order to prevent injuries and damage. Observe students' performance and record relevant data to assess progress. Organize and label materials and display students' work in a manner appropriate for their eye levels and perceptual skills. Organize and supervise games and other recreational activities to promote physical, mental, and social development. Participate in teacher-parent conferences regarding students' progress or problems. Plan, prepare, and develop various teaching aids such as bibliographies, charts, and graphs. Prepare lesson outlines and plans in assigned subject areas and submit outlines to teachers for review. Provide extra assistance to students with special needs, such as non-English-speaking students or those with physical and mental disabilities. Take class attendance and maintain attendance records. Assist in bus loading and unloading. Assist librarians in school libraries. Attend staff meetings and serve on committees as required. Carry out therapeutic regimens such as behavior modification and personal development programs under the supervision of special education instructors, psychologists, or speech-language pathologists. Collect money from students for school-related projects. Laminate teaching materials to increase their durability under repeated use. Maintain computers in classrooms and laboratories and assist students with hardware and software use. Monitor classroom viewing of live or recorded courses transmitted by communication satellites. Operate and maintain audiovisual equipment. Provide disabled students with assistive devices, supportive technology, and assistance accessing facilities such as restrooms. Requisition and stock teaching materials and supplies. Type, file, and duplicate materials. Use computers, audiovisual aids, and other equipment and materials to supplement presentations.

GOE INFORMATION—Interest Area: 12. Education and Social Service. **Work Group:** 12.03. Educational Services. **Personality Type—**Social. Social occupations frequently involve working with, communicating with, and teaching people. These occupations often involve helping or providing service to others. **Work Values—**Social Service; Authority; Pleasant Co-workers; Good Working Conditions; Achievement. **Skills—**Learning Strategies; Instructing; Speaking; Service Orientation; Active Listening; Social Perceptiveness; Complex Problem Solving; Reading Comprehension. **Abilities—***Cognitive:* Written Expression; Oral Expression; Fluency of Ideas; Originality; Oral Comprehension. *Psychomotor:* None met the criteria. *Physical:* None met the criteria. *Sensory:* Speech Clarity; Auditory Attention; Speech Recognition; Sound Localization; Peripheral Vision. **General Work Activities—***Information Input:* Getting Information; Monitoring Processes, Materials, or Surroundings; Identifying Objects, Actions, and Events. *Mental Process:* Judging Qualities of Things, Services, or Other People's Work; Organizing, Planning, and

Prioritizing; Thinking Creatively. *Work Output:* Handling and Moving Objects; Documenting or Recording Information; Performing General Physical Activities. *Interacting with Others:* Communicating with Other Workers; Establishing and Maintaining Relationships; Communicating with Persons Outside Organization. **Physical Work Conditions**—Indoors; Walking or Running; Sitting; Disease or Infections; Standing. **Other Job Characteristics**—Importance of Repeating Same Tasks; Degree of Automation; Pace Determined by Speed of Equipment.

Experience—Job Zone 3. Previous work-related skill, knowledge, or experience is required. **Job Preparation:** SVP 6.0 to less than 7.0—more than one year and less than four years. **Knowledge**—Education and Training; English Language; History and Archeology; Psychology; Sociology and Anthropology. **Instructional Programs**—Teacher Assistant/Aide; Teaching Assistants/Aides, Other.

Related DOT Jobs—099.327-010 Teacher Aide I.

25-9099.99 Education, Training, and Library Workers, All Other

- **Education/Training Required: No data available.**
- **Employed: No data available.**
- **Annual Earnings: No data available.**
- **Growth: 21.4%**
- **Annual Job Openings: 17,000**

All education, training, and library workers not listed separately.

No task data available.

GOE INFORMATION—**Interest Area:** 12. Education and Social Service. **Work Group:** 12.03. Educational Services. **Note:** The Department of Labor has not collected some data for this job, so it has fewer details than the other descriptions.

Instructional Programs—Education, Other; Library Science, Other.

Related DOT Jobs—109.267-014 Research Worker, Encyclopedia; 109.364-010 Craft Demonstrator; 249.367-074 Teacher Aide II; 249.367-086 Satellite-Instruction Facilitator.

27-0000

Arts, Design, Entertainment, Sports, and Media Occupations

27-1000 Art and Design Workers

27-1011.00 Art Directors

- Education/Training Required: **Work experience plus degree**
- Employed: 46,517
- Annual Earnings: $59,800
- Growth: 21.1%
- Annual Job Openings: 6,000

Formulate design concepts and presentation approaches and direct workers engaged in artwork, layout design, and copy writing for visual communications media, such as magazines, books, newspapers, and packaging.

Formulate basic layout design or presentation approach and specify material details, such as style and size of type, photographs, graphics, animation, video, and sound. Review and approve proofs of printed copy and art and copy materials developed by staff members. Manage own accounts and projects, working within budget and scheduling requirements. Confer with creative, art, copy-writing, or production department heads to discuss client requirements and presentation concepts and to coordinate creative activities. Present final layouts to clients for approval. Confer with clients to determine objectives, budget, background information, and presentation approaches, styles, and techniques. Hire, train, and direct staff members who develop design concepts into art layouts or who prepare layouts for printing. Work with creative directors to develop design solutions. Review illustrative material to determine if it conforms to standards and specifications. Attend photo shoots and printing sessions to ensure that the products needed are obtained. Create custom illustrations or other graphic elements. Mark up, paste, and complete layouts and write typography instructions to prepare materials for typesetting or printing. Negotiate with printers and estimators to determine what services will be performed. Conceptualize and help design interfaces for multimedia games, products, and devices. Prepare detailed storyboards showing sequence and timing of story development for television production.

GOE INFORMATION—Interest Area: 01. Arts, Entertainment, and Media. **Work Group:** 01.01. Managerial Work in Arts, Entertainment, and Media. **Personality Type**—Artistic. Artistic occupations frequently involve working with forms, designs, and patterns. They often require self-expression, and the work can be done without following a clear set of rules. **Work Values**—Creativity; Ability Utilization; Autonomy; Authority; Achievement. **Skills**—Coordination; Negotiation; Service Orientation; Persuasion; Equipment Selection; Instructing; Complex Problem Solving; Management of Financial Resources. **Abilities**—*Cognitive:* Originality; Category Flexibility; Fluency of Ideas; Visualization; Inductive Reasoning. *Psychomotor:* Finger Dexterity; Arm-Hand Steadiness. *Physical:* None met the criteria. *Sensory:* Visual Color Discrimination; Far Vision; Speech Recognition; Near Vision; Speech Clarity. **General Work Activities**—*Information Input:* Getting Information; Identifying Objects, Actions, and Events; Estimating Needed Characteristics. *Mental Process:* Thinking Creatively; Updating and Using Relevant Knowledge; Organizing, Planning, and Prioritizing. *Work Output:* Interacting with Computers; Documenting or Recording Information; Handling and Moving Objects. *Interacting with Others:* Providing Consultation and Advice to Others; Establishing and Maintaining Relationships; Communicating with Other Workers. **Physical Work Conditions**—Sitting; Indoors; Walking or Running; Bending or Twisting the Body; Disease or Infections. **Other Job Characteristics**—Importance of Being Exact or Accurate; Consequence of Error; Degree of Automation.

Experience—Job Zone 4. A minimum of two to four years of work-related skill, knowledge, or experience is needed. **Job Preparation:** SVP 7.0 to less than 8.0—two years to less than 10 years. **Knowledge**—Design; Fine Arts; Computers and Electronics; Communications and Media; Production and Processing. **Instructional Programs**—Graphic Design; Intermedia/Multimedia.

Related DOT Jobs—141.031-010 Art Director; 141.067-010 Creative Director; 141.137-010 Production Manager, Advertising.

27-1012.00 Craft Artists

- Education/Training Required: **Associate's degree**
- Employed: No data available.
- Annual Earnings: No data available.
- Growth: 16.8%
- Annual Job Openings: 15,000

Create or reproduce hand-made objects for sale and exhibition using a variety of techniques, such as welding, weaving, pottery, and needlecraft.

No task data available.

GOE INFORMATION—Interest Area: 01. Arts, Entertainment, and Media. **Work Group:** 01.06. Craft Arts. **Note:** The Department of Labor has not collected some data for this job, so it has fewer details than the other descriptions.

Instructional Programs—Art/Art Studies, General; Ceramic Arts and Ceramics; Crafts/Craft Design, Folk Art, and Artisanry; Drawing; Fiber, Textile, and Weaving Arts; Metal and Jewelry Arts; Painting; Printmaking; Sculpture; Visual and Performing Arts, General.

Related DOT Jobs—199.261-010 Taxidermist.

27-1013.00 Fine Artists, Including Painters, Sculptors, and Illustrators

- Education/Training Required: **Long-term on-the-job training**
- Employed: 30,813
- Annual Earnings: $32,870
- Growth: 13.4%
- Annual Job Openings: 4,000

Create original artwork using any of a wide variety of mediums and techniques, such as painting and sculpture.

No task data available.

GOE INFORMATION—Interest Area: 01. Arts, Entertainment, and Media. **Work Group:** 01.04. Visual Arts. **Note:** The Department of Labor has not collected some data for this job, so it has fewer details than the other descriptions.

Instructional Programs—Art/Art Studies, General; Ceramic Arts and Ceramics; Drawing; Fine Arts and Art Studies, Other; Fine/Studio Arts, General; Intermedia/Multimedia; Medical Illustration/Medical Illustrator; Painting; Printmaking; Sculpture; Visual and Performing Arts, General.

Related DOT Jobs—102.261-014 Paintings Restorer; 141.061-010 Cartoonist; 141.061-014 Fashion Artist; 141.061-022 Illustrator; 141.061-026 Illustrator, Medical and Scientific; 141.061-030 Illustrator, Set; 141.061-034 Police Artist; 141.081-010 Cartoonist, Motion Pictures; 144.061-010 Painter; 144.061-014 Printmaker; 144.061-018 Sculptor; 149.041-010 Quick Sketch Artist; 149.051-010 Silhouette Artist; 149.261-010 Exhibit Artist; 970.281-014 Delineator; 970.361-018 Artist, Suspect.

27-1013.01 Painters and Illustrators

- **Education/Training Required: Long-term on-the-job training**
- **Employed: No data available.**
- **Annual Earnings: $32,870**
- **Growth: 13.4%**
- **Annual Job Openings: 4,000**

Paint or draw subject material to produce original artwork or illustrations, using watercolors, oils, acrylics, tempera, or other paint mediums.

Renders drawings, illustrations, and sketches of buildings, manufactured products, or models, working from sketches, blueprints, memory, or reference materials. Paints scenic backgrounds, murals, and portraiture for motion picture and television production sets, glass artworks, and exhibits. Etches, carves, paints, or draws artwork on material such as stone, glass, canvas, wood, and linoleum. Develops drawings, paintings, diagrams, and models of medical or biological subjects for use in publications, exhibits, consultations, research, and teaching. Integrates and develops visual elements, such as line, space, mass, color, and perspective, to produce desired effect. Brushes or sprays protective or decorative finish on completed background panels, informational legends, exhibit accessories, or finished painting. Confers with professional personnel or client to discuss objectives of artwork, develop illustration ideas, and develop theme to be portrayed. Studies style, techniques, colors, textures, and materials used by artist to maintain consistency in reconstruction or retouching procedures. Performs tests to determine factors such as age, structure, pigment stability, and probable reaction to various cleaning agents and solvents. Removes painting from frame or paint layer from canvas to restore artwork, following specified technique and equipment. Applies select solvents and cleaning agents to clean surface of painting and remove accretions, discolorations, and deteriorated varnish. Examines surfaces of paintings and proofs of artwork, using magnifying device, to determine method of restoration or needed corrections. Assembles, leads, and solders finished glass to fabricate stained glass article. Installs finished stained glass in window or door frame.

GOE INFORMATION—Interest Area: 01. Arts, Entertainment, and Media. **Work Group:** 01.04. Visual Arts. **Personality Type—**Artistic. Artistic occupations frequently involve working with forms, designs, and patterns. They often require self-expression, and the work can be done without following a clear set of rules. **Work Values—**Creativity; Ability Utilization; Autonomy; Achievement; Independence. **Skills—**Operations Analysis; Equipment Selection. **Abilities—***Cognitive:* Originality; Visualization; Fluency of Ideas; Inductive Reasoning; Deductive Reasoning. *Psychomotor:* Arm-Hand Steadiness; Finger Dexterity; Wrist-Finger Speed; Manual Dexterity; Multilimb Coordination. *Physical:* Extent Flexibility; Trunk Strength; Gross Body Equilibrium; Dynamic Flexibility; Gross Body Coordination. *Sensory:* Visual Color Discrimination; Depth Perception. **General Work Activities—***Information Input:* Getting Information; Identifying Objects, Actions, and Events; Inspecting Equipment, Structures, or Materials. *Mental Process:* Thinking Creatively; Judging Qualities of Things, Services, or Other People's Work; Organizing, Planning, and Prioritizing. *Work Output:* Handling and Moving Objects; Drafting and Specifying Technical Devices; Performing General Physical Activities. *Interacting with Others:* Communicating with Persons Outside Organization; Providing Consultation and Advice to Others; Communicating with Other Workers. **Physical Work Conditions—**Making Repetitive Motions; Sitting; Using Hands on Objects, Tools, or Controls; Indoors; Outdoors. **Other Job Characteristics—**Importance of Repeating Same Tasks; Pace Determined by Speed of Equipment; Consequence of Error.

Experience—Job Zone 4. A minimum of two to four years of work-related skill, knowledge, or experience is needed. **Job Preparation:** SVP 7.0 to less than 8.0—two years to less than 10 years. **Knowledge—**Fine Arts; Design; Chemistry; History and Archeology; Communications and Media. **Instructional Programs—**Art/Art Studies, General; Drawing; Fine Arts and Art Studies, Other; Fine/Studio Arts, General; Medical Illustration/Medical Illustrator; Painting; Visual and Performing Arts, General.

Related DOT Jobs—102.261-014 Paintings Restorer; 141.061-014 Fashion Artist; 141.061-022 Illustrator; 141.061-026 Illustrator, Medical and Scientific; 141.061-030 Illustrator, Set; 144.061-010 Painter; 144.061-014 Printmaker; 149.261-010 Exhibit Artist; 970.281-014 Delineator.

27-1013.02 Sketch Artists

- **Education/Training Required: Long-term on-the-job training**
- **Employed: No data available.**
- **Annual Earnings: $32,870**
- **Growth: 13.4%**
- **Annual Job Openings: 4,000**

Sketch likenesses of subjects according to observation or descriptions either to assist law enforcement agencies in identifying suspects, to depict courtroom scenes, or for entertainment purposes of patrons, using mediums such as pencil, charcoal, and pastels.

Draws sketch, profile, or likeness of posed subject or photograph, using pencil, charcoal, pastels, or other medium. Assembles and arranges outlines of features to form composite image according to information provided by witness or victim. Alters copy of composite image until witness or victim is satisfied that composite is best possible representation of suspect. Interviews crime victims and witnesses to obtain descriptive information concerning physical build, sex, nationality, and facial features of unidentified suspect. Prepares series of simple line drawings conforming to description of suspect and presents drawings to informant for selection of sketch. Poses subject to accentuate most pleasing features or profile. Classifies and codes components of image, using established system, to help identify suspect. Measures distances and develops sketches of crime scene from photograph and measurements. Operates photocopy or similar machine to reproduce composite image. Searches police photograph records, using classification and coding system to determine if existing photograph of suspects is available.

GOE INFORMATION—Interest Area: 01. Arts, Entertainment, and Media. **Work Group:** 01.04. Visual Arts. **Personality Type—**Artistic. Artistic occupations frequently involve working with forms, designs, and patterns. They often require self-expression, and the work can be done without following a clear set of rules. **Work Values—**Creativity; Ability Utilization; Achievement; Autonomy; Variety. **Skills—**Active Listening. **Abilities—***Cognitive:* Visualization; Flexibility of Closure; Originality; Oral Comprehension; Fluency of Ideas. *Psychomotor:* Finger Dexterity; Arm-Hand Steadiness; Manual Dexterity. *Physical:* None met the criteria. *Sensory:* Auditory Attention; Hearing Sensitivity. **General Work Activities—***Information Input:* Getting Information; Identifying Objects, Actions, and Events; Estimating Needed Characteristics. *Mental Process:* Thinking Creatively; Making Decisions and Solving Problems; Organizing, Planning, and Prioritizing. *Work Output:* Handling and Moving Objects; Documenting or Recording Information; Controlling Machines and Processes. *Interacting with Others:* Communicating with Persons Outside Organization; Establishing and Maintaining Relationships; Communicating with Other Workers. **Physical Work Conditions—**Sitting; Making Repetitive Motions; Indoors; Extremely Bright or Inadequate Lighting; Using Hands on Objects, Tools, or Controls. **Other Job Characteristics—**Importance of Repeating Same Tasks; Importance of Being Exact or Accurate; Pace Determined by Speed of Equipment.

Experience—Job Zone 3. Previous work-related skill, knowledge, or experience is required. **Job Preparation:** SVP 6.0 to less than 7.0—more than one year and less than four years. **Knowledge**—Fine Arts; Design; Customer and Personal Service; Foreign Language. **Instructional Programs**—Art/Art Studies, General; Drawing; Fine Arts and Art Studies, Other; Fine/Studio Arts, General; Medical Illustration/Medical Illustrator; Visual and Performing Arts, General.

Related DOT Jobs—141.061-034 Police Artist; 149.041-010 Quick Sketch Artist; 149.051-010 Silhouette Artist; 970.361-018 Artist, Suspect.

27-1013.03 Cartoonists

- **Education/Training Required: Long-term on-the-job training**
- **Employed: 30,813**
- **Annual Earnings: $32,870**
- **Growth: 13.4%**
- **Annual Job Openings: 4,000**

Create original artwork using any of a wide variety of mediums and techniques, such as painting and sculpture.

Renders sequential drawings of characters or other subject material which, when photographed and projected at specific speed, become animated. Creates and prepares sketches and model drawings of characters, providing details from memory, live models, manufactured products, or reference material. Develops personal ideas for cartoons, comic strips, or animations or reads written material to develop ideas. Makes changes and corrections to cartoon, comic strip, or animation as necessary. Develops color patterns and moods and paints background layouts to dramatize action for animated cartoon scenes. Labels each section with designated colors when colors are used. Discusses ideas for cartoons, comic strips, or animations with editor or publisher's representative. Sketches and submits cartoon or animation for approval.

GOE INFORMATION—Interest Area: 01. Arts, Entertainment, and Media. **Work Group:** 01.04. Visual Arts. **Personality Type**—Artistic. Artistic occupations frequently involve working with forms, designs, and patterns. They often require self-expression, and the work can be done without following a clear set of rules. **Work Values**—Creativity; Recognition; Autonomy; Ability Utilization; Achievement. **Skills**—None met the criteria. **Abilities**—*Cognitive:* Originality; Fluency of Ideas; Visualization; Oral Comprehension; Written Comprehension. *Psychomotor:* Arm-Hand Steadiness; Finger Dexterity. *Physical:* None met the criteria. *Sensory:* Visual Color Discrimination; Near Vision. **General Work Activities**—*Information Input:* Getting Information; Identifying Objects, Actions, and Events; Estimating Needed Characteristics. *Mental Process:* Thinking Creatively; Organizing, Planning, and Prioritizing; Judging Qualities of Things, Services, or Other People's Work. *Work Output:* Handling and Moving Objects; Drafting and Specifying Technical Devices; Documenting or Recording Information. *Interacting with Others:* Communicating with Other Workers; Communicating with Persons Outside Organization; Establishing and Maintaining Relationships. **Physical Work Conditions**—Sitting; Indoors; Making Repetitive Motions. **Other Job Characteristics**—Importance of Repeating Same Tasks; Pace Determined by Speed of Equipment; Degree of Automation.

Experience—Job Zone 4. A minimum of two to four years of work-related skill, knowledge, or experience is needed. **Job Preparation:** SVP 7.0 to less than 8.0—two years to less than 10 years. **Knowledge**—Fine Arts; Communications and Media; Sales and Marketing; Design; History and Archeology. **Instructional Programs**—Art/Art Studies, General; Drawing; Fine Arts and Art Studies, Other; Fine/Studio Arts, General; Intermedia/Multimedia; Medical Illustration/Medical Illustrator; Painting; Visual and Performing Arts, General.

Related DOT Jobs—141.061-010 Cartoonist; 141.081-010 Cartoonist, Motion Pictures.

27-1013.04 Sculptors

- **Education/Training Required: Long-term on-the-job training**
- **Employed: No data available.**
- **Annual Earnings: $32,870**
- **Growth: 13.4%**
- **Annual Job Openings: 4,000**

Design and construct three-dimensional artwork, using materials such as stone, wood, plaster, and metal and employing various manual and tool techniques.

Carves objects from stone, concrete, plaster, wood, or other material, using abrasives and tools, such as chisels, gouges, and mall. Constructs artistic forms from metal or stone, using metalworking, welding, or masonry tools and equipment. Cuts, bends, laminates, arranges, and fastens individual or mixed raw and manufactured materials and products to form works of art. Models substances, such as clay or wax, using fingers and small hand tools to form objects.

GOE INFORMATION—Interest Area: 01. Arts, Entertainment, and Media. **Work Group:** 01.04. Visual Arts. **Personality Type**—Artistic. Artistic occupations frequently involve working with forms, designs, and patterns. They often require self-expression, and the work can be done without following a clear set of rules. **Work Values**—Creativity; Independence; Ability Utilization; Autonomy; Responsibility. **Skills**—None met the criteria. **Abilities**—*Cognitive:* Originality; Visualization; Fluency of Ideas. *Psychomotor:* Manual Dexterity; Finger Dexterity; Multilimb Coordination; Arm-Hand Steadiness. *Physical:* Gross Body Coordination; Extent Flexibility; Static Strength; Stamina; Trunk Strength. *Sensory:* Depth Perception. **General Work Activities**—*Information Input:* Estimating Needed Characteristics; Getting Information; Monitoring Processes, Materials, or Surroundings. *Mental Process:* Thinking Creatively; Judging Qualities of Things, Services, or Other People's Work; Organizing, Planning, and Prioritizing. *Work Output:* Handling and Moving Objects; Performing General Physical Activities; Controlling Machines and Processes. *Interacting with Others:* Influencing Others or Selling; Monitoring and Controlling Resources; Communicating with Persons Outside Organization. **Physical Work Conditions**—Using Hands on Objects, Tools, or Controls; Making Repetitive Motions; Bending or Twisting the Body; Specialized Protective or Safety Attire; Kneeling, Crouching, or Crawling. **Other Job Characteristics**—Pace Determined by Speed of Equipment; Importance of Repeating Same Tasks; Degree of Automation.

Experience—Job Zone 5. Extensive skill, knowledge, and experience are needed for these occupations. **Job Preparation:** SVP 8.0 and above—four years to more than 10 years. **Knowledge**—Fine Arts; Design; Engineering and Technology; Building and Construction; History and Archeology. **Instructional Programs**—Art/Art Studies, General; Ceramic Arts and Ceramics; Fine Arts and Art Studies, Other; Fine/Studio Arts, General; Sculpture; Visual and Performing Arts, General.

Related DOT Jobs—144.061-018 Sculptor.

27-1014.00 Multi-Media Artists and Animators

- **Education/Training Required: Bachelor's degree**
- **Employed: 69,449**
- **Annual Earnings: $42,270**
- **Growth: 22.2%**
- **Annual Job Openings: 8,000**

Create special effects, animation, or other visual images using film, video, computers, or other electronic tools and media for use in products or creations such as computer games, movies, music videos, and commercials.

Apply story development, directing, cinematography, and editing to animation to create storyboards that show the flow of the animation and map out key scenes and characters. Assemble, typeset, scan, and produce digital camera–ready art or film negatives and printer's proofs. Convert real objects to animated objects through modeling, using techniques such as optical scanning. Create and install special effects as required by the script, mixing chemicals and fabricating needed parts from wood, metal, plaster, and clay. Create basic designs, drawings, and illustrations for product labels, cartons, direct mail, or television. Create pen-and-paper images to be scanned, edited, colored, textured, or animated by computer. Create two-dimensional and three-dimensional images depicting objects in motion or illustrating a process, using computer animation or modeling programs. Design complex graphics and animation, using independent judgment, creativity, and computer equipment. Develop briefings, brochures, multimedia presentations, Web pages, promotional products, technical illustrations, and computer artwork for use in products, technical manuals, literature, newsletters, and slide shows. Implement and maintain configuration control systems. Make objects or characters appear lifelike by manipulating light, color, texture, shadow, and transparency and/or manipulating static images to give the illusion of motion. Script, plan, and create animated narrative sequences under tight deadlines, using computer software and hand drawing techniques. Use models to simulate the behavior of animated objects in the finished sequence. Participate in design and production of multimedia campaigns, handling budgeting and scheduling, and assisting with such responsibilities as production coordination, background design, and progress tracking.

GOE INFORMATION—Interest Area: 01. Arts, Entertainment, and Media. **Work Group:** 01.04. Visual Arts. **Note:** The Department of Labor has not collected some data for this job, so it has fewer details than the other descriptions.

Instructional Programs—Animation, Interactive Technology, Video Graphics and Special Effects; Drawing; Graphic Design; Intermedia/Multimedia; Painting; Printmaking; Web Page, Digital/Multimedia, and Information Resources Design.

Related DOT Jobs—141.081-010 Cartoonist, Motion Pictures.

27-1019.99 Artists and Related Workers, All Other

- **Education/Training Required: Long-term on-the-job training**
- **Employed: No data available.**
- **Annual Earnings: No data available.**
- **Growth: 16.8%**
- **Annual Job Openings: 15,000**

All artists and related workers not listed separately.

No task data available.

GOE INFORMATION—Interest Area: 01. Arts, Entertainment, and Media. **Work Group:** 01.04. Visual Arts; 01.06. Craft Arts; 01.07. Graphic Arts. **Note:** The Department of Labor has not collected some data for this job, so it has fewer details than the other descriptions.

Instructional Programs—Commercial and Advertising Art; Crafts/Craft Design, Folk Art, and Artisanry; Fine Arts and Art Studies, Other; Fine/

Studio Arts, General; Graphic Design; Illustration; Visual and Performing Arts, General.

Related DOT Jobs—191.287-014 Appraiser, Art.

27-1021.00 Commercial and Industrial Designers

- **Education/Training Required: Bachelor's degree**
- **Employed: 50,036**
- **Annual Earnings: $49,820**
- **Growth: 23.8%**
- **Annual Job Openings: 7,000**

Develop and design manufactured products, such as cars, home appliances, and children's toys. Combine artistic talent with research on product use, marketing, and materials to create the most functional and appealing product design.

Confer with engineering, marketing, production, and/or sales departments or with customers to establish and evaluate design concepts for manufactured products. Coordinate the look and function of product lines. Design graphic material for use as ornamentation, illustration, or advertising on manufactured materials and packaging or containers. Direct and coordinate the fabrication of models or samples and the drafting of working drawings and specification sheets from sketches. Modify and refine designs, using working models, to conform with customer specifications, production limitations, or changes in design trends. Prepare sketches of ideas, detailed drawings, illustrations, artwork, and/or blueprints, using drafting instruments, paints and brushes, or computer-aided design equipment. Present designs and reports to customers or design committees for approval and discuss need for modification. Read publications, attend showings, and study competing products and design styles and motifs to obtain perspective and generate design concepts. Advise corporations on issues involving corporate image projects or problems. Evaluate feasibility of design ideas, based on factors such as appearance, safety, function, serviceability, budget, production costs/methods, and market characteristics. Fabricate models or samples in paper, wood, glass, fabric, plastic, metal, or other materials, using hand and/or power tools. Research production specifications, costs, production materials, and manufacturing methods and provide cost estimates and itemized production requirements. Supervise assistants' work throughout the design process. Develop industrial standards and regulatory guidelines. Develop manufacturing procedures and monitor the manufacture of their designs in a factory to improve operations and product quality. Investigate product characteristics such as the product's safety and handling qualities, its market appeal, how efficiently it can be produced, and ways of distributing, using, and maintaining it. Participate in new product planning or market research, including studying the potential need for new products.

GOE INFORMATION—Interest Area: 01. Arts, Entertainment, and Media. **Work Group:** 01.04. Visual Arts. **Personality Type—**Artistic. Artistic occupations frequently involve working with forms, designs, and patterns. They often require self-expression, and the work can be done without following a clear set of rules. **Work Values—**Creativity; Ability Utilization; Achievement; Recognition; Autonomy. **Skills—**Equipment Selection; Operations Analysis; Complex Problem Solving; Systems Analysis; Systems Evaluation; Reading Comprehension; Management of Financial Resources; Critical Thinking. **Abilities—***Cognitive:* Visualization; Fluency of Ideas; Originality; Mathematical Reasoning; Deductive Reasoning. *Psychomotor:* Arm-Hand Steadiness; Finger Dexterity; Wrist-Finger Speed; Multilimb Coordination; Manual Dexterity. *Physical:* Gross Body Coordination; Gross Body Equilibrium; Explosive Strength. *Sen-*

sory: Visual Color Discrimination; Speech Recognition; Near Vision; Far Vision; Speech Clarity. **General Work Activities**—*Information Input:* Getting Information; Identifying Objects, Actions, and Events; Estimating Needed Characteristics. *Mental Process:* Thinking Creatively; Organizing, Planning, and Prioritizing; Updating and Using Relevant Knowledge. *Work Output:* Drafting and Specifying Technical Devices; Handling and Moving Objects; Controlling Machines and Processes. *Interacting with Others:* Communicating with Persons Outside Organization; Communicating with Other Workers; Establishing and Maintaining Relationships. **Physical Work Conditions**—Indoors; Sitting; Hazardous Equipment; Using Hands on Objects, Tools, or Controls; Disease or Infections. **Other Job Characteristics**—Importance of Being Exact or Accurate; Consequence of Error; Degree of Automation.

Experience—Job Zone 4. A minimum of two to four years of work-related skill, knowledge, or experience is needed. **Job Preparation:** SVP 7.0 to less than 8.0—two years to less than 10 years. **Knowledge**—Design; Fine Arts; Production and Processing; Sales and Marketing; Education and Training. **Instructional Programs**—Commercial and Advertising Art; Design and Applied Arts, Other; Design and Visual Communications, General; Industrial Design.

Related DOT Jobs—141.061-038 Commercial Designer; 142.061-010 Bank-Note Designer; 142.061-014 Cloth Designer; 142.061-022 Furniture Designer; 142.061-026 Industrial Designer; 142.061-030 Memorial Designer; 142.061-034 Ornamental-Metalwork Designer; 142.061-038 Safety-Clothing-and-Equipment Developer; 142.061-054 Stained Glass Artist; 142.081-018 Package Designer.

27-1022.00 *Fashion Designers*

- **Education/Training Required: Bachelor's degree**
- **Employed: 16,111**
- **Annual Earnings: $49,530**
- **Growth: 20.3%**
- **Annual Job Openings: 2,000**

Design clothing and accessories. Create original garments or design garments that follow well established fashion trends. May develop the line of color and kinds of materials.

Designs custom garments for clients. Integrates findings of analysis and discussion, and personal tastes and knowledge of design, to originate design ideas. Sketches rough and detailed drawings of apparel or accessories and writes specifications, such as color scheme, construction, or material type. Draws pattern for article designed, cuts pattern, and cuts material according to pattern, using measuring and drawing instruments and scissors. Examines sample garment on and off model and modifies design to achieve desired effect. Attends fashion shows and reviews garment magazines and manuals to analyze fashion trends, predictions, and consumer preferences. Confers with sales and management executives or clients regarding design ideas. Sews together sections to form mockup or sample of garment or article, using sewing equipment. Arranges for showing of sample garments at sales meetings or fashion shows. Directs and coordinates workers who draw and cut patterns and construct sample or finished garment.

GOE INFORMATION—**Interest Area:** 01. Arts, Entertainment, and Media. **Work Group:** 01.04. Visual Arts. **Personality Type**—Artistic. Artistic occupations frequently involve working with forms, designs, and patterns. They often require self-expression, and the work can be done without following a clear set of rules. **Work Values**—Creativity; Ability Utilization; Achievement; Recognition; Responsibility. **Skills**—Systems Analysis; Operations Analysis; Persuasion; Management of Financial Resources; Complex Problem Solving; Systems Evaluation; Management of

Material Resources; Negotiation. **Abilities**—*Cognitive:* Originality; Fluency of Ideas; Visualization; Time Sharing; Oral Expression. *Psychomotor:* Finger Dexterity; Arm-Hand Steadiness; Manual Dexterity; Wrist-Finger Speed; Multilimb Coordination. *Physical:* Gross Body Equilibrium; Dynamic Flexibility. *Sensory:* Visual Color Discrimination; Speech Recognition; Speech Clarity; Auditory Attention; Near Vision. **General Work Activities**—*Information Input:* Getting Information; Identifying Objects, Actions, and Events; Estimating Needed Characteristics. *Mental Process:* Thinking Creatively; Judging Qualities of Things, Services, or Other People's Work; Updating and Using Relevant Knowledge. *Work Output:* Drafting and Specifying Technical Devices; Handling and Moving Objects; Controlling Machines and Processes. *Interacting with Others:* Communicating with Other Workers; Establishing and Maintaining Relationships; Communicating with Persons Outside Organization. **Physical Work Conditions**—Kneeling, Crouching, or Crawling; Indoors; Sitting; Using Hands on Objects, Tools, or Controls; Keeping or Regaining Balance. **Other Job Characteristics**—Pace Determined by Speed of Equipment; Consequence of Error; Importance of Repeating Same Tasks.

Experience—Job Zone 3. Previous work-related skill, knowledge, or experience is required. **Job Preparation:** SVP 6.0 to less than 7.0—more than one year and less than four years. **Knowledge**—Fine Arts; Design; Production and Processing; Sales and Marketing; Education and Training. **Instructional Programs**—Apparel and Textile Manufacture; Fashion and Fabric Consultant; Fashion/Apparel Design; Textile Science.

Related DOT Jobs—142.061-018 Fashion Designer; 142.081-014 Fur Designer; 142.281-010 Copyist.

27-1023.00 *Floral Designers*

- **Education/Training Required: Moderate-term on-the-job training**
- **Employed: 102,447**
- **Annual Earnings: $19,280**
- **Growth: 14.9%**
- **Annual Job Openings: 15,000**

Design, cut, and arrange live, dried, or artificial flowers and foliage.

Confer with clients regarding price and type of arrangement desired and the date, time, and place of delivery. Inform customers about the care, maintenance, and handling of various flowers and foliage, indoor plants, and other items. Plan arrangement according to client's requirements, utilizing knowledge of design and properties of materials, or select appropriate standard design pattern. Select flora and foliage for arrangements, working with numerous combinations to synthesize and develop new creations. Trim material and arrange bouquets, wreaths, terrariums, and other items using trimmers, shapers, wire, pins, floral tape, foam, and other materials. Water plants and cut, condition, and clean flowers and foliage for storage. Wrap and price completed arrangements. Conduct classes or demonstrations or train other workers. Create and change in-store and window displays, designs, and looks to enhance a shop's image. Decorate or supervise the decoration of buildings, halls, churches, or other facilities for parties, weddings, and other occasions. Grow flowers for use in arrangements or for sale in shop. Order and purchase flowers and supplies from wholesalers and growers. Perform general cleaning duties in the store to ensure the shop is clean and tidy. Perform office and retail service duties such as keeping financial records, serving customers, answering telephones, selling giftware items, and receiving payment. Unpack stock as it comes into the shop.

GOE INFORMATION—**Interest Area:** 01. Arts, Entertainment, and Media. **Work Group:** 01.04. Visual Arts. **Personality Type**—Artistic. Artistic occupations frequently involve working with forms, designs, and patterns. They often require self-expression, and the work can be done without following a clear set of rules. **Work Values**—Creativity; Achievement; Ability Utilization; Autonomy; Recognition. **Skills**—Management of Material Resources; Service Orientation; Management of Financial Resources. **Abilities**—*Cognitive:* Visualization; Originality; Fluency of Ideas; Oral Expression; Category Flexibility. *Psychomotor:* Arm-Hand Steadiness; Finger Dexterity; Multilimb Coordination. *Physical:* Extent Flexibility; Gross Body Equilibrium; Gross Body Coordination. *Sensory:* Visual Color Discrimination; Speech Recognition; Speech Clarity; Auditory Attention; Night Vision. **General Work Activities**—*Information Input:* Getting Information; Estimating Needed Characteristics; Identifying Objects, Actions, and Events. *Mental Process:* Organizing, Planning, and Prioritizing; Thinking Creatively; Judging Qualities of Things, Services, or Other People's Work. *Work Output:* Handling and Moving Objects; Performing General Physical Activities; Documenting or Recording Information. *Interacting with Others:* Communicating with Persons Outside Organization; Establishing and Maintaining Relationships; Performing for or Working with the Public. **Physical Work Conditions**—Using Hands on Objects, Tools, or Controls; Bending or Twisting the Body; Keeping or Regaining Balance; Making Repetitive Motions; Standing. **Other Job Characteristics**—Importance of Repeating Same Tasks; Pace Determined by Speed of Equipment; Consequence of Error.

Experience—Job Zone 2. Some previous work-related skill, knowledge, or experience may be helpful, but usually is not needed. **Job Preparation:** SVP 4.0 to less than 6.0—six months to less than two years. **Knowledge**—Fine Arts; Customer and Personal Service; Education and Training; Biology; Design. **Instructional Programs**—Floriculture/Floristry Operations and Management.

Related DOT Jobs—142.081-010 Floral Designer; 899.364-014 Artificial-Foliage Arranger.

27-1024.00 Graphic Designers

- **Education/Training Required: Bachelor's degree**
- **Employed: 189,911**
- **Annual Earnings: $36,020**
- **Growth: 26.7%**
- **Annual Job Openings: 28,000**

Design or create graphics to meet specific commercial or promotional needs, such as packaging, displays, or logos. May use a variety of mediums to achieve artistic or decorative effects.

Create designs, concepts, and sample layouts based on knowledge of layout principles and esthetic design concepts. Determine size and arrangement of illustrative material and copy; select style and size of type. Use computer software to generate new images. Mark up, paste, and assemble final layouts to prepare layouts for printer. Draw and print charts, graphs, illustrations, and other artwork, using computer. Review final layouts and suggest improvements as needed. Confer with clients to discuss and determine layout design. Develop graphics and layouts for product illustrations, company logos, and Internet Web sites. Key information into computer equipment to create layouts for client or supervisor. Prepare illustrations or rough sketches of material, discussing them with clients and/or supervisors and making necessary changes. Study illustrations and photographs to plan presentation of materials, products, or services. Prepare notes and instructions for workers who assemble and prepare final layouts for printing. Develop negatives and prints to produce layout photographs, using negative- and print-developing equipment and tools. Photograph layouts, using camera, to make layout prints for supervisors or clients. Produce still and animated

graphics for on-air and taped portions of television news broadcasts, using electronic video equipment.

GOE INFORMATION—**Interest Area:** 01. Arts, Entertainment, and Media. **Work Group:** 01.04. Visual Arts. **Personality Type**—Artistic. Artistic occupations frequently involve working with forms, designs, and patterns. They often require self-expression, and the work can be done without following a clear set of rules. **Work Values**—Creativity; Ability Utilization; Achievement; Recognition; Good Working Conditions. **Skills**—Persuasion; Complex Problem Solving; Equipment Selection; Troubleshooting; Time Management; Instructing; Operations Analysis; Coordination. **Abilities**—*Cognitive:* Originality; Visualization; Category Flexibility; Fluency of Ideas; Inductive Reasoning. *Psychomotor:* Finger Dexterity; Arm-Hand Steadiness; Manual Dexterity; Control Precision. *Physical:* None met the criteria. *Sensory:* Visual Color Discrimination; Near Vision; Speech Recognition; Far Vision; Speech Clarity. **General Work Activities**—*Information Input:* Getting Information; Identifying Objects, Actions, and Events; Estimating Needed Characteristics. *Mental Process:* Thinking Creatively; Updating and Using Relevant Knowledge; Organizing, Planning, and Prioritizing. *Work Output:* Interacting with Computers; Handling and Moving Objects; Drafting and Specifying Technical Devices. *Interacting with Others:* Establishing and Maintaining Relationships; Communicating with Persons Outside Organization; Communicating with Other Workers. **Physical Work Conditions**—Sitting; Making Repetitive Motions; Indoors; Climbing Ladders, Scaffolds, Poles, etc.; Using Hands on Objects, Tools, or Controls. **Other Job Characteristics**—Importance of Repeating Same Tasks; Pace Determined by Speed of Equipment; Consequence of Error.

Experience—Job Zone 4. A minimum of two to four years of work-related skill, knowledge, or experience is needed. **Job Preparation:** SVP 7.0 to less than 8.0—two years to less than 10 years. **Knowledge**—Fine Arts; Design; Computers and Electronics; Sales and Marketing; Communications and Media. **Instructional Programs**—Agricultural Communication/Journalism; Commercial and Advertising Art; Computer Graphics; Design and Visual Communications, General; Graphic Design; Industrial Design; Web Page, Digital/Multimedia, and Information Resources Design.

Related DOT Jobs—141.061-018 Graphic Designer.

27-1025.00 Interior Designers

- **Education/Training Required: Bachelor's degree**
- **Employed: 45,615**
- **Annual Earnings: $39,580**
- **Growth: 17.4%**
- **Annual Job Openings: 7,000**

Plan, design, and furnish interiors of residential, commercial, or industrial buildings. Formulate design that is practical, aesthetic, and conducive to intended purposes, such as raising productivity, selling merchandise, or improving lifestyle. May specialize in a particular field, style, or phase of interior design.

Formulate environmental plan to be practical, esthetic, and conducive to intended purposes, such as raising productivity or selling merchandise. Design or select and purchase furnishings, artwork, and accessories. Confer with client to determine factors affecting planning interior environments, such as budget, architectural preferences, and purpose and function. Plan and design interior environments for boats, planes, buses, trains, and other enclosed spaces. Advise client on interior design factors, such as space planning, layout and utilization of furnishings and equipment, and color coordination. Render design ideas in form of paste-ups or drawings. Estimate material requirements and costs and present design to client for approval. Subcontract fabrication, installation, and arrangement of carpeting, fixtures, accessories, draperies, paint and wall coverings, artwork, furniture, and related items.

GOE INFORMATION—Interest Area: 01. Arts, Entertainment, and Media. **Work Group:** 01.04. Visual Arts. **Personality Type**—Artistic. Artistic occupations frequently involve working with forms, designs, and patterns. They often require self-expression, and the work can be done without following a clear set of rules. **Work Values**—Creativity; Recognition; Ability Utilization; Achievement; Autonomy. **Skills**—Management of Financial Resources; Operations Analysis; Management of Material Resources; Negotiation; Coordination; Complex Problem Solving; Mathematics; Persuasion. **Abilities**—*Cognitive:* Originality; Visualization; Fluency of Ideas; Oral Expression; Oral Comprehension. *Psychomotor:* None met the criteria. *Physical:* None met the criteria. *Sensory:* Visual Color Discrimination; Speech Recognition; Depth Perception. **General Work Activities**—*Information Input:* Getting Information; Estimating Needed Characteristics; Identifying Objects, Actions, and Events. *Mental Process:* Thinking Creatively; Organizing, Planning, and Prioritizing; Making Decisions and Solving Problems. *Work Output:* Drafting and Specifying Technical Devices; Documenting or Recording Information; Performing General Physical Activities. *Interacting with Others:* Establishing and Maintaining Relationships; Monitoring and Controlling Resources; Communicating with Persons Outside Organization. **Physical Work Conditions**—Indoors; Sitting. **Other Job Characteristics**—Consequence of Error; Importance of Being Exact or Accurate; Pace Determined by Speed of Equipment.

Experience—Job Zone 4. A minimum of two to four years of work-related skill, knowledge, or experience is needed. **Job Preparation:** SVP 7.0 to less than 8.0—two years to less than 10 years. **Knowledge**—Design; Fine Arts; Sales and Marketing; Administration and Management; Customer and Personal Service. **Instructional Programs**—Facilities Planning and Management; Interior Architecture; Interior Design; Textile Science.

Related DOT Jobs—141.051-010 Color Expert; 142.051-014 Interior Designer.

27-1026.00 Merchandise Displayers and Window Trimmers

- **Education/Training Required: Moderate-term on-the-job training**
- **Employed: 75,787**
- **Annual Earnings: $21,870**
- **Annual Job Openings: 11,000**

Plan and erect commercial displays, such as those in windows and interiors of retail stores and at trade exhibitions.

Arrange properties, furniture, merchandise, backdrops, and other accessories as shown in prepared sketches. Change or rotate window displays, interior display areas, and signage to reflect changes in inventory or promotion. Construct or assemble displays and display components from fabric, glass, paper, and plastic according to specifications, using hand tools and woodworking power tools. Consult with advertising and sales staff to determine type of merchandise to be featured and time and place for each display. Cut out designs on cardboard, hardboard, and plywood according to motif of event. Develop ideas or plans for merchandise displays or window decorations. Obtain plans from display designers or display managers and discuss their implementation with clients or supervisors. Place prices and descriptive signs on backdrops, fixtures, merchandise, or floor. Plan and erect commercial displays to entice and appeal to customers. Prepare sketches, floor plans, or models of proposed displays. Select themes, lighting, colors, and props to be used. Attend training sessions and corporate planning meetings to obtain new ideas for product launches. Collaborate with others to obtain products and other display items. Create and enhance mannequin faces by mixing and applying paint and attaching measured eyelash strips, using artist's brush, airbrush, pins, ruler, and scissors. Dress mannequins for displays. Install booths, exhibits, displays, carpets, and drapes as guided by floor plan of building and specifications. Install decorations such as flags, banners, festive lights, and bunting on or in building, street, exhibit hall, or booth. Instruct sales staff in color-coordination of clothing racks and counter displays. Maintain props and mannequins, inspecting them for imperfections and applying preservative coatings as necessary. Store, pack, and maintain records of props and display items. Take photographs of displays and signage. Use computers to produce signage.

GOE INFORMATION—Interest Area: 01. Arts, Entertainment, and Media. **Work Group:** 01.04. Visual Arts. **Personality Type**—Artistic. Artistic occupations frequently involve working with forms, designs, and patterns. They often require self-expression, and the work can be done without following a clear set of rules. **Work Values**—Creativity; Ability Utilization; Achievement; Recognition; Good Working Conditions. **Skills**—Installation; Equipment Selection. **Abilities**—*Cognitive:* Visualization; Originality; Category Flexibility; Fluency of Ideas; Perceptual Speed. *Psychomotor:* Speed of Limb Movement; Multilimb Coordination; Manual Dexterity. *Physical:* Extent Flexibility; Explosive Strength; Gross Body Equilibrium; Dynamic Flexibility; Static Strength. *Sensory:* Visual Color Discrimination; Depth Perception; Glare Sensitivity; Sound Localization; Peripheral Vision. **General Work Activities**—*Information Input:* Getting Information; Estimating Needed Characteristics; Identifying Objects, Actions, and Events. *Mental Process:* Thinking Creatively; Organizing, Planning, and Prioritizing; Judging Qualities of Things, Services, or Other People's Work. *Work Output:* Handling and Moving Objects; Performing General Physical Activities; Drafting and Specifying Technical Devices. *Interacting with Others:* Communicating with Other Workers; Influencing Others or Selling; Communicating with Persons Outside Organization. **Physical Work Conditions**—Climbing Ladders, Scaffolds, Poles, etc.; Cramped Work Space or Awkward Positions; Keeping or Regaining Balance; Minor Burns, Cuts, Bites, or Stings; Bending or Twisting the Body. **Other Job Characteristics**—Importance of Repeating Same Tasks; Pace Determined by Speed of Equipment; Degree of Automation.

Experience—Job Zone 3. Previous work-related skill, knowledge, or experience is required. **Job Preparation:** SVP 6.0 to less than 7.0—more than one year and less than four years. **Knowledge**—Sales and Marketing; Fine Arts; Design; Sociology and Anthropology; Communications and Media. **Instructional Programs**—No data available.

Related DOT Jobs—142.031-014 Manager, Display; 298.081-010 Displayer, Merchandise; 298.381-010 Decorator.

27-1027.00 Set and Exhibit Designers

- **Education/Training Required: Bachelor's degree**
- **Employed: 11,935**
- **Annual Earnings: $33,460**
- **Growth: 27.0%**
- **Annual Job Openings: 2,000**

Design special exhibits and movie, television, and theater sets. May study scripts, confer with directors, and conduct research to determine appropriate architectural styles.

Confer with clients and staff in order to gather information about exhibit space, proposed themes and content, timelines, budgets, materials, and/or promotion requirements. Confer with conservators in order to determine how to handle an exhibit's environmental aspects, such as lighting, temperature, and humidity, so that objects will be protected and exhibits will be enhanced. Coordinate the removal of sets, props, and exhibits after productions or events are complete. Design and produce displays and materials that can be used to decorate windows, interior displays, or event locations such as streets and fairgrounds. Develop set designs based on evaluation of scripts, budgets, research information, and available locations. Direct and coordinate construction, erection, or decoration activities in order to ensure that sets or exhibits meet design, budget, and schedule requirements. Examine objects to be included in exhibits in order to plan where and how to display them. Inspect installed exhibits for conformance to specifications and satisfactory operation of special effects components. Observe sets during rehearsals in order to ensure that set elements do not interfere with performance aspects such as cast movement and camera angles. Plan for location-specific issues such as space limitations, traffic flow patterns, and safety concerns. Prepare preliminary renderings of proposed exhibits, including detailed construction, layout, and material specifications and diagrams relating to aspects such as special effects and/or lighting. Prepare rough drafts and scale working drawings of sets, including floor plans, scenery, and properties to be constructed. Read scripts in order to determine location, set, and design requirements. Research architectural and stylistic elements appropriate to the time period to be depicted, consulting experts for information as necessary. Select set props such as furniture, pictures, lamps, and rugs. Submit plans for approval and adapt plans to serve intended purposes or to conform to budget or fabrication restrictions. Acquire or arrange for acquisition of specimens or graphics required to complete exhibits. Arrange for outside contractors to construct exhibit structures. Assign staff to complete design ideas and prepare sketches, illustrations, and detailed drawings of sets or graphics and animation. Attend rehearsals and production meetings in order to obtain and share information related to sets. Collaborate with those in charge of lighting and sound so that those production aspects can be coordinated with set designs or exhibit layouts. Coordinate the transportation of sets that are built off-site and coordinate their setup at the site of use. Design and build scale models of set designs or miniature sets used in filming backgrounds or special effects. Estimate set- or exhibit-related costs, including materials, construction, and rental of props or locations. Incorporate security systems into exhibit layouts. Provide supportive materials for exhibits and displays, such as press kits and advertising, posters, brochures, catalogues, and invitations and publicity notices.

GOE INFORMATION—Interest Area: 01. Arts, Entertainment, and Media. **Work Group:** 01.04. Visual Arts. **Note:** The Department of Labor has not collected some data for this job, so it has fewer details than the other descriptions.

Instructional Programs—Design and Applied Arts, Other; Design and Visual Communications, General; Illustration; Technical Theatre/Theatre Design and Technology.

Related DOT Jobs—142.051-010 Display Designer; 142.061-042 Set Decorator; 142.061-046 Set Designer; 142.061-050 Set Designer; 142.061-058 Exhibit Designer; 142.061-062 Art Director; 149.031-010 Supervisor, Scenic Arts.

27-1027.01 Set Designers

- **Education/Training Required: Bachelor's degree**
- **Employed: No data available.**
- **Annual Earnings: $33,460**
- **Growth: 27.0%**
- **Annual Job Openings: 2,000**

Design sets for theatrical, motion picture, and television productions.

Integrates requirements, including script, research, budget, and available locations to develop design. Prepares rough draft and scale working drawings of sets, including floor plans, scenery, and properties to be constructed. Presents drawings for approval and makes changes and corrections as directed. Designs and builds scale models of set design or miniature sets used in filming backgrounds or special effects. Selects furniture, draperies, pictures, lamps, and rugs for decorative quality and appearance. Researches and consults experts to determine architectural and furnishing styles to depict given periods or locations. Confers with heads of production and direction to establish budget and schedules and discuss design ideas. Estimates costs of design materials and construction or rental of location or props. Directs and coordinates set construction, erection, or decoration activities to ensure conformance to design, budget, and schedule requirements. Reads script to determine location, set, or decoration requirements. Examines dressed set to ensure props and scenery do not interfere with movements of cast or view of camera. Assigns staff to complete design ideas and prepare sketches, illustrations, and detailed drawings of sets or graphics and animation.

GOE INFORMATION—Interest Area: 01. Arts, Entertainment, and Media. **Work Group:** 01.04. Visual Arts. **Personality Type**—Artistic. Artistic occupations frequently involve working with forms, designs, and patterns. They often require self-expression, and the work can be done without following a clear set of rules. **Work Values**—Creativity; Ability Utilization; Achievement; Autonomy; Authority. **Skills**—Management of Material Resources; Management of Financial Resources; Systems Evaluation; Management of Personnel Resources; Equipment Selection; Operations Analysis; Complex Problem Solving; Persuasion. **Abilities**—*Cognitive:* Visualization; Originality; Fluency of Ideas; Time Sharing; Speed of Closure. *Psychomotor:* Arm-Hand Steadiness; Finger Dexterity; Wrist-Finger Speed; Manual Dexterity; Multilimb Coordination. *Physical:* Gross Body Equilibrium; Gross Body Coordination; Stamina; Explosive Strength; Dynamic Strength. *Sensory:* Visual Color Discrimination; Auditory Attention; Far Vision; Sound Localization; Night Vision. **General Work Activities**—*Information Input:* Getting Information; Identifying Objects, Actions, and Events; Estimating Needed Characteristics. *Mental Process:* Thinking Creatively; Organizing, Planning, and Prioritizing; Scheduling Work and Activities. *Work Output:* Drafting and Specifying Technical Devices; Handling and Moving Objects; Performing General Physical Activities. *Interacting with Others:* Coordinating the Work and Activities of Others; Communicating with Other Workers; Establishing and Maintaining Relationships. **Physical Work Conditions**—High Places; Climbing Ladders, Scaffolds, Poles, etc.; Keeping or Regaining Balance; Walking or Running; Bending or Twisting the Body. **Other Job Characteristics**—Consequence of Error; Importance of Being Exact or Accurate; Pace Determined by Speed of Equipment.

Experience—Job Zone 5. Extensive skill, knowledge, and experience are needed for these occupations. **Job Preparation:** SVP 8.0 and above—four years to more than 10 years. **Knowledge**—Fine Arts; Design; Building and Construction; History and Archeology; Geography. **Instructional Programs**—Design and Applied Arts, Other; Design and Visual Communications, General; Illustration; Technical Theatre/Theatre Design and Technology.

Related DOT Jobs—142.061-042 Set Decorator; 142.061-046 Set Designer; 142.061-050 Set Designer; 142.061-062 Art Director; 149.031-010 Supervisor, Scenic Arts.

27-1027.02 Exhibit Designers

- Education/Training Required: Bachelor's degree
- Employed: No data available.
- Annual Earnings: $33,460
- Growth: 27.0%
- Annual Job Openings: 2,000

Plan, design, and oversee construction and installation of permanent and temporary exhibits and displays.

Prepares preliminary drawings of proposed exhibit, including detailed construction, layout, material specifications, or special effects diagrams. Designs display to decorate streets, fairgrounds, building, or other places for celebrations, using paper, cloth, plastic, or other materials. Designs, draws, paints, or sketches backgrounds and fixtures for use in windows or interior displays. Oversees preparation of artwork, construction of exhibit components, and placement of collection to ensure intended interpretation of concepts and conformance to specifications. Confers with client or staff regarding theme, interpretative or informational purpose, planned location, budget, materials, or promotion. Submits plans for approval and adapts plan to serve intended purpose or to conform to budget or fabrication restrictions. Arranges for acquisition of specimens or graphics or building of exhibit structures by outside contractors to complete exhibit. Inspects installed exhibit for conformance to specifications and satisfactory operation of special effects components.

GOE INFORMATION—Interest Area: 01. Arts, Entertainment, and Media. **Work Group:** 01.04. Visual Arts. **Personality Type—**Artistic. Artistic occupations frequently involve working with forms, designs, and patterns. They often require self-expression, and the work can be done without following a clear set of rules. **Work Values—**Creativity; Ability Utilization; Autonomy; Achievement; Recognition. **Skills—**Management of Material Resources; Management of Financial Resources; Systems Evaluation; Equipment Selection; Systems Analysis; Complex Problem Solving; Operations Analysis; Negotiation. **Abilities—***Cognitive:* Visualization; Originality; Fluency of Ideas; Oral Expression; Time Sharing. *Psychomotor:* Arm-Hand Steadiness; Wrist-Finger Speed; Control Precision; Manual Dexterity; Finger Dexterity. *Physical:* Extent Flexibility; Gross Body Coordination; Gross Body Equilibrium; Stamina. *Sensory:* Visual Color Discrimination; Far Vision; Near Vision; Night Vision; Depth Perception. **General Work Activities—***Information Input:* Getting Information; Identifying Objects, Actions, and Events; Monitoring Processes, Materials, or Surroundings. *Mental Process:* Thinking Creatively; Organizing, Planning, and Prioritizing; Evaluating Information Against Standards. *Work Output:* Drafting and Specifying Technical Devices; Handling and Moving Objects; Performing General Physical Activities. *Interacting with Others:* Establishing and Maintaining Relationships; Coordinating the Work and Activities of Others; Monitoring and Controlling Resources. **Physical Work Conditions—**High Places; Climbing Ladders, Scaffolds, Poles, etc.; Keeping or Regaining Balance; Walking or Running; Kneeling, Crouching, or Crawling. **Other Job Characteristics—**Consequence of Error; Pace Determined by Speed of Equipment; Importance of Being Exact or Accurate.

Experience—Job Zone 4. A minimum of two to four years of work-related skill, knowledge, or experience is needed. **Job Preparation:** SVP 7.0 to less than 8.0—two years to less than 10 years. **Knowledge—**Fine Arts; Design; Building and Construction; Sales and Marketing; Customer and Personal Service. **Instructional Programs—**Design and Applied Arts, Other; Design and Visual Communications, General; Illustration; Technical Theatre/Theatre Design and Technology.

Related DOT Jobs—142.051-010 Display Designer; 142.061-058 Exhibit Designer.

27-1029.99 Designers, All Other

- Education/Training Required: No data available.
- Employed: No data available.
- Annual Earnings: No data available.
- Growth: 21.2%
- Annual Job Openings: 15,000

All designers not listed separately.

No task data available.

GOE INFORMATION—Interest Area: 01. Arts, Entertainment, and Media. **Work Group:** 01.04. Visual Arts. **Note:** The Department of Labor has not collected some data for this job, so it has fewer details than the other descriptions.

Instructional Programs—Design and Applied Arts, Other; Design and Visual Communications, General; Illustration; Industrial Design.

Related DOT Jobs—No related DOT jobs.

27-2000 Entertainers and Performers, Sports and Related Workers

27-2011.00 Actors

- Education/Training Required: Long-term on-the-job training
- Employed: 99,181
- Annual Earnings: $20,540
- Growth: 26.7%
- Annual Job Openings: 20,000

Play parts in stage, television, radio, video, or motion picture productions for entertainment, information, or instruction. Interpret serious or comic role by speech, gesture, and body movement to entertain or inform audience. May dance and sing.

Attend auditions and casting calls in order to audition for roles. Collaborate with other actors as part of an ensemble. Learn about characters in scripts and their relationships to each other in order to develop role interpretations. Perform humorous and serious interpretations of emotions, actions, and situations, using body movements, facial expressions, and gestures. Portray and interpret roles, using speech, gestures, and body movements in order to entertain, inform, or instruct radio, film, television, or live audiences. Sing and/or dance during dramatic or comedic performances. Study and rehearse roles from scripts in order to interpret, learn, and memorize lines, stunts, and cues as directed. Work closely with directors, other actors, and playwrights to find the interpretation most suited to the role. Manipulate strings, wires, rods, or fingers to animate puppets or dummies in synchronization with talking, singing, or recorded programs. Perform original and stock tricks of illusion to entertain and mystify audiences, occasionally including audience members as participants. Promote productions using means such as interviews about plays or movies. Read from scripts or books to narrate action or to inform or entertain audiences, utilizing few or no stage props. Tell jokes; perform comic dances, songs, and skits; impersonate mannerisms and voices of others; contort face; and use other devices to amuse audiences. Work with other crewmembers responsible for lighting, costumes, makeup, and props. Write original or adapted material for dramas, comedies, puppet shows, narration, or other performances.

Construct puppets and ventriloquist dummies and sew accessory clothing, using hand tools and machines. Dress in comical clown costumes and makeup; and perform comedy routines to entertain audiences. Introduce performances and performers in order to stimulate excitement and coordinate smooth transition of acts during events. Prepare and perform action stunts for motion picture, television, or stage productions.

GOE INFORMATION—Interest Area: 01. Arts, Entertainment, and Media. **Work Group:** 01.05. Performing Arts. **Personality Type**—Artistic. Artistic occupations frequently involve working with forms, designs, and patterns. They often require self-expression, and the work can be done without following a clear set of rules. **Work Values**—Ability Utilization; Recognition; Creativity; Variety; Achievement. **Skills**—Speaking; Monitoring; Repairing. **Abilities**—*Cognitive:* Memorization; Originality; Spatial Orientation; Oral Expression; Visualization. *Psychomotor:* Reaction Time; Speed of Limb Movement; Response Orientation; Multilimb Coordination; Wrist-Finger Speed. *Physical:* Gross Body Coordination; Explosive Strength; Dynamic Flexibility; Gross Body Equilibrium; Stamina. *Sensory:* Speech Clarity; Near Vision; Glare Sensitivity; Peripheral Vision; Far Vision. **General Work Activities**—*Information Input:* Getting Information; Identifying Objects, Actions, and Events; Monitoring Processes, Materials, or Surroundings. *Mental Process:* Thinking Creatively; Organizing, Planning, and Prioritizing; Judging Qualities of Things, Services, or Other People's Work. *Work Output:* Performing General Physical Activities; Handling and Moving Objects; Controlling Machines and Processes. *Interacting with Others:* Performing for or Working with the Public; Communicating with Persons Outside Organization; Communicating with Other Workers. **Physical Work Conditions**—Outdoors; High Places; Keeping or Regaining Balance; Extremely Bright or Inadequate Lighting; Very Hot or Cold. **Other Job Characteristics**—Importance of Being Exact or Accurate; Importance of Repeating Same Tasks; Consequence of Error.

Experience—Job Zone 3. Previous work-related skill, knowledge, or experience is required. **Job Preparation:** SVP 6.0 to less than 7.0—more than one year and less than four years. **Knowledge**—Fine Arts; Communications and Media; English Language; Psychology; Building and Construction. **Instructional Programs**—Acting; Directing and Theatrical Production; Drama and Dramatics/Theatre Arts, General; Dramatic/Theatre Arts and Stagecraft, Other.

Related DOT Jobs—150.047-010 Actor; 150.147-010 Narrator; 159.041-010 Magician; 159.041-014 Puppeteer; 159.044-010 Ventriloquist; 159.047-010 Clown; 159.047-014 Comedian; 159.047-018 Impersonator; 159.047-022 Mime; 159.341-014 Stunt Performer; 159.367-010 Ring Conductor.

27-2012.00 Producers and Directors

- **Education/Training Required: Work experience plus degree**
- **Employed: 58,489**
- **Annual Earnings: $45,090**
- **Growth: 27.1%**
- **Annual Job Openings: 11,000**

Produce or direct stage, television, radio, video, or motion picture productions for entertainment, information, or instruction. Responsible for creative decisions, such as interpretation of script, choice of guests, set design, sound, special effects, and choreography.

No task data available.

GOE INFORMATION—Interest Area: 01. Arts, Entertainment, and Media. **Work Group:** 01.01. Managerial Work in Arts, Entertainment, and Media. **Note:** The Department of Labor has not collected some data for this job, so it has fewer details than the other descriptions.

Instructional Programs—Cinematography and Film/Video Production; Directing and Theatrical Production; Drama and Dramatics/Theatre Arts, General; Dramatic/Theatre Arts and Stagecraft, Other; Film/Cinema Studies; Radio and Television; Theatre/Theatre Arts Management.

Related DOT Jobs—139.167-010 Program Coordinator; 150.027-010 Dramatic Coach; 150.067-010 Director, Stage; 159.067-010 Director, Motion Picture; 159.067-014 Director, Television; 159.117-010 Producer; 159.167-010 Artist and Repertoire Manager; 159.167-014 Director, Radio; 159.167-018 Manager, Stage; 159.267-010 Director, Casting; 166.167-010 Contestant Coordinator; 169.167-070 Director, Educational Programming; 184.117-010 Director, Public Service; 184.162-010 Manager, Production; 184.167-014 Director, News; 184.167-022 Director, Operations, Broadcast; 184.167-030 Director, Program; 184.167-034 Director, Sports; 187.167-174 Producer; 187.167-178 Producer; others.

27-2012.01 Producers

- **Education/Training Required: Work experience plus degree**
- **Employed: No data available.**
- **Annual Earnings: $45,090**
- **Growth: 27.1%**
- **Annual Job Openings: 11,000**

Plan and coordinate various aspects of radio, television, stage, or motion picture production, such as selecting script; coordinating writing, directing, and editing; and arranging financing.

Arrange financing for productions. Conduct meetings with staff to discuss production progress and to ensure production objectives are attained. Coordinate the activities of writers, directors, managers, and other personnel throughout the production process. Determine production size, content, and budget, establishing details such as production schedules and management policies. Hire directors, principal cast members, and key production staff members. Monitor post-production processes in order to ensure accurate completion of all details. Negotiate contracts with artistic personnel, often in accordance with collective bargaining agreements. Perform management activities such as budgeting, scheduling, planning, and marketing. Plan and coordinate the production of musical recordings, selecting music and directing performers. Repay investors when completed projects begin to generate revenue. Resolve personnel problems that arise during the production process by acting as liaisons between dissenting parties when necessary. Select plays, scripts, books, or ideas to be produced. Compose and edit scripts or provide screenwriters with story outlines from which scripts can be written. Determine and direct the content of radio programming. Develop marketing plans for finished products, collaborating with sales associates to supervise product distribution. Distribute residual payments to artists. Maintain knowledge of minimum wages and working conditions established by unions and/or associations of actors and technicians. Negotiate with parties, including independent producers and the distributors and broadcasters who will be handling completed productions. Obtain rights to scripts or to such items as existing video footage. Perform administrative duties such as preparing operational reports, distributing rehearsal call sheets and script copies, and arranging for rehearsal quarters. Review film, recordings, or rehearsals to ensure conformance to production and broadcast standards. Write and submit proposals to bid on contracts for projects. Edit and write news stories from information collected by reporters. Obtain and distribute costumes, props, music, and studio equipment needed to complete productions. Produce shows for special occasions, such as holidays or testimonials.

GOE INFORMATION—Interest Area: 01. Arts, Entertainment, and Media. **Work Group:** 01.01. Managerial Work in Arts, Entertainment, and Media. **Personality Type**—Artistic. Artistic occupations frequently involve working with forms, designs, and patterns. They often require self-expression, and the work can be done without following a clear set of rules. **Work Values**—Authority; Creativity; Recognition; Responsibility; Autonomy. **Skills**—Management of Personnel Resources; Coordination; Management of Material Resources; Management of Financial Resources; Speaking; Operations Analysis; Reading Comprehension; Writing. **Abilities**—*Cognitive:* Originality; Written Expression; Fluency of Ideas; Problem Sensitivity; Oral Comprehension. *Psychomotor:* None met the criteria. *Physical:* None met the criteria. *Sensory:* Speech Clarity; Speech Recognition; Far Vision; Near Vision; Glare Sensitivity. **General Work Activities**—*Information Input:* Getting Information; Identifying Objects, Actions, and Events; Monitoring Processes, Materials, or Surroundings. *Mental Process:* Organizing, Planning, and Prioritizing; Scheduling Work and Activities; Thinking Creatively. *Work Output:* Documenting or Recording Information; Drafting and Specifying Technical Devices; Handling and Moving Objects. *Interacting with Others:* Communicating with Other Workers; Resolving Conflict and Negotiating with Others; Communicating with Persons Outside Organization. **Physical Work Conditions**—Sitting; Indoors; Extremely Bright or Inadequate Lighting. **Other Job Characteristics**—Importance of Being Exact or Accurate; Consequence of Error; Importance of Repeating Same Tasks.

Experience—Job Zone 4. A minimum of two to four years of work-related skill, knowledge, or experience is needed. **Job Preparation:** SVP 7.0 to less than 8.0—two years to less than 10 years. **Knowledge**—Communications and Media; Fine Arts; Personnel and Human Resources; Administration and Management; English Language. **Instructional Programs**—Cinematography and Film/Video Production; Directing and Theatrical Production; Drama and Dramatics/Theatre Arts, General; Dramatic/Theatre Arts and Stagecraft, Other; Film/Cinema Studies; Radio and Television; Theatre/Theatre Arts Management.

Related DOT Jobs—159.117-010 Producer; 187.167-174 Producer; 187.167-178 Producer; 187.167-182 Producer, Assistant; 962.167-014 Program Assistant.

27-2012.02 Directors—Stage, Motion Pictures, Television, and Radio

- **Education/Training Required: Work experience plus degree**
- **Employed: No data available.**
- **Annual Earnings: $45,090**
- **Growth: 27.1%**
- **Annual Job Openings: 11,000**

Interpret script, conduct rehearsals, and direct activities of cast and technical crew for stage, motion pictures, television, or radio programs.

Choose settings and locations for films and determine how scenes will be shot in these settings. Collaborate with producers in order to hire crew members such as art directors, cinematographers, and costume designers. Communicate to actors the approach, characterization, and movement needed for each scene in such a way that rehearsals and takes are minimized. Confer with stage managers in order to arrange schedules for rehearsals, costume fittings, and sound/light development. Confer with technical directors, managers, crew members, and writers to discuss details of production, such as photography, script, music, sets, and costumes. Consult with writers, producers, and/or actors about script changes, or "workshop" scripts, through rehearsal with writers and actors to create final drafts. Direct live broadcasts, films and recordings, or non-broadcast programming for public entertainment or education. Establish pace of programs and sequences of scenes according to time requirements and cast and set accessibility. Hold auditions for parts and/or negotiate contracts

with actors determined suitable for specific roles, working in conjunction with producers. Plan details such as framing, composition, camera movement, sound, and actor movement for each shot or scene. Select plays or scripts for production and determine how material should be interpreted and performed. Study and research scripts in order to determine how they should be directed. Supervise and coordinate the work of camera, lighting, design, and sound crew members. Collaborate with film and sound editors during the post-production process as films are edited and soundtracks are added. Compile cue words and phrases; cue announcers, cast members, and technicians during performances. Compile scripts, program notes, and other material related to productions. Create and approve storyboards in conjunction with art directors. Cut and edit film or tape in order to integrate component parts into desired sequences. Identify and approve equipment and elements required for productions, such as scenery, lights, props, costumes, choreography, and music. Interpret stage-set diagrams to determine stage layouts; supervise placement of equipment and scenery. Promote and market productions by giving interviews, participating in talk shows, and making other public appearances. Review film daily in order to check on work in progress and to plan for future filming. Introduce plays and meet with audiences after shows in order to explain how the play was interpreted. Perform producers' duties such as securing financial backing, establishing and administering budgets, and recruiting cast and crew.

GOE INFORMATION—**Interest Area:** 01. Arts, Entertainment, and Media. **Work Group:** 01.05. Performing Arts. **Personality Type**—Artistic. Artistic occupations frequently involve working with forms, designs, and patterns. They often require self-expression, and the work can be done without following a clear set of rules. **Work Values**—Authority; Creativity; Recognition; Responsibility; Achievement. **Skills**—Coordination; Management of Personnel Resources; Instructing; Equipment Selection; Management of Material Resources; Speaking; Operation and Control; Complex Problem Solving. **Abilities**—*Cognitive:* Originality; Oral Expression; Visualization; Fluency of Ideas; Time Sharing. *Psychomotor:* Reaction Time; Response Orientation; Rate Control. *Physical:* Gross Body Coordination; Gross Body Equilibrium; Dynamic Flexibility. *Sensory:* Far Vision; Auditory Attention; Speech Clarity; Sound Localization; Hearing Sensitivity. **General Work Activities**—*Information Input:* Getting Information; Identifying Objects, Actions, and Events; Monitoring Processes, Materials, or Surroundings. *Mental Process:* Organizing, Planning, and Prioritizing; Thinking Creatively; Scheduling Work and Activities. *Work Output:* Documenting or Recording Information; Drafting and Specifying Technical Devices; Performing General Physical Activities. *Interacting with Others:* Coordinating the Work and Activities of Others; Guiding, Directing, and Motivating Subordinates; Monitoring and Controlling Resources. **Physical Work Conditions**—Outdoors; Extremely Bright or Inadequate Lighting; High Places; Radiation; Distracting Sounds and Noise Levels. **Other Job Characteristics**—Consequence of Error; Pace Determined by Speed of Equipment; Importance of Repeating Same Tasks.

Experience—Job Zone 4. A minimum of two to four years of work-related skill, knowledge, or experience is needed. **Job Preparation:** SVP 7.0 to less than 8.0—two years to less than 10 years. **Knowledge**—Fine Arts; Communications and Media; Administration and Management; Personnel and Human Resources; English Language. **Instructional Programs**—Cinematography and Film/Video Production; Directing and Theatrical Production; Drama and Dramatics/Theatre Arts, General; Dramatic/Theatre Arts and Stagecraft, Other; Film/Cinema Studies; Radio and Television; Theatre/Theatre Arts Management.

Related DOT Jobs—139.167-010 Program Coordinator; 150.027-010 Dramatic Coach; 150.067-010 Director, Stage; 159.067-010 Director, Motion Picture; 159.067-014 Director, Television; 159.167-014 Director, Radio; 159.167-018 Manager, Stage.

27-2012.03 Program Directors

- **Education/Training Required: Work experience plus degree**
- **Employed: 58,489**
- **Annual Earnings: $45,090**
- **Growth: 27.1%**
- **Annual Job Openings: 11,000**

Direct and coordinate activities of personnel engaged in preparation of radio or television station program schedules and programs such as sports or news.

Check completed program logs for accuracy and conformance with FCC rules and regulations and resolve program log inaccuracies. Confer with directors and production staff to discuss issues such as production and casting problems, budgets, policies, and news coverage. Coordinate activities between departments, such as news and programming. Cue announcers, actors, performers, and guests. Develop promotions for current programs and specials. Direct and coordinate activities of personnel engaged in broadcast news, sports, or programming. Establish work schedules and assign work to staff members. Evaluate new and existing programming for suitability and in order to assess the need for changes, using information such as audience surveys and feedback. Monitor and review programming in order to ensure that schedules are met, guidelines are adhered to, and performances are of adequate quality. Monitor network transmissions for advisories concerning daily program schedules, program content, special feeds, and/or program changes. Perform personnel duties such as hiring staff and evaluating work performance. Plan and schedule programming and event coverage based on broadcast length, time availability, and other factors such as community needs, ratings data, and viewer demographics. Act as a liaison between talent and directors, providing information that performers/guests need to prepare for appearances and communicating relevant information from guests, performers, or staff to directors. Conduct interviews for broadcasts. Develop budgets for programming and broadcasting activities and monitor expenditures to ensure that they remain within budgetary limits. Develop ideas for programs and features that a station could produce. Operate and maintain on-air and production audio equipment. Prepare copy and edit tape so that material is ready for broadcasting. Read news, read and/or record public service and promotional announcements, and otherwise participate as a member of an on-air shift as required. Review information about programs and schedules in order to ensure accuracy and provide such information to local media outlets as necessary. Select, acquire, and maintain programs, music, films, and other needed materials and obtain legal clearances for their use as necessary. Direct setup of remote facilities and install or cancel programs at remote stations. Participate in the planning and execution of fundraising activities.

GOE INFORMATION—Interest Area: 01. Arts, Entertainment, and Media. **Work Group:** 01.01. Managerial Work in Arts, Entertainment, and Media. **Personality Type**—Enterprising. Enterprising occupations frequently involve starting up and carrying out projects. These occupations can involve leading people and making many decisions. They sometimes require risk taking and often deal with business. **Work Values**—Authority; Creativity; Variety; Autonomy; Responsibility. **Skills**—Management of Personnel Resources; Coordination; Management of Financial Resources; Writing; Management of Material Resources; Complex Problem Solving; Time Management; Systems Analysis. **Abilities**—*Cognitive:* Written Expression; Originality; Oral Expression; Fluency of Ideas; Oral Comprehension. *Psychomotor:* Wrist-Finger Speed; Response Orientation. *Physical:* Trunk Strength. *Sensory:* Near Vision; Far Vision; Speech Clarity; Night Vision; Sound Localization. **General Work Activities**—*Information Input:* Getting Information; Identifying Objects, Actions, and Events; Monitoring Processes, Materials, or Surroundings.

Mental Process: Organizing, Planning, and Prioritizing; Scheduling Work and Activities; Making Decisions and Solving Problems. *Work Output:* Documenting or Recording Information; Interacting with Computers; Controlling Machines and Processes. *Interacting with Others:* Communicating with Other Workers; Monitoring and Controlling Resources; Guiding, Directing, and Motivating Subordinates. **Physical Work Conditions**—Indoors; Sitting. **Other Job Characteristics**—Importance of Being Exact or Accurate; Consequence of Error; Importance of Repeating Same Tasks.

Experience—Job Zone 5. Extensive skill, knowledge, and experience are needed for these occupations. **Job Preparation:** SVP 8.0 and above—four years to more than 10 years. **Knowledge**—Communications and Media; Administration and Management; Personnel and Human Resources; Economics and Accounting; English Language. **Instructional Programs**—Cinematography and Film/Video Production; Directing and Theatrical Production; Drama and Dramatics/Theatre Arts, General; Dramatic/Theatre Arts and Stagecraft, Other; Film/Cinema Studies; Radio and Television; Theatre/Theatre Arts Management.

Related DOT Jobs—184.117-010 Director, Public Service; 184.167-014 Director, News; 184.167-022 Director, Operations, Broadcast; 184.167-030 Director, Program; 184.167-034 Director, Sports.

27-2012.04 Talent Directors

- **Education/Training Required: Long-term on-the-job training**
- **Employed: No data available.**
- **Annual Earnings: $45,090**
- **Growth: 27.1%**
- **Annual Job Openings: 11,000**

Audition and interview performers to select most appropriate talent for parts in stage, television, radio, or motion picture productions.

Arrange for and/or design screen tests or auditions for prospective performers. Attend or view productions in order to maintain knowledge of available actors. Audition and interview performers in order to match their attributes to specific roles or to increase the pool of available acting talent. Contact agents and actors in order to provide notification of audition and performance opportunities and to set up audition times. Locate performers or extras for crowd and background scenes, and stand-ins or photo doubles for actors by direct contact or through agents. Maintain talent files that include information such as performers' specialties, past performances, and availability. Negotiate contract agreements with performers, with agents, or between performers and agents or production companies. Prepare actors for auditions by providing scripts and information about roles and casting requirements. Read scripts and confer with producers in order to determine the types and numbers of performers required for a given production. Review performer information such as photos, resumes, voice tapes, videos, and union membership in order to decide whom to audition for parts. Select performers for roles or submit lists of suitable performers to producers or directors for final selection. Hire and supervise workers who help locate people with specified attributes and talents. Serve as liaisons between directors, actors, and agents.

GOE INFORMATION—Interest Area: 01. Arts, Entertainment, and Media. **Work Group:** 01.05. Performing Arts. **Personality Type**—Artistic. Artistic occupations frequently involve working with forms, designs, and patterns. They often require self-expression, and the work can be done without following a clear set of rules. **Work Values**—Authority; Responsibility; Autonomy; Creativity; Variety. **Skills**—Negotiation; Speaking; Management of Personnel Resources; Social Perceptiveness; Active Listening. **Abilities**—*Cognitive:* Memorization; Oral Expression; Deductive Reasoning; Perceptual Speed; Inductive Reasoning. *Psychomotor:* None met the criteria. *Physical:* None met the criteria. *Sensory:* Hearing Sensitivity; Speech Clarity; Auditory Attention; Night Vision; Far Vision. **General Work Activities**—*Information Input:* Identifying Objects, Actions, and Events; Getting Information; Monitoring Processes, Materials, or Surroundings. *Mental Process:* Judging Qualities of Things, Services, or Other People's Work; Organizing, Planning, and Prioritizing; Thinking Creatively. *Work Output:* Documenting or Recording Information; Performing General Physical Activities; Handling and Moving Objects. *Interacting with Others:* Resolving Conflict and Negotiating with Others; Communicating with Persons Outside Organization; Influencing Others or Selling. **Physical Work Conditions**—Indoors; Sitting. **Other Job Characteristics**—Importance of Repeating Same Tasks; Importance of Being Exact or Accurate; Consequence of Error.

Experience—Job Zone 3. Previous work-related skill, knowledge, or experience is required. **Job Preparation:** SVP 6.0 to less than 7.0—more than one year and less than four years. **Knowledge**—Fine Arts; Sales and Marketing; Personnel and Human Resources; Administration and Management; Communications and Media. **Instructional Programs**—Cinematography and Film/Video Production; Directing and Theatrical Production; Drama and Dramatics/Theatre Arts, General; Dramatic/Theatre Arts and Stagecraft, Other; Film/Cinema Studies; Radio and Television; Theatre/Theatre Arts Management.

Related DOT Jobs—159.167-010 Artist and Repertoire Manager; 159.267-010 Director, Casting; 166.167-010 Contestant Coordinator.

27-2012.05 Technical Directors/ Managers

- **Education/Training Required: Long-term on-the-job training**
- **Employed: No data available.**
- **Annual Earnings: $45,090**
- **Growth: 27.1%**
- **Annual Job Openings: 11,000**

Coordinate activities of technical departments, such as taping, editing, engineering, and maintenance, to produce radio or television programs.

Confer with operations directors in order to formulate and maintain fair and attainable technical policies for programs. Direct technical aspects of newscasts and other productions, checking and switching between video sources and taking responsibility for the on-air product, including camera shots and graphics. Discuss filter options, lens choices, and the visual effects of objects being filmed with photography directors and video operators. Follow instructions from production managers and directors during productions, such as commands for camera cuts, effects, graphics, and takes. Monitor broadcasts in order to ensure that programs conform to station or network policies and regulations. Observe pictures through monitors and direct camera and video staff concerning shading and composition. Supervise and assign duties to workers engaged in technical control and production of radio and television programs. Test equipment in order to ensure proper operation. Train workers in use of equipment such as switchers, cameras, monitors, microphones, and lights. Act as liaisons between engineering and production departments. Collaborate with promotions directors to produce on-air station promotions. Operate equipment to produce programs or broadcast live programs from remote locations. Schedule use of studio and editing facilities for producers and engineering and maintenance staff. Set up and execute video transitions and special effects such as fades, dissolves, cuts, keys, and supers, using computers to manipulate pictures as necessary. Switch between video sources in a studio or on multi-camera remotes, using equipment such as switchers, video slide projectors, and video effects generators.

GOE INFORMATION—**Interest Area:** 01. Arts, Entertainment, and Media. **Work Group:** 01.01. Managerial Work in Arts, Entertainment, and Media. **Personality Type**—Realistic. Realistic occupations frequently involve work activities that include practical, hands-on problems and solutions. They often deal with plants, animals, and real-world materials like wood, tools, and machinery. Many of the occupations require working outside and do not involve a lot of paperwork or working closely with others. **Work Values**—Authority; Autonomy; Creativity; Variety; Ability Utilization. **Skills**—Operation Monitoring; Operation and Control; Management of Personnel Resources; Equipment Selection; Management of Material Resources; Coordination; Operations Analysis; Systems Analysis. **Abilities**—*Cognitive:* Selective Attention; Time Sharing; Speed of Closure; Perceptual Speed; Fluency of Ideas. *Psychomotor:* Reaction Time; Response Orientation; Rate Control; Control Precision. *Physical:* Gross Body Coordination; Gross Body Equilibrium; Dynamic Flexibility. *Sensory:* Far Vision; Sound Localization; Visual Color Discrimination; Auditory Attention; Hearing Sensitivity. **General Work Activities**—*Information Input:* Identifying Objects, Actions, and Events; Getting Information; Monitoring Processes, Materials, or Surroundings. *Mental Process:* Scheduling Work and Activities; Organizing, Planning, and Prioritizing; Judging Qualities of Things, Services, or Other People's Work. *Work Output:* Controlling Machines and Processes; Handling and Moving Objects; Performing General Physical Activities. *Interacting with Others:* Communicating with Other Workers; Guiding, Directing, and Motivating Subordinates; Coordinating the Work and Activities of Others. **Physical Work Conditions**—Outdoors; Indoors; Radiation; Sitting; Extremely Bright or Inadequate Lighting. **Other Job Characteristics**—Consequence of Error; Pace Determined by Speed of Equipment; Degree of Automation.

Experience—Job Zone 4. A minimum of two to four years of work-related skill, knowledge, or experience is needed. **Job Preparation:** SVP 7.0 to less than 8.0—two years to less than 10 years. **Knowledge**—Communications and Media; Administration and Management; Education and Training; Telecommunications; Personnel and Human Resources. **Instructional Programs**—Cinematography and Film/Video Production; Directing and Theatrical Production; Drama and Dramatics/Theatre Arts, General; Dramatic/Theatre Arts and Stagecraft, Other; Film/Cinema Studies; Radio and Television; Theatre/Theatre Arts Management.

Related DOT Jobs—184.162-010 Manager, Production; 962.162-010 Director, Technical.

27-2021.00 Athletes and Sports Competitors

- **Education/Training Required: Long-term on-the-job training**
- **Employed: 17,735**
- **Annual Earnings: $43,730**
- **Growth: 22.5%**
- **Annual Job Openings: 3,000**

Compete in athletic events.

Participates in athletic events and competitive sports according to established rules and regulations. Plays professional sport and is identified according to sport played, such as football, basketball, baseball, hockey, or boxing. Exercises and practices under direction of athletic trainer or professional coach to prepare and train for competitive events. Represents team or professional sports club, speaking to groups involved in activities such as sports clinics and fundraisers.

GOE INFORMATION—**Interest Area:** 01. Arts, Entertainment, and Media. **Work Group:** 01.10. Sports: Coaching, Instructing, Officiating, and Performing. **Personality Type**—Enterprising. Enterprising occupations frequently involve starting up and carrying out projects. These occupations can involve leading people and making many decisions. They sometimes require risk taking and often deal with business. **Work Values**—Recognition; Ability Utilization; Social Status; Compensation; Achievement. **Skills**—Monitoring. **Abilities**—*Cognitive:* Spatial Orientation; Time Sharing; Selective Attention; Visualization; Oral Comprehension. *Psychomotor:* Speed of Limb Movement; Reaction Time; Multilimb Coordination; Rate Control; Response Orientation. *Physical:* Stamina; Dynamic Strength; Dynamic Flexibility; Gross Body Coordination; Explosive Strength. *Sensory:* Depth Perception; Auditory Attention; Glare Sensitivity; Peripheral Vision; Far Vision. **General Work Activities**—*Information Input:* Monitoring Processes, Materials, or Surroundings; Getting Information; Identifying Objects, Actions, and Events. *Mental Process:* Updating and Using Relevant Knowledge; Organizing, Planning, and Prioritizing; Making Decisions and Solving Problems. *Work Output:* Performing General Physical Activities; Handling and Moving Objects; Repairing and Maintaining Electronic Equipment. *Interacting with Others:* Communicating with Persons Outside Organization; Performing for or Working with the Public; Establishing and Maintaining Relationships. **Physical Work Conditions**—Minor Burns, Cuts, Bites, or Stings; Walking or Running; Keeping or Regaining Balance; Outdoors; Bending or Twisting the Body. **Other Job Characteristics**—Importance of Repeating Same Tasks; Consequence of Error; Pace Determined by Speed of Equipment.

Experience—Job Zone 3. Previous work-related skill, knowledge, or experience is required. **Job Preparation:** SVP 6.0 to less than 7.0—more than one year and less than four years. **Knowledge**—Biology; Medicine and Dentistry; Communications and Media; Psychology; Sales and Marketing. **Instructional Programs**—Health and Physical Education, General.

Related DOT Jobs—153.341-010 Professional Athlete.

27-2022.00 Coaches and Scouts

- **Education/Training Required: Long-term on-the-job training**
- **Employed: 99,391**
- **Annual Earnings: $29,020**
- **Growth: 17.6%**
- **Annual Job Openings: 19,000**

Instruct or coach groups or individuals in the fundamentals of sports. Demonstrate techniques and methods of participation. May evaluate athletes' strengths and weaknesses as possible recruits or to improve the athletes' technique to prepare them for competition. Those required to hold teaching degrees should be reported in the appropriate teaching category.

Adjust coaching techniques based on the strengths and weaknesses of athletes. Analyze the strengths and weaknesses of opposing teams in order to develop game strategies. Evaluate athletes' skills and review performance records in order to determine their fitness and potential in a particular area of athletics. Explain and demonstrate the use of sports and training equipment, such as trampolines or weights. Explain and enforce safety rules and regulations. File scouting reports that detail player assessments, provide recommendations on athlete recruitment, and identify locations and individuals to be targeted for future recruitment efforts. Identify and recruit potential athletes, arranging and offering incentives such as athletic scholarships. Instruct individuals or groups in sports rules, game strategies, and performance principles such as specific ways of moving the body, hands, and/or feet in order to achieve desired results. Keep abreast of changing rules, techniques, technologies, and philosophies relevant to their sport. Monitor athletes' use of equipment in order to ensure safe and proper use. Plan and direct physical conditioning programs that will enable athletes to achieve maximum performance. Plan strategies and choose team members for individual games and/or sports seasons. Plan, organize, and conduct practice sessions. Provide training direction, encouragement, and motivation in order to prepare athletes for games, competitive events, and/or tours. Arrange and conduct sports-related activities such as training camps, skill-improvement courses, clinics, and/or pre-season try-outs. Develop and arrange competition schedules and programs. Keep records of athlete, team, and opposing team performance. Negotiate with professional athletes or their representatives in order to obtain services and arrange contracts. Perform activities that support a team or a specific sport, such as meeting with media representatives and appearing at fundraising events. Select, acquire, store, and issue equipment and other materials as necessary. Serve as organizer, leader, instructor, or referee for outdoor and indoor games, such as volleyball, football, and soccer.

GOE INFORMATION—**Interest Area:** 01. Arts, Entertainment, and Media. **Work Group:** 01.10. Sports: Coaching, Instructing, Officiating, and Performing. **Personality Type**—Enterprising. Enterprising occupations frequently involve starting up and carrying out projects. These occupations can involve leading people and making many decisions. They sometimes require risk taking and often deal with business. **Work Values**—Authority; Responsibility; Recognition; Autonomy; Creativity. **Skills**—Negotiation; Management of Personnel Resources; Instructing; Systems Analysis; Systems Evaluation; Complex Problem Solving; Time Management; Writing. **Abilities**—*Cognitive:* Fluency of Ideas; Originality; Visualization; Oral Expression; Perceptual Speed. *Psychomotor:* Speed of Limb Movement; Reaction Time; Manual Dexterity; Response Orientation; Multilimb Coordination. *Physical:* Explosive Strength; Gross Body Coordination; Stamina; Gross Body Equilibrium; Dynamic Flexibility. *Sensory:* Depth Perception; Peripheral Vision; Far Vision; Glare Sensitivity; Night Vision. **General Work Activities**—*Information Input:* Getting Information; Identifying Objects, Actions, and Events; Monitoring Processes, Materials, or Surroundings. *Mental Process:* Making Decisions and Solving Problems; Judging Qualities of Things, Services, or Other People's Work; Organizing, Planning, and Prioritizing. *Work Output:* Performing General Physical Activities; Documenting or Recording Information; Handling and Moving Objects. *Interacting with Others:* Coaching and Developing Others; Resolving Conflict and Negotiating with Others; Developing and Building Teams. **Physical Work Conditions**—Outdoors; Walking or Running; Very Hot or Cold; Kneeling, Crouching, or Crawling; Keeping or Regaining Balance. **Other Job Characteristics**—Consequence of Error; Importance of Repeating Same Tasks; Importance of Being Exact or Accurate.

Experience—Job Zone 5. Extensive skill, knowledge, and experience are needed for these occupations. **Job Preparation:** SVP 8.0 and above—four years to more than 10 years. **Knowledge**—Sales and Marketing; Education and Training; Therapy and Counseling; Administration and Management; Psychology. **Instructional Programs**—Health and Physical Education, General; Physical Education Teaching and Coaching; Sport and Fitness Administration/Management.

Related DOT Jobs—153.117-010 Head Coach; 153.117-018 Scout, Professional Sports; 153.227-010 Coach, Professional Athletes.

27-2023.00 Umpires, Referees, and Other Sports Officials

- **Education/Training Required: Long-term on-the-job training**
- **Employed: 11,472**
- **Annual Earnings: $20,650**
- **Growth: 22.7%**
- **Annual Job Openings: 2,000**

Officiate at competitive athletic or sporting events. Detect infractions of rules and decide penalties according to established regulations.

Confer with other sporting officials, coaches, players, and facility managers in order to provide information, coordinate activities, and discuss problems. Direct participants to assigned areas such as starting blocks or penalty areas. Inspect sporting equipment and/or examine participants in order to ensure compliance with event and safety regulations. Judge performances in sporting competitions in order to award points, impose scoring penalties, and determine results. Keep track of event times, including race times and elapsed time during game segments, starting or stopping play when necessary. Officiate at sporting events, games, or competitions to maintain standards of play and to ensure that game rules are observed. Resolve claims of rule infractions or complaints by participants and assess any necessary penalties according to regulations. Signal participants or other officials to make them aware of infractions or to otherwise regulate play or competition. Start races and competitions. Verify credentials of participants in sporting events and make other qualifying determinations such as starting order or handicap number. Verify scoring calculations before competition winners are announced. Compile scores and other athletic records. Report to regulating organizations regarding sporting activities, complaints made, and actions taken or needed, such as fines or other disciplinary actions. Research and study players and teams in order to anticipate issues that might arise in future engagements. Teach and explain the rules and regulations governing a specific sport.

GOE INFORMATION—Interest Area: 01. Arts, Entertainment, and Media. **Work Group:** 01.10. Sports: Coaching, Instructing, Officiating, and Performing. **Personality Type—**Enterprising. Enterprising occupations frequently involve starting up and carrying out projects. These occupations can involve leading people and making many decisions. They sometimes require risk taking and often deal with business. **Work Values—**Authority; Responsibility; Ability Utilization; Achievement; Autonomy. **Skills—**None met the criteria. **Abilities—***Cognitive:* Perceptual Speed; Memorization; Time Sharing; Selective Attention; Spatial Orientation. *Psychomotor:* Reaction Time; Response Orientation; Rate Control; Speed of Limb Movement; Multilimb Coordination. *Physical:* Stamina; Gross Body Coordination; Gross Body Equilibrium; Trunk Strength; Extent Flexibility. *Sensory:* Far Vision; Glare Sensitivity; Peripheral Vision; Speech Clarity; Auditory Attention. **General Work Activities—***Information Input:* Identifying Objects, Actions, and Events; Getting Information; Monitoring Processes, Materials, or Surroundings. *Mental Process:* Making Decisions and Solving Problems; Evaluating Information Against Standards; Judging Qualities of Things, Services, or Other People's Work. *Work Output:* Performing General Physical Activities; Documenting or Recording Information; Handling and Moving Objects. *Interacting with Others:* Communicating with Other Workers; Resolving Conflict and Negotiating with Others; Communicating with Persons Outside Organization. **Physical Work Conditions—**Walking or Running; Outdoors; Standing; Very Hot or Cold; Distracting Sounds and Noise Levels. **Other Job Characteristics—**Importance of Repeating Same Tasks; Importance of Being Exact or Accurate; Consequence of Error.

Experience—Job Zone 3. Previous work-related skill, knowledge, or experience is required. **Job Preparation:** SVP 6.0 to less than 7.0—more than one year and less than four years. **Knowledge—**Administration and Management; Public Safety and Security; Clerical; Biology; Psychology. **Instructional Programs—**No data available.

Related DOT Jobs—153.117-022 Steward, Racetrack; 153.167-010 Paddock Judge; 153.167-014 Pit Steward; 153.167-018 Racing Secretary and Handicapper; 153.267-010 Horse-Race Starter; 153.267-014 Patrol Judge; 153.267-018 Umpire; 153.287-010 Hoof and Shoe Inspector; 153.367-010 Clocker; 153.367-014 Horse-Race Timer; 153.387-010 Identifier, Horse; 153.387-014 Scorer; 153.467-010 Clerk-of-Scales; 153.667-010 Starter; 219.267-010 Handicapper, Harness Racing; 349.367-010 Kennel Manager, Dog Track; 349.367-014 Receiving-Barn Custodian; 349.665-010 Scoreboard Operator.

27-2031.00 Dancers

- **Education/Training Required: Long-term on-the-job training**
- **Employed: 15,243**
- **Annual Earnings: $23,110**
- **Growth: 17.3%**
- **Annual Job Openings: 2,000**

Perform dances. May also sing or act.

Attend costume fittings, photography sessions, and makeup calls associated with dance performances. Collaborate with choreographers in order to refine or modify dance steps. Coordinate dancing with that of partners or dance ensembles. Develop self-understanding of physical capabilities and limitations and choose dance styles accordingly. Harmonize body movements to rhythm of musical accompaniment. Perform classical, modern, or acrobatic dances in productions, expressing stories, rhythm, and sound with their bodies. Perform in productions, singing or acting in addition to dancing if required. Study and practice dance moves required in roles. Train, exercise, and attend dance classes to maintain high levels of technical proficiency, physical ability, and physical fitness. Audition for dance roles or for membership in dance companies. Devise and choreograph dance for self or others. Monitor the field of dance to remain aware of current trends and innovations. Teach dance students.

GOE INFORMATION—Interest Area: 01. Arts, Entertainment, and Media. **Work Group:** 01.05. Performing Arts. **Personality Type—**Artistic. Artistic occupations frequently involve working with forms, designs, and patterns. They often require self-expression, and the work can be done without following a clear set of rules. **Work Values—**Ability Utilization; Recognition; Achievement; Creativity; Moral Values. **Skills—**None met the criteria. **Abilities—***Cognitive:* Memorization; Originality; Spatial Orientation; Fluency of Ideas; Oral Comprehension. *Psychomotor:* Speed of Limb Movement; Multilimb Coordination; Arm-Hand Steadiness; Reaction Time. *Physical:* Gross Body Coordination; Dynamic Strength; Stamina; Dynamic Flexibility; Explosive Strength. *Sensory:* Peripheral Vision; Depth Perception; Auditory Attention; Hearing Sensitivity; Night Vision. **General Work Activities—***Information Input:* Getting Information; Monitoring Processes, Materials, or Surroundings; Identifying Objects, Actions, and Events. *Mental Process:* Thinking Creatively; Updating and Using Relevant Knowledge; Organizing, Planning, and Prioritizing. *Work Output:* Performing General Physical Activities; Drafting and Specifying Technical Devices; Handling and Moving Objects. *Interacting with Others:* Performing for or Working with the Public; Coordinating the Work and Activities of Others; Communicating with Other Workers. **Physical Work Conditions—**Keeping or Regaining Balance; Walking or Running; Bending or Twisting the Body; Making Repetitive Motions; Kneeling, Crouching, or Crawling. **Other Job Characteristics—**Importance of Repeating Same Tasks; Importance of Being Exact or Accurate; Pace Determined by Speed of Equipment.

Experience—Job Zone 4. A minimum of two to four years of work-related skill, knowledge, or experience is needed. **Job Preparation:** SVP 7.0 to less than 8.0—two years to less than 10 years. **Knowledge—**Fine Arts; Therapy and Counseling; Medicine and Dentistry; Sales and Marketing; Biology. **Instructional Programs—**Ballet; Dance, General; Dance, Other.

Related DOT Jobs—151.047-010 Dancer.

27-2032.00 Choreographers

- **Education/Training Required: Work experience in a related occupation**
- **Employed: 10,808**
- **Annual Earnings: $28,670**
- **Growth: 14.9%**
- **Annual Job Openings: 2,000**

Create and teach dance. May direct and stage presentations.

Determines dance movements designed to suggest story, interpret emotion, or enliven show. Creates original dance routines for ballets, musicals, or other forms of entertainment. Instructs cast in dance movements at rehearsals to achieve desired effect. Studies story line and music to envision and devise dance movements. Directs and stages dance presentations for various forms of entertainment. Auditions performers for one or more dance parts.

GOE INFORMATION—Interest Area: 01. Arts, Entertainment, and Media. **Work Group:** 01.05. Performing Arts. **Personality Type**—Artistic. Artistic occupations frequently involve working with forms, designs, and patterns. They often require self-expression, and the work can be done without following a clear set of rules. **Work Values**—Creativity; Authority; Responsibility; Ability Utilization; Autonomy. **Skills**—Instructing; Coordination. **Abilities**—*Cognitive:* Originality; Spatial Orientation; Visualization; Fluency of Ideas; Memorization. *Psychomotor:* Speed of Limb Movement; Multilimb Coordination; Reaction Time; Arm-Hand Steadiness. *Physical:* Gross Body Coordination; Dynamic Flexibility; Dynamic Strength; Stamina; Gross Body Equilibrium. *Sensory:* Peripheral Vision; Depth Perception; Far Vision; Auditory Attention; Glare Sensitivity. **General Work Activities**—*Information Input:* Monitoring Processes, Materials, or Surroundings; Getting Information; Identifying Objects, Actions, and Events. *Mental Process:* Thinking Creatively; Judging Qualities of Things, Services, or Other People's Work; Organizing, Planning, and Prioritizing. *Work Output:* Performing General Physical Activities; Documenting or Recording Information; Handling and Moving Objects. *Interacting with Others:* Coaching and Developing Others; Teaching Others; Coordinating the Work and Activities of Others. **Physical Work Conditions**—Keeping or Regaining Balance; Bending or Twisting the Body; Walking or Running; Making Repetitive Motions; Kneeling, Crouching, or Crawling. **Other Job Characteristics**—Importance of Repeating Same Tasks; Consequence of Error; Degree of Automation.

Experience—Job Zone 5. Extensive skill, knowledge, and experience are needed for these occupations. **Job Preparation:** SVP 8.0 and above—four years to more than 10 years. **Knowledge**—Fine Arts; Education and Training; Personnel and Human Resources; Communications and Media; Sociology and Anthropology. **Instructional Programs**—Dance, General; Dance, Other.

Related DOT Jobs—151.027-010 Choreographer.

27-2041.00 Music Directors and Composers

- **Education/Training Required: Master's degree**
- **Employed: 49,685**
- **Annual Earnings: $33,720**
- **Growth: 13.1%**
- **Annual Job Openings: 9,000**

Conduct, direct, plan, and lead instrumental or vocal performances by musical groups such as orchestras, choirs, and glee clubs. Includes arrangers, composers, choral directors, and orchestrators.

No task data available.

GOE INFORMATION—Interest Area: 01. Arts, Entertainment, and Media. **Work Group:** 01.05. Performing Arts. **Note:** The Department of Labor has not collected some data for this job, so it has fewer details than the other descriptions.

Instructional Programs—Conducting; Music Management and Merchandising; Music Performance, General; Music Theory and Composition; Music, Other; Musicology and Ethnomusicology; Religious/Sacred Music; Voice and Opera.

Related DOT Jobs—152.047-010 Choral Director; 152.047-014 Conductor, Orchestra; 152.047-018 Director, Music; 152.067-010 Arranger; 152.067-014 Composer; 152.067-022 Orchestrator; 152.267-010 Copyist.

27-2041.01 Music Directors

- **Education/Training Required: Master's degree**
- **Employed: No data available.**
- **Annual Earnings: $33,720**
- **Growth: 13.1%**
- **Annual Job Openings: 9,000**

Direct and conduct instrumental or vocal performances by musical groups such as orchestras or choirs.

Directs group at rehearsals and live or recorded performances to achieve desired effects, such as tonal and harmonic balance, dynamics, rhythm, and tempo. Selects vocal, instrumental, and recorded music suitable to type of performance requirements to accommodate ability of group. Issues assignments and reviews work of staff in such areas as scoring, arranging, and copying music and lyric and vocal coaching. Positions members within group to obtain balance among instrumental sections. Auditions and selects vocal and instrumental groups for musical presentations. Transcribes musical compositions and melodic lines to adapt them to or create particular style for group. Engages services of composer to write score.

GOE INFORMATION—Interest Area: 01. Arts, Entertainment, and Media. **Work Group:** 01.05. Performing Arts. **Personality Type**—Artistic. Artistic occupations frequently involve working with forms, designs, and patterns. They often require self-expression, and the work can be done without following a clear set of rules. **Work Values**—Creativity; Authority; Ability Utilization; Responsibility; Autonomy. **Skills**—Management of Personnel Resources; Coordination; Time Management; Instructing; Monitoring; Speaking; Learning Strategies; Operations Analysis. **Abilities**—*Cognitive:* Originality; Oral Expression; Flexibility of Closure; Fluency of Ideas; Written Expression. *Psychomotor:* None met the criteria. *Physical:* Dynamic Flexibility. *Sensory:* Hearing Sensitivity; Sound Localization; Auditory Attention; Speech Recognition; Speech Clarity. **General Work Activities**—*Information Input:* Getting Information; Identifying Objects, Actions, and Events; Monitoring Processes, Materials, or Surroundings. *Mental Process:* Thinking Creatively; Organizing, Planning, and Prioritizing; Scheduling Work and Activities. *Work Output:* Performing General Physical Activities; Handling and Moving Objects; Documenting or Recording Information. *Interacting with Others:* Coordinating the Work and Activities of Others; Establishing and Maintaining Relationships; Guiding, Directing, and Motivating Subordinates. **Physical Work Conditions**—Making Repetitive Motions; Standing; Sitting; Indoors; Distracting Sounds and Noise Levels. **Other Job Characteristics**—Importance of Repeating Same Tasks; Importance of Being Exact or Accurate; Pace Determined by Speed of Equipment.

Experience—Job Zone 5. Extensive skill, knowledge, and experience are needed for these occupations. **Job Preparation:** SVP 8.0 and above—

four years to more than 10 years. **Knowledge**—Fine Arts; Personnel and Human Resources; Administration and Management; Foreign Language; English Language. **Instructional Programs**—Conducting; Music Management and Merchandising; Music Performance, General; Music Theory and Composition; Music, Other; Musicology and Ethnomusicology; Religious/Sacred Music; Voice and Opera.

Related DOT Jobs—152.047-010 Choral Director; 152.047-014 Conductor, Orchestra; 152.047-018 Director, Music.

27-2041.02 Music Arrangers and Orchestrators

- **Education/Training Required: Bachelor's degree**
- **Employed: No data available.**
- **Annual Earnings: $33,720**
- **Growth: 13.1%**
- **Annual Job Openings: 9,000**

Write and transcribe musical scores.

Composes musical scores for orchestra, band, choral group, or individual instrumentalist or vocalist, using knowledge of music theory and instrumental and vocal capabilities. Transposes music from one voice or instrument to another to accommodate particular musician in musical group. Adapts musical composition for orchestra, band, choral group, or individual to style for which it was not originally written. Transcribes musical parts from score written by arranger or orchestrator for each instrument or voice, using knowledge of music composition. Copies parts from score for individual performers. Determines voice, instrument, harmonic structure, rhythm, tempo, and tone balance to achieve desired effect.

GOE INFORMATION—**Interest Area:** 01. Arts, Entertainment, and Media. **Work Group:** 01.05. Performing Arts. **Personality Type**—Artistic. Artistic occupations frequently involve working with forms, designs, and patterns. They often require self-expression, and the work can be done without following a clear set of rules. **Work Values**—Creativity; Ability Utilization; Autonomy; Achievement; Responsibility. **Skills**—Coordination; Complex Problem Solving. **Abilities**—*Cognitive:* Originality; Fluency of Ideas; Written Expression; Written Comprehension; Inductive Reasoning. *Psychomotor:* None met the criteria. *Physical:* None met the criteria. *Sensory:* Hearing Sensitivity; Sound Localization; Auditory Attention; Speech Recognition. **General Work Activities**—*Information Input:* Identifying Objects, Actions, and Events; Getting Information; Monitoring Processes, Materials, or Surroundings. *Mental Process:* Thinking Creatively; Judging Qualities of Things, Services, or Other People's Work; Organizing, Planning, and Prioritizing. *Work Output:* Documenting or Recording Information; Handling and Moving Objects; Performing General Physical Activities. *Interacting with Others:* Establishing and Maintaining Relationships; Interpreting Meaning of Information for Others; Communicating with Persons Outside Organization. **Physical Work Conditions**—Sitting; Indoors; High Places. **Other Job Characteristics**—Importance of Repeating Same Tasks; Pace Determined by Speed of Equipment; Importance of Being Exact or Accurate.

Experience—Job Zone 4. A minimum of two to four years of work-related skill, knowledge, or experience is needed. **Job Preparation:** SVP 7.0 to less than 8.0—two years to less than 10 years. **Knowledge**—Fine Arts; Foreign Language; Communications and Media. **Instructional Programs**—Conducting; Music Management and Merchandising; Music Performance, General; Music Theory and Composition; Music, Other; Musicology and Ethnomusicology; Religious/Sacred Music; Voice and Opera.

Related DOT Jobs—152.067-010 Arranger; 152.067-022 Orchestrator; 152.267-010 Copyist.

27-2041.03 Composers

- **Education/Training Required: Master's degree**
- **Employed: 49,685**
- **Annual Earnings: $33,720**
- **Growth: 13.1%**
- **Annual Job Openings: 9,000**

Compose music for orchestra, choral group, or band.

Creates original musical form or writes within circumscribed musical form, such as sonata, symphony, or opera. Creates musical and tonal structure, applying elements of music theory such as instrumental and vocal capabilities. Develops pattern of harmony, applying knowledge of music theory. Synthesizes ideas for melody of musical scores for choral group or band. Determines basic pattern of melody, applying knowledge of music theory. Transcribes or records musical ideas into notes on scored music paper.

GOE INFORMATION—**Interest Area:** 01. Arts, Entertainment, and Media. **Work Group:** 01.05. Performing Arts. **Personality Type**—Artistic. Artistic occupations frequently involve working with forms, designs, and patterns. They often require self-expression, and the work can be done without following a clear set of rules. **Work Values**—Creativity; Ability Utilization; Autonomy; Independence; Responsibility. **Skills**—Equipment Selection. **Abilities**—*Cognitive:* Originality; Fluency of Ideas; Flexibility of Closure; Written Expression; Category Flexibility. *Psychomotor:* None met the criteria. *Physical:* None met the criteria. *Sensory:* Hearing Sensitivity; Auditory Attention; Sound Localization; Speech Recognition. **General Work Activities**—*Information Input:* Getting Information; Identifying Objects, Actions, and Events; Monitoring Processes, Materials, or Surroundings. *Mental Process:* Thinking Creatively; Judging Qualities of Things, Services, or Other People's Work; Making Decisions and Solving Problems. *Work Output:* Documenting or Recording Information; Handling and Moving Objects; Performing General Physical Activities. *Interacting with Others:* Interpreting Meaning of Information for Others; Performing for or Working with the Public; Communicating with Persons Outside Organization. **Physical Work Conditions**—Sitting; Indoors. **Other Job Characteristics**—Importance of Repeating Same Tasks; Pace Determined by Speed of Equipment; Degree of Automation.

Experience—Job Zone 5. Extensive skill, knowledge, and experience are needed for these occupations. **Job Preparation:** SVP 8.0 and above—four years to more than 10 years. **Knowledge**—Fine Arts; History and Archeology; Foreign Language; Communications and Media; Clerical. **Instructional Programs**—Conducting; Music Management and Merchandising; Music Performance, General; Music Theory and Composition; Music, Other; Musicology and Ethnomusicology; Religious/Sacred Music; Voice and Opera.

Related DOT Jobs—152.067-014 Composer.

27-2042.00 Musicians and Singers

- **Education/Training Required: Long-term on-the-job training**
- **Employed: 190,533**
- **Annual Earnings: $40,320**
- **Growth: 20.1%**
- **Annual Job Openings: 33,000**

Play one or more musical instruments or entertain by singing songs in recital, in accompaniment, or as a member of an orchestra, band, or other musical group. Musical performers may entertain on stage, radio, TV, film, or video or record in studios.

No task data available.

GOE INFORMATION—Interest Area: 01. Arts, Entertainment, and Media. **Work Group:** 01.05. Performing Arts. **Note:** The Department of Labor has not collected some data for this job, so it has fewer details than the other descriptions.

Instructional Programs—Jazz/Jazz Studies; Music Pedagogy; Music Performance, General; Music, General; Music, Other; Piano and Organ; Violin, Viola, Guitar, and Other Stringed Instruments; Voice and Opera.

Related DOT Jobs—152.041-010 Musician, Instrumental; 152.047-022 Singer; 230.647-010 Singing Messenger.

27-2042.01 Singers

- **Education/Training Required: Long-term on-the-job training**
- **Employed: No data available.**
- **Annual Earnings: $40,320**
- **Growth: 20.1%**
- **Annual Job Openings: 33,000**

Sing songs on stage, radio, or television or in motion pictures.

Sings before audience or recipient of message as soloist or in group, as member of vocal ensemble. Sings a cappella or with musical accompaniment. Memorizes musical selections and routines or sings following printed text, musical notation, or customer instructions. Interprets or modifies music, applying knowledge of harmony, melody, rhythm, and voice production, to individualize presentation and maintain audience interest. Observes choral leader or prompter for cues or directions in vocal presentation. Practices songs and routines to maintain and improve vocal skills.

GOE INFORMATION—Interest Area: 01. Arts, Entertainment, and Media. **Work Group:** 01.05. Performing Arts. **Personality Type**—Artistic. Artistic occupations frequently involve working with forms, designs, and patterns. They often require self-expression, and the work can be done without following a clear set of rules. **Work Values**—Ability Utilization; Achievement; Recognition; Creativity; Autonomy. **Skills**—None met the criteria. **Abilities**—*Cognitive:* Originality; Memorization; Oral Expression; Oral Comprehension; Written Comprehension. *Psychomotor:* None met the criteria. *Physical:* None met the criteria. *Sensory:* Hearing Sensitivity; Auditory Attention; Sound Localization; Speech Clarity. **General Work Activities**—*Information Input:* Getting Information; Identifying Objects, Actions, and Events; Monitoring Processes, Materials, or Surroundings. *Mental Process:* Thinking Creatively; Organizing, Planning, and Prioritizing; Making Decisions and Solving Problems. *Work Output:* Performing General Physical Activities; Handling and Moving Objects; Documenting or Recording Information. *Interacting with Others:* Performing for or Working with the Public; Communicating with Persons Outside Organization; Establishing and Maintaining Relationships. **Physical Work Conditions**—Standing; Indoors. **Other Job Characteristics**—Importance of Repeating Same Tasks; Pace Determined by Speed of Equipment; Degree of Automation.

Experience—Job Zone 2. Some previous work-related skill, knowledge, or experience may be helpful, but usually is not needed. **Job Preparation:** SVP 4.0 to less than 6.0—six months to less than two years. **Knowledge**—Fine Arts; Foreign Language; Communications and Media; Biology.

Instructional Programs—Jazz/Jazz Studies; Music Pedagogy; Music Performance, General; Music, General; Music, Other; Piano and Organ; Voice and Opera.

Related DOT Jobs—152.047-022 Singer; 230.647-010 Singing Messenger.

27-2042.02 Musicians, Instrumental

- **Education/Training Required: Long-term on-the-job training**
- **Employed: No data available.**
- **Annual Earnings: $40,320**
- **Growth: 20.1%**
- **Annual Job Openings: 33,000**

Play one or more musical instruments in recital, in accompaniment, or as members of an orchestra, band, or other musical group.

Plays musical instrument as soloist or as member of musical group, such as orchestra or band, to entertain audience. Plays from memory or by following score. Studies and rehearses music to learn and interpret score. Improvises music during performance. Practices performance on musical instrument to maintain and improve skills. Memorizes musical scores. Transposes music to play in alternate key or to fit individual style or purposes. Composes new musical scores. Teaches music for specific instruments. Directs band/orchestra.

GOE INFORMATION—Interest Area: 01. Arts, Entertainment, and Media. **Work Group:** 01.05. Performing Arts. **Personality Type**—Artistic. Artistic occupations frequently involve working with forms, designs, and patterns. They often require self-expression, and the work can be done without following a clear set of rules. **Work Values**—Ability Utilization; Achievement; Creativity; Recognition; Autonomy. **Skills**—Instructing; Coordination; Learning Strategies; Monitoring; Systems Analysis; Management of Personnel Resources. **Abilities**—*Cognitive:* Memorization; Originality; Perceptual Speed; Selective Attention; Fluency of Ideas. *Psychomotor:* Wrist-Finger Speed; Multilimb Coordination; Finger Dexterity; Response Orientation; Speed of Limb Movement. *Physical:* Trunk Strength; Gross Body Coordination; Explosive Strength; Dynamic Flexibility; Static Strength. *Sensory:* Hearing Sensitivity; Sound Localization; Auditory Attention; Night Vision; Speech Clarity. **General Work Activities**—*Information Input:* Identifying Objects, Actions, and Events; Getting Information; Monitoring Processes, Materials, or Surroundings. *Mental Process:* Thinking Creatively; Organizing, Planning, and Prioritizing; Scheduling Work and Activities. *Work Output:* Handling and Moving Objects; Documenting or Recording Information; Performing General Physical Activities. *Interacting with Others:* Performing for or Working with the Public; Coaching and Developing Others; Coordinating the Work and Activities of Others. **Physical Work Conditions**—Making Repetitive Motions; Sitting; Using Hands on Objects, Tools, or Controls; Indoors; Extremely Bright or Inadequate Lighting. **Other Job Characteristics**—Importance of Being Exact or Accurate; Importance of Repeating Same Tasks; Pace Determined by Speed of Equipment.

Experience—Job Zone 5. Extensive skill, knowledge, and experience are needed for these occupations. **Job Preparation:** SVP 8.0 and above—four years to more than 10 years. **Knowledge**—Fine Arts; Education and Training; Psychology; History and Archeology; Communications and Media. **Instructional Programs**—Jazz/Jazz Studies; Music Pedagogy; Music Performance, General; Music, General; Music, Other; Piano and Organ; Violin, Viola, Guitar, and Other Stringed Instruments.

Related DOT Jobs—152.041-010 Musician, Instrumental.

27-2099.99 Entertainers and Performers, Sports and Related Workers, All Other

- Education/Training Required: No data available.
- Employed: No data available.
- Annual Earnings: No data available.
- Growth: 21.8%
- Annual Job Openings: 11,000

All entertainers and performers, sports and related workers not listed separately.

No task data available.

GOE INFORMATION—Interest Area: 01. Arts, Entertainment, and Media. **Work Group:** 01.05. Performing Arts; 01.09. Modeling and Personal Appearance; 01.10. Sports: Coaching, Instructing, Officiating, and Performing. **Note:** The Department of Labor has not collected some data for this job, so it has fewer details than the other descriptions.

Instructional Programs—Directing and Theatrical Production; Drama and Dramatics/Theatre Arts, General; Dramatic/Theatre Arts and Stagecraft, Other.

Related DOT Jobs—152.367-010 Prompter; 159.207-010 Astrologer; 159.647-018 Psychic Reader.

27-3000 Media and Communication Workers

27-3011.00 Radio and Television Announcers

- Education/Training Required: Moderate-term on-the-job training
- Employed: No data available.
- Annual Earnings: $20,270
- Growth: –5.5%
- Annual Job Openings: 4,000

Talk on radio or television. May interview guests, act as master of ceremonies, read news flashes, identify station by giving call letters, or announce song title and artist.

Announce musical selections, station breaks, commercials, or public service information and accept requests from listening audience. Comment on music and other matters, such as weather or traffic conditions. Coordinate games, contests, or other on-air competitions, performing such duties as asking questions and awarding prizes. Identify stations and introduce or close shows, using memorized or read scripts and/or ad-libs. Interview show guests about their lives, their work, or topics of current interest. Keep daily program logs to provide information on all elements aired during broadcast, such as musical selections and station promotions. Operate control consoles. Prepare and deliver news, sports, and/or weather reports, gathering and rewriting material so that it will convey required information and fit specific time slots. Read news flashes to inform audiences of important events. Select program content in conjunction with producers and assistants, based on factors such as program specialties, audience tastes, or requests from the public. Discuss various topics over the telephone with viewers or listeners. Give network cues permitting selected stations to receive programs. Host civic, charitable, or promotional events that are broadcast over television or radio. Locate guests to appear on talk or interview shows. Make promotional appearances at public or private events in order to represent their employers. Moderate panels or discussion shows on topics such as current affairs, art, or education. Provide commentary and conduct interviews during sporting events, parades, conventions, and other events. Record commercials for later broadcast. Study background information in order to prepare for programs or interviews. Attend press conferences in order to gather information for broadcast. Describe or demonstrate products that viewers may purchase through specific shows or in stores.

GOE INFORMATION—Interest Area: 01. Arts, Entertainment, and Media. **Work Group:** 01.05. Performing Arts. **Personality Type**—Artistic. Artistic occupations frequently involve working with forms, designs, and patterns. They often require self-expression, and the work can be done without following a clear set of rules. **Work Values**—Recognition; Good Working Conditions; Creativity; Variety; Social Status. **Skills**—Speaking; Active Listening; Writing; Complex Problem Solving; Reading Comprehension; Operation and Control. **Abilities**—*Cognitive:* Memorization; Oral Expression; Oral Comprehension; Fluency of Ideas; Originality. *Psychomotor:* None met the criteria. *Physical:* None met the criteria. *Sensory:* Speech Clarity; Speech Recognition; Auditory Attention. **General Work Activities**—*Information Input:* Getting Information; Identifying Objects, Actions, and Events; Estimating Needed Characteristics. *Mental Process:* Organizing, Planning, and Prioritizing; Updating and Using Relevant Knowledge; Thinking Creatively. *Work Output:* Documenting or Recording Information; Controlling Machines and Processes; Handling and Moving Objects. *Interacting with Others:* Performing for or Working with the Public; Communicating with Persons Outside Organization; Communicating with Other Workers. **Physical Work Conditions**—Sitting; Indoors. **Other Job Characteristics**—Importance of Being Exact or Accurate; Importance of Repeating Same Tasks; Consequence of Error.

Experience—Job Zone 2. Some previous work-related skill, knowledge, or experience may be helpful, but usually is not needed. **Job Preparation:** SVP 4.0 to less than 6.0—six months to less than two years. **Knowledge**—Communications and Media; Sales and Marketing; Telecommunications; Computers and Electronics; English Language. **Instructional Programs**—Broadcast Journalism; Radio and Television.

Related DOT Jobs—159.147-010 Announcer; 159.147-014 Disc Jockey; 159.147-018 Show Host/Hostess.

27-3012.00 Public Address System and Other Announcers

- Education/Training Required: Associate's degree
- Employed: No data available.
- Annual Earnings: $20,270
- Growth: –5.5%
- Annual Job Openings: 4,000

Make announcements over loudspeaker at sporting or other public events. May act as master of ceremonies or disc jockey at weddings, parties, clubs, or other gathering places.

Announce programs and player substitutions or other changes to patrons. Instruct and calm crowds during emergencies. Learn to pronounce the names of players, coaches, institutional personnel, officials, and other individuals involved in an event. Improvise commentary on items of interest, such as background and history of an event or past records of participants. Meet with event directors in order to review schedules and exchange information about details, such as national anthem performers and starting lineups. Provide running commentaries of event activities, such as play-by-play descriptions or explanations of official decisions. Read prepared scripts describing acts or tricks presented during performances. Furnish information concerning plays to scoreboard operators. Greet attendees and serve as master of ceremonies at banquets, store openings, and other events. Inform patrons of coming events at a specific venue. Organize team information, such as statistics and tournament records, in order to ensure accessibility for use during events. Preview any music intended to be broadcast over the public address system. Review and announce crowd control procedures before the beginning of each event. Study the layout of an event venue in order to be able to give accurate directions in the event of an emergency.

GOE INFORMATION—Interest Area: 01. Arts, Entertainment, and Media. **Work Group:** 01.05. Performing Arts. **Personality Type—**Social. Social occupations frequently involve working with, communicating with, and teaching people. These occupations often involve helping or providing service to others. **Work Values—**Recognition; Creativity; Variety; Social Status; Good Working Conditions. **Skills—**None met the criteria. **Abilities—***Cognitive:* Time Sharing; Selective Attention; Oral Expression; Flexibility of Closure; Speed of Closure. *Psychomotor:* Reaction Time; Response Orientation. *Physical:* None met the criteria. *Sensory:* Speech Clarity; Far Vision; Peripheral Vision; Night Vision; Glare Sensitivity. **General Work Activities—***Information Input:* Getting Information; Monitoring Processes, Materials, or Surroundings; Identifying Objects, Actions, and Events. *Mental Process:* Updating and Using Relevant Knowledge; Organizing, Planning, and Prioritizing; Thinking Creatively. *Work Output:* Handling and Moving Objects; Performing General Physical Activities; Repairing and Maintaining Electronic Equipment. *Interacting with Others:* Performing for or Working with the Public; Communicating with Persons Outside Organization; Communicating with Other Workers. **Physical Work Conditions—**Sitting; Outdoors; Extremely Bright or Inadequate Lighting; High Places; Very Hot or Cold. **Other Job Characteristics—**Degree of Automation; Importance of Repeating Same Tasks; Pace Determined by Speed of Equipment.

Experience—Job Zone 3. Previous work-related skill, knowledge, or experience is required. **Job Preparation:** SVP 6.0 to less than 7.0—more than one year and less than four years. **Knowledge—**Communications and Media; Geography; Sales and Marketing; Food Production; History and Archeology. **Instructional Programs—**Communication Studies/Speech Communication and Rhetoric.

Related DOT Jobs—159.347-010 Announcer.

27-3021.00 Broadcast News Analysts
- **Education/Training Required: Bachelor's degree**
- **Employed: No data available.**
- **Annual Earnings: $30,060**
- **Growth: 2.8%**
- **Annual Job Openings: 9,000**

Analyze, interpret, and broadcast news received from various sources.

Analyze and interpret news and information received from various sources in order to be able to broadcast the information. Edit news material to ensure that it fits within available time or space. Examine news items of local, national, and international significance in order to determine topics to address or obtain assignments from editorial staff members. Gather information and develop perspectives about news subjects through research, interviews, observation, and experience. Select material most pertinent to presentation and organize this material into appropriate formats. Write commentaries, columns, or scripts, using computers. Coordinate and serve as an anchor on news broadcast programs. Present

news stories and introduce in-depth videotaped segments or live transmissions from on-the-scene reporters.

GOE INFORMATION—Interest Area: 01. Arts, Entertainment, and Media. **Work Group:** 01.03. News, Broadcasting, and Public Relations. **Personality Type—**Artistic. Artistic occupations frequently involve working with forms, designs, and patterns. They often require self-expression, and the work can be done without following a clear set of rules. **Work Values—**Creativity; Recognition; Social Status; Achievement; Good Working Conditions. **Skills—**Speaking; Writing; Reading Comprehension; Active Listening; Complex Problem Solving; Critical Thinking. **Abilities—***Cognitive:* Written Expression; Oral Expression; Oral Comprehension; Written Comprehension; Flexibility of Closure. *Psychomotor:* None met the criteria. *Physical:* None met the criteria. *Sensory:* Speech Clarity; Auditory Attention; Speech Recognition. **General Work Activities—***Information Input:* Getting Information; Identifying Objects, Actions, and Events; Monitoring Processes, Materials, or Surroundings. *Mental Process:* Organizing, Planning, and Prioritizing; Judging Qualities of Things, Services, or Other People's Work; Analyzing Data or Information. *Work Output:* Documenting or Recording Information; Handling and Moving Objects; Interacting with Computers. *Interacting with Others:* Performing for or Working with the Public; Communicating with Persons Outside Organization; Establishing and Maintaining Relationships. **Physical Work Conditions—**Sitting; Cramped Work Space or Awkward Positions; Indoors. **Other Job Characteristics—**Importance of Being Exact or Accurate; Importance of Repeating Same Tasks; Pace Determined by Speed of Equipment.

Experience—Job Zone 4. A minimum of two to four years of work-related skill, knowledge, or experience is needed. **Job Preparation:** SVP 7.0 to less than 8.0—two years to less than 10 years. **Knowledge—**Communications and Media; English Language; Telecommunications; Computers and Electronics; Fine Arts. **Instructional Programs—**Broadcast Journalism; Journalism; Political Communication; Radio and Television.

Related DOT Jobs—131.067-010 Columnist/Commentator; 131.262-010 Newscaster.

27-3022.00 Reporters and Correspondents
- **Education/Training Required: Bachelor's degree**
- **Employed: No data available.**
- **Annual Earnings: $30,060**
- **Growth: 2.8%**
- **Annual Job Openings: 9,000**

Collect and analyze facts about newsworthy events by interview, investigation, or observation. Report and write stories for newspaper, news magazine, radio, or television.

Arrange interviews with people who can provide information about a particular story. Check reference materials such as books, news files, and public records in order to obtain relevant facts. Conduct taped or filmed interviews or narratives. Determine a story's emphasis, length, and format; organize material accordingly. Gather information about events through research, interviews, experience, and attendance at political, news, sports, artistic, social, and other functions. Investigate breaking news developments such as disasters, crimes, and human interest stories. Receive assignments or evaluate leads and tips in order to develop story ideas. Report and write news stories for publication or broadcast, describing the background and details of events. Research and analyze background information related to stories in order to be able to provide complete and accurate information. Review and evaluate notes taken about event aspects in order to isolate pertinent facts and details. Review copy and correct errors in content, grammar, and punctuation, following prescribed editorial style and formatting guidelines. Revise work in order to meet editorial approval or to fit time or space requirements. Develop ideas and material for columns or commentaries by analyzing and interpreting news, current issues, and personal experiences. Discuss issues with editors in order to establish priorities and positions. Edit or assist in editing videos for broadcast. Photograph or videotape news events or request that a photographer be assigned to provide such coverage. Present live or recorded commentary via broadcast media. Research and report on specialized fields such as medicine, science and technology, politics, foreign affairs, sports, arts, consumer affairs, business, religion, crime, or education. Transmit news stories or reporting information from remote locations, using equipment such as satellite phones, telephones, fax machines, or modems. Write columns, editorials, commentaries, or reviews that interpret events or offer opinions. Write reviews of literary, musical, and other artwork based on knowledge, judgment, and experience.

GOE INFORMATION—Interest Area: 01. Arts, Entertainment, and Media. **Work Group:** 01.03. News, Broadcasting, and Public Relations. **Personality Type**—Artistic. Artistic occupations frequently involve working with forms, designs, and patterns. They often require self-expression, and the work can be done without following a clear set of rules. **Work Values**—Creativity; Recognition; Ability Utilization; Advancement; Variety. **Skills**—Writing; Complex Problem Solving; Active Listening; Speaking; Reading Comprehension; Critical Thinking; Social Perceptiveness. **Abilities**—*Cognitive:* Written Expression; Oral Expression; Fluency of Ideas; Written Comprehension; Time Sharing. *Psychomotor:* None met the criteria. *Physical:* Stamina. *Sensory:* Speech Recognition; Speech Clarity; Far Vision; Near Vision; Night Vision. **General Work Activities**—*Information Input:* Getting Information; Identifying Objects, Actions, and Events; Monitoring Processes, Materials, or Surroundings. *Mental Process:* Updating and Using Relevant Knowledge; Analyzing Data or Information; Judging Qualities of Things, Services, or Other People's Work. *Work Output:* Documenting or Recording Information; Handling and Moving Objects; Controlling Machines and Processes. *Interacting with Others:* Communicating with Persons Outside Organization; Establishing and Maintaining Relationships; Performing for or Working with the Public. **Physical Work Conditions**—Outdoors; Walking or Running; Standing; Extremely Bright or Inadequate Lighting; Very Hot or Cold. **Other Job Characteristics**—Importance of Being Exact or Accurate; Consequence of Error; Pace Determined by Speed of Equipment.

Experience—Job Zone 4. A minimum of two to four years of work-related skill, knowledge, or experience is needed. **Job Preparation:** SVP 7.0 to less than 8.0—two years to less than 10 years. **Knowledge**—Communications and Media; English Language; Telecommunications; Computers and Electronics; Sociology and Anthropology. **Instructional Programs**—Agricultural Communication/Journalism; Broadcast Journalism; Journalism; Journalism, Other; Mass Communication/Media Studies; Photojournalism; Political Communication.

Related DOT Jobs—131.262-014 Newswriter; 131.262-018 Reporter.

27-3031.00 Public Relations Specialists

- ● **Education/Training Required: Bachelor's degree**
- ● **Employed: 136,687**
- ● **Annual Earnings: $41,010**
- ● **Growth: 36.1%**
- ● **Annual Job Openings: 19,000**

Engage in promoting or creating goodwill for individuals, groups, or organizations by writing or selecting favorable publicity material and releasing it through various communications media. May prepare and arrange displays and make speeches.

Arrange public appearances, lectures, contests, or exhibits for clients to increase product and service awareness and to promote goodwill. Consult with advertising agencies or staff to arrange promotional campaigns in all types of media for products, organizations, or individuals. Establish and maintain cooperative relationships with representatives of community, consumer, employee, and public interest groups. Plan and direct development and communication of informational programs to maintain favorable public and stockholder perceptions of an organization's accomplishments and agenda. Prepare or edit organizational publications for internal and external audiences, including employee newsletters and stockholders' reports. Respond to requests for information from the media or designate another appropriate spokesperson or information source. Study the objectives, promotional policies, and needs of organizations to develop public relations strategies that will influence public opinion or promote ideas, products, and services. Confer with other managers to identify trends and key group interests and concerns or to provide advice on business decisions. Confer with production and support personnel to produce or coordinate production of advertisements and promotions. Prepare and deliver speeches to further public relations objectives. Purchase advertising space and time as required to promote client's product or agenda. Coach client representatives in effective communication with the public and with employees. Plan and conduct market and public opinion research to test products or determine potential for product success, communicating results to client or management.

GOE INFORMATION—Interest Area: 01. Arts, Entertainment, and Media. **Work Group:** 01.03. News, Broadcasting, and Public Relations. **Personality Type**—Enterprising. Enterprising occupations frequently involve starting up and carrying out projects. These occupations can involve leading people and making many decisions. They sometimes require risk taking and often deal with business. **Work Values**—Creativity; Recognition; Ability Utilization; Achievement; Variety. **Skills**—Systems Analysis; Speaking; Persuasion; Complex Problem Solving; Writing; Service Orientation; Systems Evaluation; Management of Material Resources. **Abilities**—*Cognitive:* Originality; Written Expression; Oral Expression; Fluency of Ideas; Mathematical Reasoning. *Psychomotor:* None met the criteria. *Physical:* None met the criteria. *Sensory:* Speech Clarity; Speech Recognition; Near Vision; Auditory Attention; Far Vision. **General Work Activities**—*Information Input:* Getting Information; Identifying Objects, Actions, and Events; Estimating Needed Characteristics. *Mental Process:* Organizing, Planning, and Prioritizing; Judging Qualities of Things, Services, or Other People's Work; Making Decisions and Solving Problems. *Work Output:* Documenting or Recording Information; Handling and Moving Objects; Performing General Physical Activities. *Interacting with Others:* Communicating with Persons Outside Organization; Communicating with Other Workers; Providing Consultation and Advice to Others. **Physical Work Conditions**—Outdoors; Sitting; Walking or Running; Disease or Infections; Indoors. **Other Job Characteristics**—Degree of Automation; Importance of Repeating Same Tasks; Consequence of Error.

Experience—Job Zone 4. A minimum of two to four years of work-related skill, knowledge, or experience is needed. **Job Preparation:** SVP 7.0 to less than 8.0—two years to less than 10 years. **Knowledge**—Sales and Marketing; Communications and Media; Psychology; Education and Training; Clerical. **Instructional Programs**—Communication Studies/Speech Communication and Rhetoric; Family and Consumer Sciences/Human Sciences Communication; Health Communication; Political Communication; Public Relations/Image Management.

Related DOT Jobs—165.017-010 Lobbyist; 165.167-010 Sales-Service Promoter; 165.167-014 Public-Relations Representative.

27-3041.00 Editors

- **Education/Training Required: Bachelor's degree**
- **Employed: 121,648**
- **Annual Earnings: $39,960**
- **Growth: 22.6%**
- **Annual Job Openings: 14,000**

Perform variety of editorial duties, such as laying out, indexing, and revising content of written materials, in preparation for final publication.

Allocate print space for story text, photos, and illustrations according to space parameters and copy significance, using knowledge of layout principles. Assign topics, events, and stories to individual writers or reporters for coverage. Confer with management and editorial staff members regarding placement and emphasis of developing news stories. Develop story or content ideas, considering reader or audience appeal. Make manuscript acceptance or revision recommendations to the publisher. Meet frequently with artists, typesetters, layout personnel, marketing directors, and production managers to discuss projects and resolve problems. Monitor news-gathering operations to ensure utilization of all news sources, such as press releases, telephone contacts, radio, television, wire services, and other reporters. Oversee publication production, including artwork, layout, computer typesetting, and printing, ensuring adherence to deadlines and budget requirements. Plan the contents of publications according to the publication's style, editorial policy, and publishing requirements. Prepare, rewrite, and edit copy to improve readability or supervise others who do this work. Read copy or proof to detect and correct errors in spelling, punctuation, and syntax. Read, evaluate, and edit manuscripts or other materials submitted for publication and confer with authors regarding changes in content, style, organization, or publication. Review and approve proofs submitted by composing room prior to publication production. Select local, state, national, and international news items received from wire services, based on assessment of items' significance and interest value. Supervise and coordinate work of reporters and other editors. Arrange for copyright permissions. Direct the policies and departments of newspapers, magazines, and other publishing establishments. Interview and hire writers and reporters or negotiate contracts, royalties, and payments for authors or freelancers. Read material to determine index items and arrange them alphabetically or topically, indicating page or chapter location. Verify facts, dates, and statistics, using standard reference sources.

GOE INFORMATION—Interest Area: 01. Arts, Entertainment, and Media. **Work Group:** 01.02. Writing and Editing. **Personality Type**—Artistic. Artistic occupations frequently involve working with forms, designs, and patterns. They often require self-expression, and the work can be done without following a clear set of rules. **Work Values**—Creativity; Recognition; Ability Utilization; Responsibility; Autonomy. **Skills**—Writing; Reading Comprehension; Critical Thinking. **Abilities**—*Cognitive:* Written Comprehension; Written Expression; Originality; Information Ordering; Visualization. *Psychomotor:* None met the criteria. *Physical:* None met the criteria. *Sensory:* Near Vision; Speech Clarity. **General Work Activities**—*Information Input:* Getting Information; Identifying Objects, Actions, and Events; Monitoring Processes, Materials, or Surroundings. *Mental Process:* Judging Qualities of Things, Services, or Other People's Work; Organizing, Planning, and Prioritizing; Making Decisions and Solving Problems. *Work Output:* Handling and Moving Objects; Drafting and Specifying Technical Devices; Documenting or Recording Information. *Interacting with Others:* Communicating with Other Workers; Establishing and Maintaining Relationships; Providing Consultation and Advice to Others. **Physical Work Conditions**—Indoors; Sitting. **Other Job Characteristics**—Importance of Being Exact or Accurate; Importance of Repeating Same Tasks; Consequence of Error.

Experience—Job Zone 4. A minimum of two to four years of work-related skill, knowledge, or experience is needed. **Job Preparation:** SVP 7.0 to less than 8.0—two years to less than 10 years. **Knowledge**—Communications and Media; English Language; Clerical; Computers and Electronics; Administration and Management. **Instructional Programs**—Broadcast Journalism; Business/Corporate Communications; Communication, Journalism, and Related Programs, Other; Creative Writing; Journalism; Mass Communication/Media Studies; Publishing; Technical and Business Writing.

Related DOT Jobs—132.067-022 Editor, Greeting Card; 132.067-026 Editor, News; 132.267-010 Editor, Telegraph; 132.267-014 Editorial Assistant; 132.367-010 Editor, Index.

27-3042.00 Technical Writers

- **Education/Training Required: Bachelor's degree**
- **Employed: 57,483**
- **Annual Earnings: $49,360**
- **Growth: 29.6%**
- **Annual Job Openings: 5,000**

Write technical materials, such as equipment manuals, appendices, or operating and maintenance instructions. May assist in layout work.

Organize material and complete writing assignment according to set standards regarding order, clarity, conciseness, style, and terminology. Study drawings, specifications, mockups, and product samples to integrate and delineate technology, operating procedure, and production sequence and detail. Review published materials and recommend revisions or changes in scope, format, content, and methods of reproduction and binding. Assist in laying out material for publication. Interview production and engineering personnel and read journals and other material to become familiar with product technologies and production methods. Review manufacturer's and trade catalogs, drawings, and other data relative to operation, maintenance, and service of equipment. Edit, standardize, or make changes to material prepared by other writers or establishment personnel. Analyze developments in specific field to determine need for revisions in previously published materials and development of new material. Observe production, developmental, and experimental activities to determine operating procedure and detail. Select photographs, drawings, sketches, diagrams, and charts to illustrate material. Maintain records and files of work and revisions. Draw sketches to illustrate specified materials or assembly sequence. Arrange for typing, duplication, and distribution of material. Confer with customer representatives, vendors, plant executives, or publisher to establish technical specifications and to determine subject material to be developed for publication.

GOE INFORMATION—Interest Area: 01. Arts, Entertainment, and Media. **Work Group:** 01.02. Writing and Editing. **Personality Type**—Artistic. Artistic occupations frequently involve working with forms, designs, and patterns. They often require self-expression, and the work can be done without following a clear set of rules. **Work Values**—Creativity; Ability Utilization; Achievement; Responsibility; Recognition. **Skills**—Writing; Reading Comprehension; Complex Problem Solving; Active Listening; Critical Thinking; Speaking; Systems Analysis; Learning Strategies. **Abilities**—*Cognitive:* Written Expression; Originality; Information Ordering; Written Comprehension; Speed of Closure. *Psychomotor:* None met the criteria. *Physical:* None met the criteria. *Sensory:* Near Vision; Visual Color Discrimination; Speech Recognition; Glare Sensitivity; Speech Clarity. **General Work Activities**—*Information Input:* Getting Information; Monitoring Processes, Materials, or Surroundings; Identifying Objects, Actions, and Events. *Mental Process:* Processing

Information; Updating and Using Relevant Knowledge; Organizing, Planning, and Prioritizing. *Work Output:* Documenting or Recording Information; Drafting and Specifying Technical Devices; Handling and Moving Objects. *Interacting with Others:* Communicating with Other Workers; Interpreting Meaning of Information for Others; Communicating with Persons Outside Organization. **Physical Work Conditions**—Sitting; Indoors; Disease or Infections; Hazardous Equipment; Contaminants. **Other Job Characteristics**—Importance of Being Exact or Accurate; Importance of Repeating Same Tasks; Pace Determined by Speed of Equipment.

Experience—Job Zone 5. Extensive skill, knowledge, and experience are needed for these occupations. **Job Preparation:** SVP 8.0 and above—four years to more than 10 years. **Knowledge**—Communications and Media; Design; English Language; Education and Training; Engineering and Technology. **Instructional Programs**—Business/Corporate Communications; Family and Consumer Sciences/Human Sciences Communication; Technical and Business Writing.

Related DOT Jobs—019.267-010 Specification Writer; 131.267-026 Writer, Technical Publications; 132.017-018 Editor, Technical and Scientific Publications.

27-3043.00 Writers and Authors
- **Education/Training Required: Bachelor's degree**
- **Employed: 125,957**
- **Annual Earnings: $42,450**
- **Growth: 28.4%**
- **Annual Job Openings: 18,000**

Originate and prepare written material, such as scripts, stories, advertisements, and other material.

No task data available.

GOE INFORMATION—Interest Area: 01. Arts, Entertainment, and Media. **Work Group:** 01.02. Writing and Editing. **Note:** The Department of Labor has not collected some data for this job, so it has fewer details than the other descriptions.

Instructional Programs—Broadcast Journalism; Business/Corporate Communications; Communication Studies/Speech Communication and Rhetoric; Communication, Journalism, and Related Programs, Other; Creative Writing; English Composition; Family and Consumer Sciences/Human Sciences Communication; Journalism; Mass Communication/Media Studies; Playwriting and Screenwriting; Technical and Business Writing.

Related DOT Jobs—052.067-010 Biographer; 131.067-010 Columnist/Commentator; 131.067-014 Copy Writer; 131.067-018 Critic; 131.067-022 Editorial Writer; 131.067-026 Humorist; 131.067-030 Librettist; 131.067-034 Lyricist; 131.067-038 Playwright; 131.067-042 Poet; 131.067-046 Writer, Prose, Fiction and Nonfiction; 131.067-050 Screen Writer; 131.087-010 Continuity Writer; 139.087-010 Crossword-Puzzle Maker; 203.362-026 Caption Writer.

27-3043.01 Poets and Lyricists
- **Education/Training Required: Bachelor's degree**
- **Employed: No data available.**
- **Annual Earnings: $42,450**
- **Growth: 28.4%**
- **Annual Job Openings: 18,000**

Write poetry or song lyrics for publication or performance.

Writes words to fit musical compositions, including lyrics for operas, musical plays, and choral works. Writes narrative, dramatic, lyric, or other types of poetry for publication. Adapts text to accommodate musical requirements of composer and singer. Chooses subject matter and suitable form to express personal feeling and experience or ideas or to narrate story or event.

GOE INFORMATION—Interest Area: 01. Arts, Entertainment, and Media. **Work Group:** 01.02. Writing and Editing. **Personality Type**—Artistic. Artistic occupations frequently involve working with forms, designs, and patterns. They often require self-expression, and the work can be done without following a clear set of rules. **Work Values**—Creativity; Independence; Ability Utilization; Autonomy; Recognition. **Skills**—Writing; Reading Comprehension. **Abilities**—*Cognitive:* Originality; Fluency of Ideas; Written Expression; Category Flexibility; Memorization. *Psychomotor:* None met the criteria. *Physical:* None met the criteria. *Sensory:* Hearing Sensitivity; Auditory Attention. **General Work Activities**—*Information Input:* Getting Information; Identifying Objects, Actions, and Events; Monitoring Processes, Materials, or Surroundings. *Mental Process:* Thinking Creatively; Judging Qualities of Things, Services, or Other People's Work; Organizing, Planning, and Prioritizing. *Work Output:* Handling and Moving Objects; Documenting or Recording Information; Interacting with Computers. *Interacting with Others:* Communicating with Persons Outside Organization; Establishing and Maintaining Relationships; Communicating with Other Workers. **Physical Work Conditions**—Sitting; Indoors. **Other Job Characteristics**—Degree of Automation; Importance of Repeating Same Tasks; Pace Determined by Speed of Equipment.

Experience—Job Zone 4. A minimum of two to four years of work-related skill, knowledge, or experience is needed. **Job Preparation:** SVP 7.0 to less than 8.0—two years to less than 10 years. **Knowledge**—Fine Arts; Communications and Media; English Language; Sociology and Anthropology. **Instructional Programs**—Broadcast Journalism; Business/Corporate Communications; Communication Studies/Speech Communication and Rhetoric; Communication, Journalism, and Related Programs, Other; Creative Writing; English Composition; Family and Consumer Sciences/Human Sciences Communication; Journalism; Mass Communication/Media Studies; Playwriting and Screenwriting; Technical and Business Writing.

Related DOT Jobs—131.067-030 Librettist; 131.067-034 Lyricist; 131.067-042 Poet.

27-3043.02 Creative Writers
- **Education/Training Required: Bachelor's degree**
- **Employed: No data available.**
- **Annual Earnings: $42,450**
- **Growth: 28.4%**
- **Annual Job Openings: 18,000**

Create original written works, such as plays or prose, for publication or performance.

Writes fiction or nonfiction prose work, such as short story, novel, biography, article, descriptive or critical analysis, or essay. Writes play or script for moving pictures or television, based on original ideas or adapted from fictional, historical, or narrative sources. Writes humorous material for publication or performance, such as comedy routines, gags, comedy shows, or scripts for entertainers. Organizes material for project, plans arrangement or outline, and writes synopsis. Develops factors such as theme, plot, characterization, psychological analysis, historical environment, action, and dialogue to create material. Selects subject or theme for writing project based on personal interest and writing specialty or assignment from publisher, client, producer, or director. Reviews, submits for approval, and revises written material to meet personal standards and satisfy needs of client, publisher, director, or producer. Conducts research to obtain factual information and authentic detail, utilizing sources such as newspaper accounts, diaries, and interviews. Confers with client, publisher, or producer to discuss development changes or revisions. Collaborates with other writers on specific projects.

GOE INFORMATION—Interest Area: 01. Arts, Entertainment, and Media. **Work Group:** 01.02. Writing and Editing. **Personality Type**—Artistic. Artistic occupations frequently involve working with forms, designs, and patterns. They often require self-expression, and the work can be done without following a clear set of rules. **Work Values**—Creativity; Ability Utilization; Achievement; Recognition; Autonomy. **Skills**—Writing; Reading Comprehension; Complex Problem Solving; Critical Thinking; Coordination. **Abilities**—*Cognitive:* Originality; Written Expression; Fluency of Ideas; Oral Comprehension; Written Comprehension. *Psychomotor:* None met the criteria. *Physical:* None met the criteria. *Sensory:* Near Vision. **General Work Activities**—*Information Input:* Getting Information; Identifying Objects, Actions, and Events; Monitoring Processes, Materials, or Surroundings. *Mental Process:* Thinking Creatively; Judging Qualities of Things, Services, or Other People's Work; Organizing, Planning, and Prioritizing. *Work Output:* Documenting or Recording Information; Interacting with Computers; Handling and Moving Objects. *Interacting with Others:* Communicating with Persons Outside Organization; Communicating with Other Workers; Establishing and Maintaining Relationships. **Physical Work Conditions**—Sitting; Indoors. **Other Job Characteristics**—Degree of Automation; Importance of Repeating Same Tasks; Consequence of Error.

Experience—Job Zone 4. A minimum of two to four years of work-related skill, knowledge, or experience is needed. **Job Preparation:** SVP 7.0 to less than 8.0—two years to less than 10 years. **Knowledge**—English Language; Communications and Media; Fine Arts; Sociology and Anthropology; Computers and Electronics. **Instructional Programs**—Broadcast Journalism; Business/Corporate Communications; Communication Studies/Speech Communication and Rhetoric; Communication, Journalism, and Related Programs, Other; Creative Writing; English Composition; Family and Consumer Sciences/Human Sciences Communication; Journalism; Mass Communication/Media Studies; Playwriting and Screenwriting; Technical and Business Writing.

Related DOT Jobs—052.067-010 Biographer; 131.067-026 Humorist; 131.067-038 Playwright; 131.067-046 Writer, Prose, Fiction and Nonfiction; 131.067-050 Screen Writer; 131.087-010 Continuity Writer; 139.087-010 Crossword-Puzzle Maker.

27-3043.03 Caption Writers

- ● **Education/Training Required: Moderate-term on-the-job training**
- ● **Employed: No data available.**
- ● **Annual Earnings: $42,450**
- ● **Growth: 28.4%**
- ● **Annual Job Openings: 18,000**

Write caption phrases of dialogue for hearing-impaired and foreign language-speaking viewers of movie or television productions.

Writes captions to describe music and background noises. Watches production and reviews captions simultaneously to determine which caption phrases require editing. Translates foreign language dialogue into English language captions or English dialogue into foreign language captions. Enters commands to synchronize captions with dialogue and place on the screen. Operates computerized captioning system for movies or television productions for hearing-impaired and foreign language-speaking viewers. Edits translations for correctness of grammar, punctuation, and clarity of expression. Oversees encoding of captions to master tape of television production. Discusses captions with directors or producers of movie and television productions.

GOE INFORMATION—Interest Area: 01. Arts, Entertainment, and Media. **Work Group:** 01.03. News, Broadcasting, and Public Relations. **Personality Type**—Artistic. Artistic occupations frequently involve working with forms, designs, and patterns. They often require self-expression, and the work can be done without following a clear set of rules. **Work Values**—Good Working Conditions; Ability Utilization; Variety; Achievement; Recognition. **Skills**—Writing; Operation and Control. **Abilities**—*Cognitive:* Written Expression; Oral Comprehension; Written Comprehension; Speed of Closure; Oral Expression. *Psychomotor:* Wrist-Finger Speed. *Physical:* None met the criteria. *Sensory:* Near Vision; Speech Recognition; Speech Clarity; Hearing Sensitivity; Auditory Attention. **General Work Activities**—*Information Input:* Identifying Objects, Actions, and Events; Getting Information; Monitoring Processes, Materials, or Surroundings. *Mental Process:* Judging Qualities of Things, Services, or Other People's Work; Organizing, Planning, and Prioritizing; Evaluating Information Against Standards. *Work Output:* Interacting with Computers; Handling and Moving Objects; Controlling Machines and Processes. *Interacting with Others:* Communicating with Other Workers; Interpreting Meaning of Information for Others; Establishing and Maintaining Relationships. **Physical Work Conditions**—Sitting; Indoors; Making Repetitive Motions. **Other Job Characteristics**—Importance of Being Exact or Accurate; Pace Determined by Speed of Equipment; Degree of Automation.

Experience—Job Zone 3. Previous work-related skill, knowledge, or experience is required. **Job Preparation:** SVP 6.0 to less than 7.0—more than one year and less than four years. **Knowledge**—Foreign Language; Communications and Media; English Language; Computers and Electronics; Fine Arts. **Instructional Programs**—Broadcast Journalism; Business/Corporate Communications; Communication Studies/Speech Communication and Rhetoric; Communication, Journalism, and Related Programs, Other; Creative Writing; English Composition; Family and Consumer Sciences/Human Sciences Communication; Journalism; Mass Communication/Media Studies; Playwriting and Screenwriting; Technical and Business Writing.

Related DOT Jobs—203.362-026 Caption Writer.

27-3043.04 Copy Writers

- ● **Education/Training Required: Bachelor's degree**
- ● **Employed: 125,957**
- ● **Annual Earnings: $42,450**
- ● **Growth: 28.4%**
- ● **Annual Job Openings: 18,000**

Write advertising copy for use by publication or broadcast media to promote sale of goods and services.

Conduct research and interviews to determine which of a product's selling features should be promoted. Consult with sales, media, and marketing representatives to obtain information on product or service and discuss style and length of advertising copy. Discuss with the client the product, advertising themes and methods, and any changes that should be made in advertising copy. Edit or rewrite existing copy as necessary and submit copy for approval by supervisor. Present drafts and ideas to clients. Review advertising trends, consumer surveys, and other data regarding marketing of goods and services to determine the best way to promote products. Vary language and tone of messages based on product and medium.

Write advertising copy for use by publication, broadcast, or Internet media to promote the sale of goods and services. Write articles, bulletins, sales letters, speeches, and other related informative, marketing, and promotional material. Write to customers in their terms and on their level so that the advertiser's sales message is more readily received. Develop advertising campaigns for a wide range of clients, working with an advertising agency's creative director and art director to determine the best way to present advertising information. Invent names for products and write the slogans that appear on packaging, brochures, and other promotional material.

GOE INFORMATION—Interest Area: 01. Arts, Entertainment, and Media. **Work Group:** 01.02. Writing and Editing. **Personality Type—**Artistic. Artistic occupations frequently involve working with forms, designs, and patterns. They often require self-expression, and the work can be done without following a clear set of rules. **Work Values—**Creativity; Recognition; Advancement; Ability Utilization; Responsibility. **Skills—**Writing; Reading Comprehension; Critical Thinking; Persuasion. **Abilities—***Cognitive:* Written Expression; Fluency of Ideas; Written Comprehension; Originality; Oral Comprehension. *Psychomotor:* Wrist-Finger Speed. *Physical:* Trunk Strength. *Sensory:* Near Vision; Speech Clarity; Sound Localization. **General Work Activities—***Information Input:* Getting Information; Identifying Objects, Actions, and Events; Monitoring Processes, Materials, or Surroundings. *Mental Process:* Judging Qualities of Things, Services, or Other People's Work; Thinking Creatively; Organizing, Planning, and Prioritizing. *Work Output:* Handling and Moving Objects; Interacting with Computers; Documenting or Recording Information. *Interacting with Others:* Communicating with Other Workers; Establishing and Maintaining Relationships; Communicating with Persons Outside Organization. **Physical Work Conditions—**Sitting; Indoors. **Other Job Characteristics—**Importance of Being Exact or Accurate; Degree of Automation; Importance of Repeating Same Tasks.

Experience—Job Zone 4. A minimum of two to four years of work-related skill, knowledge, or experience is needed. **Job Preparation:** SVP 7.0 to less than 8.0—two years to less than 10 years. **Knowledge—**Sales and Marketing; Communications and Media; English Language; Computers and Electronics; Clerical. **Instructional Programs—**Broadcast Journalism; Business/Corporate Communications; Communication Studies/Speech Communication and Rhetoric; Communication, Journalism, and Related Programs, Other; Creative Writing; English Composition; Family and Consumer Sciences/Human Sciences Communication; Journalism; Mass Communication/Media Studies; Playwriting and Screenwriting; Technical and Business Writing.

Related DOT Jobs—131.067-014 Copy Writer.

27-3091.00 Interpreters and Translators

- **Education/Training Required: Long-term on-the-job training**
- **Employed: 21,816**
- **Annual Earnings: $32,000**
- **Growth: 23.8%**
- **Annual Job Openings: 3,000**

Translate or interpret written, oral, or sign language text into another language for others.

Translates approximate or exact message of speaker into specified language, orally or by using hand signs for hearing impaired. Translates responses from second language to first. Reads written material, such as legal documents, scientific works, or news reports, and rewrites material into specified language according to established rules of grammar. Listens to statements of speaker to ascertain meaning and to remember what is said, using electronic audio system. Receives information on subject to be discussed prior to interpreting session.

GOE INFORMATION—Interest Area: 01. Arts, Entertainment, and Media. **Work Group:** 01.03. News, Broadcasting, and Public Relations. **Personality Type—**Artistic. Artistic occupations frequently involve working with forms, designs, and patterns. They often require self-expression, and the work can be done without following a clear set of rules. **Work Values—**Social Service; Ability Utilization; Achievement; Good Working Conditions; Autonomy. **Skills—**Active Listening; Writing; Speaking; Reading Comprehension. **Abilities—***Cognitive:* Written Expression; Oral Expression; Written Comprehension; Selective Attention; Oral Comprehension. *Psychomotor:* None met the criteria. *Physical:* None met the criteria. *Sensory:* Speech Recognition; Speech Clarity; Auditory Attention; Sound Localization. **General Work Activities—***Information Input:* Getting Information; Identifying Objects, Actions, and Events; Monitoring Processes, Materials, or Surroundings. *Mental Process:* Processing Information; Updating and Using Relevant Knowledge; Thinking Creatively. *Work Output:* Documenting or Recording Information; Handling and Moving Objects; Interacting with Computers. *Interacting with Others:* Interpreting Meaning of Information for Others; Establishing and Maintaining Relationships; Communicating with Persons Outside Organization. **Physical Work Conditions—**Sitting; Outdoors; Indoors. **Other Job Characteristics—**Importance of Being Exact or Accurate; Importance of Repeating Same Tasks; Consequence of Error.

Experience—Job Zone 3. Previous work-related skill, knowledge, or experience is required. **Job Preparation:** SVP 6.0 to less than 7.0—more than one year and less than four years. **Knowledge—**Foreign Language; English Language; Communications and Media; Sociology and Anthropology; History and Archeology. **Instructional Programs—**African Languages, Literatures, and Linguistics; Albanian Language and Literature; American Indian/Native American Languages, Literatures, and Linguistics; Ancient Near Eastern and Biblical Languages, Literatures, and Linguistics; Ancient/Classical Greek Language and Literature; Arabic Language and Literature; Australian/Oceanic/Pacific Languages, Literatures, and Linguistics; Bahasa Indonesian/Bahasa Malay Languages and Literatures; Baltic Languages, Literatures, and Linguistics; Bengali Language and Literature; Bulgarian Language and Literature; Burmese Language and Literature; Catalan Language and Literature; Celtic Languages, Literatures, and Linguistics; Chinese Language and Literature; Classics and Classical Languages, Literatures, and Linguistics, General; Classics and Classical Languages, Literatures, and Linguistics, Other; Czech Language and Literature; Danish Language and Literature; Dutch/Flemish Language and Literature; East Asian Languages, Literatures, and Linguistics, General; East Asian Languages, Literatures, and Linguistics, Other; Filipino/Tagalog Language and Literature; Finnish and Related Languages, Literatures, and Linguistics; Foreign Languages and Literatures, General; Foreign Languages, Literatures, and Linguistics, Other; French Language and Literature; German Language and Literature; Germanic Languages, Literatures, and Linguistics, General; Germanic Languages, Literatures, and Linguistics, Other; Hebrew Language and Literature; Hindi Language and Literature; Hungarian/Magyar Language and Literature; Iranian/Persian Languages, Literatures, and Linguistics; Italian Language and Literature; Japanese Language and Literature; Khmer/Cambodian Language and Literature; Korean Language and Literature; Language Interpretation and Translation; Lao/Laotian Language and Literature; Latin Language and Literature; Latin Teacher Education; Linguistics; Middle/Near Eastern and Semitic Languages, Literatures, and Linguistics, Other; others.

Related DOT Jobs—137.267-010 Interpreter; 137.267-014 Interpreter, Deaf; 137.267-018 Translator.

27-3099.99 Media and Communication Workers, All Other

- Education/Training Required: Long-term on-the-job training
- Employed: No data available.
- Annual Earnings: No data available.
- Growth: 22.1%
- Annual Job Openings: 13,000

All media and communication workers not listed separately.

No task data available.

GOE INFORMATION—Interest Area: 01. Arts, Entertainment, and Media. **Work Group:** 01.02. Writing and Editing. **Note:** The Department of Labor has not collected some data for this job, so it has fewer details than the other descriptions.

Instructional Programs—Audiovisual Communications Technologies/Technicians, Other; Communication, Journalism, and Related Programs, Other; Communications Technology/Technician.

Related DOT Jobs—131.087-014 Reader; 199.267-038 Graphologist.

27-4000 Media and Communication Equipment Workers

27-4011.00 Audio and Video Equipment Technicians

- Education/Training Required: Long-term on-the-job training
- Employed: 37,010
- Annual Earnings: $30,170
- Growth: 16.8%
- Annual Job Openings: 3,000

Set up or set up and operate audio and video equipment, including microphones, sound speakers, video screens, projectors, video monitors, recording equipment, connecting wires and cables, sound and mixing boards, and related electronic equipment for concerts, sports events, meetings and conventions, presentations, and news conferences. May also set up and operate associated spotlights and other custom lighting systems.

Compress, digitize, duplicate, and store audio and video data. Control the lights and sound of events, such as live concerts, before and after performances and during intermissions. Design layouts of audio and video equipment and perform upgrades and maintenance. Diagnose and resolve media system problems in classrooms. Install, adjust, and operate electronic equipment used to record, edit, and transmit radio and television programs, cable programs, and motion pictures. Maintain inventories of audio- and videotapes and related supplies. Meet with directors and senior members of camera crews to discuss assignments and determine filming sequences, camera movements, and picture composition. Mix and regulate sound inputs and feeds or coordinate audio feeds with television pictures. Monitor incoming and outgoing pictures and sound feeds to ensure quality; notify directors of any possible problems. Obtain, set up, and load videotapes for scheduled productions or broadcasts. Perform minor repairs and routine cleaning of audio and video equipment. Record and edit audio material such as movie soundtracks, using audio recording and editing equipment. Record and label contents of exposed film. Switch sources of video input from one camera or studio to another, from film to live programming, or from network to local programming. Conduct training sessions on selection, use, and design of audiovisual materials and on operation of presentation equipment. Construct and position properties, sets, lighting equipment, and other equipment. Determine formats, approaches, content, levels, and mediums to effectively meet objectives within budgetary constraints, utilizing research, knowledge, and training. Develop manuals, texts, workbooks, or related materials for use in conjunction with production materials or for training. Direct and coordinate activities of assistants and other personnel during production. Edit videotapes by erasing and removing portions of programs and adding video and/or sound as required. Inform users of audio- and videotaping service policies and procedures. Locate and secure settings, properties, effects, and other production necessities. Notify supervisors when major equipment repairs are needed. Obtain and preview musical performance programs prior to events in order to become familiar with the order and approximate times of pieces. Organize and maintain compliance, license, and warranty information related to audio and video facilities. Perform narration of productions or present announcements.

GOE INFORMATION—Interest Area: 01. Arts, Entertainment, and Media. **Work Group:** 01.08. Media Technology. **Personality Type**—Conventional. Conventional occupations frequently involve following set procedures and routines. These occupations can include working with data and details more than with ideas. Usually there is a clear line of authority to follow. **Work Values**—Good Working Conditions; Authority; Pleasant Co-workers; Ability Utilization; Social Service. **Skills**—Complex Problem Solving; Learning Strategies; Writing; Instructing; Speaking; Operations Analysis; Management of Material Resources; Technology Design. **Abilities**—*Cognitive:* Originality; Fluency of Ideas; Visualization; Time Sharing; Written Expression. *Psychomotor:* Rate Control; Control Precision; Reaction Time; Speed of Limb Movement; Wrist-Finger Speed. *Physical:* Explosive Strength; Dynamic Flexibility; Extent Flexibility; Gross Body Equilibrium; Static Strength. *Sensory:* Speech Clarity; Glare Sensitivity; Hearing Sensitivity; Sound Localization; Peripheral Vision. **General Work Activities**—*Information Input:* Getting Information; Monitoring Processes, Materials, or Surroundings; Identifying Objects, Actions, and Events. *Mental Process:* Thinking Creatively; Organizing, Planning, and Prioritizing; Updating and Using Relevant Knowledge. *Work Output:* Handling and Moving Objects; Drafting and Specifying Technical Devices; Performing General Physical Activities. *Interacting with Others:* Communicating with Other Workers; Establishing and Maintaining Relationships; Coordinating the Work and Activities of Others. **Physical Work Conditions**—Cramped Work Space or Awkward Positions; Kneeling, Crouching, or Crawling; Bending or Twisting the Body; Using Hands on Objects, Tools, or Controls; Disease or Infections. **Other Job Characteristics**—Degree of Automation; Pace Determined by Speed of Equipment; Consequence of Error.

Experience—Job Zone 4. A minimum of two to four years of work-related skill, knowledge, or experience is needed. **Job Preparation:** SVP 7.0 to less than 8.0—two years to less than 10 years. **Knowledge**—Communications and Media; Education and Training; Fine Arts; Telecommunications; Administration and Management. **Instructional Programs**—Agricultural Communication/Journalism; Photographic and Film/Video Technology/Technician and Assistant; Recording Arts Technology/Technician.

Related DOT Jobs—159.042-010 Laserist; 194.262-014 Sound Controller; 962.261-010 Planetarium Technician; 962.261-014 Stage Technician; 962.267-010 Sight-Effects Specialist; 962.281-018 Special Effects Specialist; 962.362-010 Communications Technician; 962.362-014 Light Technician; 962.381-014 Lighting-Equipment Operator.

27-4012.00 Broadcast Technicians

- **Education/Training Required: Postsecondary vocational training**
- **Employed: 36,153**
- **Annual Earnings: $27,750**
- **Growth: 10.2%**
- **Annual Job Openings: 3,000**

Set up, operate, and maintain the electronic equipment used to transmit radio and television programs. Control audio equipment to regulate volume level and quality of sound during radio and television broadcasts. Operate radio transmitter to broadcast radio and television programs.

Align antennae with receiving dishes in order to obtain the clearest signal for transmission of broadcasts from field locations. Control audio equipment in order to regulate the volume and sound quality during radio and television broadcasts. Monitor strength, clarity, and reliability of incoming and outgoing signals and adjust equipment as necessary to maintain quality broadcasts. Observe monitors and converse with station personnel in order to determine audio and video levels and to ascertain that programs are airing. Preview scheduled programs to ensure that signals are functioning and programs are ready for transmission. Regulate the fidelity, brightness, and contrast of video transmissions, using video console control panels. Report equipment problems and ensure that repairs are made; make emergency repairs to equipment when necessary and possible. Schedule programming and/or read television programming logs in order to determine which programs are to be recorded or aired. Select sources from which programming will be received or through which programming will be transmitted. Set up and operate portable field transmission equipment outside the studio. Substitute programs in cases where signals fail. Design and modify equipment to employer specifications. Determine the number, type, and approximate location of microphones needed for best sound recording or transmission quality and position them appropriately. Discuss production requirements with clients. Edit broadcast material electronically, using computers. Give technical directions to other personnel during filming. Maintain programming logs as required by station management and the Federal Communications Commission. Organize recording sessions and prepare areas such as radio booths and television stations for recording. Perform preventive and minor equipment maintenance, using hand tools. Prepare reports outlining past and future programs, including content. Record sound onto tape or film for radio or television, checking its quality and making adjustments where necessary. Instruct trainees in how to use television production equipment, how to film events, and how to copy/edit graphics or sound onto videotape. Produce educational and training films and videotapes by performing activities such as selecting equipment and preparing scripts.

GOE INFORMATION—Interest Area: 01. Arts, Entertainment, and Media. **Work Group:** 01.08. Media Technology. **Personality Type—**Realistic. Realistic occupations frequently involve work activities that include practical, hands-on problems and solutions. They often deal with plants, animals, and real-world materials like wood, tools, and machinery. Many of the occupations require working outside and do not involve a lot of paperwork or working closely with others. **Work Values—**Variety; Advancement; Recognition; Good Working Conditions; Ability Utilization. **Skills—**Instructing; Installation; Operation and Control; Operation Monitoring; Troubleshooting; Technology Design; Equipment Selection; Repairing. **Abilities—***Cognitive:* Time Sharing; Selective Attention; Oral Expression; Deductive Reasoning; Oral Comprehension. *Psychomotor:* Response Orientation; Reaction Time; Control Precision; Rate Control;

Multilimb Coordination. *Physical:* Static Strength; Gross Body Coordination; Gross Body Equilibrium; Stamina; Explosive Strength. *Sensory:* Hearing Sensitivity; Night Vision; Auditory Attention; Speech Recognition; Visual Color Discrimination. **General Work Activities—***Information Input:* Monitoring Processes, Materials, or Surroundings; Inspecting Equipment, Structures, or Materials; Getting Information. *Mental Process:* Organizing, Planning, and Prioritizing; Making Decisions and Solving Problems; Judging Qualities of Things, Services, or Other People's Work. *Work Output:* Handling and Moving Objects; Repairing and Maintaining Mechanical Equipment; Performing General Physical Activities. *Interacting with Others:* Communicating with Other Workers; Teaching Others; Establishing and Maintaining Relationships. **Physical Work Conditions—**Outdoors; Hazardous Conditions; Extremely Bright or Inadequate Lighting; Climbing Ladders, Scaffolds, Poles, etc.; Hazardous Equipment. **Other Job Characteristics—**Degree of Automation; Importance of Being Exact or Accurate; Consequence of Error.

Experience—Job Zone 4. A minimum of two to four years of work-related skill, knowledge, or experience is needed. **Job Preparation:** SVP 7.0 to less than 8.0—two years to less than 10 years. **Knowledge—**Telecommunications; Geography; Computers and Electronics; Education and Training; Communications and Media. **Instructional Programs—**Audiovisual Communications Technologies/Technicians, Other; Communications Technology/Technician; Radio and Television Broadcasting Technology/Technician.

Related DOT Jobs—193.167-014 Field Supervisor, Broadcast; 193.262-018 Field Engineer; 194.062-010 Television Technician; 194.122-010 Access Coordinator, Cable Television; 194.262-010 Audio Operator; 194.262-022 Master Control Operator; 194.282-010 Video Operator; 194.362-018 Telecine Operator; 194.362-022 Technician, News Gathering; 194.381-010 Technical Testing Engineer; 194.382-018 Videotape Operator.

27-4013.00 Radio Operators

- **Education/Training Required: Long-term on-the-job training**
- **Employed: 2,934**
- **Annual Earnings: $31,940**
- **Growth: 6.2%**
- **Annual Job Openings: Fewer than 500**

Receive and transmit communications using radiotelegraph or radiotelephone equipment in accordance with government regulations. May repair equipment.

Communicate with receiving operators in order to exchange transmission instructions. Determine and obtain bearings of sources from which signals originate, using direction-finding procedures and equipment. Maintain station logs of messages transmitted and received for activities such as flight testing and fire locations. Monitor emergency frequencies in order to detect distress calls and respond by dispatching emergency equipment. Operate radio equipment in order to communicate with ships, aircraft, mining crews, offshore oil rigs, logging camps, and other remote operations. Turn controls or throw switches in order to activate power, adjust voice volume and modulation, and set transmitters on specified frequencies. Broadcast weather reports and warnings. Conduct periodic equipment inspections and routine tests in order to ensure that operations standards are met. Coordinate radio-related aspects of locating and contacting airplanes and ships that are missing or in distress. Examine and operate new equipment prior to installation in order to ensure that it performs properly. Operate sound-recording equipment in order to record signals and preserve broadcasts for purposes such as analysis by intelligence personnel. Repair radio equipment as necessary, using electronic testing equipment, hand tools, and power tools. Review applicable regulations regarding radio communications and report violations. Send, receive, and interpret coded messages. Set up antennas and mobile communication units during military field exercises.

GOE INFORMATION—Interest Area: 01. Arts, Entertainment, and Media. **Work Group:** 01.08. Media Technology. **Personality Type—**Realistic. Realistic occupations frequently involve work activities that include practical, hands-on problems and solutions. They often deal with plants, animals, and real-world materials like wood, tools, and machinery. Many of the occupations require working outside and do not involve a lot of paperwork or working closely with others. **Work Values—**Supervision, Human Relations; Achievement; Variety; Company Policies and Practices; Good Working Conditions. **Skills—**Operation Monitoring; Operation and Control; Speaking; Active Listening; Repairing. **Abilities—***Cognitive:* Time Sharing; Flexibility of Closure; Oral Expression; Selective Attention; Speed of Closure. *Psychomotor:* Response Orientation; Reaction Time; Control Precision; Finger Dexterity. *Physical:* None met the criteria. *Sensory:* Auditory Attention; Sound Localization; Speech Recognition; Speech Clarity; Hearing Sensitivity. **General Work Activities—***Information Input:* Getting Information; Monitoring Processes, Materials, or Surroundings; Identifying Objects, Actions, and Events. *Mental Process:* Processing Information; Making Decisions and Solving Problems; Updating and Using Relevant Knowledge. *Work Output:* Documenting or Recording Information; Repairing and Maintaining Electronic Equipment; Controlling Machines and Processes. *Interacting with Others:* Communicating with Other Workers; Interpreting Meaning of Information for Others; Establishing and Maintaining Relationships. **Physical Work Conditions—**Sitting; Using Hands on Objects, Tools, or Controls; Indoors. **Other Job Characteristics—**Importance of Repeating Same Tasks; Pace Determined by Speed of Equipment; Importance of Being Exact or Accurate.

Experience—Job Zone 3. Previous work-related skill, knowledge, or experience is required. **Job Preparation:** SVP 6.0 to less than 7.0—more than one year and less than four years. **Knowledge—**Telecommunications; Computers and Electronics; Geography; Communications and Media; Engineering and Technology. **Instructional Programs—**Communications Systems Installation and Repair Technology.

Related DOT Jobs—193.162-022 Airline-Radio Operator, Chief; 193.262-010 Airline-Radio Operator; 193.262-014 Dispatcher; 193.262-022 Radio Officer; 193.262-026 Radio Station Operator; 193.262-030 Radiotelegraph Operator; 193.262-034 Radiotelephone Operator; 193.362-010 Photoradio Operator; 193.362-014 Radio-Intelligence Operator; 193.382-010 Electronic Intelligence Operations Specialist.

27-4014.00 Sound Engineering Technicians

- **Education/Training Required: Postsecondary vocational training**
- **Employed: 10,991**
- **Annual Earnings: $35,130**
- **Growth: 19.0%**
- **Annual Job Openings: 1,000**

Operate machines and equipment to record, synchronize, mix, or reproduce music, voices, or sound effects in sporting arenas, theater productions, recording studios, or movie and video productions.

Confer with producers, performers, and others in order to determine and achieve the desired sound for a production such as a musical recording or a film. Mix and edit voices, music, and taped sound effects for live performances and for prerecorded events, using sound mixing boards. Record speech, music, and other sounds on recording media, using recording equipment. Regulate volume level and sound quality during recording sessions, using control consoles. Reproduce and duplicate sound recordings from original recording media, using sound editing and duplication equipment. Separate instruments, vocals, and other sounds and then combine sounds later during the mixing or post-production stage. Set up, test, and adjust recording equipment for recording sessions and live performances; tear down equipment after event completion. Synchronize and equalize prerecorded dialogue, music, and sound effects with visual action of motion pictures or television productions, using control consoles. Create musical instrument digital interface programs for music projects, commercials, or film post-production. Keep logs of recordings. Prepare for recording sessions by performing activities such as selecting and setting up microphones. Report equipment problems and ensure that required repairs are made.

GOE INFORMATION—Interest Area: 01. Arts, Entertainment, and Media. **Work Group:** 01.08. Media Technology. **Personality Type—**Realistic. Realistic occupations frequently involve work activities that include practical, hands-on problems and solutions. They often deal with plants, animals, and real-world materials like wood, tools, and machinery. Many of the occupations require working outside and do not involve a lot of paperwork or working closely with others. **Work Values—**Good Working Conditions; Authority; Creativity; Moral Values; Company Policies and Practices. **Skills—**Operation and Control; Operation Monitoring; Equipment Selection; Troubleshooting; Management of Personnel Resources. **Abilities—***Cognitive:* Flexibility of Closure; Selective Attention; Speed of Closure; Originality; Perceptual Speed. *Psychomotor:* Reaction Time; Response Orientation; Speed of Limb Movement; Rate Control; Multilimb Coordination. *Physical:* Gross Body Coordination; Dynamic Flexibility; Gross Body Equilibrium. *Sensory:* Hearing Sensitivity; Auditory Attention; Sound Localization; Night Vision; Far Vision. **General Work Activities—***Information Input:* Identifying Objects, Actions, and Events; Monitoring Processes, Materials, or Surroundings; Getting Information. *Mental Process:* Thinking Creatively; Judging Qualities of Things, Services, or Other People's Work; Organizing, Planning, and Prioritizing. *Work Output:* Controlling Machines and Processes; Repairing and Maintaining Electronic Equipment; Repairing and Maintaining Mechanical Equipment. *Interacting with Others:* Communicating with Other Workers; Establishing and Maintaining Relationships; Guiding, Directing, and Motivating Subordinates. **Physical Work Conditions—**Using Hands on Objects, Tools, or Controls; Sitting; Indoors; Making Repetitive Motions; Distracting Sounds and Noise Levels. **Other Job Characteristics—**Degree of Automation; Importance of Being Exact or Accurate; Pace Determined by Speed of Equipment.

Experience—Job Zone 3. Previous work-related skill, knowledge, or experience is required. **Job Preparation:** SVP 6.0 to less than 7.0—more than one year and less than four years. **Knowledge—**Computers and Electronics; Engineering and Technology; Telecommunications; Communications and Media; Administration and Management. **Instructional Programs—**Communications Technology/Technician; Recording Arts Technology/Technician.

Related DOT Jobs—194.262-014 Sound Controller; 194.262-018 Sound Mixer; 194.362-010 Recording Engineer; 194.362-014 Rerecording Mixer; 194.382-014 Tape Transferrer; 962.167-010 Manager, Sound Effects; 962.382-010 Recordist.

27-4021.00 Photographers

- **Education/Training Required: Long-term on-the-job training**
- **Employed: 130,637**
- **Annual Earnings: $23,040**
- **Growth: 17.0%**
- **Annual Job Openings: 13,000**

Photograph persons, subjects, merchandise, or other commercial products. May develop negatives and produce finished prints.

No task data available.

GOE INFORMATION—Interest Area: 01. Arts, Entertainment, and Media. **Work Group:** 01.08. Media Technology. **Note:** The Department of Labor has not collected some data for this job, so it has fewer details than the other descriptions.

Instructional Programs—Art/Art Studies, General; Commercial Photography; Film/Video and Photographic Arts, Other; Photography; Photojournalism; Visual and Performing Arts, General.

Related DOT Jobs—029.280-010 Photo-Optics Technician; 143.062-014 Photographer, Aerial; 143.062-018 Photographer, Apprentice; 143.062-026 Photographer, Scientific; 143.062-030 Photographer, Still; 143.062-034 Photojournalist; 143.362-010 Biological Photographer; 143.362-014 Ophthalmic Photographer; 143.382-014 Photographer, Finish.

27-4021.01 Professional Photographers

- **Education/Training Required: Long-term on-the-job training**
- **Employed: No data available.**
- **Annual Earnings: $23,040**
- **Growth: 17.0%**
- **Annual Job Openings: 13,000**

Photograph subjects or newsworthy events, using still cameras, color or black-and-white film, and variety of photographic accessories.

Frames subject matter and background in lens to capture desired image. Focuses camera and adjusts settings based on lighting, subject material, distance, and film speed. Estimates or measures light level, distance, and number of exposures needed, using measuring devices and formulas. Selects and assembles equipment and required background properties according to subject, materials, and conditions. Arranges subject material in desired position. Directs activities of workers assisting in setting up photographic.

GOE INFORMATION—Interest Area: 01. Arts, Entertainment, and Media. **Work Group:** 01.08. Media Technology. **Personality Type**—Artistic. Artistic occupations frequently involve working with forms, designs, and patterns. They often require self-expression, and the work can be done without following a clear set of rules. **Work Values**—Creativity; Ability Utilization; Achievement; Autonomy; Recognition. **Skills**—Equipment Selection; Operation and Control; Management of Material Resources. **Abilities**—*Cognitive:* Originality; Fluency of Ideas; Visualization; Spatial Orientation; Time Sharing. *Psychomotor:* Rate Control; Response Orientation; Reaction Time; Arm-Hand Steadiness; Control Precision. *Physical:* Gross Body Coordination; Extent Flexibility; Dynamic Strength; Gross Body Equilibrium; Dynamic Flexibility. *Sensory:* Depth Perception; Glare Sensitivity; Far Vision; Peripheral Vision; Night Vision. **General Work Activities**—*Information Input:* Getting Information; Identifying Objects, Actions, and Events; Monitoring Processes, Materials, or Surroundings. *Mental Process:* Judging Qualities of Things, Services, or Other People's Work; Thinking Creatively; Updating and Using Relevant Knowledge. *Work Output:* Controlling Machines and Processes; Handling and Moving Objects; Performing General Physical Activities. *Interacting with Others:* Establishing and Maintaining Relationships; Communicating with Persons Outside Organization; Coordinating the Work and Activities of Others. **Physical Work Conditions**—Extremely Bright or Inadequate Lighting; Outdoors; Very Hot or Cold; Hazardous Conditions; Kneeling, Crouching, or Crawling. **Other Job Characteristics**—Importance of Being Exact or Accurate; Degree of Automation; Consequence of Error.

Experience—Job Zone 3. Previous work-related skill, knowledge, or experience is required. **Job Preparation:** SVP 6.0 to less than 7.0—more than one year and less than four years. **Knowledge**—Fine Arts; Communications and Media; Chemistry; Geography; History and Archeology. **Instructional Programs**—Art/Art Studies, General; Commercial Photography; Film/Video and Photographic Arts, Other; Photography; Photojournalism; Visual and Performing Arts, General.

Related DOT Jobs—143.062-014 Photographer, Aerial; 143.062-018 Photographer, Apprentice; 143.062-030 Photographer, Still; 143.062-034 Photojournalist; 143.382-014 Photographer, Finish.

27-4021.02 Photographers, Scientific

- **Education/Training Required: Long-term on-the-job training**
- **Employed: No data available.**
- **Annual Earnings: $23,040**
- **Growth: 17.0%**
- **Annual Job Openings: 13,000**

Photograph variety of subject material to illustrate or record scientific/medical data or phenomena, utilizing knowledge of scientific procedures and photographic technology and techniques.

Photographs variety of subject material to illustrate or record scientific or medical data or phenomena related to an area of interest. Sights and focuses camera to take picture of subject material to illustrate or record scientific or medical data or phenomena. Plans methods and procedures for photographing subject material and setup of required equipment. Observes and arranges subject material to desired position. Removes exposed film and develops film, using chemicals, touch-up tools, and equipment. Engages in research to develop new photographic procedure, materials, and scientific data. Sets up, mounts, or installs photographic equipment and cameras.

GOE INFORMATION—Interest Area: 02. Science, Math, and Engineering. **Work Group:** 02.05. Laboratory Technology. **Personality Type**—Artistic. Artistic occupations frequently involve working with forms, designs, and patterns. They often require self-expression, and the work can be done without following a clear set of rules. **Work Values**—Creativity; Ability Utilization; Achievement; Autonomy; Recognition. **Skills**—Equipment Selection; Reading Comprehension; Science; Operation and Control; Technology Design. **Abilities**—*Cognitive:* Fluency of Ideas; Speed of Closure; Originality; Category Flexibility; Perceptual Speed. *Psychomotor:* Rate Control; Reaction Time; Arm-Hand Steadiness; Response Orientation; Control Precision. *Physical:* Gross Body Equilibrium; Gross Body Coordination; Trunk Strength; Static Strength; Dynamic Strength. *Sensory:* Visual Color Discrimination; Night Vision; Far Vision; Glare Sensitivity; Peripheral Vision. **General Work Activities**—*Information Input:* Getting Information; Identifying Objects, Actions, and Events; Monitoring Processes, Materials, or Surroundings. *Mental Process:* Organizing, Planning, and Prioritizing; Thinking Creatively; Updating and Using Relevant Knowledge. *Work Output:* Handling and Moving Objects; Performing General Physical Activities; Controlling Machines and Processes. *Interacting with Others:* Communicating with Persons Outside Organization; Communicating with Other Workers; Establishing and Maintaining Relationships. **Physical Work Conditions**—Hazardous Conditions; Extremely Bright or Inadequate Lighting; Outdoors; Standing; Using Hands on Objects, Tools, or Controls. **Other Job Characteristics**—Degree of Automation; Importance of Being Exact or Accurate; Pace Determined by Speed of Equipment.

Experience—Job Zone 3. Previous work-related skill, knowledge, or experience is required. **Job Preparation:** SVP 6.0 to less than 7.0—more than one year and less than four years. **Knowledge**—Fine Arts; Chemistry;

Physics; Engineering and Technology; Biology. **Instructional Programs**—Art/Art Studies, General; Commercial Photography; Film/Video and Photographic Arts, Other; Photography; Photojournalism; Visual and Performing Arts, General.

Related DOT Jobs—029.280-010 Photo-Optics Technician; 143.062-026 Photographer, Scientific; 143.362-010 Biological Photographer; 143.362-014 Ophthalmic Photographer.

27-4031.00 Camera Operators, Television, Video, and Motion Picture

- **Education/Training Required: Moderate-term on-the-job training**
- **Employed: 26,526**
- **Annual Earnings: $28,980**
- **Growth: 25.8%**
- **Annual Job Openings: 3,000**

Operate television, video, or motion picture camera to photograph images or scenes for various purposes, such as TV broadcasts, advertising, video production, or motion pictures.

Adjust positions and controls of cameras, printers, and related equipment in order to change focus, exposure, and lighting. Compose and frame each shot, applying the technical aspects of light, lenses, film, filters, and camera settings in order to achieve the effects sought by directors. Confer with directors, sound and lighting technicians, electricians, and other crew members to discuss assignments and determine filming sequences, desired effects, camera movements, and lighting requirements. Observe sets or locations for potential problems and to determine filming and lighting requirements. Operate television or motion picture cameras to record scenes for television broadcasts, advertising, or motion pictures. Operate zoom lenses, changing images according to specifications and rehearsal instructions. Read and analyze work orders and specifications to determine locations of subject material, work procedures, sequences of operations, and machine setups. Read charts and compute ratios to determine variables such as lighting, shutter angles, filter factors, and camera distances. Reload camera magazines with fresh raw film stock. Select and assemble cameras, accessories, equipment, and film stock to be used during filming, using knowledge of filming techniques, requirements, and computations. Set up cameras, optical printers, and related equipment to produce photographs and special effects. Test, clean, and maintain equipment to ensure proper working condition. Use cameras in any of several different camera mounts, such as stationary, track-mounted, or crane-mounted. View films to resolve problems of exposure control, subject and camera movement, changes in subject distance, and related variables. Download exposed film for shipment to processing labs. Gather and edit raw footage on location to send to television affiliates for broadcast, using electronic news-gathering or film-production equipment. Instruct camera operators regarding camera setups, angles, distances, movement, and variables and cues for starting and stopping filming. Label and record contents of exposed film and note details on report forms. Prepare slates that describe the scenes being filmed. Receive raw film stock and maintain film inventories.

GOE INFORMATION—Interest Area: 01. Arts, Entertainment, and Media. **Work Group:** 01.08. Media Technology. **Personality Type**—Artistic. Artistic occupations frequently involve working with forms, designs, and patterns. They often require self-expression, and the work can be done without following a clear set of rules. **Work Values**—Ability Utilization; Recognition; Variety; Creativity; Achievement. **Skills**—Technology Design; Operation and Control; Equipment Selection; Operation

Monitoring. **Abilities**—*Cognitive:* Spatial Orientation; Visualization; Flexibility of Closure; Perceptual Speed; Time Sharing. *Psychomotor:* Rate Control; Arm-Hand Steadiness; Control Precision; Response Orientation; Reaction Time. *Physical:* Dynamic Strength; Gross Body Coordination; Explosive Strength; Dynamic Flexibility; Static Strength. *Sensory:* Far Vision; Visual Color Discrimination; Depth Perception; Peripheral Vision; Night Vision. **General Work Activities**—*Information Input:* Identifying Objects, Actions, and Events; Getting Information; Monitoring Processes, Materials, or Surroundings. *Mental Process:* Updating and Using Relevant Knowledge; Thinking Creatively; Making Decisions and Solving Problems. *Work Output:* Controlling Machines and Processes; Handling and Moving Objects; Performing General Physical Activities. *Interacting with Others:* Communicating with Other Workers; Providing Consultation and Advice to Others; Establishing and Maintaining Relationships. **Physical Work Conditions**—High Places; Outdoors; Extremely Bright or Inadequate Lighting; Climbing Ladders, Scaffolds, Poles, etc.; Cramped Work Space or Awkward Positions. **Other Job Characteristics**—Importance of Repeating Same Tasks; Pace Determined by Speed of Equipment; Degree of Automation.

Experience—Job Zone 4. A minimum of two to four years of work-related skill, knowledge, or experience is needed. **Job Preparation:** SVP 7.0 to less than 8.0—two years to less than 10 years. **Knowledge**—Fine Arts; Communications and Media; Telecommunications; Physics; Design. **Instructional Programs**—Audiovisual Communications Technologies/Technicians, Other; Cinematography and Film/Video Production; Radio and Television Broadcasting Technology/Technician.

Related DOT Jobs—143.062-010 Director of Photography; 143.062-022 Camera Operator; 143.260-010 Optical-Effects-Camera Operator; 143.382-010 Camera Operator, Animation; 976.382-010 Camera Operator, Title.

27-4032.00 Film and Video Editors

- **Education/Training Required: Bachelor's degree**
- **Employed: 15,999**
- **Annual Earnings: $36,910**
- **Growth: 25.8%**
- **Annual Job Openings: 2,000**

Edit motion picture soundtracks, film, and video.

Confer with producers and directors concerning layout or editing approaches needed to increase dramatic or entertainment value of productions. Cut shot sequences to different angles at specific points in scenes, making each individual cut as fluid and seamless as possible. Determine the specific audio and visual effects and music necessary to complete films. Edit films and videotapes to insert music, dialogue, and sound effects; to arrange films into sequences; and to correct errors, using editing equipment. Manipulate plot, score, sound, and graphics to make the parts into a continuous whole, working closely with people in audio, visual, music, optical, and/or special effects departments. Mark frames where a particular shot or piece of sound is to begin or end. Organize and string together raw footage into a continuous whole according to scripts and/or the instructions of directors and producers. Piece sounds together to develop film soundtracks. Review assembled films or edited videotapes on screens or monitors in order to determine if corrections are necessary. Review footage sequence by sequence in order to become familiar with it before assembling it into a final product. Select and combine the most effective shots of each scene in order to form a logical and smoothly running story. Set up and operate computer editing systems, electronic titling systems, video switching equipment, and digital video effects units in order to produce a final product. Study scripts to become familiar with production concepts and requirements. Trim film segments to specified lengths and reassemble segments in sequences that present stories with maximum effect. Collaborate with music editors to select appropriate passages of music and develop production scores. Conduct film screenings for directors and members of production staffs. Develop post-production models for films. Discuss the sound requirements of pictures with sound effects editors. Estimate how long audiences watching comedies will laugh at each gag line or situation in order to space scenes appropriately. Program computerized graphic effects. Record needed sounds or obtain them from sound effects libraries. Supervise and coordinate activities of workers engaged in film editing, assembling, and recording activities. Verify key numbers and time codes on materials.

GOE INFORMATION—Interest Area: 01. Arts, Entertainment, and Media. **Work Group:** 01.08. Media Technology. **Personality Type—**Artistic. Artistic occupations frequently involve working with forms, designs, and patterns. They often require self-expression, and the work can be done without following a clear set of rules. **Work Values—**Creativity; Authority; Recognition; Social Status; Autonomy. **Skills—**Management of Personnel Resources; Monitoring; Operations Analysis; Critical Thinking; Complex Problem Solving; Operation and Control; Speaking; Coordination. **Abilities—***Cognitive:* Visualization; Information Ordering; Speed of Closure; Originality; Fluency of Ideas. *Psychomotor:* Rate Control; Reaction Time; Arm-Hand Steadiness; Control Precision; Response Orientation. *Physical:* Gross Body Coordination; Dynamic Flexibility; Gross Body Equilibrium; Stamina. *Sensory:* Night Vision; Hearing Sensitivity; Sound Localization; Auditory Attention; Far Vision. **General Work Activities—***Information Input:* Getting Information; Identifying Objects, Actions, and Events; Monitoring Processes, Materials, or Surroundings. *Mental Process:* Judging Qualities of Things, Services, or Other People's Work; Thinking Creatively; Organizing, Planning, and Prioritizing. *Work Output:* Controlling Machines and Processes; Handling and Moving Objects; Documenting or Recording Information. *Interacting with Others:* Communicating with Other Workers; Coordinating the Work and Activities of Others; Establishing and Maintaining Relationships. **Physical Work Conditions—**Sitting; Minor Burns, Cuts, Bites, or Stings; Using Hands on Objects, Tools, or Controls; Extremely Bright or Inadequate Lighting; Indoors. **Other Job Characteristics—**Degree of Automation; Pace Determined by Speed of Equipment; Importance of Being Exact or Accurate.

Experience—Job Zone 4. A minimum of two to four years of work-related skill, knowledge, or experience is needed. **Job Preparation:** SVP 7.0 to less than 8.0—two years to less than 10 years. **Knowledge—**Fine Arts; Communications and Media; Computers and Electronics; Telecommunications; Education and Training. **Instructional Programs—**Audiovisual Communications Technologies/Technicians, Other; Cinematography and Film/Video Production; Communications Technology/Technician; Photojournalism; Radio and Television; Radio and Television Broadcasting Technology/Technician.

Related DOT Jobs—962.132-010 Supervising Film-or-Videotape Editor; 962.262-010 Film or Videotape Editor; 962.361-010 Optical-Effects Layout Person; 962.382-014 Sound Cutter.

27-4099.99 Media and Communication Equipment Workers, All Other

- **Education/Training Required: Moderate-term on-the-job training**
- **Employed: No data available.**
- **Annual Earnings: No data available.**
- **Growth: 18.1%**
- **Annual Job Openings: 13,000**

All media and communication equipment workers not listed separately.

No task data available.

GOE INFORMATION—Interest Area: 01. Arts, Entertainment, and Media. **Work Group:** 01.08. Media Technology. **Note:** The Department of Labor has not collected some data for this job, so it has fewer details than the other descriptions.

Instructional Programs—Audiovisual Communications Technologies/Technicians, Other.

Related DOT Jobs—No related DOT jobs.

29-0000

Healthcare Practitioners and Technical Occupations

29-1000 Health Diagnosing and Treating Practitioners

29-1011.00 Chiropractors

- **Education/Training Required: First professional degree**
- **Employed: 49,949**
- **Annual Earnings: $68,420**
- **Growth: 23.4%**
- **Annual Job Openings: 3,000**

Adjust spinal column and other articulations of the body to correct abnormalities of the human body believed to be caused by interference with the nervous system. Examine patient to determine nature and extent of disorder. Manipulate spine or other involved area. May utilize supplementary measures, such as exercise, rest, water, light, heat, and nutritional therapy.

Advise patients about recommended courses of treatment. Consult with and refer patients to appropriate health practitioners when necessary. Counsel patients about nutrition, exercise, sleeping habits, stress management, and other matters. Diagnose health problems by reviewing patients' health and medical histories; questioning, observing and examining patients; and interpreting X rays. Evaluate the functioning of the neuromuscularskeletal system and the spine using systems of chiropractic diagnosis. Maintain accurate case histories of patients. Obtain and record patients' medical histories. Perform a series of manual adjustments to the spine, or other articulations of the body, in order to correct the musculoskeletal system. Suggest and apply the use of supports such as straps, tapes, bandages, and braces if necessary. Analyze X rays in order to locate the sources of patients' difficulties and to rule out fractures or diseases as sources of problems. Arrange for diagnostic X rays to be taken.

GOE INFORMATION—Interest Area: 14. Medical and Health Services. **Work Group:** 14.04. Health Specialties. **Personality Type—**Investigative. Investigative occupations frequently involve working with ideas and require an extensive amount of thinking. These occupations can involve searching for facts and figuring out problems mentally. **Work Values—**Social Service; Responsibility; Autonomy; Recognition; Social Status. **Skills—**Complex Problem Solving; Reading Comprehension; Science; Judgment and Decision Making; Systems Analysis; Critical Thinking; Active Listening; Equipment Selection. **Abilities—***Cognitive:* Problem Sensitivity; Inductive Reasoning; Deductive Reasoning; Oral Comprehension; Perceptual Speed. *Psychomotor:* Manual Dexterity; Finger Dexterity; Speed of Limb Movement; Multilimb Coordination; Wrist-Finger Speed. *Physical:* Dynamic Strength; Static Strength; Explosive Strength; Extent Flexibility; Dynamic Flexibility. *Sensory:* Sound Localization; Night Vision; Glare Sensitivity; Visual Color Discrimination; Near Vision. **General Work Activities—***Information Input:* Identifying Objects, Actions, and Events; Getting Information; Monitoring Processes, Materials, or Surroundings. *Mental Process:* Updating and Using Relevant Knowledge; Making Decisions and Solving Problems; Analyzing Data or Information. *Work Output:* Handling and Moving Objects; Performing General Physical Activities; Documenting or Recording Information. *Interacting with Others:* Assisting and Caring for Others; Establishing and Maintaining Relationships; Communicating with Persons Outside Organization. **Physical Work Conditions—**Disease or Infections; Radiation; Bending or Twisting the Body; Common Protective or Safety Attire; Indoors. **Other Job Characteristics—**Consequence of Error; Importance of Being Exact or Accurate; Degree of Automation.

Experience—Job Zone 5. Extensive skill, knowledge, and experience are needed for these occupations. **Job Preparation:** SVP 8.0 and above—four years to more than 10 years. **Knowledge—**Medicine and Dentistry; Biology; Therapy and Counseling; Customer and Personal Service; English Language. **Instructional Programs—**Chiropractic (DC).

Related DOT Jobs—079.101-010 Chiropractor.

29-1021.00 Dentists, General

- **Education/Training Required: First professional degree**
- **Employed: No data available.**
- **Annual Earnings: $128,910**
- **Growth: 5.7%**
- **Annual Job Openings: 6,000**

Diagnose and treat diseases, injuries, and malformations of teeth and gums and related oral structures. May treat diseases of nerve, pulp, and other dental tissues affecting vitality of teeth.

Administer anesthetics to limit the amount of pain experienced by patients during procedures. Advise and instruct patients regarding preventive dental care, the causes and treatment of dental problems, and oral health care services. Analyze and evaluate dental needs to determine changes and trends in patterns of dental disease. Apply fluoride and sealants to teeth. Bleach, clean or polish teeth to restore natural color. Design, make, and fit prosthodontic appliances such as space maintainers, bridges, and dentures or write fabrication instructions or prescriptions for denturists and dental technicians. Diagnose and treat diseases, injuries, and malformations of teeth, gums, and related oral structures and provide preventive and corrective services. Eliminate irritating margins of fillings and correct occlusions, using dental instruments. Examine teeth, gums, and related tissues, using dental instruments, X rays, and other diagnostic equipment, to evaluate dental health, diagnose diseases or abnormalities and plan appropriate treatments. Fill pulp chamber and canal with endodontic materials. Formulate plan of treatment for patient's teeth and mouth tissue. Manage business, employing and supervising staff and handling paperwork and insurance claims. Perform oral and periodontal surgery on the jaw or mouth. Remove diseased tissue using surgical instruments. Treat exposure of pulp by pulp capping, removal of pulp from pulp chamber, or root canal, using dental instruments. Plan, organize, and maintain dental health programs. Produce and evaluate dental health educational materials. Write prescriptions for antibiotics and other medications. Use air turbine and hand instruments, dental appliances, and surgical implements. Use masks, gloves, and safety glasses to protect themselves and their patients from infectious diseases.

GOE INFORMATION—Interest Area: 14. Medical and Health Services. **Work Group:** 14.03. Dentistry. **Personality Type—**Investigative. Investigative occupations frequently involve working with ideas and require an extensive amount of thinking. These occupations can involve searching for facts and figuring out problems mentally. **Work Values—**Social Service; Social Status; Responsibility; Recognition; Ability Utilization. **Skills—**Reading Comprehension; Science; Critical Thinking; Equipment Selection; Service Orientation; Complex Problem Solving; Operation and Control; Judgment and Decision Making. **Abilities—***Cognitive:* Oral Expression; Problem Sensitivity; Oral Comprehension; Written Expression; Fluency of Ideas. *Psychomotor:* Arm-Hand Steadiness; Control Precision; Finger Dexterity; Manual Dexterity; Reaction Time. *Physical:* None met the criteria. *Sensory:* Visual Color Discrimination; Near Vision. **General Work Activities—***Information Input:* Getting Information; Identifying Objects, Actions, and Events; Monitoring Processes, Materials, or Surroundings. *Mental Process:* Updating and Using Relevant Knowledge; Making Decisions and Solving Problems; Analyzing Data or Information. *Work Output:* Handling and Moving Objects; Documenting or

Recording Information; Controlling Machines and Processes. *Interacting with Others:* Assisting and Caring for Others; Establishing and Maintaining Relationships; Communicating with Persons Outside Organization. **Physical Work Conditions**—Common Protective or Safety Attire; Radiation; Disease or Infections; Indoors; Using Hands on Objects, Tools, or Controls. **Other Job Characteristics**—Importance of Being Exact or Accurate; Consequence of Error; Pace Determined by Speed of Equipment.

Experience—Job Zone 5. Extensive skill, knowledge, and experience are needed for these occupations. **Job Preparation:** SVP 8.0 and above—four years to more than 10 years. **Knowledge**—Medicine and Dentistry; Biology; Chemistry; English Language; Administration and Management. **Instructional Programs**—Advanced General Dentistry (Cert, MS, PhD); Dental Public Health and Education (Cert, MS/MPH, PhD/DPH); Dental Public Health Specialty; Dentistry (DDS, DMD); Pediatric Dentistry/Pedodontics (Cert, MS, PhD); Pedodontics Specialty.

Related DOT Jobs—072.101-010 Dentist; 072.101-014 Endodontist; 072.101-026 Pediatric Dentist; 072.101-030 Periodontist; 072.101-038 Public-Health Dentist.

29-1022.00 Oral and Maxillofacial Surgeons

- Education/Training Required: First professional degree
- Employed: No data available.
- Annual Earnings: $128,910
- Growth: 5.7%
- Annual Job Openings: 6,000

Perform surgery on mouth, jaws, and related head and neck structure to execute difficult and multiple extractions of teeth, to remove tumors and other abnormal growths, to correct abnormal jaw relations by mandibular or maxillary revision, to prepare mouth for insertion of dental prosthesis, or to treat fractured jaws.

Administer general and local anesthetics. Collaborate with other professionals such as restorative dentists and orthodontists in order to plan treatment. Perform surgery on the mouth and jaws in order to treat conditions such as cleft lip and palate and jaw growth problems. Perform surgery to prepare the mouth for dental implants and to aid in the regeneration of deficient bone and gum tissues. Provide emergency treatment of facial injuries, including facial lacerations, intra-oral lacerations, and fractured facial bones. Remove impacted, damaged, and non-restorable teeth. Remove tumors and other abnormal growths of the oral and facial regions, using surgical instruments. Restore form and function by moving skin, bone, nerves, and other tissues from other parts of the body in order to reconstruct the jaws and face. Evaluate the position of the wisdom teeth in order to determine whether problems exist currently or might occur in the future. Perform minor cosmetic procedures, such as chin and cheek-bone enhancements, and minor facial rejuvenation procedures, including the use of Botox and laser technology. Treat infections of the oral cavity, salivary glands, jaws, and neck. Treat problems affecting the oral mucosa, such as mouth ulcers and infections. Treat snoring problems, using laser surgery.

GOE INFORMATION—Interest Area: 14. Medical and Health Services. **Work Group:** 14.03. Dentistry. **Personality Type**—Investigative. Investigative occupations frequently involve working with ideas and require an extensive amount of thinking. These occupations can involve searching for facts and figuring out problems mentally. **Work Values**—Social Service; Social Status; Recognition; Responsibility; Achievement. **Skills**—Science; Reading Comprehension; Judgment and Decision Making; Criti-

cal Thinking; Speaking; Learning Strategies; Complex Problem Solving; Monitoring. **Abilities**—*Cognitive:* Visualization; Problem Sensitivity; Flexibility of Closure; Written Expression; Deductive Reasoning. *Psychomotor:* Arm-Hand Steadiness; Finger Dexterity; Control Precision; Manual Dexterity; Reaction Time. *Physical:* None met the criteria. *Sensory:* Near Vision. **General Work Activities**—*Information Input:* Getting Information; Monitoring Processes, Materials, or Surroundings; Identifying Objects, Actions, and Events. *Mental Process:* Making Decisions and Solving Problems; Updating and Using Relevant Knowledge; Analyzing Data or Information. *Work Output:* Handling and Moving Objects; Documenting or Recording Information; Controlling Machines and Processes. *Interacting with Others:* Assisting and Caring for Others; Providing Consultation and Advice to Others; Establishing and Maintaining Relationships. **Physical Work Conditions**—Common Protective or Safety Attire; Disease or Infections; Indoors; Using Hands on Objects, Tools, or Controls; Radiation. **Other Job Characteristics**—Importance of Being Exact or Accurate; Consequence of Error; Pace Determined by Speed of Equipment.

Experience—Job Zone 5. Extensive skill, knowledge, and experience are needed for these occupations. **Job Preparation:** SVP 8.0 and above—four years to more than 10 years. **Knowledge**—Medicine and Dentistry; Biology; Chemistry; Therapy and Counseling; Psychology. **Instructional Programs**—Dental/Oral Surgery Specialty; Oral/Maxillofacial Surgery (Cert, MS, PhD).

Related DOT Jobs—072.101-018 Oral and Maxillofacial Surgeon.

29-1023.00 Orthodontists

- Education/Training Required: First professional degree
- Employed: No data available.
- Annual Earnings: $128,910
- Growth: 5.7%
- Annual Job Openings: 6,000

Examine, diagnose, and treat dental malocclusions and oral cavity anomalies. Design and fabricate appliances to realign teeth and jaws to produce and maintain normal function and to improve appearance.

Adjust dental appliances periodically in order to produce and maintain normal function. Coordinate orthodontic services with other dental and medical services. Design and fabricate appliances, such as space maintainers, retainers, and labial and lingual arch wires. Diagnose teeth and jaw or other dental-facial abnormalities. Examine patients in order to assess abnormalities of jaw development, tooth position, and other dental-facial structures. Fit dental appliances in patients' mouths in order to alter the position and relationship of teeth and jaws and to realign teeth. Prepare diagnostic and treatment records. Provide patients with proposed treatment plans and cost estimates. Study diagnostic records such as medical/dental histories, plaster models of the teeth, photos of a patient's face and teeth, and X rays in order to develop patient treatment plans. Instruct dental officers and technical assistants in orthodontic procedures and techniques.

GOE INFORMATION—Interest Area: 14. Medical and Health Services. **Work Group:** 14.03. Dentistry. **Personality Type**—Investigative. Investigative occupations frequently involve working with ideas and require an extensive amount of thinking. These occupations can involve searching for facts and figuring out problems mentally. **Work Values**—Social Service; Social Status; Responsibility; Recognition; Ability Utilization. **Skills**—Science; Technology Design; Reading Comprehension; Equipment Selection; Complex Problem Solving; Critical Thinking; Operations Analysis; Service Orientation. **Abilities**—*Cognitive:* Problem

Sensitivity; Fluency of Ideas; Selective Attention; Information Ordering; Oral Expression. *Psychomotor:* Arm-Hand Steadiness; Control Precision; Manual Dexterity; Finger Dexterity; Reaction Time. *Physical:* None met the criteria. *Sensory:* None met the criteria. **General Work Activities**—*Information Input:* Getting Information; Identifying Objects, Actions, and Events; Monitoring Processes, Materials, or Surroundings. *Mental Process:* Updating and Using Relevant Knowledge; Making Decisions and Solving Problems; Judging Qualities of Things, Services, or Other People's Work. *Work Output:* Handling and Moving Objects; Documenting or Recording Information; Drafting and Specifying Technical Devices. *Interacting with Others:* Assisting and Caring for Others; Establishing and Maintaining Relationships; Communicating with Other Workers. **Physical Work Conditions**—Common Protective or Safety Attire; Disease or Infections; Indoors; Radiation; Standing. **Other Job Characteristics**—Importance of Being Exact or Accurate; Consequence of Error; Importance of Repeating Same Tasks.

Experience—Job Zone 5. Extensive skill, knowledge, and experience are needed for these occupations. **Job Preparation:** SVP 8.0 and above—four years to more than 10 years. **Knowledge**—Medicine and Dentistry; Biology; Therapy and Counseling; Customer and Personal Service; Chemistry. **Instructional Programs**—Orthodontics Specialty; Orthodontics/Orthodontology (Cert, MS, PhD).

Related DOT Jobs—072.101-022 Orthodontist.

29-1024.00 Prosthodontists

- ● **Education/Training Required: First professional degree**
- ● **Employed: No data available.**
- ● **Annual Earnings: $128,910**
- ● **Growth: 5.7%**
- ● **Annual Job Openings: 6,000**

Construct oral prostheses to replace missing teeth and other oral structures to correct natural and acquired deformation of mouth and jaws; to restore and maintain oral function, such as chewing and speaking; and to improve appearance.

Collaborate with general dentists, specialists, and other health professionals in order to develop solutions to dental and oral health concerns. Design and fabricate dental prostheses or supervise dental technicians and laboratory bench workers who construct the devices. Fit prostheses to patients, making any necessary adjustments and modifications. Measure and take impressions of patients' jaws and teeth in order to determine the shape and size of dental prostheses, using face bows, dental articulators, recording devices, and other materials. Replace missing teeth and associated oral structures with permanent fixtures, such as crowns and bridges, or removable fixtures, such as dentures. Restore function and aesthetics to traumatic injury victims or to individuals with diseases or birth defects. Bleach discolored teeth in order to brighten and whiten them. Place veneers onto teeth in order to conceal defects. Repair, reline, and/or rebase dentures. Treat facial pain and jaw joint problems. Use bonding technology on the surface of the teeth in order to change tooth shape or to close gaps.

GOE INFORMATION—**Interest Area:** 14. Medical and Health Services. **Work Group:** 14.03. Dentistry. **Personality Type**—Investigative. Investigative occupations frequently involve working with ideas and require an extensive amount of thinking. These occupations can involve searching for facts and figuring out problems mentally. **Work Values**—Social Service; Responsibility; Ability Utilization; Achievement; Autonomy. **Skills**—Technology Design; Science; Equipment Selection; Reading Comprehension; Critical Thinking; Mathematics; Judgment and Decision Making; Complex Problem Solving. **Abilities**—*Cognitive:* Visualiza-

tion; Fluency of Ideas; Information Ordering. *Psychomotor:* Finger Dexterity; Arm-Hand Steadiness; Control Precision; Wrist-Finger Speed. *Physical:* None met the criteria. *Sensory:* Near Vision; Visual Color Discrimination. **General Work Activities**—*Information Input:* Getting Information; Identifying Objects, Actions, and Events; Monitoring Processes, Materials, or Surroundings. *Mental Process:* Updating and Using Relevant Knowledge; Analyzing Data or Information; Making Decisions and Solving Problems. *Work Output:* Handling and Moving Objects; Documenting or Recording Information; Controlling Machines and Processes. *Interacting with Others:* Assisting and Caring for Others; Communicating with Persons Outside Organization; Establishing and Maintaining Relationships. **Physical Work Conditions**—Common Protective or Safety Attire; Indoors; Sitting; Bending or Twisting the Body; Disease or Infections. **Other Job Characteristics**—Importance of Being Exact or Accurate; Consequence of Error; Importance of Repeating Same Tasks.

Experience—Job Zone 5. Extensive skill, knowledge, and experience are needed for these occupations. **Job Preparation:** SVP 8.0 and above—four years to more than 10 years. **Knowledge**—Medicine and Dentistry; Biology; Chemistry; Design; English Language. **Instructional Programs**—Prosthodontics Specialty; Prosthodontics/Prosthodontology (Cert, MS, PhD).

Related DOT Jobs—072.101-034 Prosthodontist.

29-1029.99 Dentists, All Other Specialists

- ● **Education/Training Required: First professional degree**
- ● **Employed: No data available.**
- ● **Annual Earnings: No data available.**
- ● **Growth: 5.7%**
- ● **Annual Job Openings: 6,000**

All dentists not listed separately.

No task data available.

GOE INFORMATION—**Interest Area:** 14. Medical and Health Services. **Work Group:** 14.03. Dentistry. **Note:** The Department of Labor has not collected some data for this job, so it has fewer details than the other descriptions.

Instructional Programs—Advanced/Graduate Dentistry and Oral Sciences, Other; Dental Clinical Sciences, General (MS, PhD); Dental Materials (MS, PhD); Dental Public Health Specialty; Dental Residency Program, Other; Endodontics Specialty; Endodontics/Endodontology (Cert, MS, PhD); Oral Biology and Oral Pathology (MS, PhD); Oral Pathology Specialty; Periodontics Specialty; Periodontics/Periodontology (Cert, MS, PhD).

Related DOT Jobs—072.061-010 Oral Pathologist.

29-1031.00 Dietitians and Nutritionists

- ● **Education/Training Required: Bachelor's degree**
- ● **Employed: 48,740**
- ● **Annual Earnings: $40,410**
- ● **Growth: 15.2%**
- ● **Annual Job Openings: 5,000**

Plan and conduct food service or nutritional programs to assist in the promotion of health and control of disease. May supervise activities of a department providing quantity food services, counsel individuals, or conduct nutritional research.

Assess nutritional needs, diet restrictions, and current health plans to develop and implement dietary-care plans and provide nutritional counseling. Consult with physicians and health care personnel to determine nutritional needs and diet restrictions of patient or client. Advise patients and their families on nutritional principles, dietary plans and diet modifications, and food selection and preparation. Counsel individuals and groups on basic rules of good nutrition, healthy eating habits, and nutrition monitoring to improve their quality of life. Monitor food service operations to ensure conformance to nutritional, safety, sanitation, and quality standards. Coordinate recipe development and standardization and develop new menus for independent food service operations. Develop policies for food service or nutritional programs to assist in health promotion and disease control. Inspect meals served for conformance to prescribed diets and standards of palatability and appearance. Develop curriculum and prepare manuals, visual aids, course outlines, and other materials used in teaching. Prepare and administer budgets for food, equipment, and supplies. Purchase food in accordance with health and safety codes. Select, train, and supervise workers who plan, prepare, and serve meals. Manage quantity food service departments or clinical and community nutrition services. Coordinate diet counseling services. Advise food service managers and organizations on sanitation, safety procedures, menu development, budgeting, and planning to assist with the establishment, operation, and evaluation of food service facilities and nutrition programs. Organize, develop, analyze, test, and prepare special meals such as low-fat, low-cholesterol, and chemical-free meals. Plan, conduct, and evaluate dietary, nutritional, and epidemiological research. Plan and conduct training programs in dietetics, nutrition, and institutional management and administration for medical students, health-care personnel, and the general public. Make recommendations regarding public policy, such as nutrition labeling, food fortification, and nutrition standards for school programs. Write research reports and other publications to document and communicate research findings. Plan and prepare grant proposals to request program funding. Test new food products and equipment. Confer with design, building, and equipment personnel to plan for construction and remodeling of food service units.

GOE INFORMATION—Interest Area: 14. Medical and Health Services. **Work Group:** 14.08. Health Protection and Promotion. **Personality Type**—Investigative. Investigative occupations frequently involve working with ideas and require an extensive amount of thinking. These occupations can involve searching for facts and figuring out problems mentally. **Work Values**—Social Service; Authority; Creativity; Ability Utilization; Achievement. **Skills**—Instructing; Social Perceptiveness; Speaking; Learning Strategies; Writing; Reading Comprehension; Active Listening; Critical Thinking. **Abilities**—*Cognitive:* Category Flexibility; Written Expression; Deductive Reasoning; Inductive Reasoning; Originality. *Psychomotor:* None met the criteria. *Physical:* Trunk Strength. *Sensory:* Speech Recognition; Speech Clarity; Far Vision; Near Vision; Visual Color Discrimination. **General Work Activities**—*Information Input:* Identifying Objects, Actions, and Events; Getting Information; Monitoring Processes, Materials, or Surroundings. *Mental Process:* Updating and Using Relevant Knowledge; Organizing, Planning, and Prioritizing; Analyzing Data or Information. *Work Output:* Documenting or Recording Information; Interacting with Computers; Handling and Moving Objects. *Interacting with Others:* Communicating with Other Workers; Establishing and Maintaining Relationships; Teaching Others. **Physical Work Conditions**—Disease or Infections; Indoors; Walking or Running; Minor Burns, Cuts, Bites, or Stings. **Other Job Characteristics**—Importance of Repeating Same Tasks; Importance of Being Exact or Accurate; Degree of Automation.

Experience—Job Zone 5. Extensive skill, knowledge, and experience are needed for these occupations. **Job Preparation:** SVP 7.0 to less than 8.0—two years to less than 10 years. **Knowledge**—Food Production; Education and Training; Therapy and Counseling; Customer and Personal Service; Sociology and Anthropology. **Instructional Programs**—Clinical Nutrition/Nutritionist; Dietetics and Clinical Nutrition Services, Other; Dietetics/Dietitian (RD); Foods, Nutrition, and Related Services, Other; Foods, Nutrition, and Wellness Studies, General; Foodservice Systems Administration/Management; Human Nutrition; Nutrition Sciences.

Related DOT Jobs—077.061-010 Dietitian, Research; 077.117-010 Dietitian, Chief; 077.127-010 Community Dietitian; 077.127-014 Dietitian, Clinical; 077.127-018 Dietitian, Consultant; 077.127-022 Dietitian, Teaching.

29-1041.00 Optometrists

- **Education/Training Required: First professional degree**
- **Employed: 31,417**
- **Annual Earnings: $85,650**
- **Growth: 18.7%**
- **Annual Job Openings: 1,000**

Diagnose, manage, and treat conditions and diseases of the human eye and visual system. Examine eyes and visual system, diagnose problems or impairments, prescribe corrective lenses, and provide treatment. May prescribe therapeutic drugs to treat specific eye conditions.

Examine eyes, using observation, instruments, and pharmaceutical agents, to determine visual acuity and perception, focus, and coordination and to diagnose diseases and other abnormalities such as glaucoma or color blindness. Analyze test results and develop a treatment plan. Prescribe, supply, fit, and adjust eyeglasses, contact lenses, and other vision aids. Prescribe medications to treat eye diseases if state laws permit. Educate and counsel patients on contact lens care, visual hygiene, lighting arrangements, and safety factors. Consult with and refer patients to ophthalmologist or other health care practitioner if additional medical treatment is determined necessary. Remove foreign bodies from the eye. Provide patients undergoing eye surgeries, such as cataract and laser vision correction, with pre- and post-operative care. Prescribe therapeutic procedures to correct or conserve vision. Provide vision therapy and low vision rehabilitation.

GOE INFORMATION—Interest Area: 14. Medical and Health Services. **Work Group:** 14.04. Health Specialties. **Personality Type**—Investigative. Investigative occupations frequently involve working with ideas and require an extensive amount of thinking. These occupations can involve searching for facts and figuring out problems mentally. **Work Values**—Social Service; Responsibility; Social Status; Recognition; Ability Utilization. **Skills**—Active Listening; Judgment and Decision Making; Reading Comprehension; Science; Critical Thinking; Management of Personnel Resources; Complex Problem Solving; Service Orientation. **Abilities**—*Cognitive:* Inductive Reasoning; Problem Sensitivity; Flexibility of Closure; Speed of Closure; Deductive Reasoning. *Psychomotor:* Arm-Hand Steadiness; Finger Dexterity; Control Precision; Manual Dexterity; Multilimb Coordination. *Physical:* Trunk Strength. *Sensory:* Near Vision; Depth Perception; Far Vision; Speech Recognition; Visual Color Discrimination. **General Work Activities**—*Information Input:* Identifying Objects, Actions, and Events; Getting Information; Monitoring Processes, Materials, or Surroundings. *Mental Process:* Making Decisions and Solving Problems; Evaluating Information Against Standards; Processing Information. *Work Output:* Handling and Moving Objects; Documenting or Recording Information; Interacting with Computers. *Interacting with Others:* Performing for or Working with the Public; Establishing and Maintaining Relationships; Teaching Others. **Physical Work Condi-**

tions—Indoors; Specialized Protective or Safety Attire; Sitting; Disease or Infections. **Other Job Characteristics**—Importance of Being Exact or Accurate; Consequence of Error; Degree of Automation.

Experience—Job Zone 5. Extensive skill, knowledge, and experience are needed for these occupations. **Job Preparation:** SVP 7.0 to less than 8.0—two years to less than 10 years. **Knowledge**—Medicine and Dentistry; Customer and Personal Service; Biology; Psychology; Personnel and Human Resources. **Instructional Programs**—Optometry (OD).

Related DOT Jobs—079.101-018 Optometrist.

29-1051.00 Pharmacists

- **Education/Training Required: First professional degree**
- **Employed: 216,865**
- **Annual Earnings: $74,890**
- **Growth: 24.3%**
- **Annual Job Openings: 20,000**

Compound and dispense medications following prescriptions issued by physicians, dentists, or other authorized medical practitioners.

Assay radiopharmaceuticals, verify rates of disintegration, and calculate the volume required to produce the desired results to ensure proper dosages. Assess the identity, strength, and purity of medications. Compound and dispense medications as prescribed by doctors and dentists by calculating, weighing, measuring, and mixing ingredients or oversee these activities. Prepare sterile solutions and infusions for use in surgical procedures, emergency rooms, or patients' homes. Review prescriptions to assure accuracy, to ascertain the needed ingredients, and to evaluate their suitability. Advise customers on the selection of medication brands, medical equipment, and health care supplies. Analyze prescribing trends to monitor patient compliance and to prevent excessive usage or harmful interactions. Collaborate with other health care professionals to plan, monitor, review, and evaluate the quality and effectiveness of drugs and drug regimens, providing advice on drug applications and characteristics. Compound radioactive substances and reagents to prepare radiopharmaceuticals, following radiopharmacy laboratory procedures. Maintain records, such as pharmacy files, patient profiles, charge system files, inventories, control records for radioactive nuclei, and registries of poisons, narcotics, and controlled drugs. Manage pharmacy operations, hiring and supervising staff, performing administrative duties, and buying and selling non-pharmaceutical merchandise. Order and purchase pharmaceutical supplies, medical supplies, and drugs, maintaining stock and storing and handling it properly. Offer health promotion and prevention activities; for example, training people to use devices such as blood pressure or diabetes monitors. Plan, implement, and maintain procedures for mixing, packaging, and labeling pharmaceuticals according to policy and legal requirements to ensure quality, security, and proper disposal. Provide information and advice regarding drug interactions, side effects, dosage, and proper medication storage. Provide specialized services to help patients manage conditions such as diabetes, asthma, smoking cessation, or high blood pressure. Publish educational information for other pharmacists, doctors, and/or patients. Refer patients to other health professionals and agencies when appropriate. Research and develop drug products and drug therapies, such as radiopharmaceuticals or therapies for psychiatric disorders. Teach pharmacy students serving as interns in preparation for their graduation or licensure. Work for pharmaceutical firms in production, marketing, quality control, or sales. Work in hospitals, in clinics, or for HMOs, dispensing prescriptions, serving as a medical team consultants, or specializing in specific drug therapy areas such as oncology or nuclear pharmacotherapy.

GOE INFORMATION—**Interest Area:** 14. Medical and Health Services. **Work Group:** 14.02. Medicine and Surgery. **Personality Type**—Investigative. Investigative occupations frequently involve working with ideas and require an extensive amount of thinking. These occupations can involve searching for facts and figuring out problems mentally. **Work Values**—Social Service; Authority; Social Status; Ability Utilization; Good Working Conditions. **Skills**—Science; Management of Financial Resources; Instructing; Mathematics; Writing; Reading Comprehension; Management of Personnel Resources; Systems Analysis. **Abilities**—*Cognitive:* Oral Expression; Mathematical Reasoning; Oral Comprehension; Written Expression; Information Ordering. *Psychomotor:* Control Precision. *Physical:* None met the criteria. *Sensory:* Speech Recognition. **General Work Activities**—*Information Input:* Identifying Objects, Actions, and Events; Getting Information; Monitoring Processes, Materials, or Surroundings. *Mental Process:* Updating and Using Relevant Knowledge; Processing Information; Analyzing Data or Information. *Work Output:* Handling and Moving Objects; Documenting or Recording Information; Interacting with Computers. *Interacting with Others:* Teaching Others; Communicating with Other Workers; Providing Consultation and Advice to Others. **Physical Work Conditions**—Radiation; Indoors; Disease or Infections; Using Hands on Objects, Tools, or Controls; Standing. **Other Job Characteristics**—Consequence of Error; Importance of Being Exact or Accurate; Pace Determined by Speed of Equipment.

Experience—Job Zone 4. A minimum of two to four years of work-related skill, knowledge, or experience is needed. **Job Preparation:** SVP 7.0 to less than 8.0—two years to less than 10 years. **Knowledge**—Chemistry; Medicine and Dentistry; Biology; Personnel and Human Resources; Education and Training. **Instructional Programs**—Clinical and Industrial Drug Development (MS, PhD); Clinical, Hospital, and Managed Care Pharmacy (MS, PhD); Industrial and Physical Pharmacy and Cosmetic Sciences (MS, PhD); Medicinal and Pharmaceutical Chemistry (MS, PhD); Natural Products Chemistry and Pharmacognosy (MS, PhD); Pharmaceutics and Drug Design (MS, PhD); Pharmacoeconomics/Pharmaceutical Economics (MS, PhD); Pharmacy (PharmD [USA] PharmD, BS/BPharm [Canada]); Pharmacy Administration and Pharmacy Policy and Regulatory Affairs (MS, PhD); Pharmacy, Pharmaceutical Sciences, and Administration, Other.

Related DOT Jobs—074.161-010 Pharmacist; 074.161-014 Radiopharmacist; 074.167-010 Director, Pharmacy Services.

29-1061.00 Anesthesiologists

- **Education/Training Required: First professional degree**
- **Employed: No data available.**
- **Annual Earnings: Greater than $145,600**
- **Growth: 17.9%**
- **Annual Job Openings: 27,000**

Administer anesthetics during surgery or other medical procedures.

Administer anesthetic or sedation during medical procedures, using local, intravenous, spinal, or caudal methods. Confer with other medical professionals to determine type and method of anesthetic or sedation to render patient insensible to pain. Coordinate administration of anesthetics with surgeons during operation. Decide when patients have recovered or stabilized enough to be sent to another room or ward or to be sent home following outpatient surgery. Examine patient, obtain medical history, and use diagnostic tests to determine risk during surgical, obstetrical, and other medical procedures. Monitor patient before, during, and after anesthesia and counteract adverse reactions or complications. Record type and amount of anesthesia and patient condition throughout procedure. Conduct medical research to aid in controlling and curing disease, to investigate new medications, and to develop and test new medical techniques. Coordinate and direct work of nurses, medical technicians, and other health care providers. Diagnose illnesses, using examinations, tests, and reports. Inform students and staff of types and methods of anesthesia administration, signs of complications, and emergency methods to counteract reactions. Manage anesthesiological services, coordinating them with other medical activities and formulating plans and procedures. Order laboratory tests, X rays and other diagnostic procedures. Position patient on operating table to maximize patient comfort and surgical accessibility. Provide and maintain life support and airway management and help prepare patients for emergency surgery. Provide medical care and consultation in many settings, prescribing medication and treatment and referring patients for surgery. Instruct individuals and groups on ways to preserve health and prevent disease. Schedule and maintain use of surgical suite, including operating, wash-up, waiting rooms, and anesthetic and sterilizing equipment.

GOE INFORMATION—Interest Area: 14. Medical and Health Services. **Work Group:** 14.02. Medicine and Surgery. **Personality Type**—Investigative. Investigative occupations frequently involve working with ideas and require an extensive amount of thinking. These occupations can involve searching for facts and figuring out problems mentally. **Work Values**—Social Service; Social Status; Ability Utilization; Compensation; Achievement. **Skills**—Operation Monitoring; Operation and Control; Equipment Selection; Reading Comprehension; Judgment and Decision Making; Critical Thinking; Complex Problem Solving; Speaking. **Abilities**—*Cognitive:* Problem Sensitivity; Oral Expression; Time Sharing; Deductive Reasoning; Flexibility of Closure. *Psychomotor:* Control Precision; Reaction Time; Response Orientation; Arm-Hand Steadiness. *Physical:* None met the criteria. *Sensory:* Speech Clarity. **General Work Activities**—*Information Input:* Monitoring Processes, Materials, or Surroundings; Getting Information; Identifying Objects, Actions, and Events. *Mental Process:* Updating and Using Relevant Knowledge; Making Decisions and Solving Problems; Analyzing Data or Information. *Work Output:* Controlling Machines and Processes; Handling and Moving Objects; Documenting or Recording Information. *Interacting with Others:* Assisting and Caring for Others; Communicating with Other Workers; Interpreting Meaning of Information for Others. **Physical Work Conditions**—Disease or Infections; Common Protective or Safety Attire; Indoors; Radiation; Hazardous Conditions. **Other Job Characteristics**—Consequence of Error; Importance of Being Exact or Accurate; Degree of Automation.

Experience—Job Zone 5. Extensive skill, knowledge, and experience are needed for these occupations. **Job Preparation:** SVP 8.0 and above—four years to more than 10 years. **Knowledge**—Medicine and Dentistry; Biology; Chemistry; English Language; Psychology. **Instructional Programs**—Anesthesiology; Critical Care Anesthesiology.

Related DOT Jobs—070.101-010 Anesthesiologist.

29-1062.00 Family and General Practitioners

- **Education/Training Required: First professional degree**
- **Employed: No data available.**
- **Annual Earnings: $118,390**
- **Growth: 17.9%**
- **Annual Job Openings: 27,000**

Diagnose, treat, and help prevent diseases and injuries that commonly occur in the general population.

Advise patients and community members concerning diet, activity, hygiene, and disease prevention. Collect, record, and maintain patient information, such as medical history, reports, and examination results.

Explain procedures and discuss test results or prescribed treatments with patients. Monitor the patients' conditions and progress and re-evaluate treatments as necessary. Order, perform, and interpret tests and analyze records, reports, and examination information to diagnose patients' condition. Prescribe or administer treatment, therapy, medication, vaccination, and other specialized medical care to treat or prevent illness, disease, or injury. Refer patients to medical specialists or other practitioners when necessary. Conduct research to study anatomy and develop or test medications, treatments, or procedures to prevent or control disease or injury. Coordinate work with nurses, social workers, rehabilitation therapists, pharmacists, psychologists, and other health care providers. Deliver babies. Direct and coordinate activities of nurses, students, assistants, specialists, therapists, and other medical staff. Operate on patients to remove, repair, or improve functioning of diseased or injured body parts and systems. Plan, implement, or administer health programs or standards in hospital, business, or community for information, prevention, or treatment of injury or illness. Prepare reports for government or management of birth, death, and disease statistics; workforce evaluations; or medical status of individuals.

GOE INFORMATION—Interest Area: 14. Medical and Health Services. **Work Group:** 14.02. Medicine and Surgery. **Personality Type**—Investigative. Investigative occupations frequently involve working with ideas and require an extensive amount of thinking. These occupations can involve searching for facts and figuring out problems mentally. **Work Values**—Social Service; Social Status; Recognition; Ability Utilization; Responsibility. **Skills**—Science; Reading Comprehension; Systems Evaluation; Complex Problem Solving; Judgment and Decision Making; Systems Analysis; Mathematics; Management of Personnel Resources. **Abilities**—*Cognitive:* Inductive Reasoning; Oral Expression; Speed of Closure; Problem Sensitivity; Written Expression. *Psychomotor:* Manual Dexterity; Arm-Hand Steadiness; Finger Dexterity; Multilimb Coordination; Response Orientation. *Physical:* Static Strength; Dynamic Strength; Gross Body Equilibrium; Stamina; Dynamic Flexibility. *Sensory:* Speech Clarity; Visual Color Discrimination; Auditory Attention; Near Vision; Hearing Sensitivity. **General Work Activities**—*Information Input:* Getting Information; Monitoring Processes, Materials, or Surroundings; Identifying Objects, Actions, and Events. *Mental Process:* Analyzing Data or Information; Updating and Using Relevant Knowledge; Making Decisions and Solving Problems. *Work Output:* Documenting or Recording Information; Performing General Physical Activities; Handling and Moving Objects. *Interacting with Others:* Assisting and Caring for Others; Communicating with Persons Outside Organization; Performing for or Working with the Public. **Physical Work Conditions**—Disease or Infections; Common Protective or Safety Attire; Radiation; Indoors; Walking or Running. **Other Job Characteristics**—Consequence of Error; Importance of Being Exact or Accurate; Degree of Automation.

Experience—Job Zone 5. Extensive skill, knowledge, and experience are needed for these occupations. **Job Preparation:** SVP 8.0 and above—four years to more than 10 years. **Knowledge**—Medicine and Dentistry; Biology; Therapy and Counseling; Chemistry; Administration and Management. **Instructional Programs**—Family Medicine; Medicine (MD); Osteopathic Medicine/Osteopathy (DO).

Related DOT Jobs—070.101-022 General Practitioner; 070.101-026 Family Practitioner; 070.101-046 Public Health Physician; 070.101-078 Physician, Occupational; 070.101-082 Police Surgeon.

29-1063.00 Internists, General

- **Education/Training Required: First professional degree**
- **Employed: No data available.**
- **Annual Earnings: Greater than $145,600**
- **Growth: 17.9%**
- **Annual Job Openings: 27,000**

Diagnose and provide non-surgical treatment of diseases and injuries of internal organ systems. Provide care mainly for adults who have a wide range of problems associated with the internal organs.

Advise patients and community members concerning diet, activity, hygiene, and disease prevention. Analyze records, reports, test results, or examination information to diagnose medical condition of patient. Collect, record, and maintain patient information, such as medical history, reports, and examination results. Make diagnoses when different illnesses occur together or in situations where the diagnosis may be obscure. Explain procedures and discuss test results or prescribed treatments with patients. Immunize patients to protect them from preventable diseases. Manage and treat common health problems, such as infections, influenza, and pneumonia, as well as serious, chronic, and complex illnesses, in adolescents, adults, and the elderly. Monitor patients' conditions and progress and re-evaluate treatments as necessary. Prescribe or administer medication, therapy, and other specialized medical care to treat or prevent illness, disease, or injury. Provide and manage long-term, comprehensive medical care, including diagnosis and non-surgical treatment of diseases, for adult patients in an office or hospital. Refer patient to medical specialist or other practitioner when necessary. Treat internal disorders, such as hypertension, heart disease, diabetes, and problems of the lung, brain, kidney, and gastrointestinal tract. Advise surgeon of a patient's risk status and recommend appropriate intervention to minimize risk. Conduct research to develop or test medications, treatments, or procedures to prevent or control disease or injury. Direct and coordinate activities of nurses, students, assistants, specialists, therapists, and other medical staff. Operate on patients to remove, repair, or improve functioning of diseased or injured body parts and systems. Provide consulting services to other doctors caring for patients with special or difficult problems. Plan, implement, or administer health programs in hospitals, businesses, or communities for prevention and treatment of injuries or illnesses. Prepare government or organizational reports on birth, death, and disease statistics; workforce evaluations; or the medical status of individuals.

GOE INFORMATION—Interest Area: 14. Medical and Health Services. **Work Group:** 14.02. Medicine and Surgery. **Personality Type—**Investigative. Investigative occupations frequently involve working with ideas and require an extensive amount of thinking. These occupations can involve searching for facts and figuring out problems mentally. **Work Values—**Social Service; Social Status; Recognition; Ability Utilization; Responsibility. **Skills—**Science; Reading Comprehension; Systems Evaluation; Complex Problem Solving; Judgment and Decision Making; Systems Analysis; Mathematics; Management of Personnel Resources. **Abilities—***Cognitive:* Inductive Reasoning; Oral Expression; Speed of Closure; Problem Sensitivity; Written Expression. *Psychomotor:* Manual Dexterity; Arm-Hand Steadiness; Finger Dexterity; Multilimb Coordination; Response Orientation. *Physical:* Static Strength; Dynamic Strength; Gross Body Equilibrium; Stamina; Dynamic Flexibility. *Sensory:* Speech Clarity; Visual Color Discrimination; Auditory Attention; Near Vision; Hearing Sensitivity. **General Work Activities—***Information Input:* Getting Information; Monitoring Processes, Materials, or Surroundings; Identifying Objects, Actions, and Events. *Mental Process:* Analyzing Data or Information; Updating and Using Relevant Knowledge; Making Decisions and Solving Problems. *Work Output:* Documenting or Recording Information; Performing General Physical Activities; Handling and Moving Objects. *Interacting with Others:* Assisting and Caring for Others; Communicating with Persons Outside Organization; Performing for or Working with the Public. **Physical Work Conditions—**Disease or Infections; Common Protective or Safety Attire; Radiation; Indoors; Walking or Running. **Other Job Characteristics—**Consequence of Error; Importance of Being Exact or Accurate; Degree of Automation.

Experience—Job Zone 5. Extensive skill, knowledge, and experience are needed for these occupations. **Job Preparation:** SVP 8.0 and above—four years to more than 10 years. **Knowledge—**Medicine and Dentistry; Biology; Therapy and Counseling; Chemistry; Administration and Management. **Instructional Programs—**Cardiology; Critical Care Medicine; Endocrinology and Metabolism; Gastroenterology; Geriatric Medicine; Hematology; Infectious Disease; Internal Medicine; Nephrology; Neurology; Nuclear Medicine; Oncology; Pulmonary Disease; Rheumatology.

Related DOT Jobs—070.101-042 Internist.

29-1064.00 Obstetricians and Gynecologists

- **Education/Training Required: First professional degree**
- **Employed: No data available.**
- **Annual Earnings: Greater than $145,600**
- **Growth: 17.9%**
- **Annual Job Openings: 27,000**

Diagnose, treat, and help prevent diseases of women, especially those affecting the reproductive system and the process of childbirth.

Advise patients and community members concerning diet, activity, hygiene, and disease prevention. Analyze records, reports, test results, or examination information to diagnose medical condition of patient. Care for and treat women during prenatal, natal, and post-natal periods. Collect, record, and maintain patient information, such as medical histories, reports, and examination results. Explain procedures and discuss test results or prescribed treatments with patients. Monitor patients' condition and progress and re-evaluate treatments as necessary. Perform cesarean sections or other surgical procedures as needed to preserve patients' health and deliver babies safely. Prescribe or administer therapy, medication, and other specialized medical care to treat or prevent illness, disease, or injury. Refer patient to medical specialist or other practitioner when necessary. Treat diseases of female organs. Conduct research to develop or test medications, treatments, or procedures to prevent or control disease or injury. Consult with, or provide consulting services to, other physicians. Direct and coordinate activities of nurses, students, assistants, specialists, therapists, and other medical staff. Plan, implement, or administer health programs in hospitals, businesses, or communities for prevention and treatment of injuries or illnesses. Prepare government and organizational reports on birth, death, and disease statistics; workforce evaluations; or the medical status of individuals.

GOE INFORMATION—Interest Area: 14. Medical and Health Services. **Work Group:** 14.02. Medicine and Surgery. **Personality Type—**Investigative. Investigative occupations frequently involve working with ideas and require an extensive amount of thinking. These occupations can involve searching for facts and figuring out problems mentally. **Work Values—**Social Service; Social Status; Recognition; Ability Utilization; Responsibility. **Skills—**Science; Reading Comprehension; Systems Evaluation; Complex Problem Solving; Judgment and Decision Making; Systems Analysis; Mathematics; Management of Personnel Resources. **Abilities—***Cognitive:* Inductive Reasoning; Oral Expression; Speed of Closure; Problem Sensitivity; Written Expression. *Psychomotor:* Manual Dexterity; Arm-Hand Steadiness; Finger Dexterity; Multilimb Coordination; Response Orientation. *Physical:* Static Strength; Dynamic Strength; Gross Body Equilibrium; Stamina; Dynamic Flexibility. *Sensory:* Speech Clarity; Visual Color Discrimination; Auditory Attention; Near Vision; Hearing Sensitivity. **General Work Activities—***Information Input:* Getting Information; Monitoring Processes, Materials, or Surroundings; Identifying Objects, Actions, and Events. *Mental Process:* Analyzing Data or

Information; Making Decisions and Solving Problems; Updating and Using Relevant Knowledge. *Work Output:* Documenting or Recording Information; Performing General Physical Activities; Handling and Moving Objects. *Interacting with Others:* Assisting and Caring for Others; Communicating with Persons Outside Organization; Performing for or Working with the Public. **Physical Work Conditions**—Disease or Infections; Common Protective or Safety Attire; Radiation; Indoors; Walking or Running. **Other Job Characteristics**—Consequence of Error; Importance of Being Exact or Accurate; Degree of Automation.

Experience—Job Zone 5. Extensive skill, knowledge, and experience are needed for these occupations. **Job Preparation:** SVP 8.0 and above—four years to more than 10 years. **Knowledge**—Medicine and Dentistry; Biology; Therapy and Counseling; Chemistry; Administration and Management. **Instructional Programs**—Neonatal-Perinatal Medicine; Obstetrics and Gynecology.

Related DOT Jobs—070.101-034 Gynecologist; 070.101-054 Obstetrician.

29-1065.00 *Pediatricians, General*

- Education/Training Required: First professional degree
- Employed: No data available.
- Annual Earnings: $126,430
- Growth: 17.9%
- Annual Job Openings: 27,000

Diagnose, treat, and help prevent children's diseases and injuries.

Advise patients, parents or guardians, and community members concerning diet, activity, hygiene, and disease prevention. Collect, record, and maintain patient information, such as medical history, reports, and examination results. Examine children regularly to assess their growth and development. Examine patients or order, perform, and interpret diagnostic tests to obtain information on medical condition and determine diagnosis. Explain procedures and discuss test results or prescribed treatments with patients and parents or guardians. Monitor patients' condition and progress and re-evaluate treatments as necessary. Plan and execute medical care programs to aid in the mental and physical growth and development of children and adolescents. Prescribe or administer treatment, therapy, medication, vaccination, and other specialized medical care to treat or prevent illness, disease, or injury in infants and children. Refer patient to medical specialist or other practitioner when necessary. Treat children who have minor illnesses, acute and chronic health problems, and growth and development concerns. Conduct research to study anatomy and develop or test medications, treatments, or procedures to prevent or control disease or injury. Direct and coordinate activities of nurses, students, assistants, specialists, therapists, and other medical staff. Operate on patients to remove, repair, or improve functioning of diseased or injured body parts and systems. Plan, implement, or administer health programs or standards in hospital, business, or community for information, prevention, or treatment of injury or illness. Provide consulting services to other physicians. Prepare reports for government or management of birth, death, and disease statistics; workforce evaluations; or medical status of individuals.

GOE INFORMATION—Interest Area: 14. Medical and Health Services. **Work Group:** 14.02. Medicine and Surgery. **Personality Type**—Investigative. Investigative occupations frequently involve working with ideas and require an extensive amount of thinking. These occupations can involve searching for facts and figuring out problems mentally. **Work Values**—Social Service; Social Status; Recognition; Ability Utilization; Responsibility. **Skills**—Science; Reading Comprehension; Systems Evaluation; Complex Problem Solving; Judgment and Decision Making; Systems Analysis; Mathematics; Management of Personnel Resources.

Abilities—*Cognitive:* Inductive Reasoning; Oral Expression; Speed of Closure; Problem Sensitivity; Written Expression. *Psychomotor:* Manual Dexterity; Arm-Hand Steadiness; Finger Dexterity; Multilimb Coordination; Response Orientation. *Physical:* Static Strength; Dynamic Strength; Gross Body Equilibrium; Stamina; Dynamic Flexibility. *Sensory:* Speech Clarity; Visual Color Discrimination; Auditory Attention; Near Vision; Hearing Sensitivity. **General Work Activities**—*Information Input:* Getting Information; Monitoring Processes, Materials, or Surroundings; Identifying Objects, Actions, and Events. *Mental Process:* Analyzing Data or Information; Updating and Using Relevant Knowledge; Making Decisions and Solving Problems. *Work Output:* Documenting or Recording Information; Performing General Physical Activities; Handling and Moving Objects. *Interacting with Others:* Assisting and Caring for Others; Communicating with Persons Outside Organization; Communicating with Other Workers. **Physical Work Conditions**—Disease or Infections; Common Protective or Safety Attire; Radiation; Indoors; Walking or Running. **Other Job Characteristics**—Consequence of Error; Importance of Being Exact or Accurate; Degree of Automation.

Experience—Job Zone 5. Extensive skill, knowledge, and experience are needed for these occupations. **Job Preparation:** SVP 8.0 and above—four years to more than 10 years. **Knowledge**—Medicine and Dentistry; Biology; Therapy and Counseling; Chemistry; Administration and Management. **Instructional Programs**—Child/Pediatric Neurology; Family Medicine; Neonatal-Perinatal Medicine; Pediatric Cardiology; Pediatric Endocrinology; Pediatric Hemato-Oncology; Pediatric Nephrology; Pediatric Orthopedics; Pediatric Surgery; Pediatrics.

Related DOT Jobs—070.101-066 Pediatrician.

29-1066.00 *Psychiatrists*

- Education/Training Required: First professional degree
- Employed: No data available.
- Annual Earnings: $126,460
- Growth: 17.9%
- Annual Job Openings: 27,000

Diagnose, treat, and help prevent disorders of the mind.

Analyze and evaluate patient data and test or examination findings to diagnose nature and extent of mental disorder. Collaborate with physicians, psychologists, social workers, psychiatric nurses, or other professionals to discuss treatment plans and progress. Counsel outpatients and other patients during office visits. Design individualized care plans, using a variety of treatments. Examine or conduct laboratory or diagnostic tests on patient to provide information on general physical condition and mental disorder. Gather and maintain patient information and records, including social and medical history obtained from patients, relatives, and other professionals. Prescribe, direct, and administer psychotherapeutic treatments or medications to treat mental, emotional, or behavioral disorders. Review and evaluate treatment procedures and outcomes of other psychiatrists and medical professionals. Advise and inform guardians, relatives, and significant others of patients' conditions and treatment. Prepare and submit case reports and summaries to government and mental health agencies. Teach, conduct research, and publish findings to increase understanding of mental, emotional, and behavioral states and disorders. Serve on committees to promote and maintain community mental health services and delivery systems.

GOE INFORMATION—Interest Area: 14. Medical and Health Services. **Work Group:** 14.02. Medicine and Surgery. **Personality Type**—Investigative. Investigative occupations frequently involve working with ideas and require an extensive amount of thinking. These occupations can involve searching for facts and figuring out problems mentally. **Work**

Values—Social Service; Responsibility; Ability Utilization; Autonomy; Social Status. **Skills**—Social Perceptiveness; Service Orientation; Systems Analysis; Reading Comprehension; Judgment and Decision Making; Writing; Complex Problem Solving; Systems Evaluation. **Abilities**—*Cognitive:* Written Expression; Problem Sensitivity; Oral Expression; Written Comprehension; Oral Comprehension. *Psychomotor:* None met the criteria. *Physical:* None met the criteria. *Sensory:* Speech Clarity; Speech Recognition; Auditory Attention; Near Vision. **General Work Activities**—*Information Input:* Getting Information; Identifying Objects, Actions, and Events; Monitoring Processes, Materials, or Surroundings. *Mental Process:* Analyzing Data or Information; Judging Qualities of Things, Services, or Other People's Work; Updating and Using Relevant Knowledge. *Work Output:* Documenting or Recording Information; Performing General Physical Activities; Handling and Moving Objects. *Interacting with Others:* Providing Consultation and Advice to Others; Assisting and Caring for Others; Establishing and Maintaining Relationships. **Physical Work Conditions**—Sitting; Indoors; Disease or Infections. **Other Job Characteristics**—Consequence of Error; Importance of Being Exact or Accurate; Importance of Repeating Same Tasks.

Experience—Job Zone 5. Extensive skill, knowledge, and experience are needed for these occupations. **Job Preparation:** SVP 8.0 and above—four years to more than 10 years. **Knowledge**—Therapy and Counseling; Psychology; Medicine and Dentistry; Education and Training; Philosophy and Theology. **Instructional Programs**—Child Psychiatry; Physical Medical and Rehabilitation/Psychiatry; Psychiatry.

Related DOT Jobs—070.107-014 Psychiatrist.

29-1067.00 Surgeons

- **Education/Training Required: First professional degree**
- **Employed: No data available.**
- **Annual Earnings: Greater than $145,600**
- **Growth: 17.9%**
- **Annual Job Openings: 27,000**

Treat diseases, injuries, and deformities by invasive methods, such as manual manipulation or by using instruments and appliances.

Analyze patient's medical history, medication allergies, physical condition, and examination results to verify operation's necessity and to determine best procedure. Prescribe preoperative and postoperative treatments and procedures, such as sedatives, diets, antibiotics, and preparation and treatment of the patient's operative area. Direct and coordinate activities of nurses, assistants, specialists, residents, and other medical staff. Examine patient to provide information on medical condition and surgical risk. Follow established surgical techniques during the operation. Operate on patients to correct deformities, repair injuries, prevent and treat diseases, or improve or restore patients' functions. Refer patient to medical specialist or other practitioners when necessary. Conduct research to develop and test surgical techniques that can improve operating procedures and outcomes. Examine instruments, equipment, and operating room to ensure sterility. Manage surgery services, including planning, scheduling and coordination, determination of procedures, and procurement of supplies and equipment. Prepare case histories. Provide consultation and surgical assistance to other physicians and surgeons. Diagnose bodily disorders and orthopedic conditions and provide treatments, such as medicines and surgeries, in clinics, hospital wards, and operating rooms.

GOE INFORMATION—**Interest Area:** 14. Medical and Health Services. **Work Group:** 14.02. Medicine and Surgery. **Personality Type**—Investigative. Investigative occupations frequently involve working with ideas and require an extensive amount of thinking. These occupations can involve searching for facts and figuring out problems mentally. **Work**

Values—Social Service; Social Status; Recognition; Ability Utilization; Achievement. **Skills**—Science; Operation and Control; Systems Evaluation; Systems Analysis; Reading Comprehension; Judgment and Decision Making; Management of Personnel Resources; Equipment Selection. **Abilities**—*Cognitive:* Flexibility of Closure; Speed of Closure; Inductive Reasoning; Memorization; Problem Sensitivity. *Psychomotor:* Manual Dexterity; Arm-Hand Steadiness; Finger Dexterity; Control Precision; Reaction Time. *Physical:* Dynamic Strength; Explosive Strength; Stamina; Trunk Strength; Gross Body Equilibrium. *Sensory:* Depth Perception; Sound Localization; Speech Clarity; Near Vision; Visual Color Discrimination. **General Work Activities**—*Information Input:* Getting Information; Identifying Objects, Actions, and Events; Monitoring Processes, Materials, or Surroundings. *Mental Process:* Analyzing Data or Information; Making Decisions and Solving Problems; Updating and Using Relevant Knowledge. *Work Output:* Handling and Moving Objects; Performing General Physical Activities; Documenting or Recording Information. *Interacting with Others:* Assisting and Caring for Others; Communicating with Other Workers; Coordinating the Work and Activities of Others. **Physical Work Conditions**—Disease or Infections; Common Protective or Safety Attire; Specialized Protective or Safety Attire; Using Hands on Objects, Tools, or Controls; Indoors. **Other Job Characteristics**—Consequence of Error; Importance of Being Exact or Accurate; Importance of Repeating Same Tasks.

Experience—Job Zone 5. Extensive skill, knowledge, and experience are needed for these occupations. **Job Preparation:** SVP 8.0 and above—four years to more than 10 years. **Knowledge**—Medicine and Dentistry; Biology; Chemistry; Administration and Management; Therapy and Counseling. **Instructional Programs**—Adult Reconstructive Orthopedics (Orthopedic Surgery); Colon and Rectal Surgery; Critical Care Surgery; General Surgery; Hand Surgery; Neurological Surgery/Neurosurgery; Orthopedic Surgery of the Spine; Orthopedics/Orthopedic Surgery; Otolaryngology; Pediatric Orthopedics; Pediatric Surgery; Plastic Surgery; Sports Medicine; Thoracic Surgery; Urology; Vascular Surgery.

Related DOT Jobs—070.101-094 Surgeon.

29-1069.99 Physicians and Surgeons, All Other

- **Education/Training Required: First professional degree**
- **Employed: No data available.**
- **Annual Earnings: No data available.**
- **Growth: 17.9%**
- **Annual Job Openings: 27,000**

All physicians and surgeons not listed separately.

No task data available.

GOE INFORMATION—**Interest Area:** 14. Medical and Health Services. **Work Group:** 14.02. Medicine and Surgery. **Note:** The Department of Labor has not collected some data for this job, so it has fewer details than the other descriptions.

Instructional Programs—Aerospace Medicine; Allergies and Immunology; Blood Banking; Chemical Pathology; Child Neurology; Child/Pediatric Neurology; Cytopathology; Dermatology; Dermatopathology; Diagnostic Radiology; Emergency Medicine; Endocrinology and Metabolism; Forensic Pathology; Gastroenterology; Geriatric Medicine (Internal Medicine); Hematological Pathology; Hematology; Immunopathology; Laboratory Medicine; Medical Residency Programs, Other; Medicine (MD); Musculoskeletal Oncology; Nephrology; Neurology; Neuropathology; Nuclear Medicine; Nuclear Radiology; Occupational

Medicine; Oncology; Ophthalmology; Orthopedic Surgery of the Spine; Osteopathic Medicine/Osteopathy (DO); Otolaryngology; Pathology; Pediatric Urology; Physical and Rehabilitation Medicine; Physical Medical and Rehabilitation/Psychiatry; Preventive Medicine; Public Health Medicine; Pulmonary Disease; Radiation Oncology; Radioisotopic Pathology; Rheumatology; Sports Medicine; Urology.

Related DOT Jobs—070.061-010 Pathologist; 070.101-014 Cardiologist; 070.101-018 Dermatologist; 070.101-050 Neurologist; 070.101-058 Ophthalmologist; 070.101-062 Otolaryngologist; 070.101-070 Physiatrist; 070.101-086 Proctologist; 070.101-098 Urologist; 070.101-102 Allergist-Immunologist; 071.101-010 Osteopathic Physician.

29-1071.00 Physician Assistants

- **Education/Training Required: Bachelor's degree**
- **Employed: 57,813**
- **Annual Earnings: $63,970**
- **Growth: 53.5%**
- **Annual Job Openings: 5,000**

Provide health care services typically performed by a physician under the supervision of a physician. Conduct complete physicals, provide treatment, and counsel patients. May, in some cases, prescribe medication. Must graduate from an accredited educational program for physician assistants.

Administer or order diagnostic tests, such as X-ray, electrocardiogram, and laboratory tests. Examine patients to obtain information about their physical condition. Instruct and counsel patients about prescribed therapeutic regimens, normal growth and development, family planning, emotional problems of daily living, and health maintenance. Interpret diagnostic test results for deviations from normal. Make tentative diagnoses and decisions about management and treatment of patients. Obtain, compile, and record patient medical data, including health history, progress notes, and results of physical examination. Perform therapeutic procedures, such as injections, immunizations, suturing and wound care, and infection management. Prescribe therapy or medication with physician approval. Provide physicians with assistance during surgery or complicated medical procedures. Visit and observe patients on hospital rounds or house calls, updating charts, ordering therapy, and reporting back to physician. Order medical and laboratory supplies and equipment. Supervise and coordinate activities of technicians and technical assistants.

GOE INFORMATION—Interest Area: 14. Medical and Health Services. **Work Group:** 14.02. Medicine and Surgery. **Personality Type**—Investigative. Investigative occupations frequently involve working with ideas and require an extensive amount of thinking. These occupations can involve searching for facts and figuring out problems mentally. **Work Values**—Social Service; Achievement; Pleasant Co-workers; Ability Utilization; Social Status. **Skills**—Science; Reading Comprehension; Service Orientation; Speaking; Complex Problem Solving; Critical Thinking; Active Listening; Social Perceptiveness. **Abilities**—*Cognitive:* Inductive Reasoning; Problem Sensitivity; Speed of Closure; Oral Comprehension; Oral Expression. *Psychomotor:* Arm-Hand Steadiness; Manual Dexterity; Finger Dexterity; Control Precision; Reaction Time. *Physical:* None met the criteria. *Sensory:* Near Vision; Speech Clarity; Speech Recognition; Hearing Sensitivity; Auditory Attention. **General Work Activities**—*Information Input:* Identifying Objects, Actions, and Events; Getting Information; Monitoring Processes, Materials, or Surroundings. *Mental Process:* Updating and Using Relevant Knowledge; Judging Qualities of Things, Services, or Other People's Work; Processing Information. *Work Output:* Handling and Moving Objects; Documenting or Recording Information; Performing General Physical Activities. *Interacting with*

Others: Assisting and Caring for Others; Establishing and Maintaining Relationships; Communicating with Other Workers. **Physical Work Conditions**—Disease or Infections; Common Protective or Safety Attire; Radiation; Indoors; Standing. **Other Job Characteristics**—Importance of Being Exact or Accurate; Consequence of Error; Importance of Repeating Same Tasks.

Experience—Job Zone 4. A minimum of two to four years of work-related skill, knowledge, or experience is needed. **Job Preparation:** SVP 7.0 to less than 8.0—two years to less than 10 years. **Knowledge**—Medicine and Dentistry; Biology; Therapy and Counseling; Chemistry; Psychology. **Instructional Programs**—Physician Assistant.

Related DOT Jobs—079.364-018 Physician Assistant; 079.367-018 Medical-Service Technician.

29-1081.00 Podiatrists

- **Education/Training Required: First professional degree**
- **Employed: 17,909**
- **Annual Earnings: $95,390**
- **Growth: 14.2%**
- **Annual Job Openings: 1,000**

Diagnose and treat diseases and deformities of the human foot.

Advise patients about treatments and foot care techniques necessary for prevention of future problems. Correct deformities by means of plaster casts and strapping. Diagnose diseases and deformities of the foot by using medical histories, physical examinations, X rays, and laboratory test results. Make and fit prosthetic appliances. Prescribe medications, corrective devices, physical therapy, or surgery. Refer patients to physicians when symptoms indicative of systemic disorders, such as arthritis or diabetes, are observed in feet and legs. Treat bone, muscle, and joint disorders affecting the feet. Treat conditions such as corns, calluses, ingrown nails, tumors, shortened tendons, bunions, cysts, and abscesses by surgical methods. Treat deformities using mechanical methods, such as whirlpool or paraffin baths, and electrical methods, such as shortwave and low-voltage currents. Educate the public about the benefits of foot care through techniques such as speaking engagements, advertising, and other forums. Perform administrative duties such as hiring employees, ordering supplies, and keeping records.

GOE INFORMATION—Interest Area: 14. Medical and Health Services. **Work Group:** 14.04. Health Specialties. **Personality Type**—Social. Social occupations frequently involve working with, communicating with, and teaching people. These occupations often involve helping or providing service to others. **Work Values**—Social Service; Responsibility; Recognition; Autonomy; Social Status. **Skills**—Equipment Selection; Reading Comprehension; Technology Design; Complex Problem Solving; Judgment and Decision Making; Critical Thinking; Active Listening; Systems Evaluation. **Abilities**—*Cognitive:* Inductive Reasoning; Speed of Closure; Fluency of Ideas; Selective Attention; Problem Sensitivity. *Psychomotor:* Manual Dexterity; Finger Dexterity; Control Precision; Arm-Hand Steadiness; Wrist-Finger Speed. *Physical:* Static Strength; Dynamic Strength; Explosive Strength; Extent Flexibility. *Sensory:* Depth Perception; Night Vision; Visual Color Discrimination; Glare Sensitivity; Near Vision. **General Work Activities**—*Information Input:* Identifying Objects, Actions, and Events; Getting Information; Monitoring Processes, Materials, or Surroundings. *Mental Process:* Updating and Using Relevant Knowledge; Analyzing Data or Information; Making Decisions and Solving Problems. *Work Output:* Handling and Moving Objects; Performing General Physical Activities; Documenting or Recording Information. *Interacting with Others:* Assisting and Caring for Others; Communicating with Persons Outside Organization; Performing for or

Working with the Public. **Physical Work Conditions**—Disease or Infections; Common Protective or Safety Attire; Radiation; Minor Burns, Cuts, Bites, or Stings; Indoors. **Other Job Characteristics**—Consequence of Error; Importance of Being Exact or Accurate; Degree of Automation.

Experience—Job Zone 4. A minimum of two to four years of work-related skill, knowledge, or experience is needed. **Job Preparation:** SVP 7.0 to less than 8.0—two years to less than 10 years. **Knowledge**—Medicine and Dentistry; Biology; Chemistry; Therapy and Counseling; English Language. **Instructional Programs**—Podiatric Medicine/Podiatry (DPM).

Related DOT Jobs—079.101-022 Podiatrist.

29-1111.00 Registered Nurses

- **Education/Training Required: Associate's degree**
- **Employed: 2,194,224**
- **Annual Earnings: $46,670**
- **Growth: 25.6%**
- **Annual Job Openings: 140,000**

Assess patient health problems and needs, develop and implement nursing care plans, and maintain medical records. Administer nursing care to ill, injured, convalescent, or disabled patients. May advise patients on health maintenance and disease prevention or provide case management. Licensing or registration required. Includes advance practice nurses such as nurse practitioners, clinical nurse specialists, certified nurse midwives, and certified registered nurse anesthetists. Advanced practice nursing is practiced by RNs who have specialized, formal post-basic education and who function in highly autonomous and specialized roles.

Consult and coordinate with health care team members to assess, plan, implement, and evaluate patient care plans. Maintain accurate, detailed reports and records. Modify patient treatment plans as indicated by patients' responses and conditions. Monitor all aspects of patient care, including diet and physical activity. Monitor, record and report symptoms and changes in patients' conditions. Observe nurses and visit patients to ensure that proper nursing care is provided. Prepare patients for, and assist with, examinations and treatments. Prepare rooms, sterile instruments, equipment, and supplies and ensure that stock of supplies is maintained. Provide health care, first aid, immunizations, and assistance in convalescence and rehabilitation in locations such as schools, hospitals, and industry. Record patients' medical information and vital signs. Assess the needs of individuals, families, and/or communities, including assessment of individuals' home and/or work environments to identify potential health or safety problems. Conduct specified laboratory tests. Consult with institutions or associations regarding issues and concerns relevant to the practice and profession of nursing. Direct and supervise less skilled nursing/health care personnel or supervise a particular unit on one shift. Hand items to surgeons during operations. Instruct individuals, families, and other groups on topics such as health education, disease prevention, and childbirth; develop health improvement programs. Order, interpret, and evaluate diagnostic tests to identify and assess patient's condition. Prescribe or recommend drugs, medical devices, or other forms of treatment, such as physical therapy, inhalation therapy, or related therapeutic procedures. Provide or arrange for training/instruction of auxiliary personnel or students. Refer students or patients to specialized health resources or community agencies furnishing assistance. Work with individuals, groups, and families to plan and implement programs designed to improve the overall health of communities. Administer local, inhalation, intravenous, and other anesthetics. Contract independently to render nursing care, usually to one patient, in hospital or private home. Deliver infants and provide prenatal and postpartum care and treatment under obstetrician's supervision. Direct and coordinate infection control programs, advising and consulting with specified personnel about necessary precautions. Engage in research activities related to nursing.

GOE INFORMATION—Interest Area: 14. Medical and Health Services. **Work Group:** 14.02. Medicine and Surgery. **Personality Type**—Social. Social occupations frequently involve working with, communicating with, and teaching people. These occupations often involve helping or providing service to others. **Work Values**—Social Service; Pleasant Coworkers; Ability Utilization; Achievement; Activity. **Skills**—Service Orientation; Reading Comprehension; Instructing; Speaking; Social Perceptiveness; Active Listening; Science; Complex Problem Solving. **Abilities**—*Cognitive:* Speed of Closure; Inductive Reasoning; Oral Comprehension; Memorization; Written Expression. *Psychomotor:* Reaction Time; Arm-Hand Steadiness; Response Orientation; Finger Dexterity; Manual Dexterity. *Physical:* Static Strength; Extent Flexibility; Trunk Strength; Explosive Strength; Stamina. *Sensory:* Visual Color Discrimination; Speech Recognition; Night Vision; Speech Clarity; Near Vision. **General Work Activities**—*Information Input:* Monitoring Processes, Materials, or Surroundings; Identifying Objects, Actions, and Events; Getting Information. *Mental Process:* Updating and Using Relevant Knowledge; Making Decisions and Solving Problems; Judging Qualities of Things, Services, or Other People's Work. *Work Output:* Performing General Physical Activities; Handling and Moving Objects; Documenting or Recording Information. *Interacting with Others:* Assisting and Caring for Others; Communicating with Other Workers; Establishing and Maintaining Relationships. **Physical Work Conditions**—Disease or Infections; Common Protective or Safety Attire; Walking or Running; Standing; Indoors. **Other Job Characteristics**—Consequence of Error; Importance of Being Exact or Accurate; Degree of Automation.

Experience—Job Zone 4. A minimum of two to four years of work-related skill, knowledge, or experience is needed. **Job Preparation:** SVP 7.0 to less than 8.0—two years to less than 10 years. **Knowledge**—Medicine and Dentistry; Therapy and Counseling; Biology; Customer and Personal Service; Chemistry. **Instructional Programs**—Adult Health Nurse/Nursing; Clinical Nurse Specialist; Critical Care Nursing; Family Practice Nurse/Nurse Practitioner; Maternal/Child Health and Neonatal Nurse/Nursing; Nurse Anesthetist; Nurse Midwife/Nursing Midwifery; Nursing—Registered Nurse Training (RN, ASN, BSN, MSN); Nursing Science (MS, PhD); Nursing, Other; Occupational and Environmental Health Nursing; Pediatric Nurse/Nursing; Perioperative/Operating Room and Surgical Nurse/Nursing; Psychiatric/Mental Health Nurse/Nursing; Public Health/Community Nurse/Nursing.

Related DOT Jobs—075.124-010 Nurse, School; 075.124-014 Nurse, Community Health; 075.127-014 Nurse, Consultant; 075.127-026 Nurse Supervisor, Community-Health Nursing; 075.127-030 Nurse Supervisor, Evening-or-Night; 075.127-034 Nurse, Infection Control; 075.137-010 Nurse Supervisor, Occupational Health Nursing; 075.137-014 Nurse, Head; 075.167-010 Nurse, Supervisor; 075.264-010 Nurse Practitioner; 075.264-014 Nurse-Midwife; 075.364-010 Nurse, General Duty; 075.371-010 Nurse Anesthetist; 075.374-014 Nurse, Office; 075.374-018 Nurse, Private Duty; 075.374-022 Nurse, Staff, Occupational Health Nursing.

29-1121.00 Audiologists

- **Education/Training Required: Master's degree**
- **Employed: 12,790**
- **Annual Earnings: $46,900**
- **Growth: 44.7%**
- **Annual Job Openings: 1,000**

Assess and treat persons with hearing and related disorders. May fit hearing aids and provide auditory training. May perform research related to hearing problems.

Administer hearing or speech/language evaluations, tests, or examinations to patients to collect information on type and degree of impairment, using specialized instruments and electronic equipment. Counsel and instruct clients in techniques to improve hearing or speech impairment, including sign language or lip-reading. Evaluate hearing and speech/language disorders to determine diagnoses and courses of treatment. Examine and clean patients' ear canals. Fit and dispense assistive devices, such as hearing aids. Maintain client records at all stages, including initial evaluation and discharge. Monitor clients' progress and discharge them from treatment when goals have been attained. Plan and conduct treatment programs for clients' hearing or speech problems, consulting with physicians, nurses, psychologists, and other health care personnel as necessary. Recommend assistive devices according to clients' needs or nature of impairments. Refer clients to additional medical or educational services if needed. Advise educators or other medical staff on speech or hearing topics. Conduct or direct research on hearing or speech topics and report findings to help in the development of procedures, technology, or treatments. Develop and supervise hearing screening programs. Educate and supervise audiology students and health care personnel. Fit and tune cochlear implants, providing rehabilitation for adjustment to listening with implant amplification systems. Instruct clients, parents, teachers, or employers in how to avoid behavior patterns that lead to miscommunication. Participate in conferences or training to update or share knowledge of new hearing or speech disorder treatment methods or technologies. Measure noise levels in workplaces and conduct hearing protection programs in industry, schools, and communities. Work with multi-disciplinary teams to assess and rehabilitate recipients of implanted hearing devices.

GOE INFORMATION—Interest Area: 14. Medical and Health Services. **Work Group:** 14.06. Medical Therapy. **Personality Type—**Social. Social occupations frequently involve working with, communicating with, and teaching people. These occupations often involve helping or providing service to others. **Work Values—**Social Service; Authority; Creativity; Achievement; Pleasant Co-workers. **Skills—**Instructing; Writing; Management of Personnel Resources; Complex Problem Solving; Speaking; Learning Strategies; Reading Comprehension; Management of Financial Resources. **Abilities—***Cognitive:* Oral Expression; Oral Comprehension; Written Expression; Written Comprehension; Fluency of Ideas. *Psychomotor:* None met the criteria. *Physical:* None met the criteria. *Sensory:* Speech Clarity; Speech Recognition; Hearing Sensitivity; Auditory Attention; Sound Localization. **General Work Activities—***Information Input:* Getting Information; Identifying Objects, Actions, and Events; Monitoring Processes, Materials, or Surroundings. *Mental Process:* Processing Information; Analyzing Data or Information; Updating and Using Relevant Knowledge. *Work Output:* Documenting or Recording Information; Interacting with Computers; Handling and Moving Objects. *Interacting with Others:* Interpreting Meaning of Information for Others; Assisting and Caring for Others; Coordinating the Work and Activities of Others. **Physical Work Conditions—**Indoors; Sitting; Disease or Infections. **Other Job Characteristics—**Importance of Being Exact or Accurate; Importance of Repeating Same Tasks; Pace Determined by Speed of Equipment.

Experience—Job Zone 4. A minimum of two to four years of work-related skill, knowledge, or experience is needed. **Job Preparation:** SVP 7.0 to less than 8.0—two years to less than 10 years. **Knowledge—**Therapy and Counseling; Education and Training; Medicine and Dentistry; Personnel and Human Resources; Biology. **Instructional Programs—**Audiology/Audiologist and Hearing Sciences; Audiology/Audiologist and

Speech-Language Pathology/Pathologist; Communication Disorders Sciences and Services, Other; Communication Disorders, General.

Related DOT Jobs—076.101-010 Audiologist; 076.101-014 Director, Speech-and-Hearing Clinic.

29-1122.00 Occupational Therapists

- **Education/Training Required: Bachelor's degree**
- **Employed: 78,306**
- **Annual Earnings: $51,370**
- **Growth: 33.9%**
- **Annual Job Openings: 4,000**

Assess, plan, organize, and participate in rehabilitative programs that help restore vocational, homemaking, and daily living skills, as well as general independence, to disabled persons.

Complete and maintain necessary records. Evaluate patients' progress and prepare reports that detail progress. Test and evaluate patients' physical and mental abilities and analyze medical data to determine realistic rehabilitation goals for patients. Select activities that will help individuals learn work and life-management skills within limits of their mental and physical capabilities. Plan, organize, and conduct occupational therapy programs in hospital, institutional, or community settings to help rehabilitate those impaired because of illness, injury, or psychological or developmental problems. Recommend changes in patients' work or living environments consistent with their needs and capabilities. Consult with rehabilitation team to select activity programs and coordinate occupational therapy with other therapeutic activities. Help clients improve decision making, abstract reasoning, memory, sequencing, coordination, and perceptual skills, using computer programs. Develop and participate in health promotion programs, group activities, or discussions to promote client health, facilitate social adjustment, alleviate stress, and prevent physical or mental disability. Provide training and supervision in therapy techniques and objectives for students and nurses and other medical staff. Requisition or design and create special supplies and equipment, such as splints, braces, and computer-aided adaptive equipment. Plan and implement programs and social activities to help patients learn work and school skills and adjust to handicaps. Lay out materials such as puzzles, scissors, and eating utensils for use in therapy and clean and repair these tools after therapy sessions. Advise on health risks in the workplace and on health-related transition to retirement. Conduct research in occupational therapy. Provide patients with assistance in locating and holding jobs.

GOE INFORMATION—Interest Area: 14. Medical and Health Services. **Work Group:** 14.06. Medical Therapy. **Personality Type—**Social. Social occupations frequently involve working with, communicating with, and teaching people. These occupations often involve helping or providing service to others. **Work Values—**Social Service; Achievement; Pleasant Co-workers; Ability Utilization; Authority. **Skills—**Service Orientation; Social Perceptiveness; Reading Comprehension; Technology Design; Instructing; Coordination; Complex Problem Solving; Learning Strategies. **Abilities—***Cognitive:* Inductive Reasoning; Problem Sensitivity; Originality; Deductive Reasoning; Speed of Closure. *Psychomotor:* Finger Dexterity; Multilimb Coordination. *Physical:* Trunk Strength. *Sensory:* Speech Recognition; Speech Clarity; Far Vision; Near Vision; Visual Color Discrimination. **General Work Activities—***Information Input:* Identifying Objects, Actions, and Events; Monitoring Processes, Materials, or Surroundings; Getting Information. *Mental Process:* Updating and Using Relevant Knowledge; Making Decisions and Solving Problems; Organizing, Planning, and Prioritizing. *Work Output:* Handling and Moving Objects; Documenting or Recording Information;

Performing General Physical Activities. *Interacting with Others:* Establishing and Maintaining Relationships; Assisting and Caring for Others; Communicating with Other Workers. **Physical Work Conditions**—Disease or Infections; Sitting; Bending or Twisting the Body; Making Repetitive Motions; Specialized Protective or Safety Attire. **Other Job Characteristics**—Importance of Repeating Same Tasks; Consequence of Error; Pace Determined by Speed of Equipment.

Experience—Job Zone 4. A minimum of two to four years of work-related skill, knowledge, or experience is needed. **Job Preparation:** SVP 7.0 to less than 8.0—two years to less than 10 years. **Knowledge**—Therapy and Counseling; Psychology; Customer and Personal Service; Medicine and Dentistry; Education and Training. **Instructional Programs**—Occupational Therapy/Therapist.

Related DOT Jobs—076.121-010 Occupational Therapist; 076.167-010 Industrial Therapist.

29-1123.00 Physical Therapists

- **Education/Training Required: Master's degree**
- **Employed: 131,822**
- **Annual Earnings: $56,570**
- **Growth: 33.3%**
- **Annual Job Openings: 6,000**

Assess, plan, organize, and participate in rehabilitative programs that improve mobility, relieve pain, increase strength, and decrease or prevent deformity of patients suffering from disease or injury.

Plan, prepare, and carry out individually designed programs of physical treatment to maintain, improve, or restore physical functioning, alleviate pain, and prevent physical dysfunction in patients. Perform and document an initial exam, evaluating the data to identify problems and determine a diagnosis prior to intervention. Evaluate effects of treatment at various stages and adjust treatments to achieve maximum benefit. Administer manual exercises, massage, and/or traction to help relieve pain, increase the patient's strength, and decrease or prevent deformity and crippling. Instruct patient and family in treatment procedures to be continued at home. Confer with the patient, medical practitioners, and appropriate others to plan, implement, and assess the intervention program. Review physician's referral and patient's medical records to help determine diagnosis and physical therapy treatment required. Record prognosis, treatment, response, and progress in patient's chart or enter information into computer. Obtain patients' informed consent to proposed interventions. Discharge patient from physical therapy when goals or projected outcomes have been attained and provide for appropriate followup care or referrals. Test and measure patient's strength, motor development and function, sensory perception, functional capacity, and respiratory and circulatory efficiency and record data. Identify and document goals, anticipated progress, and plans for reevaluation. Provide information to the patient about the proposed intervention, its material risks and expected benefits, and any reasonable alternatives. Inform the patient when diagnosis reveals findings outside their scope and refer to an appropriate practitioner. Direct and supervise supportive personnel, assessing their competence, delegating specific tasks to them, and establishing channels of communication. Administer treatment involving application of physical agents, using equipment, moist packs, ultraviolet and infrared lamps, and ultrasound machines. Teach physical therapy students as well as those in other health professions. Evaluate, fit, and adjust prosthetic and orthotic devices and recommend modification to orthotist. Provide educational information about physical therapy and physical therapists, injury prevention, ergonomics, and ways to promote health. Refer clients to community resources and services. Conduct and support research and apply research findings to practice. Participate in

community and community agency activities and help to formulate public policy. Construct, maintain, and repair medical supportive devices. Direct group rehabilitation activities.

GOE INFORMATION—**Interest Area:** 14. Medical and Health Services. **Work Group:** 14.06. Medical Therapy. **Personality Type**—Social. Social occupations frequently involve working with, communicating with, and teaching people. These occupations often involve helping or providing service to others. **Work Values**—Social Service; Achievement; Pleasant Co-workers; Ability Utilization; Authority. **Skills**—Reading Comprehension; Instructing; Learning Strategies; Complex Problem Solving; Social Perceptiveness; Service Orientation; Monitoring; Equipment Selection. **Abilities**—*Cognitive:* Problem Sensitivity; Inductive Reasoning; Deductive Reasoning; Speed of Closure; Flexibility of Closure. *Psychomotor:* Manual Dexterity; Finger Dexterity; Multilimb Coordination; Speed of Limb Movement; Arm-Hand Steadiness. *Physical:* Dynamic Strength; Stamina; Gross Body Coordination; Static Strength; Extent Flexibility. *Sensory:* Speech Recognition; Far Vision; Near Vision; Speech Clarity; Depth Perception. **General Work Activities**—*Information Input:* Identifying Objects, Actions, and Events; Monitoring Processes, Materials, or Surroundings; Getting Information. *Mental Process:* Organizing, Planning, and Prioritizing; Updating and Using Relevant Knowledge; Analyzing Data or Information. *Work Output:* Handling and Moving Objects; Performing General Physical Activities; Documenting or Recording Information. *Interacting with Others:* Assisting and Caring for Others; Establishing and Maintaining Relationships; Communicating with Other Workers. **Physical Work Conditions**—Indoors; Disease or Infections; Standing; Bending or Twisting the Body; Kneeling, Crouching, or Crawling. **Other Job Characteristics**—Consequence of Error; Importance of Being Exact or Accurate; Importance of Repeating Same Tasks.

Experience—Job Zone 5. Extensive skill, knowledge, and experience are needed for these occupations. **Job Preparation:** SVP 7.0 to less than 8.0—two years to less than 10 years. **Knowledge**—Psychology; Therapy and Counseling; Customer and Personal Service; Medicine and Dentistry; Biology. **Instructional Programs**—Kinesiotherapy/Kinesiotherapist; Physical Therapy/Therapist.

Related DOT Jobs—076.121-014 Physical Therapist.

29-1124.00 Radiation Therapists

- **Education/Training Required: Associate's degree**
- **Employed: 15,572**
- **Annual Earnings: $49,050**
- **Growth: 22.8%**
- **Annual Job Openings: 1,000**

Provide radiation therapy to patients as prescribed by a radiologist according to established practices and standards. Duties may include reviewing prescription and diagnosis; acting as liaison with physician and supportive care personnel; preparing equipment, such as immobilization, treatment, and protection devices; and maintaining records, reports, and files. May assist in dosimetry procedures and tumor localization.

Administer prescribed doses of radiation to specific body parts, using radiation therapy equipment according to established practices and standards. Assist in the preparation of sealed radioactive materials, such as cobalt, radium, cesium, and isotopes, for use in radiation treatments. Calculate actual treatment dosages delivered during each session. Check radiation therapy equipment to ensure proper operation. Conduct most treatment sessions independently in accordance with the long-term treatment plan and under the general direction of the patient's physician.

Enter data into computer and set controls to operate and adjust equipment and regulate dosage. Follow principles of radiation protection for patient, self, and others. Help physicians, radiation oncologists, and clinical physicists to prepare physical and technical aspects of radiation treatment plans, using information about patient condition and anatomy. Maintain records, reports, and files as required, including such information as radiation dosages, equipment settings, and patients' reactions. Observe and reassure patients during treatment and report unusual reactions to physician or turn equipment off if unexpected adverse reactions occur. Prepare and construct equipment, such as immobilization, treatment, and protection devices. Position patients for treatment with accuracy according to prescription. Review prescription, diagnosis, patient chart, and identification. Store, sterilize, or prepare the special applicators containing the radioactive substance implanted by the physician. Act as liaison with physicist and supportive care personnel. Check for side effects such as skin irritation, nausea, and hair loss to assess patients' reaction to treatment. Educate, prepare, and reassure patients and their families by answering questions, providing physical assistance, and reinforcing physicians' advice regarding treatment reactions and post-treatment care. Implement appropriate follow-up care plans. Photograph treated area of patient and process film. Provide assistance to other health care personnel during dosimetry procedures and tumor localization. Train and supervise student or subordinate radiotherapy technologists.

GOE INFORMATION—Interest Area: 14. Medical and Health Services. Work Group: 14.06. Medical Therapy. Personality Type—Social. Social occupations frequently involve working with, communicating with, and teaching people. These occupations often involve helping or providing service to others. Work Values—Social Service; Pleasant Co-workers; Ability Utilization; Security; Achievement. Skills—Operation and Control; Operation Monitoring; Science; Reading Comprehension. Abilities—Cognitive: Speed of Closure; Oral Comprehension; Visualization; Flexibility of Closure; Category Flexibility. Psychomotor: Response Orientation; Reaction Time; Control Precision; Multilimb Coordination; Wrist-Finger Speed. Physical: Gross Body Equilibrium; Explosive Strength; Gross Body Coordination; Dynamic Flexibility; Dynamic Strength. Sensory: Speech Clarity; Hearing Sensitivity; Far Vision; Sound Localization; Near Vision. General Work Activities—Information Input: Monitoring Processes, Materials, or Surroundings; Getting Information; Identifying Objects, Actions, and Events. Mental Process: Updating and Using Relevant Knowledge; Making Decisions and Solving Problems; Processing Information. Work Output: Performing General Physical Activities; Controlling Machines and Processes; Handling and Moving Objects. Interacting with Others: Assisting and Caring for Others; Communicating with Other Workers; Establishing and Maintaining Relationships. Physical Work Conditions—Radiation; Disease or Infections; Common Protective or Safety Attire; Specialized Protective or Safety Attire; Indoors. Other Job Characteristics—Consequence of Error; Importance of Being Exact or Accurate; Degree of Automation.

Experience—Job Zone 4. A minimum of two to four years of work-related skill, knowledge, or experience is needed. Job Preparation: SVP 7.0 to less than 8.0—two years to less than 10 years. Knowledge—Medicine and Dentistry; Therapy and Counseling; Biology; Computers and Electronics; Clerical. Instructional Programs—Medical Radiologic Technology/Science—Radiation Therapist.

Related DOT Jobs—078.361-034 Radiation Therapist.

29-1125.00 Recreational Therapists

- Education/Training Required: Bachelor's degree
- Employed: 29,078
- Annual Earnings: $30,030
- Growth: 8.6%
- Annual Job Openings: 1,000

Plan, direct, or coordinate medically approved recreation programs for patients in hospitals, nursing homes, or other institutions. Activities include sports, trips, dramatics, social activities, and arts and crafts. May assess patient condition and recommend appropriate recreational activity.

Observe, analyze, and record patients' participation, reactions, and progress during treatment sessions, modifying treatment programs as needed. Develop treatment plan to meet needs of patient, based on needs assessment, patient interests, and objectives of therapy. Encourage clients with special needs and circumstances to acquire new skills and get involved in health-promoting leisure activities, such as sports, games, arts and crafts, and gardening. Counsel and encourage patients to develop leisure activities. Confer with members of treatment team to plan and evaluate therapy programs. Conduct therapy sessions to improve patients' mental and physical well-being. Instruct patient in activities and techniques, such as sports, dance, music, art, or relaxation techniques, designed to meet their specific physical or psychological needs. Obtain information from medical records, medical staff, family members, and the patients themselves to assess patients' capabilities, needs, and interests. Plan, organize, direct, and participate in treatment programs and activities to facilitate patients' rehabilitation, help them integrate into the community, and prevent further medical problems. Prepare and submit reports and charts to treatment team to reflect patients' reactions and evidence of progress or regression.

GOE INFORMATION—Interest Area: 14. Medical and Health Services. Work Group: 14.06. Medical Therapy. Personality Type—Social. Social occupations frequently involve working with, communicating with, and teaching people. These occupations often involve helping or providing service to others. Work Values—Social Service; Pleasant Co-workers; Creativity; Achievement; Social Status. Skills—Social Perceptiveness; Instructing; Writing; Learning Strategies; Coordination; Active Listening; Persuasion; Service Orientation. Abilities—Cognitive: Originality; Problem Sensitivity; Written Expression; Inductive Reasoning; Deductive Reasoning. Psychomotor: Reaction Time; Response Orientation; Multilimb Coordination; Control Precision; Finger Dexterity. Physical: Gross Body Coordination; Stamina; Gross Body Equilibrium; Dynamic Strength; Explosive Strength. Sensory: Speech Recognition; Speech Clarity; Depth Perception; Auditory Attention; Far Vision. General Work Activities—Information Input: Monitoring Processes, Materials, or Surroundings; Getting Information; Identifying Objects, Actions, and Events. Mental Process: Organizing, Planning, and Prioritizing; Thinking Creatively; Making Decisions and Solving Problems. Work Output: Documenting or Recording Information; Handling and Moving Objects; Performing General Physical Activities. Interacting with Others: Assisting and Caring for Others; Establishing and Maintaining Relationships; Communicating with Other Workers. Physical Work Conditions—Disease or Infections; Outdoors; Walking or Running; Bending or Twisting the Body; Keeping or Regaining Balance. Other Job Characteristics—Consequence of Error; Pace Determined by Speed of Equipment; Importance of Repeating Same Tasks.

Experience—Job Zone 4. A minimum of two to four years of work-related skill, knowledge, or experience is needed. Job Preparation: SVP 7.0 to less than 8.0—two years to less than 10 years. Knowledge—Psychology; Therapy and Counseling; Customer and Personal Service; Philosophy and Theology; Sociology and Anthropology. Instructional Programs—Therapeutic Recreation/Recreational Therapy.

Related DOT Jobs—076.124-014 Recreational Therapist; 076.124-018 Horticultural Therapist; 076.127-010 Art Therapist; 076.127-014 Music Therapist; 076.127-018 Dance Therapist.

29-1126.00 Respiratory Therapists

- **Education/Training Required: Associate's degree**
- **Employed: 83,010**
- **Annual Earnings: $39,370**
- **Growth: 34.8%**
- **Annual Job Openings: 4,000**

Assess, treat, and care for patients with breathing disorders. Assume primary responsibility for all respiratory care modalities, including the supervision of respiratory therapy technicians. Initiate and conduct therapeutic procedures; maintain patient records; and select, assemble, check, and operate equipment.

Set up and operate devices such as mechanical ventilators, therapeutic gas administration apparatus, environmental control systems, and aerosol generators, following specified parameters of treatment. Provide emergency care, including artificial respiration, external cardiac massage, and assistance with cardiopulmonary resuscitation. Determine requirements for treatment, such as type, method, and duration of therapy; precautions to be taken; and medication and dosages, compatible with physicians' orders. Monitor patient's physiological responses to therapy, such as vital signs, arterial blood gases, and blood chemistry changes, and consult with physician if adverse reactions occur. Read prescription, measure arterial blood gases, and review patient information to assess patient condition. Work as part of a team of physicians, nurses, and other health care professionals to manage patient care. Enforce safety rules and ensure careful adherence to physicians' orders. Maintain charts that contain patients' pertinent identification and therapy information. Inspect, clean, test, and maintain respiratory therapy equipment to ensure equipment is functioning safely and efficiently, ordering repairs when necessary. Educate patients and their families about their conditions and teach appropriate disease management techniques, such as breathing exercises and the use of medications and respiratory equipment. Explain treatment procedures to patients to gain cooperation and allay fears. Relay blood analysis results to a physician. Perform pulmonary function and adjust equipment to obtain optimum results in therapy. Perform bronchopulmonary drainage and assist or instruct patients in performance of breathing exercises. Demonstrate respiratory care procedures to trainees and other health care personnel. Teach, train, supervise, and utilize the assistance of students, respiratory therapy technicians, and assistants. Use a variety of testing techniques to assist doctors in cardiac and pulmonary research and to diagnose disorders. Make emergency visits to resolve equipment problems. Conduct tests, such as electrocardiograms, stress testing, and lung capacity tests, to evaluate patients' cardiopulmonary functions.

GOE INFORMATION—Interest Area: 14. Medical and Health Services. **Work Group:** 14.06. Medical Therapy. **Personality Type**—Investigative. Investigative occupations frequently involve working with ideas and require an extensive amount of thinking. These occupations can involve searching for facts and figuring out problems mentally. **Work Values**—Social Service; Pleasant Co-workers; Achievement; Social Status; Ability Utilization. **Skills**—Instructing; Operation Monitoring; Reading Comprehension; Troubleshooting; Science; Service Orientation; Mathematics; Complex Problem Solving. **Abilities**—*Cognitive:* Inductive Reasoning; Problem Sensitivity; Speed of Closure; Flexibility of Closure; Category Flexibility. *Psychomotor:* Control Precision; Response Orientation; Arm-Hand Steadiness; Manual Dexterity; Finger Dexterity. *Physical:* Trunk Strength; Stamina; Gross Body Coordination; Dynamic Strength; Extent Flexibility. *Sensory:* Speech Recognition; Hearing Sensitivity; Auditory Attention; Speech Clarity; Far Vision. **General Work Activities**—*Information Input:* Getting Information; Identifying Objects,

Actions, and Events; Monitoring Processes, Materials, or Surroundings. *Mental Process:* Making Decisions and Solving Problems; Updating and Using Relevant Knowledge; Organizing, Planning, and Prioritizing. *Work Output:* Documenting or Recording Information; Controlling Machines and Processes; Performing General Physical Activities. *Interacting with Others:* Assisting and Caring for Others; Establishing and Maintaining Relationships; Communicating with Other Workers. **Physical Work Conditions**—Disease or Infections; Indoors; Using Hands on Objects, Tools, or Controls; Standing; Common Protective or Safety Attire. **Other Job Characteristics**—Importance of Being Exact or Accurate; Consequence of Error; Pace Determined by Speed of Equipment.

Experience—Job Zone 3. Previous work-related skill, knowledge, or experience is required. **Job Preparation:** SVP 6.0 to less than 7.0—more than one year and less than four years. **Knowledge**—Customer and Personal Service; Medicine and Dentistry; Psychology; Education and Training; Biology. **Instructional Programs**—Respiratory Care Therapy/Therapist.

Related DOT Jobs—076.361-014 Respiratory Therapist.

29-1127.00 Speech-Language Pathologists

- **Education/Training Required: Master's degree**
- **Employed: 87,931**
- **Annual Earnings: $48,520**
- **Growth: 39.2%**
- **Annual Job Openings: 4,000**

Assess and treat persons with speech, language, voice, and fluency disorders. May select alternative communication systems and teach their use. May perform research related to speech and language problems.

Administer hearing or speech/language evaluations, tests, or examinations to patients to collect information on type and degree of impairments, using written and oral tests and special instruments. Develop and implement treatment plans for problems such as stuttering, delayed language, swallowing disorders, and inappropriate pitch or harsh voice problems, based on own assessments and recommendations of physicians, psychologists, and social workers. Develop speech exercise programs to reduce disabilities. Evaluate hearing and speech/language test results and medical or background information to diagnose and plan treatment for speech, language, fluency, voice, and swallowing disorders. Instruct clients in techniques for more effective communication, including sign language, lip reading, and voice improvement. Monitor patients' progress and adjust treatments accordingly. Record information on the initial evaluation, treatment, progress, and discharge of clients. Refer clients to additional medical or educational services if needed. Teach clients to control or strengthen tongue, jaw, face muscles, and breathing mechanisms. Communicate with non-speaking students, using sign language or computer technology. Conduct lessons and direct educational or therapeutic games to assist teachers dealing with speech problems. Conduct or direct research on speech or hearing topics and report findings for use in developing procedures, technologies, or treatments. Consult with and advise educators or medical staff on speech or hearing topics such as communication strategies and speech and language stimulation. Develop individual or group programs in schools to deal with speech or language problems. Instruct patients and family members in strategies to cope with or avoid communication-related misunderstandings. Participate in conferences or training or publish research results to share knowledge of new hearing or speech disorder treatment methods or technologies. Provide communication instruction to dialect speakers or students with limited English proficiency. Use computer applications to identify and assist with communication disabilities. Design, develop, and employ alternative diagnostic or communication devices and strategies.

GOE INFORMATION—Interest Area: 14. Medical and Health Services. **Work Group:** 14.06. Medical Therapy. **Personality Type**—Social. Social occupations frequently involve working with, communicating with, and teaching people. These occupations often involve helping or providing service to others. **Work Values**—Social Service; Authority; Creativity; Achievement; Pleasant Co-workers. **Skills**—Instructing; Writing; Management of Personnel Resources; Complex Problem Solving; Speaking; Learning Strategies; Reading Comprehension; Management of Financial Resources. **Abilities**—*Cognitive:* Oral Expression; Oral Comprehension; Written Expression; Written Comprehension; Fluency of Ideas. *Psychomotor:* None met the criteria. *Physical:* None met the criteria. *Sensory:* Speech Clarity; Speech Recognition; Hearing Sensitivity; Auditory Attention; Sound Localization. **General Work Activities**—*Information Input:* Getting Information; Identifying Objects, Actions, and Events; Monitoring Processes, Materials, or Surroundings. *Mental Process:* Processing Information; Analyzing Data or Information; Updating and Using Relevant Knowledge. *Work Output:* Documenting or Recording Information; Interacting with Computers; Handling and Moving Objects. *Interacting with Others:* Interpreting Meaning of Information for Others; Assisting and Caring for Others; Coordinating the Work and Activities of Others. **Physical Work Conditions**—Indoors; Sitting; Disease or Infections. **Other Job Characteristics**—Importance of Being Exact or Accurate; Importance of Repeating Same Tasks; Pace Determined by Speed of Equipment.

Experience—Job Zone 4. A minimum of two to four years of work-related skill, knowledge, or experience is needed. **Job Preparation:** SVP 7.0 to less than 8.0—two years to less than 10 years. **Knowledge**—Therapy and Counseling; Education and Training; Medicine and Dentistry; Personnel and Human Resources; Biology. **Instructional Programs**—Audiology/Audiologist and Speech-Language Pathology/Pathologist; Communication Disorders Sciences and Services, Other; Communication Disorders, General; Speech-Language Pathology/Pathologist.

Related DOT Jobs—076.101-014 Director, Speech-and-Hearing Clinic; 076.104-010 Voice Pathologist; 076.107-010 Speech Pathologist.

29-1129.99 Therapists, All Other

- **Education/Training Required: No data available.**
- **Employed: No data available.**
- **Annual Earnings: No data available.**
- **Growth: 33.2%**
- **Annual Job Openings: 3,000**

All therapists not listed separately.

No task data available.

GOE INFORMATION—Interest Area: 14. Medical and Health Services. **Work Group:** 14.06. Medical Therapy. **Note:** The Department of Labor has not collected some data for this job, so it has fewer details than the other descriptions.

Instructional Programs—Art Therapy/Therapist; Dance Therapy/Therapist; Hypnotherapy/Hypnotherapist; Kinesiology and Exercise Science; Movement Therapy and Movement Education; Music Therapy/Therapist; Rehabilitation and Therapeutic Professions, Other.

Related DOT Jobs—076.121-018 Exercise Physiologist; 076.124-010 Manual-Arts Therapist; 076.224-018 Movement Therapist; 076.264-010 Physical-Integration Practitioner; 076.361-010 Corrective Therapist; 079.157-010 Hypnotherapist.

29-1131.00 Veterinarians

- **Education/Training Required: First professional degree**
- **Employed: 58,634**
- **Annual Earnings: $62,000**
- **Growth: 31.8%**
- **Annual Job Openings: 2,000**

Diagnose and treat diseases and dysfunctions of animals. May engage in a particular function, such as research and development, consultation, administration, technical writing, sale or production of commercial products, or rendering of technical services to commercial firms or other organizations. Includes veterinarians who inspect livestock.

Advise animal owners regarding sanitary measures, feeding, and general care necessary to promote health of animals. Collect body tissue, feces, blood, urine, or other body fluids for examination and analysis. Establish and conduct quarantine and testing procedures that prevent the spread of diseases to other animals or to humans and that comply with applicable government regulations. Euthanize animals. Examine animals to detect and determine the nature of diseases or injuries. Inoculate animals against various diseases such as rabies and distemper. Inspect and test horses, sheep, poultry, and other animals to detect the presence of communicable diseases. Operate diagnostic equipment, such as radiographic and ultrasound equipment, and interpret the resulting images. Provide care to a wide range of animals or specialize in a particular species, such as horses or exotic birds. Specialize in a particular type of treatment, such as dentistry, pathology, nutrition, surgery, microbiology, or internal medicine. Treat sick or injured animals by prescribing medication, setting bones, dressing wounds, or performing surgery. Conduct postmortem studies and analyses to determine the causes of animals' deaths. Determine the effects of drug therapies, antibiotics, or new surgical techniques by testing them on animals. Direct activities concerned with the feeding, care, and housing of laboratory animals to ensure compliance with laboratory regulations. Direct the overall operations of animal hospitals, clinics, or mobile services to farms. Educate the public about diseases that can be spread from animals to humans. Enforce government regulations in disease control and food production by performing such tasks as inspecting meat packing plants and inspecting food animals before and after slaughter. Inspect animal housing facilities to determine their cleanliness and adequacy. Monitor scientific research programs to ensure compliance with regulations governing humane and ethical treatment of animals. Perform administrative duties such as scheduling appointments, accepting payments from clients, and maintaining business records. Plan and execute animal nutrition and reproduction programs. Research diseases to which animals could be susceptible. Train and supervise workers who handle and care for animals. Drive mobile clinic vans to farms so that health problems can be treated and/or prevented. Exchange information with zoos and aquariums concerning care, transfer, sale, or trade of animals in order to maintain species inventories. Teach in colleges of veterinary medicine.

GOE INFORMATION—Interest Area: 03. Plants and Animals. **Work Group:** 03.02. Animal Care and Training. **Personality Type**—Investigative. Investigative occupations frequently involve working with ideas and require an extensive amount of thinking. These occupations can involve searching for facts and figuring out problems mentally. **Work Values**—Recognition; Ability Utilization; Responsibility; Autonomy; Social Status. **Skills**—Science; Complex Problem Solving; Reading Comprehension; Instructing; Systems Evaluation; Critical Thinking; Learning Strategies; Monitoring. **Abilities**—*Cognitive:* Speed of Closure; Inductive Reasoning; Originality; Fluency of Ideas; Problem Sensitivity. *Psychomotor:* Manual Dexterity; Finger Dexterity; Arm-Hand Steadiness;

Control Precision; Response Orientation. *Physical:* Static Strength; Extent Flexibility; Explosive Strength; Dynamic Strength; Dynamic Flexibility. *Sensory:* Hearing Sensitivity; Speech Clarity; Visual Color Discrimination; Glare Sensitivity; Near Vision. **General Work Activities**—*Information Input:* Getting Information; Identifying Objects, Actions, and Events; Monitoring Processes, Materials, or Surroundings. *Mental Process:* Updating and Using Relevant Knowledge; Making Decisions and Solving Problems; Analyzing Data or Information. *Work Output:* Performing General Physical Activities; Handling and Moving Objects; Documenting or Recording Information. *Interacting with Others:* Teaching Others; Communicating with Persons Outside Organization; Assisting and Caring for Others. **Physical Work Conditions**—Disease or Infections; Minor Burns, Cuts, Bites, or Stings; Common Protective or Safety Attire; Radiation; Contaminants. **Other Job Characteristics**—Consequence of Error; Importance of Being Exact or Accurate; Pace Determined by Speed of Equipment.

Experience—Job Zone 5. Extensive skill, knowledge, and experience are needed for these occupations. **Job Preparation:** SVP 8.0 and above—four years to more than 10 years. **Knowledge**—Biology; Education and Training; Medicine and Dentistry; Chemistry; English Language. **Instructional Programs**—Comparative and Laboratory Animal Medicine (Cert, MS, PhD); Laboratory Animal Medicine; Large Animal/Food Animal and Equine Surgery and Medicine (Cert, MS, PhD); Small/Companion Animal Surgery and Medicine (Cert, MS, PhD); Theriogenology; Veterinary Anatomy (Cert, MS, PhD); Veterinary Anesthesiology; Veterinary Biomedical and Clinical Sciences, Other (Cert, MS. PhD); Veterinary Dentistry; Veterinary Dermatology; Veterinary Emergency and Critical Care Medicine; Veterinary Infectious Diseases (Cert, MS, PhD); Veterinary Internal Medicine; Veterinary Medicine (DVM); Veterinary Microbiology; Veterinary Microbiology and Immunobiology (Cert, MS, PhD); Veterinary Nutrition; Veterinary Ophthalmology; Veterinary Pathology; Veterinary Pathology and Pathobiology (Cert, MS, PhD); Veterinary Physiology (Cert, MS, PhD); Veterinary Practice; Veterinary Preventive Medicine; Veterinary Preventive Medicine Epidemiology and Public Health (Cert, MS, PhD); Veterinary Radiology; Veterinary Residency Programs, Other; Veterinary Sciences/Veterinary Clinical Sciences, General (Cert, MS, PhD); Veterinary Surgery; Veterinary Toxicology; Veterinary Toxicology and Pharmacology (Cert, MS, PhD); Zoological Medicine.

Related DOT Jobs—073.061-010 Veterinarian, Laboratory Animal Care; 073.101-010 Veterinarian; 073.101-014 Veterinarian, Poultry; 073.101-018 Zoo Veterinarian.

29-1199.99 Health Diagnosing and Treating Practitioners, All Other

- Education/Training Required: No data available.
- Employed: No data available.
- Annual Earnings: No data available.
- Growth: 24.8%
- Annual Job Openings: 3,000

All health diagnosing and treating practitioners not listed separately.

No task data available.

GOE INFORMATION—**Interest Area:** 14. Medical and Health Services. **Work Group:** 14.06. Medical Therapy. **Note:** The Department of Labor has not collected some data for this job, so it has fewer details than the other descriptions.

Instructional Programs—Acupuncture; Alternative and Complementary Medicine and Medical Systems, Other; Aromatherapy; Ayurvedic Medicine/Ayurveda; Direct Entry Midwifery (LM, CPM); Herbalism/Herbalist; Homeopathic Medicine/Homeopathy; Naturopathic Medicine/Naturopathy (ND); Phlebotomy/Phlebotomist; Traditional Chinese/Asian Medicine and Chinese Herbology.

Related DOT Jobs—070.101-090 Radiologist; 079.101-014 Doctor, Naturopathic; 079.271-010 Acupuncturist; 079.271-014 Acupressurist.

29-2000 Health Technologists and Technicians

29-2011.00 Medical and Clinical Laboratory Technologists

- Education/Training Required: Bachelor's degree
- Employed: 148,380
- Annual Earnings: $42,240
- Growth: 17.0%
- Annual Job Openings: 19,000

Perform complex medical laboratory tests for diagnosis, treatment, and prevention of disease. May train or supervise staff.

Analyze laboratory findings to check the accuracy of the results. Analyze samples of biological material for chemical content or reaction. Conduct chemical analysis of body fluids, including blood, urine, and spinal fluid, to determine presence of normal and abnormal components. Cultivate, isolate, and assist in identifying microbial organisms and perform various tests on these microorganisms. Enter data from analysis of medical tests and clinical results into computer for storage. Harvest cell cultures at optimum time based on knowledge of cell cycle differences and culture conditions. Obtain, cut, stain, and mount biological material on slides for microscopic study and diagnosis, following standard laboratory procedures. Operate, calibrate, and maintain equipment used in quantitative and qualitative analysis, such as spectrophotometers, calorimeters, flame photometers, and computer-controlled analyzers. Prepare slide of cell culture to identify chromosomes, view and photograph slide under photo-microscope, and print picture. Provide technical information about test results to physicians, family members, and researchers. Select and prepare specimen and media for cell culture, using aseptic technique and knowledge of medium components and cell requirements. Set up, clean, and maintain laboratory equipment. Study blood samples to determine the number of cells and their morphology, as well as the blood group, type, and compatibility for transfusion purposes, using microscopic technique. Cut images of chromosomes from photograph and identify and arrange them in numbered pairs on karyotype chart, using standard practices. Develop, standardize, evaluate, and modify procedures, techniques, and tests used in the analysis of specimens and in medical laboratory experiments. Establish and monitor programs to ensure the accuracy of laboratory results. Prepare vaccines and biological serums for disease prevention. Supervise, train, and direct lab assistants, medical and clinical laboratory technicians and technologists, and other medical laboratory workers engaged in laboratory testing. Conduct medical research under direction of microbiologist or biochemist.

GOE INFORMATION—**Interest Area:** 14. Medical and Health Services. **Work Group:** 14.05. Medical Technology. **Personality Type**—Investigative. Investigative occupations frequently involve working with ideas and require an extensive amount of thinking. These occupations can involve searching for facts and figuring out problems mentally. **Work Values**—Ability Utilization; Variety; Social Service; Achievement; Social

Status. **Skills**—Science; Reading Comprehension; Writing; Speaking; Complex Problem Solving; Learning Strategies; Management of Material Resources; Critical Thinking. **Abilities**—*Cognitive:* Written Expression; Oral Expression; Inductive Reasoning; Flexibility of Closure; Oral Comprehension. *Psychomotor:* Arm-Hand Steadiness; Control Precision; Finger Dexterity; Reaction Time; Wrist-Finger Speed. *Physical:* None met the criteria. *Sensory:* Visual Color Discrimination; Speech Clarity; Near Vision; Far Vision; Speech Recognition. **General Work Activities**—*Information Input:* Identifying Objects, Actions, and Events; Getting Information; Monitoring Processes, Materials, or Surroundings. *Mental Process:* Updating and Using Relevant Knowledge; Evaluating Information Against Standards; Analyzing Data or Information. *Work Output:* Documenting or Recording Information; Controlling Machines and Processes; Handling and Moving Objects. *Interacting with Others:* Communicating with Other Workers; Communicating with Persons Outside Organization; Providing Consultation and Advice to Others. **Physical Work Conditions**—Disease or Infections; Common Protective or Safety Attire; Hazardous Conditions; Sitting; Making Repetitive Motions. **Other Job Characteristics**—Importance of Being Exact or Accurate; Degree of Automation; Consequence of Error.

Experience—Job Zone 4. A minimum of two to four years of work-related skill, knowledge, or experience is needed. **Job Preparation:** SVP 7.0 to less than 8.0—two years to less than 10 years. **Knowledge**—Biology; Chemistry; Medicine and Dentistry; Education and Training; English Language. **Instructional Programs**—Clinical Laboratory Science/Medical Technology/Technologist; Clinical/Medical Laboratory Science and Allied Professions, Other; Cytogenetics/Genetics/Clinical Genetics Technology/Technologist; Cytotechnology/Cytotechnologist; Histologic Technology/Histotechnologist; Renal/Dialysis Technologist/Technician.

Related DOT Jobs—078.121-010 Medical Technologist, Teaching Supervisor; 078.161-010 Medical Technologist, Chief; 078.261-010 Biochemistry Technologist; 078.261-014 Microbiology Technologist; 078.261-026 Cytogenetic Technologist; 078.261-030 Histotechnologist; 078.261-038 Medical Technologist; 078.261-046 Immunohematologist; 078.281-010 Cytotechnologist.

29-2012.00 Medical and Clinical Laboratory Technicians

- **Education/Training Required: Associate's degree**
- **Employed: 146,793**
- **Annual Earnings: $28,810**
- **Growth: 19.0%**
- **Annual Job Openings: 19,000**

Perform routine medical laboratory tests for the diagnosis, treatment, and prevention of disease. May work under the supervision of a medical technologist.

Analyze and record test data to issue reports that use charts, graphs, and narratives. Analyze the results of tests and experiments to ensure conformity to specifications, using special mechanical and electrical devices. Conduct blood tests for transfusion purposes and perform blood counts. Conduct chemical analyses of body fluids, such as blood and urine, using microscope or automatic analyzer to detect abnormalities or diseases; enter findings into computer. Consult with a pathologist to determine a final diagnosis when abnormal cells are found. Cut, stain, and mount tissue samples for examination by pathologists. Examine cells stained with dye to locate abnormalities. Inoculate fertilized eggs, broths, or other bacteriological media with organisms. Obtain specimens, cultivating, isolating, and identifying microorganisms for analysis. Prepare standard volumetric solutions and reagents to be combined with samples, following standardized formulas or experimental procedures. Prepare vaccines and serums by standard laboratory methods, testing for virus inactivity and sterility. Collect blood or tissue samples from patients, observing principles of asepsis to obtain blood sample. Perform medical research to further control and cure disease. Set up, adjust, maintain, and clean medical laboratory equipment. Supervise and instruct other technicians and laboratory assistants. Test raw materials, processes, and finished products to determine quality and quantity of materials or characteristics of a substance.

GOE INFORMATION—**Interest Area:** 14. Medical and Health Services. **Work Group:** 14.05. Medical Technology. **Personality Type**—Realistic. Realistic occupations frequently involve work activities that include practical, hands-on problems and solutions. They often deal with plants, animals, and real-world materials like wood, tools, and machinery. Many of the occupations require working outside and do not involve a lot of paperwork or working closely with others. **Work Values**—Ability Utilization; Pleasant Co-workers; Social Service; Achievement; Security. **Skills**—Science; Quality Control Analysis; Equipment Selection; Operation Monitoring; Operation and Control. **Abilities**—*Cognitive:* Flexibility of Closure; Perceptual Speed; Speed of Closure; Information Ordering; Memorization. *Psychomotor:* Arm-Hand Steadiness; Wrist-Finger Speed; Finger Dexterity; Control Precision; Reaction Time. *Physical:* Extent Flexibility; Trunk Strength. *Sensory:* Visual Color Discrimination; Near Vision; Speech Clarity; Speech Recognition; Hearing Sensitivity. **General Work Activities**—*Information Input:* Identifying Objects, Actions, and Events; Monitoring Processes, Materials, or Surroundings; Getting Information. *Mental Process:* Evaluating Information Against Standards; Updating and Using Relevant Knowledge; Judging Qualities of Things, Services, or Other People's Work. *Work Output:* Handling and Moving Objects; Controlling Machines and Processes; Documenting or Recording Information. *Interacting with Others:* Communicating with Other Workers; Assisting and Caring for Others; Establishing and Maintaining Relationships. **Physical Work Conditions**—Disease or Infections; Common Protective or Safety Attire; Indoors; Specialized Protective or Safety Attire; Contaminants. **Other Job Characteristics**—Importance of Being Exact or Accurate; Consequence of Error; Degree of Automation.

Experience—Job Zone 2. Some previous work-related skill, knowledge, or experience may be helpful, but usually is not needed. **Job Preparation:** SVP 4.0 to less than 6.0—six months to less than two years. **Knowledge**—Biology; Chemistry; Medicine and Dentistry; Mathematics; Psychology. **Instructional Programs**—Blood Bank Technology Specialist; Clinical/Medical Laboratory Assistant; Clinical/Medical Laboratory Technician; Hematology Technology/Technician; Histologic Technician.

Related DOT Jobs—078.367-014 Specimen Processor; 078.381-014 Medical-Laboratory Technician; 078.687-010 Laboratory Assistant, Blood and Plasma; 559.361-010 Laboratory Technician, Pharmaceutical.

29-2021.00 Dental Hygienists

- **Education/Training Required: Associate's degree**
- **Employed: 146,629**
- **Annual Earnings: $54,700**
- **Growth: 37.1%**
- **Annual Job Openings: 5,000**

Clean teeth and examine oral areas, head, and neck for signs of oral disease. May educate patients on oral hygiene, take and develop X rays, or apply fluoride or sealants.

Clean calcareous deposits, accretions, and stains from teeth and beneath margins of gums, using dental instruments. Feel and visually examine gums for sores and signs of disease. Chart conditions of decay and disease for diagnosis and treatment by dentist. Feel lymph nodes under patient's chin to detect swelling or tenderness that could indicate presence of oral cancer. Apply fluorides and other cavity-preventing agents to arrest dental decay. Examine gums, using probes, to locate periodontal recessed gums and signs of gum disease. Expose and develop X-ray film. Provide clinical services and health education to improve and maintain oral health of schoolchildren. Remove excess cement from coronal surfaces of teeth. Make impressions for study casts. Place, carve, and finish amalgam restorations. Administer local anesthetic agents. Conduct dental health clinics for community groups to augment services of dentist. Remove sutures and dressings. Place and remove rubber dams, matrices, and temporary restorations.

GOE INFORMATION—Interest Area: 14. Medical and Health Services. Work Group: 14.03. Dentistry. Personality Type—Social. Social occupations frequently involve working with, communicating with, and teaching people. These occupations often involve helping or providing service to others. Work Values—Social Service; Pleasant Co-workers; Social Status; Security; Authority. Skills—Equipment Selection; Time Management; Instructing; Reading Comprehension; Social Perceptiveness; Learning Strategies; Critical Thinking; Active Listening. Abilities—*Cognitive:* Problem Sensitivity; Inductive Reasoning; Flexibility of Closure; Speed of Closure; Category Flexibility. *Psychomotor:* Finger Dexterity; Control Precision; Manual Dexterity; Arm-Hand Steadiness; Multilimb Coordination. *Physical:* Extent Flexibility; Dynamic Strength. *Sensory:* Near Vision; Speech Recognition; Speech Clarity; Visual Color Discrimination; Depth Perception. General Work Activities—*Information Input:* Identifying Objects, Actions, and Events; Getting Information; Monitoring Processes, Materials, or Surroundings. *Mental Process:* Updating and Using Relevant Knowledge; Organizing, Planning, and Prioritizing; Making Decisions and Solving Problems. *Work Output:* Documenting or Recording Information; Handling and Moving Objects; Controlling Machines and Processes. *Interacting with Others:* Establishing and Maintaining Relationships; Assisting and Caring for Others; Performing for or Working with the Public. Physical Work Conditions—Radiation; Common Protective or Safety Attire; Disease or Infections; Indoors; Standing. Other Job Characteristics—Importance of Being Exact or Accurate; Consequence of Error; Pace Determined by Speed of Equipment.

Experience—Job Zone 3. Previous work-related skill, knowledge, or experience is required. Job Preparation: SVP 6.0 to less than 7.0—more than one year and less than four years. Knowledge—Biology; Medicine and Dentistry; Customer and Personal Service; Psychology; Chemistry. Instructional Programs—Dental Hygiene/Hygienist.

Related DOT Jobs—078.361-010 Dental Hygienist.

29-2031.00 Cardiovascular Technologists and Technicians

- Education/Training Required: Associate's degree
- Employed: 38,663
- Annual Earnings: $35,010
- Growth: 34.9%
- Annual Job Openings: 3,000

Conduct tests on pulmonary or cardiovascular systems of patients for diagnostic purposes. May conduct or assist in electrocardiograms, cardiac catheterizations, pulmonary-functions, lung capacity, and similar tests.

Activate fluoroscope and camera to produce images used to guide catheter through cardiovascular system. Adjust equipment and controls according to physicians' orders or established protocol. Assess cardiac physiology and calculate valve areas from blood flow velocity measurements. Assist physicians in diagnosis and treatment of cardiac and peripheral vascular treatments; for example, assisting with balloon angioplasties to treat blood vessel blockages. Attach electrodes to the patients' chests, arms, and legs; connect electrodes to leads from the electrocardiogram (EKG) machine; and operate the EKG machine to obtain a reading. Compare measurements of heart wall thickness and chamber sizes to standard norms to identify abnormalities. Conduct electrocardiogram, phonocardiogram, echocardiogram, stress testing, and other cardiovascular tests to record patients' cardiac activity, using specialized electronic test equipment, recording devices, and laboratory instruments. Enter factors such as amount and quality of radiation beam and filming sequence into computer. Explain testing procedures to patient to obtain cooperation and reduce anxiety. Monitor patients' comfort and safety during tests, alerting physicians to abnormalities or changes in patient responses. Monitor patients' blood pressure and heart rate using electrocardiogram (EKG) equipment during diagnostic and therapeutic procedures in order to notify the physician if something appears wrong. Observe gauges, recorder, and video screens of data analysis system during imaging of cardiovascular system. Observe ultrasound display screen and listen to signals to record vascular information such as blood pressure, limb volume changes, oxygen saturation, and cerebral circulation. Operate diagnostic imaging equipment to produce contrast-enhanced radiographs of heart and cardiovascular system. Prepare and position patients for testing. Prepare reports of diagnostic procedures for interpretation by physician. Check, test, and maintain cardiology equipment, making minor repairs when necessary to ensure proper operation. Conduct tests of pulmonary system, using spirometer and other respiratory testing equipment. Inject contrast medium into patients' blood vessels. Obtain and record patient identification, medical history, and test results. Reprogram pacemakers according to required standards. Supervise and train other cardiology technologists and students.

GOE INFORMATION—Interest Area: 14. Medical and Health Services. Work Group: 14.05. Medical Technology. Personality Type—Investigative. Investigative occupations frequently involve working with ideas and require an extensive amount of thinking. These occupations can involve searching for facts and figuring out problems mentally. Work Values—Social Service; Social Status; Recognition; Compensation; Ability Utilization. Skills—Operation Monitoring; Operation and Control; Science; Mathematics; Reading Comprehension; Equipment Selection. Abilities—*Cognitive:* Oral Comprehension; Written Comprehension; Problem Sensitivity; Oral Expression; Perceptual Speed. *Psychomotor:* Control Precision; Reaction Time; Finger Dexterity. *Physical:* None met the criteria. *Sensory:* Hearing Sensitivity; Auditory Attention. General Work Activities—*Information Input:* Monitoring Processes, Materials, or Surroundings; Getting Information; Identifying Objects, Actions, and Events. *Mental Process:* Updating and Using Relevant Knowledge; Processing Information; Evaluating Information Against Standards. *Work Output:* Documenting or Recording Information; Controlling Machines and Processes; Handling and Moving Objects. *Interacting with Others:* Assisting and Caring for Others; Communicating with Other Workers; Establishing and Maintaining Relationships. Physical Work Conditions—Specialized Protective or Safety Attire; Disease or Infections; Indoors; Radiation; Standing. Other Job Characteristics—Importance of Being Exact or Accurate; Consequence of Error; Degree of Automation.

Experience—Job Zone 3. Previous work-related skill, knowledge, or experience is required. Job Preparation: SVP 6.0 to less than 7.0—more than one year and less than four years. Knowledge—Medicine and Dentistry; Biology; Computers and Electronics; Therapy and Counseling; Chemistry. Instructional Programs—Cardiopulmonary Technology/Technologist; Cardiovascular Technology/Technologist; Electrocardiograph Technology/Technician; Perfusion Technology/Perfusionist.

Related DOT Jobs—078.161-014 Cardiopulmonary Technologist, Chief; 078.262-010 Pulmonary-Function Technician; 078.264-010 Holter Scanning Technician; 078.362-030 Cardiopulmonary Technologist; 078.362-034 Perfusionist; 078.362-050 Special Procedures Technologist, Cardiac Catheterization; 078.362-062 Stress Test Technician; 078.364-014 Echocardiograph Technician; 078.365-010 Cardiac Monitor Technician.

29-2032.00 Diagnostic Medical Sonographers

- Education/Training Required: Associate's degree
- Employed: 32,815
- Annual Earnings: $46,980
- Growth: 26.1%
- Annual Job Openings: 3,000

Produce ultrasonic recordings of internal organs for use by physicians.

Decide which images to include, looking for differences between healthy and pathological areas. Observe screen during scan to ensure that image produced is satisfactory for diagnostic purposes, making adjustments to equipment as required. Observe and care for patients throughout examinations to ensure their safety and comfort. Provide sonogram and oral or written summary of technical findings to physician for use in medical diagnosis. Operate ultrasound equipment to produce and record images of the motion, shape, and composition of blood, organs, tissues, and bodily masses such as fluid accumulations. Select appropriate equipment settings and adjust patient positions to obtain the best sites and angles. Determine whether scope of exam should be extended, based on findings. Process and code film from procedures and complete appropriate documentation. Obtain and record accurate patient history, including prior test results and information from physical examinations. Prepare patient for exam by explaining procedure, transferring them to ultrasound table, scrubbing skin and applying gel, and positioning them properly. Record and store suitable images, using camera unit connected to the ultrasound equipment. Coordinate work with physicians and other health care team members, including providing assistance during invasive procedures. Maintain records that include patient information, sonographs and interpretations, files of correspondence, publications and regulations, and quality assurance records (e.g., pathology, biopsy, post-operative reports). Perform legal and ethical duties, including preparing safety and accident reports, obtaining written consent from patient to perform invasive procedures, and reporting symptoms of abuse and neglect. Supervise and train students and other medical sonographers. Maintain stock and supplies, preparing supplies for special examinations and ordering supplies when necessary. Clean, check, and maintain sonographic equipment, submitting maintenance requests or performing minor repairs as necessary. Perform clerical duties such as scheduling exams and special procedures, keeping records, and archiving computerized images. Perform medical procedures such as administering oxygen, inserting and removing airways, taking vital signs, and giving emergency treatment such as first aid or cardiopulmonary resuscitation. Load and unload film cassettes used to record images from procedures.

GOE INFORMATION—**Interest Area:** 14. Medical and Health Services. **Work Group:** 14.05. Medical Technology. **Personality Type**—No data available. **Work Values**—None met the criteria. **Skills**—Reading Comprehension; Social Perceptiveness; Operation and Control; Learning Strategies; Instructing; Active Listening; Speaking; Equipment Selection. **Abilities**—*Cognitive:* Flexibility of Closure; Problem Sensitivity; Inductive Reasoning; Perceptual Speed; Speed of Closure. *Psychomotor:* Control Precision; Reaction Time; Response Orientation; Finger Dexterity; Multilimb Coordination. *Physical:* Extent Flexibility; Gross Body Coordination; Static Strength; Stamina; Trunk Strength. *Sensory:* Near Vision; Far Vision; Depth Perception; Speech Recognition; Visual Color Discrimination. **General Work Activities**—*Information Input:* Identifying Objects, Actions, and Events; Monitoring Processes, Materials, or Surroundings; Getting Information. *Mental Process:* Organizing, Planning, and Prioritizing; Updating and Using Relevant Knowledge; Making Decisions and Solving Problems. *Work Output:* Handling and Moving Objects; Controlling Machines and Processes; Documenting or Recording Information. *Interacting with Others:* Assisting and Caring for Others; Establishing and Maintaining Relationships; Communicating with Other Workers. **Physical Work Conditions**—No data available. **Other Job Characteristics**—No data available.

Experience—Job Zone 3. Previous work-related skill, knowledge, or experience is required. **Job Preparation:** No data available. **Knowledge**—Medicine and Dentistry; Customer and Personal Service; Biology; Education and Training; Physics. **Instructional Programs**—Allied Health Diagnostic, Intervention, and Treatment Professions, Other; Diagnostic Medical Sonography/Sonographer and Ultrasound Technician.

Related DOT Jobs—078.364-010 Ultrasound Technologist.

29-2033.00 Nuclear Medicine Technologists

- Education/Training Required: Associate's degree
- Employed: 18,219
- Annual Earnings: $47,400
- Growth: 22.4%
- Annual Job Openings: 1,000

Prepare, administer, and measure radioactive isotopes in therapeutic, diagnostic, and tracer studies utilizing a variety of radioisotope equipment. Prepare stock solutions of radioactive materials and calculate doses to be administered by radiologists. Subject patients to radiation. Execute blood volume, red cell survival, and fat absorption studies following standard laboratory techniques.

Add radioactive substances to biological specimens, such as blood, urine, and feces, to determine therapeutic drug or hormone levels. Calculate, measure, and record radiation dosage or radiopharmaceuticals received, used, and disposed, using computer and following physician's prescription. Detect and map radiopharmaceuticals in patients' bodies, using a camera to produce photographic or computer images. Dispose of radioactive materials and store radiopharmaceuticals, following radiation safety procedures. Explain test procedures and safety precautions to patients and provide them with assistance during test procedures. Measure glandular activity, blood volume, red cell survival, and radioactivity of patient, using scanners, Geiger counters, scintillometers, and other laboratory equipment. Position radiation fields, radiation beams, and patient to allow for most effective treatment of patient's disease, using computer. Administer radiopharmaceuticals or radiation to patients to detect or treat diseases, using radioisotope equipment, under direction of physician. Prepare stock radiopharmaceuticals, adhering to safety standards that minimize radiation exposure to workers and patients. Process cardiac function studies, using computer. Produce a computer-generated or film image for interpretation by a physician. Record and process results of procedures. Develop treatment procedures for nuclear medicine treatment programs. Gather information on patients' illnesses and medical history to guide the choice of diagnostic procedures for therapy. Maintain and calibrate radioisotope and laboratory equipment. Train and supervise student or subordinate nuclear medicine technologists.

GOE INFORMATION—**Interest Area:** 14. Medical and Health Services. **Work Group:** 14.05. Medical Technology. **Personality Type**—Investigative. Investigative occupations frequently involve working with ideas and require an extensive amount of thinking. These occupations can involve searching for facts and figuring out problems mentally. **Work Values**—Social Service; Ability Utilization; Variety; Achievement; Social Status. **Skills**—Operation Monitoring; Operation and Control; Reading Comprehension; Science; Mathematics; Equipment Selection; Instructing; Management of Personnel Resources. **Abilities**—*Cognitive:* Oral Comprehension; Written Comprehension; Written Expression; Problem Sensitivity; Oral Expression. *Psychomotor:* Control Precision; Multilimb Coordination; Finger Dexterity; Arm-Hand Steadiness. *Physical:* Trunk Strength; Extent Flexibility. *Sensory:* Speech Recognition. **General Work Activities**—*Information Input:* Monitoring Processes, Materials, or Surroundings; Getting Information; Identifying Objects, Actions, and Events. *Mental Process:* Updating and Using Relevant Knowledge; Processing Information; Evaluating Information Against Standards. *Work Output:* Interacting with Computers; Controlling Machines and Processes; Documenting or Recording Information. *Interacting with Others:* Communicating with Other Workers; Interpreting Meaning of Information for Others; Assisting and Caring for Others. **Physical Work Conditions**—Radiation; Specialized Protective or Safety Attire; Disease or Infections; Common Protective or Safety Attire; Indoors. **Other Job Characteristics**—Importance of Being Exact or Accurate; Consequence of Error; Importance of Repeating Same Tasks.

Experience—Job Zone 4. A minimum of two to four years of work-related skill, knowledge, or experience is needed. **Job Preparation:** SVP 7.0 to less than 8.0—two years to less than 10 years. **Knowledge**—Medicine and Dentistry; Biology; Chemistry; Computers and Electronics; Therapy and Counseling. **Instructional Programs**—Nuclear Medical Technology/Technologist; Radiation Protection/Health Physics Technician.

Related DOT Jobs—078.131-010 Chief Technologist, Nuclear Medicine; 078.261-034 Medical Radiation Dosimetrist; 078.361-018 Nuclear Medicine Technologist.

29-2034.00 Radiologic Technologists and Technicians

- **Education/Training Required: Associate's degree**
- **Employed: 167,413**
- **Annual Earnings: $37,680**
- **Growth: 23.1%**
- **Annual Job Openings: 13,000**

Take X rays and CAT scans or administer nonradioactive materials into patient's bloodstream for diagnostic purposes. Includes technologists who specialize in other modalities, such as computed tomography and magnetic resonance. Includes workers whose primary duties are to demonstrate portions of the human body on X-ray film or fluoroscopic screen.

No task data available.

GOE INFORMATION—Interest Area: 14. Medical and Health Services. **Work Group:** 14.05. Medical Technology. **Note:** The Department of Labor has not collected some data for this job, so it has fewer details than the other descriptions.

Instructional Programs—Allied Health Diagnostic, Intervention, and Treatment Professions, Other; Medical Radiologic Technology/Science—Radiation Therapist; Radiologic Technology/Science—Radiographer.

Related DOT Jobs—078.162-010 Radiologic Technologist, Chief; 078.362-026 Radiologic Technologist; 078.362-046 Special Procedures Technolo-

gist, Angiogram; 078.362-054 Special Procedures Technologist, CT Scan; 078.362-058 Special Procedures Technologist, Magnetic Resonance Imaging (MRI); 078.364-010 Ultrasound Technologist.

29-2034.01 Radiologic Technologists

- **Education/Training Required: Associate's degree**
- **Employed: No data available.**
- **Annual Earnings: $37,680**
- **Growth: 23.1%**
- **Annual Job Openings: 13,000**

Take X rays and CAT scans or administer nonradioactive materials into patient's bloodstream for diagnostic purposes. Includes technologists who specialize in other modalities, such as computed tomography, ultrasound, and magnetic resonance.

Review and evaluate developed X rays, videotape, or computer-generated information to determine if images are satisfactory for diagnostic purposes. Use radiation safety measures and protection devices to comply with government regulations and to ensure safety of patients and staff. Explain procedures and observe patients to ensure safety and comfort during scan. Operate or oversee operation of radiologic and magnetic imaging equipment to produce images of the body for diagnostic purposes. Position and immobilize patient on examining table. Position imaging equipment and adjust controls to set exposure time and distance according to specification of examination. Key commands and data into computer to document and specify scan sequences, adjust transmitters and receivers, or photograph certain images. Monitor video display of area being scanned and adjust density or contrast to improve picture quality. Monitor patients' conditions and reactions, reporting abnormal signs to physician. Set up examination rooms, ensuring that all necessary equipment is ready. Prepare and administer oral or injected contrast media to patients. Take thorough and accurate patient medical histories. Remove and process film. Record, process, and maintain patient data and treatment records; prepare reports. Coordinate work with clerical personnel and other technologists. Demonstrate new equipment, procedures, and techniques to staff and provide technical assistance. Provide assistance with such tasks as dressing and changing to seriously ill, injured, or disabled patients. Move ultrasound scanner over patient's body and watch pattern produced on video screen. Measure thickness of section to be radiographed, using instruments similar to measuring tapes. Operate fluoroscope to aid physician to view and guide wire or catheter through blood vessels to area of interest. Assign duties to radiologic staff to maintain patient flows and achieve production goals. Collaborate with other medical team members, such as physicians and nurses, to conduct angiography or special vascular procedures. Perform administrative duties such as developing departmental operating budget, coordinating purchases of supplies and equipment, and preparing work schedules. Perform scheduled maintenance and minor emergency repairs on radiographic equipment.

GOE INFORMATION—Interest Area: 14. Medical and Health Services. **Work Group:** 14.05. Medical Technology. **Personality Type**—Realistic. Realistic occupations frequently involve work activities that include practical, hands-on problems and solutions. They often deal with plants, animals, and real-world materials like wood, tools, and machinery. Many of the occupations require working outside and do not involve a lot of paperwork or working closely with others. **Work Values**—Social Service; Ability Utilization; Authority; Pleasant Co-workers; Security. **Skills**—Instructing; Operation Monitoring; Social Perceptiveness; Reading Comprehension; Service Orientation; Active Listening; Speaking; Critical Thinking. **Abilities**—*Cognitive:* Flexibility of Closure; Speed of Closure; Perceptual Speed; Inductive Reasoning; Category Flexibility. *Psychomotor:* Rate Control; Control Precision; Reaction Time; Finger Dexterity;

Arm-Hand Steadiness. *Physical:* Static Strength; Extent Flexibility; Trunk Strength; Stamina; Gross Body Coordination. *Sensory:* Far Vision; Depth Perception; Speech Recognition; Visual Color Discrimination; Near Vision. **General Work Activities**—*Information Input:* Identifying Objects, Actions, and Events; Monitoring Processes, Materials, or Surroundings; Getting Information. *Mental Process:* Updating and Using Relevant Knowledge; Making Decisions and Solving Problems; Processing Information. *Work Output:* Handling and Moving Objects; Performing General Physical Activities; Controlling Machines and Processes. *Interacting with Others:* Assisting and Caring for Others; Performing for or Working with the Public; Establishing and Maintaining Relationships. **Physical Work Conditions**—Radiation; Disease or Infections; Indoors; Common Protective or Safety Attire; Specialized Protective or Safety Attire. **Other Job Characteristics**—Importance of Being Exact or Accurate; Consequence of Error; Pace Determined by Speed of Equipment.

Experience—Job Zone 3. Previous work-related skill, knowledge, or experience is required. **Job Preparation:** SVP 7.0 to less than 8.0—two years to less than 10 years. **Knowledge**—Customer and Personal Service; Medicine and Dentistry; Psychology; Biology; Chemistry. **Instructional Programs**—Allied Health Diagnostic, Intervention, and Treatment Professions, Other; Medical Radiologic Technology/Science—Radiation Therapist; Radiologic Technology/Science—Radiographer.

Related DOT Jobs—078.162-010 Radiologic Technologist, Chief; 078.362-026 Radiologic Technologist; 078.362-046 Special Procedures Technologist, Angiogram; 078.362-054 Special Procedures Technologist, CT Scan; 078.362-058 Special Procedures Technologist, Magnetic Resonance Imaging (MRI).

29-2034.02 Radiologic Technicians

- Education/Training Required: **Associate's degree**
- Employed: **No data available.**
- Annual Earnings: **$37,680**
- Growth: **23.1%**
- Annual Job Openings: **13,000**

Maintain and use equipment and supplies necessary to demonstrate portions of the human body on X-ray film or fluoroscopic screen for diagnostic purposes.

Determine patients' X ray needs by reading requests or instructions from physicians. Explain procedures to patients to reduce anxieties and obtain cooperation. Make exposures necessary for the requested procedures, rejecting and repeating work that does not meet established standards. Monitor equipment operation and report malfunctioning equipment to supervisor. Operate mobile X-ray equipment in operating room, in emergency room, or at patient's bedside. Perform procedures such as linear tomography, mammography, sonograms, joint and cyst aspirations, routine contrast studies, routine fluoroscopy, and examinations of the head, trunk, and extremities under supervision of physician. Position patient on examining table and set up and adjust equipment to obtain optimum view of specific body area as requested by physician. Position X-ray equipment and adjust controls to set exposure factors, such as time and distance. Prepare contrast material, radiopharmaceuticals, and anesthetic or antispasmodic drugs under the direction of a radiologist. Provide assistance in radiopharmaceutical administration, monitoring patients' vital signs and notifying the radiologist of any relevant changes. Provide assistance to physicians or other technologists in the performance of more complex procedures. Process exposed radiographs, using film processors or computer-generated methods. Use beam-restrictive devices and patient-shielding techniques to minimize radiation exposure to patient and staff. Assure that sterile supplies, contrast materials, catheters, and other required equipment are present and in working order, requisitioning materials as necessary. Coordinate work of other technicians or technologists when procedures require more than one person. Maintain a current file of examination protocols. Maintain records of patients examined, examinations performed, views taken, and technical factors used. Operate digital picture archiving communications systems. Prepare and set up X-ray room for patient. Assist with on-the-job training of new employees and students and provide input to supervisors regarding training performance. Provide students and other technologists with suggestions of additional views, alternate positioning, or improved techniques to ensure the images produced are of the highest quality.

GOE INFORMATION—Interest Area: 14. Medical and Health Services. **Work Group:** 14.05. Medical Technology. **Personality Type**—Realistic. Realistic occupations frequently involve work activities that include practical, hands-on problems and solutions. They often deal with plants, animals, and real-world materials like wood, tools, and machinery. Many of the occupations require working outside and do not involve a lot of paperwork or working closely with others. **Work Values**—Social Service; Pleasant Co-workers; Moral Values; Security; Supervision, Human Relations. **Skills**—Operation and Control; Operation Monitoring. **Abilities**—*Cognitive:* Oral Expression; Oral Comprehension; Written Comprehension. *Psychomotor:* Control Precision; Multilimb Coordination. *Physical:* Gross Body Coordination; Static Strength; Extent Flexibility. *Sensory:* None met the criteria. **General Work Activities**—*Information Input:* Monitoring Processes, Materials, or Surroundings; Getting Information; Identifying Objects, Actions, and Events. *Mental Process:* Updating and Using Relevant Knowledge; Processing Information; Organizing, Planning, and Prioritizing. *Work Output:* Performing General Physical Activities; Controlling Machines and Processes; Handling and Moving Objects. *Interacting with Others:* Communicating with Other Workers; Establishing and Maintaining Relationships; Assisting and Caring for Others. **Physical Work Conditions**—Radiation; Specialized Protective or Safety Attire; Disease or Infections; Indoors; Common Protective or Safety Attire. **Other Job Characteristics**—Consequence of Error; Importance of Being Exact or Accurate; Pace Determined by Speed of Equipment.

Experience—Job Zone 4. A minimum of two to four years of work-related skill, knowledge, or experience is needed. **Job Preparation:** SVP 7.0 to less than 8.0—two years to less than 10 years. **Knowledge**—Medicine and Dentistry; Biology; Customer and Personal Service; Psychology; Therapy and Counseling. **Instructional Programs**—Allied Health Diagnostic, Intervention, and Treatment Professions, Other; Medical Radiologic Technology/Science—Radiation Therapist; Radiologic Technology/Science—Radiographer.

Related DOT Jobs—078.362-026 Radiologic Technologist.

29-2041.00 Emergency Medical Technicians and Paramedics

- Education/Training Required: **Postsecondary vocational training**
- Employed: **172,110**
- Annual Earnings: **$23,170**
- Growth: **31.3%**
- Annual Job Openings: **19,000**

Assess injuries, administer emergency medical care, and extricate trapped individuals. Transport injured or sick persons to medical facilities.

Administer first-aid treatment and life-support care to sick or injured persons in prehospital setting. Operate equipment such as EKGs, external defibrillators, and bag-valve mask resuscitators in advanced life-support environments. Assess nature and extent of illness or injury to establish and prioritize medical procedures. Maintain vehicles and medical and communication equipment; replenish first-aid equipment and supplies. Observe, record, and report to physician the patient's condition or injury, the treatment provided, and reactions to drugs and treatment. Perform emergency diagnostic and treatment procedures, such as stomach suction, airway management, and heart monitoring, during ambulance ride. Administer drugs, orally or by injection, and perform intravenous procedures under a physician's direction. Comfort and reassure patients. Coordinate work with other emergency medical team members and police and fire department personnel. Communicate with dispatchers and treatment center personnel to provide information about situation, to arrange reception of victims, and to receive instructions for further treatment. Immobilize patient for placement on stretcher and ambulance transport, using backboard or other spinal immobilization device. Decontaminate ambulance interior following treatment of patient with infectious disease and report case to proper authorities. Drive mobile intensive care unit to specified location, following instructions from emergency medical dispatcher. Coordinate with treatment center personnel to obtain patients' vital statistics and medical history, to determine the circumstances of the emergency, and to administer emergency treatment.

GOE INFORMATION—Interest Area: 04. Law, Law Enforcement, and Public Safety. **Work Group:** 04.04. Public Safety. **Personality Type—** Social. Social occupations frequently involve working with, communicating with, and teaching people. These occupations often involve helping or providing service to others. **Work Values—**Social Service; Achievement; Pleasant Co-workers; Variety; Ability Utilization. **Skills—**Equipment Selection; Service Orientation; Coordination; Social Perceptiveness; Instructing; Operation Monitoring; Complex Problem Solving; Speaking. **Abilities—***Cognitive:* Flexibility of Closure; Problem Sensitivity; Speed of Closure; Time Sharing; Perceptual Speed. *Psychomotor:* Reaction Time; Rate Control; Response Orientation; Manual Dexterity; Control Precision. *Physical:* Stamina; Static Strength; Extent Flexibility; Gross Body Equilibrium; Gross Body Coordination. *Sensory:* Glare Sensitivity; Auditory Attention; Peripheral Vision; Night Vision; Far Vision. **General Work Activities—***Information Input:* Identifying Objects, Actions, and Events; Monitoring Processes, Materials, or Surroundings; Getting Information. *Mental Process:* Making Decisions and Solving Problems; Updating and Using Relevant Knowledge; Processing Information. *Work Output:* Performing General Physical Activities; Handling and Moving Objects; Documenting or Recording Information. *Interacting with Others:* Assisting and Caring for Others; Performing for or Working with the Public; Establishing and Maintaining Relationships. **Physical Work Conditions—**Disease or Infections; Specialized Protective or Safety Attire; Common Protective or Safety Attire; Kneeling, Crouching, or Crawling; Very Hot or Cold. **Other Job Characteristics—**Consequence of Error; Importance of Being Exact or Accurate; Pace Determined by Speed of Equipment.

Experience—Job Zone 2. Some previous work-related skill, knowledge, or experience may be helpful, but usually is not needed. **Job Preparation:** SVP 4.0 to less than 6.0—six months to less than two years. **Knowledge—**Customer and Personal Service; Medicine and Dentistry; Psychology; Therapy and Counseling; Public Safety and Security. **Instructional Programs—**Emergency Care Attendant (EMT Ambulance); Emergency Medical Technology/Technician (EMT Paramedic).

Related DOT Jobs—079.364-026 Paramedic; 079.374-010 Emergency Medical Technician.

29-2051.00 Dietetic Technicians

- **Education/Training Required: Moderate-term on-the-job training**
- **Employed: 25,648**
- **Annual Earnings: $21,790**
- **Growth: 27.6%**
- **Annual Job Openings: 3,000**

Assist dietitians in the provision of food service and nutritional programs. Under the supervision of dietitians, may plan and produce meals based on established guidelines, teach principles of food and nutrition, or counsel individuals.

Analyze menus and recipes, standardize recipes, and test new products. Observe patient food intake and report progress and dietary problems to dietician. Obtain and evaluate dietary histories of individuals to plan nutritional programs. Plan menus and diets or guide individuals and families in food selection, preparation, and menu planning, based upon nutritional needs and established guidelines. Prepare a major meal, following recipes and determining group food quantities. Deliver speeches on diet, nutrition, and health to promote healthy eating habits and illness prevention and treatment. Determine food and beverage costs and assist in implementing cost control procedures. Provide dietitians with assistance researching food, nutrition, and food service systems. Refer patients to other relevant services to provide continuity of care. Supervise food production and service or assist dietitians and nutritionists in food service supervision and planning. Develop job specifications, job descriptions, and work schedules. Select, schedule, and conduct orientation and in-service education programs.

GOE INFORMATION—Interest Area: 14. Medical and Health Services. **Work Group:** 14.08. Health Protection and Promotion. **Personality Type—**Social. Social occupations frequently involve working with, communicating with, and teaching people. These occupations often involve helping or providing service to others. **Work Values—**Social Service; Pleasant Co-workers; Good Working Conditions; Authority; Variety. **Skills—**Service Orientation; Complex Problem Solving; Instructing; Learning Strategies; Speaking; Writing; Reading Comprehension; Management of Personnel Resources. **Abilities—***Cognitive:* Originality; Fluency of Ideas; Oral Expression; Written Expression; Information Ordering. *Psychomotor:* Multilimb Coordination. *Physical:* None met the criteria. *Sensory:* Speech Clarity; Far Vision; Auditory Attention; Glare Sensitivity; Night Vision. **General Work Activities—***Information Input:* Identifying Objects, Actions, and Events; Getting Information; Monitoring Processes, Materials, or Surroundings. *Mental Process:* Scheduling Work and Activities; Analyzing Data or Information; Organizing, Planning, and Prioritizing. *Work Output:* Performing General Physical Activities; Documenting or Recording Information; Handling and Moving Objects. *Interacting with Others:* Communicating with Persons Outside Organization; Assisting and Caring for Others; Establishing and Maintaining Relationships. **Physical Work Conditions—**Disease or Infections; Minor Burns, Cuts, Bites, or Stings; Indoors; Common Protective or Safety Attire; Sitting. **Other Job Characteristics—**Importance of Being Exact or Accurate; Consequence of Error; Degree of Automation.

Experience—Job Zone 4. A minimum of two to four years of work-related skill, knowledge, or experience is needed. **Job Preparation:** SVP 7.0 to less than 8.0—two years to less than 10 years. **Knowledge—**Customer and Personal Service; Biology; Education and Training; Economics and Accounting; Administration and Management. **Instructional Programs—**Dietetic Technician (DTR); Dietetics/Dietitian (RD); Dietitian Assistant; Foods, Nutrition, and Wellness Studies, General; Nutrition Sciences.

Related DOT Jobs—077.124-010 Dietetic Technician.

29-2052.00 Pharmacy Technicians

- **Education/Training Required:** Moderate-term on-the-job training
- **Employed:** 189,847
- **Annual Earnings:** $21,630
- **Growth:** 36.4%
- **Annual Job Openings:** 22,000

Prepare medications under the direction of a pharmacist. May measure, mix, count out, label, and record amounts and dosages of medications.

Add measured drugs or nutrients to intravenous solutions under sterile conditions to prepare intravenous (IV) packs under pharmacist supervision. Compute charges for medication and equipment dispensed to hospital patients and enter data in computer. Fill bottles with prescribed medications and type and affix labels. Mix pharmaceutical preparations according to written prescriptions. Price and file prescriptions that have been filled. Receive written prescription or refill requests and verify that information is complete and accurate. Supply and monitor robotic machines that dispense medicine into containers; label the containers. Transfer medication from vials to the appropriate number of sterile, disposable syringes, using aseptic techniques. Answer telephones, responding to questions or requests. Assist customers by answering simple questions, locating items, or referring them to the pharmacist for medication information. Clean and help maintain equipment and work areas and sterilize glassware according to prescribed methods. Deliver medications and pharmaceutical supplies to patients, nursing stations, or surgery. Maintain proper storage and security conditions for drugs. Operate cash registers to accept payment from customers. Order, label, and count stock of medications, chemicals, and supplies and enter inventory data into computer. Price stock and mark items for sale. Receive and store incoming supplies, verify quantities against invoices, and inform supervisors of stock needs and shortages. Establish and maintain patient profiles, including lists of medications taken by individual patients. Maintain and merchandise home health care products and services. Prepare and process medical insurance claim forms and records.

GOE INFORMATION—Interest Area: 14. Medical and Health Services. **Work Group:** 14.02. Medicine and Surgery. **Personality Type—**Conventional. Conventional occupations frequently involve following set procedures and routines. These occupations can include working with data and details more than with ideas. Usually there is a clear line of authority to follow. **Work Values—**Good Working Conditions; Social Service; Pleasant Co-workers; Security; Activity. **Skills—**Science; Mathematics; Reading Comprehension. **Abilities—***Cognitive:* None met the criteria. *Psychomotor:* None met the criteria. *Physical:* None met the criteria. *Sensory:* Near Vision. **General Work Activities—***Information Input:* Getting Information; Identifying Objects, Actions, and Events; Monitoring Processes, Materials, or Surroundings. *Mental Process:* Updating and Using Relevant Knowledge; Processing Information; Evaluating Information Against Standards. *Work Output:* Handling and Moving Objects; Documenting or Recording Information; Performing General Physical Activities. *Interacting with Others:* Establishing and Maintaining Relationships; Communicating with Persons Outside Organization; Communicating with Other Workers. **Physical Work Conditions—**Indoors; Sitting; Standing. **Other Job Characteristics—**Importance of Being Exact or Accurate; Consequence of Error; Importance of Repeating Same Tasks.

Experience—Job Zone 2. Some previous work-related skill, knowledge, or experience may be helpful, but usually is not needed. **Job Preparation:** SVP 4.0 to less than 6.0—six months to less than two years. **Knowledge—**Clerical; Medicine and Dentistry; Chemistry; Computers and Electronics; Biology. **Instructional Programs—**Pharmacy Technician/Assistant.

Related DOT Jobs—074.381-010 Pharmacist Assistant; 074.382-010 Pharmacy Technician.

29-2053.00 Psychiatric Technicians

- **Education/Training Required:** Postsecondary vocational training
- **Employed:** 53,955
- **Annual Earnings:** $25,300
- **Growth:** 8.5%
- **Annual Job Openings:** 6,000

Care for mentally impaired or emotionally disturbed individuals, following physician instructions and hospital procedures. Monitor patients' physical and emotional well-being and report to medical staff. May participate in rehabilitation and treatment programs, help with personal hygiene, and administer oral medications and hypodermic injections.

Administer oral medications and hypodermic injections, following physician's prescriptions and hospital procedures. Aid patients in performing tasks such as bathing and keeping beds, clothing, and living areas clean. Collaborate with and assist doctors, psychologists, and rehabilitation therapists working with mentally ill, emotionally disturbed, or developmentally disabled patients in order to treat patients, rehabilitate them, and return them to the community. Encourage patients to develop work skills and to participate in social, recreational, and other therapeutic activities that enhance interpersonal skills and develop social relationships. Monitor patients' physical and emotional well-being and report unusual behavior or physical ailments to medical staff. Observe and influence patients' behavior, communicating and interacting with them and teaching, counseling, and befriending them. Provide nursing, psychiatric and personal care to mentally ill, emotionally disturbed, or mentally retarded patients. Develop and teach strategies to promote client wellness and independence. Interview new patients to complete admission forms, to assess their mental health status, and to obtain their mental health and treatment history. Issue medications from dispensary and maintain records in accordance with specified procedures. Lead prescribed individual or group therapy sessions as part of specific therapeutic procedures. Restrain violent, potentially violent, or suicidal patients by verbal or physical means as required. Contact patients' relatives to arrange family conferences. Take and record measures of patients' physical condition, using devices such as thermometers and blood pressure gauges.

GOE INFORMATION—Interest Area: 14. Medical and Health Services. **Work Group:** 14.07. Patient Care and Assistance. **Personality Type—**Social. Social occupations frequently involve working with, communicating with, and teaching people. These occupations often involve helping or providing service to others. **Work Values—**Social Service; Pleasant Co-workers; Supervision, Human Relations; Security; Company Policies and Practices. **Skills—**Social Perceptiveness; Service Orientation; Speaking; Active Listening; Reading Comprehension; Critical Thinking; Monitoring; Science. **Abilities—***Cognitive:* Problem Sensitivity; Time Sharing; Oral Expression; Oral Comprehension. *Psychomotor:* Reaction Time. *Physical:* Explosive Strength. *Sensory:* Speech Recognition. **General Work Activities—***Information Input:* Monitoring Processes, Materials, or Surroundings; Getting Information; Identifying Objects, Actions, and Events. *Mental Process:* Judging Qualities of Things, Services, or Other People's Work; Updating and Using Relevant Knowledge; Processing Information. *Work Output:* Performing General Physical Activities;

Documenting or Recording Information; Handling and Moving Objects. *Interacting with Others:* Assisting and Caring for Others; Communicating with Other Workers; Establishing and Maintaining Relationships. **Physical Work Conditions**—Disease or Infections; Indoors; Common Protective or Safety Attire; Minor Burns, Cuts, Bites, or Stings. **Other Job Characteristics**—Consequence of Error; Importance of Being Exact or Accurate; Importance of Repeating Same Tasks.

Experience—Job Zone 3. Previous work-related skill, knowledge, or experience is required. **Job Preparation:** SVP 6.0 to less than 7.0—more than one year and less than four years. **Knowledge**—Therapy and Counseling; Psychology; Customer and Personal Service; Medicine and Dentistry; Biology. **Instructional Programs**—Psychiatric/Mental Health Services Technician.

Related DOT Jobs—079.374-026 Psychiatric Technician.

29-2054.00 Respiratory Therapy Technicians

- **Education/Training Required: Postsecondary vocational training**
- **Employed: 26,818**
- **Annual Earnings: $33,840**
- **Growth: 34.6%**
- **Annual Job Openings: 3,000**

Provide specific, well-defined respiratory care procedures under the direction of respiratory therapists and physicians.

Use ventilators and various oxygen devices and aerosol and breathing treatments in the provision of respiratory therapy. Work with patients in areas such as the emergency room, neonatal/pediatric intensive care, and surgical intensive care, treating conditions including emphysema, chronic bronchitis, asthma, cystic fibrosis, and pneumonia. Read and evaluate physicians' orders and patients' chart information to determine patients' condition and treatment protocols. Keep records of patients' therapy, completing all necessary forms. Set equipment controls to regulate the flow of oxygen, gases, mists, or aerosols. Provide respiratory care involving the application of well-defined therapeutic techniques under the supervision of a respiratory therapist and a physician. Assess patients' response to treatments and modify treatments according to protocol if necessary. Prepare and test devices such as mechanical ventilators, therapeutic gas administration apparatus, environmental control systems, aerosol generators, and EKG machines. Monitor patients during treatment and report any unusual reactions to the respiratory therapist. Explain treatment procedures to patients. Clean, sterilize, check, and maintain respiratory therapy equipment. Perform diagnostic procedures to assess the severity of respiratory dysfunction in patients. Follow and enforce safety rules applying to equipment. Administer breathing and oxygen procedures such as intermittent positive pressure breathing treatments, ultrasonic nebulizer treatments, and incentive spirometer treatments. Recommend and review bedside procedures, X rays, and laboratory tests. Interview and examine patients to collect clinical data. Teach patients how to use respiratory equipment at home. Teach or oversee other workers who provide respiratory care services.

GOE INFORMATION—**Interest Area:** 14. Medical and Health Services. **Work Group:** 14.06. Medical Therapy. **Personality Type**—No data available. **Work Values**—None met the criteria. **Skills**—Operation Monitoring; Operation and Control; Troubleshooting; Equipment Selection; Time Management; Learning Strategies; Instructing; Social Perceptiveness. **Abilities**—*Cognitive:* Perceptual Speed; Inductive Reasoning; Flexibility of Closure; Problem Sensitivity; Speed of Closure. *Psychomotor:* Reaction

Time; Control Precision; Response Orientation; Finger Dexterity; Arm-Hand Steadiness. *Physical:* Extent Flexibility; Stamina; Static Strength; Gross Body Coordination; Trunk Strength. *Sensory:* Auditory Attention; Speech Recognition; Hearing Sensitivity; Visual Color Discrimination; Speech Clarity. **General Work Activities**—*Information Input:* Monitoring Processes, Materials, or Surroundings; Identifying Objects, Actions, and Events; Inspecting Equipment, Structures, or Materials. *Mental Process:* Making Decisions and Solving Problems; Updating and Using Relevant Knowledge; Processing Information. *Work Output:* Controlling Machines and Processes; Handling and Moving Objects; Documenting or Recording Information. *Interacting with Others:* Assisting and Caring for Others; Establishing and Maintaining Relationships; Communicating with Other Workers. **Physical Work Conditions**—No data available. **Other Job Characteristics**—No data available.

Experience—Job Zone 3. Previous work-related skill, knowledge, or experience is required. **Job Preparation:** No data available. **Knowledge**—Medicine and Dentistry; Customer and Personal Service; Psychology; Chemistry; Biology. **Instructional Programs**—Respiratory Care Therapy/Therapist; Respiratory Therapy Technician/Assistant.

Related DOT Jobs—355.674-022 Respiratory-Therapy Aide.

29-2055.00 Surgical Technologists

- **Education/Training Required: Postsecondary vocational training**
- **Employed: 71,185**
- **Annual Earnings: $30,090**
- **Growth: 34.7%**
- **Annual Job Openings: 8,000**

Assist in operations under the supervision of surgeons, registered nurses, or other surgical personnel. May help set up operating room, prepare and transport patients for surgery, adjust lights and equipment, pass instruments and other supplies to surgeons and surgeon's assistants, hold retractors, cut sutures, and help count sponges, needles, supplies, and instruments.

Clean and restock the operating room, placing equipment and supplies and arranging instruments according to instruction. Count sponges, needles, and instruments before and after operation. Hand instruments and supplies to surgeons and surgeons' assistants, hold retractors and cut sutures, and perform other tasks as directed by surgeon during operation. Maintain supply of fluids, such as plasma, saline, blood, and glucose, for use during operations. Monitor and continually assess operating room conditions, including patient and surgical team needs. Observe patients' vital signs to assess physical condition. Operate, assemble, adjust, or monitor sterilizers, lights, suction machines, and diagnostic equipment to ensure proper operation. Position patients on the operating table and cover them with sterile surgical drapes to prevent exposure. Provide technical assistance to surgeons, surgical nurses, and anesthesiologists. Scrub arms and hands and assist the surgical team to scrub and put on gloves, masks, and surgical clothing. Maintain files and records of surgical procedures. Prepare, care for, and dispose of tissue specimens taken for laboratory analysis. Prepare dressings or bandages and apply or assist with their application following surgery. Wash and sterilize equipment, using germicides and sterilizers.

GOE INFORMATION—**Interest Area:** 14. Medical and Health Services. **Work Group:** 14.02. Medicine and Surgery. **Personality Type**—Realistic. Realistic occupations frequently involve work activities that include practical, hands-on problems and solutions. They often deal with plants, animals, and real-world materials like wood, tools, and machinery. Many of the occupations require working outside and do not involve a lot of paperwork or working closely with others. **Work Values**—Social Service; Security; Supervision, Human Relations; Pleasant Co-workers; Company Policies and Practices. **Skills**—Active Listening; Reading Comprehension. **Abilities**—*Cognitive:* Oral Comprehension. *Psychomotor:* Arm-Hand Steadiness; Reaction Time; Finger Dexterity; Speed of Limb Movement. *Physical:* None met the criteria. *Sensory:* None met the criteria. **General Work Activities**—*Information Input:* Getting Information; Monitoring Processes, Materials, or Surroundings; Estimating Needed Characteristics. *Mental Process:* Updating and Using Relevant Knowledge; Evaluating Information Against Standards; Processing Information. *Work Output:* Handling and Moving Objects; Performing General Physical Activities; Controlling Machines and Processes. *Interacting with Others:* Assisting and Caring for Others; Communicating with Other Workers; Establishing and Maintaining Relationships. **Physical Work Conditions**—Disease or Infections; Indoors; Standing; Common Protective or Safety Attire. **Other Job Characteristics**—Consequence of Error; Importance of Being Exact or Accurate; Pace Determined by Speed of Equipment.

Experience—Job Zone 3. Previous work-related skill, knowledge, or experience is required. **Job Preparation:** SVP 6.0 to less than 7.0—more than one year and less than four years. **Knowledge**—Medicine and Dentistry; Biology; Chemistry; Customer and Personal Service. **Instructional Programs**—Pathology/Pathologist Assistant; Surgical Technology/Technologist.

Related DOT Jobs—079.374-022 Surgical Technician.

29-2056.00 Veterinary Technologists and Technicians

- ● Education/Training Required: Associate's degree
- ● Employed: 49,408
- ● Annual Earnings: $22,430
- ● Growth: 39.3%
- ● Annual Job Openings: 6,000

Perform medical tests in a laboratory environment for use in the treatment and diagnosis of diseases in animals. Prepare vaccines and serums for prevention of diseases. Prepare tissue samples, take blood samples, and execute laboratory tests, such as urinalysis and blood counts. Clean and sterilize instruments and materials and maintain equipment and machines.

Administer anesthesia to animals, under the direction of a veterinarian, and monitor animals' responses to anesthetics so that dosages can be adjusted. Administer emergency first aid, such as performing emergency resuscitation or other lifesaving procedures. Clean and sterilize instruments, equipment, and materials. Collect, prepare, and label samples for laboratory testing, culture, or microscopic examination. Maintain instruments, equipment, and machinery to ensure proper working condition. Maintain laboratory, research, and treatment records as well as inventories of pharmaceuticals, equipment, and supplies. Perform laboratory tests on blood, urine, and feces, such as urinalyses and blood counts, to assist in the diagnosis and treatment of animal health problems. Prepare and administer medications, vaccines, serums, and treatments as prescribed by veterinarians. Provide veterinarians with the correct equipment and instruments as needed. Take and develop diagnostic radiographs, using X-ray equipment. Bathe animals, clip nails or claws, and brush and cut animals' hair. Care for and monitor the condition of animals recovering from surgery. Clean kennels, animal holding areas, surgery suites, examination rooms, and animal loading/unloading facilities to control the spread of disease. Conduct specialized procedures such as animal branding or tattooing and hoof trimming. Dress and suture wounds and apply splints and other protective devices. Fill prescriptions, measuring medications and labeling containers. Give enemas and perform catheterizations, ear flushes, intravenous feedings, and gavages. Observe the behavior and condition of animals and monitor their clinical symptoms. Perform a variety of office, clerical, and accounting duties, such as reception, billing, bookkeeping, and/or selling products. Perform dental work such as cleaning, polishing, and extracting teeth. Prepare animals for surgery, performing such tasks as shaving surgical areas. Prepare treatment rooms for surgery. Provide assistance with animal euthanasia and the disposal of remains. Provide information and counseling regarding issues such as animal health care, behavior problems, and nutrition. Take animals into treatment areas and assist with physical examinations by performing such duties as obtaining temperature, pulse, and respiration data.

GOE INFORMATION—Interest Area: 03. Plants and Animals. **Work Group:** 03.02. Animal Care and Training. **Note:** The Department of Labor has not collected some data for this job, so it has fewer details than the other descriptions.

Instructional Programs—Veterinary/Animal Health Technology/Technician and Veterinary Assistant.

Related DOT Jobs—079.361-014 Veterinary Technician.

29-2061.00 Licensed Practical and Licensed Vocational Nurses

- ● Education/Training Required: Postsecondary vocational training
- ● Employed: 699,600
- ● Annual Earnings: $30,670
- ● Growth: 20.3%
- ● Annual Job Openings: 58,000

Care for ill, injured, convalescent, or disabled persons in hospitals, nursing homes, clinics, private homes, group homes, and similar institutions. May work under the supervision of a registered nurse. Licensing required.

Observe patients, charting and reporting changes in patients' conditions, such as adverse reactions to medication or treatment, and taking any necessary action. Administer prescribed medications or start intravenous fluids and note times and amounts on patients' charts. Answer patients' calls and determine how to assist them. Measure and record patients' vital signs, such as height, weight, temperature, blood pressure, pulse, and respiration. Provide basic patient care and treatments, such as taking temperatures and blood pressure; dressing wounds; treating bedsores; giving enemas, douches, alcohol rubs, and massages; or performing catheterizations. Help patients with bathing, dressing, personal hygiene, moving in bed, and standing and walking. Supervise nurses' aides and assistants. Work as part of a health care team to assess patient needs, plan and modify care, and implement interventions. Record food and fluid intake and output. Evaluate nursing intervention outcomes, conferring with other health care team members as necessary. Assemble and use equipment such as catheters, tracheotomy tubes, and oxygen suppliers. Collect samples such as blood, urine, and sputum from patients and perform routine laboratory tests on samples. Prepare patients for examinations, tests, and treatments and explain procedures. Prepare food trays and examine them for conformance to prescribed diet. Apply compresses, ice bags, and hot water bottles. Clean rooms and make beds. Inventory and requisition supplies and instruments. Provide medical treatment and personal care to patients in private home settings, such as cooking, keeping rooms orderly, seeing that patients are comfortable and in good spirits, and instructing family members in simple nursing tasks. Sterilize equipment and supplies, using germicides, sterilizer, or autoclave. Assist in delivery, care, and feeding of infants. Wash and dress bodies of deceased persons. Make appointments, keep records, and perform other clerical duties in doctors' offices and clinics. Set up equipment and prepare medical treatment rooms.

GOE INFORMATION—Interest Area: 14. Medical and Health Services. **Work Group:** 14.07. Patient Care and Assistance. **Personality Type—** Social. Social occupations frequently involve working with, communicating with, and teaching people. These occupations often involve helping or providing service to others. **Work Values—**Social Service; Pleasant Coworkers; Achievement; Ability Utilization; Social Status. **Skills—**Service Orientation; Operation Monitoring; Active Listening; Judgment and Decision Making; Time Management; Science; Instructing; Writing. **Abilities—***Cognitive:* Problem Sensitivity; Speed of Closure; Inductive Reasoning; Perceptual Speed; Deductive Reasoning. *Psychomotor:* Finger Dexterity; Manual Dexterity; Arm-Hand Steadiness; Reaction Time; Speed of Limb Movement. *Physical:* Static Strength; Trunk Strength; Dynamic Strength; Stamina; Gross Body Coordination. *Sensory:* Speech Recognition; Visual Color Discrimination; Hearing Sensitivity; Speech Clarity; Near Vision. **General Work Activities—***Information Input:* Monitoring Processes, Materials, or Surroundings; Identifying Objects, Actions, and Events; Getting Information. *Mental Process:* Updating and Using Relevant Knowledge; Making Decisions and Solving Problems; Organizing, Planning, and Prioritizing. *Work Output:* Documenting or Recording Information; Repairing and Maintaining Electronic Equipment; Performing General Physical Activities. *Interacting with Others:* Assisting and Caring for Others; Teaching Others; Establishing and Maintaining Relationships. **Physical Work Conditions—**Disease or Infections; Indoors; Common Protective or Safety Attire; Standing; Walking or Running. **Other Job Characteristics—**Consequence of Error; Importance of Being Exact or Accurate; Pace Determined by Speed of Equipment.

Experience—Job Zone 3. Previous work-related skill, knowledge, or experience is required. **Job Preparation:** SVP 6.0 to less than 7.0—more than one year and less than four years. **Knowledge—**Psychology; Customer and Personal Service; Therapy and Counseling; Medicine and Dentistry; Education and Training. **Instructional Programs—**Licensed Practical/Vocational Nurse Training (LPN, LVN, Cert, Dipl, AAS).

Related DOT Jobs—079.374-014 Nurse, Licensed Practical.

29-2071.00 Medical Records and Health Information Technicians

- ● **Education/Training Required: Associate's degree**
- ● **Employed: 135,733**
- ● **Annual Earnings: $23,530**
- ● **Growth: 49.0%**
- ● **Annual Job Openings: 14,000**

Compile, process, and maintain medical records of hospital and clinic patients in a manner consistent with medical, administrative, ethical, legal, and regulatory requirements of the health care system. Process, maintain, compile, and report patient information for health requirements and standards.

Protect the security of medical records to ensure that confidentiality is maintained. Process patient admission and discharge documents. Review records for completeness, accuracy, and compliance with regulations.

Compile and maintain patients' medical records to document condition and treatment and to provide data for research or cost control and care improvement efforts. Enter data, such as demographic characteristics, history and extent of disease, diagnostic procedures, and treatment, into computer. Release information to persons and agencies according to regulations. Plan, develop, maintain, and operate a variety of health record indexes and storage and retrieval systems to collect, classify, store, and analyze information. Manage the department and supervise clerical workers, directing and controlling activities of personnel in the medical records department. Transcribe medical reports. Identify, compile, abstract, and code patient data, using standard classification systems. Resolve/clarify codes and diagnoses with conflicting, missing, or unclear information by consulting with doctors or others to get additional information and by participating in the coding team's regular meetings. Train medical records staff. Assign the patient to one of several hundred "diagnosis-related groups," or DRGs, using appropriate computer software. Post medical insurance billings. Process and prepare business and government forms. Contact discharged patients, their families, and physicians to maintain registry with follow-up information, such as quality of life and length of survival of cancer patients. Prepare statistical reports, narrative reports, and graphic presentations of information such as tumor registry data for use by hospital staff, researchers, and other users. Consult classification manuals to locate information about disease processes. Compile medical care and census data for statistical reports on diseases treated, surgery performed, and use of hospital beds. Develop in-service educational materials.

GOE INFORMATION—Interest Area: 09. Business Detail. **Work Group:** 09.07. Records Processing. **Personality Type—**Conventional. Conventional occupations frequently involve following set procedures and routines. These occupations can include working with data and details more than with ideas. Usually there is a clear line of authority to follow. **Work Values—**Good Working Conditions; Moral Values; Security; Activity; Social Service. **Skills—**Instructing; Active Listening; Critical Thinking; Systems Evaluation; Learning Strategies; Reading Comprehension; Time Management; Service Orientation. **Abilities—***Cognitive:* Category Flexibility; Perceptual Speed; Inductive Reasoning; Information Ordering; Written Expression. *Psychomotor:* Finger Dexterity. *Physical:* None met the criteria. *Sensory:* Speech Recognition; Near Vision; Speech Clarity; Auditory Attention. **General Work Activities—***Information Input:* Getting Information; Monitoring Processes, Materials, or Surroundings; Identifying Objects, Actions, and Events. *Mental Process:* Updating and Using Relevant Knowledge; Evaluating Information Against Standards; Organizing, Planning, and Prioritizing. *Work Output:* Handling and Moving Objects; Interacting with Computers; Documenting or Recording Information. *Interacting with Others:* Communicating with Other Workers; Establishing and Maintaining Relationships; Communicating with Persons Outside Organization. **Physical Work Conditions—**Sitting; Indoors; Disease or Infections; Making Repetitive Motions. **Other Job Characteristics—**Importance of Being Exact or Accurate; Consequence of Error; Degree of Automation.

Experience—Job Zone 3. Previous work-related skill, knowledge, or experience is required. **Job Preparation:** SVP 6.0 to less than 7.0—more than one year and less than four years. **Knowledge—**Clerical; Customer and Personal Service; Personnel and Human Resources; Medicine and Dentistry; Administration and Management. **Instructional Programs—**Health Information/Medical Records Technology/Technician; Medical Insurance Coding Specialist/Coder.

Related DOT Jobs—079.262-014 Medical Record Coder; 079.362-014 Medical Record Technician; 079.362-018 Tumor Registrar; 169.167-046 Public Health Registrar.

29-2081.00 Opticians, Dispensing

- ● **Education/Training Required: Long-term on-the-job training**
- ● **Employed: 67,803**
- ● **Annual Earnings: $26,100**
- ● **Growth: 19.0%**
- ● **Annual Job Openings: 1,000**

Design, measure, fit, and adapt lenses and frames for client according to written optical prescription or specification. Assist client with selecting frames. Measure customer for size of eyeglasses and coordinate frames with facial and eye measurements and optical prescription. Prepare work order for optical laboratory containing instructions for grinding and mounting lenses in frames. Verify exactness of finished lens spectacles. Adjust frame and lens position to fit client. May shape or reshape frames.

Measure clients' bridge and eye size, temple length, vertex distance, pupillary distance, and optical centers of eyes, using measuring devices. Prepare work orders and instructions for grinding lenses and fabricating eyeglasses. Verify that finished lenses are ground to specifications. Determine clients' current lens prescriptions, when necessary, using lensometers or lens analyzers and clients' eyeglasses. Recommend specific lenses, lens coatings, and frames to suit client needs. Assist clients in selecting frames according to style and color; ensure that frames are coordinated with facial and eye measurements and optical prescriptions. Heat, shape, or bend plastic or metal frames in order to adjust eyeglasses to fit clients, using pliers and hands. Evaluate prescriptions in conjunction with clients' vocational and avocational visual requirements. Repair damaged frames. Fabricate lenses to meet prescription specifications. Instruct clients in how to wear and care for eyeglasses. Grind lens edges or apply coatings to lenses. Arrange and maintain displays of optical merchandise. Assemble eyeglasses by cutting and edging lenses and then fitting the lenses into frames. Fit contact lenses by measuring the shape and size of the eye, using various measuring instruments. Maintain records of customer prescriptions, work orders, and payments. Obtain a customer's previous record or verify a prescription with the examining optometrist or ophthalmologist. Perform administrative duties such as tracking inventory and sales, submitting patient insurance information, and performing simple bookkeeping. Sell goods such as contact lenses, spectacles, sunglasses, and other goods related to eyes in general. Show customers how to insert, remove, and care for their contact lenses. Supervise the training of student opticians.

GOE INFORMATION—Interest Area: 14. Medical and Health Services. **Work Group:** 14.04. Health Specialties. **Personality Type—**Enterprising. Enterprising occupations frequently involve starting up and carrying out projects. These occupations can involve leading people and making many decisions. They sometimes require risk taking and often deal with business. **Work Values—**Social Service; Social Status; Achievement; Responsibility; Authority. **Skills—**Management of Financial Resources; Technology Design; Management of Material Resources; Management of Personnel Resources; Quality Control Analysis; Equipment Selection; Science; Critical Thinking. **Abilities—***Cognitive:* Oral Expression; Oral Comprehension. *Psychomotor:* Control Precision; Arm-Hand Steadiness; Finger Dexterity. *Physical:* None met the criteria. *Sensory:* Speech Recognition. **General Work Activities—***Information Input:* Getting Information; Identifying Objects, Actions, and Events; Estimating Needed Characteristics. *Mental Process:* Evaluating Information Against Standards; Updating and Using Relevant Knowledge; Processing Information. *Work Output:* Handling and Moving Objects; Documenting or Recording Information; Controlling Machines and Processes. *Interacting with Others:* Performing for or Working with the Public; Establishing and Maintaining Relationships; Communicating with Persons Outside Organization. **Physical Work Conditions—**Indoors; Sitting. **Other Job Characteristics—**Importance of Being Exact or Accurate; Consequence of Error; Pace Determined by Speed of Equipment.

Experience—Job Zone 4. A minimum of two to four years of work-related skill, knowledge, or experience is needed. **Job Preparation:** SVP 7.0 to less than 8.0—two years to less than 10 years. **Knowledge—**Administration and Management; Sales and Marketing; Customer and Personal Service; Economics and Accounting; Personnel and Human Resources. **Instructional Programs—**Opticianry/Ophthalmic Dispensing Optician.

Related DOT Jobs—299.361-010 Optician, Dispensing; 299.361-014 Optician Apprentice, Dispensing.

29-2091.00 Orthotists and Prosthetists

- ● **Education/Training Required: Bachelor's degree**
- ● **Employed: 5,329**
- ● **Annual Earnings: $47,120**
- ● **Growth: 17.3%**
- ● **Annual Job Openings: 1,000**

Assist patients with disabling conditions of limbs and spine or with partial or total absence of limb by fitting and preparing orthopedic braces or prostheses.

Confer with physicians in order to formulate specifications and prescriptions for orthopedic and/or prosthetic devices. Construct and fabricate appliances or supervise others who are constructing the appliances. Design orthopedic and prosthetic devices based on physicians' prescriptions and examination and measurement of patients. Examine, interview, and measure patients in order to determine their appliance needs and to identify factors that could affect appliance fit. Fit, test, and evaluate devices on patients, and make adjustments for proper fit, function, and comfort. Instruct patients in the use and care of orthoses and prostheses. Make and modify plaster casts of areas that will be fitted with prostheses or orthoses for use in the device construction process. Repair, rebuild, and modify prosthetic and orthopedic appliances. Select materials and components to be used, based on device design. Maintain patients' records. Publish research findings and present them at conferences and seminars. Research new ways to construct and use orthopedic and prosthetic devices. Show and explain orthopedic and prosthetic appliances to health care workers. Train and supervise orthopedic and prosthetic assistants and technicians and other support staff. Update skills and knowledge by attending conferences and seminars.

GOE INFORMATION—Interest Area: 14. Medical and Health Services. **Work Group:** 14.05. Medical Technology. **Personality Type—**Social. Social occupations frequently involve working with, communicating with, and teaching people. These occupations often involve helping or providing service to others. **Work Values—**Social Service; Achievement; Ability Utilization; Authority; Recognition. **Skills—**Technology Design; Speaking; Social Perceptiveness; Quality Control Analysis; Active Listening; Instructing; Equipment Selection; Installation. **Abilities—***Cognitive:* Oral Expression; Originality; Deductive Reasoning; Oral Comprehension; Visualization. *Psychomotor:* Control Precision; Arm-Hand Steadiness; Manual Dexterity; Finger Dexterity; Multilimb Coordination. *Physical:* Extent Flexibility; Stamina; Explosive Strength; Dynamic Flexibility; Gross Body Coordination. *Sensory:* Speech Clarity; Near Vision; Speech Recognition; Visual Color Discrimination; Auditory Attention. **General Work Activities—***Information Input:* Getting Information; Inspecting Equipment, Structures, or Materials; Monitoring Processes, Materials, or Surroundings. *Mental Process:* Updating and Using Relevant Knowledge; Analyzing Data or Information; Thinking Creatively. *Work Output:* Handling and Moving Objects; Drafting and Specifying Technical Devices;

Performing General Physical Activities. *Interacting with Others:* Assisting and Caring for Others; Communicating with Persons Outside Organization; Communicating with Other Workers. **Physical Work Conditions—** Disease or Infections; Indoors; Kneeling, Crouching, or Crawling; Bending or Twisting the Body; Using Hands on Objects, Tools, or Controls. **Other Job Characteristics—**Importance of Being Exact or Accurate; Consequence of Error; Importance of Repeating Same Tasks.

Experience—Job Zone 3. Previous work-related skill, knowledge, or experience is required. **Job Preparation:** SVP 6.0 to less than 7.0—more than one year and less than four years. **Knowledge—**Medicine and Dentistry; Therapy and Counseling; Building and Construction; Design; Customer and Personal Service. **Instructional Programs—**Assistive/Augmentative Technology and Rehabilitation Engineering; Orthotist/Prosthetist.

Related DOT Jobs—078.261-018 Orthotist; 078.261-022 Prosthetist; 078.361-022 Orthotics Assistant; 078.361-026 Prosthetics Assistant; 078.664-010 Orthopedic Assistant.

29-2099.99 Health Technologists and Technicians, All Other

- Education/Training Required: No data available.
- Employed: No data available.
- Annual Earnings: No data available.
- Growth: 25.7%
- Annual Job Openings: 17,000

All health technologists and technicians not listed separately.

No task data available.

GOE INFORMATION—Interest Area: 14. Medical and Health Services. **Work Group:** 14.05. Medical Technology. **Note:** The Department of Labor has not collected some data for this job, so it has fewer details than the other descriptions.

Instructional Programs—Allied Health and Medical Assisting Services, Other; Allied Health Diagnostic, Intervention, and Treatment Professions, Other; Electroneurodiagnostic/Electroencephalographic Technology/Technologist; Gene/Genetic Therapy; Health Professions and Related Clinical Sciences, Other.

Related DOT Jobs—078.361-038 Ophthalmic Technician; 078.362-010 Audiometrist; 078.362-014 Dialysis Technician; 078.362-022 Electroencephalographic Technologist; 078.362-038 Electromyographic Technician; 078.362-042 Polysomnographic Technician; 078.384-010 Cephalometric Analyst; 079.364-014 Optometric Assistant; 079.364-641 Health Care Sanitary Technician; 079.371-014 Orthoptist; 354.677-010 First-Aid Attendant.

29-9000 Other Healthcare Practitioners and Technical Occupations

29-9011.00 Occupational Health and Safety Specialists

- Education/Training Required: Master's degree
- Employed: No data available.
- Annual Earnings: No data available.
- Growth: 15.0%
- Annual Job Openings: 4,000

Review, evaluate, and analyze work environments; design programs and procedures to control, eliminate, and prevent disease or injury caused by chemical, physical, and biological agents or ergonomic factors. May conduct inspections and enforce adherence to laws and regulations governing the health and safety of individuals. May be employed in the public or private sector.

Investigates adequacy of ventilation, exhaust equipment, lighting, and other conditions which may affect employee health, comfort, or efficiency. Conducts evaluations of exposure to ionizing and nonionizing radiation and to noise. Collects samples of dust, gases, vapors, and other potentially toxic materials for analysis. Recommends measures to ensure maximum employee protection. Collaborates with engineers and physicians to institute control and remedial measures for hazardous and potentially hazardous conditions of equipment. Participates in educational meetings to instruct employees in matters pertaining to occupational health and prevention of accidents. Prepares reports including observations, analysis of contaminants, and recommendation for control and correction of hazards. Reviews physicians' reports and conducts worker studies to determine if diseases or illnesses are job-related. Prepares and calibrates equipment used to collect and analyze samples. Prepares documents to be used in legal proceedings and gives testimony in court proceedings. Uses cost-benefit analysis to justify money spent.

GOE INFORMATION—Interest Area: 04. Law, Law Enforcement, and Public Safety. **Work Group:** 04.04. Public Safety. **Personality Type—** Social. Social occupations frequently involve working with, communicating with, and teaching people. These occupations often involve helping or providing service to others. **Work Values—**Autonomy; Creativity; Authority; Recognition; Variety. **Skills—**Science; Speaking; Writing; Mathematics; Operation Monitoring; Operation and Control; Complex Problem Solving; Reading Comprehension. **Abilities—***Cognitive:* Written Expression; Number Facility; Written Comprehension; Oral Expression; Mathematical Reasoning. *Psychomotor:* Manual Dexterity; Finger Dexterity; Multilimb Coordination; Control Precision; Wrist-Finger Speed. *Physical:* Gross Body Coordination; Trunk Strength; Dynamic Flexibility. *Sensory:* Sound Localization; Near Vision; Speech Clarity; Hearing Sensitivity; Visual Color Discrimination. **General Work Activities—** *Information Input:* Getting Information; Identifying Objects, Actions, and Events; Inspecting Equipment, Structures, or Materials. *Mental Process:* Analyzing Data or Information; Updating and Using Relevant Knowledge; Evaluating Information Against Standards. *Work Output:* Documenting or Recording Information; Drafting and Specifying Technical Devices; Handling and Moving Objects. *Interacting with Others:* Communicating with Other Workers; Communicating with Persons Outside Organization; Providing Consultation and Advice to Others. **Physical Work Conditions—**Disease or Infections; Contaminants; Common Protective or Safety Attire; Hazardous Conditions; Walking or Running. **Other Job Characteristics—**Importance of Being Exact or Accurate; Consequence of Error; Importance of Repeating Same Tasks.

Experience—Job Zone 5. Extensive skill, knowledge, and experience are needed for these occupations. **Job Preparation:** SVP 8.0 and above—four years to more than 10 years. **Knowledge—**Public Safety and Security; Medicine and Dentistry; Chemistry; Law and Government; Education and Training. **Instructional Programs—**Environmental Health; Industrial Safety Technology/Technician; Occupational Health and Industrial Hygiene; Occupational Safety and Health Technology/Technician; Quality Control and Safety Technologies/Technicians, Other.

Related DOT Jobs—079.161-010 Industrial Hygienist.

29-9012.00 Occupational Health and Safety Technicians

- Education/Training Required: Associate's degree
- Employed: No data available.
- Annual Earnings: No data available.
- Growth: 15.0%
- Annual Job Openings: 4,000

Collect data on work environments for analysis by occupational health and safety specialists. Implement and conduct evaluation of programs designed to limit chemical, physical, biological, and ergonomic risks to workers.

No task data available.

GOE INFORMATION—Interest Area: 04. Law, Law Enforcement, and Public Safety. **Work Group:** 04.04. Public Safety. **Note:** The Department of Labor has not collected some data for this job, so it has fewer details than the other descriptions.

Instructional Programs—Environmental Health; Occupational Health and Industrial Hygiene; Radiation Protection/Health Physics Technician.

Related DOT Jobs—199.167-010 Radiation Monitor.

29-9091.00 Athletic Trainers

- Education/Training Required: Bachelor's degree
- Employed: 14,508
- Annual Earnings: $33,450
- Growth: 18.5%
- Annual Job Openings: 2,000

Evaluate, advise, and treat athletes to assist recovery from injury, avoid injury, or maintain peak physical fitness.

Advise athletes on the proper use of equipment. Apply protective or injury preventive devices such as tape, bandages, or braces to body parts such as ankles, fingers, or wrists. Assess and report the progress of recovering athletes to coaches and physicians. Care for athletic injuries using physical therapy equipment, techniques, and medication. Collaborate with physicians in order to develop and implement comprehensive rehabilitation programs for athletic injuries. Conduct an initial assessment of an athlete's injury or illness in order to provide emergency or continued care and to determine whether they should be referred to physicians for definitive diagnosis and treatment. Develop training programs and routines designed to improve athletic performance. Massage body parts in order to relieve soreness, strains, and bruises. Plan and implement comprehensive athletic injury and illness prevention programs. Accompany injured athletes to hospitals. Conduct research and provide instruction on subject matter related to athletic training or sports medicine. Confer with coaches in order to select protective equipment. Evaluate athletes' readiness to play; provide participation clearances when necessary and warranted. Inspect playing fields in order to locate any items that could injure players. Instruct coaches, athletes, parents, medical personnel, and community members in the care and prevention of athletic injuries. Lead stretching exercises for team members prior to games and practices. Perform team-support duties such as running errands, maintaining equipment, and stocking supplies. Recommend special diets in order to improve athletes' health, increase their stamina, and/or alter their weight. Travel with athletic teams in order to be available at sporting events.

GOE INFORMATION—Interest Area: 14. Medical and Health Services. **Work Group:** 14.08. Health Protection and Promotion. **Personality Type—**Social. Social occupations frequently involve working with, communicating with, and teaching people. These occupations often involve helping or providing service to others. **Work Values—**Social Service; Authority; Variety; Creativity; Autonomy. **Skills—**Service Orientation. **Abilities—***Cognitive:* Problem Sensitivity; Speed of Closure; Inductive Reasoning; Fluency of Ideas; Oral Expression. *Psychomotor:* Speed of Limb Movement; Multilimb Coordination; Wrist-Finger Speed; Manual Dexterity; Rate Control. *Physical:* Stamina; Dynamic Flexibility; Extent Flexibility; Static Strength; Dynamic Strength. *Sensory:* Speech Clarity; Auditory Attention; Sound Localization; Speech Recognition. **General Work Activities—***Information Input:* Identifying Objects, Actions, and Events; Getting Information; Monitoring Processes, Materials, or Surroundings. *Mental Process:* Updating and Using Relevant Knowledge; Judging Qualities of Things, Services, or Other People's Work; Making Decisions and Solving Problems. *Work Output:* Performing General Physical Activities; Handling and Moving Objects; Controlling Machines and Processes. *Interacting with Others:* Assisting and Caring for Others; Establishing and Maintaining Relationships; Coaching and Developing Others. **Physical Work Conditions—**Kneeling, Crouching, or Crawling; Outdoors; Walking or Running; Disease or Infections; Very Hot or Cold. **Other Job Characteristics—**Consequence of Error; Importance of Being Exact or Accurate; Importance of Repeating Same Tasks.

Experience—Job Zone 5. Extensive skill, knowledge, and experience are needed for these occupations. **Job Preparation:** SVP 8.0 and above—four years to more than 10 years. **Knowledge—**Therapy and Counseling; Biology; Medicine and Dentistry; Customer and Personal Service; Psychology. **Instructional Programs—**Athletic Training/Trainer.

Related DOT Jobs—153.224-010 Athletic Trainer.

29-9099.99 Healthcare Practitioners and Technical Workers, All Other

- Education/Training Required: No data available.
- Employed: No data available.
- Annual Earnings: No data available.
- Growth: 19.7%
- Annual Job Openings: 17,000

All health care practitioners and technical workers not listed separately.

No task data available.

GOE INFORMATION—Interest Area: 14. Medical and Health Services. **Work Group:** 14.08. Health Protection and Promotion. **Note:** The Department of Labor has not collected some data for this job, so it has fewer details than the other descriptions.

Instructional Programs—Allied Health and Medical Assisting Services, Other; Allied Health Diagnostic, Intervention, and Treatment Professions, Other; Health Professions and Related Clinical Sciences, Other.

Related DOT Jobs—078.261-042 Pheresis Specialist; 079.151-010 Transplant Coordinator; 079.262-010 Utilization-Review Coordinator; 079.267-010 Utilization-Review Coordinator.

31-0000

Healthcare Support Occupations

31-1000 Nursing, Psychiatric, and Home Health Aides

31-1011.00 Home Health Aides

- Education/Training Required: Short-term on-the-job training
- Employed: 615,381
- Annual Earnings: $17,590
- Growth: 47.3%
- Annual Job Openings: 120,000

Provide routine, personal health care, such as bathing, dressing, or grooming, to elderly, convalescent, or disabled persons in the home of patients or in a residential care facility.

Administer prescribed oral medications under written direction of physician or as directed by home care nurse and aide. Change dressings. Check patients' pulse, temperature, and respiration. Direct patients in simple prescribed exercises and in the use of braces or artificial limbs. Maintain records of patient care, condition, progress, and problems in order to report and discuss observations with a supervisor or case manager. Massage patients and apply preparations and treatments, such as liniment, alcohol rubs, and heat-lamp stimulation. Provide patients with help moving in and out of beds, baths, wheelchairs, or automobiles and with dressing and grooming. Accompany clients to doctors' offices and on other trips outside the home, providing transportation, assistance, and companionship. Care for children who are disabled or who have sick or disabled parents. Change bed linens, wash and iron patients' laundry, and clean patients' quarters. Entertain, converse with, or read aloud to patients to keep them mentally healthy and alert. Perform a variety of duties as requested by client, such as obtaining household supplies and running errands. Plan, purchase, prepare, and serve meals to patients and other family members, according to prescribed diets. Provide patients and families with emotional support and instruction in areas such as infant care, preparing healthy meals, independent living, and adaptation to disability or illness.

GOE INFORMATION—Interest Area: 14. Medical and Health Services. **Work Group:** 14.07. Patient Care and Assistance. **Personality Type—**Social. Social occupations frequently involve working with, communicating with, and teaching people. These occupations often involve helping or providing service to others. **Work Values—**Social Service; Variety. **Skills—**Service Orientation. **Abilities—***Cognitive:* Time Sharing; Oral Comprehension; Oral Expression. *Psychomotor:* Finger Dexterity. *Physical:* Static Strength; Dynamic Strength; Stamina; Trunk Strength. *Sensory:* Sound Localization. **General Work Activities—***Information Input:* Monitoring Processes, Materials, or Surroundings; Getting Information; Identifying Objects, Actions, and Events. *Mental Process:* Organizing, Planning, and Prioritizing; Updating and Using Relevant Knowledge; Making Decisions and Solving Problems. *Work Output:* Performing General Physical Activities; Handling and Moving Objects; Documenting or Recording Information. *Interacting with Others:* Assisting and Caring for Others; Establishing and Maintaining Relationships; Monitoring and Controlling Resources. **Physical Work Conditions—**Disease or Infections; Indoors; Standing; Sitting; Outdoors. **Other Job Characteristics—**Consequence of Error; Importance of Being Exact or Accurate; Importance of Repeating Same Tasks.

Experience—Job Zone 1. No previous work-related skill, knowledge, or experience is needed. **Job Preparation:** SVP below 4.0—less than six months. **Knowledge—**Customer and Personal Service; Medicine and Dentistry; Therapy and Counseling; Psychology; Food Production. **Instructional Programs—**Home Health Aide/Home Attendant.

Related DOT Jobs—354.377-014 Home Attendant.

31-1012.00 Nursing Aides, Orderlies, and Attendants

- Education/Training Required: Short-term on-the-job training
- Employed: 1,373,206
- Annual Earnings: $19,290
- Growth: 23.5%
- Annual Job Openings: 268,000

Provide basic patient care under direction of nursing staff. Perform duties such as feeding, bathing, dressing, grooming, or moving patients or changing linens.

Administer medications and treatments, such as catheterizations, suppositories, irrigations, enemas, massages, and douches, as directed by a physician or nurse. Answer patients' call signals. Bathe, groom, shave, dress, and/or drape patients to prepare them for surgery, treatment, or examination. Clean rooms and change linens. Feed patients who are unable to feed themselves. Prepare, serve, and collect food trays. Provide patient care by supplying and emptying bed pans, applying dressings, and supervising exercise routines. Provide patients with help walking, exercising, and moving in and out of bed. Transport patients to treatment units, using a wheelchair or stretcher. Turn and re-position bedridden patients, alone or with assistance, to prevent bedsores. Work as part of a medical team that examines and treats clinic outpatients. Answer phones and direct visitors. Collect specimens such as urine, feces, or sputum. Deliver messages, documents, and specimens. Explain medical instructions to patients and family members. Maintain inventory by storing, preparing, sterilizing, and issuing supplies such as dressing packs and treatment trays. Observe patients' conditions, measuring and recording food and liquid intake and output and vital signs, and report changes to professional staff. Perform clerical duties such as processing documents and scheduling appointments. Restrain patients if necessary. Set up equipment such as oxygen tents, portable X-ray machines, and overhead irrigation bottles.

GOE INFORMATION—Interest Area: 14. Medical and Health Services. **Work Group:** 14.07. Patient Care and Assistance. **Personality Type—**Social. Social occupations frequently involve working with, communicating with, and teaching people. These occupations often involve helping or providing service to others. **Work Values—**Social Service; Pleasant Co-workers; Supervision, Technical; Security; Variety. **Skills—**Operation Monitoring; Social Perceptiveness; Service Orientation; Operation and Control. **Abilities—***Cognitive:* Spatial Orientation; Perceptual Speed; Selective Attention; Memorization; Problem Sensitivity. *Psychomotor:* Reaction Time; Arm-Hand Steadiness; Response Orientation; Manual Dexterity; Multilimb Coordination. *Physical:* Static Strength; Extent Flexibility; Trunk Strength; Dynamic Flexibility; Dynamic Strength. *Sensory:* Night Vision; Speech Recognition; Peripheral Vision; Sound Localization; Visual Color Discrimination. **General Work Activities—***Information Input:* Monitoring Processes, Materials, or Surroundings; Identifying Objects, Actions, and Events; Getting Information. *Mental Process:* Evaluating Information Against Standards; Updating and Using Relevant Knowledge; Analyzing Data or Information. *Work Output:* Performing General Physical Activities; Handling and Moving Objects; Controlling Machines and Processes. *Interacting with Others:* Assisting and Caring for Others; Establishing and Maintaining Relationships; Performing for or Working with the Public. **Physical Work Conditions—**Disease or Infections; Common Protective or Safety Attire; Walking or Running; Indoors; Standing. **Other Job Characteristics—**Consequence of Error; Importance of Being Exact or Accurate; Degree of Automation.

Experience—Job Zone 2. Some previous work-related skill, knowledge, or experience may be helpful, but usually is not needed. **Job Preparation:** SVP 4.0 to less than 6.0—six months to less than two years. **Knowledge**—Medicine and Dentistry; Therapy and Counseling; Psychology; Customer and Personal Service; Biology. **Instructional Programs**—Health Aide; Nurse/Nursing Assistant/Aide and Patient Care Assistant.

Related DOT Jobs—354.374-010 Nurse, Practical; 355.374-014 Certified Medication Technician; 355.674-014 Nurse Assistant; 355.674-018 Orderly.

31-1013.00 Psychiatric Aides

- **Education/Training Required: Short-term on-the-job training**
- **Employed: 64,705**
- **Annual Earnings: $23,040**
- **Growth: 13.2%**
- **Annual Job Openings: 13,000**

Assist mentally impaired or emotionally disturbed patients, working under direction of nursing and medical staff.

Accompany patients to and from wards for medical and dental treatments, shopping trips, and religious and recreational events. Aid patients in becoming accustomed to hospital routine. Maintain patients' restrictions to assigned areas. Monitor patients in order to detect unusual behavior and report observations to professional staff. Organize, supervise, and encourage patient participation in social, educational, and recreational activities. Participate in recreational activities with patients, including card games, sports, or television viewing. Perform nursing duties such as administering medications, measuring vital signs, collecting specimens, and drawing blood samples. Provide mentally impaired or emotionally disturbed patients with routine physical, emotional, psychological, or rehabilitation care under the direction of nursing and medical staff. Provide patients with assistance in bathing, dressing, and grooming, demonstrating these skills as necessary. Restrain or aid patients as necessary to prevent injury. Serve meals and feed patients needing assistance or persuasion. Clean and disinfect rooms and furnishings to maintain a safe and orderly environment. Interview patients upon admission and record information. Record and maintain records of patient condition and activity, including vital signs, eating habits, and behavior. Work as part of a team that may include psychiatrists, psychologists, psychiatric nurses, and social workers.

GOE INFORMATION—Interest Area: 14. Medical and Health Services. **Work Group:** 14.07. Patient Care and Assistance. **Personality Type**—Social. Social occupations frequently involve working with, communicating with, and teaching people. These occupations often involve helping or providing service to others. **Work Values**—Social Service; Pleasant Co-workers; Supervision, Human Relations; Security; Supervision, Technical. **Skills**—Speaking; Social Perceptiveness; Active Listening. **Abilities**—*Cognitive:* Time Sharing; Spatial Orientation; Problem Sensitivity; Speed of Closure; Category Flexibility. *Psychomotor:* Speed of Limb Movement; Reaction Time; Arm-Hand Steadiness; Multilimb Coordination; Manual Dexterity. *Physical:* Static Strength; Gross Body Coordination; Trunk Strength; Explosive Strength; Dynamic Flexibility. *Sensory:* Peripheral Vision; Speech Recognition; Sound Localization; Visual Color Discrimination; Hearing Sensitivity. **General Work Activities**—*Information Input:* Monitoring Processes, Materials, or Surroundings; Identifying Objects, Actions, and Events; Getting Information. *Mental Process:* Judging Qualities of Things, Services, or Other People's Work; Updating and Using Relevant Knowledge; Organizing, Planning, and Prioritizing. *Work Output:* Performing General Physical Activities; Handling and Moving Objects; Documenting or Recording Information. *Interacting with Others:* Assisting and Caring for Others; Establishing and Maintaining Relationships; Communicating with Other Workers. **Physical Work**

Conditions—Disease or Infections; Walking or Running; Common Protective or Safety Attire; Minor Burns, Cuts, Bites, or Stings; Indoors. **Other Job Characteristics**—Consequence of Error; Importance of Repeating Same Tasks; Degree of Automation.

Experience—Job Zone 2. Some previous work-related skill, knowledge, or experience may be helpful, but usually is not needed. **Job Preparation:** SVP 4.0 to less than 6.0—six months to less than two years. **Knowledge**—Psychology; Customer and Personal Service; Therapy and Counseling; Medicine and Dentistry; Chemistry. **Instructional Programs**—Health Aide; Psychiatric/Mental Health Services Technician.

Related DOT Jobs—355.377-014 Psychiatric Aide; 355.377-018 Mental-Retardation Aide.

31-2000 Occupational and Physical Therapist Assistants and Aides

31-2011.00 Occupational Therapist Assistants

- **Education/Training Required: Associate's degree**
- **Employed: 16,537**
- **Annual Earnings: $35,840**
- **Growth: 39.7%**
- **Annual Job Openings: 3,000**

Assist occupational therapists in providing occupational therapy treatments and procedures. May, in accordance with state laws, assist in development of treatment plans, carry out routine functions, direct activity programs, and document the progress of treatments. Generally requires formal training.

Alter treatment programs to obtain better results if treatment is not having the intended effect. Assemble, clean, and maintain equipment and materials for patient use. Design, fabricate, and repair assistive devices and make adaptive changes to equipment and environments. Demonstrate therapy techniques, such as manual and creative arts and games. Evaluate the daily living skills and capacities of physically, developmentally, or emotionally disabled clients. Implement, or assist occupational therapists with implementing, treatment plans designed to help clients function independently. Instruct, or assist in instructing, patients and families in home programs, basic living skills, and the care and use of adaptive equipment. Monitor patients' performance in therapy activities, providing encouragement. Observe and record patients' progress, attitudes, and behavior and maintain this information in client records. Order any needed educational or treatment supplies. Report to supervisors, verbally or in writing, on patients' progress, attitudes, and behavior. Select therapy activities to fit patients' needs and capabilities. Work under the direction of occupational therapists to plan, implement, and administer educational, vocational, and recreational programs that restore and enhance performance in individuals with functional impairments. Assist educational specialists or clinical psychologists in administering situational or diagnostic tests to measure client's abilities or progress. Aid patients in dressing and grooming themselves. Maintain and promote a positive attitude toward clients and their treatment programs. Perform clerical duties such as scheduling appointments, collecting data, and documenting health insurance billings. Teach patients how to deal constructively with their emotions. Transport patients to and from the occupational therapy work area.

GOE INFORMATION—Interest Area: 14. Medical and Health Services. Work Group: 14.06. Medical Therapy. Personality Type—Social. Social occupations frequently involve working with, communicating with, and teaching people. These occupations often involve helping or providing service to others. Work Values—Social Service; Achievement; Pleasant Co-workers; Security; Supervision, Human Relations. Skills—Social Perceptiveness; Service Orientation; Equipment Selection; Technology Design; Speaking; Reading Comprehension; Instructing. Abilities—*Cognitive:* Problem Sensitivity; Oral Expression; Written Expression; Oral Comprehension; Deductive Reasoning. *Psychomotor:* Rate Control; Multilimb Coordination. *Physical:* Static Strength; Gross Body Coordination; Extent Flexibility; Gross Body Equilibrium; Trunk Strength. *Sensory:* Speech Recognition; Hearing Sensitivity. General Work Activities—*Information Input:* Getting Information; Monitoring Processes, Materials, or Surroundings; Identifying Objects, Actions, and Events. *Mental Process:* Judging Qualities of Things, Services, or Other People's Work; Updating and Using Relevant Knowledge; Organizing, Planning, and Prioritizing. *Work Output:* Performing General Physical Activities; Documenting or Recording Information; Handling and Moving Objects. *Interacting with Others:* Assisting and Caring for Others; Establishing and Maintaining Relationships; Communicating with Other Workers. Physical Work Conditions—Disease or Infections; Kneeling, Crouching, or Crawling; Bending or Twisting the Body; Specialized Protective or Safety Attire; Making Repetitive Motions. Other Job Characteristics—Importance of Repeating Same Tasks; Consequence of Error; Pace Determined by Speed of Equipment.

Experience—Job Zone 2. Some previous work-related skill, knowledge, or experience may be helpful, but usually is not needed. Job Preparation: SVP 4.0 to less than 6.0—six months to less than two years. Knowledge—Therapy and Counseling; Medicine and Dentistry; Psychology; Education and Training; Customer and Personal Service. Instructional Programs—Occupational Therapist Assistant.

Related DOT Jobs—076.364-010 Occupational Therapy Assistant.

31-2012.00 Occupational Therapist Aides

- Education/Training Required: Short-term on-the-job training
- Employed: 8,508
- Annual Earnings: $21,570
- Growth: 45.2%
- Annual Job Openings: 2,000

Under close supervision of an occupational therapist or occupational therapy assistant, perform only delegated, selected, or routine tasks in specific situations. These duties include preparing patient and treatment room.

Accompany patients on outings, providing transportation when necessary. Assist educational specialists or clinical psychologists in administering situational or diagnostic tests to measure client's abilities or progress. Assist occupational therapists in planning, implementing, and administering therapy programs to restore, reinforce, and enhance performance, using selected activities and special equipment. Demonstrate therapy techniques, such as manual and creative arts and games. Encourage patients and attend to their physical needs to facilitate the attainment of therapeutic goals. Evaluate the living skills and capacities of physically, developmentally, or emotionally disabled clients. Instruct patients and families in work, social, and living skills; the care and use of adaptive equipment; and other skills to facilitate home and work adjustment to disability. Observe patients' attendance, progress, attitudes, and accomplishments; record and maintain information in client records. Perform clerical, administrative, and secretarial duties such as answering phones, restocking and ordering supplies, filling out paperwork, and scheduling appointments. Prepare and maintain work area, materials, and equipment; maintain inventory of treatment and educational supplies. Report to supervisors or therapists, verbally or in writing, on patients' progress, attitudes, attendance, and accomplishments. Supervise patients in choosing and completing work details or arts and crafts projects. Transport patients to and from the occupational therapy work area. Adjust and repair assistive devices and make adaptive changes to other equipment and to environments. Manage intra-departmental infection control and equipment security.

GOE INFORMATION—Interest Area: 14. Medical and Health Services. Work Group: 14.06. Medical Therapy. Personality Type—Social. Social occupations frequently involve working with, communicating with, and teaching people. These occupations often involve helping or providing service to others. Work Values—Social Service; Achievement; Pleasant Co-workers; Security; Supervision, Human Relations. Skills—Social Perceptiveness; Service Orientation; Equipment Selection; Technology Design; Speaking; Reading Comprehension; Instructing. Abilities—*Cognitive:* Problem Sensitivity; Oral Expression; Written Expression; Oral Comprehension; Deductive Reasoning. *Psychomotor:* Rate Control; Multilimb Coordination. *Physical:* Static Strength; Gross Body Coordination; Extent Flexibility; Gross Body Equilibrium; Trunk Strength. *Sensory:* Speech Recognition; Hearing Sensitivity. General Work Activities—*Information Input:* Getting Information; Identifying Objects, Actions, and Events; Monitoring Processes, Materials, or Surroundings. *Mental Process:* Updating and Using Relevant Knowledge; Judging Qualities of Things, Services, or Other People's Work; Organizing, Planning, and Prioritizing. *Work Output:* Performing General Physical Activities; Documenting or Recording Information; Handling and Moving Objects. *Interacting with Others:* Assisting and Caring for Others; Establishing and Maintaining Relationships; Communicating with Other Workers. Physical Work Conditions—Disease or Infections; Kneeling, Crouching, or Crawling; Bending or Twisting the Body; Specialized Protective or Safety Attire; Making Repetitive Motions. Other Job Characteristics—Importance of Repeating Same Tasks; Consequence of Error; Pace Determined by Speed of Equipment.

Experience—Job Zone 2. Some previous work-related skill, knowledge, or experience may be helpful, but usually is not needed. Job Preparation: SVP 4.0 to less than 6.0—six months to less than two years. Knowledge—Therapy and Counseling; Medicine and Dentistry; Psychology; Education and Training; Customer and Personal Service. Instructional Programs—Occupational Therapist Assistant.

Related DOT Jobs—355.377-010 Occupational Therapy Aide.

31-2021.00 Physical Therapist Assistants

- Education/Training Required: Associate's degree
- Employed: 43,937
- Annual Earnings: $35,280
- Growth: 44.8%
- Annual Job Openings: 9,000

Assist physical therapists in providing physical therapy treatments and procedures. May, in accordance with state laws, assist in the development of treatment plans, carry out routine functions, document the progress of treatment, and modify specific treatments in accordance with patient status and within the scope of treatment plans established by a physical therapist. Generally requires formal training.

Administer active and passive manual therapeutic exercises, therapeutic massage, and heat, light, sound, water, and electrical modality treatments, such as ultrasound. Administer traction to relieve neck and back pain, using intermittent and static traction equipment. Assist patients to dress, undress, and put on and remove supportive devices, such as braces, splints, and slings. Confer with physical therapy staff and others to discuss and evaluate patient information for planning, modifying, and coordinating treatment. Fit patients for orthopedic braces, prostheses, and supportive devices, such as crutches. Instruct, motivate, safeguard, and assist patients as they practice exercises and functional activities. Measure patients' range of joint motion, body parts, and vital signs to determine effects of treatments or for patient evaluations. Monitor operation of equipment and record use of equipment and administration of treatment. Observe patients during treatments to compile and evaluate data on patients' responses and progress; report to physical therapist. Train patients in the use of orthopedic braces, prostheses, and supportive devices. Secure patients into or onto therapy equipment. Clean work area and check and store equipment after treatment. Perform clerical duties, such as taking inventory, ordering supplies, answering telephone, taking messages, and filling out forms. Perform postural drainage, percussions, and vibrations and teach deep breathing exercises to treat respiratory conditions. Prepare treatment areas and electrotherapy equipment for use by physiotherapists. Transport patients to and from treatment areas, lifting and transferring them according to positioning requirements.

GOE INFORMATION—Interest Area: 14. Medical and Health Services. **Work Group:** 14.06. Medical Therapy. **Personality Type—**Social. Social occupations frequently involve working with, communicating with, and teaching people. These occupations often involve helping or providing service to others. **Work Values—**Social Service; Achievement; Pleasant Co-workers; Security; Supervision, Human Relations. **Skills—**Service Orientation; Instructing; Learning Strategies; Operation and Control; Speaking; Reading Comprehension. **Abilities—***Cognitive:* Oral Expression; Oral Comprehension. *Psychomotor:* Wrist-Finger Speed; Arm-Hand Steadiness. *Physical:* Static Strength; Stamina. *Sensory:* Speech Recognition. **General Work Activities—***Information Input:* Monitoring Processes, Materials, or Surroundings; Identifying Objects, Actions, and Events; Estimating Needed Characteristics. *Mental Process:* Judging Qualities of Things, Services, or Other People's Work; Updating and Using Relevant Knowledge; Organizing, Planning, and Prioritizing. *Work Output:* Handling and Moving Objects; Performing General Physical Activities; Documenting or Recording Information. *Interacting with Others:* Assisting and Caring for Others; Establishing and Maintaining Relationships; Communicating with Other Workers. **Physical Work Conditions—**Disease or Infections; Indoors; Standing; Bending or Twisting the Body; Walking or Running. **Other Job Characteristics—**Consequence of Error; Importance of Being Exact or Accurate; Importance of Repeating Same Tasks.

Experience—Job Zone 2. Some previous work-related skill, knowledge, or experience may be helpful, but usually is not needed. **Job Preparation:** SVP 4.0 to less than 6.0—six months to less than two years. **Knowledge—**Therapy and Counseling; Customer and Personal Service; Psychology; Biology; Education and Training. **Instructional Programs—**Physical Therapist Assistant.

Related DOT Jobs—076.224-010 Physical Therapist Assistant.

31-2022.00 Physical Therapist Aides
- **Education/Training Required: Associate's degree**
- **Employed: 35,902**
- **Annual Earnings: $20,300**
- **Growth: 46.3%**
- **Annual Job Openings: 7,000**

Under close supervision of a physical therapist or physical therapy assistant, perform only delegated, selected, or routine tasks in specific situations. These duties include preparing the patient and the treatment area.

Administer active and passive manual therapeutic exercises, therapeutic massage, and heat, light, sound, water, and electrical modality treatments, such as ultrasound. Arrange treatment supplies to keep them in order. Assist patients to dress, undress, and put on and remove supportive devices, such as braces, splints, and slings. Clean and organize work area and disinfect equipment after treatment. Instruct, motivate, safeguard, and assist patients practicing exercises and functional activities, under direction of medical staff. Maintain equipment and furniture to keep it in good working condition, including performing the assembly and disassembly of equipment and accessories. Observe patients during treatment to compile and evaluate data on patients' responses and progress; report to physical therapist. Perform clerical duties, such as taking inventory, ordering supplies, answering telephone, taking messages, and filling out forms. Record treatment given and equipment used. Secure patients into or onto therapy equipment. Transport patients to and from treatment areas, using wheelchairs or providing standing support. Administer traction to relieve neck and back pain, using intermittent and static traction equipment. Change linens, such as bedsheets and pillowcases. Confer with physical therapy staff and others to discuss and evaluate patient information for planning, modifying, and coordinating treatment. Fit patients for orthopedic braces, prostheses, and supportive devices, adjusting fit as needed. Measure patient's range of jt motion, body parts, and vital signs to determine effects of treatments or for patient evaluations. Participate in patient care tasks, such as assisting with passing food trays and feeding residents and bathing residents on bed rest. Train patients to use orthopedic braces, prostheses, and supportive devices.

GOE INFORMATION—Interest Area: 14. Medical and Health Services. **Work Group:** 14.06. Medical Therapy. **Personality Type—**Social. Social occupations frequently involve working with, communicating with, and teaching people. These occupations often involve helping or providing service to others. **Work Values—**Social Service; Achievement; Pleasant Co-workers; Security; Supervision, Human Relations. **Skills—**Service Orientation; Instructing; Learning Strategies; Operation and Control; Speaking; Reading Comprehension. **Abilities—***Cognitive:* Oral Expression; Oral Comprehension. *Psychomotor:* Wrist-Finger Speed; Arm-Hand Steadiness. *Physical:* Static Strength; Stamina. *Sensory:* Speech Recognition. **General Work Activities—***Information Input:* Monitoring Processes, Materials, or Surroundings; Identifying Objects, Actions, and Events; Getting Information. *Mental Process:* Judging Qualities of Things, Services, or Other People's Work; Organizing, Planning, and Prioritizing; Updating and Using Relevant Knowledge. *Work Output:* Handling and Moving Objects; Performing General Physical Activities; Documenting or Recording Information. *Interacting with Others:* Assisting and Caring for Others; Establishing and Maintaining Relationships; Communicating with Other Workers. **Physical Work Conditions—**Disease or Infections; Indoors; Standing; Bending or Twisting the Body; Walking or Running. **Other Job Characteristics—**Consequence of Error; Importance of Being Exact or Accurate; Importance of Repeating Same Tasks.

Experience—Job Zone 2. Some previous work-related skill, knowledge, or experience may be helpful, but usually is not needed. **Job Preparation:** SVP 4.0 to less than 6.0—six months to less than two years. **Knowledge—**Therapy and Counseling; Customer and Personal Service; Psychology; Biology; Education and Training. **Instructional Programs—**Physical Therapist Assistant.

Related DOT Jobs—355.354-010 Physical Therapy Aide.

31-9000 Other Healthcare Support Occupations

31-9011.00 Massage Therapists

- Education/Training Required: Postsecondary vocational training
- Employed: 34,400
- Annual Earnings: $28,050
- Growth: 30.4%
- Annual Job Openings: 7,000

Massage customers for hygienic or remedial purposes.

Apply finger and hand pressure to specific points of the body. Assess clients' soft tissue condition, joint quality and function, muscle strength, and range of motion. Confer with clients about their medical histories and any problems with stress and/or pain in order to determine whether massage would be helpful. Develop and propose client treatment plans that specify which types of massage are to be used. Massage and knead the muscles and soft tissues of the human body in order to provide courses of treatment for medical conditions and injuries or wellness maintenance. Prepare and blend oils and apply the blends to clients' skin. Consult with other health care professionals such as physiotherapists, chiropractors, physicians, and psychologists in order to develop treatment plans for clients. Maintain treatment records. Provide clients with guidance and information about techniques for postural improvement and stretching, strengthening, relaxation and rehabilitative exercises. Refer clients to other types of therapists when necessary. Use complementary aids, such as infrared lamps, wet compresses, ice, and whirlpool baths in order to promote clients' recovery, relaxation and well-being. Treat clients in own offices or travel to clients' offices and homes.

GOE INFORMATION—Interest Area: 14. Medical and Health Services. **Work Group:** 14.06. Medical Therapy. **Note:** The Department of Labor has not collected some data for this job, so it has fewer details than the other descriptions.

Instructional Programs—Asian Bodywork Therapy; Massage Therapy/Therapeutic Massage; Somatic Bodywork; Somatic Bodywork and Related Therapeutic Services, Other.

Related DOT Jobs—334.374-010 Masseur/Masseuse.

31-9091.00 Dental Assistants

- Education/Training Required: Moderate-term on-the-job training
- Employed: 246,970
- Annual Earnings: $26,720
- Growth: 37.2%
- Annual Job Openings: 16,000

Assist dentist, set up patient and equipment, and keep records.

Prepare patient, sterilize and disinfect instruments, set up instrument trays, prepare materials, and assist dentist during dental procedures. Expose dental diagnostic X rays. Record treatment information in patient records. Take and record medical and dental histories and vital signs of patients. Provide postoperative instructions prescribed by dentist. Assist dentist in management of medical and dental emergencies. Pour, trim, and polish study casts. Instruct patients in oral hygiene and plaque control programs. Make preliminary impressions for study casts and occlusal registrations for mounting study casts. Clean and polish removable appliances. Clean teeth, using dental instruments. Apply protective coating of fluoride to teeth. Fabricate temporary restorations and custom impressions from preliminary impressions. Schedule appointments, prepare bills and receive payment for dental services, complete insurance forms, and maintain records, manually or using computer.

GOE INFORMATION—Interest Area: 14. Medical and Health Services. **Work Group:** 14.03. Dentistry. **Personality Type**—Social. Social occupations frequently involve working with, communicating with, and teaching people. These occupations often involve helping or providing service to others. **Work Values**—Social Service; Good Working Conditions; Security; Pleasant Co-workers; Recognition. **Skills**—Social Perceptiveness; Equipment Selection; Operation and Control; Operation Monitoring; Instructing; Management of Material Resources; Time Management; Troubleshooting. **Abilities**—*Cognitive:* Flexibility of Closure; Time Sharing; Oral Comprehension; Category Flexibility; Perceptual Speed. *Psychomotor:* Finger Dexterity; Arm-Hand Steadiness; Manual Dexterity; Control Precision; Rate Control. *Physical:* Extent Flexibility; Trunk Strength; Stamina; Gross Body Coordination. *Sensory:* Speech Recognition; Near Vision; Depth Perception; Glare Sensitivity; Speech Clarity. **General Work Activities**—*Information Input:* Identifying Objects, Actions, and Events; Monitoring Processes, Materials, or Surroundings; Getting Information. *Mental Process:* Organizing, Planning, and Prioritizing; Updating and Using Relevant Knowledge; Processing Information. *Work Output:* Handling and Moving Objects; Documenting or Recording Information; Controlling Machines and Processes. *Interacting with Others:* Assisting and Caring for Others; Communicating with Other Workers; Coordinating the Work and Activities of Others. **Physical Work Conditions**—Common Protective or Safety Attire; Indoors; Radiation; Disease or Infections; Bending or Twisting the Body. **Other Job Characteristics**—Importance of Being Exact or Accurate; Consequence of Error; Importance of Repeating Same Tasks.

Experience—Job Zone 2. Some previous work-related skill, knowledge, or experience may be helpful, but usually is not needed. **Job Preparation:** SVP 6.0 to less than 7.0—more than one year and less than four years. **Knowledge**—Medicine and Dentistry; Customer and Personal Service; Clerical; Chemistry; Psychology. **Instructional Programs**—Dental Assisting/Assistant.

Related DOT Jobs—079.361-018 Dental Assistant.

31-9092.00 Medical Assistants

- Education/Training Required: Moderate-term on-the-job training
- Employed: 328,649
- Annual Earnings: $23,610
- Growth: 57.0%
- Annual Job Openings: 19,000

Perform administrative and certain clinical duties under the direction of physician. Administrative duties may include scheduling appointments, maintaining medical records, billing, and coding for insurance purposes. Clinical duties may include taking and recording vital signs and medical histories, preparing patients for examination, drawing blood, and administering medications as directed by physician.

Collect blood, tissue, or other laboratory specimens; log the specimens; and prepare them for testing. Contact medical facilities or departments to schedule patients for tests and/or admission. Greet and log in patients arriving at office or clinic. Help physicians examine and treat patients, handing them instruments and materials or performing such tasks as giving injections and removing sutures. Interview patients to obtain medical information and measure their vital signs, weight, and height. Inventory and order medical, lab, and office supplies and equipment. Keep financial records and perform other bookkeeping duties, such as handling credit and collections and mailing monthly statements to patients. Perform general office duties such as answering telephones, taking dictation, and completing insurance forms. Record patients' medical history, vital statistics, and information such as test results in medical records. Schedule appointments for patients. Show patients to examination rooms and prepare them for the physician. Authorize drug refills and provide prescription information to pharmacies. Change dressings on wounds. Clean and sterilize instruments and dispose of contaminated supplies. Explain treatment procedures, medications, diets, and physicians' instructions to patients. Give physiotherapy treatments, such as diathermy, galvanics, and hydrotherapy. Operate X-ray, electrocardiogram (EKG), and other equipment to administer routine diagnostic tests. Perform routine laboratory tests and sample analyses. Prepare and administer medications as directed by a physician. Prepare treatment rooms for patient examinations, keeping the rooms neat and clean. Set up medical laboratory equipment. Assist ophthalmologists with fitting contact lenses or performing office surgery. Prepare bodies for release to funeral home by cleaning and sewing as necessary.

GOE INFORMATION—Interest Area: 14. Medical and Health Services. **Work Group:** 14.02. Medicine and Surgery. **Personality Type**—Social. Social occupations frequently involve working with, communicating with, and teaching people. These occupations often involve helping or providing service to others. **Work Values**—Social Service; Pleasant Co-workers; Variety; Compensation; Supervision, Human Relations. **Skills**—Service Orientation; Operation and Control; Active Listening; Speaking; Reading Comprehension. **Abilities**—*Cognitive:* Category Flexibility; Memorization; Problem Sensitivity; Information Ordering; Flexibility of Closure. *Psychomotor:* Arm-Hand Steadiness; Response Orientation; Control Precision; Reaction Time; Finger Dexterity. *Physical:* Static Strength; Trunk Strength; Extent Flexibility; Gross Body Coordination; Dynamic Strength. *Sensory:* Speech Recognition; Sound Localization; Night Vision; Visual Color Discrimination; Hearing Sensitivity. **General Work Activities**—*Information Input:* Getting Information; Monitoring Processes, Materials, or Surroundings; Identifying Objects, Actions, and Events. *Mental Process:* Updating and Using Relevant Knowledge; Processing Information; Evaluating Information Against Standards. *Work Output:* Performing General Physical Activities; Handling and Moving Objects; Documenting or Recording Information. *Interacting with Others:* Assisting and Caring for Others; Establishing and Maintaining Relationships; Communicating with Persons Outside Organization. **Physical Work Conditions**—Disease or Infections; Radiation; Common Protective or Safety Attire; Indoors; Specialized Protective or Safety Attire. **Other Job Characteristics**—Consequence of Error; Importance of Being Exact or Accurate; Degree of Automation.

Experience—Job Zone 3. Previous work-related skill, knowledge, or experience is required. **Job Preparation:** SVP 6.0 to less than 7.0—more than one year and less than four years. **Knowledge**—Medicine and Dentistry; Biology; Therapy and Counseling; Clerical; Chemistry. **Instructional Programs**—Allied Health and Medical Assisting Services, Other; Anesthesiologist Assistant; Chiropractic Assistant/Technician; Medical Administrative/Executive Assistant and Medical Secretary; Medical Insurance Coding Specialist/Coder; Medical Office Assistant/Specialist; Medical Office Management/Administration; Medical Reception/Receptionist; Medical/Clinical Assistant; Opthalmic Technician/Technologist; Optomeric Technician/Assistant; Orthoptics/Orthoptist.

Related DOT Jobs—079.362-010 Medical Assistant; 079.364-010 Chiropractor Assistant; 079.374-018 Podiatric Assistant.

31-9093.00 Medical Equipment Preparers

- **Education/Training Required:** Short-term on-the-job training
- **Employed:** 33,267
- **Annual Earnings:** $22,490
- **Growth:** 18.2%
- **Annual Job Openings:** 5,000

Prepare, sterilize, install, or clean laboratory or health care equipment. May perform routine laboratory tasks and operate or inspect equipment.

Check sterile supplies to ensure that they are not outdated. Clean instruments in order to prepare them for sterilization. Disinfect and sterilize equipment such as respirators, hospital beds, and oxygen and dialysis equipment, using sterilizers, aerators, and washers. Examine equipment to detect leaks, worn or loose parts, or other indications of disrepair. Install and set up medical equipment, using hand tools. Operate and maintain steam autoclaves, keeping records of loads completed, items in loads, and maintenance procedures performed. Organize and assemble routine and specialty surgical instrument trays and other sterilized supplies, filling special requests as needed. Purge wastes from equipment by connecting equipment to water sources and flushing water through systems. Report defective equipment to appropriate supervisors or staff. Start equipment and observe gauges and equipment operation in order to detect malfunctions and to ensure equipment is operating to prescribed standards. Attend hospital in-service programs related to areas of work specialization. Deliver equipment to specified hospital locations or to patients' residences. Maintain records of inventory and equipment usage. Record sterilizer test results. Assist hospital staff with patient care duties such as providing transportation and setting up traction.

GOE INFORMATION—Interest Area: 14. Medical and Health Services. **Work Group:** 14.05. Medical Technology. **Personality Type**—Realistic. Realistic occupations frequently involve work activities that include practical, hands-on problems and solutions. They often deal with plants, animals, and real-world materials like wood, tools, and machinery. Many of the occupations require working outside and do not involve a lot of paperwork or working closely with others. **Work Values**—Independence; Supervision, Technical; Moral Values; Security; Supervision, Human Relations. **Skills**—Installation; Operation Monitoring; Technology Design; Troubleshooting; Operation and Control; Equipment Selection. **Abilities**—*Cognitive:* Problem Sensitivity. *Psychomotor:* Rate Control; Response Orientation; Reaction Time; Control Precision; Manual Dexterity. *Physical:* Static Strength; Stamina; Dynamic Flexibility; Dynamic Strength; Extent Flexibility. *Sensory:* Glare Sensitivity; Hearing Sensitivity. **General Work Activities**—*Information Input:* Monitoring Processes, Materials, or Surroundings; Inspecting Equipment, Structures, or Materials; Getting Information. *Mental Process:* Updating and Using Relevant Knowledge; Evaluating Information Against Standards; Organizing, Planning, and Prioritizing. *Work Output:* Handling and Moving Objects; Controlling Machines and Processes; Repairing and Maintaining Mechanical Equipment. *Interacting with Others:* Performing Administrative Activities; Communicating with Other Workers; Establishing and Maintaining Relationships. **Physical Work Conditions**—Disease or Infections; Common Protective or Safety Attire; Kneeling, Crouching, or Crawling; Walking or Running; Using Hands on Objects, Tools, or Controls. **Other Job Characteristics**—Consequence of Error; Pace Determined by Speed of Equipment; Degree of Automation.

Experience—Job Zone 2. Some previous work-related skill, knowledge, or experience may be helpful, but usually is not needed. **Job Preparation:** SVP 4.0 to less than 6.0—six months to less than two years. **Knowledge**—Chemistry; Mechanical; Customer and Personal Service; Geography; Public

Safety and Security. **Instructional Programs**—Allied Health and Medical Assisting Services, Other; Medical/Clinical Assistant.

Related DOT Jobs—355.674-022 Respiratory-Therapy Aide; 359.363-010 Health-Equipment Servicer; 599.584-010 Reuse Technician.

31-9094.00 Medical Transcriptionists

- **Education/Training Required: Associate's degree**
- **Employed: 101,864**
- **Annual Earnings: $26,460**
- **Growth: 29.8%**
- **Annual Job Openings: 15,000**

Use transcribing machines with headset and foot pedal to listen to recordings by physicians and other health care professionals dictating a variety of medical reports, such as emergency room visits, diagnostic imaging studies, operations, chart reviews, and final summaries. Transcribe dictated reports and translate medical jargon and abbreviations into their expanded forms. Edit as necessary and return reports in either printed or electronic form to the dictator for review and signature or correction.

No task data available.

GOE INFORMATION—**Interest Area:** 09. Business Detail. **Work Group:** 09.07. Records Processing. **Note:** The Department of Labor has not collected some data for this job, so it has fewer details than the other descriptions.

Instructional Programs—Medical Transcription/Transcriptionist.

Related DOT Jobs—203.582-058 Transcribing-Machine Operator.

31-9095.00 Pharmacy Aides

- **Education/Training Required: Moderate-term on-the-job training**
- **Employed: 56,797**
- **Annual Earnings: $18,010**
- **Growth: 19.5%**
- **Annual Job Openings: 9,000**

Record drugs delivered to the pharmacy, store incoming merchandise, and inform the supervisor of stock needs. May operate cash register and accept prescriptions for filling.

Accept prescriptions for filling, gathering, and processing necessary information. Answer telephone inquiries, referring callers to pharmacist when necessary. Greet customers and help them locate merchandise. Operate cash register to process cash and credit sales. Perform clerical tasks such as filing, compiling and maintaining prescription records, and composing letters. Prepare prescription labels by typing and/or operating a computer and printer. Provide customers with information about the uses and effects of drugs. Receive, store, and inventory pharmaceutical supplies, notifying pharmacist when levels are low. Restock storage areas, replenishing items on shelves. Unpack, sort, count, and label incoming merchandise, including items requiring special handling or refrigeration. Calculate anticipated drug usage for a prescribed period. Compound, package, and label pharmaceutical products under direction of pharmacist. Deliver medication to treatment areas, living units, residences, and clinics, using various means of transportation. Maintain and clean equipment, work areas, and shelves. Operate capsule- and tablet-counting machine that automatically distributes a certain number of capsules or tablets into smaller containers. Prepare solid and liquid dosage medications for dispensing into bottles and unit dose packaging. Prepare, maintain, and record records of inventories, receipts, purchases, and deliveries, using a variety of computer screen formats. Process medical insurance claims, posting bill amounts and calculating co-payments.

GOE INFORMATION—**Interest Area:** 14. Medical and Health Services. **Work Group:** 14.02. Medicine and Surgery. **Note:** The Department of Labor has not collected some data for this job, so it has fewer details than the other descriptions.

Instructional Programs—Pharmacy Technician/Assistant.

Related DOT Jobs—074.381-010 Pharmacist Assistant.

31-9096.00 Veterinary Assistants and Laboratory Animal Caretakers

- **Education/Training Required: Short-term on-the-job training**
- **Employed: 55,219**
- **Annual Earnings: $17,470**
- **Growth: 39.8%**
- **Annual Job Openings: 8,000**

Feed, water, and examine pets and other nonfarm animals for signs of illness, disease, or injury in laboratories and animal hospitals and clinics. Clean and disinfect cages and work areas; sterilize laboratory and surgical equipment. May provide routine post-operative care, administer medication orally or topically, or prepare samples for laboratory examination under the supervision of veterinary or laboratory animal technologists or technicians, veterinarians, or scientists.

Administer anesthetics during surgery and monitor the effects on animals. Administer medication, immunizations, and blood plasma to animals as prescribed by veterinarians. Assist veterinarians in examining animals to determine the nature of illnesses or injuries. Clean and maintain kennels, animal holding areas, examination and operating rooms, and animal loading/unloading facilities to control the spread of disease. Clean, maintain, and sterilize instruments and equipment. Collect laboratory specimens such as blood, urine, and feces for testing. Examine animals to detect behavioral changes or clinical symptoms that could indicate illness or injury. Fill medication prescriptions. Hold or restrain animals during veterinary procedures. Monitor animals recovering from surgery and notify veterinarians of any unusual changes or symptoms. Perform enemas, catheterization, ear flushes, intravenous feedings, and gavages. Perform hygiene-related duties such as clipping animals' claws and cleaning and polishing teeth. Perform routine laboratory tests or diagnostic tests such as taking and developing X rays. Prepare examination or treatment rooms by stocking them with appropriate supplies. Prepare feed for animals according to specific instructions such as diet lists and schedules. Prepare surgical equipment and pass instruments and materials to veterinarians during surgical procedures. Provide emergency first aid to sick or injured animals. Assist professional personnel with research projects in commercial, public health, or research laboratories. Dust, spray, or bathe animals to control insect pests. Educate and advise clients on animal health care, nutrition, and behavior problems. Exercise animals and provide them with companionship. Groom, trim, or clip animals' coats. Perform accounting duties, including bookkeeping, billing customers for services, and maintaining inventories. Perform office reception duties such as scheduling appointments and helping customers. Provide assistance with euthanasia of animals and disposal of corpses. Record information relating to animal genealogy, feeding schedules, appearance, behavior, and breeding.

GOE INFORMATION—**Interest Area:** 03. Plants and Animals. **Work Group:** 03.02. Animal Care and Training. **Personality Type**—Realistic. Realistic occupations frequently involve work activities that include practical, hands-on problems and solutions. They often deal with plants, animals, and real-world materials like wood, tools, and machinery. Many of the occupations require working outside and do not involve a lot of paperwork or working closely with others. **Work Values**—Variety; Supervision, Technical. **Skills**—Equipment Selection; Science; Quality Control Analysis. **Abilities**—*Cognitive:* Oral Comprehension; Flexibility of Closure; Speed of Closure; Perceptual Speed; Memorization. *Psychomotor:* Response Orientation; Finger Dexterity; Speed of Limb Movement; Arm-Hand Steadiness; Reaction Time. *Physical:* Static Strength; Explosive Strength; Extent Flexibility; Dynamic Flexibility; Dynamic Strength. *Sensory:* Visual Color Discrimination; Peripheral Vision; Night Vision; Depth Perception; Speech Recognition. **General Work Activities**—*Information Input:* Identifying Objects, Actions, and Events; Getting Information; Monitoring Processes, Materials, or Surroundings. *Mental Process:* Evaluating Information Against Standards; Updating and Using Relevant Knowledge; Processing Information. *Work Output:* Performing General Physical Activities; Handling and Moving Objects; Documenting or Recording Information. *Interacting with Others:* Assisting and Caring for Others; Establishing and Maintaining Relationships; Communicating with Other Workers. **Physical Work Conditions**—Disease or Infections; Minor Burns, Cuts, Bites, or Stings; Common Protective or Safety Attire; Hazardous Conditions; Radiation. **Other Job Characteristics**—Consequence of Error; Importance of Being Exact or Accurate; Pace Determined by Speed of Equipment.

Experience—Job Zone 3. Previous work-related skill, knowledge, or experience is required. **Job Preparation:** SVP 6.0 to less than 7.0—more than one year and less than four years. **Knowledge**—Biology; Medicine and Dentistry; Food Production; Therapy and Counseling; Chemistry. **Instructional Programs**—Veterinary/Animal Health Technology/Technician and Veterinary Assistant.

Related DOT Jobs—079.361-014 Veterinary Technician.

31-9099.99 Healthcare Support Workers, All Other

- **Education/Training Required: No data available.**
- **Employed: No data available.**
- **Annual Earnings: No data available.**
- **Growth: 21.1%**
- **Annual Job Openings: 27,000**

All health care support workers not listed separately.

No task data available.

GOE INFORMATION—Interest Area: 14. Medical and Health Services. **Work Group:** 14.02. Medicine and Surgery; 14.03. Dentistry. **Note:** The Department of Labor has not collected some data for this job, so it has fewer details than the other descriptions.

Instructional Programs—Aromatherapy; Energy and Biologically Based Therapies, Other; Health Aides/Attendants/Orderlies, Other; Herbalism/Herbalist; Medication Aide; Polarity Therapy; Reiki; Yoga Teacher Training/Yoga Therapy.

Related DOT Jobs—079.364-022 Phlebotomist; 354.377-010 Birth Attendant; 355.667-010 Morgue Attendant; 355.677-014 Transporter, Patients.

33-0000

Protective Service Occupations

33-1000 First-Line Supervisors/ Managers, Protective Service Workers

33-1011.00 First-Line Supervisors/ Managers of Correctional Officers

- Education/Training Required: Work experience in a related occupation
- Employed: 29,692
- Annual Earnings: $44,640
- Growth: 29.6%
- Annual Job Openings: 3,000

Supervise and coordinate activities of correctional officers and jailers.

No task data available.

GOE INFORMATION—Interest Area: 04. Law, Law Enforcement, and Public Safety. **Work Group:** 04.01. Managerial Work in Law, Law Enforcement, and Public Safety. **Note:** The Department of Labor has not collected some data for this job, so it has fewer details than the other descriptions.

Instructional Programs—Corrections; Corrections Administration.

Related DOT Jobs—372.137-010 Correction Officer, Head; 372.167-018 Jailer, Chief.

33-1012.00 First-Line Supervisors/ Managers of Police and Detectives

- Education/Training Required: Work experience in a related occupation
- Employed: 120,522
- Annual Earnings: $59,300
- Growth: 13.1%
- Annual Job Openings: 9,000

Supervise and coordinate activities of members of police force.

Explain police operations to subordinates to assist them in performing their job duties. Inform personnel of changes in regulations and policies, implications of new or amended laws, and new techniques of police work. Supervise and coordinate the investigation of criminal cases, offering guidance and expertise to investigators and ensuring that procedures are conducted in accordance with laws and regulations. Investigate and resolve personnel problems within organization and charges of misconduct against staff. Train staff in proper police work procedures. Maintain logs, prepare reports, and direct the preparation, handling, and maintenance of departmental records. Monitor and evaluate the job performance of subordinates and authorize promotions and transfers. Direct collection, preparation, and handling of evidence and personal property of prisoners. Develop, implement, and revise departmental policies and procedures. Conduct raids and order detention of witnesses and suspects for questioning. Prepare work schedules and assign duties to subordinates. Discipline staff for violation of department rules and regulations. Cooperate with court personnel and officials from other law enforcement agencies and testify in court as necessary. Review contents of written orders to ensure adherence to legal requirements. Inspect facilities, supplies, vehicles, and equipment to ensure conformance to standards. Prepare news releases and respond to police correspondence. Requisition and issue equipment and supplies. Meet with civic, educational, and community groups to develop community programs and events and to discuss law enforcement subjects. Direct release or transfer of prisoners. Prepare budgets and manage expenditures of department funds.

GOE INFORMATION—Interest Area: 04. Law, Law Enforcement, and Public Safety. **Work Group:** 04.01. Managerial Work in Law, Law Enforcement, and Public Safety. **Personality Type—**Enterprising. Enterprising occupations frequently involve starting up and carrying out projects. These occupations can involve leading people and making many decisions. They sometimes require risk taking and often deal with business. **Work Values—**Authority; Social Status; Social Service; Responsibility; Autonomy. **Skills—**Management of Personnel Resources; Persuasion; Negotiation; Social Perceptiveness; Equipment Selection; Service Orientation; Complex Problem Solving; Monitoring. **Abilities—***Cognitive:* Flexibility of Closure; Category Flexibility; Time Sharing; Inductive Reasoning; Speed of Closure. *Psychomotor:* Reaction Time; Response Orientation; Rate Control; Multilimb Coordination; Control Precision. *Physical:* Explosive Strength; Stamina; Static Strength; Gross Body Coordination; Dynamic Strength. *Sensory:* Glare Sensitivity; Night Vision; Far Vision; Peripheral Vision; Speech Recognition. **General Work Activities—***Information Input:* Monitoring Processes, Materials, or Surroundings; Getting Information; Identifying Objects, Actions, and Events. *Mental Process:* Making Decisions and Solving Problems; Updating and Using Relevant Knowledge; Organizing, Planning, and Prioritizing. *Work Output:* Documenting or Recording Information; Performing General Physical Activities; Operating Vehicles or Equipment. *Interacting with Others:* Guiding, Directing, and Motivating Subordinates; Performing for or Working with the Public; Resolving Conflict and Negotiating with Others. **Physical Work Conditions—**Outdoors; Keeping or Regaining Balance; Very Hot or Cold; Distracting Sounds and Noise Levels; Specialized Protective or Safety Attire. **Other Job Characteristics—**Consequence of Error; Degree of Automation; Importance of Being Exact or Accurate.

Experience—Job Zone 4. A minimum of two to four years of work-related skill, knowledge, or experience is needed. **Job Preparation:** SVP 7.0 to less than 8.0—two years to less than 10 years. **Knowledge—**Public Safety and Security; Customer and Personal Service; Psychology; Education and Training; Law and Government. **Instructional Programs—**Corrections; Criminal Justice/Law Enforcement Administration; Criminal Justice/Safety Studies.

Related DOT Jobs—375.133-010 Police Sergeant, Precinct I; 375.137-010 Commander, Identification and Records; 375.137-014 Desk Officer; 375.137-018 Police Lieutenant, Community Relations; 375.137-026 Traffic Sergeant; 375.137-030 Commander, Police Reserves; 375.137-034 Commanding Officer, Police; 375.163-010 Commanding Officer, Motorized Squad; 375.167-010 Commanding Officer, Homicide Squad; 375.167-014 Commanding Officer, Investigation Division; 375.167-022 Detective Chief; 375.167-030 Launch Commander, Harbor Police; 375.167-034 Police Captain, Precinct; 375.167-038 Police Lieutenant, Patrol; 375.167-046 Traffic Lieutenant; 375.167-050 Commander, Internal Affairs; 377.134-010 Supervisor, Identification and Communications; 377.137-010 Deputy Sheriff, Commander, Civil Division; 377.137-014 Deputy Sheriff, Commander, Criminal and Patrol Division; 377.137-018 Deputy, Court; others.

33-1021.00 First-Line Supervisors/ Managers of Fire Fighting and Prevention Workers

- Education/Training Required: Work experience in a related occupation
- Employed: 61,664
- Annual Earnings: $53,420
- Growth: 7.2%
- Annual Job Openings: 5,000

Supervise and coordinate activities of workers engaged in firefighting and fire prevention and control.

No task data available.

GOE INFORMATION—Interest Area: 04. Law, Law Enforcement, and Public Safety. **Work Group:** 04.01. Managerial Work in Law, Law Enforcement, and Public Safety. **Note:** The Department of Labor has not collected some data for this job, so it has fewer details than the other descriptions.

Instructional Programs—Fire Protection and Safety Technology/Technician; Fire Services Administration.

Related DOT Jobs—373.134-010 Fire Captain; 373.167-010 Battalion Chief; 373.167-014 Captain, Fire-Prevention Bureau; 373.167-018 Fire Marshal; 452.134-010 Smoke Jumper Supervisor.

33-1021.01 Municipal Fire Fighting and Prevention Supervisors

- Education/Training Required: Work experience in a related occupation
- Employed: No data available.
- Annual Earnings: $53,420
- Growth: 16.7%
- Annual Job Openings: 5,000

Supervise firefighters who control and extinguish municipal fires, protect life and property, and conduct rescue efforts.

Identify corrective actions needed to bring properties into compliance with applicable fire codes and ordinances and conduct follow-up inspections to see if corrective actions have been taken. Maintain required maps and records. Oversee review of new building plans to ensure compliance with laws, ordinances, and administrative rules for public fire safety. Present and interpret fire prevention and fire code information to citizens' groups, organizations, contractors, engineers, and developers. Recommend to proper authorities possible fire code revisions, additions, and deletions. Report and issue citations for fire code violations found during inspections, testifying in court about violations when required to do so. Study and interpret fire safety codes to establish procedures for issuing permits regulating storage or use of hazardous or flammable substances. Write and submit proposals for repair, modification, or replacement of firefighting equipment. Assess nature and extent of fire, condition of building, danger to adjacent buildings, and water supply status in order to determine crew or company requirements. Assign firefighters to jobs at strategic locations in order to facilitate rescue of persons and maximize application of extinguishing agents. Attend in-service training classes to remain current in knowledge of codes, laws, ordinances, and regulations. Direct the training of firefighters, assigning of instructors to training classes, and providing of supervisors with reports on training progress and status. Evaluate fire station procedures in order to ensure efficiency and enforcement of departmental regulations. Evaluate the performance of assigned firefighting personnel. Inspect and test new and existing fire protection systems, fire detection systems, and fire safety equipment in order to ensure that they are operating properly. Instruct and drill fire department personnel in assigned duties, including firefighting, medical care, hazardous materials response, fire prevention, and related subjects. Participate in creating fire safety guidelines and evacuation schemes for non-residential buildings. Prepare activity reports listing fire call locations, actions taken, fire types and probable causes, damage estimates, and situation dispositions. Provide emergency medical services as required and perform light to heavy rescue functions at emergencies. Recommend personnel actions related to disciplinary procedures, performance, leaves of absence, and grievances. Supervise and participate in the inspection of properties in order to ensure that they are in compliance with applicable fire codes, ordinances, laws, regulations, and standards. Compile and maintain equipment and personnel records, including accident reports. Conduct fire drills for building occupants and report on the outcomes of such drills. Coordinate the distribution of fire prevention promotional materials. Develop or review building fire exit plans. Direct firefighters in station maintenance duties and participate in these duties.

GOE INFORMATION—Interest Area: 04. Law, Law Enforcement, and Public Safety. **Work Group:** 04.01. Managerial Work in Law, Law Enforcement, and Public Safety. **Personality Type—**Realistic. Realistic occupations frequently involve work activities that include practical, hands-on problems and solutions. They often deal with plants, animals, and real-world materials like wood, tools, and machinery. Many of the occupations require working outside and do not involve a lot of paperwork or working closely with others. **Work Values—**Authority; Social Status; Achievement; Pleasant Co-workers; Social Service. **Skills—**Management of Personnel Resources; Management of Material Resources; Systems Evaluation; Systems Analysis; Service Orientation; Coordination; Complex Problem Solving; Management of Financial Resources. **Abilities—***Cognitive:* Time Sharing; Spatial Orientation; Speed of Closure; Deductive Reasoning; Oral Expression. *Psychomotor:* Response Orientation; Reaction Time; Rate Control; Speed of Limb Movement; Multilimb Coordination. *Physical:* Stamina; Explosive Strength; Dynamic Strength; Static Strength; Gross Body Equilibrium. *Sensory:* Auditory Attention; Sound Localization; Night Vision; Far Vision; Peripheral Vision. **General Work Activities—***Information Input:* Getting Information; Inspecting Equipment, Structures, or Materials; Monitoring Processes, Materials, or Surroundings. *Mental Process:* Analyzing Data or Information; Evaluating Information Against Standards; Organizing, Planning, and Prioritizing. *Work Output:* Documenting or Recording Information; Performing General Physical Activities; Handling and Moving Objects. *Interacting with Others:* Communicating with Other Workers; Communicating with Persons Outside Organization; Establishing and Maintaining Relationships. **Physical Work Conditions—**Specialized Protective or Safety Attire; Very Hot or Cold; High Places; Outdoors; Extremely Bright or Inadequate Lighting. **Other Job Characteristics—**Consequence of Error; Importance of Repeating Same Tasks; Degree of Automation.

Experience—Job Zone 4. A minimum of two to four years of work-related skill, knowledge, or experience is needed. **Job Preparation:** SVP 7.0 to less than 8.0—two years to less than 10 years. **Knowledge—**Education and Training; Public Safety and Security; Personnel and Human Resources; Building and Construction; Administration and Management. **Instructional Programs—**Fire Protection and Safety Technology/Technician; Fire Services Administration.

Related DOT Jobs—373.134-010 Fire Captain; 373.167-010 Battalion Chief; 373.167-014 Captain, Fire-Prevention Bureau; 373.167-018 Fire Marshal.

33-1021.02 Forest Fire Fighting and Prevention Supervisors

- **Education/Training Required: Work experience in a related occupation**
- **Employed: No data available.**
- **Annual Earnings: $53,420**
- **Growth: 16.7%**
- **Annual Job Openings: 5,000**

Supervise firefighters who control and suppress fires in forests or vacant public land.

Communicate fire details to superiors, subordinates, and interagency dispatch centers, using two-way radios. Direct investigations of suspected arsons in wildfires, working closely with other investigating agencies. Direct the loading of fire suppression equipment into aircraft and the parachuting of equipment to crews on the ground. Evaluate size, location, and condition of forest fires in order to request and dispatch crews and position equipment so fires can be contained safely and effectively. Identify staff training and development needs in order to ensure that appropriate training can be arranged. Maintain fire suppression equipment in good condition, checking equipment periodically in order to ensure that it is ready for use. Maintain knowledge of forest fire laws and fire prevention techniques and tactics. Monitor prescribed burns to ensure that they are conducted safely and effectively. Observe fires and crews from air to determine fire-fighting force requirements and to note changing conditions that will affect fire-fighting efforts. Operate wildland fire engines and hoselays. Perform administrative duties such as compiling and maintaining records, completing forms, preparing reports, and composing correspondence. Recruit and hire forest fire-fighting personnel. Review and evaluate employee performance. Schedule employee work assignments and set work priorities. Serve as working leader of an engine, hand, helicopter, or prescribed fire crew of three or more firefighters. Train workers in such skills as parachute jumping, fire suppression, aerial observation, and radio communication, both in the classroom and on the job. Appraise damage caused by fires in order to prepare damage reports. Direct and supervise prescribed burn projects and prepare post-burn reports analyzing burn conditions and results. Drive crew carriers in order to transport firefighters to fire sites. Educate the public about forest fire prevention by participating in activities such as exhibits and presentations and by distributing promotional materials. Inspect all stations, uniforms, equipment, and recreation areas in order to ensure compliance with safety standards, taking corrective action as necessary. Monitor fire suppression expenditures in order to ensure that they are necessary and reasonable. Parachute to major fire locations in order to direct fire containment and suppression activities. Recommend equipment modifications or new equipment purchases. Regulate open burning by issuing burning permits, inspecting problem sites, issuing citations for violations of laws and ordinances, and educating the public in proper burning practices. Lead work crews in the maintenance of structures and access roads in forest areas.

GOE INFORMATION—Interest Area: 04. Law, Law Enforcement, and Public Safety. **Work Group:** 04.01. Managerial Work in Law, Law Enforcement, and Public Safety. **Personality Type—**Realistic. Realistic occupations frequently involve work activities that include practical, hands-on problems and solutions. They often deal with plants, animals, and real-world materials like wood, tools, and machinery. Many of the occupations require working outside and do not involve a lot of paperwork or working closely with others. **Work Values—**Authority; Social Status; Responsibility; Autonomy; Achievement. **Skills—**Management of Personnel Resources; Management of Material Resources; Systems Analysis; Systems Evaluation; Service Orientation; Coordination; Instructing; Judgment and Decision Making. **Abilities—***Cognitive:* Spatial Orientation; Time Sharing; Speed of Closure; Flexibility of Closure; Selective Attention. *Psychomotor:* Rate Control; Speed of Limb Movement; Reaction Time; Response Orientation; Multilimb Coordination. *Physical:* Stamina; Gross Body Equilibrium; Static Strength; Gross Body Coordination; Explosive Strength. *Sensory:* Far Vision; Night Vision; Auditory Attention; Glare Sensitivity; Peripheral Vision. **General Work Activities—***Information Input:* Monitoring Processes, Materials, or Surroundings; Identifying Objects, Actions, and Events; Getting Information. *Mental Process:* Making Decisions and Solving Problems; Scheduling Work and Activities; Analyzing Data or Information. *Work Output:* Performing General Physical Activities; Operating Vehicles or Equipment; Handling and Moving Objects. *Interacting with Others:* Coordinating the Work and Activities of Others; Communicating with Other Workers; Teaching Others. **Physical Work Conditions—**Specialized Protective or Safety Attire; Common Protective or Safety Attire; Outdoors; Very Hot or Cold; Minor Burns, Cuts, Bites, or Stings. **Other Job Characteristics—**Consequence of Error; Importance of Repeating Same Tasks; Importance of Being Exact or Accurate.

Experience—Job Zone 5. Extensive skill, knowledge, and experience are needed for these occupations. **Job Preparation:** SVP 8.0 and above—four years to more than 10 years. **Knowledge—**Public Safety and Security; Education and Training; Administration and Management; Geography; Chemistry. **Instructional Programs—**Fire Protection and Safety Technology/Technician; Fire Services Administration.

Related DOT Jobs—452.134-010 Smoke Jumper Supervisor.

33-1099.99 First-Line Supervisors/ Managers, Protective Service Workers, All Other

- **Education/Training Required: Work experience in a related occupation**
- **Employed: No data available.**
- **Annual Earnings: No data available.**
- **Growth: 27.1%**
- **Annual Job Openings: 5,000**

All protective service supervisors not listed separately above.

No task data available.

GOE INFORMATION—Interest Area: 04. Law, Law Enforcement, and Public Safety. **Work Group:** 04.01. Managerial Work in Law, Law Enforcement, and Public Safety. **Note:** The Department of Labor has not collected some data for this job, so it has fewer details than the other descriptions.

Instructional Programs—Securities Services Administration/Management; Security and Protective Services, Other.

Related DOT Jobs—372.167-014 Guard, Chief; 376.137-010 Manager, Internal Security.

33-2000 Fire Fighting and Prevention Workers

33-2011.00 Fire Fighters

- Education/Training Required: Long-term on-the-job training
- Employed: 257,568
- Annual Earnings: $34,680
- Growth: 8.9%
- Annual Job Openings: 12,000

Control and extinguish fires or respond to emergency situations where life, property, or the environment is at risk. Duties may include fire prevention, emergency medical service, hazardous material response, search and rescue, and disaster management.

No task data available.

GOE INFORMATION—Interest Area: 04. Law, Law Enforcement, and Public Safety. **Work Group:** 04.04. Public Safety. **Note:** The Department of Labor has not collected some data for this job, so it has fewer details than the other descriptions.

Instructional Programs—Fire Protection, Other; Fire Science/Firefighting.

Related DOT Jobs—373.363-010 Fire Chief's Aide; 373.364-010 Fire Fighter; 373.364-640 Fire Apparatus Engineer; 373.364-641 Fire Engineer; 373.663-010 Fire Fighter, Crash, Fire, and Rescue; 379.374-580 Fire Medic; 452.364-014 Smoke Jumper; 452.687-014 Forest-Fire Fighter; 452.687-640 Wildland Fire Fighter Specialist.

33-2011.01 Municipal Fire Fighters

- Education/Training Required: Long-term on-the-job training
- Employed: No data available.
- Annual Earnings: $34,680
- Growth: 8.9%
- Annual Job Openings: 12,000

Control and extinguish municipal fires, protect life and property, and conduct rescue efforts.

Collaborate with police to respond to accidents, disasters, and arson investigation calls. Establish fire lines to prevent unauthorized persons from entering areas near fires. Inform and educate the public on fire prevention. Inspect buildings for fire hazards and compliance with fire prevention ordinances, testing and checking smoke alarms and fire suppression equipment as necessary. Administer first aid and cardiopulmonary resuscitation to injured persons. Assess fires and situations and report conditions to superiors in order to receive instructions, using two-way radios. Create openings in buildings for ventilation or entrance, using axes, chisels, crowbars, electric saws, or core cutters. Drive and operate fire-fighting vehicles and equipment. Inspect fire sites after flames have been extinguished in order to ensure that there is no further danger. Lay hose lines and connect them to water supplies. Move toward the source of a fire, using knowledge of types of fires, construction design, building materials, and physical layout of properties. Operate pumps connected to high-pressure hoses. Participate in physical training activities in order to maintain a high level of physical fitness. Position and climb ladders in order to gain access to upper levels of buildings or to rescue individuals from burning structures. Rescue victims from burning buildings and accident sites. Respond to fire alarms and other calls for assistance, such as automobile and industrial accidents.

Search burning buildings to locate fire victims. Select and attach hose nozzles, depending on fire type, and direct streams of water or chemicals onto fires. Protect property from water and smoke using waterproof salvage covers, smoke ejectors, and deodorants. Spray foam onto runways, extinguish fires, and rescue aircraft crew and passengers in air-crash emergencies. Clean and maintain fire stations and fire-fighting equipment and apparatus. Participate in courses, seminars, and conferences and study fire science literature in order to learn fire-fighting techniques. Participate in fire drills and demonstrations of fire-fighting techniques. Prepare written reports that detail specifics of fire incidents. Salvage property by removing broken glass, pumping out water, and ventilating buildings to remove smoke. Take action to contain hazardous chemicals that might catch fire, leak, or spill.

GOE INFORMATION—Interest Area: 04. Law, Law Enforcement, and Public Safety. **Work Group:** 04.04. Public Safety. **Personality Type—**Realistic. Realistic occupations frequently involve work activities that include practical, hands-on problems and solutions. They often deal with plants, animals, and real-world materials like wood, tools, and machinery. Many of the occupations require working outside and do not involve a lot of paperwork or working closely with others. **Work Values—**Social Status; Social Service; Achievement; Pleasant Co-workers; Supervision, Technical. **Skills—**Service Orientation; Repairing; Coordination; Operation and Control; Systems Analysis; Equipment Selection; Critical Thinking; Operation Monitoring. **Abilities—***Cognitive:* Spatial Orientation; Flexibility of Closure; Time Sharing; Speed of Closure; Selective Attention. *Psychomotor:* Reaction Time; Response Orientation; Rate Control; Speed of Limb Movement; Multilimb Coordination. *Physical:* Explosive Strength; Dynamic Strength; Stamina; Static Strength; Gross Body Equilibrium. *Sensory:* Sound Localization; Peripheral Vision; Night Vision; Auditory Attention; Far Vision. **General Work Activities—***Information Input:* Monitoring Processes, Materials, or Surroundings; Inspecting Equipment, Structures, or Materials; Identifying Objects, Actions, and Events. *Mental Process:* Making Decisions and Solving Problems; Judging Qualities of Things, Services, or Other People's Work; Evaluating Information Against Standards. *Work Output:* Performing General Physical Activities; Handling and Moving Objects; Operating Vehicles or Equipment. *Interacting with Others:* Assisting and Caring for Others; Communicating with Other Workers; Performing for or Working with the Public. **Physical Work Conditions—**Specialized Protective or Safety Attire; Common Protective or Safety Attire; Hazardous Conditions; Climbing Ladders, Scaffolds, Poles, etc.; Minor Burns, Cuts, Bites, or Stings. **Other Job Characteristics—**Consequence of Error; Importance of Repeating Same Tasks; Pace Determined by Speed of Equipment.

Experience—Job Zone 2. Some previous work-related skill, knowledge, or experience may be helpful, but usually is not needed. **Job Preparation:** SVP 4.0 to less than 6.0—six months to less than two years. **Knowledge—**Public Safety and Security; Medicine and Dentistry; Geography; Therapy and Counseling; Chemistry. **Instructional Programs—**Fire Protection, Other; Fire Science/Firefighting.

Related DOT Jobs—373.363-010 Fire Chief's Aide; 373.364-010 Fire Fighter; 373.663-010 Fire Fighter, Crash, Fire, and Rescue.

33-2011.02 Forest Fire Fighters

- Education/Training Required: Long-term on-the-job training
- Employed: No data available.
- Annual Earnings: $34,680
- Growth: 8.9%
- Annual Job Openings: 12,000

Control and suppress fires in forests or vacant public land.

Collaborate with other firefighters as a member of a fire-fighting crew. Establish water supplies, connect hoses, and direct water onto fires. Extinguish flames and embers to suppress fires, using shovels or engine- or hand-driven water or chemical pumps. Fell trees, cut and clear brush, and dig trenches in order to create fire lines, using axes, chain saws or shovels. Maintain contact with fire dispatchers at all times in order to notify them of the need for additional firefighters and supplies or to detail any difficulties encountered. Operate pumps connected to high-pressure hoses. Orient self in relation to fire, using compass and map, and collect supplies and equipment dropped by parachute. Participate in physical training in order to maintain high levels of physical fitness. Patrol burned areas after fires to locate and eliminate hot spots that may restart fires. Test and maintain tools, equipment, jump gear, and parachutes in order to ensure readiness for fire suppression activities. Observe forest areas from fire lookout towers in order to spot potential problems. Organize fire caches, positioning equipment for the most effective response. Parachute from aircraft into remote areas for initial attack on wildland fires. Participate in fire prevention and inspection programs. Perform forest maintenance and improvement tasks such as cutting brush, planting trees, building trails, and marking timber. Rescue fire victims and administer emergency medical aid. Take action to contain any hazardous chemicals that could catch fire, leak, or spill. Transport personnel and cargo to and from fire areas. Drop weighted paper streamers from aircraft to determine the speed and direction of the wind at fire sites. Inform and educate the public about fire prevention. Maintain fire equipment and firehouse living quarters. Maintain knowledge of current fire-fighting practices by participating in drills and by attending seminars, conventions, and conferences. Serve as fully trained lead helicopter crew member and as helispot manager.

GOE INFORMATION—Interest Area: 04. Law, Law Enforcement, and Public Safety. Work Group: 04.04. Public Safety. Personality Type—Realistic. Realistic occupations frequently involve work activities that include practical, hands-on problems and solutions. They often deal with plants, animals, and real-world materials like wood, tools, and machinery. Many of the occupations require working outside and do not involve a lot of paperwork or working closely with others. Work Values—Achievement; Pleasant Co-workers; Social Status; Supervision, Technical; Supervision, Human Relations. Skills—Service Orientation; Coordination; Technology Design; Equipment Selection; Systems Analysis. Abilities—Cognitive: Spatial Orientation; Time Sharing; Speed of Closure; Flexibility of Closure; Problem Sensitivity. Psychomotor: Response Orientation; Speed of Limb Movement; Reaction Time; Multilimb Coordination; Rate Control. Physical: Stamina; Explosive Strength; Static Strength; Gross Body Coordination; Dynamic Strength. Sensory: Far Vision; Night Vision; Auditory Attention; Sound Localization; Glare Sensitivity. General Work Activities—Information Input: Monitoring Processes, Materials, or Surroundings; Getting Information; Estimating Needed Characteristics. Mental Process: Organizing, Planning, and Prioritizing; Making Decisions and Solving Problems; Judging Qualities of Things, Services, or Other People's Work. Work Output: Performing General Physical Activities; Handling and Moving Objects; Controlling Machines and Processes. Interacting with Others: Communicating with Other Workers; Assisting and Caring for Others; Establishing and Maintaining Relationships. Physical Work Conditions—Specialized Protective or Safety Attire; Outdoors; Common Protective or Safety Attire; Very Hot or Cold; Minor Burns, Cuts, Bites, or Stings. Other Job Characteristics—Importance of Repeating Same Tasks; Consequence of Error; Pace Determined by Speed of Equipment.

Experience—Job Zone 2. Some previous work-related skill, knowledge, or experience may be helpful, but usually is not needed. Job Preparation: SVP 4.0 to less than 6.0—six months to less than two years. Knowledge—Public Safety and Security; Biology; Geography; Therapy and Counsel-

ing; Telecommunications. Instructional Programs—Fire Protection, Other; Fire Science/Firefighting.

Related DOT Jobs—452.364-014 Smoke Jumper; 452.687-014 Forest-Fire Fighter.

33-2021.00 Fire Inspectors and Investigators
- Education/Training Required: Moderate-term on-the-job training
- Employed: No data available.
- Annual Earnings: $42,870
- Growth: 15.1%
- Annual Job Openings: 1,000

Inspect buildings to detect fire hazards and enforce local ordinances and state laws. Investigate and gather facts to determine cause of fires and explosions.

No task data available.

GOE INFORMATION—Interest Area: 04. Law, Law Enforcement, and Public Safety. Work Group: 04.04. Public Safety. Note: The Department of Labor has not collected some data for this job, so it has fewer details than the other descriptions.

Instructional Programs—Fire Protection and Safety Technology/Technician; Fire Science/Firefighting.

Related DOT Jobs—168.267-010 Building Inspector; 373.267-010 Fire Inspector; 373.267-014 Fire Marshal; 373.267-018 Fire-Investigation Lieutenant; 373.267-640 Arson And Bomb Investigator; 373.367-010 Fire Inspector; 379.687-010 Fire-Extinguisher-Sprinkler Inspector.

33-2021.01 Fire Inspectors
- Education/Training Required: Moderate-term on-the-job training
- Employed: 12,644
- Annual Earnings: $42,870
- Growth: 15.1%
- Annual Job Openings: 1,000

Inspect buildings and equipment to detect fire hazards and enforce state and local regulations.

Attend training classes in order to maintain current knowledge of fire prevention, safety, and fire-fighting procedures. Conduct fire code compliance follow-ups to ensure that corrective actions have been taken in cases where violations were found. Conduct fire exit drills to monitor and evaluate evacuation procedures. Conduct inspections and acceptance testing of newly installed fire protection systems. Develop or review fire exit plans. Identify corrective actions necessary to bring properties into compliance with applicable fire codes, laws, regulations, and standards and explain these measures to property owners or their representatives. Inspect and test fire protection and/or fire detection systems to verify that such systems are installed in accordance with appropriate laws, codes, ordinances, regulations, and standards. Inspect buildings to locate hazardous conditions and fire code violations such as accumulations of combustible material, electrical wiring problems, and inadequate or nonfunctional fire exits. Inspect liquefied petroleum installations, storage containers, and transportation and delivery systems for compliance with fire laws. Inspect properties that store, handle, and use hazardous materials to ensure compliance with laws, codes, and regulations and issue hazardous materials permits to facilities found in compliance. Issue permits for public assemblies. Review blueprints and plans for new or remodeled buildings in order to ensure that structures meet fire safety codes. Search for clues as to the cause of a fire once the fire is completely extinguished. Write detailed reports of fire inspections performed, fire code violations observed, and corrective recommendations offered. Arrange for the replacement of defective fire-fighting equipment and for repair of fire alarm and sprinkler systems, making minor repairs such as servicing fire extinguishers when feasible. Collect fees for permits and licenses. Develop and coordinate fire prevention programs such as false alarm billing, fire inspection reporting, and hazardous materials management. Investigate causes of fires, collecting and preparing evidence and presenting it in court when necessary. Present and explain fire code requirements and fire prevention information to architects, contractors, attorneys, engineers, developers, fire service personnel, and the general public. Recommend changes to fire prevention, inspection, and fire code endorsement procedures. Serve court appearance summonses and/or condemnation notices on parties responsible for violations of fire codes, laws, and ordinances. Supervise staff, training them, planning their work, and evaluating their performance. Testify in court regarding fire code and fire safety issues.

GOE INFORMATION—Interest Area: 04. Law, Law Enforcement, and Public Safety. **Work Group:** 04.04. Public Safety. **Personality Type—** Conventional. Conventional occupations frequently involve following set procedures and routines. These occupations can include working with data and details more than with ideas. Usually there is a clear line of authority to follow. **Work Values—**Social Status; Achievement; Security; Authority; Ability Utilization. **Skills—**Troubleshooting; Writing; Systems Analysis; Quality Control Analysis; Complex Problem Solving; Persuasion; Critical Thinking; Service Orientation. **Abilities—**Cognitive: Flexibility of Closure; Oral Expression; Written Expression; Spatial Orientation; Problem Sensitivity. Psychomotor: Reaction Time; Speed of Limb Movement; Response Orientation; Multilimb Coordination; Arm-Hand Steadiness. Physical: Stamina; Gross Body Equilibrium; Explosive Strength; Static Strength; Gross Body Coordination. Sensory: Visual Color Discrimination; Far Vision; Sound Localization; Night Vision; Auditory Attention. **General Work Activities—**Information Input: Inspecting Equipment, Structures, or Materials; Getting Information; Identifying Objects, Actions, and Events. Mental Process: Evaluating Information Against Standards; Organizing, Planning, and Prioritizing; Updating and Using Relevant Knowledge. Work Output: Performing General Physical Activities; Documenting or Recording Information; Handling and Moving Objects. Interacting with Others: Assisting and Caring for Others; Communicating with Persons Outside Organization; Providing Consultation and Advice to Others. **Physical Work Conditions—**Climbing Ladders, Scaffolds, Poles, etc.; Keeping or Regaining Balance; Hazardous Conditions; Cramped Work Space or Awkward Positions; High Places. **Other Job Characteristics—**Consequence of Error; Importance of Being Exact or Accurate; Importance of Repeating Same Tasks.

Experience—Job Zone 2. Some previous work-related skill, knowledge, or experience may be helpful, but usually is not needed. **Job Preparation:** SVP 4.0 to less than 6.0—six months to less than two years. **Knowledge—** Public Safety and Security; Law and Government; Medicine and Dentistry; Education and Training; Engineering and Technology. **Instructional Programs—**Fire Protection and Safety Technology/Technician; Fire Science/Firefighting.

Related DOT Jobs—168.267-010 Building Inspector; 373.267-010 Fire Inspector; 373.367-010 Fire Inspector; 379.687-010 Fire-Extinguisher-Sprinkler Inspector.

33-2021.02 Fire Investigators

- **Education/Training Required: Bachelor's degree**
- **Employed: No data available.**
- **Annual Earnings: $42,870**
- **Growth: 15.1%**
- **Annual Job Openings: 1,000**

Conduct investigations to determine causes of fires and explosions.

Analyze evidence and other information to determine probable cause of fire or explosion. Examine fire sites and collect evidence such as glass, metal fragments, charred wood, and accelerant residue for use in determining the cause of a fire. Package collected pieces of evidence in securely closed containers such as bags, crates, or boxes in order to protect them. Photograph damage and evidence related to causes of fires or explosions in order to document investigation findings. Prepare and maintain reports of investigation results and records of convicted arsonists and arson suspects. Subpoena and interview witnesses, property owners, and building occupants to obtain information and sworn testimony. Dust evidence or portions of fire scenes for latent fingerprints. Instruct children about the dangers of fire. Test sites and materials to establish facts, such as burn patterns and flash points of materials, using test equipment. Testify in court cases involving fires, suspected arson, and false alarms. Conduct internal investigation to determine negligence and violation of laws and regulations by fire department employees. Swear out warrants and arrest and process suspected arsonists.

GOE INFORMATION—Interest Area: 04. Law, Law Enforcement, and Public Safety. **Work Group:** 04.03. Law Enforcement. **Personality Type—** Investigative. Investigative occupations frequently involve working with ideas and require an extensive amount of thinking. These occupations can involve searching for facts and figuring out problems mentally. **Work Values—**Achievement; Ability Utilization; Responsibility; Social Status; Variety. **Skills—**Active Listening; Critical Thinking; Systems Evaluation; Speaking; Complex Problem Solving; Writing; Science; Judgment and Decision Making. **Abilities—**Cognitive: Inductive Reasoning; Flexibility of Closure; Speed of Closure; Written Expression; Spatial Orientation. Psychomotor: Speed of Limb Movement; Arm-Hand Steadiness. Physical: Gross Body Equilibrium; Stamina; Gross Body Coordination; Dynamic Strength; Extent Flexibility. Sensory: Far Vision; Night Vision; Speech Clarity; Visual Color Discrimination; Auditory Attention. **General Work Activities—**Information Input: Getting Information; Identifying Objects, Actions, and Events; Inspecting Equipment, Structures, or Materials. Mental Process: Analyzing Data or Information; Making Decisions and Solving Problems; Organizing, Planning, and Prioritizing. Work Output: Documenting or Recording Information; Handling and Moving Objects; Performing General Physical Activities. Interacting with Others: Communicating with Persons Outside Organization; Communicating with Other Workers; Performing Administrative Activities. **Physical Work Conditions—**Keeping or Regaining Balance; Climbing Ladders, Scaffolds, Poles, etc.; High Places; Very Hot or Cold; Kneeling, Crouching, or Crawling. **Other Job Characteristics—**Importance of Being Exact or Accurate; Consequence of Error; Pace Determined by Speed of Equipment.

Experience—Job Zone 4. A minimum of two to four years of work-related skill, knowledge, or experience is needed. **Job Preparation:** SVP 7.0 to less than 8.0—two years to less than 10 years. **Knowledge—**Public Safety and Security; Law and Government; Education and Training; Building and Construction; Chemistry. **Instructional Programs—**Fire Protection and Safety Technology/Technician; Fire Science/Firefighting.

Related DOT Jobs—373.267-014 Fire Marshal; 373.267-018 Fire-Investigation Lieutenant.

33-2022.00 Forest Fire Inspectors and Prevention Specialists

- **Education/Training Required: Moderate-term on-the-job training**
- **Employed: No data available.**
- **Annual Earnings: $35,120**
- **Growth: 15.1%**
- **Annual Job Openings: 1,000**

Enforce fire regulations and inspect for forest fire hazards. Report forest fires and weather conditions.

Administer regulations regarding sanitation, fire prevention, violation corrections, and related forest regulations. Compile and report meteorological data, such as temperature, relative humidity, wind direction and velocity, and types of cloud formations. Estimate sizes and characteristics of fires and report findings to base camps by radio or telephone. Extinguish smaller fires with portable extinguishers, shovels, and axes. Inspect campsites to ensure that campers are in compliance with forest use regulations. Inspect forest tracts and logging areas for fire hazards such as accumulated wastes or mishandling of combustibles and recommend appropriate fire prevention measures. Locate forest fires on area maps, using azimuth sighters and known landmarks. Patrol assigned areas, looking for forest fires, hazardous conditions, and weather phenomena. Relay messages about emergencies, accidents, locations of crew and personnel, and fire hazard conditions. Restrict public access and recreational use of forest lands during critical fire seasons. Direct crews working on fire lines during forest fires. Direct maintenance and repair of fire-fighting equipment or requisition new equipment. Examine and inventory fire-fighting equipment such as axes, fire hoses, shovels, pumps, buckets, and fire extinguishers in order to determine amount and condition. Maintain records and logbooks.

GOE INFORMATION—Interest Area: 04. Law, Law Enforcement, and Public Safety. **Work Group:** 04.04. Public Safety. **Personality Type—** Realistic. Realistic occupations frequently involve work activities that include practical, hands-on problems and solutions. They often deal with plants, animals, and real-world materials like wood, tools, and machinery. Many of the occupations require working outside and do not involve a lot of paperwork or working closely with others. **Work Values—**Achievement; Authority; Ability Utilization; Social Status; Responsibility. **Skills—** Management of Personnel Resources; Equipment Selection; Management of Material Resources; Service Orientation; Monitoring; Systems Analysis; Critical Thinking; Coordination. **Abilities—***Cognitive:* Flexibility of Closure; Speed of Closure; Spatial Orientation; Problem Sensitivity; Perceptual Speed. *Psychomotor:* Reaction Time; Speed of Limb Movement; Multilimb Coordination; Response Orientation; Rate Control. *Physical:* Stamina; Explosive Strength; Static Strength; Trunk Strength; Dynamic Strength. *Sensory:* Night Vision; Glare Sensitivity; Far Vision; Sound Localization; Peripheral Vision. **General Work Activities—***Information Input:* Getting Information; Monitoring Processes, Materials, or Surroundings; Identifying Objects, Actions, and Events. *Mental Process:* Judging Qualities of Things, Services, or Other People's Work; Making Decisions and Solving Problems; Analyzing Data or Information. *Work Output:* Performing General Physical Activities; Handling and Moving Objects; Documenting or Recording Information. *Interacting with Others:* Communicating with Persons Outside Organization; Assisting and Caring for Others; Establishing and Maintaining Relationships. **Physical Work Conditions—**Outdoors; Very Hot or Cold; High Places; Specialized Protective or Safety Attire; Contaminants. **Other Job Characteristics—**Consequence of Error; Importance of Being Exact or Accurate; Importance of Repeating Same Tasks.

Experience—Job Zone 2. Some previous work-related skill, knowledge, or experience may be helpful, but usually is not needed. **Job Preparation:** SVP 4.0 to less than 6.0—six months to less than two years. **Knowledge—** Geography; Public Safety and Security; Physics; Education and Training; Biology. **Instructional Programs—**Fire Science/Firefighting.

Related DOT Jobs—452.167-010 Fire Warden; 452.367-010 Fire Lookout; 452.367-014 Fire Ranger.

33-3000 Law Enforcement Workers

33-3011.00 Bailiffs

- **Education/Training Required: Moderate-term on-the-job training**
- **Employed: 13,625**
- **Annual Earnings: $31,390**
- **Growth: 12.5%**
- **Annual Job Openings: 1,000**

Maintain order in courts of law.

Maintain order in courtroom during trial and guard jury from outside contact. Enforce courtroom rules of behavior and warn persons not to smoke or disturb court procedure. Announce entrance of judge. Stop people from entering courtroom while judge charges jury. Guard lodging of sequestered jury. Report need for police or medical assistance to sheriff's office. Check courtroom for security and cleanliness and assure availability of sundry supplies for use of judge. Provide jury escort to restaurant and other areas outside of courtroom to prevent jury contact with public. Collect and retain unauthorized firearms from persons entering courtroom.

GOE INFORMATION—Interest Area: 04. Law, Law Enforcement, and Public Safety. **Work Group:** 04.03. Law Enforcement. **Personality Type—** Social. Social occupations frequently involve working with, communicating with, and teaching people. These occupations often involve helping or providing service to others. **Work Values—**Security; Supervision, Human Relations; Authority; Company Policies and Practices; Pleasant Co-workers. **Skills—**None met the criteria. **Abilities—***Cognitive:* Selective Attention; Time Sharing; Flexibility of Closure; Originality; Spatial Orientation. *Psychomotor:* Reaction Time; Speed of Limb Movement; Response Orientation. *Physical:* Static Strength; Gross Body Coordination; Explosive Strength; Stamina; Dynamic Flexibility. *Sensory:* Peripheral Vision; Far Vision; Night Vision; Sound Localization; Auditory Attention. **General Work Activities—***Information Input:* Getting Information; Monitoring Processes, Materials, or Surroundings; Identifying Objects, Actions, and Events. *Mental Process:* Judging Qualities of Things, Services, or Other People's Work; Making Decisions and Solving Problems; Evaluating Information Against Standards. *Work Output:* Performing General Physical Activities; Handling and Moving Objects; Documenting or Recording Information. *Interacting with Others:* Performing for or Working with the Public; Establishing and Maintaining Relationships; Resolving Conflict and Negotiating with Others. **Physical Work Conditions—**Indoors; Walking or Running; Standing; Disease or Infections; Specialized Protective or Safety Attire. **Other Job Characteristics—**Consequence of Error; Importance of Repeating Same Tasks; Pace Determined by Speed of Equipment.

Experience—Job Zone 1. No previous work-related skill, knowledge, or experience is needed. **Job Preparation:** SVP below 4.0—less than six months. **Knowledge—**Public Safety and Security; Law and Government;

Psychology; Sociology and Anthropology; Geography. **Instructional Programs**—Criminal Justice/Police Science.

Related DOT Jobs—377.667-010 Bailiff.

33-3012.00 Correctional Officers and Jailers

- **Education/Training Required: Moderate-term on-the-job training**
- **Employed: 413,781**
- **Annual Earnings: $32,010**
- **Growth: 32.4%**
- **Annual Job Openings: 30,000**

Guard inmates in penal or rehabilitative institution in accordance with established regulations and procedures. May guard prisoners in transit between jail, courtroom, prison, or other point. Includes deputy sheriffs and police who spend the majority of their time guarding prisoners in correctional institutions.

Monitor conduct of prisoners, according to established policies, regulations, and procedures, in order to prevent escape or violence. Take prisoners into custody and escort to locations within and outside of facility, such as visiting room, courtroom, or airport. Inspect conditions of locks, window bars, grills, doors, and gates at correctional facilities in order to ensure that they will prevent escapes. Use weapons, handcuffs, and physical force to maintain discipline and order among prisoners. Search prisoners, cells, and vehicles for weapons, valuables, or drugs. Guard facility entrances in order to screen visitors. Record information, such as prisoner identification, charges, and incidences of inmate disturbance. Serve meals and distribute commissary items to prisoners. Settle disputes between inmates. Arrange daily schedules for prisoners, including library visits, work assignments, family visits, and counseling appointments. Assign duties to inmates, providing instructions as needed. Conduct fire, safety, and sanitation inspections. Drive passenger vehicles and trucks used to transport inmates to other institutions, courtrooms, hospitals, and work sites. Inspect mail for the presence of contraband. Investigate crimes that have occurred within an institution or assist police in their investigations of crimes and inmates. Issue clothing, tools, and other authorized items to inmates. Maintain records of prisoners' identification and charges. Provide to supervisors oral and written reports of the quality and quantity of work performed by inmates, inmate disturbances and rule violations, and unusual occurrences. Supervise and coordinate work of other correctional service officers. Search for and recapture escapees. Sponsor inmate recreational activities such as newspapers and self-help groups.

GOE INFORMATION—**Interest Area:** 04. Law, Law Enforcement, and Public Safety. **Work Group:** 04.03. Law Enforcement. **Personality Type**—Realistic. Realistic occupations frequently involve work activities that include practical, hands-on problems and solutions. They often deal with plants, animals, and real-world materials like wood, tools, and machinery. Many of the occupations require working outside and do not involve a lot of paperwork or working closely with others. **Work Values**—Security; Authority; Supervision, Human Relations; Company Policies and Practices; Pleasant Co-workers. **Skills**—Social Perceptiveness. **Abilities**—*Cognitive:* Problem Sensitivity; Spatial Orientation; Selective Attention; Time Sharing; Flexibility of Closure. *Psychomotor:* Speed of Limb Movement; Reaction Time; Response Orientation; Rate Control; Multilimb Coordination. *Physical:* Explosive Strength; Static Strength; Dynamic Strength; Stamina; Gross Body Coordination. *Sensory:* Peripheral Vision; Night Vision; Far Vision; Sound Localization; Hearing Sensitivity. **General Work Activities**—*Information Input:* Getting Information; Monitoring Processes, Materials, or Surroundings; Identifying Objects, Actions, and Events. *Mental Process:* Evaluating Information Against Standards; Analyzing Data or Information; Processing Information. *Work Output:* Performing General Physical Activities; Handling and Moving Objects; Documenting or Recording Information. *Interacting with Others:* Assisting and Caring for Others; Resolving Conflict and Negotiating with Others; Performing for or Working with the Public. **Physical Work Conditions**—Walking or Running; Climbing Ladders, Scaffolds, Poles, etc.; Outdoors; Specialized Protective or Safety Attire; Standing. **Other Job Characteristics**—Consequence of Error; Importance of Repeating Same Tasks; Importance of Being Exact or Accurate.

Experience—Job Zone 2. Some previous work-related skill, knowledge, or experience may be helpful, but usually is not needed. **Job Preparation:** SVP 4.0 to less than 6.0—six months to less than two years. **Knowledge**—Public Safety and Security; Law and Government; Medicine and Dentistry; Sociology and Anthropology; Psychology. **Instructional Programs**—Corrections; Corrections and Criminal Justice, Other; Juvenile Corrections.

Related DOT Jobs—372.367-014 Jailer; 372.567-014 Guard, Immigration; 372.667-018 Correction Officer; 372.677-010 Patrol Conductor; 375.367-010 Police Officer II.

33-3021.00 Detectives and Criminal Investigators

- **Education/Training Required: Work experience in a related occupation**
- **Employed: 93,206**
- **Annual Earnings: $50,960**
- **Growth: 16.4%**
- **Annual Job Openings: 4,000**

Conduct investigations related to suspected violations of federal, state, or local laws to prevent or solve crimes.

No task data available.

GOE INFORMATION—**Interest Area:** 04. Law, Law Enforcement, and Public Safety. **Work Group:** 04.03. Law Enforcement. **Note:** The Department of Labor has not collected some data for this job, so it has fewer details than the other descriptions.

Instructional Programs—Criminal Justice/Police Science; Criminalistics and Criminal Science.

Related DOT Jobs—168.167-022 Immigration Inspector; 168.267-018 Customs Import Specialist; 168.267-022 Customs Inspector; 168.387-010 Opener-Verifier-Packer, Customs; 188.167-090 Special Agent, Customs; 195.267-022 Child Support Officer; 375.167-042 Special Agent; 375.267-010 Detective; 375.267-014 Detective, Narcotics and Vice; 375.267-018 Investigator, Narcotics; 375.267-022 Investigator, Vice; 375.267-034 Investigator, Internal Affairs; 375.267-038 Police Officer III; 375.384-010 Police Officer, Identification and Records; 375.387-010 Fingerprint Classifier; 377.264-010 Identification Officer.

33-3021.01 Police Detectives

- **Education/Training Required: Work experience in a related occupation**
- **Employed: No data available.**
- **Annual Earnings: $50,960**
- **Growth: 16.4%**
- **Annual Job Openings: 4,000**

Conduct investigations to prevent crimes or solve criminal cases.

Examine crime scenes to obtain clues and evidence, such as loose hairs, fibers, clothing, or weapons. Secure deceased body and obtain evidence from it, preventing bystanders from tampering with it prior to medical examiner's arrival. Obtain evidence from suspects. Provide testimony as a witness in court. Analyze completed police reports to determine what additional information and investigative work is needed. Prepare charges, responses to charges, or information for court cases according to formalized procedures. Note, mark, and photograph location of objects found, such as footprints, tire tracks, bullets, and bloodstains, and take measurements of the scene. Obtain facts or statements from complainants, witnesses, and accused persons and record interviews, using recording device. Obtain summary of incident from officer in charge at crime scene, taking care to avoid disturbing evidence. Examine records and governmental agency files to find identifying data about suspects. Prepare and serve search and arrest warrants. Block or rope off scene and check perimeter to ensure that entire scene is secured. Summon medical help for injured individuals and alert medical personnel to take statements from them. Provide information to lab personnel concerning the source of an item of evidence and tests to be performed. Monitor conditions of victims who are unconscious so that arrangements can be made to take statements if consciousness is regained. Secure persons at scene, keeping witnesses from conversing or leaving the scene before investigators arrive. Preserve, process, and analyze items of evidence obtained from crime scenes and suspects, placing them in proper containers and destroying evidence no longer needed. Record progress of investigation, maintain informational files on suspects, and submit reports to commanding officer or magistrate to authorize warrants. Take photographs from all angles of relevant parts of a crime scene, including entrance and exit routes and streets and intersections. Organize scene search, assigning specific tasks and areas of search to individual officers and obtaining adequate lighting as necessary. Question individuals or observe persons and establishments to confirm information given to patrol officers. Notify or request notification of medical examiner or district attorney representative. Note relevant details upon arrival at scene, such as time of day and weather conditions. Participate or assist in raids and arrests. Videotape scenes where possible, including collection of evidence, examination of victim at scene, and defendants and witnesses. Coordinate with outside agencies and serve on interagency task forces to combat specific types of crime.

GOE INFORMATION—Interest Area: 04. Law, Law Enforcement, and Public Safety. **Work Group:** 04.03. Law Enforcement. **Personality Type—**Enterprising. Enterprising occupations frequently involve starting up and carrying out projects. These occupations can involve leading people and making many decisions. They sometimes require risk taking and often deal with business. **Work Values—**Variety; Responsibility; Ability Utilization; Social Service; Social Status. **Skills—**Persuasion; Negotiation; Social Perceptiveness; Speaking; Coordination; Active Listening; Complex Problem Solving; Critical Thinking. **Abilities—***Cognitive:* Flexibility of Closure; Speed of Closure; Fluency of Ideas; Inductive Reasoning; Category Flexibility. *Psychomotor:* Response Orientation; Reaction Time; Rate Control; Multilimb Coordination; Arm-Hand Steadiness. *Physical:* Explosive Strength; Static Strength; Gross Body Coordination; Stamina; Dynamic Strength. *Sensory:* Speech Recognition; Night Vision; Auditory Attention; Speech Clarity; Near Vision. **General Work Activities—***Information Input:* Getting Information; Identifying Objects, Actions, and Events; Monitoring Processes, Materials, or Surroundings. *Mental Process:* Making Decisions and Solving Problems; Updating and Using Relevant Knowledge; Organizing, Planning, and Prioritizing. *Work Output:* Performing General Physical Activities; Documenting or Recording Information; Interacting with Computers. *Interacting with Others:* Communicating with Persons Outside Organization; Performing for or Working with the Public; Establishing and Maintaining Relation-

ships. **Physical Work Conditions—**Specialized Protective or Safety Attire; Outdoors; Extremely Bright or Inadequate Lighting; Common Protective or Safety Attire; Very Hot or Cold. **Other Job Characteristics—**Importance of Being Exact or Accurate; Consequence of Error; Importance of Repeating Same Tasks.

Experience—Job Zone 4. A minimum of two to four years of work-related skill, knowledge, or experience is needed. **Job Preparation:** SVP 7.0 to less than 8.0—two years to less than 10 years. **Knowledge—**Public Safety and Security; Psychology; Law and Government; Customer and Personal Service; Education and Training. **Instructional Programs—**Criminal Justice/Police Science; Criminalistics and Criminal Science.

Related DOT Jobs—375.267-010 Detective; 375.267-014 Detective, Narcotics and Vice; 375.267-018 Investigator, Narcotics; 375.267-022 Investigator, Vice; 375.267-034 Investigator, Internal Affairs.

33-3021.02 Police Identification and Records Officers

- **Education/Training Required: Work experience in a related occupation**
- **Employed: No data available.**
- **Annual Earnings: $50,960**
- **Growth: 16.4%**
- **Annual Job Openings: 4,000**

Collect evidence at crime scene, classify and identify fingerprints, and photograph evidence for use in criminal and civil cases.

Analyze and process evidence at crime scenes and in the laboratory, wearing protective equipment and using powders and chemicals. Dust selected areas of crime scene and lift latent fingerprints, adhering to proper preservation procedures. Identify, classify, and file fingerprints, using systems such as the Henry Classification system. Look for trace evidence, such as fingerprints, hairs, fibers, or shoe impressions, using alternative light sources when necessary. Package, store, and retrieve evidence. Photograph crime or accident scenes for evidence records. Process film and prints from crime or accident scenes. Submit evidence to supervisors. Testify in court and present evidence. Perform emergency work during off-hours. Serve as technical advisor and coordinate with other law enforcement workers to exchange information on crime scene collection activities.

GOE INFORMATION—Interest Area: 04. Law, Law Enforcement, and Public Safety. **Work Group:** 04.03. Law Enforcement. **Personality Type—**Conventional. Conventional occupations frequently involve following set procedures and routines. These occupations can include working with data and details more than with ideas. Usually there is a clear line of authority to follow. **Work Values—**Supervision, Human Relations; Advancement; Pleasant Co-workers; Supervision, Technical; Company Policies and Practices. **Skills—**Operation and Control; Equipment Selection; Operation Monitoring. **Abilities—***Cognitive:* Category Flexibility; Information Ordering; Spatial Orientation. *Psychomotor:* Control Precision; Arm-Hand Steadiness; Multilimb Coordination. *Physical:* Extent Flexibility; Trunk Strength. *Sensory:* Night Vision; Near Vision. **General Work Activities—***Information Input:* Getting Information; Identifying Objects, Actions, and Events; Monitoring Processes, Materials, or Surroundings. *Mental Process:* Processing Information; Updating and Using Relevant Knowledge; Analyzing Data or Information. *Work Output:* Documenting or Recording Information; Performing General Physical Activities; Handling and Moving Objects. *Interacting with Others:* Communicating with Other Workers; Communicating with Persons Outside Organization; Interpreting Meaning of Information for Others. **Physical Work Conditions—**Outdoors; Kneeling, Crouching, or Crawling; Climbing Ladders, Scaffolds, Poles, etc.; High Places; Bending or Twisting the Body. **Other Job Characteristics**—Importance of Being Exact or Accurate; Consequence of Error; Importance of Repeating Same Tasks.

Experience—Job Zone 3. Previous work-related skill, knowledge, or experience is required. **Job Preparation:** SVP 6.0 to less than 7.0—more than one year and less than four years. **Knowledge**—Public Safety and Security; Clerical; Chemistry; Law and Government; Telecommunications. **Instructional Programs**—Criminal Justice/Police Science; Criminalistics and Criminal Science.

Related DOT Jobs—375.384-010 Police Officer, Identification and Records; 375.387-010 Fingerprint Classifier.

33-3021.03 Criminal Investigators and Special Agents

- **Education/Training Required: Work experience in a related occupation**
- **Employed: No data available.**
- **Annual Earnings: $50,960**
- **Growth: 16.4%**
- **Annual Job Openings: 4,000**

Investigate alleged or suspected criminal violations of federal, state, or local laws to determine if evidence is sufficient to recommend prosecution.

Determine scope, timing, and direction of investigations. Develop relationships with informants in order to obtain information related to cases. Examine records in order to locate links in chains of evidence or information. Identify case issues and evidence needed, based on analysis of charges, complaints, or allegations of law violations. Obtain and use search and arrest warrants. Obtain and verify evidence by interviewing and observing suspects and witnesses or by analyzing records. Perform undercover assignments and maintain surveillance, including monitoring authorized wiretaps. Prepare reports that detail investigation findings. Analyze evidence in laboratories or in the field. Collaborate with other authorities on activities such as surveillance, transcription, and research. Collaborate with other offices and agencies in order to exchange information and coordinate activities. Collect and record physical information about arrested suspects, including fingerprints, height and weight measurements, and photographs. Compare crime scene fingerprints with those from suspects or fingerprint files to identify perpetrators, using computers. Investigate organized crime, public corruption, financial crime, copyright infringement, civil rights violations, bank robbery, extortion, kidnapping, and other violations of federal or state statutes. Manage security programs designed to protect personnel, facilities, and information. Record evidence and documents, using equipment such as cameras and photocopy machines. Search for and collect evidence such as fingerprints, using investigative equipment. Serve subpoenas or other official papers. Testify before grand juries concerning criminal activity investigations. Administer counter-terrorism and counter-narcotics reward programs. Issue security clearances. Provide protection for individuals such as government leaders, political candidates, and visiting foreign dignitaries. Train foreign civilian police.

GOE INFORMATION—**Interest Area:** 04. Law, Law Enforcement, and Public Safety. **Work Group:** 04.03. Law Enforcement. **Personality Type**—Enterprising. Enterprising occupations frequently involve starting up and carrying out projects. These occupations can involve leading people and making many decisions. They sometimes require risk taking and often deal with business. **Work Values**—Achievement; Social Status; Ability Utilization; Security; Authority. **Skills**—Speaking; Complex Problem Solving; Social Perceptiveness; Active Listening; Critical Thinking; Writing; Judgment and Decision Making; Coordination. **Abilities**—*Cognitive:* Inductive Reasoning; Flexibility of Closure; Oral Expression; Written Expression; Fluency of Ideas. *Psychomotor:* Response Orientation; Rate Control; Multilimb Coordination; Speed of Limb Movement. *Physical:* Explosive Strength; Dynamic Flexibility; Gross Body Coordination; Stamina. *Sensory:* Night Vision; Speech Recognition; Far Vision; Sound Localization; Glare Sensitivity. **General Work Activities**—*Information Input:* Getting Information; Identifying Objects, Actions, and Events; Monitoring Processes, Materials, or Surroundings. *Mental Process:* Analyzing Data or Information; Judging Qualities of Things, Services, or Other People's Work; Organizing, Planning, and Prioritizing. *Work Output:* Documenting or Recording Information; Performing General Physical Activities; Handling and Moving Objects. *Interacting with Others:* Communicating with Other Workers; Establishing and Maintaining Relationships; Interpreting Meaning of Information for Others. **Physical Work Conditions**—Outdoors; Walking or Running; Kneeling, Crouching, or Crawling; Specialized Protective or Safety Attire; Hazardous Conditions. **Other Job Characteristics**—Importance of Being Exact or Accurate; Consequence of Error; Importance of Repeating Same Tasks.

Experience—Job Zone 4. A minimum of two to four years of work-related skill, knowledge, or experience is needed. **Job Preparation:** SVP 7.0 to less than 8.0—two years to less than 10 years. **Knowledge**—Public Safety and Security; Law and Government; Psychology; Sociology and Anthropology; Telecommunications. **Instructional Programs**—Criminal Justice/Police Science; Criminalistics and Criminal Science.

Related DOT Jobs—375.167-042 Special Agent; 377.264-010 Identification Officer.

33-3021.04 Child Support, Missing Persons, and Unemployment Insurance Fraud Investigators

- **Education/Training Required: Work experience in a related occupation**
- **Employed: No data available.**
- **Annual Earnings: $50,960**
- **Growth: 16.4%**
- **Annual Job Openings: 4,000**

Conduct investigations to locate, arrest, and return fugitives and persons wanted for non-payment of support payments and unemployment insurance fraud and to locate missing persons.

Serves warrants and makes arrests to return persons sought in connection with crimes or for non-payment of child support. Contacts employers, neighbors, relatives, and law enforcement agencies to locate person sought and verify information gathered about case. Interviews client to obtain information, such as relocation of absent parent, amount of child support awarded, and names of witnesses. Interviews and discusses case with parent charged with non-payment of support to resolve issues in lieu of filing court proceedings. Reviews files and criminal records to develop possible leads, such as previous addresses and aliases. Obtains extradition papers to bring about return of fugitive. Prepares file indicating data, such as wage records of accused, witnesses, and blood test results. Confers with prosecuting attorney to prepare court case and with court clerk to obtain arrest warrant and schedule court date. Determines types of court jurisdiction, according to facts and circumstances surrounding case, and files court action. Monitors child support payments awarded by court to ensure compliance and enforcement of child support laws. Completes reports to document information acquired during criminal and child support cases and actions taken. Examines case file to determine that divorce decree and court-ordered judgment for payment are in order. Examines medical and dental X rays, fingerprints, and other information to identify bodies held in morgue. Testifies in court to present evidence regarding cases. Computes amount of child support payments.

GOE INFORMATION—Interest Area: 04. Law, Law Enforcement, and Public Safety. **Work Group:** 04.03. Law Enforcement. **Personality Type—** Enterprising. Enterprising occupations frequently involve starting up and carrying out projects. These occupations can involve leading people and making many decisions. They sometimes require risk taking and often deal with business. **Work Values—**Achievement; Social Service; Ability Utilization; Social Status; Variety. **Skills—**Speaking; Active Listening; Complex Problem Solving; Critical Thinking; Negotiation; Reading Comprehension; Writing; Judgment and Decision Making. **Abilities—***Cognitive:* Oral Expression; Problem Sensitivity; Oral Comprehension; Written Comprehension; Written Expression. *Psychomotor:* None met the criteria. *Physical:* None met the criteria. *Sensory:* Speech Clarity; Speech Recognition; Near Vision; Auditory Attention; Peripheral Vision. **General Work Activities—***Information Input:* Getting Information; Identifying Objects, Actions, and Events; Monitoring Processes, Materials, or Surroundings. *Mental Process:* Processing Information; Organizing, Planning, and Prioritizing; Evaluating Information Against Standards. *Work Output:* Documenting or Recording Information; Performing General Physical Activities; Handling and Moving Objects. *Interacting with Others:* Communicating with Persons Outside Organization; Establishing and Maintaining Relationships; Communicating with Other Workers. **Physical Work Conditions—**Sitting; Walking or Running; Outdoors; Indoors; Radiation. **Other Job Characteristics—**Consequence of Error; Importance of Being Exact or Accurate; Degree of Automation.

Experience—Job Zone 4. A minimum of two to four years of work-related skill, knowledge, or experience is needed. **Job Preparation:** SVP 7.0 to less than 8.0—two years to less than 10 years. **Knowledge—**Law and Government; Public Safety and Security; Geography; Economics and Accounting; Therapy and Counseling. **Instructional Programs—**Criminal Justice/Police Science; Criminalistics and Criminal Science.

Related DOT Jobs—195.267-022 Child Support Officer; 375.267-038 Police Officer III.

33-3021.05 Immigration and Customs Inspectors

- Education/Training Required: Work experience in a related occupation
- Employed: 93,206
- Annual Earnings: $50,960
- Growth: 16.4%
- Annual Job Openings: 4,000

Investigate and inspect persons, common carriers, goods, and merchandise arriving in or departing from the United States or between states to detect violations of immigration and customs laws and regulations.

Detain persons found to be in violation of customs or immigration laws and arrange for legal action such as deportation. Determine duty and taxes to be paid on goods. Examine immigration applications, visas, and passports and interview persons in order to determine eligibility for admission, residence, and travel in U.S. Inspect cargo, baggage, and personal articles entering or leaving U.S. for compliance with revenue laws and U.S. Customs Service regulations. Interpret and explain laws and regulations to travelers, prospective immigrants, shippers, and

manufacturers. Investigate applications for duty refunds and petition for remission or mitigation of penalties when warranted. Locate and seize contraband, undeclared merchandise, and vehicles, aircraft, or boats that contain such merchandise. Record and report job-related activities, findings, transactions, violations, discrepancies, and decisions. Collect samples of merchandise for examination, appraisal, or testing. Institute civil and criminal prosecutions and cooperate with other law enforcement agencies in the investigation and prosecution of those in violation of immigration or customs laws. Testify regarding decisions at immigration appeals or in federal court.

GOE INFORMATION—Interest Area: 04. Law, Law Enforcement, and Public Safety. **Work Group:** 04.03. Law Enforcement. **Personality Type—** Conventional. Conventional occupations frequently involve following set procedures and routines. These occupations can include working with data and details more than with ideas. Usually there is a clear line of authority to follow. **Work Values—**Supervision, Technical; Supervision, Human Relations; Advancement; Security; Authority. **Skills—**Speaking. **Abilities—***Cognitive:* Memorization; Problem Sensitivity; Written Comprehension; Written Expression; Oral Expression. *Psychomotor:* None met the criteria. *Physical:* Stamina; Gross Body Coordination; Explosive Strength; Extent Flexibility; Dynamic Strength. *Sensory:* Far Vision; Near Vision; Speech Clarity; Speech Recognition; Peripheral Vision. **General Work Activities—***Information Input:* Getting Information; Identifying Objects, Actions, and Events; Monitoring Processes, Materials, or Surroundings. *Mental Process:* Judging Qualities of Things, Services, or Other People's Work; Evaluating Information Against Standards; Making Decisions and Solving Problems. *Work Output:* Documenting or Recording Information; Handling and Moving Objects; Performing General Physical Activities. *Interacting with Others:* Communicating with Other Workers; Interpreting Meaning of Information for Others; Communicating with Persons Outside Organization. **Physical Work Conditions—**Walking or Running; Climbing Ladders, Scaffolds, Poles, etc.; Standing; Kneeling, Crouching, or Crawling; Keeping or Regaining Balance. **Other Job Characteristics—**Importance of Repeating Same Tasks; Importance of Being Exact or Accurate; Consequence of Error.

Experience—Job Zone 3. Previous work-related skill, knowledge, or experience is required. **Job Preparation:** SVP 6.0 to less than 7.0—more than one year and less than four years. **Knowledge—**Law and Government; Geography; Public Safety and Security; Foreign Language; Communications and Media. **Instructional Programs—**Criminal Justice/Police Science; Criminalistics and Criminal Science.

Related DOT Jobs—168.167-022 Immigration Inspector; 168.267-018 Customs Import Specialist; 168.267-022 Customs Inspector; 168.387-010 Opener-Verifier-Packer, Customs; 188.167-090 Special Agent, Customs.

33-3031.00 Fish and Game Wardens

- Education/Training Required: Long-term on-the-job training
- Employed: 8,136
- Annual Earnings: $41,230
- Growth: 11.4%
- Annual Job Openings: Fewer than 500

Patrol assigned area to prevent fish and game law violations. Investigate reports of damage to crops or property by wildlife. Compile biological data.

Patrols assigned area by car, boat, airplane, or horse or on foot to observe persons engaged in taking fish and game. Ensures method and equipment used are lawful and apprehends violators. Investigates hunting accidents and reports of fish and game law violations, issues warnings or citations, and files reports. Collects and reports information on population and condition of fish and wildlife in their habitat, availability of game food and cover, and suspected pollution. Searches area of reported property damage for animal tracks, leavings, and other evidence to identify species of animal responsible. Serves warrants, makes arrests, and prepares and presents evidence in court actions. Seizes equipment used in fish and game law violations and arranges for disposition of fish and game illegally taken or possessed. Resurveys area and totals bag counts of hunters to determine effectiveness of control measures. Recommends revisions or changes in hunting and trapping regulations or seasons and animal relocation and release to obtain balance of wildlife and habitat. Assists in promoting hunter safety training. Traps beavers, dynamites beaver dams, and tranquilizes animals to implement approved control measures. Photographs extent of damage, documents other evidence, estimates financial loss, and recommends compensation. Addresses schools and civic groups to disseminate wildlife information and promote public relations.

GOE INFORMATION—**Interest Area:** 04. Law, Law Enforcement, and Public Safety. **Work Group:** 04.03. Law Enforcement. **Personality Type**—Realistic. Realistic occupations frequently involve work activities that include practical, hands-on problems and solutions. They often deal with plants, animals, and real-world materials like wood, tools, and machinery. Many of the occupations require working outside and do not involve a lot of paperwork or working closely with others. **Work Values**—Responsibility; Authority; Variety; Security; Social Status. **Skills**—Speaking; Complex Problem Solving; Systems Analysis; Systems Evaluation; Persuasion; Negotiation; Critical Thinking; Active Listening. **Abilities**—*Cognitive:* Spatial Orientation; Fluency of Ideas; Flexibility of Closure; Originality; Inductive Reasoning. *Psychomotor:* Rate Control; Speed of Limb Movement; Reaction Time; Response Orientation; Multilimb Coordination. *Physical:* Stamina; Dynamic Strength; Static Strength; Explosive Strength; Gross Body Equilibrium. *Sensory:* Night Vision; Peripheral Vision; Speech Clarity; Sound Localization; Far Vision. **General Work Activities**—*Information Input:* Getting Information; Monitoring Processes, Materials, or Surroundings; Identifying Objects, Actions, and Events. *Mental Process:* Organizing, Planning, and Prioritizing; Analyzing Data or Information; Making Decisions and Solving Problems. *Work Output:* Performing General Physical Activities; Documenting or Recording Information; Operating Vehicles or Equipment. *Interacting with Others:* Performing for or Working with the Public; Communicating with Persons Outside Organization; Resolving Conflict and Negotiating with Others. **Physical Work Conditions**—Outdoors; Minor Burns, Cuts, Bites, or Stings; Hazardous Conditions; Extremely Bright or Inadequate Lighting; Very Hot or Cold. **Other Job Characteristics**—Consequence of Error; Importance of Repeating Same Tasks; Pace Determined by Speed of Equipment.

Experience—Job Zone 3. Previous work-related skill, knowledge, or experience is required. **Job Preparation:** SVP 6.0 to less than 7.0—more than one year and less than four years. **Knowledge**—Biology; Law and Government; Geography; Public Safety and Security; Food Production. **Instructional Programs**—Fishing and Fisheries Sciences and Management; Natural Resource Economics; Wildlife and Wildlands Science and Management.

Related DOT Jobs—379.167-010 Fish and Game Warden; 379.267-010 Wildlife Control Agent.

33-3041.00 Parking Enforcement Workers

- **Education/Training Required: Short-term on-the-job training**
- **Employed: 8,574**
- **Annual Earnings: $26,820**
- **Growth: 13.2%**
- **Annual Job Openings: Fewer than 500**

Patrol assigned area, such as public parking lot or section of city, to issue tickets to overtime parking violators and illegally parked vehicles.

Enter and retrieve information pertaining to vehicle registration, identification, and status, using handheld computers. Identify vehicles in violation of parking codes, checking with dispatchers when necessary to confirm identities or to determine whether vehicles need to be booted or towed. Make arrangements for illegally parked or abandoned vehicles to be towed and direct tow-truck drivers to the correct vehicles. Mark tires of parked vehicles with chalk, record time of marking, and return at regular intervals to ensure that parking time limits are not exceeded. Patrol an assigned area by vehicle or on foot to ensure public compliance with existing parking ordinance. Perform traffic control duties such as setting up barricades and temporary signs, placing bags on parking meters to limit their use, or directing traffic. Prepare and maintain required records, including logs of parking enforcement activities and records of contested citations. Write warnings and citations for illegally parked vehicles. Appear in court at hearings regarding contested traffic citations. Assign and review the work of subordinates. Collect coins deposited in meters. Deliver money to be used as change at attended parking facilities. Investigate and answer complaints regarding contested parking citations, determining their validity and routing them appropriately. Locate lost, stolen, and counterfeit parking permits and take necessary enforcement action. Maintain assigned equipment and supplies such as handheld citation computers, citation books, rain gear, tire-marking chalk, and street cones. Maintain close communications with dispatching personnel, using two-way radios or cell phones. Observe and report hazardous conditions such as missing traffic signals or signs and street markings that need to be repainted. Perform simple vehicle maintenance procedures such as checking oil and gas and report mechanical problems to supervisors. Provide assistance to motorists needing help with problems such as flat tires, keys locked in cars, or dead batteries. Provide information to the public regarding parking regulations and facilities and the location of streets, buildings and points of interest. Remove handbills within patrol areas. Respond to and make radio dispatch calls regarding parking violations and complaints. Train new or temporary staff. Wind parking meter clocks.

GOE INFORMATION—**Interest Area:** 04. Law, Law Enforcement, and Public Safety. **Work Group:** 04.03. Law Enforcement. **Personality Type**—Conventional. Conventional occupations frequently involve following set procedures and routines. These occupations can include working with data and details more than with ideas. Usually there is a clear line of authority to follow. **Work Values**—Independence; Security; Supervision, Technical; Supervision, Human Relations; Company Policies and Practices. **Skills**—None met the criteria. **Abilities**—*Cognitive:* Spatial Orientation. *Psychomotor:* Finger Dexterity. *Physical:* Gross Body Coordination; Stamina. *Sensory:* Glare Sensitivity. **General Work Activities**—*Information Input:* Getting Information; Monitoring Processes, Materials, or Surroundings; Identifying Objects, Actions, and Events. *Mental Process:* Processing Information; Making Decisions and Solving Problems; Evaluating Information Against Standards. *Work Output:* Performing General Physical Activities; Documenting or Recording Information; Handling and Moving Objects. *Interacting with Others:* Communicating with Other Workers; Communicating with Persons Outside Organization; Performing for or Working with the Public. **Physical Work Conditions**—Outdoors; Very Hot or Cold; Walking or Running; Extremely Bright or Inadequate Lighting; Standing. **Other Job Characteristics**—Importance of Repeating Same Tasks; Pace Determined by Speed of Equipment; Degree of Automation.

Experience—Job Zone 1. No previous work-related skill, knowledge, or experience is needed. **Job Preparation:** SVP below 4.0—less than six months. **Knowledge**—Law and Government; Geography; Clerical; Foreign Language; Public Safety and Security. **Instructional Programs—**Security and Protective Services, Other.

Related DOT Jobs—375.587-010 Parking Enforcement Officer.

33-3051.00 Police and Sheriff's Patrol Officers

- **Education/Training Required: Long-term on-the-job training**
- **Employed: 606,800**
- **Annual Earnings: $40,970**
- **Growth: 23.2%**
- **Annual Job Openings: 21,000**

Maintain order, enforce laws and ordinances, and protect life and property in an assigned patrol district. Perform combination of following duties: Patrol a specific area on foot or in a vehicle; direct traffic; issue traffic summonses; investigate accidents; apprehend and arrest suspects, or serve legal processes of courts.

No task data available.

GOE INFORMATION—Interest Area: 04. Law, Law Enforcement, and Public Safety. **Work Group:** 04.03. Law Enforcement. **Note:** The Department of Labor has not collected some data for this job, so it has fewer details than the other descriptions.

Instructional Programs—Criminal Justice/Police Science; Criminalistics and Criminal Science.

Related DOT Jobs—168.167-010 Customs Patrol Officer; 169.167-042 Park Ranger; 372.363-010 Protective Officer; 375.163-014 Pilot, Highway Patrol; 375.263-010 Accident-Prevention-Squad Police Officer; 375.263-014 Police Officer I; 375.263-018 State-Highway Police Officer; 375.264-010 Police Officer, Crime Prevention; 375.267-030 Police Inspector II; 375.267-042 Police Officer, Safety Instruction; 375.363-010 Border Guard; 375.367-014 Complaint Evaluation Officer; 375.367-018 Police Officer, Booking; 377.263-010 Sheriff, Deputy; 377.363-010 Deputy Sheriff, Grand Jury; 377.667-014 Deputy Sheriff, Building Guard; 377.667-018 Deputy Sheriff, Civil Division; 379.263-014 Public-Safety Officer.

33-3051.01 Police Patrol Officers

- **Education/Training Required: Long-term on-the-job training**
- **Employed: No data available.**
- **Annual Earnings: $40,970**
- **Growth: 23.2%**
- **Annual Job Openings: 21,000**

Patrol assigned area to enforce laws and ordinances, regulate traffic, control crowds, prevent crime, and arrest violators.

Provide for public safety by maintaining order, responding to emergencies, protecting people and property, enforcing motor vehicle and criminal laws, and promoting good community relations. Identify, pursue, and arrest suspects and perpetrators of criminal acts. Record facts to prepare reports that document incidents and activities. Review facts of incidents to determine if criminal act or statute violations were involved. Render aid to accident victims and other persons requiring first aid for physical injuries. Testify in court to present evidence or act as witness in traffic and criminal cases. Evaluate complaint and emergency-request information to determine response requirements. Patrol specific area on foot, horseback, or motorized conveyance, responding promptly to calls for assistance. Monitor, note, report, and investigate suspicious persons and situations, safety hazards, and unusual or illegal activity in patrol area. Investigate traffic accidents and other accidents to determine causes

and to determine if a crime has been committed. Photograph or draw diagrams of crime or accident scenes and interview principals and eyewitnesses. Monitor traffic to ensure motorists observe traffic regulations and exhibit safe driving procedures. Relay complaint and emergency-request information to appropriate agency dispatchers. Issue citations or warnings to violators of motor vehicle ordinances. Direct traffic flow and reroute traffic in case of emergencies. Inform citizens of community services and recommend options to facilitate longer-term problem resolution. Provide road information to assist motorists. Process prisoners and prepare and maintain records of prisoner bookings and prisoner status during booking and pre-trial process. Inspect public establishments to ensure compliance with rules and regulations. Act as official escorts, such as when leading funeral processions or firefighters.

GOE INFORMATION—Interest Area: 04. Law, Law Enforcement, and Public Safety. **Work Group:** 04.03. Law Enforcement. **Personality Type—**Social. Social occupations frequently involve working with, communicating with, and teaching people. These occupations often involve helping or providing service to others. **Work Values—**Variety; Social Service; Security; Social Status; Authority. **Skills—**Persuasion; Negotiation; Social Perceptiveness; Judgment and Decision Making; Service Orientation; Complex Problem Solving; Active Listening; Critical Thinking. **Abilities—***Cognitive:* Flexibility of Closure; Time Sharing; Spatial Orientation; Speed of Closure; Perceptual Speed. *Psychomotor:* Reaction Time; Rate Control; Response Orientation; Speed of Limb Movement; Multilimb Coordination. *Physical:* Stamina; Explosive Strength; Gross Body Equilibrium; Gross Body Coordination; Static Strength. *Sensory:* Night Vision; Far Vision; Glare Sensitivity; Peripheral Vision; Sound Localization. **General Work Activities—***Information Input:* Identifying Objects, Actions, and Events; Monitoring Processes, Materials, or Surroundings; Getting Information. *Mental Process:* Making Decisions and Solving Problems; Evaluating Information Against Standards; Updating and Using Relevant Knowledge. *Work Output:* Performing General Physical Activities; Documenting or Recording Information; Operating Vehicles or Equipment. *Interacting with Others:* Resolving Conflict and Negotiating with Others; Performing for or Working with the Public; Communicating with Persons Outside Organization. **Physical Work Conditions—**Outdoors; Very Hot or Cold; Walking or Running; Common Protective or Safety Attire; Disease or Infections. **Other Job Characteristics—**Consequence of Error; Importance of Being Exact or Accurate; Degree of Automation.

Experience—Job Zone 3. Previous work-related skill, knowledge, or experience is required. **Job Preparation:** SVP 6.0 to less than 7.0—more than one year and less than four years. **Knowledge—**Public Safety and Security; Customer and Personal Service; Law and Government; Psychology; Education and Training. **Instructional Programs—**Criminal Justice/Police Science; Criminalistics and Criminal Science.

Related DOT Jobs—168.167-010 Customs Patrol Officer; 169.167-042 Park Ranger; 372.363-010 Protective Officer; 375.263-010 Accident-Prevention-Squad Police Officer; 375.263-014 Police Officer I; 375.263-018 State-Highway Police Officer; 375.264-010 Police Officer, Crime Prevention; 375.267-030 Police Inspector II; 375.267-042 Police Officer, Safety Instruction; 375.363-010 Border Guard; 375.367-014 Complaint Evaluation Officer; 375.367-018 Police Officer, Booking; 379.263-014 Public-Safety Officer.

33-3051.02 Highway Patrol Pilots

- **Education/Training Required: Long-term on-the-job training**
- **Employed: No data available.**
- **Annual Earnings: $40,970**
- **Growth: 23.2%**
- **Annual Job Openings: 21,000**

Pilot aircraft to patrol highway and enforce traffic laws.

Pilots airplane to maintain order, respond to emergencies, enforce traffic and criminal laws, and apprehend criminals. Informs ground personnel of traffic congestion or unsafe driving conditions to ensure traffic flow and reduce incidence of accidents. Informs ground personnel where to reroute traffic in case of emergencies. Arrests perpetrator of criminal act or submits citation or warning to violator of motor vehicle ordinance. Investigates traffic accidents and other accidents to determine causes and to determine if crime was committed. Reviews facts to determine if criminal act or statute violation was involved. Records facts, photographs and diagrams crime or accident scene, and interviews witnesses to gather information for possible use in legal action or safety programs. Testifies in court to present evidence or act as witness in traffic and criminal cases. Renders aid to accident victims and other persons requiring first aid for physical injuries. Evaluates complaint and emergency request information to determine response requirements. Relays complaint and emergency request information to appropriate agency dispatcher. Prepares reports to document activities. Expedites processing of prisoners, prepares and maintains records of prisoner bookings, and maintains record of prisoner status during booking and pre-trial process.

GOE INFORMATION—Interest Area: 04. Law, Law Enforcement, and Public Safety. **Work Group:** 04.03. Law Enforcement. **Personality Type—**Realistic. Realistic occupations frequently involve work activities that include practical, hands-on problems and solutions. They often deal with plants, animals, and real-world materials like wood, tools, and machinery. Many of the occupations require working outside and do not involve a lot of paperwork or working closely with others. **Work Values—**Social Service; Achievement; Security; Authority; Variety. **Skills—**Operation and Control; Social Perceptiveness; Operation Monitoring; Service Orientation; Active Listening; Judgment and Decision Making; Critical Thinking; Speaking. **Abilities—***Cognitive:* Flexibility of Closure; Speed of Closure; Spatial Orientation; Memorization; Time Sharing. *Psychomotor:* Rate Control; Response Orientation; Reaction Time; Multilimb Coordination; Control Precision. *Physical:* Explosive Strength; Static Strength; Dynamic Strength; Extent Flexibility; Dynamic Flexibility. *Sensory:* Far Vision; Glare Sensitivity; Night Vision; Depth Perception; Peripheral Vision. **General Work Activities—***Information Input:* Monitoring Processes, Materials, or Surroundings; Getting Information; Identifying Objects, Actions, and Events. *Mental Process:* Analyzing Data or Information; Judging Qualities of Things, Services, or Other People's Work; Updating and Using Relevant Knowledge. *Work Output:* Operating Vehicles or Equipment; Performing General Physical Activities; Documenting or Recording Information. *Interacting with Others:* Performing for or Working with the Public; Assisting and Caring for Others; Communicating with Persons Outside Organization. **Physical Work Conditions—**Outdoors; High Places; Distracting Sounds and Noise Levels; Common Protective or Safety Attire; Very Hot or Cold. **Other Job Characteristics—**Consequence of Error; Degree of Automation; Importance of Being Exact or Accurate.

Experience—Job Zone 3. Previous work-related skill, knowledge, or experience is required. **Job Preparation:** SVP 6.0 to less than 7.0—more than one year and less than four years. **Knowledge—**Public Safety and Security; Customer and Personal Service; Law and Government; Medicine and Dentistry; Psychology. **Instructional Programs—**Criminal Justice/Police Science; Criminalistics and Criminal Science.

Related DOT Jobs—375.163-014 Pilot, Highway Patrol.

33-3051.03 Sheriffs and Deputy Sheriffs

- **Education/Training Required: Long-term on-the-job training**
- **Employed: No data available.**
- **Annual Earnings: $40,970**
- **Growth: 23.2%**
- **Annual Job Openings: 21,000**

Enforce law and order in rural or unincorporated districts or serve legal processes of courts. May patrol courthouse, guard court or grand jury, or escort defendants.

Serves subpoenas and summonses. Executes arrest warrants, locating and taking persons into custody, and issues citations. Transports or escorts prisoners or defendants between courtroom, prison or jail, District Attorney's offices, or medical facilities. Patrols and guards courthouse, grand jury room, or assigned areas to provide security, enforce laws, maintain order, and arrest violators. Investigates illegal or suspicious activities of persons. Takes control of accident scene to maintain traffic flow, assist accident victims, and investigate causes. Confiscates real or personal property by court order and posts notices in public places. Questions individuals entering secured areas to determine purpose of business and directs or reroutes individuals to destinations. Notifies patrol units to take violators into custody or provide needed assistance or medical aid. Arranges delivery of prisoner's arrest records from criminal investigation unit at District Attorney's request. Maintains records and submits reports of dispositions and logs daily activities.

GOE INFORMATION—Interest Area: 04. Law, Law Enforcement, and Public Safety. **Work Group:** 04.03. Law Enforcement. **Personality Type—**Social. Social occupations frequently involve working with, communicating with, and teaching people. These occupations often involve helping or providing service to others. **Work Values—**Authority; Security; Variety; Social Service; Responsibility. **Skills—**Social Perceptiveness; Speaking; Active Listening; Service Orientation. **Abilities—***Cognitive:* Inductive Reasoning; Selective Attention; Spatial Orientation; Oral Comprehension; Oral Expression. *Psychomotor:* Rate Control; Multilimb Coordination; Reaction Time; Response Orientation; Speed of Limb Movement. *Physical:* Stamina; Gross Body Coordination; Explosive Strength; Trunk Strength; Dynamic Strength. *Sensory:* Night Vision; Glare Sensitivity; Far Vision; Depth Perception; Hearing Sensitivity. **General Work Activities—***Information Input:* Getting Information; Identifying Objects, Actions, and Events; Monitoring Processes, Materials, or Surroundings. *Mental Process:* Judging Qualities of Things, Services, or Other People's Work; Making Decisions and Solving Problems; Analyzing Data or Information. *Work Output:* Performing General Physical Activities; Documenting or Recording Information; Handling and Moving Objects. *Interacting with Others:* Performing for or Working with the Public; Assisting and Caring for Others; Communicating with Other Workers. **Physical Work Conditions—**Specialized Protective or Safety Attire; Outdoors; Minor Burns, Cuts, Bites, or Stings; Kneeling, Crouching, or Crawling; Walking or Running. **Other Job Characteristics—**Consequence of Error; Importance of Repeating Same Tasks; Importance of Being Exact or Accurate.

Experience—Job Zone 2. Some previous work-related skill, knowledge, or experience may be helpful, but usually is not needed. **Job Preparation:** SVP 4.0 to less than 6.0—six months to less than two years. **Knowledge—**Public Safety and Security; Law and Government; Psychology; Geography; Sociology and Anthropology. **Instructional Programs—**Criminal Justice/Police Science; Criminalistics and Criminal Science.

Related DOT Jobs—377.263-010 Sheriff, Deputy; 377.363-010 Deputy Sheriff, Grand Jury; 377.667-014 Deputy Sheriff, Building Guard; 377.667-018 Deputy Sheriff, Civil Division.

33-3052.00 Transit and Railroad Police

- **Education/Training Required: Long-term on-the-job training**
- **Employed: 5,756**
- **Annual Earnings: $43,110**
- **Growth: 16.5%**
- **Annual Job Openings: Fewer than 500**

Protect and police railroad and transit property, employees, or passengers.

Apprehend or remove trespassers or thieves from railroad property or coordinate with law enforcement agencies in apprehensions and removals. Direct and coordinate the daily activities and training of security staff. Direct security activities at derailments, fires, floods, and strikes involving railroad property. Examine credentials of unauthorized persons attempting to enter secured areas. Investigate or direct investigations of freight theft, suspicious damage or loss of passengers' valuables, and other crimes on railroad property. Patrol railroad yards, cars, stations, and other facilities in order to protect company property and shipments and to maintain order. Plan and implement special safety and preventive programs, such as fire and accident prevention. Prepare reports documenting investigation activities and results. Record and verify seal numbers from boxcars containing frequently pilfered items, such as cigarettes and liquor, in order to detect tampering. Seal empty boxcars by twisting nails in door hasps, using nail twisters. Interview neighbors, associates, and former employers of job applicants in order to verify personal references and to obtain work history data.

GOE INFORMATION—**Interest Area:** 04. Law, Law Enforcement, and Public Safety. **Work Group:** 04.03. Law Enforcement. **Personality Type**—Enterprising. Enterprising occupations frequently involve starting up and carrying out projects. These occupations can involve leading people and making many decisions. They sometimes require risk taking and often deal with business. **Work Values**—Authority; Responsibility; Creativity; Variety; Social Status. **Skills**—Speaking; Active Listening; Management of Personnel Resources; Complex Problem Solving; Operation and Control; Social Perceptiveness; Critical Thinking. **Abilities**—*Cognitive:* Inductive Reasoning; Time Sharing; Flexibility of Closure; Oral Expression; Speed of Closure. *Psychomotor:* Speed of Limb Movement; Response Orientation; Reaction Time; Rate Control; Multilimb Coordination. *Physical:* Explosive Strength; Stamina; Static Strength; Gross Body Coordination; Gross Body Equilibrium. *Sensory:* Night Vision; Sound Localization; Far Vision; Peripheral Vision; Auditory Attention. **General Work Activities**—*Information Input:* Getting Information; Monitoring Processes, Materials, or Surroundings; Identifying Objects, Actions, and Events. *Mental Process:* Organizing, Planning, and Prioritizing; Judging Qualities of Things, Services, or Other People's Work; Making Decisions and Solving Problems. *Work Output:* Performing General Physical Activities; Documenting or Recording Information; Handling and Moving Objects. *Interacting with Others:* Communicating with Other Workers; Establishing and Maintaining Relationships; Coordinating the Work and Activities of Others. **Physical Work Conditions**—Outdoors; Walking or Running; Keeping or Regaining Balance; Bending or Twisting the Body; Extremely Bright or Inadequate Lighting. **Other Job Characteristics**—Consequence of Error; Importance of Repeating Same Tasks; Pace Determined by Speed of Equipment.

Experience—Job Zone 2. Some previous work-related skill, knowledge, or experience may be helpful, but usually is not needed. **Job Preparation:** SVP 4.0 to less than 6.0—six months to less than two years. **Knowledge**—Public Safety and Security; Law and Government; Administration and Management; Personnel and Human Resources; Sociology and Anthro-

pology. **Instructional Programs**—Security and Loss Prevention Services; Security and Protective Services, Other.

Related DOT Jobs—372.267-010 Special Agent; 376.167-010 Special Agent-in-Charge; 376.667-018 Patroller.

33-9000 Other Protective Service Workers

33-9011.00 Animal Control Workers

- **Education/Training Required: Moderate-term on-the-job training**
- **Employed: 8,608**
- **Annual Earnings: $24,250**
- **Growth: 12.8%**
- **Annual Job Openings: 4,000**

Handle animals for the purpose of investigations of mistreatment or control of abandoned, dangerous, or unattended animals.

Capture and remove stray, uncontrolled, or abused animals from undesirable conditions, using nets, nooses, or tranquilizer darts as necessary. Euthanize rabid, unclaimed, or severely injured animals. Examine animal licenses and inspect establishments housing animals for compliance with laws. Examine animals for injuries or malnutrition and arrange for any necessary medical treatment. Investigate reports of animal attacks or animal cruelty, interviewing witnesses, collecting evidence, and writing reports. Issue warnings or citations in connection with animal-related offenses or contact police to report violations and request arrests. Remove captured animals from animal-control service vehicles and place animals in shelter cages or other enclosures. Supply animals with food, water, and personal care. Write reports of activities and maintain files of impoundments and dispositions of animals. Answer inquiries from the public concerning animal control operations. Clean facilities and equipment such as dog pens and animal control trucks. Contact animal owners to inform them that their pets are at animal holding facilities. Educate the public about animal welfare and animal control laws and regulations. Organize the adoption of unclaimed animals. Prepare for prosecutions related to animal treatment and give evidence in court. Train police officers in dog handling and training techniques for tracking, crowd control, and narcotics and bomb detection.

GOE INFORMATION—**Interest Area:** 04. Law, Law Enforcement, and Public Safety. **Work Group:** 04.03. Law Enforcement. **Personality Type**—Social. Social occupations frequently involve working with, communicating with, and teaching people. These occupations often involve helping or providing service to others. **Work Values**—Authority; Social Service; Supervision, Technical; Variety; Security. **Skills**—Instructing; Critical Thinking; Learning Strategies; Active Listening; Speaking; Social Perceptiveness. **Abilities**—*Cognitive:* Oral Expression; Written Expression; Inductive Reasoning; Deductive Reasoning; Flexibility of Closure. *Psychomotor:* Rate Control; Reaction Time; Speed of Limb Movement; Multilimb Coordination; Response Orientation. *Physical:* Explosive Strength; Stamina; Dynamic Strength; Static Strength; Gross Body Coordination. *Sensory:* Far Vision; Sound Localization; Auditory Attention; Speech Clarity; Glare Sensitivity. **General Work Activities**—*Information Input:* Getting Information; Identifying Objects, Actions, and Events; Monitoring Processes, Materials, or Surroundings. *Mental Process:* Judging Qualities of Things, Services, or Other People's Work; Organizing, Planning, and Prioritizing; Evaluating Information Against Standards. *Work Output:* Performing General Physical Activities; Handling and Moving Objects; Documenting or Recording Information. *Interacting with Others:* Assisting and Caring for Others; Communicating with Persons Outside Organization; Teaching Others. **Physical Work Conditions**—Minor Burns, Cuts, Bites, or Stings; Outdoors; Common Protective or Safety Attire; Kneeling, Crouching, or Crawling; Walking or Running. **Other Job Characteristics**—Importance of Repeating Same Tasks; Consequence of Error; Pace Determined by Speed of Equipment.

Experience—Job Zone 2. Some previous work-related skill, knowledge, or experience may be helpful, but usually is not needed. **Job Preparation:** SVP 4.0 to less than 6.0—six months to less than two years. **Knowledge**—Education and Training; Biology; Sales and Marketing; Public Safety and Security; Communications and Media. **Instructional Programs**—Security and Protective Services, Other.

Related DOT Jobs—379.137-010 Supervisor, Animal Cruelty Investigation; 379.227-010 Instructor-Trainer, Canine Service; 379.263-010 Animal Treatment Investigator; 379.673-010 Dog Catcher.

33-9021.00 Private Detectives and Investigators

- **Education/Training Required: Work experience in a related occupation**
- **Employed: 38,972**
- **Annual Earnings: $28,380**
- **Growth: 23.5%**
- **Annual Job Openings: 9,000**

Detect occurrences of unlawful acts or infractions of rules in private establishment or seek, examine, and compile information for client.

Enforces conformance to establishment rules and protects persons or property. Observes employees or customers and patrols premises to detect violations and obtain evidence, using binoculars, cameras, and television. Questions persons to obtain evidence for cases of divorce, child custody, or missing persons or individual's character or financial status. Examines crime scene for clues or fingerprints and submits evidence to laboratory for analysis. Warns and ejects troublemakers from premises and apprehends and releases suspects to authorities or security personnel. Obtains and analyzes information on suspects, crimes, and disturbances to solve cases, identify criminal activity, and maintain public peace and order. Counts cash and reviews transactions, sales checks, and register tapes to verify amount of cash and shortages. Confers with establishment officials, security department, police, or postal officials to identify problems, provide information, and receive instructions. Alerts staff and superiors of presence of suspect in establishment. Writes reports and case summaries to document investigations or inform supervisors. Testifies at hearings and court trials to present evidence. Locates persons using phone or mail directories to collect money owed or to serve legal papers. Evaluates performance and honesty of employees by posing as customer or employee and comparing employee to standards. Assists victims, police, fire department, and others during emergencies.

GOE INFORMATION—Interest Area: 04. Law, Law Enforcement, and Public Safety. **Work Group:** 04.03. Law Enforcement. **Personality Type**—Enterprising. Enterprising occupations frequently involve starting up and carrying out projects. These occupations can involve leading people and making many decisions. They sometimes require risk taking and often deal with business. **Work Values**—Ability Utilization; Responsibility; Achievement; Authority; Creativity. **Skills**—Systems Evaluation; Critical Thinking; Active Listening; Speaking; Persuasion; Systems Analysis; Writing; Social Perceptiveness. **Abilities**—*Cognitive:* Fluency of Ideas; Inductive Reasoning; Speed of Closure; Flexibility of Closure; Selective

Attention. *Psychomotor:* Speed of Limb Movement; Reaction Time; Response Orientation; Rate Control; Multilimb Coordination. *Physical:* Explosive Strength; Stamina; Static Strength; Gross Body Coordination; Gross Body Equilibrium. *Sensory:* Night Vision; Far Vision; Sound Localization; Peripheral Vision; Auditory Attention. **General Work Activities**—*Information Input:* Getting Information; Identifying Objects, Actions, and Events; Monitoring Processes, Materials, or Surroundings. *Mental Process:* Analyzing Data or Information; Judging Qualities of Things, Services, or Other People's Work; Making Decisions and Solving Problems. *Work Output:* Documenting or Recording Information; Performing General Physical Activities; Handling and Moving Objects. *Interacting with Others:* Communicating with Other Workers; Assisting and Caring for Others; Communicating with Persons Outside Organization. **Physical Work Conditions**—Outdoors; Walking or Running; Climbing Ladders, Scaffolds, Poles, etc.; Standing; Keeping or Regaining Balance. **Other Job Characteristics**—Consequence of Error; Importance of Being Exact or Accurate; Importance of Repeating Same Tasks.

Experience—Job Zone 2. Some previous work-related skill, knowledge, or experience may be helpful, but usually is not needed. **Job Preparation:** SVP 4.0 to less than 6.0—six months to less than two years. **Knowledge**—Public Safety and Security; Psychology; Law and Government; Medicine and Dentistry; Therapy and Counseling. **Instructional Programs**—Criminal Justice/Police Science.

Related DOT Jobs—186.267-010 Bonding Agent; 241.367-026 Skip Tracer; 343.367-014 Gambling Monitor; 376.267-010 Investigator, Cash Shortage; 376.267-014 Investigator, Fraud; 376.267-018 Investigator, Private; 376.267-022 Shopping Investigator; 376.367-010 Alarm Investigator; 376.367-014 Detective I; 376.367-018 House Officer; 376.367-022 Investigator; 376.367-026 Undercover Operator; 376.667-014 Detective II.

33-9031.00 Gaming Surveillance Officers and Gaming Investigators

- **Education/Training Required: Long-term on-the-job training**
- **Employed: 10,989**
- **Annual Earnings: $22,140**
- **Growth: 16.8%**
- **Annual Job Openings: 2,000**

Act as oversight and security agent for management and customers. Observe casino or casino hotel operation for irregular activities such as cheating or theft by either employees or patrons. May utilize one-way mirrors above the casino floor, cashier's cage, and from desk. Use of audio/video equipment is also common to observe operation of the business. Usually required to provide verbal and written reports of all violations and suspicious behavior to supervisor.

Act as oversight and security agents for management and customers. Monitor establishment activities to ensure adherence to all state gaming regulations and company policies and procedures. Observe casino or casino hotel operations for irregular activities such as cheating or theft by employees or patrons, using audio/video equipment and one-way mirrors. Report all violations and suspicious behaviors to supervisors verbally or in writing. Supervise and train surveillance observers.

GOE INFORMATION—Interest Area: 04. Law, Law Enforcement, and Public Safety. **Work Group:** 04.03. Law Enforcement. **Note:** The Department of Labor has not collected some data for this job, so it has fewer details than the other descriptions.

Instructional Programs—No data available.

Related DOT Jobs—343.367-014 Gambling Monitor; 379.367-010 Surveillance-System Monitor.

33-9032.00 Security Guards

- **Education/Training Required: Short-term on-the-job training**
- **Employed: 1,105,530**
- **Annual Earnings: $18,600**
- **Growth: 35.4%**
- **Annual Job Openings: 242,000**

Guard, patrol, or monitor premises to prevent theft, violence, or infractions of rules.

Patrol industrial and commercial premises to prevent and detect signs of intrusion and ensure security of doors, windows, and gates. Answer alarms and investigate disturbances. Call police or fire departments in cases of emergency, such as fire or presence of unauthorized persons. Operate detecting devices to screen individuals and prevent passage of prohibited articles into restricted areas. Answer telephone calls to take messages, answer questions, and provide information during non-business hours or when switchboard is closed. Drive and guard armored vehicle to transport money and valuables to prevent theft and ensure safe delivery. Monitor and adjust controls that regulate building systems, such as air conditioning, furnace, or boiler. Escort or drive motor vehicle to transport individuals to specified locations and to provide personal protection. Write reports of daily activities and irregularities, such as equipment or property damage, theft, presence of unauthorized persons, or unusual occurrences. Inspect and adjust security systems, equipment, and machinery to ensure operational use and to detect evidence of tampering. Circulate among visitors, patrons, and employees to preserve order and protect property. Warn persons of rule infractions or violations and apprehend or evict violators from premises, using force when necessary. Monitor and authorize entrance and departure of employees, visitors, and other persons to guard against theft and maintain security of premises.

GOE INFORMATION—Interest Area: 04. Law, Law Enforcement, and Public Safety. **Work Group:** 04.03. Law Enforcement. **Personality Type—**Social. Social occupations frequently involve working with, communicating with, and teaching people. These occupations often involve helping or providing service to others. **Work Values—**Social Service; Authority; Supervision, Human Relations; Supervision, Technical. **Skills—**Operation and Control; Operation Monitoring. **Abilities—***Cognitive:* Spatial Orientation; Selective Attention; Time Sharing; Flexibility of Closure; Perceptual Speed. *Psychomotor:* Response Orientation; Reaction Time; Rate Control; Speed of Limb Movement; Multilimb Coordination. *Physical:* Explosive Strength; Static Strength; Stamina; Dynamic Strength; Trunk Strength. *Sensory:* Sound Localization; Night Vision; Peripheral Vision; Far Vision; Speech Recognition. **General Work Activities—***Information Input:* Monitoring Processes, Materials, or Surroundings; Getting Information; Identifying Objects, Actions, and Events. *Mental Process:* Judging Qualities of Things, Services, or Other People's Work; Evaluating Information Against Standards; Analyzing Data or Information. *Work Output:* Performing General Physical Activities; Documenting or Recording Information; Handling and Moving Objects. *Interacting with Others:* Communicating with Other Workers; Communicating with Persons Outside Organization; Resolving Conflict and Negotiating with Others. **Physical Work Conditions—**Outdoors; Walking or Running; Very Hot or Cold; Climbing Ladders, Scaffolds, Poles, etc.; Extremely Bright or Inadequate Lighting. **Other Job Characteristics—**Consequence of Error; Importance of Repeating Same Tasks; Degree of Automation.

Experience—Job Zone 1. No previous work-related skill, knowledge, or experience is needed. **Job Preparation:** SVP below 4.0—less than six months. **Knowledge—**Public Safety and Security; Customer and Per-

sonal Service; Law and Government; Telecommunications; Psychology. **Instructional Programs—**Securities Services Administration/Management; Security and Loss Prevention Services.

Related DOT Jobs—372.563-010 Armored-Car Guard and Driver; 372.567-010 Armored-Car Guard; 372.667-010 Airline Security Representative; 372.667-014 Bodyguard; 372.667-030 Gate Guard; 372.667-034 Guard, Security; 372.667-038 Merchant Patroller; 376.667-010 Bouncer; 379.667-010 Golf-Course Ranger.

33-9091.00 Crossing Guards

- **Education/Training Required: Short-term on-the-job training**
- **Employed: 74,079**
- **Annual Earnings: $17,780**
- **Growth: 8.7%**
- **Annual Job Openings: 18,000**

Guide or control vehicular or pedestrian traffic at such places as streets, schools, railroad crossings, or construction sites.

Direct or escort pedestrians across streets, stopping traffic as necessary. Guide or control vehicular or pedestrian traffic at such places as street and railroad crossings and construction sites. Communicate traffic and crossing rules and other information to students and adults. Direct traffic movement or warn of hazards, using signs, flags, lanterns, and hand signals. Inform drivers of detour routes through construction sites. Learn the location and purpose of street traffic signs within assigned patrol areas. Monitor traffic flow to locate safe gaps through which pedestrians can cross streets. Activate railroad warning signal lights, lower crossing gates until trains pass, and raise gates when crossings are clear. Discuss traffic routing plans and control point locations with superiors. Distribute traffic control signs and markers at designated points. Record license numbers of vehicles disregarding traffic signals and report infractions to appropriate authorities. Report unsafe behavior of children to school officials. Stop speeding vehicles to warn drivers of traffic laws.

GOE INFORMATION—Interest Area: 04. Law, Law Enforcement, and Public Safety. **Work Group:** 04.03. Law Enforcement. **Personality Type—**Social. Social occupations frequently involve working with, communicating with, and teaching people. These occupations often involve helping or providing service to others. **Work Values—**Independence; Social Service; Authority; Supervision, Technical; Moral Values. **Skills—**None met the criteria. **Abilities—***Cognitive:* Selective Attention; Spatial Orientation; Time Sharing; Problem Sensitivity; Oral Expression. *Psychomotor:* Reaction Time; Response Orientation; Rate Control; Multilimb Coordination; Speed of Limb Movement. *Physical:* Gross Body Coordination; Stamina; Dynamic Flexibility; Gross Body Equilibrium. *Sensory:* Peripheral Vision; Night Vision; Far Vision; Glare Sensitivity; Sound Localization. **General Work Activities—***Information Input:* Getting Information; Identifying Objects, Actions, and Events; Monitoring Processes, Materials, or Surroundings. *Mental Process:* Making Decisions and Solving Problems; Thinking Creatively; Analyzing Data or Information. *Work Output:* Handling and Moving Objects; Performing General Physical Activities; Controlling Machines and Processes. *Interacting with Others:* Performing for or Working with the Public; Communicating with Other Workers; Communicating with Persons Outside Organization. **Physical Work Conditions—**Outdoors; Distracting Sounds and Noise Levels; Contaminants; Common Protective or Safety Attire; Making Repetitive Motions. **Other Job Characteristics—**Consequence of Error; Importance of Repeating Same Tasks; Importance of Being Exact or Accurate.

Experience—Job Zone 1. No previous work-related skill, knowledge, or experience is needed. **Job Preparation:** SVP below 4.0—less than six months. **Knowledge—**Public Safety and Security; Law and Government;

Customer and Personal Service; Geography; English Language. **Instructional Programs**—Security and Protective Services, Other.

Related DOT Jobs—371.567-010 Guard, School-Crossing; 371.667-010 Crossing Tender; 372.667-022 Flagger.

33-9092.00 Lifeguards, Ski Patrol, and Other Recreational Protective Service Workers

- **Education/Training Required: Short-term on-the-job training**
- **Employed: No data available.**
- **Annual Earnings: No data available.**
- **Growth: 21.7%**
- **Annual Job Openings: 72,000**

Monitor recreational areas, such as pools, beaches, or ski slopes, to provide assistance and protection to participants.

Contact emergency medical personnel in case of serious injury. Examine injured persons and administer first aid or cardiopulmonary resuscitation if necessary, utilizing training and medical supplies and equipment. Observe activities in assigned areas, using binoculars in order to detect hazards, disturbances, or safety infractions. Patrol or monitor recreational areas such as trails, slopes, and swimming areas on foot, in vehicles, or from towers. Provide assistance in the safe use of equipment such as ski lifts. Rescue distressed persons, using rescue techniques and equipment. Warn recreational participants of inclement weather, unsafe areas, or illegal conduct. Complete and maintain records of weather and beach conditions, emergency medical treatments performed, and other relevant incident information. Inspect recreational equipment, such as rope tows, T-bars, J-bars, and chair lifts, for safety hazards and damage or wear. Inspect recreational facilities for cleanliness. Instruct participants in skiing, swimming, or other recreational activities and provide safety precaution information. Provide assistance with staff selection, training, and supervision. Drive a four-wheel-drive vehicle equipped for major emergencies such as beached boats or cliff accidents. Operate underwater recovery units. Participate in recreational demonstrations to entertain resort guests.

GOE INFORMATION—Interest Area: 04. Law, Law Enforcement, and Public Safety. **Work Group:** 04.03. Law Enforcement. **Personality Type**—Realistic. Realistic occupations frequently involve work activities that include practical, hands-on problems and solutions. They often deal with plants, animals, and real-world materials like wood, tools, and machinery. Many of the occupations require working outside and do not involve a lot of paperwork or working closely with others. **Work Values**—Social Service; Authority; Supervision, Technical; Variety; Achievement. **Skills**—Service Orientation; Instructing; Learning Strategies; Social Perceptiveness. **Abilities**—*Cognitive:* Spatial Orientation; Time Sharing; Flexibility of Closure; Selective Attention; Oral Expression. *Psychomotor:* Reaction Time; Response Orientation; Speed of Limb Movement; Multilimb Coordination; Control Precision. *Physical:* Stamina; Explosive Strength; Gross Body Coordination; Gross Body Equilibrium; Dynamic Strength. *Sensory:* Glare Sensitivity; Sound Localization; Night Vision; Far Vision; Peripheral Vision. **General Work Activities**—*Information Input:* Monitoring Processes, Materials, or Surroundings; Getting Information; Identifying Objects, Actions, and Events. *Mental Process:* Making Decisions and Solving Problems; Updating and Using Relevant Knowledge; Organizing, Planning, and Prioritizing. *Work Output:* Performing General Physical Activities; Handling and Moving Objects; Documenting or Recording Information. *Interacting with Others:* Assisting and Caring for Others; Performing for or Working with the Public; Communicating with Persons Outside Organization. **Physical Work Conditions**—Outdoors; High Places; Climbing Ladders, Scaffolds, Poles, etc.; Very Hot or Cold; Walking or Running. **Other Job Characteristics**—Consequence of Error; Importance of Repeating Same Tasks; Importance of Being Exact or Accurate.

Experience—Job Zone 2. Some previous work-related skill, knowledge, or experience may be helpful, but usually is not needed. **Job Preparation:** SVP 4.0 to less than 6.0—six months to less than two years. **Knowledge**—Medicine and Dentistry; Public Safety and Security; Customer and Personal Service; Psychology; Biology. **Instructional Programs**—Security and Protective Services, Other.

Related DOT Jobs—379.364-014 Beach Lifeguard; 379.664-010 Ski Patroller; 379.667-014 Lifeguard.

33-9099.99 Protective Service Workers, All Other

- **Education/Training Required: No data available.**
- **Employed: No data available.**
- **Annual Earnings: No data available.**
- **Growth: 21.7%**
- **Annual Job Openings: 72,000**

All protective service workers not listed separately.

No task data available.

GOE INFORMATION—Interest Area: 04. Law, Law Enforcement, and Public Safety. **Work Group:** 04.03. Law Enforcement; 04.04. Public Safety. **Note:** The Department of Labor has not collected some data for this job, so it has fewer details than the other descriptions.

Instructional Programs—Securities Services Administration/Management; Security and Protective Services, Other.

Related DOT Jobs—199.267-026 Polygraph Examiner; 372.367-010 Community Service Officer, Patrol; 372.667-042 School Bus Monitor; 377.267-010 Deputy United States Marshal; 379.367-010 Surveillance-System Monitor.

35-0000

Food Preparation and Serving Related Occupations

35-1000 Supervisors, Food Preparation and Serving Workers

35-1011.00 Chefs and Head Cooks

- Education/Training Required: Postsecondary vocational training
- Employed: 138,572
- Annual Earnings: $26,800
- Growth: 9.0%
- Annual Job Openings: 35,000

Direct the preparation, seasoning, and cooking of salads, soups, fish, meats, vegetables, desserts, or other foods. May plan and price menu items, order supplies, and keep records and accounts. May participate in cooking.

Prepare and cook foods of all types, either on a regular basis or for special guests or functions. Supervise and coordinate activities of cooks and workers engaged in food preparation. Collaborate with other personnel to plan and develop recipes and menus, taking into account such factors as seasonal availability of ingredients and the likely number of customers. Check the quality of raw and cooked food products to ensure that standards are met. Check the quantity and quality of received products. Demonstrate new cooking techniques and equipment to staff. Determine how food should be presented and create decorative food displays. Determine production schedules and staff requirements necessary to ensure timely delivery of services. Estimate amounts and costs of required supplies, such as food and ingredients. Inspect supplies, equipment, and work areas to ensure conformance to established standards. Instruct cooks and other workers in the preparation, cooking, garnishing, and presentation of food. Monitor sanitation practices to ensure that employees follow standards and regulations. Order or requisition food and other supplies needed to ensure efficient operation. Recruit and hire staff, including cooks and other kitchen workers. Analyze recipes to assign prices to menu items, based on food, labor, and overhead costs. Arrange for equipment purchases and repairs. Meet with customers to discuss menus for special occasions such as weddings, parties, and banquets. Meet with sales representatives in order to negotiate prices and order supplies. Record production and operational data on specified forms. Coordinate planning, budgeting, and purchasing for all the food operations within establishments such as clubs, hotels, or restaurant chains. Plan, direct, and supervise the food preparation and cooking activities of multiple kitchens or restaurants in an establishment such as a restaurant chain, hospital, or hotel.

GOE INFORMATION—**Interest Area:** 11. Recreation, Travel, and Other Personal Services. **Work Group:** 11.05. Food and Beverage Services. **Personality Type**—Enterprising. Enterprising occupations frequently involve starting up and carrying out projects. These occupations can involve leading people and making many decisions. They sometimes require risk taking and often deal with business. **Work Values**—Authority; Responsibility; Creativity; Autonomy; Pleasant Co-workers. **Skills**—Management of Material Resources; Management of Financial Resources; Management of Personnel Resources; Coordination; Instructing; Equipment Selection; Systems Evaluation; Time Management. **Abilities**—*Cognitive:* Perceptual Speed; Originality; Time Sharing; Visualization; Spatial Orientation. *Psychomotor:* Manual Dexterity; Finger Dexterity; Wrist-Finger Speed; Reaction Time; Response Orientation. *Physical:* Explosive Strength; Dynamic Flexibility; Gross Body Coordination; Dynamic Strength; Extent Flexibility. *Sensory:* Sound Localization; Peripheral Vision; Visual Color Discrimination; Depth Perception; Auditory Atten-

tion. **General Work Activities**—*Information Input:* Monitoring Processes, Materials, or Surroundings; Identifying Objects, Actions, and Events; Getting Information. *Mental Process:* Scheduling Work and Activities; Organizing, Planning, and Prioritizing; Thinking Creatively. *Work Output:* Handling and Moving Objects; Documenting or Recording Information; Performing General Physical Activities. *Interacting with Others:* Establishing and Maintaining Relationships; Communicating with Other Workers; Monitoring and Controlling Resources. **Physical Work Conditions**—Minor Burns, Cuts, Bites, or Stings; Hazardous Equipment; Using Hands on Objects, Tools, or Controls; Very Hot or Cold; Standing. **Other Job Characteristics**—Importance of Repeating Same Tasks; Importance of Being Exact or Accurate; Consequence of Error.

Experience—Job Zone 4. A minimum of two to four years of work-related skill, knowledge, or experience is needed. **Job Preparation:** SVP 7.0 to less than 8.0—two years to less than 10 years. **Knowledge**—Administration and Management; Personnel and Human Resources; Education and Training; Economics and Accounting; Food Production. **Instructional Programs**—Cooking and Related Culinary Arts, General; Culinary Arts/Chef Training.

Related DOT Jobs—313.131-010 Baker, Head; 313.131-014 Chef; 313.131-018 Cook, Head, School Cafeteria; 313.131-022 Pastry Chef; 313.131-026 Sous Chef; 315.131-010 Cook, Chief; 315.131-014 Pastry Chef; 315.137-010 Chef, Passenger Vessel; 315.137-014 Sous Chef.

35-1012.00 First-Line Supervisors/ Managers of Food Preparation and Serving Workers

- Education/Training Required: Work experience in a related occupation
- Employed: 648,944
- Annual Earnings: $23,600
- Growth: 12.7%
- Annual Job Openings: 136,000

Supervise workers engaged in preparing and serving food.

Assign duties, responsibilities, and work stations to employees in accordance with work requirements. Forecast staff, equipment, and supply requirements based on a master menu. Inspect supplies, equipment, and work areas in order to ensure efficient service and conformance to standards. Observe and evaluate workers and work procedures in order to ensure quality standards and service. Perform personnel actions such as hiring and firing staff, consulting with other managers as necessary. Recommend measures for improving work procedures and worker performance in order to increase service quality and enhance job safety. Resolve customer complaints regarding food service. Train workers in food preparation and in service, sanitation, and safety procedures. Analyze operational problems, such as theft and wastage, and establish procedures to alleviate these problems. Collaborate with other personnel in order to plan menus, serving arrangements, and related details. Compile and balance cash receipts at the end of the day or shift. Control inventories of food, equipment, smallware, and liquor and report shortages to designated personnel. Develop departmental objectives, budgets, policies, procedures, and strategies. Develop equipment maintenance schedules and arrange for repairs. Estimate ingredients and supplies required to prepare a recipe. Purchase or requisition supplies and equipment needed to ensure quality and timely delivery of services. Record production and operational data on specified forms. Specify food portions and courses, production and time sequences, and workstation and equipment arrangements. Evaluate new products for usefulness and suitability. Greet and seat guests and present menus and wine lists. Perform serving duties such as carving meat, preparing flambe dishes, or serving wine and liquor. Present bills and accept payments. Schedule parties and take reservations. Supervise and check the assembly of regular and special diet trays and the delivery of food trolleys to hospital patients.

GOE INFORMATION—Interest Area: 11. Recreation, Travel, and Other Personal Services. **Work Group:** 11.01. Managerial Work in Recreation, Travel, and Other Personal Services. **Personality Type**—Enterprising. Enterprising occupations frequently involve starting up and carrying out projects. These occupations can involve leading people and making many decisions. They sometimes require risk taking and often deal with business. **Work Values**—Authority; Responsibility; Pleasant Co-workers; Creativity; Autonomy. **Skills**—Management of Personnel Resources; Management of Material Resources; Management of Financial Resources; Systems Analysis; Systems Evaluation; Time Management; Coordination; Speaking. **Abilities**—*Cognitive:* Originality; Time Sharing; Deductive Reasoning; Oral Expression; Fluency of Ideas. *Psychomotor:* Response Orientation. *Physical:* Dynamic Flexibility; Gross Body Equilibrium; Stamina. *Sensory:* Auditory Attention; Speech Clarity; Speech Recognition; Sound Localization; Hearing Sensitivity. **General Work Activities**—*Information Input:* Monitoring Processes, Materials, or Surroundings; Identifying Objects, Actions, and Events; Getting Information. *Mental Process:* Scheduling Work and Activities; Making Decisions and Solving Problems; Judging Qualities of Things, Services, or Other People's Work. *Work Output:* Documenting or Recording Information; Performing General Physical Activities; Handling and Moving Objects. *Interacting with Others:* Monitoring and Controlling Resources; Establishing and Maintaining Relationships; Guiding, Directing, and Motivating Subordinates. **Physical Work Conditions**—Walking or Running; Minor Burns, Cuts, Bites, or Stings; Disease or Infections; Indoors; Keeping or Regaining Balance. **Other Job Characteristics**—Importance of Repeating Same Tasks; Pace Determined by Speed of Equipment; Consequence of Error.

Experience—Job Zone 3. Previous work-related skill, knowledge, or experience is required. **Job Preparation:** SVP 6.0 to less than 7.0—more than one year and less than four years. **Knowledge**—Customer and Personal Service; Personnel and Human Resources; Administration and Management; Food Production; Production and Processing. **Instructional Programs**—Cooking and Related Culinary Arts, General; Foodservice Systems Administration/Management; Restaurant, Culinary, and Catering Management/Manager.

Related DOT Jobs—310.137-018 Steward/Stewardess; 310.137-022 Steward/Stewardess, Banquet; 310.137-026 Steward/Stewardess, Railroad Dining Car; 311.137-010 Counter Supervisor; 311.137-014 Waiter/Waitress, Banquet, Head; 311.137-018 Waiter/Waitress, Captain; 311.137-022 Waiter/Waitress, Head; 318.137-010 Kitchen Steward/Stewardess; 319.137-010 Food-Service Supervisor; 319.137-022 Supervisor, Commissary Production; 319.137-026 Supervisor, Kosher Dietary Service; 319.137-030 Kitchen Supervisor; 350.137-010 Headwaiter/Headwaitress; 350.137-014 Steward/Stewardess, Chief, Cargo Vessel.

35-2000 Cooks and Food Preparation Workers

35-2011.00 Cooks, Fast Food

- Education/Training Required: Short-term on-the-job training
- Employed: 521,560
- Annual Earnings: $13,940
- Growth: –0.7%
- Annual Job Openings: 124,000

Prepare and cook food in a fast-food restaurant with a limited menu. Duties of the cooks are limited to preparation of a few basic items and normally involve operating large-volume single-purpose cooking equipment.

Clean food preparation areas, cooking surfaces, and utensils. Cook and package batches of food, such as hamburgers and fried chicken, which are prepared to order or kept warm until sold. Cook the exact number of items ordered by each customer, working on several different orders simultaneously. Maintain sanitation, health, and safety standards in work areas. Measure ingredients required for specific food items being prepared. Mix ingredients such as pancake or waffle batters. Operate large-volume cooking equipment such as grills, deep-fat fryers, or griddles. Pre-cook items such as bacon in order to prepare them for later use. Prepare and serve beverages such as coffee and fountain drinks. Prepare specialty foods such as pizzas, fish and chips, sandwiches, and tacos, following specific methods that usually require short preparation time. Read food order slips or receive verbal instructions as to food required by patron and prepare and cook food according to instructions. Verify that prepared food meets requirements for quality and quantity. Wash, cut, and prepare foods designated for cooking. Clean, stock, and restock workstations and display cases. Order and take delivery of supplies. Prepare dough, following recipe. Schedule activities and equipment use with managers, using information about daily menus to help coordinate cooking times. Serve orders to customers at windows, counters, or tables. Take food and drink orders and receive payment from customers.

GOE INFORMATION—Interest Area: 11. Recreation, Travel, and Other Personal Services. **Work Group:** 11.05. Food and Beverage Services. **Personality Type**—Realistic. Realistic occupations frequently involve work activities that include practical, hands-on problems and solutions. They often deal with plants, animals, and real-world materials like wood, tools, and machinery. Many of the occupations require working outside and do not involve a lot of paperwork or working closely with others. **Work Values**—Moral Values; Pleasant Co-workers; Supervision, Technical; Activity; Social Service. **Skills**—None met the criteria. **Abilities**—*Cognitive:* None met the criteria. *Psychomotor:* Wrist-Finger Speed. *Physical:* None met the criteria. *Sensory:* None met the criteria. **General Work Activities**—*Information Input:* Identifying Objects, Actions, and Events; Monitoring Processes, Materials, or Surroundings; Getting Information. *Mental Process:* Judging Qualities of Things, Services, or Other People's Work; Processing Information; Updating and Using Relevant Knowledge. *Work Output:* Handling and Moving Objects; Performing General Physical Activities; Controlling Machines and Processes. *Interacting with Others:* Performing for or Working with the Public; Communicating with Persons Outside Organization; Establishing and Maintaining Relationships. **Physical Work Conditions**—Standing; Minor Burns, Cuts, Bites, or Stings; Indoors; Making Repetitive Motions; Very Hot or Cold. **Other Job Characteristics**—Pace Determined by Speed of Equipment; Importance of Repeating Same Tasks; Degree of Automation.

Experience—Job Zone 2. Some previous work-related skill, knowledge, or experience may be helpful, but usually is not needed. **Job Preparation:** SVP 4.0 to less than 6.0—six months to less than two years. **Knowledge**—Customer and Personal Service; Food Production. **Instructional Programs**—Food Preparation/Professional Cooking/Kitchen Assistant; Institutional Food Workers.

Related DOT Jobs—313.361-026 Cook, Specialty; 313.374-010 Cook, Fast Food; 313.381-014 Baker, Pizza.

35-2012.00 Cooks, Institution and Cafeteria

- Education/Training Required: Short-term on-the-job training
- Employed: 464,756
- Annual Earnings: $17,750
- Growth: 7.6%
- Annual Job Openings: 110,000

Prepare and cook large quantities of food for institutions, such as schools, hospitals, or cafeterias.

Cook foodstuffs according to menus, special dietary or nutritional restrictions, and numbers of portions to be served. Clean and inspect galley equipment, kitchen appliances, and work areas in order to ensure cleanliness and functional operation. Direct activities of one or more workers who assist in preparing and serving meals. Bake breads, rolls, and other pastries. Clean, cut, and cook meat, fish, and poultry. Compile and maintain records of food use and expenditures. Determine meal prices based on calculations of ingredient prices. Requisition food supplies, kitchen equipment, and appliances, based on estimates of future needs. Apportion and serve food to facility residents, employees, or patrons. Monitor menus and spending in order to ensure that meals are prepared economically. Monitor use of government food commodities to ensure that proper procedures are followed. Plan menus that are varied, nutritionally balanced, and appetizing, taking advantage of foods in season and local availability. Take inventory of supplies and equipment. Train new employees. Wash pots, pans, dishes, utensils, and other cooking equipment.

GOE INFORMATION—Interest Area: 11. Recreation, Travel, and Other Personal Services. **Work Group:** 11.05. Food and Beverage Services. **Personality Type**—Realistic. Realistic occupations frequently involve work activities that include practical, hands-on problems and solutions. They often deal with plants, animals, and real-world materials like wood, tools, and machinery. Many of the occupations require working outside and do not involve a lot of paperwork or working closely with others. **Work Values**—Pleasant Co-workers; Authority; Supervision, Technical; Social Service; Responsibility. **Skills**—Management of Personnel Resources; Management of Material Resources; Management of Financial Resources. **Abilities**—*Cognitive:* Originality; Oral Expression; Fluency of Ideas; Time Sharing. *Psychomotor:* Wrist-Finger Speed; Manual Dexterity. *Physical:* Stamina. *Sensory:* Visual Color Discrimination. **General Work Activities**—*Information Input:* Identifying Objects, Actions, and Events; Estimating Needed Characteristics; Getting Information. *Mental Process:* Organizing, Planning, and Prioritizing; Thinking Creatively; Judging Qualities of Things, Services, or Other People's Work. *Work Output:* Handling and Moving Objects; Performing General Physical Activities; Controlling Machines and Processes. *Interacting with Others:* Monitoring and Controlling Resources; Coordinating the Work and Activities of Others; Establishing and Maintaining Relationships. **Physical Work Conditions**—Standing; Minor Burns, Cuts, Bites, or Stings; Using Hands on Objects, Tools, or Controls; Very Hot or Cold; Indoors. **Other Job Characteristics**—Importance of Repeating Same Tasks; Pace Determined by Speed of Equipment; Degree of Automation.

Experience—Job Zone 2. Some previous work-related skill, knowledge, or experience may be helpful, but usually is not needed. **Job Preparation:** SVP 4.0 to less than 6.0—six months to less than two years. **Knowledge**—Customer and Personal Service; Food Production; Administration and Management; Economics and Accounting; Personnel and Human Resources. **Instructional Programs**—Cooking and Related Culinary Arts, General; Culinary Arts and Related Services, Other; Food Preparation/

Professional Cooking/Kitchen Assistant; Foodservice Systems Administration/Management; Institutional Food Workers.

Related DOT Jobs—313.381-030 Cook, School Cafeteria; 315.361-010 Cook; 315.371-010 Cook, Mess; 315.381-010 Cook; 315.381-022 Cook, Third; 315.381-026 Second Cook and Baker.

35-2013.00 Cooks, Private Household

- Education/Training Required: Short-term on-the-job training
- Employed: 5,250
- Annual Earnings: No data available.
- Growth: –18.0%
- Annual Job Openings: 1,000

Prepare meals in private homes.

No task data available.

GOE INFORMATION—Interest Area: 11. Recreation, Travel, and Other Personal Services. **Work Group:** 11.08. Other Personal Services. **Note:** The Department of Labor has not collected some data for this job, so it has fewer details than the other descriptions.

Instructional Programs—Culinary Arts/Chef Training; Food Preparation/Professional Cooking/Kitchen Assistant.

Related DOT Jobs—305.281-010 Cook.

35-2014.00 Cooks, Restaurant

- Education/Training Required: Long-term on-the-job training
- Employed: 667,748
- Annual Earnings: $18,480
- Growth: 21.7%
- Annual Job Openings: 158,000

Prepare, season, and cook soups, meats, vegetables, desserts, or other foodstuffs in restaurants. May order supplies, keep records and accounts, price items on menu, or plan menu.

Bake breads, rolls, cakes, and pastries. Bake, roast, broil, and steam meats, fish, vegetables, and other foods. Carve and trim meats such as beef, veal, ham, pork, and lamb for hot or cold service or for sandwiches. Coordinate and supervise work of kitchen staff. Estimate expected food consumption and then requisition or purchase supplies or procure food from storage. Observe and test foods to determine if they have been cooked sufficiently, using methods such as tasting, smelling, or piercing them with utensils. Portion, arrange, and garnish food and serve food to waiters or patrons. Prepare relishes and hors d'oeuvres. Regulate temperature of ovens, broilers, grills, and roasters. Season and cook food according to recipes or personal judgment and experience. Turn or stir foods to ensure even cooking. Wash, peel, cut, and seed fruits and vegetables to prepare them for consumption. Weigh, measure, and mix ingredients according to recipes or personal judgment, using various kitchen utensils and equipment. Butcher and dress animals, fowl, or shellfish or cut and bone meat prior to cooking. Consult with supervisory staff to plan menus, taking into consideration factors such as costs and special event needs. Inspect food preparation and serving areas to ensure observance of safe, sanitary food-handling practices. Keep records and accounts. Plan and price menu items. Substitute for or assist other cooks during emergencies or rush periods.

GOE INFORMATION—Interest Area: 11. Recreation, Travel, and Other Personal Services. **Work Group:** 11.05. Food and Beverage Services. **Personality Type**—Realistic. Realistic occupations frequently involve work activities that include practical, hands-on problems and solutions. They often deal with plants, animals, and real-world materials like wood, tools, and machinery. Many of the occupations require working outside and do not involve a lot of paperwork or working closely with others. **Work Values**—Creativity; Pleasant Co-workers; Authority; Social Service; Responsibility. **Skills**—Management of Personnel Resources. **Abilities**—*Cognitive:* Fluency of Ideas; Memorization; Originality; Time Sharing; Category Flexibility. *Psychomotor:* Wrist-Finger Speed; Arm-Hand Steadiness; Manual Dexterity; Speed of Limb Movement; Response Orientation. *Physical:* Static Strength; Explosive Strength; Extent Flexibility; Trunk Strength; Gross Body Equilibrium. *Sensory:* Peripheral Vision; Night Vision; Visual Color Discrimination; Sound Localization; Near Vision. **General Work Activities**—*Information Input:* Identifying Objects, Actions, and Events; Getting Information; Monitoring Processes, Materials, or Surroundings. *Mental Process:* Thinking Creatively; Organizing, Planning, and Prioritizing; Judging Qualities of Things, Services, or Other People's Work. *Work Output:* Handling and Moving Objects; Performing General Physical Activities; Controlling Machines and Processes. *Interacting with Others:* Monitoring and Controlling Resources; Staffing Organizational Units; Coaching and Developing Others. **Physical Work Conditions**—Minor Burns, Cuts, Bites, or Stings; Standing; Making Repetitive Motions; Indoors; Using Hands on Objects, Tools, or Controls. **Other Job Characteristics**—Pace Determined by Speed of Equipment; Degree of Automation; Importance of Repeating Same Tasks.

Experience—Job Zone 3. Previous work-related skill, knowledge, or experience is required. **Job Preparation:** SVP 6.0 to less than 7.0—more than one year and less than four years. **Knowledge**—Customer and Personal Service; Personnel and Human Resources; Food Production; Education and Training; Administration and Management. **Instructional Programs**—Cooking and Related Culinary Arts, General; Culinary Arts/Chef Training.

Related DOT Jobs—313.281-010 Chef De Froid; 313.361-014 Cook; 313.361-018 Cook Apprentice; 313.361-030 Cook, Specialty, Foreign Food; 313.361-034 Garde Manger; 313.381-022 Cook, Barbecue; 313.381-034 Ice-Cream Chef; 315.361-022 Cook, Station; 315.381-014 Cook, Larder; 315.381-018 Cook, Railroad.

35-2015.00 Cooks, Short Order

- Education/Training Required: **Short-term on-the-job training**
- Employed: **205,003**
- Annual Earnings: **$15,750**
- Growth: **6.8%**
- Annual Job Openings: **49,000**

Prepare and cook to order a variety of foods that require only a short preparation time. May take orders from customers and serve patrons at counters or tables.

Complete orders from steam tables, placing food on plates and serving customers at tables or counters. Grill and garnish hamburgers or other meats such as steaks and chops. Grill, cook, and fry foods such as french fries, eggs, and pancakes. Perform simple food preparation tasks such as making sandwiches, carving meats, and brewing coffee. Plan work on orders so that items served together are finished at the same time. Take orders from customers and cook foods requiring short preparation times according to customer requirements. Accept payments and make change or write charge slips as necessary. Clean food preparation equipment, work areas, and counters or tables. Order supplies and stock them on shelves.

GOE INFORMATION—**Interest Area:** 11. Recreation, Travel, and Other Personal Services. **Work Group:** 11.05. Food and Beverage Services. **Personality Type**—Realistic. Realistic occupations frequently involve work

activities that include practical, hands-on problems and solutions. They often deal with plants, animals, and real-world materials like wood, tools, and machinery. Many of the occupations require working outside and do not involve a lot of paperwork or working closely with others. **Work Values**—Social Service; Moral Values; Pleasant Co-workers; Activity. **Skills**—None met the criteria. **Abilities**—*Cognitive:* Time Sharing. *Psychomotor:* Wrist-Finger Speed. *Physical:* None met the criteria. *Sensory:* None met the criteria. **General Work Activities**—*Information Input:* Getting Information; Monitoring Processes, Materials, or Surroundings; Estimating Needed Characteristics. *Mental Process:* Judging Qualities of Things, Services, or Other People's Work; Processing Information; Updating and Using Relevant Knowledge. *Work Output:* Handling and Moving Objects; Performing General Physical Activities; Controlling Machines and Processes. *Interacting with Others:* Performing for or Working with the Public; Communicating with Persons Outside Organization; Establishing and Maintaining Relationships. **Physical Work Conditions**—Standing; Minor Burns, Cuts, Bites, or Stings; Indoors; Very Hot or Cold; Using Hands on Objects, Tools, or Controls. **Other Job Characteristics**—Pace Determined by Speed of Equipment; Importance of Repeating Same Tasks; Degree of Automation.

Experience—Job Zone 1. No previous work-related skill, knowledge, or experience is needed. **Job Preparation:** SVP below 4.0—less than six months. **Knowledge**—Customer and Personal Service; Food Production; Sales and Marketing; Biology. **Instructional Programs**—Food Preparation/Professional Cooking/Kitchen Assistant; Institutional Food Workers.

Related DOT Jobs—313.374-014 Cook, Short Order.

35-2019.99 Cooks, All Other

- Education/Training Required: **No data available.**
- Employed: **No data available.**
- Annual Earnings: **No data available.**
- Growth: **10.2%**
- Annual Job Openings: **43,000**

All cooks not listed separately.

No task data available.

GOE INFORMATION—**Interest Area:** 11. Recreation, Travel, and Other Personal Services. **Work Group:** 11.05. Food and Beverage Services. **Note:** The Department of Labor has not collected some data for this job, so it has fewer details than the other descriptions.

Instructional Programs—Cooking and Related Culinary Arts, General; Culinary Arts/Chef Training.

Related DOT Jobs—No related DOT jobs.

35-2021.00 Food Preparation Workers

- Education/Training Required: **Short-term on-the-job training**
- Employed: **844,403**
- Annual Earnings: **$15,910**
- Growth: **16.9%**
- Annual Job Openings: **231,000**

Perform a variety of food preparation duties other than cooking, such as preparing cold foods and shellfish, slicing meat, and brewing coffee or tea.

Assist cooks and kitchen staff with various tasks as needed and provide cooks with needed items. Carry food supplies, equipment, and utensils to and from storage and work areas. Clean work areas, equipment, utensils, dishes, and silverware. Cut, slice, and/or grind meat, poultry, and seafood to prepare for cooking. Distribute food to waiters and waitresses to serve to customers. Package take-out foods and/or serve food to customers. Portion and wrap the food or place it directly on plates for service to patrons. Prepare a variety of foods according to customers' orders or supervisors' instructions, following approved procedures. Prepare and serve a variety of beverages such as coffee, tea, and soft drinks. Stock cupboards and refrigerators and tend salad bars and buffet meals. Store food in designated containers and storage areas to prevent spoilage. Use manual and/or electric appliances to clean, peel, slice, and trim foods. Wash, peel, and/or cut various foods to prepare for cooking or serving. Weigh or measure ingredients. Butcher and clean fowl, fish, poultry, and shellfish to prepare for cooking or serving. Distribute menus to hospital patients, collect diet sheets, and deliver food trays and snacks to nursing units or directly to patients. Inform supervisors when supplies are getting low or equipment is not working properly. Keep records of the quantities of food used. Load dishes, glasses, and tableware into dishwashing machines. Make special dressings and sauces as condiments for sandwiches. Mix ingredients for green salads, molded fruit salads, vegetable salads, and pasta salads. Place food trays over food warmers for immediate service or store them in refrigerated storage cabinets. Receive and store food supplies, equipment, and utensils in refrigerators, cupboards, and other storage areas. Remove trash and clean kitchen garbage containers. Scrape leftovers from dishes into garbage containers. Stir and strain soups and sauces.

GOE INFORMATION—Interest Area: 11. Recreation, Travel, and Other Personal Services. **Work Group:** 11.05. Food and Beverage Services. **Personality Type**—Realistic. Realistic occupations frequently involve work activities that include practical, hands-on problems and solutions. They often deal with plants, animals, and real-world materials like wood, tools, and machinery. Many of the occupations require working outside and do not involve a lot of paperwork or working closely with others. **Work Values**—Pleasant Co-workers; Supervision, Technical; Social Service; Moral Values. **Skills**—None met the criteria. **Abilities**—*Cognitive:* Memorization; Information Ordering; Perceptual Speed; Spatial Orientation; Time Sharing. *Psychomotor:* Wrist-Finger Speed; Manual Dexterity; Arm-Hand Steadiness; Reaction Time; Speed of Limb Movement. *Physical:* Trunk Strength; Extent Flexibility; Static Strength; Explosive Strength; Stamina. *Sensory:* Visual Color Discrimination; Hearing Sensitivity; Peripheral Vision; Sound Localization; Speech Recognition. **General Work Activities**—*Information Input:* Monitoring Processes, Materials, or Surroundings; Getting Information; Identifying Objects, Actions, and Events. *Mental Process:* Organizing, Planning, and Prioritizing; Evaluating Information Against Standards; Thinking Creatively. *Work Output:* Handling and Moving Objects; Performing General Physical Activities; Controlling Machines and Processes. *Interacting with Others:* Establishing and Maintaining Relationships; Communicating with Other Workers; Performing for or Working with the Public. **Physical Work Conditions**—Minor Burns, Cuts, Bites, or Stings; Disease or Infections; Making Repetitive Motions; Indoors; Standing. **Other Job Characteristics**—Importance of Repeating Same Tasks; Pace Determined by Speed of Equipment; Degree of Automation.

Experience—Job Zone 1. No previous work-related skill, knowledge, or experience is needed. **Job Preparation:** SVP below 4.0—less than six months. **Knowledge**—Food Production; Customer and Personal Service; Biology; Public Safety and Security; Chemistry. **Instructional Programs**—Cooking and Related Culinary Arts, General; Food Preparation/Professional Cooking/Kitchen Assistant; Institutional Food Workers.

Related DOT Jobs—311.674-014 Raw Shellfish Preparer; 313.684-010 Baker Helper; 313.687-010 Cook Helper, Pastry; 316.661-010 Carver; 316.684-010 Butcher, Chicken and Fish; 316.684-014 Deli Cutter-Slicer; 317.384-010 Salad Maker; 317.664-010 Sandwich Maker; 317.684-010 Coffee Maker; 317.684-014 Pantry Goods Maker; 317.687-010 Cook Helper; 319.484-010 Food Assembler, Kitchen; 319.677-010 Caterer Helper.

35-3000 Food and Beverage Serving Workers

35-3011.00 Bartenders

- **Education/Training Required: Short-term on-the-job training**
- **Employed: 386,890**
- **Annual Earnings: $14,610**
- **Growth: 13.4%**
- **Annual Job Openings: 84,000**

Mix and serve drinks to patrons directly or through waitstaff.

Mix ingredients, such as liquor, soda, water, sugar, and bitters, in order to prepare cocktails and other drinks. Serve wine and bottled or draft beer. Collect money for drinks served. Arrange bottles and glasses to make attractive displays. Slice and pit fruit for garnishing drinks. Order or requisition liquors and supplies. Clean glasses, utensils, and bar equipment. Prepare appetizers, such as pickles, cheese, and cold meats. Ask customers who become loud and obnoxious to leave or physically remove them. Attempt to limit problems and liability related to customers' excessive drinking by taking steps such as persuading customers to stop drinking or ordering taxis or other transportation for intoxicated patrons. Balance cash receipts. Check identification of customers in order to verify age requirements for purchase of alcohol. Clean bars, work areas, and tables. Create drink recipes. Plan bar menus. Plan, organize, and control the operations of a cocktail lounge or bar. Serve snacks or food items to customers seated at the bar. Supervise the work of bar staff and other bartenders. Take beverage orders from serving staff or directly from patrons.

GOE INFORMATION—Interest Area: 11. Recreation, Travel, and Other Personal Services. **Work Group:** 11.05. Food and Beverage Services. **Personality Type**—Enterprising. Enterprising occupations frequently involve starting up and carrying out projects. These occupations can involve leading people and making many decisions. They sometimes require risk taking and often deal with business. **Work Values**—Social Service; Supervision, Technical; Pleasant Co-workers; Good Working Conditions. **Skills**—None met the criteria. **Abilities**—*Cognitive:* Memorization; Time Sharing; Information Ordering; Category Flexibility; Spatial Orientation. *Psychomotor:* Speed of Limb Movement; Wrist-Finger Speed; Manual Dexterity; Arm-Hand Steadiness; Response Orientation. *Physical:* Extent Flexibility; Trunk Strength; Gross Body Equilibrium; Stamina; Static Strength. *Sensory:* Night Vision; Auditory Attention; Speech Recognition; Visual Color Discrimination; Peripheral Vision. **General Work Activities**—*Information Input:* Getting Information; Identifying Objects, Actions, and Events; Monitoring Processes, Materials, or Surroundings. *Mental Process:* Judging Qualities of Things, Services, or Other People's Work; Evaluating Information Against Standards; Analyzing Data or Information. *Work Output:* Handling and Moving Objects; Performing General Physical Activities; Controlling Machines and Processes. *Interacting with Others:* Establishing and Maintaining Relationships; Performing for or Working with the Public; Monitoring and Controlling Resources. **Physical Work Conditions**—Extremely Bright or Inadequate Lighting; Standing; Distracting Sounds and Noise Levels; Walking or Running; Making Repetitive Motions. **Other Job Characteristics**—Importance of Repeating Same Tasks; Importance of Being Exact or Accurate; Pace Determined by Speed of Equipment.

Experience—Job Zone 1. No previous work-related skill, knowledge, or experience is needed. **Job Preparation:** SVP below 4.0—less than six months. **Knowledge**—Psychology; Sales and Marketing; Customer and Personal Service; Law and Government; Philosophy and Theology. **Instructional Programs**—Bartending/Bartender.

Related DOT Jobs—312.474-010 Bartender; 312.477-010 Bar Attendant; 312.677-010 Taproom Attendant.

35-3021.00 Combined Food Preparation and Serving Workers, Including Fast Food

- Education/Training Required: Short-term on-the-job training
- Employed: 2,206,226
- Annual Earnings: $14,120
- Growth: 30.5%
- Annual Job Openings: 737,000

Perform duties which combine both food preparation and food service.

Accept payment from customers and make change as necessary. Cook or reheat food items such as french fries. Distribute food to servers. Notify kitchen personnel of shortages or special orders. Prepare and serve cold drinks or frozen milk drinks or desserts, using drink-dispensing, milkshake, or frozen custard machines. Prepare simple foods and beverages such as sandwiches, salads, and coffee. Relay food orders to cooks. Request and record customer orders and compute bills using cash registers, multicounting machines, or pencil and paper. Select food items from serving or storage areas and place them in dishes, on serving trays, or in takeout bags. Serve customers in eating places that specialize in fast service and inexpensive carry-out food. Arrange tables and decorations according to instructions. Clean and organize eating and service areas. Collect and return dirty dishes to the kitchen for washing. Pack food, dishes, utensils, tablecloths, and accessories for transportation from catering or food preparation establishments to locations designated by customers. Provide caterers with assistance in food preparation or service. Serve food and beverages to guests at banquets or other social functions. Wash dishes, glassware, and silverware after meals.

GOE INFORMATION—**Interest Area:** 11. Recreation, Travel, and Other Personal Services. **Work Group:** 11.05. Food and Beverage Services. **Personality Type**—Realistic. Realistic occupations frequently involve work activities that include practical, hands-on problems and solutions. They often deal with plants, animals, and real-world materials like wood, tools, and machinery. Many of the occupations require working outside and do not involve a lot of paperwork or working closely with others. **Work Values**—Moral Values; Pleasant Co-workers; Advancement. **Skills**—None met the criteria. **Abilities**—*Cognitive:* Spatial Orientation. *Psychomotor:* Reaction Time; Wrist-Finger Speed; Arm-Hand Steadiness; Manual Dexterity; Speed of Limb Movement. *Physical:* Static Strength; Extent Flexibility; Trunk Strength; Gross Body Equilibrium; Dynamic Flexibility. *Sensory:* Peripheral Vision; Speech Recognition; Hearing Sensitivity; Visual Color Discrimination. **General Work Activities**—*Information Input:* Identifying Objects, Actions, and Events; Getting Information; Monitoring Processes, Materials, or Surroundings. *Mental Process:* Processing Information; Updating and Using Relevant Knowledge; Analyzing Data or Information. *Work Output:* Performing General Physical Activities; Handling and Moving Objects; Controlling Machines and Processes. *Interacting with Others:* Establishing and Maintaining Relationships; Performing for or Working with the Public; Communicating with Persons Outside Organization. **Physical Work Conditions**—Walking or Running; Standing; Minor Burns, Cuts, Bites, or Stings; Indoors;

Extremely Bright or Inadequate Lighting. **Other Job Characteristics**—Degree of Automation; Pace Determined by Speed of Equipment; Importance of Repeating Same Tasks.

Experience—Job Zone 1. No previous work-related skill, knowledge, or experience is needed. **Job Preparation:** SVP below 4.0—less than six months. **Knowledge**—Customer and Personal Service; Sales and Marketing; Food Production; Medicine and Dentistry; Public Safety and Security. **Instructional Programs**—Food Preparation/Professional Cooking/Kitchen Assistant; Institutional Food Workers.

Related DOT Jobs—311.472-010 Fast-Foods Worker.

35-3022.00 Counter Attendants, Cafeteria, Food Concession, and Coffee Shop

- Education/Training Required: Short-term on-the-job training
- Employed: 420,804
- Annual Earnings: $14,760
- Growth: 14.4%
- Annual Job Openings: 216,000

Serve food to diners at counter or from a steam table.

Deliver orders to kitchens and pick up and serve food when it is ready. Prepare food such as sandwiches, salads, and ice cream dishes, using standard formulas or following directions. Serve food, beverages, or desserts to customers in such settings as take-out counters of restaurants or lunchrooms, business or industrial establishments, hotel rooms, and cars. Serve salads, vegetables, meat, breads, and cocktails; ladle soups and sauces; portion desserts; and fill beverage cups and glasses. Take customers' orders and write ordered items on tickets, giving ticket stubs to customers when needed to identify filled orders. Wrap menu items such as sandwiches, hot entrees, and desserts for serving or for takeout. Arrange reservations for patrons of dining establishments. Balance receipts and payments in cash registers. Carve meat. Order items needed to replenish supplies. Prepare bills for food, using cash registers, calculators, or adding machines, and accept payment and make change. Replenish foods at serving stations. Scrub and polish counters, steam tables, and other equipment and clean glasses, dishes, and fountain equipment. Set up dining areas for meals and clear them following meals. Add relishes and garnishes to food orders according to instructions. Brew coffee and tea and fill containers with requested beverages.

GOE INFORMATION—**Interest Area:** 11. Recreation, Travel, and Other Personal Services. **Work Group:** 11.05. Food and Beverage Services. **Personality Type**—Social. Social occupations frequently involve working with, communicating with, and teaching people. These occupations often involve helping or providing service to others. **Work Values**—Social Service; Pleasant Co-workers; Supervision, Technical; Moral Values. **Skills**—None met the criteria. **Abilities**—*Cognitive:* None met the criteria. *Psychomotor:* Wrist-Finger Speed; Speed of Limb Movement. *Physical:* Stamina. *Sensory:* None met the criteria. **General Work Activities**—*Information Input:* Getting Information; Identifying Objects, Actions, and Events; Monitoring Processes, Materials, or Surroundings. *Mental Process:* Processing Information; Updating and Using Relevant Knowledge; Judging Qualities of Things, Services, or Other People's Work. *Work Output:* Handling and Moving Objects; Performing General Physical Activities; Documenting or Recording Information. *Interacting with Others:* Performing for or Working with the Public; Communicating with Persons Outside Organization; Establishing and Maintaining Relationships. **Physical Work Conditions**—Standing; Walking or Running; Indoors; Making Repetitive Motions; Minor Burns, Cuts, Bites, or Stings. **Other Job Characteristics**—Importance of Being Exact or Accurate;

Importance of Repeating Same Tasks; Pace Determined by Speed of Equipment.

Experience—Job Zone 1. No previous work-related skill, knowledge, or experience is needed. **Job Preparation:** SVP below 4.0—less than six months. **Knowledge**—Customer and Personal Service; Sales and Marketing; Food Production. **Instructional Programs**—Food Service, Waiter/Waitress, and Dining Room Management/Manager.

Related DOT Jobs—311.477-014 Counter Attendant, Lunchroom or Coffee Shop; 311.477-038 Waiter/Waitress, Take Out; 311.674-010 Canteen Operator; 311.677-014 Counter Attendant, Cafeteria; 319.474-010 Fountain Server.

35-3031.00 *Waiters and Waitresses*

- **Education/Training Required: Short-term on-the-job training**
- **Employed: 1,982,964**
- **Annual Earnings: $13,720**
- **Growth: 18.3%**
- **Annual Job Openings: 596,000**

Take orders and serve food and beverages to patrons at tables in dining establishment.

Check patrons' identification in order to ensure that they meet minimum age requirements for consumption of alcoholic beverages. Check with customers to ensure that they are enjoying their meals and take action to correct any problems. Escort customers to their tables. Explain how various menu items are prepared, describing ingredients and cooking methods. Inform customers of daily specials. Prepare checks that itemize and total meal costs and sales taxes. Present menus to patrons and answer questions about menu items, making recommendations upon request. Remove dishes and glasses from tables or counters and take them to kitchen for cleaning. Serve food and/or beverages to patrons; prepare and serve specialty dishes at tables as required. Stock service areas with supplies such as coffee, food, tableware, and linens. Take orders from patrons for food or beverages. Write patrons' food orders on order slips, memorize orders, or enter orders into computers for transmittal to kitchen staff. Bring wine selections to tables with appropriate glasses and pour the wines for customers. Clean tables and/or counters after patrons have finished dining. Describe and recommend wines to customers. Fill salt, pepper, sugar, cream, condiment, and napkin containers. Garnish and decorate dishes in preparation for serving. Collect payments from customers. Prepare hot, cold, and mixed drinks for patrons and chill bottles of wine. Perform food preparation duties such as preparing salads, appetizers, and cold dishes; portioning desserts; and brewing coffee. Prepare tables for meals, including setting up items such as linens, silverware, and glassware.

GOE INFORMATION—**Interest Area:** 11. Recreation, Travel, and Other Personal Services. **Work Group:** 11.05. Food and Beverage Services. **Personality Type**—Social. Social occupations frequently involve working with, communicating with, and teaching people. These occupations often involve helping or providing service to others. **Work Values**—Social Service; Supervision, Technical; Pleasant Co-workers. **Skills**—None met the criteria. **Abilities**—*Cognitive:* Memorization; Spatial Orientation; Category Flexibility; Time Sharing; Selective Attention. *Psychomotor:* Speed of Limb Movement; Reaction Time; Arm-Hand Steadiness; Response Orientation; Wrist-Finger Speed. *Physical:* Stamina; Trunk Strength; Dynamic Flexibility; Static Strength; Dynamic Strength. *Sensory:* Peripheral Vision; Night Vision; Auditory Attention; Speech Recognition; Sound Localization. **General Work Activities**—*Information Input:* Identifying Objects, Actions, and Events; Monitoring Processes, Materials, or Surroundings; Getting Information. *Mental Process:* Analyzing Data or Information; Processing Information; Evaluating Information

Against Standards. *Work Output:* Handling and Moving Objects; Performing General Physical Activities; Documenting or Recording Information. *Interacting with Others:* Performing for or Working with the Public; Establishing and Maintaining Relationships; Communicating with Persons Outside Organization. **Physical Work Conditions**—Walking or Running; Standing; Minor Burns, Cuts, Bites, or Stings; Indoors; Extremely Bright or Inadequate Lighting. **Other Job Characteristics**—Importance of Repeating Same Tasks; Pace Determined by Speed of Equipment; Degree of Automation.

Experience—Job Zone 1. No previous work-related skill, knowledge, or experience is needed. **Job Preparation:** SVP below 4.0—less than six months. **Knowledge**—Customer and Personal Service; Food Production; Sales and Marketing; Foreign Language; Psychology. **Instructional Programs**—Food Service, Waiter/Waitress, and Dining Room Management/Manager.

Related DOT Jobs—311.477-018 Waiter/Waitress, Bar; 311.477-022 Waiter/Waitress, Dining Car; 311.477-026 Waiter/Waitress, Formal; 311.477-030 Waiter/Waitress, Informal; 311.674-018 Waiter/Waitress, Buffet; 350.677-010 Mess Attendant; 350.677-026 Steward/Stewardess, Wine; 350.677-030 Waiter/Waitress; 352.677-018 Waiter/Waitress, Club.

35-3041.00 *Food Servers, Nonrestaurant*

- **Education/Training Required: Short-term on-the-job training**
- **Employed: 204,515**
- **Annual Earnings: $15,310**
- **Growth: 16.4%**
- **Annual Job Openings: 85,000**

Serve food to patrons outside of a restaurant environment, such as in hotels, hospital rooms, or cars.

Carry food, silverware, and/or linen on trays or use carts to carry trays. Place food servings on plates and trays according to orders or instructions. Prepare food items such as sandwiches, salads, soups, and beverages. Examine trays to ensure that they contain required items. Load trays with accessories such as eating utensils, napkins, and condiments. Monitor food distribution, ensuring that meals are delivered to the correct recipients and that guidelines such as those for special diets are followed. Remove trays and stack dishes for return to kitchen after meals are finished. Stock service stations with items such as ice, napkins, and straws. Take food orders and relay orders to kitchens or serving counters so they can be filled. Clean and sterilize dishes, kitchen utensils, equipment, and facilities. Determine where patients or patrons would like to eat their meals and help them get situated. Monitor food preparation and serving techniques to ensure that proper procedures are followed. Record amounts and types of special food items served to customers. Total checks, present them to customers, and accept payment for services.

GOE INFORMATION—**Interest Area:** 11. Recreation, Travel, and Other Personal Services. **Work Group:** 11.05. Food and Beverage Services. **Personality Type**—Social. Social occupations frequently involve working with, communicating with, and teaching people. These occupations often involve helping or providing service to others. **Work Values**—Social Service; Supervision, Technical; Pleasant Co-workers; Moral Values. **Skills**—None met the criteria. **Abilities**—*Cognitive:* None met the criteria. *Psychomotor:* Wrist-Finger Speed; Speed of Limb Movement. *Physical:* Stamina; Static Strength. *Sensory:* Sound Localization. **General Work Activities**—*Information Input:* Getting Information; Identifying Objects, Actions, and Events; Monitoring Processes, Materials, or Surroundings. *Mental Process:* Judging Qualities of Things, Services, or Other People's Work; Evaluating Information Against Standards; Processing Information. *Work Output:* Handling and Moving Objects; Performing

General Physical Activities; Documenting or Recording Information. *Interacting with Others:* Performing for or Working with the Public; Communicating with Persons Outside Organization; Assisting and Caring for Others. **Physical Work Conditions**—Standing; Outdoors; Walking or Running; Very Hot or Cold; Extremely Bright or Inadequate Lighting. **Other Job Characteristics**—Importance of Repeating Same Tasks; Pace Determined by Speed of Equipment; Importance of Being Exact or Accurate.

Experience—Job Zone 1. No previous work-related skill, knowledge, or experience is needed. **Job Preparation:** SVP below 4.0—less than six months. **Knowledge**—Customer and Personal Service; Sales and Marketing; Food Production. **Instructional Programs**—Food Service, Waiter/Waitress, and Dining Room Management/Manager.

Related DOT Jobs—311.477-010 Car Hop; 311.477-034 Waiter/Waitress, Room Service; 319.677-014 Food-Service Worker, Hospital.

35-9000 Other Food Preparation and Serving Related Workers

35-9011.00 Dining Room and Cafeteria Attendants and Bartender Helpers

- Education/Training Required: Short-term on-the-job training
- Employed: 430,819
- Annual Earnings: $14,150
- Growth: −6.7%
- Annual Job Openings: 161,000

Facilitate food service. Clean tables; carry dirty dishes; replace soiled table linens; set tables; replenish supply of clean linens, silverware, glassware, and dishes; supply service bar with food; and serve water, butter, and coffee to patrons.

Perform serving, cleaning, and stocking duties in establishments such as cafeterias or dining rooms in order to facilitate customer service. Clean up spilled food, drink, and broken dishes and remove empty bottles and trash. Carry food, dishes, trays, and silverware from kitchens and supply departments to serving counters. Carry trays from food counters to tables for cafeteria patrons. Fill beverage and ice dispensers. Garnish foods and position them on tables to make them visible and accessible. Maintain adequate supplies of items such as clean linens, silverware, glassware, dishes, and trays. Mix and prepare flavors for mixed drinks. Replenish supplies of food and equipment at steam tables and service bars. Scrape and stack dirty dishes and carry dishes and other tableware to kitchens for cleaning. Serve food to customers when waiters and waitresses need assistance. Serve ice water, coffee, rolls, and butter to patrons. Set tables with clean linens, condiments, and other supplies. Slice and pit fruit used to garnish drinks. Stock cabinets and serving areas with condiments and refill condiment containers as necessary. Stock refrigerating units with wines and bottled beer and replace empty beer kegs. Wash glasses and other serving equipment at bars. Wipe tables and seats with dampened cloths and replace dirty tablecloths. Carry linens to and from laundry areas. Clean and polish counters, shelves, walls, furniture, and equipment in food service areas and other areas of restaurants and mop and vacuum floors. Locate items requested by customers. Run cash registers. Stock vending machines with food.

GOE INFORMATION—Interest Area: 11. Recreation, Travel, and Other Personal Services. **Work Group:** 11.05. Food and Beverage Services. **Personality Type**—Realistic. Realistic occupations frequently involve work

activities that include practical, hands-on problems and solutions. They often deal with plants, animals, and real-world materials like wood, tools, and machinery. Many of the occupations require working outside and do not involve a lot of paperwork or working closely with others. **Work Values**—Supervision, Technical; Social Service; Pleasant Co-workers; Moral Values. **Skills**—None met the criteria. **Abilities**—*Cognitive:* None met the criteria. *Psychomotor:* Wrist-Finger Speed; Speed of Limb Movement. *Physical:* Static Strength; Stamina; Gross Body Coordination. *Sensory:* Peripheral Vision. **General Work Activities**—*Information Input:* Getting Information; Monitoring Processes, Materials, or Surroundings; Estimating Needed Characteristics. *Mental Process:* Making Decisions and Solving Problems; Judging Qualities of Things, Services, or Other People's Work; Organizing, Planning, and Prioritizing. *Work Output:* Handling and Moving Objects; Performing General Physical Activities; Controlling Machines and Processes. *Interacting with Others:* Communicating with Persons Outside Organization; Performing for or Working with the Public; Establishing and Maintaining Relationships. **Physical Work Conditions**—Standing; Walking or Running; Indoors; Bending or Twisting the Body; Making Repetitive Motions. **Other Job Characteristics**—Importance of Repeating Same Tasks; Pace Determined by Speed of Equipment; Degree of Automation.

Experience—Job Zone 1. No previous work-related skill, knowledge, or experience is needed. **Job Preparation:** SVP below 4.0—less than six months. **Knowledge**—Customer and Personal Service; Food Production. **Instructional Programs**—Food Service, Waiter/Waitress, and Dining Room Management/Manager.

Related DOT Jobs—311.677-010 Cafeteria Attendant; 311.677-018 Dining Room Attendant; 312.687-010 Bartender Helper; 319.687-010 Counter-Supply Worker.

35-9021.00 Dishwashers

- Education/Training Required: Short-term on-the-job training
- Employed: 524,549
- Annual Earnings: $14,520
- Growth: −8.0%
- Annual Job Openings: 156,000

Clean dishes, kitchen, food preparation equipment, or utensils.

Wash dishes, glassware, flatware, pots, and/or pans, using dishwashers or by hand. Clean garbage cans with water or steam. Maintain kitchen work areas, equipment, and utensils in clean and orderly condition. Place clean dishes, utensils, and cooking equipment in storage areas. Prepare and package individual place settings. Sort and remove trash, placing it in designated pickup areas. Sweep and scrub floors. Clean and prepare various foods for cooking or serving. Load or unload trucks that deliver or pick up food and supplies. Receive and store supplies. Set up banquet tables. Stock supplies such as food and utensils in serving stations, cupboards, refrigerators, and salad bars. Transfer supplies and equipment between storage and work areas by hand or using handtrucks.

GOE INFORMATION—Interest Area: 11. Recreation, Travel, and Other Personal Services. **Work Group:** 11.05. Food and Beverage Services. **Personality Type**—Realistic. Realistic occupations frequently involve work activities that include practical, hands-on problems and solutions. They often deal with plants, animals, and real-world materials like wood, tools, and machinery. Many of the occupations require working outside and do not involve a lot of paperwork or working closely with others. **Work Values**—Moral Values; Pleasant Co-workers. **Skills**—None met the criteria. **Abilities**—*Cognitive:* Spatial Orientation; Category Flexibility; Perceptual Speed. *Psychomotor:* Speed of Limb Movement; Wrist-Finger Speed; Multilimb Coordination; Manual Dexterity; Response Orientation. *Physical:* Dynamic Strength; Trunk Strength; Extent Flexibility; Dynamic Flexibility; Static Strength. *Sensory:* Peripheral Vision; Far Vision; Depth Perception; Hearing Sensitivity; Night Vision. **General Work Activities**—*Information Input:* Getting Information; Monitoring Processes, Materials, or Surroundings; Inspecting Equipment, Structures, or Materials. *Mental Process:* Evaluating Information Against Standards; Judging Qualities of Things, Services, or Other People's Work; Organizing, Planning, and Prioritizing. *Work Output:* Handling and Moving Objects; Performing General Physical Activities; Controlling Machines and Processes. *Interacting with Others:* Establishing and Maintaining Relationships; Communicating with Other Workers; Assisting and Caring for Others. **Physical Work Conditions**—Standing; Walking or Running; Minor Burns, Cuts, Bites, or Stings; Making Repetitive Motions; Indoors. **Other Job Characteristics**—Importance of Repeating Same Tasks; Degree of Automation; Pace Determined by Speed of Equipment.

Experience—Job Zone 1. No previous work-related skill, knowledge, or experience is needed. **Job Preparation:** SVP below 4.0—less than six months. **Knowledge**—Food Production; Biology; Customer and Personal Service; Public Safety and Security. **Instructional Programs**—Food Preparation/Professional Cooking/Kitchen Assistant.

Related DOT Jobs—318.687-010 Kitchen Helper; 318.687-014 Scullion; 318.687-018 Silver Wrapper.

35-9031.00 Hosts and Hostesses, Restaurant, Lounge, and Coffee Shop
- **Education/Training Required: Short-term on-the-job training**
- **Employed: 343,380**
- **Annual Earnings: $14,920**
- **Growth: 13.0%**
- **Annual Job Openings: 84,000**

Welcome patrons, seat them at tables or in lounge, and help ensure quality of facilities and service.

Assign patrons to tables suitable for their needs. Direct patrons to coatrooms and waiting areas such as lounges. Greet guests and seat them at tables or in waiting areas. Inform patrons of establishment specialties and features. Inspect dining and serving areas to ensure cleanliness and proper setup. Maintain contact with kitchen staff, management, serving staff, and customers to ensure that dining details are handled properly and customers' concerns are addressed. Provide guests with menus. Receive and record patrons' dining reservations. Supervise and coordinate activities of dining room staff to ensure that patrons receive prompt and courteous service. Hire, train, and supervise food and beverage service staff. Maintain records of time worked by staff and prepare payrolls. Operate cash registers to accept payments for food and beverages. Order or requisition supplies and equipment for tables and serving stations. Plan parties or other special events and services. Prepare cash receipts after establishments close; make bank deposits. Prepare staff work schedules. Speak with patrons to ensure satisfaction with food and service and to respond to complaints. Confer with other staff to help plan establishments' menus. Perform marketing and advertising services.

GOE INFORMATION—**Interest Area:** 11. Recreation, Travel, and Other Personal Services. **Work Group:** 11.05. Food and Beverage Services. **Personality Type**—Enterprising. Enterprising occupations frequently involve starting up and carrying out projects. These occupations can involve leading people and making many decisions. They sometimes require risk taking and often deal with business. **Work Values**—Supervision, Technical; Social Service; Pleasant Co-workers; Authority; Good Working Conditions. **Skills**—Management of Personnel Resources; Time Management. **Abilities**—*Cognitive:* Oral Comprehension; Oral Expression; Spatial Orientation. *Psychomotor:* None met the criteria. *Physical:* None met the criteria. *Sensory:* Speech Clarity; Sound Localization; Far Vision; Speech Recognition. **General Work Activities**—*Information Input:* Identifying Objects, Actions, and Events; Estimating Needed Characteristics; Monitoring Processes, Materials, or Surroundings. *Mental Process:* Scheduling Work and Activities; Judging Qualities of Things, Services, or Other People's Work; Organizing, Planning, and Prioritizing. *Work Output:* Handling and Moving Objects; Performing General Physical Activities; Documenting or Recording Information. *Interacting with Others:* Establishing and Maintaining Relationships; Performing for or Working with the Public; Staffing Organizational Units. **Physical Work Conditions**—Walking or Running; Standing; Indoors. **Other Job Characteristics**—Importance of Being Exact or Accurate; Consequence of Error; Importance of Repeating Same Tasks.

Experience—Job Zone 3. Previous work-related skill, knowledge, or experience is required. **Job Preparation:** SVP 6.0 to less than 7.0—more than one year and less than four years. **Knowledge**—Personnel and Human Resources; Customer and Personal Service; Administration and Management; Sales and Marketing; Education and Training. **Instructional Programs**—Food Service, Waiter/Waitress, and Dining Room Management/Manager.

Related DOT Jobs—310.137-010 Host/Hostess, Restaurant.

35-9099.99 Food Preparation and Serving Related Workers, All Other
- **Education/Training Required: No data available.**
- **Employed: No data available.**
- **Annual Earnings: No data available.**
- **Growth: –2.3%**
- **Annual Job Openings: 43,000**

All food preparation and serving related workers not listed separately.

No task data available.

GOE INFORMATION—**Interest Area:** 11. Recreation, Travel, and Other Personal Services. **Work Group:** 11.05. Food and Beverage Services. **Note:** The Department of Labor has not collected some data for this job, so it has fewer details than the other descriptions.

Instructional Programs—No data available.

Related DOT Jobs—211.482-018 Food-And-Beverage Checker; 319.464-010 Automat-Car Attendant; 319.464-014 Vending-Machine Attendant; 319.467-010 Food Order Expediter; 319.567-010 Mini Bar Attendant.

37-0000
Building and Grounds Cleaning and Maintenance Occupations

37-1000 Supervisors, Building and Grounds Cleaning and Maintenance Workers

37-1011.00 First-Line Supervisors/ Managers of Housekeeping and Janitorial Workers

- **Education/Training Required: Work experience in a related occupation**
- **Employed: 218,904**
- **Annual Earnings: $27,200**
- **Growth: 14.2%**
- **Annual Job Openings: 18,000**

Supervise work activities of cleaning personnel in hotels, hospitals, offices, and other establishments.

No task data available.

GOE INFORMATION—Interest Area: 11. Recreation, Travel, and Other Personal Services. **Work Group:** 11.01. Managerial Work in Recreation, Travel, and Other Personal Services. **Note:** The Department of Labor has not collected some data for this job, so it has fewer details than the other descriptions.

Instructional Programs—No data available.

Related DOT Jobs—187.167-046 Executive Housekeeper; 301.137-010 Housekeeper, Home; 309.137-010 Butler; 321.137-010 Housekeeper; 381.137-010 Supervisor, Janitorial Services; 382.137-010 Supervisor, Maintenance; 389.137-010 Supervisor, Home Restoration Service.

37-1011.01 Housekeeping Supervisors

- **Education/Training Required: Work experience in a related occupation**
- **Employed: No data available.**
- **Annual Earnings: $27,200**
- **Growth: 14.2%**
- **Annual Job Openings: 18,000**

Supervise work activities of cleaning personnel to ensure clean, orderly, and attractive rooms in hotels, hospitals, educational institutions, and similar establishments. Assign duties, inspect work, and investigate complaints regarding housekeeping service and equipment and take corrective action. May purchase housekeeping supplies and equipment, take periodic inventories, screen applicants, train new employees, and recommend dismissals.

Assigns workers their duties and inspects work for conformance to prescribed standards of cleanliness. Investigates complaints regarding housekeeping service and equipment and takes corrective action. Obtains list of rooms to be cleaned immediately and list of prospective check-outs or discharges to prepare work assignments. Coordinates work activities among departments. Screens job applicants, hires new employees, and recommends promotions, transfers, and dismissals. Records data regarding work assignments, personnel actions, and time cards and prepares periodic reports. Advises manager, desk clerk, or admitting personnel of rooms ready for occupancy. Conducts orientation training and in-service training to explain policies and work procedures and to demonstrate use and maintenance of equipment. Establishes standards and procedures for work of housekeeping staff. Inventories stock to ensure adequate supplies. Issues supplies and equipment to workers. Evaluates records to forecast department personnel requirements. Attends staff meetings to discuss company policies and patrons' complaints. Makes recommendations to improve service and ensure more efficient operation. Examines building to determine need for repairs or replacement of furniture or equipment and makes recommendations to management. Prepares reports concerning room occupancy, payroll, and department expenses. Performs cleaning duties in cases of emergency or staff shortage. Selects and purchases new furnishings.

GOE INFORMATION—Interest Area: 11. Recreation, Travel, and Other Personal Services. **Work Group:** 11.01. Managerial Work in Recreation, Travel, and Other Personal Services. **Personality Type**—Enterprising. Enterprising occupations frequently involve starting up and carrying out projects. These occupations can involve leading people and making many decisions. They sometimes require risk taking and often deal with business. **Work Values**—Authority; Pleasant Co-workers; Creativity; Variety; Social Service. **Skills**—Management of Personnel Resources; Time Management; Management of Material Resources; Speaking; Management of Financial Resources; Coordination; Systems Analysis; Systems Evaluation. **Abilities**—*Cognitive:* Oral Expression; Written Expression; Oral Comprehension; Written Comprehension; Spatial Orientation. *Psychomotor:* None met the criteria. *Physical:* None met the criteria. *Sensory:* None met the criteria. **General Work Activities**—*Information Input:* Getting Information; Identifying Objects, Actions, and Events; Monitoring Processes, Materials, or Surroundings. *Mental Process:* Scheduling Work and Activities; Updating and Using Relevant Knowledge; Making Decisions and Solving Problems. *Work Output:* Handling and Moving Objects; Performing General Physical Activities; Documenting or Recording Information. *Interacting with Others:* Communicating with Other Workers; Guiding, Directing, and Motivating Subordinates; Coordinating the Work and Activities of Others. **Physical Work Conditions**—Indoors; Sitting; Climbing Ladders, Scaffolds, Poles, etc.; Walking or Running; Contaminants. **Other Job Characteristics**—Importance of Repeating Same Tasks; Importance of Being Exact or Accurate; Pace Determined by Speed of Equipment.

Experience—Job Zone 4. A minimum of two to four years of work-related skill, knowledge, or experience is needed. **Job Preparation:** SVP 7.0 to less than 8.0—two years to less than 10 years. **Knowledge**—Personnel and Human Resources; Customer and Personal Service; Administration and Management; Education and Training; Clerical. **Instructional Programs**—No data available.

Related DOT Jobs—187.167-046 Executive Housekeeper; 321.137-010 Housekeeper.

37-1011.02 Janitorial Supervisors

- **Education/Training Required: Work experience in a related occupation**
- **Employed: No data available.**
- **Annual Earnings: $27,200**
- **Growth: 14.2%**
- **Annual Job Openings: 18,000**

Supervise work activities of janitorial personnel in commercial and industrial establishments. Assign duties, inspect work, and investigate complaints regarding janitorial services and take corrective action. May purchase janitorial supplies and equipment, take periodic inventories, screen applicants, train new employees, and recommend dismissals.

Supervises and coordinates activities of workers engaged in janitorial services. Assigns janitorial work to employees, following material and work requirements. Trains workers in janitorial methods and procedures and proper operation of equipment. Inspects work performed to ensure conformance to specifications and established standards. Confers with staff to resolve production and personnel problems. Recommends personnel actions, such as hires and discharges, to ensure proper staffing. Records personnel data on specified forms. Issues janitorial supplies and equipment to workers to ensure quality and timely delivery of services.

GOE INFORMATION—Interest Area: 11. Recreation, Travel, and Other Personal Services. **Work Group:** 11.01. Managerial Work in Recreation, Travel, and Other Personal Services. **Personality Type**—Enterprising. Enterprising occupations frequently involve starting up and carrying out projects. These occupations can involve leading people and making many decisions. They sometimes require risk taking and often deal with business. **Work Values**—Authority; Autonomy; Responsibility; Pleasant Co-workers; Activity. **Skills**—Management of Personnel Resources; Co-ordination; Time Management; Speaking; Social Perceptiveness; Management of Material Resources. **Abilities**—*Cognitive:* Oral Expression; Problem Sensitivity; Perceptual Speed; Spatial Orientation. *Psychomotor:* Manual Dexterity; Multilimb Coordination. *Physical:* Dynamic Strength; Trunk Strength. *Sensory:* None met the criteria. **General Work Activities**—*Information Input:* Getting Information; Monitoring Processes, Materials, or Surroundings; Identifying Objects, Actions, and Events. *Mental Process:* Scheduling Work and Activities; Making Decisions and Solving Problems; Processing Information. *Work Output:* Handling and Moving Objects; Performing General Physical Activities; Documenting or Recording Information. *Interacting with Others:* Establishing and Maintaining Relationships; Staffing Organizational Units; Communicating with Other Workers. **Physical Work Conditions**—Contaminants; Walking or Running; Standing; Kneeling, Crouching, or Crawling; Outdoors. **Other Job Characteristics**—Importance of Repeating Same Tasks; Consequence of Error; Pace Determined by Speed of Equipment.

Experience—Job Zone 3. Previous work-related skill, knowledge, or experience is required. **Job Preparation:** SVP 6.0 to less than 7.0—more than one year and less than four years. **Knowledge**—Personnel and Human Resources; Administration and Management; Customer and Personal Service; Education and Training; Building and Construction. **Instructional Programs**—No data available.

Related DOT Jobs—381.137-010 Supervisor, Janitorial Services; 382.137-010 Supervisor, Maintenance; 389.137-010 Supervisor, Home Restoration Service.

37-1012.00 First-Line Supervisors/ Managers of Landscaping, Lawn Service, and Groundskeeping Workers

- **Education/Training Required: Work experience in a related occupation**
- **Employed: 159,092**
- **Annual Earnings: $32,100**
- **Growth: 20.1%**
- **Annual Job Openings: 10,000**

Plan, organize, direct, or coordinate activities of workers engaged in landscaping or groundskeeping activities, such as planting and maintaining ornamental trees, shrubs, flowers, and lawns and applying fertilizers, pesticides, and other chemicals, according to contract specifications. May also coordinate activities of workers

engaged in terracing hillsides, building retaining walls, constructing pathways, installing patios, and similar activities in following a landscape design plan. Work may involve reviewing contracts to ascertain service, machine, and work force requirements; answering inquiries from potential customers regarding methods, material, and price ranges; and preparing estimates according to labor, material, and machine costs.

No task data available.

GOE INFORMATION—Interest Area: 03. Plants and Animals. **Work Group:** 03.01. Managerial Work in Plants and Animals. **Note:** The Department of Labor has not collected some data for this job, so it has fewer details than the other descriptions.

Instructional Programs—Landscaping and Groundskeeping; Ornamental Horticulture; Turf and Turfgrass Management.

Related DOT Jobs—406.134-010 Supervisor, Cemetery Workers; 406.134-014 Supervisor, Landscape; 406.137-010 Greenskeeper I; 406.137-014 Superintendent, Greens; 408.131-010 Supervisor, Spray, Lawn and Tree Service; 408.137-014 Supervisor, Tree-Trimming.

37-1012.01 Lawn Service Managers

- **Education/Training Required: Work experience in a related occupation**
- **Employed: No data available.**
- **Annual Earnings: $32,100**
- **Growth: 20.1%**
- **Annual Job Openings: 10,000**

Plan, direct, and coordinate activities of workers engaged in pruning trees and shrubs, cultivating lawns, and applying pesticides and other chemicals according to service contract specifications.

Supervises workers who provide groundskeeping services on a contract basis. Reviews contracts to ascertain service, machine, and work force requirements for job. Answers customers' questions about groundskeeping care requirements. Prepares service cost estimates for customers. Schedules work for crew according to weather conditions, availability of equipment, and seasonal limitations. Investigates customer complaints. Spot-checks completed work to improve quality of service and to ensure contract compliance. Suggests changes in work procedures and orders corrective work done. Prepares work activity and personnel reports.

GOE INFORMATION—Interest Area: 03. Plants and Animals. **Work Group:** 03.01. Managerial Work in Plants and Animals. **Personality Type**—Enterprising. Enterprising occupations frequently involve starting up and carrying out projects. These occupations can involve leading people and making many decisions. They sometimes require risk taking and often deal with business. **Work Values**—Authority; Autonomy; Responsibility; Social Service; Creativity. **Skills**—Management of Personnel Resources; Time Management; Management of Financial Resources; Systems Evaluation; Mathematics; Systems Analysis; Coordination; Speaking. **Abilities**—*Cognitive:* Oral Expression; Number Facility; Written Expression; Information Ordering; Oral Comprehension. *Psychomotor:* None met the criteria. *Physical:* None met the criteria. *Sensory:* Glare Sensitivity. **General Work Activities**—*Information Input:* Getting Information; Identifying Objects, Actions, and Events; Estimating Needed Characteristics. *Mental Process:* Organizing, Planning, and Prioritizing; Making Decisions and Solving Problems; Scheduling Work and Activities. *Work Output:* Performing General Physical Activities; Handling and Moving Objects; Documenting or Recording Information.

Interacting with Others: Guiding, Directing, and Motivating Subordinates; Communicating with Persons Outside Organization; Establishing and Maintaining Relationships. **Physical Work Conditions**—Outdoors; Very Hot or Cold; Extremely Bright or Inadequate Lighting; Minor Burns, Cuts, Bites, or Stings; Contaminants. **Other Job Characteristics**—Pace Determined by Speed of Equipment; Degree of Automation; Importance of Repeating Same Tasks.

Experience—Job Zone 4. A minimum of two to four years of work-related skill, knowledge, or experience is needed. **Job Preparation:** SVP 7.0 to less than 8.0—two years to less than 10 years. **Knowledge**—Customer and Personal Service; Administration and Management; Personnel and Human Resources; Economics and Accounting; Sales and Marketing. **Instructional Programs**—Landscaping and Groundskeeping; Ornamental Horticulture; Turf and Turfgrass Management.

Related DOT Jobs—408.131-010 Supervisor, Spray, Lawn and Tree Service.

37-1012.02 First-Line Supervisors and Manager/Supervisors—Landscaping Workers

- **Education/Training Required: Work experience in a related occupation**
- **Employed: No data available.**
- **Annual Earnings: $32,100**
- **Growth: 20.1%**
- **Annual Job Openings: 10,000**

Directly supervise and coordinate activities of landscaping workers. Manager/Supervisors are generally found in smaller establishments, where they perform both supervisory and management functions, such as accounting, marketing, and personnel work, and may also engage in the same landscaping work as the workers they supervise.

Directs workers in maintenance and repair of driveways, walkways, benches, graves, and mausoleums. Observes ongoing work to ascertain if work is being performed according to instructions and will be completed on time. Determines work priority and crew and equipment requirements and assigns workers tasks such as planting, fertilizing, irrigating, and mowing. Directs and assists workers engaged in maintenance and repair of equipment such as power mower and backhoe, using hand tools and power tools. Mixes and prepares spray and dust solutions and directs application of fertilizer, insecticide, and fungicide. Confers with manager to develop plans and schedules for maintenance and improvement of grounds. Trains workers in tasks such as transplanting and pruning trees and shrubs, finishing cement, using equipment, and caring for turf. Keeps employee time records; records daily work performed. Tours grounds, such as park, botanical garden, cemetery, or golf course, to inspect conditions. Assists workers in performing work when completion is critical. Interviews, hires, and discharges workers.

GOE INFORMATION—**Interest Area:** 03. Plants and Animals. **Work Group:** 03.01. Managerial Work in Plants and Animals. **Personality Type**—Realistic. Realistic occupations frequently involve work activities that include practical, hands-on problems and solutions. They often deal with plants, animals, and real-world materials like wood, tools, and machinery. Many of the occupations require working outside and do not involve a lot of paperwork or working closely with others. **Work Values**—Authority; Responsibility; Autonomy; Creativity; Pleasant Co-workers. **Skills**—Management of Personnel Resources; Management of Material

Resources; Coordination; Equipment Selection; Systems Analysis; Systems Evaluation; Instructing; Speaking. **Abilities**—*Cognitive:* Time Sharing; Spatial Orientation; Information Ordering; Visualization; Category Flexibility. *Psychomotor:* Speed of Limb Movement; Multilimb Coordination; Manual Dexterity; Control Precision; Wrist-Finger Speed. *Physical:* Static Strength; Gross Body Coordination; Dynamic Strength; Stamina; Trunk Strength. *Sensory:* Visual Color Discrimination; Speech Clarity; Far Vision; Glare Sensitivity; Auditory Attention. **General Work Activities**—*Information Input:* Monitoring Processes, Materials, or Surroundings; Getting Information; Identifying Objects, Actions, and Events. *Mental Process:* Organizing, Planning, and Prioritizing; Scheduling Work and Activities; Making Decisions and Solving Problems. *Work Output:* Performing General Physical Activities; Handling and Moving Objects; Repairing and Maintaining Mechanical Equipment. *Interacting with Others:* Communicating with Other Workers; Coordinating the Work and Activities of Others; Guiding, Directing, and Motivating Subordinates. **Physical Work Conditions**—Outdoors; Contaminants; Walking or Running; Minor Burns, Cuts, Bites, or Stings; Extremely Bright or Inadequate Lighting. **Other Job Characteristics**—Importance of Repeating Same Tasks; Pace Determined by Speed of Equipment; Consequence of Error.

Experience—Job Zone 3. Previous work-related skill, knowledge, or experience is required. **Job Preparation:** SVP 6.0 to less than 7.0—more than one year and less than four years. **Knowledge**—Personnel and Human Resources; Administration and Management; Chemistry; Biology; Education and Training. **Instructional Programs**—Landscaping and Groundskeeping; Ornamental Horticulture; Turf and Turfgrass Management.

Related DOT Jobs—406.134-010 Supervisor, Cemetery Workers; 406.134-014 Supervisor, Landscape; 406.137-010 Greenskeeper I; 406.137-014 Superintendent, Greens; 408.137-014 Supervisor, Tree-Trimming.

37-2000 Building Cleaning and Pest Control Workers

37-2011.00 Janitors and Cleaners, Except Maids and Housekeeping Cleaners

- **Education/Training Required: Short-term on-the-job training**
- **Employed: 2,348,069**
- **Annual Earnings: $17,900**
- **Growth: 13.5%**
- **Annual Job Openings: 507,000**

Keep buildings in clean and orderly condition. Perform heavy cleaning duties, such as cleaning floors, shampooing rugs, washing walls and glass, and removing rubbish. Duties may include tending furnace and boiler, performing routine maintenance activities, notifying management of need for repairs, and cleaning snow or debris from sidewalk.

Clean building floors by sweeping, mopping, scrubbing, or vacuuming them. Gather and empty trash. Service, clean, and supply restrooms. Clean and polish furniture and fixtures. Clean windows, glass partitions, and mirrors, using soapy water or other cleaners, sponges, and squeegees. Dust furniture, walls, machines, and equipment. Make adjustments and minor repairs to heating, cooling, ventilating, plumbing, and electrical systems. Mix water and detergents or acids in containers to prepare cleaning solutions according to specifications. Steam-clean or shampoo carpets. Strip, seal, finish, and polish floors. Clean and restore building interiors damaged by fire, smoke, or water, using commercial cleaning equipment. Clean chimneys, flues, and connecting pipes, using power and hand tools. Clean laboratory equipment, such as glassware and metal instruments, using solvents, brushes, rags, and power cleaning equipment. Drive vehicles required to perform or travel to cleaning work, including vans, industrial trucks, or industrial vacuum cleaners. Follow procedures for the use of chemical cleaners and power equipment in order to prevent damage to floors and fixtures. Monitor building security and safety by performing such tasks as locking doors after operating hours and checking electrical appliance use to ensure that hazards are not created. Move heavy furniture, equipment, and supplies, either manually or by using handtrucks. Mow and trim lawns and shrubbery, using mowers and hand and power trimmers, and clear debris from grounds. Notify managers concerning the need for major repairs or additions to building operating systems. Remove snow from sidewalks, driveways, and parking areas, using snowplows, snow blowers, and snow shovels, and spread snow-melting chemicals. Requisition supplies and equipment needed for cleaning and maintenance duties. Set up, arrange, and remove decorations, tables, chairs, ladders, and scaffolding to prepare facilities for events such as banquets and meetings. Spray insecticides and fumigants to prevent insect and rodent infestation.

GOE INFORMATION—Interest Area: 11. Recreation, Travel, and Other Personal Services. **Work Group:** 11.07. Cleaning and Building Services. **Personality Type—**Realistic. Realistic occupations frequently involve work activities that include practical, hands-on problems and solutions. They often deal with plants, animals, and real-world materials like wood, tools, and machinery. Many of the occupations require working outside and do not involve a lot of paperwork or working closely with others. **Work Values—**Independence; Moral Values; Pleasant Co-workers. **Skills—**Repairing; Installation. **Abilities—***Cognitive:* Spatial Orientation; Visualization; Information Ordering; Flexibility of Closure. *Psychomotor:* Multilimb Coordination; Manual Dexterity; Rate Control; Speed of Limb Movement; Reaction Time. *Physical:* Static Strength; Extent Flexibility; Stamina; Trunk Strength; Dynamic Strength. *Sensory:* Depth Perception; Hearing Sensitivity; Sound Localization; Visual Color Discrimination; Glare Sensitivity. **General Work Activities—***Information Input:* Inspecting Equipment, Structures, or Materials; Getting Information; Monitoring Processes, Materials, or Surroundings. *Mental Process:* Judging Qualities of Things, Services, or Other People's Work; Evaluating Information Against Standards; Analyzing Data or Information. *Work Output:* Performing General Physical Activities; Handling and Moving Objects; Controlling Machines and Processes. *Interacting with Others:* Communicating with Other Workers; Establishing and Maintaining Relationships; Monitoring and Controlling Resources. **Physical Work Conditions—**Contaminants; Hazardous Conditions; Climbing Ladders, Scaffolds, Poles, etc.; Very Hot or Cold; Extremely Bright or Inadequate Lighting. **Other Job Characteristics—**Pace Determined by Speed of Equipment; Importance of Repeating Same Tasks; Degree of Automation.

Experience—Job Zone 1. No previous work-related skill, knowledge, or experience is needed. **Job Preparation:** SVP below 4.0—less than six months. **Knowledge—**Mechanical; Chemistry; Building and Construction; Customer and Personal Service; Public Safety and Security. **Instructional Programs—**No data available.

Related DOT Jobs—358.687-010 Change-House Attendant; 381.687-014 Cleaner, Commercial or Institutional; 381.687-018 Cleaner, Industrial; 381.687-022 Cleaner, Laboratory Equipment; 381.687-026 Cleaner, Wall; 381.687-030 Patch Worker; 381.687-034 Waxer, Floor; 382.664-010 Janitor; 389.664-010 Cleaner, Home Restoration Service; 389.667-010 Sexton; 389.683-010 Sweeper-Cleaner, Industrial; 389.687-014 Cleaner, Window; 891.684-018 Swimming-Pool Servicer; 891.687-010 Chimney Sweep; 891.687-018 Project-Crew Worker.

37-2012.00 Maids and Housekeeping Cleaners

- **Education/Training Required: Short-term on-the-job training**
- **Employed: 1,633,057**
- **Annual Earnings: $16,040**
- **Growth: 5.1%**
- **Annual Job Openings: 346,000**

Perform any combination of light cleaning duties to maintain private households or commercial establishments, such as hotels, restaurants, and hospitals, in a clean and orderly manner. Duties include making beds, replenishing linens, cleaning rooms and halls, and vacuuming.

Clean rooms, hallways, lobbies, lounges, restrooms, corridors, elevators, stairways, locker rooms, and other work areas so that health standards are met. Clean rugs, carpets, upholstered furniture, and/or draperies, using vacuum cleaners and/or shampooers. Empty wastebaskets, empty and clean ashtrays, and transport other trash and waste to disposal areas. Sweep, scrub, wax, and/or polish floors, using brooms, mops, and/or powered scrubbing and waxing machines. Dust and polish furniture and equipment. Keep storage areas and carts well-stocked, clean, and tidy. Polish silver accessories and metalwork such as fixtures and fittings. Remove debris from driveways, garages, and swimming pool areas. Replace light bulbs. Replenish supplies such as drinking glasses, linens, writing supplies, and bathroom items. Sort clothing and other articles, load washing machines, and iron and fold dried items. Sort, count, and mark clean linens and store them in linen closets. Wash windows, walls, ceilings, and woodwork, waxing and polishing as necessary. Assign duties to other staff and give instructions regarding work methods and routines. Request repair services and wait for repair workers to arrive. Deliver television sets, ironing boards, baby cribs, and rollaway beds to guests' rooms. Disinfect equipment and supplies, using germicides or steam-operated sterilizers. Hang draperies and dust window blinds. Move and arrange furniture, and turn mattresses. Observe precautions required to protect hotel and guest property and report damage, theft, and found articles to supervisors. Plan menus and cook and serve meals and refreshments, following employer's instructions or own methods. Prepare rooms for meetings and arrange decorations, media equipment, and furniture for social or business functions. Take care of pets by grooming, exercising, and/or feeding them. Wash dishes and clean kitchens, cooking utensils, and silverware. Answer telephones and doorbells. Care for children and/or elderly persons by overseeing their activities, providing companionship, and assisting them with dressing, bathing, eating, and other needs. Carry linens, towels, toilet items, and cleaning supplies, using wheeled carts. Purchase or order groceries and household supplies to keep kitchens stocked and record expenditures. Run errands such as taking laundry to the cleaners and buying groceries.

GOE INFORMATION—Interest Area: 11. Recreation, Travel, and Other Personal Services. **Work Group:** 11.07. Cleaning and Building Services. **Personality Type—**Realistic. Realistic occupations frequently involve work activities that include practical, hands-on problems and solutions. They often deal with plants, animals, and real-world materials like wood, tools, and machinery. Many of the occupations require working outside and do not involve a lot of paperwork or working closely with others. **Work Values—**Independence; Moral Values; Social Service; Pleasant Co-workers; Activity. **Skills—**None met the criteria. **Abilities—***Cognitive:* Spatial Orientation. *Psychomotor:* Wrist-Finger Speed; Speed of Limb Movement; Multilimb Coordination. *Physical:* Stamina; Trunk Strength; Dynamic Strength; Static Strength. *Sensory:* None met the criteria. **General Work Activities—***Information Input:* Estimating Needed Characteristics; Getting Information; Monitoring Processes, Materials, or

Surroundings. *Mental Process:* Judging Qualities of Things, Services, or Other People's Work; Making Decisions and Solving Problems; Organizing, Planning, and Prioritizing. *Work Output:* Performing General Physical Activities; Handling and Moving Objects; Controlling Machines and Processes. *Interacting with Others:* Assisting and Caring for Others; Communicating with Other Workers; Performing for or Working with the Public. **Physical Work Conditions**—Standing; Walking or Running; Kneeling, Crouching, or Crawling; Making Repetitive Motions; Bending or Twisting the Body. **Other Job Characteristics**—Importance of Repeating Same Tasks; Pace Determined by Speed of Equipment; Degree of Automation.

Experience—Job Zone 1. No previous work-related skill, knowledge, or experience is needed. **Job Preparation:** SVP below 4.0—less than six months. **Knowledge**—Customer and Personal Service; Chemistry. **Instructional Programs**—No data available.

Related DOT Jobs—323.687-010 Cleaner, Hospital; 323.687-014 Cleaner, Housekeeping; 323.687-018 Housecleaner.

37-2019.99 Building Cleaning Workers, All Other

- **Education/Training Required: No data available.**
- **Employed: No data available.**
- **Annual Earnings: No data available.**
- **Growth: 19.6%**
- **Annual Job Openings: 34,000**

All building cleaning workers not listed separately.

No task data available.

GOE INFORMATION—Interest Area: 11. Recreation, Travel, and Other Personal Services. **Work Group:** 11.07. Cleaning and Building Services. **Note:** The Department of Labor has not collected some data for this job, so it has fewer details than the other descriptions.

Instructional Programs—No data available.

Related DOT Jobs—369.384-014 Rug Cleaner, Hand; 389.687-010 Air Purifier Servicer; 389.687-018 Light-Fixture Servicer.

37-2021.00 Pest Control Workers

- **Education/Training Required: Moderate-term on-the-job training**
- **Employed: 57,817**
- **Annual Earnings: $23,150**
- **Growth: 22.1%**
- **Annual Job Openings: 7,000**

Spray or release chemical solutions or toxic gases and set traps to kill pests and vermin, such as mice, termites, and roaches, that infest buildings and surrounding areas.

Spray or dust chemical solutions, powders, or gases into rooms; onto clothing, furnishings, or wood; and over marshlands, ditches, and catchbasins. Set mechanical traps and place poisonous paste or bait in sewers, burrows, and ditches. Inspect premises to identify infestation source and extent of damage to property, wall and roof porosity, and access to infested locations. Cut or bore openings in building or surrounding concrete, access infested areas, insert nozzle, and inject pesticide to impregnate ground. Study preliminary reports and diagrams of infested area and determine treatment type required to eliminate and prevent recurrence of infestation. Direct and/or assist other workers in treatment and extermination processes to eliminate and control rodents, insects, and weeds. Measure area dimensions requiring treatment, using rule; calculate fumigant requirements; and estimate cost for service. Clean and remove blockages from infested areas to facilitate spraying procedure and provide drainage, using broom, mop, shovel, and rake. Position and fasten edges of tarpaulins over building and tape vents to ensure airtight environment and check for leaks. Post warning signs and lock building doors to secure area to be fumigated. Drive truck equipped with power spraying equipment. Record work activities performed. Clean work site after completion of job. Either dig up weeds and burn them or spray them with herbicides.

GOE INFORMATION—Interest Area: 03. Plants and Animals. **Work Group:** 03.03. Hands-on Work in Plants and Animals. **Personality Type**—Realistic. Realistic occupations frequently involve work activities that include practical, hands-on problems and solutions. They often deal with plants, animals, and real-world materials like wood, tools, and machinery. Many of the occupations require working outside and do not involve a lot of paperwork or working closely with others. **Work Values**—Independence; Supervision, Technical; Social Service. **Skills**—Operation and Control; Mathematics; Equipment Selection. **Abilities**—*Cognitive:* Information Ordering. *Psychomotor:* Multilimb Coordination. *Physical:* Extent Flexibility; Trunk Strength; Gross Body Coordination; Gross Body Equilibrium; Dynamic Flexibility. *Sensory:* Depth Perception; Peripheral Vision. **General Work Activities**—*Information Input:* Getting Information; Inspecting Equipment, Structures, or Materials; Estimating Needed Characteristics. *Mental Process:* Analyzing Data or Information; Organizing, Planning, and Prioritizing; Making Decisions and Solving Problems. *Work Output:* Performing General Physical Activities; Handling and Moving Objects; Controlling Machines and Processes. *Interacting with Others:* Establishing and Maintaining Relationships; Communicating with Other Workers; Communicating with Persons Outside Organization. **Physical Work Conditions**—Specialized Protective or Safety Attire; Hazardous Conditions; Contaminants; Kneeling, Crouching, or Crawling; Minor Burns, Cuts, Bites, or Stings. **Other Job Characteristics**—Pace Determined by Speed of Equipment; Importance of Repeating Same Tasks; Degree of Automation.

Experience—Job Zone 2. Some previous work-related skill, knowledge, or experience may be helpful, but usually is not needed. **Job Preparation:** SVP 4.0 to less than 6.0—six months to less than two years. **Knowledge**—Chemistry; Mechanical; Biology; Customer and Personal Service; Building and Construction. **Instructional Programs**—Agricultural/Farm Supplies Retailing and Wholesaling.

Related DOT Jobs—379.687-014 Mosquito Sprayer; 383.361-010 Fumigator; 383.364-010 Exterminator, Termite; 383.684-010 Exterminator Helper; 383.687-018 Exterminator Helper, Termite; 389.684-010 Exterminator.

37-3000 Grounds Maintenance Workers

37-3011.00 Landscaping and Groundskeeping Workers

- **Education/Training Required: Short-term on-the-job training**
- **Employed: 894,187**
- **Annual Earnings: $19,120**
- **Growth: 29.0%**
- **Annual Job Openings: 193,000**

Landscape or maintain grounds of property, using hand or power tools or equipment. Workers typically perform a variety of tasks, which may include any combination of the following: sod laying, mowing, trimming, planting, watering, fertilizing, digging, raking, sprinkler installation, and installation of mortarless segmental concrete masonry wall units.

Care for established lawns by mulching, raking, weeding, grubbing and removing thatch, and trimming and edging around flower beds, walks, and walls. Mix and spray or spread fertilizers, herbicides, or insecticides onto grass, shrubs, and trees, using hand or automatic sprayers or spreaders. Mow and edge lawns, using power mowers and edgers. Plant seeds, bulbs, foliage, flowering plants, grass, ground covers, trees, and shrubs and apply mulch for protection, using gardening tools. Attach wires from planted trees to support stakes. Decorate gardens with stones and plants. Follow planned landscaping designs to determine where to lay sod, sow grass, or plant flowers and foliage. Gather and remove litter. Haul or spread topsoil and spread straw over seeded soil to hold soil in place. Maintain irrigation systems, including winterizing the systems and starting them up in spring. Plan and cultivate lawns and gardens. Prune and trim trees, shrubs, and hedges, using shears, pruners, or chain saws. Rake, mulch, and compost leaves. Trim and pick flowers and clean flower beds. Water lawns, trees, and plants, using portable sprinkler systems, hoses, or watering cans. Advise customers on plant selection and care. Build forms and mix and pour cement to form garden borders. Install rock gardens, ponds, decks, drainage systems, irrigation systems, retaining walls, fences, planters, and/or playground equipment. Maintain and repair tools, equipment, and structures such as buildings, greenhouses, fences, and benches, using hand and power tools. Provide proper upkeep of sidewalks, driveways, parking lots, fountains, planters, burial sites, and other grounds features. Shovel snow from walks, driveways, and parking lots and spread salt in those areas. Use irrigation methods to adjust the amount of water consumption and to prevent waste. Care for artificial turf fields, periodically removing the turf and replacing cushioning pads and vacuuming and disinfecting the turf after use to prevent the growth of harmful bacteria. Care for natural turf fields, making sure the underlying soil has the required composition to allow proper drainage and to support the grasses used on the fields. Mark design boundaries and paint natural and artificial turf fields with team logos and names before events. Operate powered equipment such as mowers, tractors, twin-axle vehicles, snowblowers, chain saws, electric clippers, sod cutters, and pruning saws. Use hand tools such as shovels, rakes, pruning saws, saws, hedge and brush trimmers, and axes.

GOE INFORMATION—Interest Area: 03. Plants and Animals. **Work Group:** 03.03. Hands-on Work in Plants and Animals. **Personality Type—** Realistic. Realistic occupations frequently involve work activities that include practical, hands-on problems and solutions. They often deal with plants, animals, and real-world materials like wood, tools, and machinery. Many of the occupations require working outside and do not involve a lot of paperwork or working closely with others. **Work Values—**Moral Values; Independence. **Skills—**Operation and Control. **Abilities—***Cognitive:* Visualization; Category Flexibility. *Psychomotor:* Speed of Limb Movement; Multilimb Coordination; Manual Dexterity; Rate Control. *Physical:* Stamina; Trunk Strength; Explosive Strength; Dynamic Strength; Dynamic Flexibility. *Sensory:* Glare Sensitivity; Peripheral Vision. **General Work Activities—***Information Input:* Getting Information; Monitoring Processes, Materials, or Surroundings; Inspecting Equipment, Structures, or Materials. *Mental Process:* Thinking Creatively; Judging Qualities of Things, Services, or Other People's Work; Updating and Using Relevant Knowledge. *Work Output:* Performing General Physical Activities; Handling and Moving Objects; Repairing and Maintaining Mechanical Equipment. *Interacting with Others:* Communicating with Other Workers; Establishing and Maintaining Relationships; Communi-

cating with Persons Outside Organization. **Physical Work Conditions—** Outdoors; Kneeling, Crouching, or Crawling; Walking or Running; Bending or Twisting the Body; Minor Burns, Cuts, Bites, or Stings. **Other Job Characteristics—**Pace Determined by Speed of Equipment; Importance of Repeating Same Tasks; Degree of Automation.

Experience—Job Zone 1. No previous work-related skill, knowledge, or experience is needed. **Job Preparation:** SVP below 4.0—less than six months. **Knowledge—**Chemistry; Building and Construction; Biology; Mechanical. **Instructional Programs—**Landscaping and Groundskeeping; Turf and Turfgrass Management.

Related DOT Jobs—405.684-014 Horticultural Worker I; 405.687-010 Flower Picker; 405.687-018 Transplanter, Orchid; 408.364-010 Plant-Care Worker; 408.687-014 Laborer, Landscape; 408.687-018 Tree-Surgeon Helper II; 952.687-010 Hydroelectric-Plant Maintainer.

37-3012.00 Pesticide Handlers, Sprayers, and Applicators, Vegetation

- **Education/Training Required: Moderate-term on-the-job training**
- **Employed: 26,809**
- **Annual Earnings: $24,180**
- **Growth: 13.6%**
- **Annual Job Openings: 6,000**

Mix or apply pesticides, herbicides, fungicides, or insecticides through sprays, dusts, vapors, soil incorporation, or chemical application on trees, shrubs, lawns, or botanical crops. Usually requires specific training and state or federal certification.

Lifts, pushes, and swings nozzle, hose, and tube to direct spray over designated area. Covers area to specified depth, applying knowledge of weather conditions, droplet size, elevation-to-distance ratio, and obstructions. Fills sprayer tank with water and chemicals according to formula. Connects hoses and nozzles selected according to terrain, distribution pattern requirements, type of infestation, and velocity. Starts motor and engages machinery, such as sprayer agitator and pump. Gives driving instructions to truck driver, using hand and horn signals, to ensure complete coverage of designated area. Cleans and services machinery to ensure operating efficiency, using water, gasoline, lubricants, and hand tools. Sprays livestock with pesticides. Plants grass with seed spreader and operates straw blower to cover seeded area with asphalt and straw mixture.

GOE INFORMATION—Interest Area: 03. Plants and Animals. **Work Group:** 03.03. Hands-on Work in Plants and Animals. **Personality Type—** Realistic. Realistic occupations frequently involve work activities that include practical, hands-on problems and solutions. They often deal with plants, animals, and real-world materials like wood, tools, and machinery. Many of the occupations require working outside and do not involve a lot of paperwork or working closely with others. **Work Values—**Independence; Supervision; Technical; Moral Values. **Skills—**Operation and Control. **Abilities—***Cognitive:* Spatial Orientation; Information Ordering. *Psychomotor:* Manual Dexterity; Multilimb Coordination; Wrist-Finger Speed; Finger Dexterity; Arm-Hand Steadiness. *Physical:* Explosive Strength; Dynamic Flexibility; Dynamic Strength; Stamina; Static Strength. *Sensory:* None met the criteria. **General Work Activities—** *Information Input:* Getting Information; Estimating Needed Characteristics; Identifying Objects, Actions, and Events. *Mental Process:* Evaluating Information Against Standards; Making Decisions and Solving Problems; Judging Qualities of Things, Services, or Other People's Work. *Work Output:* Performing General Physical Activities; Handling and Moving Objects; Repairing and Maintaining Mechanical Equipment. *Interacting* *with Others:* Communicating with Other Workers; Establishing and Maintaining Relationships; Communicating with Persons Outside Organization. **Physical Work Conditions**—Outdoors; Contaminants; Hazardous Conditions; Very Hot or Cold; Specialized Protective or Safety Attire. **Other Job Characteristics**—Importance of Repeating Same Tasks; Pace Determined by Speed of Equipment; Degree of Automation.

Experience—Job Zone 2. Some previous work-related skill, knowledge, or experience may be helpful, but usually is not needed. **Job Preparation:** SVP 4.0 to less than 6.0—six months to less than two years. **Knowledge**—Chemistry; Mechanical; Food Production; Engineering and Technology; Physics. **Instructional Programs**—Landscaping and Groundskeeping; Plant Nursery Operations and Management; Turf and Turfgrass Management.

Related DOT Jobs—408.662-010 Hydro-Sprayer Operator; 408.684-014 Sprayer, Hand.

37-3013.00 Tree Trimmers and Pruners

- **Education/Training Required: Short-term on-the-job training**
- **Employed: 52,149**
- **Annual Earnings: $23,950**
- **Growth: 16.3%**
- **Annual Job Openings: 11,000**

Cut away dead or excess branches from trees or shrubs to maintain right-of-way for roads, sidewalks, or utilities or to improve appearance, health, and value of tree. Prune or treat trees or shrubs using handsaws, pruning hooks, shears, and clippers. May use truck-mounted lifts and power pruners. May fill cavities in trees to promote healing and prevent deterioration.

Cuts away dead and excess branches from trees, using handsaws, pruning hooks, shears, and clippers. Uses truck-mounted hydraulic lifts and pruners and power pruners. Scrapes decayed matter from cavities in trees and fills holes with cement to promote healing and to prevent further deterioration. Applies tar or other protective substances to cut surfaces to seal surfaces against insects. Prunes, cuts down, fertilizes, and sprays trees as directed by tree surgeon. Climbs trees, using climbing hooks and belts, or climbs ladders to gain access to work area.

GOE INFORMATION—Interest Area: 03. Plants and Animals. **Work Group:** 03.03. Hands-on Work in Plants and Animals. **Personality Type**—Realistic. Realistic occupations frequently involve work activities that include practical, hands-on problems and solutions. They often deal with plants, animals, and real-world materials like wood, tools, and machinery. Many of the occupations require working outside and do not involve a lot of paperwork or working closely with others. **Work Values**—Moral Values; Independence. **Skills**—Operation and Control. **Abilities**—*Cognitive:* None met the criteria. *Psychomotor:* Multilimb Coordination; Speed of Limb Movement; Manual Dexterity; Arm-Hand Steadiness. *Physical:* Explosive Strength; Dynamic Strength; Dynamic Flexibility; Extent Flexibility; Gross Body Coordination. *Sensory:* Glare Sensitivity. **General Work Activities**—*Information Input:* Getting Information; Identifying Objects, Actions, and Events; Estimating Needed Characteristics. *Mental Process:* Judging Qualities of Things, Services, or Other People's Work; Organizing, Planning, and Prioritizing; Making Decisions and Solving Problems. *Work Output:* Performing General Physical Activities; Handling and Moving Objects; Controlling Machines and Processes. *Interacting with Others:* Communicating with Other Workers; Communicating with Persons Outside Organization; Establishing and Maintaining Relationships. **Physical Work Conditions**—Outdoors; High Places; Climbing Ladders, Scaffolds, Poles, etc.; Minor Burns, Cuts, Bites, or Stings; Specialized Protective or Safety Attire. **Other Job Characteristics**—Importance of Repeating Same Tasks; Pace Determined by Speed of Equipment; Degree of Automation.

Experience—Job Zone 2. Some previous work-related skill, knowledge, or experience may be helpful, but usually is not needed. **Job Preparation:** SVP 4.0 to less than 6.0—six months to less than two years. **Knowledge**—Biology; Chemistry; Mechanical; Engineering and Technology. **Instructional Programs**—Applied Horticulture/Horticultural Business Services, Other.

Related DOT Jobs—408.181-010 Tree Surgeon; 408.684-018 Tree Pruner.

37-3019.99 Grounds Maintenance Workers, All Other

- **Education/Training Required: No data available.**
- **Employed: No data available.**
- **Annual Earnings: No data available.**
- **Growth: 19.6%**
- **Annual Job Openings: 34,000**

All grounds maintenance workers not listed separately.

No task data available.

GOE INFORMATION—Interest Area: 03. Plants and Animals. **Work Group:** 03.03. Hands-on Work in Plants and Animals. **Note:** The Department of Labor has not collected some data for this job, so it has fewer details than the other descriptions.

Instructional Programs—Applied Horticulture/Horticultural Business Services, Other; Applied Horticulture/Horticultural Operations, General; Landscaping and Groundskeeping; Turf and Turfgrass Management.

Related DOT Jobs—329.683-010 Attendant, Campground; 406.381-010 Gardener, Special Effects And Instruction Models; 406.684-010 Cemetery Worker; 406.684-018 Garden Worker; 454.684-022 River.

39-0000

Personal Care and Service Occupations

39-1000 Supervisors, Personal Care and Service Workers

39-1011.00 Gaming Supervisors

- **Education/Training Required: Postsecondary vocational training**
- **Employed: 31,488**
- **Annual Earnings: $39,240**
- **Growth: 18.4%**
- **Annual Job Openings: 2,000**

Supervise gaming operations and personnel in an assigned area. Circulate among tables and observe operations. Ensure that stations and games are covered for each shift. May explain and interpret operating rules of house to patrons. May plan and organize activities and create friendly atmosphere for guests in hotels/casinos. May adjust service complaints.

Determine how many gaming tables to open each day and schedule staff accordingly. Establish and maintain banks and table limits for each game. Evaluate workers' performance and prepare written performance evaluations. Explain and interpret house rules, such as game rules and betting limits, for patrons. Greet customers and ask about the quality of service they are receiving. Maintain familiarity with the games at a facility and with strategies and tricks used by cheaters at such games. Monitor and verify the counting, wrapping, weighing, and distribution of currency and coins. Monitor game operations to ensure that house rules are followed; that tribal, state, and federal regulations are adhered to; and that employees provide prompt and courteous service. Monitor stations and games and move dealers from game to game to ensure adequate staffing. Observe gamblers' behavior for signs of cheating, such as marking, switching, or counting cards; notify security staff of suspected cheating. Perform paperwork required for monetary transactions. Report customer-related incidents occurring in gaming areas to supervisors. Resolve customer and employee complaints. Direct workers compiling summary sheets for each race or event to record amounts wagered and amounts to be paid to winners. Establish policies on types of gambling offered, odds, and extension of credit. Interview, hire, and train workers. Monitor patrons for signs of compulsive gambling, offering assistance if necessary. Provide fire protection and first-aid assistance when necessary. Record, issue receipts for, and pay off bets. Review operational expenses, budget estimates, betting accounts, and collection reports for accuracy. Supervise the distribution of complimentary meals, hotel rooms, discounts, and other items given to players based on length of play and amount bet.

GOE INFORMATION—Interest Area: 11. Recreation, Travel, and Other Personal Services. **Work Group:** 11.01. Managerial Work in Recreation, Travel, and Other Personal Services. **Personality Type—**Enterprising. Enterprising occupations frequently involve starting up and carrying out projects. These occupations can involve leading people and making many decisions. They sometimes require risk taking and often deal with business. **Work Values—**Authority; Social Service; Responsibility; Creativity; Autonomy. **Skills—**Management of Financial Resources; Management of Personnel Resources; Management of Material Resources; Speaking; Negotiation; Critical Thinking; Systems Evaluation; Time Management. **Abilities—***Cognitive:* Mathematical Reasoning; Number Facility; Time Sharing; Problem Sensitivity; Oral Comprehension. *Psychomotor:* None met the criteria. *Physical:* None met the criteria. *Sensory:* Far Vision; Near Vision; Night Vision; Sound Localization; Peripheral Vision. **General Work Activities—***Information Input:* Getting Information; Identifying Objects, Actions, and Events; Monitoring Processes, Materials, or Surroundings. *Mental Process:* Analyzing Data or Information; Organizing, Planning, and Prioritizing; Scheduling Work and Activities. *Work Output:* Documenting or Recording Information; Performing General Physical Activities; Handling and Moving Objects. *Interacting with Others:* Monitoring and Controlling Resources; Communicating with Other Workers; Establishing and Maintaining Relationships. **Physical Work Conditions—**Indoors; Sitting; Walking or Running; Standing. **Other Job Characteristics—**Consequence of Error; Importance of Being Exact or Accurate; Degree of Automation.

Experience—Job Zone 3. Previous work-related skill, knowledge, or experience is required. **Job Preparation:** SVP 6.0 to less than 7.0—more than one year and less than four years. **Knowledge—**Economics and Accounting; Administration and Management; Personnel and Human Resources; Customer and Personal Service; Mathematics. **Instructional Programs—**No data available.

Related DOT Jobs—343.137-014 Supervisor, Cardroom.

39-1012.00 Slot Key Persons

- **Education/Training Required: Short-term on-the-job training**
- **Employed: 14,494**
- **Annual Earnings: $22,510**
- **Growth: 23.3%**
- **Annual Job Openings: 1,000**

Coordinate/supervise functions of slot department workers to provide service to patrons. Handle and settle complaints of players. Verify and pay off jackpots. Reset slot machines after payoffs. Make minor repairs or adjustments to slot machines. Recommend removal of slot machines for repair. Report hazards and enforce safety rules.

Answer patrons' questions about gaming machine functions and payouts. Attach "out of order" signs to malfunctioning machines and notify technicians when machines need to be repaired or removed. Coordinate and oversee the work of slot department workers, including change runners and slot technicians. Enforce safety rules and report or remove safety hazards as well as guests who are underage, intoxicated, disruptive, or cheating. Monitor functioning of slot machine coin dispensers and fill coin hoppers when necessary. Monitor payment of hand-delivered jackpots to ensure promptness. Patrol assigned areas to ensure that players are following rules and that machines are functioning correctly. Perform minor repairs or make adjustments to slot machines, resolving problems such as machine tilts and coin jams. Record the specifics of malfunctioning machines and document malfunctions needing repair. Reset slot machines after payoffs. Respond to and resolve patrons' complaints. Exchange currency for customers, converting currency into requested combinations of bills and coins.

GOE INFORMATION—Interest Area: 11. Recreation, Travel, and Other Personal Services. **Work Group:** 11.02. Recreational Services. **Note:** The Department of Labor has not collected some data for this job, so it has fewer details than the other descriptions.

Instructional Programs—No data available.

Related DOT Jobs—343.137-014 Supervisor, Cardroom.

39-1021.00 First-Line Supervisors/ Managers of Personal Service Workers

- **Education/Training Required: Work experience in a related occupation**
- **Employed: 124,726**
- **Annual Earnings: $28,040**
- **Growth: 15.1%**
- **Annual Job Openings: 8,000**

Supervise and coordinate activities of personal service workers, such as supervisors of flight attendants, hairdressers, or caddies.

Supervises and coordinates activities of workers engaged in lodging and personal services. Observes and evaluates workers' appearance and performance to ensure quality service and compliance with specifications. Assigns work schedules, following work requirements, to ensure quality and timely delivery of services. Trains workers in proper operational procedures and functions; explains company policy. Resolves customer complaints regarding worker performance and services rendered. Collaborates with personnel to plan and develop programs of events, schedules of activities, and menus. Analyzes and records personnel and operational data and writes activity reports. Inspects work areas and operating equipment to ensure conformance to established standards. Requisitions supplies, equipment, and designated services to ensure quality and timely service and efficient operations. Informs workers about interests of specific groups. Furnishes customers with information on events and activities.

GOE INFORMATION—Interest Area: 11. Recreation, Travel, and Other Personal Services. **Work Group:** 11.01. Managerial Work in Recreation, Travel, and Other Personal Services. **Personality Type**—Enterprising. Enterprising occupations frequently involve starting up and carrying out projects. These occupations can involve leading people and making many decisions. They sometimes require risk taking and often deal with business. **Work Values**—Authority; Autonomy; Pleasant Co-workers; Good Working Conditions; Responsibility. **Skills**—Service Orientation; Coordination; Management of Personnel Resources; Time Management; Speaking; Active Listening; Management of Material Resources; Management of Financial Resources. **Abilities**—*Cognitive:* Time Sharing; Fluency of Ideas; Originality; Written Expression; Perceptual Speed. *Psychomotor:* Response Orientation. *Physical:* Trunk Strength. *Sensory:* Far Vision; Speech Recognition; Near Vision; Speech Clarity; Auditory Attention. **General Work Activities**—*Information Input:* Getting Information; Identifying Objects, Actions, and Events; Monitoring Processes, Materials, or Surroundings. *Mental Process:* Organizing, Planning, and Prioritizing; Scheduling Work and Activities; Judging Qualities of Things, Services, or Other People's Work. *Work Output:* Performing General Physical Activities; Handling and Moving Objects; Documenting or Recording Information. *Interacting with Others:* Coordinating the Work and Activities of Others; Communicating with Other Workers; Establishing and Maintaining Relationships. **Physical Work Conditions**—Indoors; Standing; Sitting. **Other Job Characteristics**—Importance of Being Exact or Accurate; Importance of Repeating Same Tasks; Consequence of Error.

Experience—Job Zone 3. Previous work-related skill, knowledge, or experience is required. **Job Preparation:** SVP 6.0 to less than 7.0—more than one year and less than four years. **Knowledge**—Customer and Personal Service; Administration and Management; Personnel and Human Resources; Education and Training; Psychology. **Instructional Programs**—No data available.

Related DOT Jobs—321.137-014 Inspector; 323.137-010 Supervisor, Housecleaner; 324.137-010 Baggage Porter, Head; 324.137-014 Bell Captain; 329.137-010 Superintendent, Service; 344.137-010 Usher, Head; 350.137-018 Steward/Stewardess, Chief, Passenger Ship; 350.137-022 Steward/Stewardess, Second; 350.137-026 Steward/Stewardess, Third; 352.137-010 Supervisor, Airplane-Flight Attendant; 353.137-010 Guide, Chief Airport; 358.137-010 Checkroom Chief; 388.367-010 Elevator Starter.

39-2000 Animal Care and Service Workers

39-2011.00 Animal Trainers

- **Education/Training Required: Moderate-term on-the-job training**
- **Employed: 14,579**
- **Annual Earnings: $23,280**
- **Growth: 18.4%**
- **Annual Job Openings: 2,000**

Train animals for riding, harness, security, performance, obedience, or assisting persons with disabilities. Accustom animals to human voice and contact; condition animals to respond to commands. Train animals according to prescribed standards for show or competition. May train animals to carry pack loads or work as part of pack team.

Conduct training programs in order to develop and maintain desired animal behaviors for competition, entertainment, obedience, security, riding, and related areas. Cue or signal animals during performances. Evaluate animals in order to determine their temperaments, abilities, and aptitude for training. Feed and exercise animals and provide other general care such as cleaning and maintaining holding and performance areas. Observe animals' physical conditions in order to detect illness or unhealthy conditions requiring medical care. Train and rehearse animals, according to scripts, for motion picture, television, film, stage, or circus performances. Train dogs in human-assistance or property protection duties. Train horses or other equines for riding, harness, show, racing, or other work, using knowledge of breed characteristics, training methods, performance standards, and the peculiarities of each animal. Administer prescribed medications to animals. Advise animal owners regarding the purchase of specific animals. Arrange for mating of stallions and mares; assist mares during foaling. Keep records documenting animal health, diet, and behavior. Place tack or harnesses on horses in order to accustom horses to the feel of equipment. Retrain horses to break bad habits, such as kicking, bolting, and resisting bridling and grooming. Talk to and interact with animals in order to familiarize them to human voices and contact. Use oral, spur, rein, and/or hand commands in order to condition horses to carry riders or to pull horse-drawn equipment. Instruct jockeys in handling specific horses during races. Organize and conduct animal shows.

GOE INFORMATION—Interest Area: 03. Plants and Animals. **Work Group:** 03.02. Animal Care and Training. **Personality Type**—Social. Social occupations frequently involve working with, communicating with, and teaching people. These occupations often involve helping or providing service to others. **Work Values**—Responsibility; Creativity; Autonomy; Independence; Compensation. **Skills**—Instructing; Learning Strategies; Monitoring. **Abilities**—*Cognitive:* Flexibility of Closure; Memorization; Speed of Closure; Originality; Time Sharing. *Psychomotor:* Speed of Limb Movement; Rate Control; Reaction Time; Response Orientation. *Physical:* Dynamic Flexibility; Static Strength; Gross Body

Coordination; Gross Body Equilibrium; Dynamic Strength. *Sensory:* Far Vision; Peripheral Vision; Hearing Sensitivity; Auditory Attention; Sound Localization. **General Work Activities**—*Information Input:* Identifying Objects, Actions, and Events; Getting Information; Monitoring Processes, Materials, or Surroundings. *Mental Process:* Judging Qualities of Things, Services, or Other People's Work; Thinking Creatively; Organizing, Planning, and Prioritizing. *Work Output:* Performing General Physical Activities; Handling and Moving Objects; Documenting or Recording Information. *Interacting with Others:* Providing Consultation and Advice to Others; Communicating with Persons Outside Organization; Establishing and Maintaining Relationships. **Physical Work Conditions**—Minor Burns, Cuts, Bites, or Stings; Disease or Infections; Kneeling, Crouching, or Crawling; Outdoors; Contaminants. **Other Job Characteristics**—Importance of Repeating Same Tasks; Pace Determined by Speed of Equipment; Degree of Automation.

Experience—Job Zone 3. Previous work-related skill, knowledge, or experience is required. **Job Preparation:** SVP 6.0 to less than 7.0—more than one year and less than four years. **Knowledge**—Education and Training; Biology; Customer and Personal Service; Sales and Marketing; Therapy and Counseling. **Instructional Programs**—Animal Training; Equestrian/Equine Studies.

Related DOT Jobs—159.224-010 Animal Trainer; 419.224-010 Horse Trainer.

39-2021.00 Nonfarm Animal Caretakers

- **Education/Training Required: Short-term on-the-job training**
- **Employed: 130,612**
- **Annual Earnings: $16,570**
- **Growth: 21.6%**
- **Annual Job Openings: 20,000**

Feed, water, groom, bathe, exercise, or otherwise care for pets and other nonfarm animals, such as dogs, cats, ornamental fish or birds, zoo animals, and mice. Work in settings such as kennels, animal shelters, zoos, circuses, and aquariums. May keep records of feedings, treatments, and animals received or discharged. May clean, disinfect, and repair cages, pens, or fish tanks.

Adjust controls to regulate specified temperature and humidity of animal quarters, nurseries, or exhibit areas. Clean, organize, and disinfect animal quarters such as pens, stables, cages, and yards and animal equipment such as saddles and bridles. Collect and record animal information such as weight, size, physical condition, treatments received, medications given, and food intake. Examine and observe animals in order to detect signs of illness, disease, or injury. Exercise animals in order to maintain their physical and mental health. Feed and water animals according to schedules and feeding instructions. Mix food, liquid formulas, medications, or food supplements according to instructions, prescriptions, and knowledge of animal species. Perform animal grooming duties such as washing, brushing, clipping, and trimming coats, cutting nails, and cleaning ears. Provide treatment to sick or injured animals or contact veterinarians in order to secure treatment. Administer laboratory tests to experimental animals and keep records of responses. Anesthetize and inoculate animals according to instructions. Answer telephones and schedule appointments. Clean and disinfect surgical equipment. Discuss with clients their pets' grooming needs. Install, maintain, and repair animal care facility equipment such as infrared lights, feeding devices, and cages. Observe and caution children petting and feeding animals in designated areas in order to ensure the safety of humans and animals. Order, unload, and store feed and supplies. Respond to questions from patrons and provide information about animals, such as behavior, habitat, breeding habits, or facility activities. Saddle and shoe animals. Train animals to perform certain tasks. Transfer animals between enclosures in order to facilitate

breeding, birthing, shipping, or rearrangement of exhibits. Find homes for stray or unwanted animals. Sell pet food and supplies. Teach obedience classes.

GOE INFORMATION—**Interest Area:** 03. Plants and Animals. **Work Group:** 03.02. Animal Care and Training. **Personality Type**—Realistic. Realistic occupations frequently involve work activities that include practical, hands-on problems and solutions. They often deal with plants, animals, and real-world materials like wood, tools, and machinery. Many of the occupations require working outside and do not involve a lot of paperwork or working closely with others. **Work Values**—Independence; Supervision, Technical; Activity; Moral Values. **Skills**—Repairing; Installation. **Abilities**—*Cognitive:* Spatial Orientation; Time Sharing. *Psychomotor:* Rate Control; Speed of Limb Movement; Reaction Time; Control Precision. *Physical:* Dynamic Strength; Explosive Strength; Static Strength; Dynamic Flexibility; Gross Body Coordination. *Sensory:* Sound Localization; Speech Clarity; Hearing Sensitivity. **General Work Activities**—*Information Input:* Identifying Objects, Actions, and Events; Getting Information; Monitoring Processes, Materials, or Surroundings. *Mental Process:* Updating and Using Relevant Knowledge; Judging Qualities of Things, Services, or Other People's Work; Analyzing Data or Information. *Work Output:* Performing General Physical Activities; Handling and Moving Objects; Controlling Machines and Processes. *Interacting with Others:* Communicating with Persons Outside Organization; Establishing and Maintaining Relationships; Communicating with Other Workers. **Physical Work Conditions**—Outdoors; Disease or Infections; Contaminants; Minor Burns, Cuts, Bites, or Stings; Distracting Sounds and Noise Levels. **Other Job Characteristics**—Pace Determined by Speed of Equipment; Importance of Repeating Same Tasks; Consequence of Error.

Experience—Job Zone 1. No previous work-related skill, knowledge, or experience is needed. **Job Preparation:** SVP below 4.0—less than six months. **Knowledge**—Medicine and Dentistry; Biology; Building and Construction; Chemistry; Clerical. **Instructional Programs**—Agricultural/Farm Supplies Retailing and Wholesaling; Dog/Pet/Animal Grooming.

Related DOT Jobs—410.674-010 Animal Caretaker; 410.674-022 Stable Attendant; 412.674-010 Animal Keeper; 412.674-014 Animal-Nursery Worker.

39-3000 Entertainment Attendants and Related Workers

39-3011.00 Gaming Dealers

- **Education/Training Required: Postsecondary vocational training**
- **Employed: 87,648**
- **Annual Earnings: $13,680**
- **Growth: 32.4%**
- **Annual Job Openings: 28,000**

Operate table games. Stand or sit behind table and operate games of chance by dispensing the appropriate number of cards or blocks to players or operating other gaming equipment. Compare the house's hand against players' hands and pay off or collect players' money or chips.

Answer questions about game rules and casino policies. Apply rule variations to card games such as poker, in which players bet on the value of their hands. Check to ensure that all players have placed bets before play begins. Compute amounts of players' wins or losses or scan winning tickets presented by patrons to calculate the amount of money won. Conduct gambling games such as dice, roulette, cards, or keno, following all applicable rules and regulations. Deal cards to house hands and compare these with players' hands to determine winners, as in blackjack. Inspect cards and equipment to be used in games to ensure that they are in good condition. Open and close cash floats and game tables. Pay winnings or collect losing bets as established by the rules and procedures of a specific game. Receive, verify, and record patrons' cash wagers. Refer patrons to gaming cashiers to collect winnings. Seat patrons at gaming tables. Stand behind a gaming table and deal the appropriate number of cards to each player. Start and control games and gaming equipment and announce winning numbers or colors. Exchange paper currency for playing chips or coin money. Monitor gambling tables and supervise staff. Participate in games for gambling establishments in order to provide the minimum complement of players at a table. Prepare collection reports for submission to supervisors. Sell food, beverages, and tobacco to players. Train new dealers. Work as part of a team of dealers in games such as baccarat or craps.

GOE INFORMATION—Interest Area: 11. Recreation, Travel, and Other Personal Services. **Work Group:** 11.02. Recreational Services. **Personality Type**—Enterprising. Enterprising occupations frequently involve starting up and carrying out projects. These occupations can involve leading people and making many decisions. They sometimes require risk taking and often deal with business. **Work Values**—Supervision, Technical; Pleasant Co-workers; Good Working Conditions; Compensation. **Skills**—None met the criteria. **Abilities**—*Cognitive:* Perceptual Speed; Memorization; Time Sharing; Selective Attention; Number Facility. *Psychomotor:* Wrist-Finger Speed; Response Orientation; Speed of Limb Movement; Reaction Time; Finger Dexterity. *Physical:* Dynamic Strength. *Sensory:* Auditory Attention; Peripheral Vision; Speech Recognition; Night Vision; Sound Localization. **General Work Activities**—*Information Input:* Identifying Objects, Actions, and Events; Getting Information; Monitoring Processes, Materials, or Surroundings. *Mental Process:* Processing Information; Judging Qualities of Things, Services, or Other People's Work; Evaluating Information Against Standards. *Work Output:* Handling and Moving Objects; Performing General Physical Activities; Documenting or Recording Information. *Interacting with Others:* Performing for or Working with the Public; Establishing and Maintaining Relationships; Communicating with Persons Outside Organization. **Physical Work Conditions**—Making Repetitive Motions; Indoors; Standing; Walking or Running; Sitting. **Other Job Characteristics**—Importance of Being Exact or Accurate; Importance of Repeating Same Tasks; Consequence of Error.

Experience—Job Zone 2. Some previous work-related skill, knowledge, or experience may be helpful, but usually is not needed. **Job Preparation:** SVP 4.0 to less than 6.0—six months to less than two years. **Knowledge**—Sales and Marketing; Customer and Personal Service; Law and Government; Psychology; Foreign Language. **Instructional Programs**—No data available.

Related DOT Jobs—343.464-010 Gambling Dealer.

39-3012.00 Gaming and Sports Book Writers and Runners

- **Education/Training Required: Postsecondary vocational training**
- **Employed: 12,154**
- **Annual Earnings: $18,240**
- **Growth: 21.6%**
- **Annual Job Openings: 4,000**

Assist in the operation of games such as keno and bingo. Scan winning tickets presented by patrons, calculate amount of winnings, and pay patrons. May operate keno and bingo equipment. May start gaming equipment that randomly selects numbers. May announce number selected until total numbers specified for each game are selected. May pick up tickets from players, collect bets, and receive, verify, and record patrons' cash wages.

Answer questions about game rules and casino policies. Check to ensure that all players have placed their bets before play begins. Collect bets in the form of cash or chips, verifying and recording amounts. Collect cards or tickets from players. Compare the house hand with players' hands in order to determine the winner. Compute and verify amounts won and lost and then pay out winnings or refer patrons to workers such as gaming cashiers so that winnings can be collected. Conduct gambling tables or games, such as dice, roulette, cards, or keno, and ensure that game rules are followed. Inspect cards and equipment to be used in games to ensure they are in proper condition. Open and close cash floats and game tables. Operate games in which players bet that a ball will come to rest in a particular slot on a rotating wheel, performing actions such as spinning the wheel and releasing the ball. Pay off or move bets as established by game rules and procedures. Push dice to shooters and retrieve thrown dice. Seat patrons at gaming tables. Start gaming equipment that randomly selects numbered balls; announce winning numbers and colors. Take the house percentage from each pot. Deliver tickets, cards, and money to bingo callers. Exchange paper currency for playing chips or coins. Participate in games for gambling establishments in order to provide the minimum complement of players at a table. Prepare collection reports for submission to supervisors. Record the number of tickets cashed and the amount paid out after each race or event. Sell food, beverages, and tobacco to players. Supervise staff and games; mediate disputes.

GOE INFORMATION—Interest Area: 11. Recreation, Travel, and Other Personal Services. **Work Group:** 11.02. Recreational Services. **Personality Type**—Enterprising. Enterprising occupations frequently involve starting up and carrying out projects. These occupations can involve leading people and making many decisions. They sometimes require risk taking and often deal with business. **Work Values**—Supervision, Technical; Pleasant Co-workers; Good Working Conditions; Compensation. **Skills**—None met the criteria. **Abilities**—*Cognitive:* Perceptual Speed; Memorization; Time Sharing; Selective Attention; Number Facility. *Psychomotor:* Wrist-Finger Speed; Response Orientation; Speed of Limb Movement; Reaction Time; Finger Dexterity. *Physical:* Dynamic Strength. *Sensory:* Auditory Attention; Peripheral Vision; Speech Recognition; Night Vision; Sound Localization. **General Work Activities**—*Information Input:* Identifying Objects, Actions, and Events; Getting Information; Monitoring Processes, Materials, or Surroundings. *Mental Process:* Processing Information; Judging Qualities of Things, Services, or Other People's Work; Evaluating Information Against Standards. *Work Output:* Handling and Moving Objects; Documenting or Recording Information; Performing General Physical Activities. *Interacting with Others:* Performing for or Working with the Public; Establishing and Maintaining Relationships; Communicating with Persons Outside Organization. **Physical Work Conditions**—Making Repetitive Motions; Indoors; Standing; Walking or Running; Sitting. **Other Job Characteristics**—Importance of Being Exact or Accurate; Importance of Repeating Same Tasks; Consequence of Error.

Experience—Job Zone 2. Some previous work-related skill, knowledge, or experience may be helpful, but usually is not needed. **Job Preparation:** SVP 4.0 to less than 6.0—six months to less than two years. **Knowledge**—Sales and Marketing; Customer and Personal Service; Law and Government; Psychology; Foreign Language. **Instructional Programs**—No data available.

Related DOT Jobs—343.467-010 Cardroom Attendant I; 343.467-022 Keno Writer.

39-3019.99 Gaming Service Workers, All Other

- Education/Training Required: No data available.
- Employed: No data available.
- Annual Earnings: No data available.
- Growth: 31.1%
- Annual Job Openings: 7,000

All Gaming Service Workers not listed separately.

No task data available.

GOE INFORMATION—Interest Area: 11. Recreation, Travel, and Other Personal Services. **Work Group:** 11.02. Recreational Services. **Note:** The Department of Labor has not collected some data for this job, so it has fewer details than the other descriptions.

Instructional Programs—No data available.

Related DOT Jobs—343.367-010 Card Player.

39-3021.00 Motion Picture Projectionists

- Education/Training Required: Short-term on-the-job training
- Employed: 11,110
- Annual Earnings: $16,310
- Growth: −27.0%
- Annual Job Openings: 2,000

Set up and operate motion picture projection and related sound reproduction equipment.

Insert film into top magazine reel or thread film through a series of sprockets and guide rollers, attaching the end to a take-up reel. Inspect movie films to ensure that they are complete and in good condition. Inspect projection equipment prior to operation in order to ensure proper working order. Install and connect auxiliary equipment, such as microphones, amplifiers, disc playback machines, and lights. Monitor operations to ensure that standards for sound and image projection quality are met. Observe projector operation in order to anticipate need to transfer operations from one projector to another. Operate equipment in order to show films in a number of theaters simultaneously. Perform minor repairs such as replacing worn sprockets or notify maintenance personnel of the need for major repairs. Perform regular maintenance tasks such as rotating or replacing xenon bulbs, cleaning lenses, lubricating machinery, and keeping electrical contacts clean and tight. Remove film splicing in order to prepare films for shipment after showings and return films to their sources. Splice and rewind film onto reels automatically or by hand to repair faulty or broken sections of film. Remove full take-up reels and run film through rewinding machines to rewind projected films so they may be shown again. Set up and adjust picture projectors and screens to achieve proper size, illumination, and focus of images and proper volume and tone of sound. Splice separate film reels, advertisements, and movie trailers together to form a feature-length presentation on one continuous reel. Start projectors and open shutters to project images onto screens. Coordinate equipment operation with presentation of supplemental material, such as music, oral commentaries, or sound effects. Open and close facilities according to rules and schedules. Operate special-effects equipment, such as stereopticons, to project pictures onto screens. Prepare film inspection reports, attendance sheets, and log-books. Project motion pictures onto back screens for inclusion in scenes within film or stage productions. Set up and inspect curtain and screen controls.

GOE INFORMATION—Interest Area: 11. Recreation, Travel, and Other Personal Services. **Work Group:** 11.02. Recreational Services. **Personality Type**—Realistic. Realistic occupations frequently involve work activities that include practical, hands-on problems and solutions. They often deal with plants, animals, and real-world materials like wood, tools, and machinery. Many of the occupations require working outside and do not involve a lot of paperwork or working closely with others. **Work Values**—Independence; Good Working Conditions; Moral Values; Supervision, Technical; Supervision, Human Relations. **Skills**—Installation; Repairing; Operation Monitoring; Operation and Control. **Abilities**—*Cognitive:* Selective Attention. *Psychomotor:* Rate Control; Arm-Hand Steadiness; Response Orientation; Control Precision; Reaction Time. *Physical:* None met the criteria. *Sensory:* Hearing Sensitivity; Sound Localization; Night Vision; Auditory Attention; Visual Color Discrimination. **General Work Activities**—*Information Input:* Identifying Objects, Actions, and Events; Inspecting Equipment, Structures, or Materials; Estimating Needed Characteristics. *Mental Process:* Updating and Using Relevant Knowledge; Organizing, Planning, and Prioritizing; Analyzing Data or Information. *Work Output:* Handling and Moving Objects; Controlling Machines and Processes; Repairing and Maintaining Mechanical Equipment. *Interacting with Others:* Communicating with Other Workers; Establishing and Maintaining Relationships; Performing for or Working with the Public. **Physical Work Conditions**—Distracting Sounds and Noise Levels; Extremely Bright or Inadequate Lighting; Sitting; Indoors; Making Repetitive Motions. **Other Job Characteristics**—Pace Determined by Speed of Equipment; Degree of Automation; Importance of Repeating Same Tasks.

Experience—Job Zone 2. Some previous work-related skill, knowledge, or experience may be helpful, but usually is not needed. **Job Preparation:** SVP 4.0 to less than 6.0–six months to less than two years. **Knowledge**—Communications and Media; Fine Arts; Telecommunications; Computers and Electronics. **Instructional Programs**—No data available.

Related DOT Jobs—960.362-010 Motion-Picture Projectionist; 960.382-010 Audiovisual Technician.

39-3031.00 Ushers, Lobby Attendants, and Ticket Takers

- Education/Training Required: Short-term on-the-job training
- Employed: 111,941
- Annual Earnings: $14,100
- Growth: 11.0%
- Annual Job Openings: 26,000

Assist patrons at entertainment events by performing duties such as collecting admission tickets and passes from patrons, assisting in finding seats, searching for lost articles, and locating such facilities as rest rooms and telephones.

Assist patrons in finding seats, lighting the way with flashlights if necessary. Count and record number of tickets collected. Direct patrons to rest rooms, concession stands, and telephones. Distribute programs to patrons. Examine tickets or passes to verify authenticity, using criteria such as color and date issued. Give door checks to patrons who are temporarily leaving establishments. Greet patrons attending entertainment events. Provide assistance with patrons' special needs, such as helping those with wheelchairs. Refuse admittance to undesirable persons or persons without tickets or passes. Search for lost articles or for parents of lost children. Sell and collect admission tickets and passes from patrons at entertainment events. Settle seating disputes and help solve other customer concerns. Verify credentials of patrons desiring entrance into press box and permit only authorized persons to enter. Guide patrons to exits or provide other instructions or assistance in case of emergency. Maintain order and ensure adherence to safety rules. Operate refreshment stands during intermission or obtain refreshments for press box patrons during performances. Page individuals wanted at the box office. Work with others to change advertising displays. Manage informational kiosk and display of event signs and posters. Manage inventory and sale of artist merchandise. Schedule and manage volunteer usher corps.

GOE INFORMATION—Interest Area: 11. Recreation, Travel, and Other Personal Services. **Work Group:** 11.02. Recreational Services. **Personality Type**—Social. Social occupations frequently involve working with, communicating with, and teaching people. These occupations often involve helping or providing service to others. **Work Values**—Social Service; Pleasant Co-workers; Supervision, Technical; Good Working Conditions. **Skills**—None met the criteria. **Abilities**—*Cognitive:* Spatial Orientation. *Psychomotor:* None met the criteria. *Physical:* None met the criteria. *Sensory:* Night Vision. **General Work Activities**—*Information Input:* Getting Information; Identifying Objects, Actions, and Events; Monitoring Processes, Materials, or Surroundings. *Mental Process:* Processing Information; Making Decisions and Solving Problems; Evaluating Information Against Standards. *Work Output:* Performing General Physical Activities; Handling and Moving Objects; Documenting or Recording Information. *Interacting with Others:* Performing for or Working with the Public; Establishing and Maintaining Relationships; Assisting and Caring for Others. **Physical Work Conditions**—Standing; Walking or Running; Bending or Twisting the Body; Disease or Infections; Indoors. **Other Job Characteristics**—Importance of Repeating Same Tasks; Pace Determined by Speed of Equipment; Degree of Automation.

Experience—Job Zone 1. No previous work-related skill, knowledge, or experience is needed. **Job Preparation:** SVP below 4.0—less than six months. **Knowledge**—Customer and Personal Service; Sales and Marketing; Foreign Language; Psychology; Telecommunications. **Instructional Programs**—No data available.

Related DOT Jobs—344.667-010 Ticket Taker; 344.677-010 Press-Box Custodian; 344.677-014 Usher; 349.673-010 Drive-in Theater Attendant; 349.677-018 Children's Attendant.

39-3091.00 Amusement and Recreation Attendants

- **Education/Training Required: Short-term on-the-job training**
- **Employed: 196,794**
- **Annual Earnings: $14,600**
- **Growth: 32.4%**
- **Annual Job Openings: 62,000**

Perform variety of attending duties at amusement or recreation facility. May schedule use of recreation facilities, maintain and provide equipment to participants of sporting events or recreational pursuits, or operate amusement concessions and rides.

Operate machines to clean, smooth, and prepare the ice surfaces of rinks for activities such as skating, hockey, and curling. Provide caddying and other services to golfers. Announce and describe amusement park attractions to patrons in order to entice customers to games and other entertainment. Tend amusement booths in parks, carnivals, or stadiums, performing duties such as conducting games, photographing patrons, and awarding prizes. Direct patrons to rides, seats, or attractions. Fasten safety devices for patrons or provide them with directions for fastening devices. Maintain inventories of equipment, storing and retrieving items and assembling and disassembling equipment as necessary. Monitor activities to ensure adherence to rules and safety procedures and arrange for the removal of unruly patrons. Operate, drive, or explain the use of mechanical riding devices or other automatic equipment in amusement parks, carnivals, or recreation areas. Provide assistance to patrons entering or exiting amusement rides, boats, or ski lifts or mounting or dismounting animals. Provide information about facilities, entertainment options, and rules and regulations. Rent, sell, or issue sporting equipment and supplies such as bowling shoes, golf balls, swimming suits, and beach chairs. Schedule the use of recreation facilities such as golf courses, tennis courts, bowling alleys, and softball diamonds. Sell tickets and collect fees from customers. Verify, collect, or punch tickets before admitting patrons to venues such as amusement parks and rides. Clean sporting equipment, vehicles, rides, booths, facilities, and grounds. Inspect equipment to detect wear and damage and perform minor repairs, adjustments, and maintenance tasks such as oiling parts. Keep informed of shut-down and emergency evacuation procedures. Operate and demonstrate the use of boats, such as rowboats, canoes, and motorboats. Record details of attendance, sales, receipts, reservations, and repair activities. Sell and serve refreshments to customers. Tend animals, performing such tasks as harnessing, saddling, feeding, watering, and grooming; drive horse-drawn vehicles for entertainment or advertising purposes.

GOE INFORMATION—Interest Area: 11. Recreation, Travel, and Other Personal Services. **Work Group:** 11.02. Recreational Services. **Personality Type**—Realistic. Realistic occupations frequently involve work activities that include practical, hands-on problems and solutions. They often deal with plants, animals, and real-world materials like wood, tools, and machinery. Many of the occupations require working outside and do not involve a lot of paperwork or working closely with others. **Work Values**—Social Service; Pleasant Co-workers; Supervision, Technical; Moral Values; Variety. **Skills**—Repairing; Operation and Control; Operation Monitoring. **Abilities**—*Cognitive:* Spatial Orientation; Perceptual Speed; Time Sharing; Oral Expression; Memorization. *Psychomotor:* Rate Control; Reaction Time; Response Orientation; Control Precision; Multilimb Coordination. *Physical:* Static Strength; Dynamic Strength; Gross Body Coordination; Extent Flexibility; Gross Body Equilibrium. *Sensory:* Peripheral Vision; Night Vision; Speech Recognition; Auditory Attention; Hearing Sensitivity. **General Work Activities**—*Information Input:* Monitoring Processes, Materials, or Surroundings; Inspecting Equipment, Structures, or Materials; Identifying Objects, Actions, and Events. *Mental Process:* Scheduling Work and Activities; Evaluating Information Against Standards; Processing Information. *Work Output:* Handling and Moving Objects; Performing General Physical Activities; Controlling Machines and Processes. *Interacting with Others:* Performing for or Working with the Public; Establishing and Maintaining Relationships; Communicating with Persons Outside Organization. **Physical Work Conditions**—Outdoors; Very Hot or Cold; Walking or Running; Distracting Sounds and Noise Levels; Extremely Bright or Inadequate Lighting. **Other Job Characteristics**—Degree of Automation; Pace Determined by Speed of Equipment; Importance of Repeating Same Tasks.

Experience—Job Zone 1. No previous work-related skill, knowledge, or experience is needed. **Job Preparation:** SVP below 4.0—less than six months. **Knowledge**—Customer and Personal Service; Sales and Marketing; Mechanical; Public Safety and Security; Psychology. **Instructional Programs**—No data available.

Related DOT Jobs—195.367-030 Recreation Aide; 340.367-010 Desk Clerk, Bowling Floor; 340.477-010 Racker; 341.367-010 Recreation-Facility Attendant; 341.464-010 Skate-Shop Attendant; 341.665-010 Ski-Tow Operator; 341.677-010 Caddie; 341.683-010 Golf-Range Attendant; 342.357-010 Weight Guesser; 342.657-010 Barker; 342.657-014 Game Attendant; 342.663-010 Ride Operator; 342.665-010 Fun-House Operator; 342.667-

010 Wharf Attendant; 342.667-014 Attendant, Arcade; 342.677-010 Ride Attendant; 343.467-014 Floor Attendant; 343.577-010 Cardroom Attendant II; 349.477-010 Jinrikisha Driver; 349.664-010 Amusement Park Worker; others.

39-3092.00 Costume Attendants

- **Education/Training Required: Moderate-term on-the-job training**
- **Employed: No data available.**
- **Annual Earnings: $23,570**
- **Growth: 19.1%**
- **Annual Job Openings: 8,000**

Select, fit, and take care of costumes for cast members; aid entertainers.

Arrange costumes in order of use to facilitate quick-change procedures for performances. Assign lockers to employees and maintain locker rooms, dressing rooms, wig rooms, and costume storage and laundry areas. Care for non-clothing items such as flags, table skirts, and draperies. Check the appearance of costumes on stage and under lights in order to determine whether desired effects are being achieved. Clean and press costumes before and after performances and perform any minor repairs. Collaborate with production designers, costume designers, and other production staff in order to discuss and execute costume design details. Create worksheets for dressing lists, show notes, and costume checks. Distribute costumes and related equipment and keep records of item status. Examine costume fit on cast members and sketch or write notes for alterations. Inventory stock in order to determine types and conditions of available costuming. Monitor, maintain, and secure inventories of costumes, wigs, and makeup, providing keys or access to assigned directors, costume designers, and wardrobe mistresses/masters. Provide assistance to cast members in wearing costumes or assign cast dressers to assist specific cast members with costume changes. Return borrowed or rented items when productions are complete and return other items to storage. Design and construct costumes or send them to tailors for construction, major repairs, or alterations. Direct the work of wardrobe crews during dress rehearsals and performances. Participate in the hiring, training, scheduling, and supervision of alteration workers. Provide managers with budget recommendations and take responsibility for budgetary line items related to costumes, storage, and makeup needs. Purchase, rent, or requisition costumes and other wardrobe necessities. Recommend vendors and monitor their work. Review scripts or other production information in order to determine a story's locale and period, as well as the number of characters and required costumes. Study books, pictures, and examples of period clothing in order to determine styles worn during specific periods in history.

GOE INFORMATION—Interest Area: 01. Arts, Entertainment, and Media. **Work Group:** 01.09. Modeling and Personal Appearance. **Personality Type**—Artistic. Artistic occupations frequently involve working with forms, designs, and patterns. They often require self-expression, and the work can be done without following a clear set of rules. **Work Values**—Creativity; Social Service; Autonomy; Variety; Responsibility. **Skills**—None met the criteria. **Abilities**—*Cognitive:* Originality; Category Flexibility; Fluency of Ideas; Selective Attention; Visualization. *Psychomotor:* Arm-Hand Steadiness; Wrist-Finger Speed; Finger Dexterity; Speed of Limb Movement; Control Precision. *Physical:* Dynamic Flexibility; Extent Flexibility; Dynamic Strength; Gross Body Equilibrium; Gross Body Coordination. *Sensory:* Visual Color Discrimination; Far Vision; Night Vision; Auditory Attention; Glare Sensitivity. **General Work Activities**—*Information Input:* Getting Information; Identifying Objects, Actions, and Events; Inspecting Equipment, Structures, or Materials.

Mental Process: Thinking Creatively; Organizing, Planning, and Prioritizing; Analyzing Data or Information. *Work Output:* Handling and Moving Objects; Performing General Physical Activities; Controlling Machines and Processes. *Interacting with Others:* Monitoring and Controlling Resources; Establishing and Maintaining Relationships; Communicating with Other Workers. **Physical Work Conditions**—Indoors; Kneeling, Crouching, or Crawling; Standing; Using Hands on Objects, Tools, or Controls. **Other Job Characteristics**—Consequence of Error; Degree of Automation; Importance of Being Exact or Accurate.

Experience—Job Zone 4. A minimum of two to four years of work-related skill, knowledge, or experience is needed. **Job Preparation:** SVP 7.0 to less than 8.0—two years to less than 10 years. **Knowledge**—Fine Arts; Design; Geography; History and Archeology; Sociology and Anthropology. **Instructional Programs**—No data available.

Related DOT Jobs—346.261-010 Costumer; 346.361-010 Wardrobe Supervisor.

39-3093.00 Locker Room, Coatroom, and Dressing Room Attendants

- **Education/Training Required: Short-term on-the-job training**
- **Employed: No data available.**
- **Annual Earnings: $16,430**
- **Growth: 19.1%**
- **Annual Job Openings: 8,000**

Provide personal items to patrons or customers in locker rooms, dressing rooms, or coatrooms.

Answer customer inquiries and explain cost, availability, policies, and procedures of facilities. Assign dressing room facilities, locker space, or clothing containers to patrons of athletic or bathing establishments. Check supplies to ensure adequate availability and order new supplies when necessary. Collect soiled linen or clothing for laundering. Issue gym clothes, uniforms, towels, athletic equipment, and special athletic apparel. Monitor patrons' facility use in order to ensure that rules and regulations are followed and safety and order are maintained. Operate controls that regulate temperatures or room environments. Provide towels and sheets to clients in public baths, steam rooms, and rest rooms. Store personal possessions for patrons, issue claim checks for articles stored, and return articles on receipt of checks. Activate emergency action plans and administer first aid as necessary. Bathe or massage customers in tubs or steam rooms, using water, brushes, mitts, sponges, and towels. Clean and polish footwear, using brushes, sponges, cleaning fluid, polishes, waxes, liquid or sole dressing, and daubers. Maintain a lost-and-found collection. Maintain inventories of clothing or uniforms, accessories, equipment, and/or linens. Operate washing machines and dryers in order to clean soiled apparel and towels. Procure beverages, food, and other items as requested. Provide assistance to patrons by performing duties such as opening doors and carrying bags. Provide or arrange for services such as clothes pressing, cleaning, and repair. Refer guest problems or complaints to supervisors. Report and document safety hazards, potentially hazardous conditions, and unsafe practices and procedures. Set up various apparatus or athletic equipment. Stencil identifying information on equipment. Attend to needs of athletic teams in clubhouses.

GOE INFORMATION—Interest Area: 11. Recreation, Travel, and Other Personal Services. **Work Group:** 11.07. Cleaning and Building Services. **Personality Type**—Social. Social occupations frequently involve working with, communicating with, and teaching people. These occupations often involve helping or providing service to others. **Work Values**—Social Service; Good Working Conditions; Variety; Pleasant Co-workers.

Skills—Service Orientation; Speaking; Active Listening. **Abilities**—*Cognitive:* Oral Expression; Time Sharing; Memorization; Fluency of Ideas; Spatial Orientation. *Psychomotor:* Reaction Time; Response Orientation; Rate Control; Multilimb Coordination. *Physical:* Gross Body Coordination; Stamina; Dynamic Strength; Gross Body Equilibrium; Extent Flexibility. *Sensory:* Auditory Attention; Speech Recognition; Night Vision; Glare Sensitivity; Speech Clarity. **General Work Activities**—*Information Input:* Getting Information; Identifying Objects, Actions, and Events; Inspecting Equipment, Structures, or Materials. *Mental Process:* Judging Qualities of Things, Services, or Other People's Work; Scheduling Work and Activities; Updating and Using Relevant Knowledge. *Work Output:* Performing General Physical Activities; Handling and Moving Objects; Documenting or Recording Information. *Interacting with Others:* Assisting and Caring for Others; Performing for or Working with the Public; Establishing and Maintaining Relationships. **Physical Work Conditions**—Walking or Running; Outdoors; Bending or Twisting the Body; Very Hot or Cold; Standing. **Other Job Characteristics**—Importance of Repeating Same Tasks; Pace Determined by Speed of Equipment; Degree of Automation.

Experience—Job Zone 1. No previous work-related skill, knowledge, or experience is needed. **Job Preparation:** SVP below 4.0—less than six months. **Knowledge**—Customer and Personal Service; Sales and Marketing; Biology; Economics and Accounting; Therapy and Counseling. **Instructional Programs**—No data available.

Related DOT Jobs—324.577-010 Room-Service Clerk; 324.677-014 Doorkeeper; 329.467-010 Attendant, Lodging Facilities; 329.677-010 Porter, Marina; 334.374-010 Masseur/Masseuse; 334.677-010 Rubber; 358.677-010 Checkroom Attendant; 358.677-014 Locker-Room Attendant; 359.367-014 Weight-Reduction Specialist; 359.567-010 Reducing-Salon Attendant; 359.567-014 Tanning Salon Attendant; 366.677-010 Shoe Shiner.

39-3099.99 Entertainment Attendants and Related Workers, All Other

- Education/Training Required: No data available.
- Employed: No data available.
- Annual Earnings: No data available.
- Growth: 22.5%
- Annual Job Openings: 27,000

All entertainment attendants and related workers not listed separately.

No task data available.

GOE INFORMATION—**Interest Area:** 11. Recreation, Travel, and Other Personal Services. **Work Group:** 11.02. Recreational Services. **Note:** The Department of Labor has not collected some data for this job, so it has fewer details than the other descriptions.

Instructional Programs—No data available.

Related DOT Jobs—No related DOT jobs.

39-4000 Funeral Service Workers

39-4011.00 Embalmers

- Education/Training Required: Postsecondary vocational training
- Employed: 7,180
- Annual Earnings: $33,030
- Growth: –0.6%
- Annual Job Openings: 1,000

Prepare bodies for interment in conformity with legal requirements.

Apply cosmetics to impart lifelike appearance to the deceased. Attach trocar to pump tube, start pump, and repeat probing to force embalming fluid into organs. Close incisions, using needles and sutures. Conform to laws of health and sanitation and ensure that legal requirements concerning embalming are met. Dress bodies and place them in caskets. Incise stomach and abdominal walls and probe internal organs, using trocar, to withdraw blood and waste matter from organs. Insert convex celluloid or cotton between eyeballs and eyelids to prevent slipping and sinking of eyelids. Join lips, using needles and thread or wire. Make incisions in arms or thighs and drain blood from circulatory system and replace it with embalming fluid, using pump. Pack body orifices with cotton saturated with embalming fluid to prevent escape of gases or waste matter. Press diaphragm to evacuate air from lungs. Reshape or reconstruct disfigured or maimed bodies when necessary, using derma-surgery techniques and materials such as clay, cotton, plaster of paris, and wax. Wash and dry bodies, using germicidal soap and towels or hot air dryers. Arrange for transporting the deceased to another state for interment. Assist coroners at death scenes or at autopsies, file police reports, and testify at inquests or in court if employed by a coroner. Maintain records such as itemized lists of clothing or valuables delivered with body and names of persons embalmed. Perform special procedures necessary for remains that are to be transported to other states or overseas or where death was caused by infectious disease. Supervise funeral attendants and other funeral home staff. Arrange funeral home equipment and perform general maintenance. Assist with placing caskets in hearses and organize cemetery processions. Conduct interviews to arrange for the preparation of obituary notices, to assist with the selection of caskets or urns, and to determine the location and time of burials or cremations. Direct casket and floral display placement and arrange guest seating. Perform the duties of funeral directors, including coordinating funeral activities. Serve as pallbearers, attend visiting rooms, and provide other assistance to the bereaved.

GOE INFORMATION—**Interest Area:** 11. Recreation, Travel, and Other Personal Services. **Work Group:** 11.08. Other Personal Services. **Personality Type**—Realistic. Realistic occupations frequently involve work activities that include practical, hands-on problems and solutions. They often deal with plants, animals, and real-world materials like wood, tools, and machinery. Many of the occupations require working outside and do not involve a lot of paperwork or working closely with others. **Work Values**—Independence; Social Service; Autonomy; Security; Supervision, Technical. **Skills**—Equipment Selection. **Abilities**—*Cognitive:* None met the criteria. *Psychomotor:* Finger Dexterity; Arm-Hand Steadiness; Manual Dexterity; Multilimb Coordination; Wrist-Finger Speed. *Physical:* Static Strength; Extent Flexibility; Dynamic Flexibility; Dynamic Strength; Explosive Strength. *Sensory:* Visual Color Discrimination; Glare Sensitivity; Night Vision; Depth Perception; Hearing Sensitivity. **General Work Activities**—*Information Input:* Getting Information; Identifying Objects, Actions, and Events; Monitoring Processes, Materials, or Surroundings. *Mental Process:* Organizing, Planning, and Prioritizing; Updating and Using Relevant Knowledge; Analyzing Data or Information. *Work Output:* Handling and Moving Objects; Performing General Physical Activities; Documenting or Recording Information. *Interacting with Others:* Assisting and Caring for Others; Communicating with Persons Outside Organization; Performing for or Working with the Public. **Physical Work Conditions**—Contaminants; Common Protective or Safety Attire; Hazardous Conditions; Disease or Infections; Using Hands on Objects, Tools, or Controls. **Other Job Characteristics**—Pace Determined by Speed of Equipment; Degree of Automation; Consequence of Error.

Experience—Job Zone 4. A minimum of two to four years of work-related skill, knowledge, or experience is needed. **Job Preparation:** SVP

7.0 to less than 8.0—two years to less than 10 years. **Knowledge**—Biology; Chemistry; Customer and Personal Service; Medicine and Dentistry; Law and Government. **Instructional Programs**—Funeral Service and Mortuary Science, General; Mortuary Science and Embalming/Embalmer.

Related DOT Jobs—338.371-010 Embalmer Apprentice; 338.371-014 Embalmer.

39-4021.00 Funeral Attendants

- **Education/Training Required:** Short-term on-the-job training
- **Employed:** 26,139
- **Annual Earnings:** $17,630
- **Growth:** 17.8%
- **Annual Job Openings:** 5,000

Perform variety of tasks during funeral, such as placing casket in parlor or chapel prior to service; arranging floral offerings or lights around casket; directing or escorting mourners; closing casket; and issuing and storing funeral equipment.

Act as pallbearers. Arrange floral offerings or lights around caskets. Carry flowers to hearses or limousines for transportation to places of interment. Clean and drive funeral vehicles such as cars or hearses in funeral processions. Direct or escort mourners to parlors or chapels in which wakes or funerals are being held. Greet people at the funeral home. Perform a variety of tasks during funerals to assist funeral directors and to ensure that services run smoothly and as planned. Place caskets in parlors or chapels prior to wakes or funerals. Assist with cremations and with the processing and packaging of cremated remains. Close caskets at appropriate point in services. Issue and store funeral equipment. Obtain burial permits and register deaths. Offer assistance to mourners as they enter or exit limousines. Transfer the deceased to funeral homes. Clean funeral parlors and chapels. Perform general maintenance duties for funeral homes. Provide advice to mourners on how to make charitable donations in honor of the deceased.

GOE INFORMATION—Interest Area: 11. Recreation, Travel, and Other Personal Services. **Work Group:** 11.08. Other Personal Services. **Personality Type**—Social. Social occupations frequently involve working with, communicating with, and teaching people. These occupations often involve helping or providing service to others. **Work Values**—Social Service; Security; Moral Values. **Skills**—Social Perceptiveness. **Abilities**—*Cognitive:* None met the criteria. *Psychomotor:* Rate Control; Speed of Limb Movement. *Physical:* Static Strength; Dynamic Strength; Gross Body Coordination; Extent Flexibility; Stamina. *Sensory:* Glare Sensitivity; Peripheral Vision; Night Vision; Speech Clarity; Depth Perception. **General Work Activities**—*Information Input:* Getting Information; Monitoring Processes, Materials, or Surroundings; Estimating Needed Characteristics. *Mental Process:* Thinking Creatively; Making Decisions and Solving Problems; Scheduling Work and Activities. *Work Output:* Handling and Moving Objects; Performing General Physical Activities; Operating Vehicles or Equipment. *Interacting with Others:* Assisting and Caring for Others; Communicating with Persons Outside Organization; Establishing and Maintaining Relationships. **Physical Work Conditions**—Walking or Running; Outdoors; Disease or Infections; Standing; Bending or Twisting the Body. **Other Job Characteristics**—Importance of Repeating Same Tasks; Pace Determined by Speed of Equipment; Consequence of Error.

Experience—Job Zone 1. No previous work-related skill, knowledge, or experience is needed. **Job Preparation:** SVP below 4.0—less than six months. **Knowledge**—Customer and Personal Service; Psychology; Soci-

ology and Anthropology; Therapy and Counseling. **Instructional Programs**—Funeral Service and Mortuary Science, General.

Related DOT Jobs—359.677-014 Funeral Attendant; 359.687-010 Pallbearer.

39-5000 Personal Appearance Workers

39-5011.00 Barbers

- **Education/Training Required:** Postsecondary vocational training
- **Employed:** 72,727
- **Annual Earnings:** $18,500
- **Growth:** −11.5%
- **Annual Job Openings:** 3,000

Provide barbering services, such as cutting, trimming, shampooing, and styling hair; trimming beards; or giving shaves.

Apply lather and shave beards or neck and temple hair contours, using razors. Clean and sterilize scissors, combs, clippers, and other instruments. Clean work stations and sweep floors. Curl, color, or straighten hair, using special chemical solutions and equipment. Cut and trim hair according to clients' instructions and/or current hairstyles, using clippers, combs, hand-held blow driers, and scissors. Drape and pin protective cloths around customers' shoulders. Question patrons regarding desired services and haircut styles. Record services provided on cashiers' tickets or receive payment from customers. Shampoo hair. Shape and trim beards and moustaches, using scissors. Stay informed of the latest styles and hair care techniques. Suggest treatments to alleviate hair problems. Keep card files on clientele, recording notes of work done, products used, and fees charged after each visit. Measure, fit, and groom hairpieces. Order supplies. Perform clerical and administrative duties such as keeping records, paying bills, and hiring and supervising personnel. Provide face, neck, and scalp massages. Recommend and sell lotions, tonics, or other cosmetic supplies. Identify hair problems, using microscopes and testing devices or by sending clients' hair samples out to independent laboratories for analysis. Provide skin care and nail treatments.

GOE INFORMATION—Interest Area: 11. Recreation, Travel, and Other Personal Services. **Work Group:** 11.04. Barber and Beauty Services. **Personality Type**—Realistic. Realistic occupations frequently involve work activities that include practical, hands-on problems and solutions. They often deal with plants, animals, and real-world materials like wood, tools, and machinery. Many of the occupations require working outside and do not involve a lot of paperwork or working closely with others. **Work Values**—Social Service; Autonomy; Recognition; Creativity; Moral Values. **Skills**—None met the criteria. **Abilities**—*Cognitive:* Visualization; Selective Attention. *Psychomotor:* Finger Dexterity; Arm-Hand Steadiness; Manual Dexterity; Wrist-Finger Speed; Multilimb Coordination. *Physical:* Extent Flexibility; Gross Body Coordination; Gross Body Equilibrium; Trunk Strength. *Sensory:* Visual Color Discrimination; Speech Recognition. **General Work Activities**—*Information Input:* Getting Information; Monitoring Processes, Materials, or Surroundings; Identifying Objects, Actions, and Events. *Mental Process:* Thinking Creatively; Judging Qualities of Things, Services, or Other People's Work; Organizing, Planning, and Prioritizing. *Work Output:* Handling and Moving Objects; Performing General Physical Activities; Controlling Machines and Processes. *Interacting with Others:* Establishing and Maintaining Relationships; Performing for or Working with the Public; Monitoring and Controlling Resources. **Physical Work Conditions**—Making Repetitive Motions; Minor Burns, Cuts, Bites, or Stings; Standing; Indoors; Using Hands on Objects, Tools, or Controls. **Other Job Characteristics**—Importance of Repeating Same Tasks; Pace Determined by Speed of Equipment; Degree of Automation.

Experience—Job Zone 3. Previous work-related skill, knowledge, or experience is required. **Job Preparation:** SVP 6.0 to less than 7.0—more than one year and less than four years. **Knowledge**—Customer and Personal Service; Sales and Marketing; Economics and Accounting; Biology. **Instructional Programs**—Barbering/Barber; Cosmetology, Barber/Styling, and Nail Instructor; Hair Styling/Stylist and Hair Design; Salon/Beauty Salon Management/Manager.

Related DOT Jobs—330.371-010 Barber; 330.371-014 Barber Apprentice.

39-5012.00 Hairdressers, Hairstylists, and Cosmetologists

- Education/Training Required: Postsecondary vocational training
- Employed: 636,112
- Annual Earnings: $18,260
- Growth: 13.0%
- Annual Job Openings: 78,000

Provide beauty services, such as shampooing, cutting, coloring, and styling hair and massaging and treating scalp. May also apply makeup, dress wigs, perform hair removal, and provide nail and skin care services.

Keep work stations clean and sanitize tools such as scissors and combs. Cut, trim, and shape hair or hairpieces, based on customers' instructions, hair type, and facial features, using clippers, scissors, trimmers and razors. Analyze patrons' hair and other physical features to determine and recommend beauty treatment or suggest hairstyles. Schedule client appointments. Bleach, dye, or tint hair, using applicator or brush. Update and maintain customer information records, such as beauty services provided. Shampoo, rinse, condition, and dry hair and scalp or hairpieces with water, liquid soap, or other solutions. Operate cash registers to receive payments from patrons. Demonstrate and sell hair care products and cosmetics. Develop new styles and techniques. Apply water, setting, straightening, or waving solutions to hair and use curlers, rollers, hot combs, and curling irons to press and curl hair. Comb, brush, and spray hair or wigs to set style. Shape eyebrows and remove facial hair, using depilatory cream, tweezers, electrolysis, or wax. Administer therapeutic medication and advise patron to seek medical treatment for chronic or contagious scalp conditions. Massage and treat scalp for hygienic and remedial purposes, using hands, fingers, or vibrating equipment. Shave, trim, and shape beards and moustaches. Train or supervise other hairstylists, hairdressers, and assistants. Recommend and explain the use of cosmetics, lotions, and creams to soften and lubricate skin and enhance and restore natural appearance. Give facials to patrons, using special compounds such as lotions and creams. Clean, shape, and polish fingernails and toenails, using files and nail polish. Apply artificial fingernails. Attach wigs or hairpieces to model heads and dress wigs and hairpieces according to instructions, samples, sketches or photographs.

GOE INFORMATION—**Interest Area:** 11. Recreation, Travel, and Other Personal Services. **Work Group:** 11.04. Barber and Beauty Services. **Personality Type**—Enterprising. Enterprising occupations frequently involve starting up and carrying out projects. These occupations can involve leading people and making many decisions. They sometimes require risk taking and often deal with business. **Work Values**—Social Service; Cre-

ativity; Autonomy; Achievement; Recognition. **Skills**—Equipment Selection; Learning Strategies; Speaking; Social Perceptiveness; Time Management; Operations Analysis; Critical Thinking; Service Orientation. **Abilities**—*Cognitive:* Visualization; Originality; Fluency of Ideas; Time Sharing; Flexibility of Closure. *Psychomotor:* Arm-Hand Steadiness; Finger Dexterity; Manual Dexterity; Multilimb Coordination; Control Precision. *Physical:* Trunk Strength; Extent Flexibility; Dynamic Strength; Stamina. *Sensory:* Visual Color Discrimination; Speech Recognition; Far Vision; Auditory Attention; Near Vision. **General Work Activities**—*Information Input:* Getting Information; Identifying Objects, Actions, and Events; Monitoring Processes, Materials, or Surroundings. *Mental Process:* Thinking Creatively; Updating and Using Relevant Knowledge; Organizing, Planning, and Prioritizing. *Work Output:* Handling and Moving Objects; Performing General Physical Activities; Documenting or Recording Information. *Interacting with Others:* Performing for or Working with the Public; Providing Consultation and Advice to Others; Establishing and Maintaining Relationships. **Physical Work Conditions**—Standing; Using Hands on Objects, Tools, or Controls; Contaminants; Hazardous Conditions; Indoors. **Other Job Characteristics**—Importance of Repeating Same Tasks; Pace Determined by Speed of Equipment; Degree of Automation.

Experience—Job Zone 3. Previous work-related skill, knowledge, or experience is required. **Job Preparation:** SVP 6.0 to less than 7.0—more than one year and less than four years. **Knowledge**—Customer and Personal Service; Chemistry; Sales and Marketing; Education and Training; Administration and Management. **Instructional Programs**—Cosmetology and Related Personal Grooming Arts, Other; Cosmetology, Barber/Styling, and Nail Instructor; Cosmetology/Cosmetologist, General; Electrolysis/Electrology and Electrolysis Technician; Hair Styling/Stylist and Hair Design; Make-Up Artist/Specialist; Permanent Cosmetics/Makeup and Tattooing; Salon/Beauty Salon Management/Manager.

Related DOT Jobs—332.271-010 Cosmetologist; 332.271-014 Cosmetologist Apprentice; 332.271-018 Hair Stylist; 332.361-010 Wig Dresser; 339.361-010 Mortuary Beautician.

39-5091.00 Makeup Artists, Theatrical and Performance

- Education/Training Required: Postsecondary vocational training
- Employed: No data available.
- Annual Earnings: $30,240
- Growth: 11.4%
- Annual Job Openings: 27,000

Apply makeup to performers to reflect period, setting, and situation of their role.

Alter or maintain makeup during productions as necessary to compensate for lighting changes or to achieve continuity of effect. Analyze a script, noting events that affect each character's appearance, so that plans can be made for each scene. Apply makeup to enhance and/or alter the appearance of people appearing in productions such as movies. Assess performers' skin type in order to ensure that makeup will not cause breakouts or skin irritations. Attach prostheses to performers and apply makeup in order to create special features or effects such as scars, aging, or illness. Cleanse and tone the skin in order to prepare it for makeup application. Confer with stage or motion picture officials and performers in order to determine desired effects. Design rubber or plastic prostheses that can be used to change performers' appearances. Duplicate work precisely in order to replicate characters' appearances on a daily basis. Evaluate environmental characteristics such as venue size and lighting plans in order to determine makeup requirements. Examine sketches, photographs, and plaster models in order to obtain desired character image depiction. Provide performers with makeup removal assistance after performances have been completed. Requisition or acquire needed materials for special effects, including wigs, beards, and special cosmetics. Select desired makeup shades from stock or mix oil, grease, and coloring in order to achieve specific color effects. Study production information such as character descriptions, period settings, and situations in order to determine makeup requirements. Write makeup sheets and take photos in order to document specific looks and the products that were used to achieve the looks. Advise hairdressers on the hairstyles required for character parts. Create character drawings or models based upon independent research in order to augment period production files. Demonstrate products to clients and provide instruction in makeup application. Establish budgets and work within budgetary limits. Wash and reset wigs.

GOE INFORMATION—Interest Area: 01. Arts, Entertainment, and Media. **Work Group:** 01.09. Modeling and Personal Appearance. **Personality Type**—Artistic. Artistic occupations frequently involve working with forms, designs, and patterns. They often require self-expression, and the work can be done without following a clear set of rules. **Work Values**—Social Service; Creativity; Recognition; Ability Utilization; Autonomy. **Skills**—Equipment Selection. **Abilities**—*Cognitive:* Originality; Visualization; Fluency of Ideas; Information Ordering; Deductive Reasoning. *Psychomotor:* Arm-Hand Steadiness; Finger Dexterity; Manual Dexterity; Multilimb Coordination; Wrist-Finger Speed. *Physical:* Trunk Strength; Dynamic Flexibility; Dynamic Strength; Gross Body Coordination; Gross Body Equilibrium. *Sensory:* Visual Color Discrimination; Night Vision; Depth Perception; Glare Sensitivity; Near Vision. **General Work Activities**—*Information Input:* Getting Information; Identifying Objects, Actions, and Events; Monitoring Processes, Materials, or Surroundings. *Mental Process:* Thinking Creatively; Judging Qualities of Things, Services, or Other People's Work; Organizing, Planning, and Prioritizing. *Work Output:* Handling and Moving Objects; Drafting and Specifying Technical Devices; Performing General Physical Activities. *Interacting with Others:* Assisting and Caring for Others; Communicating with Other Workers; Establishing and Maintaining Relationships. **Physical Work Conditions**—Using Hands on Objects, Tools, or Controls; Contaminants; Indoors; Hazardous Conditions; Extremely Bright or Inadequate Lighting. **Other Job Characteristics**—Importance of Repeating Same Tasks; Importance of Being Exact or Accurate; Degree of Automation.

Experience—Job Zone 2. Some previous work-related skill, knowledge, or experience may be helpful, but usually is not needed. **Job Preparation:** SVP 4.0 to less than 6.0—six months to less than two years. **Knowledge**—Fine Arts; Sociology and Anthropology; Design; History and Archeology; Customer and Personal Service. **Instructional Programs**—Cosmetology/Cosmetologist, General; Make-Up Artist/Specialist; Permanent Cosmetics/Makeup and Tattooing.

Related DOT Jobs—333.071-010 Make-Up Artist; 333.271-010 Body-Make-Up Artist.

39-5092.00 *Manicurists and Pedicurists*

- **Education/Training Required: Postsecondary vocational training**
- **Employed:** 40,232
- **Annual Earnings:** $16,700
- **Growth:** 26.5%
- **Annual Job Openings:** 5,000

Clean and shape customers' fingernails and toenails. May polish or decorate nails.

Apply undercoat and clear or colored polish onto nails with brush. Attach paper forms to tips of customers' fingers to support and shape artificial nails. Brush powder and solvent onto nails and paper forms to maintain nail appearance and to extend nails and then remove forms and shape and smooth nail edges using rotary abrasive wheel. Clean and sanitize tools and work environment. Clean customers' nails in soapy water, using swabs, files, and orange sticks. Polish nails, using powdered polish and buffer. Remove previously applied nail polish, using liquid remover and swabs. Roughen surfaces of fingernails, using abrasive wheel. Shape and smooth ends of nails, using scissors, files, and emery boards. Soften nail cuticles with water and oil; push back cuticles, using cuticle knife; and trim cuticles, using scissors or nippers. Treat nails to repair or improve strength and resilience by wrapping or provide treatment to nail biters. Whiten underside of nails with white paste or pencil. Advise clients on nail care and use of products and colors. Assess the condition of clients' hands, remove dead skin from the hands, and massage them. Decorate clients' nails by piercing them or attaching ornaments or designs. Maintain supply inventories and records of client services. Promote and sell nail care products. Schedule client appointments and accept payments.

GOE INFORMATION—Interest Area: 11. Recreation, Travel, and Other Personal Services. **Work Group:** 11.04. Barber and Beauty Services. **Personality Type**—Enterprising. Enterprising occupations frequently involve starting up and carrying out projects. These occupations can involve leading people and making many decisions. They sometimes require risk taking and often deal with business. **Work Values**—Social Service; Autonomy; Moral Values; Independence; Good Working Conditions. **Skills**—None met the criteria. **Abilities**—*Cognitive:* None met the criteria. *Psychomotor:* Arm-Hand Steadiness; Finger Dexterity. *Physical:* None met the criteria. *Sensory:* Visual Color Discrimination; Glare Sensitivity; Hearing Sensitivity; Night Vision. **General Work Activities**—*Information Input:* Getting Information; Identifying Objects, Actions, and Events; Monitoring Processes, Materials, or Surroundings. *Mental Process:* Thinking Creatively; Judging Qualities of Things, Services, or Other People's Work; Scheduling Work and Activities. *Work Output:* Handling and Moving Objects; Performing General Physical Activities; Controlling Machines and Processes. *Interacting with Others:* Performing for or Working with the Public; Establishing and Maintaining Relationships; Assisting and Caring for Others. **Physical Work Conditions**—Sitting; Using Hands on Objects, Tools, or Controls; Hazardous Conditions; Indoors; Disease or Infections. **Other Job Characteristics**—Importance of Repeating Same Tasks; Importance of Being Exact or Accurate; Pace Determined by Speed of Equipment.

Experience—Job Zone 1. No previous work-related skill, knowledge, or experience is needed. **Job Preparation:** SVP below 4.0—less than six months. **Knowledge**—Customer and Personal Service; Chemistry; Sociology and Anthropology; Medicine and Dentistry; Sales and Marketing. **Instructional Programs**—Cosmetology/Cosmetologist, General; Nail Technician/Specialist and Manicurist.

Related DOT Jobs—331.674-010 Manicurist; 331.674-014 Fingernail Former.

39-5093.00 *Shampooers*

- **Education/Training Required: Short-term on-the-job training**
- **Employed:** 19,775
- **Annual Earnings:** $13,730
- **Growth:** 13.2%
- **Annual Job Openings:** 2,000

Shampoo and rinse customers' hair.

Massage, shampoo, and condition patron's hair and scalp to clean them and remove excess oil. Advise patrons with chronic or potentially contagious scalp conditions to seek medical treatment. Maintain treatment records. Treat scalp conditions and hair loss, using specialized lotions, shampoos, or equipment such as infrared lamps or vibrating equipment.

GOE INFORMATION—Interest Area: 11. Recreation, Travel, and Other Personal Services. **Work Group:** 11.04. Barber and Beauty Services. **Note:** The Department of Labor has not collected some data for this job, so it has fewer details than the other descriptions.

Instructional Programs—Hair Styling/Stylist and Hair Design.

Related DOT Jobs—332.271-010 Cosmetologist.

39-5094.00 Skin Care Specialists

- **Education/Training Required: Short-term on-the-job training**
- **Employed: 21,334**
- **Annual Earnings: $22,060**
- **Growth: 13.3%**
- **Annual Job Openings: 3,000**

Provide skin care treatments to face and body to enhance an individual's appearance.

Advise clients about colors and types of makeup and instruct them in makeup application techniques. Apply chemical peels in order to reduce fine lines and age spots. Cleanse clients' skin with water, creams, and/or lotions. Demonstrate how to clean and care for skin properly and recommend skin-care regimens. Determine which products or colors will improve clients' skin quality and appearance. Examine clients' skin, using magnifying lamps or visors when necessary, in order to evaluate skin condition and appearance. Keep records of client needs and preferences and the services provided. Perform simple extractions to remove blackheads. Remove body and facial hair by applying wax. Select and apply cosmetic products such as creams, lotions, and tonics. Sterilize equipment and clean work areas. Treat the facial skin to maintain and improve its appearance, using specialized techniques and products such as peels and masks. Collaborate with plastic surgeons and dermatologists in order to provide patients with preoperative and postoperative skin care. Give manicures and pedicures and apply artificial nails. Provide facial and body massages. Refer clients to medical personnel for treatment of serious skin problems. Sell makeup to clients. Tint eyelashes and eyebrows.

GOE INFORMATION—Interest Area: 11. Recreation, Travel, and Other Personal Services. **Work Group:** 11.04. Barber and Beauty Services. **Note:** The Department of Labor has not collected some data for this job, so it has fewer details than the other descriptions.

Instructional Programs—Cosmetology/Cosmetologist, General; Facial Treatment Specialist/Facialist.

Related DOT Jobs—No related DOT jobs.

39-6000 Transportation, Tourism, and Lodging Attendants

39-6011.00 Baggage Porters and Bellhops

- **Education/Training Required: Short-term on-the-job training**
- **Employed: 50,897**
- **Annual Earnings: $17,320**
- **Growth: 12.6%**
- **Annual Job Openings: 12,000**

Handle baggage for travelers at transportation terminals or for guests at hotels or similar establishments.

Assist physically challenged travelers and other guests with special needs. Complete baggage insurance forms. Greet incoming guests and escort them to their rooms. Receive and mark baggage by completing and attaching claim checks. Transfer luggage, trunks, and packages to and from rooms, loading areas, vehicles, or transportation terminals by hand or using baggage carts. Act as part of the security team at transportation terminals, hotels, or similar establishments. Arrange for shipments of baggage, express mail, and parcels by providing weighing and billing services. Compute and complete charge slips for services rendered and maintain records. Deliver messages and room service orders; run errands for guests. Explain the operation of room features such as locks, ventilation systems, and televisions. Inspect guests' rooms to ensure that they are adequately stocked, orderly, and comfortable. Maintain clean lobbies or entrance areas for travelers or guests. Page guests in hotel lobbies, dining rooms, or other areas. Pick up and return items for laundry and valet service. Set up conference rooms, display tables, racks, or shelves and arrange merchandise displays for sales personnel. Supply guests or travelers with directions, travel information, and other information such as available services and points of interest. Transport guests about premises and local areas or arrange for transportation.

GOE INFORMATION—Interest Area: 11. Recreation, Travel, and Other Personal Services. **Work Group:** 11.03. Transportation and Lodging Services. **Personality Type**—Enterprising. Enterprising occupations frequently involve starting up and carrying out projects. These occupations can involve leading people and making many decisions. They sometimes require risk taking and often deal with business. **Work Values**—Social Service; Supervision, Technical; Independence; Pleasant Co-workers; Good Working Conditions. **Skills**—None met the criteria. **Abilities**—*Cognitive:* Spatial Orientation; Oral Expression. *Psychomotor:* None met the criteria. *Physical:* Static Strength; Stamina; Trunk Strength; Dynamic Strength; Gross Body Coordination. *Sensory:* None met the criteria. **General Work Activities**—*Information Input:* Inspecting Equipment, Structures, or Materials; Identifying Objects, Actions, and Events; Estimating Needed Characteristics. *Mental Process:* Processing Information; Updating and Using Relevant Knowledge; Evaluating Information Against Standards. *Work Output:* Handling and Moving Objects; Performing General Physical Activities; Controlling Machines and Processes. *Interacting with Others:* Assisting and Caring for Others; Performing for or Working with the Public; Communicating with Persons Outside Organization. **Physical Work Conditions**—Standing; Walking or Running; Outdoors; Using Hands on Objects, Tools, or Controls; Bending or Twisting the Body. **Other Job Characteristics**—Importance of Repeating Same Tasks; Importance of Being Exact or Accurate; Consequence of Error.

Experience—Job Zone 1. No previous work-related skill, knowledge, or experience is needed. **Job Preparation:** SVP below 4.0—less than six months. **Knowledge**—Customer and Personal Service; Geography; Sales and Marketing; Foreign Language; Sociology and Anthropology. **Instructional Programs**—No data available.

Related DOT Jobs—324.477-010 Porter, Baggage; 324.677-010 Bellhop; 357.477-010 Baggage Checker; 357.677-010 Porter.

39-6012.00 Concierges

- **Education/Training Required: Short-term on-the-job training**
- **Employed: 17,536**
- **Annual Earnings: $21,050**
- **Growth: 15.7%**
- **Annual Job Openings: 4,000**

Assist patrons at hotel, apartment, or office building with personal services. May take messages; arrange or give advice on transportation, business services or entertainment; or monitor guest requests for housekeeping and maintenance.

Arrange for the replacement of items lost by travelers. Carry out unusual requests such as searching for hard-to-find items and arranging for exotic services such as hot-air balloon rides. Make dining and other reservations for patrons and obtain tickets for events. Make travel arrangements for sightseeing and other tours. Pick up and deliver items or run errands for guests. Provide information about local features such as shopping, dining, nightlife, and recreational destinations. Receive, store, and deliver luggage and mail. Arrange for interpreters or translators when patrons require such services. Perform office duties on a temporary basis when needed. Plan special events, parties, and meetings, which may include booking musicians or celebrities to appear.

GOE INFORMATION—**Interest Area:** 11. Recreation, Travel, and Other Personal Services. **Work Group:** 11.03. Transportation and Lodging Services. **Note:** The Department of Labor has not collected some data for this job, so it has fewer details than the other descriptions.

Instructional Programs—No data available.

Related DOT Jobs—No related DOT jobs.

39-6021.00 Tour Guides and Escorts

- **Education/Training Required: Short-term on-the-job training**
- **Employed: No data available.**
- **Annual Earnings: $18,360**
- **Growth: 9.5%**
- **Annual Job Openings: 10,000**

Escort individuals or groups on sightseeing tours or through places of interest, such as industrial establishments, public buildings, and art galleries.

Arrange for the transportation of clients, equipment, and supplies, using horses, land vehicles, motorboats, and/or airplanes. Assemble and check the required supplies and equipment prior to departure. Collect fees and tickets from group members. Describe tour points of interest to group members and respond to questions. Distribute brochures, show audiovisual presentations, and explain establishment processes and operations at tour sites. Escort individuals or groups on cruises, on sightseeing tours, or through places of interest such as industrial establishments, public buildings, and art galleries. Greet and register visitors and issue any required identification badges and/or safety devices. Monitor visitors' activities in order to ensure compliance with establishment or tour regulations and safety practices. Plan rest stops and meals, preparing meals or teaching clients how to prepare meals on such trips as hunting expeditions. Provide directions and other pertinent information to visitors. Select travel routes and sites to be visited based on knowledge of specific areas. Carry equipment and luggage for visitors and provide errand service. Conduct educational activities for schoolchildren. Drive motor vehicles in order to transport visitors to establishments and tour site locations. Perform clerical duties such as filing, typing, operating switchboards, and routing mail and messages. Plan and conduct itineraries and activities on specialized trips such as mountain expeditions, rafting trips, hunting trips, fishing trips, photo safaris, nature study expeditions, and trail rides. Provide for physical safety of groups, performing such activities as providing first aid and directing emergency evacuations. Provide information about wildlife varieties and habitats as well as any relevant regulations, such as those pertaining to hunting and fishing. Research environmental conditions and clients' skill and ability levels in order to plan expeditions, instruction, and commentary that are appropriate. Secure any equipment required by a specific type of expedition, such as camping or climbing equipment. Solicit tour patronage and sell souvenirs. Teach skills, such as proper climbing methods, and demonstrate and advise on the use of equipment. Select and care for any animals required on an expedition, such as horses or dogs. Set up camp on overnight outdoors expeditions and prepare base camps for longer expeditions. Speak foreign languages in order to communicate with foreign visitors.

GOE INFORMATION—**Interest Area:** 11. Recreation, Travel, and Other Personal Services. **Work Group:** 11.02. Recreational Services. **Personality Type**—Social. Social occupations frequently involve working with, communicating with, and teaching people. These occupations often involve helping or providing service to others. **Work Values**—Social Service; Authority; Variety; Recognition; Supervision, Technical. **Skills**—Service Orientation. **Abilities**—*Cognitive:* Memorization; Spatial Orientation; Oral Comprehension; Oral Expression; Time Sharing. *Psychomotor:* Reaction Time; Rate Control; Response Orientation; Speed of Limb Movement. *Physical:* None met the criteria. *Sensory:* Speech Recognition; Speech Clarity; Night Vision; Far Vision; Depth Perception. **General Work Activities**—*Information Input:* Monitoring Processes, Materials, or Surroundings; Identifying Objects, Actions, and Events; Getting Information. *Mental Process:* Thinking Creatively; Judging Qualities of Things, Services, or Other People's Work; Organizing, Planning, and Prioritizing. *Work Output:* Performing General Physical Activities; Handling and Moving Objects; Operating Vehicles or Equipment. *Interacting with Others:* Communicating with Persons Outside Organization; Establishing and Maintaining Relationships; Performing for or Working with the Public. **Physical Work Conditions**—Outdoors; Walking or Running; Very Hot or Cold; Sitting; Extremely Bright or Inadequate Lighting. **Other Job Characteristics**—Importance of Repeating Same Tasks; Consequence of Error; Pace Determined by Speed of Equipment.

Experience—Job Zone 1. No previous work-related skill, knowledge, or experience is needed. **Job Preparation:** SVP below 4.0—less than six months. **Knowledge**—Foreign Language; Customer and Personal Service; History and Archeology; Sales and Marketing; Geography. **Instructional Programs**—Tourism and Travel Services Management.

Related DOT Jobs—109.367-010 Museum Attendant; 353.363-010 Guide, Sightseeing; 353.367-010 Guide; 353.367-014 Guide, Establishment; 353.367-018 Guide, Plant; 353.367-022 Page; 353.667-010 Escort.

39-6022.00 Travel Guides

- **Education/Training Required: Moderate-term on-the-job training**
- **Employed: No data available.**
- **Annual Earnings: $27,180**
- **Growth: 9.5%**
- **Annual Job Openings: 10,000**

Plan, organize, and conduct long-distance cruises, tours, and expeditions for individuals and groups.

Plans tour itinerary, applying knowledge of travel routes and destination sites. Arranges for transportation, accommodations, activity equipment, and services of medical personnel. Selects activity tour sites, leads individuals or groups to location, and describes points of interest. Verifies quantity and quality of equipment to ensure prerequisite needs for expeditions and tours have been met. Instructs novices in climbing techniques, mountaineering, and wilderness survival and demonstrates use of hunting, fishing, and climbing equipment. Obtains or assists tourists to obtain permits and documents, such as visas, passports, and health certificates, and to convert currency. Pitches camp and prepares meals for tour group members. Explains hunting and fishing laws to group to ensure compliance. Pilots airplane or drives land and water vehicles to transport tourists to activity/tour site. Administers first aid to injured group participants. Sells or rents equipment, clothing, and supplies.

GOE INFORMATION—Interest Area: 11. Recreation, Travel, and Other Personal Services. **Work Group:** 11.02. Recreational Services. **Personality Type**—Enterprising. Enterprising occupations frequently involve starting up and carrying out projects. These occupations can involve leading people and making many decisions. They sometimes require risk taking and often deal with business. **Work Values**—Social Service; Variety; Creativity; Autonomy; Authority. **Skills**—Service Orientation; Management of Material Resources; Operation and Control; Equipment Selection; Instructing; Time Management. **Abilities**—*Cognitive:* Time Sharing; Memorization; Spatial Orientation; Oral Comprehension; Oral Expression. *Psychomotor:* Reaction Time; Rate Control; Response Orientation; Multilimb Coordination; Speed of Limb Movement. *Physical:* Stamina; Dynamic Strength; Gross Body Coordination; Gross Body Equilibrium; Trunk Strength. *Sensory:* Glare Sensitivity; Night Vision; Auditory Attention; Peripheral Vision; Sound Localization. **General Work Activities—***Information Input:* Getting Information; Identifying Objects, Actions, and Events; Estimating Needed Characteristics. *Mental Process:* Scheduling Work and Activities; Organizing, Planning, and Prioritizing; Making Decisions and Solving Problems. *Work Output:* Performing General Physical Activities; Handling and Moving Objects; Operating Vehicles or Equipment. *Interacting with Others:* Performing for or Working with the Public; Assisting and Caring for Others; Communicating with Persons Outside Organization. **Physical Work Conditions**—Outdoors; Walking or Running; High Places; Specialized Protective or Safety Attire; Climbing Ladders, Scaffolds, Poles, etc. **Other Job Characteristics**—Consequence of Error; Pace Determined by Speed of Equipment; Degree of Automation.

Experience—Job Zone 2. Some previous work-related skill, knowledge, or experience may be helpful, but usually is not needed. **Job Preparation:** SVP 4.0 to less than 6.0—six months to less than two years. **Knowledge**—Geography; Customer and Personal Service; Sales and Marketing; Medicine and Dentistry; Foreign Language. **Instructional Programs**—Selling Skills and Sales Operations.

Related DOT Jobs—353.161-010 Guide, Hunting and Fishing; 353.164-010 Guide, Alpine; 353.167-010 Guide, Travel; 353.364-010 Dude Wrangler.

39-6031.00 Flight Attendants

- **Education/Training Required: Long-term on-the-job training**
- **Employed: 124,088**
- **Annual Earnings: $40,600**
- **Growth: 18.4%**
- **Annual Job Openings: 8,000**

Provide personal services to ensure the safety and comfort of airline passengers during flight. Greet passengers, verify tickets, explain use of safety equipment, and serve food or beverages.

Greets passengers, verifies tickets, records destinations, and directs passengers to assigned seats. Explains use of safety equipment to passengers. Serves prepared meals and beverages. Assists passengers in storing carry-on luggage in overhead, garment, or under-seat storage. Walks aisle of plane to verify that passengers have complied with federal regulations prior to takeoff. Administers first aid to passengers in distress when needed. Collects money for meals and beverages. Prepares reports showing place of departure and destination, passenger ticket numbers, meal and beverages inventories, and lost and found articles.

GOE INFORMATION—Interest Area: 11. Recreation, Travel, and Other Personal Services. **Work Group:** 11.03. Transportation and Lodging Services. **Personality Type**—Enterprising. Enterprising occupations frequently involve starting up and carrying out projects. These occupations can involve leading people and making many decisions. They sometimes require risk taking and often deal with business. **Work Values**—Social Service; Supervision, Technical; Pleasant Co-workers; Supervision, Human Relations; Company Policies and Practices. **Skills**—Service Orientation; Social Perceptiveness. **Abilities**—*Cognitive:* Oral Expression; Time Sharing; Spatial Orientation. *Psychomotor:* Reaction Time; Response Orientation. *Physical:* Gross Body Equilibrium; Gross Body Coordination; Stamina. *Sensory:* Speech Recognition; Speech Clarity; Auditory Attention; Night Vision. **General Work Activities—***Information Input:* Monitoring Processes, Materials, or Surroundings; Estimating Needed Characteristics; Getting Information. *Mental Process:* Organizing, Planning, and Prioritizing; Evaluating Information Against Standards; Updating and Using Relevant Knowledge. *Work Output:* Handling and Moving Objects; Performing General Physical Activities; Documenting or Recording Information. *Interacting with Others:* Performing for or Working with the Public; Assisting and Caring for Others; Establishing and Maintaining Relationships. **Physical Work Conditions**—High Places; Walking or Running; Whole Body Vibration; Standing; Keeping or Regaining Balance. **Other Job Characteristics**—Importance of Repeating Same Tasks; Consequence of Error; Importance of Being Exact or Accurate.

Experience—Job Zone 2. Some previous work-related skill, knowledge, or experience may be helpful, but usually is not needed. **Job Preparation:** SVP 4.0 to less than 6.0—six months to less than two years. **Knowledge**—Customer and Personal Service; Medicine and Dentistry; Geography; Public Safety and Security; Therapy and Counseling. **Instructional Programs**—Airline Flight Attendant.

Related DOT Jobs—352.367-010 Airplane-Flight Attendant; 352.367-014 Flight Attendant, Ramp.

39-6032.00 Transportation Attendants, Except Flight Attendants and Baggage Porters

- Education/Training Required: Short-term on-the-job training
- Employed: 22,725
- Annual Earnings: $18,080
- Growth: 20.0%
- Annual Job Openings: 1,000

Provide services to ensure the safety and comfort of passengers aboard ships, buses, or trains or within the station or terminal. Perform duties such as greeting passengers, explaining the use of safety equipment, serving meals or beverages, or answering questions related to travel.

Greets passengers boarding mode of transportation and announces stops. Demonstrates safety procedures. Provides seating arrangements and straightens and adjusts window shades and seat cushions to accommodate requests of passengers. Serves snacks, lunch, and refreshments. Distributes sports and game equipment, magazines, newspapers, pillows, blankets, and other items to passengers and guests. Responds to passengers' questions, requests, or complaints. Carries baggage to assigned rooms or to station platform. Mails letters or arranges for dispatch of telegrams to assist passengers. Issues and collects passenger boarding passes and transfers and tears or punches tickets to prevent reuse. Counts and verifies tickets and seat reservations and records number of passengers boarding and leaving mode of transportation. Signals transportation operator to stop or proceed, opens and closes doors, and establishes order among passengers. Inspects kitchen and dining area to ensure adherence to sanitation requirements. Cleans rooms and bathroom facilities, changes linens, and replenishes supplies to washroom.

GOE INFORMATION—Interest Area: 11. Recreation, Travel, and Other Personal Services. Work Group: 11.03. Transportation and Lodging Services. Personality Type—Enterprising. Enterprising occupations frequently involve starting up and carrying out projects. These occupations can involve leading people and making many decisions. They sometimes require risk taking and often deal with business. Work Values—Social Service; Pleasant Co-workers; Supervision, Technical; Security; Supervision, Human Relations. Skills—Service Orientation. Abilities—*Cognitive:* Oral Expression; Memorization; Spatial Orientation; Oral Comprehension; Perceptual Speed. *Psychomotor:* Reaction Time. *Physical:* Gross Body Equilibrium; Static Strength; Dynamic Flexibility; Extent Flexibility; Gross Body Coordination. *Sensory:* Glare Sensitivity; Night Vision; Speech Clarity; Speech Recognition; Sound Localization. General Work Activities—*Information Input:* Monitoring Processes, Materials, or Surroundings; Getting Information; Inspecting Equipment, Structures, or Materials. *Mental Process:* Organizing, Planning, and Prioritizing; Scheduling Work and Activities; Analyzing Data or Information. *Work Output:* Performing General Physical Activities; Handling and Moving Objects; Documenting or Recording Information. *Interacting with Others:* Performing for or Working with the Public; Assisting and Caring for Others; Establishing and Maintaining Relationships. Physical Work Conditions—Walking or Running; Bending or Twisting the Body; Whole Body Vibration; Kneeling, Crouching, or Crawling; Keeping or Regaining Balance. Other Job Characteristics—Pace Determined by Speed of Equipment; Consequence of Error; Degree of Automation.

Experience—Job Zone 1. No previous work-related skill, knowledge, or experience is needed. Job Preparation: SVP below 4.0—less than six months. Knowledge—Customer and Personal Service; Foreign Language;

Public Safety and Security; Geography; Communications and Media. Instructional Programs—Selling Skills and Sales Operations.

Related DOT Jobs—350.677-014 Passenger Attendant; 350.677-018 Steward/Stewardess, Bath; 350.677-022 Steward/Stewardess; 351.677-010 Service Attendant, Sleeping Car; 352.577-010 Bus Attendant; 352.677-010 Passenger Service Representative I; 910.367-026 Passenger Representative; 910.667-014 Conductor; 910.677-010 Passenger Service Representative II.

39-9000 Other Personal Care and Service Workers

39-9011.00 Child Care Workers

- Education/Training Required: Short-term on-the-job training
- Employed: 1,192,578
- Annual Earnings: $16,030
- Growth: 10.6%
- Annual Job Openings: 370,000

Attend to children at schools, businesses, private households, and child care institutions. Perform a variety of tasks, such as dressing, feeding, bathing, and overseeing play.

Care for children in institutional setting, such as group homes, nursery schools, private businesses, or schools for the handicapped. Organize and participate in recreational activities, such as games. Discipline children and recommend or initiate other measures to control behavior, such as caring for own clothing and picking up toys and books. Place or hoist children into baths or pools. Instruct children in health and personal habits such as eating, resting, and toilet habits. Assist in preparing food for children, serve meals and refreshments to children, and regulate rest periods. Read to children and teach them simple painting, drawing, handicrafts, and songs. Wheel handicapped children to classes or other areas of facility, secure in equipment such as chairs and slings. Monitor children on life-support equipment to detect malfunctioning of equipment and call for medical assistance when needed. Accompany children to and from school, on outings, and to medical appointments. Dress children and change diapers. Keep records on individual children, including daily observations and information about activities, meals served, and medications administered. Observe and monitor children's play activities. Sterilize bottles and prepare formulas. Help children with homework and schoolwork. Identify signs of emotional or developmental problems in children and bring them to parents' or guardians' attention. Organize and store toys and materials to ensure order in activity areas. Perform housekeeping duties such as laundry, cleaning, dishwashing, and changing of linens. Sanitize toys and play equipment. Support children's emotional and social development, encouraging understanding of others and positive self-concepts. Operate in-house day care centers within businesses. Provide counseling or therapy to mentally disturbed, delinquent, or handicapped children.

GOE INFORMATION—Interest Area: 12. Education and Social Service. Work Group: 12.03. Educational Services. Personality Type—Social. Social occupations frequently involve working with, communicating with, and teaching people. These occupations often involve helping or providing service to others. Work Values—Social Service; Activity; Variety; Pleasant Co-workers; Authority. Skills—None met the criteria. Abilities—*Cognitive:* Time Sharing; Oral Expression; Originality. *Psychomotor:* None met the criteria. *Physical:* Stamina; Static Strength; Trunk Strength. *Sensory:* Sound Localization; Peripheral Vision; Speech Clarity. General Work Activities—*Information Input:* Monitoring Processes, Materials, or

Surroundings; Identifying Objects, Actions, and Events; Getting Information. *Mental Process:* Organizing, Planning, and Prioritizing; Thinking Creatively; Judging Qualities of Things, Services, or Other People's Work. *Work Output:* Performing General Physical Activities; Handling and Moving Objects; Documenting or Recording Information. *Interacting with Others:* Assisting and Caring for Others; Establishing and Maintaining Relationships; Communicating with Other Workers. **Physical Work Conditions**—Disease or Infections; Standing; Outdoors; Walking or Running. **Other Job Characteristics**—Consequence of Error; Importance of Being Exact or Accurate; Importance of Repeating Same Tasks.

Experience—Job Zone 1. No previous work-related skill, knowledge, or experience is needed. **Job Preparation:** SVP below 4.0—less than six months. **Knowledge**—Customer and Personal Service; Psychology; Therapy and Counseling; Education and Training; Medicine and Dentistry. **Instructional Programs**—Child Care Provider/Assistant.

Related DOT Jobs—355.674-010 Child-Care Attendant, School; 359.677-010 Attendant, Children's Institution; 359.677-018 Nursery School Attendant; 359.677-026 Playroom Attendant.

39-9021.00 Personal and Home Care Aides

- **Education/Training Required: Short-term on-the-job training**
- **Employed: 413,633**
- **Annual Earnings: $16,140**
- **Growth: 62.5%**
- **Annual Job Openings: 84,000**

Assist elderly or disabled adults with daily living activities at the person's home or in a daytime non-residential facility. Duties performed at a place of residence may include keeping house (making beds, doing laundry, washing dishes) and preparing meals. May provide meals and supervised activities at non-residential care facilities. May advise families, the elderly, and disabled people on such things as nutrition, cleanliness, and household utilities.

Administer bedside and personal care, such as ambulation and personal hygiene assistance. Care for individuals and families during periods of incapacitation, family disruption, or convalescence, providing companionship, personal care, and help in adjusting to new lifestyles. Instruct and advise clients on issues such as household cleanliness, utilities, hygiene, nutrition, and infant care. Provide clients with communication assistance, typing their correspondence and obtaining information for them. Participate in case reviews, consulting with the team caring for the client, to evaluate the client's needs and plan for continuing services. Perform healthcare–related tasks, such as monitoring vital signs and medication, under the direction of registered nurses and physiotherapists. Perform housekeeping duties, such as cooking, cleaning, washing clothes and dishes, and running errands. Plan, shop for, and prepare meals, including special diets, and assist families in planning, shopping for, and preparing nutritious meals. Train family members to provide bedside care. Transport clients to locations outside the home, such as to physicians' offices or on outings, using a motor vehicle. Assist in training children, such as by helping to establish good study habits and by assigning duties according to children's capabilities. Prepare and maintain records of client progress and services performed, reporting changes in client condition to manager or supervisor.

GOE INFORMATION—**Interest Area:** 11. Recreation, Travel, and Other Personal Services. **Work Group:** 11.08. Other Personal Services. **Personality Type**—Social. Social occupations frequently involve working with, communicating with, and teaching people. These occupations often involve helping or providing service to others. **Work Values**—Social Service; Authority; Variety; Autonomy; Supervision, Technical. **Skills**—Service Orientation; Social Perceptiveness; Learning Strategies; Speaking; Systems Evaluation; Complex Problem Solving; Systems Analysis. **Abilities**—*Cognitive:* Oral Expression; Fluency of Ideas; Originality; Oral Comprehension; Time Sharing. *Psychomotor:* Response Orientation. *Physical:* Static Strength. *Sensory:* None met the criteria. **General Work Activities**—*Information Input:* Getting Information; Monitoring Processes, Materials, or Surroundings; Estimating Needed Characteristics. *Mental Process:* Organizing, Planning, and Prioritizing; Making Decisions and Solving Problems; Judging Qualities of Things, Services, or Other People's Work. *Work Output:* Performing General Physical Activities; Handling and Moving Objects; Documenting or Recording Information. *Interacting with Others:* Assisting and Caring for Others; Establishing and Maintaining Relationships; Communicating with Persons Outside Organization. **Physical Work Conditions**—Walking or Running; Disease or Infections; Outdoors; Indoors; Standing. **Other Job Characteristics**—Importance of Repeating Same Tasks; Consequence of Error; Pace Determined by Speed of Equipment.

Experience—Job Zone 2. Some previous work-related skill, knowledge, or experience may be helpful, but usually is not needed. **Job Preparation:** SVP 4.0 to less than 6.0—six months to less than two years. **Knowledge**—Customer and Personal Service; Medicine and Dentistry; Psychology; Therapy and Counseling; Clerical. **Instructional Programs**—No data available.

Related DOT Jobs—309.354-010 Homemaker; 359.573-010 Blind Aide.

39-9031.00 Fitness Trainers and Aerobics Instructors

- **Education/Training Required: Postsecondary vocational training**
- **Employed: 158,314**
- **Annual Earnings: $23,340**
- **Growth: 40.3%**
- **Annual Job Openings: 19,000**

Instruct or coach groups or individuals in exercise activities and the fundamentals of sports. Demonstrate techniques and methods of participation. Observe participants and inform them of corrective measures necessary to improve their skills. Those required to hold teaching degrees should be reported in the appropriate teaching category.

Conduct therapeutic, recreational, or athletic activities. Evaluate individuals' abilities, needs, and physical conditions and develop suitable training programs to meet any special requirements. Explain and enforce safety rules and regulations governing sports, recreational activities, and the use of exercise equipment. Instruct participants in maintaining exertion levels in order to maximize benefits from exercise routines. Monitor participants' progress and adapt programs as needed. Observe participants and inform them of corrective measures necessary for skill improvement. Offer alternatives during classes to accommodate different levels of fitness. Organize, lead, and referee indoor and outdoor games such as volleyball, baseball, and basketball. Plan physical education programs to promote development of participants' physical attributes and social skills. Plan routines, choose appropriate music, and choose different movements for each set of muscles, depending on participants' capabilities and limitations. Teach and demonstrate use of gymnastic and training equipment such as trampolines and weights. Teach individual and team sports to participants through instruction and demonstration, utilizing knowledge of sports techniques and of participants' physical capabilities. Teach proper breathing techniques used during physical exertion. Administer emergency first aid, wrap injuries, treat minor chronic disabilities, or refer injured persons to physicians. Advise clients about proper clothing and shoes. Advise participants in use of heat or ultraviolet treatments and hot baths. Maintain equipment inventories and select, store, and issue equipment as needed. Maintain fitness equipment. Massage body parts to relieve soreness, strains, and bruises. Organize and conduct competitions and tournaments. Provide students with information and resources regarding nutrition, weight control, and lifestyle issues. Wrap ankles, fingers, wrists, or other body parts with synthetic skin, gauze, or adhesive tape in order to support muscles and ligaments. Promote health clubs through membership sales and record member information.

GOE INFORMATION—Interest Area: 01. Arts, Entertainment, and Media. **Work Group:** 01.10. Sports: Coaching, Instructing, Officiating, and Performing. **Personality Type**—Social. Social occupations frequently involve working with, communicating with, and teaching people. These occupations often involve helping or providing service to others. **Work Values**—Authority; Creativity; Social Service; Responsibility; Achievement. **Skills**—Instructing; Learning Strategies; Coordination; Speaking; Management of Material Resources; Monitoring; Management of Personnel Resources; Social Perceptiveness. **Abilities**—*Cognitive:* Time Sharing; Visualization; Memorization; Spatial Orientation; Oral Expression. *Psychomotor:* Speed of Limb Movement; Multilimb Coordination; Response Orientation; Rate Control; Manual Dexterity. *Physical:* Stamina; Explosive Strength; Dynamic Strength; Dynamic Flexibility; Gross Body Coordination. *Sensory:* Peripheral Vision; Depth Perception; Auditory Attention; Far Vision; Glare Sensitivity. **General Work Activities**—*Information Input:* Identifying Objects, Actions, and Events; Getting Information; Monitoring Processes, Materials, or Surroundings. *Mental Process:* Organizing, Planning, and Prioritizing; Making Decisions and Solving Problems; Scheduling Work and Activities. *Work Output:* Performing General Physical Activities; Handling and Moving Objects; Documenting or Recording Information. *Interacting with Others:* Coaching and Developing Others; Establishing and Maintaining Relationships; Teaching Others. **Physical Work Conditions**—Outdoors; Walking or Running; Extremely Bright or Inadequate Lighting; Kneeling, Crouching, or Crawling; Keeping or Regaining Balance. **Other Job Characteristics**—Consequence of Error; Importance of Repeating Same Tasks; Pace Determined by Speed of Equipment.

Experience—Job Zone 3. Previous work-related skill, knowledge, or experience is required. **Job Preparation:** SVP 6.0 to less than 7.0—more than one year and less than four years. **Knowledge**—Education and Training; Psychology; Therapy and Counseling; Customer and Personal Service; Medicine and Dentistry. **Instructional Programs**—Health and Physical Education, General; Physical Education Teaching and Coaching; Sport and Fitness Administration/Management.

Related DOT Jobs—099.224-010 Instructor, Physical Education; 153.227-014 Instructor, Physical; 153.227-018 Instructor, Sports.

39-9032.00 Recreation Workers

- **Education/Training Required: Bachelor's degree**
- **Employed: 268,801**
- **Annual Earnings: $17,850**
- **Growth: 20.1%**
- **Annual Job Openings: 32,000**

Conduct recreation activities with groups in public, private, or volunteer agencies or recreation facilities. Organize and promote activities such as arts and crafts, sports, games, music, dramatics, social recreation, camping, and hobbies, taking into account the needs and interests of individual members.

Ascertain and interpret group interests, evaluate equipment and facilities, and adapt activities to meet participant needs. Complete and maintain time and attendance forms and inventory lists. Enforce rules and regulations of recreational facilities in order to maintain discipline and ensure safety. Explain principles, techniques, and safety procedures to participants in recreational activities and demonstrate use of materials and equipment. Greet new arrivals to activities, introducing them to other participants, explaining facility rules, and encouraging their participation. Manage the daily operations of recreational facilities. Meet with staff to discuss rules, regulations, and work-related problems. Organize, lead, and promote interest in recreational activities such as arts, crafts, sports, games, camping, and hobbies. Provide for entertainment and set up related decorations and equipment. Schedule maintenance and use of facilities. Serve as liaison between park or recreation administrators and activity instructors. Supervise and coordinate the work activities of personnel, such as training staff members and assigning work duties. Administer first aid according to prescribed procedures and notify emergency medical personnel when necessary. Confer with management in order to discuss and resolve participant complaints. Direct special activities or events such as aquatics, gymnastics, or performing arts. Encourage participants to develop their own activities and leadership skills through group discussions. Evaluate recreation areas, facilities, and services in order to determine if they are producing desired results. Evaluate staff performance, recording evaluations on appropriate forms. Meet and collaborate with agency personnel, community organizations, and other professional personnel to plan balanced recreational programs for participants. Oversee the purchase, planning, design, construction, and upkeep of recreation facilities and areas.

GOE INFORMATION—Interest Area: 11. Recreation, Travel, and Other Personal Services. **Work Group:** 11.02. Recreational Services. **Personality Type**—Social. Social occupations frequently involve working with, communicating with, and teaching people. These occupations often involve helping or providing service to others. **Work Values**—Social Service; Creativity; Autonomy; Pleasant Co-workers; Authority. **Skills**—Coordination; Management of Personnel Resources; Service Orientation; Management of Material Resources; Social Perceptiveness; Speaking; Time Management; Complex Problem Solving. **Abilities**—*Cognitive:* Fluency of Ideas; Originality; Memorization; Oral Expression; Time Sharing. *Psychomotor:* Response Orientation; Speed of Limb Movement; Multilimb Coordination. *Physical:* Gross Body Coordination; Gross Body Equilibrium; Stamina; Trunk Strength; Explosive Strength. *Sensory:* Speech Recognition; Speech Clarity; Far Vision; Night Vision; Peripheral Vision. **General Work Activities**—*Information Input:* Getting Information; Identifying Objects, Actions, and Events; Monitoring Processes, Materials, or Surroundings. *Mental Process:* Organizing, Planning, and Prioritizing; Scheduling Work and Activities; Thinking Creatively. *Work Output:* Handling and Moving Objects; Performing General Physical Activities; Documenting or Recording Information. *Interacting with Others:* Communicating with Other Workers; Coordinating the Work and Activities of Others; Communicating with Persons Outside Organization. **Physical Work Conditions**—Outdoors; Very Hot or Cold; Walking or Running; Kneeling, Crouching, or Crawling; Minor Burns, Cuts, Bites, or Stings. **Other Job Characteristics**—Degree of Automation; Consequence of Error; Pace Determined by Speed of Equipment.

Experience—Job Zone 3. Previous work-related skill, knowledge, or experience is required. **Job Preparation:** SVP 6.0 to less than 7.0—more than one year and less than four years. **Knowledge**—Customer and Personal Service; Personnel and Human Resources; Administration and Management; Psychology; Education and Training. **Instructional Programs**—Health and Physical Education/Fitness, Other; Parks, Recreation and Leisure Facilities Management; Parks, Recreation, and Leisure Studies; Parks, Recreation, Leisure, and Fitness Studies, Other; Sport and Fitness Administration/Management.

Related DOT Jobs—159.124-010 Counselor, Camp; 187.167-238 Recreation Supervisor; 195.167-026 Director, Recreation Center; 195.227-010 Program Aide, Group Work; 195.227-014 Recreation Leader; 352.167-010 Director, Social.

39-9041.00 *Residential Advisors*

- **Education/Training Required: Moderate-term on-the-job training**
- **Employed: 44,015**
- **Annual Earnings: $19,680**
- **Growth: 24.0%**
- **Annual Job Openings: 9,000**

Coordinate activities for residents of boarding schools, college fraternities or sororities, college dormitories, or similar establishments. Order supplies and determine need for maintenance, repairs, and furnishings. May maintain household records and assign rooms. May refer residents to counseling resources if needed.

Counsel students in the handling of issues such as family, financial, and educational problems. Enforce rules and regulations to ensure the smooth and orderly operation of dormitory programs. Observe students in order to detect and report unusual behavior. Administer, coordinate, or recommend disciplinary and corrective actions. Assign rooms to students. Communicate with other staff to resolve problems with individual students. Compile information such as residents' daily activities and the quantities of supplies used to prepare required reports. Determine the need for facility maintenance and repair; notify appropriate personnel. Direct and participate in on- and off-campus recreational activities for residents of institutions, boarding schools, fraternities or sororities, children's homes, or similar establishments. Hold regular meetings with each assigned unit. Make regular rounds to ensure that residents and areas are safe and secure. Mediate interpersonal problems between residents. Order supplies for facilities. Accompany and supervise students during meals. Answer telephones and route calls or deliver messages. Chaperone group-sponsored trips and social functions. Collaborate with counselors to develop counseling programs that address the needs of individual students. Collect laundry and send it to be cleaned. Confer with medical personnel to better understand the backgrounds and needs of individual residents. Develop program plans for individuals or assist in plan development. Inventory, pack, and remove items left behind by former residents. Plan meal menus for establishment residents. Process contract cancellations for students who are unable to follow residence hall policies and procedures. Provide emergency first aid and summon medical assistance when necessary. Provide requested information on students' progress and the development of case plans. Provide transportation and/or escort for expeditions such as shopping trips or visits to doctors or dentists. Sort and distribute mail. Supervise participants in work-study programs. Supervise students' housekeeping work to ensure that it is done properly. Supervise the activities of housekeeping personnel.

GOE INFORMATION—**Interest Area:** 12. Education and Social Service. **Work Group:** 12.02. Social Services. **Personality Type**—Social. Social occupations frequently involve working with, communicating with, and teaching people. These occupations often involve helping or providing service to others. **Work Values**—Social Service; Supervision, Human Relations; Authority; Good Working Conditions; Autonomy. **Skills**—Social Perceptiveness; Management of Personnel Resources; Negotiation; Complex Problem Solving; Speaking; Management of Material Resources; Active Listening; Coordination. **Abilities**—*Cognitive:* Originality; Fluency of Ideas; Speed of Closure; Memorization; Perceptual Speed. *Psychomotor:* Reaction Time; Response Orientation; Rate Control. *Physical:* None met the criteria. *Sensory:* Night Vision; Far Vision; Glare Sensitivity; Peripheral Vision; Speech Recognition. **General Work Activities**—*Information Input:* Monitoring Processes, Materials, or Surroundings; Getting Information; Identifying Objects, Actions, and Events. *Mental Process:* Judging Qualities of Things, Services, or Other People's Work; Scheduling Work and Activities; Making Decisions and Solving Problems. *Work Output:* Performing General Physical Activities; Handling and Moving Objects; Documenting or Recording Information. *Interacting with Others:* Establishing and Maintaining Relationships; Providing Consultation and Advice to Others; Assisting and Caring for Others. **Physical Work Conditions**—Disease or Infections; Outdoors; Walking or Running; Sitting; Keeping or Regaining Balance. **Other Job Characteristics**—Pace Determined by Speed of Equipment; Consequence of Error; Degree of Automation.

Experience—Job Zone 3. Previous work-related skill, knowledge, or experience is required. **Job Preparation:** SVP 6.0 to less than 7.0—more than one year and less than four years. **Knowledge**—Customer and Personal Service; Therapy and Counseling; Psychology; Personnel and Human Resources; Administration and Management. **Instructional Programs**—Hotel/Motel Administration/Management.

Related DOT Jobs—187.167-186 Residence Supervisor.

39-9099.99 *Personal Care and Service Workers, All Other*

- **Education/Training Required: No data available.**
- **Employed: No data available.**
- **Annual Earnings: No data available.**
- **Growth: 21.7%**
- **Annual Job Openings: 27,000**

All personal care and service workers not listed separately.

No task data available.

GOE INFORMATION—**Interest Area:** 11. Recreation, Travel, and Other Personal Services. **Work Group:** 11.08. Other Personal Services. **Note:** The Department of Labor has not collected some data for this job, so it has fewer details than the other descriptions.

Instructional Programs—No data available.

Related DOT Jobs—143.457-010 Photographer; 309.367-010 House Sitter; 339.371-010 Electrologist; 339.371-014 Scalp-Treatment Operator; 339.571-010 Tattoo Artist; 346.374-010 Costumer Assistant; 346.674-010 Dresser; 349.667-010 Host/Hostess, Dance Hall; 349.667-014 Host/Hostess, Head; 352.377-010 Host/Hostess, Ground; 352.667-014 Parlor Chaperone; 352.677-014 Receptionist, Airline Lounge; 355.687-014 Graves Registration Specialist; 359.367-010 Escort; 359.667-010 Chaperon; 359.677-022 Passenger Service Representative; 359.677-030 Research Subject; 359.685-010 Cremator.

41-0000
Sales and Related Occupations

41-1000 Supervisors, Sales Workers

41-1011.00 First-Line Supervisors/ Managers of Retail Sales Workers

- **Education/Training Required: Work experience in a related occupation**
- Employed: 2,071,641
- Annual Earnings: $28,590
- Growth: 8.1%
- Annual Job Openings: 206,000

Directly supervise sales workers in a retail establishment or department. Duties may include management functions, such as purchasing, budgeting, accounting, and personnel work, in addition to supervisory duties.

Provide customer service by greeting and assisting customers and responding to customer inquiries and complaints. Monitor sales activities to ensure that customers receive satisfactory service and quality goods. Assign employees to specific duties. Direct and supervise employees engaged in sales, inventory-taking, reconciling cash receipts, or performing services for customers. Inventory stock and reorder when inventory drops to a specified level. Keep records of purchases, sales, and requisitions. Enforce safety, health, and security rules. Examine products purchased for resale or received for storage to assess the condition of each product or item. Hire, train, and evaluate personnel in sales or marketing establishments, promoting or firing workers when appropriate. Perform work activities of subordinates, such as cleaning and organizing shelves and displays and selling merchandise. Establish and implement policies, goals, objectives, and procedures for their department. Instruct staff on how to handle difficult and complicated sales. Formulate pricing policies for merchandise according to profitability requirements. Estimate consumer demand and determine the types and amounts of goods to be sold. Examine merchandise to ensure that it is correctly priced and displayed and that it functions as advertised. Plan and prepare work schedules and keep records of employees' work schedules and time cards. Review inventory and sales records to prepare reports for management and budget departments. Plan and coordinate advertising campaigns and sales promotions and prepare merchandise displays and advertising copy. Confer with company officials to develop methods and procedures to increase sales, expand markets, and promote business. Establish credit policies and operating procedures. Plan budgets and authorize payments and merchandise returns.

GOE INFORMATION—Interest Area: 10. Sales and Marketing. **Work Group:** 10.01. Managerial Work in Sales and Marketing. **Personality Type**—Enterprising. Enterprising occupations frequently involve starting up and carrying out projects. These occupations can involve leading people and making many decisions. They sometimes require risk taking and often deal with business. **Work Values**—Authority; Responsibility; Creativity; Autonomy; Good Working Conditions. **Skills**—Management of Personnel Resources; Instructing; Persuasion; Monitoring; Speaking; Time Management; Troubleshooting; Repairing. **Abilities**—*Cognitive:* Originality; Time Sharing; Mathematical Reasoning; Category Flexibility; Written Expression. *Psychomotor:* Speed of Limb Movement; Finger Dexterity. *Physical:* Extent Flexibility; Trunk Strength; Stamina; Gross Body Coordination; Static Strength. *Sensory:* Speech Recognition; Far Vision; Speech Clarity; Auditory Attention; Near Vision. **General Work Activities**—*Information Input:* Inspecting Equipment, Structures, or Materials; Getting Information; Monitoring Processes, Materials, or Surroundings. *Mental Process:* Organizing, Planning, and Prioritizing; Thinking Creatively; Updating and Using Relevant Knowledge. *Work Output:* Handling and Moving Objects; Performing General Physical Activities; Documenting or Recording Information. *Interacting with Others:* Establishing and Maintaining Relationships; Communicating with Other Workers; Performing for or Working with the Public. **Physical Work Conditions**—Walking or Running. **Other Job Characteristics**—Importance of Being Exact or Accurate; Consequence of Error; Pace Determined by Speed of Equipment.

Experience—Job Zone 2. Some previous work-related skill, knowledge, or experience may be helpful, but usually is not needed. **Job Preparation:** SVP 6.0 to less than 7.0—more than one year and less than four years. **Knowledge**—Customer and Personal Service; Sales and Marketing; Personnel and Human Resources; Administration and Management; Food Production. **Instructional Programs**—Business, Management, Marketing, and Related Support Services, Other; Consumer Merchandising/Retailing Management; E-Commerce/Electronic Commerce; Floriculture/Floristry Operations and Management; Retailing and Retail Operations; Selling Skills and Sales Operations; Special Products Marketing Operations; Specialized Merchandising, Sales, and Related Marketing Operations, Other.

Related DOT Jobs—185.167-010 Commissary Manager; 185.167-014 Manager, Automobile Service Station; 185.167-022 Manager, Food Concession; 185.167-026 Manager, Machinery-or-Equipment, Rental and Leasing; 185.167-030 Manager, Meat Sales and Storage; 185.167-038 Manager, Parts; 185.167-046 Manager, Retail Store; 185.167-066 Vending-Stand Supervisor; 299.137-010 Manager, Department; 299.137-022 Supervisor, Ice Storage, Sale, and Delivery; 299.137-026 Supervisor, Marina Sales and Service.

41-1012.00 First-Line Supervisors/ Managers of Non-Retail Sales Workers

- **Education/Training Required: Work experience in a related occupation**
- Employed: 432,285
- Annual Earnings: $51,490
- Growth: 5.8%
- Annual Job Openings: 41,000

Directly supervise and coordinate activities of sales workers other than retail sales workers. May perform duties such as budgeting, accounting, and personnel work in addition to supervisory duties.

Prepares sales and inventory reports for management and budget departments. Assists sales staff in completing complicated and difficult sales. Listens to and resolves customer complaints regarding service, product, or personnel. Keeps records pertaining to purchases, sales, and requisitions. Examines merchandise to ensure that it is correctly priced and displayed or functions as advertised. Formulates pricing policies on merchandise according to requirements for profitability of store operations. Inventories stock and reorders when inventories drop to specified level. Prepares rental or lease agreement specifying charges and payment procedures for use of machinery, tools, or other such items. Examines products purchased for resale or received for storage to determine condition of product or item. Directs and supervises employees engaged in sales, inventory-taking, reconciling cash receipts, or performing specific service such as pumping gasoline for customers. Plans and prepares work schedules and assigns employees to specific duties. Hires, trains, and evaluates personnel in sales or marketing establishment. Coordinates sales promotion activities and prepares merchandise displays and advertising copy. Confers with company officials to develop methods and procedures to increase sales, expand markets, and promote business.

GOE INFORMATION—Interest Area: 10. Sales and Marketing. **Work Group:** 10.01. Managerial Work in Sales and Marketing. **Personality Type**—Enterprising. Enterprising occupations frequently involve starting up and carrying out projects. These occupations can involve leading people and making many decisions. They sometimes require risk taking and often deal with business. **Work Values**—Authority; Responsibility; Creativity; Autonomy; Good Working Conditions. **Skills**—Management of Personnel Resources; Management of Material Resources; Management of Financial Resources; Systems Evaluation; Systems Analysis; Speaking; Mathematics; Complex Problem Solving. **Abilities**—*Cognitive:* Oral Expression; Fluency of Ideas; Originality; Number Facility; Written Expression. *Psychomotor:* None met the criteria. *Physical:* None met the criteria. *Sensory:* Speech Clarity. **General Work Activities**—*Information Input:* Getting Information; Identifying Objects, Actions, and Events; Monitoring Processes, Materials, or Surroundings. *Mental Process:* Scheduling Work and Activities; Organizing, Planning, and Prioritizing; Making Decisions and Solving Problems. *Work Output:* Handling and Moving Objects; Documenting or Recording Information; Performing General Physical Activities. *Interacting with Others:* Monitoring and Controlling Resources; Communicating with Other Workers; Staffing Organizational Units. **Physical Work Conditions**—Walking or Running. **Other Job Characteristics**—Importance of Being Exact or Accurate; Consequence of Error; Pace Determined by Speed of Equipment.

Experience—Job Zone 3. Previous work-related skill, knowledge, or experience is required. **Job Preparation:** SVP 6.0 to less than 7.0—more than one year and less than four years. **Knowledge**—Sales and Marketing; Economics and Accounting; Personnel and Human Resources; Administration and Management; Customer and Personal Service. **Instructional Programs**—Business, Management, Marketing, and Related Support Services, Other; General Merchandising, Sales, and Related Marketing Operations, Other; Special Products Marketing Operations; Specialized Merchandising, Sales, and Related Marketing Operations, Other.

Related DOT Jobs—163.167-014 Manager, Circulation; 169.167-038 Order Department Supervisor; 180.167-010 Artificial-Breeding Distributor; 185.157-018 Wholesaler II; 185.167-038 Manager, Parts; 185.167-050 Manager, Textile Conversion; 185.167-054 Manager, Tobacco Warehouse; 185.167-070 Wholesaler I; 186.167-034 Manager, Insurance Office; 187.167-098 Manager, Employment Agency; 187.167-138 Manager, Sales; 230.137-010 Supervisor, Advertising-Material Distributors; 291.157-010 Subscription Crew Leader; 293.137-010 Supervisor, Blood-Donor Recruiters; 299.137-014 Sales Supervisor, Malt Liquors.

41-2000 Retail Sales Workers

41-2011.00 Cashiers

- **Education/Training Required: Short-term on-the-job training**
- **Employed: 3,363,102**
- **Annual Earnings: $14,950**
- **Growth: 14.5%**
- **Annual Job Openings: 1,125,000**

Receive and disburse money in establishments other than financial institutions. Usually involves use of electronic scanners, cash registers, or related equipment. Often involved in processing credit or debit card transactions and validating checks.

Answer customers' questions and provide information on procedures or policies. Bag, box, wrap, or gift-wrap merchandise and prepare packages for shipment. Compute and record totals of transactions. Count money in cash drawers at the beginning of shifts to ensure that amounts are correct and that there is adequate change. Establish or identify prices of goods, services, or admission and tabulate bills using calculators, cash registers, or optical price scanners. Greet customers entering establishments. Issue receipts, refunds, credits, or change due to customers. Issue trading stamps and redeem food stamps and coupons. Maintain clean and orderly checkout areas. Monitor checkout stations to ensure that they have adequate cash available and that they are staffed appropriately. Offer customers carry-out service at the completion of transactions. Process merchandise returns and exchanges. Receive payment by cash, check, credit cards, vouchers, or automatic debits. Request information or assistance using paging systems. Resolve customer complaints. Sort, count, and wrap currency and coins. Weigh items sold by weight in order to determine prices. Accept reservations or requests for take-out orders. Calculate total payments received during a time period and reconcile this with total sales. Cash checks for customers. Compile and maintain non-monetary reports and records. Keep periodic balance sheets of amounts and numbers of transactions. Post charges against guests' or patients' accounts. Sell tickets and other items to customers. Stock shelves and mark prices on shelves and items. Pay company bills by cash, vouchers, or checks.

GOE INFORMATION—Interest Area: 09. Business Detail. **Work Group:** 09.05. Customer Service. **Personality Type**—Conventional. Conventional occupations frequently involve following set procedures and routines. These occupations can include working with data and details more than with ideas. Usually there is a clear line of authority to follow. **Work Values**—Supervision, Technical; Pleasant Co-workers; Social Service; Supervision, Human Relations; Advancement. **Skills**—None met the criteria. **Abilities**—*Cognitive:* Memorization; Mathematical Reasoning; Perceptual Speed; Number Facility; Category Flexibility. *Psychomotor:* Wrist-Finger Speed; Finger Dexterity; Response Orientation; Reaction Time; Manual Dexterity. *Physical:* Trunk Strength; Dynamic Flexibility; Extent Flexibility. *Sensory:* Visual Color Discrimination; Speech Recognition; Peripheral Vision; Near Vision; Auditory Attention. **General Work Activities**—*Information Input:* Identifying Objects, Actions, and Events; Getting Information; Monitoring Processes, Materials, or Surroundings. *Mental Process:* Processing Information; Evaluating Information Against Standards; Making Decisions and Solving Problems. *Work Output:* Handling and Moving Objects; Performing General Physical Activities; Documenting or Recording Information. *Interacting with Others:* Establishing and Maintaining Relationships; Performing for or Working with the Public; Communicating with Persons Outside Organization. **Physical Work Conditions**—Making Repetitive Motions; Standing; Indoors; Walking or Running. **Other Job Characteristics**—Importance of Being Exact or Accurate; Degree of Automation; Importance of Repeating Same Tasks.

Experience—Job Zone 1. No previous work-related skill, knowledge, or experience is needed. **Job Preparation:** SVP below 4.0—less than six months. **Knowledge**—Clerical; Customer and Personal Service; Sales and Marketing; Economics and Accounting; Computers and Electronics. **Instructional Programs**—Retailing and Retail Operations.

Related DOT Jobs—211.367-010 Paymaster of Purses; 211.462-010 Cashier II; 211.462-014 Cashier-Checker; 211.462-018 Cashier-Wrapper; 211.462-022 Cashier, Gambling; 211.462-026 Check Cashier; 211.462-030 Drivers's-Cash Clerk; 211.462-034 Teller; 211.462-038 Toll Collector; 211.467-010 Cashier, Courtesy Booth; 211.467-014 Money Counter; 211.467-018 Parimutuel-Ticket Cashier; 211.467-022 Parimutuel-Ticket Seller; 211.467-026 Sheet Writer; 211.467-030 Ticket Seller; 211.467-034 Change Person; 211.482-010 Cashier, Tube Room; 211.482-014 Food Checker; 249.467-010 Information Clerk-Cashier; 294.567-010 Auction Clerk.

41-2012.00 Gaming Change Persons and Booth Cashiers

- **Education/Training Required: Short-term on-the-job training**
- **Employed: 38,123**
- **Annual Earnings: $18,990**
- **Growth: 36.1%**
- **Annual Job Openings: 13,000**

Exchange coins and tokens for patrons' money. May issue payoffs and obtain customer's signature on receipt when winnings exceed the amount held in the slot machine. May operate a booth in the slot machine area and furnish change persons with money bank at the start of the shift or count and audit money in drawers.

Calculate the value of chips won or lost by players. Count money and audit money drawers. Exchange money, credit, and casino chips and make change for customers. Keep accurate records of monetary exchanges, authorization forms, and transaction reconciliations. Listen for jackpot alarm bells and issue payoffs to winners. Obtain customers' signatures on receipts when winnings exceed the amount held in a slot machine. Sell gambling chips, tokens, or tickets to patrons or to other workers for resale to patrons. Work in and monitor an assigned area on the casino floor where slot machines are located. Accept credit applications and verify credit references in order to provide check-cashing authorization or to establish house credit accounts. Furnish change persons with a money bank at the start of each shift. Maintain cage security according to rules. Reconcile daily summaries of transactions to balance books.

GOE INFORMATION—Interest Area: 09. Business Detail. **Work Group:** 09.05. Customer Service. **Note:** The Department of Labor has not collected some data for this job, so it has fewer details than the other descriptions.

Instructional Programs—Retailing and Retail Operations.

Related DOT Jobs—211.467-034 Change Person.

41-2021.00 Counter and Rental Clerks

- **Education/Training Required: Short-term on-the-job training**
- **Employed: 423,463**
- **Annual Earnings: $16,750**
- **Growth: 19.4%**
- **Annual Job Openings: 150,000**

Receive orders for repairs, rentals, and services. May describe available options, compute cost, and accept payment.

Compute charges for merchandise or services and receive payments. Prepare merchandise for display or for purchase or rental. Recommend and provide advice on a wide variety of products and services. Answer telephones to provide information and receive orders. Greet customers and discuss the type, quality, and quantity of merchandise sought for rental. Keep records of transactions and of the number of customers entering an establishment. Prepare rental forms, obtaining customer signature and other information, such as required licenses. Receive, examine, and tag articles to be altered, cleaned, stored, or repaired. Inspect and adjust rental items to meet needs of customer. Explain rental fees, policies, and procedures. Reserve items for requested times and keep records of items rented. Receive orders for services, such as rentals, repairs, dry cleaning, and storage. Rent items, arrange for provision of services to customers, and accept returns. Provide information about rental items, such as availability, operation, or description. Advise customers on use

and care of merchandise. Allocate equipment to participants in sporting events or recreational activities.

GOE INFORMATION—Interest Area: 09. Business Detail. **Work Group:** 09.05. Customer Service. **Personality Type—**Conventional. Conventional occupations frequently involve following set procedures and routines. These occupations can include working with data and details more than with ideas. Usually there is a clear line of authority to follow. **Work Values—**Social Service; Good Working Conditions; Supervision, Technical; Pleasant Co-workers; Advancement. **Skills—**None met the criteria. **Abilities—***Cognitive:* Category Flexibility; Oral Expression; Selective Attention; Oral Comprehension. *Psychomotor:* Finger Dexterity. *Physical:* Extent Flexibility; Trunk Strength; Gross Body Coordination; Stamina. *Sensory:* Speech Recognition; Speech Clarity; Near Vision; Auditory Attention. **General Work Activities—***Information Input:* Identifying Objects, Actions, and Events; Monitoring Processes, Materials, or Surroundings; Getting Information. *Mental Process:* Updating and Using Relevant Knowledge; Evaluating Information Against Standards; Judging Qualities of Things, Services, or Other People's Work. *Work Output:* Handling and Moving Objects; Performing General Physical Activities; Documenting or Recording Information. *Interacting with Others:* Performing for or Working with the Public; Establishing and Maintaining Relationships; Coaching and Developing Others. **Physical Work Conditions—**Standing; Indoors; Walking or Running. **Other Job Characteristics—**Degree of Automation; Pace Determined by Speed of Equipment; Importance of Repeating Same Tasks.

Experience—Job Zone 1. No previous work-related skill, knowledge, or experience is needed. **Job Preparation:** SVP below 4.0–less than six months. **Knowledge—**Food Production; Administration and Management; Sales and Marketing; Customer and Personal Service; Personnel and Human Resources. **Instructional Programs—**Selling Skills and Sales Operations.

Related DOT Jobs—216.482-030 Laundry Pricing Clerk; 249.362-010 Counter Clerk; 249.366-010 Counter Clerk; 290.477-010 Coupon-Redemption Clerk; 290.477-018 Sales Clerk, Food; 295.357-010 Apparel-Rental Clerk; 295.357-014 Tool-and-Equipment-Rental Clerk; 295.357-018 Furniture-Rental Consultant; 295.367-010 Airplane-Charter Clerk; 295.367-014 Baby-Stroller and Wheelchair Rental Clerk; 295.367-026 Storage-Facility Rental Clerk; 295.467-010 Bicycle-Rental Clerk; 295.467-014 Boat-Rental Clerk; 295.467-018 Hospital-Television-Rental Clerk; 295.467-022 Trailer-Rental Clerk; 295.467-026 Automobile Rental Clerk; 299.367-018 Watch-and-Clock-Repair Clerk; 369.367-010 Fur-Storage Clerk; 369.367-014 Rug Measurer; 369.467-010 Manager, Branch Store; others.

41-2022.00 Parts Salespersons

- **Education/Training Required: Moderate-term on-the-job training**
- **Employed: 259,866**
- **Annual Earnings: $23,300**
- **Growth: –4.4%**
- **Annual Job Openings: 21,000**

Sell spare and replacement parts and equipment in repair shop or parts store.

Determine replacement parts required, according to inspections of old parts, customer requests, or customers' descriptions of malfunctions. Read catalogs, microfiche viewers, or computer displays in order to determine replacement part stock numbers and prices. Fill customer orders from stock. Advise customers on substitution or modification of parts when identical replacements are not available. Examine returned parts for defects and exchange defective parts or refund money. Prepare sales slips or sales contracts. Receive payment or obtain credit authorization. Receive and fill telephone orders for parts. Demonstrate equipment to customers and explain functioning of equipment. Discuss use and features of various parts based on knowledge of machines or equipment. Measure parts, using precision measuring instruments, in order to determine whether similar parts may be machined to required sizes. Place new merchandise on display. Mark and store parts in stockrooms according to prearranged systems. Take inventory of stock. Repair parts or equipment.

GOE INFORMATION—Interest Area: 10. Sales and Marketing. **Work Group:** 10.03. General Sales. **Personality Type**—Enterprising. Enterprising occupations frequently involve starting up and carrying out projects. These occupations can involve leading people and making many decisions. They sometimes require risk taking and often deal with business. **Work Values**—Social Service; Pleasant Co-workers; Good Working Conditions; Supervision, Technical; Advancement. **Skills**—Repairing; Troubleshooting; Quality Control Analysis. **Abilities**—*Cognitive:* Visualization; Deductive Reasoning; Memorization; Perceptual Speed; Oral Expression. *Psychomotor:* Finger Dexterity; Wrist-Finger Speed; Manual Dexterity; Arm-Hand Steadiness; Response Orientation. *Physical:* Extent Flexibility; Gross Body Equilibrium; Static Strength; Explosive Strength; Trunk Strength. *Sensory:* Speech Recognition; Visual Color Discrimination; Auditory Attention; Sound Localization; Near Vision. **General Work Activities**—*Information Input:* Inspecting Equipment, Structures, or Materials; Identifying Objects, Actions, and Events; Getting Information. *Mental Process:* Updating and Using Relevant Knowledge; Evaluating Information Against Standards; Analyzing Data or Information. *Work Output:* Repairing and Maintaining Mechanical Equipment; Performing General Physical Activities; Handling and Moving Objects. *Interacting with Others:* Communicating with Persons Outside Organization; Influencing Others or Selling; Performing for or Working with the Public. **Physical Work Conditions**—Indoors; Standing; Hazardous Equipment; Walking or Running; Climbing Ladders, Scaffolds, Poles, etc. **Other Job Characteristics**—Degree of Automation; Importance of Being Exact or Accurate; Pace Determined by Speed of Equipment.

Experience—Job Zone 2. Some previous work-related skill, knowledge, or experience may be helpful, but usually is not needed. **Job Preparation:** SVP 4.0 to less than 6.0—six months to less than two years. **Knowledge**—Sales and Marketing; Mechanical; Customer and Personal Service; Economics and Accounting; Clerical. **Instructional Programs**—Selling Skills and Sales Operations; Vehicle and Vehicle Parts and Accessories Marketing Operations.

Related DOT Jobs—279.357-062 Salesperson, Parts.

41-2031.00 *Retail Salespersons*

- **Education/Training Required: Short-term on-the-job training**
- **Employed: 4,109,460**
- **Annual Earnings: $17,150**
- **Growth: 12.4%**
- **Annual Job Openings: 1,124,000**

Sell merchandise such as furniture, motor vehicles, appliances, or apparel in a retail establishment.

Greet customers and ascertain what each customer wants or needs. Open and close cash registers, performing tasks such as counting money; separating charge slips, coupons, and vouchers; balancing cash drawers; and making deposits. Maintain knowledge of current sales and promotions, policies regarding payment and exchanges, and security practices. Compute sales prices and total purchases and receive and process cash or credit payment. Maintain records related to sales. Watch for and

recognize security risks and thefts and know how to prevent or handle these situations. Recommend, select, and help locate or obtain merchandise based on customer needs and desires. Answer questions regarding the store and its merchandise. Describe merchandise and explain use, operation, and care of merchandise to customers. Ticket, arrange, and display merchandise to promote sales. Prepare sales slips or sales contracts. Place special orders or call other stores to find desired items. Demonstrate use or operation of merchandise. Clean shelves, counters, and tables. Exchange merchandise for customers and accept returns. Bag or package purchases and wrap gifts. Help customers try on or fit merchandise. Inventory stock and requisition new stock. Prepare merchandise for purchase or rental. Sell or arrange for delivery, insurance, financing, or service contracts for merchandise. Estimate and quote trade-in allowances. Estimate cost of repair or alteration of merchandise. Estimate quantity and cost of merchandise required, such as paint or floor covering. Rent merchandise to customers.

GOE INFORMATION—Interest Area: 10. Sales and Marketing. **Work Group:** 10.03. General Sales. **Personality Type**—Enterprising. Enterprising occupations frequently involve starting up and carrying out projects. These occupations can involve leading people and making many decisions. They sometimes require risk taking and often deal with business. **Work Values**—Supervision, Technical; Social Service; Advancement; Pleasant Co-workers; Good Working Conditions. **Skills**—Speaking; Social Perceptiveness; Writing; Critical Thinking. **Abilities**—*Cognitive:* Category Flexibility; Memorization; Oral Expression; Problem Sensitivity; Time Sharing. *Psychomotor:* None met the criteria. *Physical:* Trunk Strength; Extent Flexibility; Gross Body Coordination; Gross Body Equilibrium; Static Strength. *Sensory:* Speech Recognition; Far Vision; Speech Clarity; Near Vision. **General Work Activities**—*Information Input:* Monitoring Processes, Materials, or Surroundings; Identifying Objects, Actions, and Events; Getting Information. *Mental Process:* Updating and Using Relevant Knowledge; Organizing, Planning, and Prioritizing; Thinking Creatively. *Work Output:* Handling and Moving Objects; Performing General Physical Activities; Interacting with Computers. *Interacting with Others:* Performing for or Working with the Public; Establishing and Maintaining Relationships; Influencing Others or Selling. **Physical Work Conditions**—Standing; Walking or Running; Indoors; Kneeling, Crouching, or Crawling; Bending or Twisting the Body. **Other Job Characteristics**—Degree of Automation; Pace Determined by Speed of Equipment; Importance of Repeating Same Tasks.

Experience—Job Zone 2. Some previous work-related skill, knowledge, or experience may be helpful, but usually is not needed. **Job Preparation:** SVP 4.0 to less than 6.0—six months to less than two years. **Knowledge**—Sales and Marketing; Customer and Personal Service; Education and Training; Administration and Management; Personnel and Human Resources. **Instructional Programs**—Floriculture/Floristry Operations and Management; Retailing and Retail Operations; Sales, Distribution, and Marketing Operations, General; Selling Skills and Sales Operations.

Related DOT Jobs—260.357-026 Salesperson, Flowers; 261.351-010 Salesperson, Wigs; 261.354-010 Salesperson, Corsets; 261.357-042 Salesperson, Furs; 261.357-046 Salesperson, Infants' and Children's Wear; 261.357-050 Salesperson, Men's and Boys' Clothing; 261.357-054 Salesperson, Men's Furnishings; 261.357-058 Salesperson, Millinery; 261.357-062 Salesperson, Shoes; 261.357-066 Salesperson, Women's Apparel and Accessories; 261.357-070 Salesperson, Yard Goods; 261.357-074 Salesperson, Leather-and-Suede Apparel-and-Accessories; 262.357-018 Salesperson, Cosmetics and Toiletries; 270.352-010 Salesperson, Sewing Machines; 270.357-018 Salesperson, China and Silverware; 270.357-022 Salesperson, Curtains and Draperies; 270.357-026 Salesperson, Floor Coverings; 270.357-030 Salesperson, Furniture; 270.357-034 Salesperson, Household Appliances; 270.357-038 Salesperson, Stereo Equipment; others.

41-3000 Sales Representatives, Services

41-3011.00 Advertising Sales Agents

- **Education/Training Required: Moderate-term on-the-job training**
- **Employed: 155,066**
- **Annual Earnings: $36,560**
- **Growth: 26.3%**
- **Annual Job Openings: 25,000**

Sell or solicit advertising, including graphic art, advertising space in publications, custom-made signs, or TV and radio advertising time. May obtain leases for outdoor advertising sites or persuade retailer to use sales promotion display items.

Consult with company officials, sales departments, and advertising agencies in order to develop promotional plans. Deliver advertising or illustration proofs to customers for approval. Draw up contracts for advertising work and collect payments due. Explain to customers how specific types of advertising will help promote their products or services in the most effective way possible. Identify new advertising markets and propose products to serve them. Locate and contact potential clients in order to offer advertising services. Maintain assigned account bases while developing new accounts. Obtain and study information about clients' products, needs, problems, advertising history, and business practices in order to offer effective sales presentations and appropriate product assistance. Prepare and deliver sales presentations to new and existing customers in order to sell new advertising programs and to protect and increase existing advertising. Prepare promotional plans, sales literature, media kits, and sales contracts, using computer. Process all correspondence and paperwork related to accounts. Provide clients with estimates of the costs of advertising products or services. Recommend appropriate sizes and formats for advertising, depending on medium being used. Arrange for commercial taping sessions and accompany clients to sessions. Attend sales meetings, industry trade shows, and training seminars in order to gather information, promote products, expand network of contacts, and increase knowledge. Determine advertising medium to be used and prepare sample advertisements within the selected medium for presentation to customers. Gather all relevant material for bid processes and coordinate bidding and contract approval. Inform customers of available options for advertisement artwork and provide samples. Write copy as part of layout. Write sales outlines for use by staff.

GOE INFORMATION—Interest Area: 10. Sales and Marketing. **Work Group:** 10.02. Sales Technology. **Personality Type**—Enterprising. Enterprising occupations frequently involve starting up and carrying out projects. These occupations can involve leading people and making many decisions. They sometimes require risk taking and often deal with business. **Work Values**—Creativity; Variety; Good Working Conditions; Ability Utilization; Autonomy. **Skills**—Persuasion; Speaking; Writing; Complex Problem Solving; Negotiation; Reading Comprehension; Critical Thinking; Active Listening. **Abilities**—*Cognitive:* Oral Expression; Originality; Written Expression; Visualization; Fluency of Ideas. *Psychomotor:* None met the criteria. *Physical:* None met the criteria. *Sensory:* Speech Recognition; Speech Clarity; Near Vision; Visual Color Discrimination. **General Work Activities**—*Information Input:* Getting Information; Identifying Objects, Actions, and Events; Estimating Needed Characteristics. *Mental Process:* Organizing, Planning, and Prioritizing; Thinking Creatively; Updating and Using Relevant Knowledge. *Work Output:* Documenting or Recording Information; Interacting with Computers; Handling and Moving Objects. *Interacting with Others:* Influencing Others or Selling; Communicating with Persons Outside Organization; Establishing and Maintaining Relationships. **Physical Work Conditions**—Sitting; Indoors. **Other Job Characteristics**—Importance of Being Exact or Accurate; Consequence of Error; Importance of Repeating Same Tasks.

Experience—Job Zone 3. Previous work-related skill, knowledge, or experience is required. **Job Preparation:** SVP 6.0 to less than 7.0—more than one year and less than four years. **Knowledge**—Sales and Marketing; Fine Arts; Communications and Media; English Language; Psychology. **Instructional Programs**—Advertising.

Related DOT Jobs—254.251-010 Sales Representative, Graphic Art; 254.257-010 Sales Representative, Signs and Displays; 254.357-014 Sales Representative, Advertising; 254.357-022 Sales Representative, Signs; 259.357-018 Sales Representative, Radio and Television Time.

41-3021.00 Insurance Sales Agents

- **Education/Training Required: Bachelor's degree**
- **Employed: 377,750**
- **Annual Earnings: $38,890**
- **Growth: 3.3%**
- **Annual Job Openings: 43,000**

Sell life, property, casualty, health, automotive, or other types of insurance. May refer clients to independent brokers, work as independent broker, or be employed by an insurance company.

Call on policyholders to deliver and explain policy, to analyze insurance program and suggest additions or changes, or to change beneficiaries. Calculate premiums and establish payment method. Customize insurance programs to suit individual customers, often covering a variety of risks. Sell various types of insurance policies to businesses and individuals on behalf of insurance companies, including automobile, fire, life, property, medical, and dental insurance or specialized policies such as marine, farm/crop, and medical malpractice. Interview prospective clients to obtain data about their financial resources and needs and the physical condition of the person or property to be insured and to discuss any existing coverage. Seek out new clients and develop clientele by networking to find new customers and generate lists of prospective clients. Explain features, advantages, and disadvantages of various policies to promote sale of insurance plans. Contact underwriter and submit forms to obtain binder coverage. Ensure that policy requirements are fulfilled, including any necessary medical examinations and the completion of appropriate forms. Confer with clients to obtain and provide information when claims are made on a policy. Perform administrative tasks, such as maintaining records and handling policy renewals. Select company that offers type of coverage requested by client to underwrite policy. Monitor insurance claims to ensure they are settled equitably for both the client and the insurer. Develop marketing strategies to compete with other individuals or companies who sell insurance. Attend meetings, seminars, and programs to learn about new products and services, learn new skills, and receive technical assistance in developing new accounts. Inspect property, examining its general condition, type of construction, age, and other characteristics, to decide if it is a good insurance risk. Install bookkeeping systems and resolve system problems. Plan and oversee incorporation of insurance program into bookkeeping system of company. Explain necessary bookkeeping requirements for customer to implement and provide group insurance program.

GOE INFORMATION—Interest Area: 10. Sales and Marketing. **Work Group:** 10.02. Sales Technology. **Personality Type**—Enterprising. Enterprising occupations frequently involve starting up and carrying out projects. These occupations can involve leading people and making many decisions. They sometimes require risk taking and often deal with business. **Work Values**—Good Working Conditions; Advancement; Responsibility; Social Service; Autonomy. **Skills**—Persuasion; Time Management; Speaking; Negotiation; Service Orientation; Complex Problem Solving; Active Listening; Judgment and Decision Making. **Abilities**—*Cognitive:* Deductive Reasoning; Category Flexibility; Inductive Reasoning; Oral Expression; Originality. *Psychomotor:* Finger Dexterity. *Physical:* None met the criteria. *Sensory:* Speech Recognition; Near Vision; Far Vision; Speech Clarity; Depth Perception. **General Work Activities**—*Information Input:* Getting Information; Identifying Objects, Actions, and Events; Monitoring Processes, Materials, or Surroundings. *Mental Process:* Processing Information; Making Decisions and Solving Problems; Evaluating Information Against Standards. *Work Output:* Documenting or Recording Information; Interacting with Computers; Performing General Physical Activities. *Interacting with Others:* Establishing and Maintaining Relationships; Communicating with Persons Outside Organization; Resolving Conflict and Negotiating with Others. **Physical Work Conditions**—Sitting; Indoors. **Other Job Characteristics**—Importance of Being Exact or Accurate; Consequence of Error; Degree of Automation.

Experience—Job Zone 3. Previous work-related skill, knowledge, or experience is required. **Job Preparation:** SVP 6.0 to less than 7.0—more than one year and less than four years. **Knowledge**—Customer and Personal Service; Sales and Marketing; Economics and Accounting; Computers and Electronics; Clerical. **Instructional Programs**—Insurance.

Related DOT Jobs—169.167-050 Special Agent, Group Insurance; 186.167-010 Estate Planner; 239.267-010 Placer; 250.257-010 Sales Agent, Insurance.

41-3031.00 Securities, Commodities, and Financial Services Sales Agents

- **Education/Training Required: Bachelor's degree**
- **Employed: 367,337**
- **Annual Earnings: $59,690**
- **Growth: 22.3%**
- **Annual Job Openings: 55,000**

Buy and sell securities in investment and trading firms or call upon businesses and individuals to sell financial services. Provide financial services such as loan, tax, and securities counseling. May advise securities customers about such things as stocks, bonds, and market conditions.

No task data available.

GOE INFORMATION—Interest Area: 10. Sales and Marketing. **Work Group:** 10.02. Sales Technology. **Note:** The Department of Labor has not collected some data for this job, so it has fewer details than the other descriptions.

Instructional Programs—Business and Personal/Financial Services Marketing Operations; Financial Planning and Services; Investments and Securities.

Related DOT Jobs—162.157-010 Broker-and-Market Operator, Grain; 162.167-034 Floor Broker; 162.167-038 Securities Trader; 250.257-014 Financial Planner; 250.257-018 Registered Representative; 250.257-022 Sales Representative, Financial Services; 250.357-026 Sales Agent, Financial-Report Service.

41-3031.01 Sales Agents, Securities and Commodities

- **Education/Training Required: Bachelor's degree**
- **Employed: No data available.**
- **Annual Earnings: $59,690**
- **Growth: 22.3%**
- **Annual Job Openings: 55,000**

Buy and sell securities in investment and trading firms and develop and implement financial plans for individuals, businesses, and organizations.

Develop financial plans based on analysis of clients' financial status and discuss financial options with clients. Relay buy or sell orders to securities exchanges or to firm trading departments. Record transactions accurately and keep clients informed about transactions. Analyze market conditions in order to determine optimum times to execute securities transactions. Review financial periodicals, stock and bond reports, business publications, and other material in order to identify potential investments for clients and to keep abreast of trends affecting market conditions. Read corporate reports and calculate ratios to determine best prospects for profit on stock purchases and to monitor client accounts. Interview clients to determine clients' assets, liabilities, cash flow, insurance coverage, tax status, and financial objectives. Review all securities transactions to ensure accuracy of information and ensure that trades conform to regulations of governing agencies. Prepare documents needed to implement plans selected by clients. Complete sales order tickets and submit for processing of client requested transactions. Inform and advise concerned parties regarding fluctuations and securities transactions affecting plans or accounts. Prepare financial reports to monitor client or corporate finances. Identify potential clients, using advertising campaigns, mailing lists, and personal contacts. Contact prospective customers to determine customer needs, present information, and explain available services. Explain stock market terms and trading practices to clients. Offer advice on the purchase or sale of particular securities. Supply the latest price quotes on any security, as well as information on the activities and financial positions of the corporations issuing these securities. Calculate costs for billings and commissions purposes.

GOE INFORMATION—Interest Area: 10. Sales and Marketing. **Work Group:** 10.02. Sales Technology. **Personality Type**—Enterprising. Enterprising occupations frequently involve starting up and carrying out projects. These occupations can involve leading people and making many decisions. They sometimes require risk taking and often deal with business. **Work Values**—Recognition; Compensation; Responsibility; Good Working Conditions; Autonomy. **Skills**—Management of Financial Resources; Systems Analysis; Systems Evaluation; Persuasion; Service Orientation; Complex Problem Solving; Mathematics; Judgment and Decision Making. **Abilities**—*Cognitive:* Number Facility; Deductive Reasoning; Written Expression; Mathematical Reasoning; Speed of Closure. *Psychomotor:* None met the criteria. *Physical:* None met the criteria. *Sensory:* Speech Recognition; Near Vision; Speech Clarity; Auditory Attention. **General Work Activities**—*Information Input:* Getting Information; Identifying Objects, Actions, and Events; Monitoring Processes, Materials, or Surroundings. *Mental Process:* Updating and Using Relevant Knowledge; Analyzing Data or Information; Making Decisions and Solving Problems. *Work Output:* Documenting or Recording Information; Interacting with Computers; Handling and Moving Objects. *Interacting with Others:* Communicating with Persons Outside Organization; Monitoring and Controlling Resources; Providing Consultation and Advice to Others. **Physical Work Conditions**—Sitting; Indoors; Disease or Infections. **Other Job Characteristics**—Consequence of Error; Importance of Being Exact or Accurate; Importance of Repeating Same Tasks.

Experience—Job Zone 4. A minimum of two to four years of work-related skill, knowledge, or experience is needed. **Job Preparation:** SVP 7.0 to less than 8.0—two years to less than 10 years. **Knowledge**—Economics and Accounting; Sales and Marketing; Customer and Personal Service; Mathematics; Personnel and Human Resources. **Instructional Programs**—Business and Personal/Financial Services Marketing Operations; Financial Planning and Services; Investments and Securities.

Related DOT Jobs—162.157-010 Broker-and-Market Operator, Grain; 162.167-034 Floor Broker; 162.167-038 Securities Trader; 250.257-014 Financial Planner; 250.257-018 Registered Representative.

41-3031.02 Sales Agents, Financial Services

- **Education/Training Required: Bachelor's degree**
- **Employed: No data available.**
- **Annual Earnings: $59,690**
- **Growth: 22.3%**
- **Annual Job Openings: 55,000**

Sell financial services such as loan, tax, and securities counseling to customers of financial institutions and business establishments.

Contact prospective customers in order to present information and explain available services. Determine customers' financial services needs and prepare proposals to sell services that address these needs. Develop prospects from current commercial customers, referral leads, and sales and trade meetings. Prepare forms or agreements to complete sales. Sell services and equipment such as trusts, investments, and check processing services. Evaluate costs and revenue of agreements in order to determine continued profitability. Make presentations on financial services to groups in order to attract new clients. Review business trends in order to advise customers regarding expected fluctuations.

GOE INFORMATION—Interest Area: 10. Sales and Marketing. **Work Group:** 10.02. Sales Technology. **Personality Type**—Enterprising. Enterprising occupations frequently involve starting up and carrying out projects. These occupations can involve leading people and making many decisions. They sometimes require risk taking and often deal with business. **Work Values**—Recognition; Compensation; Good Working Conditions; Responsibility; Autonomy. **Skills**—Systems Analysis; Persuasion; Management of Financial Resources; Service Orientation; Systems Evaluation; Complex Problem Solving; Monitoring; Negotiation. **Abilities**—*Cognitive:* Mathematical Reasoning; Number Facility; Written Expression; Deductive Reasoning; Oral Expression. *Psychomotor:* None met the criteria. *Physical:* None met the criteria. *Sensory:* Speech Recognition; Speech Clarity; Near Vision; Auditory Attention; Far Vision. **General Work Activities**—*Information Input:* Identifying Objects, Actions, and Events; Getting Information; Monitoring Processes, Materials, or Surroundings. *Mental Process:* Making Decisions and Solving Problems; Organizing, Planning, and Prioritizing; Updating and Using Relevant Knowledge. *Work Output:* Documenting or Recording Information; Performing General Physical Activities; Interacting with Computers. *Interacting with Others:* Communicating with Persons Outside Organization; Establishing and Maintaining Relationships; Influencing Others or Selling. **Physical Work Conditions**—Sitting; Indoors; Disease or Infections. **Other Job Characteristics**—Importance of Repeating Same Tasks; Importance of Being Exact or Accurate; Consequence of Error.

Experience—Job Zone 3. Previous work-related skill, knowledge, or experience is required. **Job Preparation:** SVP 6.0 to less than 7.0—more than one year and less than four years. **Knowledge**—Economics and Accounting; Sales and Marketing; Computers and Electronics; Customer and

Personal Service; Administration and Management. **Instructional Programs**—Business and Personal/Financial Services Marketing Operations; Financial Planning and Services; Investments and Securities.

Related DOT Jobs—250.257-022 Sales Representative, Financial Services; 250.357-026 Sales Agent, Financial-Report Service.

41-3041.00 Travel Agents

- **Education/Training Required: Postsecondary vocational training**
- **Employed: 134,666**
- **Annual Earnings: $25,580**
- **Growth: 3.2%**
- **Annual Job Openings: 23,000**

Plan and sell transportation and accommodations for travel agency customers. Determine destination, modes of transportation, travel dates, costs, and accommodations required.

Collect payment for transportation and accommodations from customer. Converse with customer to determine destination, mode of transportation, travel dates, financial considerations, and accommodations required. Compute cost of travel and accommodations, using calculator, computer, carrier tariff books, and hotel rate books, or quote package tour's costs. Book transportation and hotel reservations, using computer terminal or telephone. Plan, describe, arrange, and sell itinerary tour packages and promotional travel incentives offered by various travel carriers. Provide customer with brochures and publications containing travel information, such as local customs, points of interest, or foreign country regulations. Print or request transportation carrier tickets, using computer printer system or system link to travel carrier.

GOE INFORMATION—Interest Area: 10. Sales and Marketing. **Work Group:** 10.03. General Sales. **Personality Type**—Enterprising. Enterprising occupations frequently involve starting up and carrying out projects. These occupations can involve leading people and making many decisions. They sometimes require risk taking and often deal with business. **Work Values**—Social Service; Good Working Conditions; Autonomy; Recognition; Variety. **Skills**—Service Orientation; Persuasion; Active Listening; Speaking; Time Management; Critical Thinking; Complex Problem Solving; Negotiation. **Abilities**—*Cognitive:* Fluency of Ideas; Time Sharing; Originality; Category Flexibility; Oral Expression. *Psychomotor:* None met the criteria. *Physical:* None met the criteria. *Sensory:* Speech Recognition; Near Vision; Auditory Attention; Speech Clarity. **General Work Activities**—*Information Input:* Getting Information; Identifying Objects, Actions, and Events; Estimating Needed Characteristics. *Mental Process:* Organizing, Planning, and Prioritizing; Updating and Using Relevant Knowledge; Processing Information. *Work Output:* Documenting or Recording Information; Interacting with Computers; Handling and Moving Objects. *Interacting with Others:* Performing for or Working with the Public; Establishing and Maintaining Relationships; Communicating with Persons Outside Organization. **Physical Work Conditions**—Sitting; Indoors. **Other Job Characteristics**—Importance of Being Exact or Accurate; Consequence of Error; Importance of Repeating Same Tasks.

Experience—Job Zone 3. Previous work-related skill, knowledge, or experience is required. **Job Preparation:** SVP 4.0 to less than 6.0—six months to less than two years. **Knowledge**—Geography; Sales and Marketing; Customer and Personal Service; Clerical; Computers and Electronics. **Instructional Programs**—Selling Skills and Sales Operations; Tourism and Travel Services Marketing Operations.

Related DOT Jobs—252.152-010 Travel Agent.

41-3099.99 Sales Representatives, Services, All Other

- Education/Training Required: No data available.
- Employed: No data available.
- Annual Earnings: No data available.
- Growth: 11.9%
- Annual Job Openings: 99,000

All services sales representatives not listed separately.

No task data available.

GOE INFORMATION—Interest Area: 10. Sales and Marketing. Work Group: 10.02. Sales Technology. Note: The Department of Labor has not collected some data for this job, so it has fewer details than the other descriptions.

Instructional Programs—Business, Management, Marketing, and Related Support Services, Other; Retailing and Retail Operations; Selling Skills and Sales Operations.

Related DOT Jobs—165.157-010 Song Plugger; 236.252-010 Representative, Personal Service; 250.357-022 Sales Representative; 251.157-014 Sales Representative, Data Processing Services; 251.257-014 Sales Agent, Psychological Tests And Industrial Relations; 251.357-010 Sales Agent, Business Services; 251.357-018 Sales Agent, Pest Control Service; 251.357-022 Sales Representative, Franchise; 251.357-026 Sales Representative, Herbicide Service; 252.257-010 Traffic Agent; 252.357-010 Crating-And-Moving Estimator; 252.357-014 Sales Representative, Shipping Services; 253.157-010 Communications Consultant; 253.257-010 Sales Representative, Telephone Services; 253.357-010 Sales Representative, Public Utilities; 254.357-018 Sales Representative, Printing; 259.157-010 Sales Representative, Audiovisual Program Productions; 259.157-014 Sales Representative, Hotel Services; 259.257-010 Sales Representative, Education Courses; 259.257-018 Service Representative, Elevators, Escalators, And Dumbwaiters; others.

41-4000 Sales Representatives, Wholesale and Manufacturing

41-4011.00 Sales Representatives, Wholesale and Manufacturing, Technical and Scientific Products

- Education/Training Required: Moderate-term on-the-job training
- Employed: 395,860
- Annual Earnings: $54,360
- Growth: 7.5%
- Annual Job Openings: 24,000

Sell goods for wholesalers or manufacturers where technical or scientific knowledge is required in such areas as biology, engineering, chemistry, and electronics, normally obtained from at least two years of postsecondary education.

No task data available.

GOE INFORMATION—Interest Area: 10. Sales and Marketing. Work Group: 10.02. Sales Technology. Note: The Department of Labor has not collected some data for this job, so it has fewer details than the other descriptions.

Instructional Programs—Business, Management, Marketing, and Related Support Services, Other; Selling Skills and Sales Operations.

Related DOT Jobs—259.257-014 Sales Representative, Electroplating; 262.157-010 Pharmaceutical Detailer; 262.357-010 Sales Representative, Chemicals and Drugs; 262.357-022 Sales Representative, Water-Treatment Chemicals; 271.257-010 Sales Representative, Communication Equipment; 271.352-010 Sales Representative, Radiographic-Inspection Equipment and Services; 271.352-014 Sales Representative, Ultrasonic Equipment; 271.357-010 Sales Representative, Electronics Parts; 272.357-010 Sales Representative, Animal-Feed Products; 272.357-014 Sales Representative, Farm and Garden Equipment and Supplies; 272.357-018 Sales Representative, Poultry Equipment and Supplies; 273.253-010 Sales Representative, Aircraft; 273.357-010 Sales Representative, Aircraft Equipment and Parts; 273.357-026 Sales Representative, Railroad Equipment and Supplies; 274.157-010 Sales Representative, Elevators, Escalators, and Dumbwaiters; 274.257-010 Sales Representative, Foundry and Machine Shop Products; 274.357-010 Sales Representative, Abrasives; 274.357-018 Sales Representative, Building Equipment and Supplies; 274.357-022 Sales Representative, Construction Machinery; 274.357-030 Sales Representative, Dairy Supplies; others.

41-4011.01 Sales Representatives, Agricultural

- Education/Training Required: Moderate-term on-the-job training
- Employed: No data available.
- Annual Earnings: $54,360
- Growth: 7.5%
- Annual Job Openings: 24,000

Sell agricultural products and services, such as animal feeds, farm and garden equipment, and dairy, poultry, and veterinarian supplies.

Demonstrates use of agricultural equipment or machines. Prepares reports of business transactions. Recommends changes in customer use of agricultural products to improve production. Solicits orders from customers in person or by phone. Displays or shows customer agricultural related products. Quotes prices and credit terms. Compiles lists of prospective customers for use as sales leads. Prepares sales contracts for orders obtained. Consults with customer regarding installation, setup, or layout of agricultural equipment and machines. Informs customer of estimated delivery schedule, service contracts, warranty, or other information pertaining to purchased products.

GOE INFORMATION—Interest Area: 10. Sales and Marketing. Work Group: 10.02. Sales Technology. Personality Type—Enterprising. Enterprising occupations frequently involve starting up and carrying out projects. These occupations can involve leading people and making many decisions. They sometimes require risk taking and often deal with business. Work Values—Creativity; Responsibility; Advancement; Achievement; Recognition. Skills—Speaking; Persuasion; Negotiation; Active Listening; Writing. Abilities—*Cognitive:* Oral Expression; Written Comprehension; Fluency of Ideas; Written Expression; Oral Comprehension. *Psychomotor:* None met the criteria. *Physical:* None met the criteria. *Sensory:* Speech Recognition. General Work Activities—*Information Input:* Getting Information; Identifying Objects, Actions, and Events; Estimating Needed Characteristics. *Mental Process:* Organizing, Planning, and Prioritizing; Updating and Using Relevant Knowledge; Thinking

Creatively. *Work Output:* Controlling Machines and Processes; Handling and Moving Objects; Documenting or Recording Information. *Interacting with Others:* Influencing Others or Selling; Communicating with Persons Outside Organization; Establishing and Maintaining Relationships. **Physical Work Conditions**—Outdoors; Hazardous Equipment; Standing. **Other Job Characteristics**—Consequence of Error; Importance of Being Exact or Accurate; Importance of Repeating Same Tasks.

Experience—Job Zone 2. Some previous work-related skill, knowledge, or experience may be helpful, but usually is not needed. **Job Preparation:** SVP 4.0 to less than 6.0—six months to less than two years. **Knowledge**—Sales and Marketing; Economics and Accounting; Customer and Personal Service; Food Production; Mathematics. **Instructional Programs**—Business, Management, Marketing, and Related Support Services, Other; Selling Skills and Sales Operations.

Related DOT Jobs—272.357-010 Sales Representative, Animal-Feed Products; 272.357-014 Sales Representative, Farm and Garden Equipment and Supplies; 272.357-018 Sales Representative, Poultry Equipment and Supplies; 274.357-030 Sales Representative, Dairy Supplies; 276.357-018 Sales Representative, Veterinarian Supplies; 299.251-010 Sales-Service Representative, Milking Machines.

41-4011.02 Sales Representatives, Chemical and Pharmaceutical

- **Education/Training Required: Moderate-term on-the-job training**
- **Employed: No data available.**
- **Annual Earnings: $54,360**
- **Growth: 7.5%**
- **Annual Job Openings: 24,000**

Sell chemical or pharmaceutical products or services, such as acids, industrial chemicals, agricultural chemicals, medicines, drugs, and water treatment supplies.

Promotes and sells pharmaceutical and chemical products to potential customers. Explains water treatment package benefits to customer and sells chemicals to treat and resolve water process problems. Distributes drug samples to customer and takes orders for pharmaceutical supply items from customer. Discusses characteristics and clinical studies pertaining to pharmaceutical products with physicians, dentists, hospitals, and retail/wholesale establishments. Estimates and advises customer of service costs to correct water-treatment process problems. Inspects, tests, and observes chemical changes in water system equipment, utilizing test kit, reference manual, and knowledge of chemical treatment.

GOE INFORMATION—**Interest Area:** 10. Sales and Marketing. **Work Group:** 10.02. Sales Technology. **Personality Type**—Enterprising. Enterprising occupations frequently involve starting up and carrying out projects. These occupations can involve leading people and making many decisions. They sometimes require risk taking and often deal with business. **Work Values**—Recognition; Compensation; Creativity; Ability Utilization; Variety. **Skills**—Speaking; Persuasion; Science. **Abilities**—*Cognitive:* Oral Expression; Written Comprehension; Oral Comprehension; Number Facility; Memorization. *Psychomotor:* None met the criteria. *Physical:* None met the criteria. *Sensory:* Speech Clarity; Speech Recognition. **General Work Activities**—*Information Input:* Getting Information; Identifying Objects, Actions, and Events; Inspecting Equipment, Structures, or Materials. *Mental Process:* Updating and Using Relevant Knowledge; Organizing, Planning, and Prioritizing; Analyzing Data or Information. *Work Output:* Controlling Machines and Processes; Handling and Moving Objects; Documenting or Recording Information.

Interacting with Others: Communicating with Persons Outside Organization; Influencing Others or Selling; Establishing and Maintaining Relationships. **Physical Work Conditions**—Sitting; Standing. **Other Job Characteristics**—Pace Determined by Speed of Equipment; Consequence of Error; Degree of Automation.

Experience—Job Zone 3. Previous work-related skill, knowledge, or experience is required. **Job Preparation:** SVP 6.0 to less than 7.0—more than one year and less than four years. **Knowledge**—Sales and Marketing; Chemistry; Biology; Medicine and Dentistry; Economics and Accounting. **Instructional Programs**—Business, Management, Marketing, and Related Support Services, Other; Selling Skills and Sales Operations.

Related DOT Jobs—262.157-010 Pharmaceutical Detailer; 262.357-010 Sales Representative, Chemicals and Drugs; 262.357-022 Sales Representative, Water-Treatment Chemicals.

41-4011.03 Sales Representatives, Electrical/Electronic

- **Education/Training Required: Moderate-term on-the-job training**
- **Employed: No data available.**
- **Annual Earnings: $54,360**
- **Growth: 7.5%**
- **Annual Job Openings: 24,000**

Sell electrical, electronic, or related products or services, such as communication equipment, radiographic-inspection equipment and services, ultrasonic equipment, electronics parts, computers, and EDP systems.

Analyzes communication needs of customer and consults with staff engineers regarding technical problems. Recommends equipment to meet customer requirements, considering salable features such as flexibility, cost, capacity, and economy of operation. Sells electrical or electronic equipment, such as computers, data processing, and radiographic equipment to businesses and industrial establishments. Negotiates terms of sale and services with customer. Trains establishment personnel in equipment use, utilizing knowledge of electronics and product sold.

GOE INFORMATION—**Interest Area:** 10. Sales and Marketing. **Work Group:** 10.02. Sales Technology. **Personality Type**—Enterprising. Enterprising occupations frequently involve starting up and carrying out projects. These occupations can involve leading people and making many decisions. They sometimes require risk taking and often deal with business. **Work Values**—Recognition; Variety; Advancement; Good Working Conditions; Compensation. **Skills**—Persuasion; Equipment Selection; Negotiation; Operations Analysis; Instructing. **Abilities**—*Cognitive:* Oral Expression; Oral Comprehension; Memorization; Number Facility; Selective Attention. *Psychomotor:* Control Precision. *Physical:* None met the criteria. *Sensory:* Speech Clarity; Speech Recognition. **General Work Activities**—*Information Input:* Getting Information; Identifying Objects, Actions, and Events; Estimating Needed Characteristics. *Mental Process:* Updating and Using Relevant Knowledge; Analyzing Data or Information; Organizing, Planning, and Prioritizing. *Work Output:* Handling and Moving Objects; Interacting with Computers; Controlling Machines and Processes. *Interacting with Others:* Communicating with Persons Outside Organization; Influencing Others or Selling; Performing for or Working with the Public. **Physical Work Conditions**—Indoors; Walking or Running; Standing. **Other Job Characteristics**—Degree of Automation; Consequence of Error; Pace Determined by Speed of Equipment.

Experience—Job Zone 2. Some previous work-related skill, knowledge, or experience may be helpful, but usually is not needed. **Job Preparation:**

SVP 4.0 to less than 6.0—six months to less than two years. **Knowledge**—Sales and Marketing; Computers and Electronics; Education and Training; Economics and Accounting; Psychology. **Instructional Programs**—Business, Management, Marketing, and Related Support Services, Other; Selling Skills and Sales Operations.

Related DOT Jobs—271.257-010 Sales Representative, Communication Equipment; 271.352-010 Sales Representative, Radiographic-Inspection Equipment and Services; 271.352-014 Sales Representative, Ultrasonic Equipment; 271.357-010 Sales Representative, Electronics Parts; 275.257-010 Sales Representative, Computers and EDP Systems.

41-4011.04 Sales Representatives, Mechanical Equipment and Supplies

- Education/Training Required: Moderate-term on-the-job training
- Employed: No data available.
- Annual Earnings: $54,360
- Growth: 7.5%
- Annual Job Openings: 24,000

Sell mechanical equipment, machinery, materials, and supplies, such as aircraft and railroad equipment and parts, construction machinery, material-handling equipment, industrial machinery, and welding equipment.

Recommends and sells textile, industrial, construction, railroad, and oil field machinery, equipment, materials, supplies, and services, utilizing knowledge of machine operations. Contacts current and potential customers, visits establishments to evaluate needs, and promotes sale of products and services. Computes installation or production costs, estimates savings, and prepares and submits bid specifications to customer for review and approval. Submits orders for product and follows up on order to verify material list accuracy and verify that delivery schedule meets project deadline. Arranges for installation and test-operation of machinery and recommends solutions to product-related problems. Appraises equipment and verifies customer credit rating to establish trade-in value and contract terms. Demonstrates and explains use of installed equipment and production processes. Reviews existing machinery/equipment placement and diagrams proposal to illustrate efficient space utilization, using standard measuring devices and templates. Inspects establishment premises to verify installation feasibility and obtains building blueprints and elevator specifications to submit to engineering department for bid. Attends sales and trade meetings and reads related publications to obtain current market condition information, business trends, and industry developments.

GOE INFORMATION—Interest Area: 10. Sales and Marketing. **Work Group:** 10.02. Sales Technology. **Personality Type**—Enterprising. Enterprising occupations frequently involve starting up and carrying out projects. These occupations can involve leading people and making many decisions. They sometimes require risk taking and often deal with business. **Work Values**—Autonomy; Variety; Recognition; Compensation; Achievement. **Skills**—Equipment Selection; Operations Analysis; Speaking; Persuasion; Negotiation; Active Listening; Instructing; Reading Comprehension. **Abilities**—*Cognitive:* Oral Expression; Written Expression; Memorization; Mathematical Reasoning; Problem Sensitivity. *Psychomotor:* None met the criteria. *Physical:* None met the criteria. *Sensory:* Speech Clarity; Speech Recognition; Auditory Attention. **General Work Activities**—*Information Input:* Getting Information; Inspecting Equipment, Structures, or Materials; Identifying Objects, Actions, and Events. *Mental Process:* Processing Information; Updating and Using Relevant Knowledge; Organizing, Planning, and Prioritizing. *Work Output:* Controlling

Machines and Processes; Performing General Physical Activities; Drafting and Specifying Technical Devices. *Interacting with Others:* Influencing Others or Selling; Communicating with Persons Outside Organization; Establishing and Maintaining Relationships. **Physical Work Conditions**—Walking or Running; Indoors; Standing; Sitting; Outdoors. **Other Job Characteristics**—Degree of Automation; Importance of Repeating Same Tasks; Pace Determined by Speed of Equipment.

Experience—Job Zone 2. Some previous work-related skill, knowledge, or experience may be helpful, but usually is not needed. **Job Preparation:** SVP 4.0 to less than 6.0—six months to less than two years. **Knowledge**—Sales and Marketing; Economics and Accounting; Mathematics; Customer and Personal Service; Design. **Instructional Programs**—Business, Management, Marketing, and Related Support Services, Other; Selling Skills and Sales Operations.

Related DOT Jobs—259.257-014 Sales Representative, Electroplating; 273.253-010 Sales Representative, Aircraft; 273.357-010 Sales Representative, Aircraft Equipment and Parts; 273.357-026 Sales Representative, Railroad Equipment and Supplies; 274.157-010 Sales Representative, Elevators, Escalators, and Dumbwaiters; 274.257-010 Sales Representative, Foundry and Machine Shop Products; 274.357-010 Sales Representative, Abrasives; 274.357-018 Sales Representative, Building Equipment and Supplies; 274.357-022 Sales Representative, Construction Machinery; 274.357-038 Sales Representative, Industrial Machinery; 274.357-046 Sales Representative, Lubricating Equipment; 274.357-050 Sales Representative, Material-Handling Equipment; 274.357-054 Sales Representative, Metals; 274.357-058 Sales Representative, Oil Field Supplies and Equipment; 274.357-070 Sales Representative, Textile Machinery; 274.357-074 Sales Representative, Welding Equipment; 274.357-078 Sales Representative, Wire Rope.

41-4011.05 Sales Representatives, Medical

- Education/Training Required: Moderate-term on-the-job training
- Employed: No data available.
- Annual Earnings: $54,360
- Growth: 7.5%
- Annual Job Openings: 24,000

Sell medical equipment, products, and services. Does not include pharmaceutical sales representatives.

Promotes sale of medical and dental equipment, supplies, and services to doctors, dentists, hospitals, medical schools, and retail establishments. Selects surgical appliances from stock and fits and sells appliance to customer. Studies data describing new products to accurately recommend purchase of equipment and supplies. Writes specifications to order custom-made surgical appliances, using customer measurements and physician prescriptions. Advises customer regarding office layout, legal and insurance regulations, cost analysis, and collection methods. Designs and fabricates custom-made medical appliances.

GOE INFORMATION—Interest Area: 10. Sales and Marketing. **Work Group:** 10.02. Sales Technology. **Personality Type**—Enterprising. Enterprising occupations frequently involve starting up and carrying out projects. These occupations can involve leading people and making many decisions. They sometimes require risk taking and often deal with business. **Work Values**—Autonomy; Recognition; Compensation; Creativity; Variety. **Skills**—Technology Design; Equipment Selection; Operations Analysis; Active Listening; Speaking; Writing; Persuasion; Negotiation. **Abilities**—*Cognitive:* Oral Comprehension; Oral Expression; Mathematical Reasoning; Written Comprehension; Fluency of Ideas. *Psychomotor:*

None met the criteria. *Physical:* None met the criteria. *Sensory:* Speech Recognition. **General Work Activities**—*Information Input:* Getting Information; Identifying Objects, Actions, and Events; Estimating Needed Characteristics. *Mental Process:* Updating and Using Relevant Knowledge; Analyzing Data or Information; Organizing, Planning, and Prioritizing. *Work Output:* Handling and Moving Objects; Drafting and Specifying Technical Devices; Controlling Machines and Processes. *Interacting with Others:* Influencing Others or Selling; Communicating with Persons Outside Organization; Establishing and Maintaining Relationships. **Physical Work Conditions**—Indoors; Walking or Running; Radiation; Standing. **Other Job Characteristics**—Consequence of Error; Pace Determined by Speed of Equipment; Importance of Being Exact or Accurate.

Experience—Job Zone 3. Previous work-related skill, knowledge, or experience is required. **Job Preparation:** SVP 6.0 to less than 7.0—more than one year and less than four years. **Knowledge**—Sales and Marketing; Design; Mathematics; Economics and Accounting; Engineering and Technology. **Instructional Programs**—Business, Management, Marketing, and Related Support Services, Other; Selling Skills and Sales Operations.

Related DOT Jobs—276.257-010 Sales Representative, Dental and Medical Equipment and Supplies; 276.257-022 Salesperson, Surgical Appliances.

41-4011.06 Sales Representatives, Instruments

- **Education/Training Required: Moderate-term on-the-job training**
- **Employed: 395,860**
- **Annual Earnings: $54,360**
- **Growth: 7.5%**
- **Annual Job Openings: 24,000**

Sell precision instruments, such as dynamometers and spring scales, and laboratory, navigation, and surveying instruments.

Assists customer with product selection, utilizing knowledge of engineering specifications and catalog resources. Sells weighing and other precision instruments, such as spring scales, dynamometers, and laboratory, navigational, and surveying instruments, to customer. Evaluates customer needs and emphasizes product features based on technical knowledge of product capabilities and limitations.

GOE INFORMATION—**Interest Area:** 10. Sales and Marketing. **Work Group:** 10.02. Sales Technology. **Personality Type**—Enterprising. Enterprising occupations frequently involve starting up and carrying out projects. These occupations can involve leading people and making many decisions. They sometimes require risk taking and often deal with business. **Work Values**—Autonomy; Recognition; Creativity; Good Working Conditions; Variety. **Skills**—Persuasion. **Abilities**—*Cognitive:* Oral Expression; Mathematical Reasoning; Oral Comprehension. *Psychomotor:* None met the criteria. *Physical:* None met the criteria. *Sensory:* Speech Recognition. **General Work Activities**—*Information Input:* Identifying Objects, Actions, and Events; Getting Information; Estimating Needed Characteristics. *Mental Process:* Updating and Using Relevant Knowledge; Analyzing Data or Information; Processing Information. *Work Output:* Controlling Machines and Processes; Handling and Moving Objects; Performing General Physical Activities. *Interacting with Others:* Influencing Others or Selling; Communicating with Persons Outside Organization; Establishing and Maintaining Relationships. **Physical Work Conditions**—Standing; Sitting; Indoors. **Other Job Characteristics**—Pace Determined by Speed of Equipment; Importance of Repeating Same Tasks; Consequence of Error.

Experience—Job Zone 3. Previous work-related skill, knowledge, or experience is required. **Job Preparation:** SVP 6.0 to less than 7.0—more than one year and less than four years. **Knowledge**—Sales and Marketing; Customer and Personal Service; Engineering and Technology; Psychology; Philosophy and Theology. **Instructional Programs**—Business, Management, Marketing, and Related Support Services, Other; Selling Skills and Sales Operations.

Related DOT Jobs—276.257-014 Sales Representative, Weighing and Force-Measurement Instruments; 276.357-014 Sales Representative, Precision Instruments.

41-4012.00 Sales Representatives, Wholesale and Manufacturing, Except Technical and Scientific Products

- **Education/Training Required: Moderate-term on-the-job training**
- **Employed: 1,425,125**
- **Annual Earnings: $41,520**
- **Growth: 5.7%**
- **Annual Job Openings: 86,000**

Sell goods for wholesalers or manufacturers to businesses or groups of individuals. Work requires substantial knowledge of items sold.

Contacts regular and prospective customers to solicit orders. Recommends products to customers based on customer's specific needs and interests. Answers questions about products, prices, durability, and credit terms. Meets with customers to demonstrate and explain features of products. Prepares lists of prospective customers. Reviews sales records and current market information to determine value or sales potential of product. Estimates delivery dates and arranges delivery schedules. Completes sales contracts or forms to record sales information. Instructs customers in use of products. Assists and advises retail dealers in use of sales promotion techniques. Investigates and resolves customer complaints. Forwards orders to manufacturer. Assembles and stocks product displays in retail stores. Writes reports on sales and products. Prepares drawings, estimates, and bids to meet specific needs of customer. Obtains credit information on prospective customers. Oversees delivery or installation of products or equipment.

GOE INFORMATION—**Interest Area:** 10. Sales and Marketing. **Work Group:** 10.03. General Sales. **Personality Type**—Enterprising. Enterprising occupations frequently involve starting up and carrying out projects. These occupations can involve leading people and making many decisions. They sometimes require risk taking and often deal with business. **Work Values**—Autonomy; Recognition; Variety; Creativity; Compensation. **Skills**—Management of Material Resources; Negotiation; Speaking; Service Orientation; Persuasion; Complex Problem Solving; Writing; Active Listening. **Abilities**—*Cognitive:* Memorization; Fluency of Ideas; Originality; Category Flexibility; Mathematical Reasoning. *Psychomotor:* Response Orientation; Speed of Limb Movement; Reaction Time; Multilimb Coordination; Rate Control. *Physical:* Static Strength; Extent Flexibility; Trunk Strength; Explosive Strength; Gross Body Coordination. *Sensory:* Speech Recognition; Speech Clarity; Far Vision; Night Vision; Near Vision. **General Work Activities**—*Information Input:* Getting Information; Identifying Objects, Actions, and Events; Estimating Needed Characteristics. *Mental Process:* Organizing, Planning, and Prioritizing; Analyzing Data or Information; Updating and Using Relevant Knowledge. *Work Output:* Documenting or Recording Information; Drafting and Specifying Technical Devices; Interacting with Computers. *Interacting with Others:* Influencing Others or Selling; Communicating with Persons Outside Organization; Communicating with Other Workers. **Physical Work Conditions**—Walking or Running; Sitting; Outdoors; Indoors; Kneeling, Crouching, or Crawling. **Other Job Characteristics**—Consequence of Error; Degree of Automation; Importance of Being Exact or Accurate.

Experience—Job Zone 2. Some previous work-related skill, knowledge, or experience may be helpful, but usually is not needed. **Job Preparation:** SVP 4.0 to less than 6.0—six months to less than two years. **Knowledge**—Sales and Marketing; Customer and Personal Service; Communications and Media; Economics and Accounting; Psychology. **Instructional Programs**—Apparel and Accessories Marketing Operations; Business, Management, Marketing, and Related Support Services, Other; Fashion Merchandising; General Merchandising, Sales, and Related Marketing Operations, Other; Sales, Distribution, and Marketing Operations, General; Special Products Marketing Operations; Specialized Merchandising, Sales, and Related Marketing Operations, Other.

Related DOT Jobs—162.157-026 Commission Agent, Livestock; 260.257-010 Sales Representative, Livestock; 260.357-010 Commission Agent, Agricultural Produce; 260.357-014 Sales Representative, Food Products; 260.357-018 Sales Representative, Malt Liquors; 260.357-022 Sales Representative, Tobacco Products and Smoking Supplies; 261.357-010 Sales Representative, Apparel Trimmings; 261.357-014 Sales Representative, Canvas Products; 261.357-018 Sales Representative, Footwear; 261.357-022 Sales Representative, Men's and Boys' Apparel; 261.357-026 Sales Representative, Safety Apparel and Equipment; 261.357-030 Sales Representative, Textiles; 261.357-034 Sales Representative, Uniforms; 261.357-038 Sales Representative, Women's and Girls' Apparel; 262.357-014 Sales Representative, Toilet Preparations; 269.357-010 Sales Representative, Fuels; 269.357-014 Sales Representative, Petroleum Products; 270.357-010 Sales Representative, Home Furnishings; 270.357-014 Sales Representative, Household Appliances; 271.357-014 Sales Representative, Videotape; others.

41-9000 Other Sales and Related Workers

41-9011.00 Demonstrators and Product Promoters

- **Education/Training Required: Moderate-term on-the-job training**
- **Employed: 117,613**
- **Annual Earnings: $20,690**
- **Growth: 24.9%**
- **Annual Job Openings: 34,000**

Demonstrate merchandise and answer questions for the purpose of creating public interest in buying the product. May sell demonstrated merchandise.

Demonstrates and explains products, methods, or services to persuade customers to purchase products or utilize services available; answers questions. Visits homes, community organizations, stores, and schools to demonstrate products or services. Attends trade, traveling, promotional, educational, or amusement exhibit to answer visitors' questions and to protect exhibit against theft or damage. Sets up and arranges display to attract attention of prospective customers. Suggests product improvements to employer and product to purchase to customer. Gives product samples or token gifts to customers and distributes handbills,

brochures, or gift certificates to passers-by. Answers telephone and written requests from customers for information about product use and writes articles and pamphlets on product. Lectures and shows slides to users of company product. Advises customers on homemaking problems related to products or services offered by company. Wears costume or sign boards and walks in public to attract attention to advertise merchandise, services, or belief. Contacts businesses and civic establishments and arranges to exhibit and sell merchandise made by disadvantaged persons. Instructs customers in alteration of products. Develops list of prospective clients from sources such as newspaper items, company records, local merchants, and customers. Solicits new organization membership. Trains demonstrators to present company's products or services. Conducts guided tours of plant where product is made. Prepares reports of services rendered and visits made. Drives truck and trailer to transport exhibit. Collects fees or accepts donations.

GOE INFORMATION—**Interest Area:** 10. Sales and Marketing. **Work Group:** 10.04. Personal Soliciting. **Personality Type**—Enterprising. Enterprising occupations frequently involve starting up and carrying out projects. These occupations can involve leading people and making many decisions. They sometimes require risk taking and often deal with business. **Work Values**—Variety; Social Service; Independence; Supervision, Technical. **Skills**—Persuasion; Speaking; Social Perceptiveness; Instructing; Learning Strategies; Complex Problem Solving; Writing; Critical Thinking. **Abilities**—*Cognitive:* Fluency of Ideas; Originality; Written Expression; Oral Expression; Memorization. *Psychomotor:* Response Orientation; Multilimb Coordination; Rate Control; Control Precision. *Physical:* Static Strength; Gross Body Equilibrium; Stamina; Dynamic Flexibility. *Sensory:* Speech Clarity; Night Vision; Far Vision; Speech Recognition; Glare Sensitivity. **General Work Activities**—*Information Input:* Identifying Objects, Actions, and Events; Getting Information; Estimating Needed Characteristics. *Mental Process:* Organizing, Planning, and Prioritizing; Scheduling Work and Activities; Judging Qualities of Things, Services, or Other People's Work. *Work Output:* Handling and Moving Objects; Performing General Physical Activities; Documenting or Recording Information. *Interacting with Others:* Communicating with Persons Outside Organization; Establishing and Maintaining Relationships; Performing for or Working with the Public. **Physical Work Conditions**—Outdoors; Walking or Running; Keeping or Regaining Balance; Extremely Bright or Inadequate Lighting; Distracting Sounds and Noise Levels. **Other Job Characteristics**—Importance of Repeating Same Tasks; Pace Determined by Speed of Equipment; Degree of Automation.

Experience—Job Zone 1. No previous work-related skill, knowledge, or experience is needed. **Job Preparation:** SVP below 4.0—less than six months. **Knowledge**—Sales and Marketing; Education and Training; Communications and Media; English Language; Clerical. **Instructional Programs**—Retailing and Retail Operations.

Related DOT Jobs—279.357-010 Sales Exhibitor; 293.357-018 Goodwill Ambassador; 297.354-010 Demonstrator; 297.354-014 Demonstrator, Knitting; 297.357-010 Demonstrator, Electric-Gas Appliances; 297.367-010 Exhibit-Display Representative; 297.451-010 Instructor, Painting; 297.454-010 Demonstrator, Sewing Techniques; 299.687-014 Sandwich-Board Carrier.

41-9012.00 Models

- **Education/Training Required: Moderate-term on-the-job training**
- **Employed: 3,734**
- **Annual Earnings: $19,010**
- **Growth: 26.0%**
- **Annual Job Openings: 1,000**

Model garments and other apparel to display clothing before prospective buyers at fashion shows, private showings, retail establishments, or photographer. May pose for photos to be used for advertising purposes. May pose as subject for paintings, sculptures, and other types of artistic expression.

Poses as subject for paintings, sculptures, and other types of art for translation into plastic or pictorial values. Poses as directed or strikes suitable interpretive poses for promoting and selling merchandise or fashions during photo session. Wears character costumes and impersonates characters portrayed to amuse children and adults. Stands, turns, and walks to demonstrate features of garment to observers at fashion shows, private showings, and retail establishments. Hands out samples or presents, demonstrates toys, and converses with children and adults while dressed in costume. Dresses in sample or completed garments and selects own accessories. Applies makeup to face and styles hair to enhance appearance, considering such factors as color, camera techniques, and facial features. Informs prospective purchasers as to model, number, and price of garments and department where garment can be purchased.

GOE INFORMATION—Interest Area: 01. Arts, Entertainment, and Media. **Work Group:** 01.09. Modeling and Personal Appearance. **Personality Type**—Artistic. Artistic occupations frequently involve working with forms, designs, and patterns. They often require self-expression, and the work can be done without following a clear set of rules. **Work Values**—Recognition; Compensation; Social Status. **Skills**—None met the criteria. **Abilities**—*Cognitive:* Spatial Orientation; Originality. *Psychomotor:* Speed of Limb Movement; Arm-Hand Steadiness; Finger Dexterity. *Physical:* Gross Body Coordination; Dynamic Flexibility; Gross Body Equilibrium; Stamina. *Sensory:* Glare Sensitivity; Peripheral Vision; Visual Color Discrimination; Auditory Attention; Night Vision. **General Work Activities**—*Information Input:* Monitoring Processes, Materials, or Surroundings; Getting Information; Identifying Objects, Actions, and Events. *Mental Process:* Organizing, Planning, and Prioritizing; Thinking Creatively; Updating and Using Relevant Knowledge. *Work Output:* Performing General Physical Activities; Handling and Moving Objects; Documenting or Recording Information. *Interacting with Others:* Performing for or Working with the Public; Establishing and Maintaining Relationships; Communicating with Persons Outside Organization. **Physical Work Conditions**—Walking or Running; Keeping or Regaining Balance; Extremely Bright or Inadequate Lighting; Outdoors; Standing. **Other Job Characteristics**—Importance of Repeating Same Tasks; Pace Determined by Speed of Equipment; Degree of Automation.

Experience—Job Zone 1. No previous work-related skill, knowledge, or experience is needed. **Job Preparation:** SVP below 4.0—less than six months. **Knowledge**—Fine Arts; Sales and Marketing; Communications and Media; Sociology and Anthropology; Customer and Personal Service. **Instructional Programs**—Fashion Modeling.

Related DOT Jobs—297.667-014 Model; 299.647-010 Impersonator, Character; 961.367-010 Model, Photographer's; 961.667-010 Model, Artist's.

41-9021.00 *Real Estate Brokers*

- **Education/Training Required: Work experience in a related occupation**
- **Employed: 92,751**
- **Annual Earnings: $51,370**
- **Growth: 9.6%**
- **Annual Job Openings: 8,000**

Operate real estate office or work for commercial real estate firm, overseeing real estate transactions. Other duties usually include selling real estate or renting properties and arranging loans.

Act as an intermediary in negotiations between buyers and sellers over property prices and settlement details and during the closing of sales. Appraise property values, assessing income potential when relevant. Arrange for title searches of properties being sold. Check work completed by loan officers, attorneys, and other professionals to ensure that it is performed properly. Compare a property with similar properties that have recently sold in order to determine its competitive market price. Generate lists of properties for sale, their locations and descriptions, and available financing options, using computers. Maintain awareness of current income tax regulations; local zoning, building, and tax laws; and growth possibilities of the area where a property is located. Maintain knowledge of real estate law, local economies, fair housing laws, and types of available mortgages, financing options, and government programs. Manage and operate real estate offices, handling associated business details. Monitor fulfillment of purchase contract terms to ensure that they are handled in a timely manner. Obtain agreements from property owners to place properties for sale with real estate firms. Sell, for a fee, real estate owned by others. Arrange for financing of property purchases. Develop, sell, or lease property used for industry or manufacturing. Give buyers virtual tours of properties in which they are interested, using computers. Maintain working knowledge of various factors that determine a farm's capacity to produce, including agricultural variables and proximity to market centers and transportation facilities. Rent properties or manage rental properties. Review property details to ensure that environmental regulations are met. Supervise agents who handle real estate transactions.

GOE INFORMATION—Interest Area: 10. Sales and Marketing. **Work Group:** 10.03. General Sales. **Note:** The Department of Labor has not collected some data for this job, so it has fewer details than the other descriptions.

Instructional Programs—Real Estate.

Related DOT Jobs—250.357-018 Real-Estate Broker (UR).

41-9022.00 *Real Estate Sales Agents*

- **Education/Training Required: Postsecondary vocational training**
- **Employed: 339,058**
- **Annual Earnings: $28,570**
- **Growth: 9.5%**
- **Annual Job Openings: 28,000**

Rent, buy, or sell property for clients. Perform duties, such as study property listings, interview prospective clients, accompany clients to property site, discuss conditions of sale, and draw up real estate contracts. Includes agents who represent buyer.

Accompany buyers during visits to and inspections of property, advising them on the suitability and value of the homes they are visiting. Act as an intermediary in negotiations between buyers and sellers, generally representing one or the other. Advise clients on market conditions, prices, mortgages, legal requirements, and related matters. Advise sellers on how to make homes more appealing to potential buyers. Answer clients' questions regarding construction work, financing, maintenance, repairs, and appraisals. Arrange for title searches to determine whether clients have clear property titles. Arrange meetings between buyers and sellers when details of transactions need to be negotiated. Compare a property with similar properties that have recently sold in order to determine its competitive market price. Confer with escrow companies, lenders, home inspectors, and pest control operators to ensure that terms and conditions of purchase agreements are met before closing dates. Contact property owners and advertise services in order to solicit property sales listings. Coordinate appointments to show homes to prospective buyers. Coordinate property closings, overseeing signing of documents and disbursement of funds. Display commercial, industrial, agricultural, and residential properties to clients and explain their features. Generate lists of properties that are compatible with buyers' needs and financial resources. Interview clients to determine what kinds of properties they are seeking. Prepare documents such as representation contracts, purchase agreements, closing statements, deeds, and leases. Present purchase offers to sellers for consideration. Promote sales of properties through advertisements, open houses, and participation in multiple listing services. Review plans for new construction with clients, enumerating and recommending available options and features. Review property listings, trade journals, and relevant literature and attend conventions, seminars, and staff and association meetings in order to remain knowledgeable about real estate markets. Solicit and compile listings of available rental properties. Visit properties to assess them before showing them to clients. Appraise properties to determine loan values. Conduct seminars and training sessions for sales agents in order to improve sales techniques. Contact utility companies for service hookups to clients' property. Develop networks of attorneys, mortgage lenders, and contractors to whom clients may be referred.

GOE INFORMATION—Interest Area: 10. Sales and Marketing. Work Group: 10.03. General Sales. Personality Type—Enterprising. Enterprising occupations frequently involve starting up and carrying out projects. These occupations can involve leading people and making many decisions. They sometimes require risk taking and often deal with business. Work Values—Responsibility; Recognition; Compensation; Variety; Social Service. Skills—Persuasion; Speaking; Active Listening; Mathematics; Negotiation; Complex Problem Solving; Management of Financial Resources; Judgment and Decision Making. Abilities—Cognitive: Number Facility; Mathematical Reasoning; Spatial Orientation; Oral Expression; Written Comprehension. Psychomotor: None met the criteria. Physical: None met the criteria. Sensory: Speech Recognition; Far Vision; Speech Clarity; Near Vision. General Work Activities—Information Input: Getting Information; Identifying Objects, Actions, and Events; Inspecting Equipment, Structures, or Materials. Mental Process: Judging Qualities of Things, Services, or Other People's Work; Organizing, Planning, and Prioritizing; Updating and Using Relevant Knowledge. Work Output: Documenting or Recording Information; Performing General Physical Activities; Handling and Moving Objects. Interacting with Others: Influencing Others or Selling; Communicating with Persons Outside Organization; Establishing and Maintaining Relationships. Physical Work Conditions—Sitting; Outdoors; Walking or Running; Indoors. Other Job Characteristics—Importance of Being Exact or Accurate; Consequence of Error; Importance of Repeating Same Tasks.

Experience—Job Zone 2. Some previous work-related skill, knowledge, or experience may be helpful, but usually is not needed. Job Preparation: SVP 4.0 to less than 6.0—six months to less than two years. Knowledge—Sales and Marketing; Economics and Accounting; Law and Government; Communications and Media; Geography. Instructional Programs—Real Estate.

Related DOT Jobs—250.157-010 Superintendent, Sales; 250.357-010 Building Consultant; 250.357-014 Leasing Agent, Residence; 250.357-018 Sales Agent, Real Estate.

41-9031.00 Sales Engineers

- **Education/Training Required:** Bachelor's degree
- **Employed:** 85,164
- **Annual Earnings:** $59,720
- **Growth:** 17.7%
- **Annual Job Openings:** 4,000

Sell business goods or services, the selling of which requires a technical background equivalent to a baccalaureate degree in engineering.

Calls on management representatives at commercial, industrial, and other establishments to convince prospective client to buy products or services offered. Assists sales force in sale of company products. Demonstrates and explains product or service to customer representatives, such as engineers, architects, and other professionals. Draws up sales or service contract for products or services. Provides technical services to clients relating to use, operation, and maintenance of equipment. Arranges for trial installations of equipment. Designs and drafts variations of standard products in order to meet customer needs. Reviews customer documents to develop and prepare cost estimates or projected production increases from use of proposed equipment or services. Draws up or proposes changes in equipment, processes, materials, or services resulting in cost reduction or improvement in customer operations. Assists in development of custom-made machinery. Diagnoses problems with equipment installed. Provides technical training to employees of client.

GOE INFORMATION—Interest Area: 02. Science, Math, and Engineering. Work Group: 02.07. Engineering. Personality Type—Enterprising. Enterprising occupations frequently involve starting up and carrying out projects. These occupations can involve leading people and making many decisions. They sometimes require risk taking and often deal with business. Work Values—Ability Utilization; Creativity; Recognition; Variety; Social Service. Skills—Technology Design; Troubleshooting; Operations Analysis; Speaking; Equipment Selection; Persuasion; Management of Material Resources; Negotiation. Abilities—Cognitive: Mathematical Reasoning; Visualization; Written Expression; Written Comprehension; Fluency of Ideas. Psychomotor: Reaction Time; Response Orientation; Rate Control; Control Precision; Arm-Hand Steadiness. Physical: Extent Flexibility; Static Strength; Gross Body Equilibrium; Trunk Strength; Gross Body Coordination. Sensory: Speech Clarity; Hearing Sensitivity; Speech Recognition; Visual Color Discrimination; Sound Localization. General Work Activities—Information Input: Getting Information; Identifying Objects, Actions, and Events; Estimating Needed Characteristics. Mental Process: Updating and Using Relevant Knowledge; Analyzing Data or Information; Organizing, Planning, and Prioritizing. Work Output: Drafting and Specifying Technical Devices; Documenting or Recording Information; Handling and Moving Objects. Interacting with Others: Communicating with Persons Outside Organization; Providing Consultation and Advice to Others; Influencing Others or Selling. Physical Work Conditions—Walking or Running; Indoors; Sitting. Other Job Characteristics—Degree of Automation; Importance of Being Exact or Accurate; Consequence of Error.

Experience—Job Zone 5. Extensive skill, knowledge, and experience are needed for these occupations. Job Preparation: SVP 8.0 and above—four years to more than 10 years. Knowledge—Sales and Marketing; Design; Engineering and Technology; Production and Processing; Customer and Personal Service. Instructional Programs—Selling Skills and Sales Operations.

Related DOT Jobs—010.151-010 Sales Engineer, Mining-and-Oil-Well Equipment and Services; 013.151-010 Sales Engineer, Agricultural Equipment; 014.151-010 Sales Engineer, Marine Equipment; 015.151-010 Sales Engineer, Nuclear Equipment; 215.101-010 Sales Engineer, Aeronautical Products; 315.101-010 Sales-Engineer, Electrical Products; 315.101-014 Sales-Engineer, Electronics Products and Systems; 615.101-010 Sales Engineer, Ceramic Products; 715.101-010 Sales Engineer, Mechanical Equipment; 815.101-010 Chemical-Equipment Sales Engineer.

41-9041.00 Telemarketers

- **Education/Training Required: Short-term on-the-job training**
- **Employed: 571,820**
- **Annual Earnings: $19,210**
- **Growth: 22.2%**
- **Annual Job Openings: 145,000**

Solicit orders for goods or services over the telephone.

Adjust sales scripts to better target the needs and interests of specific individuals. Answer telephone calls from potential customers who have been solicited through advertisements. Contact businesses or private individuals by telephone in order to solicit sales for goods or services or to request donations for charitable causes. Deliver prepared sales talks, reading from scripts that describe products or services, in order to persuade potential customers to purchase a product or service or to make a donation. Explain products or services and prices and answer questions from customers. Maintain records of contacts, accounts, and orders. Obtain customer information such as name, address, and payment method and enter orders into computers. Record names, addresses, purchases, and reactions of prospects contacted. Schedule appointments for sales representatives to meet with prospective customers or for customers to attend sales presentations. Conduct client or market surveys in order to obtain information about potential customers. Obtain names and telephone numbers of potential customers from sources such as telephone directories, magazine reply cards, and lists purchased from other organizations. Telephone or write letters to respond to correspondence from customers or to follow up on initial sales contacts.

GOE INFORMATION—Interest Area: 10. Sales and Marketing. Work Group: 10.04. Personal Soliciting. Personality Type—Enterprising. Enterprising occupations frequently involve starting up and carrying out projects. These occupations can involve leading people and making many decisions. They sometimes require risk taking and often deal with business. Work Values—Independence; Social Service. Skills—Persuasion. Abilities—*Cognitive:* Originality; Memorization; Time Sharing; Number Facility; Oral Comprehension. *Psychomotor:* None met the criteria. *Physical:* Stamina. *Sensory:* Speech Clarity; Speech Recognition; Auditory Attention; Glare Sensitivity; Night Vision. General Work Activities—*Information Input:* Getting Information; Estimating Needed Characteristics; Inspecting Equipment, Structures, or Materials. *Mental Process:* Thinking Creatively; Organizing, Planning, and Prioritizing; Updating and Using Relevant Knowledge. *Work Output:* Performing General Physical Activities; Handling and Moving Objects; Documenting or Recording Information. *Interacting with Others:* Influencing Others or Selling; Communicating with Persons Outside Organization; Performing for or Working with the Public. Physical Work Conditions—Outdoors; Walking or Running; Extremely Bright or Inadequate Lighting; Very Hot or Cold; Kneeling, Crouching, or Crawling. Other Job Characteristics—Importance of Repeating Same Tasks; Pace Determined by Speed of Equipment; Degree of Automation.

Experience—Job Zone 1. No previous work-related skill, knowledge, or experience is needed. Job Preparation: SVP below 4.0—less than six months. Knowledge—Sales and Marketing; Customer and Personal Service; Economics and Accounting; Communications and Media; Geography. Instructional Programs—Sales, Distribution, and Marketing Operations, General; Selling Skills and Sales Operations.

Related DOT Jobs—299.357-014 Telephone Solicitor.

41-9091.00 Door-To-Door Sales Workers, News and Street Vendors, and Related Workers

- **Education/Training Required: Short-term on-the-job training**
- **Employed: 165,861**
- **Annual Earnings: $24,830**
- **Growth: –6.2%**
- **Annual Job Openings: 42,000**

Sell goods or services door-to-door or on the street.

Contacts customers by phone, by mail, or in person to offer or persuade them to purchase merchandise or services. Explains products or services and prices and demonstrates use of products. Writes orders for merchandise or enters order into computer. Circulates among potential customers or travels by foot, truck, automobile, or bicycle to deliver or sell merchandise or services. Arranges buying party and solicits sponsorship of parties to sell merchandise. Delivers merchandise, serves customer, collects money, and makes change. Distributes product samples or literature that details products or services. Maintains records of accounts and orders and develops prospect lists. Orders or purchases supplies and stocks cart or stand. Sets up and displays sample merchandise at parties or stands.

GOE INFORMATION—Interest Area: 10. Sales and Marketing. Work Group: 10.04. Personal Soliciting. Personality Type—Enterprising. Enterprising occupations frequently involve starting up and carrying out projects. These occupations can involve leading people and making many decisions. They sometimes require risk taking and often deal with business. Work Values—Independence; Social Service. Skills—Persuasion. Abilities—*Cognitive:* Originality; Memorization; Time Sharing; Number Facility; Oral Comprehension. *Psychomotor:* None met the criteria. *Physical:* Stamina. *Sensory:* Speech Clarity; Speech Recognition; Auditory Attention; Glare Sensitivity; Night Vision. General Work Activities—*Information Input:* Getting Information; Estimating Needed Characteristics; Identifying Objects, Actions, and Events. *Mental Process:* Thinking Creatively; Organizing, Planning, and Prioritizing; Updating and Using Relevant Knowledge. *Work Output:* Performing General Physical Activities; Handling and Moving Objects; Documenting or Recording Information. *Interacting with Others:* Influencing Others or Selling; Communicating with Persons Outside Organization; Performing for or Working with the Public. Physical Work Conditions—Outdoors; Walking or Running; Extremely Bright or Inadequate Lighting; Very Hot or Cold; Kneeling, Crouching, or Crawling. Other Job Characteristics—Importance of Repeating Same Tasks; Pace Determined by Speed of Equipment; Degree of Automation.

Experience—Job Zone 1. No previous work-related skill, knowledge, or experience is needed. Job Preparation: SVP below 4.0—less than six months. Knowledge—Sales and Marketing; Customer and Personal Service; Economics and Accounting; Communications and Media; Geography. Instructional Programs—Selling Skills and Sales Operations.

Related DOT Jobs—279.357-038 Salesperson-Demonstrator, Party Plan; 291.357-010 Sales Representative, Door-To-Door; 291.454-010 Lei Seller; 291.457-010 Cigarette Vendor; 291.457-014 Lounge-Car Attendant; 291.457-018 Peddler; 291.457-022 Vendor; 292.457-010 Newspaper Carrier.

41-9099.99 Sales and Related Workers, All Other

- **Education/Training Required: No data available.**
- **Employed: No data available.**
- **Annual Earnings: No data available.**
- **Growth: 22.0%**
- **Annual Job Openings: 99,000**

All sales and related workers not listed separately.

No task data available.

GOE INFORMATION—Interest Area: 10. Sales and Marketing. **Work Group:** 10.02. Sales Technology; 10.03. General Sales. **Note:** The Department of Labor has not collected some data for this job, so it has fewer details than the other descriptions.

Instructional Programs—Auctioneering; Business, Management, Marketing, and Related Support Services, Other; General Merchandising, Sales, and Related Marketing Operations, Other; Retailing and Retail Operations; Selling Skills and Sales Operations; Special Products Marketing Operations; Specialized Merchandising, Sales, and Related Marketing Operations, Other.

Related DOT Jobs—191.157-010 Pawnbroker; 191.287-010 Appraiser; 259.357-034 Ticket Broker; 294.257-010 Auctioneer; 296.357-010 Personal Shopper; 296.367-010 Automobile Locator; 296.367-014 Comparison Shopper; 299.357-018 Wedding Consultant; 299.364-010 Drapery And Upholstery Measurer; 299.364-014 Gift Wrapper; 299.367-010 Customer-Service Clerk; 299.387-010 Drapery And Upholstery Estimator; 299.387-018 Stamp Classifier; 299.667-014 Stock Checker, Apparel; 869.367-014 Measurer.

43-0000
Office and Administrative Support Occupations

43-1000 Supervisors, Office and Administrative Support Workers

43-1011.00 First-Line Supervisors/ Managers of Office and Administrative Support Workers

- Education/Training Required: Work experience in a related occupation
- Employed: 1,391,544
- Annual Earnings: $37,990
- Growth: 9.4%
- Annual Job Openings: 146,000

Supervise and coordinate the activities of clerical and administrative support workers.

No task data available.

GOE INFORMATION—Interest Area: 09. Business Detail. Work Group: 09.01. Managerial Work in Business Detail. Note: The Department of Labor has not collected some data for this job, so it has fewer details than the other descriptions.

Instructional Programs—Agricultural Business Technology; Customer Service Management; Medical/Health Management and Clinical Assistant/Specialist; Office Management and Supervision.

Related DOT Jobs—109.137-010 Shelving Supervisor; 168.167-058 Manager, Customer Service; 168.167-070 Regulatory Administrator; 202.132-010 Supervisor, Steno Pool; 203.132-010 Supervisor, Telegraphic-Typewriter Operators; 203.132-014 Supervisor, Transcribing Operators; 203.137-010 Supervisor, Word Processing; 203.137-014 Typing Section Chief; 205.137-014 Supervisor, Survey Workers; 205.162-010 Admitting Officer; 206.137-010 Supervisor, Files; 207.137-010 Chief Clerk, Print Shop; 209.132-010 Supervisor, Personnel Clerks; 209.132-014 Technical Coordinator; 209.137-010 Mailroom Supervisor; 209.137-014 Meter Reader, Chief; 209.137-018 Supervisor, Agency Appointments; 209.137-026 Supervisor, Marking Room; 210.132-010 Supervisor, Audit Clerks; 211.132-010 Teller, Head; others.

43-1011.01 First-Line Supervisors, Customer Service

- Education/Training Required: Work experience in a related occupation
- Employed: No data available.
- Annual Earnings: $37,990
- Growth: 9.4%
- Annual Job Openings: 146,000

Supervise and coordinate activities of workers involved in providing customer service.

Supervises and coordinates activities of workers engaged in customer service activities. Plans, prepares, and devises work schedules according to budgets and workloads. Observes and evaluates workers' performance. Issues instructions and assigns duties to workers. Trains and instructs employees. Hires and discharges workers. Communicates with other departments and management to resolve problems and expedite work. Interprets and communicates work procedures and company policies to staff. Helps workers in resolving problems and completing work. Resolves complaints and answers questions of customers regarding services and procedures. Reviews and checks work of subordinates, such as reports, records, and applications, for accuracy and content; corrects errors. Prepares, maintains, and submits reports and records, such as budgets and operational and personnel reports. Makes recommendations to management concerning staff and improvement of procedures. Plans and develops improved procedures. Requisitions or purchases supplies.

GOE INFORMATION—Interest Area: 09. Business Detail. Work Group: 09.01. Managerial Work in Business Detail. Personality Type—Enterprising. Enterprising occupations frequently involve starting up and carrying out projects. These occupations can involve leading people and making many decisions. They sometimes require risk taking and often deal with business. Work Values—Authority; Autonomy; Creativity; Social Service; Good Working Conditions. Skills—Management of Personnel Resources; Management of Financial Resources; Service Orientation; Systems Evaluation; Coordination; Speaking; Social Perceptiveness; Monitoring. Abilities—*Cognitive:* Memorization; Written Expression; Originality; Mathematical Reasoning; Fluency of Ideas. *Psychomotor:* Wrist-Finger Speed; Response Orientation; Finger Dexterity. *Physical:* Trunk Strength. *Sensory:* Speech Recognition; Speech Clarity; Near Vision; Auditory Attention; Hearing Sensitivity. General Work Activities—*Information Input:* Getting Information; Identifying Objects, Actions, and Events; Estimating Needed Characteristics. *Mental Process:* Scheduling Work and Activities; Organizing, Planning, and Prioritizing; Making Decisions and Solving Problems. *Work Output:* Documenting or Recording Information; Handling and Moving Objects; Performing General Physical Activities. *Interacting with Others:* Guiding, Directing, and Motivating Subordinates; Communicating with Other Workers; Resolving Conflict and Negotiating with Others. Physical Work Conditions—Walking or Running; Indoors; Sitting. Other Job Characteristics—Degree of Automation; Consequence of Error; Importance of Repeating Same Tasks.

Experience—Job Zone 3. Previous work-related skill, knowledge, or experience is required. Job Preparation: SVP 6.0 to less than 7.0—more than one year and less than four years. Knowledge—Customer and Personal Service; Personnel and Human Resources; Education and Training; Administration and Management; Clerical. Instructional Programs—Agricultural Business Technology; Customer Service Management; Medical/ Health Management and Clinical Assistant/Specialist; Office Management and Supervision.

Related DOT Jobs—168.167-058 Manager, Customer Service; 205.137-014 Supervisor, Survey Workers; 205.162-010 Admitting Officer; 209.132-014 Technical Coordinator; 209.137-014 Meter Reader, Chief; 211.132-010 Teller, Head; 211.137-010 Supervisor, Cashiers; 211.137-014 Supervisor, Food Checkers and Cashiers; 211.137-022 Supervisor, Tellers; 214.137-010 Documentation Supervisor; 214.137-014 Supervisor, Statement Clerks; 214.137-022 Supervisor, Accounts Receivable; 216.137-014 Transfer Clerk, Head; 222.137-014 Linen-Room Supervisor; 222.137-026 Petroleum-Inspector Supervisor; 230.137-018 Supervisor, Mail Carriers; 235.132-010 Central-Office-Operator Supervisor; 237.137-010 Supervisor, Telephone Information; 237.137-014 Supervisor, Travel-Information Center; 238.137-010 Manager, Reservations; others.

43-1011.02 First-Line Supervisors, Administrative Support

- Education/Training Required: Work experience in a related occupation
- Employed: No data available.
- Annual Earnings: $37,990
- Growth: 9.4%
- Annual Job Openings: 146,000

Supervise and coordinate activities of workers involved in providing administrative support.

Supervises and coordinates activities of workers engaged in clerical or administrative support activities. Plans, prepares, and revises work schedules and duty assignments according to budget allotments, customer needs, problems, work loads, and statistical forecasts. Evaluates subordinate job performance and conformance to regulations and recommends appropriate personnel action. Oversees, coordinates, or performs activities associated with shipping, receiving, distribution, and transportation. Verifies completeness and accuracy of subordinates' work, computations, and records. Interviews, selects, and discharges employees. Consults with supervisor and other personnel to resolve problems, such as equipment performance, output quality, and work schedules. Reviews records and reports pertaining to such activities as production, operation, payroll, customer accounts, and shipping. Trains employees in work and safety procedures and company policies. Participates in work of subordinates to facilitate productivity or overcome difficult aspects of work. Examines procedures and recommends changes to save time, labor, and other costs and to improve quality control and operating efficiency. Maintains records of such matters as inventory, personnel, orders, supplies, and machine maintenance. Identifies and resolves discrepancies or errors. Compiles reports and information required by management or governmental agencies. Plans layout of stockroom, warehouse, or other storage areas, considering turnover, size, weight, and related factors pertaining to items stored. Inspects equipment for defects and notifies maintenance personnel or outside service contractors for repairs. Analyzes financial activities of establishment or department and assists in planning budget. Computes figures such as balances, totals, and commissions. Requisitions supplies.

GOE INFORMATION—Interest Area: 09. Business Detail. **Work Group:** 09.01. Managerial Work in Business Detail. **Personality Type—**Enterprising. Enterprising occupations frequently involve starting up and carrying out projects. These occupations can involve leading people and making many decisions. They sometimes require risk taking and often deal with business. **Work Values—**Authority; Autonomy; Creativity; Social Service; Responsibility. **Skills—**Management of Personnel Resources; Management of Material Resources; Management of Financial Resources; Complex Problem Solving; Monitoring; Systems Evaluation; Time Management; Speaking. **Abilities—***Cognitive:* Number Facility; Written Expression; Mathematical Reasoning; Memorization; Oral Expression. *Psychomotor:* Wrist-Finger Speed; Finger Dexterity; Response Orientation; Reaction Time; Manual Dexterity. *Physical:* Extent Flexibility; Gross Body Equilibrium; Explosive Strength; Static Strength; Dynamic Flexibility. *Sensory:* Speech Recognition; Speech Clarity; Near Vision; Peripheral Vision; Sound Localization. **General Work Activities—***Information Input:* Getting Information; Identifying Objects, Actions, and Events; Monitoring Processes, Materials, or Surroundings. *Mental Process:* Making Decisions and Solving Problems; Scheduling Work and Activities; Processing Information. *Work Output:* Documenting or Recording Information; Interacting with Computers; Handling and Moving Objects. *Interacting with Others:* Communicating with Other Workers; Resolving Conflict and Negotiating with Others; Guiding, Directing, and Motivating Subordinates. **Physical Work Conditions—**Sitting; Indoors; Walking or Running. **Other Job Characteristics—**Degree of Automation; Importance of Being Exact or Accurate; Consequence of Error.

Experience—Job Zone 3. Previous work-related skill, knowledge, or experience is required. **Job Preparation:** SVP 6.0 to less than 7.0—more than one year and less than four years. **Knowledge—**Clerical; Personnel and Human Resources; Administration and Management; Economics and Accounting; Education and Training. **Instructional Programs—**Agricultural Business Technology; Customer Service Management; Medical/

Health Management and Clinical Assistant/Specialist; Office Management and Supervision.

Related DOT Jobs—109.137-010 Shelving Supervisor; 202.132-010 Supervisor, Steno Pool; 203.132-010 Supervisor, Telegraphic-Typewriter Operators; 203.132-014 Supervisor, Transcribing Operators; 203.137-010 Supervisor, Word Processing; 203.137-014 Typing Section Chief; 206.137-010 Supervisor, Files; 207.137-010 Chief Clerk, Print Shop; 209.132-010 Supervisor, Personnel Clerks; 209.137-010 Mailroom Supervisor; 209.137-018 Supervisor, Agency Appointments; 209.137-026 Supervisor, Marking Room; 210.132-010 Supervisor, Audit Clerks; 211.137-018 Supervisor, Money-Room; 213.132-010 Supervisor, Computer Operations; 214.137-018 Rate Supervisor; 215.137-010 Crew Scheduler, Chief; 215.137-014 Supervisor, Payroll; 215.137-018 Supervisor, Force Adjustment; 216.132-010 Supervisor, Accounting Clerks; others.

43-2000 Communications Equipment Operators

43-2011.00 Switchboard Operators, Including Answering Service

- ● **Education/Training Required: Short-term on-the-job training**
- ● **Employed: 259,108**
- ● **Annual Earnings: $20,650**
- ● **Growth: –15.7%**
- ● **Annual Job Openings: 48,000**

Operate telephone business systems equipment or switchboards to relay incoming, outgoing, and interoffice calls. May supply information to callers and record messages.

Answer incoming calls, greeting callers, providing information, transferring calls, and/or taking messages as necessary. Answer simple questions about clients' businesses, using reference files. Keep records of calls placed and charges incurred. Operate communication systems, such as telephone, switchboard, intercom, two-way radio, or public address. Page individuals to inform them of telephone calls, using paging and interoffice communication equipment. Place telephone calls or arrange conference calls as instructed. Record messages, suggesting rewording for clarity and conciseness. Relay and route written and verbal messages. Route emergency calls appropriately. Stamp messages with time and date; file them appropriately. Complete forms for sales orders. Contact security staff members when necessary, using radio-telephones. Monitor alarm systems in order to ensure that secure conditions are maintained. Perform clerical duties, such as typing, proofreading, accepting orders, scheduling appointments, and sorting mail.

GOE INFORMATION—Interest Area: 09. Business Detail. **Work Group:** 09.06. Communications. **Personality Type—**Conventional. Conventional occupations frequently involve following set procedures and routines. These occupations can include working with data and details more than with ideas. Usually there is a clear line of authority to follow. **Work Values—**Independence; Activity; Supervision, Technical; Supervision, Human Relations; Good Working Conditions. **Skills—**None met the criteria. **Abilities—***Cognitive:* Oral Comprehension; Oral Expression; Selective Attention. *Psychomotor:* Wrist-Finger Speed; Response Orientation; Reaction Time; Multilimb Coordination. *Physical:* None met the criteria. *Sensory:* Speech Recognition; Auditory Attention; Hearing Sensitivity; Sound Localization; Speech Clarity. **General Work Activities—***Information Input:* Getting Information; Identifying Objects, Actions, and Events; Monitoring Processes, Materials, or Surroundings. *Mental Process:* Processing Information; Evaluating Information Against Standards; Scheduling Work and Activities. *Work Output:* Documenting or Recording Information; Controlling Machines and Processes; Handling and Moving Objects. *Interacting with Others:* Communicating with Persons Outside Organization; Establishing and Maintaining Relationships; Communicating with Other Workers. **Physical Work Conditions**—Sitting; Indoors; Making Repetitive Motions; Using Hands on Objects, Tools, or Controls. **Other Job Characteristics**—Importance of Repeating Same Tasks; Degree of Automation; Pace Determined by Speed of Equipment.

Experience—Job Zone 1. No previous work-related skill, knowledge, or experience is needed. **Job Preparation:** SVP below 4.0—less than six months. **Knowledge**—Clerical; Telecommunications; Computers and Electronics; Customer and Personal Service; Communications and Media. **Instructional Programs**—Receptionist.

Related DOT Jobs—235.562-014 Switchboard Operator, Police District; 235.662-014 Communication-Center Operator; 235.662-022 Telephone Operator; 235.662-026 Telephone-Answering-Service Operator; 239.362-010 Telephone Clerk, Telegraph Office.

43-2021.00 Telephone Operators

- **Education/Training Required: Short-term on-the-job training**
- **Employed: 53,600**
- **Annual Earnings: $29,540**
- **Growth: –35.3%**
- **Annual Job Openings: 10,000**

Provide information by accessing alphabetical and geographical directories. Assist customers with special billing requests, such as charges to a third party and credits or refunds for incorrectly dialed numbers or bad connections. May handle emergency calls and assist children or people with physical disabilities to make telephone calls.

No task data available.

GOE INFORMATION—**Interest Area:** 09. Business Detail. **Work Group:** 09.06. Communications. **Note:** The Department of Labor has not collected some data for this job, so it has fewer details than the other descriptions.

Instructional Programs—Customer Service Support/Call Center/Teleservice Operation; Receptionist.

Related DOT Jobs—235.462-010 Central-Office Operator; 235.662-018 Directory-Assistance Operator.

43-2021.01 Directory Assistance Operators

- **Education/Training Required: Short-term on-the-job training**
- **Employed: No data available.**
- **Annual Earnings: $29,540**
- **Growth: –35.3%**
- **Annual Job Openings: 10,000**

Provide telephone information from central office switchboard. Refer to alphabetical or geographical reels or directories to answer questions or suggest answer sources.

Refers to alphabetical or geographical reels or directories to answer questions and provide telephone information. Types location and spelling of name on computer terminal keyboard and scans directory or microfilm viewer to locate number. Suggests alternate locations and spellings under which number could be listed. Plugs in headphones when signal light flashes on cord switchboard or pushes switch keys on cordless switchboard to make connections. Maintains record of calls received. Keeps reels and directories up-to-date.

GOE INFORMATION—**Interest Area:** 09. Business Detail. **Work Group:** 09.06. Communications. **Personality Type**—Conventional. Conventional occupations frequently involve following set procedures and routines. These occupations can include working with data and details more than with ideas. Usually there is a clear line of authority to follow. **Work Values**—Supervision, Technical; Independence; Social Service; Activity; Supervision, Human Relations. **Skills**—None met the criteria. **Abilities**—*Cognitive:* Perceptual Speed; Category Flexibility; Memorization; Oral Expression; Speed of Closure. *Psychomotor:* Reaction Time; Wrist-Finger Speed; Response Orientation; Finger Dexterity; Speed of Limb Movement. *Physical:* Extent Flexibility. *Sensory:* Speech Recognition; Speech Clarity; Auditory Attention; Hearing Sensitivity; Near Vision. **General Work Activities**—*Information Input:* Getting Information; Identifying Objects, Actions, and Events; Monitoring Processes, Materials, or Surroundings. *Mental Process:* Processing Information; Updating and Using Relevant Knowledge; Evaluating Information Against Standards. *Work Output:* Handling and Moving Objects; Interacting with Computers; Documenting or Recording Information. *Interacting with Others:* Communicating with Persons Outside Organization; Assisting and Caring for Others; Establishing and Maintaining Relationships. **Physical Work Conditions**—Sitting; Indoors; Making Repetitive Motions. **Other Job Characteristics**—Degree of Automation; Importance of Repeating Same Tasks; Pace Determined by Speed of Equipment.

Experience—Job Zone 1. No previous work-related skill, knowledge, or experience is needed. **Job Preparation:** SVP below 4.0—less than six months. **Knowledge**—Telecommunications; Geography; Clerical; Computers and Electronics; Customer and Personal Service. **Instructional Programs**—Customer Service Support/Call Center/Teleservice Operation; Receptionist.

Related DOT Jobs—235.662-018 Directory-Assistance Operator.

43-2021.02 Central Office Operators

- **Education/Training Required: Short-term on-the-job training**
- **Employed: No data available.**
- **Annual Earnings: $29,540**
- **Growth: –35.3%**
- **Annual Job Openings: 10,000**

Operate telephone switchboard to establish or assist customers in establishing local or long-distance telephone connections.

Observes signal light on switchboard, plugs cords into trunk-jack, and dials or presses button to make connections. Consults charts to determine charges for pay-telephone calls. Inserts tickets in calculagraph (time-stamping device) to record time of toll calls. Requests coin deposits for calls. Gives information regarding subscribers' telephone numbers. Calculates and quotes charges on long-distance connections.

GOE INFORMATION—**Interest Area:** 09. Business Detail. **Work Group:** 09.06. Communications. **Personality Type**—Conventional. Conventional occupations frequently involve following set procedures and routines. These occupations can include working with data and details more than with ideas. Usually there is a clear line of authority to follow. **Work Values**—Supervision, Technical; Independence; Social Service; Supervision, Human Relations; Activity. **Skills**—Operation and Control. **Abilities**—*Cognitive:* Oral Expression. *Psychomotor:* Wrist-Finger Speed. *Physical:* None met the criteria. *Sensory:* Speech Recognition; Speech Clarity.

General Work Activities—*Information Input:* Getting Information; Identifying Objects, Actions, and Events; Monitoring Processes, Materials, or Surroundings. *Mental Process:* Processing Information; Updating and Using Relevant Knowledge; Organizing, Planning, and Prioritizing. *Work Output:* Handling and Moving Objects; Controlling Machines and Processes; Documenting or Recording Information. *Interacting with Others:* Communicating with Persons Outside Organization; Performing for or Working with the Public; Assisting and Caring for Others. **Physical Work Conditions**—Sitting; Indoors; Using Hands on Objects, Tools, or Controls. **Other Job Characteristics**—Importance of Being Exact or Accurate; Importance of Repeating Same Tasks; Degree of Automation.

Experience—Job Zone 1. No previous work-related skill, knowledge, or experience is needed. **Job Preparation:** SVP below 4.0—less than six months. **Knowledge**—Telecommunications; Customer and Personal Service; Geography. **Instructional Programs**—Customer Service Support/Call Center/Teleservice Operation; Receptionist.

Related DOT Jobs—235.462-010 Central-Office Operator.

43-2099.99 *Communications Equipment Operators, All Other*

- Education/Training Required: No data available.
- Employed: No data available.
- Annual Earnings: No data available.
- Growth: –21.8%
- Annual Job Openings: 5,000

All communications equipment operators not listed separately.

No task data available.

GOE INFORMATION—**Interest Area:** 09. Business Detail. **Work Group:** 09.06. Communications. **Note:** The Department of Labor has not collected some data for this job, so it has fewer details than the other descriptions.

Instructional Programs—Communications Systems Installation and Repair Technology.

Related DOT Jobs—203.562-010 Wire-Transfer Clerk; 235.562-010 Clerk, Route; 236.562-010 Telegrapher; 236.562-014 Telegrapher Agent; 237.367-034 Pay-Station Attendant; 239.382-010 Wire-Photo Operator, News.

43-3000 **Financial Clerks**

43-3011.00 *Bill and Account Collectors*

- Education/Training Required: Short-term on-the-job training
- Employed: 400,233
- Annual Earnings: $25,960
- Growth: 25.3%
- Annual Job Openings: 71,000

Locate and notify customers of delinquent accounts by mail, telephone, or personal visit to solicit payment. Duties include receiving payment and posting amount to customer's account, preparing statements to credit department if customer fails to respond, initiating repossession proceedings or service disconnection, and keeping records of collection and status of accounts.

Arrange for debt repayment or establish repayment schedules based on customers' financial situations. Confer with customers by telephone or in person to determine reasons for overdue payments and to review the terms of sales, service, or credit contracts. Locate and monitor overdue accounts, using computers and a variety of automated systems. Locate and notify customers of delinquent accounts by mail, telephone, or personal visits in order to solicit payment. Negotiate credit extensions when necessary. Notify credit departments, order merchandise repossession or service disconnection, and turn over account records to attorneys when customers fail to respond to collection attempts. Perform various administrative functions for assigned accounts, such as recording address changes and purging the records of deceased customers. Persuade customers to pay amounts due on credit accounts, damage claims, or nonpayable checks or to return merchandise. Receive payments and post amounts paid to customer accounts. Record information about financial status of customers and status of collection efforts. Trace delinquent customers to new addresses by inquiring at post offices, telephone companies, or credit bureaus or through the questioning of neighbors. Advise customers of necessary actions and strategies for debt repayment. Drive vehicles to visit customers, return merchandise to creditors, or deliver bills. Sort and file correspondence and perform miscellaneous clerical duties such as answering correspondence and writing reports.

GOE INFORMATION—**Interest Area:** 09. Business Detail. **Work Group:** 09.05. Customer Service. **Personality Type**—Conventional. Conventional occupations frequently involve following set procedures and routines. These occupations can include working with data and details more than with ideas. Usually there is a clear line of authority to follow. **Work Values**—Supervision, Human Relations; Authority; Supervision, Technical; Variety; Advancement. **Skills**—Persuasion; Active Listening; Speaking. **Abilities**—*Cognitive:* Written Expression; Number Facility; Oral Expression; Oral Comprehension; Written Comprehension. *Psychomotor:* Rate Control; Wrist-Finger Speed; Response Orientation. *Physical:* None met the criteria. *Sensory:* Speech Recognition; Speech Clarity; Glare Sensitivity; Auditory Attention. **General Work Activities**—*Information Input:* Getting Information; Identifying Objects, Actions, and Events; Monitoring Processes, Materials, or Surroundings. *Mental Process:* Organizing, Planning, and Prioritizing; Making Decisions and Solving Problems; Judging Qualities of Things, Services, or Other People's Work. *Work Output:* Documenting or Recording Information; Handling and Moving Objects; Operating Vehicles or Equipment. *Interacting with Others:* Resolving Conflict and Negotiating with Others; Influencing Others or Selling; Performing for or Working with the Public. **Physical Work Conditions**—Sitting; Outdoors; Indoors. **Other Job Characteristics**—Importance of Repeating Same Tasks; Consequence of Error; Degree of Automation.

Experience—Job Zone 2. Some previous work-related skill, knowledge, or experience may be helpful, but usually is not needed. **Job Preparation:** SVP 4.0 to less than 6.0—six months to less than two years. **Knowledge**—Clerical; Economics and Accounting; Law and Government; Computers and Electronics; Administration and Management. **Instructional Programs**—Banking and Financial Support Services.

Related DOT Jobs—241.357-010 Collection Clerk; 241.367-010 Collector; 241.367-022 Repossessor.

43-3021.00 *Billing and Posting Clerks and Machine Operators*

- Education/Training Required: Moderate-term on-the-job training
- Employed: 506,221
- Annual Earnings: $25,350
- Growth: 8.5%
- Annual Job Openings: 69,000

Compile, compute, and record billing, accounting, statistical, and other numerical data for billing purposes. Prepare billing invoices for services rendered or for delivery or shipment of goods.

No task data available.

GOE INFORMATION—Interest Area: 09. Business Detail. **Work Group:** 09.03. Bookkeeping, Auditing, and Accounting. **Note:** The Department of Labor has not collected some data for this job, so it has fewer details than the other descriptions.

Instructional Programs—Accounting Technology/Technician and Bookkeeping.

Related DOT Jobs—184.387-010 Wharfinger; 191.367-010 Personal Property Assessor; 214.267-010 Rate Analyst, Freight; 214.362-010 Demurrage Clerk; 214.362-014 Documentation-Billing Clerk; 214.362-022 Insurance Clerk; 214.362-026 Invoice-Control Clerk; 214.362-038 Traffic-Rate Clerk; 214.362-042 Billing Clerk; 214.362-046 Statement Clerk; 214.382-014 Billing Typist; 214.382-018 C.O.D. Clerk; 214.382-022 Interline Clerk; 214.382-026 Revising Clerk; 214.382-030 Settlement Clerk; 214.387-010 Billing-Control Clerk; 214.387-014 Rate Reviewer; 214.387-018 Services Clerk; 214.462-010 Accounts-Adjustable Clerk; 214.467-010 Foreign Clerk; others.

43-3021.01 *Statement Clerks*

- **Education/Training Required: Short-term on-the-job training**
- **Employed: No data available.**
- **Annual Earnings: $25,350**
- **Growth: 8.5%**
- **Annual Job Openings: 69,000**

Prepare and distribute bank statements to customers, answer inquiries, and reconcile discrepancies in records and accounts.

Compare previously prepared bank statements with canceled checks and reconcile discrepancies. Encode and cancel checks, using bank machines. Load machines with statements, cancelled checks, and envelopes in order to prepare statements for distribution to customers or stuff envelopes by hand. Maintain files of canceled checks and customers' signatures. Match statements with batches of canceled checks by account numbers. Monitor equipment in order to ensure proper operation. Retrieve checks returned to customers in error, adjusting customer accounts and answering inquiries about errors as necessary. Route statements for mailing or over-the-counter delivery to customers. Verify signatures and required information on checks. Weigh envelopes containing statements in order to determine correct postage and affix postage using stamps or metering equipment. Fix minor problems, such as equipment jams, and notify repair personnel of major equipment problems. Post stop-payment notices in order to prevent payment of protested checks. Take orders for imprinted checks.

GOE INFORMATION—Interest Area: 09. Business Detail. **Work Group:** 09.03. Bookkeeping, Auditing, and Accounting. **Personality Type—** Conventional. Conventional occupations frequently involve following set procedures and routines. These occupations can include working with data and details more than with ideas. Usually there is a clear line of authority to follow. **Work Values**—Good Working Conditions; Supervision, Human Relations; Supervision, Technical; Social Service; Advancement. **Skills**—None met the criteria. **Abilities**—*Cognitive:* Perceptual Speed; Written Comprehension; Number Facility. *Psychomotor:* Multilimb Coordination; Control Precision. *Physical:* None met the criteria. *Sensory:* Hearing Sensitivity; Glare Sensitivity; Near Vision. **General Work Activities**—*Information Input:* Identifying Objects, Actions, and Events; Getting Information; Monitoring Processes, Materials, or Surroundings.

Mental Process: Processing Information; Analyzing Data or Information; Evaluating Information Against Standards. *Work Output:* Handling and Moving Objects; Documenting or Recording Information; Performing General Physical Activities. *Interacting with Others:* Communicating with Persons Outside Organization; Establishing and Maintaining Relationships; Performing for or Working with the Public. **Physical Work Conditions**—Indoors; Sitting; Making Repetitive Motions. **Other Job Characteristics**—Importance of Being Exact or Accurate; Degree of Automation; Pace Determined by Speed of Equipment.

Experience—Job Zone 2. Some previous work-related skill, knowledge, or experience may be helpful, but usually is not needed. **Job Preparation:** SVP 4.0 to less than 6.0—six months to less than two years. **Knowledge—** Clerical; Computers and Electronics; Economics and Accounting; Customer and Personal Service; Telecommunications. **Instructional Programs**—Accounting Technology/Technician and Bookkeeping.

Related DOT Jobs—214.362-046 Statement Clerk.

43-3021.02 *Billing, Cost, and Rate Clerks*

- **Education/Training Required: Short-term on-the-job training**
- **Employed: No data available.**
- **Annual Earnings: $25,350**
- **Growth: 8.5%**
- **Annual Job Openings: 69,000**

Compile data, compute fees and charges, and prepare invoices for billing purposes. Duties include computing costs and calculating rates for goods, services, and shipment of goods; posting data; and keeping other relevant records. May involve use of computer or typewriter, calculator, and adding and bookkeeping machines.

Compile reports of cost factors, such as labor, production, storage, and equipment. Compute credit terms, discounts, shipment charges, and rates for goods and services in order to complete billing documents. Consult sources such as rate books, manuals, and insurance company representatives in order to determine specific charges and information such as rules, regulations, and government tax and tariff information. Keep records of invoices and support documents. Prepare itemized statements, bills, or invoices and record amounts due for items purchased or services rendered. Review documents such as purchase orders, sales tickets, charge slips, or hospital records in order to compute fees and charges due. Track accumulated hours and dollar amounts charged to each client job in order to calculate client fees for professional services such as legal and accounting services. Verify accuracy of billing data and revise any errors. Answer mail and telephone inquiries regarding rates, routing, and procedures. Contact customers in order to obtain or relay account information. Estimate market value of products or services. Perform bookkeeping work, including posting data and keeping other records concerning costs of goods and services and the shipment of goods. Resolve discrepancies in accounting records. Review compiled data on operating costs and revenues in order to set rates. Type billing documents, shipping labels, credit memorandums, and credit forms, using typewriters or computers. Update manuals when rates, rules, or regulations are amended. Operate typing, adding, calculating, and billing machines.

GOE INFORMATION—Interest Area: 09. Business Detail. **Work Group:** 09.03. Bookkeeping, Auditing, and Accounting. **Personality Type—** Conventional. Conventional occupations frequently involve following set procedures and routines. These occupations can include working with data and details more than with ideas. Usually there is a clear line of authority to follow. **Work Values**—Good Working Conditions;

Independence; Advancement; Activity; Supervision, Technical. **Skills—**Mathematics. **Abilities—***Cognitive:* Number Facility; Mathematical Reasoning; Written Expression; Perceptual Speed; Category Flexibility. *Psychomotor:* Wrist-Finger Speed; Finger Dexterity; Control Precision; Response Orientation. *Physical:* Trunk Strength. *Sensory:* Near Vision; Speech Recognition; Speech Clarity; Auditory Attention; Glare Sensitivity. **General Work Activities—***Information Input:* Getting Information; Identifying Objects, Actions, and Events; Estimating Needed Characteristics. *Mental Process:* Processing Information; Evaluating Information Against Standards; Updating and Using Relevant Knowledge. *Work Output:* Documenting or Recording Information; Handling and Moving Objects; Interacting with Computers. *Interacting with Others:* Communicating with Persons Outside Organization; Performing Administrative Activities; Establishing and Maintaining Relationships. **Physical Work Conditions—**Sitting; Making Repetitive Motions; Indoors; Walking or Running. **Other Job Characteristics—**Degree of Automation; Importance of Repeating Same Tasks; Importance of Being Exact or Accurate.

Experience—Job Zone 2. Some previous work-related skill, knowledge, or experience may be helpful, but usually is not needed. **Job Preparation:** SVP 4.0 to less than 6.0–six months to less than two years. **Knowledge—**Clerical; Economics and Accounting; Law and Government; Computers and Electronics; Mathematics. **Instructional Programs—**Accounting Technology/Technician and Bookkeeping.

Related DOT Jobs—184.387-010 Wharfinger; 191.367-010 Personal Property Assessor; 214.267-010 Rate Analyst, Freight; 214.362-010 Demurrage Clerk; 214.362-014 Documentation-Billing Clerk; 214.362-022 Insurance Clerk; 214.362-026 Invoice-Control Clerk; 214.362-038 Traffic-Rate Clerk; 214.362-042 Billing Clerk; 214.382-014 Billing Typist; 214.382-018 C.O.D. Clerk; 214.382-022 Interline Clerk; 214.382-026 Revising Clerk; 214.382-030 Settlement Clerk; 214.387-010 Billing-Control Clerk; 214.387-014 Rate Reviewer; 214.387-018 Services Clerk; 214.467-010 Foreign Clerk; 214.467-014 Pricer, Message and Delivery Service; 214.482-014 Deposit-Refund Clerk; others.

43-3021.03 Billing, Posting, and Calculating Machine Operators

- **Education/Training Required: Short-term on-the-job training**
- **Employed: No data available.**
- **Annual Earnings: $25,350**
- **Growth: 8.5%**
- **Annual Job Openings: 69,000**

Operate machines that automatically perform mathematical processes, such as addition, subtraction, multiplication, and division, to calculate and record billing, accounting, statistical, and other numerical data. Duties include operating special billing machines to prepare statements, bills, and invoices and operating bookkeeping machines to copy and post data, make computations, and compile records of transactions.

Balance and reconcile batch control totals with source documents or computer listings in order to locate errors, encode correct amounts, or prepare correction records. Compute monies due on personal and real property, inventories, redemption payments, and other amounts, applying specialized knowledge of tax rates, formulas, interest rates, and other relevant information. Compute payroll and retirement amounts, applying knowledge of payroll deductions, actuarial tables, disability factors, and survivor allowances. Encode and add amounts of transaction documents, such as checks or money orders, using encoding machines. Enter into machines all information needed for bill generation. Observe operation of sorters to locate documents that machines cannot read; manually record amounts of these documents. Reconcile and post receipts for cash received by various departments. Send completed bills to billing clerks for information verification. Sort and microfilm transaction documents, such as checks, using sorting machines. Transcribe data from office records, using specified forms, billing machines, and transcribing machines. Transfer data from machines, such as encoding machines, to computers. Verify completeness and accuracy of original documents such as business property statements, tax rolls, invoices, bonds and coupons, and redemption certificates. Assign purchase order numbers to invoices, requisitions, and formal and informal bids. Bundle sorted documents to prepare those drawn on other banks for collection. Clean machines and replace ribbons, film, and tape. Compile, code, and verify requisition, production, statistical, mileage, and other reports which require specialized knowledge in selecting the totals used. Compute and record inventory data from audio transcription, using transcribing machines and calculators. Maintain ledgers and registers, posting charges and refunds to individual funds and computing and verifying balances. Prepare transmittal reports for changes to assessment and tax rolls, for redemption file changes, and for warrants, deposits, and invoices. Sort and list items for proof or collection. Train other calculating machine operators and review their work. Verify and post to ledgers purchase orders, reports of goods received, invoices, paid vouchers, and other information. Operate bookkeeping machines to copy and post data, make computations, and compile records of transactions. Operate special billing machines to prepare statements, bills, and invoices.

GOE INFORMATION—Interest Area: 09. Business Detail. **Work Group:** 09.09. Clerical Machine Operation. **Personality Type—**Conventional. Conventional occupations frequently involve following set procedures and routines. These occupations can include working with data and details more than with ideas. Usually there is a clear line of authority to follow. **Work Values—**Independence; Supervision, Technical; Supervision, Human Relations; Advancement; Activity. **Skills—**Mathematics; Operation and Control; Operation Monitoring. **Abilities—***Cognitive:* Mathematical Reasoning; Selective Attention; Number Facility; Time Sharing; Category Flexibility. *Psychomotor:* Wrist-Finger Speed. *Physical:* Dynamic Flexibility. *Sensory:* Near Vision. **General Work Activities—***Information Input:* Monitoring Processes, Materials, or Surroundings; Identifying Objects, Actions, and Events; Getting Information. *Mental Process:* Processing Information; Analyzing Data or Information; Updating and Using Relevant Knowledge. *Work Output:* Handling and Moving Objects; Controlling Machines and Processes; Documenting or Recording Information. *Interacting with Others:* Communicating with Other Workers; Communicating with Persons Outside Organization; Establishing and Maintaining Relationships. **Physical Work Conditions—**Making Repetitive Motions; Indoors; Sitting. **Other Job Characteristics—**Importance of Repeating Same Tasks; Pace Determined by Speed of Equipment; Importance of Being Exact or Accurate.

Experience—Job Zone 1. No previous work-related skill, knowledge, or experience is needed. **Job Preparation:** SVP below 4.0—less than six months. **Knowledge—**Clerical; Economics and Accounting; Computers and Electronics; Mathematics. **Instructional Programs—**Accounting Technology/Technician and Bookkeeping.

Related DOT Jobs—214.462-010 Accounts-Adjustable Clerk; 214.482-010 Billing-Machine Operator; 216.482-018 Audit-Machine Operator; 216.482-022 Calculating-Machine Operator; 217.382-010 Proof-Machine Operator.

43-3031.00 Bookkeeping, Accounting, and Auditing Clerks

- Education/Training Required: Moderate-term on-the-job training
- Employed: 1,990,762
- Annual Earnings: $26,540
- Growth: 2.0%
- Annual Job Openings: 298,000

Compute, classify, and record numerical data to keep financial records complete. Perform any combination of routine calculating, posting, and verifying duties to obtain primary financial data for use in maintaining accounting records. May also check the accuracy of figures, calculations, and postings pertaining to business transactions recorded by other workers.

Calculate and prepare checks for utilities, taxes, and other payments. Calculate, prepare, and issue bills, invoices, account statements, and other financial statements according to established procedures. Check figures, postings, and documents for correct entry, mathematical accuracy, and proper codes. Classify, record, and summarize numerical and financial data in order to compile and keep financial records, using journals and ledgers or computers. Compare computer printouts to manually maintained journals in order to determine if they match. Compile statistical, financial, accounting, or auditing reports and tables pertaining to such matters as cash receipts, expenditures, accounts payable and receivable, and profits and losses. Complete and submit tax forms and returns, workers' compensation forms, pension contribution forms, and other government documents. Compute deductions for income and social security taxes. Debit, credit, and total accounts on computer spreadsheets and databases, using specialized accounting software. Monitor status of loans and accounts to ensure that payments are up to date. Operate computers programmed with accounting software to record, store, and analyze information. Perform financial calculations such as amounts due, interest charges, balances, discounts, equity, and principal. Prepare bank deposits by compiling data from cashiers, verifying and balancing receipts, and sending cash, checks, or other forms of payment to banks. Prepare purchase orders and expense reports. Prepare trial balances of books. Receive, record, and bank cash, checks, and vouchers. Reconcile or note and report discrepancies found in records. Reconcile records of bank transactions. Transfer details from separate journals to general ledgers and/or data processing sheets. Access computerized financial information to answer general questions as well as those related to specific accounts. Calculate costs of materials, overhead, and other expenses, based on estimates, quotations, and price lists. Code documents according to company procedures. Compile budget data and documents, based on estimated revenues and expenses and previous budgets. Comply with federal, state, and company policies, procedures, and regulations. Maintain inventory records. Match order forms with invoices and record the necessary information.

GOE INFORMATION—**Interest Area:** 09. Business Detail. **Work Group:** 09.03. Bookkeeping, Auditing, and Accounting. **Personality Type**—Conventional. Conventional occupations frequently involve following set procedures and routines. These occupations can include working with data and details more than with ideas. Usually there is a clear line of authority to follow. **Work Values**—Good Working Conditions; Independence; Advancement; Autonomy; Company Policies and Practices. **Skills**—Mathematics; Management of Financial Resources; Reading Comprehension. **Abilities**—*Cognitive:* Number Facility; Perceptual Speed; Mathematical Reasoning; Written Expression; Category Flexibility. *Psychomotor:* Wrist-Finger Speed; Finger Dexterity; Response Orientation;

Control Precision. *Physical:* None met the criteria. *Sensory:* Near Vision; Speech Recognition; Speech Clarity; Glare Sensitivity; Auditory Attention. **General Work Activities**—*Information Input:* Getting Information; Identifying Objects, Actions, and Events; Estimating Needed Characteristics. *Mental Process:* Processing Information; Analyzing Data or Information; Evaluating Information Against Standards. *Work Output:* Documenting or Recording Information; Interacting with Computers; Handling and Moving Objects. *Interacting with Others:* Communicating with Other Workers; Performing Administrative Activities; Establishing and Maintaining Relationships. **Physical Work Conditions**—Sitting; Indoors; Making Repetitive Motions. **Other Job Characteristics**—Importance of Being Exact or Accurate; Importance of Repeating Same Tasks; Degree of Automation.

Experience—Job Zone 2. Some previous work-related skill, knowledge, or experience may be helpful, but usually is not needed. **Job Preparation:** SVP 4.0 to less than 6.0—six months to less than two years. **Knowledge**—Clerical; Economics and Accounting; Law and Government; Computers and Electronics; Mathematics. **Instructional Programs**—Accounting and Related Services, Other; Accounting Technology/Technician and Bookkeeping.

Related DOT Jobs—210.362-010 Distribution-Accounting Clerk; 210.367-010 Account-Information Clerk; 210.367-014 Foreign-Exchange-Position Clerk; 210.382-010 Audit Clerk; 210.382-014 Bookkeeper; 210.382-042 Fixed-Capital Clerk; 210.382-046 General-Ledger Bookkeeper; 210.382-054 Night Auditor; 210.382-062 Securities Clerk; 216.362-014 Collection Clerk; 216.362-022 Food-and-Beverage Controller; 216.362-034 Reserves Clerk; 216.362-038 Electronic Funds Transfer Coordinator; 216.362-042 Margin Clerk I; 216.367-014 Trust-Vault Clerk; 216.382-022 Budget Clerk; 216.482-010 Accounting Clerk; 219.367-042 Canceling and Cutting Control Clerk; 219.367-050 Letter-of-Credit Clerk.

43-3041.00 Gaming Cage Workers

- Education/Training Required: Moderate-term on-the-job training
- Employed: 21,837
- Annual Earnings: $21,540
- Growth: 25.2%
- Annual Job Openings: 7,000

In a gaming establishment, conduct financial transactions for patrons. May reconcile daily summaries of transactions to balance books. Accept patron's credit application and verify credit references to provide check-cashing authorization or to establish house credit accounts. May sell gambling chips, tokens, or tickets to patrons or to other workers for resale to patrons. May convert gaming chips, tokens, or tickets to currency upon patron's request. May use a cash register or computer to record transaction.

Cash checks and process credit card advances for patrons. Convert gaming checks, coupons, tokens, and coins to currency for gaming patrons. Count funds and reconcile daily summaries of transactions to balance books. Determine cash requirements for windows and order all necessary currency, coins, and chips. Follow all gaming regulations. Provide customers with information about casino operations. Record casino exchange transactions, using cash registers. Sell gambling chips, tokens, or tickets to patrons or to other workers for resale to patrons. Supply currency, coins, chips, and gaming checks to other departments as needed. Verify accuracy of reports such as authorization forms, transaction reconciliations, and exchange summary reports. Establish new computer accounts. Maintain cage security. Maintain confidentiality of customers' transactions. Perform removal and rotation of cash, coin, and chip inventories as necessary. Prepare bank deposits, balancing assigned funds as necessary. Prepare reports, including assignment of company funds and recording of department revenues. Provide assistance in the training and orientation of new cashiers.

GOE INFORMATION—Interest Area: 09. Business Detail. **Work Group:** 09.05. Customer Service. **Note:** The Department of Labor has not collected some data for this job, so it has fewer details than the other descriptions.

Instructional Programs—Accounting Technology/Technician and Bookkeeping.

Related DOT Jobs—211.462-022 Cashier, Gambling.

43-3051.00 *Payroll and Timekeeping Clerks*

- Education/Training Required: **Short-term on-the-job training**
- Employed: **200,907**
- Annual Earnings: **$28,250**
- Growth: **2.3%**
- Annual Job Openings: **26,000**

Compile and post employee time and payroll data. May compute employees' time worked, production, and commission. May compute and post wages and deductions. May prepare paychecks.

Compile employee time, production, and payroll data from time sheets and other records. Complete time sheets showing employees' arrival and departure times. Complete, verify, and process forms and documentation for administration of benefits such as pension plans and unemployment and medical insurance. Compute wages and deductions and enter data into computers. Issue and record adjustments to pay related to previous errors or retroactive increases. Post relevant work hours to client files in order to bill clients properly. Process and issue employee paychecks and statements of earnings and deductions. Record employee information, such as exemptions, transfers, and resignations, in order to maintain and update payroll records. Review time sheets, work charts, wage computation, and other information in order to detect and reconcile payroll discrepancies. Verify attendance, hours worked, and pay adjustments; post information onto designated records. Compile statistical reports, statements, and summaries related to pay and benefits accounts and submit them to appropriate departments. Coordinate special programs, such as United Way campaigns, that involve payroll deductions. Distribute and collect timecards each pay period. Keep informed about changes in tax and deduction laws that apply to the payroll process. Prepare and balance period-end reports and reconcile issued payrolls to bank statements. Provide information to employees and managers on payroll matters, tax issues, benefit plans, and collective agreement provisions.

GOE INFORMATION—Interest Area: 09. Business Detail. **Work Group:** 09.03. Bookkeeping, Auditing, and Accounting. **Personality Type—** Conventional. Conventional occupations frequently involve following set procedures and routines. These occupations can include working with data and details more than with ideas. Usually there is a clear line of authority to follow. **Work Values**—Good Working Conditions; Independence; Advancement; Supervision, Technical; Supervision, Human Relations. **Skills**—Mathematics. **Abilities**—*Cognitive:* Number Facility; Mathematical Reasoning. *Psychomotor:* Wrist-Finger Speed; Finger Dexterity. *Physical:* Trunk Strength. *Sensory:* None met the criteria. **General Work Activities**—*Information Input:* Getting Information; Identifying Objects, Actions, and Events; Monitoring Processes, Materials, or Surroundings. *Mental Process:* Processing Information; Updating and Using Relevant Knowledge; Organizing, Planning, and Prioritizing. *Work Out-*

put: Documenting or Recording Information; Interacting with Computers; Handling and Moving Objects. *Interacting with Others:* Communicating with Other Workers; Performing Administrative Activities; Establishing and Maintaining Relationships. **Physical Work Conditions**—Sitting; Indoors; Making Repetitive Motions. **Other Job Characteristics**—Importance of Being Exact or Accurate; Importance of Repeating Same Tasks; Consequence of Error.

Experience—Job Zone 2. Some previous work-related skill, knowledge, or experience may be helpful, but usually is not needed. **Job Preparation:** SVP 4.0 to less than 6.0—six months to less than two years. **Knowledge**—Clerical; Economics and Accounting; Personnel and Human Resources; Mathematics; Law and Government. **Instructional Programs**—Accounting Technology/Technician and Bookkeeping.

Related DOT Jobs—215.362-018 Flight-Crew-Time Clerk; 215.362-022 Timekeeper; 215.382-014 Payroll Clerk.

43-3061.00 *Procurement Clerks*

- Education/Training Required: **Short-term on-the-job training**
- Employed: **76,278**
- Annual Earnings: **$28,790**
- Growth: **−12.2%**
- Annual Job Openings: **13,000**

Compile information and records to draw up purchase orders for procurement of materials and services.

Approve bills for payment. Calculate costs of orders and charge or forward invoices to appropriate accounts. Check shipments when they arrive to ensure that orders have been filled correctly and that goods meet specifications. Compare prices, specifications, and delivery dates in order to determine the best bid among potential suppliers. Compare suppliers' bills with bids and purchase orders in order to verify accuracy. Contact suppliers in order to schedule or expedite deliveries and to resolve shortages, missed or late deliveries, and other problems. Determine if inventory quantities are sufficient for needs, ordering more materials when necessary. Locate suppliers, using sources such as catalogs and the Internet, and interview them to gather information about products to be ordered. Prepare, maintain, and review purchasing files, reports, and price lists. Prepare purchase orders and send copies to suppliers and to departments originating requests. Respond to customer and supplier inquiries about order status, changes, or cancellations. Review requisition orders in order to verify accuracy, terminology, and specifications. Track the status of requisitions, contracts, and orders. Maintain knowledge of all organizational and governmental rules affecting purchases and provide information about these rules to organization staff members and to vendors. Monitor contractor performance, recommending contract modifications when necessary. Monitor in-house inventory movement and complete inventory transfer forms for bookkeeping purposes. Perform buying duties when necessary. Prepare invitation-of-bid forms and mail forms to supplier firms or distribute forms for public posting.

GOE INFORMATION—Interest Area: 09. Business Detail. **Work Group:** 09.07. Records Processing. **Personality Type**—Conventional. Conventional occupations frequently involve following set procedures and routines. These occupations can include working with data and details more than with ideas. Usually there is a clear line of authority to follow. **Work Values**—Good Working Conditions; Supervision, Technical; Advancement; Independence; Pleasant Co-workers. **Skills**—Management of Material Resources; Speaking; Management of Financial Resources; Negotiation; Complex Problem Solving. **Abilities**—*Cognitive:* Written Expression; Number Facility; Selective Attention; Perceptual Speed; Category Flexibility. *Psychomotor:* Finger Dexterity. *Physical:* None met the criteria. *Sensory:* Near Vision. **General Work Activities—***Information Input:* Identifying Objects, Actions, and Events; Getting Information; Estimating Needed Characteristics. *Mental Process:* Processing Information; Evaluating Information Against Standards; Judging Qualities of Things, Services, or Other People's Work. *Work Output:* Documenting or Recording Information; Handling and Moving Objects; Performing General Physical Activities. *Interacting with Others:* Establishing and Maintaining Relationships; Communicating with Other Workers; Communicating with Persons Outside Organization. **Physical Work Conditions—**Sitting; Indoors; Walking or Running. **Other Job Characteristics—**Importance of Repeating Same Tasks; Importance of Being Exact or Accurate; Pace Determined by Speed of Equipment.

Experience—Job Zone 1. No previous work-related skill, knowledge, or experience is needed. **Job Preparation:** SVP below 4.0—less than six months. **Knowledge—**Clerical; Economics and Accounting; Computers and Electronics; Mathematics; Telecommunications. **Instructional Programs—**General Office Occupations and Clerical Services.

Related DOT Jobs—249.367-066 Procurement Clerk; 976.567-010 Film-Replacement Orderer.

43-3071.00 Tellers

- **Education/Training Required: Short-term on-the-job training**
- **Employed: 499,440**
- **Annual Earnings: $19,830**
- **Growth: –11.8%**
- **Annual Job Openings: 98,000**

Receive and pay out money. Keep records of money and negotiable instruments involved in a financial institution's various transactions.

Arrange monies received in cash boxes and coin dispensers according to denomination. Balance currency, coin, and checks in cash drawers at ends of shifts and calculate daily transactions using computers, calculators, or adding machines. Cash checks and pay out money after verifying that signatures are correct, that written and numerical amounts agree, and that accounts have sufficient funds. Count currency, coins, and checks received, by hand or using currency-counting machine, in order to prepare them for deposit or shipment to branch banks or the Federal Reserve Bank. Count, verify, and post armored car deposits. Enter customers' transactions into computers in order to record transactions and issue computer-generated receipts. Examine checks for endorsements and to verify other information such as dates, bank names, identification of the persons receiving payments, and the legality of the documents. Identify transaction mistakes when debits and credits do not balance. Order a supply of cash to meet daily needs. Prepare and verify cashier's checks. Process transactions such as term deposits, retirement savings plan contributions, automated teller transactions, night deposits, and mail deposits. Quote unit exchange rates, following daily international rate sheets or computer displays. Receive and count daily inventories of cash, drafts, and travelers' checks. Receive checks and cash for deposit, verify amounts, and check accuracy of deposit slips. Receive mortgage, loan, or public utility bill payments, verifying payment dates and amounts due. Sort and file deposit slips and checks. Carry out special services for customers, such as ordering bank cards and checks. Compose, type, and mail customer statements and other correspondence related to issues such as discrepancies and outstanding unpaid items. Compute financial fees, interest, and service charges. Explain, promote, or sell products or services such as travelers' checks, savings bonds, money orders, and cashier's checks, using computerized information about customers to tailor recommendations. Inform customers about foreign currency regulations and compute transaction fees for currency exchanges. Issue checks to bond owners in settlement of transactions. Monitor bank vaults to ensure cash balances are correct. Obtain and process information required for the provision of services, such as opening accounts and savings plans and purchasing bonds. Perform clerical tasks such as typing, filing, and microfilm photography. Process and maintain records of customer loans.

GOE INFORMATION—Interest Area: 09. Business Detail. **Work Group:** 09.05. Customer Service. **Personality Type—**Conventional. Conventional occupations frequently involve following set procedures and routines. These occupations can include working with data and details more than with ideas. Usually there is a clear line of authority to follow. **Work Values—**Good Working Conditions; Pleasant Co-workers; Social Service; Supervision, Technical; Supervision, Human Relations. **Skills—**None met the criteria. **Abilities—***Cognitive:* Perceptual Speed; Number Facility; Mathematical Reasoning; Memorization; Written Expression. *Psychomotor:* Wrist-Finger Speed; Response Orientation. *Physical:* Extent Flexibility; Trunk Strength. *Sensory:* Speech Recognition; Near Vision; Speech Clarity; Auditory Attention; Visual Color Discrimination. **General Work Activities—***Information Input:* Identifying Objects, Actions, and Events; Getting Information; Monitoring Processes, Materials, or Surroundings. *Mental Process:* Processing Information; Evaluating Information Against Standards; Updating and Using Relevant Knowledge. *Work Output:* Handling and Moving Objects; Documenting or Recording Information; Interacting with Computers. *Interacting with Others:* Performing for or Working with the Public; Communicating with Persons Outside Organization; Establishing and Maintaining Relationships. **Physical Work Conditions—**Making Repetitive Motions; Indoors; Sitting; Walking or Running. **Other Job Characteristics—**Degree of Automation; Importance of Being Exact or Accurate; Consequence of Error.

Experience—Job Zone 2. Some previous work-related skill, knowledge, or experience may be helpful, but usually is not needed. **Job Preparation:** SVP 4.0 to less than 6.0—six months to less than two years. **Knowledge—**Clerical; Economics and Accounting; Sales and Marketing; Customer and Personal Service; Law and Government. **Instructional Programs—**Banking and Financial Support Services.

Related DOT Jobs—211.362-014 Foreign Banknote Teller-Trader; 211.362-018 Teller; 211.382-010 Teller, Vault; 219.462-010 Coupon Clerk.

43-4000 Information and Record Clerks

43-4011.00 Brokerage Clerks

- **Education/Training Required: Moderate-term on-the-job training**
- **Employed: 69,537**
- **Annual Earnings: $32,470**
- **Growth: –1.4%**
- **Annual Job Openings: 7,000**

Perform clerical duties involving the purchase or sale of securities. Duties include writing orders for stock purchases and sales, computing transfer taxes, verifying stock transactions, accepting and delivering securities, tracking stock price fluctuations, computing equity, distributing dividends, and keeping records of daily transactions and holdings.

Record and document security transactions, such as purchases, sales, conversions, redemptions, and payments, using computers, accounting ledgers, and certificate records. Prepare reports summarizing daily transactions and earnings for individual customer accounts. Compute total holdings, dividends, interest, transfer taxes, brokerage fees, and commissions and allocate appropriate payments to customers. Prepare forms, such as receipts, withdrawal orders, transmittal papers, and transfer confirmations, based on transaction requests from stockholders. Correspond with customers and confer with co-workers in order to answer inquiries, discuss market fluctuations, and resolve account problems. Schedule and coordinate transfer and delivery of security certificates between companies, departments, and customers. Monitor daily stock prices and compute fluctuations in order to determine the need for additional collateral to secure loans. Verify ownership and transaction information and dividend distribution instructions to ensure conformance with governmental regulations, using stock records and reports. File, type, and operate standard office machines.

GOE INFORMATION—Interest Area: 09. Business Detail. **Work Group:** 09.03. Bookkeeping, Auditing, and Accounting. **Personality Type—**Conventional. Conventional occupations frequently involve following set procedures and routines. These occupations can include working with data and details more than with ideas. Usually there is a clear line of authority to follow. **Work Values—**Good Working Conditions; Pleasant Co-workers; Activity; Supervision, Human Relations; Advancement. **Skills—**Mathematics; Active Listening; Service Orientation; Speaking. **Abilities—***Cognitive:* Mathematical Reasoning; Number Facility; Written Comprehension; Written Expression; Oral Expression. *Psychomotor:* Wrist-Finger Speed. *Physical:* None met the criteria. *Sensory:* Speech Recognition; Near Vision. **General Work Activities—***Information Input:* Getting Information; Identifying Objects, Actions, and Events; Estimating Needed Characteristics. *Mental Process:* Processing Information; Evaluating Information Against Standards; Updating and Using Relevant Knowledge. *Work Output:* Documenting or Recording Information; Interacting with Computers; Handling and Moving Objects. *Interacting with Others:* Communicating with Persons Outside Organization; Communicating with Other Workers; Establishing and Maintaining Relationships. **Physical Work Conditions—**Sitting; Indoors; Walking or Running. **Other Job Characteristics—**Consequence of Error; Importance of Being Exact or Accurate; Importance of Repeating Same Tasks.

Experience—Job Zone 2. Some previous work-related skill, knowledge, or experience may be helpful, but usually is not needed. **Job Preparation:** SVP 4.0 to less than 6.0—six months to less than two years. **Knowledge—**Clerical; Economics and Accounting; Sales and Marketing; Mathematics; Computers and Electronics. **Instructional Programs—**Accounting Technology/Technician and Bookkeeping.

Related DOT Jobs—216.362-046 Transfer Clerk; 216.382-046 Margin Clerk II; 216.482-034 Dividend Clerk; 219.362-018 Brokerage Clerk II; 219.362-054 Securities Clerk; 219.482-010 Brokerage Clerk I.

43-4021.00 *Correspondence Clerks*

- **Education/Training Required: Short-term on-the-job training**
- **Employed: 38,360**
- **Annual Earnings: $25,230**
- **Growth: 9.1%**
- **Annual Job Openings: 5,000**

Compose letters in reply to requests for merchandise, damage claims, credit and other information, delinquent accounts, incorrect billings, or unsatisfactory services. Duties may include gathering data to formulate reply and typing correspondence.

Complete form letters in response to requests or problems identified by correspondence. Compose letters in reply to correspondence concerning such items as requests for merchandise, damage claims, credit information requests, delinquent accounts, incorrect billing, or unsatisfactory service. Compute costs of records furnished to requesters and write letters to obtain payment. Gather records pertinent to specific problems, review them for completeness and accuracy, and attach records to correspondence as necessary. Maintain files and control records to show correspondence activities. Prepare documents and correspondence such as damage claims, credit and billing inquiries, invoices, and service complaints. Prepare records for shipment by certified mail. Present clear and concise explanations of governing rules and regulations. Read incoming correspondence to ascertain nature of writers' concerns and to determine disposition of correspondence. Review correspondence for format and typographical accuracy, assemble the information into a prescribed form with the correct number of copies, and submit it to an authorized official for signature. Route correspondence to other departments for reply. Type acknowledgment letters to persons sending correspondence. Compile data from records to prepare periodic reports. Compile data pertinent to manufacture of special products for customers. Compose correspondence requesting medical information and records. Confer with company personnel regarding feasibility of complying with writers' requests. Ensure that money collected is properly recorded and secured. Obtain written authorization to access required medical information. Process orders for goods requested in correspondence. Respond to internal and external requests for the release of information contained in medical records, copying medical records, and selective extracts in accordance with laws and regulations. Submit completed documents to typists for typing in final form and instruct typists in matters such as format, addresses, addressees, and the necessary number of copies.

GOE INFORMATION—Interest Area: 09. Business Detail. **Work Group:** 09.07. Records Processing. **Personality Type—**Conventional. Conventional occupations frequently involve following set procedures and routines. These occupations can include working with data and details more than with ideas. Usually there is a clear line of authority to follow. **Work Values—**Good Working Conditions; Social Service; Supervision, Human Relations; Company Policies and Practices; Activity. **Skills—**Writing; Reading Comprehension. **Abilities—***Cognitive:* Written Expression; Written Comprehension; Fluency of Ideas. *Psychomotor:* Wrist-Finger Speed. *Physical:* None met the criteria. *Sensory:* Near Vision. **General Work Activities—***Information Input:* Getting Information; Identifying Objects, Actions, and Events; Monitoring Processes, Materials, or Surroundings. *Mental Process:* Processing Information; Evaluating Information Against Standards; Analyzing Data or Information. *Work Output:* Handling and Moving Objects; Documenting or Recording Information; Interacting with Computers. *Interacting with Others:* Communicating with Other Workers; Communicating with Persons Outside Organization; Establishing and Maintaining Relationships. **Physical Work Conditions—**Sitting; Indoors. **Other Job Characteristics—**Importance of Being Exact or Accurate; Consequence of Error; Importance of Repeating Same Tasks.

Experience—Job Zone 2. Some previous work-related skill, knowledge, or experience may be helpful, but usually is not needed. **Job Preparation:** SVP 4.0 to less than 6.0—six months to less than two years. **Knowledge—**Clerical; Communications and Media; Computers and Electronics; Economics and Accounting; English Language. **Instructional Programs—**General Office Occupations and Clerical Services.

Related DOT Jobs—209.362-034 Correspondence Clerk; 209.367-018 Correspondence-Review Clerk; 209.387-034 Suggestion Clerk; 221.367-062 Sales Correspondent.

43-4031.00 Court, Municipal, and License Clerks

- **Education/Training Required: Short-term on-the-job training**
- **Employed: 104,709**
- **Annual Earnings: $27,090**
- **Growth: 12.0%**
- **Annual Job Openings: 14,000**

Perform clerical duties in courts of law, municipalities, and governmental licensing agencies and bureaus. May prepare docket of cases to be called; secure information for judges and court; prepare draft agendas or bylaws for town or city council; answer official correspondence; keep fiscal records and accounts; issue licenses or permits; record data, administer tests, or collect fees.

No task data available.

GOE INFORMATION—Interest Area: 09. Business Detail. **Work Group:** 09.02. Administrative Detail. **Note:** The Department of Labor has not collected some data for this job, so it has fewer details than the other descriptions.

Instructional Programs—General Office Occupations and Clerical Services.

Related DOT Jobs—205.367-034 License Clerk; 243.362-010 Court Clerk; 243.367-018 Town Clerk; 249.367-030 Dog Licenser; 379.137-014 Supervisor, Dog License Officer.

43-4031.01 Court Clerks

- **Education/Training Required: Short-term on-the-job training**
- **Employed: No data available.**
- **Annual Earnings: $27,090**
- **Growth: 12.0%**
- **Annual Job Openings: 14,000**

Perform clerical duties in court of law; prepare docket of cases to be called; secure information for judges; and contact witnesses, attorneys, and litigants to obtain information for court.

Amend indictments when necessary and endorse indictments with pertinent information. Conduct roll calls and poll jurors. Examine legal documents submitted to courts for adherence to laws or court procedures. Explain procedures or forms to parties in cases or to the general public. Instruct parties about timing of court appearances. Meet with judges, lawyers, parole officers, police, and social agency officials in order to coordinate the functions of the court. Open courts, calling them to order and announcing judges. Prepare and issue orders of the court, including probation orders, release documentation, sentencing information, and summonses. Prepare and mark all applicable court exhibits and evidence. Prepare courtrooms with paper, pens, water, easels, and electronic equipment and ensure that recording equipment is working. Prepare dockets or calendars of cases to be called, using typewriters or computers. Prepare documents recording the outcomes of court proceedings. Read charges and related information to the court and, if necessary, record defendants' pleas. Record case dispositions, court orders, and arrangements made for payment of court fees. Search files and contact witnesses, attorneys, and litigants in order to obtain information for the court. Answer inquiries from the general public regarding judicial procedures, court appearances, trial dates, adjournments, outstanding warrants, summonses, subpoenas, witness fees, and payment of fines. Arrange transportation and accommodation

for witnesses and jurors if required. Collect court fees or fines and record amounts collected. Direct support staff in handling of paperwork processed by clerks' offices. Follow procedures to secure courtrooms and exhibits such as money, drugs, and weapons. Record court proceedings, using recording equipment, or record minutes of court proceedings, using stenotype machines or shorthand. Swear in jury members, interpreters, witnesses, and defendants.

GOE INFORMATION—Interest Area: 09. Business Detail. **Work Group:** 09.02. Administrative Detail. **Personality Type—**Conventional. Conventional occupations frequently involve following set procedures and routines. These occupations can include working with data and details more than with ideas. Usually there is a clear line of authority to follow. **Work Values—**Good Working Conditions; Supervision, Human Relations; Security; Authority; Activity. **Skills—**Active Listening; Speaking; Reading Comprehension. **Abilities—***Cognitive:* Oral Comprehension; Written Expression; Oral Expression; Written Comprehension. *Psychomotor:* Wrist-Finger Speed; Finger Dexterity. *Physical:* None met the criteria. *Sensory:* Near Vision; Speech Recognition. **General Work Activities—***Information Input:* Getting Information; Monitoring Processes, Materials, or Surroundings; Identifying Objects, Actions, and Events. *Mental Process:* Evaluating Information Against Standards; Organizing, Planning, and Prioritizing; Processing Information. *Work Output:* Documenting or Recording Information; Handling and Moving Objects; Controlling Machines and Processes. *Interacting with Others:* Communicating with Persons Outside Organization; Communicating with Other Workers; Performing for or Working with the Public. **Physical Work Conditions—**Sitting; Making Repetitive Motions; Indoors. **Other Job Characteristics—**Importance of Repeating Same Tasks; Importance of Being Exact or Accurate; Consequence of Error.

Experience—Job Zone 3. Previous work-related skill, knowledge, or experience is required. **Job Preparation:** SVP 6.0 to less than 7.0—more than one year and less than four years. **Knowledge—**Clerical; Law and Government; English Language; Computers and Electronics; Telecommunications. **Instructional Programs—**General Office Occupations and Clerical Services.

Related DOT Jobs—243.362-010 Court Clerk.

43-4031.02 Municipal Clerks

- **Education/Training Required: Short-term on-the-job training**
- **Employed: No data available.**
- **Annual Earnings: $27,090**
- **Growth: 12.0%**
- **Annual Job Openings: 14,000**

Draft agendas and bylaws for town or city council; record minutes of council meetings; answer official correspondence; keep fiscal records and accounts; and prepare reports on civic needs.

Issue public notification of all official activities and meetings. Issue various permits and licenses, including marriage, fishing, hunting, and dog licenses, and collect appropriate fees. Maintain and update documents such as municipal codes and city charters. Maintain fiscal records and accounts. Perform general office duties such as taking and transcribing dictation, typing and proofreading correspondence, distributing and filing official forms, and scheduling appointments. Plan and direct the maintenance, filing, safekeeping, and computerization of all municipal documents. Prepare meeting agendas and packets of related information. Prepare ordinances, resolutions, and proclamations so that they can be executed, recorded, archived, and distributed. Record and edit the minutes of meetings and then distribute them to appropriate officials and staff members. Respond to requests for information from the public, other municipalities, state officials, and state and federal legislative offices.

Collaborate with other staff to assist in the development and implementation of goals, objectives, policies, and priorities. Coordinate and maintain office-tracking systems for correspondence and follow-up actions. Participate in the administration of municipal elections, including preparation and distribution of ballots, appointment and training of election officers, and tabulation and certification of results. Perform budgeting duties, including assisting in budget preparation, expenditure review, and budget administration. Perform contract administration duties, assisting with bid openings and the awarding of contracts. Prepare reports on civic needs. Process claims against the municipality, maintaining files and log of claims, and coordinate claim response and handling with municipal claims administrators. Represent municipalities at community events and serve as liaisons on community committees. Research information in the municipal archives upon request of public officials and private citizens. Serve as a notary of the public. Develop and conduct orientation programs for candidates for political office. Provide assistance to persons with disabilities in reaching less accessible areas of municipal facilities. Provide assistance with events such as police department auctions of abandoned automobiles.

GOE INFORMATION—Interest Area: 09. Business Detail. **Work Group:** 09.02. Administrative Detail. **Personality Type—**Conventional. Conventional occupations frequently involve following set procedures and routines. These occupations can include working with data and details more than with ideas. Usually there is a clear line of authority to follow. **Work Values—**Good Working Conditions; Supervision, Human Relations; Company Policies and Practices; Security; Social Service. **Skills—**Writing; Active Listening; Mathematics; Critical Thinking; Reading Comprehension. **Abilities—***Cognitive:* Selective Attention; Written Expression; Speed of Closure; Memorization; Written Comprehension. *Psychomotor:* Wrist-Finger Speed; Reaction Time. *Physical:* None met the criteria. *Sensory:* Night Vision; Auditory Attention; Far Vision; Speech Recognition; Hearing Sensitivity. **General Work Activities—***Information Input:* Getting Information; Monitoring Processes, Materials, or Surroundings; Identifying Objects, Actions, and Events. *Mental Process:* Processing Information; Organizing, Planning, and Prioritizing; Scheduling Work and Activities. *Work Output:* Documenting or Recording Information; Handling and Moving Objects; Interacting with Computers. *Interacting with Others:* Communicating with Other Workers; Communicating with Persons Outside Organization; Performing Administrative Activities. **Physical Work Conditions—**Sitting; Indoors. **Other Job Characteristics—**Importance of Being Exact or Accurate; Degree of Automation; Importance of Repeating Same Tasks.

Experience—Job Zone 2. Some previous work-related skill, knowledge, or experience may be helpful, but usually is not needed. **Job Preparation:** SVP 4.0 to less than 6.0—six months to less than two years. **Knowledge—**Economics and Accounting; Clerical; English Language; Law and Government; Communications and Media. **Instructional Programs—**General Office Occupations and Clerical Services.

Related DOT Jobs—243.367-018 Town Clerk.

43-4031.03 License Clerks

- Education/Training Required: **Short-term on-the-job training**
- Employed: **No data available.**
- Annual Earnings: **$27,090**
- Growth: **12.0%**
- Annual Job Openings: **14,000**

Issue licenses or permits to qualified applicants. Obtain necessary information; record data; advise applicants on requirements; collect fees; and issue licenses. May conduct oral, written, visual, or performance testing.

Answer questions and provide advice to the public regarding licensing policies, procedures, and regulations. Assemble photographs with printed license information in order to produce completed documents. Collect prescribed fees for licenses. Conduct and score oral, visual, written, or performance tests to determine applicant qualifications and notify applicants of their scores. Evaluate information on applications to verify completeness and accuracy and to determine whether applicants are qualified to obtain desired licenses. Instruct customers in the completion of driver's license application forms and other forms such as voter registration cards and organ donor forms. Maintain records of applications made and licensing fees collected. Operate specialized photographic equipment in order to obtain photographs for driver's licenses and photo identification cards. Perform routine data entry and other office support activities, including creating, sorting, photocopying, distributing, and filing documents. Question applicants to obtain required information, such as name, address, and age, and record data on prescribed forms. Stock counters with adequate supplies of forms, film, licenses, and other required materials. Update operational records and licensing information, using computer terminals. Code information on license applications for entry into computers. Inform customers by mail or telephone of additional steps they need to take to obtain licenses. Perform record checks on past and current licensees as required by investigations. Prepare bank deposits and take them to banks. Prepare lists of overdue accounts and license suspensions and issuances. Train other workers and coordinate their work as necessary. Send driver's licenses to out-of-county or out-of-state applicants by mail. Enforce canine licensing regulations, contacting noncompliant owners in person or by mail to inform them of the required regulations and potential enforcement actions. Perform driver education program enrollments for participating schools. Provide assistance in the preparation of insurance examinations covering a variety of types of insurance. Respond to correspondence from insurance companies regarding the licensure of agents, brokers, and adjusters.

GOE INFORMATION—Interest Area: 09. Business Detail. **Work Group:** 09.02. Administrative Detail. **Personality Type—**Conventional. Conventional occupations frequently involve following set procedures and routines. These occupations can include working with data and details more than with ideas. Usually there is a clear line of authority to follow. **Work Values—**Social Service; Supervision, Human Relations; Good Working Conditions; Supervision, Technical; Activity. **Skills—**Speaking. **Abilities—***Cognitive:* Perceptual Speed; Written Expression. *Psychomotor:* None met the criteria. *Physical:* None met the criteria. *Sensory:* Far Vision; Glare Sensitivity; Night Vision; Auditory Attention. **General Work Activities—***Information Input:* Getting Information; Identifying Objects, Actions, and Events; Monitoring Processes, Materials, or Surroundings. *Mental Process:* Evaluating Information Against Standards; Processing Information; Analyzing Data or Information. *Work Output:* Documenting or Recording Information; Handling and Moving Objects; Performing General Physical Activities. *Interacting with Others:* Performing for or Working with the Public; Communicating with Persons Outside Organization; Establishing and Maintaining Relationships. **Physical Work Conditions—**Disease or Infections; Indoors; Sitting; Whole Body Vibration; Keeping or Regaining Balance. **Other Job Characteristics—**Degree of Automation; Importance of Repeating Same Tasks; Importance of Being Exact or Accurate.

Experience—Job Zone 2. Some previous work-related skill, knowledge, or experience may be helpful, but usually is not needed. **Job Preparation:** SVP 4.0 to less than 6.0—six months to less than two years. **Knowledge—**Clerical; Law and Government; Economics and Accounting; Customer and Personal Service; Sociology and Anthropology. **Instructional Programs—**General Office Occupations and Clerical Services.

Related DOT Jobs—205.367-034 License Clerk; 249.367-030 Dog Licenser; 379.137-014 Supervisor, Dog License Officer.

43-4041.00 Credit Authorizers, Checkers, and Clerks

- **Education/Training Required: Short-term on-the-job training**
- **Employed: 86,473**
- **Annual Earnings: $25,870**
- **Growth: 4.1%**
- **Annual Job Openings: 17,000**

Authorize credit charges against customers' accounts. Investigate history and credit standing of individuals or business establishments applying for credit. May interview applicants to obtain personal and financial data, determine creditworthiness, process applications, and notify customers of acceptance or rejection of credit.

No task data available.

GOE INFORMATION—Interest Area: 09. Business Detail. **Work Group:** 09.07. Records Processing. **Note:** The Department of Labor has not collected some data for this job, so it has fewer details than the other descriptions.

Instructional Programs—Banking and Financial Support Services.

Related DOT Jobs—209.362-018 Credit Reference Clerk; 237.367-014 Call-Out Operator; 241.267-030 Investigator; 249.367-022 Credit Authorizer.

43-4041.01 Credit Authorizers

- **Education/Training Required: Short-term on-the-job training**
- **Employed: No data available.**
- **Annual Earnings: $25,870**
- **Growth: 4.1%**
- **Annual Job Openings: 17,000**

Authorize credit charges against customers' accounts.

Evaluate customers' computerized credit records and payment histories to decide whether to approve new credit, based on predetermined standards. File sales slips in customers' ledgers for billing purposes. Keep records of customers' charges and payments. Receive charge slips or credit applications by mail or receive information from salespeople or merchants by telephone. Mail charge statements to customers. Prepare credit cards or charge account plates.

GOE INFORMATION—Interest Area: 09. Business Detail. **Work Group:** 09.07. Records Processing. **Personality Type—**Conventional. Conventional occupations frequently involve following set procedures and routines. These occupations can include working with data and details more than with ideas. Usually there is a clear line of authority to follow. **Work Values—**Good Working Conditions; Supervision, Human Relations; Security; Supervision, Technical; Social Service. **Skills—**None met the criteria. **Abilities—***Cognitive:* Perceptual Speed; Number Facility. *Psychomotor:* Wrist-Finger Speed. *Physical:* None met the criteria. *Sensory:* Glare Sensitivity. **General Work Activities—***Information Input:* Getting Information; Identifying Objects, Actions, and Events; Estimating Needed Characteristics. *Mental Process:* Analyzing Data or Information; Evaluating Information Against Standards; Judging Qualities of Things, Services, or Other People's Work. *Work Output:* Documenting or Recording Information; Handling and Moving Objects; Interacting with Computers. *Interacting with Others:* Establishing and Maintaining Relationships; Communicating with Persons Outside Organization; Communicating with Other Workers. **Physical Work Conditions—**Sitting; Indoors. **Other Job Characteristics—**Importance of Being Exact or Accurate; Degree of Automation; Importance of Repeating Same Tasks.

Experience—Job Zone 1. No previous work-related skill, knowledge, or experience is needed. **Job Preparation:** SVP below 4.0—less than six months. **Knowledge—**Clerical; Computers and Electronics; Economics and Accounting; Telecommunications; Customer and Personal Service. **Instructional Programs—**Banking and Financial Support Services.

Related DOT Jobs—249.367-022 Credit Authorizer.

43-4041.02 Credit Checkers

- **Education/Training Required: Short-term on-the-job training**
- **Employed: No data available.**
- **Annual Earnings: $25,870**
- **Growth: 4.1%**
- **Annual Job Openings: 17,000**

Investigate history and credit standing of individuals or business establishments applying for credit. Telephone or write to credit departments of business and service establishments to obtain information about applicant's credit standing.

Compile and analyze credit information gathered by investigation. Contact former employers and other acquaintances to verify applicants' references, employment, health history, and social behavior. Examine city directories and public records in order to verify residence property ownership, bankruptcies, liens, arrest record, or unpaid taxes of applicants. Interview credit applicants by telephone or in person in order to obtain personal and financial data needed to complete credit report. Obtain information about potential creditors from banks, credit bureaus, and other credit services and provide reciprocal information if requested. Prepare reports of findings and recommendations, using typewriters or computers. Relay credit report information to subscribers by mail or by telephone.

GOE INFORMATION—Interest Area: 09. Business Detail. **Work Group:** 09.07. Records Processing. **Personality Type—**Conventional. Conventional occupations frequently involve following set procedures and routines. These occupations can include working with data and details more than with ideas. Usually there is a clear line of authority to follow. **Work Values—**Good Working Conditions; Supervision, Human Relations; Advancement; Pleasant Co-workers; Activity. **Skills—**Speaking; Active Listening. **Abilities—***Cognitive:* Written Expression; Oral Comprehension; Oral Expression; Number Facility; Problem Sensitivity. *Psychomotor:* Wrist-Finger Speed. *Physical:* Gross Body Equilibrium. *Sensory:* Speech Clarity. **General Work Activities—***Information Input:* Getting Information; Identifying Objects, Actions, and Events; Estimating Needed Characteristics. *Mental Process:* Processing Information; Judging Qualities of Things, Services, or Other People's Work; Making Decisions and Solving Problems. *Work Output:* Documenting or Recording Information; Handling and Moving Objects; Interacting with Computers. *Interacting with Others:* Communicating with Persons Outside Organization; Establishing and Maintaining Relationships; Communicating with Other Workers. **Physical Work Conditions—**Sitting; Indoors. **Other Job Characteristics—**Importance of Repeating Same Tasks; Importance of Being Exact or Accurate; Consequence of Error.

Experience—Job Zone 1. No previous work-related skill, knowledge, or experience is needed. **Job Preparation:** SVP below 4.0—less than six months. **Knowledge—**Clerical; Economics and Accounting; Computers and Electronics; Law and Government; Mathematics. **Instructional Programs—**Banking and Financial Support Services.

Related DOT Jobs—209.362-018 Credit Reference Clerk; 237.367-014 Call-Out Operator; 241.267-030 Investigator.

43-4051.00 Customer Service Representatives

- Education/Training Required: Moderate-term on-the-job training
- Employed: 1,945,945
- Annual Earnings: $25,430
- Growth: 32.4%
- Annual Job Openings: 359,000

Interact with customers to provide information in response to inquiries about products and services and to handle and resolve complaints.

Complete contract forms, prepare change of address records, and issue service discontinuance orders, using computers. Confer with customers by telephone or in person in order to provide information about products and services, to take orders or cancel accounts, or to obtain details of complaints. Contact customers in order to respond to inquiries or to notify them of claim investigation results and any planned adjustments. Determine charges for services requested, collect deposits or payments, and/or arrange for billing. Obtain and examine all relevant information in order to assess validity of complaints and to determine possible causes, such as extreme weather conditions that could increase utility bills. Refer unresolved customer grievances to designated departments for further investigation. Resolve customers' service or billing complaints by performing activities such as exchanging merchandise, refunding money, and adjusting bills. Check to ensure that appropriate changes were made to resolve customers' problems. Compare disputed merchandise with original requisitions and information from invoices and prepare invoices for returned goods. Keep records of customer interactions and transactions, recording details of inquiries, complaints, and comments as well as actions taken. Recommend improvements in products, packaging, shipping, service, or billing methods and procedures in order to prevent future problems. Review insurance policy terms in order to determine whether a particular loss is covered by insurance. Review claims adjustments with dealers, examining parts claimed to be defective and approving or disapproving dealers' claims. Order tests that could determine the causes of product malfunctions. Solicit sale of new or additional services or products.

GOE INFORMATION—Interest Area: 09. Business Detail. **Work Group:** 09.05. Customer Service. **Note:** The Department of Labor has not collected some data for this job, so it has fewer details than the other descriptions.

Instructional Programs—Customer Service Support/Call Center/Teleservice Operation; Receptionist.

Related DOT Jobs—191.167-022 Service Representative; 209.587-042 Return-To-Factory Clerk; 221.387-014 Complaint Clerk; 239.362-014 Customer Service Representative; 241.267-034 Investigator, Utility-Bill Complaints; 241.367-014 Customer-Complaint Clerk; 241.367-034 Tire Adjuster; 241.387-010 Claims Clerk.

43-4051.01 Adjustment Clerks

- Education/Training Required: Moderate-term on-the-job training
- Employed: No data available.
- Annual Earnings: $25,430
- Growth: 32.4%
- Annual Job Openings: 359,000

Investigate and resolve customers' inquiries concerning merchandise, service, billing, or credit rating. Examine pertinent information to determine accuracy of customers' complaints and responsibility for errors. Notify customers and appropriate personnel of findings, adjustments, and recommendations, such as exchange of merchandise, refund of money, credit to customers' accounts, or adjustment to customers' bills.

Reviews claims adjustments with dealer, examines parts claimed to be defective, and approves or disapproves of dealer's claim. Notifies customer and designated personnel of findings and recommendations, such as exchanging merchandise, refunding money, or adjustment of bill. Examines weather conditions and number of days in billing period and reviews meter accounts for errors which might explain high utility charges. Writes work order. Prepares reports showing volume, types, and disposition of claims handled. Compares merchandise with original requisition and information on invoice and prepares invoice for returned goods. Orders tests to detect product malfunction and determines if defect resulted from faulty construction. Trains dealers or service personnel in construction of products, service operations, and customer service.

GOE INFORMATION—Interest Area: 09. Business Detail. **Work Group:** 09.05. Customer Service. **Personality Type—**Conventional. Conventional occupations frequently involve following set procedures and routines. These occupations can include working with data and details more than with ideas. Usually there is a clear line of authority to follow. **Work Values—**Good Working Conditions; Social Service; Supervision, Human Relations; Pleasant Co-workers; Authority. **Skills—**Speaking; Instructing. **Abilities—***Cognitive:* Number Facility; Oral Comprehension; Written Expression; Deductive Reasoning; Oral Expression. *Psychomotor:* Wrist-Finger Speed. *Physical:* None met the criteria. *Sensory:* Speech Recognition; Near Vision; Speech Clarity; Far Vision. **General Work Activities—***Information Input:* Getting Information; Identifying Objects, Actions, and Events; Monitoring Processes, Materials, or Surroundings. *Mental Process:* Analyzing Data or Information; Processing Information; Making Decisions and Solving Problems. *Work Output:* Documenting or Recording Information; Handling and Moving Objects; Performing General Physical Activities. *Interacting with Others:* Performing for or Working with the Public; Communicating with Persons Outside Organization; Resolving Conflict and Negotiating with Others. **Physical Work Conditions—**Sitting; Indoors. **Other Job Characteristics—**Importance of Being Exact or Accurate; Consequence of Error; Importance of Repeating Same Tasks.

Experience—Job Zone 2. Some previous work-related skill, knowledge, or experience may be helpful, but usually is not needed. **Job Preparation:** SVP 4.0 to less than 6.0—six months to less than two years. **Knowledge—**Economics and Accounting; Education and Training; Customer and Personal Service; Clerical; Administration and Management. **Instructional Programs—**Customer Service Support/Call Center/Teleservice Operation; Receptionist.

Related DOT Jobs—191.167-022 Service Representative; 209.587-042 Return-To-Factory Clerk; 221.387-014 Complaint Clerk; 241.267-034 Investigator, Utility-Bill Complaints; 241.367-014 Customer-Complaint Clerk; 241.367-034 Tire Adjuster; 241.387-010 Claims Clerk.

43-4051.02 Customer Service Representatives, Utilities

- Education/Training Required: Moderate-term on-the-job training
- Employed: No data available.
- Annual Earnings: $25,430
- Growth: 32.4%
- Annual Job Openings: 359,000

Interview applicants for water, gas, electric, or telephone service. Talk with customer by phone or in person and receive orders for installation, turn-on, discontinuance, or change in services.

Confers with customer by phone or in person to receive orders for installation, turn-on, discontinuance, or change in service. Completes contract forms, prepares change of address records, and issues discontinuance orders, using computer. Resolves billing or service complaints and refers grievances to designated departments for investigation. Determines charges for service requested and collects deposits. Solicits sale of new or additional utility services.

GOE INFORMATION—Interest Area: 09. Business Detail. **Work Group:** 09.05. Customer Service. **Personality Type—**Conventional. Conventional occupations frequently involve following set procedures and routines. These occupations can include working with data and details more than with ideas. Usually there is a clear line of authority to follow. **Work Values—**Supervision, Technical; Social Service; Supervision, Human Relations; Security; Good Working Conditions. **Skills—**Speaking; Active Listening; Service Orientation. **Abilities—***Cognitive:* Number Facility; Oral Expression; Mathematical Reasoning; Speed of Closure. *Psychomotor:* Wrist-Finger Speed. *Physical:* None met the criteria. *Sensory:* Auditory Attention; Speech Clarity; Speech Recognition; Near Vision. **General Work Activities—***Information Input:* Getting Information; Identifying Objects, Actions, and Events; Estimating Needed Characteristics. *Mental Process:* Processing Information; Analyzing Data or Information; Making Decisions and Solving Problems. *Work Output:* Handling and Moving Objects; Documenting or Recording Information; Interacting with Computers. *Interacting with Others:* Performing for or Working with the Public; Communicating with Persons Outside Organization; Resolving Conflict and Negotiating with Others. **Physical Work Conditions—**Sitting; Indoors; Making Repetitive Motions; Disease or Infections; Using Hands on Objects, Tools, or Controls. **Other Job Characteristics—**Importance of Repeating Same Tasks; Degree of Automation; Pace Determined by Speed of Equipment.

Experience—Job Zone 2. Some previous work-related skill, knowledge, or experience may be helpful, but usually is not needed. **Job Preparation:** SVP 4.0 to less than 6.0—six months to less than two years. **Knowledge—**Sales and Marketing; Customer and Personal Service; Economics and Accounting; Clerical; Telecommunications. **Instructional Programs—**Customer Service Support/Call Center/Teleservice Operation; Receptionist.

Related DOT Jobs—239.362-014 Customer Service Representative.

43-4061.00 Eligibility Interviewers, Government Programs

- **Education/Training Required: Moderate-term on-the-job training**
- **Employed: 116,921**
- **Annual Earnings: $30,020**
- **Growth: –9.3%**
- **Annual Job Openings: 13,000**

Determine eligibility of persons applying to receive assistance from government programs and agency resources, such as welfare, unemployment benefits, social security, and public housing.

No task data available.

GOE INFORMATION—Interest Area: 09. Business Detail. **Work Group:** 09.02. Administrative Detail. **Note:** The Department of Labor has not collected some data for this job, so it has fewer details than the other descriptions.

Instructional Programs—Community Organization and Advocacy.

Related DOT Jobs—168.267-038 Eligibility-and-Occupancy Interviewer; 169.167-018 Contact Representative; 169.367-010 Employment-and-Claims Aide; 195.267-010 Eligibility Worker; 195.267-018 Patient-Resources-and-Reimbursement Agent; 205.367-046 Rehabilitation Clerk.

43-4061.01 Claims Takers, Unemployment Benefits

- **Education/Training Required: Moderate-term on-the-job training**
- **Employed: No data available.**
- **Annual Earnings: $30,020**
- **Growth: –9.3%**
- **Annual Job Openings: 13,000**

Interview unemployed workers and compile data to determine eligibility for unemployment benefits.

Interviews claimants returning at specified intervals to certify claimants for continuing benefits. Reviews data on job application or claim forms to ensure completeness. Assists applicants completing application forms for job referrals or unemployment compensation claims. Answers questions concerning registration for jobs or application for unemployment benefits. Assists applicants in filling out forms, using knowledge of information required or native language of applicant. Schedules unemployment insurance claimants for adjudication interview when question of eligibility arises. Refers applicants to job opening or interview with other staff, in accordance with administrative guidelines or office procedure.

GOE INFORMATION—Interest Area: 09. Business Detail. **Work Group:** 09.02. Administrative Detail. **Personality Type—**Conventional. Conventional occupations frequently involve following set procedures and routines. These occupations can include working with data and details more than with ideas. Usually there is a clear line of authority to follow. **Work Values—**Social Service; Supervision, Technical; Security; Authority; Supervision, Human Relations. **Skills—**Speaking; Active Listening. **Abilities—***Cognitive:* Written Expression; Oral Comprehension; Oral Expression; Written Comprehension; Fluency of Ideas. *Psychomotor:* None met the criteria. *Physical:* None met the criteria. *Sensory:* Speech Clarity; Speech Recognition; Near Vision. **General Work Activities—***Information Input:* Getting Information; Identifying Objects, Actions, and Events; Monitoring Processes, Materials, or Surroundings. *Mental Process:* Processing Information; Judging Qualities of Things, Services, or Other People's Work; Making Decisions and Solving Problems. *Work Output:* Handling and Moving Objects; Documenting or Recording Information; Performing General Physical Activities. *Interacting with Others:* Communicating with Persons Outside Organization; Performing for or Working with the Public; Interpreting Meaning of Information for Others. **Physical Work Conditions—**Sitting; Indoors. **Other Job Characteristics—**Importance of Being Exact or Accurate; Importance of Repeating Same Tasks; Consequence of Error.

Experience—Job Zone 2. Some previous work-related skill, knowledge, or experience may be helpful, but usually is not needed. **Job Preparation:** SVP 4.0 to less than 6.0—six months to less than two years. **Knowledge—**Personnel and Human Resources; Therapy and Counseling; Clerical; Customer and Personal Service; Foreign Language. **Instructional Programs—**Community Organization and Advocacy.

Related DOT Jobs—169.367-010 Employment-and-Claims Aide.

43-4061.02 Welfare Eligibility Workers and Interviewers

- **Education/Training Required:** Moderate-term on-the-job training
- **Employed:** No data available.
- **Annual Earnings:** $30,020
- **Growth:** –9.3%
- **Annual Job Openings:** 13,000

Interview and investigate applicants and recipients to determine eligibility for use of social programs and agency resources. Duties include recording and evaluating personal and financial data obtained from individuals; initiating procedures to grant, modify, deny, or terminate eligibility for various aid programs; authorizing grant amounts; and preparing reports. These workers generally receive specialized training and assist social service caseworkers.

Interviews and investigates applicants for public assistance to gather information pertinent to their application. Selects and refers eligible applicants to public assistance or public housing agencies. Records and evaluates personal and financial data to determine initial or continuing eligibility. Initiates procedures to grant, modify, deny, or terminate eligibility and grants for various assistance programs. Authorizes amounts of grants, money payments, food stamps, medical care, or other general assistance. Prepares regular and special reports, keeps records of assigned cases, and submits individual recommendations. Computes public housing rent in proportion to eligible tenant's income. Prepares and assists applicants in completion of routine intake and personnel forms. Conducts annual, interim, and special housing reviews and home visits to ensure conformance to regulations. Explains eligibility requirements, form completion requirements, community resources for financial assistance, housing opportunities, and tenant selection methods. Reviews training approval forms and payment vouchers for completeness and accuracy. Interprets and explains rules and regulations governing eligibility and grants, payment methods, and applicant's legal rights. Receives and records security deposits and advance rents from selected tenants.

GOE INFORMATION—Interest Area: 09. Business Detail. **Work Group:** 09.02. Administrative Detail. **Personality Type—**Social. Social occupations frequently involve working with, communicating with, and teaching people. These occupations often involve helping or providing service to others. **Work Values—**Social Service; Achievement; Security; Authority; Supervision, Technical. **Skills—**Service Orientation; Systems Evaluation; Judgment and Decision Making; Speaking; Active Listening; Writing; Complex Problem Solving; Systems Analysis. **Abilities—***Cognitive:* Written Expression; Oral Expression; Written Comprehension; Oral Comprehension; Memorization. *Psychomotor:* None met the criteria. *Physical:* None met the criteria. *Sensory:* Speech Clarity; Speech Recognition. **General Work Activities—***Information Input:* Getting Information; Identifying Objects, Actions, and Events; Monitoring Processes, Materials, or Surroundings. *Mental Process:* Processing Information; Analyzing Data or Information; Making Decisions and Solving Problems. *Work Output:* Documenting or Recording Information; Performing General Physical Activities; Handling and Moving Objects. *Interacting with Others:* Communicating with Persons Outside Organization; Assisting and Caring for Others; Establishing and Maintaining Relationships. **Physical Work Conditions—**Sitting; Indoors; Walking or Running. **Other Job Characteristics—**Importance of Being Exact or Accurate; Consequence of Error; Pace Determined by Speed of Equipment.

Experience—Job Zone 2. Some previous work-related skill, knowledge, or experience may be helpful, but usually is not needed. **Job Preparation:** SVP 4.0 to less than 6.0—six months to less than two years. **Knowledge—**Therapy and Counseling; Administration and Management; Sociology and Anthropology; Psychology; Law and Government. **Instructional Programs—**Community Organization and Advocacy.

Related DOT Jobs—168.267-038 Eligibility-and-Occupancy Interviewer; 169.167-018 Contact Representative; 195.267-010 Eligibility Worker; 195.267-018 Patient-Resources-and-Reimbursement Agent; 205.367-046 Rehabilitation Clerk.

43-4071.00 File Clerks

- **Education/Training Required:** Short-term on-the-job training
- **Employed:** 287,725
- **Annual Earnings:** $19,490
- **Growth:** 9.1%
- **Annual Job Openings:** 49,000

File correspondence, cards, invoices, receipts, and other records in alphabetical or numerical order or according to the filing system used. Locate and remove material from file when requested.

Add new material to file records and create new records as necessary. Answer questions about records and files. Assign and record or stamp identification numbers or codes in order to index materials for filing. Eliminate outdated or unnecessary materials, destroying them or transferring them to inactive storage according to file maintenance guidelines and/or legal requirements. Enter document identification codes into systems in order to determine locations of documents to be retrieved. Find and retrieve information from files in response to requests from authorized users. Keep records of materials filed or removed, using logbooks or computers. Modify and improve filing systems or implement new filing systems. Perform periodic inspections of materials or files in order to ensure correct placement, legibility, and proper condition. Place materials into storage receptacles, such as file cabinets, boxes, bins, or drawers, according to classification and identification information. Scan or read incoming materials in order to determine how and where they should be classified or filed. Sort or classify information according to guidelines such as content; purpose; user criteria; or chronological, alphabetical, or numerical order. Track materials removed from files in order to ensure that borrowed files are returned. Convert documents to films for storage on microforms such as microfilm or microfiche. Design forms related to filing systems. Gather materials to be filed from departments and employees. Operate mechanized files that rotate to bring needed records to a particular location. Perform general office duties such as typing, operating office machines, and sorting mail. Retrieve documents stored in microfilm or microfiche and place them in viewers for reading.

GOE INFORMATION—Interest Area: 09. Business Detail. **Work Group:** 09.07. Records Processing. **Personality Type—**Conventional. Conventional occupations frequently involve following set procedures and routines. These occupations can include working with data and details more than with ideas. Usually there is a clear line of authority to follow. **Work Values—**Good Working Conditions; Moral Values; Supervision, Human Relations; Company Policies and Practices; Activity. **Skills—**None met the criteria. **Abilities—***Cognitive:* Category Flexibility. *Psychomotor:* None met the criteria. *Physical:* None met the criteria. *Sensory:* Near Vision. **General Work Activities—***Information Input:* Identifying Objects, Actions, and Events; Getting Information; Inspecting Equipment, Structures, or Materials. *Mental Process:* Processing Information; Judging Qualities of Things, Services, or Other People's Work; Evaluating Information Against Standards. *Work Output:* Handling and Moving Objects; Documenting or Recording Information; Performing General Physical Activities. *Interacting with Others:* Communicating with Other Workers;

Performing Administrative Activities; Establishing and Maintaining Relationships. **Physical Work Conditions**—Sitting; Indoors; Making Repetitive Motions. **Other Job Characteristics**—Importance of Being Exact or Accurate; Importance of Repeating Same Tasks; Consequence of Error.

Experience—Job Zone 1. No previous work-related skill, knowledge, or experience is needed. **Job Preparation:** SVP below 4.0—less than six months. **Knowledge**—Clerical; Computers and Electronics. **Instructional Programs**—General Office Occupations and Clerical Services.

Related DOT Jobs—206.367-014 File Clerk II; 206.367-018 Tape Librarian; 206.387-010 Classification Clerk; 206.387-014 Fingerprint Clerk II; 206.387-022 Record Clerk; 206.387-034 File Clerk I.

43-4081.00 Hotel, Motel, and Resort Desk Clerks

- **Education/Training Required: Short-term on-the-job training**
- **Employed: 176,738**
- **Annual Earnings: $16,920**
- **Growth: 33.4%**
- **Annual Job Openings: 73,000**

Accommodate hotel, motel, and resort patrons by registering and assigning rooms to guests, issuing room keys, transmitting and receiving messages, keeping records of occupied rooms and guests' accounts, making and confirming reservations, and presenting statements to and collecting payments from departing guests.

Greet, register, and assign rooms to guests of hotels or motels. Keep records of room availability and guests' accounts, manually or using computers. Compute bills, collect payments, and make change for guests. Make and confirm reservations. Post charges, such those for rooms, food, liquor, or telephone calls, to ledgers manually or by using computers. Transmit and receive messages, using telephones or telephone switchboards. Issue room keys and escort instructions to bellhops. Date-stamp, sort, and rack incoming mail and messages. Answer inquiries pertaining to hotel services, registration of guests, and shopping, dining, entertainment, and travel directions. Deposit guests' valuables in hotel safes or safe-deposit boxes. Advise housekeeping staff when rooms have been vacated and are ready for cleaning. Arrange tours, taxis, and restaurants for customers. Contact housekeeping or maintenance staff when guests report problems. Perform simple bookkeeping activities, such as balancing cash accounts. Record guest comments or complaints, referring customers to managers as necessary. Review accounts and charges with guests during the checkout process. Verify customers' credit and establish how the customer will pay for the accommodation.

GOE INFORMATION—**Interest Area:** 11. Recreation, Travel, and Other Personal Services. **Work Group:** 11.03. Transportation and Lodging Services. **Personality Type**—Conventional. Conventional occupations frequently involve following set procedures and routines. These occupations can include working with data and details more than with ideas. Usually there is a clear line of authority to follow. **Work Values**—Social Service; Good Working Conditions; Supervision, Human Relations; Supervision, Technical; Pleasant Co-workers. **Skills**—Service Orientation. **Abilities**—*Cognitive:* Oral Expression; Oral Comprehension; Time Sharing. *Psychomotor:* None met the criteria. *Physical:* None met the criteria. *Sensory:* Speech Recognition. **General Work Activities**—*Information Input:* Identifying Objects, Actions, and Events; Getting Information; Monitoring Processes, Materials, or Surroundings. *Mental Process:* Processing Information; Making Decisions and Solving Problems; Evaluating Information Against Standards. *Work Output:* Handling and Moving Objects;

Documenting or Recording Information; Interacting with Computers. *Interacting with Others:* Establishing and Maintaining Relationships; Assisting and Caring for Others; Performing for or Working with the Public. **Physical Work Conditions**—Standing. **Other Job Characteristics**—Importance of Being Exact or Accurate; Importance of Repeating Same Tasks; Degree of Automation.

Experience—Job Zone 2. Some previous work-related skill, knowledge, or experience may be helpful, but usually is not needed. **Job Preparation:** SVP 4.0 to less than 6.0—six months to less than two years. **Knowledge**—Customer and Personal Service; Clerical; Computers and Electronics; Sales and Marketing; Geography. **Instructional Programs**—Selling Skills and Sales Operations.

Related DOT Jobs—238.367-038 Hotel Clerk.

43-4111.00 Interviewers, Except Eligibility and Loan

- **Education/Training Required: Short-term on-the-job training**
- **Employed: 153,888**
- **Annual Earnings: $21,880**
- **Growth: 33.4%**
- **Annual Job Openings: 53,000**

Interview persons by telephone, by mail, in person, or by other means for the purpose of completing forms, applications, or questionnaires. Ask specific questions, record answers, and assist persons with completing form. May sort, classify, and file forms.

Ask questions in accordance with instructions to obtain various specified information, such as person's name, address, age, religious preference, and state of residency. Assist individuals in filling out applications or questionnaires. Compile, record, and code results and data from interview or survey, using computer or specified form. Contact individuals to be interviewed at home, place of business, or field location by telephone, by mail, or in person. Explain survey objectives and procedures to interviewees and interpret survey questions to help interviewees' comprehension. Identify and report problems in obtaining valid data. Identify and resolve inconsistencies in interviewees' responses by means of appropriate questioning and/or explanation. Locate and list addresses and households. Review data obtained from interview for completeness and accuracy. Collect and analyze data, such as studying old records, tallying the number of outpatients entering each day or week, or participating in federal, state, or local population surveys as a Census Enumerator. Meet with supervisor daily to submit completed assignments and discuss progress. Prepare reports to provide answers in response to specific problems. Ensure payment for services by verifying benefits with the person's insurance provider or working out financing options. Perform other office duties as needed, such as telemarketing and customer service inquiries, billing patients, and receiving payments. Perform patient services, such as answering the telephone and assisting patients with financial and medical questions.

GOE INFORMATION—**Interest Area:** 09. Business Detail. **Work Group:** 09.02. Administrative Detail. **Personality Type**—Conventional. Conventional occupations frequently involve following set procedures and routines. These occupations can include working with data and details more than with ideas. Usually there is a clear line of authority to follow. **Work Values**—Good Working Conditions; Supervision, Technical; Independence. **Skills**—Speaking; Active Listening. **Abilities**—*Cognitive:* Oral Expression. *Psychomotor:* Wrist-Finger Speed. *Physical:* None met the criteria. *Sensory:* Speech Recognition; Speech Clarity. **General Work Activities**—*Information Input:* Getting Information; Identifying Objects,

Actions, and Events; Monitoring Processes, Materials, or Surroundings. *Mental Process:* Processing Information; Evaluating Information Against Standards; Making Decisions and Solving Problems. *Work Output:* Documenting or Recording Information; Handling and Moving Objects; Interacting with Computers. *Interacting with Others:* Communicating with Persons Outside Organization; Performing for or Working with the Public; Establishing and Maintaining Relationships. **Physical Work Conditions**—Sitting; Indoors. **Other Job Characteristics**—Importance of Repeating Same Tasks; Importance of Being Exact or Accurate; Pace Determined by Speed of Equipment.

Experience—Job Zone 1. No previous work-related skill, knowledge, or experience is needed. **Job Preparation:** SVP below 4.0—less than six months. **Knowledge**—Clerical; Personnel and Human Resources; Telecommunications; Computers and Electronics; Communications and Media. **Instructional Programs**—Receptionist.

Related DOT Jobs—205.362-018 Hospital-Admitting Clerk; 205.367-014 Charge-Account Clerk; 205.367-026 Creel Clerk; 205.367-042 Registration Clerk; 205.367-054 Survey Worker; 205.367-058 Traffic Checker.

43-4121.00 *Library Assistants, Clerical*

- **Education/Training Required: Short-term on-the-job training**
- **Employed: 98,348**
- **Annual Earnings: $18,580**
- **Growth: 19.7%**
- **Annual Job Openings: 26,000**

Compile records, sort and shelve books, and issue and receive library materials such as pictures, cards, slides, and microfilm. Locate library materials for loan and replace material in shelving area, stacks, or files according to identification number and title. Register patrons to permit them to borrow books, periodicals, and other library materials.

Answer routine inquiries and refer patrons in need of professional assistance to librarians. Deliver and retrieve items to and from departments by hand or using push carts. Enter and update patrons' records on computers. Inspect returned books for condition and due-date status and compute any applicable fines. Lend and collect books, periodicals, videotapes, and other materials at circulation desks. Locate library materials for patrons, including books, periodicals, tape cassettes, Braille volumes, and pictures. Maintain records of items received, stored, issued, and returned; file catalog cards according to system used. Operate and maintain audiovisual equipment. Perform clerical activities such as filing, typing, word processing, photocopying and mailing out material, and mail sorting. Process new materials, including books, audiovisual materials, and computer software. Provide assistance to librarians in the maintenance of collections of books, periodicals, magazines, newspapers, and audiovisual and other materials. Repair books, using mending tape, paste, and brushes. Review records, such as microfilm and issue cards, in order to identify titles of overdue materials and delinquent borrowers. Send out notices and accept fine payments for lost or overdue books. Sort books, publications, and other items according to established procedure and return them to shelves, files, or other designated storage areas. Assist in the preparation of book displays. Classify and catalog items according to content and purpose. Drive bookmobiles to specified off-site locations, following library service schedules, and to garages for preventive maintenance and repairs. Facilitate the acquisition of books, pamphlets, periodicals, and audiovisual materials by checking prices, figuring costs, and preparing appropriate order forms. Instruct patrons on how to use reference sources, card catalogs, and automated information systems. Place books in mailing containers, affix address labels, and secure containers with straps for mailing to blind library patrons. Prepare, store,

and retrieve classification and catalog information, lecture notes, or other information related to stored documents, using computers. Register new patrons and issue borrower identification cards that permit patrons to borrow books and other materials. Schedule and supervise clerical workers, volunteers, and student assistants. Select substitute titles when requested materials are unavailable, following criteria such as age, education, and interests. Take action to deal with disruptive or problem patrons.

GOE INFORMATION—**Interest Area:** 12. Education and Social Service. **Work Group:** 12.03. Educational Services. **Personality Type**—Conventional. Conventional occupations frequently involve following set procedures and routines. These occupations can include working with data and details more than with ideas. Usually there is a clear line of authority to follow. **Work Values**—Supervision, Technical; Good Working Conditions; Social Service; Supervision, Human Relations; Moral Values. **Skills**—None met the criteria. **Abilities**—*Cognitive:* Category Flexibility; Memorization; Time Sharing; Perceptual Speed; Written Comprehension. *Psychomotor:* Wrist-Finger Speed; Reaction Time; Rate Control; Response Orientation. *Physical:* Dynamic Flexibility; Extent Flexibility; Gross Body Equilibrium. *Sensory:* Speech Clarity; Near Vision; Night Vision; Visual Color Discrimination; Auditory Attention. **General Work Activities**—*Information Input:* Getting Information; Identifying Objects, Actions, and Events; Monitoring Processes, Materials, or Surroundings. *Mental Process:* Updating and Using Relevant Knowledge; Processing Information; Analyzing Data or Information. *Work Output:* Handling and Moving Objects; Performing General Physical Activities; Documenting or Recording Information. *Interacting with Others:* Communicating with Persons Outside Organization; Performing for or Working with the Public; Establishing and Maintaining Relationships. **Physical Work Conditions**—Bending or Twisting the Body; Kneeling, Crouching, or Crawling; Climbing Ladders, Scaffolds, Poles, etc.; Indoors; Walking or Running. **Other Job Characteristics**—Importance of Repeating Same Tasks; Degree of Automation; Pace Determined by Speed of Equipment.

Experience—Job Zone 1. No previous work-related skill, knowledge, or experience is needed. **Job Preparation:** SVP below 4.0—less than six months. **Knowledge**—Clerical; Customer and Personal Service; Communications and Media; Computers and Electronics; History and Archeology. **Instructional Programs**—Library Assistant/Technician.

Related DOT Jobs—209.387-026 Library Clerk, Talking Books; 222.367-026 Film-or-Tape Librarian; 222.587-014 Braille-and-Talking Books Clerk; 249.363-010 Bookmobile Driver; 249.365-010 Registration Clerk; 249.367-046 Library Assistant; 249.687-014 Page.

43-4131.00 *Loan Interviewers and Clerks*

- **Education/Training Required: Short-term on-the-job training**
- **Employed: 138,939**
- **Annual Earnings: $27,070**
- **Growth: -27.6%**
- **Annual Job Openings: 25,000**

Interview loan applicants to elicit information; investigate applicants' backgrounds and verify references; prepare loan request papers; and forward findings, reports, and documents to appraisal department. Review loan papers to ensure completeness and complete transactions between loan establishment, borrowers, and sellers upon approval of loan.

Verify and examine information and accuracy of loan application and closing documents. Prepare and type loan applications, closing documents, legal documents, letters, forms, government notices, and checks, using computers. Interview loan applicants in order to obtain personal and financial data and to assist in completing applications. Assemble and compile documents for loan closings, such as title abstracts, insurance forms, loan forms, and tax receipts. Record applications for loan and credit, loan information, and disbursements of funds, using computers. Submit loan applications with recommendation for underwriting approval. Contact customers by mail, by telephone, or in person concerning acceptance or rejection of applications. Contact credit bureaus, employers, and other sources in order to check applicants' credit and personal references. Check value of customer collateral to be held as loan security. Calculate, review, and correct errors on interest, principal, payment, and closing costs, using computers or calculators. Answer questions and advise customers regarding loans and transactions. Schedule and conduct closings of mortgage transactions. Present loan and repayment schedules to customers. Establish credit limits and grant extensions of credit on overdue accounts. File and maintain loan records. Order property insurance or mortgage insurance policies in order to ensure protection against loss on mortgaged property. Accept payment on accounts. Review customer accounts in order to determine whether payments are made on time and ensure that other loan terms are being followed.

GOE INFORMATION—Interest Area: 09. Business Detail. Work Group: 09.02. Administrative Detail. Personality Type—Conventional. Conventional occupations frequently involve following set procedures and routines. These occupations can include working with data and details more than with ideas. Usually there is a clear line of authority to follow. Work Values—Good Working Conditions; Social Service; Advancement; Pleasant Co-workers; Supervision, Human Relations. Skills—Speaking; Mathematics; Active Listening. Abilities—*Cognitive:* Number Facility; Mathematical Reasoning; Perceptual Speed; Written Expression; Written Comprehension. *Psychomotor:* Wrist-Finger Speed; Response Orientation. *Physical:* Trunk Strength. *Sensory:* Near Vision; Speech Recognition; Speech Clarity; Auditory Attention. General Work Activities—*Information Input:* Getting Information; Identifying Objects, Actions, and Events; Monitoring Processes, Materials, or Surroundings. *Mental Process:* Processing Information; Evaluating Information Against Standards; Analyzing Data or Information. *Work Output:* Documenting or Recording Information; Interacting with Computers; Handling and Moving Objects. *Interacting with Others:* Communicating with Persons Outside Organization; Establishing and Maintaining Relationships; Performing Administrative Activities. Physical Work Conditions—Sitting; Indoors. Other Job Characteristics—Degree of Automation; Importance of Being Exact or Accurate; Pace Determined by Speed of Equipment.

Experience—Job Zone 2. Some previous work-related skill, knowledge, or experience may be helpful, but usually is not needed. Job Preparation: SVP 4.0 to less than 6.0—six months to less than two years. Knowledge—Clerical; Economics and Accounting; Law and Government; Customer and Personal Service; Computers and Electronics. Instructional Programs—Banking and Financial Support Services.

Related DOT Jobs—205.367-022 Credit Clerk; 219.362-038 Mortgage-Closing Clerk; 219.367-046 Disbursement Clerk; 249.362-014 Mortgage Clerk; 249.362-018 Mortgage Loan Closer; 249.362-022 Mortgage Loan Processor.

43-4141.00 New Accounts Clerks

- Education/Training Required: Work experience in a related occupation
- Employed: 86,589
- Annual Earnings: $24,670
- Growth: 2.7%
- Annual Job Openings: 30,000

Interview persons desiring to open bank accounts. Explain banking services available to prospective customers and assist them in preparing application form.

Answer customers' questions and explain available services, such as deposit accounts, bonds, and securities. Collect and record customer deposits and fees; issue receipts using computers. Compile information about new accounts, enter account information into computers, and file related forms or other documents. Inform customers of procedures for applying for services such as ATM cards, direct deposit of checks, and certificates of deposit. Interview customers in order to obtain information needed for opening accounts or renting safe-deposit boxes. Refer customers to appropriate bank personnel in order to meet their financial needs. Duplicate records for distribution to branch offices. Execute wire transfers of funds. Investigate and correct errors upon customers' request, according to customer and bank records. Issue initial and replacement safe-deposit keys to customers and admit customers to vaults. Obtain credit records from reporting agencies. Perform foreign currency transactions and sell traveler's checks. Perform teller duties as required. Schedule repairs for locks on safe-deposit boxes.

GOE INFORMATION—Interest Area: 09. Business Detail. Work Group: 09.05. Customer Service. Personality Type—Conventional. Conventional occupations frequently involve following set procedures and routines. These occupations can include working with data and details more than with ideas. Usually there is a clear line of authority to follow. Work Values—Good Working Conditions; Social Service; Pleasant Co-workers; Supervision, Technical; Supervision, Human Relations. Skills—Speaking. Abilities—*Cognitive:* Number Facility; Oral Expression; Memorization; Mathematical Reasoning; Oral Comprehension. *Psychomotor:* Wrist-Finger Speed. *Physical:* None met the criteria. *Sensory:* Speech Recognition; Near Vision. General Work Activities—*Information Input:* Getting Information; Identifying Objects, Actions, and Events; Estimating Needed Characteristics. *Mental Process:* Processing Information; Updating and Using Relevant Knowledge; Evaluating Information Against Standards. *Work Output:* Handling and Moving Objects; Documenting or Recording Information; Interacting with Computers. *Interacting with Others:* Communicating with Persons Outside Organization; Performing for or Working with the Public; Establishing and Maintaining Relationships. Physical Work Conditions—Sitting; Indoors; Disease or Infections. Other Job Characteristics—Importance of Being Exact or Accurate; Importance of Repeating Same Tasks; Consequence of Error.

Experience—Job Zone 2. Some previous work-related skill, knowledge, or experience may be helpful, but usually is not needed. Job Preparation: SVP 4.0 to less than 6.0—six months to less than two years. Knowledge—Economics and Accounting; Clerical; Customer and Personal Service; Computers and Electronics; Sales and Marketing. Instructional Programs—Banking and Financial Support Services.

Related DOT Jobs—205.362-026 Customer Service Representative; 295.367-022 Safe-Deposit-Box Rental Clerk.

43-4151.00 Order Clerks

- Education/Training Required: Short-term on-the-job training
- Employed: 348,231
- Annual Earnings: $24,250
- Growth: −20.4%
- Annual Job Openings: 49,000

Receive and process incoming orders for materials, merchandise, classified ads, or services such as repairs, installations, or rental of facilities. Duties include informing customers of receipt, prices, shipping dates, and delays; preparing contracts; and handling complaints.

Check inventory records to determine availability of requested merchandise. Compute total charges for merchandise or services and shipping charges. Direct specified departments or units to prepare and ship orders to designated locations. File copies of orders received or post orders on records. Inform customers by mail or telephone of order information, such as unit prices, shipping dates, and any anticipated delays. Obtain customers' names, addresses, and billing information; product numbers; and specifications of items to be purchased and enter this information on order forms. Prepare invoices, shipping documents, and contracts. Review orders for completeness according to reporting procedures and forward incomplete orders for further processing. Verify customer and order information for correctness, checking it against previously obtained information as necessary. Adjust inventory records to reflect product movement. Attempt to sell additional merchandise or services to prospective or current customers by telephone or through visits. Calculate and compile order-related statistics and prepare reports for management. Collect payment for merchandise, record transactions, and send items such as checks or money orders for further processing. Confer with production, sales, shipping, warehouse, or common carrier personnel in order to expedite or trace shipments. Inspect outgoing work for compliance with customers' specifications. Notify departments when supplies of specific items are low or when orders would deplete available supplies. Receive and respond to customer complaints. Recommend merchandise or services that will meet customers' needs. Recommend type of packing or labeling needed on order.

GOE INFORMATION—Interest Area: 09. Business Detail. **Work Group:** 09.05. Customer Service. **Personality Type**—Conventional. Conventional occupations frequently involve following set procedures and routines. These occupations can include working with data and details more than with ideas. Usually there is a clear line of authority to follow. **Work Values**—Supervision, Technical; Advancement; Social Service; Supervision, Human Relations; Pleasant Co-workers. **Skills**—None met the criteria. **Abilities**—*Cognitive:* Mathematical Reasoning; Number Facility; Problem Sensitivity; Oral Expression; Oral Comprehension. *Psychomotor:* None met the criteria. *Physical:* None met the criteria. *Sensory:* Speech Recognition; Speech Clarity; Auditory Attention. **General Work Activities**—*Information Input:* Getting Information; Identifying Objects, Actions, and Events; Estimating Needed Characteristics. *Mental Process:* Processing Information; Analyzing Data or Information; Updating and Using Relevant Knowledge. *Work Output:* Handling and Moving Objects; Documenting or Recording Information; Interacting with Computers. *Interacting with Others:* Communicating with Other Workers; Influencing Others or Selling; Communicating with Persons Outside Organization. **Physical Work Conditions**—Sitting; Indoors. **Other Job Characteristics**—Importance of Repeating Same Tasks; Pace Determined by Speed of Equipment; Degree of Automation.

Experience—Job Zone 2. Some previous work-related skill, knowledge, or experience may be helpful, but usually is not needed. **Job Preparation:** SVP 4.0 to less than 6.0—six months to less than two years. **Knowledge**—Clerical; Sales and Marketing; Economics and Accounting; Customer and Personal Service; Communications and Media. **Instructional Programs**—General Office Occupations and Clerical Services.

Related DOT Jobs—209.387-018 Contact Clerk; 209.567-014 Order Clerk, Food and Beverage; 245.367-026 Order-Control Clerk, Blood Bank; 249.362-026 Order Clerk; 249.367-042 Gas-Distribution-and-Emergency Clerk; 295.367-018 Film-Rental Clerk; 659.462-010 Electrotype Servicer.

43-4161.00 Human Resources Assistants, Except Payroll and Timekeeping

- **Education/Training Required: Short-term on-the-job training**
- **Employed: 177,187**
- **Annual Earnings: $29,470**
- **Growth: 19.3%**
- **Annual Job Openings: 25,000**

Compile and keep personnel records. Record data for each employee, such as address, weekly earnings, absences, amount of sales or production, supervisory reports on ability, and date of and reason for termination. Compile and type reports from employment records. File employment records. Search employee files and furnish information to authorized persons.

Answer questions regarding examinations, eligibility, salaries, benefits, and other pertinent information. Arrange for advertising or posting of job vacancies and notify eligible workers of position availability. Compile and prepare reports and documents pertaining to personnel activities. Examine employee files to answer inquiries and provide information for personnel actions. Explain company personnel policies, benefits, and procedures to employees or job applicants. Gather personnel records from other departments and/or employees. Inform job applicants of their acceptance or rejection of employment. Process and review employment applications in order to evaluate qualifications or eligibility of applicants. Process, verify, and maintain documentation relating to personnel activities such as staffing, recruitment, training, grievances, performance evaluations, and classifications. Provide assistance in administering employee benefit programs and worker's compensation plans. Record data for each employee, including such information as addresses, weekly earnings, absences, amount of sales or production, supervisory reports on performance, and dates of and reasons for terminations. Request information from law enforcement officials, previous employers, and other references in order to determine applicants' employment acceptability. Administer and score applicant and employee aptitude, personality, and interest assessment instruments. Arrange for in-house and external training activities. Interview job applicants to obtain and verify information used to screen and evaluate them. Prepare badges, passes, and identification cards and perform other security-related duties. Search employee files in order to obtain information for authorized persons and organizations, such as credit bureaus and finance companies. Select applicants meeting specified job requirements and refer them to hiring personnel.

GOE INFORMATION—Interest Area: 09. Business Detail. **Work Group:** 09.07. Records Processing. **Personality Type**—Conventional. Conventional occupations frequently involve following set procedures and routines. These occupations can include working with data and details more than with ideas. Usually there is a clear line of authority to follow. **Work Values**—Good Working Conditions; Social Service; Supervision, Human Relations; Supervision, Technical; Company Policies and Practices. **Skills**—Equipment Selection; Speaking; Reading Comprehension. **Abilities**—*Cognitive:* Written Expression; Oral Comprehension; Oral Expression; Written Comprehension; Number Facility. *Psychomotor:* Response Orientation. *Physical:* Gross Body Equilibrium; Gross Body Coordination. *Sensory:* Speech Recognition; Speech Clarity; Hearing Sensitivity; Auditory Attention; Far Vision. **General Work Activities**—*Information Input:* Getting Information; Identifying Objects, Actions, and Events; Monitoring Processes, Materials, or Surroundings. *Mental Process:* Evaluating Information Against Standards; Judging Qualities of Things, Services, or Other People's Work; Processing Information. *Work Output:* Documenting or Recording Information; Interacting with Computers; Handling and Moving Objects. *Interacting with Others:* Establishing and Maintaining Relationships; Staffing Organizational Units; Communicating with Persons Outside Organization. **Physical Work Conditions**—Sitting; Indoors; Making Repetitive Motions; Using Hands on Objects, Tools, or Controls. **Other Job Characteristics**—Importance of Repeating Same Tasks; Importance of Being Exact or Accurate; Pace Determined by Speed of Equipment.

Experience—Job Zone 2. Some previous work-related skill, knowledge, or experience may be helpful, but usually is not needed. **Job Preparation:** SVP 4.0 to less than 6.0—six months to less than two years. **Knowledge**—Clerical; Personnel and Human Resources; English Language; Computers and Electronics; Mathematics. **Instructional Programs**—General Office Occupations and Clerical Services.

Related DOT Jobs—205.362-010 Civil-Service Clerk; 205.362-014 Employment Clerk; 205.362-022 Identification Clerk; 205.367-062 Referral Clerk, Temporary Help Agency; 205.567-010 Benefits Clerk II; 209.362-026 Personnel Clerk; 241.267-010 Agent-Contract Clerk; 249.367-090 Assignment Clerk.

43-4171.00 Receptionists and Information Clerks

- **Education/Training Required: Short-term on-the-job training**
- **Employed: 1,078,457**
- **Annual Earnings: $20,650**
- **Growth: 23.7%**
- **Annual Job Openings: 269,000**

Answer inquiries and obtain information for general public, customers, visitors, and other interested parties. Provide information regarding activities conducted at establishment, location of departments and offices, and employees within organization.

Operate telephone switchboard to answer, screen, and forward calls, providing information, taking messages, and scheduling appointments. Receive payment and record receipts for services. Perform administrative support tasks such as proofreading, transcribing handwritten information, and operating calculators or computers to work with pay records, invoices, balance sheets, and other documents. Greet persons entering establishment, determine nature and purpose of visit, and direct or escort them to specific destinations. Hear and resolve complaints from customers and public. File and maintain records. Transmit information or documents to customers, using computer, mail, or facsimile machine. Schedule appointments and maintain and update appointment calendars. Analyze data to determine answers to questions from customers or members of the public. Provide information about establishment, such as location of departments or offices, employees within the organization, or services provided. Keep a current record of staff members' whereabouts and availability. Collect, sort, distribute, and prepare mail, messages, and courier deliveries. Calculate and quote rates for tours, stocks, insurance policies, and other products and services. Take orders for merchandise or materials and send them to the proper departments to be filled. Process and prepare memos, correspondence, travel vouchers, or other documents. Schedule space and equipment for special programs and prepare lists of participants. Enroll individuals to participate in programs and notify them of their acceptance. Conduct tours or deliver talks describing features of public facility, such as historic site or national park. Perform duties such as taking care of plants and straightening magazines to maintain lobby or reception area.

GOE INFORMATION—**Interest Area:** 09. Business Detail. **Work Group:** 09.05. Customer Service. **Personality Type**—Conventional. Conven-

tional occupations frequently involve following set procedures and routines. These occupations can include working with data and details more than with ideas. Usually there is a clear line of authority to follow. **Work Values**—Social Service; Good Working Conditions; Supervision, Technical; Company Policies and Practices; Activity. **Skills**—Active Listening; Service Orientation; Social Perceptiveness; Speaking; Critical Thinking; Reading Comprehension; Writing; Learning Strategies. **Abilities**—*Cognitive:* Oral Expression; Category Flexibility; Perceptual Speed; Inductive Reasoning; Speed of Closure. *Psychomotor:* Finger Dexterity. *Physical:* None met the criteria. *Sensory:* Speech Recognition; Speech Clarity; Far Vision; Near Vision. **General Work Activities**—*Information Input:* Getting Information; Monitoring Processes, Materials, or Surroundings; Identifying Objects, Actions, and Events. *Mental Process:* Organizing, Planning, and Prioritizing; Updating and Using Relevant Knowledge; Making Decisions and Solving Problems. *Work Output:* Interacting with Computers; Handling and Moving Objects; Documenting or Recording Information. *Interacting with Others:* Establishing and Maintaining Relationships; Communicating with Other Workers; Communicating with Persons Outside Organization. **Physical Work Conditions**—Sitting; Outdoors; Very Hot or Cold; Walking or Running; Making Repetitive Motions. **Other Job Characteristics**—Degree of Automation; Importance of Repeating Same Tasks; Pace Determined by Speed of Equipment.

Experience—Job Zone 2. Some previous work-related skill, knowledge, or experience may be helpful, but usually is not needed. **Job Preparation:** SVP below 4.0—less than six months. **Knowledge**—Customer and Personal Service; Clerical; Computers and Electronics; Administration and Management; English Language. **Instructional Programs**—General Office Occupations and Clerical Services; Health Unit Coordinator/Ward Clerk; Medical Reception/Receptionist; Receptionist.

Related DOT Jobs—203.362-014 Credit Reporting Clerk; 205.367-038 Registrar; 237.267-010 Information Clerk, Automobile Club; 237.367-010 Appointment Clerk; 237.367-018 Information Clerk; 237.367-022 Information Clerk; 237.367-038 Receptionist; 237.367-042 Referral-and-Information Aide; 237.367-046 Telephone Quotation Clerk; 238.367-022 Space Scheduler; 238.367-034 Scheduler; 239.367-034 Utility Clerk; 249.262-010 Policyholder-Information Clerk; 249.367-082 Park Aide.

43-4181.00 Reservation and Transportation Ticket Agents and Travel Clerks

- **Education/Training Required: Short-term on-the-job training**
- **Employed: 190,916**
- **Annual Earnings: $24,090**
- **Growth: 14.5%**
- **Annual Job Openings: 39,000**

Make and confirm reservations and sell tickets to passengers for large hotel or motel chains. May check baggage and direct passengers to designated concourse, pier, or track; make reservations; deliver tickets; arrange for visas; contact individuals and groups to inform them of package tours; or provide tourists with travel information, such as points of interest, restaurants, rates, and emergency service.

No task data available.

GOE INFORMATION—**Interest Area:** 11. Recreation, Travel, and Other Personal Services. **Work Group:** 11.03. Transportation and Lodging Services. **Note:** The Department of Labor has not collected some data for this job, so it has fewer details than the other descriptions.

Instructional Programs—Selling Skills and Sales Operations; Tourism and Travel Services Marketing Operations; Tourism Promotion Operations.

Related DOT Jobs—214.362-030 Rate Clerk, Passenger; 237.367-050 Tourist-Information Assistant; 238.167-010 Travel Clerk; 238.167-014 Travel Counselor, Automobile Club; 238.362-014 Reservation Clerk; 238.367-010 Gate Agent; 238.367-014 Reservation Clerk; 238.367-018 Reservations Agent; 238.367-026 Ticket Agent; 238.367-030 Travel Clerk; 248.382-010 Ticketing Clerk.

43-4181.01 Travel Clerks

- **Education/Training Required: Short-term on-the-job training**
- **Employed: No data available.**
- **Annual Earnings: $24,090**
- **Growth: 14.5%**
- **Annual Job Openings: 39,000**

Provide tourists with travel information, such as points of interest, restaurants, rates, and emergency service. Duties include answering inquiries, offering suggestions, and providing literature pertaining to trips, excursions, sporting events, concerts, and plays. May make reservations, deliver tickets, arrange for visas, or contact individuals and groups to inform them of package tours.

Provides customers with travel suggestions and information such as guides, directories, brochures, and maps. Confers with customers by telephone, in writing, or in person to answer questions regarding services and determine travel preferences. Provides information concerning fares, availability of travel, and accommodations, either orally or by using guides, brochures, and maps. Informs client of travel dates, times, connections, baggage limits, medical and visa requirements, and emergency information. Obtains reservations for air, train, or car travel and hotel or other housing accommodations. Confirms travel arrangements and reservations. Plans itinerary for travel and accommodations, using knowledge of routes, types of carriers, and regulations. Assists client in preparing required documents and forms for travel, such as visas. Calculates estimated travel rates and expenses, using items such as rate tables and calculators. Studies maps, directories, routes, and rate tables to determine travel route and cost and availability of accommodations. Contacts motel, hotel, resort, and travel operators by mail or telephone to obtain advertising literature.

GOE INFORMATION—**Interest Area:** 09. Business Detail. **Work Group:** 09.05. Customer Service. **Personality Type**—Conventional. Conventional occupations frequently involve following set procedures and routines. These occupations can include working with data and details more than with ideas. Usually there is a clear line of authority to follow. **Work Values**—Social Service; Good Working Conditions; Supervision, Human Relations; Activity; Supervision, Technical. **Skills**—Service Orientation; Speaking; Active Listening. **Abilities**—*Cognitive:* Fluency of Ideas; Oral Expression; Oral Comprehension; Memorization; Written Comprehension. *Psychomotor:* Wrist-Finger Speed. *Physical:* Trunk Strength. *Sensory:* Near Vision; Speech Clarity; Auditory Attention. **General Work Activities**—*Information Input:* Getting Information; Identifying Objects, Actions, and Events; Estimating Needed Characteristics. *Mental Process:* Scheduling Work and Activities; Organizing, Planning, and Prioritizing; Processing Information. *Work Output:* Documenting or Recording Information; Interacting with Computers; Handling and Moving Objects. *Interacting with Others:* Assisting and Caring for Others; Establishing and Maintaining Relationships; Performing for or Working with the Public. **Physical Work Conditions**—Sitting; Indoors. **Other Job Char-**

acteristics—Importance of Repeating Same Tasks; Importance of Being Exact or Accurate; Degree of Automation.

Experience—Job Zone 2. Some previous work-related skill, knowledge, or experience may be helpful, but usually is not needed. **Job Preparation:** SVP 4.0 to less than 6.0—six months to less than two years. **Knowledge**—Geography; Customer and Personal Service; Sales and Marketing; Clerical; Telecommunications. **Instructional Programs**—Selling Skills and Sales Operations; Tourism and Travel Services Marketing Operations; Tourism Promotion Operations.

Related DOT Jobs—214.362-030 Rate Clerk, Passenger; 237.367-050 Tourist-Information Assistant; 238.167-010 Travel Clerk; 238.167-014 Travel Counselor, Automobile Club; 238.362-014 Reservation Clerk; 238.367-030 Travel Clerk.

43-4181.02 Reservation and Transportation Ticket Agents

- **Education/Training Required: Short-term on-the-job training**
- **Employed: No data available.**
- **Annual Earnings: $24,090**
- **Growth: 14.5%**
- **Annual Job Openings: 39,000**

Make and confirm reservations for passengers and sell tickets for transportation agencies such as airlines, bus companies, railroads, and steamship lines. May check baggage and direct passengers to designated concourse, pier, or track.

Arranges reservations and routing for passengers at request of Ticket Agent. Assigns specified space to customers and maintains computerized inventory of passenger space available. Determines whether space is available on travel dates requested by customer. Checks baggage and directs passenger to designated location for loading. Examines passenger ticket or pass to direct passenger to specified area for loading. Answers inquiries made to travel agencies or transportation firms, such as airlines, bus companies, railroad companies, and steamship lines. Plans route and computes ticket cost, using schedules, rate books, and computer. Sells and assembles tickets for transmittal or mailing to customers. Reads coded data on tickets to ascertain destination, marks tickets, and assigns boarding pass. Telephones customer or Ticket Agent to advise of changes with travel conveyance or to confirm reservation. Assists passengers requiring special assistance to board or depart conveyance. Announces arrival and departure information, using public-address system. Informs travel agents in other locations of space reserved or available. Sells travel insurance.

GOE INFORMATION—**Interest Area:** 11. Recreation, Travel, and Other Personal Services. **Work Group:** 11.03. Transportation and Lodging Services. **Personality Type**—Conventional. Conventional occupations frequently involve following set procedures and routines. These occupations can include working with data and details more than with ideas. Usually there is a clear line of authority to follow. **Work Values**—Social Service; Supervision, Human Relations; Good Working Conditions; Supervision, Technical; Company Policies and Practices. **Skills**—Service Orientation; Active Listening. **Abilities**—*Cognitive:* Memorization; Oral Expression; Mathematical Reasoning; Perceptual Speed; Number Facility. *Psychomotor:* Wrist-Finger Speed; Speed of Limb Movement; Finger Dexterity; Response Orientation; Arm-Hand Steadiness. *Physical:* Static Strength; Trunk Strength. *Sensory:* Speech Recognition; Speech Clarity; Auditory Attention; Near Vision; Sound Localization. **General Work Activities**—*Information Input:* Getting Information; Monitoring Processes, Materials, or Surroundings; Identifying Objects, Actions, and Events. *Mental*

Process: Scheduling Work and Activities; Updating and Using Relevant Knowledge; Processing Information. *Work Output:* Handling and Moving Objects; Documenting or Recording Information; Performing General Physical Activities. *Interacting with Others:* Assisting and Caring for Others; Performing for or Working with the Public; Communicating with Persons Outside Organization. **Physical Work Conditions**—Indoors; Standing; Making Repetitive Motions; Walking or Running. **Other Job Characteristics**—Degree of Automation; Consequence of Error; Pace Determined by Speed of Equipment.

Experience—Job Zone 2. Some previous work-related skill, knowledge, or experience may be helpful, but usually is not needed. **Job Preparation:** SVP 4.0 to less than 6.0—six months to less than two years. **Knowledge**—Geography; Sales and Marketing; Clerical; Customer and Personal Service; Computers and Electronics. **Instructional Programs**—Selling Skills and Sales Operations; Tourism and Travel Services Marketing Operations; Tourism Promotion Operations.

Related DOT Jobs—238.367-010 Gate Agent; 238.367-014 Reservation Clerk; 238.367-018 Reservations Agent; 238.367-026 Ticket Agent; 248.382-010 Ticketing Clerk.

43-4199.99 Information and Record Clerks, All Other

- **Education/Training Required: Short-term on-the-job training**
- **Employed: No data available.**
- **Annual Earnings: No data available.**
- **Growth: 19.3%**
- **Annual Job Openings: 23,000**

All information and record clerks not listed separately.

No task data available.

GOE INFORMATION—**Interest Area:** 09. Business Detail. **Work Group:** 09.07. Records Processing. **Note:** The Department of Labor has not collected some data for this job, so it has fewer details than the other descriptions.

Instructional Programs—General Office Occupations and Clerical Services.

Related DOT Jobs—214.362-034 Tariff Inspector; 241.367-038 Investigator, Dealer Accounts; 249.387-018 Pedigree Tracer.

43-5000 Material Recording, Scheduling, Dispatching, and Distributing Workers

43-5011.00 Cargo and Freight Agents

- **Education/Training Required: Moderate-term on-the-job training**
- **Employed: 60,047**
- **Annual Earnings: $30,640**
- **Growth: 8.3%**
- **Annual Job Openings: 9,000**

Expedite and route movement of incoming and outgoing cargo and freight shipments in airline, train, and trucking terminals and shipping docks. Take orders from customers and arrange pickup of freight and cargo for delivery to loading platform. Prepare and examine bills of lading to determine shipping charges and tariffs.

Advise clients on transportation and payment methods. Arrange insurance coverage for goods. Check import/export documentation to determine cargo contents and classify goods into different fee or tariff groups, using a tariff coding system. Contact vendors and/or claims adjustment departments in order to resolve problems with shipments or contact service depots to arrange for repairs. Determine method of shipment and prepare bills of lading, invoices, and other shipping documents. Direct delivery trucks to shipping doors or designated marshalling areas and help load and unload goods safely. Direct or participate in cargo loading in order to ensure completeness of load and even distribution of weight. Enter shipping information into a computer by hand or by using a hand-held scanner that reads bar codes on goods. Estimate freight or postal rates and record shipment costs and weights. Inspect and count items received and check them against invoices or other documents, recording shortages and rejecting damaged goods. Keep records of all goods shipped, received, and stored. Negotiate and arrange transport of goods with shipping or freight companies. Notify consignees, passengers, or customers of the arrival of freight or baggage and arrange for delivery. Retrieve stored items and trace lost shipments as necessary. Route received goods to first available flight or to appropriate storage areas or departments, using forklifts, handtrucks, or other equipment. Assemble containers and crates used to transport items such as machines or vehicles. Attach address labels, identification codes, and shipping instructions to containers. Coordinate and supervise activities of workers engaged in packing and shipping merchandise. Inspect trucks and vans to ensure cleanliness when shipping such items as grain, flour, and milk. Install straps, braces, and padding to loads in order to prevent shifting or damage during shipment. Maintain a supply of packing materials. Obtain flight numbers, airplane numbers, and names of crew members from dispatchers and record data on airplane flight papers. Open cargo containers and unwrap contents, using steel cutters, crowbars, or other hand tools. Pack goods for shipping, using tools such as staplers, strapping machines, and hammers. Position ramps for loading of airplanes. Prepare manifests showing baggage, mail, and freight weights and number of passengers on airplanes; transmit data to destinations.

GOE INFORMATION—**Interest Area:** 09. Business Detail. **Work Group:** 09.08. Records and Materials Processing. **Personality Type**—Conventional. Conventional occupations frequently involve following set procedures and routines. These occupations can include working with data and details more than with ideas. Usually there is a clear line of authority to follow. **Work Values**—Supervision, Technical; Supervision, Human Relations; Company Policies and Practices; Moral Values; Advancement. **Skills**—Operation and Control. **Abilities**—*Cognitive:* Oral Expression; Spatial Orientation. *Psychomotor:* Manual Dexterity. *Physical:* Static Strength; Trunk Strength; Dynamic Strength; Stamina. *Sensory:* None met the criteria. **General Work Activities**—*Information Input:* Monitoring Processes, Materials, or Surroundings; Getting Information; Identifying Objects, Actions, and Events. *Mental Process:* Evaluating Information Against Standards; Processing Information; Updating and Using Relevant Knowledge. *Work Output:* Handling and Moving Objects; Performing General Physical Activities; Documenting or Recording Information. *Interacting with Others:* Communicating with Persons Outside Organization; Assisting and Caring for Others; Communicating with Other Workers. **Physical Work Conditions**—Distracting Sounds and Noise Levels; Outdoors; Walking or Running; Very Hot or Cold; Contaminants. **Other Job Characteristics**—Pace Determined by Speed of Equipment; Consequence of Error; Importance of Repeating Same Tasks.

Experience—Job Zone 2. Some previous work-related skill, knowledge, or experience may be helpful, but usually is not needed. **Job Preparation:** SVP 4.0 to less than 6.0—six months to less than two years. **Knowledge**—Geography; Clerical; Customer and Personal Service; Telecommunications; Public Safety and Security. **Instructional Programs**—General Office Occupations and Clerical Services.

Related DOT Jobs—248.367-018 Cargo Agent; 912.367-014 Transportation Agent.

43-5021.00 Couriers and Messengers

- **Education/Training Required: Short-term on-the-job training**
- **Employed: 140,893**
- **Annual Earnings: $19,140**
- **Growth: –3.9%**
- **Annual Job Openings: 37,000**

Pick up and carry messages, documents, packages, and other items between offices or departments within an establishment or to other business concerns, traveling by foot, bicycle, motorcycle, automobile, or public conveyance.

Check with home offices after completed deliveries in order to confirm deliveries and collections and to receive instructions for other deliveries. Deliver messages and items such as newspapers, documents, and packages between establishment departments and to other establishments and private homes. Obtain signatures and payments or arrange for recipients to make payments. Plan and follow the most efficient routes for delivering goods. Receive messages or materials to be delivered and information on recipients, such as names, addresses, telephone numbers, and delivery instructions, communicated via telephone, two-way radio, or in person. Record information such as items received and delivered and recipients' responses to messages. Sort items to be delivered according to the delivery route. Unload and sort items collected along delivery routes. Walk, ride bicycles, drive vehicles, or use public conveyances in order to reach destinations to deliver messages or materials. Call by telephone in order to deliver verbal messages. Collect, seal, and stamp outgoing mail, using postage meters and envelope sealers. Load vehicles with listed goods, ensuring that goods are loaded correctly and taking precautions with hazardous goods. Open, sort, and distribute incoming mail. Perform routine maintenance on delivery vehicles, such as monitoring fluid levels and replenishing fuel. Unload goods from large trucks and load them onto smaller delivery vehicles. Perform general office or clerical work such as filing materials, operating duplicating machines, or running errands.

GOE INFORMATION—**Interest Area:** 09. Business Detail. **Work Group:** 09.08. Records and Materials Processing. **Personality Type**—Realistic. Realistic occupations frequently involve work activities that include practical, hands-on problems and solutions. They often deal with plants, animals, and real-world materials like wood, tools, and machinery. Many of the occupations require working outside and do not involve a lot of paperwork or working closely with others. **Work Values**—Independence; Social Service. **Skills**—None met the criteria. **Abilities**—*Cognitive:* Spatial Orientation; Memorization; Time Sharing. *Psychomotor:* Response Orientation; Reaction Time; Rate Control; Speed of Limb Movement; Multilimb Coordination. *Physical:* Stamina; Gross Body Coordination; Extent Flexibility; Gross Body Equilibrium; Dynamic Flexibility. *Sensory:* Night Vision; Far Vision; Speech Recognition; Glare Sensitivity; Peripheral Vision. **General Work Activities**—*Information Input:* Getting Information; Estimating Needed Characteristics; Monitoring Processes, Materials, or Surroundings. *Mental Process:* Organizing, Planning, and Prioritizing; Evaluating Information Against Standards; Making Decisions and Solving Problems. *Work Output:* Performing General Physical

Activities; Handling and Moving Objects; Documenting or Recording Information. *Interacting with Others:* Communicating with Persons Outside Organization; Establishing and Maintaining Relationships; Communicating with Other Workers. **Physical Work Conditions**—Outdoors; Hazardous Equipment; Walking or Running; Very Hot or Cold; Radiation. **Other Job Characteristics**—Importance of Repeating Same Tasks; Pace Determined by Speed of Equipment; Importance of Being Exact or Accurate.

Experience—Job Zone 1. No previous work-related skill, knowledge, or experience is needed. **Job Preparation:** SVP below 4.0—less than six months. **Knowledge**—Geography; Food Production; Customer and Personal Service; Public Safety and Security; Telecommunications. **Instructional Programs**—No data available.

Related DOT Jobs—215.563-010 Caller; 230.663-010 Deliverer, Outside; 239.567-010 Office Helper; 239.677-010 Messenger, Copy; 239.687-010 Route Aide; 239.687-014 Tube Operator; 299.477-010 Deliverer, Merchandise.

43-5031.00 Police, Fire, and Ambulance Dispatchers

- **Education/Training Required: Moderate-term on-the-job training**
- **Employed: 85,979**
- **Annual Earnings: $26,690**
- **Growth: 14.5%**
- **Annual Job Openings: 4,000**

Receive complaints from public concerning crimes and police emergencies. Broadcast orders to police patrol units in vicinity of complaint to investigate. Operate radio, telephone, or computer equipment to receive reports of fires and medical emergencies and relay information or orders to proper officials.

Answer routine inquiries and refer calls not requiring dispatches to appropriate departments and agencies. Determine response requirements and relative priorities of situations and dispatch units in accordance with established procedures. Maintain files of information relating to emergency calls, such as personnel rosters and emergency call-out and pager files. Monitor various radio frequencies such as those used by public works departments, school security, and civil defense in order to keep apprised of developing situations. Observe alarm registers and scan maps in order to determine whether a specific emergency is in the dispatch service area. Question callers to determine their locations and the nature of their problems in order to determine type of response needed. Read and effectively interpret small-scale maps and information from a computer screen in order to determine locations and provide directions. Receive incoming telephone or alarm system calls regarding emergency and non-emergency police and fire service, emergency ambulance service, information, and after-hours calls for departments within a city. Record details of calls, dispatches, and messages. Relay information and messages to and from emergency sites, to law enforcement agencies, and to all other individuals or groups requiring notification. Scan status charts and computer screens and contact emergency response field units in order to determine emergency units available for dispatch. Enter, update, and retrieve information from teletype networks and computerized data systems regarding such things as wanted persons, stolen property, vehicle registration, and stolen vehicles. Learn material and pass required tests for certification. Monitor alarm systems to detect emergencies such as fires and illegal entry into establishments. Provide emergency medical instructions to callers. Test and adjust communication and alarm systems and report malfunctions to maintenance units. Maintain access to, and security of, highly sensitive materials. Operate and maintain mobile dispatch vehicles and equipment.

GOE INFORMATION—Interest Area: 09. Business Detail. **Work Group:** 09.06. Communications. **Personality Type—**Social. Social occupations frequently involve working with, communicating with, and teaching people. These occupations often involve helping or providing service to others. **Work Values—**Social Service; Authority; Supervision, Technical; Supervision, Human Relations; Security. **Skills—**Service Orientation; Active Listening; Speaking; Operation and Control; Coordination; Judgment and Decision Making. **Abilities—***Cognitive:* Speed of Closure; Time Sharing; Selective Attention; Oral Comprehension; Oral Expression. *Psychomotor:* Reaction Time; Wrist-Finger Speed; Multilimb Coordination; Response Orientation; Speed of Limb Movement. *Physical:* None met the criteria. *Sensory:* Speech Recognition; Speech Clarity; Auditory Attention; Sound Localization; Near Vision. **General Work Activities—***Information Input:* Monitoring Processes, Materials, or Surroundings; Getting Information; Identifying Objects, Actions, and Events. *Mental Process:* Making Decisions and Solving Problems; Judging Qualities of Things, Services, or Other People's Work; Processing Information. *Work Output:* Documenting or Recording Information; Handling and Moving Objects; Controlling Machines and Processes. *Interacting with Others:* Assisting and Caring for Others; Communicating with Persons Outside Organization; Performing for or Working with the Public. **Physical Work Conditions—**Sitting; Indoors; Making Repetitive Motions; Disease or Infections; Distracting Sounds and Noise Levels. **Other Job Characteristics—**Consequence of Error; Importance of Being Exact or Accurate; Importance of Repeating Same Tasks.

Experience—Job Zone 2. Some previous work-related skill, knowledge, or experience may be helpful, but usually is not needed. **Job Preparation:** SVP 4.0 to less than 6.0—six months to less than two years. **Knowledge—**Telecommunications; Geography; Computers and Electronics; Public Safety and Security; Customer and Personal Service. **Instructional Programs—**No data available.

Related DOT Jobs—379.162-010 Alarm Operator; 379.362-010 Dispatcher, Radio; 379.362-014 Protective-Signal Operator; 379.362-018 Telecommunicator.

43-5032.00 Dispatchers, Except Police, Fire, and Ambulance

- **Education/Training Required: Moderate-term on-the-job training**
- **Employed: 168,294**
- **Annual Earnings: $30,070**
- **Growth: 22.2%**
- **Annual Job Openings: 8,000**

Schedule and dispatch workers, work crews, equipment, or service vehicles for conveyance of materials, freight, or passengers or for normal installation, service, or emergency repairs rendered outside the place of business. Duties may include using radio, telephone, or computer to transmit assignments and compiling statistics and reports on work progress.

Confer with customers or supervising personnel in order to address questions, problems, and requests for service or equipment. Determine types or amounts of equipment, vehicles, materials, or personnel required according to work orders or specifications. Monitor personnel and/or equipment locations and utilization in order to coordinate service and schedules. Oversee all communications within specifically assigned

territories. Prepare daily work and run schedules. Receive or prepare work orders. Record and maintain files and records of customer requests, work or services performed, charges, expenses, inventory, and other dispatch information. Relay work orders, messages, and information to or from work crews, supervisors, and field inspectors, using telephones or two-way radios. Advise personnel about traffic problems such as construction areas, accidents, congestion, weather conditions, and other hazards. Arrange for necessary repairs in order to restore service and schedules. Schedule and dispatch workers, work crews, equipment, or service vehicles to appropriate locations according to customer requests, specifications, or needs, using radios or telephones. Ensure timely and efficient movement of trains according to train orders and schedules. Order supplies and equipment and issue them to personnel.

GOE INFORMATION—Interest Area: 09. Business Detail. **Work Group:** 09.06. Communications. **Personality Type—**Conventional. Conventional occupations frequently involve following set procedures and routines. These occupations can include working with data and details more than with ideas. Usually there is a clear line of authority to follow. **Work Values—**Authority; Supervision, Technical; Social Service; Supervision, Human Relations; Security. **Skills—**Equipment Selection; Management of Material Resources. **Abilities—***Cognitive:* Oral Expression; Oral Comprehension; Time Sharing; Selective Attention. *Psychomotor:* Reaction Time; Response Orientation. *Physical:* None met the criteria. *Sensory:* Speech Recognition; Speech Clarity; Auditory Attention. **General Work Activities—***Information Input:* Identifying Objects, Actions, and Events; Getting Information; Monitoring Processes, Materials, or Surroundings. *Mental Process:* Organizing, Planning, and Prioritizing; Scheduling Work and Activities; Analyzing Data or Information. *Work Output:* Documenting or Recording Information; Handling and Moving Objects; Interacting with Computers. *Interacting with Others:* Communicating with Other Workers; Performing for or Working with the Public; Coordinating the Work and Activities of Others. **Physical Work Conditions—**Sitting; Indoors. **Other Job Characteristics—**Importance of Repeating Same Tasks; Consequence of Error; Importance of Being Exact or Accurate.

Experience—Job Zone 2. Some previous work-related skill, knowledge, or experience may be helpful, but usually is not needed. **Job Preparation:** SVP 4.0 to less than 6.0—six months to less than two years. **Knowledge—**Telecommunications; Customer and Personal Service; Geography; Clerical; Economics and Accounting. **Instructional Programs—**No data available.

Related DOT Jobs—215.167-010 Car Clerk, Pullman; 215.367-018 Taxicab Coordinator; 221.362-014 Dispatcher, Relay; 221.367-070 Service Clerk; 221.367-082 Work-Order-Sorting Clerk; 239.167-014 Dispatcher; 239.367-014 Dispatcher, Maintenance Service; 239.367-022 Receiver-Dispatcher; 239.367-030 Dispatcher, Street Department; 248.367-026 Dispatcher, Ship Pilot; 249.167-014 Dispatcher, Motor Vehicle; 249.367-070 Routing Clerk; 910.167-014 Train Dispatcher, Assistant Chief; 910.367-018 Engine Dispatcher; 911.167-010 Dispatcher, Tugboat; 913.167-010 Bus Dispatcher, Interstate; 913.367-010 Taxicab Starter; 914.167-014 Dispatcher, Oil; 919.162-010 Dispatcher, Traffic or System; 932.167-010 Dispatcher; others.

43-5041.00 Meter Readers, Utilities

- **Education/Training Required: Short-term on-the-job training**
- **Employed: 48,763**
- **Annual Earnings: $28,360**
- **Growth: −26.0%**
- **Annual Job Openings: 8,000**

Read meter and record consumption of electricity, gas, water, or steam.

Walks or drives truck over established route and takes readings of meter dials. Reads electric meter. Reads gas meter. Reads steam meter. Reads water meter. Indicates irregularities on forms for necessary action by service department. Verifies readings to locate abnormal consumption and records reasons for fluctuations. Returns route book to business office for billing purposes. Collects bills in arrears. Inspects meters for defects, damage, and unauthorized connections. Turns service off for nonpayment of charges in vacant premises or on for new occupants.

GOE INFORMATION—Interest Area: 09. Business Detail. **Work Group:** 09.04. Material Control. **Personality Type—**Conventional. Conventional occupations frequently involve following set procedures and routines. These occupations can include working with data and details more than with ideas. Usually there is a clear line of authority to follow. **Work Values—**Independence; Supervision, Technical; Supervision, Human Relations; Company Policies and Practices; Security. **Skills—**None met the criteria. **Abilities—***Cognitive:* Spatial Orientation. *Psychomotor:* Rate Control. *Physical:* Stamina. *Sensory:* None met the criteria. **General Work Activities—***Information Input:* Inspecting Equipment, Structures, or Materials; Getting Information; Identifying Objects, Actions, and Events. *Mental Process:* Evaluating Information Against Standards; Processing Information; Judging Qualities of Things, Services, or Other People's Work. *Work Output:* Performing General Physical Activities; Handling and Moving Objects; Documenting or Recording Information. *Interacting with Others:* Communicating with Persons Outside Organization; Communicating with Other Workers; Performing Administrative Activities. **Physical Work Conditions—**Outdoors; Very Hot or Cold; Walking or Running; Standing; Extremely Bright or Inadequate Lighting. **Other Job Characteristics—**Importance of Being Exact or Accurate; Importance of Repeating Same Tasks; Consequence of Error.

Experience—Job Zone 1. No previous work-related skill, knowledge, or experience is needed. **Job Preparation:** SVP below 4.0—less than six months. **Knowledge—**Geography; Economics and Accounting; Clerical. **Instructional Programs—**No data available.

Related DOT Jobs—209.567-010 Meter Reader.

43-5051.00 Postal Service Clerks

- **Education/Training Required: Short-term on-the-job training**
- **Employed: 74,466**
- **Annual Earnings: $39,070**
- **Growth: 2.4%**
- **Annual Job Openings: 3,000**

Perform any combination of tasks in a post office, such as receiving letters and parcels; selling postage and revenue stamps, postal cards, and stamped envelopes; filling out and selling money orders; placing mail in pigeonholes of mail rack or in bags according to state, address, or other scheme; and examining mail for correct postage.

Answer questions regarding mail regulations and procedures, postage rates, and post office boxes. Check mail in order to ensure correct postage and that packages and letters are in proper condition for mailing. Complete forms regarding changes of address or theft or loss of mail or for special services such as registered or priority mail. Feed mail into postage-canceling devices or hand-stamp mail to cancel postage. Keep money drawers in order and record and balance daily transactions. Obtain signatures from recipients of registered or special delivery mail. Provide customers with assistance in filing claims for mail theft or lost or damaged mail. Put undelivered parcels away, retrieve them when customers come to claim them, and complete any related documentation. Receive letters and parcels and place mail into bags. Register, certify, and insure letters and parcels. Rent post office boxes to customers. Respond to complaints regarding mail theft, delivery problems, and lost or damaged mail, filling out forms and making appropriate referrals for investigation. Sell and collect payment for products such as stamps, prepaid mail envelopes, and money orders. Set postage meters and calibrate them to ensure correct operation. Sort incoming and outgoing mail according to type and destination by hand or by operating electronic mail-sorting and scanning devices. Transport mail from one workstation to another. Weigh letters and parcels; compute mailing costs based on type, weight, and destination; and affix correct postage. Cash money orders. Post announcements or government information on public bulletin boards. Provide assistance to the public in complying with federal regulations of Postal Service and other federal agencies.

GOE INFORMATION—Interest Area: 09. Business Detail. **Work Group:** 09.09. Clerical Machine Operation. **Personality Type—**Conventional. Conventional occupations frequently involve following set procedures and routines. These occupations can include working with data and details more than with ideas. Usually there is a clear line of authority to follow. **Work Values—**Security; Supervision, Technical; Supervision, Human Relations; Social Service; Company Policies and Practices. **Skills—**None met the criteria. **Abilities—***Cognitive:* Perceptual Speed; Time Sharing; Oral Expression; Memorization; Spatial Orientation. *Psychomotor:* Rate Control. *Physical:* Dynamic Flexibility; Extent Flexibility; Dynamic Strength; Static Strength; Trunk Strength. *Sensory:* Speech Clarity; Glare Sensitivity; Near Vision. **General Work Activities—***Information Input:* Identifying Objects, Actions, and Events; Getting Information; Monitoring Processes, Materials, or Surroundings. *Mental Process:* Processing Information; Analyzing Data or Information; Updating and Using Relevant Knowledge. *Work Output:* Handling and Moving Objects; Performing General Physical Activities; Controlling Machines and Processes. *Interacting with Others:* Performing for or Working with the Public; Assisting and Caring for Others; Establishing and Maintaining Relationships. **Physical Work Conditions—**Making Repetitive Motions; Standing; Bending or Twisting the Body; Indoors; Kneeling, Crouching, or Crawling. **Other Job Characteristics—**Importance of Repeating Same Tasks; Importance of Being Exact or Accurate; Pace Determined by Speed of Equipment.

Experience—Job Zone 2. Some previous work-related skill, knowledge, or experience may be helpful, but usually is not needed. **Job Preparation:** SVP 4.0 to less than 6.0—six months to less than two years. **Knowledge—**Clerical; Customer and Personal Service; Geography; Law and Government; Sales and Marketing. **Instructional Programs—**General Office Occupations and Clerical Services.

Related DOT Jobs—209.687-014 Mail Handler; 243.367-014 Post-Office Clerk.

43-5052.00 Postal Service Mail Carriers

- **Education/Training Required: Short-term on-the-job training**
- **Employed: 324,321**
- **Annual Earnings: $38,700**
- **Growth: 2.4%**
- **Annual Job Openings: 13,000**

Sort mail for delivery. Deliver mail on established route by vehicle or on foot.

Bundle mail in preparation for delivery or transportation to relay boxes. Deliver mail to residences and business establishments along specified routes by walking and/or driving, using a combination of satchels, carts, cars, and small trucks. Enter change-of-address orders into computers that process forwarding address stickers. Hold mail for customers who are away from delivery locations. Leave notices telling patrons where to collect mail that could not be delivered. Maintain accurate records of deliveries. Meet schedules for the collection and return of mail. Record address changes and redirect mail for those addresses. Return incorrectly addressed mail to senders. Return to the post office with mail collected from homes, businesses, and public mailboxes. Sign for cash-on-delivery and registered mail before leaving the post office. Sort mail for delivery, arranging it in delivery sequence. Travel to post offices to pick up the mail for routes and/or pick up mail from postal relay boxes. Turn in money and receipts collected along mail routes. Answer customers' questions about postal services and regulations. Complete forms that notify publishers of address changes. Obtain signed receipts for registered, certified, and insured mail; collect associated charges; and complete any necessary paperwork. Provide customers with change of address cards and other forms. Register, certify, and insure parcels and letters. Report any unusual circumstances concerning mail delivery, including the condition of street letter boxes. Sell stamps and money orders.

GOE INFORMATION—Interest Area: 09. Business Detail. **Work Group:** 09.08. Records and Materials Processing. **Personality Type**—Conventional. Conventional occupations frequently involve following set procedures and routines. These occupations can include working with data and details more than with ideas. Usually there is a clear line of authority to follow. **Work Values**—Independence; Security; Supervision, Human Relations; Social Service; Company Policies and Practices. **Skills**—None met the criteria. **Abilities**—*Cognitive:* Spatial Orientation; Perceptual Speed. *Psychomotor:* Rate Control; Response Orientation. *Physical:* Static Strength; Stamina. *Sensory:* Glare Sensitivity; Far Vision. **General Work Activities**—*Information Input:* Getting Information; Identifying Objects, Actions, and Events; Estimating Needed Characteristics. *Mental Process:* Processing Information; Evaluating Information Against Standards; Updating and Using Relevant Knowledge. *Work Output:* Performing General Physical Activities; Handling and Moving Objects; Operating Vehicles or Equipment. *Interacting with Others:* Communicating with Persons Outside Organization; Performing for or Working with the Public; Establishing and Maintaining Relationships. **Physical Work Conditions**—Outdoors; Walking or Running; Very Hot or Cold; Minor Burns, Cuts, Bites, or Stings; Making Repetitive Motions. **Other Job Characteristics**—Importance of Being Exact or Accurate; Importance of Repeating Same Tasks; Pace Determined by Speed of Equipment.

Experience—Job Zone 1. No previous work-related skill, knowledge, or experience is needed. **Job Preparation:** SVP below 4.0—less than six months. **Knowledge**—Geography; Clerical; Sales and Marketing; Law and Government; Customer and Personal Service. **Instructional Programs**—General Office Occupations and Clerical Services.

Related DOT Jobs—230.363-010 Rural Mail Carrier; 230.367-010 Mail Carrier.

43-5053.00 Postal Service Mail Sorters, Processors, and Processing Machine Operators

- **Education/Training Required: Short-term on-the-job training**
- **Employed: 288,753**
- **Annual Earnings: $35,260**
- **Growth: –4.9%**
- **Annual Job Openings: 12,000**

Prepare incoming and outgoing mail for distribution. Examine, sort, and route mail by state, type of mail, or other scheme. Load, operate, and occasionally adjust and repair mail processing, sorting, and canceling machinery. Keep records of shipments, pouches, and sacks and other duties related to mail handling within the postal service. Must complete a competitive exam.

Accept and check containers of mail from large-volume mailers, couriers, and contractors. Bundle, label, and route sorted mail to designated areas depending on destinations and according to established procedures and deadlines. Cancel letter or parcel post stamps by hand. Check items to ensure that addresses are legible and correct, that sufficient postage has been paid or the appropriate documentation is attached, and that items are in a suitable condition for processing. Clear jams in sorting equipment. Direct items according to established routing schemes, using computer-controlled keyboards or voice recognition equipment. Distribute incoming mail into the correct boxes or pigeonholes. Dump sacks of mail onto conveyors for culling and sorting. Load and unload mail trucks, sometimes lifting containers of mail onto equipment that transports items to sorting stations. Move containers of mail, using equipment such as forklifts and automated "trains". Open and label mail containers. Operate machines that seal envelopes and print postage and postmarks. Operate various types of equipment, such as computer scanning equipment, addressographs, mimeographs, optical character readers, and bar-code sorters. Remove envelopes or tape from postmarking machines. Sort odd-sized mail by hand, sort mail that other workers have been unable to sort, and segregate items requiring special handling. Weigh articles to determine required postage. Rewrap soiled or broken parcels. Search directories to find correct addresses for redirected mail. Serve the public at counters or windows, such as by selling stamps and weighing parcels. Supervise other mail sorters. Train new workers.

GOE INFORMATION—Interest Area: 09. Business Detail. **Work Group:** 09.08. Records and Materials Processing. **Note:** The Department of Labor has not collected some data for this job, so it has fewer details than the other descriptions.

Instructional Programs—General Office Occupations and Clerical Services.

Related DOT Jobs—209.687-014 Mail Handler.

43-5061.00 Production, Planning, and Expediting Clerks

- **Education/Training Required: Short-term on-the-job training**
- **Employed: 331,962**
- **Annual Earnings: $32,420**
- **Growth: 17.9%**
- **Annual Job Openings: 36,000**

Coordinate and expedite the flow of work and materials within or between departments of an establishment according to production schedule. Duties include reviewing and distributing production, work, and shipment schedules; conferring with department supervisors to determine progress of work and completion dates; and compiling reports on progress of work, inventory levels, costs, and production problems.

Reviews documents, such as production schedules, staffing tables, and specifications to obtain information, such as materials, priorities, and personnel requirements. Confers with establishment personnel, vendors, and customers to coordinate processing and shipping and to resolve complaints. Completes status reports, such as production progress, customer information, and materials inventory. Compiles schedules and orders, such as personnel assignments, production, work flow, transportation, and maintenance and repair. Examines documents, materials, and products; monitors work processes for completeness, accuracy, and conformance to standards and specifications. Monitors work progress; provides services such as furnishing permits, tickets, and union information; and directs workers to expedite work flow. Arranges for delivery and distributes supplies and parts to expedite flow of materials to meet production schedules. Requisitions and maintains inventory of materials and supplies to meet production demands. Maintains files, such as maintenance records, bills of lading, and cost reports. Calculates figures, such as labor and materials amounts, manufacturing costs, and wages, using pricing schedules, adding machine, or calculator.

GOE INFORMATION—Interest Area: 09. Business Detail. **Work Group:** 09.04. Material Control. **Personality Type—**Conventional. Conventional occupations frequently involve following set procedures and routines. These occupations can include working with data and details more than with ideas. Usually there is a clear line of authority to follow. **Work Values—**Supervision, Technical; Supervision, Human Relations; Advancement; Activity; Company Policies and Practices. **Skills—**Management of Material Resources; Management of Personnel Resources; Systems Analysis; Management of Financial Resources; Systems Evaluation; Complex Problem Solving; Time Management; Writing. **Abilities—***Cognitive:* Number Facility; Mathematical Reasoning; Perceptual Speed; Speed of Closure; Deductive Reasoning. *Psychomotor:* Wrist-Finger Speed. *Physical:* Dynamic Flexibility. *Sensory:* Near Vision; Speech Recognition; Auditory Attention; Sound Localization. **General Work Activities—***Information Input:* Getting Information; Identifying Objects, Actions, and Events; Monitoring Processes, Materials, or Surroundings. *Mental Process:* Processing Information; Organizing, Planning, and Prioritizing; Evaluating Information Against Standards. *Work Output:* Documenting or Recording Information; Handling and Moving Objects; Performing General Physical Activities. *Interacting with Others:* Communicating with Other Workers; Establishing and Maintaining Relationships; Coordinating the Work and Activities of Others. **Physical Work Conditions—**Sitting; Indoors; Walking or Running; Disease or Infections; Climbing Ladders, Scaffolds, Poles, etc. **Other Job Characteristics—**Importance of Repeating Same Tasks; Consequence of Error; Importance of Being Exact or Accurate.

Experience—Job Zone 2. Some previous work-related skill, knowledge, or experience may be helpful, but usually is not needed. **Job Preparation:** SVP 4.0 to less than 6.0—six months to less than two years. **Knowledge—**Clerical; Production and Processing; Economics and Accounting; Administration and Management; Computers and Electronics. **Instructional Programs—**Parts, Warehousing, and Inventory Management Operations.

Related DOT Jobs—199.382-010 Television-Schedule Coordinator; 215.362-010 Crew Scheduler; 215.362-014 Dispatcher Clerk; 215.367-010 Assignment Clerk; 215.367-014 Personnel Scheduler; 219.362-030 Extension Clerk; 219.387-010 Assignment Clerk; 221.162-010 Production Scheduler, Paperboard Products; 221.167-010 Copy Cutter; 221.167-014 Material Coordinator; 221.167-018 Production Coordinator; 221.167-022 Retort-Load Expediter; 221.167-026 Customer Services Coordinator; 221.362-018 Estimator, Paperboard Boxes; 221.362-022 Progress Clerk; 221.362-030 Computer Processing Scheduler; 221.367-010 Alterations Workroom Clerk; 221.367-014 Estimator, Printing; 221.367-018 Follow-Up Clerk; 221.367-026 Line-Up Worker; others.

43-5071.00 Shipping, Receiving, and Traffic Clerks

- Education/Training Required: **Short-term on-the-job training**
- Employed: **889,666**
- Annual Earnings: **$22,710**
- Growth: **9.3%**
- Annual Job Openings: **133,000**

Verify and keep records on incoming and outgoing shipments. Prepare items for shipment. Duties include assembling, addressing, stamping, and shipping merchandise or material; receiving, unpacking, verifying, and recording incoming merchandise or material; and arranging for the transportation of products.

Examine contents and compare with records such as manifests, invoices, or orders to verify accuracy of incoming or outgoing shipment. Determine shipping method for materials, using knowledge of shipping procedures, routes, and rates. Prepare documents such as work orders, bills of lading, and shipping orders to route materials. Confer and correspond with establishment representatives to rectify problems such as damages, shortages, and nonconformance to specifications. Requisition and store shipping materials and supplies to maintain inventory of stock. Deliver or route materials to departments, using work devices such as handtruck, conveyor, or sorting bins. Pack, seal, label, and affix postage to prepare materials for shipping, using work devices such as hand tools, power tools, and postage meter. Contact carrier representative to make arrangements and to issue instructions for shipping and delivery of materials. Record shipment data, such as weight, charges, space availability, and damages and discrepancies, for reporting, accounting, and record-keeping purposes. Compute amounts, such as space available and shipping, storage, and demurrage charges, using calculator or price list.

GOE INFORMATION—Interest Area: 09. Business Detail. **Work Group:** 09.08. Records and Materials Processing. **Personality Type—**Conventional. Conventional occupations frequently involve following set procedures and routines. These occupations can include working with data and details more than with ideas. Usually there is a clear line of authority to follow. **Work Values—**Moral Values; Supervision, Human Relations; Supervision, Technical; Advancement; Pleasant Co-workers. **Skills—**Service Orientation. **Abilities—***Cognitive:* Spatial Orientation; Perceptual Speed; Oral Expression; Category Flexibility; Mathematical Reasoning. *Psychomotor:* Rate Control; Manual Dexterity; Reaction Time; Speed of Limb Movement; Wrist-Finger Speed. *Physical:* Static Strength; Stamina; Gross Body Coordination; Dynamic Flexibility; Gross Body Equilibrium. *Sensory:* Speech Recognition; Auditory Attention; Speech Clarity; Far Vision; Near Vision. **General Work Activities—***Information Input:* Getting Information; Identifying Objects, Actions, and Events; Inspecting Equipment, Structures, or Materials. *Mental Process:* Evaluating Information Against Standards; Making Decisions and Solving Problems; Processing Information. *Work Output:* Handling and Moving Objects; Performing General Physical Activities; Documenting or Recording Information. *Interacting with Others:* Communicating with Persons Outside Organization; Monitoring and Controlling Resources; Communicating with Other Workers. **Physical Work Conditions—**Indoors; Kneeling, Crouching, or Crawling; Climbing Ladders, Scaffolds, Poles, etc.; Keeping or Regaining Balance; Making Repetitive Motions. **Other Job Characteristics—**Importance of Repeating Same Tasks; Degree of Automation; Importance of Being Exact or Accurate.

Experience—Job Zone 1. No previous work-related skill, knowledge, or experience is needed. **Job Preparation:** SVP below 4.0—less than six months. **Knowledge—**Clerical; Economics and Accounting; Production and Processing; Philosophy and Theology; Geography. **Instructional Programs—**General Office Occupations and Clerical Services; Traffic, Customs, and Transportation Clerk/Technician.

Related DOT Jobs—209.367-042 Reconsignment Clerk; 214.587-014 Traffic Clerk; 219.367-022 Paper-Control Clerk; 219.367-030 Shipping-Order Clerk; 221.367-022 Industrial-Order Clerk; 222.367-066 Truckload Checker; 222.387-014 Car Checker; 222.387-022 Gun-Repair Clerk; 222.387-050 Shipping and Receiving Clerk; 222.567-010 Grain Elevator Clerk; 222.567-014 Ship Runner; 222.587-018 Distributing Clerk; 222.587-034 Route-

Delivery Clerk; 222.587-058 Vault Worker; 222.687-022 Routing Clerk; 222.687-030 Shipping Checker; 248.362-010 Incoming-Freight Clerk; 248.367-014 Booking Clerk; 248.367-022 Container Coordinator; 976.687-018 Photofinishing Laboratory Worker.

43-5081.00 Stock Clerks and Order Fillers

- **Education/Training Required: Short-term on-the-job training**
- **Employed: 1,678,730**
- **Annual Earnings: $19,060**
- **Growth: 8.5%**
- **Annual Job Openings: 467,000**

Receive, store, and issue sales floor merchandise, materials, equipment, and other items from stockroom, warehouse, or storage yard to fill shelves, racks, tables, or customers' orders. May mark prices on merchandise and set up sales displays.

No task data available.

GOE INFORMATION—Interest Area: 09. Business Detail. **Work Group:** 09.08. Records and Materials Processing. **Note:** The Department of Labor has not collected some data for this job, so it has fewer details than the other descriptions.

Instructional Programs—Retailing and Retail Operations.

Related DOT Jobs—209.587-034 Marker; 216.567-010 Ticket Marker; 219.367-018 Merchandise Distributor; 219.387-026 Space-and-Storage Clerk; 219.387-030 Stock Control Clerk; 221.587-018 Odd-Piece Checker; 221.587-022 Outsole Scheduler; 222.367-014 Cut-File Clerk; 222.367-038 Magazine Keeper; 222.367-042 Parts Clerk; 222.367-050 Prescription Clerk, Lens-and-Frames; 222.367-062 Tool-Crib Attendant; 222.387-018 Fuel-Oil Clerk; 222.387-026 Inventory Clerk; 222.387-030 Linen-Room Attendant; 222.387-034 Material Clerk; 222.387-042 Property Custodian; 222.387-054 Sorter-Pricer; 222.387-058 Stock Clerk; 222.387-062 Storekeeper; others.

43-5081.01 Stock Clerks, Sales Floor

- **Education/Training Required: Short-term on-the-job training**
- **Employed: No data available.**
- **Annual Earnings: $19,060**
- **Growth: 8.5%**
- **Annual Job Openings: 467,000**

Receive, store, and issue sales floor merchandise. Stock shelves, racks, cases, bins, and tables with merchandise and arrange merchandise displays to attract customers. May periodically take physical count of stock or check and mark merchandise.

Compare merchandise invoices to items actually received to ensure that shipments are correct. Design and set up advertising signs and displays of merchandise on shelves, counters, or tables to attract customers and promote sales. Receive, open, unpack, and issue sales floor merchandise. Stock shelves, racks, cases, bins, and tables with new or transferred merchandise. Take inventory or examine merchandise to identify items to be reordered or replenished. Answer customers' questions about merchandise and advise customers on merchandise selection. Clean display cases, shelves, and aisles. Itemize and total customer merchandise selection at checkout counter, using cash register, and accept cash or charge card for purchases. Pack customer purchases in bags or cartons. Requisition merchandise from supplier based on available space, merchandise on hand, customer demand, or advertised specials. Stamp, attach, or change price tags on merchandise, referring to price list. Transport packages to customers' vehicles. Cut lumber, screening, glass, and related materials to size requested by customer.

GOE INFORMATION—Interest Area: 10. Sales and Marketing. **Work Group:** 10.03. General Sales. **Personality Type—**Realistic. Realistic occupations frequently involve work activities that include practical, hands-on problems and solutions. They often deal with plants, animals, and real-world materials like wood, tools, and machinery. Many of the occupations require working outside and do not involve a lot of paperwork or working closely with others. **Work Values—**Supervision, Technical; Independence; Advancement; Moral Values; Activity. **Skills—**None met the criteria. **Abilities—***Cognitive:* Spatial Orientation; Category Flexibility; Memorization; Visualization; Perceptual Speed. *Psychomotor:* Speed of Limb Movement; Manual Dexterity; Multilimb Coordination; Finger Dexterity; Arm-Hand Steadiness. *Physical:* Static Strength; Extent Flexibility; Dynamic Strength; Trunk Strength; Gross Body Equilibrium. *Sensory:* Far Vision; Speech Recognition; Depth Perception; Peripheral Vision; Night Vision. **General Work Activities—***Information Input:* Getting Information; Identifying Objects, Actions, and Events; Monitoring Processes, Materials, or Surroundings. *Mental Process:* Processing Information; Updating and Using Relevant Knowledge; Thinking Creatively. *Work Output:* Handling and Moving Objects; Performing General Physical Activities; Documenting or Recording Information. *Interacting with Others:* Establishing and Maintaining Relationships; Performing for or Working with the Public; Communicating with Persons Outside Organization. **Physical Work Conditions—**Walking or Running; Standing; Climbing Ladders, Scaffolds, Poles, etc.; Hazardous Equipment; Kneeling, Crouching, or Crawling. **Other Job Characteristics—**Importance of Repeating Same Tasks; Degree of Automation; Pace Determined by Speed of Equipment.

Experience—Job Zone 1. No previous work-related skill, knowledge, or experience is needed. **Job Preparation:** SVP below 4.0—less than six months. **Knowledge—**Sales and Marketing; Clerical; Building and Construction; Customer and Personal Service; Fine Arts. **Instructional Programs—**Retailing and Retail Operations.

Related DOT Jobs—299.367-014 Stock Clerk; 299.677-014 Sales Attendant, Building Materials.

43-5081.02 Marking Clerks

- **Education/Training Required: Short-term on-the-job training**
- **Employed: No data available.**
- **Annual Earnings: $19,060**
- **Growth: 8.5%**
- **Annual Job Openings: 467,000**

Print and attach price tickets to articles of merchandise using one or several methods, such as marking price on tickets by hand or using ticket-printing machine.

Compare printed price tickets with entries on purchase orders to verify accuracy and notify supervisor of discrepancies. Indicate item size, style, color, and inspection results on tags, tickets, and labels, using rubber stamp or writing instrument. Mark selling price by hand on boxes containing merchandise. Pin, paste, sew, tie, or staple tickets, tags, or labels to article. Put price information on tickets, marking by hand or using ticket-printing machine. Keep records of production, returned goods, and related transactions. Record number and types of articles marked and pack articles in boxes. Record price, buyer, and grade of product on tickets attached to products auctioned. Change the price of books in a warehouse.

GOE INFORMATION—Interest Area: 09. Business Detail. **Work Group:** 09.08. Records and Materials Processing. **Personality Type—**Conventional. Conventional occupations frequently involve following set procedures and routines. These occupations can include working with data and details more than with ideas. Usually there is a clear line of authority to follow. **Work Values**—Independence; Moral Values; Supervision, Technical. **Skills**—None met the criteria. **Abilities**—*Cognitive:* Category Flexibility. *Psychomotor:* None met the criteria. *Physical:* None met the criteria. *Sensory:* None met the criteria. **General Work Activities**—*Information Input:* Inspecting Equipment, Structures, or Materials; Identifying Objects, Actions, and Events; Getting Information. *Mental Process:* Evaluating Information Against Standards; Updating and Using Relevant Knowledge; Organizing, Planning, and Prioritizing. *Work Output:* Handling and Moving Objects; Performing General Physical Activities; Documenting or Recording Information. *Interacting with Others:* Communicating with Other Workers; Performing Administrative Activities; Communicating with Persons Outside Organization. **Physical Work Conditions**—Making Repetitive Motions; Indoors; Using Hands on Objects, Tools, or Controls; Standing; Walking or Running. **Other Job Characteristics**—Importance of Repeating Same Tasks; Importance of Being Exact or Accurate; Consequence of Error.

Experience—Job Zone 1. No previous work-related skill, knowledge, or experience is needed. **Job Preparation:** SVP below 4.0—less than six months. **Knowledge**—Clerical. **Instructional Programs**—Retailing and Retail Operations.

Related DOT Jobs—209.587-034 Marker; 216.567-010 Ticket Marker; 222.387-054 Sorter-Pricer; 229.587-018 Ticketer.

43-5081.03 Stock Clerks—Stockroom, Warehouse, or Storage Yard

- Education/Training Required: Moderate-term on-the-job training
- Employed: No data available.
- Annual Earnings: $19,060
- Growth: 8.5%
- Annual Job Openings: 467,000

Receive, store, and issue materials, equipment, and other items from stockroom, warehouse, or storage yard. Keep records and compile stock reports.

Clean and maintain supplies, tools, equipment, and storage areas in order to ensure compliance with safety regulations. Compile, review, and maintain data from contracts, purchase orders, requisitions, and other documents in order to assess supply needs. Determine proper storage methods, identification, and stock location based on turnover, environmental factors, and physical capabilities of facilities. Examine and inspect stock items for wear or defects, reporting any damage to supervisors. Keep records on the use and/or damage of stock or stock handling equipment. Mark stock items using identification tags, stamps, electric marking tools, or other labeling equipment. Pack and unpack items to be stocked on shelves in stockrooms, warehouses, or storage yards. Prepare and maintain records and reports of inventories, price lists, shortages, shipments, expenditures, and goods used or issued. Prepare products, supplies, equipment, or other items for use by adjusting, repairing, or assembling them as necessary. Issue or distribute materials, products, parts, and supplies to customers or co-workers, based on information from incoming requisitions. Receive and count stock items; record data manually or using computer. Store items in an orderly and accessible manner in warehouses, tool rooms, supply rooms, or other areas. Verify inventory computations by comparing them to physical counts of stock; investigate discrepancies or adjust errors. Advise retail customers or internal users on the appropriateness of parts, supplies, or materials requested. Confer with engineering and purchasing personnel and vendors regarding stock procurement and availability. Determine

sequence and release of back orders according to stock availability. Dispose of damaged or defective items or return them to vendors. Drive trucks in order to pick up incoming stock or to deliver parts to designated locations. Provide assistance or direction to other stockroom, warehouse, or storage yard workers. Purchase new or additional stock or prepare documents that provide for such purchases. Recommend disposal of excess, defective, or obsolete stock. Sell materials, equipment, and other items from stock in retail settings.

GOE INFORMATION—**Interest Area:** 09. Business Detail. **Work Group:** 09.08. Records and Materials Processing. **Personality Type**—Conventional. Conventional occupations frequently involve following set procedures and routines. These occupations can include working with data and details more than with ideas. Usually there is a clear line of authority to follow. **Work Values**—Moral Values; Supervision, Technical; Independence; Supervision, Human Relations; Advancement. **Skills**—Management of Material Resources. **Abilities**—*Cognitive:* Spatial Orientation; Category Flexibility; Perceptual Speed; Memorization; Information Ordering. *Psychomotor:* Manual Dexterity; Multilimb Coordination; Wrist-Finger Speed; Speed of Limb Movement; Response Orientation. *Physical:* Dynamic Flexibility; Extent Flexibility; Static Strength; Gross Body Coordination; Gross Body Equilibrium. *Sensory:* Far Vision; Near Vision; Visual Color Discrimination; Speech Recognition; Night Vision. **General Work Activities**—*Information Input:* Monitoring Processes, Materials, or Surroundings; Identifying Objects, Actions, and Events; Inspecting Equipment, Structures, or Materials. *Mental Process:* Evaluating Information Against Standards; Judging Qualities of Things, Services, or Other People's Work; Processing Information. *Work Output:* Handling and Moving Objects; Documenting or Recording Information; Performing General Physical Activities. *Interacting with Others:* Monitoring and Controlling Resources; Communicating with Other Workers; Communicating with Persons Outside Organization. **Physical Work Conditions**—Climbing Ladders, Scaffolds, Poles, etc.; Walking or Running; Kneeling, Crouching, or Crawling; Keeping or Regaining Balance; Hazardous Equipment. **Other Job Characteristics**—Importance of Repeating Same Tasks; Degree of Automation; Pace Determined by Speed of Equipment.

Experience—Job Zone 2. Some previous work-related skill, knowledge, or experience may be helpful, but usually is not needed. **Job Preparation:** SVP 4.0 to less than 6.0—six months to less than two years. **Knowledge**—Clerical; Computers and Electronics; Economics and Accounting; Sales and Marketing; Building and Construction. **Instructional Programs**—Retailing and Retail Operations.

Related DOT Jobs—219.367-018 Merchandise Distributor; 219.387-026 Space-and-Storage Clerk; 219.387-030 Stock Control Clerk; 221.587-018 Odd-Piece Checker; 221.587-022 Outsole Scheduler; 222.367-014 Cut-File Clerk; 222.367-038 Magazine Keeper; 222.367-042 Parts Clerk; 222.367-050 Prescription Clerk, Lens-and-Frames; 222.367-062 Tool-Crib Attendant; 222.387-018 Fuel-Oil Clerk; 222.387-026 Inventory Clerk; 222.387-030 Linen-Room Attendant; 222.387-034 Material Clerk; 222.387-042 Property Custodian; 222.387-058 Stock Clerk; 222.387-062 Storekeeper; 222.487-010 Checker, Bakery Products; 222.587-022 Kitchen Clerk; 222.587-054 Transformer-Stock Clerk; others.

43-5081.04 Order Fillers, Wholesale and Retail Sales

- Education/Training Required: Moderate-term on-the-job training
- Employed: No data available.
- Annual Earnings: $19,060
- Growth: 8.5%
- Annual Job Openings: 467,000

Fill customers' mail and telephone orders from stored merchandise in accordance with specifications on sales slips or order forms. Duties include computing prices of items, completing order receipts, keeping records of outgoing orders, and requisitioning additional materials, supplies, and equipment.

Complete order receipts. Compute prices of items or groups of items. Keep records of outgoing orders. Obtain merchandise from bins or shelves. Place merchandise on conveyors leading to wrapping areas. Read orders to ascertain catalog numbers, sizes, colors, and quantities of merchandise. Requisition additional materials, supplies, and equipment.

GOE INFORMATION—Interest Area: 09. Business Detail. **Work Group:** 09.08. Records and Materials Processing. **Personality Type**—Conventional. Conventional occupations frequently involve following set procedures and routines. These occupations can include working with data and details more than with ideas. Usually there is a clear line of authority to follow. **Work Values**—Moral Values; Supervision, Human Relations. **Skills**—None met the criteria. **Abilities**—*Cognitive:* None met the criteria. *Psychomotor:* None met the criteria. *Physical:* Static Strength. *Sensory:* Speech Recognition. **General Work Activities**—*Information Input:* Identifying Objects, Actions, and Events; Getting Information; Estimating Needed Characteristics. *Mental Process:* Processing Information; Evaluating Information Against Standards; Organizing, Planning, and Prioritizing. *Work Output:* Handling and Moving Objects; Performing General Physical Activities; Documenting or Recording Information. *Interacting with Others:* Monitoring and Controlling Resources; Communicating with Persons Outside Organization; Communicating with Other Workers. **Physical Work Conditions**—Indoors; Making Repetitive Motions; Climbing Ladders, Scaffolds, Poles, etc.; Standing; Bending or Twisting the Body. **Other Job Characteristics**—Importance of Being Exact or Accurate; Pace Determined by Speed of Equipment; Importance of Repeating Same Tasks.

Experience—Job Zone 2. Some previous work-related skill, knowledge, or experience may be helpful, but usually is not needed. **Job Preparation:** SVP 4.0 to less than 6.0—six months to less than two years. **Knowledge**—Clerical; Production and Processing; Telecommunications. **Instructional Programs**—Retailing and Retail Operations.

Related DOT Jobs—222.487-014 Order Filler; 299.387-014 Stamp Analyst.

43-5111.00 Weighers, Measurers, Checkers, and Samplers, Recordkeeping

- **Education/Training Required: Short-term on-the-job training**
- **Employed: 82,839**
- **Annual Earnings: $24,690**
- **Growth: 17.9%**
- **Annual Job Openings: 13,000**

Weigh, measure, and check materials, supplies, and equipment for the purpose of keeping relevant records. Duties are primarily clerical by nature.

Weighs or measures materials or products, using volume meters, scales, rules, and calipers. Documents quantity, quality, type, weight, and value of materials or products to maintain shipping, receiving, and production records and files. Counts or estimates quantities of materials, parts, or products received or shipped. Examines products or materials, parts, and subassemblies for damage, defects, or shortages, using specification sheets, gauges, and standards charts. Collects, prepares, or attaches measurement, weight, or identification labels or tickets to products. Compares product labels, tags, or tickets; shipping manifests; purchase orders; and bills of lading to verify that the contents, quantity, or weight of shipments is accurate. Computes product totals and charges for shipments, using calculator. Prepares measurement tables and conversion charts, using standard formulae. Sorts products or materials into predetermined sequence or groupings for packing, shipping, or storage. Maintains perpetual inventory of samples and replenishes stock to maintain required levels. Collects and prepares product samples for laboratory analysis or testing. Fills orders for products and samples, following order tickets, and forwards or mails items. Unloads or unpacks incoming shipments or arranges, packs, or prepares materials and products for display, distribution, outgoing shipment, or storage. Transports materials, products, or samples to processing, shipping, or storage areas manually or by using conveyors, pumps, or handtrucks. Removes products or loads not meeting quality standards from stock and notifies supervisor or appropriate department of discrepancy or shortage. Examines blueprints and prepares plans, layouts, or drawings of facility or finished products to identify storage locations or verify parts assemblies. Collects fees and issues receipts for payments. Operates or tends machines to clean or sanitize equipment or manually washes equipment, using detergent, brushes, and hoses. Communicates with customers and vendors to exchange information regarding products, materials, and services. Works with, signals, or instructs other workers to weigh, move, or check products.

GOE INFORMATION—Interest Area: 09. Business Detail. **Work Group:** 09.08. Records and Materials Processing. **Personality Type**—Conventional. Conventional occupations frequently involve following set procedures and routines. These occupations can include working with data and details more than with ideas. Usually there is a clear line of authority to follow. **Work Values**—Supervision, Technical; Supervision, Human Relations; Moral Values; Independence; Pleasant Co-workers. **Skills**—Operation and Control; Operation Monitoring; Equipment Selection. **Abilities**—*Cognitive:* Selective Attention; Perceptual Speed; Number Facility; Spatial Orientation; Flexibility of Closure. *Psychomotor:* Multilimb Coordination; Manual Dexterity; Control Precision; Response Orientation; Finger Dexterity. *Physical:* Gross Body Equilibrium; Explosive Strength; Extent Flexibility; Static Strength; Gross Body Coordination. *Sensory:* Hearing Sensitivity; Depth Perception; Sound Localization; Auditory Attention; Peripheral Vision. **General Work Activities**—*Information Input:* Getting Information; Identifying Objects, Actions, and Events; Monitoring Processes, Materials, or Surroundings. *Mental Process:* Evaluating Information Against Standards; Judging Qualities of Things, Services, or Other People's Work; Processing Information. *Work Output:* Handling and Moving Objects; Performing General Physical Activities; Drafting and Specifying Technical Devices. *Interacting with Others:* Communicating with Persons Outside Organization; Communicating with Other Workers; Establishing and Maintaining Relationships. **Physical Work Conditions**—Using Hands on Objects, Tools, or Controls; Making Repetitive Motions; High Places; Indoors; Standing. **Other Job Characteristics**—Importance of Repeating Same Tasks; Degree of Automation; Importance of Being Exact or Accurate.

Experience—Job Zone 1. No previous work-related skill, knowledge, or experience is needed. **Job Preparation:** SVP below 4.0—less than six months. **Knowledge**—Clerical; Design; Production and Processing. **Instructional Programs**—General Office Occupations and Clerical Services.

Related DOT Jobs—206.587-010 Brand Recorder; 209.587-046 Sample Clerk, Paper; 216.462-010 Booking Prizer; 219.367-010 Checker, Dump Grounds; 221.467-010 Gin Clerk; 221.482-018 Ticket Worker; 221.487-010 Lumber Scaler; 221.587-010 Checker; 221.587-026 Recorder; 221.587-030 Tallier; 221.587-034 Tare Weigher; 221.587-046 Wheel-Press Clerk; 221.687-014 Ticket Puller; 222.367-010 Cargo Checker; 222.387-010 Aircraft-Shipping Checker; 222.387-066 Sample Clerk; 222.387-074 Shipping-and-Receiving Weigher; 222.485-010 Milk-Receiver, Tank Truck; 222.585-010 Milk Receiver; 222.587-042 Sampler, Wool; others.

43-6000 Secretaries and Administrative Assistants

43-6011.00 Executive Secretaries and Administrative Assistants

- Education/Training Required: Moderate-term on-the-job training
- Employed: 1,445,097
- Annual Earnings: $32,380
- Growth: 11.5%
- Annual Job Openings: 185,000

Provide high-level administrative support by conducting research, preparing statistical reports, handling information requests, and performing clerical functions such as preparing correspondence, receiving visitors, arranging conference calls, and scheduling meetings. May also train and supervise lower-level clerical staff.

Attend meetings in order to record minutes. Compile, transcribe, and distribute minutes of meetings. Coordinate and direct office services, such as records and budget preparation, personnel, and housekeeping, in order to aid executives. Greet visitors and determine whether they should be given access to specific individuals. Make travel arrangements for executives. Manage and maintain executives' schedules. Open, sort, and distribute incoming correspondence, including faxes and e-mail. Prepare agendas and make arrangements for committee, board, and other meetings. Prepare invoices, reports, memos, letters, financial statements, and other documents, using word-processing, spreadsheet, database, and/or presentation software. Prepare responses to correspondence containing routine inquiries. Read and analyze incoming memos, submissions, and reports in order to determine their significance and plan their distribution. Supervise and train other clerical staff. Conduct research, compile data, and prepare papers for consideration and presentation by executives, committees, and boards of directors. File and retrieve corporate documents, records, and reports. Interpret administrative and operating policies and procedures for employees. Meet with individuals, special interest groups, and others on behalf of executives, committees, and boards of directors. Perform general office duties such as ordering supplies, maintaining records management systems, and performing basic bookkeeping work. Review operating practices and procedures in order to determine whether improvements can be made in areas such as workflow, reporting procedures, or expenditures. Set up and oversee administrative policies and procedures for offices and/or organizations.

GOE INFORMATION—Interest Area: 09. Business Detail. **Work Group:** 09.02. Administrative Detail. **Personality Type**—Conventional. Conventional occupations frequently involve following set procedures and routines. These occupations can include working with data and details more than with ideas. Usually there is a clear line of authority to follow. **Work Values**—Social Service; Good Working Conditions; Company Policies and Practices; Supervision, Human Relations; Advancement. **Skills**—Management of Financial Resources; Systems Analysis; Management of Material Resources; Coordination; Complex Problem Solving; Writing; Management of Personnel Resources; Reading Comprehension. **Abilities**—*Cognitive:* Written Comprehension; Inductive Reasoning; Originality; Written Expression; Oral Comprehension. *Psychomotor:* Wrist-Finger Speed. *Physical:* Trunk Strength. *Sensory:* Near Vision; Speech Clarity; Far Vision; Speech Recognition. **General Work Activities**—*Information Input:* Getting Information; Identifying Objects, Actions, and Events; Monitoring Processes, Materials, or Surroundings. *Mental Process:* Scheduling Work and Activities; Organizing, Planning, and Prioritizing; Pro-

cessing Information. *Work Output:* Documenting or Recording Information; Interacting with Computers; Handling and Moving Objects. *Interacting with Others:* Establishing and Maintaining Relationships; Communicating with Other Workers; Performing Administrative Activities. **Physical Work Conditions**—Sitting; Indoors; Making Repetitive Motions; Radiation. **Other Job Characteristics**—Consequence of Error; Importance of Being Exact or Accurate; Importance of Repeating Same Tasks.

Experience—Job Zone 4. A minimum of two to four years of work-related skill, knowledge, or experience is needed. **Job Preparation:** SVP 7.0 to less than 8.0—two years to less than 10 years. **Knowledge**—Clerical; Administration and Management; Economics and Accounting; Computers and Electronics; Personnel and Human Resources. **Instructional Programs**—Administrative Assistant and Secretarial Science, General; Executive Assistant/Executive Secretary; Medical Administrative/Executive Assistant and Medical Secretary.

Related DOT Jobs—169.167-010 Administrative Assistant; 169.167-014 Administrative Secretary.

43-6012.00 Legal Secretaries

- Education/Training Required: Postsecondary vocational training
- Employed: 279,164
- Annual Earnings: $34,610
- Growth: 20.3%
- Annual Job Openings: 36,000

Perform secretarial duties, utilizing legal terminology, procedures, and documents. Prepare legal papers and correspondence, such as summonses, complaints, motions, and subpoenas. May also assist with legal research.

Prepare and process legal documents and papers, such as summonses, subpoenas, complaints, appeals, motions, and pretrial agreements. Mail, fax, or arrange for delivery of legal correspondence to clients, witnesses, and court officials. Receive and place telephone calls. Schedule and make appointments. Make photocopies of correspondence, documents, and other printed matter. Organize and maintain law libraries and document and case files. Assist attorneys in collecting information such as employment, medical, and other records. Attend legal meetings, such as client interviews, hearings, or depositions, and take notes. Draft and type office memos. Review legal publications and perform database searches to identify laws and court decisions relevant to pending cases. Submit articles and information from searches to attorneys for review and approval for use. Complete various forms, such as accident reports, trial and courtroom requests, and applications for clients.

GOE INFORMATION—Interest Area: 09. Business Detail. **Work Group:** 09.02. Administrative Detail. **Personality Type**—Conventional. Conventional occupations frequently involve following set procedures and routines. These occupations can include working with data and details more than with ideas. Usually there is a clear line of authority to follow. **Work Values**—Good Working Conditions; Activity; Company Policies and Practices; Supervision, Technical; Social Service. **Skills**—Writing; Time Management; Reading Comprehension; Active Listening; Speaking; Social Perceptiveness; Learning Strategies; Instructing. **Abilities**—*Cognitive:* Written Expression; Oral Comprehension; Written Comprehension; Time Sharing; Oral Expression. *Psychomotor:* Wrist-Finger Speed. *Physical:* None met the criteria. *Sensory:* Speech Recognition; Near Vision; Speech Clarity; Far Vision. **General Work Activities**—*Information Input:* Getting Information; Monitoring Processes, Materials, or Surroundings; Identifying Objects, Actions, and

Events. *Mental Process:* Organizing, Planning, and Prioritizing; Updating and Using Relevant Knowledge; Scheduling Work and Activities. *Work Output:* Interacting with Computers; Documenting or Recording Information; Handling and Moving Objects. *Interacting with Others:* Performing Administrative Activities; Establishing and Maintaining Relationships; Communicating with Persons Outside Organization. **Physical Work Conditions**—Sitting; Making Repetitive Motions; Walking or Running; Disease or Infections; Indoors. **Other Job Characteristics**—Importance of Repeating Same Tasks; Importance of Being Exact or Accurate; Degree of Automation.

Experience—Job Zone 3. Previous work-related skill, knowledge, or experience is required. **Job Preparation:** SVP 6.0 to less than 7.0—more than one year and less than four years. **Knowledge**—Clerical; Law and Government; Customer and Personal Service; Economics and Accounting; Computers and Electronics. **Instructional Programs**—Legal Administrative Assistant/Secretary.

Related DOT Jobs—201.362-010 Legal Secretary.

43-6013.00 Medical Secretaries

- **Education/Training Required: Postsecondary vocational training**
- **Employed: 313,902**
- **Annual Earnings: $24,670**
- **Growth: 19.0%**
- **Annual Job Openings: 40,000**

Perform secretarial duties, utilizing specific knowledge of medical terminology and hospital, clinic, or laboratory procedures. Duties include scheduling appointments, billing patients, and compiling and recording medical charts, reports, and correspondence.

Schedule and confirm patient diagnostic appointments, surgeries, and medical consultations. Compile and record medical charts, reports, and correspondence, using typewriter or personal computer. Answer telephones and direct calls to appropriate staff. Receive and route messages and documents such as laboratory results to appropriate staff. Greet visitors, ascertain purpose of visit, and direct them to appropriate staff. Interview patients in order to complete documents, case histories, and forms such as intake and insurance forms. Maintain medical records, technical library, and correspondence files. Operate office equipment such as voice mail messaging systems and use word-processing, spreadsheet, and other software applications to prepare reports, invoices, financial statements, letters, case histories, and medical records. Transmit correspondence and medical records by mail, e-mail, or fax. Perform various clerical and administrative functions, such as ordering and maintaining an inventory of supplies. Arrange hospital admissions for patients. Transcribe recorded messages and practitioners' diagnoses and recommendations into patients' medical records. Perform bookkeeping duties, such as credits and collections, preparing and sending financial statements and bills, and keeping financial records. Complete insurance and other claim forms. Prepare correspondence and assist physicians or medical scientists with preparation of reports, speeches, articles, and conference proceedings.

GOE INFORMATION—**Interest Area:** 09. Business Detail. **Work Group:** 09.02. Administrative Detail. **Personality Type**—Conventional. Conventional occupations frequently involve following set procedures and routines. These occupations can include working with data and details more than with ideas. Usually there is a clear line of authority to follow. **Work Values**—Good Working Conditions; Activity; Company Policies and Practices; Supervision, Technical; Security. **Skills**—Equipment Selection; Active Listening; Speaking; Social Perceptiveness; Reading Comprehension; Instructing; Writing; Time Management. **Abilities**—*Cognitive:* Category Flexibility; Information Ordering; Time Sharing; Oral Comprehension; Originality. *Psychomotor:* Finger Dexterity. *Physical:* Trunk Strength. *Sensory:* Speech Recognition; Near Vision; Auditory Attention; Speech Clarity. **General Work Activities**—*Information Input:* Getting Information; Monitoring Processes, Materials, or Surroundings; Identifying Objects, Actions, and Events. *Mental Process:* Organizing, Planning, and Prioritizing; Processing Information; Updating and Using Relevant Knowledge. *Work Output:* Documenting or Recording Information; Interacting with Computers; Handling and Moving Objects. *Interacting with Others:* Establishing and Maintaining Relationships; Assisting and Caring for Others; Communicating with Other Workers. **Physical Work Conditions**—Sitting; Indoors; Making Repetitive Motions; Disease or Infections; Radiation. **Other Job Characteristics**—Importance of Being Exact or Accurate; Importance of Repeating Same Tasks; Consequence of Error.

Experience—Job Zone 2. Some previous work-related skill, knowledge, or experience may be helpful, but usually is not needed. **Job Preparation:** SVP 6.0 to less than 7.0—more than one year and less than four years. **Knowledge**—Customer and Personal Service; Clerical; Computers and Electronics; English Language; Telecommunications. **Instructional Programs**—Medical Administrative/Executive Assistant and Medical Secretary; Medical Insurance Specialist/Medical Biller; Medical Office Assistant/Specialist.

Related DOT Jobs—201.362-014 Medical Secretary.

43-6014.00 Secretaries, Except Legal, Medical, and Executive

- **Education/Training Required: Moderate-term on-the-job training**
- **Employed: 1,863,668**
- **Annual Earnings: $24,640**
- **Growth: –1.0%**
- **Annual Job Openings: 239,000**

Perform routine clerical and administrative functions such as drafting correspondence, scheduling appointments, organizing and maintaining paper and electronic files, or providing information to callers.

Answer telephones and give information to callers, take messages, or transfer calls to appropriate individuals. Arrange conferences, meetings, and travel reservations for office personnel. Complete forms in accordance with company procedures. Compose, type, and distribute meeting notes, routine correspondence, and reports. Greet visitors and callers, handle their inquiries, and direct them to the appropriate persons according to their needs. Locate and attach appropriate files to incoming correspondence requiring replies. Mail newsletters, promotional material, and other information. Maintain scheduling and event calendars. Make copies of correspondence and other printed material. Open, read, route, and distribute incoming mail and other material and prepare answers to routine letters. Schedule and confirm appointments for clients, customers, or supervisors. Set up and maintain paper and electronic filing systems for records, correspondence, and other material. Take dictation in shorthand or by machine and transcribe information. Collect and disburse funds from cash accounts, and keep records of collections and disbursements. Conduct searches to find needed information, using such sources as the Internet. Coordinate conferences and meetings. Establish work procedures and schedules and keep track of the daily work of clerical staff. Learn to operate new office technologies as they are developed and implemented. Manage projects and contribute to work of committees and teams. Operate electronic mail systems and coordinate the flow of information both internally and with other organizations. Order and dispense supplies. Prepare and mail checks. Provide services to customers, such as order placement and account information. Review work done by others to check for correct spelling and grammar, ensure that company format policies are followed, and recommend revisions. Supervise other clerical staff and provide training and orientation to new staff. Operate office equipment such as fax machines, copiers, and phone systems; use computers for spreadsheet, word-processing, database management, and other applications.

GOE INFORMATION—Interest Area: 09. Business Detail. **Work Group:** 09.02. Administrative Detail. **Personality Type**—Conventional. Conventional occupations frequently involve following set procedures and routines. These occupations can include working with data and details more than with ideas. Usually there is a clear line of authority to follow. **Work Values**—Good Working Conditions; Activity; Company Policies and Practices; Supervision, Technical; Social Service. **Skills**—Service Orientation. **Abilities**—*Cognitive:* Perceptual Speed; Speed of Closure; Category Flexibility; Memorization; Oral Comprehension. *Psychomotor:* Wrist-Finger Speed; Finger Dexterity; Speed of Limb Movement; Response Orientation; Manual Dexterity. *Physical:* Dynamic Strength; Gross Body Equilibrium; Trunk Strength. *Sensory:* Speech Recognition; Near Vision; Speech Clarity; Auditory Attention; Sound Localization. **General Work Activities**—*Information Input:* Getting Information; Identifying Objects, Actions, and Events; Monitoring Processes, Materials, or Surroundings. *Mental Process:* Scheduling Work and Activities; Processing Information; Organizing, Planning, and Prioritizing. *Work Output:* Handling and Moving Objects; Documenting or Recording Information; Interacting with Computers. *Interacting with Others:* Establishing and Maintaining Relationships; Communicating with Other Workers; Performing Administrative Activities. **Physical Work Conditions**—Sitting; Indoors; Making Repetitive Motions; Walking or Running; Kneeling, Crouching, or Crawling. **Other Job Characteristics**—Importance of Repeating Same Tasks; Degree of Automation; Importance of Being Exact or Accurate.

Experience—Job Zone 2. Some previous work-related skill, knowledge, or experience may be helpful, but usually is not needed. **Job Preparation:** SVP 4.0 to less than 6.0—six months to less than two years. **Knowledge**—Clerical; Economics and Accounting; Computers and Electronics; Customer and Personal Service; Geography. **Instructional Programs**—Administrative Assistant and Secretarial Science, General; Executive Assistant/Executive Secretary.

Related DOT Jobs—201.162-010 Social Secretary; 201.362-018 Membership Secretary; 201.362-022 School Secretary; 201.362-026 Script Supervisor; 201.362-030 Secretary; 219.362-074 Trust Operations Assistant.

43-9000 Other Office and Administrative Support Workers

43-9011.00 Computer Operators

- **Education/Training Required: Moderate-term on-the-job training**
- **Employed: 194,438**
- **Annual Earnings: $28,880**
- **Growth: –17.1%**
- **Annual Job Openings: 31,000**

Monitor and control electronic computer and peripheral electronic data processing equipment to process business, scientific, engineering, and other data according to operating instructions. May enter commands at a computer terminal and set controls on computer and peripheral devices. Monitor and respond to operating and error messages.

Clear equipment at end of operating run and review schedule to determine next assignment. Enter commands, using computer terminal, and activate controls on computer and peripheral equipment to integrate and operate equipment. Load peripheral equipment with selected materials for operating runs or oversee loading of peripheral equipment by peripheral equipment operators. Monitor the system for equipment failure or errors in performance. Notify supervisor or computer maintenance technicians of equipment malfunctions. Read job setup instructions to determine equipment to be used, order of use, material such as disks and paper to be loaded, and control settings. Record information such as computer operating time, problems that occurred, and actions taken. Respond to program error messages by finding and correcting problems or terminating the program. Retrieve, separate, and sort program output as needed and send data to specified users. Type command on keyboard to transfer encoded data from memory unit to magnetic tape and assist in labeling, classifying, cataloging, and maintaining tapes. Answer telephone calls to assist computer users encountering problems. Help programmers and systems analysts test and debug new programs. Oversee the operation of computer hardware systems, including coordinating and scheduling the use of computer terminals and networks to ensure efficient use. Supervise and train peripheral equipment operators and computer operator trainees. Operate encoding machine to trace coordinates on documents such as maps or drawings and to encode document points into computer. Operate spreadsheet programs and other types of software to load and manipulate data and to produce reports.

GOE INFORMATION—Interest Area: 09. Business Detail. **Work Group:** 09.09. Clerical Machine Operation. **Personality Type**—Conventional. Conventional occupations frequently involve following set procedures and routines. These occupations can include working with data and details more than with ideas. Usually there is a clear line of authority to follow. **Work Values**—Good Working Conditions; Supervision, Human Relations; Independence; Recognition; Company Policies and Practices. **Skills**—Equipment Selection; Troubleshooting; Programming; Reading Comprehension; Operation Monitoring; Critical Thinking; Active Listening; Operation and Control. **Abilities**—*Cognitive:* Speed of Closure; Category Flexibility; Memorization; Oral Expression; Written Comprehension. *Psychomotor:* Wrist-Finger Speed; Reaction Time; Finger Dexterity; Response Orientation; Control Precision. *Physical:* Extent Flexibility; Trunk Strength; Dynamic Flexibility. *Sensory:* Speech Recognition; Near Vision; Sound Localization; Speech Clarity; Far Vision. **General Work Activities**—*Information Input:* Monitoring Processes, Materials, or Surroundings; Getting Information; Identifying Objects, Actions, and Events. *Mental Process:* Updating and Using Relevant Knowledge; Evaluating Information Against Standards; Processing Information. *Work Output:* Handling and Moving Objects; Interacting with Computers; Repairing and Maintaining Electronic Equipment. *Interacting with Others:* Communicating with Other Workers; Establishing and Maintaining Relationships; Providing Consultation and Advice to Others. **Physical Work Conditions**—Sitting; Indoors; Making Repetitive Motions. **Other Job Characteristics**—Degree of Automation; Pace Determined by Speed of Equipment; Importance of Being Exact or Accurate.

Experience—Job Zone 3. Previous work-related skill, knowledge, or experience is required. **Job Preparation:** SVP 6.0 to less than 7.0—more than one year and less than four years. **Knowledge**—Computers and Electronics; Clerical; Customer and Personal Service; Telecommunications; Education and Training. **Instructional Programs**—Data Processing and Data Processing Technology/Technician.

Related DOT Jobs—213.362-010 Computer Operator.

43-9021.00 Data Entry Keyers

- **Education/Training Required: Moderate-term on-the-job training**
- **Employed: 509,404**
- **Annual Earnings: $21,960**
- **Growth: 4.9%**
- **Annual Job Openings: 90,000**

Operate data entry device, such as keyboard or photo composing perforator. Duties may include verifying data and preparing materials for printing.

Enters data from source documents into computer or onto tape or disk for subsequent entry, using keyboard or scanning device. Compiles, sorts, and verifies accuracy of data to be entered. Compares data entered with source documents. Deletes incorrectly entered data. Re-enters data in verification format to detect errors. Keeps record of completed work. Selects materials needed to complete work assignment. Loads machine with required input or output media, such as paper, cards, disk, tape or Braille media. Resolves garbled or indecipherable messages, using cryptographic procedures and equipment. Files completed documents.

GOE INFORMATION—Interest Area: 09. Business Detail. **Work Group:** 09.09. Clerical Machine Operation. **Personality Type—**Conventional. Conventional occupations frequently involve following set procedures and routines. These occupations can include working with data and details more than with ideas. Usually there is a clear line of authority to follow. **Work Values—**Independence; Moral Values; Activity; Supervision, Human Relations; Good Working Conditions. **Skills—**None met the criteria. **Abilities—***Cognitive:* Written Comprehension; Category Flexibility. *Psychomotor:* Wrist-Finger Speed. *Physical:* None met the criteria. *Sensory:* Near Vision. **General Work Activities—***Information Input:* Identifying Objects, Actions, and Events; Getting Information; Monitoring Processes, Materials, or Surroundings. *Mental Process:* Processing Information; Evaluating Information Against Standards; Organizing, Planning, and Prioritizing. *Work Output:* Handling and Moving Objects; Interacting with Computers; Documenting or Recording Information. *Interacting with Others:* Interpreting Meaning of Information for Others; Performing Administrative Activities; Communicating with Other Workers. **Physical Work Conditions—**Making Repetitive Motions; Sitting; Indoors; Using Hands on Objects, Tools, or Controls. **Other Job Characteristics—**Importance of Repeating Same Tasks; Importance of Being Exact or Accurate; Pace Determined by Speed of Equipment.

Experience—Job Zone 2. Some previous work-related skill, knowledge, or experience may be helpful, but usually is not needed. **Job Preparation:** SVP 4.0 to less than 6.0—six months to less than two years. **Knowledge—**Clerical; Computers and Electronics. **Instructional Programs—**Business/Office Automation/Technology/Data Entry; Data Entry/Microcomputer Applications, General; Graphic and Printing Equipment Operator, General Production.

Related DOT Jobs—203.582-010 Braille Operator; 203.582-014 Braille Typist; 203.582-018 Cryptographic-Machine Operator; 203.582-038 Perforator Typist; 203.582-054 Data Entry Clerk.

43-9022.00 Word Processors and Typists

- **Education/Training Required: Moderate-term on-the-job training**
- **Employed: 296,730**
- **Annual Earnings: $26,000**
- **Growth: −19.1%**
- **Annual Job Openings: 47,000**

Use word processor/computer or typewriter to type letters, reports, forms, or other material from rough draft, corrected copy, or voice recording. May perform other clerical duties as assigned.

Check completed work for spelling, grammar, punctuation, and format. Perform other clerical duties such as answering telephone, sorting and distributing mail, running errands, or sending faxes. Gather, register, and arrange the material to be typed, following instructions. Type correspondence, reports, text, and other written material from rough drafts, corrected copies, voice recordings, dictation, or previous versions, using a computer, word processor, or typewriter. File and store completed documents on computer hard drive or disk and/or maintain a computer filing system to store, retrieve, update, and delete documents. Print and make copies of work. Keep records of work performed. Compute and verify totals on report forms, requisitions, or bills, using adding machine or calculator. Collate pages of reports and other documents prepared. Electronically sort and compile text and numerical data, retrieving, updating, and merging documents as required. Reformat documents, moving paragraphs and/or columns. Search for specific sets of stored, typed characters in order to make changes. Adjust settings for format, page layout, line spacing, and other style requirements. Address envelopes or prepare envelope labels, using typewriter or computer. Operate and resupply printers and computers, changing print wheels or fluid cartridges, adding paper, and loading blank tapes, cards, or disks into equipment. Transmit work electronically to other locations. Work with technical material, preparing statistical reports, planning and typing statistical tables, and combining and rearranging material from different sources. Use data entry devices, such as optical scanners, to input data into computers for revision or editing. Transcribe stenotyped notes of court proceedings.

GOE INFORMATION—Interest Area: 09. Business Detail. **Work Group:** 09.09. Clerical Machine Operation. **Personality Type—**Conventional. Conventional occupations frequently involve following set procedures and routines. These occupations can include working with data and details more than with ideas. Usually there is a clear line of authority to follow. **Work Values—**Good Working Conditions; Company Policies and Practices; Independence; Supervision, Human Relations; Moral Values. **Skills—**Equipment Selection; Persuasion; Learning Strategies; Social Perceptiveness; Speaking; Instructing; Coordination; Repairing. **Abilities—***Cognitive:* Perceptual Speed; Category Flexibility; Flexibility of Closure; Time Sharing; Oral Comprehension. *Psychomotor:* Wrist-Finger Speed; Finger Dexterity. *Physical:* None met the criteria. *Sensory:* Speech Recognition; Near Vision; Hearing Sensitivity; Auditory Attention; Speech Clarity. **General Work Activities—***Information Input:* Getting Information; Identifying Objects, Actions, and Events; Monitoring Processes, Materials, or Surroundings. *Mental Process:* Organizing, Planning, and Prioritizing; Thinking Creatively; Updating and Using Relevant Knowledge. *Work Output:* Interacting with Computers; Documenting or Recording Information; Handling and Moving Objects. *Interacting with Others:* Establishing and Maintaining Relationships; Performing Administrative Activities; Communicating with Other Workers. **Physical Work Conditions—**Sitting; Making Repetitive Motions; Indoors; Walking or Running. **Other Job Characteristics—**Importance of Repeating Same Tasks; Degree of Automation; Pace Determined by Speed of Equipment.

Experience—Job Zone 2. Some previous work-related skill, knowledge, or experience may be helpful, but usually is not needed. **Job Preparation:** SVP 4.0 to less than 6.0—six months to less than two years. **Knowledge—**Clerical; Customer and Personal Service; Computers and Electronics; English Language; Sales and Marketing. **Instructional Programs—**General Office Occupations and Clerical Services; Word Processing.

Related DOT Jobs—203.362-010 Clerk-Typist; 203.382-030 Word Processing Machine Operator; 203.582-058 Transcribing-Machine Operator;

203.582-066 Typist; 203.582-078 Notereader; 209.382-010 Continuity Clerk; 209.587-010 Addresser.

43-9031.00 Desktop Publishers

- **Education/Training Required: Postsecondary vocational training**
- **Employed: 37,956**
- **Annual Earnings: $31,200**
- **Growth: 66.7%**
- **Annual Job Openings: 5,000**

Format typescript and graphic elements using computer software to produce publication-ready material.

Check preliminary and final proofs for errors and make necessary corrections. Edit graphics and photos using pixel or bitmap editing, airbrushing, masking, or image retouching. Enter data, such as coordinates of images and color specifications, into system to retouch and make color corrections. Enter digitized data into electronic prepress system computer memory, using scanner, camera, keyboard, or mouse. Enter text into computer keyboard and select the size and style of type, column width, and appropriate spacing for printed materials. Import text and art elements such as electronic clip art or electronic files from photographs that have been scanned or produced with a digital camera, using computer software. Load floppy disks or tapes containing information into system. Operate desktop publishing software and equipment to design, lay out, and produce camera-ready copy. Position text and art elements from a variety of databases in a visually appealing way in order to design print or Web pages, using knowledge of type styles and size and layout patterns. Prepare sample layouts for approval, using computer software. Select number of colors and determine color separations. Study layout or other design instructions to determine work to be done and sequence of operations. Transmit, deliver, or mail publication master to printer for production into film and plates. View monitors for visual representation of work in progress and for instructions and feedback throughout process, making modifications as necessary. Collaborate with graphic artists, editors, and writers to produce master copies according to design specifications. Convert various types of files for printing or for the Internet, using computer software. Create special effects such as vignettes, mosaics, and image combining and add elements such as sound and animation to electronic publications. Store copies of publications on paper, magnetic tape, film, or diskette.

GOE INFORMATION—Interest Area: 01. Arts, Entertainment, and Media. **Work Group:** 01.07. Graphic Arts. **Personality Type**—Realistic. Realistic occupations frequently involve work activities that include practical, hands-on problems and solutions. They often deal with plants, animals, and real-world materials like wood, tools, and machinery. Many of the occupations require working outside and do not involve a lot of paperwork or working closely with others. **Work Values**—Good Working Conditions; Independence; Variety; Supervision, Human Relations; Autonomy. **Skills**—Equipment Selection; Operation and Control. **Abilities**—*Cognitive:* Visualization; Speed of Closure; Flexibility of Closure; Perceptual Speed; Originality. *Psychomotor:* Wrist-Finger Speed; Control Precision; Response Orientation; Finger Dexterity; Arm-Hand Steadiness. *Physical:* None met the criteria. *Sensory:* Visual Color Discrimination; Near Vision; Glare Sensitivity; Night Vision. **General Work Activities**—*Information Input:* Getting Information; Identifying Objects, Actions, and Events; Monitoring Processes, Materials, or Surroundings. *Mental Process:* Updating and Using Relevant Knowledge; Thinking Creatively; Processing Information. *Work Output:* Handling and Moving Objects; Interacting with Computers; Documenting or Recording Information. *Interacting with Others:* Communicating with Other Workers;

Establishing and Maintaining Relationships; Providing Consultation and Advice to Others. **Physical Work Conditions**—Sitting; Indoors; Using Hands on Objects, Tools, or Controls; Extremely Bright or Inadequate Lighting; Making Repetitive Motions. **Other Job Characteristics**—Degree of Automation; Pace Determined by Speed of Equipment; Importance of Being Exact or Accurate.

Experience—Job Zone 4. A minimum of two to four years of work-related skill, knowledge, or experience is needed. **Job Preparation:** SVP 7.0 to less than 8.0—two years to less than 10 years. **Knowledge**—Computers and Electronics; Communications and Media; Clerical; English Language; Fine Arts. **Instructional Programs**—Prepress/Desktop Publishing and Digital Imaging Design.

Related DOT Jobs—979.282-010 Electronic Prepress System Operator.

43-9041.00 Insurance Claims and Policy Processing Clerks

- **Education/Training Required: Short-term on-the-job training**
- **Employed: 289,155**
- **Annual Earnings: $28,480**
- **Growth: −20.2%**
- **Annual Job Openings: 36,000**

Process new insurance policies, modifications to existing policies, and claims forms. Obtain information from policyholders to verify the accuracy and completeness of information on claims forms, applications and related documents, and company records. Update existing policies and company records to reflect changes requested by policyholders and insurance company representatives.

No task data available.

GOE INFORMATION—Interest Area: 09. Business Detail. **Work Group:** 09.07. Records Processing. **Note:** The Department of Labor has not collected some data for this job, so it has fewer details than the other descriptions.

Instructional Programs—General Office Occupations and Clerical Services.

Related DOT Jobs—203.382-014 Cancellation Clerk; 205.367-018 Claims Clerk II; 209.382-014 Special-Certificate Dictator; 209.687-018 Reviewer; 219.362-042 Policy-Change Clerk; 219.362-050 Revival Clerk; 219.482-014 Insurance Checker; 241.362-010 Claims Clerk I.

43-9041.01 Insurance Claims Clerks

- **Education/Training Required: Moderate-term on-the-job training**
- **Employed: No data available.**
- **Annual Earnings: $28,480**
- **Growth: −20.2%**
- **Annual Job Openings: 36,000**

Obtain information from insured or designated persons for purpose of settling claim with insurance carrier.

Apply insurance rating systems. Calculate amount of claim. Contact insured or other involved persons to obtain missing information. Post or attach information to claim file. Prepare and review insurance-claim forms and related documents for completeness. Provide customer service, such as giving limited instructions on how to proceed with claims or providing referrals to auto repair facilities or local contractors. Review insurance policy to determine coverage. Transmit claims for payment or further investigation. Organize and work with detailed office or warehouse records, using computers to enter, access, search, and retrieve data. Pay small claims.

GOE INFORMATION—Interest Area: 09. Business Detail. **Work Group:** 09.07. Records Processing. **Personality Type**—Conventional. Conventional occupations frequently involve following set procedures and routines. These occupations can include working with data and details more than with ideas. Usually there is a clear line of authority to follow. **Work Values**—Supervision, Human Relations; Good Working Conditions; Advancement; Moral Values; Company Policies and Practices. **Skills**—Speaking. **Abilities**—*Cognitive:* Number Facility; Mathematical Reasoning; Written Comprehension; Perceptual Speed; Oral Expression. *Psychomotor:* Wrist-Finger Speed. *Physical:* None met the criteria. *Sensory:* Speech Recognition; Near Vision; Speech Clarity; Auditory Attention. **General Work Activities**—*Information Input:* Getting Information; Identifying Objects, Actions, and Events; Monitoring Processes, Materials, or Surroundings. *Mental Process:* Evaluating Information Against Standards; Processing Information; Analyzing Data or Information. *Work Output:* Documenting or Recording Information; Handling and Moving Objects; Interacting with Computers. *Interacting with Others:* Communicating with Persons Outside Organization; Establishing and Maintaining Relationships; Performing Administrative Activities. **Physical Work Conditions**—Sitting; Indoors. **Other Job Characteristics**—Degree of Automation; Importance of Being Exact or Accurate; Importance of Repeating Same Tasks.

Experience—Job Zone 2. Some previous work-related skill, knowledge, or experience may be helpful, but usually is not needed. **Job Preparation:** SVP 4.0 to less than 6.0—six months to less than two years. **Knowledge**—Clerical; Law and Government; Economics and Accounting; Customer and Personal Service; Telecommunications. **Instructional Programs**—General Office Occupations and Clerical Services.

Related DOT Jobs—205.367-018 Claims Clerk II; 241.362-010 Claims Clerk I.

43-9041.02 Insurance Policy Processing Clerks

- **Education/Training Required: Moderate-term on-the-job training**
- **Employed: No data available.**
- **Annual Earnings: $28,480**
- **Growth: –20.2%**
- **Annual Job Openings: 36,000**

Process applications for, changes to, reinstatement of, and cancellation of insurance policies. Duties include reviewing insurance applications to ensure that all questions have been answered, compiling data on insurance policy changes, changing policy records to conform to insured party's specifications, compiling data on lapsed insurance policies to determine automatic reinstatement according to company policies, canceling insurance policies as requested by agents, and verifying the accuracy of insurance company records.

Modify, update, and process existing policies and claims to reflect any change in beneficiary, amount of coverage, or type of insurance. Process and record new insurance policies and claims. Review and verify data such as age, name, address, and principal sum and value of property on insurance applications and policies. Organize and work with detailed office or warehouse records, maintaining files for each policyholder, including policies that are to be reinstated or cancelled. Examine letters from policyholders or agents, original insurance applications, and other company documents to determine if changes are needed and effects of changes. Correspond with insured or agent to obtain information or inform them of account status or changes. Transcribe data to worksheets and enter data into computer for use in preparing documents and adjusting accounts. Notify insurance agent and accounting department of policy cancellation. Interview clients and take their calls in order to provide customer service and obtain information on claims. Compare information from application to criteria for policy reinstatement and approve reinstatement when criteria are met. Process, prepare, and submit business or government forms, such as submitting applications for coverage to insurance carriers. Collect initial premiums and issue receipts. Calculate premiums, refunds, commissions, adjustments, and new reserve requirements, using insurance rate standards. Obtain computer printout of policy cancellations or retrieve cancellation cards from file. Compose business correspondence for supervisors, managers, and professionals. Check computations of interest accrued, premiums due, and settlement surrender on loan values.

GOE INFORMATION—Interest Area: 09. Business Detail. **Work Group:** 09.07. Records Processing. **Personality Type**—Conventional. Conventional occupations frequently involve following set procedures and routines. These occupations can include working with data and details more than with ideas. Usually there is a clear line of authority to follow. **Work Values**—Good Working Conditions; Supervision, Human Relations; Advancement; Pleasant Co-workers; Supervision, Technical. **Skills**—Critical Thinking; Learning Strategies; Complex Problem Solving; Social Perceptiveness; Service Orientation; Instructing; Reading Comprehension; Speaking. **Abilities**—*Cognitive:* Deductive Reasoning; Inductive Reasoning; Category Flexibility; Mathematical Reasoning; Flexibility of Closure. *Psychomotor:* Finger Dexterity. *Physical:* None met the criteria. *Sensory:* Speech Recognition; Near Vision; Speech Clarity. **General Work Activities**—*Information Input:* Getting Information; Identifying Objects, Actions, and Events; Monitoring Processes, Materials, or Surroundings. *Mental Process:* Organizing, Planning, and Prioritizing; Updating and Using Relevant Knowledge; Making Decisions and Solving Problems. *Work Output:* Interacting with Computers; Documenting or Recording Information; Performing General Physical Activities. *Interacting with Others:* Communicating with Other Workers; Establishing and Maintaining Relationships; Communicating with Persons Outside Organization. **Physical Work Conditions**—Sitting; Indoors. **Other Job Characteristics**—Importance of Repeating Same Tasks; Importance of Being Exact or Accurate; Pace Determined by Speed of Equipment.

Experience—Job Zone 2. Some previous work-related skill, knowledge, or experience may be helpful, but usually is not needed. **Job Preparation:** SVP 4.0 to less than 6.0—six months to less than two years. **Knowledge**—Clerical; Customer and Personal Service; Computers and Electronics; Sales and Marketing; Economics and Accounting. **Instructional Programs**—General Office Occupations and Clerical Services.

Related DOT Jobs—203.382-014 Cancellation Clerk; 209.382-014 Special-Certificate Dictator; 209.687-018 Reviewer; 219.362-042 Policy-Change Clerk; 219.362-050 Revival Clerk; 219.482-014 Insurance Checker.

43-9051.00 Mail Clerks and Mail Machine Operators, Except Postal Service

- **Education/Training Required: Short-term on-the-job training**
- **Employed: 187,948**
- **Annual Earnings: $20,610**
- **Growth: 9.9%**
- **Annual Job Openings: 22,000**

Prepare incoming and outgoing mail for distribution. Use hand or mail-handling machines to time-stamp, open, read, sort, and route incoming mail and address, seal, stamp, fold, stuff, and affix postage to outgoing mail or packages. Duties may also include keeping necessary records and completed forms.

No task data available.

GOE INFORMATION—Interest Area: 09. Business Detail. **Work Group:** 09.09. Clerical Machine Operation. **Note:** The Department of Labor has not collected some data for this job, so it has fewer details than the other descriptions.

Instructional Programs—General Office Occupations and Clerical Services.

Related DOT Jobs—208.462-010 Mailing-Machine Operator; 208.582-010 Addressing-Machine Operator; 208.685-014 Folding-Machine Operator; 208.685-018 Inserting-Machine Operator; 208.685-026 Sealing-and-Canceling-Machine Operator; 208.685-034 Wing-Mailer-Machine Operator; 209.587-018 Direct-Mail Clerk; 209.687-026 Mail Clerk; 222.367-022 Express Clerk; 222.387-038 Parcel Post Clerk; 222.567-018 Slot-Tag Inserter; 222.587-030 Mailer; 222.587-032 Mailer Apprentice; 249.687-010 Office Copy Selector.

43-9051.01 Mail Machine Operators, Preparation and Handling

- Education/Training Required: **Short-term on-the-job training**
- Employed: **No data available.**
- Annual Earnings: **$20,610**
- Growth: **9.9%**
- Annual Job Openings: **22,000**

Operate machines that emboss names, addresses, and other matter onto metal plates for use in addressing machines; print names, addresses, and similar information onto items such as envelopes, accounting forms, and advertising literature; address, fold, stuff, seal, and stamp mail; and open envelopes.

Inserts material for printing or addressing into loading rack on machine. Starts machine. Operates embossing machine or typewriter to make corrections, additions, and changes on address plates. Removes printed material from machine, such as labeled articles, postmarked envelopes or tape, and folded sheets. Selects type of die size. Adjusts machine guides, rollers, and card insert prior to starting machine. Changes machine ribbon. Checks ink level, adds ink, and fills paste reservoir. Observes machine operation to detect evidence of malfunctions during production run. Makes adjustments to machine and inspects output for defects. Positions plates, stencils, or tapes in machine magazine. Places folded sheets into envelopes preparatory to mailing. Reads production order to determine type and size of items scheduled for printing and mailing.

GOE INFORMATION—Interest Area: 09. Business Detail. **Work Group:** 09.09. Clerical Machine Operation. **Personality Type**—Realistic. Realistic occupations frequently involve work activities that include practical, hands-on problems and solutions. They often deal with plants, animals, and real-world materials like wood, tools, and machinery. Many of the occupations require working outside and do not involve a lot of paperwork or working closely with others. **Work Values**—Supervision, Technical; Independence; Moral Values; Supervision, Human Relations. **Skills**—Operation and Control. **Abilities**—*Cognitive:* Perceptual Speed; Flexibility of Closure; Category Flexibility. *Psychomotor:* Rate Control;

Manual Dexterity; Reaction Time; Response Orientation; Speed of Limb Movement. *Physical:* Dynamic Flexibility. *Sensory:* Peripheral Vision; Near Vision. **General Work Activities—***Information Input:* Monitoring Processes, Materials, or Surroundings; Identifying Objects, Actions, and Events; Inspecting Equipment, Structures, or Materials. *Mental Process:* Organizing, Planning, and Prioritizing; Judging Qualities of Things, Services, or Other People's Work; Updating and Using Relevant Knowledge. *Work Output:* Handling and Moving Objects; Controlling Machines and Processes; Performing General Physical Activities. *Interacting with Others:* Communicating with Other Workers; Establishing and Maintaining Relationships; Interpreting Meaning of Information for Others. **Physical Work Conditions**—Making Repetitive Motions; Using Hands on Objects, Tools, or Controls; Indoors; Standing; Bending or Twisting the Body. **Other Job Characteristics**—Pace Determined by Speed of Equipment; Degree of Automation; Importance of Repeating Same Tasks.

Experience—Job Zone 1. No previous work-related skill, knowledge, or experience is needed. **Job Preparation:** SVP below 4.0—less than six months. **Knowledge**—Production and Processing; Engineering and Technology. **Instructional Programs**—General Office Occupations and Clerical Services.

Related DOT Jobs—208.462-010 Mailing-Machine Operator; 208.582-010 Addressing-Machine Operator; 208.685-014 Folding-Machine Operator; 208.685-018 Inserting-Machine Operator; 208.685-026 Sealing-and-Canceling-Machine Operator; 208.685-034 Wing-Mailer-Machine Operator.

43-9051.02 Mail Clerks, Except Mail Machine Operators and Postal Service

- Education/Training Required: **Short-term on-the-job training**
- Employed: **No data available.**
- Annual Earnings: **$20,610**
- Growth: **9.9%**
- Annual Job Openings: **22,000**

Prepare incoming and outgoing mail for distribution. Duties include time-stamping, opening, reading, sorting, and routing incoming mail; sealing, stamping, and affixing postage to outgoing mail or packages; and keeping necessary records and completed forms.

Sorts letters or packages into sacks or bins and places identifying tag on sack or bin according to destination and type. Affixes postage to packages or letter by hand, or stamps with postage meter, and dispatches mail. Stamps date and time of receipt of incoming mail and distributes and collects mail. Seals or opens envelopes by hand or machine. Records and maintains records of information such as charges and destination of insured, registered, or C.O.D. packages. Wraps packages or bundles by hand or using tying machine. Weighs packages or letters, computes charges, and accepts payment, using weight scale and rate chart. Inspects wrapping, address, and appearance of outgoing package or letter for conformance to standards and accuracy. Addresses packages or letters by hand or using addressing machine, label, or stamp. Stacks bundles of bulk printed matter for shipment and loads and unloads from trucks and conveyors. Releases packages or letters to customer upon presentation of written notice or other identification. Receives request for merchandise samples or promotional literature, prepares shipping slips, and mails samples or literature. Answers inquiries regarding shipping or mailing policies.

* * * * * * * * * * * * © JIST Works

GOE INFORMATION—Interest Area: 09. Business Detail. **Work Group:** 09.08. Records and Materials Processing. **Personality Type—**Conventional. Conventional occupations frequently involve following set procedures and routines. These occupations can include working with data and details more than with ideas. Usually there is a clear line of authority to follow. **Work Values—**Supervision, Technical; Security; Supervision, Human Relations; Activity; Moral Values. **Skills—**None met the criteria. **Abilities—***Cognitive:* Perceptual Speed; Speed of Closure; Category Flexibility. *Psychomotor:* Wrist-Finger Speed; Response Orientation; Multilimb Coordination; Rate Control; Manual Dexterity. *Physical:* Dynamic Flexibility; Stamina; Extent Flexibility; Gross Body Coordination; Gross Body Equilibrium. *Sensory:* Auditory Attention. **General Work Activities—***Information Input:* Inspecting Equipment, Structures, or Materials; Getting Information; Monitoring Processes, Materials, or Surroundings. *Mental Process:* Processing Information; Evaluating Information Against Standards; Organizing, Planning, and Prioritizing. *Work Output:* Handling and Moving Objects; Performing General Physical Activities; Controlling Machines and Processes. *Interacting with Others:* Communicating with Persons Outside Organization; Communicating with Other Workers; Performing for or Working with the Public. **Physical Work Conditions—**Making Repetitive Motions; Indoors; Walking or Running; Using Hands on Objects, Tools, or Controls; Disease or Infections. **Other Job Characteristics—**Importance of Repeating Same Tasks; Degree of Automation; Pace Determined by Speed of Equipment.

Experience—Job Zone 1. No previous work-related skill, knowledge, or experience is needed. **Job Preparation:** SVP below 4.0—less than six months. **Knowledge—**Geography; Clerical; Customer and Personal Service; Philosophy and Theology; Sales and Marketing. **Instructional Programs—**General Office Occupations and Clerical Services.

Related DOT Jobs—209.587-018 Direct-Mail Clerk; 209.687-026 Mail Clerk; 222.367-022 Express Clerk; 222.387-038 Parcel Post Clerk; 222.567-018 Slot-Tag Inserter; 222.587-030 Mailer; 222.587-032 Mailer Apprentice; 249.687-010 Office Copy Selector.

43-9061.00 Office Clerks, General

- **Education/Training Required: Short-term on-the-job training**
- **Employed: 2,704,897**
- **Annual Earnings: $21,780**
- **Growth: 15.9%**
- **Annual Job Openings: 676,000**

Perform duties too varied and diverse to be classified in any specific office clerical occupation, requiring limited knowledge of office management systems and procedures. Clerical duties may be assigned in accordance with the office procedures of individual establishments and may include a combination of answering telephones, bookkeeping, typing or word processing, stenography, office machine operation, and filing.

Collect, count, and disburse money; do basic bookkeeping; and complete banking transactions. Communicate with customers, employees, and other individuals to answer questions, disseminate or explain information, take orders, and address complaints. Answer telephones, direct calls, and take messages. Compile, copy, sort, and file records of office activities, business transactions, and other activities. Complete and mail bills, contracts, policies, invoices, or checks. Operate office machines, such as photocopiers and scanners, facsimile machines, voice mail systems, and personal computers. Compute, record, and proofread data and other information, such as records or reports. Maintain and update filing, inventory, mailing, and database systems, either manually or using a computer. Open, sort, and route incoming mail, answer correspondence, and prepare outgoing mail. Review files, records, and other documents to obtain information to respond to requests. Deliver messages and run errands. Inventory and order materials, supplies, and services. Complete work schedules, manage calendars, and arrange appointments. Process and prepare documents such as business or government forms and expense reports. Monitor and direct the work of lower-level clerks. Type, format, proofread, and edit correspondence and other documents from notes or dictating machines, using computers or typewriters. Count, weigh, measure, and/or organize materials. Train other staff members to perform work activities such as using computer applications. Prepare meeting agendas, attend meetings, and record and transcribe minutes. Troubleshoot problems involving office equipment, such as computer hardware and software. Make travel arrangements for office personnel.

GOE INFORMATION—Interest Area: 09. Business Detail. **Work Group:** 09.07. Records Processing. **Personality Type—**Conventional. Conventional occupations frequently involve following set procedures and routines. These occupations can include working with data and details more than with ideas. Usually there is a clear line of authority to follow. **Work Values—**Advancement; Pleasant Co-workers; Good Working Conditions; Supervision, Technical; Supervision, Human Relations. **Skills—**Active Listening; Reading Comprehension. **Abilities—***Cognitive:* Category Flexibility; Flexibility of Closure; Perceptual Speed; Oral Expression; Time Sharing. *Psychomotor:* Wrist-Finger Speed; Manual Dexterity; Finger Dexterity. *Physical:* None met the criteria. *Sensory:* Speech Recognition; Far Vision; Near Vision; Speech Clarity. **General Work Activities—***Information Input:* Getting Information; Identifying Objects, Actions, and Events; Monitoring Processes, Materials, or Surroundings. *Mental Process:* Organizing, Planning, and Prioritizing; Processing Information; Updating and Using Relevant Knowledge. *Work Output:* Interacting with Computers; Documenting or Recording Information; Handling and Moving Objects. *Interacting with Others:* Establishing and Maintaining Relationships; Communicating with Other Workers; Performing for or Working with the Public. **Physical Work Conditions—**Sitting; Making Repetitive Motions; Indoors; Walking or Running. **Other Job Characteristics—**Importance of Repeating Same Tasks; Degree of Automation; Pace Determined by Speed of Equipment.

Experience—Job Zone 2. Some previous work-related skill, knowledge, or experience may be helpful, but usually is not needed. **Job Preparation:** SVP below 4.0—less than six months. **Knowledge—**Clerical; Customer and Personal Service; Economics and Accounting; Personnel and Human Resources; Computers and Electronics. **Instructional Programs—**General Office Occupations and Clerical Services.

Related DOT Jobs—162.167-026 Prize Coordinator; 205.367-010 Admissions Evaluator; 205.367-030 Election Clerk; 209.362-010 Circulation Clerk; 209.362-014 Control Clerk, Auditing; 209.362-022 Identification Clerk; 209.362-030 Congressional-District Aide; 209.367-010 Agent-Licensing Clerk; 209.367-026 Fingerprint Clerk I; 209.367-034 Lost-Charge-Card Clerk; 209.367-038 News Assistant; 209.367-050 Trip Follower; 209.367-054 Yard Clerk; 209.382-022 Traffic Clerk; 209.387-022 Data-Examination Clerk; 209.562-010 Clerk, General; 209.587-014 Credit-Card Clerk; 209.587-022 History-Card Clerk; 209.587-030 Map Clerk; 209.587-050 Wrong-Address Clerk; others.

43-9071.00 Office Machine Operators, Except Computer

- **Education/Training Required: Short-term on-the-job training**
- **Employed: 83,771**
- **Annual Earnings: $21,740**
- **Growth: –18.8%**
- **Annual Job Openings: 18,000**

Operate one or more of a variety of office machines, such as photocopying, photographic, and duplicating machines or other office machines.

No task data available.

GOE INFORMATION—Interest Area: 09. Business Detail. **Work Group:** 09.09. Clerical Machine Operation. **Note:** The Department of Labor has not collected some data for this job, so it has fewer details than the other descriptions.

Instructional Programs—Agricultural Business Technology; General Office Occupations and Clerical Services.

Related DOT Jobs—207.682-010 Duplicating-Machine Operator I; 207.682-014 Duplicating-Machine Operator II; 207.682-018 Offset-Duplicating-Machine Operator; 207.685-010 Braille-Duplicating-Machine Operator; 207.685-014 Photocopying-Machine Operator; 207.685-018 Photographic-Machine Operator.

43-9071.01 Duplicating Machine Operators

- **Education/Training Required: Short-term on-the-job training**
- **Employed: No data available.**
- **Annual Earnings: $21,740**
- **Growth: –18.8%**
- **Annual Job Openings: 18,000**

Operate one of a variety of office machines such as photocopying, photographic, mimeograph, and duplicating machines to make copies.

Sets controls for number of copies and presses buttons to start machine. Selects type, embossed plate, or paper stock according to size, color, thickness, and quantity specified. Places original copy in feed tray, feeds originals into feed rolls, or positions originals on table beneath camera lens. Adjusts machine to regulate ink flow, speed, paper size, focus, exposure, and camera distance from document. Loads machine with blank paper or film and places paper roll in holding tray or rack of machine. Moves heat unit and clamping frame over screen bed to form Braille impression on page. Cuts copies apart and writes identifying information on copies. Cleans and oils machine and printing plate. Records number of copies made.

GOE INFORMATION—Interest Area: 09. Business Detail. **Work Group:** 09.09. Clerical Machine Operation. **Personality Type—**Conventional. Conventional occupations frequently involve following set procedures and routines. These occupations can include working with data and details more than with ideas. Usually there is a clear line of authority to follow. **Work Values—**Independence; Supervision, Technical; Moral Values; Supervision, Human Relations. **Skills—**Repairing. **Abilities—***Cognitive:* Spatial Orientation. *Psychomotor:* Control Precision; Finger Dexterity. *Physical:* None met the criteria. *Sensory:* Visual Color Discrimination; Glare Sensitivity. **General Work Activities—***Information Input:* Getting Information; Monitoring Processes, Materials, or Surroundings; Inspecting Equipment, Structures, or Materials. *Mental Process:* Updating and Using Relevant Knowledge; Judging Qualities of Things, Services, or Other People's Work; Organizing, Planning, and Prioritizing. *Work Output:* Handling and Moving Objects; Performing General Physical Activities; Controlling Machines and Processes. *Interacting with Others:* Performing Administrative Activities; Assisting and Caring for Others; Communicating with Other Workers. **Physical Work Conditions—**Making Repetitive Motions; Using Hands on Objects, Tools, or Controls;

Indoors; Standing; Kneeling, Crouching, or Crawling. **Other Job Characteristics—**Pace Determined by Speed of Equipment; Degree of Automation; Importance of Repeating Same Tasks.

Experience—Job Zone 1. No previous work-related skill, knowledge, or experience is needed. **Job Preparation:** SVP below 4.0—less than six months. **Knowledge—**Computers and Electronics. **Instructional Programs—**Agricultural Business Technology; General Office Occupations and Clerical Services.

Related DOT Jobs—207.682-010 Duplicating-Machine Operator I; 207.682-014 Duplicating-Machine Operator II; 207.682-018 Offset-Duplicating-Machine Operator; 207.685-010 Braille-Duplicating-Machine Operator; 207.685-014 Photocopying-Machine Operator; 207.685-018 Photographic-Machine Operator.

43-9081.00 Proofreaders and Copy Markers

- **Education/Training Required: Short-term on-the-job training**
- **Employed: 35,282**
- **Annual Earnings: $23,860**
- **Growth: –5.5%**
- **Annual Job Openings: 7,000**

Read transcript or proof type setup to detect and mark for correction any grammatical, typographical, or compositional errors.

Compare information or figures on one record against same data on other records, or with original copy, to detect errors. Consult reference books or secure aid of readers to check references with rules of grammar and composition. Correct or record omissions, errors, or inconsistencies found. Mark copy to indicate and correct errors in type, arrangement, grammar, punctuation, or spelling, using standard printers' marks. Read corrected copies or proofs in order to ensure that all corrections have been made. Route proofs with marked corrections to authors, editors, typists, or typesetters for correction and/or reprinting. Measure dimensions, spacing, and positioning of page elements (copy and illustrations) in order to verify conformance to specifications, using printer's ruler. Read proof sheets aloud, calling out punctuation marks and spelling unusual words and proper names.

GOE INFORMATION—Interest Area: 09. Business Detail. **Work Group:** 09.07. Records Processing. **Personality Type—**Conventional. Conventional occupations frequently involve following set procedures and routines. These occupations can include working with data and details more than with ideas. Usually there is a clear line of authority to follow. **Work Values—**Good Working Conditions; Independence; Moral Values; Supervision, Human Relations; Company Policies and Practices. **Skills—**Reading Comprehension. **Abilities—***Cognitive:* Written Comprehension; Memorization; Perceptual Speed; Written Expression; Flexibility of Closure. *Psychomotor:* None met the criteria. *Physical:* None met the criteria. *Sensory:* Near Vision; Speech Clarity. **General Work Activities—***Information Input:* Identifying Objects, Actions, and Events; Getting Information; Inspecting Equipment, Structures, or Materials. *Mental Process:* Evaluating Information Against Standards; Judging Qualities of Things, Services, or Other People's Work; Processing Information. *Work Output:* Handling and Moving Objects; Interacting with Computers; Documenting or Recording Information. *Interacting with Others:* Communicating with Other Workers; Providing Consultation and Advice to Others; Establishing and Maintaining Relationships. **Physical Work Conditions—**Sitting; Indoors; Making Repetitive Motions; Radiation. **Other Job Characteristics—**Importance of Repeating Same Tasks; Importance of Being Exact or Accurate; Consequence of Error.

Experience—Job Zone 2. Some previous work-related skill, knowledge, or experience may be helpful, but usually is not needed. **Job Preparation:** SVP 4.0 to less than 6.0—six months to less than two years. **Knowledge**—English Language; Computers and Electronics; Philosophy and Theology; Sales and Marketing; Fine Arts. **Instructional Programs**—Graphic and Printing Equipment Operator, General Production.

Related DOT Jobs—209.387-030 Proofreader; 209.667-010 Copy Holder; 209.687-010 Checker II; 247.667-010 Production Proofreader.

43-9111.00 Statistical Assistants

- **Education/Training Required: Moderate-term on-the-job training**
- **Employed: 21,160**
- **Annual Earnings: $28,990**
- **Growth: 2.1%**
- **Annual Job Openings: 2,000**

Compile and compute data according to statistical formulas for use in statistical studies. May perform actuarial computations and compile charts and graphs for use by actuaries. Includes actuarial clerks.

Check source data in order to verify its completeness and accuracy. Check survey responses for errors such as the use of pens instead of pencils and set aside response forms that cannot be used. Code data as necessary prior to computer entry, using lists of codes. Compile reports, charts, and graphs that describe and interpret findings of analyses. Compile statistics from source materials, such as production and sales records, quality-control and test records, time sheets, and survey sheets. Compute and analyze data, using statistical formulas and computers or calculators. Enter data into computers for use in analyses and reports. Feed response sheets through optical scanners that read responses and store data in a format that computers can read. File data and related information; maintain and update databases. Organize paperwork such as survey forms and reports for distribution and for analysis. Select statistical tests for analyzing data. Discuss data presentation requirements with clients. Interview people and keep track of their responses. Participate in the publication of data and information. Send out surveys.

GOE INFORMATION—**Interest Area:** 02. Science, Math, and Engineering. **Work Group:** 02.06. Mathematics and Computers. **Personality Type**—Conventional. Conventional occupations frequently involve following set procedures and routines. These occupations can include working with data and details more than with ideas. Usually there is a clear line of authority to follow. **Work Values**—Independence; Good Working Conditions; Advancement; Supervision, Human Relations; Autonomy. **Skills**—Mathematics; Writing. **Abilities**—*Cognitive:* Mathematical Reasoning; Number Facility; Category Flexibility; Written Expression; Perceptual Speed. *Psychomotor:* Wrist-Finger Speed. *Physical:* None met the criteria. *Sensory:* Glare Sensitivity. **General Work Activities**—*Information Input:* Getting Information; Identifying Objects, Actions, and Events; Estimating Needed Characteristics. *Mental Process:* Analyzing Data or Information; Processing Information; Updating and Using Relevant Knowledge. *Work Output:* Interacting with Computers; Documenting or Recording Information; Handling and Moving Objects. *Interacting with Others:* Interpreting Meaning of Information for Others; Communicating with Other Workers; Providing Consultation and Advice to Others. **Physical Work Conditions**—Sitting; Making Repetitive Motions; Indoors. **Other Job Characteristics**—Importance of Repeating Same Tasks; Importance of Being Exact or Accurate; Pace Determined by Speed of Equipment.

Experience—Job Zone 2. Some previous work-related skill, knowledge, or experience may be helpful, but usually is not needed. **Job Preparation:** SVP 4.0 to less than 6.0—six months to less than two years. **Knowledge**—Mathematics; Computers and Electronics; Clerical; Communications and Media. **Instructional Programs**—Accounting Technology/Technician and Bookkeeping.

Related DOT Jobs—209.387-014 Compiler; 214.487-010 Chart Calculator; 216.382-062 Statistical Clerk; 216.382-066 Statistical Clerk, Advertising; 219.387-022 Planimeter Operator; 221.382-010 Chart Clerk; 221.584-010 Chart Changer.

43-9199.99 Office and Administrative Support Workers, All Other

- **Education/Training Required: No data available.**
- **Employed: No data available.**
- **Annual Earnings: No data available.**
- **Growth: –0.9%**
- **Annual Job Openings: 89,000**

All office and administrative support workers not listed separately.

No task data available.

GOE INFORMATION—**Interest Area:** 09. Business Detail. **Work Group:** 09.02. Administrative Detail; 09.03. Bookkeeping, Auditing, and Accounting; 09.07. Records Processing; 09.08. Records and Materials Processing; 09.09. Clerical Machine Operation. **Note:** The Department of Labor has not collected some data for this job, so it has fewer details than the other descriptions.

Instructional Programs—Business Operations Support and Secretarial Services, Other; General Office Occupations and Clerical Services.

Related DOT Jobs—206.367-010 Engineering-Document-Control Clerk; 208.582-014 Embossing-Machine Operator I; 208.682-010 Embossing-Machine Operator II; 208.685-010 Collator Operator; 208.685-022 Microfilm Mounter; 211.362-010 Cashier I; 216.587-010 Booking Clerk; 216.685-010 Gas Usage Meter Clerk; 217.485-010 Currency Counter; 217.585-010 Coin-Counter-And-Wrapper; 219.367-014 Insurance Clerk; 221.362-010 Aircraft-Log Clerk; 221.362-026 Railroad-Maintenance Clerk; 229.267-010 Parts Cataloger; 237.367-026 Land-Leasing Examiner; 239.367-026 Service Observer; 243.367-010 Mail Censor; 248.367-030 Waterway Traffic Checker; 976.682-022 Microfilm-Camera Operator.

45-0000

Farming, Fishing, and Forestry Occupations

45-1000 Supervisors, Farming, Fishing, and Forestry Workers

45-1011.00 First-Line Supervisors/ Managers of Farming, Fishing, and Forestry Workers

- Education/Training Required: Work experience in a related occupation
- Employed: No data available.
- Annual Earnings: $33,330
- Growth: 13.0%
- Annual Job Openings: 89,000

Directly supervise and coordinate the activities of agricultural, forestry, aquacultural, and related workers.

No task data available.

GOE INFORMATION—Interest Area: 03. Plants and Animals. **Work Group:** 03.01. Managerial Work in Plants and Animals. **Note:** The Department of Labor has not collected some data for this job, so it has fewer details than the other descriptions.

Instructional Programs—Agricultural Animal Breeding; Agricultural Business and Management, Other; Agricultural Production Operations, General; Agricultural Production Operations, Other; Agriculture, Agriculture Operations, and Related Sciences, Other; Agronomy and Crop Science; Animal Nutrition; Animal Sciences, General; Animal/Livestock Husbandry and Production; Aquaculture; Crop Production; Dairy Husbandry and Production; Dairy Science; Farm/Farm and Ranch Management; Fishing and Fisheries Sciences and Management; Horse Husbandry/Equine Science and Management; Livestock Management; Plant Sciences, General; Poultry Science; Range Science and Management.

Related DOT Jobs—180.167-014 Field Supervisor, Seed Production; 180.167-022 Group Leader; 180.167-038 Manager, Game Preserve; 180.167-050 Migrant Leader; 183.167-038 Superintendent, Logging; 187.167-218 Manager, Animal Shelter; 401.137-010 Supervisor, Area; 401.137-014 Supervisor, Detasseling Crew; 402.131-010 Supervisor, Vegetable Farming; 403.131-010 Supervisor, Tree-Fruit-and-Nut Farming; 403.131-014 Supervisor, Vine-Fruit Farming; 404.131-010 Supervisor, Field-Crop Farming; 404.131-014 Supervisor, Shed Workers; 405.131-010 Supervisor, Horticultural-Specialty Farming; 405.137-010 Supervisor, Rose-Grading; 407.131-010 Supervisor, Diversified Crops; 408.137-010 Supervisor, Insect and Disease Inspection; 409.117-010 Harvest Contractor; 409.131-010 Supervisor, Picking Crew; 409.137-010 Irrigator, Head; others.

45-1011.01 First-Line Supervisors and Manager/Supervisors—Agricultural Crop Workers

- Education/Training Required: Associate's degree
- Employed: No data available.
- Annual Earnings: $33,330
- Growth: 13.0%
- Annual Job Openings: 8,000

Directly supervise and coordinate activities of agricultural crop workers. Manager/Supervisors are generally found in smaller establishments, where they perform both supervisory and management functions, such as accounting, marketing, and personnel work, and may also engage in the same agricultural work as the workers they supervise.

Assigns duties, such as tilling soil, planting, irrigating, storing crops, and maintaining machines, and assigns fields or rows to workers. Determines number and kind of workers needed to perform required work and schedules activities. Observes workers to detect inefficient and unsafe work procedures or identify problems and initiates actions to correct improper procedure or solve problem. Inspects crops and fields to determine maturity, yield, infestation, or work requirements, such as cultivating, spraying, weeding, or harvesting. Issues farm implements and machinery, ladders, or containers to workers and collects them at end of workday. Recruits, hires, and discharges workers. Investigates grievances and settles disputes to maintain harmony among workers. Contracts with seasonal workers and farmers to provide employment and arranges for transportation, equipment, and living quarters. Trains workers in methods of field work and safety regulations and briefs them on identifying characteristics of insects and diseases. Directs or assists in adjustment, repair, and maintenance of farm machinery and equipment. Prepares time, payroll, and production reports, such as farm conditions, amount of yield, machinery breakdowns, and labor problems. Confers with manager to evaluate weather and soil conditions and to develop and revise plans and procedures. Requisitions and purchases farm supplies, such as insecticides, machine parts or lubricants, and tools. Drives and operates farm machinery, such as trucks, tractors, or self-propelled harvesters, to transport workers or cultivate and harvest fields. Opens gate to permit entry of water into ditches or pipes and signals worker to start flow of water to irrigate fields.

GOE INFORMATION—Interest Area: 03. Plants and Animals. **Work Group:** 03.01. Managerial Work in Plants and Animals. **Personality Type**—Enterprising. Enterprising occupations frequently involve starting up and carrying out projects. These occupations can involve leading people and making many decisions. They sometimes require risk taking and often deal with business. **Work Values**—Authority; Responsibility; Autonomy; Variety; Activity. **Skills**—Management of Personnel Resources; Management of Material Resources; Equipment Selection; Repairing; Coordination; Speaking; Time Management; Instructing. **Abilities**—*Cognitive:* Number Facility; Problem Sensitivity; Oral Comprehension; Oral Expression; Deductive Reasoning. *Psychomotor:* Multilimb Coordination; Control Precision; Response Orientation; Wrist-Finger Speed. *Physical:* Static Strength; Extent Flexibility; Gross Body Coordination; Trunk Strength; Dynamic Strength. *Sensory:* Far Vision; Depth Perception; Speech Recognition; Sound Localization; Glare Sensitivity. **General Work Activities**—*Information Input:* Monitoring Processes, Materials, or Surroundings; Getting Information; Identifying Objects, Actions, and Events. *Mental Process:* Scheduling Work and Activities; Processing Information; Making Decisions and Solving Problems. *Work Output:* Repairing and Maintaining Mechanical Equipment; Performing General Physical Activities; Handling and Moving Objects. *Interacting with Others:* Communicating with Other Workers; Guiding, Directing, and Motivating Subordinates; Coordinating the Work and Activities of Others. **Physical Work Conditions**—Outdoors; Hazardous Equipment; Contaminants; Hazardous Conditions; Minor Burns, Cuts, Bites, or Stings. **Other Job Characteristics**—Consequence of Error; Pace Determined by Speed of Equipment; Importance of Repeating Same Tasks.

Experience—Job Zone 3. Previous work-related skill, knowledge, or experience is required. **Job Preparation:** SVP 6.0 to less than 7.0—more than one year and less than four years. **Knowledge**—Food Production; Personnel and Human Resources; Administration and Management; Biology; Mechanical. **Instructional Programs**—Agricultural Business and Management, Other; Agricultural Production Operations, General; Agricultural Production Operations, Other; Agriculture, Agriculture Operations, and Related Sciences, Other; Agronomy and Crop Science; Aquaculture; Crop Production; Farm/Farm and Ranch Management; Fishing and Fisheries Sciences and Management; Plant Sciences, General; Range Science and Management.

Related DOT Jobs—180.167-014 Field Supervisor, Seed Production; 180.167-022 Group Leader; 180.167-050 Migrant Leader; 401.137-010 Supervisor, Area; 401.137-014 Supervisor, Detasseling Crew; 402.131-010 Supervisor, Vegetable Farming; 403.131-010 Supervisor, Tree-Fruit-and-Nut Farming; 403.131-014 Supervisor, Vine-Fruit Farming; 404.131-010 Supervisor, Field-Crop Farming; 404.131-014 Supervisor, Shed Workers; 407.131-010 Supervisor, Diversified Crops; 408.137-010 Supervisor, Insect and Disease Inspection; 409.117-010 Harvest Contractor; 409.131-010 Supervisor, Picking Crew; 409.137-010 Irrigator, Head; 409.137-014 Row Boss, Hoeing; 929.137-034 Yard Supervisor, Cotton Gin.

45-1011.02 First-Line Supervisors and Manager/Supervisors—Animal Husbandry Workers

- **Education/Training Required: Associate's degree**
- **Employed: No data available.**
- **Annual Earnings: $33,330**
- **Growth: 13.0%**
- **Annual Job Openings: 8,000**

Directly supervise and coordinate activities of animal husbandry workers. Manager/Supervisors are generally found in smaller establishments, where they perform both supervisory and management functions, such as accounting, marketing, and personnel work, and may also engage in the same animal husbandry work as the workers they supervise.

Assigns workers to tasks such as feeding and treating animals, cleaning quarters, transferring animals, and maintaining facilities. Oversees animal care, maintenance, breeding, or packing and transfer activities to ensure work is done correctly and to identify and solve problems. Plans and prepares work schedules. Studies feed, weight, health, genetic, or milk production records to determine feed formula and rations or breeding schedule. Recruits, hires, and pays workers. Confers with manager to discuss and ascertain production requirements, condition of equipment and supplies, and work schedules. Inspects buildings, fences, fields or range, supplies, and equipment to determine work to be done. Observes animals, such as cattle, sheep, poultry, or game animals, for signs of illness, injury, nervousness, or unnatural behavior. Notifies veterinarian and manager of serious illnesses or injuries to animals. Trains workers in animal care, artificial insemination techniques, egg candling and sorting, and transfer of animals. Prepares animal condition, production, feed consumption, and worker attendance reports. Requisitions equipment, materials, and supplies. Transports or arranges for transport of animals, equipment, food, animal feed, and other supplies to and from work site. Inseminates livestock artificially to produce desired offspring and to demonstrate techniques to farmers. Treats animal illness or injury, following experience or instructions of veterinarian. Monitors eggs and adjusts incubator thermometer and gauges to ascertain hatching progress and maintain specified conditions.

GOE INFORMATION—Interest Area: 03. Plants and Animals. **Work Group:** 03.01. Managerial Work in Plants and Animals. **Personality Type**—Enterprising. Enterprising occupations frequently involve starting up and carrying out projects. These occupations can involve leading people and making many decisions. They sometimes require risk taking and often deal with business. **Work Values**—Authority; Responsibility; Autonomy; Variety; Activity. **Skills**—Management of Personnel Resources; Equipment Selection; Management of Material Resources; Systems Evaluation; Instructing; Systems Analysis; Time Management; Coordination. **Abilities**—*Cognitive:* Perceptual Speed; Problem Sensitivity; Memorization; Category Flexibility; Spatial Orientation. *Psychomotor:* Manual Dexterity; Speed of Limb Movement; Reaction Time; Finger Dexterity; Arm-Hand Steadiness. *Physical:* Dynamic Strength; Gross Body Coordination; Explosive Strength; Dynamic Flexibility; Static Strength. *Sensory:* Peripheral Vision; Night Vision; Glare Sensitivity; Visual Color Discrimination; Depth Perception. **General Work Activities**—*Information Input:* Identifying Objects, Actions, and Events; Getting Information; Monitoring Processes, Materials, or Surroundings. *Mental Process:* Scheduling Work and Activities; Judging Qualities of Things, Services, or Other People's Work; Updating and Using Relevant Knowledge. *Work Output:* Handling and Moving Objects; Performing General Physical Activities; Documenting or Recording Information. *Interacting with Others:* Establishing and Maintaining Relationships; Staffing Organizational Units; Communicating with Other Workers. **Physical Work Conditions**—Outdoors; Disease or Infections; Contaminants; Very Hot or Cold; Walking or Running. **Other Job Characteristics**—Importance of Being Exact or Accurate; Consequence of Error; Importance of Repeating Same Tasks.

Experience—Job Zone 3. Previous work-related skill, knowledge, or experience is required. **Job Preparation:** SVP 6.0 to less than 7.0—more than one year and less than four years. **Knowledge**—Food Production; Biology; Personnel and Human Resources; Administration and Management; Medicine and Dentistry. **Instructional Programs**—Agricultural Animal Breeding; Agricultural Business and Management, Other; Agricultural Production Operations, General; Agricultural Production Operations, Other; Agriculture, Agriculture Operations, and Related Sciences, Other; Animal Nutrition; Animal Sciences, General; Animal/Livestock Husbandry and Production; Aquaculture; Dairy Husbandry and Production; Dairy Science; Farm/Farm and Ranch Management; Fishing and Fisheries Sciences and Management; Horse Husbandry/Equine Science and Management; Livestock Management; Poultry Science; Range Science and Management.

Related DOT Jobs—410.131-010 Barn Boss; 410.131-014 Supervisor, Artificial Breeding Ranch; 410.131-018 Supervisor, Dairy Farm; 410.131-022 Supervisor, Stock Ranch; 410.134-010 Supervisor, Livestock-Yard; 410.134-014 Supervisor, Wool-Shearing; 410.134-022 Supervisor, Research Dairy Farm; 410.137-010 Camp Tender; 410.137-014 Top Screw; 411.131-010 Supervisor, Poultry Farm; 411.137-010 Supervisor, Poultry Hatchery; 412.131-010 Supervisor, Game Farm.

45-1011.03 First-Line Supervisors and Manager/Supervisors—Animal Care Workers, Except Livestock

- **Education/Training Required: Associate's degree**
- **Employed: No data available.**
- **Annual Earnings: $33,330**
- **Growth: 13.0%**
- **Annual Job Openings: 8,000**

Directly supervise and coordinate activities of animal care workers. Manager/Supervisors are generally found in smaller establishments, where they perform both supervisory and management functions, such as accounting, marketing, and personnel work, and may also engage in the same animal care work as the workers they supervise.

Assigns workers to tasks such as feeding and treatment of animals and cleaning and maintenance of animal quarters. Establishes work schedule and procedures of animal care. Monitors animal care and inspects facilities to identify problems and discusses solutions with workers. Trains workers in animal care procedures, maintenance duties, and safety precautions. Directs and assists workers in maintenance and repair of facilities. Plans budget and arranges for purchase of animals, feed, or supplies. Observes and examines animals to detect signs of illness and determine need of services from veterinarian. Prepares reports concerning activity of facility, employees' time records, and animal treatment. Investigates complaints of animal neglect or cruelty and follows up on complaints appearing to justify prosecution. Operates euthanasia equipment to destroy animals. Delivers lectures to public to stimulate interest in animals and communicate humane philosophy to public.

GOE INFORMATION—Interest Area: 03. Plants and Animals. **Work Group:** 03.01. Managerial Work in Plants and Animals. **Personality Type—**Realistic. Realistic occupations frequently involve work activities that include practical, hands-on problems and solutions. They often deal with plants, animals, and real-world materials like wood, tools, and machinery. Many of the occupations require working outside and do not involve a lot of paperwork or working closely with others. **Work Values—**Authority; Responsibility; Autonomy; Creativity; Activity. **Skills—**Management of Financial Resources; Instructing; Management of Personnel Resources; Management of Material Resources; Speaking; Systems Evaluation; Writing; Systems Analysis. **Abilities—***Cognitive:* Problem Sensitivity; Speed of Closure; Written Expression; Oral Expression; Written Comprehension. *Psychomotor:* Manual Dexterity; Control Precision; Response Orientation; Speed of Limb Movement; Reaction Time. *Physical:* Gross Body Coordination; Static Strength; Explosive Strength; Extent Flexibility; Trunk Strength. *Sensory:* Peripheral Vision; Far Vision; Auditory Attention; Sound Localization; Night Vision. **General Work Activities—***Information Input:* Identifying Objects, Actions, and Events; Monitoring Processes, Materials, or Surroundings; Getting Information. *Mental Process:* Organizing, Planning, and Prioritizing; Scheduling Work and Activities; Making Decisions and Solving Problems. *Work Output:* Performing General Physical Activities; Handling and Moving Objects; Documenting or Recording Information. *Interacting with Others:* Communicating with Other Workers; Coordinating the Work and Activities of Others; Communicating with Persons Outside Organization. **Physical Work Conditions—**Disease or Infections; Minor Burns, Cuts, Bites, or Stings; Outdoors; Hazardous Conditions; Kneeling, Crouching, or Crawling. **Other Job Characteristics—**Importance of Being Exact or Accurate; Consequence of Error; Importance of Repeating Same Tasks.

Experience—Job Zone 3. Previous work-related skill, knowledge, or experience is required. **Job Preparation:** SVP 6.0 to less than 7.0—more than one year and less than four years. **Knowledge—**Administration and Management; Biology; Medicine and Dentistry; Education and Training; Personnel and Human Resources. **Instructional Programs—**Agricultural Business and Management, Other; Agricultural Production Operations, General; Agricultural Production Operations, Other; Agriculture, Agriculture Operations, and Related Sciences, Other; Animal Nutrition; Animal Sciences, General; Aquaculture; Farm/Farm and Ranch Management; Fishing and Fisheries Sciences and Management; Range Science and Management.

Related DOT Jobs—180.167-038 Manager, Game Preserve; 187.167-218 Manager, Animal Shelter; 410.134-018 Supervisor, Kennel; 410.137-018 Supervisor, Animal Maintenance; 412.137-010 Animal Keeper, Head; 418.137-010 Supervisor, Laboratory Animal Facility; 418.137-014 Supervisor, Research Kennel.

45-1011.04 First-Line Supervisors and Manager/Supervisors—Horticultural Workers

- **Education/Training Required: Associate's degree**
- **Employed: No data available.**
- **Annual Earnings: $33,330**
- **Growth: 13.0%**
- **Annual Job Openings: 8,000**

Directly supervise and coordinate activities of horticultural workers. Manager/Supervisors are generally found in smaller establishments, where they perform both supervisory and management functions, such as accounting, marketing, and personnel work, and may also engage in the same horticultural work as the workers they supervise.

Assigns workers to duties such as cultivation, harvesting, maintenance, grading and packing products, or altering greenhouse environmental conditions. Reviews employees' work to ascertain quality and quantity of work performed. Estimates work-hour requirements to plant, cultivate, or harvest and prepares work schedule. Reads inventory records, customer orders, and shipping schedules to ascertain day's activities. Confers with management to report conditions, plan planting and harvesting schedules, and discuss changes in fertilizer, herbicides, or cultivating techniques. Observes plants, flowers, shrubs, and trees in greenhouses, cold frames, or fields to ascertain condition. Inspects facilities to determine maintenance needs, such as malfunctioning environmental- control system, clogged sprinklers, or missing glass panes in greenhouse. Trains employees in horticultural techniques, such as transplanting and weeding, shearing and harvesting trees, and grading and packing flowers. Prepares and submits written or oral reports of personnel actions, such as performance evaluations, hires, promotions, and discipline. Maintains records of employees' hours worked and work completed. Drives and operates heavy machinery, such as dump truck, tractor, or growth-media tiller, to transport materials and supplies.

GOE INFORMATION—Interest Area: 03. Plants and Animals. **Work Group:** 03.01. Managerial Work in Plants and Animals. **Personality Type—**Realistic. Realistic occupations frequently involve work activities that include practical, hands-on problems and solutions. They often deal with plants, animals, and real-world materials like wood, tools, and machinery. Many of the occupations require working outside and do not involve a lot of paperwork or working closely with others. **Work Values—**Authority; Responsibility; Autonomy; Creativity; Variety. **Skills—**Management of Personnel Resources; Operation Monitoring; Equipment Selection; Management of Material Resources; Instructing; Repairing; Troubleshooting; Coordination. **Abilities—***Cognitive:* Spatial Orientation; Oral Expression; Fluency of Ideas; Category Flexibility; Mathematical Reasoning. *Psychomotor:* Multilimb Coordination; Control Precision; Response Orientation; Manual Dexterity; Reaction Time. *Physical:* Static Strength; Dynamic Flexibility; Dynamic Strength; Gross Body Coordination; Gross Body Equilibrium. *Sensory:* Visual Color Discrimination; Glare Sensitivity; Speech Clarity; Far Vision; Auditory Attention. **General Work Activities—***Information Input:* Identifying Objects, Actions, and Events; Getting Information; Inspecting Equipment, Structures, or Materials. *Mental Process:* Organizing, Planning, and Prioritizing; Updating and Using Relevant Knowledge; Making Decisions and Solving Problems. *Work Output:* Performing General Physical Activities; Handling and Moving Objects; Documenting or Recording Information. *Interacting with Others:* Communicating with Other Workers; Establishing and Maintaining Relationships; Coordinating the Work and Activities of Others. **Physical Work Conditions—**Outdoors; Very Hot or Cold; Extremely Bright or Inadequate Lighting; Minor Burns, Cuts, Bites, or Stings; Kneeling, Crouching, or Crawling. **Other Job Characteristics—**Consequence of Error; Importance of Repeating Same Tasks; Pace Determined by Speed of Equipment.

Experience—Job Zone 3. Previous work-related skill, knowledge, or experience is required. **Job Preparation:** SVP 6.0 to less than 7.0—more than one year and less than four years. **Knowledge—**Biology; Personnel and Human Resources; Food Production; Administration and Management; Chemistry. **Instructional Programs—**Agricultural Business and Management, Other; Agricultural Production Operations, General; Agricultural Production Operations, Other; Agriculture, Agriculture Operations, and Related Sciences, Other; Agronomy and Crop Science; Crop Production; Farm/Farm and Ranch Management; Plant Sciences, General.

Related DOT Jobs—405.131-010 Supervisor, Horticultural-Specialty Farming; 405.137-010 Supervisor, Rose-Grading; 451.137-010 Forest Nursery Supervisor; 451.137-014 Supervisor, Christmas-Tree Farm.

45-1011.05 First-Line Supervisors and Manager/Supervisors—Logging Workers

- Education/Training Required: Bachelor's degree
- Employed: No data available.
- Annual Earnings: $33,330
- Growth: 13.0%
- Annual Job Openings: 8,000

Directly supervise and coordinate activities of logging workers. Manager/Supervisors are generally found in smaller establishments, where they perform both supervisory and management functions, such as accounting, marketing, and personnel work, and may also engage in the same logging work as the workers they supervise.

Plans and schedules logging operations, such as felling and bucking trees, grading and sorting logs, and yarding and loading logs. Assigns workers to duties such as trees to be cut, cutting sequence and specifications, and loading of trucks, rail cars, or rafts. Oversees logging operations to identify and solve problems and ensure safety and company regulations are being followed. Coordinates dismantling, moving, and setting up equipment at new work site. Determines methods for logging operations, size of crew, and equipment requirements. Coordinates selection and movement of logs from storage areas according to transportation schedules or production requirements of wood products plant. Changes logging operations or methods to eliminate unsafe conditions and warns or disciplines workers disregarding safety regulations. Confers with mill, company, and government forestry officials to determine safest and most efficient method of logging tract. Trains workers in felling and bucking trees, operating tractors and loading machines, yarding and loading techniques, and safety regulations. Prepares production and personnel time records for management.

GOE INFORMATION—Interest Area: 03. Plants and Animals. **Work Group:** 03.01. Managerial Work in Plants and Animals. **Personality Type—**Realistic. Realistic occupations frequently involve work activities that include practical, hands-on problems and solutions. They often deal with plants, animals, and real-world materials like wood, tools, and machinery. Many of the occupations require working outside and do not involve a lot of paperwork or working closely with others. **Work Values—**Authority; Responsibility; Autonomy; Creativity; Activity. **Skills—**Management of Personnel Resources; Management of Material Resources; Operation and Control; Instructing; Time Management; Coordination; Systems Analysis; Equipment Selection. **Abilities—***Cognitive:* Spatial Orientation; Time Sharing; Originality; Fluency of Ideas; Mathematical

Reasoning. *Psychomotor:* Rate Control; Multilimb Coordination; Speed of Limb Movement; Response Orientation; Reaction Time. *Physical:* Static Strength; Explosive Strength; Dynamic Strength; Stamina; Gross Body Equilibrium. *Sensory:* Auditory Attention; Far Vision; Sound Localization; Depth Perception; Glare Sensitivity. **General Work Activities—***Information Input:* Identifying Objects, Actions, and Events; Getting Information; Inspecting Equipment, Structures, or Materials. *Mental Process:* Scheduling Work and Activities; Making Decisions and Solving Problems; Organizing, Planning, and Prioritizing. *Work Output:* Performing General Physical Activities; Handling and Moving Objects; Controlling Machines and Processes. *Interacting with Others:* Communicating with Other Workers; Coordinating the Work and Activities of Others; Communicating with Persons Outside Organization. **Physical Work Conditions—**Outdoors; Hazardous Equipment; Minor Burns, Cuts, Bites, or Stings; Very Hot or Cold; Distracting Sounds and Noise Levels. **Other Job Characteristics—**Pace Determined by Speed of Equipment; Consequence of Error; Importance of Repeating Same Tasks.

Experience—Job Zone 4. A minimum of two to four years of work-related skill, knowledge, or experience is needed. **Job Preparation:** SVP 7.0 to less than 8.0—two years to less than 10 years. **Knowledge—**Administration and Management; Production and Processing; Education and Training; Personnel and Human Resources; Public Safety and Security. **Instructional Programs—**Agricultural Business and Management, Other; Agricultural Production Operations, General; Agricultural Production Operations, Other; Agriculture, Agriculture Operations, and Related Sciences, Other; Agronomy and Crop Science; Crop Production; Farm/Farm and Ranch Management; Plant Sciences, General.

Related DOT Jobs—183.167-038 Superintendent, Logging; 454.134-010 Supervisor, Felling-Bucking; 455.134-010 Supervisor, Log Sorting; 459.133-010 Supervisor, Logging; 459.137-010 Woods Boss; 921.131-010 Hook Tender.

45-1011.06 First-Line Supervisors and Manager/Supervisors—Fishery Workers

- Education/Training Required: Associate's degree
- Employed: No data available.
- Annual Earnings: $33,330
- Growth: 13.0%
- Annual Job Openings: 8,000

Directly supervise and coordinate activities of fishery workers. Manager/Supervisors are generally found in smaller establishments, where they perform both supervisory and management functions, such as accounting, marketing, and personnel work, and may also engage in the same fishery work as the workers they supervise.

Assigns workers to duties such as fertilizing and incubating spawn, feeding and transferring fish, and planting, cultivating, and harvesting shellfish beds. Oversees worker activities such as treatment and rearing of fingerlings, maintenance of equipment, and harvesting of fish or shellfish. Directs workers to correct deviations or problems, such as disease, quality of seed distribution, or adequacy of cultivation. Plans work schedules according to availability of personnel and equipment, tidal levels, feeding schedules, or need for transfer or harvest. Trains workers in spawning, rearing, cultivating, and harvesting methods and use of equipment. Observes fish and beds or ponds to detect diseases, determine quality of fish, or determine completeness of harvesting. Confers with manager to determine time and place of seed planting and cultivating, feeding, or harvesting of fish or shellfish. Records number and type of fish or shellfish reared and harvested and keeps workers' time records.

GOE INFORMATION—Interest Area: 03. Plants and Animals. Work Group: 03.01. Managerial Work in Plants and Animals. Personality Type—Realistic. Realistic occupations frequently involve work activities that include practical, hands-on problems and solutions. They often deal with plants, animals, and real-world materials like wood, tools, and machinery. Many of the occupations require working outside or working closely with others. Work Values—Authority; Responsibility; Autonomy; Creativity; Achievement. Skills—Management of Personnel Resources; Instructing; Operation and Control; Systems Analysis; Management of Material Resources; Time Management; Equipment Selection. Abilities—*Cognitive:* Flexibility of Closure; Speed of Closure; Category Flexibility; Deductive Reasoning; Perceptual Speed. *Psychomotor:* Wrist-Finger Speed; Speed of Limb Movement; Arm-Hand Steadiness; Rate Control; Control Precision. *Physical:* Gross Body Coordination; Gross Body Equilibrium; Trunk Strength; Dynamic Strength; Static Strength. *Sensory:* Depth Perception; Far Vision; Glare Sensitivity; Visual Color Discrimination; Hearing Sensitivity. General Work Activities—*Information Input:* Monitoring Processes, Materials, or Surroundings; Identifying Objects, Actions, and Events; Getting Information. *Mental Process:* Scheduling Work and Activities; Organizing, Planning, and Prioritizing; Updating and Using Relevant Knowledge. *Work Output:* Performing General Physical Activities; Handling and Moving Objects; Documenting or Recording Information. *Interacting with Others:* Coordinating the Work and Activities of Others; Communicating with Other Workers; Establishing and Maintaining Relationships. Physical Work Conditions—Outdoors; Walking or Running; Disease or Infections; Extremely Bright or Inadequate Lighting; Very Hot or Cold. Other Job Characteristics—Consequence of Error; Degree of Automation; Importance of Repeating Same Tasks.

Experience—Job Zone 3. Previous work-related skill, knowledge, or experience is required. Job Preparation: SVP 6.0 to less than 7.0—more than one year and less than four years. Knowledge—Food Production; Biology; Personnel and Human Resources; Administration and Management; Production and Processing. Instructional Programs—Agricultural Animal Breeding; Agricultural Business and Management, Other; Agricultural Production Operations, General; Agricultural Production Operations, Other; Agriculture, Agriculture Operations, and Related Sciences, Other; Animal Nutrition; Animal Sciences, General; Animal/Livestock Husbandry and Production; Farm/Farm and Ranch Management; Fishing and Fisheries Sciences and Management.

Related DOT Jobs—446.133-010 Supervisor, Shellfish Farming; 446.134-010 Supervisor, Fish Hatchery.

45-1012.00 Farm Labor Contractors

- Education/Training Required: Work experience in a related occupation
- Employed: No data available.
- Annual Earnings: $14,760
- Growth: 13.0%
- Annual Job Openings: 8,000

Recruit, hire, furnish, and supervise seasonal or temporary agricultural laborers for a fee. May transport, house, and provide meals for workers.

No task data available.

GOE INFORMATION—Interest Area: 03. Plants and Animals. Work Group: 03.01. Managerial Work in Plants and Animals. Note: The Department of Labor has not collected some data for this job, so it has fewer details than the other descriptions.

Instructional Programs—Agricultural and Domestic Animal Services, Other.

Related DOT Jobs—409.117-010 Harvest Contractor.

45-2000 Agricultural Workers

45-2011.00 Agricultural Inspectors

- Education/Training Required: Work experience in a related occupation
- Employed: 14,964
- Annual Earnings: $27,400
- Growth: 6.6%
- Annual Job Openings: 1,000

Inspect agricultural commodities, processing equipment, and facilities and fish and logging operations to ensure compliance with regulations and laws governing health, quality, and safety.

Inspects facilities and equipment for adequacy, sanitation, and compliance with regulations. Inspects horticultural products or livestock to detect harmful disease, infestation, or growth rate. Examines, weighs, and measures commodities such as poultry, eggs, meat, and seafood to certify wholesomeness, grade, and weight. Inspects livestock to determine effectiveness of medication and feeding programs. Writes reports of findings and recommendations and advises farmer, grower, or processor of corrective action to be taken. Collects sample of pests or suspected diseased animals or materials and routes to laboratory for identification and analysis. Advises farmers and growers of development programs or new equipment and techniques to aid in quality production, applying agricultural knowledge. Testifies in legal proceedings.

GOE INFORMATION—Interest Area: 04. Law, Law Enforcement, and Public Safety. Work Group: 04.04. Public Safety. Personality Type—Realistic. Realistic occupations frequently involve work activities that include practical, hands-on problems and solutions. They often deal with plants, animals, and real-world materials like wood, tools, and machinery. Many of the occupations require working outside and do not involve a lot of paperwork or working closely with others. Work Values—Responsibility; Autonomy; Security; Independence; Variety. Skills—Quality Control Analysis; Operation Monitoring; Reading Comprehension; Writing; Speaking; Science; Complex Problem Solving; Critical Thinking. Abilities—*Cognitive:* Written Expression; Problem Sensitivity; Inductive Reasoning; Flexibility of Closure; Originality. *Psychomotor:* Wrist-Finger Speed; Arm-Hand Steadiness; Manual Dexterity; Finger Dexterity; Control Precision. *Physical:* Gross Body Coordination; Gross Body Equilibrium; Explosive Strength; Stamina; Trunk Strength. *Sensory:* Speech Clarity; Near Vision; Visual Color Discrimination; Far Vision; Speech Recognition. General Work Activities—*Information Input:* Identifying Objects, Actions, and Events; Inspecting Equipment, Structures, or Materials; Getting Information. *Mental Process:* Evaluating Information Against Standards; Making Decisions and Solving Problems; Judging Qualities of Things, Services, or Other People's Work. *Work Output:* Documenting or Recording Information; Handling and Moving Objects; Drafting and Specifying Technical Devices. *Interacting with Others:* Providing Consultation and Advice to Others; Communicating with Persons Outside Organization; Interpreting Meaning of Information for Others. Physical Work Conditions—Outdoors; Walking or Running; Disease or Infections; Very Hot or Cold; Distracting Sounds and Noise Levels. Other Job Characteristics—Consequence of Error; Importance of Being Exact or Accurate; Importance of Repeating Same Tasks.

Experience—Job Zone 4. A minimum of two to four years of work-related skill, knowledge, or experience is needed. **Job Preparation:** SVP 7.0 to less than 8.0—two years to less than 10 years. **Knowledge**—Food Production; Biology; Production and Processing; Law and Government; Chemistry. **Instructional Programs**—Agricultural and Food Products Processing.

Related DOT Jobs—168.287-010 Inspector, Agricultural Commodities; 411.267-010 Field Service Technician, Poultry.

45-2021.00 Animal Breeders

- Education/Training Required: Associate's degree
- Employed: No data available.
- Annual Earnings: $22,650
- Growth: 3.7%
- Annual Job Openings: 39,000

Breed animals, including cattle, goats, horses, sheep, swine, poultry, dogs, cats, or pet birds. Select and breed animals according to their genealogy, characteristics, and offspring. May require a knowledge of artificial insemination techniques and equipment use. May involve keeping records on heats, birth intervals, or pedigree.

Adjust controls in order to maintain specific building temperatures required for animals' health and safety. Attach rubber collecting sheaths to genitals of tethered bull and stimulate animal's organ in order to induce ejaculation. Confine roosters (pinioning) in order to collect semen in vial. Examine animals in order to detect symptoms of illness or injury. Examine semen microscopically in order to assess and record density and motility of gametes and dilute semen with prescribed diluents according to formulas. Incubate eggs to induce hatching. Inject prepared animal semen into female animals for breeding purposes by inserting nozzle of syringe into vagina and depressing syringe plunger. Inject semen into hens' oviducts or through holes in eggshells. Maintain logs of semen specimens used and animals bred. Measure specified amounts of semen into calibrated syringes and insert syringes into inseminating guns. Observe animals in heat in order to detect approach of estrus and exercise animals to induce or hasten estrus, if necessary. Package and label semen to be used for artificial insemination, recording information such as the date, source, quality, and concentration. Prepare containers of semen for freezing and storage or shipment, placing them in dry ice or liquid nitrogen. Record animal characteristics such as weights, growth patterns, and diets. Select animals to be bred and semen specimens to be used according to knowledge of animals, genealogies, traits, and desired offspring characteristics. Arrange for sale of animals and eggs to hospitals, research centers, pet shops, and food processing plants. Brand, tattoo, or tag animals in order to allow animal identification. Build hutches, pens, and fenced yards. Clip or shear hair on animals. Exhibit animals at shows. Feed and water animals and clean and disinfect pens, cages, yards, and hutches. Kill animals, remove their pelts, and arrange for sale of pelts. Milk cows and goats. Perform procedures such as animal dehorning or castration. Place vaccines in drinking water, inject vaccines, or dust air with vaccine powder in order to protect animals from diseases. Treat minor injuries and ailments and contact veterinarians in order to obtain treatment for animals with serious illnesses or injuries.

GOE INFORMATION—Interest Area: 03. Plants and Animals. Work Group: 03.02. Animal Care and Training. Personality Type—Realistic. Realistic occupations frequently involve work activities that include practical, hands-on problems and solutions. They often deal with plants, animals, and real-world materials like wood, tools, and machinery. Many of the occupations require working outside and do not involve a lot of paperwork or working closely with others. Work Values—Responsibil-ity; Independence; Autonomy; Creativity; Activity. **Skills**—Equipment Selection. **Abilities**—*Cognitive:* Deductive Reasoning. *Psychomotor:* Control Precision; Speed of Limb Movement. *Physical:* Static Strength; Explosive Strength; Dynamic Strength; Extent Flexibility; Trunk Strength. *Sensory:* Peripheral Vision. **General Work Activities**—*Information Input:* Identifying Objects, Actions, and Events; Monitoring Processes, Materials, or Surroundings; Getting Information. *Mental Process:* Judging Qualities of Things, Services, or Other People's Work; Updating and Using Relevant Knowledge; Organizing, Planning, and Prioritizing. *Work Output:* Performing General Physical Activities; Handling and Moving Objects; Documenting or Recording Information. *Interacting with Others:* Monitoring and Controlling Resources; Influencing Others or Selling; Communicating with Persons Outside Organization. **Physical Work Conditions**—Minor Burns, Cuts, Bites, or Stings; Outdoors; Kneeling, Crouching, or Crawling; Distracting Sounds and Noise Levels; Bending or Twisting the Body. **Other Job Characteristics**—Importance of Repeating Same Tasks; Consequence of Error; Pace Determined by Speed of Equipment.

Experience—Job Zone 3. Previous work-related skill, knowledge, or experience is required. **Job Preparation:** SVP 6.0 to less than 7.0—more than one year and less than four years. **Knowledge**—Food Production; Sales and Marketing; Biology; Medicine and Dentistry; Building and Construction. **Instructional Programs**—Animal/Livestock Husbandry and Production; Horse Husbandry/Equine Science and Management.

Related DOT Jobs—410.161-010 Animal Breeder; 410.161-014 Fur Farmer; 410.161-018 Livestock Rancher; 410.161-022 Hog-Confinement-System Manager; 411.161-010 Canary Breeder; 411.161-014 Poultry Breeder; 413.161-014 Reptile Farmer.

45-2041.00 Graders and Sorters, Agricultural Products

- Education/Training Required: Work experience in a related occupation
- Employed: 63,257
- Annual Earnings: $15,440
- Growth: 9.1%
- Annual Job Openings: 12,000

Grade, sort, or classify unprocessed food and other agricultural products by size, weight, color, or condition.

Grades and sorts products according to factors such as color, length, width, appearance, feel, and smell. Segregates products on conveyor belt or table according to grade, color, size, fiber quality, species, deformities, and sex. Weighs and places products in containers according to grade and marks grade on containers. Estimates weight of product visually and by feel. Records grade on tag or shipping, receiving, or sales sheet. Examines product fibers through microscope to determine maturity and spirality of fibers. Pulls product sample apart between fingers to determine fiber quality. Discards inferior or defective products and foreign matter and places acceptable products in containers for further processing.

GOE INFORMATION—Interest Area: 08. Industrial Production. Work Group: 08.03. Production Work. Personality Type—Realistic. Realistic occupations frequently involve work activities that include practical, hands-on problems and solutions. They often deal with plants, animals, and real-world materials like wood, tools, and machinery. Many of the occupations require working outside and do not involve a lot of paperwork or working closely with others. Work Values—Independence; Supervision, Technical; Moral Values; Supervision, Human Relations; Responsibility. **Skills**—None met the criteria. **Abilities**—*Cognitive:* Perceptual Speed; Category Flexibility; Flexibility of Closure; Speed of Closure; Selective Attention. *Psychomotor:* Speed of Limb Movement; Finger Dexterity; Rate Control; Manual Dexterity; Arm-Hand Steadiness. *Physical:* Explosive Strength; Dynamic Flexibility; Dynamic Strength; Extent Flexibility; Static Strength. *Sensory:* Visual Color Discrimination; Depth Perception; Hearing Sensitivity; Peripheral Vision; Sound Localization. **General Work Activities**—*Information Input:* Identifying Objects, Actions, and Events; Inspecting Equipment, Structures, or Materials; Getting Information. *Mental Process:* Judging Qualities of Things, Services, or Other People's Work; Evaluating Information Against Standards; Processing Information. *Work Output:* Handling and Moving Objects; Performing General Physical Activities; Controlling Machines and Processes. *Interacting with Others:* Establishing and Maintaining Relationships; Communicating with Other Workers; Monitoring and Controlling Resources. **Physical Work Conditions**—Making Repetitive Motions; Using Hands on Objects, Tools, or Controls; Indoors; Standing; Contaminants. **Other Job Characteristics**—Importance of Repeating Same Tasks; Pace Determined by Speed of Equipment; Degree of Automation.

Experience—Job Zone 1. No previous work-related skill, knowledge, or experience is needed. **Job Preparation:** SVP below 4.0—less than six months. **Knowledge**—Production and Processing; Food Production. **Instructional Programs**—Agricultural/Farm Supplies Retailing and Wholesaling.

Related DOT Jobs—409.687-010 Inspector-Grader, Agricultural Establishment; 410.687-026 Wool-Fleece Sorter; 411.687-010 Chick Grader; 411.687-014 Chick Sexer; 429.387-010 Cotton Classer; 429.587-010 Cotton Classer Aide; 446.687-010 Clam Sorter; 522.384-010 Fish Roe Technician; 529.687-074 Egg Candler; 529.687-186 Sorter, Agricultural Produce; 589.387-014 Wool Sorter; 589.687-054 Wool-Fleece Grader.

45-2091.00 Agricultural Equipment Operators

- ● **Education/Training Required: Moderate-term on-the-job training**
- ● **Employed: No data available.**
- ● **Annual Earnings: $16,640**
- ● **Growth: 3.3%**
- ● **Annual Job Openings: 39,000**

Drive and control farm equipment to till soil and to plant, cultivate, and harvest crops. May perform tasks such as crop baling or hay bucking. May operate stationary equipment to perform post-harvest tasks, such as husking, shelling, threshing, and ginning.

Drives tractor with implements to plow, plant, cultivate, or harvest crops and to move trailers for crop harvest. Manipulates controls to set, activate, and regulate mechanisms on machinery such as self-propelled machines, conveyors, separators, cleaners, and dryers. Drives truck to haul harvested crops, supplies, tools, or farm workers. Drives truck, or tractor with trailer attached, alongside crew loading crop or adjacent to harvesting machine. Sprays fertilizer or pesticide solutions, using hand sprayer, to control insects, fungus and weed growth, and diseases. Observes and listens to machinery operation to detect equipment malfunction and removes obstruction to avoid damage to product or machinery. Attaches farm implements, such as plow, disc, sprayer, or harvester, to tractor, using bolts and mechanic's hand tools. Discards diseased or rotting product and guides product on conveyor to regulate flow through machine. Positions boxes or attaches bags at discharge end of machinery to catch products,

places lids on boxes, and closes sacks. Thins, hoes, weeds, or prunes row crops, fruit trees, or vines, using hand implements. Loads hoppers, containers, or conveyor to feed machine with products, using suction gates, shovel, or pitchfork. Adjusts, repairs, lubricates, and services farm machinery and notifies supervisor or appropriate personnel when machinery malfunctions. Walks beside or rides on planting machine while inserting plants in planter mechanism at specified intervals. Irrigates soil, using portable pipe or ditch system, and maintains ditch or pipe and pumps. Mixes specified materials or chemicals and dumps solutions, powders, or seeds into planter or sprayer machinery. Loads and unloads crops or containers of materials manually or using conveyors, handtruck, forklift, or transfer auger. Weighs crop-filled containers and records weights and other identifying information. Hand-picks fruit, such as apples, oranges, or strawberries. Oversees work crew engaged in planting, weeding, or harvesting activities.

GOE INFORMATION—**Interest Area:** 03. Plants and Animals. **Work Group:** 03.03. Hands-on Work in Plants and Animals. **Personality Type**—Realistic. Realistic occupations frequently involve work activities that include practical, hands-on problems and solutions. They often deal with plants, animals, and real-world materials like wood, tools, and machinery. Many of the occupations require working outside and do not involve a lot of paperwork or working closely with others. **Work Values**—Moral Values; Authority; Variety; Independence; Autonomy. **Skills**—Repairing; Operation and Control; Operation Monitoring; Equipment Selection; Installation; Systems Analysis. **Abilities**—*Cognitive:* Spatial Orientation; Information Ordering; Time Sharing; Visualization; Category Flexibility. *Psychomotor:* Multilimb Coordination; Rate Control; Control Precision; Manual Dexterity; Reaction Time. *Physical:* Static Strength; Stamina; Dynamic Strength; Explosive Strength; Trunk Strength. *Sensory:* Hearing Sensitivity; Far Vision; Night Vision; Peripheral Vision; Sound Localization. **General Work Activities**—*Information Input:* Monitoring Processes, Materials, or Surroundings; Inspecting Equipment, Structures, or Materials; Identifying Objects, Actions, and Events. *Mental Process:* Judging Qualities of Things, Services, or Other People's Work; Organizing, Planning, and Prioritizing; Making Decisions and Solving Problems. *Work Output:* Performing General Physical Activities; Handling and Moving Objects; Controlling Machines and Processes. *Interacting with Others:* Coordinating the Work and Activities of Others; Communicating with Other Workers; Establishing and Maintaining Relationships. **Physical Work Conditions**—Outdoors; Hazardous Equipment; Minor Burns, Cuts, Bites, or Stings; Very Hot or Cold; Contaminants. **Other Job Characteristics**—Pace Determined by Speed of Equipment; Degree of Automation; Importance of Repeating Same Tasks.

Experience—Job Zone 2. Some previous work-related skill, knowledge, or experience may be helpful, but usually is not needed. **Job Preparation:** SVP 4.0 to less than 6.0—six months to less than two years. **Knowledge**—Food Production; Chemistry; Mechanical; Physics; Biology. **Instructional Programs**—Agricultural Power Machinery Operation.

Related DOT Jobs—401.683-010 Farmworker, Grain I; 401.683-014 Farmworker, Rice; 402.663-010 Farmworker, Vegetable I; 403.683-010 Farmworker, Fruit I; 404.663-010 Farmworker, Field Crop I; 404.685-010 Seed-Potato Arranger; 405.683-010 Farmworker, Bulbs; 405.683-014 Growth-Media Mixer, Mushroom; 407.663-010 Farmworker, Diversified Crops I; 409.683-010 Farm-Machine Operator; 409.683-014 Field Hauler; 409.685-010 Farm-Machine Tender; 409.686-010 Farmworker, Machine; 421.683-010 Farmworker, General I; 429.685-010 Ginner; 429.685-014 Thresher, Broomcorn.

45-2092.00 Farmworkers and Laborers, Crop, Nursery, and Greenhouse

- **Education/Training Required: Short-term on-the-job training**
- **Employed: No data available.**
- **Annual Earnings: $14,500**
- **Growth: 3.3%**
- **Annual Job Openings: 192,000**

Manually plant, cultivate, and harvest vegetables, fruits, nuts, horticultural specialties, and field crops. Use hand tools, such as shovels, trowels, hoes, tampers, pruning hooks, shears, and knives. Duties may include tilling soil and applying fertilizers; transplanting, weeding, thinning, or pruning crops; applying pesticides; and cleaning, grading, sorting, packing, and loading harvested products. May construct trellises, repair fences and farm buildings, or participate in irrigation activities.

No task data available.

GOE INFORMATION—Interest Area: 03. Plants and Animals. **Work Group:** 03.03. Hands-on Work in Plants and Animals. **Note:** The Department of Labor has not collected some data for this job, so it has fewer details than the other descriptions.

Instructional Programs—Agricultural Production Operations, General; Crop Production.

Related DOT Jobs—401.687-010 Farmworker, Grain II; 402.687-010 Farmworker, Vegetable II; 402.687-014 Harvest Worker, Vegetable; 403.687-010 Farmworker, Fruit II; 403.687-014 Fig Caprifier; 403.687-018 Harvest Worker, Fruit; 404.686-010 Seed Cutter; 404.687-010 Farmworker, Field Crop II; 404.687-014 Harvest Worker, Field Crop; 405.684-010 Budder; 405.687-014 Horticultural Worker II; 407.687-010 Farmworker, Diversified Crops II; 409.684-010 Irrigator, Valve Pipe; 409.685-014 Irrigator, Sprinkling System; 409.687-014 Irrigator, Gravity Flow; 409.687-018 Weeder-Thinner; 421.683-010 Farmworker, General I; 421.687-010 Farmworker, General II; 954.362-010 Ditch Rider.

45-2092.01 Nursery Workers

- **Education/Training Required: Short-term on-the-job training**
- **Employed: No data available.**
- **Annual Earnings: $14,500**
- **Growth: 3.3%**
- **Annual Job Openings: 192,000**

Work in nursery facilities or at customer location planting, cultivating, harvesting, and transplanting trees, shrubs, or plants.

Hauls and spreads topsoil, fertilizer, peat moss, and other materials to condition soil, using wheelbarrow or cart and shovel. Digs, rakes, and screens soil and fills cold frames and hot beds to prepare them for planting. Sows grass seed or plants plugs of grass and cuts, rolls, and stacks sod. Plants, sprays, weeds, and waters plants, shrubs, and trees, using hand tools and gardening tools. Cuts and opens incision in rootstock, using budding knife, and inserts and ties bud. Fills growing tanks with water. Inspects bud tie to ensure quality. Moves containerized shrubs, plants, and trees, using wheelbarrow. Traps and destroys pests, such as moles, gophers, and mice, using pesticides. Ties, bunches, wraps roots of, and packs flowers, plants, shrubs, and trees to fill orders. Folds and staples corrugated forms to make boxes used for packing horticultural products. Dips rose cuttings into vat to disinfect prior to storage.

GOE INFORMATION—Interest Area: 03. Plants and Animals. **Work Group:** 03.03. Hands-on Work in Plants and Animals. **Personality Type—**Realistic. Realistic occupations frequently involve work activities that include practical, hands-on problems and solutions. They often deal with plants, animals, and real-world materials like wood, tools, and machinery. Many of the occupations require working outside and do not involve a lot of paperwork or working closely with others. **Work Values—**Moral Values; Supervision, Technical; Independence; Supervision, Human Relations; Company Policies and Practices. **Skills—**None met the criteria. **Abilities—***Cognitive:* Flexibility of Closure; Spatial Orientation; Perceptual Speed; Visualization; Speed of Closure. *Psychomotor:* Speed of Limb Movement; Arm-Hand Steadiness; Multilimb Coordination; Wrist-Finger Speed; Manual Dexterity. *Physical:* Dynamic Flexibility; Dynamic Strength; Extent Flexibility; Static Strength; Trunk Strength. *Sensory:* Hearing Sensitivity; Glare Sensitivity; Depth Perception; Peripheral Vision; Night Vision. **General Work Activities—***Information Input:* Inspecting Equipment, Structures, or Materials; Identifying Objects, Actions, and Events; Getting Information. *Mental Process:* Organizing, Planning, and Prioritizing; Judging Qualities of Things, Services, or Other People's Work; Evaluating Information Against Standards. *Work Output:* Performing General Physical Activities; Handling and Moving Objects; Controlling Machines and Processes. *Interacting with Others:* Communicating with Persons Outside Organization; Performing for or Working with the Public; Communicating with Other Workers. **Physical Work Conditions—**Outdoors; Kneeling, Crouching, or Crawling; Common Protective or Safety Attire; Minor Burns, Cuts, Bites, or Stings; Using Hands on Objects, Tools, or Controls. **Other Job Characteristics—**Importance of Repeating Same Tasks; Pace Determined by Speed of Equipment; Degree of Automation.

Experience—Job Zone 1. No previous work-related skill, knowledge, or experience is needed. **Job Preparation:** SVP below 4.0—less than six months. **Knowledge—**Biology; Food Production. **Instructional Programs—**Agricultural Production Operations, General; Crop Production.

Related DOT Jobs—405.684-010 Budder; 405.687-014 Horticultural Worker II.

45-2092.02 General Farmworkers

- **Education/Training Required: Short-term on-the-job training**
- **Employed: No data available.**
- **Annual Earnings: $14,500**
- **Growth: 3.3%**
- **Annual Job Openings: 192,000**

Apply pesticides, herbicides, and fertilizer to crops and livestock; plant, maintain, and harvest food crops; and tend livestock and poultry. Repair farm buildings and fences. Duties may include operating milking machines and other dairy processing equipment, supervising seasonal help, irrigating crops, and hauling livestock products to market.

Operates tractors, tractor-drawn machinery, and self-propelled machinery to plow, harrow, and fertilize soil and plant, cultivate, spray, and harvest crops. Feeds, waters, grooms, and otherwise cares for livestock and poultry. Harvests fruits and vegetables by hand. Digs and transplants seedlings by hand. Repairs farm buildings, fences, and other structures. Sets up and operates irrigation equipment. Clears and maintains irrigation ditches. Operates truck to haul livestock and products to market. Loads agricultural products into trucks for transport. Cleans barns, stables, pens, and kennels. Administers simple medications to animals and fowl. Repairs and maintains farm vehicles, implements, and mechanical equipment. Oversees casual and seasonal help during planting and harvesting.

GOE INFORMATION—Interest Area: 03. Plants and Animals. **Work Group:** 03.03. Hands-on Work in Plants and Animals. **Personality Type—**Realistic. Realistic occupations frequently involve work activities that include practical, hands-on problems and solutions. They often deal with plants, animals, and real-world materials like wood, tools, and machinery. Many of the occupations require working outside and do not involve a lot of paperwork or working closely with others. **Work Values—**Independence; Variety; Moral Values. **Skills—**Repairing; Operation and Control; Operation Monitoring; Installation; Equipment Selection; Troubleshooting; Management of Personnel Resources. **Abilities—***Cognitive:* Spatial Orientation; Information Ordering; Time Sharing; Category Flexibility; Visualization. *Psychomotor:* Rate Control; Response Orientation; Multilimb Coordination; Control Precision; Reaction Time. *Physical:* Static Strength; Extent Flexibility; Explosive Strength; Dynamic Strength; Trunk Strength. *Sensory:* Hearing Sensitivity; Depth Perception; Peripheral Vision; Sound Localization; Night Vision. **General Work Activities—***Information Input:* Identifying Objects, Actions, and Events; Monitoring Processes, Materials, or Surroundings; Estimating Needed Characteristics. *Mental Process:* Organizing, Planning, and Prioritizing; Making Decisions and Solving Problems; Judging Qualities of Things, Services, or Other People's Work. *Work Output:* Performing General Physical Activities; Handling and Moving Objects; Repairing and Maintaining Mechanical Equipment. *Interacting with Others:* Coordinating the Work and Activities of Others; Monitoring and Controlling Resources; Communicating with Other Workers. **Physical Work Conditions—**Outdoors; Very Hot or Cold; Hazardous Equipment; Contaminants; Extremely Bright or Inadequate Lighting. **Other Job Characteristics—**Pace Determined by Speed of Equipment; Importance of Repeating Same Tasks; Consequence of Error.

Experience—Job Zone 1. No previous work-related skill, knowledge, or experience is needed. **Job Preparation:** SVP below 4.0—less than six months. **Knowledge—**Food Production; Building and Construction; Mechanical; Chemistry; Biology. **Instructional Programs—**Agricultural Production Operations, General; Crop Production.

Related DOT Jobs—421.683-010 Farmworker, General I; 421.687-010 Farmworker, General II.

45-2093.00 Farmworkers, Farm and Ranch Animals

- Education/Training Required: **Short-term on-the-job training**
- Employed: **No data available.**
- Annual Earnings: **$16,490**
- Growth: **3.3%**
- Annual Job Openings: **192,000**

Attend to live farm, ranch, or aquacultural animals that may include cattle, sheep, swine, goats, horses and other equines, poultry, finfish, shellfish, and bees. Attend to animals produced for animal products, such as meat, fur, skins, feathers, eggs, milk, and honey. Duties may include feeding, watering, herding, grazing, castrating, branding, debeaking, weighing, catching, and loading animals. May maintain records on animals; examine animals to detect diseases and injuries; assist in birth deliveries; and administer medications, vaccinations, or insecticides as appropriate. May clean and maintain animal housing areas.

Waters livestock. Herds livestock to pasture for grazing or to scales, trucks, or other enclosures. Examines animals to detect disease and injuries. Applies or administers medications and vaccinates animals. Sprays livestock with disinfectants and insecticides. Cleans stalls, pens, and equipment, using disinfectant solutions, brushes, shovels, and water hoses. Castrates

or docks ears and tails of animals. Marks livestock to identify ownership and grade, using brands, tags, paint, or tattoos. Assists with birthing of animals. Debeaks and trims wings of poultry. Fills feed troughs with feed. Milks farm animals, such as cows and goats, by hand or using milking machine. Collects, inspects, or packs eggs or places them in incubator. Mixes feed, additives, and medicines in prescribed portions. Maintains growth, feeding, production, and cost records. Inspects and repairs fences, stalls, and pens. Moves equipment, poultry, or livestock manually or using truck or cart from one location to another. Grooms, clips, and trims animals. Segregates animals according to weight, age, color, and physical condition. Maintains equipment and machinery.

GOE INFORMATION—Interest Area: 03. Plants and Animals. **Work Group:** 03.03. Hands-on Work in Plants and Animals. **Personality Type—**Realistic. Realistic occupations frequently involve work activities that include practical, hands-on problems and solutions. They often deal with plants, animals, and real-world materials like wood, tools, and machinery. Many of the occupations require working outside and do not involve a lot of paperwork or working closely with others. **Work Values—**Variety; Moral Values; Independence. **Skills—**Repairing. **Abilities—***Cognitive:* Spatial Orientation. *Psychomotor:* Multilimb Coordination; Speed of Limb Movement; Rate Control; Manual Dexterity; Reaction Time. *Physical:* Static Strength; Dynamic Strength; Trunk Strength; Explosive Strength; Gross Body Coordination. *Sensory:* Glare Sensitivity; Night Vision; Sound Localization; Peripheral Vision. **General Work Activities—***Information Input:* Monitoring Processes, Materials, or Surroundings; Inspecting Equipment, Structures, or Materials; Getting Information. *Mental Process:* Updating and Using Relevant Knowledge; Judging Qualities of Things, Services, or Other People's Work; Making Decisions and Solving Problems. *Work Output:* Handling and Moving Objects; Performing General Physical Activities; Controlling Machines and Processes. *Interacting with Others:* Monitoring and Controlling Resources; Communicating with Other Workers; Performing Administrative Activities. **Physical Work Conditions—**Outdoors; Minor Burns, Cuts, Bites, or Stings; Kneeling, Crouching, or Crawling; Walking or Running; Cramped Work Space or Awkward Positions. **Other Job Characteristics—**Importance of Repeating Same Tasks; Consequence of Error; Pace Determined by Speed of Equipment.

Experience—Job Zone 1. No previous work-related skill, knowledge, or experience is needed. **Job Preparation:** SVP below 4.0—less than six months. **Knowledge—**Food Production; Biology; Medicine and Dentistry; Building and Construction; Chemistry. **Instructional Programs—**Animal/Livestock Husbandry and Production; Aquaculture; Plant Nursery Operations and Management.

Related DOT Jobs—410.364-010 Lamber; 410.664-010 Farmworker, Livestock; 410.674-014 Cowpuncher; 410.674-018 Livestock-Yard Attendant; 410.684-010 Farmworker, Dairy; 410.684-014 Sheep Shearer; 410.685-010 Milker, Machine; 410.687-010 Fleece Tier; 410.687-014 Goat Herder; 410.687-022 Sheep Herder; 411.161-018 Poultry Farmer; 411.364-014 Poultry Tender; 411.584-010 Farmworker, Poultry; 411.684-010 Caponizer; 411.684-014 Poultry Vaccinator; 411.687-018 Laborer, Poultry Farm; 411.687-022 Laborer, Poultry Hatchery; 411.687-026 Poultry Debeaker; 412.684-010 Game-Farm Helper; 413.687-014 Worm-Farm Laborer; others.

45-2099.99 Agricultural Workers, All Other

- Education/Training Required: **No data available.**
- Employed: **No data available.**
- Annual Earnings: **No data available.**
- Growth: **4.9%**
- Annual Job Openings: **39,000**

All agricultural workers not listed separately.

No task data available.

GOE INFORMATION—Interest Area: 03. Plants and Animals. **Work Group:** 03.02. Animal Care and Training; 03.03. Hands-on Work in Plants and Animals. **Note:** The Department of Labor has not collected some data for this job, so it has fewer details than the other descriptions.

Instructional Programs—Agricultural Production Operations, General.

Related DOT Jobs—408.381-010 Scout; 408.687-010 Field Inspector, Disease And Insect Control; 413.687-010 Worm Picker.

45-3000 Fishing and Hunting Workers

45-3011.00 Fishers and Related Fishing Workers

- Education/Training Required: Short-term on-the-job training
- Employed: No data available.
- Annual Earnings: No data available.
- Growth: –12.2%
- Annual Job Openings: 5,000

Use nets, fishing rods, traps, or other equipment to catch and gather fish or other aquatic animals from rivers, lakes, or oceans for human consumption or other uses. May haul game onto ship.

Cultivates and harvests or gathers marine life, such as sponges, abalone, or oysters, from sea bottom, using diving or dredging equipment or barge. Connects accessories, such as floats, weights, flags, lights, or markers, to nets, lines, or traps. Puts fishing equipment into water and anchors or tows equipment according to method of fishing. Pulls and guides nets, traps, and lines onto vessel by hand or using hoisting equipment. Attaches nets, slings, hooks, blades, and lifting devices to cables, booms, hoists, and dredges. Hits fish with club or hooks fish with gaff to assist in hauling large fish from water. Removes catch from fishing equipment and uses measuring equipment to ensure compliance with legal size. Loads and unloads equipment and supplies aboard vessel by hand or using hoisting equipment. Stands lookout for schools of fish and for steering and engine-room watches. Sorts and cleans marine life and returns undesirable or illegal catch to sea. Signals other workers to move, hoist, and position loads. Places catch in containers and stows in hold with salt and ice. Steers vessel in fishing area. Rows boats and dinghies and operates skiffs to transport fishers, divers, and sponge hookers and to tow and position fishing equipment. Records date, harvest area, and yield in logbook. Washes deck, conveyors, knives, and other equipment, using brush, detergent, and water. Lubricates, adjusts, and makes minor repairs to engines and fishing equipment. Negotiates with buyers for sale of catch.

GOE INFORMATION—Interest Area: 03. Plants and Animals. **Work Group:** 03.03. Hands-on Work in Plants and Animals. **Personality Type—**Realistic. Realistic occupations frequently involve work activities that include practical, hands-on problems and solutions. They often deal with plants, animals, and real-world materials like wood, tools, and machinery. Many of the occupations require working outside and do not involve a lot of paperwork or working closely with others. **Work Values**—None met the criteria. **Skills**—Repairing; Equipment Selection; Operation and Control; Negotiation. **Abilities**—*Cognitive:* Spatial Orientation; Flexibil-ity of Closure; Selective Attention; Perceptual Speed; Speed of Closure. *Psychomotor:* Multilimb Coordination; Speed of Limb Movement; Manual Dexterity; Rate Control; Reaction Time. *Physical:* Static Strength; Dynamic Strength; Extent Flexibility; Stamina; Trunk Strength. *Sensory:* Glare Sensitivity; Far Vision; Depth Perception; Auditory Attention; Peripheral Vision. **General Work Activities**—*Information Input:* Identifying Objects, Actions, and Events; Monitoring Processes, Materials, or Surroundings; Inspecting Equipment, Structures, or Materials. *Mental Process:* Organizing, Planning, and Prioritizing; Judging Qualities of Things, Services, or Other People's Work; Evaluating Information Against Standards. *Work Output:* Performing General Physical Activities; Handling and Moving Objects; Operating Vehicles or Equipment. *Interacting with Others:* Resolving Conflict and Negotiating with Others; Influencing Others or Selling; Communicating with Persons Outside Organization. **Physical Work Conditions**—Outdoors; Contaminants; Minor Burns, Cuts, Bites, or Stings; Using Hands on Objects, Tools, or Controls; Hazardous Equipment. **Other Job Characteristics**—Importance of Repeating Same Tasks; Pace Determined by Speed of Equipment; Consequence of Error.

Experience—Job Zone 1. No previous work-related skill, knowledge, or experience is needed. **Job Preparation:** SVP below 4.0—less than six months. **Knowledge**—Food Production; Biology; Sales and Marketing. **Instructional Programs**—Fishing and Fisheries Sciences and Management.

Related DOT Jobs—441.132-010 Boatswain, Otter Trawler; 441.683-010 Skiff Operator; 441.684-010 Fisher, Net; 441.684-014 Fisher, Pot; 441.684-018 Fisher, Terrapin; 441.684-022 Fisher, Weir; 442.684-010 Fisher, Line; 443.664-010 Fisher, Diving; 443.684-010 Fisher, Spear; 446.161-014 Shellfish Grower; 446.663-010 Shellfish Dredge Operator; 446.684-014 Shellfish-Bed Worker; 449.664-010 Net Repairer; 449.667-010 Deckhand, Fishing Vessel; 449.687-010 Oyster Floater.

45-3021.00 Hunters and Trappers

- Education/Training Required: Moderate-term on-the-job training
- Employed: No data available.
- Annual Earnings: No data available.
- Growth: 4.9%
- Annual Job Openings: 5,000

Hunt and trap wild animals for human consumption, fur, feed, bait, or other purposes.

Traps or captures quarry alive for identification, relocation, or live sale. Select, baits, and sets traps according to species, size, habits, and environs of bird or animal and reason for trapping. Drives quarry into traps, nets, or killing area, using dogs or prods. Kills quarry for pelts or bounty, using club, poison, gun, or drowning method. Patrols trapline or nets to inspect settings, remove catch, and reset or relocate traps. Restrains quarry with arms or nets and rigs net or sling under catch to permit hoisting without bodily injury. Releases quarry from trap or net and transfers it to cage or secures identification tag to quarry and releases it. Skins quarry, using knife, and stretches pelts on frames to be cured. Scrapes fat, blubber, or flesh from skin side of pelt with knife or hand scraper and cures pelts with salt and boric acid. Washes and sorts pelts according to species, color, and quality. Packs pelts in containers and loads containers onto trucks for transporting. Removes designated parts, such as ears or tail, from slain quarry as evidence for killing bounty, using knife. Trains dogs for hunting. Stands watch to observe behavior of captured quarry.

GOE INFORMATION—Interest Area: 03. Plants and Animals. **Work Group:** 03.03. Hands-on Work in Plants and Animals. **Personality Type—**

Realistic. Realistic occupations frequently involve work activities that include practical, hands-on problems and solutions. They often deal with plants, animals, and real-world materials like wood, tools, and machinery. Many of the occupations require working outside and do not involve a lot of paperwork or working closely with others. **Work Values**—Independence; Autonomy; Variety; Creativity. **Skills**—None met the criteria. **Abilities**—*Cognitive:* Spatial Orientation; Flexibility of Closure; Category Flexibility; Selective Attention. *Psychomotor:* Speed of Limb Movement; Rate Control; Wrist-Finger Speed; Reaction Time; Response Orientation. *Physical:* Static Strength; Explosive Strength; Dynamic Strength; Gross Body Equilibrium; Gross Body Coordination. *Sensory:* Night Vision; Peripheral Vision; Depth Perception; Far Vision; Visual Color Discrimination. **General Work Activities**—*Information Input:* Getting Information; Identifying Objects, Actions, and Events; Monitoring Processes, Materials, or Surroundings. *Mental Process:* Judging Qualities of Things, Services, or Other People's Work; Organizing, Planning, and Prioritizing; Making Decisions and Solving Problems. *Work Output:* Handling and Moving Objects; Performing General Physical Activities; Controlling Machines and Processes. *Interacting with Others:* Monitoring and Controlling Resources; Communicating with Other Workers; Establishing and Maintaining Relationships. **Physical Work Conditions**—Outdoors; Minor Burns, Cuts, Bites, or Stings; Kneeling, Crouching, or Crawling; Common Protective or Safety Attire; Bending or Twisting the Body. **Other Job Characteristics**—Consequence of Error; Importance of Repeating Same Tasks; Pace Determined by Speed of Equipment.

Experience—Job Zone 2. Some previous work-related skill, knowledge, or experience may be helpful, but usually is not needed. **Job Preparation:** SVP 4.0 to less than 6.0—six months to less than two years. **Knowledge**—Sales and Marketing; Public Safety and Security; Food Production; Geography. **Instructional Programs**—No data available.

Related DOT Jobs—461.134-010 Expedition Supervisor; 461.661-010 Predatory-Animal Hunter; 461.664-010 Underwater Hunter-Trapper; 461.684-010 Sealer; 461.684-014 Trapper, Animal; 461.684-018 Trapper, Bird.

45-4000 Forest, Conservation, and Logging Workers

45-4011.00 Forest and Conservation Workers

- **Education/Training Required: Moderate-term on-the-job training**
- **Employed: 21,334**
- **Annual Earnings: $19,000**
- **Growth: 3.9%**
- **Annual Job Openings: 4,000**

Under supervision, perform manual labor necessary to develop, maintain, or protect forest, forested areas, and woodlands through such activities as raising and transporting tree seedlings; combating insects, pests, and diseases harmful to trees; building erosion and water control structures; and leaching of forest soil. Includes forester aides, seedling pullers, and tree planters.

Select tree seedlings, prepare the ground, and plant the trees in reforestation areas, using manual planting tools. Sort and separate tree seedlings, discarding substandard seedlings, according to standard charts and verbal instructions. Spray or inject vegetation with insecticides to kill insects and to protect against disease and with herbicides to reduce competing vegetation. Thin and space trees, using power thinning saws. Check equipment to ensure that it is operating properly. Confer with other workers to discuss issues such as safety, cutting heights, and work needs. Erect signs and fences, using posthole diggers, shovels, or other hand tools. Explain and enforce regulations regarding camping, vehicle use, fires, use of building, and sanitation. Fight forest fires or perform prescribed burning tasks under the direction of fire suppression officers or forestry technicians. Maintain campsites and recreational areas, replenishing firewood and other supplies and cleaning kitchens and restrooms. Operate a skidder, bulldozer, or other prime mover to pull a variety of scarification or site preparation equipment over areas to be regenerated. Provide assistance to forest survey crews by clearing sitelines, holding measuring tools, and setting stakes. Sow and harvest cover crops such as alfalfa. Gather, package, and deliver forest products to buyers. Drag cut trees from cutting areas and load trees onto trucks. Examine and grade trees according to standard charts and staple color-coded grade tags to limbs. Identify diseased or undesirable trees and remove them, using power saws or hand saws. Maintain tallies of trees examined and counted during tree marking and measuring efforts. Perform fire protection and suppression duties such as constructing fire breaks and disposing of brush. Prune or shear tree tops and limbs in order to control growth, increase density, and improve shape. Select and cut trees according to markings or sizes, types, and grades.

GOE INFORMATION—**Interest Area:** 03. Plants and Animals. **Work Group:** 03.03. Hands-on Work in Plants and Animals. **Personality Type**—Realistic. Realistic occupations frequently involve work activities that include practical, hands-on problems and solutions. They often deal with plants, animals, and real-world materials like wood, tools, and machinery. Many of the occupations require working outside and do not involve a lot of paperwork or working closely with others. **Work Values**—Achievement; Independence; Moral Values; Variety; Responsibility. **Skills**—None met the criteria. **Abilities**—*Cognitive:* Spatial Orientation; Flexibility of Closure; Category Flexibility; Problem Sensitivity. *Psychomotor:* Speed of Limb Movement; Manual Dexterity; Multilimb Coordination; Reaction Time. *Physical:* Static Strength; Dynamic Strength; Explosive Strength; Stamina; Dynamic Flexibility. *Sensory:* Far Vision; Night Vision. **General Work Activities**—*Information Input:* Identifying Objects, Actions, and Events; Estimating Needed Characteristics; Monitoring Processes, Materials, or Surroundings. *Mental Process:* Judging Qualities of Things, Services, or Other People's Work; Organizing, Planning, and Prioritizing; Making Decisions and Solving Problems. *Work Output:* Handling and Moving Objects; Performing General Physical Activities; Controlling Machines and Processes. *Interacting with Others:* Communicating with Persons Outside Organization; Communicating with Other Workers; Establishing and Maintaining Relationships. **Physical Work Conditions**—Outdoors; Minor Burns, Cuts, Bites, or Stings; Common Protective or Safety Attire; Walking or Running; Very Hot or Cold. **Other Job Characteristics**—Importance of Repeating Same Tasks; Consequence of Error; Pace Determined by Speed of Equipment.

Experience—Job Zone 1. No previous work-related skill, knowledge, or experience is needed. **Job Preparation:** SVP below 4.0—less than six months. **Knowledge**—Biology; Chemistry; Food Production; Public Safety and Security; Geography. **Instructional Programs**—Forest Management/Forest Resources Management; Forest Resources Production and Management; Forest Sciences and Biology; Forestry, General; Forestry, Other; Natural Resources and Conservation, Other; Natural Resources Management and Policy, Other; Natural Resources/Conservation, General; Urban Forestry; Wood Science and Wood Products/Pulp and Paper Technology.

Related DOT Jobs—451.687-010 Christmas-Tree Farm Worker; 451.687-014 Christmas-Tree Grader; 451.687-018 Seedling Puller; 451.687-022 Seedling Sorter; 452.687-010 Forest Worker; 452.687-018 Tree Planter; 453.687-010 Forest-Products Gatherer; 453.687-014 Laborer, Tree Tapping.

45-4021.00 *Fallers*

- **Education/Training Required: Moderate-term on-the-job training**
- **Employed: 13,415**
- **Annual Earnings: $26,750**
- **Growth: –8.7%**
- **Annual Job Openings: 2,000**

Use axes or chain saws to fell trees, using knowledge of tree characteristics and cutting techniques to control direction of fall and minimize tree damage.

Scores cutting lines with ax, saws undercut along scored lines with chain saw, and knocks slabs from cuts with ax. Saws back-cuts, leaving sufficient sound wood to control direction of fall. Inserts jacks or drives wedge behind saw to prevent binding of saw and start tree falling. Cuts limbs from felled trees, using chain saw or ax. Cuts felled trees into log lengths, using chain saw and ax. Determines position, direction, and depth of cuts to be made and placement of wedges or jacks. Stops saw engine as tree falls, pulls cutting bar from cut, and runs to safe location to avoid injury. Measures and marks felled trees for cutting into log lengths. Splits logs, using ax, wedges, and maul, and stacks wood in rick or cord lots. Places supporting limbs or poles under felled tree to avoid splitting underside and to prevent log from rolling. Clears brush from work area and escape route and cuts sapling and other trees from direction of fall, using ax and chain saw. Appraises tree for characteristics such as twist, rot, and heavy limb growth and gauges amount and direction of lean. Secures cables to logs and drives tractor to drag logs to landing. Loads logs or wood onto trucks, by hand or using winch. Tags unsafe trees with high-visibility ribbon.

GOE INFORMATION—Interest Area: 03. Plants and Animals. **Work Group:** 03.03. Hands-on Work in Plants and Animals. **Personality Type—**Realistic. Realistic occupations frequently involve work activities that include practical, hands-on problems and solutions. They often deal with plants, animals, and real-world materials like wood, tools, and machinery. Many of the occupations require working outside and do not involve a lot of paperwork or working closely with others. **Work Values—**Moral Values; Supervision, Technical; Activity. **Skills—**Equipment Selection; Operation and Control. **Abilities—***Cognitive:* Spatial Orientation; Visualization; Time Sharing; Category Flexibility; Flexibility of Closure. *Psychomotor:* Speed of Limb Movement; Reaction Time; Response Orientation; Multilimb Coordination; Control Precision. *Physical:* Explosive Strength; Static Strength; Dynamic Strength; Stamina; Trunk Strength. *Sensory:* Depth Perception; Far Vision; Peripheral Vision; Sound Localization; Glare Sensitivity. **General Work Activities—***Information Input:* Identifying Objects, Actions, and Events; Estimating Needed Characteristics; Getting Information. *Mental Process:* Judging Qualities of Things, Services, or Other People's Work; Making Decisions and Solving Problems; Organizing, Planning, and Prioritizing. *Work Output:* Performing General Physical Activities; Handling and Moving Objects; Operating Vehicles or Equipment. *Interacting with Others:* Communicating with Other Workers; Establishing and Maintaining Relationships; Monitoring and Controlling Resources. **Physical Work Conditions—**Outdoors; Hazardous Equipment; Whole Body Vibration; Minor Burns, Cuts, Bites, or Stings; Distracting Sounds and Noise Levels. **Other Job Characteristics—**Importance of Repeating Same Tasks; Pace Determined by Speed of Equipment; Consequence of Error.

Experience—Job Zone 1. No previous work-related skill, knowledge, or experience is needed. **Job Preparation:** SVP below 4.0—less than six months. **Knowledge—**Public Safety and Security; Mechanical; Fine Arts; Foreign Language; Biology. **Instructional Programs—**Forest Resources Production and Management.

Related DOT Jobs—454.384-010 Faller I; 454.684-010 Bucker; 454.684-014 Faller II; 454.684-018 Logger, All-Round; 454.684-026 Tree Cutter; 454.687-010 Chain Saw Operator.

45-4022.00 *Logging Equipment Operators*

- **Education/Training Required: Moderate-term on-the-job training**
- **Employed: 47,117**
- **Annual Earnings: $26,140**
- **Growth: –2.0%**
- **Annual Job Openings: 7,000**

Drive logging tractor or wheeled vehicle equipped with one or more accessories, such as bulldozer blade, frontal shear, grapple, logging arch, cable winches, hoisting rack, or crane boom, to fell tree; to skid, load, unload, or stack logs; or to pull stumps or clear brush.

No task data available.

GOE INFORMATION—Interest Area: 03. Plants and Animals. **Work Group:** 03.03. Hands-on Work in Plants and Animals. **Note:** The Department of Labor has not collected some data for this job, so it has fewer details than the other descriptions.

Instructional Programs—Forest Resources Production and Management.

Related DOT Jobs—454.683-010 Tree-Shear Operator; 929.663-010 Logging-Tractor Operator.

45-4022.01 *Logging Tractor Operators*

- **Education/Training Required: Moderate-term on-the-job training**
- **Employed: No data available.**
- **Annual Earnings: $26,140**
- **Growth: –2.0%**
- **Annual Job Openings: 7,000**

Drive tractor equipped with one or more accessories, such as bulldozer blade, frontal hydraulic shear, grapple, logging arch, cable winches, hoisting rack, or crane boom, to fell tree; to skid, load and unload, or stack logs; or to pull stumps or clear brush.

Drives and maneuvers tractor and activates shear to cut and fell trees. Controls hydraulic tractor equipped with tree clamp and boom to lift, swing, and bunch sheared trees. Controls equipment to load, unload, or stack logs; pull stumps; and clear brush. Drives tractor to build or repair logging and skid roads. Saws felled trees into lengths. Gives or receives signals from co-workers to move logs.

GOE INFORMATION—Interest Area: 03. Plants and Animals. **Work Group:** 03.03. Hands-on Work in Plants and Animals. **Personality Type—**Realistic. Realistic occupations frequently involve work activities that include practical, hands-on problems and solutions. They often deal with plants, animals, and real-world materials like wood, tools, and machinery. Many of the occupations require working outside and do not involve a lot of paperwork or working closely with others. **Work Values—**Moral

Values; Pleasant Co-workers; Supervision, Technical; Supervision, Human Relations. **Skills**—Operation and Control; Operation Monitoring. **Abilities**—*Cognitive:* Spatial Orientation. *Psychomotor:* Control Precision; Reaction Time; Multilimb Coordination; Response Orientation; Rate Control. *Physical:* Trunk Strength; Gross Body Coordination; Explosive Strength; Extent Flexibility; Static Strength. *Sensory:* Depth Perception; Peripheral Vision; Glare Sensitivity; Far Vision. **General Work Activities**—*Information Input:* Getting Information; Monitoring Processes, Materials, or Surroundings; Inspecting Equipment, Structures, or Materials. *Mental Process:* Making Decisions and Solving Problems; Organizing, Planning, and Prioritizing; Analyzing Data or Information. *Work Output:* Controlling Machines and Processes; Performing General Physical Activities; Handling and Moving Objects. *Interacting with Others:* Communicating with Other Workers; Establishing and Maintaining Relationships; Monitoring and Controlling Resources. **Physical Work Conditions**—Outdoors; Whole Body Vibration; Hazardous Equipment; Climbing Ladders, Scaffolds, Poles, etc.; Minor Burns, Cuts, Bites, or Stings. **Other Job Characteristics**—Importance of Repeating Same Tasks; Pace Determined by Speed of Equipment; Consequence of Error.

Experience—Job Zone 2. Some previous work-related skill, knowledge, or experience may be helpful, but usually is not needed. **Job Preparation:** SVP 4.0 to less than 6.0—six months to less than two years. **Knowledge**—Mechanical; Food Production; Engineering and Technology; Physics. **Instructional Programs**—Forest Resources Production and Management.

Related DOT Jobs—454.683-010 Tree-Shear Operator; 929.663-010 Logging-Tractor Operator.

45-4023.00 Log Graders and Scalers

- **Education/Training Required: Moderate-term on-the-job training**
- **Employed: 7,996**
- **Annual Earnings: $26,970**
- **Growth: −4.0%**
- **Annual Job Openings: 1,000**

Grade logs or estimate the marketable content or value of logs or pulpwood in sorting yards, millpond, log deck, or similar locations. Inspect logs for defects or measure logs to determine volume.

Estimates and calculates total volume, waste volume, and marketable volume of log, using measurements and conversion table, and records results. Measures wood to determine dimensions or quantity, using measuring device and conversion table. Jabs log with scale stick and inspects log for defects and to ascertain characteristics. Evaluates log's characteristics and determines grade, using established criteria. Paints mark on logs to identify grade and species or calls out grade. Weighs log trucks before and after unloading and records weight and identity of supplier. Tends conveyor chain to move logs to and from scaling station.

GOE INFORMATION—Interest Area: 08. Industrial Production. **Work Group:** 08.02. Production Technology. **Personality Type**—Realistic. Realistic occupations frequently involve work activities that include practical, hands-on problems and solutions. They often deal with plants, animals, and real-world materials like wood, tools, and machinery. Many of the occupations require working outside and do not involve a lot of paperwork or working closely with others. **Work Values**—Independence; Moral Values; Supervision, Technical; Responsibility; Supervision, Human Relations. **Skills**—Mathematics. **Abilities**—*Cognitive:* Mathematical Reasoning; Number Facility; Spatial Orientation. *Psychomotor:* Rate Control; Reaction Time; Arm-Hand Steadiness; Speed of Limb Movement; Multilimb Coordination. *Physical:* Explosive Strength; Gross Body Coordination; Gross Body Equilibrium; Stamina; Static Strength. *Sensory:* Peripheral Vision; Night Vision; Depth Perception; Glare Sensitivity. **General Work Activities**—*Information Input:* Identifying Objects, Actions, and Events; Inspecting Equipment, Structures, or Materials; Getting Information. *Mental Process:* Processing Information; Judging Qualities of Things, Services, or Other People's Work; Analyzing Data or Information. *Work Output:* Performing General Physical Activities; Handling and Moving Objects; Controlling Machines and Processes. *Interacting with Others:* Communicating with Other Workers; Communicating with Persons Outside Organization; Establishing and Maintaining Relationships. **Physical Work Conditions**—Outdoors; Whole Body Vibration; Common Protective or Safety Attire; Climbing Ladders, Scaffolds, Poles, etc.; High Places. **Other Job Characteristics**—Pace Determined by Speed of Equipment; Importance of Being Exact or Accurate; Importance of Repeating Same Tasks.

Experience—Job Zone 2. Some previous work-related skill, knowledge, or experience may be helpful, but usually is not needed. **Job Preparation:** SVP 4.0 to less than 6.0—six months to less than two years. **Knowledge**—Biology; Building and Construction; Production and Processing. **Instructional Programs**—Forest Resources Production and Management.

Related DOT Jobs—455.367-010 Log Grader; 455.487-010 Log Scaler.

45-4029.99 Logging Workers, All Other

- **Education/Training Required: Moderate-term on-the-job training**
- **Employed: No data available.**
- **Annual Earnings: No data available.**
- **Growth: −1.8%**
- **Annual Job Openings: 7,000**

All logging workers not listed separately.

No task data available.

GOE INFORMATION—Interest Area: 03. Plants and Animals. **Work Group:** 03.03. Hands-on Work in Plants and Animals. **Note:** The Department of Labor has not collected some data for this job, so it has fewer details than the other descriptions.

Instructional Programs—Forest Resources Production and Management.

Related DOT Jobs—168.267-070 Logging-Operations Inspector; 454.687-018 Log Marker; 455.664-010 Rafter; 455.684-010 Log Sorter; 455.687-010 Log Marker; 459.387-010 Cruiser; 669.485-010 Power-Barker Operator; 669.687-022 Picker; 921.364-010 Rigging Slinger; 921.667-014 Chaser; 921.686-018 Log-Haul Chain Feeder; 921.686-022 Pond Worker; 921.687-014 Choke Setter; 921.687-022 Log Loader Helper; 921.687-030 Rigger, Third; 922.687-082 Pulp Piler.

47-0000
Construction and Extraction Occupations

47-1000 Supervisors, Construction and Extraction Workers

47-1011.00 First-Line Supervisors/ Managers of Construction Trades and Extraction Workers

- **Education/Training Required: Work experience in a related occupation**
- **Employed: 792,225**
- **Annual Earnings: $46,570**
- **Growth: 16.5%**
- **Annual Job Openings: 43,000**

Directly supervise and coordinate activities of construction or extraction workers.

No task data available.

GOE INFORMATION—Interest Area: 06. Construction, Mining, and Drilling. **Work Group:** 06.01. Managerial Work in Construction, Mining, and Drilling. **Note:** The Department of Labor has not collected some data for this job, so it has fewer details than the other descriptions.

Instructional Programs—Blasting/Blaster; Building/Construction Finishing, Management, and Inspection, Other; Building/Construction Site Management/Manager; Building/Home/Construction Inspection/Inspector; Building/Property Maintenance and Management; Carpentry/Carpenter; Concrete Finishing/Concrete Finisher; Construction Trades, Other; Drywall Installation/Drywaller; Electrical and Power Transmission Installation/Installer, General; Electrical and Power Transmission Installers, Other; Electrician; Glazier; Lineworker; Mason/Masonry; Painting/Painter and Wall Coverer; Plumbing Technology/Plumber; Roofer; Well Drilling/Driller.

Related DOT Jobs—184.167-234 Supervisor of Way; 801.131-010 Supervisor, Chimney Construction; 801.134-010 Supervisor, Reinforced-Steel-Placing; 809.131-014 Supervisor, Ornamental Ironworking; 809.131-018 Supervisor, Structural-Steel Erection; 821.131-022 Steel-Post-Installer Supervisor; 824.137-010 Electrician, Chief; 825.131-010 Electrician Supervisor; 829.131-014 Electrician Supervisor; 840.131-010 Supervisor, Painting; 840.131-014 Supervisor, Painting, Shipyard; 841.137-010 Supervisor, Billposting; 842.131-010 Supervisor, Dry-Wall Application; 842.131-014 Supervisor, Lathing; 842.131-018 Supervisor, Plastering; 842.134-010 Supervisor, Taping; 843.134-010 Supervisor, Doping; 843.137-010 Supervisor, Waterproofing; 850.133-010 Supervisor, Reclamation; 850.137-010 Supervisor, Core Drilling; others.

47-1011.01 First-Line Supervisors and Manager/Supervisors—Construction Trades Workers

- **Education/Training Required: Work experience in a related occupation**
- **Employed: No data available.**
- **Annual Earnings: $46,570**
- **Growth: 16.5%**
- **Annual Job Openings: 43,000**

Directly supervise and coordinate activities of construction trades workers and their helpers. Manager/Supervisors are generally found in smaller establishments, where they perform both supervisory and management functions, such as accounting, marketing, and personnel work, and may also engage in the same construction trades work as the workers they supervise.

Supervises and coordinates activities of construction trades workers. Directs and leads workers engaged in construction activities. Assigns work to employees, using material and worker requirements data. Confers with staff and worker to ensure that production and personnel problems are resolved. Suggests and initiates personnel actions, such as promotions, transfers, and hires. Analyzes and resolves worker problems and recommends motivational plans. Examines and inspects work progress, equipment, and construction sites to verify safety and ensure that specifications are met. Estimates material and worker requirements to complete job. Reads specifications, such as blueprints and data, to determine construction requirements. Analyzes and plans installation and construction of equipment and structures. Locates, measures, and marks location and placement of structures and equipment. Records information, such as personnel, production, and operational data, on specified forms and reports. Trains workers in construction methods and operation of equipment. Recommends measures to improve production methods and equipment performance to increase efficiency and safety. Assists workers engaged in construction activities, using hand tools and equipment.

GOE INFORMATION—Interest Area: 06. Construction, Mining, and Drilling. **Work Group:** 06.01. Managerial Work in Construction, Mining, and Drilling. **Personality Type**—Enterprising. Enterprising occupations frequently involve starting up and carrying out projects. These occupations can involve leading people and making many decisions. They sometimes require risk taking and often deal with business. **Work Values**—Authority; Responsibility; Autonomy; Variety; Pleasant Co-workers. **Skills**—Management of Personnel Resources; Management of Material Resources; Equipment Selection; Installation; Quality Control Analysis; Systems Analysis; Troubleshooting; Systems Evaluation. **Abilities**—*Cognitive:* Spatial Orientation; Speed of Closure; Information Ordering; Problem Sensitivity; Perceptual Speed. *Psychomotor:* Manual Dexterity; Reaction Time; Control Precision; Response Orientation; Speed of Limb Movement. *Physical:* Explosive Strength; Gross Body Equilibrium; Dynamic Strength; Static Strength; Stamina. *Sensory:* Far Vision; Glare Sensitivity; Peripheral Vision; Depth Perception; Night Vision. **General Work Activities**—*Information Input:* Getting Information; Inspecting Equipment, Structures, or Materials; Monitoring Processes, Materials, or Surroundings. *Mental Process:* Updating and Using Relevant Knowledge; Scheduling Work and Activities; Organizing, Planning, and Prioritizing. *Work Output:* Performing General Physical Activities; Handling and Moving Objects; Controlling Machines and Processes. *Interacting with Others:* Coordinating the Work and Activities of Others; Communicating with Other Workers; Establishing and Maintaining Relationships. **Physical Work Conditions**—High Places; Outdoors; Keeping or Regaining Balance; Common Protective or Safety Attire; Climbing Ladders, Scaffolds, Poles, etc. **Other Job Characteristics**—Importance of Repeating Same Tasks; Importance of Being Exact or Accurate; Consequence of Error.

Experience—Job Zone 4. A minimum of two to four years of work-related skill, knowledge, or experience is needed. **Job Preparation:** SVP 7.0 to less than 8.0—two years to less than 10 years. **Knowledge**—Building and Construction; Personnel and Human Resources; Administration and Management; Design; Education and Training. **Instructional Programs**—Building/Construction Finishing, Management, and Inspection,

Other; Building/Construction Site Management/Manager; Building/Home/Construction Inspection/Inspector; Building/Property Maintenance and Management; Carpentry/Carpenter; Concrete Finishing/Concrete Finisher; Construction Trades, Other; Drywall Installation/Drywaller; Electrical and Power Transmission Installation/Installer, General; Electrical and Power Transmission Installers, Other; Electrician; Glazier; Lineworker; Mason/Masonry; Painting/Painter and Wall Coverer; Plumbing Technology/Plumber; Roofer; Well Drilling/Driller.

Related DOT Jobs—184.167-234 Supervisor of Way; 801.131-010 Supervisor, Chimney Construction; 801.134-010 Supervisor, Reinforced-Steel-Placing; 809.131-014 Supervisor, Ornamental Ironworking; 809.131-018 Supervisor, Structural-Steel Erection; 821.131-022 Steel-Post-Installer Supervisor; 824.137-010 Electrician, Chief; 825.131-010 Electrician Supervisor; 829.131-014 Electrician Supervisor; 840.131-010 Supervisor, Painting; 840.131-014 Supervisor, Painting, Shipyard; 841.137-010 Supervisor, Billposting; 842.131-010 Supervisor, Dry-Wall Application; 842.131-014 Supervisor, Lathing; 842.131-018 Supervisor, Plastering; 842.134-010 Supervisor, Taping; 843.134-010 Supervisor, Doping; 843.137-010 Supervisor, Waterproofing; 850.133-010 Supervisor, Reclamation; 850.137-014 Supervisor, Labor Gang; others.

47-1011.02 First-Line Supervisors and Manager/Supervisors—Extractive Workers

- **Education/Training Required: Work experience in a related occupation**
- **Employed: No data available.**
- **Annual Earnings: $46,570**
- **Growth: 16.5%**
- **Annual Job Openings: 43,000**

Directly supervise and coordinate activities of extractive workers and their helpers. Manager/Supervisors are generally found in smaller establishments, where they perform both supervisory and management functions, such as accounting, marketing, and personnel work, and may also engage in the same extractive work as the workers they supervise.

Supervises and coordinates activities of workers engaged in the extraction of geological materials. Directs and leads workers engaged in extraction of geological materials. Assigns work to employees, using material and worker requirements data. Confers with staff and workers to ensure that production personnel problems are resolved. Analyzes and resolves worker problems and recommends motivational plans. Analyzes and plans extraction process of geological materials. Trains workers in construction methods and operation of equipment. Examines and inspects equipment, site, and materials to verify that specifications are met. Recommends measures to improve production methods and equipment performance to increase efficiency and safety. Suggests and initiates personnel actions, such as promotions, transfers, and hires. Records information such as personnel, production, and operational data on specified forms. Assists workers engaged in extraction activities, using hand tools and equipment. Locates, measures, and marks materials and site location, using measuring and marking equipment. Orders materials, supplies, and repair of equipment and machinery.

GOE INFORMATION—Interest Area: 06. Construction, Mining, and Drilling. **Work Group:** 06.01. Managerial Work in Construction, Mining, and Drilling. **Personality Type—**Enterprising. Enterprising occupations frequently involve starting up and carrying out projects. These occupations can involve leading people and making many decisions.

They sometimes require risk taking and often deal with business. **Work Values—**Authority; Responsibility; Variety; Autonomy; Pleasant Co-workers. **Skills—**Management of Personnel Resources; Management of Material Resources; Instructing; Operation Monitoring; Equipment Selection; Systems Evaluation; Systems Analysis; Operation and Control. **Abilities—***Cognitive:* Deductive Reasoning; Problem Sensitivity; Visualization; Inductive Reasoning; Written Expression. *Psychomotor:* Manual Dexterity; Control Precision; Response Orientation; Speed of Limb Movement. *Physical:* Stamina; Trunk Strength; Dynamic Flexibility; Dynamic Strength. *Sensory:* Far Vision; Speech Recognition; Near Vision; Peripheral Vision; Speech Clarity. **General Work Activities—***Information Input:* Getting Information; Identifying Objects, Actions, and Events; Monitoring Processes, Materials, or Surroundings. *Mental Process:* Updating and Using Relevant Knowledge; Making Decisions and Solving Problems; Scheduling Work and Activities. *Work Output:* Performing General Physical Activities; Handling and Moving Objects; Documenting or Recording Information. *Interacting with Others:* Communicating with Other Workers; Coordinating the Work and Activities of Others; Guiding, Directing, and Motivating Subordinates. **Physical Work Conditions—**Common Protective or Safety Attire; Outdoors; Whole Body Vibration; Specialized Protective or Safety Attire; Contaminants. **Other Job Characteristics—**Consequence of Error; Importance of Being Exact or Accurate; Pace Determined by Speed of Equipment.

Experience—Job Zone 3. Previous work-related skill, knowledge, or experience is required. **Job Preparation:** SVP 6.0 to less than 7.0—more than one year and less than four years. **Knowledge—**Personnel and Human Resources; Administration and Management; Engineering and Technology; Education and Training; Production and Processing. **Instructional Programs—**Blasting/Blaster; Well Drilling/Driller.

Related DOT Jobs—850.137-010 Supervisor, Core Drilling; 930.130-010 Tool Pusher; 930.131-010 Field Supervisor, Oil-Well Services; 930.134-010 Quarry Supervisor, Dimension Stone; 932.132-010 Bank Boss; 939.131-010 Quarry Supervisor, Open Pit; 939.132-010 Dredge Operator Supervisor; 939.132-014 Oil-Well-Services Supervisor; 939.137-014 Pit Supervisor; 939.137-018 Section Supervisor; 939.137-022 Supervisor, Harvesting.

47-2000 Construction Trades Workers

47-2011.00 Boilermakers

- **Education/Training Required: Long-term on-the-job training**
- **Employed: 26,960**
- **Annual Earnings: $39,640**
- **Growth: 2.1%**
- **Annual Job Openings: 2,000**

Construct, assemble, maintain, and repair stationary steam boilers and boiler house auxiliaries. Align structures or plate sections to assemble boiler frame tanks or vats, following blueprints. Work involves use of hand and power tools, plumb bobs, levels, wedges, dogs, or turnbuckles. Assist in testing assembled vessels. Direct cleaning of boilers and boiler furnaces. Inspect and repair boiler fittings, such as safety valves, regulators, automatic-control mechanisms, water columns, and auxiliary machines.

Positions, aligns, and secures structural parts and related assemblies of pressure vessels, using plumb bobs, levels, wedges, and turnbuckles. Bolts or arc-welds pressure vessel structures and parts together, using wrenches and welding equipment. Straightens or reshapes bent pressure vessel plates and structure parts, using hammer, jacks, and torch. Bells, beads with power hammer, or welds pressure vessel tube ends to ensure leakproof joints. Installs manholes, handholes, valves, gauges, and feedwater connections in drums of water tube boilers, using hand tools. Inspects assembled vessels for faulty accessories and pressure tests for leakage. Repairs or replaces defective pressure vessel parts, using torch, jacks, caulking hammers, power saw, threading die, and welding equipment. Maintains and repairs stationary steam boilers and boiler house auxiliaries, using hand tools and power tools. Shapes seams, joints, and irregular edges of pressure vessel sections and structural parts to attain specified fit, using cutting torch, file, and power grinder. Repairs insulation of pressure vessel with cement. Studies blueprints to determine location, relationship, and dimensions of parts to assemble pressure vessels, such as boilers, tanks and vats. Locates and marks reference points for columns or plates on foundation, using master straightedge, square, transit, and measuring instruments. Installs refractory brick and other heat-resistant materials in firebox of pressure vessel. Fabricates parts, such as stacks, uptakes, and chutes, to adapt pressure vessel to premises. Cleans pressure vessel equipment, using scrapers, wire brush, and cleaning solvent. Attaches rigging and signals crane operator to lift pressure vessel parts to specified position.

GOE INFORMATION—Interest Area: 06. Construction, Mining, and Drilling. **Work Group:** 06.02. Construction. **Personality Type—**Realistic. Realistic occupations frequently involve work activities that include practical, hands-on problems and solutions. They often deal with plants, animals, and real-world materials like wood, tools, and machinery. Many of the occupations require working outside and do not involve a lot of paperwork or working closely with others. **Work Values—**Supervision, Technical; Compensation; Supervision, Human Relations; Moral Values; Creativity. **Skills—**Installation; Repairing; Quality Control Analysis; Troubleshooting; Operation and Control; Equipment Selection; Operation Monitoring; Systems Analysis. **Abilities—***Cognitive:* Visualization; Selective Attention; Flexibility of Closure; Speed of Closure; Memorization. *Psychomotor:* Manual Dexterity; Multilimb Coordination; Finger Dexterity; Control Precision; Speed of Limb Movement. *Physical:* Static Strength; Extent Flexibility; Dynamic Flexibility; Dynamic Strength; Explosive Strength. *Sensory:* Auditory Attention; Night Vision; Depth Perception; Sound Localization; Glare Sensitivity. **General Work Activities—***Information Input:* Inspecting Equipment, Structures, or Materials; Getting Information; Identifying Objects, Actions, and Events. *Mental Process:* Evaluating Information Against Standards; Organizing, Planning, and Prioritizing; Judging Qualities of Things, Services, or Other People's Work. *Work Output:* Repairing and Maintaining Mechanical Equipment; Handling and Moving Objects; Performing General Physical Activities. *Interacting with Others:* Communicating with Other Workers; Establishing and Maintaining Relationships; Coordinating the Work and Activities of Others. **Physical Work Conditions—**Hazardous Equipment; Minor Burns, Cuts, Bites, or Stings; Common Protective or Safety Attire; Cramped Work Space or Awkward Positions; Distracting Sounds and Noise Levels. **Other Job Characteristics—**Consequence of Error; Importance of Being Exact or Accurate; Degree of Automation.

Experience—Job Zone 4. A minimum of two to four years of work-related skill, knowledge, or experience is needed. **Job Preparation:** SVP 7.0 to less than 8.0—two years to less than 10 years. **Knowledge—**Building and Construction; Mechanical; Engineering and Technology; Physics; Design. **Instructional Programs—**Boilermaking/Boilermaker.

Related DOT Jobs—805.261-010 Boilermaker Apprentice; 805.261-014 Boilermaker I; 805.361-010 Boilerhouse Mechanic; 805.361-014 Boilermaker Fitter; 805.381-010 Boilermaker II.

47-2021.00 Brickmasons and Blockmasons

- **Education/Training Required: Long-term on-the-job training**
- **Employed: 144,380**
- **Annual Earnings: $41,590**
- **Growth: 12.5%**
- **Annual Job Openings: 18,000**

Lay and bind building materials, such as brick, structural tile, concrete block, cinder block, glass block, and terra-cotta block, with mortar and other substances to construct or repair walls, partitions, arches, sewers, and other structures.

Apply and smooth mortar or other mixture over work surface. Break or cut bricks, tiles, or blocks to size, using trowel edge, hammer, or power saw. Calculate angles and courses and determine vertical and horizontal alignment of courses. Construct corners by fastening in plumb position a corner pole or building a corner pyramid of bricks and then filling in between the corners, using a line from corner to corner to guide each course, or layer, of brick. Fasten or fuse brick or other building material to structure with wire clamps, anchor holes, torch, or cement. Interpret blueprints and drawings to determine specifications and to calculate the materials required. Lay and align bricks, blocks, or tiles to build or repair structures or high-temperature equipment, such as cupola, kilns, ovens, or furnaces. Measure distance from reference points and mark guidelines to lay out work, using plumb bobs and levels. Mix specified amounts of sand, clay, dirt, or mortar powder with water to form refractory mixtures. Remove burned or damaged brick or mortar, using sledgehammer, crowbar, chipping gun, or chisel. Remove excess mortar with trowels and hand tools and finish mortar joints with jointing tools for a sealed, uniform appearance. Clean working surface to remove scale, dust, soot, or chips of brick and mortar, using broom, wire brush, or scraper. Examine brickwork or structure to determine need for repair. Spray or spread refractory material over brickwork to protect against deterioration.

GOE INFORMATION—Interest Area: 06. Construction, Mining, and Drilling. **Work Group:** 06.02. Construction. **Personality Type—**Realistic. Realistic occupations frequently involve work activities that include practical, hands-on problems and solutions. They often deal with plants, animals, and real-world materials like wood, tools, and machinery. Many of the occupations require working outside and do not involve a lot of paperwork or working closely with others. **Work Values—**Moral Values; Compensation; Independence; Variety; Ability Utilization. **Skills—**Repairing; Equipment Selection; Mathematics. **Abilities—***Cognitive:* Visualization; Information Ordering; Inductive Reasoning; Mathematical Reasoning; Number Facility. *Psychomotor:* Manual Dexterity; Speed of Limb Movement; Arm-Hand Steadiness; Multilimb Coordination; Wrist-Finger Speed. *Physical:* Dynamic Strength; Extent Flexibility; Trunk Strength; Explosive Strength; Static Strength. *Sensory:* Peripheral Vision; Depth Perception; Glare Sensitivity. **General Work Activities—***Information Input:* Estimating Needed Characteristics; Getting Information; Identifying Objects, Actions, and Events. *Mental Process:* Analyzing Data or Information; Thinking Creatively; Organizing, Planning, and Prioritizing. *Work Output:* Performing General Physical Activities; Handling and Moving Objects; Controlling Machines and Processes. *Interacting with Others:* Communicating with Other Workers; Establishing and Maintaining Relationships; Monitoring and Controlling Resources. **Physical Work Conditions—**Outdoors; Contaminants; Making Repetitive Motions; Cramped Work Space or Awkward Positions; Climbing Ladders, Scaffolds, Poles, etc. **Other Job Characteristics—**Importance of Repeating Same Tasks; Importance of Being Exact or Accurate; Consequence of Error.

Experience—Job Zone 3. Previous work-related skill, knowledge, or experience is required. **Job Preparation:** SVP 6.0 to less than 7.0—more than one year and less than four years. **Knowledge**—Building and Construction; Mechanical; Physics. **Instructional Programs**—Mason/Masonry.

Related DOT Jobs—573.684-010 Kiln-Door Builder; 709.684-046 Hot-Top Liner; 861.381-010 Acid-Tank Liner; 861.381-014 Bricklayer; 861.381-018 Bricklayer; 861.381-022 Bricklayer Apprentice; 861.381-026 Bricklayer, Firebrick and Refractory Tile; 861.684-010 Cupola Patcher; 861.684-014 Patcher; 861.684-022 Repairer, Kiln Car; 899.364-010 Chimney Repairer.

47-2022.00 Stonemasons

- Education/Training Required: Long-term on-the-job training
- Employed: 13,710
- Annual Earnings: $32,470
- Growth: 20.8%
- Annual Job Openings: 2,000

Build stone structures, such as piers, walls, and abutments. Lay walks, curbstones, or special types of masonry for vats, tanks, and floors.

Clean excess mortar or grout from surface of marble, stone, or monument, using sponge, brush, water, or acid. Drill holes in marble or ornamental stone and anchor brackets in holes. Lay out wall patterns or foundations, using straight edge, rule, or staked lines. Mix mortar or grout and pour or spread mortar or grout on marble slabs, stone, or foundation. Remove wedges; fill joints between stones; finish joints between stones, using a trowel; and smooth the mortar to an attractive finish, using a tuck pointer. Set stone or marble in place according to layout or pattern. Shape, trim, face, and cut marble or stone preparatory to setting, using power saws, cutting equipment, and hand tools. Smooth, polish, and bevel surfaces, using hand tools and power tools. Dig trench for foundation of monument, using pick and shovel. Line interiors of molds with treated paper and fill molds with composition-stone mixture. Position mold along guidelines of wall, press mold in place, and remove mold and paper from wall. Remove sections of monument from truck bed and guide stone onto foundation, using skids, hoist, or truck crane. Repair cracked or chipped areas of stone or marble, using blowtorch and mastic, and remove rough or defective spots from concrete, using power grinder or chisel and hammer. Set vertical and horizontal alignment of structures, using plumb bob, gauge line, and level. Construct and install prefabricated masonry units. Lay brick to build shells of chimneys and smokestacks or to line or reline industrial furnaces, kilns, boilers, and similar installations. Replace broken or missing masonry units in walls or floors.

GOE INFORMATION—Interest Area: 06. Construction, Mining, and Drilling. **Work Group:** 06.02. Construction. **Personality Type**—Realistic. Realistic occupations frequently involve work activities that include practical, hands-on problems and solutions. They often deal with plants, animals, and real-world materials like wood, tools, and machinery. Many of the occupations require working outside and do not involve a lot of paperwork or working closely with others. **Work Values**—Moral Values; Compensation; Independence; Achievement; Ability Utilization. **Skills**—Repairing; Operation and Control; Equipment Selection. **Abilities**—*Cognitive:* Visualization. *Psychomotor:* Speed of Limb Movement; Wrist-Finger Speed; Multilimb Coordination. *Physical:* Static Strength; Dynamic Strength; Explosive Strength; Stamina; Dynamic Flexibility. *Sensory:* Glare Sensitivity; Depth Perception; Peripheral Vision; Night Vision. **General Work Activities**—*Information Input:* Inspecting Equipment, Structures, or Materials; Estimating Needed Characteristics; Identifying Objects, Actions, and Events. *Mental Process:* Thinking Creatively; Organizing, Planning, and Prioritizing; Processing Information. *Work Output:* Performing General Physical Activities; Handling and Moving Objects; Controlling Machines and Processes. *Interacting with Others:*

Communicating with Other Workers; Establishing and Maintaining Relationships; Assisting and Caring for Others. **Physical Work Conditions**—Outdoors; Kneeling, Crouching, or Crawling; Common Protective or Safety Attire; Making Repetitive Motions; Bending or Twisting the Body. **Other Job Characteristics**—Importance of Repeating Same Tasks; Pace Determined by Speed of Equipment; Importance of Being Exact or Accurate.

Experience—Job Zone 4. A minimum of two to four years of work-related skill, knowledge, or experience is needed. **Job Preparation:** SVP 7.0 to less than 8.0—two years to less than 10 years. **Knowledge**—Building and Construction; Design; Mechanical; Fine Arts. **Instructional Programs**—Mason/Masonry.

Related DOT Jobs—861.361-010 Composition-Stone Applicator; 861.361-014 Monument Setter; 861.381-030 Marble Setter; 861.381-038 Stonemason; 861.381-042 Stonemason Apprentice.

47-2031.00 Carpenters

- Education/Training Required: Long-term on-the-job training
- Employed: 1,204,050
- Annual Earnings: $33,470
- Growth: 8.2%
- Annual Job Openings: 161,000

Construct, erect, install, or repair structures and fixtures made of wood, such as concrete forms; building frameworks, including partitions, joists, studding, and rafters; wood stairways; window and door frames; and hardwood floors. May also install cabinets, siding, drywall, and batt or roll insulation. Includes brattice builders who build doors or brattices (ventilation walls or partitions) in underground passageways to control the proper circulation of air through the passageways and to the working places.

No task data available.

GOE INFORMATION—Interest Area: 06. Construction, Mining, and Drilling. **Work Group:** 06.02. Construction. **Note:** The Department of Labor has not collected some data for this job, so it has fewer details than the other descriptions.

Instructional Programs—Carpentry/Carpenter.

Related DOT Jobs—739.684-190 Casket Assembler; 764.684-022 Cooper; 764.684-026 Hogshead Cooper I; 769.684-038 Repairer, Assembled Wood Products; 806.281-058 Carpenter, Prototype; 807.361-014 Boat Repairer; 842.361-010 Lather; 842.361-014 Lather Apprentice; 860.281-010 Carpenter, Maintenance; 860.281-014 Carpenter, Ship; 860.361-010 Boatbuilder, Wood; 860.361-014 Boatbuilder Apprentice, Wood; 860.381-022 Carpenter; 860.381-026 Carpenter Apprentice; 860.381-030 Carpenter, Bridge; 860.381-034 Carpenter, Mold; 860.381-038 Carpenter, Railcar; 860.381-042 Carpenter, Rough; 860.381-046 Form Builder; 860.381-050 Joiner; others.

47-2031.01 Construction Carpenters

- Education/Training Required: Long-term on-the-job training
- Employed: No data available.
- Annual Earnings: $33,470
- Growth: 8.2%
- Annual Job Openings: 161,000

Construct, erect, install, and repair structures and fixtures of wood, plywood, and wallboard, using carpenter's hand tools and power tools.

Measure and mark cutting lines on materials, using ruler, pencil, chalk, and marking gauge. Follow established safety rules and regulations and maintain a safe and clean environment. Verify trueness of structure, using plumb bob and level. Shape or cut materials to specified measurements, using hand tools, machines, or power saw. Study specifications in blueprints, sketches, or building plans to prepare project layout and determine dimensions and materials required. Assemble and fasten materials to make framework or props, using hand tools and wood screws, nails, dowel pins, or glue. Build or repair cabinets, doors, frameworks, floors, and other wooden fixtures used in buildings, using woodworking machines, carpenter's hand tools, and power tools. Erect scaffolding and ladders for assembling structures above ground level. Remove damaged or defective parts or sections of structures and repair or replace, using hand tools. Install structures and fixtures, such as windows, frames, floorings, and trim, or hardware, using carpenter's hand and power tools. Select and order lumber and other required materials. Maintain records, document actions, and present written progress reports. Finish surfaces of woodwork or wallboard in houses and buildings, using paint, hand tools, and paneling. Prepare cost estimates for clients or employers. Arrange for subcontractors to deal with special areas such as heating and electrical wiring work. Inspect ceiling or floor tile, wall coverings, siding, glass, or woodwork to detect broken or damaged structures. Work with and/or remove hazardous material. Construct forms and chutes for pouring concrete. Cover subfloors with building paper to keep out moisture and lay hardwood, parquet, and wood-strip-block floors by nailing floors to subfloor or cementing them to mastic or asphalt base. Fill cracks and other defects in plaster or plasterboard and sand patch, using patching plaster, trowel, and sanding tool. Perform minor plumbing, welding, and/or concrete mixing work. Apply shock-absorbing, sound-deadening, and decorative paneling to ceilings and walls.

GOE INFORMATION—Interest Area: 06. Construction, Mining, and Drilling. **Work Group:** 06.02. Construction. **Personality Type—**Realistic. Realistic occupations frequently involve work activities that include practical, hands-on problems and solutions. They often deal with plants, animals, and real-world materials like wood, tools, and machinery. Many of the occupations require working outside and do not involve a lot of paperwork or working closely with others. **Work Values—**Creativity; Variety; Compensation; Moral Values; Ability Utilization. **Skills—**Management of Personnel Resources; Management of Material Resources; Repairing; Management of Financial Resources; Quality Control Analysis; Equipment Selection; Speaking; Mathematics. **Abilities—***Cognitive:* Visualization; Information Ordering; Flexibility of Closure; Originality; Category Flexibility. *Psychomotor:* Multilimb Coordination; Manual Dexterity; Arm-Hand Steadiness; Control Precision; Reaction Time. *Physical:* Gross Body Equilibrium; Extent Flexibility; Dynamic Strength; Static Strength; Stamina. *Sensory:* Depth Perception; Glare Sensitivity; Far Vision; Auditory Attention; Speech Recognition. **General Work Activities—***Information Input:* Monitoring Processes, Materials, or Surroundings; Identifying Objects, Actions, and Events; Inspecting Equipment, Structures, or Materials. *Mental Process:* Organizing, Planning, and Prioritizing; Updating and Using Relevant Knowledge; Judging Qualities of Things, Services, or Other People's Work. *Work Output:* Handling and Moving Objects; Performing General Physical Activities; Controlling Machines and Processes. *Interacting with Others:* Coordinating the Work and Activities of Others; Teaching Others; Communicating with Other Workers. **Physical Work Conditions—**Hazardous Equipment; High Places; Common Protective or Safety Attire; Climbing Ladders, Scaffolds, Poles, etc.; Kneeling, Crouching, or Crawling. **Other Job Characteristics—**Importance of Repeating Same Tasks; Importance of Being Exact or Accurate; Degree of Automation.

Experience—Job Zone 3. Previous work-related skill, knowledge, or experience is required. **Job Preparation:** SVP 7.0 to less than 8.0—two years to less than 10 years. **Knowledge—**Building and Construction; Production and Processing; Design; Public Safety and Security; Engineering and Technology. **Instructional Programs—**Carpentry/Carpenter.

Related DOT Jobs—860.281-010 Carpenter, Maintenance; 860.381-022 Carpenter; 860.381-026 Carpenter Apprentice; 860.381-034 Carpenter, Mold; 860.381-038 Carpenter, Railcar; 869.381-010 House Repairer; 962.281-010 Prop Maker.

47-2031.02 Rough Carpenters

- **Education/Training Required: Moderate-term on-the-job training**
- **Employed: No data available.**
- **Annual Earnings: $33,470**
- **Growth: 8.2%**
- **Annual Job Openings: 161,000**

Build rough wooden structures, such as concrete forms; scaffolds; tunnel, bridge, or sewer supports; billboard signs; and temporary frame shelters, according to sketches, blueprints, or oral instructions.

Anchor and brace forms and other structures in place, using nails, bolts, anchor rods, steel cables, planks, wedges, and timbers. Assemble and fasten material together to construct wood or metal framework of structure, using bolts, nails, or screws. Bore boltholes in timber, masonry, or concrete walls, using power drill. Cut or saw boards, timbers, or plywood to required size, using handsaw, power saw, or woodworking machine. Erect forms, framework, scaffolds, hoists, roof supports, or chutes, using hand tools, plumb rule, and level. Install rough door and window frames, subflooring, fixtures, or temporary supports in structures undergoing construction or repair. Mark cutting lines on materials, using pencil and scriber. Measure materials or distances, using square, measuring tape, or rule to lay out work. Study blueprints and diagrams to determine dimensions of structure or form to be constructed. Build chutes for pouring concrete. Dig or direct digging of postholes and set poles to support structures. Examine structural timbers and supports to detect decay and replace timbers as required, using hand tools, nuts, and bolts. Fabricate parts, using woodworking and metalworking machines. Build sleds from logs and timbers for use in hauling camp buildings and machinery through wooded areas.

GOE INFORMATION—Interest Area: 06. Construction, Mining, and Drilling. **Work Group:** 06.02. Construction. **Personality Type—**Realistic. Realistic occupations frequently involve work activities that include practical, hands-on problems and solutions. They often deal with plants, animals, and real-world materials like wood, tools, and machinery. Many of the occupations require working outside and do not involve a lot of paperwork or working closely with others. **Work Values—**Variety; Moral Values; Creativity; Compensation; Recognition. **Skills—**Installation; Repairing; Operation and Control. **Abilities—***Cognitive:* Visualization; Oral Comprehension; Flexibility of Closure; Speed of Closure; Number Facility. *Psychomotor:* Manual Dexterity; Speed of Limb Movement; Multilimb Coordination; Control Precision; Wrist-Finger Speed. *Physical:* Static Strength; Trunk Strength; Extent Flexibility; Explosive Strength; Dynamic Strength. *Sensory:* Depth Perception; Far Vision; Near Vision; Peripheral Vision. **General Work Activities—***Information Input:* Inspecting Equipment, Structures, or Materials; Getting Information; Identifying Objects, Actions, and Events. *Mental Process:* Judging Qualities of Things, Services, or Other People's Work; Updating and Using Relevant Knowledge; Evaluating Information Against Standards. *Work Output:* Performing General Physical Activities; Handling and Moving

Objects; Controlling Machines and Processes. *Interacting with Others:* Communicating with Other Workers; Coordinating the Work and Activities of Others; Establishing and Maintaining Relationships. **Physical Work Conditions**—Outdoors; Climbing Ladders, Scaffolds, Poles, etc.; High Places; Hazardous Equipment; Common Protective or Safety Attire. **Other Job Characteristics**—Importance of Being Exact or Accurate; Consequence of Error; Importance of Repeating Same Tasks.

Experience—Job Zone 3. Previous work-related skill, knowledge, or experience is required. **Job Preparation:** SVP 6.0 to less than 7.0—more than one year and less than four years. **Knowledge**—Building and Construction; Design; Fine Arts; Engineering and Technology; Physics. **Instructional Programs**—Carpentry/Carpenter.

Related DOT Jobs—860.381-030 Carpenter, Bridge; 860.381-042 Carpenter, Rough; 860.381-046 Form Builder; 869.361-018 Sign Erector-and-Repairer; 869.381-034 Timber Framer.

47-2031.03 Carpenter Assemblers and Repairers

- Education/Training Required: Moderate-term on-the-job training
- Employed: No data available.
- Annual Earnings: $33,470
- Growth: 8.2%
- Annual Job Openings: 161,000

Perform a variety of tasks requiring a limited knowledge of carpentry, such as applying siding and weatherboard to building exteriors or assembling and erecting prefabricated buildings.

Measures and marks location of studs, leaders, and receptacle openings, using tape measure, template, and marker. Cuts sidings and moldings, sections of weatherboard, openings in sheetrock, and lumber, using hand tools and power tools. Aligns and fastens materials together, using hand tools and power tools, to form building or bracing. Lays out and aligns materials on worktable or in assembly jig according to specified instructions. Installs prefabricated windows and doors; insulation; wall, ceiling, and floor panels; or siding, using adhesives, hoists, hand tools, and power tools. Trims overlapping edges of wood or weatherboard, using portable router or power saw and hand tools. Removes surface defects, using knife, scraper, wet sponge, electric iron, and sanding tools. Repairs or replaces defective locks, hinges, cranks, and pieces of wood, using glue, hand tools, and power tools. Realigns windows and screens to fit casements and oils moving parts. Measures cut materials to determine conformance to specifications, using tape measure. Examines wood surfaces for defects, such as nicks, cracks, or blisters. Fills cracks, seams, depressions, and nail holes with filler. Studies blueprints, specification sheets, and drawings to determine style and type of window or wall panel required. Moves panel or roof section to other workstations or to storage or shipping area, using electric hoist. Directs crane operator in positioning floor, wall, ceiling, and roof panel on house foundation. Applies stain, paint, or crayons to defects and filter to touch up the repaired area.

GOE INFORMATION—Interest Area: 06. Construction, Mining, and Drilling. **Work Group:** 06.04. Hands-on Work in Construction, Extraction, and Maintenance. **Personality Type**—Realistic. Realistic occupations frequently involve work activities that include practical, hands-on problems and solutions. They often deal with plants, animals, and real-world materials like wood, tools, and machinery. Many of the occupations require working outside and do not involve a lot of paperwork or working closely with others. **Work Values**—Moral Values; Variety; Pleasant Co-workers; Activity; Supervision, Technical. **Skills**—Repairing; In-

stallation; Operation and Control. **Abilities**—*Cognitive:* Spatial Orientation; Visualization; Perceptual Speed; Memorization; Time Sharing. *Psychomotor:* Manual Dexterity; Multilimb Coordination; Arm-Hand Steadiness; Speed of Limb Movement; Control Precision. *Physical:* Gross Body Equilibrium; Explosive Strength; Dynamic Strength; Static Strength; Gross Body Coordination. *Sensory:* Depth Perception; Glare Sensitivity; Peripheral Vision; Far Vision; Visual Color Discrimination. **General Work Activities**—*Information Input:* Getting Information; Identifying Objects, Actions, and Events; Inspecting Equipment, Structures, or Materials. *Mental Process:* Updating and Using Relevant Knowledge; Analyzing Data or Information; Evaluating Information Against Standards. *Work Output:* Performing General Physical Activities; Handling and Moving Objects; Controlling Machines and Processes. *Interacting with Others:* Communicating with Other Workers; Coordinating the Work and Activities of Others; Assisting and Caring for Others. **Physical Work Conditions**—High Places; Hazardous Equipment; Cramped Work Space or Awkward Positions; Climbing Ladders, Scaffolds, Poles, etc.; Kneeling, Crouching, or Crawling. **Other Job Characteristics**—Importance of Repeating Same Tasks; Pace Determined by Speed of Equipment; Degree of Automation.

Experience—Job Zone 2. Some previous work-related skill, knowledge, or experience may be helpful, but usually is not needed. **Job Preparation:** SVP 4.0 to less than 6.0—six months to less than two years. **Knowledge**—Building and Construction; Design; Engineering and Technology; Mechanical. **Instructional Programs**—Carpentry/Carpenter.

Related DOT Jobs—769.684-038 Repairer, Assembled Wood Products; 860.664-010 Carpenter I; 860.681-010 Carpenter II; 860.684-010 Builder, Beam; 860.684-014 Sider; 863.684-010 Composition-Weatherboard Applier; 863.684-014 Sider; 869.684-018 Assembler, Subassembly; 869.684-034 Lay-Out Worker; 869.684-038 Panel Installer; 869.684-042 Roof Assembler I; 869.684-062 Stull Installer; 869.684-066 Trimmer; 899.684-042 Window Repairer; 920.684-010 Crater.

47-2031.04 Ship Carpenters and Joiners

- Education/Training Required: Moderate-term on-the-job training
- Employed: No data available.
- Annual Earnings: $33,470
- Growth: 8.2%
- Annual Job Openings: 161,000

Fabricate, assemble, install, or repair wooden furnishings in ships or boats.

Reads blueprints to determine dimensions of furnishings in ships or boats. Shapes and laminates wood to form parts of ship, using steam chambers, clamps, glue, and jigs. Assembles and installs hardware, gaskets, floors, furnishings, or insulation, using adhesive, hand tools, and power tools. Repairs structural woodwork and replaces defective parts and equipment, using hand tools and power tools. Cuts wood or glass to specified dimensions, using hand tools and power tools. Constructs floors, doors, and partitions, using woodworking machines, hand tools, and power tools. Shapes irregular parts and trims excess material from bulkhead and furnishings to ensure fit meets specifications. Transfers dimensions or measurements of wood parts or bulkhead on plywood, using measuring instruments and marking devices. Greases gears and other moving parts of machines on ship.

GOE INFORMATION—Interest Area: 06. Construction, Mining, and Drilling. **Work Group:** 06.02. Construction. **Personality Type**—Realistic. Realistic occupations frequently involve work activities that include practical, hands-on problems and solutions. They often deal with plants, animals, and real-world materials like wood, tools, and machinery. Many of the occupations require working outside and do not involve a lot of paperwork or working closely with others. **Work Values**—Independence; Variety; Compensation; Moral Values; Activity. **Skills**—Installation; Repairing. **Abilities**—*Cognitive:* Visualization; Number Facility; Spatial Orientation. *Psychomotor:* Manual Dexterity; Speed of Limb Movement; Control Precision; Multilimb Coordination; Wrist-Finger Speed. *Physical:* Dynamic Flexibility; Stamina; Static Strength; Explosive Strength; Extent Flexibility. *Sensory:* Depth Perception; Far Vision; Near Vision. **General Work Activities**—*Information Input:* Getting Information; Monitoring Processes, Materials, or Surroundings; Identifying Objects, Actions, and Events. *Mental Process:* Making Decisions and Solving Problems; Evaluating Information Against Standards; Updating and Using Relevant Knowledge. *Work Output:* Handling and Moving Objects; Performing General Physical Activities; Controlling Machines and Processes. *Interacting with Others:* Communicating with Other Workers; Coordinating the Work and Activities of Others; Performing Administrative Activities. **Physical Work Conditions**—Climbing Ladders, Scaffolds, Poles, etc.; Hazardous Equipment; Using Hands on Objects, Tools, or Controls; Kneeling, Crouching, or Crawling; Keeping or Regaining Balance. **Other Job Characteristics**—Importance of Being Exact or Accurate; Consequence of Error; Importance of Repeating Same Tasks.

Experience—Job Zone 3. Previous work-related skill, knowledge, or experience is required. **Job Preparation:** SVP 6.0 to less than 7.0—more than one year and less than four years. **Knowledge**—Building and Construction; Design; Engineering and Technology; Mechanical; Fine Arts. **Instructional Programs**—Carpentry/Carpenter.

Related DOT Jobs—806.281-058 Carpenter, Prototype; 860.281-014 Carpenter, Ship; 860.381-050 Joiner; 860.381-054 Joiner Apprentice.

47-2031.05 Boat Builders and Shipwrights

- Education/Training Required: **Long-term on-the-job training**
- Employed: **No data available.**
- Annual Earnings: **$33,470**
- Growth: **8.2%**
- Annual Job Openings: **161,000**

Construct and repair ships or boats according to blueprints.

Cuts and forms parts, such as keel, ribs, sidings, and support structures and blocks, using woodworking hand tools and power tools. Constructs and shapes wooden frames, structures, and other parts according to blueprint specifications, using hand tools, power tools, and measuring instruments. Assembles and installs hull timbers and other structures in ship, using adhesive, measuring instruments, and hand tools or power tools. Attaches metal parts, such as fittings, plates, and bulkheads, to ship, using brace and bits, augers, and wrenches. Cuts out defect, using power tools and hand tools, and fits and secures replacement part, using caulking gun, adhesive, or hand tools. Smoothes and finishes ship surfaces, using power sander, broadax, adze, and paint, and waxes and buffs surface to specified finish. Establishes dimensional reference points on layout and hull to make template of parts and locate machinery and equipment. Measures and marks dimensional lines on lumber, following template and using scriber. Positions and secures support structures on construction area. Inspects boat to determine location and extent of defect. Marks outline of boat on building dock, shipway, or mold loft according to blueprint specifications, using measuring instruments and crayon. Attaches hoist to sections of hull and directs hoist operator to align parts over blocks according to layout of boat. Consults with customer or supervisor and reads blueprint to determine necessary repairs.

GOE INFORMATION—Interest Area: 06. Construction, Mining, and Drilling. **Work Group:** 06.02. Construction. **Personality Type**—Realistic. Realistic occupations frequently involve work activities that include practical, hands-on problems and solutions. They often deal with plants, animals, and real-world materials like wood, tools, and machinery. Many of the occupations require working outside and do not involve a lot of paperwork or working closely with others. **Work Values**—Ability Utilization; Achievement; Supervision, Technical; Variety; Compensation. **Skills**—Repairing; Installation; Equipment Selection; Operations Analysis; Technology Design. **Abilities**—*Cognitive:* Visualization; Information Ordering; Oral Comprehension; Number Facility; Spatial Orientation. *Psychomotor:* Manual Dexterity; Arm-Hand Steadiness; Control Precision; Speed of Limb Movement; Wrist-Finger Speed. *Physical:* Static Strength; Dynamic Strength; Extent Flexibility; Gross Body Equilibrium; Trunk Strength. *Sensory:* Near Vision; Depth Perception; Speech Recognition; Peripheral Vision. **General Work Activities**—*Information Input:* Inspecting Equipment, Structures, or Materials; Estimating Needed Characteristics; Getting Information. *Mental Process:* Updating and Using Relevant Knowledge; Processing Information; Evaluating Information Against Standards. *Work Output:* Performing General Physical Activities; Handling and Moving Objects; Repairing and Maintaining Mechanical Equipment. *Interacting with Others:* Communicating with Other Workers; Communicating with Persons Outside Organization; Establishing and Maintaining Relationships. **Physical Work Conditions**—Outdoors; Climbing Ladders, Scaffolds, Poles, etc.; Cramped Work Space or Awkward Positions; Hazardous Equipment; High Places. **Other Job Characteristics**—Importance of Being Exact or Accurate; Consequence of Error; Importance of Repeating Same Tasks.

Experience—Job Zone 4. A minimum of two to four years of work-related skill, knowledge, or experience is needed. **Job Preparation:** SVP 7.0 to less than 8.0—two years to less than 10 years. **Knowledge**—Building and Construction; Design; Mechanical; Production and Processing; Engineering and Technology. **Instructional Programs**—Carpentry/Carpenter.

Related DOT Jobs—807.361-014 Boat Repairer; 860.361-010 Boatbuilder, Wood; 860.361-014 Boatbuilder Apprentice, Wood; 860.381-058 Shipwright; 860.381-062 Shipwright Apprentice.

47-2031.06 Brattice Builders

- Education/Training Required: **Moderate-term on-the-job training**
- Employed: **No data available.**
- Annual Earnings: **$33,470**
- Growth: **8.2%**
- Annual Job Openings: **161,000**

Build doors or brattices (ventilation walls or partitions) in underground passageways to control the proper circulation of air through the passageways and to the working places.

Installs rigid and flexible air ducts to transport air to work areas. Erects partitions to support roof in areas unsuited to timbering or bolting. Drills and blasts obstructing boulders to reopen ventilation shafts.

GOE INFORMATION—Interest Area: 06. Construction, Mining, and Drilling. **Work Group:** 06.02. Construction. **Personality Type**—Realistic. Realistic occupations frequently involve work activities that include practical, hands-on problems and solutions. They often deal with plants, animals, and real-world materials like wood, tools, and machinery. Many of the occupations require working outside and do not involve a lot of paperwork or working closely with others. **Work Values**—Moral Values;

Supervision, Technical; Supervision, Human Relations. **Skills**—Installation; Equipment Selection; Technology Design. **Abilities**—*Cognitive:* None met the criteria. *Psychomotor:* Multilimb Coordination; Speed of Limb Movement; Control Precision; Arm-Hand Steadiness; Wrist-Finger Speed. *Physical:* Dynamic Strength; Extent Flexibility; Explosive Strength; Static Strength; Stamina. *Sensory:* Depth Perception. **General Work Activities**—*Information Input:* Inspecting Equipment, Structures, or Materials; Monitoring Processes, Materials, or Surroundings; Identifying Objects, Actions, and Events. *Mental Process:* Making Decisions and Solving Problems; Evaluating Information Against Standards; Analyzing Data or Information. *Work Output:* Performing General Physical Activities; Handling and Moving Objects; Controlling Machines and Processes. *Interacting with Others:* Communicating with Other Workers; Teaching Others; Coaching and Developing Others. **Physical Work Conditions**—Cramped Work Space or Awkward Positions; Hazardous Conditions; Whole Body Vibration; Specialized Protective or Safety Attire; Common Protective or Safety Attire. **Other Job Characteristics**—Consequence of Error; Importance of Repeating Same Tasks; Importance of Being Exact or Accurate.

Experience—Job Zone 2. Some previous work-related skill, knowledge, or experience may be helpful, but usually is not needed. **Job Preparation:** SVP 4.0 to less than 6.0—six months to less than two years. **Knowledge**—Building and Construction; Physics; Mechanical; Engineering and Technology; Design. **Instructional Programs**—Carpentry/Carpenter.

Related DOT Jobs—869.684-058 Stopping Builder.

47-2041.00 *Carpet Installers*

- **Education/Training Required: Moderate-term on-the-job training**
- **Employed: 76,007**
- **Annual Earnings: $31,470**
- **Growth: 10.5%**
- **Annual Job Openings: 7,000**

Lay and install carpet from rolls or blocks on floors. Install padding and trim flooring materials.

Cut and trim carpet to fit along wall edges, openings, and projections, finishing the edges with a wall trimmer. Cut carpet padding to size and install padding, following prescribed method. Fasten metal treads across door openings or where carpet meets flooring to hold carpet in place. Inspect the surface to be covered to determine its condition and correct any imperfections that might show through carpet or cause carpet to wear unevenly. Install carpet on some floors using adhesive, following prescribed method. Nail tack strips around area to be carpeted or use old strips to attach edges of new carpet. Plan the layout of the carpet, allowing for expected traffic patterns and placing seams for best appearance and longest wear. Roll out, measure, mark, and cut carpeting to size with a carpet knife, following floor sketches and allowing extra carpet for final fitting. Stretch carpet to align with walls and ensure a smooth surface and press carpet in place over tack strips or use staples, tape, tacks, or glue to hold carpet in place. Take measurements and study floor sketches to calculate the area to be carpeted and the amount of material needed. Cut and bind material. Draw building diagrams and record dimensions. Join edges of carpet and seam edges where necessary by sewing or by using tape with glue and heated carpet iron. Measure, cut, and install tackless strips along the baseboard or wall. Move furniture from area to be carpeted and remove old carpet and padding.

GOE INFORMATION—**Interest Area:** 06. Construction, Mining, and Drilling. **Work Group:** 06.02. Construction. **Personality Type**—Realistic. Realistic occupations frequently involve work activities that include practical, hands-on problems and solutions. They often deal with plants,

animals, and real-world materials like wood, tools, and machinery. Many of the occupations require working outside and do not involve a lot of paperwork or working closely with others. **Work Values**—Moral Values; Social Service. **Skills**—Installation; Mathematics. **Abilities**—*Cognitive:* Visualization; Spatial Orientation; Mathematical Reasoning. *Psychomotor:* Speed of Limb Movement; Multilimb Coordination; Arm-Hand Steadiness; Wrist-Finger Speed; Manual Dexterity. *Physical:* Static Strength; Explosive Strength; Dynamic Flexibility; Dynamic Strength; Stamina. *Sensory:* Visual Color Discrimination; Depth Perception; Far Vision; Glare Sensitivity; Night Vision. **General Work Activities**—*Information Input:* Identifying Objects, Actions, and Events; Estimating Needed Characteristics; Getting Information. *Mental Process:* Evaluating Information Against Standards; Organizing, Planning, and Prioritizing; Updating and Using Relevant Knowledge. *Work Output:* Performing General Physical Activities; Handling and Moving Objects; Controlling Machines and Processes. *Interacting with Others:* Communicating with Persons Outside Organization; Performing for or Working with the Public; Establishing and Maintaining Relationships. **Physical Work Conditions**—Kneeling, Crouching, or Crawling; Bending or Twisting the Body; Cramped Work Space or Awkward Positions; Making Repetitive Motions; Minor Burns, Cuts, Bites, or Stings. **Other Job Characteristics**—Importance of Repeating Same Tasks; Consequence of Error; Pace Determined by Speed of Equipment.

Experience—Job Zone 4. A minimum of two to four years of work-related skill, knowledge, or experience is needed. **Job Preparation:** SVP 7.0 to less than 8.0—two years to less than 10 years. **Knowledge**—Building and Construction; Design; Therapy and Counseling; Fine Arts; Philosophy and Theology. **Instructional Programs**—Construction Trades, Other.

Related DOT Jobs—864.381-010 Carpet Layer.

47-2042.00 *Floor Layers, Except Carpet, Wood, and Hard Tiles*

- **Education/Training Required: Moderate-term on-the-job training**
- **Employed: 23,236**
- **Annual Earnings: $31,490**
- **Growth: 15.8%**
- **Annual Job Openings: 2,000**

Apply blocks, strips, or sheets of shock-absorbing, sound-deadening, or decorative coverings to floors.

Apply adhesive cement to floor or wall material to join and adhere foundation material. Cut covering and foundation materials according to blueprints and sketches. Cut flooring material to fit around obstructions. Determine traffic areas and decide location of seams. Form a smooth foundation by stapling plywood or Masonite over the floor or by brushing waterproof compound onto surface and filling cracks with plaster, putty, or grout to seal pores. Heat and soften floor covering materials to patch cracks or fit floor coverings around irregular surfaces, using blowtorch. Inspect surface to be covered to ensure that it is firm and dry. Lay out, position, and apply shock-absorbing, sound-deadening, or decorative coverings to floors, walls, and cabinets, following guidelines to keep courses straight and create designs. Measure and mark guidelines on surfaces or foundations, using chalk lines and dividers. Remove excess cement to clean finished surface. Roll and press sheet wall and floor covering into cement base to smooth and finish surface, using hand roller. Sweep, scrape, sand, or chip dirt and irregularities to clean base surfaces, correcting imperfections that may show through the covering. Trim excess covering materials, tack edges, and join sections of covering material to form tight joint. Disconnect and remove appliances, light fixtures, and worn floor and wall covering from floors, walls, and cabinets.

GOE INFORMATION—Interest Area: 06. Construction, Mining, and Drilling. **Work Group:** 06.02. Construction. **Personality Type**—Realistic. Realistic occupations frequently involve work activities that include practical, hands-on problems and solutions. They often deal with plants, animals, and real-world materials like wood, tools, and machinery. Many of the occupations require working outside and do not involve a lot of paperwork or working closely with others. **Work Values**—Moral Values. **Skills**—Installation. **Abilities**—*Cognitive:* Visualization. *Psychomotor:* Multilimb Coordination; Manual Dexterity; Control Precision; Finger Dexterity; Speed of Limb Movement. *Physical:* Extent Flexibility; Explosive Strength; Static Strength; Trunk Strength; Dynamic Strength. *Sensory:* Depth Perception. **General Work Activities**—*Information Input:* Estimating Needed Characteristics; Getting Information; Identifying Objects, Actions, and Events. *Mental Process:* Organizing, Planning, and Prioritizing; Evaluating Information Against Standards; Judging Qualities of Things, Services, or Other People's Work. *Work Output:* Handling and Moving Objects; Performing General Physical Activities; Controlling Machines and Processes. *Interacting with Others:* Communicating with Other Workers; Communicating with Persons Outside Organization; Establishing and Maintaining Relationships. **Physical Work Conditions**—Kneeling, Crouching, or Crawling; Cramped Work Space or Awkward Positions; Bending or Twisting the Body; Minor Burns, Cuts, Bites, or Stings; Indoors. **Other Job Characteristics**—Importance of Repeating Same Tasks; Consequence of Error; Pace Determined by Speed of Equipment.

Experience—Job Zone 3. Previous work-related skill, knowledge, or experience is required. **Job Preparation:** SVP 6.0 to less than 7.0—more than one year and less than four years. **Knowledge**—Building and Construction; Design; Mechanical; Physics. **Instructional Programs**—Construction Trades, Other.

Related DOT Jobs—622.381-026 Floor-Covering Layer; 861.381-034 Soft-Tile Setter; 864.481-010 Floor Layer; 864.481-014 Floor-Layer Apprentice.

47-2043.00 Floor Sanders and Finishers

- **Education/Training Required: Moderate-term on-the-job training**
- **Employed: 13,709**
- **Annual Earnings: $25,930**
- **Growth: 14.7%**
- **Annual Job Openings: 1,000**

Scrape and sand wooden floors to smooth surfaces, using floor scraper and floor sanding machine, and apply coats of finish.

Guides machine over surface of floor until surface is smooth. Scrapes and sands floor edges and areas inaccessible to floor sander, using scraper and disk-type sander. Attaches sandpaper to roller of sanding machine. Applies filler compound to floor to seal wood.

GOE INFORMATION—Interest Area: 06. Construction, Mining, and Drilling. **Work Group:** 06.02. Construction. **Personality Type**—Realistic. Realistic occupations frequently involve work activities that include practical, hands-on problems and solutions. They often deal with plants, animals, and real-world materials like wood, tools, and machinery. Many of the occupations require working outside and do not involve a lot of paperwork or working closely with others. **Work Values**—Moral Values. **Skills**—Equipment Selection. **Abilities**—*Cognitive:* Spatial Orientation. *Psychomotor:* Speed of Limb Movement; Multilimb Coordination; Manual Dexterity; Rate Control; Control Precision. *Physical:* Stamina; Dynamic

Strength; Dynamic Flexibility; Static Strength; Gross Body Coordination. *Sensory:* Depth Perception; Far Vision; Peripheral Vision. **General Work Activities**—*Information Input:* Monitoring Processes, Materials, or Surroundings; Inspecting Equipment, Structures, or Materials; Getting Information. *Mental Process:* Judging Qualities of Things, Services, or Other People's Work; Organizing, Planning, and Prioritizing; Evaluating Information Against Standards. *Work Output:* Performing General Physical Activities; Handling and Moving Objects; Controlling Machines and Processes. *Interacting with Others:* Communicating with Other Workers; Communicating with Persons Outside Organization; Performing for or Working with the Public. **Physical Work Conditions**—Contaminants; Whole Body Vibration; Making Repetitive Motions; Using Hands on Objects, Tools, or Controls; Common Protective or Safety Attire. **Other Job Characteristics**—Degree of Automation; Importance of Repeating Same Tasks; Pace Determined by Speed of Equipment.

Experience—Job Zone 2. Some previous work-related skill, knowledge, or experience may be helpful, but usually is not needed. **Job Preparation:** SVP 4.0 to less than 6.0—six months to less than two years. **Knowledge**—Mechanical; Building and Construction; Philosophy and Theology. **Instructional Programs**—Construction Trades, Other.

Related DOT Jobs—869.664-014 Construction Worker I.

47-2044.00 Tile and Marble Setters

- **Education/Training Required: Long-term on-the-job training**
- **Employed: 53,990**
- **Annual Earnings: $35,390**
- **Growth: 15.6%**
- **Annual Job Openings: 5,000**

Apply hard tile, marble, and wood tile to walls, floors, ceilings, and roof decks.

Align and straighten tile, using levels, squares and straightedges. Apply a sealer to make grout stain- and water-resistant. Apply mortar to tile back, position the tile, and press or tap with trowel handle to affix tile to base. Build underbeds and install anchor bolts, wires, and brackets. Cut and shape tile to fit around obstacles and into odd spaces and corners, using hand and power cutting tools. Cut tile backing to required size, using shears. Determine and implement the best layout to achieve a desired pattern. Finish and dress the joints and wipe excess grout from between tiles, using damp sponge. Install and anchor fixtures in designated positions, using hand tools. Lay and set mosaic tiles to create decorative wall, mural, and floor designs. Measure and cut metal lath to size for walls and ceilings, using tin snips. Measure and mark surfaces to be tiled, following blueprints. Mix and apply mortar or cement to edges and ends of drain tiles to seal halves and joints. Mix, apply, and spread plaster, concrete, mortar, cement, mastic, glue, or other adhesives to form a bed for the tiles, using brush, trowel and screed. Prepare surfaces for tiling by attaching lath or waterproof paper or by applying a cement mortar coat onto a metal screen. Study blueprints and examine surface to be covered to determine amount of material needed. Assist customers in selection of tile and grout. Brush glue onto manila paper on which design has been drawn and position tiles finished side down onto paper. Cut, surface, polish, and install marble and granite and/or install pre-cast terrazzo, granite, or marble units. Level concrete and allow to dry. Prepare cost and labor estimates based on calculations of time and materials needed for project. Remove and replace cracked or damaged tile. Remove any old tile, grout, and adhesive, using chisels and scrapers, and clean the surface carefully. Select and order tile and other items to be installed, such as bathroom accessories, walls, panels, and cabinets, according to specifications. Spread mastic or other adhesive base on roof deck to form base for promenade tile, using serrated spreader.

GOE INFORMATION—**Interest Area:** 06. Construction, Mining, and Drilling. **Work Group:** 06.02. Construction. **Personality Type**—Realistic. Realistic occupations frequently involve work activities that include practical, hands-on problems and solutions. They often deal with plants, animals, and real-world materials like wood, tools, and machinery. Many of the occupations require working outside and do not involve a lot of paperwork or working closely with others. **Work Values**—Moral Values; Independence; Compensation; Supervision, Technical; Achievement. **Skills**—Installation. **Abilities**—*Cognitive:* Visualization; Information Ordering; Spatial Orientation. *Psychomotor:* Arm-Hand Steadiness; Multilimb Coordination; Manual Dexterity; Finger Dexterity; Speed of Limb Movement. *Physical:* Explosive Strength; Dynamic Strength; Extent Flexibility; Dynamic Flexibility; Static Strength. *Sensory:* Night Vision; Depth Perception; Glare Sensitivity; Visual Color Discrimination; Peripheral Vision. **General Work Activities**—*Information Input:* Getting Information; Estimating Needed Characteristics; Identifying Objects, Actions, and Events. *Mental Process:* Organizing, Planning, and Prioritizing; Analyzing Data or Information; Evaluating Information Against Standards. *Work Output:* Handling and Moving Objects; Performing General Physical Activities; Controlling Machines and Processes. *Interacting with Others:* Monitoring and Controlling Resources; Communicating with Persons Outside Organization; Establishing and Maintaining Relationships. **Physical Work Conditions**—High Places; Minor Burns, Cuts, Bites, or Stings; Climbing Ladders, Scaffolds, Poles, etc.; Cramped Work Space or Awkward Positions; Using Hands on Objects, Tools, or Controls. **Other Job Characteristics**—Importance of Being Exact or Accurate; Importance of Repeating Same Tasks; Pace Determined by Speed of Equipment.

Experience—Job Zone 2. Some previous work-related skill, knowledge, or experience may be helpful, but usually is not needed. **Job Preparation:** SVP 4.0 to less than 6.0—six months to less than two years. **Knowledge**—Building and Construction; Design; Physics; Fine Arts; Mechanical. **Instructional Programs**—Building/Construction Finishing, Management, and Inspection, Other.

Related DOT Jobs—779.381-014 Mosaic Worker; 861.381-054 Tile Setter; 861.381-058 Tile Setter Apprentice; 861.381-062 Tile-Conduit Layer; 861.684-018 Tile Setter.

47-2051.00 Cement Masons and Concrete Finishers

- **Education/Training Required: Long-term on-the-job training**
- **Employed:** 162,485
- **Annual Earnings:** $29,650
- **Growth:** 3.0%
- **Annual Job Openings:** 4,000

Smooth and finish surfaces of poured concrete, such as floors, walks, sidewalks, roads, or curbs, using a variety of hand and power tools. Align forms for sidewalks, curbs, or gutters; patch voids; use saws to cut expansion joints.

Apply hardening and sealing compounds to cure surface of concrete and waterproof or restore surface. Apply muriatic acid to clean surface and rinse with water. Check the forms that hold the concrete to see that they are properly constructed. Chip, scrape, and grind high spots, ridges, and rough projections to finish concrete, using pneumatic chisels, power grinders, or hand tools. Clean chipped area, using wire brush, and feel and observe surface to determine if it is rough or uneven. Mix cement, sand, and water to produce concrete, grout, or slurry, using hoe, trowel, tamper, scraper, or concrete-mixing machine. Mold expansion joints and edges, using edging tools, jointers, and straightedge. Monitor how the wind, heat, or cold affect the curing of the concrete throughout the entire process. Set the forms that hold concrete to the desired pitch and depth and align them. Spread, level, and smooth concrete, using rake, shovel, hand or power trowel, hand or power screed, and float. Waterproof or restore concrete surfaces, using appropriate compounds. Wet concrete surface and rub with stone to smooth surface and obtain specified finish. Wet surface to prepare for bonding, fill holes and cracks with grout or slurry, and smooth, using trowel. Build wooden molds and clamp molds around area to be repaired, using hand tools. Cut out damaged areas, drill holes for reinforcing rods, and position reinforcing rods to repair concrete, using power saw and drill. Direct the casting of the concrete and supervise laborers who use shovels or special tools to spread it. Install anchor bolts, steel plates, door sills, and other fixtures in freshly poured concrete and/or pattern or stamp the surface to provide a decorative finish. Polish surface, using polishing or surfacing machine. Produce rough concrete surface, using broom. Push roller over surface to embed chips in surface. Signal truck driver to position truck to facilitate pouring concrete and move chute to direct concrete on forms. Sprinkle colored marble or stone chips, powdered steel, or coloring powder over surface to produce prescribed finish. Cut metal division strips and press them into terrazzo base so that top edges form desired design or pattern. Fabricate concrete beams, columns, and panels. Operate power vibrator to compact concrete. Spread roofing paper on surface of foundation and spread concrete onto roofing paper with trowel to form terrazzo base.

GOE INFORMATION—**Interest Area:** 06. Construction, Mining, and Drilling. **Work Group:** 06.02. Construction. **Personality Type**—Realistic. Realistic occupations frequently involve work activities that include practical, hands-on problems and solutions. They often deal with plants, animals, and real-world materials like wood, tools, and machinery. Many of the occupations require working outside and do not involve a lot of paperwork or working closely with others. **Work Values**—Moral Values; Compensation; Pleasant Co-workers; Supervision, Technical; Ability Utilization. **Skills**—Repairing. **Abilities**—*Cognitive:* Spatial Orientation; Visualization. *Psychomotor:* Manual Dexterity; Speed of Limb Movement; Multilimb Coordination; Wrist-Finger Speed; Arm-Hand Steadiness. *Physical:* Static Strength; Stamina; Trunk Strength; Dynamic Flexibility; Explosive Strength. *Sensory:* Visual Color Discrimination; Glare Sensitivity; Auditory Attention; Far Vision; Peripheral Vision. **General Work Activities**—*Information Input:* Getting Information; Inspecting Equipment, Structures, or Materials; Monitoring Processes, Materials, or Surroundings. *Mental Process:* Organizing, Planning, and Prioritizing; Judging Qualities of Things, Services, or Other People's Work; Evaluating Information Against Standards. *Work Output:* Performing General Physical Activities; Handling and Moving Objects; Controlling Machines and Processes. *Interacting with Others:* Communicating with Other Workers; Establishing and Maintaining Relationships; Communicating with Persons Outside Organization. **Physical Work Conditions**—Outdoors; Kneeling, Crouching, or Crawling; Keeping or Regaining Balance; Bending or Twisting the Body; Climbing Ladders, Scaffolds, Poles, etc. **Other Job Characteristics**—Importance of Repeating Same Tasks; Pace Determined by Speed of Equipment; Consequence of Error.

Experience—Job Zone 3. Previous work-related skill, knowledge, or experience is required. **Job Preparation:** SVP 6.0 to less than 7.0—more than one year and less than four years. **Knowledge**—Building and Construction; Fine Arts; Design; Engineering and Technology; Geography. **Instructional Programs**—Concrete Finishing/Concrete Finisher.

Related DOT Jobs—844.364-010 Cement Mason; 844.364-014 Cement-Mason Apprentice; 844.461-010 Concrete-Stone Finisher; 844.684-010 Concrete Rubber.

47-2053.00 Terrazzo Workers and Finishers

- **Education/Training Required: Long-term on-the-job training**
- **Employed: 3,493**
- **Annual Earnings: $28,690**
- **Growth: 2.0%**
- **Annual Job Openings: Fewer than 500**

Apply a mixture of cement, sand, pigment, or marble chips to floors, stairways, and cabinet fixtures to fashion durable and decorative surfaces.

Blend marble chip mixtures and place into panels and then push a roller over the surface to embed the chips. Cut metal division strips and press them into the terrazzo base wherever there is to be a joint or change of color, to form desired designs or patterns, and to help prevent cracks. Grind curved surfaces and areas inaccessible to surfacing machine, such as stairways and cabinet tops, with portable hand grinder. Grind surfaces with a power grinder and polish surfaces with polishing or surfacing machines. Measure designated amounts of ingredients for terrazzo or grout according to standard formulas and specifications, using graduated containers and scale, and load ingredients into portable mixer. Mix cement, sand, and water to produce concrete, grout, or slurry, using hoe, trowel, tamper, scraper, or concrete-mixing machine. Modify mixing, grouting, grinding, and cleaning procedures according to type of installation or material used. Mold expansion joints and edges, using edging tools, jointers, and straightedges. Position and secure moisture membrane and wire mesh prior to pouring base materials for terrazzo installation. Spread roofing paper on surface of foundation and spread concrete onto roofing paper with trowel to form terrazzo base. Spread, level, and smooth concrete and terrazzo mixtures to form bases and finished surfaces, using rakes, shovels, hand or power trowels, hand or power screeds, and floats. Sprinkle colored marble or stone chips, powdered steel, or coloring powder over surface to produce prescribed finish. Wash polished terrazzo surface, using cleaner and water, and apply sealer and curing agent according to manufacturer's specifications, using brush or sprayer. Wet surface to prepare for bonding, fill holes and cracks with grout or slurry, and smooth, using trowel. Build wooden molds, clamping molds around areas to be repaired and setting up frames to the proper depth and alignment. Chip, scrape, and grind high spots, ridges, and rough projections to finish concrete, using pneumatic chisel, hand chisel, or other hand tools. Clean chipped area, using wire brush, and feel and observe surface to determine if it is rough or uneven. Clean installation site, mixing and storage areas, tools, machines, and equipment, and store materials and equipment. Cut out damaged areas, drill holes for reinforcing rods, and position reinforcing rods to repair concrete, using power saw and drill. Fill slight depressions left by grinding with a matching grout material and then hand-trowel for a smooth, uniform surface. Move terrazzo installation materials, tools, machines, and work devices to work areas, manually or using wheelbarrow. Precast terrazzo blocks in wooden forms. Produce rough concrete surface, using broom. Remove frames once the foundation is dry. Signal truck driver to position truck to facilitate pouring concrete and move chute to direct concrete on forms. Wet concrete surface and rub with stone to smooth surface and obtain specified finish.

GOE INFORMATION—Interest Area: 06. Construction, Mining, and Drilling. **Work Group:** 06.02. Construction. **Personality Type**—Realistic. Realistic occupations frequently involve work activities that include practical, hands-on problems and solutions. They often deal with plants, animals, and real-world materials like wood, tools, and machinery. Many of the occupations require working outside and do not involve a lot of paperwork or working closely with others. **Work Values**—Moral Values; Compensation; Pleasant Co-workers; Supervision, Technical; Ability Utilization. **Skills**—Repairing. **Abilities**—*Cognitive:* Spatial Orientation; Visualization. *Psychomotor:* Manual Dexterity; Speed of Limb Movement; Multilimb Coordination; Wrist-Finger Speed; Arm-Hand Steadiness. *Physical:* Static Strength; Stamina; Trunk Strength; Dynamic Flexibility; Explosive Strength. *Sensory:* Visual Color Discrimination; Glare Sensitivity; Auditory Attention; Far Vision; Peripheral Vision. **General Work Activities**—*Information Input:* Inspecting Equipment, Structures, or Materials; Getting Information; Monitoring Processes, Materials, or Surroundings. *Mental Process:* Organizing, Planning, and Prioritizing; Judging Qualities of Things, Services, or Other People's Work; Updating and Using Relevant Knowledge. *Work Output:* Performing General Physical Activities; Handling and Moving Objects; Controlling Machines and Processes. *Interacting with Others:* Communicating with Other Workers; Establishing and Maintaining Relationships; Coordinating the Work and Activities of Others. **Physical Work Conditions**—Outdoors; Kneeling, Crouching, or Crawling; Keeping or Regaining Balance; Bending or Twisting the Body; Climbing Ladders, Scaffolds, Poles, etc. **Other Job Characteristics**—Importance of Repeating Same Tasks; Pace Determined by Speed of Equipment; Consequence of Error.

Experience—Job Zone 3. Previous work-related skill, knowledge, or experience is required. **Job Preparation:** SVP 6.0 to less than 7.0—more than one year and less than four years. **Knowledge**—Building and Construction; Fine Arts; Design; Engineering and Technology; Geography. **Instructional Programs**—Building/Construction Finishing, Management, and Inspection, Other.

Related DOT Jobs—861.381-046 Terrazzo Worker; 861.381-050 Terrazzo-Worker Apprentice.

47-2061.00 Construction Laborers

- **Education/Training Required: Moderate-term on-the-job training**
- **Employed: 791,324**
- **Annual Earnings: $24,070**
- **Growth: 17.0%**
- **Annual Job Openings: 236,000**

Perform tasks involving physical labor at building, highway, and heavy construction projects, tunnel and shaft excavations, and demolition sites. May operate hand and power tools of all types: air hammers, earth tampers, cement mixers, small mechanical hoists, surveying and measuring equipment, and a variety of other equipment and instruments. May clean and prepare sites, dig trenches, set braces to support the sides of excavations, erect scaffolding, clean up rubble and debris, and remove asbestos, lead, and other hazardous waste materials. May assist other craft workers.

Tends pumps, compressors, and generators to provide power for tools, machinery, and equipment or to heat and move materials such as asphalt. Mops, brushes, or spreads paints, cleaning solutions, or other compounds over surfaces to clean or provide protection. Cleans construction site to eliminate possible hazards. Tends machine that pumps concrete, grout, cement, sand, plaster, or stucco through spray gun for application to ceilings and walls. Lubricates, cleans, and repairs machinery, equipment, and tools. Sprays materials such as water, sand, steam, vinyl, paint, or stucco through hose to clean, coat, or seal surfaces. Mixes ingredients to create compounds used to cover or clean surfaces. Razes buildings and salvages useful materials. Loads and unloads trucks and hauls and hoists materials. Mixes concrete, using portable mixer. Erects and disassembles scaffolding, shoring, braces, and other temporary structures. Grinds, scrapes, sands, or polishes surfaces, such as concrete, marble, terrazzo, or wood flooring, using abrasive tools or machines. Builds and positions forms for pouring concrete and dismantles forms after use, using saws, hammers, nails, or bolts. Signals equipment operators to facilitate alignment, movement, and adjustment of machinery, equipment, and materials. Digs ditches and levels earth to grade specifications, using pick and shovel. Positions, joins, aligns, and seals structural components, such as concrete wall sections and pipes. Applies caulking compounds by hand or with caulking gun to seal crevices. Smooth and finishes freshly poured cement or concrete, using float, trowel, screed, or powered cement finishing tool. Measures, marks, and records openings and distances to lay out area to be graded or to erect building structures.

GOE INFORMATION—Interest Area: 06. Construction, Mining, and Drilling. **Work Group:** 06.04. Hands-on Work in Construction, Extraction, and Maintenance. **Personality Type—**Realistic. Realistic occupations frequently involve work activities that include practical, hands-on problems and solutions. They often deal with plants, animals, and real-world materials like wood, tools, and machinery. Many of the occupations require working outside and do not involve a lot of paperwork or working closely with others. **Work Values—**Pleasant Co-workers; Supervision, Technical. **Skills—**None met the criteria. **Abilities—***Cognitive:* None met the criteria. *Psychomotor:* Speed of Limb Movement; Multilimb Coordination; Response Orientation; Control Precision; Arm-Hand Steadiness. *Physical:* Static Strength; Trunk Strength; Dynamic Strength; Stamina; Explosive Strength. *Sensory:* Glare Sensitivity. **General Work Activities—***Information Input:* Monitoring Processes, Materials, or Surroundings; Inspecting Equipment, Structures, or Materials; Identifying Objects, Actions, and Events. *Mental Process:* Updating and Using Relevant Knowledge; Making Decisions and Solving Problems; Evaluating Information Against Standards. *Work Output:* Performing General Physical Activities; Handling and Moving Objects; Controlling Machines and Processes. *Interacting with Others:* Communicating with Other Workers; Establishing and Maintaining Relationships; Assisting and Caring for Others. **Physical Work Conditions—**Outdoors; Hazardous Equipment; Minor Burns, Cuts, Bites, or Stings; Very Hot or Cold; Distracting Sounds and Noise Levels. **Other Job Characteristics—**Importance of Repeating Same Tasks; Pace Determined by Speed of Equipment; Consequence of Error.

Experience—Job Zone 2. Some previous work-related skill, knowledge, or experience may be helpful, but usually is not needed. **Job Preparation:** SVP 4.0 to less than 6.0—six months to less than two years. **Knowledge—**Building and Construction; Mechanical; Production and Processing; Engineering and Technology; Physics. **Instructional Programs—**Construction Trades, Other.

Related DOT Jobs—800.684-010 Riveter; 800.684-014 Riveter, Pneumatic; 842.665-010 Plaster-Machine Tender; 849.665-010 Pump Tender, Cement Based Materials; 850.467-010 Grade Checker; 853.665-010 Asphalt-Distributor Tender; 853.685-010 Asphalt-Heater Tender; 864.684-010 Floor and Wall Applier, Liquid; 869.487-010 Measurer; 869.664-010 Concrete-Building Assembler; 869.664-014 Construction Worker I; 869.665-010 Auxiliary-Equipment Tender; 869.667-010 Column Precaster; 869.684-082 Asbestos Removal Worker; 891.684-022 Building Cleaner; 891.685-010 Steam-Cleaning-Machine Operator; 899.684-046 Maintenance Worker, Municipal.

47-2071.00 Paving, Surfacing, and Tamping Equipment Operators

- ● **Education/Training Required:** Moderate-term on-the-job training
- ● **Employed:** 54,528
- ● **Annual Earnings:** $28,290
- ● **Growth:** 15.5%
- ● **Annual Job Openings:** 6,000

Operate equipment used for applying concrete, asphalt, or other materials to road beds, parking lots, or airport runways and taxiways or equipment used for tamping gravel, dirt, or other materials. Includes concrete and asphalt paving machine operators, form tampers, tamping machine operators, and stone spreader operators.

Control paving machines to push dump trucks and to maintain a constant flow of asphalt or other material into hoppers or screeds. Drive and operate curbing machines to extrude concrete or asphalt curbing. Fill tanks, hoppers, or machines with paving materials. Install dies, cutters, and extensions to screeds onto machines, using hand tools. Light burners or start heating units of machines and regulate screed temperatures and asphalt flow rates. Observe distribution of paving material in order to adjust machine settings or material flow and indicate low spots for workers to add material. Operate machines that clean or cut expansion joints in concrete or asphalt and that rout out cracks in pavement. Operate tamping machines or manually roll surfaces to compact earth fills, foundation forms, and finished road materials according to grade specifications. Place strips of material such as cork, asphalt, or steel into joints or place rolls of expansion-joint material on machines that automatically insert material. Set up and tear down equipment. Start machine, engage clutch, and push and move levers to guide machine along forms or guidelines and to control the operation of machine attachments. Operate machines to spread, smooth, level, or steel-reinforce stone, concrete, or asphalt on road beds. Coordinate truck dumping. Cut or break up pavement and drive guardrail posts, using machines equipped with interchangeable hammers. Drive machines onto truck trailers and drive trucks to transport machines and material to and from job sites. Inspect, clean, maintain, and repair equipment, using mechanics' hand tools, or report malfunctions to supervisors. Operate oil distributors, loaders, chip spreaders, dump trucks, and snow plows. Set up forms and lay out guidelines for curbs, according to written specifications, using string, spray paint, and concrete/water mixes. Shovel blacktop.

GOE INFORMATION—Interest Area: 06. Construction, Mining, and Drilling. **Work Group:** 06.02. Construction. **Personality Type—**Realistic. Realistic occupations frequently involve work activities that include practical, hands-on problems and solutions. They often deal with plants, animals, and real-world materials like wood, tools, and machinery. Many of the occupations require working outside and do not involve a lot of paperwork or working closely with others. **Work Values—**Moral Values; Supervision, Technical; Independence. **Skills—**Operation and Control; Operation Monitoring; Equipment Selection. **Abilities—***Cognitive:* Spatial Orientation; Visualization; Time Sharing; Selective Attention. *Psychomotor:* Control Precision; Reaction Time; Rate Control; Multilimb Coordination; Manual Dexterity. *Physical:* Explosive Strength; Dynamic Strength; Static Strength; Stamina; Dynamic Flexibility. *Sensory:* Depth Perception; Peripheral Vision; Far Vision; Glare Sensitivity; Night Vision. **General Work Activities—***Information Input:* Monitoring Processes, Materials, or Surroundings; Inspecting Equipment, Structures, or Materials; Identifying Objects, Actions, and Events. *Mental Process:* Making Decisions and Solving Problems; Judging Qualities of Things, Services, or Other People's Work; Updating and Using Relevant Knowledge. *Work*

Output: Controlling Machines and Processes; Handling and Moving Objects; Operating Vehicles or Equipment. *Interacting with Others:* Communicating with Other Workers; Coordinating the Work and Activities of Others; Interpreting Meaning of Information for Others. **Physical Work Conditions**—Outdoors; Hazardous Equipment; Whole Body Vibration; Distracting Sounds and Noise Levels; Using Hands on Objects, Tools, or Controls. **Other Job Characteristics**—Degree of Automation; Pace Determined by Speed of Equipment; Importance of Repeating Same Tasks.

Experience—Job Zone 2. Some previous work-related skill, knowledge, or experience may be helpful, but usually is not needed. **Job Preparation:** SVP 4.0 to less than 6.0—six months to less than two years. **Knowledge**—Mechanical; Production and Processing; Building and Construction; Physics; Design. **Instructional Programs**—Construction/Heavy Equipment/Earthmoving Equipment Operation.

Related DOT Jobs—853.663-010 Asphalt-Paving-Machine Operator; 853.663-014 Concrete-Paving-Machine Operator; 853.663-018 Road-Oiling-Truck Driver; 853.663-022 Stone-Spreader Operator; 853.683-010 Curb-Machine Operator; 853.683-014 Heater-Planer Operator; 853.683-018 Joint-Cleaning-and-Grooving-Machine Operator; 859.683-022 Reinforcing-Steel-Machine Operator; 859.683-026 Road-Mixer Operator; 859.683-030 Road-Roller Operator; 869.683-010 Form-Tamper Operator; 869.683-018 Tamping-Machine Operator.

47-2072.00 Pile-Driver Operators

- **Education/Training Required: Moderate-term on-the-job training**
- **Employed: 4,423**
- **Annual Earnings: $41,310**
- **Growth: 14.0%**
- **Annual Job Openings: 1,000**

Operate pile drivers mounted on skids, barges, crawler treads, or locomotive cranes to drive pilings for retaining walls, bulkheads, and foundations of structures, such as buildings, bridges, and piers.

Moves hand and foot levers to control hoisting equipment to position piling leads, hoist piling into leads, and position hammer over piling. Moves levers and turns valves to activate power hammer or raise and lower drophammer which drives piles to required depth.

GOE INFORMATION—**Interest Area:** 06. Construction, Mining, and Drilling. **Work Group:** 06.02. Construction. **Personality Type**—Realistic. Realistic occupations frequently involve work activities that include practical, hands-on problems and solutions. They often deal with plants, animals, and real-world materials like wood, tools, and machinery. Many of the occupations require working outside and do not involve a lot of paperwork or working closely with others. **Work Values**—Moral Values; Independence. **Skills**—Operation and Control; Operation Monitoring. **Abilities**—*Cognitive:* Spatial Orientation. *Psychomotor:* Multilimb Coordination; Control Precision; Speed of Limb Movement; Rate Control. *Physical:* Explosive Strength; Dynamic Flexibility; Extent Flexibility; Gross Body Coordination. *Sensory:* Depth Perception; Far Vision; Glare Sensitivity; Peripheral Vision; Night Vision. **General Work Activities**—*Information Input:* Monitoring Processes, Materials, or Surroundings; Getting Information; Inspecting Equipment, Structures, or Materials. *Mental Process:* Evaluating Information Against Standards; Organizing, Planning, and Prioritizing; Processing Information. *Work Output:* Controlling Machines and Processes; Operating Vehicles or Equipment; Handling and Moving Objects. *Interacting with Others:* Communicating with Other Workers; Coordinating the Work and Activities of Others; Establishing and Maintaining Relationships. **Physical Work Conditions**—Whole Body

Vibration; Outdoors; Hazardous Equipment; Distracting Sounds and Noise Levels; Extremely Bright or Inadequate Lighting. **Other Job Characteristics**—Degree of Automation; Pace Determined by Speed of Equipment; Consequence of Error.

Experience—Job Zone 2. Some previous work-related skill, knowledge, or experience may be helpful, but usually is not needed. **Job Preparation:** SVP 4.0 to less than 6.0—six months to less than two years. **Knowledge**—Building and Construction; Engineering and Technology; Mechanical; Physics; Public Safety and Security. **Instructional Programs**—Construction/Heavy Equipment/Earthmoving Equipment Operation.

Related DOT Jobs—859.682-018 Pile-Driver Operator.

47-2073.00 Operating Engineers and Other Construction Equipment Operators

- **Education/Training Required: Moderate-term on-the-job training**
- **Employed: 357,206**
- **Annual Earnings: $34,160**
- **Growth: 6.9%**
- **Annual Job Openings: 25,000**

Operate one or several types of power construction equipment, such as motor graders, bulldozers, scrapers, compressors, pumps, derricks, shovels, tractors, or front-end loaders to excavate, move, and grade earth, erect structures, or pour concrete or other hard-surface pavement. May repair and maintain equipment in addition to other duties.

No task data available.

GOE INFORMATION—**Interest Area:** 06. Construction, Mining, and Drilling. **Work Group:** 06.02. Construction. **Note:** The Department of Labor has not collected some data for this job, so it has fewer details than the other descriptions.

Instructional Programs—Construction/Heavy Equipment/Earthmoving Equipment Operation; Mobil Crane Operation/Operator.

Related DOT Jobs—850.663-014 Elevating-Grader Operator; 850.663-022 Motor-Grader Operator; 850.683-010 Bulldozer Operator I; 850.683-014 Ditcher Operator; 850.683-022 Form-Grader Operator; 850.683-038 Scraper Operator; 850.683-046 Utility-Tractor Operator; 859.683-010 Operating Engineer; 859.683-014 Operating-Engineer Apprentice; 955.463-010 Sanitary Landfill Operator.

47-2073.01 Grader, Bulldozer, and Scraper Operators

- **Education/Training Required: Moderate-term on-the-job training**
- **Employed: No data available.**
- **Annual Earnings: $34,160**
- **Growth: 6.9%**
- **Annual Job Openings: 25,000**

Operate machines or vehicles equipped with blades to remove, distribute, level, or grade earth.

Starts engine; moves throttle, switches, and levers; and depresses pedals to operate machines, equipment, and attachments. Drives equipment in successive passes over working area to achieve specified result, such as grading terrain or removing, dumping, or spreading earth and rock. Aligns machine, cutterhead, or depth gauge marker with reference stakes and guidelines on ground or positions equipment following hand signals of assistant. Fastens bulldozer blade or other attachment to tractor, using hitches. Connects hydraulic hoses, belts, mechanical linkage, or power takeoff shaft to tractor. Signals operator to guide movement of tractor-drawn machine. Greases, oils, and performs minor repairs on tractor, using grease gun, oilcans, and hand tools.

GOE INFORMATION—Interest Area: 06. Construction, Mining, and Drilling. **Work Group:** 06.02. Construction. **Personality Type**—Realistic. Realistic occupations frequently involve work activities that include practical, hands-on problems and solutions. They often deal with plants, animals, and real-world materials like wood, tools, and machinery. Many of the occupations require working outside and do not involve a lot of paperwork or working closely with others. **Work Values**—Moral Values; Supervision, Technical; Independence. **Skills**—Operation and Control; Repairing; Operation Monitoring; Equipment Selection. **Abilities**—*Cognitive:* Spatial Orientation. *Psychomotor:* Control Precision; Reaction Time; Rate Control; Response Orientation; Speed of Limb Movement. *Physical:* Explosive Strength; Dynamic Strength; Static Strength; Stamina; Trunk Strength. *Sensory:* Depth Perception; Far Vision; Glare Sensitivity; Peripheral Vision; Hearing Sensitivity. **General Work Activities**—*Information Input:* Monitoring Processes, Materials, or Surroundings; Getting Information; Identifying Objects, Actions, and Events. *Mental Process:* Updating and Using Relevant Knowledge; Evaluating Information Against Standards; Judging Qualities of Things, Services, or Other People's Work. *Work Output:* Operating Vehicles or Equipment; Handling and Moving Objects; Controlling Machines and Processes. *Interacting with Others:* Communicating with Other Workers; Assisting and Caring for Others; Coordinating the Work and Activities of Others. **Physical Work Conditions**—Whole Body Vibration; Outdoors; Hazardous Equipment; Distracting Sounds and Noise Levels; Very Hot or Cold. **Other Job Characteristics**—Degree of Automation; Pace Determined by Speed of Equipment; Importance of Repeating Same Tasks.

Experience—Job Zone 2. Some previous work-related skill, knowledge, or experience may be helpful, but usually is not needed. **Job Preparation:** SVP 4.0 to less than 6.0—six months to less than two years. **Knowledge**—Mechanical; Building and Construction; Physics; Philosophy and Theology. **Instructional Programs**—Construction/Heavy Equipment/Earthmoving Equipment Operation; Mobil Crane Operation/Operator.

Related DOT Jobs—850.663-014 Elevating-Grader Operator; 850.663-022 Motor-Grader Operator; 850.683-010 Bulldozer Operator I; 850.683-014 Ditcher Operator; 850.683-022 Form-Grader Operator; 850.683-038 Scraper Operator; 850.683-046 Utility-Tractor Operator; 955.463-010 Sanitary Landfill Operator.

47-2073.02 Operating Engineers

- **Education/Training Required: Moderate-term on-the-job training**
- **Employed: No data available.**
- **Annual Earnings: $34,160**
- **Growth: 6.9%**
- **Annual Job Openings: 25,000**

Operate several types of power construction equipment, such as compressors, pumps, hoists, derricks, cranes, shovels, tractors, scrapers, or motor graders, to excavate, move, and grade earth; erect structures; or pour concrete or other hard-surface pavement. May repair and maintain equipment in addition to other duties.

Adjusts handwheels and depresses pedals to drive machines and control attachments, such as blades, buckets, scrapers, and swing booms. Turns valves to control air and water output of compressors and pumps. Repairs and maintains equipment.

GOE INFORMATION—Interest Area: 06. Construction, Mining, and Drilling. **Work Group:** 06.02. Construction. **Personality Type**—Realistic. Realistic occupations frequently involve work activities that include practical, hands-on problems and solutions. They often deal with plants, animals, and real-world materials like wood, tools, and machinery. Many of the occupations require working outside and do not involve a lot of paperwork or working closely with others. **Work Values**—Supervision, Technical; Independence; Moral Values. **Skills**—Operation and Control; Repairing; Operation Monitoring; Troubleshooting. **Abilities**—*Cognitive:* Visualization. *Psychomotor:* Multilimb Coordination; Control Precision; Response Orientation; Reaction Time; Rate Control. *Physical:* Explosive Strength; Static Strength; Gross Body Coordination; Trunk Strength. *Sensory:* Depth Perception. **General Work Activities**—*Information Input:* Inspecting Equipment, Structures, or Materials; Monitoring Processes, Materials, or Surroundings; Identifying Objects, Actions, and Events. *Mental Process:* Organizing, Planning, and Prioritizing; Judging Qualities of Things, Services, or Other People's Work; Updating and Using Relevant Knowledge. *Work Output:* Controlling Machines and Processes; Handling and Moving Objects; Repairing and Maintaining Mechanical Equipment. *Interacting with Others:* Communicating with Persons Outside Organization; Influencing Others or Selling; Coordinating the Work and Activities of Others. **Physical Work Conditions**—Whole Body Vibration; Hazardous Equipment; Outdoors; Common Protective or Safety Attire; Very Hot or Cold. **Other Job Characteristics**—Pace Determined by Speed of Equipment; Degree of Automation; Importance of Repeating Same Tasks.

Experience—Job Zone 3. Previous work-related skill, knowledge, or experience is required. **Job Preparation:** SVP 6.0 to less than 7.0—more than one year and less than four years. **Knowledge**—Mechanical; Building and Construction; Sales and Marketing; Engineering and Technology; Physics. **Instructional Programs**—Construction/Heavy Equipment/Earthmoving Equipment Operation; Mobil Crane Operation/Operator.

Related DOT Jobs—859.683-010 Operating Engineer; 859.683-014 Operating-Engineer Apprentice.

47-2081.00 Drywall and Ceiling Tile Installers

- **Education/Training Required: Moderate-term on-the-job training**
- **Employed: 143,472**
- **Annual Earnings: $33,000**
- **Growth: 9.4%**
- **Annual Job Openings: 19,000**

Apply plasterboard or other wallboard to ceilings or interior walls of buildings. Apply or mount acoustical tiles or blocks, strips, or sheets of shock-absorbing materials to ceilings and walls of buildings to reduce or reflect sound. Materials may be of decorative quality. Includes lathers who fasten wooden, metal, or rockboard lath to walls, ceilings, or partitions of buildings to provide support base for plaster, fireproofing, or acoustical material.

No task data available.

GOE INFORMATION—Interest Area: 06. Construction, Mining, and Drilling. **Work Group:** 06.02. Construction. **Note:** The Department of

Labor has not collected some data for this job, so it has fewer details than the other descriptions.

Instructional Programs—Drywall Installation/Drywaller.

Related DOT Jobs—842.361-030 Dry-Wall Applicator; 842.684-014 Dry-Wall Applicator; 860.381-010 Acoustical Carpenter; 869.684-050 Sheetrock Applicator.

47-2081.01 Ceiling Tile Installers

- **Education/Training Required: Moderate-term on-the-job training**
- **Employed: No data available.**
- **Annual Earnings: $33,000**
- **Growth: 9.4%**
- **Annual Job Openings: 19,000**

Apply or mount acoustical tiles or blocks, strips, or sheets of shock-absorbing materials to ceilings and walls of buildings to reduce or reflect sound. Materials may be of decorative quality. Includes lathers who fasten wooden, metal, or rockboard lath to walls, ceilings, or partitions of buildings to provide support base for plaster, fireproofing, or acoustical material.

Applies acoustical tiles or shock-absorbing materials to ceilings and walls of buildings to reduce or reflect sound and to decorate rooms. Applies cement to back of tile and presses tile into place, aligning with layout marks and joints of previously laid tile. Nails or screws molding to wall to support and seals joint between ceiling tile and wall. Scribes and cuts edges of tile to fit wall where wall molding is not specified. Nails channels or wood furring strips to surfaces to provide mounting for tile. Cuts tiles for fixture and borders, using keyhole saw, and inserts tiles into supporting framework. Measures and marks surface to lay out work according to blueprints and drawings. Hangs dry lines (stretched string) to wall molding to guide positioning of main runners. Inspects furrings, mechanical mountings, and masonry surface for plumbness and level, using spirit or water level. Washes concrete surfaces with washing soda and zinc sulfate solution before mounting tile to increase adhesive qualities of surfaces.

GOE INFORMATION—**Interest Area:** 06. Construction, Mining, and Drilling. **Work Group:** 06.02. Construction. **Personality Type**—Realistic. Realistic occupations frequently involve work activities that include practical, hands-on problems and solutions. They often deal with plants, animals, and real-world materials like wood, tools, and machinery. Many of the occupations require working outside and do not involve a lot of paperwork or working closely with others. **Work Values**—Independence; Supervision, Human Relations; Moral Values; Supervision, Technical; Compensation. **Skills**—None met the criteria. **Abilities**—*Cognitive:* Visualization; Spatial Orientation. *Psychomotor:* Multilimb Coordination; Speed of Limb Movement; Arm-Hand Steadiness; Manual Dexterity; Wrist-Finger Speed. *Physical:* Extent Flexibility; Gross Body Equilibrium; Dynamic Flexibility; Explosive Strength; Dynamic Strength. *Sensory:* Depth Perception; Peripheral Vision; Night Vision; Glare Sensitivity. **General Work Activities**—*Information Input:* Getting Information; Inspecting Equipment, Structures, or Materials; Estimating Needed Characteristics. *Mental Process:* Making Decisions and Solving Problems; Organizing, Planning, and Prioritizing; Processing Information. *Work Output:* Performing General Physical Activities; Handling and Moving Objects; Controlling Machines and Processes. *Interacting with Others:* Establishing and Maintaining Relationships; Communicating with Other Workers; Communicating with Persons Outside Organization. **Physical Work Conditions**—Climbing Ladders, Scaffolds, Poles, etc.; High Places; Minor Burns, Cuts, Bites, or Stings; Hazardous Equipment; Common Protective or Safety Attire. **Other Job Characteristics**—Importance of Being

Exact or Accurate; Importance of Repeating Same Tasks; Pace Determined by Speed of Equipment.

Experience—Job Zone 4. A minimum of two to four years of work-related skill, knowledge, or experience is needed. **Job Preparation:** SVP 7.0 to less than 8.0—two years to less than 10 years. **Knowledge**—Building and Construction; Design; Mathematics; Physics; Fine Arts. **Instructional Programs**—Drywall Installation/Drywaller.

Related DOT Jobs—860.381-010 Acoustical Carpenter.

47-2081.02 Drywall Installers

- **Education/Training Required: Moderate-term on-the-job training**
- **Employed: No data available.**
- **Annual Earnings: $33,000**
- **Growth: 9.4%**
- **Annual Job Openings: 19,000**

Apply plasterboard or other wallboard to ceilings and interior walls of buildings.

Trims rough edges from wallboard to maintain even joints, using knife. Fits and fastens wallboard or sheetrock into specified position, using hand tools, portable power tools, or adhesive. Measures and marks cutting lines on framing, drywall, and trim, using tape measure, straightedge or square, and marking devices. Cuts openings into board for electrical outlets, windows, vents, or fixtures, using keyhole saw or other cutting tools. Cuts metal or wood framing, angle and channel iron, and trim to size, using cutting tools. Installs horizontal and vertical metal or wooden studs for attachment of wallboard on interior walls, using hand tools. Suspends angle iron grid and channel iron from ceiling, using wire. Lays out reference lines and points, computes position of framing and furring channels, and marks position, using chalkline. Reads blueprints and other specifications to determine method of installation, work procedures, and material and tool requirements. Assembles and installs metal framing and decorative trim for windows, doorways, and bents. Removes plaster, drywall, or paneling, using crowbar and hammer. Installs blanket insulation between studs and tacks plastic moisture barrier over insulation.

GOE INFORMATION—**Interest Area:** 06. Construction, Mining, and Drilling. **Work Group:** 06.02. Construction. **Personality Type**—Realistic. Realistic occupations frequently involve work activities that include practical, hands-on problems and solutions. They often deal with plants, animals, and real-world materials like wood, tools, and machinery. Many of the occupations require working outside and do not involve a lot of paperwork or working closely with others. **Work Values**—Supervision, Technical; Supervision, Human Relations; Moral Values; Independence. **Skills**—Installation; Equipment Selection. **Abilities**—*Cognitive:* Visualization. *Psychomotor:* Control Precision; Multilimb Coordination; Manual Dexterity; Wrist-Finger Speed; Speed of Limb Movement. *Physical:* Explosive Strength; Extent Flexibility; Gross Body Equilibrium; Static Strength; Trunk Strength. *Sensory:* None met the criteria. **General Work Activities**—*Information Input:* Getting Information; Inspecting Equipment, Structures, or Materials; Identifying Objects, Actions, and Events. *Mental Process:* Organizing, Planning, and Prioritizing; Making Decisions and Solving Problems; Evaluating Information Against Standards. *Work Output:* Handling and Moving Objects; Performing General Physical Activities; Controlling Machines and Processes. *Interacting with Others:* Communicating with Other Workers; Establishing and Maintaining Relationships; Communicating with Persons Outside Organization. **Physical Work Conditions**—Cramped Work Space or Awkward Positions; Climbing Ladders, Scaffolds, Poles, etc.; Contaminants; Hazardous Equipment; Minor Burns, Cuts, Bites, or Stings. **Other Job**

Characteristics—Importance of Repeating Same Tasks; Pace Determined by Speed of Equipment; Consequence of Error.

Experience—Job Zone 2. Some previous work-related skill, knowledge, or experience may be helpful, but usually is not needed. **Job Preparation:** SVP 4.0 to less than 6.0—six months to less than two years. **Knowledge—** Building and Construction; Design; Engineering and Technology; Mechanical; Fine Arts. **Instructional Programs**—Drywall Installation/ Drywaller.

Related DOT Jobs—842.361-030 Dry-Wall Applicator; 842.684-014 Dry-Wall Applicator; 869.684-050 Sheetrock Applicator.

47-2082.00 Tapers

- **Education/Training Required: Moderate-term on-the-job training**
- **Employed: 44,125**
- **Annual Earnings: $37,850**
- **Growth: 8.3%**
- **Annual Job Openings: 6,000**

Seal joints between plasterboard or other wallboard to prepare wall surface for painting or papering.

Spreads sealing compound between boards, using trowel, broadknife, or spatula. Presses paper tape over joint to embed tape into sealing compound and seal joint. Tapes joint, using mechanical applicator that spreads compound and embeds tape in one operation. Spreads and smoothes cementing material over tape, using trowel or floating machine to blend joint with wall surface. Sands rough spots after cement has dried. Fills cracks and holes in walls and ceiling with sealing compound. Installs metal molding at corners in lieu of sealant and tape. Mixes sealing compound by hand or with portable electric mixer. Applies texturizing compound and primer to walls and ceiling preparatory to final finishing, using brushes, roller, or spray gun. Countersinks nails or screws below surface of wall prior to applying sealing compound, using hammer or screwdriver.

GOE INFORMATION—Interest Area: 06. Construction, Mining, and Drilling. **Work Group:** 06.02. Construction. **Personality Type**—Realistic. Realistic occupations frequently involve work activities that include practical, hands-on problems and solutions. They often deal with plants, animals, and real-world materials like wood, tools, and machinery. Many of the occupations require working outside and do not involve a lot of paperwork or working closely with others. **Work Values**—Moral Values; Supervision, Technical; Independence; Supervision, Human Relations. **Skills**—None met the criteria. **Abilities**—*Cognitive:* None met the criteria. *Psychomotor:* Manual Dexterity; Speed of Limb Movement; Arm-Hand Steadiness; Wrist-Finger Speed; Finger Dexterity. *Physical:* Explosive Strength; Gross Body Equilibrium; Dynamic Flexibility; Extent Flexibility; Dynamic Strength. *Sensory:* Depth Perception; Night Vision; Glare Sensitivity; Peripheral Vision. **General Work Activities**—*Information Input:* Getting Information; Inspecting Equipment, Structures, or Materials; Estimating Needed Characteristics. *Mental Process:* Evaluating Information Against Standards; Organizing, Planning, and Prioritizing; Thinking Creatively. *Work Output:* Performing General Physical Activities; Handling and Moving Objects; Controlling Machines and Processes. *Interacting with Others:* Communicating with Other Workers; Establishing and Maintaining Relationships; Communicating with Persons Outside Organization. **Physical Work Conditions**—Climbing Ladders, Scaffolds, Poles, etc.; Contaminants; High Places; Common Protective or Safety Attire; Hazardous Conditions. **Other Job Characteristics**—Importance of Repeating Same Tasks; Pace Determined by Speed of Equipment; Degree of Automation.

Experience—Job Zone 2. Some previous work-related skill, knowledge, or experience may be helpful, but usually is not needed. **Job Preparation:** SVP 4.0 to less than 6.0—six months to less than two years. **Knowledge—** Building and Construction; Chemistry. **Instructional Programs**—Construction Trades, Other.

Related DOT Jobs—842.664-010 Taper.

47-2111.00 Electricians

- **Education/Training Required: Long-term on-the-job training**
- **Employed: 698,398**
- **Annual Earnings: $40,770**
- **Growth: 17.3%**
- **Annual Job Openings: 66,000**

Install, maintain, and repair electrical wiring, equipment, and fixtures. Ensure that work is in accordance with relevant codes. May install or service street lights, intercom systems, or electrical control systems.

Assemble, install, test, and maintain electrical or electronic wiring, equipment, appliances, apparatus, and fixtures, using hand tools and power tools. Connect wires to circuit breakers, transformers, or other components. Construct and fabricate parts, using hand tools and specifications. Diagnose malfunctioning systems, apparatus, and components, using test equipment and hand tools, to locate the cause of a breakdown and correct the problem. Fasten small metal or plastic boxes to walls to house electrical switches or outlets. Inspect electrical systems, equipment, and components to identify hazards, defects, and the need for adjustment or repair and to ensure compliance with codes. Install ground leads and connect power cables to equipment such as motors. Maintain current electrician's license or identification card to meet governmental regulations. Place conduit (pipes or tubing) inside designated partitions, walls, or other concealed areas, and pull insulated wires or cables through the conduit to complete circuits between boxes. Plan layout and installation of electrical wiring, equipment, and fixtures, based on job specifications and local codes. Repair or replace wiring, equipment, and fixtures, using hand tools and power tools. Prepare sketches or follow blueprints to determine the location of wiring and equipment and to ensure conformance to building and safety codes. Test electrical systems and continuity of circuits in electrical wiring, equipment, and fixtures, using testing devices such as ohmmeters, voltmeters, and oscilloscopes to ensure compatibility and safety of system. Advise management on whether continued operation of equipment could be hazardous. Direct and train workers to install, maintain, or repair electrical wiring, equipment, and fixtures. Perform business management duties such as maintaining records and files, preparing reports, and ordering supplies and equipment. Perform physically demanding tasks, such as digging trenches to lay conduit and moving and lifting heavy objects. Provide assistance during emergencies by operating floodlights and generators, placing flares, and driving needed vehicles. Provide preliminary sketches and cost estimates for materials and services. Use a variety of tools and equipment such as power construction equipment, measuring devices, power tools, and testing equipment, including oscilloscopes, ammeters, and test lamps. Work from ladders, scaffolds, and roofs to install, maintain, or repair electrical wiring, equipment, and fixtures.

GOE INFORMATION—Interest Area: 06. Construction, Mining, and Drilling. **Work Group:** 06.02. Construction. **Personality Type**—Realistic. Realistic occupations frequently involve work activities that include practical, hands-on problems and solutions. They often deal with plants, animals, and real-world materials like wood, tools, and machinery. Many of the occupations require working outside and do not involve a lot of paperwork or working closely with others. **Work Values**—Authority; Ability Utilization; Creativity; Variety; Compensation. **Skills**—Installation; Repairing; Equipment Selection; Troubleshooting; Quality Control Analysis; Mathematics. **Abilities**—*Cognitive:* Memorization; Spatial Orientation; Oral Expression; Visualization; Information Ordering. *Psychomotor:* Finger Dexterity; Arm-Hand Steadiness; Manual Dexterity; Multilimb Coordination; Wrist-Finger Speed. *Physical:* Extent Flexibility; Dynamic Flexibility; Gross Body Equilibrium; Trunk Strength; Dynamic Strength. *Sensory:* Visual Color Discrimination; Night Vision; Depth Perception; Near Vision; Peripheral Vision. **General Work Activities**—*Information Input:* Monitoring Processes, Materials, or Surroundings; Getting Information; Inspecting Equipment, Structures, or Materials. *Mental Process:* Updating and Using Relevant Knowledge; Judging Qualities of Things, Services, or Other People's Work; Evaluating Information Against Standards. *Work Output:* Repairing and Maintaining Electronic Equipment; Drafting and Specifying Technical Devices; Performing General Physical Activities. *Interacting with Others:* Communicating with Other Workers; Coordinating the Work and Activities of Others; Teaching Others. **Physical Work Conditions**—Hazardous Conditions; Hazardous Equipment; Climbing Ladders, Scaffolds, Poles, etc.; Common Protective or Safety Attire; Using Hands on Objects, Tools, or Controls. **Other Job Characteristics**—Consequence of Error; Importance of Being Exact or Accurate; Importance of Repeating Same Tasks.

Experience—Job Zone 3. Previous work-related skill, knowledge, or experience is required. **Job Preparation:** SVP 6.0 to less than 7.0—more than one year and less than four years. **Knowledge**—Design; Engineering and Technology; Computers and Electronics; Building and Construction; Education and Training. **Instructional Programs**—Electrician.

Related DOT Jobs—729.381-018 Street-Light Repairer; 822.361-018 Protective-Signal Installer; 822.361-022 Protective-Signal Repairer; 824.261-010 Electrician; 824.261-014 Electrician Apprentice; 824.281-010 Airport Electrician; 824.281-018 Neon-Sign Servicer; 824.381-010 Street-Light Servicer; 824.681-010 Electrician; 825.281-014 Electrician; 825.381-030 Electrician; 825.381-034 Electrician Apprentice; 829.261-018 Electrician, Maintenance.

47-2121.00 *Glaziers*

- ⦾ Education/Training Required: **Long-term on-the-job training**
- ⦾ Employed: 48,670
- ⦾ Annual Earnings: $30,540
- ⦾ Growth: 14.8%
- ⦾ Annual Job Openings: 6,000

Install glass in windows, skylights, store fronts, and display cases or on surfaces such as building fronts, interior walls, ceilings, and tabletops.

Fastens glass panes into wood sash and spreads and smoothes putty around edge of pane with knife to seal joints. Installs pre-assembled framework for windows or doors designed to be fitted with glass panels, including stained glass windows, using hand tools. Attaches backing and leveling devices to wall surface, using nails and screws, and cuts mounting strips and moldings to required lengths. Marks outline or pattern on glass, cuts glass, and breaks off excess glass by hand or with notched tool. Sets glass doors into frame and bolts metal hinges, handles, locks, and other hardware onto glass doors. Assembles, fits, and attaches metal-framed glass enclosures for showers or bathtubs to framing around bath enclosure. Measures mirror and dimensions of area to be covered and determines plumb of walls or ceilings, using plumb-line and level. Attaches mounting strips and moldings to surface and applies mastic cement, putty, or screws to secure mirrors into position. Measures, cuts, fits, and

presses anti-glare adhesive film to glass or sprays glass with tinting solution to prevent light glare. Covers mirrors with protective material to prevent damage. Loads and arranges mirrors on truck, following sequence of deliveries. Drives truck to installation site and unloads mirrors, equipment, and tools. Moves furniture to clear work site and covers floors and furnishings with drop cloths.

GOE INFORMATION—**Interest Area:** 06. Construction, Mining, and Drilling. **Work Group:** 06.02. Construction. **Personality Type**—Realistic. Realistic occupations frequently involve work activities that include practical, hands-on problems and solutions. They often deal with plants, animals, and real-world materials like wood, tools, and machinery. Many of the occupations require working outside and do not involve a lot of paperwork or working closely with others. **Work Values**—Moral Values. **Skills**—Installation; Technology Design; Repairing. **Abilities**—*Cognitive:* Spatial Orientation; Category Flexibility; Visualization; Mathematical Reasoning. *Psychomotor:* Reaction Time; Speed of Limb Movement; Multilimb Coordination; Arm-Hand Steadiness; Response Orientation. *Physical:* Static Strength; Gross Body Coordination; Gross Body Equilibrium; Stamina; Extent Flexibility. *Sensory:* Glare Sensitivity; Peripheral Vision; Far Vision; Night Vision; Depth Perception. **General Work Activities**—*Information Input:* Inspecting Equipment, Structures, or Materials; Getting Information; Monitoring Processes, Materials, or Surroundings. *Mental Process:* Organizing, Planning, and Prioritizing; Updating and Using Relevant Knowledge; Judging Qualities of Things, Services, or Other People's Work. *Work Output:* Handling and Moving Objects; Performing General Physical Activities; Operating Vehicles or Equipment. *Interacting with Others:* Communicating with Persons Outside Organization; Establishing and Maintaining Relationships; Communicating with Other Workers. **Physical Work Conditions**—Minor Burns, Cuts, Bites, or Stings; Climbing Ladders, Scaffolds, Poles, etc.; Keeping or Regaining Balance; High Places; Kneeling, Crouching, or Crawling. **Other Job Characteristics**—Importance of Repeating Same Tasks; Importance of Being Exact or Accurate; Pace Determined by Speed of Equipment.

Experience—Job Zone 3. Previous work-related skill, knowledge, or experience is required. **Job Preparation:** SVP 6.0 to less than 7.0—more than one year and less than four years. **Knowledge**—Building and Construction; Production and Processing; Design; Geography; Fine Arts. **Instructional Programs**—Glazier.

Related DOT Jobs—865.361-010 Mirror Installer; 865.381-010 Glazier; 865.381-014 Glazier Apprentice.

47-2131.00 *Insulation Workers, Floor, Ceiling, and Wall*

- ● Education/Training Required: **Moderate-term on-the-job training**
- ● Employed: No data available.
- ● Annual Earnings: $28,000
- ● Growth: 13.6%
- ● Annual Job Openings: 12,000

Line and cover structures with insulating materials. May work with batt, roll, or blown insulation materials.

Fits, wraps, or attaches insulating materials to structures of surfaces, using hand tools or wires and following blueprint specifications. Evenly distributes insulating materials into small spaces within floors, ceilings, or walls, using blower and hose attachments or cement mortar. Covers, seals, or finishes insulated surfaces or access holes with plastic covers, canvas ships, sealant, tape, cement, or asphalt mastic. Prepare surfaces for insulation application by brushing or spreading on adhesives, cement, or asphalt or attaching metal pins to surfaces. Reads blueprints and selects appropriate insulation, based on the heat-retaining or -excluding characteristics of the material. Measures and cuts insulation for covering surfaces, using tape measure, handsaw, knife, or scissors. Moves controls, buttons, or levers to start blower and regulate flow of materials through nozzle. Fills blower hopper with insulating materials.

GOE INFORMATION—Interest Area: 06. Construction, Mining, and Drilling. **Work Group:** 06.02. Construction. **Personality Type**—Realistic. Realistic occupations frequently involve work activities that include practical, hands-on problems and solutions. They often deal with plants, animals, and real-world materials like wood, tools, and machinery. Many of the occupations require working outside and do not involve a lot of paperwork or working closely with others. **Work Values**—Moral Values; Independence. **Skills**—None met the criteria. **Abilities**—*Cognitive:* None met the criteria. *Psychomotor:* Control Precision. *Physical:* Static Strength; Trunk Strength; Gross Body Coordination; Dynamic Flexibility. *Sensory:* None met the criteria. **General Work Activities**—*Information Input:* Getting Information; Monitoring Processes, Materials, or Surroundings; Estimating Needed Characteristics. *Mental Process:* Organizing, Planning, and Prioritizing; Making Decisions and Solving Problems; Judging Qualities of Things, Services, or Other People's Work. *Work Output:* Handling and Moving Objects; Performing General Physical Activities; Controlling Machines and Processes. *Interacting with Others:* Communicating with Other Workers; Monitoring and Controlling Resources; Establishing and Maintaining Relationships. **Physical Work Conditions**—Common Protective or Safety Attire; High Places; Contaminants; Standing; Climbing Ladders, Scaffolds, Poles, etc. **Other Job Characteristics**—Importance of Repeating Same Tasks; Pace Determined by Speed of Equipment; Consequence of Error.

Experience—Job Zone 3. Previous work-related skill, knowledge, or experience is required. **Job Preparation:** SVP 6.0 to less than 7.0—more than one year and less than four years. **Knowledge**—Building and Construction; Mechanical. **Instructional Programs**—Construction Trades, Other.

Related DOT Jobs—863.364-010 Insulation-Worker Apprentice; 863.364-014 Insulation Worker; 863.381-010 Cork Insulator, Refrigeration Plant; 863.664-010 Blower Insulator; 863.685-010 Insulation-Power-Unit Tender.

47-2132.00 Insulation Workers, Mechanical

- **Education/Training Required: Moderate-term on-the-job training**
- **Employed: No data available.**
- **Annual Earnings: $28,000**
- **Growth: 13.6%**
- **Annual Job Openings: 12,000**

Apply insulating materials to pipes or ductwork or other mechanical systems in order to help control and maintain temperature.

Fits, wraps, or attaches insulating materials to structures of surfaces, using hand tools or wires and following blueprint specifications. Evenly distributes insulating materials into small spaces within floors, ceilings, or walls, using blower and hose attachments or cement mortar. Covers, seals, or finishes insulated surfaces or access holes with plastic covers, canvas ships, sealant, tape, cement, or asphalt mastic. Prepare surfaces for insulation application by brushing or spreading on adhesives, cement, or asphalt or attaching metal pins to surfaces. Reads blueprints and selects appropriate insulation, based on the heat-retaining or -excluding

characteristics of the material. Measures and cuts insulation for covering surfaces, using tape measure, handsaw, knife, or scissors. Moves controls, buttons, or levers to start blower and regulate flow of materials through nozzle. Fills blower hopper with insulating materials.

GOE INFORMATION—Interest Area: 06. Construction, Mining, and Drilling. **Work Group:** 06.02. Construction. **Personality Type**—Realistic. Realistic occupations frequently involve work activities that include practical, hands-on problems and solutions. They often deal with plants, animals, and real-world materials like wood, tools, and machinery. Many of the occupations require working outside and do not involve a lot of paperwork or working closely with others. **Work Values**—Moral Values; Independence. **Skills**—None met the criteria. **Abilities**—*Cognitive:* None met the criteria. *Psychomotor:* Control Precision. *Physical:* Static Strength; Trunk Strength; Gross Body Coordination; Dynamic Flexibility. *Sensory:* None met the criteria. **General Work Activities**—*Information Input:* Getting Information; Monitoring Processes, Materials, or Surroundings; Estimating Needed Characteristics. *Mental Process:* Organizing, Planning, and Prioritizing; Making Decisions and Solving Problems; Judging Qualities of Things, Services, or Other People's Work. *Work Output:* Handling and Moving Objects; Performing General Physical Activities; Controlling Machines and Processes. *Interacting with Others:* Communicating with Other Workers; Monitoring and Controlling Resources; Establishing and Maintaining Relationships. **Physical Work Conditions**—Common Protective or Safety Attire; High Places; Contaminants; Standing; Climbing Ladders, Scaffolds, Poles, etc. **Other Job Characteristics**—Importance of Repeating Same Tasks; Pace Determined by Speed of Equipment; Consequence of Error.

Experience—Job Zone 3. Previous work-related skill, knowledge, or experience is required. **Job Preparation:** SVP 6.0 to less than 7.0—more than one year and less than four years. **Knowledge**—Building and Construction; Mechanical. **Instructional Programs**—Construction Trades, Other.

Related DOT Jobs—863.364-010 Insulation-Worker Apprentice; 863.364-014 Insulation Worker; 863.381-014 Pipe Coverer and Insulator.

47-2141.00 Painters, Construction and Maintenance

- **Education/Training Required: Moderate-term on-the-job training**
- **Employed: 491,401**
- **Annual Earnings: $28,420**
- **Growth: 19.1%**
- **Annual Job Openings: 67,000**

Paint walls, equipment, buildings, bridges, and other structural surfaces, using brushes, rollers, and spray guns. May remove old paint to prepare surface prior to painting. May mix colors or oils to obtain desired color or consistency.

Paints surfaces, using brushes, spray gun, or rollers. Applies paint to simulate wood grain, marble, brick, or stonework. Bakes finish on painted and enameled articles in baking oven. Sands surfaces between coats and polishes final coat to specified finish. Cuts stencils; brushes and sprays lettering and decorations on surfaces. Washes and treats surfaces with oil, turpentine, mildew remover, or other preparations. Smoothes surfaces, using sandpaper, scrapers, brushes, steel wool, or sanding machine. Mixes and matches colors of paint, stain, or varnish. Sprays or brushes hot plastics or pitch onto surfaces. Fills cracks, holes, and joints with caulk putty, plaster, or other filler, using caulking gun or putty knife. Removes fixtures, such as pictures and electric switchcovers, from walls prior to painting. Burns off old paint, using blowtorch. Covers surfaces with drop cloths or masking tape and paper to protect surface during painting. Erects scaffolding or sets up ladders to work above ground level. Reads work order or receives instructions from supervisor or homeowner.

GOE INFORMATION—Interest Area: 06. Construction, Mining, and Drilling. **Work Group:** 06.02. Construction. **Personality Type—**Realistic. Realistic occupations frequently involve work activities that include practical, hands-on problems and solutions. They often deal with plants, animals, and real-world materials like wood, tools, and machinery. Many of the occupations require working outside and do not involve a lot of paperwork or working closely with others. **Work Values—**Moral Values; Supervision, Technical; Independence. **Skills—**None met the criteria. **Abilities—***Cognitive:* Spatial Orientation. *Psychomotor:* Wrist-Finger Speed; Arm-Hand Steadiness; Multilimb Coordination. *Physical:* Dynamic Strength; Stamina; Static Strength; Dynamic Flexibility; Extent Flexibility. *Sensory:* Visual Color Discrimination. **General Work Activities—***Information Input:* Getting Information; Identifying Objects, Actions, and Events; Estimating Needed Characteristics. *Mental Process:* Organizing, Planning, and Prioritizing; Thinking Creatively; Updating and Using Relevant Knowledge. *Work Output:* Handling and Moving Objects; Performing General Physical Activities; Controlling Machines and Processes. *Interacting with Others:* Communicating with Other Workers; Communicating with Persons Outside Organization; Performing for or Working with the Public. **Physical Work Conditions—**High Places; Climbing Ladders, Scaffolds, Poles, etc.; Making Repetitive Motions; Contaminants; Standing. **Other Job Characteristics—**Importance of Repeating Same Tasks; Importance of Being Exact or Accurate; Consequence of Error.

Experience—Job Zone 4. A minimum of two to four years of work-related skill, knowledge, or experience is needed. **Job Preparation:** SVP 7.0 to less than 8.0—two years to less than 10 years. **Knowledge—**Building and Construction; Fine Arts; Customer and Personal Service; Chemistry; Design. **Instructional Programs—**Painting/Painter and Wall Coverer.

Related DOT Jobs—840.381-010 Painter; 840.381-014 Painter Apprentice, Shipyard; 840.381-018 Painter, Shipyard; 840.681-010 Painter, Stage Settings.

47-2142.00 Paperhangers

- **Education/Training Required: Moderate-term on-the-job training**
- **Employed: 26,820**
- **Annual Earnings: $31,330**
- **Growth: 20.2%**
- **Annual Job Openings: 3,000**

Cover interior walls and ceilings of rooms with decorative wallpaper or fabric or attach advertising posters on surfaces, such as walls and billboards. Duties include removing old materials from surface to be papered.

Applies thinned glue to waterproof porous surfaces, using brush, roller, or pasting machine. Measures and cuts strips from roll of wallpaper or fabric, using shears or razor. Mixes paste, using paste-powder and water, and brushes paste onto surface. Trims rough edges from strips, using straightedge and trimming knife. Aligns and places strips or poster sections of billboard on surface to match adjacent edges. Smoothes strips or poster sections with brush or roller to remove wrinkles and bubbles and to smooth joints. Trims excess material at ceiling or baseboard, using knife. Marks vertical guideline on wall to align first strip, using plumb bob and chalkline. Applies acetic acid to damp plaster to prevent lime from bleeding through paper. Staples or tacks advertising posters onto

fences, walls, or poles. Measures walls and ceiling to compute number and length of strips required to cover surface. Smoothes rough spots on walls and ceilings, using sandpaper. Fills holes and cracks with plaster, using trowel. Removes old paper, using water, steam machine, or chemical remover and scraper. Removes paint, varnish, and grease from surfaces, using paint remover and water soda solution. Erects and works from scaffold.

GOE INFORMATION—Interest Area: 06. Construction, Mining, and Drilling. **Work Group:** 06.02. Construction. **Personality Type—**Realistic. Realistic occupations frequently involve work activities that include practical, hands-on problems and solutions. They often deal with plants, animals, and real-world materials like wood, tools, and machinery. Many of the occupations require working outside and do not involve a lot of paperwork or working closely with others. **Work Values—**Moral Values; Supervision, Technical. **Skills—**None met the criteria. **Abilities—***Cognitive:* None met the criteria. *Psychomotor:* Multilimb Coordination; Arm-Hand Steadiness; Manual Dexterity; Speed of Limb Movement. *Physical:* Stamina; Extent Flexibility; Gross Body Equilibrium; Dynamic Strength; Static Strength. *Sensory:* None met the criteria. **General Work Activities—***Information Input:* Monitoring Processes, Materials, or Surroundings; Getting Information; Inspecting Equipment, Structures, or Materials. *Mental Process:* Organizing, Planning, and Prioritizing; Processing Information; Thinking Creatively. *Work Output:* Handling and Moving Objects; Performing General Physical Activities; Controlling Machines and Processes. *Interacting with Others:* Communicating with Other Workers; Monitoring and Controlling Resources; Communicating with Persons Outside Organization. **Physical Work Conditions—**Climbing Ladders, Scaffolds, Poles, etc.; High Places; Standing; Making Repetitive Motions; Keeping or Regaining Balance. **Other Job Characteristics—**Importance of Repeating Same Tasks; Importance of Being Exact or Accurate; Pace Determined by Speed of Equipment.

Experience—Job Zone 2. Some previous work-related skill, knowledge, or experience may be helpful, but usually is not needed. **Job Preparation:** SVP 4.0 to less than 6.0—six months to less than two years. **Knowledge—**Building and Construction; Design; Chemistry. **Instructional Programs—**Painting/Painter and Wall Coverer.

Related DOT Jobs—841.381-010 Paperhanger; 841.684-010 Billposter.

47-2151.00 Pipelayers

- **Education/Training Required: Moderate-term on-the-job training**
- **Employed: 65,480**
- **Annual Earnings: $28,190**
- **Growth: 11.9%**
- **Annual Job Openings: 6,000**

Lay pipe for storm or sanitation sewers, drains, and water mains. Perform any combination of the following tasks: grade trenches or culverts, position pipe, or seal joints.

Grades and levels base of trench, using tamping machine and hand tools. Lays pipes in trenches and welds, cements, glues, or otherwise connects pieces together. Lays out route of pipe, following written instructions or blueprints. Checks slope, using carpenter's level or lasers. Digs trenches to desired or required depth by hand or using trenching tool. Taps and drills holes into pipe to introduce auxiliary lines or devices. Covers pipe with earth or other materials.

GOE INFORMATION—Interest Area: 06. Construction, Mining, and Drilling. **Work Group:** 06.02. Construction. **Personality Type—**Realistic. Realistic occupations frequently involve work activities that include practical, hands-on problems and solutions. They often deal with plants, animals, and real-world materials like wood, tools, and machinery. Many of the occupations require working outside and do not involve a lot of paperwork or working closely with others. **Work Values**—Moral Values; Supervision, Technical. **Skills**—Equipment Selection; Operation and Control; Installation. **Abilities**—*Cognitive:* Spatial Orientation; Visualization. *Psychomotor:* Speed of Limb Movement; Multilimb Coordination; Manual Dexterity; Arm-Hand Steadiness; Rate Control. *Physical:* Trunk Strength; Dynamic Flexibility; Dynamic Strength; Stamina; Static Strength. *Sensory:* Glare Sensitivity; Depth Perception; Peripheral Vision; Night Vision; Far Vision. **General Work Activities**—*Information Input:* Monitoring Processes, Materials, or Surroundings; Getting Information; Identifying Objects, Actions, and Events. *Mental Process:* Judging Qualities of Things, Services, or Other People's Work; Analyzing Data or Information; Making Decisions and Solving Problems. *Work Output:* Performing General Physical Activities; Handling and Moving Objects; Controlling Machines and Processes. *Interacting with Others:* Communicating with Other Workers; Coordinating the Work and Activities of Others; Assisting and Caring for Others. **Physical Work Conditions**—Outdoors; Extremely Bright or Inadequate Lighting; Hazardous Equipment; Very Hot or Cold; Making Repetitive Motions. **Other Job Characteristics**—Importance of Repeating Same Tasks; Degree of Automation; Pace Determined by Speed of Equipment.

Experience—Job Zone 2. Some previous work-related skill, knowledge, or experience may be helpful, but usually is not needed. **Job Preparation:** SVP 4.0 to less than 6.0—six months to less than two years. **Knowledge**—Building and Construction; Mechanical; Design; Physics; Geography. **Instructional Programs**—Plumbing Technology/Plumber.

Related DOT Jobs—851.383-010 Irrigation System Installer; 869.664-014 Construction Worker I.

47-2152.00 Plumbers, Pipefitters, and Steamfitters

- **Education/Training Required: Long-term on-the-job training**
- **Employed: 502,616**
- **Annual Earnings: $38,710**
- **Growth: 10.2%**
- **Annual Job Openings: 49,000**

Assemble, install, alter, and repair pipelines or pipe systems that carry water, steam, air, or other liquids or gases. May install heating and cooling equipment and mechanical control systems.

No task data available.

GOE INFORMATION—**Interest Area:** 06. Construction, Mining, and Drilling. **Work Group:** 06.02. Construction. **Note:** The Department of Labor has not collected some data for this job, so it has fewer details than the other descriptions.

Instructional Programs—Pipefitting/Pipefitter and Sprinkler Fitter; Plumbing and Related Water Supply Services, Other; Plumbing Technology/Plumber.

Related DOT Jobs—862.261-010 Pipe Fitter; 862.281-010 Coppersmith; 862.281-014 Coppersmith Apprentice; 862.281-022 Pipe Fitter; 862.281-026 Pipe-Fitter Apprentice; 862.361-014 Gas-Main Fitter; 862.361-018 Pipe Fitter, Diesel Engine I; 862.361-022 Steam Service Inspector; 862.381-014 Industrial-Gas Fitter; 862.381-022 Pipe Fitter, Diesel Engine II; 862.381-030 Plumber; 862.381-034 Plumber Apprentice; 862.681-010 Plumber; 862.684-034 Water-Softener Servicer-And-Installer; 869.664-014 Construction Worker I.

47-2152.01 Pipe Fitters

- **Education/Training Required: Long-term on-the-job training**
- **Employed: No data available.**
- **Annual Earnings: $38,710**
- **Growth: 10.2%**
- **Annual Job Openings: 49,000**

Lay out, assemble, install, and maintain pipe systems, pipe supports, and related hydraulic and pneumatic equipment for steam, hot water, heating, cooling, lubricating, sprinkling, and industrial production and processing systems.

Assemble and secure pipes, tubes, fittings, and related equipment according to specifications by welding, brazing, cementing, soldering, and threading joints. Attach pipes to walls, structures, and fixtures, such as radiators or tanks, using brackets, clamps, tools, or welding equipment. Cut and bore holes in structures such as bulkheads, decks, walls, and mains prior to pipe installation, using hand and power tools. Cut, thread, and hammer pipe to specifications, using tools such as saws, cutting torches, and pipe threaders and benders. Inspect, examine, and test installed systems and pipe lines, using pressure gauge, hydrostatic testing, observation, or other methods. Lay out full-scale drawings of pipe systems, supports, and related equipment, following blueprints. Measure and mark pipes for cutting and threading. Modify, clean, and maintain pipe systems, units, fittings, and related machines and equipment, following specifications and using hand and power tools. Plan pipe system layout, installation, or repair according to specifications. Select pipe sizes and types and related materials, such as supports, hangers, and hydraulic cylinders, according to specifications. Dip nonferrous piping materials in a mixture of molten tin and lead to obtain a coating that prevents erosion or galvanic and electrolytic action. Inspect work sites for obstructions and to ensure that holes will not cause structural weakness. Install automatic controls used to regulate pipe systems. Operate motorized pumps to remove water from flooded manholes, basements, or facility floors. Prepare cost estimates for clients. Remove and replace worn components. Turn valves to shut off steam, water, or other gases or liquids from pipe sections, using valve keys or wrenches.

GOE INFORMATION—**Interest Area:** 06. Construction, Mining, and Drilling. **Work Group:** 06.02. Construction. **Personality Type**—Realistic. Realistic occupations frequently involve work activities that include practical, hands-on problems and solutions. They often deal with plants, animals, and real-world materials like wood, tools, and machinery. Many of the occupations require working outside and do not involve a lot of paperwork or working closely with others. **Work Values**—Moral Values; Independence; Supervision, Technical; Ability Utilization; Variety. **Skills**—Installation; Repairing; Operation and Control; Quality Control Analysis; Equipment Selection. **Abilities**—*Cognitive:* Visualization; Spatial Orientation; Perceptual Speed; Flexibility of Closure; Information Ordering. *Psychomotor:* Speed of Limb Movement; Arm-Hand Steadiness; Multilimb Coordination; Finger Dexterity; Wrist-Finger Speed. *Physical:* Static Strength; Extent Flexibility; Stamina; Explosive Strength; Dynamic Strength. *Sensory:* Depth Perception; Sound Localization; Far Vision; Peripheral Vision; Near Vision. **General Work Activities**—*Information Input:* Inspecting Equipment, Structures, or Materials; Getting Information; Monitoring Processes, Materials, or Surroundings. *Mental Process:* Organizing, Planning, and Prioritizing; Updating and Using Relevant Knowledge; Evaluating Information Against Standards. *Work Output:* Performing General Physical Activities; Handling and Moving Objects; Repairing and Maintaining Mechanical Equipment. *Interacting with Others:* Communicating with Other Workers; Assisting and Caring for Others; Monitoring and Controlling Resources. **Physical Work Conditions**—Common Protective or Safety Attire; Cramped Work Space or Awkward Positions; Kneeling, Crouching, or Crawling; Using Hands on Objects, Tools, or Controls; Very Hot or Cold. **Other Job Characteristics**—Importance of Being Exact or Accurate; Consequence of Error; Pace Determined by Speed of Equipment.

Experience—Job Zone 4. A minimum of two to four years of work-related skill, knowledge, or experience is needed. **Job Preparation:** SVP 7.0 to less than 8.0—two years to less than 10 years. **Knowledge**—Building and Construction; Mechanical; Design; Physics; Production and Processing. **Instructional Programs**—Pipefitting/Pipefitter and Sprinkler Fitter; Plumbing and Related Water Supply Services, Other; Plumbing Technology/Plumber.

Related DOT Jobs—862.261-010 Pipe Fitter; 862.281-010 Coppersmith; 862.281-014 Coppersmith Apprentice; 862.281-022 Pipe Fitter; 862.281-026 Pipe-Fitter Apprentice; 862.361-014 Gas-Main Fitter; 862.361-018 Pipe Fitter, Diesel Engine I; 862.361-022 Steam Service Inspector; 862.381-014 Industrial-Gas Fitter; 862.381-022 Pipe Fitter, Diesel Engine II.

47-2152.02 Plumbers

- **Education/Training Required: Long-term on-the-job training**
- **Employed: No data available.**
- **Annual Earnings: $38,710**
- **Growth: 10.2%**
- **Annual Job Openings: 49,000**

Assemble, install, and repair pipes, fittings, and fixtures of heating, water, and drainage systems according to specifications and plumbing codes.

Assemble pipe sections, tubing, and fittings, using couplings, clamps, screws, bolts, cement, plastic solvent, caulking, or soldering, brazing, and welding equipment. Cut openings in structures to accommodate pipes and pipe fittings, using hand and power tools. Fill pipes or plumbing fixtures with water or air and observe pressure gauges to detect and locate leaks. Hang steel supports from ceiling joists to hold pipes in place. Install pipe assemblies, fittings, valves, appliances such as dishwashers and water heaters, and fixtures such as sinks and toilets, using hand and power tools. Install underground storm, sanitary, and water piping systems and extend piping to connect fixtures and plumbing to these systems. Locate and mark the position of pipe installations, connections, passage holes, and fixtures in structures, using measuring instruments such as rulers and levels. Measure, cut, thread, and bend pipe to required angle, using hand and power tools or machines such as pipe cutters, pipe-threading machines, and pipe-bending machines. Repair and maintain plumbing, replacing defective washers, replacing or mending broken pipes, and opening clogged drains. Study building plans and inspect structures to assess material and equipment needs, to establish the sequence of pipe installations, and to plan installation around obstructions such as electrical wiring. Clear away debris in a renovation. Direct workers engaged in pipe cutting and preassembly and installation of plumbing systems and components. Keep records of assignments and produce detailed work reports. Perform complex calculations and planning for special or very large jobs. Prepare written work cost estimates and negotiate contracts. Install oxygen and medical gas in hospitals. Review blueprints and building codes and specifications to determine work details and procedures. Use specialized techniques, equipment, or materials, such as performing computer-assisted welding of small pipes or working with the special piping used in microchip fabrication.

GOE INFORMATION—**Interest Area:** 06. Construction, Mining, and Drilling. **Work Group:** 06.02. Construction. **Personality Type**—Realistic. Realistic occupations frequently involve work activities that include practical, hands-on problems and solutions. They often deal with plants,

animals, and real-world materials like wood, tools, and machinery. Many of the occupations require working outside and do not involve a lot of paperwork or working closely with others. **Work Values**—Compensation; Authority; Social Service; Responsibility; Moral Values. **Skills**—Installation; Repairing; Operation and Control; Equipment Selection; Technology Design; Operation Monitoring; Troubleshooting. **Abilities**—*Cognitive:* Visualization; Perceptual Speed; Spatial Orientation; Flexibility of Closure; Oral Expression. *Psychomotor:* Speed of Limb Movement; Finger Dexterity; Arm-Hand Steadiness; Manual Dexterity; Multilimb Coordination. *Physical:* Extent Flexibility; Explosive Strength; Dynamic Strength; Static Strength; Trunk Strength. *Sensory:* Night Vision; Near Vision; Far Vision; Depth Perception; Sound Localization. **General Work Activities**—*Information Input:* Getting Information; Inspecting Equipment, Structures, or Materials; Monitoring Processes, Materials, or Surroundings. *Mental Process:* Organizing, Planning, and Prioritizing; Updating and Using Relevant Knowledge; Making Decisions and Solving Problems. *Work Output:* Performing General Physical Activities; Handling and Moving Objects; Controlling Machines and Processes. *Interacting with Others:* Communicating with Other Workers; Establishing and Maintaining Relationships; Coordinating the Work and Activities of Others. **Physical Work Conditions**—Cramped Work Space or Awkward Positions; Kneeling, Crouching, or Crawling; Using Hands on Objects, Tools, or Controls; Bending or Twisting the Body; Hazardous Conditions. **Other Job Characteristics**—Importance of Being Exact or Accurate; Consequence of Error; Pace Determined by Speed of Equipment.

Experience—Job Zone 3. Previous work-related skill, knowledge, or experience is required. **Job Preparation:** SVP 6.0 to less than 7.0—more than one year and less than four years. **Knowledge**—Building and Construction; Mechanical; Design; Physics; Engineering and Technology. **Instructional Programs**—Pipefitting/Pipefitter and Sprinkler Fitter; Plumbing and Related Water Supply Services, Other; Plumbing Technology/Plumber.

Related DOT Jobs—862.381-030 Plumber; 862.381-034 Plumber Apprentice; 862.681-010 Plumber.

47-2152.03 Pipelaying Fitters

- **Education/Training Required: Moderate-term on-the-job training**
- **Employed: No data available.**
- **Annual Earnings: $38,710**
- **Growth: 10.2%**
- **Annual Job Openings: 49,000**

Align pipeline section in preparation for welding. Signal tractor driver for placement of pipeline sections in proper alignment. Insert steel spacer.

Correct misalignments of pipe, using a sledgehammer. Guide pipe into trench and signal hoist operator to move pipe until alignment is achieved so that pipes can be welded together. Insert spacers between pipe ends. Inspect joints to ensure uniform spacing and proper alignment of pipe surfaces.

GOE INFORMATION—**Interest Area:** 06. Construction, Mining, and Drilling. **Work Group:** 06.02. Construction. **Personality Type**—Realistic. Realistic occupations frequently involve work activities that include practical, hands-on problems and solutions. They often deal with plants, animals, and real-world materials like wood, tools, and machinery. Many of the occupations require working outside and do not involve a lot of paperwork or working closely with others. **Work Values**—Moral Values; Supervision, Technical; Advancement. **Skills**—Installation. **Abilities**—*Cognitive:* Spatial Orientation; Visualization. *Psychomotor:* Speed of Limb Movement; Reaction Time; Arm-Hand Steadiness; Multilimb Coordination; Manual Dexterity. *Physical:* Explosive Strength; Gross Body Coordination; Dynamic Flexibility; Static Strength; Trunk Strength. *Sensory:* Depth Perception; Far Vision; Peripheral Vision; Glare Sensitivity; Night Vision. **General Work Activities**—*Information Input:* Inspecting Equipment, Structures, or Materials; Monitoring Processes, Materials, or Surroundings; Identifying Objects, Actions, and Events. *Mental Process:* Judging Qualities of Things, Services, or Other People's Work; Organizing, Planning, and Prioritizing; Evaluating Information Against Standards. *Work Output:* Handling and Moving Objects; Performing General Physical Activities; Controlling Machines and Processes. *Interacting with Others:* Communicating with Other Workers; Coordinating the Work and Activities of Others; Assisting and Caring for Others. **Physical Work Conditions**—Outdoors; Kneeling, Crouching, or Crawling; Hazardous Equipment; Very Hot or Cold; Common Protective or Safety Attire. **Other Job Characteristics**—Importance of Repeating Same Tasks; Pace Determined by Speed of Equipment; Degree of Automation.

Experience—Job Zone 2. Some previous work-related skill, knowledge, or experience may be helpful, but usually is not needed. **Job Preparation:** SVP 4.0 to less than 6.0—six months to less than two years. **Knowledge**—Building and Construction; Mechanical; Food Production. **Instructional Programs**—Pipefitting/Pipefitter and Sprinkler Fitter; Plumbing and Related Water Supply Services, Other; Plumbing Technology/Plumber.

Related DOT Jobs—869.664-014 Construction Worker I.

47-2161.00 *Plasterers and Stucco Masons*

- **Education/Training Required: Long-term on-the-job training**
- **Employed: 54,096**
- **Annual Earnings: $32,840**
- **Growth: 11.9%**
- **Annual Job Openings: 7,000**

Apply interior or exterior plaster, cement, stucco, or similar materials. May also set ornamental plaster.

Apply coats of plaster or stucco to walls, ceilings, or partitions of buildings, using trowels, brushes, or spray guns. Apply weatherproof, decorative coverings to exterior surfaces of buildings, such as troweling or spraying on coats of stucco. Clean and prepare surfaces for applications of plaster, cement, stucco, or similar materials, such as by drywall taping. Cure freshly plastered surfaces. Install guidewires on exterior surfaces of buildings to indicate thickness of plaster or stucco and nail wire mesh, lath, or similar materials to the outside surface to hold stucco in place. Mix mortar and plaster to desired consistency or direct workers who perform mixing. Mold and install ornamental plaster pieces, panels, and trim. Rough the undercoat surface with a scratcher so the finish coat will adhere. Spray acoustic materials or texture finish over walls and ceilings. Apply insulation to building exteriors by installing prefabricated insulation systems over existing walls or by covering the outer wall with insulation board, reinforcing mesh, and a base coat. Create decorative textures in finish coat, using brushes or trowels, sand, pebbles, or stones.

GOE INFORMATION—**Interest Area:** 06. Construction, Mining, and Drilling. **Work Group:** 06.02. Construction. **Personality Type**—Realistic. Realistic occupations frequently involve work activities that include practical, hands-on problems and solutions. They often deal with plants, animals, and real-world materials like wood, tools, and machinery. Many of the occupations require working outside and do not involve a lot of paperwork or working closely with others. **Work Values**—Moral Values; Pleasant Co-workers; Supervision, Technical; Compensation. **Skills**—Installation. **Abilities**—*Cognitive:* None met the criteria. *Psychomotor:* Manual Dexterity; Speed of Limb Movement; Multilimb Coordination; Wrist-Finger Speed; Arm-Hand Steadiness. *Physical:* Dynamic Flexibility; Dynamic Strength; Gross Body Equilibrium; Explosive Strength;

Extent Flexibility. *Sensory:* Glare Sensitivity; Depth Perception; Peripheral Vision; Night Vision. **General Work Activities**—*Information Input:* Getting Information; Monitoring Processes, Materials, or Surroundings; Inspecting Equipment, Structures, or Materials. *Mental Process:* Thinking Creatively; Organizing, Planning, and Prioritizing; Judging Qualities of Things, Services, or Other People's Work. *Work Output:* Handling and Moving Objects; Performing General Physical Activities; Controlling Machines and Processes. *Interacting with Others:* Establishing and Maintaining Relationships; Coordinating the Work and Activities of Others; Communicating with Other Workers. **Physical Work Conditions**—Climbing Ladders, Scaffolds, Poles, etc.; High Places; Contaminants; Cramped Work Space or Awkward Positions; Common Protective or Safety Attire. **Other Job Characteristics**—Importance of Repeating Same Tasks; Importance of Being Exact or Accurate; Pace Determined by Speed of Equipment.

Experience—Job Zone 4. A minimum of two to four years of work-related skill, knowledge, or experience is needed. **Job Preparation:** SVP 7.0 to less than 8.0—two years to less than 10 years. **Knowledge**—Building and Construction; Design; Fine Arts; Engineering and Technology; Education and Training. **Instructional Programs**—Construction Trades, Other.

Related DOT Jobs—842.361-018 Plasterer; 842.361-022 Plasterer Apprentice; 842.361-026 Plasterer, Molding; 842.381-014 Stucco Mason.

47-2171.00 *Reinforcing Iron and Rebar Workers*

- **Education/Training Required: Long-term on-the-job training**
- **Employed: 27,455**
- **Annual Earnings: $34,750**
- **Growth: 17.5%**
- **Annual Job Openings: 4,000**

Position and secure steel bars or mesh in concrete forms in order to reinforce concrete. Use a variety of fasteners, rod-bending machines, blowtorches, and hand tools.

Determines number, sizes, shapes, and locations of reinforcing rods from blueprints, sketches, or oral instructions. Selects and places rods in forms, spacing and fastening them together, using wire and pliers. Welds reinforcing bars together, using arch-welding equipment. Bends steel rods with hand tools and rod-bending machine. Reinforces concrete with wire mesh. Cuts rods to required lengths, using hacksaw, bar cutters, or acetylene torch.

GOE INFORMATION—**Interest Area:** 06. Construction, Mining, and Drilling. **Work Group:** 06.02. Construction. **Personality Type**—Realistic. Realistic occupations frequently involve work activities that include practical, hands-on problems and solutions. They often deal with plants, animals, and real-world materials like wood, tools, and machinery. Many of the occupations require working outside and do not involve a lot of paperwork or working closely with others. **Work Values**—Moral Values; Supervision, Technical; Independence. **Skills**—None met the criteria. **Abilities**—*Cognitive:* Visualization; Spatial Orientation. *Psychomotor:* Speed of Limb Movement; Multilimb Coordination; Control Precision; Wrist-Finger Speed. *Physical:* Explosive Strength; Static Strength; Dynamic Strength; Extent Flexibility; Dynamic Flexibility. *Sensory:* Glare Sensitivity; Night Vision; Depth Perception; Sound Localization; Peripheral Vision. **General Work Activities**—*Information Input:* Getting Information; Monitoring Processes, Materials, or Surroundings; Inspecting Equipment, Structures, or Materials. *Mental Process:* Organizing, Planning, and Prioritizing; Evaluating Information Against Standards; Analyzing Data or Information. *Work Output:* Handling and Moving Objects;

Performing General Physical Activities; Controlling Machines and Processes. *Interacting with Others:* Communicating with Other Workers; Establishing and Maintaining Relationships; Monitoring and Controlling Resources. **Physical Work Conditions**—Minor Burns, Cuts, Bites, or Stings; Common Protective or Safety Attire; Outdoors; Hazardous Equipment; Cramped Work Space or Awkward Positions. **Other Job Characteristics**—Consequence of Error; Pace Determined by Speed of Equipment; Degree of Automation.

Experience—Job Zone 3. Previous work-related skill, knowledge, or experience is required. **Job Preparation:** SVP 6.0 to less than 7.0—more than one year and less than four years. **Knowledge**—Building and Construction; Physics; Design; Engineering and Technology; Public Safety and Security. **Instructional Programs**—Construction Trades, Other.

Related DOT Jobs—801.684-026 Reinforcing-Metal Worker.

47-2181.00 Roofers

- **Education/Training Required: Moderate-term on-the-job training**
- **Employed: 157,776**
- **Annual Earnings: $29,460**
- **Growth: 19.4%**
- **Annual Job Openings: 38,000**

Cover roofs of structures with shingles, slate, asphalt, aluminum, wood, and related materials. May spray roofs, sidings, and walls with material to bind, seal, insulate, or soundproof sections of structures.

Fastens composition shingles or sheets to roof with asphalt, cement, or nails. Applies alternate layers of hot asphalt or tar and roofing paper until roof covering is completed as specified. Aligns roofing material with edge of roof. Overlaps successive layers of roofing material, determining distance of overlap, using chalkline, gauge on shingling hatchet, or lines on shingles. Cuts strips of flashing and fits them into angles formed by walls, vents, and intersecting roof surfaces. Mops or pours hot asphalt or tar onto roof base when applying asphalt or tar and gravel to roof. Applies gravel or pebbles over top layer, using rake or stiff-bristled broom. Cuts roofing paper to size and nails or staples paper to roof in overlapping strips to form base for roofing materials. Punches holes in slate, tile, terra cotta, or wooden shingles, using punch and hammer. Insulates, soundproofs, and seals buildings with foam, using spray gun, air compressor, and heater. Removes snow, water, or debris from roofs prior to applying roofing materials. Cleans and maintains equipment.

GOE INFORMATION—**Interest Area:** 06. Construction, Mining, and Drilling. **Work Group:** 06.02. Construction. **Personality Type**—Realistic. Realistic occupations frequently involve work activities that include practical, hands-on problems and solutions. They often deal with plants, animals, and real-world materials like wood, tools, and machinery. Many of the occupations require working outside and do not involve a lot of paperwork or working closely with others. **Work Values**—Moral Values. **Skills**—Repairing; Equipment Selection; Installation; Operation and Control. **Abilities**—*Cognitive:* Spatial Orientation. *Psychomotor:* Speed of Limb Movement; Multilimb Coordination; Manual Dexterity; Wrist-Finger Speed; Finger Dexterity. *Physical:* Gross Body Equilibrium; Extent Flexibility; Static Strength; Stamina; Dynamic Strength. *Sensory:* Peripheral Vision; Depth Perception; Glare Sensitivity. **General Work Activities**—*Information Input:* Identifying Objects, Actions, and Events; Getting Information; Estimating Needed Characteristics. *Mental Process:* Organizing, Planning, and Prioritizing; Judging Qualities of Things, Services, or Other People's Work; Making Decisions and Solving Problems. *Work Output:* Performing General Physical Activities; Handling and Moving Objects; Controlling Machines and Processes. *Interacting*

with Others: Communicating with Other Workers; Establishing and Maintaining Relationships; Communicating with Persons Outside Organization. **Physical Work Conditions**—High Places; Outdoors; Keeping or Regaining Balance; Cramped Work Space or Awkward Positions; Climbing Ladders, Scaffolds, Poles, etc. **Other Job Characteristics**—Importance of Repeating Same Tasks; Consequence of Error; Importance of Being Exact or Accurate.

Experience—Job Zone 3. Previous work-related skill, knowledge, or experience is required. **Job Preparation:** SVP 6.0 to less than 7.0—more than one year and less than four years. **Knowledge**—Building and Construction; Mechanical; Chemistry. **Instructional Programs**—Roofer.

Related DOT Jobs—866.381-010 Roofer; 866.381-014 Roofer Apprentice; 866.684-010 Roofer Applicator.

47-2211.00 Sheet Metal Workers

- **Education/Training Required: Moderate-term on-the-job training**
- **Employed: 224,024**
- **Annual Earnings: $33,210**
- **Growth: 23.0%**
- **Annual Job Openings: 13,000**

Fabricate, assemble, install, and repair sheet metal products and equipment, such as ducts, control boxes, drainpipes, and furnace casings. Work may involve any of the following: setting up and operating fabricating machines to cut, bend, and straighten sheet metal; shaping metal over anvils, blocks, or forms, using hammer; operating soldering and welding equipment to join sheet metal parts; inspecting, assembling, and smoothing seams and joints of burred surfaces.

Finish parts, using hacksaws and hand, rotary, or squaring shears. Inspect individual parts, assemblies, and installations for conformance to specifications and building codes, using measuring instruments such as calipers, scales, and micrometers. Install assemblies, such as flashing, pipes, tubes, heating and air conditioning ducts, furnace casings, rain gutters, and downspouts, in supportive frameworks. Lay out, measure, and mark dimensions and reference lines on material such as roofing panels according to drawings or templates, using calculators, scribes, dividers, squares, and rulers. Select gauges and types of sheet metal or non-metallic material according to product specifications. Shape metal material over anvils, blocks, or other forms, using hand tools. Trim, file, grind, deburr, buff, and smooth surfaces, seams, and joints of assembled parts, using hand tools and portable power tools. Convert blueprints into shop drawings to be followed in the construction and assembly of sheet metal products. Develop and lay out patterns that use materials most efficiently, using computerized metalworking equipment to experiment with different layouts. Fabricate or alter parts at construction sites, using shears, hammers, punches, and drills. Fasten roof panel edges and machine-made molding to structures, nailing or welding pieces into place. Maintain equipment, making repairs and modifications when necessary. Maneuver completed units into position for installation and anchor the units. Secure metal roof panels in place and then interlock and fasten grooved panel edges. Transport prefabricated parts to construction sites for assembly and installation. Determine project requirements, including scope, assembly sequences, and required methods and materials, according to blueprints, drawings, and written or verbal instructions. Drill and punch holes in metal for screws, bolts, and rivets. Fasten seams and joints together with welds, bolts, cement, rivets, solder, caulks, metal drive clips, and bonds in order to assemble components into products or to repair sheet metal items.

GOE INFORMATION—**Interest Area:** 06. Construction, Mining, and Drilling. **Work Group:** 06.02. Construction. **Personality Type**—Realistic. Realistic occupations frequently involve work activities that include practical, hands-on problems and solutions. They often deal with plants, animals, and real-world materials like wood, tools, and machinery. Many of the occupations require working outside and do not involve a lot of paperwork or working closely with others. **Work Values**—Moral Values; Advancement; Supervision, Technical; Supervision, Human Relations; Independence. **Skills**—Installation; Equipment Selection; Operation and Control; Repairing; Quality Control Analysis; Technology Design; Mathematics. **Abilities**—*Cognitive:* Information Ordering. *Psychomotor:* Control Precision; Arm-Hand Steadiness; Manual Dexterity; Multilimb Coordination. *Physical:* Static Strength; Explosive Strength; Stamina; Trunk Strength; Dynamic Strength. *Sensory:* None met the criteria. **General Work Activities**—*Information Input:* Inspecting Equipment, Structures, or Materials; Getting Information; Monitoring Processes, Materials, or Surroundings. *Mental Process:* Evaluating Information Against Standards; Judging Qualities of Things, Services, or Other People's Work; Organizing, Planning, and Prioritizing. *Work Output:* Handling and Moving Objects; Performing General Physical Activities; Controlling Machines and Processes. *Interacting with Others:* Communicating with Other Workers; Monitoring and Controlling Resources; Performing Administrative Activities. **Physical Work Conditions**—Hazardous Equipment; Distracting Sounds and Noise Levels; Common Protective or Safety Attire; Indoors; Whole Body Vibration. **Other Job Characteristics**—Pace Determined by Speed of Equipment; Degree of Automation; Importance of Repeating Same Tasks.

Experience—Job Zone 3. Previous work-related skill, knowledge, or experience is required. **Job Preparation:** SVP 6.0 to less than 7.0—more than one year and less than four years. **Knowledge**—Production and Processing; Building and Construction; Design; Computers and Electronics; Mechanical. **Instructional Programs**—Sheet Metal Technology/Sheetworking.

Related DOT Jobs—804.281-010 Sheet-Metal Worker; 804.281-014 Sheet-Metal-Worker Apprentice; 804.481-010 Hood Maker.

47-2221.00 *Structural Iron and Steel Workers*

- Education/Training Required: Long-term on-the-job training
- Employed: 83,633
- Annual Earnings: $38,950
- Growth: 18.4%
- Annual Job Openings: 12,000

Raise, place, and unite iron or steel girders, columns, and other structural members to form completed structures or structural frameworks. May erect metal storage tanks and assemble prefabricated metal buildings.

Guides structural-steel member, using tab line (rope), or rides on member in order to guide it into position. Pulls, pushes, or pries structural-steel member into approximate position while member is supported by hoisting device. Forces structural-steel members into final position, using turnbuckles, crowbars, jacks, and hand tools. Drives drift pins through rivet holes to align rivet holes in structural-steel member with corresponding holes in previously placed member. Bolts aligned structural-steel members in position until they can be permanently riveted, bolted, or welded in place. Fastens structural-steel members to cable of hoist, using chain, cable, or rope. Verifies vertical and horizontal alignment of structural-steel members, using plumb bob and level. Signals worker operating hoisting equipment to lift and place structural-steel member.

Catches hot rivets tossed by Rivet Heater in bucket and inserts rivets in holes, using tongs. Bucks (holds) rivets while Riveter, Pneumatic uses air-hammer to form heads on rivets. Cuts and welds steel members to make alterations, using oxyacetylene welding equipment. Inserts sealing strips, wiring, insulating material, ladders, flanges, gauges, and valves, depending on type of structure being assembled. Sets up hoisting equipment for raising and placing structural-steel members.

GOE INFORMATION—**Interest Area:** 06. Construction, Mining, and Drilling. **Work Group:** 06.02. Construction. **Personality Type**—Realistic. Realistic occupations frequently involve work activities that include practical, hands-on problems and solutions. They often deal with plants, animals, and real-world materials like wood, tools, and machinery. Many of the occupations require working outside and do not involve a lot of paperwork or working closely with others. **Work Values**—Moral Values; Pleasant Co-workers; Supervision, Technical; Compensation; Supervision, Human Relations. **Skills**—Installation; Equipment Selection; Repairing; Operation and Control. **Abilities**—*Cognitive:* Visualization; Spatial Orientation; Information Ordering; Perceptual Speed; Oral Comprehension. *Psychomotor:* Manual Dexterity; Multilimb Coordination; Response Orientation; Reaction Time; Speed of Limb Movement. *Physical:* Gross Body Equilibrium; Static Strength; Dynamic Strength; Explosive Strength; Trunk Strength. *Sensory:* Depth Perception; Peripheral Vision; Far Vision; Sound Localization; Glare Sensitivity. **General Work Activities**—*Information Input:* Inspecting Equipment, Structures, or Materials; Monitoring Processes, Materials, or Surroundings; Estimating Needed Characteristics. *Mental Process:* Updating and Using Relevant Knowledge; Judging Qualities of Things, Services, or Other People's Work; Evaluating Information Against Standards. *Work Output:* Performing General Physical Activities; Handling and Moving Objects; Controlling Machines and Processes. *Interacting with Others:* Communicating with Other Workers; Coordinating the Work and Activities of Others; Establishing and Maintaining Relationships. **Physical Work Conditions**—Common Protective or Safety Attire; Climbing Ladders, Scaffolds, Poles, etc.; High Places; Outdoors; Distracting Sounds and Noise Levels. **Other Job Characteristics**—Consequence of Error; Pace Determined by Speed of Equipment; Importance of Repeating Same Tasks.

Experience—Job Zone 3. Previous work-related skill, knowledge, or experience is required. **Job Preparation:** SVP 6.0 to less than 7.0—more than one year and less than four years. **Knowledge**—Building and Construction; Mechanical; Public Safety and Security; Engineering and Technology; Design. **Instructional Programs**—Construction Trades, Other; Metal Building Assembly/Assembler.

Related DOT Jobs—801.361-014 Structural-Steel Worker; 801.361-018 Structural-Steel-Worker Apprentice; 801.361-022 Tank Setter; 801.381-010 Assembler, Metal Building.

47-3000 Helpers, Construction Trades

47-3011.00 *Helpers—Brickmasons, Blockmasons, Stonemasons, and Tile and Marble Setters*

- Education/Training Required: Short-term on-the-job training
- Employed: No data available.
- Annual Earnings: $23,620
- Growth: 14.1%
- Annual Job Openings: 14,000

Help brickmasons, blockmasons, stonemasons, or tile and marble setters by performing duties of lesser skill. Duties include using, supplying, or holding materials or tools and cleaning work area and equipment.

Assists in the preparation, installation, repair, or rebuilding of tile, brick, or stone surfaces. Removes damaged tile, brick, or mortar and prepares installation surfaces, using pliers, chipping hammers, chisels, drills, and metal wire anchors. Applies grout between joints of bricks or tiles, using grouting trowel. Removes excess grout and residue from tile or brick joints with wet sponge or trowel. Applies caulk, sealants, or other agents to installed surface. Cleans installation surfaces, equipment, tools, work site, and storage areas, using water, chemical solutions, oxygen lance, or polishing machines. Corrects surface imperfections or fills chipped, cracked, or broken bricks or tiles, using fillers, adhesives, and grouting materials. Modifies material moving, mixing, grouting, grinding, polishing, or cleaning procedures according to the type of installation or materials required. Transports materials, tools, and machines to installation site manually or using conveyance equipment. Manually mixes or machine-mixes mortar, plaster, and grout according to standard formulae. Selects materials for installation, following numbered sequence or drawings. Cuts materials to specified size for installation, using power saw or tile cutter. Moves or positions marble slabs and ingot covers, using crane, hoist, or dolly. Arranges and stores materials, machines, tools, and equipment. Erects scaffolding or other installation structures.

GOE INFORMATION—Interest Area: 06. Construction, Mining, and Drilling. **Work Group:** 06.04. Hands-on Work in Construction, Extraction, and Maintenance. **Personality Type**—Realistic. Realistic occupations frequently involve work activities that include practical, hands-on problems and solutions. They often deal with plants, animals, and real-world materials like wood, tools, and machinery. Many of the occupations require working outside and do not involve a lot of paperwork or working closely with others. **Work Values**—Supervision, Technical; Moral Values; Advancement; Pleasant Co-workers. **Skills**—Installation. **Abilities**—*Cognitive:* None met the criteria. *Psychomotor:* Speed of Limb Movement; Multilimb Coordination; Rate Control; Wrist-Finger Speed; Reaction Time. *Physical:* Dynamic Strength; Static Strength; Stamina; Extent Flexibility; Explosive Strength. *Sensory:* Sound Localization; Glare Sensitivity; Peripheral Vision. **General Work Activities**—*Information Input:* Getting Information; Monitoring Processes, Materials, or Surroundings; Inspecting Equipment, Structures, or Materials. *Mental Process:* Judging Qualities of Things, Services, or Other People's Work; Organizing, Planning, and Prioritizing; Analyzing Data or Information. *Work Output:* Handling and Moving Objects; Performing General Physical Activities; Controlling Machines and Processes. *Interacting with Others:* Communicating with Other Workers; Establishing and Maintaining Relationships; Assisting and Caring for Others. **Physical Work Conditions**—Outdoors; High Places; Kneeling, Crouching, or Crawling; Climbing Ladders, Scaffolds, Poles, etc.; Cramped Work Space or Awkward Positions. **Other Job Characteristics**—Importance of Repeating Same Tasks; Consequence of Error; Pace Determined by Speed of Equipment.

Experience—Job Zone 1. No previous work-related skill, knowledge, or experience is needed. **Job Preparation:** SVP below 4.0—less than six months. **Knowledge**—Building and Construction; Mechanical; Design. **Instructional Programs**—Mason/Masonry.

Related DOT Jobs—709.687-018 Hot-Top-Liner Helper; 861.664-010 Marble Finisher; 861.664-018 Tile Finisher; 861.687-010 Bricklayer Helper, Firebrick and Refractory Tile; 861.687-014 Patcher Helper.

47-3012.00 Helpers—Carpenters

- **Education/Training Required: Short-term on-the-job training**
- **Employed: No data available.**
- **Annual Earnings: $21,200**
- **Growth: 6.6%**
- **Annual Job Openings: 24,000**

Help carpenters by performing duties of lesser skill. Duties include using, supplying, or holding materials or tools and cleaning work area and equipment.

Clean work areas, machines, and equipment to maintain a clean and safe job site. Cover surfaces with laminated plastic covering material. Cut timbers, lumber, and/or paneling to specified dimensions and drill holes in timbers or lumber. Hold plumb bobs, sighting rods, and other equipment to aid in establishing reference points and lines. Position and hold timbers, lumber, and paneling in place for fastening or cutting. Select tools, equipment, and materials from storage and transport items to work site. Align, straighten, plumb, and square forms for installation. Cut and install insulating or sound-absorbing material. Cut tile or linoleum to fit and spread adhesives on flooring to install tile or linoleum. Erect scaffolding, shoring, and braces. Fasten timbers and/or lumber with glue, screws, pegs, or nails and install hardware. Glue and clamp edges or joints of assembled parts. Construct forms and then assist in raising them to the required elevation. Install handrails under the direction of a carpenter. Perform tie spacing layout and then measure, mark, drill, and/or cut. Secure stakes to grids for constructions of footings, nail scabs to footing forms, and vibrate and float concrete. Smooth and sand surfaces to remove ridges, tool marks, glue, or caulking.

GOE INFORMATION—Interest Area: 06. Construction, Mining, and Drilling. **Work Group:** 06.04. Hands-on Work in Construction, Extraction, and Maintenance. **Personality Type**—Realistic. Realistic occupations frequently involve work activities that include practical, hands-on problems and solutions. They often deal with plants, animals, and real-world materials like wood, tools, and machinery. Many of the occupations require working outside and do not involve a lot of paperwork or working closely with others. **Work Values**—Advancement; Pleasant Co-workers; Supervision, Technical; Moral Values. **Skills**—Repairing. **Abilities**—*Cognitive:* Spatial Orientation; Visualization; Category Flexibility. *Psychomotor:* Speed of Limb Movement; Reaction Time; Manual Dexterity; Multilimb Coordination; Arm-Hand Steadiness. *Physical:* Static Strength; Dynamic Strength; Explosive Strength; Stamina; Trunk Strength. *Sensory:* Peripheral Vision; Far Vision; Depth Perception; Glare Sensitivity; Sound Localization. **General Work Activities**—*Information Input:* Monitoring Processes, Materials, or Surroundings; Getting Information; Inspecting Equipment, Structures, or Materials. *Mental Process:* Organizing, Planning, and Prioritizing; Evaluating Information Against Standards; Making Decisions and Solving Problems. *Work Output:* Performing General Physical Activities; Handling and Moving Objects; Controlling Machines and Processes. *Interacting with Others:* Establishing and Maintaining Relationships; Communicating with Other Workers; Assisting and Caring for Others. **Physical Work Conditions**—Common Protective or Safety Attire; Hazardous Equipment; Kneeling, Crouching, or Crawling; Outdoors; Very Hot or Cold. **Other Job Characteristics**—Importance of Repeating Same Tasks; Pace Determined by Speed of Equipment; Degree of Automation.

Experience—Job Zone 1. No previous work-related skill, knowledge, or experience is needed. **Job Preparation:** SVP below 4.0—less than six months. **Knowledge**—Building and Construction; Mechanical; Design; Public Safety and Security; Medicine and Dentistry. **Instructional Programs**—Carpentry/Carpenter.

Related DOT Jobs—764.687-050 Cooper Helper; 860.664-014 Joiner Helper; 860.664-018 Shipwright Helper; 869.664-014 Construction Worker I; 869.687-026 Construction Worker II; 869.687-042 Timber-Framer Helper.

47-3013.00 Helpers—Electricians

- **Education/Training Required: Short-term on-the-job training**
- **Employed: No data available.**
- **Annual Earnings: $22,160**
- **Growth: 13.3%**
- **Annual Job Openings: 27,000**

Help electricians by performing duties of lesser skill. Duties include using, supplying, or holding materials or tools and cleaning work area and equipment.

Bolt component parts together to form tower assemblies, using hand tools. Construct controllers and panels, using power drills, drill presses, taps, saws, and punches. Disassemble defective electrical equipment, replace defective or worn parts, and reassemble equipment, using hand tools. Drill holes and pull or push wiring through openings, using hand and power tools. Erect electrical system components and barricades and rig scaffolds, hoists, and shoring. Examine electrical units for loose connections and broken insulation and tighten connections, using hand tools. Maintain tools, vehicles, and equipment and keep parts and supplies in order. Measure, cut, and bend wire and conduit, using measuring instruments and hand tools. Perform semi-skilled and unskilled laboring duties related to the installation, maintenance, and repair of a wide variety of electrical systems and equipment. Raise, lower, or position equipment, tools, and materials, using hoist, hand line, or block and tackle. Solder electrical connections, using soldering iron. String transmission lines or cables through ducts or conduits, under the ground, through equipment, or to towers. Strip insulation from wire ends, using wire-stripping pliers, and attach wires to terminals for subsequent soldering. Thread conduit ends, connect couplings, and fabricate and secure conduit support brackets, using hand tools. Trace out short circuits in wiring, using test meter. Transport tools, materials, equipment, and supplies to work site by hand, handtruck, or heavy, motorized truck. Break up concrete, using airhammer, to facilitate installation, construction, or repair of equipment. Clean work area and wash parts. Dig trenches or holes for installation of conduit or supports. Install copper-clad ground rods, using a manual post driver. Paint a variety of objects related to electrical functions. Requisition materials, using warehouse requisition or release forms. Trim trees and clear undergrowth along right-of-way. Operate cutting torches and welding equipment while working with conduit and metal components to construct devices associated with electrical functions.

GOE INFORMATION—**Interest Area:** 05. Mechanics, Installers, and Repairers. **Work Group:** 05.03. Mechanical Work. **Personality Type**—Realistic. Realistic occupations frequently involve work activities that include practical, hands-on problems and solutions. They often deal with plants, animals, and real-world materials like wood, tools, and machinery. Many of the occupations require working outside and do not involve a lot of paperwork or working closely with others. **Work Values**—Supervision, Technical; Advancement; Moral Values; Pleasant Co-workers. **Skills**—Repairing; Installation. **Abilities**—*Cognitive:* Spatial Orientation; Visualization. *Psychomotor:* Manual Dexterity; Speed of Limb Movement; Multilimb Coordination; Arm-Hand Steadiness; Finger Dexterity. *Physical:* Explosive Strength; Dynamic Strength; Static Strength; Gross Body Equilibrium; Stamina. *Sensory:* Visual Color Discrimination; Depth Perception; Peripheral Vision; Night Vision; Glare Sensitivity. **General Work Activities**—*Information Input:* Monitoring Processes, Materials, or Surroundings; Inspecting Equipment, Structures, or Materials; Getting In-

formation. *Mental Process:* Judging Qualities of Things, Services, or Other People's Work; Updating and Using Relevant Knowledge; Organizing, Planning, and Prioritizing. *Work Output:* Handling and Moving Objects; Performing General Physical Activities; Repairing and Maintaining Electronic Equipment. *Interacting with Others:* Assisting and Caring for Others; Communicating with Other Workers; Establishing and Maintaining Relationships. **Physical Work Conditions**—High Places; Hazardous Conditions; Climbing Ladders, Scaffolds, Poles, etc.; Hazardous Equipment; Keeping or Regaining Balance. **Other Job Characteristics**—Degree of Automation; Importance of Repeating Same Tasks; Pace Determined by Speed of Equipment.

Experience—Job Zone 2. Some previous work-related skill, knowledge, or experience may be helpful, but usually is not needed. **Job Preparation:** SVP 4.0 to less than 6.0—six months to less than two years. **Knowledge**—Computers and Electronics; Mechanical; Building and Construction; Engineering and Technology; Public Safety and Security. **Instructional Programs**—Electrician.

Related DOT Jobs—821.667-010 Helper, Electrical; 821.684-014 Tower Erector Helper; 822.664-010 Protective-Signal-Installer Helper; 822.684-014 Protective-Signal-Repairer Helper; 825.684-010 Electrician Helper, Automotive; 829.684-022 Electrician Helper; 829.684-026 Electrician Helper.

47-3014.00 Helpers—Painters, Paperhangers, Plasterers, and Stucco Masons

- **Education/Training Required: Short-term on-the-job training**
- **Employed: No data available.**
- **Annual Earnings: $19,480**
- **Growth: 12.9%**
- **Annual Job Openings: 6,000**

Help painters, paperhangers, plasterers, or stucco masons by performing duties of lesser skill. Duties include using, supplying, or holding materials or tools and cleaning work area and equipment.

Performs any combination of support duties to assist painter, paperhanger, plasterer, or mason. Pours specified amounts of chemical solutions into stripping tanks. Places articles to be stripped into stripping tanks. Removes articles, such as cabinets, metal furniture, and paint containers, from stripping tanks after prescribed period of time. Covers surfaces of articles not to be painted with masking tape prior to painting. Fills cracks or breaks in surfaces of plaster articles with putty or epoxy compounds. Smoothes surfaces of articles to be painted, using sanding and buffing tools and equipment.

GOE INFORMATION—**Interest Area:** 06. Construction, Mining, and Drilling. **Work Group:** 06.04. Hands-on Work in Construction, Extraction, and Maintenance. **Personality Type**—Realistic. Realistic occupations frequently involve work activities that include practical, hands-on problems and solutions. They often deal with plants, animals, and real-world materials like wood, tools, and machinery. Many of the occupations require working outside and do not involve a lot of paperwork or working closely with others. **Work Values**—Supervision, Technical; Moral Values; Advancement; Pleasant Co-workers. **Skills**—None met the criteria. **Abilities**—*Cognitive:* None met the criteria. *Psychomotor:* Manual Dexterity. *Physical:* Static Strength; Dynamic Strength; Explosive Strength; Extent Flexibility; Dynamic Flexibility. *Sensory:* Visual Color Discrimination. **General Work Activities**—*Information Input:* Getting Information; Monitoring Processes, Materials, or Surroundings; Inspecting Equipment, Structures, or Materials. *Mental Process:* Updating and

Using Relevant Knowledge; Organizing, Planning, and Prioritizing; Thinking Creatively. *Work Output:* Handling and Moving Objects; Performing General Physical Activities; Controlling Machines and Processes. *Interacting with Others:* Communicating with Other Workers; Establishing and Maintaining Relationships; Assisting and Caring for Others. **Physical Work Conditions**—Climbing Ladders, Scaffolds, Poles, etc.; High Places; Contaminants; Cramped Work Space or Awkward Positions; Common Protective or Safety Attire. **Other Job Characteristics**—Importance of Repeating Same Tasks; Pace Determined by Speed of Equipment; Consequence of Error.

Experience—Job Zone 1. No previous work-related skill, knowledge, or experience is needed. **Job Preparation:** SVP below 4.0—less than six months. **Knowledge**—Building and Construction; Chemistry. **Instructional Programs**—Painting/Painter and Wall Coverer.

Related DOT Jobs—840.687-010 Painter Helper, Shipyard.

47-3015.00 Helpers—Pipelayers, Plumbers, Pipefitters, and Steamfitters

- **Education/Training Required: Short-term on-the-job training**
- **Employed: No data available.**
- **Annual Earnings: $21,830**
- **Growth: 11.5%**
- **Annual Job Openings: 20,000**

Help plumbers, pipefitters, steamfitters, or pipelayers by performing duties of lesser skill. Duties include using, supplying, or holding materials or tools and cleaning work area and equipment.

Clean and renew steam traps. Assist pipefitters in the layout, assembly, and installation of piping for air, ammonia, gas, and water systems. Assist plumbers by performing rough-ins, repairing and replacing fixtures, and locating and repairing leaking or broken pipes. Clean shop, work area, and machines, using solvent and rags. Cut pipe and lift up to fitters. Disassemble and remove damaged or worn pipe. Excavate and grade ditches and lay and join pipe for water and sewer service. Fill pipes with sand or resin to prevent distortion and hold pipes during bending and installation. Fit or assist in fitting valves, couplings, or assemblies to tanks, pumps, or systems, using hand tools. Immerse pipe in chemical solution to remove dirt, oil, and scale. Requisition tools and equipment, select type and size of pipe, and collect and transport materials and equipment to work site. Cut or drill holes in walls or floors to accommodate the passage of pipes. Measure, cut, thread, and assemble new pipe, placing the assembled pipe in hangers or other supports. Mount brackets and hangers on walls and ceilings to hold pipes and set sleeves or inserts to provide support for pipes. Install gas burners to convert furnaces from wood, coal, or oil.

GOE INFORMATION—Interest Area: 06. Construction, Mining, and Drilling. **Work Group:** 06.04. Hands-on Work in Construction, Extraction, and Maintenance. **Personality Type**—Realistic. Realistic occupations frequently involve work activities that include practical, hands-on problems and solutions. They often deal with plants, animals, and real-world materials like wood, tools, and machinery. Many of the occupations require working outside and do not involve a lot of paperwork or working closely with others. **Work Values**—Advancement; Supervision, Technical; Moral Values; Pleasant Co-workers. **Skills**—Repairing; Equipment Selection; Installation. **Abilities**—*Cognitive:* Spatial Orientation; Visualization. *Psychomotor:* Manual Dexterity; Multilimb Coordination; Arm-Hand Steadiness; Control Precision; Finger Dexterity. *Physical:* Explosive Strength; Dynamic Strength; Static Strength; Stamina; Dynamic Flexibility. *Sensory:* Depth Perception; Far Vision; Glare Sensitivity; Night Vision; Visual Color Discrimination. **General Work Activities**—*Information Input:* Getting Information; Monitoring Processes, Materials, or Surroundings; Identifying Objects, Actions, and Events. *Mental Process:* Updating and Using Relevant Knowledge; Judging Qualities of Things, Services, or Other People's Work; Organizing, Planning, and Prioritizing. *Work Output:* Handling and Moving Objects; Performing General Physical Activities; Controlling Machines and Processes. *Interacting with Others:* Communicating with Other Workers; Establishing and Maintaining Relationships; Assisting and Caring for Others. **Physical Work Conditions**—Climbing Ladders, Scaffolds, Poles, etc.; Hazardous Equipment; Keeping or Regaining Balance; Cramped Work Space or Awkward Positions; Contaminants. **Other Job Characteristics**—Degree of Automation; Importance of Repeating Same Tasks; Pace Determined by Speed of Equipment.

Experience—Job Zone 2. Some previous work-related skill, knowledge, or experience may be helpful, but usually is not needed. **Job Preparation:** SVP 4.0 to less than 6.0—six months to less than two years. **Knowledge**—Building and Construction; Mechanical; Production and Processing; Chemistry; Physics. **Instructional Programs**—Plumbing Technology/Plumber.

Related DOT Jobs—862.684-018 Pipe-Fitter Helper; 862.684-022 Pipe-Fitter Helper.

47-3016.00 Helpers—Roofers

- **Education/Training Required: Short-term on-the-job training**
- **Employed: No data available.**
- **Annual Earnings: $19,950**
- **Growth: 19.3%**
- **Annual Job Openings: 6,000**

Help roofers by performing duties of lesser skill. Duties include using, supplying, or holding materials or tools and cleaning work area and equipment.

No task data available.

GOE INFORMATION—Interest Area: 06. Construction, Mining, and Drilling. **Work Group:** 06.04. Hands-on Work in Construction, Extraction, and Maintenance. **Note:** The Department of Labor has not collected some data for this job, so it has fewer details than the other descriptions.

Instructional Programs—Roofer.

Related DOT Jobs—869.687-026 Construction Worker II.

47-3019.99 Helpers, Construction Trades, All Other

- **Education/Training Required: Short-term on-the-job training**
- **Employed: No data available.**
- **Annual Earnings: No data available.**
- **Growth: 29.1%**
- **Annual Job Openings: 10,000**

All construction trades helpers not listed separately.

No task data available.

GOE INFORMATION—Interest Area: 06. Construction, Mining, and Drilling. **Work Group:** 06.04. Hands-on Work in Construction, Extraction, and Maintenance. **Note:** The Department of Labor has not collected some data for this job, so it has fewer details than the other descriptions.

Instructional Programs—Concrete Finishing/Concrete Finisher; Drywall Installation/Drywaller; Glazier.

Related DOT Jobs—844.687-010 Cement Sprayer Helper, Nozzle; 850.684-014 Horizontal-Earth-Boring-Machine-Operator Helper; 864.687-010 Carpet-Layer Helper; 869.567-010 Surveyor Helper; 869.687-010 Awning-Hanger Helper; 869.687-034 House-Mover Helper; 899.664-010 Diver Helper; 911.667-018 Sounder; 930.687-014 Core-Drill-Operator Helper.

47-4000 Other Construction and Related Workers

47-4011.00 Construction and Building Inspectors

- Education/Training Required: Work experience in a related occupation
- Employed: 74,590
- Annual Earnings: $40,190
- Growth: 15.0%
- Annual Job Openings: 2,000

Inspect structures, using engineering skills to determine structural soundness and compliance with specifications, building codes, and other regulations. Inspections may be general in nature or may be limited to a specific area, such as electrical systems or plumbing.

Use survey instruments, metering devices, tape measures, and test equipment, such as concrete strength measurers, to perform inspections. Inspect bridges, dams, highways, buildings, wiring, plumbing, electrical circuits, sewers, heating systems, and foundations during and after construction for structural quality, general safety, and conformance to specifications and codes. Maintain daily logs and supplement inspection records with photographs. Review and interpret plans, blueprints, site layouts, specifications, and construction methods to ensure compliance with legal requirements and safety regulations. Inspect and monitor construction sites to ensure adherence to safety standards, building codes, and specifications. Measure dimensions and verify level, alignment, and elevation of structures and fixtures to ensure compliance to building plans and codes. Issue violation notices and stop-work orders, conferring with owners, violators, and authorities to explain regulations and recommend rectifications. Issue permits for construction, relocation, demolition, and occupancy. Approve and sign plans that meet required specifications. Compute estimates of work completed or of needed renovations or upgrades and approve payment for contractors. Monitor installation of plumbing, wiring, equipment, and appliances to ensure that installation is performed properly and is in compliance with applicable regulations. Examine lifting and conveying devices, such as elevators, escalators, moving sidewalks, lifts and hoists, inclined railways, ski lifts, and amusement rides, to ensure safety and proper functioning. Train, direct, and supervise other construction inspectors. Evaluate premises for cleanliness, including proper garbage disposal and lack of vermin infestation.

GOE INFORMATION—Interest Area: 02. Science, Math, and Engineering. **Work Group:** 02.08. Engineering Technology. **Personality Type**—Conventional. Conventional occupations frequently involve following set procedures and routines. These occupations can include working with data and details more than with ideas. Usually there is a clear line of authority to follow. **Work Values**—Responsibility; Autonomy; Supervision, Technical; Independence; Advancement. **Skills**—Mathematics; Equipment Selection; Persuasion; Critical Thinking; Reading Compre-

hension; Time Management; Active Listening; Coordination. **Abilities**—*Cognitive:* Problem Sensitivity; Deductive Reasoning; Flexibility of Closure; Perceptual Speed; Speed of Closure. *Psychomotor:* Control Precision; Multilimb Coordination; Reaction Time; Arm-Hand Steadiness; Rate Control. *Physical:* Gross Body Equilibrium; Extent Flexibility; Gross Body Coordination; Trunk Strength; Stamina. *Sensory:* Auditory Attention; Speech Recognition; Visual Color Discrimination; Glare Sensitivity; Far Vision. **General Work Activities**—*Information Input:* Monitoring Processes, Materials, or Surroundings; Identifying Objects, Actions, and Events; Inspecting Equipment, Structures, or Materials. *Mental Process:* Updating and Using Relevant Knowledge; Evaluating Information Against Standards; Organizing, Planning, and Prioritizing. *Work Output:* Documenting or Recording Information; Handling and Moving Objects; Performing General Physical Activities. *Interacting with Others:* Communicating with Other Workers; Resolving Conflict and Negotiating with Others; Establishing and Maintaining Relationships. **Physical Work Conditions**—Outdoors; Climbing Ladders, Scaffolds, Poles, etc.; High Places; Cramped Work Space or Awkward Positions; Kneeling, Crouching, or Crawling. **Other Job Characteristics**—Consequence of Error; Importance of Being Exact or Accurate; Importance of Repeating Same Tasks.

Experience—Job Zone 3. Previous work-related skill, knowledge, or experience is required. **Job Preparation:** SVP 6.0 to less than 7.0—more than one year and less than four years. **Knowledge**—Building and Construction; Design; Engineering and Technology; Customer and Personal Service; Public Safety and Security. **Instructional Programs**—Building/Home/Construction Inspection/Inspector.

Related DOT Jobs—168.167-030 Inspector, Building; 168.167-034 Inspector, Electrical; 168.167-046 Inspector, Heating and Refrigeration; 168.167-050 Inspector, Plumbing; 168.267-102 Plan Checker; 168.367-018 Code Inspector; 182.267-010 Construction Inspector.

47-4021.00 Elevator Installers and Repairers

- Education/Training Required: Long-term on-the-job training
- Employed: 23,076
- Annual Earnings: $51,630
- Growth: 17.2%
- Annual Job Openings: 2,000

Assemble, install, repair, or maintain electric or hydraulic freight or passenger elevators, escalators, or dumbwaiters.

Studies blueprints to determine layout of framework and foundations. Cuts prefabricated sections of framework, rails, and other components to specified dimensions. Completes service reports to verify conformance to prescribed standards. Locates malfunction in brakes, motor, switches, and signal and control systems, using test equipment. Disassembles defective unit and repairs or replaces parts, such as locks, gears, cables, and electric wiring. Installs safety and control devices, cables, drives, rails, motors, and elevator cars. Connects electrical wiring to control panels and electric motors. Inspects wiring connections, control panel hookups, door installation, and alignment and clearance of car hoistway. Adjusts safety controls, counterweights, and mechanism of doors. Operates elevator to determine power demand and tests power consumption to detect overload factors. Lubricates bearings and other parts to minimize friction.

GOE INFORMATION—Interest Area: 05. Mechanics, Installers, and Repairers. **Work Group:** 05.02. Electrical and Electronic Systems. **Personality Type**—Realistic. Realistic occupations frequently involve work activities that include practical, hands-on problems and solutions. They often deal with plants, animals, and real-world materials like wood, tools, and machinery. Many of the occupations require working outside and do not involve a lot of paperwork or working closely with others. **Work Values**—Independence; Moral Values; Supervision, Technical; Creativity; Compensation. **Skills**—Installation; Repairing; Troubleshooting; Quality Control Analysis; Operation Monitoring; Operation and Control; Equipment Selection; Systems Analysis. **Abilities**—*Cognitive:* Visualization; Information Ordering; Deductive Reasoning; Problem Sensitivity; Perceptual Speed. *Psychomotor:* Manual Dexterity; Speed of Limb Movement; Control Precision; Multilimb Coordination; Finger Dexterity. *Physical:* Dynamic Strength; Extent Flexibility; Gross Body Equilibrium; Static Strength; Stamina. *Sensory:* Night Vision; Hearing Sensitivity; Peripheral Vision; Depth Perception; Sound Localization. **General Work Activities**—*Information Input:* Inspecting Equipment, Structures, or Materials; Monitoring Processes, Materials, or Surroundings; Getting Information. *Mental Process:* Updating and Using Relevant Knowledge; Organizing, Planning, and Prioritizing; Evaluating Information Against Standards. *Work Output:* Repairing and Maintaining Mechanical Equipment; Handling and Moving Objects; Performing General Physical Activities. *Interacting with Others:* Communicating with Other Workers; Communicating with Persons Outside Organization; Establishing and Maintaining Relationships. **Physical Work Conditions**—High Places; Hazardous Equipment; Climbing Ladders, Scaffolds, Poles, etc.; Hazardous Conditions; Minor Burns, Cuts, Bites, or Stings. **Other Job Characteristics**—Consequence of Error; Importance of Being Exact or Accurate; Degree of Automation.

Experience—Job Zone 4. A minimum of two to four years of work-related skill, knowledge, or experience is needed. **Job Preparation:** SVP 7.0 to less than 8.0—two years to less than 10 years. **Knowledge**—Building and Construction; Mechanical; Engineering and Technology; Physics; Public Safety and Security. **Instructional Programs**—Industrial Mechanics and Maintenance Technology.

Related DOT Jobs—825.261-014 Elevator Examiner-and-Adjuster; 825.281-030 Elevator Repairer; 825.281-034 Elevator-Repairer Apprentice; 825.361-010 Elevator Constructor.

47-4031.00 Fence Erectors

- **Education/Training Required: Moderate-term on-the-job training**
- **Employed:** 28,957
- **Annual Earnings:** $21,830
- **Growth:** 4.6%
- **Annual Job Openings:** 5,000

Erect and repair metal and wooden fences and fence gates around highways, industrial establishments, residences, or farms, using hand and power tools.

Sets metal or wooden post in upright position in posthole. Attaches fence rail support to post, using hammer and pliers. Inserts metal tubing through rail supports. Completes top fence rail of metal fence by connecting tube sections, using metal sleeves. Attaches rails or tension wire along bottoms of posts to form fencing frame. Stretches wire, wire mesh, or chain link fencing between posts. Attaches fencing to frame. Nails top and bottom rails to fence posts or inserts them in slots on posts. Nails pointed slats to rails to construct picket fence. Erects alternate panel, basket weave, and louvered fences. Mixes and pours concrete around base of post or tamps soil into posthole to embed post. Assembles gate and fastens gate in position, using hand tools. Saws required lengths of lumber to make rails for wooden fence. Digs postholes with spade, posthole digger, or power-driven auger. Aligns posts, using line or by sighting, and verifies vertical

alignment of posts with plumb bob or spirit level. Lays out fence line, using tape measure, and marks positions for postholes. Cuts metal tubing, using pipe cutter. Welds metal parts together, using portable gas welding equipment. Blasts rock formations with dynamite to facilitate digging of postholes.

GOE INFORMATION—**Interest Area:** 06. Construction, Mining, and Drilling. **Work Group:** 06.02. Construction. **Personality Type**—Realistic. Realistic occupations frequently involve work activities that include practical, hands-on problems and solutions. They often deal with plants, animals, and real-world materials like wood, tools, and machinery. Many of the occupations require working outside and do not involve a lot of paperwork or working closely with others. **Work Values**—Moral Values. **Skills**—Repairing; Equipment Selection. **Abilities**—*Cognitive:* Spatial Orientation. *Psychomotor:* Speed of Limb Movement; Multilimb Coordination; Manual Dexterity; Wrist-Finger Speed; Arm-Hand Steadiness. *Physical:* Static Strength; Extent Flexibility; Trunk Strength; Explosive Strength; Dynamic Strength. *Sensory:* Depth Perception; Glare Sensitivity; Peripheral Vision; Night Vision; Sound Localization. **General Work Activities**—*Information Input:* Estimating Needed Characteristics; Getting Information; Identifying Objects, Actions, and Events. *Mental Process:* Organizing, Planning, and Prioritizing; Making Decisions and Solving Problems; Processing Information. *Work Output:* Handling and Moving Objects; Performing General Physical Activities; Controlling Machines and Processes. *Interacting with Others:* Performing for or Working with the Public; Establishing and Maintaining Relationships; Communicating with Other Workers. **Physical Work Conditions**—Outdoors; Using Hands on Objects, Tools, or Controls; Hazardous Conditions; Minor Burns, Cuts, Bites, or Stings; Distracting Sounds and Noise Levels. **Other Job Characteristics**—Importance of Repeating Same Tasks; Pace Determined by Speed of Equipment; Degree of Automation.

Experience—Job Zone 2. Some previous work-related skill, knowledge, or experience may be helpful, but usually is not needed. **Job Preparation:** SVP 4.0 to less than 6.0—six months to less than two years. **Knowledge**—Building and Construction; Geography; Design; Public Safety and Security; Mechanical. **Instructional Programs**—Construction Trades, Other.

Related DOT Jobs—869.684-022 Fence Erector.

47-4041.00 Hazardous Materials Removal Workers

- **Education/Training Required: Moderate-term on-the-job training**
- **Employed:** 36,920
- **Annual Earnings:** $31,800
- **Growth:** 32.8%
- **Annual Job Openings:** 9,000

Identify, remove, pack, transport, or dispose of hazardous materials, including asbestos, lead-based paint, waste oil, fuel, transmission fluid, radioactive materials, contaminated soil, etc. Specialized training and certification in hazardous materials handling or a confined entry permit are generally required. May operate earth-moving equipment or trucks.

No task data available.

GOE INFORMATION—**Interest Area:** 06. Construction, Mining, and Drilling. **Work Group:** 06.02. Construction. **Note:** The Department of Labor has not collected some data for this job, so it has fewer details than the other descriptions.

Instructional Programs—Construction Trades, Other; Hazardous Materials Management and Waste Technology/Technician; Mechanic and Repair Technologies/Technicians, Other.

Related DOT Jobs—921.663-034 Irradiated-Fuel Handler; 955.383-010 Waste-Disposal Attendant.

47-4041.01 Irradiated-Fuel Handlers

- **Education/Training Required: Moderate-term on-the-job training**
- **Employed: No data available.**
- **Annual Earnings: $31,800**
- **Growth: 32.8%**
- **Annual Job Openings: 9,000**

Package, store, and convey irradiated fuels and wastes, using hoists, mechanical arms, shovels, and industrial truck.

Operates machines and equipment to package, store, or transport loads of waste materials. Loads and unloads materials into containers and onto trucks, using hoists or forklift. Drives truck to convey contaminated waste to designated sea or ground location. Mixes and pours concrete into forms to encase waste material for disposal. Follows prescribed safety procedures and complies with federal laws regulating waste disposal methods. Records number of containers stored at disposal site and specifies amount and type of equipment and waste disposed. Cleans contaminated equipment for reuse, using detergents and solvents, sandblasters, filter pumps, and steam cleaners.

GOE INFORMATION—**Interest Area:** 08. Industrial Production. **Work Group:** 08.07. Hands-on Work: Loading, Moving, Hoisting, and Conveying. **Personality Type**—Realistic. Realistic occupations frequently involve work activities that include practical, hands-on problems and solutions. They often deal with plants, animals, and real-world materials like wood, tools, and machinery. Many of the occupations require working outside and do not involve a lot of paperwork or working closely with others. **Work Values**—Supervision, Technical; Independence; Supervision, Human Relations; Compensation; Advancement. **Skills**—Operation and Control. **Abilities**—*Cognitive:* Spatial Orientation; Information Ordering. *Psychomotor:* Control Precision; Rate Control; Multilimb Coordination; Reaction Time. *Physical:* Static Strength; Gross Body Coordination. *Sensory:* None met the criteria. **General Work Activities**—*Information Input:* Inspecting Equipment, Structures, or Materials; Identifying Objects, Actions, and Events; Getting Information. *Mental Process:* Evaluating Information Against Standards; Updating and Using Relevant Knowledge; Processing Information. *Work Output:* Handling and Moving Objects; Controlling Machines and Processes; Performing General Physical Activities. *Interacting with Others:* Establishing and Maintaining Relationships; Assisting and Caring for Others; Communicating with Other Workers. **Physical Work Conditions**—Radiation; Contaminants; Specialized Protective or Safety Attire; Outdoors; Common Protective or Safety Attire. **Other Job Characteristics**—Consequence of Error; Importance of Being Exact or Accurate; Pace Determined by Speed of Equipment.

Experience—Job Zone 2. Some previous work-related skill, knowledge, or experience may be helpful, but usually is not needed. **Job Preparation:** SVP 4.0 to less than 6.0—six months to less than two years. **Knowledge**—Production and Processing; Chemistry; Public Safety and Security; Law and Government; Building and Construction. **Instructional Programs**—Hazardous Materials Management and Waste Technology/Technician.

Related DOT Jobs—921.663-034 Irradiated-Fuel Handler; 955.383-010 Waste-Disposal Attendant.

47-4051.00 Highway Maintenance Workers

- **Education/Training Required: Moderate-term on-the-job training**
- **Employed: 151,167**
- **Annual Earnings: $27,510**
- **Growth: 5.2%**
- **Annual Job Openings: 31,000**

Maintain highways, municipal and rural roads, airport runways, and rights-of-way. Duties include patching broken or eroded pavement and repairing guardrails, highway markers, and snow fences. May also mow or clear brush from along road or plow snow from roadway.

Apply oil to road surfaces, using sprayers. Apply poisons along roadsides and in animal burrows to eliminate unwanted roadside vegetation and rodents. Clean and clear debris from culverts, catch basins, drop inlets, ditches, and other drain structures. Drive trucks or tractors with adjustable attachments to sweep debris from paved surfaces, mow grass and weeds, and remove snow and ice. Dump, spread, and tamp asphalt, using pneumatic tampers, to repair joints and patch broken pavement. Erect, install, or repair guardrails, road shoulders, berms, highway markers, warning signals, and highway lighting, using hand tools and power tools. Haul and spread sand, gravel, and clay to fill washouts and repair road shoulders. Inspect markers to verify accurate installation. Measure and mark locations for installation of markers, using tape, string, or chalk. Paint traffic control lines and place pavement traffic messages by hand or using machines. Perform roadside landscaping work, such as clearing weeds and brush and planting and trimming trees. Place and remove snow fences used to prevent the accumulation of drifting snow on highways. Remove litter and debris from roadways, including debris from rock slides and mudslides. Set out signs and cones around work areas to divert traffic. Blend compounds to form adhesive mixtures used for marker installation. Drive trucks to transport crews and equipment to work sites. Flag motorists to warn them of obstacles or repair work ahead. Inspect, clean, and repair drainage systems, bridges, tunnels, and other structures.

GOE INFORMATION—**Interest Area:** 06. Construction, Mining, and Drilling. **Work Group:** 06.04. Hands-on Work in Construction, Extraction, and Maintenance. **Personality Type**—Realistic. Realistic occupations frequently involve work activities that include practical, hands-on problems and solutions. They often deal with plants, animals, and real-world materials like wood, tools, and machinery. Many of the occupations require working outside and do not involve a lot of paperwork or working closely with others. **Work Values**—Moral Values; Supervision, Human Relations; Pleasant Co-workers. **Skills**—Repairing; Operation and Control; Installation. **Abilities**—*Cognitive:* Spatial Orientation; Selective Attention. *Psychomotor:* Rate Control; Reaction Time; Response Orientation; Multilimb Coordination; Manual Dexterity. *Physical:* Dynamic Strength; Static Strength; Trunk Strength; Explosive Strength; Stamina. *Sensory:* Glare Sensitivity; Depth Perception; Sound Localization; Peripheral Vision; Far Vision. **General Work Activities**—*Information Input:* Getting Information; Monitoring Processes, Materials, or Surroundings; Identifying Objects, Actions, and Events. *Mental Process:* Updating and Using Relevant Knowledge; Judging Qualities of Things, Services, or Other People's Work; Evaluating Information Against Standards. *Work Output:* Performing General Physical Activities; Handling and Moving Objects; Controlling Machines and Processes. *Interacting with Others:* Establishing and Maintaining Relationships; Communicating with Other Workers; Assisting and Caring for Others. **Physical Work Conditions**—Outdoors; Very Hot or Cold; Contaminants; Common

Protective or Safety Attire; Distracting Sounds and Noise Levels. **Other Job Characteristics**—Importance of Repeating Same Tasks; Pace Determined by Speed of Equipment; Consequence of Error.

Experience—Job Zone 1. No previous work-related skill, knowledge, or experience is needed. **Job Preparation:** SVP below 4.0—less than six months. **Knowledge**—Building and Construction; Public Safety and Security; Mechanical; Geography; Physics. **Instructional Programs**—Construction/Heavy Equipment/Earthmoving Equipment Operation.

Related DOT Jobs—859.684-010 Lane-Marker Installer; 899.684-014 Highway-Maintenance Worker.

47-4061.00 Rail-Track Laying and Maintenance Equipment Operators

- Education/Training Required: Moderate-term on-the-job training
- Employed: 11,756
- Annual Earnings: $33,900
- Growth: −26.1%
- Annual Job Openings: 3,000

Lay, repair, and maintain track for standard or narrow-gauge railroad equipment used in regular railroad service or in plant yards, quarries, sand and gravel pits, and mines. Includes ballast cleaning machine operators and road bed tamping machine operators.

Drives vehicle that automatically moves and lays track or rails over section of track to be constructed, repaired, or maintained. Pushes control to close grasping device on track or rail section to raise or move section to specified location. Engages mechanism that lays track or rail to specified gauge. Adjusts controls of machines that spread, shape, raise, level, and align track, according to specifications. Turns wheels of machine, using lever controls, to adjust guidelines for track alignments and grades, following specifications. Strings and attaches wire-guidelines machine to rails to level or align track or rails. Drives graders, tamping machines, brooms, and ballast-cleaning-spreading machines to redistribute gravel and ballast between rails. Observes leveling indicator arms to verify levelness and alignment of track. Lubricates machines, changes oil, and fills hydraulic reservoirs to specified levels.

GOE INFORMATION—**Interest Area:** 06. Construction, Mining, and Drilling. **Work Group:** 06.02. Construction. **Personality Type**—Realistic. Realistic occupations frequently involve work activities that include practical, hands-on problems and solutions. They often deal with plants, animals, and real-world materials like wood, tools, and machinery. Many of the occupations require working outside and do not involve a lot of paperwork or working closely with others. **Work Values**—Moral Values; Supervision, Technical; Supervision, Human Relations. **Skills**—Operation and Control; Operation Monitoring. **Abilities**—*Cognitive:* Spatial Orientation. *Psychomotor:* Multilimb Coordination; Control Precision; Rate Control; Reaction Time; Response Orientation. *Physical:* Explosive Strength; Gross Body Coordination; Dynamic Flexibility; Dynamic Strength; Static Strength. *Sensory:* Depth Perception; Peripheral Vision; Glare Sensitivity; Sound Localization; Night Vision. **General Work Activities**—*Information Input:* Getting Information; Monitoring Processes, Materials, or Surroundings; Identifying Objects, Actions, and Events. *Mental Process:* Evaluating Information Against Standards; Judging Qualities of Things, Services, or Other People's Work; Analyzing Data or Information. *Work Output:* Handling and Moving Objects; Controlling Machines and Processes; Operating Vehicles or Equipment. *Interacting with Others:* Establishing and Maintaining Relationships; Communicating with Other Workers; Coordinating the Work and Activities of Oth-

ers. **Physical Work Conditions**—Outdoors; Whole Body Vibration; Hazardous Equipment; Distracting Sounds and Noise Levels; Minor Burns, Cuts, Bites, or Stings. **Other Job Characteristics**—Degree of Automation; Consequence of Error; Pace Determined by Speed of Equipment.

Experience—Job Zone 1. No previous work-related skill, knowledge, or experience is needed. **Job Preparation:** SVP below 4.0—less than six months. **Knowledge**—Building and Construction; Mechanical; Engineering and Technology; Geography; Physics. **Instructional Programs**—Construction/Heavy Equipment/Earthmoving Equipment Operation.

Related DOT Jobs—859.683-018 Railway-Equipment Operator; 910.663-010 Track-Moving-Machine Operator; 910.683-018 Track-Surfacing-Machine Operator.

47-4071.00 Septic Tank Servicers and Sewer Pipe Cleaners

- Education/Training Required: Moderate-term on-the-job training
- Employed: 15,349
- Annual Earnings: $27,260
- Growth: 16.5%
- Annual Job Openings: 4,000

Clean and repair septic tanks, sewer lines, or drains. May patch walls and partitions of tank, replace damaged drain tile, or repair breaks in underground piping.

Rotates cleaning rods manually with turning pin. Operates sewer cleaning equipment, including power rodder, high-velocity water jet, sewer flusher, bucket machine, wayne ball, and vac-all. Cleans sewage collection points and sanitary lines and repairs catch basins, manholes, culverts, and storm drains. Cuts damaged section of pipe with cutters, removes broken section from ditch, and replaces pipe section, using pipe sleeve. Starts machine to feed revolving cable or rods into opening, stopping machine and changing knives to conform to pipe size. Withdraws cable and observes residue for evidence of mud, roots, grease, and other deposits indicating broken or clogged sewer line. Cleans and disinfects domestic basements and other areas flooded as result of sewer stoppages. Installs rotary knives on flexible cable, mounted on reel of machine, according to diameter of pipe to be cleaned. Measures distance of excavation site, using plumbers' snake, tapeline, or length of cutting head within sewer, and marks trenching area. Inspects manholes to locate stoppage of sewer line and repaired sewer line joints to ensure tightness prior to backfilling. Covers repaired pipe with dirt and packs backfilled excavation, using air and gasoline tamper. Breaks asphalt and other pavement, using airhammer, pick, and shovel. Notifies co-workers to dig out ruptured line or digs out shallow sewers, using shovel. Requisitions tools and equipment and prepares records showing actions taken. Taps mainline sewers to install sewer saddles. Drives pickup trucks to haul crew, materials, and equipment. Services, adjusts, and makes minor repairs to equipment, machines, and attachments. Updates sewer maps and manhole charting. Communicates with supervisor and other workers, using radio telephone.

GOE INFORMATION—**Interest Area:** 06. Construction, Mining, and Drilling. **Work Group:** 06.04. Hands-on Work in Construction, Extraction, and Maintenance. **Personality Type**—Realistic. Realistic occupations frequently involve work activities that include practical, hands-on problems and solutions. They often deal with plants, animals, and real-world materials like wood, tools, and machinery. Many of the occupations require working outside and do not involve a lot of paperwork or working closely with others. **Work Values**—Supervision, Technical; Independence; Moral Values. **Skills**—Installation; Operation and Control; Repairing; Equipment Selection; Management of Material Resources. **Abilities**—*Cognitive:* Spatial Orientation. *Psychomotor:* Speed of Limb Movement; Multilimb Coordination; Wrist-Finger Speed; Manual Dexterity; Arm-Hand Steadiness. *Physical:* Static Strength; Explosive Strength; Trunk Strength; Extent Flexibility; Dynamic Strength. *Sensory:* None met the criteria. **General Work Activities**—*Information Input:* Inspecting Equipment, Structures, or Materials; Identifying Objects, Actions, and Events; Getting Information. *Mental Process:* Organizing, Planning, and Prioritizing; Making Decisions and Solving Problems; Judging Qualities of Things, Services, or Other People's Work. *Work Output:* Performing General Physical Activities; Handling and Moving Objects; Repairing and Maintaining Mechanical Equipment. *Interacting with Others:* Communicating with Other Workers; Communicating with Persons Outside Organization; Coordinating the Work and Activities of Others. **Physical Work Conditions**—Outdoors; Contaminants; Cramped Work Space or Awkward Positions; Whole Body Vibration; Kneeling, Crouching, or Crawling. **Other Job Characteristics**—Pace Determined by Speed of Equipment; Consequence of Error; Importance of Repeating Same Tasks.

Experience—Job Zone 2. Some previous work-related skill, knowledge, or experience may be helpful, but usually is not needed. **Job Preparation:** SVP 4.0 to less than 6.0—six months to less than two years. **Knowledge**—Mechanical; Building and Construction; Economics and Accounting; Engineering and Technology; Geography. **Instructional Programs**—Plumbing Technology/Plumber.

Related DOT Jobs—869.664-018 Sewer-Line Repairer; 899.664-014 Sewer-Pipe Cleaner.

47-4091.00 Segmental Pavers

- **Education/Training Required: Moderate-term on-the-job training**
- **Employed: No data available.**
- **Annual Earnings: $26,170**
- **Growth: 26.7%**
- **Annual Job Openings: 21,000**

Lay out, cut, and paste segmental paving units. Includes installers of bedding and restraining materials for the paving units.

Cement the edges of the paved area. Cut paving stones to size and for edges, using a splitter and a masonry saw. Design paver installation layout pattern and create markings for directional references of joints and stringlines. Compact bedding sand and pavers to finish the paved area, using a plate compactor. Prepare base for installation by removing unstable or unsuitable materials, compacting and grading the soil, draining or stabilizing weak or saturated soils, and taking measures to prevent water penetration and migration of bedding sand. Resurface an outside area with cobblestones, terra cotta tiles, concrete, or other materials. Screed sand level to an even thickness and recheck sand exposed to elements, raking and rescreeding if necessary. Set pavers, aligning and spacing them correctly. Supply and place base materials, edge restraints, bedding sand, and jointing sand. Sweep sand into the joints and compact pavement until the joints are full. Discuss the design with the client. Sweep sand from the surface prior to opening to traffic.

GOE INFORMATION—Interest Area: 06. Construction, Mining, and Drilling. **Work Group:** 06.02. Construction. **Note:** The Department of Labor has not collected some data for this job, so it has fewer details than the other descriptions.

Instructional Programs—Concrete Finishing/Concrete Finisher.

Related DOT Jobs—No related DOT jobs.

47-4099.99 Construction and Related Workers, All Other

- **Education/Training Required: Moderate-term on-the-job training**
- **Employed: No data available.**
- **Annual Earnings: No data available.**
- **Growth: 26.7%**
- **Annual Job Openings: 21,000**

All construction and related workers not listed separately.

No task data available.

GOE INFORMATION—Interest Area: 06. Construction, Mining, and Drilling. **Work Group:** 06.02. Construction. **Note:** The Department of Labor has not collected some data for this job, so it has fewer details than the other descriptions.

Instructional Programs—Construction Trades, Other; Construction/Heavy Equipment/Earthmoving Equipment Operation.

Related DOT Jobs—168.364-640 Hazardous-Waste Material Technician; 779.684-058 Stone Repairer; 809.381-022 Ornamental-Iron Worker; 809.381-026 Ornamental-Iron-Worker Apprentice; 821.687-010 Steel-Post Installer; 851.262-010 Sewer-Line Repairer, Tele-Grout; 862.662-010 Pipe-Cleaning-And-Priming-Machine Operator; 862.682-014 Pipe-Wrapping-Machine Operator; 869.261-010 House Mover; 869.261-018 Poured-Concrete-Wall Technician; 869.281-014 House Builder; 869.361-010 Conduit Mechanic; 869.361-014 Hydraulic-Jack Adjuster; 869.381-026 Sign Erector I; 869.381-030 Steeple Jack; 869.662-010 Lift-Slab Operator; 869.681-010 Concrete-Fence Builder; 869.684-054 Sign Erector II; 899.684-026 Pipeliner.

47-5000 Extraction Workers

47-5011.00 Derrick Operators, Oil and Gas

- **Education/Training Required: Moderate-term on-the-job training**
- **Employed: 16,109**
- **Annual Earnings: $28,500**
- **Growth: 0.1%**
- **Annual Job Openings: 1,000**

Rig derrick equipment and operate pumps to circulate mud through drill hole.

Clamp holding fixtures on ends of hoisting cables. Control the viscosity and weight of the drilling fluid. Guide lengths of pipe into and out of elevators. Inspect derricks for flaws; clean and oil derricks in order to maintain proper working conditions. Inspect derricks or order their inspection prior to being raised or lowered. Listen to mud pumps and check regularly for vibration and other problems in order to ensure that rig pumps and drilling mud systems are working properly. Position and align derrick elements, using harnesses and platform climbing devices. Set and bolt crown blocks to posts at tops of derricks. Start pumps that circulate mud through drill pipes and boreholes to cool drill bits and flush out drill-cuttings. Steady pipes during connection to or disconnection from drill or casing strings. String cables through pulleys and blocks. Prepare mud reports and instruct crews about the handling of any chemical additives. Repair pumps, mud tanks, and related equipment. Supervise crew members and provide assistance in training them. Weigh clay and mix with water and chemicals in order to make drilling mud, using portable mixers.

GOE INFORMATION—Interest Area: 06. Construction, Mining, and Drilling. **Work Group:** 06.03. Mining and Drilling. **Personality Type—** Realistic. Realistic occupations frequently involve work activities that include practical, hands-on problems and solutions. They often deal with plants, animals, and real-world materials like wood, tools, and machinery. Many of the occupations require working outside and do not involve a lot of paperwork or working closely with others. **Work Values—**Moral Values; Supervision, Technical; Supervision, Human Relations; Company Policies and Practices. **Skills—**Repairing; Operation and Control; Troubleshooting; Operation Monitoring. **Abilities—***Cognitive:* None met the criteria. *Psychomotor:* Multilimb Coordination; Speed of Limb Movement; Rate Control. *Physical:* Static Strength; Extent Flexibility; Explosive Strength; Dynamic Strength; Gross Body Equilibrium. *Sensory:* Peripheral Vision; Depth Perception; Glare Sensitivity. **General Work Activities—***Information Input:* Inspecting Equipment, Structures, or Materials; Monitoring Processes, Materials, or Surroundings; Getting Information. *Mental Process:* Updating and Using Relevant Knowledge; Judging Qualities of Things, Services, or Other People's Work; Making Decisions and Solving Problems. *Work Output:* Performing General Physical Activities; Handling and Moving Objects; Controlling Machines and Processes. *Interacting with Others:* Communicating with Other Workers; Establishing and Maintaining Relationships; Monitoring and Controlling Resources. **Physical Work Conditions—**Outdoors; Hazardous Equipment; Whole Body Vibration; Distracting Sounds and Noise Levels; Contaminants. **Other Job Characteristics—**Degree of Automation; Pace Determined by Speed of Equipment; Consequence of Error.

Experience—Job Zone 2. Some previous work-related skill, knowledge, or experience may be helpful, but usually is not needed. **Job Preparation:** SVP 4.0 to less than 6.0—six months to less than two years. **Knowledge—**Mechanical; Physics; Building and Construction; Public Safety and Security; Geography. **Instructional Programs—**Well Drilling/Driller.

Related DOT Jobs—930.382-022 Rotary Derrick Operator.

47-5012.00 Rotary Drill Operators, Oil and Gas

- Education/Training Required: Moderate-term on-the-job training
- Employed: 18,087
- Annual Earnings: $33,010
- Growth: –8.0%
- Annual Job Openings: 1,000

Set up or operate a variety of drills to remove petroleum products from the earth and to find and remove core samples for testing during oil and gas exploration.

Bolt together pump and engine parts; connect tanks and flow lines. Cap wells with packers or turn valves in order to regulate outflow of oil from wells. Clean and oil pulleys, blocks, and cables. Connect sections of drill pipe, using hand tools and powered wrenches and tongs. Count sections of drill rod in order to determine depths of boreholes. Dig holes, set forms, and mix and pour concrete for foundations of steel or wooden derricks. Direct rig crews in drilling and other activities, such as setting up rigs and completing or servicing wells. Line drilled holes with pipes and install all necessary hardware in order to prepare new wells. Lower and explode charges in boreholes in order to start flow of oil from wells. Monitor progress of drilling operations and select and change drill bits according to the nature of strata, using hand tools. Observe pressure gauge and move throttles and levers in order to control the speed of rotary tables and to regulate pressure of tools at bottoms of boreholes. Position and prepare truck-mounted derricks at drilling areas that are specified on field maps. Push levers and brake pedals in order to control gasoline, diesel, electric, or steam draw works that lower and raise drill pipes and casings in and out of wells. Remove core samples during drilling in order to determine the nature of the strata being drilled. Start and examine operation of slush pumps in order to ensure circulation and consistency of drilling fluid or mud in well. Weigh clay and mix with water and chemicals to make drilling mud. Locate and recover lost or broken bits, casings, and drill pipes from wells, using special tools. Maintain and adjust machinery in order to ensure proper performance. Maintain records of footage drilled, location and nature of strata penetrated, materials and tools used, services rendered, and time required. Plug observation wells and restore sites. Repair or replace defective parts of machinery, such as rotary drill rigs, water trucks, air compressors, and pumps, using hand tools. Train crews and introduce procedures to make drill work more safe and effective.

GOE INFORMATION—Interest Area: 06. Construction, Mining, and Drilling. **Work Group:** 06.03. Mining and Drilling. **Personality Type—** Realistic. Realistic occupations frequently involve work activities that include practical, hands-on problems and solutions. They often deal with plants, animals, and real-world materials like wood, tools, and machinery. Many of the occupations require working outside and do not involve a lot of paperwork or working closely with others. **Work Values—**Compensation; Supervision, Technical; Supervision, Human Relations; Company Policies and Practices; Advancement. **Skills—**Repairing; Operation Monitoring; Operation and Control; Equipment Selection. **Abilities—***Cognitive:* Spatial Orientation; Flexibility of Closure; Perceptual Speed; Speed of Closure. *Psychomotor:* Multilimb Coordination; Control Precision; Rate Control; Response Orientation; Speed of Limb Movement. *Physical:* Static Strength; Explosive Strength; Extent Flexibility; Dynamic Flexibility; Gross Body Coordination. *Sensory:* Depth Perception; Far Vision; Peripheral Vision; Visual Color Discrimination; Sound Localization. **General Work Activities—***Information Input:* Monitoring Processes, Materials, or Surroundings; Inspecting Equipment, Structures, or Materials; Getting Information. *Mental Process:* Making Decisions and Solving Problems; Analyzing Data or Information; Updating and Using Relevant Knowledge. *Work Output:* Handling and Moving Objects; Performing General Physical Activities; Controlling Machines and Processes. *Interacting with Others:* Establishing and Maintaining Relationships; Communicating with Other Workers; Performing Administrative Activities. **Physical Work Conditions—**Outdoors; Hazardous Equipment; Whole Body Vibration; Hazardous Conditions; Minor Burns, Cuts, Bites, or Stings. **Other Job Characteristics—**Degree of Automation; Consequence of Error; Pace Determined by Speed of Equipment.

Experience—Job Zone 3. Previous work-related skill, knowledge, or experience is required. **Job Preparation:** SVP 6.0 to less than 7.0—more than one year and less than four years. **Knowledge—**Mechanical; Physics; Geography; Engineering and Technology; Building and Construction. **Instructional Programs—**Well Drilling/Driller.

Related DOT Jobs—930.382-018 Prospecting Driller; 930.382-026 Rotary Driller; 950.382-022 Rotary-Rig Engine Operator.

47-5013.00 Service Unit Operators, Oil, Gas, and Mining

- **Education/Training Required: Moderate-term on-the-job training**
- **Employed: 10,963**
- **Annual Earnings: $27,270**
- **Growth: –1.2%**
- **Annual Job Openings: 1,000**

Operate equipment to increase oil flow from producing wells or to remove stuck pipe, casing, tools, or other obstructions from drilling wells. May also perform similar services in mining exploration operations.

Analyze conditions of unserviceable wells in order to determine actions to be taken to improve well conditions. Assemble and lower detection instruments into wells with obstructions. Assemble and operate sound-wave generating and detecting mechanisms in order to determine well fluid levels. Confer with other personnel in order to gather information regarding pipe and tool sizes and borehole conditions in wells. Direct drilling crews performing such activities as assembling and connecting pipe, applying weights to drill pipes, and drilling around lodged obstacles. Direct lowering of specialized equipment to point of obstruction and push switches or pull levers in order to back off or sever pipes by chemical or explosive action. Interpret instrument readings in order to ascertain the depth of obstruction. Observe load variations on strain gauges, mud pumps, and motor pressure indicators and listen to engines, rotary chains, and other equipment in order to detect faulty operations or unusual well conditions. Plan fishing methods and select tools for removing obstacles such as liners, broken casing, screens, and drill pipe from wells. Start pumps that circulate water, oil, or other fluids through wells in order to remove sand and other materials obstructing the free flow of oil. Close and seal wells no longer in use. Drive truck-mounted units to well sites. Install pressure-control devices onto well heads. Operate controls that raise derricks and level rigs. Perforate well casings or sidewalls of boreholes with explosive charges. Quote prices to customers and prepare reports of services rendered, tools used, and time required so that bills can be produced. Thread cables through pulleys in derricks and connect hydraulic lines, using hand tools.

GOE INFORMATION—Interest Area: 06. Construction, Mining, and Drilling. **Work Group:** 06.03. Mining and Drilling. **Personality Type—** Realistic. Realistic occupations frequently involve work activities that include practical, hands-on problems and solutions. They often deal with plants, animals, and real-world materials like wood, tools, and machinery. Many of the occupations require working outside and do not involve a lot of paperwork or working closely with others. **Work Values—**Authority; Supervision, Technical; Compensation; Supervision, Human Relations; Pleasant Co-workers. **Skills—**Operation Monitoring; Operation and Control; Equipment Selection; Troubleshooting; Management of Personnel Resources; Monitoring; Systems Analysis; Critical Thinking. **Abilities—***Cognitive:* Flexibility of Closure; Originality; Fluency of Ideas; Visualization; Inductive Reasoning. *Psychomotor:* Control Precision; Multilimb Coordination; Reaction Time; Rate Control; Response Orientation. *Physical:* Dynamic Flexibility; Static Strength; Gross Body Equilibrium; Explosive Strength; Dynamic Strength. *Sensory:* Depth Perception; Hearing Sensitivity; Auditory Attention; Sound Localization; Glare Sensitivity. **General Work Activities—***Information Input:* Getting Information; Monitoring Processes, Materials, or Surroundings; Identifying Objects, Actions, and Events. *Mental Process:* Analyzing Data or Information; Making Decisions and Solving Problems; Organizing, Planning, and Prioritizing. *Work Output:* Controlling Machines and Pro-

cesses; Performing General Physical Activities; Handling and Moving Objects. *Interacting with Others:* Coordinating the Work and Activities of Others; Communicating with Other Workers; Guiding, Directing, and Motivating Subordinates. **Physical Work Conditions—**Outdoors; Hazardous Equipment; Hazardous Conditions; Distracting Sounds and Noise Levels; Extremely Bright or Inadequate Lighting. **Other Job Characteristics—**Degree of Automation; Consequence of Error; Pace Determined by Speed of Equipment.

Experience—Job Zone 4. A minimum of two to four years of work-related skill, knowledge, or experience is needed. **Job Preparation:** SVP 7.0 to less than 8.0—two years to less than 10 years. **Knowledge—**Mechanical; Physics; Engineering and Technology; Geography; Economics and Accounting. **Instructional Programs—**Mining Technology/Technician.

Related DOT Jobs—930.261-010 Fishing-Tool Technician, Oil Well; 930.361-010 Service-Unit Operator, Oil Well.

47-5021.00 Earth Drillers, Except Oil and Gas

- **Education/Training Required: Moderate-term on-the-job training**
- **Employed: 23,649**
- **Annual Earnings: $32,000**
- **Growth: 12.6%**
- **Annual Job Openings: 3,000**

Operate a variety of drills—such as rotary, churn, and pneumatic—to tap sub-surface water and salt deposits, to remove core samples during mineral exploration or soil testing, and to facilitate the use of explosives in mining or construction. May use explosives. Includes horizontal and earth boring machine operators.

No task data available.

GOE INFORMATION—Interest Area: 06. Construction, Mining, and Drilling. **Work Group:** 06.03. Mining and Drilling. **Note:** The Department of Labor has not collected some data for this job, so it has fewer details than the other descriptions.

Instructional Programs—Construction/Heavy Equipment/Earthmoving Equipment Operation; Well Drilling/Driller.

Related DOT Jobs—850.662-010 Horizontal-Earth-Boring-Machine Operator; 850.662-014 Rock-Drill Operator II; 850.683-034 Rock-Drill Operator I; 859.362-010 Well-Drill Operator; 859.682-010 Earth-Boring-Machine Operator; 859.682-014 Foundation-Drill Operator; 930.662-014 Core-Drill Operator; 930.682-010 Core-Drill Operator.

47-5021.01 Construction Drillers

- **Education/Training Required: Moderate-term on-the-job training**
- **Employed: No data available.**
- **Annual Earnings: $32,000**
- **Growth: 12.6%**
- **Annual Job Openings: 3,000**

Operate machine to drill or bore through earth or rock.

Monitors drilling operation and strata being drilled to determine need to adjust drilling or insert casing into hole. Starts, stops, and controls drilling speed of machine and insertion of casing into hole. Retracts auger to force discharge dirt from hole. Operates machine to flush earth cuttings or blows dust from hole. Assembles and positions machine, augers, and casing pipes. Verifies depth and level of boring position. Operates hoist to lift power line poles into position. Signals crane operator to move equipment. Drives truck or tractor to work site.

GOE INFORMATION—Interest Area: 06. Construction, Mining, and Drilling. **Work Group:** 06.03. Mining and Drilling. **Personality Type—** Realistic. Realistic occupations frequently involve work activities that include practical, hands-on problems and solutions. They often deal with plants, animals, and real-world materials like wood, tools, and machinery. Many of the occupations require working outside and do not involve a lot of paperwork or working closely with others. **Work Values—**Moral Values; Supervision, Technical. **Skills—**Operation Monitoring; Operation and Control. **Abilities—***Cognitive:* Spatial Orientation; Visualization; Information Ordering; Perceptual Speed; Flexibility of Closure. *Psychomotor:* Response Orientation; Reaction Time; Rate Control; Control Precision; Speed of Limb Movement. *Physical:* Static Strength; Dynamic Strength; Explosive Strength; Trunk Strength; Stamina. *Sensory:* Depth Perception; Peripheral Vision; Auditory Attention; Sound Localization; Hearing Sensitivity. **General Work Activities—***Information Input:* Monitoring Processes, Materials, or Surroundings; Identifying Objects, Actions, and Events; Inspecting Equipment, Structures, or Materials. *Mental Process:* Updating and Using Relevant Knowledge; Judging Qualities of Things, Services, or Other People's Work; Making Decisions and Solving Problems. *Work Output:* Controlling Machines and Processes; Operating Vehicles or Equipment; Performing General Physical Activities. *Interacting with Others:* Communicating with Other Workers; Establishing and Maintaining Relationships; Coordinating the Work and Activities of Others. **Physical Work Conditions—**Outdoors; Hazardous Equipment; Whole Body Vibration; Contaminants; Common Protective or Safety Attire. **Other Job Characteristics—**Pace Determined by Speed of Equipment; Degree of Automation; Importance of Repeating Same Tasks.

Experience—Job Zone 2. Some previous work-related skill, knowledge, or experience may be helpful, but usually is not needed. **Job Preparation:** SVP 4.0 to less than 6.0—six months to less than two years. **Knowledge—**Mechanical; Engineering and Technology; Public Safety and Security; Geography; Physics. **Instructional Programs—**Construction/Heavy Equipment/Earthmoving Equipment Operation; Well Drilling/Driller.

Related DOT Jobs—850.662-010 Horizontal-Earth-Boring-Machine Operator; 850.662-014 Rock-Drill Operator II; 850.683-034 Rock-Drill Operator I; 859.682-010 Earth-Boring-Machine Operator; 859.682-014 Foundation-Drill Operator.

47-5021.02 Well and Core Drill Operators

- Education/Training Required: **Long-term on-the-job training**
- Employed: **No data available.**
- Annual Earnings: **$32,000**
- Growth: **12.6%**
- Annual Job Openings: **3,000**

Operate machine to drill wells and take samples or cores for analysis of strata.

Starts and controls drilling action and lowering of well casing into well bore. Monitors operation of drilling equipment to determine changes in strata or variations in drilling. Withdraws drill rod from hole and extracts core sample. Couples additional lengths of drill rod as bit advances. Assembles non-truck-mounted drilling equipment, using hand tools and power tools. Changes drill bits as needed. Inspects core samples to determine nature of strata or takes samples to laboratory for analysis. Pours water into well or pumps water or slush into well to cool drill bit and remove drillings. Drives or guides truck-mounted equipment into position, levels and stabilizes rig, and extends telescoping derrick. Retrieves lost equipment from boreholes, using retrieval tools and equipment. Lubricates machine, splices worn or broken cables, replaces parts, and builds up and repairs drill bits. Records drilling progress and geological data. Fabricates well casings.

GOE INFORMATION—Interest Area: 06. Construction, Mining, and Drilling. **Work Group:** 06.03. Mining and Drilling. **Personality Type—** Realistic. Realistic occupations frequently involve work activities that include practical, hands-on problems and solutions. They often deal with plants, animals, and real-world materials like wood, tools, and machinery. Many of the occupations require working outside and do not involve a lot of paperwork or working closely with others. **Work Values—**Moral Values; Supervision, Technical; Advancement. **Skills—**Operation Monitoring; Operation and Control; Repairing; Equipment Selection. **Abilities—***Cognitive:* Spatial Orientation; Perceptual Speed; Selective Attention; Information Ordering; Flexibility of Closure. *Psychomotor:* Response Orientation; Control Precision; Reaction Time; Multilimb Coordination; Speed of Limb Movement. *Physical:* Static Strength; Explosive Strength; Trunk Strength; Extent Flexibility; Dynamic Strength. *Sensory:* Depth Perception; Peripheral Vision; Visual Color Discrimination; Hearing Sensitivity; Auditory Attention. **General Work Activities—***Information Input:* Monitoring Processes, Materials, or Surroundings; Identifying Objects, Actions, and Events; Inspecting Equipment, Structures, or Materials. *Mental Process:* Judging Qualities of Things, Services, or Other People's Work; Updating and Using Relevant Knowledge; Evaluating Information Against Standards. *Work Output:* Handling and Moving Objects; Performing General Physical Activities; Controlling Machines and Processes. *Interacting with Others:* Communicating with Other Workers; Monitoring and Controlling Resources; Establishing and Maintaining Relationships. **Physical Work Conditions—**Distracting Sounds and Noise Levels; Common Protective or Safety Attire; Outdoors; Hazardous Equipment; Whole Body Vibration. **Other Job Characteristics—**Pace Determined by Speed of Equipment; Degree of Automation; Consequence of Error.

Experience—Job Zone 3. Previous work-related skill, knowledge, or experience is required. **Job Preparation:** SVP 6.0 to less than 7.0—more than one year and less than four years. **Knowledge—**Mechanical; Physics; Engineering and Technology; Geography; Public Safety and Security. **Instructional Programs—**Construction/Heavy Equipment/ Earthmoving Equipment Operation; Well Drilling/Driller.

Related DOT Jobs—859.362-010 Well-Drill Operator; 930.662-014 Core-Drill Operator.

47-5031.00 Explosives Workers, Ordnance Handling Experts, and Blasters

- Education/Training Required: **Moderate-term on-the-job training**
- Employed: **5,081**
- Annual Earnings: **$33,940**
- Growth: **1.9%**
- Annual Job Openings: **Fewer than 500**

Place and detonate explosives to demolish structures or to loosen, remove, or displace earth, rock, or other materials. May perform specialized handling, storage, and accounting procedures. Includes seismograph shooters.

Assembles equipment, primer, explosives, and blasting cap or loads perforating gun with explosives. Loads specified amount of explosives into blast holes manually or using rope or hoist. Lights fuse, drops detonating device into well, or connects wires to firing device and activates device to set off blast. Plants explosive charge in structures or outside, using rope and safety harness for climbing. Cuts specified lengths of primacord and attaches primer to end of cord. Lays primacord between rows of charged blast holes and ties cord into main line to form blast pattern. Ties specified lengths of delaying fuses into pattern to time sequence of explosions. Fills and tamps blasting hole. Observes control panel to verify detonation of charge or listens for sound of blast. Examines blast area to determine amount and kind of explosive needed and to ensure safety prior to detonation. Marks location and depth of charge holes for drilling and measures depth of drilled blast holes. Sets up and operates pneumatic drilling equipment to dill blast holes. Operates equipment, such as hoist, jackhammer, or drill, to bore charge holes. Sets up and operates radio or telephone equipment to receive blast information. Signals workers to clear area and hoist operator to raise equipment and sample from blast hole after detonation. Places safety cones around blast area to alert other workers. Drives truck to transport explosives and blasting equipment to blasting site. Moves, stores, and maintains inventories of high explosives. Repairs and services blasting and automotive equipment and electrical instruments, using hand tools.

GOE INFORMATION—Interest Area: 06. Construction, Mining, and Drilling. Work Group: 06.02. Construction. Personality Type—Realistic. Realistic occupations frequently involve work activities that include practical, hands-on problems and solutions. They often deal with plants, animals, and real-world materials like wood, tools, and machinery. Many of the occupations require working outside and do not involve a lot of paperwork or working closely with others. Work Values—Supervision, Technical; Moral Values; Authority; Compensation. Skills—Operation Monitoring; Operation and Control; Equipment Selection; Repairing; Troubleshooting; Installation. Abilities—Cognitive: Spatial Orientation; Information Ordering; Visualization; Time Sharing; Selective Attention. Psychomotor: Reaction Time; Response Orientation; Speed of Limb Movement; Rate Control; Multilimb Coordination. Physical: Extent Flexibility; Gross Body Equilibrium; Explosive Strength; Static Strength; Gross Body Coordination. Sensory: Depth Perception; Visual Color Discrimination; Far Vision; Sound Localization; Glare Sensitivity. General Work Activities—Information Input: Monitoring Processes, Materials, or Surroundings; Identifying Objects, Actions, and Events; Getting Information. Mental Process: Making Decisions and Solving Problems; Updating and Using Relevant Knowledge; Thinking Creatively. Work Output: Performing General Physical Activities; Handling and Moving Objects; Repairing and Maintaining Mechanical Equipment. Interacting with Others: Communicating with Other Workers; Monitoring and Controlling Resources; Establishing and Maintaining Relationships. Physical Work Conditions—Hazardous Conditions; Outdoors; Whole Body Vibration; Distracting Sounds and Noise Levels; Common Protective or Safety Attire. Other Job Characteristics—Consequence of Error; Importance of Being Exact or Accurate; Pace Determined by Speed of Equipment.

Experience—Job Zone 2. Some previous work-related skill, knowledge, or experience may be helpful, but usually is not needed. Job Preparation: SVP 4.0 to less than 6.0—six months to less than two years. Knowledge—Public Safety and Security; Physics; Engineering and Technology; Building and Construction; Telecommunications. Instructional Programs—Blasting/Blaster.

Related DOT Jobs—850.381-010 Miner; 859.261-010 Blaster; 931.261-010 Blaster; 931.361-010 Sample-Taker Operator; 931.361-014 Shooter; 931.361-018 Shooter, Seismograph; 931.382-010 Perforator Operator, Oil Well; 931.664-010 Tier-and-Detonator; 931.667-010 Powder Loader.

47-5041.00 Continuous Mining Machine Operators

- **Education/Training Required: Moderate-term on-the-job training**
- **Employed: 9,530**
- **Annual Earnings: $33,640**
- **Growth: −13.4%**
- **Annual Job Openings: 1,000**

Operate self-propelled mining machines that rip coal, metal and nonmetal ores, rock, stone, or sand from the face and load it onto conveyors or into shuttle cars in a continuous operation.

Moves levers to sump (advance) ripper bar or boring head into face of coal seam. Starts machine to gather coal and convey it to floor or shuttle car. Moves lever to raise and lower hydraulic safety bar that supports roof above machine until other workers complete their framing. Drives machine into position at working face. Repairs, oils, and adjusts machine and changes cutting teeth, using wrench.

GOE INFORMATION—Interest Area: 06. Construction, Mining, and Drilling. Work Group: 06.03. Mining and Drilling. Personality Type—Realistic. Realistic occupations frequently involve work activities that include practical, hands-on problems and solutions. They often deal with plants, animals, and real-world materials like wood, tools, and machinery. Many of the occupations require working outside and do not involve a lot of paperwork or working closely with others. Work Values—Supervision, Technical; Supervision, Human Relations; Moral Values; Company Policies and Practices. Skills—Repairing; Operation and Control; Operation Monitoring. Abilities—Cognitive: Spatial Orientation. Psychomotor: Multilimb Coordination; Reaction Time; Rate Control; Control Precision; Response Orientation. Physical: Static Strength; Explosive Strength; Gross Body Coordination; Gross Body Equilibrium. Sensory: Depth Perception; Night Vision; Peripheral Vision; Sound Localization; Hearing Sensitivity. General Work Activities—Information Input: Monitoring Processes, Materials, or Surroundings; Getting Information; Inspecting Equipment, Structures, or Materials. Mental Process: Updating and Using Relevant Knowledge; Analyzing Data or Information; Organizing, Planning, and Prioritizing. Work Output: Controlling Machines and Processes; Operating Vehicles or Equipment; Handling and Moving Objects. Interacting with Others: Communicating with Other Workers; Establishing and Maintaining Relationships; Coordinating the Work and Activities of Others. Physical Work Conditions—Outdoors; Whole Body Vibration; Hazardous Equipment; Common Protective or Safety Attire; Distracting Sounds and Noise Levels. Other Job Characteristics—Pace Determined by Speed of Equipment; Degree of Automation; Consequence of Error.

Experience—Job Zone 2. Some previous work-related skill, knowledge, or experience may be helpful, but usually is not needed. Job Preparation: SVP 4.0 to less than 6.0—six months to less than two years. Knowledge—Mechanical; Engineering and Technology; Building and Construction; Public Safety and Security; Physics. Instructional Programs—Construction/Heavy Equipment/Earthmoving Equipment Operation.

Related DOT Jobs—930.683-010 Continuous-Mining-Machine Operator.

47-5042.00 Mine Cutting and Channeling Machine Operators

- **Education/Training Required: Moderate-term on-the-job training**
- **Employed: No data available.**
- **Annual Earnings: $35,350**
- **Growth: –13.4%**
- **Annual Job Openings: 1,000**

Operate machinery—such as longwall shears, plows, and cutting machines—to cut or channel along the face or seams of coal mines, stone quarries, or other mining surfaces to facilitate blasting, separating, or removing minerals or materials from mines or from the earth's surface.

Advance plow blades through coal strata by remote control according to electronic or radio signals from the tailer. Cut slots along working faces of coal, salt, or other non-metal deposits in order to facilitate blasting by moving levers to start the machine and to control the vertical reciprocating drills. Determine locations, boundaries, and depths of holes or channels to be cut. Drive mobile, truck-mounted, or track-mounted drilling or cutting machine in mines and quarries or on construction sites. Move controls to start and position drill cutters or torches and to advance tools into mines or quarry faces in order to complete horizontal or vertical cuts. Move planer levers to control and adjust the movement of equipment and the speed, height, and depth of cuts and to rotate swivel cutting booms. Observe indicator lights and gauges and listen to machine operation in order to detect binding or stoppage of tools or other equipment problems. Reposition machines and move controls in order to make additional holes or cuts. Signal that machine plow blades are properly positioned, using electronic buzzers or two-way radios. Charge and set off explosives in blasting holes. Cut and move shale from open pits. Cut entries between rooms and haulage-ways. Free jams in planer hoppers, using metal pinch bars. Guide and assist crews in laying track for machines and resetting planer rails, supports, and blocking, using jacks, shovels, sledges, picks, and pinch bars. Monitor movement of shale along conveyors from hoppers to trucks or rail cars. Position jacks, timbers, or roof supports and install casings in order to prevent cave-ins. Press buttons to activate conveyor belts and push or pull chain handles to regulate conveyor movement so that material can be moved or loaded into dinkey cars or dump trucks. Remove debris such as loose shale from channels and planer travel areas. Replace worn or broken tools and machine bits and parts, using wrenches, pry bars, and other hand tools, and lubricate machines, using grease guns. Signal crew members to adjust the speed of equipment to the rate of installation of roof supports and to adjust the speed of conveyors to the volume of coal. Signal truck drivers to position their vehicles for receiving shale from planer hoppers.

GOE INFORMATION—Interest Area: 06. Construction, Mining, and Drilling. **Work Group:** 06.03. Mining and Drilling. **Personality Type—**Realistic. Realistic occupations frequently involve work activities that include practical, hands-on problems and solutions. They often deal with plants, animals, and real-world materials like wood, tools, and machinery. Many of the occupations require working outside and do not involve a lot of paperwork or working closely with others. **Work Values—**Supervision, Technical; Moral Values; Supervision, Human Relations; Pleasant Co-workers; Advancement. **Skills—**Operation and Control; Operation Monitoring; Repairing. **Abilities—***Cognitive:* Spatial Orientation; Flexibility of Closure; Time Sharing. *Psychomotor:* Multilimb Coordination; Rate Control; Speed of Limb Movement; Control Precision; Reaction Time. *Physical:* Explosive Strength; Static Strength; Dynamic Flexibility; Extent Flexibility; Gross Body Coordination. *Sensory:* Depth Perception; Hearing Sensitivity; Night Vision; Peripheral Vision; Auditory Attention. **General Work Activities—***Information Input:* Monitoring Processes, Materials, or Surroundings; Getting Information; Identifying Objects, Actions, and Events. *Mental Process:* Organizing, Planning, and Prioritizing; Making Decisions and Solving Problems; Updating and Using Relevant Knowledge. *Work Output:* Controlling Machines and Processes; Operating Vehicles or Equipment; Performing General Physical Activities. *Interacting with Others:* Communicating with Other Workers; Coordinating the Work and Activities of Others; Establishing and Maintaining Relationships. **Physical Work Conditions—**Outdoors; Common Protective or Safety Attire; Whole Body Vibration; Hazardous Conditions; Distracting Sounds and Noise Levels. **Other Job Characteristics—**Consequence of Error; Degree of Automation; Pace Determined by Speed of Equipment.

Experience—Job Zone 2. Some previous work-related skill, knowledge, or experience may be helpful, but usually is not needed. **Job Preparation:** SVP 4.0 to less than 6.0–six months to less than two years. **Knowledge—**Mechanical; Building and Construction; Engineering and Technology; Public Safety and Security; Physics. **Instructional Programs—**Construction/Heavy Equipment/Earthmoving Equipment Operation.

Related DOT Jobs—930.382-010 Driller, Machine; 930.383-010 Channeling-Machine Runner; 930.482-010 Drilling-Machine Operator; 930.662-010 Long-Wall Shear Operator; 930.663-010 Shale Planer Operator; 930.683-014 Cutter Operator; 930.684-010 Flame Channeler.

47-5049.99 Mining Machine Operators, All Other

- **Education/Training Required: Moderate-term on-the-job training**
- **Employed: No data available.**
- **Annual Earnings: No data available.**
- **Growth: –13.4%**
- **Annual Job Openings: 1,000**

All mining machine operators not listed separately.

No task data available.

GOE INFORMATION—Interest Area: 06. Construction, Mining, and Drilling. **Work Group:** 06.03. Mining and Drilling. **Note:** The Department of Labor has not collected some data for this job, so it has fewer details than the other descriptions.

Instructional Programs—Construction/Heavy Equipment/Earthmoving Equipment Operation.

Related DOT Jobs—No related DOT jobs.

47-5051.00 Rock Splitters, Quarry

- **Education/Training Required: Moderate-term on-the-job training**
- **Employed: No data available.**
- **Annual Earnings: $26,940**
- **Growth: –13.4%**
- **Annual Job Openings: 1,000**

Separate blocks of rough-dimension stone from quarry mass, using jackhammer and wedges.

Inserts wedges and feathers into holes and drives wedges with sledgehammer to split stone from mass. Marks desired dimensions on stone, using rule and chalkline. Cuts groove along outline, using chisel. Drills holes along outline with jackhammer.

GOE INFORMATION—Interest Area: 06. Construction, Mining, and Drilling. **Work Group:** 06.03. Mining and Drilling. **Personality Type—**Realistic. Realistic occupations frequently involve work activities that include practical, hands-on problems and solutions. They often deal with plants, animals, and real-world materials like wood, tools, and machinery. Many of the occupations require working outside and do not involve a lot of paperwork or working closely with others. **Work Values—**Moral Values; Independence. **Skills—**Operation and Control. **Abilities—***Cognitive:* None met the criteria. *Psychomotor:* Speed of Limb Movement; Wrist-Finger Speed. *Physical:* Static Strength; Explosive Strength; Dynamic Strength; Trunk Strength; Stamina. *Sensory:* Depth Perception; Glare Sensitivity; Peripheral Vision; Sound Localization; Auditory Attention. **General Work Activities—***Information Input:* Getting Information; Inspecting Equipment, Structures, or Materials; Identifying Objects, Actions, and Events. *Mental Process:* Judging Qualities of Things, Services, or Other People's Work; Making Decisions and Solving Problems; Organizing, Planning, and Prioritizing. *Work Output:* Performing General Physical Activities; Handling and Moving Objects; Controlling Machines and Processes. *Interacting with Others:* Communicating with Other Workers; Coordinating the Work and Activities of Others; Establishing and Maintaining Relationships. **Physical Work Conditions—**Outdoors; Common Protective or Safety Attire; Whole Body Vibration; Distracting Sounds and Noise Levels; Hazardous Conditions. **Other Job Characteristics—**Consequence of Error; Importance of Being Exact or Accurate; Pace Determined by Speed of Equipment.

Experience—Job Zone 2. Some previous work-related skill, knowledge, or experience may be helpful, but usually is not needed. **Job Preparation:** SVP 4.0 to less than 6.0—six months to less than two years. **Knowledge—**Mechanical; Public Safety and Security; Building and Construction; Physics; Engineering and Technology. **Instructional Programs—**No data available.

Related DOT Jobs—930.684-022 Quarry Plug-and-Feather Driller.

47-5061.00 Roof Bolters, Mining

- **Education/Training Required: Moderate-term on-the-job training**
- **Employed: No data available.**
- **Annual Earnings: $37,480**
- **Growth: –13.4%**
- **Annual Job Openings: 1,000**

Operate machinery to install roof support bolts in underground mine.

Drill bolt holes into roofs at specified distances from ribs or adjacent bolts. Force bolts into holes, using hydraulic mechanisms of self-propelled bolting machines. Install truss bolts traversing entire ceiling spans. Position bolting machines and insert drill bits into chucks. Position safety jacks to support underground mine roofs until bolts can be installed. Remove drill bits from chucks after drilling holes and then insert bolts into chucks. Rotate chucks to turn bolts and open expansion heads against rock formations. Test bolts for specified tension, using torque wrenches. Tighten ends of anchored truss bolts, using turnbuckles.

GOE INFORMATION—Interest Area: 06. Construction, Mining, and Drilling. **Work Group:** 06.03. Mining and Drilling. **Personality Type—**Realistic. Realistic occupations frequently involve work activities that include practical, hands-on problems and solutions. They often deal with

plants, animals, and real-world materials like wood, tools, and machinery. Many of the occupations require working outside and do not involve a lot of paperwork or working closely with others. **Work Values—**Supervision, Technical; Moral Values; Supervision, Human Relations. **Skills—**Operation and Control; Installation. **Abilities—***Cognitive:* None met the criteria. *Psychomotor:* Control Precision; Manual Dexterity; Arm-Hand Steadiness; Multilimb Coordination. *Physical:* Extent Flexibility; Dynamic Strength; Explosive Strength; Gross Body Coordination; Static Strength. *Sensory:* Depth Perception; Night Vision. **General Work Activities—***Information Input:* Getting Information; Monitoring Processes, Materials, or Surroundings; Inspecting Equipment, Structures, or Materials. *Mental Process:* Evaluating Information Against Standards; Judging Qualities of Things, Services, or Other People's Work; Analyzing Data or Information. *Work Output:* Performing General Physical Activities; Handling and Moving Objects; Controlling Machines and Processes. *Interacting with Others:* Communicating with Other Workers; Establishing and Maintaining Relationships; Coordinating the Work and Activities of Others. **Physical Work Conditions—**Outdoors; Specialized Protective or Safety Attire; Extremely Bright or Inadequate Lighting; Common Protective or Safety Attire; Whole Body Vibration. **Other Job Characteristics—**Consequence of Error; Importance of Repeating Same Tasks; Importance of Being Exact or Accurate.

Experience—Job Zone 2. Some previous work-related skill, knowledge, or experience may be helpful, but usually is not needed. **Job Preparation:** SVP 4.0 to less than 6.0—six months to less than two years. **Knowledge—**Mechanical; Building and Construction; Physics; Engineering and Technology; Public Safety and Security. **Instructional Programs—**No data available.

Related DOT Jobs—930.683-026 Roof Bolter.

47-5071.00 Roustabouts, Oil and Gas

- **Education/Training Required: Short-term on-the-job training**
- **Employed: 41,343**
- **Annual Earnings: $21,140**
- **Growth: –4.2%**
- **Annual Job Openings: 3,000**

Assemble or repair oil field equipment, using hand and power tools. Perform other tasks as needed.

Bolt or nail together wood or steel framework in order to erect derricks. Bolt together pump and engine parts. Dig holes, set forms, and mix and pour concrete into forms in order to make foundations for wood or steel derricks. Dismantle and repair oil field machinery, boilers, and steam engine parts, using hand tools and power tools. Unscrew or tighten pipes, casing, tubing, and pump rods, using hand and power wrenches and tongs. Clean up spilled oil by bailing it into barrels. Cut down and remove trees and brush to clear drill sites in order to reduce fire hazards and to make way for roads to sites. Dig drainage ditches around wells and storage tanks. Guide cranes to move loads about decks. Keep pipe deck and main deck areas clean and tidy. Move pipes to and from trucks, using truck winches and motorized lifts or by hand. Supply equipment to rig floors as requested and provide assistance to roughnecks. Walk flow lines to locate leaks, using electronic detectors and making visual inspections.

GOE INFORMATION—Interest Area: 06. Construction, Mining, and Drilling. **Work Group:** 06.03. Mining and Drilling. **Personality Type—**Realistic. Realistic occupations frequently involve work activities that include practical, hands-on problems and solutions. They often deal with plants, animals, and real-world materials like wood, tools, and machinery. Many of the occupations require working outside and do not involve a lot of paperwork or working closely with others. **Work Values—**Moral

Values; Supervision, Technical; Supervision, Human Relations. **Skills—**Repairing; Installation; Troubleshooting. **Abilities—***Cognitive:* Perceptual Speed. *Psychomotor:* Speed of Limb Movement; Multilimb Coordination; Manual Dexterity; Finger Dexterity; Rate Control. *Physical:* Dynamic Strength; Static Strength; Explosive Strength; Stamina; Trunk Strength. *Sensory:* Glare Sensitivity; Peripheral Vision; Depth Perception; Hearing Sensitivity; Auditory Attention. **General Work Activities—***Information Input:* Getting Information; Identifying Objects, Actions, and Events; Inspecting Equipment, Structures, or Materials. *Mental Process:* Updating and Using Relevant Knowledge; Analyzing Data or Information; Making Decisions and Solving Problems. *Work Output:* Performing General Physical Activities; Handling and Moving Objects; Repairing and Maintaining Mechanical Equipment. *Interacting with Others:* Establishing and Maintaining Relationships; Assisting and Caring for Others; Communicating with Other Workers. **Physical Work Conditions—**Outdoors; Hazardous Equipment; Cramped Work Space or Awkward Positions; Distracting Sounds and Noise Levels; Kneeling, Crouching, or Crawling. **Other Job Characteristics—**Consequence of Error; Importance of Repeating Same Tasks; Degree of Automation.

Experience—Job Zone 2. Some previous work-related skill, knowledge, or experience may be helpful, but usually is not needed. **Job Preparation:** SVP 4.0 to less than 6.0—six months to less than two years. **Knowledge—**Mechanical; Building and Construction; Engineering and Technology; Geography; Physics. **Instructional Programs—**Heavy/Industrial Equipment Maintenance Technologies, Other.

Related DOT Jobs—869.684-046 Roustabout.

47-5081.00 Helpers—Extraction Workers

- **Education/Training Required: Short-term on-the-job training**
- **Employed: No data available.**
- **Annual Earnings: $24,430**
- **Growth: 2.4%**
- **Annual Job Openings: 6,000**

Help extraction craft workers, such as earth drillers, blasters and explosives workers, derrick operators, and mining machine operators, by performing duties of lesser skill. Duties include supplying equipment or cleaning work area.

Clean and prepare sites for excavation or boring. Clean up work areas and remove debris after extraction activities are complete. Dismantle extracting and boring equipment used for excavation, using hand tools. Drive moving equipment in order to transport materials and parts to excavation sites. Load materials into well holes or into equipment, using hand tools. Observe and monitor equipment operation during the extraction process in order to detect any problems. Organize materials in order to prepare for use. Provide assistance to extraction craft workers such as earth drillers and derrick operators. Set up and adjust equipment used to excavate geological materials. Signal workers to start geological material extraction or boring. Unload materials, devices, and machine parts, using hand tools. Collect and examine geological matter, using hand tools and testing devices. Dig trenches. Repair and maintain automotive and drilling equipment, using hand tools.

GOE INFORMATION—Interest Area: 06. Construction, Mining, and Drilling. **Work Group:** 06.04. Hands-on Work in Construction, Extraction, and Maintenance. **Personality Type—**Realistic. Realistic occupations frequently involve work activities that include practical, hands-on

problems and solutions. They often deal with plants, animals, and real-world materials like wood, tools, and machinery. Many of the occupations require working outside and do not involve a lot of paperwork or working closely with others. **Work Values—**Supervision, Technical; Advancement; Moral Values; Pleasant Co-workers; Supervision, Human Relations. **Skills—**Repairing; Operation Monitoring; Operation and Control. **Abilities—***Cognitive:* Flexibility of Closure; Spatial Orientation. *Psychomotor:* Speed of Limb Movement; Rate Control; Multilimb Coordination; Reaction Time; Wrist-Finger Speed. *Physical:* Explosive Strength; Static Strength; Stamina; Dynamic Strength; Dynamic Flexibility. *Sensory:* Auditory Attention; Glare Sensitivity; Night Vision. **General Work Activities—***Information Input:* Monitoring Processes, Materials, or Surroundings; Inspecting Equipment, Structures, or Materials; Getting Information. *Mental Process:* Organizing, Planning, and Prioritizing; Updating and Using Relevant Knowledge; Judging Qualities of Things, Services, or Other People's Work. *Work Output:* Performing General Physical Activities; Handling and Moving Objects; Repairing and Maintaining Mechanical Equipment. *Interacting with Others:* Communicating with Other Workers; Assisting and Caring for Others; Establishing and Maintaining Relationships. **Physical Work Conditions—**Whole Body Vibration; Outdoors; Extremely Bright or Inadequate Lighting; Distracting Sounds and Noise Levels; Contaminants. **Other Job Characteristics—**Pace Determined by Speed of Equipment; Consequence of Error; Importance of Repeating Same Tasks.

Experience—Job Zone 1. No previous work-related skill, knowledge, or experience is needed. **Job Preparation:** SVP below 4.0—less than six months. **Knowledge—**Physics; Mechanical; Production and Processing; Public Safety and Security; Engineering and Technology. **Instructional Programs—**No data available.

Related DOT Jobs—859.687-010 Blaster Helper; 930.664-014 Clean-Out-Driller Helper; 930.666-010 Driller Helper; 930.666-014 Tailer; 930.667-010 Shale Planer Operator Helper; 930.684-026 Rotary-Driller Helper; 930.687-010 Bottom-Hole-Pressure-Recording-Operator Helper; 939.364-010 Observer Helper, Seismic Prospecting; 939.663-010 Observer Helper, Gravity Prospecting.

47-5099.99 Extraction Workers, All Other

- **Education/Training Required: No data available.**
- **Employed: No data available.**
- **Annual Earnings: No data available.**
- **Growth: –2.1%**
- **Annual Job Openings: 1,000**

All extraction workers not listed separately.

No task data available.

GOE INFORMATION—Interest Area: 06. Construction, Mining, and Drilling. **Work Group:** 06.03. Mining and Drilling; 06.04. Hands-on Work in Construction, Extraction, and Maintenance. **Note:** The Department of Labor has not collected some data for this job, so it has fewer details than the other descriptions.

Instructional Programs—Construction/Heavy Equipment/Earthmoving Equipment Operation.

Related DOT Jobs—850.682-010 Shield Runner; 930.664-010 Caser; 933.664-010 Crusher Setter; 939.667-014 Quarry Worker; 939.687-026 Rock-Dust Sprayer.

49-0000

Installation, Maintenance, and Repair Occupations

49-1000 Supervisors of Installation, Maintenance, and Repair Workers

49-1011.00 First-Line Supervisors/ Managers of Mechanics, Installers, and Repairers

- Education/Training Required: Work experience in a related occupation
- Employed: 442,039
- Annual Earnings: $46,320
- Growth: 16.0%
- Annual Job Openings: 38,000

Supervise and coordinate the activities of mechanics, installers, and repairers.

Compile operational and personnel records, such as time and production records, inventory data, repair and maintenance statistics, and test results. Compute estimates and actual costs of factors such as materials, labor, and outside contractors. Conduct or arrange for worker training in safety, repair, and maintenance techniques; operational procedures; and equipment use. Counsel employees about work-related issues and assist employees to correct job-skill deficiencies. Determine schedules, sequences, and assignments for work activities, based on work priority, quantity of equipment, and skill of personnel. Develop, implement, and evaluate maintenance policies and procedures. Inspect, test, and measure completed work, using devices such as hand tools and gauges to verify conformance to standards and repair requirements. Interpret specifications, blueprints, and job orders in order to construct templates and lay out reference points for workers. Monitor employees' work levels and review work performance. Patrol and monitor work areas and examine tools and equipment in order to detect unsafe conditions or violations of procedures or safety rules. Recommend or initiate personnel actions, such as hires, promotions, transfers, discharges, and disciplinary measures. Requisition materials and supplies, such as tools, equipment, and replacement parts. Confer with personnel, such as management, engineering, quality control, customer, and union workers' representatives, in order to coordinate work activities, resolve employee grievances, and identify and review resource needs. Develop and implement electronic maintenance programs and computer information management systems. Examine objects, systems, or facilities and analyze information to determine needed installations, services, or repairs. Investigate accidents and injuries and prepare reports of findings. Monitor tool inventories and the condition and maintenance of shops in order to ensure adequate working conditions. Participate in budget preparation and administration, coordinating purchasing and documentation and monitoring departmental expenditures. Design equipment configurations to meet personnel needs. Meet with vendors and suppliers in order to discuss products used in repair work. Perform skilled repair and maintenance operations, using equipment such as hand and power tools, hydraulic presses and shears, and welding equipment.

GOE INFORMATION—**Interest Area:** 05. Mechanics, Installers, and Repairers. **Work Group:** 05.01. Managerial Work in Mechanics, Installers, and Repairers. **Personality Type**—Enterprising. Enterprising occupations frequently involve starting up and carrying out projects. These occupations can involve leading people and making many decisions. They sometimes require risk taking and often deal with business. **Work**

Values—Authority; Responsibility; Autonomy; Variety; Pleasant Co-workers. **Skills**—Management of Personnel Resources; Management of Material Resources; Management of Financial Resources; Repairing; Installation; Systems Analysis; Coordination; Quality Control Analysis. **Abilities**—*Cognitive:* Oral Expression; Information Ordering; Inductive Reasoning; Deductive Reasoning; Oral Comprehension. *Psychomotor:* Manual Dexterity; Finger Dexterity; Wrist-Finger Speed; Response Orientation; Control Precision. *Physical:* Trunk Strength; Static Strength; Dynamic Flexibility. *Sensory:* Hearing Sensitivity; Sound Localization; Near Vision; Speech Clarity. **General Work Activities**—*Information Input:* Getting Information; Monitoring Processes, Materials, or Surroundings; Identifying Objects, Actions, and Events. *Mental Process:* Organizing, Planning, and Prioritizing; Updating and Using Relevant Knowledge; Making Decisions and Solving Problems. *Work Output:* Performing General Physical Activities; Handling and Moving Objects; Documenting or Recording Information. *Interacting with Others:* Coordinating the Work and Activities of Others; Communicating with Other Workers; Establishing and Maintaining Relationships. **Physical Work Conditions**—Hazardous Conditions; Common Protective or Safety Attire; Distracting Sounds and Noise Levels; High Places; Contaminants. **Other Job Characteristics**—Consequence of Error; Importance of Being Exact or Accurate; Pace Determined by Speed of Equipment.

Experience—Job Zone 4. A minimum of two to four years of work-related skill, knowledge, or experience is needed. **Job Preparation:** SVP 7.0 to less than 8.0—two years to less than 10 years. **Knowledge**—Mechanical; Administration and Management; Personnel and Human Resources; Economics and Accounting; Public Safety and Security. **Instructional Programs**—Operations Management and Supervision.

Related DOT Jobs—169.167-074 Preventive Maintenance Coordinator; 184.167-050 Maintenance Supervisor; 184.167-194 Superintendent, Meters; 185.164-010 Service Manager; 185.167-058 Service Manager; 185.167-074 Manager, Auto Specialty Services; 187.167-010 Appliance-Service Supervisor; 187.167-130 Manager, Marine Service; 187.167-142 Manager, Service Department; 189.167-046 Superintendent, Maintenance; 375.167-018 Commanding Officer, Motor Equipment; 620.131-010 Supervisor, Endless Track Vehicle; 620.131-014 Supervisor, Garage; 620.131-018 Supervisor, Motorcycle Repair Shop; 620.137-010 Tank and Amphibian Tractor Operations Chief; 621.131-010 Supercharger-Repair Supervisor; 621.131-014 Supervisor, Aircraft Maintenance; 622.131-010 Supervisor, Railroad Car Repair; 622.131-014 Supervisor, Roundhouse; 622.131-018 Supervisor, Wheel Shop; others.

49-2000 Electrical and Electronic Equipment Mechanics, Installers, and Repairers

49-2011.00 Computer, Automated Teller, and Office Machine Repairers

- Education/Training Required: Postsecondary vocational training
- Employed: 172,253
- Annual Earnings: $32,890
- Growth: 14.2%
- Annual Job Openings: 24,000

Repair, maintain, or install computers, word processing systems, automated teller machines, and electronic office machines, such as duplicating and fax machines.

No task data available.

GOE INFORMATION—Interest Area: 05. Mechanics, Installers, and Repairers. **Work Group:** 05.02. Electrical and Electronic Systems. **Note:** The Department of Labor has not collected some data for this job, so it has fewer details than the other descriptions.

Instructional Programs—Business Machine Repair; Computer Installation and Repair Technology/Technician.

Related DOT Jobs—211.367-014 Automatic Teller Machine (ATM) Servicer; 633.261-010 Assembly Technician; 633.261-014 Mail-Processing-Equipment Mechanic; 633.281-010 Cash-Register Servicer; 633.281-014 Dictating-Transcribing-Machine Servicer; 633.281-018 Office-Machine Servicer; 633.281-022 Office-Machine-Servicer Apprentice; 633.281-030 Statistical-Machine Servicer; 706.381-010 Aligner, Typewriter; 706.381-030 Repairer, Typewriter; 828.261-022 Electronics Mechanic; 828.261-026 Electronics-Mechanic Apprentice.

49-2011.01 Automatic Teller Machine Servicers

- Education/Training Required: Long-term on-the-job training
- Employed: No data available.
- Annual Earnings: $32,890
- Growth: 14.2%
- Annual Job Openings: 24,000

Collect deposits and replenish automatic teller machines with cash and supplies.

Removes money canisters from ATM and replenishes machine supplies, such as deposit envelopes, receipt paper, and cash. Counts cash and items deposited by customers and compares to transactions indicated on transaction tape from ATM. Records transaction information on form or log and notifies designated personnel of discrepancies. Tests machine functions and balances machine cash account, using electronic keypad. Corrects malfunctions, such as jammed cash or paper, or calls repair personnel when ATM needs repair.

GOE INFORMATION—Interest Area: 09. Business Detail. **Work Group:** 09.09. Clerical Machine Operation. **Personality Type**—Realistic. Realistic occupations frequently involve work activities that include practical, hands-on problems and solutions. They often deal with plants, animals, and real-world materials like wood, tools, and machinery. Many of the occupations require working outside and do not involve a lot of paperwork or working closely with others. **Work Values**—Independence; Supervision, Technical; Supervision, Human Relations; Company Policies and Practices; Security. **Skills**—None met the criteria. **Abilities**—*Cognitive:* Number Facility; Perceptual Speed; Time Sharing; Speed of Closure; Spatial Orientation. *Psychomotor:* Manual Dexterity; Finger Dexterity; Multilimb Coordination. *Physical:* Stamina. *Sensory:* Visual Color Discrimination; Sound Localization; Glare Sensitivity; Near Vision; Peripheral Vision. **General Work Activities**—*Information Input:* Inspecting Equipment, Structures, or Materials; Getting Information; Monitoring Processes, Materials, or Surroundings. *Mental Process:* Processing Information; Evaluating Information Against Standards; Organizing, Planning, and Prioritizing. *Work Output:* Handling and Moving Objects; Documenting or Recording Information; Performing General Physical Activities. *Interacting with Others:* Communicating with Other Workers; Performing Administrative Activities; Establishing and Maintaining Relationships. **Physical Work Conditions**—Outdoors; Standing; Making Repetitive Motions; Very Hot or Cold; Kneeling, Crouching, or Crawling. **Other Job Characteristics**—Importance of Repeating Same Tasks; Importance of Being Exact or Accurate; Degree of Automation.

Experience—Job Zone 3. Previous work-related skill, knowledge, or experience is required. **Job Preparation:** SVP 6.0 to less than 7.0—more than one year and less than four years. **Knowledge**—Computers and Electronics; Philosophy and Theology; Fine Arts; Geography; Foreign Language. **Instructional Programs**—Business Machine Repair; Computer Installation and Repair Technology/Technician.

Related DOT Jobs—211.367-014 Automatic Teller Machine (ATM) Servicer.

49-2011.02 Data Processing Equipment Repairers

- Education/Training Required: Postsecondary vocational training
- Employed: No data available.
- Annual Earnings: $32,890
- Growth: 14.2%
- Annual Job Openings: 24,000

Repair, maintain, and install computer hardware, such as peripheral equipment and word-processing systems.

Replaces defective components and wiring. Tests faulty equipment and applies knowledge of functional operation of electronic units and systems to diagnose cause of malfunction. Tests electronic components and circuits to locate defects, using oscilloscopes, signal generators, ammeters, and voltmeters. Aligns, adjusts, and calibrates equipment according to specifications. Converses with equipment operators to ascertain problems with equipment before breakdown or cause of breakdown. Adjusts mechanical parts, using hand tools and soldering iron. Calibrates testing instruments. Maintains records of repairs, calibrations, and tests. Enters information into computer to copy program from one electronic component to another or to draw, modify, or store schematics.

GOE INFORMATION—Interest Area: 05. Mechanics, Installers, and Repairers. **Work Group:** 05.02. Electrical and Electronic Systems. **Personality Type**—Realistic. Realistic occupations frequently involve work activities that include practical, hands-on problems and solutions. They often deal with plants, animals, and real-world materials like wood, tools, and machinery. Many of the occupations require working outside and do not involve a lot of paperwork or working closely with others. **Work Values**—Variety; Supervision, Technical; Advancement; Moral Values; Security. **Skills**—Installation; Repairing; Troubleshooting; Operation Monitoring; Quality Control Analysis; Science; Operation and Control; Equipment Selection. **Abilities**—*Cognitive:* Visualization; Inductive Reasoning; Mathematical Reasoning; Speed of Closure; Perceptual Speed. *Psychomotor:* Finger Dexterity; Control Precision; Response Orientation; Manual Dexterity; Wrist-Finger Speed. *Physical:* Extent Flexibility; Explosive Strength; Trunk Strength; Gross Body Equilibrium; Gross Body Coordination. *Sensory:* Hearing Sensitivity; Visual Color Discrimination; Sound Localization; Near Vision; Auditory Attention. **General Work Activities**—*Information Input:* Getting Information; Inspecting Equipment, Structures, or Materials; Monitoring Processes, Materials, or Surroundings. *Mental Process:* Updating and Using Relevant Knowledge; Analyzing Data or Information; Making Decisions and Solving Problems. *Work Output:* Repairing and Maintaining Electronic Equipment; Interacting with Computers; Handling and Moving Objects. *Interacting with Others:* Communicating with Other Workers; Establishing and Maintaining Relationships; Interpreting Meaning of Information for Others. **Physical Work Conditions**—Hazardous Conditions; Indoors; Kneeling, Crouching, or Crawling; Using Hands on Objects, Tools, or Controls; Common Protective or Safety Attire. **Other Job Characteristics**—Degree of Automation; Importance of Being Exact or Accurate; Consequence of Error.

Experience—Job Zone 4. A minimum of two to four years of work-related skill, knowledge, or experience is needed. **Job Preparation:** SVP 7.0 to less than 8.0—two years to less than 10 years. **Knowledge**—Computers and Electronics; Telecommunications; Design; Mechanical; Physics. **Instructional Programs**—Business Machine Repair; Computer Installation and Repair Technology/Technician.

Related DOT Jobs—828.261-022 Electronics Mechanic; 828.261-026 Electronics-Mechanic Apprentice.

49-2011.03 Office Machine and Cash Register Servicers

- Education/Training Required: Long-term on-the-job training
- Employed: No data available.
- Annual Earnings: $32,890
- Growth: 14.2%
- Annual Job Openings: 24,000

Repair and service office machines, such as adding, accounting, calculating, duplicating, and typewriting machines. Includes the repair of manual, electrical, and electronic office machines.

Tests machine to locate cause of electrical problems, using testing devices such as voltmeter, ohmmeter, and circuit test equipment. Disassembles machine and examines parts such as wires, gears, and bearings for wear and defects, using hand tools, power tools, and measuring devices. Repairs, adjusts, or replaces electrical and mechanical components and parts, using hand tools, power tools, and soldering or welding equipment. Operates machine such as typewriter, cash-register, or adding machine to test functioning of parts and mechanisms. Reads specifications such as blueprints, charts, and schematics to determine machine settings and adjustments. Cleans and oils mechanical parts to maintain machine. Assembles and installs machine according to specifications, using hand tools, power tools, and measuring devices. Instructs operators and servicers in operation, maintenance, and repair of machine.

GOE INFORMATION—Interest Area: 05. Mechanics, Installers, and Repairers. **Work Group:** 05.02. Electrical and Electronic Systems. **Personality Type**—Realistic. Realistic occupations frequently involve work activities that include practical, hands-on problems and solutions. They often deal with plants, animals, and real-world materials like wood, tools, and machinery. Many of the occupations require working outside and do not involve a lot of paperwork or working closely with others. **Work Values**—Supervision, Technical; Moral Values; Independence; Responsibility; Supervision, Human Relations. **Skills**—Repairing; Installation; Instructing; Troubleshooting; Technology Design; Operation and Control; Quality Control Analysis; Operation Monitoring. **Abilities**—*Cognitive:* Visualization; Oral Expression; Speed of Closure; Selective Attention; Information Ordering. *Psychomotor:* Finger Dexterity; Arm-Hand Steadiness; Control Precision; Manual Dexterity; Speed of Limb Movement. *Physical:* Static Strength; Dynamic Flexibility; Explosive Strength; Gross Body Coordination; Stamina. *Sensory:* Visual Color Discrimination; Speech Clarity; Hearing Sensitivity; Auditory Attention; Sound Localization. **General Work Activities**—*Information Input:* Inspecting Equipment, Structures, or Materials; Monitoring Processes, Materials, or Surroundings; Getting Information. *Mental Process:* Updating and Using Relevant Knowledge; Organizing, Planning, and Prioritizing; Evaluating Information Against Standards. *Work Output:* Repairing and Maintaining Electronic Equipment; Repairing and Maintaining Mechanical Equipment; Handling and Moving Objects. *Interacting with Others:* Teaching Others; Communicating with Other Workers; Communicating with Persons Outside Organization. **Physical Work Conditions**—Hazardous Equipment; Using Hands on Objects, Tools, or Controls;

Indoors; Making Repetitive Motions; Bending or Twisting the Body. **Other Job Characteristics**—Degree of Automation; Pace Determined by Speed of Equipment; Importance of Repeating Same Tasks.

Experience—Job Zone 3. Previous work-related skill, knowledge, or experience is required. **Job Preparation:** SVP 6.0 to less than 7.0—more than one year and less than four years. **Knowledge**—Computers and Electronics; Mechanical; Design; Education and Training; Engineering and Technology. **Instructional Programs**—Business Machine Repair; Computer Installation and Repair Technology/Technician.

Related DOT Jobs—633.261-010 Assembly Technician; 633.261-014 Mail-Processing-Equipment Mechanic; 633.281-010 Cash-Register Servicer; 633.281-014 Dictating-Transcribing-Machine Servicer; 633.281-018 Office-Machine Servicer; 633.281-022 Office-Machine-Servicer Apprentice; 633.281-030 Statistical-Machine Servicer; 706.381-010 Aligner, Typewriter; 706.381-030 Repairer, Typewriter.

49-2021.00 Radio Mechanics

- Education/Training Required: Postsecondary vocational training
- Employed: 6,947
- Annual Earnings: $34,040
- Growth: –24.2%
- Annual Job Openings: Fewer than 500

Test or repair mobile or stationary radio transmitting and receiving equipment and two-way radio communications systems used in ship-to-shore communications and found in service and emergency vehicles.

Locates defects, such as loose connections, broken wires, or burned-out components, using schematic diagrams, test equipment, and inspection tags. Inspects wiring and soldering and performs repairs, using soldering iron, wire cutters, pliers, and wiring diagram. Tests equipment for power output, frequency, and calibration, using oscilloscope, circuit analyzer, frequency meter, wattmeter, ammeter, and voltmeter. Replaces defective components, such as conductors, resistors, semiconductors, and integrated circuits, using soldering iron, wire cutters, and hand tools. Tests batteries with hydrometer and ammeter and charges batteries. Tests noise level and audio quality, using audiometer. Monitors radio range station to detect flaws in transmission and adjusts controls to eliminate flaws. Removes and replaces defective units that are not repairable. Adjusts receivers for maximum sensitivity and transmitters for maximum output, using frequency meter. Installs, tests, adjusts, modifies, and repairs intercommunication systems. Inserts plugs into receptacles and bolts or screws leads to terminals to connect equipment to power source, using hand tools. Tests emergency transmitter to ensure readiness for immediate use.

GOE INFORMATION—Interest Area: 05. Mechanics, Installers, and Repairers. **Work Group:** 05.02. Electrical and Electronic Systems. **Personality Type**—Realistic. Realistic occupations frequently involve work activities that include practical, hands-on problems and solutions. They often deal with plants, animals, and real-world materials like wood, tools, and machinery. Many of the occupations require working outside and do not involve a lot of paperwork or working closely with others. **Work Values**—Independence; Moral Values; Supervision, Technical; Variety; Security. **Skills**—Repairing; Installation; Troubleshooting; Quality Control Analysis; Operation Monitoring; Equipment Selection; Operation and Control. **Abilities**—*Cognitive:* Speed of Closure; Flexibility of Closure; Perceptual Speed; Visualization; Memorization. *Psychomotor:* Finger Dexterity; Manual Dexterity; Response Orientation; Arm-Hand Steadiness; Multilimb Coordination. *Physical:* Explosive Strength; Dynamic Strength; Static Strength; Dynamic Flexibility. *Sensory:* Visual Color Discrimination; Hearing Sensitivity; Night Vision; Auditory Attention; Sound Localization. **General Work Activities**—*Information Input:* Monitoring Processes, Materials, or Surroundings; Getting Information; Identifying Objects, Actions, and Events. *Mental Process:* Updating and Using Relevant Knowledge; Evaluating Information Against Standards; Analyzing Data or Information. *Work Output:* Repairing and Maintaining Electronic Equipment; Handling and Moving Objects; Performing General Physical Activities. *Interacting with Others:* Communicating with Other Workers; Providing Consultation and Advice to Others; Communicating with Persons Outside Organization. **Physical Work Conditions**—Minor Burns, Cuts, Bites, or Stings; Using Hands on Objects, Tools, or Controls; Cramped Work Space or Awkward Positions; Kneeling, Crouching, or Crawling; Hazardous Conditions. **Other Job Characteristics**—Degree of Automation; Importance of Being Exact or Accurate; Consequence of Error.

Experience—Job Zone 3. Previous work-related skill, knowledge, or experience is required. **Job Preparation:** SVP 6.0 to less than 7.0—more than one year and less than four years. **Knowledge**—Telecommunications; Computers and Electronics; Engineering and Technology; Physics; Design. **Instructional Programs**—Communications Systems Installation and Repair Technology.

Related DOT Jobs—726.381-014 Electronic Equipment Repairer; 823.261-018 Radio Mechanic; 823.281-014 Electrician, Radio.

49-2022.00 Telecommunications Equipment Installers and Repairers, Except Line Installers

- **Education/Training Required: Postsecondary vocational training**
- **Employed: 188,722**
- **Annual Earnings: $46,390**
- **Growth: –3.1%**
- **Annual Job Openings: 9,000**

Set-up, rearrange, or remove switching and dialing equipment used in central offices. Service or repair telephones and other communication equipment on customers' property. May install equipment in new locations or install wiring and telephone jacks in buildings under construction.

No task data available.

GOE INFORMATION—**Interest Area:** 05. Mechanics, Installers, and Repairers. **Work Group:** 05.02. Electrical and Electronic Systems. **Note:** The Department of Labor has not collected some data for this job, so it has fewer details than the other descriptions.

Instructional Programs—Communications Systems Installation and Repair Technology.

Related DOT Jobs—722.281-010 Instrument Repairer; 821.261-010 Cable Television Line Technician; 822.261-010 Electrician, Office; 822.261-022 Station Installer-and-Repairer; 822.281-010 Automatic-Equipment Technician; 822.281-014 Central-Office Repairer; 822.281-018 Maintenance Mechanic, Telephone; 822.281-022 Private-Branch-Exchange Repairer; 822.281-030 Technician, Plant and Maintenance; 822.281-034 Technician, Submarine Cable Equipment; 822.361-014 Central-Office Installer; 822.381-010 Equipment Installer; 822.381-018 Private-Branch-Exchange Installer; 822.381-022 Telegraph-Plant Maintainer; 822.684-010 Frame Wirer; 823.261-010 Public-Address Servicer; 823.261-022 Antenna Installer,

Satellite Communications; 823.261-030 Data Communications Technician; 823.281-022 Rigger; 823.281-720 Telecommunications Technician; others.

49-2022.01 Central Office and PBX Installers and Repairers

- **Education/Training Required: Postsecondary vocational training**
- **Employed: No data available.**
- **Annual Earnings: $46,390**
- **Growth: –3.1%**
- **Annual Job Openings: 9,000**

Test, analyze, and repair telephone or telegraph circuits and equipment at a central office location using test meters and hand tools. Analyze and repair defects in communications equipment on customers' premises using circuit diagrams, polarity probes, meters, and a telephone test set. May install equipment.

Tests circuits and components of malfunctioning telecommunication equipment to isolate source of malfunction, using test instruments and circuit diagrams. Analyzes test readings, computer printouts, and trouble reports to determine method of repair. Repairs or replaces defective components, such as switches, relays, amplifiers, and circuit boards, using hand tools and soldering iron. Tests and adjusts installed equipment to ensure circuit continuity and operational performance, using test instruments. Retests repaired equipment to ensure that malfunction has been corrected. Installs preassembled or partially assembled switching equipment, switchboards, wiring frames, and power apparatus according to floor plans. Connects wires to equipment, using hand tools, soldering iron, or wire wrap gun. Removes and remakes connections on wire distributing frame to change circuit layout, following diagrams. Enters codes to correct programming of electronic switching systems. Routes cables and trunklines from entry points to specified equipment, following diagrams.

GOE INFORMATION—**Interest Area:** 05. Mechanics, Installers, and Repairers. **Work Group:** 05.02. Electrical and Electronic Systems. **Personality Type**—Realistic. Realistic occupations frequently involve work activities that include practical, hands-on problems and solutions. They often deal with plants, animals, and real-world materials like wood, tools, and machinery. Many of the occupations require working outside and do not involve a lot of paperwork or working closely with others. **Work Values**—Supervision, Technical; Company Policies and Practices; Moral Values; Security; Variety. **Skills**—Repairing; Installation; Troubleshooting; Operation Monitoring; Operation and Control; Technology Design; Equipment Selection; Quality Control Analysis. **Abilities**—*Cognitive:* Flexibility of Closure; Inductive Reasoning; Spatial Orientation. *Psychomotor:* Finger Dexterity; Arm-Hand Steadiness; Control Precision; Manual Dexterity. *Physical:* Stamina; Explosive Strength. *Sensory:* Hearing Sensitivity; Visual Color Discrimination; Auditory Attention; Sound Localization; Near Vision. **General Work Activities**—*Information Input:* Inspecting Equipment, Structures, or Materials; Getting Information; Monitoring Processes, Materials, or Surroundings. *Mental Process:* Analyzing Data or Information; Updating and Using Relevant Knowledge; Evaluating Information Against Standards. *Work Output:* Repairing and Maintaining Electronic Equipment; Handling and Moving Objects; Performing General Physical Activities. *Interacting with Others:* Communicating with Other Workers; Communicating with Persons Outside Organization; Performing Administrative Activities. **Physical Work Conditions**—Kneeling, Crouching, or Crawling; Hazardous Conditions; Cramped Work Space or Awkward Positions; Climbing Ladders, Scaffolds, Poles, etc.;

Hazardous Equipment. **Other Job Characteristics**—Importance of Being Exact or Accurate; Consequence of Error; Pace Determined by Speed of Equipment.

Experience—Job Zone 4. A minimum of two to four years of work-related skill, knowledge, or experience is needed. **Job Preparation:** SVP 7.0 to less than 8.0—two years to less than 10 years. **Knowledge**—Telecommunications; Computers and Electronics; Design; Engineering and Technology; Physics. **Instructional Programs**—Communications Systems Installation and Repair Technology.

Related DOT Jobs—822.281-014 Central-Office Repairer; 822.281-022 Private-Branch-Exchange Repairer; 822.361-014 Central-Office Installer; 822.381-018 Private-Branch-Exchange Installer; 822.381-022 Telegraph-Plant Maintainer.

49-2022.02 Frame Wirers, Central Office

- Education/Training Required: Postsecondary vocational training
- Employed: No data available.
- Annual Earnings: $46,390
- Growth: –3.1%
- Annual Job Openings: 9,000

Connect wires from telephone lines and cables to distributing frames in telephone company central office, using soldering iron and other hand tools.

Solders connections, following diagram or oral instructions. Strings distributing frames with connecting wires. Removes and remakes connections to change circuit layouts. Tests circuit connections, using voltmeter or ammeter. Cleans switches and replaces contact points, using vacuum hose, solvents, and hand tools. Lubricates moving switch parts. Assists in locating and correcting malfunction in wiring on distributing frame.

GOE INFORMATION—**Interest Area:** 05. Mechanics, Installers, and Repairers. **Work Group:** 05.02. Electrical and Electronic Systems. **Personality Type**—Realistic. Realistic occupations frequently involve work activities that include practical, hands-on problems and solutions. They often deal with plants, animals, and real-world materials like wood, tools, and machinery. Many of the occupations require working outside and do not involve a lot of paperwork or working closely with others. **Work Values**—Supervision, Technical; Moral Values; Security; Supervision, Human Relations; Company Policies and Practices. **Skills**—Installation; Repairing; Quality Control Analysis; Operation Monitoring; Troubleshooting; Equipment Selection. **Abilities**—*Cognitive:* Visualization; Deductive Reasoning. *Psychomotor:* Arm-Hand Steadiness; Multilimb Coordination; Finger Dexterity. *Physical:* Extent Flexibility; Trunk Strength; Explosive Strength; Dynamic Flexibility. *Sensory:* None met the criteria. **General Work Activities**—*Information Input:* Monitoring Processes, Materials, or Surroundings; Inspecting Equipment, Structures, or Materials; Getting Information. *Mental Process:* Making Decisions and Solving Problems; Analyzing Data or Information; Judging Qualities of Things, Services, or Other People's Work. *Work Output:* Repairing and Maintaining Electronic Equipment; Handling and Moving Objects; Performing General Physical Activities. *Interacting with Others:* Communicating with Other Workers; Establishing and Maintaining Relationships; Performing Administrative Activities. **Physical Work Conditions**—Climbing Ladders, Scaffolds, Poles, etc.; Hazardous Conditions; Cramped Work Space or Awkward Positions; High Places; Kneeling, Crouching, or Crawling. **Other Job Characteristics**—Importance of Being Exact or Accurate; Importance of Repeating Same Tasks; Consequence of Error.

Experience—Job Zone 2. Some previous work-related skill, knowledge, or experience may be helpful, but usually is not needed. **Job Preparation:** SVP 4.0 to less than 6.0—six months to less than two years. **Knowledge**—Telecommunications; Engineering and Technology; Mechanical; Computers and Electronics; Physics. **Instructional Programs**—Communications Systems Installation and Repair Technology.

Related DOT Jobs—822.684-010 Frame Wirer.

49-2022.03 Communication Equipment Mechanics, Installers, and Repairers

- Education/Training Required: Postsecondary vocational training
- Employed: No data available.
- Annual Earnings: $46,390
- Growth: –3.1%
- Annual Job Openings: 9,000

Install, maintain, test, and repair communication cables and equipment.

Examines and tests malfunctioning equipment to determine defects, using blueprints and electrical measuring instruments. Disassembles equipment to adjust, repair, or replace parts, using hand tools. Repairs, replaces, or adjusts defective components. Assembles and installs communication equipment, such as data communication lines and equipment, computer systems, and antennas and towers, using hand tools. Tests installed equipment for conformance to specifications, using test equipment. Evaluates quality of performance of installed equipment by observance and using test equipment. Measures, cuts, splices, connects, solders, and installs wires and cables. Performs routine maintenance on equipment, which includes adjustment, repair, and painting. Adjusts or modifies equipment in accordance with customer request or to enhance performance of equipment. Reviews work orders, building permits, manufacturer's instructions, and ordinances to move, change, install, repair, or remove communication equipment. Plans layout and installation of data communications equipment. Climbs poles and ladders; constructs pole, roof mounts, or reinforcements; and mixes concrete to enable equipment installation. Measures distance from landmarks to identify exact installation site. Determines viability of site through observation and discusses site location and construction requirements with customer. Demonstrates equipment and instructs customer in use of equipment. Communicates with base, using telephone or two-way radio to receive instructions or technical advice or to report unauthorized use of equipment. Cleans and maintains tools, test equipment, and motor vehicle. Answers customers' inquiries or complaints. Digs holes or trenches.

GOE INFORMATION—**Interest Area:** 05. Mechanics, Installers, and Repairers. **Work Group:** 05.02. Electrical and Electronic Systems. **Personality Type**—Realistic. Realistic occupations frequently involve work activities that include practical, hands-on problems and solutions. They often deal with plants, animals, and real-world materials like wood, tools, and machinery. Many of the occupations require working outside and do not involve a lot of paperwork or working closely with others. **Work Values**—Supervision, Technical; Variety; Security; Social Service; Compensation. **Skills**—Repairing; Installation; Troubleshooting; Quality Control Analysis; Technology Design; Operation Monitoring; Equipment Selection; Operation and Control. **Abilities**—*Cognitive:* Visualization; Problem Sensitivity; Spatial Orientation; Perceptual Speed; Flexibility of Closure. *Psychomotor:* Manual Dexterity; Response Orientation; Rate Control; Finger Dexterity; Multilimb Coordination. *Physical:* Dynamic Strength; Gross Body Equilibrium; Stamina; Explosive Strength; Gross Body Coordination. *Sensory:* Depth Perception; Visual

Color Discrimination; Hearing Sensitivity; Sound Localization; Glare Sensitivity. **General Work Activities**—*Information Input:* Inspecting Equipment, Structures, or Materials; Getting Information; Monitoring Processes, Materials, or Surroundings. *Mental Process:* Updating and Using Relevant Knowledge; Evaluating Information Against Standards; Making Decisions and Solving Problems. *Work Output:* Performing General Physical Activities; Repairing and Maintaining Electronic Equipment; Handling and Moving Objects. *Interacting with Others:* Communicating with Persons Outside Organization; Establishing and Maintaining Relationships; Communicating with Other Workers. **Physical Work Conditions**—High Places; Hazardous Conditions; Outdoors; Climbing Ladders, Scaffolds, Poles, etc.; Kneeling, Crouching, or Crawling. **Other Job Characteristics**—Importance of Being Exact or Accurate; Consequence of Error; Pace Determined by Speed of Equipment.

Experience—Job Zone 3. Previous work-related skill, knowledge, or experience is required. **Job Preparation:** SVP 6.0 to less than 7.0—more than one year and less than four years. **Knowledge**—Telecommunications; Computers and Electronics; Design; Mechanical; Engineering and Technology. **Instructional Programs**—Communications Systems Installation and Repair Technology.

Related DOT Jobs—722.281-010 Instrument Repairer; 821.261-010 Cable Television Line Technician; 822.261-010 Electrician, Office; 822.281-030 Technician, Plant and Maintenance; 822.281-034 Technician, Submarine Cable Equipment; 823.261-022 Antenna Installer, Satellite Communications; 823.261-030 Data Communications Technician; 823.281-022 Rigger.

49-2022.04 Telecommunications Facility Examiners

- **Education/Training Required: Long-term on-the-job training**
- **Employed: No data available.**
- **Annual Earnings: $46,390**
- **Growth: –3.1%**
- **Annual Job Openings: 9,000**

Examine telephone transmission facilities to determine equipment requirements for providing subscribers with new or additional telephone services.

Examines telephone transmission facilities to determine requirements for new or additional telephone services. Climbs telephone poles or stands on truck-mounted boom to examine terminal boxes for available connections. Designates cables available for use. Visits subscribers' premises to arrange for new installations, such as telephone booths and telephone poles.

GOE INFORMATION—Interest Area: 05. Mechanics, Installers, and Repairers. **Work Group:** 05.02. Electrical and Electronic Systems. **Personality Type**—Realistic. Realistic occupations frequently involve work activities that include practical, hands-on problems and solutions. They often deal with plants, animals, and real-world materials like wood, tools, and machinery. Many of the occupations require working outside and do not involve a lot of paperwork or working closely with others. **Work Values**—Supervision, Technical; Responsibility; Moral Values; Independence; Supervision, Human Relations. **Skills**—None met the criteria. **Abilities**—*Cognitive:* Spatial Orientation. *Psychomotor:* Multilimb Coordination; Arm-Hand Steadiness. *Physical:* Dynamic Strength; Gross Body Coordination; Gross Body Equilibrium; Stamina; Extent Flexibility. *Sensory:* Night Vision; Visual Color Discrimination; Glare Sensitivity; Hearing Sensitivity; Sound Localization. **General Work Activities**—*Information Input:* Inspecting Equipment, Structures, or Materials; Getting Informa-

tion; Identifying Objects, Actions, and Events. *Mental Process:* Organizing, Planning, and Prioritizing; Making Decisions and Solving Problems; Updating and Using Relevant Knowledge. *Work Output:* Performing General Physical Activities; Handling and Moving Objects; Controlling Machines and Processes. *Interacting with Others:* Communicating with Persons Outside Organization; Establishing and Maintaining Relationships; Providing Consultation and Advice to Others. **Physical Work Conditions**—High Places; Climbing Ladders, Scaffolds, Poles, etc.; Hazardous Conditions; Outdoors; Keeping or Regaining Balance. **Other Job Characteristics**—Consequence of Error; Importance of Being Exact or Accurate; Importance of Repeating Same Tasks.

Experience—Job Zone 3. Previous work-related skill, knowledge, or experience is required. **Job Preparation:** SVP 6.0 to less than 7.0—more than one year and less than four years. **Knowledge**—Telecommunications; Computers and Electronics; Geography; Engineering and Technology; Design. **Instructional Programs**—Communications Systems Installation and Repair Technology.

Related DOT Jobs—959.367-014 Facility Examiner.

49-2022.05 Station Installers and Repairers, Telephone

- **Education/Training Required: Postsecondary vocational training**
- **Employed: No data available.**
- **Annual Earnings: $46,390**
- **Growth: –3.1%**
- **Annual Job Openings: 9,000**

Install and repair telephone station equipment, such as telephones, coin collectors, telephone booths, and switching-key equipment.

Installs communication equipment, such as intercommunication systems and related apparatus, using schematic diagrams, testing devices, and hand tools. Assembles telephone equipment, mounts brackets, and connects wire leads, using hand tools and following installation diagrams or work order. Repairs cables, lays out plans for new equipment, and estimates material required. Analyzes equipment operation, using testing devices to locate and diagnose nature of malfunction and ascertain needed repairs. Disassembles components and replaces, cleans, adjusts, and repairs parts, wires, switches, relays, circuits, or signaling units, using hand tools. Operates and tests equipment to ensure elimination of malfunction. Climbs poles to install or repair outside service lines.

GOE INFORMATION—Interest Area: 05. Mechanics, Installers, and Repairers. **Work Group:** 05.02. Electrical and Electronic Systems. **Personality Type**—Realistic. Realistic occupations frequently involve work activities that include practical, hands-on problems and solutions. They often deal with plants, animals, and real-world materials like wood, tools, and machinery. Many of the occupations require working outside and do not involve a lot of paperwork or working closely with others. **Work Values**—Supervision, Technical; Moral Values; Security; Advancement; Independence. **Skills**—Repairing; Troubleshooting; Installation; Operation and Control; Quality Control Analysis; Operation Monitoring; Equipment Selection. **Abilities**—*Cognitive:* Spatial Orientation; Problem Sensitivity. *Psychomotor:* Finger Dexterity; Arm-Hand Steadiness; Control Precision; Manual Dexterity; Multilimb Coordination. *Physical:* Dynamic Strength; Gross Body Equilibrium; Stamina; Gross Body Coordination; Static Strength. *Sensory:* Visual Color Discrimination; Sound Localization; Glare Sensitivity. **General Work Activities**—*Information Input:* Getting Information; Inspecting Equipment, Structures, or Materials; Monitoring Processes, Materials, or Surroundings. *Mental*

Process: Analyzing Data or Information; Making Decisions and Solving Problems; Organizing, Planning, and Prioritizing. *Work Output:* Performing General Physical Activities; Repairing and Maintaining Electronic Equipment; Handling and Moving Objects. *Interacting with Others:* Communicating with Other Workers; Establishing and Maintaining Relationships; Performing for or Working with the Public. **Physical Work Conditions**—Climbing Ladders, Scaffolds, Poles, etc.; High Places; Keeping or Regaining Balance; Common Protective or Safety Attire; Very Hot or Cold. **Other Job Characteristics**—Importance of Being Exact or Accurate; Pace Determined by Speed of Equipment; Consequence of Error.

Experience—Job Zone 4. A minimum of two to four years of work-related skill, knowledge, or experience is needed. **Job Preparation:** SVP 7.0 to less than 8.0—two years to less than 10 years. **Knowledge**—Telecommunications; Computers and Electronics; Mechanical; Engineering and Technology; Design. **Instructional Programs**—Communications Systems Installation and Repair Technology.

Related DOT Jobs—822.261-022 Station Installer-and-Repairer; 822.281-018 Maintenance Mechanic, Telephone.

49-2091.00 Avionics Technicians
- **Education/Training Required: Postsecondary vocational training**
- **Employed: 15,534**
- **Annual Earnings: $41,450**
- **Growth: 9.8%**
- **Annual Job Openings: 2,000**

Install, inspect, test, adjust, or repair avionics equipment, such as radar, radio, navigation, and missile control systems in aircraft or space vehicles.

Assembles components, such as switches, electrical controls, and junction boxes, using hand tools and soldering iron. Connects components to assemblies, such as radio systems, instruments, magnetos, inverters, and in-flight refueling systems, using hand tools and soldering iron. Tests components or assemblies, using circuit tester, oscilloscope, and voltmeter. Adjusts, repairs, or replaces malfunctioning components or assemblies, using hand tools and soldering iron. Lays out installation of assemblies and systems in aircraft according to blueprints and wiring diagrams, using scribe, scale, and protractor. Installs electrical and electronic components, assemblies, and systems in aircraft, using hand tools, power tools, and soldering iron. Sets up and operates ground support and test equipment to perform functional flight test of electrical and electronic systems. Interprets flight test data to diagnose malfunctions and systemic performance problems. Fabricates parts and test aids as required.

GOE INFORMATION—Interest Area: 05. Mechanics, Installers, and Repairers. **Work Group:** 05.02. Electrical and Electronic Systems. **Personality Type**—Realistic. Realistic occupations frequently involve work activities that include practical, hands-on problems and solutions. They often deal with plants, animals, and real-world materials like wood, tools, and machinery. Many of the occupations require working outside and do not involve a lot of paperwork or working closely with others. **Work Values**—Supervision, Technical; Variety; Compensation; Supervision, Human Relations; Moral Values. **Skills**—Repairing; Installation; Operation Monitoring; Troubleshooting; Operation and Control; Quality Control Analysis; Equipment Selection; Systems Analysis. **Abilities**—*Cognitive:* Spatial Orientation; Visualization; Mathematical Reasoning; Number Facility; Information Ordering. *Psychomotor:* Finger Dexterity; Arm-Hand Steadiness; Manual Dexterity; Multilimb Coordination; Reaction Time. *Physical:* Extent Flexibility; Explosive Strength; Dynamic Flexibility; Gross Body Equilibrium; Dynamic Strength. *Sensory:* Visual Color Discrimination; Depth Perception; Far Vision; Sound Localization; Near Vision. **General Work Activities**—*Information Input:* Inspecting Equipment, Structures, or Materials; Monitoring Processes, Materials, or Surroundings; Getting Information. *Mental Process:* Updating and Using Relevant Knowledge; Evaluating Information Against Standards; Judging Qualities of Things, Services, or Other People's Work. *Work Output:* Repairing and Maintaining Electronic Equipment; Handling and Moving Objects; Controlling Machines and Processes. *Interacting with Others:* Interpreting Meaning of Information for Others; Communicating with Other Workers; Coordinating the Work and Activities of Others. **Physical Work Conditions**—Hazardous Conditions; Cramped Work Space or Awkward Positions; Using Hands on Objects, Tools, or Controls; Distracting Sounds and Noise Levels; Kneeling, Crouching, or Crawling. **Other Job Characteristics**—Importance of Being Exact or Accurate; Consequence of Error; Degree of Automation.

Experience—Job Zone 4. A minimum of two to four years of work-related skill, knowledge, or experience is needed. **Job Preparation:** SVP 7.0 to less than 8.0—two years to less than 10 years. **Knowledge**—Computers and Electronics; Design; Physics; Engineering and Technology; Telecommunications. **Instructional Programs**—Airframe Mechanics and Aircraft Maintenance Technology/Technician; Avionics Maintenance Technology/Technician.

Related DOT Jobs—825.261-018 Electrician, Aircraft; 825.381-010 Aircraft Mechanic, Electrical and Radio; 829.281-018 In-Flight Refueling System Repairer.

49-2092.00 Electric Motor, Power Tool, and Related Repairers
- **Education/Training Required: Long-term on-the-job training**
- **Employed: 36,853**
- **Annual Earnings: $31,010**
- **Growth: 7.9%**
- **Annual Job Openings: 3,000**

Repair, maintain, or install electric motors, wiring, or switches.

No task data available.

GOE INFORMATION—Interest Area: 05. Mechanics, Installers, and Repairers. **Work Group:** 05.02. Electrical and Electronic Systems. **Note:** The Department of Labor has not collected some data for this job, so it has fewer details than the other descriptions.

Instructional Programs—Electrical/Electronics Equipment Installation and Repair, General.

Related DOT Jobs—519.684-026 Tool Repairer; 620.261-026 Electric-Golf-Cart Repairer; 637.261-010 Air-Conditioning Installer-Servicer, Window Unit; 701.381-010 Repairer, Handtools; 701.384-010 Tool-Maintenance Worker; 701.684-010 Calibrator; 721.261-010 Electric-Motor Analyst; 721.281-010 Automotive-Generator-and-Starter Repairer; 721.281-014 Electric-Motor Assembler and Tester; 721.281-018 Electric-Motor Repairer; 721.281-026 Propulsion-Motor-and-Generator Repairer; 721.381-010 Electric-Motor Fitter; 723.381-010 Electrical-Appliance Repairer; 723.381-014 Vacuum Cleaner Repairer; 723.584-010 Appliance Repairer; 724.381-010 Adjuster, Electrical Contacts; 724.381-018 Transformer Repairer; 724.684-018 Armature Winder, Repair; 727.381-014 Battery Repairer; 727.684-018 Cell Repairer; others.

49-2092.01 Electric Home Appliance and Power Tool Repairers

- **Education/Training Required: Long-term on-the-job training**
- **Employed: No data available.**
- **Annual Earnings: $31,010**
- **Growth: 7.9%**
- **Annual Job Openings: 3,000**

Repair, adjust, and install all types of electric household appliances.

Disassembles appliance to examine specific mechanical and electrical parts to diagnose problem. Replaces worn and defective parts, such as switches, bearings, transmissions, belts, gears, circuit boards, or defective wiring. Reassembles unit, making necessary adjustments to ensure efficient operation. Connects appliance to power source and uses test instruments to calibrate timers and thermostats and to adjust contact points. Observes and examines appliance during operation to detect specific malfunction, such as loose parts or leaking fluid. Traces electrical circuits, following diagram, to locate shorts and grounds, using electrical circuit testers. Instructs customer regarding operation and care of appliance and provides emergency service number. Cleans, lubricates, and touches up minor scratches on newly installed or repaired appliance. Maintains stock of parts used in on-site installation, maintenance, and repair of appliance. Records nature of maintenance or repair in log and returns to business office for further assignments. Measures and performs minor carpentry procedures to area where appliance is to be installed.

GOE INFORMATION—Interest Area: 05. Mechanics, Installers, and Repairers. **Work Group:** 05.02. Electrical and Electronic Systems. **Personality Type**—Realistic. Realistic occupations frequently involve work activities that include practical, hands-on problems and solutions. They often deal with plants, animals, and real-world materials like wood, tools, and machinery. Many of the occupations require working outside and do not involve a lot of paperwork or working closely with others. **Work Values**—Variety; Social Service; Supervision, Technical; Independence; Moral Values. **Skills**—Installation; Repairing; Troubleshooting; Operation Monitoring; Technology Design; Quality Control Analysis; Operation and Control. **Abilities**—*Cognitive:* Visualization. *Psychomotor:* Arm-Hand Steadiness; Finger Dexterity; Control Precision. *Physical:* Static Strength; Dynamic Strength; Extent Flexibility; Stamina; Trunk Strength. *Sensory:* Visual Color Discrimination. **General Work Activities**—*Information Input:* Monitoring Processes, Materials, or Surroundings; Inspecting Equipment, Structures, or Materials; Getting Information. *Mental Process:* Updating and Using Relevant Knowledge; Evaluating Information Against Standards; Judging Qualities of Things, Services, or Other People's Work. *Work Output:* Handling and Moving Objects; Repairing and Maintaining Electronic Equipment; Performing General Physical Activities. *Interacting with Others:* Communicating with Persons Outside Organization; Performing for or Working with the Public; Performing Administrative Activities. **Physical Work Conditions**—Using Hands on Objects, Tools, or Controls; Indoors; Kneeling, Crouching, or Crawling; Cramped Work Space or Awkward Positions; Hazardous Equipment. **Other Job Characteristics**—Importance of Being Exact or Accurate; Pace Determined by Speed of Equipment; Consequence of Error.

Experience—Job Zone 3. Previous work-related skill, knowledge, or experience is required. **Job Preparation:** SVP 6.0 to less than 7.0—more than one year and less than four years. **Knowledge**—Mechanical; Building and Construction; Design; Engineering and Technology; Computers and Electronics. **Instructional Programs**—Electrical/Electronics Equipment Installation and Repair, General.

Related DOT Jobs—637.261-010 Air-Conditioning Installer-Servicer, Window Unit; 723.381-010 Electrical-Appliance Repairer; 723.381-014 Vacuum Cleaner Repairer; 723.584-010 Appliance Repairer; 729.281-022 Electric-Tool Repairer; 827.261-010 Electrical-Appliance Servicer; 827.261-014 Electrical-Appliance-Servicer Apprentice.

49-2092.02 Electric Motor and Switch Assemblers and Repairers

- **Education/Training Required: Long-term on-the-job training**
- **Employed: No data available.**
- **Annual Earnings: $31,010**
- **Growth: 7.9%**
- **Annual Job Openings: 3,000**

Test, repair, rebuild, and assemble electric motors, generators, and equipment.

Assembles electrical parts, such as alternators, generators, starting devices, and switches, following schematic drawings, using hand, machine, and power tools. Repairs and rebuilds defective mechanical parts in electric motors, generators, and related equipment, using hand tools and power tools. Tests for overheating, using speed gauges and thermometers. Rewinds coils on core while core is in slots or makes replacement coils, using coil-winding machine. Replaces defective parts, such as coil leads, carbon brushes, and connecting wires, using soldering equipment. Installs, secures, and aligns parts, using hand tools, welding equipment, and electrical meters. Rewires electrical systems and repairs or replaces electrical accessories. Reassembles repaired electric motors to specified requirements and ratings, using hand tools and electrical meters. Disassembles defective unit, using hand tools. Measures velocity, horsepower, r.p.m., amperage, circuitry, and voltage of unit or parts, using electrical meters and mechanical testing devices. Cuts and removes parts, such as defective coils and insulation. Adjusts working parts, such as fan belt tension, voltage output, contacts, and springs, using hand tools, and verifies corrections, using gauges. Tests charges and replaces batteries. Inspects parts for wear or damage or reads work order or schematic drawings to determine required repairs. Cuts and forms insulation and inserts insulation into armature, rotor, or stator slots. Refaces, reams, and polishes commutators and machine parts to specified tolerances, using machine tools. Records repairs required, parts used, and labor time. Scrapes and cleans units or parts, using cleaning solvent, and lubricates moving parts. Lifts units or parts, such as motors or generators, using crane or chain hoist.

GOE INFORMATION—Interest Area: 05. Mechanics, Installers, and Repairers. **Work Group:** 05.02. Electrical and Electronic Systems. **Personality Type**—Realistic. Realistic occupations frequently involve work activities that include practical, hands-on problems and solutions. They often deal with plants, animals, and real-world materials like wood, tools, and machinery. Many of the occupations require working outside and do not involve a lot of paperwork or working closely with others. **Work Values**—Supervision, Technical; Moral Values; Independence; Variety; Compensation. **Skills**—Repairing; Installation; Operation Monitoring; Troubleshooting; Operation and Control; Quality Control Analysis; Technology Design; Science. **Abilities**—*Cognitive:* Speed of Closure; Visualization; Flexibility of Closure; Information Ordering; Written Comprehension. *Psychomotor:* Finger Dexterity; Arm-Hand Steadiness; Speed of Limb Movement; Multilimb Coordination; Response Orientation. *Physical:* Extent Flexibility; Explosive Strength; Stamina; Static Strength; Dynamic Strength. *Sensory:* Visual Color Discrimination; Hearing Sensitivity; Sound Localization; Auditory Attention; Near Vision. **General Work Activities**—*Information Input:* Inspecting Equipment, Structures, or Materials; Monitoring Processes, Materials, or Surroundings; Getting Information. *Mental Process:* Judging Qualities of Things, Services, or Other People's Work; Evaluating Information Against Standards; Updating and Using Relevant Knowledge. *Work Output:* Handling and Moving Objects; Repairing and Maintaining Mechanical Equipment; Performing General Physical Activities. *Interacting with Others:* Communicating with Other Workers; Performing Administrative Activities; Establishing and Maintaining Relationships. **Physical Work Conditions**—Hazardous Conditions; Hazardous Equipment; Using Hands on Objects, Tools, or Controls; Minor Burns, Cuts, Bites, or Stings; Common Protective or Safety Attire. **Other Job Characteristics**—Degree of Automation; Pace Determined by Speed of Equipment; Importance of Repeating Same Tasks.

Experience—Job Zone 3. Previous work-related skill, knowledge, or experience is required. **Job Preparation:** SVP 6.0 to less than 7.0—more than one year and less than four years. **Knowledge**—Computers and Electronics; Mechanical; Design; Engineering and Technology; Public Safety and Security. **Instructional Programs**—Electrical/Electronics Equipment Installation and Repair, General.

Related DOT Jobs—620.261-026 Electric-Golf-Cart Repairer; 721.261-010 Electric-Motor Analyst; 721.281-010 Automotive-Generator-and-Starter Repairer; 721.281-014 Electric-Motor Assembler and Tester; 721.281-018 Electric-Motor Repairer; 721.281-026 Propulsion-Motor-and-Generator Repairer; 721.381-010 Electric-Motor Fitter; 724.381-010 Adjuster, Electrical Contacts; 729.684-038 Repairer, Switchgear; 821.381-018 Wind-Generating-Electric-Power Installer.

49-2092.03 *Battery Repairers*

- Education/Training Required: **Moderate-term on-the-job training**
- Employed: **No data available.**
- Annual Earnings: **$31,010**
- Growth: **7.9%**
- Annual Job Openings: **3,000**

Inspect, repair, recharge, and replace batteries.

Inspects electrical connections, wiring charging relays, charging resistance box, and storage batteries, following wiring diagram. Inspects battery for defects, such as dented cans, damaged carbon rods and terminals, and defective seals. Removes and disassembles cells and cathode assembly, using tension handles, prybars, and hoist, and cuts wires to faulty cells. Tests condition, fluid level, and specific gravity of electrolyte cells, using voltmeter, hydrometer, and thermometer. Connects battery to battery charger and adjusts rheostat to start flow of electricity into battery. Replaces defective parts, such as cell plates, fuses, lead parts, switches, wires, anodes, cathodes, and rheostat. Repairs or adjusts defective parts, using hand tools or power tools. Adds water and acid to battery cells to obtain specified concentration. Disconnects electrical leads and removes battery, using hand tools and hoist. Cleans cells, cell assemblies, glassware, leads, electrical connections, and battery poles, using scraper, steam, water, emery cloth, power grinder, or acid. Installs recharged or repaired battery or cells, using hand tools. Positions and levels, or signals worker to position and level, cell, anode, or cathode, using hoist and leveling jacks. Secures cell on rocker mechanism or attaches assemblies, using bolts or cement. Measures cathode blade and anode, using ruler, and rate of mercury flow, using stopwatch. Repairs battery-charging equipment. Seals joints with putty, mortar, and asbestos, using putty extruder and knife. Compiles operating and maintenance records. Fabricates and assembles electrolytic cell parts for storage batteries.

GOE INFORMATION—Interest Area: 05. Mechanics, Installers, and Repairers. **Work Group:** 05.02. Electrical and Electronic Systems. **Person-**

ality Type—Realistic. Realistic occupations frequently involve work activities that include practical, hands-on problems and solutions. They often deal with plants, animals, and real-world materials like wood, tools, and machinery. Many of the occupations require working outside and do not involve a lot of paperwork or working closely with others. **Work Values**—Supervision, Technical; Moral Values; Security; Independence; Supervision, Human Relations. **Skills**—Repairing; Installation; Quality Control Analysis; Troubleshooting; Operation and Control; Equipment Selection. **Abilities**—*Cognitive:* Spatial Orientation. *Psychomotor:* Manual Dexterity; Reaction Time; Multilimb Coordination; Finger Dexterity; Speed of Limb Movement. *Physical:* Explosive Strength; Dynamic Strength; Dynamic Flexibility; Static Strength; Gross Body Equilibrium. *Sensory:* Visual Color Discrimination; Peripheral Vision. **General Work Activities**—*Information Input:* Monitoring Processes, Materials, or Surroundings; Inspecting Equipment, Structures, or Materials; Getting Information. *Mental Process:* Judging Qualities of Things, Services, or Other People's Work; Updating and Using Relevant Knowledge; Analyzing Data or Information. *Work Output:* Handling and Moving Objects; Repairing and Maintaining Electronic Equipment; Performing General Physical Activities. *Interacting with Others:* Communicating with Other Workers; Establishing and Maintaining Relationships; Performing Administrative Activities. **Physical Work Conditions**—Cramped Work Space or Awkward Positions; Minor Burns, Cuts, Bites, or Stings; Kneeling, Crouching, or Crawling; Contaminants; Hazardous Conditions. **Other Job Characteristics**—Importance of Repeating Same Tasks; Consequence of Error; Pace Determined by Speed of Equipment.

Experience—Job Zone 2. Some previous work-related skill, knowledge, or experience may be helpful, but usually is not needed. **Job Preparation:** SVP 4.0 to less than 6.0—six months to less than two years. **Knowledge**—Computers and Electronics; Chemistry; Mechanical; Engineering and Technology; Physics. **Instructional Programs**—Electrical/Electronics Equipment Installation and Repair, General.

Related DOT Jobs—727.381-014 Battery Repairer; 727.684-018 Cell Repairer; 820.381-010 Battery Maintainer, Large Emergency Storage; 825.684-018 Battery Charger; 826.384-010 Cell Repairer; 826.684-014 Cell Changer; 826.684-018 Cell Installer; 829.684-010 Battery Inspector.

49-2092.04 *Transformer Repairers*

- Education/Training Required: **Long-term on-the-job training**
- Employed: **No data available.**
- Annual Earnings: **$31,010**
- Growth: **7.9%**
- Annual Job Openings: **3,000**

Clean and repair electrical transformers.

Cleans transformer case, using scrapers and solvent. Disassembles distribution, streetlight, or instrument transformers. Drains and filters transformer oil. Reassembles transformer. Fills reassembled transformer with oil until coils are submerged. Replaces worn or defective parts, using hand tools. Dismantles lamination assembly preparatory to cleaning and inspection. Inspects transformer for defects, such as cracked weldments. Secures input and output wires in position. Signals crane operator to raise heavy transformer component subassemblies. Winds replacement coils, using coil-winding machine.

GOE INFORMATION—Interest Area: 05. Mechanics, Installers, and Repairers. **Work Group:** 05.02. Electrical and Electronic Systems. **Personality Type**—Realistic. Realistic occupations frequently involve work activities that include practical, hands-on problems and solutions. They often deal with plants, animals, and real-world materials like wood, tools, and machinery. Many of the occupations require working outside and do not involve a lot of paperwork or working closely with others. **Work Values**—Supervision, Technical; Moral Values; Security; Supervision, Human Relations; Independence. **Skills**—Repairing; Installation; Troubleshooting. **Abilities**—*Cognitive:* Spatial Orientation; Problem Sensitivity. *Psychomotor:* Manual Dexterity; Reaction Time; Speed of Limb Movement; Finger Dexterity; Multilimb Coordination. *Physical:* Dynamic Strength; Dynamic Flexibility; Gross Body Equilibrium; Stamina; Explosive Strength. *Sensory:* Night Vision; Depth Perception; Visual Color Discrimination. **General Work Activities**—*Information Input:* Inspecting Equipment, Structures, or Materials; Identifying Objects, Actions, and Events; Getting Information. *Mental Process:* Updating and Using Relevant Knowledge; Judging Qualities of Things, Services, or Other People's Work; Evaluating Information Against Standards. *Work Output:* Handling and Moving Objects; Performing General Physical Activities; Repairing and Maintaining Mechanical Equipment. *Interacting with Others:* Communicating with Other Workers; Coordinating the Work and Activities of Others; Establishing and Maintaining Relationships. **Physical Work Conditions**—Outdoors; Hazardous Conditions; Climbing Ladders, Scaffolds, Poles, etc.; High Places; Common Protective or Safety Attire. **Other Job Characteristics**—Consequence of Error; Importance of Being Exact or Accurate; Pace Determined by Speed of Equipment.

Experience—Job Zone 4. A minimum of two to four years of work-related skill, knowledge, or experience is needed. **Job Preparation:** SVP 7.0 to less than 8.0—two years to less than 10 years. **Knowledge**—Mechanical; Engineering and Technology; Computers and Electronics; Telecommunications; Building and Construction. **Instructional Programs**—Electrical/Electronics Equipment Installation and Repair, General.

Related DOT Jobs—724.381-018 Transformer Repairer; 821.361-034 Power-Transformer Repairer.

49-2092.05 Electrical Parts Reconditioners

- **Education/Training Required: Moderate-term on-the-job training**
- **Employed: No data available.**
- **Annual Earnings: $31,010**
- **Growth: 7.9%**
- **Annual Job Openings: 3,000**

Recondition and rebuild salvaged electrical parts of equipment and wind new coils on armatures of used generators and motors.

Solders, wraps, and coats wires to ensure proper insulation. Replaces broken and defective parts. Cuts insulating material to fit slots on armature core and places material in bottom of core slots. Winds new coils on armatures of generators and motors. Disassembles salvaged equipment used in electric-power systems, such as air circuit breakers and lightning arresters, using hand tools, and discards non-repairable parts. Inserts and hammers ready-made coils in place. Cleans and polishes parts, using solvent and buffing wheel. Bolts porcelain insulators to wood parts to assemble hot stools. Solders ends of coils to commutator segments. Tests armatures and motors to ensure proper operation.

GOE INFORMATION—Interest Area: 05. Mechanics, Installers, and Repairers. **Work Group:** 05.02. Electrical and Electronic Systems. **Personality Type**—Realistic. Realistic occupations frequently involve work activities that include practical, hands-on problems and solutions. They often deal with plants, animals, and real-world materials like wood, tools, and machinery. Many of the occupations require working outside and do not involve a lot of paperwork or working closely with others. **Work**

Values—Independence; Moral Values; Supervision, Technical; Responsibility; Supervision, Human Relations. **Skills**—Repairing; Installation; Quality Control Analysis; Equipment Selection. **Abilities**—*Cognitive:* None met the criteria. *Psychomotor:* Finger Dexterity; Speed of Limb Movement; Manual Dexterity; Rate Control; Wrist-Finger Speed. *Physical:* Explosive Strength; Dynamic Flexibility; Dynamic Strength; Extent Flexibility; Static Strength. *Sensory:* Visual Color Discrimination; Sound Localization. **General Work Activities**—*Information Input:* Inspecting Equipment, Structures, or Materials; Getting Information; Identifying Objects, Actions, and Events. *Mental Process:* Updating and Using Relevant Knowledge; Judging Qualities of Things, Services, or Other People's Work; Making Decisions and Solving Problems. *Work Output:* Handling and Moving Objects; Performing General Physical Activities; Repairing and Maintaining Mechanical Equipment. *Interacting with Others:* Communicating with Other Workers; Interpreting Meaning of Information for Others; Establishing and Maintaining Relationships. **Physical Work Conditions**—Common Protective or Safety Attire; Making Repetitive Motions; Minor Burns, Cuts, Bites, or Stings; Outdoors; Hazardous Equipment. **Other Job Characteristics**—Importance of Being Exact or Accurate; Importance of Repeating Same Tasks; Pace Determined by Speed of Equipment.

Experience—Job Zone 2. Some previous work-related skill, knowledge, or experience may be helpful, but usually is not needed. **Job Preparation:** SVP 4.0 to less than 6.0—six months to less than two years. **Knowledge**—Mechanical; Engineering and Technology; Building and Construction. **Instructional Programs**—Electrical/Electronics Equipment Installation and Repair, General.

Related DOT Jobs—724.684-018 Armature Winder, Repair; 729.384-018 Salvage Repairer II.

49-2092.06 Hand and Portable Power Tool Repairers

- **Education/Training Required: Moderate-term on-the-job training**
- **Employed: No data available.**
- **Annual Earnings: $31,010**
- **Growth: 7.9%**
- **Annual Job Openings: 3,000**

Repair and adjust hand and power tools.

Repairs or replaces tools and defective parts, such as handles, vises, pliers, or metal buckets, using soldering tool, gas torch, power tools, or hand tools. Examines and tests tools to determine defects or cause of malfunction, using hand and power tools, observation, and experience. Disassembles and reassembles tools, using hand tools, power tools, or arbor press. Verifies and adjusts alignment and dimensions of parts, using gauges and tracing lathe. Sharpens tools, such as picks, shovels, screwdrivers, and scoops, using bench grinder and emery wheel. Sprays, brushes, or recoats surface of polishing wheel and places it in oven to dry. Cleans polishing and buffing wheels, using steam cleaning machine, to remove abrasives and bonding materials and salvages cloth from wheel. Records nature and extent of repairs performed. Maintains stock of parts.

GOE INFORMATION—Interest Area: 05. Mechanics, Installers, and Repairers. **Work Group:** 05.03. Mechanical Work. **Personality Type**—Realistic. Realistic occupations frequently involve work activities that include practical, hands-on problems and solutions. They often deal with plants, animals, and real-world materials like wood, tools, and machinery. Many of the occupations require working outside and do not involve a lot of paperwork or working closely with others. **Work Values**—Independence;

Moral Values; Activity; Supervision, Technical; Responsibility. **Skills—**Repairing; Operation and Control. **Abilities—***Cognitive:* Visualization; Flexibility of Closure; Memorization. *Psychomotor:* Manual Dexterity; Finger Dexterity; Wrist-Finger Speed; Speed of Limb Movement; Control Precision. *Physical:* Stamina; Trunk Strength; Explosive Strength; Dynamic Flexibility. *Sensory:* Hearing Sensitivity; Depth Perception; Sound Localization. **General Work Activities—***Information Input:* Inspecting Equipment, Structures, or Materials; Getting Information; Monitoring Processes, Materials, or Surroundings. *Mental Process:* Updating and Using Relevant Knowledge; Judging Qualities of Things, Services, or Other People's Work; Processing Information. *Work Output:* Handling and Moving Objects; Performing General Physical Activities; Repairing and Maintaining Mechanical Equipment. *Interacting with Others:* Monitoring and Controlling Resources; Performing Administrative Activities; Communicating with Other Workers. **Physical Work Conditions—**Common Protective or Safety Attire; Hazardous Equipment; Using Hands on Objects, Tools, or Controls; Making Repetitive Motions; Minor Burns, Cuts, Bites, or Stings. **Other Job Characteristics—**Importance of Repeating Same Tasks; Consequence of Error; Pace Determined by Speed of Equipment.

Experience—Job Zone 2. Some previous work-related skill, knowledge, or experience may be helpful, but usually is not needed. **Job Preparation:** SVP 4.0 to less than 6.0—six months to less than two years. **Knowledge—**Mechanical; Engineering and Technology; Design; Clerical; Physics. **Instructional Programs—**Electrical/Electronics Equipment Installation and Repair, General.

Related DOT Jobs—519.684-026 Tool Repairer; 701.381-010 Repairer, Handtools; 701.384-010 Tool-Maintenance Worker; 701.684-010 Calibrator; 739.684-030 Buffing-and-Polishing-Wheel Repairer.

49-2093.00 Electrical and Electronics Installers and Repairers, Transportation Equipment

- Education/Training Required: Postsecondary vocational training
- Employed: 13,594
- Annual Earnings: $37,910
- Growth: 13.6%
- Annual Job Openings: 1,000

Install, adjust, or maintain mobile electronics communication equipment, including sound, sonar, security, navigation, and surveillance systems on trains, watercraft, or other mobile equipment.

Visually inspects and tests electrical system or equipment, using testing devices such as oscilloscope, voltmeter, and ammeter, to determine malfunctions. Cuts openings and drills holes for fixtures, outlet boxes, and fuse holders, using electric drill and router. Installs electrical equipment, such as air-conditioning, heating, or ignition systems, generator brushes, and commutators, using hand tools. Confers with customer to determine nature of malfunction. Installs fixtures, outlets, terminal boards, switches, and wall boxes, using hand tools. Estimates cost of repairs based on parts and labor charges. Measures, cuts, and installs framework and conduit to support and connect wiring, control panels, and junction boxes, using hand tools. Adjusts, repairs, or replaces defective wiring and relays in ignition, lighting, air-conditioning, and safety control systems, using electrician's tools. Splices wires with knife or cutting pliers and solders connections to fixtures, outlets, and equipment. Repairs or rebuilds starters, generators, distributors, or door controls, using electrician's tools.

GOE INFORMATION—Interest Area: 05. Mechanics, Installers, and Repairers. **Work Group:** 05.02. Electrical and Electronic Systems. **Personality Type—**Realistic. Realistic occupations frequently involve work activities that include practical, hands-on problems and solutions. They often deal with plants, animals, and real-world materials like wood, tools, and machinery. Many of the occupations require working outside and do not involve a lot of paperwork or working closely with others. **Work Values—**Supervision, Technical; Variety; Supervision, Human Relations; Moral Values; Advancement. **Skills—**Repairing; Installation; Equipment Selection. **Abilities—***Cognitive:* Memorization; Visualization; Selective Attention; Problem Sensitivity; Flexibility of Closure. *Psychomotor:* Manual Dexterity; Finger Dexterity; Arm-Hand Steadiness; Control Precision; Multilimb Coordination. *Physical:* Extent Flexibility; Explosive Strength; Dynamic Flexibility; Trunk Strength; Static Strength. *Sensory:* Visual Color Discrimination; Hearing Sensitivity; Near Vision; Night Vision; Depth Perception. **General Work Activities—***Information Input:* Inspecting Equipment, Structures, or Materials; Monitoring Processes, Materials, or Surroundings; Getting Information. *Mental Process:* Updating and Using Relevant Knowledge; Judging Qualities of Things, Services, or Other People's Work; Evaluating Information Against Standards. *Work Output:* Repairing and Maintaining Electronic Equipment; Handling and Moving Objects; Controlling Machines and Processes. *Interacting with Others:* Communicating with Persons Outside Organization; Interpreting Meaning of Information for Others; Communicating with Other Workers. **Physical Work Conditions—**Hazardous Conditions; Cramped Work Space or Awkward Positions; Hazardous Equipment; Kneeling, Crouching, or Crawling; Using Hands on Objects, Tools, or Controls. **Other Job Characteristics—**Degree of Automation; Importance of Being Exact or Accurate; Consequence of Error.

Experience—Job Zone 3. Previous work-related skill, knowledge, or experience is required. **Job Preparation:** SVP 6.0 to less than 7.0—more than one year and less than four years. **Knowledge—**Computers and Electronics; Mechanical; Building and Construction; Engineering and Technology; Public Safety and Security. **Instructional Programs—**Automobile/Automotive Mechanics Technology/Technician.

Related DOT Jobs—825.281-026 Electrician, Locomotive; 825.381-018 Controller Repairer-and-Tester; 829.684-014 Body Wirer.

49-2094.00 Electrical and Electronics Repairers, Commercial and Industrial Equipment

- Education/Training Required: Postsecondary vocational training
- Employed: 89,699
- Annual Earnings: $38,800
- Growth: 9.2%
- Annual Job Openings: 10,000

Repair, test, adjust, or install electronic equipment, such as industrial controls, transmitters, and antennas.

Perform scheduled preventive maintenance tasks, such as checking, cleaning, and repairing equipment, to detect and prevent problems. Examine work orders and converse with equipment operators to detect equipment problems and to ascertain whether mechanical or human errors contributed to the problems. Set up and test industrial equipment to ensure that it functions properly. Operate equipment to demonstrate proper use and to analyze malfunctions. Test faulty equipment to diagnose malfunctions, using test equipment and software and applying knowledge of the functional operation of electronic units and systems. Repair and adjust equipment, machines, and defective components, replacing worn parts such as gaskets and seals in watertight electrical equipment. Calibrate testing instruments and installed or repaired equipment to prescribed specifications. Advise management regarding customer satisfaction, product performance, and suggestions for product improvements. Inspect components of industrial equipment for accurate assembly and installation and for defects such as loose connections and frayed wires. Study blueprints, schematics, manuals, and other specifications to determine installation procedures. Maintain equipment logs that record performance problems, repairs, calibrations, and tests. Coordinate efforts with other workers involved in installing and maintaining equipment or components. Maintain inventory of spare parts. Consult with customers, supervisors, and engineers to plan layout of equipment and to resolve problems in system operation and maintenance. Send defective units to the manufacturer or to a specialized repair shop for repair. Install repaired equipment in various settings, such as industrial or military establishments. Determine feasibility of using standardized equipment and develop specifications for equipment required to perform additional functions. Enter information into computer to copy program or to draw, modify, or store schematics, applying knowledge of software package used. Sign overhaul documents for equipment replaced or repaired. Develop or modify industrial electronic devices, circuits, and equipment according to available specifications.

GOE INFORMATION—Interest Area: 05. Mechanics, Installers, and Repairers. **Work Group:** 05.02. Electrical and Electronic Systems. **Personality Type—**Realistic. Realistic occupations frequently involve work activities that include practical, hands-on problems and solutions. They often deal with plants, animals, and real-world materials like wood, tools, and machinery. Many of the occupations require working outside and do not involve a lot of paperwork or working closely with others. **Work Values—**Authority; Variety; Creativity; Compensation; Advancement. **Skills—**Installation; Repairing; Operation Monitoring; Troubleshooting; Operation and Control; Equipment Selection; Complex Problem Solving; Systems Analysis. **Abilities—***Cognitive:* Visualization; Perceptual Speed; Selective Attention; Flexibility of Closure; Inductive Reasoning. *Psychomotor:* Finger Dexterity; Control Precision; Arm-Hand Steadiness; Multilimb Coordination; Reaction Time. *Physical:* Extent Flexibility; Gross Body Coordination; Trunk Strength; Static Strength; Stamina. *Sensory:* Visual Color Discrimination; Auditory Attention; Hearing Sensitivity; Depth Perception; Speech Recognition. **General Work Activities—***Information Input:* Monitoring Processes, Materials, or Surroundings; Getting Information; Identifying Objects, Actions, and Events. *Mental Process:* Updating and Using Relevant Knowledge; Organizing, Planning, and Prioritizing; Making Decisions and Solving Problems. *Work Output:* Repairing and Maintaining Electronic Equipment; Interacting with Computers; Handling and Moving Objects. *Interacting with Others:* Communicating with Other Workers; Establishing and Maintaining Relationships; Communicating with Persons Outside Organization. **Physical Work Conditions—**Hazardous Conditions; Cramped Work Space or Awkward Positions; Common Protective or Safety Attire; Radiation; Sitting. **Other Job Characteristics—**Importance of Being Exact or Accurate; Consequence of Error; Pace Determined by Speed of Equipment.

Experience—Job Zone 3. Previous work-related skill, knowledge, or experience is required. **Job Preparation:** SVP 6.0 to less than 7.0—more than one year and less than four years. **Knowledge—**Computers and Electronics; Mechanical; Telecommunications; Customer and Personal Service; Design. **Instructional Programs—**Computer Installation and Repair Technology/Technician; Industrial Electronics Technology/Technician.

Related DOT Jobs—823.261-026 Avionics Technician; 828.251-010 Electronic-Sales-and-Service Technician; 828.261-014 Field Service Engineer; 828.261-022 Electronics Mechanic; 828.261-026 Electronics-Mechanic Apprentice; 828.281-022 Radioactivity-Instrument Maintenance Technician; 828.281-026 Computerized Environmental Control Installer.

49-2095.00 Electrical and Electronics Repairers, Powerhouse, Substation, and Relay

- **Education/Training Required:** Postsecondary vocational training
- **Employed:** 18,101
- **Annual Earnings:** $50,420
- **Growth:** –2.3%
- **Annual Job Openings:** 2,000

Inspect, test, repair, or maintain electrical equipment in generating stations, substations, and in-service relays.

Repairs, replaces, and cleans equipment, such as brushes, commutators, windings, bearings, relays, switches, controls, and instruments. Repairs or rebuilds circuit breakers, transformers, and lightning arresters by replacing worn parts. Inspects and tests equipment and circuits to identify malfunction or defect, using wiring diagrams and testing devices such as ohmmeters, voltmeters, or ammeters. Tests oil in circuit breakers and transformers for dielectric strength and periodically refills. Tests insulators and bushings of equipment by inducing voltage across insulation, using testing apparatus, and calculating insulation loss. Disconnects voltage regulators, bolts, and screws and connects replacement regulators to high-voltage lines. Analyzes test data to diagnose malfunctions and evaluate effect of system modifications. Prepares reports of work performed. Notifies personnel of need for equipment shutdown requiring changes from normal operation to maintain service. Paints, repairs, and maintains buildings and sets forms and pours concrete footings for installation of heavy equipment.

GOE INFORMATION—Interest Area: 05. Mechanics, Installers, and Repairers. **Work Group:** 05.02. Electrical and Electronic Systems. **Personality Type—**Realistic. Realistic occupations frequently involve work activities that include practical, hands-on problems and solutions. They often deal with plants, animals, and real-world materials like wood, tools, and machinery. Many of the occupations require working outside and do not involve a lot of paperwork or working closely with others. **Work Values—**Variety; Moral Values; Supervision, Technical; Responsibility; Compensation. **Skills—**Repairing; Installation; Troubleshooting; Operation Monitoring; Equipment Selection; Quality Control Analysis; Science; Mathematics. **Abilities—***Cognitive:* Perceptual Speed; Number Facility; Selective Attention; Spatial Orientation; Visualization. *Psychomotor:* Reaction Time; Control Precision; Manual Dexterity; Response Orientation; Finger Dexterity. *Physical:* Gross Body Equilibrium; Dynamic Strength; Extent Flexibility; Explosive Strength; Dynamic Flexibility. *Sensory:* Visual Color Discrimination; Hearing Sensitivity; Auditory Attention; Sound Localization; Glare Sensitivity. **General Work Activities—***Information Input:* Monitoring Processes, Materials, or Surroundings; Inspecting Equipment, Structures, or Materials; Getting Information. *Mental Process:* Updating and Using Relevant Knowledge; Analyzing Data or Information; Making Decisions and Solving Problems. *Work Output:* Repairing and Maintaining Electronic Equipment; Performing General Physical Activities; Handling and Moving Objects. *Interacting with Others:* Communicating with Other Workers; Performing Administrative Activities; Establishing and Maintaining Relationships. **Physical Work Conditions—**Hazardous Conditions; High Places; Using Hands on Objects, Tools, or Controls; Common Protective or Safety Attire; Outdoors. **Other Job Characteristics—**Consequence of Error; Importance of Being Exact or Accurate; Importance of Repeating Same Tasks.

Experience—Job Zone 5. Extensive skill, knowledge, and experience are needed for these occupations. **Job Preparation: SVP 8.0 and above—** four years to more than 10 years. **Knowledge—**Computers and Electronics; Mechanical; Physics; Engineering and Technology; Mathematics. **Instructional Programs—**No data available.

Related DOT Jobs—820.261-010 Electrician Apprentice, Powerhouse; 820.261-014 Electrician, Powerhouse; 820.261-018 Electrician, Substation; 821.261-018 Relay Technician.

49-2096.00 Electronic Equipment Installers and Repairers, Motor Vehicles

- **Education/Training Required: Postsecondary vocational training**
- **Employed: 12,809**
- **Annual Earnings: $25,250**
- **Growth: 15.6%**
- **Annual Job Openings: 1,000**

Install, diagnose, or repair communications, sound, security, or navigation equipment in motor vehicles.

Adjusts, repairs, or replaces defective wiring and relays in ignition, lighting, air-conditioning, and safety control systems, using electrician's tools. Repairs or rebuilds starters, generators, distributors, or door controls, using electrician's tools. Installs electrical equipment, such as air-conditioning, heating, or ignition systems, generator brushes, and commutators, using hand tools. Installs fixtures, outlets, terminal boards, switches, and wall boxes, using hand tools. Measures, cuts, and installs framework and conduit to support and connect wiring, control panels, and junction boxes, using hand tools. Splices wires with knife or cutting pliers and solders connections to fixtures, outlets, and equipment. Visually inspects and tests electrical system or equipment, using testing devices such as oscilloscope, voltmeter, and ammeter, to determine malfunctions. Cuts openings and drills holes for fixtures, outlet boxes, and fuse holders, using electric drill and router. Confers with customer to determine nature of malfunction. Estimates cost of repairs based on parts and labor charges.

GOE INFORMATION—Interest Area: 05. Mechanics, Installers, and Repairers. **Work Group:** 05.02. Electrical and Electronic Systems. **Personality Type—**Realistic. Realistic occupations frequently involve work activities that include practical, hands-on problems and solutions. They often deal with plants, animals, and real-world materials like wood, tools, and machinery. Many of the occupations require working outside and do not involve a lot of paperwork or working closely with others. **Work Values—**Supervision, Technical; Variety; Supervision, Human Relations; Moral Values; Advancement. **Skills—**Repairing; Installation; Equipment Selection. **Abilities—***Cognitive:* Memorization; Visualization; Selective Attention; Problem Sensitivity; Flexibility of Closure. *Psychomotor:* Manual Dexterity; Finger Dexterity; Arm-Hand Steadiness; Control Precision; Multilimb Coordination. *Physical:* Extent Flexibility; Explosive Strength; Dynamic Flexibility; Trunk Strength; Static Strength. *Sensory:* Visual Color Discrimination; Hearing Sensitivity; Near Vision; Night Vision; Depth Perception. **General Work Activities—***Information Input:* Inspecting Equipment, Structures, or Materials; Monitoring Processes, Materials, or Surroundings; Getting Information. *Mental Process:* Updating and Using Relevant Knowledge; Judging Qualities of Things, Services, or Other People's Work; Evaluating Information Against Standards. *Work Output:* Repairing and Maintaining Electronic Equipment; Handling and Moving Objects; Repairing and Maintaining Mechanical Equipment. *Interacting with Others:* Communicating with Persons Outside Organization; Interpreting Meaning of Information for Others; Com-

municating with Other Workers. **Physical Work Conditions—**Hazardous Conditions; Cramped Work Space or Awkward Positions; Hazardous Equipment; Kneeling, Crouching, or Crawling; Using Hands on Objects, Tools, or Controls. **Other Job Characteristics—**Degree of Automation; Importance of Being Exact or Accurate; Consequence of Error.

Experience—Job Zone 3. Previous work-related skill, knowledge, or experience is required. **Job Preparation: SVP 6.0 to less than 7.0—**more than one year and less than four years. **Knowledge—**Computers and Electronics; Mechanical; Building and Construction; Engineering and Technology; Public Safety and Security. **Instructional Programs—**Automobile/Automotive Mechanics Technology/Technician.

Related DOT Jobs—825.281-022 Electrician, Automotive; 828.381-010 Equipment Installer.

49-2097.00 Electronic Home Entertainment Equipment Installers and Repairers

- **Education/Training Required: Postsecondary vocational training**
- **Employed: 36,779**
- **Annual Earnings: $26,960**
- **Growth: –17.9%**
- **Annual Job Openings: 4,000**

Repair, adjust, or install audio or television receivers, stereo systems, camcorders, video systems, or other electronic home entertainment equipment.

Disassembles equipment and repairs or replaces loose, worn, or defective components and wiring, using hand tools and soldering iron. Tunes or adjusts equipment and instruments according to specifications to obtain optimum visual or auditory reception. Analyzes and tests products and parts to locate defects or source of trouble. Tests circuits, using schematic diagrams, service manuals, and testing instruments such as voltmeters, oscilloscopes, and audiogenerators. Confers with customers to determine nature of problem or to explain repairs. Makes service calls and repairs units in customers' homes or returns unit to shop for major repair. Installs electronic equipment or instruments, such as televisions, radios, audiovisual equipment, and organs, using hand tools. Computes cost estimates for labor and materials. Positions or mounts speakers and wires speakers to console.

GOE INFORMATION—Interest Area: 05. Mechanics, Installers, and Repairers. **Work Group:** 05.02. Electrical and Electronic Systems. **Personality Type—**Realistic. Realistic occupations frequently involve work activities that include practical, hands-on problems and solutions. They often deal with plants, animals, and real-world materials like wood, tools, and machinery. Many of the occupations require working outside and do not involve a lot of paperwork or working closely with others. **Work Values—**Variety; Supervision, Technical; Independence; Social Service; Compensation. **Skills—**Installation; Repairing; Troubleshooting; Science; Technology Design; Quality Control Analysis; Operation Monitoring; Operation and Control. **Abilities—***Cognitive:* Visualization; Speed of Closure; Flexibility of Closure; Information Ordering; Written Comprehension. *Psychomotor:* Finger Dexterity; Arm-Hand Steadiness; Control Precision; Manual Dexterity; Multilimb Coordination. *Physical:* Static Strength; Gross Body Equilibrium; Extent Flexibility; Gross Body Coordination; Trunk Strength. *Sensory:* Visual Color Discrimination; Sound Localization; Hearing Sensitivity; Near Vision; Auditory Attention. **Gen-**

eral Work Activities—*Information Input:* Monitoring Processes, Materials, or Surroundings; Inspecting Equipment, Structures, or Materials; Getting Information. *Mental Process:* Updating and Using Relevant Knowledge; Analyzing Data or Information; Organizing, Planning, and Prioritizing. *Work Output:* Repairing and Maintaining Electronic Equipment; Handling and Moving Objects; Controlling Machines and Processes. *Interacting with Others:* Communicating with Persons Outside Organization; Establishing and Maintaining Relationships; Performing for or Working with the Public. **Physical Work Conditions**—Keeping or Regaining Balance; Cramped Work Space or Awkward Positions; Climbing Ladders, Scaffolds, Poles, etc.; Bending or Twisting the Body; Kneeling, Crouching, or Crawling. **Other Job Characteristics**—Degree of Automation; Importance of Being Exact or Accurate; Importance of Repeating Same Tasks.

Experience—Job Zone 3. Previous work-related skill, knowledge, or experience is required. **Job Preparation:** SVP 6.0 to less than 7.0—more than one year and less than four years. **Knowledge**—Computers and Electronics; Design; Telecommunications; Mechanical; Customer and Personal Service. **Instructional Programs**—Communications Systems Installation and Repair Technology.

Related DOT Jobs—720.281-010 Radio Repairer; 720.281-014 Tape-Recorder Repairer; 720.281-018 Television-and-Radio Repairer; 729.281-010 Audio-Video Repairer; 730.281-018 Electric-Organ Inspector and Repairer; 823.361-010 Television Installer; 828.261-010 Electronic-Organ Technician.

49-2098.00 Security and Fire Alarm Systems Installers

- **Education/Training Required: Postsecondary vocational training**
- **Employed: 43,943**
- **Annual Earnings: $30,490**
- **Growth: 23.4%**
- **Annual Job Openings: 4,000**

Install, program, maintain, and repair security and fire alarm wiring and equipment. Ensure that work is in accordance with relevant codes.

No task data available.

GOE INFORMATION—Interest Area: 06. Construction, Mining, and Drilling. **Work Group:** 06.02. Construction. **Note:** The Department of Labor has not collected some data for this job, so it has fewer details than the other descriptions.

Instructional Programs—Electrician; Security System Installation, Repair, and Inspection Technology/Technician.

Related DOT Jobs—822.361-018 Protective-Signal Installer; 822.361-022 Protective-Signal Repairer.

49-3000 Vehicle and Mobile Equipment Mechanics, Installers, and Repairers

49-3011.00 Aircraft Mechanics and Service Technicians

- **Education/Training Required: Postsecondary vocational training**
- **Employed: 157,884**
- **Annual Earnings: $41,990**
- **Growth: 16.7%**
- **Annual Job Openings: 11,000**

Diagnose, adjust, repair, or overhaul aircraft engines and assemblies, such as hydraulic and pneumatic systems.

No task data available.

GOE INFORMATION—Interest Area: 05. Mechanics, Installers, and Repairers. **Work Group:** 05.03. Mechanical Work. **Note:** The Department of Labor has not collected some data for this job, so it has fewer details than the other descriptions.

Instructional Programs—Agricultural Mechanics and Equipment/Machine Technology; Aircraft Powerplant Technology/Technician; Airframe Mechanics and Aircraft Maintenance Technology/Technician.

Related DOT Jobs—621.261-022 Experimental Aircraft Mechanic; 621.281-014 Airframe-and-Power-Plant Mechanic; 621.281-018 Airframe-and-Power-Plant-Mechanic Apprentice; 621.281-030 Rocket-Engine-Component Mechanic; 807.261-010 Aircraft Body Repairer; 807.381-014 Bonded Structures Repairer; 825.281-038 Experimental-Rocket-Sled Mechanic.

49-3011.01 Airframe-and-Power-Plant Mechanics

- **Education/Training Required: Postsecondary vocational training**
- **Employed: No data available.**
- **Annual Earnings: $41,990**
- **Growth: 16.7%**
- **Annual Job Openings: 11,000**

Inspect, test, repair, maintain, and service aircraft.

Adjusts, aligns, and calibrates aircraft systems, using hand tools, gauges, and test equipment. Examines and inspects engines or other components for cracks, breaks, or leaks. Tests engine and system operations, using testing equipment, and listens to engine sounds to detect and diagnose malfunctions. Disassembles and inspects parts for wear, warping, or other defects. Repairs, replaces, and rebuilds aircraft structures, functional components, and parts, such as wings and fuselage, rigging, and hydraulic units. Services and maintains aircraft systems by performing tasks such as flushing crankcase, cleaning screens, greasing moving parts, and checking brakes. Assembles and installs electrical, plumbing, mechanical, hydraulic, and structural components and accessories, using hand tools and power tools. Removes engine from aircraft or installs engine, using hoist or forklift truck. Reads and interprets aircraft maintenance manuals and specifications to determine feasibility and method of repairing or replacing malfunctioning or damaged components. Modifies aircraft structures, space vehicles, systems, or components, following drawings, engineering orders, and technical publications.

GOE INFORMATION—Interest Area: 05. Mechanics, Installers, and Repairers. **Work Group:** 05.03. Mechanical Work. **Personality Type—**Realistic. Realistic occupations frequently involve work activities that include practical, hands-on problems and solutions. They often deal with plants, animals, and real-world materials like wood, tools, and machinery. Many of the occupations require working outside and do not involve a lot of paperwork or working closely with others. **Work Values—**Compensation; Moral Values; Security; Variety; Advancement. **Skills—**Installation; Repairing; Operation Monitoring; Troubleshooting; Quality Control Analysis; Equipment Selection; Operation and Control; Science. **Abilities—***Cognitive:* Deductive Reasoning; Perceptual Speed; Speed of Closure; Visualization; Inductive Reasoning. *Psychomotor:* Manual Dexterity; Control Precision; Multilimb Coordination; Reaction Time; Finger Dexterity. *Physical:* Explosive Strength; Extent Flexibility; Static Strength; Dynamic Flexibility; Dynamic Strength. *Sensory:* Visual Color Discrimination; Hearing Sensitivity; Depth Perception; Sound Localization; Auditory Attention. **General Work Activities—***Information Input:* Inspecting Equipment, Structures, or Materials; Monitoring Processes, Materials, or Surroundings; Getting Information. *Mental Process:* Updating and Using Relevant Knowledge; Evaluating Information Against Standards; Judging Qualities of Things, Services, or Other People's Work. *Work Output:* Repairing and Maintaining Mechanical Equipment; Repairing and Maintaining Electronic Equipment; Handling and Moving Objects. *Interacting with Others:* Communicating with Other Workers; Performing Administrative Activities; Coordinating the Work and Activities of Others. **Physical Work Conditions—**Hazardous Equipment; Kneeling, Crouching, or Crawling; Common Protective or Safety Attire; Cramped Work Space or Awkward Positions; High Places. **Other Job Characteristics—**Consequence of Error; Importance of Being Exact or Accurate; Degree of Automation.

Experience—Job Zone 4. A minimum of two to four years of work-related skill, knowledge, or experience is needed. **Job Preparation:** SVP 7.0 to less than 8.0—two years to less than 10 years. **Knowledge—**Mechanical; Building and Construction; Engineering and Technology; Design; Physics. **Instructional Programs—**Agricultural Mechanics and Equipment/Machine Technology; Aircraft Powerplant Technology/Technician; Airframe Mechanics and Aircraft Maintenance Technology/Technician.

Related DOT Jobs—621.261-022 Experimental Aircraft Mechanic; 621.281-014 Airframe-and-Power-Plant Mechanic; 621.281-018 Airframe-and-Power-Plant-Mechanic Apprentice.

49-3011.02 Aircraft Engine Specialists

- **Education/Training Required: Postsecondary vocational training**
- **Employed: No data available.**
- **Annual Earnings: $41,990**
- **Growth: 16.7%**
- **Annual Job Openings: 11,000**

Repair and maintain the operating condition of aircraft engines. Includes helicopter engine mechanics.

Replaces or repairs worn, defective, or damaged components, using hand tools, gauges, and testing equipment. Disassembles and inspects engine parts, such as turbine blades and cylinders, for wear, warping, cracks, and leaks. Reassembles engine and installs engine in aircraft. Listens to operating engine to detect and diagnose malfunctions, such as sticking or burned valves. Tests engine operation, using test equipment such as ignition analyzer, compression checker, distributor timer, and ammeter to identify malfunction. Removes engine from aircraft, using hoist or forklift truck. Services and maintains aircraft and related apparatus by performing activities such as flushing crankcase, cleaning screens, and lubricating moving parts. Reads and interprets manufacturers' maintenance manuals, service bulletins, and other specifications to determine feasibility and methods of repair. Adjusts, repairs, or replaces electrical wiring system and aircraft accessories. Services, repairs, and rebuilds aircraft structures, such as wings, fuselage, rigging, and surface and hydraulic controls, using hand or power tools and equipment.

GOE INFORMATION—Interest Area: 05. Mechanics, Installers, and Repairers. **Work Group:** 05.03. Mechanical Work. **Personality Type—**Realistic. Realistic occupations frequently involve work activities that include practical, hands-on problems and solutions. They often deal with plants, animals, and real-world materials like wood, tools, and machinery. Many of the occupations require working outside and do not involve a lot of paperwork or working closely with others. **Work Values—**Compensation; Moral Values; Ability Utilization; Security; Company Policies and Practices. **Skills—**Repairing; Installation; Troubleshooting; Operation Monitoring; Quality Control Analysis; Equipment Selection; Judgment and Decision Making; Systems Analysis. **Abilities—***Cognitive:* Inductive Reasoning; Written Comprehension; Flexibility of Closure; Speed of Closure; Problem Sensitivity. *Psychomotor:* Multilimb Coordination; Control Precision; Manual Dexterity; Finger Dexterity; Wrist-Finger Speed. *Physical:* Extent Flexibility; Static Strength; Explosive Strength; Dynamic Strength; Dynamic Flexibility. *Sensory:* Hearing Sensitivity; Sound Localization; Auditory Attention; Depth Perception; Night Vision. **General Work Activities—***Information Input:* Getting Information; Inspecting Equipment, Structures, or Materials; Monitoring Processes, Materials, or Surroundings. *Mental Process:* Updating and Using Relevant Knowledge; Evaluating Information Against Standards; Analyzing Data or Information. *Work Output:* Repairing and Maintaining Mechanical Equipment; Handling and Moving Objects; Performing General Physical Activities. *Interacting with Others:* Communicating with Other Workers; Coaching and Developing Others; Teaching Others. **Physical Work Conditions—**Hazardous Equipment; Hazardous Conditions; Minor Burns, Cuts, Bites, or Stings; High Places; Cramped Work Space or Awkward Positions. **Other Job Characteristics—**Consequence of Error; Importance of Being Exact or Accurate; Degree of Automation.

Experience—Job Zone 4. A minimum of two to four years of work-related skill, knowledge, or experience is needed. **Job Preparation:** SVP 7.0 to less than 8.0—two years to less than 10 years. **Knowledge—**Mechanical; Engineering and Technology; Physics; Building and Construction; Computers and Electronics. **Instructional Programs—**Agricultural Mechanics and Equipment/Machine Technology; Aircraft Powerplant Technology/Technician.

Related DOT Jobs—621.281-014 Airframe-and-Power-Plant Mechanic; 621.281-030 Rocket-Engine-Component Mechanic; 825.281-038 Experimental-Rocket-Sled Mechanic.

49-3011.03 Aircraft Body and Bonded Structure Repairers

- **Education/Training Required: Postsecondary vocational training**
- **Employed: No data available.**
- **Annual Earnings: $41,990**
- **Growth: 16.7%**
- **Annual Job Openings: 11,000**

Repair body or structure of aircraft according to specifications.

Reinstalls repaired or replacement parts for subsequent riveting or welding, using clamps and wrenches. Repairs or fabricates defective section or part, using metal fabricating machines, saws, brakes, shears, and grinders. Trims and shapes replacement section to specified size and fits and secures section in place, using adhesives, hand tools, and power tools. Reads work orders, blueprints, and specifications or examines sample or damaged part or structure to determine repair or fabrication procedures and sequence of operations. Locates and marks dimension and reference lines on defective or replacement part, using templates, scribes, compass, and steel rule. Removes or cuts out defective part or drills holes to gain access to internal defect or damage, using drill and punch. Communicates with other workers to fit and align heavy parts or expedite processing of repair parts. Cleans, strips, primes, and sands structural surfaces and materials prior to bonding. Cures bonded structure, using portable or stationary curing equipment. Spreads plastic film over area to be repaired to prevent damage to surrounding area.

GOE INFORMATION—Interest Area: 05. Mechanics, Installers, and Repairers. **Work Group:** 05.03. Mechanical Work. **Personality Type—**Realistic. Realistic occupations frequently involve work activities that include practical, hands-on problems and solutions. They often deal with plants, animals, and real-world materials like wood, tools, and machinery. Many of the occupations require working outside and do not involve a lot of paperwork or working closely with others. **Work Values—**Moral Values; Compensation; Security; Supervision, Technical; Variety. **Skills—**Repairing; Installation; Equipment Selection; Operation and Control. **Abilities—***Cognitive:* Information Ordering; Visualization; Spatial Orientation; Inductive Reasoning; Memorization. *Psychomotor:* Finger Dexterity; Wrist-Finger Speed; Manual Dexterity; Speed of Limb Movement; Rate Control. *Physical:* Extent Flexibility; Gross Body Equilibrium; Explosive Strength; Gross Body Coordination; Dynamic Flexibility. *Sensory:* Depth Perception; Visual Color Discrimination; Far Vision; Peripheral Vision; Hearing Sensitivity. **General Work Activities—***Information Input:* Inspecting Equipment, Structures, or Materials; Monitoring Processes, Materials, or Surroundings; Identifying Objects, Actions, and Events. *Mental Process:* Updating and Using Relevant Knowledge; Judging Qualities of Things, Services, or Other People's Work; Evaluating Information Against Standards. *Work Output:* Handling and Moving Objects; Repairing and Maintaining Mechanical Equipment; Performing General Physical Activities. *Interacting with Others:* Communicating with Other Workers; Coordinating the Work and Activities of Others; Establishing and Maintaining Relationships. **Physical Work Conditions—**Hazardous Equipment; Climbing Ladders, Scaffolds, Poles, etc.; Cramped Work Space or Awkward Positions; Using Hands on Objects, Tools, or Controls; Kneeling, Crouching, or Crawling. **Other Job Characteristics—**Degree of Automation; Consequence of Error; Importance of Being Exact or Accurate.

Experience—Job Zone 3. Previous work-related skill, knowledge, or experience is required. **Job Preparation:** SVP 6.0 to less than 7.0—more than one year and less than four years. **Knowledge—**Mechanical; Building and Construction; Design; Production and Processing; Engineering and Technology. **Instructional Programs—**Agricultural Mechanics and Equipment/Machine Technology; Airframe Mechanics and Aircraft Maintenance Technology/Technician.

Related DOT Jobs—807.261-010 Aircraft Body Repairer; 807.381-014 Bonded Structures Repairer.

49-3021.00 Automotive Body and Related Repairers

- **Education/Training Required: Long-term on-the-job training**
- **Employed: 198,955**
- **Annual Earnings: $32,490**
- **Growth: 10.2%**
- **Annual Job Openings: 18,000**

Repair and refinish automotive vehicle bodies and straighten vehicle frames.

Fill small dents that cannot be worked out with plastic or solder. Apply heat to plastic panels, using hot-air welding guns or immersion in hot water, and press the softened panels back into shape by hand. Chain or clamp frames and sections to alignment machines that use hydraulic pressure to align damaged components. File, grind, sand, and smooth filled or repaired surfaces, using power tools and hand tools. Fit and secure windows, vinyl roofs, and metal trim to vehicle bodies, using caulking guns, adhesive brushes, and mallets. Fit and weld replacement parts into place, using wrenches and welding equipment, and grind down welds to smooth them, using power grinders and other tools. Inspect repaired vehicles for dimensional accuracy and test drive them to ensure proper alignment and handling. Position dolly blocks against surfaces of dented areas and beat opposite surfaces to remove dents, using hammers. Read specifications or confer with customers in order to determine the desired custom modifications for altering the appearance of vehicles. Remove damaged panels and identify the family and properties of the plastic used on a vehicle. Remove damaged sections of vehicles, using metal-cutting guns, air grinders, and wrenches, and install replacement parts, using wrenches or welding equipment. Remove small pits and dimples in body metal using pick hammers and punches. Remove upholstery, accessories, electrical window-and-seat-operating equipment, and trim in order to gain access to vehicle bodies and fenders. Review damage reports, prepare or review repair cost estimates, and plan work to be performed. Sand body areas to be painted and cover bumpers, windows, and trim with masking tape or paper to protect them from the paint. Adjust or align headlights, wheels, and brake systems. Clean work areas, using air hoses, in order to remove damaged material and discarded fiberglass strips used in repair procedures. Cut and tape plastic separating film to outside repair areas in order to avoid damaging surrounding surfaces during repair procedure and remove tape and wash surfaces after repairs are complete. Cut openings in vehicle bodies for the installation of customized windows, using templates and power shears or chisels. Follow supervisors' instructions as to which parts to restore or replace and how much time the job should take. Measure and mark vinyl material and cut material to size for roof installation, using rules, straightedges, and hand shears. Mix polyester resins and hardeners to be used in restoring damaged areas. Prime and paint repaired surfaces, using paint spray guns and motorized sanders. Replace damaged glass on vehicles. Soak fiberglass matting in resin mixtures and apply layers of matting over repair areas to specified thicknesses.

GOE INFORMATION—Interest Area: 05. Mechanics, Installers, and Repairers. **Work Group:** 05.03. Mechanical Work. **Personality Type—**Realistic. Realistic occupations frequently involve work activities that include practical, hands-on problems and solutions. They often deal with plants, animals, and real-world materials like wood, tools, and machinery. Many of the occupations require working outside and do not involve a lot of paperwork or working closely with others. **Work Values—**Independence; Variety; Compensation; Moral Values; Ability Utilization. **Skills—**Repairing; Installation; Technology Design; Quality Control Analysis; Operation Monitoring; Troubleshooting; Operation and Control.

Abilities—*Cognitive:* Visualization; Selective Attention; Information Ordering; Spatial Orientation; Fluency of Ideas. *Psychomotor:* Speed of Limb Movement; Control Precision; Manual Dexterity; Finger Dexterity; Arm-Hand Steadiness. *Physical:* Extent Flexibility; Static Strength; Trunk Strength; Dynamic Strength; Explosive Strength. *Sensory:* Visual Color Discrimination; Hearing Sensitivity; Auditory Attention; Sound Localization; Night Vision. **General Work Activities—***Information Input:* Getting Information; Inspecting Equipment, Structures, or Materials; Monitoring Processes, Materials, or Surroundings. *Mental Process:* Updating and Using Relevant Knowledge; Judging Qualities of Things, Services, or Other People's Work; Evaluating Information Against Standards. *Work Output:* Handling and Moving Objects; Performing General Physical Activities; Controlling Machines and Processes. *Interacting with Others:* Communicating with Persons Outside Organization; Communicating with Other Workers; Performing for or Working with the Public. **Physical Work Conditions—**Cramped Work Space or Awkward Positions; Distracting Sounds and Noise Levels; Kneeling, Crouching, or Crawling; Hazardous Equipment; Common Protective or Safety Attire. **Other Job Characteristics—**Pace Determined by Speed of Equipment; Importance of Being Exact or Accurate; Consequence of Error.

Experience—Job Zone 3. Previous work-related skill, knowledge, or experience is required. **Job Preparation:** SVP 6.0 to less than 7.0—more than one year and less than four years. **Knowledge—**Mechanical; Engineering and Technology; Building and Construction; Foreign Language; Fine Arts. **Instructional Programs—**Autobody/Collision and Repair Technology/Technician.

Related DOT Jobs—807.361-010 Automobile-Body Customizer; 807.381-010 Automobile-Body Repairer; 807.381-030 Auto-Body Repairer, Fiberglass.

49-3022.00 Automotive Glass Installers and Repairers

- Education/Training Required: **Long-term on-the-job training**
- Employed: 21,955
- Annual Earnings: $27,160
- Growth: 10.5%
- Annual Job Openings: 2,000

Replace or repair broken windshields and window glass in motor vehicles.

Allow all glass parts installed with urethane ample time to cure, taking temperature and humidity into account. Apply a bead of urethane around the perimeter of each pinchweld and dress the remaining urethane on the pinchwelds so that it is of uniform level and thickness all the way around. Check for moisture or contamination in damaged areas, dry out any moisture prior to making repairs, and keep damaged areas dry until repairs are complete. Cool or warm glass in the event of temperature extremes. Hold cut or uneven edges of glass against automated abrasive belts in order to shape or smooth edges. Install new foam dams on pinchwelds if required. Install replacement glass in vehicles after old glass has been removed and all necessary preparations have been made. Install rubber-channeling strips around edges of glass or frames in order to weatherproof windows or to prevent rattling. Install, repair, and replace safety glass and related materials, such as backglass heating-elements, on vehicles and equipment. Obtain windshields or windows for specific automobile makes and models from stock and examine them for defects prior to installation. Prime all scratches on pinchwelds with primer and allow primed scratches to dry. Remove all dirt, foreign matter, and loose glass from damaged areas and then apply primer along windshield or window edges and allow it to dry. Remove all moldings, clips, windshield wipers, screws, bolts, and inside A-pillar moldings and then lower headliners

prior to beginning installation or repair work. Remove broken or damaged glass windshields or window-glass from motor vehicles, using hand tools to remove screws from frames holding glass. Replace all moldings, clips, windshield wipers, and any other parts that were removed prior to glass replacement or repair. Replace or adjust motorized or manual window-raising mechanisms. Select appropriate tools, safety equipment, and parts according to job requirements. Cut flat safety glass according to specified patterns or perform precision pattern-making and glass-cutting to custom-fit replacement windows.

GOE INFORMATION—Interest Area: 05. Mechanics, Installers, and Repairers. **Work Group:** 05.03. Mechanical Work. **Personality Type—**Realistic. Realistic occupations frequently involve work activities that include practical, hands-on problems and solutions. They often deal with plants, animals, and real-world materials like wood, tools, and machinery. Many of the occupations require working outside and do not involve a lot of paperwork or working closely with others. **Work Values—**Independence; Moral Values; Security; Supervision, Technical; Compensation. **Skills—**Installation; Repairing. **Abilities—***Cognitive:* Visualization. *Psychomotor:* Arm-Hand Steadiness; Multilimb Coordination; Finger Dexterity; Manual Dexterity; Control Precision. *Physical:* Static Strength; Extent Flexibility; Stamina; Gross Body Coordination; Gross Body Equilibrium. *Sensory:* Night Vision; Glare Sensitivity. **General Work Activities—***Information Input:* Inspecting Equipment, Structures, or Materials; Getting Information; Identifying Objects, Actions, and Events. *Mental Process:* Judging Qualities of Things, Services, or Other People's Work; Evaluating Information Against Standards; Updating and Using Relevant Knowledge. *Work Output:* Handling and Moving Objects; Performing General Physical Activities; Repairing and Maintaining Mechanical Equipment. *Interacting with Others:* Communicating with Persons Outside Organization; Communicating with Other Workers; Performing for or Working with the Public. **Physical Work Conditions—**Common Protective or Safety Attire; Minor Burns, Cuts, Bites, or Stings; Keeping or Regaining Balance; Outdoors; Using Hands on Objects, Tools, or Controls. **Other Job Characteristics—**Importance of Being Exact or Accurate; Pace Determined by Speed of Equipment; Importance of Repeating Same Tasks.

Experience—Job Zone 2. Some previous work-related skill, knowledge, or experience may be helpful, but usually is not needed. **Job Preparation:** SVP 4.0 to less than 6.0—six months to less than two years. **Knowledge—**Mechanical; Engineering and Technology; Fine Arts; Building and Construction; Foreign Language. **Instructional Programs—**Autobody/Collision and Repair Technology/Technician.

Related DOT Jobs—865.684-010 Glass Installer.

49-3023.00 Automotive Service Technicians and Mechanics

- Education/Training Required: **Postsecondary vocational training**
- Employed: 839,689
- Annual Earnings: $29,510
- Growth: 18.0%
- Annual Job Openings: 104,000

Diagnose, adjust, repair, or overhaul automotive vehicles.

No task data available.

GOE INFORMATION—Interest Area: 05. Mechanics, Installers, and Repairers. **Work Group:** 05.03. Mechanical Work. **Note:** The Department of Labor has not collected some data for this job, so it has fewer details than the other descriptions.

Instructional Programs—Alternative Fuel Vehicle Technology/Technician; Automobile/Automotive Mechanics Technology/Technician; Automotive Engineering Technology/Technician; Medium/Heavy Vehicle and Truck Technology/Technician; Vehicle Emissions Inspection and Maintenance Technology/Technician.

Related DOT Jobs—619.380-018 Spring Repairer, Hand; 620.261-010 Automobile Mechanic; 620.261-012 Automobile-Mechanic Apprentice; 620.261-030 Automobile-Service-Station Mechanic; 620.261-034 Automotive-Cooling-System Diagnostic Technician; 620.281-010 Air-Conditioning Mechanic; 620.281-026 Brake Repairer; 620.281-034 Carburetor Mechanic; 620.281-038 Front-End Mechanic; 620.281-062 Transmission Mechanic; 620.281-066 Tune-Up Mechanic; 620.281-070 Vehicle-Fuel-Systems Converter; 620.364-010 Squeak, Rattle, and Leak Repairer; 620.381-010 Automobile-Radiator Mechanic; 620.381-022 Repairer, Heavy; 620.682-010 Brake-Drum-Lathe Operator; 620.684-018 Brake Adjuster; 620.684-022 Clutch Rebuilder; 625.281-022 Fuel-Injection Servicer; 706.381-046 Wheelwright; others.

49-3023.01 Automotive Master Mechanics

- **Education/Training Required: Postsecondary vocational training**
- **Employed: No data available.**
- **Annual Earnings: $29,510**
- **Growth: 18.0%**
- **Annual Job Openings: 104,000**

Repair automobiles, trucks, buses, and other vehicles. Master mechanics repair virtually any part on the vehicle or specialize in the transmission system.

Align vehicles' front ends. Confer with customers to obtain descriptions of vehicle problems and to discuss work to be performed and future repair requirements. Disassemble units and inspect parts for wear, using micrometers, calipers, and gauges. Examine vehicles to determine extent of damage or malfunctions. Install and repair accessories such as radios, heaters, mirrors, and windshield wipers. Overhaul or replace carburetors, blowers, generators, distributors, starters, and pumps. Perform routine and scheduled maintenance services such as oil changes, lubrications, and tune-ups. Plan work procedures, using charts, technical manuals, and experience. Rebuild parts such as crankshafts and cylinder blocks. Repair and service air conditioning, heating, engine-cooling, and electrical systems. Repair damaged automobile bodies. Repair manual and automatic transmissions. Repair or replace parts such as pistons, rods, gears, valves, and bearings. Repair or replace shock absorbers. Repair radiator leaks. Repair, reline, replace, and adjust brakes. Replace and adjust headlights. Rewire ignition systems, lights, and instrument panels. Tear down, repair, and rebuild faulty assemblies such as power systems, steering systems, and linkages. Test and adjust repaired systems to meet manufacturers' performance specifications. Test drive vehicles and test components and systems, using equipment such as infrared engine analyzers, compression gauges, and computerized diagnostic devices. Follow checklists to ensure all important parts are examined, including belts, hoses, steering systems, spark plugs, brake and fuel systems, wheel bearings, and other potentially troublesome areas. Review work orders and discuss work with supervisors.

GOE INFORMATION—**Interest Area:** 05. Mechanics, Installers, and Repairers. **Work Group:** 05.03. Mechanical Work. **Personality Type**—Realistic. Realistic occupations frequently involve work activities that include practical, hands-on problems and solutions. They often deal with plants, animals, and real-world materials like wood, tools, and machinery. Many

of the occupations require working outside and do not involve a lot of paperwork or working closely with others. **Work Values**—Compensation; Independence; Ability Utilization; Responsibility; Variety. **Skills**—Repairing; Troubleshooting; Installation; Operation Monitoring; Quality Control Analysis; Operation and Control; Technology Design; Equipment Selection. **Abilities**—*Cognitive:* Visualization; Information Ordering; Originality; Spatial Orientation; Inductive Reasoning. *Psychomotor:* Reaction Time; Response Orientation; Control Precision; Wrist-Finger Speed; Rate Control. *Physical:* Extent Flexibility; Static Strength; Dynamic Flexibility; Explosive Strength; Trunk Strength. *Sensory:* Hearing Sensitivity; Visual Color Discrimination; Sound Localization; Auditory Attention; Depth Perception. **General Work Activities**—*Information Input:* Inspecting Equipment, Structures, or Materials; Monitoring Processes, Materials, or Surroundings; Estimating Needed Characteristics. *Mental Process:* Updating and Using Relevant Knowledge; Evaluating Information Against Standards; Making Decisions and Solving Problems. *Work Output:* Repairing and Maintaining Mechanical Equipment; Handling and Moving Objects; Performing General Physical Activities. *Interacting with Others:* Communicating with Persons Outside Organization; Establishing and Maintaining Relationships; Communicating with Other Workers. **Physical Work Conditions**—Hazardous Equipment; Cramped Work Space or Awkward Positions; Common Protective or Safety Attire; Kneeling, Crouching, or Crawling; Extremely Bright or Inadequate Lighting. **Other Job Characteristics**—Consequence of Error; Importance of Being Exact or Accurate; Importance of Repeating Same Tasks.

Experience—Job Zone 3. Previous work-related skill, knowledge, or experience is required. **Job Preparation:** SVP 6.0 to less than 7.0—more than one year and less than four years. **Knowledge**—Mechanical; Computers and Electronics; Engineering and Technology; Customer and Personal Service; Physics. **Instructional Programs**—Alternative Fuel Vehicle Technology/Technician; Automobile/Automotive Mechanics Technology/Technician; Automotive Engineering Technology/Technician; Medium/Heavy Vehicle and Truck Technology/Technician; Vehicle Emissions Inspection and Maintenance Technology/Technician.

Related DOT Jobs—620.261-010 Automobile Mechanic; 620.261-012 Automobile-Mechanic Apprentice; 620.281-062 Transmission Mechanic; 620.364-010 Squeak, Rattle, and Leak Repairer; 620.381-022 Repairer, Heavy.

49-3023.02 Automotive Specialty Technicians

- **Education/Training Required: Postsecondary vocational training**
- **Employed: No data available.**
- **Annual Earnings: $29,510**
- **Growth: 18.0%**
- **Annual Job Openings: 104,000**

Repair only one system or component on a vehicle, such as brakes, suspension, or radiator.

Align and repair wheels, axles, frames, torsion bars, and steering mechanisms of automobiles, using special alignment equipment and wheel-balancing machines. Examine vehicles, compile estimates of repair costs, and secure customers' approval to perform repairs. Install and repair air conditioners; service components such as compressors, condensers, and controls. Rebuild, repair, and test automotive fuel injection units. Remove and replace defective mufflers and tailpipes. Repair and rebuild clutch systems. Repair and replace automobile leaf springs. Repair and replace defective ball joint suspensions, brake shoes, and wheel bearings. Repair, overhaul, and adjust automobile brake systems. Repair, replace, and adjust defective carburetor parts and gasoline filters. Test electronic computer components in automobiles to ensure that they are working properly. Tune automobile engines to ensure proper and efficient functioning. Use electronic test equipment to locate and correct malfunctions in fuel, ignition, and emissions control systems. Convert vehicle fuel systems from gasoline to butane gas operations and repair and service operating butane fuel units. Inspect and test new vehicles for damage and then record findings so that necessary repairs can be made. Repair, install, and adjust hydraulic and electromagnetic automatic lift mechanisms used to raise and lower automobile windows, seats, and tops.

GOE INFORMATION—Interest Area: 05. Mechanics, Installers, and Repairers. **Work Group:** 05.03. Mechanical Work. **Personality Type—**Realistic. Realistic occupations frequently involve work activities that include practical, hands-on problems and solutions. They often deal with plants, animals, and real-world materials like wood, tools, and machinery. Many of the occupations require working outside and do not involve a lot of paperwork or working closely with others. **Work Values—**Responsibility; Independence; Ability Utilization; Compensation; Achievement. **Skills—**Repairing; Installation; Troubleshooting; Operation Monitoring; Operation and Control; Quality Control Analysis. **Abilities—***Cognitive:* Visualization; Information Ordering; Perceptual Speed; Flexibility of Closure; Spatial Orientation. *Psychomotor:* Reaction Time; Manual Dexterity; Multilimb Coordination; Rate Control; Response Orientation. *Physical:* Extent Flexibility; Explosive Strength; Static Strength; Trunk Strength; Dynamic Flexibility. *Sensory:* Hearing Sensitivity; Sound Localization; Auditory Attention; Visual Color Discrimination; Peripheral Vision. **General Work Activities—***Information Input:* Inspecting Equipment, Structures, or Materials; Getting Information; Monitoring Processes, Materials, or Surroundings. *Mental Process:* Updating and Using Relevant Knowledge; Evaluating Information Against Standards; Judging Qualities of Things, Services, or Other People's Work. *Work Output:* Repairing and Maintaining Mechanical Equipment; Handling and Moving Objects; Performing General Physical Activities. *Interacting with Others:* Communicating with Persons Outside Organization; Establishing and Maintaining Relationships; Communicating with Other Workers. **Physical Work Conditions—**Common Protective or Safety Attire; Contaminants; Cramped Work Space or Awkward Positions; Kneeling, Crouching, or Crawling; Distracting Sounds and Noise Levels. **Other Job Characteristics—**Consequence of Error; Pace Determined by Speed of Equipment; Importance of Repeating Same Tasks.

Experience—Job Zone 2. Some previous work-related skill, knowledge, or experience may be helpful, but usually is not needed. **Job Preparation:** SVP 4.0 to less than 6.0—six months to less than two years. **Knowledge—**Mechanical; Computers and Electronics; Design; Physics; Engineering and Technology. **Instructional Programs—**Alternative Fuel Vehicle Technology/Technician; Automobile/Automotive Mechanics Technology/Technician; Automotive Engineering Technology/Technician; Medium/Heavy Vehicle and Truck Technology/Technician; Vehicle Emissions Inspection and Maintenance Technology/Technician.

Related DOT Jobs—619.380-018 Spring Repairer, Hand; 620.261-030 Automobile-Service-Station Mechanic; 620.261-034 Automotive-Cooling-System Diagnostic Technician; 620.281-010 Air-Conditioning Mechanic; 620.281-026 Brake Repairer; 620.281-034 Carburetor Mechanic; 620.281-038 Front-End Mechanic; 620.281-066 Tune-Up Mechanic; 620.281-070 Vehicle-Fuel-Systems Converter; 620.381-010 Automobile-Radiator Mechanic; 620.682-010 Brake-Drum-Lathe Operator; 620.684-018 Brake Adjuster; 620.684-022 Clutch Rebuilder; 625.281-022 Fuel-Injection Servicer; 706.381-046 Wheelwright; 806.361-026 New-Car Get-Ready Mechanic; 807.664-010 Muffler Installer; 807.684-022 Floor Service Worker, Spring; 825.381-014 Automatic-Window-Seat-and-Top-Lift Repairer.

49-3031.00 Bus and Truck Mechanics and Diesel Engine Specialists

- **Education/Training Required: Postsecondary vocational training**
- **Employed: 285,208**
- **Annual Earnings: $33,570**
- **Growth: 14.2%**
- **Annual Job Openings: 20,000**

Diagnose, adjust, repair, or overhaul trucks, buses, and all types of diesel engines. Includes mechanics working primarily with automobile diesel engines.

Adjust and reline brakes, align wheels, tighten bolts and screws, and reassemble equipment. Align front ends and suspension systems. Attach test instruments to equipment and read dials and gauges in order to diagnose malfunctions. Disassemble and overhaul internal combustion engines, pumps, generators, transmissions, clutches, and differential units. Examine and adjust protective guards, loose bolts, and specified safety devices. Inspect brake systems, steering mechanisms, wheel bearings, and other important parts to ensure that they are in proper operating condition. Inspect, repair, and maintain automotive and mechanical equipment and machinery such as pumps and compressors. Inspect, test, and listen to defective equipment to diagnose malfunctions, using test instruments such as handheld computers, motor analyzers, chassis charts, and pressure gauges. Operate valve-grinding machines to grind and reset valves. Perform routine maintenance such as changing oil, checking batteries, and lubricating equipment and machinery. Raise trucks, buses, and heavy parts or equipment, using hydraulic jacks or hoists. Rebuild gas and/or diesel engines. Recondition and replace parts, pistons, bearings, gears, and valves. Repair and adjust seats, doors, and windows and install and repair accessories. Rewire ignition systems, lights, and instrument panels. Inspect and verify dimensions and clearances of parts to ensure conformance to factory specifications. Specialize in repairing and maintaining parts of the engine, such as fuel injection systems. Test drive trucks and buses to diagnose malfunctions or to ensure that they are working properly. Use hand tools, such as screwdrivers, pliers, wrenches, pressure gauges, and precision instruments, as well as power tools, such as pneumatic wrenches, lathes, welding equipment, and jacks and hoists.

GOE INFORMATION—Interest Area: 05. Mechanics, Installers, and Repairers. **Work Group:** 05.03. Mechanical Work. **Personality Type—**Realistic. Realistic occupations frequently involve work activities that include practical, hands-on problems and solutions. They often deal with plants, animals, and real-world materials like wood, tools, and machinery. Many of the occupations require working outside and do not involve a lot of paperwork or working closely with others. **Work Values—**Independence; Variety; Compensation; Responsibility; Achievement. **Skills—**Repairing; Installation; Troubleshooting; Quality Control Analysis; Operation Monitoring; Operation and Control; Equipment Selection. **Abilities—***Cognitive:* Problem Sensitivity; Inductive Reasoning; Deductive Reasoning; Information Ordering. *Psychomotor:* Control Precision; Finger Dexterity; Rate Control; Reaction Time; Arm-Hand Steadiness. *Physical:* Static Strength; Dynamic Strength; Extent Flexibility; Trunk Strength; Explosive Strength. *Sensory:* Hearing Sensitivity; Sound Localization. **General Work Activities—***Information Input:* Inspecting Equipment, Structures, or Materials; Getting Information; Monitoring Processes, Materials, or Surroundings. *Mental Process:* Updating and Using Relevant Knowledge; Evaluating Information Against Standards; Judging Qualities of Things, Services, or Other People's Work. *Work Output:* Handling and Moving Objects; Repairing and Maintaining Mechanical Equipment; Performing

General Physical Activities. *Interacting with Others:* Performing Administrative Activities; Communicating with Other Workers; Communicating with Persons Outside Organization. **Physical Work Conditions**—Kneeling, Crouching, or Crawling; Hazardous Equipment; Cramped Work Space or Awkward Positions; Very Hot or Cold; Using Hands on Objects, Tools, or Controls. **Other Job Characteristics**—Degree of Automation; Importance of Being Exact or Accurate; Pace Determined by Speed of Equipment.

Experience—Job Zone 3. Previous work-related skill, knowledge, or experience is required. **Job Preparation:** SVP 6.0 to less than 7.0—more than one year and less than four years. **Knowledge**—Mechanical; Engineering and Technology; Physics; Design; Public Safety and Security. **Instructional Programs**—Diesel Mechanics Technology/Technician; Medium/Heavy Vehicle and Truck Technology/Technician.

Related DOT Jobs—620.281-046 Maintenance Mechanic; 620.281-050 Mechanic, Industrial Truck; 620.281-058 Tractor Mechanic; 625.281-010 Diesel Mechanic; 625.281-014 Diesel-Mechanic Apprentice; 629.381-014 Oil-Field Equipment Mechanic.

49-3041.00 Farm Equipment Mechanics

- **Education/Training Required: Postsecondary vocational training**
- **Employed: 41,172**
- **Annual Earnings: $26,360**
- **Growth: 0.9%**
- **Annual Job Openings: 3,000**

Diagnose, adjust, repair, or overhaul farm machinery and vehicles, such as tractors, harvesters, dairy equipment, and irrigation systems.

Repairs or replaces defective parts, using hand tools, milling and woodworking machines, lathes, welding equipment, grinders, or saws. Reassembles, adjusts, and lubricates machines and equipment, using hand tools. Dismantles defective machines, using hand tools. Installs and repairs agricultural plumbing systems. Installs and maintains self-propelled irrigation system, using truck-mounted crane, wrenches, tube cutter, and pipe threader. Tests and replaces electrical components and wiring, using test meter, soldering equipment, and wire strippers. Examines and listens to machines, motors, gas and diesel engines, and equipment to detect malfunctioning. Reads inspection reports and examines equipment to determine type and extent of defect. Fabricates new metal parts, using drill press, engine lathe, and other machine tools. Drives truck to haul tools and equipment to work site. Records type and cause of defect on agricultural equipment.

GOE INFORMATION—Interest Area: 05. Mechanics, Installers, and Repairers. **Work Group:** 05.03. Mechanical Work. **Personality Type**—Realistic. Realistic occupations frequently involve work activities that include practical, hands-on problems and solutions. They often deal with plants, animals, and real-world materials like wood, tools, and machinery. Many of the occupations require working outside and do not involve a lot of paperwork or working closely with others. **Work Values**—Moral Values; Independence; Variety; Responsibility; Ability Utilization. **Skills**—Installation; Repairing; Operation Monitoring; Troubleshooting; Technology Design; Quality Control Analysis; Operation and Control; Equipment Selection. **Abilities**—*Cognitive:* Visualization; Speed of Closure; Inductive Reasoning; Flexibility of Closure; Deductive Reasoning. *Psychomotor:* Control Precision; Multilimb Coordination; Arm-Hand Steadiness; Response Orientation; Finger Dexterity. *Physical:* Extent Flexibility; Explosive Strength; Static Strength; Stamina; Dynamic Strength. *Sensory:* Hearing Sensitivity; Visual Color Discrimination; Sound Localization; Auditory Attention; Night Vision. **General Work Activities**—*Information Input:* Monitoring Processes, Materials, or Surroundings; Inspecting Equipment, Structures, or Materials; Getting Information. *Mental Process:* Updating and Using Relevant Knowledge; Evaluating Information Against Standards; Making Decisions and Solving Problems. *Work Output:* Repairing and Maintaining Mechanical Equipment; Handling and Moving Objects; Performing General Physical Activities. *Interacting with Others:* Communicating with Other Workers; Performing for or Working with the Public; Providing Consultation and Advice to Others. **Physical Work Conditions**—Hazardous Equipment; Outdoors; Cramped Work Space or Awkward Positions; Minor Burns, Cuts, Bites, or Stings; Using Hands on Objects, Tools, or Controls. **Other Job Characteristics**—Consequence of Error; Degree of Automation; Pace Determined by Speed of Equipment.

Experience—Job Zone 3. Previous work-related skill, knowledge, or experience is required. **Job Preparation:** SVP 6.0 to less than 7.0—more than one year and less than four years. **Knowledge**—Mechanical; Engineering and Technology; Computers and Electronics; Physics; Chemistry. **Instructional Programs**—Agricultural Mechanics and Equipment/Machine Technology; Agricultural Mechanization, General; Agricultural Mechanization, Other; Agricultural Power Machinery Operation.

Related DOT Jobs—624.281-010 Farm-Equipment Mechanic I; 624.281-014 Farm-Equipment-Mechanic Apprentice; 624.361-014 Sprinkler-Irrigation-Equipment Mechanic; 624.381-010 Assembly Repairer; 624.381-014 Farm-Equipment Mechanic II; 629.281-018 Dairy-Equipment Repairer; 809.381-018 Milking-System Installer.

49-3042.00 Mobile Heavy Equipment Mechanics, Except Engines

- **Education/Training Required: Postsecondary vocational training**
- **Employed: 130,086**
- **Annual Earnings: $35,190**
- **Growth: 14.0%**
- **Annual Job Openings: 11,000**

Diagnose, adjust, repair, or overhaul mobile mechanical, hydraulic, and pneumatic equipment, such as cranes, bulldozers, graders, and conveyors, used in construction, logging, and surface mining.

Adjust, maintain, and repair or replace subassemblies, such as transmissions and crawler heads, using hand tools, jacks, and cranes. Assemble gear systems and align frames and gears. Clean parts by spraying them with grease solvent or immersing them in tanks of solvent. Clean, lubricate, and perform other routine maintenance work on equipment and vehicles. Diagnose faults or malfunctions to determine required repairs, using engine diagnostic equipment such as computerized test equipment and calibration devices. Dismantle and reassemble heavy equipment, using hoists and hand tools. Examine parts for damage or excessive wear, using micrometers and gauges. Fit bearings to adjust, repair, or overhaul mobile mechanical, hydraulic, and pneumatic equipment. Operate and inspect machines or heavy equipment in order to diagnose defects. Overhaul and test machines or equipment to ensure operating efficiency. Repair and replace damaged or worn parts. Test mechanical products and equipment after repair or assembly to ensure proper performance and compliance with manufacturers' specifications. Weld or solder broken parts and structural members, using electric or gas welders and soldering tools. Direct workers who are assembling or disassembling equipment or cleaning parts. Fabricate needed parts or items from sheet metal. Schedule maintenance for industrial machines and equipment; keep equipment service records. Adjust and maintain industrial machinery, using control and regulating devices. Read and understand operating manuals, blueprints, and technical drawings.

GOE INFORMATION—**Interest Area:** 05. Mechanics, Installers, and Repairers. **Work Group:** 05.03. Mechanical Work. **Personality Type**—Realistic. Realistic occupations frequently involve work activities that include practical, hands-on problems and solutions. They often deal with plants, animals, and real-world materials like wood, tools, and machinery. Many of the occupations require working outside and do not involve a lot of paperwork or working closely with others. **Work Values**—Compensation; Moral Values; Authority; Variety; Ability Utilization. **Skills**—Repairing; Troubleshooting; Operation and Control; Quality Control Analysis; Operation Monitoring; Equipment Selection; Installation. **Abilities**—*Cognitive:* Problem Sensitivity. *Psychomotor:* Multilimb Coordination; Control Precision; Arm-Hand Steadiness; Manual Dexterity; Wrist-Finger Speed. *Physical:* Extent Flexibility; Explosive Strength; Dynamic Strength; Static Strength; Gross Body Coordination. *Sensory:* Hearing Sensitivity; Sound Localization. **General Work Activities**—*Information Input:* Inspecting Equipment, Structures, or Materials; Getting Information; Monitoring Processes, Materials, or Surroundings. *Mental Process:* Updating and Using Relevant Knowledge; Judging Qualities of Things, Services, or Other People's Work; Evaluating Information Against Standards. *Work Output:* Repairing and Maintaining Mechanical Equipment; Controlling Machines and Processes; Performing General Physical Activities. *Interacting with Others:* Communicating with Other Workers; Coordinating the Work and Activities of Others; Establishing and Maintaining Relationships. **Physical Work Conditions**—Cramped Work Space or Awkward Positions; Hazardous Equipment; Kneeling, Crouching, or Crawling; Outdoors; Bending or Twisting the Body. **Other Job Characteristics**—Pace Determined by Speed of Equipment; Consequence of Error; Importance of Repeating Same Tasks.

Experience—Job Zone 4. A minimum of two to four years of work-related skill, knowledge, or experience is needed. **Job Preparation:** SVP 7.0 to less than 8.0—two years to less than 10 years. **Knowledge**—Mechanical; Engineering and Technology; Building and Construction; Physics; Chemistry. **Instructional Programs**—Agricultural Mechanics and Equipment/Machine Technology; Heavy Equipment Maintenance Technology/Technician.

Related DOT Jobs—620.261-022 Construction-Equipment Mechanic; 620.281-042 Logging-Equipment Mechanic; 620.381-014 Mechanic, Endless Track Vehicle.

49-3043.00 Rail Car Repairers

- **Education/Training Required: Long-term on-the-job training**
- **Employed: 13,974**
- **Annual Earnings: $38,390**
- **Growth: –7.6%**
- **Annual Job Openings: 1,000**

Diagnose, adjust, repair, or overhaul railroad rolling stock, mine cars, or mass transit rail cars.

Repairs, reassembles, and replaces defective parts, metal sections, or components, using hand tools, torque wrench, power tools, and welding equipment. Examines car roof for wear and damage and repairs defective sections, using roofing material, cement, nails, and waterproof paint. Installs and repairs interior flooring, fixtures, walls, plumbing, steps, and platforms. Inspects components, such as bearings, seals, gaskets, wheels, truck and brake assemblies, air cylinder reservoirs, valves, and coupler assemblies. Aligns car sides for installation of car ends and crossties, using width gauge, turnbuckle, and wrench. Replaces defective wiring and insulation and tightens electrical connections, using hand tools. Disassembles units, such as water pump, control valve, governor, distributor, windshield wiper motor, compressor, and roller bearings. Tests units before and after repairs for operability. Adjusts repaired or replaced units as needed, following diagrams. Repairs window sash frames, attaches weather stripping and channels to frame, and replaces window glass, using hand tools. Measures sections and drills holes to prepare replacement sections for reassembly. Measures diameter of axle wheel seats, using micrometer, and marks dimension on axle for boring of wheels to specified dimensions. Tests electric systems of cars, using ammeter and by operating light and signal switches. Removes locomotive, car mechanical unit, or other component, using pneumatic hoist and jack, pinch bar, hand tools, and cutting torch. Records condition of cars, repairs made, and other repair work to be performed. Cleans units and components, using compressed air blower.

GOE INFORMATION—**Interest Area:** 05. Mechanics, Installers, and Repairers. **Work Group:** 05.03. Mechanical Work. **Personality Type**—Realistic. Realistic occupations frequently involve work activities that include practical, hands-on problems and solutions. They often deal with plants, animals, and real-world materials like wood, tools, and machinery. Many of the occupations require working outside and do not involve a lot of paperwork or working closely with others. **Work Values**—Variety; Moral Values; Independence; Compensation; Ability Utilization. **Skills**—Repairing; Installation; Troubleshooting; Quality Control Analysis; Equipment Selection; Operation Monitoring. **Abilities**—*Cognitive:* Visualization; Inductive Reasoning; Information Ordering; Perceptual Speed; Flexibility of Closure. *Psychomotor:* Multilimb Coordination; Control Precision; Finger Dexterity; Manual Dexterity; Speed of Limb Movement. *Physical:* Extent Flexibility; Static Strength; Explosive Strength; Dynamic Strength; Gross Body Equilibrium. *Sensory:* Depth Perception; Glare Sensitivity; Peripheral Vision; Night Vision; Visual Color Discrimination. **General Work Activities**—*Information Input:* Getting Information; Inspecting Equipment, Structures, or Materials; Monitoring Processes, Materials, or Surroundings. *Mental Process:* Updating and Using Relevant Knowledge; Analyzing Data or Information; Evaluating Information Against Standards. *Work Output:* Repairing and Maintaining Mechanical Equipment; Handling and Moving Objects; Performing General Physical Activities. *Interacting with Others:* Communicating with Other Workers; Establishing and Maintaining Relationships; Assisting and Caring for Others. **Physical Work Conditions**—Outdoors; Hazardous Equipment; Minor Burns, Cuts, Bites, or Stings; Cramped Work Space or Awkward Positions; Distracting Sounds and Noise Levels. **Other Job Characteristics**—Consequence of Error; Importance of Being Exact or Accurate; Degree of Automation.

Experience—Job Zone 3. Previous work-related skill, knowledge, or experience is required. **Job Preparation:** SVP 6.0 to less than 7.0—more than one year and less than four years. **Knowledge**—Mechanical; Building and Construction; Engineering and Technology; Design; Physics. **Instructional Programs**—Heavy Equipment Maintenance Technology/Technician.

Related DOT Jobs—620.381-018 Mechanical-Unit Repairer; 622.381-014 Car Repairer; 622.381-018 Car Repairer, Pullman; 622.381-022 Car-Repairer Apprentice; 622.684-010 Air-Compressor Mechanic; 807.381-026 Streetcar Repairer.

49-3051.00 Motorboat Mechanics

- **Education/Training Required: Long-term on-the-job training**
- **Employed: 25,016**
- **Annual Earnings: $28,200**
- **Growth: 9.0%**
- **Annual Job Openings: 5,000**

Repairs and adjusts electrical and mechanical equipment of gasoline- or diesel-powered inboard or inboard-outboard boat engines.

Tests motor for conformance to specifications and operations while motor is running in tank, using tachometers, monometers, voltmeters, ammeter, and stroboscope. Replaces parts such as gears, magneto points, piston rings, and spark plugs and reassembles engine. Repairs mechanical equipment of engines, such as power-tilt, bilge pumps, or power take-offs. Idles motor and observes thermometer to determine effectiveness of cooling system. Analyzes test results and disassembles and inspects motor for defective parts, using mechanic's hand tools and gauges. Examines propeller and propeller shafts and aligns, repairs, or replaces defective parts. Adjusts generator and replaces faulty wiring, using hand tools and soldering iron. Starts motor and listens to and inspects it for signs of malfunctioning, such as smoke, excessive vibration, misfiring, and missing or broken parts. Adjusts carburetor mixture, electrical point settings, and timing while motor is running in water-filled test tank. Operates machine tools, such as lathes, mills, drills, and grinders, to repair or rework parts, such as cams, rods, crankshaft, and propeller. Sets starter lock and aligns and repairs steering or throttle controls, using gauges, screwdrivers, and wrenches. Mounts motor to boat and operates boat at various speeds on waterway to conduct operational tests. Writes test report to indicate acceptance or reason for rejection of motor.

GOE INFORMATION—Interest Area: 05. Mechanics, Installers, and Repairers. **Work Group:** 05.03. Mechanical Work. **Personality Type**—Realistic. Realistic occupations frequently involve work activities that include practical, hands-on problems and solutions. They often deal with plants, animals, and real-world materials like wood, tools, and machinery. Many of the occupations require working outside and do not involve a lot of paperwork or working closely with others. **Work Values**—Moral Values; Variety; Compensation; Security; Ability Utilization. **Skills**—Repairing; Quality Control Analysis; Troubleshooting; Installation; Operation Monitoring; Operation and Control; Equipment Selection. **Abilities**—*Cognitive:* Deductive Reasoning; Inductive Reasoning; Visualization. *Psychomotor:* Control Precision; Multilimb Coordination; Arm-Hand Steadiness; Manual Dexterity. *Physical:* Static Strength; Dynamic Strength; Extent Flexibility; Gross Body Coordination; Trunk Strength. *Sensory:* Hearing Sensitivity; Sound Localization; Glare Sensitivity; Depth Perception. **General Work Activities**—*Information Input:* Inspecting Equipment, Structures, or Materials; Monitoring Processes, Materials, or Surroundings; Getting Information. *Mental Process:* Updating and Using Relevant Knowledge; Making Decisions and Solving Problems; Organizing, Planning, and Prioritizing. *Work Output:* Repairing and Maintaining Mechanical Equipment; Performing General Physical Activities; Handling and Moving Objects. *Interacting with Others:* Performing Administrative Activities; Communicating with Other Workers; Communicating with Persons Outside Organization. **Physical Work Conditions**—Outdoors; Kneeling, Crouching, or Crawling; Hazardous Conditions; Cramped Work Space or Awkward Positions; Using Hands on Objects, Tools, or Controls. **Other Job Characteristics**—Importance of Being Exact or Accurate; Consequence of Error; Degree of Automation.

Experience—Job Zone 3. Previous work-related skill, knowledge, or experience is required. **Job Preparation:** SVP 6.0 to less than 7.0—more than one year and less than four years. **Knowledge**—Mechanical; Engineering and Technology; Physics; Building and Construction. **Instructional Programs**—Marine Maintenance/Fitter and Ship Repair Technology/Technician; Small Engine Mechanics and Repair Technology/Technician.

Related DOT Jobs—623.261-010 Experimental Mechanic, Outboard Motors; 623.261-014 Outboard-Motor Tester; 623.281-038 Motorboat Mechanic; 623.281-042 Outboard-Motor Mechanic.

49-3052.00 Motorcycle Mechanics

- **Education/Training Required: Long-term on-the-job training**
- **Employed: 14,461**
- **Annual Earnings: $26,400**
- **Growth: 8.6%**
- **Annual Job Openings: 3,000**

Diagnose, adjust, repair, or overhaul motorcycles, scooters, mopeds, dirt bikes, or similar motorized vehicles.

Dismantle engines and repair or replace defective parts, such as magnetos, carburetors, and generators. Remove cylinder heads, grind valves, and scrape off carbon and replace defective valves, pistons, cylinders, and rings, using hand tools and power tools. Hammer out dents and bends in frames, weld tears and breaks; then reassemble frames and reinstall engines. Repair or replace other parts, such as headlights, horns, handlebar controls, gasoline and oil tanks, starters, and mufflers. Repair and adjust motorcycle subassemblies such as forks, transmissions, brakes, and drive chains, according to specifications. Replace defective parts, using hand tools, arbor presses, flexible power presses, or power tools. Reassemble and test subassembly units. Disassemble subassembly units and examine condition, movement, or alignment of parts visually or using gauges. Listen to engines, examine vehicle frames, and confer with customers in order to determine nature and extent of malfunction or damage. Connect test panels to engines and measure generator output, ignition timing, and other engine performance indicators.

GOE INFORMATION—Interest Area: 05. Mechanics, Installers, and Repairers. **Work Group:** 05.03. Mechanical Work. **Personality Type**—Realistic. Realistic occupations frequently involve work activities that include practical, hands-on problems and solutions. They often deal with plants, animals, and real-world materials like wood, tools, and machinery. Many of the occupations require working outside and do not involve a lot of paperwork or working closely with others. **Work Values**—Variety; Independence; Compensation; Responsibility; Achievement. **Skills**—Repairing; Troubleshooting; Installation; Operation and Control; Operation Monitoring; Technology Design; Quality Control Analysis. **Abilities**—*Cognitive:* Visualization; Deductive Reasoning; Information Ordering. *Psychomotor:* Control Precision; Finger Dexterity; Manual Dexterity; Arm-Hand Steadiness; Multilimb Coordination. *Physical:* Static Strength; Gross Body Coordination; Dynamic Flexibility; Dynamic Strength; Explosive Strength. *Sensory:* Hearing Sensitivity; Depth Perception; Sound Localization. **General Work Activities**—*Information Input:* Monitoring Processes, Materials, or Surroundings; Inspecting Equipment, Structures, or Materials; Getting Information. *Mental Process:* Updating and Using Relevant Knowledge; Making Decisions and Solving Problems; Judging Qualities of Things, Services, or Other People's Work. *Work Output:* Repairing and Maintaining Mechanical Equipment; Handling and Moving Objects; Performing General Physical Activities. *Interacting with Others:* Providing Consultation and Advice to Others; Communicating with Persons Outside Organization; Interpreting Meaning of Information for Others. **Physical Work Conditions**—Kneeling, Crouching, or Crawling; Cramped Work Space or Awkward Positions; Contaminants; Minor Burns, Cuts, Bites, or Stings; Using Hands on Objects, Tools, or Controls. **Other Job Characteristics**—Pace Determined by Speed of Equipment; Degree of Automation; Importance of Being Exact or Accurate.

Experience—Job Zone 2. Some previous work-related skill, knowledge, or experience may be helpful, but usually is not needed. **Job Preparation:** SVP 4.0 to less than 6.0—six months to less than two years. **Knowledge**—Mechanical; Engineering and Technology; Customer and Personal Service; Physics. **Instructional Programs**—Motorcycle Maintenance and Repair Technology/Technician.

Related DOT Jobs—620.281-054 Motorcycle Repairer; 620.684-026 Motorcycle Subassembly Repairer; 807.381-018 Frame Repairer; 807.484-010 Frame Straightener.

49-3053.00 Outdoor Power Equipment and Other Small Engine Mechanics

- Education/Training Required: Moderate-term on-the-job training
- Employed: 33,190
- Annual Earnings: $24,180
- Growth: 8.2%
- Annual Job Openings: 7,000

Diagnose, adjust, repair, or overhaul small engines used to power lawn mowers, chain saws, and related equipment.

Repairs or replaces defective parts, such as water pump, carburetor, thermostat, gears, solenoid, pistons, valves, and crankshaft, using hand tools. Adjusts points, valves, carburetor, distributor, and spark plug gaps, using feeler gauges. Repairs fractional-horsepower gasoline engines used to power lawn mowers, garden tractors, and similar machines. Tests and repairs magnetos used in gasoline and diesel engines, using meters, gauges, and hand tools. Repairs and maintains portable saws powered by internal combustion engines, following manufacturer's repair manuals and using hand tools. Dismantles engines, using hand tools; examines parts for defects; and cleans parts. Tests and repairs turbo or superchargers. Reassembles engines and listens to engines in action to detect operational difficulties. Repairs and maintains gas internal combustion engines that power electric generators, compressors, and similar equipment. Tests and inspects engine to determine malfunctions and locate missing and broken parts, using diagnostic instruments. Grinds, reams, rebores, and retaps parts to obtain specified clearances, using grinders, lathes, taps, reamers, boring machines, and micrometer. Positions and bolts engine to engine stand. Records repairs made, time spent, and parts used.

GOE INFORMATION—Interest Area: 05. Mechanics, Installers, and Repairers. Work Group: 05.03. Mechanical Work. Personality Type—Realistic. Realistic occupations frequently involve work activities that include practical, hands-on problems and solutions. They often deal with plants, animals, and real-world materials like wood, tools, and machinery. Many of the occupations require working outside and do not involve a lot of paperwork or working closely with others. Work Values—Moral Values; Company Policies and Practices; Variety; Compensation; Security. Skills—Repairing; Troubleshooting; Quality Control Analysis; Installation; Operation and Control; Operation Monitoring. Abilities—*Cognitive:* Visualization; Flexibility of Closure. *Psychomotor:* Finger Dexterity; Multilimb Coordination; Control Precision; Arm-Hand Steadiness; Wrist-Finger Speed. *Physical:* Extent Flexibility; Static Strength; Explosive Strength; Gross Body Coordination; Trunk Strength. *Sensory:* Sound Localization; Hearing Sensitivity. General Work Activities—*Information Input:* Getting Information; Inspecting Equipment, Structures, or Materials; Monitoring Processes, Materials, or Surroundings. *Mental Process:* Updating and Using Relevant Knowledge; Evaluating Information Against Standards; Analyzing Data or Information. *Work Output:* Repairing and Maintaining Mechanical Equipment; Handling and Moving Objects; Performing General Physical Activities. *Interacting with Others:* Communicating with Persons Outside Organization; Interpreting Meaning of Information for Others; Communicating with Other Workers. Physical Work Conditions—Kneeling, Crouching, or Crawling; Hazardous Equipment; Contaminants; Distracting Sounds and Noise Levels; Cramped Work Space or Awkward Positions. Other Job Characteristics—Pace Determined by Speed of Equipment; Degree of Automation; Importance of Repeating Same Tasks.

Experience—Job Zone 3. Previous work-related skill, knowledge, or experience is required. Job Preparation: SVP 6.0 to less than 7.0—more than one year and less than four years. Knowledge—Mechanical; Engineering and Technology; Customer and Personal Service; Physics. Instructional Programs—Small Engine Mechanics and Repair Technology/Technician.

Related DOT Jobs—625.281-018 Engine Repairer, Service; 625.281-026 Gas-Engine Repairer; 625.281-030 Power-Saw Mechanic; 625.281-034 Small-Engine Mechanic; 625.381-010 Engine Repairer, Production; 721.281-022 Magneto Repairer.

49-3091.00 Bicycle Repairers

- Education/Training Required: Moderate-term on-the-job training
- Employed: 8,536
- Annual Earnings: $18,820
- Growth: 17.7%
- Annual Job Openings: 3,000

Repair and service bicycles.

Install, repair, and replace equipment or accessories, such as handlebars, stands, lights, and seats. Align wheels. Disassemble axles in order to repair, adjust, and replace defective parts, using hand tools. Install and adjust speed and gear mechanisms. Weld broken or cracked frames together, using oxyacetylene torches and welding rods. Repair holes in tire tubes, using scrapers and patches. Paint bicycle frames, using spray guns or brushes. Shape replacement parts, using bench grinders. Assemble new bicycles.

GOE INFORMATION—Interest Area: 05. Mechanics, Installers, and Repairers. Work Group: 05.03. Mechanical Work. Personality Type—Realistic. Realistic occupations frequently involve work activities that include practical, hands-on problems and solutions. They often deal with plants, animals, and real-world materials like wood, tools, and machinery. Many of the occupations require working outside and do not involve a lot of paperwork or working closely with others. Work Values—Social Service; Independence; Responsibility; Moral Values; Creativity. Skills—Repairing; Installation; Technology Design. Abilities—*Cognitive:* Visualization. *Psychomotor:* Finger Dexterity; Manual Dexterity; Arm-Hand Steadiness; Speed of Limb Movement; Rate Control. *Physical:* Extent Flexibility; Static Strength; Explosive Strength; Dynamic Flexibility; Dynamic Strength. *Sensory:* Glare Sensitivity; Speech Clarity; Sound Localization; Visual Color Discrimination; Depth Perception. General Work Activities—*Information Input:* Getting Information; Inspecting Equipment, Structures, or Materials; Identifying Objects, Actions, and Events. *Mental Process:* Updating and Using Relevant Knowledge; Organizing, Planning, and Prioritizing; Evaluating Information Against Standards. *Work Output:* Handling and Moving Objects; Repairing and Maintaining Mechanical Equipment; Performing General Physical Activities. *Interacting with Others:* Influencing Others or Selling; Performing for or Working with the Public; Communicating with Persons Outside Organization. Physical Work Conditions—Kneeling, Crouching, or Crawling; Hazardous Equipment; Using Hands on Objects, Tools, or Controls; Hazardous Conditions; Minor Burns, Cuts, Bites, or Stings. Other Job Characteristics—Degree of Automation; Pace Determined by Speed of Equipment; Consequence of Error.

Experience—Job Zone 2. Some previous work-related skill, knowledge, or experience may be helpful, but usually is not needed. Job Preparation: SVP 4.0 to less than 6.0—six months to less than two years. Knowledge—Sales and Marketing; Mechanical; Engineering and Technology; Physics; Building and Construction. Instructional Programs—Bicycle Mechanics and Repair Technology/Technician.

Related DOT Jobs—639.681-010 Bicycle Repairer.

49-3092.00 Recreational Vehicle Service Technicians

- **Education/Training Required: Long-term on-the-job training**
- **Employed: 12,280**
- **Annual Earnings: $26,410**
- **Growth: 25.4%**
- **Annual Job Openings: 4,000**

Diagnose, inspect, adjust, repair, or overhaul recreational vehicles, including travel trailers. May specialize in maintaining gas, electrical, hydraulic, plumbing, or chassis/towing systems as well as repairing generators, appliances, and interior components.

Locates and repairs frayed wiring, broken connections, or incorrect wiring, using ohmmeter, soldering iron, tape, and hand tools. Repairs plumbing and propane gas lines, using caulking compounds and plastic or copper pipe. Inspects, examines, and tests operation of parts or systems to be repaired and to verify completeness of work performed. Removes damaged exterior panels, repairs and replaces structural frame members, and seals leaks, using hand tools. Repairs leaks with caulking compound or replaces pipes, using pipe wrench. Connects electrical system to outside power source and activates switches to test operation of appliances and light fixtures. Connects water hose to inlet pipe of plumbing system and tests operation of toilets and sinks. Confers with customer or reads work order to determine nature and extent of damage to unit. Lists parts needed, estimates costs, and plans work procedure, using parts list, technical manuals, and diagrams. Opens and closes doors, windows, and drawers to test their operation and trims edges to fit, using jack-plane or drawknife. Refinishes wood surfaces on cabinets, doors, moldings, and floors, using power sander, putty, spray equipment, brush, paints, or varnishes. Resets hardware, using chisel, mallet, and screwdriver. Seals open side of modular units to prepare them for shipment, using polyethylene sheets, nails, and hammer.

GOE INFORMATION—Interest Area: 05. Mechanics, Installers, and Repairers. **Work Group:** 05.03. Mechanical Work. **Personality Type—**Realistic. Realistic occupations frequently involve work activities that include practical, hands-on problems and solutions. They often deal with plants, animals, and real-world materials like wood, tools, and machinery. Many of the occupations require working outside and do not involve a lot of paperwork or working closely with others. **Work Values—**Supervision, Technical; Variety; Moral Values; Supervision, Human Relations. **Skills—**Installation; Repairing; Troubleshooting; Equipment Selection; Quality Control Analysis. **Abilities—***Cognitive:* Visualization; Flexibility of Closure; Spatial Orientation. *Psychomotor:* Control Precision; Manual Dexterity; Speed of Limb Movement; Multilimb Coordination; Arm-Hand Steadiness. *Physical:* Extent Flexibility; Static Strength; Trunk Strength; Explosive Strength; Dynamic Strength. *Sensory:* Depth Perception. **General Work Activities—***Information Input:* Monitoring Processes, Materials, or Surroundings; Getting Information; Inspecting Equipment, Structures, or Materials. *Mental Process:* Judging Qualities of Things, Services, or Other People's Work; Evaluating Information Against Standards; Updating and Using Relevant Knowledge. *Work Output:* Performing General Physical Activities; Handling and Moving Objects; Repairing and Maintaining Mechanical Equipment. *Interacting with Others:* Establishing and Maintaining Relationships; Communicating with Other Workers; Communicating with Persons Outside Organization. **Physical Work Conditions—**Hazardous Conditions; Outdoors; Whole Body Vibration; Climbing Ladders, Scaffolds, Poles, etc.; Kneeling, Crouching, or Crawling. **Other Job Characteristics—**Consequence of Error; Pace Determined by Speed of Equipment; Importance of Being Exact or Accurate.

Experience—Job Zone 2. Some previous work-related skill, knowledge, or experience may be helpful, but usually is not needed. **Job Preparation:** SVP 4.0 to less than 6.0—six months to less than two years. **Knowledge—**Building and Construction; Mechanical; Design; Engineering and Technology; Physics. **Instructional Programs—**Vehicle Maintenance and Repair Technologies, Other.

Related DOT Jobs—806.381-070 Custom Van Converter; 869.261-022 Repairer, Recreational Vehicle.

49-3093.00 Tire Repairers and Changers

- **Education/Training Required: Short-term on-the-job training**
- **Employed: 89,031**
- **Annual Earnings: $19,710**
- **Growth: 6.8%**
- **Annual Job Openings: 27,000**

Repair and replace tires.

Apply rubber cement to buffed tire casings prior to vulcanization process. Buff defective areas of inner tubes, using scrapers. Glue boots (tire patches) over ruptures in tire casings, using rubber cement. Hammer required counterweights onto rims of wheels. Inflate inner tubes and immerse them in water to locate leaks. Inspect tire casings for defects, such as holes and tears. Locate punctures in tubeless tires by visual inspection or by immersing inflated tires in water baths and observing air bubbles. Patch tubes with adhesive rubber patches or seal rubber patches to tubes using hot vulcanizing plates. Place casing-camelback assemblies in tire molds for the vulcanization process and exert pressure on the camelbacks to ensure good adhesion. Place wheels on balancing machines to determine counterweights required to balance wheels. Prepare rims and wheel drums for reassembly by scraping, grinding, or sandblasting. Raise vehicles using hydraulic jacks. Reassemble tires onto wheels. Remount wheels onto vehicles. Replace valve stems and remove puncturing objects. Roll new rubber treads, known as camelbacks, over tire casings, and mold the semi-raw rubber treads onto the buffed casings. Rotate tires to different positions on vehicles, using hand tools. Seal punctures in tubeless tires by inserting adhesive material and expanding rubber plugs into punctures, using hand tools. Separate tubed tires from wheels, using rubber mallets and metal bars or mechanical tire changers. Unbolt wheels from vehicles and remove them, using lug wrenches and other hand and power tools. Assist mechanics and perform other duties as directed. Clean sides of whitewall tires. Drive automobile or service trucks to industrial sites in order to provide services and respond to emergency calls. Identify and inflate tires correctly for the size and ply. Order replacements for tires and tubes.

GOE INFORMATION—Interest Area: 05. Mechanics, Installers, and Repairers. **Work Group:** 05.03. Mechanical Work. **Personality Type—**Realistic. Realistic occupations frequently involve work activities that include practical, hands-on problems and solutions. They often deal with plants, animals, and real-world materials like wood, tools, and machinery. Many of the occupations require working outside and do not involve a lot of paperwork or working closely with others. **Work Values—**Moral Values; Supervision, Technical; Independence; Social Service; Security. **Skills—**Repairing; Installation; Operation and Control. **Abilities—***Cognitive:* None met the criteria. *Psychomotor:* Control Precision; Response Orientation; Wrist-Finger Speed; Finger Dexterity; Multilimb Coordination. *Physical:* Static Strength; Explosive Strength; Extent Flexibility; Stamina; Trunk Strength. *Sensory:* None met the criteria. **General Work Activities—***Information Input:* Monitoring Processes, Materials, or Surroundings; Inspecting Equipment, Structures, or Materials; Estimating Needed Characteristics. *Mental Process:* Making Decisions and Solving Problems; Judging Qualities of Things, Services, or Other People's Work; Updating and Using Relevant Knowledge. *Work Output:* Handling and Moving Objects; Performing General Physical Activities; Controlling Machines and Processes. *Interacting with Others:* Performing for or Working with the Public; Communicating with Persons Outside Organization; Assisting and Caring for Others. **Physical Work Conditions**—Kneeling, Crouching, or Crawling; Using Hands on Objects, Tools, or Controls; Outdoors; Standing; Distracting Sounds and Noise Levels. **Other Job Characteristics**—Importance of Repeating Same Tasks; Pace Determined by Speed of Equipment; Consequence of Error.

Experience—Job Zone 1. No previous work-related skill, knowledge, or experience is needed. **Job Preparation:** SVP below 4.0—less than six months. **Knowledge**—Customer and Personal Service; Mechanical; Geography; Engineering and Technology. **Instructional Programs**—No data available.

Related DOT Jobs—750.681-010 Tire Repairer; 915.684-010 Tire Repairer.

49-9000 Other Installation, Maintenance, and Repair Occupations

49-9011.00 Mechanical Door Repairers

- Education/Training Required: Moderate-term on-the-job training
- Employed: 11,263
- Annual Earnings: $28,760
- Growth: 12.7%
- Annual Job Openings: 1,000

Install, service, or repair opening and closing mechanisms of automatic doors and hydraulic door closers. Includes garage door mechanics.

Adjust doors to open or close with the correct amount of effort and make simple adjustments to electric openers. Apply hardware to door sections, such as drilling holes to install locks. Assemble and fasten tracks to structures or bucks, using impact wrenches or welding equipment. Bore and cut holes in flooring as required for installation, using hand tools and power tools. Carry springs to tops of doors, using ladders or scaffolding, and attach springs to tracks in order to install spring systems. Clean door closer parts, using caustic soda, rotary brushes, and grinding wheels. Cover treadles with carpeting or other floor covering materials and test systems by operating treadles. Cut door stops and angle irons to fit openings. Fasten angle iron back-hangers to ceilings and tracks, using fasteners or welding equipment. Inspect job sites, assessing headroom, side room, and other conditions in order to determine appropriateness of door for a given location. Install dock seals, bumpers, and shelters. Install door frames, rails, steel rolling curtains, electronic-eye mechanisms, and electric door openers and closers, using power tools, hand tools, and electronic test equipment. Lubricate door closer oil chambers and pack spindles with leather washers. Remove or disassemble defective automatic mechanical door closers, using hand tools. Repair or replace worn or broken door parts, using hand tools. Run low-voltage wiring on ceiling surfaces, using insulated staples. Set doors into place or stack hardware sections into openings after rail or track installation. Set in and secure floor treadles for door activating mechanisms; then connect power packs and electrical panelboards to treadles. Study blueprints and schematic diagrams in order to determine appropriate methods of installing and repairing automated door openers. Wind large springs with upward motion of arm. Collect payment upon job completion. Complete required paperwork, such as work orders, according to services performed or required. Fabricate replacements for worn or broken parts, using welders, lathes, drill presses, and shaping and milling machines. Operate lifts, winches, or chain falls in order to move heavy curtain doors. Order replacement springs, sections, and slats.

GOE INFORMATION—**Interest Area:** 05. Mechanics, Installers, and Repairers. **Work Group:** 05.03. Mechanical Work. **Personality Type**—Realistic. Realistic occupations frequently involve work activities that include practical, hands-on problems and solutions. They often deal with plants, animals, and real-world materials like wood, tools, and machinery. Many of the occupations require working outside and do not involve a lot of paperwork or working closely with others. **Work Values**—Independence; Moral Values; Supervision, Technical; Responsibility; Supervision, Human Relations. **Skills**—Repairing; Installation. **Abilities**—*Cognitive:* Visualization; Information Ordering; Spatial Orientation. *Psychomotor:* Speed of Limb Movement; Arm-Hand Steadiness; Multilimb Coordination; Manual Dexterity; Finger Dexterity. *Physical:* Extent Flexibility; Dynamic Strength; Gross Body Equilibrium; Stamina; Explosive Strength. *Sensory:* Visual Color Discrimination; Hearing Sensitivity; Sound Localization; Far Vision; Night Vision. **General Work Activities**—*Information Input:* Getting Information; Inspecting Equipment, Structures, or Materials; Identifying Objects, Actions, and Events. *Mental Process:* Evaluating Information Against Standards; Updating and Using Relevant Knowledge; Organizing, Planning, and Prioritizing. *Work Output:* Performing General Physical Activities; Handling and Moving Objects; Repairing and Maintaining Mechanical Equipment. *Interacting with Others:* Communicating with Other Workers; Performing Administrative Activities; Communicating with Persons Outside Organization. **Physical Work Conditions**—Hazardous Equipment; Kneeling, Crouching, or Crawling; Outdoors; Bending or Twisting the Body; Climbing Ladders, Scaffolds, Poles, etc. **Other Job Characteristics**—Pace Determined by Speed of Equipment; Importance of Repeating Same Tasks; Degree of Automation.

Experience—Job Zone 3. Previous work-related skill, knowledge, or experience is required. **Job Preparation:** SVP 6.0 to less than 7.0—more than one year and less than four years. **Knowledge**—Mechanical; Building and Construction; Engineering and Technology; Design; Physics. **Instructional Programs**—No data available.

Related DOT Jobs—630.381-014 Door-Closer Mechanic; 829.281-010 Automatic-Door Mechanic.

49-9012.00 Control and Valve Installers and Repairers, Except Mechanical Door

- Education/Training Required: Moderate-term on-the-job training
- Employed: 34,264
- Annual Earnings: $42,950
- Growth: 2.7%
- Annual Job Openings: 4,000

Install, repair, and maintain mechanical regulating and controlling devices, such as electric meters, gas regulators, thermostats, safety and flow valves, and other mechanical governors.

No task data available.

GOE INFORMATION—**Interest Area:** 05. Mechanics, Installers, and Repairers. **Work Group:** 05.03. Mechanical Work. **Note:** The Department of Labor has not collected some data for this job, so it has fewer details than the other descriptions.

Instructional Programs—Electromechanical and Instrumentation and Maintenance Technologies/Technicians, Other.

Related DOT Jobs—622.381-010 Air-Valve Repairer; 630.381-030 Valve Repairer; 637.261-022 Industrial-Gas Servicer; 709.684-070 Salvager; 710.281-022 Gas-Meter Prover; 710.281-034 Meter Repairer; 710.381-022 Gas-Meter Mechanic I; 710.381-026 Gas-Regulator Repairer; 710.381-050 Thermostat Repairer; 710.684-026 Gas-Meter Mechanic II; 729.281-014 Electric-Meter Repairer; 729.281-018 Electric-Meter-Repairer Apprentice; 729.281-034 Inside-Meter Tester; 821.361-014 Electric-Meter Installer I; 821.684-010 Electric-Meter Installer II; 862.684-030 Water Regulator and Valve Repairer; 953.281-010 Field-Mechanical-Meter Tester; 953.384-640 Gas Utility Worker; 954.564-010 Water-Meter Installer.

49-9012.01 Electric Meter Installers and Repairers

- **Education/Training Required: Moderate-term on-the-job training**
- **Employed: No data available.**
- **Annual Earnings: $42,950**
- **Growth: 2.7%**
- **Annual Job Openings: 4,000**

Install electric meters on customers' premises or on pole. Test meters and perform necessary repairs. Turn current on/off by connecting/disconnecting service drop.

Mounts and installs meter and other electric equipment, such as time clocks, transformers, and circuit breakers, using electrician's hand tools. Inspects and tests electric meters, relays, and power to detect cause of malfunction and inaccuracy, using hand tools and testing equipment. Repairs electric meters and components, such as transformers and relays, and changes faulty or incorrect wiring, using hand tools. Splices and connects cable from meter or current transformer to pull box or switchboard, using hand tools, to provide power. Makes adjustments to meter components, such as setscrews or timing mechanism, to conform to specifications. Disconnects and removes electric power meters when defective or when customer accounts are in default, using hand tools. Cleans meter parts, using chemical solutions, brushes, sandpaper, and soap and water. Records meter reading and installation data on meter cards, work orders, or field service orders.

GOE INFORMATION—**Interest Area:** 05. Mechanics, Installers, and Repairers. **Work Group:** 05.02. Electrical and Electronic Systems. **Personality Type**—Realistic. Realistic occupations frequently involve work activities that include practical, hands-on problems and solutions. They often deal with plants, animals, and real-world materials like wood, tools, and machinery. Many of the occupations require working outside and do not involve a lot of paperwork or working closely with others. **Work Values**—Independence; Moral Values; Supervision, Technical; Security; Supervision, Human Relations. **Skills**—Installation; Repairing; Troubleshooting; Quality Control Analysis; Technology Design; Operation Monitoring; Operation and Control. **Abilities**—*Cognitive:* Spatial Orientation; Information Ordering; Visualization; Flexibility of Closure; Speed of Closure. *Psychomotor:* Finger Dexterity; Arm-Hand Steadiness; Reaction Time; Manual Dexterity; Multilimb Coordination. *Physical:* Gross Body Equilibrium; Extent Flexibility; Gross Body Coordination; Explosive Strength; Stamina. *Sensory:* Visual Color Discrimination; Far Vision;

Glare Sensitivity; Near Vision; Night Vision. **General Work Activities**—*Information Input:* Inspecting Equipment, Structures, or Materials; Monitoring Processes, Materials, or Surroundings; Getting Information. *Mental Process:* Organizing, Planning, and Prioritizing; Updating and Using Relevant Knowledge; Judging Qualities of Things, Services, or Other People's Work. *Work Output:* Repairing and Maintaining Electronic Equipment; Performing General Physical Activities; Handling and Moving Objects. *Interacting with Others:* Communicating with Other Workers; Performing Administrative Activities; Establishing and Maintaining Relationships. **Physical Work Conditions**—Hazardous Conditions; Outdoors; Minor Burns, Cuts, Bites, or Stings; Climbing Ladders, Scaffolds, Poles, etc.; High Places. **Other Job Characteristics**—Importance of Being Exact or Accurate; Consequence of Error; Degree of Automation.

Experience—Job Zone 3. Previous work-related skill, knowledge, or experience is required. **Job Preparation:** SVP 6.0 to less than 7.0—more than one year and less than four years. **Knowledge**—Computers and Electronics; Mechanical; Engineering and Technology; Design; Geography. **Instructional Programs**—Electromechanical and Instrumentation and Maintenance Technologies/Technicians, Other.

Related DOT Jobs—729.281-014 Electric-Meter Repairer; 729.281-018 Electric-Meter-Repairer Apprentice; 729.281-034 Inside-Meter Tester; 821.361-014 Electric-Meter Installer I; 821.684-010 Electric-Meter Installer II.

49-9012.02 Valve and Regulator Repairers

- **Education/Training Required: Moderate-term on-the-job training**
- **Employed: No data available.**
- **Annual Earnings: $42,950**
- **Growth: 2.7%**
- **Annual Job Openings: 4,000**

Test, repair, and adjust mechanical regulators and valves.

Replaces, repairs, or adjusts defective valve or regulator parts and tightens attachments, using hand tools, power tools, and welder. Tests valves and regulators for leaks, temperature, and pressure settings, using precision testing equipment. Disassembles mechanical control devices or valves, such as regulators, thermostats, or hydrants, using power tools, hand tools, and cutting torch. Examines valves or mechanical control device parts for defects, dents, or loose attachments. Lubricates wearing surfaces of mechanical parts, using oils or other lubricants. Measures salvageable parts removed from mechanical control devices for conformance to standards or specifications, using gauges, micrometers, and calipers. Cleans corrosives and other deposits from serviceable parts, using solvents, wire brushes, or sandblaster. Dips valves and regulators in molten lead to prevent leakage and paints valves, fittings, and other devices, using spray gun. Correlates testing data, performs technical calculations, and writes test reports to record data. Records repair work, inventories parts, and orders new parts. Advises customers on proper installation of valves or regulators and related equipment.

GOE INFORMATION—**Interest Area:** 05. Mechanics, Installers, and Repairers. **Work Group:** 05.03. Mechanical Work. **Personality Type**—Realistic. Realistic occupations frequently involve work activities that include practical, hands-on problems and solutions. They often deal with plants, animals, and real-world materials like wood, tools, and machinery. Many of the occupations require working outside and do not involve a lot of paperwork or working closely with others. **Work Values**—Supervision, Technical; Moral Values; Independence; Responsibility; Supervision, Human Relations. **Skills**—Repairing; Installation; Quality Control Analysis; Operation and Control; Equipment Selection; Troubleshooting; Mathematics. **Abilities**—*Cognitive:* Spatial Orientation; Visualization; Flexibility of Closure; Perceptual Speed; Speed of Closure. *Psychomotor:* Manual Dexterity; Finger Dexterity; Wrist-Finger Speed; Arm-Hand Steadiness; Multilimb Coordination. *Physical:* Extent Flexibility; Explosive Strength; Dynamic Flexibility; Dynamic Strength; Static Strength. *Sensory:* Depth Perception; Hearing Sensitivity; Sound Localization; Glare Sensitivity; Peripheral Vision. **General Work Activities**—*Information Input:* Getting Information; Identifying Objects, Actions, and Events; Inspecting Equipment, Structures, or Materials. *Mental Process:* Updating and Using Relevant Knowledge; Judging Qualities of Things, Services, or Other People's Work; Analyzing Data or Information. *Work Output:* Handling and Moving Objects; Repairing and Maintaining Mechanical Equipment; Performing General Physical Activities. *Interacting with Others:* Communicating with Persons Outside Organization; Providing Consultation and Advice to Others; Establishing and Maintaining Relationships. **Physical Work Conditions**—Hazardous Equipment; Hazardous Conditions; Climbing Ladders, Scaffolds, Poles, etc.; Using Hands on Objects, Tools, or Controls; Distracting Sounds and Noise Levels. **Other Job Characteristics**—Degree of Automation; Importance of Repeating Same Tasks; Pace Determined by Speed of Equipment.

Experience—Job Zone 3. Previous work-related skill, knowledge, or experience is required. **Job Preparation:** SVP 6.0 to less than 7.0—more than one year and less than four years. **Knowledge**—Mechanical; Physics; Engineering and Technology; Mathematics; Building and Construction. **Instructional Programs**—Electromechanical and Instrumentation and Maintenance Technologies/Technicians, Other.

Related DOT Jobs—622.381-010 Air-Valve Repairer; 630.381-030 Valve Repairer; 637.261-022 Industrial-Gas Servicer; 709.684-070 Salvager; 710.381-026 Gas-Regulator Repairer; 710.381-050 Thermostat Repairer; 862.684-030 Water Regulator and Valve Repairer; 953.281-010 Field-Mechanical-Meter Tester.

49-9012.03 Meter Mechanics

- Education/Training Required: Moderate-term on-the-job training
- Employed: No data available.
- Annual Earnings: $42,950
- Growth: 2.7%
- Annual Job Openings: 4,000

Test, adjust, and repair gas, water, and oil meters.

Adjusts meter and repeats test until meter registration is within specified limits. Connects gas, oil, water, or air meter to test apparatus to detect leaks. Dismantles meter and replaces defective parts, such as case, shafts, gears, disks, and recording mechanisms, using soldering iron and hand tools. Inspects, repairs, and maintains gas meters at wells or processing plants. Reassembles meter and meter parts, using soldering gun, power tools, and hand tools. Analyzes test results to determine cause of persistent meter registration errors. Lubricates moving meter parts, using oil gun. Cleans plant growth, scale, and rust from meter housing, using wire brush, buffer, sandblaster, or cleaning compounds. Records test results, materials used, and meters needing repair on log or card and segregates meters requiring repair. Caps meter housing and activates controls on paint booth to spray paint meter case.

GOE INFORMATION—**Interest Area:** 05. Mechanics, Installers, and Repairers. **Work Group:** 05.03. Mechanical Work. **Personality Type**—Realistic. Realistic occupations frequently involve work activities that include practical, hands-on problems and solutions. They often deal with plants, animals, and real-world materials like wood, tools, and machinery. Many

of the occupations require working outside and do not involve a lot of paperwork or working closely with others. **Work Values**—Independence; Moral Values; Supervision, Technical; Security; Supervision, Human Relations. **Skills**—Repairing; Installation; Quality Control Analysis; Operation and Control; Operation Monitoring; Troubleshooting. **Abilities**—*Cognitive:* Visualization; Flexibility of Closure; Spatial Orientation; Speed of Closure; Number Facility. *Psychomotor:* Finger Dexterity; Arm-Hand Steadiness; Control Precision; Speed of Limb Movement; Multilimb Coordination. *Physical:* Dynamic Flexibility; Extent Flexibility; Stamina; Explosive Strength; Dynamic Strength. *Sensory:* Visual Color Discrimination; Glare Sensitivity; Night Vision; Near Vision. **General Work Activities**—*Information Input:* Inspecting Equipment, Structures, or Materials; Getting Information; Monitoring Processes, Materials, or Surroundings. *Mental Process:* Making Decisions and Solving Problems; Evaluating Information Against Standards; Updating and Using Relevant Knowledge. *Work Output:* Performing General Physical Activities; Handling and Moving Objects; Repairing and Maintaining Mechanical Equipment. *Interacting with Others:* Performing Administrative Activities; Interpreting Meaning of Information for Others; Communicating with Other Workers. **Physical Work Conditions**—Outdoors; Kneeling, Crouching, or Crawling; Cramped Work Space or Awkward Positions; Minor Burns, Cuts, Bites, or Stings; Walking or Running. **Other Job Characteristics**—Importance of Being Exact or Accurate; Consequence of Error; Importance of Repeating Same Tasks.

Experience—Job Zone 2. Some previous work-related skill, knowledge, or experience may be helpful, but usually is not needed. **Job Preparation:** SVP 4.0 to less than 6.0—six months to less than two years. **Knowledge**—Mechanical; Engineering and Technology; Clerical; Telecommunications. **Instructional Programs**—Electromechanical and Instrumentation and Maintenance Technologies/Technicians, Other.

Related DOT Jobs—710.281-022 Gas-Meter Prover; 710.281-034 Meter Repairer; 710.381-022 Gas-Meter Mechanic I; 710.684-026 Gas-Meter Mechanic II.

49-9021.00 Heating, Air Conditioning, and Refrigeration Mechanics and Installers

- Education/Training Required: Long-term on-the-job training
- Employed: 243,058
- Annual Earnings: $34,020
- Growth: 22.3%
- Annual Job Openings: 21,000

Install or repair heating, central air conditioning, or refrigeration systems, including oil burners, hot-air furnaces, and heating stoves.

No task data available.

GOE INFORMATION—**Interest Area:** 05. Mechanics, Installers, and Repairers. **Work Group:** 05.03. Mechanical Work. **Note:** The Department of Labor has not collected some data for this job, so it has fewer details than the other descriptions.

Instructional Programs—Heating, Air Conditioning, Ventilation, and Refrigeration Maintenance Technology/Technician (HAC, HACR, HVAC, HVACR); Heating, Air Conditioning, and Refrigeration Technology/Technician (ACH/ACR/ACHR/HRAC/HVAC/AC Technology); Solar Energy Technology/Technician.

Related DOT Jobs—637.261-014 Heating-and-Air-Conditioning Installer-Servicer; 637.261-026 Refrigeration Mechanic; 637.261-030 Solar-Energy-System Installer; 637.261-034 Air and Hydronic Balancing

Technician; 637.381-010 Evaporative-Cooler Installer; 637.381-014 Refrigeration Unit Repairer; 827.361-014 Refrigeration Mechanic; 862.281-018 Oil-Burner-Servicer-and-Installer; 862.361-010 Furnace Installer; 869.281-010 Furnace Installer-and-Repairer, Hot Air.

49-9021.01 Heating and Air Conditioning Mechanics

- **Education/Training Required: Long-term on-the-job training**
- **Employed: No data available.**
- **Annual Earnings: $34,020**
- **Growth: 22.3%**
- **Annual Job Openings: 21,000**

Install, service, and repair heating and air conditioning systems in residences and commercial establishments.

Obtain and maintain required certification(s). Comply with all applicable standards, policies, and procedures, including safety procedures and the maintenance of a clean work area. Repair or replace defective equipment, components, or wiring. Test electrical circuits and components for continuity, using electrical test equipment. Reassemble and test equipment following repairs. Inspect and test system to verify system compliance with plans and specifications and to detect and locate malfunctions. Discuss heating-cooling system malfunctions with users to isolate problems or to verify that malfunctions have been corrected. Record and report all faults, deficiencies, and other unusual occurrences, as well as the time and materials expended on work orders. Test pipe or tubing joints and connections for leaks, using pressure gauge or soap-and-water solution. Adjust system controls to setting recommended by manufacturer to balance system, using hand tools. Recommend, develop, and perform preventive and general maintenance procedures such as cleaning, power-washing, and vacuuming equipment, oiling parts, and changing filters. Lay out and connect electrical wiring between controls and equipment according to wiring diagram, using electrician's hand tools. Install auxiliary components to heating-cooling equipment, such as expansion and discharge valves, air ducts, pipes, blowers, dampers, flues, and stokers, following blueprints. Assist with other work in coordination with repair and maintenance teams. Install, connect, and adjust thermostats, humidistats and timers, using hand tools. Generate work orders that address deficiencies in need of correction. Join pipes or tubing to equipment and to fuel, water, or refrigerant source to form complete circuit. Assemble, position, and mount heating or cooling equipment, following blueprints. Study blueprints, design specifications, and manufacturers' recommendations to ascertain the configuration of heating or cooling equipment components and to ensure the proper installation of components. Cut and drill holes in floors, walls, and roof to install equipment, using power saws and drills. Wrap pipes in insulation, securing it in place with cement or wire bands. Measure, cut, thread, and bend pipe or tubing, using pipefitter's tools. Fabricate, assemble, and install duct work and chassis parts, using portable metal-working tools and welding equipment.

GOE INFORMATION—Interest Area: 05. Mechanics, Installers, and Repairers. **Work Group:** 05.03. Mechanical Work. **Personality Type**—Realistic. Realistic occupations frequently involve work activities that include practical, hands-on problems and solutions. They often deal with plants, animals, and real-world materials like wood, tools, and machinery. Many of the occupations require working outside and do not involve a lot of paperwork or working closely with others. **Work Values**—Independence; Variety; Moral Values; Supervision, Technical; Responsibility. **Skills**—Repairing; Installation; Troubleshooting; Coordination; Systems Evaluation; Operation Monitoring; Negotiation; Equipment Selection. **Abilities**—*Cognitive:* Visualization; Speed of Closure; Flexibility of Clo-

sure; Inductive Reasoning; Perceptual Speed. *Psychomotor:* Finger Dexterity; Manual Dexterity; Reaction Time; Control Precision; Multilimb Coordination. *Physical:* Extent Flexibility; Gross Body Equilibrium; Stamina; Gross Body Coordination; Trunk Strength. *Sensory:* Hearing Sensitivity; Visual Color Discrimination; Glare Sensitivity; Depth Perception; Auditory Attention. **General Work Activities**—*Information Input:* Getting Information; Monitoring Processes, Materials, or Surroundings; Identifying Objects, Actions, and Events. *Mental Process:* Making Decisions and Solving Problems; Organizing, Planning, and Prioritizing; Thinking Creatively. *Work Output:* Handling and Moving Objects; Performing General Physical Activities; Repairing and Maintaining Mechanical Equipment. *Interacting with Others:* Establishing and Maintaining Relationships; Performing for or Working with the Public; Communicating with Persons Outside Organization. **Physical Work Conditions**—Kneeling, Crouching, or Crawling; Cramped Work Space or Awkward Positions; Climbing Ladders, Scaffolds, Poles, etc.; Using Hands on Objects, Tools, or Controls; Very Hot or Cold. **Other Job Characteristics**—Importance of Being Exact or Accurate; Pace Determined by Speed of Equipment; Consequence of Error.

Experience—Job Zone 3. Previous work-related skill, knowledge, or experience is required. **Job Preparation:** SVP 7.0 to less than 8.0—two years to less than 10 years. **Knowledge**—Mechanical; Building and Construction; Design; Customer and Personal Service; Sales and Marketing. **Instructional Programs**—Heating, Air Conditioning, and Refrigeration Technology/Technician (HAC, HACR, HVAC, HVACR); Heating, Air Conditioning, Ventilation, and Refrigeration Maintenance Technology/Technician (ACH/ACR/ACHR/HRAC/HVAC/AC Technology); Solar Energy Technology/Technician.

Related DOT Jobs—637.261-014 Heating-and-Air-Conditioning Installer-Servicer; 637.261-030 Solar-Energy-System Installer; 637.261-034 Air and Hydronic Balancing Technician; 637.381-010 Evaporative-Cooler Installer; 862.281-018 Oil-Burner-Servicer-and-Installer; 862.361-010 Furnace Installer; 869.281-010 Furnace Installer-and-Repairer, Hot Air.

49-9021.02 Refrigeration Mechanics

- **Education/Training Required: Long-term on-the-job training**
- **Employed: No data available.**
- **Annual Earnings: $34,020**
- **Growth: 22.3%**
- **Annual Job Openings: 21,000**

Install and repair industrial and commercial refrigerating systems.

Adjust or replace worn or defective mechanisms and parts and reassemble repaired systems. Adjust valves according to specifications and charge system with proper type of refrigerant by pumping the specified gas or fluid into the system. Braze or solder parts to repair defective joints and leaks. Cut, bend, thread, and connect pipe to functional components and water, power, or refrigeration system. Dismantle malfunctioning systems and test components, using electrical, mechanical, and pneumatic testing equipment. Drill holes and install mounting brackets and hangers into floor and walls of building. Fabricate and assemble structural and functional components of refrigeration system, using hand tools, power tools, and welding equipment. Install expansion and control valves, using acetylene torches and wrenches. Install wiring to connect components to an electric power source. Lay out reference points for installation of structural and functional components, using measuring instruments. Lift and align components into position, using hoist or block and tackle. Mount compressor, condenser, and other components in specified locations on frames, using hand tools and acetylene welding equipment. Observe and test system operation, using gauges and instruments. Perform mechanical overhauls and refrigerant reclaiming. Read blueprints to determine location, size, capacity, and type of components needed to build refrigeration system. Test lines, components, and connections for leaks. Estimate, order, pick up, deliver, and install materials and supplies needed to maintain equipment in good working condition. Insulate shells and cabinets of systems. Keep records of repairs and replacements made and causes of malfunctions. Schedule work with customers and initiate work orders; house requisitions and orders from stock. Supervise and instruct assistants.

GOE INFORMATION—Interest Area: 05. Mechanics, Installers, and Repairers. **Work Group:** 05.03. Mechanical Work. **Personality Type—**Realistic. Realistic occupations frequently involve work activities that include practical, hands-on problems and solutions. They often deal with plants, animals, and real-world materials like wood, tools, and machinery. Many of the occupations require working outside and do not involve a lot of paperwork or working closely with others. **Work Values—**Moral Values; Independence; Supervision, Technical; Variety; Compensation. **Skills—**Repairing; Installation; Troubleshooting; Quality Control Analysis; Operation Monitoring; Equipment Selection; Operation and Control. **Abilities—***Cognitive:* Problem Sensitivity; Visualization; Written Comprehension; Inductive Reasoning; Memorization. *Psychomotor:* Control Precision; Multilimb Coordination; Manual Dexterity; Finger Dexterity. *Physical:* Extent Flexibility; Explosive Strength; Static Strength; Dynamic Strength; Gross Body Coordination. *Sensory:* None met the criteria. **General Work Activities—***Information Input:* Monitoring Processes, Materials, or Surroundings; Getting Information; Inspecting Equipment, Structures, or Materials. *Mental Process:* Updating and Using Relevant Knowledge; Evaluating Information Against Standards; Judging Qualities of Things, Services, or Other People's Work. *Work Output:* Repairing and Maintaining Mechanical Equipment; Performing General Physical Activities; Handling and Moving Objects. *Interacting with Others:* Establishing and Maintaining Relationships; Performing Administrative Activities; Communicating with Other Workers. **Physical Work Conditions—**Hazardous Equipment; Kneeling, Crouching, or Crawling; Hazardous Conditions; Using Hands on Objects, Tools, or Controls; Cramped Work Space or Awkward Positions. **Other Job Characteristics—**Importance of Being Exact or Accurate; Consequence of Error; Pace Determined by Speed of Equipment.

Experience—Job Zone 4. A minimum of two to four years of work-related skill, knowledge, or experience is needed. **Job Preparation:** SVP 7.0 to less than 8.0—two years to less than 10 years. **Knowledge—**Mechanical; Engineering and Technology; Building and Construction; Design; Physics. **Instructional Programs—**Heating, Air Conditioning, and Refrigeration Technology/Technician (ACH/ACR/ACHR/HRAC/HVAC/AC Technology); Heating, Air Conditioning, Ventilation, and Refrigeration Maintenance Technology/Technician (HAC, HACR, HVAC, HVACR).

Related DOT Jobs—637.261-026 Refrigeration Mechanic; 637.381-014 Refrigeration Unit Repairer; 827.361-014 Refrigeration Mechanic.

49-9031.00 Home Appliance Repairers

- Education/Training Required: **Postsecondary vocational training**
- Employed: **42,999**
- Annual Earnings: **$29,570**
- Growth: **6.2%**
- Annual Job Openings: **5,000**

Repair, adjust, or install all types of electric or gas household appliances, such as refrigerators, washers, dryers, and ovens.

No task data available.

GOE INFORMATION—Interest Area: 05. Mechanics, Installers, and Repairers. **Work Group:** 05.02. Electrical and Electronic Systems. **Note:** The Department of Labor has not collected some data for this job, so it has fewer details than the other descriptions.

Instructional Programs—Appliance Installation and Repair Technology/Technician; Home Furnishings and Equipment Installers.

Related DOT Jobs—637.261-018 Gas-Appliance Servicer; 827.661-010 Household-Appliance Installer; 959.361-010 Customer Service Representative.

49-9031.01 Home Appliance Installers

- Education/Training Required: **Long-term on-the-job training**
- Employed: **No data available.**
- Annual Earnings: **$29,570**
- Growth: **6.2%**
- Annual Job Openings: **5,000**

Install household appliances, such as refrigerators, washing machines, and stoves, in mobile homes or customers' homes.

Observes and tests operation of appliances, such as refrigerators, washers, and dryers, and makes initial installation adjustments accordingly. Levels refrigerators, adjusts doors, and connects water lines to water pipes for ice makers and water dispensers, using hand tools. Levels washing machines and connects hoses to water pipes, using plumbing and other hand tools. Lights and adjusts pilot lights on gas stoves and examines valves and burners for gas leakage and specified flame. Advises customers regarding use and care of appliance and provides them with emergency service number. Disassembles and re-installs existing kitchen cabinets and assembles and installs prefabricated kitchen cabinets in conjunction with appliance installation.

GOE INFORMATION—Interest Area: 05. Mechanics, Installers, and Repairers. **Work Group:** 05.02. Electrical and Electronic Systems. **Personality Type—**Realistic. Realistic occupations frequently involve work activities that include practical, hands-on problems and solutions. They often deal with plants, animals, and real-world materials like wood, tools, and machinery. Many of the occupations require working outside and do not involve a lot of paperwork or working closely with others. **Work Values—**Social Service; Moral Values; Supervision, Technical; Advancement; Security. **Skills—**Installation; Troubleshooting; Repairing; Operation Monitoring. **Abilities—***Cognitive:* Visualization. *Psychomotor:* Wrist-Finger Speed; Finger Dexterity; Speed of Limb Movement. *Physical:* Static Strength; Dynamic Strength; Explosive Strength; Extent Flexibility; Gross Body Coordination. *Sensory:* Hearing Sensitivity; Sound Localization. **General Work Activities—***Information Input:* Inspecting Equipment, Structures, or Materials; Monitoring Processes, Materials, or Surroundings; Getting Information. *Mental Process:* Updating and Using Relevant Knowledge; Organizing, Planning, and Prioritizing; Evaluating Information Against Standards. *Work Output:* Handling and Moving Objects; Performing General Physical Activities; Repairing and Maintaining Mechanical Equipment. *Interacting with Others:* Communicating with Persons Outside Organization; Performing for or Working with the Public; Interpreting Meaning of Information for Others. **Physical Work Conditions—**Cramped Work Space or Awkward Positions; Using Hands on Objects, Tools, or Controls; Kneeling, Crouching, or Crawling; Bending or Twisting the Body; Standing. **Other Job Characteristics—**Importance of Repeating Same Tasks; Consequence of Error; Importance of Being Exact or Accurate.

Experience—Job Zone 3. Previous work-related skill, knowledge, or experience is required. **Job Preparation:** SVP 6.0 to less than 7.0—more than one year and less than four years. **Knowledge**—Building and Construction; Mechanical; Engineering and Technology; Production and Processing; Public Safety and Security. **Instructional Programs**—Appliance Installation and Repair Technology/Technician; Home Furnishings and Equipment Installers.

Related DOT Jobs—827.661-010 Household-Appliance Installer.

49-9031.02 Gas Appliance Repairers

- **Education/Training Required: Long-term on-the-job training**
- **Employed: No data available.**
- **Annual Earnings: $29,570**
- **Growth: 6.2%**
- **Annual Job Openings: 5,000**

Repair and install gas appliances and equipment, such as ovens, dryers, and hot water heaters.

Measures, cuts, and threads pipe and connects it to feeder lines and equipment or appliance, using rule and hand tools. Dismantles meters and regulators and replaces defective pipes, thermocouples, thermostats, valves, and indicator spindles, using hand tools. Assembles new or reconditioned appliances. Tests and examines pipelines and equipment to locate leaks and faulty connections and to determine pressure and flow of gas.

GOE INFORMATION—**Interest Area:** 05. Mechanics, Installers, and Repairers. **Work Group:** 05.03. Mechanical Work. **Personality Type**—Realistic. Realistic occupations frequently involve work activities that include practical, hands-on problems and solutions. They often deal with plants, animals, and real-world materials like wood, tools, and machinery. Many of the occupations require working outside and do not involve a lot of paperwork or working closely with others. **Work Values**—Independence; Moral Values; Supervision, Technical; Responsibility; Variety. **Skills**—Repairing; Installation; Troubleshooting; Operation Monitoring; Operation and Control; Quality Control Analysis. **Abilities**—*Cognitive:* Visualization; Speed of Closure; Perceptual Speed; Flexibility of Closure. *Psychomotor:* Manual Dexterity; Multilimb Coordination; Reaction Time; Finger Dexterity; Speed of Limb Movement. *Physical:* Extent Flexibility; Static Strength; Explosive Strength; Dynamic Flexibility; Dynamic Strength. *Sensory:* Sound Localization; Depth Perception; Night Vision; Hearing Sensitivity; Glare Sensitivity. **General Work Activities**—*Information Input:* Inspecting Equipment, Structures, or Materials; Monitoring Processes, Materials, or Surroundings; Getting Information. *Mental Process:* Updating and Using Relevant Knowledge; Evaluating Information Against Standards; Organizing, Planning, and Prioritizing. *Work Output:* Handling and Moving Objects; Performing General Physical Activities; Repairing and Maintaining Mechanical Equipment. *Interacting with Others:* Communicating with Persons Outside Organization; Performing for or Working with the Public; Establishing and Maintaining Relationships. **Physical Work Conditions**—Hazardous Conditions; Cramped Work Space or Awkward Positions; Kneeling, Crouching, or Crawling; Using Hands on Objects, Tools, or Controls; Minor Burns, Cuts, Bites, or Stings. **Other Job Characteristics**—Consequence of Error; Degree of Automation; Importance of Repeating Same Tasks.

Experience—Job Zone 4. A minimum of two to four years of work-related skill, knowledge, or experience is needed. **Job Preparation:** SVP 7.0 to less than 8.0—two years to less than 10 years. **Knowledge**—Mechanical; Building and Construction; Physics; Chemistry; Economics and Accounting. **Instructional Programs**—Appliance Installation and Repair Technology/Technician; Home Furnishings and Equipment Installers.

Related DOT Jobs—637.261-018 Gas-Appliance Servicer.

49-9041.00 Industrial Machinery Mechanics

- **Education/Training Required: Long-term on-the-job training**
- **Employed: 198,276**
- **Annual Earnings: $37,600**
- **Growth: 3.4%**
- **Annual Job Openings: 7,000**

Repair, install, adjust, or maintain industrial production and processing machinery or refinery and pipeline distribution systems.

Confers with operators and observes, tests, and evaluates operation of machinery and equipment to diagnose cause of malfunction. Disassembles machinery and equipment to remove parts and make repairs. Examines parts for defects, such as breakage or excessive wear. Repairs, replaces, adjusts, and aligns components of machinery and equipment. Cleans and lubricates parts, equipment, and machinery. Test-runs repaired machinery and equipment to verify adequacy of repairs. Fabricates replacement parts. Welds to repair broken metal parts, fabricate new parts, and assemble new equipment. Orders or requisitions parts and materials. Repairs and replaces electrical wiring and components of machinery. Enters codes and instructions to program computer-controlled machinery. Records repairs and maintenance performed.

GOE INFORMATION—**Interest Area:** 05. Mechanics, Installers, and Repairers. **Work Group:** 05.03. Mechanical Work. **Personality Type**—Realistic. Realistic occupations frequently involve work activities that include practical, hands-on problems and solutions. They often deal with plants, animals, and real-world materials like wood, tools, and machinery. Many of the occupations require working outside and do not involve a lot of paperwork or working closely with others. **Work Values**—Moral Values; Independence; Variety; Advancement; Activity. **Skills**—Repairing; Troubleshooting; Operation Monitoring; Quality Control Analysis; Installation; Operation and Control; Equipment Selection; Technology Design. **Abilities**—*Cognitive:* Visualization; Information Ordering; Spatial Orientation; Category Flexibility; Memorization. *Psychomotor:* Control Precision; Reaction Time; Finger Dexterity; Speed of Limb Movement; Wrist-Finger Speed. *Physical:* Extent Flexibility; Static Strength; Dynamic Strength; Trunk Strength; Explosive Strength. *Sensory:* Hearing Sensitivity; Auditory Attention; Visual Color Discrimination; Sound Localization; Peripheral Vision. **General Work Activities**—*Information Input:* Inspecting Equipment, Structures, or Materials; Getting Information; Monitoring Processes, Materials, or Surroundings. *Mental Process:* Updating and Using Relevant Knowledge; Making Decisions and Solving Problems; Analyzing Data or Information. *Work Output:* Repairing and Maintaining Mechanical Equipment; Performing General Physical Activities; Controlling Machines and Processes. *Interacting with Others:* Communicating with Other Workers; Monitoring and Controlling Resources; Interpreting Meaning of Information for Others. **Physical Work Conditions**—Hazardous Equipment; Common Protective or Safety Attire; Distracting Sounds and Noise Levels; Cramped Work Space or Awkward Positions; Kneeling, Crouching, or Crawling. **Other Job Characteristics**—Importance of Being Exact or Accurate; Degree of Automation; Consequence of Error.

Experience—Job Zone 3. Previous work-related skill, knowledge, or experience is required. **Job Preparation:** SVP 6.0 to less than 7.0—more than one year and less than four years. **Knowledge**—Mechanical; Engineering and Technology; Computers and Electronics; Physics; Public Safety and Security. **Instructional Programs**—Heavy/Industrial Equipment Maintenance Technologies, Other; Industrial Mechanics and Maintenance Technology.

Related DOT Jobs—601.281-030 Tool and Fixture Repairer; 620.281-018 Automotive-Maintenance-Equipment Servicer; 626.261-010 Forge-Shop-Machine Repairer; 626.261-014 Repairer, Welding Systems and Equipment; 626.361-010 Repairer, Welding, Brazing, and Burning Machines; 626.381-014 Gas-Welding-Equipment Mechanic; 626.381-018 Hydraulic-Press Servicer; 626.384-010 Repairer, Welding Equipment; 627.261-010 Composing-Room Machinist; 627.261-014 Machinist Apprentice, Composing Room; 627.261-018 Machinist Apprentice, Linotype; 627.261-022 Machinist, Linotype; 629.261-010 Laundry-Machine Mechanic; 629.261-014 Miller, Head, Wet Process; 629.261-018 Powder-Line Repairer; 629.261-022 Electronic-Production-Line-Maintenance Mechanic; 629.280-010 Maintenance Mechanic; 629.281-010 Bakery-Machine Mechanic; 629.281-014 Cellophane-Casting-Machine Repairer; 629.281-030 Maintenance Mechanic; others.

49-9042.00 *Maintenance and Repair Workers, General*

- **Education/Training Required: Long-term on-the-job training**
- **Employed: 1,251,271**
- **Annual Earnings: $28,740**
- **Growth: 4.7%**
- **Annual Job Openings: 103,000**

Perform work involving the skills of two or more maintenance or craft occupations to keep machines, mechanical equipment, or the structure of an establishment in repair. Duties may involve pipe fitting; boiler making; insulating; welding; machining; carpentry; repairing electrical or mechanical equipment; installing, aligning, and balancing new equipment; and repairing buildings, floors, or stairs.

Adjust functional parts of devices and control instruments, using hand tools, levels, plumb bobs, and straightedges. Align and balance new equipment after installation. Assemble, install, and/or repair wiring, electrical and electronic components, pipe systems and plumbing, machinery, and equipment. Clean and lubricate shafts, bearings, gears, and other parts of machinery. Diagnose mechanical problems and determine how to correct them, checking blueprints, repair manuals, and parts catalogs as necessary. Dismantle devices to gain access to and remove defective parts, using hoists, cranes, hand tools, and power tools. Inspect, operate, and test machinery and equipment in order to diagnose machine malfunctions. Lay brick to repair and maintain buildings, walls, arches, and other structures. Maintain and repair specialized equipment and machinery found in cafeterias, laundries, hospitals, stores, offices, and factories. Paint and repair roofs, windows, doors, floors, woodwork, plaster, drywall, and other parts of building structures. Perform routine preventive maintenance to ensure that machines continue to run smoothly, building systems operate efficiently, and the physical condition of buildings does not deteriorate. Plan and lay out repair work, using diagrams, drawings, blueprints, maintenance manuals, and schematic diagrams. Repair or replace defective equipment parts, using hand tools and power tools, and reassemble equipment. Estimate repair costs. Fabricate and repair counters, benches, partitions, and other wooden structures such as sheds and outbuildings. Grind and reseat valves, using valve-grinding machines. Inspect drives, motors, and belts; check fluid levels; replace filters; and perform other maintenance actions, following checklists. Inspect used parts to determine changes in dimensional requirements, using rules, calipers, micrometers, and other measuring instruments. Order parts, supplies, and equipment from catalogs and suppliers or obtain them from storerooms. Record maintenance and repair work performed and the costs of the work. Operate cutting torches or welding equipment to cut or join metal parts. Set up and operate machine tools to repair or fabricate machine parts, jigs and fixtures, and

tools. Use tools ranging from common hand and power tools, such as hammers, hoists, saws, drills, and wrenches, to precision measuring instruments and electrical and electronic testing devices.

GOE INFORMATION—**Interest Area:** 05. Mechanics, Installers, and Repairers. **Work Group:** 05.03. Mechanical Work. **Personality Type**—Realistic. Realistic occupations frequently involve work activities that include practical, hands-on problems and solutions. They often deal with plants, animals, and real-world materials like wood, tools, and machinery. Many of the occupations require working outside and do not involve a lot of paperwork or working closely with others. **Work Values**—Variety; Moral Values; Supervision, Technical; Independence; Supervision, Human Relations. **Skills**—Repairing; Installation; Troubleshooting; Operation Monitoring; Equipment Selection; Quality Control Analysis; Operation and Control. **Abilities**—*Cognitive:* Visualization; Perceptual Speed; Memorization; Spatial Orientation; Speed of Closure. *Psychomotor:* Reaction Time; Control Precision; Speed of Limb Movement; Finger Dexterity; Multilimb Coordination. *Physical:* Static Strength; Extent Flexibility; Dynamic Strength; Explosive Strength; Trunk Strength. *Sensory:* Hearing Sensitivity; Visual Color Discrimination; Sound Localization; Depth Perception; Auditory Attention. **General Work Activities**—*Information Input:* Getting Information; Inspecting Equipment, Structures, or Materials; Monitoring Processes, Materials, or Surroundings. *Mental Process:* Updating and Using Relevant Knowledge; Organizing, Planning, and Prioritizing; Analyzing Data or Information. *Work Output:* Repairing and Maintaining Mechanical Equipment; Performing General Physical Activities; Handling and Moving Objects. *Interacting with Others:* Monitoring and Controlling Resources; Establishing and Maintaining Relationships; Performing Administrative Activities. **Physical Work Conditions**—Common Protective or Safety Attire; Hazardous Equipment; Cramped Work Space or Awkward Positions; Distracting Sounds and Noise Levels; Climbing Ladders, Scaffolds, Poles, etc. **Other Job Characteristics**—Importance of Repeating Same Tasks; Importance of Being Exact or Accurate; Consequence of Error.

Experience—Job Zone 3. Previous work-related skill, knowledge, or experience is required. **Job Preparation:** SVP 6.0 to less than 7.0—more than one year and less than four years. **Knowledge**—Building and Construction; Mechanical; Design; Engineering and Technology; Public Safety and Security. **Instructional Programs**—Building/Construction Site Management/Manager.

Related DOT Jobs—638.281-010 Fire-Fighting-Equipment Specialist; 899.261-014 Maintenance Repairer, Industrial; 899.381-010 Maintenance Repairer, Building; 899.484-010 Mobile-Home-Lot Utility Worker; 912.364-010 Airport Attendant.

49-9043.00 *Maintenance Workers, Machinery*

- **Education/Training Required: Long-term on-the-job training**
- **Employed: 113,805**
- **Annual Earnings: $31,950**
- **Growth: 5.8%**
- **Annual Job Openings: 4,000**

Lubricate machinery, change parts, or perform other routine machinery maintenance.

Sets up and operates machine and adjusts controls that regulate operational functions to ensure conformance to specifications. Installs, replaces, or changes machine parts and attachments according to production specifications. Lubricates, oils, or applies adhesive or other material to machines, machine parts, or other equipment according to specified procedures. Starts machine and observes mechanical operation to determine efficiency and to detect defects, malfunctions, or other machine damage. Replaces or repairs metal, wood, leather, glass, or other lining in machine or equipment compartments or containers. Inspects or tests damaged machine parts and marks defective area or advises supervisor of need for repair. Dismantles machine, removes machine parts, and reassembles machine, using hand tools, chain falls, jack, crane, or hoist. Cuts, shapes, smoothes, attaches, or assembles pieces of metal, wood, rubber, or other material to repair and maintenance machines and equipment. Cleans machine and machine parts, using cleaning solvent, cloth, air gun, hose, vacuum, or other equipment. Reads work orders and specifications to determine machines and equipment requiring repair or maintenance. Removes hardened material from machine or machine parts, using abrasives, power and hand tools, jackhammer, sledgehammer, or other equipment. Replaces, empties, or replenishes empty machine and equipment containers, such as gas tanks or boxes. Communicates with or assists other workers to repair or move machines, machine parts, or equipment. Measures, mixes, prepares, and tests chemical solutions used to clean or repair machinery and equipment according to product specifications. Marks, separates, ties, aligns, threads, attaches, or inserts material or product preparatory to machine operation or to identify machine process. Records and maintains production, repair, and machine maintenance information. Inventories and requisitions machine parts, equipment, and other supplies to replenish and maintain stock. Transports machine parts, tools, equipment, and other material between work areas and storage, using crane, hoist, or dolly. Collects and discards worn machine parts and other garbage to maintain machinery and work areas.

GOE INFORMATION—Interest Area: 05. Mechanics, Installers, and Repairers. Work Group: 05.03. Mechanical Work. Personality Type—Realistic. Realistic occupations frequently involve work activities that include practical, hands-on problems and solutions. They often deal with plants, animals, and real-world materials like wood, tools, and machinery. Many of the occupations require working outside and do not involve a lot of paperwork or working closely with others. Work Values—Variety; Moral Values; Supervision, Human Relations; Pleasant Co-workers; Supervision, Technical. Skills—Repairing; Operation Monitoring; Installation; Troubleshooting; Operation and Control; Technology Design; Equipment Selection; Quality Control Analysis. Abilities—Cognitive: Perceptual Speed; Visualization; Information Ordering; Inductive Reasoning. Psychomotor: Reaction Time; Rate Control; Arm-Hand Steadiness; Control Precision; Manual Dexterity. Physical: Extent Flexibility; Static Strength; Dynamic Strength; Explosive Strength; Dynamic Flexibility. Sensory: Sound Localization; Hearing Sensitivity; Auditory Attention; Depth Perception; Peripheral Vision. General Work Activities—Information Input: Inspecting Equipment, Structures, or Materials; Getting Information; Monitoring Processes, Materials, or Surroundings. Mental Process: Updating and Using Relevant Knowledge; Making Decisions and Solving Problems; Evaluating Information Against Standards. Work Output: Repairing and Maintaining Mechanical Equipment; Performing General Physical Activities; Handling and Moving Objects. Interacting with Others: Communicating with Other Workers; Establishing and Maintaining Relationships; Assisting and Caring for Others. Physical Work Conditions—Hazardous Equipment; Distracting Sounds and Noise Levels; Common Protective or Safety Attire; Cramped Work Space or Awkward Positions; Kneeling, Crouching, or Crawling. Other Job Characteristics—Pace Determined by Speed of Equipment; Degree of Automation; Importance of Repeating Same Tasks.

Experience—Job Zone 1. No previous work-related skill, knowledge, or experience is needed. Job Preparation: SVP below 4.0—less than six months. Knowledge—Mechanical; Chemistry; Production and Processing; Engineering and Technology; Physics. Instructional Programs—Heavy/Industrial Equipment Maintenance Technologies, Other; Industrial Mechanics and Maintenance Technology.

Related DOT Jobs—514.684-018 Nozzle-and-Sleeve Worker; 519.664-014 Pot Liner; 519.667-010 Carbon Setter; 519.684-014 Leaf Coverer; 529.667-014 Mash-Filter-Cloth Changer; 564.684-010 Knife Setter, Grinder Machine; 590.384-014 Production Technician, Semiconductor Processing Equipment; 622.684-018 Switch Repairer; 628.684-010 Binder and Box Builder; 628.684-014 Frame Bander; 628.684-022 Overhead Cleaner Maintainer; 628.684-042 Spindle Repairer; 628.684-046 Texturing-Machine Fixer; 628.687-010 Flyer Repairer; 629.684-010 Curing-Press Maintainer; 630.584-010 Equipment Cleaner-and-Tester; 638.684-010 Knife Changer; 638.684-014 Knife Setter; 652.385-010 Printing-Roller Handler; 680.684-010 Card Grinder Helper; others.

49-9044.00 Millwrights

- **Education/Training Required: Long-term on-the-job training**
- **Employed: 72,378**
- **Annual Earnings: $41,960**
- **Growth: 3.9%**
- **Annual Job Openings: 7,000**

Install, dismantle, or move machinery and heavy equipment according to layout plans, blueprints, or other drawings.

Dismantle machines, using hammers, wrenches, crowbars, and other hand tools. Assemble machines and bolt, weld, rivet, or otherwise fasten them to foundation or other structures, using hand tools and power tools. Move machinery and equipment, using hoists, dollies, rollers, and trucks. Dismantle machinery and equipment for shipment to installation site, usually performing installation and maintenance work as part of team. Construct foundation for machines, using hand tools and building materials such as wood, cement, and steel. Install robot and modify its program, using teach pendant. Shrink-fit bushings, sleeves, rings, liners, gears, and wheels to specified items, using portable gas heating equipment. Level bedplate and establish centerline, using straightedge, levels, and transit. Insert shims, adjust tension on nuts and bolts, or position parts, using hand tools and measuring instruments, to set specified clearances between moving and stationary parts. Lay out mounting holes, using measuring instruments, and drill holes with power drill. Position steel beams to support bedplates of machines and equipment, using blueprints and schematic drawings to determine work procedures. Connect power unit to machines or steam piping to equipment and test unit to evaluate its mechanical operation. Replace defective parts of machine or adjust clearances and alignment of moving parts. Repair and lubricate machines and equipment. Operate engine lathe to grind, file, and turn machine parts to dimensional specifications. Signal crane operator to lower basic assembly units to bedplate and align unit to centerline. Align machines and equipment, using hoists, jacks, hand tools, squares, rules, micrometers, and plumb bobs. Attach moving parts and subassemblies to basic assembly unit, using hand tools and power tools. Assemble and install equipment, using hand tools and power tools. Bolt parts, such as side and deck plates, jaw plates, and journals, to basic assembly unit.

GOE INFORMATION—Interest Area: 05. Mechanics, Installers, and Repairers. Work Group: 05.03. Mechanical Work. Personality Type—Realistic. Realistic occupations frequently involve work activities that include practical, hands-on problems and solutions. They often deal with plants, animals, and real-world materials like wood, tools, and machinery. Many of the occupations require working outside and do not involve a lot of paperwork or working closely with others. Work Values—Variety; Moral Values; Compensation; Supervision, Human Relations; Supervision, Technical. Skills—Installation; Repairing; Troubleshooting; Quality Control Analysis; Operation and Control; Operation Monitoring; Equipment Selection. Abilities—Cognitive: Visualization; Spatial Orientation; Information Ordering; Time Sharing; Perceptual Speed. Psychomotor: Response

Orientation; Multilimb Coordination; Control Precision; Reaction Time; Manual Dexterity. *Physical:* Static Strength; Extent Flexibility; Explosive Strength; Dynamic Strength; Trunk Strength. *Sensory:* Depth Perception; Peripheral Vision; Hearing Sensitivity; Auditory Attention; Visual Color Discrimination. **General Work Activities**—*Information Input:* Inspecting Equipment, Structures, or Materials; Getting Information; Monitoring Processes, Materials, or Surroundings. *Mental Process:* Updating and Using Relevant Knowledge; Making Decisions and Solving Problems; Evaluating Information Against Standards. *Work Output:* Handling and Moving Objects; Performing General Physical Activities; Controlling Machines and Processes. *Interacting with Others:* Establishing and Maintaining Relationships; Communicating with Other Workers; Coordinating the Work and Activities of Others. **Physical Work Conditions**—Hazardous Equipment; Common Protective or Safety Attire; Distracting Sounds and Noise Levels; Cramped Work Space or Awkward Positions; Bending or Twisting the Body. **Other Job Characteristics**—Pace Determined by Speed of Equipment; Importance of Being Exact or Accurate; Consequence of Error.

Experience—Job Zone 4. A minimum of two to four years of work-related skill, knowledge, or experience is needed. **Job Preparation:** SVP 7.0 to less than 8.0—two years to less than 10 years. **Knowledge**—Mechanical; Building and Construction; Design; Engineering and Technology; Physics. **Instructional Programs**—Heavy/Industrial Equipment Maintenance Technologies, Other; Industrial Mechanics and Maintenance Technology.

Related DOT Jobs—638.261-014 Machinery Erector; 638.281-018 Millwright; 638.281-022 Millwright Apprentice.

49-9045.00 Refractory Materials Repairers, Except Brickmasons

- Education/Training Required: **Short-term on-the-job training**
- Employed: **No data available.**
- Annual Earnings: **$35,130**
- Growth: **11.5%**
- Annual Job Openings: **16,000**

Build or repair furnaces, kilns, cupolas, boilers, converters, ladles, soaking pits, ovens, etc., using refractory materials.

Relines or repairs ladle and pouring spout with refractory clay, using trowel. Dries and bakes new lining by placing inverted lining over burner, by building fire in ladle, or by using blowtorch. Drills holes in furnace wall, bolts overlapping layers of plastic to walls, and hammers surface to compress layers into solid sheets. Fastens stopper head to rod with metal pin to assemble refractory stopper used to plug pouring nozzles of steel ladles. Spreads mortar on stopper head and rod, using trowel, and slides brick sleeves over rod to form refractory jacket. Tightens locknuts holding assembly together, spreads mortar on jacket to seal sleeve joints, and dries mortar in oven. Mixes specified amounts of sand, clay, mortar powder, and water to form refractory clay or mortar, using shovel or mixing machine. Dumps and tamps clay in mold, using tamping tool. Disassembles mold and cuts, chips, and smoothes clay structures, such as floaters, drawbars, and L-blocks, using square rule and hand tools. Removes worn or damaged plastic block refractory lining of furnace, using hand tools. Bolts sections of wooden mold together, using wrench, and lines mold with paper to prevent adherence of clay to mold. Measures furnace wall and cuts required number of sheets from plastic block, using saw. Installs clay structures in melting tanks and drawing kilns to control flow and temperature of molten glass, using hoists and hand tools. Climbs scaffolding with hose and sprays surfaces of cupola with refractory mixture, using spray equipment. Transfers clay structures to curing ovens, melting tanks, and drawing kilns, using electric forklift truck. Chips slag from lining of ladle, or entire lining when beyond repair, using hammer and chisel. Installs preformed metal scaffolding in interior of cupola, using hand tools.

GOE INFORMATION—**Interest Area:** 06. Construction, Mining, and Drilling. **Work Group:** 06.02. Construction. **Personality Type**—Realistic. Realistic occupations frequently involve work activities that include practical, hands-on problems and solutions. They often deal with plants, animals, and real-world materials like wood, tools, and machinery. Many of the occupations require working outside and do not involve a lot of paperwork or working closely with others. **Work Values**—Independence; Moral Values; Variety; Company Policies and Practices; Supervision, Technical. **Skills**—Repairing; Installation; Operation and Control; Equipment Selection. **Abilities**—*Cognitive:* Spatial Orientation; Visualization; Information Ordering. *Psychomotor:* Multilimb Coordination; Speed of Limb Movement; Control Precision; Wrist-Finger Speed; Manual Dexterity. *Physical:* Dynamic Strength; Explosive Strength; Extent Flexibility; Static Strength; Stamina. *Sensory:* Depth Perception; Peripheral Vision; Auditory Attention; Far Vision; Glare Sensitivity. **General Work Activities**—*Information Input:* Monitoring Processes, Materials, or Surroundings; Inspecting Equipment, Structures, or Materials; Getting Information. *Mental Process:* Judging Qualities of Things, Services, or Other People's Work; Making Decisions and Solving Problems; Evaluating Information Against Standards. *Work Output:* Handling and Moving Objects; Performing General Physical Activities; Repairing and Maintaining Mechanical Equipment. *Interacting with Others:* Communicating with Other Workers; Establishing and Maintaining Relationships; Providing Consultation and Advice to Others. **Physical Work Conditions**—Climbing Ladders, Scaffolds, Poles, etc.; Hazardous Equipment; High Places; Very Hot or Cold; Common Protective or Safety Attire. **Other Job Characteristics**—Importance of Repeating Same Tasks; Pace Determined by Speed of Equipment; Consequence of Error.

Experience—Job Zone 1. No previous work-related skill, knowledge, or experience is needed. **Job Preparation:** SVP below 4.0—less than six months. **Knowledge**—Building and Construction; Production and Processing; Mechanical; Fine Arts; Chemistry. **Instructional Programs**—Industrial Mechanics and Maintenance Technology.

Related DOT Jobs—519.684-010 Ladle Liner; 519.684-022 Stopper Maker; 579.664-010 Clay-Structure Builder and Servicer; 849.484-010 Boiler Reliner, Plastic Block; 899.684-010 Bondactor-Machine Operator.

49-9051.00 Electrical Power-Line Installers and Repairers

- Education/Training Required: **Long-term on-the-job training**
- Employed: **99,181**
- Annual Earnings: **$47,210**
- Growth: **9.3%**
- Annual Job Openings: **5,000**

Install or repair cables or wires used in electrical power or distribution systems. May erect poles and light- or heavy-duty transmission towers.

Splices, solders, and insulates conductors and wiring to join sections of power line and to connect transformers and electrical accessories. Tests electric power lines and auxiliary equipment, using direct reading and testing instruments to identify cause of disturbances. Strings wire conductors and cable between erected poles and adjusts slack, using winch. Climbs poles and removes and installs hardware, wires, and other equipment. Opens switches or clamps grounding device to de-energize disturbed or fallen lines to facilitate repairs or to remove electrical hazards.

Replaces and straightens poles and attaches crossarms, insulators, and auxiliary equipment to wood poles preparatory to erection. Cuts and peels lead sheath and insulation from defective or newly installed cables and conducts prior to splicing. Cleans, tins, and splices corresponding conductors by twisting ends together or by joining ends with metal clamps and soldering connection. Tests conductors to identify corresponding conductors and to prevent incorrect connections according to electrical diagrams and specifications. Installs watt-hour meters and connects service drops between power line and consumer. Covers conductors with insulating or fireproofing materials. Works on energized lines to avoid interruption of service. Drives conveyance equipped with tools and materials to job site. Repairs electrical power cables and auxiliary equipment for electrical power lines. Installs and repairs conduits, cables, wires, and auxiliary equipment, following blueprints. Splices cables together or to overhead transmission line, customer service line, or street light line.

GOE INFORMATION—Interest Area: 05. Mechanics, Installers, and Repairers. **Work Group:** 05.02. Electrical and Electronic Systems. **Personality Type**—Realistic. Realistic occupations frequently involve work activities that include practical, hands-on problems and solutions. They often deal with plants, animals, and real-world materials like wood, tools, and machinery. Many of the occupations require working outside and do not involve a lot of paperwork or working closely with others. **Work Values**—Supervision, Technical; Moral Values; Security; Advancement; Supervision, Human Relations. **Skills**—Installation; Repairing; Troubleshooting; Quality Control Analysis; Operation and Control; Technology Design; Science; Equipment Selection. **Abilities**—*Cognitive:* Visualization; Spatial Orientation; Information Ordering; Perceptual Speed; Flexibility of Closure. *Psychomotor:* Arm-Hand Steadiness; Multilimb Coordination; Response Orientation; Manual Dexterity; Finger Dexterity. *Physical:* Dynamic Strength; Extent Flexibility; Gross Body Equilibrium; Explosive Strength; Gross Body Coordination. *Sensory:* Visual Color Discrimination; Far Vision; Depth Perception; Near Vision; Hearing Sensitivity. **General Work Activities**—*Information Input:* Inspecting Equipment, Structures, or Materials; Monitoring Processes, Materials, or Surroundings; Getting Information. *Mental Process:* Updating and Using Relevant Knowledge; Evaluating Information Against Standards; Making Decisions and Solving Problems. *Work Output:* Performing General Physical Activities; Handling and Moving Objects; Repairing and Maintaining Electronic Equipment. *Interacting with Others:* Communicating with Other Workers; Coordinating the Work and Activities of Others; Coaching and Developing Others. **Physical Work Conditions**—Hazardous Conditions; High Places; Outdoors; Common Protective or Safety Attire; Climbing Ladders, Scaffolds, Poles, etc. **Other Job Characteristics**—Consequence of Error; Importance of Being Exact or Accurate; Importance of Repeating Same Tasks.

Experience—Job Zone 4. A minimum of two to four years of work-related skill, knowledge, or experience is needed. **Job Preparation:** SVP 7.0 to less than 8.0—two years to less than 10 years. **Knowledge**—Public Safety and Security; Mechanical; Design; Building and Construction; Engineering and Technology. **Instructional Programs**—Electrical and Power Transmission Installation/Installer, General; Electrical and Power Transmission Installers, Other; Lineworker.

Related DOT Jobs—821.261-014 Line Maintainer; 821.261-022 Service Restorer, Emergency; 821.261-026 Trouble Shooter II; 821.361-010 Cable Installer-Repairer; 821.361-018 Line Erector; 821.361-022 Line Installer, Street Railway; 821.361-026 Line Repairer; 821.361-030 Line-Erector Apprentice; 821.361-038 Tower Erector; 821.684-022 Trolley-Wire Installer; 825.381-038 Third-Rail Installer; 829.361-010 Cable Splicer; 829.361-014 Cable-Splicer Apprentice.

49-9052.00 Telecommunications Line Installers and Repairers

- **Education/Training Required: Long-term on-the-job training**
- **Employed: 163,719**
- **Annual Earnings: $39,200**
- **Growth: 27.6%**
- **Annual Job Openings: 9,000**

String and repair telephone and television cable, including fiber optics and other equipment for transmitting messages or television programming.

Installs terminal boxes and strings lead-in-wires, using electrician's tools. Repairs cable system, defective lines, and auxiliary equipment. Ascends poles or enters tunnels and sewers to string lines and install terminal boxes, auxiliary equipment, and appliances according to diagrams. Pulls lines through ducts by hand or with use of winch. Computes impedance of wire from pole to house to determine additional resistance needed for reducing signal to desired level. Connects television set to cable system, evaluates incoming signal, and adjusts system to ensure optimum reception. Measures signal strength at utility pole, using electronic test equipment. Installs and removes plant equipment, such as callboxes and clocks. Digs holes, using power auger or shovel, and hoists poles upright into holes, using truck-mounted winch. Fills and tamps holes, using cement, earth, and tamping device. Cleans and maintains tools and test equipment. Explains cable service to subscriber. Collects installation fees.

GOE INFORMATION—Interest Area: 05. Mechanics, Installers, and Repairers. **Work Group:** 05.02. Electrical and Electronic Systems. **Personality Type**—Realistic. Realistic occupations frequently involve work activities that include practical, hands-on problems and solutions. They often deal with plants, animals, and real-world materials like wood, tools, and machinery. Many of the occupations require working outside and do not involve a lot of paperwork or working closely with others. **Work Values**—Supervision, Technical; Independence; Security; Variety; Social Service. **Skills**—Installation; Repairing; Troubleshooting; Operation Monitoring; Operation and Control; Equipment Selection. **Abilities**—*Cognitive:* Mathematical Reasoning; Oral Comprehension; Oral Expression; Spatial Orientation. *Psychomotor:* Manual Dexterity; Control Precision; Arm-Hand Steadiness; Finger Dexterity; Multilimb Coordination. *Physical:* Gross Body Coordination; Gross Body Equilibrium; Explosive Strength; Static Strength; Trunk Strength. *Sensory:* Visual Color Discrimination. **General Work Activities**—*Information Input:* Monitoring Processes, Materials, or Surroundings; Inspecting Equipment, Structures, or Materials; Getting Information. *Mental Process:* Updating and Using Relevant Knowledge; Judging Qualities of Things, Services, or Other People's Work; Making Decisions and Solving Problems. *Work Output:* Performing General Physical Activities; Repairing and Maintaining Electronic Equipment; Handling and Moving Objects. *Interacting with Others:* Communicating with Other Workers; Communicating with Persons Outside Organization; Establishing and Maintaining Relationships. **Physical Work Conditions**—Outdoors; High Places; Cramped Work Space or Awkward Positions; Climbing Ladders, Scaffolds, Poles, etc.; Very Hot or Cold. **Other Job Characteristics**—Importance of Repeating Same Tasks; Importance of Being Exact or Accurate; Pace Determined by Speed of Equipment.

Experience—Job Zone 3. Previous work-related skill, knowledge, or experience is required. **Job Preparation:** SVP 6.0 to less than 7.0—more than one year and less than four years. **Knowledge**—Telecommunications; Computers and Electronics; Sales and Marketing; Mechanical; Physics. **Instructional Programs**—Communications Systems Installation and Repair Technology.

Related DOT Jobs—821.281-010 Cable Television Installer; 822.381-014 Line Installer-Repairer.

49-9061.00 Camera and Photographic Equipment Repairers

- **Education/Training Required: Moderate-term on-the-job training**
- **Employed: 7,199**
- **Annual Earnings: $30,080**
- **Growth: −2.1%**
- **Annual Job Openings: 1,000**

Repair and adjust cameras and photographic equipment, including commercial video and motion picture camera equipment.

Measure parts to verify specified dimensions/settings, such as camera shutter speed and light meter reading accuracy, using measuring instruments. Test equipment performance, focus of lens system, alignment of diaphragm, lens mounts, and film transport, using precision gauges. Fabricate or modify defective electronic, electrical, and mechanical components, using bench lathe, milling machine, shaper, grinder, and precision hand tools according to specifications. Recommend design changes or upgrades of micro-filming, film-developing, and photographic equipment. Requisition parts and materials. Record test data and document fabrication techniques on reports. Clean and lubricate cameras and polish camera lenses, using cleaning materials and work aids. Lay out reference points and dimensions on parts and metal stock to be machined, using precision measuring instruments. Install film in aircraft camera and electrical assemblies and wiring in camera housing, following blueprints and using hand tools and soldering equipment. Assemble aircraft cameras, still and motion picture cameras, photographic equipment, and frames, using diagrams, blueprints, bench machines, hand tools, and power tools. Read and interpret engineering drawings, diagrams, instructions, and specifications to determine needed repairs, fabrication method, and operation sequence. Examine cameras, equipment, processed film, and laboratory reports to diagnose malfunction, using work aids and specifications. Disassemble equipment to gain access to defect, using hand tools. Adjust cameras, photographic mechanisms, and equipment, such as range and view finders, shutters, light meters, and lens systems, using hand tools. Calibrate and verify accuracy of light meters, shutter diaphragm operation, and lens carriers, using timing instruments.

GOE INFORMATION—Interest Area: 05. Mechanics, Installers, and Repairers. **Work Group:** 05.03. Mechanical Work. **Personality Type—**Realistic. Realistic occupations frequently involve work activities that include practical, hands-on problems and solutions. They often deal with plants, animals, and real-world materials like wood, tools, and machinery. Many of the occupations require working outside and do not involve a lot of paperwork or working closely with others. **Work Values—**Good Working Conditions; Autonomy; Independence; Ability Utilization; Variety. **Skills—**Repairing; Troubleshooting; Installation; Quality Control Analysis; Operation Monitoring; Technology Design; Equipment Selection; Speaking. **Abilities—***Cognitive:* Written Comprehension; Visualization; Speed of Closure; Originality; Oral Expression. *Psychomotor:* Finger Dexterity; Control Precision; Arm-Hand Steadiness; Multilimb Coordination; Manual Dexterity. *Physical:* Dynamic Flexibility; Dynamic Strength; Extent Flexibility; Gross Body Equilibrium; Explosive Strength. *Sensory:* Visual Color Discrimination; Night Vision; Depth Perception; Glare Sensitivity; Speech Clarity. **General Work Activities—***Information Input:* Getting Information; Identifying Objects, Actions, and Events; Inspecting Equipment, Structures, or Materials. *Mental Process:* Updating and Using Relevant Knowledge; Analyzing Data or Information; Evaluating Information Against Standards. *Work Output:* Repairing and Maintaining Mechanical Equipment; Handling and Moving Objects; Controlling Machines and Processes. *Interacting with Others:* Communicating with Persons Outside Organization; Establishing and Maintaining Relationships; Providing Consultation and Advice to Others. **Physical Work Conditions—**Using Hands on Objects, Tools, or Controls; Minor Burns, Cuts, Bites, or Stings; Hazardous Conditions; Extremely Bright or Inadequate Lighting; Hazardous Equipment. **Other Job Characteristics—**Degree of Automation; Importance of Repeating Same Tasks; Importance of Being Exact or Accurate.

Experience—Job Zone 4. A minimum of two to four years of work-related skill, knowledge, or experience is needed. **Job Preparation:** SVP 7.0 to less than 8.0—two years to less than 10 years. **Knowledge—**Mechanical; Engineering and Technology; Design; Fine Arts; Physics. **Instructional Programs—**Communications Systems Installation and Repair Technology.

Related DOT Jobs—714.281-010 Aircraft-Photographic-Equipment Mechanic; 714.281-014 Camera Repairer; 714.281-018 Machinist, Motion-Picture Equipment; 714.281-022 Photographic Equipment Technician; 714.281-026 Photographic-Equipment-Maintenance Technician; 714.281-030 Service Technician, Computerized-Photofinishing Equipment; 826.261-010 Field-Service Engineer.

49-9062.00 Medical Equipment Repairers

- **Education/Training Required: Moderate-term on-the-job training**
- **Employed: 28,482**
- **Annual Earnings: $35,540**
- **Growth: 14.9%**
- **Annual Job Openings: 3,000**

Test, adjust, or repair biomedical or electromedical equipment.

Contribute expertise to develop medical maintenance standard operating procedures. Evaluate technical specifications to identify equipment and systems best suited for intended use and possible purchase based on specifications, user needs, and technical requirements. Fabricate, dress down, or substitute parts or major new items to modify equipment to meet unique operational or research needs, working from job orders, sketches, modification orders, samples, or discussions with operating officials. Make computations relating to load requirements of wiring and equipment, using algebraic expressions and standard formulas. Research catalogs and repair part lists to locate sources for repair parts, requisitioning parts and recording their receipt. Supervise and advise subordinate personnel. Repair shop equipment, metal furniture, and hospital equipment, including welding broken parts and replacing missing parts, or bring item into local shop for major repairs. Test, evaluate, and classify excess or in-use medical equipment and determine serviceability, condition, and disposition in accordance with regulations. Compute power and space requirements for installing medical, dental, or related equipment and install units to manufacturers' specifications. Disassemble malfunctioning equipment and remove, repair, and replace defective parts such as motors, clutches, or transformers. Examine medical equipment and facility's structural environment and check for proper use of equipment to protect patients and staff from electrical or mechanical hazards and to ensure compliance with safety regulations. Explain and demonstrate correct operation and preventive maintenance of medical equipment to personnel. Inspect and test malfunctioning medical and related equipment following manufacturers' specifications, using test and analysis instruments. Keep records of maintenance, repair, and required updates of equipment. Perform preventive maintenance or service such as cleaning, lubricating, and adjusting equipment. Plan and carry out work assignments, using blueprints, schematic drawings, technical manuals, wiring diagrams, and liquid and air flow sheets, while following prescribed regulations, directives, and other instructions as required. Solder loose connections, using soldering iron. Study technical manuals and attend training sessions provided by equipment manufacturers to maintain current knowledge. Test and calibrate components and equipment, following manufacturers' manuals and troubleshooting techniques and using hand tools, power tools, and measuring devices.

GOE INFORMATION—Interest Area: 05. Mechanics, Installers, and Repairers. **Work Group:** 05.03. Mechanical Work. **Personality Type**—Realistic. Realistic occupations frequently involve work activities that include practical, hands-on problems and solutions. They often deal with plants, animals, and real-world materials like wood, tools, and machinery. Many of the occupations require working outside and do not involve a lot of paperwork or working closely with others. **Work Values**—Compensation; Moral Values; Supervision, Technical; Variety; Pleasant Co-workers. **Skills**—Installation; Repairing; Troubleshooting; Operation Monitoring; Technology Design; Quality Control Analysis; Instructing; Equipment Selection. **Abilities**—*Cognitive:* Visualization; Written Comprehension; Speed of Closure; Originality; Oral Comprehension. *Psychomotor:* Finger Dexterity; Control Precision; Arm-Hand Steadiness; Response Orientation; Manual Dexterity. *Physical:* Explosive Strength; Extent Flexibility; Static Strength; Dynamic Strength; Gross Body Equilibrium. *Sensory:* Speech Clarity; Sound Localization; Hearing Sensitivity; Visual Color Discrimination; Auditory Attention. **General Work Activities**—*Information Input:* Monitoring Processes, Materials, or Surroundings; Inspecting Equipment, Structures, or Materials; Getting Information. *Mental Process:* Updating and Using Relevant Knowledge; Analyzing Data or Information; Evaluating Information Against Standards. *Work Output:* Repairing and Maintaining Electronic Equipment; Repairing and Maintaining Mechanical Equipment; Handling and Moving Objects. *Interacting with Others:* Communicating with Persons Outside Organization; Influencing Others or Selling; Communicating with Other Workers. **Physical Work Conditions**—Hazardous Equipment; Minor Burns, Cuts, Bites, or Stings; Disease or Infections; Using Hands on Objects, Tools, or Controls; Hazardous Conditions. **Other Job Characteristics**—Importance of Being Exact or Accurate; Consequence of Error; Degree of Automation.

Experience—Job Zone 3. Previous work-related skill, knowledge, or experience is required. **Job Preparation:** SVP 6.0 to less than 7.0—more than one year and less than four years. **Knowledge**—Mechanical; Engineering and Technology; Computers and Electronics; Design; Biology. **Instructional Programs**—Biomedical Technology/Technician.

Related DOT Jobs—019.261-010 Biomedical Equipment Technician; 639.281-022 Medical-Equipment Repairer; 719.261-014 Radiological-Equipment Specialist; 729.281-030 Electromedical-Equipment Repairer; 829.261-014 Dental-Equipment Installer and Servicer.

49-9063.00 *Musical Instrument Repairers and Tuners*

- Education/Training Required: Long-term on-the-job training
- Employed: 7,068
- Annual Earnings: $29,420
- Growth: 9.4%
- Annual Job Openings: 1,000

Repair percussion, stringed, reed, or wind instruments. May specialize in one area, such as piano tuning.

No task data available.

GOE INFORMATION—Interest Area: 05. Mechanics, Installers, and Repairers. **Work Group:** 05.03. Mechanical Work. **Note:** The Department of Labor has not collected some data for this job, so it has fewer details than the other descriptions.

Instructional Programs—Musical Instrument Fabrication and Repair.

Related DOT Jobs—730.281-014 Accordion Repairer; 730.281-026 Fretted-Instrument Repairer; 730.281-038 Piano Technician; 730.281-050 Violin Repairer; 730.281-054 Wind-Instrument Repairer; 730.361-010 Piano Tuner; 730.361-014 Pipe-Organ Tuner and Repairer; 730.381-010 Accordion Tuner; 730.381-026 Harp Regulator; 730.381-034 Metal-Reed Tuner; 730.381-038 Organ-Pipe Voicer; 730.381-042 Percussion-Instrument Repairer; 730.381-058 Tuner, Percussion; 730.681-010 Piano Regulator-Inspector; 730.684-022 Bow Rehairer; 730.684-026 Chip Tuner; 730.684-094 Tone Regulator.

49-9063.01 *Keyboard Instrument Repairers and Tuners*

- Education/Training Required: Long-term on-the-job training
- Employed: No data available.
- Annual Earnings: $29,420
- Growth: 9.4%
- Annual Job Openings: 1,000

Repair, adjust, refinish, and tune musical keyboard instruments.

Repairs or replaces defective, broken, or worn parts, using hand tools, power tools, glue, and nails. Adjusts lips, reeds, or toe hole of organ pipes, using hand tools, to regulate airflow and loudness of sound. Adjusts felt hammers on piano to increase tonal mellowness or brilliance, using sanding paddle, lacquer, or needles. Adjusts alignment, string spacing, and striking point of hammers of piano, using wrench, burner, shims, and bushings. Disassembles and reassembles instruments and parts to tune and repair, using hand tools and power tools. Compares pitch of instruments with specified pitch of tuning tool to tune instrument. Removes irregularities from tuning pins, strings, and hammers of piano, using wood block or filing tool. Inspects and tests parts of pianos, pipe organs, accordions, and concertinas to determine defects, using hand tools, gauges, and electronic testing equipment. Assembles and installs new pipe organs and pianos in buildings. Makes wood replacement parts, using woodworking machines and hand tools. Mixes and measures glue. Cleans instruments, using vacuum cleaner.

GOE INFORMATION—Interest Area: 05. Mechanics, Installers, and Repairers. **Work Group:** 05.03. Mechanical Work. **Personality Type**—Realistic. Realistic occupations frequently involve work activities that include practical, hands-on problems and solutions. They often deal with plants, animals, and real-world materials like wood, tools, and machinery. Many of the occupations require working outside and do not involve a lot of paperwork or working closely with others. **Work Values**—Independence; Moral Values; Good Working Conditions; Autonomy; Supervision, Technical. **Skills**—Repairing; Installation; Equipment Selection. **Abilities**—*Cognitive:* Visualization; Flexibility of Closure; Speed of Closure; Selective Attention; Spatial Orientation. *Psychomotor:* Wrist-Finger Speed; Finger Dexterity; Control Precision; Speed of Limb Movement; Arm-Hand Steadiness. *Physical:* Extent Flexibility; Dynamic Flexibility; Dynamic Strength; Static Strength; Gross Body Coordination. *Sensory:* Hearing Sensitivity; Sound Localization; Auditory Attention; Depth Perception; Visual Color Discrimination. **General Work Activities**—*Information Input:* Inspecting Equipment, Structures, or Materials; Identifying Objects, Actions, and Events; Getting Information. *Mental Process:* Judging Qualities of Things, Services, or Other People's Work; Organizing, Planning, and Prioritizing; Evaluating Information Against Standards. *Work Output:*

Repairing and Maintaining Mechanical Equipment; Handling and Moving Objects; Performing General Physical Activities. *Interacting with Others:* Communicating with Persons Outside Organization; Monitoring and Controlling Resources; Assisting and Caring for Others. **Physical Work Conditions**—Using Hands on Objects, Tools, or Controls; Cramped Work Space or Awkward Positions; Making Repetitive Motions; Indoors; Kneeling, Crouching, or Crawling. **Other Job Characteristics**—Importance of Being Exact or Accurate; Importance of Repeating Same Tasks; Pace Determined by Speed of Equipment.

Experience—Job Zone 3. Previous work-related skill, knowledge, or experience is required. **Job Preparation:** SVP 6.0 to less than 7.0—more than one year and less than four years. **Knowledge**—Mechanical; Fine Arts; Engineering and Technology; Building and Construction. **Instructional Programs**—Musical Instrument Fabrication and Repair.

Related DOT Jobs—730.281-014 Accordion Repairer; 730.281-038 Piano Technician; 730.361-010 Piano Tuner; 730.361-014 Pipe-Organ Tuner and Repairer; 730.381-010 Accordion Tuner; 730.381-038 Organ-Pipe Voicer; 730.681-010 Piano Regulator-Inspector; 730.684-026 Chip Tuner; 730.684-094 Tone Regulator.

49-9063.02 Stringed Instrument Repairers and Tuners

- Education/Training Required: Long-term on-the-job training
- Employed: No data available.
- Annual Earnings: $29,420
- Growth: 9.4%
- Annual Job Openings: 1,000

Repair, adjust, refinish, and tune musical stringed instruments.

Repairs broken parts, using glue, clamp, and handpress. Refinishes instruments to protect and decorate them, using hand tools, buffing tools, and varnish. Strings instrument and adjusts truss and bridge of instrument to obtain specified string tension and height. Adjusts string tension to tune instrument, using hand tools and electronic tuning device. Reassembles instrument or bow with new or repaired part, using glue, hairs, yarn, resin, and clamps. Disassembles instrument or bow, using hand tools. Inspects musical instruments, such as cellos, violins, guitars, and mandolins, to determine defects. Removes cracked, worn, or broken parts of instrument, using heated knife and hand tools. Carves wood replacement parts, such as wedges or plugs, according to the shape and dimensions of the instrument or bow. Assembles instruments according to specifications, using hand tools. Plays instrument to determine pitch. Tests tubes and pickups in electronic amplifier units and solders parts and connections.

GOE INFORMATION—Interest Area: 05. Mechanics, Installers, and Repairers. **Work Group:** 05.03. Mechanical Work. **Personality Type**—Realistic. Realistic occupations frequently involve work activities that include practical, hands-on problems and solutions. They often deal with plants, animals, and real-world materials like wood, tools, and machinery. Many of the occupations require working outside and do not involve a lot of paperwork or working closely with others. **Work Values**—Independence; Moral Values; Good Working Conditions; Autonomy; Ability Utilization. **Skills**—Repairing; Technology Design. **Abilities**—*Cognitive:* Visualization; Flexibility of Closure; Speed of Closure; Memorization; Perceptual Speed. *Psychomotor:* Speed of Limb Movement; Arm-Hand Steadiness; Control Precision; Finger Dexterity; Wrist-Finger Speed. *Physical:* Explosive Strength; Dynamic Flexibility; Extent Flexibility; Static Strength; Dynamic Strength. *Sensory:* Hearing Sensitivity; Auditory Attention; Sound Localization; Visual Color Discrimination; Depth Perception. **General Work Activities**—*Information Input:* Identifying Objects,

Actions, and Events; Inspecting Equipment, Structures, or Materials; Getting Information. *Mental Process:* Judging Qualities of Things, Services, or Other People's Work; Thinking Creatively; Evaluating Information Against Standards. *Work Output:* Handling and Moving Objects; Repairing and Maintaining Mechanical Equipment; Repairing and Maintaining Electronic Equipment. *Interacting with Others:* Monitoring and Controlling Resources; Communicating with Other Workers; Communicating with Persons Outside Organization. **Physical Work Conditions**—Using Hands on Objects, Tools, or Controls; Indoors; Making Repetitive Motions; Bending or Twisting the Body; Radiation. **Other Job Characteristics**—Importance of Being Exact or Accurate; Importance of Repeating Same Tasks; Consequence of Error.

Experience—Job Zone 3. Previous work-related skill, knowledge, or experience is required. **Job Preparation:** SVP 6.0 to less than 7.0—more than one year and less than four years. **Knowledge**—Fine Arts; Building and Construction. **Instructional Programs**—Musical Instrument Fabrication and Repair.

Related DOT Jobs—730.281-026 Fretted-Instrument Repairer; 730.281-050 Violin Repairer; 730.381-026 Harp Regulator; 730.684-022 Bow Rehairer.

49-9063.03 Reed or Wind Instrument Repairers and Tuners

- Education/Training Required: Long-term on-the-job training
- Employed: No data available.
- Annual Earnings: $29,420
- Growth: 9.4%
- Annual Job Openings: 1,000

Repair, adjust, refinish, and tune musical reed and wind instruments.

Disassembles instrument parts, such as keys, pistons, and other parts, to tune or repair, using gas torch and hand tools. Repairs cracks in wood or metal instruments, using wire, lathe, filler, clamps, or soldering iron. Files reed until pitch corresponds with standard pitch of tuning bar. Replaces worn pads and springs, using hand tools. Lubricates and reassembles instrument, using hand tools and soldering iron or torch. Inspects mechanical parts of instrument to determine defects. Removes dents and burrs from metal instruments, using mallet and burnishing tool. Shapes old parts and replacement parts to improve tone or intonation, using hand tools, lathe, or soldering iron. Operates bellows to sound metal reed and ascertain its pitch. Compares pitch of reed with pitch of tuning bar. Polishes instrument, using rag and polishing compound, buffing wheel, or burnishing tool. Washes metal instruments in lacquer-stripping and cyanide solution to remove lacquer and tarnish.

GOE INFORMATION—Interest Area: 05. Mechanics, Installers, and Repairers. **Work Group:** 05.03. Mechanical Work. **Personality Type**—Realistic. Realistic occupations frequently involve work activities that include practical, hands-on problems and solutions. They often deal with plants, animals, and real-world materials like wood, tools, and machinery. Many of the occupations require working outside and do not involve a lot of paperwork or working closely with others. **Work Values**—Independence; Moral Values; Good Working Conditions; Autonomy; Responsibility. **Skills**—Repairing; Troubleshooting. **Abilities**—*Cognitive:* Flexibility of Closure; Speed of Closure; Perceptual Speed; Visualization; Selective Attention. *Psychomotor:* Finger Dexterity; Speed of Limb Movement; Arm-Hand Steadiness; Wrist-Finger Speed; Manual Dexterity. *Physical:* Dynamic Strength; Explosive Strength; Dynamic Flexibility; Extent Flexibility; Static Strength. *Sensory:* Hearing Sensitivity; Auditory Attention; Sound Localization; Depth Perception; Visual Color Discrimination. **General Work Activities**—*Information Input:* Identifying Objects, Actions, and Events; Inspecting Equipment, Structures, or Materials; Getting Information. *Mental Process:* Evaluating Information Against Standards; Judging Qualities of Things, Services, or Other People's Work; Analyzing Data or Information. *Work Output:* Handling and Moving Objects; Repairing and Maintaining Mechanical Equipment; Controlling Machines and Processes. *Interacting with Others:* Communicating with Persons Outside Organization; Monitoring and Controlling Resources; Providing Consultation and Advice to Others. **Physical Work Conditions**— Using Hands on Objects, Tools, or Controls; Indoors; Common Protective or Safety Attire; Making Repetitive Motions; Contaminants. **Other Job Characteristics**—Importance of Being Exact or Accurate; Consequence of Error; Importance of Repeating Same Tasks.

Experience—Job Zone 4. A minimum of two to four years of work-related skill, knowledge, or experience is needed. **Job Preparation:** SVP 7.0 to less than 8.0—two years to less than 10 years. **Knowledge**—Mechanical; Fine Arts. **Instructional Programs**—Musical Instrument Fabrication and Repair.

Related DOT Jobs—730.281-054 Wind-Instrument Repairer; 730.381-034 Metal-Reed Tuner.

49-9063.04 Percussion Instrument Repairers and Tuners

- **Education/Training Required: Long-term on-the-job training**
- **Employed: No data available.**
- **Annual Earnings: $29,420**
- **Growth: 9.4%**
- **Annual Job Openings: 1,000**

Repair and tune musical percussion instruments.

Stretches skin over rim hoop, using hand-tucking tool. Places rim hoop back onto drum shell to allow drumhead to dry and become taut. Repairs breaks in percussion instruments, such as drums and cymbals, using drill press, power saw, glues, clamps, or other hand tools. Strikes wood, fiberglass, or metal bars of instruments, such as xylophone or vibraharp, to ascertain tone. Compares tone of bar with tuned block, stroboscope, or electronic tuner. Removes dents in tympani, using steel block and hammer. Removes drumhead, using drum key and cutting tools. Cuts new drumhead from animal skin, using scissors. Soaks drumhead in water to make it pliable. Removes material from bar, using band saw, sanding machine, machine grinder, or hand files and scrapers, to obtain the specified tone. Assembles bar onto instruments. Solders or welds frames of mallet instruments and metal drum parts. Cleans, sands, and paints parts of percussion instruments to maintain their condition in accordance with blueprints and shop drawings.

GOE INFORMATION—**Interest Area:** 05. Mechanics, Installers, and Repairers. **Work Group:** 05.03. Mechanical Work. **Personality Type**—Realistic. Realistic occupations frequently involve work activities that include practical, hands-on problems and solutions. They often deal with plants, animals, and real-world materials like wood, tools, and machinery. Many of the occupations require working outside and do not involve a lot of paperwork or working closely with others. **Work Values**—Independence; Moral Values; Good Working Conditions; Autonomy; Responsibility. **Skills**—Repairing; Equipment Selection. **Abilities**—*Cognitive:* None met the criteria. *Psychomotor:* Speed of Limb Movement; Finger Dexterity; Manual Dexterity; Control Precision; Wrist-Finger Speed. *Physical:* Explosive Strength; Trunk Strength; Extent Flexibility; Static Strength; Dynamic Flexibility. *Sensory:* Hearing Sensitivity; Auditory Attention; Near Vision; Sound Localization. **General Work Activities**—*Information Input:* Inspecting Equipment, Structures, or Materials; Identifying Objects, Actions, and Events; Getting Information. *Mental Process:* Judging

Qualities of Things, Services, or Other People's Work; Evaluating Information Against Standards; Thinking Creatively. *Work Output:* Handling and Moving Objects; Controlling Machines and Processes; Repairing and Maintaining Mechanical Equipment. *Interacting with Others:* Monitoring and Controlling Resources; Providing Consultation and Advice to Others; Communicating with Other Workers. **Physical Work Conditions**—Using Hands on Objects, Tools, or Controls; Hazardous Equipment; Minor Burns, Cuts, Bites, or Stings; Indoors; Making Repetitive Motions. **Other Job Characteristics**—Importance of Being Exact or Accurate; Importance of Repeating Same Tasks; Consequence of Error.

Experience—Job Zone 3. Previous work-related skill, knowledge, or experience is required. **Job Preparation:** SVP 6.0 to less than 7.0—more than one year and less than four years. **Knowledge**—Fine Arts; Mechanical; Building and Construction; Design; Engineering and Technology. **Instructional Programs**—Musical Instrument Fabrication and Repair.

Related DOT Jobs—730.381-042 Percussion-Instrument Repairer; 730.381-058 Tuner, Percussion.

49-9064.00 Watch Repairers

- **Education/Training Required: Long-term on-the-job training**
- **Employed: 5,242**
- **Annual Earnings: $25,930**
- **Growth: 6.2%**
- **Annual Job Openings: 1,000**

Repair, clean, and adjust mechanisms of timing instruments, such as watches and clocks.

Repairs or replaces broken, damaged, or worn parts, using watchmaker's lathe, drill press, and hand tools. Assembles mechanism, oils moving parts, and demagnetizes mechanism, using demagnetizing machine. Cleans, rinses, and dries parts, using watch-cleaning machine. Tests accuracy of balance wheel assembly and adjusts timing regulator, using truing calipers, watch-rate recorder, and tweezers. Removes mechanism from case and disassembles parts, such as hands, springs, or wheels, using hand tools. Tests and replaces batteries and other electronic components. Examines watch mechanism, case, and parts for defects or foreign matter, using loupe (magnifier). Repairs watch cases, surface defects of clocks, and watch bands. Estimates cost of watch for repair. Records quantity and type of clocks repaired.

GOE INFORMATION—**Interest Area:** 05. Mechanics, Installers, and Repairers. **Work Group:** 05.03. Mechanical Work. **Personality Type**—Realistic. Realistic occupations frequently involve work activities that include practical, hands-on problems and solutions. They often deal with plants, animals, and real-world materials like wood, tools, and machinery. Many of the occupations require working outside and do not involve a lot of paperwork or working closely with others. **Work Values**—Independence; Good Working Conditions; Moral Values; Ability Utilization; Compensation. **Skills**—Repairing; Troubleshooting; Quality Control Analysis; Equipment Selection. **Abilities**—*Cognitive:* Flexibility of Closure; Number Facility. *Psychomotor:* Finger Dexterity; Arm-Hand Steadiness; Manual Dexterity; Control Precision; Wrist-Finger Speed. *Physical:* None met the criteria. *Sensory:* Near Vision; Glare Sensitivity. **General Work Activities**—*Information Input:* Inspecting Equipment, Structures, or Materials; Monitoring Processes, Materials, or Surroundings; Identifying Objects, Actions, and Events. *Mental Process:* Evaluating Information Against Standards; Updating and Using Relevant Knowledge; Analyzing Data or Information. *Work Output:* Repairing and Maintaining Mechanical Equipment; Handling and Moving Objects; Controlling Machines and Processes. *Interacting with Others:* Communicating with Persons Outside Organization; Performing for or Working with the Public; Performing

Administrative Activities. **Physical Work Conditions**—Using Hands on Objects, Tools, or Controls; Sitting; Making Repetitive Motions; Indoors; Minor Burns, Cuts, Bites, or Stings. **Other Job Characteristics**—Importance of Being Exact or Accurate; Pace Determined by Speed of Equipment; Importance of Repeating Same Tasks.

Experience—Job Zone 3. Previous work-related skill, knowledge, or experience is required. **Job Preparation:** SVP 6.0 to less than 7.0—more than one year and less than four years. **Knowledge**—Customer and Personal Service; Mechanical; Production and Processing; Sales and Marketing; Clerical. **Instructional Programs**—Watchmaking and Jewelrymaking.

Related DOT Jobs—715.281-010 Watch Repairer; 715.281-014 Watch Repairer Apprentice; 715.584-014 Repairer, Auto Clocks.

49-9069.99 Precision Instrument and Equipment Repairers, All Other

- Education/Training Required: Long-term on-the-job training
- Employed: No data available.
- Annual Earnings: No data available.
- Growth: 6.8%
- Annual Job Openings: 2,000

All precision instrument and equipment repairers not listed separately.

No task data available.

GOE INFORMATION—**Interest Area:** 05. Mechanics, Installers, and Repairers. **Work Group:** 05.03. Mechanical Work. **Note:** The Department of Labor has not collected some data for this job, so it has fewer details than the other descriptions.

Instructional Programs—Electromechanical and Instrumentation and Maintenance Technologies/Technicians, Other; Instrumentation Technology/Technician.

Related DOT Jobs—710.281-038 Taximeter Repairer; 710.381-054 Repairer, Gyroscope.

49-9091.00 Coin, Vending, and Amusement Machine Servicers and Repairers

- Education/Training Required: Moderate-term on-the-job training
- Employed: 36,803
- Annual Earnings: $26,510
- Growth: 18.5%
- Annual Job Openings: 4,000

Install, service, adjust, or repair coin, vending, or amusement machines, including video games, jukeboxes, pinball machines, or slot machines.

Adjusts and repairs vending machines and meters and replaces defective mechanical and electrical parts, using hand tools, soldering iron, and diagrams. Tests dispensing, coin-handling, electrical, refrigeration, carbonation, or ice-making systems of machine. Examines and inspects vending machines and meters to determine cause of malfunction. Disassembles and assembles machines, following specifications and using hand tools and power tools. Cleans and oils parts with soap and water, gasoline, kerosene, or carbon tetrachloride. Replenishes vending machines with ingredients or products. Shellacs or paints dial markings or mechanisms' exterior, using brush or spray gun. Collects coins from

machine and makes settlements with concessionaires. Keeps records of machine maintenance and repair.

GOE INFORMATION—**Interest Area:** 05. Mechanics, Installers, and Repairers. **Work Group:** 05.03. Mechanical Work. **Personality Type**—Realistic. Realistic occupations frequently involve work activities that include practical, hands-on problems and solutions. They often deal with plants, animals, and real-world materials like wood, tools, and machinery. Many of the occupations require working outside and do not involve a lot of paperwork or working closely with others. **Work Values**—Independence; Supervision, Technical; Moral Values; Responsibility; Security. **Skills**—Repairing; Installation; Troubleshooting. **Abilities**—*Cognitive:* Spatial Orientation; Number Facility. *Psychomotor:* Finger Dexterity; Control Precision; Wrist-Finger Speed; Multilimb Coordination; Manual Dexterity. *Physical:* Static Strength; Trunk Strength; Dynamic Flexibility; Extent Flexibility; Gross Body Equilibrium. *Sensory:* Peripheral Vision; Visual Color Discrimination; Auditory Attention; Sound Localization; Night Vision. **General Work Activities**—*Information Input:* Inspecting Equipment, Structures, or Materials; Getting Information; Monitoring Processes, Materials, or Surroundings. *Mental Process:* Making Decisions and Solving Problems; Evaluating Information Against Standards; Organizing, Planning, and Prioritizing. *Work Output:* Handling and Moving Objects; Repairing and Maintaining Mechanical Equipment; Performing General Physical Activities. *Interacting with Others:* Communicating with Persons Outside Organization; Establishing and Maintaining Relationships; Communicating with Other Workers. **Physical Work Conditions**—Kneeling, Crouching, or Crawling; Bending or Twisting the Body; Making Repetitive Motions; Outdoors; Walking or Running. **Other Job Characteristics**—Importance of Repeating Same Tasks; Pace Determined by Speed of Equipment; Importance of Being Exact or Accurate.

Experience—Job Zone 2. Some previous work-related skill, knowledge, or experience may be helpful, but usually is not needed. **Job Preparation:** SVP 4.0 to less than 6.0—six months to less than two years. **Knowledge**—Mechanical; Engineering and Technology; Computers and Electronics; Chemistry. **Instructional Programs**—Electrical/Electronics Maintenance and Repair Technology, Other.

Related DOT Jobs—349.680-010 Ticket-Dispenser Changer; 639.281-014 Coin-Machine-Service Repairer; 710.384-026 Parking-Meter Servicer; 710.681-018 Register Repairer; 729.381-014 Pin-Game-Machine Inspector; 729.384-014 Fare-Register Repairer.

49-9092.00 Commercial Divers

- Education/Training Required: Moderate-term on-the-job training
- Employed: No data available.
- Annual Earnings: $32,770
- Growth: 11.5%
- Annual Job Openings: 16,000

Work below surface of water, using scuba gear, to inspect, repair, remove, or install equipment and structures. May use a variety of power and hand tools, such as drills, sledgehammers, torches, and welding equipment. May conduct tests or experiments, rig explosives, or photograph structures or marine life.

Descends into water with aid of diver helper, using scuba gear or diving suit. Communicates with surface while underwater by signal line or telephone. Searches for lost or sunken objects, such as bodies, torpedoes, equipment, and ships. Recovers objects by placing rigging around sunken objects and hooking rigging to crane lines. Inspects docks, hulls, and propellers of ships and underwater pipelines, cables, and sewers. Repairs ships and other structures below the water line, using caulk, bolts, and hand tools. Cuts and welds steel, using underwater welding equipment. Removes obstructions from strainers and marine railway or launching ways, using pneumatic and power hand tools. Sets or guides placement of pilings and sandbags to provide support for structures such as docks, bridges, cofferdams, and platforms. Drills holes in rock and rigs explosives for underwater demolitions. Photographs underwater structures or marine life. Levels rails, using wedges and maul or sledgehammer.

GOE INFORMATION—Interest Area: 06. Construction, Mining, and Drilling. Work Group: 06.02. Construction. Personality Type—Realistic. Realistic occupations frequently involve work activities that include practical, hands-on problems and solutions. They often deal with plants, animals, and real-world materials like wood, tools, and machinery. Many of the occupations require working outside and do not involve a lot of paperwork or working closely with others. Work Values—Variety; Ability Utilization; Responsibility; Achievement; Moral Values. Skills—Repairing; Installation; Operation and Control. Abilities—Cognitive: Spatial Orientation; Flexibility of Closure; Perceptual Speed; Speed of Closure; Time Sharing. Psychomotor: Speed of Limb Movement; Manual Dexterity; Rate Control; Multilimb Coordination; Reaction Time. Physical: Gross Body Coordination; Stamina; Dynamic Strength; Dynamic Flexibility; Explosive Strength. Sensory: Night Vision; Depth Perception; Peripheral Vision; Far Vision; Visual Color Discrimination. General Work Activities—Information Input: Identifying Objects, Actions, and Events; Inspecting Equipment, Structures, or Materials; Getting Information. Mental Process: Making Decisions and Solving Problems; Updating and Using Relevant Knowledge; Organizing, Planning, and Prioritizing. Work Output: Performing General Physical Activities; Repairing and Maintaining Mechanical Equipment; Handling and Moving Objects. Interacting with Others: Communicating with Other Workers; Establishing and Maintaining Relationships; Interpreting Meaning of Information for Others. Physical Work Conditions—Specialized Protective or Safety Attire; Common Protective or Safety Attire; Outdoors; Extremely Bright or Inadequate Lighting; Very Hot or Cold. Other Job Characteristics—Consequence of Error; Importance of Repeating Same Tasks; Importance of Being Exact or Accurate.

Experience—Job Zone 2. Some previous work-related skill, knowledge, or experience may be helpful, but usually is not needed. Job Preparation: SVP 4.0 to less than 6.0—six months to less than two years. Knowledge—Building and Construction; Mechanical; Physics; Fine Arts; Engineering and Technology. Instructional Programs—Diver, Professional and Instructor.

Related DOT Jobs—379.384-010 Scuba Diver; 899.261-010 Diver.

49-9093.00 Fabric Menders, Except Garment

- Education/Training Required: Short-term on-the-job training
- Employed: No data available.
- Annual Earnings: $23,700
- Growth: 11.5%
- Annual Job Openings: 16,000

Repair tears, holes, and other defects in fabrics, such as draperies, linens, parachutes, and tents.

Operates sewing machine to restitch defective seams, sew up holes, or replace garment pockets or blanket binding ribbons. Patches holes, sews tears and ripped seams, or darns defects in items, using needle and thread or sewing machine. Reknits runs and replaces broken threads, using latch needle. Repairs holes by weaving thread over them, using needle. Pulls knots to wrong side of garment, using hook. Spreads out articles or material and examines for holes, tears, worn areas, and other marked or

unmarked defects. Replaces defective shrouds and splices connections between shrouds and harness, using hand tools. Trims edges of cut or torn fabric, using scissors or knife, and stitches together. Sews fringe, tassels, and ruffles onto drapes and curtains and buttons and trimming onto garments. Measures and hems curtains, garments, and canvas coverings to size, using tape measure. Sews labels and emblems on articles for identification. Stamps grommets into canvas, using mallet and punch or eyelet machine. Cleans stains from fabric or garment, using spray gun and cleaning fluid.

GOE INFORMATION—Interest Area: 11. Recreation, Travel, and Other Personal Services. Work Group: 11.06. Apparel, Shoes, Leather, and Fabric Care. Personality Type—Realistic. Realistic occupations frequently involve work activities that include practical, hands-on problems and solutions. They often deal with plants, animals, and real-world materials like wood, tools, and machinery. Many of the occupations require working outside and do not involve a lot of paperwork or working closely with others. Work Values—Moral Values; Independence; Supervision, Technical; Activity. Skills—None met the criteria. Abilities—Cognitive: None met the criteria. Psychomotor: Finger Dexterity; Arm-Hand Steadiness; Wrist-Finger Speed; Manual Dexterity; Control Precision. Physical: None met the criteria. Sensory: Visual Color Discrimination; Near Vision. General Work Activities—Information Input: Monitoring Processes, Materials, or Surroundings; Inspecting Equipment, Structures, or Materials; Identifying Objects, Actions, and Events. Mental Process: Judging Qualities of Things, Services, or Other People's Work; Evaluating Information Against Standards; Organizing, Planning, and Prioritizing. Work Output: Handling and Moving Objects; Controlling Machines and Processes; Performing General Physical Activities. Interacting with Others: Communicating with Other Workers; Communicating with Persons Outside Organization; Establishing and Maintaining Relationships. Physical Work Conditions—Making Repetitive Motions; Sitting; Using Hands on Objects, Tools, or Controls; Indoors; Contaminants. Other Job Characteristics—Importance of Repeating Same Tasks; Pace Determined by Speed of Equipment; Degree of Automation.

Experience—Job Zone 1. No previous work-related skill, knowledge, or experience is needed. Job Preparation: SVP below 4.0—less than six months. Knowledge—Fine Arts; Philosophy and Theology; Foreign Language; History and Archeology. Instructional Programs—No data available.

Related DOT Jobs—782.684-010 Canvas Repairer; 782.684-046 Mender, Knit Goods; 784.684-046 Mender; 787.682-030 Mender; 789.684-038 Parachute Mender.

49-9094.00 Locksmiths and Safe Repairers

- Education/Training Required: Moderate-term on-the-job training
- Employed: 23,324
- Annual Earnings: $28,990
- Growth: 8.7%
- Annual Job Openings: 3,000

Repair and open locks, make keys, change locks and safe combinations, and install and repair safes.

Disassemble mechanical or electrical locking devices and repair or replace worn tumblers, springs, and other parts, using hand tools. Insert new or repaired tumblers into locks in order to change combinations. Repair and adjust safes, vault doors, and vault components, using hand tools, lathes, drill presses, and welding and acetylene cutting apparatus. Cut new or duplicate keys, using key-cutting machines. Install safes, vault doors, and deposit boxes according to blueprints, using equipment such as powered drills, taps, dies, truck cranes, and dollies. Open safe locks by drilling. Move picklocks in cylinders in order to open door locks without keys. Remove interior and exterior finishes on safes and vaults and spray on new finishes. Keep records of company locks and keys.

GOE INFORMATION—**Interest Area:** 05. Mechanics, Installers, and Repairers. **Work Group:** 05.03. Mechanical Work. **Personality Type**—Realistic. Realistic occupations frequently involve work activities that include practical, hands-on problems and solutions. They often deal with plants, animals, and real-world materials like wood, tools, and machinery. Many of the occupations require working outside and do not involve a lot of paperwork or working closely with others. **Work Values**—Independence; Responsibility; Supervision, Technical; Moral Values; Security. **Skills**—Installation; Repairing. **Abilities**—*Cognitive:* None met the criteria. *Psychomotor:* Finger Dexterity; Arm-Hand Steadiness; Control Precision; Manual Dexterity. *Physical:* Gross Body Coordination. *Sensory:* None met the criteria. **General Work Activities**—*Information Input:* Inspecting Equipment, Structures, or Materials; Getting Information; Identifying Objects, Actions, and Events. *Mental Process:* Updating and Using Relevant Knowledge; Making Decisions and Solving Problems; Judging Qualities of Things, Services, or Other People's Work. *Work Output:* Handling and Moving Objects; Performing General Physical Activities; Controlling Machines and Processes. *Interacting with Others:* Communicating with Persons Outside Organization; Establishing and Maintaining Relationships; Performing Administrative Activities. **Physical Work Conditions**—Using Hands on Objects, Tools, or Controls; Kneeling, Crouching, or Crawling; Cramped Work Space or Awkward Positions; Minor Burns, Cuts, Bites, or Stings; Very Hot or Cold. **Other Job Characteristics**—Importance of Being Exact or Accurate; Pace Determined by Speed of Equipment; Importance of Repeating Same Tasks.

Experience—Job Zone 3. Previous work-related skill, knowledge, or experience is required. **Job Preparation:** SVP 6.0 to less than 7.0—more than one year and less than four years. **Knowledge**—Mechanical; Clerical; Engineering and Technology; Building and Construction; Physics. **Instructional Programs**—Locksmithing and Safe Repair.

Related DOT Jobs—709.281-010 Locksmith; 709.281-014 Locksmith Apprentice; 869.381-022 Safe-and-Vault Service Mechanic.

49-9095.00 Manufactured Building and Mobile Home Installers

- ● **Education/Training Required: Moderate-term on-the-job training**
- ● **Employed: 17,001**
- ● **Annual Earnings: $22,940**
- ● **Growth: 19.1%**
- ● **Annual Job Openings: 2,000**

Move or install mobile homes or prefabricated buildings.

Locates and repairs frayed wiring, broken connections, or incorrect wiring, using ohmmeter, soldering iron, tape, and hand tools. Repairs plumbing and propane gas lines, using caulking compounds and plastic or copper pipe. Inspects, examines, and tests operation of parts or systems to be repaired and verifies completeness of work performed. Removes damaged exterior panels, repairs and replaces structural frame members, and seals leaks, using hand tools. Repairs leaks with caulking compound or replaces pipes, using pipe wrench. Connects electrical system to outside power source and activates switches to test operation of appliances and light fixtures. Connects water hose to inlet pipe of plumbing system and tests operation of toilets and sinks. Confers with customer or reads work order

to determine nature and extent of damage to unit. Lists parts needed, estimates costs, and plans work procedure, using parts list, technical manuals, and diagrams. Opens and closes doors, windows, and drawers to test their operation and trims edges to fit, using jack-plane or drawknife. Refinishes wood surfaces on cabinets, doors, moldings, and floors, using power sander, putty, spray equipment, brush, paints, or varnishes. Resets hardware, using chisel, mallet, and screwdriver. Seals open side of modular units to prepare them for shipment, using polyethylene sheets, nails, and hammer.

GOE INFORMATION—**Interest Area:** 06. Construction, Mining, and Drilling. **Work Group:** 06.02. Construction. **Personality Type**—Realistic. Realistic occupations frequently involve work activities that include practical, hands-on problems and solutions. They often deal with plants, animals, and real-world materials like wood, tools, and machinery. Many of the occupations require working outside and do not involve a lot of paperwork or working closely with others. **Work Values**—Supervision, Technical; Variety; Moral Values; Supervision, Human Relations. **Skills**—Installation; Repairing; Troubleshooting; Equipment Selection; Quality Control Analysis. **Abilities**—*Cognitive:* Visualization; Flexibility of Closure; Spatial Orientation. *Psychomotor:* Control Precision; Manual Dexterity; Speed of Limb Movement; Multilimb Coordination; Arm-Hand Steadiness. *Physical:* Extent Flexibility; Static Strength; Trunk Strength; Explosive Strength; Dynamic Strength. *Sensory:* Depth Perception. **General Work Activities**—*Information Input:* Getting Information; Monitoring Processes, Materials, or Surroundings; Inspecting Equipment, Structures, or Materials. *Mental Process:* Judging Qualities of Things, Services, or Other People's Work; Evaluating Information Against Standards; Updating and Using Relevant Knowledge. *Work Output:* Performing General Physical Activities; Handling and Moving Objects; Repairing and Maintaining Mechanical Equipment. *Interacting with Others:* Establishing and Maintaining Relationships; Communicating with Persons Outside Organization; Communicating with Other Workers. **Physical Work Conditions**—Hazardous Conditions; Outdoors; Whole Body Vibration; Climbing Ladders, Scaffolds, Poles, etc.; Kneeling, Crouching, or Crawling. **Other Job Characteristics**—Consequence of Error; Pace Determined by Speed of Equipment; Importance of Being Exact or Accurate.

Experience—Job Zone 2. Some previous work-related skill, knowledge, or experience may be helpful, but usually is not needed. **Job Preparation:** SVP 4.0 to less than 6.0—six months to less than two years. **Knowledge**—Building and Construction; Mechanical; Design; Engineering and Technology; Physics. **Instructional Programs**—Building/Construction Site Management/Manager.

Related DOT Jobs—869.384-010 Repairer, Manufactured Buildings; 869.684-074 Utility Worker.

49-9096.00 Riggers

- ● **Education/Training Required: Short-term on-the-job training**
- ● **Employed: 20,417**
- ● **Annual Earnings: $32,690**
- ● **Growth: 10.1%**
- ● **Annual Job Openings: 2,000**

Set up or repair rigging for construction projects, manufacturing plants, logging yards, or ships and shipyards or for the entertainment industry.

Selects gear, such as cables, pulleys, and winches, according to load weight and size, facilities, and work schedule. Fabricates and repairs rigging, such as slings, tackle, and ladders, using hand and power tools. Assembles and installs supporting structures, rigging, hoists, and pulling gear, using hand and power tools. Attaches pulleys and blocks to fixed overhead structures, such as beams, ceilings, and gin pole booms with bolts and clamps. Attaches load to rigging to provide support or prepare for moving, using hand and power tools. Signals or gives verbal directions to workers engaged in hoisting and moving loads to ensure safety of workers and materials. Tests rigging to ensure safety and reliability. Dismantles, maintains, and stores rigging equipment. Manipulates rigging lines, hoists, and pulling gear to move or support materials, such as heavy equipment, ships, or theatrical sets. Aligns, levels, and anchors machinery. Controls movement of heavy equipment through narrow openings or confined spaces. Cleans and dresses machine surfaces and component parts.

GOE INFORMATION—Interest Area: 06. Construction, Mining, and Drilling. **Work Group:** 06.02. Construction. **Personality Type**—Realistic. Realistic occupations frequently involve work activities that include practical, hands-on problems and solutions. They often deal with plants, animals, and real-world materials like wood, tools, and machinery. Many of the occupations require working outside and do not involve a lot of paperwork or working closely with others. **Work Values**—Authority; Moral Values; Supervision, Technical; Pleasant Co-workers; Responsibility. **Skills**—Repairing; Technology Design; Operation and Control; Equipment Selection; Operation Monitoring; Installation; Coordination; Quality Control Analysis. **Abilities**—*Cognitive:* Visualization; Spatial Orientation; Time Sharing; Information Ordering; Selective Attention. *Psychomotor:* Reaction Time; Multilimb Coordination; Response Orientation; Speed of Limb Movement; Manual Dexterity. *Physical:* Gross Body Equilibrium; Dynamic Strength; Extent Flexibility; Stamina; Static Strength. *Sensory:* Depth Perception; Far Vision; Peripheral Vision; Sound Localization; Auditory Attention. **General Work Activities**—*Information Input:* Identifying Objects, Actions, and Events; Inspecting Equipment, Structures, or Materials; Monitoring Processes, Materials, or Surroundings. *Mental Process:* Organizing, Planning, and Prioritizing; Making Decisions and Solving Problems; Updating and Using Relevant Knowledge. *Work Output:* Handling and Moving Objects; Performing General Physical Activities; Controlling Machines and Processes. *Interacting with Others:* Coordinating the Work and Activities of Others; Communicating with Other Workers; Establishing and Maintaining Relationships. **Physical Work Conditions**—High Places; Climbing Ladders, Scaffolds, Poles, etc.; Keeping or Regaining Balance; Outdoors; Cramped Work Space or Awkward Positions. **Other Job Characteristics**—Importance of Repeating Same Tasks; Consequence of Error; Importance of Being Exact or Accurate.

Experience—Job Zone 3. Previous work-related skill, knowledge, or experience is required. **Job Preparation:** SVP 6.0 to less than 7.0—more than one year and less than four years. **Knowledge**—Public Safety and Security; Mechanical; Engineering and Technology; Building and Construction; Fine Arts. **Instructional Programs**—Construction/Heavy Equipment/Earthmoving Equipment Operation.

Related DOT Jobs—623.381-010 Gear Repairer; 806.261-014 Rigger; 806.261-018 Rigger Apprentice; 921.260-010 Rigger; 921.664-014 Rigger; 962.664-010 High Rigger; 962.684-010 Acrobatic Rigger; 962.684-014 Grip.

49-9097.00 Signal and Track Switch Repairers

- **Education/Training Required: Postsecondary vocational training**
- **Employed: No data available.**
- **Annual Earnings: $42,390**
- **Growth: 11.5%**
- **Annual Job Openings: 16,000**

Install, inspect, test, maintain, or repair electric gate crossings, signals, signal equipment, track switches, section lines, or intercommunications systems within a railroad system.

Installs and inspects switch-controlling mechanism on trolley wire and switch in bed of track bed, using hand tools and test equipment. Inspects and tests gate crossings, signals, and signal equipment, such as interlocks and hotbox detectors. Inspects electrical units of railroad grade crossing gates to detect loose bolts, defective electrical connections and parts. Tests signal circuit connections, using standard electrical testing equipment. Replaces defective wiring, broken lenses, or burned-out light bulbs. Tightens loose bolts, using wrench, and tests circuits and connections by opening and closing gate. Tests air lines and air cylinders on pneumatically operated gates. Inspects batteries to ensure that batteries are filled with battery water or to determine need for replacement. Lubricates moving parts on gate crossing mechanisms and swinging signals. Maintains high-tension lines, deenergizing lines for power company as repairs are requested. Cleans lenses of lamps with cloths and solvent. Compiles reports indicating mileage or track inspected, repairs made, and equipment requiring replacement.

GOE INFORMATION—Interest Area: 05. Mechanics, Installers, and Repairers. **Work Group:** 05.02. Electrical and Electronic Systems. **Personality Type**—Realistic. Realistic occupations frequently involve work activities that include practical, hands-on problems and solutions. They often deal with plants, animals, and real-world materials like wood, tools, and machinery. Many of the occupations require working outside and do not involve a lot of paperwork or working closely with others. **Work Values**—Supervision, Technical; Moral Values; Supervision, Human Relations; Security; Variety. **Skills**—Installation; Repairing; Troubleshooting; Operation Monitoring; Quality Control Analysis; Equipment Selection; Science; Systems Evaluation. **Abilities**—*Cognitive:* Perceptual Speed; Visualization; Flexibility of Closure; Speed of Closure. *Psychomotor:* Finger Dexterity; Control Precision; Response Orientation; Speed of Limb Movement; Rate Control. *Physical:* Gross Body Equilibrium; Extent Flexibility; Static Strength; Explosive Strength; Dynamic Flexibility. *Sensory:* Peripheral Vision; Sound Localization; Visual Color Discrimination; Depth Perception; Night Vision. **General Work Activities**—*Information Input:* Getting Information; Inspecting Equipment, Structures, or Materials; Monitoring Processes, Materials, or Surroundings. *Mental Process:* Updating and Using Relevant Knowledge; Making Decisions and Solving Problems; Analyzing Data or Information. *Work Output:* Performing General Physical Activities; Repairing and Maintaining Mechanical Equipment; Handling and Moving Objects. *Interacting with Others:* Communicating with Other Workers; Establishing and Maintaining Relationships; Monitoring and Controlling Resources. **Physical Work Conditions**—Outdoors; Hazardous Conditions; Hazardous Equipment; Minor Burns, Cuts, Bites, or Stings; Common Protective or Safety Attire. **Other Job Characteristics**—Consequence of Error; Degree of Automation; Importance of Being Exact or Accurate.

Experience—Job Zone 4. A minimum of two to four years of work-related skill, knowledge, or experience is needed. **Job Preparation:** SVP 7.0 to less than 8.0—two years to less than 10 years. **Knowledge**—Mechanical; Telecommunications; Engineering and Technology; Public Safety and Security; Physics. **Instructional Programs**—Electrician.

Related DOT Jobs—822.281-026 Signal Maintainer; 825.261-010 Electric-Track-Switch Maintainer.

49-9098.00 Helpers—Installation, Maintenance, and Repair Workers

- **Education/Training Required: Short-term on-the-job training**
- **Employed: No data available.**
- **Annual Earnings: $21,210**
- **Growth: 18.5%**
- **Annual Job Openings: 35,000**

Help installation, maintenance, and repair workers in maintenance, parts replacement, and repair of vehicles, industrial machinery, and electrical and electronic equipment. Perform duties such as furnishing tools, materials, and supplies to other workers; cleaning work area, machines, and tools; and holding materials or tools for other workers.

Disassemble broken or defective equipment in order to facilitate repair; reassemble equipment when repairs are complete. Hold or supply tools, parts, equipment, and supplies for other workers. Position vehicles, machinery, equipment, physical structures, and other objects for assembly or installation, using hand tools, power tools, and moving equipment. Prepare workstations so mechanics and repairers can conduct work. Provide assistance to more skilled workers involved in the adjustment, maintenance, part replacement, and repair of tools, equipment, and machines. Tend and observe equipment and machinery in order to verify efficient and safe operation. Transfer tools, parts, equipment, and supplies to and from workstations and other areas. Adjust, connect, or disconnect wiring, piping, tubing, and other parts, using hand tools or power tools. Apply protective materials to equipment, components, and parts in order to prevent defects and corrosion. Assemble and maintain physical structures, using hand tools or power tools. Clean or lubricate vehicles, machinery, equipment, instruments, tools, work areas, and other objects, using hand tools, power tools, and cleaning equipment. Examine and test machinery, equipment, components, and parts for defects and to ensure proper functioning. Install or replace machinery, equipment, and new or replacement parts and instruments, using hand tools or power tools.

GOE INFORMATION—Interest Area: 05. Mechanics, Installers, and Repairers. **Work Group:** 05.03. Mechanical Work. **Personality Type**—Realistic. Realistic occupations frequently involve work activities that include practical, hands-on problems and solutions. They often deal with plants, animals, and real-world materials like wood, tools, and machinery. Many of the occupations require working outside and do not involve a lot of paperwork or working closely with others. **Work Values**—Advancement; Supervision, Technical; Moral Values; Pleasant Co-workers; Variety. **Skills**—Repairing; Installation; Operation and Control; Operation Monitoring; Quality Control Analysis. **Abilities**—*Cognitive:* Spatial Orientation; Information Ordering; Visualization; Flexibility of Closure; Selective Attention. *Psychomotor:* Speed of Limb Movement; Arm-Hand Steadiness; Wrist-Finger Speed; Manual Dexterity; Reaction Time. *Physical:* Extent Flexibility; Static Strength; Dynamic Strength; Gross Body Equilibrium; Trunk Strength. *Sensory:* Hearing Sensitivity; Auditory Attention; Visual Color Discrimination; Sound Localization; Depth Perception. **General Work Activities**—*Information Input:* Monitoring Processes, Materials, or Surroundings; Inspecting Equipment, Structures, or Materials; Identifying Objects, Actions, and Events. *Mental Process:* Evaluating Information Against Standards; Updating and Using Relevant Knowledge; Judging Qualities of Things, Services, or Other People's Work. *Work Output:* Handling and Moving Objects; Repairing and Maintaining Mechanical Equipment; Performing General Physical Activities. *Interacting with Others:* Communicating with Other Workers; Establishing and Maintaining Relationships; Assisting and Caring for Others. **Physical Work Conditions**—Hazardous Equipment; Cramped Work Space or Awkward Positions; Bending or Twisting the Body; Minor Burns, Cuts, Bites, or Stings; Using Hands on Objects, Tools, or Controls. **Other Job Characteristics**—Importance of Repeating Same Tasks; Pace Determined by Speed of Equipment; Degree of Automation.

Experience—Job Zone 1. No previous work-related skill, knowledge, or experience is needed. **Job Preparation:** SVP below 4.0—less than six months. **Knowledge**—Mechanical; Building and Construction; Engineering and Technology; Physics; Production and Processing. **Instructional Programs**—Industrial Mechanics and Maintenance Technology.

Related DOT Jobs—620.664-010 Construction-Equipment-Mechanic Helper; 620.664-014 Maintenance Mechanic Helper; 620.684-014 Automobile-Mechanic Helper; 620.684-030 Tractor-Mechanic Helper; 621.684-010 Airframe-and-Power-Plant-Mechanic Helper; 622.684-014 Car-Repairer Helper; 623.684-010 Motorboat-Mechanic Helper; 623.687-010 Machinist Helper, Outside; 625.684-010 Diesel-Mechanic Helper; 628.664-010 Overhauler Helper; 630.664-010 Repairer Helper; 630.664-018 Service-Mechanic Helper, Compressed-Gas Equipment; 630.684-022 Pump-Servicer Helper; 630.684-034 Spray-Gun-Repairer Helper; 631.364-010 Hydroelectric-Machinery-Mechanic Helper; 631.684-010 Powerhouse-Mechanic Helper; 632.684-010 Ordnance-Artificer Helper; 637.384-010 Industrial-Gas-Servicer Helper; 637.664-010 Heating-and-Air-Conditioning Installer-Servicer Helper; 637.684-010 Gas-Appliance-Servicer Helper; others.

49-9099.99 Installation, Maintenance, and Repair Workers, All Other

- **Education/Training Required: No data available.**
- **Employed: No data available.**
- **Annual Earnings: No data available.**
- **Growth: 11.5%**
- **Annual Job Openings: 16,000**

All mechanical, installation, and repair workers and helpers not listed separately.

No task data available.

GOE INFORMATION—Interest Area: 05. Mechanics, Installers, and Repairers. **Work Group:** 05.02. Electrical and Electronic Systems; 05.03. Mechanical Work. **Note:** The Department of Labor has not collected some data for this job, so it has fewer details than the other descriptions.

Instructional Programs—Gunsmithing/Gunsmith; Parts and Warehousing Operations and Maintenance Technology/Technician; Precision Systems Maintenance and Repair Technologies, Other.

Related DOT Jobs—369.684-018 Umbrella Repairer; 616.662-010 Hydraulic Press Operator; 619.281-010 Casting Repairer; 620.684-010 Automobile Wrecker; 621.261-520 Aviation Safety Equipment Technician; 621.684-014 Reclamation Worker; 630.684-018 Pump Installer; 632.381-010 Gun Synchronizer; 705.684-042 Mother Repairer; 709.364-014 Towel-Cabinet Repairer; 709.384-010 Fire-Extinguisher Repairer; 709.684-034 Cigarette-Lighter Repairer; 709.684-062 Repairer; 719.381-014 Hearing-Aid Repairer; 729.684-042 Safety-Lamp Keeper; 731.684-014 Doll Repairer; 731.684-022 Toy-Electric-Train Repairer; 732.364-014 Ski-Binding Fitter-And-Repairer; 732.381-022 Golf-Club Repairer; 732.684-102 Roller-Skate Repairer; others.

51-0000
Production Occupations

51-1000 Supervisors, Production Workers

51-1011.00 First-Line Supervisors/ Managers of Production and Operating Workers

- **Education/Training Required: Work experience in a related occupation**
- **Employed: 818,756**
- **Annual Earnings: $42,000**
- **Growth: 1.0%**
- **Annual Job Openings: 71,000**

Supervise and coordinate the activities of production and operating workers, such as inspectors, precision workers, machine setters and operators, assemblers, fabricators, and plant and system operators.

Direct and coordinate the activities of employees engaged in production or processing of goods. Plans and establishes work schedules, assignments, and production sequences to meet production goals. Calculates labor and equipment requirements and production specifications, using standard formulas. Determines standards, production, and rates based on company policy, equipment and labor availability, and workload. Reviews operations and accounting records or reports to determine the feasibility of production estimates and evaluate current production. Confers with management or subordinates to resolve worker problems, complaints, or grievances. Confers with other supervisors to coordinate operations and activities within departments or between departments. Reads and analyzes charts, work orders, or production schedules to determine production requirements. Maintains operations data, such as time, production, and cost records, and prepares management reports. Recommends or implements measures to motivate employees and improve production methods, equipment performance, product quality, or efficiency. Requisitions materials, supplies, equipment parts, or repair services. Interprets specifications, blueprints, job orders, and company policies and procedures for workers. Inspects materials, products, or equipment to detect defects or malfunctions. Demonstrates equipment operations or work procedures to new employees or assigns employees to experienced workers for training. Monitors or patrols work area and enforces safety or sanitation regulations. Monitors gauges, dials, and other indicators to ensure operators conform to production or processing standards. Sets up and adjusts machines and equipment.

GOE INFORMATION—Interest Area: 08. Industrial Production. **Work Group:** 08.01. Managerial Work in Industrial Production. **Personality Type**—Enterprising. Enterprising occupations frequently involve starting up and carrying out projects. These occupations can involve leading people and making many decisions. They sometimes require risk taking and often deal with business. **Work Values**—Authority; Responsibility; Variety; Pleasant Co-workers; Autonomy. **Skills**—Management of Personnel Resources; Management of Material Resources; Systems Analysis; Operation Monitoring; Operation and Control; Coordination; Complex Problem Solving; Mathematics. **Abilities**—*Cognitive:* Oral Comprehension; Oral Expression; Time Sharing; Mathematical Reasoning; Number Facility. *Psychomotor:* Response Orientation; Rate Control; Control Precision. *Physical:* Explosive Strength; Dynamic Flexibility; Gross Body Equilibrium. *Sensory:* Auditory Attention; Speech Clarity; Sound Localization; Speech Recognition; Hearing Sensitivity. **General Work Activities**—*Information Input:* Monitoring Processes, Materials, or Surroundings; Getting Information; Identifying Objects, Actions, and Events. *Mental Process:* Organizing, Planning, and Prioritizing; Scheduling Work and Activities; Updating and Using Relevant Knowledge. *Work Output:* Controlling Machines and Processes; Documenting or Recording Information; Performing General Physical Activities. *Interacting with Others:* Communicating with Other Workers; Monitoring and Controlling Resources; Coordinating the Work and Activities of Others. **Physical Work Conditions**—Walking or Running; Indoors; Hazardous Equipment; Distracting Sounds and Noise Levels; Sitting. **Other Job Characteristics**—Consequence of Error; Degree of Automation; Pace Determined by Speed of Equipment.

Experience—Job Zone 3. Previous work-related skill, knowledge, or experience is required. **Job Preparation:** SVP 6.0 to less than 7.0—more than one year and less than four years. **Knowledge**—Production and Processing; Personnel and Human Resources; Administration and Management; Economics and Accounting; Education and Training. **Instructional Programs**—Operations Management and Supervision.

Related DOT Jobs—184.167-046 Incinerator-Plant-General Supervisor; 184.167-142 Superintendent, Cold Storage; 299.137-018 Sample-Room Supervisor; 361.137-010 Supervisor, Laundry; 369.137-010 Supervisor, Dry Cleaning; 369.137-014 Supervisor, Rug Cleaning; 369.167-010 Manager, Laundromat; 500.131-010 Supervisor; 500.132-010 Supervisor, Sheet Manufacturing; 500.134-010 Supervisor, Matrix; 501.130-010 Supervisor, Hot-Dip-Tinning; 501.137-010 Supervisor, Hot-Dip Plating; 502.130-010 Supervisor, Casting-and-Pasting; 503.137-010 Supervisor, Sandblaster; 504.131-010 Heat-Treat Supervisor; 505.130-010 Supervisor, Metalizing; 505.130-014 Supervisor, Vacuum Metalizing; 509.130-010 Supervisor, Powdered Metal; 509.130-014 Supervisor, Power-Reactor; 509.132-010 Supervisor, Soaking Pits; others.

51-2000 Assemblers and Fabricators

51-2011.00 Aircraft Structure, Surfaces, Rigging, and Systems Assemblers

- **Education/Training Required: Long-term on-the-job training**
- **Employed: 20,057**
- **Annual Earnings: $37,190**
- **Growth: 14.2%**
- **Annual Job Openings: 2,000**

Assemble, fit, fasten, and install parts of airplanes, space vehicles, or missiles, such as tails, wings, fuselage, bulkheads, stabilizers, landing gear, rigging and control equipment, or heating and ventilating systems.

No task data available.

GOE INFORMATION—Interest Area: 08. Industrial Production. **Work Group:** 08.02. Production Technology. **Note:** The Department of Labor has not collected some data for this job, so it has fewer details than the other descriptions.

Instructional Programs—Aircraft Powerplant Technology/Technician; Airframe Mechanics and Aircraft Maintenance Technology/Technician; Avionics Maintenance Technology/Technician.

Related DOT Jobs—806.361-014 Assembler-Installer, General; 806.361-030 Aircraft Mechanic, Armament; 806.380-010 Riveting Machine Operator, Automatic; 806.381-014 Aircraft Mechanic, Environmental Control

System; 806.381-018 Aircraft Mechanic, Rigging and Controls; 806.381-026 Assembler, Aircraft, Structures and Surfaces; 806.381-034 Assembler, Tubing; 806.381-042 Cable Assembler and Swager; 806.381-066 Aircraft Mechanic, Plumbing and Hydraulics; 806.381-082 Precision Assembler.

51-2011.01 Aircraft Structure Assemblers, Precision

- Education/Training Required: Long-term on-the-job training
- Employed: No data available.
- Annual Earnings: $37,190
- Growth: 14.2%
- Annual Job Openings: 2,000

Assemble tail, wing, fuselage, or other structural section of aircraft, space vehicles, and missiles from parts, subassemblies, and components and install functional units, parts, or equipment, such as landing gear, control surfaces, doors, and floorboards.

Installs units, parts, equipment, and components in structural assembly according to blueprints and specifications, using hand tools and power tools. Bolts, screws, or rivets accessories to fasten, support, or hang components and subassemblies. Drills holes in structure and subassemblies and attaches brackets, hinges, or clips to secure installation or to fasten subassemblies. Locates and marks reference points and holes for installation of parts and components, using jigs, templates, and measuring instruments. Aligns structural assemblies. Cuts, trims, and files parts and verifies fitting tolerances to prepare for installation. Positions and aligns subassemblies in jigs or fixtures, using measuring instruments and following blueprint lines and index points. Inspects and tests installed units, parts, and equipment for fit, performance, and compliance with standards, using measuring instruments and test equipment.

GOE INFORMATION—Interest Area: 08. Industrial Production. **Work Group:** 08.02. Production Technology. **Personality Type—**Realistic. Realistic occupations frequently involve work activities that include practical, hands-on problems and solutions. They often deal with plants, animals, and real-world materials like wood, tools, and machinery. Many of the occupations require working outside and do not involve a lot of paperwork or working closely with others. **Work Values—**Moral Values; Independence; Advancement; Supervision, Technical; Supervision, Human Relations. **Skills—**Installation; Equipment Selection; Repairing; Quality Control Analysis; Troubleshooting; Operation and Control. **Abilities—***Cognitive:* Visualization; Spatial Orientation; Perceptual Speed; Information Ordering; Problem Sensitivity. *Psychomotor:* Arm-Hand Steadiness; Manual Dexterity; Finger Dexterity; Speed of Limb Movement; Rate Control. *Physical:* Extent Flexibility; Gross Body Equilibrium; Dynamic Flexibility; Explosive Strength; Static Strength. *Sensory:* Depth Perception; Visual Color Discrimination; Far Vision; Peripheral Vision; Sound Localization. **General Work Activities—***Information Input:* Inspecting Equipment, Structures, or Materials; Monitoring Processes, Materials, or Surroundings; Identifying Objects, Actions, and Events. *Mental Process:* Updating and Using Relevant Knowledge; Evaluating Information Against Standards; Judging Qualities of Things, Services, or Other People's Work. *Work Output:* Handling and Moving Objects; Repairing and Maintaining Mechanical Equipment; Controlling Machines and Processes. *Interacting with Others:* Communicating with Other Workers; Coordinating the Work and Activities of Others; Performing Administrative Activities. **Physical Work Conditions—**Outdoors; Cramped Work Space or Awkward Positions; Hazardous Equipment; Using Hands on Objects, Tools, or Controls; Distracting Sounds and Noise Levels. **Other Job Characteristics—**Importance of Being Exact or Accurate; Consequence of Error; Degree of Automation.

Experience—Job Zone 3. Previous work-related skill, knowledge, or experience is required. **Job Preparation:** SVP 6.0 to less than 7.0—more than one year and less than four years. **Knowledge—**Mechanical; Production and Processing; Building and Construction; Engineering and Technology; Design. **Instructional Programs—**Aircraft Powerplant Technology/Technician; Airframe Mechanics and Aircraft Maintenance Technology/Technician; Avionics Maintenance Technology/Technician.

Related DOT Jobs—806.361-014 Assembler-Installer, General; 806.381-026 Assembler, Aircraft, Structures and Surfaces.

51-2011.02 Aircraft Systems Assemblers, Precision

- Education/Training Required: Long-term on-the-job training
- Employed: No data available.
- Annual Earnings: $37,190
- Growth: 14.2%
- Annual Job Openings: 2,000

Lay out, assemble, install, and test aircraft systems, such as armament, environmental control, plumbing, and hydraulic.

Aligns, fits, and assembles system components, such as armament, structural, and mechanical components, using jigs, fixtures, measuring instruments, hand tools, and power tools. Lays out location of parts and assemblies according to specifications. Assembles and installs parts, fittings, and assemblies on aircraft, using layout tools, hand tools, power tools, and fasteners. Tests systems and assemblies for functional performance and adjusts, repairs, or replaces malfunctioning units or parts. Installs mechanical linkages and actuators and verifies tension of cables, using tensiometer. Examines parts for defects and for conformance to specifications, using precision measuring instruments. Reworks, replaces, realigns, and adjusts parts and assemblies according to specifications. Cleans, oils, assembles, and attaches system components to aircraft, using hand tools, power tools, and measuring instruments. Reads and interprets blueprints, illustrations, and specifications to determine layout, sequence of operations, or identity and relationship of parts. Measures, drills, files, cuts, bends, and smoothes materials to ensure fit and clearance of parts.

GOE INFORMATION—Interest Area: 08. Industrial Production. **Work Group:** 08.02. Production Technology. **Personality Type—**Realistic. Realistic occupations frequently involve work activities that include practical, hands-on problems and solutions. They often deal with plants, animals, and real-world materials like wood, tools, and machinery. Many of the occupations require working outside and do not involve a lot of paperwork or working closely with others. **Work Values—**Moral Values; Independence; Advancement; Compensation; Supervision, Technical. **Skills—**Installation; Repairing; Troubleshooting; Quality Control Analysis; Operation and Control; Equipment Selection; Operation Monitoring; Technology Design. **Abilities—***Cognitive:* Visualization; Spatial Orientation; Information Ordering; Flexibility of Closure; Category Flexibility. *Psychomotor:* Manual Dexterity; Arm-Hand Steadiness; Multilimb Coordination; Reaction Time; Speed of Limb Movement. *Physical:* Explosive Strength; Dynamic Strength; Static Strength; Dynamic Flexibility; Extent Flexibility. *Sensory:* Depth Perception; Peripheral Vision; Visual Color Discrimination; Hearing Sensitivity; Near Vision. **General Work Activities—***Information Input:* Inspecting Equipment, Structures, or Materials; Getting Information; Identifying Objects, Actions, and Events. *Mental Process:* Updating and Using Relevant Knowledge; Evaluating Information Against Standards; Judging Qualities of Things, Services, or Other People's Work. *Work Output:* Handling and Moving Objects; Repairing and Maintaining Mechanical Equipment; Performing General Physical Activities. *Interacting with Others:* Communicating with Other

Workers; Coordinating the Work and Activities of Others; Performing Administrative Activities. **Physical Work Conditions**—Hazardous Equipment; Distracting Sounds and Noise Levels; Kneeling, Crouching, or Crawling; Cramped Work Space or Awkward Positions; Using Hands on Objects, Tools, or Controls. **Other Job Characteristics**—Degree of Automation; Importance of Being Exact or Accurate; Importance of Repeating Same Tasks.

Experience—Job Zone 3. Previous work-related skill, knowledge, or experience is required. **Job Preparation:** SVP 6.0 to less than 7.0—more than one year and less than four years. **Knowledge**—Mechanical; Design; Production and Processing; Building and Construction; Engineering and Technology. **Instructional Programs**—Aircraft Powerplant Technology/Technician; Airframe Mechanics and Aircraft Maintenance Technology/Technician; Avionics Maintenance Technology/Technician.

Related DOT Jobs—806.361-030 Aircraft Mechanic, Armament; 806.381-014 Aircraft Mechanic, Environmental Control System; 806.381-018 Aircraft Mechanic, Rigging and Controls; 806.381-066 Aircraft Mechanic, Plumbing and Hydraulics; 806.381-082 Precision Assembler.

51-2011.03 Aircraft Rigging Assemblers

- **Education/Training Required: Long-term on-the-job training**
- **Employed: No data available.**
- **Annual Earnings: $37,190**
- **Growth: 14.2%**
- **Annual Job Openings: 2,000**

Fabricate and assemble aircraft tubing or cable components or assemblies.

Sets up and operates machines and systems to crimp, cut, bend, form, swage, flare, bead, burr, and straighten tubing according to specifications. Assembles and attaches fittings onto cable and tubing components, using hand tools. Measures, cuts, and inspects cable and tubing, using master template, measuring instruments, and cable cutter or saw. Welds tubing and fittings and solders cable ends, using tack-welder, induction brazing chamber, or other equipment. Swages fittings onto cable, using swaging machine. Forms loops or splices in cables, using clamps and fittings, or reweaves cable strands. Marks location of cutouts, holes, and trim lines of parts and relationship of parts, using measuring instruments. Fabricates cable templates. Reads and interprets blueprints, work orders, data charts, and specifications to determine operations and type, quantity, dimensions, configuration, and finish of tubing, cable, and fittings. Verifies dimensions of cable assembly and position of fittings, using measuring instruments, and repairs and reworks defective assemblies. Selects and installs accessories in swaging machine, using hand tools. Marks identifying information on tubing or cable assemblies, using electro-chemical etching device, label, rubber stamp, or other methods. Tests tubing and cable assemblies for defects, using pressure testing equipment and proofloading machines. Cleans, lubricates, and coats tubing and cable assemblies.

GOE INFORMATION—Interest Area: 08. Industrial Production. **Work Group:** 08.02. Production Technology. **Personality Type**—Realistic. Realistic occupations frequently involve work activities that include practical, hands-on problems and solutions. They often deal with plants, animals, and real-world materials like wood, tools, and machinery. Many of the occupations require working outside and do not involve a lot of paperwork or working closely with others. **Work Values**—Moral Values; Independence; Supervision, Technical; Advancement; Supervision, Human Relations. **Skills**—Installation; Repairing; Operation and Control; Equipment Selection; Operation Monitoring. **Abilities**—*Cognitive:* Visualization; Spatial Orientation; Written Comprehension; Information

Ordering; Memorization. *Psychomotor:* Manual Dexterity; Arm-Hand Steadiness; Speed of Limb Movement; Multilimb Coordination; Control Precision. *Physical:* Explosive Strength; Dynamic Flexibility; Dynamic Strength; Static Strength; Gross Body Equilibrium. *Sensory:* Depth Perception; Visual Color Discrimination; Peripheral Vision; Far Vision; Night Vision. **General Work Activities**—*Information Input:* Inspecting Equipment, Structures, or Materials; Monitoring Processes, Materials, or Surroundings; Identifying Objects, Actions, and Events. *Mental Process:* Updating and Using Relevant Knowledge; Judging Qualities of Things, Services, or Other People's Work; Evaluating Information Against Standards. *Work Output:* Handling and Moving Objects; Controlling Machines and Processes; Repairing and Maintaining Mechanical Equipment. *Interacting with Others:* Communicating with Other Workers; Coordinating the Work and Activities of Others; Assisting and Caring for Others. **Physical Work Conditions**—Hazardous Equipment; Using Hands on Objects, Tools, or Controls; Outdoors; Minor Burns, Cuts, Bites, or Stings; Making Repetitive Motions. **Other Job Characteristics**—Importance of Repeating Same Tasks; Degree of Automation; Importance of Being Exact or Accurate.

Experience—Job Zone 3. Previous work-related skill, knowledge, or experience is required. **Job Preparation:** SVP 6.0 to less than 7.0—more than one year and less than four years. **Knowledge**—Production and Processing; Physics; Design; Engineering and Technology; Mechanical. **Instructional Programs**—Aircraft Powerplant Technology/Technician; Airframe Mechanics and Aircraft Maintenance Technology/Technician; Avionics Maintenance Technology/Technician.

Related DOT Jobs—806.381-034 Assembler, Tubing; 806.381-042 Cable Assembler and Swager.

51-2021.00 Coil Winders, Tapers, and Finishers

- **Education/Training Required: Short-term on-the-job training**
- **Employed: 55,998**
- **Annual Earnings: $22,090**
- **Growth: 8.2%**
- **Annual Job Openings: 10,000**

Wind wire coils used in electrical components, such as resistors and transformers, and in electrical equipment and instruments, such as field cores, bobbins, armature cores, electrical motors, generators, and control equipment.

Operates or tends wire-coiling machine. Attaches, alters, and trims materials such as wire, insulation, and coils, using hand tools. Reviews work orders and specifications to ascertain material needed and type of part to be processed. Observes gauges and stops machine to remove completed components, using hand tools. Selects and loads materials such as workpieces, objects, and machine parts onto equipment used in coiling process. Examines and tests wired electrical components, using measuring devices. Applies solutions or paints to wired electrical components, using hand tools. Records production and operational data on specified forms. Repairs and maintains electrical components and machinery parts, using hand tools.

GOE INFORMATION—Interest Area: 08. Industrial Production. **Work Group:** 08.03. Production Work. **Personality Type**—Realistic. Realistic occupations frequently involve work activities that include practical, hands-on problems and solutions. They often deal with plants, animals, and real-world materials like wood, tools, and machinery. Many of the occupations require working outside and do not involve a lot of paperwork or working closely with others. **Work Values**—Supervision, Technical; Moral Values; Company Policies and Practices; Activity;

Independence. **Skills**—Repairing; Operation Monitoring; Operation and Control; Equipment Selection; Installation. **Abilities**—*Cognitive:* Spatial Orientation; Perceptual Speed; Memorization. *Psychomotor:* Control Precision; Manual Dexterity; Speed of Limb Movement; Rate Control; Arm-Hand Steadiness. *Physical:* Explosive Strength; Dynamic Strength; Static Strength; Dynamic Flexibility; Extent Flexibility. *Sensory:* Depth Perception; Peripheral Vision; Visual Color Discrimination. **General Work Activities**—*Information Input:* Monitoring Processes, Materials, or Surroundings; Inspecting Equipment, Structures, or Materials; Getting Information. *Mental Process:* Evaluating Information Against Standards; Judging Qualities of Things, Services, or Other People's Work; Updating and Using Relevant Knowledge. *Work Output:* Handling and Moving Objects; Controlling Machines and Processes; Repairing and Maintaining Mechanical Equipment. *Interacting with Others:* Communicating with Other Workers; Performing Administrative Activities; Coordinating the Work and Activities of Others. **Physical Work Conditions**—Hazardous Equipment; Using Hands on Objects, Tools, or Controls; Distracting Sounds and Noise Levels; Indoors; Common Protective or Safety Attire. **Other Job Characteristics**—Degree of Automation; Pace Determined by Speed of Equipment; Importance of Repeating Same Tasks.

Experience—Job Zone 2. Some previous work-related skill, knowledge, or experience may be helpful, but usually is not needed. **Job Preparation:** SVP 4.0 to less than 6.0—six months to less than two years. **Knowledge**—Production and Processing; Mechanical; Building and Construction; Physics; Clerical. **Instructional Programs**—Industrial Electronics Technology/Technician.

Related DOT Jobs—721.684-018 Coil Connector; 724.362-010 Wire Coiler; 724.381-014 Coil Winder, Repair; 724.684-010 Armature Bander; 724.684-014 Armature Connector II; 724.684-026 Coil Winder; 724.685-010 Element Winding Machine Tender; 726.682-014 Wire-Wrapping-Machine Operator.

51-2022.00 Electrical and Electronic Equipment Assemblers

- **Education/Training Required: Short-term on-the-job training**
- **Employed: 378,772**
- **Annual Earnings: $22,270**
- **Growth: –6.3%**
- **Annual Job Openings: 66,000**

Assemble or modify electrical or electronic equipment, such as computers, test equipment telemetering systems, electric motors, and batteries.

Assembles systems and support structures and installs components, units, and printed circuit boards, following specifications and using hand tools and power tools. Reads and interprets schematic drawings, diagrams, blueprints, specifications, work orders, and reports to determine materials requirements and assembly instructions. Drills and taps holes in specified locations to mount control units and to provide openings for elements, wiring, and instruments. Inspects units to detect malfunctions and adjusts, repairs, or replaces component parts to ensure conformance to specifications. Measures and adjusts voltages to specified value to determine operational accuracy of instruments. Fabricates and forms parts, coils, and structures according to specifications, using drill, calipers, cutters, and saws. Tests wiring installations, assemblies, and circuits for resistance factors and operational defects and records results. Positions, aligns, and adjusts workpieces and electrical parts to facilitate wiring and assembly. Selects or distributes materials, supplies, and subassemblies to work area. Assists or confers with supervisor or engineer to plan and review work activities and to resolve production problems. Completes, reviews, and

maintains production, time, and component waste reports. Cleans parts, using cleaning solution, air hose, and cloth. Packs finished assemblies for shipment and transports to storage areas, using hoists or handtrucks. Instructs customers in installation, repair, and maintenance of products and explains assembly procedures or techniques to workers. Paints structures as specified, using paint sprayer. Marks and tags components to track and identify stock inventory.

GOE INFORMATION—**Interest Area:** 08. Industrial Production. **Work Group:** 08.02. Production Technology. **Personality Type**—Realistic. Realistic occupations frequently involve work activities that include practical, hands-on problems and solutions. They often deal with plants, animals, and real-world materials like wood, tools, and machinery. Many of the occupations require working outside and do not involve a lot of paperwork or working closely with others. **Work Values**—Moral Values; Company Policies and Practices; Advancement; Authority; Supervision; Technical. **Skills**—Installation; Quality Control Analysis; Equipment Selection; Science; Operation Monitoring; Operation and Control; Repairing; Instructing. **Abilities**—*Cognitive:* Visualization; Perceptual Speed; Flexibility of Closure; Speed of Closure; Selective Attention. *Psychomotor:* Finger Dexterity; Control Precision; Manual Dexterity; Speed of Limb Movement; Arm-Hand Steadiness. *Physical:* Dynamic Flexibility; Extent Flexibility; Explosive Strength; Dynamic Strength; Static Strength. *Sensory:* Visual Color Discrimination; Hearing Sensitivity; Auditory Attention; Sound Localization; Glare Sensitivity. **General Work Activities**—*Information Input:* Inspecting Equipment, Structures, or Materials; Getting Information; Monitoring Processes, Materials, or Surroundings. *Mental Process:* Updating and Using Relevant Knowledge; Judging Qualities of Things, Services, or Other People's Work; Processing Information. *Work Output:* Repairing and Maintaining Electronic Equipment; Handling and Moving Objects; Controlling Machines and Processes. *Interacting with Others:* Communicating with Other Workers; Communicating with Persons Outside Organization; Providing Consultation and Advice to Others. **Physical Work Conditions**—Using Hands on Objects, Tools, or Controls; Hazardous Equipment; Indoors; Common Protective or Safety Attire; Hazardous Conditions. **Other Job Characteristics**—Importance of Being Exact or Accurate; Importance of Repeating Same Tasks; Consequence of Error.

Experience—Job Zone 3. Previous work-related skill, knowledge, or experience is required. **Job Preparation:** SVP 6.0 to less than 7.0—more than one year and less than four years. **Knowledge**—Computers and Electronics; Production and Processing; Engineering and Technology; Design; Mechanical. **Instructional Programs**—Communications Systems Installation and Repair Technology; Industrial Electronics Technology/Technician.

Related DOT Jobs—693.381-026 Electrical and Radio Mock-Up Mechanic; 710.281-010 Assembler and Tester, Electronics; 721.381-014 Electric-Motor-Control Assembler; 722.381-010 Assembler; 726.361-014 Group Leader, Printed Circuit Board Assembly; 729.281-042 Wirer; 729.381-022 Wirer, Cable; 730.381-022 Electric-Organ Assembler and Checker; 759.261-010 Prototype-Deicer Assembler; 820.381-014 Transformer Assembler I; 826.361-010 Assembler and Wirer, Industrial Equipment; 826.381-010 Fabricator, Industrial Furnace.

51-2023.00 Electromechanical Equipment Assemblers

- **Education/Training Required: Short-term on-the-job training**
- **Employed: 72,976**
- **Annual Earnings: $24,690**
- **Growth: 4.5%**
- **Annual Job Openings: 13,000**

Assemble or modify electromechanical equipment or devices, such as servomechanisms, gyros, dynamometers, magnetic drums, tape drives, brakes, control linkage, actuators, and appliances.

Assembles parts or unit and attaches unit to assembly, subassembly, or frame, using hand tools and power tools. Inspects, tests, and adjusts completed unit to ensure that unit meets specifications, tolerances, and customer order requirements. Connects electrical wiring according to circuit diagram, using soldering iron. Measures parts to determine tolerances, using precision measuring instruments such as micrometers, calipers, and verniers. Drills, taps, reams, countersinks, and spotfaces bolt holes in parts, using drill press and portable power drill. Positions and aligns parts, using fixtures, jigs, and templates. Reads blueprints and specifications to determine component parts and assembly sequence of electromechanical unit. Files, laps, and buffs parts to fit, using hand tools and power tools. Disassembles unit to replace parts or to crate for shipping. Cleans and lubricates parts and subassemblies. Attaches name plates and marks identifying information on parts.

GOE INFORMATION—Interest Area: 08. Industrial Production. **Work Group:** 08.02. Production Technology. **Personality Type**—Realistic. Realistic occupations frequently involve work activities that include practical, hands-on problems and solutions. They often deal with plants, animals, and real-world materials like wood, tools, and machinery. Many of the occupations require working outside and do not involve a lot of paperwork or working closely with others. **Work Values**—Independence; Advancement; Supervision, Technical; Moral Values; Company Policies and Practices. **Skills**—Installation; Quality Control Analysis; Operation Monitoring; Operation and Control; Repairing; Equipment Selection; Technology Design. **Abilities**—*Cognitive:* Visualization; Problem Sensitivity; Number Facility; Spatial Orientation; Flexibility of Closure. *Psychomotor:* Manual Dexterity; Arm-Hand Steadiness; Multilimb Coordination; Finger Dexterity; Speed of Limb Movement. *Physical:* Explosive Strength; Dynamic Strength; Dynamic Flexibility; Extent Flexibility; Static Strength. *Sensory:* Visual Color Discrimination; Depth Perception; Peripheral Vision; Near Vision. **General Work Activities**—*Information Input:* Inspecting Equipment, Structures, or Materials; Getting Information; Monitoring Processes, Materials, or Surroundings. *Mental Process:* Updating and Using Relevant Knowledge; Evaluating Information Against Standards; Judging Qualities of Things, Services, or Other People's Work. *Work Output:* Handling and Moving Objects; Repairing and Maintaining Electronic Equipment; Controlling Machines and Processes. *Interacting with Others:* Communicating with Other Workers; Coordinating the Work and Activities of Others; Performing Administrative Activities. **Physical Work Conditions**—Hazardous Equipment; Distracting Sounds and Noise Levels; Hazardous Conditions; Using Hands on Objects, Tools, or Controls; Minor Burns, Cuts, Bites, or Stings. **Other Job Characteristics**—Degree of Automation; Importance of Repeating Same Tasks; Importance of Being Exact or Accurate.

Experience—Job Zone 3. Previous work-related skill, knowledge, or experience is required. **Job Preparation:** SVP 6.0 to less than 7.0—more than one year and less than four years. **Knowledge**—Computers and Electronics; Mechanical; Production and Processing; Design; Building and Construction. **Instructional Programs**—Electromechanical and Instrumentation and Maintenance Technologies/Technicians, Other; Electromechanical Technology/Electromechanical Engineering Technology; Robotics Technology/Technician.

Related DOT Jobs—706.381-018 Final Assembler; 706.381-050 Precision Assembler, Bench; 714.381-010 Assembler, Photographic Equipment; 721.381-018 Governor Assembler, Hydraulic.

51-2031.00 Engine and Other Machine Assemblers

- **Education/Training Required: Short-term on-the-job training**
- **Employed: 67,239**
- **Annual Earnings: $28,100**
- **Growth: 7.1%**
- **Annual Job Openings: 11,000**

Construct, assemble, or rebuild machines, such as engines, turbines, and similar equipment used in such industries as construction, extraction, textiles, and paper manufacturing.

Fastens components or parts together, using hand tools, rivet gun, and welding equipment. Positions and aligns components for assembly, manually or with hoist. Reworks, repairs, and replaces damaged parts or assemblies. Analyzes assembly blueprint and specifications manual and plans assembly or building operations. Fastens and installs piping, fixtures, or wiring and electrical components to specifications. Inspects and tests parts and accessories for leakage, defect, or functionality, using test equipment. Sets and verifies clearance of parts. Verifies conformance of parts to stock list and blueprints, using measuring instruments such as calipers, gauges, and micrometers. Lays out and drills, reams, taps, and cuts parts for assembly. Operates machine to verify functioning, machine capabilities, and conformance to customer's specifications. Removes rough spots and smoothes surfaces to fit, trim, or clean parts or components, using hand tools and power tools. Sets up and operates metalworking machines, such as milling and grinding machines, to shape or fabricate parts. Maintains and lubricates parts and components.

GOE INFORMATION—Interest Area: 08. Industrial Production. **Work Group:** 08.02. Production Technology. **Personality Type**—Realistic. Realistic occupations frequently involve work activities that include practical, hands-on problems and solutions. They often deal with plants, animals, and real-world materials like wood, tools, and machinery. Many of the occupations require working outside and do not involve a lot of paperwork or working closely with others. **Work Values**—Moral Values; Independence; Advancement; Supervision, Technical; Supervision, Human Relations. **Skills**—Operation and Control; Repairing; Quality Control Analysis; Operation Monitoring; Installation; Technology Design; Equipment Selection; Troubleshooting. **Abilities**—*Cognitive:* Visualization; Information Ordering; Category Flexibility; Deductive Reasoning; Written Comprehension. *Psychomotor:* Multilimb Coordination; Control Precision; Finger Dexterity; Speed of Limb Movement; Arm-Hand Steadiness. *Physical:* Extent Flexibility; Static Strength; Explosive Strength; Dynamic Strength; Gross Body Equilibrium. *Sensory:* Visual Color Discrimination; Hearing Sensitivity; Depth Perception; Sound Localization; Near Vision. **General Work Activities**—*Information Input:* Monitoring Processes, Materials, or Surroundings; Inspecting Equipment, Structures, or Materials; Getting Information. *Mental Process:* Evaluating Information Against Standards; Analyzing Data or Information; Judging Qualities of Things, Services, or Other People's Work. *Work Output:* Repairing and Maintaining Mechanical Equipment; Handling and Moving Objects; Controlling Machines and Processes. *Interacting with Others:* Communicating with Other Workers; Establishing and Maintaining Relationships; Communicating with Persons Outside Organization. **Physical Work Conditions**—Hazardous Equipment; Minor Burns, Cuts, Bites, or Stings; Cramped Work Space or Awkward Positions; Kneeling, Crouching, or Crawling; Distracting Sounds and Noise Levels. **Other Job Characteristics**—Consequence of Error; Pace Determined by Speed of Equipment; Degree of Automation.

Experience—Job Zone 3. Previous work-related skill, knowledge, or experience is required. **Job Preparation:** SVP 6.0 to less than 7.0—more than one year and less than four years. **Knowledge**—Mechanical; Design; Building and Construction; Public Safety and Security; Engineering and Technology. **Instructional Programs**—Engine Machinist; Heavy Equipment Maintenance Technology/Technician; Industrial Mechanics and Maintenance Technology.

Related DOT Jobs—600.261-010 Assembler, Steam-and-Gas Turbine; 600.281-022 Machine Builder; 600.380-026 Turbine-Blade Assembler; 624.381-018 Farm-Machinery Set-Up Mechanic; 638.361-010 Machine Assembler; 706.361-010 Assembler; 706.381-034 Sewing-Machine Assembler; 706.381-038 Subassembler; 706.381-042 Turbine Subassembler; 706.481-010 Internal-Combustion-Engine Subassembler; 801.261-010 Assembler, Mining Machinery; 801.261-018 Rotary-Engine Assembler; 801.361-010 Blower and Compressor Assembler; 806.381-022 Assembler, Aircraft Power Plant; 806.481-014 Assembler, Internal Combustion Engine; 820.361-014 Electric-Motor-and-Generator Assembler.

51-2041.00 Structural Metal Fabricators and Fitters

- Education/Training Required: Moderate-term on-the-job training
- Employed: 100,655
- Annual Earnings: $28,000
- Growth: 19.5%
- Annual Job Openings: 20,000

Fabricate, lay out, position, align, and fit parts of structural metal products.

No task data available.

GOE INFORMATION—**Interest Area:** 08. Industrial Production. **Work Group:** 08.03. Production Work. **Note:** The Department of Labor has not collected some data for this job, so it has fewer details than the other descriptions.

Instructional Programs—Machine Shop Technology/Assistant.

Related DOT Jobs—619.361-010 Former, Hand; 619.361-014 Metal Fabricator; 619.361-018 Metal-Fabricator Apprentice; 623.281-720 Ship Propeller Finisher; 801.261-014 Fitter I; 801.381-014 Fitter; 809.261-010 Assembler, Ground Support Equipment; 809.381-010 Fabricator-Assembler Metal Products.

51-2041.01 Metal Fabricators, Structural Metal Products

- Education/Training Required: Moderate-term on-the-job training
- Employed: No data available.
- Annual Earnings: $28,000
- Growth: 19.5%
- Annual Job Openings: 20,000

Fabricate and assemble structural metal products, such as frameworks or shells for machinery, ovens, tanks, and stacks and metal parts for buildings and bridges according to job order or blueprints.

Develops layout and plans sequence of operations for fabricating and assembling structural metal products, applying trigonometry and knowledge of metal. Locates and marks bending and cutting lines onto workpiece, allowing for stock thickness and machine and welding shrinkage. Sets up and operates fabricating machines, such as brakes, rolls, shears, flame cutters, and drill presses. Hammers, chips, and grinds workpiece to cut, bend, and straighten metal. Positions, aligns, fits, and welds together parts, using jigs, welding torch, and hand tools. Preheats workpieces to render them malleable, using hand torch or furnace. Verifies conformance of workpiece to specifications, using square, ruler, and measuring tape. Sets up and operates machine tools associated with fabricating shops, such as radial drill, end mill, and edge planer. Designs and constructs templates and fixtures, using hand tools.

GOE INFORMATION—**Interest Area:** 08. Industrial Production. **Work Group:** 08.03. Production Work. **Personality Type**—Realistic. Realistic occupations frequently involve work activities that include practical, hands-on problems and solutions. They often deal with plants, animals, and real-world materials like wood, tools, and machinery. Many of the occupations require working outside and do not involve a lot of paperwork or working closely with others. **Work Values**—Independence; Supervision, Human Relations; Moral Values; Company Policies and Practices; Activity. **Skills**—Operation and Control; Mathematics; Equipment Selection; Quality Control Analysis; Operation Monitoring. **Abilities**—*Cognitive:* Visualization; Mathematical Reasoning; Number Facility. *Psychomotor:* Control Precision; Multilimb Coordination; Arm-Hand Steadiness; Manual Dexterity; Finger Dexterity. *Physical:* Extent Flexibility; Static Strength; Explosive Strength; Dynamic Strength; Gross Body Coordination. *Sensory:* None met the criteria. **General Work Activities**—*Information Input:* Identifying Objects, Actions, and Events; Getting Information; Monitoring Processes, Materials, or Surroundings. *Mental Process:* Evaluating Information Against Standards; Making Decisions and Solving Problems; Judging Qualities of Things, Services, or Other People's Work. *Work Output:* Handling and Moving Objects; Controlling Machines and Processes; Performing General Physical Activities. *Interacting with Others:* Communicating with Other Workers; Establishing and Maintaining Relationships; Monitoring and Controlling Resources. **Physical Work Conditions**—Hazardous Equipment; Common Protective or Safety Attire; Whole Body Vibration; Distracting Sounds and Noise Levels; Using Hands on Objects, Tools, or Controls. **Other Job Characteristics**—Pace Determined by Speed of Equipment; Importance of Repeating Same Tasks; Importance of Being Exact or Accurate.

Experience—Job Zone 4. A minimum of two to four years of work-related skill, knowledge, or experience is needed. **Job Preparation:** SVP 7.0 to less than 8.0—two years to less than 10 years. **Knowledge**—Design; Building and Construction; Production and Processing; Mechanical; Engineering and Technology. **Instructional Programs**—Machine Shop Technology/Assistant.

Related DOT Jobs—619.361-014 Metal Fabricator; 619.361-018 Metal-Fabricator Apprentice.

51-2041.02 Fitters, Structural Metal— Precision

- Education/Training Required: Moderate-term on-the-job training
- Employed: No data available.
- Annual Earnings: $28,000
- Growth: 19.5%
- Annual Job Openings: 20,000

Lay out, position, align, and fit together fabricated parts of structural metal products preparatory to welding or riveting.

Aligns parts, using jack, turnbuckles, wedges, drift pins, pry bars, and hammer. Moves parts into position manually or by hoist or crane. Marks reference points onto floor or face block and transposes them to workpiece, using measuring devices, squares, chalk, and soapstone. Positions or tightens braces, jacks, clamps, ropes, or bolt straps or bolts parts in positions for welding or riveting. Tack-welds fitted parts together. Examines blueprints and plans sequence of operation, applying knowledge of geometry, effects of heat, weld shrinkage, machining, and metal thickness. Sets up face block, jigs, and fixtures. Removes high spots and cuts bevels, using hand files, portable grinders, and cutting torch. Locates reference points, using transit, and erects ladders and scaffolding to fit together large assemblies. Straightens warped or bent parts, using sledge, hand torch, straightening press, or bulldozer. Heat-treats parts with acetylene torch. Gives directions to welder to build up low spots or short pieces with weld.

GOE INFORMATION—Interest Area: 08. Industrial Production. Work Group: 08.03. Production Work. Personality Type—Realistic. Realistic occupations frequently involve work activities that include practical, hands-on problems and solutions. They often deal with plants, animals, and real-world materials like wood, tools, and machinery. Many of the occupations require working outside and do not involve a lot of paperwork or working closely with others. Work Values—Moral Values; Supervision, Technical; Independence; Supervision, Human Relations; Company Policies and Practices. Skills—Mathematics; Equipment Selection. Abilities—Cognitive: Number Facility; Originality; Mathematical Reasoning; Visualization; Flexibility of Closure. Psychomotor: Multilimb Coordination; Control Precision; Manual Dexterity; Speed of Limb Movement; Arm-Hand Steadiness. Physical: Static Strength; Explosive Strength; Dynamic Flexibility; Extent Flexibility; Dynamic Strength. Sensory: Depth Perception; Glare Sensitivity; Peripheral Vision; Night Vision; Sound Localization. General Work Activities—Information Input: Getting Information; Monitoring Processes, Materials, or Surroundings; Identifying Objects, Actions, and Events. Mental Process: Analyzing Data or Information; Evaluating Information Against Standards; Updating and Using Relevant Knowledge. Work Output: Handling and Moving Objects; Performing General Physical Activities; Controlling Machines and Processes. Interacting with Others: Communicating with Other Workers; Coordinating the Work and Activities of Others; Guiding, Directing, and Motivating Subordinates. Physical Work Conditions—Hazardous Equipment; Minor Burns, Cuts, Bites, or Stings; Common Protective or Safety Attire; Distracting Sounds and Noise Levels; High Places. Other Job Characteristics—Importance of Being Exact or Accurate; Consequence of Error; Degree of Automation.

Experience—Job Zone 4. A minimum of two to four years of work-related skill, knowledge, or experience is needed. Job Preparation: SVP 7.0 to less than 8.0—two years to less than 10 years. Knowledge—Building and Construction; Mechanical; Design; Physics; Mathematics. Instructional Programs—Machine Shop Technology/Assistant.

Related DOT Jobs—801.261-014 Fitter I; 801.381-014 Fitter; 809.261-010 Assembler, Ground Support Equipment.

51-2091.00 Fiberglass Laminators and Fabricators

- Education/Training Required: Moderate-term on-the-job training
- Employed: 47,951
- Annual Earnings: $23,810
- Growth: 11.4%
- Annual Job Openings: 9,000

Laminate layers of fiberglass on molds to form boat decks and hulls, bodies for golf carts, automobiles, or other products.

No task data available.

GOE INFORMATION—Interest Area: 08. Industrial Production. Work Group: 08.03. Production Work. Note: The Department of Labor has not collected some data for this job, so it has fewer details than the other descriptions.

Instructional Programs—Marine Maintenance/Fitter and Ship Repair Technology/Technician.

Related DOT Jobs—806.684-054 Fiberglass Laminator.

51-2092.00 Team Assemblers

- Education/Training Required: Moderate-term on-the-job training
- Employed: 1,458,353
- Annual Earnings: $22,260
- Growth: 5.9%
- Annual Job Openings: 283,000

Work as part of a team having responsibility for assembling an entire product or component of a product. Team assemblers can perform all tasks conducted by the team in the assembly process and rotate through all or most of them rather than being assigned to a specific task on a permanent basis. May participate in making management decisions affecting the work. Team leaders who work as part of the team should be included.

No task data available.

GOE INFORMATION—Interest Area: 08. Industrial Production. Work Group: 08.03. Production Work. Note: The Department of Labor has not collected some data for this job, so it has fewer details than the other descriptions.

Instructional Programs—No data available.

Related DOT Jobs—726.261-560 Production Technologist; 806.684-010 Assembler, Motor Vehicle.

51-2093.00 Timing Device Assemblers, Adjusters, and Calibrators

- Education/Training Required: Moderate-term on-the-job training
- Employed: 11,855
- Annual Earnings: $23,550
- Growth: 2.5%
- Annual Job Openings: 2,000

Perform precision assembling or adjusting within narrow tolerances of timing devices, such as watches, clocks, or chronometers.

Adjusts size or positioning of timepiece parts to achieve specified fit or function, using calipers, fixture, and loupe. Assembles and installs components of timepieces, using watchmaker's tools and loupe, to complete mechanism. Disassembles timepieces, such as watches, clocks, and chronometers, to diagnose and repair malfunctions. Replaces specified parts to repair malfunctioning timepieces, using watchmaker's tools, loupe, and holding fixture. Tests operation and fit of timepiece parts and subassemblies, using electronic testing equipment, tweezers, watchmaker's tools, and loupe. Screws parts or assemblies into position. Reviews blueprints, sketches, or work orders to gather information about task to be completed. Examines components of timepieces, such as watches, clocks, or chronometers, for defects, using loupe or microscope. Observes operation of timepiece parts and subassemblies to determine accuracy of movement and diagnose cause of defects. Bends parts, such as hairsprings, pallets, barrel covers, and bridges, to correct deficiencies in truing or endshake, using tweezers. Cleans and lubricates timepiece parts and assemblies, using solvent, buff stick, and oil.

GOE INFORMATION—Interest Area: 08. Industrial Production. **Work Group:** 08.02. Production Technology. **Personality Type**—Realistic. Realistic occupations frequently involve work activities that include practical, hands-on problems and solutions. They often deal with plants, animals, and real-world materials like wood, tools, and machinery. Many of the occupations require working outside and do not involve a lot of paperwork or working closely with others. **Work Values**—Independence; Moral Values; Good Working Conditions; Ability Utilization; Achievement. **Skills**—Repairing; Installation; Technology Design; Equipment Selection. **Abilities**—*Cognitive:* Visualization; Inductive Reasoning; Speed of Closure; Deductive Reasoning. *Psychomotor:* Finger Dexterity; Manual Dexterity; Arm-Hand Steadiness; Wrist-Finger Speed; Control Precision. *Physical:* Trunk Strength. *Sensory:* Near Vision. **General Work Activities**—*Information Input:* Inspecting Equipment, Structures, or Materials; Getting Information; Monitoring Processes, Materials, or Surroundings. *Mental Process:* Updating and Using Relevant Knowledge; Evaluating Information Against Standards; Analyzing Data or Information. *Work Output:* Repairing and Maintaining Mechanical Equipment; Repairing and Maintaining Electronic Equipment; Handling and Moving Objects. *Interacting with Others:* Communicating with Persons Outside Organization; Establishing and Maintaining Relationships; Communicating with Other Workers. **Physical Work Conditions**—Using Hands on Objects, Tools, or Controls; Sitting; Indoors; Making Repetitive Motions. **Other Job Characteristics**—Importance of Repeating Same Tasks; Importance of Being Exact or Accurate; Pace Determined by Speed of Equipment.

Experience—Job Zone 2. Some previous work-related skill, knowledge, or experience may be helpful, but usually is not needed. **Job Preparation:** SVP 4.0 to less than 6.0—six months to less than two years. **Knowledge**—Mechanical; Design; Engineering and Technology. **Instructional Programs**—Watchmaking and Jewelrymaking.

Related DOT Jobs—715.381-010 Assembler; 715.381-014 Assembler, Watch Train; 715.381-018 Banking Pin Adjuster; 715.381-022 Barrel Assembler; 715.381-026 Barrel-Bridge Assembler; 715.381-030 Barrel-Endshake Adjuster; 715.381-038 Chronometer Assembler and Adjuster; 715.381-042 Chronometer-Balance-and-Hairspring Assembler; 715.381-054 Hairspring Assembler; 715.381-062 Hairspring Vibrator; 715.381-082 Pallet-Stone Inserter; 715.381-086 Pallet-Stone Positioner; 715.381-094 Watch Assembler; 715.681-010 Timing Adjuster.

51-2099.99 Assemblers and Fabricators, All Other

- **Education/Training Required: No data available.**
- **Employed: No data available.**
- **Annual Earnings: No data available.**
- **Growth: 15.4%**
- **Annual Job Openings: 85,000**

All assemblers and fabricators not listed separately.

No task data available.

GOE INFORMATION—Interest Area: 08. Industrial Production. **Work Group:** 08.03. Production Work. **Note:** The Department of Labor has not collected some data for this job, so it has fewer details than the other descriptions.

Instructional Programs—No data available.

Related DOT Jobs—692.685-230 Trim Attacher; 699.685-026 Power-Screwdriver Operator; 706.381-014 Bench Hand; 706.381-026 Operating-Table Assembler; 706.684-046 Bench Hand; 709.381-010 Atomic-Fuel Assembler; 709.381-030 Organ-Pipe Maker, Metal; 709.381-038 Reed Maker; 709.381-046 Wire-Mesh-Filter Fabricator; 709.684-098 Wire-Frame-Lamp-Shade Maker; 710.381-010 Assembler II; 710.681-026 Thermometer Maker; 730.381-014 Bell Maker; 730.381-018 Brass-Wind-Instrument Maker; 730.381-030 Harp-Action Assembler; 730.381-046 Pipe-Organ Installer; 730.381-050 Player-Piano Technician; 730.381-054 Trombone-Slide Assembler; 730.681-014 Piston Maker; 730.681-018 Valve Maker II; others.

51-3000 Food Processing Workers

51-3011.00 Bakers

- **Education/Training Required: Long-term on-the-job training**
- **Employed: 159,912**
- **Annual Earnings: $20,440**
- **Growth: 16.8%**
- **Annual Job Openings: 25,000**

Mix and bake ingredients according to recipes to produce breads, rolls, cookies, cakes, pies, pastries, or other baked goods.

No task data available.

GOE INFORMATION—Interest Area: 11. Recreation, Travel, and Other Personal Services. **Work Group:** 11.05. Food and Beverage Services. **Note:** The Department of Labor has not collected some data for this job, so it has fewer details than the other descriptions.

Instructional Programs—Baking and Pastry Arts/Baker/Pastry Chef.

Related DOT Jobs—313.361-010 Baker, Second; 313.361-038 Pie Maker; 313.381-010 Baker; 313.381-018 Cook Apprentice, Pastry; 313.381-026 Cook, Pastry; 520.384-010 Bench Hand; 526.381-010 Baker; 526.381-014 Baker Apprentice.

51-3011.01 Bakers, Bread and Pastry

- **Education/Training Required: Long-term on-the-job training**
- **Employed: No data available.**
- **Annual Earnings: $20,440**
- **Growth: 16.8%**
- **Annual Job Openings: 25,000**

Mix and bake ingredients according to recipes to produce small quantities of breads, pastries, and other baked goods for consumption on premises or for sale as specialty baked goods.

Weighs and measures ingredients, using measuring cups and spoons. Mixes ingredients to form dough or batter by hand or using electric mixer. Rolls and shapes dough, using rolling pin, and cuts dough in uniform portions with knife, divider, or cookie cutter. Molds dough in desired shapes, places dough in greased or floured pans, and trims overlapping edges with knife. Mixes and cooks pie fillings, pours fillings into pie shells, and tops filling with meringue or cream. Checks production schedule to determine variety and quantity of goods to bake. Spreads or sprinkles toppings on loaves or specialties and places dough in oven, using long-handled paddle (peel). Covers filling with top crust, places pies in oven, and adjust drafts or thermostatic controls to regulate oven temperatures. Mixes ingredients to make icings, decorates cakes and pastries, and blends colors for icings, shaped ornaments, and statuaries. Cuts, peels, and prepares fruit for pie fillings.

GOE INFORMATION—Interest Area: 11. Recreation, Travel, and Other Personal Services. **Work Group:** 11.05. Food and Beverage Services. **Personality Type**—Realistic. Realistic occupations frequently involve work activities that include practical, hands-on problems and solutions. They often deal with plants, animals, and real-world materials like wood, tools, and machinery. Many of the occupations require working outside and do not involve a lot of paperwork or working closely with others. **Work Values**—Moral Values; Supervision, Technical; Independence; Supervision, Human Relations. **Skills**—None met the criteria. **Abilities**—*Cognitive:* None met the criteria. *Psychomotor:* Finger Dexterity. *Physical:* Dynamic Flexibility. *Sensory:* None met the criteria. **General Work Activities**—*Information Input:* Identifying Objects, Actions, and Events; Getting Information; Monitoring Processes, Materials, or Surroundings. *Mental Process:* Organizing, Planning, and Prioritizing; Thinking Creatively; Updating and Using Relevant Knowledge. *Work Output:* Handling and Moving Objects; Controlling Machines and Processes; Performing General Physical Activities. *Interacting with Others:* Communicating with Persons Outside Organization; Performing for or Working with the Public; Communicating with Other Workers. **Physical Work Conditions**—Standing; Minor Burns, Cuts, Bites, or Stings; Indoors; Making Repetitive Motions; Very Hot or Cold. **Other Job Characteristics**—Pace Determined by Speed of Equipment; Importance of Repeating Same Tasks; Degree of Automation.

Experience—Job Zone 3. Previous work-related skill, knowledge, or experience is required. **Job Preparation:** SVP 6.0 to less than 7.0—more than one year and less than four years. **Knowledge**—Food Production; Production and Processing; Sales and Marketing; Customer and Personal Service. **Instructional Programs**—Baking and Pastry Arts/Baker/Pastry Chef.

Related DOT Jobs—313.361-010 Baker, Second; 313.361-038 Pie Maker; 313.381-010 Baker; 313.381-018 Cook Apprentice, Pastry; 313.381-026 Cook, Pastry.

51-3011.02 Bakers, Manufacturing

- ● **Education/Training Required: Long-term on-the-job training**
- ● **Employed: No data available.**
- ● **Annual Earnings: $20,440**
- ● **Growth: 16.8%**
- ● **Annual Job Openings: 25,000**

Mix and bake ingredients according to recipes to produce breads, pastries, and other baked goods. Goods are produced in large quantities for sale through establishments such as grocery stores. Generally, high-volume production equipment is used.

Measures flour and other ingredients to prepare batters, dough, fillings, and icings, using scale and graduated containers. Places dough in pans, in molds, or on sheets and bakes dough in oven or on grill. Observes color of products being baked and adjusts oven temperature. Dumps ingredients into mixing-machine bowl or steam kettle to mix or cook ingredients according to specific instructions. Rolls, cuts, and shapes dough to form sweet rolls, pie crusts, tarts, cookies, and related products prior to baking. Applies glaze, icing, or other topping to baked goods, using spatula or brush. Decorates cakes. Develops new recipes for cakes and icings.

GOE INFORMATION—Interest Area: 08. Industrial Production. **Work Group:** 08.03. Production Work. **Personality Type**—Realistic. Realistic occupations frequently involve work activities that include practical, hands-on problems and solutions. They often deal with plants, animals, and real-world materials like wood, tools, and machinery. Many of the

occupations require working outside and do not involve a lot of paperwork or working closely with others. **Work Values**—Supervision, Technical; Moral Values; Independence; Company Policies and Practices; Supervision, Human Relations. **Skills**—None met the criteria. **Abilities**—*Cognitive:* Information Ordering; Originality. *Psychomotor:* Manual Dexterity; Rate Control; Multilimb Coordination. *Physical:* Gross Body Coordination; Dynamic Flexibility. *Sensory:* Visual Color Discrimination. **General Work Activities**—*Information Input:* Getting Information; Identifying Objects, Actions, and Events; Monitoring Processes, Materials, or Surroundings. *Mental Process:* Thinking Creatively; Making Decisions and Solving Problems; Judging Qualities of Things, Services, or Other People's Work. *Work Output:* Performing General Physical Activities; Handling and Moving Objects; Controlling Machines and Processes. *Interacting with Others:* Monitoring and Controlling Resources; Communicating with Other Workers; Establishing and Maintaining Relationships. **Physical Work Conditions**—Minor Burns, Cuts, Bites, or Stings; Very Hot or Cold; Indoors; Standing; Making Repetitive Motions. **Other Job Characteristics**—Pace Determined by Speed of Equipment; Importance of Repeating Same Tasks; Degree of Automation.

Experience—Job Zone 3. Previous work-related skill, knowledge, or experience is required. **Job Preparation:** SVP 6.0 to less than 7.0—more than one year and less than four years. **Knowledge**—Production and Processing; Food Production. **Instructional Programs**—Baking and Pastry Arts/Baker/Pastry Chef.

Related DOT Jobs—520.384-010 Bench Hand; 526.381-010 Baker; 526.381-014 Baker Apprentice.

51-3021.00 Butchers and Meat Cutters

- ● **Education/Training Required: Long-term on-the-job training**
- ● **Employed: 141,071**
- ● **Annual Earnings: $24,800**
- ● **Growth: −8.9%**
- ● **Annual Job Openings: 16,000**

Cut, trim, or prepare consumer-sized portions of meat for use or sale in retail establishments.

Cure, smoke, tenderize, and preserve meat. Cut, trim, bone, tie, and grind meats, such as beef, pork, poultry, and fish, to prepare meat in cooking form. Prepare and place meat cuts and products in display counter so they will appear attractive and catch the shopper's eye. Prepare special cuts of meat ordered by customers. Shape, lace, and tie roasts, using boning knife, skewer, and twine. Total sales and collect money from customers. Wrap, weigh, label, and price cuts of meat. Estimate requirements and order or requisition meat supplies to maintain inventories. Negotiate with representatives from supply companies to determine order details. Receive, inspect, and store meat upon delivery to ensure meat quality. Record quantity of meat received and issued to cooks and/or keep records of meat sales. Supervise other butchers or meat cutters.

GOE INFORMATION—Interest Area: 11. Recreation, Travel, and Other Personal Services. **Work Group:** 11.05. Food and Beverage Services. **Personality Type**—Realistic. Realistic occupations frequently involve work activities that include practical, hands-on problems and solutions. They often deal with plants, animals, and real-world materials like wood, tools, and machinery. Many of the occupations require working outside and do not involve a lot of paperwork or working closely with others. **Work Values**—Independence; Social Service; Moral Values; Responsibility; Security. **Skills**—None met the criteria. **Abilities**—*Cognitive:* None met the criteria. *Psychomotor:* Manual Dexterity; Finger Dexterity. *Physical:* Dynamic Strength; Dynamic Flexibility. *Sensory:* None met the criteria.

General Work Activities—*Information Input:* Identifying Objects, Actions, and Events; Estimating Needed Characteristics; Getting Information. *Mental Process:* Judging Qualities of Things, Services, or Other People's Work; Evaluating Information Against Standards; Making Decisions and Solving Problems. *Work Output:* Handling and Moving Objects; Performing General Physical Activities; Documenting or Recording Information. *Interacting with Others:* Performing for or Working with the Public; Monitoring and Controlling Resources; Communicating with Persons Outside Organization. **Physical Work Conditions—**Minor Burns, Cuts, Bites, or Stings; Hazardous Equipment; Standing; Indoors; Making Repetitive Motions. **Other Job Characteristics—**Importance of Repeating Same Tasks; Pace Determined by Speed of Equipment; Degree of Automation.

Experience—Job Zone 3. Previous work-related skill, knowledge, or experience is required. **Job Preparation:** SVP 6.0 to less than 7.0—more than one year and less than four years. **Knowledge—**Food Production; Biology; Sales and Marketing; Personnel and Human Resources; Customer and Personal Service. **Instructional Programs—**Meat Cutting/Meat Cutter.

Related DOT Jobs—316.681-010 Butcher, Meat; 316.684-018 Meat Cutter; 316.684-022 Meat-Cutter Apprentice.

51-3022.00 Meat, Poultry, and Fish Cutters and Trimmers

- Education/Training Required: **Short-term on-the-job training**
- Employed: **147,920**
- Annual Earnings: **$17,350**
- Growth: **9.5%**
- Annual Job Openings: **16,000**

Use hand tools to perform routine cutting and trimming of meat, poultry, and fish.

Clean, trim, slice, and section carcasses for future processing. Cut and trim meat to prepare for packing. Inspect meat products for defects, bruises, or blemishes and remove them along with any excess fat. Obtain and distribute specified meat or carcass. Process primal parts into cuts that are ready for retail use. Produce hamburger meat and meat trimmings. Remove parts, such as skin, feathers, scales, or bones, from carcass. Separate meats and byproducts into specified containers and seal containers. Weigh meats and tag containers for weight and contents. Clean and salt hides. Prepare ready-to-heat foods by filleting meat or fish or cutting it into bite-sized pieces, preparing and adding vegetables or applying sauces or breading. Prepare sausages, luncheon meats, hot dogs, and other fabricated meat products, using meat trimmings and hamburger meat. Slaughter live animals, using stunning devices and knives. Use knives, cleavers, meat saws, band saws, or other equipment to perform meat cutting and trimming.

GOE INFORMATION—Interest Area: 08. Industrial Production. **Work Group:** 08.03. Production Work. **Personality Type—**Realistic. Realistic occupations frequently involve work activities that include practical, hands-on problems and solutions. They often deal with plants, animals, and real-world materials like wood, tools, and machinery. Many of the occupations require working outside and do not involve a lot of paperwork or working closely with others. **Work Values—**Supervision, Technical; Independence; Moral Values. **Skills—**None met the criteria. **Abilities—***Cognitive:* Spatial Orientation; Category Flexibility; Perceptual Speed. *Psychomotor:* Wrist-Finger Speed; Manual Dexterity; Speed of Limb Movement; Arm-Hand Steadiness; Reaction Time. *Physical:* Static

Strength; Dynamic Strength; Dynamic Flexibility; Extent Flexibility; Trunk Strength. *Sensory:* Peripheral Vision; Visual Color Discrimination; Depth Perception. **General Work Activities—***Information Input:* Identifying Objects, Actions, and Events; Monitoring Processes, Materials, or Surroundings; Inspecting Equipment, Structures, or Materials. *Mental Process:* Judging Qualities of Things, Services, or Other People's Work; Organizing, Planning, and Prioritizing; Evaluating Information Against Standards. *Work Output:* Handling and Moving Objects; Performing General Physical Activities; Controlling Machines and Processes. *Interacting with Others:* Communicating with Other Workers; Monitoring and Controlling Resources; Performing Administrative Activities. **Physical Work Conditions—**Making Repetitive Motions; Minor Burns, Cuts, Bites, or Stings; Contaminants; Common Protective or Safety Attire; Disease or Infections. **Other Job Characteristics—**Importance of Repeating Same Tasks; Pace Determined by Speed of Equipment; Degree of Automation.

Experience—Job Zone 1. No previous work-related skill, knowledge, or experience is needed. **Job Preparation:** SVP below 4.0—less than six months. **Knowledge—**Food Production; Biology; Production and Processing; Law and Government; Public Safety and Security. **Instructional Programs—**Meat Cutting/Meat Cutter.

Related DOT Jobs—521.687-058 Fish Chopper, Gang Knife; 521.687-106 Sausage-Meat Trimmer; 521.687-126 Skin Lifter, Bacon; 522.687-046 Fish Roe Processor; 525.684-010 Boner, Meat; 525.684-014 Butcher, Fish; 525.684-018 Carcass Splitter; 525.684-022 Crab Butcher; 525.684-026 Final-Dressing Cutter; 525.684-030 Fish Cleaner; 525.684-034 Head Trimmer; 525.684-038 Offal Separator; 525.684-042 Poultry Killer; 525.684-046 Skinner; 525.684-050 Sticker, Animal; 525.684-054 Trimmer, Meat; 525.684-058 Turkey-Roll Maker; 525.687-010 Animal Eviscerator; 525.687-014 Casing Splitter; 525.687-030 Gambreler; others.

51-3023.00 Slaughterers and Meat Packers

- Education/Training Required: **Moderate-term on-the-job training**
- Employed: **121,642**
- Annual Earnings: **$19,960**
- Growth: **2.6%**
- Annual Job Openings: **13,000**

Work in slaughtering, meat packing, or wholesale establishments performing precision functions involving the preparation of meat. Work may include specialized slaughtering tasks, cutting standard or premium cuts of meat for marketing, making sausage, or wrapping meats.

Trims headmeat and otherwise severs or removes parts of animals' heads or skulls. Wraps dressed carcasses and/or meat cuts. Trims, cleans, and/or cures animal hides. Removes bone and cuts meat into standard cuts to prepare meat for marketing. Skins sections of animals or whole animals. Grinds meat into sausage. Stuns animals prior to slaughtering. Slaughters animals in accordance with religious law and determines that carcasses meet specified religious standards when slaughtering is performed for religious purposes. Saws, splits, or scribes slaughtered animals to reduce carcasses. Slits open, eviscerates, and trims carcasses of slaughtered animals. Severs jugular vein to drain blood and facilitate slaughtering. Cuts, trims, skins, sorts, and washes viscera of slaughtered animals to separate edible portions from offal. Shackles hind legs of animals to raise them for slaughtering or skinning. Washes and/or shaves carcasses.

GOE INFORMATION—Interest Area: 08. Industrial Production. Work Group: 08.03. Production Work. Personality Type—Realistic. Realistic occupations frequently involve work activities that include practical, hands-on problems and solutions. They often deal with plants, animals, and real-world materials like wood, tools, and machinery. Many of the occupations require working outside and do not involve a lot of paperwork or working closely with others. Work Values—Independence; Security. Skills—None met the criteria. Abilities—*Cognitive:* Flexibility of Closure; Perceptual Speed; Spatial Orientation; Category Flexibility; Selective Attention. *Psychomotor:* Manual Dexterity; Arm-Hand Steadiness; Wrist-Finger Speed; Speed of Limb Movement; Reaction Time. *Physical:* Static Strength; Dynamic Strength; Extent Flexibility; Trunk Strength; Dynamic Flexibility. *Sensory:* Visual Color Discrimination; Peripheral Vision; Far Vision; Depth Perception; Hearing Sensitivity. General Work Activities—*Information Input:* Identifying Objects, Actions, and Events; Monitoring Processes, Materials, or Surroundings; Inspecting Equipment, Structures, or Materials. *Mental Process:* Evaluating Information Against Standards; Judging Qualities of Things, Services, or Other People's Work; Updating and Using Relevant Knowledge. *Work Output:* Handling and Moving Objects; Performing General Physical Activities; Controlling Machines and Processes. *Interacting with Others:* Communicating with Other Workers; Assisting and Caring for Others; Establishing and Maintaining Relationships. Physical Work Conditions—Common Protective or Safety Attire; Minor Burns, Cuts, Bites, or Stings; Making Repetitive Motions; Disease or Infections; Distracting Sounds and Noise Levels. Other Job Characteristics—Importance of Repeating Same Tasks; Pace Determined by Speed of Equipment; Consequence of Error.

Experience—Job Zone 2. Some previous work-related skill, knowledge, or experience may be helpful, but usually is not needed. Job Preparation: SVP 4.0 to less than 6.0—six months to less than two years. Knowledge—Food Production; Biology; Philosophy and Theology; Public Safety and Security; Production and Processing. Instructional Programs—Meat Cutting/Meat Cutter.

Related DOT Jobs—525.361-010 Slaughterer, Religious Ritual; 525.381-010 Butcher Apprentice; 525.381-014 Butcher, All-Round; 525.664-010 Meat Dresser.

51-3091.00 Food and Tobacco Roasting, Baking, and Drying Machine Operators and Tenders

- Education/Training Required: Short-term on-the-job training
- Employed: 18,236
- Annual Earnings: $23,210
- Growth: −9.0%
- Annual Job Openings: 3,000

Operate or tend food or tobacco roasting, baking, or drying equipment, including hearth ovens, kiln driers, roasters, char kilns, and vacuum drying equipment.

Clear or dislodge blockages in bins, screens, or other equipment, using poles, brushes, or mallets. Fill or remove product from trays, carts, hoppers, or equipment, using scoops, peels, or shovels or by hand. Observe flow of materials; listen for machine malfunctions, such as jamming or spillage; and notify supervisors if corrective actions fail. Observe temperature, humidity, pressure gauges, and product samples and adjust controls, such as thermostats and valves, in order to maintain prescribed operating conditions for specific stages. Observe, feel, taste, or otherwise examine products during and after processing in order to ensure conformance to standards. Open valves, gates, or chutes or use shovels in order to load or remove products from ovens or other equipment. Operate or tend equipment that roasts, bakes, dries, or cures food items such as cocoa and coffee beans, grains, nuts, and bakery products. Push racks or carts in order to transfer products to storage, cooling stations, or the next stage of processing. Read work orders in order to determine quantities and types of products to be baked, dried, or roasted. Set temperature and time controls; light ovens, burners, driers, or roasters; and start equipment, such as conveyors, cylinders, blowers, driers, or pumps. Smooth out products in bins, pans, trays, or conveyors, using rakes or shovels. Test products for moisture content, using moisture meters. Weigh or measure products, using scale hoppers or scale conveyors. Clean equipment with steam, hot water, and hoses. Dump sugar dust from collectors into melting tanks and add water in order to reclaim sugar lost during processing. Install equipment, such as spray units, cutting blades, or screens, using hand tools. Record production data, such as weight and amount of product processed, type of product, and time and temperature of processing. Signal co-workers in order to synchronize flow of materials. Start conveyors to move roasted grain to cooling pans and agitate grain with rakes as blowers force air through perforated bottoms of pans. Take product samples during and/or after processing for laboratory analyses. Lift racks of fish from washing tanks and place racks in smoke chambers. Remove salt-cured fish from barrels, hang fish on racks, and place racks in washing tank, turning valves to regulate fresh water flow.

GOE INFORMATION—Interest Area: 08. Industrial Production. Work Group: 08.03. Production Work. Personality Type—Realistic. Realistic occupations frequently involve work activities that include practical, hands-on problems and solutions. They often deal with plants, animals, and real-world materials like wood, tools, and machinery. Many of the occupations require working outside and do not involve a lot of paperwork or working closely with others. Work Values—Moral Values; Supervision, Technical; Independence; Company Policies and Practices; Supervision, Human Relations. Skills—Operation and Control; Operation Monitoring; Installation; Quality Control Analysis. Abilities—*Cognitive:* Time Sharing; Selective Attention; Perceptual Speed; Visualization; Spatial Orientation. *Psychomotor:* Reaction Time; Control Precision; Manual Dexterity; Response Orientation; Finger Dexterity. *Physical:* Static Strength; Explosive Strength; Dynamic Strength; Gross Body Equilibrium; Trunk Strength. *Sensory:* Hearing Sensitivity; Sound Localization; Visual Color Discrimination; Auditory Attention; Depth Perception. General Work Activities—*Information Input:* Identifying Objects, Actions, and Events; Getting Information; Monitoring Processes, Materials, or Surroundings. *Mental Process:* Evaluating Information Against Standards; Judging Qualities of Things, Services, or Other People's Work; Organizing, Planning, and Prioritizing. *Work Output:* Handling and Moving Objects; Performing General Physical Activities; Controlling Machines and Processes. *Interacting with Others:* Communicating with Other Workers; Establishing and Maintaining Relationships; Performing Administrative Activities. Physical Work Conditions—Minor Burns, Cuts, Bites, or Stings; Hazardous Equipment; Common Protective or Safety Attire; Using Hands on Objects, Tools, or Controls; Very Hot or Cold. Other Job Characteristics—Degree of Automation; Pace Determined by Speed of Equipment; Importance of Repeating Same Tasks.

Experience—Job Zone 1. No previous work-related skill, knowledge, or experience is needed. Job Preparation: SVP below 4.0—less than six months. Knowledge—Food Production; Production and Processing; Chemistry; Mechanical; Fine Arts. Instructional Programs—Agricultural and Food Products Processing.

Related DOT Jobs—522.662-014 Redrying-Machine Operator; 522.685-038 Curing-Bin Operator; 522.685-066 Fish Smoker; 523.362-010 Cocoa-Bean Roaster I; 523.362-014 Drier Operator; 523.382-010 Gunner; 523.585-022 Drier, Long Goods; 523.585-030 Pulp-Drier Firer; 523.585-034 Roaster, Grain; 523.662-010 Bone-Char Kiln Operator; 523.665-010 Sugar Drier; 523.682-014 Coffee Roaster; 523.682-022 Drier Operator; 523.682-026 Drum Drier; 523.682-030 Kiln Operator, Malt House; 523.682-038 Tobacco Curer; 523.685-026 Coffee Roaster, Continuous Process; 523.685-054 Dehydrator Tender; 523.685-058 Drier Attendant; 523.685-062 Drier Operator; others.

51-3092.00 Food Batchmakers

- **Education/Training Required: Short-term on-the-job training**
- **Employed: 65,800**
- **Annual Earnings: $21,690**
- **Growth: 1.4%**
- **Annual Job Openings: 9,000**

Set up and operate equipment that mixes or blends ingredients used in the manufacturing of food products. Includes candy makers and cheese makers.

Determine mixing sequences, based on knowledge of temperature effects and of the solubility of specific ingredients. Examine, feel, and taste product samples during production in order to evaluate quality, color, texture, flavor, and bouquet; document the results. Fill processing or cooking containers, such as kettles, rotating cookers, pressure cookers, or vats, with ingredients by opening valves, by starting pumps or injectors, or by hand. Follow recipes to produce food products of specified flavor, texture, clarity, bouquet, and/or color. Manipulate products by hand or using machines in order to separate, spread, knead, spin, cast, cut, pull, or roll products. Mix or blend ingredients according to recipes, using a paddle or an agitator or by controlling vats that heat and mix ingredients. Modify cooking and forming operations based on the results of sampling processes, adjusting time cycles and ingredients in order to achieve desired qualities such as firmness or texture. Observe and listen to equipment in order to detect possible malfunctions, such as leaks or plugging, and report malfunctions or undesirable tastes to supervisors. Observe gauges and thermometers to determine if the mixing chamber temperature is within specified limits and turn valves to control the temperature. Press switches and turn knobs to start, adjust, and regulate equipment such as beaters, extruders, discharge pipes, and salt pumps. Select and measure or weigh ingredients, using English or metric measures and balance scales. Set up, operate, and tend equipment that cooks, mixes, blends, or processes ingredients in the manufacturing of food products according to formulas or recipes. Test food product samples for moisture content, acidity level, specific gravity, and/or butter-fat content and continue processing until desired levels are reached. Turn valve controls to start equipment and to adjust operation in order to maintain product quality. Clean and sterilize vats and factory processing areas. Cool food product batches on slabs or in water-cooled kettles. Formulate and/or modify recipes for specific kinds of food products. Give directions to other workers who are assisting in the batchmaking process. Grade food products according to government regulations or according to type, color, bouquet, and moisture content. Homogenize or pasteurize material to prevent separation or to obtain prescribed butterfat content, using a homogenizing device. Inspect and pack the final product. Inspect vats after cleaning in order to ensure that fermentable residue has been removed. Operate refining machines in order to reduce the particle size of cooked batches. Place products on carts or conveyors in order to transfer them to the next stage of processing. Record production and test data for each food product batch, such as the ingredients used, temperature, test results, and time cycle.

GOE INFORMATION—**Interest Area:** 08. Industrial Production. **Work Group:** 08.03. Production Work. **Personality Type**—Realistic. Realistic occupations frequently involve work activities that include practical, hands-on problems and solutions. They often deal with plants, animals, and real-world materials like wood, tools, and machinery. Many of the occupations require working outside and do not involve a lot of paperwork or working closely with others. **Work Values**—Supervision, Technical; Authority; Variety; Supervision, Human Relations; Company Policies and Practices. **Skills**—Operation and Control. **Abilities**—*Cognitive:* Information Ordering; Memorization; Flexibility of Closure; Perceptual Speed; Number Facility. *Psychomotor:* Manual Dexterity; Wrist-Finger Speed; Speed of Limb Movement; Response Orientation; Multilimb Coordination. *Physical:* Extent Flexibility; Explosive Strength. *Sensory:* Visual Color Discrimination; Near Vision; Hearing Sensitivity. **General Work Activities**—*Information Input:* Identifying Objects, Actions, and Events; Monitoring Processes, Materials, or Surroundings; Getting Information. *Mental Process:* Judging Qualities of Things, Services, or Other People's Work; Evaluating Information Against Standards; Updating and Using Relevant Knowledge. *Work Output:* Handling and Moving Objects; Controlling Machines and Processes; Performing General Physical Activities. *Interacting with Others:* Establishing and Maintaining Relationships; Monitoring and Controlling Resources; Communicating with Other Workers. **Physical Work Conditions**—Standing; Making Repetitive Motions; Using Hands on Objects, Tools, or Controls; Indoors; Very Hot or Cold. **Other Job Characteristics**—Pace Determined by Speed of Equipment; Importance of Repeating Same Tasks; Degree of Automation.

Experience—Job Zone 3. Previous work-related skill, knowledge, or experience is required. **Job Preparation:** SVP 6.0 to less than 7.0—more than one year and less than four years. **Knowledge**—Food Production; Production and Processing. **Instructional Programs**—Agricultural and Food Products Processing; Foodservice Systems Administration/Management.

Related DOT Jobs—520.361-010 Honey Grader-and-Blender; 529.361-010 Almond-Paste Mixer; 529.361-014 Candy Maker; 529.361-018 Cheesemaker; 529.381-010 Compounder, Flavorings.

51-3093.00 Food Cooking Machine Operators and Tenders

- **Education/Training Required: Short-term on-the-job training**
- **Employed: 37,120**
- **Annual Earnings: $21,420**
- **Growth: 0.6%**
- **Annual Job Openings: 7,000**

Operate or tend cooking equipment, such as steam cooking vats, deep fry cookers, pressure cookers, kettles, and boilers, to prepare food products.

Operate auxiliary machines and equipment, such as grinders, canners, and molding presses, in order to prepare or further process products. Place products on conveyors or carts and monitor product flow. Record production and test data, such as processing steps, temperature and steam readings, cooking time, batches processed, and test results. Activate agitators and paddles in order to mix or stir ingredients, stopping machines when ingredients are thoroughly mixed. Admit required amounts of water, steam, cooking oils, or compressed air into equipment, such as by opening water valves to cool mixtures to the desired consistency. Collect and examine product samples during production in order to test them for quality, color, content, consistency, viscosity, acidity, and/or specific gravity. Measure or weigh ingredients, using scales or measuring containers. Observe gauges, dials, and product characteristics and adjust controls in order to maintain appropriate temperature, pressure, and flow of ingredients. Pour, dump, or load prescribed quantities of ingredients or products into cooking equipment manually or using a hoist. Read work orders, recipes, or formulas in order to determine cooking times and temperatures and ingredient specifications. Remove cooked material or products from equipment. Set temperature, pressure, and time controls; start conveyers, machines, or pumps. Tend or operate and control equipment such as kettles, cookers, vats and tanks, and boilers in order to cook ingredients or prepare products for further processing. Turn valves or start pumps to add ingredients or drain products from equipment and to transfer products for storage, cooling, or further processing. Clean, wash, and sterilize equipment and cooking area, using water hoses, cleaning or sterilizing solutions, or rinses. Listen for malfunction alarms and shut down equipment and notify supervisors when necessary. Notify or signal other workers to operate equipment or when processing is complete.

GOE INFORMATION—Interest Area: 08. Industrial Production. Work Group: 08.03. Production Work. Personality Type—Realistic. Realistic occupations frequently involve work activities that include practical, hands-on problems and solutions. They often deal with plants, animals, and real-world materials like wood, tools, and machinery. Many of the occupations require working outside and do not involve a lot of paperwork or working closely with others. Work Values—Moral Values; Supervision, Technical; Supervision, Human Relations; Company Policies and Practices; Independence. Skills—Operation Monitoring; Operation and Control; Quality Control Analysis. Abilities—*Cognitive:* Selective Attention. *Psychomotor:* Reaction Time; Response Orientation; Rate Control; Control Precision; Arm-Hand Steadiness. *Physical:* Static Strength; Dynamic Flexibility. *Sensory:* Auditory Attention; Sound Localization; Visual Color Discrimination. General Work Activities—*Information Input:* Identifying Objects, Actions, and Events; Inspecting Equipment, Structures, or Materials; Getting Information. *Mental Process:* Judging Qualities of Things, Services, or Other People's Work; Evaluating Information Against Standards; Updating and Using Relevant Knowledge. *Work Output:* Handling and Moving Objects; Performing General Physical Activities; Controlling Machines and Processes. *Interacting with Others:* Communicating with Other Workers; Establishing and Maintaining Relationships; Performing Administrative Activities. Physical Work Conditions—Very Hot or Cold; Minor Burns, Cuts, Bites, or Stings; Indoors; Standing; Common Protective or Safety Attire. Other Job Characteristics—Pace Determined by Speed of Equipment; Degree of Automation; Consequence of Error.

Experience—Job Zone 1. No previous work-related skill, knowledge, or experience is needed. Job Preparation: SVP below 4.0—less than six months. Knowledge—Food Production; Production and Processing. Instructional Programs—Agricultural and Food Products Processing.

Related DOT Jobs—520.685-082 Cooker, Casing; 521.687-090 Nut Steamer; 522.362-010 Yeast Distiller; 522.382-010 Cottage-Cheese Maker; 522.382-022 Mash-Tub-Cooker Operator; 522.382-034 Sugar Boiler; 522.482-010 Masher; 522.682-010 Kettle Operator; 522.682-014 Ordering-Machine Operator; 522.685-018 Brine Maker I; 522.685-034 Corn Cooker; 522.685-094 Steam-Conditioner Operator; 522.685-102 Vacuum-Conditioner Operator; 523.382-022 Processor, Instant Potato; 523.682-010 Chocolate Temperer; 523.682-018 Dextrine Mixer; 523.685-014 Blanching-Machine Operator; 523.685-022 Chocolate Temperer; 523.685-030 Cook-Box Filler; 523.685-034 Cooker, Meal; others.

51-4000 Metal Workers and Plastic Workers

51-4011.00 Computer-Controlled Machine Tool Operators, Metal and Plastic

- Education/Training Required: Moderate-term on-the-job training
- Employed: 161,979
- Annual Earnings: $28,390
- Growth: 19.7%
- Annual Job Openings: 15,000

Operate computer-controlled machines or robots to perform one or more machine functions on metal or plastic workpieces.

No task data available.

GOE INFORMATION—Interest Area: 08. Industrial Production. Work Group: 08.03. Production Work. Note: The Department of Labor has not collected some data for this job, so it has fewer details than the other descriptions.

Instructional Programs—Machine Shop Technology/Assistant.

Related DOT Jobs—604.362-010 Lathe Operator, Numerical Control; 605.360-010 Router Set-Up Operator, Numerical Control; 605.380-010 Milling-Machine Set-Up Operator, Numerical Control; 605.382-046 Numerical-Control Router Operator; 606.362-010 Drill-Press Operator, Numerical Control; 606.382-014 Jig-Boring Machine Operator, Numerical Control; 606.382-018 Numerical-Control Drill Operator, Printed Circuit Boards; 606.382-026 Robotic Machine Operator; 609.360-010 Numerical Control Machine Set-Up Operator; 609.362-010 Numerical Control Machine Operator; 617.280-010 Shot-Peening Operator; 699.362-010 Automated Cutting Machine Operator; 726.682-010 Laser-Beam-Trim Operator.

51-4011.01 Numerical Control Machine Tool Operators and Tenders, Metal and Plastic

- Education/Training Required: Long-term on-the-job training
- Employed: No data available.
- Annual Earnings: $28,390
- Growth: 19.7%
- Annual Job Openings: 15,000

Set up and operate numerical control (magnetic- or punched-tape-controlled) machine tools that automatically mill, drill, broach, and ream metal and plastic parts. May adjust machine feed and speed, change cutting tools, or adjust machine controls when automatic programming is faulty or if machine malfunctions.

Selects, measures, assembles, and sets machine tools, such as drill bits and milling or cutting tools, using precision gauges and instruments. Mounts, installs, aligns, and secures tools, attachments, fixtures, and workpiece on machine, using hand tools and precision measuring instruments. Loads control media, such as tape, card, or disk, in machine controller or enters commands to retrieve programmed instructions. Determines specifications or procedures for tooling setup, machine operation, workpiece dimensions, or numerical control sequences, using blueprints, instructions, and machine knowledge. Positions and secures workpiece on machine bed, indexing table, fixture, or dispensing or holding device. Lays out and marks areas of part to be shot-peened and fills hopper with shot. Calculates and sets machine controls to position tools, synchronize tape and tool, or regulate cutting depth, speed, feed, or coolant flow. Starts automatic operation of numerical control machine to machine parts or test setup, workpiece dimensions, or programming. Monitors machine operation and control panel displays to detect malfunctions and compare readings to specifications. Stops machine to remove finished workpiece or change tooling, setup, or workpiece placement according to required machining sequence. Enters commands or manually adjusts machine controls to correct malfunctions or tolerances. Lifts workpiece to machine manually, with hoist or crane, or with tweezers. Measures dimensions of finished workpiece to ensure conformance to specifications, using precision measuring instruments, templates, and fixtures. Operates lathe, drill press, jig-boring machine, or other machines manually or semiautomatically. Examines electronic components for defects and completeness of laser-beam trimming, using microscope. Maintains machines and removes and replaces broken or worn machine tools, using hand tools. Confers with supervisor or programmer to resolve machine malfunctions and production errors and obtains approval to continue production. Cleans machine, tooling, and parts, using solvent or solution and rag.

GOE INFORMATION—Interest Area: 08. Industrial Production. **Work Group:** 08.03. Production Work. **Personality Type**—Realistic. Realistic occupations frequently involve work activities that include practical, hands-on problems and solutions. They often deal with plants, animals, and real-world materials like wood, tools, and machinery. Many of the occupations require working outside and do not involve a lot of paperwork or working closely with others. **Work Values**—Moral Values; Supervision, Technical; Activity; Independence; Supervision, Human Relations. **Skills**—Operation Monitoring; Operation and Control; Equipment Selection; Quality Control Analysis; Installation; Mathematics; Troubleshooting. **Abilities**—*Cognitive:* Perceptual Speed; Visualization; Selective Attention; Problem Sensitivity; Time Sharing. *Psychomotor:* Rate Control; Reaction Time; Control Precision; Wrist-Finger Speed; Response Orientation. *Physical:* Dynamic Strength; Explosive Strength; Dynamic Flexibility; Static Strength; Gross Body Coordination. *Sensory:* Sound Localization; Speech Recognition; Peripheral Vision. **General Work Activities**—*Information Input:* Inspecting Equipment, Structures, or Materials; Monitoring Processes, Materials, or Surroundings; Identifying Objects, Actions, and Events. *Mental Process:* Updating and Using Relevant Knowledge; Judging Qualities of Things, Services, or Other People's Work; Processing Information. *Work Output:* Handling and Moving Objects; Controlling Machines and Processes; Repairing and Maintaining Mechanical Equipment. *Interacting with Others:* Communicating with Other Workers; Establishing and Maintaining Relationships; Coordinating the Work and Activities of Others. **Physical Work Conditions**—Hazardous Equipment; Distracting Sounds and Noise Levels; Common Protective or Safety Attire; Minor Burns, Cuts, Bites, or Stings; Indoors. **Other Job Characteristics**—Pace Determined by Speed of Equipment; Degree of Automation; Importance of Being Exact or Accurate.

Experience—Job Zone 2. Some previous work-related skill, knowledge, or experience may be helpful, but usually is not needed. **Job Preparation:** SVP 4.0 to less than 6.0—six months to less than two years. **Knowledge**—Production and Processing; Design; Mechanical; Engineering and Technology; Computers and Electronics. **Instructional Programs**—Machine Shop Technology/Assistant.

Related DOT Jobs—604.362-010 Lathe Operator, Numerical Control; 605.360-010 Router Set-Up Operator, Numerical Control; 605.380-010 Milling-Machine Set-Up Operator, Numerical Control; 605.382-046 Numerical-Control Router Operator; 606.362-010 Drill-Press Operator, Numerical Control; 606.382-014 Jig-Boring Machine Operator, Numerical Control; 606.382-018 Numerical-Control Drill Operator, Printed Circuit Boards; 606.382-026 Robotic Machine Operator; 609.360-010 Numerical Control Machine Set-Up Operator; 609.362-010 Numerical Control Machine Operator; 617.280-010 Shot-Peening Operator; 699.362-010 Automated Cutting Machine Operator; 726.682-010 Laser-Beam-Trim Operator.

51-4012.00 Numerical Tool and Process Control Programmers

- **Education/Training Required: Long-term on-the-job training**
- **Employed: 23,774**
- **Annual Earnings: $37,290**
- **Growth: 16.6%**
- **Annual Job Openings: 2,000**

Develop programs to control machining or processing of parts by automatic machine tools, equipment, or systems.

Prepares geometric layout from graphic displays, using computer-assisted drafting software or drafting instruments and graph paper. Writes instruction sheets, cutter lists, and machine instructions programs to guide setup and encode numerical control tape. Analyzes drawings, specifications, printed circuit board pattern film, and design data to calculate dimensions, tool selection, machine speeds, and feed rates. Determines reference points, machine cutting paths, or hole locations and computes angular and linear dimensions, radii, and curvatures. Compares encoded tape or computer printout with original program sheet to verify accuracy of instructions. Draws machine tool paths on pattern film, using colored markers and following guidelines for tool speed and efficiency. Revises numerical control machine tape programs to eliminate instruction errors and omissions. Enters computer commands to store or retrieve parts patterns, graphic displays, or programs to transfer data to other media. Aligns and secures pattern film on reference table of optical programmer and observes enlarger scope view of printed circuit board. Moves reference table to align pattern film over circuit board holes with reference marks on enlarger scope. Depresses pedal or button of programmer to enter coordinates of each hole location into program memory. Loads and unloads disks or tapes and observes operation of machine on trial run to test taped or programmed instructions. Reviews shop orders to determine job specifications and requirements. Sorts shop orders into groups to maximize materials utilization and minimize machine setup.

GOE INFORMATION—Interest Area: 02. Science, Math, and Engineering. **Work Group:** 02.08. Engineering Technology. **Personality Type**—Realistic. Realistic occupations frequently involve work activities that include practical, hands-on problems and solutions. They often deal with plants, animals, and real-world materials like wood, tools, and machinery. Many of the occupations require working outside and do not involve a lot of paperwork or working closely with others. **Work Values**—Creativity; Compensation; Independence; Autonomy; Advancement. **Skills**—Programming; Troubleshooting; Operation Monitoring; Operation and Control; Quality Control Analysis; Mathematics; Technology Design; Equipment Selection. **Abilities**—*Cognitive:* Mathematical Reasoning; Number Facility; Information Ordering; Speed of Closure; Deductive Reasoning. *Psychomotor:* Reaction Time; Control Precision; Finger Dexterity; Wrist-Finger Speed; Arm-Hand Steadiness. *Physical:* Gross Body Equilibrium. *Sensory:* Near Vision; Auditory Attention; Visual Color Discrimination; Hearing Sensitivity; Peripheral Vision. **General Work Activities**—*Information Input:* Identifying Objects, Actions, and Events; Getting Information; Monitoring Processes, Materials, or Surroundings. *Mental Process:* Analyzing Data or Information; Making Decisions and Solving Problems; Processing Information. *Work Output:* Drafting and Specifying Technical Devices; Interacting with Computers; Handling and Moving Objects. *Interacting with Others:* Communicating with Other Workers; Providing Consultation and Advice to Others; Performing Administrative Activities. **Physical Work Conditions**—Sitting; Indoors; Using Hands on Objects, Tools, or Controls; Keeping or Regaining Balance; Making Repetitive Motions. **Other Job Characteristics**—Degree of Automation; Importance of Being Exact or Accurate; Pace Determined by Speed of Equipment.

Experience—Job Zone 3. Previous work-related skill, knowledge, or experience is required. **Job Preparation:** SVP 6.0 to less than 7.0—more than one year and less than four years. **Knowledge**—Design; Computers and Electronics; Mathematics; Production and Processing; Engineering and Technology. **Instructional Programs**—Computer Programming/Programmer, General; Data Processing and Data Processing Technology/Technician.

Related DOT Jobs—609.262-010 Tool Programmer, Numerical Control; 716.701-018 Tool Programmer, Numerical Control; 736.201-010 Nesting Operator, Numerical Control.

51-4021.00 Extruding and Drawing Machine Setters, Operators, and Tenders, Metal and Plastic

- Education/Training Required: Moderate-term on-the-job training
- Employed: 125,987
- Annual Earnings: $25,170
- Growth: 13.5%
- Annual Job Openings: 23,000

Set up, operate, or tend machines to extrude or draw thermoplastic or metal materials into tubes, rods, hoses, wire, bars, or structural shapes.

Installs dies, machine screws, and sizing rings on machine extruding thermoplastic or metal materials. Starts machine and sets controls to regulate vacuum, air pressure, sizing rings, and temperature and synchronizes speed of extrusion. Selects nozzles, spacers, and wire guides according to diameter and length of rod. Loads machine hopper with mixed materials, using auger, or stuffs rolls of plastic dough into machine cylinders. Adjusts controls to draw or press metal into specified shape and diameter. Studies specifications, determines setup procedures, and selects machine dies and parts. Operates shearing mechanism to cut rods to specified length. Weighs and mixes pelletized, granular, or powdered thermoplastic materials and coloring pigments. Replaces worn dies when products vary from specifications. Examines extruded product for defects, such as wrinkles, bubbles, and splits. Measures extruded articles for conformance to specifications and adjusts controls to obtain product of specified dimensions. Tests physical properties of product with testing devices such as acid-bath tester, burst tester, and impact tester. Reels extruded product into rolls of specified length and weight.

GOE INFORMATION—**Interest Area:** 08. Industrial Production. **Work Group:** 08.02. Production Technology. **Personality Type**—Realistic. Realistic occupations frequently involve work activities that include practical, hands-on problems and solutions. They often deal with plants, animals, and real-world materials like wood, tools, and machinery. Many of the occupations require working outside and do not involve a lot of paperwork or working closely with others. **Work Values**—Moral Values; Independence; Supervision, Technical; Activity; Supervision, Human Relations. **Skills**—Operation and Control; Quality Control Analysis; Operation Monitoring; Installation; Equipment Selection; Repairing. **Abilities**—*Cognitive:* Visualization. *Psychomotor:* Control Precision; Rate Control; Multilimb Coordination. *Physical:* Static Strength; Stamina; Dynamic Strength. *Sensory:* None met the criteria. **General Work Activities**—*Information Input:* Monitoring Processes, Materials, or Surroundings; Inspecting Equipment, Structures, or Materials; Getting Information. *Mental Process:* Updating and Using Relevant Knowledge; Judging Qualities of Things, Services, or Other People's Work; Evaluating Information Against Standards. *Work Output:* Handling and Moving Objects; Performing General Physical Activities; Controlling Machines and Processes. *Interacting with Others:* Communicating with Other Workers; Monitoring and Controlling Resources; Establishing and Maintaining Relationships. **Physical Work Conditions**—Hazardous Equipment; Common Protective or Safety Attire; Distracting Sounds and Noise Levels; Indoors; Standing. **Other Job Characteristics**—Pace Determined by Speed of Equipment; Degree of Automation; Importance of Repeating Same Tasks.

Experience—Job Zone 2. Some previous work-related skill, knowledge, or experience may be helpful, but usually is not needed. **Job Preparation:** SVP 4.0 to less than 6.0—six months to less than two years. **Knowledge**—Production and Processing; Mechanical; Physics; Engineering and Technology; Public Safety and Security. **Instructional Programs**—Machine Tool Technology/Machinist.

Related DOT Jobs—557.382-010 Extruder Operator; 614.380-010 Extrusion-Press Adjuster; 614.382-010 Wire Drawer; 614.482-010 Draw-Bench Operator; 614.482-014 Extruder Operator; 614.482-018 Extrusion-Press Operator I.

51-4022.00 Forging Machine Setters, Operators, and Tenders, Metal and Plastic

- Education/Training Required: Moderate-term on-the-job training
- Employed: 53,706
- Annual Earnings: $25,880
- Growth: 9.1%
- Annual Job Openings: 6,000

Set up, operate, or tend forging machines to taper, shape, or form metal or plastic parts.

Starts machine, produces sample workpiece, and observes operations to detect machine malfunction and ensure setup conforms to specifications. Selects, aligns, and bolts positioning fixtures and stops and specified dies to ram and anvil, forging rolls, or presses and hammers. Turns handles or knobs to set pressure and depth of ram stroke and synchronize machine operations. Installs and adjusts or removes and replaces dies, synchronizing cams, forging hammer, and stop guides according to specifications. Reads blueprints to determine specified tolerances and sequence of operations to set up machines. Marks layout; verifies dimensions; and measures, weighs, and inspects machined parts to ensure conformance to product specifications. Positions and moves metal wire or workpiece through series of dies to compress and shape stock to form die impressions. Trims and compresses finished forgings to specified tolerances. Adjust temperature controls of furnace in which rods are heated. Sharpens cutting tools and drill bits, using bench grinder. Confers with other workers regarding setup and operational specifications of machines.

GOE INFORMATION—**Interest Area:** 08. Industrial Production. **Work Group:** 08.02. Production Technology. **Personality Type**—Realistic. Realistic occupations frequently involve work activities that include practical, hands-on problems and solutions. They often deal with plants, animals, and real-world materials like wood, tools, and machinery. Many of the occupations require working outside and do not involve a lot of paperwork or working closely with others. **Work Values**—Moral Values; Supervision, Technical; Independence; Supervision, Human Relations; Company Policies and Practices. **Skills**—Operation Monitoring; Operation and Control; Installation; Repairing; Equipment Selection; Quality Control Analysis. **Abilities**—*Cognitive:* Visualization; Selective Attention; Information Ordering; Number Facility; Inductive Reasoning. *Psychomotor:* Control Precision; Manual Dexterity; Arm-Hand Steadiness; Reaction Time; Speed of Limb Movement. *Physical:* Static Strength; Extent Flexibility; Gross Body Equilibrium; Trunk Strength; Stamina. *Sensory:* None met the criteria. **General Work Activities**—*Information Input:* Monitoring Processes, Materials, or Surroundings; Inspecting Equipment, Structures, or Materials; Getting Information. *Mental Process:* Evaluating Information Against Standards; Judging Qualities of Things, Services, or Other People's Work; Updating and Using Relevant Knowledge. *Work Output:* Handling and Moving Objects; Controlling Machines and Processes; Repairing and Maintaining Mechanical Equipment. *Interacting with Others:* Communicating with Other Workers; Establishing and Maintaining Relationships; Providing Consultation and Advice to Others. **Physical Work Conditions**—Using Hands on Objects, Tools, or Controls; Common Protective or Safety Attire; Hazardous Equipment; Distracting Sounds and Noise Levels; Very Hot or Cold. **Other Job Characteristics**—Pace Determined by Speed of Equipment; Degree of Automation; Importance of Repeating Same Tasks.

Experience—Job Zone 2. Some previous work-related skill, knowledge, or experience may be helpful, but usually is not needed. **Job Preparation:** SVP 4.0 to less than 6.0—six months to less than two years. **Knowledge**—Design; Mechanical; Physics; Engineering and Technology; Production and Processing. **Instructional Programs**—Machine Tool Technology/Machinist.

Related DOT Jobs—610.362-010 Drophammer Operator; 611.482-010 Forging-Press Operator I; 611.662-010 Upsetter; 611.682-010 Steel-Shot-Header Operator; 612.260-010 Fastener Technologist; 612.360-010 Die Setter; 612.361-010 Heavy Forger; 612.462-010 Multi-Operation-Machine Operator; 612.462-014 Nut Former; 612.662-010 Spike-Machine Operator; 612.682-010 Buckshot-Swage Operator; 612.682-014 Forging-Roll Operator.

51-4023.00 Rolling Machine Setters, Operators, and Tenders, Metal and Plastic

- **Education/Training Required: Moderate-term on-the-job training**
- **Employed: 49,162**
- **Annual Earnings: $27,670**
- **Growth: 1.4%**
- **Annual Job Openings: 6,000**

Set up, operate, or tend machines to roll steel or plastic, forming bends, beads, knurls, rolls, or plate or to flatten, temper, or reduce gauge of material.

Starts operation of rolling and milling machines to flatten, temper, form, and reduce sheet metal sections and produce steel strips. Manipulates controls and observes dial indicators to monitor, adjust, and regulate speed of machine mechanisms. Resets, adjusts, and corrects machine setup to reduce thickness, reshape products, and eliminate product defects. Monitors machine cycles and mill operation to detect jamming and to ensure fabricated products conform to specifications. Selects rolls, dies, roll stands, and chucks from data charts to form specified contours and to fabricate products. Sets distance points between rolls, guides, meters,

and stops according to specifications. Positions, aligns, and secures arbor, spindle, coils, mandrel, dies, and slitting knives onto machine. Installs equipment, such as guides, guards, gears, cooling equipment, and rolls, using hand tools. Fills oil cups, adjusts valves, and observes gauges to control flow of metal coolant and lubricants onto workpiece. Examines, inspects, measures, and feels raw materials and finished product to verify conformance to specifications visually or using measurement instruments. Reads rolling order and mill schedules to determine setup specifications, work sequence, product dimensions, and installation procedures. Calculates draft space and roll speed for each mill stand to plan rolling sequence and specified dimensions and temper. Threads or feeds sheets or rods through rolling mechanism or starts and controls mechanism that automatically feeds steel into rollers. Activates shear and grinder to trim workpiece, cut steel strips, and monitor forming of gears to specified length and diameter. Disassembles sizing mills removed from rolling line and sorts and stores parts. Removes scratches and polishes roll surface, using polishing stone and electric buffer. Records mill production on schedule sheet. Directs and trains other workers to change rolls, operate mill equipment, remove coils and cobbles, and band and load material. Signals and assists other workers to remove and position equipment, fill hoppers, and feed materials into machine.

GOE INFORMATION—**Interest Area:** 08. Industrial Production. **Work Group:** 08.02. Production Technology. **Personality Type**—Realistic. Realistic occupations frequently involve work activities that include practical, hands-on problems and solutions. They often deal with plants, animals, and real-world materials like wood, tools, and machinery. Many of the occupations require working outside and do not involve a lot of paperwork or working closely with others. **Work Values**—Supervision, Technical; Supervision, Human Relations; Moral Values; Activity; Independence. **Skills**—Operation and Control; Operation Monitoring; Installation; Quality Control Analysis; Repairing; Mathematics. **Abilities**—*Cognitive:* Perceptual Speed; Spatial Orientation; Time Sharing; Flexibility of Closure; Visualization. *Psychomotor:* Rate Control; Manual Dexterity; Control Precision; Multilimb Coordination; Reaction Time. *Physical:* Static Strength; Dynamic Flexibility; Extent Flexibility; Explosive Strength; Dynamic Strength. *Sensory:* Peripheral Vision; Depth Perception; Visual Color Discrimination; Hearing Sensitivity; Sound Localization. **General Work Activities**—*Information Input:* Monitoring Processes, Materials, or Surroundings; Inspecting Equipment, Structures, or Materials; Getting Information. *Mental Process:* Evaluating Information Against Standards; Organizing, Planning, and Prioritizing; Updating and Using Relevant Knowledge. *Work Output:* Handling and Moving Objects; Controlling Machines and Processes; Performing General Physical Activities. *Interacting with Others:* Guiding, Directing, and Motivating Subordinates; Communicating with Other Workers; Coordinating the Work and Activities of Others. **Physical Work Conditions**—Hazardous Equipment; Distracting Sounds and Noise Levels; Using Hands on Objects, Tools, or Controls; Common Protective or Safety Attire; Standing. **Other Job Characteristics**—Degree of Automation; Pace Determined by Speed of Equipment; Importance of Repeating Same Tasks.

Experience—Job Zone 2. Some previous work-related skill, knowledge, or experience may be helpful, but usually is not needed. **Job Preparation:** SVP 4.0 to less than 6.0—six months to less than two years. **Knowledge**—Production and Processing; Mechanical; Education and Training; Physics; Personnel and Human Resources. **Instructional Programs**—Machine Tool Technology/Machinist; Sheet Metal Technology/Sheetworking.

Related DOT Jobs—613.360-010 Roll-Forming-Machine Set-Up Mechanic; 613.360-014 Roll-Tube Setter; 613.360-018 Tin Roller, Hot Mill; 613.361-010 Guide Setter; 613.382-014 Finisher; 613.462-018 Rolling-Mill Operator; 613.482-014 Piercing-Machine Operator; 613.662-018 Cold-Mill Operator; 613.682-014 Reeling-Machine Operator; 613.682-022 Strip Roller;

613.682-030 Mill Operator, Rolls; 617.480-010 Job Setter, Spline-Rolling Machine; 617.482-014 Forming-Roll Operator I; 617.482-018 Roll-Forming-Machine Operator I; 617.682-022 Setter, Cold-Rolling Machine; 619.462-010 Roll-Threader Operator.

51-4031.00 Cutting, Punching, and Press Machine Setters, Operators, and Tenders, Metal and Plastic

- **Education/Training Required: Moderate-term on-the-job training**
- **Employed: 371,706**
- **Annual Earnings: $24,080**
- **Growth: –4.0%**
- **Annual Job Openings: 35,000**

Set up, operate, or tend machines to saw, cut, shear, slit, punch, crimp, notch, bend, or straighten metal or plastic material.

No task data available.

GOE INFORMATION—Interest Area: 08. Industrial Production. **Work Group:** 08.02. Production Technology. **Note:** The Department of Labor has not collected some data for this job, so it has fewer details than the other descriptions.

Instructional Programs—Machine Tool Technology/Machinist; Sheet Metal Technology/Sheetworking.

Related DOT Jobs—607.382-010 Contour-Band-Saw Operator, Vertical; 607.382-014 Saw Operator; 607.682-010 Cut-Off-Saw Operator, Metal; 607.682-014 Profile Trimmer; 607.685-010 Cut-Off Saw Tender, Metal; 607.685-014 Debridging-Machine Operator; 609.280-010 Trim-Machine Adjuster; 609.682-030 Screwmaker, Automatic; 612.685-014 Spring Tester I; 615.280-010 Slitter Service and Setter; 615.380-010 Shear Setter; 615.382-010 Punch-Press Operator I; 615.482-010 Angle Shear Operator; 615.482-014 Duplicator-Punch Operator; 615.482-018 Ironworker-Machine Operator; 615.482-026 Punch-Press Operator, Automatic; 615.482-030 Rotary-Shear Operator; 615.482-038 Turret-Punch-Press Operator; 615.662-010 Slitting-Machine Operator II; 615.682-010 Flying-Shear Operator; others.

51-4031.01 Sawing Machine Tool Setters and Set-Up Operators, Metal and Plastic

- **Education/Training Required: Moderate-term on-the-job training**
- **Employed: No data available.**
- **Annual Earnings: $24,080**
- **Growth: –4.0%**
- **Annual Job Openings: 35,000**

Set up or set up and operate metal or plastic sawing machines to cut straight, curved, irregular, or internal patterns in metal or plastic stock or to trim edges of metal or plastic objects. Involves the use of such machines as band saws, circular saws, friction saws, hacksawing machines, and jigsaws.

Turns valves to start flow of coolant against cutting area and to start airflow which blows cuttings away from kerf. Selects blade according to specifications and installs on machine, using hand tools. Positions guides, stops, holding blocks, or other fixtures to secure and direct workpiece, using hand tools and measuring devices. Scribes reference lines on workpiece as guide for sawing operations according to blueprints, templates, sample parts, or specifications. Reads work order for specifications, such as materials to be used, location of cutting lines, and dimensions and tolerances. Replaces defective blades or wheels, using hand tools. Measures completed workpiece to verify conformance to specifications, using micrometers, gauges, calipers, templates, or rulers. Places workpiece on cutting table manually or using hoist and clamps workpiece into position. Sharpens dulled blades, using bench grinder, abrasive wheel, or lathe. Removes housings, feed tubes, tool holders, and other accessories to replace worn or broken parts, such as springs and bushings. Examines completed workpieces for defects, such as chipped edges and marred surfaces, and sorts defective pieces according to defect. Marks identifying data on workpieces. Turns controls to set cutting speed, feed rate, and table angle for specified operation. Starts machine and feeds workpiece against blade, guiding along layout lines, to cut workpiece to specified dimensions. Sets blade tension, height, and angle to perform prescribed cut, using wrench.

GOE INFORMATION—Interest Area: 08. Industrial Production. **Work Group:** 08.02. Production Technology. **Personality Type**—Realistic. Realistic occupations frequently involve work activities that include practical, hands-on problems and solutions. They often deal with plants, animals, and real-world materials like wood, tools, and machinery. Many of the occupations require working outside and do not involve a lot of paperwork or working closely with others. **Work Values**—Moral Values; Supervision, Technical; Independence; Supervision, Human Relations; Company Policies and Practices. **Skills**—Operation Monitoring; Operation and Control; Equipment Selection; Installation; Repairing; Quality Control Analysis. **Abilities**—*Cognitive:* Perceptual Speed; Visualization; Spatial Orientation; Memorization; Selective Attention. *Psychomotor:* Rate Control; Arm-Hand Steadiness; Control Precision; Manual Dexterity; Finger Dexterity. *Physical:* Explosive Strength; Static Strength; Stamina; Dynamic Strength; Extent Flexibility. *Sensory:* Depth Perception; Peripheral Vision; Hearing Sensitivity; Sound Localization; Near Vision. **General Work Activities**—*Information Input:* Monitoring Processes, Materials, or Surroundings; Inspecting Equipment, Structures, or Materials; Getting Information. *Mental Process:* Updating and Using Relevant Knowledge; Judging Qualities of Things, Services, or Other People's Work; Evaluating Information Against Standards. *Work Output:* Handling and Moving Objects; Controlling Machines and Processes; Repairing and Maintaining Mechanical Equipment. *Interacting with Others:* Communicating with Other Workers; Performing Administrative Activities; Coordinating the Work and Activities of Others. **Physical Work Conditions**—Hazardous Equipment; Distracting Sounds and Noise Levels; Minor Burns, Cuts, Bites, or Stings; Common Protective or Safety Attire; Using Hands on Objects, Tools, or Controls. **Other Job Characteristics**—Degree of Automation; Pace Determined by Speed of Equipment; Importance of Repeating Same Tasks.

Experience—Job Zone 2. Some previous work-related skill, knowledge, or experience may be helpful, but usually is not needed. **Job Preparation:** SVP 4.0 to less than 6.0–six months to less than two years. **Knowledge**—Production and Processing; Mechanical; Design; Engineering and Technology; Building and Construction. **Instructional Programs**—Machine Tool Technology/Machinist; Sheet Metal Technology/Sheetworking.

Related DOT Jobs—607.382-010 Contour-Band-Saw Operator, Vertical; 607.382-014 Saw Operator; 607.682-010 Cut-Off-Saw Operator, Metal; 609.280-010 Trim-Machine Adjuster; 690.482-010 Sawyer; 700.682-018 Profile-Saw Operator.

51-4031.02 Punching Machine Setters and Set-Up Operators, Metal and Plastic

- Education/Training Required: Moderate-term on-the-job training
- Employed: No data available.
- Annual Earnings: $24,080
- Growth: –4.0%
- Annual Job Openings: 35,000

Set up or set up and operate machines to punch, crimp, cut blanks, or notch metal or plastic workpieces between preset dies according to specifications.

Activates machine and observes operation to detect misalignment or machine malfunctions. Installs, aligns, and locks specified punches, dies, and cutting blades in ram or bed of machine, using gauges and hand tools. Adjusts ram stroke of press to specified length, using hand tools. Sets stops or guides or installs jigs or fixtures for positioning successive workpieces. Sets controls or installs gears to synchronize action of feed bar or rollers. Reads job order to determine location of holes or cutting lines. Measures workpiece with rule or tape or traces from template and marks location with scribe, soapstone, or center punch. Positions, aligns, and secures workpiece against fixtures or stops on machine bed or on die. Inspects workpieces for conformance to specifications visually or using gauges or templates, scale, or compass and adjusts machine to correct errors. Cleans and lubricates machines.

GOE INFORMATION—Interest Area: 08. Industrial Production. **Work Group:** 08.02. Production Technology. **Personality Type**—Realistic. Realistic occupations frequently involve work activities that include practical, hands-on problems and solutions. They often deal with plants, animals, and real-world materials like wood, tools, and machinery. Many of the occupations require working outside and do not involve a lot of paperwork or working closely with others. **Work Values**—Independence; Moral Values; Supervision, Technical; Activity; Supervision, Human Relations. **Skills**—Operation and Control; Installation. **Abilities**—*Cognitive:* Visualization; Perceptual Speed; Spatial Orientation; Information Ordering. *Psychomotor:* Control Precision; Manual Dexterity; Finger Dexterity; Reaction Time; Response Orientation. *Physical:* Extent Flexibility; Static Strength; Trunk Strength. *Sensory:* Near Vision. **General Work Activities**—*Information Input:* Monitoring Processes, Materials, or Surroundings; Getting Information; Inspecting Equipment, Structures, or Materials. *Mental Process:* Evaluating Information Against Standards; Making Decisions and Solving Problems; Analyzing Data or Information. *Work Output:* Handling and Moving Objects; Controlling Machines and Processes; Performing General Physical Activities. *Interacting with Others:* Monitoring and Controlling Resources; Coordinating the Work and Activities of Others; Teaching Others. **Physical Work Conditions**—Hazardous Equipment; Using Hands on Objects, Tools, or Controls; Common Protective or Safety Attire; Indoors; Standing. **Other Job Characteristics**—Pace Determined by Speed of Equipment; Importance of Repeating Same Tasks; Degree of Automation.

Experience—Job Zone 2. Some previous work-related skill, knowledge, or experience may be helpful, but usually is not needed. **Job Preparation:** SVP 4.0 to less than 6.0—six months to less than two years. **Knowledge**—Mechanical; Production and Processing; Physics; Engineering and Technology; Design. **Instructional Programs**—Machine Tool Technology/Machinist; Sheet Metal Technology/Sheetworking.

Related DOT Jobs—615.382-010 Punch-Press Operator I; 615.482-014 Duplicator-Punch Operator; 615.482-018 Ironworker-Machine Operator; 615.482-026 Punch-Press Operator, Automatic; 619.380-014 Punch-Press Setter; 699.380-010 Die Set-Up Operator, Printed Circuit Boards.

51-4031.03 Press and Press Brake Machine Setters and Set-Up Operators, Metal and Plastic

- Education/Training Required: Moderate-term on-the-job training
- Employed: No data available.
- Annual Earnings: $24,080
- Growth: –4.0%
- Annual Job Openings: 35,000

Set up or set up and operate power-press machines or power-brake machines to bend, form, stretch, notch, punch, or straighten metal or plastic plate and structural shapes as specified by work order, blueprints, drawing, templates, or layout.

Operates power press, power brake, apron brake, swaging machine, foot-powered press, hydraulic press, or arbor press according to specifications. Selects and positions flat, block, radius, or special-purpose die sets into ram and bed of machine, using hoist, crane, measuring instruments, and hand tools. Installs, aligns, and secures gears, holding fixtures, and dies to machine bed, using gauges, templates, feelers, shims, and hand tools. Measures workpiece and verifies dimensions and weight, using micrometer, template, straightedge, and scale. Inspects workpiece for defects. Plans sequence of operations, applying knowledge of physical properties of metal. Preheats workpiece, using heating furnace or hand torch. Lifts, positions, and secures workpiece between dies of machine, using crane and sledge. Lubricates workpiece with oil. Grinds out burrs and sharp edges, using portable grinder, speed lathe, and polishing jack. Hand forms, cuts, or finishes workpiece, using tools such as table saw, hand sledge and anvil, flaring tool, and gauge. Sets stops on machine bed, changes dies, and adjusts components, such as ram or power press, when making multiple or successive passes.

GOE INFORMATION—Interest Area: 08. Industrial Production. **Work Group:** 08.02. Production Technology. **Personality Type**—Realistic. Realistic occupations frequently involve work activities that include practical, hands-on problems and solutions. They often deal with plants, animals, and real-world materials like wood, tools, and machinery. Many of the occupations require working outside and do not involve a lot of paperwork or working closely with others. **Work Values**—Independence; Moral Values; Activity; Supervision, Technical; Supervision, Human Relations. **Skills**—Operation Monitoring; Operation and Control; Installation; Science; Technology Design; Quality Control Analysis; Equipment Selection; Repairing. **Abilities**—*Cognitive:* Visualization; Information Ordering; Spatial Orientation; Time Sharing; Originality. *Psychomotor:* Multilimb Coordination; Manual Dexterity; Control Precision; Arm-Hand Steadiness; Reaction Time. *Physical:* Dynamic Strength; Explosive Strength; Extent Flexibility; Static Strength; Stamina. *Sensory:* Depth Perception; Auditory Attention; Peripheral Vision; Sound Localization; Hearing Sensitivity. **General Work Activities**—*Information Input:* Inspecting Equipment, Structures, or Materials; Monitoring Processes, Materials, or Surroundings; Getting Information. *Mental Process:* Evaluating Information Against Standards; Organizing, Planning, and Prioritizing; Updating and Using Relevant Knowledge. *Work Output:* Handling and Moving Objects; Controlling Machines and Processes; Performing General Physical Activities. *Interacting with Others:* Communicating with Other Workers; Providing Consultation and Advice to Others; Coordinating the Work and Activities of Others. **Physical Work Conditions**—

Hazardous Equipment; Common Protective or Safety Attire; Distracting Sounds and Noise Levels; Minor Burns, Cuts, Bites, or Stings; Whole Body Vibration. **Other Job Characteristics**—Pace Determined by Speed of Equipment; Importance of Repeating Same Tasks; Degree of Automation.

Experience—Job Zone 2. Some previous work-related skill, knowledge, or experience may be helpful, but usually is not needed. **Job Preparation:** SVP 4.0 to less than 6.0—six months to less than two years. **Knowledge**—Mechanical; Building and Construction; Production and Processing; Public Safety and Security; Design. **Instructional Programs**—Machine Tool Technology/Machinist; Sheet Metal Technology/Sheetworking.

Related DOT Jobs—616.682-010 Arbor-Press Operator I; 616.682-026 Kick-Press Operator I; 617.260-010 Press Operator, Heavy Duty; 617.360-010 Brake Operator I; 617.360-014 Swaging-Machine Adjuster; 617.380-010 Kick Press Setter; 617.382-010 Tube Bender, Brass-Wind Instruments; 617.480-014 Press Setter; 617.482-010 Bending-Machine Operator I; 807.684-010 Automobile-Bumper Straightener.

51-4031.04 Shear and Slitter Machine Setters and Set-Up Operators, Metal and Plastic

- **Education/Training Required: Moderate-term on-the-job training**
- **Employed: No data available.**
- **Annual Earnings: $24,080**
- **Growth: –4.0%**
- **Annual Job Openings: 35,000**

Set up or set up and operate power-shear or slitting machines to cut metal or plastic material, such as plates, sheets, slabs, billets, or bars, to specified dimensions and angles.

Installs and aligns knives, disk cutters, or fixtures to shear, bevel, or trim fabricated items. Starts machine; adjusts blade and controls, using wrenches, rule, gauge, or template; and monitors operation. Tests and adjusts cutting speed and action according to specified length of product, using gauges and hand tools. Selects, cleans, and installs spacers, rubber sleeves, and cutter on arbors. Operates shear or slitter that cuts or shears metal, such as plates, sheets, slabs, billets, or bars, to size. Reads production schedule to determine setup or adjustment of equipment. Threads end of metal coil from reel through slitter and secures ends on recoiler. Observes machine operation and examines cut strips for flatness, holes, burrs, and surface defects. Hones cutters with oilstone to remove nicks. Measures dimensions of workpiece, using tape, gauge, template, or rule and square, for conformance to specifications. Lays out cutting lines on metal stock to obtain maximum number of pieces from stock. Lifts workpiece manually or by hoist and positions and secures against guides and stops. Lubricates and cleans machine.

GOE INFORMATION—Interest Area: 08. Industrial Production. **Work Group:** 08.02. Production Technology. **Personality Type**—Realistic. Realistic occupations frequently involve work activities that include practical, hands-on problems and solutions. They often deal with plants, animals, and real-world materials like wood, tools, and machinery. Many of the occupations require working outside and do not involve a lot of paperwork or working closely with others. **Work Values**—Moral Values; Independence; Activity; Supervision, Technical; Supervision, Human Relations. **Skills**—Operation Monitoring; Operation and Control; Installation; Quality Control Analysis; Troubleshooting; Technology Design; Repairing. **Abilities**—*Cognitive:* Visualization; Selective Attention;

Perceptual Speed; Spatial Orientation; Information Ordering. *Psychomotor:* Reaction Time; Control Precision; Finger Dexterity; Arm-Hand Steadiness; Multilimb Coordination. *Physical:* Extent Flexibility; Static Strength; Explosive Strength; Stamina; Dynamic Strength. *Sensory:* Depth Perception; Peripheral Vision; Visual Color Discrimination; Sound Localization; Auditory Attention. **General Work Activities**—*Information Input:* Inspecting Equipment, Structures, or Materials; Getting Information; Monitoring Processes, Materials, or Surroundings. *Mental Process:* Evaluating Information Against Standards; Updating and Using Relevant Knowledge; Organizing, Planning, and Prioritizing. *Work Output:* Controlling Machines and Processes; Handling and Moving Objects; Performing General Physical Activities. *Interacting with Others:* Communicating with Other Workers; Establishing and Maintaining Relationships; Coordinating the Work and Activities of Others. **Physical Work Conditions**—Hazardous Equipment; Common Protective or Safety Attire; Minor Burns, Cuts, Bites, or Stings; Distracting Sounds and Noise Levels; Making Repetitive Motions. **Other Job Characteristics**—Pace Determined by Speed of Equipment; Degree of Automation; Importance of Repeating Same Tasks.

Experience—Job Zone 2. Some previous work-related skill, knowledge, or experience may be helpful, but usually is not needed. **Job Preparation:** SVP 4.0 to less than 6.0—six months to less than two years. **Knowledge**—Mechanical; Production and Processing; Building and Construction; Fine Arts; Public Safety and Security. **Instructional Programs**—Machine Tool Technology/Machinist; Sheet Metal Technology/Sheetworking.

Related DOT Jobs—615.280-010 Slitter Service and Setter; 615.380-010 Shear Setter; 615.482-010 Angle Shear Operator; 615.662-010 Slitting-Machine Operator II; 615.682-010 Flying-Shear Operator; 615.682-018 Shear Operator I.

51-4032.00 Drilling and Boring Machine Tool Setters, Operators, and Tenders, Metal and Plastic

- **Education/Training Required: Moderate-term on-the-job training**
- **Employed: 71,162**
- **Annual Earnings: $26,670**
- **Growth: –4.5%**
- **Annual Job Openings: 8,000**

Set up, operate, or tend drilling machines to drill, bore, ream, mill, or countersink metal or plastic workpieces.

Operates single- or multiple-spindle drill press to bore holes to perform machining operations on metal, nonmetallic, or plastic workpieces. Installs tool in spindle. Studies machining instructions to determine dimensional and finish specifications, sequence of operation, setup, and tooling requirements. Lays out reference lines and machining locations on work, applying knowledge of shop math and layout techniques and using layout tools. Selects cutting tool according to instructions and knowledge of metal properties. Positions and secures workpiece on table with bolts, jigs, clamps, shims, or other holding devices, using machining hand tools. Operates tracing attachment to duplicate contours from templates or models. Verifies conformance of machined work to specifications, using measuring instruments such as calipers, micrometers, and fixed and telescoping gauges. Lifts workpiece either manually or with hoist onto machine table or directs crane operator to lift and position workpiece.

GOE INFORMATION—Interest Area: 08. Industrial Production. **Work Group:** 08.02. Production Technology. **Personality Type**—Realistic.

Realistic occupations frequently involve work activities that include practical, hands-on problems and solutions. They often deal with plants, animals, and real-world materials like wood, tools, and machinery. Many of the occupations require working outside and do not involve a lot of paperwork or working closely with others. **Work Values**—Independence; Supervision, Technical; Moral Values; Supervision, Human Relations; Activity. **Skills**—Operation Monitoring; Operation and Control; Quality Control Analysis; Installation; Equipment Selection; Mathematics. **Abilities**—*Cognitive:* Visualization; Selective Attention; Information Ordering; Perceptual Speed; Mathematical Reasoning. *Psychomotor:* Arm-Hand Steadiness; Multilimb Coordination; Control Precision; Manual Dexterity; Finger Dexterity. *Physical:* Static Strength; Dynamic Strength; Stamina; Explosive Strength; Extent Flexibility. *Sensory:* Hearing Sensitivity; Depth Perception; Sound Localization. **General Work Activities**—*Information Input:* Getting Information; Inspecting Equipment, Structures, or Materials; Monitoring Processes, Materials, or Surroundings. *Mental Process:* Evaluating Information Against Standards; Updating and Using Relevant Knowledge; Organizing, Planning, and Prioritizing. *Work Output:* Performing General Physical Activities; Handling and Moving Objects; Controlling Machines and Processes. *Interacting with Others:* Communicating with Other Workers; Establishing and Maintaining Relationships; Coordinating the Work and Activities of Others. **Physical Work Conditions**—Hazardous Equipment; Distracting Sounds and Noise Levels; Common Protective or Safety Attire; Minor Burns, Cuts, Bites, or Stings; Using Hands on Objects, Tools, or Controls. **Other Job Characteristics**—Pace Determined by Speed of Equipment; Importance of Repeating Same Tasks; Degree of Automation.

Experience—Job Zone 2. Some previous work-related skill, knowledge, or experience may be helpful, but usually is not needed. **Job Preparation:** SVP 4.0 to less than 6.0—six months to less than two years. **Knowledge**—Mechanical; Building and Construction; Design; Foreign Language; Fine Arts. **Instructional Programs**—Machine Tool Technology/Machinist.

Related DOT Jobs—606.280-010 Boring-Machine Set-Up Operator, Jig; 606.280-014 Boring-Mill Set-Up Operator, Horizontal; 606.380-010 Drill-Press Set-Up Operator, Multiple Spindle; 606.380-014 Drill-Press Set-Up Operator, Radial; 606.380-018 Drill-Press Set-Up Operator, Radial, Tool; 606.382-022 Boring-Machine Operator; 606.682-018 Drill-Press Set-Up Operator, Single Spindle; 606.682-022 Tapper Operator; 676.382-010 Drill-Press Operator, Printed Circuit Boards; 731.381-010 Dice Maker.

51-4033.00 Grinding, Lapping, Polishing, and Buffing Machine Tool Setters, Operators, and Tenders, Metal and Plastic

- **Education/Training Required: Moderate-term on-the-job training**
- **Employed: 145,245**
- **Annual Earnings: $25,530**
- **Growth: 7.3%**
- **Annual Job Openings: 26,000**

Set up, operate, or tend grinding and related tools that remove excess material or burrs from surfaces, sharpen edges or corners, or buff, hone, or polish metal or plastic workpieces.

No task data available.

GOE INFORMATION—**Interest Area:** 08. Industrial Production. **Work Group:** 08.02. Production Technology. **Note:** The Department of Labor has not collected some data for this job, so it has fewer details than the other descriptions.

Instructional Programs—Machine Shop Technology/Assistant; Machine Tool Technology/Machinist.

Related DOT Jobs—No related DOT jobs.

51-4033.01 Grinding, Honing, Lapping, and Deburring Machine Set-Up Operators

- **Education/Training Required: Moderate-term on-the-job training**
- **Employed: No data available.**
- **Annual Earnings: $25,530**
- **Growth: 7.3%**
- **Annual Job Openings: 26,000**

Set up and operate grinding, honing, lapping, or deburring machines to remove excess materials or burrs from internal and external surfaces.

Moves machine controls to index workpiece and adjust machine for preselected operational settings. Activates machine start-up switches to grind, lap, hone, debar, shear, or cut workpiece according to specifications. Threads and hand-feeds materials through machine cutters or abraders. Computes machine indexing and settings for specified dimension and base reference points. Selects machine tooling to be used in machine operation, utilizing knowledge of machine and production requirements. Observes and adjusts machine operation. Studies blueprints, work order, or machining instructions to determine product dimensions and tooling and to plan operational sequence. Mounts and positions tools in machine chuck, spindle, or other tool-holding device to specifications, using hand tools. Measures workpieces and lays out work, using precision measuring devices. Grinds, sharpens, or hones tools, dies, and products to prescribed dimensions, using power tools, hand tools, and precision measuring instruments. Inspects or measures workpiece, using measuring instruments such as gauges or micrometers for conformance to specifications. Lifts and positions workpiece manually or with hoist and secures in hopper or on machine table, faceplate, or chuck, using clamps. Brushes or sprays lubricating compound on workpiece or turns valve handle and directs flow of coolant against tool and workpiece. Repairs or replaces machine parts, using hand tools, or notifies engineering personnel when corrective action is required. Maintains stock of machine parts and machining tools.

GOE INFORMATION—**Interest Area:** 08. Industrial Production. **Work Group:** 08.02. Production Technology. **Personality Type**—Realistic. Realistic occupations frequently involve work activities that include practical, hands-on problems and solutions. They often deal with plants, animals, and real-world materials like wood, tools, and machinery. Many of the occupations require working outside and do not involve a lot of paperwork or working closely with others. **Work Values**—Independence; Moral Values; Supervision, Technical; Activity; Supervision, Human Relations. **Skills**—Operation and Control; Repairing; Operation Monitoring; Installation; Equipment Selection; Troubleshooting. **Abilities**—*Cognitive:* Visualization; Mathematical Reasoning; Number Facility; Selective Attention. *Psychomotor:* Control Precision; Manual Dexterity; Finger Dexterity; Speed of Limb Movement; Arm-Hand Steadiness. *Physical:* Static Strength; Trunk Strength; Stamina; Extent Flexibility; Explosive Strength. *Sensory:* Depth Perception; Hearing Sensitivity; Near Vision; Sound Localization. **General Work Activities**—*Information Input:* Monitoring Processes, Materials, or Surroundings; Getting Information; Inspecting Equipment, Structures, or Materials. *Mental Process:* Evaluating Information Against Standards; Updating and Using Relevant Knowledge; Judging Qualities of Things, Services, or Other People's Work. *Work Output:* Handling and Moving Objects; Controlling Machines and Processes; Repairing and Maintaining Mechanical Equipment. *Interacting with Others:* Monitoring and Controlling Resources; Communicating with Other Workers; Coordinating the Work and Activities of Others. **Physical Work Conditions**—Hazardous Equipment; Using Hands on Objects, Tools, or Controls; Distracting Sounds and Noise Levels; Indoors; Contaminants. **Other Job Characteristics**—Pace Determined by Speed of Equipment; Degree of Automation; Importance of Repeating Same Tasks.

Experience—Job Zone 3. Previous work-related skill, knowledge, or experience is required. **Job Preparation:** SVP 6.0 to less than 7.0—more than one year and less than four years. **Knowledge**—Mechanical; Production and Processing; Engineering and Technology; Physics; Design. **Instructional Programs**—Machine Shop Technology/Assistant; Machine Tool Technology/Machinist.

Related DOT Jobs—601.482-010 Profile-Grinder Technician; 602.360-010 Grinder Set-Up Operator, Gear, Tool; 602.382-034 Grinder, Gear; 602.482-010 Gear-Lapping-Machine Operator; 603.260-010 Grinder Set-Up Operator, Thread Tool; 603.280-026 Grinder Set-Up Operator, Jig; 603.280-034 Job Setter, Honing; 603.380-010 Grinder Machine Setter; 603.382-014 Grinder Set-Up Operator, Centerless; 603.382-018 Honing-Machine Set-Up Operator; 603.382-022 Honing-Machine Set-Up Operator, Tool; 603.382-026 Lapping-Machine Set-Up Operator; 603.382-034 Grinder Set-Up Operator; 603.382-038 Knife Grinder; 603.482-010 Deburrer, Strip; 609.682-026 Nicking-Machine Operator; 628.382-014 Shear-Grinder Operator; 629.682-010 Roll Grinder; 690.280-010 Deburring-and-Tooling-Machine Operator.

51-4033.02 Buffing and Polishing Set-Up Operators

- **Education/Training Required: Moderate-term on-the-job training**
- **Employed: No data available.**
- **Annual Earnings: $25,530**
- **Growth: 7.3%**
- **Annual Job Openings: 26,000**

Set up and operate buffing or polishing machine.

Sets and adjusts machine controls according to product specifications, utilizing knowledge of machine operation. Starts and observes machine operation for conformance to specifications. Selects buffing or polishing tools and positions and mounts tools to machine tool, chuck, or jig, using hand tools. Reads work order to determine parts to be buffed or polished. Selects and attaches workpiece holding fixture to drive mechanism and positions or clamps workpiece to fixture. Holds stick of buffing compound or turns valve and depresses pedal to administer coolant to workpiece surface. Removes workpiece and examines finish or luster to ensure surface meets specifications. Repairs or replaces machine parts to maintain machine in operational condition.

GOE INFORMATION—Interest Area: 08. Industrial Production. **Work Group:** 08.02. Production Technology. **Personality Type**—Realistic. Realistic occupations frequently involve work activities that include practical, hands-on problems and solutions. They often deal with plants, animals, and real-world materials like wood, tools, and machinery. Many of the occupations require working outside and do not involve a lot of paperwork or working closely with others. **Work Values**—Independence; Moral Values; Supervision, Technical; Activity; Supervision, Human Relations. **Skills**—Repairing; Operation and Control; Operation Monitoring; Installation. **Abilities**—*Cognitive:* Spatial Orientation; Visualization. *Psychomotor:* Rate Control; Control Precision; Speed of Limb

Movement; Manual Dexterity; Arm-Hand Steadiness. *Physical:* Dynamic Flexibility; Explosive Strength; Dynamic Strength; Extent Flexibility; Stamina. *Sensory:* Depth Perception; Peripheral Vision. **General Work Activities**—*Information Input:* Monitoring Processes, Materials, or Surroundings; Inspecting Equipment, Structures, or Materials; Getting Information. *Mental Process:* Evaluating Information Against Standards; Making Decisions and Solving Problems; Updating and Using Relevant Knowledge. *Work Output:* Handling and Moving Objects; Controlling Machines and Processes; Performing General Physical Activities. *Interacting with Others:* Communicating with Other Workers; Coordinating the Work and Activities of Others; Performing Administrative Activities. **Physical Work Conditions**—Hazardous Equipment; Using Hands on Objects, Tools, or Controls; Distracting Sounds and Noise Levels; Standing; Common Protective or Safety Attire. **Other Job Characteristics**—Degree of Automation; Pace Determined by Speed of Equipment; Importance of Repeating Same Tasks.

Experience—Job Zone 2. Some previous work-related skill, knowledge, or experience may be helpful, but usually is not needed. **Job Preparation:** SVP 4.0 to less than 6.0—six months to less than two years. **Knowledge**—Mechanical; Production and Processing. **Instructional Programs**—Machine Shop Technology/Assistant; Machine Tool Technology/Machinist.

Related DOT Jobs—603.360-010 Buffing-Line Set-Up Worker; 603.382-010 Buffing-Machine Operator; 603.682-010 Buffing-Machine Operator, Silverware; 603.682-022 Mirror-Finishing-Machine Operator; 603.682-026 Polishing-Machine Operator.

51-4034.00 Lathe and Turning Machine Tool Setters, Operators, and Tenders, Metal and Plastic

- **Education/Training Required: Moderate-term on-the-job training**
- **Employed: 83,718**
- **Annual Earnings: $29,620**
- **Growth: −7.4%**
- **Annual Job Openings: 12,000**

Set up, operate, or tend lathe and turning machines to turn, bore, thread, form, or face metal or plastic materials, such as wire, rod, or bar stock.

Moves controls to set cutting speeds and depths and feed rates and to position tool in relation to workplace. Cranks machine through cycle, stopping to adjust tool positions and machine controls to ensure specified timing, clearance, and tolerances. Starts machine and turns valve handle to direct flow of coolant on work area or coats disk with spinning compound. Installs holding fixtures, cams, gears, and stops to control stock and tool movement, using hand tools, power tools, and measuring instruments. Moves toolholder manually or by turning handwheel or engages automatic feeding mechanism to feed tools to and along workpiece. Selects cutting tools and tooling instructions according to knowledge of metal properties and shop mathematics or written specifications. Positions, secures, and aligns cutting tools in toolholders on machine, using hand tools, and verifies their position with measuring instruments. Observes operation and stops machine to inspect finished workpiece and verify conformance with specifications of first run, using measuring instruments. Mounts attachments, such as relieving or tracing attachments, to perform operations such as duplicating contours of template or trimming workpiece. Studies blueprint, layout, or chart to visualize work and determine materials needed, sequence of operations, dimensions, and tooling instructions. Computes unspecified dimensions and machine settings, using knowledge of metal properties and shop mathematics. Lifts metal stock or workpiece manually or using hoist and positions and secures it in machine, using fasteners and hand tools. Replaces worn tools and sharpens dull cutting tools and dies.

GOE INFORMATION—Interest Area: 08. Industrial Production. **Work Group:** 08.02. Production Technology. **Personality Type**—Realistic. Realistic occupations frequently involve work activities that include practical, hands-on problems and solutions. They often deal with plants, animals, and real-world materials like wood, tools, and machinery. Many of the occupations require working outside and do not involve a lot of paperwork or working closely with others. **Work Values**—Moral Values; Supervision, Technical; Independence; Supervision, Human Relations; Company Policies and Practices. **Skills**—Installation; Operation Monitoring; Operation and Control; Equipment Selection; Technology Design; Repairing; Quality Control Analysis. **Abilities**—*Cognitive:* Visualization; Mathematical Reasoning; Number Facility; Written Comprehension; Information Ordering. *Psychomotor:* Control Precision; Multilimb Coordination; Rate Control; Reaction Time; Arm-Hand Steadiness. *Physical:* Static Strength; Stamina; Dynamic Strength; Trunk Strength; Explosive Strength. *Sensory:* Hearing Sensitivity. **General Work Activities**—*Information Input:* Monitoring Processes, Materials, or Surroundings; Inspecting Equipment, Structures, or Materials; Identifying Objects, Actions, and Events. *Mental Process:* Evaluating Information Against Standards; Judging Qualities of Things, Services, or Other People's Work; Updating and Using Relevant Knowledge. *Work Output:* Controlling Machines and Processes; Handling and Moving Objects; Performing General Physical Activities. *Interacting with Others:* Communicating with Other Workers; Establishing and Maintaining Relationships; Assisting and Caring for Others. **Physical Work Conditions**—Hazardous Equipment; Distracting Sounds and Noise Levels; Common Protective or Safety Attire; Using Hands on Objects, Tools, or Controls; Indoors. **Other Job Characteristics**—Degree of Automation; Pace Determined by Speed of Equipment; Importance of Being Exact or Accurate.

Experience—Job Zone 3. Previous work-related skill, knowledge, or experience is required. **Job Preparation:** SVP 6.0 to less than 7.0—more than one year and less than four years. **Knowledge**—Production and Processing; Mechanical; Engineering and Technology; Physics; Design. **Instructional Programs**—Machine Tool Technology/Machinist.

Related DOT Jobs—604.260-010 Screw-Machine Set-Up Operator, Swiss-Type; 604.280-010 Engine-Lathe Set-Up Operator, Tool; 604.280-014 Screw-Machine Set-Up Operator, Multiple Spindle; 604.280-018 Screw-Machine Set-Up Operator, Single Spindle; 604.280-022 Turret-Lathe Set-Up Operator, Tool; 604.360-010 Setter, Automatic-Spinning Lathe; 604.380-010 Chucking-Machine Set-Up Operator; 604.380-014 Chucking-Machine Set-Up Operator, Multiple Spindle, Vertical; 604.380-018 Engine-Lathe Set-Up Operator; 604.380-022 Screw-Machine Set-Up Operator; 604.380-026 Turret-Lathe Set-Up Operator; 604.682-014 Threading-Machine Operator; 609.380-014 Threading-Machine Setter; 619.362-018 Spinner, Hand; 619.362-022 Spinner, Hydraulic.

51-4035.00 Milling and Planing Machine Setters, Operators, and Tenders, Metal and Plastic

- Education/Training Required: Moderate-term on-the-job training
- Employed: 34,259
- Annual Earnings: $28,750
- Growth: –6.7%
- Annual Job Openings: 4,000

Set up, operate, or tend milling or planing machines to mill, plane, shape, groove, or profile metal or plastic workpieces.

Selects and installs cutting tool, stylus, and other accessories according to specifications, using hand tools or power tools. Moves controls to set cutting specifications, position cutting tool and workpiece in relation to each other, and start machine. Moves cutter or material manually or by turning handwheel or engages automatic feeding mechanism to mill workpiece to specifications. Observes machine operation and adjusts controls to ensure conformance with specified tolerances. Selects cutting speed, feed rate, and depth of cut, applying knowledge of metal properties and shop mathematics. Verifies alignment of workpiece on machine, using measuring instruments such as rules, gauges, or calipers. Turns valve to begin and regulate the flow of coolant on work area. Studies blueprint, layout, sketch, or other specifications to determine materials needed, sequence of operations, dimensions, and tooling instructions. Computes dimensions, tolerances, and angles of workpiece or machine according to specifications and knowledge of metal properties and shop mathematics. Positions and secures workpiece on machine, using holding devices, measuring instruments, hand tools, and hoists. Verifies conformance of finished workpiece to specifications, using measuring instruments such as microscopes, gauges, calipers, and micrometers. Removes workpiece and template or model from machine. Mounts attachments and other tools, such as pantograph, engraver, or router, to perform other operations, such as drilling or boring. Replaces worn tools, using hand tools. Sharpens dull tools, using bench grinder. Makes templates or cutting tools. Records production output.

GOE INFORMATION—Interest Area: 08. Industrial Production. **Work Group:** 08.02. Production Technology. **Personality Type**—Realistic. Realistic occupations frequently involve work activities that include practical, hands-on problems and solutions. They often deal with plants, animals, and real-world materials like wood, tools, and machinery. Many of the occupations require working outside and do not involve a lot of paperwork or working closely with others. **Work Values**—Independence; Moral Values; Supervision, Technical; Supervision, Human Relations; Company Policies and Practices. **Skills**—Operation and Control; Operation Monitoring; Equipment Selection; Repairing; Installation; Technology Design; Mathematics. **Abilities**—*Cognitive:* Mathematical Reasoning. *Psychomotor:* Control Precision; Reaction Time; Rate Control; Wrist-Finger Speed; Manual Dexterity. *Physical:* Static Strength; Stamina; Dynamic Flexibility; Dynamic Strength; Gross Body Coordination. *Sensory:* Auditory Attention. **General Work Activities**—*Information Input:* Monitoring Processes, Materials, or Surroundings; Inspecting Equipment, Structures, or Materials; Identifying Objects, Actions, and Events. *Mental Process:* Evaluating Information Against Standards; Updating and Using Relevant Knowledge; Judging Qualities of Things, Services, or Other People's Work. *Work Output:* Controlling Machines and Processes; Handling and Moving Objects; Performing General Physical Activities. *Interacting with Others:* Establishing and Maintaining Relationships; Communicating with Other Workers; Coaching and Developing Others. **Physical Work Conditions**—Hazardous Equipment; Common Protective or Safety Attire; Distracting Sounds and Noise Levels; Making Repetitive Motions; Using Hands on Objects, Tools, or Controls. **Other Job Characteristics**—Degree of Automation; Pace Determined by Speed of Equipment; Importance of Repeating Same Tasks.

Experience—Job Zone 3. Previous work-related skill, knowledge, or experience is required. **Job Preparation:** SVP 6.0 to less than 7.0—more than one year and less than four years. **Knowledge**—Production and Processing; Mechanical; Physics; Design; Engineering and Technology. **Instructional Programs**—Machine Tool Technology/Machinist.

Related DOT Jobs—605.280-010 Milling-Machine Set-Up Operator I; 605.280-014 Profiling-Machine Set-Up Operator I; 605.280-018 Profiling-

Machine Set-Up Operator, Tool; 605.282-010 Milling-Machine Set-Up Operator II; 605.282-014 Planer Set-Up Operator, Tool; 605.282-018 Planer-Type-Milling-Machine Set-Up Operator; 605.382-010 Broaching-Machine Set-Up Operator; 605.382-014 Engraver, Tire Mold; 605.382-018 Keyseating-Machine Set-Up Operator; 605.382-022 Pantograph-Machine Set-Up Operator; 605.382-026 Profiling-Machine Set-Up Operator II; 605.382-030 Rotary-Head-Milling-Machine Set-Up Operator; 605.382-034 Router Operator; 605.382-038 Shaper Set-Up Operator, Tool; 605.382-042 Thread-Milling-Machine Set-Up Operator; 605.482-010 Steel-Wool-Machine Operator; 605.682-010 Barrel-Rib Matting-Machine Operator; 605.682-022 Scalper Operator; 605.682-026 Tooth Cutter, Escape Wheel.

51-4041.00 Machinists

- **Education/Training Required: Long-term on-the-job training**
- **Employed: 429,564**
- **Annual Earnings: $32,090**
- **Growth: 9.1%**
- **Annual Job Openings: 28,000**

Set up and operate a variety of machine tools to produce precision parts and instruments. Includes precision instrument makers who fabricate, modify, or repair mechanical instruments. May also fabricate and modify parts to make or repair machine tools or maintain industrial machines, applying knowledge of mechanics, shop mathematics, metal properties, layout, and machining procedures.

Align and secure holding fixtures, cutting tools, attachments, accessories, and materials onto machines. Calculate dimensions and tolerances, using knowledge of mathematics and instruments such as micrometers and vernier calipers. Check workpieces to ensure that they are properly lubricated and cooled. Dismantle machines or equipment, using hand tools and power tools, in order to examine parts for defects and replace defective parts where needed. Fit and assemble parts to make or repair machine tools. Lay out, measure, and mark metal stock in order to display placement of cuts. Machine parts to specifications, using machine tools such as lathes, milling machines, shapers, or grinders. Maintain industrial machines, applying knowledge of mechanics, shop mathematics, metal properties, layout, and machining procedures. Measure, examine, and test completed units in order to detect defects and ensure conformance to specifications, using precision instruments such as micrometers. Monitor the feed and speed of machines during the machining process. Operate equipment to verify operational efficiency. Position and fasten workpieces. Select the appropriate tools, machines, and materials to be used in preparation of machinery work. Set controls to regulate machining or enter commands to retrieve, input, or edit computerized machine control media. Set up, adjust, and operate all of the basic machine tools and many specialized or advanced variation tools in order to perform precision machining operations. Study sample parts, blueprints, drawings, and engineering information in order to determine methods and sequences of operations needed to fabricate products and determine product dimensions and tolerances. Clean and lubricate machines, tools, and equipment in order to remove grease, rust, stains, and foreign matter. Confer with engineering, supervisory, and manufacturing personnel in order to exchange technical information. Confer with numerical control programmers in order to check and ensure that new programs or machinery will function properly and that output will meet specifications. Design fixtures, tooling, and experimental parts to meet special engineering needs. Establish work procedures for fabricating new structural products, using a variety of metalworking machines. Evaluate experimental procedures and recommend changes or modifications for improved efficiency and adaptability to setup and production. Install experimental parts and assemblies such as hydraulic systems, electrical wiring, lubricants, and batteries into machines and mechanisms. Install repaired parts into equipment or install new equipment. Observe and listen to operating machines or equipment in order to diagnose machine malfunctions and to determine need for adjustments or repairs. Prepare working sketches for the illustration of product appearance.

GOE INFORMATION—Interest Area: 08. Industrial Production. **Work Group:** 08.04. Metal and Plastics Machining Technology. **Personality Type**—Realistic. Realistic occupations frequently involve work activities that include practical, hands-on problems and solutions. They often deal with plants, animals, and real-world materials like wood, tools, and machinery. Many of the occupations require working outside and do not involve a lot of paperwork or working closely with others. **Work Values**—Moral Values; Supervision, Technical; Company Policies and Practices; Creativity; Compensation. **Skills**—Installation; Operation Monitoring; Repairing; Technology Design; Equipment Selection; Quality Control Analysis; Operation and Control; Troubleshooting. **Abilities**—*Cognitive:* Visualization; Originality; Perceptual Speed; Mathematical Reasoning; Number Facility. *Psychomotor:* Control Precision; Arm-Hand Steadiness; Reaction Time; Finger Dexterity; Response Orientation. *Physical:* Dynamic Strength; Explosive Strength; Extent Flexibility; Static Strength; Trunk Strength. *Sensory:* Hearing Sensitivity; Visual Color Discrimination; Sound Localization; Auditory Attention; Near Vision. **General Work Activities**—*Information Input:* Getting Information; Inspecting Equipment, Structures, or Materials; Monitoring Processes, Materials, or Surroundings. *Mental Process:* Updating and Using Relevant Knowledge; Analyzing Data or Information; Evaluating Information Against Standards. *Work Output:* Controlling Machines and Processes; Handling and Moving Objects; Repairing and Maintaining Mechanical Equipment. *Interacting with Others:* Communicating with Other Workers; Providing Consultation and Advice to Others; Establishing and Maintaining Relationships. **Physical Work Conditions**—Common Protective or Safety Attire; Hazardous Equipment; Distracting Sounds and Noise Levels; Making Repetitive Motions; Cramped Work Space or Awkward Positions. **Other Job Characteristics**—Degree of Automation; Pace Determined by Speed of Equipment; Importance of Being Exact or Accurate.

Experience—Job Zone 4. A minimum of two to four years of work-related skill, knowledge, or experience is needed. **Job Preparation:** SVP 7.0 to less than 8.0—two years to less than 10 years. **Knowledge**—Mechanical; Design; Production and Processing; Engineering and Technology; Physics. **Instructional Programs**—Machine Shop Technology/Assistant; Machine Tool Technology/Machinist.

Related DOT Jobs—019.161-014 Test Technician; 600.260-022 Machinist, Experimental; 600.280-022 Machinist; 600.280-026 Machinist Apprentice; 600.280-030 Machinist Apprentice, Automotive; 600.280-034 Machinist, Automotive; 600.280-042 Maintenance Machinist; 600.281-010 Fluid-Power Mechanic; 600.380-010 Fixture Maker; 693.261-014 Development Mechanic; 693.261-022 Rocket-Motor Mechanic; 806.281-014 Experimental Mechanic, Electrical.

51-4051.00 Metal-Refining Furnace Operators and Tenders

- **Education/Training Required: Moderate-term on-the-job training**
- **Employed: 23,914**
- **Annual Earnings: $29,880**
- **Growth: 7.4%**
- **Annual Job Openings: 3,000**

Operate or tend furnaces, such as gas, oil, coal, electric-arc or electric induction, open-hearth, or oxygen furnaces, to melt and refine metal before casting or to produce specified types of steel.

Manipulates controls to ignite burners, adjust fuel mixtures, open and close furnace doors, or load and discharge materials into or from furnace. Observes air and temperature gauges or metal color and turns fuel valves or adjusts controls to maintain required temperature. Regulates supply of fuel and air or controls flow of electric current and water coolant to heat furnaces. Observes inside of furnace operations by television screen and operates controls to move or discharge metal workpiece. Drains, transfers, or removes molten metal from furnace or into molds by hoist or pumps or ladles. Observes color and fluidity of molten metal and obtains test sample of metal from furnace or kettle for analysis. Kindles fire and shovels fuels and other materials into furnaces or onto conveyors by hand, with hoists, or by directing crane operator. Sprinkles chemicals over molten metal to bring impurities to surface and removes impurities, using strainers. Analyzes metal test sample according to specific instructions and for specific and for specific element content. Inspects furnace and equipment for defects and wear and directs work crew in cleaning and repairing furnace walls and flooring. Examines and prepares material to load into furnace, including cleaning, crushing, or applying chemicals, using crushing machine, shovel, rake, or sprayer. Draws smelted metal samples from furnace for analysis and calculates type and amount of material required to correct smelting process. Weighs materials to be charged into furnace or to maintain prescribed weight, using scales. Scrapes accumulations of metal oxides from floors, molds, and crucibles and sifts and stores for reclamation. Records data and maintains production logs.

GOE INFORMATION—Interest Area: 08. Industrial Production. **Work Group:** 08.03. Production Work. **Personality Type—**Realistic. Realistic occupations frequently involve work activities that include practical, hands-on problems and solutions. They often deal with plants, animals, and real-world materials like wood, tools, and machinery. Many of the occupations require working outside and do not involve a lot of paperwork or working closely with others. **Work Values—**Independence; Moral Values; Supervision, Human Relations; Company Policies and Practices; Activity. **Skills—**Operation Monitoring; Operation and Control. **Abilities—***Cognitive:* Perceptual Speed; Time Sharing; Memorization; Spatial Orientation; Information Ordering. *Psychomotor:* Control Precision; Manual Dexterity; Multilimb Coordination; Rate Control; Speed of Limb Movement. *Physical:* Static Strength; Dynamic Flexibility; Dynamic Strength; Stamina; Explosive Strength. *Sensory:* Visual Color Discrimination; Glare Sensitivity; Depth Perception; Peripheral Vision; Far Vision. **General Work Activities—***Information Input:* Inspecting Equipment, Structures, or Materials; Monitoring Processes, Materials, or Surroundings; Getting Information. *Mental Process:* Processing Information; Judging Qualities of Things, Services, or Other People's Work; Analyzing Data or Information. *Work Output:* Handling and Moving Objects; Controlling Machines and Processes; Performing General Physical Activities. *Interacting with Others:* Communicating with Other Workers; Performing Administrative Activities; Coordinating the Work and Activities of Others. **Physical Work Conditions—**Hazardous Equipment; Very Hot or Cold; Hazardous Conditions; Minor Burns, Cuts, Bites, or Stings; Contaminants. **Other Job Characteristics—**Degree of Automation; Pace Determined by Speed of Equipment; Importance of Repeating Same Tasks.

Experience—Job Zone 2. Some previous work-related skill, knowledge, or experience may be helpful, but usually is not needed. **Job Preparation:** SVP 4.0 to less than 6.0—six months to less than two years. **Knowledge—**Production and Processing; Mechanical; Physics; Chemistry; Engineering and Technology. **Instructional Programs—**No data available.

Related DOT Jobs—504.665-014 Charger Operator; 512.362-010 First Helper; 512.362-014 Furnace Operator; 512.362-018 Furnace Operator; 512.382-010 Oxygen-Furnace Operator; 512.382-014 Stove Tender; 512.382-018 Tin Recovery Worker; 512.662-010 Cupola Tender; 512.684-014 Furnace Charger; 512.685-010 Furnace Tender; 512.685-022 Reclamation Kettle Tender, Metal; 553.685-114 Cadmium Burner.

51-4052.00 Pourers and Casters, Metal

- **Education/Training Required: Moderate-term on-the-job training**
- **Employed: 16,475**
- **Annual Earnings: $27,590**
- **Growth: 6.9%**
- **Annual Job Openings: 2,000**

Operate hand-controlled mechanisms to pour and regulate the flow of molten metal into molds to produce castings or ingots.

Pours molten metal into molds and forms, using ladle. Adds metal to molds to compensate for shrinkage. Skims slag or removes excess metal from ingots or equipment, using hand tools, strainers, rakes, or burners, and recycles scrap. Positions equipment or signals workers to position equipment such as ladles, grinding wheels, or crucibles. Reads temperature gauges, observes color changes, and adjusts furnace flame, torch, or electrical heating unit to melt metal. Loads specified amount of metal and flux into furnace or clay crucible. Turns valves to circulate water through core or sprays water on filled molds to cool and solidify metal. Examines molds to ensure they are clean, smooth, and properly coated. Assembles and imbeds cores in casting frames, using hand tools and equipment. Removes metal ingots or cores from molds, using hand tools, cranes, and chain hoists. Collects samples or signals workers to sample metal for analysis. Stencils identifying information on ingots and pigs, using special hand tools. Repairs and maintains metal forms and equipment, using hand tools, sledges, and bars. Transports metal ingots to storage areas, using forklift.

GOE INFORMATION—Interest Area: 08. Industrial Production. **Work Group:** 08.03. Production Work. **Personality Type—**Realistic. Realistic occupations frequently involve work activities that include practical, hands-on problems and solutions. They often deal with plants, animals, and real-world materials like wood, tools, and machinery. Many of the occupations require working outside and do not involve a lot of paperwork or working closely with others. **Work Values—**Moral Values; Supervision, Technical; Independence; Supervision, Human Relations; Company Policies and Practices. **Skills—**Operation Monitoring; Operation and Control; Repairing; Installation. **Abilities—***Cognitive:* Perceptual Speed; Visualization; Flexibility of Closure; Selective Attention; Spatial Orientation. *Psychomotor:* Speed of Limb Movement; Arm-Hand Steadiness; Control Precision; Manual Dexterity; Reaction Time. *Physical:* Explosive Strength; Dynamic Flexibility; Dynamic Strength; Static Strength; Gross Body Coordination. *Sensory:* Depth Perception; Visual Color Discrimination; Hearing Sensitivity; Sound Localization; Auditory Attention. **General Work Activities—***Information Input:* Monitoring Processes, Materials, or Surroundings; Inspecting Equipment, Structures, or Materials; Getting Information. *Mental Process:* Evaluating Information Against Standards; Judging Qualities of Things, Services, or Other People's Work; Making Decisions and Solving Problems. *Work Output:* Handling and Moving Objects; Performing General Physical Activities; Controlling Machines and Processes. *Interacting with Others:* Communicating with Other Workers; Establishing and Maintaining Relationships; Assisting and Caring for Others. **Physical Work Conditions—**Common Protective or Safety Attire; Minor Burns, Cuts, Bites, or Stings; Very Hot or Cold; Using Hands on Objects, Tools, or Controls; Hazardous Conditions. **Other Job Characteristics**—Pace Determined by Speed of Equipment; Importance of Repeating Same Tasks; Consequence of Error.

Experience—Job Zone 1. No previous work-related skill, knowledge, or experience is needed. **Job Preparation:** SVP below 4.0—less than six months. **Knowledge**—Production and Processing; Mechanical; Physics; Building and Construction. **Instructional Programs**—No data available.

Related DOT Jobs—502.664-014 Steel Pourer; 502.687-014 Busher; 514.584-010 Ingot Header; 514.684-010 Caster; 514.684-014 Ladle Pourer; 514.684-022 Pourer, Metal; 518.664-010 Mold Maker; 700.687-042 Melter.

51-4061.00 Model Makers, Metal and Plastic

- **Education/Training Required: Moderate-term on-the-job training**
- **Employed: 10,616**
- **Annual Earnings: $36,770**
- **Growth: −3.2%**
- **Annual Job Openings: 1,000**

Set up and operate machines such as lathes, milling and engraving machines, and jig borers to make working models of metal or plastic objects.

Sets up and operates machines, such as lathes, drill presses, punch presses, or band saw, to fabricate prototypes or models. Determines fixtures, machines, tooling and sequence of operations to fabricate parts, dies, and tooling, according to drawings and sketches. Drills, countersinks, and reams holes in parts and assemblies for bolts, screws, and other fasteners, using power tools. Lays out and marks reference points and dimension on materials, using measuring instruments and drawing or scribing tools. Cuts, shapes, and forms metal parts, using lathe, power saw, snips, power brakes and shear, files, and mallets. Grinds, files, and sands parts to finished dimensions. Studies blueprint, drawings, or sketches and computes dimensions for laying out materials and planning model production. Fabricates metal or plastic parts, using hand tools. Aligns, fits, and joins parts, using bolts or screws or by welding or gluing. Assembles mechanical, electrical, and electronic components into models or prototypes, using hand tools, power tools, and fabricating machines. Wires and solders electrical and electronic connections and components. Reworks or alters component model or parts as required to ensure performance of equipment or ensure that parts meet standards. Inspects and tests model or other product to verify conformance to specifications, using precision measuring instruments or circuit tester. Devises and constructs own tools, dies, molds, jigs, and fixtures or modifies existing tools and equipment. Makes bridges, plates, wheels, cutting teeth on wheels and pinions, and threaded screws. Consults and confers with engineering personnel to discuss developmental problems and recommend modifications to correct or improve performance of product. Records specifications, production operations, and final dimensions of model for use in establishing operating standards and machinery procedures.

GOE INFORMATION—**Interest Area:** 08. Industrial Production. **Work Group:** 08.04. Metal and Plastics Machining Technology. **Personality Type**—Realistic. Realistic occupations frequently involve work activities that include practical, hands-on problems and solutions. They often deal with plants, animals, and real-world materials like wood, tools, and machinery. Many of the occupations require working outside and do not involve a lot of paperwork or working closely with others. **Work Values**—Creativity; Ability Utilization; Moral Values; Variety; Compensation. **Skills**—Technology Design; Equipment Selection; Quality Control

Analysis; Operation Monitoring; Troubleshooting; Operation and Control; Operations Analysis; Repairing. **Abilities**—*Cognitive:* Visualization; Mathematical Reasoning; Oral Expression; Originality; Number Facility. *Psychomotor:* Control Precision; Reaction Time; Arm-Hand Steadiness; Manual Dexterity; Finger Dexterity. *Physical:* Gross Body Coordination; Trunk Strength; Explosive Strength; Dynamic Strength; Extent Flexibility. *Sensory:* Visual Color Discrimination; Auditory Attention; Far Vision; Near Vision; Hearing Sensitivity. **General Work Activities**—*Information Input:* Getting Information; Inspecting Equipment, Structures, or Materials; Identifying Objects, Actions, and Events. *Mental Process:* Making Decisions and Solving Problems; Judging Qualities of Things, Services, or Other People's Work; Processing Information. *Work Output:* Handling and Moving Objects; Controlling Machines and Processes; Drafting and Specifying Technical Devices. *Interacting with Others:* Communicating with Other Workers; Providing Consultation and Advice to Others; Performing Administrative Activities. **Physical Work Conditions**—Hazardous Equipment; Minor Burns, Cuts, Bites, or Stings; Common Protective or Safety Attire; Using Hands on Objects, Tools, or Controls; Indoors. **Other Job Characteristics**—Pace Determined by Speed of Equipment; Importance of Being Exact or Accurate; Degree of Automation.

Experience—Job Zone 4. A minimum of two to four years of work-related skill, knowledge, or experience is needed. **Job Preparation:** SVP 7.0 to less than 8.0—two years to less than 10 years. **Knowledge**—Design; Mechanical; Building and Construction; Computers and Electronics; Engineering and Technology. **Instructional Programs**—Sheet Metal Technology/Sheetworking.

Related DOT Jobs—600.260-014 Experimental Mechanic; 600.260-018 Model Maker, Firearms; 600.280-054 Sample Maker, Appliances; 693.260-018 Engineering Model Maker; 693.361-014 Mock-Up Builder; 693.380-010 Model Maker; 709.381-014 Model Builder; 710.361-010 Model Maker, Scale; 723.361-010 Model Maker, Fluorescent Lighting.

51-4062.00 Patternmakers, Metal and Plastic

- **Education/Training Required: Moderate-term on-the-job training**
- **Employed: 8,843**
- **Annual Earnings: $32,740**
- **Growth: −8.4%**
- **Annual Job Openings: 1,000**

Lay out, machine, fit, and assemble castings and parts to metal or plastic foundry patterns, core boxes, or match plates.

Sets up and operates machine tools, such as milling machines, lathes, drill presses, and grinders, to machine castings or pattern. Cuts, trims, shapes, and forms patterns or templates, using hand tools and power tools. Designs and develops template or pattern according to work orders, sample parts, or mockups. Lays out and draws or scribes pattern onto material, using compass, protractor, ruler, scribe, or other instruments. Verifies conformance of pattern or template dimensions to specifications, using measuring instruments such as calipers, scales, and micrometers. Studies blueprint of part to be cast or pattern to be made, computes dimensions, and plans sequence of operations. Operates welding equipment to weld pattern together. Assembles pattern sections, using hand tools, bolts, screws, rivets, or glue. Cleans and fine-finishes pattern or template, using emery cloth, files, scrapers, and power grinders. Repairs and reworks templates and patterns. Marks identification numbers or symbols onto pattern or template. Makes templates or files for own use in inspection and finishing of particular shape. Constructs platforms, fixtures, and jigs for holding and placing patterns. Covers or sprays pattern used in producing plastic with plastic-impregnated fabric or coat of sealing lacquer or wax.

GOE INFORMATION—Interest Area: 08. Industrial Production. **Work Group:** 08.04. Metal and Plastics Machining Technology. **Personality Type**—Realistic. Realistic occupations frequently involve work activities that include practical, hands-on problems and solutions. They often deal with plants, animals, and real-world materials like wood, tools, and machinery. Many of the occupations require working outside and do not involve a lot of paperwork or working closely with others. **Work Values**—Moral Values; Supervision, Technical; Independence; Company Policies and Practices; Creativity. **Skills**—Operation and Control; Operation Monitoring; Repairing; Quality Control Analysis; Technology Design. **Abilities**—*Cognitive:* Visualization; Information Ordering; Mathematical Reasoning; Selective Attention. *Psychomotor:* Arm-Hand Steadiness; Control Precision; Wrist-Finger Speed; Finger Dexterity; Speed of Limb Movement. *Physical:* Dynamic Strength; Static Strength; Explosive Strength; Gross Body Equilibrium; Stamina. *Sensory:* Auditory Attention; Near Vision; Peripheral Vision. **General Work Activities**—*Information Input:* Getting Information; Inspecting Equipment, Structures, or Materials; Estimating Needed Characteristics. *Mental Process:* Organizing, Planning, and Prioritizing; Evaluating Information Against Standards; Judging Qualities of Things, Services, or Other People's Work. *Work Output:* Handling and Moving Objects; Controlling Machines and Processes; Drafting and Specifying Technical Devices. *Interacting with Others:* Establishing and Maintaining Relationships; Communicating with Other Workers; Teaching Others. **Physical Work Conditions**—Hazardous Equipment; Common Protective or Safety Attire; Minor Burns, Cuts, Bites, or Stings; Distracting Sounds and Noise Levels; Using Hands on Objects, Tools, or Controls. **Other Job Characteristics**—Pace Determined by Speed of Equipment; Degree of Automation; Importance of Being Exact or Accurate.

Experience—Job Zone 4. A minimum of two to four years of work-related skill, knowledge, or experience is needed. **Job Preparation:** SVP 7.0 to less than 8.0—two years to less than 10 years. **Knowledge**—Design; Production and Processing; Mechanical; Foreign Language; Fine Arts. **Instructional Programs**—Sheet Metal Technology/Sheetworking.

Related DOT Jobs—600.280-046 Patternmaker Apprentice, Metal; 600.280-050 Patternmaker, Metal; 601.280-038 Template Maker, Extrusion Die; 601.381-038 Template Maker; 693.281-014 Patternmaker; 693.281-018 Patternmaker, Metal, Bench; 693.281-022 Patternmaker, Sample; 703.381-010 Patternmaker; 709.381-034 Patternmaker; 751.381-010 Patternmaker; 754.381-014 Patternmaker, Plastics.

51-4071.00 Foundry Mold and Coremakers

- **Education/Training Required: Moderate-term on-the-job training**
- **Employed: 59,308**
- **Annual Earnings: $25,570**
- **Growth: –1.2%**
- **Annual Job Openings: 13,000**

Make or form wax or sand cores or molds used in the production of metal castings in foundries.

Forms and assembles slab cores around pattern and positions wire in mold sections to reinforce mold, using hand tools and glue. Sifts sand and packs sand into mold sections, core box, and pattern contours, using hand or pneumatic ramming tools. Positions cores into lower section of mold and reassembles mold for pouring. Cuts spouts, runner holes, and sprue holes into mold. Sprinkles or sprays parting agent onto pattern and mold sections to facilitate removal of pattern from mold. Positions patterns inside mold sections and clamps sections together. Operates ovens to bake cores or furnaces to melt, skim, and flux metal. Lifts upper mold section from lower and removes molded patterns. Rotates sweep board around spindle to make symmetrical molds for convex impressions. Cleans and smoothes molds, cores, and core boxes and repairs surface imperfections. Pours molten metal into mold, manually or using crane ladle. Moves and positions workpieces, such as mold sections, patterns, and bottom boards, using cranes, or signals others to move workpieces.

GOE INFORMATION—Interest Area: 08. Industrial Production. **Work Group:** 08.02. Production Technology. **Personality Type**—Realistic. Realistic occupations frequently involve work activities that include practical, hands-on problems and solutions. They often deal with plants, animals, and real-world materials like wood, tools, and machinery. Many of the occupations require working outside and do not involve a lot of paperwork or working closely with others. **Work Values**—Moral Values; Supervision, Technical; Supervision, Human Relations; Advancement; Company Policies and Practices. **Skills**—Operation and Control; Operation Monitoring. **Abilities**—*Cognitive:* Visualization; Selective Attention; Spatial Orientation; Information Ordering. *Psychomotor:* Arm-Hand Steadiness; Multilimb Coordination; Speed of Limb Movement; Control Precision; Reaction Time. *Physical:* Static Strength; Stamina; Explosive Strength; Gross Body Coordination; Gross Body Equilibrium. *Sensory:* Glare Sensitivity; Auditory Attention; Sound Localization; Night Vision; Visual Color Discrimination. **General Work Activities**—*Information Input:* Monitoring Processes, Materials, or Surroundings; Estimating Needed Characteristics; Getting Information. *Mental Process:* Judging Qualities of Things, Services, or Other People's Work; Updating and Using Relevant Knowledge; Evaluating Information Against Standards. *Work Output:* Handling and Moving Objects; Performing General Physical Activities; Controlling Machines and Processes. *Interacting with Others:* Communicating with Other Workers; Establishing and Maintaining Relationships; Coordinating the Work and Activities of Others. **Physical Work Conditions**—Common Protective or Safety Attire; Hazardous Equipment; Very Hot or Cold; Minor Burns, Cuts, Bites, or Stings; Extremely Bright or Inadequate Lighting. **Other Job Characteristics**—Pace Determined by Speed of Equipment; Importance of Repeating Same Tasks; Degree of Automation.

Experience—Job Zone 2. Some previous work-related skill, knowledge, or experience may be helpful, but usually is not needed. **Job Preparation:** SVP 4.0 to less than 6.0—six months to less than two years. **Knowledge**—Building and Construction; Mechanical; Design; Production and Processing; Fine Arts. **Instructional Programs**—Ironworking/Ironworker.

Related DOT Jobs—518.361-010 Molder; 518.361-014 Molder Apprentice; 518.361-018 Molder, Sweep; 518.381-014 Coremaker; 518.381-018 Coremaker Apprentice.

51-4072.00 Molding, Coremaking, and Casting Machine Setters, Operators, and Tenders, Metal and Plastic

- **Education/Training Required: Moderate-term on-the-job training**
- **Employed: 176,092**
- **Annual Earnings: $22,340**
- **Growth: 9.8%**
- **Annual Job Openings: 38,000**

Set up, operate, or tend metal or plastic molding, casting, or coremaking machines to mold or cast metal or thermoplastic parts or products.

No task data available.

GOE INFORMATION—Interest Area: 08. Industrial Production. **Work Group:** 08.02. Production Technology. **Note:** The Department of Labor has not collected some data for this job, so it has fewer details than the other descriptions.

Instructional Programs—No data available.

Related DOT Jobs—502.362-010 Shot Dropper; 502.382-010 Bullet-Slug-Casting-Machine Operator; 502.482-010 Caster; 502.482-014 Casting-Machine Operator, Automatic; 502.482-018 Rotor Casting-Machine Operator; 502.682-010 Bullet-Casting Operator; 502.682-014 Casting-Machine Operator; 502.685-010 Molder, Lead Ingot; 502.685-014 Remelter; 514.360-010 Die-Casting-Machine Setter; 514.362-010 Pig-Machine Operator; 514.382-010 Die-Casting-Machine Operator I; 514.562-010 Centrifugal-Casting-Machine Operator III; 514.582-010 Vacuum Caster; 514.662-010 Casting Operator; 514.682-010 Casting-Wheel Operator; 514.685-010 Centrifugal-Casting-Machine Operator I; 514.685-014 Centrifugal-Casting-Machine Operator II; 514.685-018 Die-Casting-Machine Operator II; 518.380-010 Setter, Molding-and-Coremaking Machines; others.

51-4072.01 Plastic Molding and Casting Machine Setters and Set-Up Operators

- Education/Training Required: Moderate-term on-the-job training
- Employed: No data available.
- Annual Earnings: $22,340
- Growth: 9.8%
- Annual Job Openings: 38,000

Set up or set up and operate plastic molding machines, such as compression or injection molding machines, to mold, form, or cast thermoplastic materials to specified shape.

Positions, aligns, and secures assembled mold, mold components, and machine accessories onto machine press bed and attaches connecting lines. Installs dies onto machine or press and coats dies with parting agent according to work order specifications. Sets machine controls to regulate molding temperature, volume, pressure, and time according to knowledge of plastics and molding procedures. Presses button or pulls lever to activate machine to inject dies and compress compounds to form and cure specified products. Reads specifications to determine setup and prescribed temperature and time settings to mold, form, or cast plastic materials. Weighs premixed compounds and dumps compound into die well or fills hoppers of machines that automatically supply compound to die. Observes and adjusts machine setup and operations to eliminate production of defective parts and products. Mixes catalysts, thermoplastic materials, and coloring pigments according to formula, using paddle and mixing machine. Measures and visually inspects products for surface and dimension defects, using precision measuring instruments, to ensure conformance to specifications. Removes finished or cured product from dies or mold, using hand tools and air hose. Trims excess material from part, using knife, and grinds scrap plastic into powder for reuse. Repairs and maintains machines and auxiliary equipment, using hand tools and power tools.

GOE INFORMATION—Interest Area: 08. Industrial Production. **Work Group:** 08.02. Production Technology. **Personality Type**—Realistic. Realistic occupations frequently involve work activities that include practical, hands-on problems and solutions. They often deal with plants, animals, and real-world materials like wood, tools, and machinery. Many of the occupations require working outside and do not involve a lot of

paperwork or working closely with others. **Work Values**—Moral Values; Independence; Supervision, Human Relations; Company Policies and Practices; Activity. **Skills**—Operation Monitoring; Repairing; Operation and Control; Troubleshooting. **Abilities**—*Cognitive:* Visualization; Information Ordering. *Psychomotor:* Control Precision; Reaction Time; Wrist-Finger Speed; Manual Dexterity; Finger Dexterity. *Physical:* Explosive Strength; Static Strength; Dynamic Flexibility; Dynamic Strength; Extent Flexibility. *Sensory:* Visual Color Discrimination; Depth Perception; Near Vision. **General Work Activities**—*Information Input:* Monitoring Processes, Materials, or Surroundings; Inspecting Equipment, Structures, or Materials; Identifying Objects, Actions, and Events. *Mental Process:* Updating and Using Relevant Knowledge; Evaluating Information Against Standards; Organizing, Planning, and Prioritizing. *Work Output:* Handling and Moving Objects; Controlling Machines and Processes; Performing General Physical Activities. *Interacting with Others:* Communicating with Other Workers; Establishing and Maintaining Relationships; Assisting and Caring for Others. **Physical Work Conditions**—Hazardous Equipment; Contaminants; Distracting Sounds and Noise Levels; Common Protective or Safety Attire; Hazardous Conditions. **Other Job Characteristics**—Pace Determined by Speed of Equipment; Degree of Automation; Consequence of Error.

Experience—Job Zone 2. Some previous work-related skill, knowledge, or experience may be helpful, but usually is not needed. **Job Preparation:** SVP 4.0 to less than 6.0–six months to less than two years. **Knowledge**—Mechanical; Production and Processing; Chemistry. **Instructional Programs**—No data available.

Related DOT Jobs—556.380-010 Mold Setter; 556.382-014 Injection-Molding-Machine Operator; 556.682-014 Compression-Molding-Machine Operator.

51-4072.02 Plastic Molding and Casting Machine Operators and Tenders

- Education/Training Required: Short-term on-the-job training
- Employed: No data available.
- Annual Earnings: $22,340
- Growth: 9.8%
- Annual Job Openings: 38,000

Operate or tend plastic molding machines, such as compression or injection molding machines, to mold, form, or cast thermoplastic materials to specified shape.

Starts machine that automatically liquefies plastic material in heating chamber, injects liquefied material into mold, and ejects molded product. Turns valves and dials of machines to regulate pressure and temperature, to set press-cycle time, and to close press. Observes meters and gauges to verify specified temperatures, pressures, and press-cycle times. Observes continuous operation of automatic machine and width and alignment of plastic sheeting to ensure side flanges. Dumps plastic powder, preformed plastic pellets, or preformed rubber slugs into hopper of molding machine. Pulls level and toggle latches to fill mold and regulate tension on sheeting and to release mold covers. Mixes and pours liquid plastic into rotating drum of machine that spreads, hardens, and shapes mixture. Fills tubs, molds, or cavities of machine with plastic material in solid or liquid form prior to activating machine. Examines molded product for surface defects, such as dents, bubbles, thin areas, and cracks. Positions mold frame to correct alignment and tubs containing mixture on top of mold to facilitate loading of molds. Removes product from mold or conveyor and cleans and reloads mold. Weighs prescribed amounts of material for molded part and finished product to ensure specifications are maintained. Heats plastic material prior to forming product or cools product after processing to prevent distortion. Breaks seals that hold plastic product in molds, using hand tool, and removes product from mold. Feels stiffness and consistency of molded sheeting to detect machinery malfunction. Stacks molded parts in boxes or on conveyor for subsequent processing or leaves parts in mold to cool. Reports defect in molds to supervisor. Throws flash and rejected parts into grinder machine to be recycled. Signals co-worker to synchronize feed of materials into molding process. Trims flashing from product.

GOE INFORMATION—Interest Area: 08. Industrial Production. **Work Group:** 08.02. Production Technology. **Personality Type—**Realistic. Realistic occupations frequently involve work activities that include practical, hands-on problems and solutions. They often deal with plants, animals, and real-world materials like wood, tools, and machinery. Many of the occupations require working outside and do not involve a lot of paperwork or working closely with others. **Work Values—**Moral Values; Independence; Company Policies and Practices; Supervision, Technical; Supervision, Human Relations. **Skills—**Operation Monitoring; Operation and Control; Quality Control Analysis. **Abilities—***Cognitive:* Perceptual Speed; Time Sharing; Selective Attention; Spatial Orientation; Problem Sensitivity. *Psychomotor:* Rate Control; Control Precision; Reaction Time; Speed of Limb Movement; Manual Dexterity. *Physical:* Static Strength; Dynamic Strength; Explosive Strength; Dynamic Flexibility; Gross Body Coordination. *Sensory:* Hearing Sensitivity; Sound Localization; Peripheral Vision; Visual Color Discrimination; Depth Perception. **General Work Activities—***Information Input:* Monitoring Processes, Materials, or Surroundings; Inspecting Equipment, Structures, or Materials; Estimating Needed Characteristics. *Mental Process:* Judging Qualities of Things, Services, or Other People's Work; Evaluating Information Against Standards; Analyzing Data or Information. *Work Output:* Handling and Moving Objects; Controlling Machines and Processes; Performing General Physical Activities. *Interacting with Others:* Communicating with Other Workers; Coordinating the Work and Activities of Others; Establishing and Maintaining Relationships. **Physical Work Conditions—**Hazardous Equipment; Distracting Sounds and Noise Levels; Using Hands on Objects, Tools, or Controls; Standing; Hazardous Conditions. **Other Job Characteristics—**Pace Determined by Speed of Equipment; Degree of Automation; Importance of Repeating Same Tasks.

Experience—Job Zone 1. No previous work-related skill, knowledge, or experience is needed. **Job Preparation:** SVP below 4.0—less than six months. **Knowledge—**Production and Processing; Mechanical; Physics; Philosophy and Theology. **Instructional Programs—**No data available.

Related DOT Jobs—556.385-010 Centrifugal-Casting-Machine Tender; 556.665-010 Cake-Press Operator; 556.665-014 Corrugator Operator; 556.665-018 Molder, Pipe Covering; 556.685-022 Compression-Molding-Machine Tender; 556.685-038 Injection-Molding-Machine Tender; 556.685-082 Vacuum Plastic-Forming-Machine Operator; 556.685-086 Blow-Molding-Machine Tender; 556.685-090 Centrifugal-Casting-Machine Tender; 690.685-090 Contact-Lens Molder.

51-4072.03 Metal Molding, Coremaking, and Casting Machine Setters and Set-Up Operators

- **Education/Training Required: Moderate-term on-the-job training**
- **Employed: No data available.**
- **Annual Earnings: $22,340**
- **Growth: 9.8%**
- **Annual Job Openings: 38,000**

Set up or set up and operate metal casting, molding, and coremaking machines to mold or cast metal parts and products, such as tubes, rods, automobile trim, carburetor housings, and motor parts. Machines include die casting and continuous casting machines and roll-over, squeeze, and shell molding machines.

Moves controls to start, set, or adjust casting, molding, or pressing machines. Loads die sections into machine, using equipment such as chain fall or hoist, and secures in position, using hand tools. Pours molten metal into cold-chamber machine or cylinders, using hand ladle. Connects water hose to cooling system of die, using hand tools. Loads metal ingots or aluminum bars into melting furnace and transfers molten metal to reservoir of die casting machine. Lines cylinder pot with asbestos strips and disk to prevent chilling. Stacks and mounts rotor core laminations over keyed mandrel of casting machine and removes and stamps rotor with identifying data. Preheats die sections with torch or electric heater. Removes castings from dies and dips castings in water to cool, using pliers or tongs. Obtains and moves specified pattern to workstation, manually or using hoist, and secures pattern to machine, using wrenches. Repairs or replaces worn or defective machine parts and dies. Inspects castings and core slots for defects, using fixed gauges. Cleans and lubricates casting machine and dies, using air hose and brushes.

GOE INFORMATION—Interest Area: 08. Industrial Production. **Work Group:** 08.02. Production Technology. **Personality Type—**Realistic. Realistic occupations frequently involve work activities that include practical, hands-on problems and solutions. They often deal with plants, animals, and real-world materials like wood, tools, and machinery. Many of the occupations require working outside and do not involve a lot of paperwork or working closely with others. **Work Values—**Independence; Moral Values; Supervision, Human Relations; Company Policies and Practices; Supervision, Technical. **Skills—**Operation Monitoring; Operation and Control; Equipment Selection; Installation; Repairing; Quality Control Analysis. **Abilities—***Cognitive:* Perceptual Speed; Time Sharing; Spatial Orientation; Flexibility of Closure; Memorization. *Psychomotor:* Control Precision; Arm-Hand Steadiness; Rate Control; Manual Dexterity; Reaction Time. *Physical:* Explosive Strength; Static Strength; Gross Body Coordination; Dynamic Strength; Extent Flexibility. *Sensory:* Depth Perception; Peripheral Vision; Visual Color Discrimination; Far Vision; Glare Sensitivity. **General Work Activities—***Information Input:* Monitoring Processes, Materials, or Surroundings; Inspecting Equipment, Structures, or Materials; Getting Information. *Mental Process:* Updating and Using Relevant Knowledge; Judging Qualities of Things, Services, or Other People's Work; Organizing, Planning, and Prioritizing. *Work Output:* Handling and Moving Objects; Controlling Machines and Processes; Repairing and Maintaining Mechanical Equipment. *Interacting with Others:* Communicating with Other Workers; Coordinating the Work and Activities of Others; Assisting and Caring for Others. **Physical Work Conditions—**Hazardous Equipment; Common Protective or Safety Attire; Minor Burns, Cuts, Bites, or Stings; Very Hot or Cold; Using Hands on Objects, Tools, or Controls. **Other Job Characteristics—**Degree of Automation; Pace Determined by Speed of Equipment; Importance of Repeating Same Tasks.

Experience—Job Zone 2. Some previous work-related skill, knowledge, or experience may be helpful, but usually is not needed. **Job Preparation:** SVP 4.0 to less than 6.0—six months to less than two years. **Knowledge—**Production and Processing; Mechanical; Physics; Building and Construction; Philosophy and Theology. **Instructional Programs—**No data available.

Related DOT Jobs—502.482-018 Rotor Casting-Machine Operator; 502.682-014 Casting-Machine Operator; 514.360-010 Die-Casting-Machine Setter; 514.382-010 Die-Casting-Machine Operator I; 518.380-010 Setter, Molding-and-Coremaking Machines.

51-4072.04 Metal Molding, Coremaking, and Casting Machine Operators and Tenders

- Education/Training Required: Short-term on-the-job training
- Employed: No data available.
- Annual Earnings: $22,340
- Growth: 9.8%
- Annual Job Openings: 38,000

Operate or tend metal molding, casting, or coremaking machines to mold or cast metal products, such as pipes, brake drums, and rods, and metal parts, such as automobile trim, carburetor housings, and motor parts. Machines include centrifugal casting machines, vacuum casting machines, turnover draw-type coremaking machines, conveyor-screw coremaking machines, and die casting machines.

Starts and operates furnace, oven, die casting, coremaking, metal molding, or rotating machines to pour metal or create molds and casts. Positions ladles or pourers and adjusts controls to regulate the flow of metal, sand, or coolant into mold. Positions, aligns, and secures molds or core boxes in holding devices or under pouring spouts and tubes, using hand tools. Removes casting from mold, mold from press, or core from core box, using tongs, pliers, or hydraulic ram or by inversion. Observes and records data from pyrometers, lights, and gauges to monitor molding process and adjust furnace temperature. Pours or loads metal or sand into melting pot, furnace, mold, core box, or hopper, using shovel, ladle, or machine. Fills core boxes and mold patterns with sand or powders, using ramming tools or pneumatic hammers, and removes excess. Inspects metal casts and molds for cracks, bubbles, or other defects and measures castings to ensure specifications are met. Assembles shell halves, patterns, and foundry flasks and reinforces core boxes, using glue, clamps, wire, bolts, rams, or machines. Skims or pours dross, slag, or impurities from molten metal, using ladle, rake, hoe, spatula, or spoon. Sprays, smokes, or coats molds with compounds to lubricate or insulate mold, using acetylene torches or sprayers. Smoothes and cleans inner surface of mold, using brush, scraper, air hose, or grinding wheel, and fills imperfections with refractory material. Weighs metals and powders and computes amounts of materials necessary to produce mixture of specified content. Requisitions molds and supplies; inventories and records finished products. Signals or directs other workers to load conveyor, spray molds, or remove ingots. Cuts spouts and pouring holes in molds and sizes hardened cores, using saws. Cleans, glues, and racks cores, ingots, or finished products for storage. Repairs or replaces damaged molds, pipes, belts, chains, or other equipment, using hand tools, hand-powered press, or jib crane.

GOE INFORMATION—Interest Area: 08. Industrial Production. **Work Group:** 08.02. Production Technology. **Personality Type**—Realistic. Realistic occupations frequently involve work activities that include practical, hands-on problems and solutions. They often deal with plants, animals, and real-world materials like wood, tools, and machinery. Many of the occupations require working outside and do not involve a lot of paperwork or working closely with others. **Work Values**—Moral Values; Supervision, Human Relations; Company Policies and Practices; Activity; Supervision, Technical. **Skills**—Operation Monitoring; Operation and Control; Repairing; Quality Control Analysis; Installation; Equipment Selection; Troubleshooting. **Abilities**—*Cognitive:* Selective Attention; Perceptual Speed; Flexibility of Closure; Time Sharing; Information Ordering. *Psychomotor:* Reaction Time; Response Orientation; Arm-Hand Steadiness; Multilimb Coordination; Speed of Limb Movement. *Physical:* Static Strength; Gross Body Equilibrium; Stamina; Dynamic Strength; Gross Body Coordination. *Sensory:* Auditory Attention; Visual Color Discrimination; Sound Localization; Hearing Sensitivity; Far Vision. **General Work Activities**—*Information Input:* Inspecting Equipment, Structures, or Materials; Monitoring Processes, Materials, or Surroundings; Identifying Objects, Actions, and Events. *Mental Process:* Evaluating Information Against Standards; Processing Information; Judging Qualities of Things, Services, or Other People's Work. *Work Output:* Handling and Moving Objects; Performing General Physical Activities; Controlling Machines and Processes. *Interacting with Others:* Communicating with Other Workers; Monitoring and Controlling Resources; Coordinating the Work and Activities of Others. **Physical Work Conditions**—Hazardous Equipment; Common Protective or Safety Attire; Very Hot or Cold; Hazardous Conditions; Minor Burns, Cuts, Bites, or Stings. **Other Job Characteristics**—Pace Determined by Speed of Equipment; Degree of Automation; Importance of Repeating Same Tasks.

Experience—Job Zone 1. No previous work-related skill, knowledge, or experience is needed. **Job Preparation:** SVP below 4.0—less than six months. **Knowledge**—Mechanical; Production and Processing; Building and Construction; Public Safety and Security; Foreign Language. **Instructional Programs**—No data available.

Related DOT Jobs—502.362-010 Shot Dropper; 502.382-010 Bullet-Slug-Casting-Machine Operator; 502.482-010 Caster; 502.482-014 Casting-Machine Operator, Automatic; 502.682-010 Bullet-Casting Operator; 502.685-010 Molder, Lead Ingot; 502.685-014 Remelter; 514.362-010 Pig-Machine Operator; 514.562-010 Centrifugal-Casting-Machine Operator III; 514.582-010 Vacuum Caster; 514.662-010 Casting Operator; 514.682-010 Casting-Wheel Operator; 514.685-010 Centrifugal-Casting-Machine Operator I; 514.685-014 Centrifugal-Casting-Machine Operator II; 514.685-018 Die-Casting-Machine Operator II; 518.682-010 Machine Molder; 518.685-014 Coremaker, Machine I; 518.685-018 Coremaker, Machine II; 518.685-022 Coremaker, Machine III; 518.685-026 Shell Molder; others.

51-4072.05 Casting Machine Set-Up Operators

- Education/Training Required: Postsecondary vocational training
- Employed: No data available.
- Annual Earnings: $22,340
- Growth: 9.8%
- Annual Job Openings: 38,000

Set up and operate machines to cast and assemble printing type.

Sets up matrices in assembly stick by hand according to specifications. Starts machine and monitors operation for proper functioning. Stops machine when galley is full or when strip is completed. Positions composing stick to length of line specified in casting instructions. Inserts and locks galley or matrix case into place on machine. Places reel of controller paper on holder, threads around reels, and attaches to winding roll. Removes and stores assembly stick, controller reel, and matrix case. Forwards galley to appropriate personnel for proofing.

GOE INFORMATION—Interest Area: 08. Industrial Production. **Work Group:** 08.02. Production Technology. **Personality Type**—Realistic. Realistic occupations frequently involve work activities that include practical, hands-on problems and solutions. They often deal with plants, animals, and real-world materials like wood, tools, and machinery. Many of the occupations require working outside and do not involve a lot of paperwork or working closely with others. **Work Values**—Independence; Moral Values; Supervision, Technical; Supervision, Human Relations; Company Policies and Practices. **Skills**—Operation Monitoring; Operation and Control; Installation. **Abilities**—*Cognitive:* Perceptual Speed.

Psychomotor: Manual Dexterity; Reaction Time; Arm-Hand Steadiness; Control Precision; Rate Control. *Physical:* Dynamic Flexibility; Dynamic Strength; Extent Flexibility; Static Strength; Gross Body Coordination. *Sensory:* Depth Perception; Peripheral Vision. **General Work Activities**—*Information Input:* Monitoring Processes, Materials, or Surroundings; Identifying Objects, Actions, and Events; Getting Information. *Mental Process:* Evaluating Information Against Standards; Updating and Using Relevant Knowledge; Analyzing Data or Information. *Work Output:* Handling and Moving Objects; Controlling Machines and Processes; Performing General Physical Activities. *Interacting with Others:* Communicating with Other Workers; Establishing and Maintaining Relationships; Coordinating the Work and Activities of Others. **Physical Work Conditions**—Hazardous Equipment; Distracting Sounds and Noise Levels; Using Hands on Objects, Tools, or Controls; Indoors; Standing. **Other Job Characteristics**—Pace Determined by Speed of Equipment; Degree of Automation; Importance of Repeating Same Tasks.

Experience—Job Zone 3. Previous work-related skill, knowledge, or experience is required. **Job Preparation:** SVP 6.0 to less than 7.0—more than one year and less than four years. **Knowledge**—Production and Processing; Mechanical. **Instructional Programs**—No data available.

Related DOT Jobs—654.382-010 Casting-Machine Operator; 654.582-010 Type-Casting Machine Operator.

51-4081.00 Multiple Machine Tool Setters, Operators, and Tenders, Metal and Plastic

- **Education/Training Required: Postsecondary vocational training**
- **Employed: 105,068**
- **Annual Earnings: $27,910**
- **Growth: 14.7%**
- **Annual Job Openings: 21,000**

Set up, operate, or tend more than one type of cutting or forming machine tool or robot.

No task data available.

GOE INFORMATION—**Interest Area:** 08. Industrial Production. **Work Group:** 08.02. Production Technology. **Note:** The Department of Labor has not collected some data for this job, so it has fewer details than the other descriptions.

Instructional Programs—Machine Shop Technology/Assistant; Machine Tool Technology/Machinist.

Related DOT Jobs—600.360-010 Machine Try-Out Setter; 600.360-014 Machine Setter; 600.380-018 Machine Set-Up Operator; 600.380-022 Machine Setter; 601.280-054 Tool-Machine Set-Up Operator; 602.280-010 Gear-Cutting-Machine Set-Up Operator, Tool; 602.380-010 Gear-Cutting-Machine Set-Up Operator; 602.382-010 Gear Hobber Set-Up Operator; 602.382-014 Gear-Generator Set-Up Operator, Spiral Bevel; 602.382-018 Gear-Generator Set-Up Operator, Straight Bevel; 602.382-022 Gear-Milling-Machine Set-Up Operator; 602.382-026 Gear-Shaper Set-Up Operator; 602.382-030 Gear-Shaver Set-Up Operator; 602.685-010 Gear-Cutting-Machine Operator, Production; 609.260-010 Gunsmith, Ballistics Laboratory; 609.682-010 Automatic-Wheel-Line Operator; 609.682-022 Machine Operator, Centrifugal-Control Switches; 609.685-018 Production Machine Tender; 609.685-022 Transfer-Machine Operator; 609.685-026 Trim-Machine Operator; others.

51-4081.01 Combination Machine Tool Setters and Set-Up Operators, Metal and Plastic

- **Education/Training Required: Moderate-term on-the-job training**
- **Employed: No data available.**
- **Annual Earnings: $27,910**
- **Growth: 14.7%**
- **Annual Job Openings: 21,000**

Set up or set up and operate more than one type of cutting or forming machine tool, such as gear hobbers, lathes, press brakes, and shearing and boring machines.

Sets up and operates lathes, cutters, borers, millers, grinders, presses, drills, and auxiliary machines to make metallic and plastic workpieces. Moves controls or mounts gears, cams, or templates in machine to set feed rate and cutting speed, depth, and angle. Monitors machine operation and moves controls to align and adjust position of workpieces and action of cutting tools. Selects, installs, and adjusts alignment of drills, cutters, dies, guides, and holding devices, using template, measuring instruments, and hand tools. Starts machine and turns handwheels or valves to engage feeding, cooling, and lubricating mechanisms. Reads blueprint or job order to determine product specifications and tooling instructions and to plan operational sequences. Measures and marks reference points and cutting lines on workpiece, using traced templates, compasses, and rules. Computes data, such as gear dimensions and machine settings, applying knowledge of shop mathematics. Inspects first-run workpieces and verifies conformance to specifications to check accuracy of machine setup. Lifts, positions, and secures workpieces in holding devices, using hoists and hand tools. Makes minor electrical and mechanical repairs and adjustments to machines and notifies supervisor when major service is required. Records operational data such as pressure readings, length of stroke, feeds, and speeds. Instructs operators or other workers in machine setup and operation.

GOE INFORMATION—**Interest Area:** 08. Industrial Production. **Work Group:** 08.02. Production Technology. **Personality Type**—Realistic. Realistic occupations frequently involve work activities that include practical, hands-on problems and solutions. They often deal with plants, animals, and real-world materials like wood, tools, and machinery. Many of the occupations require working outside and do not involve a lot of paperwork or working closely with others. **Work Values**—Moral Values; Supervision, Technical; Company Policies and Practices; Activity; Supervision, Human Relations. **Skills**—Operation Monitoring; Operation and Control; Quality Control Analysis; Repairing; Installation; Equipment Selection; Mathematics; Troubleshooting. **Abilities**—*Cognitive:* Selective Attention; Visualization; Perceptual Speed; Time Sharing; Mathematical Reasoning. *Psychomotor:* Reaction Time; Control Precision; Speed of Limb Movement; Manual Dexterity; Rate Control. *Physical:* Static Strength; Extent Flexibility; Gross Body Equilibrium; Trunk Strength; Explosive Strength. *Sensory:* Visual Color Discrimination; Auditory Attention; Hearing Sensitivity; Far Vision; Sound Localization. **General Work Activities**—*Information Input:* Monitoring Processes, Materials, or Surroundings; Getting Information; Inspecting Equipment, Structures, or Materials. *Mental Process:* Evaluating Information Against Standards; Processing Information; Analyzing Data or Information. *Work Output:* Handling and Moving Objects; Controlling Machines and Processes; Performing General Physical Activities. *Interacting with Others:* Teaching Others; Communicating with Other Workers; Establishing and Maintaining Relationships. **Physical Work Conditions**—Hazardous Equipment; Distracting Sounds and Noise Levels; Common Protective or Safety Attire; Minor Burns, Cuts, Bites, or Stings; Using Hands on Objects, Tools, or Controls. **Other Job Characteristics**—Degree of Automation; Pace Determined by Speed of Equipment; Importance of Repeating Same Tasks.

Experience—Job Zone 3. Previous work-related skill, knowledge, or experience is required. **Job Preparation:** SVP 6.0 to less than 7.0—more than one year and less than four years. **Knowledge**—Mechanical; Design; Production and Processing; Education and Training; Building and Construction. **Instructional Programs**—Machine Shop Technology/Assistant; Machine Tool Technology/Machinist.

Related DOT Jobs—600.360-010 Machine Try-Out Setter; 600.360-014 Machine Setter; 600.380-018 Machine Set-Up Operator; 600.380-022 Machine Setter; 601.280-054 Tool-Machine Set-Up Operator; 602.280-010 Gear-Cutting-Machine Set-Up Operator, Tool; 602.380-010 Gear-Cutting-Machine Set-Up Operator; 602.382-010 Gear Hobber Set-Up Operator; 602.382-014 Gear-Generator Set-Up Operator, Spiral Bevel; 602.382-018 Gear-Generator Set-Up Operator, Straight Bevel; 602.382-022 Gear-Milling-Machine Set-Up Operator; 602.382-026 Gear-Shaper Set-Up Operator; 602.382-030 Gear-Shaver Set-Up Operator; 616.360-022 Machine Setter; 616.380-018 Machine Operator I; 692.682-034 Electrode Turner-and-Finisher.

51-4081.02 Combination Machine Tool Operators and Tenders, Metal and Plastic

- **Education/Training Required: Moderate-term on-the-job training**
- **Employed: No data available.**
- **Annual Earnings: $27,910**
- **Growth: 14.7%**
- **Annual Job Openings: 21,000**

Operate or tend more than one type of cutting or forming machine tool which has been previously set up. Includes such machine tools as band saws, press brakes, slitting machines, drills, lathes, and boring machines.

Activates and tends or operates machines to cut, shape, thread, bore, drill, tap, bend, or mill metal or non-metallic material. Observes machine operation to detect workpiece defects or machine malfunction. Positions, adjusts, and secures workpiece against stops, on arbor, or in chuck, fixture, or automatic feeding mechanism manually or using hoist. Reads job specifications to determine machine adjustments and material requirements. Aligns layout marks with die or blade. Extracts or lifts jammed pieces from machine, using fingers, wire hooks, or lift bar. Inspects workpiece for defects and measures workpiece, using rule, template, or other measuring instruments to determine accuracy of machine operation. Adjusts machine components and changes worn accessories, such as cutting tools and brushes, using hand tools. Sets machine stops or guides to specified length as indicated by scale, rule, or template. Installs machine components, such as chucks, boring bars, or cutting tools, according to specifications, using hand tools. Removes burrs, sharp edges, rust, or scale from workpiece, using file, hand grinder, wire brush, or power tools. Performs minor machine maintenance, such as oiling or cleaning machines, dies, or workpieces or adding coolant to machine reservoir.

GOE INFORMATION—**Interest Area:** 08. Industrial Production. **Work Group:** 08.03. Production Work. **Personality Type**—Realistic. Realistic occupations frequently involve work activities that include practical, hands-on problems and solutions. They often deal with plants, animals, and real-world materials like wood, tools, and machinery. Many of the

occupations require working outside and do not involve a lot of paperwork or working closely with others. **Work Values**—Moral Values; Independence; Company Policies and Practices; Supervision, Human Relations; Activity. **Skills**—Operation Monitoring; Operation and Control; Installation; Quality Control Analysis. **Abilities**—*Cognitive:* Perceptual Speed; Problem Sensitivity; Spatial Orientation; Time Sharing; Memorization. *Psychomotor:* Rate Control; Manual Dexterity; Control Precision; Multilimb Coordination; Reaction Time. *Physical:* Explosive Strength; Dynamic Flexibility; Static Strength; Extent Flexibility; Gross Body Coordination. *Sensory:* Peripheral Vision; Depth Perception. **General Work Activities**—*Information Input:* Inspecting Equipment, Structures, or Materials; Monitoring Processes, Materials, or Surroundings; Getting Information. *Mental Process:* Updating and Using Relevant Knowledge; Evaluating Information Against Standards; Judging Qualities of Things, Services, or Other People's Work. *Work Output:* Handling and Moving Objects; Controlling Machines and Processes; Performing General Physical Activities. *Interacting with Others:* Communicating with Other Workers; Performing Administrative Activities; Coordinating the Work and Activities of Others. **Physical Work Conditions**—Hazardous Equipment; Distracting Sounds and Noise Levels; Minor Burns, Cuts, Bites, or Stings; Common Protective or Safety Attire; Using Hands on Objects, Tools, or Controls. **Other Job Characteristics**—Pace Determined by Speed of Equipment; Degree of Automation; Importance of Repeating Same Tasks.

Experience—Job Zone 2. Some previous work-related skill, knowledge, or experience may be helpful, but usually is not needed. **Job Preparation:** SVP 4.0 to less than 6.0—six months to less than two years. **Knowledge**—Production and Processing; Mechanical; Building and Construction; Design; Engineering and Technology. **Instructional Programs**—Machine Shop Technology/Assistant; Machine Tool Technology/Machinist.

Related DOT Jobs—602.685-010 Gear-Cutting-Machine Operator, Production; 609.682-010 Automatic-Wheel-Line Operator; 609.682-022 Machine Operator, Centrifugal-Control Switches; 609.685-018 Production Machine Tender; 609.685-022 Transfer-Machine Operator; 609.685-026 Trim-Machine Operator; 619.685-062 Machine Operator II.

51-4111.00 Tool and Die Makers

- **Education/Training Required: Long-term on-the-job training**
- **Employed: 129,579**
- **Annual Earnings: $41,620**
- **Growth: 2.2%**
- **Annual Job Openings: 6,000**

Analyze specifications, lay out metal stock, set up and operate machine tools, and fit and assemble parts to make and repair dies, cutting tools, jigs, fixtures, gauges, and machinists' hand tools.

Studies blueprints or specifications and visualizes shape of die, part, or tool. Computes dimensions of assembly and plans sequence of operations. Measures, marks, and scribes metal or plastic stock to lay out machining, using instruments such as protractors, micrometers, scribes, and rulers. Sets up and operates machine tools, such as lathes, milling machines, shapers, and grinders, to machine parts. Lifts, positions, and secures machined parts on surface plate or worktable, using hoist, vises, v-blocks, or angle plates. Smoothes and polishes flat and contoured surfaces of parts or tools, using scrapers, abrasive stones, files, emery cloth, or power grinder. Verifies dimensions, alignments, and clearances of finished parts, using measuring instruments such as calipers, gauge blocks, micrometers, and dial indicators. Fits and assembles parts, using bolts, glue, and other fasteners and hand tools, such as hammers and wrenches. Sets pyrometer controls of heat-treating furnace and feeds or places parts, tools, or assemblies into furnace to harden. Repairs or modifies tools and dies, using machine tools and hand tools. Designs tools, jigs, fixtures, and templates for use as work aids. Cuts, shapes, and trims blank or block to specified length or shape, using power saws, power shears, rule, and hand tools. Casts plastic tools or parts or tungsten-carbide cutting tips, using pre-made molds. Sets up and operates drill press to drill and tap holes in parts for assembly. Operates power press to test completed dies and applies pigment to die to indicate high spots that require reworking. Inspects die for smoothness, contour conformity, and defects by touch or visually, using loupe or microscope. Connects wiring and hydraulic lines to install electrical and hydraulic components. Fabricates saw blades, using power roller to straighten blade stock, punch press to cut teeth, and power grinder to sharpen teeth.

GOE INFORMATION—Interest Area: 08. Industrial Production. **Work Group:** 08.04. Metal and Plastics Machining Technology. **Personality Type**—Realistic. Realistic occupations frequently involve work activities that include practical, hands-on problems and solutions. They often deal with plants, animals, and real-world materials like wood, tools, and machinery. Many of the occupations require working outside and do not involve a lot of paperwork or working closely with others. **Work Values**—Moral Values; Supervision, Technical; Company Policies and Practices; Advancement; Independence. **Skills**—Operation and Control; Repairing; Equipment Selection; Installation; Technology Design; Quality Control Analysis; Operation Monitoring. **Abilities**—*Cognitive:* Mathematical Reasoning; Number Facility; Visualization; Information Ordering; Perceptual Speed. *Psychomotor:* Manual Dexterity; Control Precision; Wrist-Finger Speed; Finger Dexterity; Speed of Limb Movement. *Physical:* Static Strength; Dynamic Strength; Trunk Strength; Dynamic Flexibility; Explosive Strength. *Sensory:* Near Vision. **General Work Activities**—*Information Input:* Getting Information; Monitoring Processes, Materials, or Surroundings; Inspecting Equipment, Structures, or Materials. *Mental Process:* Updating and Using Relevant Knowledge; Organizing, Planning, and Prioritizing; Evaluating Information Against Standards. *Work Output:* Handling and Moving Objects; Controlling Machines and Processes; Performing General Physical Activities. *Interacting with Others:* Communicating with Other Workers; Coordinating the Work and Activities of Others; Performing Administrative Activities. **Physical Work Conditions**—Hazardous Equipment; Using Hands on Objects, Tools, or Controls; Common Protective or Safety Attire; Indoors; Making Repetitive Motions. **Other Job Characteristics**—Pace Determined by Speed of Equipment; Importance of Repeating Same Tasks; Importance of Being Exact or Accurate.

Experience—Job Zone 4. A minimum of two to four years of work-related skill, knowledge, or experience is needed. **Job Preparation:** SVP 7.0 to less than 8.0—two years to less than 10 years. **Knowledge**—Mechanical; Production and Processing; Building and Construction; Design; Engineering and Technology. **Instructional Programs**—Tool and Die Technology/Technician.

Related DOT Jobs—601.260-010 Tool-and-Die Maker; 601.260-014 Tool-and-Die-Maker Apprentice; 601.280-010 Die Maker, Stamping; 601.280-014 Die Maker, Trim; 601.280-018 Die Maker, Wire Drawing; 601.280-022 Die Sinker; 601.280-030 Mold Maker, Die-Casting and Plastic Molding; 601.280-034 Tap-and-Die-Maker Technician; 601.280-042 Tool Maker; 601.280-058 Tool-Maker Apprentice; 601.281-010 Die Maker, Bench, Stamping; 601.281-014 Die-Try-Out Worker, Stamping; 601.281-026 Tool Maker, Bench; 601.380-010 Carbide Operator; 601.381-010 Die Finisher; 601.381-014 Die Maker; 601.381-022 Die-Maker Apprentice; 601.381-026 Plastic Tool Maker; 601.381-030 Plastic-Fixture Builder; 601.381-034 Saw Maker; others.

51-4121.00 Welders, Cutters, Solderers, and Brazers

- **Education/Training Required: Long-term on-the-job training**
- **Employed: 446,482**
- **Annual Earnings: $28,490**
- **Growth: 19.3%**
- **Annual Job Openings: 51,000**

Use hand-welding, flame-cutting, hand-soldering, or brazing equipment to weld or join metal components or to fill holes, indentations, or seams of fabricated metal products.

No task data available.

GOE INFORMATION—Interest Area: 08. Industrial Production. **Work Group:** 08.03. Production Work. **Note:** The Department of Labor has not collected some data for this job, so it has fewer details than the other descriptions.

Instructional Programs—Welding Technology/Welder.

Related DOT Jobs—No related DOT jobs.

51-4121.01 Welders, Production

- **Education/Training Required: Short-term on-the-job training**
- **Employed: No data available.**
- **Annual Earnings: $28,490**
- **Growth: 19.3%**
- **Annual Job Openings: 51,000**

Assemble and weld metal parts on production line, using welding equipment requiring only a limited knowledge of welding techniques.

Welds or tack welds metal parts together, using spot-welding gun or hand, electric, or gas welding equipment. Guides and directs flame or electrodes on or across workpiece to straighten, bend, melt, or build up metal. Fuses parts together, seals tension points, and adds metal to build up parts. Connects hoses from torch to tanks of oxygen and fuel gas and turns valves to release mixture. Ignites torch and regulates flow of gas and air to obtain desired temperature, size, and color of flame. Selects, positions, and secures torch, cutting tips, or welding rod according to type, thickness, area, and desired temperature of metal. Preheats workpieces preparatory to welding or bending, using torch. Positions and secures workpiece, using hoist, crane, wire and banding machine, or hand tools. Fills cavities or corrects malformation in lead parts and hammers out bulges and bends in metal workpieces. Dismantles metal assemblies or cuts scrap metal, using thermal-cutting equipment such as flame-cutting torch or plasma-arc equipment. Examines workpiece for defects and measures workpiece with straightedge or template to ensure conformance with specifications. Signals crane operator to move large workpieces. Climbs ladders or works on scaffolds to disassemble structures.

GOE INFORMATION—Interest Area: 08. Industrial Production. **Work Group:** 08.03. Production Work. **Personality Type**—Realistic. Realistic occupations frequently involve work activities that include practical, hands-on problems and solutions. They often deal with plants, animals, and real-world materials like wood, tools, and machinery. Many of the occupations require working outside and do not involve a lot of paperwork or working closely with others. **Work Values**—Moral Values; Company Policies and Practices; Activity; Supervision, Technical; Independence. **Skills**—Operation Monitoring; Operation and Control; Equipment Selection. **Abilities**—*Cognitive:* Perceptual Speed; Spatial Orientation; Visualization; Selective Attention. *Psychomotor:* Arm-Hand

Steadiness; Manual Dexterity; Rate Control; Control Precision; Speed of Limb Movement. *Physical:* Dynamic Strength; Explosive Strength; Gross Body Equilibrium; Dynamic Flexibility; Extent Flexibility. *Sensory:* Depth Perception; Visual Color Discrimination; Glare Sensitivity; Peripheral Vision; Near Vision. **General Work Activities**—*Information Input:* Inspecting Equipment, Structures, or Materials; Monitoring Processes, Materials, or Surroundings; Getting Information. *Mental Process:* Updating and Using Relevant Knowledge; Evaluating Information Against Standards; Judging Qualities of Things, Services, or Other People's Work. *Work Output:* Handling and Moving Objects; Performing General Physical Activities; Controlling Machines and Processes. *Interacting with Others:* Communicating with Other Workers; Coordinating the Work and Activities of Others; Assisting and Caring for Others. **Physical Work Conditions**—Common Protective or Safety Attire; Hazardous Equipment; Distracting Sounds and Noise Levels; Climbing Ladders, Scaffolds, Poles, etc.; High Places. **Other Job Characteristics**—Pace Determined by Speed of Equipment; Degree of Automation; Importance of Repeating Same Tasks.

Experience—Job Zone 1. No previous work-related skill, knowledge, or experience is needed. **Job Preparation:** SVP below 4.0—less than six months. **Knowledge**—Mechanical; Production and Processing; Building and Construction; Physics; Public Safety and Security. **Instructional Programs**—Welding Technology/Welder.

Related DOT Jobs—613.667-010 Liner Assembler; 709.684-086 Torch-Straightener-and-Heater; 727.684-022 Lead Burner; 810.664-010 Welder, Gun; 810.684-010 Welder, Tack; 816.684-010 Thermal Cutter, Hand II; 819.684-010 Welder, Production Line.

51-4121.02 *Welders and Cutters*

- **Education/Training Required: Long-term on-the-job training**
- **Employed: No data available.**
- **Annual Earnings: $28,490**
- **Growth: 19.3%**
- **Annual Job Openings: 51,000**

Use hand-welding and flame-cutting equipment to weld together metal components and parts or to cut, trim, or scarf metal objects to dimensions as specified by layouts, work orders, or blueprints.

Welds metal parts or components together, using brazing, gas, or arc-welding equipment. Guides electrodes or torch along weld line at specified speed and angle to weld, melt, cut, or trim metal. Reviews layouts, blueprints, diagrams, or work orders in preparation for welding or cutting metal components. Selects and inserts electrode or gas nozzle into holder and connects hoses and cables to obtain gas or specified amperage, voltage, or polarity. Selects and installs torch, torch tip, filler rod, and flux according to welding chart specifications or type and thickness of metal. Connects and turns regulator valves to activate and adjust gas flow and pressure to obtain desired flame. Ignites torch or starts power supply and strikes arc. Repairs broken or cracked parts, fills holes, and increases size of metal parts, using welding equipment. Preheats workpiece, using hand torch or heating furnace. Welds in flat, horizontal, vertical, or overhead position. Positions workpieces and clamps together or assembles in jigs or fixtures. Chips or grinds off excess weld, slag, or spatter, using hand scraper or power chipper, portable grinder, or arc-cutting equipment. Inspects finished workpiece for conformance to specifications. Cleans or degreases parts, using wire brush, portable grinder, or chemical bath.

GOE INFORMATION—Interest Area: 08. Industrial Production. **Work Group:** 08.03. Production Work. **Personality Type**—Realistic. Realistic occupations frequently involve work activities that include practical, hands-on problems and solutions. They often deal with plants, animals, and real-world materials like wood, tools, and machinery. Many of the occupations require working outside and do not involve a lot of paperwork or working closely with others. **Work Values**—Moral Values; Activity; Company Policies and Practices; Advancement; Supervision, Technical. **Skills**—Operation Monitoring; Operation and Control; Repairing; Installation; Equipment Selection. **Abilities**—*Cognitive:* Visualization; Spatial Orientation; Perceptual Speed; Memorization; Selective Attention. *Psychomotor:* Arm-Hand Steadiness; Rate Control; Control Precision; Manual Dexterity; Multilimb Coordination. *Physical:* Explosive Strength; Dynamic Flexibility; Dynamic Strength; Extent Flexibility; Trunk Strength. *Sensory:* Glare Sensitivity; Depth Perception; Near Vision; Peripheral Vision; Visual Color Discrimination. **General Work Activities**—*Information Input:* Monitoring Processes, Materials, or Surroundings; Getting Information; Identifying Objects, Actions, and Events. *Mental Process:* Judging Qualities of Things, Services, or Other People's Work; Updating and Using Relevant Knowledge; Evaluating Information Against Standards. *Work Output:* Handling and Moving Objects; Controlling Machines and Processes; Performing General Physical Activities. *Interacting with Others:* Communicating with Other Workers; Performing Administrative Activities; Coordinating the Work and Activities of Others. **Physical Work Conditions**—Hazardous Equipment; Minor Burns, Cuts, Bites, or Stings; Common Protective or Safety Attire; Hazardous Conditions; Using Hands on Objects, Tools, or Controls. **Other Job Characteristics**—Importance of Repeating Same Tasks; Degree of Automation; Pace Determined by Speed of Equipment.

Experience—Job Zone 2. Some previous work-related skill, knowledge, or experience may be helpful, but usually is not needed. **Job Preparation:** SVP 4.0 to less than 6.0—six months to less than two years. **Knowledge**—Building and Construction; Mechanical; Design; Production and Processing; Physics. **Instructional Programs**—Welding Technology/Welder.

Related DOT Jobs—810.384-010 Welder Apprentice, Arc; 810.384-014 Welder, Arc; 811.684-010 Welder Apprentice, Gas; 811.684-014 Welder, Gas; 816.364-010 Arc Cutter; 816.464-010 Thermal Cutter, Hand I; 819.384-010 Welder, Combination; 819.384-014 Welder Apprentice, Combination.

51-4121.03 *Welder-Fitters*

- **Education/Training Required: Long-term on-the-job training**
- **Employed: No data available.**
- **Annual Earnings: $28,490**
- **Growth: 19.3%**
- **Annual Job Openings: 51,000**

Lay out, fit, and fabricate metal components to assemble structural forms, such as machinery frames, bridge parts, and pressure vessels, using knowledge of welding techniques, metallurgy, and engineering requirements. Includes experimental welders who analyze engineering drawings and specifications to plan welding operations where procedural information is unavailable.

Installs or repairs equipment, such as lead pipes, valves, floors, and tank linings. Lays out, positions, and secures parts and assemblies according to specifications, using straightedge, combination square, calipers, and ruler. Analyzes engineering drawings and specifications to plan layout, assembly, and welding operations. Inspects grooves, angles, or gap allowances, using micrometer, caliper, and precision measuring instruments. Determines required equipment and welding method, applying knowledge of metallurgy, geometry, and welding techniques. Observes tests on welded surfaces such as hydrostatic, X-ray, and dimension tolerance to evaluate weld quality and conformance to specifications. Develops templates and other work aids to hold and align parts. Ignites torch and adjusts valves, amperage, or voltage to obtain desired flame or arc. Tack-welds or welds components and assemblies, using electric, gas, arc, or other welding equipment. Heats, forms, and dresses metal parts, using hand tools, torch, or arc-welding equipment. Cuts workpiece, using powered saws, hand shears, or chipping knife. Welds components in flat, vertical, or overhead positions. Melts lead bar, wire, or scrap to add lead to joint or to extrude melted scrap into reusable form. Removes rough spots from workpiece, using portable grinder, hand file, or scraper.

GOE INFORMATION—Interest Area: 08. Industrial Production. **Work Group:** 08.03. Production Work. **Personality Type—**Realistic. Realistic occupations frequently involve work activities that include practical, hands-on problems and solutions. They often deal with plants, animals, and real-world materials like wood, tools, and machinery. Many of the occupations require working outside and do not involve a lot of paperwork or working closely with others. **Work Values—**Company Policies and Practices; Activity; Advancement; Moral Values; Supervision, Technical. **Skills—**Repairing; Equipment Selection; Installation; Quality Control Analysis; Mathematics. **Abilities—***Cognitive:* Originality; Spatial Orientation; Visualization; Number Facility; Memorization. *Psychomotor:* Arm-Hand Steadiness; Rate Control; Multilimb Coordination; Manual Dexterity; Speed of Limb Movement. *Physical:* Gross Body Equilibrium; Extent Flexibility; Dynamic Strength; Stamina; Dynamic Flexibility. *Sensory:* Depth Perception; Far Vision; Glare Sensitivity; Near Vision; Peripheral Vision. **General Work Activities—***Information Input:* Getting Information; Monitoring Processes, Materials, or Surroundings; Inspecting Equipment, Structures, or Materials. *Mental Process:* Judging Qualities of Things, Services, or Other People's Work; Analyzing Data or Information; Making Decisions and Solving Problems. *Work Output:* Handling and Moving Objects; Controlling Machines and Processes; Performing General Physical Activities. *Interacting with Others:* Communicating with Other Workers; Coordinating the Work and Activities of Others; Teaching Others. **Physical Work Conditions—**Hazardous Equipment; Minor Burns, Cuts, Bites, or Stings; Common Protective or Safety Attire; Hazardous Conditions; Very Hot or Cold. **Other Job Characteristics—**Importance of Repeating Same Tasks; Degree of Automation; Importance of Being Exact or Accurate.

Experience—Job Zone 4. A minimum of two to four years of work-related skill, knowledge, or experience is needed. **Job Preparation:** SVP 7.0 to less than 8.0—two years to less than 10 years. **Knowledge—**Design; Building and Construction; Production and Processing; Mechanical; Engineering and Technology. **Instructional Programs—**Welding Technology/Welder.

Related DOT Jobs—819.281-010 Lead Burner; 819.281-014 Lead-Burner Apprentice; 819.281-022 Welder, Experimental; 819.361-010 Welder-Fitter; 819.361-014 Welder-Fitter Apprentice; 819.381-010 Welder-Assembler.

51-4121.04 *Solderers*

- **Education/Training Required: Short-term on-the-job training**
- **Employed: No data available.**
- **Annual Earnings: $28,490**
- **Growth: 19.3%**
- **Annual Job Openings: 51,000**

Solder together components to assemble fabricated metal products, using soldering iron.

Melts and applies solder along adjoining edges of workpieces to solder joints, using soldering iron, gas torch, or electric-ultrasonic equipment. Melts and applies solder to fill holes, indentations, and seams of fabricated metal products, using soldering equipment. Heats soldering iron or workpiece to specified temperature for soldering, using gas flame or electric current. Dips workpieces into molten solder or places solder strip

between seams and heats seam with iron to band items together. Aligns and clamps workpieces together, using rule, square, or hand tools, or positions items in fixtures, jigs, or vise. Applies flux to workpiece surfaces in preparation for soldering. Grinds, cuts, buffs, or bends edges of workpieces to be joined to ensure snug fit, using power grinder and hand tools. Melts and separates soldered joints to repair misaligned or damaged assemblies, using soldering equipment. Removes workpieces from molten solder and holds parts together until color indicates that solder has set. Cleans tip of soldering iron, using chemical solution or cleaning compound. Cleans workpieces, using chemical solution, file, wire brush, or grinder.

GOE INFORMATION—Interest Area: 08. Industrial Production. **Work Group:** 08.03. Production Work. **Personality Type—**Realistic. Realistic occupations frequently involve work activities that include practical, hands-on problems and solutions. They often deal with plants, animals, and real-world materials like wood, tools, and machinery. Many of the occupations require working outside and do not involve a lot of paperwork or working closely with others. **Work Values—**Moral Values; Activity; Independence; Company Policies and Practices; Supervision, Technical. **Skills—**Operation and Control; Equipment Selection; Operation Monitoring; Installation. **Abilities—***Cognitive:* Visualization; Spatial Orientation. *Psychomotor:* Manual Dexterity; Finger Dexterity; Arm-Hand Steadiness; Wrist-Finger Speed; Speed of Limb Movement. *Physical:* Dynamic Strength; Extent Flexibility; Static Strength; Explosive Strength; Dynamic Flexibility. *Sensory:* Visual Color Discrimination; Near Vision; Sound Localization; Glare Sensitivity. **General Work Activities—***Information Input:* Monitoring Processes, Materials, or Surroundings; Inspecting Equipment, Structures, or Materials; Identifying Objects, Actions, and Events. *Mental Process:* Analyzing Data or Information; Thinking Creatively; Organizing, Planning, and Prioritizing. *Work Output:* Handling and Moving Objects; Controlling Machines and Processes; Performing General Physical Activities. *Interacting with Others:* Monitoring and Controlling Resources; Establishing and Maintaining Relationships; Communicating with Other Workers. **Physical Work Conditions—**Common Protective or Safety Attire; Using Hands on Objects, Tools, or Controls; Contaminants; Making Repetitive Motions; Hazardous Equipment. **Other Job Characteristics—**Importance of Repeating Same Tasks; Pace Determined by Speed of Equipment; Degree of Automation.

Experience—Job Zone 1. No previous work-related skill, knowledge, or experience is needed. **Job Preparation:** SVP below 4.0—less than six months. **Knowledge—**Building and Construction; Production and Processing; Mechanical; Chemistry; Engineering and Technology. **Instructional Programs—**Welding Technology/Welder.

Related DOT Jobs—736.684-038 Solderer, Barrel Ribs; 739.684-054 Deicer Finisher; 813.684-014 Solderer-Assembler; 813.684-018 Solderer-Dipper; 813.684-022 Solderer, Production Line; 813.684-026 Solderer, Torch I; 813.684-030 Solderer, Ultrasonic, Hand.

51-4121.05 *Brazers*

- **Education/Training Required: Short-term on-the-job training**
- **Employed: No data available.**
- **Annual Earnings: $28,490**
- **Growth: 19.3%**
- **Annual Job Openings: 51,000**

Braze together components to assemble fabricated metal parts, using torch or welding machine and flux.

Guides torch and rod along joint of workpieces to heat to brazing temperature, melt braze alloy, and bond workpieces together. Adjusts electric current and timing cycle of resistance-welding machine to heat metal to bonding temperature. Selects torch tip, flux, and brazing alloy from data charts or work order. Connects hoses from torch to regulator valves and cylinders of oxygen and specified fuel gas—acetylene or natural. Turns valves to start flow of gases, lights flame, and adjusts valves to obtain desired color and size of flame. Brushes flux onto joint of workpiece or dips braze rod into flux to prevent oxidation of metal. Melts and separates brazed joints to remove and straighten damaged or misaligned components, using hand torch or furnace. Aligns and secures workpieces in fixtures, jigs, or vise, using rule, square, or template. Examines seam and rebrazes defective joints or broken parts. Cleans joints of workpieces, using wire brush or by dipping them into cleaning solution. Removes workpiece from fixture, using tongs, and cools workpiece, using air or water. Cuts carbon electrodes to specified size and shape, using cutoff saw.

GOE INFORMATION—Interest Area: 08. Industrial Production. **Work Group:** 08.03. Production Work. **Personality Type—**Realistic. Realistic occupations frequently involve work activities that include practical, hands-on problems and solutions. They often deal with plants, animals, and real-world materials like wood, tools, and machinery. Many of the occupations require working outside and do not involve a lot of paperwork or working closely with others. **Work Values—**Moral Values; Activity; Independence; Company Policies and Practices; Supervision, Technical. **Skills—**Operation and Control; Operation Monitoring; Equipment Selection; Installation. **Abilities—***Cognitive:* Visualization; Perceptual Speed. *Psychomotor:* Arm-Hand Steadiness; Speed of Limb Movement; Control Precision; Reaction Time; Manual Dexterity. *Physical:* Dynamic Strength; Extent Flexibility; Static Strength; Gross Body Equilibrium; Stamina. *Sensory:* Glare Sensitivity; Visual Color Discrimination; Near Vision. **General Work Activities—***Information Input:* Monitoring Processes, Materials, or Surroundings; Inspecting Equipment, Structures, or Materials; Identifying Objects, Actions, and Events. *Mental Process:* Evaluating Information Against Standards; Analyzing Data or Information; Updating and Using Relevant Knowledge. *Work Output:* Handling and Moving Objects; Controlling Machines and Processes; Performing General Physical Activities. *Interacting with Others:* Communicating with Other Workers; Establishing and Maintaining Relationships; Coordinating the Work and Activities of Others. **Physical Work Conditions—**Common Protective or Safety Attire; Hazardous Conditions; Hazardous Equipment; Using Hands on Objects, Tools, or Controls; Specialized Protective or Safety Attire. **Other Job Characteristics—**Consequence of Error; Importance of Repeating Same Tasks; Importance of Being Exact or Accurate.

Experience—Job Zone 2. Some previous work-related skill, knowledge, or experience may be helpful, but usually is not needed. **Job Preparation:** SVP 4.0 to less than 6.0—six months to less than two years. **Knowledge—**Engineering and Technology; Building and Construction; Mechanical; Chemistry; Production and Processing. **Instructional Programs—**Welding Technology/Welder.

Related DOT Jobs—813.682-010 Brazer, Resistance; 813.684-010 Brazer, Assembler.

51-4122.00 Welding, Soldering, and Brazing Machine Setters, Operators, and Tenders

- Education/Training Required: Moderate-term on-the-job training
- Employed: 74,361
- Annual Earnings: $28,220
- Growth: 15.1%
- Annual Job Openings: 9,000

Set up, operate, or tend welding, soldering, or brazing machines or robots that weld, braze, solder, or heat-treat metal products, components, or assemblies.

No task data available.

GOE INFORMATION—Interest Area: 08. Industrial Production. **Work Group:** 08.02. Production Technology. **Note:** The Department of Labor has not collected some data for this job, so it has fewer details than the other descriptions.

Instructional Programs—Welding Technology/Welder.

Related DOT Jobs—614.684-010 Billet Assembler; 706.685-010 Type-Soldering-Machine Tender; 715.685-058 Solderer; 726.362-014 Wave-Soldering Machine Operator; 726.684-094 Solder Deposit Operator; 726.685-038 Reflow Operator; 727.662-010 Lead Burner, Machine; 810.382-010 Welding-Machine Operator, Arc; 811.482-010 Welding-Machine Operator, Gas; 812.360-010 Welder Setter, Resistance Machine; 812.682-010 Welding-Machine Operator, Resistance; 813.360-010 Brazing-Machine Setter; 813.360-014 Setter, Induction-Heating Equipment; 813.382-010 Brazer, Induction; 813.382-014 Brazing-Machine Operator; 813.482-010 Brazer, Furnace; 813.685-010 Brazer, Controlled Atmospheric Furnace; 814.382-010 Welding-Machine Operator, Friction; 814.682-010 Welding-Machine Operator, Ultrasonic; 814.684-010 Welder, Explosion; others.

51-4122.01 Welding Machine Setters and Set-Up Operators

- Education/Training Required: Postsecondary vocational training
- Employed: No data available.
- Annual Earnings: $28,220
- Growth: 15.1%
- Annual Job Openings: 9,000

Set up or set up and operate welding machines that join or bond together components to fabricate metal products or assemblies according to specifications and blueprints.

Tests products and records test results and operational data on specified forms. Sets up and operates welding machines that join or bond components to fabricate metal products or assemblies. Turns and presses controls, such as cranks, knobs, and buttons, to adjust and activate welding process. Feeds workpiece into welding machine to join or bond components. Observes and listens to welding machine and its gauges to ensure welding process meets specifications. Operates welding machine to produce trial workpieces used to examine and test. Positions and adjusts fixtures, attachments, or workpieces on machine, using hand tools. Lays out, fits, or tacks workpieces together, using hand tools. Stops and opens holding device on welding machine, using hand tools. Examines metal product or assemblies to ensure specifications are met. Adds components, chemicals, and solutions to welding machine, using hand tools. Tends auxiliary equipment used in welding process. Cleans and maintains workpieces and welding machine parts, using hand tools and equipment. Devises and builds fixtures used to bond components during the welding process.

GOE INFORMATION—Interest Area: 08. Industrial Production. **Work Group:** 08.02. Production Technology. **Personality Type—**Realistic. Realistic occupations frequently involve work activities that include practical, hands-on problems and solutions. They often deal with plants, animals, and real-world materials like wood, tools, and machinery. Many of the occupations require working outside and do not involve a lot of paperwork or working closely with others. **Work Values—**Moral Values;

Independence; Company Policies and Practices; Supervision, Technical; Supervision, Human Relations. **Skills**—Equipment Selection; Operation Monitoring; Operation and Control; Quality Control Analysis; Installation. **Abilities**—*Cognitive:* Perceptual Speed; Spatial Orientation; Visualization; Information Ordering; Time Sharing. *Psychomotor:* Manual Dexterity; Rate Control; Reaction Time; Arm-Hand Steadiness; Multilimb Coordination. *Physical:* Dynamic Flexibility; Static Strength; Explosive Strength; Dynamic Strength; Extent Flexibility. *Sensory:* Hearing Sensitivity; Sound Localization; Auditory Attention; Depth Perception; Peripheral Vision. **General Work Activities**—*Information Input:* Inspecting Equipment, Structures, or Materials; Monitoring Processes, Materials, or Surroundings; Identifying Objects, Actions, and Events. *Mental Process:* Judging Qualities of Things, Services, or Other People's Work; Evaluating Information Against Standards; Updating and Using Relevant Knowledge. *Work Output:* Handling and Moving Objects; Controlling Machines and Processes; Performing General Physical Activities. *Interacting with Others:* Communicating with Other Workers; Performing Administrative Activities; Establishing and Maintaining Relationships. **Physical Work Conditions**—Hazardous Equipment; Distracting Sounds and Noise Levels; Common Protective or Safety Attire; Hazardous Conditions; Using Hands on Objects, Tools, or Controls. **Other Job Characteristics**—Pace Determined by Speed of Equipment; Degree of Automation; Importance of Repeating Same Tasks.

Experience—Job Zone 3. Previous work-related skill, knowledge, or experience is required. **Job Preparation:** SVP 6.0 to less than 7.0—more than one year and less than four years. **Knowledge**—Mechanical; Production and Processing; Chemistry; Building and Construction; Design. **Instructional Programs**—Welding Technology/Welder.

Related DOT Jobs—727.662-010 Lead Burner, Machine; 810.382-010 Welding-Machine Operator, Arc; 811.482-010 Welding-Machine Operator, Gas; 812.360-010 Welder Setter, Resistance Machine; 812.682-010 Welding-Machine Operator, Resistance; 815.380-010 Welder Setter, Electron-Beam Machine; 815.382-010 Welding-Machine Operator, Electron Beam.

51-4122.02 Welding Machine Operators and Tenders

- **Education/Training Required: Moderate-term on-the-job training**
- **Employed: No data available.**
- **Annual Earnings: $28,220**
- **Growth: 15.1%**
- **Annual Job Openings: 9,000**

Operate or tend welding machines that join or bond together components to fabricate metal products and assemblies according to specifications and blueprints.

Operates or tends welding machines that join or bond components to fabricate metal products and assemblies. Turns and presses knobs and buttons to adjust and start welding machine. Observes and listens to welding machine and its controls to ensure welding process meets specifications. Enters operating instructions into computer to adjust and start welding machine. Positions and adjusts fixtures, attachments, or workpiece on machine, using hand tools and measuring devices. Reads production schedule and specifications to ascertain product to be fabricated. Stops and opens holding device on welding machine, using hand tools. Inspects metal workpiece to ensure specifications are met, using measuring devices. Tends auxiliary equipment used in the welding process. Adds chemicals or solutions to welding machine to join or bind components. Cleans and maintains workpieces and welding machine

parts, using hand tools and equipment. Transfers components, metal products, and assemblies, using moving equipment.

GOE INFORMATION—**Interest Area:** 08. Industrial Production. **Work Group:** 08.03. Production Work. **Personality Type**—Realistic. Realistic occupations frequently involve work activities that include practical, hands-on problems and solutions. They often deal with plants, animals, and real-world materials like wood, tools, and machinery. Many of the occupations require working outside and do not involve a lot of paperwork or working closely with others. **Work Values**—Moral Values; Independence; Company Policies and Practices; Supervision, Human Relations; Activity. **Skills**—Operation and Control; Operation Monitoring; Equipment Selection. **Abilities**—*Cognitive:* Perceptual Speed; Spatial Orientation; Memorization; Information Ordering; Problem Sensitivity. *Psychomotor:* Control Precision; Manual Dexterity; Reaction Time; Speed of Limb Movement; Arm-Hand Steadiness. *Physical:* Explosive Strength; Static Strength; Dynamic Strength; Gross Body Coordination; Stamina. *Sensory:* Hearing Sensitivity; Sound Localization; Peripheral Vision; Glare Sensitivity; Depth Perception. **General Work Activities**—*Information Input:* Monitoring Processes, Materials, or Surroundings; Inspecting Equipment, Structures, or Materials; Getting Information. *Mental Process:* Evaluating Information Against Standards; Updating and Using Relevant Knowledge; Judging Qualities of Things, Services, or Other People's Work. *Work Output:* Handling and Moving Objects; Controlling Machines and Processes; Performing General Physical Activities. *Interacting with Others:* Communicating with Other Workers; Coordinating the Work and Activities of Others; Performing Administrative Activities. **Physical Work Conditions**—Hazardous Equipment; Distracting Sounds and Noise Levels; Common Protective or Safety Attire; Using Hands on Objects, Tools, or Controls; Contaminants. **Other Job Characteristics**—Pace Determined by Speed of Equipment; Degree of Automation; Importance of Repeating Same Tasks.

Experience—Job Zone 2. Some previous work-related skill, knowledge, or experience may be helpful, but usually is not needed. **Job Preparation:** SVP 4.0 to less than 6.0—six months to less than two years. **Knowledge**—Production and Processing; Chemistry; Building and Construction; Design; Engineering and Technology. **Instructional Programs**—Welding Technology/Welder.

Related DOT Jobs—614.684-010 Billet Assembler; 814.382-010 Welding-Machine Operator, Friction; 814.682-010 Welding-Machine Operator, Ultrasonic; 814.684-010 Welder, Explosion; 815.382-014 Welding-Machine Operator, Electroslag; 815.682-010 Laser-Beam-Machine Operator; 815.682-014 Welding-Machine Operator, Thermit; 819.685-010 Welding-Machine Tender.

51-4122.03 Soldering and Brazing Machine Setters and Set-Up Operators

- **Education/Training Required: Moderate-term on-the-job training**
- **Employed: No data available.**
- **Annual Earnings: $28,220**
- **Growth: 15.1%**
- **Annual Job Openings: 9,000**

Set up or set up and operate soldering or brazing machines to braze, solder, heat-treat, or spot-weld fabricated metal products or components as specified by work orders, blueprints, and layout specifications.

Selects torch tips, alloy, flux, coil, tubing, and wire according to metal type and thickness, data charts, and records. Connects, forms, and installs parts to braze, heat-treat, and spot-weld workpiece, metal parts, and components. Sets dials and timing controls to regulate electrical current, gas flow pressure, heating/cooling cycles, and shutoff. Positions, aligns, and bolts holding fixtures, guides, and stops onto or into brazing machine to position and hold workpieces. Fills hoppers and positions spout to direct flow of flux or manually brushes flux onto seams of workpieces. Starts machine to complete trial run, readjusts machine, and records setup data. Assembles, aligns, and clamps workpieces into holding fixture to bond, heat-treat, or solder fabricated metal components. Manipulates levers to synchronize brazing action or to move workpiece through brazing process. Operates and trains workers to operate heat-treating equipment to bond fabricated metal components according to blueprints, work orders, or specifications. Disconnects electrical current and removes and immerses workpiece into water or acid bath to cool and clean component. Examines workpiece for defective seams, solidification, and adherence to specifications and anneals finished workpiece to relieve internal stress. Cleans, lubricates, and adjusts equipment to maintain efficient operation, using air hose, cleaning fluid, and hand tools.

GOE INFORMATION—Interest Area: 08. Industrial Production. **Work Group:** 08.02. Production Technology. **Personality Type—**Realistic. Realistic occupations frequently involve work activities that include practical, hands-on problems and solutions. They often deal with plants, animals, and real-world materials like wood, tools, and machinery. Many of the occupations require working outside and do not involve a lot of paperwork or working closely with others. **Work Values—**Moral Values; Independence; Company Policies and Practices; Supervision, Technical; Supervision, Human Relations. **Skills—**Operation Monitoring; Operation and Control; Installation; Quality Control Analysis; Repairing; Equipment Selection; Troubleshooting. **Abilities—***Cognitive:* Visualization. *Psychomotor:* Reaction Time; Rate Control; Manual Dexterity; Speed of Limb Movement; Control Precision. *Physical:* Explosive Strength; Static Strength; Dynamic Flexibility. *Sensory:* Sound Localization; Glare Sensitivity. **General Work Activities—***Information Input:* Monitoring Processes, Materials, or Surroundings; Inspecting Equipment, Structures, or Materials; Getting Information. *Mental Process:* Evaluating Information Against Standards; Analyzing Data or Information; Processing Information. *Work Output:* Handling and Moving Objects; Controlling Machines and Processes; Performing General Physical Activities. *Interacting with Others:* Coaching and Developing Others; Communicating with Other Workers; Teaching Others. **Physical Work Conditions—**Common Protective or Safety Attire; Hazardous Conditions; Hazardous Equipment; Cramped Work Space or Awkward Positions; Extremely Bright or Inadequate Lighting. **Other Job Characteristics—**Pace Determined by Speed of Equipment; Degree of Automation; Consequence of Error.

Experience—Job Zone 2. Some previous work-related skill, knowledge, or experience may be helpful, but usually is not needed. **Job Preparation:** SVP 4.0 to less than 6.0—six months to less than two years. **Knowledge—**Mechanical; Building and Construction; Design; Production and Processing; Engineering and Technology. **Instructional Programs—**Welding Technology/Welder.

Related DOT Jobs—813.360-010 Brazing-Machine Setter; 813.360-014 Setter, Induction-Heating Equipment; 813.382-010 Brazer, Induction; 813.382-014 Brazing-Machine Operator.

51-4122.04 Soldering and Brazing Machine Operators and Tenders

- **Education/Training Required:** Short-term on-the-job training
- **Employed:** No data available.
- **Annual Earnings:** $28,220
- **Growth:** 15.1%
- **Annual Job Openings:** 9,000

Operate or tend soldering and brazing machines that braze, solder, or spot-weld fabricated metal products or components as specified by work orders, blueprints, and layout specifications.

Operates or tends soldering and brazing machines that braze, solder, or spot-weld fabricated products or components. Moves controls to activate and adjust soldering and brazing machines. Observes meters, gauges, and machine to ensure solder or brazing process meets specifications. Loads and adjusts workpieces, clamps, and parts onto machine, using hand tools. Adds chemicals and materials to workpieces or machines, using hand tools. Removes workpieces and parts from machinery, using hand tools. Cleans and maintains workpieces and machines, using equipment and hand tools. Examines and tests soldered or brazed products or components, using testing devices. Reads and records operational information on specified production reports.

GOE INFORMATION—Interest Area: 08. Industrial Production. **Work Group:** 08.03. Production Work. **Personality Type—**Realistic. Realistic occupations frequently involve work activities that include practical, hands-on problems and solutions. They often deal with plants, animals, and real-world materials like wood, tools, and machinery. Many of the occupations require working outside and do not involve a lot of paperwork or working closely with others. **Work Values—**Moral Values; Independence; Company Policies and Practices; Supervision, Human Relations; Activity. **Skills—**Operation Monitoring; Operation and Control; Repairing; Equipment Selection; Quality Control Analysis. **Abilities—***Cognitive:* Perceptual Speed; Information Ordering; Flexibility of Closure. *Psychomotor:* Control Precision; Multilimb Coordination; Wrist-Finger Speed; Arm-Hand Steadiness; Manual Dexterity. *Physical:* Extent Flexibility; Static Strength; Trunk Strength; Dynamic Flexibility. *Sensory:* Glare Sensitivity; Near Vision; Sound Localization. **General Work Activities—***Information Input:* Monitoring Processes, Materials, or Surroundings; Inspecting Equipment, Structures, or Materials; Getting Information. *Mental Process:* Evaluating Information Against Standards; Organizing, Planning, and Prioritizing; Judging Qualities of Things, Services, or Other People's Work. *Work Output:* Handling and Moving Objects; Controlling Machines and Processes; Performing General Physical Activities. *Interacting with Others:* Performing Administrative Activities; Communicating with Other Workers; Monitoring and Controlling Resources. **Physical Work Conditions—**Common Protective or Safety Attire; Hazardous Equipment; Using Hands on Objects, Tools, or Controls; Very Hot or Cold; Indoors. **Other Job Characteristics—**Pace Determined by Speed of Equipment; Importance of Repeating Same Tasks; Degree of Automation.

Experience—Job Zone 1. No previous work-related skill, knowledge, or experience is needed. **Job Preparation:** SVP below 4.0—less than six months. **Knowledge—**Mechanical; Production and Processing; Chemistry; Building and Construction. **Instructional Programs—**Welding Technology/Welder.

Related DOT Jobs—706.685-010 Type-Soldering-Machine Tender; 715.685-058 Solderer; 726.362-014 Wave-Soldering Machine Operator; 726.684-094 Solder Deposit Operator; 726.685-038 Reflow Operator; 813.482-010 Brazer, Furnace; 813.685-010 Brazer, Controlled Atmospheric Furnace.

51-4191.00 Heat Treating Equipment Setters, Operators, and Tenders, Metal and Plastic

- **Education/Training Required: Moderate-term on-the-job training**
- **Employed: 42,902**
- **Annual Earnings: $27,540**
- **Growth: 13.4%**
- **Annual Job Openings: 9,000**

Set up, operate, or tend heating equipment, such as heat-treating furnaces, flame-hardening machines, induction machines, soaking pits, or vacuum equipment to temper, harden, anneal, or heat-treat metal or plastic objects.

No task data available.

GOE INFORMATION—Interest Area: 08. Industrial Production. **Work Group:** 08.02. Production Technology. **Note:** The Department of Labor has not collected some data for this job, so it has fewer details than the other descriptions.

Instructional Programs—Machine Shop Technology/Assistant; Machine Tool Technology/Machinist.

Related DOT Jobs—504.360-010 Flame-Annealing-Machine Setter; 504.380-010 Flame-Hardening-Machine Setter; 504.380-014 Induction-Machine Setter; 504.382-010 Hardener; 504.382-014 Heat Treater I; 504.382-018 Heat-Treater Apprentice; 504.682-010 Annealer; 504.682-014 Case Hardener; 504.682-018 Heat Treater II; 504.682-022 Heat-Treating Bluer; 504.682-026 Temperer; 504.685-010 Base-Draw Operator; 504.685-014 Flame-Hardening-Machine Operator; 504.685-022 Induction-Machine Operator; 504.685-026 Production Hardener; 504.687-010 Annealer; 509.382-014 Dental-Amalgam Processor; 553.685-014 Bagger; 613.362-010 Heater I; 613.462-014 Furnace Operator; others.

51-4191.01 Heating Equipment Setters and Set-Up Operators, Metal and Plastic

- **Education/Training Required: Postsecondary vocational training**
- **Employed: No data available.**
- **Annual Earnings: $27,540**
- **Growth: 13.4%**
- **Annual Job Openings: 9,000**

Set up or set up and operate heating equipment, such as heat-treating furnaces, flame-hardening machines, and induction machines, that anneal or heat-treat metal objects.

Mounts fixtures and industrial coil on machine and workpieces in fixture, using hand tools. Lights gas burners and adjusts flow of gas and coolant water. Sets frequency of current and automatic timer. Starts conveyors and dial feeder plates and turns setscrews in nozzles to direct flames which anneal specific area of object. Estimates flame temperature and heating cycle based on degree of hardness-required and metal to be treated. Reads work order to determine processing specifications. Visually examines or tests objects, using hardness-testing equipment, to determine flame temperature and degree of hardness. Crushes random samples between fingers to determine hardness. Replaces worn dial-feed, burner, and conveyor parts, using hand tools. Instruct new workers in machine operation.

GOE INFORMATION—Interest Area: 08. Industrial Production. **Work Group:** 08.02. Production Technology. **Personality Type**—Realistic. Realistic occupations frequently involve work activities that include practical, hands-on problems and solutions. They often deal with plants, animals, and real-world materials like wood, tools, and machinery. Many of the occupations require working outside and do not involve a lot of paperwork or working closely with others. **Work Values**—Moral Values; Supervision, Technical; Supervision, Human Relations; Company Policies and Practices; Activity. **Skills**—Operation Monitoring; Operation and Control. **Abilities**—*Cognitive:* Perceptual Speed; Spatial Orientation; Category Flexibility; Memorization; Information Ordering. *Psychomotor:* Control Precision; Manual Dexterity; Arm-Hand Steadiness; Rate Control; Reaction Time. *Physical:* Explosive Strength; Dynamic Flexibility; Dynamic Strength; Static Strength; Gross Body Equilibrium. *Sensory:* Peripheral Vision; Depth Perception; Near Vision; Visual Color Discrimination; Hearing Sensitivity. **General Work Activities**—*Information Input:* Inspecting Equipment, Structures, or Materials; Monitoring Processes, Materials, or Surroundings; Identifying Objects, Actions, and Events. *Mental Process:* Updating and Using Relevant Knowledge; Making Decisions and Solving Problems; Judging Qualities of Things, Services, or Other People's Work. *Work Output:* Handling and Moving Objects; Controlling Machines and Processes; Repairing and Maintaining Mechanical Equipment. *Interacting with Others:* Communicating with Other Workers; Teaching Others; Assisting and Caring for Others. **Physical Work Conditions**—Hazardous Equipment; Common Protective or Safety Attire; Minor Burns, Cuts, Bites, or Stings; Using Hands on Objects, Tools, or Controls; Very Hot or Cold. **Other Job Characteristics**—Degree of Automation; Pace Determined by Speed of Equipment; Importance of Repeating Same Tasks.

Experience—Job Zone 3. Previous work-related skill, knowledge, or experience is required. **Job Preparation:** SVP 6.0 to less than 7.0—more than one year and less than four years. **Knowledge**—Mechanical; Production and Processing; Physics; Education and Training; Building and Construction. **Instructional Programs**—Machine Shop Technology/Assistant; Machine Tool Technology/Machinist.

Related DOT Jobs—504.360-010 Flame-Annealing-Machine Setter; 504.380-010 Flame-Hardening-Machine Setter; 504.380-014 Induction-Machine Setter.

51-4191.02 Heat Treating, Annealing, and Tempering Machine Operators and Tenders, Metal and Plastic

- **Education/Training Required: Moderate-term on-the-job training**
- **Employed: No data available.**
- **Annual Earnings: $27,540**
- **Growth: 13.4%**
- **Annual Job Openings: 9,000**

Operate or tend machines, such as furnaces, baths, flame-hardening machines, and electronic induction machines, to harden, anneal, and heat-treat metal products or metal parts.

Sets automatic controls, observes gauges, and operates gas or electric furnace used to harden, temper, or anneal metal parts. Positions part in fixture, presses buttons to light burners, and tends flame-hardening machine, according to procedures, to case-harden metal part. Activates and tends electric furnace that anneals base sections of hardened parts for subsequent machining. Adjusts speed and operates continuous furnace through which parts are passed by means of reels and conveyors. Sets up and operates die-quenching machine to prevent parts from warping. Reads production schedule to determine processing sequence and furnace temperature requirements for objects to be heat-treated. Reduces heat and allows parts to cool in furnace. Loads parts into containers, closes furnace door, and inserts parts into furnace when specified temperature is reached. Removes parts from furnace after specified time and air-dries or cools parts in water or oil brine or other baths. Examines parts to ensure that metal shade and color conform to specifications, utilizing knowledge of metal heat-treating. Tests parts for hardness, using hardness-testing equipment, and stamps heat-treatment identification mark on part, using hammer and punch. Signals forklift operator to deposit or extract containers of parts into and from furnaces and quenching rinse tanks. Cleans oxides and scale from parts or fittings, using steam spray or immersing parts in chemical and water baths. Covers parts with charcoal before inserting in furnace to prevent discoloration caused by rapid heating.

GOE INFORMATION—Interest Area: 08. Industrial Production. **Work Group:** 08.02. Production Technology. **Personality Type**—Realistic. Realistic occupations frequently involve work activities that include practical, hands-on problems and solutions. They often deal with plants, animals, and real-world materials like wood, tools, and machinery. Many of the occupations require working outside and do not involve a lot of paperwork or working closely with others. **Work Values**—Moral Values; Independence; Supervision, Technical; Supervision, Human Relations; Company Policies and Practices. **Skills**—Operation Monitoring; Quality Control Analysis; Operation and Control; Equipment Selection; Installation. **Abilities**—*Cognitive:* Perceptual Speed; Memorization; Problem Sensitivity; Selective Attention; Spatial Orientation. *Psychomotor:* Rate Control; Control Precision; Reaction Time; Speed of Limb Movement; Multilimb Coordination. *Physical:* Dynamic Strength; Static Strength; Explosive Strength; Dynamic Flexibility; Extent Flexibility. *Sensory:* Visual Color Discrimination; Depth Perception; Peripheral Vision; Far Vision; Glare Sensitivity. **General Work Activities**—*Information Input:* Monitoring Processes, Materials, or Surroundings; Inspecting Equipment, Structures, or Materials; Getting Information. *Mental Process:* Judging Qualities of Things, Services, or Other People's Work; Evaluating Information Against Standards; Making Decisions and Solving Problems. *Work Output:* Handling and Moving Objects; Controlling Machines and Processes; Performing General Physical Activities. *Interacting with Others:* Communicating with Other Workers; Coordinating the Work and Activities of Others; Establishing and Maintaining Relationships. **Physical Work Conditions**—Hazardous Equipment; Hazardous Conditions; Minor Burns, Cuts, Bites, or Stings; Very Hot or Cold; Contaminants. **Other Job Characteristics**—Degree of Automation; Pace Determined by Speed of Equipment; Importance of Repeating Same Tasks.

Experience—Job Zone 2. Some previous work-related skill, knowledge, or experience may be helpful, but usually is not needed. **Job Preparation:** SVP 4.0 to less than 6.0—six months to less than two years. **Knowledge**—Production and Processing; Mechanical; Physics; Chemistry; Building and Construction. **Instructional Programs**—Machine Shop Technology/Assistant; Machine Tool Technology/Machinist.

Related DOT Jobs—504.382-010 Hardener; 504.382-014 Heat Treater I; 504.382-018 Heat-Treater Apprentice; 504.682-010 Annealer; 504.682-014 Case Hardener; 504.682-018 Heat Treater II; 504.682-022 Heat-Treating Bluer; 504.682-026 Temperer; 504.685-010 Base-Draw Operator; 504.685-014 Flame-Hardening-Machine Operator; 504.685-022 Induction-Machine Operator; 504.685-026 Production Hardener; 504.687-010 Annealer.

51-4191.03 Heaters, Metal and Plastic

- **Education/Training Required: Moderate-term on-the-job training**
- **Employed: No data available.**
- **Annual Earnings: $27,540**
- **Growth: 13.4%**
- **Annual Job Openings: 9,000**

Operate or tend heating equipment, such as soaking pits, reheating furnaces, and heating and vacuum equipment, to heat metal sheets, blooms, billets, bars, plate, and rods to a specified temperature for rolling or processing or to heat and cure preformed plastic parts.

Ignites furnace with torch and turns valve to regulate flow of fuel and air to burners. Starts conveyors and opens furnace doors to load stock or signals crane operator to uncover soaking pits and lower ingots into them. Adjusts controls to maintain temperature and heating time, using thermal instruments and charts, dials and gauges of furnace, and color of stock. Sets oven controls or turns air-pressure valve or autoclave. Adjusts controls to synchronize speed of feed and take-off conveyors of furnace. Inserts vacuum tube into bag and seals bag around tube with tape. Places part on cart, connects vacuum line to tube, and smoothes bag around part to ensure vacuum. Positions plastic sheet and mold in plastic bag, heats material under lamps, and forces confrontation of sheet to mold by vacuum pressure. Positions stock in furnace, using tongs, chain hoist, or pry bar. Removes material from furnace, using crane, or signals crane operator to transfer to next station. Removes stock from furnace, using cold rod, tongs or chain hoist, and places stock on conveyor for transport to work area. Positions part in plastic bag and seals bag with iron. Removes part and cuts away plastic bag. Pushes cart to curing oven or places part in autoclave. Impregnates fabric with plastic resins and cuts fabric into strips. Signals co-worker to charge steel into furnace. Records time and production data. Assists workers in repairing, replacing, cleaning, lubricating, or adjusting furnace equipment, using hand tools.

GOE INFORMATION—Interest Area: 08. Industrial Production. **Work Group:** 08.03. Production Work. **Personality Type**—Realistic. Realistic occupations frequently involve work activities that include practical, hands-on problems and solutions. They often deal with plants, animals, and real-world materials like wood, tools, and machinery. Many of the occupations require working outside and do not involve a lot of paperwork or working closely with others. **Work Values**—Moral Values; Supervision, Technical; Supervision, Human Relations; Company Policies and Practices; Activity. **Skills**—Repairing; Operation and Control; Operation Monitoring. **Abilities**—*Cognitive:* None met the criteria. *Psychomotor:* Control Precision; Multilimb Coordination; Arm-Hand Steadiness; Rate Control. *Physical:* Extent Flexibility; Static Strength; Gross Body Coordination. *Sensory:* None met the criteria. **General Work Activities**—*Information Input:* Monitoring Processes, Materials, or Surroundings; Identifying Objects, Actions, and Events; Inspecting Equipment, Structures, or Materials. *Mental Process:* Evaluating Information Against Standards; Judging Qualities of Things, Services, or Other People's Work; Making Decisions and Solving Problems. *Work Output:* Handling and Moving Objects; Controlling Machines and Processes; Performing General Physical Activities. *Interacting with Others:* Communicating with Other Workers; Assisting and Caring for Others; Establishing and Maintaining Relationships. **Physical Work Conditions**—Hazardous Equipment; Hazardous Conditions; Minor Burns, Cuts, Bites, or Stings; Very Hot or Cold; Common Protective or Safety Attire. **Other Job Characteristics**—Pace Determined by Speed of Equipment; Degree of Automation; Consequence of Error.

Experience—Job Zone 2. Some previous work-related skill, knowledge, or experience may be helpful, but usually is not needed. **Job Preparation:**

SVP 4.0 to less than 6.0—six months to less than two years. **Knowledge**—Production and Processing; Mechanical; Physics; Engineering and Technology; Building and Construction. **Instructional Programs**—Machine Shop Technology/Assistant; Machine Tool Technology/Machinist.

Related DOT Jobs—553.685-014 Bagger; 613.362-010 Heater I; 613.462-014 Furnace Operator; 619.682-022 Heater; 619.686-026 Spike-Machine Heater.

51-4192.00 Lay-Out Workers, Metal and Plastic

- **Education/Training Required: Postsecondary vocational training**
- **Employed: 18,378**
- **Annual Earnings: $30,580**
- **Growth: –6.0%**
- **Annual Job Openings: 1,000**

Lay out reference points and dimensions on metal or plastic stock or workpieces, such as sheets, plates, tubes, structural shapes, castings, or machine parts, for further processing. Includes shipfitters.

Determines reference points and computes layout dimensions and works to tolerances as close as 0.001 inch. Locates center line and verifies template position, using measuring instruments, including gauge blocks, height gauges, and dial indicators. Examines workpiece and verifies such requirements as dimensions and squareness, using rule, square, and straightedge. Details location and sequence of cutting, drilling, bending, rolling, punching, and welding operations, using compass, protractor, dividers, and rule. Marks curves, lines, holes, dimensions, and welding symbols onto workpiece, using scribes, soapstone, punches, and hand drill. Plans and develops layout from blueprints and templates, applying knowledge of trigonometry, design, effects of heat, and properties of metal. Lifts and positions workpiece in relation to surface plate manually or with hoist, using parallel blocks and angle plates. Adds dimensional details to blueprints or drawings by other workers and designs templates of wood, paper, or metal. Fits and aligns fabricated parts for welding or assembly operations. Inspects machined parts to verify conformance to specifications. Applies pigment to layout surfaces, using paint brush.

GOE INFORMATION—Interest Area: 08. Industrial Production. **Work Group:** 08.04. Metal and Plastics Machining Technology. **Personality Type**—Realistic. Realistic occupations frequently involve work activities that include practical, hands-on problems and solutions. They often deal with plants, animals, and real-world materials like wood, tools, and machinery. Many of the occupations require working outside and do not involve a lot of paperwork or working closely with others. **Work Values**—Moral Values; Independence; Supervision, Technical; Company Policies and Practices; Advancement. **Skills**—Mathematics; Technology Design; Equipment Selection. **Abilities**—*Cognitive:* Mathematical Reasoning; Visualization; Number Facility; Information Ordering; Deductive Reasoning. *Psychomotor:* Multilimb Coordination; Arm-Hand Steadiness; Manual Dexterity; Finger Dexterity; Control Precision. *Physical:* Static Strength; Extent Flexibility; Dynamic Strength; Explosive Strength; Gross Body Coordination. *Sensory:* Depth Perception; Near Vision. **General Work Activities**—*Information Input:* Inspecting Equipment, Structures, or Materials; Getting Information; Identifying Objects, Actions, and Events. *Mental Process:* Evaluating Information Against Standards; Judging Qualities of Things, Services, or Other People's Work; Processing Information. *Work Output:* Handling and Moving Objects; Performing General Physical Activities; Drafting and Specifying Technical Devices. *Interacting with Others:* Communicating with Other Workers; Establishing and Maintaining Relationships; Coordinating the Work

and Activities of Others. **Physical Work Conditions**—Using Hands on Objects, Tools, or Controls; Hazardous Equipment; Standing; Distracting Sounds and Noise Levels; Kneeling, Crouching, or Crawling. **Other Job Characteristics**—Importance of Being Exact or Accurate; Degree of Automation; Pace Determined by Speed of Equipment.

Experience—Job Zone 3. Previous work-related skill, knowledge, or experience is required. **Job Preparation:** SVP 6.0 to less than 7.0—more than one year and less than four years. **Knowledge**—Design; Production and Processing; Mathematics; Physics; Engineering and Technology. **Instructional Programs**—Machine Shop Technology/Assistant; Machine Tool Technology/Machinist.

Related DOT Jobs—600.281-018 Lay-Out Worker; 809.281-010 Lay-Out Worker I; 809.381-014 Lay-Out Worker II.

51-4193.00 Plating and Coating Machine Setters, Operators, and Tenders, Metal and Plastic

- **Education/Training Required: Moderate-term on-the-job training**
- **Employed: 65,356**
- **Annual Earnings: $24,810**
- **Growth: 10.2%**
- **Annual Job Openings: 14,000**

Set up, operate, or tend plating or coating machines to coat metal or plastic products with chromium, zinc, copper, cadmium, nickel, or other metal to protect or decorate surfaces. Includes electrolytic processes.

No task data available.

GOE INFORMATION—Interest Area: 08. Industrial Production. **Work Group:** 08.03. Production Work. **Note:** The Department of Labor has not collected some data for this job, so it has fewer details than the other descriptions.

Instructional Programs—No data available.

Related DOT Jobs—500.362-010 Electrogalvanizing-Machine Operator; 500.362-014 Plater, Barrel; 500.380-010 Plater; 500.380-014 Plater Apprentice; 500.384-010 Matrix Plater; 500.384-014 Matrix-Bath Attendant; 500.485-010 Zinc-Plating-Machine Operator; 500.682-010 Anodizer; 500.684-010 Electroformer; 500.684-018 Plate Former; 500.684-026 Plater, Printed Circuit Board Panels; 500.684-030 Plater, Semiconductor Wafers and Components; 500.684-034 Plater; 500.685-014 Plating Equipment Tender; 501.362-010 Coating-Machine Operator; 501.485-010 Wire-Coating Operator, Metal; 501.685-010 Plater, Hot Dip; 501.685-014 Tinning-Equipment Tender; 501.685-018 Black Oxide Coating Equipment Tender; 501.685-022 Electroless Plater, Printed Circuit Board Panels; others.

51-4193.01 Electrolytic Plating and Coating Machine Setters and Set-Up Operators, Metal and Plastic

- **Education/Training Required: Postsecondary vocational training**
- **Employed: No data available.**
- **Annual Earnings: $24,810**
- **Growth: 10.2%**
- **Annual Job Openings: 14,000**

Set up or set up and operate electrolytic plating or coating machines, such as continuous multistrand electrogalvanizing machines, to coat metal or plastic products electrolytically with chromium, copper, cadmium, or other metal to provide protective or decorative surfaces or to build up worn surfaces.

Moves controls to permit electrodeposition of metal on object or to regulate movement of wire strand to obtain specified thickness. Adjusts voltage and amperage based on observations. Determines size and composition of object to be plated and amount of electrical current and time required, following work order. Suspends object, such as part or mold, from cathode rod (negative terminal) and immerses object in plating solution. Suspends stick or piece of plating metal from anode (positive terminal) and immerses metal in plating solution. Mixes chemical solutions, fills tanks, and charges furnaces. Removes plated object from solution at periodic intervals and observes object to ensure conformance to specifications. Plates small objects, such as nuts or bolts, using motor-driven barrel. Immerses object in cleaning and rinsing baths to complete plating process. Examines object at end of process to determine thickness of metal deposit or measures thickness, using instruments such as micrometers. Measures, marks, and masks areas excluded from plating. Grinds, polishes, or rinses object in water and dries object to maintain clean, even surface.

GOE INFORMATION—Interest Area: 08. Industrial Production. **Work Group:** 08.03. Production Work. **Personality Type**—Realistic. Realistic occupations frequently involve work activities that include practical, hands-on problems and solutions. They often deal with plants, animals, and real-world materials like wood, tools, and machinery. Many of the occupations require working outside and do not involve a lot of paperwork or working closely with others. **Work Values**—Moral Values; Independence; Supervision, Human Relations; Supervision, Technical; Activity. **Skills**—Operation and Control; Operation Monitoring. **Abilities**—*Cognitive:* None met the criteria. *Psychomotor:* Control Precision; Multilimb Coordination; Manual Dexterity; Wrist-Finger Speed; Finger Dexterity. *Physical:* Static Strength; Gross Body Coordination; Explosive Strength; Extent Flexibility; Trunk Strength. *Sensory:* None met the criteria. **General Work Activities**—*Information Input:* Getting Information; Monitoring Processes, Materials, or Surroundings; Inspecting Equipment, Structures, or Materials. *Mental Process:* Evaluating Information Against Standards; Analyzing Data or Information; Making Decisions and Solving Problems. *Work Output:* Handling and Moving Objects; Controlling Machines and Processes; Performing General Physical Activities. *Interacting with Others:* Communicating with Other Workers; Establishing and Maintaining Relationships; Coaching and Developing Others. **Physical Work Conditions**—Common Protective or Safety Attire; Hazardous Conditions; Minor Burns, Cuts, Bites, or Stings; Specialized Protective or Safety Attire; Indoors. **Other Job Characteristics**—Pace Determined by Speed of Equipment; Importance of Repeating Same Tasks; Consequence of Error.

Experience—Job Zone 3. Previous work-related skill, knowledge, or experience is required. **Job Preparation:** SVP 6.0 to less than 7.0—more than one year and less than four years. **Knowledge**—Chemistry; Mechanical; Production and Processing; Physics; Engineering and Technology. **Instructional Programs**—No data available.

Related DOT Jobs—500.362-010 Electrogalvanizing-Machine Operator; 500.380-010 Plater; 500.380-014 Plater Apprentice.

51-4193.02 Electrolytic Plating and Coating Machine Operators and Tenders, Metal and Plastic

- **Education/Training Required: Moderate-term on-the-job training**
- **Employed: No data available.**
- **Annual Earnings: $24,810**
- **Growth: 10.2%**
- **Annual Job Openings: 14,000**

Operate or tend electrolytic plating or coating machines, such as zinc-plating machines and anodizing machines, to coat metal or plastic products electrolytically with chromium, zinc, copper, cadmium, or other metal to provide protective or decorative surfaces or to build up worn surfaces.

Measures or estimates amounts of electric current needed and time required to coat objects. Adjusts dials to regulate flow of current and voltage supplied to terminals to control plating process. Positions objects to be plated in frame or suspends them from positive or negative terminals of power supply. Removes objects from plating solution after specified time or when desired thickness of metal is deposited on them. Mixes and tests plating solution to specified formula and turns valves to fill tank with solution. Monitors and measures thickness of electroplating on component part to verify conformance to specifications, using micrometer. Mixes forming acid solution, treats battery plates, and removes and rinses formed plates. Immerses objects to be coated or plated into cleaning solutions or sprays with conductive solution to prepare object for plating. Rinses coated object in cleansing liquids and dries with cloth, with centrifugal driers, or by tumbling in sawdust-filled barrels. Lubricates moving parts of plating conveyor and cleans plating and cleaning solution tanks.

GOE INFORMATION—Interest Area: 08. Industrial Production. **Work Group:** 08.03. Production Work. **Personality Type**—Realistic. Realistic occupations frequently involve work activities that include practical, hands-on problems and solutions. They often deal with plants, animals, and real-world materials like wood, tools, and machinery. Many of the occupations require working outside and do not involve a lot of paperwork or working closely with others. **Work Values**—Moral Values; Independence; Supervision, Human Relations; Activity; Supervision, Technical. **Skills**—Operation and Control; Quality Control Analysis; Operation Monitoring. **Abilities**—*Cognitive:* Mathematical Reasoning; Number Facility; Information Ordering. *Psychomotor:* Control Precision; Reaction Time; Rate Control; Wrist-Finger Speed; Speed of Limb Movement. *Physical:* Dynamic Flexibility; Dynamic Strength; Explosive Strength. *Sensory:* None met the criteria. **General Work Activities**—*Information Input:* Estimating Needed Characteristics; Monitoring Processes, Materials, or Surroundings; Inspecting Equipment, Structures, or Materials. *Mental Process:* Updating and Using Relevant Knowledge; Judging Qualities of Things, Services, or Other People's Work; Organizing, Planning, and Prioritizing. *Work Output:* Handling and Moving Objects; Controlling Machines and Processes; Performing General Physical Activities. *Interacting with Others:* Communicating with Other Workers; Establishing and Maintaining Relationships; Coordinating the Work and Activities of Others. **Physical Work Conditions**—Hazardous Conditions; Common Protective or Safety Attire; Using Hands on Objects, Tools, or Controls; Indoors; Distracting Sounds and Noise Levels. **Other Job Characteristics**—Pace Determined by Speed of Equipment; Degree of Automation; Importance of Repeating Same Tasks.

Experience—Job Zone 2. Some previous work-related skill, knowledge, or experience may be helpful, but usually is not needed. **Job Preparation:** SVP 4.0 to less than 6.0—six months to less than two years. **Knowledge**—Chemistry; Production and Processing; Mechanical; Physics; Computers and Electronics. **Instructional Programs**—No data available.

Related DOT Jobs—500.362-014 Plater, Barrel; 500.384-010 Matrix Plater; 500.384-014 Matrix-Bath Attendant; 500.485-010 Zinc-Plating-Machine Operator; 500.682-010 Anodizer; 500.684-010 Electroformer; 500.684-018 Plate Former; 500.684-026 Plater, Printed Circuit Board Panels; 500.684-030 Plater, Semiconductor Wafers and Components; 500.684-034 Plater; 500.685-014 Plating Equipment Tender.

51-4193.03 Nonelectrolytic Plating and Coating Machine Setters and Set-Up Operators, Metal and Plastic

- **Education/Training Required: Postsecondary vocational training**
- **Employed: No data available.**
- **Annual Earnings: $24,810**
- **Growth: 10.2%**
- **Annual Job Openings: 14,000**

Set up or set up and operate nonelectrolytic plating or coating machines, such as hot-dip lines and metal-spraying machines, to coat metal or plastic products or parts with metal.

Measures and sets stops, rolls, brushes, and guides on automatic feeder and conveying equipment or coating machines, using micrometer, rule, and hand tools. Adjusts controls to set temperatures of coating substance and adjusts speeds of machines and equipment. Attaches nozzle, positions gun, connects hoses, and threads wire to set up metal-spraying machine. Ignites gun and adjusts controls to regulate wire feed, air pressure, and flow of oxygen and fuel to operate metal-spraying machine. Installs gears and holding devices on conveyor equipment. Reads production schedule to determine setup of equipment and machines. Mixes alodize solution in tank of machine according to formula and verifies solution concentration, using gauge. Positions workpieces, starts operation of machines and conveyors, and feeds workpieces into machines to be coated. Adjusts controls to synchronize equipment speed with speed of coating or spraying machine. Operates hoist to place workpieces onto machine feed carriage or spindle. Inspects coated products for defects and specified color and coverage. Operates sandblasting equipment to roughen and clean surface of workpieces. Preheats workpieces in oven.

GOE INFORMATION—**Interest Area:** 08. Industrial Production. **Work Group:** 08.03. Production Work. **Personality Type**—Realistic. Realistic occupations frequently involve work activities that include practical, hands-on problems and solutions. They often deal with plants, animals, and real-world materials like wood, tools, and machinery. Many of the occupations require working outside and do not involve a lot of paperwork or working closely with others. **Work Values**—Moral Values; Independence; Supervision, Human Relations; Supervision, Technical; Company Policies and Practices. **Skills**—Operation and Control; Operation Monitoring; Installation; Equipment Selection. **Abilities**—*Cognitive:* Visualization; Number Facility; Selective Attention; Information Ordering; Problem Sensitivity. *Psychomotor:* Control Precision; Rate Control; Manual Dexterity; Reaction Time; Multilimb Coordination. *Physical:* Explosive Strength; Dynamic Strength; Static Strength; Dynamic Flexibility; Extent Flexibility. *Sensory:* Visual Color Discrimination; Depth Perception; Glare Sensitivity; Peripheral Vision. **General Work Activities**—*Information Input:* Monitoring Processes, Materials, or Surround-

ings; Inspecting Equipment, Structures, or Materials; Getting Information. *Mental Process:* Updating and Using Relevant Knowledge; Evaluating Information Against Standards; Organizing, Planning, and Prioritizing. *Work Output:* Handling and Moving Objects; Controlling Machines and Processes; Performing General Physical Activities. *Interacting with Others:* Communicating with Other Workers; Establishing and Maintaining Relationships; Coordinating the Work and Activities of Others. **Physical Work Conditions**—Common Protective or Safety Attire; Hazardous Equipment; Minor Burns, Cuts, Bites, or Stings; Cramped Work Space or Awkward Positions; Using Hands on Objects, Tools, or Controls. **Other Job Characteristics**—Pace Determined by Speed of Equipment; Degree of Automation; Importance of Being Exact or Accurate.

Experience—Job Zone 3. Previous work-related skill, knowledge, or experience is required. **Job Preparation:** SVP 6.0 to less than 7.0—more than one year and less than four years. **Knowledge**—Production and Processing; Chemistry; Mechanical; Physics; Engineering and Technology. **Instructional Programs**—No data available.

Related DOT Jobs—501.362-010 Coating-Machine Operator; 505.382-010 Metal-Spraying-Machine Operator, Automatic I; 509.462-010 Alodize-Machine Operator.

51-4193.04 Nonelectrolytic Plating and Coating Machine Operators and Tenders, Metal and Plastic

- **Education/Training Required: Short-term on-the-job training**
- **Employed: No data available.**
- **Annual Earnings: $24,810**
- **Growth: 10.2%**
- **Annual Job Openings: 14,000**

Operate or tend nonelectrolytic plating or coating machines, such as metal-spraying machines and vacuum metalizing machines, to coat metal or plastic products or parts with metal.

Observes gauges and adjusts controls of machine to regulate functions such as speed and temperature according to specifications. Sprays coating in specified pattern according to instructions and inspects area for defects, such as air bubbles or uneven coverage. Presses or turns controls to activate and set equipment operation according to specifications. Positions and feeds materials on plate into machine manually or automatically for processing. Fills machine receptacle with coating material or solution. Immerses workpieces in coating solution for specified time. Mixes coating material or solution according to formula or uses premixed solutions. Places materials on racks and transfers to oven to dry for a specified period of time. Removes excess material or impurities from objects, using air hose or grinding machine. Cuts metal or other materials, using shears or band saw. Measures or weighs materials, using ruler, calculator, and scale. Positions containers to receive parts and loads or unloads materials in containers, using dolly or handtruck. Cleans and maintains equipment, using water hose and scraper. Solders equipment and visually examines for completeness. Cleans workpieces, using wire brush. Maintains production records. Replaces worn parts and adjusts equipment components, using hand tools.

GOE INFORMATION—**Interest Area:** 08. Industrial Production. **Work Group:** 08.03. Production Work. **Personality Type**—Realistic. Realistic occupations frequently involve work activities that include practical, hands-on problems and solutions. They often deal with plants, animals, and real-world materials like wood, tools, and machinery. Many of the occupations require working outside and do not involve a lot of paperwork or working closely with others. **Work Values**—Moral Values; Independence; Supervision, Human Relations; Supervision, Technical; Company Policies and Practices. **Skills**—Operation Monitoring; Operation and Control; Repairing. **Abilities**—*Cognitive:* None met the criteria. *Psychomotor:* Speed of Limb Movement; Multilimb Coordination; Control Precision; Arm-Hand Steadiness. *Physical:* Extent Flexibility; Trunk Strength; Explosive Strength; Dynamic Strength; Static Strength. *Sensory:* None met the criteria. **General Work Activities**—*Information Input:* Monitoring Processes, Materials, or Surroundings; Inspecting Equipment, Structures, or Materials; Getting Information. *Mental Process:* Evaluating Information Against Standards; Updating and Using Relevant Knowledge; Judging Qualities of Things, Services, or Other People's Work. *Work Output:* Handling and Moving Objects; Performing General Physical Activities; Controlling Machines and Processes. *Interacting with Others:* Communicating with Other Workers; Establishing and Maintaining Relationships; Coaching and Developing Others. **Physical Work Conditions**—Common Protective or Safety Attire; Minor Burns, Cuts, Bites, or Stings; Indoors; Using Hands on Objects, Tools, or Controls; Standing. **Other Job Characteristics**—Pace Determined by Speed of Equipment; Importance of Repeating Same Tasks; Degree of Automation.

Experience—Job Zone 1. No previous work-related skill, knowledge, or experience is needed. **Job Preparation:** SVP below 4.0—less than six months. **Knowledge**—Production and Processing; Chemistry; Mechanical; Physics; Engineering and Technology. **Instructional Programs**—No data available.

Related DOT Jobs—501.485-010 Wire-Coating Operator, Metal; 501.685-010 Plater, Hot Dip; 501.685-014 Tinning-Equipment Tender; 501.685-018 Black Oxide Coating Equipment Tender; 501.685-022 Electroless Plater, Printed Circuit Board Panels; 503.685-010 Coater; 505.382-014 Welding-Rod Coater; 505.482-010 Pasting-Machine Operator; 505.682-010 Sprayer Operator; 505.685-010 Browning Processor; 505.685-014 Metal-Spraying-Machine Operator, Automatic II; 505.685-018 Vacuum-Metalizer Operator; 509.382-010 Coater Operator; 509.685-022 Ceramic Coater, Machine; 509.685-026 Gettering-Filament-Machine Operator; 509.685-030 Impregnator; 509.685-034 Lacquer-Dipping-Machine Operator; 509.685-038 Lubricating-Machine Tender; 554.382-014 Plastics-Spreading-Machine Operator; 554.585-014 Coater Operator; others.

51-4194.00 Tool Grinders, Filers, and Sharpeners

- **Education/Training Required: Moderate-term on-the-job training**
- **Employed: 29,457**
- **Annual Earnings: $28,630**
- **Growth: −7.7%**
- **Annual Job Openings: 2,000**

Perform precision smoothing, sharpening, polishing, or grinding of metal objects.

Sets up, operates, and adjusts grinding or polishing machines to grind metal workpieces, such as dies, parts, and tools. Dresses grinding wheel according to specifications. Tends machine that grinds, files, or polishes workpiece. Files or finishes surface of workpiece, using prescribed hand tool. Observes and listens to machine operation to determine whether adjustments are necessary to ensure that workpieces meet specifications. Selects and mounts grinding wheels on machines, according to specifications, using hand tools and applying knowledge of abrasive and grinding procedures. Examines and feels surface of workpiece to verify that grinding meets specifications. Straightens workpiece and removes dents in workpiece, using straightening press and hammers. Turns valves to direct flow of coolant against cutting wheel and workpiece. Computes number, width, and angle of cutting tool, micrometer, scales, and gauges and adjusts tool to produce specified cuts. Measures and examines workpiece to verify that dimensions meet specifications. Studies blueprint or layout of metal workpiece to visualize grinding procedure and plan sequences of operations. Places workpiece in electroplating solution or applies pigment to surfaces of workpiece to highlight ridges and grooves. Duplicates workpiece contours, using tracer attachment. Removes and replaces machine parts, using hand tools. Forms specified section of workpiece and repairs cracks in workpiece, using welding or brazing equipment. Fits parts together in preassembly to ensure dimensions are accurate. Inspects dies to detect defects, assess wear, and verify specifications, using micrometers, steel gauge pins, and loupe. Removes finished workpiece from machine and places in boxes or racks, depending on size of workpiece. Cleans and lubricates machine parts.

GOE INFORMATION—**Interest Area:** 08. Industrial Production. **Work Group:** 08.04. Metal and Plastics Machining Technology. **Personality Type**—Realistic. Realistic occupations frequently involve work activities that include practical, hands-on problems and solutions. They often deal with plants, animals, and real-world materials like wood, tools, and machinery. Many of the occupations require working outside and do not involve a lot of paperwork or working closely with others. **Work Values**—Moral Values; Supervision, Technical; Supervision, Human Relations; Company Policies and Practices; Independence. **Skills**—Operation Monitoring; Operation and Control; Quality Control Analysis; Equipment Selection; Technology Design; Repairing; Mathematics; Troubleshooting. **Abilities**—*Cognitive:* Visualization; Selective Attention; Flexibility of Closure; Mathematical Reasoning; Inductive Reasoning. *Psychomotor:* Speed of Limb Movement; Control Precision; Wrist-Finger Speed; Manual Dexterity; Arm-Hand Steadiness. *Physical:* Static Strength; Extent Flexibility; Gross Body Coordination; Stamina; Explosive Strength. *Sensory:* Hearing Sensitivity; Auditory Attention; Sound Localization; Glare Sensitivity; Near Vision. **General Work Activities**—*Information Input:* Inspecting Equipment, Structures, or Materials; Getting Information; Monitoring Processes, Materials, or Surroundings. *Mental Process:* Evaluating Information Against Standards; Judging Qualities of Things, Services, or Other People's Work; Organizing, Planning, and Prioritizing. *Work Output:* Handling and Moving Objects; Controlling Machines and Processes; Performing General Physical Activities. *Interacting with Others:* Establishing and Maintaining Relationships; Communicating with Other Workers; Coordinating the Work and Activities of Others. **Physical Work Conditions**—Hazardous Equipment; Minor Burns, Cuts, Bites, or Stings; Common Protective or Safety Attire; Distracting Sounds and Noise Levels; Indoors. **Other Job Characteristics**—Pace Determined by Speed of Equipment; Degree of Automation; Importance of Repeating Same Tasks.

Experience—Job Zone 3. Previous work-related skill, knowledge, or experience is required. **Job Preparation:** SVP 6.0 to less than 7.0—more than one year and less than four years. **Knowledge**—Design; Mechanical; Building and Construction; Public Safety and Security; Foreign Language. **Instructional Programs**—Machine Shop Technology/Assistant.

Related DOT Jobs—500.381-010 Cylinder Grinder; 601.381-018 Die Polisher; 603.280-010 Grinder Operator, External, Tool; 603.280-014 Grinder Operator, Surface, Tool; 603.280-018 Grinder Operator, Tool; 603.280-022 Grinder Set-Up Operator, Internal; 603.280-030 Grinder Set-Up Operator, Universal; 603.280-038 Tool-Grinder Operator; 680.380-010 Card Grinder; 701.381-014 Saw Filer; 701.381-018 Tool Grinder I; 701.684-030 Tool Filer; 705.381-010 Die Barber; 705.481-010 Filer, Finish; 705.481-014 Lapper, Hand, Tool.

51-4199.99 Metal Workers and Plastic Workers, All Other

- Education/Training Required: No data available.
- Employed: No data available.
- Annual Earnings: No data available.
- Growth: 16.4%
- Annual Job Openings: 20,000

All metalworkers and plastic workers not listed separately.

No task data available.

GOE INFORMATION—Interest Area: 08. Industrial Production. **Work Group:** 08.04. Metal and Plastics Machining Technology. **Note:** The Department of Labor has not collected some data for this job, so it has fewer details than the other descriptions.

Instructional Programs—Machine Shop Technology/Assistant; Machine Tool Technology/Machinist; Precision Metal Working, Other.

Related DOT Jobs—500.685-010 Etcher, Electrolytic; 503.362-014 Shotblast-Equipment Operator; 503.685-018 Drifter; 503.685-038 Sandblast Operator; 503.685-042 Sandblast-Or-Shotblast-Equipment Tender; 503.685-046 Strip-Tank Tender; 505.380-010 Metal Sprayer, Machined Parts; 509.362-010 Mixer Operator, Hot Metal; 509.384-010 Case Preparer-And-Liner; 509.485-014 Shot Polisher And Inspector; 509.685-042 Lubricator-Granulator; 509.685-054 Tank Tender; 511.682-010 Dust Collector, Ore Crushing; 512.683-010 Charging-Machine Operator; 514.682-014 Press Operator, Carbon Blocks; 514.685-026 Tube-Cleaning Operator; 518.685-030 Shell-Mold-Bonding-Machine Operator; 519.362-010 Nickel-Plant Operator; 519.362-014 Tank-House Operator; 519.484-010 Carnallite-Plant Operator; others.

51-5000 Printing Workers

51-5011.00 Bindery Workers

- Education/Training Required: Moderate-term on-the-job training
- Employed: 105,476
- Annual Earnings: $21,480
- Growth: 7.3%
- Annual Job Openings: 13,000

Set up or operate binding machines that produce books and other printed materials.

No task data available.

GOE INFORMATION—Interest Area: 08. Industrial Production. **Work Group:** 08.02. Production Technology. **Note:** The Department of Labor has not collected some data for this job, so it has fewer details than the other descriptions.

Instructional Programs—Graphic Communications, Other.

Related DOT Jobs—653.360-010 Casing-in-Line Setter; 653.360-018 Bindery-Machine Setter; 653.382-010 Folding-Machine Operator; 653.382-014 Collating-Machine Operator; 653.662-010 Stitching-Machine Operator; 653.682-010 Book-Sewing-Machine Operator II; 653.682-014 Covering-Machine Operator; 653.682-018 Head-Bander-and-Liner Operator; 653.682-022 Tinning-Machine Set-Up Operator; 653.685-010 Bindery Worker; 653.685-014 Book-Sewing-Machine Operator I; 653.685-022 Magazine Repairer; 653.685-026 Rounding-and-Backing-Machine Operator; 653.685-030 Spiral Binder; 692.685-146 Saddle-and-Side Wire Stitcher.

51-5011.01 Bindery Machine Setters and Set-Up Operators

- Education/Training Required: Moderate-term on-the-job training
- Employed: No data available.
- Annual Earnings: $21,480
- Growth: 7.3%
- Annual Job Openings: 13,000

Set up or set up and operate machines that perform some or all of the following functions in order to produce books, magazines, pamphlets, catalogs, and other printed materials: gathering, folding, cutting, stitching, rounding and backing, supering, casing in, lining, pressing, and trimming.

Installs bindery machine devices such as knives, guides, and clamps to accommodate sheets, signatures, or books of specified sizes. Sets machine controls to adjust length and thickness of folds, stitches, or cuts and to adjust speed and pressure. Mounts and secures rolls or reels of wire, cloth, paper, or other material onto machine spindles and fills paper feed. Positions and clamps stitching heads on crossarms to space stitches to specified lengths. Starts machines and makes trial runs to verify accuracy of machine setup. Observes and monitors machine operations to detect malfunctions and makes required adjustments. Fills glue pot and adjusts flow of glue and speed of conveyors. Threads wire into machine to load stitcher head for stapling. Reads work order to determine work instructions. Examines product samples for defects. Cleans and lubricates machinery parts and makes minor repairs. Removes books or products from machine and stacks them. Trains workers to set up, operate, and use automatic bindery machines. Records time spent on specific tasks and number of items produced for daily production sheet. Manually stocks supplies such as signatures, books, or paper.

GOE INFORMATION—Interest Area: 08. Industrial Production. **Work Group:** 08.02. Production Technology. **Personality Type**—Realistic. Realistic occupations frequently involve work activities that include practical, hands-on problems and solutions. They often deal with plants, animals, and real-world materials like wood, tools, and machinery. Many of the occupations require working outside and do not involve a lot of paperwork or working closely with others. **Work Values**—Moral Values; Supervision, Technical; Independence; Activity; Supervision, Human Relations. **Skills**—Operation Monitoring; Operation and Control; Repairing; Installation. **Abilities**—*Cognitive:* Perceptual Speed; Selective Attention; Information Ordering; Oral Expression; Visualization. *Psychomotor:* Control Precision; Arm-Hand Steadiness; Response Orientation; Reaction Time; Speed of Limb Movement. *Physical:* Static Strength; Dynamic Flexibility; Extent Flexibility. *Sensory:* Hearing Sensitivity. **General Work Activities**—*Information Input:* Monitoring Processes, Materials, or Surroundings; Inspecting Equipment, Structures, or Materials; Identifying Objects, Actions, and Events. *Mental Process:* Updating and Using Relevant Knowledge; Judging Qualities of Things, Services, or Other People's Work; Making Decisions and Solving Problems. *Work Output:* Handling and Moving Objects; Controlling Machines and Processes; Performing General Physical Activities. *Interacting with Others:* Communicating with Other Workers; Teaching Others; Performing Administrative Activities. **Physical Work Conditions**—Using Hands on Objects, Tools, or Controls; Making Repetitive Motions; Indoors; Hazardous Equipment; Standing. **Other Job Characteristics**—Pace Determined by Speed of Equipment; Degree of Automation; Importance of Repeating Same Tasks.

Experience—Job Zone 2. Some previous work-related skill, knowledge, or experience may be helpful, but usually is not needed. **Job Preparation:** SVP 4.0 to less than 6.0—six months to less than two years. **Knowledge**—Production and Processing; Mechanical; Education and Training; Clerical; Personnel and Human Resources. **Instructional Programs**—Graphic Communications, Other.

Related DOT Jobs—653.360-010 Casing-in-Line Setter; 653.360-018 Bindery-Machine Setter; 653.382-010 Folding-Machine Operator; 653.382-014 Collating-Machine Operator; 653.662-010 Stitching-Machine Operator; 653.682-010 Book-Sewing-Machine Operator II; 653.682-018 Head-Bander-and-Liner Operator; 653.682-022 Tinning-Machine Set-Up Operator.

51-5011.02 Bindery Machine Operators and Tenders

- **Education/Training Required: Short-term on-the-job training**
- **Employed: No data available.**
- **Annual Earnings: $21,480**
- **Growth: 7.3%**
- **Annual Job Openings: 13,000**

Operate or tend binding machines that round, back, case, line-stitch, press, fold, trim, or perform other binding operations on books and related articles.

Operates or tends machines that perform binding operations, such as pressing, folding, and trimming, on books and related articles. Moves controls to adjust and activate bindery machine to meet specifications. Selects, loads, and adjusts workpieces and machine parts, using hand tools. Feeds books and related articles, such as periodicals and pamphlets, into binding machines, following specifications. Inserts illustrated pages, extra sheets, and collated sets into catalogs, periodicals, directories, and other printed products and applies labels to envelopes, using hands or machine. Stitches or fastens endpapers or bindings, stitches signatures, and applies glue along binding edge of first and last signatures of books. Opens machine and removes and replaces damaged covers and book, using hand tools. Threads spirals in perforated holes of items to be bound, using spindle or rollers. Removes broken wire pieces from machine and loads machine with spool of wire. Punches holes in paper sheets and fastens sheets, signatures, or other material, using hand or machine punch or stapler. Examines printed material and related products for defects and to ensure conformance to specifications. Creases or compresses signatures before affixing covers and places paper jackets on finished books. Applies materials on books or related articles, using machine. Removes printed material or finished products from machines or conveyor belts and stacks material on pallets or skids. Rolls, bends, smoothes, and folds sheets, using hands, and stacks sheets to be returned to binding machines. Wraps product in plastic, using machine, and packs products in boxes. Maintains records of daily production, using specified forms. Cleans work area and maintains equipment and workstations, using hand tools.

GOE INFORMATION—**Interest Area:** 08. Industrial Production. **Work Group:** 08.03. Production Work. **Personality Type**—Realistic. Realistic occupations frequently involve work activities that include practical, hands-on problems and solutions. They often deal with plants, animals, and real-world materials like wood, tools, and machinery. Many of the occupations require working outside and do not involve a lot of paperwork or working closely with others. **Work Values**—Moral Values; Independence; Supervision, Technical; Supervision, Human Relations; Activity. **Skills**—Operation Monitoring; Operation and Control; Quality Control Analysis. **Abilities**—*Cognitive:* Perceptual Speed; Spatial Orientation; Memorization. *Psychomotor:* Rate Control; Control Precision;

Manual Dexterity; Speed of Limb Movement; Arm-Hand Steadiness. *Physical:* Explosive Strength; Dynamic Strength; Dynamic Flexibility; Static Strength; Extent Flexibility. *Sensory:* Peripheral Vision; Depth Perception; Far Vision. **General Work Activities**—*Information Input:* Monitoring Processes, Materials, or Surroundings; Inspecting Equipment, Structures, or Materials; Identifying Objects, Actions, and Events. *Mental Process:* Judging Qualities of Things, Services, or Other People's Work; Updating and Using Relevant Knowledge; Evaluating Information Against Standards. *Work Output:* Handling and Moving Objects; Controlling Machines and Processes; Performing General Physical Activities. *Interacting with Others:* Communicating with Other Workers; Performing Administrative Activities; Coordinating the Work and Activities of Others. **Physical Work Conditions**—Hazardous Equipment; Distracting Sounds and Noise Levels; Using Hands on Objects, Tools, or Controls; Making Repetitive Motions; Minor Burns, Cuts, Bites, or Stings. **Other Job Characteristics**—Pace Determined by Speed of Equipment; Degree of Automation; Importance of Repeating Same Tasks.

Experience—Job Zone 1. No previous work-related skill, knowledge, or experience is needed. **Job Preparation:** SVP below 4.0—less than six months. **Knowledge**—Production and Processing; Mechanical; Clerical; Building and Construction; Design. **Instructional Programs**—Graphic Communications, Other.

Related DOT Jobs—653.682-014 Covering-Machine Operator; 653.685-010 Bindery Worker; 653.685-014 Book-Sewing-Machine Operator I; 653.685-022 Magazine Repairer; 653.685-026 Rounding-and-Backing-Machine Operator; 653.685-030 Spiral Binder; 692.685-146 Saddle-and-Side Wire Stitcher.

51-5012.00 Bookbinders

- **Education/Training Required: Moderate-term on-the-job training**
- **Employed: 9,636**
- **Annual Earnings: $24,660**
- **Growth: 8.2%**
- **Annual Job Openings: 1,000**

Perform highly skilled hand-finishing operations, such as grooving and lettering, to bind books.

Applies glue to back of book, using brush or glue machine, and attaches cloth backing and headband. Cuts binder board to specified dimension, using board shears, hand cutter, or cutting machine. Cuts cover material to specified dimensions and fits and glues material to binder board manually or by machine. Glues outside endpapers to cover. Attaches endpapers to top and bottom of book body, using sewing machine, or glues endpapers and signatures together along spine, using brush or glue machine. Trims edges of book to size, using cutting or book-trimming machine or hand cutter. Inserts book body in device that forms back edge of book into convex shape and produces grooves to facilitate attachment of cover. Applies color to edges of signatures, using brush, pad, or atomizer. Imprints and embosses lettering, designs, or numbers on cover, using gold, silver, or colored foil and stamping machine. Compresses sewed or glued signatures to reduce book to required thickness, using handpress or smashing machine. Folds printed sheets to form signatures (pages) and assembles signatures in numerical order to form book body. Places bound book in press that exerts pressure on cover until glue dries. Packs, weighs, and stacks books on pallet for shipment.

GOE INFORMATION—**Interest Area:** 08. Industrial Production. **Work Group:** 08.02. Production Technology. **Personality Type**—Realistic. Realistic occupations frequently involve work activities that include practical, hands-on problems and solutions. They often deal with plants, animals, and real-world materials like wood, tools, and machinery. Many of the occupations require working outside and do not involve a lot of paperwork or working closely with others. **Work Values**—Supervision, Technical; Moral Values; Independence; Good Working Conditions; Supervision, Human Relations. **Skills**—Operation and Control. **Abilities**—*Cognitive:* None met the criteria. *Psychomotor:* Manual Dexterity; Wrist-Finger Speed; Speed of Limb Movement; Arm-Hand Steadiness; Finger Dexterity. *Physical:* Static Strength; Explosive Strength; Dynamic Flexibility; Dynamic Strength; Trunk Strength. *Sensory:* Visual Color Discrimination; Depth Perception; Peripheral Vision; Glare Sensitivity; Near Vision. **General Work Activities**—*Information Input:* Getting Information; Identifying Objects, Actions, and Events; Monitoring Processes, Materials, or Surroundings. *Mental Process:* Analyzing Data or Information; Evaluating Information Against Standards; Updating and Using Relevant Knowledge. *Work Output:* Handling and Moving Objects; Performing General Physical Activities; Controlling Machines and Processes. *Interacting with Others:* Communicating with Other Workers; Establishing and Maintaining Relationships; Teaching Others. **Physical Work Conditions**—Minor Burns, Cuts, Bites, or Stings; Contaminants; Hazardous Conditions; Indoors; Using Hands on Objects, Tools, or Controls. **Other Job Characteristics**—Degree of Automation; Pace Determined by Speed of Equipment; Importance of Repeating Same Tasks.

Experience—Job Zone 4. A minimum of two to four years of work-related skill, knowledge, or experience is needed. **Job Preparation:** SVP 7.0 to less than 8.0—two years to less than 10 years. **Knowledge**—Production and Processing; Mechanical; Communications and Media; Engineering and Technology; Fine Arts. **Instructional Programs**—Precision Production, Other.

Related DOT Jobs—977.381-010 Bookbinder; 977.381-014 Bookbinder Apprentice.

51-5021.00 Job Printers

- **Education/Training Required: Long-term on-the-job training**
- **Employed: 55,601**
- **Annual Earnings: $29,220**
- **Growth: 6.4%**
- **Annual Job Openings: 6,000**

Set type according to copy, operate press to print job order, read proof for errors and clarity of impression, and correct imperfections. Job printers are often found in small establishments where work combines several job skills.

Selects type from type case and inserts type in printer's stick to reproduce material in copy. Reads proof for errors and clarity of impression. Runs proof sheet through press and examines sheet for clarity of impression. Inserts spacers between words and leads between lines. Lays form on proof press, inks type, fastens paper to press roller, and pulls roller over form to make proof copy. Corrects errors by resetting type and improves impression by tapping face of type with hammer. Pushes button to start press, examines printed sheets, and adjusts press when printing is defective. Slides type from stick into galley. Places chase over type, inserts quoins, and locks chase to hold type. Removes assembled type from galley and places type on composing stone. Positions form (type in locked chase) on bed of press and tightens clamps, using wrench. Fills ink fountain and moves lever to adjust flow of ink. Sets feed guides according to size and thickness of paper. Cleans ink rollers at end of run.

GOE INFORMATION—**Interest Area:** 08. Industrial Production. **Work Group:** 08.03. Production Work. **Personality Type**—Realistic. Realistic occupations frequently involve work activities that include practical, hands-on problems and solutions. They often deal with plants, animals,

and real-world materials like wood, tools, and machinery. Many of the occupations require working outside and do not involve a lot of paperwork or working closely with others. **Work Values**—Independence; Moral Values; Supervision, Technical; Variety; Activity. **Skills**—Operation and Control; Operation Monitoring. **Abilities**—*Cognitive:* Perceptual Speed; Speed of Closure. *Psychomotor:* Finger Dexterity; Manual Dexterity; Wrist-Finger Speed; Control Precision; Speed of Limb Movement. *Physical:* Explosive Strength; Dynamic Flexibility; Extent Flexibility. *Sensory:* Near Vision; Visual Color Discrimination; Glare Sensitivity. **General Work Activities**—*Information Input:* Monitoring Processes, Materials, or Surroundings; Identifying Objects, Actions, and Events; Inspecting Equipment, Structures, or Materials. *Mental Process:* Judging Qualities of Things, Services, or Other People's Work; Evaluating Information Against Standards; Making Decisions and Solving Problems. *Work Output:* Handling and Moving Objects; Controlling Machines and Processes; Performing General Physical Activities. *Interacting with Others:* Establishing and Maintaining Relationships; Monitoring and Controlling Resources; Communicating with Other Workers. **Physical Work Conditions**—Hazardous Equipment; Hazardous Conditions; Contaminants; Distracting Sounds and Noise Levels; Common Protective or Safety Attire. **Other Job Characteristics**—Degree of Automation; Pace Determined by Speed of Equipment; Importance of Being Exact or Accurate.

Experience—Job Zone 5. Extensive skill, knowledge, and experience are needed for these occupations. **Job Preparation:** SVP 8.0 and above—four years to more than 10 years. **Knowledge**—Production and Processing; Communications and Media; English Language; Mechanical; Clerical. **Instructional Programs**—Graphic and Printing Equipment Operator, General Production; Printing Management.

Related DOT Jobs—973.381-018 Job Printer; 973.381-022 Job-Printer Apprentice.

51-5022.00 Prepress Technicians and Workers

- **Education/Training Required: Long-term on-the-job training**
- **Employed: 106,844**
- **Annual Earnings: $30,790**
- **Growth: –15.6%**
- **Annual Job Openings: 12,000**

Set up and prepare material for printing presses.

No task data available.

GOE INFORMATION—**Interest Area:** 08. Industrial Production. **Work Group:** 08.03. Production Work. **Note:** The Department of Labor has not collected some data for this job, so it has fewer details than the other descriptions.

Instructional Programs—Graphic and Printing Equipment Operator, General Production; Graphic Communications, General; Graphic Communications, Other; Graphic Design; Platemaker/Imager; Prepress/Desktop Publishing and Digital Imaging Design; Printing Management.

Related DOT Jobs—208.382-010 Terminal-Makeup Operator; 650.582-010 Linotype Operator; 650.582-014 Monotype-Keyboard Operator; 650.582-018 Photocomposing-Machine Operator; 650.582-022 Phototype-setter Operator; 650.682-010 Equipment Monitor, Phototypesetting; 650.685-010 Typesetting-Machine Tender; 652.585-010 Photolettering-Machine Operator; 652.685-106 Type-Proof Reproducer; 659.360-010 Plate Finisher; 714.381-018 Photographic-Plate Maker; 970.361-014 Repeat Chief; 970.381-018 Lay-Out Former; 970.381-030 Retoucher, Photoengraving; 971.261-010 Etcher, Hand; 971.381-010 Etcher Apprentice, Photoengraving; 971.381-014 Etcher, Photoengraving; 971.381-022 Photoengraver;

971.381-026 Photoengraver Apprentice; 971.381-030 Photoengraving Finisher; others.

51-5022.01 Hand Compositors and Typesetters

- ● **Education/Training Required: Long-term on-the-job training**
- ● **Employed: No data available.**
- ● **Annual Earnings: $30,790**
- ● **Growth: –15.6%**
- ● **Annual Job Openings: 12,000**

Set up and arrange type by hand. Assemble and lock setup of type, cuts, and headings. Pull proofs.

Inserts spacers between words or units to balance and justify lines. Inserts lead, slugs, or lines of quads between lines to adjust length of setup. Arranges, groups, and locks galley setups of type, cuts, and headings in chases according to dummy makeup sheet. Selects type from type case and sets it in compositional sequence, reading from copy. Prepares proof copy of setup, using proof press. Arranges galleys of linotype slugs (takes) in sequence on correction table. Measures copy with line gauge to determine length of line. Transfers type from stick to galley when setup is complete. Compares corrected type slugs against proof to detect errors. Compares symbols on proof with galley symbol and reads portion of text to locate positions for insertion of corrected slugs. Removes incorrect portion and manually inserts corrections. Cleans type after use and distributes it to specified boxes in type case.

GOE INFORMATION—Interest Area: 08. Industrial Production. **Work Group:** 08.03. Production Work. **Personality Type—**Realistic. Realistic occupations frequently involve work activities that include practical, hands-on problems and solutions. They often deal with plants, animals, and real-world materials like wood, tools, and machinery. Many of the occupations require working outside and do not involve a lot of paperwork or working closely with others. **Work Values—**Moral Values; Supervision, Technical; Independence; Good Working Conditions; Supervision, Human Relations. **Skills—**None met the criteria. **Abilities—***Cognitive:* Perceptual Speed; Visualization. *Psychomotor:* Finger Dexterity; Wrist-Finger Speed; Arm-Hand Steadiness. *Physical:* Dynamic Flexibility. *Sensory:* Glare Sensitivity; Near Vision; Peripheral Vision; Depth Perception; Night Vision. **General Work Activities—***Information Input:* Inspecting Equipment, Structures, or Materials; Getting Information; Monitoring Processes, Materials, or Surroundings. *Mental Process:* Evaluating Information Against Standards; Updating and Using Relevant Knowledge; Making Decisions and Solving Problems. *Work Output:* Handling and Moving Objects; Performing General Physical Activities; Controlling Machines and Processes. *Interacting with Others:* Establishing and Maintaining Relationships; Communicating with Other Workers; Monitoring and Controlling Resources. **Physical Work Conditions—**Using Hands on Objects, Tools, or Controls; Hazardous Equipment; Indoors; Distracting Sounds and Noise Levels; Making Repetitive Motions. **Other Job Characteristics—**Importance of Repeating Same Tasks; Importance of Being Exact or Accurate; Pace Determined by Speed of Equipment.

Experience—Job Zone 4. A minimum of two to four years of work-related skill, knowledge, or experience is needed. **Job Preparation:** SVP 7.0 to less than 8.0—two years to less than 10 years. **Knowledge—**Production and Processing; Communications and Media; English Language; Clerical; Engineering and Technology. **Instructional Programs—**Graphic and Printing Equipment Operator, General Production; Graphic Communications, General; Graphic Communications, Other; Graphic Design; Platemaker/Imager; Prepress/Desktop Publishing and Digital Imaging Design; Printing Management.

Related DOT Jobs—973.381-010 Compositor; 973.381-014 Compositor Apprentice; 973.381-026 Make-Up Arranger; 973.381-030 Proofsheet Corrector; 973.681-010 Galley Stripper.

51-5022.02 Paste-Up Workers

- ● **Education/Training Required: Long-term on-the-job training**
- ● **Employed: No data available.**
- ● **Annual Earnings: $30,790**
- ● **Growth: –15.6%**
- ● **Annual Job Openings: 12,000**

Arrange and mount typeset material and illustrations into pasteup for printing reproduction based on artist's or editor's layout.

Measures and marks board according to layout to indicate position of artwork, typeset copy, page edges, folds, and colors. Cuts typeset copy and artwork to size, applies adhesive, and aligns artwork and typeset copy on board, following position marks. Measures artwork and layout space of artwork on pasteup. Compares measurements, using ruler and proportion wheel, to determine proportions needed to make reduced or enlarged photographic prints for pasteup. Tapes transparent plastic overlay to board and positions and applies copy to plastic. Operates electronic plotter to draw artwork positions on pasteup. Operates phototypesetter to prepare typeset copy for pasteup. Applies masking film to artwork layout space on overlay to create clear space on negative for subsequent addition of artwork. Indicates crop marks and enlargement or reduction measurements on photographs with grease pencil to facilitate processing. Makes negatives or prints of artwork, using photographic equipment, to prepare artwork for pasteup. Removes excess adhesive from board, using scissors, artist's knife, and drafting instruments. Covers photographs and artwork with tissue or tracing paper for protection. Draws functional and decorative borders around layout, using marking and measuring instruments. Writes specifications on tracing paper to provide information for other workers.

GOE INFORMATION—Interest Area: 01. Arts, Entertainment, and Media. **Work Group:** 01.07. Graphic Arts. **Personality Type—**Realistic. Realistic occupations frequently involve work activities that include practical, hands-on problems and solutions. They often deal with plants, animals, and real-world materials like wood, tools, and machinery. Many of the occupations require working outside and do not involve a lot of paperwork or working closely with others. **Work Values—**Good Working Conditions; Independence; Moral Values; Variety; Advancement. **Skills—**Operation and Control; Operation Monitoring. **Abilities—***Cognitive:* Perceptual Speed; Visualization. *Psychomotor:* Arm-Hand Steadiness; Wrist-Finger Speed; Manual Dexterity; Multilimb Coordination; Control Precision. *Physical:* None met the criteria. *Sensory:* Visual Color Discrimination; Glare Sensitivity; Night Vision; Sound Localization; Near Vision. **General Work Activities—***Information Input:* Getting Information; Monitoring Processes, Materials, or Surroundings; Estimating Needed Characteristics. *Mental Process:* Thinking Creatively; Evaluating Information Against Standards; Making Decisions and Solving Problems. *Work Output:* Handling and Moving Objects; Controlling Machines and Processes; Drafting and Specifying Technical Devices. *Interacting with Others:* Communicating with Other Workers; Establishing and Maintaining Relationships; Interpreting Meaning of Information for Others. **Physical Work Conditions—**Minor Burns, Cuts, Bites, or Stings; Contaminants; Indoors; Using Hands on Objects, Tools, or Controls; Sitting. **Other Job Characteristics—**Importance of Being Exact or Accurate; Degree of Automation; Importance of Repeating Same Tasks.

Experience—Job Zone 4. A minimum of two to four years of work-related skill, knowledge, or experience is needed. **Job Preparation:** SVP 7.0 to less than 8.0—two years to less than 10 years. **Knowledge—**Design;

Communications and Media; Fine Arts; Clerical; Production and Processing. **Instructional Programs**—Graphic and Printing Equipment Operator, General Production; Graphic Communications, General; Graphic Communications, Other; Graphic Design; Platemaker/Imager; Prepress/Desktop Publishing and Digital Imaging Design; Printing Management.

Related DOT Jobs—970.381-018 Lay-Out Former; 972.381-030 Paste-Up Artist; 972.381-038 Paste-Up Artist Apprentice.

51-5022.03 Photoengravers

- ● **Education/Training Required: Long-term on-the-job training**
- ● **Employed: No data available.**
- ● **Annual Earnings: $30,790**
- ● **Growth: –15.6%**
- ● **Annual Job Openings: 12,000**

Photograph copy, develop negatives, and prepare photosensitized metal plates for use in letterpress and gravure printing.

Develops and prints negatives, positives, film, or plates by controlled exposure to light, using exposure equipment, chemical baths, and vacuum. Transfers images, designs, or patterns onto rollers, plates, or film, using photographic or pantographic equipment and techniques and hand tools. Positions, loads, or mounts copy, plates, film, or rollers and secures into place. Washes rollers and plates preparatory to etching or to remove resistant solution and photographic emulsion, using water, cleaning solution, and brush. Brushes protective solution and powder on plate and starts machine to distribute acid or photosensitizing solution over plate or rollers. Computes camera machine settings for film exposure or reproduction, using equipment meter, computer, worksheets, and standard formulas and tables. Etches designs on metal rollers and plates, using etching machines, hand tools, and acidic chemicals, to produce printing plates and rollers. Mixes caustic or acid solutions. Modifies or repairs plates or film, using etching and artist's brush, acid, and hand tools. Examines developed film, proof, or engravings, using magnifier, chalk, or charcoal to evaluate quality and detect errors. Matches colors with original to produce balanced color values or intensity design. Studies and compares film negatives or positives with originals or design to determine photographic requirements and verify reproduction.

GOE INFORMATION—Interest Area: 01. Arts, Entertainment, and Media. **Work Group:** 01.07. Graphic Arts. **Personality Type**—Realistic. Realistic occupations frequently involve work activities that include practical, hands-on problems and solutions. They often deal with plants, animals, and real-world materials like wood, tools, and machinery. Many of the occupations require working outside and do not involve a lot of paperwork or working closely with others. **Work Values**—Independence; Supervision, Technical; Autonomy; Moral Values; Variety. **Skills**—Operation and Control. **Abilities**—*Cognitive:* Flexibility of Closure; Perceptual Speed; Visualization; Spatial Orientation; Category Flexibility. *Psychomotor:* Finger Dexterity; Arm-Hand Steadiness; Manual Dexterity; Wrist-Finger Speed; Rate Control. *Physical:* Dynamic Flexibility. *Sensory:* Night Vision; Visual Color Discrimination; Near Vision; Glare Sensitivity; Depth Perception. **General Work Activities**—*Information Input:* Monitoring Processes, Materials, or Surroundings; Identifying Objects, Actions, and Events; Getting Information. *Mental Process:* Updating and Using Relevant Knowledge; Thinking Creatively; Evaluating Information Against Standards. *Work Output:* Handling and Moving Objects; Controlling Machines and Processes; Performing General Physical Activities. *Interacting with Others:* Establishing and Maintaining Relationships; Communicating with Other Workers; Assisting and Caring for Others. **Physical Work Conditions**—Contaminants; Hazardous Conditions; Common Protective or Safety Attire; Making Repetitive Motions; Extremely Bright or Inad-

equate Lighting. **Other Job Characteristics**—Degree of Automation; Pace Determined by Speed of Equipment; Importance of Being Exact or Accurate.

Experience—Job Zone 4. A minimum of two to four years of work-related skill, knowledge, or experience is needed. **Job Preparation:** SVP 7.0 to less than 8.0—two years to less than 10 years. **Knowledge**—Fine Arts; Chemistry; Computers and Electronics; Design; Physics. **Instructional Programs**—Graphic and Printing Equipment Operator, General Production; Graphic Communications, General; Graphic Communications, Other; Graphic Design; Platemaker/Imager; Prepress/Desktop Publishing and Digital Imaging Design; Printing Management.

Related DOT Jobs—970.361-014 Repeat Chief; 970.381-030 Retoucher, Photoengraving; 971.261-010 Etcher, Hand; 971.381-010 Etcher Apprentice, Photoengraving; 971.381-014 Etcher, Photoengraving; 971.381-022 Photoengraver; 971.381-026 Photoengraver Apprentice; 971.381-030 Photoengraving Finisher; 971.381-034 Photoengraving Printer; 971.381-038 Photoengraving Proofer; 971.381-040 Photoengraving-Proofer Apprentice; 971.382-014 Photographer, Photoengraving; 971.382-018 Repeat-Photocomposing-Machine Operator; 972.382-018 Photo Mask Maker, Electron-Beam.

51-5022.04 Camera Operators

- ● **Education/Training Required: Long-term on-the-job training**
- ● **Employed: No data available.**
- ● **Annual Earnings: $30,790**
- ● **Growth: –15.6%**
- ● **Annual Job Openings: 12,000**

Operate process camera and related darkroom equipment to photograph and develop negatives of material to be printed.

Feeds film into automatic film processor that develops, fixes, washes, and dries film. Adjusts camera settings, lights, and lens. Selects and installs screens and filters in camera to produce desired effects. Exposes high-contrast film for predetermined exposure time. Immerses film in series of chemical baths to develop images and hangs film on rack to dry. Performs exposure tests to determine line, halftone, and color reproduction exposure lengths for various photographic factors. Measures density of continuous tone images to be photographed to set exposure time for halftone images. Mounts material to be photographed on copyboard of camera. Measures original layouts and determines proportions needed to make reduced or enlarged photographic prints for pasteup.

GOE INFORMATION—Interest Area: 01. Arts, Entertainment, and Media. **Work Group:** 01.07. Graphic Arts. **Personality Type**—Realistic. Realistic occupations frequently involve work activities that include practical, hands-on problems and solutions. They often deal with plants, animals, and real-world materials like wood, tools, and machinery. Many of the occupations require working outside and do not involve a lot of paperwork or working closely with others. **Work Values**—Independence; Creativity; Autonomy; Moral Values; Social Status. **Skills**—Technology Design; Equipment Selection; Operation and Control; Quality Control Analysis. **Abilities**—*Cognitive:* Visualization; Information Ordering; Spatial Orientation. *Psychomotor:* Arm-Hand Steadiness; Multilimb Coordination; Control Precision. *Physical:* Gross Body Coordination; Extent Flexibility; Gross Body Equilibrium. *Sensory:* Visual Color Discrimination; Night Vision; Glare Sensitivity; Near Vision. **General Work Activities**—*Information Input:* Monitoring Processes, Materials, or Surroundings; Getting Information; Identifying Objects, Actions, and Events. *Mental Process:* Processing Information; Making Decisions and Solving Problems; Thinking Creatively. *Work Output:* Handling and Moving Objects; Controlling Machines and Processes; Performing General Physical Activities. *Interacting with Others:* Communicating with Other Workers; Communicating with Persons Outside Organization; Establishing and Maintaining Relationships. **Physical Work Conditions**—Indoors; Extremely Bright or Inadequate Lighting; Cramped Work Space or Awkward Positions; Bending or Twisting the Body; Using Hands on Objects, Tools, or Controls. **Other Job Characteristics**—Pace Determined by Speed of Equipment; Importance of Repeating Same Tasks; Importance of Being Exact or Accurate.

Experience—Job Zone 4. A minimum of two to four years of work-related skill, knowledge, or experience is needed. **Job Preparation:** SVP 7.0 to less than 8.0—two years to less than 10 years. **Knowledge**—Fine Arts; Chemistry; Production and Processing. **Instructional Programs**—Graphic and Printing Equipment Operator, General Production; Graphic Communications, General; Graphic Communications, Other; Graphic Design; Platemaker/Imager; Prepress/Desktop Publishing and Digital Imaging Design; Printing Management.

Related DOT Jobs—972.382-010 Photographer Apprentice, Lithographic; 972.382-014 Photographer, Lithographic.

51-5022.05 Scanner Operators

- ● **Education/Training Required: Long-term on-the-job training**
- ● **Employed: No data available.**
- ● **Annual Earnings: $30,790**
- ● **Growth: –15.6%**
- ● **Annual Job Openings: 12,000**

Operate electronic or computerized scanning equipment to produce and screen film separations of photographs or art for use in producing lithographic printing plates. Evaluate and correct for deficiencies in the film.

Activates scanner to produce positive or negative films for each primary color and black in original copy. Types on scanner keyboard or touches mouse to symbols on scanner video display unit to input software or moves controls to set scanner to specific color density, size, screen ruling, and exposure adjustments. Loads film into holder, places holder in exposing chamber, and starts mechanism that loads and secures film on scanner drum. Unloads exposed film from scanner and places film in automatic processor to develop image on film. Inspects developed film for specified results and quality and forwards acceptable negatives or positives to other workers or customer. Analyzes original to evaluate color density, gradation highlights, middle tones, and shadows, using densitometer and knowledge of light and color. Performs tests to determine exposure adjustments on scanner and adjusts scanner controls until specified results are obtained. Positions color transparency, negative, or reflection copy on scanning drum and mounts drum and head on scanner.

GOE INFORMATION—**Interest Area:** 08. Industrial Production. **Work Group:** 08.03. Production Work. **Personality Type**—Realistic. Realistic occupations frequently involve work activities that include practical, hands-on problems and solutions. They often deal with plants, animals, and real-world materials like wood, tools, and machinery. Many of the occupations require working outside and do not involve a lot of paperwork or working closely with others. **Work Values**—Moral Values; Independence; Autonomy; Good Working Conditions; Creativity. **Skills**—Quality Control Analysis; Operation and Control. **Abilities**—*Cognitive:* Perceptual Speed; Memorization. *Psychomotor:* Control Precision; Response Orientation; Finger Dexterity; Rate Control. *Physical:* None met the criteria. *Sensory:* Visual Color Discrimination; Night Vision; Near Vision; Glare Sensitivity; Depth Perception. **General Work Activities**—*Information Input:* Identifying Objects, Actions, and Events;

Monitoring Processes, Materials, or Surroundings; Getting Information. *Mental Process:* Thinking Creatively; Judging Qualities of Things, Services, or Other People's Work; Evaluating Information Against Standards. *Work Output:* Handling and Moving Objects; Controlling Machines and Processes; Interacting with Computers. *Interacting with Others:* Communicating with Persons Outside Organization; Communicating with Other Workers; Establishing and Maintaining Relationships. **Physical Work Conditions**—Using Hands on Objects, Tools, or Controls; Sitting; Extremely Bright or Inadequate Lighting; Contaminants; Making Repetitive Motions. **Other Job Characteristics**—Degree of Automation; Pace Determined by Speed of Equipment; Importance of Being Exact or Accurate.

Experience—Job Zone 4. A minimum of two to four years of work-related skill, knowledge, or experience is needed. **Job Preparation:** SVP 7.0 to less than 8.0—two years to less than 10 years. **Knowledge**—Fine Arts; Production and Processing; Computers and Electronics; Chemistry; Communications and Media. **Instructional Programs**—Graphic and Printing Equipment Operator, General Production; Graphic Communications, General; Graphic Communications, Other; Graphic Design; Platemaker/Imager; Prepress/Desktop Publishing and Digital Imaging Design; Printing Management.

Related DOT Jobs—972.282-010 Scanner Operator.

51-5022.06 Strippers

- ● **Education/Training Required: Long-term on-the-job training**
- ● **Employed: No data available.**
- ● **Annual Earnings: $30,790**
- ● **Growth: –15.6%**
- ● **Annual Job Openings: 12,000**

Cut and arrange film into flats (layout sheets resembling a film negative of text in its final form) which are used to make plates. Prepare separate flat for each color.

Cuts image window area to allow exposure to plate or film, using razor or artist's knife. Applies rubber solution and collodion to toughen negative, cuts to size, and immerses in acid bath to prepare negative for stripping. Positions film negatives or positives on light table according to art layout, blueprint, and color register to form film flat. Selects and inserts screen tints in film flat, using knowledge of dot percentages required to obtain specific colors. Cuts masks and arranges negatives to prepare for contact printing, plate exposure, or proof making. Aligns negatives and masks over unexposed film in vacuum frame to make negatives or positives for final film of each color. Assembles and aligns negatives or positives to assure register and fit with units of color. Strips negative from base. Examines pasteup, artwork, film, prints, and instructions to determine size and dimensions, number of job colors, and camera work needed. Makes proof from film flat to determine accuracy of flat. Determines proportions needed to reduce or enlarge photographs and graphics to fit in designated area, using calculator or proportion scale. Examines negatives and photographs to detect defective areas, using lighted viewing table. Determines or approves plans and page sequences to lay out job for specific printing press. Touches up imperfections, using opaque and brush on negatives and needle and crayon pencil on photographs. Examines proof returned by customer and makes corrections according to customer specifications. Sends completed flat to proofing area or platemaking area for preparation of final proof or lithographic plate. Draws ruled lines and borders around negatives or positives.

GOE INFORMATION—**Interest Area:** 08. Industrial Production. **Work Group:** 08.03. Production Work. **Personality Type**—Realistic. Realistic occupations frequently involve work activities that include practical, hands-on problems and solutions. They often deal with plants, animals, and real-world materials like wood, tools, and machinery. Many of the occupations require working outside and do not involve a lot of paperwork or working closely with others. **Work Values**—Independence; Creativity; Moral Values; Supervision, Technical; Responsibility. **Skills**—Equipment Selection; Operation and Control. **Abilities**—*Cognitive:* Visualization; Fluency of Ideas; Information Ordering. *Psychomotor:* Arm-Hand Steadiness; Finger Dexterity. *Physical:* None met the criteria. *Sensory:* Visual Color Discrimination; Night Vision; Near Vision. **General Work Activities**—*Information Input:* Getting Information; Identifying Objects, Actions, and Events; Monitoring Processes, Materials, or Surroundings. *Mental Process:* Updating and Using Relevant Knowledge; Judging Qualities of Things, Services, or Other People's Work; Evaluating Information Against Standards. *Work Output:* Handling and Moving Objects; Performing General Physical Activities; Controlling Machines and Processes. *Interacting with Others:* Communicating with Other Workers; Communicating with Persons Outside Organization; Performing Administrative Activities. **Physical Work Conditions**—Indoors; Sitting; Extremely Bright or Inadequate Lighting; Making Repetitive Motions; Using Hands on Objects, Tools, or Controls. **Other Job Characteristics**—Importance of Being Exact or Accurate; Degree of Automation; Importance of Repeating Same Tasks.

Experience—Job Zone 4. A minimum of two to four years of work-related skill, knowledge, or experience is needed. **Job Preparation:** SVP 7.0 to less than 8.0—two years to less than 10 years. **Knowledge**—Fine Arts; Chemistry; Production and Processing; Design. **Instructional Programs**—Graphic and Printing Equipment Operator, General Production; Graphic Communications, General; Graphic Communications, Other; Graphic Design; Platemaker/Imager; Prepress/Desktop Publishing and Digital Imaging Design; Printing Management.

Related DOT Jobs—971.381-050 Stripper; 971.381-054 Stripper Apprentice; 972.281-022 Stripper, Lithographic I; 972.381-022 Stripper, Lithographic II.

51-5022.07 Platemakers

- **Education/Training Required: Long-term on-the-job training**
- **Employed: No data available.**
- **Annual Earnings: $30,790**
- **Growth: –15.6%**
- **Annual Job Openings: 12,000**

Produce printing plates by exposing sensitized metal sheets to special light through a photographic negative. May operate machines that process plates automatically.

Mounts negative and plate in camera that exposes exposed plate to artificial light through photographic negative, thus transferring image. Transfers image from master plate to unexposed plate and immerses plate in developing solution to develop image on plate. Transfers images by hand and covers surface of plates with photosensitive chemical, using brush, and allows plate to dry. Lowers vacuum frame onto plate-film assembly to establish contact between positive-negative film and plate and sets timer to expose plate. Removes plate-film assembly from vacuum frame and places exposed plate in automatic processor to develop image and dry plate. Mixes and applies chemical-based developing solution to plates and replenishes solution in processor to maintain it in working order. Examines unexposed photographic plate to detect flaws or foreign particles prior to printing pattern of aperture masks on sensitized steel. Examines plate, using light-box and microscope to detect flaws, verify conformity with master plate, and measure dot size and center. Installs and aligns plates in printing case. Repairs defective plates with missing dots, using photographic touch-up tool and ink. Punches holes in light-sensitive

plate and inserts pins in holes to prepare plate for contact with positive or negative film. Places plate in vacuum frame to align positives or negatives with each other and places masking paper over uncovered areas. Performs tests to determine time required for exposure by exposing plates and compares exposure to scale which measures tone ranges.

GOE INFORMATION—**Interest Area:** 08. Industrial Production. **Work Group:** 08.03. Production Work. **Personality Type**—Realistic. Realistic occupations frequently involve work activities that include practical, hands-on problems and solutions. They often deal with plants, animals, and real-world materials like wood, tools, and machinery. Many of the occupations require working outside and do not involve a lot of paperwork or working closely with others. **Work Values**—Independence; Creativity; Moral Values; Supervision, Technical; Responsibility. **Skills**—Quality Control Analysis; Operation and Control; Operation Monitoring; Installation. **Abilities**—*Cognitive:* Visualization. *Psychomotor:* Arm-Hand Steadiness; Multilimb Coordination. *Physical:* Extent Flexibility. *Sensory:* Glare Sensitivity. **General Work Activities**—*Information Input:* Monitoring Processes, Materials, or Surroundings; Identifying Objects, Actions, and Events; Inspecting Equipment, Structures, or Materials. *Mental Process:* Evaluating Information Against Standards; Judging Qualities of Things, Services, or Other People's Work; Organizing, Planning, and Prioritizing. *Work Output:* Handling and Moving Objects; Controlling Machines and Processes; Performing General Physical Activities. *Interacting with Others:* Communicating with Other Workers; Establishing and Maintaining Relationships; Coordinating the Work and Activities of Others. **Physical Work Conditions**—Using Hands on Objects, Tools, or Controls; Minor Burns, Cuts, Bites, or Stings; Making Repetitive Motions; Indoors. **Other Job Characteristics**—Importance of Being Exact or Accurate; Pace Determined by Speed of Equipment; Degree of Automation.

Experience—Job Zone 3. Previous work-related skill, knowledge, or experience is required. **Job Preparation:** SVP 6.0 to less than 7.0—more than one year and less than four years. **Knowledge**—Chemistry; Production and Processing; Fine Arts; Physics; Engineering and Technology. **Instructional Programs**—Graphic and Printing Equipment Operator, General Production; Graphic Communications, General; Graphic Communications, Other; Graphic Design; Platemaker/Imager; Prepress/Desktop Publishing and Digital Imaging Design; Printing Management.

Related DOT Jobs—714.381-018 Photographic-Plate Maker; 972.381-010 Lithographic Platemaker; 972.381-014 Lithographic-Plate-Maker Apprentice; 972.381-026 Transferrer.

51-5022.08 Dot Etchers

- **Education/Training Required: Long-term on-the-job training**
- **Employed: No data available.**
- **Annual Earnings: $30,790**
- **Growth: –15.6%**
- **Annual Job Openings: 12,000**

Increase or reduce size of photographic dots by chemical or photomechanical methods to make color corrections on halftone negatives or positives to be used in preparation of lithographic printing plates.

Places masks over separation negatives or positives and exposes film for specified time, using contact frame and automatic film processor to reduce size of photographic dots to increase or reduce color. Prepares dyes and other chemical solutions according to standard and applies solution to inaccurately colored areas of film to correct color by chemical method. Blocks out or modifies color shades of film, using template, brushes, and opaque. Prepares photographic masks to protect areas of film not needing correction, using contact frame and automatic film processor or by manually cutting masking material, to correct color by photomechanical method. Determines extent of correction and exposure length needed based on experience or predetermined exposure and color charts. Compares proof print of color separation negative or positive with customer's original copy and standard color chart to determine accuracy of reproduction. Applies opaque to defective areas of film to block out blemishes and pinholes. Examines film on light table to determine specified color and color balance, using magnifying glass or densitometer. Identifies and marks color discrepancies on print and film.

GOE INFORMATION—Interest Area: 01. Arts, Entertainment, and Media. **Work Group:** 01.07. Graphic Arts. **Personality Type**—Realistic. Realistic occupations frequently involve work activities that include practical, hands-on problems and solutions. They often deal with plants, animals, and real-world materials like wood, tools, and machinery. Many of the occupations require working outside and do not involve a lot of paperwork or working closely with others. **Work Values**—Independence; Moral Values; Autonomy; Good Working Conditions; Creativity. **Skills**—Equipment Selection. **Abilities**—*Cognitive:* Flexibility of Closure; Visualization; Category Flexibility; Speed of Closure; Information Ordering. *Psychomotor:* Arm-Hand Steadiness. *Physical:* None met the criteria. *Sensory:* Visual Color Discrimination; Night Vision; Near Vision; Depth Perception; Glare Sensitivity. **General Work Activities**—*Information Input:* Monitoring Processes, Materials, or Surroundings; Getting Information; Identifying Objects, Actions, and Events. *Mental Process:* Thinking Creatively; Updating and Using Relevant Knowledge; Making Decisions and Solving Problems. *Work Output:* Handling and Moving Objects; Controlling Machines and Processes; Repairing and Maintaining Mechanical Equipment. *Interacting with Others:* Communicating with Other Workers; Monitoring and Controlling Resources; Establishing and Maintaining Relationships. **Physical Work Conditions**—Radiation; Extremely Bright or Inadequate Lighting; Using Hands on Objects, Tools, or Controls; Hazardous Conditions; Specialized Protective or Safety Attire. **Other Job Characteristics**—Pace Determined by Speed of Equipment; Importance of Being Exact or Accurate; Importance of Repeating Same Tasks.

Experience—Job Zone 5. Extensive skill, knowledge, and experience are needed for these occupations. **Job Preparation:** SVP 8.0 and above—four years to more than 10 years. **Knowledge**—Fine Arts; Chemistry; Production and Processing; Customer and Personal Service. **Instructional Programs**—Graphic and Printing Equipment Operator, General Production; Graphic Communications, General; Graphic Communications, Other; Graphic Design; Platemaker/Imager; Prepress/Desktop Publishing and Digital Imaging Design; Printing Management.

Related DOT Jobs—972.281-010 Dot Etcher; 972.281-018 Dot Etcher Apprentice.

51-5022.09 Electronic Masking System Operators

- **Education/Training Required: Long-term on-the-job training**
- **Employed: 106,844**
- **Annual Earnings: $30,790**
- **Growth: −15.6%**
- **Annual Job Openings: 12,000**

Operate computerized masking system to produce stripping masks used in production of offset lithographic printing plates.

Views monitors for feedback and error prompts, for visual representations of work in progress, and for numerical information such as width of line and last point plotted. Selects options on menu of electronic masking system, such as shape, dimensions of designs to be drawn, register marks, and retrieval of stored designs. Touches symbol of option selected on menu and activates option with mouse. Touches reference points of designs on layout sheet, using mouse, and presses button of mouse to enter coordinates of design in system memory. Presses button to activate vacuum to hold masking in place and to activate drafting unit that scores masking material with programmed figures. Activates plotting drum to make photographic mask exposures. Presses button to transfer data from system memory to disk. Loads drafting unit with masking material to prepare for plotting and scoring of programmed figures or loads film into plotting drum to make photographic mask exposure. Studies layout sheet to determine shapes of windows drawn on layout sheet. Positions artist's layout on digitizing tables of electronic masking system to prepare for data entry in system memory. Removes film from plotting drum and puts film in automatic film processor to create masks. Removes scored masking material from drafting table. Places material on light table and peels scored figures from masking material, using needle and tape.

GOE INFORMATION—Interest Area: 01. Arts, Entertainment, and Media. **Work Group:** 01.07. Graphic Arts. **Personality Type**—Realistic. Realistic occupations frequently involve work activities that include practical, hands-on problems and solutions. They often deal with plants, animals, and real-world materials like wood, tools, and machinery. Many of the occupations require working outside and do not involve a lot of paperwork or working closely with others. **Work Values**—Independence; Moral Values; Good Working Conditions; Supervision, Technical; Social Status. **Skills**—Operation and Control. **Abilities**—*Cognitive:* Visualization; Fluency of Ideas; Information Ordering. *Psychomotor:* Arm-Hand Steadiness. *Physical:* None met the criteria. *Sensory:* None met the criteria. **General Work Activities**—*Information Input:* Monitoring Processes, Materials, or Surroundings; Getting Information; Identifying Objects, Actions, and Events. *Mental Process:* Updating and Using Relevant Knowledge; Thinking Creatively; Processing Information. *Work Output:* Interacting with Computers; Handling and Moving Objects; Controlling Machines and Processes. *Interacting with Others:* Communicating with Other Workers; Establishing and Maintaining Relationships; Assisting and Caring for Others. **Physical Work Conditions**—Sitting; Using Hands on Objects, Tools, or Controls; Indoors. **Other Job Characteristics**—Degree of Automation; Pace Determined by Speed of Equipment; Importance of Being Exact or Accurate.

Experience—Job Zone 4. A minimum of two to four years of work-related skill, knowledge, or experience is needed. **Job Preparation:** SVP 7.0 to less than 8.0—two years to less than 10 years. **Knowledge**—Design; Computers and Electronics; Production and Processing; Fine Arts; Engineering and Technology. **Instructional Programs**—Graphic and Printing Equipment Operator, General Production; Graphic Communications, General; Graphic Communications, Other; Graphic Design; Platemaker/Imager; Prepress/Desktop Publishing and Digital Imaging Design; Printing Management.

Related DOT Jobs—972.282-018 Electronic Masking System Operator; 972.382-022 Photo Mask Technician, Electron-Beam.

51-5022.10 Electrotypers and Stereotypers

- **Education/Training Required: Long-term on-the-job training**
- **Employed: No data available.**
- **Annual Earnings: $30,790**
- **Growth: −15.6%**
- **Annual Job Openings: 12,000**

Fabricate and finish electrotype and stereotype printing plates.

Inserts pins in base to register stereotype plates to key plate for mat molding. Pours metal into casting box or plated mold by hand to produce electrotype or stereotype printing plates. Drills matching holes in series of mounted color stereotype plates to be duplicated. Forms mold of composed type, using plastic sheet-molding or wood-fiber mat and hydraulic press. Operates automatic casting machine to produce electrotype or stereotype printing plates. Corrects defects on plate, using engraver's hand tools, punches, and hammers. Removes excess metal from edges, back, and nonprinting surface areas of plate, using power shear, milling machines, or routing machine. Aligns and notches mats of color series with key color mat, using matching machine with monocolor magnifier attachment. Trims mat, using trimming machine, by aligning notches of mat with pins on trimming machine. Sprays plastic mold with silver solution and immerses mold in plating tank. Examines plate to detect imperfect formation of lines, type, and halftone dots, using magnifier. Operates proof press to obtain proof of plate reproduction and registration. Cuts and pastes pieces of paper-felt or cardboard in nonprinting areas of wood-fiber mat to prevent collapse during casting. Curves plates for cylinder presses, using plate-curving machine. Mounts finished plates on wood or metal blocks for flatbed presses, using hammer, nails, or bonding press.

GOE INFORMATION—Interest Area: 08. Industrial Production. Work Group: 08.03. Production Work. Personality Type—Realistic. Realistic occupations frequently involve work activities that include practical, hands-on problems and solutions. They often deal with plants, animals, and real-world materials like wood, tools, and machinery. Many of the occupations require working outside and do not involve a lot of paperwork or working closely with others. Work Values—Independence; Supervision, Technical; Moral Values; Supervision, Human Relations; Good Working Conditions. Skills—Operation and Control. Abilities—Cognitive: Visualization; Category Flexibility; Information Ordering. Psychomotor: Arm-Hand Steadiness; Manual Dexterity; Rate Control; Finger Dexterity; Control Precision. Physical: Explosive Strength; Extent Flexibility; Static Strength; Dynamic Flexibility; Dynamic Strength. Sensory: Visual Color Discrimination; Near Vision. General Work Activities—Information Input: Monitoring Processes, Materials, or Surroundings; Getting Information; Identifying Objects, Actions, and Events. Mental Process: Evaluating Information Against Standards; Judging Qualities of Things, Services, or Other People's Work; Analyzing Data or Information. Work Output: Handling and Moving Objects; Controlling Machines and Processes; Performing General Physical Activities. Interacting with Others: Establishing and Maintaining Relationships; Coordinating the Work and Activities of Others; Communicating with Other Workers. Physical Work Conditions—Hazardous Equipment; Common Protective or Safety Attire; Using Hands on Objects, Tools, or Controls; Making Repetitive Motions; Distracting Sounds and Noise Levels. Other Job Characteristics—Pace Determined by Speed of Equipment; Importance of Repeating Same Tasks; Degree of Automation.

Experience—Job Zone 5. Extensive skill, knowledge, and experience are needed for these occupations. Job Preparation: SVP 8.0 and above—four years to more than 10 years. Knowledge—Mechanical; Production and Processing; Engineering and Technology; Building and Construction; Chemistry. Instructional Programs—Graphic and Printing Equipment Operator, General Production; Graphic Communications, General; Graphic Communications, Other; Graphic Design; Platemaker/Imager; Prepress/Desktop Publishing and Digital Imaging Design; Printing Management.

Related DOT Jobs—974.381-010 Electrotyper; 974.381-014 Electrotyper Apprentice; 974.382-010 Stereotyper Apprentice; 974.382-014 Stereotyper.

51-5022.11 Plate Finishers

- Education/Training Required: Long-term on-the-job training
- Employed: No data available.
- Annual Earnings: $30,790
- Growth: −15.6%
- Annual Job Openings: 12,000

Set up and operate equipment to trim and mount electrotype or stereotype plates.

Selects cutting position and sets controls of saws, milling machines, and routers, following specifications. Operates cutting tools to shave and smooth plates to specified thickness. Operates plate curving machine to cut plates to fit printing press. Mounts finished plates on wood or metal blocks, using hammer and nails or thermoplastic adhesive and heat press. Operates press to print proof of plate, observing printing quality. Rubs surface with finishing material to reveal unevenness. Taps plate with hammer and block to flatten until even. Examines plates with magnifier or microscope to detect flaws, using engraver's tools.

GOE INFORMATION—Interest Area: 08. Industrial Production. Work Group: 08.03. Production Work. Personality Type—Realistic. Realistic occupations frequently involve work activities that include practical, hands-on problems and solutions. They often deal with plants, animals, and real-world materials like wood, tools, and machinery. Many of the occupations require working outside and do not involve a lot of paperwork or working closely with others. Work Values—Independence; Moral Values; Supervision, Technical; Supervision, Human Relations; Company Policies and Practices. Skills—Operation and Control. Abilities—Cognitive: Flexibility of Closure; Spatial Orientation; Perceptual Speed. Psychomotor: Rate Control; Reaction Time; Control Precision; Manual Dexterity; Arm-Hand Steadiness. Physical: Explosive Strength; Dynamic Strength; Static Strength; Stamina; Trunk Strength. Sensory: Depth Perception; Near Vision; Peripheral Vision; Visual Color Discrimination; Sound Localization. General Work Activities—Information Input: Inspecting Equipment, Structures, or Materials; Identifying Objects, Actions, and Events; Getting Information. Mental Process: Judging Qualities of Things, Services, or Other People's Work; Evaluating Information Against Standards; Updating and Using Relevant Knowledge. Work Output: Handling and Moving Objects; Controlling Machines and Processes; Performing General Physical Activities. Interacting with Others: Communicating with Other Workers; Assisting and Caring for Others; Coordinating the Work and Activities of Others. Physical Work Conditions—Hazardous Equipment; Using Hands on Objects, Tools, or Controls; Making Repetitive Motions; Distracting Sounds and Noise Levels; Common Protective or Safety Attire. Other Job Characteristics—Degree of Automation; Pace Determined by Speed of Equipment; Importance of Being Exact or Accurate.

Experience—Job Zone 5. Extensive skill, knowledge, and experience are needed for these occupations. Job Preparation: SVP 8.0 and above—four years to more than 10 years. Knowledge—Production and Processing; Mechanical; Engineering and Technology. Instructional Programs—Graphic and Printing Equipment Operator, General Production; Graphic Communications, General; Graphic Communications, Other; Graphic Design; Platemaker/Imager; Prepress/Desktop Publishing and Digital Imaging Design; Printing Management.

Related DOT Jobs—659.360-010 Plate Finisher.

51-5022.12 Typesetting and Composing Machine Operators and Tenders

- Education/Training Required: Moderate-term on-the-job training
- Employed: No data available.
- Annual Earnings: $30,790
- Growth: −15.6%
- Annual Job Openings: 12,000

Operate or tend typesetting and composing equipment, such as phototypesetters, linotype or monotype keyboard machines, photocomposers, linocasters, and photoletterers.

Monitors machines and gauges to ensure and maintain standards. Mounts materials to be printed onto feed mechanisms and threads materials through guides on machine. Adjusts feed guides, gauges, and rollers, using hand tools. Installs printing plates, cylinders, or rollers on machine, using hand tools and gauges. Fills reservoirs with paint or ink. Selects printing plates, dies, or type according to work order. Adjusts and changes gears, using hand tools. Mixes colors of paint according to formulas. Inspects product to detect defects. Measures and records amount of product produced. Cleans and lubricates equipment. Repairs or replaces worn or broken parts, using hand tools.

GOE INFORMATION—Interest Area: 09. Business Detail. **Work Group:** 09.09. Clerical Machine Operation. **Personality Type—**Realistic. Realistic occupations frequently involve work activities that include practical, hands-on problems and solutions. They often deal with plants, animals, and real-world materials like wood, tools, and machinery. Many of the occupations require working outside and do not involve a lot of paperwork or working closely with others. **Work Values—**Independence; Moral Values; Supervision, Technical; Supervision, Human Relations; Company Policies and Practices. **Skills—**Operation and Control; Operation Monitoring. **Abilities—***Cognitive:* Information Ordering; Visualization; Selective Attention. *Psychomotor:* Arm-Hand Steadiness; Reaction Time; Control Precision; Wrist-Finger Speed; Manual Dexterity. *Physical:* Stamina; Explosive Strength; Dynamic Flexibility; Extent Flexibility; Static Strength. *Sensory:* Visual Color Discrimination; Near Vision; Hearing Sensitivity; Auditory Attention; Sound Localization. **General Work Activities—***Information Input:* Inspecting Equipment, Structures, or Materials; Monitoring Processes, Materials, or Surroundings; Getting Information. *Mental Process:* Evaluating Information Against Standards; Updating and Using Relevant Knowledge; Judging Qualities of Things, Services, or Other People's Work. *Work Output:* Handling and Moving Objects; Controlling Machines and Processes; Performing General Physical Activities. *Interacting with Others:* Communicating with Other Workers; Establishing and Maintaining Relationships; Teaching Others. **Physical Work Conditions—**Hazardous Equipment; Using Hands on Objects, Tools, or Controls; Indoors; Hazardous Conditions; Minor Burns, Cuts, Bites, or Stings. **Other Job Characteristics—**Pace Determined by Speed of Equipment; Degree of Automation; Importance of Repeating Same Tasks.

Experience—Job Zone 2. Some previous work-related skill, knowledge, or experience may be helpful, but usually is not needed. **Job Preparation:** SVP 4.0 to less than 6.0—six months to less than two years. **Knowledge—**Computers and Electronics; Production and Processing. **Instructional Programs—**Graphic and Printing Equipment Operator, General Production; Graphic Communications, General; Graphic Communications, Other; Graphic Design; Platemaker/Imager; Prepress/Desktop Publishing and Digital Imaging Design; Printing Management.

Related DOT Jobs—650.582-010 Linotype Operator; 650.582-014 Monotype-Keyboard Operator; 650.582-018 Photocomposing-Machine Operator; 650.582-022 Phototypesetter Operator; 650.682-010 Equipment Monitor, Phototypesetting; 650.685-010 Typesetting-Machine Tender; 652.585-010 Photolettering-Machine Operator; 652.685-106 Type-Proof Reproducer.

51-5022.13 Photoengraving and Lithographing Machine Operators and Tenders

- Education/Training Required: Moderate-term on-the-job training
- Employed: No data available.
- Annual Earnings: $30,790
- Growth: −15.6%
- Annual Job Openings: 12,000

Operate or tend photoengraving and lithographing equipment, such as plate graining, pantograph, roll varnishing, and routing machines.

Operates machinery, such as film processor, graining machine, and varnishing equipment. Cuts excess metal and bevels edges of printing plates, using routing machine. Mounts finished plates on wood, synthetic, or metal blocks either by hand or using automatic plate-mounting equipment. Immerses and turns printing roller in bath solutions to dissolve coating, develop image, and dye, using electric hoist. Grains printing plates by wet or dry sandblasting or using glass marbles. Paints over pinholes, scratches, and reference points on roller, using brush and acid-resistant paint. Applies acid-resistant ink to varnished copper roller and examines for ink smears or cavities filled with ink. Copies printed materials, such as documents and drawings, using blueprint machine. Maintains machinery in working order, such as automatic film processor and exposure machine. Rolls out and hammers used printing plates to remove gripper marks and bent corners. Examines printing plates with magnifier for uniformity, size, and structures of grain and washes off excess sediment. Cuts printing plates from sheets of aluminum and zinc, using power shears. Examines finished blueprint for specified color, intensity, and sharpness of line.

GOE INFORMATION—Interest Area: 08. Industrial Production. **Work Group:** 08.03. Production Work. **Personality Type—**Realistic. Realistic occupations frequently involve work activities that include practical, hands-on problems and solutions. They often deal with plants, animals, and real-world materials like wood, tools, and machinery. Many of the occupations require working outside and do not involve a lot of paperwork or working closely with others. **Work Values—**Moral Values; Independence; Supervision, Technical; Supervision, Human Relations; Activity. **Skills—**Operation and Control. **Abilities—***Cognitive:* Visualization; Information Ordering. *Psychomotor:* Control Precision; Finger Dexterity; Speed of Limb Movement; Arm-Hand Steadiness. *Physical:* None met the criteria. *Sensory:* Visual Color Discrimination; Near Vision. **General Work Activities—***Information Input:* Monitoring Processes, Materials, or Surroundings; Inspecting Equipment, Structures, or Materials; Getting Information. *Mental Process:* Judging Qualities of Things, Services, or Other People's Work; Evaluating Information Against Standards; Thinking Creatively. *Work Output:* Handling and Moving Objects; Controlling Machines and Processes; Repairing and Maintaining Mechanical Equipment. *Interacting with Others:* Communicating with Other Workers; Coaching and Developing Others; Establishing and Maintaining Relationships. **Physical Work Conditions—**Hazardous Equipment; Indoors; Using Hands on Objects, Tools, or Controls; Distracting Sounds and Noise Levels; Sitting. **Other Job Characteristics—**Degree of Automation; Pace Determined by Speed of Equipment; Importance of Being Exact or Accurate.

Experience—Job Zone 2. Some previous work-related skill, knowledge, or experience may be helpful, but usually is not needed. **Job Preparation:** SVP 4.0 to less than 6.0—six months to less than two years. **Knowledge**—Production and Processing; Chemistry; Physics; Fine Arts; Mechanical. **Instructional Programs**—Graphic and Printing Equipment Operator, General Production; Graphic Communications, General; Graphic Communications, Other; Graphic Design; Platemaker/Imager; Prepress/Desktop Publishing and Digital Imaging Design; Printing Management.

Related DOT Jobs—971.685-010 Roller-Print Tender; 972.384-014 Platemaker, Semiconductor Packages; 972.682-010 Plate Grainer; 972.682-014 Plate-Grainer Apprentice; 979.382-022 Pantographer; 979.682-014 Blueprinting-Machine Operator; 979.682-022 Roller Varnisher; 979.682-026 Router.

51-5023.00 Printing Machine Operators

- Education/Training Required: Moderate-term on-the-job training
- Employed: 222,249
- Annual Earnings: $29,010
- Growth: 5.5%
- Annual Job Openings: 24,000

Set up or operate various types of printing machines, such as offset, letterset, intaglio, or gravure presses or screen printers, to produce print on paper or other materials.

No task data available.

GOE INFORMATION—Interest Area: 08. Industrial Production. **Work Group:** 08.03. Production Work. **Note:** The Department of Labor has not collected some data for this job, so it has fewer details than the other descriptions.

Instructional Programs—Graphic and Printing Equipment Operator, General Production; Graphic Communications, Other; Printing Management; Printing Press Operator.

Related DOT Jobs—209.582-010 Music Copyist; 209.584-010 Braille Transcriber, Hand; 617.685-018 Embossing-Machine Operator; 651.362-010 Cylinder-Press Operator; 651.362-014 Cylinder-Press-Operator Apprentice; 651.362-018 Platen-Press Operator; 651.362-022 Platen-Press-Operator Apprentice; 651.362-026 Rotogravure-Press Operator; 651.362-030 Web-Press Operator; 651.362-034 Web-Press-Operator Apprentice; 651.382-010 Engraving Press Operator; 651.382-014 Lithograph-Press Operator, Tinware; 651.382-026 Printer, Plastic; 651.382-030 Steel-Die Printer; 651.382-034 Tab-Card-Press Operator; 651.382-042 Offset-Press Operator I; 651.382-046 Offset-Press-Operator Apprentice; 651.582-010 Proof-Press Operator; 651.582-014 Lithographic-Proofer Apprentice; 651.585-010 Assistant-Press Operator; others.

51-5023.01 Precision Printing Workers

- Education/Training Required: Moderate-term on-the-job training
- Employed: No data available.
- Annual Earnings: $29,010
- Growth: 5.5%
- Annual Job Openings: 24,000

Perform variety of precision printing activities, such as duplication of microfilm and reproduction of graphic arts materials.

Operates automatic processor to develop photographs, plates, or base material used in single or multicolor proofs. Sets up and operates various types of cameras to produce negatives, photostats, or plastic or paper printing plates. Immerses exposed materials into chemical solutions to hand-develop single or multicolor proofs or printing plates. Operates offset-duplicating machine or small printing press to reproduce single or multicolor copies of line, drawings, graphs, or similar materials. Prepares microfiche duplicates of microfilm, using contact printer and developing machine. Positions and aligns negatives to assemble flats for reproduction. Puts flats into vacuum frame to produce aluminum plate, microfiche print, or single or multicolor proof. Compares test exposures to quality control color guides or exposure guides to determine data for exposure settings. Hand-rubs paper against printing plate to transfer specified design onto paper for use in etching glassware. Enters, positions, and alters size of text, using computer, to make up and arrange pages to produce printed materials. Scans artwork, using optical scanner, which changes image into computer-readable form. Prints paper or film copies of completed material from computer. Measures density levels of colors or color guides on proofs, using densitometer, and compares readings to set standards. Reviews layout and customer order to determine size and style of type. Mixes powdered ink pigments, using matching book and measuring and mixing tools. Examines and inspects printed material for clarity of print and specified color. Maintains printing machinery and equipment. Sets up and operates bindery equipment to cut, assemble, staple, or bind materials.

GOE INFORMATION—Interest Area: 08. Industrial Production. **Work Group:** 08.03. Production Work. **Personality Type**—Realistic. Realistic occupations frequently involve work activities that include practical, hands-on problems and solutions. They often deal with plants, animals, and real-world materials like wood, tools, and machinery. Many of the occupations require working outside and do not involve a lot of paperwork or working closely with others. **Work Values**—Supervision, Technical; Independence; Variety; Moral Values; Autonomy. **Skills**—Operation and Control; Equipment Selection; Quality Control Analysis. **Abilities**—*Cognitive:* Visualization; Flexibility of Closure; Fluency of Ideas; Information Ordering. *Psychomotor:* Control Precision; Reaction Time; Finger Dexterity; Rate Control; Arm-Hand Steadiness. *Physical:* Dynamic Flexibility; Extent Flexibility. *Sensory:* Visual Color Discrimination; Depth Perception; Near Vision; Glare Sensitivity; Night Vision. **General Work Activities**—*Information Input:* Identifying Objects, Actions, and Events; Inspecting Equipment, Structures, or Materials; Monitoring Processes, Materials, or Surroundings. *Mental Process:* Updating and Using Relevant Knowledge; Judging Qualities of Things, Services, or Other People's Work; Evaluating Information Against Standards. *Work Output:* Handling and Moving Objects; Controlling Machines and Processes; Interacting with Computers. *Interacting with Others:* Communicating with Persons Outside Organization; Communicating with Other Workers; Establishing and Maintaining Relationships. **Physical Work Conditions**—Making Repetitive Motions; Using Hands on Objects, Tools, or Controls; Radiation; Kneeling, Crouching, or Crawling; Standing. **Other Job Characteristics**—Degree of Automation; Pace Determined by Speed of Equipment; Importance of Repeating Same Tasks.

Experience—Job Zone 2. Some previous work-related skill, knowledge, or experience may be helpful, but usually is not needed. **Job Preparation:** SVP 4.0 to less than 6.0—six months to less than two years. **Knowledge**—Computers and Electronics; Chemistry; Fine Arts; Production and Processing; Communications and Media. **Instructional Programs**—Graphic and Printing Equipment Operator, General Production; Graphic Communications, Other; Printing Management; Printing Press Operator.

Related DOT Jobs—971.381-046 Screen Maker, Textile; 972.381-034 Proofer, Prepress; 976.381-014 Microfiche Duplicator; 979.381-014 Line-Up Examiner; 979.382-018 Printer; 979.382-026 Computer Typesetter-Keyliner; 979.384-010 Screen Maker, Photographic Process; 979.681-014 Printer.

51-5023.02 Offset Lithographic Press Setters and Set-Up Operators

- Education/Training Required: Long-term on-the-job training
- Employed: No data available.
- Annual Earnings: $29,010
- Growth: 5.5%
- Annual Job Openings: 24,000

Set up or set up and operate offset printing press, either sheet or web fed, to print single and multicolor copy from lithographic plates. Examine job order to determine press operating time, quantity to be printed, and stock specifications.

Examines job order to determine quantity to be printed, stock specifications, colors, and special printing instructions. Starts press and examines printed copy for ink density, position on paper, and registration. Makes adjustments to press throughout production run to maintain specific registration and color density. Installs and locks plate into position, using hand tools, to achieve pressure required for printing. Measures paper thickness and adjusts space between blanket and impression cylinders according to thickness of paper stock. Measures plate thickness and inserts packing sheets on plate cylinder to build up plate to printing height. Washes plate to remove protective gum coating. Fills ink and dampening-solution fountains and adjusts controls to regulate flow of ink and dampening solution to plate cylinder. Applies packing sheets to blanket cylinder to build up blanket thickness to diameter of plate cylinder. Loads paper into feeder or installs rolls of paper, adjusts feeder and delivery mechanisms, and unloads printed material from delivery mechanism. Removes and cleans plate and cylinders.

GOE INFORMATION—Interest Area: 08. Industrial Production. **Work Group:** 08.03. Production Work. **Personality Type—**Realistic. Realistic occupations frequently involve work activities that include practical, hands-on problems and solutions. They often deal with plants, animals, and real-world materials like wood, tools, and machinery. Many of the occupations require working outside and do not involve a lot of paperwork or working closely with others. **Work Values—**Independence; Moral Values; Activity; Supervision, Technical; Company Policies and Practices. **Skills—**Operation Monitoring; Operation and Control; Installation; Equipment Selection. **Abilities—***Cognitive:* None met the criteria. *Psychomotor:* Control Precision; Finger Dexterity. *Physical:* None met the criteria. *Sensory:* Visual Color Discrimination. **General Work Activities—***Information Input:* Monitoring Processes, Materials, or Surroundings; Estimating Needed Characteristics; Getting Information. *Mental Process:* Judging Qualities of Things, Services, or Other People's Work; Updating and Using Relevant Knowledge; Evaluating Information Against Standards. *Work Output:* Handling and Moving Objects; Controlling Machines and Processes; Performing General Physical Activities. *Interacting with Others:* Guiding, Directing, and Motivating Subordinates; Coordinating the Work and Activities of Others; Communicating with Other Workers. **Physical Work Conditions—**Indoors; Standing; Distracting Sounds and Noise Levels; Hazardous Equipment; Making Repetitive Motions. **Other Job Characteristics—**Pace Determined by Speed of Equipment; Degree of Automation; Importance of Repeating Same Tasks.

Experience—Job Zone 5. Extensive skill, knowledge, and experience are needed for these occupations. **Job Preparation:** SVP 8.0 and above—four years to more than 10 years. **Knowledge—**Production and Processing; Mechanical; Personnel and Human Resources; Communications

and Media; Administration and Management. **Instructional Programs—**Graphic and Printing Equipment Operator, General Production; Graphic Communications, Other; Printing Management; Printing Press Operator.

Related DOT Jobs—651.382-042 Offset-Press Operator I; 651.382-046 Offset-Press-Operator Apprentice.

51-5023.03 Letterpress Setters and Set-Up Operators

- Education/Training Required: Moderate-term on-the-job training
- Employed: No data available.
- Annual Earnings: $29,010
- Growth: 5.5%
- Annual Job Openings: 24,000

Set up or set up and operate direct relief letterpresses, either sheet or roll (web) fed, to produce single- or multicolor printed material, such as newspapers, books, and periodicals.

Moves controls to set or adjust ink flow, tension rollers, paper guides, and feed controls. Positions and installs printing plates, cylinder packing, die, and type forms in press according to specifications, using hand tools. Loads, positions, and adjusts unprinted materials on holding fixtures or in feeding mechanism of press. Pushes buttons or moves controls to start printing press and control operation. Monitors feeding and printing operations to maintain specified operating levels and detect malfunctions. Mixes colors or inks and fills reservoirs. Dismantles and reassembles printing unit or parts, using hand tools, to repair, clean, maintain, or adjust press. Operates specially equipped presses and auxiliary equipment, such as cutting, folding, numbering, and pasting devices. Reads work orders and job specifications to select ink and paper stock. Inspects printed materials for irregularities such as off-level areas, variations in ink volume, register slippage, and poor color register. Record and maintain production logsheet. Directs and monitors activities of apprentices and feeding or stacking workers.

GOE INFORMATION—Interest Area: 08. Industrial Production. **Work Group:** 08.03. Production Work. **Personality Type—**Realistic. Realistic occupations frequently involve work activities that include practical, hands-on problems and solutions. They often deal with plants, animals, and real-world materials like wood, tools, and machinery. Many of the occupations require working outside and do not involve a lot of paperwork or working closely with others. **Work Values—**Independence; Supervision, Technical; Moral Values; Activity; Company Policies and Practices. **Skills—**Operation Monitoring; Operation and Control; Installation; Equipment Selection; Quality Control Analysis; Troubleshooting. **Abilities—***Cognitive:* Perceptual Speed; Information Ordering; Inductive Reasoning; Time Sharing; Selective Attention. *Psychomotor:* Control Precision; Speed of Limb Movement; Wrist-Finger Speed; Manual Dexterity; Multilimb Coordination. *Physical:* Static Strength; Trunk Strength; Dynamic Flexibility. *Sensory:* Visual Color Discrimination; Near Vision; Night Vision. **General Work Activities—***Information Input:* Monitoring Processes, Materials, or Surroundings; Inspecting Equipment, Structures, or Materials; Identifying Objects, Actions, and Events. *Mental Process:* Judging Qualities of Things, Services, or Other People's Work; Evaluating Information Against Standards; Organizing, Planning, and Prioritizing. *Work Output:* Handling and Moving Objects; Controlling Machines and Processes; Repairing and Maintaining Mechanical Equipment. *Interacting with Others:* Communicating with Other Workers; Establishing and Maintaining Relationships; Coaching and Developing Others. **Physical Work Conditions—**Hazardous Equipment; Using

Hands on Objects, Tools, or Controls; Indoors; Standing; Common Protective or Safety Attire. **Other Job Characteristics**—Pace Determined by Speed of Equipment; Degree of Automation; Importance of Repeating Same Tasks.

Experience—Job Zone 3. Previous work-related skill, knowledge, or experience is required. **Job Preparation:** SVP 6.0 to less than 7.0—more than one year and less than four years. **Knowledge**—Production and Processing. **Instructional Programs**—Graphic and Printing Equipment Operator, General Production; Graphic Communications, Other; Printing Management; Printing Press Operator.

Related DOT Jobs—651.362-010 Cylinder-Press Operator; 651.362-014 Cylinder-Press-Operator Apprentice; 651.362-018 Platen-Press Operator; 651.362-022 Platen-Press-Operator Apprentice; 651.362-030 Web-Press Operator; 651.362-034 Web-Press-Operator Apprentice; 651.382-034 Tab-Card-Press Operator.

51-5023.04 Design Printing Machine Setters and Set-Up Operators

- **Education/Training Required: Postsecondary vocational training**
- **Employed: No data available.**
- **Annual Earnings: $29,010**
- **Growth: 5.5%**
- **Annual Job Openings: 24,000**

Set up or set up and operate machines to print designs on materials.

Installs printing plates, cylinders, or rollers on machine, using hand tools and gauges. Adjusts feed guides, gauges, and rollers, using hand tools. Adjusts and changes gears, using hand tools. Fills reservoirs with paint or ink. Monitors machines and gauges to ensure and maintain standards. Mixes colors of paint according to formulas. Inspects product to detect defects. Cleans and lubricates equipment. Repairs or replaces worn or broken parts, using hand tools. Measures and records amount of product produced.

GOE INFORMATION—**Interest Area:** 08. Industrial Production. **Work Group:** 08.03. Production Work. **Personality Type**—Realistic. Realistic occupations frequently involve work activities that include practical, hands-on problems and solutions. They often deal with plants, animals, and real-world materials like wood, tools, and machinery. Many of the occupations require working outside and do not involve a lot of paperwork or working closely with others. **Work Values**—Independence; Moral Values; Supervision, Technical; Company Policies and Practices; Activity. **Skills**—Repairing; Operation Monitoring; Operation and Control; Installation; Equipment Selection; Technology Design; Troubleshooting. **Abilities**—*Cognitive:* Visualization; Perceptual Speed. *Psychomotor:* Rate Control; Multilimb Coordination; Control Precision; Reaction Time; Finger Dexterity. *Physical:* Dynamic Strength; Dynamic Flexibility; Gross Body Equilibrium; Explosive Strength; Gross Body Coordination. *Sensory:* Visual Color Discrimination; Sound Localization; Depth Perception; Glare Sensitivity; Peripheral Vision. **General Work Activities**—*Information Input:* Monitoring Processes, Materials, or Surroundings; Inspecting Equipment, Structures, or Materials; Estimating Needed Characteristics. *Mental Process:* Processing Information; Evaluating Information Against Standards; Judging Qualities of Things, Services, or Other People's Work. *Work Output:* Handling and Moving Objects; Repairing and Maintaining Mechanical Equipment; Performing General Physical Activities. *Interacting with Others:* Communicating with Other Workers; Performing Administrative Activities; Communicating with Persons Outside Organization. **Physical Work Conditions**—Hazardous

Equipment; Making Repetitive Motions; Indoors; Kneeling, Crouching, or Crawling; Common Protective or Safety Attire. **Other Job Characteristics**—Pace Determined by Speed of Equipment; Degree of Automation; Importance of Being Exact or Accurate.

Experience—Job Zone 3. Previous work-related skill, knowledge, or experience is required. **Job Preparation:** SVP 6.0 to less than 7.0—more than one year and less than four years. **Knowledge**—Mechanical; Production and Processing; Engineering and Technology; Fine Arts. **Instructional Programs**—Graphic and Printing Equipment Operator, General Production; Graphic Communications, Other; Printing Management; Printing Press Operator.

Related DOT Jobs—651.382-014 Lithograph-Press Operator, Tinware; 651.382-026 Printer, Plastic; 652.382-010 Cloth Printer; 652.662-014 Wallpaper Printer I.

51-5023.05 Marking and Identification Printing Machine Setters and Set-Up Operators

- **Education/Training Required: Short-term on-the-job training**
- **Employed: No data available.**
- **Annual Earnings: $29,010**
- **Growth: 5.5%**
- **Annual Job Openings: 24,000**

Set up or set up and operate machines to print trademarks, labels, or multicolored identification symbols on materials.

Adjusts machine as needed, using hand tools. Selects printing plates, dies, or type according to work order. Mounts printing plates, dies, or type onto machine. Mounts materials to be printed onto feed mechanisms and threads materials through guides on machine. Fills reservoirs with ink or specified coloring agents. Sets rate of flow of coloring agent and speed and spacing of materials to achieve desired product. Monitors printing process to detect machine malfunctions. Examines product to detect defects. Cleans machine and equipment, using solvent and rags.

GOE INFORMATION—**Interest Area:** 08. Industrial Production. **Work Group:** 08.03. Production Work. **Personality Type**—Realistic. Realistic occupations frequently involve work activities that include practical, hands-on problems and solutions. They often deal with plants, animals, and real-world materials like wood, tools, and machinery. Many of the occupations require working outside and do not involve a lot of paperwork or working closely with others. **Work Values**—Independence; Moral Values; Supervision, Technical; Company Policies and Practices; Activity. **Skills**—Operation and Control; Operation Monitoring. **Abilities**—*Cognitive:* None met the criteria. *Psychomotor:* Rate Control; Speed of Limb Movement; Arm-Hand Steadiness; Response Orientation; Finger Dexterity. *Physical:* Dynamic Flexibility; Dynamic Strength; Extent Flexibility. *Sensory:* Visual Color Discrimination. **General Work Activities**—*Information Input:* Monitoring Processes, Materials, or Surroundings; Identifying Objects, Actions, and Events; Inspecting Equipment, Structures, or Materials. *Mental Process:* Evaluating Information Against Standards; Updating and Using Relevant Knowledge; Judging Qualities of Things, Services, or Other People's Work. *Work Output:* Handling and Moving Objects; Controlling Machines and Processes; Performing General Physical Activities. *Interacting with Others:* Communicating with Other Workers; Establishing and Maintaining Relationships; Communicating with Persons Outside Organization. **Physical Work Conditions**—Making Repetitive Motions; Using Hands on Objects, Tools, or Controls; Kneeling, Crouching, or Crawling; Hazardous Equipment; Cramped Work Space or Awkward Positions. **Other Job Characteristics**—Pace Determined by Speed of Equipment; Degree of Automation; Importance of Being Exact or Accurate.

Experience—Job Zone 1. No previous work-related skill, knowledge, or experience is needed. **Job Preparation:** SVP below 4.0—less than six months. **Knowledge**—Production and Processing; Mechanical; Chemistry. **Instructional Programs**—Graphic and Printing Equipment Operator, General Production; Graphic Communications, Other; Printing Management; Printing Press Operator.

Related DOT Jobs—651.682-022 Tip Printer; 652.662-010 Printing-Machine Operator, Tape Rules; 652.682-010 Box Printer; 652.682-026 Striping-Machine Operator.

51-5023.06 Screen Printing Machine Setters and Set-Up Operators

- **Education/Training Required: Moderate-term on-the-job training**
- **Employed: No data available.**
- **Annual Earnings: $29,010**
- **Growth: 5.5%**
- **Annual Job Openings: 24,000**

Set up or set up and operate screen-printing machines to print designs onto articles and materials such as glass or plasticware, cloth, and paper.

Sets and adjusts feed rollers, spindle reel, printing screens, and bolts to specifications. Starts dyeing oven and sets thermostat to temperature specified for printing run. Reviews print order to determine settings and adjustments required to set up manually controlled or automatic screen-printing machine or decorating equipment. Measures, centers, and aligns and positions screen, using gauge and hand tools. Determines from orders type and color of designs to print. Mixes paints according to formula, using bench mixer. Examines product for paint smears, position of design, or other defects and adjusts equipment. Compares ink or paint prepared for printing run with master color swatch to confirm accuracy of match. Inspects printing equipment and replaces damaged or defective parts, such as switches, pulleys, fixtures, screws, and bolts. Patrols printing area to monitor production activities and to detect problems, such as mechanical breakdowns or malfunctions. Counts and records quantities printed in production log. Trains workers in use of printing equipment and in quality standards. Adjusts position of design or screen to ensure specified color print registration.

GOE INFORMATION—Interest Area: 08. Industrial Production. **Work Group:** 08.02. Production Technology. **Personality Type**—Realistic. Realistic occupations frequently involve work activities that include practical, hands-on problems and solutions. They often deal with plants, animals, and real-world materials like wood, tools, and machinery. Many of the occupations require working outside and do not involve a lot of paperwork or working closely with others. **Work Values**—Company Policies and Practices; Authority; Supervision, Technical; Moral Values; Activity. **Skills**—Repairing; Operation and Control; Operation Monitoring; Troubleshooting; Quality Control Analysis; Instructing. **Abilities**—*Cognitive:* Perceptual Speed; Visualization; Flexibility of Closure. *Psychomotor:* Finger Dexterity; Multilimb Coordination; Control Precision; Arm-Hand Steadiness; Wrist-Finger Speed. *Physical:* Extent Flexibility; Explosive Strength; Dynamic Flexibility. *Sensory:* Visual Color Discrimination; Speech Clarity; Depth Perception; Auditory Attention; Glare Sensitivity. **General Work Activities**—*Information Input:* Inspecting Equipment, Structures, or Materials; Monitoring Processes, Materials, or Surroundings; Identifying Objects, Actions, and Events. *Mental Process:*

Evaluating Information Against Standards; Updating and Using Relevant Knowledge; Judging Qualities of Things, Services, or Other People's Work. *Work Output:* Handling and Moving Objects; Controlling Machines and Processes; Repairing and Maintaining Mechanical Equipment. *Interacting with Others:* Establishing and Maintaining Relationships; Teaching Others; Communicating with Other Workers. **Physical Work Conditions**—Hazardous Equipment; Hazardous Conditions; Distracting Sounds and Noise Levels; Contaminants; Common Protective or Safety Attire. **Other Job Characteristics**—Degree of Automation; Pace Determined by Speed of Equipment; Importance of Being Exact or Accurate.

Experience—Job Zone 3. Previous work-related skill, knowledge, or experience is required. **Job Preparation:** SVP 6.0 to less than 7.0—more than one year and less than four years. **Knowledge**—Production and Processing; Fine Arts; Education and Training; Mechanical; Design. **Instructional Programs**—Graphic and Printing Equipment Operator, General Production; Graphic Communications, Other; Printing Management; Printing Press Operator.

Related DOT Jobs—652.260-010 Section Leader, Screen Printing; 652.380-010 Decorating-Equipment Setter; 979.360-010 Screen-Printing-Equipment Setter.

51-5023.07 Embossing Machine Set-Up Operators

- **Education/Training Required: Postsecondary vocational training**
- **Employed: No data available.**
- **Annual Earnings: $29,010**
- **Growth: 5.5%**
- **Annual Job Openings: 24,000**

Set up and operate embossing machines.

Sets guides to hold cover in position and adjusts table height to obtain correct depth of impression. Starts machine to lower ram and impress cardboard. Stamps embossing design on workpiece, using heated work tools. Positions, installs, and locks embossed plate in chase and locks chase in bed of press. Makes impression of embossing to desired depth in composition on platen, trims off excess, and allows composition to harden. Sets sheets singly in gauge pins and starts press. Mixes embossing composition to putty-like consistency, spreads glue on paten, and applies thin pad of composition over glue. Scrapes high spots on counter die to prevent from puncturing paper. Cuts surface of cardboard, leaving design or letters, using hand tools. Removes and stacks embossed covers.

GOE INFORMATION—Interest Area: 08. Industrial Production. **Work Group:** 08.03. Production Work. **Personality Type**—Realistic. Realistic occupations frequently involve work activities that include practical, hands-on problems and solutions. They often deal with plants, animals, and real-world materials like wood, tools, and machinery. Many of the occupations require working outside and do not involve a lot of paperwork or working closely with others. **Work Values**—Independence; Moral Values; Supervision, Technical; Supervision, Human Relations; Activity. **Skills**—Operation and Control; Installation. **Abilities**—*Cognitive:* None met the criteria. *Psychomotor:* Manual Dexterity; Control Precision; Speed of Limb Movement; Multilimb Coordination. *Physical:* Trunk Strength; Dynamic Flexibility. *Sensory:* None met the criteria. **General Work Activities**—*Information Input:* Monitoring Processes, Materials, or Surroundings; Getting Information; Identifying Objects, Actions, and Events. *Mental Process:* Evaluating Information Against Standards; Analyzing Data or Information; Updating and Using Relevant Knowledge. *Work Output:* Handling and Moving Objects; Controlling Machines and Processes; Performing General Physical Activities. *Interacting with Others:* Communicating with Other Workers; Coordinating the Work and Activities of Others; Monitoring and Controlling Resources. **Physical Work Conditions**—Hazardous Equipment; Using Hands on Objects, Tools, or Controls; Common Protective or Safety Attire; Indoors; Making Repetitive Motions. **Other Job Characteristics**—Pace Determined by Speed of Equipment; Degree of Automation; Importance of Repeating Same Tasks.

Experience—Job Zone 3. Previous work-related skill, knowledge, or experience is required. **Job Preparation:** SVP 6.0 to less than 7.0—more than one year and less than four years. **Knowledge**—Production and Processing. **Instructional Programs**—Graphic and Printing Equipment Operator, General Production; Graphic Communications, Other; Printing Management; Printing Press Operator.

Related DOT Jobs—659.382-010 Embosser; 659.682-014 Embossing-Press Operator; 659.682-018 Embossing-Press-Operator Apprentice.

51-5023.08 Engraver Set-Up Operators

- **Education/Training Required: Long-term on-the-job training**
- **Employed: No data available.**
- **Annual Earnings: $29,010**
- **Growth: 5.5%**
- **Annual Job Openings: 24,000**

Set up and operate machines to transfer printing designs.

Positions machine mechanisms and depresses levers to apply marks on roller. Aligns plate with markings on machine table and tacks to table. Adjusts and tightens levers in position, using hand tools. Turns screws to align machine components. Inserts mandrel through roller and lifts into position on machine. Determines ground setting according to weight of fabric, type of design, and colors in design. Measures depth of engraving and weighs diamond points, using gauges and scales. Examines marks on roller to verify alignment and detect defects. Records ground setting, length of roller, width of engraving, and circumference of roller on production sheet.

GOE INFORMATION—Interest Area: 08. Industrial Production. **Work Group:** 08.03. Production Work. **Personality Type**—Realistic. Realistic occupations frequently involve work activities that include practical, hands-on problems and solutions. They often deal with plants, animals, and real-world materials like wood, tools, and machinery. Many of the occupations require working outside and do not involve a lot of paperwork or working closely with others. **Work Values**—Independence; Moral Values; Supervision, Technical; Supervision, Human Relations; Company Policies and Practices. **Skills**—Operation and Control; Operation Monitoring. **Abilities**—*Cognitive:* Flexibility of Closure; Perceptual Speed; Visualization; Information Ordering; Deductive Reasoning. *Psychomotor:* Control Precision; Arm-Hand Steadiness; Manual Dexterity; Multilimb Coordination; Wrist-Finger Speed. *Physical:* Dynamic Flexibility; Extent Flexibility; Gross Body Coordination; Gross Body Equilibrium. *Sensory:* Visual Color Discrimination; Auditory Attention; Near Vision; Sound Localization. **General Work Activities**—*Information Input:* Getting Information; Identifying Objects, Actions, and Events; Inspecting Equipment, Structures, or Materials. *Mental Process:* Analyzing Data or Information; Updating and Using Relevant Knowledge; Making Decisions and Solving Problems. *Work Output:* Handling and Moving Objects; Controlling Machines and Processes; Performing General Physical Activities. *Interacting with Others:* Performing Administrative Activities; Communicating with Other Workers; Establishing and Maintaining Relationships. **Physical Work Conditions**—Hazardous Equipment; Minor Burns, Cuts, Bites, or Stings; Using Hands on Objects, Tools, or Controls; Indoors; Distracting Sounds and Noise Levels. **Other Job Char-

acteristics**—Pace Determined by Speed of Equipment; Degree of Automation; Importance of Repeating Same Tasks.

Experience—Job Zone 4. A minimum of two to four years of work-related skill, knowledge, or experience is needed. **Job Preparation:** SVP 7.0 to less than 8.0—two years to less than 10 years. **Knowledge**—Production and Processing; Mechanical; Clerical; Physics; Design. **Instructional Programs**—Graphic and Printing Equipment Operator, General Production; Graphic Communications, Other; Printing Management; Printing Press Operator.

Related DOT Jobs—979.380-010 Pantograph Setter; 979.382-014 Engraver, Machine.

51-5023.09 Printing Press Machine Operators and Tenders

- **Education/Training Required: Short-term on-the-job training**
- **Employed: 222,249**
- **Annual Earnings: $29,010**
- **Growth: 5.5%**
- **Annual Job Openings: 24,000**

Operate or tend various types of printing machines, such as offset lithographic presses, letter or letterset presses, and flexographic or gravure presses, to produce print on paper or other materials such as plastic, cloth, or rubber.

Pushes buttons, turns handles, or moves controls and levers to start printing machine or manually controls equipment operation. Turns, pushes, or moves controls to set and adjust speed, temperature, inkflow, and position and pressure tolerances of press. Selects and installs printing plates, rollers, screens, stencils, type, die, and cylinders in machine according to specifications, using hand tools. Loads, positions, and adjusts unprinted materials on holding fixture or in loading and feeding mechanisms of press. Monitors feeding, printing, and racking processes of press to maintain specified operating levels and detect malfunctions. Reviews work order to determine ink, stock, and equipment needed for production. Monitors and controls operation of auxiliary equipment, such as cutters, folders, drying ovens, and sanders, to assemble and finish product. Blends and tests paint, inks, stains, and solvents according to type of material being printed and work order specifications. Pours or spreads paint, ink, color compounds, and other materials into reservoirs, troughs, hoppers, or color holders of printing unit. Inspects and examines printed products for print clarity, color accuracy, conformance to specifications, and external defects. Removes printed materials from press, using handtruck, electric lift, or hoist, and transports them to drying, storage, or finishing areas. Cleans and lubricates printing machine and components (e.g., rollers, screens, typesetting, reservoirs) using oil, solvents, brushes, rags, and hoses. Dismantles and reassembles printing unit or parts, using hand and power tools, to repair, maintain, or adjust machine. Discards or corrects misprinted materials, using ink eradicators or solvents. Accepts orders, calculates and quotes prices, and receives payments from customers. Packs and labels cartons, boxes, or bins of finished products. Keeps daily time and materials usage reports and records identifying information printed on manufactured products and parts. Directs and monitors activities of workers feeding, inspecting, and tending printing machines and materials.

GOE INFORMATION—Interest Area: 08. Industrial Production. **Work Group:** 08.03. Production Work. **Personality Type**—Realistic. Realistic occupations frequently involve work activities that include practical, hands-on problems and solutions. They often deal with plants, animals, and real-world materials like wood, tools, and machinery. Many of the occupations require working outside and do not involve a lot of paperwork or working closely with others. **Work Values**—Advancement; Authority; Supervision, Technical; Supervision, Human Relations; Company Policies and Practices. **Skills**—Operation Monitoring; Operation and Control; Repairing; Quality Control Analysis; Installation; Management of Personnel Resources; Equipment Selection. **Abilities**—*Cognitive:* Visualization; Perceptual Speed; Category Flexibility; Oral Comprehension; Oral Expression. *Psychomotor:* Manual Dexterity; Control Precision; Finger Dexterity; Reaction Time; Arm-Hand Steadiness. *Physical:* Static Strength; Dynamic Flexibility; Explosive Strength; Dynamic Strength. *Sensory:* Visual Color Discrimination; Near Vision. **General Work Activities**—*Information Input:* Monitoring Processes, Materials, or Surroundings; Getting Information; Inspecting Equipment, Structures, or Materials. *Mental Process:* Processing Information; Updating and Using Relevant Knowledge; Making Decisions and Solving Problems. *Work Output:* Handling and Moving Objects; Controlling Machines and Processes; Repairing and Maintaining Mechanical Equipment. *Interacting with Others:* Establishing and Maintaining Relationships; Communicating with Other Workers; Coordinating the Work and Activities of Others. **Physical Work Conditions**—Common Protective or Safety Attire; Hazardous Equipment; Indoors; Distracting Sounds and Noise Levels; Bending or Twisting the Body. **Other Job Characteristics**—Pace Determined by Speed of Equipment; Degree of Automation; Importance of Repeating Same Tasks.

Experience—Job Zone 1. No previous work-related skill, knowledge, or experience is needed. **Job Preparation:** SVP below 4.0—less than six months. **Knowledge**—Production and Processing; Mechanical; Chemistry; Customer and Personal Service; Engineering and Technology. **Instructional Programs**—Graphic and Printing Equipment Operator, General Production; Graphic Communications, Other; Printing Management; Printing Press Operator.

Related DOT Jobs—651.582-010 Proof-Press Operator; 651.582-014 Lithographic-Proofer Apprentice; 651.585-010 Assistant-Press Operator; 651.682-014 Offset-Duplicating-Machine Operator; 651.682-018 Striper; 651.685-010 Bag Printer; 651.685-014 Design Printer, Balloon; 651.685-018 Offset-Press Operator II; 651.685-022 Platen-Press Feeder; 651.685-026 Assistant Press Operator, Offset; 652.462-010 Rubber-Printing-Machine Operator; 652.582-010 Marker; 652.582-014 Rotary-Screen-Printing-Machine Operator; 652.662-018 Print-Line Operator; 652.682-014 Embossograph Operator; 652.682-018 Screen-Printing-Machine Operator; 652.682-030 Stamping-Press Operator; 652.685-010 Back Tender, Cloth Printing; 652.685-014 Binding Printer; 652.685-018 Carton Marker, Machine; others.

51-6000 Textile, Apparel, and Furnishings Workers

51-6011.00 Laundry and Dry-Cleaning Workers

- **Education/Training Required: Short-term on-the-job training**
- **Employed: 235,708**
- **Annual Earnings: $16,360**
- **Growth: 11.4%**
- **Annual Job Openings: 62,000**

Operate or tend washing or dry-cleaning machines to wash or dry-clean industrial or household articles, such as cloth garments, suede, leather, furs, blankets, draperies, fine linens, rugs, and carpets.

No task data available.

GOE INFORMATION—**Interest Area:** 11. Recreation, Travel, and Other Personal Services. **Work Group:** 11.06. Apparel, Shoes, Leather, and Fabric Care. **Note:** The Department of Labor has not collected some data for this job, so it has fewer details than the other descriptions.

Instructional Programs—No data available.

Related DOT Jobs—361.665-010 Washer, Machine; 361.682-010 Rug Cleaner, Machine; 361.684-010 Launderer, Hand; 361.684-014 Laundry Worker I; 361.684-018 Spotter I; 361.685-014 Continuous-Towel Roller; 361.685-018 Laundry Worker II; 362.381-010 Spotter II; 362.382-010 Dry-Cleaner Apprentice; 362.382-014 Dry Cleaner; 362.684-014 Fur Cleaner; 362.684-026 Leather Cleaner; 362.685-010 Feather Renovator; 364.361-010 Dyer; 364.361-014 Rug Dyer I; 364.684-010 Rug Dyer II; 369.684-014 Laundry Operator; 369.685-010 Fur Blower; 369.685-014 Fur Cleaner, Machine; 369.685-022 Fur-Glazing-and-Polishing-Machine Operator; others.

51-6011.01 Spotters, Dry Cleaning

- **Education/Training Required: Short-term on-the-job training**
- **Employed: No data available.**
- **Annual Earnings: $16,360**
- **Growth: 11.4%**
- **Annual Job Openings: 62,000**

Identify stains in wool, synthetic, and silk garments and household fabrics and apply chemical solutions to remove stain. Determine spotting procedures on basis of type of fabric and nature of stain.

Inspects spots to ascertain composition and select solvent. Sprinkles chemical solvents over stain and pats area with brush or sponge until stain is removed. Applies bleaching powder to spot and sprays with steam to remove stains from certain fabrics which do not respond to other cleaning solvents. Applies chemicals to neutralize effect of solvents. Sprays steam, water, or air over spot to flush out chemicals, dry material, raise nap, or brighten color. Cleans fabric using vacuum or air hose. Mixes bleaching agent with hot water in vats and soaks material until it is bleached. Spreads article on worktable and positions stain over vacuum head or on marble slab. Operates dry-cleaning machine.

GOE INFORMATION—**Interest Area:** 11. Recreation, Travel, and Other Personal Services. **Work Group:** 11.06. Apparel, Shoes, Leather, and Fabric Care. **Personality Type**—Realistic. Realistic occupations frequently involve work activities that include practical, hands-on problems and solutions. They often deal with plants, animals, and real-world materials like wood, tools, and machinery. Many of the occupations require working outside and do not involve a lot of paperwork or working closely with others. **Work Values**—Independence; Moral Values; Supervision, Technical; Security. **Skills**—Operation Monitoring. **Abilities**—*Cognitive:* None met the criteria. *Psychomotor:* Wrist-Finger Speed. *Physical:* Dynamic Flexibility. *Sensory:* Visual Color Discrimination; Glare Sensitivity; Hearing Sensitivity; Peripheral Vision. **General Work Activities**—*Information Input:* Getting Information; Inspecting Equipment, Structures, or Materials; Identifying Objects, Actions, and Events. *Mental Process:* Judging Qualities of Things, Services, or Other People's Work; Making Decisions and Solving Problems; Analyzing Data or Information. *Work Output:* Handling and Moving Objects; Performing General Physical Activities; Controlling Machines and Processes. *Interacting with Others:* Establishing and Maintaining Relationships; Monitoring and Controlling Resources; Assisting and Caring for Others. **Physical Work Conditions**—Hazardous Conditions; Contaminants; Using Hands on Objects, Tools, or Controls; Minor Burns, Cuts, Bites, or Stings; Indoors. **Other Job Characteristics**—Degree of Automation; Pace Determined by Speed of Equipment; Importance of Repeating Same Tasks.

Experience—Job Zone 1. No previous work-related skill, knowledge, or experience is needed. **Job Preparation:** SVP below 4.0—less than six months. **Knowledge**—Chemistry; Customer and Personal Service; Public Safety and Security. **Instructional Programs**—No data available.

Related DOT Jobs—361.684-018 Spotter I; 362.381-010 Spotter II; 582.684-014 Spot Cleaner; 780.687-058 Upholstery Cleaner.

51-6011.02 Precision Dyers

- **Education/Training Required: Postsecondary vocational training**
- **Employed: No data available.**
- **Annual Earnings: $16,360**
- **Growth: 11.4%**
- **Annual Job Openings: 62,000**

Change or restore the color of articles, such as garments, drapes, and slipcovers, by means of dyes. Work requires knowledge of the composition of the textiles being dyed or restored, the chemical properties of bleaches and dyes, and their effects upon such textiles.

Matches sample color, applying knowledge of bleaching agent and dye properties and type, construction, condition, and color of article. Examines article to identify fabric and original dye by sight, by touch, or by testing sample with fire or chemical reagent. Tests dye on swatch of fabric to ensure color match. Immerses article in bleaching bath to strip colors. Immerses article in dye solution and stirs with stick or dyes article in rotary-drum or paddle-dyeing machine. Applies dye to article, using spray gun, electrically rotated brush, or handbrush. Rinses article in water and acetic acid solution to remove excess dye and to fix colors. Measures and mixes amounts of bleaches, dyes, oils, and acids, following formulas. Dissolves dye or bleaching chemicals in water. Sprays or brushes article with prepared solution to remove stains. Operates or directs operation of extractor and drier.

GOE INFORMATION—**Interest Area:** 11. Recreation, Travel, and Other Personal Services. **Work Group:** 11.06. Apparel, Shoes, Leather, and Fabric Care. **Personality Type**—Realistic. Realistic occupations frequently involve work activities that include practical, hands-on problems and solutions. They often deal with plants, animals, and real-world materials like wood, tools, and machinery. Many of the occupations require working outside and do not involve a lot of paperwork or working closely with others. **Work Values**—Supervision, Technical; Independence; Moral Values; Security. **Skills**—Science. **Abilities**—*Cognitive:* Category Flexibility; Information Ordering. *Psychomotor:* Control Precision. *Physical:* Extent Flexibility; Trunk Strength; Gross Body Coordination; Dynamic Flexibility. *Sensory:* Visual Color Discrimination. **General Work Activities**—*Information Input:* Estimating Needed Characteristics; Getting Information; Identifying Objects, Actions, and Events. *Mental Process:* Making Decisions and Solving Problems; Judging Qualities of Things, Services, or Other People's Work; Organizing, Planning, and Prioritizing. *Work Output:* Handling and Moving Objects; Controlling Machines and Processes; Performing General Physical Activities. *Interacting with Others:* Communicating with Other Workers; Performing Administrative Activities; Coordinating the Work and Activities of Others. **Physical Work Conditions**—Bending or Twisting the Body; Indoors; Standing; Hazardous Conditions; Specialized Protective or Safety Attire. **Other Job Characteristics**—Importance of Repeating Same Tasks; Pace Determined by Speed of Equipment; Importance of Being Exact or Accurate.

Experience—Job Zone 3. Previous work-related skill, knowledge, or experience is required. **Job Preparation:** SVP 6.0 to less than 7.0—more than one year and less than four years. **Knowledge**—Chemistry; Production and Processing; Fine Arts. **Instructional Programs**—No data available.

Related DOT Jobs—364.361-010 Dyer; 364.361-014 Rug Dyer I; 364.684-010 Rug Dyer II.

51-6011.03 Laundry and Drycleaning Machine Operators and Tenders, Except Pressing

- **Education/Training Required: Moderate-term on-the-job training**
- **Employed: No data available.**
- **Annual Earnings: $16,360**
- **Growth: 11.4%**
- **Annual Job Openings: 62,000**

Operate or tend washing or dry-cleaning machines to wash or dry-clean commercial, industrial, or household articles, such as cloth garments, suede, leather, furs, blankets, draperies, fine linens, rugs, and carpets.

Starts washer, dry cleaner, drier, or extractor, and turns valves or levers to regulate and monitor cleaning or drying operations. Loads or directs other workers to load articles into washer or dry-cleaning machine. Mixes and adds detergents, dyes, bleach, starch, and other solutions and chemicals to clean, color, dry, or stiffen articles. Starts pumps to operate distilling system that drains and reclaims dry-cleaning solvents. Tends variety of automatic machines that comb and polish furs; clean, sterilize, and fluff feathers and blankets; and roll and package towels. Adjusts switches to tend and regulate equipment that fumigates and removes foreign matter from furs. Removes or directs other workers to remove items from washer or dry-cleaning machine and into extractor or tumbler. Cleans machine filters and lubricates equipment. Washes, dry cleans, or glazes delicate articles or fur garment linings by hand, using mild detergent or dry-cleaning solutions. Pre-soaks, sterilizes, scrubs, spot-cleans, and dries contaminated or stained articles, using neutralizer solutions and portable machines. Examines and sorts articles to be cleaned into lots, according to color, fabric, dirt content, and cleaning technique required. Sorts and counts articles removed from dryer and folds, wraps, or hangs items for airing out, pickup, or delivery. Receives and marks articles for laundry or dry cleaning with identifying code number or name, using hand or machine marker. Irons or presses articles, fabrics, and furs, using hand iron or pressing machine. Hangs curtains, drapes, blankets, pants, and other garments on stretch frames to dry and transports items between specified locations. Mends and sews articles, using hand stitching, adhesive patch, or power sewing machine.

GOE INFORMATION—**Interest Area:** 11. Recreation, Travel, and Other Personal Services. **Work Group:** 11.06. Apparel, Shoes, Leather, and Fabric Care. **Personality Type**—Realistic. Realistic occupations frequently involve work activities that include practical, hands-on problems and solutions. They often deal with plants, animals, and real-world materials like wood, tools, and machinery. Many of the occupations require working outside and do not involve a lot of paperwork or working closely with others. **Work Values**—Supervision, Technical; Company Policies and Practices; Moral Values; Supervision, Human Relations; Independence. **Skills**—Operation Monitoring; Operation and Control. **Abilities**—*Cognitive:* Category Flexibility. *Psychomotor:* Speed of Limb Movement; Manual Dexterity; Arm-Hand Steadiness; Rate Control; Multilimb Coordination. *Physical:* Dynamic Strength; Gross Body Coordination; Trunk Strength; Stamina; Dynamic Flexibility. *Sensory:* Visual Color Discrimination; Depth Perception; Peripheral Vision. **General Work Activities**—*Information Input:* Monitoring Processes, Materials, or Surroundings; Identifying Objects, Actions, and Events; Inspecting Equipment, Structures, or Materials. *Mental Process:* Making Decisions and Solving Problems; Judging Qualities of Things, Services, or Other People's Work; Processing Information. *Work Output:* Handling and Moving Objects; Performing General Physical Activities; Controlling Machines and Processes. *Interacting with Others:* Communicating with Other Workers; Guiding, Directing, and Motivating Subordinates; Coordinating the Work and Activities of Others. **Physical Work Conditions**—Hazardous Equipment; Very Hot or Cold; Contaminants; Hazardous Conditions; Using Hands on Objects, Tools, or Controls. **Other Job Characteristics**—Degree of Automation; Pace Determined by Speed of Equipment; Importance of Repeating Same Tasks.

Experience—Job Zone 1. No previous work-related skill, knowledge, or experience is needed. **Job Preparation:** SVP below 4.0—less than six months. **Knowledge**—Chemistry; Production and Processing; Customer and Personal Service; Mechanical; Philosophy and Theology. **Instructional Programs**—No data available.

Related DOT Jobs—361.665-010 Washer, Machine; 361.682-010 Rug Cleaner, Machine; 361.684-010 Launderer, Hand; 361.684-014 Laundry Worker I; 361.685-014 Continuous-Towel Roller; 361.685-018 Laundry Worker II; 362.382-010 Dry-Cleaner Apprentice; 362.382-014 Dry Cleaner; 362.684-014 Fur Cleaner; 362.684-026 Leather Cleaner; 362.685-010 Feather Renovator; 369.684-014 Laundry Operator; 369.685-010 Fur Blower; 369.685-014 Fur Cleaner, Machine; 369.685-022 Fur-Glazing-and-Polishing-Machine Operator; 589.685-038 Dry Cleaner.

51-6021.00 Pressers, Textile, Garment, and Related Materials

- Education/Training Required: **Moderate-term on-the-job training**
- Employed: **110,064**
- Annual Earnings: **$16,600**
- Growth: **1.7%**
- Annual Job Openings: **19,000**

Press or shape articles by hand or machine.

No task data available.

GOE INFORMATION—**Interest Area:** 11. Recreation, Travel, and Other Personal Services. **Work Group:** 11.06. Apparel, Shoes, Leather, and Fabric Care. **Note:** The Department of Labor has not collected some data for this job, so it has fewer details than the other descriptions.

Instructional Programs—No data available.

Related DOT Jobs—361.685-022 Patching-Machine Operator; 363.681-010 Silk Finisher; 363.682-010 Leather Finisher; 363.682-014 Presser, All-Around; 363.682-018 Presser, Machine; 363.684-010 Blocker; 363.684-014 Hat Blocker; 363.684-018 Presser, Hand; 363.685-010 Press Operator; 363.685-014 Presser, Automatic; 363.685-018 Presser, Form; 363.685-022 Presser, Handkerchief; 363.685-026 Shirt Presser; 369.685-018 Fur Ironer; 580.685-042 Molder; 583.585-010 Calender-Machine Operator; 583.685-018 Brim Presser I; 583.685-022 Brim-and-Crown Presser; 583.685-050 Hat-Lining Blocker; 583.685-054 Hydraulic-Press Operator; others.

51-6021.01 Pressers, Delicate Fabrics

- Education/Training Required: **Moderate-term on-the-job training**
- Employed: **No data available.**
- Annual Earnings: **$16,600**
- Growth: **1.7%**
- Annual Job Openings: **19,000**

Press dry-cleaned and wet-cleaned silk and synthetic fiber garments by hand or machine, applying knowledge of fabrics and heat to produce high-quality finish. Finish pleated or fancy garments, normally by hand.

Operates machine presses to finish parts that can be pressed flat and completes other parts by pressing with hand iron. Finishes velvet garments by steaming them on buck of hot-head press or steam table and brushing pile (nap) with handbrush. Finishes fancy garments with hand iron to produce high-quality finishes which cannot be obtained on machine presses. Finishes parts difficult to reach, such as flounces, by fitting parts over puff irons. Finishes pleated garments, determining size of pleat from evidence of old pleat or from work order, using machine press or hand iron. Presses ties on small pressing machine. Inserts heated metal form into tie and touches up rough places with hand iron.

GOE INFORMATION—**Interest Area:** 11. Recreation, Travel, and Other Personal Services. **Work Group:** 11.06. Apparel, Shoes, Leather, and Fabric Care. **Personality Type**—Realistic. Realistic occupations frequently involve work activities that include practical, hands-on problems and solutions. They often deal with plants, animals, and real-world materials like wood, tools, and machinery. Many of the occupations require working outside and do not involve a lot of paperwork or working closely with others. **Work Values**—Moral Values; Supervision, Technical; Independence; Security. **Skills**—None met the criteria. **Abilities**—*Cognitive:* None met the criteria. *Psychomotor:* Manual Dexterity; Reaction Time; Speed of Limb Movement; Arm-Hand Steadiness. *Physical:* Dynamic Flexibility; Explosive Strength; Dynamic Strength. *Sensory:* Visual Color Discrimination; Depth Perception; Glare Sensitivity. **General Work Activities**—*Information Input:* Getting Information; Monitoring Processes, Materials, or Surroundings; Inspecting Equipment, Structures, or Materials. *Mental Process:* Making Decisions and Solving Problems; Judging Qualities of Things, Services, or Other People's Work; Evaluating Information Against Standards. *Work Output:* Handling and Moving Objects; Performing General Physical Activities; Controlling Machines and Processes. *Interacting with Others:* Monitoring and Controlling Resources; Communicating with Other Workers; Establishing and Maintaining Relationships. **Physical Work Conditions**—Minor Burns, Cuts, Bites, or Stings; Very Hot or Cold; Indoors; Contaminants; Using Hands on Objects, Tools, or Controls. **Other Job Characteristics**—Degree of Automation; Pace Determined by Speed of Equipment; Importance of Repeating Same Tasks.

Experience—Job Zone 2. Some previous work-related skill, knowledge, or experience may be helpful, but usually is not needed. **Job Preparation:** SVP 4.0 to less than 6.0—six months to less than two years. **Knowledge**—Customer and Personal Service; Fine Arts. **Instructional Programs**—No data available.

Related DOT Jobs—363.681-010 Silk Finisher.

51-6021.02 Pressing Machine Operators and Tenders—Textile, Garment, and Related Materials

- Education/Training Required: **Short-term on-the-job training**
- Employed: **No data available.**
- Annual Earnings: **$16,600**
- Growth: **1.7%**
- Annual Job Openings: **19,000**

Operate or tend pressing machines, such as hot-head pressing, steam pressing, automatic pressing, ironing, plunger pressing, and hydraulic pressing machines, to press and shape articles such as leather, fur, and cloth garments, drapes, slipcovers, handkerchiefs, and millinery.

Activates pressing machine to remove wrinkles from garments and flatwork items or shape, form, or patch articles. Activates and adjusts machine controls to regulate temperature and pressure of rollers, ironing shoe, or plates, according to specifications. Lowers iron, ram, or pressing head of machine into position over material to be pressed. Selects, installs, and adjusts machine components, including pressing forms, rollers, and guides, according to pressing instructions, using hoist and hand tools. Positions materials such as cloth garments, felt, or straw on table, die, or feeding mechanism of pressing machine. Removes finished pieces from pressing machine and hangs or stacks for cooling or forwards for additional processing. Presses materials, such as garments, drapes, and slipcovers, using hand iron. Moistens materials to soften and smoothes and straightens materials with hands to prepare for machine pressing. Examines and measures finished articles to verify conformance to standards, using measuring devices, including tape measure and micrometer. Sews end of new material to leader or to end of material in pressing machine, using sewing machine. Shrinks, stretches, or blocks articles by hand to conform to original measurements, using forms, blocks, and steam. Applies cleaning solvents and brushes materials made of suede, leather, and felt to remove spots and raise and smooth nap. Hangs, folds, packages, and tags finished articles for delivery to customer. Cleans and maintains pressing machines, using cleaning solutions and lubricants.

GOE INFORMATION—Interest Area: 08. Industrial Production. **Work Group:** 08.03. Production Work. **Personality Type**—Realistic. Realistic occupations frequently involve work activities that include practical, hands-on problems and solutions. They often deal with plants, animals, and real-world materials like wood, tools, and machinery. Many of the occupations require working outside and do not involve a lot of paperwork or working closely with others. **Work Values**—Moral Values; Independence; Company Policies and Practices; Supervision, Technical; Supervision, Human Relations. **Skills**—Operation and Control; Operation Monitoring; Quality Control Analysis. **Abilities**—*Cognitive:* Perceptual Speed; Visualization; Category Flexibility; Information Ordering. *Psychomotor:* Arm-Hand Steadiness; Control Precision; Manual Dexterity; Reaction Time; Speed of Limb Movement. *Physical:* Dynamic Strength; Gross Body Coordination; Gross Body Equilibrium; Dynamic Flexibility; Extent Flexibility. *Sensory:* Visual Color Discrimination; Sound Localization. **General Work Activities**—*Information Input:* Monitoring Processes, Materials, or Surroundings; Getting Information; Inspecting Equipment, Structures, or Materials. *Mental Process:* Evaluating Information Against Standards; Judging Qualities of Things, Services, or Other People's Work; Organizing, Planning, and Prioritizing. *Work Output:* Handling and Moving Objects; Performing General Physical Activities; Controlling Machines and Processes. *Interacting with Others:* Communicating with Other Workers; Establishing and Maintaining Relationships; Monitoring and Controlling Resources. **Physical Work Conditions**—Minor Burns, Cuts, Bites, or Stings; Very Hot or Cold; Hazardous Equipment; Hazardous Conditions; Making Repetitive Motions. **Other Job Characteristics**—Importance of Repeating Same Tasks; Pace Determined by Speed of Equipment; Degree of Automation.

Experience—Job Zone 1. No previous work-related skill, knowledge, or experience is needed. **Job Preparation:** SVP below 4.0—less than six months. **Knowledge**—Fine Arts; Engineering and Technology; Foreign Language; Philosophy and Theology; Chemistry. **Instructional Programs**—No data available.

Related DOT Jobs—361.685-022 Patching-Machine Operator; 363.682-010 Leather Finisher; 363.682-014 Presser, All-Around; 363.682-018 Presser, Machine; 363.684-010 Blocker; 363.684-014 Hat Blocker; 363.685-010 Press

Operator; 363.685-014 Presser, Automatic; 363.685-018 Presser, Form; 363.685-022 Presser, Handkerchief; 363.685-026 Shirt Presser; 369.685-018 Fur Ironer; 580.685-042 Molder; 583.585-010 Calender-Machine Operator; 583.685-018 Brim Presser I; 583.685-022 Brim-and-Crown Presser; 583.685-050 Hat-Lining Blocker; 583.685-054 Hydraulic-Press Operator; 583.685-058 Hydraulic-Press Operator; 583.685-070 Mangler; others.

51-6021.03 Pressers, Hand

- **Education/Training Required: Short-term on-the-job training**
- **Employed: No data available.**
- **Annual Earnings: $16,600**
- **Growth: 1.7%**
- **Annual Job Openings: 19,000**

Press articles to remove wrinkles, flatten seams, and give shape by using hand iron. Articles pressed include drapes, knit goods, millinery parts, parachutes, garments, slip covers, and textiles such as lace, rayon, and silk. May block (shape) knitted garments after cleaning. May press leather goods.

Pushes and pulls iron over surface of article according to type of fabric. Adjusts temperature of iron according to fabric type and uses covering cloths to prevent scorching or sheen on delicate fabrics. Fits odd-shaped pieces which cannot be pressed flat over puff iron. Smoothes and shapes fabric prior to pressing. Places article in position on ironing board or worktable. Measures fabric to specifications, cuts uneven edges with shears, folds material, and presses with iron to form heading. Sprays water over fabric to soften fibers when not using steam iron. Pins, folds, and hangs article after pressing.

GOE INFORMATION—Interest Area: 11. Recreation, Travel, and Other Personal Services. **Work Group:** 11.06. Apparel, Shoes, Leather, and Fabric Care. **Personality Type**—Realistic. Realistic occupations frequently involve work activities that include practical, hands-on problems and solutions. They often deal with plants, animals, and real-world materials like wood, tools, and machinery. Many of the occupations require working outside and do not involve a lot of paperwork or working closely with others. **Work Values**—Moral Values; Independence. **Skills**—None met the criteria. **Abilities**—*Cognitive:* None met the criteria. *Psychomotor:* Manual Dexterity; Speed of Limb Movement; Multilimb Coordination; Wrist-Finger Speed; Reaction Time. *Physical:* Dynamic Strength; Trunk Strength; Dynamic Flexibility. *Sensory:* Depth Perception; Glare Sensitivity. **General Work Activities**—*Information Input:* Inspecting Equipment, Structures, or Materials; Getting Information; Monitoring Processes, Materials, or Surroundings. *Mental Process:* Judging Qualities of Things, Services, or Other People's Work; Evaluating Information Against Standards; Analyzing Data or Information. *Work Output:* Handling and Moving Objects; Performing General Physical Activities; Controlling Machines and Processes. *Interacting with Others:* Communicating with Other Workers; Establishing and Maintaining Relationships; Monitoring and Controlling Resources. **Physical Work Conditions**—Minor Burns, Cuts, Bites, or Stings; Using Hands on Objects, Tools, or Controls; Indoors; Contaminants; Making Repetitive Motions. **Other Job Characteristics**—Importance of Repeating Same Tasks; Degree of Automation; Pace Determined by Speed of Equipment.

Experience—Job Zone 1. No previous work-related skill, knowledge, or experience is needed. **Job Preparation:** SVP below 4.0—less than six months. **Knowledge**—Customer and Personal Service; Production and Processing. **Instructional Programs**—No data available.

Related DOT Jobs—363.684-018 Presser, Hand; 781.684-030 Drapery-Head Former.

51-6031.00 Sewing Machine Operators

- **Education/Training Required: Moderate-term on-the-job training**
- **Employed: 398,891**
- **Annual Earnings: $16,810**
- **Growth: –12.9%**
- **Annual Job Openings: 81,000**

Operate or tend sewing machines to join, reinforce, decorate, or perform related sewing operations in the manufacture of garment or nongarment products.

No task data available.

GOE INFORMATION—Interest Area: 08. Industrial Production. **Work Group:** 08.03. Production Work. **Note:** The Department of Labor has not collected some data for this job, so it has fewer details than the other descriptions.

Instructional Programs—Apparel and Textile Manufacture.

Related DOT Jobs—684.682-014 Sewer and Inspector; 689.662-014 Stripe Matcher; 689.682-018 Splicing-Machine Operator; 689.682-022 Stitcher; 689.685-026 Bouffant-Curtain-Machine Tender; 689.685-106 Quilting-Machine Operator; 689.685-118 Sewing-Machine Operator, Special Equipment; 689.685-126 Stitch-Bonding-Machine Tender; 689.685-150 Watcher, Automat; 689.685-154 Watcher, Pantograph; 692.685-254 Window-Shade-Ring Sewer; 731.685-010 Rooter Operator; 780.682-010 Sewing-Machine Operator; 780.682-014 Slip-Cover Sewer; 780.682-018 Upholstery Sewer; 782.687-046 Sack Repairer; 783.381-014 Fur Finisher; 783.682-010 Fur-Machine Operator; 783.682-014 Sewing Machine Operator; 784.682-010 Glove Sewer; others.

51-6031.01 Sewing Machine Operators, Garment

- **Education/Training Required: Moderate-term on-the-job training**
- **Employed: No data available.**
- **Annual Earnings: $16,810**
- **Growth: –12.9%**
- **Annual Job Openings: 81,000**

Operate or tend sewing machines to perform garment-sewing operations, such as joining, reinforcing, or decorating garments or garment parts.

Starts and operates or tends machines that automatically join, reinforce, or decorate material or fabricated articles. Draws thread through guides, tensions, and needles and adjusts machine functions according to fabric type. Positions item under needle, using marks on machine, clamp or template, edges of cloth, or markings on cloth as guides. Turns knobs, screws, and dials to adjust settings of machine, according to garment style and observation of operation. Replaces and rethreads needles. Guides garment or garment parts under machine needle and presser foot to sew parts together. Positions material or article in clamps, template, or hoop frame prior to automatic operation of machine. Sews replacement parts or missing stitches according to repair tickets. Observes sewing machine operation to detect defects in stitching or machine malfunction and notifies supervisor. Attaches buttons or fasteners to fabric, using feeding hopper or clamp holder. Folds or stretches edges or length of items, while sewing, to facilitate forming specified sections. Attaches tape, trim, or elastic to specified garments or garment parts according to item specifications. Removes holding devices and finished item from machine. Selects supplies, such as fasteners and thread, according to specifications or characteristics of fabric. Bastes edges of material to align and temporarily secure garment parts for final assembly. Draws markings or pins applique on fabric to obtain variation in design and marks stitching errors with pins or tape. Replaces sewing machine parts and performs basic maintenance, such as oiling machine. Cuts material and threads, using scissors. Inspects garments and examines repair tags and markings on garment to locate defects or damage. Records number of garment parts or complete garments sewn.

GOE INFORMATION—Interest Area: 08. Industrial Production. **Work Group:** 08.03. Production Work. **Personality Type**—Realistic. Realistic occupations frequently involve work activities that include practical, hands-on problems and solutions. They often deal with plants, animals, and real-world materials like wood, tools, and machinery. Many of the occupations require working outside and do not involve a lot of paperwork or working closely with others. **Work Values**—Moral Values; Activity; Independence; Supervision, Human Relations; Company Policies and Practices. **Skills**—Operation and Control; Equipment Selection; Repairing. **Abilities**—*Cognitive:* Selective Attention; Perceptual Speed; Visualization; Spatial Orientation. *Psychomotor:* Arm-Hand Steadiness; Reaction Time; Manual Dexterity; Speed of Limb Movement; Rate Control. *Physical:* Dynamic Flexibility; Extent Flexibility; Dynamic Strength; Gross Body Coordination; Gross Body Equilibrium. *Sensory:* Visual Color Discrimination; Hearing Sensitivity; Sound Localization; Depth Perception; Near Vision. **General Work Activities**—*Information Input:* Inspecting Equipment, Structures, or Materials; Identifying Objects, Actions, and Events; Monitoring Processes, Materials, or Surroundings. *Mental Process:* Evaluating Information Against Standards; Thinking Creatively; Judging Qualities of Things, Services, or Other People's Work. *Work Output:* Handling and Moving Objects; Controlling Machines and Processes; Performing General Physical Activities. *Interacting with Others:* Establishing and Maintaining Relationships; Communicating with Other Workers; Monitoring and Controlling Resources. **Physical Work Conditions**—Making Repetitive Motions; Sitting; Hazardous Equipment; Using Hands on Objects, Tools, or Controls; Distracting Sounds and Noise Levels. **Other Job Characteristics**—Importance of Repeating Same Tasks; Pace Determined by Speed of Equipment; Degree of Automation.

Experience—Job Zone 1. No previous work-related skill, knowledge, or experience is needed. **Job Preparation:** SVP below 4.0—less than six months. **Knowledge**—Production and Processing. **Instructional Programs**—Apparel and Textile Manufacture.

Related DOT Jobs—684.682-014 Sewer and Inspector; 689.685-150 Watcher, Automat; 689.685-154 Watcher, Pantograph; 784.682-010 Glove Sewer; 784.682-014 Hat-and-Cap Sewer; 784.685-014 Brim Stitcher I; 786.682-010 Appliquer, Zigzag; 786.682-014 Armhole Baster, Jumpbasting; 786.682-018 Armhole Feller, Handstitching Machine; 786.682-022 Armhole-Sew-and-Trim Operator, Lockstitch; 786.682-026 Back Maker, Lockstitch; 786.682-030 Basting-Machine Operator; 786.682-034 Binder, Chainstitch; 786.682-038 Binder, Coverstitch; 786.682-042 Binder, Lockstitch; 786.682-046 Blindstitch-Machine Operator; 786.682-050 Canvas Baster, Jumpbasting; 786.682-054 Chainstitch Sewing Machine Operator; 786.682-058 Coat Joiner, Lockstitch; 786.682-062 Collar Baster, Jumpbasting; others.

51-6031.02 Sewing Machine Operators, Non-Garment

- Education/Training Required: Moderate-term on-the-job training
- Employed: No data available.
- Annual Earnings: $16,810
- Growth: –12.9%
- Annual Job Openings: 81,000

Operate or tend sewing machines to join together, reinforce, decorate, or perform related sewing operations in the manufacture of nongarment products, such as upholstery, draperies, linens, carpets, and mattresses.

Activates and adjusts machine controls to regulate stitching speed and length, dimensions of gathers and tucks, and material or thread tension. Activates sewing machine to join, gather, hem, reinforce, or decorate materials or fabricated articles, such as linens, toys, or luggage. Monitors machine operation to detect problems such as defective stitching, breaks in thread, or machine malfunction. Positions materials through feed rollers and guides or positions and maneuvers under sewing machine presser foot and needle during operation. Mounts attachments, such as needles, cutting blades, or pattern plates, and adjusts machine guides according to specifications. Examines and measures finished articles to verify conformance to standards, using ruler. Selects supplies, such as binding, cord, or thread, according to specifications or color of material. Places spools of thread, cord, or other materials on spindles, inserts bobbin, and threads ends through machine guides and components. Folds or fits together materials, such as cloth, foam rubber, or leather, to prepare for machine sewing. Cuts materials according to specifications or cuts excess material or thread from finished product, using blade, scissors, or electric knife. Replaces needles, sands rough areas of needles with sandpaper, and cleans and oils sewing machines to maintain equipment. Positions and marks patterns on materials to prepare for sewing. Tapes or twists together thread or cord to repair breaks. Removes finished materials from sewing machine. Records amount of materials processed in production logs. Sews materials by hand, using needle and thread.

GOE INFORMATION—Interest Area: 08. Industrial Production. Work Group: 08.03. Production Work. Personality Type—Realistic. Realistic occupations frequently involve work activities that include practical, hands-on problems and solutions. They often deal with plants, animals, and real-world materials like wood, tools, and machinery. Many of the occupations require working outside and do not involve a lot of paperwork or working closely with others. Work Values—Moral Values; Independence; Supervision, Human Relations; Activity; Company Policies and Practices. Skills—Operation and Control. Abilities—*Cognitive:* Visualization; Perceptual Speed; Spatial Orientation. *Psychomotor:* Rate Control; Manual Dexterity; Arm-Hand Steadiness; Finger Dexterity; Control Precision. *Physical:* Trunk Strength; Dynamic Flexibility; Dynamic Strength; Extent Flexibility; Stamina. *Sensory:* Visual Color Discrimination; Near Vision; Depth Perception; Peripheral Vision. General Work Activities—*Information Input:* Monitoring Processes, Materials, or Surroundings; Inspecting Equipment, Structures, or Materials; Estimating Needed Characteristics. *Mental Process:* Evaluating Information Against Standards; Judging Qualities of Things, Services, or Other People's Work; Updating and Using Relevant Knowledge. *Work Output:* Handling and Moving Objects; Controlling Machines and Processes; Documenting or Recording Information. *Interacting with Others:* Performing Administrative Activities; Communicating with Other Workers; Coordinating the Work and Activities of Others. Physical Work Conditions—Hazardous Equipment; Making Repetitive Motions; Using Hands on Objects, Tools,

or Controls; Sitting; Indoors. Other Job Characteristics—Pace Determined by Speed of Equipment; Degree of Automation; Importance of Repeating Same Tasks.

Experience—Job Zone 1. No previous work-related skill, knowledge, or experience is needed. Job Preparation: SVP below 4.0—less than six months. Knowledge—Production and Processing; Mechanical; Clerical; Fine Arts; Philosophy and Theology. Instructional Programs—Apparel and Textile Manufacture.

Related DOT Jobs—689.662-014 Stripe Matcher; 689.682-018 Splicing-Machine Operator; 689.682-022 Stitcher; 689.685-026 Bouffant-Curtain-Machine Tender; 689.685-106 Quilting-Machine Operator; 689.685-118 Sewing-Machine Operator, Special Equipment; 689.685-126 Stitch-Bonding-Machine Tender; 692.685-254 Window-Shade-Ring Sewer; 731.685-010 Rooter Operator; 780.682-010 Sewing-Machine Operator; 780.682-014 Slip-Cover Sewer; 780.682-018 Upholstery Sewer; 782.687-046 Sack Repairer; 783.682-010 Fur-Machine Operator; 783.682-014 Sewing Machine Operator; 787.682-010 Binder; 787.682-014 Carpet Sewer; 787.682-018 Drapery Operator; 787.682-026 Hemmer; 787.682-034 Overedge Sewer; others.

51-6041.00 Shoe and Leather Workers and Repairers

- Education/Training Required: Long-term on-the-job training
- Employed: 18,867
- Annual Earnings: $18,100
- Growth: –21.4%
- Annual Job Openings: 3,000

Construct, decorate, or repair leather and leather-like products, such as luggage, shoes, and saddles.

Assembles product according to specifications, utilizing sewing machine, needle and thread, or leather lacing, glue, clamps, or rivets. Attaches accessories or ornamentation to decorate or protect product. Sews rips or patches holes by hand or machine to repair articles such as purses, shoes, and luggage. Selects material and cuts parts along pattern or outline with knife, shears, or scissors. Dyes, soaks, paints, stamps, or engraves leather or other materials to obtain desired effect or shape. Inserts and positions padding, foam cushioning, or lining and glues or stitches into place. Fabricates articles such as purses, wallets, belts, luggage frames, and shoes. Repairs and reconditions products such as trunks, luggage, shoes, and saddles. Aligns and stitches or glues materials such as fabric, fleece, leather, or wood to join parts. Drills or punches holes and inserts metal rings, handles, and hardware. Reads prescription or specifications and measures item, using calipers, tape measures, or rule. Draws pattern, using measurements, plaster cast, or customer specifications, and positions or outlines pattern on workpiece. Trims and buffs, bevels, or flares workpiece to specified size and shape. Inspects article for defects and removes damaged or worn parts, using hand tools.

GOE INFORMATION—Interest Area: 11. Recreation, Travel, and Other Personal Services. Work Group: 11.06. Apparel, Shoes, Leather, and Fabric Care. Personality Type—Realistic. Realistic occupations frequently involve work activities that include practical, hands-on problems and solutions. They often deal with plants, animals, and real-world materials like wood, tools, and machinery. Many of the occupations require working outside and do not involve a lot of paperwork or working closely with others. Work Values—Independence; Moral Values; Creativity; Ability Utilization; Autonomy. Skills—Repairing. Abilities—*Cognitive:* Visualization; Information Ordering; Category Flexibility. *Psychomotor:* Arm-Hand Steadiness; Finger Dexterity; Wrist-Finger Speed; Manual Dexterity; Control Precision. *Physical:* Extent Flexibility; Static Strength; Stamina;

Explosive Strength; Dynamic Flexibility. *Sensory:* Visual Color Discrimination; Near Vision. **General Work Activities**—*Information Input:* Getting Information; Monitoring Processes, Materials, or Surroundings; Identifying Objects, Actions, and Events. *Mental Process:* Evaluating Information Against Standards; Organizing, Planning, and Prioritizing; Judging Qualities of Things, Services, or Other People's Work. *Work Output:* Handling and Moving Objects; Controlling Machines and Processes; Performing General Physical Activities. *Interacting with Others:* Performing for or Working with the Public; Communicating with Persons Outside Organization; Communicating with Other Workers. **Physical Work Conditions**—Making Repetitive Motions; Using Hands on Objects, Tools, or Controls; Sitting; Indoors; Hazardous Equipment. **Other Job Characteristics**—Importance of Repeating Same Tasks; Pace Determined by Speed of Equipment; Degree of Automation.

Experience—Job Zone 2. Some previous work-related skill, knowledge, or experience may be helpful, but usually is not needed. **Job Preparation:** SVP 4.0 to less than 6.0—six months to less than two years. **Knowledge**—Production and Processing; Fine Arts; Design; Foreign Language; Engineering and Technology. **Instructional Programs**—Leatherworking and Upholstery, Other; Shoe, Boot and Leather Repair.

Related DOT Jobs—365.361-010 Luggage Repairer; 365.361-014 Shoe Repairer; 739.684-114 Last-Repairer Helper; 753.381-010 Bootmaker, Hand; 753.684-026 Repairer; 780.381-030 Pad Hand; 781.381-018 Leather Stamper; 783.361-010 Custom-Leather-Products Maker; 783.381-018 Harness Maker; 783.381-022 Luggage Maker; 783.381-026 Saddle Maker; 788.261-010 Orthopedic-Boot-and-Shoe Designer and Maker; 788.381-010 Cobbler; 788.381-014 Shoemaker, Custom; 788.684-046 Finger Cobbler; 788.684-098 Sample Shoe Inspector and Reworker.

51-6042.00 Shoe Machine Operators and Tenders

- **Education/Training Required: Moderate-term on-the-job training**
- **Employed: 9,058**
- **Annual Earnings: $19,180**
- **Growth: −53.6%**
- **Annual Job Openings: 2,000**

Operate or tend a variety of machines to join, decorate, reinforce, or finish shoes and shoe parts.

Turns setscrew on needle bar and positions required number of needles in designated stitching machines. Aligns parts to be stitched, following seams, edges, or markings, and positions parts under needle. Draws thread through machine guide slots and needles. Selects and inserts specified cassettes into consoles of stitching machine to stitch decorative designs onto shoe parts. Lowers pressure foot or roller to secure parts and starts machine stitching, using hand, foot, or knee controls. Guides shoe into feeding mechanism that attaches, stitches, joins, or reinforces shoe parts according to instructions. Selects and places spools of thread or prewound bobbins into shuttles or onto spindles or loupers of stitching machines. Reads shoe part tags to identify appropriate instruction cassette and style and color of thread. Removes and examines shoe parts and design to verify conformance to specifications. Cuts excess thread or material from shoe part, using scissors or knife.

GOE INFORMATION—**Interest Area:** 08. Industrial Production. **Work Group:** 08.03. Production Work. **Personality Type**—Realistic. Realistic occupations frequently involve work activities that include practical, hands-on problems and solutions. They often deal with plants, animals, and real-world materials like wood, tools, and machinery. Many of the occupations require working outside and do not involve a lot of paper-

work or working closely with others. **Work Values**—Moral Values; Independence; Activity; Supervision, Human Relations; Company Policies and Practices. **Skills**—Operation and Control. **Abilities**—*Cognitive:* None met the criteria. *Psychomotor:* Finger Dexterity; Arm-Hand Steadiness; Manual Dexterity; Wrist-Finger Speed; Multilimb Coordination. *Physical:* Dynamic Strength; Explosive Strength; Dynamic Flexibility. *Sensory:* Visual Color Discrimination; Glare Sensitivity. **General Work Activities**—*Information Input:* Monitoring Processes, Materials, or Surroundings; Inspecting Equipment, Structures, or Materials; Getting Information. *Mental Process:* Evaluating Information Against Standards; Updating and Using Relevant Knowledge; Organizing, Planning, and Prioritizing. *Work Output:* Handling and Moving Objects; Performing General Physical Activities; Controlling Machines and Processes. *Interacting with Others:* Communicating with Other Workers; Establishing and Maintaining Relationships; Performing Administrative Activities. **Physical Work Conditions**—Making Repetitive Motions; Minor Burns, Cuts, Bites, or Stings; Sitting; Hazardous Equipment; Indoors. **Other Job Characteristics**—Importance of Repeating Same Tasks; Pace Determined by Speed of Equipment; Degree of Automation.

Experience—Job Zone 1. No previous work-related skill, knowledge, or experience is needed. **Job Preparation:** SVP below 4.0—less than six months. **Knowledge**—Production and Processing. **Instructional Programs**—Shoe, Boot and Leather Repair.

Related DOT Jobs—690.682-078 Stitcher, Special Machine; 690.682-082 Stitcher, Standard Machine; 690.685-494 Stitcher, Tape-Controlled Machine; 788.684-114 Thread Laster.

51-6051.00 Sewers, Hand

- **Education/Training Required: Short-term on-the-job training**
- **Employed: 42,576**
- **Annual Earnings: $17,540**
- **Growth: −6.6%**
- **Annual Job Openings: 8,000**

Sew, join, reinforce, or finish, usually with needle and thread, a variety of manufactured items. Includes weavers and stitchers.

Sews using various types of stitches, such as felling, tacking, basting, embroidery, and fagoting. Joins and reinforces parts of articles, such as garments, books, mattresses, toys, and wigs. Selects thread, twine, cord, or yarn and threads needles. Folds, twists, stretches, or drapes material and secures article in preparation for sewing. Measures and aligns parts, fasteners, or trimmings, following seams, edges, or markings on parts. Trims excess threads or edges of parts, using scissors or knife. Ties, knits, weaves, or knots ribbon, yarn, or decorative materials. Smoothes seams with heated iron, flat bone, or rubbing stick. Attaches trimmings and labels to article with cement, using brush or cement gun. Draws and cuts pattern according to specifications. Waxes thread by drawing it through ball of wax. Softens leather or shoe material with water.

GOE INFORMATION—**Interest Area:** 08. Industrial Production. **Work Group:** 08.03. Production Work. **Personality Type**—Realistic. Realistic occupations frequently involve work activities that include practical, hands-on problems and solutions. They often deal with plants, animals, and real-world materials like wood, tools, and machinery. Many of the occupations require working outside and do not involve a lot of paperwork or working closely with others. **Work Values**—Independence; Moral Values; Activity. **Skills**—None met the criteria. **Abilities**—*Cognitive:* Visualization; Selective Attention. *Psychomotor:* Arm-Hand Steadiness; Wrist-Finger Speed; Finger Dexterity; Speed of Limb Movement; Multilimb Coordination. *Physical:* None met the criteria. *Sensory:* Visual Color Discrimination; Near Vision. **General Work Activities**—*Information Input:*

Getting Information; Identifying Objects, Actions, and Events; Estimating Needed Characteristics. *Mental Process:* Making Decisions and Solving Problems; Analyzing Data or Information; Updating and Using Relevant Knowledge. *Work Output:* Handling and Moving Objects; Performing General Physical Activities; Drafting and Specifying Technical Devices. *Interacting with Others:* Communicating with Other Workers; Monitoring and Controlling Resources; Coordinating the Work and Activities of Others. **Physical Work Conditions**—Making Repetitive Motions; Using Hands on Objects, Tools, or Controls; Sitting; Indoors; Common Protective or Safety Attire. **Other Job Characteristics**—Importance of Repeating Same Tasks; Pace Determined by Speed of Equipment; Importance of Being Exact or Accurate.

Experience—Job Zone 1. No previous work-related skill, knowledge, or experience is needed. **Job Preparation:** SVP below 4.0—less than six months. **Knowledge**—Production and Processing; Fine Arts; Design. **Instructional Programs**—No data available.

Related DOT Jobs—529.687-030 Casing Sewer; 732.684-034 Baseball Sewer, Hand; 732.684-050 Feather Stitcher; 732.684-090 Pelota Maker; 739.384-014 Foundation Maker; 739.684-162 Umbrella Tipper, Hand; 780.684-070 Mattress Finisher; 782.684-030 Hosiery Mender; 782.684-050 Passementerie Worker; 782.684-058 Sewer, Hand; 782.687-018 Cloth-Bale Header; 782.687-058 Thread Marker; 784.684-022 Decorator; 784.684-042 Hat Maker; 787.381-010 Lamp-Shade Sewer; 788.684-054 Hand Sewer, Shoes; 788.684-110 Sole Sewer, Hand; 789.381-010 Beadworker; 789.484-014 Finisher, Hand; 920.687-022 Bale Sewer; others.

51-6052.00 Tailors, Dressmakers, and Custom Sewers

- **Education/Training Required: Work experience in a related occupation**
- **Employed: 58,005**
- **Annual Earnings: $21,590**
- **Growth: −11.4%**
- **Annual Job Openings: 11,000**

Design, make, alter, repair, or fit garments.

No task data available.

GOE INFORMATION—**Interest Area:** 11. Recreation, Travel, and Other Personal Services. **Work Group:** 11.06. Apparel, Shoes, Leather, and Fabric Care. **Note:** The Department of Labor has not collected some data for this job, so it has fewer details than the other descriptions.

Instructional Programs—No data available.

Related DOT Jobs—782.361-010 Corset Fitter; 782.381-010 Hat Trimmer; 783.261-010 Furrier; 785.261-010 Alteration Tailor; 785.261-014 Custom Tailor; 785.261-018 Tailor Apprentice, Alteration; 785.261-022 Tailor Apprentice, Custom; 785.361-010 Dressmaker; 785.361-014 Garment Fitter; 785.361-018 Sample Stitcher; 785.361-022 Shop Tailor; 785.361-026 Shop Tailor Apprentice; 969.381-010 Wardrobe-Specialty Worker.

51-6052.01 Shop and Alteration Tailors

- **Education/Training Required: Work experience in a related occupation**
- **Employed: No data available.**
- **Annual Earnings: $21,590**
- **Growth: −11.4%**
- **Annual Job Openings: 11,000**

Make tailored garments from existing patterns. Alter, repair, or fit made-to-measure or ready-to-wear garments.

Repairs or replaces defective garment parts, such as pockets, pocket flaps, and linings. Measures and marks alteration lines. Pins altering folds or marks on cloth at seams, darts, or necklines to indicate alterations to be made. Shortens or lengthens garment parts, such as sleeves or legs. Expands or narrows garment parts, such as waist or chest. Raises or lowers garment parts, such as collars or lapels. Resews garment, using needle and thread or sewing machine. Examines tag on garment to ascertain necessary alterations. Fits garment on customer to determine required alterations. Studies garment on customer and measures pieces, such as sleeves, pants, and hems, using tape measure. Removes stitches from garment, using ripper or razor blade. Inserts or eliminates padding in shoulders while maintaining drape and proportions of garment. Records required alterations and instructions. Presses garment, using hand iron or pressing machine.

GOE INFORMATION—**Interest Area:** 11. Recreation, Travel, and Other Personal Services. **Work Group:** 11.06. Apparel, Shoes, Leather, and Fabric Care. **Personality Type**—Realistic. Realistic occupations frequently involve work activities that include practical, hands-on problems and solutions. They often deal with plants, animals, and real-world materials like wood, tools, and machinery. Many of the occupations require working outside and do not involve a lot of paperwork or working closely with others. **Work Values**—Good Working Conditions; Independence; Social Service; Autonomy; Variety. **Skills**—None met the criteria. **Abilities**—*Cognitive:* None met the criteria. *Psychomotor:* Arm-Hand Steadiness; Finger Dexterity; Control Precision; Wrist-Finger Speed; Manual Dexterity. *Physical:* None met the criteria. *Sensory:* None met the criteria. **General Work Activities**—*Information Input:* Getting Information; Identifying Objects, Actions, and Events; Estimating Needed Characteristics. *Mental Process:* Evaluating Information Against Standards; Thinking Creatively; Judging Qualities of Things, Services, or Other People's Work. *Work Output:* Handling and Moving Objects; Performing General Physical Activities; Controlling Machines and Processes. *Interacting with Others:* Performing for or Working with the Public; Communicating with Persons Outside Organization; Establishing and Maintaining Relationships. **Physical Work Conditions**—Sitting; Making Repetitive Motions; Indoors; Kneeling, Crouching, or Crawling; Hazardous Equipment. **Other Job Characteristics**—Importance of Being Exact or Accurate; Pace Determined by Speed of Equipment; Importance of Repeating Same Tasks.

Experience—Job Zone 3. Previous work-related skill, knowledge, or experience is required. **Job Preparation:** SVP 6.0 to less than 7.0—more than one year and less than four years. **Knowledge**—Customer and Personal Service; Production and Processing; Design. **Instructional Programs**—No data available.

Related DOT Jobs—782.361-010 Corset Fitter; 785.261-010 Alteration Tailor; 785.261-018 Tailor Apprentice, Alteration; 785.361-014 Garment Fitter; 785.361-018 Sample Stitcher; 785.361-022 Shop Tailor; 785.361-026 Shop Tailor Apprentice; 969.381-010 Wardrobe-Specialty Worker.

51-6052.02 Custom Tailors

- **Education/Training Required: Work experience in a related occupation**
- **Employed: No data available.**
- **Annual Earnings: $21,590**
- **Growth: −11.4%**
- **Annual Job Openings: 11,000**

Design/make tailored garments, applying knowledge of garment design, construction, styling, and fabrics.

Develops design for garment, adapts existing design for garment, or copies existing design for garment. Assembles garment parts and joins parts with basting stitches, using needle and thread or sewing machine. Fits basted garment on customer and marks areas requiring alterations. Alters garment and joins parts, using needle and thread or sewing machine, to form finished garment. Measures customer for size, using tape measure, and records measurements. Draws individual pattern or alters existing pattern to fit customer's measurements. Positions pattern of garment parts on fabric and cuts fabric along outlines, using scissors. Sews buttons and buttonholes to finish garment. Confers with customer to determine type of material and garment style desired. Presses garment, using hand iron or pressing machine.

GOE INFORMATION—Interest Area: 11. Recreation, Travel, and Other Personal Services. **Work Group:** 11.06. Apparel, Shoes, Leather, and Fabric Care. **Personality Type—**Realistic. Realistic occupations frequently involve work activities that include practical, hands-on problems and solutions. They often deal with plants, animals, and real-world materials like wood, tools, and machinery. Many of the occupations require working outside and do not involve a lot of paperwork or working closely with others. **Work Values—**Autonomy; Creativity; Good Working Conditions; Social Service; Ability Utilization. **Skills—**Operation and Control. **Abilities—***Cognitive:* Originality; Fluency of Ideas; Visualization. *Psychomotor:* Arm-Hand Steadiness; Finger Dexterity. *Physical:* None met the criteria. *Sensory:* None met the criteria. **General Work Activities—***Information Input:* Getting Information; Identifying Objects, Actions, and Events; Inspecting Equipment, Structures, or Materials. *Mental Process:* Thinking Creatively; Making Decisions and Solving Problems; Organizing, Planning, and Prioritizing. *Work Output:* Handling and Moving Objects; Controlling Machines and Processes; Performing General Physical Activities. *Interacting with Others:* Communicating with Persons Outside Organization; Performing for or Working with the Public; Establishing and Maintaining Relationships. **Physical Work Conditions—**Indoors; Sitting; Using Hands on Objects, Tools, or Controls; Making Repetitive Motions; Kneeling, Crouching, or Crawling. **Other Job Characteristics—**Importance of Being Exact or Accurate; Importance of Repeating Same Tasks; Pace Determined by Speed of Equipment.

Experience—Job Zone 4. A minimum of two to four years of work-related skill, knowledge, or experience is needed. **Job Preparation:** SVP 7.0 to less than 8.0—two years to less than 10 years. **Knowledge—**Design; Customer and Personal Service; Production and Processing; Fine Arts; Sales and Marketing. **Instructional Programs—**No data available.

Related DOT Jobs—785.261-014 Custom Tailor; 785.261-022 Tailor Apprentice, Custom; 785.361-010 Dressmaker.

51-6061.00 Textile Bleaching and Dyeing Machine Operators and Tenders

- **Education/Training Required: Moderate-term on-the-job training**
- **Employed: 36,573**
- **Annual Earnings: $20,340**
- **Growth: 10.8%**
- **Annual Job Openings: 2,000**

Operate or tend machines to bleach, shrink, wash, dye, or finish textiles or synthetic or glass fibers.

Starts machines and equipment to process and finish textile goods prior to further processing, following instructions. Observes display screen, control panel and equipment, and cloth entering or exiting process to determine equipment adjustments. Adjusts equipment controls to maintain standards. Mixes or adds dyes, water, detergents, or chemicals to tanks to dilute or strengthen solutions as indicated by tests. Mounts roll of cloth on machine, using hoist, or places textile goods in machines or pieces of equipment. Threads ends of cloth or twine through specified sections of equipment prior to processing. Removes items such as dyed articles, cloth, cones, and bobbins from tanks and machines for drying and further processing. Creels machine with bobbins or twine. Keys in processing instructions to program electronic equipment. Soaks specified textile products for designated time. Tests solutions used to process textile goods to detect variations from standards, using standard procedures. Weighs ingredient to be mixed together to process textiles. Examines and feels products to determine variation from processing standards. Sews ends of cloth together by hand or using machine to form endless length of cloth to facilitate processing. Records information such as fabric yardage processed, temperature readings, fabric tensions, machine speeds, and delays caused by range malfunctions. Notifies supervisor of equipment malfunctions and co-workers to initiate steps in processing of textile goods. Confers with co-workers to ascertain information regarding customer orders, process steps to be completed during shift, or reason for delays. Ravels seams connecting cloth ends after processing is completed. Cleans machines and equipment.

GOE INFORMATION—Interest Area: 08. Industrial Production. **Work Group:** 08.03. Production Work. **Personality Type—**Realistic. Realistic occupations frequently involve work activities that include practical, hands-on problems and solutions. They often deal with plants, animals, and real-world materials like wood, tools, and machinery. Many of the occupations require working outside and do not involve a lot of paperwork or working closely with others. **Work Values—**Moral Values; Supervision, Technical; Supervision, Human Relations; Company Policies and Practices; Advancement. **Skills—**Operation and Control; Operation Monitoring. **Abilities—***Cognitive:* Perceptual Speed; Spatial Orientation; Problem Sensitivity; Time Sharing; Memorization. *Psychomotor:* Rate Control; Arm-Hand Steadiness; Control Precision; Wrist-Finger Speed; Manual Dexterity. *Physical:* Dynamic Flexibility; Dynamic Strength; Static Strength; Explosive Strength; Extent Flexibility. *Sensory:* Visual Color Discrimination; Depth Perception; Near Vision; Peripheral Vision; Far Vision. **General Work Activities—***Information Input:* Monitoring Processes, Materials, or Surroundings; Identifying Objects, Actions, and Events; Inspecting Equipment, Structures, or Materials. *Mental Process:* Evaluating Information Against Standards; Updating and Using Relevant Knowledge; Processing Information. *Work Output:* Controlling Machines and Processes; Handling and Moving Objects; Performing General Physical Activities. *Interacting with Others:* Communicating with Other Workers; Establishing and Maintaining Relationships; Performing Administrative Activities. **Physical Work Conditions—**Hazardous Equipment; Hazardous Conditions; Contaminants; Minor Burns, Cuts, Bites, or Stings; Using Hands on Objects, Tools, or Controls. **Other Job Characteristics—**Pace Determined by Speed of Equipment; Degree of Automation; Importance of Repeating Same Tasks.

Experience—Job Zone 1. No previous work-related skill, knowledge, or experience is needed. **Job Preparation:** SVP below 4.0—less than six months. **Knowledge—**Production and Processing; Chemistry; Mechanical; Computers and Electronics; Philosophy and Theology. **Instructional Programs—**No data available.

Related DOT Jobs—582.362-010 Panelboard Operator; 582.362-014 Dye Automation Operator; 582.582-010 Dye-Range Operator, Cloth; 582.665-014 Dye-Reel Operator; 582.665-018 Jigger; 582.685-014 Beam-Dyer Operator; 582.685-018 Bleach-Range Operator; 582.685-022 Boil-Off-Machine Operator, Cloth; 582.685-030 Cloth-Washer Operator; 582.685-034 Coloring-Machine Operator; 582.685-054 Dye-Tank Tender; 582.685-058 Dyed-Yarn Operator; 582.685-070 Felt-Washing-Machine Tender; 582.685-090

Jet-Dyeing-Machine Tender; 582.685-094 Knit-Goods Washer; 582.685-098 Open-Developer Operator; 582.685-102 Package-Dyeing-Machine Operator; 582.685-106 Padding-Machine Operator; 582.685-110 Patch Washer; 582.685-114 Rope-Silica-Machine Operator; others.

51-6062.00 Textile Cutting Machine Setters, Operators, and Tenders

- **Education/Training Required: Moderate-term on-the-job training**
- **Employed: 37,628**
- **Annual Earnings: $19,360**
- **Growth: –6.5%**
- **Annual Job Openings: 7,000**

Set up, operate, or tend machines that cut textiles.

Installs, levels, and aligns components, such as gears, chains, guides, dies, cutters, and needles, to set up machinery for operation. Adjusts heating mechanisms, tension, and speed of machine operation to produce product meeting desired specifications. Starts machine, monitors operation, makes adjustments as needed, and stops machine when specified amount of product has been produced. Threads yarn, thread, and fabric through guides, needles, and rollers of machines. Operates machine for test run to verify adjustments and to obtain sample of product. Studies guides, samples, charts, and specification sheets or confers with supervisor or engineering staff to determine setup requirements. Inspects product to ensure product meets specifications and to determine need for machine adjustment. Inspects machinery to determine adjustments or repairs needed. Repairs or replaces worn or defective parts or components, using hand tools. Cleans, oils, and lubricates machines, using air hose, cleaning solutions, rags, oilcan, and grease gun.

GOE INFORMATION—Interest Area: 08. Industrial Production. **Work Group:** 08.02. Production Technology. **Personality Type—**Realistic. Realistic occupations frequently involve work activities that include practical, hands-on problems and solutions. They often deal with plants, animals, and real-world materials like wood, tools, and machinery. Many of the occupations require working outside and do not involve a lot of paperwork or working closely with others. **Work Values—**Moral Values; Supervision, Technical; Supervision, Human Relations; Independence; Company Policies and Practices. **Skills—**Operation Monitoring; Operation and Control; Installation; Repairing; Quality Control Analysis; Troubleshooting. **Abilities—***Cognitive:* Visualization; Information Ordering; Time Sharing; Flexibility of Closure; Speed of Closure. *Psychomotor:* Control Precision; Arm-Hand Steadiness; Finger Dexterity; Reaction Time; Manual Dexterity. *Physical:* Extent Flexibility; Gross Body Equilibrium; Dynamic Flexibility; Static Strength; Gross Body Coordination. *Sensory:* Auditory Attention; Hearing Sensitivity; Sound Localization; Visual Color Discrimination; Near Vision. **General Work Activities—***Information Input:* Inspecting Equipment, Structures, or Materials; Monitoring Processes, Materials, or Surroundings; Identifying Objects, Actions, and Events. *Mental Process:* Updating and Using Relevant Knowledge; Evaluating Information Against Standards; Organizing, Planning, and Prioritizing. *Work Output:* Repairing and Maintaining Mechanical Equipment; Handling and Moving Objects; Controlling Machines and Processes. *Interacting with Others:* Communicating with Other Workers; Establishing and Maintaining Relationships; Providing Consultation and Advice to Others. **Physical Work Conditions—**Hazardous Equipment; Minor Burns, Cuts, Bites, or Stings; Common Protective or Safety Attire; Using Hands on Objects, Tools, or Controls; Indoors. **Other Job Characteristics—**Degree of Automation; Pace Determined by Speed of Equipment; Importance of Repeating Same Tasks.

Experience—Job Zone 3. Previous work-related skill, knowledge, or experience is required. **Job Preparation:** SVP 6.0 to less than 7.0—more than one year and less than four years. **Knowledge—**Mechanical; Design; Fine Arts; Public Safety and Security; Foreign Language. **Instructional Programs—**Industrial Mechanics and Maintenance Technology.

Related DOT Jobs—585.380-010 Cutting-Machine Fixer.

51-6063.00 Textile Knitting and Weaving Machine Setters, Operators, and Tenders

- **Education/Training Required: Long-term on-the-job training**
- **Employed: 70,045**
- **Annual Earnings: $22,480**
- **Growth: –2.4%**
- **Annual Job Openings: 14,000**

Set up, operate, or tend machines that knit, loop, weave, or draw in textiles.

Installs, levels, and aligns components, such as gears, chains, guides, dies, cutters, and needles, to set up machinery for operation. Adjusts heating mechanisms, tension, and speed of machine operation to produce product meeting desired specifications. Starts machine, monitors operation, makes adjustments as needed, and stops machine when specified amount of product has been produced. Threads yarn, thread, and fabric through guides, needles, and rollers of machines. Operates machine for test run to verify adjustments and to obtain sample of product. Studies guides, samples, charts, and specification sheets, or confers with supervisor or engineering staff to determine setup requirements. Inspects product to ensure product meets specifications and to determine need for machine adjustment. Inspects machinery to determine adjustments or repairs needed. Repairs or replaces worn or defective parts or components, using hand tools. Cleans, oils, and lubricates machines, using air hose, cleaning solutions, rags, oilcan, and grease gun.

GOE INFORMATION—Interest Area: 08. Industrial Production. **Work Group:** 08.02. Production Technology. **Personality Type—**Realistic. Realistic occupations frequently involve work activities that include practical, hands-on problems and solutions. They often deal with plants, animals, and real-world materials like wood, tools, and machinery. Many of the occupations require working outside and do not involve a lot of paperwork or working closely with others. **Work Values—**Moral Values; Supervision, Technical; Supervision, Human Relations; Independence; Company Policies and Practices. **Skills—**Operation Monitoring; Operation and Control; Installation; Repairing; Quality Control Analysis; Troubleshooting. **Abilities—***Cognitive:* Visualization; Information Ordering; Time Sharing; Flexibility of Closure; Speed of Closure. *Psychomotor:* Control Precision; Arm-Hand Steadiness; Finger Dexterity; Reaction Time; Manual Dexterity. *Physical:* Extent Flexibility; Gross Body Equilibrium; Dynamic Flexibility; Static Strength; Gross Body Coordination. *Sensory:* Auditory Attention; Hearing Sensitivity; Sound Localization; Visual Color Discrimination; Near Vision. **General Work Activities—***Information Input:* Inspecting Equipment, Structures, or Materials; Monitoring Processes, Materials, or Surroundings; Identifying Objects, Actions, and Events. *Mental Process:* Updating and Using Relevant Knowledge; Evaluating Information Against Standards; Analyzing Data or Information. *Work Output:* Repairing and Maintaining Mechanical Equipment; Handling and Moving Objects; Controlling Machines and Processes. *Interacting with Others:* Communicating with Other Workers; Establishing and Maintaining Relationships; Providing Consultation and Advice to Others. **Physical Work Conditions—**Hazardous Equipment; Minor Burns, Cuts, Bites, or Stings; Common Protective or Safety Attire; Using

Hands on Objects, Tools, or Controls; Indoors. **Other Job Characteristics**—Degree of Automation; Pace Determined by Speed of Equipment; Importance of Repeating Same Tasks.

Experience—Job Zone 3. Previous work-related skill, knowledge, or experience is required. **Job Preparation:** SVP 6.0 to less than 7.0—more than one year and less than four years. **Knowledge**—Mechanical; Design; Fine Arts; Public Safety and Security; Foreign Language. **Instructional Programs**—Industrial Mechanics and Maintenance Technology.

Related DOT Jobs—683.260-014 Carpet-Loom Fixer; 683.260-018 Loom Fixer; 683.360-010 Loom Changer; 683.381-010 Chain Builder, Loom Control; 683.680-010 Harness Placer; 683.680-014 Heddles Tier, Jacquard Loom; 683.682-018 Drawing-in-Machine Tender; 685.360-010 Knitter Mechanic; 685.380-010 Link-and-Link-Knitting-Machine Operator; 685.381-010 Jacquard-Plate Maker; 685.680-010 Threader; 689.260-014 Quilter Fixer; 689.260-026 Knitting-Machine Fixer; 689.360-010 Needle-Loom Setter; 689.362-010 Needle-Felt-Making-Machine Operator; 689.380-010 Emblem Drawer-in; 689.382-010 Automatic-Pad-Making-Machine Operator.

51-6064.00 Textile Winding, Twisting, and Drawing Out Machine Setters, Operators, and Tenders

- **Education/Training Required: Moderate-term on-the-job training**
- **Employed: 89,868**
- **Annual Earnings: $21,330**
- **Growth: –4.4%**
- **Annual Job Openings: 19,000**

Set up, operate, or tend machines that wind or twist textiles or draw out and combine sliver, such as wool, hemp, or synthetic fibers.

Installs, levels, and aligns components, such as gears, chains, guides, dies, cutters, and needles, to set up machinery for operation. Adjusts heating mechanisms, tension, and speed of machine operation to produce product meeting desired specifications. Starts machine, monitors operation, makes adjustments as needed, and stops machine when specified amount of product has been produced. Threads yarn, thread, and fabric through guides, needles, and rollers of machines. Operates machine for test run to verify adjustments and to obtain sample of product. Studies guides, samples, charts, and specification sheets or confers with supervisor or engineering staff to determine setup requirements. Inspects product to ensure product meets specifications and to determine need for machine adjustment. Inspects machinery to determine adjustments or repairs needed. Repairs or replaces worn or defective parts or components, using hand tools. Cleans, oils, and lubricates machines, using air hose, cleaning solutions, rags, oilcan, and grease gun.

GOE INFORMATION—**Interest Area:** 08. Industrial Production. **Work Group:** 08.02. Production Technology. **Personality Type**—Realistic. Realistic occupations frequently involve work activities that include practical, hands-on problems and solutions. They often deal with plants, animals, and real-world materials like wood, tools, and machinery. Many of the occupations require working outside and do not involve a lot of paperwork or working closely with others. **Work Values**—Moral Values; Supervision, Technical; Supervision, Human Relations; Independence; Company Policies and Practices. **Skills**—Operation Monitoring; Operation and Control; Installation; Repairing; Quality Control Analysis; Troubleshooting. **Abilities**—*Cognitive:* Visualization; Information Ordering; Time Sharing; Flexibility of Closure; Speed of Closure. *Psychomotor:*

Control Precision; Arm-Hand Steadiness; Finger Dexterity; Reaction Time; Manual Dexterity. *Physical:* Extent Flexibility; Gross Body Equilibrium; Dynamic Flexibility; Static Strength; Gross Body Coordination. *Sensory:* Auditory Attention; Hearing Sensitivity; Sound Localization; Visual Color Discrimination; Near Vision. **General Work Activities**—*Information Input:* Inspecting Equipment, Structures, or Materials; Monitoring Processes, Materials, or Surroundings; Identifying Objects, Actions, and Events. *Mental Process:* Evaluating Information Against Standards; Updating and Using Relevant Knowledge; Organizing, Planning, and Prioritizing. *Work Output:* Repairing and Maintaining Mechanical Equipment; Handling and Moving Objects; Controlling Machines and Processes. *Interacting with Others:* Communicating with Other Workers; Establishing and Maintaining Relationships; Providing Consultation and Advice to Others. **Physical Work Conditions**—Hazardous Equipment; Minor Burns, Cuts, Bites, or Stings; Common Protective or Safety Attire; Using Hands on Objects, Tools, or Controls; Indoors. **Other Job Characteristics**—Degree of Automation; Pace Determined by Speed of Equipment; Importance of Repeating Same Tasks.

Experience—Job Zone 3. Previous work-related skill, knowledge, or experience is required. **Job Preparation:** SVP 6.0 to less than 7.0—more than one year and less than four years. **Knowledge**—Mechanical; Design; Fine Arts; Public Safety and Security; Foreign Language. **Instructional Programs**—Industrial Mechanics and Maintenance Technology.

Related DOT Jobs—589.360-010 Bonding-Machine Setter; 681.380-010 Rope-Machine Setter; 683.260-010 Braid-Pattern Setter; 689.260-010 Machine Fixer; 689.260-018 Section Leader and Machine Setter; 689.260-022 Section Leader and Machine Setter, Polishing; 689.280-010 Box Tender.

51-6091.00 Extruding and Forming Machine Setters, Operators, and Tenders, Synthetic and Glass Fibers

- **Education/Training Required: Moderate-term on-the-job training**
- **Employed: 41,356**
- **Annual Earnings: $27,120**
- **Growth: 5.7%**
- **Annual Job Openings: 6,000**

Set up, operate, or tend machines that extrude and form continuous filaments from synthetic materials, such as liquid polymer, rayon, and fiberglass.

No task data available.

GOE INFORMATION—**Interest Area:** 08. Industrial Production. **Work Group:** 08.03. Production Work. **Note:** The Department of Labor has not collected some data for this job, so it has fewer details than the other descriptions.

Instructional Programs—No data available.

Related DOT Jobs—557.565-014 Synthetic-Filament Extruder; 557.665-010 Synthetic-Staple Extruder; 557.685-018 Processor; 557.685-022 Second-Floor Operator; 557.685-026 Spinner; 575.685-030 Fiber-Machine Tender; 575.685-082 Test-Skein Winder.

51-6091.01 Extruding and Forming Machine Operators and Tenders, Synthetic or Glass Fibers

- Education/Training Required: Moderate-term on-the-job training
- Employed: No data available.
- Annual Earnings: $27,120
- Growth: 5.7%
- Annual Job Openings: 6,000

Operate or tend machines that extrude and form continuous filaments from synthetic materials, such as liquid polymer, rayon, and fiberglass, preparatory to further processing.

Operates or tends machines that extrude and form filaments from synthetic materials. Loads and adjusts materials into extruding and forming machines, using hand tools. Moves controls to activate and adjust extruding and forming machines. Presses buttons to stop machine when process is completed or malfunction is detected. Observes machine operation, control board, and gauges to detect malfunctions. Removes excess or completed filament from machine, using hand tools. Notifies workers of defects and to adjust extruding and forming machines. Cleans and maintains extruding and forming machines, using hand tools. Records operational data on tag and attaches to machine.

GOE INFORMATION—Interest Area: 08. Industrial Production. **Work Group:** 08.03. Production Work. **Personality Type**—Realistic. Realistic occupations frequently involve work activities that include practical, hands-on problems and solutions. They often deal with plants, animals, and real-world materials like wood, tools, and machinery. Many of the occupations require working outside and do not involve a lot of paperwork or working closely with others. **Work Values**—Moral Values; Supervision, Technical; Independence; Supervision, Human Relations; Company Policies and Practices. **Skills**—Operation Monitoring; Operation and Control. **Abilities**—*Cognitive:* Perceptual Speed; Selective Attention; Flexibility of Closure. *Psychomotor:* Control Precision; Wrist-Finger Speed; Response Orientation; Manual Dexterity; Reaction Time. *Physical:* Static Strength; Extent Flexibility; Trunk Strength. *Sensory:* Hearing Sensitivity; Sound Localization; Near Vision; Auditory Attention. **General Work Activities**—*Information Input:* Monitoring Processes, Materials, or Surroundings; Inspecting Equipment, Structures, or Materials; Getting Information. *Mental Process:* Evaluating Information Against Standards; Organizing, Planning, and Prioritizing; Making Decisions and Solving Problems. *Work Output:* Handling and Moving Objects; Controlling Machines and Processes; Repairing and Maintaining Mechanical Equipment. *Interacting with Others:* Communicating with Other Workers; Establishing and Maintaining Relationships; Coordinating the Work and Activities of Others. **Physical Work Conditions**—Using Hands on Objects, Tools, or Controls; Common Protective or Safety Attire; Making Repetitive Motions; Indoors; Hazardous Equipment. **Other Job Characteristics**—Pace Determined by Speed of Equipment; Degree of Automation; Importance of Repeating Same Tasks.

Experience—Job Zone 1. No previous work-related skill, knowledge, or experience is needed. **Job Preparation:** SVP below 4.0—less than six months. **Knowledge**—Production and Processing; Mechanical; Engineering and Technology. **Instructional Programs**—No data available.

Related DOT Jobs—557.565-014 Synthetic-Filament Extruder; 557.665-010 Synthetic-Staple Extruder; 557.685-018 Processor; 557.685-022 Second-Floor Operator; 557.685-026 Spinner; 575.685-030 Fiber-Machine Tender; 575.685-082 Test-Skein Winder.

51-6092.00 Fabric and Apparel Patternmakers

- Education/Training Required: Long-term on-the-job training
- Employed: 15,031
- Annual Earnings: $24,930
- Growth: –5.4%
- Annual Job Openings: 2,000

Draw and construct sets of precision master fabric patterns or layouts. May also mark and cut fabrics and apparel.

Draws outline of pattern parts, using drafting instruments such as calipers, squares, and straight and curved rules. Draws details on outlined parts to indicate guides in joining parts. Draws patterns for range of garment sizes, grading master pattern for each size, using charts or grading device. Draws lines between reference points, producing outline of graded pattern. Positions and cuts out pattern, using scissors and knife. Traces outline of specified pattern onto material and cuts fabric, using scissors. Traces outline of paper onto cardboard pattern and cuts pattern into parts to make template. Examines sketches or sample articles and design specifications to ascertain number, shape, and size of pattern parts. Calculates dimensions and specifications from sales order and enters data on worksheet. Positions master pattern on paperboard and drafts reference points based on data from charts. Positions master pattern in clamp of grading device, places paperboard under pattern, sets device to specified size, and marks reference points. Computes dimensions of pattern according to size, considering stretching of material, and measures and marks pattern. Makes drawings of garments and patterns and writes instructions for use in reproducing commercial patterns. Lays out large patterns on floor and cuts material according to markings. Positions and pins pattern sections onto model form and discusses style lines, details, and revisions with designer. Marks finished pattern with garment size, section, and style information.

GOE INFORMATION—Interest Area: 08. Industrial Production. **Work Group:** 08.03. Production Work. **Personality Type**—Realistic. Realistic occupations frequently involve work activities that include practical, hands-on problems and solutions. They often deal with plants, animals, and real-world materials like wood, tools, and machinery. Many of the occupations require working outside and do not involve a lot of paperwork or working closely with others. **Work Values**—Independence; Moral Values; Good Working Conditions; Advancement; Achievement. **Skills**—None met the criteria. **Abilities**—*Cognitive:* Visualization; Mathematical Reasoning; Fluency of Ideas; Originality; Number Facility. *Psychomotor:* Arm-Hand Steadiness; Wrist-Finger Speed; Manual Dexterity; Finger Dexterity; Multilimb Coordination. *Physical:* Stamina; Dynamic Flexibility. *Sensory:* Visual Color Discrimination; Near Vision. **General Work Activities**—*Information Input:* Getting Information; Estimating Needed Characteristics; Identifying Objects, Actions, and Events. *Mental Process:* Processing Information; Evaluating Information Against Standards; Thinking Creatively. *Work Output:* Handling and Moving Objects; Drafting and Specifying Technical Devices; Performing General Physical Activities. *Interacting with Others:* Communicating with Other Workers; Providing Consultation and Advice to Others; Establishing and Maintaining Relationships. **Physical Work Conditions**—Using Hands on Objects, Tools, or Controls; Indoors; Sitting; Minor Burns, Cuts, Bites, or Stings; Making Repetitive Motions. **Other Job Characteristics**—Importance of Repeating Same Tasks; Pace Determined by Speed of Equipment; Importance of Being Exact or Accurate.

Experience—Job Zone 2. Some previous work-related skill, knowledge, or experience may be helpful, but usually is not needed. **Job Preparation:** SVP 4.0 to less than 6.0—six months to less than two years. **Knowledge**—

Design; Fine Arts; Production and Processing; Philosophy and Theology; Therapy and Counseling. **Instructional Programs**—Apparel and Textile Manufacture.

Related DOT Jobs—781.361-010 Assistant Designer; 781.361-014 Patternmaker; 781.381-022 Pattern Grader-Cutter; 781.381-030 Sail-Lay-Out Worker; 781.381-034 Grader Marker; 781.484-010 Pleat Patternmaker; 788.281-010 Designer and Patternmaker; 789.381-014 Pattern Chart-Writer; 962.381-010 Draper.

51-6093.00 *Upholsterers*

- **Education/Training Required: Long-term on-the-job training**
- **Employed: 58,480**
- **Annual Earnings: $24,540**
- **Growth: –9.5%**
- **Annual Job Openings: 9,000**

Make, repair, or replace upholstery for household furniture or transportation vehicles.

Measures and cuts new covering material, using pattern and measuring and cutting instruments. Operates sewing machine to seam cushions and join various sections of covering material. Fits, installs, and secures material on workpiece, using hand tools, power tools, glue, cement, or staples. Adjusts or replaces webbing, padding, and springs and secures them in place. Attaches binding or applies solutions to edges of cut material to prevent raveling. Sews rips or tears in material or creates tufting, using needle and thread. Reads order and applies knowledge and experience with materials to determine type and amount of material required to cover workpiece. Draws cutting lines on material following pattern, templates, sketches, or blueprints, using chalk, pencil, paint, or other method. Attaches fasteners, grommets, buckles, ornamental trim, and other accessories to cover or frame, using hand tools. Examines upholstery to locate defects. Removes covering, webbing, padding, and defective springs from workpiece, using hand tools. Repairs frame of workpiece. Stacks, aligns, and smoothes material on cutting table. Drills or punches holes in material. Designs upholstery cover patterns. Maintains records of time required to perform each job. Refinishes wood surfaces on upholstered or reupholstered furniture.

GOE INFORMATION—Interest Area: 11. Recreation, Travel, and Other Personal Services. **Work Group:** 11.06. Apparel, Shoes, Leather, and Fabric Care. **Personality Type**—Realistic. Realistic occupations frequently involve work activities that include practical, hands-on problems and solutions. They often deal with plants, animals, and real-world materials like wood, tools, and machinery. Many of the occupations require working outside and do not involve a lot of paperwork or working closely with others. **Work Values**—Autonomy; Creativity; Good Working Conditions; Independence; Moral Values. **Skills**—Repairing. **Abilities**—*Cognitive:* Visualization; Perceptual Speed; Flexibility of Closure; Mathematical Reasoning. *Psychomotor:* Finger Dexterity; Manual Dexterity; Wrist-Finger Speed; Arm-Hand Steadiness; Speed of Limb Movement. *Physical:* Static Strength; Extent Flexibility; Dynamic Strength; Trunk Strength; Explosive Strength. *Sensory:* Visual Color Discrimination; Near Vision. **General Work Activities**—*Information Input:* Estimating Needed Characteristics; Getting Information; Inspecting Equipment, Structures, or Materials. *Mental Process:* Thinking Creatively; Organizing, Planning, and Prioritizing; Judging Qualities of Things, Services, or Other People's Work. *Work Output:* Handling and Moving Objects; Performing General Physical Activities; Drafting and Specifying Technical Devices. *Interacting with Others:* Communicating with Other Workers; Establishing and Maintaining Relationships; Performing Administrative Activities. **Physical Work Conditions**—Using Hands on Objects, Tools, or Controls;

Kneeling, Crouching, or Crawling; Bending or Twisting the Body; Making Repetitive Motions; Indoors. **Other Job Characteristics**—Importance of Being Exact or Accurate; Consequence of Error; Importance of Repeating Same Tasks.

Experience—Job Zone 3. Previous work-related skill, knowledge, or experience is required. **Job Preparation:** SVP 6.0 to less than 7.0—more than one year and less than four years. **Knowledge**—Building and Construction; Production and Processing; Design. **Instructional Programs**—Upholstery/Upholsterer.

Related DOT Jobs—780.381-010 Automobile Upholsterer; 780.381-014 Automobile-Upholsterer Apprentice; 780.381-018 Furniture Upholsterer; 780.381-022 Furniture-Upholsterer Apprentice; 780.381-026 Upholsterer, Limousine and Hearse; 780.381-034 Slipcover Cutter; 780.381-038 Upholsterer, Inside; 780.384-014 Upholsterer; 780.684-122 Upholstery Repairer.

51-6099.99 *Textile, Apparel, and Furnishings Workers, All Other*

- **Education/Training Required: No data available.**
- **Employed: No data available.**
- **Annual Earnings: No data available.**
- **Growth: 18.0%**
- **Annual Job Openings: 19,000**

All textile, apparel, and furnishings workers not listed separately.

No task data available.

GOE INFORMATION—Interest Area: 11. Recreation, Travel, and Other Personal Services. **Work Group:** 11.06. Apparel, Shoes, Leather, and Fabric Care. **Note:** The Department of Labor has not collected some data for this job, so it has fewer details than the other descriptions.

Instructional Programs—Apparel and Textile Manufacture.

Related DOT Jobs—580.380-010 Fixer, Boarding Room; 585.681-010 Flesher; 585.681-014 Fur Plucker; 589.361-010 Fur Dresser; 589.685-086 Rolling-Down-Machine Operator; 683.582-010 Card Cutter, Jacquard; 712.281-014 Designer; 782.381-014 Oriental-Rug Repairer; 782.381-018 Rug Repairer; 782.684-042 Mender; 784.261-010 Milliner; 789.261-010 Boat-Canvas Maker-Installer; 789.381-018 Trawl Net Maker.

51-7000 Woodworkers

51-7011.00 *Cabinetmakers and Bench Carpenters*

- **Education/Training Required: Long-term on-the-job training**
- **Employed: 159,274**
- **Annual Earnings: $23,500**
- **Growth: 9.8%**
- **Annual Job Openings: 8,000**

Cut, shape, and assemble wooden articles or set up and operate a variety of woodworking machines, such as power saws, jointers, and mortisers, to surface, cut, or shape lumber or to fabricate parts for wood products.

Sets up and operates machines, including power saws, jointers, mortisers, tenoners, molders, and shapers, to cut and shape woodstock. Trims component parts of joints to ensure snug fit, using hand tools such as planes, chisels, or wood files. Glues, fits, and clamps parts and subassemblies together to form complete unit. Drives nails or other fasteners to joints of articles to prepare articles for finishing. Bores holes for insertion of screws or dowel by hand or using boring machine. Marks dimensions of parts on paper or lumber stock, following blueprints, and matches lumber for color, grain, and texture. Sands and scrapes surfaces and joints of articles to prepare articles for finishing. Studies blueprints, drawings, and written specifications of articles to be constructed or repaired and plans sequence of performing such operations. Dips, brushes, or sprays assembled articles with protective or decorative materials, such as stain, varnish, or lacquer. Installs hardware, such as hinges, catches, and drawer pulls, using hand tools.

GOE INFORMATION—Interest Area: 08. Industrial Production. **Work Group:** 08.05. Woodworking Technology. **Personality Type**—Realistic. Realistic occupations frequently involve work activities that include practical, hands-on problems and solutions. They often deal with plants, animals, and real-world materials like wood, tools, and machinery. Many of the occupations require working outside and do not involve a lot of paperwork or working closely with others. **Work Values**—Recognition; Independence; Moral Values; Social Status; Supervision, Technical. **Skills**—Operation and Control; Installation; Equipment Selection. **Abilities**—*Cognitive:* Visualization. *Psychomotor:* Arm-Hand Steadiness; Control Precision; Multilimb Coordination; Manual Dexterity; Wrist-Finger Speed. *Physical:* Explosive Strength; Extent Flexibility; Dynamic Strength; Static Strength; Trunk Strength. *Sensory:* Depth Perception. **General Work Activities**—*Information Input:* Monitoring Processes, Materials, or Surroundings; Estimating Needed Characteristics; Identifying Objects, Actions, and Events. *Mental Process:* Organizing, Planning, and Prioritizing; Making Decisions and Solving Problems; Processing Information. *Work Output:* Handling and Moving Objects; Performing General Physical Activities; Controlling Machines and Processes. *Interacting with Others:* Communicating with Other Workers; Teaching Others; Coordinating the Work and Activities of Others. **Physical Work Conditions**—Kneeling, Crouching, or Crawling; Hazardous Equipment; Using Hands on Objects, Tools, or Controls; Cramped Work Space or Awkward Positions; Whole Body Vibration. **Other Job Characteristics**—Importance of Being Exact or Accurate; Pace Determined by Speed of Equipment; Importance of Repeating Same Tasks.

Experience—Job Zone 3. Previous work-related skill, knowledge, or experience is required. **Job Preparation:** SVP 6.0 to less than 7.0—more than one year and less than four years. **Knowledge**—Building and Construction; Design; Production and Processing; Engineering and Technology; Mechanical. **Instructional Programs**—Cabinetmaking and Millwork/Millwright.

Related DOT Jobs—660.280-010 Cabinetmaker; 660.280-014 Cabinetmaker Apprentice.

51-7021.00 Furniture Finishers

- **Education/Training Required: Long-term on-the-job training**
- **Employed: 45,403**
- **Annual Earnings: $22,350**
- **Growth: 8.4%**
- **Annual Job Openings: 4,000**

Shape, finish, and refinish damaged, worn, or used furniture or new high-grade furniture to specified color or finish.

Disassembles item, masks areas adjacent to those being refinished, and removes accessories, using hand tools, to prepare for finishing. Removes old finish and damaged or deteriorated parts, using hand tools, abrasives, or solvents. Fills cracks, blemishes, or depressions and repairs broken

parts, using plastic or wood putty, glue, nails, or screws. Treats warped or stained surfaces to restore original contour and color. Smoothes and shapes surfaces with sandpaper, pumice stone, steel wool, or chisel. Washes or bleaches surface to return to natural color or prepare for application of finish. Brushes, sprays, or hand rubs finishing ingredients onto and into grain of wood. Finishes surfaces of new furniture pieces to replicate antiques by distressing surfaces with abrasives before staining. Examines furniture to determine extent of damage or deterioration and determines method of repair or restoration. Selects appropriate finishing ingredients, such as paint, stain, lacquer, shellac, or varnish, for wood surface. Mixes finish ingredients to obtain desired color or shade of existing finish. Stencils, gilds, embosses, or paints designs or borders on restored pieces to reproduce original appearance. Polishes, sprays, or waxes finished pieces to match surrounding finish. Replaces and refurbishes upholstery of item, using tacks, adhesives, softeners, solvents, stains, or polish. Spreads graining ink over metal portions of furniture to simulate wood-grain finish.

GOE INFORMATION—Interest Area: 08. Industrial Production. **Work Group:** 08.05. Woodworking Technology. **Personality Type**—Realistic. Realistic occupations frequently involve work activities that include practical, hands-on problems and solutions. They often deal with plants, animals, and real-world materials like wood, tools, and machinery. Many of the occupations require working outside and do not involve a lot of paperwork or working closely with others. **Work Values**—Independence; Recognition; Creativity; Autonomy; Moral Values. **Skills**—Equipment Selection; Repairing. **Abilities**—*Cognitive:* Visualization; Information Ordering. *Psychomotor:* Speed of Limb Movement; Finger Dexterity; Arm-Hand Steadiness; Multilimb Coordination; Wrist-Finger Speed. *Physical:* Dynamic Flexibility; Extent Flexibility; Explosive Strength; Dynamic Strength; Static Strength. *Sensory:* Visual Color Discrimination; Glare Sensitivity; Night Vision; Peripheral Vision; Depth Perception. **General Work Activities**—*Information Input:* Getting Information; Identifying Objects, Actions, and Events; Inspecting Equipment, Structures, or Materials. *Mental Process:* Judging Qualities of Things, Services, or Other People's Work; Thinking Creatively; Updating and Using Relevant Knowledge. *Work Output:* Handling and Moving Objects; Performing General Physical Activities; Controlling Machines and Processes. *Interacting with Others:* Communicating with Persons Outside Organization; Monitoring and Controlling Resources; Communicating with Other Workers. **Physical Work Conditions**—Hazardous Conditions; Kneeling, Crouching, or Crawling; Contaminants; Minor Burns, Cuts, Bites, or Stings; Using Hands on Objects, Tools, or Controls. **Other Job Characteristics**—Importance of Repeating Same Tasks; Pace Determined by Speed of Equipment; Degree of Automation.

Experience—Job Zone 2. Some previous work-related skill, knowledge, or experience may be helpful, but usually is not needed. **Job Preparation:** SVP 4.0 to less than 6.0—six months to less than two years. **Knowledge**—Building and Construction; Fine Arts; Chemistry; Production and Processing; History and Archeology. **Instructional Programs**—Furniture Design and Manufacturing.

Related DOT Jobs—763.380-010 Furniture Restorer; 763.381-010 Furniture Finisher; 763.381-014 Furniture-Finisher Apprentice; 763.681-010 Frame Repairer; 763.684-022 Caner II; 763.684-034 Finish Patcher.

51-7031.00 Model Makers, Wood

- **Education/Training Required: Long-term on-the-job training**
- **Employed: No data available.**
- **Annual Earnings: $24,990**
- **Growth: 16.0%**
- **Annual Job Openings: 1,000**

Construct full-size and scale wooden precision models of products. Includes wood jig builders and loft workers.

Plans, lays out, and draws outline of unit, sectional patterns, or full-scale mock-up of products. Trims, smoothes, and shapes surfaces and planes, shaves, files, scrapes, and sands models to attain specified shapes, using hand tools. Fits, fastens, and assembles wood parts together to form pattern, model, or section, using glue, nails, dowels, bolts, and screws. Sets up, operates, and adjusts variety of woodworking machines to cut and shape sections, parts, and patterns according to specifications. Constructs wooden models, templates, full scale mock-up, and molds for parts of products. Reads blueprints, drawing, or written specifications to determine size and shape of pattern and required machine setup. Shellacs, lacquers, or waxes finished pattern or model. Marks identifying information such as colors or codes on patterns, parts, and templates to indicate assembly method. Issues patterns to designated machine operators and maintains pattern record for reference.

GOE INFORMATION—Interest Area: 08. Industrial Production. **Work Group:** 08.05. Woodworking Technology. **Personality Type**—Realistic. Realistic occupations frequently involve work activities that include practical, hands-on problems and solutions. They often deal with plants, animals, and real-world materials like wood, tools, and machinery. Many of the occupations require working outside and do not involve a lot of paperwork or working closely with others. **Work Values**—Moral Values; Independence; Supervision, Technical; Ability Utilization. **Skills**—Equipment Selection; Operation and Control. **Abilities**—*Cognitive:* Visualization. *Psychomotor:* Multilimb Coordination; Control Precision; Speed of Limb Movement; Arm-Hand Steadiness; Finger Dexterity. *Physical:* Extent Flexibility; Explosive Strength; Gross Body Coordination; Trunk Strength; Dynamic Flexibility. *Sensory:* None met the criteria. **General Work Activities**—*Information Input:* Getting Information; Estimating Needed Characteristics; Identifying Objects, Actions, and Events. *Mental Process:* Evaluating Information Against Standards; Making Decisions and Solving Problems; Processing Information. *Work Output:* Handling and Moving Objects; Performing General Physical Activities; Drafting and Specifying Technical Devices. *Interacting with Others:* Communicating with Other Workers; Establishing and Maintaining Relationships; Providing Consultation and Advice to Others. **Physical Work Conditions**—Minor Burns, Cuts, Bites, or Stings; Hazardous Equipment; Indoors; Making Repetitive Motions; Using Hands on Objects, Tools, or Controls. **Other Job Characteristics**—Importance of Being Exact or Accurate; Importance of Repeating Same Tasks; Pace Determined by Speed of Equipment.

Experience—Job Zone 4. A minimum of two to four years of work-related skill, knowledge, or experience is needed. **Job Preparation:** SVP 7.0 to less than 8.0–two years to less than 10 years. **Knowledge**—Design; Building and Construction; Engineering and Technology; Mechanical; Production and Processing. **Instructional Programs**—Cabinetmaking and Millwork/Millwright.

Related DOT Jobs—661.380-010 Model Maker, Wood.

51-7032.00 Patternmakers, Wood

- Education/Training Required: Long-term on-the-job training
- Employed: No data available.
- Annual Earnings: $28,690
- Growth: 16.0%
- Annual Job Openings: 1,000

Plan, lay out, and construct wooden unit or sectional patterns used in forming sand molds for castings.

Plans, lays out, and draws outline of unit, sectional patterns, or full-scale mock-up of products. Trims, smoothes, and shapes surfaces and planes, shaves, files, scrapes, and sands models to attain specified shapes, using hand tools. Fits, fastens, and assembles wood parts together to form pattern, model, or section, using glue, nails, dowels, bolts, and screws. Sets up, operates, and adjusts variety of woodworking machines to cut and shape sections, parts, and patterns according to specifications. Constructs wooden models, templates, full scale mock-up, and molds for parts of products. Reads blueprints, drawing, or written specifications to determine size and shape of pattern and required machine setup. Shellacs, lacquers, or waxes finished pattern or model. Marks identifying information such as colors or codes on patterns, parts, and templates to indicate assembly method. Issues patterns to designated machine operators and maintains pattern record for reference.

GOE INFORMATION—Interest Area: 08. Industrial Production. **Work Group:** 08.05. Woodworking Technology. **Personality Type**—Realistic. Realistic occupations frequently involve work activities that include practical, hands-on problems and solutions. They often deal with plants, animals, and real-world materials like wood, tools, and machinery. Many of the occupations require working outside and do not involve a lot of paperwork or working closely with others. **Work Values**—Moral Values; Independence; Supervision, Technical; Ability Utilization. **Skills**—Equipment Selection; Operation and Control. **Abilities**—*Cognitive:* Visualization. *Psychomotor:* Multilimb Coordination; Control Precision; Speed of Limb Movement; Arm-Hand Steadiness; Finger Dexterity. *Physical:* Extent Flexibility; Explosive Strength; Gross Body Coordination; Trunk Strength; Dynamic Flexibility. *Sensory:* None met the criteria. **General Work Activities**—*Information Input:* Getting Information; Estimating Needed Characteristics; Identifying Objects, Actions, and Events. *Mental Process:* Evaluating Information Against Standards; Making Decisions and Solving Problems; Processing Information. *Work Output:* Handling and Moving Objects; Performing General Physical Activities; Drafting and Specifying Technical Devices. *Interacting with Others:* Communicating with Other Workers; Establishing and Maintaining Relationships; Providing Consultation and Advice to Others. **Physical Work Conditions**—Minor Burns, Cuts, Bites, or Stings; Hazardous Equipment; Indoors; Making Repetitive Motions; Using Hands on Objects, Tools, or Controls. **Other Job Characteristics**—Importance of Being Exact or Accurate; Importance of Repeating Same Tasks; Pace Determined by Speed of Equipment.

Experience—Job Zone 4. A minimum of two to four years of work-related skill, knowledge, or experience is needed. **Job Preparation:** SVP 7.0 to less than 8.0–two years to less than 10 years. **Knowledge**—Design; Building and Construction; Engineering and Technology; Mechanical; Production and Processing. **Instructional Programs**—Cabinetmaking and Millwork/Millwright.

Related DOT Jobs—661.281-018 Patternmaker Apprentice, Wood; 661.281-022 Patternmaker, Wood.

51-7041.00 Sawing Machine Setters, Operators, and Tenders, Wood

- Education/Training Required: Moderate-term on-the-job training
- Employed: 57,318
- Annual Earnings: $21,740
- Growth: 11.7%
- Annual Job Openings: 9,000

Set up, operate, or tend wood-sawing machines. Includes head sawyers.

No task data available.

GOE INFORMATION—Interest Area: 08. Industrial Production. **Work Group:** 08.03. Production Work. **Note:** The Department of Labor has not collected some data for this job, so it has fewer details than the other descriptions.

Instructional Programs—Cabinetmaking and Millwork/Millwright.

Related DOT Jobs—665.685-046 Shaping Machine Tender; 667.382-010 Stock Grader; 667.482-014 Pocket Cutter; 667.482-018 Stock Cutter; 667.485-010 Shingle Sawyer; 667.662-010 Head Sawyer; 667.662-014 Machine-Tank Operator; 667.682-010 Band-Scroll-Saw Operator; 667.682-014 Bottom-Saw Operator; 667.682-018 Corner-Trimmer Operator; 667.682-022 Cut-Off-Saw Operator I; 667.682-026 Edger, Automatic; 667.682-030 Gang Sawyer; 667.682-034 Head Sawyer, Automatic; 667.682-038 Heading-Saw Operator; 667.682-042 Jigsaw Operator; 667.682-046 Packager, Head; 667.682-050 Pony Edger; 667.682-054 Radial-Arm-Saw Operator; 667.682-058 Resaw Operator; others.

51-7041.01 Sawing Machine Setters and Set-Up Operators

- **Education/Training Required:** Moderate-term on-the-job training
- **Employed:** No data available.
- **Annual Earnings:** $21,740
- **Growth:** 11.7%
- **Annual Job Openings:** 9,000

Set up or set up and operate wood-sawing machines. Examine blueprints, drawings, work orders, and patterns to determine size and shape of items to be sawed, sawing machines to set up, and sequence of sawing operations.

Selects knives to achieve specified diameter of cut or installs bit and dado saw according to work ticket. Aligns and bolts knives in cutterhead and screws it on spindle, using wrenches. Adjusts angle of table by turning handwheel and bolts or clamps holding jigs to table. Places stock in jig and pushes table containing stock into saw or lays stock on conveyor that carries it into machine. Pulls table back against stops and depresses pedal to advance cutterhead that shapes end of stock.

GOE INFORMATION—Interest Area: 08. Industrial Production. **Work Group:** 08.03. Production Work. **Personality Type**—Realistic. Realistic occupations frequently involve work activities that include practical, hands-on problems and solutions. They often deal with plants, animals, and real-world materials like wood, tools, and machinery. Many of the occupations require working outside and do not involve a lot of paperwork or working closely with others. **Work Values**—Independence; Moral Values; Company Policies and Practices; Supervision, Technical; Supervision, Human Relations. **Skills**—Operation and Control; Equipment Selection. **Abilities**—*Cognitive:* Visualization. *Psychomotor:* Control Precision; Manual Dexterity; Speed of Limb Movement; Arm-Hand Steadiness; Multilimb Coordination. *Physical:* Static Strength; Explosive Strength; Extent Flexibility; Dynamic Flexibility. *Sensory:* Depth Perception; Hearing Sensitivity; Peripheral Vision; Glare Sensitivity; Night Vision. **General Work Activities**—*Information Input:* Getting Information; Monitoring Processes, Materials, or Surroundings; Identifying Objects, Actions, and Events. *Mental Process:* Organizing, Planning, and Prioritizing; Analyzing Data or Information; Making Decisions and Solving Problems. *Work Output:* Handling and Moving Objects; Controlling Machines and Processes; Performing General Physical Activities. *Interacting with Others:* Communicating with Other Workers; Coaching and Developing Others; Establishing and Maintaining Relationships. **Physical Work Conditions**—Hazardous Equipment; Minor Burns, Cuts, Bites, or Stings; Common Protective or Safety Attire; Distracting Sounds and Noise Levels; Contaminants. **Other Job Characteristics**—Degree of Automation; Pace Determined by Speed of Equipment; Importance of Repeating Same Tasks.

Experience—Job Zone 2. Some previous work-related skill, knowledge, or experience may be helpful, but usually is not needed. **Job Preparation:** SVP 4.0 to less than 6.0—six months to less than two years. **Knowledge**—Building and Construction; Design; Mechanical; Production and Processing; Engineering and Technology. **Instructional Programs**—Cabinetmaking and Millwork/Millwright.

Related DOT Jobs—669.682-026 Chucking-and-Sawing-Machine Operator; 669.682-030 Corner-Brace-Block-Machine Operator.

51-7041.02 Sawing Machine Operators and Tenders

- **Education/Training Required:** Moderate-term on-the-job training
- **Employed:** No data available.
- **Annual Earnings:** $21,740
- **Growth:** 11.7%
- **Annual Job Openings:** 9,000

Operate or tend wood-sawing machines, such as circular saws, band saws, multiple-blade sawing machines, scroll saws, ripsaws, equalizer saws, power saws, and crozer machines. Duties include sawing logs to specifications; cutting lumber to specified dimensions; sawing curved or irregular designs; trimming edges and removing defects from lumber; or cutting grooves, bevel, and miter according to specifications or work orders.

Operates and tends saws and machines to cut stock and to adjust machine speed and tension, moving levers and handwheels. Guides workpiece against saw or saw over workpiece or operates automatic feeding device to guide cuts. Operates panelboard of saw and conveyor system to cut stock to specified dimensions and to move stock through process. Trims defects from stock or workpiece to straighten rough edges of lumber, using circular power saw. Turns knobs, handwheels, setscrews, and panel controls or uses hand tools to position and adjust cutting stops and guides. Adjusts saw blades by turning handwheels; pressing pedals, levers, and panel buttons; or using wrenches and rulers. Observes approaching lumber on conveyor to determine cut that will produce highest grade. Determines sawing blade, type and grade of stock needed, and cutting procedures according to work order or supervisor's instructions. Mounts and bolts sawing blade or attachments to machine shaft and turns handwheels to set blade tension. Positions and clamps stock on table, conveyor, or carriage, using hoists, guides, stops, dogs, wedges, and wrench. Moves machine table to specified angle and height by turning handwheels, cranks, or knobs. Measures workpiece to mark for cuts and to verify accuracy of cuts, using ruler, square, or caliper rule. Clears machine jams, using hand tools. Unclamps and removes finished workpiece from table. Sharpens blades or replaces defective or worn blades and bands, using hand tools. Inspects stock for imperfections and estimates grade or quality of stock or workpiece. Lubricates and cleans machines, using wrench, grease gun, and solvents. Unloads and rolls logs from truck to sawmill deck or to carriage or moves logs in pond, using pike pole. Counts, sorts, and stacks finished workpieces and disposes of waste material.

GOE INFORMATION—**Interest Area:** 08. Industrial Production. **Work Group:** 08.03. Production Work. **Personality Type**—Realistic. Realistic occupations frequently involve work activities that include practical, hands-on problems and solutions. They often deal with plants, animals, and real-world materials like wood, tools, and machinery. Many of the occupations require working outside and do not involve a lot of paperwork or working closely with others. **Work Values**—Independence; Moral Values; Supervision, Technical; Activity; Company Policies and Practices. **Skills**—Operation and Control; Repairing; Equipment Selection; Operation Monitoring. **Abilities**—*Cognitive:* Spatial Orientation; Perceptual Speed; Category Flexibility; Visualization; Flexibility of Closure. *Psychomotor:* Rate Control; Control Precision; Manual Dexterity; Speed of Limb Movement; Arm-Hand Steadiness. *Physical:* Static Strength; Stamina; Dynamic Strength; Gross Body Coordination; Dynamic Flexibility. *Sensory:* Peripheral Vision; Depth Perception; Far Vision; Near Vision; Visual Color Discrimination. **General Work Activities**—*Information Input:* Monitoring Processes, Materials, or Surroundings; Inspecting Equipment, Structures, or Materials; Identifying Objects, Actions, and Events. *Mental Process:* Judging Qualities of Things, Services, or Other People's Work; Updating and Using Relevant Knowledge; Organizing, Planning, and Prioritizing. *Work Output:* Handling and Moving Objects; Performing General Physical Activities; Controlling Machines and Processes. *Interacting with Others:* Communicating with Other Workers; Performing Administrative Activities; Interpreting Meaning of Information for Others. **Physical Work Conditions**—Hazardous Equipment; Minor Burns, Cuts, Bites, or Stings; Distracting Sounds and Noise Levels; Contaminants; Common Protective or Safety Attire. **Other Job Characteristics**—Pace Determined by Speed of Equipment; Degree of Automation; Importance of Repeating Same Tasks.

Experience—Job Zone 2. Some previous work-related skill, knowledge, or experience may be helpful, but usually is not needed. **Job Preparation:** SVP 4.0 to less than 6.0—six months to less than two years. **Knowledge**—Production and Processing; Mechanical; Building and Construction; Design; Medicine and Dentistry. **Instructional Programs**—Cabinetmaking and Millwork/Millwright.

Related DOT Jobs—665.685-046 Shaping Machine Tender; 667.382-010 Stock Grader; 667.482-014 Pocket Cutter; 667.482-018 Stock Cutter; 667.485-010 Shingle Sawyer; 667.662-014 Machine-Tank Operator; 667.682-010 Band-Scroll-Saw Operator; 667.682-014 Bottom-Saw Operator; 667.682-018 Corner-Trimmer Operator; 667.682-022 Cut-Off-Saw Operator I; 667.682-026 Edger, Automatic; 667.682-030 Gang Sawyer; 667.682-042 Jigsaw Operator; 667.682-046 Packager, Head; 667.682-050 Pony Edger; 667.682-054 Radial-Arm-Saw Operator; 667.682-058 Resaw Operator; 667.682-062 Rip-and-Groove-Machine Operator; 667.682-066 Ripsaw Operator; 667.682-070 Shake Sawyer; others.

51-7042.00 Woodworking Machine Setters, Operators, and Tenders, Except Sawing

- **Education/Training Required: Moderate-term on-the-job training**
- **Employed: 102,702**
- **Annual Earnings: $21,600**
- **Growth: 5.3%**
- **Annual Job Openings: 15,000**

Set up, operate, or tend woodworking machines, such as drill presses, lathes, shapers, routers, sanders, planers, and wood nailing machines.

No task data available.

GOE INFORMATION—**Interest Area:** 08. Industrial Production. **Work Group:** 08.02. Production Technology. **Note:** The Department of Labor has not collected some data for this job, so it has fewer details than the other descriptions.

Instructional Programs—Cabinetmaking and Millwork/Millwright; Woodworking, General.

Related DOT Jobs—564.682-010 Chipping-Machine Operator; 569.662-010 Incising-Machine Operator; 569.685-014 Bender, Machine; 662.682-010 Molding Sander; 662.682-014 Multiple-Drum Sander; 662.682-018 Stroke-Belt-Sander Operator; 662.685-010 Cork Grinder; 662.685-014 Cylinder-Sander Operator; 662.685-018 Last Scourer; 662.685-022 Sanding-Machine Buffer; 662.685-026 Sanding-Machine Tender; 662.685-030 Sizing-Machine Tender; 662.685-034 Speed-Belt-Sander Tender; 662.685-038 Turning-Sander Tender; 662.685-042 Wood-Heel Back-Liner; 663.380-010 Knife Setter; 663.585-010 Clipper, Automatic; 663.682-010 Barker Operator; 663.682-018 Veneer-Slicing-Machine Operator; 663.685-014 Excelsior-Machine Tender; others.

51-7042.01 Woodworking Machine Setters and Set-Up Operators, Except Sawing

- **Education/Training Required: Moderate-term on-the-job training**
- **Employed: No data available.**
- **Annual Earnings: $21,600**
- **Growth: 5.3%**
- **Annual Job Openings: 15,000**

Set up or set up and operate woodworking machines, such as lathes, drill presses, sanders, shapers, and planing machines, to perform woodworking operations.

Installs knives, sanding apparatus, cams, cutting heads, bits, chisels, and blades, using hand tools. Attaches and adjusts guides, stops, clamps, chucks, and feed mechanisms, using hand tools. Starts machine and feeds stock into machine through feed mechanisms or conveyors. Monitors operation of automatic machines and makes adjustments as needed to correct problems and ensure conformance to specifications. Examines blueprints, drawings, and work orders to determine characteristics of finished item, materials to be used, and machine setup requirements. Adjusts machine table or cutting devices to produce specified cut or operation. Pushes or holds workpiece against, under, or through cutting, boring or shaping mechanism. Selects knives, sanding apparatus, cams, cutting heads, bits, chisels, and blades. Mounts or clamps stock onto machine. Removes and replaces worn machine parts, knives, bits, belts, and sandpaper. Examines workpiece visually, by touch, or using tape rule, calipers, or gauges to ensure product meets desired standards. Unclamps and removes workpiece from machine and stacks workpiece on pallet or in box. Sharpens knives, bits, and other cutting and shaping tools. Cleans product, machine, or work area, using rags and air hose.

GOE INFORMATION—**Interest Area:** 08. Industrial Production. **Work Group:** 08.02. Production Technology. **Personality Type**—Realistic. Realistic occupations frequently involve work activities that include practical, hands-on problems and solutions. They often deal with plants, animals, and real-world materials like wood, tools, and machinery. Many of the occupations require working outside and do not involve a lot of paperwork or working closely with others. **Work Values**—Independence; Moral Values; Supervision, Technical; Activity; Company Policies and

Practices. **Skills**—Operation Monitoring; Operation and Control; Installation; Equipment Selection; Repairing; Troubleshooting. **Abilities**—*Cognitive:* Visualization; Selective Attention. *Psychomotor:* Rate Control; Control Precision; Manual Dexterity; Reaction Time; Finger Dexterity. *Physical:* Dynamic Strength; Dynamic Flexibility; Explosive Strength; Static Strength; Gross Body Equilibrium. *Sensory:* Peripheral Vision; Depth Perception; Glare Sensitivity. **General Work Activities**—*Information Input:* Inspecting Equipment, Structures, or Materials; Estimating Needed Characteristics; Getting Information. *Mental Process:* Evaluating Information Against Standards; Analyzing Data or Information; Organizing, Planning, and Prioritizing. *Work Output:* Handling and Moving Objects; Controlling Machines and Processes; Performing General Physical Activities. *Interacting with Others:* Communicating with Other Workers; Establishing and Maintaining Relationships; Monitoring and Controlling Resources. **Physical Work Conditions**—Hazardous Equipment; Common Protective or Safety Attire; Minor Burns, Cuts, Bites, or Stings; Using Hands on Objects, Tools, or Controls; Making Repetitive Motions. **Other Job Characteristics**—Pace Determined by Speed of Equipment; Degree of Automation; Importance of Repeating Same Tasks.

Experience—Job Zone 2. Some previous work-related skill, knowledge, or experience may be helpful, but usually is not needed. **Job Preparation:** SVP 4.0 to less than 6.0—six months to less than two years. **Knowledge**—Mechanical; Design; Production and Processing; Engineering and Technology; Building and Construction. **Instructional Programs**—Cabinetmaking and Millwork/Millwright; Woodworking, General.

Related DOT Jobs—662.682-010 Molding Sander; 662.682-014 Multiple-Drum Sander; 663.380-010 Knife Setter; 664.382-010 Swing-Type-Lathe Operator; 664.382-018 Trimming Machine Set-Up Operator; 664.662-010 Veneer-Lathe Operator; 665.382-010 Chucking-Machine Operator; 665.382-018 Wood-Carving-Machine Operator; 665.482-014 Mortising-Machine Operator; 665.682-010 Dowel-Machine Operator; 665.682-018 Molder Operator; 665.682-022 Planer Operator; 665.682-026 Profile-Shaper Operator, Automatic; 665.682-030 Router Operator; 665.682-034 Shaper Operator; 665.682-038 Veneer Jointer; 665.682-042 Jointer Operator; 666.382-010 Boring-Machine Operator; 669.280-010 Machine Setter; 669.360-010 Checkering-Machine Adjuster; others.

51-7042.02 Woodworking Machine Operators and Tenders, Except Sawing

- Education/Training Required: **Moderate-term on-the-job training**
- Employed: **No data available.**
- Annual Earnings: **$21,600**
- Growth: **5.3%**
- Annual Job Openings: **15,000**

Operate or tend woodworking machines, such as drill presses, lathes, shapers, routers, sanders, planers, and wood-nailing machines, to perform woodworking operations.

Starts machine, adjusts controls, and moves lever or depresses pedal to bore, shape, smooth, shave, chip, slice, or cut woodstock. Starts machine and moves lever to engage hydraulic lift to press woodstock into desired form, allows for drying time, and removes. Re-adjusts and re-aligns guides of sanding, cutting, or boring machines to correct defects in finished product, using hand tools. Installs and adjusts blades, cutterheads, boring bits, or sanding belts in machines according to workpiece, machine function, and specifications, using hand tools. Selects knives, blades, cutterheads, boring bits, or sanding belts according to workpiece, machine function, and specifications. Places or secures woodstock against guide

or into holding device prior to feeding into machine. Examines blueprints, drawings, or samples to determine size, type, and setting of machine tools, stops, jigs, and guides to use. Places water-soaked woodstock into form under hydraulic lift to shape for use in making such items as musical instruments. Examines finished workpiece for smoothness, shape, angle, depth of cut, and conformity to specifications visually and using hands, rule, or other gauges. Examines raw woodstock for defects and to ensure conformity to size and other specification standards. Examines rollers, sanding belts, knives, cutting or boring devices, and conveyor mechanisms and sharpens or replaces worn parts, using hand tools. Cleans machines, workstation, or conveyor, using air hose, wax, solvents, brushes, and rags. Marks or otherwise identifies completed and inspected workpiece. Hand-stacks on pallet or conveyor or controls hoist to remove part or product from workstation.

GOE INFORMATION—**Interest Area:** 08. Industrial Production. **Work Group:** 08.03. Production Work. **Personality Type**—Realistic. Realistic occupations frequently involve work activities that include practical, hands-on problems and solutions. They often deal with plants, animals, and real-world materials like wood, tools, and machinery. Many of the occupations require working outside and do not involve a lot of paperwork or working closely with others. **Work Values**—Independence; Moral Values; Supervision, Technical; Activity; Company Policies and Practices. **Skills**—Operation and Control; Operation Monitoring; Quality Control Analysis; Repairing; Installation; Equipment Selection. **Abilities**—*Cognitive:* Visualization; Selective Attention; Information Ordering; Perceptual Speed. *Psychomotor:* Arm-Hand Steadiness; Speed of Limb Movement; Reaction Time; Multilimb Coordination; Control Precision. *Physical:* Static Strength; Explosive Strength; Dynamic Strength; Extent Flexibility; Stamina. *Sensory:* Auditory Attention; Sound Localization; Far Vision; Visual Color Discrimination; Hearing Sensitivity. **General Work Activities**—*Information Input:* Inspecting Equipment, Structures, or Materials; Getting Information; Monitoring Processes, Materials, or Surroundings. *Mental Process:* Judging Qualities of Things, Services, or Other People's Work; Evaluating Information Against Standards; Updating and Using Relevant Knowledge. *Work Output:* Handling and Moving Objects; Controlling Machines and Processes; Performing General Physical Activities. *Interacting with Others:* Communicating with Other Workers; Establishing and Maintaining Relationships; Monitoring and Controlling Resources. **Physical Work Conditions**—Hazardous Equipment; Common Protective or Safety Attire; Minor Burns, Cuts, Bites, or Stings; Distracting Sounds and Noise Levels; Contaminants. **Other Job Characteristics**—Pace Determined by Speed of Equipment; Degree of Automation; Importance of Repeating Same Tasks.

Experience—Job Zone 1. No previous work-related skill, knowledge, or experience is needed. **Job Preparation:** SVP below 4.0—less than six months. **Knowledge**—Building and Construction; Production and Processing; Design; Mechanical; Fine Arts. **Instructional Programs**—Cabinetmaking and Millwork/Millwright; Woodworking, General.

Related DOT Jobs—564.682-010 Chipping-Machine Operator; 569.662-010 Incising-Machine Operator; 569.685-014 Bender, Machine; 662.682-018 Stroke-Belt-Sander Operator; 662.685-010 Cork Grinder; 662.685-014 Cylinder-Sander Operator; 662.685-018 Last Scourer; 662.685-022 Sanding-Machine Buffer; 662.685-026 Sanding-Machine Tender; 662.685-030 Sizing-Machine Tender; 662.685-034 Speed-Belt-Sander Tender; 662.685-038 Turning-Sander Tender; 662.685-042 Wood-Heel Back-Liner; 663.585-010 Clipper, Automatic; 663.682-010 Barker Operator; 663.682-018 Veneer-Slicing-Machine Operator; 663.685-014 Excelsior-Machine Tender; 663.685-018 Molding Cutter; 663.685-022 Puncher; 663.685-026 Rounding-Machine Tender; others.

51-7099.99 Woodworkers, All Other

- Education/Training Required: **No data available.**
- Employed: **No data available.**
- Annual Earnings: **No data available.**
- Growth: **10.6%**
- Annual Job Openings: **4,000**

All woodworkers not listed separately.

No task data available.

GOE INFORMATION—Interest Area: 08. Industrial Production. **Work Group:** 08.02. Production Technology. **Note:** The Department of Labor has not collected some data for this job, so it has fewer details than the other descriptions.

Instructional Programs—Furniture Design and Manufacturing; Woodworking, General; Woodworking, Other.

Related DOT Jobs—149.281-010 Furniture Reproducer; 661.280-010 Patternmaker; 661.281-014 Loft Worker Apprentice; 761.381-022 Pattern Marker I.

51-8000 Plant and System Operators

51-8011.00 Nuclear Power Reactor Operators

- Education/Training Required: **Long-term on-the-job training**
- Employed: **3,763**
- Annual Earnings: **$60,180**
- Growth: **−3.4%**
- Annual Job Openings: **Fewer than 500**

Control nuclear reactors.

Regulates equipment according to data provided by recording and indicating instruments or computers. Monitors gauges to determine effects of generator loading on other power equipment. Monitors computer-operated equipment. Adjusts controls to regulate flow of power between generating and substations. Notes malfunctions of equipment, instruments, or controls. Corrects abnormal conditions, following standard practices. Monitors and operates boilers, turbines, wells, and auxiliary power plant equipment. Dispatches orders and instructions to personnel through radiotelephone or intercommunication system to coordinate operation of auxiliary equipment.

GOE INFORMATION—Interest Area: 08. Industrial Production. **Work Group:** 08.06. Systems Operation. **Personality Type**—Realistic. Realistic occupations frequently involve work activities that include practical, hands-on problems and solutions. They often deal with plants, animals, and real-world materials like wood, tools, and machinery. Many of the occupations require working outside and do not involve a lot of paperwork or working closely with others. **Work Values**—Supervision, Technical; Authority; Supervision, Human Relations; Advancement; Pleasant Co-workers. **Skills**—Operation Monitoring; Operation and Control; Speaking; Systems Analysis. **Abilities**—*Cognitive:* Written Comprehension; Oral Comprehension; Information Ordering; Problem Sensitivity; Oral Expression. *Psychomotor:* Control Precision; Multilimb Coordina-

tion; Reaction Time; Arm-Hand Steadiness; Response Orientation. *Physical:* Explosive Strength. *Sensory:* Speech Clarity; Hearing Sensitivity; Peripheral Vision. **General Work Activities**—*Information Input:* Monitoring Processes, Materials, or Surroundings; Getting Information; Identifying Objects, Actions, and Events. *Mental Process:* Updating and Using Relevant Knowledge; Evaluating Information Against Standards; Making Decisions and Solving Problems. *Work Output:* Handling and Moving Objects; Controlling Machines and Processes; Performing General Physical Activities. *Interacting with Others:* Communicating with Other Workers; Establishing and Maintaining Relationships; Coordinating the Work and Activities of Others. **Physical Work Conditions**—Hazardous Conditions; Specialized Protective or Safety Attire; Radiation; Using Hands on Objects, Tools, or Controls; Common Protective or Safety Attire. **Other Job Characteristics**—Degree of Automation; Pace Determined by Speed of Equipment; Consequence of Error.

Experience—Job Zone 4. A minimum of two to four years of work-related skill, knowledge, or experience is needed. **Job Preparation:** SVP 7.0 to less than 8.0—two years to less than 10 years. **Knowledge**—Engineering and Technology; Telecommunications; Physics; Chemistry; Computers and Electronics. **Instructional Programs**—Nuclear/Nuclear Power Technology/Technician.

Related DOT Jobs—952.362-022 Power-Reactor Operator.

51-8012.00 Power Distributors and Dispatchers

- Education/Training Required: **Long-term on-the-job training**
- Employed: **14,857**
- Annual Earnings: **$52,220**
- Growth: **−5.1%**
- Annual Job Openings: **1,000**

Coordinate, regulate, or distribute electricity or steam.

Controls and operates equipment to regulate or distribute electricity or steam according to data provided by recording or indicating instruments or computers. Adjusts controls to regulate the flow of power between generating stations, substations, and distribution lines. Turns and moves controls to adjust and activate power distribution equipment and machines. Calculates and determines load estimates or equipment requirements to control electrical distribution equipment or stations. Monitors switchboard and control board to ensure equipment operation and electrical and steam distribution. Directs activities of personnel engaged in the controlling and operating of electrical distribution equipment and machinery. Compiles and records operational data, such as chart and meter readings, power demands, and usage and operating time. Tends auxiliary equipment used in the power distribution process. Notifies workers or utilities of electrical and steam distribution process changes. Inspects equipment to ensure specifications are met and to detect defects. Repairs, maintains, and cleans equipment and machines, using hand tools.

GOE INFORMATION—Interest Area: 08. Industrial Production. **Work Group:** 08.06. Systems Operation. **Personality Type**—Realistic. Realistic occupations frequently involve work activities that include practical, hands-on problems and solutions. They often deal with plants, animals, and real-world materials like wood, tools, and machinery. Many of the occupations require working outside and do not involve a lot of paperwork or working closely with others. **Work Values**—Authority; Supervision, Technical; Security; Compensation; Supervision, Human Relations. **Skills**—Operation Monitoring; Repairing; Operation and Control; Management of Personnel Resources; Troubleshooting; Installation. **Abilities**—*Cognitive:* Perceptual Speed; Selective Attention; Number Facility; Time Sharing; Speed of Closure. *Psychomotor:* Reaction Time; Response Orientation; Manual Dexterity; Finger Dexterity; Control Precision. *Physical:* Gross Body Equilibrium; Explosive Strength; Gross Body Coordination; Dynamic Flexibility; Extent Flexibility. *Sensory:* Sound Localization; Hearing Sensitivity; Auditory Attention; Far Vision; Visual Color Discrimination. **General Work Activities**—*Information Input:* Monitoring Processes, Materials, or Surroundings; Inspecting Equipment, Structures, or Materials; Getting Information. *Mental Process:* Processing Information; Making Decisions and Solving Problems; Organizing, Planning, and Prioritizing. *Work Output:* Controlling Machines and Processes; Repairing and Maintaining Mechanical Equipment; Documenting or Recording Information. *Interacting with Others:* Communicating with Other Workers; Coordinating the Work and Activities of Others; Guiding, Directing, and Motivating Subordinates. **Physical Work Conditions**—Hazardous Conditions; Cramped Work Space or Awkward Positions; Using Hands on Objects, Tools, or Controls; Bending or Twisting the Body; Extremely Bright or Inadequate Lighting. **Other Job Characteristics**—Consequence of Error; Pace Determined by Speed of Equipment; Degree of Automation.

Experience—Job Zone 4. A minimum of two to four years of work-related skill, knowledge, or experience is needed. **Job Preparation:** SVP 7.0 to less than 8.0—two years to less than 10 years. **Knowledge**—Mechanical; Physics; Engineering and Technology; Telecommunications; Computers and Electronics. **Instructional Programs**—No data available.

Related DOT Jobs—820.662-010 Motor-Room Controller; 952.167-014 Load Dispatcher; 952.362-014 Feeder-Switchboard Operator; 952.362-026 Substation Operator; 952.362-030 Substation Operator Apprentice; 952.362-034 Switchboard Operator; 952.362-038 Switchboard Operator; 952.367-014 Switchboard Operator Assistant.

51-8013.00 Power Plant Operators

- **Education/Training Required: Long-term on-the-job training**
- **Employed: 36,242**
- **Annual Earnings: $48,560**
- **Growth: 1.8%**
- **Annual Job Openings: 3,000**

Control, operate, or maintain machinery to generate electric power. Includes auxiliary equipment operators.

No task data available.

GOE INFORMATION—**Interest Area:** 08. Industrial Production. **Work Group:** 08.06. Systems Operation. **Note:** The Department of Labor has not collected some data for this job, so it has fewer details than the other descriptions.

Instructional Programs—No data available.

Related DOT Jobs—951.685-010 Firer, High Pressure; 952.362-010 Auxiliary-Equipment Operator; 952.362-018 Hydroelectric-Station Operator; 952.362-042 Turbine Operator; 952.382-010 Diesel-Plant Operator; 952.382-014 Power Operator; 952.382-018 Power-Plant Operator.

51-8013.01 Power Generating Plant Operators, Except Auxiliary Equipment Operators

- **Education/Training Required: Long-term on-the-job training**
- **Employed: No data available.**
- **Annual Earnings: $48,560**
- **Growth: 1.8%**
- **Annual Job Openings: 3,000**

Control or operate machinery, such as steam-driven turbogenerators, to generate electric power, often through the use of panelboards, control boards, or semi-automatic equipment.

Operates or controls machinery that generates electric power, using control boards or semiautomatic equipment. Adjusts controls on equipment to generate specified electrical power. Monitors control and switchboard gauges to determine electrical power distribution meets specifications. Compiles and records operational data on specified forms. Examines and tests electrical power distribution machinery and equipment, using testing devices. Maintains and repairs electrical power distribution machinery and equipment, using hand tools.

GOE INFORMATION—**Interest Area:** 08. Industrial Production. **Work Group:** 08.06. Systems Operation. **Personality Type**—Realistic. Realistic occupations frequently involve work activities that include practical, hands-on problems and solutions. They often deal with plants, animals, and real-world materials like wood, tools, and machinery. Many of the occupations require working outside and do not involve a lot of paperwork or working closely with others. **Work Values**—Supervision, Technical; Supervision, Human Relations; Moral Values; Independence; Security. **Skills**—Operation Monitoring; Operation and Control; Troubleshooting; Repairing; Quality Control Analysis; Equipment Selection; Science. **Abilities**—*Cognitive:* Selective Attention; Perceptual Speed; Speed of Closure; Spatial Orientation; Flexibility of Closure. *Psychomotor:* Reaction Time; Response Orientation; Control Precision; Wrist-Finger Speed; Speed of Limb Movement. *Physical:* Gross Body Coordination; Gross Body Equilibrium; Static Strength; Explosive Strength; Dynamic Flexibility. *Sensory:* Sound Localization; Hearing Sensitivity; Auditory Attention; Depth Perception; Far Vision. **General Work Activities**—*Information Input:* Monitoring Processes, Materials, or Surroundings; Inspecting Equipment, Structures, or Materials; Identifying Objects, Actions, and Events. *Mental Process:* Processing Information; Evaluating Information Against Standards; Updating and Using Relevant Knowledge. *Work Output:* Controlling Machines and Processes; Repairing and Maintaining Electronic Equipment; Repairing and Maintaining Mechanical Equipment. *Interacting with Others:* Establishing and Maintaining Relationships; Performing Administrative Activities; Communicating with Other Workers. **Physical Work Conditions**—Common Protective or Safety Attire; Cramped Work Space or Awkward Positions; Hazardous Conditions; Climbing Ladders, Scaffolds, Poles, etc.; Hazardous Equipment. **Other Job Characteristics**—Consequence of Error; Degree of Automation; Pace Determined by Speed of Equipment.

Experience—Job Zone 4. A minimum of two to four years of work-related skill, knowledge, or experience is needed. **Job Preparation:** SVP 7.0 to less than 8.0—two years to less than 10 years. **Knowledge**—Mechanical; Engineering and Technology; Physics; Computers and Electronics. **Instructional Programs**—No data available.

Related DOT Jobs—952.362-018 Hydroelectric-Station Operator; 952.362-042 Turbine Operator; 952.382-010 Diesel-Plant Operator; 952.382-014 Power Operator; 952.382-018 Power-Plant Operator.

51-8013.02 Auxiliary Equipment Operators, Power

- Education/Training Required: Long-term on-the-job training
- Employed: No data available.
- Annual Earnings: $48,560
- Growth: 1.8%
- Annual Job Openings: 3,000

Control and maintain auxiliary equipment, such as pumps, fans, compressors, condensers, feedwater heaters, filters, and chlorinators, that supplies water, fuel, lubricants, air, and auxiliary power for turbines, generators, boilers, and other power-generating plant facilities.

Tends portable or stationary high pressure boilers that supply heat or power for engines , turbines, and steam-powered equipment. Opens and closes valves and switches in sequence upon signal from other worker to start or shut down auxiliary units. Replenishes electrolyte in batteries and oil in voltage transformers and resets tripped electric relays. Tightens leaking gland and pipe joints and reports need for major equipment repairs. Reads gauges to verify that units are operating at specified capacity and listens for sounds warning of mechanical malfunction. Cleans and lubricates equipment and collects oil, water, and electrolyte samples for laboratory analysis to prevent equipment failure or deterioration. Assists in making electrical repairs.

GOE INFORMATION—Interest Area: 08. Industrial Production. **Work Group:** 08.06. Systems Operation. **Personality Type**—Realistic. Realistic occupations frequently involve work activities that include practical, hands-on problems and solutions. They often deal with plants, animals, and real-world materials like wood, tools, and machinery. Many of the occupations require working outside and do not involve a lot of paperwork or working closely with others. **Work Values**—Supervision, Technical; Supervision, Human Relations; Moral Values; Advancement; Security. **Skills**—Operation Monitoring; Operation and Control; Repairing; Troubleshooting. **Abilities**—*Cognitive:* Selective Attention; Deductive Reasoning. *Psychomotor:* Control Precision; Reaction Time; Multilimb Coordination. *Physical:* Extent Flexibility; Gross Body Coordination; Trunk Strength. *Sensory:* Sound Localization; Hearing Sensitivity. **General Work Activities**—*Information Input:* Monitoring Processes, Materials, or Surroundings; Getting Information; Identifying Objects, Actions, and Events. *Mental Process:* Evaluating Information Against Standards; Making Decisions and Solving Problems; Analyzing Data or Information. *Work Output:* Performing General Physical Activities; Handling and Moving Objects; Controlling Machines and Processes. *Interacting with Others:* Communicating with Other Workers; Performing Administrative Activities; Communicating with Persons Outside Organization. **Physical Work Conditions**—Hazardous Conditions; Hazardous Equipment; Kneeling, Crouching, or Crawling; Cramped Work Space or Awkward Positions; Whole Body Vibration. **Other Job Characteristics**—Degree of Automation; Pace Determined by Speed of Equipment; Importance of Repeating Same Tasks.

Experience—Job Zone 2. Some previous work-related skill, knowledge, or experience may be helpful, but usually is not needed. **Job Preparation:** SVP 4.0 to less than 6.0—six months to less than two years. **Knowledge**—Mechanical; Physics; Engineering and Technology; Chemistry. **Instructional Programs**—No data available.

Related DOT Jobs—951.685-010 Firer, High Pressure; 952.362-010 Auxiliary-Equipment Operator.

51-8021.00 Stationary Engineers and Boiler Operators

- Education/Training Required: Moderate-term on-the-job training
- Employed: 57,183
- Annual Earnings: $41,470
- Growth: −1.3%
- Annual Job Openings: 4,000

Operate or maintain stationary engines, boilers, or other mechanical equipment to provide utilities for buildings or industrial processes. Operate equipment, such as steam engines, generators, motors, turbines, and steam boilers.

No task data available.

GOE INFORMATION—Interest Area: 08. Industrial Production. **Work Group:** 08.06. Systems Operation. **Note:** The Department of Labor has not collected some data for this job, so it has fewer details than the other descriptions.

Instructional Programs—No data available.

Related DOT Jobs—553.685-066 Firer, Retort; 950.362-014 Refrigerating Engineer; 950.382-010 Boiler Operator; 950.382-018 Gas-Engine Operator; 950.382-026 Stationary Engineer; 950.382-030 Stationary-Engineer Apprentice; 950.485-010 Humidifier Attendant; 950.585-014 Boiler-Operator Helper; 950.685-010 Air-Compressor Operator; 950.685-014 Boiler-Room Helper; 951.685-014 Firer, Low Pressure; 951.685-018 Firer, Marine.

51-8021.01 Boiler Operators and Tenders, Low Pressure

- Education/Training Required: Moderate-term on-the-job training
- Employed: No data available.
- Annual Earnings: $41,470
- Growth: −1.3%
- Annual Job Openings: 4,000

Operate or tend low-pressure stationary steam boilers and auxiliary steam equipment, such as pumps, compressors, and air-conditioning equipment, to supply steam heat for office buildings, apartment houses, or industrial establishments; to maintain steam at specified pressure aboard marine vessels; or to generate and supply compressed air for operation of pneumatic tools, hoists, and air lances.

Tends boilers and equipment to supply and maintain steam or heat for buildings, marine vessels, or operation of pneumatic tools. Moves controls and observes gauges to regulate heat and steam. Ignites fuel in burner, using torch or flame. Installs burners and auxiliary equipment, using hand tools. Shovels coal or coke into firebox to feed fuel, using hand tools. Obtains samples from designated location on boiler and carries samples to testing laboratory. Tests sample quality to ensure sample meets specifications, using testing devices. Cleans and maintains heating and steam boilers and equipment, using hand tools. Records test results on specified form and gives to worker or supervisor.

GOE INFORMATION—Interest Area: 08. Industrial Production. **Work Group:** 08.06. Systems Operation. **Personality Type**—Realistic. Realistic occupations frequently involve work activities that include practical, hands-on problems and solutions. They often deal with plants, animals, and real-world materials like wood, tools, and machinery. Many of the occupations require working outside and do not involve a lot of paperwork or working closely with others. **Work Values**—Moral Values; Supervision, Technical; Independence; Company Policies and Practices. **Skills**—Operation Monitoring; Operation and Control; Installation; Repairing; Equipment Selection. **Abilities**—*Cognitive:* Perceptual Speed; Spatial Orientation; Selective Attention; Information Ordering; Problem Sensitivity. *Psychomotor:* Control Precision; Reaction Time; Arm-Hand Steadiness; Multilimb Coordination; Manual Dexterity. *Physical:* Explosive Strength; Dynamic Strength; Trunk Strength; Extent Flexibility; Static Strength. *Sensory:* Depth Perception; Peripheral Vision; Hearing Sensitivity; Far Vision; Night Vision. **General Work Activities**—*Information Input:* Monitoring Processes, Materials, or Surroundings; Inspecting Equipment, Structures, or Materials; Identifying Objects, Actions, and Events. *Mental Process:* Updating and Using Relevant Knowledge; Evaluating Information Against Standards; Judging Qualities of Things, Services, or Other People's Work. *Work Output:* Performing General Physical Activities; Handling and Moving Objects; Controlling Machines and Processes. *Interacting with Others:* Communicating with Other Workers; Performing Administrative Activities; Coordinating the Work and Activities of Others. **Physical Work Conditions**—Very Hot or Cold; Hazardous Equipment; Distracting Sounds and Noise Levels; Contaminants; Hazardous Conditions. **Other Job Characteristics**—Importance of Repeating Same Tasks; Pace Determined by Speed of Equipment; Degree of Automation.

Experience—Job Zone 2. Some previous work-related skill, knowledge, or experience may be helpful, but usually is not needed. **Job Preparation:** SVP 4.0 to less than 6.0—six months to less than two years. **Knowledge**—Mechanical; Physics; Production and Processing; Engineering and Technology; Building and Construction. **Instructional Programs**—No data available.

Related DOT Jobs—553.685-066 Firer, Retort; 950.585-014 Boiler-Operator Helper; 950.685-014 Boiler-Room Helper; 951.685-014 Firer, Low Pressure; 951.685-018 Firer, Marine.

51-8021.02 Stationary Engineers

- Education/Training Required: **Long-term on-the-job training**
- Employed: **No data available.**
- Annual Earnings: **$41,470**
- Growth: **–1.3%**
- Annual Job Openings: **4,000**

Operate and maintain stationary engines and mechanical equipment to provide utilities for buildings or industrial processes. Operate equipment such as steam engines, generators, motors, turbines, and steam boilers.

Adjusts controls and valves on equipment to provide power and regulate and set operations of system and industrial processes. Inspects equipment to determine need for repair, lubrication, or adjustment. Lights burners and opens valves on equipment, such as condensers, pumps, and compressors, to prepare system for operation. Reads dials of temperature, pressure, and ampere gauges and meters to detect malfunctions and ensure specified operation of equipment. Lubricates, maintains, and repairs equipment, using hand tools and power tools. Adds chemicals or tends equipment to maintain temperature of fluids or atmosphere or to prevent scale buildup. Tests electrical system to determine voltage, using voltage meter. Records temperature, pressure, water levels, fuel consumption, and other data at specified intervals in logbook. Cleans equipment, using air hose, brushes, and rags, and drains water from pipes and air reservoir.

GOE INFORMATION—**Interest Area:** 08. Industrial Production. **Work Group:** 08.06. Systems Operation. **Personality Type**—Realistic. Realistic occupations frequently involve work activities that include practical, hands-on problems and solutions. They often deal with plants, animals, and real-world materials like wood, tools, and machinery. Many of the occupations require working outside and do not involve a lot of paperwork or working closely with others. **Work Values**—Supervision, Technical; Supervision, Human Relations; Moral Values; Autonomy; Independence. **Skills**—Operation Monitoring; Operation and Control; Repairing; Troubleshooting; Quality Control Analysis. **Abilities**—*Cognitive:* Problem Sensitivity. *Psychomotor:* Control Precision; Finger Dexterity; Manual Dexterity; Arm-Hand Steadiness; Multilimb Coordination. *Physical:* Static Strength; Explosive Strength. *Sensory:* Sound Localization. **General Work Activities**—*Information Input:* Inspecting Equipment, Structures, or Materials; Monitoring Processes, Materials, or Surroundings; Getting Information. *Mental Process:* Processing Information; Evaluating Information Against Standards; Analyzing Data or Information. *Work Output:* Repairing and Maintaining Mechanical Equipment; Controlling Machines and Processes; Handling and Moving Objects. *Interacting with Others:* Communicating with Other Workers; Interpreting Meaning of Information for Others; Establishing and Maintaining Relationships. **Physical Work Conditions**—Distracting Sounds and Noise Levels; Hazardous Conditions; Specialized Protective or Safety Attire; Contaminants; Minor Burns, Cuts, Bites, or Stings. **Other Job Characteristics**—Degree of Automation; Consequence of Error; Pace Determined by Speed of Equipment.

Experience—Job Zone 3. Previous work-related skill, knowledge, or experience is required. **Job Preparation:** SVP 6.0 to less than 7.0—more than one year and less than four years. **Knowledge**—Mechanical; Physics; Engineering and Technology; Computers and Electronics; Chemistry. **Instructional Programs**—No data available.

Related DOT Jobs—950.362-014 Refrigerating Engineer; 950.382-010 Boiler Operator; 950.382-018 Gas-Engine Operator; 950.382-026 Stationary Engineer; 950.382-030 Stationary-Engineer Apprentice; 950.485-010 Humidifier Attendant; 950.685-010 Air-Compressor Operator.

51-8031.00 Water and Liquid Waste Treatment Plant and System Operators

- Education/Training Required: **Long-term on-the-job training**
- Employed: **88,328**
- Annual Earnings: **$32,560**
- Growth: **18.1%**
- Annual Job Openings: **6,000**

Operate or control an entire process or system of machines, often through the use of control boards, to transfer or treat water or liquid waste.

Add chemicals, such as ammonia, chlorine, and lime, to disinfect and deodorize water and other liquids. Operate and adjust controls on equipment to purify and clarify water, process or dispose of sewage, and generate power. Inspect equipment and monitor operating conditions, meters, and gauges to determine load requirements and detect malfunctions. Collect and test water and sewage samples, using test equipment and color analysis standards. Record operational data, personnel attendance, and meter and gauge readings on specified forms. Maintain, repair, and lubricate equipment, using hand tools and power tools. Clean and maintain tanks and filter beds, using hand tools and power tools. Direct and coordinate plant workers engaged in routine operations and maintenance activities.

GOE INFORMATION—**Interest Area:** 08. Industrial Production. **Work Group:** 08.06. Systems Operation. **Personality Type**—Realistic. Realistic occupations frequently involve work activities that include practical, hands-on problems and solutions. They often deal with plants, animals, and real-world materials like wood, tools, and machinery. Many of the occupations require working outside and do not involve a lot of paperwork or working closely with others. **Work Values**—Security; Authority; Supervision, Technical; Company Policies and Practices; Pleasant Co-workers. **Skills**—Operation Monitoring; Operation and Control; Installation; Troubleshooting; Management of Material Resources; Operations Analysis; Mathematics; Management of Personnel Resources. **Abilities**—*Cognitive:* Flexibility of Closure; Selective Attention; Perceptual Speed; Time Sharing; Inductive Reasoning. *Psychomotor:* Multilimb Coordination; Control Precision; Reaction Time; Rate Control; Response Orientation. *Physical:* Extent Flexibility; Gross Body Coordination; Trunk Strength; Gross Body Equilibrium; Stamina. *Sensory:* Depth Perception; Auditory Attention; Glare Sensitivity; Far Vision; Visual Color Discrimination. **General Work Activities**—*Information Input:* Monitoring Processes, Materials, or Surroundings; Identifying Objects, Actions, and Events; Inspecting Equipment, Structures, or Materials. *Mental Process:* Updating and Using Relevant Knowledge; Making Decisions and Solving Problems; Organizing, Planning, and Prioritizing. *Work Output:* Handling and Moving Objects; Performing General Physical Activities; Documenting or Recording Information. *Interacting with Others:* Communicating with Other Workers; Establishing and Maintaining Relationships; Monitoring and Controlling Resources. **Physical Work Conditions**—Contaminants; Hazardous Conditions; Disease or Infections; Common Protective or Safety Attire; Hazardous Equipment. **Other Job Characteristics**—Degree of Automation; Consequence of Error; Pace Determined by Speed of Equipment.

Experience—Job Zone 3. Previous work-related skill, knowledge, or experience is required. **Job Preparation:** SVP 4.0 to less than 6.0—six months to less than two years. **Knowledge**—Biology; Chemistry; Public Safety and Security; Physics; Law and Government. **Instructional Programs**—Water Quality and Wastewater Treatment Management and Recycling Technology/Technician.

Related DOT Jobs—954.382-010 Pump-Station Operator, Waterworks; 954.382-014 Water-Treatment-Plant Operator; 955.362-010 Wastewater-Treatment-Plant Operator; 955.382-010 Clarifying-Plant Operator; 955.382-014 Waste-Treatment Operator.

51-8091.00 Chemical Plant and System Operators

- **Education/Training Required: Long-term on-the-job training**
- **Employed: 71,256**
- **Annual Earnings: $41,990**
- **Growth: –3.3%**
- **Annual Job Openings: 5,000**

Control or operate an entire chemical process or system of machines.

Turns valves to regulate flow of product or byproducts through agitator tanks, storage drums, or neutralizer tanks according to process. Starts pumps to wash and rinse reactor vessels, to exhaust gases and vapors, and to mix product with water. Moves control settings to make control adjustments on equipment units affecting speed of chemical reactions and quality and yield. Monitors recording instruments, flowmeters, panel lights, and other indicators and listens for warning signals to verify conformity of process conditions. Interprets chemical reactions visible through sight glasses or on television monitor and reviews laboratory test reports for process adjustments. Manually regulates or shuts down

equipment during emergency situations as directed by supervisory personnel. Records operating data, such as process conditions, test results, and instrument readings, calculating material requirements or yield according to formulas. Defrosts frozen valves, using steam hose. Patrols work area to observe level of carbon in thickener tank and wash solutions in overflow troughs to prevent spills. Gauges tank levels, using calibrated rod. Notifies maintenance, stationary-engineering, and other auxiliary personnel to correct equipment malfunction and adjust power, steam, water, or air supply. Inspects equipment for potential and actual hazards, wear, leaks, and other conditions requiring maintenance shutdown. Confers with technical and supervisory personnel to report or resolve conditions affecting safety, efficiency, and product quality. Draws samples of products and conducts quality control tests to monitor processing and ensure standards are met.

GOE INFORMATION—**Interest Area:** 08. Industrial Production. **Work Group:** 08.06. Systems Operation. **Personality Type**—Realistic. Realistic occupations frequently involve work activities that include practical, hands-on problems and solutions. They often deal with plants, animals, and real-world materials like wood, tools, and machinery. Many of the occupations require working outside and do not involve a lot of paperwork or working closely with others. **Work Values**—Supervision, Technical; Compensation; Security; Supervision, Human Relations; Company Policies and Practices. **Skills**—Operation Monitoring; Operation and Control; Science; Troubleshooting; Quality Control Analysis; Mathematics; Systems Analysis; Systems Evaluation. **Abilities**—*Cognitive:* Information Ordering; Oral Comprehension; Written Comprehension; Flexibility of Closure; Selective Attention. *Psychomotor:* Reaction Time; Control Precision; Response Orientation; Finger Dexterity. *Physical:* None met the criteria. *Sensory:* Near Vision; Auditory Attention. **General Work Activities**—*Information Input:* Monitoring Processes, Materials, or Surroundings; Inspecting Equipment, Structures, or Materials; Getting Information. *Mental Process:* Evaluating Information Against Standards; Updating and Using Relevant Knowledge; Analyzing Data or Information. *Work Output:* Controlling Machines and Processes; Handling and Moving Objects; Performing General Physical Activities. *Interacting with Others:* Communicating with Other Workers; Establishing and Maintaining Relationships; Performing Administrative Activities. **Physical Work Conditions**—Hazardous Conditions; Common Protective or Safety Attire; Standing; Sitting; Disease or Infections. **Other Job Characteristics**—Consequence of Error; Importance of Being Exact or Accurate; Degree of Automation.

Experience—Job Zone 2. Some previous work-related skill, knowledge, or experience may be helpful, but usually is not needed. **Job Preparation:** SVP 4.0 to less than 6.0—six months to less than two years. **Knowledge**—Production and Processing; Chemistry; Public Safety and Security; Mechanical; Engineering and Technology. **Instructional Programs**—Chemical Technology/Technician.

Related DOT Jobs—558.260-010 Chief Operator; 559.165-010 Checker; 559.382-010 Ammonia-Still Operator; 559.382-038 Naphtha-Washing-System Operator; 559.662-014 Wash Operator.

51-8092.00 Gas Plant Operators

- **Education/Training Required: Long-term on-the-job training**
- **Employed: 12,087**
- **Annual Earnings: $46,930**
- **Growth: –6.3%**
- **Annual Job Openings: 1,000**

Distribute or process gas for utility companies and others by controlling compressors to maintain specified pressures on main pipelines.

No task data available.

GOE INFORMATION—Interest Area: 08. Industrial Production. **Work Group:** 08.06. Systems Operation. **Note:** The Department of Labor has not collected some data for this job, so it has fewer details than the other descriptions.

Instructional Programs—No data available.

Related DOT Jobs—552.362-014 Oxygen-Plant Operator; 559.362-018 Liquefaction-Plant Operator; 953.362-010 Fuel Attendant; 953.362-014 Liquefaction-and-Regasification-Plant Operator; 953.362-018 Pressure Controller.

51-8092.01 Gas Processing Plant Operators

- **Education/Training Required: Long-term on-the-job training**
- **Employed: No data available.**
- **Annual Earnings: $46,930**
- **Growth: –6.3%**
- **Annual Job Openings: 1,000**

Control equipment, such as compressors, evaporators, heat exchangers, and refrigeration equipment to process gas for utility companies and for industrial use.

Controls fractioning columns, compressors, purifying towers, heat exchangers, and related equipment to extract nitrogen and oxygen from air. Adjusts temperature, pressure, vacuum, level, flow rate, or transfer of gas according to test results and knowledge of process and equipment. Controls operation of compressors, scrubbers, evaporators, and refrigeration equipment to liquefy, compress, or regasify natural gas. Observes pressure, temperature, level, and flow gauges to ensure standard operation. Tests oxygen for purity and moisture content at various stages of process, using burette and moisture meter. Reads logsheet to ascertain demand and disposition of product or to detect equipment malfunctions. Calculates gas ratios, using testing apparatus, to detect deviations from specifications. Records gauge readings and test results. Cleans and repairs equipment, using hand tools. Signals or directs workers tending auxiliary equipment.

GOE INFORMATION—Interest Area: 08. Industrial Production. **Work Group:** 08.06. Systems Operation. **Personality Type**—Realistic. Realistic occupations frequently involve work activities that include practical, hands-on problems and solutions. They often deal with plants, animals, and real-world materials like wood, tools, and machinery. Many of the occupations require working outside and do not involve a lot of paperwork or working closely with others. **Work Values**—Security; Supervision, Human Relations; Supervision, Technical; Company Policies and Practices; Advancement. **Skills**—Operation Monitoring; Repairing; Operation and Control; Mathematics; Quality Control Analysis; Troubleshooting. **Abilities**—*Cognitive:* Mathematical Reasoning. *Psychomotor:* Control Precision. *Physical:* Gross Body Coordination. *Sensory:* None met the criteria. **General Work Activities**—*Information Input:* Inspecting Equipment, Structures, or Materials; Monitoring Processes, Materials, or Surroundings; Identifying Objects, Actions, and Events. *Mental Process:* Judging Qualities of Things, Services, or Other People's Work; Processing Information; Evaluating Information Against Standards. *Work Output:* Repairing and Maintaining Mechanical Equipment; Performing General Physical Activities; Handling and Moving Objects. *Interacting with Others:* Communicating with Other Workers; Performing Administrative Activities; Coordinating the Work and Activities of Others. **Physical Work Conditions**—Specialized Protective or Safety Attire; Hazardous Conditions; Contaminants; Common Protective or Safety Attire; Bending or Twisting the Body. **Other Job Characteristics**—Degree of Automation; Consequence of Error; Importance of Being Exact or Accurate.

Experience—Job Zone 2. Some previous work-related skill, knowledge, or experience may be helpful, but usually is not needed. **Job Preparation:** SVP 4.0 to less than 6.0—six months to less than two years. **Knowledge**—Mechanical; Chemistry; Engineering and Technology; Production and Processing; Physics. **Instructional Programs**—No data available.

Related DOT Jobs—552.362-014 Oxygen-Plant Operator; 559.362-018 Liquefaction-Plant Operator; 953.362-014 Liquefaction-and-Regasification-Plant Operator.

51-8092.02 Gas Distribution Plant Operators

- **Education/Training Required: Long-term on-the-job training**
- **Employed: No data available.**
- **Annual Earnings: $46,930**
- **Growth: –6.3%**
- **Annual Job Openings: 1,000**

Control equipment to regulate flow and pressure of gas for utility companies and industrial use. May control distribution of gas for a municipal or industrial plant or a single process in an industrial plant.

Controls equipment to regulate flow and pressure of gas to feedlines of boilers, furnaces, and related steam-generating or heating equipment. Determines required governor adjustments according to customer-demand estimates. Adjusts governors to maintain specified gas pressure and volume. Observes, records, and reports flow and pressure gauge readings on gas mains and fuel feedlines. Determines causes of abnormal pressure variances and makes corrective recommendations, such as installation of pipe to relieve overloading. Changes charts in recording meters.

GOE INFORMATION—Interest Area: 08. Industrial Production. **Work Group:** 08.06. Systems Operation. **Personality Type**—Realistic. Realistic occupations frequently involve work activities that include practical, hands-on problems and solutions. They often deal with plants, animals, and real-world materials like wood, tools, and machinery. Many of the occupations require working outside and do not involve a lot of paperwork or working closely with others. **Work Values**—Security; Supervision, Technical; Supervision, Human Relations; Advancement; Company Policies and Practices. **Skills**—Operation and Control; Operation Monitoring; Troubleshooting; Repairing; Operations Analysis. **Abilities**—*Cognitive:* Inductive Reasoning. *Psychomotor:* Control Precision. *Physical:* Extent Flexibility. *Sensory:* None met the criteria. **General Work Activities**—*Information Input:* Monitoring Processes, Materials, or Surroundings; Inspecting Equipment, Structures, or Materials; Getting Information. *Mental Process:* Evaluating Information Against Standards; Making Decisions and Solving Problems; Analyzing Data or Information. *Work Output:* Repairing and Maintaining Mechanical Equipment; Performing General Physical Activities; Handling and Moving Objects. *Interacting with Others:* Communicating with Other Workers; Performing Administrative Activities; Interpreting Meaning of Information for Others. **Physical Work Conditions**—Hazardous Conditions; Contaminants; Common Protective or Safety Attire; Walking or Running; Cramped Work Space or Awkward Positions. **Other Job Characteristics**—Degree of Automation; Importance of Repeating Same Tasks; Importance of Being Exact or Accurate.

Experience—Job Zone 3. Previous work-related skill, knowledge, or experience is required. **Job Preparation:** SVP 6.0 to less than 7.0—more than one year and less than four years. **Knowledge**—Mechanical; Physics; Production and Processing; Engineering and Technology; Clerical. **Instructional Programs**—No data available.

Related DOT Jobs—953.362-010 Fuel Attendant; 953.362-018 Pressure Controller.

51-8093.00 Petroleum Pump System Operators, Refinery Operators, and Gaugers

- Education/Training Required: Long-term on-the-job training
- Employed: 35,262
- Annual Earnings: $47,970
- Growth: −4.1%
- Annual Job Openings: 2,000

Control the operation of petroleum refining or processing units. May specialize in controlling manifold and pumping systems, gauging or testing oil in storage tanks, or regulating the flow of oil into pipelines.

No task data available.

GOE INFORMATION—Interest Area: 08. Industrial Production. **Work Group:** 08.06. Systems Operation. **Note:** The Department of Labor has not collected some data for this job, so it has fewer details than the other descriptions.

Instructional Programs—No data available.

Related DOT Jobs—546.382-010 Control-Panel Operator; 549.260-010 Refinery Operator; 549.360-010 Pumper; 914.384-010 Gauger.

51-8093.01 Petroleum Pump System Operators

- Education/Training Required: Long-term on-the-job training
- Employed: No data available.
- Annual Earnings: $47,970
- Growth: −4.1%
- Annual Job Openings: 2,000

Control or operate manifold and pumping systems to circulate liquids through a petroleum refinery.

Starts battery of pumps, observes pressure meters and flowmeters, and turns valves to regulate pumping speeds according to schedules. Turns handwheels to open line valves and direct flow of product. Synchronizes activities with other pumphouses to ensure continuous flow of products and minimum of contamination between products. Plans movement of products through lines to processing, storage, and shipping units, utilizing knowledge of interconnections and capacities system. Reads operating schedules or instructions from dispatcher. Signals other workers by telephone or radio to operate pumps, open and close valves, and check temperatures. Records operating data, such as products and quantities pumped, stocks used, gauging results, and operating time.

GOE INFORMATION—Interest Area: 08. Industrial Production. **Work Group:** 08.06. Systems Operation. **Personality Type**—Realistic. Realistic occupations frequently involve work activities that include practical, hands-on problems and solutions. They often deal with plants, animals, and real-world materials like wood, tools, and machinery. Many of the occupations require working outside and do not involve a lot of paperwork or working closely with others. **Work Values**—Supervision, Technical; Supervision, Human Relations; Compensation; Company Policies and Practices; Security. **Skills**—Operation and Control; Operation Monitoring; Repairing; Troubleshooting; Coordination. **Abilities**—*Cognitive:*

Information Ordering. *Psychomotor:* Rate Control; Control Precision. *Physical:* Gross Body Coordination; Explosive Strength; Extent Flexibility; Static Strength; Trunk Strength. *Sensory:* None met the criteria. **General Work Activities**—*Information Input:* Inspecting Equipment, Structures, or Materials; Getting Information; Monitoring Processes, Materials, or Surroundings. *Mental Process:* Evaluating Information Against Standards; Processing Information; Organizing, Planning, and Prioritizing. *Work Output:* Repairing and Maintaining Mechanical Equipment; Controlling Machines and Processes; Handling and Moving Objects. *Interacting with Others:* Communicating with Other Workers; Establishing and Maintaining Relationships; Performing Administrative Activities. **Physical Work Conditions**—Contaminants; Hazardous Conditions; Climbing Ladders, Scaffolds, Poles, etc.; Specialized Protective or Safety Attire; Kneeling, Crouching, or Crawling. **Other Job Characteristics**—Degree of Automation; Pace Determined by Speed of Equipment; Importance of Repeating Same Tasks.

Experience—Job Zone 3. Previous work-related skill, knowledge, or experience is required. **Job Preparation:** SVP 6.0 to less than 7.0—more than one year and less than four years. **Knowledge**—Mechanical; Chemistry; Production and Processing; Clerical; Telecommunications. **Instructional Programs**—No data available.

Related DOT Jobs—549.360-010 Pumper.

51-8093.02 Petroleum Refinery and Control Panel Operators

- Education/Training Required: Long-term on-the-job training
- Employed: No data available.
- Annual Earnings: $47,970
- Growth: −4.1%
- Annual Job Openings: 2,000

Analyze specifications and control continuous operation of petroleum refining and processing units. Operate control panel to regulate temperature, pressure, rate of flow, and tank level in petroleum refining unit according to process schedules.

Reads and analyzes specifications, schedules, logs, and test results to determine changes to equipment controls required to produce specified product. Operates control panel to coordinate and regulate process variables and to direct product flow rate according to prescribed schedules. Monitors and adjusts unit controls to ensure safe and efficient operating conditions. Observes instruments, gauges, and meters to verify conformance to specified quality and quantity of product. Operates auxiliary equipment and controls multiple processing units during distilling or treating operations. Inspects equipment and listens for automated warning signals to determine location and nature of malfunction, such as leaks and breakage. Samples and tests liquids and gases for chemical characteristics and color of products or sends products to laboratory for analysis. Repairs, lubricates, and maintains equipment or reports malfunctioning equipment to supervisor to schedule needed repairs. Cleans interior of processing units by circulating chemicals and solvents within unit. Compiles and records operating data, instrument readings, documents, and results of laboratory analyses.

GOE INFORMATION—Interest Area: 08. Industrial Production. **Work Group:** 08.06. Systems Operation. **Personality Type**—Realistic. Realistic occupations frequently involve work activities that include practical, hands-on problems and solutions. They often deal with plants, animals, and real-world materials like wood, tools, and machinery. Many of the occupations require working outside and do not involve a lot of paperwork or working closely with others. **Work Values**—Supervision, Technical; Supervision, Human Relations; Company Policies and Practices; Advancement; Moral Values. **Skills**—Operation Monitoring; Operation and Control; Repairing; Troubleshooting; Quality Control Analysis; Mathematics; Science. **Abilities**—*Cognitive:* Time Sharing; Mathematical Reasoning; Problem Sensitivity; Category Flexibility; Flexibility of Closure. *Psychomotor:* Rate Control; Reaction Time; Control Precision; Speed of Limb Movement; Response Orientation. *Physical:* Explosive Strength; Dynamic Flexibility; Extent Flexibility; Dynamic Strength; Gross Body Equilibrium. *Sensory:* Sound Localization; Auditory Attention; Hearing Sensitivity; Far Vision. **General Work Activities**—*Information Input:* Inspecting Equipment, Structures, or Materials; Getting Information; Monitoring Processes, Materials, or Surroundings. *Mental Process:* Updating and Using Relevant Knowledge; Analyzing Data or Information; Judging Qualities of Things, Services, or Other People's Work. *Work Output:* Controlling Machines and Processes; Handling and Moving Objects; Repairing and Maintaining Mechanical Equipment. *Interacting with Others:* Communicating with Other Workers; Interpreting Meaning of Information for Others; Establishing and Maintaining Relationships. **Physical Work Conditions**—Hazardous Conditions; Distracting Sounds and Noise Levels; Contaminants; Keeping or Regaining Balance; Common Protective or Safety Attire. **Other Job Characteristics**—Degree of Automation; Pace Determined by Speed of Equipment; Consequence of Error.

Experience—Job Zone 4. A minimum of two to four years of work-related skill, knowledge, or experience is needed. **Job Preparation:** SVP 7.0 to less than 8.0—two years to less than 10 years. **Knowledge**—Chemistry; Mechanical; Physics; Production and Processing; Public Safety and Security. **Instructional Programs**—No data available.

Related DOT Jobs—546.382-010 Control-Panel Operator; 549.260-010 Refinery Operator.

51-8093.03 Gaugers

- Education/Training Required: Long-term on-the-job training
- Employed: No data available.
- Annual Earnings: $47,970
- Growth: –4.1%
- Annual Job Openings: 2,000

Gauge and test oil in storage tanks. Regulate flow of oil into pipelines at wells, tank farms, refineries, and marine and rail terminals, following prescribed standards and regulations.

Gauges quality of oil in storage tanks before and after delivery, using calibrated steel tape and conversion. Tests oil to determine amount of bottom sediment, water, and foreign materials, using centrifugal tester. Regulates flow of products into pipelines, using automated pumping equipment. Starts pumps and opens valves to regulate flow of oil into and out of tanks according to delivery schedules. Reads automatic gauges at specified intervals to determine flow rate of oil into or from tanks and amount of oil in tanks. Gauges tank containing petroleum and natural gas byproducts, such as condensate or natural gasoline. Operates pumps, teletype, and mobile radio. Calculates test results, using standard formulas. Turns bleeder valves or lowers sample container into tank to obtain oil sample. Records readings and test results. Lowers thermometer into tanks to obtain temperature reading. Records meter and pressure readings at gas well. Reports leaks or defective valves to maintenance. Clamps seal around valves to secure tanks. Inspects pipelines, valves, and flanges to detect malfunctions, such as loose connections and leaks. Tightens connections with wrenches and greases and oils valves, using grease gum and oil can.

GOE INFORMATION—**Interest Area:** 08. Industrial Production. **Work Group:** 08.06. Systems Operation. **Personality Type**—Realistic. Realistic occupations frequently involve work activities that include practical, hands-on problems and solutions. They often deal with plants, animals, and real-world materials like wood, tools, and machinery. Many of the occupations require working outside and do not involve a lot of paperwork or working closely with others. **Work Values**—Supervision, Technical; Independence; Moral Values; Supervision, Human Relations. **Skills**—Operation Monitoring; Operation and Control; Mathematics; Quality Control Analysis; Troubleshooting; Repairing; Science; Equipment Selection. **Abilities**—*Cognitive:* Perceptual Speed; Flexibility of Closure; Spatial Orientation; Speed of Closure. *Psychomotor:* Response Orientation; Control Precision; Rate Control; Reaction Time; Speed of Limb Movement. *Physical:* Static Strength; Extent Flexibility; Explosive Strength; Dynamic Flexibility; Gross Body Equilibrium. *Sensory:* Auditory Attention; Sound Localization; Glare Sensitivity; Peripheral Vision; Night Vision. **General Work Activities**—*Information Input:* Identifying Objects, Actions, and Events; Inspecting Equipment, Structures, or Materials; Getting Information. *Mental Process:* Evaluating Information Against Standards; Processing Information; Analyzing Data or Information. *Work Output:* Handling and Moving Objects; Performing General Physical Activities; Controlling Machines and Processes. *Interacting with Others:* Communicating with Other Workers; Establishing and Maintaining Relationships; Monitoring and Controlling Resources. **Physical Work Conditions**—Hazardous Conditions; Contaminants; Outdoors; Common Protective or Safety Attire; Climbing Ladders, Scaffolds, Poles, etc. **Other Job Characteristics**—Degree of Automation; Consequence of Error; Importance of Being Exact or Accurate.

Experience—Job Zone 3. Previous work-related skill, knowledge, or experience is required. **Job Preparation:** SVP 6.0 to less than 7.0—more than one year and less than four years. **Knowledge**—Mechanical; Physics; Engineering and Technology; Public Safety and Security; Production and Processing. **Instructional Programs**—No data available.

Related DOT Jobs—914.384-010 Gauger.

51-8099.99 Plant and System Operators, All Other

- Education/Training Required: No data available.
- Employed: No data available.
- Annual Earnings: No data available.
- Growth: 11.4%
- Annual Job Openings: 3,000

All plant and system operators not listed separately.

No task data available.

GOE INFORMATION—**Interest Area:** 08. Industrial Production. **Work Group:** 08.06. Systems Operation. **Note:** The Department of Labor has not collected some data for this job, so it has fewer details than the other descriptions.

Instructional Programs—No data available.

Related DOT Jobs—590.362-010 Forming-Process Worker; 850.663-018 Lock Tender II; 914.362-010 Coal Pipeline Operator; 921.662-014 Charge-Machine Operator; 921.665-010 Cement-Boat-And-Barge Loader; 939.362-014 Panelboard Operator; 950.562-010 Panelboard Operator; 950.585-010 Ventilation Equipment Tender; 954.382-018 Watershed Tender; 955.362-014 Incinerator Operator II; 955.585-010 Wastewater-Treatment-Plant Attendant.

51-9000 Other Production Occupations

51-9011.00 Chemical Equipment Operators and Tenders

- **Education/Training Required: Moderate-term on-the-job training**
- **Employed: 61,007**
- **Annual Earnings: $36,810**
- **Growth: 14.9%**
- **Annual Job Openings: 9,000**

Operate or tend equipment to control chemical changes or reactions in the processing of industrial or consumer products. Equipment used includes devulcanizers, steam-jacketed kettles, and reactor vessels.

No task data available.

GOE INFORMATION—Interest Area: 08. Industrial Production. **Work Group:** 08.03. Production Work. **Note:** The Department of Labor has not collected some data for this job, so it has fewer details than the other descriptions.

Instructional Programs—Chemical Technology/Technician.

Related DOT Jobs—521.685-190 Ion Exchange Operator; 546.385-010 Gas Treater; 551.465-010 Purification-Operator Helper; 551.585-018 Pan Helper; 551.685-094 Lye Treater; 553.685-026 Cadmium-Liquor Maker; 558.385-010 Cd-Reactor Operator; 558.385-014 Tower Helper; 558.485-010 Caustic Operator; 558.565-010 Acid-Plant Helper; 558.585-010 Catalytic-Converter-Operator Helper; 558.585-018 Contact-Acid-Plant Operator; 558.585-022 Cuprous-Chloride Helper; 558.585-026 Devulcanizer Tender; 558.585-034 Neutralizer; 558.585-042 Twitchell Operator; 558.685-010 Acid-Polymerization Operator; 558.685-014 Ball-Mill Operator; 558.685-030 Ion-Exchange Operator; 558.685-034 Ion-Exchange Operator; others.

51-9011.01 Chemical Equipment Controllers and Operators

- **Education/Training Required: Moderate-term on-the-job training**
- **Employed: No data available.**
- **Annual Earnings: $36,810**
- **Growth: 14.9%**
- **Annual Job Openings: 9,000**

Control or operate equipment to control chemical changes or reactions in the processing of industrial or consumer products. Typical equipment used are reaction kettles, catalytic converters, continuous or batch-treating equipment, saturator tanks, electrolytic cells, reactor vessels, recovery units, and fermentation chambers.

Sets and adjusts indicating, controlling, or timing devices, such as gauging instruments, thermostat, gas analyzers, or recording calorimeter. Starts pumps, agitators, reactors, blowers, or automatic feed of materials. Opens valves or operates pumps to admit or drain specified amounts of materials, impurities, or treating agents to or from equipment. Moves controls to adjust feed and flow of liquids and gases through equipment in specified sequence. Adjusts controls to regulate temperature, pressure, and time of prescribed reaction according to knowledge of equipment and process.

Monitors gauges, recording instruments, flowmeters, or product to regulate or maintain specified conditions. Operates or tends auxiliary equipment, such as heaters, scrubbers, filters, or driers, to prepare or further process materials. Mixes chemicals according to proportion tables or prescribed formulas. Adds treating or neutralizing agent to product and pumps product through filter or centrifuge to remove impurities or precipitate product. Dumps or scoops prescribed solid, granular, or powdered materials into equipment. Reads plant specifications to ascertain product, ingredient, and prescribed modifications of plant procedures. Weighs or measures specified amounts of materials. Patrols and inspects equipment or unit to detect leaks and malfunctions. Tests sample for specific gravity, chemical characteristics, pH level, concentration, or viscosity. Draws samples of product and sends to laboratory for analysis. Flushes or cleans equipment, using steamhose or mechanical reamer. Records operational data such as temperature, pressure, ingredients used, processing time, or test results, in operating log. Makes minor repairs and lubricates and maintains equipment, using hand tools. Directs activities of workers assisting in control or verification of process or in unloading materials.

GOE INFORMATION—Interest Area: 08. Industrial Production. **Work Group:** 08.03. Production Work. **Personality Type**—Realistic. Realistic occupations frequently involve work activities that include practical, hands-on problems and solutions. They often deal with plants, animals, and real-world materials like wood, tools, and machinery. Many of the occupations require working outside and do not involve a lot of paperwork or working closely with others. **Work Values**—Supervision, Technical; Moral Values; Company Policies and Practices; Supervision, Human Relations; Advancement. **Skills**—Operation Monitoring; Operation and Control; Quality Control Analysis; Science; Repairing; Management of Personnel Resources; Equipment Selection; Mathematics. **Abilities**—*Cognitive:* Information Ordering; Selective Attention; Perceptual Speed; Oral Expression; Written Comprehension. *Psychomotor:* Reaction Time; Control Precision; Response Orientation; Finger Dexterity; Arm-Hand Steadiness. *Physical:* Gross Body Equilibrium; Extent Flexibility; Stamina; Dynamic Strength; Static Strength. *Sensory:* Sound Localization; Visual Color Discrimination; Hearing Sensitivity; Peripheral Vision; Night Vision. **General Work Activities**—*Information Input:* Inspecting Equipment, Structures, or Materials; Monitoring Processes, Materials, or Surroundings; Identifying Objects, Actions, and Events. *Mental Process:* Updating and Using Relevant Knowledge; Making Decisions and Solving Problems; Evaluating Information Against Standards. *Work Output:* Controlling Machines and Processes; Handling and Moving Objects; Repairing and Maintaining Mechanical Equipment. *Interacting with Others:* Coordinating the Work and Activities of Others; Communicating with Other Workers; Establishing and Maintaining Relationships. **Physical Work Conditions**—Hazardous Conditions; Common Protective or Safety Attire; Minor Burns, Cuts, Bites, or Stings; Hazardous Equipment; Using Hands on Objects, Tools, or Controls. **Other Job Characteristics**—Degree of Automation; Pace Determined by Speed of Equipment; Consequence of Error.

Experience—Job Zone 2. Some previous work-related skill, knowledge, or experience may be helpful, but usually is not needed. **Job Preparation:** SVP 4.0 to less than 6.0—six months to less than two years. **Knowledge**—Chemistry; Mechanical; Public Safety and Security; Production and Processing; Engineering and Technology. **Instructional Programs**—Chemical Technology/Technician.

Related DOT Jobs—No related DOT jobs.

51-9011.02 Chemical Equipment Tenders

- **Education/Training Required: Moderate-term on-the-job training**
- **Employed: No data available.**
- **Annual Earnings: $36,810**
- **Growth: 14.9%**
- **Annual Job Openings: 9,000**

Tend equipment in which a chemical change or reaction takes place in the processing of industrial or consumer products. Typical equipment used are devulcanizers, batch stills, fermenting tanks, steam-jacketed kettles, and reactor vessels.

Starts pumps and agitators, turns valves, or moves controls of processing equipment to admit, transfer, filter, or mix chemicals. Adjusts valves or controls to maintain system within specified operating conditions. Observes gauges, meters, and panel lights to monitor operating conditions, such as temperature or pressure. Loads specified amounts of chemicals into processing equipment. Patrols work area to detect leaks and equipment malfunctions and monitor operating conditions. Weighs, measures, or mixes prescribed quantities of materials. Drains equipment and pumps water or other solution through to flush and clean tanks or equipment. Draws sample of products for analysis to aid in process adjustments and maintain production standards. Replaces filtering media or makes minor repairs to equipment, using hand tools. Tests samples to determine specific gravity, composition, or acidity, using chemical test equipment such as hydrometer or pH meter. Records data in log from instruments and gauges concerning temperature, pressure, materials used, treating time, and shift production. Notifies maintenance engineer of equipment malfunction. Observes safety precautions to prevent fires and explosions. Assists other workers in preparing and maintaining equipment. Inventories supplies received and consumed.

GOE INFORMATION—Interest Area: 08. Industrial Production. **Work Group:** 08.03. Production Work. **Personality Type—**Realistic. Realistic occupations frequently involve work activities that include practical, hands-on problems and solutions. They often deal with plants, animals, and real-world materials like wood, tools, and machinery. Many of the occupations require working outside and do not involve a lot of paperwork or working closely with others. **Work Values—**Moral Values; Supervision, Technical; Advancement; Company Policies and Practices; Supervision, Human Relations. **Skills—**Operation Monitoring; Operation and Control; Repairing; Quality Control Analysis; Science; Troubleshooting. **Abilities—***Cognitive:* Selective Attention; Problem Sensitivity; Information Ordering; Flexibility of Closure; Spatial Orientation. *Psychomotor:* Reaction Time; Speed of Limb Movement; Control Precision; Rate Control; Response Orientation. *Physical:* Dynamic Flexibility; Gross Body Equilibrium; Explosive Strength; Dynamic Strength; Stamina. *Sensory:* Sound Localization; Visual Color Discrimination; Speech Recognition; Glare Sensitivity. **General Work Activities—***Information Input:* Monitoring Processes, Materials, or Surroundings; Inspecting Equipment, Structures, or Materials; Getting Information. *Mental Process:* Updating and Using Relevant Knowledge; Processing Information; Evaluating Information Against Standards. *Work Output:* Controlling Machines and Processes; Handling and Moving Objects; Documenting or Recording Information. *Interacting with Others:* Communicating with Other Workers; Assisting and Caring for Others; Establishing and Maintaining Relationships. **Physical Work Conditions—**Hazardous Conditions; Common Protective or Safety Attire; Contaminants; Hazardous Equipment; Specialized Protective or Safety Attire. **Other Job Characteristics—**Degree of Automation; Pace Determined by Speed of Equipment; Importance of Being Exact or Accurate.

Experience—Job Zone 2. Some previous work-related skill, knowledge, or experience may be helpful, but usually is not needed. **Job Preparation:** SVP 4.0 to less than 6.0—six months to less than two years. **Knowledge—**Chemistry; Public Safety and Security; Mechanical; Production and Processing; Clerical. **Instructional Programs—**Chemical Technology/Technician.

Related DOT Jobs—521.685-190 Ion Exchange Operator; 546.385-010 Gas Treater; 551.465-010 Purification-Operator Helper; 551.585-018 Pan Helper; 551.685-094 Lye Treater; 553.685-026 Cadmium-Liquor Maker; 558.385-010 Cd-Reactor Operator; 558.385-014 Tower Helper; 558.485-010 Caustic Operator; 558.565-010 Acid-Plant Helper; 558.585-010 Catalytic-Converter-Operator Helper; 558.585-018 Contact-Acid-Plant Operator; 558.585-022 Cuprous-Chloride Helper; 558.585-026 Devulcanizer Tender; 558.585-034 Neutralizer; 558.585-042 Twitchell Operator; 558.685-010 Acid-Polymerization Operator; 558.685-014 Ball-Mill Operator; 558.685-030 Ion-Exchange Operator; 558.685-034 Ion-Exchange Operator; others.

51-9012.00 Separating, Filtering, Clarifying, Precipitating, and Still Machine Setters, Operators, and Tenders

- **Education/Training Required: Moderate-term on-the-job training**
- **Employed: 38,967**
- **Annual Earnings: $29,210**
- **Growth: 2.2%**
- **Annual Job Openings: 5,000**

Set up, operate, or tend continuous-flow or vat-type equipment; filter presses; shaker screens; centrifuges; condenser tubes; precipitating, fermenting, or evaporating tanks; scrubbing towers; or batch stills. These machines extract, sort, or separate liquids, gases, or solids from other materials to recover a refined product. Includes dairy processing equipment operators.

Starts agitators, shakers, conveyors, pumps, or centrifuge machines; turns valves; or moves controls to admit, drain, filter, mix, or transfer materials. Sets or adjusts machine controls to regulate conditions such as material flow, temperature, and pressure according to specified operating procedures. Monitors material flow and control instruments, such as gauges, indicators, and meters, to ensure optimal processing conditions and results. Dumps, pours, or loads specified amounts of refined or unrefined materials into equipment or containers for further processing or storage. Removes clogs, defects, and impurities from machines, tanks, conveyors, screen, or other processing equipment. Measures or weighs materials to be refined, mixed, transferred, stored, or otherwise processed. Examines samples visually or by hand to verify quality, such as clarity, cleanliness, consistency, dryness, and texture. Inspects machines and equipment for hazards, operating efficiency, mechanical malfunctions, wear, and leaks. Lubricates, connects, installs, replaces, or makes minor adjustments or repairs to hoses, pumps, filters, or screens to maintain processing equipment, using hand tools. Cleans tanks, screens, inflow pipes, and other processing equipment, using hoses, brushes, scrappers, or chemical solutions. Collects samples of material or product for laboratory analysis. Tests samples to determine viscosity, acidity, specific gravity, or degree of concentration, using test equipment such as viscometer, pH meter, and hydrometer. Removes full bags or containers from discharge outlets and replaces them with empty ones. Maintains log of instrument readings, test results, and shift production. Communicates or signals processing instructions to other workers.

GOE INFORMATION—**Interest Area:** 08. Industrial Production. **Work Group:** 08.03. Production Work. **Personality Type**—Realistic. Realistic occupations frequently involve work activities that include practical, hands-on problems and solutions. They often deal with plants, animals, and real-world materials like wood, tools, and machinery. Many of the occupations require working outside and do not involve a lot of paperwork or working closely with others. **Work Values**—Moral Values; Supervision, Technical; Supervision, Human Relations; Company Policies and Practices; Advancement. **Skills**—Operation Monitoring; Repairing; Operation and Control; Quality Control Analysis. **Abilities**—*Cognitive:* Perceptual Speed; Flexibility of Closure; Speed of Closure; Selective Attention. *Psychomotor:* Control Precision; Response Orientation; Wrist-Finger Speed; Reaction Time; Rate Control. *Physical:* Trunk Strength; Static Strength; Stamina; Dynamic Flexibility. *Sensory:* Near Vision; Sound Localization. **General Work Activities**—*Information Input:* Monitoring Processes, Materials, or Surroundings; Identifying Objects, Actions, and Events; Inspecting Equipment, Structures, or Materials. *Mental Process:* Evaluating Information Against Standards; Judging Qualities of Things, Services, or Other People's Work; Updating and Using Relevant Knowledge. *Work Output:* Handling and Moving Objects; Controlling Machines and Processes; Repairing and Maintaining Mechanical Equipment. *Interacting with Others:* Communicating with Other Workers; Performing Administrative Activities; Coordinating the Work and Activities of Others. **Physical Work Conditions**—Contaminants; Common Protective or Safety Attire; Using Hands on Objects, Tools, or Controls; Hazardous Conditions; Making Repetitive Motions. **Other Job Characteristics**—Pace Determined by Speed of Equipment; Degree of Automation; Importance of Repeating Same Tasks.

Experience—Job Zone 1. No previous work-related skill, knowledge, or experience is needed. **Job Preparation:** SVP below 4.0—less than six months. **Knowledge**—Chemistry; Mechanical; Production and Processing; Clerical; Physics. **Instructional Programs**—No data available.

Related DOT Jobs—509.685-050 Scrap Handler; 511.385-010 Zinc-Chloride Operator; 511.462-010 Concentrator Operator; 511.465-010 Top-Precipitator Operator; 511.482-014 Cryolite-Recovery Operator; 511.485-010 Molybdenum-Steamer Operator; 511.485-014 Thickener Operator; 511.562-010 Classifier Operator; 511.565-010 Dewaterer Operator; 511.565-018 Iron-Launder Operator; 511.582-010 Leacher; 511.585-010 Hydrate-Control Tender; 511.662-010 Clarifier Operator; 511.664-010 Bottom-Precipitator Operator; 511.685-010 Amalgamator; 511.685-014 Classifier Tender; 511.685-018 Condenser-Tube Tender; 511.685-026 Flotation Tender; 511.685-030 Kettle Tender II; 511.685-034 Kettle Tender, Platinum and Palladium; others.

51-9021.00 Crushing, Grinding, and Polishing Machine Setters, Operators, and Tenders

- **Education/Training Required: Moderate-term on-the-job training**
- **Employed: 44,353**
- **Annual Earnings: $25,670**
- **Growth: 9.8%**
- **Annual Job Openings: 4,000**

Set up, operate, or tend machines to crush, grind, or polish materials, such as coal, glass, grain, stone, food, or rubber.

Operates or tends machines and equipment that crush, grind, polish, or blend materials. Moves controls to start, stop, or adjust machinery and equipment that crush, grind, polish, or blend materials. Observes production monitoring equipment to ensure safety and efficient operation. Loads materials into machinery and equipment, using hand tools. Adds or mixes chemicals and ingredients for processing, using hand tools or other devices. Dislodges and clears jammed materials or other items from machinery and equipment, using hand tools. Tends accessory equipment, such as pumps and conveyors, to move materials or ingredients through production process. Weighs or measures materials, ingredients, and products to ensure conformance to requirements. Reads work orders to ascertain production specifications and information. Examines or feels materials, ingredients, or products to ensure conformance to established standards. Collects samples of materials or products for laboratory testing. Cleans and maintains machinery, equipment, materials, and products, using hand tools. Tests samples of materials or products to ensure compliance with specifications, using test equipment. Transfers materials, supplies, and products between work areas, using moving equipment and hand tools. Records operational and production data on specified forms.

GOE INFORMATION—**Interest Area:** 08. Industrial Production. **Work Group:** 08.03. Production Work. **Personality Type**—Realistic. Realistic occupations frequently involve work activities that include practical, hands-on problems and solutions. They often deal with plants, animals, and real-world materials like wood, tools, and machinery. Many of the occupations require working outside and do not involve a lot of paperwork or working closely with others. **Work Values**—Moral Values; Supervision, Technical; Independence; Supervision, Human Relations; Company Policies and Practices. **Skills**—Operation Monitoring; Operation and Control; Quality Control Analysis. **Abilities**—*Cognitive:* Perceptual Speed. *Psychomotor:* Control Precision; Reaction Time; Rate Control; Speed of Limb Movement; Manual Dexterity. *Physical:* Static Strength; Explosive Strength; Dynamic Flexibility; Dynamic Strength; Stamina. *Sensory:* Sound Localization. **General Work Activities**—*Information Input:* Inspecting Equipment, Structures, or Materials; Monitoring Processes, Materials, or Surroundings; Identifying Objects, Actions, and Events. *Mental Process:* Evaluating Information Against Standards; Judging Qualities of Things, Services, or Other People's Work; Updating and Using Relevant Knowledge. *Work Output:* Handling and Moving Objects; Controlling Machines and Processes; Performing General Physical Activities. *Interacting with Others:* Communicating with Other Workers; Establishing and Maintaining Relationships; Interpreting Meaning of Information for Others. **Physical Work Conditions**—Common Protective or Safety Attire; Hazardous Equipment; Distracting Sounds and Noise Levels; Contaminants; Extremely Bright or Inadequate Lighting. **Other Job Characteristics**—Pace Determined by Speed of Equipment; Degree of Automation; Importance of Repeating Same Tasks.

Experience—Job Zone 1. No previous work-related skill, knowledge, or experience is needed. **Job Preparation:** SVP below 4.0—less than six months. **Knowledge**—Production and Processing; Mechanical; Chemistry; Physics; Food Production. **Instructional Programs**—No data available.

Related DOT Jobs—515.585-010 Scale-Reclamation Tender; 515.685-010 Batch Maker; 515.685-014 Crusher Tender; 515.685-018 Stamping-Mill Tender; 515.687-010 Hammer-Mill Operator; 519.485-010 Grinder-Mill Operator; 519.685-030 Rod-Mill Tender; 521.362-014 Miller, Distillery; 521.585-014 Miller; 521.585-018 Powder-Mill Operator; 521.662-010 Miller, Wet Process; 521.682-022 Flake Miller, Wheat and Oats; 521.682-026 Grinder Operator; 521.682-034 Refining-Machine Operator; 521.685-074 Cocoa-Room Operator; 521.685-078 Coffee Grinder; 521.685-082 Corn Grinder; 521.685-086 Corn-Grinder Operator, Automatic; 521.685-090 Crusher Operator; 521.685-094 Crushing-Machine Operator; others.

51-9022.00 Grinding and Polishing Workers, Hand

- **Education/Training Required:** Moderate-term on-the-job training
- **Employed:** 48,707
- **Annual Earnings:** $22,540
- **Growth:** 13.7%
- **Annual Job Openings:** 5,000

Grind, sand, or polish, using hand tools or hand-held power tools, a variety of metal, wood, stone, clay, plastic, or glass objects.

Grinds, sands, cleans, or polishes objects or parts, using hand tools or equipment. Moves controls to adjust, start, or stop equipment during grinding and polishing process. Trims, scrapes, or deburrs objects or parts, using hand tools or equipment. Selects, loads, and adjusts workpiece or abrasive parts onto equipment or worktable, using hand tools. Observes and inspects equipment, objects, or parts to ensure specifications are met. Measures and marks equipment, objects, or parts to ensure grinding and polishing standards are met. Applies solutions and chemicals to equipment, objects, or parts, using hand tools. Removes workpiece from equipment or worktable, using hand tools. Repairs and maintains equipment, objects, or parts, using hand tools. Sharpens abrasive grinding tools, using machines and hand tools. Transfers equipment, objects, or parts to specified work areas, using moving devices. Records product and processing data on specified forms.

GOE INFORMATION—Interest Area: 08. Industrial Production. **Work Group:** 08.03. Production Work. **Personality Type—**Realistic. Realistic occupations frequently involve work activities that include practical, hands-on problems and solutions. They often deal with plants, animals, and real-world materials like wood, tools, and machinery. Many of the occupations require working outside and do not involve a lot of paperwork or working closely with others. **Work Values—**Moral Values; Supervision, Technical; Independence. **Skills—**Operation Monitoring; Operation and Control; Repairing. **Abilities—***Cognitive:* None met the criteria. *Psychomotor:* Control Precision; Wrist-Finger Speed; Multilimb Coordination; Manual Dexterity. *Physical:* Trunk Strength; Extent Flexibility; Stamina; Dynamic Flexibility; Dynamic Strength. *Sensory:* None met the criteria. **General Work Activities—***Information Input:* Monitoring Processes, Materials, or Surroundings; Inspecting Equipment, Structures, or Materials; Getting Information. *Mental Process:* Evaluating Information Against Standards; Judging Qualities of Things, Services, or Other People's Work; Updating and Using Relevant Knowledge. *Work Output:* Handling and Moving Objects; Performing General Physical Activities; Controlling Machines and Processes. *Interacting with Others:* Communicating with Other Workers; Performing Administrative Activities; Establishing and Maintaining Relationships. **Physical Work Conditions—**Common Protective or Safety Attire; Hazardous Equipment; Distracting Sounds and Noise Levels; Making Repetitive Motions; Contaminants. **Other Job Characteristics—**Importance of Repeating Same Tasks; Pace Determined by Speed of Equipment; Degree of Automation.

Experience—Job Zone 1. No previous work-related skill, knowledge, or experience is needed. **Job Preparation:** SVP below 4.0—less than six months. **Knowledge—**Production and Processing; Chemistry; Mechanical; Physics; Design. **Instructional Programs—**No data available.

Related DOT Jobs—519.684-018 Mold Dresser; 700.684-034 Filer; 700.687-058 Polisher; 703.687-022 Steel-Barrel Reamer; 705.384-010 Scraper, Hand; 705.484-010 Filer, Hand, Tool; 705.484-014 Final Finisher, Forging Dies; 705.684-022 Grease Buffer; 705.684-026 Grinder I; 705.684-030 Grinder-Chipper I; 705.684-034 Metal Finisher; 705.684-038 Mold Finisher; 705.684-046 Needle Polisher; 705.684-050 Nib Finisher; 705.684-054 Pipe Buffer; 705.684-062 Polisher and Buffer II; 705.687-014 Laborer, Grinding and Polishing; 705.687-018 Metal Sander and Finisher; 706.684-098 Valve Grinder; 709.381-026 Mold Stamper and Repairer; others.

51-9023.00 Mixing and Blending Machine Setters, Operators, and Tenders

- **Education/Training Required:** Moderate-term on-the-job training
- **Employed:** 108,628
- **Annual Earnings:** $26,860
- **Growth:** 9.0%
- **Annual Job Openings:** 11,000

Set up, operate, or tend machines to mix or blend materials, such as chemicals, tobacco, liquids, color pigments, or explosive ingredients.

Operates or tends machines and equipment that crush, grind, polish, or blend materials. Moves controls to start, stop, or adjust machinery and equipment that crush, grind, polish, or blend materials. Observes production monitoring equipment to ensure safety and efficient operation. Loads materials into machinery and equipment, using hand tools. Adds or mixes chemicals and ingredients for processing, using hand tools or other devices. Dislodges and clears jammed materials or other items from machinery and equipment, using hand tools. Tends accessory equipment, such as pumps and conveyors, to move materials or ingredients through production process. Weighs or measures materials, ingredients, and products to ensure conformance to requirements. Reads work orders to ascertain production specifications and information. Examines or feels materials, ingredients, or products to ensure conformance to established standards. Collects samples of materials or products for laboratory testing. Cleans and maintains machinery, equipment, materials, and products, using hand tools. Tests samples of materials or products to ensure compliance with specifications, using test equipment. Transfers materials, supplies, and products between work areas, using moving equipment and hand tools. Records operational and production data on specified forms.

GOE INFORMATION—Interest Area: 08. Industrial Production. **Work Group:** 08.03. Production Work. **Personality Type—**Realistic. Realistic occupations frequently involve work activities that include practical, hands-on problems and solutions. They often deal with plants, animals, and real-world materials like wood, tools, and machinery. Many of the occupations require working outside and do not involve a lot of paperwork or working closely with others. **Work Values—**Moral Values; Supervision, Technical; Independence; Supervision, Human Relations; Company Policies and Practices. **Skills—**Operation Monitoring; Operation and Control; Quality Control Analysis. **Abilities—***Cognitive:* Perceptual Speed. *Psychomotor:* Control Precision; Reaction Time; Rate Control; Speed of Limb Movement; Manual Dexterity. *Physical:* Static Strength; Explosive Strength; Dynamic Flexibility; Dynamic Strength; Stamina. *Sensory:* Sound Localization. **General Work Activities—***Information Input:* Inspecting Equipment, Structures, or Materials; Monitoring Processes, Materials, or Surroundings; Identifying Objects, Actions, and Events. *Mental Process:* Evaluating Information Against Standards; Judging Qualities of Things, Services, or Other People's Work; Updating and Using Relevant Knowledge. *Work Output:* Performing General Physical Activities; Handling and Moving Objects; Controlling Machines and Processes. *Interacting with Others:* Communicating with Other Workers; Establishing and Maintaining Relationships; Interpreting Meaning of Information for Others. **Physical Work Conditions—**Common Protective or Safety Attire; Hazardous Equipment; Distracting Sounds and

Noise Levels; Contaminants; Extremely Bright or Inadequate Lighting. **Other Job Characteristics**—Pace Determined by Speed of Equipment; Degree of Automation; Importance of Repeating Same Tasks.

Experience—Job Zone 1. No previous work-related skill, knowledge, or experience is needed. **Job Preparation:** SVP below 4.0—less than six months. **Knowledge**—Production and Processing; Mechanical; Chemistry; Physics; Food Production. **Instructional Programs**—Agricultural and Food Products Processing.

Related DOT Jobs—510.465-010 Carbide-Powder Processor; 510.465-014 Slurry-Control Tender; 510.685-010 Dust Mixer; 510.685-014 Mix-House Tender; 510.685-018 Mixer; 510.685-022 Pug-Mill Operator; 510.685-026 Sinter-Machine Operator; 510.685-030 Slime-Plant Operator I; 511.685-046 Reagent Tender; 514.685-022 Lime Mixer Tender; 519.685-026 Mud-Mill Tender; 520.362-010 Bulk-Plant Operator; 520.362-014 Dry-Starch Operator; 520.382-010 Cistern-Room Operator; 520.382-014 Liquid-Sugar Melter; 520.385-010 Mixer, Whipped Topping; 520.462-010 Dough-Mixer Operator; 520.485-010 Flour Mixer; 520.485-014 Grain Mixer; 520.485-022 Refined-Syrup Operator; others.

51-9031.00 Cutters and Trimmers, Hand

- **Education/Training Required: Short-term on-the-job training**
- **Employed: 32,399**
- **Annual Earnings: $21,760**
- **Growth: 2.2%**
- **Annual Job Openings: 6,000**

Use hand tools or hand-held power tools to cut and trim a variety of manufactured items, such as carpet, fabric, stone, glass, or rubber.

Cuts materials, such as textiles, food, and metal, using hand tools, portable power tools, or bench-mounted tools. Lowers table-mounted cutter, such as knife blade, cutting wheel, or saw, to cut items to specified size. Adjusts guides and stops to control depth and width of cuts. Routes items to provide cutouts for parts, using portable router, grinder, and hand tools. Positions template or measures material to locate specified point of cut or to obtain maximum yield, using rule, scale, or pattern. Marks cutting lines around pattern or template or follows layout points, using square, rule, straightedge and chalk, pencil, or scribe. Reads work order to determine dimensions, cutting locations, and quantity to cut. Unrolls, lays out, attaches, or mounts material or item on cutting table or machine. Folds or shapes materials preparatory to or after cutting. Observes and marks or discards items with defects, such as spots, stains, scars, snags, chips, scratches, or unacceptable shape or finish. Marks identification numbers, trademark, grade, marketing data, size, or model number on products. Replaces or sharpens dulled cutting tools, such as saws. Separates materials or products according to size, weight, type, condition, color, or shade. Stacks cut items and loads them on racks, on conveyors, or onto truck. Cleans, treats, buffs, or polishes finished items, using grinder, brush, chisel, and cleaning solutions and polishing materials. Counts or weighs and bundles items. Transports items to work or storage area by pushing or pulling carts.

GOE INFORMATION—**Interest Area:** 08. Industrial Production. **Work Group:** 08.03. Production Work. **Personality Type**—Realistic. Realistic occupations frequently involve work activities that include practical, hands-on problems and solutions. They often deal with plants, animals, and real-world materials like wood, tools, and machinery. Many of the occupations require working outside and do not involve a lot of paperwork or working closely with others. **Work Values**—Independence; Moral Values; Supervision, Technical. **Skills**—None met the criteria. **Abilities**—*Cognitive:* Visualization; Number Facility; Category Flexibility. *Psychomotor:* Manual Dexterity; Wrist-Finger Speed; Speed of Limb Movement;

Arm-Hand Steadiness; Control Precision. *Physical:* Trunk Strength; Static Strength; Dynamic Flexibility; Dynamic Strength; Extent Flexibility. *Sensory:* Visual Color Discrimination. **General Work Activities**—*Information Input:* Getting Information; Monitoring Processes, Materials, or Surroundings; Identifying Objects, Actions, and Events. *Mental Process:* Evaluating Information Against Standards; Judging Qualities of Things, Services, or Other People's Work; Processing Information. *Work Output:* Handling and Moving Objects; Performing General Physical Activities; Controlling Machines and Processes. *Interacting with Others:* Communicating with Other Workers; Monitoring and Controlling Resources; Performing Administrative Activities. **Physical Work Conditions**—Hazardous Equipment; Minor Burns, Cuts, Bites, or Stings; Using Hands on Objects, Tools, or Controls; Common Protective or Safety Attire; Making Repetitive Motions. **Other Job Characteristics**—Importance of Repeating Same Tasks; Importance of Being Exact or Accurate; Pace Determined by Speed of Equipment.

Experience—Job Zone 1. No previous work-related skill, knowledge, or experience is needed. **Job Preparation:** SVP below 4.0—less than six months. **Knowledge**—Production and Processing; Building and Construction; Mechanical; Fine Arts; Physics. **Instructional Programs**—No data available.

Related DOT Jobs—521.687-014 Binder Cutter, Hand; 521.687-026 Bunch Trimmer, Mold; 521.687-066 Fruit Cutter; 524.687-010 Cherry Cutter; 525.687-046 Hide Trimmer; 539.686-010 Cutter, Wet Machine; 569.684-010 Log Peeler; 569.687-026 Wood Hacker; 575.684-022 Crosscutter, Rolled Glass; 579.684-030 Cutter; 585.684-010 Trimmer, Hand; 590.687-022 Rug Cutter; 673.666-014 Stripper; 689.687-090 Lapper; 700.684-018 Bright Cutter; 700.684-038 Gold Cutter; 700.684-050 Mesh Cutter; 701.687-030 Power-Chisel Operator; 703.684-018 Template Cutter; 709.684-074 Shearer and Trimmer, Wire Screen and Fabric; others.

51-9032.00 Cutting and Slicing Machine Setters, Operators, and Tenders

- **Education/Training Required: Moderate-term on-the-job training**
- **Employed: 82,725**
- **Annual Earnings: $24,940**
- **Growth: 1.7%**
- **Annual Job Openings: 16,000**

Set up, operate, or tend machines that cut or slice materials, such as glass, stone, cork, rubber, tobacco, food, paper, or insulating material.

No task data available.

GOE INFORMATION—**Interest Area:** 08. Industrial Production. **Work Group:** 08.03. Production Work. **Note:** The Department of Labor has not collected some data for this job, so it has fewer details than the other descriptions.

Instructional Programs—No data available.

Related DOT Jobs—520.682-022 Gum-Scoring-Machine Operator; 521.685-018 Almond-Cutting-Machine Tender; 521.685-098 Cutter, Frozen Meat; 521.685-102 Cutting-Machine Operator; 521.685-158 Granulating-Machine Operator; 521.685-170 Hasher Operator; 521.685-298 Slice-Plug-Cutter Operator; 521.685-302 Slicing-Machine Operator; 521.685-306 Slicing-Machine Operator; 521.685-310 Smoking-Tobacco-Cutter Operator; 521.685-338 Strip-Cutting-Machine Operator; 521.685-342 Stripper-Cutter, Machine; 521.685-354 Sugar-Chipper-Machine Operator; 521.685-386 Scaling Machine Operator; 525.685-010 Band-Saw

Operator; 529.585-010 Cheese Cutter; 529.685-018 Binder Layer; 529.685-082 Cutter; 529.685-090 Defective-Cigarette Slitter; 529.685-110 Filler Shredder, Machine; others.

51-9032.01 Fiber Product Cutting Machine Setters and Set-Up Operators

- **Education/Training Required: Moderate-term on-the-job training**
- **Employed: No data available.**
- **Annual Earnings: $24,940**
- **Growth: 1.7%**
- **Annual Job Openings: 16,000**

Set up and operate machine to cut or slice fiber material, such as paper, wallboard, and insulation material.

Adjusts machine controls to position and align and to regulate speed and pressure of components. Activates machine to cut, slice, slit, perforate, or score fiber products, such as paperboard sheets, rubber shoe soles, or plaster wallboard. Selects and installs machine components, such as cutting blades, rollers, and templates, according to specifications, using hand tools. Monitors operation of cutting or slicing machine to detect malfunctions, removes defective or substandard materials, and readjusts machine components to conform to standards. Reviews work order, blueprints, specifications, or job sample to determine components, settings, and adjustments for cutting and slicing machines. Positions materials such as rubber, paper, or leather on feeding mechanism of cutting or slicing machine. Examines, measures, and weighs materials or products to verify conformance to specifications, using measuring devices such as ruler, micrometer, or scale. Replaces worn or broken parts, and cleans and lubricates cutting or slicing machine to maintain equipment in working order. Removes completed materials or products from cutting or slicing machine and stacks or stores for additional processing. Maintains production records, such as quantity, type, and dimensions of materials produced.

GOE INFORMATION—Interest Area: 08. Industrial Production. **Work Group:** 08.03. Production Work. **Personality Type—**Realistic. Realistic occupations frequently involve work activities that include practical, hands-on problems and solutions. They often deal with plants, animals, and real-world materials like wood, tools, and machinery. Many of the occupations require working outside and do not involve a lot of paperwork or working closely with others. **Work Values—**Moral Values; Supervision, Technical; Independence; Activity; Supervision, Human Relations. **Skills—**Operation and Control; Operation Monitoring; Repairing. **Abilities—***Cognitive:* Perceptual Speed; Visualization; Selective Attention; Spatial Orientation; Flexibility of Closure. *Psychomotor:* Rate Control; Control Precision; Reaction Time; Manual Dexterity; Multilimb Coordination. *Physical:* Explosive Strength; Static Strength; Dynamic Flexibility; Dynamic Strength; Extent Flexibility. *Sensory:* Depth Perception; Peripheral Vision; Far Vision. **General Work Activities—***Information Input:* Inspecting Equipment, Structures, or Materials; Monitoring Processes, Materials, or Surroundings; Getting Information. *Mental Process:* Judging Qualities of Things, Services, or Other People's Work; Updating and Using Relevant Knowledge; Evaluating Information Against Standards. *Work Output:* Handling and Moving Objects; Controlling Machines and Processes; Performing General Physical Activities. *Interacting with Others:* Communicating with Other Workers; Performing Administrative Activities; Establishing and Maintaining Relationships. **Physical Work Conditions—**Hazardous Equipment; Minor Burns, Cuts, Bites, or Stings; Distracting Sounds and Noise Levels; Using Hands on Objects, Tools, or Controls; Indoors. **Other Job Characteristics—**Degree of Automation; Pace Determined by Speed of Equipment; Importance of Repeating Same Tasks.

Experience—Job Zone 2. Some previous work-related skill, knowledge, or experience may be helpful, but usually is not needed. **Job Preparation:** SVP 4.0 to less than 6.0—six months to less than two years. **Knowledge—**Production and Processing; Mechanical; Design; Building and Construction; Clerical. **Instructional Programs—**No data available.

Related DOT Jobs—579.382-018 Knife Operator; 640.360-010 Panel-Machine Setter; 640.682-018 Cutting-Machine Operator; 649.682-026 Platen-Press Operator; 649.682-038 Slitter-Scorer-Cut-Off Operator; 649.682-042 Tablet-Making-Machine Operator; 677.382-010 Batting-Machine Operator, Insulation; 677.682-026 Tenoner Operator; 690.462-010 Outsole Cutter, Automatic; 690.682-010 Arch-Cushion-Skiving-Machine Operator; 690.682-038 Foxing-Cutting-Machine Operator, Automatic; 690.682-042 Heel Breaster, Leather; 690.682-046 Heel-Seat Fitter, Machine; 690.682-050 Hot-Die-Press Operator; 692.360-014 Brush-Machine Setter; 699.382-010 Fluid Jet Cutter Operator.

51-9032.02 Stone Sawyers

- **Education/Training Required: Moderate-term on-the-job training**
- **Employed: No data available.**
- **Annual Earnings: $24,940**
- **Growth: 1.7%**
- **Annual Job Openings: 16,000**

Set up and operate gang saws, reciprocating saws, circular saws, or wire saws to cut blocks of stone into specified dimensions.

Changes or replaces saw blades, cables, and grinding wheels, using wrench. Turns crank or presses button to move car under sawing cable or saw frame. Aligns cable or blades with marks on stone and presses button or turns lever to lower sawing cable or blades to stone. Observes operation to detect uneven sawing and exhausted abrasive supply and tightens pulleys or adds abrasive to maintain cutting speed. Marks dimensions or traces on stone according to diagram, using chisel and hammer, straightedge, rule, and chalked string. Builds bed of timbers on car and aligns and levels stone on bed, using crowbar, sledgehammer, wedges, blocks, rule, and spirit level. Washes stone, using water hose, and verifies width or thickness of cut stone, using rule. Operates crane or signals crane operator to position or remove stone from car or saw bed. Starts saw and moves blade across surface of material, such as stone, concrete slabs, and asbestos-cement sheets and pipes, to saw. Adjusts blade pressure against stone, using ammeter, and lowers blade in stone as cut depth increases. Starts pump to circulate water and abrasive onto blade or cable during cutting.

GOE INFORMATION—Interest Area: 08. Industrial Production. **Work Group:** 08.03. Production Work. **Personality Type—**Realistic. Realistic occupations frequently involve work activities that include practical, hands-on problems and solutions. They often deal with plants, animals, and real-world materials like wood, tools, and machinery. Many of the occupations require working outside and do not involve a lot of paperwork or working closely with others. **Work Values—**Moral Values; Supervision, Technical; Company Policies and Practices; Activity; Independence. **Skills—**Operation Monitoring; Operation and Control; Equipment Selection. **Abilities—***Cognitive:* Spatial Orientation; Selective Attention; Problem Sensitivity; Visualization; Time Sharing. *Psychomotor:* Control Precision; Reaction Time; Rate Control; Multilimb Coordination; Speed of Limb Movement. *Physical:* Stamina; Explosive Strength; Dynamic Strength; Static Strength; Gross Body Coordination. *Sensory:* Depth Perception; Peripheral Vision; Hearing Sensitivity; Sound Localization; Glare Sensitivity. **General Work Activities—***Information Input:* Monitoring Processes, Materials, or Surroundings; Inspecting Equipment, Structures, or Materials; Identifying Objects, Actions, and Events. *Mental Process:* Evaluating Information Against Standards; Judging Qualities of Things, Services, or Other People's Work; Updating and Using Relevant Knowledge. *Work Output:* Handling and Moving Objects; Controlling Machines and Processes; Performing General Physical Activities. *Interacting with Others:* Communicating with Other Workers; Coordinating the Work and Activities of Others; Assisting and Caring for Others. **Physical Work Conditions**—Hazardous Equipment; Distracting Sounds and Noise Levels; Common Protective or Safety Attire; Contaminants; Minor Burns, Cuts, Bites, or Stings. **Other Job Characteristics**—Degree of Automation; Pace Determined by Speed of Equipment; Importance of Repeating Same Tasks.

Experience—Job Zone 2. Some previous work-related skill, knowledge, or experience may be helpful, but usually is not needed. **Job Preparation:** SVP 4.0 to less than 6.0–six months to less than two years. **Knowledge**—Mechanical; Building and Construction; Production and Processing; Physics; Design. **Instructional Programs**—No data available.

Related DOT Jobs—670.362-010 Gang Sawyer, Stone; 677.462-010 Circular Sawyer, Stone; 677.462-014 Wire Sawyer.

51-9032.03 Glass Cutting Machine Setters and Set-Up Operators

- **Education/Training Required: Short-term on-the-job training**
- **Employed: No data available.**
- **Annual Earnings: $24,940**
- **Growth: 1.7%**
- **Annual Job Openings: 16,000**

Set up and operate machines to cut glass.

Operates single cut machine to cut glass. Starts machine to verify setup. Adjusts position, height, and stroke of cutting bridges, manually or by turning controls, to score glass to specific dimensions. Adjusts timing mechanism to synchronize breaker bar to snap glass at score. Removes and replaces worn cutter heads, using hand tools. Starts vacuum-cupped crane to lift and transfer glass. Measures glass with tape to verify dimensions and observes glass to detect defects. Reviews work order and maintains record of production, using counter. Directs workers on cutting team.

GOE INFORMATION—Interest Area: 08. Industrial Production. **Work Group:** 08.03. Production Work. **Personality Type**—Realistic. Realistic occupations frequently involve work activities that include practical, hands-on problems and solutions. They often deal with plants, animals, and real-world materials like wood, tools, and machinery. Many of the occupations require working outside and do not involve a lot of paperwork or working closely with others. **Work Values**—Authority; Supervision, Technical; Moral Values; Pleasant Co-workers; Activity. **Skills**—Operation and Control; Operation Monitoring. **Abilities**—*Cognitive:* Perceptual Speed; Visualization; Memorization. *Psychomotor:* Arm-Hand Steadiness; Rate Control; Manual Dexterity; Control Precision; Reaction Time. *Physical:* Explosive Strength; Dynamic Flexibility; Dynamic Strength; Extent Flexibility; Trunk Strength. *Sensory:* Depth Perception; Visual Color Discrimination; Far Vision; Speech Recognition; Sound Localization. **General Work Activities**—*Information Input:* Monitoring Processes, Materials, or Surroundings; Inspecting Equipment, Structures, or Materials; Getting Information. *Mental Process:* Judging Qualities of Things, Services, or Other People's Work; Evaluating Information Against Standards; Analyzing Data or Information. *Work Output:* Handling and Moving Objects; Controlling Machines and Processes; Repairing and Maintaining Mechanical Equipment. *Interacting with Others:* Guiding, Directing, and Motivating Subordinates; Communicating with

Other Workers; Coordinating the Work and Activities of Others. **Physical Work Conditions**—Hazardous Equipment; Minor Burns, Cuts, Bites, or Stings; Using Hands on Objects, Tools, or Controls; Distracting Sounds and Noise Levels; Common Protective or Safety Attire. **Other Job Characteristics**—Degree of Automation; Pace Determined by Speed of Equipment; Importance of Repeating Same Tasks.

Experience—Job Zone 1. No previous work-related skill, knowledge, or experience is needed. **Job Preparation:** SVP below 4.0—less than six months. **Knowledge**—Production and Processing; Mechanical; Medicine and Dentistry; Philosophy and Theology. **Instructional Programs**—No data available.

Related DOT Jobs—677.562-010 Glass-Cutting-Machine Operator, Automatic.

51-9032.04 Cutting and Slicing Machine Operators and Tenders

- **Education/Training Required: Short-term on-the-job training**
- **Employed: No data available.**
- **Annual Earnings: $24,940**
- **Growth: 1.7%**
- **Annual Job Openings: 16,000**

Operate or tend machines to cut or slice any of a wide variety of products or materials, such as tobacco, food, paper, roofing slate, glass, stone, rubber, cork, and insulating material.

Starts cutting machine by pressing button, pulling lever, or depressing pedal to cut stock, following markings or specifications. Stops cutting machine when necessary, by pulling lever, pressing button, or depressing pedal, and removes debris. Adjusts feeding guides, blades, settings, or speed to regulate specified depth, length, or width of material, using hand tools or hands. Observes cutting machine in operation to ensure even flow of stock and to detect jamming, improper feeding, or foreign materials. Reads work order or receives oral instructions regarding specifications for stock to be cut. Feeds stock into cutting machine, into conveyor, or under cutting blades by threading, guiding, pushing, or turning handwheel. Positions stock along cutting lines or against stops on bed of scoring or cutting machine. Marks cutting lines or identifying information on stock, using marking pencil, ruler, or scribe. Installs or replaces cutting knives, blades, or wheels in cutting machine using hand tools. Examines and measures stock to ensure conformance to specifications, using ruler, gauge, micrometer or scale, and removes defects. Sharpens cutting blades, knives, or saws, using file, bench grinder, or honing stone. Cuts stock manually to prepare for machine cutting, using tools such as knife, cleaver, handsaw, or hammer and chisel. Cleans and lubricates cutting machine, conveyors, blades, saws, or knives, using steam hose, scrapers, brush, or oilcans. Records data concerning amount and type of stock cut from duties performed, including weight, length, and width. Moves stock or scrap to and from machine, transporting either manually or using cart, handtruck, or lift truck. Stacks and sorts cut material according to type and size for packaging, further processing, or shipping.

GOE INFORMATION—Interest Area: 08. Industrial Production. **Work Group:** 08.03. Production Work. **Personality Type**—Realistic. Realistic occupations frequently involve work activities that include practical, hands-on problems and solutions. They often deal with plants, animals, and real-world materials like wood, tools, and machinery. Many of the occupations require working outside and do not involve a lot of paperwork or working closely with others. **Work Values**—Moral Values; Supervision, Technical; Independence; Activity; Supervision, Human Relations.

Skills—Operation Monitoring; Operation and Control; Installation. **Abilities**—*Cognitive:* Perceptual Speed. *Psychomotor:* Reaction Time; Arm-Hand Steadiness; Rate Control; Control Precision; Manual Dexterity. *Physical:* Extent Flexibility; Explosive Strength; Static Strength; Dynamic Strength; Dynamic Flexibility. *Sensory:* None met the criteria. **General Work Activities**—*Information Input:* Monitoring Processes, Materials, or Surroundings; Inspecting Equipment, Structures, or Materials; Getting Information. *Mental Process:* Evaluating Information Against Standards; Judging Qualities of Things, Services, or Other People's Work; Updating and Using Relevant Knowledge. *Work Output:* Handling and Moving Objects; Controlling Machines and Processes; Performing General Physical Activities. *Interacting with Others:* Establishing and Maintaining Relationships; Communicating with Other Workers; Coordinating the Work and Activities of Others. **Physical Work Conditions**—Hazardous Equipment; Minor Burns, Cuts, Bites, or Stings; Common Protective or Safety Attire; Using Hands on Objects, Tools, or Controls; Indoors. **Other Job Characteristics**—Pace Determined by Speed of Equipment; Importance of Repeating Same Tasks; Degree of Automation.

Experience—Job Zone 1. No previous work-related skill, knowledge, or experience is needed. **Job Preparation:** SVP below 4.0—less than six months. **Knowledge**—Production and Processing; Food Production; Design; Mechanical; Physics. **Instructional Programs**—No data available.

Related DOT Jobs—520.682-022 Gum-Scoring-Machine Operator; 521.685-018 Almond-Cutting-Machine Tender; 521.685-098 Cutter, Frozen Meat; 521.685-102 Cutting-Machine Operator; 521.685-158 Granulating-Machine Operator; 521.685-170 Hasher Operator; 521.685-298 Slice-Plug-Cutter Operator; 521.685-302 Slicing-Machine Operator; 521.685-306 Slicing-Machine Operator; 521.685-310 Smoking-Tobacco-Cutter Operator; 521.685-338 Strip-Cutting-Machine Operator; 521.685-342 Stripper-Cutter, Machine; 521.685-354 Sugar-Chipper-Machine Operator; 521.685-386 Scaling Machine Operator; 525.685-010 Band-Saw Operator; 529.585-010 Cheese Cutter; 529.685-018 Binder Layer; 529.685-082 Cutter; 529.685-090 Defective-Cigarette Slitter; 529.685-110 Filler Shredder, Machine; others.

51-9041.00 Extruding, Forming, Pressing, and Compacting Machine Setters, Operators, and Tenders

- **Education/Training Required: Short-term on-the-job training**
- **Employed: 73,428**
- **Annual Earnings: $25,790**
- **Growth: 9.0%**
- **Annual Job Openings: 12,000**

Set up, operate, or tend machines, such as glass-forming machines, plodder machines, and tuber machines, to shape and form products such as glassware, food, rubber, soap, brick, tile, clay, wax, tobacco, or cosmetics.

No task data available.

GOE INFORMATION—Interest Area: 08. Industrial Production. **Work Group:** 08.02. Production Technology. **Note:** The Department of Labor has not collected some data for this job, so it has fewer details than the other descriptions.

Instructional Programs—No data available.

Related DOT Jobs—520.682-014 Center-Machine Operator; 520.682-030 Spinner; 520.682-034 Cracker-and-Cookie-Machine Operator; 520.685-038 Cake Former; 520.685-058 Casting-Machine Operator; 520.685-062 Casting-Machine Operator; 520.685-078 Confectionery-Drops-Machine Operator; 520.685-086 Dividing-Machine Operator; 520.685-102 Flaking-Roll Operator; 520.685-178 Pellet-Mill Operator; 520.685-182 Press Operator, Meat; 520.685-186 Press Tender; 520.685-190 Pretzel-Twisting-Machine Operator; 520.685-198 Rolling-Machine Operator; 520.685-214 Sweet-Goods-Machine Operator; 521.685-330 Stem-Roller-or-Crusher Operator; 521.685-350 Sugar Presser; 529.682-026 Lozenge Maker; 529.685-014 Automatic Lump Making Machine Tender; 529.685-042 Butt Maker; others.

51-9041.01 Extruding, Forming, Pressing, and Compacting Machine Setters and Set-Up Operators

- **Education/Training Required: Moderate-term on-the-job training**
- **Employed: No data available.**
- **Annual Earnings: $25,790**
- **Growth: 9.0%**
- **Annual Job Openings: 12,000**

Set up or set up and operate machines, such as glass forming machines, plodder machines, and tuber machines, to manufacture any of a wide variety of products, such as soap bars, formed rubber, glassware, food, brick, and tile, by means of extruding, compressing, or compacting.

Installs dies or molds in machines to produce products from variety of materials according to work order and specifications. Turns controls to control machine functions, such as regulate air pressure and create vacuum and coolant flow. Operates machines and notifies supervisor or setup personnel of needed adjustments to machines. Observes operation of machine and product to detect and diagnose cause of faulty operation and monitors gauges and recorders. Presses control button to activate machinery and equipment. Synchronizes speed of sections of machine when producing products involving several steps or processes. Selects and measures arbors and dies to verify size specified on work ticket. Installs, aligns, and adjusts neck rings, press plungers, and feeder tubes to molds to deliver material and form product. Couples air and gas lines to machine to maintain plasticity of material and to regulate solidification of final product. Adjusts timer drum to set size of product material and rollers, cutoff knives, and stops to regulate thickness and length. Threads extruded strip through water tank and holddown bars or attaches strands to wire and draws through tube. Pours, scoops, or dumps specified ingredients, metal assemblies, or mixtures into sections of machine prior to starting machine. Feeds product into machine by hand or conveyor. Ignites burner to preheat product or applies heat, using torch. Removes products from discharge belts and molds, mold components, and feeder tubes from machines. Cleans dies, arbors, compression chambers, and molds, using swabs, sponge, or air hose, and swabs molds with solution to prevent sticking. Collects, examines, measures, weighs, and tests product to verify machine setup and conformance of product to specifications. Records product information, such as scrap quantity, machine number, and ingredients, to complete work ticket and places tickets with product. Routes sample to lab for analysis according to procedure. Disassembles and repairs machinery and equipment.

GOE INFORMATION—Interest Area: 08. Industrial Production. **Work Group:** 08.02. Production Technology. **Personality Type**—Realistic. Realistic occupations frequently involve work activities that include practical, hands-on problems and solutions. They often deal with plants, animals, and real-world materials like wood, tools, and machinery. Many of the occupations require working outside and do not involve a lot of paperwork or working closely with others. **Work Values**—Moral Values; Supervision, Technical; Independence; Supervision, Human Relations; Company Policies and Practices. **Skills**—Operation Monitoring; Installation; Repairing; Operation and Control; Quality Control Analysis; Equipment Selection; Troubleshooting. **Abilities**—*Cognitive:* Visualization. *Psychomotor:* Rate Control; Reaction Time; Control Precision; Multilimb Coordination; Arm-Hand Steadiness. *Physical:* Static Strength; Dynamic Strength; Stamina. *Sensory:* Hearing Sensitivity. **General Work Activities**—*Information Input:* Monitoring Processes, Materials, or Surroundings; Inspecting Equipment, Structures, or Materials; Getting Information. *Mental Process:* Evaluating Information Against Standards; Making Decisions and Solving Problems; Judging Qualities of Things, Services, or Other People's Work. *Work Output:* Controlling Machines and Processes; Handling and Moving Objects; Performing General Physical Activities. *Interacting with Others:* Communicating with Other Workers; Coaching and Developing Others; Establishing and Maintaining Relationships. **Physical Work Conditions**—Hazardous Equipment; Distracting Sounds and Noise Levels; Indoors; Using Hands on Objects, Tools, or Controls; Making Repetitive Motions. **Other Job Characteristics**—Pace Determined by Speed of Equipment; Degree of Automation; Consequence of Error.

Experience—Job Zone 2. Some previous work-related skill, knowledge, or experience may be helpful, but usually is not needed. **Job Preparation:** SVP 4.0 to less than 6.0—six months to less than two years. **Knowledge**—Production and Processing; Mechanical; Physics; Chemistry; Engineering and Technology. **Instructional Programs**—No data available.

Related DOT Jobs—520.682-014 Center-Machine Operator; 556.682-018 Plodder Operator; 556.682-022 Compressor; 557.382-014 Wink-Cutter Operator; 557.682-010 Graining-Press Operator; 575.380-010 Forming-Machine Upkeep Mechanic; 575.382-010 Brick-and-Tile-Making-Machine Operator; 575.382-014 Forming-Machine Operator; 575.382-022 Glass-Rolling-Machine Operator; 575.682-010 Fiberglass-Dowel-Drawing-Machine Operator; 575.682-022 Ram-Press Operator; 649.582-014 Sizing-Machine Operator; 690.662-014 Tuber-Machine Operator; 692.362-010 Set-Up Mechanic, Crown Assembly Machine.

51-9041.02 Extruding, Forming, Pressing, and Compacting Machine Operators and Tenders

- **Education/Training Required: Short-term on-the-job training**
- **Employed: No data available.**
- **Annual Earnings: $25,790**
- **Growth: 9.0%**
- **Annual Job Openings: 12,000**

Operate or tend machines to shape and form any of a wide variety of manufactured products, such as glass bulbs, molded food and candy, rubber goods, clay products, wax products, tobacco plugs, cosmetics, or paper products, by means of extruding, compressing, or compacting.

Activates machine to shape or form products, such as candy bars, light bulbs, silver spoons, balloons, or insulation panels. Monitors machine operations and observes indicator lights and gauges such as thermometers, voltage meters, and timers to detect malfunctions. Adjusts machine components to regulate speed, pressure, and temperature of machine and amount, dimensions, and flow of materials or ingredients. Fills molds or positions ingredients or materials, such as glass rods, candy, or rolls of paper, on machine feeding mechanism. Clears jams, removes defective or substandard materials or products, and readjusts machine components to conform to specifications. Removes materials or products from mold or from extruding, forming, pressing, or compacting machine and stacks or stores for additional processing. Reviews work orders, specifications, or instructions to determine materials, ingredients, procedures, components, settings, and adjustments for extruding, forming, pressing, or compacting machine. Measures, mixes, cuts, shapes, softens, and joins materials and ingredients such as powder, cornmeal, or rubber to prepare for machine processing. Selects and installs machine components, such as dies, molds, and cutters, according to specifications, using hand tools and measuring devices. Examines, measures, and weighs materials or products to verify conformance to standards, using measuring devices, such as templates, micrometers, or scales. Moves materials, supplies, components, and finished products between storage and work areas, using work aids such as racks, hoists, and handtrucks. Replaces worn or broken parts, such as nozzles, punches, and filters, and cleans and lubricates machine components to maintain in working order. Records and maintains production data, such as meter readings and quantity, type, and dimensions of materials produced.

GOE INFORMATION—**Interest Area:** 08. Industrial Production. **Work Group:** 08.03. Production Work. **Personality Type**—Realistic. Realistic occupations frequently involve work activities that include practical, hands-on problems and solutions. They often deal with plants, animals, and real-world materials like wood, tools, and machinery. Many of the occupations require working outside and do not involve a lot of paperwork or working closely with others. **Work Values**—Moral Values; Supervision, Technical; Independence; Supervision, Human Relations; Company Policies and Practices. **Skills**—Operation and Control; Operation Monitoring; Repairing; Installation. **Abilities**—*Cognitive:* Perceptual Speed; Spatial Orientation; Visualization; Category Flexibility; Memorization. *Psychomotor:* Rate Control; Control Precision; Reaction Time; Speed of Limb Movement; Multilimb Coordination. *Physical:* Dynamic Strength; Explosive Strength; Dynamic Flexibility; Gross Body Coordination; Trunk Strength. *Sensory:* Peripheral Vision; Depth Perception; Hearing Sensitivity; Glare Sensitivity. **General Work Activities**—*Information Input:* Monitoring Processes, Materials, or Surroundings; Identifying Objects, Actions, and Events; Inspecting Equipment, Structures, or Materials. *Mental Process:* Evaluating Information Against Standards; Judging Qualities of Things, Services, or Other People's Work; Processing Information. *Work Output:* Handling and Moving Objects; Controlling Machines and Processes; Performing General Physical Activities. *Interacting with Others:* Performing Administrative Activities; Communicating with Other Workers; Interpreting Meaning of Information for Others. **Physical Work Conditions**—Hazardous Equipment; Using Hands on Objects, Tools, or Controls; Distracting Sounds and Noise Levels; Making Repetitive Motions; Standing. **Other Job Characteristics**—Pace Determined by Speed of Equipment; Degree of Automation; Importance of Repeating Same Tasks.

Experience—Job Zone 1. No previous work-related skill, knowledge, or experience is needed. **Job Preparation:** SVP below 4.0—less than six months. **Knowledge**—Production and Processing; Mechanical; Clerical. **Instructional Programs**—No data available.

Related DOT Jobs—520.682-030 Spinner; 520.682-034 Cracker-and-Cookie-Machine Operator; 520.685-038 Cake Former; 520.685-058 Casting-Machine Operator; 520.685-062 Casting-Machine Operator; 520.685-078 Confectionery-Drops-Machine Operator; 520.685-086 Dividing-Machine Operator; 520.685-102 Flaking-Roll Operator; 520.685-178 Pellet-Mill Operator; 520.685-182 Press Operator, Meat; 520.685-186 Press Tender; 520.685-190 Pretzel-Twisting-Machine Operator; 520.685-198 Rolling-Machine Operator; 520.685-214 Sweet-Goods-Machine Operator; 521.685-330 Stem-Roller-or-Crusher Operator; 521.685-350 Sugar Presser;

529.682-026 Lozenge Maker; 529.685-014 Automatic Lump Making Machine Tender; 529.685-042 Butt Maker; 529.685-054 Chocolate Molder, Machine; others.

51-9051.00 Furnace, Kiln, Oven, Drier, and Kettle Operators and Tenders

- Education/Training Required: Moderate-term on-the-job training
- Employed: 32,559
- Annual Earnings: $28,000
- Growth: 3.2%
- Annual Job Openings: 5,000

Operate or tend heating equipment other than basic metal, plastic, or food processing equipment. Includes activities such as annealing glass, drying lumber, curing rubber, removing moisture from materials, or boiling soap.

Examine or test samples of processed substances or collect samples for laboratory testing in order to ensure conformance to specifications. Load equipment receptacles or conveyors with material to be processed by hand or using hoists. Monitor equipment operation, gauges, and panel lights in order to detect deviations from standards. Press and adjust controls in order to activate, set, and regulate equipment according to specifications. Read and interpret work orders and instructions in order to determine work assignments, process specifications, and production schedules. Remove products from equipment, manually or using hoists, and prepare them for storage, shipment, or additional processing. Stop equipment and clear blockages or jams, using fingers, wire, or hand tools. Weigh or measure specified amounts of ingredients or materials for processing, using devices such as scales and calipers. Calculate amounts of materials to be loaded into furnaces, adjusting amounts as necessary for specific conditions. Clean, lubricate, and adjust equipment, using scrapers, solvents, air hoses, oil, and hand tools. Confer with supervisors or other equipment operators in order to report equipment malfunctions or to resolve production problems. Direct crane operators and crew members to load vessels with materials to be processed. Feed fuel, such as coal and coke, into fireboxes or onto conveyors and remove ashes from furnaces, using shovels and buckets. Melt or refine metal before casting, calculating required temperatures, and observe metal color and adjust controls as necessary in order to maintain required temperatures. Record gauge readings, test results, and shift production in logbooks. Replace worn or defective equipment parts, using hand tools. Sprinkle chemicals on the surface of molten metal in order to bring impurities to surface and remove impurities, using strainers. Transport materials and products to and from work areas manually or using carts, handtrucks, or hoists.

GOE INFORMATION—Interest Area: 08. Industrial Production. Work Group: 08.03. Production Work. Personality Type—Realistic. Realistic occupations frequently involve work activities that include practical, hands-on problems and solutions. They often deal with plants, animals, and real-world materials like wood, tools, and machinery. Many of the occupations require working outside and do not involve a lot of paperwork or working closely with others. Work Values—Moral Values; Supervision, Technical; Supervision, Human Relations; Company Policies and Practices; Independence. Skills—Repairing; Operation Monitoring; Operation and Control. Abilities—*Cognitive:* None met the criteria. *Psychomotor:* Control Precision; Rate Control. *Physical:* Static Strength; Stamina; Trunk Strength; Dynamic Strength. *Sensory:* None met the criteria. General Work Activities—*Information Input:* Monitoring Processes, Materials, or Surroundings; Inspecting Equipment, Structures, or Materials;

Getting Information. *Mental Process:* Evaluating Information Against Standards; Judging Qualities of Things, Services, or Other People's Work; Analyzing Data or Information. *Work Output:* Handling and Moving Objects; Controlling Machines and Processes; Performing General Physical Activities. *Interacting with Others:* Communicating with Other Workers; Establishing and Maintaining Relationships; Coaching and Developing Others. Physical Work Conditions—Hazardous Equipment; Distracting Sounds and Noise Levels; Very Hot or Cold; Common Protective or Safety Attire; Hazardous Conditions. Other Job Characteristics—Pace Determined by Speed of Equipment; Degree of Automation; Importance of Repeating Same Tasks.

Experience—Job Zone 1. No previous work-related skill, knowledge, or experience is needed. Job Preparation: SVP below 4.0—less than six months. Knowledge—Production and Processing; Mechanical; Chemistry; Engineering and Technology; Physics. Instructional Programs—No data available.

Related DOT Jobs—361.685-010 Conditioner-Tumbler Operator; 369.685-026 Rug-Dry-Room Attendant; 369.685-034 Tumbler Operator; 503.685-022 Flame Degreaser; 504.485-010 Rivet Heater; 504.685-030 Reel-Blade-Bender Furnace Tender; 509.565-010 Kiln Operator; 509.685-018 Burning-Plant Operator; 511.482-010 Control Operator; 511.565-014 Drier Tender; 512.685-018 Pot Tender; 513.362-010 Calciner Operator; 513.462-010 Furnace Operator; 513.565-010 Kiln Operator; 513.682-010 Rotary-Kiln Operator; 518.685-010 Core-Oven Tender; 519.665-014 Standpipe Tender; 519.685-010 Briquetting-Machine Operator; 519.685-018 Kettle Operator; 519.685-022 Kettle Tender I; others.

51-9061.00 Inspectors, Testers, Sorters, Samplers, and Weighers

- Education/Training Required: Postsecondary vocational training
- Employed: 602,132
- Annual Earnings: $26,690
- Growth: −1.9%
- Annual Job Openings: 91,000

Inspect, test, sort, sample, or weigh nonagricultural raw materials or processed, machined, fabricated, or assembled parts or products for defects, wear, and deviations from specifications. May use precision measuring instruments and complex test equipment.

No task data available.

GOE INFORMATION—Interest Area: 08. Industrial Production. Work Group: 08.02. Production Technology. Note: The Department of Labor has not collected some data for this job, so it has fewer details than the other descriptions.

Instructional Programs—Quality Control Technology/Technician.

Related DOT Jobs—194.387-010 Quality-Control Inspector; 194.387-014 Record Tester; 199.171-010 Proof Technician; 199.361-010 Radiographer; 222.367-046 Petroleum Inspector; 222.384-010 Inspector, Receiving; 222.687-042 Inspector, Handbag Frames; 343.687-010 Plastic-Card Grader, Cardroom; 361.587-010 Flatwork Tier; 361.687-010 Assembler, Wet Wash; 361.687-014 Classifier; 361.687-022 Linen Grader; 369.687-010 Assembler; 369.687-014 Checker; 369.687-022 Inspector; 369.687-026 Marker; 369.687-030 Rug Inspector; 500.287-010 Inspector, Plating; 502.382-014 Fluoroscope Operator; 504.281-010 Heat-Treat Inspector; others.

51-9061.01 Materials Inspectors

- **Education/Training Required: Moderate-term on-the-job training**
- **Employed: No data available.**
- **Annual Earnings: $26,690**
- **Growth: –1.9%**
- **Annual Job Openings: 91,000**

Examine and inspect materials and finished parts and products for defects and wear and to ensure conformance with work orders, diagrams, blueprints, and template specifications. Usually specialize in a single phase of inspection.

Inspects materials, products, and work in progress for conformance to specifications and adjusts process or assembly equipment to meet standards. Tests and measures finished products, components, or assemblies for functioning, operation, accuracy, or assembly to verify adherence to functional specifications. Analyzes and interprets blueprints, sample data, and other materials to determine, change, or measure specifications or inspection and testing procedures. Collects samples for testing and computes findings. Reads dials and meters to verify functioning of equipment according to specifications. Observes and monitors production operations and equipment to ensure proper assembly of parts or assists in testing and monitoring activities. Fabricates, installs, positions, or connects components, parts, finished products, or instruments for testing or operational purposes. Marks items for acceptance or rejection, records test results and inspection data, and compares findings with specifications to ensure conformance to standards. Operates or tends machinery and equipment and uses hand tools. Supervises testing or drilling activities and adjusts equipment to obtain sample fluids or to direct drilling. Confers with vendors and others regarding inspection results, recommends corrective procedures, and compiles reports of results, recommendations, and needed repairs.

GOE INFORMATION—Interest Area: 08. Industrial Production. **Work Group:** 08.02. Production Technology. **Personality Type—**Realistic. Realistic occupations frequently involve work activities that include practical, hands-on problems and solutions. They often deal with plants, animals, and real-world materials like wood, tools, and machinery. Many of the occupations require working outside and do not involve a lot of paperwork or working closely with others. **Work Values—**Responsibility; Supervision, Technical; Independence; Autonomy; Activity. **Skills—**Quality Control Analysis; Operation Monitoring; Operation and Control; Troubleshooting; Installation; Technology Design; Repairing; Mathematics. **Abilities—***Cognitive:* Perceptual Speed; Inductive Reasoning; Selective Attention; Problem Sensitivity; Flexibility of Closure. *Psychomotor:* Reaction Time; Manual Dexterity; Response Orientation; Control Precision; Finger Dexterity. *Physical:* Explosive Strength; Static Strength; Dynamic Flexibility; Extent Flexibility; Gross Body Equilibrium. *Sensory:* Visual Color Discrimination; Auditory Attention; Peripheral Vision; Hearing Sensitivity; Sound Localization. **General Work Activities—***Information Input:* Inspecting Equipment, Structures, or Materials; Monitoring Processes, Materials, or Surroundings; Identifying Objects, Actions, and Events. *Mental Process:* Updating and Using Relevant Knowledge; Evaluating Information Against Standards; Analyzing Data or Information. *Work Output:* Handling and Moving Objects; Controlling Machines and Processes; Performing General Physical Activities. *Interacting with Others:* Providing Consultation and Advice to Others; Establishing and Maintaining Relationships; Communicating with Other Workers. **Physical Work Conditions—**Hazardous Equipment; Common Protective or Safety Attire; Distracting Sounds and Noise Levels; Making Repetitive Motions; Very Hot or Cold. **Other Job Characteristics—**Degree of Automation; Pace Determined by Speed of Equipment; Importance of Being Exact or Accurate.

Experience—Job Zone 3. Previous work-related skill, knowledge, or experience is required. **Job Preparation:** SVP 6.0 to less than 7.0—more than one year and less than four years. **Knowledge—**Design; Production and Processing; Mechanical; Engineering and Technology; Physics. **Instructional Programs—**Quality Control Technology/Technician.

Related DOT Jobs—199.361-010 Radiographer; 504.281-010 Heat-Treat Inspector; 526.381-022 Cake Tester; 529.281-010 Taster; 549.261-010 Mechanical Inspector; 559.381-010 Inspector; 559.381-014 Rubber Tester; 572.360-010 Furnace-Combustion Analyst; 600.281-014 Lay-Out Inspector; 601.261-010 Inspector, Set-Up and Lay-Out; 601.281-022 Inspector, Tool; 609.361-010 Inspector, Floor; 612.261-010 Inspector; 616.361-010 Spring Inspector I; 619.261-010 Inspector, Metal Fabricating; 619.364-010 Inspector I; 619.381-010 Inspector; 619.381-014 Eddy-Current Inspector; 622.381-038 Salvage Inspector; 632.381-014 Inspector, Firearms; others.

51-9061.02 Mechanical Inspectors

- **Education/Training Required: Long-term on-the-job training**
- **Employed: No data available.**
- **Annual Earnings: $26,690**
- **Growth: –1.9%**
- **Annual Job Openings: 91,000**

Inspect and test mechanical assemblies and systems, such as motors, vehicles, and transportation equipment, for defects and wear to ensure compliance with specifications.

Tests and measures finished products, components, or assemblies for functioning, operation, accuracy, or assembly to verify adherence to functional specifications. Inspects materials, products, and work in progress for conformance to specifications and adjusts process or assembly equipment to meet standards. Starts and operates finished products for testing or inspection. Reads dials and meters to ensure that equipment is operating according to specifications. Collects samples for testing and computes findings. Marks items for acceptance or rejection, records test results and inspection data, and compares findings with specifications to ensure conformance to standards. Discards or rejects products, materials, and equipment not meeting specifications. Reads and interprets materials, such as work orders, inspection manuals, and blueprints, to determine inspection and test procedures. Analyzes and interprets sample data. Installs and positions new or replacement parts, components, and instruments. Estimates and records operational data. Completes necessary procedures to satisfy licensing requirements and indicates concurrence with acceptance or rejection decisions. Confers with vendors and others regarding inspection results, recommends corrective procedures, and compiles reports of results, recommendations, and needed repairs. Cleans and maintains test equipment and instruments to ensure proper functioning.

GOE INFORMATION—Interest Area: 08. Industrial Production. **Work Group:** 08.02. Production Technology. **Personality Type—**Realistic. Realistic occupations frequently involve work activities that include practical, hands-on problems and solutions. They often deal with plants, animals, and real-world materials like wood, tools, and machinery. Many of the occupations require working outside and do not involve a lot of paperwork or working closely with others. **Work Values—**Responsibility; Independence; Supervision, Technical; Autonomy; Activity. **Skills—**Quality Control Analysis; Operation Monitoring; Installation; Operation and Control; Science; Troubleshooting; Repairing; Writing. **Abilities—***Cognitive:* Perceptual Speed; Visualization; Flexibility of Closure; Selective Attention; Written Comprehension. *Psychomotor:* Response Orientation; Reaction Time; Control Precision; Rate Control; Manual Dexterity. *Physical:* Extent Flexibility; Static Strength; Explosive Strength; Gross Body Equilibrium; Trunk Strength. *Sensory:* Hearing Sensitivity; Sound Localization; Auditory Attention; Visual Color Discrimination; Depth Perception. **General Work Activities**—*Information Input:* Inspecting Equipment, Structures, or Materials; Monitoring Processes, Materials, or Surroundings; Identifying Objects, Actions, and Events. *Mental Process:* Evaluating Information Against Standards; Judging Qualities of Things, Services, or Other People's Work; Making Decisions and Solving Problems. *Work Output:* Handling and Moving Objects; Repairing and Maintaining Mechanical Equipment; Performing General Physical Activities. *Interacting with Others:* Communicating with Persons Outside Organization; Communicating with Other Workers; Providing Consultation and Advice to Others. **Physical Work Conditions**—Distracting Sounds and Noise Levels; Hazardous Equipment; Common Protective or Safety Attire; Walking or Running; Cramped Work Space or Awkward Positions. **Other Job Characteristics**—Importance of Being Exact or Accurate; Pace Determined by Speed of Equipment; Consequence of Error.

Experience—Job Zone 4. A minimum of two to four years of work-related skill, knowledge, or experience is needed. **Job Preparation:** SVP 7.0 to less than 8.0—two years to less than 10 years. **Knowledge**—Mechanical; Design; Engineering and Technology; Production and Processing; Public Safety and Security. **Instructional Programs**—Quality Control Technology/Technician.

Related DOT Jobs—602.362-010 Gear Inspector; 620.261-014 Automobile Tester; 620.261-018 Automobile-Repair-Service Estimator; 620.281-014 Automotive Technician, Exhaust Emissions; 620.281-030 Bus Inspector; 621.261-010 Airplane Inspector; 621.261-014 Engine Tester; 622.281-010 Locomotive Inspector; 622.381-034 Railroad Wheels and Axle Inspector; 624.361-010 Inspector and Tester; 625.261-010 Diesel-Engine Tester; 710.384-014 Inspector; 736.381-018 Process Inspector; 801.381-018 Major-Assembly Inspector; 806.261-010 Internal-Combustion-Engine Inspector; 806.261-022 Tester, Rocket Motor; 806.261-030 Inspector, Assemblies and Installations; 806.261-038 Inspector, Missile; 806.281-010 Dynamometer Tester, Engine; 806.281-018 Final Inspector, Motorcyles; others.

51-9061.03 Precision Devices Inspectors and Testers

- **Education/Training Required: Moderate-term on-the-job training**
- **Employed: No data available.**
- **Annual Earnings: $26,690**
- **Growth: –1.9%**
- **Annual Job Openings: 91,000**

Verify accuracy of and adjust precision devices, such as meters and gauges, testing instruments, and clock and watch mechanisms, to ensure operation of device is in accordance with design specifications.

Inspects materials, products, and work in progress for conformance to specifications and adjusts process or assembly equipment to meet standards. Reads dials and meters to verify functioning of equipment according to specifications. Tests and measures finished products, components, or assemblies for functioning, operation, accuracy, or assembly to verify adherence to functional specifications. Cleans and maintains test equipment and instruments and certifies that precision instruments meet standards. Marks items for acceptance or rejection, records test results and inspection data, and compares findings with specifications to ensure conformance to standards. Fabricates, installs,

positions, or connects components, parts, finished products, or instruments for testing or operational purposes. Analyzes and interprets blueprints, sample data, and other materials to determine, change, or measure specifications or inspection and testing procedures. Discards or rejects products, materials, and equipment not meeting specifications. Operates or tends machinery and equipment and uses hand tools. Estimates operational data to meet acceptable standards. Disassembles defective parts and components. Confers with vendors and others regarding inspection results and recommends corrective procedures. Computes and/or calculates data and other information. Completes necessary procedures to satisfy licensing requirements.

GOE INFORMATION—**Interest Area:** 08. Industrial Production. **Work Group:** 08.02. Production Technology. **Personality Type**—Realistic. Realistic occupations frequently involve work activities that include practical, hands-on problems and solutions. They often deal with plants, animals, and real-world materials like wood, tools, and machinery. Many of the occupations require working outside and do not involve a lot of paperwork or working closely with others. **Work Values**—Responsibility; Supervision, Technical; Independence; Autonomy; Activity. **Skills**—Quality Control Analysis; Operation Monitoring; Installation; Technology Design; Troubleshooting; Operation and Control; Science; Repairing. **Abilities**—*Cognitive:* Perceptual Speed; Selective Attention; Visualization; Inductive Reasoning; Memorization. *Psychomotor:* Control Precision; Finger Dexterity; Arm-Hand Steadiness; Reaction Time; Rate Control. *Physical:* Extent Flexibility; Explosive Strength; Gross Body Equilibrium; Dynamic Flexibility; Static Strength. *Sensory:* Visual Color Discrimination; Hearing Sensitivity; Near Vision; Sound Localization; Auditory Attention. **General Work Activities**—*Information Input:* Inspecting Equipment, Structures, or Materials; Monitoring Processes, Materials, or Surroundings; Identifying Objects, Actions, and Events. *Mental Process:* Updating and Using Relevant Knowledge; Evaluating Information Against Standards; Analyzing Data or Information. *Work Output:* Handling and Moving Objects; Repairing and Maintaining Electronic Equipment; Repairing and Maintaining Mechanical Equipment. *Interacting with Others:* Communicating with Other Workers; Communicating with Persons Outside Organization; Establishing and Maintaining Relationships. **Physical Work Conditions**—Making Repetitive Motions; Common Protective or Safety Attire; Kneeling, Crouching, or Crawling; Walking or Running; Indoors. **Other Job Characteristics**—Importance of Being Exact or Accurate; Degree of Automation; Consequence of Error.

Experience—Job Zone 3. Previous work-related skill, knowledge, or experience is required. **Job Preparation:** SVP 6.0 to less than 7.0—more than one year and less than four years. **Knowledge**—Design; Mechanical; Production and Processing; Mathematics; Engineering and Technology. **Instructional Programs**—Quality Control Technology/Technician.

Related DOT Jobs—601.281-018 Inspector, Gauge and Instrument; 710.381-014 Balancer, Scale; 710.381-030 Hydrometer Calibrator; 710.381-034 Calibrator; 710.381-042 Calibrator, Barometers; 710.384-022 Meter Inspector; 711.281-010 Inspector, Optical Instrument; 714.381-014 Inspector, Photographic Equipment; 715.261-010 Mechanical Technician, Laboratory; 715.381-050 Final Inspector; 715.381-058 Hairspring Truer; 715.381-066 Inspector, Hairspring I; 715.381-070 Inspector, Watch Assembly; 715.381-074 Inspector, Watch Train; 715.381-078 Location-and-Measurement Technician; 715.384-022 Inspector, Watch Parts; 716.381-010 Inspector, Precision; 722.381-014 Instrument Inspector; 729.281-046 X-Ray-Equipment Tester; 729.361-010 Inspector, Electromechanical; others.

51-9061.04 Electrical and Electronic Inspectors and Testers

- **Education/Training Required: Moderate-term on-the-job training**
- **Employed: No data available.**
- **Annual Earnings: $26,690**
- **Growth: −1.9%**
- **Annual Job Openings: 91,000**

Inspect and test electrical and electronic systems, such as radar navigational equipment, computer memory units, and television and radio transmitters, using precision measuring instruments.

Tests and measures finished products, components, or assemblies for functioning, operation, accuracy, or assembly to verify adherence to functional specifications. Inspects materials, products, and work in progress for conformance to specifications and adjusts process or assembly equipment to meet standards. Marks items for acceptance or rejection, records test results and inspection data, and compares findings with specifications to ensure conformance to standards. Reads dials and meters to verify functioning of equipment according to specifications. Analyzes and interprets blueprints, sample data, and other materials to determine, change, or measure specifications or inspection and testing procedures. Computes and/or calculates sample data and test results. Examines and adjusts or repairs finished products and components or parts. Confers with vendors and others regarding inspection results, recommends corrective procedures, and compiles reports of results, recommendations, and needed repairs. Operates or tends machinery and equipment and uses hand tools. Positions or directs other workers to position products, components, or parts for testing. Cleans and maintains test equipment and instruments to ensure proper functioning. Disassembles defective parts and components. Reviews maintenance records to ensure that plant equipment functions properly. Installs, positions, or connects new or replacement parts, components, and instruments. Writes and installs computer programs to control test equipment.

GOE INFORMATION—Interest Area: 08. Industrial Production. **Work Group:** 08.02. Production Technology. **Personality Type—**Realistic. Realistic occupations frequently involve work activities that include practical, hands-on problems and solutions. They often deal with plants, animals, and real-world materials like wood, tools, and machinery. Many of the occupations require working outside and do not involve a lot of paperwork or working closely with others. **Work Values—**Responsibility; Supervision, Technical; Pleasant Co-workers; Advancement; Activity. **Skills—**Quality Control Analysis; Installation; Programming; Operation Monitoring; Troubleshooting; Repairing; Operation and Control; Equipment Selection. **Abilities—***Cognitive:* Perceptual Speed; Speed of Closure; Mathematical Reasoning; Selective Attention; Number Facility. *Psychomotor:* Control Precision; Reaction Time; Finger Dexterity; Response Orientation; Multilimb Coordination. *Physical:* Explosive Strength; Extent Flexibility; Trunk Strength; Dynamic Strength; Static Strength. *Sensory:* Sound Localization; Visual Color Discrimination; Hearing Sensitivity; Depth Perception; Auditory Attention. **General Work Activities—***Information Input:* Inspecting Equipment, Structures, or Materials; Getting Information; Monitoring Processes, Materials, or Surroundings. *Mental Process:* Updating and Using Relevant Knowledge; Evaluating Information Against Standards; Processing Information. *Work Output:* Repairing and Maintaining Electronic Equipment; Handling and Moving Objects; Controlling Machines and Processes. *Interacting with Others:* Establishing and Maintaining Relationships; Communicating with Other Workers; Communicating with Persons Outside Organization. **Physical Work Conditions—**Hazardous Conditions; Common Protective or Safety Attire; Hazardous Equipment; Distracting Sounds and Noise Levels; Walking or Running. **Other Job Characteristics—**Degree of Automation; Importance of Being Exact or Accurate; Pace Determined by Speed of Equipment.

Experience—Job Zone 3. Previous work-related skill, knowledge, or experience is required. **Job Preparation:** SVP 6.0 to less than 7.0—more than one year and less than four years. **Knowledge—**Computers and Electronics; Telecommunications; Design; Mechanical; Engineering and Technology. **Instructional Programs—**Quality Control Technology/Technician.

Related DOT Jobs—710.381-046 Tester, Electronic Scale; 721.261-014 Final Tester; 721.281-030 Tester, Motors and Controls; 721.361-010 Inspector, Motors and Generators; 724.281-010 Transformer Tester; 724.364-010 Winding Inspector and Tester; 724.384-010 Armature Tester I; 726.261-018 Electronics Tester; 726.361-018 Group Leader, Printed Circuit Board Quality Control; 726.362-010 Group Leader, Semiconductor Testing; 726.364-010 Lead Hand, Inspecting and Testing; 726.381-010 Electronics Inspector; 726.384-014 Inspector, Circuitry Negative; 726.384-018 Inspector, Semiconductor Wafer Processing; 726.384-022 Photo Mask Inspector; 726.682-018 Coordinate Measuring Equipment Operator; 727.381-018 Dry-Cell Tester; 727.381-022 Storage Battery Inspector and Tester; 729.281-038 Relay Tester; 729.381-010 Electrical-Equipment Tester; others.

51-9061.05 Production Inspectors, Testers, Graders, Sorters, Samplers, Weighers

- **Education/Training Required: Short-term on-the-job training**
- **Employed: No data available.**
- **Annual Earnings: $26,690**
- **Growth: −1.9%**
- **Annual Job Openings: 91,000**

Inspect, test, grade, sort, sample, or weigh nonagricultural raw materials or processed, machined, fabricated, or assembled parts or products. Work may be performed before, during, or after processing.

Weighs materials, products, containers, or samples to verify packaging weight, to determine percentage of each ingredient, or to determine sorting. Examines product or monitors processing of product, using any or all of five senses, to determine defects or grade. Measures dimensions of product, using measuring instruments such as rulers, calipers, gauges, or micrometers, to verify conformance to specifications. Compares color, shape, texture, or grade of product or material with color chart, template, or sample to verify conformance to standards. Tests samples, materials, or products, using test equipment, such as thermometer, voltmeter, moisture meter, or tensiometer, for conformance to specifications. Grades, classifies, and sorts products according to size, weight, color, or other specifications. Marks, affixes, or stamps product or container to identify defects or denote grade or size information. Records inspection or test data, such as weight, temperature, grade, or moisture content, and number inspected or graded. Collects or selects samples for testing or for use as model. Discards or routes defective products or contaminants for rework or reuse. Notifies supervisor or specified personnel of deviations from specifications, machine malfunctions, or need for equipment maintenance. Reads work order to determine inspection criteria and to verify identification numbers and product type. Uses or operates product to test functional performance. Computes percentages or averages, using formulas and calculator, and prepares reports of inspection or test findings. Sets controls, starts machine, and observes machine which automatically sorts or inspects products. Counts number of product tested or inspected and stacks or arranges for further processing, shipping, or packing. Cleans, trims, makes adjustments, or repairs product or processing equipment to correct defects found during inspection. Transports inspected or tested products to other workstations, using handtruck or lift truck. Wraps and packages product for shipment or delivery.

GOE INFORMATION—Interest Area: 08. Industrial Production. **Work Group:** 08.02. Production Technology. **Personality Type—**Realistic. Realistic occupations frequently involve work activities that include practical, hands-on problems and solutions. They often deal with plants, animals, and real-world materials like wood, tools, and machinery. Many of the occupations require working outside and do not involve a lot of paperwork or working closely with others. **Work Values—**Supervision, Technical; Responsibility; Activity; Independence; Compensation. **Skills—**Quality Control Analysis; Operation Monitoring; Operation and Control. **Abilities—***Cognitive:* Perceptual Speed; Category Flexibility; Flexibility of Closure; Selective Attention; Speed of Closure. *Psychomotor:* Control Precision; Multilimb Coordination; Manual Dexterity; Finger Dexterity; Rate Control. *Physical:* Dynamic Flexibility; Extent Flexibility; Stamina; Dynamic Strength; Static Strength. *Sensory:* Visual Color Discrimination; Auditory Attention; Near Vision; Hearing Sensitivity; Sound Localization. **General Work Activities—***Information Input:* Monitoring Processes, Materials, or Surroundings; Identifying Objects, Actions, and Events; Getting Information. *Mental Process:* Processing Information; Evaluating Information Against Standards; Judging Qualities of Things, Services, or Other People's Work. *Work Output:* Handling and Moving Objects; Documenting or Recording Information; Controlling Machines and Processes. *Interacting with Others:* Communicating with Other Workers; Performing Administrative Activities; Interpreting Meaning of Information for Others. **Physical Work Conditions—**Using Hands on Objects, Tools, or Controls; Indoors; Making Repetitive Motions; Walking or Running; Bending or Twisting the Body. **Other Job Characteristics—**Importance of Repeating Same Tasks; Pace Determined by Speed of Equipment; Importance of Being Exact or Accurate.

Experience—Job Zone 1. No previous work-related skill, knowledge, or experience is needed. **Job Preparation:** SVP below 4.0—less than six months. **Knowledge—**Production and Processing; Engineering and Technology; Mechanical; Physics; Clerical. **Instructional Programs—**Quality Control Technology/Technician.

Related DOT Jobs—194.387-010 Quality-Control Inspector; 194.387-014 Record Tester; 199.171-010 Proof Technician; 222.367-046 Petroleum Inspector; 222.384-010 Inspector, Receiving; 222.687-042 Inspector, Handbag Frames; 343.687-010 Plastic-Card Grader, Cardroom; 361.587-010 Flatwork Tier; 361.687-010 Assembler, Wet Wash; 361.687-014 Classifier; 361.687-022 Linen Grader; 369.687-010 Assembler; 369.687-014 Checker; 369.687-022 Inspector; 369.687-026 Marker; 369.687-030 Rug Inspector; 500.287-010 Inspector, Plating; 502.382-014 Fluoroscope Operator; 504.387-010 Hardness Inspector; 509.584-010 Test Preparer; others.

51-9071.00 Jewelers and Precious Stone and Metal Workers

- Education/Training Required: Long-term on-the-job training
- Employed: 43,368
- Annual Earnings: $27,210
- Growth: 1.3%
- Annual Job Openings: 3,000

Design, fabricate, adjust, repair, or appraise jewelry, gold, silver, other precious metals, or gems. Includes diamond polishers and gem cutters and persons who perform precision casting and modeling of

molds, casting metal in molds, or setting precious and semi-precious stones for jewelry and related products.

No task data available.

GOE INFORMATION—Interest Area: 08. Industrial Production. **Work Group:** 08.02. Production Technology. **Note:** The Department of Labor has not collected some data for this job, so it has fewer details than the other descriptions.

Instructional Programs—Watchmaking and Jewelrymaking.

Related DOT Jobs—199.281-010 Gemologist; 502.381-010 Caster; 502.384-010 Pewter Caster; 502.682-018 Centrifugal-Casting-Machine Operator; 518.381-010 Bench-Molder Apprentice; 518.381-022 Molder, Bench; 700.261-010 Pewterer; 700.281-010 Jeweler; 700.281-014 Jeweler Apprentice; 700.281-018 Model Maker I; 700.281-022 Silversmith II; 700.281-026 Pewter Finisher; 700.381-010 Chain Maker, Hand; 700.381-014 Fancy-Wire Drawer; 700.381-018 Goldbeater; 700.381-022 Hammersmith; 700.381-026 Lay-Out Worker; 700.381-030 Locket Maker; 700.381-034 Mold Maker I; 700.381-038 Mold-Maker Apprentice; others.

51-9071.01 Jewelers

- Education/Training Required: Postsecondary vocational training
- Employed: No data available.
- Annual Earnings: $27,210
- Growth: 1.3%
- Annual Job Openings: 3,000

Fabricate and repair jewelry articles.

Cuts and shapes metal into jewelry pieces, using cutting and carving tools. Arranges jewelry pieces into specified design, softens metal by heating with gas torch, and shapes, using hammer and die. Solders pieces of jewelry together and enlarges or reduces size of rings, using soldering torch or iron. Repairs, reshapes, and restyles jewelry by replacing broken parts or using hand tools and machines. Ties or twists gold or silver wires together and bends to form rings. Smoothes soldered joints and rough spots, using hand file and emery paper, and polishes with polishing wheel or buffing wire. Immerses jewelry in cleaning solution or acid to remove stains or in solution of gold or other metal to color jewelry. Forms model of article from wax or metal, using carving tools. Places model in casting ring and pours plaster into ring to form mold. Forms sand or rubber mold from model for casting article. Pours molten metal into mold or operates centrifugal casting machine to cast article. Examines gemstone surfaces and internal structure to evaluate genuineness, quality, and value, using polariscope, refractometer, and other optical instruments. Immerses gemstones in chemical solutions to determine specific gravity and key properties for identification and appraisal. Grades stones for color, perfection, and quality of cut. Estimates wholesale and retail value of gemstones, following price guides and market fluctuations.

GOE INFORMATION—Interest Area: 08. Industrial Production. **Work Group:** 08.02. Production Technology. **Personality Type—**Realistic. Realistic occupations frequently involve work activities that include practical, hands-on problems and solutions. They often deal with plants, animals, and real-world materials like wood, tools, and machinery. Many of the occupations require working outside and do not involve a lot of paperwork or working closely with others. **Work Values—**Good Working Conditions; Ability Utilization; Autonomy; Creativity; Independence. **Skills—**Repairing; Quality Control Analysis; Operation Monitoring; Operation and Control; Equipment Selection; Installation. **Abilities—***Cognitive:* Visualization; Category Flexibility; Originality; Memorization; Flexibility of Closure. *Psychomotor:* Finger Dexterity; Arm-Hand Steadiness; Manual Dexterity; Control Precision; Wrist-Finger Speed. *Physical:* Explosive Strength; Dynamic Strength; Trunk Strength. *Sensory:* Visual Color Discrimination; Near Vision; Depth Perception; Glare Sensitivity. **General Work Activities**—*Information Input:* Identifying Objects, Actions, and Events; Monitoring Processes, Materials, or Surroundings; Getting Information. *Mental Process:* Judging Qualities of Things, Services, or Other People's Work; Thinking Creatively; Making Decisions and Solving Problems. *Work Output:* Handling and Moving Objects; Controlling Machines and Processes; Documenting or Recording Information. *Interacting with Others:* Communicating with Persons Outside Organization; Interpreting Meaning of Information for Others; Monitoring and Controlling Resources. **Physical Work Conditions**—Using Hands on Objects, Tools, or Controls; Hazardous Conditions; Indoors; Sitting; Making Repetitive Motions. **Other Job Characteristics**—Consequence of Error; Degree of Automation; Importance of Repeating Same Tasks.

Experience—Job Zone 4. A minimum of two to four years of work-related skill, knowledge, or experience is needed. **Job Preparation:** SVP 7.0 to less than 8.0—two years to less than 10 years. **Knowledge**—Fine Arts; Production and Processing; Design; Chemistry; Physics. **Instructional Programs**—Watchmaking and Jewelrymaking.

Related DOT Jobs—199.281-010 Gemologist; 700.281-010 Jeweler; 700.281-014 Jeweler Apprentice; 700.381-030 Locket Maker; 700.381-042 Ring Maker; 700.381-046 Sample Maker I.

51-9071.02 Silversmiths

- **Education/Training Required: Long-term on-the-job training**
- **Employed: No data available.**
- **Annual Earnings: $27,210**
- **Growth: 1.3%**
- **Annual Job Openings: 3,000**

Anneal, solder, hammer, shape, and glue silver articles.

Anneals silverware, such as coffeepots, tea sets, and trays, in gas oven for prescribed time to soften metal for reworking. Solders parts together and fills holes and cracks with silver solder, using gas torch. Hammers out deformations, selecting and using hammer and dollies with head corresponding in curvature with surface of article. Forms concavity in bottom of article to improve stability, using tracing punches and hammer. Shapes and straightens damaged or twisted articles by hand or using pliers. Strikes article with small tools or punches with hammer to indent or restore embossing. Glues plastic separators to handles of coffee and teapots. Outlines design from photographs or drawings onto surface of article, using hand tools. Positions article over snarling tool and raises design area, using foot-powered hammer. Peens edges of scratches or holes to repair defect, using peening hammer. Wires parts such as legs, spouts, and handles to body to prepare article for soldering. Pierces and cuts open design in ornamentation, using hand drill and scroll saw. Examines article to determine nature of defects, such as dents, uneven bottom, scratches, or holes, to repair. Verifies levelness of bottom edges of article, using straightedge or by rocking back and forth on flat surface.

GOE INFORMATION—**Interest Area:** 08. Industrial Production. **Work Group:** 08.02. Production Technology. **Personality Type**—Realistic. Realistic occupations frequently involve work activities that include practical, hands-on problems and solutions. They often deal with plants, animals, and real-world materials like wood, tools, and machinery. Many of the occupations require working outside and do not involve a lot of paperwork or working closely with others. **Work Values**—Independence; Creativity; Variety; Autonomy; Recognition. **Skills**—Equipment Selection. **Abilities**—*Cognitive:* Perceptual Speed; Visualization; Flexibility of

Closure; Originality; Memorization. *Psychomotor:* Arm-Hand Steadiness; Manual Dexterity; Finger Dexterity; Multilimb Coordination; Wrist-Finger Speed. *Physical:* Explosive Strength; Dynamic Strength; Gross Body Equilibrium; Static Strength; Dynamic Flexibility. *Sensory:* Depth Perception; Glare Sensitivity; Near Vision; Peripheral Vision. **General Work Activities**—*Information Input:* Inspecting Equipment, Structures, or Materials; Monitoring Processes, Materials, or Surroundings; Identifying Objects, Actions, and Events. *Mental Process:* Judging Qualities of Things, Services, or Other People's Work; Thinking Creatively; Updating and Using Relevant Knowledge. *Work Output:* Handling and Moving Objects; Controlling Machines and Processes; Performing General Physical Activities. *Interacting with Others:* Communicating with Other Workers; Communicating with Persons Outside Organization; Performing Administrative Activities. **Physical Work Conditions**—Hazardous Equipment; Very Hot or Cold; Using Hands on Objects, Tools, or Controls; Indoors; Distracting Sounds and Noise Levels. **Other Job Characteristics**—Importance of Repeating Same Tasks; Degree of Automation; Pace Determined by Speed of Equipment.

Experience—Job Zone 3. Previous work-related skill, knowledge, or experience is required. **Job Preparation:** SVP 6.0 to less than 7.0—more than one year and less than four years. **Knowledge**—Mechanical; Fine Arts; Production and Processing; Building and Construction; Design. **Instructional Programs**—Watchmaking and Jewelrymaking.

Related DOT Jobs—700.281-022 Silversmith II; 700.381-022 Hammersmith; 704.381-010 Chaser.

51-9071.03 Model and Mold Makers, Jewelry

- **Education/Training Required: Long-term on-the-job training**
- **Employed: No data available.**
- **Annual Earnings: $27,210**
- **Growth: 1.3%**
- **Annual Job Openings: 3,000**

Make models or molds to create jewelry items.

Carves, chisels, scrapes, and files plaster, wax, or other plastic materials to make mold or model according to design specifications. Fits, secures, and solders halves of molds together and drills holes in mold to attach handles and allow gases to escape during casting. Lays out design on metal stock and cuts along markings to fabricate pieces used to cast metal molds. Builds sand mold in flask, following pattern, and heats flask, using furnace or torch to dry and harden mold. Cuts design in mold or other material to be used as model to fabricate metal and jewelry products. Constructs preliminary model of wax, metal, clay, or plaster; forms sample casting in mold; and measures casting to verify dimensions. Mixes or melts clay, metal, plaster, wax, or other material and pours material into mold to cast model or mold. Examines and measures metal parts for conformance to design specifications on scale drawing. Writes or modifies design specifications, such as content, weight, and material to be used to cast article. Presses model into clay and builds up clay around exposed parts of model to retain plaster. Removes mold from cast article, cleans mold, and applies shellac and dry powder to preserve mold for reuse. Polishes metal surfaces and products, using abrasive wheel. Modifies, sharpens, repairs, or fabricates jigs, fixtures, and hand tools, such as scrapers, cutter, gougers, and shapers. Computes cost of labor and material to determine production cost of products and articles.

GOE INFORMATION—**Interest Area:** 08. Industrial Production. **Work Group:** 08.02. Production Technology. **Personality Type**—Realistic. Realistic occupations frequently involve work activities that include practical, hands-on problems and solutions. They often deal with plants, animals, and real-world materials like wood, tools, and machinery. Many of the occupations require working outside and do not involve a lot of paperwork or working closely with others. **Work Values**—Independence; Good Working Conditions; Variety; Creativity; Ability Utilization. **Skills**—Repairing; Operation and Control; Equipment Selection; Technology Design. **Abilities**—*Cognitive:* Visualization; Originality; Mathematical Reasoning; Fluency of Ideas; Number Facility. *Psychomotor:* Arm-Hand Steadiness; Finger Dexterity; Manual Dexterity; Wrist-Finger Speed; Control Precision. *Physical:* Explosive Strength; Dynamic Flexibility; Gross Body Coordination; Gross Body Equilibrium; Stamina. *Sensory:* Near Vision; Visual Color Discrimination; Glare Sensitivity; Depth Perception. **General Work Activities**—*Information Input:* Getting Information; Inspecting Equipment, Structures, or Materials; Estimating Needed Characteristics. *Mental Process:* Thinking Creatively; Judging Qualities of Things, Services, or Other People's Work; Evaluating Information Against Standards. *Work Output:* Handling and Moving Objects; Drafting and Specifying Technical Devices; Performing General Physical Activities. *Interacting with Others:* Communicating with Other Workers; Performing Administrative Activities; Interpreting Meaning of Information for Others. **Physical Work Conditions**—Minor Burns, Cuts, Bites, or Stings; Hazardous Equipment; Using Hands on Objects, Tools, or Controls; Common Protective or Safety Attire; Indoors. **Other Job Characteristics**—Importance of Repeating Same Tasks; Pace Determined by Speed of Equipment; Degree of Automation.

Experience—Job Zone 3. Previous work-related skill, knowledge, or experience is required. **Job Preparation:** SVP 6.0 to less than 7.0—more than one year and less than four years. **Knowledge**—Design; Fine Arts; Building and Construction; Production and Processing; Economics and Accounting. **Instructional Programs**—Watchmaking and Jewelrymaking.

Related DOT Jobs—518.381-010 Bench-Molder Apprentice; 518.381-022 Molder, Bench; 700.281-018 Model Maker I; 700.381-034 Mold Maker I; 700.381-038 Mold-Maker Apprentice; 709.381-018 Model Maker II; 709.381-022 Model-Maker Apprentice; 735.381-018 Sample Maker II; 777.381-022 Mold Maker II.

51-9071.04 Bench Workers, Jewelry

- Education/Training Required: **Long-term on-the-job training**
- Employed: **No data available.**
- Annual Earnings: **$27,210**
- Growth: **1.3%**
- Annual Job Openings: **3,000**

Cut, file, form, and solder parts for jewelry.

Cuts, trims, shapes, and smoothes jewelry stones, pearls, and metal pieces, using abrasives, grinding stone, and power and hand tools. Weighs, mixes, and melts metal alloys or material and pours molten material into mold to cast models of jewelry. Forms, joins, or assembles metal pieces, articles, or wire, using soldering iron, gas torch, and hand tools. Disassembles mold casting from metal or jewelry workpiece and places workpiece in water or on tray to cool. Marks and drills holes in jewelry mounting to center stones according to design specifications. Positions and aligns stones and metal pieces and sets, mounts, and secures item in place, using setting and hand tools. Manually rotates mold to distribute molten material and prevent formation of air pockets in mold. Marks, engraves, or embosses designs on metal pieces, such as castings, wire, or jewelry, following samples, sketches, or other specifications. Plates articles, such as jewelry pieces and clock and watch dials, with silver, gold, nickel, or other metals. Examines assembled or finished product, using magnifying glass or precision measuring instruments, to ensure conformance to specifications. Repairs existing jewelry mountings to reposition jewels or adjust mounting. Sands inside mold pieces, using

emery cloth and chalkdust. Assembles and secures mold sections used to cast metal articles and pieces. Brushes, buffs, cleans, and polishes metal items and jewelry pieces, using jeweler's tools, polishing wheel, and chemical bath. Operates machines, such as centrifugal-casting, routing, and lathe, to fabricate casting molds, metal parts, or wax models of products. Weighs completed pieces to determine deviation from specifications and records weight and processing time on production records. Designs and fabricates molds, models, and machine accessories and modifies hand tools used to cast metal and jewelry pieces. Researches and analyzes reference materials and consults with interested parties to develop new or modify existing products.

GOE INFORMATION—**Interest Area:** 08. Industrial Production. **Work Group:** 08.02. Production Technology. **Personality Type**—Realistic. Realistic occupations frequently involve work activities that include practical, hands-on problems and solutions. They often deal with plants, animals, and real-world materials like wood, tools, and machinery. Many of the occupations require working outside and do not involve a lot of paperwork or working closely with others. **Work Values**—Independence; Good Working Conditions; Creativity; Ability Utilization; Variety. **Skills**—Operation and Control; Quality Control Analysis. **Abilities**—*Cognitive:* Visualization; Flexibility of Closure; Written Comprehension. *Psychomotor:* Finger Dexterity; Arm-Hand Steadiness; Manual Dexterity; Control Precision; Wrist-Finger Speed. *Physical:* Dynamic Flexibility. *Sensory:* Near Vision; Visual Color Discrimination. **General Work Activities**—*Information Input:* Getting Information; Monitoring Processes, Materials, or Surroundings; Identifying Objects, Actions, and Events. *Mental Process:* Thinking Creatively; Updating and Using Relevant Knowledge; Evaluating Information Against Standards. *Work Output:* Handling and Moving Objects; Controlling Machines and Processes; Documenting or Recording Information. *Interacting with Others:* Communicating with Persons Outside Organization; Communicating with Other Workers; Establishing and Maintaining Relationships. **Physical Work Conditions**—Using Hands on Objects, Tools, or Controls; Sitting; Indoors; Making Repetitive Motions; Hazardous Equipment. **Other Job Characteristics**—Importance of Being Exact or Accurate; Importance of Repeating Same Tasks; Pace Determined by Speed of Equipment.

Experience—Job Zone 3. Previous work-related skill, knowledge, or experience is required. **Job Preparation:** SVP 6.0 to less than 7.0—more than one year and less than four years. **Knowledge**—Fine Arts; Production and Processing; Design; Chemistry; History and Archeology. **Instructional Programs**—Watchmaking and Jewelrymaking.

Related DOT Jobs—502.381-010 Caster; 502.682-018 Centrifugal-Casting-Machine Operator; 700.381-010 Chain Maker, Hand; 700.381-014 Fancy-Wire Drawer; 700.381-018 Goldbeater; 700.381-026 Lay-Out Worker; 700.381-050 Solderer; 700.381-054 Stone Setter; 700.381-058 Stone-Setter Apprentice; 704.381-018 Engine Turner; 715.381-046 Dial Maker; 735.381-010 Bench Hand; 735.381-014 Pearl Restorer; 735.681-010 Bracelet and Brooch Maker; 770.381-010 Bead Maker.

51-9071.05 Pewter Casters and Finishers

- Education/Training Required: **Postsecondary vocational training**
- Employed: **No data available.**
- Annual Earnings: **$27,210**
- Growth: **1.3%**
- Annual Job Openings: **3,000**

Cast and finish pewter alloy to form parts for goblets, candlesticks, and other pewterware.

Fills casting mold to form parts. Secures molded item in chuck of lathe, activates lathe, and finishes inner and outer surfaces of item. Rotates mold to distribute alloy in mold and to prevent formation of air pockets. Heats ingots or alloy mixture and skims off impurities. Weighs and mixes alloy ingredients. Engraves decorative lines on item, using engraving tool. Routes out location of part and solder path where part is joined to item, using routing machine. Positions and aligns auxiliary part in jig and joins parts, using solder and blowtorch. Sands inside of mold parts, applies glaze to inside surface of mold, and assembles mold. Strikes mold to separate dried casting from mold. Determines placement of auxiliary parts, such as handle and spout, and marks locations of parts. Weighs completed item to determine deviation from specified weight and records weight. Designs, drafts, and fabricates models of new casting molds and chipping and turning tools used to finish surface of products. Carries castings or finished item to storage area or next workstation. Researches reference materials, analyzes production data, and consults with interested parties to develop ideas for new products.

GOE INFORMATION—Interest Area: 08. Industrial Production. Work Group: 08.02. Production Technology. Personality Type—Realistic. Realistic occupations frequently involve work activities that include practical, hands-on problems and solutions. They often deal with plants, animals, and real-world materials like wood, tools, and machinery. Many of the occupations require working outside and do not involve a lot of paperwork or working closely with others. Work Values—Independence; Creativity; Ability Utilization; Variety; Moral Values. Skills—Operation and Control; Technology Design; Installation. Abilities—*Cognitive:* Originality; Visualization; Fluency of Ideas; Selective Attention; Information Ordering. *Psychomotor:* Arm-Hand Steadiness; Control Precision; Speed of Limb Movement; Finger Dexterity; Rate Control. *Physical:* Dynamic Strength; Extent Flexibility; Explosive Strength; Dynamic Flexibility; Static Strength. *Sensory:* Auditory Attention; Glare Sensitivity; Near Vision; Visual Color Discrimination. General Work Activities—*Information Input:* Getting Information; Identifying Objects, Actions, and Events; Monitoring Processes, Materials, or Surroundings. *Mental Process:* Thinking Creatively; Organizing, Planning, and Prioritizing; Updating and Using Relevant Knowledge. *Work Output:* Handling and Moving Objects; Performing General Physical Activities; Drafting and Specifying Technical Devices. *Interacting with Others:* Communicating with Persons Outside Organization; Communicating with Other Workers; Performing Administrative Activities. Physical Work Conditions—Very Hot or Cold; Minor Burns, Cuts, Bites, or Stings; Common Protective or Safety Attire; Extremely Bright or Inadequate Lighting; Hazardous Equipment. Other Job Characteristics—Importance of Repeating Same Tasks; Pace Determined by Speed of Equipment; Degree of Automation.

Experience—Job Zone 4. A minimum of two to four years of work-related skill, knowledge, or experience is needed. Job Preparation: SVP 7.0 to less than 8.0—two years to less than 10 years. Knowledge—Fine Arts; Design; Production and Processing; Building and Construction; Chemistry. Instructional Programs—Watchmaking and Jewelrymaking.

Related DOT Jobs—502.384-010 Pewter Caster; 700.261-010 Pewterer; 700.281-026 Pewter Finisher.

51-9071.06 Gem and Diamond Workers

- Education/Training Required: Moderate-term on-the-job training
- Employed: No data available.
- Annual Earnings: $27,210
- Growth: 1.3%
- Annual Job Openings: 3,000

Split, saw, cut, shape, polish, or drill gems and diamonds used in jewelry or industrial tools.

Holds stone, gem, die, or stylus, attached to holder or lapidary stick, against rotating plates or wheels to shape, grind, and polish. Bores, laps, and polishes holes in industrial diamonds used for dies, using drill, lathe, lapping machine, and hand tools. Splits gem along premarked lines to remove imperfections, using blade and jeweler's hammer. Grinds, drills, and finishes jewel bearings for use in precision instruments, such as compasses and chronometers. Laps girdle on rough diamonds, using diamond girdling lathe. Locates and marks drilling position on surface of diamond dies, using diamond chip and power hand drill. Measures size of stone's bore holes and cuts to ensure adherence to specifications, using precision measuring instruments. Positions gem or diamond against edge of revolving saw, lathe saw, or lapidary slitter to cut, block, or slit stone. Selects shaping wheel and mixes and applies abrasive, bort, or polishing compound. Examines diamond or gem to determine shape, cut, and width of stone. Secures gem or diamond in holder, chuck, dop, lapidary stick, or block for cutting, polishing, grinding, drilling, or shaping. Examines gem during processing to ensure accuracy of angle and position of cut or bore, using magnifying glass, loupe, or shadowgraph. Replaces, trues, and sharpens blades, drills, and plates. Lubricates, dismantles, and cleans lapping, boring, cutting, polishing, and shaping equipment and machinery.

GOE INFORMATION—Interest Area: 08. Industrial Production. Work Group: 08.02. Production Technology. Personality Type—Realistic. Realistic occupations frequently involve work activities that include practical, hands-on problems and solutions. They often deal with plants, animals, and real-world materials like wood, tools, and machinery. Many of the occupations require working outside and do not involve a lot of paperwork or working closely with others. Work Values—Independence; Supervision, Technical; Ability Utilization; Compensation; Good Working Conditions. Skills—Operation and Control; Equipment Selection. Abilities—*Cognitive:* Selective Attention; Visualization; Flexibility of Closure; Category Flexibility; Mathematical Reasoning. *Psychomotor:* Arm-Hand Steadiness; Control Precision; Finger Dexterity; Manual Dexterity; Wrist-Finger Speed. *Physical:* Explosive Strength; Dynamic Strength; Dynamic Flexibility. *Sensory:* Near Vision; Visual Color Discrimination; Depth Perception; Glare Sensitivity. General Work Activities—*Information Input:* Getting Information; Identifying Objects, Actions, and Events; Monitoring Processes, Materials, or Surroundings. *Mental Process:* Judging Qualities of Things, Services, or Other People's Work; Evaluating Information Against Standards; Thinking Creatively. *Work Output:* Handling and Moving Objects; Controlling Machines and Processes; Performing General Physical Activities. *Interacting with Others:* Monitoring and Controlling Resources; Communicating with Other Workers; Coordinating the Work and Activities of Others. Physical Work Conditions—Hazardous Equipment; Minor Burns, Cuts, Bites, or Stings; Using Hands on Objects, Tools, or Controls; Sitting; Indoors. Other Job Characteristics—Importance of Being Exact or Accurate; Importance of Repeating Same Tasks; Consequence of Error.

Experience—Job Zone 2. Some previous work-related skill, knowledge, or experience may be helpful, but usually is not needed. Job Preparation: SVP 4.0 to less than 6.0—six months to less than two years. Knowledge—Mechanical; Fine Arts; Production and Processing; Engineering and Technology; Physics. Instructional Programs—Watchmaking and Jewelrymaking.

Related DOT Jobs—770.261-010 Brilliandeer-Lopper; 770.261-014 Girdler; 770.281-014 Gem Cutter; 770.381-014 Diamond Cleaver; 770.381-018 Diamond Driller; 770.381-022 Diamond-Die Polisher; 770.381-026 Jewel Blocker and Sawyer; 770.381-030 Jewel-Bearing Maker; 770.381-034 Oliving-Machine Operator; 770.381-038 Sapphire-Stylus Grinder; 770.381-042 Spotter; 770.382-010 Lathe Operator; 770.382-014 Phonograph-Needle-Tip Maker.

51-9081.00 Dental Laboratory Technicians

- Education/Training Required: Long-term on-the-job training
- Employed: 43,017
- Annual Earnings: $27,970
- Growth: 6.3%
- Annual Job Openings: 3,000

Construct and repair full or partial dentures or dental appliances.

Apply porcelain paste or wax over prosthesis frameworks or setups, using brushes and spatulas. Build and shape wax teeth, using small hand instruments and information from observations or dentists' specifications. Fabricate, alter, and repair dental devices such as dentures, crowns, bridges, inlays, and appliances for straightening teeth. Fill chipped or low spots in surfaces of devices, using acrylic resins. Load newly constructed teeth into porcelain furnaces in order to bake the porcelain onto the metal framework. Melt metals or mix plaster, porcelain, or acrylic pastes and pour materials into molds or over frameworks in order to form dental prostheses or apparatus. Mold wax over denture setups in order to form the full contours of artificial gums. Place tooth models on apparatus that mimics bite and movement of patient's jaw to evaluate functionality of model. Prepare metal surfaces for bonding with porcelain to create artificial teeth, using small hand tools. Read prescriptions or specifications and examine models and impressions in order to determine the design of dental products to be constructed. Rebuild or replace linings, wire sections, and missing teeth in order to repair dentures. Remove excess metal or porcelain and polish surfaces of prostheses or frameworks, using polishing machines. Shape and solder wire and metal frames or bands for dental products, using soldering irons and hand tools. Test appliances for conformance to specifications and accuracy of occlusion, using articulators and micrometers. Create a model of patient's mouth by pouring plaster into a dental impression and allowing plaster to set. Prepare wax bite-blocks and impression trays for use. Train and supervise other dental technicians or dental laboratory bench workers.

GOE INFORMATION—Interest Area: 08. Industrial Production. **Work Group:** 08.02. Production Technology. **Personality Type—**Realistic. Realistic occupations frequently involve work activities that include practical, hands-on problems and solutions. They often deal with plants, animals, and real-world materials like wood, tools, and machinery. Many of the occupations require working outside and do not involve a lot of paperwork or working closely with others. **Work Values—**Independence; Good Working Conditions; Supervision, Technical; Moral Values; Recognition. **Skills—**Quality Control Analysis; Technology Design; Science; Reading Comprehension; Operations Analysis. **Abilities—***Cognitive:* Visualization; Written Comprehension; Speed of Closure; Information Ordering; Oral Comprehension. *Psychomotor:* Finger Dexterity; Arm-Hand Steadiness; Control Precision; Manual Dexterity; Wrist-Finger Speed. *Physical:* None met the criteria. *Sensory:* Near Vision; Visual Color Discrimination. **General Work Activities—***Information Input:* Getting Information; Monitoring Processes, Materials, or Surroundings; Identifying Objects, Actions, and Events. *Mental Process:* Evaluating Information Against Standards; Analyzing Data or Information; Updating and Using Relevant Knowledge. *Work Output:* Handling and Moving Objects; Controlling Machines and Processes; Performing General Physical Activities. *Interacting with Others:* Communicating with Other Workers; Communicating with Persons Outside Organization; Establishing and Maintaining Relationships. **Physical Work Conditions—**Using Hands on Objects, Tools, or Controls; Indoors; Sitting; Common Protective or Safety Attire; Making Repetitive Motions. **Other Job Characteristics—**Importance of Repeating Same Tasks; Importance of Being Exact or Accurate; Consequence of Error.

Experience—Job Zone 3. Previous work-related skill, knowledge, or experience is required. **Job Preparation:** SVP 6.0 to less than 7.0—more than one year and less than four years. **Knowledge—**Medicine and Dentistry; Design; Biology; Building and Construction; Chemistry. **Instructional Programs—**Dental Laboratory Technology/Technician.

Related DOT Jobs—712.381-014 Contour Wire Specialist, Denture; 712.381-018 Dental-Laboratory Technician; 712.381-022 Dental-Laboratory-Technician Apprentice; 712.381-026 Orthodontic Band Maker; 712.381-030 Orthodontic Technician; 712.381-042 Dental Ceramist; 712.381-046 Denture Waxer; 712.381-050 Finisher, Denture; 712.664-010 Dental Ceramist Assistant.

51-9082.00 Medical Appliance Technicians

- Education/Training Required: Long-term on-the-job training
- Employed: 12,892
- Annual Earnings: $25,850
- Growth: 19.0%
- Annual Job Openings: 1,000

Construct, fit, maintain, or repair medical supportive devices, such as braces, artificial limbs, joints, arch supports, and other surgical and medical appliances.

Bend, form, and shape fabric or material so that it conforms to prescribed contours needed to fabricate structural components. Construct or receive casts or impressions of patients' torsos or limbs for use as cutting and fabrication patterns. Cover or pad metal or plastic structures and devices, using coverings such as rubber, leather, felt, plastic, or fiberglass. Drill and tap holes for rivets and glue, weld, bolt, and rivet parts together in order to form prosthetic or orthotic devices. Fit appliances onto patients, and make any necessary adjustments. Instruct patients in use of prosthetic or orthotic devices. Lay out and mark dimensions of parts, using templates and precision measuring instruments. Make orthotic/prosthetic devices, using materials such as thermoplastic and thermosetting materials, metal alloys and leather, and hand and power tools. Mix pigments to match patients' skin coloring, according to formulas, and apply mixtures to orthotic or prosthetic devices. Polish artificial limbs, braces, and supports, using grinding and buffing wheels. Read prescriptions or specifications in order to determine the type of product or device to be fabricated and the materials and tools that will be required. Repair, modify, and maintain medical supportive devices, such as artificial limbs, braces, and surgical supports, according to specifications. Test medical supportive devices for proper alignment, movement, and biomechanical stability, using meters and alignment fixtures. Service and repair machinery used in the fabrication of appliances. Take patients' body or limb measurements for use in device construction.

GOE INFORMATION—Interest Area: 05. Mechanics, Installers, and Repairers. **Work Group:** 05.03. Mechanical Work. **Personality Type—**Realistic. Realistic occupations frequently involve work activities that include practical, hands-on problems and solutions. They often deal with plants, animals, and real-world materials like wood, tools, and machinery. Many of the occupations require working outside and do not involve a lot of paperwork or working closely with others. **Work Values—**Independence; Social Service; Achievement; Recognition; Social Status. **Skills—**Technology Design; Repairing; Operations Analysis; Equipment Selection; Quality Control Analysis; Operation and Control. **Abilities—***Cognitive:* Visualization; Information Ordering. *Psychomotor:* Manual Dexterity;

Finger Dexterity; Arm-Hand Steadiness; Control Precision; Rate Control. *Physical:* Explosive Strength. *Sensory:* Visual Color Discrimination; Speech Clarity; Speech Recognition; Glare Sensitivity; Near Vision. **General Work Activities**—*Information Input:* Getting Information; Identifying Objects, Actions, and Events; Monitoring Processes, Materials, or Surroundings. *Mental Process:* Updating and Using Relevant Knowledge; Organizing, Planning, and Prioritizing; Judging Qualities of Things, Services, or Other People's Work. *Work Output:* Handling and Moving Objects; Controlling Machines and Processes; Drafting and Specifying Technical Devices. *Interacting with Others:* Assisting and Caring for Others; Communicating with Persons Outside Organization; Teaching Others. **Physical Work Conditions**—Hazardous Equipment; Making Repetitive Motions; Minor Burns, Cuts, Bites, or Stings; Kneeling, Crouching, or Crawling; Common Protective or Safety Attire. **Other Job Characteristics**—Importance of Being Exact or Accurate; Importance of Repeating Same Tasks; Pace Determined by Speed of Equipment.

Experience—Job Zone 2. Some previous work-related skill, knowledge, or experience may be helpful, but usually is not needed. **Job Preparation:** SVP 4.0 to less than 6.0—six months to less than two years. **Knowledge**—Design; Medicine and Dentistry; Mechanical; Engineering and Technology; Therapy and Counseling. **Instructional Programs**—Assistive/Augmentative Technology and Rehabilitation Engineering; Orthotist/Prosthetist.

Related DOT Jobs—712.381-010 Arch-Support Technician; 712.381-034 Orthotics Technician; 712.381-038 Prosthetics Technician.

51-9083.00 Ophthalmic Laboratory Technicians

- **Education/Training Required: Moderate-term on-the-job training**
- **Employed: 32,407**
- **Annual Earnings: $21,350**
- **Growth: 5.7%**
- **Annual Job Openings: 2,000**

Cut, grind, and polish eyeglasses, contact lenses, or other precision optical elements. Assemble and mount lenses into frames or process other optical elements.

No task data available.

GOE INFORMATION—**Interest Area:** 05. Mechanics, Installers, and Repairers. **Work Group:** 05.03. Mechanical Work. **Note:** The Department of Labor has not collected some data for this job, so it has fewer details than the other descriptions.

Instructional Programs—Ophthalmic Laboratory Technology/Technician.

Related DOT Jobs—711.381-010 Optical-Instrument Assembler; 713.381-010 Lens-Mold Setter; 713.681-010 Lens Mounter II; 716.280-010 Optician Apprentice; 716.280-014 Optician; 716.280-018 Optician; 716.280-540 Shop Optician, Surface Room; 716.280-541 Shop Optician, Benchroom; 716.381-014 Lay-Out Technician; 716.382-010 Lathe Operator, Contact Lens; 716.382-014 Optical-Element Coater; 716.382-018 Precision-Lens Grinder; 716.382-022 Precision-Lens-Grinder Apprentice; 716.462-010 Precision-Lens Centerer and Edger; 716.681-010 Blocker and Cutter, Contact Lens; 716.681-014 Glass Cutter, Hand; 716.681-018 Lens Polisher, Hand; 716.682-010 Eyeglass-Lens Cutter; 716.682-014 Precision-Lens Generator; 716.682-018 Precision-Lens Polisher.

51-9083.01 Precision Lens Grinders and Polishers

- **Education/Training Required: Moderate-term on-the-job training**
- **Employed: No data available.**
- **Annual Earnings: $21,350**
- **Growth: 5.7%**
- **Annual Job Openings: 2,000**

Set up and operate variety of machines and equipment to grind and polish lens and other optical elements.

Adjust lenses and frames in order to correct alignment. Assemble molds used to cast contact lenses. Clean finished lenses and eyeglasses, using cloths and solvents. Control equipment that coats lenses to alter their reflective qualities. Examine prescriptions, work orders, or broken or used eyeglasses in order to determine specifications for lenses, contact lenses, and other optical elements. Inspect lens blanks in order to detect flaws, verify smoothness of surface, and ensure thickness of coating on lenses. Inspect, weigh, and measure mounted or unmounted lenses after completion in order to verify alignment and conformance to specifications, using precision instruments. Lay out lenses and trace lens outlines on glass, using templates. Mount and secure lens blanks or optical lenses in holding tools or chucks of cutting, polishing, grinding, or coating machines. Mount, secure, and align finished lenses in frames or optical assemblies, using precision hand tools. Position and adjust cutting tools to specified curvature, dimensions, and depth of cut. Remove lenses from molds and separate lenses in containers for further processing or storage. Select lens blanks, molds, tools, and polishing or grinding wheels according to production specifications. Set dials and start machines to polish lenses or hold lenses against rotating wheels in order to polish them manually. Set up machines to polish, bevel, edge, and grind lenses, flats, blanks, and other precision optical elements. Shape lenses appropriately so that they can be inserted into frames. Assemble eyeglass frames and attach shields, nose pads, and temple pieces, using pliers, screwdrivers, and drills. Immerse eyeglass frames in solutions in order to harden, soften, or dye frames. Repair broken parts, using precision hand tools and soldering irons.

GOE INFORMATION—**Interest Area:** 08. Industrial Production. **Work Group:** 08.02. Production Technology. **Personality Type**—Realistic. Realistic occupations frequently involve work activities that include practical, hands-on problems and solutions. They often deal with plants, animals, and real-world materials like wood, tools, and machinery. Many of the occupations require working outside and do not involve a lot of paperwork or working closely with others. **Work Values**—Independence; Moral Values; Good Working Conditions; Compensation; Supervision, Technical. **Skills**—Operation and Control; Equipment Selection; Operation Monitoring; Quality Control Analysis. **Abilities**—*Cognitive:* Perceptual Speed; Written Comprehension; Number Facility; Flexibility of Closure; Memorization. *Psychomotor:* Finger Dexterity; Arm-Hand Steadiness; Manual Dexterity; Control Precision; Rate Control. *Physical:* Extent Flexibility; Trunk Strength; Explosive Strength; Dynamic Flexibility. *Sensory:* Near Vision; Visual Color Discrimination; Depth Perception. **General Work Activities**—*Information Input:* Inspecting Equipment, Structures, or Materials; Monitoring Processes, Materials, or Surroundings; Identifying Objects, Actions, and Events. *Mental Process:* Updating and Using Relevant Knowledge; Evaluating Information Against Standards; Judging Qualities of Things, Services, or Other People's Work. *Work Output:* Handling and Moving Objects; Controlling Machines and Processes; Documenting or Recording Information. *Interacting with Others:* Communicating with Other Workers; Performing Administrative

Activities; Coordinating the Work and Activities of Others. **Physical Work Conditions**—Using Hands on Objects, Tools, or Controls; Indoors; Hazardous Equipment; Sitting; Common Protective or Safety Attire. **Other Job Characteristics**—Importance of Being Exact or Accurate; Degree of Automation; Pace Determined by Speed of Equipment.

Experience—Job Zone 3. Previous work-related skill, knowledge, or experience is required. **Job Preparation:** SVP 6.0 to less than 7.0—more than one year and less than four years. **Knowledge**—Physics; Mechanical; Production and Processing; Chemistry; Medicine and Dentistry. **Instructional Programs**—Ophthalmic Laboratory Technology/Technician.

Related DOT Jobs—713.381-010 Lens-Mold Setter; 713.681-010 Lens Mounter II; 716.280-010 Optician Apprentice; 716.280-014 Optician; 716.381-014 Lay-Out Technician; 716.382-010 Lathe Operator, Contact Lens; 716.382-014 Optical-Element Coater; 716.382-018 Precision-Lens Grinder; 716.382-022 Precision-Lens-Grinder Apprentice; 716.462-010 Precision-Lens Centerer and Edger; 716.681-010 Blocker and Cutter, Contact Lens; 716.681-014 Glass Cutter, Hand; 716.681-018 Lens Polisher, Hand; 716.682-010 Eyeglass-Lens Cutter; 716.682-014 Precision-Lens Generator; 716.682-018 Precision-Lens Polisher.

51-9083.02 Optical Instrument Assemblers

- **Education/Training Required: Moderate-term on-the-job training**
- **Employed: No data available.**
- **Annual Earnings: $21,350**
- **Growth: 5.7%**
- **Annual Job Openings: 2,000**

Assemble optical instruments, such as telescopes, level-transits, and gunsights.

Cement multiple lens assemblies together. Clean elements and parts, using tissue, cleaning solutions, and air compressors. Coat optical elements according to specifications, using coating equipment. Fill instrument housings with nitrogen gas in order to minimize corrosive effects on internal optical surfaces, using vacuum pumps. Grind and polish optics, using hand tools and polishing cloths. Insert and screw locking rings into housings in order to hold elements in place; apply cement to locking rings in order to prevent loosening. Measure and mark dimensions and reference points and lay out stock for machining. Measure elements and instrument parts in order to verify dimensional specifications, using precision measuring instruments. Mix holding compounds and mount workpieces or optical elements on holding fixtures. Pick up elements, using vacuum-holding devices, and position elements in mounting seats of instrument housings. Position targets in darkroom tunnels and connect optical instruments to test devices, such as oscilloscopes and collimators. Set up and operate machines in order to assemble structural, mechanical, and optical parts of instruments. Sight instruments on targets and read dials in order to determine optical centers of instrument lenses and to verify compliance to focusing power specifications. Study work orders, blueprints, and sketches in order to formulate plans and sequences for fabricating optical elements, instruments, and systems. Compute sighting instrument distances, using trigonometric formulas. Paint parts, using brushes and spray guns. Record production, inspection, and test data in logs.

GOE INFORMATION—**Interest Area:** 05. Mechanics, Installers, and Repairers. **Work Group:** 05.03. Mechanical Work. **Personality Type**—Realistic. Realistic occupations frequently involve work activities that include practical, hands-on problems and solutions. They often deal with plants,

animals, and real-world materials like wood, tools, and machinery. Many of the occupations require working outside and do not involve a lot of paperwork or working closely with others. **Work Values**—Independence; Moral Values; Good Working Conditions; Supervision, Technical; Supervision, Human Relations. **Skills**—Equipment Selection; Operation Monitoring; Operation and Control; Mathematics; Quality Control Analysis; Installation; Science; Technology Design. **Abilities**—*Cognitive:* Number Facility; Mathematical Reasoning; Memorization; Information Ordering; Deductive Reasoning. *Psychomotor:* Finger Dexterity; Arm-Hand Steadiness; Manual Dexterity; Rate Control; Reaction Time. *Physical:* Explosive Strength; Trunk Strength; Dynamic Flexibility; Extent Flexibility; Gross Body Equilibrium. *Sensory:* Near Vision; Depth Perception; Visual Color Discrimination; Far Vision. **General Work Activities**—*Information Input:* Inspecting Equipment, Structures, or Materials; Monitoring Processes, Materials, or Surroundings; Identifying Objects, Actions, and Events. *Mental Process:* Processing Information; Evaluating Information Against Standards; Judging Qualities of Things, Services, or Other People's Work. *Work Output:* Controlling Machines and Processes; Handling and Moving Objects; Performing General Physical Activities. *Interacting with Others:* Performing Administrative Activities; Communicating with Other Workers; Interpreting Meaning of Information for Others. **Physical Work Conditions**—Using Hands on Objects, Tools, or Controls; Hazardous Equipment; Indoors; Common Protective or Safety Attire; Hazardous Conditions. **Other Job Characteristics**—Degree of Automation; Pace Determined by Speed of Equipment; Importance of Being Exact or Accurate.

Experience—Job Zone 4. A minimum of two to four years of work-related skill, knowledge, or experience is needed. **Job Preparation:** SVP 7.0 to less than 8.0—two years to less than 10 years. **Knowledge**—Physics; Mathematics; Mechanical; Design; Building and Construction. **Instructional Programs**—Ophthalmic Laboratory Technology/Technician.

Related DOT Jobs—711.381-010 Optical-Instrument Assembler; 716.280-018 Optician.

51-9111.00 Packaging and Filling Machine Operators and Tenders

- **Education/Training Required: Short-term on-the-job training**
- **Employed: 378,652**
- **Annual Earnings: $20,760**
- **Growth: 14.4%**
- **Annual Job Openings: 56,000**

Operate or tend machines to prepare industrial or consumer products for storage or shipment. Includes cannery workers who pack food products.

Adjust machine components and machine tension and pressure according to size or processing angle of product. Inspect and remove defective products and packaging material. Monitor the production line, watching for problems such as pile-ups, jams, or glue that isn't sticking properly. Observe machine operations to ensure quality and conformity of filled or packaged products to standards. Package the product in the form in which it will be sent out, for example, filling bags with flour from a chute or spout. Regulate machine flow, speed, or temperature. Remove finished packaged items from machine and separate rejected items. Start machine by engaging controls. Stock and sort product for packaging or filling machine operation and replenish packaging supplies, such as wrapping paper, plastic sheet, boxes, cartons, glue, ink, or labels. Stop or reset machines when malfunctions occur, clear machine jams, and report malfunctions to a supervisor. Supply materials to spindles, conveyors, hoppers, or other feeding devices and unload packaged product. Tend or operate machine that packages product. Attach identification labels to finished packaged items or cut stencils and stencil information on containers, such as lot numbers or shipping destinations. Clean and remove damaged or otherwise inferior materials to prepare raw products for processing. Clean, oil, and make minor adjustments or repairs to machinery and equipment, such as opening valves or setting guides. Clean packaging containers and line and pad crates and/or assemble cartons to prepare for product packing. Count and record finished and rejected packaged items. Secure finished packaged items by hand-tying, sewing, gluing, stapling, or attaching fastener. Sort, grade, weigh, and inspect products, verifying and adjusting product weight or measurement to meet specifications. Stack finished packaged items or wrap protective material around each item and pack the items in cartons or containers.

GOE INFORMATION—Interest Area: 08. Industrial Production. **Work Group:** 08.03. Production Work. **Personality Type**—Realistic. Realistic occupations frequently involve work activities that include practical, hands-on problems and solutions. They often deal with plants, animals, and real-world materials like wood, tools, and machinery. Many of the occupations require working outside and do not involve a lot of paperwork or working closely with others. **Work Values**—Moral Values; Independence; Supervision, Technical; Supervision, Human Relations; Activity. **Skills**—Operation Monitoring; Operation and Control; Repairing; Quality Control Analysis; Troubleshooting. **Abilities**—*Cognitive:* Perceptual Speed; Spatial Orientation; Selective Attention; Time Sharing; Category Flexibility. *Psychomotor:* Reaction Time; Response Orientation; Control Precision; Rate Control; Manual Dexterity. *Physical:* Static Strength; Extent Flexibility; Trunk Strength; Dynamic Flexibility; Explosive Strength. *Sensory:* Hearing Sensitivity; Peripheral Vision; Sound Localization; Visual Color Discrimination; Depth Perception. **General Work Activities**—*Information Input:* Monitoring Processes, Materials, or Surroundings; Inspecting Equipment, Structures, or Materials; Getting Information. *Mental Process:* Evaluating Information Against Standards; Judging Qualities of Things, Services, or Other People's Work; Processing Information. *Work Output:* Handling and Moving Objects; Controlling Machines and Processes; Performing General Physical Activities. *Interacting with Others:* Communicating with Other Workers; Performing Administrative Activities; Monitoring and Controlling Resources. **Physical Work Conditions**—Hazardous Equipment; Distracting Sounds and Noise Levels; Making Repetitive Motions; Minor Burns, Cuts, Bites, or Stings; Indoors. **Other Job Characteristics**—Pace Determined by Speed of Equipment; Degree of Automation; Importance of Repeating Same Tasks.

Experience—Job Zone 1. No previous work-related skill, knowledge, or experience is needed. **Job Preparation:** SVP below 4.0—less than six months. **Knowledge**—Production and Processing; Mechanical; Food Production; Physics; Public Safety and Security. **Instructional Programs**—No data available.

Related DOT Jobs—509.685-046 Scrap Baller; 518.683-010 Sand-Slinger Operator; 520.685-174 Molder, Meat; 520.685-210 Stuffer; 520.685-218 Tray-Casting-Machine Operator; 524.685-030 Filling Machine Tender; 525.685-014 Casing-Running-Machine Tender; 529.665-010 Fruit-Grader Operator; 529.665-022 Yeast-Cutting-and-Wrapping-Machine Operator; 529.685-010 Auto Roller; 529.685-038 Bunch Maker, Machine; 529.685-138 Ham-Rolling-Machine Operator; 529.685-162 Linking-Machine Operator; 529.685-186 Plug-Overwrap-Machine Tender; 529.685-190 Preservative Filler, Machine; 529.685-266 Wrapper Layer; 529.685-270 Wrapper-Layer-and-Examiner, Soft Work; 529.685-282 Can-Filling-and-Closing-Machine Tender; 529.685-286 Cigar-Wrapper Tender, Automatic; 554.684-014 Foam Dispenser; others.

51-9121.00 Coating, Painting, and Spraying Machine Setters, Operators, and Tenders

- **Education/Training Required: Short-term on-the-job training**
- **Employed: 107,975**
- **Annual Earnings: $24,710**
- **Growth: 11.9%**
- **Annual Job Openings: 18,000**

Set up, operate, or tend machines to coat or paint any of a wide variety of products. including food, glassware, cloth, ceramics, metal, plastic, paper, or wood with lacquer, silver, copper, rubber, varnish, glaze, enamel, oil, or rust-proofing materials.

No task data available.

GOE INFORMATION—Interest Area: 08. Industrial Production. **Work Group:** 08.02. Production Technology. **Note:** The Department of Labor has not collected some data for this job, so it has fewer details than the other descriptions.

Instructional Programs—No data available.

Related DOT Jobs—524.382-010 Coating-Machine Operator; 524.382-014 Enrobing-Machine Operator; 524.665-010 Sanding-Machine Operator; 524.682-010 Depositing-Machine Operator; 524.685-014 Cheese Sprayer; 524.685-018 Coating Operator; 524.685-022 Cracker Sprayer; 524.685-026 Enrobing-Machine Operator; 524.685-034 Icer, Machine; 534.380-010 Carbon-Paper-Coating-Machine Setter; 534.482-010 Waxing-Machine Operator; 534.582-010 Paper-Coating-Machine Operator; 534.682-010 Air-Drier-Machine Operator; 534.682-014 Carbon-Coater-Machine Operator; 534.682-018 Coating-Machine Operator; 534.682-022 Coating-Machine Operator, Hardboard; 534.682-038 Supercalender Operator; 534.685-022 Paper Coater; 534.685-026 Paraffin-Machine Operator; 534.685-030 Varnishing-Machine Operator; others.

51-9121.01 Coating, Painting, and Spraying Machine Setters and Set-Up Operators

- **Education/Training Required: Moderate-term on-the-job training**
- **Employed: No data available.**
- **Annual Earnings: $24,710**
- **Growth: 11.9%**
- **Annual Job Openings: 18,000**

Set up or set up and operate machines to coat or paint any of a wide variety of products, such as food products, glassware, and cloth, ceramic, metal, plastic, paper, and wood products, with lacquer, silver and copper solution, rubber, paint, varnish, glaze, enamel, oil, or rust-proofing materials.

Sets up and operates machines to paint or coat products with such materials as silver and copper solution, rubber, paint, glaze, oil, or rust-proofing materials. Selects and loads materials, parts, and workpieces on machine, using hand tools. Turns valves and adjusts controls to regulate speed of conveyor, temperature, air pressure and circulation, and flow or spray of coating or paint. Starts pumps to mix solutions and to activate coating or painting machines. Operates auxiliary machines or equipment used on the coating or painting process. Weighs or measures chemicals, coatings, or paints and adds to machine. Observes and adjusts loaded workpiece or machine according to specifications. Removes materials, parts, or workpieces from painting or coating machines, using hand tools. Examines and tests solutions, paints, products, and workpieces to ensure specifications are met. Measures thickness and quality of coating, using micrometer. Cleans and maintains coating and painting machines, using hand tools. Records operational data on specified forms.

GOE INFORMATION—Interest Area: 08. Industrial Production. **Work Group:** 08.02. Production Technology. **Personality Type—**Realistic. Realistic occupations frequently involve work activities that include practical, hands-on problems and solutions. They often deal with plants, animals, and real-world materials like wood, tools, and machinery. Many of the occupations require working outside and do not involve a lot of paperwork or working closely with others. **Work Values—**Moral Values; Independence; Activity; Supervision, Technical; Supervision, Human Relations. **Skills—**Operation Monitoring; Operation and Control; Equipment Selection. **Abilities—***Cognitive:* Spatial Orientation; Perceptual Speed; Memorization. *Psychomotor:* Rate Control; Manual Dexterity; Control Precision; Speed of Limb Movement; Arm-Hand Steadiness. *Physical:* Explosive Strength; Trunk Strength; Dynamic Strength; Gross Body Coordination; Stamina. *Sensory:* Visual Color Discrimination; Peripheral Vision; Depth Perception. **General Work Activities—***Information Input:* Monitoring Processes, Materials, or Surroundings; Inspecting Equipment, Structures, or Materials; Getting Information. *Mental Process:* Judging Qualities of Things, Services, or Other People's Work; Evaluating Information Against Standards; Updating and Using Relevant Knowledge. *Work Output:* Handling and Moving Objects; Controlling Machines and Processes; Performing General Physical Activities. *Interacting with Others:* Communicating with Other Workers; Performing Administrative Activities; Coordinating the Work and Activities of Others. **Physical Work Conditions—**Contaminants; Hazardous Conditions; Common Protective or Safety Attire; Hazardous Equipment; Distracting Sounds and Noise Levels. **Other Job Characteristics—**Degree of Automation; Pace Determined by Speed of Equipment; Importance of Repeating Same Tasks.

Experience—Job Zone 2. Some previous work-related skill, knowledge, or experience may be helpful, but usually is not needed. **Job Preparation:** SVP 4.0 to less than 6.0—six months to less than two years. **Knowledge—**Production and Processing; Chemistry; Mechanical; Food Production; Building and Construction. **Instructional Programs—**No data available.

Related DOT Jobs—534.380-010 Carbon-Paper-Coating-Machine Setter; 574.462-010 Abrasive-Coating-Machine Operator; 574.582-010 Silvering Applicator; 574.682-014 Spray-Machine Operator; 599.382-010 Paint-Sprayer Operator, Automatic; 632.380-018 Primer-Waterproofing-Machine Adjuster; 632.380-026 Varnishing-Unit Tool Setter; 679.682-010 Banding-Machine Operator; 692.682-014 Bead-Forming-Machine Operator.

51-9121.02 Coating, Painting, and Spraying Machine Operators and Tenders

- **Education/Training Required: Moderate-term on-the-job training**
- **Employed: No data available.**
- **Annual Earnings: $24,710**
- **Growth: 11.9%**
- **Annual Job Openings: 18,000**

Coating Machine Operators and Tenders: Operate or tend machines to coat any of a wide variety of items: Coat food products with sugar,

chocolate, or butter; coat paper and paper products with chemical solutions, wax, or glazes; or coat fabric with rubber or plastic. Painting and Spraying Machine Operators and Tenders: Operate or tend machines to spray or paint decorative, protective, or other coating or finish, such as adhesive, lacquer, paint, stain, latex, preservative, oil, or other solutions. May apply coating or finish to any of a wide variety of items or materials, such as wood and wood products, ceramics, and glass. Includes workers who apply coating or finish to materials preparatory to further processing or to consumer use.

Observes machine operation and gauges to detect defects or deviations from standards. Turns dial, handwheel, valve, or switch to control and adjust temperature, speed, and flow of product or machine. Starts and stops operation of machine, using lever or button. Fills hopper, reservoir, trough, or pan with material used to coat, paint, or spray, using conveyor or pail. Attaches specified hose or nozzle to machine, using wrench and pliers. Measures and mixes specified quantities of substances to create coatings, paints, or sprays. Aligns or fastens machine parts such as rollers, guides, brushes, and blades to secure roll, using hand tools. Threads or feeds item or product through or around machine rollers and dryers. Places item or product on feedrack, spindle, or reel strand to coat, paint, or spray, using hands, hoist, or trucklift. Examines, measures, weighs, or tests sample product to ensure conformance to specifications. Transfers completed item or product from machine to drying or storage area, using handcart, handtruck, or crane. Cleans machine, equipment, and work area, using water, solvents, and other cleaning aids. Records production data.

GOE INFORMATION—Interest Area: 08. Industrial Production. **Work Group:** 08.03. Production Work. **Personality Type—**Realistic. Realistic occupations frequently involve work activities that include practical, hands-on problems and solutions. They often deal with plants, animals, and real-world materials like wood, tools, and machinery. Many of the occupations require working outside and do not involve a lot of paperwork or working closely with others. **Work Values—**Moral Values; Supervision, Technical; Independence; Supervision, Human Relations; Company Policies and Practices. **Skills—**Operation Monitoring; Operation and Control. **Abilities—***Cognitive:* Perceptual Speed; Spatial Orientation. *Psychomotor:* Rate Control; Reaction Time; Arm-Hand Steadiness; Multilimb Coordination; Control Precision. *Physical:* Dynamic Strength; Dynamic Flexibility; Stamina; Gross Body Coordination; Explosive Strength. *Sensory:* Visual Color Discrimination; Sound Localization; Peripheral Vision. **General Work Activities—***Information Input:* Monitoring Processes, Materials, or Surroundings; Inspecting Equipment, Structures, or Materials; Getting Information. *Mental Process:* Evaluating Information Against Standards; Organizing, Planning, and Prioritizing; Updating and Using Relevant Knowledge. *Work Output:* Handling and Moving Objects; Controlling Machines and Processes; Performing General Physical Activities. *Interacting with Others:* Communicating with Other Workers; Establishing and Maintaining Relationships; Coordinating the Work and Activities of Others. **Physical Work Conditions—**Contaminants; Hazardous Conditions; Common Protective or Safety Attire; Hazardous Equipment; Making Repetitive Motions. **Other Job Characteristics—**Pace Determined by Speed of Equipment; Degree of Automation; Importance of Repeating Same Tasks.

Experience—Job Zone 1. No previous work-related skill, knowledge, or experience is needed. **Job Preparation:** SVP below 4.0—less than six months. **Knowledge—**Chemistry; Food Production; Production and Processing; Physics; Mechanical. **Instructional Programs—**No data available.

Related DOT Jobs—524.382-010 Coating-Machine Operator; 524.382-014 Enrobing-Machine Operator; 524.665-010 Sanding-Machine Operator; 524.682-010 Depositing-Machine Operator; 524.685-014 Cheese Sprayer; 524.685-018 Coating Operator; 524.685-022 Cracker Sprayer; 524.685-026 Enrobing-Machine Operator; 524.685-034 Icer, Machine; 534.482-010 Waxing-Machine Operator; 534.582-010 Paper-Coating-Machine Operator; 534.682-010 Air-Drier-Machine Operator; 534.682-014 Carbon-Coater-Machine Operator; 534.682-018 Coating-Machine Operator; 534.682-022 Coating-Machine Operator, Hardboard; 534.682-038 Supercalender Operator; 534.685-022 Paper Coater; 534.685-026 Paraffin-Machine Operator; 534.685-030 Varnishing-Machine Operator; 539.482-010 Calender Operator, Insulation Board; others.

51-9122.00 Painters, Transportation Equipment

- **Education/Training Required: Moderate-term on-the-job training**
- **Employed: 48,884**
- **Annual Earnings: $32,330**
- **Growth: 17.5%**
- **Annual Job Openings: 8,000**

Operate or tend painting machines to paint surfaces of transportation equipment, such as automobiles, buses, trucks, trains, boats, and airplanes.

Adjust controls on infrared ovens, heat lamps, portable ventilators, and exhaust units in order to speed the drying of vehicles between coats. Allow the sprayed product to dry and then touch up any spots that may have been missed. Apply designs, lettering, or other identifying or decorative items to finished products, using paint brushes or paint sprayers. Apply primer over any repairs made to vehicle surfaces. Apply rust-resistant undercoats and caulk and seal seams. Buff and wax the finished paintwork. Fill small dents and scratches with body fillers and smooth surfaces in order to prepare vehicles for painting. Lay out logos, symbols, or designs on painted surfaces according to blueprint specifications, using measuring instruments, stencils, and patterns. Mix paints to match color specifications or vehicles' original colors and then stir and thin the paints, using spatulas or power mixing equipment. Monitor painting operations in order to identify flaws such as blisters and streaks so that their causes can be corrected. Operate lifting and moving devices in order to move equipment or materials so that areas to be painted are accessible. Paint by hand areas that cannot be reached with a spray gun or those that need retouching, using brushes. Pour paint into spray guns and adjust nozzles and paint mixes in order to get the proper paint flow and coating thickness. Remove accessories from vehicles, such as chrome or mirrors, and mask other surfaces with tape or paper in order to protect them from paint. Remove grease, dirt, paint, and rust from vehicle surfaces in preparation for paint application, using abrasives, solvents, brushes, blowtorches, washing tanks, or sandblasters. Sand the final finish and apply sealer once a vehicle has dried properly. Sand vehicle surfaces between coats of paint and/or primer in order to remove flaws and enhance adhesion for subsequent coats. Select paint according to company requirements and match colors of paint following specified color charts. Select the correct spray gun system for the material being applied. Set up portable equipment such as ventilators, exhaust units, ladders, and scaffolding. Spray prepared surfaces with specified amounts of primers and decorative or finish coatings. Disassemble, clean, and reassemble sprayers and power equipment, using solvents, wire brushes, and cloths for cleaning duties. Dispose of hazardous waste in an appropriate manner. Verify paint consistency, using a viscosity meter.

GOE INFORMATION—Interest Area: 05. Mechanics, Installers, and Repairers. **Work Group:** 05.03. Mechanical Work. **Personality Type—**Realistic. Realistic occupations frequently involve work activities that include practical, hands-on problems and solutions. They often deal with plants, animals, and real-world materials like wood, tools, and machinery. Many of the occupations require working outside and do not involve a lot of paperwork or working closely with others. **Work Values—**Moral Values; Independence; Supervision, Technical; Supervision, Human Relations; Company Policies and Practices. **Skills—**Operation and Control. **Abilities—***Cognitive:* None met the criteria. *Psychomotor:* Arm-Hand Steadiness; Control Precision; Manual Dexterity; Speed of Limb Movement. *Physical:* Dynamic Flexibility; Gross Body Equilibrium; Dynamic Strength; Static Strength; Stamina. *Sensory:* Visual Color Discrimination; Peripheral Vision; Depth Perception; Far Vision; Glare Sensitivity. **General Work Activities—***Information Input:* Monitoring Processes, Materials, or Surroundings; Getting Information; Identifying Objects, Actions, and Events. *Mental Process:* Evaluating Information Against Standards; Organizing, Planning, and Prioritizing; Thinking Creatively. *Work Output:* Handling and Moving Objects; Performing General Physical Activities; Controlling Machines and Processes. *Interacting with Others:* Communicating with Other Workers; Establishing and Maintaining Relationships; Monitoring and Controlling Resources. **Physical Work Conditions—**Making Repetitive Motions; High Places; Climbing Ladders, Scaffolds, Poles, etc.; Contaminants; Bending or Twisting the Body. **Other Job Characteristics—**Importance of Repeating Same Tasks; Importance of Being Exact or Accurate; Consequence of Error.

Experience—Job Zone 2. Some previous work-related skill, knowledge, or experience may be helpful, but usually is not needed. **Job Preparation:** SVP 4.0 to less than 6.0—six months to less than two years. **Knowledge—**Design; Fine Arts; Mechanical; Chemistry. **Instructional Programs—**Autobody/Collision and Repair Technology/Technician.

Related DOT Jobs—845.381-010 Painter Apprentice, Transportation Equipment; 845.381-014 Painter, Transportation Equipment; 845.381-018 Paint Sprayer, Sandblaster; 845.681-010 Railroad-Car Letterer.

51-9123.00 Painting, Coating, and Decorating Workers

- **Education/Training Required: Short-term on-the-job training**
- **Employed: 38,065**
- **Annual Earnings: $20,560**
- **Growth: 17.9%**
- **Annual Job Openings: 6,000**

Paint, coat, or decorate articles, such as furniture, glass, plateware, pottery, jewelry, cakes, toys, books, or leather.

Applies coating, such as paint, ink, or lacquer, to protect or decorate workpiece surface, using spray gum, pen, or brush. Immerses workpiece into coating material for specified time. Positions and glues decorative pieces in cutout section, following pattern. Reads job order and inspects workpiece to determine work procedure and materials required. Conceals blemishes in workpiece, such as nicks and dents, using filler, such as putty. Rinses coated workpiece to remove excess coating material or to facilitate setting of finish coat on workpiece. Drains or wipes workpieces to remove excess coating material or to facilitate setting of finish coat on workpiece. Examines finished surface of workpiece to verify conformance to specifications and retouches defective areas of surface. Cleans surface of workpiece in preparation for coating, using cleaning fluid, solvent, brushes, scraper, steam, sandpaper, or cloth. Cuts out sections in surface of material to be inlaid with decorative pieces, using pattern and knife or scissors. Places coated workpiece in oven or dryer for specified time to dry or harden finish. Melts or heats coating material to specified temperature. Selects and mixes ingredients to prepare coating substance according to specifications, using paddle or mechanical mixer. Cleans and maintains tools and equipment, using solvent, brushes, and rags.

GOE INFORMATION—Interest Area: 08. Industrial Production. **Work Group:** 08.03. Production Work. **Personality Type**—Realistic. Realistic occupations frequently involve work activities that include practical, hands-on problems and solutions. They often deal with plants, animals, and real-world materials like wood, tools, and machinery. Many of the occupations require working outside and do not involve a lot of paperwork or working closely with others. **Work Values**—Moral Values; Independence; Supervision, Technical. **Skills**—None met the criteria. **Abilities**—*Cognitive:* Information Ordering; Visualization; Flexibility of Closure. *Psychomotor:* Manual Dexterity; Arm-Hand Steadiness; Wrist-Finger Speed; Finger Dexterity; Speed of Limb Movement. *Physical:* Trunk Strength; Stamina; Dynamic Flexibility. *Sensory:* Visual Color Discrimination; Near Vision. **General Work Activities**—*Information Input:* Monitoring Processes, Materials, or Surroundings; Getting Information; Inspecting Equipment, Structures, or Materials. *Mental Process:* Evaluating Information Against Standards; Judging Qualities of Things, Services, or Other People's Work; Making Decisions and Solving Problems. *Work Output:* Handling and Moving Objects; Performing General Physical Activities; Controlling Machines and Processes. *Interacting with Others:* Communicating with Other Workers; Coordinating the Work and Activities of Others; Assisting and Caring for Others. **Physical Work Conditions**—Using Hands on Objects, Tools, or Controls; Contaminants; Common Protective or Safety Attire; Indoors; Making Repetitive Motions. **Other Job Characteristics**—Importance of Repeating Same Tasks; Pace Determined by Speed of Equipment; Importance of Being Exact or Accurate.

Experience—Job Zone 1. No previous work-related skill, knowledge, or experience is needed. **Job Preparation:** SVP below 4.0—less than six months. **Knowledge**—Production and Processing; Fine Arts; Building and Construction. **Instructional Programs**—Graphic Design.

Related DOT Jobs—364.381-010 Painter, Rug Touch-Up; 500.684-022 Silver Spray Worker; 505.684-010 Electroless Plater; 505.684-014 Metal Sprayer, Production; 509.684-010 Enameler; 554.384-010 Dyer; 554.684-010 Caustic Operator; 562.687-010 Dyer; 562.687-014 Resin Coater; 574.484-010 Optical-Glass Silverer; 574.684-010 Ground Layer; 574.684-014 Silverer; 584.684-010 Latexer; 584.687-010 Leather Coater; 584.687-014 Sprayer, Hand; 589.687-034 Stainer; 589.687-038 Stiffener; 599.682-010 Painter, Electrostatic; 599.687-010 Balloon Dipper; 700.684-054 Oxidizer; others.

51-9131.00 *Photographic Process Workers*

- **Education/Training Required: Moderate-term on-the-job training**
- **Employed: 26,273**
- **Annual Earnings: $19,630**
- **Growth: –8.2%**
- **Annual Job Openings: 3,000**

Perform precision work involved in photographic processing, such as editing photographic negatives and prints, using photo-mechanical, chemical, or computerized methods.

No task data available.

GOE INFORMATION—Interest Area: 08. Industrial Production. **Work Group:** 08.03. Production Work. **Note:** The Department of Labor has not collected some data for this job, so it has fewer details than the other descriptions.

Instructional Programs—Photographic and Film/Video Technology/Technician and Assistant.

Related DOT Jobs—970.281-010 Airbrush Artist; 970.281-018 Photograph Retoucher; 970.381-010 Colorist, Photography; 970.381-034 Spotter, Photographic; 976.361-010 Reproduction Technician; 976.381-010 Film Laboratory Technician I; 976.381-018 Projection Printer; 976.381-022 Template Reproduction Technician; 976.382-022 Photostat Operator; 976.681-010 Developer.

51-9131.01 *Photographic Retouchers and Restorers*

- **Education/Training Required: Moderate-term on-the-job training**
- **Employed: No data available.**
- **Annual Earnings: $19,630**
- **Growth: –8.2%**
- **Annual Job Openings: 3,000**

Retouch or restore photographic negatives and prints to accentuate desirable features of subject, using pencils, watercolors, or airbrushes.

Applies paint to retouch or enhance negative or photograph, using airbrush, pen, artist's brush, cotton swab, or gloved finger. Shades negative or photograph with pencil to smooth facial contours; conceal blemishes, stray hairs, or wrinkles; and soften highlights. Rubs eraser or cloth over photograph to reduce gloss, remove debris, or prepare specified areas of illustration for highlighting. Paints negative with retouching medium to ensure retouching pencil will mark surface of negative. Inks borders or lettering on illustration, using pen, brush, or drafting instruments. Wipes excess color from portrait to produce specified shade, using cotton swab. Examines drawing, negative, or photographic print to determine coloring, shading, accenting, and changes required to retouch or restore. Cuts out masking template, using shears, and positions templates on picture to mask selected areas. Mixes ink or paint solutions according to color specifications, color chart, and consistency desired. Trims edges of print to enhance appearance, using scissors or paper cutter.

GOE INFORMATION—Interest Area: 08. Industrial Production. **Work Group:** 08.03. Production Work. **Personality Type**—Artistic. Artistic occupations frequently involve working with forms, designs, and patterns. They often require self-expression, and the work can be done without following a clear set of rules. **Work Values**—Independence; Good Working Conditions; Creativity; Variety; Achievement. **Skills**—None met the criteria. **Abilities**—*Cognitive:* Visualization; Flexibility of Closure; Originality. *Psychomotor:* Arm-Hand Steadiness; Finger Dexterity; Wrist-Finger Speed; Manual Dexterity; Speed of Limb Movement. *Physical:* None met the criteria. *Sensory:* Visual Color Discrimination; Glare Sensitivity; Near Vision; Depth Perception. **General Work Activities**—*Information Input:* Getting Information; Identifying Objects, Actions, and Events; Monitoring Processes, Materials, or Surroundings. *Mental Process:* Thinking Creatively; Evaluating Information Against Standards; Updating and Using Relevant Knowledge. *Work Output:* Handling and Moving Objects; Controlling Machines and Processes; Performing General Physical Activities. *Interacting with Others:* Establishing and Maintaining Relationships; Communicating with Other Workers; Assisting and Caring for Others. **Physical Work Conditions**—Using Hands on Objects, Tools, or Controls; Sitting; Making Repetitive Motions; Contaminants; Hazardous Conditions. **Other Job Characteristics**—Importance of Being Exact or Accurate; Consequence of Error; Importance of Repeating Same Tasks.

Experience—Job Zone 3. Previous work-related skill, knowledge, or experience is required. **Job Preparation:** SVP 6.0 to less than 7.0—more than one year and less than four years. **Knowledge**—Fine Arts; Chemistry; Production and Processing. **Instructional Programs**—Photographic and Film/Video Technology/Technician and Assistant.

Related DOT Jobs—970.281-010 Airbrush Artist; 970.281-018 Photograph Retoucher; 970.381-010 Colorist, Photography; 970.381-034 Spotter, Photographic.

51-9131.02 *Photographic Reproduction Technicians*

- Education/Training Required: Moderate-term on-the-job training
- Employed: No data available.
- Annual Earnings: $19,630
- Growth: −8.2%
- Annual Job Openings: 3,000

Duplicate materials to produce prints on sensitized paper, cloth, or film, using photographic equipment.

Starts exposure to duplicate original, photograph, or negative. Estimates exposure time according to size of lens aperture, grade of sensitized paper, and intensity of light. Places filter over lens to make color separation when copying color work. Sets automatic timer, lens opening, and carriage of printer to specified focus and exposure time. Reprints original to enlarge or in sections to be pieced together. Examines negative for contrast to determine grade of sensitized paper required for print. Selects lens assembly according to size and type of negative or photograph to be printed. Measures material to be copied and computes percentage of enlargement or reproduction necessary, using rule, chart, or percentage scale. Mounts original photograph, negative, or other printed material in holder or vacuum frame beneath light. Mounts camera on tripod or stand and loads prescribed type and size film in camera. Reads work order to determine required processes, techniques, materials, and equipment. Places sensitized paper in frame of projection printer, photostat, or other reproduction machine. Rinses developed print in water and places in heated drying cabinet. Retouches defects in print, using chemicals, inks, brushes, and pens. Rolls exposed section of sensitized paper into developer tank inside machine. Develops exposed paper or material. Examines developed print for defects, such as broken lines, spots, and blurs. Mixes developing and processing solutions for use in developing, processing, and rinsing prints.

GOE INFORMATION—**Interest Area:** 08. Industrial Production. **Work Group:** 08.03. Production Work. **Personality Type**—Realistic. Realistic occupations frequently involve work activities that include practical, hands-on problems and solutions. They often deal with plants, animals, and real-world materials like wood, tools, and machinery. Many of the occupations require working outside and do not involve a lot of paperwork or working closely with others. **Work Values**—Independence; Moral Values; Good Working Conditions; Supervision, Technical; Variety. **Skills**—Equipment Selection; Operation and Control; Installation; Mathematics. **Abilities**—*Cognitive:* Information Ordering; Flexibility of Closure; Mathematical Reasoning; Number Facility; Speed of Closure. *Psychomotor:* Arm-Hand Steadiness; Reaction Time; Wrist-Finger Speed; Control Precision; Response Orientation. *Physical:* Stamina; Dynamic Flexibility. *Sensory:* Visual Color Discrimination; Night Vision; Near Vision; Depth Perception; Far Vision. **General Work Activities**—*Information Input:* Getting Information; Estimating Needed Characteristics; Monitoring Processes, Materials, or Surroundings. *Mental Process:* Evaluating Information Against Standards; Updating and Using Relevant Knowl-

edge; Analyzing Data or Information. *Work Output:* Handling and Moving Objects; Controlling Machines and Processes; Performing General Physical Activities. *Interacting with Others:* Communicating with Other Workers; Performing Administrative Activities; Establishing and Maintaining Relationships. **Physical Work Conditions**—Hazardous Conditions; Extremely Bright or Inadequate Lighting; Indoors; Using Hands on Objects, Tools, or Controls; Common Protective or Safety Attire. **Other Job Characteristics**—Pace Determined by Speed of Equipment; Importance of Repeating Same Tasks; Degree of Automation.

Experience—Job Zone 3. Previous work-related skill, knowledge, or experience is required. **Job Preparation:** SVP 6.0 to less than 7.0—more than one year and less than four years. **Knowledge**—Fine Arts; Chemistry; Production and Processing; Engineering and Technology. **Instructional Programs**—Photographic and Film/Video Technology/Technician and Assistant.

Related DOT Jobs—976.361-010 Reproduction Technician; 976.381-018 Projection Printer; 976.381-022 Template Reproduction Technician; 976.382-022 Photostat Operator.

51-9131.03 *Photographic Hand Developers*

- Education/Training Required: Moderate-term on-the-job training
- Employed: No data available.
- Annual Earnings: $19,630
- Growth: −8.2%
- Annual Job Openings: 3,000

Develop exposed photographic film or sensitized paper in series of chemical and water baths to produce negative or positive prints.

Immerses exposed film or photographic paper in developer solution to bring out latent image. Immerses negative paper, film, or print in stop bath to arrest developer action. Immerses negative paper, film, or print in hyposolution to fix image. Immerses negative paper, film, or print in water to remove chemicals. Dries prints or negatives, using sponge, squeegee, or mechanical air dryer. Mixes developing and fixing solutions, following formula. Produces color photographs, negatives, and slides, using color reproduction processes.

GOE INFORMATION—**Interest Area:** 08. Industrial Production. **Work Group:** 08.03. Production Work. **Personality Type**—Realistic. Realistic occupations frequently involve work activities that include practical, hands-on problems and solutions. They often deal with plants, animals, and real-world materials like wood, tools, and machinery. Many of the occupations require working outside and do not involve a lot of paperwork or working closely with others. **Work Values**—Independence; Moral Values; Supervision, Technical. **Skills**—None met the criteria. **Abilities**—*Cognitive:* Perceptual Speed; Spatial Orientation; Information Ordering. *Psychomotor:* Reaction Time; Wrist-Finger Speed; Control Precision; Manual Dexterity; Rate Control. *Physical:* Extent Flexibility; Trunk Strength. *Sensory:* Night Vision; Visual Color Discrimination; Peripheral Vision; Depth Perception; Near Vision. **General Work Activities**—*Information Input:* Monitoring Processes, Materials, or Surroundings; Getting Information; Identifying Objects, Actions, and Events. *Mental Process:* Updating and Using Relevant Knowledge; Evaluating Information Against Standards; Thinking Creatively. *Work Output:* Handling and Moving Objects; Controlling Machines and Processes; Performing General Physical Activities. *Interacting with Others:* Communicating with Other Workers; Monitoring and Controlling Resources; Performing Administrative Activities. **Physical Work Conditions**—Hazardous Conditions; Extremely Bright or Inadequate Lighting; Contaminants; Using Hands on

Objects, Tools, or Controls; Indoors. **Other Job Characteristics**—Importance of Being Exact or Accurate; Importance of Repeating Same Tasks; Consequence of Error.

Experience—Job Zone 2. Some previous work-related skill, knowledge, or experience may be helpful, but usually is not needed. **Job Preparation:** SVP 4.0 to less than 6.0—six months to less than two years. **Knowledge**—Fine Arts; Chemistry; Production and Processing. **Instructional Programs**—Photographic and Film/Video Technology/Technician and Assistant.

Related DOT Jobs—976.681-010 Developer.

51-9131.04 Film Laboratory Technicians

- **Education/Training Required: Moderate-term on-the-job training**
- **Employed: No data available.**
- **Annual Earnings: $19,630**
- **Growth: –8.2%**
- **Annual Job Openings: 3,000**

Evaluate motion picture film to determine characteristics, such as sensitivity to light, density, and exposure time required for printing.

Computes amount of light intensity needed to compensate for density of film, using standardized formulas. Exposes film strip to progressively timed lights to compare effects of various exposure times. Examines developed film strip to determine optimal exposure time and light intensity required for printing. Reads gauges on sensitometer to determine film's sensitivity to light. Threads film strip through densitometer and exposes film to light to determine density of film. Threads film strip through sensitometer and exposes film to light. Records test data and routes film to film developer and film printer for further processing.

GOE INFORMATION—**Interest Area:** 08. Industrial Production. **Work Group:** 08.03. Production Work. **Personality Type**—Realistic. Realistic occupations frequently involve work activities that include practical, hands-on problems and solutions. They often deal with plants, animals, and real-world materials like wood, tools, and machinery. Many of the occupations require working outside and do not involve a lot of paperwork or working closely with others. **Work Values**—Independence; Supervision, Technical; Moral Values; Good Working Conditions; Autonomy. **Skills**—None met the criteria. **Abilities**—*Cognitive:* Mathematical Reasoning; Number Facility; Information Ordering; Perceptual Speed; Flexibility of Closure. *Psychomotor:* Arm-Hand Steadiness; Control Precision; Finger Dexterity; Wrist-Finger Speed. *Physical:* None met the criteria. *Sensory:* Visual Color Discrimination; Night Vision; Far Vision; Near Vision; Hearing Sensitivity. **General Work Activities**—*Information Input:* Identifying Objects, Actions, and Events; Getting Information; Monitoring Processes, Materials, or Surroundings. *Mental Process:* Judging Qualities of Things, Services, or Other People's Work; Processing Information; Evaluating Information Against Standards. *Work Output:* Handling and Moving Objects; Documenting or Recording Information; Controlling Machines and Processes. *Interacting with Others:* Interpreting Meaning of Information for Others; Communicating with Other Workers; Performing Administrative Activities. **Physical Work Conditions**—Extremely Bright or Inadequate Lighting; Indoors; Using Hands on Objects, Tools, or Controls; Sitting; Minor Burns, Cuts, Bites, or Stings. **Other Job Characteristics**—Pace Determined by Speed of Equipment; Importance of Repeating Same Tasks; Degree of Automation.

Experience—Job Zone 4. A minimum of two to four years of work-related skill, knowledge, or experience is needed. **Job Preparation:** SVP 7.0 to less than 8.0—two years to less than 10 years. **Knowledge**—Fine Arts; Physics; Production and Processing; Engineering and Technology;

Clerical. **Instructional Programs**—Photographic and Film/Video Technology/Technician and Assistant.

Related DOT Jobs—976.381-010 Film Laboratory Technician I.

51-9132.00 Photographic Processing Machine Operators

- **Education/Training Required: Short-term on-the-job training**
- **Employed: 49,535**
- **Annual Earnings: $18,300**
- **Growth: 7.6%**
- **Annual Job Openings: 6,000**

Operate photographic processing machines, such as photographic printing machines, film-developing machines, and mounting presses.

Loads circuit boards, racks or rolls of film, negatives, or printing paper into processing or printing machines. Sets and adjusts machine controls according to specifications, type of operation, and material requirements. Starts and operates machines to prepare circuit boards and expose, develop, etch, fix, wash, dry, and print film or plates. Fills tanks of processing machines with solutions such as developer, dyes, stop-baths, fixers, bleaches, and washes. Monitors equipment operation to detect malfunctions. Measures and mixes chemicals according to formula to prepare solutions for processing. Removes completed work from equipment and examines circuit boards, plates, film, and prints for conformance to quality standards. Reads work orders and examines negatives and film to determine machine settings and processing requirements. Places film in labeled containers or numbers film for identification, using numbering machine or by hand. Discards or cleans and repairs defective film or circuit patterns on photographic plates, using cleaning solutions and hand tools. Cleans and maintains photoprocessing equipment, using cleaning and rinsing solutions and ultrasonic equipment. Maintains records, such as number and types of processing completed, rate of materials usage, and customer charges.

GOE INFORMATION—**Interest Area:** 08. Industrial Production. **Work Group:** 08.03. Production Work. **Personality Type**—Realistic. Realistic occupations frequently involve work activities that include practical, hands-on problems and solutions. They often deal with plants, animals, and real-world materials like wood, tools, and machinery. Many of the occupations require working outside and do not involve a lot of paperwork or working closely with others. **Work Values**—Independence; Moral Values; Good Working Conditions; Supervision, Technical; Supervision, Human Relations. **Skills**—Operation Monitoring; Operation and Control. **Abilities**—*Cognitive:* Perceptual Speed; Memorization. *Psychomotor:* Rate Control; Manual Dexterity; Arm-Hand Steadiness; Control Precision; Reaction Time. *Physical:* Dynamic Flexibility; Dynamic Strength; Gross Body Coordination; Explosive Strength; Extent Flexibility. *Sensory:* Night Vision; Visual Color Discrimination; Near Vision; Peripheral Vision. **General Work Activities**—*Information Input:* Monitoring Processes, Materials, or Surroundings; Inspecting Equipment, Structures, or Materials; Identifying Objects, Actions, and Events. *Mental Process:* Judging Qualities of Things, Services, or Other People's Work; Evaluating Information Against Standards; Updating and Using Relevant Knowledge. *Work Output:* Handling and Moving Objects; Controlling Machines and Processes; Documenting or Recording Information. *Interacting with Others:* Performing Administrative Activities; Communicating with Other Workers; Coordinating the Work and Activities of Others. **Physical Work Conditions**—Hazardous Conditions; Contaminants; Using Hands on Objects, Tools, or Controls; Extremely Bright or Inadequate Lighting; Standing. **Other Job Characteristics**—Pace Determined by Speed of Equipment; Degree of Automation; Importance of Repeating Same Tasks.

Experience—Job Zone 2. Some previous work-related skill, knowledge, or experience may be helpful, but usually is not needed. **Job Preparation:** SVP 4.0 to less than 6.0—six months to less than two years. **Knowledge**—Production and Processing; Chemistry; Fine Arts; Mechanical; Computers and Electronics. **Instructional Programs**—Photographic and Film/Video Technology/Technician and Assistant.

Related DOT Jobs—976.380-010 Computer-Controlled-Color-Photograph-Printer Operator; 976.382-014 Color-Printer Operator; 976.382-018 Film Developer; 976.382-030 Photographic Aligner, Semiconductor Wafers; 976.382-034 Step-and-Repeat Reduction Camera Operator; 976.382-038 Photo Mask Pattern Generator; 976.384-010 Photo Technician; 976.384-014 Photo Mask Processor; 976.385-010 Microfilm Processor; 976.665-010 Take-Down Sorter; 976.682-010 Film Printer; 976.682-014 Printer Operator, Black-and-White; 976.682-018 Rectification Printer; 976.684-014 Film Laboratory Technician; 976.684-030 Contact Printer, Printed Circuit Boards; 976.684-038 Contact Worker, Lithography; 976.685-014 Developer, Automatic; 976.685-018 Film Laboratory Technician II; 976.685-022 Mounter, Automatic; 976.685-026 Print Developer, Automatic; others.

51-9141.00 Semiconductor Processors

- ● **Education/Training Required: Associate's degree**
- ● **Employed: 52,168**
- ● **Annual Earnings: $26,480**
- ● **Growth: 32.4%**
- ● **Annual Job Openings: 7,000**

Perform any or all of the following functions in the manufacture of electronic semiconductors: Load semiconductor material into furnace; saw formed ingots into segments; load individual segment into crystal growing chamber and monitor controls; locate crystal axis in ingot, using X-ray equipment, and saw ingots into wafers; clean, polish, and load wafers into series of special purpose furnaces, chemical baths, and equipment used to form circuitry and change conductive properties.

Align photo mask pattern on photoresist layer, expose pattern to ultraviolet light, and develop pattern, using specialized equipment. Attach ampoule to diffusion pump to remove air from ampoule and seal ampoule, using blowtorch. Calculate etching time based on thickness of material to be removed from wafers or crystals. Clean semiconductor wafers, using cleaning equipment such as chemical baths, automatic wafer cleaners, or blow-off wands. Etch, lap, polish, or grind wafers or ingots to form circuitry and change conductive properties, using etching, lapping, polishing, or grinding equipment. Load and unload equipment chambers and transport finished product to storage or to area for further processing. Load semiconductor material into furnace. Locate crystal axis of ingot and draw orientation lines on ingot, using X-ray equipment, drill, and sanding machine. Manipulate valves, switches, and buttons or key commands into control panels to start semiconductor processing cycles. Measure and weigh amounts of crystal-growing materials, mix and grind materials, load materials into container, and monitor processing procedures to help identify crystal-growing problems. Monitor operation and adjust controls of processing machines and equipment to produce compositions with specific electronic properties, using computer terminals. Mount crystal ingots or wafers on blocks or plastic laminate, using special mounting devices, to facilitate their positioning in the holding fixtures of sawing, drilling, grinding or sanding equipment. Operate saw to cut remelt into sections of specified size or to cut ingots into wafers. Place semiconductor wafers in processing containers or equipment holders, using vacuum wand or tweezers. Scribe or separate wafers into dice. Set, adjust, and readjust computerized or mechanical equipment controls to regulate power level, temperature, vacuum, and rotation speed of furnace

according to crystal-growing specifications. Stamp, etch, or scribe identifying information on finished component according to specifications. Study work orders, instructions, formulas, and processing charts to determine specifications and sequence of operations. Clean and maintain equipment, including replacing etching and rinsing solutions and cleaning bath containers and work area. Connect reactor to computer, using hand tools and power tools. Count, sort, and weigh processed items. Inspect equipment for leaks, diagnose malfunctions, and request repairs. Inspect materials, components, or products for surface defects and measure circuitry, using electronic test equipment, precision measuring instruments, microscope, and standard procedures. Maintain processing, production, and inspection information and reports.

GOE INFORMATION—**Interest Area:** 08. Industrial Production. **Work Group:** 08.03. Production Work. **Personality Type**—Realistic. Realistic occupations frequently involve work activities that include practical, hands-on problems and solutions. They often deal with plants, animals, and real-world materials like wood, tools, and machinery. Many of the occupations require working outside and do not involve a lot of paperwork or working closely with others. **Work Values**—Independence; Moral Values; Company Policies and Practices; Supervision, Human Relations; Advancement. **Skills**—Operation Monitoring; Operation and Control; Equipment Selection; Science; Quality Control Analysis. **Abilities**—*Cognitive:* Perceptual Speed; Written Comprehension; Inductive Reasoning; Number Facility; Information Ordering. *Psychomotor:* Control Precision; Wrist-Finger Speed; Response Orientation; Finger Dexterity; Manual Dexterity. *Physical:* Trunk Strength; Dynamic Flexibility. *Sensory:* Near Vision; Glare Sensitivity; Far Vision. **General Work Activities**—*Information Input:* Monitoring Processes, Materials, or Surroundings; Inspecting Equipment, Structures, or Materials; Getting Information. *Mental Process:* Updating and Using Relevant Knowledge; Processing Information; Evaluating Information Against Standards. *Work Output:* Handling and Moving Objects; Controlling Machines and Processes; Performing General Physical Activities. *Interacting with Others:* Communicating with Other Workers; Establishing and Maintaining Relationships; Performing Administrative Activities. **Physical Work Conditions**—Using Hands on Objects, Tools, or Controls; Hazardous Equipment; Indoors; Common Protective or Safety Attire; Making Repetitive Motions. **Other Job Characteristics**—Importance of Repeating Same Tasks; Importance of Being Exact or Accurate; Pace Determined by Speed of Equipment.

Experience—Job Zone 1. No previous work-related skill, knowledge, or experience is needed. **Job Preparation:** SVP below 4.0—less than six months. **Knowledge**—Production and Processing; Computers and Electronics; Mechanical; Physics; Engineering and Technology. **Instructional Programs**—Industrial Electronics Technology/Technician.

Related DOT Jobs—590.362-018 Group Leader, Semiconductor Processing; 590.382-022 Ion Implant Machine Operator; 590.384-010 Charge Preparation Technician; 590.684-014 Electronic-Component Processor; 590.684-022 Semiconductor Processor; 590.684-042 Integrated Circuit Fabricator; 590.685-070 Diffusion Furnace Operator, Semiconductor Wafers; 590.685-086 Metallization Equipment Tender, Semiconductors.

51-9191.00 Cementing and Gluing Machine Operators and Tenders

- ● **Education/Training Required: Moderate-term on-the-job training**
- ● **Employed: 35,614**
- ● **Annual Earnings: $22,570**
- ● **Growth: 6.7%**
- ● **Annual Job Openings: 5,000**

Operate or tend cementing and gluing machines to join items for further processing or to form a completed product. Processes include joining veneer sheets into plywood; gluing paper; and joining rubber and rubberized fabric parts, plastic, simulated leather, or other materials.

Adjusts machine to apply specified amount of glue, cement, or adhesive. Starts machine and turns valves or moves controls to feed, admit, or transfer materials and adhesive. Adjusts machine components according to specifications such as width, length, and thickness of materials to be joined. Observes gauges, meters, and control panels to regulate temperature, pressure, or speed of feeder or conveyor. Monitors machine operation to detect malfunctions, remove jammed materials, and readjust machine components to conform to specifications. Monitors and fills machine with glue, cement, or adhesive as needed. Reads work orders and communicates with co-workers to determine machine and equipment settings and adjustments and supply and product specifications. Positions materials being joined to ensure accurate application of adhesive. Mounts or loads material such as paper, plastic, wood, or rubber in feeding mechanism of cementing or gluing machine. Measures and mixes ingredients according to specifications to prepare glue. Examines and measures completed materials or products to verify conformance to specifications, using measuring devices, such as tape measure, gauge, or calipers. Removes completed materials or products and restocks materials to be joined. Cleans and maintains gluing and cementing machines, using cleaning solutions, lubricants, brushes, and scrapers. Maintains production records, such as number, dimensions, and thickness of materials processed. Transports materials, supplies, and finished products between storage and work areas, using forklift.

GOE INFORMATION—Interest Area: 08. Industrial Production. **Work Group:** 08.03. Production Work. **Personality Type—**Realistic. Realistic occupations frequently involve work activities that include practical, hands-on problems and solutions. They often deal with plants, animals, and real-world materials like wood, tools, and machinery. Many of the occupations require working outside and do not involve a lot of paperwork or working closely with others. **Work Values—**Moral Values; Supervision, Technical; Supervision, Human Relations; Company Policies and Practices; Independence. **Skills—**Operation Monitoring; Operation and Control; Equipment Selection; Troubleshooting. **Abilities—***Cognitive:* Visualization; Spatial Orientation. *Psychomotor:* Arm-Hand Steadiness; Control Precision; Rate Control; Manual Dexterity; Reaction Time. *Physical:* Dynamic Flexibility; Static Strength; Dynamic Strength; Trunk Strength; Explosive Strength. *Sensory:* Depth Perception. **General Work Activities—***Information Input:* Monitoring Processes, Materials, or Surroundings; Inspecting Equipment, Structures, or Materials; Getting Information. *Mental Process:* Updating and Using Relevant Knowledge; Evaluating Information Against Standards; Organizing, Planning, and Prioritizing. *Work Output:* Handling and Moving Objects; Performing General Physical Activities; Controlling Machines and Processes. *Interacting with Others:* Communicating with Other Workers; Establishing and Maintaining Relationships; Performing Administrative Activities. **Physical Work Conditions—**Hazardous Equipment; Distracting Sounds and Noise Levels; Common Protective or Safety Attire; Minor Burns, Cuts, Bites, or Stings; Contaminants. **Other Job Characteristics—**Pace Determined by Speed of Equipment; Degree of Automation; Importance of Repeating Same Tasks.

Experience—Job Zone 1. No previous work-related skill, knowledge, or experience is needed. **Job Preparation:** SVP below 4.0—less than six months. **Knowledge—**Production and Processing; Mechanical; Chemistry; Building and Construction; Physics. **Instructional Programs—**No data available.

Related DOT Jobs—554.682-014 Masking-Machine Operator; 554.685-

030 Laminator; 569.565-010 Crew Leader, Gluing; 569.685-018 Core Feeder, Plywood Layup Line; 569.685-022 Core-Composer-Machine Tender; 569.685-026 Core-Laying-Machine Operator; 569.685-034 Edge-Glue-Machine Tender; 569.685-042 Glue Spreader, Veneer; 569.685-054 Hot-Plate-Plywood-Press Operator; 569.685-062 Splicer Operator; 579.685-022 Glass-Wool-Blanket-Machine Feeder; 584.665-014 Glue-Spreading-Machine Operator; 584.685-026 Hat-Stock-Laminating-Machine Operator; 620.685-010 Bonder, Automobile Brakes; 640.685-014 Book-Jacket-Cover-Machine Operator; 641.662-010 Box-Sealing-Machine Operator; 641.682-010 Blanket-Winder Operator; 641.682-014 Gluing-Machine Operator, Automatic; 641.685-014 Board-Liner Operator; 641.685-018 Box-Lining-Machine Feeder; others.

51-9192.00 Cleaning, Washing, and Metal Pickling Equipment Operators and Tenders

- **Education/Training Required: Moderate-term on-the-job training**
- **Employed: 20,275**
- **Annual Earnings: $22,400**
- **Growth: −14.2%**
- **Annual Job Openings: 3,000**

Operate or tend machines to wash or clean products, such as barrels or kegs, glass items, tin plate, food, pulp, coal, plastic, or rubber, to remove impurities.

Add specified amounts of chemicals to equipment at required times to maintain solution levels and concentrations. Drain, clean, and refill machines or tanks at designated intervals, using cleaning solutions or water. Load machines with objects to be processed, unload objects after cleaning, and place them on conveyors or racks. Measure, weigh, or mix cleaning solutions, using measuring tanks, calibrated rods, or suction tubes. Observe machine operations, gauges, or thermometers and adjust controls to maintain specified conditions. Operate or tend machines to wash and remove impurities from items such as barrels or kegs, glass products, tin plate surfaces, dried fruit, pulp, animal stock, coal, manufactured articles, plastic, or rubber. Set controls to regulate temperature and length of cycles and start conveyors, pumps, agitators, and machines. Adjust, clean, and lubricate mechanical parts of machines, using hand tools and grease guns. Draw samples for laboratory analysis or test solutions for conformance to specifications, such as acidity or specific gravity. Examine and inspect machines to detect malfunctions. Record gauge readings, materials used, processing times, and/or test results in production logs.

GOE INFORMATION—Interest Area: 08. Industrial Production. **Work Group:** 08.03. Production Work. **Personality Type—**Realistic. Realistic occupations frequently involve work activities that include practical, hands-on problems and solutions. They often deal with plants, animals, and real-world materials like wood, tools, and machinery. Many of the occupations require working outside and do not involve a lot of paperwork or working closely with others. **Work Values—**Moral Values; Independence; Supervision, Technical; Supervision, Human Relations; Company Policies and Practices. **Skills—**Operation Monitoring; Operation and Control; Quality Control Analysis. **Abilities—***Cognitive:* Information Ordering. *Psychomotor:* Rate Control; Control Precision; Multilimb Coordination; Arm-Hand Steadiness. *Physical:* Dynamic Flexibility. *Sensory:* None met the criteria. **General Work Activities—***Information Input:* Inspecting Equipment, Structures, or Materials; Identifying Objects, Actions, and Events; Monitoring Processes, Materials, or Surroundings.

Mental Process: Evaluating Information Against Standards; Updating and Using Relevant Knowledge; Organizing, Planning, and Prioritizing. *Work Output:* Handling and Moving Objects; Controlling Machines and Processes; Performing General Physical Activities. *Interacting with Others:* Performing Administrative Activities; Establishing and Maintaining Relationships; Communicating with Other Workers. **Physical Work Conditions**—Hazardous Equipment; Distracting Sounds and Noise Levels; Common Protective or Safety Attire; Making Repetitive Motions; Minor Burns, Cuts, Bites, or Stings. **Other Job Characteristics**—Pace Determined by Speed of Equipment; Degree of Automation; Importance of Repeating Same Tasks.

Experience—Job Zone 1. No previous work-related skill, knowledge, or experience is needed. **Job Preparation:** SVP below 4.0—less than six months. **Knowledge**—Production and Processing; Chemistry; Mechanical; Food Production. **Instructional Programs**—No data available.

Related DOT Jobs—503.685-026 Furnace-and-Wash-Equipment Operator; 503.685-030 Metal-Cleaner, Immersion; 503.685-034 Metal-Washing-Machine Operator; 509.685-014 Branner-Machine Tender; 511.685-022 Dust-Collector Attendant; 511.685-066 Trommel Tender; 521.685-110 Dried Fruit Washer; 529.665-014 Washroom Operator; 529.685-074 Container Washer, Machine; 529.685-226 Steamer; 529.685-254 Wash-House Worker; 529.685-258 Washer, Agricultural Produce; 529.685-262 Wheat Cleaner; 529.685-278 Yeast Washer; 533.362-010 Bleacher, Pulp; 533.665-010 Blow-Pit Operator; 533.685-010 Bleach-Boiler Filler; 533.685-014 Brown-Stock Washer; 533.685-034 Washer Engineer; 549.685-010 Air-Table Operator; others.

51-9193.00 Cooling and Freezing Equipment Operators and Tenders

- **Education/Training Required: Moderate-term on-the-job training**
- **Employed: 7,166**
- **Annual Earnings: $21,110**
- **Growth: −1.3%**
- **Annual Job Openings: 1,000**

Operate or tend equipment, such as cooling and freezing units, refrigerators, batch freezers, and freezing tunnels, to cool or freeze products, food, blood plasma, and chemicals.

Adjust machine or freezer speed and air intake in order to obtain desired consistency and amount of product. Correct machinery malfunctions by performing actions such as removing jams and inform supervisors of malfunctions as necessary. Insert forming fixtures and start machines that cut frozen products into measured portions or specified shapes. Load and position wrapping paper, sticks, bags, or cartons into dispensing machines. Measure or weigh specified amounts of ingredients or materials and load them into tanks, vats, hoppers, or other equipment. Monitor pressure gauges, ammeters, flowmeters, thermometers, or products and adjust controls to maintain specified conditions, such as feed rate, product consistency, temperature, air pressure, and machine speed. Place or position containers into equipment and remove containers after completion of cooling or freezing processes. Position molds on conveyors and measure and adjust level of fill, using depth gauges. Read dials and gauges on panel control boards in order to ascertain temperatures, alkalinities, and densities of mixtures and turn valves in order to obtain specified mixtures. Scrape, dislodge, or break excess frost, ice, or frozen product from equipment in order to prevent accumulation, using hands and hand tools. Start agitators to blend contents or start beater, scraper, and expeller blades to mix contents with air and prevent sticking. Start

machinery, such as pumps, feeders, or conveyors, and turn valves in order to heat, admit, or transfer products, refrigerants, or mixes. Stir material with spoons or paddles in order to mix ingredients or allow even cooling and prevent coagulation. Weigh packages and adjust freezer air valves or switches on filler heads in order to obtain specified amounts of product in each container. Activate mechanical rakes in order to regulate flow of ice from storage bins to vats. Assemble equipment and attach pipes, fittings, or valves, using hand tools. Inspect and flush lines with solutions or steam and spray equipment with sterilizing solutions. Record temperatures, amounts of materials processed, and/or test results on report forms. Sample and test product characteristics such as specific gravity, acidity, and sugar content, using hydrometers, pH meters, or refractometers.

GOE INFORMATION—Interest Area: 08. Industrial Production. **Work Group:** 08.03. Production Work. **Personality Type**—Realistic. Realistic occupations frequently involve work activities that include practical, hands-on problems and solutions. They often deal with plants, animals, and real-world materials like wood, tools, and machinery. Many of the occupations require working outside and do not involve a lot of paperwork or working closely with others. **Work Values**—Moral Values; Independence; Supervision, Technical; Supervision, Human Relations; Company Policies and Practices. **Skills**—Operation Monitoring; Repairing; Operation and Control; Quality Control Analysis; Troubleshooting; Installation. **Abilities**—*Cognitive:* Perceptual Speed; Selective Attention; Visualization; Information Ordering; Time Sharing. *Psychomotor:* Reaction Time; Manual Dexterity; Finger Dexterity; Control Precision; Speed of Limb Movement. *Physical:* Extent Flexibility; Stamina; Static Strength; Dynamic Flexibility; Gross Body Coordination. *Sensory:* Visual Color Discrimination; Sound Localization; Hearing Sensitivity; Near Vision. **General Work Activities**—*Information Input:* Monitoring Processes, Materials, or Surroundings; Inspecting Equipment, Structures, or Materials; Identifying Objects, Actions, and Events. *Mental Process:* Evaluating Information Against Standards; Making Decisions and Solving Problems; Organizing, Planning, and Prioritizing. *Work Output:* Handling and Moving Objects; Controlling Machines and Processes; Performing General Physical Activities. *Interacting with Others:* Communicating with Other Workers; Performing Administrative Activities; Communicating with Persons Outside Organization. **Physical Work Conditions**—Very Hot or Cold; Hazardous Equipment; Indoors; Cramped Work Space or Awkward Positions; Using Hands on Objects, Tools, or Controls. **Other Job Characteristics**—Degree of Automation; Pace Determined by Speed of Equipment; Importance of Repeating Same Tasks.

Experience—Job Zone 1. No previous work-related skill, knowledge, or experience is needed. **Job Preparation:** SVP below 4.0—less than six months. **Knowledge**—Chemistry; Mechanical; Food Production; Public Safety and Security; Engineering and Technology. **Instructional Programs**—No data available.

Related DOT Jobs—522.685-014 Brewery Cellar Worker; 523.585-014 Chiller Tender; 523.585-018 Crystallizer Operator; 523.685-010 Batch Freezer; 523.685-018 Chilling-Hood Operator; 523.685-038 Cooler Tender; 523.685-042 Cooling-Machine Operator; 523.685-046 Cooling-Pan Tender; 523.685-050 Crystallizer Operator; 523.685-082 Freezer Tunnel Operator; 523.685-102 Ice Maker; 529.482-010 Freezer Operator; 529.482-014 Novelty Maker I; 529.482-018 Novelty Maker II; 529.485-010 Barrel Filler; 529.685-250 Votator-Machine Operator; 551.685-042 Chiller Operator; 556.685-054 Paradichlorobenzene Tender; 559.685-090 Freezing-Machine Operator; 559.685-170 Spreading-Machine Operator.

51-9194.00 Etchers and Engravers

- Education/Training Required: **Postsecondary vocational training**
- Employed: **14,697**
- Annual Earnings: **$22,100**
- Growth: **11.1%**
- Annual Job Openings: **2,000**

Engrave or etch metal, wood, rubber, or other materials for identification or decorative purposes. Includes such workers as etcher-circuit processors, pantograph engravers, and silk screen etchers.

No task data available.

GOE INFORMATION—Interest Area: 01. Arts, Entertainment, and Media. **Work Group:** 01.07. Graphic Arts. **Note:** The Department of Labor has not collected some data for this job, so it has fewer details than the other descriptions.

Instructional Programs—Graphic Communications, Other.

Related DOT Jobs—590.684-018 Etched-Circuit Processor; 704.381-022 Engraver Apprentice, Decorative; 704.381-026 Engraver, Hand, Hard Metals; 704.381-030 Engraver, Hand, Soft Metals; 704.381-034 Engraver, Seals; 704.382-010 Engraver, Pantograph I; 704.582-010 Engraver, Machine II; 704.682-010 Engraver, Machine I; 704.682-014 Engraver, Pantograph II; 704.684-010 Etcher; 704.684-014 Silk-Screen Etcher; 704.687-014 Etcher, Hand; 716.681-022 Optical-Glass Etcher; 732.584-010 Bowling-Ball Engraver; 733.381-010 Engraver, Rubber; 754.381-010 Internal Carver; 775.381-010 Engraver; 775.381-014 Glass Decorator; 775.584-010 Glass Calibrator; 972.381-018 Sketch Maker II; others.

51-9194.01 Precision Etchers and Engravers, Hand or Machine

- Education/Training Required: **Long-term on-the-job training**
- Employed: **No data available.**
- Annual Earnings: **$22,100**
- Growth: **11.1%**
- Annual Job Openings: **2,000**

Engrave or etch flat or curved metal, wood, rubber, or other materials by hand or machine for printing, identification, or decorative purposes. Includes etchers and engravers of both hard and soft metals or materials and jewelry and seal engravers.

Engraves or cuts lettering, design, or characters in workpiece surface, using hand tools and engraving tool. Sketches, traces, or scribes layout lines and design on workpiece, plates, dies, or rollers, using compass, scriber, graver, or pencil. Determines machine settings and moves bars or levers to reproduce designs on rollers or plates. Operates machine to engrave design into steel rollers or plates. Trims precut designs or cuts around design to remove undesirable part, using graver. Reviews sketches, diagrams, blueprints, or photographs to determine design to be cut or engraved. Measures and computes dimensions of lettering, designs, or patterns to be engraved. Prints proof or examines design to verify accuracy and reworks engraving as required. Sketches original design or pattern for use in printing or engraving. Transfers design from sleet or film to die or roller by decimal staining. Casts male die from engraved female die for use in seals. Positions and clamps workpiece, plate, or roller in holding fixture. Scrapes plate or die to remove imperfections and smooth surface. Sharpens and forms cutting edge of gravers or cutter grinder. Polishes and oils surface of plate or die or brushes with acid-proof paint.

GOE INFORMATION—Interest Area: 01. Arts, Entertainment, and Media. **Work Group:** 01.07. Graphic Arts. **Personality Type**—Realistic. Realistic occupations frequently involve work activities that include practical, hands-on problems and solutions. They often deal with plants, animals, and real-world materials like wood, tools, and machinery. Many of the occupations require working outside and do not involve a lot of paperwork or working closely with others. **Work Values**—Independence; Moral Values; Creativity; Good Working Conditions; Ability Utilization. **Skills**—Operation and Control; Equipment Selection. **Abilities**—*Cognitive:* Visualization; Category Flexibility. *Psychomotor:* Arm-Hand Steadiness; Control Precision; Finger Dexterity; Manual Dexterity; Multilimb Coordination. *Physical:* Gross Body Coordination. *Sensory:* Depth Perception. **General Work Activities**—*Information Input:* Getting Information; Identifying Objects, Actions, and Events; Monitoring Processes, Materials, or Surroundings. *Mental Process:* Thinking Creatively; Judging Qualities of Things, Services, or Other People's Work; Organizing, Planning, and Prioritizing. *Work Output:* Handling and Moving Objects; Controlling Machines and Processes; Performing General Physical Activities. *Interacting with Others:* Communicating with Other Workers; Establishing and Maintaining Relationships; Communicating with Persons Outside Organization. **Physical Work Conditions**—Making Repetitive Motions; Minor Burns, Cuts, Bites, or Stings; Using Hands on Objects, Tools, or Controls; Indoors; Standing. **Other Job Characteristics**—Importance of Being Exact or Accurate; Pace Determined by Speed of Equipment; Importance of Repeating Same Tasks.

Experience—Job Zone 3. Previous work-related skill, knowledge, or experience is required. **Job Preparation:** SVP 6.0 to less than 7.0—more than one year and less than four years. **Knowledge**—Fine Arts; Design; Production and Processing; Mechanical. **Instructional Programs**—Graphic Communications, Other.

Related DOT Jobs—704.381-022 Engraver Apprentice, Decorative; 704.381-026 Engraver, Hand, Hard Metals; 704.381-030 Engraver, Hand, Soft Metals; 704.381-034 Engraver, Seals; 972.381-018 Sketch Maker II; 972.681-010 Music Engraver; 979.281-010 Die Maker; 979.281-014 Engraver, Block; 979.281-018 Engraver, Picture; 979.381-010 Engraver I; 979.381-030 Siderographer.

51-9194.02 Engravers/Carvers

- Education/Training Required: **Long-term on-the-job training**
- Employed: **No data available.**
- Annual Earnings: **$22,100**
- Growth: **11.1%**
- Annual Job Openings: **2,000**

Engrave or carve designs or lettering onto objects, using hand-held power tools.

Holds workpiece against outer edge of wheel and twists and turns workpiece to grind glass according to marked design. Carves design on workpiece, using electric hand tool. Cuts outline of impression with graver and removes excess material with knife. Traces, sketches, or presses design or facsimile signature on workpiece by hand or by using artist equipment. Selects and mounts wheel and miter on lathe and equips lathe with water to cool wheel and prevent dust. Polishes engravings, using felt and cork wheels. Prepares workpiece to be engraved or carved, such as glassware, rubber, or plastic product. Attaches engraved workpiece to mount, using cement. Dresses and shapes cutting wheels by holding dressing stone against rotating wheel. Suggests original designs to customer or management.

GOE INFORMATION—Interest Area: 01. Arts, Entertainment, and Media. **Work Group:** 01.07. Graphic Arts. **Personality Type**—Realistic. Realistic occupations frequently involve work activities that include practical, hands-on problems and solutions. They often deal with plants, animals, and real-world materials like wood, tools, and machinery. Many of the occupations require working outside and do not involve a lot of paperwork or working closely with others. **Work Values**—Independence; Moral Values; Creativity; Good Working Conditions; Variety. **Skills**—Operation and Control; Equipment Selection. **Abilities**—*Cognitive:* Originality; Visualization; Perceptual Speed; Fluency of Ideas; Spatial Orientation. *Psychomotor:* Arm-Hand Steadiness; Finger Dexterity; Manual Dexterity; Control Precision; Rate Control. *Physical:* Dynamic Flexibility; Dynamic Strength; Trunk Strength; Gross Body Coordination; Explosive Strength. *Sensory:* Depth Perception; Near Vision; Visual Color Discrimination; Peripheral Vision. **General Work Activities**—*Information Input:* Monitoring Processes, Materials, or Surroundings; Inspecting Equipment, Structures, or Materials; Getting Information. *Mental Process:* Thinking Creatively; Judging Qualities of Things, Services, or Other People's Work; Organizing, Planning, and Prioritizing. *Work Output:* Handling and Moving Objects; Controlling Machines and Processes; Performing General Physical Activities. *Interacting with Others:* Communicating with Persons Outside Organization; Communicating with Other Workers; Providing Consultation and Advice to Others. **Physical Work Conditions**—Hazardous Equipment; Using Hands on Objects, Tools, or Controls; Making Repetitive Motions; Minor Burns, Cuts, Bites, or Stings; Indoors. **Other Job Characteristics**—Importance of Being Exact or Accurate; Degree of Automation; Pace Determined by Speed of Equipment.

Experience—Job Zone 3. Previous work-related skill, knowledge, or experience is required. **Job Preparation:** SVP 6.0 to less than 7.0—more than one year and less than four years. **Knowledge**—Fine Arts; Production and Processing; Design; Communications and Media; Philosophy and Theology. **Instructional Programs**—Graphic Communications, Other.

Related DOT Jobs—733.381-010 Engraver, Rubber; 754.381-010 Internal Carver; 775.381-010 Engraver.

51-9194.03 Etchers

- **Education/Training Required: Long-term on-the-job training**
- **Employed: No data available.**
- **Annual Earnings: $22,100**
- **Growth: 11.1%**
- **Annual Job Openings: 2,000**

Etch or cut artistic designs in glass articles, using acid solutions, sandblasting equipment, and design patterns.

Immerses waxed ware in hydrofluoric acid to etch design on glass surface. Sandblasts exposed area of glass, using spray gun, to cut design in surface. Positions pattern against waxed or taped ware and sprays ink through pattern to transfer design to wax or tape. Removes wax or tape, using stylus or knife, to expose glassware surface to be etched. Coats glass in molten wax or masks glassware with tape. Immerses ware in hot water to remove wax or peels off tape.

GOE INFORMATION—Interest Area: 01. Arts, Entertainment, and Media. **Work Group:** 01.07. Graphic Arts. **Personality Type**—Realistic. Realistic occupations frequently involve work activities that include practical, hands-on problems and solutions. They often deal with plants, animals, and real-world materials like wood, tools, and machinery. Many of the occupations require working outside and do not involve a lot of paperwork or working closely with others. **Work Values**—Independence; Creativity; Moral Values; Variety; Supervision, Technical. **Skills**—Operation Monitoring; Operation and Control; Equipment Selection. **Abilities**—*Cognitive:* Visualization. *Psychomotor:* Arm-Hand Steadiness; Manual

Dexterity; Wrist-Finger Speed; Control Precision; Finger Dexterity. *Physical:* Gross Body Equilibrium; Stamina; Explosive Strength; Dynamic Flexibility; Dynamic Strength. *Sensory:* Depth Perception; Peripheral Vision; Glare Sensitivity. **General Work Activities**—*Information Input:* Monitoring Processes, Materials, or Surroundings; Inspecting Equipment, Structures, or Materials; Getting Information. *Mental Process:* Organizing, Planning, and Prioritizing; Updating and Using Relevant Knowledge; Judging Qualities of Things, Services, or Other People's Work. *Work Output:* Handling and Moving Objects; Controlling Machines and Processes; Performing General Physical Activities. *Interacting with Others:* Communicating with Other Workers; Performing for or Working with the Public; Coordinating the Work and Activities of Others. **Physical Work Conditions**—Hazardous Equipment; Using Hands on Objects, Tools, or Controls; Contaminants; Common Protective or Safety Attire; Making Repetitive Motions. **Other Job Characteristics**—Importance of Repeating Same Tasks; Importance of Being Exact or Accurate; Degree of Automation.

Experience—Job Zone 3. Previous work-related skill, knowledge, or experience is required. **Job Preparation:** SVP 6.0 to less than 7.0—more than one year and less than four years. **Knowledge**—Fine Arts; Chemistry; Production and Processing; Design; Mechanical. **Instructional Programs**—Graphic Communications, Other.

Related DOT Jobs—775.381-014 Glass Decorator.

51-9194.04 Pantograph Engravers

- **Education/Training Required: Moderate-term on-the-job training**
- **Employed: No data available.**
- **Annual Earnings: $22,100**
- **Growth: 11.1%**
- **Annual Job Openings: 2,000**

Affix identifying information onto a variety of materials and products, using engraving machines or equipment.

Starts machine and guides stylus over template, causing cutting tool to simultaneously duplicate design or letters on workpiece. Adjusts depth and size of cut by adjusting height of worktable or adjusting gauge on machine arms. Sets stylus at beginning of pattern. Selects and inserts letter or design template beneath stylus attached to machine cutting tool or router according to work order. Positions and secures workpiece, such as nameplate, stamp, seal, badge, trophy, or bowling ball, in holding fixture, using measuring instruments. Sets reduction scale to obtain required reproduction ratio on workpiece. Inserts cutting tool or bit into machine and secures with wrench. Observes action of cutting tool through microscope and adjusts movement of stylus to ensure accurate reproduction. Brushes acid over designated engraving to darken or highlight inscription. Verifies conformance to specifications, using micrometers and calipers. Examines engraving for quality of cut, burrs, rough spots, and irregular or incomplete engraving. Sharpens cutting tools on cutter grinder.

GOE INFORMATION—Interest Area: 01. Arts, Entertainment, and Media. **Work Group:** 01.07. Graphic Arts. **Personality Type**—Realistic. Realistic occupations frequently involve work activities that include practical, hands-on problems and solutions. They often deal with plants, animals, and real-world materials like wood, tools, and machinery. Many of the occupations require working outside and do not involve a lot of paperwork or working closely with others. **Work Values**—Moral Values; Independence; Supervision, Technical. **Skills**—Operation and Control; Operation Monitoring. **Abilities**—*Cognitive:* Visualization; Perceptual Speed; Selective Attention; Spatial Orientation. *Psychomotor:* Rate Control; Arm-Hand Steadiness; Control Precision; Manual Dexterity; Multilimb Coordination. *Physical:* Dynamic Strength; Dynamic Flexibility; Trunk Strength; Gross Body Coordination; Explosive Strength. *Sensory:* Near Vision; Depth Perception; Visual Color Discrimination; Peripheral Vision. **General Work Activities**—*Information Input:* Monitoring Processes, Materials, or Surroundings; Inspecting Equipment, Structures, or Materials; Identifying Objects, Actions, and Events. *Mental Process:* Judging Qualities of Things, Services, or Other People's Work; Updating and Using Relevant Knowledge; Evaluating Information Against Standards. *Work Output:* Handling and Moving Objects; Controlling Machines and Processes; Performing General Physical Activities. *Interacting with Others:* Communicating with Other Workers; Performing Administrative Activities; Establishing and Maintaining Relationships. **Physical Work Conditions**—Hazardous Equipment; Minor Burns, Cuts, Bites, or Stings; Using Hands on Objects, Tools, or Controls; Indoors; Hazardous Conditions. **Other Job Characteristics**—Degree of Automation; Pace Determined by Speed of Equipment; Importance of Being Exact or Accurate.

Experience—Job Zone 1. No previous work-related skill, knowledge, or experience is needed. **Job Preparation:** SVP below 4.0—less than six months. **Knowledge**—Production and Processing; Mechanical; Design; Fine Arts; Philosophy and Theology. **Instructional Programs**—Graphic Communications, Other.

Related DOT Jobs—704.382-010 Engraver, Pantograph I; 704.582-010 Engraver, Machine II; 704.682-010 Engraver, Machine I; 704.682-014 Engraver, Pantograph II; 732.584-010 Bowling-Ball Engraver.

51-9194.05 Etchers, Hand

- Education/Training Required: **Moderate-term on-the-job training**
- Employed: **No data available.**
- Annual Earnings: **$22,100**
- Growth: **11.1%**
- Annual Job Openings: **2,000**

Etch patterns, designs, lettering, or figures onto a variety of materials and products.

Exposes workpiece to acid to develop etch pattern, such as designs, lettering, or figures. Fills etched characters with opaque paste to improve readability. Prepares workpiece for etching by cutting, sanding, cleaning, or treating with wax, acid resist, lime, etching powder, or light-sensitive enamel. Transfers image to workpiece, using contact printer, pantograph stylus, silkscreen printing device, or stamp pad. Neutralizes workpiece to remove acid, wax, or enamel, using water or solvents. Measures and marks workpiece, such as plastic, fiberglass, epoxy board, metal, or glass, using measuring and calibrating equipment. Prepares etching solution according to formula. Inspects etched work for uniformity, using calibrated microscope and gauge. Positions and secures workpiece to be etched on setup board. Compares workpiece design, such as lettering, trademark, numerals, or lines, to sample to verify development of pattern. Reduces artwork, using reduction camera.

GOE INFORMATION—**Interest Area:** 01. Arts, Entertainment, and Media. **Work Group:** 01.07. Graphic Arts. **Personality Type**—Realistic. Realistic occupations frequently involve work activities that include practical, hands-on problems and solutions. They often deal with plants, animals, and real-world materials like wood, tools, and machinery. Many of the occupations require working outside and do not involve a lot of paperwork or working closely with others. **Work Values**—Moral Values; Independence; Supervision, Technical. **Skills**—Equipment Selection.

Abilities—*Cognitive:* Visualization; Perceptual Speed; Memorization; Spatial Orientation. *Psychomotor:* Arm-Hand Steadiness; Manual Dexterity; Control Precision; Finger Dexterity; Reaction Time. *Physical:* Dynamic Flexibility; Explosive Strength; Dynamic Strength; Static Strength; Gross Body Coordination. *Sensory:* Visual Color Discrimination; Near Vision; Depth Perception; Night Vision; Peripheral Vision. **General Work Activities**—*Information Input:* Inspecting Equipment, Structures, or Materials; Monitoring Processes, Materials, or Surroundings; Identifying Objects, Actions, and Events. *Mental Process:* Judging Qualities of Things, Services, or Other People's Work; Updating and Using Relevant Knowledge; Evaluating Information Against Standards. *Work Output:* Handling and Moving Objects; Controlling Machines and Processes; Performing General Physical Activities. *Interacting with Others:* Communicating with Other Workers; Performing Administrative Activities; Performing for or Working with the Public. **Physical Work Conditions**—Hazardous Conditions; Using Hands on Objects, Tools, or Controls; Contaminants; Minor Burns, Cuts, Bites, or Stings; Indoors. **Other Job Characteristics**—Importance of Being Exact or Accurate; Importance of Repeating Same Tasks; Pace Determined by Speed of Equipment.

Experience—Job Zone 1. No previous work-related skill, knowledge, or experience is needed. **Job Preparation:** SVP below 4.0—less than six months. **Knowledge**—Fine Arts; Design; Production and Processing; Chemistry; Computers and Electronics. **Instructional Programs**—Graphic Communications, Other.

Related DOT Jobs—590.684-018 Etched-Circuit Processor; 704.684-010 Etcher; 704.684-014 Silk-Screen Etcher; 704.687-014 Etcher, Hand; 716.681-022 Optical-Glass Etcher; 775.584-010 Glass Calibrator.

51-9194.06 Engravers, Hand

- Education/Training Required: **Long-term on-the-job training**
- Employed: **No data available.**
- Annual Earnings: **$22,100**
- Growth: **11.1%**
- Annual Job Openings: **2,000**

Engrave designs and identifying information onto rollers or plates used in printing.

Cuts grooves of specified depth and uniformity into printing roller, following lines of design impression. Cuts around drawn pattern, leaving raised design or letters, using cutting tools. Presses sketch on copper printing roller to produce impression of design. Traces pattern of design and letters in reverse on linoleum or two- or three-ply rubber, using ruler, pencil, drawing instruments, or cutting tools. Cuts strip of engraving gum (two- or three-ply rubber, cemented to cloth backing), using knife. Prepares additional rubber plates for jobs requiring colors by omitting different portions of design or lettering on each plate. Refers to sketch to ensure that lines of only one printing color are engraved into each roller. Glues rubber or linoleum pattern to wood block. Punches holes in plate to fasten plate to press, using hand tools. Inspects designs for defective engraving and re-engraves to meet specifications.

GOE INFORMATION—**Interest Area:** 01. Arts, Entertainment, and Media. **Work Group:** 01.07. Graphic Arts. **Personality Type**—Realistic. Realistic occupations frequently involve work activities that include practical, hands-on problems and solutions. They often deal with plants, animals, and real-world materials like wood, tools, and machinery. Many of the occupations require working outside and do not involve a lot of paperwork or working closely with others. **Work Values**—Moral Values; Independence; Supervision, Technical. **Skills**—None met the criteria. **Abilities**—*Cognitive:* Visualization; Spatial Orientation; Perceptual Speed;

Memorization. *Psychomotor:* Arm-Hand Steadiness; Manual Dexterity; Finger Dexterity; Speed of Limb Movement; Multilimb Coordination. *Physical:* Explosive Strength; Dynamic Flexibility; Dynamic Strength; Extent Flexibility; Trunk Strength. *Sensory:* Depth Perception; Visual Color Discrimination; Near Vision. **General Work Activities**—*Information Input:* Getting Information; Inspecting Equipment, Structures, or Materials; Monitoring Processes, Materials, or Surroundings. *Mental Process:* Thinking Creatively; Judging Qualities of Things, Services, or Other People's Work; Evaluating Information Against Standards. *Work Output:* Handling and Moving Objects; Controlling Machines and Processes; Drafting and Specifying Technical Devices. *Interacting with Others:* Coordinating the Work and Activities of Others; Communicating with Other Workers; Performing Administrative Activities. **Physical Work Conditions**—Using Hands on Objects, Tools, or Controls; Making Repetitive Motions; Hazardous Equipment; Indoors; Minor Burns, Cuts, Bites, or Stings. **Other Job Characteristics**—Importance of Being Exact or Accurate; Degree of Automation; Importance of Repeating Same Tasks.

Experience—Job Zone 3. Previous work-related skill, knowledge, or experience is required. **Job Preparation:** SVP 6.0 to less than 7.0—more than one year and less than four years. **Knowledge**—Fine Arts; Design; Production and Processing; Building and Construction; Communications and Media. **Instructional Programs**—Graphic Communications, Other.

Related DOT Jobs—979.581-010 Engraver, Rubber; 979.681-018 Roller Engraver, Hand; 979.684-014 Engraver II.

51-9195.00 Molders, Shapers, and Casters, Except Metal and Plastic

- **Education/Training Required: Postsecondary vocational training**
- **Employed: 42,282**
- **Annual Earnings: $24,670**
- **Growth: 7.4%**
- **Annual Job Openings: 6,000**

Mold, shape, form, cast, or carve products such as food products, figurines, tile, pipes, and candles consisting of clay, glass, plaster, concrete, stone, or combinations of materials.

No task data available.

GOE INFORMATION—Interest Area: 08. Industrial Production. **Work Group:** 08.02. Production Technology. **Note:** The Department of Labor has not collected some data for this job, so it has fewer details than the other descriptions.

Instructional Programs—No data available.

Related DOT Jobs—006.261-010 Scientific Glass Blower; 502.381-014 Molder, Punch; 502.684-010 Lead Caster; 502.684-014 Mill Helper; 502.684-022 Needle Leader; 518.484-010 Plaster Molder II; 518.684-014 Coremaker, Pipe; 556.484-010 Scagliola Mechanic; 556.684-014 Encapsulator; 556.684-018 Mold-Filling Operator; 556.684-026 Rubber Molder; 556.684-030 Loader-Demolder; 556.687-022 Molder, Toilet Products; 556.687-030 Mold Filler; 575.381-010 Molder; 575.461-010 Concrete-Stone Fabricator; 575.684-014 Caster; 575.684-018 Caster; 575.684-030 Handle Maker; 575.684-034 Laundry-Tub Maker; others.

51-9195.01 Precision Mold and Pattern Casters, Except Nonferrous Metals

- **Education/Training Required: Moderate-term on-the-job training**
- **Employed: No data available.**
- **Annual Earnings: $24,670**
- **Growth: 7.4%**
- **Annual Job Openings: 6,000**

Cast molds and patterns from a variety of materials except nonferrous metals, according to blueprints and specifications.

Pours, packs, spreads, or presses plaster, concrete, liquid plastic, or other materials into or around model or mold. Applies reinforcing strips and additional layers of materials to form pattern of model. Reviews specifications, blueprint, or sketch to plan and lay out work. Applies lubricant or parting agent to mold or pattern. Constructs or assembles wooden mold, using clamps and bolts, hand tools, and power tools. Locates and scribes parting line on patterns, using measuring instruments such as calipers, square, and depth gauge. Positions and secures reinforcing structure or materials, flask, mold, model, or pattern. Combines or melts ingredients to attain specified viscosity and shape. Removes casting from mold after specified time, using tools and equipment such as hand tools, power tools, and crane. Verifies dimensions, using measuring instruments such as calipers, vernier gauge, and protractor. Mixes ingredients according to standard formula. Trims or removes excess material, using scraper, knife, or band saw. Patches broken edges and fractures, using clay or plaster and molder's hand tools.

GOE INFORMATION—Interest Area: 08. Industrial Production. **Work Group:** 08.02. Production Technology. **Personality Type**—Realistic. Realistic occupations frequently involve work activities that include practical, hands-on problems and solutions. They often deal with plants, animals, and real-world materials like wood, tools, and machinery. Many of the occupations require working outside and do not involve a lot of paperwork or working closely with others. **Work Values**—Moral Values; Supervision, Technical; Independence; Supervision, Human Relations; Advancement. **Skills**—None met the criteria. **Abilities**—*Cognitive:* Visualization; Information Ordering. *Psychomotor:* Arm-Hand Steadiness; Wrist-Finger Speed; Speed of Limb Movement; Manual Dexterity; Finger Dexterity. *Physical:* Explosive Strength; Stamina. *Sensory:* None met the criteria. **General Work Activities**—*Information Input:* Inspecting Equipment, Structures, or Materials; Monitoring Processes, Materials, or Surroundings; Identifying Objects, Actions, and Events. *Mental Process:* Evaluating Information Against Standards; Updating and Using Relevant Knowledge; Thinking Creatively. *Work Output:* Handling and Moving Objects; Performing General Physical Activities; Controlling Machines and Processes. *Interacting with Others:* Communicating with Other Workers; Coaching and Developing Others; Assisting and Caring for Others. **Physical Work Conditions**—Distracting Sounds and Noise Levels; Hazardous Equipment; Indoors; Standing; Common Protective or Safety Attire. **Other Job Characteristics**—Pace Determined by Speed of Equipment; Importance of Repeating Same Tasks; Consequence of Error.

Experience—Job Zone 3. Previous work-related skill, knowledge, or experience is required. **Job Preparation:** SVP 6.0 to less than 7.0—more than one year and less than four years. **Knowledge**—Production and Processing; Building and Construction; Design; Engineering and Technology; Mechanical. **Instructional Programs**—No data available.

Related DOT Jobs—575.461-010 Concrete-Stone Fabricator; 739.381-046 Mannequin-Mold Maker; 769.381-010 Compo Caster; 777.081-010 Modeler; 777.381-034 Plaster Molder I; 777.381-038 Plaster-Pattern Caster.

51-9195.02 Precision Pattern and Die Casters, Nonferrous Metals

- Education/Training Required: Long-term on-the-job training
- Employed: No data available.
- Annual Earnings: $24,670
- Growth: 7.4%
- Annual Job Openings: 6,000

Cast metal patterns and dies according to specifications from a variety of nonferrous metals, such as aluminum or bronze.

Shapes mold to specified contours with sand, using trowel and related tools. Tilts melting pot or uses ladle to pour molten alloy, bronze, or other nonferrous metal into sand mold. Preheats dies or patterns, using blowtorch or other equipment, and applies parting compound. Lowers metal jig into molten metal in prescribed manner to attach anchor bolts to punch. Clamps metal and plywood strips around die or pattern to form mold. Operates foundry furnaces and ovens. Constructs wood patterns used to form sand molds for metal casts. Operates hoist to position dies or patterns on foundry floor. Machines metal patterns to exact dimensions.

GOE INFORMATION—Interest Area: 08. Industrial Production. **Work Group:** 08.02. Production Technology. **Personality Type**—Realistic. Realistic occupations frequently involve work activities that include practical, hands-on problems and solutions. They often deal with plants, animals, and real-world materials like wood, tools, and machinery. Many of the occupations require working outside and do not involve a lot of paperwork or working closely with others. **Work Values**—Moral Values; Independence; Supervision, Human Relations; Supervision, Technical. **Skills**—Operation and Control. **Abilities**—*Cognitive:* Selective Attention. *Psychomotor:* Manual Dexterity; Reaction Time; Multilimb Coordination; Response Orientation; Speed of Limb Movement. *Physical:* Explosive Strength; Dynamic Strength; Static Strength; Stamina; Trunk Strength. *Sensory:* Depth Perception; Glare Sensitivity; Sound Localization. **General Work Activities**—*Information Input:* Monitoring Processes, Materials, or Surroundings; Getting Information; Inspecting Equipment, Structures, or Materials. *Mental Process:* Evaluating Information Against Standards; Updating and Using Relevant Knowledge; Judging Qualities of Things, Services, or Other People's Work. *Work Output:* Performing General Physical Activities; Handling and Moving Objects; Controlling Machines and Processes. *Interacting with Others:* Communicating with Other Workers; Establishing and Maintaining Relationships; Assisting and Caring for Others. **Physical Work Conditions**—Very Hot or Cold; Contaminants; Common Protective or Safety Attire; Hazardous Conditions; Hazardous Equipment. **Other Job Characteristics**—Pace Determined by Speed of Equipment; Degree of Automation; Importance of Repeating Same Tasks.

Experience—Job Zone 4. A minimum of two to four years of work-related skill, knowledge, or experience is needed. **Job Preparation:** SVP 7.0 to less than 8.0—two years to less than 10 years. **Knowledge**—Production and Processing; Building and Construction; Design; Engineering and Technology; Physics. **Instructional Programs**—No data available.

Related DOT Jobs—502.381-014 Molder, Punch; 693.381-022 Molder, Pattern.

51-9195.03 Stone Cutters and Carvers

- Education/Training Required: Moderate-term on-the-job training
- Employed: No data available.
- Annual Earnings: $24,670
- Growth: 7.4%
- Annual Job Openings: 6,000

Cut or carve stone according to diagrams and patterns.

Guides nozzle over stone, following stencil outline, or chips along marks to create design or work surface down to desired finish. Drills holes or cuts molding and grooves in stone. Studies artistic objects or graphic materials, such as models, sketches, or blueprints, and plans carving or cutting technique. Lays out designs or dimensions on stone surface by freehand or transfer from tracing paper, using scribe or chalk and measuring instruments. Selects chisels, pneumatic or surfacing tools, or sandblasting nozzles and determines sequence of their use according to intricacy of design or figure. Removes or adds stencil during blasting to create differences in depth of cuts, intricate designs, or rough, pitted finish. Loads sandblasting equipment with abrasive, attaches nozzle to hose, and turns valves to admit compressed air and activate jet. Verifies depth and dimensions of cut or carving, using measuring instruments, to ensure adherence to specifications. Moves fingers over surface of carving to ensure smoothness of finish.

GOE INFORMATION—Interest Area: 06. Construction, Mining, and Drilling. **Work Group:** 06.02. Construction. **Personality Type**—Realistic. Realistic occupations frequently involve work activities that include practical, hands-on problems and solutions. They often deal with plants, animals, and real-world materials like wood, tools, and machinery. Many of the occupations require working outside and do not involve a lot of paperwork or working closely with others. **Work Values**—Independence; Moral Values; Recognition; Autonomy; Achievement. **Skills**—Equipment Selection; Operation and Control. **Abilities**—*Cognitive:* Visualization. *Psychomotor:* Arm-Hand Steadiness; Wrist-Finger Speed. *Physical:* Extent Flexibility; Static Strength; Trunk Strength; Dynamic Flexibility. *Sensory:* Depth Perception; Near Vision. **General Work Activities**—*Information Input:* Getting Information; Monitoring Processes, Materials, or Surroundings; Identifying Objects, Actions, and Events. *Mental Process:* Thinking Creatively; Evaluating Information Against Standards; Judging Qualities of Things, Services, or Other People's Work. *Work Output:* Handling and Moving Objects; Controlling Machines and Processes; Performing General Physical Activities. *Interacting with Others:* Coaching and Developing Others; Communicating with Other Workers; Establishing and Maintaining Relationships. **Physical Work Conditions**—Common Protective or Safety Attire; Contaminants; Whole Body Vibration; Distracting Sounds and Noise Levels; Using Hands on Objects, Tools, or Controls. **Other Job Characteristics**—Importance of Repeating Same Tasks; Pace Determined by Speed of Equipment; Importance of Being Exact or Accurate.

Experience—Job Zone 3. Previous work-related skill, knowledge, or experience is required. **Job Preparation:** SVP 6.0 to less than 7.0—more than one year and less than four years. **Knowledge**—Fine Arts; Design; Building and Construction; Physics; Engineering and Technology. **Instructional Programs**—No data available.

Related DOT Jobs—673.382-010 Sandblaster, Stone; 673.382-014 Sandblaster, Stone Apprentice; 771.281-014 Stone Carver; 771.381-010 Stonecutter Apprentice, Hand; 771.381-014 Stonecutter, Hand.

51-9195.04 Glass Blowers, Molders, Benders, and Finishers

- Education/Training Required: Long-term on-the-job training
- Employed: No data available.
- Annual Earnings: $24,670
- Growth: 7.4%
- Annual Job Openings: 6,000

Shape molten glass according to patterns.

Shapes, bends, or joins sections of glass, using paddles, pressing and flattening hand tools, or cork. Blows tubing into specified shape, using compressed air or own breath. Places glass into die or mold of press and controls press to form products such as glassware components or optical blanks. Dips end of blowpipe into molten glass to collect gob on pipe head or cuts gob from molten glass, using sheers. Preheats or melts glass pieces or anneals or cools glass products and components, using ovens and refractory powder. Heats glass to pliable stage, using gas flame or oven. Cuts length of tubing to specified size, using file or cutting wheel. Inspects and measures product to verify conformance to specifications, using instruments such as micrometers, calipers, magnifier, and ruler. Examines gob of molten glass for imperfections, utilizing knowledge of molten glass characteristics. Strikes neck of finished article to separate article from blowpipe. Determines type and quantity of glass required to fabricate product. Adjusts press stroke length and pressure and regulates oven temperatures according to glass type processed. Develops sketch of glass product into blueprint specifications, applying knowledge of glass technology and glass-blowing.

GOE INFORMATION—Interest Area: 01. Arts, Entertainment, and Media. Work Group: 01.06. Craft Arts. Personality Type—Realistic. Realistic occupations frequently involve work activities that include practical, hands-on problems and solutions. They often deal with plants, animals, and real-world materials like wood, tools, and machinery. Many of the occupations require working outside and do not involve a lot of paperwork or working closely with others. Work Values—Independence; Ability Utilization; Achievement; Moral Values; Recognition. Skills—None met the criteria. Abilities—*Cognitive:* Visualization. *Psychomotor:* Arm-Hand Steadiness; Manual Dexterity; Control Precision; Wrist-Finger Speed; Reaction Time. *Physical:* Stamina; Dynamic Flexibility; Extent Flexibility; Explosive Strength. *Sensory:* None met the criteria. General Work Activities—*Information Input:* Monitoring Processes, Materials, or Surroundings; Inspecting Equipment, Structures, or Materials; Estimating Needed Characteristics. *Mental Process:* Thinking Creatively; Evaluating Information Against Standards; Judging Qualities of Things, Services, or Other People's Work. *Work Output:* Handling and Moving Objects; Performing General Physical Activities; Controlling Machines and Processes. *Interacting with Others:* Establishing and Maintaining Relationships; Coaching and Developing Others; Communicating with Other Workers. Physical Work Conditions—Very Hot or Cold; Minor Burns, Cuts, Bites, or Stings; Making Repetitive Motions; Using Hands on Objects, Tools, or Controls; Indoors. Other Job Characteristics—Importance of Repeating Same Tasks; Degree of Automation; Pace Determined by Speed of Equipment.

Experience—Job Zone 4. A minimum of two to four years of work-related skill, knowledge, or experience is needed. Job Preparation: SVP 7.0 to less than 8.0—two years to less than 10 years. Knowledge—Production and Processing; Physics; Design; Fine Arts; Engineering and Technology. Instructional Programs—No data available.

Related DOT Jobs—575.381-010 Molder; 626.101-010 Scientific Glass Blower; 772.281-010 Glass Blower, Laboratory Apparatus; 772.381-010 Glass Bender; 772.381-018 Ware Finisher; 772.381-022 Glass Blower.

51-9195.05 Potters

- Education/Training Required: Long-term on-the-job training
- Employed: No data available.
- Annual Earnings: $24,670
- Growth: 7.4%
- Annual Job Openings: 6,000

Mold clay into ware as clay revolves on potter's wheel.

Raises and shapes clay into ware, such as vases, saggers, and pitchers, on revolving wheel, using hands, fingers, and thumbs. Smoothes surfaces of finished piece, using rubber scrapers and wet sponge. Adjusts speed of wheel according to feel of changing firmness of clay. Positions ball of clay in center of potter's wheel. Starts motor or pumps treadle with foot to revolve wheel. Pulls wire through base of article and wheel to separate finished piece. Verifies size and form, using calipers and templates. Moves piece from wheel to dry.

GOE INFORMATION—Interest Area: 01. Arts, Entertainment, and Media. Work Group: 01.06. Craft Arts. Personality Type—Realistic. Realistic occupations frequently involve work activities that include practical, hands-on problems and solutions. They often deal with plants, animals, and real-world materials like wood, tools, and machinery. Many of the occupations require working outside and do not involve a lot of paperwork or working closely with others. Work Values—Moral Values; Creativity; Independence; Autonomy; Recognition. Skills—Operation and Control. Abilities—*Cognitive:* Visualization; Originality. *Psychomotor:* Arm-Hand Steadiness; Manual Dexterity; Rate Control; Multilimb Coordination; Finger Dexterity. *Physical:* Dynamic Flexibility; Extent Flexibility. *Sensory:* None met the criteria. General Work Activities—*Information Input:* Monitoring Processes, Materials, or Surroundings; Getting Information; Estimating Needed Characteristics. *Mental Process:* Thinking Creatively; Updating and Using Relevant Knowledge; Evaluating Information Against Standards. *Work Output:* Handling and Moving Objects; Controlling Machines and Processes; Performing General Physical Activities. *Interacting with Others:* Monitoring and Controlling Resources; Communicating with Other Workers; Establishing and Maintaining Relationships. Physical Work Conditions—Making Repetitive Motions; Using Hands on Objects, Tools, or Controls; Sitting; Bending or Twisting the Body; Contaminants. Other Job Characteristics—Importance of Repeating Same Tasks; Pace Determined by Speed of Equipment; Degree of Automation.

Experience—Job Zone 4. A minimum of two to four years of work-related skill, knowledge, or experience is needed. Job Preparation: SVP 7.0 to less than 8.0—two years to less than 10 years. Knowledge—Fine Arts; Production and Processing; Design; Building and Construction; Physics. Instructional Programs—No data available.

Related DOT Jobs—774.381-010 Thrower.

51-9195.06 Mold Makers, Hand

- Education/Training Required: Moderate-term on-the-job training
- Employed: No data available.
- Annual Earnings: $24,670
- Growth: 7.4%
- Annual Job Openings: 6,000

Construct or form molds from existing forms for use in casting objects.

Constructs molds used for casting metal, clay, or plaster objects, using plaster, fiberglass, rubber, casting machine, patterns, and flasks. Assembles hardened molds and seals joints. Places form around model and separately immerses each half portion of model in plaster, wax, or other mold-making material. Covers portions of model with layers of modeling or casting material treated to harden when allowed to set or dry. Removes excess modeling or mold material, such as plaster, wax, or rubber, using straightedge. Smoothes surfaces of mold, using scraping tool and sandpaper. Covers model or pattern of object from which mold is to be made with lubricant or parting agent to prevent mold from sticking to model. Bores holes or cuts grates and risers in mold, using power tools. Separates model or pattern from mold. Examines mold for accuracy. Allows mold to harden or dry in oven and repeats process until mold is complete. Repairs cracks and broken edges of mold, using hand tools. Mixes modeling material, such as plaster powder and water or mud, sand, and loam, to specified formula. Melts metal pieces, using torch, and casts products such as inlays and crowns, using centrifugal casting machine.

GOE INFORMATION—Interest Area: 08. Industrial Production. **Work Group:** 08.03. Production Work. **Personality Type—**Realistic. Realistic occupations frequently involve work activities that include practical, hands-on problems and solutions. They often deal with plants, animals, and real-world materials like wood, tools, and machinery. Many of the occupations require working outside and do not involve a lot of paperwork or working closely with others. **Work Values—**Moral Values; Supervision, Technical; Independence; Supervision, Human Relations. **Skills—**Repairing; Equipment Selection. **Abilities—***Cognitive:* Visualization; Selective Attention; Perceptual Speed; Flexibility of Closure. *Psychomotor:* Speed of Limb Movement; Arm-Hand Steadiness; Manual Dexterity; Finger Dexterity; Multilimb Coordination. *Physical:* Explosive Strength; Dynamic Flexibility; Extent Flexibility; Dynamic Strength; Static Strength. *Sensory:* Hearing Sensitivity; Depth Perception; Glare Sensitivity; Sound Localization; Peripheral Vision. **General Work Activities—***Information Input:* Getting Information; Inspecting Equipment, Structures, or Materials; Monitoring Processes, Materials, or Surroundings. *Mental Process:* Evaluating Information Against Standards; Judging Qualities of Things, Services, or Other People's Work; Organizing, Planning, and Prioritizing. *Work Output:* Handling and Moving Objects; Controlling Machines and Processes; Performing General Physical Activities. *Interacting with Others:* Communicating with Other Workers; Establishing and Maintaining Relationships; Providing Consultation and Advice to Others. **Physical Work Conditions—**Common Protective or Safety Attire; Using Hands on Objects, Tools, or Controls; Contaminants; Hazardous Equipment; Making Repetitive Motions. **Other Job Characteristics—**Importance of Repeating Same Tasks; Consequence of Error; Importance of Being Exact or Accurate.

Experience—Job Zone 2. Some previous work-related skill, knowledge, or experience may be helpful, but usually is not needed. **Job Preparation:** SVP 4.0 to less than 6.0—six months to less than two years. **Knowledge—**Building and Construction; Production and Processing. **Instructional Programs—**No data available.

Related DOT Jobs—518.484-010 Plaster Molder II; 518.684-014 Coremaker, Pipe; 575.684-038 Mold Maker, Terra Cotta; 712.684-046 Denture-Model Maker; 777.684-014 Mold Maker; 777.684-018 Mold Maker.

51-9195.07 Molding and Casting Workers

- **Education/Training Required:** Moderate-term on-the-job training
- **Employed:** No data available.
- **Annual Earnings:** $24,670
- **Growth:** 7.4%
- **Annual Job Openings:** 6,000

Perform a variety of duties such as mixing materials, assembling mold parts, filling molds, and stacking molds to mold and cast a wide range of products.

Fills mold with mixed material or applies material to mold to specified thickness. Molds parts or products using vibrator, handpress, or casting equipment and taps or tilts mold to ensure uniformity. Operates and adjusts controls of heating equipment to melt material or to cure, dry, or bake filled molds according to specifications. Opens mold and removes finished products. Measures ingredients and mixes molding or casting material or sealing compound to prescribed consistency according to formula. Assembles, inserts, and adjusts wires, tubes, cores, fittings, rods, or patterns into mold, using hand tools and depth gauge. Removes excess material and levels and smoothes wet mold mixture. Loads or stacks filled molds in oven, drier, or curing box or on storage racks or carts. Reads work order or examines part to determine part or section of product to be produced. Selects size and type of mold according to instructions. Installs and secures mold or mold parts together. Brushes or sprays surface of mold with parting agent or inserts paper to ensure smoothness and prevent sticking or seepage. Measures and cuts product to specified dimensions, using measuring and cutting instruments. Aligns and assembles parts to produce completed product, using gauges and hand tools. Inspects and tests parts or products for defects and to verify accuracy and adherence to standards. Fastens metal inserts, such as drainage tubes, bolts, or electrical connections to product, using hand tools and power tools. Cleans, trims, smoothes, and polishes products or parts. Cleans and lubricates mold and mold parts. Engraves or stamps identifying symbols, letters, or numbers on product.

GOE INFORMATION—Interest Area: 08. Industrial Production. **Work Group:** 08.03. Production Work. **Personality Type—**Realistic. Realistic occupations frequently involve work activities that include practical, hands-on problems and solutions. They often deal with plants, animals, and real-world materials like wood, tools, and machinery. Many of the occupations require working outside and do not involve a lot of paperwork or working closely with others. **Work Values—**Moral Values; Supervision, Technical; Independence; Supervision, Human Relations; Company Policies and Practices. **Skills—**Operation Monitoring; Operation and Control; Quality Control Analysis; Equipment Selection; Repairing; Installation. **Abilities—***Cognitive:* Visualization; Memorization; Information Ordering; Perceptual Speed; Inductive Reasoning. *Psychomotor:* Manual Dexterity; Finger Dexterity; Arm-Hand Steadiness; Multilimb Coordination; Control Precision. *Physical:* Static Strength; Trunk Strength; Explosive Strength; Dynamic Flexibility; Stamina. *Sensory:* Near Vision. **General Work Activities—***Information Input:* Monitoring Processes, Materials, or Surroundings; Inspecting Equipment, Structures, or Materials; Getting Information. *Mental Process:* Evaluating Information Against Standards; Judging Qualities of Things, Services, or Other People's Work; Organizing, Planning, and Prioritizing. *Work Output:* Handling and Moving Objects; Performing General Physical Activities; Controlling Machines and Processes. *Interacting with Others:* Establishing and Maintaining Relationships; Communicating with Other Workers; Coordinating the Work and Activities of Others. **Physical Work Conditions—**Using Hands on Objects, Tools, or Controls;

Making Repetitive Motions; Indoors; Bending or Twisting the Body; Hazardous Equipment. **Other Job Characteristics**—Importance of Repeating Same Tasks; Pace Determined by Speed of Equipment; Importance of Being Exact or Accurate.

Experience—Job Zone 2. Some previous work-related skill, knowledge, or experience may be helpful, but usually is not needed. **Job Preparation:** SVP 4.0 to less than 6.0—six months to less than two years. **Knowledge**—Building and Construction; Production and Processing. **Instructional Programs**—No data available.

Related DOT Jobs—502.684-010 Lead Caster; 502.684-014 Mill Helper; 502.684-022 Needle Leader; 556.484-010 Scagliola Mechanic; 556.684-014 Encapsulator; 556.684-018 Mold-Filling Operator; 556.684-026 Rubber Molder; 556.684-030 Loader-Demolder; 556.687-022 Molder, Toilet Products; 556.687-030 Mold Filler; 575.684-014 Caster; 575.684-018 Caster; 575.684-030 Handle Maker; 575.684-034 Laundry-Tub Maker; 575.684-042 Molder, Hand; 575.684-046 Terrazzo-Tile Maker; 575.684-050 Cultured-Marble-Products Maker; 579.684-010 Concrete-Vault Maker; 579.684-018 Kiln-Furniture Caster; 579.684-026 Caster; others.

51-9196.00 Paper Goods Machine Setters, Operators, and Tenders

- **Education/Training Required: Moderate-term on-the-job training**
- **Employed: 123,089**
- **Annual Earnings: $27,760**
- **Growth: −5.4%**
- **Annual Job Openings: 18,000**

Set up, operate, or tend paper goods machines that perform a variety of functions, such as converting, sawing, corrugating, banding, wrapping, boxing, stitching, forming, or sealing paper or paperboard sheets into products.

Adjusts guide assembly and folding mechanism according to specifications, using hand tools. Measures, spaces, and sets saw blades, cutters, and perforators according to product specifications. Starts machine, regulates tension on pressure rolls, and synchronizes speed of machine components and temperature of glue or paraffin. Installs attachments to machines for gluing, folding, printing, or cutting. Places roll of paper or cardboard on machine feedtrack and threads paper through gluing, coating, and slitting rollers. Fills glue and paraffin reservoirs and loads automatic stapling mechanism. Observes operation of various machines to detect machine malfunctions and makes corrections for product to meet specifications. Examines completed work to detect defects and verify conformance to work orders. Removes finished cores and stacks or places them on conveyor for transfer to other work areas. Disassembles machines to repair or replace broken or worn parts using hand or power tools. Cuts products to specified dimensions, using hand or power cutters.

GOE INFORMATION—**Interest Area:** 08. Industrial Production. **Work Group:** 08.02. Production Technology. **Personality Type**—Realistic. Realistic occupations frequently involve work activities that include practical, hands-on problems and solutions. They often deal with plants, animals, and real-world materials like wood, tools, and machinery. Many of the occupations require working outside and do not involve a lot of paperwork or working closely with others. **Work Values**—Moral Values; Independence; Supervision, Human Relations; Supervision, Technical; Company Policies and Practices. **Skills**—Operation Monitoring; Operation and Control; Installation; Repairing; Troubleshooting; Quality Control Analysis. **Abilities**—*Cognitive:* None met the criteria. *Psychomotor:* Rate Control; Control Precision; Manual Dexterity; Finger Dexterity;

Speed of Limb Movement. *Physical:* Static Strength. *Sensory:* None met the criteria. **General Work Activities**—*Information Input:* Monitoring Processes, Materials, or Surroundings; Inspecting Equipment, Structures, or Materials; Getting Information. *Mental Process:* Evaluating Information Against Standards; Judging Qualities of Things, Services, or Other People's Work; Updating and Using Relevant Knowledge. *Work Output:* Handling and Moving Objects; Controlling Machines and Processes; Performing General Physical Activities. *Interacting with Others:* Communicating with Other Workers; Performing Administrative Activities; Monitoring and Controlling Resources. **Physical Work Conditions**—Hazardous Equipment; Distracting Sounds and Noise Levels; Common Protective or Safety Attire; Indoors; Standing. **Other Job Characteristics**—Degree of Automation; Pace Determined by Speed of Equipment; Importance of Repeating Same Tasks.

Experience—Job Zone 2. Some previous work-related skill, knowledge, or experience may be helpful, but usually is not needed. **Job Preparation:** SVP 4.0 to less than 6.0—six months to less than two years. **Knowledge**—Production and Processing; Mechanical; Engineering and Technology. **Instructional Programs**—No data available.

Related DOT Jobs—640.682-010 Convolute-Tube Winder; 640.682-022 Spiral-Tube Winder; 641.380-010 Envelope-Folding-Machine Adjuster; 649.380-010 Machine Set-Up Operator, Paper Goods; 649.682-010 Box-Folding-Machine Operator.

51-9197.00 Tire Builders

- **Education/Training Required: Moderate-term on-the-job training**
- **Employed: 18,467**
- **Annual Earnings: $38,230**
- **Growth: 8.6%**
- **Annual Job Openings: 3,000**

Operate machines to build tires from rubber components.

Depresses pedal to rotate drum and winds specified number of plies around drum to form tire body. Starts rollers that bond tread and plies as drum revolves. Activates bead setters that press prefabricated beads onto plies and position rollers that turn ply edges under and over beads. Depresses pedal to collapse drum and lifts tire onto conveyor. Aligns tread with guide, starts drum to wind tread onto plies, and slices ends. Turns ends of plies under and over beads with steel rod. Positions ply stitcher rollers and drum according to width of stock, using hand tools and gauges. Brushes solvent onto ply to ensure adhesion and repeats process as specified, alternating direction of each ply to strengthen tire. Winds chafers and breaker onto plies. Rubs cement stick on drum edge to provide adhesive surface for plies. Pulls ply from supply rack and aligns ply with edge of drum. Cuts ply at splice point and presses ends together to form continuous band.

GOE INFORMATION—**Interest Area:** 08. Industrial Production. **Work Group:** 08.03. Production Work. **Personality Type**—Realistic. Realistic occupations frequently involve work activities that include practical, hands-on problems and solutions. They often deal with plants, animals, and real-world materials like wood, tools, and machinery. Many of the occupations require working outside and do not involve a lot of paperwork or working closely with others. **Work Values**—Moral Values; Independence; Supervision, Technical; Supervision, Human Relations; Company Policies and Practices. **Skills**—Operation and Control. **Abilities**—*Cognitive:* None met the criteria. *Psychomotor:* Speed of Limb Movement; Rate Control; Wrist-Finger Speed; Manual Dexterity; Multilimb Coordination. *Physical:* Explosive Strength; Static Strength; Dynamic Strength; Dynamic Flexibility; Extent Flexibility. *Sensory:* Depth Perception; Hearing Sensitivity; Peripheral Vision; Sound Localization. **General Work Activities**—*Information Input:* Monitoring Processes, Materials, or Surroundings; Getting Information; Identifying Objects, Actions, and Events. *Mental Process:* Evaluating Information Against Standards; Analyzing Data or Information; Organizing, Planning, and Prioritizing. *Work Output:* Handling and Moving Objects; Performing General Physical Activities; Controlling Machines and Processes. *Interacting with Others:* Communicating with Other Workers; Establishing and Maintaining Relationships; Monitoring and Controlling Resources. **Physical Work Conditions**—Hazardous Equipment; Minor Burns, Cuts, Bites, or Stings; Contaminants; Hazardous Conditions; Common Protective or Safety Attire. **Other Job Characteristics**—Pace Determined by Speed of Equipment; Degree of Automation; Importance of Repeating Same Tasks.

Experience—Job Zone 1. No previous work-related skill, knowledge, or experience is needed. **Job Preparation:** SVP below 4.0—less than six months. **Knowledge**—Production and Processing; Mechanical; Physics. **Instructional Programs**—No data available.

Related DOT Jobs—750.384-010 Tire Builder, Automobile; 750.684-014 Bead Builder.

51-9198.00 Helpers—Production Workers

- **Education/Training Required: Short-term on-the-job training**
- **Employed: No data available.**
- **Annual Earnings: $18,990**
- **Growth: 11.9%**
- **Annual Job Openings: 143,000**

Help production workers by performing duties of lesser skill. Duties include supplying or holding materials or tools and cleaning work area and equipment.

No task data available.

GOE INFORMATION—**Interest Area:** 08. Industrial Production. **Work Group:** 08.03. Production Work. **Note:** The Department of Labor has not collected some data for this job, so it has fewer details than the other descriptions.

Instructional Programs—No data available.

Related DOT Jobs—230.667-014 Telephone-Directory Deliverer; 230.687-010 Advertising-Material Distributor; 299.667-010 Billposter; 299.687-010 Porter, Sample Case; 361.687-018 Laundry Laborer; 361.687-026 Shaker, Wearing Apparel; 361.687-030 Washer, Hand; 362.686-010 Dry-Cleaner Helper; 362.686-014 Rug-Cleaner Helper; 362.687-010 Glove Cleaner, Hand; 362.687-014 Lining Scrubber; 362.687-018 Shaver; 363.687-010 Glove Former; 363.687-014 Ironer, Sock; 363.687-018 Puff Ironer; 363.687-022 Stretcher-Drier Operator; 364.687-010 Dyer Helper; 364.687-014 Rug-Dyer Helper; 365.674-010 Shoe-Repairer Helper; 369.387-010 Laundry Worker III; others.

51-9198.01 Production Laborers

- **Education/Training Required: Short-term on-the-job training**
- **Employed: No data available.**
- **Annual Earnings: $18,990**
- **Growth: 11.9%**
- **Annual Job Openings: 143,000**

Perform variety of routine tasks to assist in production activities.

Carries or handtrucks supplies to workstations. Loads and unloads items from machines, conveyors, and conveyance. Lifts raw materials, final products, and items packed for shipment manually or using hoist. Breaks up defective products for reprocessing. Attaches slings, ropes, cables, or identification tags to objects, such as pipes, hoses, and bundles. Weighs raw materials for distribution. Ties product in bundles for further processing or shipment, following prescribed procedure. Threads ends of items such as thread, cloth, and lace through needles and rollers and around takeup tube. Positions spout or chute of storage bin to fill containers during processing. Places product in equipment or on work surface for further processing, inspecting, or wrapping. Cuts or breaks flashing from materials or products. Separates product according to weight, grade, size, and composition of material used to produced product. Folds parts of product and final product during processing. Washes machines, equipment, vehicles, and products such as prints, rugs, and table linens. Counts finished product to determine completion of production order. Inserts parts into partial assembly during various stages of assembly to complete product. Feeds item into processing machine. Mixes ingredients according to formula. Examines product to verify conformance to company standards. Records information, such as number of product tested, meter readings, and date and time product placed in oven.

GOE INFORMATION—**Interest Area:** 08. Industrial Production. **Work Group:** 08.03. Production Work. **Personality Type**—Realistic. Realistic occupations frequently involve work activities that include practical, hands-on problems and solutions. They often deal with plants, animals, and real-world materials like wood, tools, and machinery. Many of the occupations require working outside and do not involve a lot of paperwork or working closely with others. **Work Values**—Moral Values; Activity; Supervision, Technical; Pleasant Co-workers. **Skills**—None met the criteria. **Abilities**—*Cognitive:* Category Flexibility; Spatial Orientation. *Psychomotor:* Manual Dexterity; Speed of Limb Movement; Arm-Hand Steadiness; Rate Control; Multilimb Coordination. *Physical:* Dynamic Strength; Static Strength; Explosive Strength; Dynamic Flexibility; Stamina. *Sensory:* Depth Perception; Peripheral Vision; Glare Sensitivity; Visual Color Discrimination; Sound Localization. **General Work Activities**—*Information Input:* Inspecting Equipment, Structures, or Materials; Monitoring Processes, Materials, or Surroundings; Getting Information. *Mental Process:* Evaluating Information Against Standards; Updating and Using Relevant Knowledge; Processing Information. *Work Output:* Handling and Moving Objects; Performing General Physical Activities; Controlling Machines and Processes. *Interacting with Others:* Performing Administrative Activities; Assisting and Caring for Others; Communicating with Other Workers. **Physical Work Conditions**—Hazardous Equipment; Making Repetitive Motions; Bending or Twisting the Body; Distracting Sounds and Noise Levels; Using Hands on Objects, Tools, or Controls. **Other Job Characteristics**—Importance of Repeating Same Tasks; Pace Determined by Speed of Equipment; Degree of Automation.

Experience—Job Zone 1. No previous work-related skill, knowledge, or experience is needed. **Job Preparation:** SVP below 4.0—less than six months. **Knowledge**—Production and Processing; Clerical; Building and Construction; Chemistry. **Instructional Programs**—No data available.

Related DOT Jobs—230.667-014 Telephone-Directory Deliverer; 230.687-010 Advertising-Material Distributor; 299.667-010 Billposter; 299.687-010 Porter, Sample Case; 361.687-018 Laundry Laborer; 361.687-026 Shaker, Wearing Apparel; 361.687-030 Washer, Hand; 362.686-010 Dry-Cleaner Helper; 362.686-014 Rug-Cleaner Helper; 362.687-010 Glove Cleaner, Hand; 362.687-014 Lining Scrubber; 362.687-018 Shaver; 363.687-010 Glove Former; 363.687-014 Ironer, Sock; 363.687-018 Puff Ironer; 363.687-022 Stretcher-Drier Operator; 364.687-010 Dyer Helper; 364.687-014 Rug-Dyer Helper; 369.387-010 Laundry Worker III; 369.687-018 Folder; others.

51-9198.02 Production Helpers

- **Education/Training Required: Short-term on-the-job training**
- **Employed: No data available.**
- **Annual Earnings: $18,990**
- **Growth: 11.9%**
- **Annual Job Openings: 143,000**

Perform variety of tasks requiring limited knowledge of production processes in support of skilled production workers.

Cleans and lubricates equipment. Dumps materials into machine hopper prior to mixing. Loads and unloads processing equipment or conveyance used to receive raw materials or to ship finished products. Marks or tags identification on parts. Observes operation and notifies equipment operator of malfunctions. Places or positions equipment or partially assembled product for further processing manually or using hoist. Reads gauges and charts and records data. Removes product, machine attachments, and waste material from machine. Starts machines or equipment to begin process. Turns valves to regulate flow of liquids or air, to reverse machine, to start pump, and to regulate equipment. Mixes ingredients according to procedure. Tends equipment to facilitate process. Replaces damaged or worm equipment parts. Measures amount of ingredients, length of extruded article, or work to ensure conformance to specifications. Signals co-workers to facilitate moving product during processing.

GOE INFORMATION—Interest Area: 08. Industrial Production. **Work Group:** 08.03. Production Work. **Personality Type—**Realistic. Realistic occupations frequently involve work activities that include practical, hands-on problems and solutions. They often deal with plants, animals, and real-world materials like wood, tools, and machinery. Many of the occupations require working outside and do not involve a lot of paperwork or working closely with others. **Work Values—**Supervision, Technical; Moral Values; Supervision, Human Relations; Activity; Advancement. **Skills—**Repairing; Operation Monitoring; Operation and Control; Installation. **Abilities—***Cognitive:* Perceptual Speed; Selective Attention; Spatial Orientation. *Psychomotor:* Reaction Time; Speed of Limb Movement; Multilimb Coordination; Control Precision; Wrist-Finger Speed. *Physical:* Static Strength; Stamina; Explosive Strength; Dynamic Flexibility; Gross Body Equilibrium. *Sensory:* Auditory Attention; Hearing Sensitivity; Sound Localization; Far Vision. **General Work Activities—***Information Input:* Getting Information; Inspecting Equipment, Structures, or Materials; Monitoring Processes, Materials, or Surroundings. *Mental Process:* Updating and Using Relevant Knowledge; Processing Information; Evaluating Information Against Standards. *Work Output:* Handling and Moving Objects; Performing General Physical Activities; Controlling Machines and Processes. *Interacting with Others:* Communicating with Other Workers; Coordinating the Work and Activities of Others; Establishing and Maintaining Relationships. **Physical Work Conditions—**Hazardous Equipment; Minor Burns, Cuts, Bites, or Stings; Using Hands on Objects, Tools, or Controls; High Places; Standing. **Other Job Characteristics—**Pace Determined by Speed of Equipment; Importance of Repeating Same Tasks; Degree of Automation.

Experience—Job Zone 1. No previous work-related skill, knowledge, or experience is needed. **Job Preparation:** SVP below 4.0—less than six months. **Knowledge—**Mechanical; Production and Processing; Engineering and Technology; Building and Construction. **Instructional Programs—**No data available.

Related DOT Jobs—365.674-010 Shoe-Repairer Helper; 500.686-010 Laborer, Electroplating; 502.664-018 Steel-Pourer Helper; 503.686-010 Pickler Helper, Continuous Pickling Line; 504.685-018 Heat-Treater Helper; 509.685-010 Alodize-Machine Helper; 511.685-058 Slime-Plant-Operator Helper; 512.684-010 Second Helper; 518.684-010 Core Setter; 519.485-014 Recovery-Operator Helper; 529.685-146 Ice Cream Freezer Assistant; 540.686-010 Compounder Helper; 542.362-014 Refinery Operator Helper; 542.665-010 Oven-Heater Helper; 543.664-010 Carbon-Furnace-Operator Helper; 549.684-010 Pumper Helper; 549.685-030 Treater Helper; 549.685-034 Wash-Oil-Pump Operator Helper; 557.564-010 Extruder-Operator Helper; 558.585-038 Polymerization Helper; others.

51-9199.99 Production Workers, All Other

- **Education/Training Required: No data available.**
- **Employed: No data available.**
- **Annual Earnings: No data available.**
- **Growth: 12.7%**
- **Annual Job Openings: 101,000**

All production workers not listed separately.

No task data available.

GOE INFORMATION—Interest Area: 08. Industrial Production. **Work Group:** 08.02. Production Technology; 08.03. Production Work. **Note:** The Department of Labor has not collected some data for this job, so it has fewer details than the other descriptions.

Instructional Programs—No data available.

Related DOT Jobs—017.684-010 Taper, Printed Circuit Layout; 222.687-014 Garment Sorter; 362.684-010 Dry Cleaner, Hand; 362.684-018 Fur Cleaner, Hand; 362.684-022 Furniture Cleaner; 364.684-014 Shoe Dyer; 364.684-018 Sprayer, Leather; 369.384-010 Hatter; 369.684-010 Fur Glazer; 369.685-030 Shirt-Folding-Machine Operator; 410.687-018 Pelter; 500.684-014 Matrix Worker; 502.664-010 Blast-Furnace Keeper; 502.684-018 Mold Setter; 503.362-010 Pickler, Continuous Pickling Line; 503.684-010 Cleaner; 503.685-014 Dip-Lube Operator; 509.687-018 Stringer; 511.382-010 Tungsten Refiner; 511.482-018 Dust-Collector Operator; others.

53-0000
Transportation and Material Moving Occupations

53-1000 Supervisors, Transportation and Material Moving Workers

53-1011.00 Aircraft Cargo Handling Supervisors

- Education/Training Required: Work experience in a related occupation
- Employed: 9,949
- Annual Earnings: $37,330
- Growth: 27.7%
- Annual Job Openings: 1,000

Direct ground crew in the loading, unloading, securing, and staging of aircraft cargo or baggage. Determine the quantity and orientation of cargo and compute aircraft center of gravity. May accompany aircraft as member of flight crew, monitor and handle cargo in flight, and assist and brief passengers on safety and emergency procedures.

No task data available.

GOE INFORMATION—Interest Area: 11. Recreation, Travel, and Other Personal Services. **Work Group:** 11.01. Managerial Work in Recreation, Travel, and Other Personal Services. **Note:** The Department of Labor has not collected some data for this job, so it has fewer details than the other descriptions.

Instructional Programs—No data available.

Related DOT Jobs—912.367-014 Transportation Agent.

53-1021.00 First-Line Supervisors/ Managers of Helpers, Laborers, and Material Movers, Hand

- Education/Training Required: Work experience in a related occupation
- Employed: 153,121
- Annual Earnings: $36,090
- Growth: 18.9%
- Annual Job Openings: 14,000

Supervise and coordinate the activities of helpers, laborers, or material movers.

Supervises and coordinates activities of workers performing assigned tasks. Assigns duties and work schedules. Determines work sequence and equipment needed according to work order, shipping records, and experience. Observes work procedures to ensure quality of work. Trains and instructs workers. Records information such as daily receipts, employee time and wage data, description of freight, and inspection results. Verifies materials loaded or unloaded against work order and schedules times of shipment and mode of transportation. Examines freight to determine sequence of loading and equipment to determine compliance with specifications. Inspects equipment for wear and completed work for conformance to standards. Inventories and orders supplies. Informs designated employee or department of items loaded or reports loading deficiencies. Quotes prices to customers. Resolves customer complaints.

GOE INFORMATION—**Interest Area:** 08. Industrial Production. **Work Group:** 08.01. Managerial Work in Industrial Production. **Personality Type**—Enterprising. Enterprising occupations frequently involve starting up and carrying out projects. These occupations can involve leading people and making many decisions. They sometimes require risk taking and often deal with business. **Work Values**—Authority; Responsibility; Pleasant Co-workers; Autonomy; Variety. **Skills**—Management of Personnel Resources; Instructing; Systems Analysis; Social Perceptiveness; Systems Evaluation; Operation and Control; Mathematics; Learning Strategies. **Abilities**—*Cognitive:* Oral Expression; Mathematical Reasoning; Oral Comprehension; Fluency of Ideas; Time Sharing. *Psychomotor:* None met the criteria. *Physical:* Static Strength. *Sensory:* Speech Clarity. **General Work Activities**—*Information Input:* Getting Information; Monitoring Processes, Materials, or Surroundings; Inspecting Equipment, Structures, or Materials. *Mental Process:* Scheduling Work and Activities; Evaluating Information Against Standards; Judging Qualities of Things, Services, or Other People's Work. *Work Output:* Handling and Moving Objects; Performing General Physical Activities; Documenting or Recording Information. *Interacting with Others:* Communicating with Other Workers; Establishing and Maintaining Relationships; Guiding, Directing, and Motivating Subordinates. **Physical Work Conditions**—Indoors; Sitting; Distracting Sounds and Noise Levels. **Other Job Characteristics**—Importance of Being Exact or Accurate; Consequence of Error; Pace Determined by Speed of Equipment.

Experience—Job Zone 3. Previous work-related skill, knowledge, or experience is required. **Job Preparation:** SVP 6.0 to less than 7.0—more than one year and less than four years. **Knowledge**—Production and Processing; Economics and Accounting; Personnel and Human Resources; Administration and Management; Education and Training. **Instructional Programs**—No data available.

Related DOT Jobs—189.167-042 Superintendent, Labor Utilization; 519.137-014 Supervisor, Scrap Preparation; 559.137-050 Supervisor, Tank Cleaning; 570.132-022 Supervisor; 699.137-010 Supervisor, Cleaning; 860.137-010 Carpenter-Labor Supervisor; 891.137-014 Supervisor, Aircraft Cleaning; 891.137-018 Supervisor, Tank Cleaning; 899.131-022 Utility Supervisor, Boat and Plant; 910.137-014 Car-Cleaning Supervisor; 910.137-018 Circus-Train Supervisor; 910.137-026 Freight-Loading Supervisor; 915.137-010 Car-Wash Supervisor; 922.137-018 Supervisor, Loading and Unloading.

53-1031.00 First-Line Supervisors/ Managers of Transportation and Material-Moving Machine and Vehicle Operators

- Education/Training Required: Work experience in a related occupation
- Employed: 194,016
- Annual Earnings: $41,140
- Growth: 19.9%
- Annual Job Openings: 17,000

Directly supervise and coordinate activities of transportation and material-moving machine and vehicle operators and helpers.

Reviews orders, production schedules, and shipping/receiving notices to determine work sequence and material shipping dates, type, volume, and destinations. Plans and establishes transportation routes, work schedules, and assignments and allocates equipment to meet transportation, operations, or production goals. Directs workers in transportation or related services, such as pumping, moving, storing, and loading/unloading of materials or people. Maintains or verifies time, transportation, financial, inventory, and personnel records. Explains and demonstrates work tasks to new workers or assigns workers to experienced workers for further training. Resolves worker problems or assists workers in solving problems. Computes and estimates cash, payroll, transportation, personnel, and storage requirements, using calculator. Requisitions needed personnel, supplies, equipment, parts, or repair services. Recommends and implements measures to improve worker motivation, equipment performance, work methods, and customer services. Prepares, compiles, and submits reports on work activities, operations, production, and work-related accidents. Inspects or tests materials, stock, vehicles, equipment, and facilities to locate defects, meet maintenance or production specifications, and verify safety standards. Interprets transportation and tariff regulations, shipping orders, safety regulations, and company policies and procedures for workers. Recommends or implements personnel actions, such as hiring, firing, and performance evaluations. Receives telephone or radio reports of emergencies and dispatches personnel and vehicle in response to request. Confers with customers, supervisors, contractors, and other personnel to exchange information and resolve problems. Assists workers in performing tasks such as coupling railroad cars or loading vehicles. Repairs or schedules repair and preventive maintenance of vehicles and other equipment. Examines, measures, and weighs cargo or materials to determine specific handling requirements. Drives vehicles or operates machines or equipment.

GOE INFORMATION—Interest Area: 07. Transportation. **Work Group:** 07.01. Managerial Work in Transportation. **Personality Type—**Enterprising. Enterprising occupations frequently involve starting up and carrying out projects. These occupations can involve leading people and making many decisions. They sometimes require risk taking and often deal with business. **Work Values—**Authority; Responsibility; Variety; Autonomy; Pleasant Co-workers. **Skills—**Management of Financial Resources; Management of Personnel Resources; Management of Material Resources; Systems Analysis; Operations Analysis; Repairing; Equipment Selection; Systems Evaluation. **Abilities—***Cognitive:* Mathematical Reasoning; Number Facility; Written Expression; Oral Expression; Deductive Reasoning. *Psychomotor:* Multilimb Coordination; Control Precision; Rate Control. *Physical:* Explosive Strength; Gross Body Coordination; Trunk Strength. *Sensory:* Speech Recognition; Speech Clarity; Night Vision. **General Work Activities—***Information Input:* Getting Information; Identifying Objects, Actions, and Events; Inspecting Equipment, Structures, or Materials. *Mental Process:* Scheduling Work and Activities; Organizing, Planning, and Prioritizing; Evaluating Information Against Standards. *Work Output:* Handling and Moving Objects; Documenting or Recording Information; Controlling Machines and Processes. *Interacting with Others:* Communicating with Other Workers; Coordinating the Work and Activities of Others; Guiding, Directing, and Motivating Subordinates. **Physical Work Conditions—**Very Hot or Cold; Outdoors; Sitting; Walking or Running; Cramped Work Space or Awkward Positions. **Other Job Characteristics—**Consequence of Error; Importance of Being Exact or Accurate; Importance of Repeating Same Tasks.

Experience—Job Zone 3. Previous work-related skill, knowledge, or experience is required. **Job Preparation:** SVP 6.0 to less than 7.0—more than one year and less than four years. **Knowledge—**Personnel and Human Resources; Economics and Accounting; Administration and Management; Sales and Marketing; Production and Processing. **Instructional Programs—**No data available.

Related DOT Jobs—185.167-018 Manager, Distribution Warehouse; 187.167-150 Manager, Storage Garage; 292.137-014 Supervisor, Route Sales-Deliv-

ery Drivers; 579.137-030 Dispatcher, Concrete Products; 859.137-010 Supervisor, Grading; 909.137-010 Driver Supervisor; 909.137-014 Garbage-Collection Supervisor; 909.137-018 Truck Supervisor; 910.137-022 Conductor, Yard; 910.137-034 Road Supervisor of Engines; 910.137-046 Yard Manager; 911.131-010 Boatswain; 911.137-018 Header; 911.137-022 Superintendent, Stevedoring; 911.137-026 Supervisor, Ferry Terminal; 913.133-010 Road Supervisor; 913.133-014 Supervisor, Cab; 913.167-014 Dispatcher, Bus and Trolley; 914.131-010 Supervisor, Pumping; 914.132-010 Compressor-Station Engineer, Chief; others.

53-2000 Air Transportation Workers

53-2011.00 Airline Pilots, Copilots, and Flight Engineers

- **Education/Training Required: Bachelor's degree**
- **Employed: 98,080**
- **Annual Earnings: $109,800**
- **Growth: 6.4%**
- **Annual Job Openings: 5,000**

Pilot and navigate the flight of multi-engine aircraft in regularly scheduled service for the transport of passengers and cargo. Requires Federal Air Transport rating and certification in specific aircraft type used.

Starts engines, operates controls, and pilots airplane to transport passengers, mail, or freight, adhering to flight plan and regulations and procedures. Obtains and reviews data such as load weight, fuel supply, weather conditions, and flight schedule. Plots flight pattern and files flight plan with appropriate officials. Orders changes in fuel supply, load, route, or schedule to ensure safety of flight. Conducts preflight checks and reads gauges to verify that fluids and pressure are at prescribed levels. Operates radio equipment and contacts control tower for takeoff, clearance, arrival instructions, and other information. Coordinates flight activities with ground-crew and air-traffic control and informs crew members of flight and test procedures. Holds commercial pilot's license issued by Federal Aviation Administration. Conducts in-flight tests and evaluations at specified altitudes in all types of weather to determine receptivity and other characteristics of equipment and systems. Logs information such as flight time, altitude flown, and fuel consumption. Plans and formulates flight activities and test schedules and prepares flight evaluation reports. Gives training and instruction in aircraft operations for students and other pilots.

GOE INFORMATION—Interest Area: 07. Transportation. **Work Group:** 07.03. Air Vehicle Operation. **Personality Type—**Realistic. Realistic occupations frequently involve work activities that include practical, hands-on problems and solutions. They often deal with plants, animals, and real-world materials like wood, tools, and machinery. Many of the occupations require working outside and do not involve a lot of paperwork or working closely with others. **Work Values—**Authority; Recognition; Compensation; Ability Utilization; Social Status. **Skills—**Operation and Control; Operation Monitoring; Instructing; Science; Coordination; Systems Analysis; Systems Evaluation; Troubleshooting. **Abilities—***Cognitive:* Spatial Orientation; Speed of Closure; Selective Attention; Time Sharing; Number Facility. *Psychomotor:* Rate Control; Response Orientation; Reaction Time; Multilimb Coordination; Control Precision. *Physical:* Gross Body Coordination; Extent Flexibility; Gross Body Equilibrium;

Trunk Strength; Explosive Strength. *Sensory:* Night Vision; Far Vision; Peripheral Vision; Depth Perception; Glare Sensitivity. **General Work Activities**—*Information Input:* Monitoring Processes, Materials, or Surroundings; Getting Information; Identifying Objects, Actions, and Events. *Mental Process:* Organizing, Planning, and Prioritizing; Making Decisions and Solving Problems; Evaluating Information Against Standards. *Work Output:* Operating Vehicles or Equipment; Handling and Moving Objects; Controlling Machines and Processes. *Interacting with Others:* Teaching Others; Communicating with Other Workers; Coordinating the Work and Activities of Others. **Physical Work Conditions**—High Places; Whole Body Vibration; Hazardous Equipment; Sitting; Cramped Work Space or Awkward Positions. **Other Job Characteristics**—Consequence of Error; Degree of Automation; Importance of Being Exact or Accurate.

Experience—Job Zone 4. A minimum of two to four years of work-related skill, knowledge, or experience is needed. **Job Preparation:** SVP 7.0 to less than 8.0—two years to less than 10 years. **Knowledge**—Geography; Education and Training; Public Safety and Security; Mechanical; Computers and Electronics. **Instructional Programs**—Airline/Commercial/Professional Pilot and Flight Crew; Flight Instructor.

Related DOT Jobs—196.263-030 Executive Pilot; 196.263-034 Facilities-Flight-Check Pilot.

53-2012.00 *Commercial Pilots*

- **Education/Training Required: Postsecondary vocational training**
- **Employed: 19,256**
- **Annual Earnings: $47,420**
- **Growth: 26.9%**
- **Annual Job Openings: 1,000**

Pilot and navigate the flight of small fixed or rotary winged aircraft, primarily for the transport of cargo and passengers. Requires Commercial Rating.

Starts engines, operates controls, and pilots airplane to transport passengers, mail, or freight, adhering to flight plan and regulations and procedures. Obtains and reviews data such as load weight, fuel supply, weather conditions, and flight schedule. Plots flight pattern and files flight plan with appropriate officials. Orders changes in fuel supply, load, route, or schedule to ensure safety of flight. Conducts preflight checks and reads gauges to verify that fluids and pressure are at prescribed levels. Operates radio equipment and contacts control tower for takeoff, clearance, arrival instructions, and other information. Coordinates flight activities with ground-crew and air-traffic control and informs crew members of flight and test procedures. Holds commercial pilot's license issued by Federal Aviation Administration. Conducts in-flight tests and evaluations at specified altitudes in all types of weather to determine receptivity and other characteristics of equipment and systems. Logs information such as flight time, altitude flown, and fuel consumption. Plans and formulates flight activities and test schedules and prepares flight evaluation reports. Gives training and instruction in aircraft operations for students and other pilots.

GOE INFORMATION—**Interest Area:** 07. Transportation. **Work Group:** 07.03. Air Vehicle Operation. **Personality Type**—Realistic. Realistic occupations frequently involve work activities that include practical, hands-on problems and solutions. They often deal with plants, animals, and real-world materials like wood, tools, and machinery. Many of the occupations require working outside and do not involve a lot of paperwork or working closely with others. **Work Values**—Authority; Recognition;

Compensation; Ability Utilization; Social Status. **Skills**—Operation and Control; Operation Monitoring; Instructing; Science; Coordination; Systems Analysis; Systems Evaluation; Troubleshooting. **Abilities**—*Cognitive:* Spatial Orientation; Speed of Closure; Selective Attention; Time Sharing; Number Facility. *Psychomotor:* Rate Control; Response Orientation; Reaction Time; Multilimb Coordination; Control Precision. *Physical:* Gross Body Coordination; Extent Flexibility; Gross Body Equilibrium; Trunk Strength; Explosive Strength. *Sensory:* Night Vision; Far Vision; Peripheral Vision; Depth Perception; Glare Sensitivity. **General Work Activities**—*Information Input:* Monitoring Processes, Materials, or Surroundings; Getting Information; Inspecting Equipment, Structures, or Materials. *Mental Process:* Making Decisions and Solving Problems; Organizing, Planning, and Prioritizing; Evaluating Information Against Standards. *Work Output:* Operating Vehicles or Equipment; Handling and Moving Objects; Documenting or Recording Information. *Interacting with Others:* Teaching Others; Communicating with Other Workers; Coordinating the Work and Activities of Others. **Physical Work Conditions**—High Places; Whole Body Vibration; Hazardous Equipment; Sitting; Cramped Work Space or Awkward Positions. **Other Job Characteristics**—Consequence of Error; Degree of Automation; Importance of Being Exact or Accurate.

Experience—Job Zone 4. A minimum of two to four years of work-related skill, knowledge, or experience is needed. **Job Preparation:** SVP 7.0 to less than 8.0—two years to less than 10 years. **Knowledge**—Geography; Education and Training; Public Safety and Security; Mechanical; Computers and Electronics. **Instructional Programs**—Airline/Commercial/Professional Pilot and Flight Crew; Flight Instructor.

Related DOT Jobs—196.263-014 Airplane Pilot, Commercial.

53-2021.00 *Air Traffic Controllers*

- **Education/Training Required: Long-term on-the-job training**
- **Employed: 26,645**
- **Annual Earnings: $87,930**
- **Growth: 7.2%**
- **Annual Job Openings: 2,000**

Control air traffic on and within vicinity of airport and movement of air traffic between altitude sectors and control centers according to established procedures and policies. Authorize, regulate, and control commercial airline flights according to government or company regulations to expedite and ensure flight safety.

Communicates with, relays flight plans to, and coordinates movement of air traffic between control centers. Determines timing of and procedure for flight vector changes in sector. Issues landing and take-off authorizations and instructions and communicates other information to aircraft. Controls air traffic at and within vicinity of airport. Recommends flight path changes to planes traveling in storms or fog or in emergency situations. Relays air traffic information such as altitude, expected time of arrival, and course of aircraft to control centers. Transfers control of departing flights to traffic control center and accepts control of arriving flights from air traffic control center. Analyzes factors such as weather reports, fuel requirements, and maps to determine flights and air routes. Directs radio searches for aircraft and alerts control center's emergency facilities of flight difficulties. Inspects, adjusts, and controls radio equipment and airport lights. Completes daily activity report and keeps record of messages from aircraft. Reviews records and reports for clarity and completeness and maintains records and reports.

GOE INFORMATION—**Interest Area:** 07. Transportation. **Work Group:** 07.02. Vehicle Expediting and Coordinating. **Personality Type**—

Conventional. Conventional occupations frequently involve following set procedures and routines. These occupations can include working with data and details more than with ideas. Usually there is a clear line of authority to follow. **Work Values**—Authority; Supervision, Technical; Responsibility; Ability Utilization; Achievement. **Skills**—Operation and Control; Operation Monitoring; Active Listening; Critical Thinking; Coordination; Equipment Selection; Complex Problem Solving; Systems Analysis. **Abilities**—*Cognitive:* Perceptual Speed; Time Sharing; Selective Attention; Spatial Orientation; Flexibility of Closure. *Psychomotor:* Reaction Time; Response Orientation; Rate Control. *Physical:* Gross Body Equilibrium; Gross Body Coordination. *Sensory:* Auditory Attention; Sound Localization; Near Vision; Speech Clarity; Hearing Sensitivity. **General Work Activities**—*Information Input:* Monitoring Processes, Materials, or Surroundings; Identifying Objects, Actions, and Events; Getting Information. *Mental Process:* Making Decisions and Solving Problems; Analyzing Data or Information; Processing Information. *Work Output:* Documenting or Recording Information; Controlling Machines and Processes; Handling and Moving Objects. *Interacting with Others:* Communicating with Other Workers; Assisting and Caring for Others; Coordinating the Work and Activities of Others. **Physical Work Conditions**—Sitting; Indoors; Distracting Sounds and Noise Levels; High Places; Using Hands on Objects, Tools, or Controls. **Other Job Characteristics**—Consequence of Error; Importance of Being Exact or Accurate; Importance of Repeating Same Tasks.

Experience—Job Zone 4. A minimum of two to four years of work-related skill, knowledge, or experience is needed. **Job Preparation:** SVP 7.0 to less than 8.0—two years to less than 10 years. **Knowledge**—Physics; Telecommunications; Geography; Computers and Electronics; Clerical. **Instructional Programs**—Air Traffic Controller.

Related DOT Jobs—193.162-010 Air-Traffic Coordinator; 193.162-014 Air-Traffic-Control Specialist, Station; 193.162-018 Air-Traffic-Control Specialist, Tower; 193.167-010 Chief Controller; 912.167-010 Dispatcher.

53-2022.00 Airfield Operations Specialists

- Education/Training Required: **Short-term on-the-job training**
- Employed: **4,815**
- Annual Earnings: **$35,220**
- Growth: **27.1%**
- Annual Job Openings: **Fewer than 500**

Ensure the safe takeoff and landing of commercial and military aircraft. Duties include coordination between air-traffic control and maintenance personnel; dispatching; using airfield landing and navigational aids; implementing airfield safety procedures; monitoring and maintaining flight records; and applying knowledge of weather information.

No task data available.

GOE INFORMATION—Interest Area: 07. Transportation. **Work Group:** 07.02. Vehicle Expediting and Coordinating. **Note:** The Department of Labor has not collected some data for this job, so it has fewer details than the other descriptions.

Instructional Programs—Air Traffic Controller.

Related DOT Jobs—912.367-010 Flight-Information Expediter.

53-3000 Motor Vehicle Operators

53-3011.00 Ambulance Drivers and Attendants, Except Emergency Medical Technicians

- Education/Training Required: **Moderate-term on-the-job training**
- Employed: **15,249**
- Annual Earnings: **$18,890**
- Growth: **33.7%**
- Annual Job Openings: **3,000**

Drive ambulance or assist ambulance driver in transporting sick, injured, or convalescent persons. Assist in lifting patients.

Accompany and assist emergency medical technicians on calls. Administer first aid such as bandaging, splinting, and administering oxygen. Drive ambulances or assist ambulance drivers in transporting sick, injured, or convalescent persons. Place patients on stretchers and load stretchers into ambulances, usually with assistance from other attendants. Remove and replace soiled linens and equipment in order to maintain sanitary conditions. Replace supplies and disposable items on ambulances. Report facts concerning accidents or emergencies to hospital personnel or law enforcement officials. Earn and maintain appropriate certifications. Restrain or shackle violent patients.

GOE INFORMATION—Interest Area: 07. Transportation. **Work Group:** 07.07. Other Services Requiring Driving. **Personality Type**—Social. Social occupations frequently involve working with, communicating with, and teaching people. These occupations often involve helping or providing service to others. **Work Values**—Social Service; Variety; Security; Pleasant Co-workers; Supervision, Technical. **Skills**—Operation and Control; Service Orientation. **Abilities**—*Cognitive:* Spatial Orientation; Memorization; Selective Attention; Flexibility of Closure; Time Sharing. *Psychomotor:* Reaction Time; Response Orientation; Rate Control; Speed of Limb Movement; Control Precision. *Physical:* Static Strength; Gross Body Equilibrium; Gross Body Coordination; Explosive Strength; Stamina. *Sensory:* Sound Localization; Peripheral Vision; Far Vision; Night Vision; Glare Sensitivity. **General Work Activities**—*Information Input:* Getting Information; Monitoring Processes, Materials, or Surroundings; Identifying Objects, Actions, and Events. *Mental Process:* Updating and Using Relevant Knowledge; Judging Qualities of Things, Services, or Other People's Work; Making Decisions and Solving Problems. *Work Output:* Performing General Physical Activities; Operating Vehicles or Equipment; Handling and Moving Objects. *Interacting with Others:* Assisting and Caring for Others; Establishing and Maintaining Relationships; Performing for or Working with the Public. **Physical Work Conditions**—Disease or Infections; Outdoors; Contaminants; Hazardous Conditions; Common Protective or Safety Attire. **Other Job Characteristics**—Consequence of Error; Importance of Being Exact or Accurate; Pace Determined by Speed of Equipment.

Experience—Job Zone 1. No previous work-related skill, knowledge, or experience is needed. **Job Preparation:** SVP below 4.0—less than six months. **Knowledge**—Medicine and Dentistry; Biology; Geography; Customer and Personal Service; Therapy and Counseling. **Instructional Programs**—Emergency Medical Technology/Technician (EMT Paramedic).

Related DOT Jobs—355.374-010 Ambulance Attendant; 913.683-010 Ambulance Driver.

53-3021.00 Bus Drivers, Transit and Intercity

- **Education/Training Required: Moderate-term on-the-job training**
- **Employed: 184,547**
- **Annual Earnings: $28,060**
- **Growth: 17.4%**
- **Annual Job Openings: 24,000**

Drive bus or motor coach, including regular route operations, charters, and private carriage. May assist passengers with baggage. May collect fares or tickets.

Drive vehicles over specified routes or to specified destinations according to time schedules in order to transport passengers, complying with traffic regulations. Assist passengers with baggage and collect tickets or cash fares. Park vehicles at loading areas so that passengers can board. Load and unload baggage in baggage compartments. Regulate heating, lighting, and ventilating systems for passenger comfort. Advise passengers to be seated and orderly while on vehicles. Record cash receipts and ticket fares. Inspect vehicles and check gas, oil, and water levels prior to departure. Report delays or accidents. Make minor repairs to vehicle and change tires.

GOE INFORMATION—Interest Area: 07. Transportation. **Work Group:** 07.07. Other Services Requiring Driving. **Personality Type—**Realistic. Realistic occupations frequently involve work activities that include practical, hands-on problems and solutions. They often deal with plants, animals, and real-world materials like wood, tools, and machinery. Many of the occupations require working outside and do not involve a lot of paperwork or working closely with others. **Work Values—**Supervision, Technical; Supervision, Human Relations; Company Policies and Practices; Social Service; Independence. **Skills—**Operation and Control; Repairing; Operation Monitoring. **Abilities—***Cognitive:* Spatial Orientation. *Psychomotor:* Reaction Time; Response Orientation; Control Precision; Multilimb Coordination. *Physical:* Static Strength. *Sensory:* Night Vision; Far Vision; Peripheral Vision; Depth Perception; Sound Localization. **General Work Activities—***Information Input:* Inspecting Equipment, Structures, or Materials; Monitoring Processes, Materials, or Surroundings; Identifying Objects, Actions, and Events. *Mental Process:* Making Decisions and Solving Problems; Updating and Using Relevant Knowledge; Organizing, Planning, and Prioritizing. *Work Output:* Handling and Moving Objects; Operating Vehicles or Equipment; Repairing and Maintaining Mechanical Equipment. *Interacting with Others:* Performing for or Working with the Public; Communicating with Persons Outside Organization; Assisting and Caring for Others. **Physical Work Conditions—**Sitting; Outdoors; Extremely Bright or Inadequate Lighting; Using Hands on Objects, Tools, or Controls; Hazardous Equipment. **Other Job Characteristics—**Consequence of Error; Importance of Repeating Same Tasks; Pace Determined by Speed of Equipment.

Experience—Job Zone 1. No previous work-related skill, knowledge, or experience is needed. **Job Preparation:** SVP below 4.0—less than six months. **Knowledge—**Geography; Public Safety and Security; Mechanical; Customer and Personal Service; Law and Government. **Instructional Programs—**Truck and Bus Driver/Commercial Vehicle Operation.

Related DOT Jobs—913.363-010 Bus Driver, Day-Haul or Farm Charter; 913.463-010 Bus Driver; 913.663-014 Mobile-Lounge Driver.

53-3022.00 Bus Drivers, School

- **Education/Training Required: Short-term on-the-job training**
- **Employed: 481,163**
- **Annual Earnings: $21,990**
- **Growth: 11.6%**
- **Annual Job Openings: 63,000**

Transport students or special clients, such as the elderly or persons with disabilities. Ensure adherence to safety rules. May assist passengers in boarding or exiting.

Drive gasoline, diesel, or electrically powered multi-passenger vehicles to transport students between neighborhoods, schools, and school activities. Check the condition of a vehicle's tires, brakes, windshield wipers, lights, oil, fuel, water, and safety equipment to ensure that everything is in working order. Comply with traffic regulations in order to operate vehicles in a safe and courteous manner. Follow safety rules as students are boarding and exiting buses and as they cross streets near bus stops. Pick up and drop off students at regularly scheduled neighborhood locations, following strict time schedules. Read maps and follow written and verbal geographic directions. Regulate heating, lighting, and ventilation systems for passenger comfort. Escort small children across roads and highways. Keep bus interiors clean for passengers. Maintain knowledge of first-aid procedures. Maintain order among pupils during trips in order to ensure safety. Make minor repairs to vehicles. Prepare and submit reports that may include the number of passengers or trips, hours worked, mileage, fuel consumption, and/or fares received. Report any bus malfunctions or needed repairs. Report delays, accidents, or other traffic and transportation situations, using telephones or mobile two-way radios.

GOE INFORMATION—Interest Area: 07. Transportation. **Work Group:** 07.07. Other Services Requiring Driving. **Personality Type—**Realistic. Realistic occupations frequently involve work activities that include practical, hands-on problems and solutions. They often deal with plants, animals, and real-world materials like wood, tools, and machinery. Many of the occupations require working outside and do not involve a lot of paperwork or working closely with others. **Work Values—**Supervision, Technical; Supervision, Human Relations; Independence; Social Service; Company Policies and Practices. **Skills—**Operation and Control; Repairing; Operation Monitoring. **Abilities—***Cognitive:* Spatial Orientation; Time Sharing; Selective Attention; Memorization. *Psychomotor:* Response Orientation; Reaction Time; Rate Control; Multilimb Coordination; Speed of Limb Movement. *Physical:* Gross Body Coordination; Explosive Strength; Trunk Strength. *Sensory:* Sound Localization; Peripheral Vision; Far Vision; Auditory Attention; Hearing Sensitivity. **General Work Activities—***Information Input:* Inspecting Equipment, Structures, or Materials; Monitoring Processes, Materials, or Surroundings; Getting Information. *Mental Process:* Making Decisions and Solving Problems; Updating and Using Relevant Knowledge; Organizing, Planning, and Prioritizing. *Work Output:* Operating Vehicles or Equipment; Handling and Moving Objects; Repairing and Maintaining Mechanical Equipment. *Interacting with Others:* Performing for or Working with the Public; Resolving Conflict and Negotiating with Others; Assisting and Caring for Others. **Physical Work Conditions—**Distracting Sounds and Noise Levels; Sitting; Outdoors; Extremely Bright or Inadequate Lighting; Making Repetitive Motions. **Other Job Characteristics—**Consequence of Error; Degree of Automation; Pace Determined by Speed of Equipment.

Experience—Job Zone 2. Some previous work-related skill, knowledge, or experience may be helpful, but usually is not needed. **Job Preparation:** SVP 4.0 to less than 6.0—six months to less than two years. **Knowledge—**

Customer and Personal Service; Public Safety and Security; Psychology; Law and Government; Geography. **Instructional Programs**—Truck and Bus Driver/Commercial Vehicle Operation.

Related DOT Jobs—913.463-010 Bus Driver.

53-3031.00 Driver/Sales Workers

- **Education/Training Required: Short-term on-the-job training**
- **Employed: 401,764**
- **Annual Earnings: $20,170**
- **Growth: 7.1%**
- **Annual Job Openings: 55,000**

Drive truck or other vehicle over established routes or within an established territory and sell goods such as food products, including restaurant take-out items, or pick up and deliver items such as laundry. May also take orders and collect payments. Includes newspaper delivery drivers.

Drive trucks in order to deliver such items as food, medical supplies, or newspapers. Collect coins from vending machines, refill machines, and remove aged merchandise. Sell food specialties, such as sandwiches and beverages, to office workers and patrons of sports events. Collect money from customers, make change, and record transactions on customer receipts. Call on prospective customers in order to explain company services and to solicit new business. Record sales or delivery information on daily sales or delivery record. Inform regular customers of new products or services and price changes. Review lists of dealers, customers, or station drops and load trucks. Write customer orders and sales contracts according to company guidelines. Listen to and resolve customers' complaints regarding products or services. Maintain trucks and food-dispensing equipment and clean inside of machines that dispense food or beverages. Arrange merchandise and sales promotion displays or issue sales promotion materials to customers.

GOE INFORMATION—Interest Area: 07. Transportation. **Work Group:** 07.07. Other Services Requiring Driving. **Personality Type**—Enterprising. Enterprising occupations frequently involve starting up and carrying out projects. These occupations can involve leading people and making many decisions. They sometimes require risk taking and often deal with business. **Work Values**—Independence; Supervision, Technical; Social Service. **Skills**—None met the criteria. **Abilities**—*Cognitive:* Spatial Orientation; Oral Expression; Number Facility. *Psychomotor:* Manual Dexterity. *Physical:* Static Strength; Stamina; Trunk Strength. *Sensory:* Speech Recognition; Glare Sensitivity. **General Work Activities**—*Information Input:* Identifying Objects, Actions, and Events; Estimating Needed Characteristics; Getting Information. *Mental Process:* Processing Information; Organizing, Planning, and Prioritizing; Judging Qualities of Things, Services, or Other People's Work. *Work Output:* Handling and Moving Objects; Performing General Physical Activities; Operating Vehicles or Equipment. *Interacting with Others:* Influencing Others or Selling; Establishing and Maintaining Relationships; Performing for or Working with the Public. **Physical Work Conditions**—Outdoors; Very Hot or Cold; Walking or Running; Standing; Extremely Bright or Inadequate Lighting. **Other Job Characteristics**—Importance of Repeating Same Tasks; Pace Determined by Speed of Equipment; Degree of Automation.

Experience—Job Zone 1. No previous work-related skill, knowledge, or experience is needed. **Job Preparation:** SVP below 4.0—less than six months. **Knowledge**—Sales and Marketing; Economics and Accounting; Customer and Personal Service; Production and Processing; Geography. **Instructional Programs**—Retailing and Retail Operations.

Related DOT Jobs—292.353-010 Driver, Sales Route; 292.363-010 Newspaper-Delivery Driver; 292.463-010 Lunch-Truck Driver; 292.483-010 Coin Collector; 292.667-010 Driver Helper, Sales Route; 292.687-010 Coin-Machine Collector.

53-3032.00 Truck Drivers, Heavy and Tractor-Trailer

- **Education/Training Required: Moderate-term on-the-job training**
- **Employed: 1,749,270**
- **Annual Earnings: $32,580**
- **Growth: 19.8%**
- **Annual Job Openings: 240,000**

Drive a tractor-trailer combination or a truck with a capacity of at least 26,000 GVW to transport and deliver goods, livestock, or materials in liquid, loose, or packaged form. May be required to unload truck. May require use of automated routing equipment. Requires commercial drivers' license.

No task data available.

GOE INFORMATION—Interest Area: 07. Transportation. **Work Group:** 07.05. Truck Driving. **Note:** The Department of Labor has not collected some data for this job, so it has fewer details than the other descriptions.

Instructional Programs—Truck and Bus Driver/Commercial Vehicle Operation.

Related DOT Jobs—900.683-010 Concrete-Mixing-Truck Driver; 902.683-010 Dump-Truck Driver; 903.683-010 Explosives-Truck Driver; 903.683-014 Powder-Truck Driver; 903.683-018 Tank-Truck Driver; 904.363-010 Tractor-Trailer Moving Van Driver; 904.383-010 Tractor-Trailer-Truck Driver; 904.683-010 Log-Truck Driver; 905.363-900 Construction Driver; 905.483-010 Milk Driver; 905.663-010 Garbage Collector Driver; 905.663-014 Truck Driver, Heavy; 905.663-018 Van Driver; 905.683-010 Water-Truck Driver II; 909.663-010 Hostler; 919.663-018 Driver-Utility Worker; 919.663-026 Tow-Truck Operator; 953.583-010 Drip Pumper.

53-3032.01 Truck Drivers, Heavy

- **Education/Training Required: Short-term on-the-job training**
- **Employed: No data available.**
- **Annual Earnings: $32,580**
- **Growth: 19.8%**
- **Annual Job Openings: 240,000**

Drive truck with capacity of more than three tons to transport materials to specified destinations.

Drives truck with capacity of more than three tons to transport and deliver cargo, materials, or damaged vehicle. Maintains radio or telephone contact with base or supervisor to receive instructions or be dispatched to new location. Maintains truck log according to state and federal regulations. Keeps record of materials and products transported. Position blocks and ties rope around items to secure cargo for transport. Cleans, inspects, and services vehicle. Operates equipment on vehicle to load, unload, or disperse cargo or materials. Obtains customer signature or collects payment for goods delivered and delivery charges. Assists in loading and unloading truck manually.

GOE INFORMATION—Interest Area: 07. Transportation. **Work Group:** 07.05. Truck Driving. **Personality Type**—Realistic. Realistic occupations frequently involve work activities that include practical, hands-on problems and solutions. They often deal with plants, animals, and real-world materials like wood, tools, and machinery. Many of the occupations require working outside and do not involve a lot of paperwork or working closely with others. **Work Values**—Independence; Compensation; Company Policies and Practices; Autonomy; Supervision, Technical. **Skills**—Repairing; Operation Monitoring; Operation and Control. **Abilities**—*Cognitive:* Spatial Orientation; Time Sharing; Perceptual Speed; Flexibility of Closure; Visualization. *Psychomotor:* Response Orientation; Reaction Time; Rate Control; Control Precision; Multilimb Coordination. *Physical:* Static Strength; Explosive Strength; Extent Flexibility; Dynamic Strength; Trunk Strength. *Sensory:* Night Vision; Depth Perception; Peripheral Vision; Far Vision; Glare Sensitivity. **General Work Activities**—*Information Input:* Inspecting Equipment, Structures, or Materials; Getting Information; Identifying Objects, Actions, and Events. *Mental Process:* Evaluating Information Against Standards; Processing Information; Updating and Using Relevant Knowledge. *Work Output:* Performing General Physical Activities; Handling and Moving Objects; Operating Vehicles or Equipment. *Interacting with Others:* Communicating with Persons Outside Organization; Communicating with Other Workers; Establishing and Maintaining Relationships. **Physical Work Conditions**—Outdoors; Sitting; Whole Body Vibration; Extremely Bright or Inadequate Lighting; Very Hot or Cold. **Other Job Characteristics**—Consequence of Error; Degree of Automation; Pace Determined by Speed of Equipment.

Experience—Job Zone 1. No previous work-related skill, knowledge, or experience is needed. **Job Preparation:** SVP below 4.0—less than six months. **Knowledge**—Geography; Telecommunications; Mechanical; Public Safety and Security; Law and Government. **Instructional Programs**—Truck and Bus Driver/Commercial Vehicle Operation.

Related DOT Jobs—900.683-010 Concrete-Mixing-Truck Driver; 902.683-010 Dump-Truck Driver; 903.683-010 Explosives-Truck Driver; 903.683-014 Powder-Truck Driver; 903.683-018 Tank-Truck Driver; 905.483-010 Milk Driver; 905.663-010 Garbage Collector Driver; 905.663-014 Truck Driver, Heavy; 905.683-010 Water-Truck Driver II; 909.663-010 Hostler; 919.663-018 Driver-Utility Worker; 919.663-026 Tow-Truck Operator; 953.583-010 Drip Pumper.

53-3032.02 Tractor-Trailer Truck Drivers

- **Education/Training Required: Moderate-term on-the-job training**
- **Employed: No data available.**
- **Annual Earnings: $32,580**
- **Growth: 19.8%**
- **Annual Job Openings: 240,000**

Drive tractor-trailer truck to transport products, livestock, or materials to specified destinations.

Drives tractor-trailer combination, applying knowledge of commercial driving regulations, to transport and deliver products, livestock, or materials, usually over long distance. Maneuvers truck into loading or unloading position, following signals from loading crew as needed. Drives truck to weigh station before and after loading and along route to document weight and conform to state regulations. Maintains driver log according to I.C.C. regulations. Inspects truck before and after trips and submits report indicating truck condition. Reads bill of lading to determine assignment. Fastens chain or binders to secure load on trailer during transit. Loads or unloads or assists in loading and unloading truck. Works as member of two-person team driving tractor with sleeper bunk behind cab. Services truck with oil, fuel, and radiator fluid to maintain tractor-

trailer. Obtains customer's signature or collects payment for services. Inventories and inspects goods to be moved. Wraps goods using pads, packing paper, and containers; secures load to trailer wall, using straps. Gives directions to helper in packing and moving goods to trailer.

GOE INFORMATION—**Interest Area:** 07. Transportation. **Work Group:** 07.05. Truck Driving. **Personality Type**—Realistic. Realistic occupations frequently involve work activities that include practical, hands-on problems and solutions. They often deal with plants, animals, and real-world materials like wood, tools, and machinery. Many of the occupations require working outside and do not involve a lot of paperwork or working closely with others. **Work Values**—Compensation; Company Policies and Practices; Independence; Supervision, Human Relations; Autonomy. **Skills**—Operation and Control; Repairing; Operation Monitoring. **Abilities**—*Cognitive:* Spatial Orientation; Visualization; Time Sharing; Perceptual Speed; Flexibility of Closure. *Psychomotor:* Reaction Time; Response Orientation; Rate Control; Multilimb Coordination; Speed of Limb Movement. *Physical:* Static Strength; Explosive Strength; Extent Flexibility; Dynamic Strength; Dynamic Flexibility. *Sensory:* Depth Perception; Peripheral Vision; Night Vision; Far Vision; Hearing Sensitivity. **General Work Activities**—*Information Input:* Inspecting Equipment, Structures, or Materials; Getting Information; Identifying Objects, Actions, and Events. *Mental Process:* Evaluating Information Against Standards; Organizing, Planning, and Prioritizing; Processing Information. *Work Output:* Handling and Moving Objects; Performing General Physical Activities; Operating Vehicles or Equipment. *Interacting with Others:* Establishing and Maintaining Relationships; Communicating with Other Workers; Performing Administrative Activities. **Physical Work Conditions**—Extremely Bright or Inadequate Lighting; Outdoors; Sitting; Very Hot or Cold; Distracting Sounds and Noise Levels. **Other Job Characteristics**—Degree of Automation; Pace Determined by Speed of Equipment; Importance of Repeating Same Tasks.

Experience—Job Zone 2. Some previous work-related skill, knowledge, or experience may be helpful, but usually is not needed. **Job Preparation:** SVP 4.0 to less than 6.0—six months to less than two years. **Knowledge**—Geography; Mechanical; Law and Government; Public Safety and Security; Customer and Personal Service. **Instructional Programs**—Truck and Bus Driver/Commercial Vehicle Operation.

Related DOT Jobs—904.363-010 Tractor-Trailer Moving Van Driver; 904.383-010 Tractor-Trailer-Truck Driver; 904.683-010 Log-Truck Driver.

53-3033.00 Truck Drivers, Light or Delivery Services

- **Education/Training Required: Short-term on-the-job training**
- **Employed: 1,116,862**
- **Annual Earnings: $23,330**
- **Growth: 19.2%**
- **Annual Job Openings: 153,000**

Drive a truck or van with a capacity of under 26,000 GVW primarily to deliver or pick up merchandise or to deliver packages within a specified area. May require use of automatic routing or location software. May load and unload truck.

Drive vehicles with capacities under three tons in order to transport materials to and from specified destinations such as railroad stations, plants, residences, and offices or within industrial yards. Inspect and maintain vehicle supplies and equipment, such as gas, oil, water, tires, lights, and brakes, in order to ensure that vehicles are in proper working condition. Load and unload trucks, vans, or automobiles. Obey traffic laws and follow established traffic and transportation procedures. Read maps and follow written and verbal geographic directions. Verify the contents of inventory loads against shipping papers. Maintain records such as vehicle logs, records of cargo, or billing statements in accordance with regulations. Perform emergency repairs such as changing tires or installing light bulbs, fuses, tire chains, and spark plugs. Present bills and receipts and collect payments for goods delivered or loaded. Report any mechanical problems encountered with vehicles. Report delays, accidents, or other traffic and transportation situations to bases or other vehicles, using telephones or mobile two-way radios. Turn in receipts and money received from deliveries. Drive trucks equipped with public address systems through city streets in order to broadcast announcements for advertising or publicity purposes. Sell and keep records of sales for products from truck inventory. Use and maintain the tools and equipment found on commercial vehicles, such as weighing and measuring devices.

GOE INFORMATION—Interest Area: 07. Transportation. **Work Group:** 07.05. Truck Driving. **Personality Type**—Realistic. Realistic occupations frequently involve work activities that include practical, hands-on problems and solutions. They often deal with plants, animals, and real-world materials like wood, tools, and machinery. Many of the occupations require working outside and do not involve a lot of paperwork or working closely with others. **Work Values**—Independence; Compensation; Supervision, Technical; Company Policies and Practices; Supervision, Human Relations. **Skills**—Repairing; Operation Monitoring; Operation and Control. **Abilities**—*Cognitive:* Spatial Orientation; Time Sharing; Perceptual Speed; Flexibility of Closure; Mathematical Reasoning. *Psychomotor:* Response Orientation; Reaction Time; Rate Control; Control Precision; Multilimb Coordination. *Physical:* Static Strength; Explosive Strength; Extent Flexibility; Trunk Strength; Dynamic Strength. *Sensory:* Far Vision; Depth Perception; Hearing Sensitivity; Night Vision; Peripheral Vision. **General Work Activities**—*Information Input:* Inspecting Equipment, Structures, or Materials; Getting Information; Estimating Needed Characteristics. *Mental Process:* Processing Information; Evaluating Information Against Standards; Making Decisions and Solving Problems. *Work Output:* Handling and Moving Objects; Performing General Physical Activities; Repairing and Maintaining Mechanical Equipment. *Interacting with Others:* Communicating with Persons Outside Organization; Performing for or Working with the Public; Establishing and Maintaining Relationships. **Physical Work Conditions**—Outdoors; Very Hot or Cold; Sitting; Whole Body Vibration; Extremely Bright or Inadequate Lighting. **Other Job Characteristics**—Degree of Automation; Pace Determined by Speed of Equipment; Consequence of Error.

Experience—Job Zone 1. No previous work-related skill, knowledge, or experience is needed. **Job Preparation:** SVP below 4.0—less than six months. **Knowledge**—Geography; Telecommunications; Mechanical; Law and Government; Public Safety and Security. **Instructional Programs**—Truck and Bus Driver/Commercial Vehicle Operation.

Related DOT Jobs—906.683-010 Food-Service Driver; 906.683-014 Liquid-Fertilizer Servicer; 906.683-018 Telephone-Directory-Distributor Driver; 906.683-022 Truck Driver, Light; 913.663-018 Driver; 919.663-022 Escort-Vehicle Driver.

53-3041.00 Taxi Drivers and Chauffeurs

- Education/Training Required: **Short-term on-the-job training**
- Employed: **175,826**
- Annual Earnings: **$17,920**
- Growth: **24.4%**
- Annual Job Openings: **37,000**

Drive automobiles, vans, or limousines to transport passengers. May occasionally carry cargo.

Collect fares or vouchers from passengers; make change and/or issue receipts as necessary. Communicate with dispatchers by radio, telephone, or computer in order to exchange information and receive requests for passenger service. Determine fares based on trip distances and times, using taximeters and fee schedules, and announce fares to passengers. Drive taxicabs, limousines, company cars, or privately owned vehicles in order to transport passengers. Follow regulations governing taxi operation and ensure that passengers follow safety regulations. Notify dispatchers or company mechanics of vehicle problems. Perform routine vehicle maintenance, such as regulating tire pressure and adding gasoline, oil, and water. Pick up or meet employers according to requests, appointments, or schedules. Pick up passengers at prearranged locations, at taxi stands, or by cruising streets in high-traffic areas. Provide passengers with assistance entering and exiting vehicles and help them with any luggage. Record name, date, and taxi identification information on trip sheets, along with trip information such as time and place of pickup and drop-off and total fee. Test vehicle equipment, such as lights, brakes, horns, and windshield wipers, in order to ensure proper operation. Turn the taximeter on when passengers enter the cab and turn it off when they reach the final destination. Arrange to pick up particular customers or groups on a regular schedule. Complete accident reports when necessary. Perform errands for customers or employers, such as delivering or picking up mail and packages. Perform minor vehicle repairs, such as cleaning spark plugs, or take vehicles to mechanics for servicing. Provide passengers with information about the local area and points of interest and/or give advice on hotels and restaurants. Report to taxicab services or garages in order to receive vehicle assignments. Vacuum and clean interiors and wash and polish exteriors of automobiles. Deliver automobiles to customers from rental agencies, car dealerships, or repair shops. Drive automobiles in order to escort vehicles carrying wide loads. Operate vans with special equipment such as wheelchair lifts to transport people with special needs.

GOE INFORMATION—Interest Area: 07. Transportation. **Work Group:** 07.07. Other Services Requiring Driving. **Personality Type**—Realistic. Realistic occupations frequently involve work activities that include practical, hands-on problems and solutions. They often deal with plants, animals, and real-world materials like wood, tools, and machinery. Many of the occupations require working outside and do not involve a lot of paperwork or working closely with others. **Work Values**—Social Service; Independence. **Skills**—Operation and Control; Repairing; Service Orientation; Operation Monitoring. **Abilities**—*Cognitive:* Memorization; Spatial Orientation; Time Sharing; Number Facility; Oral Comprehension. *Psychomotor:* Reaction Time; Response Orientation; Rate Control; Multilimb Coordination; Speed of Limb Movement. *Physical:* Gross Body Coordination; Dynamic Strength; Gross Body Equilibrium. *Sensory:* Peripheral Vision; Sound Localization; Night Vision; Glare Sensitivity; Depth Perception. **General Work Activities**—*Information Input:* Monitoring Processes, Materials, or Surroundings; Getting Information; Inspecting Equipment, Structures, or Materials. *Mental Process:* Organizing, Planning, and Prioritizing; Updating and Using Relevant Knowledge; Analyzing Data or Information. *Work Output:* Performing General Physical Activities; Repairing and Maintaining Mechanical Equipment; Handling and Moving Objects. *Interacting with Others:* Establishing and Maintaining Relationships; Performing for or Working with the Public; Assisting and Caring for Others. **Physical Work Conditions**—Outdoors; Hazardous Conditions; Making Repetitive Motions; Whole Body Vibration; Distracting Sounds and Noise Levels. **Other Job Characteristics**—Pace Determined by Speed of Equipment; Degree of Automation; Importance of Repeating Same Tasks.

Experience—Job Zone 1. No previous work-related skill, knowledge, or experience is needed. **Job Preparation:** SVP below 4.0—less than six months. **Knowledge**—Customer and Personal Service; Geography; Telecommunications; Mechanical; Law and Government. **Instructional Programs**—Truck and Bus Driver/Commercial Vehicle Operation.

Related DOT Jobs—359.673-010 Chauffeur; 359.673-014 Chauffeur, Funeral Car; 913.463-018 Taxi Driver; 913.663-010 Chauffeur; 919.663-010 Deliverer, Car Rental; 919.683-014 Driver.

53-3099.99 Motor Vehicle Operators, All Other

- **Education/Training Required: No data available.**
- **Employed: No data available.**
- **Annual Earnings: No data available.**
- **Growth: 18.2%**
- **Annual Job Openings: 16,000**

All motor vehicle operators not listed separately.

No task data available.

GOE INFORMATION—Interest Area: 07. Transportation. **Work Group:** 07.07. Other Services Requiring Driving. **Note:** The Department of Labor has not collected some data for this job, so it has fewer details than the other descriptions.

Instructional Programs—Ground Transportation, Other.

Related DOT Jobs—919.683-022 Street-Sweeper Operator; 919.683-030 Driver, Starting Gate.

53-4000 Rail Transportation Workers

53-4011.00 Locomotive Engineers

- **Education/Training Required: Work experience in a related occupation**
- **Employed: No data available.**
- **Annual Earnings: $46,540**
- **Growth: 2.3%**
- **Annual Job Openings: 3,000**

Drive electric, diesel-electric, steam, or gas-turbine-electric locomotives to transport passengers or freight. Interpret train orders, electronic or manual signals, and railroad rules and regulations.

Interprets train orders, train signals, and railroad rules and regulations to drive locomotive, following safety regulations and time schedule. Observes track to detect obstructions. Receives starting signal from conductor and moves controls, such as throttle and air brakes, to drive locomotive. Confers with conductor or traffic control center personnel via radiophone to issue or receive information concerning stops, delays, or oncoming trains. Calls out train signals to assistant for verification of meaning to avoid errors in interpretation. Drives diesel-electric rail-detector car to transport rail-flaw-detecting machine over railroad. Inspects locomotive before run to verify specified fuel, sand, water, and other supplies. Synchronizes watch with that of conductor to ensure departure time from station or terminal is in accordance with time schedule. Inspects locomotive after run to detect damaged or defective equipment. Prepares reports to explain accidents, unscheduled stops, or delays.

GOE INFORMATION—Interest Area: 07. Transportation. **Work Group:** 07.06. Rail Vehicle Operation. **Personality Type**—Realistic. Realistic oc-

cupations frequently involve work activities that include practical, hands-on problems and solutions. They often deal with plants, animals, and real-world materials like wood, tools, and machinery. Many of the occupations require working outside and do not involve a lot of paperwork or working closely with others. **Work Values**—Supervision, Technical; Supervision, Human Relations; Compensation; Company Policies and Practices; Security. **Skills**—Operation and Control; Operation Monitoring; Systems Analysis; Troubleshooting. **Abilities**—*Cognitive:* Selective Attention; Time Sharing; Spatial Orientation; Perceptual Speed; Speed of Closure. *Psychomotor:* Reaction Time; Response Orientation; Rate Control; Control Precision; Speed of Limb Movement. *Physical:* Explosive Strength; Gross Body Coordination; Dynamic Strength; Gross Body Equilibrium; Dynamic Flexibility. *Sensory:* Night Vision; Sound Localization; Auditory Attention; Peripheral Vision; Depth Perception. **General Work Activities**—*Information Input:* Inspecting Equipment, Structures, or Materials; Getting Information; Monitoring Processes, Materials, or Surroundings. *Mental Process:* Evaluating Information Against Standards; Making Decisions and Solving Problems; Analyzing Data or Information. *Work Output:* Operating Vehicles or Equipment; Handling and Moving Objects; Performing General Physical Activities. *Interacting with Others:* Communicating with Other Workers; Establishing and Maintaining Relationships; Interpreting Meaning of Information for Others. **Physical Work Conditions**—Hazardous Equipment; Hazardous Conditions; Distracting Sounds and Noise Levels; Contaminants; Outdoors. **Other Job Characteristics**—Consequence of Error; Pace Determined by Speed of Equipment; Degree of Automation.

Experience—Job Zone 4. A minimum of two to four years of work-related skill, knowledge, or experience is needed. **Job Preparation:** SVP 7.0 to less than 8.0—two years to less than 10 years. **Knowledge**—Geography; Public Safety and Security; Mechanical; Engineering and Technology; Telecommunications. **Instructional Programs**—Transportation and Materials Moving, Other.

Related DOT Jobs—910.363-014 Locomotive Engineer.

53-4012.00 Locomotive Firers

- **Education/Training Required: Postsecondary vocational training**
- **Employed: No data available.**
- **Annual Earnings: $48,670**
- **Growth: 2.3%**
- **Annual Job Openings: 3,000**

Monitor locomotive instruments and watch for dragging equipment, obstacles on rights-of-way, and train signals during run. Watch for and relay traffic signals from yard workers to yard engineer in railroad yard.

Observes oil, temperature, and pressure gauges on dashboard to ascertain if engine is operating safely and efficiently. Observes track from left side of locomotive to detect obstructions on tracks. Observes train signals along route and verifies their meaning for engineer. Observes train as it goes around curves to detect dragging equipment and smoking journal boxes. Observes signal from workers in rear of train and relays information to engineer. Signals other worker to set brakes and to throw track switches when switching cars from train to way stations. Inspects locomotive to detect damaged or worn parts. Inventories supplies, such as fuel, water, and sand, to ensure safe, efficient operation during run. Operates locomotive during emergency. Starts diesel engine to warm engine before run.

GOE INFORMATION—Interest Area: 07. Transportation. **Work Group:** 07.06. Rail Vehicle Operation. **Personality Type**—Realistic. Realistic occupations frequently involve work activities that include practical, hands-on problems and solutions. They often deal with plants, animals, and real-world materials like wood, tools, and machinery. Many of the occupations require working outside and do not involve a lot of paperwork or working closely with others. **Work Values**—Supervision, Technical; Supervision, Human Relations; Company Policies and Practices; Moral Values; Advancement. **Skills**—Operation Monitoring; Operation and Control. **Abilities**—*Cognitive:* Perceptual Speed; Spatial Orientation; Time Sharing; Selective Attention; Problem Sensitivity. *Psychomotor:* Reaction Time; Response Orientation; Rate Control; Manual Dexterity; Control Precision. *Physical:* Extent Flexibility; Dynamic Flexibility; Gross Body Equilibrium; Explosive Strength; Gross Body Coordination. *Sensory:* Far Vision; Night Vision; Peripheral Vision; Glare Sensitivity; Depth Perception. **General Work Activities**—*Information Input:* Monitoring Processes, Materials, or Surroundings; Inspecting Equipment, Structures, or Materials; Getting Information. *Mental Process:* Evaluating Information Against Standards; Making Decisions and Solving Problems; Processing Information. *Work Output:* Operating Vehicles or Equipment; Handling and Moving Objects; Performing General Physical Activities. *Interacting with Others:* Establishing and Maintaining Relationships; Communicating with Other Workers; Interpreting Meaning of Information for Others. **Physical Work Conditions**—Whole Body Vibration; Hazardous Equipment; Distracting Sounds and Noise Levels; Outdoors; Very Hot or Cold. **Other Job Characteristics**—Consequence of Error; Degree of Automation; Importance of Being Exact or Accurate.

Experience—Job Zone 3. Previous work-related skill, knowledge, or experience is required. **Job Preparation:** SVP 6.0 to less than 7.0—more than one year and less than four years. **Knowledge**—Geography; Mechanical; Public Safety and Security; Physics; Engineering and Technology. **Instructional Programs**—Transportation and Materials Moving, Other.

Related DOT Jobs—910.363-010 Firer, Locomotive.

53-4013.00 Rail Yard Engineers, Dinkey Operators, and Hostlers

- Education/Training Required: Work experience in a related occupation
- Employed: 3,831
- Annual Earnings: $38,110
- Growth: –4.5%
- Annual Job Openings: Fewer than 500

Drive switching or other locomotive or dinkey engines within railroad yard, industrial plant, quarry, construction project, or similar location.

Records number of cars available or number of cars sent to repair station and type of service needed. Inspects track for defects and assists in installation or repair of rails and ties. Drives switching locomotive within railroad yard or other establishment to switch railroad cars. Operates switching diesel engine to switch railroad cars, using remote control. Drives locomotives to and from various stations in roundhouse to have locomotives cleaned, serviced, repaired, or supplied. Operates and controls dinkey engine to transport and shunt cars at industrial or mine site. Operates flatcar equipped with derrick or rail car to transport personnel or equipment. Receives switching orders from yard conductor and talks with conductor and other workers via radio-telephone to exchange switching information. Reads daily car schedule to determine number of cars needed for next day's run. Inspects engine at start and end of shift and refuels and lubricates engine as needed. Observes oil, air, and steam pressure gauges and water level to ensure operating efficiency.

GOE INFORMATION—**Interest Area:** 07. Transportation. **Work Group:** 07.06. Rail Vehicle Operation. **Personality Type**—Realistic. Realistic occupations frequently involve work activities that include practical, hands-on problems and solutions. They often deal with plants, animals, and real-world materials like wood, tools, and machinery. Many of the occupations require working outside and do not involve a lot of paperwork or working closely with others. **Work Values**—Supervision, Technical; Supervision, Human Relations; Company Policies and Practices; Security; Advancement. **Skills**—Operation and Control; Operation Monitoring; Repairing; Installation. **Abilities**—*Cognitive:* Spatial Orientation; Perceptual Speed; Time Sharing; Speed of Closure; Memorization. *Psychomotor:* Rate Control; Control Precision; Reaction Time; Response Orientation; Multilimb Coordination. *Physical:* Static Strength; Gross Body Coordination; Explosive Strength. *Sensory:* Depth Perception; Glare Sensitivity; Peripheral Vision; Night Vision; Far Vision. **General Work Activities**—*Information Input:* Inspecting Equipment, Structures, or Materials; Getting Information; Monitoring Processes, Materials, or Surroundings. *Mental Process:* Organizing, Planning, and Prioritizing; Evaluating Information Against Standards; Making Decisions and Solving Problems. *Work Output:* Operating Vehicles or Equipment; Performing General Physical Activities; Handling and Moving Objects. *Interacting with Others:* Communicating with Other Workers; Establishing and Maintaining Relationships; Interpreting Meaning of Information for Others. **Physical Work Conditions**—Outdoors; Distracting Sounds and Noise Levels; Making Repetitive Motions; Whole Body Vibration; Contaminants. **Other Job Characteristics**—Pace Determined by Speed of Equipment; Degree of Automation; Importance of Being Exact or Accurate.

Experience—Job Zone 2. Some previous work-related skill, knowledge, or experience may be helpful, but usually is not needed. **Job Preparation:** SVP 4.0 to less than 6.0—six months to less than two years. **Knowledge**—Mechanical; Public Safety and Security; Engineering and Technology; Telecommunications; Geography. **Instructional Programs**—Truck and Bus Driver/Commercial Vehicle Operation.

Related DOT Jobs—910.363-018 Yard Engineer; 910.583-010 Laborer, Car Barn; 910.683-010 Hostler; 919.663-014 Dinkey Operator.

53-4021.00 Railroad Brake, Signal, and Switch Operators

- Education/Training Required: Moderate-term on-the-job training
- Employed: 21,863
- Annual Earnings: $44,920
- Growth: –60.8%
- Annual Job Openings: 2,000

Operate railroad track switches. Couple or uncouple rolling stock to make up or break up trains. Signal engineers by hand or flagging. May inspect couplings, air hoses, journal boxes, and hand brakes.

No task data available.

GOE INFORMATION—**Interest Area:** 07. Transportation. **Work Group:** 07.02. Vehicle Expediting and Coordinating. **Note:** The Department of Labor has not collected some data for this job, so it has fewer details than the other descriptions.

Instructional Programs—Truck and Bus Driver/Commercial Vehicle Operation.

Related DOT Jobs—910.364-010 Braker, Passenger Train; 910.367-010 Brake Coupler, Road Freight; 910.367-022 Locomotive Operator Helper; 910.664-010 Yard Coupler; 910.667-026 Switch Tender; 932.664-010 Brake Holder.

53-4021.01 Train Crew Members

- Education/Training Required: Work experience in a related occupation
- Employed: No data available.
- Annual Earnings: $44,920
- Growth: –60.8%
- Annual Job Openings: 2,000

Inspect couplings, air hoses, journal boxes, and handbrakes on trains to ensure that they function properly.

Inspects couplings, air hoses, journal boxes, and handbrakes to ensure that they are securely fastened and function properly. Reports to conductor any equipment requiring major repair. Climbs ladder to top of car to set brakes or to ride atop to control its speed when shunted. Makes minor repairs to couplings, air hoses, and journal boxes, using hand tools. Signals locomotive engineer to start or stop train when coupling or uncoupling cars. Sets flares, flags, lanterns, or torpedoes in front and at rear of train during emergency stops to warn oncoming trains. Observes signals from other crew members. Pulls or pushes track switch to reroute cars. Collects tickets, fares, and passes from passengers. Answers questions from passengers concerning train rules, station, and timetable information. Assists passengers to board and leave train. Adjusts controls to regulate air conditioning, heating, and lighting on train for comfort of passengers. Places passengers' baggage in rack above seats on train.

GOE INFORMATION—Interest Area: 07. Transportation. Work Group: 07.08. Support Work. Personality Type—Realistic. Realistic occupations frequently involve work activities that include practical, hands-on problems and solutions. They often deal with plants, animals, and real-world materials like wood, tools, and machinery. Many of the occupations require working outside and do not involve a lot of paperwork or working closely with others. Work Values—Supervision, Technical; Social Service; Supervision, Human Relations; Company Policies and Practices; Advancement. Skills—Repairing; Operation and Control; Troubleshooting. Abilities—*Cognitive:* Spatial Orientation; Oral Expression; Problem Sensitivity; Perceptual Speed; Flexibility of Closure. *Psychomotor:* Reaction Time; Response Orientation; Speed of Limb Movement; Rate Control; Multilimb Coordination. *Physical:* Gross Body Equilibrium; Dynamic Strength; Gross Body Coordination; Stamina; Static Strength. *Sensory:* Auditory Attention; Far Vision; Night Vision; Sound Localization; Speech Clarity. General Work Activities—*Information Input:* Inspecting Equipment, Structures, or Materials; Getting Information; Identifying Objects, Actions, and Events. *Mental Process:* Updating and Using Relevant Knowledge; Judging Qualities of Things, Services, or Other People's Work; Making Decisions and Solving Problems. *Work Output:* Performing General Physical Activities; Handling and Moving Objects; Repairing and Maintaining Mechanical Equipment. *Interacting with Others:* Performing for or Working with the Public; Communicating with Other Workers; Communicating with Persons Outside Organization. Physical Work Conditions—Walking or Running; Outdoors; Whole Body Vibration; Climbing Ladders, Scaffolds, Poles, etc.; High Places. Other Job Characteristics—Importance of Repeating Same Tasks; Consequence of Error; Pace Determined by Speed of Equipment.

Experience—Job Zone 2. Some previous work-related skill, knowledge, or experience may be helpful, but usually is not needed. Job Preparation: SVP 4.0 to less than 6.0—six months to less than two years. Knowledge—Customer and Personal Service; Mechanical; Public Safety and Security; Geography; Building and Construction. Instructional Programs—Truck and Bus Driver/Commercial Vehicle Operation.

Related DOT Jobs—910.364-010 Braker, Passenger Train; 910.367-010 Brake Coupler, Road Freight.

53-4021.02 Railroad Yard Workers

- Education/Training Required: Work experience in a related occupation
- Employed: No data available.
- Annual Earnings: $44,920
- Growth: –18.9%
- Annual Job Openings: 2,000

Perform a variety of activities such as coupling rail cars and operating railroad track switches in railroad yard to facilitate the movement of rail cars within the yard.

Throws track switches to route cars to different sections of yard. Receives oral or written instructions indicating which cars are to be switched and track assignments. Raises lever to couple and uncouple cars for makeup and breakup of trains. Opens and closes chute gates to load and unload cars. Watches for and relays traffic signals to start and stop cars during shunting, using arm or lantern. Signals engineer to start and stop engine. Rides atop cars that have been shunted and turns handwheel to control speed or stop car at specified position. Attaches cable to cars being hoisted by cable or chain in mines, quarries, or industrial plants. Connects air hose to car, using wrench. Opens and closes ventilation doors.

GOE INFORMATION—Interest Area: 07. Transportation. Work Group: 07.08. Support Work. Personality Type—Realistic. Realistic occupations frequently involve work activities that include practical, hands-on problems and solutions. They often deal with plants, animals, and real-world materials like wood, tools, and machinery. Many of the occupations require working outside and do not involve a lot of paperwork or working closely with others. Work Values—Supervision, Technical; Supervision, Human Relations; Company Policies and Practices; Advancement; Moral Values. Skills—Operation and Control. Abilities—*Cognitive:* Spatial Orientation; Speed of Closure; Perceptual Speed; Time Sharing; Selective Attention. *Psychomotor:* Response Orientation; Rate Control; Reaction Time; Control Precision; Speed of Limb Movement. *Physical:* Gross Body Equilibrium; Dynamic Strength; Explosive Strength; Stamina; Extent Flexibility. *Sensory:* Far Vision; Night Vision; Auditory Attention; Sound Localization; Depth Perception. General Work Activities—*Information Input:* Monitoring Processes, Materials, or Surroundings; Getting Information; Identifying Objects, Actions, and Events. *Mental Process:* Analyzing Data or Information; Making Decisions and Solving Problems; Organizing, Planning, and Prioritizing. *Work Output:* Performing General Physical Activities; Handling and Moving Objects; Controlling Machines and Processes. *Interacting with Others:* Communicating with Other Workers; Coordinating the Work and Activities of Others; Establishing and Maintaining Relationships. Physical Work Conditions—Outdoors; Climbing Ladders, Scaffolds, Poles, etc.; High Places; Whole Body Vibration; Hazardous Equipment. Other Job Characteristics—Pace Determined by Speed of Equipment; Consequence of Error; Importance of Being Exact or Accurate.

Experience—Job Zone 1. No previous work-related skill, knowledge, or experience is needed. Job Preparation: SVP below 4.0—less than six months. Knowledge—Mechanical; Public Safety and Security; Engineering and Technology; Physics. Instructional Programs—Truck and Bus Driver/Commercial Vehicle Operation.

Related DOT Jobs—910.367-022 Locomotive Operator Helper; 910.664-010 Yard Coupler; 910.667-026 Switch Tender; 932.664-010 Brake Holder.

53-4031.00 Railroad Conductors and Yardmasters

- **Education/Training Required: Work experience in a related occupation**
- **Employed: 44,874**
- **Annual Earnings: $42,840**
- **Growth: −18.9%**
- **Annual Job Openings: 4,000**

Conductors coordinate activities of train crew on passenger or freight train. Coordinate activities of switch-engine crew within yard of railroad, industrial plant, or similar location. Yardmasters coordinate activities of workers engaged in railroad traffic operations, such as the makeup or breakup of trains, yard switching, and reviewing train schedules and switching orders.

Directs and instructs workers engaged in yard activities, such as switching track, coupling/uncoupling cars, and routing inbound/outbound traffic. Coordinates crew activities to transport and provide boarding, porter, maid, and meal services to passengers. Signals engineer to begin train run, stop train, or change speed, using radiotelephone, lantern, teletypewriter, or hand movement. Reviews schedules, switching orders, way bills, and shipping records to obtain cargo loading and unloading information. Observes yard traffic to determine tracks available to accommodate inbound and outbound traffic. Instructs workers to set warning signals in front and rear of train during emergency stops to warn oncoming trains. Confers with traffic control personnel, engineer, and other workers engaged in transporting freight to receive and convey instructions. Observes and communicates with passengers and instructs workers to regulate air conditioning, lighting, and heating to ensure passenger safety and comfort. Observes lights on panelboard to monitor location of trains. Operates controls to electrically activate track switches and traffic signals. Inspects or supervises workers in inspection and maintenance of mechanical equipment to ensure efficient and safe train operation. Collects tickets, fares, or passes from passengers; answers questions concerning train rules, regulations, and schedules; and provides destination information. Inspects freight cars for compliance with sealing procedures, records car and corresponding seal number, and confirms route and destination information. Verifies accuracy of timekeeping instruments with engineer to assure station departure time complies with timetable schedules. Records departure and arrival times, messages, tickets and revenue collected, and passenger accommodations and destinations. Documents and prepares reports of accidents, unscheduled stops, or delays at completion of train run. Charts train movements to estimate arrival times.

GOE INFORMATION—Interest Area: 07. Transportation. **Work Group:** 07.01. Managerial Work in Transportation. **Personality Type—**Realistic. Realistic occupations frequently involve work activities that include practical, hands-on problems and solutions. They often deal with plants, animals, and real-world materials like wood, tools, and machinery. Many of the occupations require working outside and do not involve a lot of paperwork or working closely with others. **Work Values—**Authority; Supervision, Technical; Company Policies and Practices; Autonomy; Security. **Skills—**Operation and Control; Operation Monitoring; Coordination; Management of Personnel Resources; Troubleshooting; Systems Evaluation; Systems Analysis; Equipment Selection. **Abilities—***Cognitive:* Written Expression; Oral Expression; Oral Comprehension; Deductive Reasoning; Problem Sensitivity. *Psychomotor:* Rate Control; Reaction Time; Multilimb Coordination; Control Precision; Response Orientation. *Physical:* Gross Body Equilibrium. *Sensory:* Speech Clarity; Far Vision; Night Vision; Visual Color Discrimination; Depth Perception.

General Work Activities—*Information Input:* Getting Information; Monitoring Processes, Materials, or Surroundings; Identifying Objects, Actions, and Events. *Mental Process:* Scheduling Work and Activities; Making Decisions and Solving Problems; Organizing, Planning, and Prioritizing. *Work Output:* Documenting or Recording Information; Performing General Physical Activities; Handling and Moving Objects. *Interacting with Others:* Communicating with Other Workers; Coordinating the Work and Activities of Others; Communicating with Persons Outside Organization. **Physical Work Conditions—**Keeping or Regaining Balance; Outdoors; Hazardous Conditions; Walking or Running; Distracting Sounds and Noise Levels. **Other Job Characteristics—**Degree of Automation; Pace Determined by Speed of Equipment; Consequence of Error.

Experience—Job Zone 4. A minimum of two to four years of work-related skill, knowledge, or experience is needed. **Job Preparation:** SVP 7.0 to less than 8.0—two years to less than 10 years. **Knowledge—**Administration and Management; Geography; Customer and Personal Service; Public Safety and Security; Telecommunications. **Instructional Programs—**Truck and Bus Driver/Commercial Vehicle Operation.

Related DOT Jobs—184.167-262 Train Dispatcher; 184.167-278 Yard Manager; 198.167-010 Conductor, Passenger Car; 198.167-014 Conductor, Pullman; 198.167-018 Conductor, Road Freight; 910.167-010 Car Chaser.

53-4041.00 Subway and Streetcar Operators

- **Education/Training Required: Moderate-term on-the-job training**
- **Employed: No data available.**
- **Annual Earnings: No data available.**
- **Growth: −4.1%**
- **Annual Job Openings: No data available.**

Operate subway or elevated suburban train with no separate locomotive or electric-powered streetcar to transport passengers. May handle fares.

Drive and control rail-guided public transportation, such as subways; elevated trains; and electric-powered streetcars, trams, or trolleys, in order to transport passengers. Make announcements to passengers, such as notifications of upcoming stops or schedule delays. Operate controls to open and close transit vehicle doors. Regulate vehicle speed and the time spent at each stop in order to maintain schedules. Report delays, mechanical problems, and emergencies to supervisors or dispatchers, using radios. Monitor lights indicating obstructions or other trains ahead and watch for car and truck traffic at crossings to stay alert to potential hazards. Attend meetings on driver and passenger safety in order to learn ways in which job performance might be affected. Collect fares from passengers and issue change and transfers. Complete reports, including shift summaries and incident or accident reports. Direct emergency evacuation procedures. Greet passengers, provide information, and answer questions concerning fares, schedules, transfers, and routings. Record transactions and coin receptor readings in order to verify the amount of money collected.

GOE INFORMATION—Interest Area: 07. Transportation. **Work Group:** 07.06. Rail Vehicle Operation. **Personality Type—**Realistic. Realistic occupations frequently involve work activities that include practical, hands-on problems and solutions. They often deal with plants, animals, and real-world materials like wood, tools, and machinery. Many of the occupations require working outside and do not involve a lot of paperwork or working closely with others. **Work Values—**Supervision, Technical; Supervision, Human Relations; Independence; Social Service; Company Policies and Practices. **Skills—**Operation and Control; Operation Monitoring. **Abilities**—*Cognitive:* Spatial Orientation; Oral Expression. *Psychomotor:* Reaction Time; Control Precision; Response Orientation; Rate Control; Multilimb Coordination. *Physical:* Gross Body Coordination; Trunk Strength. *Sensory:* Glare Sensitivity; Night Vision; Depth Perception; Far Vision; Peripheral Vision. **General Work Activities**—*Information Input:* Identifying Objects, Actions, and Events; Monitoring Processes, Materials, or Surroundings; Getting Information. *Mental Process:* Processing Information; Making Decisions and Solving Problems; Updating and Using Relevant Knowledge. *Work Output:* Operating Vehicles or Equipment; Handling and Moving Objects; Documenting or Recording Information. *Interacting with Others:* Performing for or Working with the Public; Communicating with Persons Outside Organization; Communicating with Other Workers. **Physical Work Conditions**—Sitting; Whole Body Vibration; Using Hands on Objects, Tools, or Controls; Making Repetitive Motions; Outdoors. **Other Job Characteristics**—Pace Determined by Speed of Equipment; Importance of Repeating Same Tasks; Consequence of Error.

Experience—Job Zone 2. Some previous work-related skill, knowledge, or experience may be helpful, but usually is not needed. **Job Preparation:** SVP 4.0 to less than 6.0—six months to less than two years. **Knowledge**—Geography; Customer and Personal Service; Clerical; Foreign Language; Telecommunications. **Instructional Programs**—Truck and Bus Driver/Commercial Vehicle Operation.

Related DOT Jobs—910.683-014 Motor Operator; 913.463-014 Streetcar Operator.

53-4099.99 Rail Transportation Workers, All Other

- Education/Training Required: No data available.
- Employed: No data available.
- Annual Earnings: No data available.
- Growth: –4.1%
- Annual Job Openings: 1,000

All rail transportation workers not listed separately.

No task data available.

GOE INFORMATION—Interest Area: 07. Transportation. **Work Group:** 07.06. Rail Vehicle Operation. **Note:** The Department of Labor has not collected some data for this job, so it has fewer details than the other descriptions.

Instructional Programs—Truck and Bus Driver/Commercial Vehicle Operation.

Related DOT Jobs—910.362-010 Tower Operator; 910.382-010 Car-Retarder Operator; 910.683-022 Transfer-Table Operator; 919.683-026 Trackmobile Operator.

53-5000 Water Transportation Workers

53-5011.00 Sailors and Marine Oilers

- Education/Training Required: Short-term on-the-job training
- Employed: 31,594
- Annual Earnings: $28,630
- Growth: 4.9%
- Annual Job Openings: 2,000

Stand watch to look for obstructions in path of vessel, measure water depth, turn wheel on bridge, or use emergency equipment as directed by captain, mate, or pilot. Break out, rig, overhaul, and store cargo-handling gear, stationary rigging, and running gear. Perform a variety of maintenance tasks to preserve the painted surface of the ship and to maintain line and ship equipment. Must hold government-issued certification and tankerman certification when working aboard liquid-carrying vessels.

No task data available.

GOE INFORMATION—Interest Area: 07. Transportation. **Work Group:** 07.04. Water Vehicle Operation. **Note:** The Department of Labor has not collected some data for this job, so it has fewer details than the other descriptions.

Instructional Programs—Marine Transportation, Other.

Related DOT Jobs—911.363-014 Quartermaster; 911.364-010 Able Seaman; 911.584-010 Marine Oiler; 911.664-014 Sailor, Pleasure Craft; 911.687-022 Deckhand; 911.687-030 Ordinary Seaman.

53-5011.01 Able Seamen

- Education/Training Required: Short-term on-the-job training
- Employed: No data available.
- Annual Earnings: $28,630
- Growth: 4.9%
- Annual Job Openings: 2,000

Stand watch at bow or on wing of bridge to look for obstructions in path of vessel. Measure water depth. Turn wheel on bridge or use emergency equipment as directed by mate. Break out, rig, overhaul, and store cargo-handling gear, stationary rigging, and running gear. Chip rust from and paint deck or ship's structure. Must hold government-issued certification. Must hold certification when working aboard liquid-carrying vessels.

Measures depth of water in shallow or unfamiliar waters, using leadline, and telephones or shouts information to bridge. Breaks out, rigs, overhauls, and stows cargo-handling gear, stationary rigging, and running gear. Paints and chips rust on deck or superstructure of ship. Stands watch from bow of ship or wing of bridge to look for obstruction in path of ship. Overhauls lifeboats and lifeboat gear and lowers or raises lifeboats with winch or falls. Steers ship under direction of ship's commander or navigating officer or directs helmsman to steer, following designated course. Steers ship and maintains visual communication with other ships. Stands by wheel when ship is on automatic pilot and verifies accuracy of course by comparing with magnetic compass. Relays specified signals to ships in vicinity, using visual signaling devices such as blinker light and semaphore. Stows or removes cargo from ship's hold. Maintains ship's log while in port and stands gangway watch to prevent unauthorized persons from boarding ship. Gives directions to crew engaged in cleaning wheelhouse and quarter deck.

GOE INFORMATION—Interest Area: 07. Transportation. **Work Group:** 07.04. Water Vehicle Operation. **Personality Type**—Realistic. Realistic occupations frequently involve work activities that include practical, hands-on problems and solutions. They often deal with plants, animals, and real-world materials like wood, tools, and machinery. Many of the occupations require working outside and do not involve a lot of paperwork or working closely with others. **Work Values**—Supervision, Technical; Advancement; Pleasant Co-workers; Authority; Recognition. **Skills**—Operation and Control; Operation Monitoring. **Abilities**—*Cognitive:* Spatial Orientation; Perceptual Speed; Time Sharing; Selective

Attention; Speed of Closure. *Psychomotor:* Rate Control; Control Precision; Reaction Time; Speed of Limb Movement; Response Orientation. *Physical:* Gross Body Equilibrium; Static Strength; Dynamic Flexibility; Extent Flexibility; Stamina. *Sensory:* Glare Sensitivity; Night Vision; Far Vision; Peripheral Vision; Depth Perception. **General Work Activities—** *Information Input:* Monitoring Processes, Materials, or Surroundings; Getting Information; Inspecting Equipment, Structures, or Materials. *Mental Process:* Processing Information; Evaluating Information Against Standards; Analyzing Data or Information. *Work Output:* Operating Vehicles or Equipment; Performing General Physical Activities; Handling and Moving Objects. *Interacting with Others:* Communicating with Other Workers; Establishing and Maintaining Relationships; Coordinating the Work and Activities of Others. **Physical Work Conditions—**Keeping or Regaining Balance; Outdoors; High Places; Climbing Ladders, Scaffolds, Poles, etc.; Extremely Bright or Inadequate Lighting. **Other Job Characteristics—**Consequence of Error; Degree of Automation; Pace Determined by Speed of Equipment.

Experience—Job Zone 2. Some previous work-related skill, knowledge, or experience may be helpful, but usually is not needed. **Job Preparation:** SVP 4.0 to less than 6.0—six months to less than two years. **Knowledge—**Geography; Mechanical; Public Safety and Security; Telecommunications; Physics. **Instructional Programs—**Marine Transportation, Other.

Related DOT Jobs—911.363-014 Quartermaster; 911.364-010 Able Seaman.

53-5011.02 Ordinary Seamen and Marine Oilers

- **Education/Training Required: Short-term on-the-job training**
- **Employed: No data available.**
- **Annual Earnings: $28,630**
- **Growth: 4.9%**
- **Annual Job Openings: 2,000**

Stand deck department watches and perform a variety of tasks to preserve the painted surface of the ship and to maintain lines and ship equipment, such as running and cargo-handling gear. May oil and grease moving parts of engines and auxiliary equipment. Must hold government-issued certification. Must hold certification when working aboard liquid-carrying vessels.

Cleans and polishes wood trim, brass, and other metal parts. Chips and cleans rust spots on deck, superstructure, and sides of ship, using wire brush and hand or air chipping machine. Paints or varnishes decks, superstructures, lifeboats, or sides of ship. Lubricates machinery, equipment, and engine parts, such as gears, shafts, and bearings. Sweeps and washes deck, using broom, mops, brushes, and hose. Splices and repairs cables and ropes, using marlinespike, wire cutters, twine, and hand tools. Handles lines to moor vessel to wharf, tie up vessel to another vessel, or rig towing lines. Stands watch from bow of ship or wing of bridge to look for obstructions in path of ship. Examines machinery for specified pressure and flow of lubricants. Loads or unloads materials from vessel. Reads pressure and temperature gauges or displays and records data in engineering log. Lowers and mans lifeboat in case of emergency. Assists engineer in overhauling and adjusting machinery. Records data in ship's log, such as weather conditions and distance traveled. Turns wheel while observing compass to maintain ship on course.

GOE INFORMATION—Interest Area: 07. Transportation. **Work Group:** 07.04. Water Vehicle Operation. **Personality Type—**Realistic. Realistic occupations frequently involve work activities that include practical, hands-on problems and solutions. They often deal with plants, animals,

and real-world materials like wood, tools, and machinery. Many of the occupations require working outside and do not involve a lot of paperwork or working closely with others. **Work Values—**Advancement; Supervision, Technical; Pleasant Co-workers. **Skills—**Repairing; Operation and Control; Operation Monitoring; Troubleshooting. **Abilities—***Cognitive:* Spatial Orientation; Flexibility of Closure; Time Sharing; Speed of Closure. *Psychomotor:* Control Precision; Speed of Limb Movement; Multilimb Coordination; Reaction Time; Rate Control. *Physical:* Gross Body Equilibrium; Stamina; Trunk Strength; Explosive Strength; Extent Flexibility. *Sensory:* Night Vision; Peripheral Vision; Depth Perception; Far Vision; Sound Localization. **General Work Activities—***Information Input:* Getting Information; Monitoring Processes, Materials, or Surroundings; Inspecting Equipment, Structures, or Materials. *Mental Process:* Updating and Using Relevant Knowledge; Analyzing Data or Information; Judging Qualities of Things, Services, or Other People's Work. *Work Output:* Performing General Physical Activities; Handling and Moving Objects; Operating Vehicles or Equipment. *Interacting with Others:* Establishing and Maintaining Relationships; Communicating with Other Workers; Assisting and Caring for Others. **Physical Work Conditions—**Outdoors; Whole Body Vibration; Keeping or Regaining Balance; Hazardous Equipment; Minor Burns, Cuts, Bites, or Stings. **Other Job Characteristics—**Consequence of Error; Degree of Automation; Importance of Being Exact or Accurate.

Experience—Job Zone 2. Some previous work-related skill, knowledge, or experience may be helpful, but usually is not needed. **Job Preparation:** SVP 4.0 to less than 6.0—six months to less than two years. **Knowledge—**Geography; Mechanical; Building and Construction; Public Safety and Security; Engineering and Technology. **Instructional Programs—**Marine Transportation, Other.

Related DOT Jobs—911.584-010 Marine Oiler; 911.664-014 Sailor, Pleasure Craft; 911.687-022 Deckhand; 911.687-030 Ordinary Seaman.

53-5021.00 Captains, Mates, and Pilots of Water Vessels

- **Education/Training Required: Long-term on-the-job training**
- **Employed: No data available.**
- **Annual Earnings: $48,680**
- **Growth: 4.9%**
- **Annual Job Openings: 2,000**

Command or supervise operations of ships and water vessels, such as tugboats and ferryboats, that travel into and out of harbors, estuaries, straits, and sounds and on rivers, lakes, bays, and oceans. Required to hold license issued by U.S. Coast Guard.

No task data available.

GOE INFORMATION—Interest Area: 07. Transportation. **Work Group:** 07.04. Water Vehicle Operation. **Note:** The Department of Labor has not collected some data for this job, so it has fewer details than the other descriptions.

Instructional Programs—Commercial Fishing; Marine Science/Merchant Marine Officer; Marine Transportation, Other.

Related DOT Jobs—197.133-010 Captain, Fishing Vessel; 197.133-014 Master, Yacht; 197.133-018 Mate, Fishing Vessel; 197.133-022 Mate, Ship; 197.133-026 Pilot, Ship; 197.133-030 Tugboat Captain; 197.133-034 Tugboat Mate; 197.137-010 Dredge Mate; 197.161-010 Dredge Captain; 197.163-010 Ferryboat Captain; 197.163-014 Master, Passenger Barge; 197.163-018 Master, Riverboat; 197.167-010 Master, Ship; 911.133-010 Cadet, Deck; 911.137-010 Barge Captain; 911.137-014 Derrick-Boat Captain;

911.263-010 Deep Submergence Vehicle Operator; 911.363-010 Ferryboat Operator.

53-5021.01 Ship and Boat Captains

- **Education/Training Required: Long-term on-the-job training**
- **Employed: No data available.**
- **Annual Earnings: $48,680**
- **Growth: 3.4%**
- **Annual Job Openings: 2,000**

Command vessels in oceans, bays, lakes, rivers, and coastal waters.

Commands water vessels, such as passenger and freight vessels, fishing vessels, yachts, tugboats, barges, deep submergence vehicles, and ferryboats. Directs and coordinates activities of crew or workers, such as loading and unloading, operating signal devices, fishing, and repairing defective equipment. Steers and operates vessel or orders helmsperson to steer vessel, using radio, depth finder, radar, lights, buoys, and lighthouses. Computes position, sets course, and determines speed, using charts, area plotting sheets, compass, sextant, and knowledge of local conditions. Inspects vessel to ensure safety of crew and passengers, efficient and safe operation of vessel and equipment, and conformance to regulations. Signals crew or deckhands to rig tow lines, open or close gates and ramps, and pull guard chains across entry. Monitors sonar and navigational aids and reads gauges to verify sufficient levels of hydraulic fluid, air pressure, and oxygen. Calculates sighting of land, using electronic sounding devices and following contour lines on chart. Maintains records of daily activities, movements, and ports-of-call and prepares progress and personnel reports. Interviews, hires, and instructs crew and assigns watches and living quarters. Tows and maneuvers barge or signals tugboat to tow barge to destination. Signals passing vessels, using whistle, flashing lights, flags, and radio. Purchases supplies and equipment, contacts buyers to sell fish, and resolves questions or problems with customs officials. Collects fares from customers or signals ferryboat helper to collect fares.

GOE INFORMATION—Interest Area: 07. Transportation. **Work Group:** 07.04. Water Vehicle Operation. **Personality Type**—Enterprising. Enterprising occupations frequently involve starting up and carrying out projects. These occupations can involve leading people and making many decisions. They sometimes require risk taking and often deal with business. **Work Values**—Authority; Responsibility; Autonomy; Recognition; Social Status. **Skills**—Management of Personnel Resources; Operation Monitoring; Operation and Control; Troubleshooting; Management of Material Resources; Coordination; Equipment Selection; Judgment and Decision Making. **Abilities**—*Cognitive:* Spatial Orientation; Time Sharing; Mathematical Reasoning; Oral Expression; Speed of Closure. *Psychomotor:* Response Orientation; Reaction Time; Rate Control; Control Precision; Multilimb Coordination. *Physical:* Gross Body Equilibrium; Gross Body Coordination; Stamina; Dynamic Flexibility. *Sensory:* Night Vision; Far Vision; Glare Sensitivity; Depth Perception; Peripheral Vision. **General Work Activities**—*Information Input:* Getting Information; Identifying Objects, Actions, and Events; Monitoring Processes, Materials, or Surroundings. *Mental Process:* Making Decisions and Solving Problems; Updating and Using Relevant Knowledge; Analyzing Data or Information. *Work Output:* Operating Vehicles or Equipment; Documenting or Recording Information; Handling and Moving Objects. *Interacting with Others:* Communicating with Other Workers; Staffing Organizational Units; Coordinating the Work and Activities of Others. **Physical Work Conditions**—Outdoors; Keeping or Regaining Balance; Extremely Bright or Inadequate Lighting; Very Hot or Cold; Making Repetitive Motions. **Other Job Characteristics**—Importance of Being Exact or Accurate; Pace Determined by Speed of Equipment; Consequence of Error.

Experience—Job Zone 4. A minimum of two to four years of work-related skill, knowledge, or experience is needed. **Job Preparation:** SVP 7.0 to less than 8.0—two years to less than 10 years. **Knowledge**—Geography; Administration and Management; Personnel and Human Resources; Physics; Law and Government. **Instructional Programs**—Commercial Fishing; Marine Science/Merchant Marine Officer; Marine Transportation, Other.

Related DOT Jobs—197.133-010 Captain, Fishing Vessel; 197.133-014 Master, Yacht; 197.133-030 Tugboat Captain; 197.161-010 Dredge Captain; 197.163-010 Ferryboat Captain; 197.163-014 Master, Passenger Barge; 197.163-018 Master, Riverboat; 197.167-010 Master, Ship; 911.137-010 Barge Captain; 911.137-014 Derrick-Boat Captain; 911.263-010 Deep Submergence Vehicle Operator; 911.363-010 Ferryboat Operator.

53-5021.02 Mates—Ship, Boat, and Barge

- **Education/Training Required: Work experience in a related occupation**
- **Employed: No data available.**
- **Annual Earnings: $48,680**
- **Growth: 3.4%**
- **Annual Job Openings: 2,000**

Supervise and coordinate activities of crew aboard ships, boats, barges, or dredges.

Supervises crew in repair or replacement of defective vessel, gear, and equipment. Supervises crew in cleaning and maintaining decks, superstructure, and bridge. Observes loading and unloading of cargo and equipment to ensure that handling and storage are according to specifications. Supervises activities of crew engaged in ship's activity, such as barging, towing, dredging, or fishing. Stands watch on vessel during specified periods while vessel is underway. Inspects equipment, such as cargo-handling gear; lifesaving equipment; fishing, towing, or dredging gear; and visual-signaling equipment, for defects. Assumes command of vessel in event ship master becomes incapacitated. Observes water from masthead and advises navigational direction. Determines geographical position of ship, using loran and azimuths of celestial bodies. Steers vessel, utilizing navigation devices such as compass and sexton and navigational aids such as lighthouses and buoys.

GOE INFORMATION—Interest Area: 07. Transportation. **Work Group:** 07.04. Water Vehicle Operation. **Personality Type**—Realistic. Realistic occupations frequently involve work activities that include practical, hands-on problems and solutions. They often deal with plants, animals, and real-world materials like wood, tools, and machinery. Many of the occupations require working outside and do not involve a lot of paperwork or working closely with others. **Work Values**—Authority; Advancement; Pleasant Co-workers; Supervision, Technical; Autonomy. **Skills**—Operation and Control; Repairing; Management of Personnel Resources; Operation Monitoring; Coordination; Systems Analysis; Systems Evaluation; Speaking. **Abilities**—*Cognitive:* Spatial Orientation; Mathematical Reasoning; Oral Comprehension; Deductive Reasoning. *Psychomotor:* Control Precision; Rate Control; Reaction Time; Response Orientation; Multilimb Coordination. *Physical:* Gross Body Equilibrium; Gross Body Coordination. *Sensory:* Far Vision; Glare Sensitivity; Night Vision; Depth Perception; Peripheral Vision. **General Work Activities**—*Information Input:* Getting Information; Monitoring Processes, Materials, or Surroundings; Inspecting Equipment, Structures, or Materials. *Mental Process:* Making Decisions and Solving Problems; Judging Qualities of Things, Services, or Other People's Work; Organizing, Planning, and Prioritizing. *Work Output:* Operating Vehicles or Equipment; Performing General Physical Activities; Handling and Moving Objects. *Interacting with Others:* Guiding, Directing, and Motivating Subordinates; Coordinating the Work and Activities of Others; Establishing and Maintaining Relationships. **Physical Work Conditions**—Outdoors; Climbing Ladders, Scaffolds, Poles, etc.; Very Hot or Cold; Keeping or Regaining Balance; High Places. **Other Job Characteristics**—Importance of Repeating Same Tasks; Pace Determined by Speed of Equipment; Consequence of Error.

Experience—Job Zone 3. Previous work-related skill, knowledge, or experience is required. **Job Preparation:** SVP 6.0 to less than 7.0—more than one year and less than four years. **Knowledge**—Geography; Mechanical; Administration and Management; Public Safety and Security; Physics. **Instructional Programs**—Commercial Fishing; Marine Science/Merchant Marine Officer; Marine Transportation, Other.

Related DOT Jobs—197.133-018 Mate, Fishing Vessel; 197.133-022 Mate, Ship; 197.133-034 Tugboat Mate; 197.137-010 Dredge Mate; 911.133-010 Cadet, Deck.

53-5021.03 Pilots, Ship

- Education/Training Required: **Work experience plus degree**
- Employed: **No data available.**
- Annual Earnings: **$48,680**
- Growth: **3.4%**
- Annual Job Openings: **2,000**

Command ships to steer them into and out of harbors, estuaries, straits, and sounds and on rivers, lakes, and bays. Must be licensed by U.S. Coast Guard with limitations indicating class and tonnage of vessels for which license is valid and route and waters that may be piloted.

Directs course and speed of ship on basis of specialized knowledge of local winds, weather, tides, and current. Orders worker at helm to steer ship. Navigates ship to avoid reefs, outlying shoals, and other hazards, utilizing aids to navigation such as lighthouses and buoys. Signals tugboat captain to berth and unberth ship.

GOE INFORMATION—**Interest Area:** 07. Transportation. **Work Group:** 07.04. Water Vehicle Operation. **Personality Type**—Realistic. Realistic occupations frequently involve work activities that include practical, hands-on problems and solutions. They often deal with plants, animals, and real-world materials like wood, tools, and machinery. Many of the occupations require working outside and do not involve a lot of paperwork or working closely with others. **Work Values**—Authority; Responsibility; Autonomy; Social Status; Recognition. **Skills**—Operation and Control; Operation Monitoring; Systems Analysis; Judgment and Decision Making; Systems Evaluation; Management of Personnel Resources; Monitoring; Complex Problem Solving. **Abilities**—*Cognitive:* Spatial Orientation; Time Sharing; Flexibility of Closure; Memorization; Selective Attention. *Psychomotor:* Rate Control; Reaction Time; Response Orientation; Control Precision; Speed of Limb Movement. *Physical:* Gross Body Equilibrium; Stamina; Dynamic Flexibility; Trunk Strength. *Sensory:* Far Vision; Night Vision; Glare Sensitivity; Depth Perception; Peripheral Vision. **General Work Activities**—*Information Input:* Monitoring Processes, Materials, or Surroundings; Getting Information; Identifying Objects, Actions, and Events. *Mental Process:* Analyzing Data or Information; Making Decisions and Solving Problems; Updating and Using Relevant Knowledge. *Work Output:* Operating Vehicles or Equipment; Performing General Physical Activities; Controlling Machines and Processes. *Interacting with Others:* Communicating with Other Workers; Communicating with Persons Outside Organization; Establishing and

Maintaining Relationships. **Physical Work Conditions**—Keeping or Regaining Balance; Very Hot or Cold; Outdoors; Climbing Ladders, Scaffolds, Poles, etc.; High Places. **Other Job Characteristics**—Consequence of Error; Pace Determined by Speed of Equipment; Degree of Automation.

Experience—Job Zone 5. Extensive skill, knowledge, and experience are needed for these occupations. **Job Preparation:** SVP 8.0 and above—four years to more than 10 years. **Knowledge**—Geography; Law and Government; Physics; Public Safety and Security; Engineering and Technology. **Instructional Programs**—Commercial Fishing; Marine Science/Merchant Marine Officer; Marine Transportation, Other.

Related DOT Jobs—197.133-026 Pilot, Ship.

53-5022.00 Motorboat Operators

- Education/Training Required: **Moderate-term on-the-job training**
- Employed: **No data available.**
- Annual Earnings: **$29,750**
- Growth: **3.4%**
- Annual Job Openings: **2,000**

Operate small motor-driven boats to carry passengers and freight between ships or from ship to shore. May patrol harbors and beach areas. May assist in navigational activities.

Follow safety procedures in order to ensure the protection of passengers, cargo, and vessels. Issue directions for loading, unloading, and seating in boats. Maintain desired courses, using compasses or electronic navigational aids. Operate engine throttles and steering mechanisms in order to guide boats on desired courses. Oversee operation of vessels used for carrying passengers, motor vehicles, or goods across rivers, harbors, lakes, and coastal waters. Secure boats to docks with mooring lines and cast off lines to enable departure. Arrange repairs, fuel, and supplies for vessels. Clean boats and repair hulls and superstructures, using hand tools, paint, and brushes. Direct safety operations in emergency situations. Maintain equipment such as range markers, fire extinguishers, boat fenders, lines, pumps, and fittings. Organize and direct the activities of crew members. Report any observed navigational hazards to authorities. Service motors by performing tasks such as changing oil and lubricating parts. Tow, push, or guide other boats, barges, logs, or rafts. Perform general labor duties such as repairing booms. Position booms around docked ships. Take depth soundings in turning basins.

GOE INFORMATION—**Interest Area:** 07. Transportation. **Work Group:** 07.04. Water Vehicle Operation. **Personality Type**—Realistic. Realistic occupations frequently involve work activities that include practical, hands-on problems and solutions. They often deal with plants, animals, and real-world materials like wood, tools, and machinery. Many of the occupations require working outside and do not involve a lot of paperwork or working closely with others. **Work Values**—Autonomy; Independence; Recognition; Authority; Responsibility. **Skills**—Repairing; Operation and Control; Operation Monitoring; Troubleshooting. **Abilities**—*Cognitive:* Spatial Orientation; Perceptual Speed; Visualization; Time Sharing; Selective Attention. *Psychomotor:* Reaction Time; Rate Control; Response Orientation; Control Precision; Speed of Limb Movement. *Physical:* Extent Flexibility; Static Strength; Gross Body Equilibrium; Explosive Strength; Dynamic Flexibility. *Sensory:* Night Vision; Sound Localization; Peripheral Vision; Far Vision; Glare Sensitivity. **General Work Activities**—*Information Input:* Monitoring Processes, Materials, or Surroundings; Inspecting Equipment, Structures, or Materials; Getting Information. *Mental Process:* Updating and Using Relevant Knowledge; Organizing, Planning, and Prioritizing; Making Decisions and Solving

Problems. *Work Output:* Repairing and Maintaining Mechanical Equipment; Operating Vehicles or Equipment; Performing General Physical Activities. *Interacting with Others:* Performing for or Working with the Public; Communicating with Persons Outside Organization; Establishing and Maintaining Relationships. **Physical Work Conditions**—Outdoors; Keeping or Regaining Balance; Common Protective or Safety Attire; Hazardous Equipment; Minor Burns, Cuts, Bites, or Stings. **Other Job Characteristics**—Consequence of Error; Pace Determined by Speed of Equipment; Degree of Automation.

Experience—Job Zone 2. Some previous work-related skill, knowledge, or experience may be helpful, but usually is not needed. **Job Preparation:** SVP 4.0 to less than 6.0—six months to less than two years. **Knowledge**—Mechanical; Geography; Customer and Personal Service; Public Safety and Security; Building and Construction. **Instructional Programs**—Marine Transportation, Other.

Related DOT Jobs—911.663-010 Motorboat Operator; 919.683-010 Dock Hand.

53-5031.00 Ship Engineers

- **Education/Training Required: Postsecondary vocational training**
- **Employed: 8,576**
- **Annual Earnings: $50,010**
- **Growth: 5.8%**
- **Annual Job Openings: 1,000**

Supervise and coordinate activities of crew engaged in operating and maintaining engines, boilers, deck machinery, and electrical, sanitary, and refrigeration equipment aboard ship.

Orders crew to repair or replace defective parts of engines and other equipment. Inspects engines and other equipment. Stands engine-room watch, observing that lubricants and water levels are maintained in machinery and load on generators is within limits. Starts engines to propel ship and regulates engines and power transmission to control speed of ship. Maintains engineering log and bellbook (orders of changes in speed and direction of ship). Repairs machinery, using hand tools and power tools.

GOE INFORMATION—Interest Area: 08. Industrial Production. **Work Group:** 08.06. Systems Operation. **Personality Type**—Realistic. Realistic occupations frequently involve work activities that include practical, hands-on problems and solutions. They often deal with plants, animals, and real-world materials like wood, tools, and machinery. Many of the occupations require working outside and do not involve a lot of paperwork or working closely with others. **Work Values**—Authority; Responsibility; Compensation; Autonomy; Social Status. **Skills**—Operation and Control; Operation Monitoring; Repairing; Management of Personnel Resources; Troubleshooting; Coordination; Systems Evaluation; Quality Control Analysis. **Abilities**—*Cognitive:* Oral Expression; Deductive Reasoning; Problem Sensitivity; Spatial Orientation; Written Comprehension. *Psychomotor:* Control Precision; Multilimb Coordination; Reaction Time. *Physical:* Explosive Strength; Gross Body Coordination; Gross Body Equilibrium; Extent Flexibility; Trunk Strength. *Sensory:* Glare Sensitivity; Auditory Attention; Night Vision; Hearing Sensitivity; Sound Localization. **General Work Activities**—*Information Input:* Inspecting Equipment, Structures, or Materials; Monitoring Processes, Materials, or Surroundings; Identifying Objects, Actions, and Events. *Mental Process:* Analyzing Data or Information; Making Decisions and Solving Problems; Updating and Using Relevant Knowledge. *Work Output:* Repairing and Maintaining Mechanical Equipment; Controlling Machines and Processes; Performing General Physical Activities. *Interacting with Others:*

Coordinating the Work and Activities of Others; Communicating with Other Workers; Guiding, Directing, and Motivating Subordinates. **Physical Work Conditions**—Cramped Work Space or Awkward Positions; Climbing Ladders, Scaffolds, Poles, etc.; Very Hot or Cold; Kneeling, Crouching, or Crawling; Keeping or Regaining Balance. **Other Job Characteristics**—Consequence of Error; Pace Determined by Speed of Equipment; Degree of Automation.

Experience—Job Zone 5. Extensive skill, knowledge, and experience are needed for these occupations. **Job Preparation:** SVP 8.0 and above—four years to more than 10 years. **Knowledge**—Mechanical; Engineering and Technology; Public Safety and Security; Telecommunications; Physics. **Instructional Programs**—No data available.

Related DOT Jobs—197.130-010 Engineer.

53-6000 Other Transportation Workers

53-6011.00 Bridge and Lock Tenders

- **Education/Training Required: Short-term on-the-job training**
- **Employed: 4,482**
- **Annual Earnings: $33,390**
- **Growth: –19.1%**
- **Annual Job Openings: Fewer than 500**

Operate and tend bridges, canal locks, and lighthouses to permit marine passage on inland waterways, near shores, and at danger points in waterway passages. May supervise such operations. Includes drawbridge operators, lock tenders and operators, and slip bridge operators.

Controls machinery to open and close canal locks and dams, railroad or highway drawbridges, or horizontally or vertically adjustable bridges. Moves levers to activate traffic signals, navigation lights, and alarms. Operates gas, steam, and hydroelectric generating units to control mechanisms to open locks or bridge. Observes approaching vessels to determine size and speed and listens for whistle signal indicating desire to pass. Signals vessels to proceed. Observes positions of vessels to ensure optimum utilization of lock space or bridge opening space. Attaches rope or cable lines to bitt on lock deck or wharf to secure vessel. Relays messages to vessels in waterway. Inspects bridge and bridge or canal auxiliary equipment. Logs data, such as water levels and weather conditions. Prepares accident reports. Cleans, oils, greases, and makes minor repairs and adjustments to equipment. Records names, type, and destinations of vessels passing through bridge opening or locks and number of trains or vehicles crossing bridge. Writes and submits maintenance work requisitions. Turns valves to increase or decrease water level in lock.

GOE INFORMATION—Interest Area: 05. Mechanics, Installers, and Repairers. **Work Group:** 05.03. Mechanical Work. **Personality Type**—Realistic. Realistic occupations frequently involve work activities that include practical, hands-on problems and solutions. They often deal with plants, animals, and real-world materials like wood, tools, and machinery. Many of the occupations require working outside and do not involve a lot of paperwork or working closely with others. **Work Values**—Independence; Supervision, Human Relations; Moral Values; Security; Autonomy. **Skills**—Repairing; Installation; Operation and Control; Operation Monitoring; Troubleshooting. **Abilities**—*Cognitive:* Spatial Orientation; Flexibility of Closure; Selective Attention; Visualization; Time Sharing. *Psychomotor:* Reaction Time; Rate Control; Control Precision; Response

Orientation; Speed of Limb Movement. *Physical:* Extent Flexibility; Static Strength; Explosive Strength; Gross Body Coordination; Gross Body Equilibrium. *Sensory:* Far Vision; Night Vision; Depth Perception; Glare Sensitivity; Hearing Sensitivity. **General Work Activities—***Information Input:* Monitoring Processes, Materials, or Surroundings; Inspecting Equipment, Structures, or Materials; Identifying Objects, Actions, and Events. *Mental Process:* Processing Information; Evaluating Information Against Standards; Analyzing Data or Information. *Work Output:* Handling and Moving Objects; Controlling Machines and Processes; Repairing and Maintaining Mechanical Equipment. *Interacting with Others:* Communicating with Persons Outside Organization; Communicating with Other Workers; Assisting and Caring for Others. **Physical Work Conditions—**Hazardous Equipment; Outdoors; Extremely Bright or Inadequate Lighting; Very Hot or Cold; High Places. **Other Job Characteristics—**Consequence of Error; Degree of Automation; Pace Determined by Speed of Equipment.

Experience—Job Zone 2. Some previous work-related skill, knowledge, or experience may be helpful, but usually is not needed. **Job Preparation:** SVP 4.0 to less than 6.0—six months to less than two years. **Knowledge—**Mechanical; Engineering and Technology; Public Safety and Security; Clerical; Building and Construction. **Instructional Programs—**No data available.

Related DOT Jobs—371.362-010 Drawbridge Operator; 911.131-014 Lock Tender, Chief Operator; 911.362-010 Lock Operator; 919.682-010 Bridge Operator, Slip.

53-6021.00 Parking Lot Attendants

- **Education/Training Required: Short-term on-the-job training**
- **Employed: 116,639**
- **Annual Earnings: $15,690**
- **Growth: 19.8%**
- **Annual Job Openings: 17,000**

Park automobiles or issue tickets for customers in a parking lot or garage. May collect fee.

Calculate parking charges and collect fees from customers. Direct motorists to parking areas or parking spaces, using hand signals or flashlights as necessary. Issue ticket stubs or place numbered tags on windshields and give customers matching tags for locating parked vehicles. Lift, position, and remove barricades in order to open or close parking areas. Park and retrieve automobiles for customers in parking lots, storage garages, or new car lots. Take numbered tags from customers, locate vehicles, and deliver vehicles or provide customers with instructions for locating vehicles. Escort customers to their vehicles in order to ensure their safety. Greet customers and open their car doors. Inspect vehicles in order to detect any damage. Keep parking areas clean and orderly to ensure that space usage is maximized. Patrol parking areas in order to prevent vehicle damage and vehicle or property thefts. Perform maintenance on cars in storage in order to protect tires, batteries, and exteriors from deterioration. Review motorists' identification before allowing them to enter parking facilities. Service vehicles with gas, oil, and water.

GOE INFORMATION—Interest Area: 07. Transportation. **Work Group:** 07.07. Other Services Requiring Driving. **Personality Type—**Realistic. Realistic occupations frequently involve work activities that include practical, hands-on problems and solutions. They often deal with plants, animals, and real-world materials like wood, tools, and machinery. Many of the occupations require working outside and do not involve a lot of paperwork or working closely with others. **Work Values—**Social Service; Independence; Moral Values. **Skills—**None met the criteria. **Abilities—***Cognitive:* Spatial Orientation. *Psychomotor:* Control Precision. *Physical:*

None met the criteria. *Sensory:* None met the criteria. **General Work Activities—***Information Input:* Monitoring Processes, Materials, or Surroundings; Identifying Objects, Actions, and Events; Inspecting Equipment, Structures, or Materials. *Mental Process:* Judging Qualities of Things, Services, or Other People's Work; Processing Information; Organizing, Planning, and Prioritizing. *Work Output:* Performing General Physical Activities; Handling and Moving Objects; Documenting or Recording Information. *Interacting with Others:* Performing for or Working with the Public; Communicating with Persons Outside Organization; Resolving Conflict and Negotiating with Others. **Physical Work Conditions—**Outdoors; Walking or Running; Very Hot or Cold; Extremely Bright or Inadequate Lighting; Standing. **Other Job Characteristics—**Importance of Repeating Same Tasks; Consequence of Error; Importance of Being Exact or Accurate.

Experience—Job Zone 1. No previous work-related skill, knowledge, or experience is needed. **Job Preparation:** SVP below 4.0—less than six months. **Knowledge—**Customer and Personal Service; Public Safety and Security; Clerical. **Instructional Programs—**No data available.

Related DOT Jobs—915.473-010 Parking-Lot Attendant; 915.583-010 Lot Attendant; 915.667-014 Parking Lot Signaler.

53-6031.00 Service Station Attendants

- **Education/Training Required: Short-term on-the-job training**
- **Employed: 112,355**
- **Annual Earnings: $16,110**
- **Growth: −1.7%**
- **Annual Job Openings: 45,000**

Service automobiles, buses, trucks, boats, and other automotive or marine vehicles with fuel, lubricants, and accessories. Collect payment for services and supplies. May lubricate vehicle, change motor oil, install antifreeze, or replace lights or other accessories, such as windshield wiper blades or fan belts. May repair or replace tires.

Check air pressure in vehicle tires and levels of fuel, motor oil, transmission, radiator, battery, and other fluids and add air, oil, water, or other fluids as required. Clean parking areas, offices, restrooms, and equipment and remove trash. Clean windshields and/or wash and wax vehicles. Collect cash payments from customers and make change or charge purchases to customers' credit cards and provide customers with receipts. Activate fuel pumps and fill fuel tanks of vehicles with gasoline or diesel fuel to specified levels. Order stock and price and shelve incoming goods. Prepare daily reports of fuel, oil, and accessory sales. Sell and install accessories, such as batteries, windshield wiper blades, fan belts, bulbs, and headlamps. Sell prepared food, groceries, and related items. Grease and lubricate vehicles or specified units, such as springs, universal joints, and steering knuckles, using grease guns or spray lubricants. Maintain customer records and follow up periodically with telephone, mail, or personal reminders of service due. Operate car washes. Perform minor repairs such as adjusting brakes, replacing spark plugs, and changing engine oil and filters. Provide customers with information about local roads and highways. Rotate, test, and repair or replace tires. Test and charge batteries.

GOE INFORMATION—Interest Area: 10. Sales and Marketing. **Work Group:** 10.03. General Sales. **Personality Type—**Realistic. Realistic occupations frequently involve work activities that include practical, hands-on problems and solutions. They often deal with plants, animals, and real-world materials like wood, tools, and machinery. Many of the occupations require working outside and do not involve a lot of paperwork or working closely with others. **Work Values—**Social Service; Pleasant Co-workers. **Skills**—Repairing; Installation. **Abilities**—*Cognitive:* Time Sharing. *Psychomotor:* Rate Control; Reaction Time; Multilimb Coordination; Response Orientation; Wrist-Finger Speed. *Physical:* Extent Flexibility; Static Strength; Dynamic Strength; Trunk Strength; Explosive Strength. *Sensory:* Hearing Sensitivity; Sound Localization; Auditory Attention; Glare Sensitivity. **General Work Activities**—*Information Input:* Getting Information; Monitoring Processes, Materials, or Surroundings; Inspecting Equipment, Structures, or Materials. *Mental Process:* Updating and Using Relevant Knowledge; Organizing, Planning, and Prioritizing; Analyzing Data or Information. *Work Output:* Handling and Moving Objects; Performing General Physical Activities; Repairing and Maintaining Mechanical Equipment. *Interacting with Others:* Communicating with Persons Outside Organization; Performing for or Working with the Public; Establishing and Maintaining Relationships. **Physical Work Conditions**—Contaminants; Hazardous Conditions; Outdoors; Kneeling, Crouching, or Crawling; Cramped Work Space or Awkward Positions. **Other Job Characteristics**—Pace Determined by Speed of Equipment; Consequence of Error; Degree of Automation.

Experience—Job Zone 1. No previous work-related skill, knowledge, or experience is needed. **Job Preparation:** SVP below 4.0—less than six months. **Knowledge**—Sales and Marketing; Customer and Personal Service; Physics; Chemistry; Mechanical. **Instructional Programs**—No data available.

Related DOT Jobs—915.467-010 Automobile-Service-Station Attendant; 915.477-010 Automobile-Self-Serve-Service-Station Attendant; 915.587-010 Gas-and-Oil Servicer; 915.687-014 Garage Servicer, Industrial; 915.687-018 Lubrication Servicer; 915.687-030 Taxi Servicer.

53-6041.00 Traffic Technicians

- **Education/Training Required: Short-term on-the-job training**
- **Employed: 4,434**
- **Annual Earnings: $31,440**
- **Growth: 14.1%**
- **Annual Job Openings: 1,000**

Conduct field studies to determine traffic volume, speed, effectiveness of signals, adequacy of lighting, and other factors influencing traffic conditions under direction of traffic engineer.

Analyze data related to traffic flow, accident rate data, and proposed development in order to determine the most efficient methods to expedite traffic flow. Compute time settings for traffic signals and speed restrictions, using standard formulas. Gather and compile data from hand count sheets, machine count tapes, and radar speed checks and code data for computer input. Interview motorists about specific intersections or highways in order to secure information regarding roadway conditions for use in planning. Lay out pavement markings for striping crews. Maintain and make minor adjustments and field repairs to equipment used in surveys, including the replacement of parts on traffic data-gathering devices. Measure and record the speed of vehicular traffic, using electrical timing devices or radar equipment. Operate counters and record data in order to assess the volume, type, and movement of vehicular and pedestrian traffic at specified times. Place and secure automatic counters, using power tools, and retrieve counters after counting periods end. Study factors affecting traffic conditions, such as lighting and sign and marking visibility, in order to assess their effectiveness. Study traffic delays by noting times of delays, the numbers of vehicles affected, and vehicle speed through the delay area. Time stoplights or other delays, using stopwatches. Develop plans and long-range strategies for providing adequate parking space. Establish procedures for street closures and for repair or construction projects. Interact with the public in order to answer traffic-related questions, respond to complaints and requests, or discuss

traffic control ordinances, plans, policies, and procedures. Monitor street and utility projects for compliance to traffic control permit conditions. Plan, design, and improve components of traffic control systems in order to accommodate current and projected traffic and to increase usability and efficiency. Prepare drawings of proposed signal installations or other control devices, using drafting instruments or computer-automated drafting equipment. Prepare graphs, charts, diagrams, and other aids in order to illustrate observations and conclusions. Prepare work orders for repair, maintenance, and changes in traffic systems. Provide technical supervision regarding traffic control devices to other traffic technicians and laborers. Review traffic control/barricade plans in order to issue permits for parades and other special events and for construction work that affects rights-of-way, providing assistance with plan preparation or revision as necessary. Visit development and work sites in order to determine projects' effect on traffic and the adequacy of plans to control traffic and maintain safety and to suggest traffic control measures.

GOE INFORMATION—**Interest Area:** 07. Transportation. **Work Group:** 07.02. Vehicle Expediting and Coordinating. **Personality Type**—Realistic. Realistic occupations frequently involve work activities that include practical, hands-on problems and solutions. They often deal with plants, animals, and real-world materials like wood, tools, and machinery. Many of the occupations require working outside and do not involve a lot of paperwork or working closely with others. **Work Values**—Independence; Variety; Supervision, Human Relations; Supervision, Technical; Company Policies and Practices. **Skills**—Mathematics; Complex Problem Solving; Critical Thinking; Systems Analysis; Writing; Equipment Selection; Operations Analysis; Systems Evaluation. **Abilities**—*Cognitive:* Number Facility; Fluency of Ideas; Inductive Reasoning; Flexibility of Closure; Mathematical Reasoning. *Psychomotor:* Reaction Time; Finger Dexterity; Rate Control; Response Orientation; Multilimb Coordination. *Physical:* Gross Body Coordination; Dynamic Flexibility; Gross Body Equilibrium. *Sensory:* Glare Sensitivity; Night Vision; Far Vision; Peripheral Vision; Depth Perception. **General Work Activities**—*Information Input:* Getting Information; Monitoring Processes, Materials, or Surroundings; Identifying Objects, Actions, and Events. *Mental Process:* Processing Information; Analyzing Data or Information; Making Decisions and Solving Problems. *Work Output:* Drafting and Specifying Technical Devices; Documenting or Recording Information; Handling and Moving Objects. *Interacting with Others:* Communicating with Other Workers; Communicating with Persons Outside Organization; Providing Consultation and Advice to Others. **Physical Work Conditions**—Very Hot or Cold; Outdoors; Extremely Bright or Inadequate Lighting; Distracting Sounds and Noise Levels; Contaminants. **Other Job Characteristics**—Importance of Being Exact or Accurate; Importance of Repeating Same Tasks; Degree of Automation.

Experience—Job Zone 4. A minimum of two to four years of work-related skill, knowledge, or experience is needed. **Job Preparation:** SVP 7.0 to less than 8.0—two years to less than 10 years. **Knowledge**—Design; Mathematics; Engineering and Technology; Public Safety and Security; Geography. **Instructional Programs**—Traffic, Customs, and Transportation Clerk/Technician.

Related DOT Jobs—199.267-030 Traffic Technician.

53-6051.00 Transportation Inspectors

- **Education/Training Required: Work experience in a related occupation**
- **Employed: 25,358**
- **Annual Earnings: $47,330**
- **Growth: 11.3%**
- **Annual Job Openings: 3,000**

Inspect equipment or goods in connection with the safe transport of cargo or people. Includes rail transport inspectors, such as freight inspectors, car inspectors, rail inspectors, and other nonprecision inspectors of other types of transportation vehicles.

No task data available.

GOE INFORMATION—Interest Area: 07. Transportation. **Work Group:** 07.08. Support Work. **Note:** The Department of Labor has not collected some data for this job, so it has fewer details than the other descriptions.

Instructional Programs—No data available.

Related DOT Jobs—168.167-082 Transportation Inspector; 168.264-010 Inspector, Air-Carrier; 168.267-058 Inspector, Motor Vehicles; 168.267-094 Marine-Cargo Surveyor; 168.287-018 Inspector, Railroad; 169.284-010 Admeasurer; 184.163-010 Traffic Inspector; 196.163-014 Supervising Airplane Pilot; 379.364-010 Automobile Tester; 910.263-010 Rail-Flaw-Detector Operator; 910.367-030 Way Inspector; 910.384-010 Tank-Car Inspector; 910.387-010 Perishable-Fruit Inspector; 910.387-014 Railroad-Car Inspector; 910.667-010 Car Inspector; 910.667-018 Loading Inspector; 910.667-022 Perishable-Freight Inspector; 919.363-010 New-Car Inspector; 919.687-018 Safety Inspector, Truck.

53-6051.01 Aviation Inspectors

- **Education/Training Required: Work experience in a related occupation**
- **Employed: No data available.**
- **Annual Earnings: $47,330**
- **Growth: 11.3%**
- **Annual Job Openings: 3,000**

Inspect aircraft, maintenance procedures, air navigational aids, air traffic controls, and communications equipment to ensure conformance with federal safety regulations.

Inspects aircraft and components to identify damage or defects and to determine structural and mechanical airworthiness, using hand tools and test instruments. Examines maintenance record and flight log to determine if service and maintenance checks and overhauls were performed at prescribed intervals. Examines access plates and doors for security. Starts aircraft and observes gauges, meters, and other instruments to detect evidence of malfunction. Conducts flight test program to test equipment, instruments, and systems under various conditions, including adverse weather, using both manual and automatic controls. Recommends purchase, repair, or modification of equipment. Schedules and coordinates in-flight testing program with ground crews and air traffic control to assure ground tracking, equipment monitoring, and related services. Prepares reports to document flight activities and inspection findings. Approves or disapproves issuance of certificate of airworthiness. Investigates air accidents to determine cause. Analyzes training program and conducts examinations to assure competency of persons operating, installing, and repairing equipment.

GOE INFORMATION—Interest Area: 04. Law, Law Enforcement, and Public Safety. **Work Group:** 04.04. Public Safety. **Personality Type—** Realistic. Realistic occupations frequently involve work activities that include practical, hands-on problems and solutions. They often deal with plants, animals, and real-world materials like wood, tools, and machinery. Many of the occupations require working outside and do not involve a lot of paperwork or working closely with others. **Work Values—**Responsibility; Supervision, Technical; Supervision, Human Relations; Authority; Compensation. **Skills—**Operation Monitoring; Quality Control Analysis; Systems Analysis; Science; Systems Evaluation; Writing; Opera-

tion and Control; Equipment Selection. **Abilities—***Cognitive:* Problem Sensitivity; Written Expression; Inductive Reasoning; Flexibility of Closure; Written Comprehension. *Psychomotor:* Response Orientation; Rate Control; Control Precision; Reaction Time; Manual Dexterity. *Physical:* Gross Body Equilibrium; Gross Body Coordination; Extent Flexibility; Stamina; Trunk Strength. *Sensory:* Far Vision; Peripheral Vision; Hearing Sensitivity; Sound Localization; Glare Sensitivity. **General Work Activities—***Information Input:* Inspecting Equipment, Structures, or Materials; Monitoring Processes, Materials, or Surroundings; Getting Information. *Mental Process:* Updating and Using Relevant Knowledge; Evaluating Information Against Standards; Analyzing Data or Information. *Work Output:* Documenting or Recording Information; Drafting and Specifying Technical Devices; Handling and Moving Objects. *Interacting with Others:* Communicating with Other Workers; Providing Consultation and Advice to Others; Coordinating the Work and Activities of Others. **Physical Work Conditions—**Distracting Sounds and Noise Levels; Outdoors; Climbing Ladders, Scaffolds, Poles, etc.; Hazardous Equipment; High Places. **Other Job Characteristics—**Importance of Being Exact or Accurate; Consequence of Error; Degree of Automation.

Experience—Job Zone 4. A minimum of two to four years of work-related skill, knowledge, or experience is needed. **Job Preparation:** SVP 7.0 to less than 8.0—two years to less than 10 years. **Knowledge—**Public Safety and Security; Engineering and Technology; Mechanical; Education and Training; Law and Government. **Instructional Programs—**No data available.

Related DOT Jobs—168.264-010 Inspector, Air-Carrier; 196.163-014 Supervising Airplane Pilot.

53-6051.02 Public Transportation Inspectors

- **Education/Training Required: Work experience in a related occupation**
- **Employed: No data available.**
- **Annual Earnings: $47,330**
- **Growth: 11.3%**
- **Annual Job Openings: 3,000**

Monitor operation of public transportation systems to ensure good service and compliance with regulations. Investigate accidents, equipment failures, and complaints.

Observes employees performing assigned duties to note their deportment, treatment of passengers, and adherence to company regulations and schedules. Observes and records time required to load and unload passengers or freight volume of traffic on vehicle and at stops. Investigates schedule delays, accidents, and complaints. Inspects company vehicles and other property for evidence of abuse, damage, and mechanical malfunction and directs repair. Determines need for changes in service, such as additional vehicles, route changes, and revised schedules to improve service and efficiency. Drives automobile along route to detect conditions hazardous to equipment and passengers and negotiates with local governments to eliminate hazards. Submits written reports to management with recommendations for improving service. Reports disruptions to service. Assists in dispatching equipment when necessary. Recommends promotions and disciplinary actions involving transportation personnel.

GOE INFORMATION—Interest Area: 04. Law, Law Enforcement, and Public Safety. **Work Group:** 04.04. Public Safety. **Personality Type—** Enterprising. Enterprising occupations frequently involve starting up and carrying out projects. These occupations can involve leading people and making many decisions. They sometimes require risk taking and often deal with business. **Work Values**—Authority; Supervision, Human Relations; Supervision, Technical; Responsibility; Company Policies and Practices. **Skills**—Operations Analysis; Writing; Systems Evaluation; Monitoring; Speaking; Management of Personnel Resources. **Abilities**—*Cognitive:* Written Expression; Oral Expression; Fluency of Ideas; Inductive Reasoning; Time Sharing. *Psychomotor:* Response Orientation; Rate Control. *Physical:* None met the criteria. *Sensory:* Far Vision; Hearing Sensitivity; Night Vision. **General Work Activities**—*Information Input:* Getting Information; Identifying Objects, Actions, and Events; Inspecting Equipment, Structures, or Materials. *Mental Process:* Analyzing Data or Information; Making Decisions and Solving Problems; Processing Information. *Work Output:* Documenting or Recording Information; Repairing and Maintaining Mechanical Equipment; Handling and Moving Objects. *Interacting with Others:* Communicating with Other Workers; Establishing and Maintaining Relationships; Performing Administrative Activities. **Physical Work Conditions**—Outdoors; Walking or Running; Sitting; Very Hot or Cold; Extremely Bright or Inadequate Lighting. **Other Job Characteristics**—Consequence of Error; Importance of Being Exact or Accurate; Pace Determined by Speed of Equipment.

Experience—Job Zone 4. A minimum of two to four years of work-related skill, knowledge, or experience is needed. **Job Preparation:** SVP 7.0 to less than 8.0—two years to less than 10 years. **Knowledge**—Personnel and Human Resources; Public Safety and Security; Law and Government; Customer and Personal Service; Administration and Management. **Instructional Programs**—No data available.

Related DOT Jobs—168.167-082 Transportation Inspector; 184.163-010 Traffic Inspector.

53-6051.03 Marine Cargo Inspectors

- **Education/Training Required: Work experience in a related occupation**
- **Employed: No data available.**
- **Annual Earnings: $47,330**
- **Growth: 11.3%**
- **Annual Job Openings: 3,000**

Inspect cargoes of seagoing vessels to certify compliance with health and safety regulations in cargo handling and stowage.

Inspects loaded cargo in holds and cargo handling devices to determine compliance with regulations and need for maintenance. Reads vessel documents to ascertain cargo capabilities according to design and cargo regulations. Calculates gross and net tonnage, hold capacities, volume of stored fuel and water, cargo weight, and ship stability factors, using mathematical formulas. Determines type of license and safety equipment required and computes applicable tolls and wharfage fees. Examines blueprints of ship and takes physical measurements to determine capacity and depth of vessel in water, using measuring instruments. Writes certificates of admeasurement, listing details such as design, length, depth, and breadth of vessel and method of propulsion. Issues certificate of compliance when violations are not detected or recommends remedial procedures to correct deficiencies. Times roll of ship, using stopwatch. Analyzes data, formulates recommendations, and writes reports of findings. Advises crew in techniques of stowing dangerous and heavy cargo according to knowledge of hazardous cargo.

GOE INFORMATION—**Interest Area:** 04. Law, Law Enforcement, and Public Safety. **Work Group:** 04.04. Public Safety. **Personality Type**—Conventional. Conventional occupations frequently involve following set procedures and routines. These occupations can include working with data and details more than with ideas. Usually there is a clear line of

authority to follow. **Work Values**—Responsibility; Autonomy; Independence; Supervision, Technical; Compensation. **Skills**—Mathematics; Writing; Speaking; Quality Control Analysis; Active Listening; Reading Comprehension; Systems Evaluation; Critical Thinking. **Abilities**—*Cognitive:* Number Facility; Mathematical Reasoning; Spatial Orientation; Perceptual Speed; Flexibility of Closure. *Psychomotor:* Multilimb Coordination. *Physical:* Gross Body Equilibrium; Gross Body Coordination; Stamina; Dynamic Flexibility; Extent Flexibility. *Sensory:* Far Vision; Depth Perception; Glare Sensitivity; Near Vision; Peripheral Vision. **General Work Activities**—*Information Input:* Inspecting Equipment, Structures, or Materials; Identifying Objects, Actions, and Events; Getting Information. *Mental Process:* Analyzing Data or Information; Processing Information; Evaluating Information Against Standards. *Work Output:* Documenting or Recording Information; Handling and Moving Objects; Performing General Physical Activities. *Interacting with Others:* Communicating with Other Workers; Interpreting Meaning of Information for Others; Communicating with Persons Outside Organization. **Physical Work Conditions**—Outdoors; Walking or Running; Extremely Bright or Inadequate Lighting; Climbing Ladders, Scaffolds, Poles, etc.; Very Hot or Cold. **Other Job Characteristics**—Importance of Being Exact or Accurate; Consequence of Error; Importance of Repeating Same Tasks.

Experience—Job Zone 5. Extensive skill, knowledge, and experience are needed for these occupations. **Job Preparation:** SVP 8.0 and above—four years to more than 10 years. **Knowledge**—Public Safety and Security; Design; Mathematics; Physics; Law and Government. **Instructional Programs**—No data available.

Related DOT Jobs—168.267-094 Marine-Cargo Surveyor; 169.284-010 Admeasurer.

53-6051.04 Railroad Inspectors

- **Education/Training Required: Work experience in a related occupation**
- **Employed: No data available.**
- **Annual Earnings: $47,330**
- **Growth: 11.3%**
- **Annual Job Openings: 3,000**

Inspect railroad equipment, roadbed, and track to ensure safe transport of people or cargo.

Inspects signals and track wiring to determine continuity of electrical connections. Examines roadbed, switches, fishplates, rails, and ties to detect damage or wear. Examines locomotives and cars to detect damage or structural defects. Inspects and tests completed work. Operates switches to determine working conditions. Tests and synchronizes rail-flaw-detection machine, using circuit tester and hand tools, and reloads machine with paper and ink. Starts machine and signals worker to operate rail-detector car. Prepares reports on repairs made and equipment, rail cars, or roadbed needing repairs. Tags rail cars needing immediate repair. Fills paint container on rail-detector car used to mark section of defective rail with paint. Directs crews to repair or replace defective equipment or to re-ballast roadbed. Places lanterns or flags in front and rear of train to signal that inspection is being performed. Seals leaks found during inspection that can be sealed with caulking compound. Replaces defective brake rod pins and tightens safety appliances. Notifies train dispatcher of rail car to be moved to shop for repair. Makes minor repairs. Packs brake bearings with grease.

GOE INFORMATION—**Interest Area:** 05. Mechanics, Installers, and Repairers. **Work Group:** 05.03. Mechanical Work. **Personality Type**—Realistic. Realistic occupations frequently involve work activities that include practical, hands-on problems and solutions. They often deal with plants, animals, and real-world materials like wood, tools, and machinery. Many of the occupations require working outside and do not involve a lot of paperwork or working closely with others. **Work Values**—Responsibility; Authority; Supervision, Technical; Pleasant Co-workers; Autonomy. **Skills**—Repairing; Operation Monitoring; Troubleshooting; Quality Control Analysis; Operation and Control; Management of Personnel Resources; Systems Analysis; Equipment Selection. **Abilities**—*Cognitive:* Inductive Reasoning; Flexibility of Closure; Speed of Closure; Problem Sensitivity; Written Expression. *Psychomotor:* Response Orientation; Control Precision; Reaction Time; Arm-Hand Steadiness; Multilimb Coordination. *Physical:* Extent Flexibility; Gross Body Coordination; Gross Body Equilibrium; Static Strength; Stamina. *Sensory:* Hearing Sensitivity; Night Vision; Far Vision; Auditory Attention; Glare Sensitivity. **General Work Activities**—*Information Input:* Monitoring Processes, Materials, or Surroundings; Inspecting Equipment, Structures, or Materials; Identifying Objects, Actions, and Events. *Mental Process:* Updating and Using Relevant Knowledge; Evaluating Information Against Standards; Making Decisions and Solving Problems. *Work Output:* Repairing and Maintaining Mechanical Equipment; Performing General Physical Activities; Handling and Moving Objects. *Interacting with Others:* Communicating with Other Workers; Coordinating the Work and Activities of Others; Establishing and Maintaining Relationships. **Physical Work Conditions**—Outdoors; Hazardous Equipment; Keeping or Regaining Balance; Very Hot or Cold; Distracting Sounds and Noise Levels. **Other Job Characteristics**—Consequence of Error; Importance of Being Exact or Accurate; Importance of Repeating Same Tasks.

Experience—Job Zone 2. Some previous work-related skill, knowledge, or experience may be helpful, but usually is not needed. **Job Preparation:** SVP 4.0 to less than 6.0–six months to less than two years. **Knowledge**—Public Safety and Security; Building and Construction; Mechanical; Engineering and Technology; Geography. **Instructional Programs**—No data available.

Related DOT Jobs—168.287-018 Inspector, Railroad; 910.263-010 Rail-Flaw-Detector Operator; 910.367-030 Way Inspector; 910.384-010 Tank-Car Inspector; 910.387-014 Railroad-Car Inspector; 910.667-010 Car Inspector.

53-6051.05 Motor Vehicle Inspectors
- **Education/Training Required:** Work experience in a related occupation
- **Employed:** No data available.
- **Annual Earnings:** $47,330
- **Growth:** 11.3%
- **Annual Job Openings:** 3,000

Inspect automotive vehicles to ensure compliance with governmental regulations and safety standards.

Inspects truck accessories, air lines, and electric circuits and reports needed repairs. Examines vehicles for damage and drives vehicle to detect malfunctions. Tests vehicle components for wear, damage, or improper adjustment, using mechanical or electrical devices. Applies inspection sticker to vehicles that pass inspection and rejection sticker to vehicles that fail. Prepares report on each vehicle for follow-up action by owner or police. Prepares and keeps record of vehicles delivered. Positions trailer and drives car onto truck trailer. Notifies authorities of owners having illegal equipment installed on vehicle. Services vehicles with fuel and water.

GOE INFORMATION—Interest Area: 08. Industrial Production. **Work Group:** 08.02. Production Technology. **Personality Type**—Realistic.

Realistic occupations frequently involve work activities that include practical, hands-on problems and solutions. They often deal with plants, animals, and real-world materials like wood, tools, and machinery. Many of the occupations require working outside and do not involve a lot of paperwork or working closely with others. **Work Values**—Responsibility; Supervision, Technical; Autonomy; Security; Independence. **Skills**—Troubleshooting; Quality Control Analysis; Operation Monitoring; Science. **Abilities**—*Cognitive:* Flexibility of Closure; Speed of Closure; Problem Sensitivity; Time Sharing; Spatial Orientation. *Psychomotor:* Control Precision; Multilimb Coordination; Response Orientation; Rate Control; Manual Dexterity. *Physical:* Extent Flexibility; Gross Body Coordination; Static Strength; Gross Body Equilibrium; Dynamic Flexibility. *Sensory:* Hearing Sensitivity; Sound Localization; Visual Color Discrimination; Auditory Attention; Far Vision. **General Work Activities**—*Information Input:* Identifying Objects, Actions, and Events; Inspecting Equipment, Structures, or Materials; Getting Information. *Mental Process:* Updating and Using Relevant Knowledge; Evaluating Information Against Standards; Judging Qualities of Things, Services, or Other People's Work. *Work Output:* Performing General Physical Activities; Handling and Moving Objects; Repairing and Maintaining Mechanical Equipment. *Interacting with Others:* Communicating with Persons Outside Organization; Performing for or Working with the Public; Communicating with Other Workers. **Physical Work Conditions**—Outdoors; Cramped Work Space or Awkward Positions; Kneeling, Crouching, or Crawling; Keeping or Regaining Balance; Bending or Twisting the Body. **Other Job Characteristics**—Degree of Automation; Importance of Being Exact or Accurate; Consequence of Error.

Experience—Job Zone 2. Some previous work-related skill, knowledge, or experience may be helpful, but usually is not needed. **Job Preparation:** SVP 4.0 to less than 6.0–six months to less than two years. **Knowledge**—Public Safety and Security; Computers and Electronics; Mechanical; Engineering and Technology; Law and Government. **Instructional Programs**—No data available.

Related DOT Jobs—168.267-058 Inspector, Motor Vehicles; 379.364-010 Automobile Tester; 919.363-010 New-Car Inspector; 919.687-018 Safety Inspector, Truck.

53-6051.06 Freight Inspectors
- **Education/Training Required:** Work experience in a related occupation
- **Employed:** No data available.
- **Annual Earnings:** $47,330
- **Growth:** 11.3%
- **Annual Job Openings:** 3,000

Inspect freight for proper storage according to specifications.

Inspects shipment to ascertain that freight is securely braced and blocked. Observes loading of freight to ensure that crews comply with procedures. Monitors temperature and humidity of freight storage area. Records freight condition and handling and notifies crews to reload freight or insert additional bracing or packing. Measures height and width of loads that will pass over bridges or through tunnels. Notifies workers of special treatment required for shipments. Prepares and submits report after trip. Posts warning signs on vehicles containing explosives or inflammatory or radioactive materials.

GOE INFORMATION—Interest Area: 07. Transportation. **Work Group:** 07.08. Support Work. **Personality Type**—Conventional. Conventional occupations frequently involve following set procedures and routines. These occupations can include working with data and details more than with ideas. Usually there is a clear line of authority to follow. **Work Values**—Supervision, Technical; Responsibility; Supervision, Human

Relations; Company Policies and Practices; Security. **Skills**—None met the criteria. **Abilities**—*Cognitive:* Category Flexibility; Spatial Orientation; Oral Expression; Perceptual Speed. *Psychomotor:* None met the criteria. *Physical:* Stamina; Gross Body Coordination; Gross Body Equilibrium; Extent Flexibility; Trunk Strength. *Sensory:* Far Vision; Sound Localization; Night Vision; Speech Recognition; Speech Clarity. **General Work Activities**—*Information Input:* Inspecting Equipment, Structures, or Materials; Getting Information; Identifying Objects, Actions, and Events. *Mental Process:* Evaluating Information Against Standards; Making Decisions and Solving Problems; Processing Information. *Work Output:* Documenting or Recording Information; Performing General Physical Activities; Handling and Moving Objects. *Interacting with Others:* Performing Administrative Activities; Communicating with Other Workers; Coordinating the Work and Activities of Others. **Physical Work Conditions**—Outdoors; Climbing Ladders, Scaffolds, Poles, etc.; High Places; Cramped Work Space or Awkward Positions; Keeping or Regaining Balance. **Other Job Characteristics**—Consequence of Error; Importance of Repeating Same Tasks; Importance of Being Exact or Accurate.

Experience—Job Zone 2. Some previous work-related skill, knowledge, or experience may be helpful, but usually is not needed. **Job Preparation:** SVP 4.0 to less than 6.0—six months to less than two years. **Knowledge**—Public Safety and Security; Production and Processing; Geography; Clerical; Philosophy and Theology. **Instructional Programs**—No data available.

Related DOT Jobs—910.387-010 Perishable-Fruit Inspector; 910.667-018 Loading Inspector; 910.667-022 Perishable-Freight Inspector.

53-6099.99 Transportation Workers, All Other

- **Education/Training Required: No data available.**
- **Employed: No data available.**
- **Annual Earnings: No data available.**
- **Growth: 17.9%**
- **Annual Job Openings: 9,000**

All transportation workers not listed separately.

No task data available.

GOE INFORMATION—**Interest Area:** 07. Transportation. **Work Group:** 07.08. Support Work. **Note:** The Department of Labor has not collected some data for this job, so it has fewer details than the other descriptions.

Instructional Programs—No data available.

Related DOT Jobs—196.223-010 Instructor, Flying I; 196.223-014 Instructor, Pilot; 196.263-022 Check Pilot; 388.663-010 Elevator Operator; 911.664-010 Ferryboat Operator, Cable; 912.663-010 Airport Utility Worker.

53-7000 Material Moving Workers

53-7011.00 Conveyor Operators and Tenders

- **Education/Training Required: Short-term on-the-job training**
- **Employed: 63,006**
- **Annual Earnings: $23,390**
- **Growth: 13.3%**
- **Annual Job Openings: 8,000**

Control or tend conveyors or conveyor systems that move materials or products to and from stockpiles, processing stations, departments, or vehicles. May control speed and routing of materials or products.

Manipulates controls, levers, and valves to start pumps, auxiliary equipment, or conveyors and adjust equipment positions, speed, timing, and material flow. Observes conveyor operations and monitors lights, dials, and gauges to maintain specified operating levels and detect equipment malfunctions. Stops equipment or machinery and clears jams, using poles, bars, and hand tools, or removes damaged materials from conveyors. Reads production and delivery schedules and confers with supervisor to determine processing procedures. Loads, unloads, or adjusts materials or products on conveyors by hand or using lifts and hoists. Inspects equipment and machinery to prevent loss of materials or products during transit. Signals workers in other departments to move materials, products, or machinery or notifies workstations of shipments en route and estimated delivery times. Moves, assembles, and connects hoses or nozzles to material hoppers, storage tanks, conveyor sections or chutes, and pumps. Repairs or replaces equipment components or parts such as blades, rolls, and pumps. Cleans, sterilizes, and maintains equipment, machinery, and workstations, using hand tools, shovels, brooms, chemicals, hoses, and lubricants. Weighs or measures materials and products, using scales or other measuring instruments, to verify specified tonnage and prevent overloads. Collects samples of materials or products for laboratory analysis and ensure conformance to specifications. Affixes identifying information to materials or products, using hand tools. Records production data, such as weight, type, quantity, and storage locations of materials, and documents equipment downtime. Distributes materials, supplies, and equipment to workstations, using lifts and trucks.

GOE INFORMATION—**Interest Area:** 08. Industrial Production. **Work Group:** 08.07. Hands-on Work: Loading, Moving, Hoisting, and Conveying. **Personality Type**—Realistic. Realistic occupations frequently involve work activities that include practical, hands-on problems and solutions. They often deal with plants, animals, and real-world materials like wood, tools, and machinery. Many of the occupations require working outside and do not involve a lot of paperwork or working closely with others. **Work Values**—Supervision, Technical; Supervision, Human Relations; Moral Values; Activity; Company Policies and Practices. **Skills**—Operation Monitoring; Operation and Control; Repairing; Troubleshooting. **Abilities**—*Cognitive:* Perceptual Speed; Selective Attention; Flexibility of Closure. *Psychomotor:* Rate Control; Multilimb Coordination; Response Orientation; Control Precision; Wrist-Finger Speed. *Physical:* Static Strength; Trunk Strength; Dynamic Flexibility; Dynamic Strength; Extent Flexibility. *Sensory:* Near Vision; Depth Perception; Peripheral Vision; Sound Localization. **General Work Activities**—*Information Input:* Monitoring Processes, Materials, or Surroundings; Inspecting Equipment, Structures, or Materials; Getting Information. *Mental Process:* Processing Information; Evaluating Information Against Standards; Making Decisions and Solving Problems. *Work Output:* Handling and Moving Objects; Controlling Machines and Processes; Performing General Physical Activities. *Interacting with Others:* Communicating with Other Workers; Establishing and Maintaining Relationships; Performing Administrative Activities. **Physical Work Conditions**—Contaminants; Making Repetitive Motions; Hazardous Equipment; Using Hands on Objects, Tools, or Controls; Bending or Twisting the Body. **Other Job Characteristics**—Pace Determined by Speed of Equipment; Degree of Automation; Importance of Repeating Same Tasks.

Experience—Job Zone 1. No previous work-related skill, knowledge, or experience is needed. **Job Preparation:** SVP below 4.0—less than six months. **Knowledge**—Production and Processing; Mechanical. **Instructional Programs**—Ground Transportation, Other.

Related DOT Jobs—524.565-010 Trolley Operator; 529.682-030 Silo Operator; 529.685-050 Char-Conveyor Tender; 553.685-078 Milled-Rubber Tender; 575.687-038 Tip-Out Worker; 579.685-050 Silo Tender; 579.685-062 Brick Unloader Tender; 613.685-034 Bed Operator; 669.685-090 Tipple Tender; 921.382-010 Conveyor Operator, Pneumatic System; 921.563-010 Coke Loader; 921.565-010 Cement Loader; 921.662-018 Conveyor-System Operator; 921.662-026 Tipple Operator; 921.682-014 Palletizer Operator I; 921.683-014 Boom-Conveyor Operator; 921.685-014 Bull-Chain Operator; 921.685-022 Chip-Bin Conveyor Tender; 921.685-026 Conveyor Tender; 921.685-030 Cooker Loader; others.

53-7021.00 Crane and Tower Operators

- **Education/Training Required: Moderate-term on-the-job training**
- **Employed: 54,585**
- **Annual Earnings: $34,610**
- **Growth: 8.6%**
- **Annual Job Openings: 5,000**

Operate mechanical boom and cable or tower and cable equipment to lift and move materials, machines, or products in many directions.

Operates cranes, cherry pickers, or other moving equipment to lift and move loads such as machinery or bulk materials. Loads and unloads bundles from trucks and moves containers to storage bins, using moving equipment. Inspects and adjusts crane mechanisms and accessory equipment to prevent malfunctions and wear. Inspects and compares load weights with lifting capacity to ensure against overload. Cleans, lubricates, and maintains mechanisms such as cables, pulleys, and grappling devices. Reviews daily truck-delivery schedule to ascertain orders, sequence of deliveries, and special loading instructions. Directs truck drivers backing vehicles into loading bays and covers, uncovers, and secures loads for delivery. Inspects cables and grappling devices for wear and installs or replaces cables. Directs helpers engaged in placing blocking and outrigging under crane when lifting loads. Weighs bundles, using floor scale, and records weight for company records. Inspects bundle packaging for conformance to customer requirements and removes and batches packaging tickets.

GOE INFORMATION—**Interest Area:** 08. Industrial Production. **Work Group:** 08.07. Hands-on Work: Loading, Moving, Hoisting, and Conveying. **Personality Type**—Realistic. Realistic occupations frequently involve work activities that include practical, hands-on problems and solutions. They often deal with plants, animals, and real-world materials like wood, tools, and machinery. Many of the occupations require working outside and do not involve a lot of paperwork or working closely with others. **Work Values**—Supervision, Technical; Moral Values; Supervision, Human Relations; Authority; Company Policies and Practices. **Skills**—Operation and Control; Repairing; Installation; Operation Monitoring; Equipment Selection. **Abilities**—*Cognitive:* Spatial Orientation; Perceptual Speed; Information Ordering. *Psychomotor:* Multilimb Coordination; Reaction Time; Control Precision; Response Orientation; Speed of Limb Movement. *Physical:* Static Strength; Dynamic Strength; Gross Body Equilibrium; Stamina; Explosive Strength. *Sensory:* Depth Perception; Far Vision; Auditory Attention; Glare Sensitivity; Peripheral Vision. **General Work Activities**—*Information Input:* Inspecting Equipment, Structures, or Materials; Getting Information; Monitoring Processes, Materials, or Surroundings. *Mental Process:* Updating and Using Relevant Knowledge; Evaluating Information Against Standards; Making Decisions and Solving Problems. *Work Output:* Controlling Machines and Processes; Performing General Physical Activities; Handling and Moving Objects. *Interacting with Others:* Communicating with Other Workers; Coordinating the Work and Activities of Others; Establishing

and Maintaining Relationships. **Physical Work Conditions**—Outdoors; Hazardous Equipment; Whole Body Vibration; Climbing Ladders, Scaffolds, Poles, etc.; High Places. **Other Job Characteristics**—Pace Determined by Speed of Equipment; Degree of Automation; Importance of Repeating Same Tasks.

Experience—Job Zone 2. Some previous work-related skill, knowledge, or experience may be helpful, but usually is not needed. **Job Preparation:** SVP 4.0 to less than 6.0—six months to less than two years. **Knowledge**—Mechanical; Building and Construction; Clerical; Physics; Public Safety and Security. **Instructional Programs**—Construction/Heavy Equipment/Earthmoving Equipment Operation; Mobil Crane Operation/Operator.

Related DOT Jobs—519.683-010 Dross Skimmer; 921.663-010 Overhead Crane Operator; 921.663-014 Cherry-Picker Operator; 921.663-022 Derrick Operator; 921.663-038 Locomotive-Crane Operator; 921.663-042 Monorail Crane Operator; 921.663-054 Tower-Crane Operator; 921.663-058 Tractor-Crane Operator; 921.663-062 Truck-Crane Operator; 921.663-070 Truck Loader, Overhead Crane; 921.683-018 Cantilever-Crane Operator; 921.683-034 Derrick-Boat Operator; 921.683-066 Sorting-Grapple Operator; 921.683-074 Tower-Loader Operator.

53-7031.00 Dredge Operators

- **Education/Training Required: Moderate-term on-the-job training**
- **Employed: No data available.**
- **Annual Earnings: $27,590**
- **Growth: No data available.**
- **Annual Job Openings: No data available.**

Operate dredge to remove sand, gravel, or other materials from lakes, rivers, or streams and to excavate and maintain navigable channels in waterways.

Starts and stops engines to operate equipment. Moves levers to position dredge for excavation, engage hydraulic pump, raise and lower suction boom, and control rotation of cutterhead. Starts power winch that draws in or lets out cable to change position of dredge or pulls in and lets out cable manually. Lowers anchor pole to verify depth of excavation, using winch, or scans depth gauge to determine depth of excavation. Directs workers placing shore anchors and cables, laying additional pipes from dredge to shore, and pumping water from pontoons.

GOE INFORMATION—**Interest Area:** 07. Transportation. **Work Group:** 07.04. Water Vehicle Operation. **Personality Type**—Realistic. Realistic occupations frequently involve work activities that include practical, hands-on problems and solutions. They often deal with plants, animals, and real-world materials like wood, tools, and machinery. Many of the occupations require working outside and do not involve a lot of paperwork or working closely with others. **Work Values**—Authority; Supervision, Technical; Moral Values. **Skills**—Operation and Control; Operation Monitoring; Management of Personnel Resources. **Abilities**—*Cognitive:* Spatial Orientation. *Psychomotor:* Multilimb Coordination; Control Precision; Speed of Limb Movement; Rate Control; Reaction Time. *Physical:* Static Strength; Dynamic Strength; Dynamic Flexibility; Extent Flexibility; Stamina. *Sensory:* Depth Perception; Glare Sensitivity; Peripheral Vision; Sound Localization; Far Vision. **General Work Activities**—*Information Input:* Monitoring Processes, Materials, or Surroundings; Getting Information; Identifying Objects, Actions, and Events. *Mental Process:* Making Decisions and Solving Problems; Updating and Using Relevant Knowledge; Evaluating Information Against Standards. *Work Output:* Controlling Machines and Processes; Handling and Moving Objects; Performing General Physical Activities. *Interacting with Others:* Communicating with Other Workers; Coordinating the Work and Activities of Others; Guiding, Directing, and Motivating Subordinates. **Physical Work Conditions**—Outdoors; Hazardous Equipment; Whole Body Vibration; Distracting Sounds and Noise Levels; Using Hands on Objects, Tools, or Controls. **Other Job Characteristics**—Degree of Automation; Pace Determined by Speed of Equipment; Consequence of Error.

Experience—Job Zone 2. Some previous work-related skill, knowledge, or experience may be helpful, but usually is not needed. **Job Preparation:** SVP 4.0 to less than 6.0—six months to less than two years. **Knowledge**—Engineering and Technology; Mechanical; Physics; Geography; Public Safety and Security. **Instructional Programs**—Construction/Heavy Equipment/Earthmoving Equipment Operation.

Related DOT Jobs—850.663-010 Dredge Operator.

53-7032.00 Excavating and Loading Machine and Dragline Operators

- **Education/Training Required: Moderate-term on-the-job training**
- **Employed: 76,455**
- **Annual Earnings: $32,000**
- **Growth: 14.8%**
- **Annual Job Openings: 5,000**

Operate or tend machinery equipped with scoops, shovels, or buckets to excavate and load loose materials.

No task data available.

GOE INFORMATION—**Interest Area:** 08. Industrial Production. **Work Group:** 08.07. Hands-on Work: Loading, Moving, Hoisting, and Conveying. **Note:** The Department of Labor has not collected some data for this job, so it has fewer details than the other descriptions.

Instructional Programs—Construction/Heavy Equipment/Earthmoving Equipment Operation.

Related DOT Jobs—850.663-026 Stripping-Shovel Operator; 850.683-018 Dragline Operator; 850.683-026 Mucking-Machine Operator; 850.683-030 Power-Shovel Operator; 850.683-042 Tower-Excavator Operator; 851.663-010 Septic-Tank Installer; 921.683-022 Coal-Equipment Operator; 930.683-022 Harvester Operator.

53-7032.01 Excavating and Loading Machine Operators

- **Education/Training Required: Moderate-term on-the-job training**
- **Employed: No data available.**
- **Annual Earnings: $32,000**
- **Growth: 14.8%**
- **Annual Job Openings: 5,000**

Operate machinery equipped with scoops, shovels, or buckets to excavate and load loose materials.

Operates power machinery, such as powered shovel, stripping shovel, scraper loader (mucking machine), or backhoe (trench-excavating machine) to excavate and load material. Observes hand signals, grade stakes, and other markings when operating machines. Receives written or oral instructions to move or excavate material. Measures and verifies levels of rock or gravel, base, and other excavated material. Lubricates and repairs machinery and replaces parts, such as gears, bearings, and bucket

teeth. Directs ground workers engaged in activities such as moving stakes or markers.

GOE INFORMATION—**Interest Area:** 06. Construction, Mining, and Drilling. **Work Group:** 06.03. Mining and Drilling. **Personality Type**—Realistic. Realistic occupations frequently involve work activities that include practical, hands-on problems and solutions. They often deal with plants, animals, and real-world materials like wood, tools, and machinery. Many of the occupations require working outside and do not involve a lot of paperwork or working closely with others. **Work Values**—Authority; Supervision, Technical; Compensation; Moral Values; Supervision, Human Relations. **Skills**—Operation and Control; Operation Monitoring; Repairing; Equipment Selection. **Abilities**—*Cognitive:* Spatial Orientation; Oral Comprehension; Written Comprehension; Time Sharing. *Psychomotor:* Multilimb Coordination; Reaction Time; Control Precision; Response Orientation; Rate Control. *Physical:* Dynamic Strength; Static Strength; Gross Body Coordination; Trunk Strength; Stamina. *Sensory:* Depth Perception; Far Vision; Peripheral Vision; Speech Clarity; Speech Recognition. **General Work Activities**—*Information Input:* Getting Information; Inspecting Equipment, Structures, or Materials; Identifying Objects, Actions, and Events. *Mental Process:* Updating and Using Relevant Knowledge; Judging Qualities of Things, Services, or Other People's Work; Evaluating Information Against Standards. *Work Output:* Operating Vehicles or Equipment; Controlling Machines and Processes; Performing General Physical Activities. *Interacting with Others:* Communicating with Other Workers; Coordinating the Work and Activities of Others; Establishing and Maintaining Relationships. **Physical Work Conditions**—Whole Body Vibration; Outdoors; Hazardous Equipment; Distracting Sounds and Noise Levels; Very Hot or Cold. **Other Job Characteristics**—Pace Determined by Speed of Equipment; Degree of Automation; Importance of Repeating Same Tasks.

Experience—Job Zone 2. Some previous work-related skill, knowledge, or experience may be helpful, but usually is not needed. **Job Preparation:** SVP 4.0 to less than 6.0—six months to less than two years. **Knowledge**—Mechanical; Engineering and Technology; Physics; Building and Construction. **Instructional Programs**—Construction/Heavy Equipment/Earthmoving Equipment Operation.

Related DOT Jobs—850.663-026 Stripping-Shovel Operator; 850.683-026 Mucking-Machine Operator; 850.683-030 Power-Shovel Operator; 850.683-042 Tower-Excavator Operator; 851.663-010 Septic-Tank Installer; 921.683-022 Coal-Equipment Operator; 930.683-022 Harvester Operator.

53-7032.02 Dragline Operators

- **Education/Training Required: Moderate-term on-the-job training**
- **Employed: No data available.**
- **Annual Earnings: $32,000**
- **Growth: 14.8%**
- **Annual Job Openings: 5,000**

Operate power-driven crane equipment with dragline bucket to excavate or move sand, gravel, mud, or other materials.

Moves controls to position boom, lower and drag bucket through material, and release material at unloading point. Directs workers engaged in placing blocks and outriggers to prevent capsizing of machine when lifting heavy loads. Drives machine to work site.

GOE INFORMATION—**Interest Area:** 08. Industrial Production. **Work Group:** 08.07. Hands-on Work: Loading, Moving, Hoisting, and Conveying. **Personality Type**—Realistic. Realistic occupations frequently involve work activities that include practical, hands-on problems and solutions. They often deal with plants, animals, and real-world materials like wood, tools, and machinery. Many of the occupations require working outside and do not involve a lot of paperwork or working closely with others. **Work Values**—Authority; Supervision, Technical; Moral Values. **Skills**—Operation and Control. **Abilities**—*Cognitive:* Spatial Orientation. *Psychomotor:* Multilimb Coordination; Control Precision; Rate Control; Reaction Time; Response Orientation. *Physical:* Static Strength; Dynamic Flexibility; Gross Body Coordination; Explosive Strength; Gross Body Equilibrium. *Sensory:* Depth Perception; Far Vision; Peripheral Vision; Glare Sensitivity; Night Vision. **General Work Activities**—*Information Input:* Getting Information; Monitoring Processes, Materials, or Surroundings; Identifying Objects, Actions, and Events. *Mental Process:* Making Decisions and Solving Problems; Organizing, Planning, and Prioritizing; Updating and Using Relevant Knowledge. *Work Output:* Controlling Machines and Processes; Operating Vehicles or Equipment; Performing General Physical Activities. *Interacting with Others:* Communicating with Other Workers; Establishing and Maintaining Relationships; Coordinating the Work and Activities of Others. **Physical Work Conditions**—Outdoors; Whole Body Vibration; Hazardous Equipment; Extremely Bright or Inadequate Lighting; Distracting Sounds and Noise Levels. **Other Job Characteristics**—Degree of Automation; Pace Determined by Speed of Equipment; Consequence of Error.

Experience—Job Zone 2. Some previous work-related skill, knowledge, or experience may be helpful, but usually is not needed. **Job Preparation:** SVP 4.0 to less than 6.0—six months to less than two years. **Knowledge**—Building and Construction; Physics; Public Safety and Security; Mechanical; Engineering and Technology. **Instructional Programs**—Construction/Heavy Equipment/Earthmoving Equipment Operation.

Related DOT Jobs—850.683-018 Dragline Operator.

53-7033.00 Loading Machine Operators, Underground Mining

- **Education/Training Required: Moderate-term on-the-job training**
- **Employed: No data available.**
- **Annual Earnings: $30,320**
- **Growth: No data available.**
- **Annual Job Openings: No data available.**

Operate underground loading machine to load coal, ore, or rock into shuttle or mine car or onto conveyors. Loading equipment may include power shovels, hoisting engines equipped with cable-drawn scraper or scoop, or machines equipped with gathering arms and conveyor.

Operates levers to move conveyor boom or shovel to move mine contents into car or onto conveyor. Advances machine to gather material and convey it into car at rear. Stops gathering arms when car is full. Drives machine into pile of material blasted from working face. Pries off loose material from roof and moves it into path of machine with crowbar. Moves trailing electrical cable clear of obstructions, using rubber safety gloves. Starts conveyor boom and gathering-arm motors.

GOE INFORMATION—**Interest Area:** 06. Construction, Mining, and Drilling. **Work Group:** 06.03. Mining and Drilling. **Personality Type**—Realistic. Realistic occupations frequently involve work activities that include practical, hands-on problems and solutions. They often deal with plants, animals, and real-world materials like wood, tools, and machinery. Many of the occupations require working outside and do not involve a lot of paperwork or working closely with others. **Work Values**—Supervision, Technical; Independence; Supervision, Human Relations; Moral

Values; Advancement. **Skills**—Repairing; Operation and Control; Operation Monitoring. **Abilities**—*Cognitive:* Spatial Orientation. *Psychomotor:* Multilimb Coordination; Control Precision; Reaction Time; Speed of Limb Movement; Rate Control. *Physical:* Static Strength; Gross Body Coordination; Dynamic Flexibility; Gross Body Equilibrium; Stamina. *Sensory:* Night Vision; Depth Perception; Peripheral Vision; Sound Localization; Auditory Attention. **General Work Activities**—*Information Input:* Inspecting Equipment, Structures, or Materials; Monitoring Processes, Materials, or Surroundings; Identifying Objects, Actions, and Events. *Mental Process:* Judging Qualities of Things, Services, or Other People's Work; Organizing, Planning, and Prioritizing; Updating and Using Relevant Knowledge. *Work Output:* Handling and Moving Objects; Operating Vehicles or Equipment; Performing General Physical Activities. *Interacting with Others:* Establishing and Maintaining Relationships; Communicating with Other Workers; Monitoring and Controlling Resources. **Physical Work Conditions**—Outdoors; Whole Body Vibration; Hazardous Equipment; Common Protective or Safety Attire; Extremely Bright or Inadequate Lighting. **Other Job Characteristics**—Degree of Automation; Pace Determined by Speed of Equipment; Consequence of Error.

Experience—Job Zone 2. Some previous work-related skill, knowledge, or experience may be helpful, but usually is not needed. **Job Preparation:** SVP 4.0 to less than 6.0—six months to less than two years. **Knowledge**—Mechanical; Engineering and Technology; Public Safety and Security; Physics; Production and Processing. **Instructional Programs**—Ground Transportation, Other.

Related DOT Jobs—932.683-014 Loading-Machine Operator; 932.683-018 Mechanical-Shovel Operator.

53-7041.00 Hoist and Winch Operators

- **Education/Training Required: Moderate-term on-the-job training**
- **Employed: 8,892**
- **Annual Earnings: $32,370**
- **Growth: 8.3%**
- **Annual Job Openings: 1,000**

Operate or tend hoists or winches to lift and pull loads, using power-operated cable equipment.

Apply hand or foot brakes and move levers to lock hoists or winches. Attach, fasten, and disconnect cables or lines to loads, materials, and equipment, using hand tools. Move levers, pedals, and throttles in order to stop, start, and regulate speeds of hoist or winch drums in response to hand, bell, buzzer, telephone, loudspeaker, or whistle signals or by observing dial indicators or cable marks. Move or reposition hoists, winches, loads, and materials manually or using equipment and machines such as trucks, cars, and handtrucks. Observe equipment gauges and indicators and hand signals of other workers in order to verify load positions and/or depths. Operate compressed air, diesel, electric, gasoline, or steam-driven hoists or winches in order to control movement of cableways, cages, derricks, draglines, loaders, rail cars, or skips. Select loads or materials according to weight and size specifications. Start engines of hoists or winches and use levers and pedals to wind or unwind cable on drums. Tend auxiliary equipment such as jacks, slings, cables, or stop blocks in order to facilitate moving items or materials for further processing. Fire boilers on steam hoists. Oil winch drums so that cables will wind smoothly. Repair, maintain, and adjust equipment, using hand tools. Signal and assist other workers loading or unloading materials. Climb ladders in order to position and set up vehicle-mounted derricks.

GOE INFORMATION—**Interest Area:** 08. Industrial Production. **Work Group:** 08.07. Hands-on Work: Loading, Moving, Hoisting, and Conveying. **Personality Type**—Realistic. Realistic occupations frequently involve work activities that include practical, hands-on problems and solutions. They often deal with plants, animals, and real-world materials like wood, tools, and machinery. Many of the occupations require working outside and do not involve a lot of paperwork or working closely with others. **Work Values**—Independence; Moral Values; Supervision, Technical; Advancement. **Skills**—Repairing; Operation Monitoring; Operation and Control; Equipment Selection; Troubleshooting. **Abilities**—*Cognitive:* Spatial Orientation; Visualization; Information Ordering. *Psychomotor:* Multilimb Coordination; Reaction Time; Control Precision; Response Orientation; Speed of Limb Movement. *Physical:* Static Strength; Dynamic Strength; Gross Body Equilibrium; Stamina; Explosive Strength. *Sensory:* Depth Perception; Peripheral Vision; Far Vision; Glare Sensitivity; Hearing Sensitivity. **General Work Activities**—*Information Input:* Monitoring Processes, Materials, or Surroundings; Identifying Objects, Actions, and Events; Estimating Needed Characteristics. *Mental Process:* Evaluating Information Against Standards; Organizing, Planning, and Prioritizing; Judging Qualities of Things, Services, or Other People's Work. *Work Output:* Handling and Moving Objects; Performing General Physical Activities; Controlling Machines and Processes. *Interacting with Others:* Communicating with Other Workers; Communicating with Persons Outside Organization; Performing Administrative Activities. **Physical Work Conditions**—Outdoors; High Places; Whole Body Vibration; Hazardous Equipment; Climbing Ladders, Scaffolds, Poles, etc. **Other Job Characteristics**—Pace Determined by Speed of Equipment; Degree of Automation; Importance of Repeating Same Tasks.

Experience—Job Zone 1. No previous work-related skill, knowledge, or experience is needed. **Job Preparation:** SVP below 4.0—less than six months. **Knowledge**—Mechanical; Public Safety and Security; Fine Arts; Foreign Language; Physics. **Instructional Programs**—Construction/ Heavy Equipment/Earthmoving Equipment Operation.

Related DOT Jobs—663.686-022 Lathe Spotter; 869.683-014 Rigger; 911.687-018 Coal Trimmer; 921.662-022 Marine Railway Operator; 921.663-026 Hoist Operator; 921.663-030 Hoisting Engineer; 921.663-046 Pneumatic-Hoist Operator; 921.663-050 Scraper-Loader Operator; 921.663-066 Yarding Engineer; 921.682-022 Transfer Controller; 921.683-010 Boat-Hoist Operator; 921.683-030 Cupola Hoist Operator; 921.683-046 Hydraulic-Boom Operator; 921.683-054 Jammer Operator; 921.683-058 Log Loader; 921.683-082 Winch Driver; 921.683-086 Yard Worker; 921.685-010 Boat Loader II; 921.685-042 Electric-Fork Operator; 930.363-010 Clean-Out Driller; others.

53-7051.00 Industrial Truck and Tractor Operators

- **Education/Training Required: Short-term on-the-job training**
- **Employed: 634,899**
- **Annual Earnings: $25,350**
- **Growth: 11.3%**
- **Annual Job Openings: 91,000**

Operate industrial trucks or tractors equipped to move materials around a warehouse, storage yard, factory, construction site, or similar location.

Move controls to drive gasoline- or electric-powered trucks, cars, or tractors and transport materials between loading, processing, and storage areas. Move levers and controls that operate lifting devices, such as forklifts, lift beams and swivel-hooks, hoists, and elevating platforms, in order to load, unload, transport, and stack material. Position lifting devices under, over, or around loaded pallets, skids, and boxes and secure material or

products for transport to designated areas. Hook tow trucks to trailer hitches and fasten attachments such as graders, plows, rollers, and winch cables to tractors, using hitchpins. Turn valves and open chutes in order to dump, spray, or release materials from dump cars or storage bins into hoppers. Perform routine maintenance on vehicles and auxiliary equipment, such as cleaning, lubricating, recharging batteries, fueling, or replacing liquefied-gas tank. Manually load or unload materials onto or off pallets, skids, platforms, cars, or lifting devices. Operate or tend automatic stacking, loading, packaging, or cutting machines. Weigh materials or products and record weight and other production data on tags or labels. Signal workers to discharge, dump, or level materials.

GOE INFORMATION—**Interest Area:** 08. Industrial Production. **Work Group:** 08.07. Hands-on Work: Loading, Moving, Hoisting, and Conveying. **Personality Type**—Realistic. Realistic occupations frequently involve work activities that include practical, hands-on problems and solutions. They often deal with plants, animals, and real-world materials like wood, tools, and machinery. Many of the occupations require working outside and do not involve a lot of paperwork or working closely with others. **Work Values**—Supervision, Technical; Supervision, Human Relations; Moral Values; Company Policies and Practices; Advancement. **Skills**—Operation and Control; Repairing; Operation Monitoring; Equipment Selection; Troubleshooting. **Abilities**—*Cognitive:* Spatial Orientation. *Psychomotor:* Multilimb Coordination; Control Precision; Speed of Limb Movement; Reaction Time; Response Orientation. *Physical:* Static Strength; Extent Flexibility; Trunk Strength; Dynamic Flexibility; Explosive Strength. *Sensory:* Depth Perception; Peripheral Vision; Far Vision; Sound Localization; Glare Sensitivity. **General Work Activities**—*Information Input:* Monitoring Processes, Materials, or Surroundings; Inspecting Equipment, Structures, or Materials; Getting Information. *Mental Process:* Evaluating Information Against Standards; Organizing, Planning, and Prioritizing; Updating and Using Relevant Knowledge. *Work Output:* Handling and Moving Objects; Performing General Physical Activities; Controlling Machines and Processes. *Interacting with Others:* Establishing and Maintaining Relationships; Communicating with Other Workers; Monitoring and Controlling Resources. **Physical Work Conditions**—Common Protective or Safety Attire; Outdoors; Using Hands on Objects, Tools, or Controls; Contaminants; Hazardous Equipment. **Other Job Characteristics**—Consequence of Error; Importance of Repeating Same Tasks; Pace Determined by Speed of Equipment.

Experience—Job Zone 1. No previous work-related skill, knowledge, or experience is needed. **Job Preparation:** SVP below 4.0—less than six months. **Knowledge**—Mechanical. **Instructional Programs**—Ground Transportation, Other.

Related DOT Jobs—519.663-014 Hot-Car Operator; 519.683-014 Larry Operator; 569.683-010 Kiln-Transfer Operator; 921.583-010 Transfer-Car Operator, Drier; 921.683-042 Front-End Loader Operator; 921.683-050 Industrial-Truck Operator; 921.683-070 Straddle-Truck Operator; 921.683-078 Transfer-Car Operator; 929.583-010 Yard Worker; 929.683-014 Tractor Operator.

53-7061.00 Cleaners of Vehicles and Equipment

- **Education/Training Required: Short-term on-the-job training**
- **Employed: 321,580**
- **Annual Earnings: $16,490**
- **Growth: 18.8%**
- **Annual Job Openings: 86,000**

Wash or otherwise clean vehicles, machinery, and other equipment. Use such materials as water, cleaning agents, brushes, cloths, and hoses.

Connect hoses and lines to pumps and other equipment. Mix cleaning solutions, abrasive compositions, and other compounds according to formulas. Monitor operation of cleaning machines and stop machines or notify supervisors when malfunctions occur. Pre-soak or rinse machine parts, equipment, or vehicles by immersing objects in cleaning solutions or water manually or using hoists. Press buttons to activate cleaning equipment or machines. Rinse objects and place them on drying racks or use cloth, squeegees, or air compressors to dry surfaces. Scrub, scrape, or spray machine parts, equipment, or vehicles, using scrapers, brushes, clothes, cleaners, disinfectants, insecticides, acid, abrasives, vacuums, and hoses. Sweep, shovel, or vacuum loose debris and salvageable scrap into containers and remove containers from work areas. Turn valves or disconnect hoses in order to eliminate water, cleaning solutions, or vapors from machinery or tanks. Turn valves or handles on equipment in order to regulate pressure and flow of water, air, steam, or abrasives from sprayer nozzles. Apply paints, dyes, polishes, reconditioners, waxes, and masking materials to vehicles in order to preserve, protect, or restore color and condition. Clean and polish vehicle windows. Clean the plastic work inside cars, using paintbrushes. Collect and test samples of cleaning solutions and vapors. Disassemble and reassemble machines or equipment or remove and reattach vehicle parts and trim, using hand tools. Drive vehicles to and from workshops and/or customers' workplaces or homes. Fit boot spoilers, side skirts, and mud flaps to cars. Inspect parts, equipment, and vehicles for cleanliness, damage, and compliance with standards or regulations. Lubricate machinery, vehicles, and equipment and perform minor repairs and adjustments, using hand tools. Maintain inventories of supplies. Transport materials, equipment, or supplies to and from work areas, using carts or hoists.

GOE INFORMATION—Interest Area: 11. Recreation, Travel, and Other Personal Services. **Work Group:** 11.08. Other Personal Services. **Personality Type**—Realistic. Realistic occupations frequently involve work activities that include practical, hands-on problems and solutions. They often deal with plants, animals, and real-world materials like wood, tools, and machinery. Many of the occupations require working outside and do not involve a lot of paperwork or working closely with others. **Work Values**—Independence; Moral Values; Supervision, Technical. **Skills**—Repairing; Operation and Control; Equipment Selection. **Abilities**—*Cognitive:* Spatial Orientation. *Psychomotor:* Speed of Limb Movement; Wrist-Finger Speed; Multilimb Coordination; Manual Dexterity; Finger Dexterity. *Physical:* Extent Flexibility; Stamina; Static Strength; Trunk Strength; Dynamic Flexibility. *Sensory:* Near Vision. **General Work Activities**—*Information Input:* Monitoring Processes, Materials, or Surroundings; Inspecting Equipment, Structures, or Materials; Getting Information. *Mental Process:* Evaluating Information Against Standards; Judging Qualities of Things, Services, or Other People's Work; Organizing, Planning, and Prioritizing. *Work Output:* Handling and Moving Objects; Performing General Physical Activities; Controlling Machines and Processes. *Interacting with Others:* Monitoring and Controlling Resources; Performing Administrative Activities; Communicating with Other Workers. **Physical Work Conditions**—Outdoors; Cramped Work Space or Awkward Positions; Using Hands on Objects, Tools, or Controls; Standing; Kneeling, Crouching, or Crawling. **Other Job Characteristics**—Importance of Repeating Same Tasks; Pace Determined by Speed of Equipment; Degree of Automation.

Experience—Job Zone 1. No previous work-related skill, knowledge, or experience is needed. **Job Preparation:** SVP below 4.0—less than six months. **Knowledge**—Chemistry; Mechanical. **Instructional Programs**—No data available.

Related DOT Jobs—503.687-010 Sandblaster; 511.687-010 Blanket Washer; 519.664-010 Assembly Cleaner; 521.687-030 Char Puller; 521.687-054 Filter-Screen Cleaner; 521.687-114 Shaker Washer; 529.685-230 Stem-Dryer Maintainer; 529.687-014 Bin Cleaner; 529.687-018 Box-Truck Washer; 529.687-054 Cooker Cleaner; 529.687-062 Die Cleaner; 529.687-190 Stone Cleaner; 529.687-194 Suction-Plate-Carrier Cleaner; 529.687-206 Trolley Cleaner; 529.687-210 Washer; 529.687-214 Washroom Cleaner; 557.684-010 Jet Handler; 559.684-022 Tank Cleaner; 559.687-018 Casting-Machine-Service Operator; 559.687-022 Cell Cleaner; others.

53-7062.00 Laborers and Freight, Stock, and Material Movers, Hand

- **Education/Training Required: Short-term on-the-job training**
- **Employed: 2,084,333**
- **Annual Earnings: $19,440**
- **Growth: 13.9%**
- **Annual Job Openings: 519,000**

Manually move freight, stock, or other materials or perform other unskilled general labor. Includes all unskilled manual laborers not elsewhere classified.

No task data available.

GOE INFORMATION—Interest Area: 08. Industrial Production. **Work Group:** 08.07. Hands-on Work: Loading, Moving, Hoisting, and Conveying. **Note:** The Department of Labor has not collected some data for this job, so it has fewer details than the other descriptions.

Instructional Programs—No data available.

Related DOT Jobs—412.687-010 Commissary Assistant; 520.687-010 Blender Laborer; 520.687-038 Gum Puller; 523.687-022 Freezing-Room Worker; 525.687-054 Offal Icer, Poultry; 525.687-086 Shackler; 529.687-138 Leaf Tier; 542.667-010 Wharf Tender; 573.687-030 Setter Helper; 575.687-026 Pipe Stripper; 579.665-014 Laborer, Concrete-Mixing Plant; 579.687-018 Floor Attendant; 669.687-018 Lumber Straightener; 677.687-010 Log Roller; 684.687-022 Collector; 727.687-030 Battery Stacker; 860.684-018 Car Blocker; 904.687-010 Tractor-Trailer Moving Van Driver Helper; 905.687-010 Truck-Driver Helper; 905.687-014 Van-Driver Helper; others.

53-7062.01 Stevedores, Except Equipment Operators

- **Education/Training Required: Short-term on-the-job training**
- **Employed: No data available.**
- **Annual Earnings: $19,440**
- **Growth: 13.9%**
- **Annual Job Openings: 519,000**

Manually load and unload ship cargo. Stack cargo in transit shed or in hold of ship, using pallet or cargo board. Attach and move slings to lift cargo. Guide load lift.

Carries or moves cargo by handtruck to wharf and stacks cargo on pallets to facilitate transfer to and from ship. Stacks cargo in transit shed or in hold of ship as directed. Attaches and moves slings used to lift cargo. Guides load being lifted to prevent swinging. Shores cargo in ship's hold to prevent shifting during voyage.

GOE INFORMATION—Interest Area: 07. Transportation. **Work Group:** 07.08. Support Work. **Personality Type**—Realistic. Realistic occupations frequently involve work activities that include practical, hands-on problems and solutions. They often deal with plants, animals, and real-world materials like wood, tools, and machinery. Many of the occupations require working outside and do not involve a lot of paperwork or working closely with others. **Work Values**—Supervision, Technical; Moral Values; Pleasant Co-workers. **Skills**—None met the criteria. **Abilities**—*Cognitive:* Spatial Orientation. *Psychomotor:* Speed of Limb Movement; Multilimb Coordination; Reaction Time; Rate Control; Manual Dexterity. *Physical:* Static Strength; Dynamic Strength; Stamina; Explosive Strength; Trunk Strength. *Sensory:* Depth Perception; Peripheral Vision; Glare Sensitivity; Night Vision; Auditory Attention. **General Work Activities**—*Information Input:* Identifying Objects, Actions, and Events; Estimating Needed Characteristics; Monitoring Processes, Materials, or Surroundings. *Mental Process:* Analyzing Data or Information; Making Decisions and Solving Problems; Organizing, Planning, and Prioritizing. *Work Output:* Handling and Moving Objects; Performing General Physical Activities; Controlling Machines and Processes. *Interacting with Others:* Communicating with Other Workers; Establishing and Maintaining Relationships; Assisting and Caring for Others. **Physical Work Conditions**—Outdoors; Bending or Twisting the Body; Hazardous Equipment; Extremely Bright or Inadequate Lighting; Very Hot or Cold. **Other Job Characteristics**—Importance of Repeating Same Tasks; Consequence of Error; Degree of Automation.

Experience—Job Zone 1. No previous work-related skill, knowledge, or experience is needed. **Job Preparation:** SVP below 4.0—less than six months. **Knowledge**—Production and Processing; Physics; Public Safety and Security. **Instructional Programs**—No data available.

Related DOT Jobs—922.687-090 Stevedore II.

53-7062.02 Grips and Set-Up Workers, Motion Picture Sets, Studios, and Stages
- **Education/Training Required: Short-term on-the-job training**
- **Employed: No data available.**
- **Annual Earnings: $19,440**
- **Growth: 13.9%**
- **Annual Job Openings: 519,000**

Arrange equipment; raise and lower scenery; move dollies, cranes, and booms; and perform other duties for motion-picture, recording, or television industry.

Arranges equipment preparatory to sessions and performances, following work order specifications, and handles props during performances. Rigs and dismantles stage or set equipment, such as frames, scaffolding, platforms, or backdrops, using carpenter's hand tools. Adjusts controls to raise and lower scenery and stage curtain during performance, following cues. Adjusts controls to guide, position, and move equipment, such as cranes, booms, and cameras. Erects canvas covers to protect equipment from weather. Reads work orders and follows oral instructions to determine specified material and equipment to be moved and its relocation. Connects electrical equipment to power source and tests equipment before performance. Orders equipment and maintains equipment storage areas. Sews and repairs items, using materials and hand tools such as canvas and sewing machines. Produces special lighting and sound effects during performances, using various machines and devices.

GOE INFORMATION—Interest Area: 06. Construction, Mining, and Drilling. **Work Group:** 06.04. Hands-on Work in Construction, Extraction, and Maintenance. **Personality Type**—Realistic. Realistic occupations frequently involve work activities that include practical, hands-on problems and solutions. They often deal with plants, animals, and real-world materials like wood, tools, and machinery. Many of the occupa-

tions require working outside and do not involve a lot of paperwork or working closely with others. **Work Values**—Supervision, Technical; Company Policies and Practices; Advancement; Moral Values; Pleasant Co-workers. **Skills**—Repairing; Operation and Control; Installation; Operation Monitoring. **Abilities**—*Cognitive:* Spatial Orientation; Visualization; Information Ordering; Oral Comprehension. *Psychomotor:* Manual Dexterity; Arm-Hand Steadiness; Multilimb Coordination; Control Precision; Finger Dexterity. *Physical:* Static Strength; Extent Flexibility; Trunk Strength; Explosive Strength; Dynamic Strength. *Sensory:* Depth Perception; Hearing Sensitivity; Auditory Attention; Sound Localization; Peripheral Vision. **General Work Activities**—*Information Input:* Identifying Objects, Actions, and Events; Getting Information; Monitoring Processes, Materials, or Surroundings. *Mental Process:* Organizing, Planning, and Prioritizing; Updating and Using Relevant Knowledge; Making Decisions and Solving Problems. *Work Output:* Performing General Physical Activities; Handling and Moving Objects; Controlling Machines and Processes. *Interacting with Others:* Monitoring and Controlling Resources; Communicating with Other Workers; Establishing and Maintaining Relationships. **Physical Work Conditions**—High Places; Climbing Ladders, Scaffolds, Poles, etc.; Using Hands on Objects, Tools, or Controls; Hazardous Conditions; Kneeling, Crouching, or Crawling. **Other Job Characteristics**—Consequence of Error; Pace Determined by Speed of Equipment; Importance of Repeating Same Tasks.

Experience—Job Zone 2. Some previous work-related skill, knowledge, or experience may be helpful, but usually is not needed. **Job Preparation:** SVP 4.0 to less than 6.0—six months to less than two years. **Knowledge**—Building and Construction; Fine Arts; Mechanical; Design; Physics. **Instructional Programs**—No data available.

Related DOT Jobs—962.384-010 Microphone-Boom Operator; 962.664-014 Recording Studio Set-Up Worker; 962.684-018 Motor-Power Connector; 962.684-022 Prop Attendant; 962.687-018 Flyer; 962.687-022 Grip.

53-7062.03 Freight, Stock, and Material Movers, Hand
- **Education/Training Required: Short-term on-the-job training**
- **Employed: No data available.**
- **Annual Earnings: $19,440**
- **Growth: 13.9%**
- **Annual Job Openings: 519,000**

Load, unload and move materials at plant, yard, or other work site.

Loads and unloads materials to and from designated storage areas, such as racks and shelves, or vehicles, such as trucks. Transports receptacles to and from designated areas by hand or using dollies, handtrucks, and wheelbarrows. Secures lifting attachments to materials and conveys load to destination, using crane or hoist. Directs spouts and positions receptacles, such as bins, carts, and containers, to receive loads. Stacks or piles materials such as lumber, boards, or pallets. Shovels materials such as gravel, ice, or spilled concrete into containers, into bins, or onto conveyors. Bundles and bands material such as fodder and tobacco leaves, using banding machines. Reads work orders or receives and listens to oral instructions to determine work assignment. Sorts and stores items according to specifications. Installs protective devices such as bracing, padding or strapping to prevent shifting or damage to items being transported. Cleans work area, using brooms, rags, and cleaning compounds. Attaches identifying tags or marks information on containers. Records number of units handled and moved, using daily production sheet or work tickets. Adjusts or replaces equipment parts such as rollers, belts, plugs and caps, using hand tools. Assembles product containers and crates, using hand tools and precut lumber.

GOE INFORMATION—**Interest Area:** 08. Industrial Production. **Work Group:** 08.07. Hands-on Work: Loading, Moving, Hoisting, and Conveying. **Personality Type**—Realistic. Realistic occupations frequently involve work activities that include practical, hands-on problems and solutions. They often deal with plants, animals, and real-world materials like wood, tools, and machinery. Many of the occupations require working outside and do not involve a lot of paperwork or working closely with others. **Work Values**—Supervision, Technical; Moral Values; Supervision, Human Relations; Advancement; Pleasant Co-workers. **Skills**—None met the criteria. **Abilities**—*Cognitive:* Category Flexibility; Spatial Orientation; Oral Comprehension. *Psychomotor:* Multilimb Coordination; Manual Dexterity. *Physical:* Static Strength; Trunk Strength; Extent Flexibility; Gross Body Equilibrium; Explosive Strength. *Sensory:* Peripheral Vision; Depth Perception. **General Work Activities**—*Information Input:* Getting Information; Inspecting Equipment, Structures, or Materials; Estimating Needed Characteristics. *Mental Process:* Evaluating Information Against Standards; Organizing, Planning, and Prioritizing; Updating and Using Relevant Knowledge. *Work Output:* Handling and Moving Objects; Performing General Physical Activities; Controlling Machines and Processes. *Interacting with Others:* Communicating with Other Workers; Performing Administrative Activities; Establishing and Maintaining Relationships. **Physical Work Conditions**—Climbing Ladders, Scaffolds, Poles, etc.; Common Protective or Safety Attire; Kneeling, Crouching, or Crawling; Keeping or Regaining Balance; Walking or Running. **Other Job Characteristics**—Importance of Repeating Same Tasks; Degree of Automation; Pace Determined by Speed of Equipment.

Experience—Job Zone 1. No previous work-related skill, knowledge, or experience is needed. **Job Preparation:** SVP below 4.0—less than six months. **Knowledge**—Production and Processing; Mechanical; Physics; Building and Construction; Engineering and Technology. **Instructional Programs**—No data available.

Related DOT Jobs—412.687-010 Commissary Assistant; 520.687-010 Blender Laborer; 520.687-038 Gum Puller; 523.687-022 Freezing-Room Worker; 525.687-054 Offal Icer, Poultry; 525.687-086 Shackler; 529.687-138 Leaf Tier; 542.667-010 Wharf Tender; 573.687-030 Setter Helper; 575.687-026 Pipe Stripper; 579.665-014 Laborer, Concrete-Mixing Plant; 579.687-018 Floor Attendant; 669.687-018 Lumber Straightener; 677.687-010 Log Roller; 684.687-022 Collector; 727.687-030 Battery Stacker; 860.684-018 Car Blocker; 904.687-010 Tractor-Trailer Moving Van Driver Helper; 905.687-010 Truck-Driver Helper; 910.667-030 Transfer-Table Operator Helper; others.

53-7063.00 *Machine Feeders and Offbearers*

- **Education/Training Required: Short-term on-the-job training**
- **Employed: 181,833**
- **Annual Earnings: $21,150**
- **Growth: –12.3%**
- **Annual Job Openings: 41,000**

Feed materials into or remove materials from machines or equipment that is automatic or tended by other workers.

Feeds materials into machines and equipment to process and manufacture products. Loads materials and products into machines and equipment, using hand tools and moving devices. Removes materials and products from machines and equipment, using hand tools and moving devices. Off-bears materials and products from machines and equipment, using hand tools. Shovels or scoops materials into containers, machines, or equipment for processing, storage, or transport. Adds chemicals, solutions, or ingredients to machines or equipment to ensure manufacturing

process meets specifications. Transfers materials and products between storage areas and machinery and equipment. Sorts and selects materials and products and rejects defective pieces, following specified instructions and standards. Fastens, packages, or stacks materials and products, using hand tools and fastening equipment. Inspects materials and products for defects and to ensure conformance to specifications. Weighs or measures materials or products to ensure conformance to specifications. Identifies and marks materials, products, and samples, following instructions. Records production and operational information and data on specified forms. Modifies materials and products during manufacturing process to meet requirements. Moves controls to start, stop, or adjust machinery and equipment. Cleans and maintains machinery, equipment, and work areas to ensure proper functioning and safe working conditions.

GOE INFORMATION—**Interest Area:** 08. Industrial Production. **Work Group:** 08.07. Hands-on Work: Loading, Moving, Hoisting, and Conveying. **Personality Type**—Realistic. Realistic occupations frequently involve work activities that include practical, hands-on problems and solutions. They often deal with plants, animals, and real-world materials like wood, tools, and machinery. Many of the occupations require working outside and do not involve a lot of paperwork or working closely with others. **Work Values**—Moral Values; Activity; Supervision, Technical; Pleasant Co-workers; Supervision, Human Relations. **Skills**—Operation and Control; Operation Monitoring. **Abilities**—*Cognitive:* Perceptual Speed; Spatial Orientation; Category Flexibility; Memorization. *Psychomotor:* Manual Dexterity; Multilimb Coordination; Reaction Time; Speed of Limb Movement; Control Precision. *Physical:* Static Strength; Dynamic Strength; Stamina; Explosive Strength; Dynamic Flexibility. *Sensory:* Depth Perception; Peripheral Vision; Glare Sensitivity; Hearing Sensitivity; Far Vision. **General Work Activities**—*Information Input:* Inspecting Equipment, Structures, or Materials; Monitoring Processes, Materials, or Surroundings; Getting Information. *Mental Process:* Evaluating Information Against Standards; Updating and Using Relevant Knowledge; Judging Qualities of Things, Services, or Other People's Work. *Work Output:* Handling and Moving Objects; Performing General Physical Activities; Controlling Machines and Processes. *Interacting with Others:* Performing Administrative Activities; Communicating with Other Workers; Coordinating the Work and Activities of Others. **Physical Work Conditions**—Hazardous Equipment; Making Repetitive Motions; Using Hands on Objects, Tools, or Controls; Distracting Sounds and Noise Levels; Standing. **Other Job Characteristics**—Pace Determined by Speed of Equipment; Degree of Automation; Importance of Repeating Same Tasks.

Experience—Job Zone 1. No previous work-related skill, knowledge, or experience is needed. **Job Preparation:** SVP below 4.0—less than six months. **Knowledge**—Production and Processing; Chemistry; Mechanical; Clerical; Foreign Language. **Instructional Programs**—No data available.

Related DOT Jobs—361.686-010 Washing-Machine Loader-and-Puller; 363.686-010 Flatwork Finisher; 369.686-010 Folding-Machine Operator; 429.686-010 Press Feeder, Broomcorn; 504.686-014 Furnace Helper; 504.686-022 Heat Treater; 509.666-010 Compound-Coating-Machine Offbearer; 509.686-014 Pasting-Machine Offbearer; 509.687-026 Laborer, General; 512.686-010 Cupola Charger; 515.686-010 Battery-Wrecker Operator; 519.686-010 Laborer, General; 520.686-010 Ball-Machine Operator; 520.686-014 Dessert-Cup-Machine Feeder; 520.686-030 Molding-Machine-Operator Helper; 520.686-034 Plug Shaper, Machine; 521.686-014 Cake Puller; 521.686-018 Chicle-Grinder Feeder; 521.686-022 Cotton Puller; 521.686-030 Cut-in Worker; others.

53-7064.00 Packers and Packagers, Hand

- **Education/Training Required: Short-term on-the-job training**
- **Employed: 1,090,520**
- **Annual Earnings: $16,280**
- **Growth: 19.3%**
- **Annual Job Openings: 242,000**

Pack or package by hand a wide variety of products and materials.

Assemble, line, and pad cartons, crates, and containers, using hand tools. Examine and inspect containers, materials, and products in order to ensure that packing specifications are met. Mark and label containers, container tags, or products, using marking tools. Obtain, move, and sort products, materials, containers, and orders, using hand tools. Place or pour products or materials into containers, using hand tools and equipment, or fill containers from spouts or chutes. Remove completed or defective products or materials, placing them on moving equipment such as conveyors or in specified areas such as loading docks. Seal containers or materials, using glues, fasteners, nails, and hand tools. Clean containers, materials, supplies, or work areas, using cleaning solutions and hand tools. Load materials and products into package processing equipment. Measure, weigh, and count products and materials. Record product, packaging, and order information on specified forms and records. Transport packages to customers' vehicles.

GOE INFORMATION—Interest Area: 08. Industrial Production. **Work Group:** 08.07. Hands-on Work: Loading, Moving, Hoisting, and Conveying. **Personality Type**—Realistic. Realistic occupations frequently involve work activities that include practical, hands-on problems and solutions. They often deal with plants, animals, and real-world materials like wood, tools, and machinery. Many of the occupations require working outside and do not involve a lot of paperwork or working closely with others. **Work Values**—Supervision, Technical; Moral Values; Activity; Pleasant Co-workers; Supervision, Human Relations. **Skills**—None met the criteria. **Abilities**—*Cognitive:* Perceptual Speed; Spatial Orientation. *Psychomotor:* Manual Dexterity; Wrist-Finger Speed; Speed of Limb Movement; Control Precision; Finger Dexterity. *Physical:* Static Strength; Dynamic Flexibility; Dynamic Strength; Extent Flexibility; Trunk Strength. *Sensory:* None met the criteria. **General Work Activities**—*Information Input:* Monitoring Processes, Materials, or Surroundings; Inspecting Equipment, Structures, or Materials; Getting Information. *Mental Process:* Organizing, Planning, and Prioritizing; Evaluating Information Against Standards; Judging Qualities of Things, Services, or Other People's Work. *Work Output:* Handling and Moving Objects; Performing General Physical Activities; Controlling Machines and Processes. *Interacting with Others:* Coordinating the Work and Activities of Others; Performing Administrative Activities; Monitoring and Controlling Resources. **Physical Work Conditions**—Making Repetitive Motions; Using Hands on Objects, Tools, or Controls; Climbing Ladders, Scaffolds, Poles, etc.; Standing; Common Protective or Safety Attire. **Other Job Characteristics**—Importance of Repeating Same Tasks; Pace Determined by Speed of Equipment; Degree of Automation.

Experience—Job Zone 1. No previous work-related skill, knowledge, or experience is needed. **Job Preparation:** SVP below 4.0—less than six months. **Knowledge**—Production and Processing; Clerical. **Instructional Programs**—No data available.

Related DOT Jobs—522.687-010 Barrel Filler I; 522.687-018 Bulker; 525.687-082 Poultry-Dressing Worker; 525.687-118 Tier; 529.687-022 Bulk Filler; 529.687-086 Fish-Egg Packer; 529.687-150 Linker; 559.687-014 Ampoule Sealer; 585.687-030 Singer; 700.687-038 Laborer, Gold Leaf; 710.687-034 Tie-Up Worker; 737.587-018 Primer Boxer; 737.687-014 Bag Loader; 737.687-030 Core Loader; 737.687-094 Packer-Fuser; 753.687-038 Packing-Line Worker; 784.687-042 Inspector-Packer; 789.687-106 Mophead Trimmer-and-Wrapper; 794.687-034 Paper-Pattern Folder; 920.587-010 Cloth-Bolt Bander; others.

53-7071.00 Gas Compressor and Gas Pumping Station Operators

- **Education/Training Required: Moderate-term on-the-job training**
- **Employed: 6,682**
- **Annual Earnings: $43,340**
- **Growth: 4.8%**
- **Annual Job Openings: 1,000**

Operate steam, gas, electric motor, or internal combustion engine–driven compressors. Transmit, compress, or recover gases, such as butane, nitrogen, hydrogen, and natural gas.

No task data available.

GOE INFORMATION—Interest Area: 08. Industrial Production. **Work Group:** 08.06. Systems Operation. **Note:** The Department of Labor has not collected some data for this job, so it has fewer details than the other descriptions.

Instructional Programs—No data available.

Related DOT Jobs—950.382-014 Gas-Compressor Operator; 953.382-010 Gas-Pumping-Station Operator.

53-7071.01 Gas Pumping Station Operators

- **Education/Training Required: Moderate-term on-the-job training**
- **Employed: No data available.**
- **Annual Earnings: $43,340**
- **Growth: 4.8%**
- **Annual Job Openings: 1,000**

Control the operation of steam, gas, or electric motor–driven compressor to maintain specified pressures on high- and low-pressure mains dispensing gas from gasholders.

Opens valve to allow gas to flow into and out of compressors. Observes pressure gauges to determine consumption rate variations and turns knobs or switches to regulate pressures. Reads gas meters and records amount of gas received and dispensed from holders. Cleans, lubricates, and adjusts compressors, using hand tools.

GOE INFORMATION—Interest Area: 08. Industrial Production. **Work Group:** 08.06. Systems Operation. **Personality Type**—Realistic. Realistic occupations frequently involve work activities that include practical, hands-on problems and solutions. They often deal with plants, animals, and real-world materials like wood, tools, and machinery. Many of the occupations require working outside and do not involve a lot of paperwork or working closely with others. **Work Values**—Independence; Supervision, Technical; Supervision, Human Relations. **Skills**—Operation Monitoring; Operation and Control. **Abilities**—*Cognitive:* None met the criteria. *Psychomotor:* Control Precision; Reaction Time. *Physical:* Static Strength. *Sensory:* Glare Sensitivity. **General Work Activities**—*Information Input:* Monitoring Processes, Materials, or Surroundings; Getting Information; Identifying Objects, Actions, and Events. *Mental Process:* Processing Information; Evaluating Information Against Standards;

Making Decisions and Solving Problems. *Work Output:* Handling and Moving Objects; Repairing and Maintaining Mechanical Equipment; Performing General Physical Activities. *Interacting with Others:* Performing Administrative Activities; Monitoring and Controlling Resources; Communicating with Other Workers. **Physical Work Conditions**—Contaminants; Outdoors; Very Hot or Cold; Standing; Hazardous Conditions. **Other Job Characteristics**—Degree of Automation; Pace Determined by Speed of Equipment; Importance of Repeating Same Tasks.

Experience—Job Zone 2. Some previous work-related skill, knowledge, or experience may be helpful, but usually is not needed. **Job Preparation:** SVP 4.0 to less than 6.0—six months to less than two years. **Knowledge**—Mechanical; Engineering and Technology; Physics; Computers and Electronics; Public Safety and Security. **Instructional Programs**—No data available.

Related DOT Jobs—953.382-010 Gas-Pumping-Station Operator.

53-7071.02 Gas Compressor Operators

- **Education/Training Required: Moderate-term on-the-job training**
- **Employed: No data available.**
- **Annual Earnings: $43,340**
- **Growth: 4.8%**
- **Annual Job Openings: 1,000**

Operate steam or internal combustion engines to transmit, compress, or recover gases, such as butane, nitrogen, hydrogen, and natural gas, in various production processes.

Moves controls and turns valves to start compressor engines, pumps, and auxiliary equipment. Operates equipment to control transmission of natural gas through pipelines. Observes operation of equipment to detect malfunctions. Monitors meters, gauges, and recording instrument charts to ensure specified temperature, pressure, and flow of gas through system. Conducts chemical tests to evaluate quality of gas. Records instrument readings and operational changes in operating log. Performs minor repairs on equipment, using hand tools. Operates or tends equipment to purify gases.

GOE INFORMATION—Interest Area: 08. Industrial Production. **Work Group:** 08.06. Systems Operation. **Personality Type**—Realistic. Realistic occupations frequently involve work activities that include practical, hands-on problems and solutions. They often deal with plants, animals, and real-world materials like wood, tools, and machinery. Many of the occupations require working outside and do not involve a lot of paperwork or working closely with others. **Work Values**—Supervision, Technical; Independence; Supervision, Human Relations; Moral Values; Security. **Skills**—Operation Monitoring; Repairing; Operation and Control; Troubleshooting. **Abilities**—*Cognitive:* None met the criteria. *Psychomotor:* Control Precision; Multilimb Coordination. *Physical:* Extent Flexibility. *Sensory:* None met the criteria. **General Work Activities**—*Information Input:* Inspecting Equipment, Structures, or Materials; Monitoring Processes, Materials, or Surroundings; Identifying Objects, Actions, and Events. *Mental Process:* Processing Information; Evaluating Information Against Standards; Analyzing Data or Information. *Work Output:* Controlling Machines and Processes; Documenting or Recording Information; Handling and Moving Objects. *Interacting with Others:* Communicating with Other Workers; Performing Administrative Activities; Establishing and Maintaining Relationships. **Physical Work Conditions**—Contaminants; Hazardous Conditions; Climbing Ladders, Scaffolds, Poles, etc.; Common Protective or Safety Attire; Specialized

Protective or Safety Attire. **Other Job Characteristics**—Degree of Automation; Pace Determined by Speed of Equipment; Consequence of Error.

Experience—Job Zone 4. A minimum of two to four years of work-related skill, knowledge, or experience is needed. **Job Preparation:** SVP 7.0 to less than 8.0—two years to less than 10 years. **Knowledge**—Chemistry; Mechanical; Physics; Production and Processing; Clerical. **Instructional Programs**—No data available.

Related DOT Jobs—950.382-014 Gas-Compressor Operator.

53-7072.00 Pump Operators, Except Wellhead Pumpers

- **Education/Training Required: Moderate-term on-the-job training**
- **Employed: 13,899**
- **Annual Earnings: $36,060**
- **Growth: 4.8%**
- **Annual Job Openings: 1,000**

Tend, control, or operate power-driven, stationary, or portable pumps and manifold systems to transfer gases, oil, other liquids, slurries, or powdered materials to and from various vessels and processes.

Turns valves and starts pump to commence or regulate flow of substances, such as gases, liquids, slurries, or powdered materials. Tends vessels that store substances such as gases, liquids, slurries, or powdered materials. Connects hoses and pipes to pumps and vessels, using hand tools. Observes gauges and flowmeter to ascertain that specifications are met, such as tank level, chemical amounts, and pressure. Adds chemicals and solutions to tank to ensure that specifications are met. Tends auxiliary equipment such as water treatment and refrigeration units and heat exchanges. Communicates with workers to start flow of materials or substance. Cleans and maintains pumps and vessels, using hand tools and equipment. Collects and delivers sample solutions for laboratory analysis. Tests materials and solutions, using testing equipment. Transfers materials to and from vessels, using moving equipment. Inspects and reports vessel and pump abnormalities such as leaks, pressure, and temperature fluctuations. Records information such as type and quantity of material and operating data.

GOE INFORMATION—Interest Area: 08. Industrial Production. **Work Group:** 08.07. Hands-on Work: Loading, Moving, Hoisting, and Conveying. **Personality Type**—Realistic. Realistic occupations frequently involve work activities that include practical, hands-on problems and solutions. They often deal with plants, animals, and real-world materials like wood, tools, and machinery. Many of the occupations require working outside and do not involve a lot of paperwork or working closely with others. **Work Values**—Supervision, Technical; Supervision, Human Relations; Moral Values; Advancement; Independence. **Skills**—Operation Monitoring; Operation and Control; Repairing. **Abilities**—*Cognitive:* Time Sharing; Perceptual Speed; Memorization; Selective Attention; Spatial Orientation. *Psychomotor:* Rate Control; Control Precision; Speed of Limb Movement; Arm-Hand Steadiness; Manual Dexterity. *Physical:* Gross Body Coordination; Stamina; Dynamic Flexibility; Trunk Strength; Dynamic Strength. *Sensory:* Depth Perception; Visual Color Discrimination; Near Vision; Hearing Sensitivity; Far Vision. **General Work Activities**—*Information Input:* Monitoring Processes, Materials, or Surroundings; Inspecting Equipment, Structures, or Materials; Getting Information. *Mental Process:* Evaluating Information Against Standards; Judging Qualities of Things, Services, or Other People's Work; Updating and Using Relevant Knowledge. *Work Output:* Controlling Machines and Processes; Handling and Moving Objects; Repairing and Maintaining Mechanical Equipment. *Interacting with Others:* Communicating with Other Workers; Coordinating the Work and Activities of Others; Establishing and Maintaining Relationships. **Physical Work Conditions**—Hazardous Equipment; Hazardous Conditions; Using Hands on Objects, Tools, or Controls; Distracting Sounds and Noise Levels; Contaminants. **Other Job Characteristics**—Pace Determined by Speed of Equipment; Degree of Automation; Importance of Repeating Same Tasks.

Experience—Job Zone 2. Some previous work-related skill, knowledge, or experience may be helpful, but usually is not needed. **Job Preparation:** SVP 4.0 to less than 6.0—six months to less than two years. **Knowledge**—Mechanical; Physics; Production and Processing; Chemistry; Building and Construction. **Instructional Programs**—No data available.

Related DOT Jobs—521.565-010 Liquor-Bridge Operator; 522.662-010 Receiver, Fermenting Cellars; 529.585-014 Tank Tender; 529.685-242 Tank Pumper, Panelboard; 529.685-246 Tapper; 549.362-010 Still-Pump Operator; 549.382-018 Wash-Oil-Pump Operator; 549.685-042 Utility Operator III; 559.585-014 Grease-and-Tallow Pumper; 559.665-038 Tank-Farm Attendant; 559.684-034 Utility Worker, Production; 559.685-026 Brine-Well Operator; 914.585-010 Gas-Transfer Operator; 914.665-010 Pigment Pumper; 914.665-014 Pumper, Brewery; 914.682-010 Pumper; 939.682-010 Monitor Car Operator; 950.362-010 Engineer, Exhauster; 952.464-010 Cable Maintainer.

53-7073.00 Wellhead Pumpers

- **Education/Training Required: Moderate-term on-the-job training**
- **Employed: 11,708**
- **Annual Earnings: $32,140**
- **Growth: –8.5%**
- **Annual Job Openings: 1,000**

Operate power pumps and auxiliary equipment to produce flow of oil or gas from wells in oil field.

Attach pumps and hoses to wellheads. Monitor control panels during pumping operations in order to ensure that materials are being pumped at the correct pressure, density, rate, and concentration. Open valves to return compressed gas to bottoms of specified wells in order to repressurize them and force oil to surface. Operate engines and pumps in order to shut off wells according to production schedules and to switch flow of oil into storage tanks. Start compressor engines and divert oil from storage tanks into compressor units and auxiliary equipment in order to recover natural gas from oil. Control pumping and blending equipment to acidize, cement, or fracture gas or oil wells and permeable rock formations. Drive trucks in order to transport high-pressure pumping equipment and chemicals, fluids, or gases to be pumped into wells. Mix acids, chemicals, or dry cement as required for a specific job. Perform routine maintenance on vehicles and equipment. Prepare trucks and equipment necessary for the type of pumping service required. Repair gas and oil meters and gauges. Supervise oil pumpers and other workers engaged in producing oil from wells. Unload and assemble pipes and pumping equipment, using hand tools.

GOE INFORMATION—Interest Area: 08. Industrial Production. **Work Group:** 08.06. Systems Operation. **Personality Type**—Realistic. Realistic occupations frequently involve work activities that include practical, hands-on problems and solutions. They often deal with plants, animals, and real-world materials like wood, tools, and machinery. Many of the occupations require working outside and do not involve a lot of paperwork or working closely with others. **Work Values**—Independence; Supervision, Technical; Supervision, Human Relations; Moral Values. **Skills**—Operation Monitoring; Operation and Control. **Abilities**—*Cog-*

nitive: None met the criteria. *Psychomotor:* Control Precision; Rate Control. *Physical:* Gross Body Coordination; Explosive Strength. *Sensory:* None met the criteria. **General Work Activities**—*Information Input:* Monitoring Processes, Materials, or Surroundings; Inspecting Equipment, Structures, or Materials; Identifying Objects, Actions, and Events. *Mental Process:* Evaluating Information Against Standards; Making Decisions and Solving Problems; Processing Information. *Work Output:* Controlling Machines and Processes; Handling and Moving Objects; Performing General Physical Activities. *Interacting with Others:* Performing Administrative Activities; Communicating with Other Workers; Establishing and Maintaining Relationships. **Physical Work Conditions**—Contaminants; Common Protective or Safety Attire; Very Hot or Cold; Hazardous Conditions; Extremely Bright or Inadequate Lighting. **Other Job Characteristics**—Pace Determined by Speed of Equipment; Degree of Automation; Importance of Repeating Same Tasks.

Experience—Job Zone 4. A minimum of two to four years of work-related skill, knowledge, or experience is needed. **Job Preparation:** SVP 7.0 to less than 8.0—two years to less than 10 years. **Knowledge**—Production and Processing; Clerical; Physics; Mechanical; Chemistry. **Instructional Programs**—No data available.

Related DOT Jobs—914.382-022 Pumper, Head.

53-7081.00 Refuse and Recyclable Material Collectors

- **Education/Training Required: Short-term on-the-job training**
- **Employed: 124,117**
- **Annual Earnings: $23,850**
- **Growth: 16.6%**
- **Annual Job Openings: 34,000**

Collect and dump refuse or recyclable materials from containers into truck. May drive truck.

Communicate with dispatchers concerning delays, unsafe sites, accidents, equipment breakdowns, and other maintenance problems. Dismount garbage trucks to collect garbage and remount trucks to ride to the next collection point. Drive to disposal sites to empty trucks that have been filled. Drive trucks along established routes through residential streets and alleys or through business and industrial areas. Operate automated or semi-automated hoisting devices that raise refuse bins and dump contents into openings in truck bodies. Operate equipment that compresses the collected refuse. Sort items set out for recycling and throw materials into designated truck compartments. Tag garbage or recycling containers to inform customers of problems such as excess garbage or inclusion of items that are not permitted. Clean trucks and compactor bodies after routes have been completed. Fill out any needed reports for defective equipment. Inspect trucks prior to beginning routes to ensure safe operating condition. Keep informed of road and weather conditions to determine how routes will be affected. Refuel trucks and add other necessary fluids, such as oil. Organize schedules for refuse collection. Provide quotes for refuse collection contracts.

GOE INFORMATION—Interest Area: 08. Industrial Production. **Work Group:** 08.07. Hands-on Work: Loading, Moving, Hoisting, and Conveying. **Personality Type**—Realistic. Realistic occupations frequently involve work activities that include practical, hands-on problems and solutions. They often deal with plants, animals, and real-world materials like wood, tools, and machinery. Many of the occupations require working outside and do not involve a lot of paperwork or working closely with others. **Work Values**—Supervision, Technical; Supervision, Human Relations; Company Policies and Practices; Security; Moral Values. **Skills**—

Operation and Control. **Abilities**—*Cognitive:* None met the criteria. *Psychomotor:* Rate Control; Multilimb Coordination. *Physical:* Static Strength; Stamina; Dynamic Strength; Gross Body Coordination; Trunk Strength. *Sensory:* Glare Sensitivity. **General Work Activities**—*Information Input:* Identifying Objects, Actions, and Events; Getting Information; Inspecting Equipment, Structures, or Materials. *Mental Process:* Organizing, Planning, and Prioritizing; Evaluating Information Against Standards; Judging Qualities of Things, Services, or Other People's Work. *Work Output:* Performing General Physical Activities; Handling and Moving Objects; Operating Vehicles or Equipment. *Interacting with Others:* Communicating with Other Workers; Establishing and Maintaining Relationships; Performing Administrative Activities. **Physical Work Conditions**—Outdoors; Very Hot or Cold; Contaminants; Distracting Sounds and Noise Levels; Minor Burns, Cuts, Bites, or Stings. **Other Job Characteristics**—Importance of Repeating Same Tasks; Pace Determined by Speed of Equipment; Degree of Automation.

Experience—Job Zone 1. No previous work-related skill, knowledge, or experience is needed. **Job Preparation:** SVP below 4.0—less than six months. **Knowledge**—Geography; Public Safety and Security. **Instructional Programs**—No data available.

Related DOT Jobs—955.687-022 Garbage Collector.

53-7111.00 Shuttle Car Operators

- **Education/Training Required: Moderate-term on-the-job training**
- **Employed: No data available.**
- **Annual Earnings: $37,460**
- **Growth: No data available.**
- **Annual Job Openings: No data available.**

Operate diesel or electric-powered shuttle car in underground mine to transport materials from working face to mine cars or conveyor.

Control conveyors that run the entire length of shuttle cars in order to distribute loads as loading progresses. Drive loaded shuttle cars to ramps and move controls in order to discharge loads into mine cars or onto conveyors. Guide and stop cars by switching, applying brakes, or placing scotches (wooden wedges) between wheels and rails. Measure, weigh, or verify levels of rock, gravel, or other excavated material in order to prevent equipment overloads. Monitor loading processes in order to ensure that materials are loaded according to specifications. Move mine cars into position for loading and unloading, using pinchbars inserted under car wheels to position cars under loading spouts. Observe hand signals, grade stakes, or other markings when operating machines. Open and close bottom doors of cars in order to dump contents. Push or ride cars down slopes or hook cars to cables and control cable drum brakes in order to ease cars down inclines. Read written instructions or confer with supervisors about schedules and materials to be moved. Clean, fuel, and service equipment; repair and replace parts as necessary. Direct other workers to move stakes, place blocks, position anchors or cables, or move materials. Maintain records of materials moved. Place planks between coke ovens and tops of railroad cars in order to provide paths for wheelbarrows.

GOE INFORMATION—**Interest Area:** 06. Construction, Mining, and Drilling. **Work Group:** 06.03. Mining and Drilling. **Personality Type**—Realistic. Realistic occupations frequently involve work activities that include practical, hands-on problems and solutions. They often deal with plants, animals, and real-world materials like wood, tools, and machinery. Many of the occupations require working outside and do not involve a lot of paperwork or working closely with others. **Work Values**—Independence; Supervision, Technical; Supervision, Human Relations; Moral

Values; Advancement. **Skills**—Operation and Control; Operation Monitoring. **Abilities**—*Cognitive:* Spatial Orientation. *Psychomotor:* Rate Control; Multilimb Coordination; Control Precision; Response Orientation; Reaction Time. *Physical:* Gross Body Coordination; Explosive Strength; Dynamic Flexibility. *Sensory:* Night Vision; Depth Perception; Peripheral Vision; Sound Localization; Far Vision. **General Work Activities**—*Information Input:* Monitoring Processes, Materials, or Surroundings; Getting Information; Estimating Needed Characteristics. *Mental Process:* Making Decisions and Solving Problems; Organizing, Planning, and Prioritizing; Evaluating Information Against Standards. *Work Output:* Operating Vehicles or Equipment; Handling and Moving Objects; Controlling Machines and Processes. *Interacting with Others:* Communicating with Other Workers; Coaching and Developing Others; Establishing and Maintaining Relationships. **Physical Work Conditions**—Outdoors; Extremely Bright or Inadequate Lighting; Distracting Sounds and Noise Levels; Whole Body Vibration; Hazardous Equipment. **Other Job Characteristics**—Degree of Automation; Pace Determined by Speed of Equipment; Consequence of Error.

Experience—Job Zone 2. Some previous work-related skill, knowledge, or experience may be helpful, but usually is not needed. **Job Preparation:** SVP 4.0 to less than 6.0—six months to less than two years. **Knowledge**—Mechanical; Engineering and Technology; Production and Processing; Geography; Physics. **Instructional Programs**—No data available.

Related DOT Jobs—932.683-022 Shuttle-Car Operator.

53-7121.00 Tank Car, Truck, and Ship Loaders

- **Education/Training Required: Moderate-term on-the-job training**
- **Employed: 18,575**
- **Annual Earnings: $31,200**
- **Growth: 13.5%**
- **Annual Job Openings: 2,000**

Load and unload chemicals and bulk solids such as coal, sand, and grain into or from tank cars, trucks, or ships, using material-moving equipment. May perform a variety of other tasks relating to shipment of products. May gauge or sample shipping tanks and test them for leaks.

Starts pumps and adjusts valves to regulate flow of product to vessel, utilizing knowledge of loading procedures. Monitors product movement to and from storage tanks and coordinates with other workers to ensure constant product flow. Unloads cars by connecting hose to outlet plugs and pumping compressed air into car, forcing liquid into storage tank. Verifies tank car, barge, or truck load number to ensure car placement accuracy based on written or verbal instructions. Weighs and inspects vessels to prevent contamination and to ensure cleanliness and compliance to loading procedures. Tests vessels for leaks, damage, and defects; repairs or replaces defective parts. Reads meter to verify content, temperature, and volume of liquid load. Copies and tacks load specifications onto tank and seals outlet valves on tank car, barge, or truck. Records operating data, such as products and quantities pumped, gauge readings, and operating time, manually or using computer. Retrieves liquid sample and performs tests on contents or delivers sample to laboratory for testing. Operates blenders and heaters to mix, blend, and heat products.

GOE INFORMATION—**Interest Area:** 08. Industrial Production. **Work Group:** 08.07. Hands-on Work: Loading, Moving, Hoisting, and Conveying. **Personality Type**—Realistic. Realistic occupations frequently involve work activities that include practical, hands-on problems and solutions. They often deal with plants, animals, and real-world materials like wood, tools, and machinery. Many of the occupations require working outside and do not involve a lot of paperwork or working closely with others. **Work Values**—Supervision, Technical; Independence; Moral Values; Supervision, Human Relations. **Skills**—Operation Monitoring; Operation and Control; Repairing; Quality Control Analysis. **Abilities**— *Cognitive:* None met the criteria. *Psychomotor:* Rate Control; Reaction Time; Response Orientation; Control Precision; Manual Dexterity. *Physical:* Static Strength; Explosive Strength; Dynamic Strength; Gross Body Coordination; Gross Body Equilibrium. *Sensory:* Sound Localization; Peripheral Vision. **General Work Activities**—*Information Input:* Getting Information; Inspecting Equipment, Structures, or Materials; Monitoring Processes, Materials, or Surroundings. *Mental Process:* Evaluating Information Against Standards; Judging Qualities of Things, Services, or Other People's Work; Processing Information. *Work Output:* Controlling Machines and Processes; Handling and Moving Objects; Performing General Physical Activities. *Interacting with Others:* Communicating with Other Workers; Coordinating the Work and Activities of Others; Monitoring and Controlling Resources. **Physical Work Conditions**—Hazardous Conditions; Contaminants; Outdoors; Common Protective or Safety Attire; Specialized Protective or Safety Attire. **Other Job Characteristics**—Consequence of Error; Pace Determined by Speed of Equipment; Importance of Being Exact or Accurate.

Experience—Job Zone 3. Previous work-related skill, knowledge, or experience is required. **Job Preparation:** SVP 6.0 to less than 7.0—more than one year and less than four years. **Knowledge**—Chemistry; Production and Processing; Mechanical; Physics; Public Safety and Security. **Instructional Programs**—No data available.

Related DOT Jobs—914.382-014 Pumper-Gauger; 914.382-018 Pumper-Gauger Apprentice; 914.667-010 Loader I.

53-7199.99 Material Moving Workers, All Other

- Education/Training Required: No data available.
- Employed: No data available.
- Annual Earnings: No data available.
- Growth: 16.4%
- Annual Job Openings: 14,000

All material moving workers not listed separately.

No task data available.

GOE INFORMATION—**Interest Area:** 08. Industrial Production. **Work Group:** 08.07. Hands-on Work: Loading, Moving, Hoisting, and Conveying. **Note:** The Department of Labor has not collected some data for this job, so it has fewer details than the other descriptions.

Instructional Programs—No data available.

Related DOT Jobs—504.665-010 Slab-Depiler Operator; 521.685-278 Routing-Equipment Tender; 521.685-366 Tipple Tender; 529.685-102 Dumping-Machine Operator; 569.685-066 Stacker, Machine; 575.683-010 Bucket Operator; 612.683-010 Manipulator Operator; 850.387-010 Inspector Of Dredging; 911.364-014 Boat Loader I; 914.685-010 Fish Bailer; 919.664-010 Teamster; 919.683-018 Rail-Tractor Operator; 921.662-010 Car-Dumper Operator; 921.663-018 Chip Unloader; 921.667-018 Dumper; 921.682-010 Loader, Malt House; 921.682-018 Stacker-And-Sorter Operator; 921.683-038 Elevator Operator, Freight; 921.683-062 Skip Operator; 921.685-018 Cager Operator; others.

55-0000
Military Specific Occupations

55-1000 Military Officer Special and Tactical Operations Leaders/Managers

55-1011.00 Air Crew Officers

- **Education/Training Required: Long-term on-the-job training**
- **Employed: No data available.**
- **Annual Earnings: No data available.**
- **Growth: No data available.**
- **Annual Job Openings: No data available.**

Perform and direct in-flight duties to ensure the successful completion of combat, reconnaissance, transport, and search and rescue missions. Duties include operating aircraft communications and radar equipment, such as establishing satellite linkages and jamming enemy communications capabilities; operating aircraft weapons and defensive systems; conducting pre-flight, in-flight, and post-flight inspections of onboard equipment; and directing cargo and personnel drops.

No task data available.

GOE INFORMATION—Interest Area: 04. Law, Law Enforcement, and Public Safety. **Work Group:** 04.05. Military. **Note:** The Department of Labor has not collected some data for this job, so it has fewer details than the other descriptions.

Instructional Programs—No data available.

Related DOT Jobs—No related DOT jobs.

55-1012.00 Aircraft Launch and Recovery Officers

- **Education/Training Required: Long-term on-the-job training**
- **Employed: No data available.**
- **Annual Earnings: No data available.**
- **Growth: No data available.**
- **Annual Job Openings: No data available.**

Plan and direct the operation and maintenance of catapults, arresting gear, and associated mechanical, hydraulic, and control systems involved primarily in aircraft carrier takeoff and landing operations. Duties include supervision of readiness and safety of arresting gear, launching equipment, barricades, and visual landing aid systems; planning and coordinating the design, development, and testing of launch and recovery systems; preparing specifications for catapult and arresting gear installations; evaluating design proposals; determining handling equipment needed for new aircraft; preparing technical data and instructions for operation of landing aids; and training personnel in carrier takeoff and landing procedures.

No task data available.

GOE INFORMATION—Interest Area: 04. Law, Law Enforcement, and Public Safety. **Work Group:** 04.05. Military. **Note:** The Department of Labor has not collected some data for this job, so it has fewer details than the other descriptions.

Instructional Programs—No data available.

Related DOT Jobs—No related DOT jobs.

55-1013.00 Armored Assault Vehicle Officers

- **Education/Training Required: Long-term on-the-job training**
- **Employed: No data available.**
- **Annual Earnings: No data available.**
- **Growth: No data available.**
- **Annual Job Openings: No data available.**

Direct the operation of tanks, light armor, and amphibious assault vehicle units during combat situations on land or in aquatic environments. Duties include directing crew members in the operation of targeting and firing systems; coordinating the operation of advanced onboard communications and navigation equipment; directing the transport of personnel and equipment during combat; formulating and implementing battle plans, including the tactical employment of armored vehicle units; and coordinating with infantry, artillery, and air support units.

No task data available.

GOE INFORMATION—Interest Area: 04. Law, Law Enforcement, and Public Safety. **Work Group:** 04.05. Military. **Note:** The Department of Labor has not collected some data for this job, so it has fewer details than the other descriptions.

Instructional Programs—No data available.

Related DOT Jobs—No related DOT jobs.

55-1014.00 Artillery and Missile Officers

- **Education/Training Required: Long-term on-the-job training**
- **Employed: No data available.**
- **Annual Earnings: No data available.**
- **Growth: No data available.**
- **Annual Job Openings: No data available.**

Manage personnel and weapons operations to destroy enemy positions, aircraft, and vessels. Duties include planning, targeting, and coordinating the tactical deployment of field artillery and air defense artillery missile systems units; directing the establishment and operation of fire control communications systems; targeting and launching intercontinental ballistic missiles; directing the storage and handling of nuclear munitions and components; overseeing security of weapons storage and launch facilities; and managing maintenance of weapons systems.

No task data available.

GOE INFORMATION—Interest Area: 04. Law, Law Enforcement, and Public Safety. **Work Group:** 04.05. Military. **Note:** The Department of Labor has not collected some data for this job, so it has fewer details than the other descriptions.

Instructional Programs—No data available.

Related DOT Jobs—378.132-010 Field Artillery Senior Sergeant.

55-1015.00 Command and Control Center Officers

- Education/Training Required: Long-term on-the-job training
- Employed: No data available.
- Annual Earnings: No data available.
- Growth: No data available.
- Annual Job Openings: No data available.

Manage the operation of communications, detection, and weapons systems essential for controlling air, ground, and naval operations. Duties include managing critical communication links between air, naval, and ground forces; formulating and implementing emergency plans for natural and wartime disasters; coordinating emergency response teams and agencies; evaluating command center information and need for high-level military and government reporting; managing the operation of surveillance and detection systems; providing technical information and advice on capabilities and operational readiness; and directing operation of weapons targeting, firing, and launch computer systems.

No task data available.

GOE INFORMATION—Interest Area: 04. Law, Law Enforcement, and Public Safety. **Work Group:** 04.05. Military. **Note:** The Department of Labor has not collected some data for this job, so it has fewer details than the other descriptions.

Instructional Programs—No data available.

Related DOT Jobs—No related DOT jobs.

55-1016.00 Infantry Officers

- Education/Training Required: Long-term on-the-job training
- Employed: No data available.
- Annual Earnings: No data available.
- Growth: No data available.
- Annual Job Openings: No data available.

Direct, train, and lead infantry units in ground combat operations. Duties include directing deployment of infantry weapons, vehicles, and equipment; directing location, construction, and camouflage of infantry positions and equipment; managing field communications operations; coordinating with armor, artillery, and air support units; performing strategic and tactical planning, including battle plan development; and leading basic reconnaissance operations.

No task data available.

GOE INFORMATION—Interest Area: 04. Law, Law Enforcement, and Public Safety. **Work Group:** 04.05. Military. **Note:** The Department of Labor has not collected some data for this job, so it has fewer details than the other descriptions.

Instructional Programs—No data available.

Related DOT Jobs—378.137-010 Infantry Unit Leader.

55-1017.00 Special Forces Officers

- Education/Training Required: Long-term on-the-job training
- Employed: No data available.
- Annual Earnings: No data available.
- Growth: No data available.
- Annual Job Openings: No data available.

Lead elite teams that implement unconventional operations by air, land, or sea during combat or peacetime. These activities include offensive raids, demolitions, reconnaissance, search and rescue, and counterterrorism. In addition to their combat training, special forces officers often have specialized training in swimming, diving, parachuting, survival, emergency medicine, and foreign languages. Duties include directing advanced reconnaissance operations and evaluating intelligence information; recruiting, training, and equipping friendly forces; leading raids and invasions on enemy territories; training personnel to implement individual missions and contingency plans; performing strategic and tactical planning for politically sensitive missions; and operating sophisticated communications equipment.

No task data available.

GOE INFORMATION—Interest Area: 04. Law, Law Enforcement, and Public Safety. **Work Group:** 04.05. Military. **Note:** The Department of Labor has not collected some data for this job, so it has fewer details than the other descriptions.

Instructional Programs—No data available.

Related DOT Jobs—No related DOT jobs.

55-1019.99 Military Officer Special and Tactical Operations Leaders/Managers, All Other

- Education/Training Required: Long-term on-the-job training
- Employed: No data available.
- Annual Earnings: No data available.
- Growth: No data available.
- Annual Job Openings: No data available.

All military officer special and tactical operations leaders/managers not listed separately.

No task data available.

GOE INFORMATION—Interest Area: 04. Law, Law Enforcement, and Public Safety. **Work Group:** 04.05. Military. **Note:** The Department of Labor has not collected some data for this job, so it has fewer details than the other descriptions.

Instructional Programs—No data available.

Related DOT Jobs—No related DOT jobs.

55-2000 First-Line Enlisted Military Supervisor/Managers

55-2011.00 First-Line Supervisors/ Managers of Air Crew Members

- Education/Training Required: Work experience in a related occupation
- Employed: No data available.
- Annual Earnings: No data available.
- Growth: No data available.
- Annual Job Openings: No data available.

Supervise and coordinate the activities of air crew members. Supervisors may also perform the same activities as the workers they supervise.

No task data available.

GOE INFORMATION—Interest Area: 04. Law, Law Enforcement, and Public Safety. **Work Group:** 04.05. Military. **Note:** The Department of Labor has not collected some data for this job, so it has fewer details than the other descriptions.

Instructional Programs—No data available.

Related DOT Jobs—No related DOT jobs.

55-2012.00 *First-Line Supervisors/ Managers of Weapons Specialists/Crew Members*

- Education/Training Required: **Work experience in a related occupation**
- Employed: **No data available.**
- Annual Earnings: **No data available.**
- Growth: **No data available.**
- Annual Job Openings: **No data available.**

Supervise and coordinate the activities of weapons specialists/crew members. Supervisors may also perform the same activities as the workers they supervise.

No task data available.

GOE INFORMATION—Interest Area: 04. Law, Law Enforcement, and Public Safety. **Work Group:** 04.05. Military. **Note:** The Department of Labor has not collected some data for this job, so it has fewer details than the other descriptions.

Instructional Programs—No data available.

Related DOT Jobs—No related DOT jobs.

55-2013.00 *First-Line Supervisors/ Managers of All Other Tactical Operations Specialists*

- Education/Training Required: **Work experience in a related occupation**
- Employed: **No data available.**
- Annual Earnings: **No data available.**
- Growth: **No data available.**
- Annual Job Openings: **No data available.**

Supervise and coordinate the activities of all other tactical operations specialists not classified separately above. Supervisors may also perform the same activities as the workers they supervise.

No task data available.

GOE INFORMATION—Interest Area: 04. Law, Law Enforcement, and Public Safety. **Work Group:** 04.05. Military. **Note:** The Department of Labor has not collected some data for this job, so it has fewer details than the other descriptions.

Instructional Programs—No data available.

Related DOT Jobs—No related DOT jobs.

55-3000 Military Enlisted Tactical Operations and Air/ Weapons Specialists and Crew Members

55-3011.00 *Air Crew Members*

- Education/Training Required: **Moderate-term on-the-job training**
- Employed: **No data available.**
- Annual Earnings: **No data available.**
- Growth: **No data available.**
- Annual Job Openings: **No data available.**

Perform in-flight duties to ensure the successful completion of combat, reconnaissance, transport, and search and rescue missions. Duties include operating aircraft communications and detection equipment, including establishing satellite linkages and jamming enemy communications capabilities; conducting pre-flight, in-flight, and post-flight inspections of onboard equipment; operating and maintaining aircraft weapons and defensive systems; operating and maintaining aircraft in-flight refueling systems; executing aircraft safety and emergency procedures; computing and verifying passenger, cargo, fuel, and emergency and special equipment weight and balance data; and conducting cargo and personnel drops.

No task data available.

GOE INFORMATION—Interest Area: 04. Law, Law Enforcement, and Public Safety. **Work Group:** 04.05. Military. **Note:** The Department of Labor has not collected some data for this job, so it has fewer details than the other descriptions.

Instructional Programs—No data available.

Related DOT Jobs—No related DOT jobs.

55-3012.00 *Aircraft Launch and Recovery Specialists*

- Education/Training Required: **Moderate-term on-the-job training**
- Employed: **No data available.**
- Annual Earnings: **No data available.**
- Growth: **No data available.**
- Annual Job Openings: **No data available.**

Operate and maintain catapults, arresting gear, and associated mechanical, hydraulic, and control systems involved primarily in aircraft carrier takeoff and landing operations. Duties include installing and maintaining visual landing aids; testing and maintaining launch and recovery equipment, using electric and mechanical test equipment and hand tools; activating airfield arresting systems, such as crash barriers and cables, during emergency landing situations; directing aircraft launch and recovery operations, using hand or light signals; and maintaining logs of airplane launches, recoveries, and equipment maintenance.

No task data available.

GOE INFORMATION—**Interest Area:** 04. Law, Law Enforcement, and Public Safety. **Work Group:** 04.05. Military. **Note:** The Department of Labor has not collected some data for this job, so it has fewer details than the other descriptions.

Instructional Programs—No data available.

Related DOT Jobs—912.682-010 Aircraft Launch And Recovery Technician.

55-3013.00 Armored Assault Vehicle Crew Members

- **Education/Training Required: Moderate-term on-the-job training**
- **Employed: No data available.**
- **Annual Earnings: No data available.**
- **Growth: No data available.**
- **Annual Job Openings: No data available.**

Operate tanks, light armor, and amphibious assault vehicles during combat situations on land or in aquatic environments. Duties include driving armored vehicles which require specialized training; operating and maintaining targeting and firing systems; operating and maintaining advanced onboard communications and navigation equipment; transporting personnel and equipment in a combat environment; and operating and maintaining auxiliary weapons, including machine guns and grenade launchers.

No task data available.

GOE INFORMATION—**Interest Area:** 04. Law, Law Enforcement, and Public Safety. **Work Group:** 04.05. Military. **Note:** The Department of Labor has not collected some data for this job, so it has fewer details than the other descriptions.

Instructional Programs—No data available.

Related DOT Jobs—378.683-018 Tank Crewmember.

55-3014.00 Artillery and Missile Crew Members

- **Education/Training Required: Moderate-term on-the-job training**
- **Employed: No data available.**
- **Annual Earnings: No data available.**
- **Growth: No data available.**
- **Annual Job Openings: No data available.**

Target, fire, and maintain weapons used to destroy enemy positions, aircraft, and vessels. Field artillery crew members predominantly use guns, cannons, and howitzers in ground combat operations, whereas air defense artillery crew members predominantly use missiles and rockets. Naval artillery crew members predominantly use torpedoes and missiles launched from a ship or submarine. Duties include testing, inspecting, and storing ammunition, missiles, and torpedoes; conducting preventive and routine maintenance on weapons and related equipment; establishing and maintaining radio and wire communications; and operating weapons-targeting, -firing, and -launch computer systems.

No task data available.

GOE INFORMATION—**Interest Area:** 04. Law, Law Enforcement, and Public Safety. **Work Group:** 04.05. Military. **Note:** The Department of Labor has not collected some data for this job, so it has fewer details than the other descriptions.

Instructional Programs—No data available.

Related DOT Jobs—378.663-010 Vulcan Crewmember; 378.682-010 Redeye Gunner; 378.684-018 Field Artillery Crewmember; 632.261-010 Aircraft-Armament Mechanic; 632.261-014 Fire-Control Mechanic; 632.261-018 Ordnance Artificer.

55-3015.00 Command and Control Center Specialists

- **Education/Training Required: Moderate-term on-the-job training**
- **Employed: No data available.**
- **Annual Earnings: No data available.**
- **Growth: No data available.**
- **Annual Job Openings: No data available.**

Operate and monitor communications, detection, and weapons systems essential for controlling air, ground, and naval operations. Duties include maintaining and relaying critical communications between air, naval, and ground forces; implementing emergency plans for natural and wartime disasters; relaying command center information to high-level military and government decision makers; monitoring surveillance and detection systems, such as air defense; interpreting and evaluating tactical situations and making recommendations to superiors; and operating weapons-targeting, -firing, and -launch computer systems.

No task data available.

GOE INFORMATION—**Interest Area:** 04. Law, Law Enforcement, and Public Safety. **Work Group:** 04.05. Military. **Note:** The Department of Labor has not collected some data for this job, so it has fewer details than the other descriptions.

Instructional Programs—No data available.

Related DOT Jobs—235.662-010 Command And Control Specialist; 378.367-026 Operations And Intelligence Assistant.

55-3016.00 Infantry

- **Education/Training Required: Moderate-term on-the-job training**
- **Employed: No data available.**
- **Annual Earnings: No data available.**
- **Growth: No data available.**
- **Annual Job Openings: No data available.**

Operate weapons and equipment in ground combat operations. Duties include operating and maintaining weapons, such as rifles, machine guns, mortars, and hand grenades; locating, constructing, and camouflaging infantry positions and equipment; evaluating terrain and recording topographical information; operating and maintaining field communications equipment; assessing need for and directing supporting fire; placing explosives and performing minesweeping activities on land; and participating in basic reconnaissance operations.

No task data available.

GOE INFORMATION—Interest Area: 04. Law, Law Enforcement, and Public Safety. **Work Group:** 04.05. Military. **Note:** The Department of Labor has not collected some data for this job, so it has fewer details than the other descriptions.

Instructional Programs—No data available.

Related DOT Jobs—378.684-014 Combat Rifle Crewmember.

55-3017.00 Radar and Sonar Technicians

- Education/Training Required: Moderate-term on-the-job training
- Employed: No data available.
- Annual Earnings: No data available.
- Growth: No data available.
- Annual Job Openings: No data available.

Operate equipment using radio or sound wave technology to identify, track, and analyze objects or natural phenomena of military interest. Includes airborne, shipboard, and terrestrial positions. May perform minor maintenance.

No task data available.

GOE INFORMATION—Interest Area: 04. Law, Law Enforcement, and Public Safety. **Work Group:** 04.05. Military. **Note:** The Department of Labor has not collected some data for this job, so it has fewer details than the other descriptions.

Instructional Programs—No data available.

Related DOT Jobs—No related DOT jobs.

55-3018.00 Special Forces

- Education/Training Required: Long-term on-the-job training
- Employed: No data available.
- Annual Earnings: No data available.
- Growth: No data available.
- Annual Job Openings: No data available.

Implement unconventional operations by air, land, or sea during combat or peacetime as members of elite teams. These activities include offensive raids, demolitions, reconnaissance, search and rescue, and counterterrorism. In addition to their combat training, special forces members often have specialized training in swimming, diving, parachuting, survival, emergency medicine, and foreign languages. Duties include conducting advanced reconnaissance operations and collecting intelligence information; recruiting, training, and equipping friendly forces; conducting raids and

invasions on enemy territories; laying and detonating explosives for demolition targets; locating, identifying, defusing, and disposing of ordnance; and operating and maintaining sophisticated communications equipment.

No task data available.

GOE INFORMATION—Interest Area: 04. Law, Law Enforcement, and Public Safety. **Work Group:** 04.05. Military. **Note:** The Department of Labor has not collected some data for this job, so it has fewer details than the other descriptions.

Instructional Programs—No data available.

Related DOT Jobs—378.227-018 Survival Specialist; 378.367-030 Reconnaissance Crewmember; 378.683-010 Amphibian Crewmember.

55-3019.99 Military Enlisted Tactical Operations and Air/Weapons Specialists and Crew Members, All Other

- Education/Training Required: No data available.
- Employed: No data available.
- Annual Earnings: No data available.
- Growth: No data available.
- Annual Job Openings: No data available.

All military enlisted tactical operations and air/weapons specialists and crew members not listed separately.

No task data available.

GOE INFORMATION—Interest Area: 04. Law, Law Enforcement, and Public Safety. **Work Group:** 04.05. Military. **Note:** The Department of Labor has not collected some data for this job, so it has fewer details than the other descriptions.

Instructional Programs—No data available.

Related DOT Jobs—199.682-010 Aerospace Physiological Technician; 248.387-010 Flight Operations Specialist; 249.387-014 Intelligence Clerk; 378.161-010 Combat Surveillance And Target Acquisition Noncommissioned Officer; 378.227-014 Recruit Instructor; 378.267-010 Counterintelligence Agent; 378.281-010 Target Aircraft Technician; 378.362-010 Sound Ranging Crewmember; 378.363-010 Armor Reconnaissance Specialist; 378.367-010 Artillery Or Naval Gunfire Observer; 378.367-014 Field Artillery Operations Specialist; 378.367-018 Flash Ranging Crewmember; 378.367-022 Infantry Operations Specialist; 378.382-010 Airborne Sensor Specialist; 378.382-014 Defensive Fire Control Systems Operator; 378.382-018 Unattended-Ground-Sensor Specialist; 378.464-010 Antitank Assault Gunner; 378.682-014 Smoke And Flame Specialist; 378.683-014 Powered Bridge Specialist; 378.684-010 Camouflage Specialist; others.

Index of O*NET Job Titles

A

F

G

H

I

J–K

L

N

O

P–Q

* * * * * * * * * * ❋ ❋   © JIST Works

R

S

T

U–Z

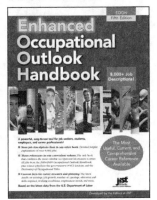
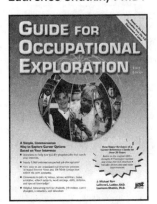
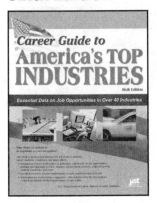